,ook is to be returned on or before
he last date stamped below.

The Dorling Kindersley

ILLUSTRATED
FAMILY
ENCYCLOPEDIA

LONDON, NEW YORK, MUNICH,
MELBOURNE AND DELHI

Senior Editor Jayne Parsons   **Senior Art Editor** Gillian Shaw

Project Editors
Marian Broderick, Gill Cooling,
Maggie Crowley, Hazel Egerton,
Cynthia O'Neill, Veronica Pennycook,
Louise Pritchard, Steve Setford, Jackie Wilson

Project Art Editors
Jane Felstead, Martyn Foote,
Neville Graham, Jamie Hanson,
Christopher Howson, Jill Plank, Floyd Sayers,
Jane Tetzlaff, Ann Thompson

Editors
Rachel Beaugié, Nic Kynaston, Sarah Levete,
Karen O'Brien, Linda Sonntag

Art Editors
Tina Borg, Diane Clouting,
Tory Gordon-Harris

DTP Designers
Andrew O'Brien, Cordelia Springer

Managing Editor Ann Kramer   **Managing Art Editor** Peter Bailey

Senior DTP Designer Mathew Birch

Picture Research Jo Walton, Kate Duncan, Liz Moore

DK Picture Library Ola Rudowska, Melanie Simmonds

Country pages by PAGE*One*: Bob Gordon, Helen Parker,
Thomas Keenes, Sarah Watson, Chris Clark

Cartographers Peter Winfield, James Anderson

Research Robert Graham, Angela Koo

Editorial Assistants Sarah-Louise Reed, Nichola Roberts

Production Louise Barratt, Charlotte Traill

First published in Great Britain in 1997
This edition published in 2005
by Dorling Kindersley Limited,
80 Strand, London WC2R 0RL

A CIP catalogue record for this book is available from the British Library

ISBN: 1 4053 1112 6

Colour reproduction by Colourscan, Singapore
Printed and bound in China by Toppan Printing Co. (Shenzhen) Ltd.

**Find out more at
www.dk.com**

LIST OF MAIN ENTRIES

See index for further topics

POWER AND SPEED

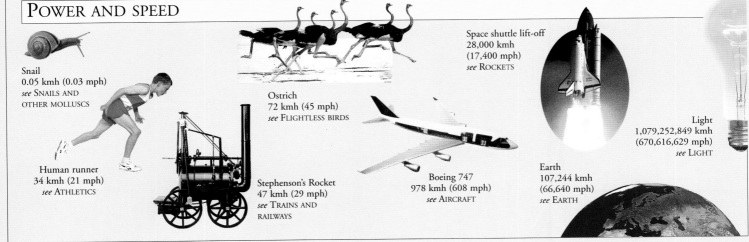

Snail
0.05 kmh (0.03 mph)
see SNAILS AND
OTHER MOLLUSCS

Human runner
34 kmh (21 mph)
see ATHLETICS

Ostrich
72 kmh (45 mph)
see FLIGHTLESS BIRDS

Stephenson's Rocket
47 kmh (29 mph)
see TRAINS AND
RAILWAYS

Boeing 747
978 kmh (608 mph)
see AIRCRAFT

Space shuttle lift-off
28,000 kmh
(17,400 mph)
see ROCKETS

Earth
107,244 kmh
(66,640 mph)
see EARTH

Light
1,079,252,849 kmh
(670,616,629 mph)
see LIGHT

Jupiter, the largest planet, comparative to the Sun

Sun see SUN AND SOLAR SYSTEM

COMPARATIVE PLANET SIZES

Uranus *see* PLANETS

Neptune *see* PLANETS

Pluto *see* PLANETS

Mars *see* PLANETS

Earth *see* EARTH

Mercury *see* PLANETS

Venus *see* PLANETS

Saturn *see* PLANETS

Jupiter *see* PLANETS

COMMUNICATION TIMELINE

490 BC
Marathon runner
see OLYMPIC
GAMES

Carrier pigeon
see BIRDS

18th century Sign language
see LANGUAGES

1840
Postage stamp
see STAMPS AND
POSTAL SERVICES

1837
Electric
telegraph
see TELECOMMUNICATIONS

1844
Morse code
see CODES AND
CIPHERS

1876
Bell telephone
see TELEPHONES

12th century Smoke signals   1784 Mail coach   1850 Pillar box   1855 Printing telegraph   1860 Semaphore and Pony Express   1861 Postcards

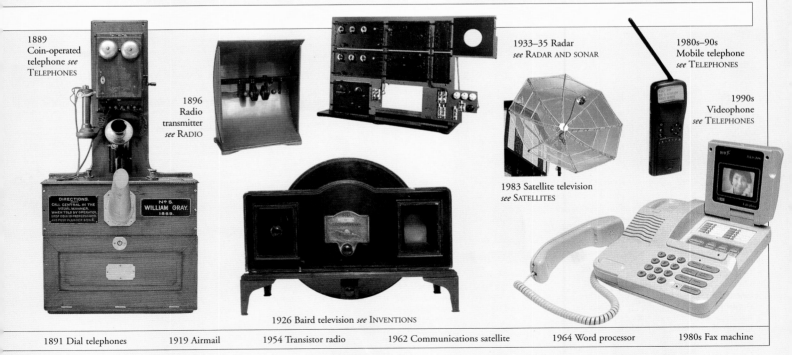

1889
Coin-operated
telephone see
TELEPHONES

1896
Radio
transmitter
see RADIO

1926 Baird television see INVENTIONS

1933–35 Radar
see RADAR AND SONAR

1983 Satellite television
see SATELLITES

1980s–90s
Mobile telephone
see TELEPHONES

1990s
Videophone
see TELEPHONES

1891 Dial telephones   1919 Airmail   1954 Transistor radio   1962 Communications satellite   1964 Word processor   1980s Fax machine

HOW TO USE THIS ENCYCLOPEDIA

THE FOLLOWING PAGES WILL HELP YOU get the most out of your copy of the *Dorling Kindersley Illustrated Family Encyclopedia*. The encyclopedia contains nearly 700 main entries organised alphabetically, from Aboriginal Australians through to Zoos. To find the entry you want, simply turn to the correct letter of the alphabet.

If you cannot find the topic you want, then turn to the index and gazetteer, which will direct you straight to the page you need. In addition, the reference section contains hundreds of reference charts, fact boxes, lists, and tables to supplement the information provided on the main entry pages.

MEASUREMENTS AND ABBREVIATIONS

Most measurements are supplied in both metric and imperial units. Some of the most common abbreviations used in the encyclopedia are shown below in **bold** type.

°C = degrees Celsius
°F = degrees Fahrenheit
K = degrees kelvin
mm = millimetre; cm = centimetre
m = metre; km = kilometre
in = inch; ft = foot; yd = yard
g = gram; kg = kilogram
oz = ounce; lb = pound
ml = millilitre; l = litre
pt = pint; gal = gallon
sq km (km²) = square kilometre
sq ft (ft²) = square foot
kmh = kilometres per hour
mph = miles per hour
mya = million years ago
BC = before Christ
AD = anno Domini (refers to any date after the birth of Christ)
c. = circa (about)
b. = born; d. = died; r. = reigned

THE PAGE LAYOUT

The pages in this encyclopedia have been carefully planned to make each subject as accessible as possible. Main entries are broken down into a hierarchy of information – from a general introduction to more specific individual topics.

Alphabet locators

Letter flashes help you find your way quickly around the encyclopedia.

Sub-entries

Sub-entries provide important additional information and expand on points made in the introduction.

This sub-entry explains how rainbows are caused by raindrops in the air.

Diagrams

Clear diagrams help explain complex processes and scientific concepts.

The diagram here shows how a raindrop splits sunlight into its constituent colours.

Introduction

Clear introductions are the starting point for each entry. The introduction defines and provides an overview of each subject.

In the main entry on COLOUR, the introduction explains that colours are different forms of light, and that sunlight contains light of many different colours.

COLOUR

A WORLD WITHOUT COLOUR would be dull and uninspiring. Colour is a form of light. Light is made up of electromagnetic waves of varying lengths. The human eye detects these different wavelengths and sees them as different colours. White light – like that from the Sun – is a mixture of all the different wavelengths. Objects look coloured because they give out or reflect only certain wavelengths of light.

White light spectrum

Passing white light through a transparent triangular block called a prism separates out the different wavelengths of light. The prism refracts (bends) each wavelength by a different amount, forming a band of colours called a white light spectrum, or a visible spectrum. The seven main colours are red, orange, yellow, green, blue, indigo, and violet. Red has the longest wavelength and violet the shortest. Here, a convex lens combines the colours back into white light.

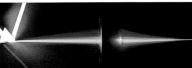

Rainbow

If it rains on a sunny day, you may well see a rainbow if you stand with your back to the Sun. A rainbow is a curved white light spectrum that forms when light is reflected and refracted by raindrops in the sky.

A rainbow at dawn

How a rainbow forms
When white sunlight passes through a raindrop, the raindrop acts like a tiny prism. The raindrop refracts the light and splits it up into its separate colours. The colours fan out and emerge as a spectrum. A rainbow is made up of spectra from millions of raindrops.

Sunlight

Spectrum

Colours refract again

Light refracts

Colours reflect off back surface

Colour and temperature

Objects at room temperature emit (give out) electromagnetic waves, but these waves are too long for human eyes to see. Heating an object, such as this steel bar, gives the waves it emits more energy and makes them shorter. The waves eventually become short enough to be seen, and the bar begins to glow. As the bar's temperature rises, it glows with different colours.

Steel bar at 630°C (1,170°F)

Steel bar at 1,530°C (2,790°F)

Spectroscope

An instrument called a spectroscope is used to analyze the light given out by hot substances. Inside the spectroscope, a prism or diffraction grating (a glass slide scored with fine lines) splits light from a glowing substance into its component wavelengths.

Light source

Diffraction grating

Cone cells

At the back of the eye there are special cells called cones that enable humans to see colours. There are three types of cone, called red, green, and blue cones. Each type of cone is sensitive to a different range of light wavelengths. White light stimulates all three types of cone.

Cone cells

Emission spectrum
Each chemical element gives out a unique range of light wavelengths when heated. Seen through a spectroscope, these wavelengths appear as a set of bright lines on a dark background. This is the element's emission spectrum. A compound's emission spectrum is a combination of spectra from the elements that make up the compound.

Emission spectrum of a sodium flame

Sodium flame

Sensitivity of red cones

Sensitivity of green cones

Sensitivity of blue cones

Visible spectrum

Sensitivity of cone cells in the human eye

Glowing white

Glowing red

Visible spectrum

Red hot and white hot
As the steel bar gets hotter, it emits more and more of the visible spectrum. At about 630°C (1,170°F), it is "red hot" and emits light from the red end of the spectrum. At about 1,530°C (2,790°F), the "white hot" bar emits the entire white light spectrum.

Hot stars
The colour of a star gives a clue to its age. To the naked eye, most stars look white, but their true colours can be seen using a telescope. Young stars are hot and glow with white light. Older stars are relatively cool and glow red or orange.

A cluster of young stars

Joseph von Fraunhofer

The German physicist Joseph von Fraunhofer (1787–1826) became interested in the nature of light while training as a mirror maker and lens polisher. His training enabled him to make spectroscopes of great precision. From 1814–17, he used them to make the first scientific study of the Sun's emission spectrum.

Munsell colour system

Describing colours exactly using words alone is not easy. To avoid confusion, manufacturing industries use standard colour-identification systems. The Munsell system is used to specify colours for dyes and pigments. It defines a colour by its value (brightness), its chroma (strength), and its hue (position in the spectrum).

Colour matching systems
Graphic designers use swatches of colour cards to match the colours in their work with those available from printers. The designer supplies the printer with the reference number of the colour, so the printer knows exactly what is wanted.

Each colour has a reference number.

226

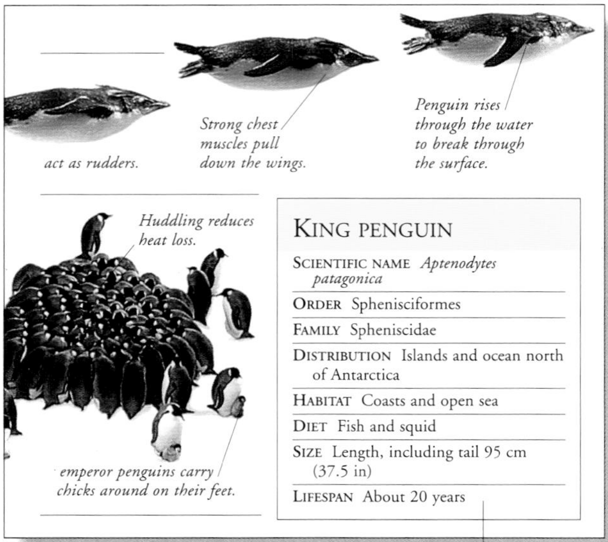

Labels help to identify images.

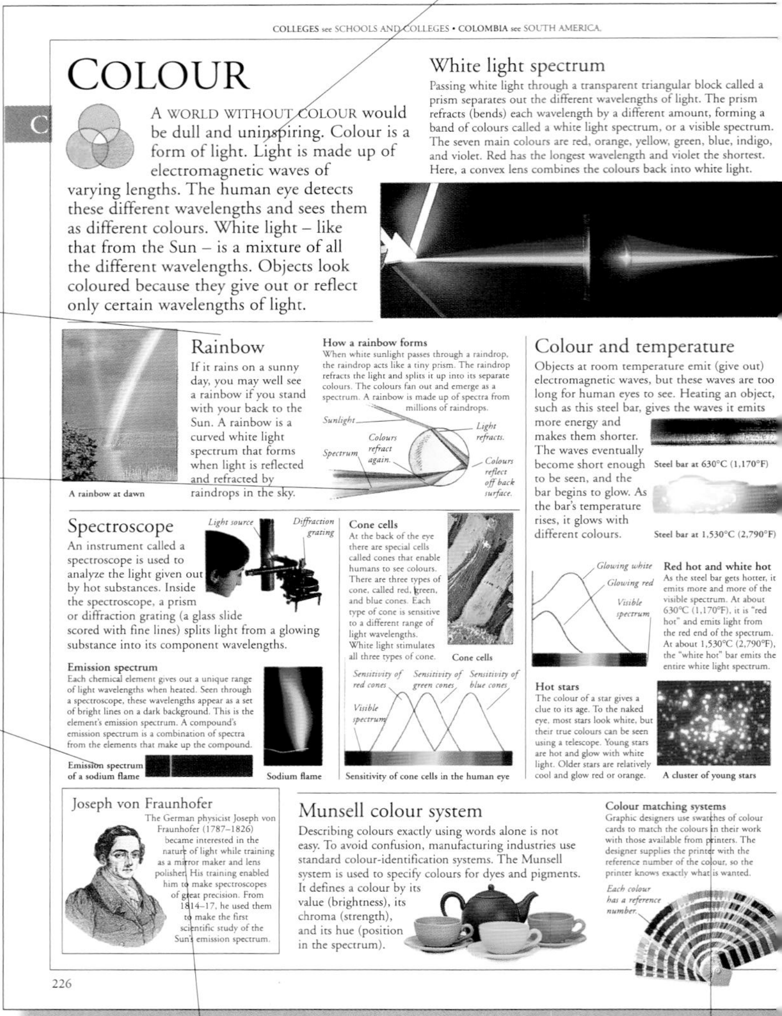

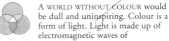

act as rudders.

Strong chest muscles pull down the wings.

Penguin rises through the water to break through the surface.

Huddling reduces heat loss.

KING PENGUIN

SCIENTIFIC NAME *Aptenodytes patagonica*

ORDER Sphenisciformes

FAMILY Spheniscidae

DISTRIBUTION Islands and ocean north of Antarctica

HABITAT Coasts and open sea

DIET Fish and squid

SIZE Length, including tail 95 cm (37.5 in)

LIFESPAN About 20 years

emperor penguins carry chicks around on their feet.

Natural history data boxes

On the natural history pages, data boxes summarize essential information about a key animal featured in the entry. The box contains information about the animal's size, diet, habitat, lifespan, distribution, and scientific name.

This data box gives you key facts about the King Penguin.

Biography boxes

Most main entry pages have biography boxes that tell you about key people who have contributed to our knowledge of the subject. The encyclopedia also has single-page entries on the life and work of more than 50 major historical figures.

This biography box describes the work of the physicist Joseph von Fraunhofer.

Headings

The topic headings enable you to see at-a-glance which subjects are covered within the main entry.

The heading Colour matching systems refers to the way designers use reference numbers to match the colours on their work to the colours of printers' inks.

INDEX
The index lists all the topics mentioned in the encyclopedia and the pages on which they can be found. The gazetteer follows on, with references to help you find all the features included on the maps.

• page numbers in **bold** type (eg Knights and heraldry **495-6**) show that the subject is a main A–Z entry.

• page numbers in plain type (eg armour 69) send you to sub-entries, text references, and the reference section.

• grid references (eg Cremona Italy 475 C3) are letter-number combinations that locate features on maps.

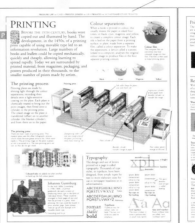

This two-page entry discusses the main types of primate.

Running head
There is an A–Z running head at the top of most pages to help you find important topics that are not main entries within the encyclopedia.

The running head on PRINTING tells you that although there is no main entry on primates, you can find the topic on MONKEYS AND OTHER PRIMATES.

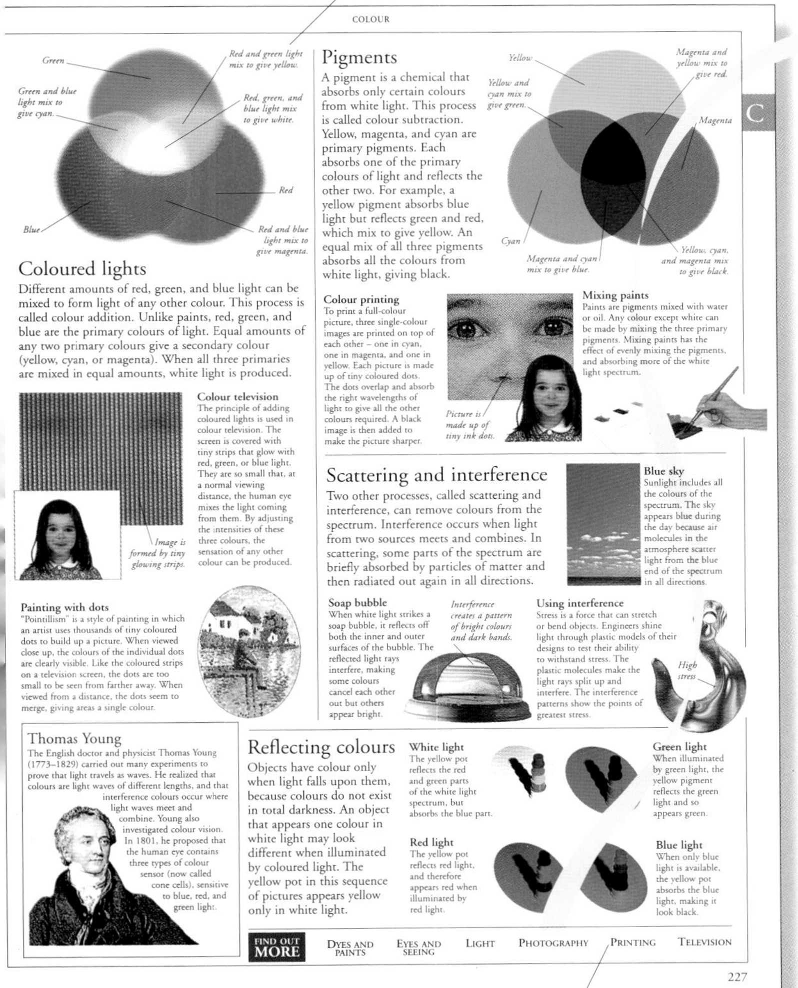

Illustrations
Each main entry is heavily illustrated with models, photographs, and artworks, adding a vibrant layer of visual information to the page.

This annotation tells you how different colours can be produced by mixing red, green, and blue light.

Annotation
The illustrations are comprehensively annotated to draw attention to details of particular interest and to explain complex points.

COLOUR

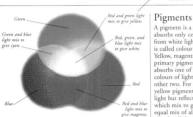

Green
Red and green light mix to give yellow.
Green and blue light mix to give cyan.
Red, green, and blue light mix to give white.
Red
Blue
Red and blue light mix to give magenta.

Coloured lights
Different amounts of red, green, and blue light can be mixed to form light of any other colour. This process is called colour addition. Unlike paints, red, green, and blue are the primary colours of light. Equal amounts of any two primary colours give a secondary colour (yellow, cyan, or magenta). When all three primaries are mixed in equal amounts, white light is produced.

Colour television
The principle of adding coloured lights is used in colour television. The screen is covered with tiny strips that glow with red, green, or blue light. They are so small that, at a normal viewing distance, the human eye mixes the light coming from them. By adjusting the intensities of these three colours, the sensation of any other colour can be produced.

Image is formed by tiny glowing strips.

Painting with dots
"Pointillism" is a style of painting in which an artist uses thousands of tiny coloured dots to build up a picture. When viewed close up, the colours of the individual dots are clearly visible. Like the coloured strips on a television screen, the dots are too small to be seen from farther away. When viewed from a distance, the dots seem to merge, giving areas a single colour.

Thomas Young
The English doctor and physicist Thomas Young (1773–1829) carried out many experiments to prove that light travels as waves. He realized that colours are light waves of different lengths, and that interference colours occur where light waves meet and combine. Young also investigated colour vision. In 1801, he proposed that the human eye contains three types of colour sensor (now called cone cells), most sensitive to blue, red, and green light.

Pigments
A pigment is a chemical that absorbs only certain colours from white light. This process is called colour subtraction. Yellow, magenta, and cyan are primary pigments. Each absorbs one of the primary colours of light and reflects the other two. For example, a yellow pigment absorbs blue light but reflects green and red, which mix to give yellow. An equal mix of all three pigments absorbs all the colours from white light, giving black.

Colour printing
To print a full-colour picture, three single-colour images are printed on top of each other – one in cyan, one in magenta, and one in yellow. Each picture is made up of tiny coloured dots. The dots overlap and absorb the right wavelengths of light to give all the other colours required. A black image is then added to make the picture sharper.

Picture is made up of tiny ink dots.

Yellow
Yellow and cyan mix to give green.
Magenta and yellow mix to give red.
Magenta
Cyan
Magenta and cyan mix to give blue.
Yellow, cyan, and magenta mix to give black.

Mixing paints
Paints are pigments mixed with water or oil. Any colour except white can be made by mixing the three primary pigments. Mixing paints has the effect of evenly mixing the pigments, and absorbing more of the white light spectrum.

Scattering and interference
Two other processes, called scattering and interference, can remove colours from the spectrum. Interference occurs when light from two sources meets and combines. In scattering, some parts of the spectrum are briefly absorbed by particles of matter and then radiated out again in all directions.

Blue sky
Sunlight includes all the colours of the spectrum. The sky appears blue during the day because air molecules in the atmosphere scatter light from the blue end of the spectrum in all directions.

Soap bubble
When white light strikes a soap bubble, it reflects off both the inner and outer surfaces of the bubble. The reflected light rays interfere, making some colours cancel each other out but others appear bright.

Interference creates a pattern of bright colours and dark bands.

Using interference
Stress is a force that can stretch or bend objects. Engineers shine light through plastic models of their designs to test their ability to withstand stress. The plastic molecules make the light rays split up and interfere. The interference patterns show the points of greatest stress.

High stress

Reflecting colours
Objects have colour only when light falls upon them, because colours do not exist in total darkness. An object that appears one colour in white light may look different when illuminated by coloured light. The yellow pot in this sequence of pictures appears yellow only in white light.

White light
The white pot reflects the red and green parts of the white light spectrum, but absorbs the blue part.

Red light
The yellow pot reflects red light, and therefore appears red when illuminated by red light.

Green light
When illuminated by green light, the yellow pigment reflects the green light and so appears green.

Blue light
When only blue light is available, the yellow pot absorbs the blue light, making it look black.

FIND OUT MORE | DYES AND PAINTS | EYES AND SEEING | LIGHT | PHOTOGRAPHY | PRINTING | TELEVISION

227

PRINTING

PRINTING

BEFORE THE 15TH CENTURY, books were copied out and illustrated by hand. The development, in the 1450s, of a printing press capable of using movable type led to an information revolution. Large numbers of books and leaflets could be copied mechanically, quickly and cheaply, allowing learning to spread rapidly. Today we are surrounded by printed material, from magazines, packaging, and posters produced in their thousands, to the smaller number of prints made by artists.

Colour separations
When a hole is printed in colour, this usually means the paper is inked four times: in black, cyan, magenta, and yellow, to create a complete colour image. Each ink is laid on the paper from a printing surface or plate, made from a separate film, called a colour separation. To make the separations, a device called a scanner, linked to a computer, analyses the original colour image to determine how it is formed from its four separate printing colours.

Printing methods
The four major types of printing methods are screen printing, relief printing, the intaglio process, and lithography. Printing may be used for commercial printing processes or to make thousands of copies, or on a smaller scale by an artist, to make a very few copies of an image.

The printing process
Printing plates are made by shining light through the colour separations, creating thin details onto a light-sensitive coating on the plate. Each plate is chemically treated to bring out the print image, then firmed onto a cylinder in the printing press. The inked image on the plate is transferred (either on another cylinder, the blanket cylinder) and from there on to the paper.

Screen printing
In this type of printing, a stencil is attached to a mesh screen. The screen is then laid on the surface to be printed and ink is pushed through the mesh, tracing an image. Screen printing is widely used or production for printing posters and packaging. Prints can be made on many different surfaces, including paper, wood, metal, and fabric.

Relief printing
With this method, the non-printing areas of a plate are cut away, leaving a raised image, which is then inked all round. Letterpress printing, once used to print newspapers, is a type of relief printing.

Intaglio process
In this process, a recessed image is engraved or etched into a metal plate. The plate is inked and wiped, so that only the grooves are filled with ink. Damp paper is laid on the plate, and both are passed through the rollers of an etching press. The paper is forced into the grooves to take up the ink, printing the design the right way round.

The printing press
This illustration shows a four-colour printing press that uses the offset lithography process, in which inked rollers transfer the image onto cylinders instead of directly onto the paper.

Typography
The design and use of letters printed on a page is called typography. Thousands of type styles, or typefaces, have been designed, from simple types for text to more elaborate ones for use in newspaper headlines or in advertisements.

ABCDEFGHIJKLMNO
PQRSTUVWXYZ
abcdefghijklmno
pqrstuvwxyz
roman
italic
bold

Johannes Gutenberg
In the mid 1400s, Gutenberg (c.1400–1468), a goldsmith from Mainz in Germany, was the first person in Europe to develop a press using movable metal type. The letters could be re-used many times.

xpH

Aa Aa

Colour separations
... (illustration labels: Black, Cyan, Magenta, Yellow) ...

FIND OUT MORE | ART | BOOKS | CHINA | COLOUR | COMPUTERS | NEWSPAPERS | TELEVISION

Timelines
An entry may include a timeline that gives the dates of key events in the history or development of the subject.

The PRINTING timeline stretches from the printing of the first books in ancient China to the computerization of modern printing.

COLLECTION PAGES
There are more than 70 pages of photographic collections, which follow main entries and provide a visual guide to the subject. They are organized under clear headings.

CHINA, HISTORY OF

CHINA is THE WORLD'S oldest continuous civilization. For more than 2,000 years, from 221 BC to AD 1911, it was united as a single vast empire under a series of all-powerful rulers. During this period, borders changed, lands were added, and the country was invaded by fierce tribes, including the Mongols. However, for most of its history, China led the world in art and technology, while its people were inventing paper, porcelain, and gunpowder. Despite its huge size, a unique system of government and a strong sense of national identity have helped to maintain a united China.

Qin Shi Huangdi
When Zheng (259–210 BC), the leader of the victorious Qin army, took control of China in 221 BC, he took the title of First Sovereign Qin Emperor, or Qin Shi Huangdi. The First Emperor ruled by very strict laws.

Ancient China
The first known Chinese dynasty, the Shang (c.1766–c.1027 BC), made a new device, and collected tribute from the lords of outlying regions.

Unification
By 400 BC, central government had broken down and many small kingdoms fought each other. In 221 BC, the state of Qin triumphed, uniting all of China under the rule of the First Emperor. This was built at this time, along with other unifications.

Han Dynasty
In 207 BC, a new dynasty took power. The Han Emperors, who ruled until AD 220, set up a national civil service to run the country. Officials studied the teachings of the philosopher Confucius (551–479 BC), and were selected by a rigorous examination system. The Han reign marked a period of peace and prosperity.

Terracotta army
The First Emperor's tomb was guarded by thousands of life-sized terracotta soldiers. The statues of warriors, horses, and chariots were carefully arranged in battle formation.

Inventions
Throughout Chinese history, emperors encouraged the development of science and technology. Paper making, gunpowder, harnesses for animals, the magnetic compass and stern-rudder, and the wheelbarrow were all invented in China.

Paper money

Gunpowder
Chinese scientists first attempted to make gold from other chemicals. They did not succeed, but one of their experiments resulted in gunpowder. Early Chinese rockets, fuelled by gunpowder, were first produced in China in the 11th century. The Chinese also created fire arrows and firing bombs using several missiles freely.

Chinese arts and crafts
Jewellery and adornment

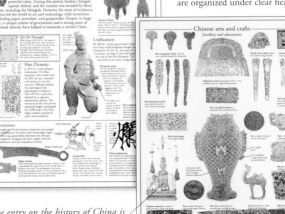

Statue artefacts

Find out more
The Find Out More lines at the end of each entry direct you to other relevant main entries in the encyclopedia. Using the Find Out More lines can help you understand an entry in its wider context.

On COLOUR, the Find Out More line directs you to the entry on PRINTING, where there is a detailed explanation of the colour printing process and how printing presses work.

PRINTING's Find Out More line sends you to CHINA, HISTORY OF, which lists ancient Chinese inventions, including printing.

The entry on the history of China is followed by a collection page showing Chinese jewellery and ornaments.

CONTINENT AND COUNTRY PAGES

The encyclopedia contains entries on all the world's continents and countries, each containing a detailed map. Continent entries focus on the physical geography of the region; country entries provide information about the society and economy of the country. Below is the single-page entry on the Netherlands

The country's flag appears by its name.

Locator map

A small map in the top left-hand corner of the page shows you where the region lies within a continent or in relation to the rest of the world.

Map of Netherlands' position in Europe.

The introduction defines the region and provides an overview to the entry.

Compass points north

Scale bar

Scale bar and compass

Each map has a scale bar that shows how distances on the map relate to actual miles and kilometers. The compass shows you which direction on the map is north (N).

Grid reference

The numbers and letters around the map help you find all the places listed in the index.

The index gives Amsterdam's grid reference as C4, so you can find it on the map by locating the third square along (C) and the fourth square down (4).

Population density

A population density diagram shows how many people there are to every square mile or square kilometer.

The Netherlands is a very densely populated country

KEY TO MAP

International border	Lake	●	Capital city
Disputed border	Seasonal lake	◉	Major town
Road	River	●	Minor town
Railroad	Canal	▲	Spot height (feet)
✈ International airport	Waterfall	▼	Spot depth (feet)

Country file

On each country page there is a fact box containing key details about the country, such as its population, capital city, area, currency, political system, and main language and religion. Other categories of information include:

Literacy – the percentage of people over 15 years old who can read and write.
People per doctor – a rough guide to the availability of medical facilities.
Life expectancy – how long an average person can expect to live.

Climate

A climate diagram gives details of rainfall levels and temperatures in the country, region, or continent.

Average summer temperature — *Average winter temperature*

Single country's average in capital city

Average summer temperature — *Average winter temperature*

Regional average is the average of all capital cities on map

Average rainfall

Average rainfall

Concise explanation of the country's main physical characteristics.

Land use

The land-use diagram tells you how much of the the country's total land area is taken up by, for example, woodland, agriculture, and urban developments such as villages, towns, and cities.

Most of the land in the Netherlands is used for farming.

Urban/rural split

A small diagram shows the percentage of people living in urban (built-up) areas and rural (country) areas.

The majority of people in the Netherlands live in urban areas.

NETHERLANDS

N

ALSO CALLED HOLLAND, the Netherlands straddles the deltas of five major rivers in northwest Europe. The Dutch people say they created their own country because they have reclaimed about one-third of the land from sea or marshland by enclosing the area with earth barriers, or dikes, and draining the water from it. Despite being one of the most densely populated countries in the world, the Netherlands enjoys high living standards. Amsterdam is the official capital, although the government is based at The Hague.

NETHERLANDS FACTS
CAPITAL CITY Amsterdam (seat of government The Hague)
AREA 37,330 sq km (14,413 sq miles)
POPULATION 15,800,000
MAIN LANGUAGE Dutch
MAJOR RELIGION Christian
CURRENCY Euro
PEOPLE PER DOCTOR 385
LIFE EXPECTANCY 78 years
GOVERNMENT Multi-party democracy
ADULT LITERACY 99%

Physical features
The Netherlands is mainly flat, with 27 per cent of the land below sea level, and protected from the sea by natural sand dunes along the coast, and by artificial dikes. Wide sandy plains cover most of the rest of the country, falling into a few, low hills in the eastern and southern parts of the country.

Canals
The Netherlands is a land of canals, which drain the land and serve as waterways for the movement of people and freight. Amsterdam alone has more than 100 canals.

Windmills
For centuries the Dutch landscape was dotted with 10,000 windmills, which powered pumps to drain water from the land. Electric pumps now do this work in the battle to keep the sea back.

37°C (99°F) / -25°C (-13°F)
16°C (62°F) / 2°C (36°F)
580 mm (23 in)

Climate
The Netherlands has mild, rainy winters and cool summers. In winter northerly gales lash the coast, damaging dikes and threatening floods. Frosts sometimes freeze canals.

Forest 3.5% / Farmland 84.5%
Built-up 12%

Land use
Almost one-third of the land has been reclaimed from the sea. These areas are known as polders and are extremely fertile. The country has large natural gas reserves in the north, and there is some offshore oil drilling in the North Sea.

Farming and industry
The Dutch economy is one of the most successful in Europe. Most imports and exports travel through Rotterdam, the world's biggest port. In addition to high-tech sectors such as electronics, telecommunications, and chemicals, the Netherlands has a successful agricultural industry. Productivity is high, and products such as vegetables, cheese, meat, and cut flowers are significant export earners.

Amsterdam
The Dutch capital is built on 70 islands, linked by about 500 bridges, which span its many canals. The best way to get around is by bicycle, and around 750,000 people cycle to school or work each day. Today, Amsterdam is a busy centre for tourism and diamond trading.

One of Amsterdam's many canals

People
The Dutch see their society as the most tolerant in Europe, with relaxed laws on sexuality, drugs, and euthanasia. The country has a long history of welcoming immigrants, often from former Dutch colonies. Most of these people are now assimilated as Dutch citizens. However, members of the small Turkish community, which makes up just one per cent of the population, do not enjoy full citizenship.

Street scene, Amsterdam

466 per sq km (1,206 per sq mile) / 89% Urban / 11% Rural

Dutch tulips

FIND OUT MORE | DAMS | EMPIRES | EUROPE | EUROPE, HISTORY OF | EUROPEAN UNION | FARMING | NETHERLANDS, HISTORY OF | PORTS AND WATERWAYS

601

REFERENCE PAGES

Volume 3 of the Encyclopedia contains an illustrated reference section with essential facts, figures, and statistical data, divided into the five main strands described here.

International world

This strand contains a double-page map showing all the countries of the world, and data on the world's population, economy, and resources.

History

The history strand features a timeline of key historical events, stretching from 40,000 BC to the present day, together with the dates of major wars, revolutions, battles, and great leaders.

Living world

The centrepiece of this strand is a detailed guide to the classification of living things, supported by lists of species in danger, and many other facts about the natural world.

People, arts, and media

This strand is crammed full of information about television, theatre, music, art, philosophy, architecture, literature, dance, and much

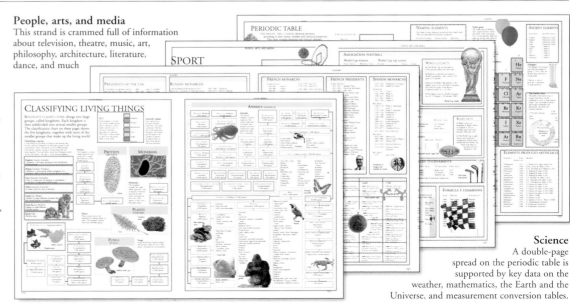

Science

A double-page spread on the periodic table is supported by key data on the weather, mathematics, the Earth and the Universe, and measurement conversion tables.

ABORIGINAL AUSTRALIANS

THE ABORIGINALS settled the Australian continent more than 40,000 years ago. They lived in total isolation from the rest of the world, existing by hunting and gathering. In the 18th century, the Europeans arrived, forcing the Aboriginals off their territories. Today, many feel isolated from white society, but still try to preserve their tribal identity.

Some early peoples crossed by means of a land bridge.

Settlers stayed near the coast and rivers where more food was available.

Aboriginal history

Aboriginals first reached Australia during the last Ice Age. Sea levels were low, and they were able to cross from southeast Asia over land bridges and small stretches of water. When the ice melted and sea levels rose again, the continent was completely cut off. Initially, the settlers clung to the coasts and rivers, but gradually moved across the continent. By the time Europeans arrived, there were about 500 different tribal groups living in Australia.

Ways of life

Traditionally, Aboriginals lived by hunting and gathering. They were nomadic, roaming over large stretches of territory, setting up temporary camps near watering places, and moving on when food supplies were exhausted. They traded with other tribes, exchanging goods such as spears.

Hunting and gathering

Aboriginals lived by hunting animals such as kangaroos, and supplemented their diet with wild plants, nuts, and berries. The hunters used spears with stone blades and wooden boomerangs, a type of missile that flies back to the thrower. Some tribes developed an elaborate sign language, so that they could send silent messages to each other when they were stalking game.

Aboriginal hunters used silent signals to avoid disturbing the game. The sign for kangaroo starts with a closed hand and moves to an open shape.

Corroborees

Aboriginal peoples have handed down stories, songs, and traditions from generation to generation. This culture is kept alive at corroborees, ceremonial dances where tribes gather together to retell the tales of Australia's past through songs, music, and dance.

Dreamtime

The Aboriginals believe that Dreamtime is a period when Ancestral Beings shaped the land, creating all species and human beings. These beings are thought to live on eternally in spirit form. Human beings are believed to be a part of nature, closely associated with all other living things. Images of spirits of Dreamtime, such as Lightning Man, cover sacred cliffs and caves in tribal areas.

Barrkinj – wife of Lightning Man

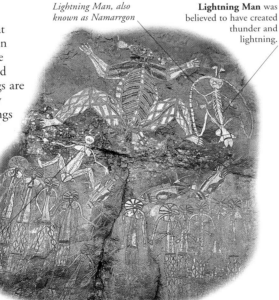

Lightning Man, also known as Namarrgon

Lightning Man was believed to have created thunder and lightning.

Aboriginals today

European colonists arrived in Australia in 1788, and displaced Aboriginal tribes from their territory. Today, there are about 250,000 Aboriginals in Australia, many of whom live in urban areas. Although there is still discrimination, Aboriginals are beginning to benefit from government aid, and to assert their civil rights.

Land rights

When the Europeans arrived in Australia they claimed that the land was *Terra nullius*, that it belonged to no one, and that they were entitled to occupy it. More recently, the Aboriginals have campaigned to regain their lost territory and sacred sites. In 1993, the Australian government reversed its *Terra nullius* policy.

Uluru (Ayers Rock)

Aboriginals believe that the Ancestral Beings created the Australian landscape, and established customs and traditions still followed today. They have left evidence of their presence in the many sacred places, such as Uluru in central Australia. This is revered as a sacred place by the local Aranda people. Once called Ayers Rock by the Australian government, the rock regained its Aboriginal name in 1988.

Education

During early contact with the Europeans, Aboriginal languages were lost or fell into disuse. In 1972, the government established a bilingual education programme. Many children are now taught in their tribal languages before learning English. Books, radio, and television broadcasts are all available in many Aboriginal languages.

FIND OUT MORE

ART, HISTORY OF   AUSTRALASIA AND OCEANIA   AUSTRALIA   AUSTRALIA, HISTORY OF   COOK, JAMES   MYTHS AND LEGENDS   RELIGIONS   SOCIETIES, HUMAN

ACIDS AND ALKALIS

LEMON JUICE AND VINEGAR taste sour because they contain weak acids. An acid is a substance that dissolves in water to form positively charged particles called hydrogen ions (H$^+$). The opposite of an acid is an alkali, which dissolves in water to form negatively charged ions of hydrogen and oxygen, called hydroxide ions (OH$^-$). Alkalis are "anti-acids" because they cancel out acidity. Toothpaste, for example, contains an alkali to cancel out acidity in the mouth that would otherwise damage teeth.

Hydrochloric acid

There is a tremendous fizzing as hydrogen gas is given off.

Zinc replaces the hydrogen in the acid to form zinc chloride.

Zinc nuggets

pH scale

The concentration of hydrogen ions in a solution is known as its pH. Scientists use the pH scale to measure acidity and alkalinity. On the pH scale, a solution with a pH lower than 7 is acidic, and a solution with a pH greater than 7 is alkaline. Water is neutral, with a pH of 7. A solution's pH can be tested with universal indicator solution or paper, which changes colour in acids and alkalis.

Universal indicator pH colour chart

Universal indicator paper

1 Strong acids
7 Neutral
14 Strong alkalis

Digestive juices: pH 1

Hydrochloric acid (pH 1)

Lemon juice: pH 3

Acid rain: pH 5

Vinegar (pH 4)

Human blood: pH 7.4

Liquid soap (pH 8–9)

Oven cleaner: pH 13

Household cleaner (pH 10)

Strong acids

The more hydrogen ions an acid forms in water, the stronger it is, and the lower its pH. Strong acids, such as sulphuric acid and nitric acid, are very dangerous and must be handled carefully.

Sulphuric acid

Carbon

Sugar

Sulphuric acid
Concentrated sulphuric acid will dehydrate (remove water from) any substance with which it comes into contact. For example, the acid dehydrates sugar, a carbohydrate, to leave a mass of smouldering black carbon.

Cork

Nitrogen dioxide gas and smoke are given off as acid reacts with cork.

Nitric acid

Nitric acid
Organic matter, such as paper, cork, rubber, fabric, and skin, is rapidly decomposed by nitric acid. The acid is so corrosive because it oxidizes (supplies oxygen to) any material with which it comes into contact.

Svante Arrhenius
Swedish scientist Svante Arrhenius (1859–1927) won acclaim for his research into how compounds form ions in solution. This work led him to realize that it is hydrogen ions that give acids their special properties.

Acids and metals

Even the weakest acids cannot be stored in metal containers because acids are corrosive to most metals. When an acid reacts with a metal, hydrogen gas is given off and the metal dissolves in the acid to form a compound called a salt. The reaction is very violent with metals such as potassium and sodium, and quite vigorous with metals such as magnesium and zinc.

Salts
When the hydrogen in an acid is replaced by a metal during a chemical reaction, a neutral compound called a salt is formed. For example, when copper reacts with nitric acid, the copper takes the place of the hydrogen to make the salt copper nitrate. Like other metals, copper forms a variety of salts when mixed with different acids. Most salts are crystals, and many are coloured. Some salts, such as sodium chloride (common salt), occur naturally.

Copper nitrate

Nitric acid

Sulphuric acid

Hydrochloric acid

Copper turnings

Copper sulphate

Copper chloride

Acid industry

Acids are widely used in industry because they react so readily with other materials. For example, sulphuric acid is used in the production of dyes and pigments, artificial fibres, plastics, soaps, and explosives. The acid is made by sulphur and oxygen reacting together.

Sulphuric acid chemical plant

Acid rain
Burning fossil fuels to produce energy for use at home and in industry releases polluting gases into the air. The gases dissolve in water in the clouds to form nitric acid and sulphuric acid. This water falls as acid rain, which erodes stone buildings and statues, kills trees and aquatic life, and reduces the soil's fertility.

Bases and alkalis

The acidity of vinegar (ethanoic acid) can be neutralized, or cancelled out, by adding chalk (calcium carbonate). Any substance that neutralizes acidity, such as chalk, is called a base. An alkali is a base that dissolves in water. An alkali's strength is measured by the number of hydroxide ions it forms in water. Strong alkalis, such as sodium hydroxide, are just as corrosive as strong acids.

Chalk and vinegar react together and release carbon dioxide gas.

The product of the reaction is a salt called calcium ethanoate.

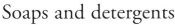

The mixture spills out of the flask.

Testing the mixture with universal indicator solution proves that it is now neutral – the acidity has been cancelled out.

Soaps and detergents

Alkalis are good at dissolving oil and grease, so they are widely used in the manufacture of soaps and detergents. Most dirt is bound to skin, clothes, or eating utensils by grease. The grease makes it difficult to remove the dirt with water alone, because water and grease do not mix. A soap or detergent, such as washing-up liquid, breaks the grease up into tiny drops and allows the water to wash away the dirt.

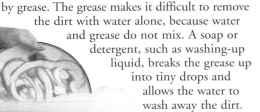

Once the washing-up liquid has broken down the grease, the water can wet the plate and dissolve the rest of the dirt.

Oil slicks

Accidents with oil tankers at sea can create huge oil slicks (spillages) on the water's surface. Detergents called dispersants are used to break up the oil and reduce environmental damage. Wildlife experts also use detergents, such as washing-up liquid, to clean the feathers of oil-coated seabirds. If the birds' feathers – which usually keep them warm and dry – become clogged with oil, the birds may lose their buoyancy and drown, or die of exposure to the cold.

Batteries

Acids, alkalis, and salts are electrolytes, meaning that they conduct electricity when in solution. Batteries consist of an electrolyte – usually in the form of a moist paste or liquid – between two rods or plates called electrodes. The most common battery is the dry cell, which uses the salt ammonium chloride as an electrolyte. Long-life batteries contain alkaline electrolytes, such as potassium hydroxide; car batteries have electrolytes of sulphuric acid.

Car battery

Long-life battery

Dry cell

Alkali industry

The main raw material in the alkali industry is brine (salt water). Sodium hydroxide, which is used to make soaps and paper, is produced from brine by electrolysis (passing electricity through it). Brine will also absorb carbon dioxide to make sodium carbonate, which is used in textile treatment, photography, and glass making.

Electrolysis of brine to make sodium hydroxide

Neutralizing acids

An alkali and an acid react together to give a neutral salt. In addition, hydroxide ions (OH^-) in the alkali combine with the acid's hydrogen ions (H^+) to produce water (H_2O). In daily life, problems of unwanted acidity are solved by adding an alkali of the appropriate strength.

Soil acidity

The pH of soil varies from area to area. Few crops grow well in highly acidic soil, because the acid dissolves vital minerals that the plants need for healthy growth and allows them to be washed away. Farmers treat acidic soil by spreading lime (calcium oxide) over their fields. This is a cheaply produced alkali made from limestone. It neutralizes the acid in the soil, making it more fertile.

Farmer liming acidic soil

Curing indigestion

The human stomach uses hydrochloric acid to break down food. Some foods cause your stomach to produce so much acid that it gives you discomfort. Stomach powders or indigestion tablets can cure this. They contain weak alkalis that neutralize the acidity, but do not harm your stomach, or react too vigorously with the acid.

Stomach powder fizzes as it reacts with lemon juice (citric acid).

Bee and wasp stings

A bee sting is painful because it is acidic. Treating the sting with a weak alkali, such as soap or bicarbonate of soda, relieves the pain by neutralizing the acid. In contrast, a wasp sting is alkaline, so it can be neutralized by a weak acid, such as vinegar or lemon juice.

Wasp

Bee

Fritz Haber

In 1908, the German chemist Fritz Haber (1868–1934) developed a process for making the alkali ammonia, which is used to make fertilizers and explosives. The Haber process involves reacting nitrogen from the air with hydrogen at high pressure and temperature. Haber later devised a way of making nitric acid by heating ammonia in air.

Timeline

c.600 BC The Phoenicians use alkaline wood ash to make soap.

11th century AD Arab chemists make sulphuric, nitric, and hydrochloric acids.

1780s World's first sulphuric acid factory opens in France.

1865 Ernest Solvay, a Belgian chemist, develops the first commercially successful process for making the alkali, sodium carbonate, on a large scale.

Sodium carbonate

1887 Svante Arrhenius proposes that it is hydrogen ions that give acids their special properties.

1908 Fritz Haber invents a process for making ammonia.

1909 The Danish chemist Søren Sørensen (1868–1939) devises the pH scale.

FIND OUT MORE   ATOMS AND MOLECULES   BEES AND WASPS   CHEMISTRY   DIGESTION   ELECTRICITY   MIXTURES AND COMPOUNDS   POLLUTION   ROCKETS   SOIL

A

ADVERTISING AND MARKETING

WHEN A COMPANY WISHES TO SELL or improve the sales of its products or services, it may decide to advertise. Newspapers and magazines carry advertisements, as do billboards, television, and radio. Marketing is the wider process of creating a product or service, advertising it, and selling it. Advertising and marketing are vast industries that affect all our lives.

Copy line gives us product information. Here, the tyre-making company Pirelli uses humour and an eye-catching image to advertise its tyres' road-holding ability.

Well-known athlete

The striking image of an athlete in high heels grabs our attention.

POWER IS NOTHING WITHOUT CONTROL.

Product name

How advertising works

Advertisements use humour and strong images to get our attention. Short, memorable catchphrases called slogans become associated with the product. An advertising campaign often combines posters and television advertisements so that repetition ensures people remember the product.

Image
Advertisers try to create a product image that will appeal to particular customers. An advertisement for perfume, for example, may project an image of beauty and sophistication. Well-known personalities may be shown endorsing a product to strengthen its image.

Public relations
Many companies use public relations, or PR, to improve their standing with the people who buy their products. The two main branches of PR are research and communication. Research tries to find out what people think about the company and its products. Companies communicate with people through press coverage, advertising, and sponsorship.

Marketing

A company's marketing strategy includes market research, product development, publicity, advertising, and point of sale displays. The marketing department researches the products people want, and works with other departments to make sure that products meet the customer's needs and expectations.

Pepsi-Cola painted Concorde blue to gain publicity.

Market research
The purpose of market research is to find out what sort of people are likely to buy a product, and what will make them buy one product rather than another. Researchers get this information from interviews, questionnaires, and government statistics.

Point of sale
Shops use posters and display units to encourage people to buy products. Point of sale displays try to catch the customer's eye where he or she can buy the product immediately. Shop window displays aim to draw customers into a shop.

Advertising agencies

Companies use advertising agencies to advise them on their advertising strategy. Advertising agencies conduct market research, plan which forms of media the client's advertisements should appear in, and finally prepare the client's advertisements.

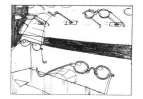

Storyboards
The first stage of producing a television advertisement is to present a storyboard of ideas to the client, showing how the final advertisement will look. A storyboard looks rather like a comic strip, with a series of pictures showing how the action will run. If the client approves the storyboard, production can go ahead.

The film is combined with a sound track, and then edited.

Production
The advertising agency hires a production team to film the advertisement. This will include a producer, who supervises the rehearsal schedule, and a director, who directs the action when the commercial is being filmed. Once the film has been shot, a sound track is added. The sound track may be a voice-over repeating the product name and a catchy tune called a jingle.

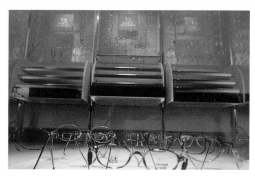

Advertisement
Once the advertisement has been completed, it is shown to the client. If the client approves the film, it is taken to the television stations to be aired. Television advertising is by far the most expensive form of advertising, but it is the most effective since it reaches people in their own homes.

FIND OUT MORE   DESIGN   FILMS AND FILM-MAKING   MONEY   SHOPS   TELEVISION   TRADE AND INDUSTRY

AFRICA

THE SECOND LARGEST CONTINENT after Asia, Africa is dominated in the north by the vast Sahara Desert and in the east by the Great Rift Valley. A belt of rainforest lies along the Equator, and grasslands provide grazing for herds of wild animals. Africa is home to many different peoples, each with their own distinctive languages and customs. Islam and Christianity are widespread, but many Africans adhere to their own traditional beliefs.

Physical features

Most of Africa is a high plateau covered with deserts, lush rainforests, and dry grasslands. It is crossed by rivers, which bring water to dry regions and provide communications. Although they lie on the Equator, the high peaks in the east are snow-capped all year. Africa has several volcanoes.

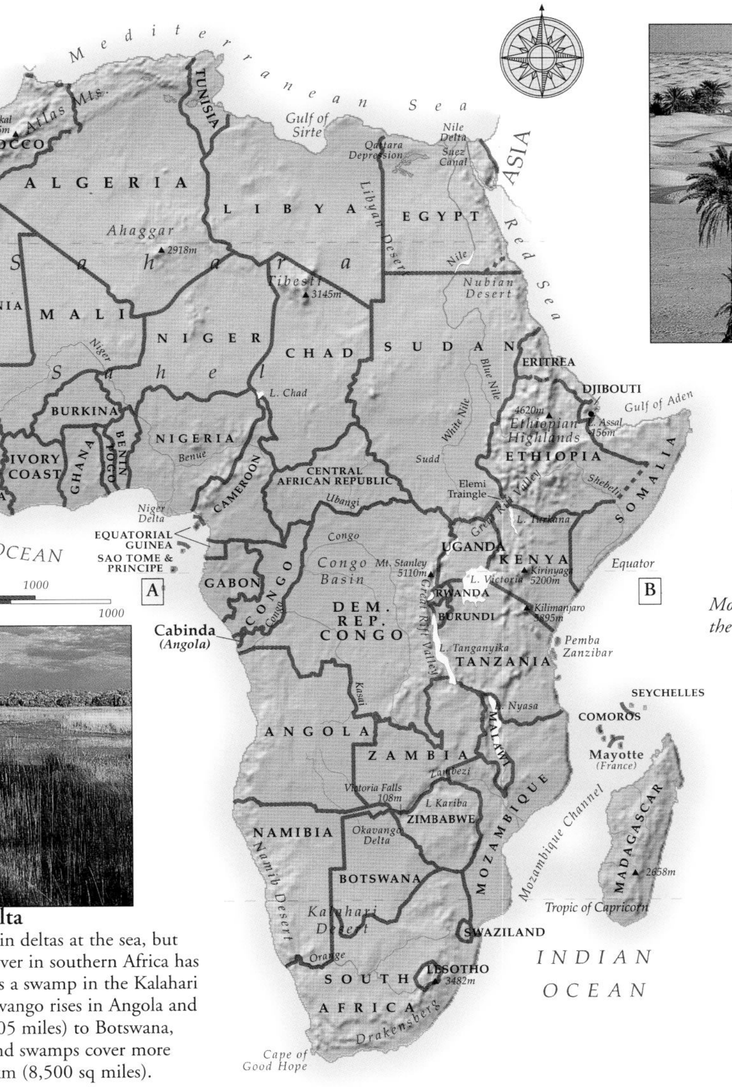

Sahara

The world's largest desert, the Sahara, covers much of northwestern Africa. It has an area of 9,065,000 sq km (3,263,400 sq miles) and is rapidly expanding as land at its edges is overgrazed. With less than 100 mm (4 in) of rainfall every year and daytime temperatures of up to 50°C (122°F), only a few specially adapted plants and animals survive here.

River Nile

The Nile is the world's longest river. From its source in Lake Victoria, it flows 6,695 km (4,160 miles) north through Uganda, Sudan, and Egypt to the Mediterranean Sea. Africa's third longest river, the Niger, flows 4,180 km (2,597 miles) in a big loop through western Africa, ending in Nigeria in a delta bigger than that of the Nile.

River Nile at Aswan in Egypt

Great Rift Valley

The mountains of Ethiopia are divided by the Great Rift Valley that stretches 6,000 km (3,750 miles) north from Mozambique, through east Africa and the Red Sea, into Syria. The valley is formed by massive cracks in the Earth's crust. It is up to 90 km (55 miles) wide, and in millions of years will eventually divide the African continent.

Mountains rise from the Great Rift Valley.

Simen Mountains, Ethiopia

Okavango Delta

Many rivers end in deltas at the sea, but the Okavango River in southern Africa has a delta that forms a swamp in the Kalahari Desert. The Okavango rises in Angola and flows 974 km (605 miles) to Botswana, where its delta and swamps cover more than 22,000 sq km (8,500 sq miles).

AFRICA FACTS

AREA	30,335,000 sq km (11,712,434 sq miles)
POPULATION	811,600,000
NUMBER OF COUNTRIES	53
BIGGEST COUNTRY	Sudan
SMALLEST COUNTRY	Seychelles
HIGHEST POINT	Kilimanjaro (Tanzania) 5,895 m (19,341 ft)
LONGEST RIVER	Nile (Uganda/Sudan/Egypt) 6,695 km (4,160 miles)
BIGGEST LAKE	Lake Victoria (East Africa) 68,880 sq km (26,560 sq miles)

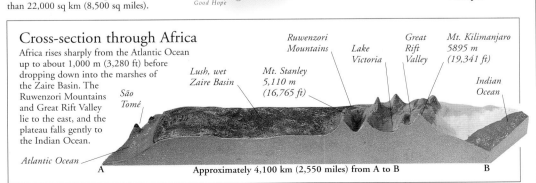

Cross-section through Africa

Africa rises sharply from the Atlantic Ocean up to about 1,000 m (3,280 ft) before dropping down into the marshes of the Zaire Basin. The Ruwenzori Mountains and Great Rift Valley lie to the east, and the plateau falls gently to the Indian Ocean.

Ruwenzori Mountains

Lake Victoria

Great Rift Valley

Mt. Kilimanjaro 5895 m (19,341 ft)

Lush, wet Zaire Basin

Mt. Stanley 5,110 m (16,765 ft)

Indian Ocean

São Tomé

Atlantic Ocean

A — Approximately 4,100 km (2,550 miles) from A to B — B

15

Climatic zones

Although most of Africa is warm or hot all year round, the climate varies greatly because of the wide range of landscapes. Parts of the north coast have hot, dry summers and cooler, moist winters. Desert regions have cold nights, scorching hot days, and almost no rain at all. On the Equator the climate is hot and humid, with high rainfall. Mountain regions have warm summers and cool winters.

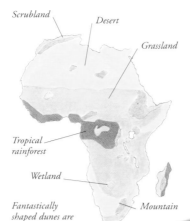

Scrubland • Desert • Grassland • Tropical rainforest • Wetland • Mountain

Fantastically shaped dunes are formed by strong desert winds.

Scrubland

Much of the northern coast of Africa has a warm Mediterranean climate. Coastal cliffs and hills are covered in sparse, low-growing, often fragrant plants and shrubs that are able to thrive in the poor, stony soils. Many of the plants have thorns and small, leathery leaves to prevent them from drying out in the fierce heat of the sun and frequent sea breezes.

Baie de Souhalias, Algeria

Evergreen plants are able to retain their moisture in the heat.

Deserts

About 40 per cent of Africa is desert. The Erg of Bilma in Niger is part of the vast Sahara. In Arabic, *erg* means a sandy expanse. The sand is blown by the wind into ripples and into huge dunes, some of which may be nearly 200 m (650 ft) high. Two other main desert areas are the Kalahari and the Namib, both in southern Africa.

Savannah

About 40 per cent of Africa is covered with savannah, which is the name given to grassland with scattered trees and shrubs. This type of land forms a wide loop around the Zaire (Congo) Basin. Vast herds of grazing animals, such as antelopes and zebras, move around the savannah seeking fresh grass to eat.

Masai Mara, Kenya

Occasional stunted trees offer animals some protection from the harsh sun.

Low shrubs cover some of the mountains' lower slopes and foothills.

Tropical rainforest

Dense, tropical rainforest covers less than 20 per cent of Africa. The most extensive areas lie close to the Equator in West Africa and in Central Africa's Zaire (Congo) Basin. Thousands of species of tree flourish in the hot, humid climate, which produces rain all year round. However, large-scale felling of trees for timber hardwoods, such as teak and mahogany, threatens to destroy this environment.

Many streams and rivers cross the rainforest.

Mahogany leaf

Mountain

Africa's highest ranges include the Drakensberg, in southeast Africa, which runs for about 1,130 km (70 miles) through South Africa and Lesotho and forms part of the rim of the great South African Plateau. The highest point is Thabana Ntlenyana at 3,482 m (11,424 ft). Even higher mountain ranges are the Atlas range in Morocco, and the Ruwenzori on the border between Uganda and Congo (Zaire).

People

One in eight of the world's people lives in Africa, mostly along the north and west coasts, and in the fertile river valleys. Although traditionally people live in small villages, a growing number are moving to towns and cities to look for work. Birth rates in many countries are high and families are large. About half the population is under 15 years old.

Ghanaian girls • Tanzanian girl • Egyptian boy

Resources

Africa has many resources, but they are unevenly distributed. Libya and Nigeria are leading oil producers, southern Africa is rich in gold and diamonds, and Zambia is a leading copper producer. Tropical forests yield valuable timber but are being felled at an alarming rate. Africa is a leading producer of cocoa beans, cassava, bananas, coffee, and tea.

Oil

Cocoa beans and pod

Diamond

FIND OUT MORE — AFRICA, HISTORY OF • AFRICAN WILDLIFE • CLIMATES • CONTINENTS • DESERTS • FORESTS • GRASSLAND WILDLIFE • MOUNTAINS AND VALLEYS • OIL • RAINFOREST WILDLIFE

AFRICA, HISTORY OF

CIVILIZATION IN AFRICA BEGAN TO appear more than 5,000 years ago with the rise of ancient Egypt. From about 2,500 years ago in sub-Saharan Africa, many other different kingdoms also developed. The Sahara acted as a barrier to keep this area separate from the rest of the world until the arrival of Arab traders in the 8th century. From the 15th century, the arrival of Europeans, the subsequent slave trade, and European imperialism had a profound effect on the continent. Since the 1950s, all African nations have reclaimed independence, although modern Africa continues to struggle with its post-colonial legacy and environmental problems.

Ancient empires

North Africa was in a good position to trade with western Asia. This caused rich empires to develop, including Meroë (modern Sudan, c.600 BC–AD 350), and Aksum (a trading state in northern Ethiopia, c.100 BC–AD 1000). The ancient empire of Ghana (in West Africa, c.500–1300) developed for similar reasons.

Meroë
From the city of Meroë, the Kushites controlled trade in the Red Sea and the Nile River from 600 BC. They exported luxury goods, such as ostrich feathers and leopard skins, and built fine temples and flat-topped pyramids over the graves of their dead.

Ruined temple, Meroë

Ghana
Ghana (then located on the borders of modern Mali and Mauritania) was one of Africa's most important empires. It controlled the trans-Saharan trade in gold, and surviving gold artefacts show the incredible wealth of this kingdom. Ghana's kings wore gold jewellery, and gold-embroidered clothes and turbans.

Heads of gold, often of royalty, played an important part in rituals.

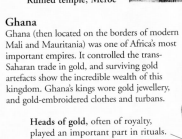

Carving was made of wood and coated with gold.

Figures were attached to royal thrones.

Bird ornament

Rings were often decorated with flowers.

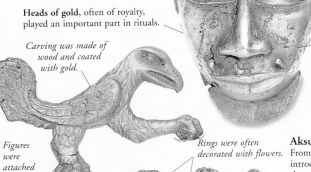

Finger rings

Head weighs 1.5 kg (3 lbs).

Stela, Aksum

Aksum
From c.300, Christianity was introduced to Aksum, which under the reign of King Ezana became known as a holy city. During this period, Aksum took over the empire based at Meroë. Aksum's people built tall, stone stelae (monuments) to mark the tombs of dead kings.

Early inhabitants

Humans have inhabited Africa for 4 million years. The Sahara was once a fertile land rich in plants and animals. But thousands of years ago, it dried up, and people moved south to the savannah to farm there.

Rock paintings
Rock and bone pictures often depicted everyday events, such as dancing, hunting animals, and fishing. Painters used animal fat coloured with vegetable dyes.

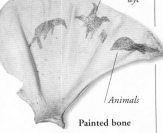

Vegetable dye

Animals

Painted bone

Nok culture
The earliest evidence of Iron Age settlement is called the Nok culture (500 BC–AD 200), which existed in what is now central Nigeria. Nok people lived in farming communities. They made iron weapons and tools for farming, and also produced fine terracotta sculptures.

Terracotta head, Nok culture

Spread of religions

From the 8th century, trade, conquests, and colonialism spread religions such as Islam in Africa. In North Africa, Islam completely replaced traditional religions, which often included the worship of ancestors.

Festival mask

Ancestor worship
In many parts of Africa, communities had sacred shrines where they placed offerings for the spirits of their dead ancestors. Today, during certain annual festivals, members of the community wear special masks, sing, dance, and tell stories in honour of their ancestors.

Islam
By c.800, Middle Eastern Arabs had taken Islam to North Africa. From the 11th century, trade helped spread Islam across the Sahara into West Africa and up the River Nile into Sudan.

Ait Benhaddou, Morocco

Slave trade
By the 1470s, the Portuguese were trading copper, brass, gold, and slaves with Benin in West Africa. In the 1480s, the Portuguese arrived in the islands of Principe and São Tomé in the Gulf of Guinea, just off the west African coast. They established sugar plantations, and forced African captives (mainly kidnapped in Senegal and Gambia) to work as slaves on the plantations. This was the beginning of European domination in Africa.

Plaque showing Portuguese soldier, 1500s

A

Colonialism

During the 1800s, Europeans colonized areas in Africa, introducing Christianity, and taking economic control. They used African workers to grow or mine precious raw materials, but sent the materials to be manufactured in Europe and America – where profits stayed. During this period, slavery was at its height and many Africans were kidnapped to work in the Americas.

African Diaspora

The slave trade scattered more than 20 million Africans throughout the Americas and Europe, undermining African culture in the process. Over the centuries, the dispersed descendents of these slaves became known as the African Diaspora.

African carving of a European

Christianity

Europe sent missionaries to Africa to set up schools and churches, and to convert Africans to Christianity. They also tried to abolish African traditional religions, often punishing those who still practised them.

Traditional witch doctors

Voodoo voice disguiser

Voodoo

In 19th-century Caribbean colonies, traditional ancestor worship combined with Christianity to produce a religion called voodoo.

Scramble for Africa

In 1884, European leaders decided that their countries could claim African territories as colonies when occupied by Europeans. This started a scramble to the interior in search of new lands. By 1902, all of Africa was colonized, except Liberia and Ethiopia.

Carving of Queen Victoria

French
British
German
Portuguese
Belgium
Spanish
Italian
Anglo-Egyptian

Morocco Tunisia
Algeria Libya
Egypt
Liberia Nigeria British Somaliland
Sierra Leone Ethiopia
British East Africa (Kenya)
Angola

World Wars I and II

Although both world wars were European, thousands of Africans lost their lives as colonial rulers forced them to join the army. One cause of World War I was German resentment against other European countries during colonization. In World War II, North Africa became a battleground, as German and Italian forces invaded British- and French-ruled territories.

Troops at El Alamein, Egypt

World War I

At the time World War I broke out in 1914, the Ottoman Empire controlled North Africa. The Egyptians colluded with the British to overthrow Turkish rule, and were helped from 1916 to 1918 by the eccentric soldier and author Thomas Edward Lawrence (1888–1935), who became famous as Lawrence of Arabia. After the war, Egypt became a British protectorate but signed a treaty for independence in 1922.

El Alamein

In 1941, Italian and German forces invaded North African territories held by the British. The British recruited soldiers from their colonies of Nigeria, Ghana, and Sierra Leone to join the fight. In 1942, the British defeated the Germans at the historic battle of El Alamein. This battle was a turning point in the war.

Herero and Nama tribes fight German colonialists, Namibia, 1904

African resistance

Africans strenuously resisted colonialism. The Ethiopians fought to stay independent and won (1896); Zimbabwe and Sudan rebelled against the British (1896 and 1920); tribes in Angola tried to overthrow the Portuguese (1902); in Namibia and Tanzania, thousands were killed in uprisings against the Germans (1904–1908); and in Nigeria, tribes resisted the French rule of surrounding areas (1920s).

TE Lawrence

African Front

Operation Torch

In 1942, American and British soldiers landed in Morocco and Algeria in an invasion called Operation Torch. Joined by the French, the Allies attacked the German and Italian armies, forcing them into Tunisia. After a bloody battle, Germany's Afrika Korps surrendered. The war on African soil was over by May 1943.

Haile Selassie

Emperor Haile Selassie of Ethiopia (r.1930–74) led his troops against the Italian invasion of 1935. The Italians forced the emperor into exile in 1936, but he returned in 1941. Haile Selassie instituted reforms, suppressed slavery, and worked with the Organization of African Unity. In 1974, the army overthrew the emperor, installed military rule, and later had him executed.

A

Independence

After World War II, many Africans wanted to end colonial rule, and govern their own countries. Colonial powers such as France, Portugal, and Britain fought to prevent this, and there were bloody wars of independence in Algeria, Mozambique, Angola, and Zimbabwe. By the late 1960s most African countries had gained independence, but political and economic problems remained.

Returning refugees, Angola

Ghanaian
Independence
Day stamps

Gold Coast
One of the first colonies to become independent was the former British colony of the Gold Coast. After World War II, anti-colonial feeling had intensified, and, in 1957, the state of Ghana (which was named after a powerful West African medieval empire) became independent. A leading nationalist, Kwame Nkrumah (1909–72) became the new country's first prime minister. In 1960, Nkrumah declared Ghana a republic and himself president for life. He became increasingly dictatorial, while drawing ever further away from the west. In 1966, a police-military coup overthrew Nkrumah.

OAU member states now number 50.

OAU
summit, Tunisia

Organization of African Unity
In 1963, the heads of 30 independent African states met to form the OAU (Organization of African Unity). Its aim was to promote political and economic co-operation between the states, and help colonies achieve independence.

Angola War
In 1961, Angola's people rose in revolt against the Portuguese colonial government. The Portuguese army crushed the rebels, who fled into exile in Zaire. While in exile, the rebels formed liberation movements, and waged guerrilla warfare in Angola. In 1974, the liberation forces staged a military uprising, and overthrew the Portuguese, who finally granted independence in 1975. After independence, a bitter civil war erupted between two political groups, both of whom wanted to govern Angola. One side was backed by South African troops, the other by Russian troops. The Angolan factions agreed to a ceasefire in 1994.

A taxi stand for whites, South Africa, 1967

Apartheid
By the 1980s, only South Africa was still trying to retain white-minority power. The white government had passed the Apartheid (separateness) Policy in 1948, which classified people according to race. Under apartheid, those classified as Black, Coloured, or Asian had few rights. Apartheid was abolished in 1994.

Electronics technician

Modern Africa

Mineral-rich Africa has a thriving mining industry. More recently, new African electronics plants are specializing in the assembly of imported electronic components.

Game park, Kenya

Tourism
A century ago, East African governments established game reserves and parks to protect wildlife from hunters. Today, tourists pay to stay in the parks and go on safari to see the wild animals. Kenya now makes more money from tourism than from any other source.

Village co-operatives
Agricultural workers (mainly women) set up village co-operatives to grow food crops, which they sell at the local market. This reverses a situation that existed under colonial governments, when small-scale farmers were forced to grow cash crops (coffee, groundnuts, cocoa, and cotton) to sell to large European companies. The farmers could not grow food crops for themselves, and had to buy expensive imports, such as rice.

Women's agricultural
co-operative, Niger

Women are the main agricultural workers.

Food crops

Deforestation, Somalia

Environmental devastation
In semi-arid areas of Africa, such as Somalia, land is gradually turning into desert. Since the 1950s, there has been a fall in the average annual rainfall, and much of the land has become very dry. The people have often over-used the land for cash crops, and cut down the trees for firewood.

Ken Saro-Wiwa
Ken Saro-Wiwa (1941–1995), a human rights campaigner, was hanged along with eight others by Nigeria's military government. His "crime" was to speak out against the pollution of tribal lands by government-backed international oil companies.

Timeline
African carving

2500 BC Climatic changes in the Sahara region force people to move southward.

c.600 BC Kushite people of Sudan expand and base their capital at Meroë.

c.AD 320–25 King Ezama of Aksum becomes Christian.

500–1300
The kingdom of Ghana controls trans-Saharan trade.

641 Arabs conquer Egypt, and convert it to Islam.

600s The empire based at Aksum begins to decline.

1497 Portuguese explorers land on east coast, after sailing around Africa.

1900 Most of the Sahara region comes under French colonial rule.

1940 Italian forces invade North Africa; Germans follow one year later.

1945 League of Arab States is founded; it includes eight African nations.

1973–75 Horn of Africa suffers a severe drought.

1994–95 In Rwanda 800,000 Hutus are massacred by Tutsis; millions flee the country.

FIND OUT MORE   BENIN EMPIRE   GREAT ZIMBABWE   MALI EMPIRE   MANDELA, NELSON   RELIGIONS   SLAVERY   SONGHAI EMPIRE   SOUTH AFRICA, HISTORY OF

AFRICA, CENTRAL

THE EQUATOR RUNS THROUGH Central Africa, affecting not only climate but also ways of life. There are ten countries. All were European colonies with a history of a cruel slave trade. Although these countries were all independent by the end of the 1960s, they have experienced mixed fortunes. Cameroon is stable, while Democratic Republic of the Congo and the Central African Republic, have suffered dictatorships. Most Central Africans live by farming.

Physical features

The landscape varies according to its distance from the Equator. Much of the region is rolling hills and valleys, with craggy mountains in the north and east. The arid Sahara desert and Sahel cover the extreme north. Farther south, is the vast equatorial basin of the River Congo, surrounded by some unspoilt tropical rainforest.

Dry woodland
Tropical rainforests give way to woodland, where the climate is much drier. Acacia and baobab trees grow in this region. The baobabs have very thick trunks that can hold water to feed themselves. Some baobabs on Cameroon's central plateau live for 1,000 years.

Tibesti
The dramatic cliffs of the volcanic Tibesti Mountains dominate the border between Chad and Libya, in the Sahara Desert. At 3,415 m (11,204 ft) above sea-level, Emi Koussi is the highest peak.

River Congo
One of the longest rivers in the world, the Congo, formerly the Zaire, flows in a great curve for 4,666 km (2,900 miles), crossing the Equator twice. It drains an area of about 3,630,000 sq km (1,400,000 sq miles).

Equatorial rainforest
The hot, humid basin of the River Congo is Africa's largest remaining region of tropical rainforest. Competing for light, a wide variety of trees grow tall, forming a protective canopy that teems with plant and animal life.

Regional climate
The north of the region, the Sahara and Sahel area, is a broad band of dry, dusty land that is starved of rain. By contrast, in the steamy equatorial forests more than 38 mm (1.5 in) of rain falls every day in places. The south experiences the monsoon season between May and October.

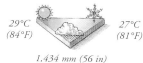

29°C (84°F)   27°C (81°F)

1,434 mm (56 in)

Ethnic diversity

There are hundreds of different peoples in Central Africa, each with their own customs and languages. Large groups include the Kongo and Luba, and there are several pygmy groups including the Twa, BaKa, and Mbuti, who live in clearings deep in the rainforests. A growing number of people are moving to towns to escape war, drought, or famine, and because larger centres offer more jobs and food.

Village chief, Brazzaville, Congo

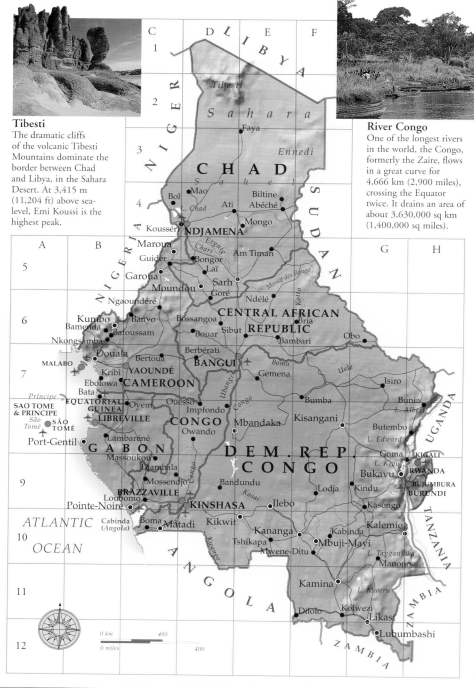

Chad

The land-locked republic of Chad is one of the world's poorest countries. Nearly half of the land is desert or lies in the Sahel, where rainfall is erratic. More than half of the people work on farmland near the Chari river in the south, but lack of food is still a problem. Chad has some valuable mineral deposits, but they are unexploited.

Muslim nomads
More than 100,000 nomadic Muslims live in the desert and northern Sahel regions of Chad. They include the Kanimbo people, who are related to the Arabs and Berbers of North Africa. Every day, Kanimbo women must walk long distances in the heat to fetch water for their families.

Camels
One of the only ways to cross the vast Sahara Desert is by camel. Camels are used as pack animals to transport forest products and minerals from Lake Chad, as well as for farming, pumping water, and carrying people. Herders value their milk, meat, and hides.

Dried gourds used as bowls for making butter.

Fulani
Throughout Africa a nomadic group called the Fulani herd cattle and roam wherever there is grazing land. They drink the cows' milk and use it to make butter and cheese. Bottle-shaped gourds, a type of fruit, are dried and decorated for use as water carriers and bowls.

CHAD FACTS
CAPITAL CITY	N'Djamena
AREA	1,284,000 sq km (495,752 sq miles)
POPULATION	8,100,000
MAIN LANGUAGES	French, Arabic, Sara
MAJOR RELIGIONS	Muslim, Christian, traditional beliefs
CURRENCY	CFA franc

Cameroon

On Africa's west coast, Cameroon was once a colony divided between the French and the British. The two parts gained independence and became a united country in 1961. Despite initial troubles, Cameroon now has one of the most successful economies in Africa, exporting oil, bauxite, and a range of natural products, including cocoa, coffee, and rubber. The country has a diverse culture with more than 230 ethnic groups.

Timber
Like many other African countries, Cameroon sells hardwood logs, including mahogany, ebony, and teak from its rainforests to earn foreign currency. Although the trade represents one tenth of the country's total exports, it poses a serious threat to the future of the forests.

CAMEROON FACTS
CAPITAL CITY	Yaoundé
AREA	475,400 sq km (183,567 sq miles)
POPULATION	15,200,000
MAIN LANGUAGES	French, English, Fang, Duala, Fulani
MAJOR RELIGIONS	Traditional beliefs, Christian, Muslim
CURRENCY	CFA franc

Dried gourds amplify sounds made by strings.

Football
One of Cameroon's leading amateur sports, football is widely enjoyed and people play it whenever they have time. Games draw large crowds of spectators. Cameroon's national football team was acclaimed as one of the best in Africa, after displaying its skills in the 1990 World Cup.

Music
Makossa is a popular style of African folk music that originated in Cameroon. It is played on traditional instruments, including this one, known as a *mvet*. It is made using a wooden stick, horsehair strings, and hollowed-out gourds. *Mvet* players are specially trained and highly regarded in the community.

Several strings are stretched along the stick and plucked to make a range of sounds.

Central African Republic

Lying in the very heart of Africa, the Central African Republic, or CAR, has a complicated history. Drought and 13 years of repressive government have made the CAR one of the poorest nations in the world. Only two per cent of the people live in the semi-arid north, and the majority are clustered in villages in the southern rainforests.

Bantu woman

Cotton
Coffee and cotton together form about 13 per cent of the country's exports. Grown on large plantations, all parts of the cotton plant are used. The fibre, known as a boll, is spun into yarn to make fabric. The seed's oil forms the base of many foods, whilst the plant's stalks and leaves are ploughed back into the soil to fertilize it.

CENTRAL AFRICAN REPUBLIC FACTS
CAPITAL CITY	Bangui
AREA	622,984 sq km (240,534 sq miles)
POPULATION	3,800,000
MAIN LANGUAGES	French, Sango, Zande, Banda, Sara, Arabic
MAJOR RELIGIONS	Traditional beliefs, Christian, Muslim
CURRENCY	CFA franc

After drying in the sun, cotton bolls are sorted by hand.

Millet

Cassava

People
Seven major Bantu language groups and many smaller ones make up the population of the CAR. Several thousand hunter-gatherers live in the rainforests in harmony with nature. They survive by eating forest fruits and build their homes from banana leaves.

Food
The people of the CAR grow nearly all their own food by subsistence farming. Root crops, such as cassava, yams, and vegetables, are cultivated alongside grains including millet, maize, and sorghum. Fish from the CAR's rivers, including the Chari and Ubangi, is a vital source of protein.

A

Congo

The Republic of Congo was a French territory until 1960. It is a hot, humid land, and its densely forested north has few inhabitants. Nearly half the country's people are members of the Kongo group; the rest include Batéké, M'Bochi, and Sangha. The mineral and timber industries have made Congo wealthy, but many people are still subsistence farmers, growing barely enough food to survive.

Animal skin is stretched across the drum.

Each cocoa pod contains about 30 beans, for use in chocolate and cosmetics.

Coffee beans

Crops
About 50 per cent of the work-force are farmers who grow cassava, maize, rice, peanuts, and fruit to feed their families. Much food is imported. The steady export of coffee and cocoa beans has saved Congo from economic problems.

Cocoa pods

Drum
An essential part of African life, drums are used for signalling as well as for music. Most drums are intricately carved out of a solid piece of wood and can be decorated with different woods and hides. Drums are made in all shapes and sizes – this one is almost as tall as the player.

Industry
Oil from the Atlantic Ocean accounts for 90 per cent of Congo's exports, contributing largely to the country's wealth. Fluctuating oil prices have caused some economic problems, but Congo's crop exports have remained strong. The felling of forests to export tropical timber is a pressing environmental concern. Huge barges on the Congo and other rivers carry timber goods as far as Brazzaville; from there the Congo Ocean Railway takes them to Pointe Noire, Congo's only port.

CONGO FACTS

CAPITAL CITY	Brazzaville
AREA	342,000 sq km (132,046 sq miles)
POPULATION	3,100,000
MAIN LANGUAGES	French, Kongo
MAJOR RELIGIONS	Christian, traditional beliefs
CURRENCY	CFA franc

Gabon

A palm-fringed sandy coastline 800 km (500 miles) long, and lush tropical vegetation dominate Gabon's landscape. The country earns 80 per cent of its foreign currency from oil and also sells timber, manganese, and uranium ore. Gabon has the potential to be wealthy, but mismanagement by the government has led to continued poverty.

Woman in Libreville, Gabon's capital

Libreville
The bustling port city of Libreville was founded in 1849 by French naval officers. Meaning "free town" in French, Libreville was a new home for liberated slaves. It is now a modern, growing city, and a centre of culture, industry, and government. Many citizens are wealthy, but poverty still exists.

People
Although Gabon is one of Africa's most thinly populated countries, it contains more than 40 different ethnic groups. The indigenous Fang people form the largest group. Once fierce warriors, they now dominate the government. Most Gabonese people are Christians, and about 90 per cent of their children attend primary schools. The Gabonese traditions of dance, song, poetry, and story-telling remain an important social and cultural part of everyday life.

The Trans-Gabon Railway runs from Libreville to Franceville.

Trans-Gabon Railway
Opened in 1986 to transport gold and manganese, the Trans-Gabon Railway has caused much controversy because it cut through rainforest, destroying many valuable and rare trees.

GABON FACTS

CAPITAL CITY	Libreville
AREA	267,667 sq km (103,346 sq miles)
POPULATION	1,300,000
MAIN LANGUAGES	French, Fang
MAJOR RELIGION	Christian
CURRENCY	CFA franc

Equatorial Guinea

Two former Spanish colonies make up the country of Equatorial Guinea, located close to the Equator. Río Muni, also called Mbini, is on mainland Africa, and Bioko Island, which has fertile, volcanic soil that is ideal for growing cocoa beans, is situated to the northwest, off the coast of neighbouring Cameroon.

Traditional healing
Like other Africans, many people in Equatorial Guinea believe that illness is due to the influence of bad spirits. Professional healers use dancing and chants to drive out the evil spirits. They keep a range of animal bones, shells, sticks, and other plant parts in their medicine bags for use in group ceremonies.

Hippopotamus tooth

Cowrie shell

Tree root

Animal bone

Extended families
Among the people of Equatorial Guinea there is a strong tradition of large, extended families, who stay together and help one another in times of hardship.

EQUATORIAL GUINEA FACTS

CAPITAL CITY	Malabo
AREA	28,051 sq km (10,830 sq miles)
POPULATION	470,000
MAIN LANGUAGES	Spanish, Bubi, Fang, French
MAJOR RELIGION	Christian
CURRENCY	CFA franc

Dem. Rep. Congo

Formerly known as Belgian Congo and then as Zaire, this country was renamed Democratic Republic of the Congo in 1997 after the overthrow of the corrupt military government. The country consists of a plateau 1,200 m (3,900 ft) above sea-level, through which the River Congo flows. The land is fertile and rich in minerals, but spendthrift governments and civil war, including conflict with Rwanda in 1996–97, have kept it poor.

Cowrie shells are sewn on to decorate the mask.

Mask
Among the many peoples of Dem. Rep. Congo are the Kuba, a small ethnic group who have lived there for many years. Their chief wears a hunting mask, known as a Mashamboy mask, made of shells, beads, and raffia, to symbolize the power of the Great Spirit.

A

Creole woman selling diamonds

Farming
Dem. Rep. Congo has much potentially cultivable land. Sixty per cent of the population are subsistence farmers, producing palm oil, coffee, tea, rubber, cotton, fruit, vegetables, and rice. Here, on the border of volcanic Virunga National Park, the land is rich and fertile.

Mining
Copper ore, cobalt, and diamonds provide 85 per cent of national exports. Dem. Rep. Congo rates second in world diamond exports, with most mining activity in the Shaba province.

River ports
The River Congo and its tributaries give the country 11,500 km (7,000 miles) of navigable waterways. There are many river ports with boat-building and repair yards, craft shops, and lively markets that sell cassava, fruits, and fish, and delicacies such as monkey and snake meat. Traders take their produce to sell at river markets in dug-out canoes made by local craftsmen.

Ethnic strife
The present country boundaries in Central Africa date back to European colonialism, and cut across logical ethnic groupings. In some places there is actual ethnic warfare, for example that between the Hutus and the Tutsis of Rwanda and Burundi. For hundreds of years, Rwanda was dominated by the Tutsis, who ruled the Hutus. In 1959, the Hutus rebelled, and widespread fighting broke out. In the mid-1990s the violence escalated, resulting in 800,000 mainly Tutsi deaths and a massive refugee exodus into other countries.

Refugee camp, Tanzania

Sao Tome and Principe

This tiny country, formed by the main volcanic islands of Sao Tome and Principe, and four smaller islands, lies 200 km (120 miles) off the coast of Gabon. Its mountains are covered with forests, and rich soil supports farms that grow cocoa beans and sugar-cane. Sea fishing has potential for development.

Rwanda

One of Africa's most densely populated countries, Rwanda has been made poor by ethnic strife that forced hundreds of thousands of people to flee to Dem. Rep. Congo for safety. Rwanda makes its money by exporting coffee, tea, and tin and tungsten ores. Most of its people just manage to feed themselves.

Burundi

Like Rwanda, its neighbour, Burundi has been torn by conflict between the Tutsis and the Hutus, which has led to riots and thousands of deaths. Burundi has massive oil and nickel reserves beneath Lake Tanganyika, but lacks the funds to begin extraction. Most people are subsistence farmers.

Pepper
The pepper plant's small, green berries redden as they ripen. Harvested straight away, the half-ripe berries are cleaned, dried in the sun, ground, and sifted to make ground black pepper.

Volcanoes Park
The *Parc des volcans* is a scenic reserve dominated by volcanic mountains, two of which are active. The park is the last refuge of the mountain gorillas, which now number around 630.

Farming
Most farmers grow cassava and maize to feed their families. Some grow coffee, tea, cotton, and bananas for export. Overplanting fertile land is causing soil erosion.

Creole culture
Nobody lived on these islands until Portuguese explorers landed in 1470. The Portuguese peopled the islands with slaves from the mainland. Their mixed descendants created a culture called creole, but the creoles now number only ten per cent because more than 4,000 left the country at independence.

FIND OUT MORE AFRICA, HISTORY OF   EMPIRES   FARMING   FORESTS   MONKEYS AND OTHER PRIMATES   MUSIC   OIL   PORTS AND WATERWAYS   SLAVERY   TRAINS AND RAILWAYS

AFRICA, EAST

ONE OF THE WORLD'S OLDEST civilizations, Egypt, occupies the northeastern corner of East Africa, while Kenya, Tanzania, and Uganda sit farther south. Along the Horn of Africa, a piece of land that juts out into the Indian Ocean, are four of the world's poorest countries – Eritrea, Somalia, Ethiopia, and Djibouti. In recent years, Somalia, Sudan, and Ethiopia have been devastated by drought and war. Most East Africans scrape a living from farming, and some rely on food aid from abroad.

Physical features

Running through eastern Africa is the Great Rift Valley, a huge gash in the Earth that continues north through the Red Sea. Other features include the Nile, the world's longest river, and Lake Victoria, Africa's largest lake. The varied landscape includes deserts, grassland, mountains, and swamps.

Savannah
The southern countries of East Africa contain large areas of savannah, or grassland scattered with acacia and baobab trees. This region is home to much of Africa's wildlife, including antelopes, giraffes, and zebras, and their predators such as lions and hyenas.

River Nile
At 6,695 km (4,160 miles) long, the Nile supports the thousands of people who live on its fertile banks. The river flows north from Lake Victoria to the Mediterranean Sea. The Blue Nile Falls is on an important branch of the Nile in Ethiopia.

Kilimanjaro
Africa's highest peak at 5,895 m (19,341 ft), the snow-capped Mount Kibo is one of the Kilimanjaro group of three volcanoes. The group dominates Arusha National Park in Tanzania, on the border with Kenya. Steam and fumes smoking from Kibo's crater indicate that the volcano is not yet extinct, adding to the attraction for mountaineers.

Regional climate
East Africa's climate is affected by altitude. Dominated by desert, Djibouti, and parts of Egypt, Eritrea, Ethiopia, Sudan, and Somalia are plagued by droughts. South Sudan and western Ethiopia receive seasonal rainfall, while parts of Tanzania, Kenya, and Uganda are hot and dry; their highlands are wet.

23°C (73°F)   20°C (68°F)

580 mm (23 in)

Nomadic herding
Many of the original peoples of eastern Africa, particularly the Dinka of Sudan, are nomads, who move from place to place with their herds of cattle in search of water and grazing land. However, competition for land is forcing many nomads to seek alternative lifestyles. Some men now take occasional work in cities or on construction sites.

Map labels:
Mediterranean Sea, Nile Delta, ISRAEL, Port Said, Alexandria, Matrûh, Tanta, Ismâ'iliya, JORDAN, CAIRO, Suez, Monkhafad el Qattâra, El Giza, Helwân, Beni Suef, El Minya, EGYPT, Asyût, Hurghada, Sohâg, Qena, El Khârga, Isna, Luxor, Idfu, Aswân, Buheiret Nâsir, Tropic of Cancer, Libyan Desert, Wadi Halfa, Red Sea, Nubian Desert, Dongola, Port Sudan, Nile, SUDAN, Atbara, Karora, Omdurman, Khartoum North, KHARTOUM, Massawa, ERITREA, Kassala, ASMARA, Wad Medani, Gedaref, Teseney, Geneina, El Fasher, Himora, Ed, El Obeid, Singa, Mek'elê, Aseb, Nyala, Dilling, Gonder, DJIBOUTI, Kadugli, Bahir Dar, Desé, DJIBOUTI, Boosaaso, Malakal, Kurmuk, Bure, Ethiopian, Berbera, Sudd, ADDIS ABABA, Dire Dawa, Hargeysa, Wau, Gore, Debre Zeyit, Nazrêt, Highlands, Garoowe, CENTRAL AFRICAN REPUBLIC, Jima, Oqadeen, Rumbek, ETHIOPIA, Dila, Gaalkacyo, Yambio, Juba, Negêlê, Shebeli, SOMALIA, Elemi Triangle, Beledweyne, Arua, Lokitaung, Lake Turkana, Moyale, Baydhabo, Gulu, Lira, Buurhakaba, Wanlaweyn, DEM. REP. CONGO, Masindi, Mbale, Eldoret, KENYA, Marka, MOGADISHU, KAMPALA, Nakuru, Meru, Jamaame, Equator, Lake Edward, Entebbe, Nyeri, Garissa, INDIAN OCEAN, Kabale, Lake Victoria, Kisumu, NAIROBI, Kismaayo, RWANDA, Machakos, BURUNDI, Mwanza, Arusha, Moshi, Shinyanga, Malindi, Kigoma, Tabora, Mombasa, Lake Tanganyika, TANZANIA, Tanga, Sumbawanga, DODOMA, Zanzibar, Morogoro, Dar es Salaam, Mbeya, Iringa, Lindi, ZAMBIA, Lake Nyasa, Songea, Mtwara, MALAWI, MOZAMBIQUE, Gulf of Aden, Darfur, White Nile, Blue Nile, Jonglei Canal

0 km 400
0 miles 400

Egypt

Today, as throughout its 5,000-year history, Egypt depends on the River Nile for much of its water, food, transport, and energy now generated at the massive Aswan Dam. Egypt controls the Suez Canal, an important shipping route that links Africa, Europe, and Asia, and brings money into the country. About 99 per cent of Egypt's people live along the lush, fertile banks of the river, and most are farmers, although the oil industry and tourist trade provide a growing number of jobs.

Water is drawn up to feed pipes that lead into the fields.

People

Several ethnic groups live in Egypt. Most people speak Arabic, but there are Berber and Nubian minorities. Until recently urban women were among the most liberated in the Arab world, but that may change with the rise of Islamic fundamentalism. In rural families, men go out to work, while women cook and fetch water.

A

Farming

Egypt is one of the world's leading producers of dates, which are mostly grown in oases, along with melons. While some farmers use modern methods, many *fellahin*, or peasant farmers, use centuries-old techniques such as this one, where the donkey drives a wheel that scoops up water for irrigation.

Food

Reputed to be as old as the Pyramids, the traditional Egyptian dish of *ful medames* is made by boiling broad beans with garlic, onion, olive oil, and spices. The beans are served with hard-boiled eggs, lemon, and unleavened bread. Food is often accompanied by sweet tea and coffee.

Ful medames

Ramesses II statue, Temple of Luxor

Tourism

Millions of people flock to Egypt every year to see the Pyramids and other remains of the country's ancient past, such as the tombs in the Valleys of the Kings and Queens, and the temples at Karnak and Luxor. The oldest pyramid is the Step Pyramid at Saqqara, which was built about 2650 BC as a tomb for King Zoser.

Soft dusters on poles are used to clean the delicate sandstone.

Cotton plant

Cairo

Egypt's ancient capital is the largest city in Africa, with a population of more than 7,000,000. It has at least 1,000 mosques, some built with stone looted from the Pyramids. Old Cairo's narrow streets heave with bustling bazaars, while the wealthy west bank has modern casinos and hotels.

The Sultan Hassan Mosque and surrounding area

Suez Canal

More than 20,000 cargo ships sail through the Suez Canal each year. The canal, built by French engineers in 1869, is 190 km (118 miles) long and provides a short cut for ships between the Gulf of Suez and the Mediterranean Sea.

Cotton

Although only five per cent of Egypt's land can be farmed, the country is a leading producer of cotton. Quality cloths are exported or made into cool garments like *jelebas*, or tunics, often worn by locals.

Cotton boll

Sudan

Sudan is the largest country in Africa, measuring 2,050 km (1,274 miles) long from north to south. Desert in the north gives way to a central, grassy plain. Marshland covers much of the south. Two branches of the Nile (the White Nile and the Blue Nile) meet at the capital, Khartoum, providing fertile soil for farming. The country has good oil and mineral resources, but war and drought have weakened it.

People

There are more than 500 Sudanese ethnic groups, speaking about 100 languages and dialects. Some are nomadic herders, many of whom have now settled on farms. Most own their own plots, and live in villages of mud huts along the Nile, where farming is combined with fishing. The produce is sold at markets. Civil war and famine in the south of Sudan have created refugees.

Religious conflict

The ruling people of the north are Arab Muslims, and the tall minarets of their beautiful mosques dominate the landscape. Farther south, the majority are divided into many ethnic groups and follow Christianity or traditional African religions. The religious, cultural, and language differences between north and south have caused bitter fighting.

Eritrea

A small, hot country on the Horn of Africa, Eritrea won independence from Ethiopia in 1993 after a 30-year war with Ethiopian troops, which left a legacy of destruction and further war. Vast, but as yet, unexploited copper resources around the rugged mountains have potential for development. Eritrea's strategic Red Sea coastal position gives it access to the sea's oil fields, fishing grounds, and useful trade routes.

ERITREA FACTS

CAPITAL CITY Asmara

AREA 121,320 sq km (46,842 sq miles)

POPULATION 3,800,000

MAIN LANGUAGES Tigrinya, Arabic

MAJOR RELIGIONS Christian, Muslim

CURRENCY Nakfa

Subsistence farming
More than 80 per cent of Eritreans live by subsistence farming, many of them as nomadic herders. Farmers depend on September rains to create seasonal rivers that water the harvest, but recurring droughts have meant that Eritrea has been forced to rely on food aid from overseas.

People
The long war of independence developed a strong sense of nationalism among the people, although they belong to several ethnic groups speaking different languages. Women, 30,000 of whom fought in the war, many at leadership level, have been pressing the government for equal rights in the country's new political constitution.

Somalia

An arid, flat country bordering the Indian Ocean, Somalia has some of the longest beaches in the world. The country gained independence in 1960, but since the late 1980s the south has been in the grip of civil war, waged by wealthy rival warlords, and has had no effective government. Most people are poor, and live in coastal towns in the north and in the south near rivers.

SOMALIA FACTS

CAPITAL CITY Mogadishu

AREA 637,657 sq km (246,199 sq miles)

POPULATION 9,200,000

MAIN LANGUAGES Somali, Arabic

MAJOR RELIGION Muslim

CURRENCY Somali shilling

Mogadishu
Conveniently situated on Somalia's coastline, Mogadishu has long been an important port. Arabs founded the capital more than 1,000 years ago, and sold it to the Italians in 1905. In 1960, it was returned to Somalia. The city's buildings are a mixture of older Arab architecture and 20th-century Italian design, but many have been damaged by war.

Civil war
Traditionally, the Somalis were organized in clans, or loyal family groups, that were controlled by elder members. The government destroyed the clan system in the 1980s, provoking bitter wars. Many people are now dependent on overseas aid.

Ethiopia

The Great Rift Valley, a high plateau, and an arid desert dominate Ethiopia. The country has suffered famine, drought, and civil war, but farming reforms and good seasonal rains have enabled Ethiopians to depend less on aid from abroad. Four-fifths of the population make their living through farming. Unique traditions like storytelling, music, and dance are an important part of everyday life.

Food
Spicy foods are standard in Ethiopia. A hot sauce, known as *wat*, is served with beef or chicken, and mopped up with bread. Usually, a soft, flat bread called *enjera* is eaten, which is made from teff, a field crop grown mainly in Ethiopia. A wide range of fish is available to those with money. Ethiopian *kaffa*, coffee flavoured with rye, is known as "health of Adam".

ETHIOPIA FACTS

CAPITAL CITY Addis Ababa

AREA 1,127,127 sq km (435,184 sq miles)

POPULATION 64,500,000

MAIN LANGUAGE Amharic

MAJOR RELIGIONS Muslim, Christian, traditional beliefs

CURRENCY Ethiopian Birr

Vegetable dish made from cabbage, carrots, garlic, and red lentils

Hard-boiled egg

Chicken stew with egg, and red peppers

Enjera

A stew of beef, cinnamon, peppers, red chilli, and tomatoes

Red onions, chillies, garlic, and ginger, make wat, *a spicy sauce.*

Orthodox Church
The Ethiopian Orthodox Church is the chief Christian faith in the country. The pilgrimage centre of Lalibela, in Ethiopia's central highlands, is known for its Christian churches, which date from the 10th century. *Timkat*, a yearly festival, is celebrated by many Ethiopian Christians.

Orthodox priests

Djibouti

A desert country on the Gulf of Aden, Djibouti serves as a port for Ethiopia. The two ethnic groups, the Afars and Issas, have a tradition of nomadic herding, but now half of them live in settled homes in the capital, Djibouti.

DJIBOUTI FACTS

CAPITAL CITY Djibouti

AREA 22,000 sq km (8,494 sq miles)

POPULATION 644,000

MAIN LANGUAGES Arabic, French

MAJOR RELIGIONS Muslim, Christian

CURRENCY Djibouti Franc

Shipping and fishing
The 19th-century city of Djibouti is one of the key Red Sea ports in the area, and generates much of the country's income. The fishing industry thrives on its rich waters.

Kenya

Lying on the Equator, Kenya has a varied landscape. The arid north is hot, but there is a rich farming region along the coast, and the southwestern highlands are warm and wet. The country has a stable, prosperous economy based on agriculture. More than 90 per cent of the Kenyan people are under the age of 45 and belong to about 70 ethnic groups. Kenya is noted for its wildlife and its spectacular national parks.

KENYA FACTS

CAPITAL CITY Nairobi

AREA 582,650 sq km (224,961 sq miles)

POPULATION 31,300,000

MAIN LANGUAGES Kiswahili, English

MAJOR RELIGIONS Christian, traditional beliefs, Muslim

CURRENCY Kenya shilling

Nairobi
Founded by British colonists as a railway town in 1899, Nairobi is Kenya's capital and a centre of business and communications. Home to 2,564,500 people, the city's high-rise buildings contrast with the surrounding plains where elephants and lions roam.

Tourism
National parks are the main attraction for the thousands of tourists who visit Kenya every year. Ten per cent of all Kenya is designated parkland, and there are more than 40 major national reserves. Amboseli, where many African animals (including lions, antelopes, and leopards) live, enjoys a spectacular view of Kilimanjaro.

Coffee beans

Tea leaves

Green beans

Crops
About 85 per cent of the population work on the land. Kenya is the world's fourth largest producer of tea, which, together with coffee, is grown on plantations. Kenya leads the world in the export of pyrethrum, a pink flower that is dried to make insecticides.

Uganda

Independence from Britain in 1962 led to ethnic conflict and poverty in Uganda, but since 1986, when peace was restored, the economy has been recovering slowly. Agriculture is still the main activity, with coffee, cotton, and cane sugar the main exports. Uganda also has good mineral deposits, including copper, gold, and cobalt. Most Ugandans live in rural villages.

UGANDA FACTS

CAPITAL CITY Kampala

AREA 236,040 sq km (91,135 sq miles)

POPULATION 24,000,000

MAIN LANGUAGES English, Kiswahili

MAJOR RELIGIONS Christian, traditional beliefs, Muslim

CURRENCY New Uganda shilling

Sweet potatoes

Market in Kampala

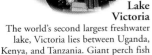

Farming
About 80 per cent of the work-force farm 43 per cent of the land. Most people own small farms, producing enough cassava, maize, millet, and sweet potatoes for themselves and to trade at market.

Kampala
Uganda's capital, Kampala, stands on hills overlooking Lake Victoria. The ancient palace of the former Buganda kings stands alongside the modern Makerere University. The 953,400 people of Kampala experience violent thunderstorms on an average of 242 days a year, and rain nearly every day.

Lake Victoria

The world's second largest freshwater lake, Victoria lies between Uganda, Kenya, and Tanzania. Giant perch fish have eaten nearly all the lake's natural fish species. A hydroelectricity project at the lake's Owen Falls aims to cut Uganda's oil imports in half.

Tanzania

The islands of Zanzibar united with mainland Tanganyika in 1964, creating Tanzania. More than half the country is covered by forests, and it has a long Indian Ocean coastline. Dar es Salaam, the largest city and chief port, was until recently the capital. Farming is the main activity, but oil, diamonds, and gas have been discovered.

TANZANIA FACTS

CAPITAL CITY Dodoma

AREA 945,087 sq km (364,898 sq miles)

POPULATION 36,000,000

MAIN LANGUAGES English, Kiswahili

MAJOR RELIGIONS Traditional beliefs, Muslim, Christian

CURRENCY Tanzania shilling

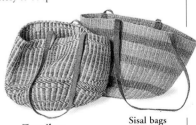

Cotton
Tea, tobacco, and cotton account for two-thirds of Tanzania's exports. Most cotton is produced on government-operated farms in the north and south highlands and around Lake Victoria. Workers carry the cotton to the factory to be spun and woven into cloth.

People
The 120 ethnic groups of Tanzania live together in harmony, as no single group is dominant. More than two thirds of the people live in small, scattered villages, but the state *Ujamaa* policy has tried to resettle them into larger communities to provide more facilities.

Sisal bags

Zanzibar
The island of Zanzibar and its small companion island of Pemba lie off the east coast of Tanzania. Zanzibar is one of the world's leading producers of cloves and sisal, a plant grown for making rope and bags for export.

FIND OUT MORE AFRICA, HISTORY OF · CHRISTIANITY · DAMS · EGYPT, ANCIENT · EMPIRES · FARMING · ISLAM · PORTS AND WATERWAYS · RIVERS · WARFARE

AFRICA, NORTHWEST

MOROCCO, ALGERIA, TUNISIA, and Libya, plus the disputed territory of Western Sahara, make up the northwest corner of Africa. The region has been dominated by Arabs and their religion, Islam, for more than 1,300 years. Algeria and Libya are huge countries, but much of the land is desert. However, they and Tunisia have abundant reserves of oil and natural gas. Farming, made possible by irrigation projects, is still important to the region. Many people lead nomadic lives roaming the land with their herds of animals.

Mediterranean coast
Once occupied by the Phoenicians, Greeks, and Romans, northwest Africa's Mediterranean coast has many ancient ruins that are particularly popular with tourists in Morocco, Algeria, and Tunisia. Most people live on the coastal plain, which has fertile land and a warm climate.

Physical features

Along the Mediterranean and Atlantic coasts is a fertile strip where most of the people live. The Atlas Mountain chain runs across Morocco and continues as rolling hills in Algeria and Tunisia. The rest of the land is desert, broken by oases and bleak mountain ranges.

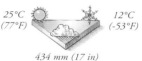

25°C (77°F)   12°C (-53°F)

434 mm (17 in)

Regional climate
Along most of the coast and on high ground, summers are hot and dry and winters are warm and wet. Daytime desert temperatures average about 38°C (100°F); at night they are low. Desert rainfall may be as little as 2.5 cm (1 in) a year, and irregular.

Sahara
The Sahara Desert covers about 9,065,000 sq km (3,263,400 sq miles). Only about one-fifth is sand. The rest includes vast, flat expanses of barren rock and gravel and mountains such as Algeria's Ahaggar range, peaking at 2,918 m (9,573 ft). Crops are grown in 90 large oases.

Atlas Mountains
The Atlas Mountains consist of several chains of mountains that stretch 2,410 km (1,500 miles) from the Atlantic coast of Morocco to Cape Bon in eastern Tunisia. The highest peak is Djebel Toubkal at 4,167 m (13,665 ft), which lies in the High Atlas range in southern Morocco.

Berbers

The original people of Northwest Africa are the Berbers. Today, about 15,000,000 Berbers still live in the mountains and deserts of the region. Most are Muslim, but retain their own language and dialects. The Tuareg are a group of nomadic Berber herders who roam the North African desert.

Berber man and child

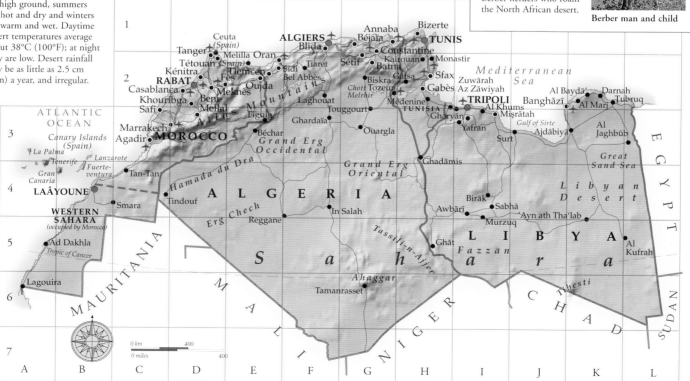

Morocco

 A mix of African, Islamic, Arab, Berber, and European influences, Morocco attracts more than four million tourists each year. The country's strengths are farming and phosphate mining. Founded in Fès, in AD 859, Karueein University is the oldest in the world.

MOROCCO FACTS

CAPITAL CITY Rabat

AREA 446,300 sq km (172,316 sq miles)

POPULATION 30,400,000

MAIN LANGUAGES Arabic, Berber, French

MAJOR RELIGION Muslim

CURRENCY Moroccan dirham

Mint tea
The traditional drink in Morocco is a refreshing mint tea, served in glasses or pots, with plenty of sugar and a sprig of mint. It is often offered free of charge in the *souks* (markets), when bargaining is about to begin.

Carpets
Hand-knotted woollen carpets are one of Morocco's great craft industries. The leading carpet factories are in Fès and Rabat. The carpets have bold colours and symbolic, abstract Islamic patterns. Though sold by men, most rugs are made by women.

Western Sahara
Morocco has occupied the ex-Spanish colony of Western Sahara since 1975. Polisario Front guerrillas began fighting for independence in 1983, to resist mass settlement of the area by Moroccans keen to hold on to the phosphate-rich territory.

Polisario soldiers keep watch

Tunisia

 A former French colony, Tunisia is the smallest country in the region and one of the more liberal Arab states. Although not admitted into politics, Tunisian women enjoy a high level of equality, making up 31 per cent of the work-force.

TUNISIA FACTS

CAPITAL CITY Tunis

AREA 163,610 sq km (63,169 sq miles)

POPULATION 9,600,000

MAIN LANGUAGES Arabic, French

MAJOR RELIGION Muslim

CURRENCY Tunisian dinar

Couscous is steamed in a special pot that sits above the stewing meat.

Couscous
The staple food in Tunisia is granules of semolina called couscous. Originally a Berber dish, couscous is served with a meat or vegetable sauce. Tunisians like their food spicy. After this main course, dates stuffed with almond paste, or sweet pastries filled with honey and nuts are served.

Souk
A feature of Tunisian cities – and indeed all northwest African cities – is the *souk*, or market. This is traditionally a tangle of narrow streets flanked by open-fronted stalls, where people can buy anything from food to carpets or hand-made jewellery.

Algeria

Under French rule from 1830, Algeria won independence in 1962. The country has a high birth rate and a young population: 86 per cent are below the age of 44. Crude oil and natural gas are an important source of income. Increasingly, fundamentalist Islamic groups pose a threat to non-Muslims.

ALGERIA FACTS

CAPITAL CITY Algiers

AREA 2,381,740 sq km (919,590 sq miles)

POPULATION 30,800,000

MAIN LANGUAGES Arabic, Berber, French, Tamazight

MAJOR RELIGION Muslim

CURRENCY Algerian dinar

Overpopulation
Since more than four-fifths of Algeria is desert, 90 per cent of Algerians live in the far north of the country, where it is cooler. However, as Algeria's population continues to increase at a rate of more than 1.7 per cent a year, many northern towns, like Constantine, are struggling to house everybody, and slum areas are growing.

Houses are built on every available piece of land.

Black dates

Yellow dates

Dates
Algeria is the world's sixth largest producer of dates. They are grown in the fertile north as well as in the many oases of the Sahara, and provide a main source of income. Date palms also yield timber; their leaves are used to thatch buildings.

Libya

Since 95 per cent of Libya is desert, the Great Man-made River Project was set up to irrigate farming land. Water is piped from beneath the Sahara to populated coastal regions.

LIBYA FACTS

CAPITAL CITY Tripoli

AREA 1,759,540 sq km (679, 358 sq miles)

POPULATION 5,400,000

MAIN LANGUAGES Arabic, Tuareg

MAJOR RELIGION Muslim

CURRENCY Libyan dinar

Oil and gas
The discovery of oil and natural gas in 1959 transformed Libya into a wealthy nation, and many people moved to the towns in search of work. In 1992, trade with the West was severely disrupted when the UN imposed sanctions because of leader Colonel Gaddafi's alleged links with international terrorist groups.

Oil workers at Calanscio

Roman ruins
Libya was abandoned by the Romans after the Arab conquest of AD 643 and was an Italian colony between 1911 and 1951. Today, some of the finest Roman ruins outside Italy can be seen at Leptis Magna, now called Labdah, to the east of the capital, Tripoli.

FIND OUT MORE   AFRICA, HISTORY OF   DESERTS   EMPIRES   FARMING   ISLAM   ISLAMIC EMPIRE   MOUNTAINS AND VALLEYS   OIL   ROMAN EMPIRE   TEXTILES AND WEAVING

AFRICA, SOUTHERN CENTRAL

SOUTHERN CENTRAL AFRICA is made up of seven countries that form part of the African mainland, and the islands of Madagascar and Comoros in the Indian Ocean. Farming is still an important source of income in these countries, but major deposits of minerals such as diamonds, copper, uranium, and iron have led many people to move to the towns and cities in search of work. A variety of tribal groups, each with its own language, customs, and beliefs, lives in the southern central region.

Physical features

Although lowlands fringe the coast, most of the region lies 400–1,500 m (1,200–4,500 ft) above sea-level. The landscape includes the Namib and Kalahari deserts in the west and centre, dry savannah and woodland, and humid, subtropical forests in the north.

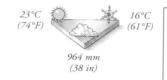

Acacia trees, Madagascar

Namib Desert
The Namib Desert extends 1,900 km (1,100 miles) in a narrow strip from southwestern Angola, along the Skeleton Coast of Namibia, and down to the border of South Africa. Although it rarely rains, the climate on the coast is humid with cold, morning fogs. Sand dunes reach down to the edge of the Atlantic and the only practical means of transport is the camel.

Savannah
Much of the region is covered by grassland, or savannah. The most common trees in these areas are thorn trees, especially acacias. They are suited to the dry conditions and grow on the edges of the Kalahari and other semi-desert regions.

Regional climate

Most of the region lies in the tropics, where the climate is always hot, but there are two seasons: wet and dry. Rain is heavy in the wet season. Most of Botswana and Namibia has a semi-arid climate, and much of Namibia is desert. Eastern Madagascar has a tropical wet climate.

23°C (74°F)   16°C (61°F)

964 mm (38 in)

Zimbabwean woman with her baby

Women's role

The traditional role of African women was to look after the home and bring up the children. Many were also expected to cultivate the crops, and some built their own houses. Today, many women in southern central Africa have additional responsibilities, because their husbands are away working in mines and cities. Despite the domestic power of women, few have official jobs or own property.

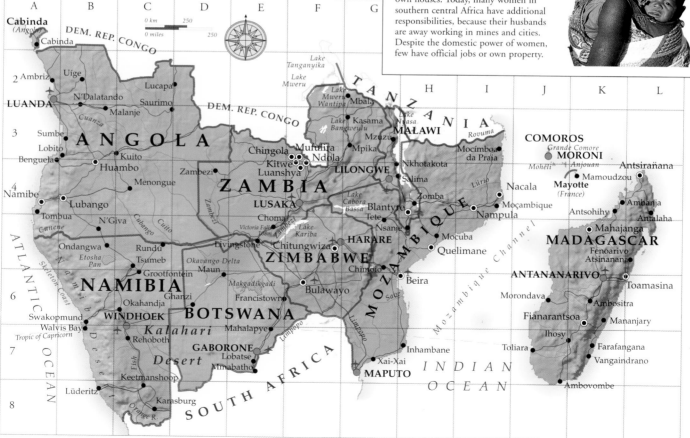

Angola

In 1975, after a long war, Angola became independent of Portuguese colonial rule. With fertile land and huge reserves of diamonds, oil, and natural gas, the country should have become prosperous. However, Angola was torn apart and economic development was restricted by the fighting that continued after independence. Civil war erupted between rival ethnic groups and continues today.

ANGOLA FACTS

CAPITAL CITY Luanda

AREA 1,246,700 sq km (481,351 sq miles)

POPULATION 13,500,000

MAIN LANGUAGE Portuguese

MAJOR RELIGIONS Christian, traditional beliefs

CURRENCY Readjusted kwanza

Oil and diamonds
Most of Angola's oil is produced in Cabinda, a tiny Angolan enclave in Dem. Rep. Congo. Petroleum provides 90 per cent of Angola's exports. Angola also ranks highly in world output of diamonds, its second largest export.

Luanda
Founded by the Portuguese in 1575, Angola's capital and largest city is home to more than 2,500,000 people. Once used for shipping slaves to Brazil, it is still a major seaport. Modern Luanda is an industrial centre with its own oil refinery.

Zambia

Bordered to the south by the Zambezi River, Zambia is a country of upland plateaus, 80 per cent of which are grassland and forest. About 50 per cent of the people live by subsistence farming, constantly threatened by drought. Tobacco is the main exported crop. Hydroelectric power provides much of Zambia's energy. Low copper prices in the 1980s upset finances.

ZAMBIA FACTS

CAPITAL CITY Lusaka

AREA 752,614 sq km (290,584 sq miles)

POPULATION 10,600,000

MAIN LANGUAGES English, Bemba, Tonga, Nyanja, Lozi, Lunda

MAJOR RELIGIONS Christian, traditional beliefs

CURRENCY Zambian kwacha

Cobalt is used in steel production.

Copper forms 90 per cent of exports.

Copper bracelets

Copper and cobalt
Zambia is the world's sixth largest producer of copper. The seam of copper ore where the metal is mined, the Copperbelt, is 320 km (200 miles) long. The second largest producer of cobalt, Zambia also mines lead, silver, and zinc.

Urban living
About half of Zambia's people, a mix of more than 70 different ethnic groups, live in towns and cities. The most populated area is the Copperbelt, where most of them work. The capital, Lusaka, a thriving industrial and business centre, is home to 1,800,000 Zambians.

Namibia

An ex-German colony, and ruled for 70 years by South Africa, Namibia won its independence in 1990. Rich mineral resources make mining the country's leading industry. One in seven people lives on the land, mainly rearing livestock, although drought and the expanding desert make farming difficult. Fishing is good off the Atlantic coast.

NAMIBIA FACTS

CAPITAL CITY Windhoek

AREA 825,418 sq km (318,694 sq miles)

POPULATION 1,800,000

MAIN LANGUAGES English, Afrikaans, Ovambo, Kavango

MAJOR RELIGION Christian

CURRENCY Namibian dollar

Uranium
The Rössing Uranium Mine in the Namib Desert is the world's largest, producing 2,000 tonnes (2,200 tons) of uranium every year. Namibia is the world's fifth largest producer of uranium and ranks among the top producers of diamonds.

People
Namibia has a peaceful multiracial society. The white minority lives mostly in Windhoek, in European-style houses. Black Namibians include many groups, the largest of which are the northern Ovambo. To the west, the semi-nomadic Himba raise cattle.

Himba woman

Hair is braided and beaded.

Botswana

Southwest Botswana is covered by the Kalahari Desert. To the north is the marshy delta of the Okavango River, a haven for wildlife. Despite this wetland, however, Botswana suffers droughts. Most people live in the more fertile east. Production of diamonds – the third largest in the world – has helped to stimulate Botswana's economy.

BOTSWANA FACTS

CAPITAL CITY Gaborone

AREA 600,370 sq km (231,803 sq miles)

POPULATION 1,600,000

MAIN LANGUAGES English, Tswana, Shona, Khoikhoi, Ndebele

MAJOR RELIGIONS Traditional beliefs, Christian

CURRENCY Pula

Beef stew with dried spinach   *Savoury porridge*

San
The original inhabitants of Botswana are the nomadic San people, once known as Kalahari Bushmen, one of Africa's only remaining groups of hunter-gatherers. There are fewer than 50,000 San today, but small groups still roam the Kalahari Desert hunting small animals and eating edible plants and insects. Many San now work on cattle ranches.

Food
The Tswana people, who make up the majority of Botswana's population, live mostly by subsistence farming, raising cattle, and growing enough maize, sorghum, and millet for their own use. Their staple diet consists of meat stews served with a kind of porridge made from cereals. Fresh vegetables are rare.

A

Zimbabwe

In 1980, the former British colony of Rhodesia became independent and took the name Zimbabwe, after the ancient city of Great Zimbabwe. About 70 per cent of Zimbabweans live from farming. Coal, gold, asbestos, and nickel are mined for export. Zimbabwe has recently suffered great disruption over the issues of government and land re-distribution.

ZIMBABWE FACTS

CAPITAL CITY	Harare
AREA	390,580 sq km (150,803 sq miles)
POPULATION	12,900,000
MAIN LANGUAGES	English, Shona, Ndebele
MAJOR RELIGIONS	Traditional beliefs, Christian
CURRENCY	Zimbabwe dollar

Tourism
Zimbabwe's main tourist attractions are the spectacular Victoria Falls, the Kariba Dam, national parks, and the ruins of the city of Great Zimbabwe. Tourists enjoy action holidays, such as canoeing and rafting, on the Zambezi.

Harare
Formerly called Salisbury, the capital is Zimbabwe's commercial and industrial centre and home to almost two million people. It is a clean and sophisticated city that is characterized by flowering trees, colourful parks, and modern buildings.

Madagascar

The fourth largest island in the world, Madagascar is home to some unique wildlife because of its isolated position off Africa's east coast. A high plateau runs the length of the island, dropping to a narrow, fertile strip in the east, where most people live. The country's economy is based on growing crops and raising livestock.

MADAGASCAR FACTS

CAPITAL CITY	Antananarivo
AREA	587,040 sq km (226,656 sq miles)
POPULATION	16,400,000
MAIN LANGUAGES	Malagasy, French
MAJOR RELIGIONS	Traditional beliefs, Christian, Muslim
CURRENCY	Malagasy franc

Vanilla
Madagascar is the world's largest exporter of vanilla. The pods of the plants are used to flavour ice-cream and chocolate. Other important cash crops are cloves, sisal, cocoa, and butter beans.

Vanilla pods grow 25 cm (10 in) long.

Rural society
Most Madagascans are descended from Asians from Malaysia and Indonesia, who began to settle on the island almost 2,000 years ago. Later waves of mainland Africans intermixed to produce a uniquely multiracial society. Three-quarters of the Madagascan labour force works on the land growing subsistence crops, such as cassava and rice.

Mozambique

As a result of years of civil war, flooding, and drought, Mozambique is now one of the world's poorest countries, with a high birth rate. The land, though largely unexploited, is fertile and rich in minerals. The ports and railways provide a trade link for land-locked Swaziland, Malawi, and Zimbabwe.

MOZAMBIQUE FACTS

CAPITAL CITY	Maputo
AREA	801,590 sq km (309,494 sq miles)
POPULATION	18,600,000
MAIN LANGUAGE	Portuguese
MAJOR RELIGIONS	Traditional beliefs, Christian, Muslim
CURRENCY	Metical

Fishing
One of Mozambique's key industries is fishing, and shrimps account for more than 40 per cent of export earnings. The country's total annual fish catch averages 24,170 tonnes (26,643 tons). Other exports include cotton, tea, and sugar.

Malawi

With few natural resources, Malawi has a rural society, despite the constant threat of drought. Light industries, such as food processing, textiles, and manufacturing farm tools, are developing. Fish from Lake Malawi, which covers one-quarter of the country, is a source of food.

MALAWI FACTS

CAPITAL CITY	Lilongwe
AREA	118,480 sq km (45,745 sq miles)
POPULATION	11,600,000
MAIN LANGUAGES	Chewa, English
MAJOR RELIGIONS	Christian, Muslim
CURRENCY	Malawian kwacha

Tea grows well in the tropical climate of Malawi's hillsides.

Farming
Almost 86 per cent of the Malawi labour force works in agriculture, growing cash crops, such as tea, tobacco, coffee, cotton, and sugar, as well as subsistence crops of maize, rice, cassava, and plantains. The country is self-sufficient in food.

Comoros

The three islands and few islets of the Comoros archipelago lie north of Madagascar in the Indian Ocean. They were governed by France until 1975. The economy is underdeveloped, and most of the people live by subsistence farming.

COMOROS FACTS

CAPITAL CITY	Moroni
AREA	2,170 sq km (838 sq miles)
POPULATION	707,000
MAIN LANGUAGES	Arabic, French, Comoran, local languages
MAJOR RELIGIONS	Muslim
CURRENCY	Comoros franc

Ylang-ylang
Comoros is the world's largest grower of ylang-ylang, an aromatic tree with greenish-yellow flowers that produce a pleasantly scented oil used to make perfume.

FIND OUT MORE AFRICA, HISTORY OF AFRICAN WILDLIFE DESERTS EMPIRES FARMING FISHING INDUSTRY GREAT ZIMBABWE OIL ROCKS AND MINERALS SOCIETIES, HUMAN

A

AFRICA, WEST

THE ATLANTIC OCEAN borders all but three
of the 15 countries that make up West Africa.
Much of the area is dominated by the Sahara
and the Sahel, a vast area of semi-desert, which
the Sahara is slowly invading. Despite their potential wealth
and rich resources, most of the countries are desperately poor.
Long-established trade routes across the Sahara link West Africa
with the Mediterranean coast to the north. For millions of
West Africans, life is a perpetual struggle against a hostile
climate, the threat of drought, and political instability.

Sahel
Immediately south of the Sahara Desert, stretching all
the way across West Africa, is a broad band of hot, arid,
semi-desert grassland called the Sahel. In Arabic, the
word Sahel means "shore" of the desert. Rainfall in this
region is sporadic and droughts are common.

Regional climate
Moving from north
to south, there are
four main climate
regions in West
Africa: desert, Sahel,
grassland, and tropical
rainforest. Rain is rare in the northern desert and Sahel
regions, yet the south is humid and tropical with a
distinct rainy season that can last for four to six months.

25°C (78°F)   26°C (80°F)
1,879 mm (74 in)

Physical features

Most of West Africa lies 200–
400 m (600–1200 ft) above
sea-level. The Sahara dominates
Niger, Mauritania, and Mali,
and the Sahel extends south
into Senegal, Burkina Faso,
and Nigeria. The rivers Senegal,
Gambia, Volta, and Niger
irrigate the west and south.

River Niger
Africa's third longest river,
the Niger flows in
a great arc for 4,180 km
(2,597 miles) from Guinea
through Mali, Niger,
Benin, and Nigeria
to a vast delta on
the Gulf of Guinea.
A valuable source of
fish and water, it is
navigable for more
than half its length.

Groundnuts
Also called peanuts,
groundnuts develop
underground. They are
widely grown in West
Africa as a source of edible
oil, and as a foodstuff that is
rich in protein and vitamins.
The plants were introduced
into West Africa from
South America.

Harvesting peanuts

Mauritania

The northern two-thirds of Mauritania are desert. The only farmland lies in a narrow, fertile strip along the bank of the River Senegal in the southwest. This area is scattered with small villages and oases. Nomadic Moors of Arab descent, from the north, live in Mauritania. They have often clashed with black farmers in the south.

Fishing
The waters off Mauritania are said to have the richest fish stocks in the world; they attract many foreign fishing fleets. All catches must be sold through the state fishing company. Fishing provides more than half of Mauritania's export earnings.

Desertification
Successive years of drought and overgrazing in the Sahel region have caused the desert to expand southwards, killing livestock and forcing many nomads to move into towns.

Government schemes are attempting to reclaim the land by reducing soil erosion.

Mineral wealth
The Mauritanian desert contains the largest deposits of gypsum – used for making plaster – and some of the largest reserves of iron ore in the world. The country also exports gold. A single rail line connects mines with Nouakchott, the country's capital and main port.

Gypsum crystal

MAURITANIA FACTS

CAPITAL CITY	Nouakchott
AREA	1,030,700 sq km (397,953 sq miles)
POPULATION	2,700,000
MAIN LANGUAGES	Arabic, French, Hassaniya, Wolof, Soninké
MAJOR RELIGION	Muslim
CURRENCY	Ouguiya

Senegal

The flat, semi-desert plains of Senegal are crossed by four rivers – the Senegal, Gambia, Saloum, and Casamance – which provide water for agriculture, the country's main source of income. Tourism is also developing. Senegal has a mix of ethnic groups, the largest of which are the Wolofs.

Music
At festivals and ceremonies, or *griots*, a mix of historians, musicians, and poets, sing and recite traditional stories, often to the accompaniment of a *kora*.

Kora

Musicians pluck the 21 strings to give a wide range of muted sounds.

Many of Senegal's fruits and vegetables are imported and expensive.

Dakar
Senegal's capital and major port, Dakar is a bustling industrial centre with good restaurants, shops, and markets. However, many of the 2,500,000 people who live here are poor and live in suburban slums.

Gourd soundbox

SENEGAL FACTS

CAPITAL CITY	Dakar
AREA	196,190 sq km (75,749 sq miles)
POPULATION	9,700,000
MAIN LANGUAGES	French, Wolof, Fulani, Sérèr, Diola, Mandinka
MAJOR RELIGIONS	Muslim, Christian, traditional beliefs
CURRENCY	CFA franc

Farming
About 60 per cent of the Senegalese labour force works on the land growing cotton and sugar-cane for export, and rice, sorghum, and millet for their food. Until droughts in the 1970s damaged yields, groundnuts were the main cash crop. Fish is now the main export.

Gambia

One of the most densely populated countries in Africa, Gambia occupies a narrow strip either side of the River Gambia and is surrounded on three sides by Senegal. With little industry, 80 per cent of the people live off the land. Groundnuts make up 80 per cent of exports. The main ethnic groups are the Mandingo, Fulani, and Wolof.

GAMBIA FACTS

CAPITAL CITY	Banjul
AREA	11,300 sq km (4,363 sq miles)
POPULATION	1,340,000
MAIN LANGUAGES	English, Mandinka
MAJOR RELIGIONS	Muslim, Christian, traditional beliefs
CURRENCY	Dalasi

Tourism
Gambia is an attractive destination for winter sun-seekers from Europe. Tourism, the country's fastest-growing industry, employs one in ten Gambians. About 10,000 of those work on a seasonal basis.

Guinea-Bissau

Rainfall in Guinea-Bissau is more reliable than in most of the rest of Africa, enabling the country to be self-sufficient in rice. However, flooding is common along the coast because farmers have cut down mangroves to plant rice fields. Most people travel by boat.

Cashew nuts

Grated coconut

Coconut

GUINEA-BISSAU FACTS

CAPITAL CITY	Bissau
AREA	36,120 sq km (13,946 sq miles)
POPULATION	1,200,000
MAIN LANGUAGES	Portuguese, Crioulo
MAJOR RELIGIONS	Traditional beliefs, Muslim, Christian
CURRENCY	CFA Franc

Cashew nuts
Farming employs 85 per cent of the work-force. Rice, cotton, groundnuts, and copra are produced as cash crops, as are cashew nuts, which make up nearly 60 per cent of the country's exports.

Guinea

With more than 30 per cent of the world's known reserves of bauxite, and deposits of diamonds, iron, copper, manganese, uranium and gold, Guinea could be a wealthy country. However, years of poor government and lack of support from former French rulers have made Guinea's economic development difficult.

Coffee beans

Bananas

Pineapple

Fruit growing
Bananas, plantains, and pineapples grow well in the fertile Fouta Djalon hills (Guinea Highlands). Farmers cultivate coffee, palm nuts, and groundnuts as cash crops and sorghum, rice, and cassava for their families.

People
Three-quarters of Guineans belong to one of three main ethnic groups – the Malinke and Fulani who live in the north and centre, and the Susu who live closer to the coast. Two-thirds live in small rural communities, where the standard of living is one of the lowest in the world. Average life expectancy is low, at only 45 years, and only about 35 per cent of people can read.

Sierra Leone

Sierra Leone was founded by the British in the early 1800s as a colony for freed slaves. Its name is Spanish for "Lion Mountains" and refers to the constant roar of thunder. Of the 12 ethnic groups, the biggest are the Mende and the Temne. A ceasefire halted civil war in 2000.

A

Industry
Mining is the mainstay of Sierra Leone's economy. The chief exports are diamonds, some of which are still mined by hand, as well as gold, bauxite, and titanium ore. Farming employs more than two-thirds of the work-force, growing coffee, cocoa, palm kernels, ginger, and cassava.

Uncut diamond looks like any other stone.

Freetown
Surrounded by green hills, Sierra Leone's capital, Freetown, is a colourful and historic port and home to more than 700,000 people. The name is a reminder of the country's former status as a haven for freed slaves. Among Freetown's attractions are a 500-year-old cotton tree, and West Africa's oldest university, built in 1827.

Ivory Coast

With 600 km (370 miles) of Atlantic coastline, and three main rivers, Ivory Coast is fertile and farming efficient. It is among the world's top producers of coffee and cocoa. Food accounts for half of all exports. Most people work in farming and forestry. Nearly all the forests have been sold off as timber to pay foreign debts.

Farmers use pesticides on cocoa plantations, but the lack of protective clothes is a serious health risk.

Yamoussoukro Basilica
Although only 29 per cent of the people of the population are Christian, Ivory Coast has one of the world's largest Christian churches. Able to seat 7,000 people, it dominates the city of Yamoussoukro, which replaced Abidjan as the country's capital in 1983.

Cocoa
Ivory Coast is the world's leading producer of cocoa beans. Cocoa trees need humid conditions, and many cocoa plantations lie in moist, tropical regions where rainforests were felled for timber. Factories have been set up in Ivory Coast to make cocoa butter, which is the basic ingredient of chocolate and some cosmetics.

Liberia

Founded by the USA in the 1820s as a home for freed black slaves, Liberia has never been colonized. About five per cent of the people descend from former slaves and American settlers. The rest are a varied mix of ethnic groups. About 70 per cent of Liberians work on the land, growing oil palms, coffee, and cocoa, and rubber for export. Civil war has damaged trade.

Civil war
Since 1990, Liberia has been torn by a chaotic and bloody civil war, and its once prosperous economy has collapsed. The war, which began as clashes between various ethnic groups, has made thousands of people homeless and many are forced to live in large refugee camps where food shortages are a part of everyday life.

Monrovia
Reputedly the world's wettest capital city, with more than 4,560 mm (183 in) of rain per year, Monrovia is a sprawling city and major port. Liberia has the world's largest commercial fleet of ships. Almost all are foreign owned, but registered in Monrovia, where taxes are low.

A

Mali

Desert and semi-desert cover the northern two-thirds of Mali, and only two per cent of the land can be cultivated. Most people live in the south, in farming settlements close to the rivers Niger and Senegal. Droughts, poor food, and an average life expectancy of only 51 years, make Mali one of the world's poorest countries. Some gold is mined, but cotton is the biggest export.

Buildings such as this granary are made from sand bricks.

MALI FACTS

CAPITAL CITY Bamako

AREA 1,240,000 sq km (478,764 sq miles)

POPULATION 11,700,000

MAIN LANGUAGES French, Bambara, Mande, Arabic, Fulani, Senufo, Soninke

MAJOR RELIGIONS Muslim, traditional beliefs

CURRENCY CFA franc

Making "mud cloth"

People

Mali's main peoples are the Bambara, Fulani, Tuareg, and Dogon, with smaller numbers of Songhai and Bozo. Bozo artists, mostly women, are noted for their "mud cloth", made by painting abstract designs on to rough cloth using differently coloured soils.

Tombouctou

Lying on the edge of the desert, Tombouctou is a city of sand still visited by camel caravans carrying salt from mines in the north for shipping up the River Niger to Mopti. This historic city is a centre of Islamic learning.

Burkina

Land-locked in the arid Sahel region and threatened by the Sahara, which is expanding southwards, Burkina (formerly Upper Volta) is one of West Africa's poorest and most overpopulated countries. Faced with droughts and lack of work, many young people are forced to leave to find jobs abroad.

Fulani

The Fulani are nomadic cattle herders who roam West Africa with their animals. In Burkina, where they number about 75,000, they are one of more than 60 ethnic groups. Fulani herders traditionally tend cattle for local farmers in exchange for sacks of rice.

BURKINA FACTS

CAPITAL CITY Ouagadougou

AREA 274,200 sq km (105,869 sq miles)

POPULATION 11,900,000

MAIN LANGUAGES French, Mossi, Mande, Fulani, Lobi, Bobo

MAJOR RELIGIONS Traditional beliefs, Muslim, Christian

CURRENCY CFA franc

Fulani children

Cotton

Burkina's most valuable cash crop is cotton, which brings in about 25 per cent of its export earnings. However, the country's farming is threatened by the mass emigration of young workers, who send money home to their families. The country has deposits of silver and manganese, and exports gold.

Ghana

Once called the "Gold Coast" by Europeans who found gold here 500 years ago, Ghana still has reserves of gold, which has recently replaced cocoa as the country's major source of income. The country is still one of the world's largest cocoa producers. Lake Volta, formed by a dam on the River Volta, is the world's largest artificial lake.

GHANA FACTS

CAPITAL CITY Accra

AREA 238,540 sq km (92,100 sq miles)

POPULATION 19,700,000

MAIN LANGUAGES English, Akan, Mossi, Ewe, Ga, Twi, Fanti, Gurma

MAJOR RELIGIONS Christian, traditional beliefs, Muslim

CURRENCY Cedi

Eseye (a kind of spinach)

Plantains

Food

A popular food in Ghana is *banku*, a mixture of maize dough and cassava. Ghanaians mix leaves of *eseye*, a type of spinach, with palm oil to make a sauce that is eaten with boiled fish or vegetables.

People

Family ties are strong in Ghana, and the extended family is important. About half of Ghanaians are Ashanti people whose ancestors developed one of the richest and most famous civilizations in Africa. Other groups include the Mole-Dagbani, Ewe, and Ga. About 38 per cent of the people live in cities and towns.

Ghanaian family

Togo

A long, narrow country, just 110 km (68 miles) at its widest point, Togo has a central forested plateau with savannah to the north and south. Nearly half the population is under 15 years of age, and few people are more than 45. Although most people are farmers, Togo's main export is phosphates, used for making fertilizers.

TOGO FACTS

CAPITAL CITY Lomé

AREA 56,785 sq km (21,924 sq miles)

POPULATION 4,700,000

MAIN LANGUAGES French, Kabye, Ewe

MAJOR RELIGIONS Traditional beliefs, Christian, Muslim

CURRENCY CFA franc

Farming

Togolese farmers produce cocoa, coffee, cotton, copra, and palm kernels mainly for export. New products include herbs, tomatoes, and sugar. For their own use, they grow millet, cassava, and maize. Fishing is important in coastal areas.

Maize

Market women

Although politics and formal employment remain the domain of men, many Togolese women work informally in part-time jobs. The Nana Benz, wealthy women traders so-called because they all seem to own Mercedes Benz cars, dominate Togo's markets and taxi businesses. Based in the market at Lomé, these formidable women fight hard for business and have a legendary capacity for haggling.

Nigeria

With large reserves of oil, natural gas, coal, iron ore, lead, tin, and zinc, and rich, fertile farmland, Nigeria looked set to prosper when it gained independence from Britain in 1960. However, the country's economy has experienced difficulty due to falling oil prices, ethnic conflicts, and corrupt government. After 16 years of military dictatorship, civilian rule was restored in 1999.

Abuja

Begun in 1980, the new, purpose-built city of Abuja replaced Lagos as Nigeria's capital in 1991, because the government believed Lagos was too influenced by the Yoruba people. By the late 1990s, much of Abuja was unfinished as money ran low during construction.

Central mosque, Abuja

People

Nigerian society consists of an uneasy mix of more than 250 ethnic groups. Two-thirds of the population belongs to one of three groups – the Hausa in the north, the Ibo in the east, and the Yoruba in the west. About 57 per cent of people live in small tight-knit villages where communal life is important.

Nigerian oil has a low sulphur content and is ideal for aircraft fuel.

Oil

Nigeria's oil production, which ranks first in Africa and highly in the world, accounts for 95 per cent of all its exports. Almost totally dependent on this new industry, which began in the 1960s, Nigeria is vulnerable to changes in world oil prices.

Plantations

Agriculture employs more than 40 per cent of all Nigerian workers. Although most farmers work on small plots with simple tools, vast plantations have been established to cultivate cash crops on a commercial scale for export, using modern machinery. Crops include cotton, coffee, cocoa beans, and oil palms.

The best cloth is a mix of cotton and silk.

Cloth

Nigeria's Yoruba and Hausa peoples produce many attractive patterned textiles, hand-dyed using natural plant colours. In the Hausa town of Kano, in the north, men dye the cloth in ancient dye pits.

NIGERIA FACTS

CAPITAL CITY	Abuja
AREA	923,768 sq km (356,667 sq miles)
POPULATION	116,900,000
DENSITY	128 per sq km (332 per sq mile)
MAIN LANGUAGES	English, Hausa, Yoruba, Ibo
MAJOR RELIGIONS	Muslim, Christian, traditional beliefs
CURRENCY	Naira
LIFE EXPECTANCY	52 years
PEOPLE PER DOCTOR	5,000
GOVERNMENT	Multiparty democracy
ADULT LITERACY	64%

Benin

A former French colony, Benin took its name from an ancient empire, in 1975, 15 years after becoming independent. It is a long, narrow country with a short coastline on the Gulf of Guinea. Most of the land is flat and forested, with a large marsh in the south. Most people live off the land, producing yams, cassava, and maize. Cotton brings in about three-quarters of the country's export income.

BENIN FACTS

CAPITAL CITY	Porto-Novo
AREA	112,620 sq km (43,483 sq miles)
POPULATION	6,400,000
MAIN LANGUAGES	French, Fon, Bariba, Yoruba, Adja, Fulani
MAJOR RELIGIONS	Traditional beliefs, Muslim, Christian
CURRENCY	CFA franc

Fishing

Every year, fishermen catch about 39,000 tonnes (42,990 tons) of fish in the lagoons along the coast of Benin.

Betamaribé

One of five main ethnic groups in Benin, the Betamaribé, or Somba, live in the northwest near the Atakora Mountains. One of the first peoples to settle in Benin, they have lived free from Western influence for hundreds of years and have managed to keep many of their traditions intact.

Niger

Although it is the largest country in West Africa, Niger is two-thirds desert. The people, who are very poor, live in the dry Sahel region, or in the southwest close to the Niger River, where they plant crops and herd animals. The country is one of the world's top producers of uranium.

NIGER FACTS

CAPITAL CITY	Niamey
AREA	1,267,000 sq km (489,188 sq miles)
POPULATION	11,200,000
MAIN LANGUAGES	French, Hausa, Djerma, Fulani, Tuareg, Teda
MAJOR RELIGION	Muslim
CURRENCY	CFA franc

Fighting the desert

The people of Niger are waging a battle against the advance of the desert into the dry Sahel where they live. They plant trees and grass in an attempt to stop the soil eroding.

Male beauty contest

Every year, in a festival known as the *gerewol*, young Wodaabé men make themselves up to try and attract a wife in an unusual beauty contest. After much dancing, the women make their choice. If a marriage proposal results, the man kidnaps the woman, and they set off into the desert for a nomadic life together.

FIND OUT MORE AFRICA, HISTORY OF | BENIN EMPIRE | CONSERVATION | DESERTS | FARMING | FISHING INDUSTRY | OIL | ROCKS AND MINERALS | SLAVERY | TEXTILES AND WEAVING

AFRICAN WILDLIFE

NO OTHER CONTINENT matches the wealth of wildlife found in Africa. Covering the full climatic spectrum from intense heat to bitter cold, its varied vegetation has given rise to a wide range of animals, including mammals, birds, reptiles, fish, and insects. Among them are more than 40 species of primate, ranging from tiny galagos to huge gorillas, a great variety of antelopes, gazelles, and other hoofed animals, and 70 species of carnivore. Bird life, too, is extraordinarily rich; more than 1,500 species live south of the Sahara. In addition, Africa is inhabited by the world's fastest land animal, the cheetah; the biggest bird, the ostrich; and the largest land animal, the elephant.

Giraffe

The giraffe's great height – males reach up to 5.5 m (18 ft) – gives it the advantage of being able to spot danger from a distance and then escape at speed. It also enables the giraffe to browse on acacia leaves that are out of the reach of most other grassland animals, giving it a near monopoly of its principal food supply.

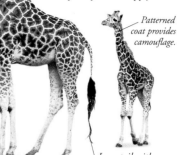

Patterned coat provides camouflage.

Long tail with coarse hair is used to deter flies.

Grassland wildlife

African grasslands (savannahs) sustain over 20 species of grazing animals, from the giant sable antelope to the tiny pygmy antelope. The herds of plains game and their predators, including lions, are pursued by scavengers such as hyenas and vultures. Grassland birds include the guineafowl and hornbills.

Long tail feathers help it balance when running.

Zebras call to each other while grazing.

Lion
The lion is the principal predator of the African savannah. Lionesses hunt together, preying on large animals, such as buffalo, zebra, and wildebeest.

Long legs for running through grass after snakes and frogs.

Secretary bird
Among the most striking of Africa's grassland birds is the secretary bird, with its long legs and feathered crest. It rarely flies, preferring to walk, nodding its head with each step. It attacks snakes, spreading its wings over its body to shield itself from venomous bites, while using its feet to stamp them to death.

Aardvark
The aardvark is a solitary, nocturnal animal. It uses its powerful claws to break into the nests of ants and termites, which it extracts with its long, sticky tongue. The aardvark can dig at an astonishing speed – faster than a person with a shovel.

Zebra
Zebras usually live in family groups of 5–20 animals, but in the dry season they may gather in herds of a few hundred, for protection against predators such as lions. Male zebras defend themselves by kicking out with their legs and hooves. Zebras eat the tough tops of the grasses.

Papyrus
The most common plant in African swamps is papyrus. It grows in clumps, often dense enough to support the weight of large animals.

Papyrus may reach 4.5 m (15 ft) in height.

Wetland wildlife

Africa's wetlands are seething with wildlife, such as crocodiles, hippos, floodplain species such as lechwes, and fish, including the Nile perch and tiger fish. The wetlands also provide stopping places for migratory birds flying south to winter in Africa.

Lesser flamingo
Three million flamingos gather at Lake Nakuru, in Kenya, forming an amazing spectacle. They feed on the plentiful algae that flourish in the salty water, sunlight, and high temperatures in and around the lake.

Hippopotamus
Hippos spend most of the day submerged in water, with only their ears, eyes, and nostrils above the surface. They become active at dusk when they emerge from the water to graze on nearby grassland.

Cichlid fish
Lakes Malawi and Tanganyika contain 265 different species of cichlid (mouth-brooding fish); all but five are unique to Africa. Great depth, isolation, and few predators have resulted in this proliferation.

Long legs for wading through water.

Webbed feet

A

Addax

The addax lives in the driest and hottest parts of the Sahara – conditions few other animals could tolerate. It rarely drinks as it obtains all its liquid from the succulent plants and tubers on which it feeds.

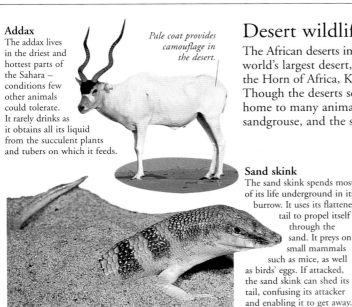

Pale coat provides camouflage in the desert.

Desert wildlife

The African deserts include the Sahara, the world's largest desert, and the deserts of the Horn of Africa, Kalahari, and Namib. Though the deserts seem barren, they are home to many animals such as bustards, sandgrouse, and the scimitar-horned oryx.

Fennec fox

The fennec lives in small colonies among sand dunes, into which it burrows to avoid the heat. It burrows so quickly, it disappears from sight in seconds.

Fox obtains all its liquid from its prey.

Sand skink

The sand skink spends most of its life underground in its burrow. It uses its flattened tail to propel itself through the sand. It preys on small mammals such as mice, as well as birds' eggs. If attacked, the sand skink can shed its tail, confusing its attacker and enabling it to get away.

Sandgrouse

Despite living in the open desert, sandgrouse must drink regularly. This often means flying long distances. Sandgrouse obtain water for their young by immersing themselves in water and carrying droplets back to their nests in their feathers.

Rainforest wildlife

Rainforests dominate western Central Africa. The warm, wet environment is home to many animals. Herbivores such as gorillas feed on leaves. Fruit that falls from the canopy provides food for pigs and porcupines, while animals such as tree pangolins forage in the trees.

Yellow back patch

Yellow-backed duiker

Standing 1 m (3.3 ft) at the shoulder, the yellow-backed duiker is the largest of the forest duikers. In West Africa it lives in the densest parts of the rain forest; in East Africa it lives in bamboo forests.

Red colobus monkey

The red colobus is one of five species of specialized leaf-eating primates spread across Africa. It lives in the forest canopy in family groups of about 20 animals, rarely descending to the ground.

Small spotted genet

This cat-like animal spends the day asleep in the branches of a tree, becoming active at night. An agile climber, it stalks its prey – birds, small mammals, and insects – like a cat, before seizing it with a sudden pounce.

Gorillas eat many types of rainforest vegetation.

Mountain gorilla

The mountain gorilla is confined to a small area of rainforest, at a point where the boundaries of Uganda, Zaire, and Rwanda meet. It is a massively built animal, but is not normally aggressive. The females build nests where they sleep with their young.

Gelada

The gelada is the sole survivor of a group of ground-dwelling primates now found only in Ethiopia. It lives in open country at high altitude, close to cliffs and rock faces, where it retreats if alarmed. It eats seeds, roots, grass, and fruit.

Mountain wildlife

The mountains of Ruwenzori, Kenya, and Kilimanjaro have distinctive plants and animals. Rodents inhabit moorland, while the scarlet-tufted malachite sunbird lives in close association with giant lobelias.

Giant plants

Africa's mountain plants include some of the most extraordinary vegetation in the world. Plants small elsewhere have grown into giants, including the giant lobelia, tree heath, and giant groundsel, which reaches 9 m (30 ft) in height.

Flower spikes of the Giant Lobelia are more than 1 m (3.3 ft) tall.

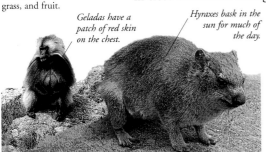

Geladas have a patch of red skin on the chest.

Hyraxes bask in the sun for much of the day.

Rock hyrax

Rock hyraxes live in colonies of 50 or more among rocky outcrops. They remain alert for signs of danger, such as eagles and leopards.

Crowned hawk eagle

One of the largest eagles, the crowned hawk eagle is widely distributed throughout the mountainous regions of East Africa and Zaire, wherever there are suitable forests containing the monkeys that are its chief food.

FIND OUT MORE | BIRDS | BIRDS OF PREY | DEER AND ANTELOPES | GIRAFFES | HIPPOPOTAMUSES | LIONS AND OTHER WILD CATS | LIZARDS | MONKEYS AND OTHER PRIMATES

AIR

WE LIVE, MOVE, AND BREATHE at the bottom of an immense ocean of air called the atmosphere. Air is an invisible mixture of gases, made up of a teeming mass of millions of tiny gas molecules that move about randomly and at high speed. Without air, the Earth would be a lifeless planet, because the gases air contains are vital to plants and animals.

The uses of air

Scuba divers use compressed air to breathe underwater. However, the gases in air can also be used separately. Nitrogen is used in explosives and oxygen in medicine. Gases are extracted from air by a process called fractional distillation. Air is cooled and compressed until it forms a blue liquid. When the liquid expands and warms up, each gas boils off at a different temperature and is collected separately.

Divers with tanks of compressed air

Carbon dioxide (CO_2)

Carbon dioxide is vital for plant life. Plants absorb carbon dioxide from the air and combine it with water gathered by their roots to form sugars, which they use for growth.

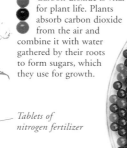

Tablets of nitrogen fertilizer

Nitrogen (N_2)

Every living cell contains nitrogen. Plants cannot take nitrogen from the air, so they get it from the soil. Fertilizers contain nitrogen to replenish what plants remove from the soil.

Composition of air

Any volume of pure, dry air is 78.09% nitrogen, 20.95% oxygen, 0.93% argon, and 0.03% carbon dioxide and other gases. These coloured balls represent the proportions of the different gases in air.

Candle burns in jar of air.

Flame goes out and water level rises as the oxygen is used up.

Red balls represent oxygen.

Green balls represent argon.

Black ball represents carbon dioxide and other gases.

Blue balls represent nitrogen.

Oxygen (O_2)

Burning is a chemical reaction of a substance with oxygen, as this experiment shows. The candle burns in the jar of air until it has used up all the oxygen. Humans and other animals use oxygen from the air to "burn" food inside their bodies and produce energy.

Argon (Ar)

The gas argon is called an "inert" gas because it is so unreactive. Electric light bulbs are often filled with argon. It prevents the bulb's filament from burning up as it would in air, giving the bulb a much longer life.

Air pollution

Air is not naturally "pure" and contains varying amounts of other substances, such as dust, water vapour, bacteria, pollen, and polluting gases. Air pollution from industry and traffic can cause serious health problems in towns and cities, as well as long-term damage to the environment.

Smog

The hazy air pollution that hangs over an urban area is called smog. Sulphurous smog is the result of burning fuels with a high sulphur content, such as coal. Photochemical smog occurs when sunlight causes car exhaust fumes to react together.

Water vapour

Up to 4 per cent of the volume of air may be water vapour. Warm air can hold more water vapour than cool air. A can of cold drink absorbs heat from the air around it. As the air cools, water vapour condenses out of the air to form droplets on the outside of the can.

Air pressure

Air exerts a force on objects because its moving molecules are constantly colliding with them. Air pressure is a measure of this force. The pressure of the open air is called atmospheric pressure. It is lower at high altitudes, where the air is less dense.

Barometer

A device that measures atmospheric pressure is called a barometer. It can be used to forecast a change in the weather, because air pressure varies slightly from day to day with changes in the air's temperature and humidity.

Sucking

When a person sucks on one end of a drinking straw, the lungs reduce the air pressure inside the straw. Atmospheric pressure on the liquid's surface does the rest, pushing down on the liquid, and making it rise up through the straw.

Compressed air

The pressure of air can be increased by compressing it – that is, pumping more and more of it into a limited space. Bicycle tyres are filled with compressed air to give a smooth, comfortable ride.

Weight of air

Air has weight, as this simple experiment proves. Identical empty balloons are attached to both ends of a stick. The balloons balance when the stick is suspended from its middle. Inflating one of the balloons tips the balance, because the balloon full of compressed air weighs more than the empty balloon.

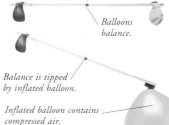

Balloons balance.

Balance is tipped by inflated balloon.

Inflated balloon contains compressed air.

Joseph Priestley

English scientist and clergyman Joseph Priestley (1733–1804) discovered oxygen in 1774. He also discovered many other gases, including nitrous oxide (laughing gas) and ammonia. Priestley studied carbon dioxide and devised a way to make carbonated (fizzy) water.

FIND OUT MORE | ATOMS AND MOLECULES | CELLS | FRICTION | GASES | LUNGS AND BREATHING | PHOTOSYNTHESIS | POLLUTION | PRESSURE | WEATHER

AIRCRAFT

ANY VEHICLE THAT travels through the air is called an aircraft. The ability to soar over obstacles such as oceans and mountains makes aircraft the fastest form of travel. An airliner (a large passenger plane) can fly a passenger thousands of kilometres in hours. The same journey would take several days by boat or car. Airliners and military aircraft are complex machines. Their frames are built with lightweight metals, such as aluminium, and hi-tech materials, such as plastics. Inside, their sophisticated electronic controls help pilots fly efficiently and safely. Smaller aircraft, such as gliders and hot-air balloons, are often used for sport and leisure.

Types of aircraft

The word aircraft covers all flying machines – from balloons to helicopters. Most aircraft are aeroplanes, which have wings, and jet engines to give them speed. Other types of aircraft are gliders, which have no engines, helicopters, balloons, and airships. An aircraft's function determines its size and shape.

Biplanes
Many planes before World War II (1939–1945) had two pairs of wings, and were called biplanes.

Transport aircraft
Armies need aircraft to transport troops and equipment. Special aircraft are designed to carry very heavy objects, such as tanks.

Balloons
Lighter-than-air craft are known as balloons. A bag is filled with gas or hot air that is lighter than the atmosphere.

Gliders
Currents of air move up and down. A glider has no engine, but flies by the effects of air currents on its wings.

Concorde
Supersonic airliners such as Concorde can travel faster than the speed of sound – about 1,240 kmh (770 mph). They can cross the Atlantic twice as fast as any other airliner, but are very noisy and need lots of fuel.

Anatomy of an airliner

Most airliners, such as this *Boeing 747-400*, have the same basic design. The main part is the fuselage, which is similar to a long, thin, metal tube. The wings are attached to the middle of the fuselage, and the tailplane and fin are attached at the back. A floor separates the passenger cabin from the baggage hold.

The **Boeing 747-400** can fly more than 13,600 km (8,451 miles) without stopping for fuel.

Main cabin, with economy-class seats

Fin

Tailplane

Upper deck with business-class seats

Fuselage

Fuel for engines in fuel tanks inside wings

Forward cabin with first-class seats

Engine controls and navigation instruments

Pilot's control column

Turbofan engines hang from wings on pylons.

Freighters
Airplanes that carry cargo are called freighters. The cargo is loaded through a huge door in the aeroplane's nose. The *Boeing 747* can be converted from a passenger plane to a freighter, then back again.

Cockpit
The aircraft is controlled from the cockpit. The pilot and co-pilot fly the plane using control columns, and instruments show the status of all the plane's equipment. The cockpit also contains radar and radio controls.

In-flight food
Pre-prepared meals are stored in trolleys, which lock into spaces in the aircraft's galleys until it is time for the cabin staff to serve them.

Entertainment
Some airliners feature video screens and headphones that can be tuned to music channels.

Howard Hughes
Hughes (1905–76) was an American industrialist, film-maker, and aviation enthusiast. He founded the airline TWA, and broke a number of aviation records in aircraft of his own design. Not all were successful; the *Spruce Goose* (1947) only flew once.

A

Forces of flight

An aircraft needs two forces to fly: lift to keep it up and thrust to propel it forward. Lift overcomes the plane's weight, and thrust overcomes the drag caused by the air flowing past the plane. When an aircraft is cruising, lift is equal to weight and thrust is equal to drag.

Lift

Thrust

Drag

Weight

Wings

An aircraft's wings create lift. To do this, they need air to flow over them.

The aerofoil shape
If you cut an aircraft wing in two and looked at the end, you would see a special cross-section called an aerofoil. The top surface is longer and more curved than the bottom surface.

The aerofoil at work
The air pressure beneath the wing is greater than above it, and lifts the wing up.

Lift

Angle of attack
At small angles, tilting the blades gives extra lift.

Lift

Flying controls

An aircraft is steered through the air by way of three main control surfaces – the elevators on the tailplane, the ailerons on the wings, and a rudder on the fin.

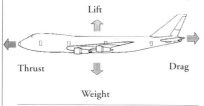

Elevators make the aircraft's nose tilt up and down.

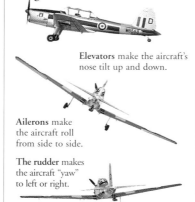

Ailerons make the aircraft roll from side to side.

The rudder makes the aircraft "yaw" to left or right.

Aero engines

An aircraft's engines drive it through the air by producing thrust. Different types of engine produce thrust in different ways. Piston and turbo-prop engines drive propellers that screw into the air, just as a ship propeller bites into water. Turbo-jet and turbo-fan engines produce a fast-moving stream of gas which pushes the aircraft forwards.

Piston engines
These work in the same way as car engines. Petrol and air vapour are mixed in the engine's cylinders and they cause an explosion. The explosions push pistons, which turn a shaft. The shaft then turns a propeller.

Shaft

Turbo-prop engines
The simplest type of jets – a turbo-jet engine with a propeller is called a turbo-prop engine. A motor turns the compressor and the propeller, which provides the main engine thrust.

Propeller spins to provide engine thrust

Turbo-jet engines
Air is drawn in and compressed, then sent to a chamber where fuel burns. The gases produced are shot out of the back of the engine, which pushes the aircraft forwards, like a deflating balloon.

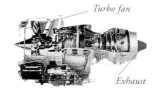

Gas shoots out

Air drawn in

Turbo-fan engines
A hybrid of turbo-jet and turbo-props, the turbo-fan engine sucks in air, which is combined with the backdraft from a fan, and also sends air around the engine, producing the same effect as a propeller.

Turbo fan

Exhaust

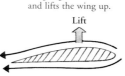
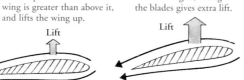

Helicopters

Unlike most aircraft, which have fixed wings, a helicopter has a spinning rotor with two or more long, thin blades attached. When the blades spin round, they lift the helicopter straight up into the air. A helicopter can take off from almost anywhere and does not need to use airport runways. It can hover in one place, and fly backwards, forwards, and sideways. This makes it the most versatile of all aircraft; it is very useful for transport, surveillance, and rescue missions.

Rotor blades twist to control the helicopter's direction.

Turbo-shaft engine

Main rotor

Main rotor

G-HUMT

Tail rotor stops fuselage spinning in opposite direction to main rotor.

Landing skids in place of undercarriage

Flying controls
A helicopter pilot has three flying controls. The collective pitch lever changes the amount of lift produced by the main rotor. The cyclic pitch control makes the helicopter move forwards, backwards, or sideways. Rudder pedals make the helicopter turn left or right.

Lifting off
Before take-off, the main and tail rotors are speeded up. When the main rotor is turning fast enough, the pilot lifts the collective pitch lever to increase the tilt of the rotor blades. The tilt produces lift, and the helicopter takes off. The higher the lever is lifted, the faster the aircraft rises.

Moving away
The cyclic pitch control makes the helicopter move in the direction the control is pushed. It tilts the main rotor so that some of the rotor's lift pulls the helicopter along. Here, the pilot has pulled the control back to make the helicopter move backwards.

Igor Ivan Sikorsky
Sikorsky (1889–1972) was born in Ukraine, where he became an aeronautical engineer. In 1919 he moved to the United States where he set up an aircraft factory. He designed the first practical helicopter, the *VS-300*, which first flew in 1939. The design had to be modified many times: at one point, the helicopter flew in every direction except forwards.

FIND OUT MORE   AIRSHIPS AND BALLOONS   ATMOSPHERE   ENGINES AND MOTORS   FLIGHT, HISTORY OF   TRANSPORT, HISTORY OF   WARPLANES   WORLD WAR I   WORLD WAR II

Types of aircraft
Military

Twin tail fins

Fighter/strike aircraft, McDonnell Douglas F/A-18E Super Hornet

Harrier can take off and land vertically.

Naval strike aircraft, McDonnell Douglas AV-8B Harrier II

Wings fold back for supersonic flight.

Swing-wing bomber, General Dynamics F-111A Aardvark

The A-10's huge array of weapons gives it a massive firepower.

Ground-attack "tankbuster" aircraft, Fairchild A-10 Thunderbolt II

Radar dome

Refuelling/electronic counter-measures aircraft, Boeing EC-135 Stratotanker

Hinged nose is raised to allow loading.

Heavy transport aircraft, Lockheed C-5A Galaxy – one of the world's largest aircraft

Twin propellers

Radar bulge

Radar aircraft, Fairey Gannet AEW-3, gives early warning of air attacks.

Extended wings for high-altitude flight.

High-level reconnaissance aircraft, Lockheed U-2

Passenger and cargo aircraft

777's engines are the most powerful aircraft engines ever built.

Wide-bodied, long-haul airliner, Boeing 777-200

737 is the world's best-selling jet airliner.

Medium-range airliner, Boeing 737-300

Low-noise engines

Short-range airliner, British Aerospace Bae 146-RJ85

More than 1,800 727s were built.

Freight transporter aircraft, Boeing 727

Seating for 8–14 passsengers

Business jet, British Aerospace Bae 125-600

Turbo-prop engines

Commuter aircraft, Fairchild Metro II

Cabin holds four people.

Single engine

Leisure aircraft, SOCATA TB-20 Trinidad

Rear-mounted engines

Wing float

Flying boat, Beriev A-50 Mermaid

Helicopters

Wings carry armaments such as rockets and guns.

Attack helicopter, Bell AH-1 Cobra

Five-bladed main rotor

Tail rotor

Radar

Passenger helicopter, Sikorsky S-61

Transport helicopter, Boeing CH-47 Chinook

Twin rotors

Osprey can fly like both a helicopter and a plane.

Rotors can tilt 90°.

Tilt-rotor aircraft, Boeing V-22 Osprey

Sport

Glider soars on warm air currents.

Pilot launches glider by running downhill.

Hang-glider is like a huge wing with a harness below to hold the pilot.

Fabric-covered wings and fuselage

Biplane training/leisure aircraft, De Havilland Tiger Moth DH8A

Wing of light woven fabric over metal frame

Propeller

Motor

Hand grip

Wheels allow microlight to take off and land like a normal aircraft.

Microlight is a kind of motorized hang-glider, with a strong frame and a streamlined fibreglass "tricycle" underneath to carry the pilot.

AIRPORTS

TODAY, MORE PEOPLE TRAVEL by air than ever before. Whether they are business people off to visit clients or families going on holiday, all air travellers leave from airports, which range in size from small local facilities to enormous international terminals. A large airport is like a city. It contains shops, offices, and hotels, in addition to all the buildings, runways, and taxiways needed to service the aircraft and their passengers. Airport security is always tight, because airports and aircraft have often been the targets of terrorist attacks.

Features of an airport

Aircraft take off and land on runways, which are linked to the terminal buildings by routes called taxiways. The passengers embark and disembark at the terminal buildings. For the aircraft, the airport has repair workshops, refuelling facilities, and storage hangars.

Runway
To take the biggest jet aircraft, runways have to be 3–4 km (1.8–2.5 miles) long and some 50 m (165 ft) wide. They need a specially toughened surface to take the pounding they get when large jets take off or land.

Terminal building at Kansai International Airport, Japan

"Landside" of terminal

Passengers enter terminal from lower level and leave it from upper level.

Road transport for passengers leaving the airport.

Access area provides escalators to all parts of the terminal building.

International arrivals floor

Curving roof truss

International departures floor

Security area and passport checkpoint

Domestic arrivals and departures are on middle 2 floors.

Boarding gates

"Airside" of terminal

Bridge connects boarding gate to aircraft.

Waiting aircraft

Service area contains boilers, ventilation equipment, and other building services.

Air traffic control

At the heart of an airport is the control tower, where air traffic controllers monitor every moment of an aircraft's arrival and departure. They make sure that each pilot follows the correct flight path, that all aircraft land in the right place, and that there is a safe amount of time between each take-off and landing.

Air traffic controllers in the control tower

Radar display screen
Airport radar tracks each aircraft as it lands, giving the controllers precise details of its position. All aircraft within 20 to 50 km (12 to 30 miles) of the airport can be tracked by radar and shown on the controllers' display screens.

Flight path
Air traffic controllers tell pilots when it is safe to land. They guide a pilot to a specific path, which the pilot must then follow as the aircraft descends to the runway. Navigation aids, such as high-frequency radio beacons, give the pilot accurate bearings.

How an aircraft lands

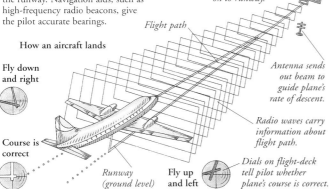

Fly down and right

Course is correct

Runway (ground level)

Fly up and left

Radar antenna sends out beam to guide plane on to runway.

Flight path

Antenna sends out beam to guide plane's rate of descent.

Radio waves carry information about flight path.

Dials on flight-deck tell pilot whether plane's course is correct.

Security

Airport security staff are always on their guard, trying to spot terrorists or smugglers. Metal detectors and other electronic devices alert staff when a passenger is carrying a gun or other type of weapon. There are also "sniffer" dogs that have been trained to detect the scent of explosives or illegal drugs.

An X-ray reveals a gun.

Passports
A person travelling from one country to another usually carries a passport, an official document that identifies the owner and their place of origin. Passports are inspected at international airports.

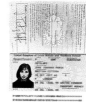

EU passport

X-ray scanner
Airport staff use X-ray machines to scan the contents of passengers' luggage. A screen on the side of the X-ray machine shows what is inside each bag. Different materials show up in different colours, enabling items such as guns to be found with ease.

Airports and the environment

A large airport can have a devastating impact on the local environment. Clearing the land to build an airport destroys carefully balanced ecosystems, while the air pollution can harm wildlife, and the noise may scare some animals away.

Kestrel

Airport ecosystems
Since airports cover such vast areas, birds and animals can also move into these areas and establish new ecosystems, undisturbed by people.

Animals can live in the large green spaces around a big airport.

FIND OUT MORE

AIRCRAFT   ECOLOGY AND ECOSYSTEMS   RADAR AND SONAR   TRAVEL

AIRSHIPS AND BALLOONS

AIRSHIPS AND BALLOONS are known as lighter-than-air aircraft because, instead of wings, they use a large envelope, or bag, full of gas or hot air that is lighter than the air in the atmosphere around it. The air pushes the envelope upwards, just as water pushes a submerged air-filled ball upwards. In 1783, the Montgolfier brothers achieved the first manned flight ever by sending a hot-air balloon over Paris. Balloons fly where the wind blows them; airships have engines and can be steered. Today, airships are used for aerial filming and coast-guard patrols, and ballooning is a popular sport.

Anatomy of a modern airship
The main part of an airship is its envelope, which contains bags of helium gas. The gas is slightly pressurized to keep the envelope in shape. A fin and tailplane keep the airship steady as it flies slowly along. The crew travels in a gondola attached to the underside of the envelope.

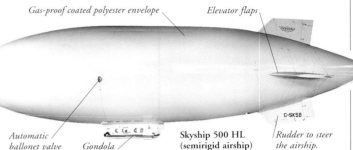

Gas-proof coated polyester envelope   Elevator flaps

Automatic ballonet valve   Gondola   Skyship 500 HL (semirigid airship)   Rudder to steer the airship.

The Hindenburg, 1937

Airship disasters
Several terrible disasters made people lose trust in airship travel. Airships were usually lost for two reasons: either they were uncontrollable in bad weather; or the highly inflammable hydrogen gas used inside the envelope exploded. Today, airship pilots use the much safer helium gas in special nylon envelopes. However, they still have to be wary of the weather.

Types of airship
Practical airships could be built only after the lightweight internal combustion engine had been developed. The earliest airships were "nonrigid" (they are still used today). These were followed by the "rigid" and the less usual "semirigid" types of airship.

Nonrigid airships have a flexible fabric envelope, from which the load hangs, suspended by ropes.

Rigid airship's envelope is built around a rigid framework. This skeleton contains bags of the lifting gas – helium.

Ferdinand von Zeppelin
German count Ferdinand von Zeppelin (1838–1917) began experimenting with air travel in 1891. In 1900, he devised the first airship, a 128-m (420-ft) rigid craft named the LZ1. During World War I, some 100 Zeppelins were built for military use.

Balloons
Balloons were first used for aerial reconnaissance during the French Revolution, and used again in the American Civil War. During World Wars I and II, balloons were used to spot targets for artillery attacks, and barrage balloons defended cities against aircraft.

Weather and research balloons
To study what is happening in the upper reaches of the atmosphere, pilots send up helium-filled weather balloons. These carry instruments which measure temperature, wind speed, and so on, and send their results to the ground or to satellites by radio.

Balloon festivals
Today, ballooning is a popular sport. During the summer, ballooning enthusiasts gather at festivals to enjoy the dazzling prospect of dozens of brightly coloured balloons flying together. Some of the balloons are owned by companies, and are made in the shapes of their products, as a form of advertising.

Flight
Hot-air ballooning requires a perfectly clear day with a gentle breeze. Too high a wind puts the balloon at risk on take-off and landing. After take-off, a ground crew follows the balloon in a vehicle to recover both it and the crew after landing.

1 The balloon is laid on the ground. Burners heat air to fill the balloon.

2 The balloon's envelope expands as the hot air starts to fill it

3 The expanding balloon becomes buoyant, and rises into the air.

4 Guy ropes hold the balloon down until the crew boards.

5 The crew blasts hot air into the envelope to keep the balloon afloat.

FIND OUT MORE   ATMOSPHERE   FLIGHT, HISTORY OF   GALILEO GALILEI   GASES   JOHNSON, AMY   RENAISSANCE   WEATHER FORECASTING

Airships and balloons

Balloons

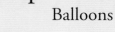

False basket

Easter egg envelope is decorated to celebrate Easter.

Golf ball, an uncomplicated, yet realistic balloon shape

Upside-down balloon, where a false basket has been attached to the balloon's top.

Fabergé egg, the trademark jewel of a famous Russian jewellers

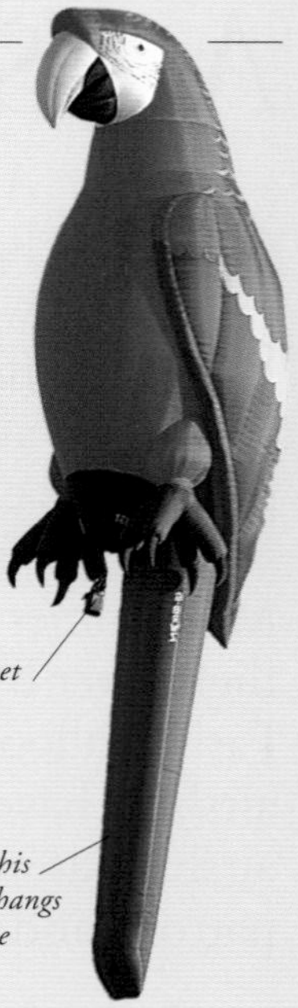

Basket

Lavishly decorated character from the *Thousand and One Nights*

Uncle Sam, a lighthearted symbol of the USA

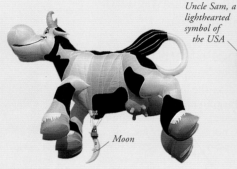

Part of this balloon hangs below the basket.

Red, blue, and yellow panels of this balloon's envelope represent the exotic plumage of a parrot.

Carmen Miranda, a 1940s' singing star

Moon

A **"cow jumps over the moon"** is a very complicated balloon shape inspired by the famous nursery rhyme.

Face-shaped balloons are relatively simple to create.

Upturned eaves

Modern tractor has its basket hanging where the back axle would be.

Japanese temple; the envelope comes complete with authentic upturned eaves and balcony rails.

Drink can, the first non-traditional balloon shape

Santa Claus, an aerial Christmas decoration

NASA rocket, celebrating space exploration.

Elephant, complete with trunk and a surprised look!

Airships

Spectacular eagle has a very complicated and realistically painted envelope.

Aerial tours are often run by companies that have both airships and balloons.

Modern airships, because of their visibility and size, are often used to advertise products or services.

Rupert the Bear, a favourite fictional character for children all over the world

ALEXANDER THE GREAT

IN LESS THAN FOUR YEARS, a brilliant young general created the largest empire the world had ever seen. The empire was the creation of Alexander the Great of Macedon, a gifted leader who inspired tremendous loyalty from his troops. It stretched from Greece in the west to India in the east. Alexander's sudden death at the age of 33 led to the empire's collapse, but it lived on in a series of towns that spread Greek culture eastwards. These cities, all called Alexandria after their founder, opened up a trade between Asia and Europe that survived for centuries.

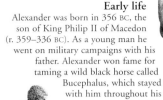

Early life
Alexander was born in 356 BC, the son of King Philip II of Macedon (r. 359–336 BC). As a young man he went on military campaigns with his father. Alexander won fame for taming a wild black horse called Bucephalus, which stayed with him throughout his whole life.

Aristotle
Alexander was taught by the Athenian philosopher Aristotle (384–322 BC). Aristotle's interests ranged from politics and morality to biology and literature. He shared his enthusiasm for new ideas with his young pupil.

Greece
The heartland of Alexander's empire was his home state of Macedon, northern Greece. Before Alexander became king, Greece was divided into rival city states, and was threatened by the powerful Persian Empire.

Terracotta figure of the Greek love goddess, Aphrodite

Alexander's empire
When Alexander became king of Macedon in 336 BC, Greece was dominated by Persia. In a series of brilliant military campaigns, Alexander defeated Persia and created his vast empire.

- Gordion
- Issus
- Gaugamela
- Alexandria ad Caucasum
- Alexandria Prophthasia
- Babylon
- Alexandria
- Persepolis

Macedonian Empire

Persia
The rich empire of Persia occupied much of modern Iraq, Turkey, and Iran. After Alexander had conquered the area, he tried to unite Macedonia and Persia by encouraging his generals to marry Persians. Alexander himself married Roxana, a princess from eastern Persia.

Stag comes from palace at Persepolis.

Persian silver stag ornament

Egypt
In 332 BC, Alexander conquered Egypt and was accepted as the new pharaoh. He founded the city of Alexandria, in northern Egypt, which became the most important city of the Greek-speaking world. When Alexander died in 323 BC, he was buried in a vast tomb in the centre of the city.

Alexander wears the pharaoh's crown

Battle of Issus
In 333 BC, the Macedonian army overwhelmed the more powerful Persian army led by Darius III (r. 336–330 BC) at the battle of Issus, Syria. The Persians were defeated again in 331 BC at Gaugamela near the River Tigris. After this battle, the Persian capital, Persepolis, was destroyed and the empire collapsed.

Relief of the Battle of Issus

Eastern empire
By 326 BC, Alexander had marched through Persia and had conquered Afghanistan and the Punjab. Although his troops were very loyal to him, they refused to go further than the River Indus.

Coin from Indus area

Death of Alexander
In 323 BC Alexander caught a fever in the city of Babylon. Although he was only 33, he died. This sudden death meant that Alexander did not have time to consolidate his rule or even name his successor. Within a few years of his death, the huge Macedonian Empire had collapsed.

Alexander's sarcophagus

Carved relief shows Alexander leading his troops.

Sarcophagus from the royal cemetery of Sidon, said to be the tomb of Alexander.

ALEXANDER THE GREAT

356 BC	Born in Macedon
336 BC	Succeeds his father to the Macedonian throne; quells rebellions in Greece
334 BC	Leads his army into Persia and defeats a Persian army at the Granicus River
333 BC	Defeats Darius III at Issus
331 BC	Defeats Darius III again at Gaugamela, completing his conquest of the Persian Empire
326 BC	Reaches the Indus, but is forced to turn back by his troops
323 BC	Dies of fever in Babylon

FIND OUT MORE ASIA, HISTORY OF | EGYPT, ANCIENT | GREECE, ANCIENT | PERSIAN EMPIRES | PHILOSOPHY

AMERICAN CIVIL WAR

LESS THAN 80 YEARS after independence, the USA split in two over the issue of slavery. The richer, industrial northern states had banned slavery, but slaves were used on plantations in the south. When Abraham Lincoln became president in 1860, the southern states, fearing he would ban slavery, seceded from the Union, and established the Confederate States of America. Fighting began in 1861 and lasted for four years. At first the sides were evenly matched, but the strength of the Union wore down the Confederacy, and it surrendered. Slavery was then abolished throughout the country.

Divided nation

Eleven southern slave states left the Union of states, declaring independence as the Confederacy. Four other slave states refused to break away; West Virginia split from the rest of the state and stayed in the Union.

Union states

Confederate states

Slave states in the union

Washington

Charleston

First modern war

The American Civil War was the first recognizably modern war. Railways transported men and supplies to the battlefield, and iron ships were used for the first time. Commanders talked to each other by field telegraph, and the war was photographed and widely reported in newspapers.

Much of the fighting was trench warfare, but troops were also prepared for a pitched battle.

Soldiers
More than three million people fought in the two opposing armies, most of them as infantrymen (foot soldiers).

Union infantry sergeant

Chevrons

Shell jacket

Sergeant's sash

Sergeant's trouser stripe

Confederate infantryman

Union soldiers and guns

Gunner

Field gun

Officer

Percussion musket

Abraham Lincoln

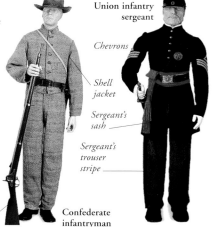

Lincoln was born in Kentucky in 1809. He was elected to the state legislature in 1834, was elected president in 1860, and led the Union states to victory in the civil war. He was assassinated in 1865.

Merrimack and Monitor
The Confederate ironclad ship *Merrimack* (renamed *Virginia*) fought the Union's vessel *Monitor* on 9 March 1862. The battle was inconclusive, but marked the first occasion on which iron ships had been used in naval warfare.

Gettysburg Address
Lincoln's fine speeches helped win the war. In 1863, he dedicated a cemetery on the site of a battlefield in Gettysburg, Pennsylvania. In his speech, he hoped that "these dead shall not have died in vain; that this nation, under God, shall have a new birth of freedom, and that government of the people, by the people, for the people, shall not perish from the earth".

Appomattox
On 9 April 1865, at Appomattox, Virginia, the Confederate general Robert E. Lee surrendered to Union general Ulysses S. Grant. More than 600,000 Americans died in the four years of fighting, and many more were injured.

Signing the surrender documents

Timeline

April 1861 After 11 states leave the Union, war breaks out when Confederate troops fire on the Union garrison at Fort Sumter, South Carolina.

1861 Confederates under generals Jackson and Beauregard win the first major battle against Unionists at Bull Run, near Washington.

Ulysses S. Grant

1862 Confederates win Seven Days' Battle (near Richmond, Virginia) and Battle of Fredericksburg, Virginia.

1863 Union wins its first major battle at Gettysburg; Emancipation Proclamation frees slaves in the Confederate states.

1864 Ulysses S. Grant becomes Union commander-in-chief.

1864 General Sherman's Union army marches through Georgia, taking Atlanta and weakening the Confederacy.

13-in Mortar

April 1865 Lee's Confederate army surrenders at Appomattox, Virginia.

May 1865 Last Confederate army surrenders.

December 1865 Slavery is banned throughout the USA by the 13th amendment.

FIND OUT MORE   AMERICAN REVOLUTION   ARMIES   NORTH AMERICA, HISTORY OF   SHIPS AND BOATS   SLAVERY   UNITED STATES, HISTORY OF   WARFARE   WASHINGTON, GEORGE

AMERICAN REVOLUTION

IN 1783, A NEW NATION WAS BORN – the United States of America. Its struggle for independence is called the American Revolution. It began in 1775, when 13 American colonies went to war against Britain. Britain governed the colonies and imposed high taxes. The colonists, who were not represented in the British Parliament, resented the taxes. Protests and demonstrations broke out, and the colonists formed a Continental Congress to negotiate with Britain. A skirmish led to war, and in 1776, the American colonists, inspired by ideals of freedom, declared independence. The British surrendered in 1781, and two years later recognized the new country.

Maine (to Massachusetts)
New Hampshire
Massachusetts
New York
Rhode Island
Pennsylvania
Connecticut
New Jersey
Delaware
Virginia
Maryland
N. Carolina
S. Carolina
Georgia

Thirteen colonies
After the Revolution, Britain's 13 original colonies formed the first 13 states of the new United States.

Stamp tax

The colonists set their own taxes. But in 1765, Britain introduced a stamp tax on legal documents. The angry colonists stated that "taxation without representation is tyranny". They refused to buy British goods.

Boston Tea Party
Britain withdrew the stamp tax, but set others on glass and tea. Three groups of protesters, dressed as Mohawk Indians, boarded tea ships in Boston Harbour and threw their cargo into the water.

Colonists pour tea into Boston Harbour, in protest at British taxes

Lexington and Concord

In April 1775, the war began with skirmishes near Lexington and Concord. American patriots forced the British to withdraw at Lexington. They marched back to Boston under continuous fire.

Paul Revere
Paul Revere (1735–1818) rode through Massachusetts on the night of 18 April 1775, to warn that the British were coming. He was part of an anti-British group called the Sons of Liberty.

Revere on horseback

Thomas Jefferson

A planter from Virginia, Thomas Jefferson (1743–1826) attended the Continental Congress in 1775. He drafted the Declaration of Independence, reformed the laws of his native state, and went on diplomatic missions to Europe. He became the third president of the USA in 1801 and served until 1809.

Revolutionary war

The war lasted for six years. Washington's leadership played a vital part in the American victory. He led his troops to victories at Brandywine (1777) and Yorktown (1781).

American soldier
- Cocked hat
- Cartridge box belt
- Knapsack strap
- Brush for musket lock
- Musket
- Gaitered trousers
- Musket

British infantryman
- Cocked hat
- Crossbelt
- Red coat
- Bayonet
- Brush for musket lock
- Breeches
- Leather spatterdash
- Shoe

Surrender at Yorktown
The fighting lasted until spring 1781, when the colonists cut the British off from their supplies at Yorktown. They finally surrendered on 19 October.

Declaration of Independence

On 4 July 1776, the 13 colonies signed the Declaration of Independence. This document stated that "all men are created equal..." and its belief in "Life, Liberty, and the Pursuit of Happiness" later inspired the French Revolution.

George Washington

The commander of the colonial army was George Washington (1732–1799). He was an inspiring general, who kept the morale of his troops high in spite of several defeats at the beginning of the war. When France joined the war on the colonial side in 1778, followed by Spain in 1779, victory was assured.

Washington

The opposing armies
The British were well trained but poorly led. Their orders came from 4,000 km (2,500 miles) away. The Americans were less well trained and equipped, but knew the terrain and had good leaders.

Timeline
1765 Britain introduces the stamp tax. Protests break out. Britain withdraws the stamp tax, but other taxes remain.

1773 Boston Tea Party. Americans, dressed as Mohawks, dump tea in Boston Harbour as a protest against heavy taxes.

1774–75 Continental Congress. Representatives draft a petition to Britain insisting on no taxation without representation.

1775 Battle of Lexington. Congress takes over government of the colonies, and appoints Washington Commander-in-Chief.

1777 British general John Burgoyne (1722–92) forced to surrender at Saratoga.

1778 France joins the war on the American side.

1781 British surrender at Yorktown.

French private soldier

FIND OUT MORE FRENCH REVOLUTION   UNITED KINGDOM, HISTORY OF   UNITED STATES, HISTORY OF   WARFARE   WASHINGTON, GEORGE

AMPHIBIANS

COLD-BLOODED animals, amphibians are vertebrates (animals with a backbone) that evolved from fish. They are adapted for life on land, but most must return to water in some form to breed. Amphibians undergo a process known as metamorphosis in their development from larvae to adult, hence the Greek origin of their name: *amphi* meaning "double"; *bios* meaning "life". There are three groups of amphibians and more than 3,000 species.

Amphibian features

Apart from the caecilians and a few species of salamander, adult amphibians have four legs, each with four or five digits. Most species take to the water to mate and produce their eggs, but some make nests on land, occasionally in burrows in the ground or in moss.

European common frog

Long legs for leaping.

Frog leaps after prey such as an insect.

Webbed toes for swimming.

Marbled newt

"Marbled" colour extends along the tail.

Couch's spadefoot toad

Amphibian groups

There are three groups of amphibians: the worm-like caecilians; the tailed amphibians, including newts and salamanders; and the tail-less frogs and toads, probably the most diverse group.

Distribution of amphibians
Amphibians live everywhere. Desert species survive the driest season by staying underground inside a membranous sac, which they secrete themselves. Some temperate species hibernate in pond mud in the winter.

Caecilians
Caecilians are legless, carnivorous amphibians most of which live in the tropics. Some species burrow in the ground; others are aquatic. They have small eyes and ears and sensory tentacles on the head.

Frogs and toads
In temperate regions, frogs are more aquatic than toads, have slimier skin and longer legs. In the tropics, some species of frog and toad are fully aquatic and live in trees or underground.

Newts and salamanders
The tailed amphibians – newts, salamanders, and the eel-like sirens of North America – live in tropical forests, temperate woods, mountain streams, and lakes. Some have very specialized lifestyles: a few even live in the total darkness of caves.

Skin

Amphibian skin is thin and scaleless. It is usually kept moist with mucus to increase its ability to allow oxygen through for skin breathing. Skin can be smooth or rough. It secretes certain chemicals: pheromones can attract potential mates, while poisons deter predators. As they grow, amphibians shed the top layer of skin.

White's tree frogs

Colour
Amphibians may have skin colours that absorb or reflect heat. Colour also varies with temperature, becoming pale when warm and darker if cold and damp.

Camouflaged tree frogs

Camouflage
Many frogs and toads are camouflaged to avoid detection by predators. Most have a combination of forest colours and disruptive patterning. Some rainforest species are shaped to look like dead leaves.

Great crested newt   Square marked toad

Mandarin salamander   Tree frog

Texture
Many frogs and toads have smooth skin covered by mucus. Other amphibians, such as the mandarin salamander and many dry-skinned toads, have raised nodules.

Poison-dart tadpoles

Defence
The bright colours of Colombian poison-dart frogs warn predators of their highly toxic skin. The tadpoles develop their skin poisons as their colours develop. Marine toads secrete a strong toxin through large glands behind the head.

Metamorphosis

The development from an aquatic larva that breathes through gills, or spiracles, to an air-breathing adult is called metamorphosis. It involves the growth of legs and the loss of the tail in frogs and toads.

Newt egg

Frog spawn

Eggs
Amphibian eggs are laid singly, in clumps, or in strings of clear "jelly" called spawn. They have no shell and require a moist environment to survive.

Tadpoles
Larvae, or tadpoles, hatch from the eggs. Salamander tadpoles have limbs, but frogs and toads develop these during metamorphosis. Salamander larvae are carnivorous, but most frog and toad tadpoles are herbivorous.

Frog tadpole

Gills

Salamander tadpole

Axolotl
Some salamanders may stay as larvae all their life. The axolotl is a form of the Mexican tiger salamander.

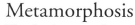

FIND OUT MORE | EVOLUTION | FROGS AND TOADS | POISONOUS ANIMALS | SALAMANDERS AND NEWTS

ANGLO-SAXONS

BY THE END of the 8th century, Britain's people, known as the Anglo-Saxons, had created a rich culture, which included masterpieces of jewellery, architecture, and literature. Originally these people had come from northern Germany and southern Denmark, where they were known as the Angles, Saxons, and Jutes. In the 3rd and 4th centuries, these tribes travelled to various parts of the Roman Empire, including Gaul, or present-day France, where their influence was short-lived. They travelled to Britain in the 5th century, where they settled, and formed several separate kingdoms. Eventually the kingdom of Wessex became the dominant power.

Culture

Cultural life centred on the monasteries and on the royal court. Alfred the Great gathered scholars and artists around him, and he himself translated many of the Latin classics into Anglo-Saxon, or Old English.

Architecture
Anglo-Saxon churches, like the one at Earls Barton, England, often have square towers decorated with stone relief. This pattern may be based on timber buildings of the period, which have all perished.

Decorated manuscripts
Monks produced quality manuscripts. One monk wrote the work, while a second illustrated it with figures, such as St Dunstan (c.909–988) kneeling before Jesus, and a third decorated it.

Kingdoms

There was always a struggle for supremacy among the kingdoms formed by the settlers. Northumbria was the earliest one to dominate under Edwin (d. 633). Then it was Mercia's turn under Aethelbald (d. 757) and Offa (d. 796). Finally, Wessex dominated under Alfred the Great. When Vikings from Denmark attacked and occupied northern England, Alfred stopped them from pushing farther south, and the Anglo-Saxons reconquered the north in the 10th century.

King Canute the Great
By 1016, the Danes ruled all England under the popular Canute (c.995–1035). Canute's sons inherited England, but the Anglo-Saxon Edward the Confessor (c.1003–1066) regained the country in 1042. He had no children and, when he died, an unsettled England was vulnerable to conquest by the Normans.

Edward the Confessor

Canute the Great

Written records

In the 7th century, missionaries from mainland Europe, such as St Augustine of Canterbury, converted the Anglo-Saxons to Christianity. The creation of monasteries meant that more people learned to read and write. Monks produced historical works, such as the *Anglo-Saxon Chronicle*, which today give insights into the events of the period.

Possible image of Alfred the Great

Jewellery
This jewel is inscribed "Alfred ordered me to be made" and may have belonged to Alfred the Great. The inscription and animal-head decoration are finely worked in gold; the portrait, perhaps of the king himself, is made of enamel.

Alfred the Great

Ruler of Wessex and Mercia, Alfred (c.849–c.899) was an able soldier who defended his kingdom against the Vikings. He loved learning and education, and arts and crafts flourished in his reign. He could not drive the Vikings from northern England, but most people saw him as their protector. He was the first English king to become a national symbol.

Anglo-Saxon Chronicle
In the ninth century, Alfred the Great ordered the *Chronicle*, a year-by-year account of the history of England. It covers the lives of kings and church leaders, military history, and major events, such as the Viking invasions, and was last updated in 1154.

Bede (c.673–735)
Bede, an English monk and teacher in Jarrow, wrote *A History of the English Church and People*, one of the most important sources of our knowledge of Anglo-Saxon times.

Timeline

450 Angles, Saxons, and Jutes from northern Germany and Denmark begin to arrive in England. They settle mainly along the eastern coast – East Anglia.

802–39 Reign of Egbert of Wessex. There are many Viking attacks.

871–99 Reign of Alfred the Great, famous for law-making, translating books into Old English, and defeating the Vikings at Edington in 878.

1016 Canute the Great, a Dane, is elected king by the British; he rules until 1035.

Anglo-Saxon buckle

1042 Anglo-Saxons regain power under Edward the Confessor.

1066 Last Anglo-Saxon king, Harold II, is killed by William of Normandy at the Battle of Hastings.

FIND OUT MORE   CELTS   EUROPE, HISTORY OF   MONASTERIES   NORMANS   UNITED KINGDOM, HISTORY OF   VIKINGS

ANIMAL BEHAVIOUR

A

ALL ANIMALS RESPOND to their surroundings. A cat, for example, will arch its back when threatening a rival, but lower its body when stalking a mouse. Everything that an animal does, and the way in which it does it, makes up its behaviour. An animal's behaviour enables it to increase its chances of survival and find a mate so that it can pass on its genes to the next generation. Some behaviours are inbuilt, or instinctive; others are learned during the animal's lifetime.

Egg-rolling
Greylag geese nest on the ground. If an egg rolls out of the nest, the female goose automatically reaches out with her neck and pulls the egg back in. By being in the wrong place, the egg acts as a sign stimulus that causes the female to carry out the fixed-action pattern of egg-rolling.

Instinctive behaviour

Instinct is a term used to describe behaviours that an animal performs automatically without having to learn them. Instinctive behaviour is programmed by an animal's genes. It consists of unchanging components called fixed-action patterns. The fixed-action pattern often begins when an animal responds to a feature in its surroundings or on another animal, called a sign stimulus.

Web spinning
Many species of spider, including this black widow spider, spin webs in order to trap their insect food. Web spinning is purely instinctive. A spider would not have time in its limited life to learn how to construct such a complex structure.

Sign stimulus
In the spring, when these freshwater fish breed, the male's throat and belly turn red. If one male intrudes into the territory of another male, its red colour acts as a sign stimulus that produces a fixed-action pattern: the occupying fish drives out the intruder.

Bright spring colours

Bright colours fade after the breeding season.

Learned behaviour

Learning occurs when an animal adapts to its surroundings by changing its behaviour. By responding to experiences and adapting to changing conditions, an animal increases its chances of survival. Learning takes time, and animals that are dependent on learned behaviour have long lives and large brains.

Learning tool use
Some animals learn to use simple "tools" in order to feed. Sea otters, found off the coast of California, USA, swim on their backs with a stone on their chests on which they smash the shells of clams and mussels to get at the juicy contents. Young otters learn tool use from their parents.

Trial and error learning
An animal will associate an action it carries out with a successful result, such as getting food or defeating a rival. This "reward" motivates the animal to alter its behaviour to improve the result of future actions.

Puppies play-fight and perfect their hunting skills.

Young ducklings follow their mother.

Imprinting
This is shown by some young animals that make a strong bond with their parent soon after hatching or birth. Young ducklings, for example, stay close to their mother and improve their chances of survival under her protection.

Insight learning
This involves a form of reasoning. Some animals can solve new problems by drawing on past experiences. Chimpanzees, having learned to extract termites or ants from a nest with a stick, can exploit any shape or size of nest.

Communication

Animals communicate by sending out signals that are recognized by other animals and alter their behaviour in some way. The signals can be sights, sounds, or scents. Communication is used, for example, to find a mate, threaten rivals or enemies, defend a territory, warn of danger, or hold a group together.

Song thrush sings from a perch.

Visual signals
Animals may use visual signals as a threat or to attract a mate. This puss moth caterpillar adopts a warning posture if threatened by an enemy. An enemy that ignores the warning is rewarded with a stinging squirt of formic acid.

Puss moth caterpillar

Bright colours add to the warning.

Sound
Many animals, including crickets, bullfrogs, peacocks, and whales, use sound to communicate. This male song thrush sings to proclaim his territory, to warn rivals to stay away, and to attract a female.

Chemicals
Some animals release chemicals called pheromones, which, when detected, affect the behaviour of other members of the same species. Female gypsy moths release pheromones that attract males from several kilometres away.

Gypsy moth

Courtship

Mating in most mammals and birds takes place only at certain times of the year. Courtship describes the behaviour used by male animals to attract a female and mate with her. It informs a potential mate that the intention is breeding and not aggression. During courtship, males usually compete with each other to attract females, advertise that they are ready to mate, and encourage females to be sexually responsive. Females select males by the quality of their courtship display.

Male is aware that the female may lash out at him.

Male is attentive to the female.

Domestic cats

A female cat comes on heat, or is sexually responsive, about twice a year. She produces scents and calls loudly to attract males. Several males may compete for her by fighting. The successful male encourages the female by touching her and calling softly.

Female is sexually responsive and rolls.

Bird of paradise

Most birds have fixed courtship displays that ensure they attract a mate of the same species. Male birds often have brighter plumage than females, and this is especially true of the emperor bird of paradise. Males compete for females by quivering their long feathers and calling loudly.

Territorial behaviour

Many animals defend their territory to maintain access to food, water, shelter, and somewhere to reproduce. Territories can be large or small and held by one animal or by a group. Birdsong or the marking of territorial boundaries may deter rivals from entering a territory and avoid conflict and possible fatal injuries.

Cats

Most cats are solitary and maintain a territory on their own. Cheetahs patrol their territory and mark its boundaries by spraying urine on trees and other landmarks. The scent warns neighbouring cheetahs not to intrude.

Kittiwakes

Like many gull species, kittiwakes nest in colonies on narrow cliff ledges. Each pair of birds defends a small territory on the ledge, just large enough for the female to lay eggs and raise their young.

Aggression

Animals show aggression to other members of their species when competing for food, water, shelter, or mates. Some animals use horns, some use teeth or claws, and others kick. In many cases, animals signal their aggressive intent. This may defuse the situation and prevent injury.

Inflated porcupine fish

Fighting bighorn sheep

Aggression within a species

These bighorn sheep use their horns to clash head-on in competition for mates. The winner of the fight gains higher social ranking and more females. Aggression like this is highly ritualized, and neither male is likely to be injured.

Aggression between species

Animals may be aggressive towards members of other species that are threatening or attacking them. Some animals use a threat display, often making themselves bigger to deter enemies. This porcupine fish inflates its body like a balloon and erects its spines.

Social behaviour

Social animals live in groups. Individuals co-operate to find food, defend themselves, and look after the young. Social groups range from shoals of fish, which are purely defensive, to societies of honeybees, where social organization affects all aspects of an individual's life.

Helping others

African wild dogs are social animals and often help each other. Male dogs will look after pups that are not their own, but were fathered by a brother or close relative. In this way they help pups to survive.

Living in large numbers

Many fish species swim close together in large numbers called shoals. A shoal moves and turns in a co-ordinated manner that mimics a single large living organism. Predators find it difficult to focus on one individual within the shoal.

Worker bee

Male bee, called a drone

Section of a bees' nest

Konrad Lorenz

Austrian zoologist Konrad Lorenz (1903-89) pioneered the study of animal behaviour. As part of his work on individual and group behaviour, Lorenz discovered imprinting. Lorenz shared a Nobel Prize in 1973 for his work.

Social insects

Within a colony of social insects, such as bees, there are groups that carry out certain tasks. In a bee colony a single queen lays eggs, while sterile female workers look after the young, collect food, and defend the colony. Male bees fertilize the queen.

FIND OUT MORE   BIRDS   FISH   GENETICS   INSECTS   MAMMALS   SONGBIRDS

ANIMALS

MORE THAN a million and a half species of animal have been identified, and there are many millions more yet to be discovered. Animals are living organisms found in nearly all of the Earth's habitats, including the depths of the oceans, the freezing Arctic, and even inside other animals and plants. The animal kingdom is divided into animals without backbones (invertebrates), such as snails and lobsters, and animals with backbones (vertebrates), such as frogs and monkeys. Invertebrates make up 97 per cent of all animal species.

Large eyes enable the leopard to see in dim light.

Body is covered with insulating fur and supported internally by a skeleton.

Long tail is a balancing aid.

Black leopard
The leopard is a mammal. Its well-defined head is equipped with sense organs, including eyes, nose, tongue, and whiskers. Sharp teeth in the mouth allow the leopard to kill prey and tear off flesh. Muscular legs enable it to walk, run, and pounce.

Air is breathed in through nostrils.

What is an animal?
Animals are made up of many cells. Most move actively, and those that are fixed in one place, or sedentary, move their body parts. Animals live by taking food into their bodies. They have sensors and nervous systems that enable them to detect what is happening around them and respond appropriately.

Animal classification
Animals are classified into groups according to their similarities and whether they have common ancestors. There are 35 major groups called phyla (singular phylum). Each phylum is divided into sub-groups. The smallest of these is the species, which contains animals of just one type.

Giant land flatworm

Sponge processed for human use

Sea anemones

Sponges
The simplest animals are sponges (phylum Porifera). There are about 5,000 species, most of which live in the sea attached to rocks and other objects. Water is drawn in through holes, or pores, in the sponge's body wall, and bits of food are filtered out and eaten by the sponge's cells.

Cnidarians
There are more than 9,000 species of cnidarians (phylum Cnidaria), most of which are found in the sea. They include jellyfish, sea anemones, hydras, and corals. Cnidarians catch food using tentacles armed with stinging threads, called nematocysts.

Flatworms
These worms (phylum Platyhelminthes) have a flattened body with one opening, the mouth, on the underside. There are about 18,500 species including those, such as tapeworms, that are parasites of humans and other animals.

Nematodes
Roundworms, or nematodes (phylum Nematoda), have a thin, cylindrical body that is pointed at both ends. Free-living nematodes are found in many habitats and occur in very large numbers in soil. Many nematodes are parasites of plants and animals.

Threadworm

Stalked eye

Coiled shell protects the soft body.

Annelids
Animals in the phylum Annelida include earthworms, marine bristleworms such as ragworms, and leeches. There are about 12,000 species, each of which has a body made up of segments with a mouth at one end and an anus at the other.

King ragworm

Snail emerging from its shell.

Molluscs
Molluscs (phylum Mollusca) form a highly diverse group of about 50,000 species. These include snails and slugs, mussels and clams, and squids and octopuses. They are soft-bodied animals that may be protected by a shell. Most live in water, but some, such as snails, are found on land.

Snail moves on a muscular foot.

Sensory tentacle

Head and foot fully extended

Echinoderms
All echinoderms (phylum Echinodermata) live in the sea. The 6,500 or so species include sea urchins and starfish. Most have five parts radiating from a central point, hard plates under the skin, and many tube-feet.

Cushion star

Bloody Henry starfish

Cushion star

Arthropods
With at least one million known species, Arthropods (phylum Arthropoda) are the largest group of animals. They include insects, crustaceans (such as crabs), arachnids (such as spiders), and centipedes.

Arthropods have hard, jointed external skeletons.

Sharp teeth to grasp food

Chordates
There are about 48,000 species of chordate (phylum Chordata). Most are vertebrates, such as fish, amphibians, reptiles, birds, and mammals. Vertebrates are the most advanced animals.

Tarantula

Tail used for movement or balance is typical of many vertebrates.

Caiman

Animal skeletons

The skeleton is a supportive framework that maintains the shape of an animal and enables it to move. Most skeletons are hard structures, either inside or outside the animal's body, to which muscles are attached. The skeleton may also protect internal organs and, in the case of an insect's external skeleton, prevent the animal from drying out.

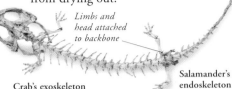

Limbs and head attached to backbone

Crab's exoskeleton

Salamander's endoskeleton

Internal skeletons

A skeleton found inside the body is called an endoskeleton. Most vertebrates have a skeleton made of cartilage and bone. Joints between the bones allow the animal to move. The endoskeleton grows with the rest of the body.

External skeletons

A hard outer skeleton that covers all or part of the body is called an exoskeleton. An insect's outer cuticle and a snail's shell are examples of an exoskeleton. An insect's exoskeleton does not grow and must be shed, or moulted, periodically to allow the animal to grow.

Earthworm

Hydrostatic skeleton

The hydrostatic skeleton is an internal skeleton found in soft-bodied animals such as earthworms. It consists of a fluid-filled core surrounded by muscles, and maintains the shape of the worm.

Worm gets longer when it contracts its muscles.

Feeding

All animals feed by taking in food. They use a range of feeding strategies and can be grouped accordingly. Some animals kill and eat others, some graze or browse on plants, others filter food particles from water. After feeding, or ingestion, food is digested so that it can be used by the body.

Giant clam

Filter feeders

These are animals that feed by sieving food particles from water that flows into their body. Many are sedentary and draw in a current of water. Some whales are filter feeders that eat small animals called krill.

Movement of an eel through water

Eel moves by throwing its body into curves that push against the water.

Animal movement

The ability to move is characteristic of animals, which move to find food, escape from predators, and find a mate. The way in which an animal moves depends on its complexity, lifestyle, and where it lives. The wide range of movement includes swimming through water, walking and creeping on land, and flying or gliding in air.

Wings sweep downward to produce forward thrust.

Movement in air

Insects, birds, and bats are capable of powered flight using wings. Birds have lightweight, streamlined bodies. They use energy to flap their wings, which pushes them forward. As air passes over the wings it creates the lift that keeps the bird in the air.

Young chaffinch in flight

Moving in water

Many aquatic animals are adapted for movement in water by having streamlined bodies. Most fish move by pushing their tail fin from side to side. This pushes the water backward and sideways, and propels the fish forward. Whales move in a similar way, except that the tail moves up and down.

Asian elephant

Feet expand under the elephant's weight as they are put down.

Movement on land

Animals move on land in a variety of ways. Many have limbs that raise the body off the ground, support it, and enable the animal to walk, run, or hop. The animals move forward by pushing the ends of their legs, or feet, backward against the ground.

Animal senses

The main senses are vision, hearing, taste, smell, and touch. Animals use their senses to find out what is going on around them. A stimulus from outside, such as a sound, is detected by a sense organ, such as the ear. Nerve impulses from sense organs are interpreted by the animal's brain which "decides" how to respond.

Mormon caterpillar consuming a leaf

Herbivores

Animals that feed solely on plants are called herbivores. Many use specialized mouthparts, such as grinding teeth, to break up tough plant tissues. Plant material is not a rich food source, and most herbivores eat a lot to obtain the necessary nutrients.

Longhorn beetle

Dragonfly eyes

Eyes

Eyes contain sensors that are sensitive to light. When stimulated they send nerve impulses to the brain, which enable it to build up a picture. Insects have compound eyes made up of many separate units, or ommatidia.

Antennae

These are found on the head of arthropods such as insects. They are used to detect odours and may detect chemicals called pheromones released by insects to communicate with each other. Antennae also detect vibrations and movements in the air or in water.

Carnivores

These types of feeders are adapted to detect prey animals, to catch and kill them, and to cut them up to eat them. They include cats, eagles, and some insects. Dragonfly larvae live in water and they can catch small fish to eat.

Dragonfly larva with stickleback

External ear flaps channel sounds into the ear.

Ears

Some animals can detect sounds with ears. The ear converts sounds into nerve impulses that can be interpreted by the animal's brain. Animals use sounds to communicate with each other and to detect approaching predators or prey.

Domestic Basenji dog

FIND OUT MORE

AMPHIBIANS   ANIMAL BEHAVIOUR   BIRDS   FISH   FLIGHT, ANIMAL   INSECTS   MAMMALS   REPTILES   SNAILS AND OTHER MOLLUSCS

ANTARCTICA

A

WITH THE SOUTH POLE at its heart, Antarctica is the world's windiest, coldest, and most southerly continent. The last region on Earth to be explored, this huge landmass is not divided into countries, but seven countries claimed territories there. In 1959, however, the Antarctic Treaty suspended those claims and stated that the continent is to be used for peaceful purposes only. Antarctica's sole inhabitants are visiting scientists, working in research stations.

Physical features

Antarctica is almost entirely covered by a vast sheet of ice, in places 4.8 km (3 miles) deep. It contains 90 per cent of the Earth's ice, and 80 per cent of the world's fresh water. The vast Ronne and Ross ice shelves are formed where the ice sheet extends over the ocean.

ANTARCTICA FACTS

AREA 13,900,000 sq km (5,366,790 sq miles)

POPULATION 4,000 international researchers

NUMBER OF COUNTRIES None

HIGHEST POINT Vinson Massif, 5,140 m (16,863 ft)

AVERAGE THICKNESS OF ICE CAP 2,450 m (8,000 ft)

Icebergs

Currents beneath Antarctica's vast ice shelves cause giant slabs of ice to break away, the largest of which may be 200 km (124 miles) long. As these enormous icebergs drift north they slowly break up and melt. Only the top third of an iceberg shows above the water.

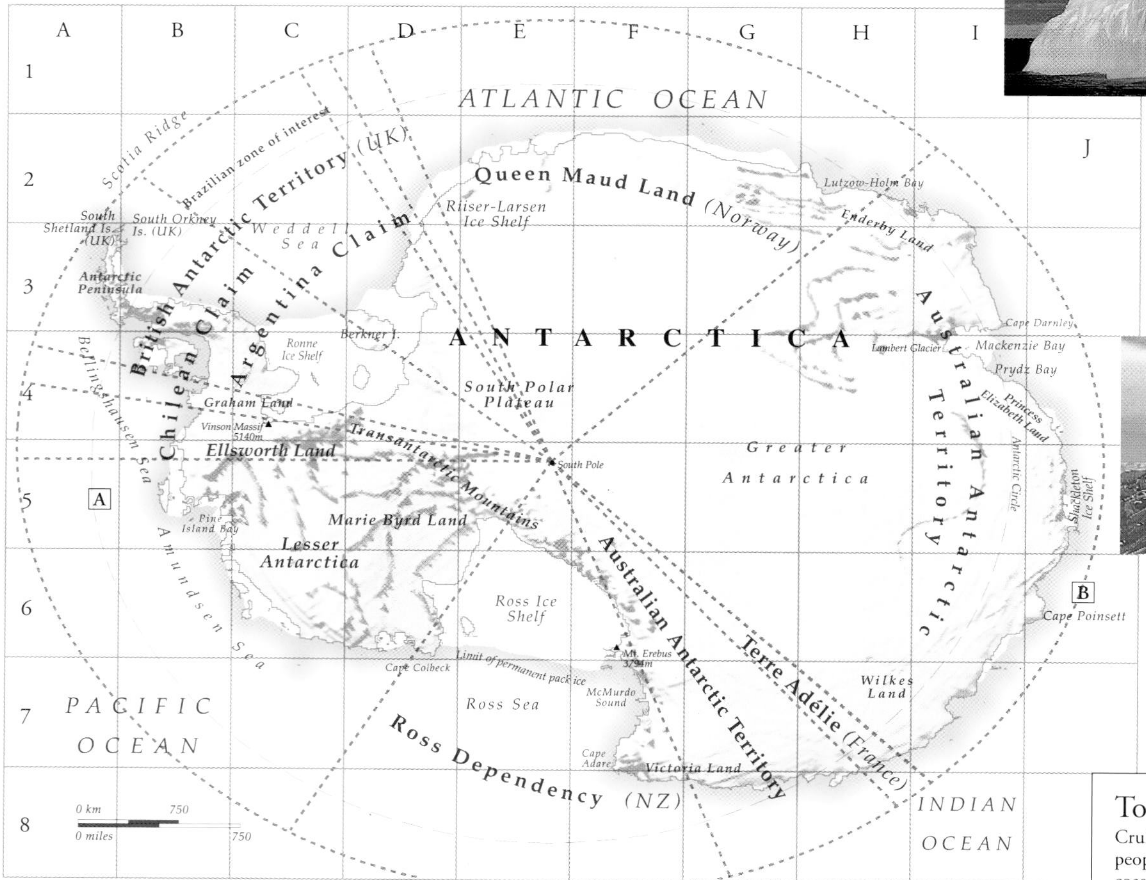

Mount Erebus

Antarctica has volcanic areas. An active volcano, Mount Erebus, lies on Ross Island on the edge of the Ross Ice Shelf. It forms part of the Transantarctic mountain chain that includes peaks up to 4,570 m (15,000 ft) high.

Map

(Map of Antarctica with grid references A–I horizontally and 1–8 vertically)

ATLANTIC OCEAN

Scotia Ridge
Brazilian zone of interest
British Antarctic Territory (UK)
Queen Maud Land (Norway)
Lützow-Holm Bay
Riiser-Larsen Ice Shelf
South Shetland Is. (UK)
South Orkney Is. (UK)
Weddell Sea
Enderby Land
Antarctic Peninsula
Chilean Claim
Argentina Claim
ANTARCTICA
Cape Darnley
Ronne Ice Shelf
Berkner I.
Lambert Glacier
Mackenzie Bay
Elizabeth Land
Prydz Bay
South Polar Plateau
Graham Land
Transantarctic Mountains
Vinson Massif 5140m
Ellsworth Land
South Pole
Greater Antarctica
Australian Antarctic Territory
Antarctic Circle
Shackleton Ice Shelf
Bellingshausen Sea
A
Pine Island Bay
Marie Byrd Land
Lesser Antarctica
Amundsen Sea
Ross Ice Shelf
Australian Antarctic Territory
Terre Adélie (France)
Cape Poinsett
B
Cape Colbeck
Limit of permanent pack ice
Mt Erebus 3795m
McMurdo Sound
Wilkes Land
PACIFIC OCEAN
Ross Sea
Ross Dependency (NZ)
Cape Adare
Victoria Land
INDIAN OCEAN

0 km 750
0 miles 750

Tourism

Cruise ships bring around 9,000 people each year to see Antarctica's coastline and wildlife. A hotel now exists on King George Island. Tourists who venture on to the ice must wear insulated clothing and goggles to protect their eyes from the glare.

Tourists shelter in a whale skull

Cross-section through Antarctica

The Transantarctic mountains divide the continent of Antarctica into Greater and Lesser Antarctica. Although the land itself is low, the depth of the ice on top of it makes Antarctica the highest continent, with an average height of 2,100 m (6,900 ft). The ice-cap was formed by the build up of snow over the last 100,000 years and contains 90 per cent of the world's ice.

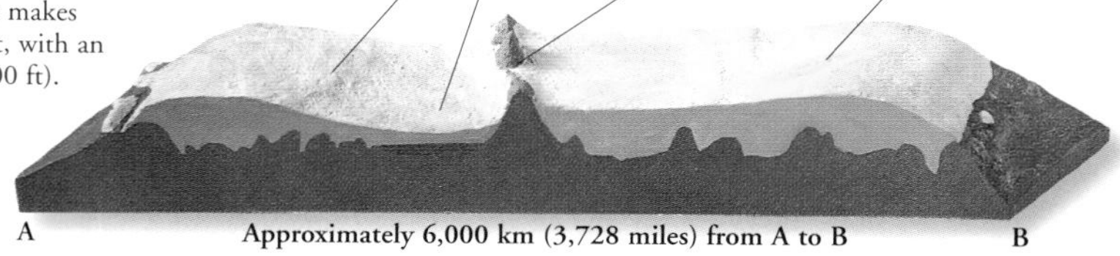

West Antarctic Ice Sheet (Lesser Antarctica)

Ross Ice Shelf

Transantarctic Mountains

East Antarctic Ice Sheet (Greater Antarctica)

A   Approximately 6,000 km (3,728 miles) from A to B   B

FIND OUT MORE | ATLANTIC OCEAN | CLIMATE | GLACIATION | INDIAN OCEAN | PACIFIC OCEAN | POLAR EXPLORATION | POLAR WILDLIFE | POLLUTION | VOLCANOES

ANTEATERS, SLOTHS AND ARMADILLOS

A BIZARRE GROUP of animals make up the order of mammals known as the edentates. They include the anteaters, armadillos, and sloths, all of which, except the nine-banded armadillo, live in the tropical regions of South and Central America. The name "edentate" means "without teeth", but it is a misleading term, as only the anteaters are toothless. In fact, some armadillos have more teeth than any other land mammal.

Young

A female anteater gives birth to a single young. The young anteater travels on its mother's back for the first year of its life, by which time it is almost half the size of its mother.

Tongue

Anteaters have long sticky tongues that can be pushed deep into termite nests. The tongue is covered in little spines that point backwards, making it very difficult for ants and termites to escape.

Curved spines on tongue

Anteater

There are four species of anteater. The giant anteater lives in grasslands; the other three species live in forests and have prehensile (grasping) tails with which they hang from trees. Anteaters have long snouts and tongues to enable them to collect the termites and ants on which they feed. They locate their prey with their acute sense of smell. Their foreclaws are so large that they need to walk on their knuckles. The claws are used to break open termite nests and for defence. If threatened, they rear up on their hind legs and try to rip their opponent with their claws.

Giant anteater breaking into a termite mound.

Long bushy tail

Giant anteater

Armadillo

Of the 21 species of armadillo, the largest is the giant armadillo, which is 91.5 cm (3 ft) in length. It has up to 100 peg-like teeth – twice as many as most mammals – which are shed when the animal reaches adulthood. The smallest species, the fairy armadillo, is less than 15 cm (6 in) long. Armadillos give birth to up to four young. The nine-banded armadillo, from North America, gives birth to quadruplets of the same sex.

Claws

Armadillos have large curved claws. They use them to dig into the ground to make burrows, to escape predators, and to find food. The giant armadillo's middle claw is the largest claw in the animal kingdom, measuring 18 cm (7 in) around the curve.

Nine-banded armadillo

Large claws

Hairy stomach

Nine-banded armadillo

Bony plates

Body armour

Armadillos are encased in "body armour" formed by separate plates made of bone. Soft skin links the plates together, giving them flexibility. In most species the plates cover only the upper part of the body. If threatened, some species, such as the three-banded armadillo, roll into a ball, while others make for their burrow or dig themselves into the ground.

Sloth

Adapted to living upside down, sloths hang by their claws from the branches of trees. They can rotate their heads through a 270° angle, allowing them to keep their head upright while their body remains inverted. They eat, mate, give birth, and spend their entire life-cycle upside down. Sloth's hair lies in the opposite direction from other animals', to allow rain to run off. Only when asleep do they adopt a more normal position, by squatting in the fork of a tree. There are seven species of sloth; all are herbivorous.

Female three-toed sloth with baby

Green algae cover the sloth's coat.

Movement

Sloths are very slow movers. They rarely descend to the ground as they can only just stand, but cannot walk. They drag themselves along with their claws. In water though, they are good swimmers.

Sloth swimming

Camouflage

Due to the high humidity levels in the rainforest, infestations of green algae grow within a sloth's fur and cover its coat. This acts as a camouflage and makes the sloth less conspicuous. As the seasons change, the algae change colour to match the colour of the trees.

Pangolin

There are seven species of pangolin, or scaly anteater. They have much in common with the edentates, but they belong to a different order called the Pholidota. They are covered with scales attached to the skin. Some species have a long, prehensile tail that is used to grasp branches and also to lash out at predators. They feed on termites, ants, and larvae which they catch with their long tongues.

Malayan pangolin

GIANT ANTEATER

SCIENTIFIC NAME
Myrmecophaga tridactyla

ORDER Edentata

FAMILY Myrmecophagidae

DISTRIBUTION South America

HABITAT Grasslands and savannahs

DIET Termites, ants, and larvae

SIZE Length, including tail: 1.83 m (6 ft)

LIFESPAN 25 years (in captivity)

FIND OUT MORE

ASIAN WILDLIFE · CAMOUFLAGE AND COLOUR · CONSERVATION · GRASSLAND WILDLIFE · MAMMALS · RAINFOREST WILDLIFE · SOUTH AMERICAN WILDLIFE

ANTS AND TERMITES

FOR EVERY HUMAN, there are 1,000,000 ants. Ants and termites are social insects that live in large colonies and have developed complex systems of communication. Ants are found worldwide, but, like termites, most of the 9,500 species of ant live in the tropics. There are more than 2,400 types of termite; many are blind, spending their lives inside nests, never seeing the light of day.

Ants

Ants have two pairs of compound eyes, three single eyes, or ocelli, two antennae, and three pairs of legs. Only queens and males have wings. A narrow waist connects the thorax and abdomen. Ants undergo complete metamorphosis, from an egg to larval and pupal stages, before emerging as adults. They live in huge groups and each ant has a particular role. The queen runs the nest and mates with male ants. Workers are female and gather food and nurse the eggs, larvae, and pupae. Soldier ants, also female, guard the nest.

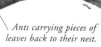

Bull ant
Antennae are used to pick up the scent of pheromones.
Eyes
Spiked jaws used to attack prey and predators.

Defence
If a nest is attacked, the ants release pheromones to warn each other. Most run for cover, but soldier ants get aggressive and defend the colony. They attack enemies with their large jaws, or sting them and inject formic acid, which causes extreme pain. Some ants even explode to shower an attacker in venom.

Communication
Ants lay trails of pheromones – chemicals that smell – so that other ants can follow them by using their sensitive antennae to pick up the smell. This helps foraging teams home in on food.

Eyes
Pheromones are released from the abdomen.
Thorax
Legs are attached to the thorax.
Wood ants

Ant nest
Most ants live in nests or colonies, usually underground. However, weaver ants build nests out of leaves in trees, and army ants build "live nests" of worker ants. Normally, there is one queen in a nest, but there are sometimes several. Nests of Australian bull ants contain up to 600 ants, while some wood ants' nests can house more than 300 million.

"Live nest" made by army ants

Feeding
Many ants are omnivores and eat seeds, nectar, and invertebrates. Army and driver ants are more carnivorous, and kill and eat prey such as worms, spiders, and even some lizards. Leaf-cutting ants are one of a few species of herbivorous ants. They feed on a type of fungus, which grows on the chewed-up remains of leaves and flowers that the ants take back to their nests.

Ants carrying pieces of leaves back to their nest.
Leaf-cutting ants

Termites

Although often called white ants, termites belong to a totally different order, the Isoptera. Like ants, termites live in large colonies. Unlike ants, termites do not have waists, and the male, called a king, does not die after mating, but lives with the queen. They do not go through complete metamorphosis, but grow up gradually through several nymphal stages.

Soldiers
Like ants, termites have soldiers. Termites cannot sting, but defend themselves in other ways. Some soldiers have large jaws that can cut through flesh; others squirt a poisonous sticky liquid from a special nozzle on their heads. Some nests have no soldiers – the termites defend themselves by vibrating their bodies against the side of their nest, making the sound of a hissing snake.

Pincers

Queen and king
A queen termite can reach more than 15 cm (6 in) in length. Her ovaries make her so large. She can lay up to 30,000 eggs a day. The king remains by the queen's side and mates with her several times to fertilize all the eggs.

Queen

Fungus
gardens are areas where fungi grow on termites' faeces and break down the cellulose within them. The termites feed on the products released and the fungi itself.

"Chimneys" allow warm air to rise and escape.

Solid outer walls are up to 50 cm (20 in) thick.

Air channel
Living quarters
Soft inner walls
Food stores
Termites spread water on walls to cool the nest.
Ground level
Nurseries
Royal chamber
Thick pillar supports nest.

Termite mounds
Each species of termite has its own type of nest. Some build towers more than 6 m (20 ft) tall, which help maintain the correct temperature and humidity of the nest at the base. Others build mushroom-shaped mounds – the domed top deflects the rain away from the nest below and has given these insects their name of umbrella termites. Many termites do not build nests above ground, but live below the soil or inside logs. Termites that live in trees build their nests on branches.

Workers
Worker termites build the nest, collect food, and feed the soldiers, king, and queen. The nest is made from saliva, soil, and their own faeces. Most workers feed on wood and have microscopic organisms in their guts to break down the wood into a more easily digested form.

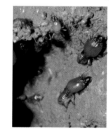

WOOD ANT
SCIENTIFIC NAME Formica rufa
ORDER Hymenoptera
FAMILY Formicidae
DISTRIBUTION Europe
HABITAT Woods and forests
DIET Omnivorous, feeding on seeds and invertebrates
SIZE Workers 6–8 mm (0.24–0.31 in) in length; queen 10–13 mm (0.4–0.5 in) in length
LIFESPAN Workers live for 3–4 months; the queen lives for about 15 years

 FIND OUT MORE | ANIMAL BEHAVIOUR | ARTHROPODS | INSECTS | MONGOOSES AND CIVETS | MUSHROOMS AND OTHER FUNGI | NESTS AND BURROWS | WOODLAND WILDLIFE

ARCHAEOLOGY

HUMANKIND HAS ALWAYS been fascinated by the question of who we are, where we came from, and how we used to live. Archaeology is the study of our past, from early prehistory onward, using the material remains of our ancestors and the possessions they left behind. Over thousands of years, evidence of human activity, such as camp fires, rubbish tips, and dwellings, become buried. Archaeological teams discover these sites and uncover this evidence by careful excavation. The material is then conserved and studied in order to help the archaeologist piece together a picture of how people lived and died in the past.

Discovery

Iron Age fort, England

Archaeological sites are found during building work, through reading historical documents, geophysical surveys (the study of the soil's structure), and field walking (recording above-ground objects).

Aerial photography
Horizontal and vertical lines seen from the air often show medieval strip fields, ancient roads, walls, and ditches. Aerial photography done when the sun is low shows varying surface levels, moisture levels, and vegetation most clearly.

Excavation

Archaeological sites are excavated by layers. Workers remove the top, most recent layer and work down, uncovering older, deeper levels. The study of these layers and the items they contain is called stratigraphy.

Stratigraphy
By revealing features such as ditches, post holes, and floors, stratigraphy gives information about the history of a site, and the people who lived there. In urban areas, such as London, surface levels rise as debris is shovelled in to level the ground before rebuilding. Because it shows a chrono-logical sequence, stratigraphy was used to date sites before radiocarbon dating was invented.

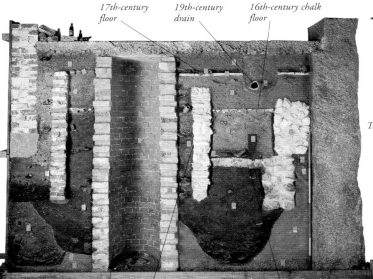

17th-century floor
19th-century drain
16th-century chalk floor

Cross section through
a dig, City of London

Brick-lined well, c.1800
14th-century chalk-lined cesspit
Roman tiled floor

Pickaxe

Trowel   Measuring tape

Tools
Archaeologists use shovels and handpicks to remove the topsoil. Then smaller hand tools are used, such as dental picks, teaspoons, and trowels, to excavate delicate objects.

Finds
Archaeologists usually draw or photograph the artefacts (objects) to make a visual record. They carefully measure and record the shapes, colours, decorations, and ages of any artefacts or features. This helps archaeologists link and relate different objects and sites.

Investigation

Buried objects are fragile, and decay quickly after excavation. To stabilize them, they are cleaned and conserved. After conservation, an object can be studied. The material of which it is made, its function, and its date are recorded. It may then be photographed and displayed in a museum.

Salt water has caused corrosion

Pewter jug

A cradle hoisted the ship from the seabed.

To conserve the wood, chilled water is sprayed on the ship 20 hours a day.

The Mary Rose in dry dock

Underwater archaeology
Sites beneath the sea or in lakes are more difficult to excavate than those on land because shifting silt or sand causes poor visibility. However, marine sites often preserve materials, such as the wood of the 16th-century ship, the Mary Rose, which would usually be lost on dry land. Conservation may involve treatment with water, sealing with chemicals, or careful drying.

Timeline

1748 Pompeii discovered.

1799 An officer in Napoleon's army discovers the Rosetta Stone, which features 6th-century BC hieroglyphs.

1812 Abu Simbel discovered.

1822 Scholars decipher Egyptian hieroglyphs.

1861 Evans and Prestwich confirm the antiquity of humans, and humans' association with extinct animals.

1891 Homo erectus material found.

1922 Howard Carter discovers the tomb of Tutankhamun.

1931 Louis Leakey begins excavations at Olduvai Gorge.

1940 Archaeologists discover prehistoric Lascaux cave paintings.

1949 Radiocarbon dating is developed.

1974 Donald Johanson discovers "Lucy", an early hominid.

Australopithecus, an early human ancestor

Mortimer Wheeler

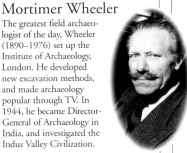

The greatest field archaeo-logist of the day, Wheeler (1890–1976) set up the Institute of Archaeology, London. He developed new excavation methods, and made archaeology popular through TV. In 1944, he became Director-General of Archaeology in India, and investigated the Indus Valley Civilization.

FIND OUT MORE

ASIA, HISTORY OF | BRONZE AGE | EUROPE, HISTORY OF | HUMAN EVOLUTION | PREHISTORIC PEOPLE | STONE AGE

Archaeological finds from the *Mary Rose*

Weapons

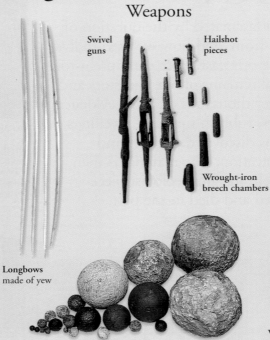

Swivel guns

Hailshot pieces

Closed hand

Lint held at this end

Wrought-iron breech chambers

Longbows made of yew

Stone, iron, and lead shot, used for cannon

Wooden linstocks held the slow match (lint), which the crew used to light gunpowder in cannon.

Linstock handle

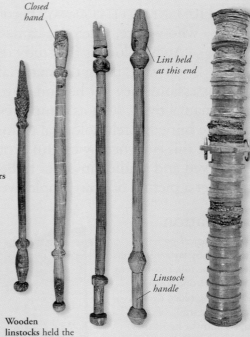

Breech loader gun, made of wrought iron

Demi cannon, a cast bronze muzzle loader

Culverin, a cast bronze muzzle loader

Shipboard equipment

Wooden razor handles

Apothecary's balance

Deadeye

Personal sundial

Ceramic medicine jar

An angel, a 1545 gold coin

Bronze cooking pot, used for communal meals

Wooden tankard

Pewter spoon and plates were used at the captain's dinner table.

Clothing and personal

Inkpot, made of horn

Manicure set, made of bone

Wooden comb

Leather jerkin

Backgammon set

Yew and spruce inlay

Leather flask for storing wine or water

Leather book cover

ARCHITECTURE

![icon]

FROM A TOWERING SKYSCRAPER to a functional factory, architecture is the art of planning a building. The word also refers to the different building styles seen throughout history. Looking at changes in architecture tells us about earlier societies: the materials that were available to their builders, the skills mastered by their engineers, and the social ideals that they wished to express in their public buildings.

Architectural features

The main structural and functional features of a building are the roof, arches and walls, doors, and windows. The architect combines the practical knowledge of how to construct these with a sense of how to combine shape, space, and light to suit the function of the building itself.

Groin
Vault

Groin vault, where two barrel vaults intersect

Main arch

Barrel vault

Round arch

Arch and vault

An arch is a curved or pointed structure that bridges a gap; it must carry the weight of the wall, floor, or roof above, and its structure allows it to support greater weight than a flat slab can. A vault is simply an arched ceiling.

Classical Europe

Classical architecture is that of the ancient Greeks and Romans. Both built by laying stones on top of each other, or by resting beams on columns. The Romans also developed the arch, vault, dome, and the use of concrete to develop curved spaces.

Use of concrete

Cheap and durable, this material allowed Roman architects to cover vast curved spaces, which were impossible to construct before.

Opening

Dome, 43 m (142 ft) across

Walls 6 m (21 ft) thick

Entrance porch, or portico

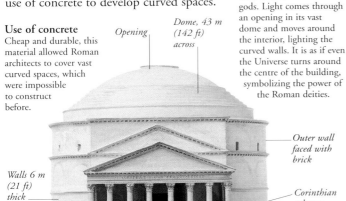

Outer wall faced with brick

Corinthian column

The Pantheon, Rome, Italy, completed c. AD 128

Brunelleschi

Italian architect Filippo Brunelleschi (1377–1446) returned to the use of Classical features, rejecting the Gothic style. Architects all across Europe followed his example.

Symbolism

The Pantheon is a temple built to all the Roman gods. Light comes through an opening in its vast dome and moves around the interior, lighting the curved walls. It is as if even the Universe turns around the centre of the building, symbolizing the power of the Roman deities.

Cross and orb

Lantern (turret with windows) provides light

Round-arched window

Dome on a circular base

Dome metalling, Church of the Sorbonne, Paris, France, 17th century

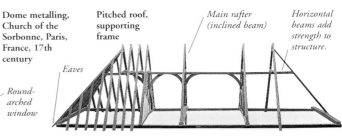

Eaves

Pitched roof, supporting frame

Main rafter (inclined beam)

Horizontal beams add strength to structure.

Ornament

Early in the 20th century, many Western architects rejected all forms of building ornament. This is rare: most buildings from other periods and cultures use it extensively, and even a simple building will usually have some decoration to reflect the taste of its owner. The ancient Greeks, for instance, carved the tops, or capitals, of columns to dignify their most prestigious buildings. The distinct decorations were based on styles called orders.

Doric order

Ionic order

Corinthian order

Dome

Domes – curved, solid roofs – were first built on palaces and religious buildings as striking symbols of the building's status. They are often difficult to build, and have been constructed in various shapes: the Dome of the Rock in Jerusalem is hemispherical; the "onion"-shaped dome is a popular feature of many Russian and Bavarian buildings.

Roof

All roofs are designed for the practical purpose of providing protection from the weather. The design and covering used will reflect the local climate: for instance, in a wet country a sloping (pitched) roof will let rain run off. Roofs can also be ingenious and beautiful, such as when crowning an ornate castle.

Gothic

This distinctive, ornate European style emerged in the 12th century, and was used mainly in cathedrals and churches. Features include pointed arches and windows, and elaborate stone tracery used to divide the openings in window arches.

Building innovations

The pointed arch and flying buttress were innovations that allowed Gothic churches to soar higher than had been possible before. Pointed arches can support heavier, taller structures than round arches. The flying buttress is a stone rib which extends down and away from the walls, transferring weight to the ground, and giving extra support to a roof or walls.

Eight-sided spire, built using scaffolding and wooden cranes

Turret-like pinnacle

Pointed arch

Flying buttress

Pointed arch filled with tracery

Pitched roof

Buttress

Old St. Paul's Cathedral, London, England, 1087–1666

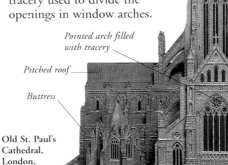

Southeast Asia and the Middle East

The traditional architectural styles of Asia and the Middle East remained the same for centuries. Both were heavily influenced by religious belief: Buddhism and Hinduism in southern Asia, and Islam in the Middle East. The style of buildings was determined by climate, and the materials available to local builders. As early as the 7th century, wooden temples and monasteries were being built in China and Japan.

Pagoda in Burmese style, 9th–10th century

Gilded crown

Islamic decoration favours geometric patterns and calligraphy.

South and East Asia
Many of the distinctive features of this area's architecture originated in Buddhist India. An example is the multi-storeyed pagoda, a temple which seems to stretch towards Heaven. It was developed initially in Japan and China but was based on the spires found on early Indian temples. An important feature of many traditional Asian buildings is their imaginative roof forms.

Minaret

Islamic architecture
The most important buildings in Islamic countries are usually mosques and tombs. The mosque is the centre of a Muslim community, and provides space for group worship. It contains a prayer hall, often with a domed roof, and may also have a courtyard. A minaret, from which the faithful are called to prayer, is a typical feature.

Early American civilizations

The Aztecs, who ruled in what is now Mexico from the 14th to 16th centuries, built stone pyramids to their gods. The remains of five separate temples have been found at Tenochtitlan, built one on top of the other as new rulers erected bigger temples on the same site.

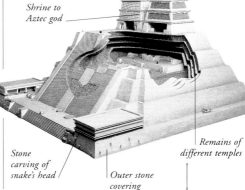

Shrine to Aztec god

Remains of different temples

Stone carving of snake's head

Outer stone covering

Baroque and Neoclassical

The Baroque style emerged in early 17th-century Europe. It introduced buildings with ornate decoration, complex shapes, and dramatic lighting. It was followed by the Neoclassical style, which revived the more restrained Classical traditions. This was partly as a reaction to Baroque excess.

Greek-style portico

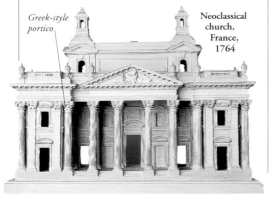

Neoclassical church, France, 1764

The 19th and 20th centuries

The development of new, very strong materials made it possible to construct buildings which were often highly original in style and owed little to the past. Helped by better technology, architects turned to glass, steel, and concrete to express their vision of modern architecture.

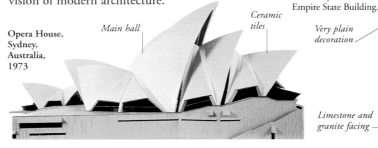

Opera House, Sydney, Australia, 1973

Main hall

Ceramic tiles

Interlocked vaults
The dramatic profile of the Opera House dominates Sydney Harbour. The building's roof of interlocked vaults, made from reinforced concrete covered with gleaming tiles, resembles a ship in sail.

Skyscrapers
The invention of the lift during the 19th century made it practical to build skyscrapers, and the first appeared in Chicago, USA, in the 1880s. Today, most are constructed for large businesses: they convey perfectly an image of wealth, size, and strength.

Steel
Following the arrival of reinforced steel, very tall structures could be built for the first time. An internal steel skeleton supports the weight of a skyscraper, such as the 102 storeys of the Empire State Building.

Empire State Building, New York, USA, 1931

Very plain decoration

Limestone and granite facing

Le Corbusier
Le Corbusier was the name used by the Swiss-French Charles Édouard Jeanneret (1887–1965), the most influential 20th-century architect. Le Corbusier promoted the use of new materials and construction techniques. His imaginative buildings favoured plain, often severe, geometric forms.

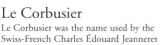

Proposed design

Architects
An architect designs a building and oversees its construction. Successful architects become very well-known. Until recently, architects drew large numbers of plans to instruct builders and engineers. Much of this work is now carried out on computer.

Timeline

2650 BC The Step Pyramid in Egypt is designed.

c.300 BC Buddhist temple mounds appear in India.

AD 82 Colosseum built in Rome. Dozens of stone arches support the walls of this stone arena.

690–850 Early Islamic buildings are designed around courtyards.

1100–1500 Gothic churches built in Europe.

c.1420 Renaissance begins in Italy; architects return to the elegant, ordered values of Classical builders.

19th century Industrial Revolution: mass-produced materials transform construction.

1920s International Modernism begins, typified by glass-and-steel towers and flat-roofed, white houses.

1970s Postmodernism develops. It refers to past styles, in a humourous way. Strong colours are popular.

1990s Eco-friendly architecture reflects environmental concerns about energy-saving and recycling.

FIND OUT MORE BUILDING AND CONSTRUCTION · CHURCHES AND CATHEDRALS · CITIES · MOSQUES

Architecture

Gothic, Renaissance, and Baroque

Carved stone lantern

Magnificent Gothic cathedral

Two lions flank the entrance.

Notre Dame, Paris, France: built from 1163 to 1250.

Palacio de las Cadenas, Ubeda, Spain: built during the mid-16th century. The Classical facade shows the elegance of Renaissance buildings.

St. Paul's Cathedral, London, Britain: built in the Baroque style.

Carved stone figures

Ribbed dome designed by Michelangelo

Facade by Carlo Maderno (c.1556–1629)

135 spires crown the roof.

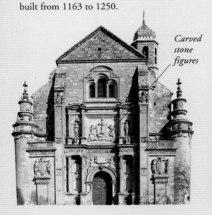

Capilla del Salvador, Ubeda, Spain: one of Spain's finest Renaissance churches, it was designed by three 16th-century architects.

St. Peter's, Rome, Italy, took over a century to build (1506–1614). It involved all the great architects of the Roman Renaissance and Baroque, including Michelangelo Buonarroti (1475–1564).

Milan Cathedral, Italy, is one of the largest Gothic churches in the world. Building began in the 14th century, but was not completed for 500 years.

Modern architecture

Windows give the effect of glass curtains.

Two towers, linked by means of a central atrium.

Framework

Arched sunburst, typical of 1920s' style known as "Art Deco"

Designed in 1942, completed in 1960

Descending spiral gallery

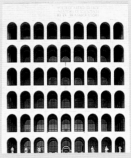

Bauhaus Building, Dessau, Germany: built from steel and concrete in the International Modern Style (1925–26).

Guggenheim Museum, New York, USA: a stunning, innovative design by the great US architect Frank Lloyd Wright (1869–1959).

Steel and concrete structure

Century Tower, Tokyo, Japan, completed in 1991.

Palace of the Statues, Rome, Italy, completed during the 1950s.

Spire of the Chrysler Building, an office block in New York, USA (completed 1930).

Great Arch, Paris, France, completed in 1989, houses an exhibition gallery.

Seagram Building, New York, USA, completed in 1958.

ARCTIC OCEAN

ONE OF THE COLDEST places on Earth, the Arctic Ocean is surrounded by the northern parts of Europe, Asia, North America, and Greenland. These icy lands are rich in minerals and wildlife, but are home to few people. In summer, when temperatures reach 0°C (32°F), warm currents from the Pacific and Atlantic melt some of the ice. With the help of icebreakers to clear their path, ships are able to sail along the coasts of Asia and North America.

Physical features

The Arctic is the smallest and shallowest of the world's oceans. Most of its surface is covered by a frozen mass of floating ice about 2 m (6 ft) thick. The North Pole lies in the centre of the Arctic Ocean on drifting pack ice.

ARCTIC OCEAN FACTS

AREA	14,089,600 sq km (5,440,000 sq miles)
AVERAGE DEPTH	1,330 m (4,360 ft)
AVERAGE ICE THICKNESS	1.5–3 m (4.9–9.8 ft)
LOWEST TEMPERATURE	-70°C (-94°F) on northeast tip of Greenland

Icebergs
Giant icebergs break off glaciers in Greenland and drift south into the North Atlantic Ocean. They rise up to 120 m (400 ft) above sea-level. As only a fraction of an iceberg shows above water, they are a shipping hazard.

Northern lights
On dark nights, spectacular coloured lights, or Aurora, can be seen in the sky. Caused by electricity in the upper atmosphere, they are brightest in mid winter when the sun never rises and invisible in summer due to 24-hour sun.

Arctic peoples
About 800,000 indigenous people live in the Arctic. The Yu'pik of Alaska are part of the Eskimo group that includes Inuit in Canada and Greenland and Yuit in Siberia. Many have given up nomadic life and now live in villages. The Arctic is the workplace of about 2,000,000 engineers and traders from the south.

Yu'pik family from Alaska

Greenland

Although Greenland is the world's largest island, its permanent ice cover means few people live there. The most populated area is the southwest coast, where the climate is less extreme than the bleak centre. The island is a self-governing territory of Denmark.

GREENLAND FACTS

CAPITAL CITY	Nuuk (Godthaab)
AREA	2,175,600 sq km (840,000 sq miles)
POPULATION	56,569
MAIN LANGUAGES	Danish, Greenlandic
MAJOR RELIGION	Christian
CURRENCY	Danish krone

Halibut

Haddock

Cod

Fishing
Cod, haddock, halibut, and shrimp fishing are the mainstay of Greenland's economy. Fish-processing factories freeze and can the fish for export to Europe and the USA. Much of the cod is made into fish fingers.

FIND OUT MORE ATMOSPHERE CLIMATE FISHING INDUSTRY GLACIATION NATIVE AMERICANS OCEANS AND SEAS POLAR EXPLORATION POLAR WILDLIFE TUNDRA

ARGENTINA, CHILE, AND URUGUAY

THE SOUTHERN PART of South America is occupied by three countries: Argentina, Chile, and Uruguay. Lying between the Pacific and Atlantic Oceans, South America's southernmost point, Cape Horn, lies only about 1,000 km (600 miles) from the northern tip of Antarctica. Once part of the Spanish Empire, all three countries still show strong European influences. Their vast mineral resources have resulted in some prosperity, but all have agricultural economies and have suffered under a series of unstable governments.

Physical features

Dominating the west of the region, the Andes Mountains form a rugged frontier between Chile and Argentina. The hot, humid land of the Gran Chaco covers the northeast, turning to rolling grassland, known as pampas, in the centre. South of this and the arid plateau of Patagonia, lie the windy islands of Tierra del Fuego.

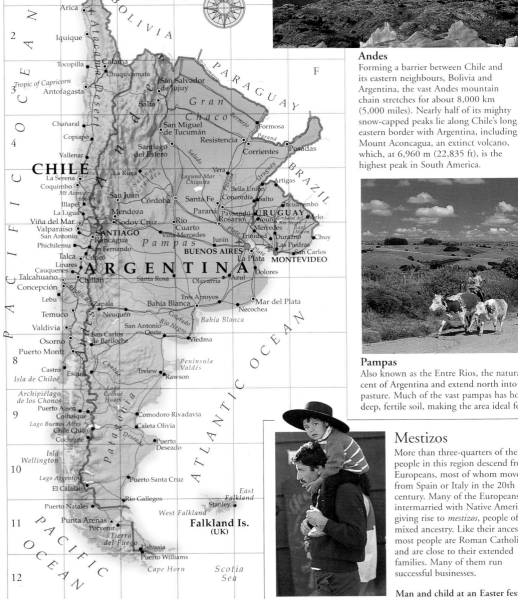

Andes
Forming a barrier between Chile and its eastern neighbours, Bolivia and Argentina, the vast Andes mountain chain stretches for about 8,000 km (5,000 miles). Nearly half of its mighty snow-capped peaks lie along Chile's long eastern border with Argentina, including Mount Aconcagua, an extinct volcano, which, at 6,960 m (22,835 ft), is the highest peak in South America.

Atacama Desert
The hot Atacama Desert is one of the world's driest places. It covers the northern 965 km (600 miles) of Chile's long coastal strip, and receives less than 13 mm (½ in) of rain in a year. By contrast, the Patagonian Desert, in the far south of Argentina, near Antarctica, is a vast, icy-cold expanse of windswept rocks.

Pampas
Also known as the Entre Rios, the natural grasslands of the pampas cover about 20 per cent of Argentina and extend north into Uruguay, where three-quarters of the land is rich pasture. Much of the vast pampas has hot summers, warm winters, plenty of rain, and deep, fertile soil, making the area ideal for growing crops and for raising cattle and sheep.

Mestizos
More than three-quarters of the people in this region descend from Europeans, most of whom moved from Spain or Italy in the 20th century. Many of the Europeans intermarried with Native Americans, giving rise to *mestizos*, people of mixed ancestry. Like their ancestors, most people are Roman Catholics and are close to their extended families. Many of them run successful businesses.

Man and child at an Easter festival

21°C (70°F)   9°C (48°F)

762 mm (30 in)

Regional climate
Chile's long, narrow shape gives it an extremely varied climate. Desert and mountains in the north give way to fertile valleys, with hot, dry summers and mild, moist winters. Argentina's southern Andean peaks and Patagonian glaciers have year-round snow; the north is hotter and wetter. Uruguay is mild and pleasant.

Map labels

PERU
BOLIVIA
PARAGUAY
BRAZIL
CHILE
ARGENTINA
URUGUAY

Arica
Iquique
Tocopilla
Calama
Chuquicamata
Antofagasta
Salta
San Salvador de Jujuy
Gran Chaco
Formosa
Resistencia
Corrientes
Posadas
Chañaral
Copiapó
San Miguel de Tucumán
Vallenar
Santiago del Estero
La Rioja
Vera
La Serena
Coquimbo
Córdoba
Santa Fe
Bella Unión
Artigas
Concordia
Salto
Tacuarembó
Mt Aconcagua 6960m
San Juan
Paraná
Paysandú
Melo
Illapel
Mendoza
Rosario
Durazno
La Ligua
Godoy Cruz
Río Cuarto
Trinidad
Mercedes
Viña del Mar
Valparaíso
Villa Mercedes
Junín
Las Piedras
Chuy
San Antonio
Phichilemu
Rancagua
San Fernando
La Plata
San Carlos
Talca
Curicó
MONTEVIDEO
Linares
BUENOS AIRES
Cauquenes
Santa Rosa
Dolores
Talcahuano
Chillán
Olavarría
Azul
Concepción
Zapala
Bahía Blanca
Tres Arroyos
Lebu
Neuquén
Mar del Plata
Temuco
Necochea
Valdivia
San Antonio Oeste
Osorno
San Carlos de Bariloche
Viedma
Puerto Montt
Castro
Esquel
Trelew
Península Valdés
Isla de Chiloé
Rawson
Archipiélago de los Chonos
Puerto Aisén
Coihaique
Comodoro Rivadavia
Lago Buenos Aires
Caleta Olivia
Chile Chico
Cochrane
Puerto Deseado
Isla Wellington
Lago Argentino
Puerto Santa Cruz
El Calafate
Río Gallegos
Puerto Natales
Stanley
West Falkland
East Falkland
Punta Arenas
Porvenir
Falkland Is. (UK)
Tierra del Fuego
Ushuaia
Puerto Williams
Cape Horn
Scotia Sea

PACIFIC OCEAN
ATLANTIC OCEAN

Pampas
Patagonia
Atacama Desert
Tropic of Capricorn

0 km 200
0 miles 200

Argentina

After Brazil, Argentina is the second largest country in South America. It is separated from Uruguay by the Río de la Plata estuary, on which its capital, Buenos Aires, stands. Argentina is one of the wealthiest countries in South America, with fertile soils, a wealth of mineral resources, and a skilled work-force. However, years of political instability have left huge overseas debts, which caused the economy to collapse at the end of 2001.

Couple dancing the tango

People

More than 89 per cent of Argentina's people live in towns and cities and most enjoy a high standard of living. However, city slums, or *orillas*, illustrate the sharp contrast between the country's rich and poor. It was in the slums that the tango, the traditional dance of Buenos Aires, originated, in the late 1800s. Many tangos contain lyrics that express the frustrations of the immigrants who came from Spain, Italy, Austria, France, Germany, and Britain. The tango is now famous worldwide.

14 per sq km
(35 per sq mile)

89%
Urban

11%
Rural

ARGENTINA FACTS

CAPITAL CITY Buenos Aires

AREA 2,766,890 sq km (1,068,296 sq miles)

POPULATION 37,500,000

MAIN LANGUAGE Spanish

MAJOR RELIGION Christian

CURRENCY Argentinian peso

LIFE EXPECTANCY 73 years

PEOPLE PER DOCTOR 370

GOVERNMENT Multi-party democracy

ADULT LITERACY 97%

Buenos Aires

Situated on the South Atlantic coast, Argentina's capital has been an important trade port since it was founded by the Spanish in 1536. Buenos Aires is a wealthy, sophisticated city, with expensive shops, fine avenues, and modern buildings, as well as a spectacular old cathedral. The city is the centre of government, industry, and culture. Almost 40 per cent of Argentinians, numbering about 14,000,000, live in the metropolitan capital, referring to it as "Baires".

Government buildings

Clarín is Argentina's best-selling newspaper.

Newspapers

More than 180 daily newspapers are published every day in Argentina. Most are in Spanish, but English, French, and German papers are widely available. In the past, dictatorships have imposed censorship on the media, and today's government withdraws advertising from those who do not support its policies.

Food

High-quality beef, which is produced throughout Argentina, is used as a base for many local dishes, such as *empanadas*, or savoury mince pastries. Every restaurant has a barbeque grill, or *parillada*. As a cheaper alternative to meat, many people eat small potato dumplings called *noquis*, which were introduced by Italian immigrants.

Noquis

Schooling

Literacy is high in Argentina, and free-state primary and secondary education is provided. Schooling is compulsory for all children between the ages of six and 14, and more than one-third of all students go on to one of Argentina's 45 universities. Buenos Aires has the largest university in South America, with 140,000 students.

Farming

Agriculture accounts for about 60 per cent of Argentina's export earnings. The country is a major producer of wheat, barley, and maize, which flourish on the pampas, and is the world's third largest producer of soya beans. Fruit, especially oranges, grows well in the warm climate, and grapes are produced for wine-making.

Harvesting barley on the fertile pampas

Gauchos

Tough, independent gauchos, or cowhands, have roamed the pampas on horseback for more than 300 years, tending cattle and horses. Modern gauchos work mainly on huge *estancias*, or ranches, owned by wealthy landlords, where they rear animals and mend fences. Gauchos are experts in handling herds and are the national heroes of Argentina.

Bolas rope used to slow down cattle

Woollen poncho, or cloak, for warmth at night

Strong boots have heels to fit into stirrups.

Industry

About 30 per cent of the labour force works in industry. Textiles, food production, and chemical products dominate business. The country is self-sufficient in oil and gas, and rich in minerals.

Falkland Islands

Britain and Argentina have fought over ownership of the Falkland Islands, or Islas Malvinas, since the British claimed the islands from the Spanish in 1833. In 1982, an Argentine invasion of the islands was overthrown, and the British continue to hold them.

These women work in a fish-packing plant and must wear hats for hygiene.

The Falkland Islands lie 480 km (300 miles) east of Argentina.

Chile

A long and extremely narrow country, Chile measures, at most, only about 430 km (267 miles) wide. Most Chileans live in cities and towns in the Central Valley, between the low coastal mountains to the west and the towering Andes on the east. The cold, stormy southern coast is flanked by thousands of islands, whose waters provide rich fishing grounds. Chile has a strong economy rooted in its natural resources: minerals, fruit, sea products, and timber.

Santiago

Located in the heart of Chile, the capital, Santiago, is a bustling, modern city. The city and suburbs house about five million people. Santiago is known for severe traffic congestion, and has one of the highest taxi densities in the world, with one per 100 inhabitants. About 3,600 km (2,236 miles) of Pan-American Highway runs through Santiago, but high smog levels over the city concern environmentalists.

Some of Santiago's 14,500 buses on Avenue Campama

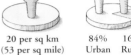

Mapuche

Descended from the original inhabitants of South America, the Mapuche people are also known as the Araucanians. About 675,000 Mapuche live in the central and southern regions of Chile. They follow the Roman Catholic religion and speak their own language, as well as Spanish. The Mapuche people have fought for independence since the 16th century and are still at odds with the Chilean government. Quechua and Aymara Indians also live in the country, in the north.

20 per sq km
(53 per sq mile)

84% Urban   16% Rural

The Chuquicamata copper mine, 670 m (2,200 ft) deep

Copper

Chile leads the world in the production of copper ore, of which it owns about 20 per cent of known reserves. The Central Valley, which extends for 1,600 km (994 miles), has the world's largest underground copper mine, located at El Teniente. Chuquicamata, in the bleak Atacama Desert, is one of the largest open-cast copper mines in the world. The country also mines iron, gold, and silver.

Wine

Vineyards first planted by Spanish colonists in the 1500s have benefited from the hot, dry summers in the Central Valley. Today, about 320,000 tonnes (350,000 tons) of Chilean wines, red from Cabernet Sauvignon grapes and white from Chardonnay grapes, are exported all over the world.

Cabernet Sauvignon grapes and wine

Crabs are put into small baskets.

Fishing

Although less than one per cent of the people work in the fishing industry, Chile leads the world in fishmeal production. In a good year, around 6,000 tonnes of sardines, anchovetas, mackerel, and salmon are caught and processed. Punta Arenas, on the Strait of Magellan in the south, is the industry's centre.

CHILE FACTS

CAPITAL CITY	Santiago
AREA	756,950 sq km (292,258 sq miles)
POPULATION	15,400,000
MAIN LANGUAGE	Spanish
MAJOR RELIGION	Christian
CURRENCY	Chilean peso
LIFE EXPECTANCY	75 years
PEOPLE PER DOCTOR	909
GOVERNMENT	Multi-party democracy
ADULT LITERACY	96%

A

Uruguay

One of the smallest countries in South America, Uruguay is also one of the most prosperous and harmonious. More than 40 per cent of its people, about 1,449,900, live in Montevideo, the capital, chief port, and largest city. The rest are scattered over the vast lowland pastures. Uruguay has a high tourist rate, mainly because of its sandy beaches and fine weather.

People

There are 11 times as many sheep, cattle, and horses as people in Uruguay. Most Uruguayans are of Spanish or Italian descent. They enjoy considerable prosperity, largely due to the wealth from earlier cattle ranching in the country.

Hydroelectricity

More than 90 per cent of Uruguay's power is generated through hydroelectricity. The main hydroelectric plants are situated on the country's major rivers, the Uruguay and its tributary, the Río Negro, which both widen out into the Río de la Plata estuary. Huge turbines have been built across the rivers, so that as the water rushes through, it turns the turbines and makes electricity.

URUGUAY FACTS

CAPITAL CITY	Montevideo
AREA	176,220 sq km (68,039 sq miles)
POPULATION	3,400,000
MAIN LANGUAGE	Spanish
MAJOR RELIGION	Christian
CURRENCY	Uruguayan peso

Wool

Three-quarters of Uruguay is rich, green pasture that provides excellent grazing land for its 25,000,000 sheep and 10,000,000 cattle. The land provides work for nearly half the population. Uruguay is the world's second biggest producer of wool, and textiles made from wool account for about 20 per cent of Uruguayan exports.

Hand-made scarf

 CHRISTIANITY   DANCE   DESERTS   ENERGY   FARMING   GRASSLAND WILDLIFE   NATIVE AMERICANS   SOUTH AMERICA, HISTORY OF   TEXTILES AND WEAVING

ARMIES

FROM ANCIENT TIMES to the present day, the role of an army has always remained the same – to attack enemy territory and defend the country from attack. Armies usually work in close partnership with air and naval forces. Throughout history, foot soldiers called infantry have done most of the fighting, supported by troops on horseback called cavalry. Today, cavalry have been replaced on the battlefield by armoured tank units.

Ancient Greece
Each Greek city-state had its own army. Greek soldiers were so well regarded that other countries hired them to fight on their behalf.

History of armies

The world's first armies, raised in Assyria, Egypt, China, and India, were ill-trained, undisciplined civilians forced to fight for their leaders. The ancient Greeks introduced compulsory military service and rigorous training for their civilian army. Later, the Romans established the first professional (paid) army to protect its empire.

Modern army

Combat troops fighting in the front line need plenty of support. Engineers, for example, repair damaged roads and bridges to help troops cross rough terrain. Other support staff includes doctors and nurses to treat wounded soldiers, caterers to feed the army, and communications experts.

British SAS personal equipment

Gas mask

Knife sheath

Balaclava

Steel fire lighter

SAS survival kit

Miniature harpoons

Wire saw

Fire-kindling tin

Leather glove

Body armour

Grenade pocket

Waist-belt loop

Magazine pouch

Thigh strap

Leather boots

Reinforced toecap

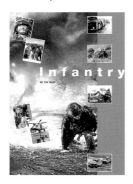

Recruitment
In some countries, the army is made up entirely of volunteer recruits who willingly join the army for a fixed period of time. In other countries, the army is made up largely of conscripts – that is, young people required by law to spend a number of years in the army.

British Army recruitment poster

Training
Modern weapons use advanced technology, so troops need to be not just physically fit but also able to make split-second decisions and operate highly complex computerized equipment. For this reason, technical instruction is just as important a part of a soldier's training as exercise and parade-ground drill.

Specialist units
Most armies have units of troops trained to carry out specialist tasks, such as reconnaissance missions and sabotage raids behind enemy lines, tackling terrorists, and rescuing hostages. These units include the US Army's Green Berets and the British Special Air Service (SAS).

Italian officer's cap badge **British officer's epaulette**

Officers
An army needs a strong chain of command, from the highest to the lowest ranks, so that orders are passed on quickly and clearly. Officers receive training in leading and inspiring their troops. Officers' ranks are shown by special symbols on their uniforms.

Terrorist armies
Sometimes, armies are set up by groups of people struggling to overthrow the existing government or achieve independence for their country or region. Their supporters call them freedom fighters, but those who oppose them call them terrorists. Such groups often stage spectacular bomb attacks to gain publicity for their cause.

Terrorist bomb damage

Non-combat roles

When a nation is at peace, its army still has a vital role to play. For example, when natural disasters occur – such as earthquakes, floods, or famines – an army can bring in medical supplies and food, and restore communications links and electricity and water supplies. Armies can also help to establish peace in other war-torn countries.

Peacekeeping
To separate warring sides in a civil war or to keep the peace once a ceasefire has been negotiated, the United Nations (UN) often sends multinational forces consisting of troops from many different armies.

Crisis response
Armies need to react quickly and efficiently in times of crisis. Huge cargo aircraft carry supplies, trucks, and even small tanks to the crisis area, while passenger planes take troops and other personnel.

FIND OUT MORE   ARMS AND ARMOUR   COLD WAR   FEUDALISM   GREECE, ANCIENT   KNIGHTS AND HERALDRY   ROMAN EMPIRE   UNITED NATIONS   WARFARE   WARSHIPS   WEAPONS

ARMS AND ARMOUR

WARRIORS OF THE PAST attacked with slashing swords, sharp spears, flying arrows, deadly axes, and crushing clubs. All of these arms, or weapons, could kill, so fighters protected themselves with armour: tough coverings of wood, leather, or metal. The invention of firearms in the 14th century made armour useless, because metal plates thick enough to deflect bullets were too heavy to wear. By the 16th century, arms and armour were strictly for show. Modern soldiers may still wear shiny breastplates and carry swords or spears on parade, but they swap them for guns and bullet-proof vests on the battlefield.

Arms

The simplest arms – clubs – are extensions of a fighter's fist, delivering a knock-out punch from a greater distance. Most hand arms, however, aim to wound by cutting the body. Swords, daggers, and lances do this for hand-to-hand fighting; arrows and boomerangs do it from afar, killing or injuring foes that may be almost out of sight.

Four circular bosses covered the handle attachment.

Defensive weapons

Shields are used for defence. Prehistoric hunters may have invented them as camouflage when hunting. Later fighters strapped shields to their left arms to fend off sword cuts. Wood and leather shields were light, and strong enough to deflect all but a direct sword thrust.

Indian shield

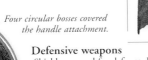

Boomerang

Parrying shield

Crescent-shaped blade

Tabars, Indian steel axes

Tiger heads studded with gems.

Mughal dagger

Sheath

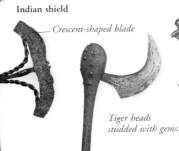

Aboriginal weapons

Club

Attacking weapons

Over the centuries, warriors have used various weapons for different kinds of fighting. Sabres (curved swords) delivered the deadliest cuts, but straight swords were better for thrusting strokes. Clubs and axes had to be heavy and sharp, yet short enough to swing easily. Small, easily hidden daggers were often used for secret assassinations.

Shamshir, a classic Indian sabre

Armour

A suit of armour had to protect against weapons, yet it also had to be comfortable enough to wear all day. Different cultures used various materials, such as leather or metal, to achieve these aims.

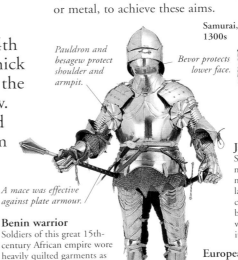

Horns

Iron mask

Samurai, 1300s

Pauldron and besagew protect shoulder and armpit.

Bevor protects lower face.

A mace was effective against plate armour.

Benin warrior

Soldiers of this great 15th-century African empire wore heavily quilted garments as armour. Light bamboo shields were easy to carry and protected warriors from glancing blows from iron-tipped spears or javelins.

Benin bronze plaque

Japanese samurai

Samurai armour was made of many small metal or leather scales laced together with coloured silks. Armour became more decorative when firearms removed its protective value.

European knight

Knights wore chain mail (linked metal rings) to protect them. In the 14th century, armourers introduced metal plates (plate armour) for extra protection.

European knight, 1300s

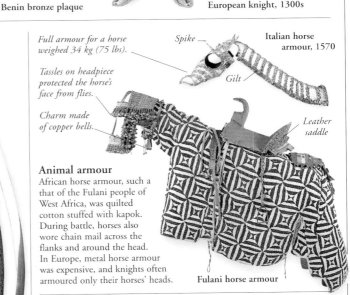

Full armour for a horse weighed 34 kg (75 lbs).

Spike

Italian horse armour, 1570

Tassles on headpiece protected the horse's face from flies.

Gilt

Charm made of copper bells.

Leather saddle

Animal armour

African horse armour, such a that of the Fulani people of West Africa, was quilted cotton stuffed with kapok. During battle, horses also wore chain mail across the flanks and around the head. In Europe, metal horse armour was expensive, and knights often armoured only their horses' heads.

Fulani horse armour

Modern armour

Artificial fabric, such as nylon, provides soldiers and police officers with more protection than thick metal armour. Bullet-proof vests are made of 16 or more layers of nylon. A bullet flattens when it hits the outer layer; lower layers slow it down so that the wearer is bruised, rather than killed or seriously injured.

Riot police

FIND OUT MORE | ABORIGINAL AUSTRALIANS | BENIN EMPIRE | EUROPE, HISTORY OF | GUNS | INDIA, HISTORY OF | JAPAN, HISTORY OF | METALS | WARFARE | WEAPONS

Arms and Armour
Helmets

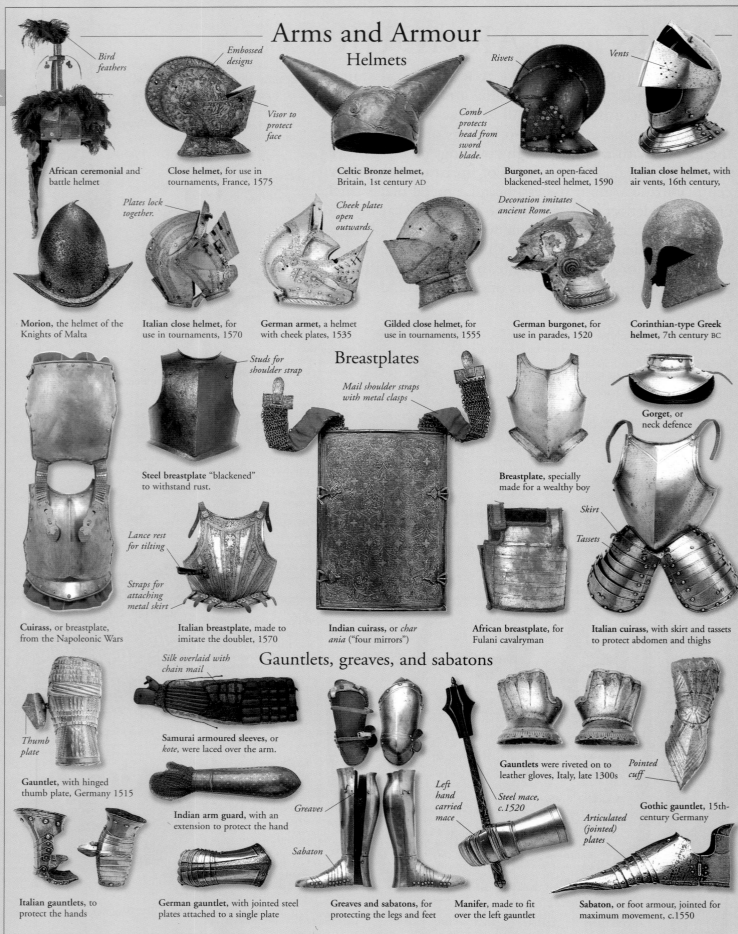

Bird feathers

African ceremonial and battle helmet

Embossed designs

Visor to protect face

Close helmet, for use in tournaments, France, 1575

Celtic Bronze helmet, Britain, 1st century AD

Rivets

Comb protects head from sword blade.

Burgonet, an open-faced blackened-steel helmet, 1590

Vents

Italian close helmet, with air vents, 16th century,

Plates lock together.

Morion, the helmet of the Knights of Malta

Italian close helmet, for use in tournaments, 1570

Cheek plates open outwards.

German armet, a helmet with cheek plates, 1535

Gilded close helmet, for use in tournaments, 1555

Decoration imitates ancient Rome.

German burgonet, for use in parades, 1520

Corinthian-type Greek helmet, 7th century BC

Breastplates

Studs for shoulder strap

Steel breastplate "blackened" to withstand rust.

Mail shoulder straps with metal clasps

Breastplate, specially made for a wealthy boy

Gorget, or neck defence

Lance rest for tilting

Straps for attaching metal skirt

Cuirass, or breastplate, from the Napoleonic Wars

Italian breastplate, made to imitate the doublet, 1570

Indian cuirass, or *char ania* ("four mirrors")

African breastplate, for Fulani cavalryman

Skirt

Tassets

Italian cuirass, with skirt and tassets to protect abdomen and thighs

Gauntlets, greaves, and sabatons

Thumb plate

Gauntlet, with hinged thumb plate, Germany 1515

Silk overlaid with chain mail

Samurai armoured sleeves, or *kote,* were laced over the arm.

Indian arm guard, with an extension to protect the hand

Greaves

Sabaton

Greaves and sabatons, for protecting the legs and feet

Left hand carried mace

Manifer, made to fit over the left gauntlet

Gauntlets were riveted on to leather gloves, Italy, late 1300s

Steel mace, c.1520

Pointed cuff

Gothic gauntlet, 15th-century Germany

Articulated (jointed) plates

Italian gauntlets, to protect the hands

German gauntlet, with jointed steel plates attached to a single plate

Sabaton, or foot armour, jointed for maximum movement, c.1550

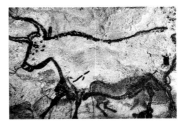

ART, HISTORY OF

FROM THE EARLIEST TIMES, people all over the world have expressed their thoughts and feelings by making art. Over the centuries, styles in the visual arts (sculpture, painting, and drawing) have changed. These differences reflect the changing beliefs and traditions people held as their societies developed. Materials have changed as well, allowing artists to try new ways of reflecting the world around them.

Early art

The earliest works of art usually seem to have had a religious or magical purpose: to represent a god, for example, or to bring a hunter luck as he stalked animals.

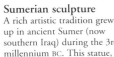

Sumerian sculpture
A rich artistic tradition grew up in ancient Sumer (now southern Iraq) during the 3rd millennium BC. This statue, which shows a Sumerian ruler, is carved from hard stone. It represents the strength and dignity of a good leader.

Caves at Lascaux
These extraordinary pictures of wild animals were painted in French caves more than 17,000 years ago. The outlines were painted by hand, and the vivid colours were filled in by spraying pigment through tubes of bone.

Classical art

Western European art stems directly from the traditions of the ancient Mediterranean world, and especially the art of ancient Greece and Rome. In particular, sculpture from these civilizations is remarkably lifelike, or naturalistic, and concentrates on the human figure.

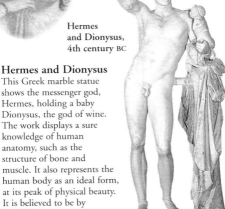

Fresco from Pompeii

Roman wall painting
Most ancient paintings have not survived. This one was preserved by volcanic ash at Pompeii. It shows figures from Roman mythology, and was painted on a wall to decorate the interior of a Roman house.

Hermes and Dionysus, 4th century BC

Hermes and Dionysus
This Greek marble statue shows the messenger god, Hermes, holding a baby Dionysus, the god of wine. The work displays a sure knowledge of human anatomy, such as the structure of bone and muscle. It also represents the human body as an ideal form, at its peak of physical beauty. It is believed to be by Praxiteles, the most famous ancient Greek sculptor.

Masaccio, *The Holy Trinity*, 1428

Painted vault gives sense of space.

Skeleton, a symbol of mortality

Perspective
The Italian Tomaso Masaccio (1401–28) was the first painter to use perspective since Classical times. Perspective creates the illusion that depth exists behind the flat surface of a painting.

Non-religious art
During the Renaissance, European painters broke with earlier tradition. Religious subject matter, such as scenes from the Bible, was still important, but artists also began to record everyday events.

Renaissance

After the fall of the Roman Empire, Classical art was considered too pagan for the Christian civilizations which began to develop in Europe. By the 15th century, painters, sculptors, and architects began to revive a classical tradition in the arts, creating highly lifelike Christian works of art. This revival is called the Renaissance, from the French for "rebirth". It began in Italy and spread through Europe. Influential artists included Michelangelo (1475–1564).

Jan Van Eyck, *The Arnolfini Marriage*, 1434

Early paint making

The materials used to produce a painting affect the way it looks. Before oil paints arrived in the 15th century, artists worked straight onto wet plaster with tempera, a mixture of egg and paint pigment. Oil paints, which were more flexible and gave a more realistic finish, soon became the favourite medium.

Mineral, ground into pigment

Egg tempera
Egg (either the yolk or both yolk and white) provides a strong medium for colours, but is sticky and quick-drying, so difficult to apply.

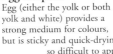

Egg yolk

Oil paint
As a medium, oil has the advantage of being slow to dry, allowing artists to make changes while they work.

Oil for binding paint pigment

Value of colour
Certain colours, such as gold, have always been more expensive than others. Until the 17th century, dark blue was the most costly because it was made from lapis lazuli, a semi-precious stone.

Lapis lazuli

Scales weigh pigment

A

Baroque art

The term "Baroque" describes a style of 17th-century European art. Rome, the centre of the Catholic church, was its birthplace. During the 16th century, the Christian church split into Roman Catholic and Protestant factions. By the 17th century, the Catholic church was using art to spread its teachings. To appeal to the viewer, it promoted a style of art that was theatrical and emotional. Painters were encouraged to use light and shade for dramatic contrasts, sculptors to show figures in dynamic poses. To achieve these effects, artists had to develop great technical skills.

Dramatic facial expression

Arrow is a symbol of God's love.

Bernini, *The ecstasy of St. Teresa*, 1652

Bernini
The Italian painter, sculptor, and architect Gianlorenzo Bernini (1598–1680) was an outstanding influence on Baroque art. He had an exceptional ability to convey great emotion and drama in stone, designed to inspire those who saw his work to greater faith. This sculpture depicts the vision of St. Teresa, in which an angel pierced her with an arrow.

Caravaggio, *The Calling of St. Matthew*, c.1598–99

Light and shade
The Italian painter Michelangelo Caravaggio (1573–1610) shows the moment when Christ calls Matthew to become a disciple. A ray of light illuminates Matthew, but Christ is hidden by shadow.

Romanticism

The early 19th century in Europe is known as the Romantic Age. It was, in part, a reaction to 18th-century art, which had emphasized balance and order. Romantic artists questioned the place of human beings in the Universe. They stressed the importance of human emotion and the imagination, and celebrated the wild power of nature in dramatic landscape paintings.

Friedrich, *Wanderer among the Mists*, 1818

The lonely universe
The German artist Caspar David Friedrich (1774–1840) was spiritually inspired by natural landscapes. There is an intense mysticism to this painting, as a solitary figure contemplates the mighty Alps.

A powerful landscape, shrouded in mist, conveys the strength and mystery of nature.

Change in the 19th century

From the mid-19th century, artists broke with the tradition established by earlier generations. Where they were once told what to depict by patrons, who paid them, they now produced what they wanted, and then tried to sell their work.

Camille Pissarro, *Place du Théâtre Français*, 1898

Selection of colours from Renoir's palette

Lead white *Vermilion*

Naples yellow *Emerald green* *Cobalt blue*

Impressionism
This school of painting grew up in France in the late 19th century. Artists such as Camille Pissarro (1830–1903), Claude Monet (1840–1926), and Auguste Renoir (1841–1919) painted their impressions of a brief moment in time, in particular, the changing effects of sunlight. They were criticized at first, for viewers expected paintings to look more detailed, but have been very influential.

20th-century art

During the 20th century, artists explored new theories about the world, religion, and the mind. They asked the public to confront things that they might wish to ignore, and explored many different styles. After nearly 2,500 years, the grip of Classical art seemed to have been broken.

Surrealism
During the 1920s, the fantastical art made by the Surrealists explored theories about the way the brain works. New ideas had suggested that people consciously only used a tiny part of their brains, and that they were unaware of subconscious activity, over which they had no rational control. The bizarre, dreamlike paintings of Surrealists, such as the Spanish artist Salvador Dali (1904–89), were inspired by these ideas.

Salvador Dali

Modern art
Much modern art is specially created to be seen in a museum or gallery, and not for houses, palaces, or churches as in the past. It often prefers to baffle, tease, and provoke its audience, rather than make its meaning obvious.

Abstract art
Abstract artists do not represent objects from the everyday world. Colour and shape alone suggest ideas or emotions. In this way, abstract art is like music: neither describe anything that can be defined in words, but both can be expressive and moving. The artists Jackson Pollock (1912–56) and Mark Rothko (1903–70) are two of the most famous abstract painters.

Jackson Pollock, *The Moon, Woman cuts the circle*, 1943

Yoki Terauchi, *Air Castle*, 1994

Ambroise Vollard

The French art dealer Ambroise Vollard (1865–1939) made a living buying, selling, and exhibiting modern art. He gave early 20th-century artists unprecedented financial and creative freedom to paint as they wished. Artists such as Paul Cezanne and Henri Matisse achieved success in Vollard's gallery in Paris in the 1900s.

Art in Africa

African art has a long tradition, although a lack of written records make its history hard to trace. Sculpture and masks are major art forms. Most art seems to have been made for religious or ritual purposes. Wood-carving and bronze-casting techniques were highly developed.

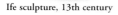

Sculpture

The rich tradition of sculpture in West Africa begins with the pottery figures made by the Nok people from 500 BC. Around the 13th century AD the Ife of Nigeria began to cast outstanding bronze heads and figures in a highly realistic style. These may have influenced sculptures made in Benin, Nigeria, from the 16th to 19th centuries.

Ife sculpture, 13th century

Masks

African masks may represent a spirit or ancestor, or be purely decorative. Their meaning comes from the masquerade (dance, drama, and music) of which they are a part. Wood, beads, ivory, and shells are important materials. This capped mask, carved in a bold, vital style, is from Cameroon.

Wooden mask, 20th century

Asia

Traditionally in Asian art, the symbolic meaning behind the subject of a painting, sculpture, or carving is more important than the illusion of realism. In China, for instance, landscape paintings are stylized to express the ideals of religious thought: natural harmony, peace, and grace. In China and Japan, calligraphy was seen as a high form of art. The inscriptions are usually of short, poetic situations.

T'ang Yin, Dreaming of Immortality in a Thatched Cottage, Ming dynasty

Chinese landscape

In China, the art of painting developed from calligraphy. Landscape artists painted on paper or silk, using brush and ink. They did not paint from real life. The flow and vigour of the brush strokes were more important.

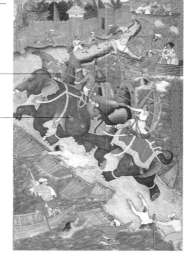

16th-century Mughal manuscript

Vividly coloured

High level of detail

Brief poetic description of the scene

Miniatures

During the Mughal Empire (16th–17th centuries), figurative miniature painting flourished in India. These were richly coloured and exceptionally delicate. This illustration comes from a contemporary chronicle of the emperor's exploits.

Hokusai

Katsushika Hokusai (1760–1849) is perhaps the best-known Japanese printmaker. His famous wood-cuts include landscapes as well as scenes of daily life (called ukiyo-e). They are dramatically coloured and composed.

The Great Wave of Kawagawa, 1831

Native American art

Sophisticated Native American societies, such as the Aztec and Maya in Mexico and the Inca in Peru, created distinct artistic and architectural styles. Nearly 3,000 years ago, nomadic peoples in North and South America marked awe-inspiring "sculptures" on to the land, or created vast earthworks whose shapes can only be seen from high in the air.

Tlingit totem pole

Totem poles

Complex in design, and carved with great skill, totem poles showed the status of many Native North American chiefs.

Sand paintings

In the Southwest, Native North Americans trickled coloured sand and ground stones on to a smooth background to create temporary symbolic paintings with a ritual importance.

Navajo sand painting represents figures from Navajo mythology.

Easter Island statues

Between AD 400 and 1680, the people of Easter Island carved huge heads, up to 12 m (40 ft) high, from volcanic rock. They commemorate the divine ancestors of tribal chiefs.

Pacific art

Contact with European Christian cultures from the 18th century onwards had a destructive effect on ancient local lifestyles in the Pacific islands. Much art has been lost, although some remarkable sculptures have survived, due to their durability. Wood and stone carvings, bark cloth paintings, spirit masks, and intricate body tattoos are among the important art forms of the Pacific area.

Statues face out to sea.

Statues, Easter Island

Timeline

30,000 BC Earliest known works of art produced.	**c.500 BC** Lifelike human figurines produced by the Nok in West Africa.	**618–907** T'ang dynasty, China: great tradition of landscape painting develops.	**16th century** Mughal dynasty holds power in India.	**19th century** Photography invented.	*Metal tubes are invented in the 1840s.*		**20th century** Time of incredible diversity of styles in the visual arts, including Cubism (1907–1920s), abstract art (1910–50), surrealism (1920s), and Pop Art (mid-1950s).
30,000–10,000 BC Cave paintings made in France.	**100 BC–AD 300s** Roman empire spreads Classical art around Europe.			**1860s–90s** Impressionism develops in France. It is very influential.			
	Warrior, Greece, 520 BC	**15th century** Beginning of the Renaissance in Europe.	**17th century** Dutch Golden Age of painting.		**19th-century oil paints**		

FIND OUT MORE

AFRICA, HISTORY OF · ARCHITECTURE · MONET · NATIVE AMERICANS · PAINTING AND DRAWING · PHOTOGRAPHY · PICASSO · RENAISSANCE · SCULPTURE

ARTHROPODS

A

MORE THAN ONE MILLION species of arthropod exist, making them the largest group in the animal kingdom. They live in almost all habitats, from mountain tops to the ocean depths. Arthropods are invertebrates – animals without backbones. They come in many shapes and sizes, from tiny mites to large crabs. Their bodies are divided into segments, and they have distinct heads with antennae or eyes. Rigid exoskeletons encase their bodies, but flexible leg joints allow them to move around, and give them their name.

Types of arthropod

Arthropods vary in size, from minute creatures a fraction of a millimetre long to outsized sea dwellers several kilograms in weight. There are four main types of arthropod – insects, arachnids, crustaceans, and myriapods. Insects are the largest group, accounting for almost 90 per cent of all arthropods.

Asian giant millipede

Two pairs of legs on each body segment

Antenna

Myriapods

Myriapods include millipedes and centipedes. They have more legs than other arthropods – as many as 200 in some species. Their bodies are long and tubular. They live in the soil or among leaf debris.

Spiders have 8 legs.

Red-kneed tarantula

Arachnids

Arachnids include spiders, scorpions, and mites. They have eight legs; scorpions use the front pair as claws. Spiders and scorpions are carnivores that live mainly on land. Spiders often kill their prey with poisonous fangs; scorpions use their venom-filled sting.

Delicate wings

Large compound eye helps it to catch prey in flight.

Broad-bodied chaser dragonfly

Insects

Insects are the most diverse group of arthropods. They live in all kinds of land and freshwater habitats. All adult insects have six legs, and most have wings – they are the only arthropods that can fly.

European lobster

Hard exoskeleton

Crustaceans

Crustaceans include crabs, shrimps, and lobsters. Most live in the sea or in freshwater and have five pairs of legs. Lobsters and crabs have very thick exoskeletons and some grow extremely large.

Exoskeleton

Exoskeletons are made mainly of the substance chitin.

Exoskeleton of a fiddler crab

The exoskeleton of an arthropod is a tough outer layer covering the entire body, including the eyes, antennae, and legs. It protects and supports the muscles and soft organs within the body and helps to retain moisture.

Moulting and growth

Exoskeletons are fixed in size. In order to grow, an arthropod must shed, or moult, this rigid layer. Its body then rapidly expands before a new exoskeleton hardens in place of the old one. Moulting is part of a process called "incomplete metamorphosis". This is where the young, called nymphs, emerge from eggs looking like tiny adults. They moult many times before reaching adult size. In "complete metamorphosis", the animal changes form as well as size.

Moulting

1 An emerging adult grasshopper has cracked open its old exoskeleton and is starting to wriggle its body free, headfirst. Before this final moult, the nymph will already have been through four previous moults.

Nymph on twig

Adult is almost free of the nymph's skin.

2 The adult has pulled its legs and most of its body out of the old skin. It is already expanding in size, now that it is free from its confines.

Old, empty exoskeleton

Adult waits as blood pumps into its wings before it flies away.

3 Moulting is now complete. The adult rests while its new exoskeleton hardens and its wings unfurl. Its old exoskeleton, now empty and brittle, still clings to the twig.

Reproduction

Breeding habits are very diverse among arthropods. Fertilization may take place inside or outside the female's body. Normally, eggs are laid; some are guarded, others are hidden and left alone. The young of some arthropods, such as garden spiders, are tiny versions of adults called nymphs; others start life as larvae and look different from the adults.

Cluster of young garden spiders

Feeding

Arthropods feed on all kinds of plant and animal matter, both living and dead. Some arthropods, such as praying mantises, have pincers to gather food; others use their front legs. Many have cutting and chewing mouthparts, while those that feed on fluids, such as true bugs, have mouths modified for sucking. Small aquatic arthropods eat by filtering food particles from water.

Herbivores

Some arthropods, such as chafer beetles, eat only plant matter. Adults feed on stems, leaves, and buds, while larvae eat plant roots.

Field chafer beetle

Carnivores

Many arthropods feed on other animals. Garden spiders, for example, feed mainly on insects. Some meat eaters also eat dead animals and are called scavengers. Sand crabs scavenge on dead birds and other debris found on the beach and seabed.

Web spun around wasp

Garden spider feeding on a wasp

Defence

As arthropods are generally small in size, they are the target for a great many predators. Their hard exoskeleton, which acts as a tiny suit of armour, provides the first line of defence. Some arthropods, such as pill millipedes, take a passive form of defence and roll up into a ball if danger threatens. Other arthropods have special protective weapons; including stings and pincers. Many ant species have glands on their abdomens from which they secrete formic acid to drive off enemies.

Stings and pincers

Some arthropods have pincers and stings which they use to defend themselves against attackers. Scorpions also use their large pincers to catch animals. They then use their venom-filled stings to paralyze their prey.

Sting

Eyes

Fat-tailed scorpion

| FIND OUT MORE | ANTS AND TERMITES | BEETLES | CAVE WILDLIFE | CRABS AND OTHER CRUSTACEANS | FLIES | GRASSHOPPERS AND CRICKETS | INSECTS | POISONOUS ANIMALS | SPIDERS AND SCORPIONS |

ASIA

STRETCHING from the frozen Arctic to the equator, Asia is the world's largest continent. It is also a continent of extremes, containing the world's highest point, Mount Everest, as well as its lowest, the Dead Sea. China has the world's greatest population, while Asia's largest country, the Russian Federation, extends into Europe. Asia is separated from North America by the Bering Sea, and from Europe by the Caspian Sea, Turkey, and the Ural Mountains. In the southeast, it breaks into a mass of tiny islands.

Physical features

Much of Southwest and Central Asia is covered with barren desert, such as the Gobi and Syrian deserts. The Himalayan Mountains separate the bleak north from the fierce heat of the Indian subcontinent and the tropical rainforests of Southeast Asia. Asia has many great rivers, including the Huang He, Mekong, and Indus, flanked by fertile plains and valleys.

Lake Baikal
Siberia, the northern region of Asia, has the oldest, deepest, and eighth largest lake in the world. Lake Baikal, which contains more than 20 per cent of the world's unfrozen fresh water, reaches a depth of 1,637 m (5,371 ft). It covers a total area of 31,468 sq km (12,150 sq miles).

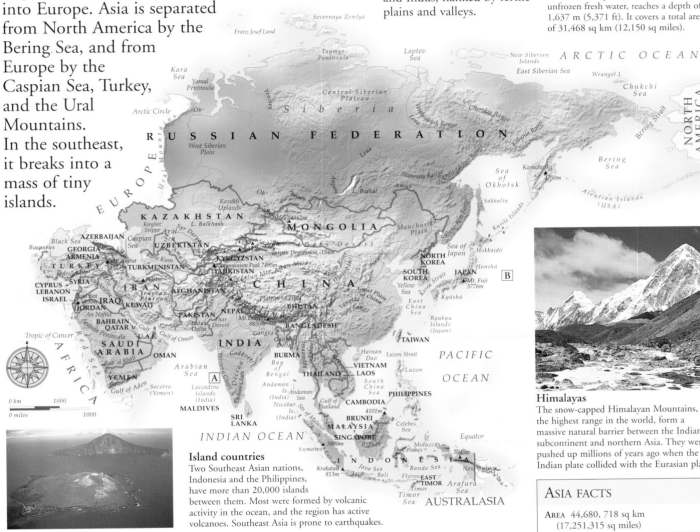

Himalayas
The snow-capped Himalayan Mountains, the highest range in the world, form a massive natural barrier between the Indian subcontinent and northern Asia. They were pushed up millions of years ago when the Indian plate collided with the Eurasian plate.

Island countries
Two Southeast Asian nations, Indonesia and the Philippines, have more than 20,000 islands between them. Most were formed by volcanic activity in the ocean, and the region has active volcanoes. Southeast Asia is prone to earthquakes.

ASIA FACTS

AREA	44,680, 718 sq km (17,251,315 sq miles)
POPULATION	3,700,700,000
NUMBER OF COUNTRIES	49
BIGGEST COUNTRY	Russian Federation
SMALLEST COUNTRY	Maldives
HIGHEST POINT	Mt. Everest (China/Nepal) 8,850 m (29,035 ft)
LOWEST POINT	Dead Sea shore (Israel) 400 m (1,312 ft) below sea-level
LONGEST RIVER	Yangtze (Chang Jiang) (China) 6,380 km (3,965 miles)
BIGGEST LAKE	Caspian Sea 378,400 sq km (146,100 sq miles)

Cross-section through Asia

From the Indian Ocean, the land rises to the Vindhya Range in central India descending to the Ganges Plain, watered by the Himalayas. In the east, the mountains drop to the Great Plain of China. Across the Yellow Sea, the Korean Peninsula juts out near to Japan in the Pacific Ocean.

Indian Ocean — A — Approximately 6,480 km (4,027 miles) from A to B — B

Labels: Ganges Plain, Mt. Everest, Himalayas, Nepal, Great Plain of China, Korean Peninsula, Mt. Fuji, Japan, Red Basin, China, Sea of Japan, Vindhya Range

Climatic zones

Asia has every kind of climate and landscape. In the far north, Siberia is covered in tundra, where part of the ground is permanently frozen. South of the tundra are coniferous forests and open grasslands (steppes). Central and southwest Asia are mostly desert and mountains, while the east has deciduous forests. Tropical rainforests cover much of the south and southeast.

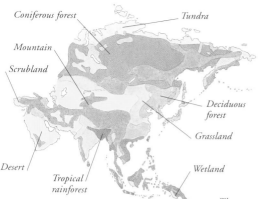

Coniferous forest *Tundra* *Mountain* *Scrubland* *Deciduous forest* *Grassland* *Desert* *Wetland* *Tropical rainforest*

Tundra

In the bitterly cold and treeless tundra region of Siberia, the subsoil remains frozen – a condition known as permafrost. With temperatures of less than -10°C (14°F) and covered by snow for six to ten months of the year, the topsoil thaws only briefly in the summer. The tundra has rich mineral resources.

Mosses, lichens, and a few flowers appear briefly during the warmer months.

Harsh conditions make trees stunted and sparse. Ice and snow cover the region for half the year.

The steppes are the Asian equivalent of the pampas and prairies of the Americas.

Taiga

The Siberian taiga, which lies to the south of the tundra, is the world's largest coniferous forest. The main trees are spruce, fir, larch, and pine. In the spring, much of the taiga becomes flooded as the lower reaches of the north-flowing rivers thaw, while their mouths remain frozen. In summer, some ground remains swampy; in winter it freezes.

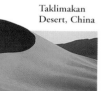

Steppes

The wide, open grasslands that cover Mongolia and southern Siberia are known as the steppes. Livestock is grazed on these broad, treeless plains, which, in places, merge into semi-desert. The soil is mostly fertile and, with irrigation, many areas have become productive farmland.

Dunes form as sand drifts in the prevailing wind.

Taklimakan Desert, China

Deserts

Asia has both hot and cold deserts, as well as many regions of semi-desert where animals can be grazed. Middle Eastern deserts are hot and dry all year, with cold nights. The Gobi and Taklimakan deserts of Central Asia have scorching summers, but are bitterly cold in winter.

Wetlands

Mangrove swamps are found along many coasts of southern Asia, from India to the Philippines. The mangrove trees have long, spreading roots, producing a forest that looks as if it is on stilts. Logging and pollution are destroying many mangroves.

Mangrove roots help stop coast eroding in storms.

Temperatures average 21°C (70°F), with 2,000 mm (79 in) of rain per year.

Tropical rainforest

There are tropical rainforests in India, Southeast Asia, and the Philippines. They flourish on the southern slopes of the Himalayas, and in Burma (Myanmar), the Malay Peninsula, and the western part of the island of Irian Jaya. Home to 40 per cent of all plant and animal species, the world's rainforests are threatened, as people cut down trees for the timber industry and to clear space for farming.

Trees lose their leaves in winter as a means of protecting themselves from wind and cold.

Deciduous forest

Asia has comparatively few broadleaf forests of deciduous trees that shed their leaves in winter. They occur mainly in eastern Asia, including China, Japan, and the Koreas, or in cooler upland areas, such as the mountains of Nepal.

People

Asia contains two-thirds of the world's population, and the birth rate is still rising in many countries. Most people live in the southern and eastern regions and in the fertile river valleys. Many are farmers, although increasing numbers are moving into expanding cities in search of work.

Israeli boy   Vietnamese girl   Japanese boy

Resources

Asia's natural resources include farmland, which provides work for 60 per cent of the people, and the fishing grounds of the Pacific Ocean. Minerals include oil and natural gas from the Gulf States, as well as bauxite, copper, coal, diamonds, gold, iron, lead, manganese, mercury, tin, and titanium.

Rice

Diamond

Tuna fish

FIND OUT MORE   ASIA, HISTORY OF   ASIAN WILDLIFE   CLIMATE   CONTINENTS   DESERTS   FORESTS   GRASSLAND WILDLIFE   LAKES   MOUNTAINS AND VALLEYS   RAINFOREST WILDLIFE   TUNDRA

ASIA, HISTORY OF

ASIA IS THE WORLD'S LARGEST continent and the birthplace of the world's earliest civilizations, such as those of the Sumerians, China, and India. The emergence of these civilizations had a profound impact on history, both ancient and modern, as did the emergence of three major world religions: Hinduism, Buddhism, and Islam. Colonial interference affected Asia's development over the centuries, but after decades of independent growth, today's Asian economies are booming. There are still conflicts, however, and those in Southeast Asia and the Middle East tend to affect world politics.

Early development
Early civilizations in Asia were largely isolated from each other and from the rest of the world by barriers of deserts, mountains, and oceans. Only the Middle East had strong connections with Europe. Therefore, Asian civilizations and cultures developed independently for thousands of years. Over time, major civilizations, such as those of India and China, began to affect other Asian countries.

Central Asia

For centuries the only travellers in the inhospitable landscape of Central Asia were traders using the Silk Road. In 1398, the Mongolian warrior Timur (1336–1405) swept down from the steppes and founded a Central Asian empire.

Typically tiled Samarkandian roof

Samarkand
In 1369, Timur moved his capital to the prosperous city of Samarkand, in modern Uzbekistan. The city experienced a golden age and became the architectural jewel of Central Asia as Timur and his descendants built palaces, astronomical observatories, and Islamic colleges. In the early 1500s, nomadic Uzbeks attacked the city.

Uleg Beg Medrasa, Uzbekistan

Swat, Pakistan

Kushan Empire
In c.170 BC, a northern Chinese clan, the Yuezhi, moved west to Central Asia. By the 3rd century AD, they had founded an empire that stretched from eastern Iran to the Ganges in India. The Kushans controlled fertile river valleys and were at the centre of the silk trade. They encouraged Buddhism and religious art, but declined in the 4th century.

Padmasambhava

A legendary sage and yoga expert from Swat, modern Pakistan, Padmasambhava founded Tibetan Buddhism. He and his consort, Yeshe Tsogyal, arrived in Tibet in 747, and established the first Buddhist monastery. The sage then spent his life writing and lecturing on the religion.

Semi-precious stones

Ancient civilizations

The Sumerians of western Asia evolved the world's first civilization, but it was the early civilizations of India and China that affected Asia the most. Their religions had special impact: Hinduism (the religion of the people of India) and Buddhism (founded by Siddhartha Gautama and one of the three great religions of China) spread over Asia.

Kogyuro openwork cup

Chola dynasty
From 850–c.1200, a powerful dynasty known as the Cholas began to dominate much of India. They built many Hindu temples and spread their religion to Sri Lanka. They extended their naval power over the seas of Southeast Asia, and this helped spread Hinduism as far as Sumatra and Bali.

Koguryo dynasty
By the 7th century China's influence was increasing, and Chinese monks converted Korea to Buddhism. The Koguryo rulers (1st century BC–AD 7th century) encouraged the spread of Buddhism. From Korea, the missionaries went to Japan, which adopted not only Buddhism but also Chinese script, architecture, and culture.

Southeast Asia

For 1,000 years, India was the major shaping force of this region, and provided a mould for Southeast Asian culture, art, and religion. Its influence declined after c.1300.

Siam
Over centuries, waves of migrants from the north entered Siam (Thailand), and intermarried with the native tribes. In the 13th century, one tribe, the Thais, unified Siam into a single nation with one monarch and one religion – Buddhism.

Sea routes
From c.300, Indian traders sailed to Thailand, Malaysia, Indonesia, and the Philippines. From the 1200s, Arabian merchants spread Islam along sea trade routes. From c.1500, the region also traded with Europe.

Dhow leaving Muscat, Oman

Thai tribal woman

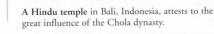

A Hindu temple in Bali, Indonesia, attests to the great influence of the Chola dynasty.

A

Trade and culture

During the 17th, 18th, and 19th centuries trade thrived, though some Asian countries were closed to outsiders. Russia and European countries bought silk, tea, and porcelain from China. India traded with the world, and was famous for its handmade textiles, such as "paisley", which was a traditional Indian pattern. During this period, Western powers became increasingly interested in annexing Asian territories for trade purposes.

Great Game

During the 1800s, Russia expanded into Central Asia. The British feared the Russians were aiming to take over India, and both sides began to spy on each other. The British called this the Great Game; to the Russians it was known as the Tournament of Shadows.

Mountains of Lake Baikal, Russia

Manchu Dynasty

China's Manchu Dynasty (1644–1911) was expansionist, and spread its culture by acquiring other territories, such as Mongolia (1697), Tibet (1751), and eastern Turkestan (1760). At home, however, economic conditions worsened.

Yellow lotus is a sacred flower.

A rich woman's silk robe, 19th century

Asian resistance

In the 17th and 18th centuries, China, Japan, Korea, and Siam (Thailand) resisted European expansion. China confined European trade to Macao and Canton, Japan traded only with Holland at Nagasaki, and Korea remained closed to the west. In 1688, a revolution in Siam ended French attempts to gain influence in Bangkok.

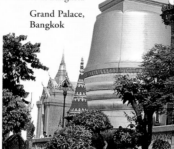

Gold-coated roof

Grand Palace, Bangkok

Nineteenth-century colonization

In the 19th century, European powers colonized much of Asia. The British took over Burma, Malaya, North Borneo, and Hong Kong; France dominated Indochina; the Dutch controlled Indonesia; and Russia annexed Central Asian provinces.

Britain
Russia
France
Netherlands
Japan

Conversion of the Philippines

In the late 1500s, the Spanish colonial government encouraged Filipinos to become Roman Catholics, and gave financial support to missionaries. By the 18th century, most Filipinos in towns and lowland areas had converted to Catholicism. The island of Mindanao, however, embraced Islam, which was brought to them by Muslim traders.

Paoay church, Ilocos Norte Province, Philippines

Engraving of Anglo-Burmese wars, 1824

Anglo-Burmese wars

In 1886, Burma lost its independence to Britain after a series of wars. This takeover was strategic rather than trade-based: the British wanted to prevent the French from gaining too much influence in Asia.

Golden East

As Europe gained in military and industrial strength in the 19th century, it expanded, and Asia became a rich source of food and raw materials. European planters developed tea, coffee, and rubber plantations, founded tin mines, exploited Asian timber, and prospected for gold, silver, and precious stones.

Indian tea

Vietnamese mahogany

Rama V

Chulalongkorn (1853–1910) became Rama V, King of Siam, in 1868. He travelled widely throughout Asia, and was determined to strengthen his country by a process of modernization. In the 1880s, he created a modern army, civil service, and education system. Although Thailand lost some provinces to Britain and France, it managed to preserve its prestige and independence.

The king and queen of Siam

Rebellion

From the 1850s, there were rebellions against European interference in Asian affairs. In 1857, the Sepoy Rebellion took place in India, and, in 1900, there was the Boxer Rebellion in China. Both revolts were protests against western strength and culture. They were crushed by western or colonial government forces.

Cover of Le Petit Parisien, 1900, "Death to Foreigners"

Timeline

4000–c.2500 BC The world's earliest civilization flourishes in Sumer, western Asia.

c.2500 BC Indus Valley period, India's earliest civilization.

1800 BC Shang period: China's earliest civilization starts to build its first cities.

c.330 BC Alexander the Great destroys the Persian Empire.

138 BC First recorded journey on the Silk Road.

c.50 Buddhism reaches China from India.

206 BC– AD 220 Height of the Chinese Han Empire.

FIND OUT MORE   ARCHITECTURE   CHINA, HISTORY OF   CONFUCIUS

Growth of nationalism

After World War I, Asian nationalism (a belief in independence) grew. In 1918, Arab leaders overthrew Turkish rule. The desire of Jews to create an independent state in Palestine gained support. By 1933, 238,000 Jews had settled in Palestine, and, in 1948, the state of Israel was created.

Living quarters

Jewish settlers in Palestine, 1930s

Independence movements

After 1945, many Asian countries threw off colonial rule. In 1947, India and Pakistan struggled for and won independence from Britain. In 1948, a Jewish homeland, Israel, came into being. Indonesia won independence from the Netherlands in 1949, after a four-year battle. France also tried to prevent Vietnamese independence, but was defeated in 1954; the other French colonies, Laos and Cambodia, became independent in 1954 and 1953 respectively.

These territories all gained independence since 1939. There were eventually 48 independent countries in post-war Asia.

World War II

In 1941–42, Japan occupied Burma, Indochina, and Indonesia. After the horrors of occupation, these areas rejected all foreign rule. In China, communist guerrillas resisting the Japanese, gained popular and political support.

Two war veterans on the Death Railway, River Kwai, Thailand, 1990s

Death Railway

During World War II, the Japanese built a railway to link Burma and Thailand to supply Japanese troops in Burma. Many thousands of Asian labourers and Western prisoners died from malnutrition, disease, and exhaustion building the 420-km (260-mile) railway, and it became known as the Death Railway.

Dragon economies

In the 1980s, Singapore, Taiwan, Hong Kong, and South Korea used their well-educated populations and high investment to become prosperous "dragon" economies. In the 1990s, Thailand, Malaysia, and Indonesia also developed rapidly.

Taiwanese factory

Taiwanese exported goods

Taiwan traditionally exported agricultural products, such as sugar, pineapples, and bananas; but by the 1980s it also exported advanced electronic products, such as personal computers, televisions, and portable phones.

Communist Asia

In 1949, the communists established the People's Republic of China – the world's largest communist state. In 1954, the North Vietnamese created an independent communist state. From the 1960s, communist movements in Indonesia and Malaysia threatened to overthrow existing governments.

US troops carrying wounded soldiers from a "chopper"

Khe Sanh, Vietnam

Middle East conflicts

Since 1948, Arab-Israeli territorial conflict, such as the war of 1973 (when Egypt and Syria attacked Israel), has dominated the Middle East. There have also been conflicts between Arab countries, such as the Iran-Iraq war (1980–88). Although the oil boom has helped this situation by lessening poverty, the situation in the Middle East remains unstable.

Oil rigs, Middle East

Vietnam War

From 1954, communist North Vietnam sought to reunite with non-communist South Vietnam by force. Originally a civil war, the Vietnam War escalated into an international conflict with the gradual intervention of the United States in the 1960s. Following defeats and heavy casualties, the USA agreed to withdraw in 1973. In 1975, northern forces unified both halves of Vietnam.

Chaim Weizmann

Weizmann (1874–1952) was born near Pinsk in Belorussia and studied chemistry in Switzerland. In his youth he became a passionate Zionist and eventually was made head of the World Zionist Movement. After World War II, Weizmann campaigned for the creation of Israel, and in 1948, became the state of Israel's first president.

Timeline

c.618–907 The sophisticated T'ang dynasty dominates China.

1211 Mongol warrior Ghengis Khan invades China.

1300s Silk Road is shut.

1368 Ming dynasty expels Mongols from China.

1397 Mongols invade India.

1350–1460 Collapse of Khmer Empire, Cambodia.

1453 Fall of Constantinople to the Turkish Ottoman Empire.

Toy dog, Thailand, 1926

c.1488 Ming emperors rebuild the Great Wall of China.

1526–1707 Domination of Mughals in India.

1600–1614 British, French, and Dutch form East India companies.

1736–96 Manchu China prospers under Emperor Qianlong.

c.1750 Cultural and artistic peak in Japan.

1757 British take control of Bengal, India.

1839–42 First Opium War.

1907 Anglo-Russian agreement ends the Great Game in Central Asia.

1949 Chinese Revolution.

1950–53 Korean War.

1954–75 Vietnam War.

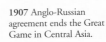

Toy robot, Japan, 1956

 FIND OUT MORE EMPIRES EXPLORATION GANDHI, MOHANDAS INDIA, HISTORY OF JAPAN, HISTORY OF MUHAMMAD PERSIAN EMPIRES WARFARE

ASIA, CENTRAL

MAINLY ARID DESERT and mountainous, Central Asia is made up of five countries. The Silk Road, an ancient trade route between China, the Middle East, and Europe, once passed through the region, boosting the textile industry, and making handwoven rugs from Central Asia world famous. From 1922 until 1991 the whole area, apart from Afghanistan, was part of the Soviet Union. Under communist rule, the countries were partly modernized. Today, however, as independent nations they face an uncertain future. In 2001 Afghanistan was linked to the terrorist attacks of September 11 in the USA and was devastated by US-led reprisal bombings.

Physical features

Much of Central Asia is covered by two hot, dry deserts: the Karakumy and the Kyzyl Kum. The rest is largely rugged mountain chains. There is a small area of farmland, which has been extended by irrigation.

Kyzyl Kum
The name Kyzyl Kum means "red sands". This desert region lies south of the Aral Sea, between the rivers Syr Daria and Amu Darya, mostly in Uzbekistan. Few people apart from nomads live here. Much of it is covered by low hills and sandy wasteland.

Tien Shan
The literal translation of Tien Shan is "Heavenly Mountains". This range of ice-capped peaks runs for about 3,000 km (1,864 miles) from eastern Kyrgyzstan into China. The highest point is Pobeda Peak, 7,439 m (24,406 ft). Mountain rivers form broad, fertile valleys, which are used for farming.

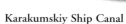

Karakumskiy Ship Canal
The Karakumskiy Ship Canal is being built from the Amu Darya, one of Central Asia's main rivers, across the Karakumy Desert. It will link the river with the Caspian Sea, 1,400 km (870 miles) away.

Nomads
Many Central Asian people are nomads who roam the land with their animal herds, constantly searching for new pastures. They live in traditional tents usually made of animal skins. Their animals – mainly sheep and goats – provide them with meat, milk, skins, and wool, some of which they sell.

Kyrgyz nomad at home with horse

27°C (81°F)   -5°C (23°F)

316 mm (12 in)

Regional climate
Most of this region is cold in winter and very hot and dry in summer. Rainfall is uniformly low, which hampers farming. The mountain regions are always cooler than the lowlands, and many of the peaks are permanently covered by snow and ice.

Turkmenistan

Only two per cent of Turkmenistan's arid land can be farmed. With irrigation, cotton, fruit, wheat, and vegetables are produced. Many people live in nomadic tribes, and there is much intertribal tension. Turkmenistan is the world's fifth largest producer of natural gas.

TURKMENISTAN FACTS

CAPITAL CITY Ashgabat

AREA 488,100 sq km (188,455 sq miles)

POPULATION 4,800,000

MAIN LANGUAGES Turkmen, Russian

MAJOR RELIGION Muslim, Eastern Orthodox

CURRENCY Manat

Akhal-Teke
Known as the "wind of heaven", Akhal-Teke race-horses have been bred in the south of the Karakumy Desert for centuries. Fast, hardy, and well suited to the hot, harsh climate, Akhal-Tekes compete in traditional horse races at the Ashgabat hippodrome.

Akhal-Teke

Carpets
For centuries, Turkmenistan has produced beautiful, velvety carpets in deep, toning shades of red, brown, and maroon. Women hand-knot each carpet using fine wool from karakul sheep. They make several sizes, including *khali* (large), *ensi* (door rug), as well as weaving curtains, sacks, bags, and pouches.

Uzbekistan

Although 80 per cent of Uzbekistan is covered by dry steppe and desert, its areas of fertile land and resources of oil, gas, gold, copper, and coal make it one of Central Asia's wealthier countries. Fruit, silk cocoons, and vegetables are exported to Moscow. Uzbekistan has the world's largest single gold mine.

UZBEKISTAN FACTS

CAPITAL CITY Tashkent

AREA 447,400 sq km (172,741 sq miles)

POPULATION 25,300,000

MAIN LANGUAGES Uzbek, Russian

MAJOR RELIGION Muslim, Eastern Orthodox

CURRENCY Som

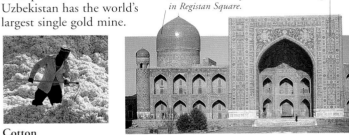

The Tillya-Kari is an Islamic seminary in Registan Square.

An intricate mosaic covers building.

Cotton
Uzbekistan is the world's fourth largest producer of cotton. However, the irrigation system used to water crops has seriously depleted the Aral Sea.

Samarkand
Home to 370,000 people, the ancient city of Samarkand was once the centre for trade in silk from China. Today, the manufacture of silk and cotton textiles is still the city's main industry. Samarkand's Registan Square contains some magnificent 14th-century Islamic architecture.

Kyrgyzstan

Dominated by the arid Tian Shan mountains, Kyrgyzstan is a mainly rural country. Only seven per cent of the land is cultivable. Half is used for growing fodder for livestock; the rest supports vegetables, wheat, fruit, cotton, and tobacco.

KYRGYZSTAN FACTS

CAPITAL CITY Bishkek

AREA 198,500 sq km (76,640 sq miles)

POPULATION 5,000,000

MAIN LANGUAGE Kyrgyz, Russian

MAJOR RELIGION Muslim

CURRENCY Som

People
The population of Kyrgyzstan is made up of 57 per cent Kyrgyz people. The rest are mainly Russians and Uzbeks. Many Russians are leaving as a result of the strong nationalist feelings that have grown in the country since the end of Soviet rule. Ethnic tension also exists with the Uzbeks.

Resources
Gold and mercury are mined for export, as well as smaller amounts of other minerals, including iron ore, tin, lead, copper, zinc, and bauxite. Kyrgyzstan also has reserves of oil, coal, and gas, and its many rivers and lakes give it great potential for hydroelectric power.

Tajikistan

The poorest of the former Soviet republics, Tajikistan has been torn by civil war ever since independence. The main conflict is between ethnic Tajiks, who make up about two-thirds of the population, and Uzbeks, who make up one-quarter. Tajikistan has rich mineral resources.

TAJIKISTAN FACTS

CAPITAL CITY Dushanbe

AREA 143,100 sq km (55,251 sq miles)

POPULATION 6,100,000

MAIN LANGUAGES Tajik, Uzbek

MAJOR RELIGION Muslim

CURRENCY Somoni

Watermelon

Uranium
Tajikistan has 14 per cent of the world's uranium, used as nuclear fuel. It is a major export, but the end of the nuclear arms race has reduced its value.

Farming
Only about six per cent of Tajikistan is suitable for farming. The main farming areas are in the northwest, near Khudzhand, and the southwest, south of Dushanbe. Melons, grapes, and peaches are grown in fertile soils washed down from the mountains into the valleys.

Afghanistan

Afghanistan has a long history of war. After years of civil strife, Afghanistan was further destroyed by a US-led 'war on terrorism' in 2001–02. Pashtuns are the majority ethnic group. Afghanistan is one of the world's poorest countries.

Taliban
An Islamic sect called the Taliban took power in 1996 and created a hardline regime which banned many freedoms. Women suffered heavily under Taliban rule as they were forbidden to receive an education, hold a job, or show their faces in public. The Taliban fled power in 2001 during western war reprisals for the September 11 terrorist attacks.

AFGHANISTAN FACTS

CAPITAL CITY Kabul

AREA 647,500 sq km (250,000 sq miles)

POPULATION 22,500,000

MAIN LANGUAGES Persian, Pashto, Dari

MAJOR RELIGION Muslim

CURRENCY Afghani

FIND OUT MORE   ASIA, HISTORY OF   DESERTS   FARMING   HORSES   ISLAM   MOUNTAINS AND VALLEYS   NUCLEAR POWER   ROCKS AND MINERALS   TEXTILES AND WEAVING   TRADE AND INDUSTRY

ASIAN WILDLIFE

ASIA STRETCHES FROM the frozen Arctic in the north to the warm tropics in the south. Although much of Asia is undulating plain, it also boasts the awesome mountain range of the Himalayas. Much of the interior receives little rain, but parts of India hold the world record for annual rainfall. This continent of contrasts provides many habitats, each with its own characteristic plants and animals. Many of the world's best known endangered species, such as giant pandas and tigers, live in Asia. But many less publicized, smaller animals and plants are also threatened by the steady spread of human populations.

Temperate forest wildlife

Asian temperate woodlands are rich in species of broadleaved trees. Summers are mild, but winters can be cold, and after the leaves have fallen, there is little food or shelter. Some animals migrate or hibernate; others, such as the Japanese macaque, are adapted to the cold.

Monkey eating snow

Thick, shaggy coat

Japanese macaque
Living throughout most of Japan, the Japanese macaque lives in a more northerly climate than any other monkey. In winter it grows a thick coat for protection, and some troops sit in hot springs to avoid the chill of a snowstorm. Roots, buds, and shoots form its winter diet.

Japanese emperor butterfly
Only the male Japanese emperor has an iridescent purple sheen, but both sexes have spotted wings. This pattern breaks up their outline, making it difficult to see where they land on sun-flecked foliage. Their caterpillars are leaf green, to camouflage them on the leaves of celtis trees, on which they feed.

Purple iridescence of male

White spots

Rainforest wildlife

Asia's rainforests are warm all year round, but they do have short dry seasons. They are festooned with lianas and epiphytes. The rainforest provides homes for animals at all levels, from fruit bats in the canopy to tigers on the forest floor.

Long aerial roots

Banyan tree
Some fig trees, such as the banyan tree, start life as a tiny seedling that grows in the crown of another rainforest tree. The banyan tree sends aerial roots down to the ground, that enmesh and kill the host tree.

Striped coat provides camouflage in forest.

Tiger
The tiger spends much of its day roaming through its rainforest territory, stalking prey. Tigers love water, and to avoid the heat of the day, they cool down by basking in shallow pools.

Saltwater crocodile
Large reptiles, such as saltwater crocodiles, lie out on the shores of rainforest rivers in the morning sun to warm up their bodies. Later on, when the Sun gets too hot, the crocodiles return to the water to cool down.

Bill is used to kill snakes and scorpions.

Rhinoceros hornbill
With its loud call and noisy wingbeats, the rhinoceros hornbill is a very noticeable rainforest inhabitant. It uses its huge bill with great dexterity to pick fruit and kill prey.

Grassland wildlife

The papery orange lanterns enclose berries.

Asia has both tropical savannahs and vast plains of temperate steppes, with hot, dry summers. However, grasses and drought-resistant shrubs do grow there. Large animals have adapted to conserve moisture; smaller ones shelter in burrows.

Chinese lantern
The Chinese lantern is a drought-resistant plant. Its roots spread deep into the soil to reach any available water. New shoots appear each spring, that bear flowers and edible fruits.

Heavy snout

Saiga antelope
Herds of saiga antelopes migrate south in winter to escape severe weather. They return north in summer, when the grasses are more plentiful. Saigas have a mucous-lined sac in the snout that warms inhaled air in winter and filters out dust in the hot, dry summer.

Tawny eagle
The tawny eagle nests in shrubs and trees by watercourses. It flies long distances over steppes and semi-arid deserts in search of food. The tawny eagle is a skilful hunter, but it increases its chances of getting enough food by feeding on carrion and stealing other predators' prey.

Hooked beak for tearing flesh of prey

Eagle has pushed off ground to launch itself into the air.

Mountain wildlife

The steep crags and valleys of the Himalayas provide many refuges for wildlife. Forests on the lower slopes give way to high altitude meadows and snowfields. Animals of the higher slopes, such as the yak, are adapted to survive the winters; others migrate to warmer, lower slopes.

Himalayan griffon

The Himalayan griffon is a large, aggressive vulture that soars over some of the highest mountain slopes in search of food. The diet of vultures is almost entirely restricted to carrion. The Himalayan griffon's powerful hooked bill is strong enough to rip open the leathery hide of a dead yak to feast on the entrails.

Hooked beak helps pull apart prey.

Rhododendron

When in flower, rhododendrons set the mountainside ablaze with a riot of colour. Their tiny seeds are readily spread by wind or water.

Yak

Domesticated for centuries, the yak is still found living wild in some parts of its mountain range. With its long, shaggy coat, a yak can survive temperatures as low as -40°C (-40°F). It grazes on whatever plants are available, including mosses and lichens, and can use snow as a source of water.

Sharp spines on head and neck provide protection.

Armoured pricklenape agama

This lizard lives in the treetops in mountain forests. Its greeny-brown scales conceal it among twigs and leaves. Pricklenape agamas have sharp claws that give them a sure grip, as they run and leap through the branches.

Long toes and claws grip when climbing.

Northern bat

In summer, this hardy bat forages for insects in the forest and even up into the Arctic Circle. To survive the winter it hibernates in caves or buildings. Its distribution is dictated by the availability of suitable roost sites.

Boreal forest wildlife

Just south of the Arctic tundra is a vast forest of conifer trees. In Asia, this boreal forest is called the taiga. Wildflowers, and animals such as the sable, are adapted to exploit the brief summers and withstand the long, harsh winters.

Norway spruce

Narrow-crowned spruces are a characteristic feature of the taiga. Snow slides easily from their curved branches without breaking them. Norway spruce grows at the western reaches of the taiga, soon giving way to Siberian spruce. The seeds of both trees provide food for birds and rodents.

Fur for warmth

Sable

The sable hunts all year round for nestlings and rodents. It also eats shoots and berries if prey is scarce. The sable sleeps, shelters, and gives birth in hollow logs or tree holes.

Thick fur covers the whole body and even the soles of the feet.

Great grey owl

To find enough food, including voles, lemmings, and other small rodents, the great grey owl hunts by day as well as night. It may travel far to a good source of food, but returns to the dense boreal forest to breed. It chooses a secure nest site in a tree, or may use another large bird's old nest.

Desert wildlife

Not all deserts are hot all year round. Temperate deserts, such as the Gobi in Central Asia, have scorching hot summers, but icy cold winters. Nights are cold even in summer, as there is no vegetation to trap the heat. To survive here, animals must be adapted both to the dry environment and extremes of temperature.

Onager

Onagers live in small herds in the desert. There is little vegetation here for grazing animals, but the onager can cope with eating tough desert grasses and straw. Wolves, although uncommon, are their main predators. To defend themselves, onagers can run fast for long distances.

Mongolian gerbil

Like many small desert animals, these gerbils escape from temperature extremes by digging underground burrows. Living below ground also helps to conserve bodily moisture. Gerbils nibble roots, shoots, seeds, and buds, and drink water if it is available. In a drought, they can get sufficient moisture from the early morning dew on their food.

Bactrian camel

Few of these desert creatures remain in the wild. A Bactrian camel has a very thick woolly coat to protect it from severe cold in winter. Fat stored in two humps on its back enables it to survive with little food or water for long periods of time.

Almost all-round vision helps them to spot danger.

Pale fur for camouflage in desert

Cheek pouches stretch so gerbil can carry food in its mouth.

FIND OUT MORE   ASIA   BATS   BIRDS OF PREY   BUFFALO AND OTHER WILD CATTLE   CAMELS   DEER AND ANTELOPES   LIONS AND OTHER WILD CATS   RATS AND OTHER RODENTS   TREES

ASSYRIAN EMPIRE

A

THE GRAND CITY OF ASHUR, beside the Tigris river in northern Mesopotamia (present-day Iraq), developed as an important trading centre; by 2000 BC, it had become the capital of a great Assyrian kingdom. From 1400 BC, Assyrian armies were marching north and west to secure trade and obtain booty and tribute. Feared for their military strength, they soon came to dominate the Near East. Assyrian kings built several capital cities after Ashur, of which Nimrud and Nineveh were the most magnificent. Assyrian civilization and culture, however, were heavily influenced by Babylonia to the south, and it was the Babylonians who eventually absorbed the Assyrians into their empire.

Extent of the empire
The greatest extent of the empire was reached in the 7th century, when the well-equipped soldiers of King Ashurbanipal conquered and held lands from Egypt to Iran. Assyrian governors controlled the provinces. They were expected to send taxes back to the Assyrian capital and recruit soldiers for the army.

Bronze armour

Army

The Assyrian army was the most efficient fighting machine of its time, and its reputation alone was often enough to frighten rebellious states into surrender. At first, the army consisted of native Assyrians, but Tiglath-Pileser III (745–727 BC) recruited men from other areas of the empire. They were armed with iron helmets, armour, spears, swords, and shields. The Assyrians also used chariots and siege engines (battering rams on wheels), the most advanced weapons of the time.

Assyrian official | King Ashurnasirpal II (r.883–859 BC) | Siege engine
Stone relief of Assyrians attacking a town on the Euphrates river

Nimrud and Nineveh
By 900 BC, the city of Ashur was overcrowded. Nimrud was built in the 9th century BC; Nineveh was constructed in the 7th century BC. These cities were famous for their splendid palaces and temples.

Exotic animals from all over the empire, such as elephants and lions, filled the wildlife parks and gardens that surrounded the city of Nineveh.

Politics

At his coronation, the Assyrian king swore to expand the empire. The Assyrians believed their god Ashur (after whom the first city was named) chose each king, so he had absolute power. He appointed all the governors of the various parts of his empire, led the army, and was responsible for all the temples. The king demonstrated his power and wealth by many ambitious building projects. A network of spies reported to the king on all matters within the empire.

Gold earrings

Precious stones

Queens of Assyria
Some Assyrian queens were so powerful they became legendary. One such, Sammurammat (Semiramis), dominated court for 42 years in the 9th century BC. Some royal jewellery has been found in tombs at Nimrud.

Art and literature

Brightly painted, stone-relief carvings, the most spectacular of all Assyrian art forms, decorated palace walls from 900 BC. Artists decorated royal furniture with carvings of real or mythical animals, such as sphinxes.

Ivory winged sphinx

Timeline

2400 BC The city of Ashur dominates trade routes.

1900 BC, Assyrians establish trading colonies in Anatolia (modern Turkey).

1250 BC Kings of Assyria campaign as far as the Mediterranean and Babylon.

879 BC Ashurnasirpal II builds a new capital at Kalhu (Nimrud).

744–727 BC King Tiglath-Pileser III creates an empire.

721–705 BC Sargon II builds capital at Khorsabad (Dur-Sharrokin).

Gold earring

701 BC Sennacherib leads his army to Jerusalem from his new capital at Nineveh.

689 BC Sennacherib destroys Babylon.

664 BC Ashurbanipal attacks and conquers Egypt.

612 BC Median and Babylonian armies destroy Nineveh.

609 BC Crown prince Nebuchadnezzar of Babylon finally defeats the Assyrians.

606 BC The Medes from Iran sack Nineveh.

Sennacherib

Sennacherib (r.704–681 BC), a strong king, spent many years building Nineveh. He established control over the coast of the Mediterranean, and destroyed Babylon, but he was murdered by his jealous sons.

FIND OUT MORE | ARMS AND ARMOUR | ASIA, HISTORY OF | BABYLONIAN EMPIRE | HITTITES | PHOENICIANS | SUMERIANS | WARFARE

ASTROLOGY

FOR CENTURIES, people have believed that the position of the stars and planets has an influence on human life. The study of this influence is known as astrology. It began about 4,000 years ago in Mesopotamia (modern Iraq) and eventually spread throughout the ancient world. In most cultures astrology was regarded as a science, and many rulers even used astrology when making important political decisions. Today, although there is no scientific proof for its accuracy, many people still believe in astrology.

Astrology and astronomy

The scientific study of stars and planets is known as astronomy. For thousands of years, astronomy and astrology were closely linked. From the 17th century onwards, however, leaps in scientific knowledge resulted in astronomy becoming increasingly important, while belief in astrology began to wane.

An early telescope

Astrological map showing the view of the universe in 1660.

Twelve signs of the zodiac

Aries
Taurus
Gemini
Cancer
Leo
Virgo
Libra
Scorpio
Sagittarius
Capricorn
Aquarius
Pisces

Celestial spheres

Ancient astrologers believed that the Universe was a gigantic sphere, with the Earth at the centre and the stars circling around it. They divided this sphere into 12 sections, each of which was named after a constellation of fixed stars – the signs of the zodiac.

Signs of the zodiac

Each sign of the zodiac takes its name from ancient mythology. Early astrologers chose names to suit the shapes formed by the constellations – the stars that make up Leo, for example, were thought to resemble a lion.

Casting a horoscope

To draw up your horoscope, or birth chart, astrologers need to know the exact date, time, and place of your birth. They then use careful calculations to plot the position of the Sun, Moon, and planets. Astrologers claim that they can interpret the finished horoscope to reveal your character.

This line represents the horizon at the time of birth.

The chart is divided into 12 houses, one for each zodiac sign.

Complicated calculations are now done with calculators.

Chinese horoscopes

Unlike Western astrology which is based on the movement of the Sun and planets, Chinese horoscopes are based on the cycle of the Moon. Each Chinese year is named after a different animal – the Rat, Ox, Tiger, Rabbit, Dragon, Snake, Horse, Ram, Monkey, Rooster, Dog, and Pig.

The five elements

☐ Water   ☐ Wood
☐ Earth   ☐ Fire   ☐ Gold

Astrological wheel

Chinese astrology features 12 animals, and each represents a different personality type. For example, people born in the year of the Snake are said to be sociable, confident, and energetic.

The black and white bands represent the Universe's balancing forces of yin and yang.

Each animal sign is linked to one of the five elements.

Associations

Each astrological animal is associated with a certain food, colour, and symbol. The Rat's symbol is the set of balances, its colour is black, and it is linked with salty-tasting foods.

Fortune telling

People's desire to see into the future has given rise to many different forms of prediction, which vary from culture to culture. They include crystal ball gazing, dream interpretation, palmistry, divination sticks, tarot reading, runes, numerology, and the *I Ching*, an ancient Chinese oracle.

Consulting a fortune teller in Hong Kong

The role of chance

Many fortune-telling systems use dice, coins, or cards to introduce an element of randomness.

Throwing dice is an ancient way of making predictions.

I Ching coins

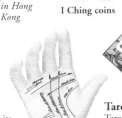

TEMPERANCE.
KING of WANDS

Palmistry

Each person's palm is unique, with its own distinctive pattern of lines. Palm readers believe these markings reveal the owner's character, past and future. As well as both palms, the palmist examines the fingers and nails.

Palmistry hand

Tarot cards

Tarot cards are found worldwide. They can be dealt in many different ways, and are thought to answer specific questions, or be a guide to the future.

FIND OUT MORE   ASTRONOMY   CHINA, HISTORY OF   SCIENCE, HISTORY OF   STARS   SUN AND SOLAR SYSTEM

ASTRONAUTS

MORE THAN 350 PEOPLE have travelled into space; 26 on missions to the Moon and the rest in orbit around Earth. For journeying into space, astronauts must be physically and mentally fit. They must also be trained to prepare them for living and working in the hostile environment of space.

Spacesuit

When astronauts work outside the spacecraft, they need to wear a suit that keeps their body at the correct temperature and protects them from fast-moving micrometeoroids. The suit must also provide oxygen for breathing and be pressurized because there is no air or atmospheric pressure in space.

Yuri Gagarin

The first person to fly into space was a Russian, Yuri Gagarin (1934–68). His flight on 12 April 1961 took him once around the Earth and lasted 108 minutes. No one knew how the space flight would affect a human, so Gagarin's spacecraft, *Vostok 1*, was controlled from the ground.

Pressure helmet

Visor

Cap

Communications headset

Communications input socket

Oxygen inlets and outlets

Liquid-cooled undergarment

Water inlet and outlet

Pressure glove

Extravehicular glove

Wrist clamp

Urine transfer connection

Snap-on fastening

Integrated thermal micrometeoroid garment

Lunar overshoe

Apollo 9 spacesuit

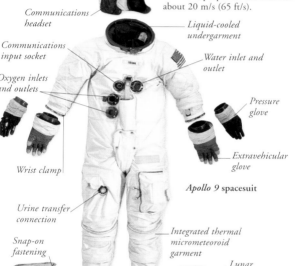

MMU

To fly free from the spacecraft, an astronaut wears a powered backpack, the Manned Manoeuvring Unit (MMU). Mini nitrogen thrusters, operated from arm rests, propel the astronaut at about 20 m/s (65 ft/s).

Living in space

Daily life for an astronaut includes all the usual things, such as breathing, eating, sleeping, and going to the bathroom. The big difference, however, is living in weightless conditions. Sleeping astronauts float around the spacecraft unless tethered down, and using the toilet has to be carefully controlled.

Astronauts need daily exercise to keep fit in the weightless conditions of space.

Meal tray strapped to leg.

Vacuum-wrapped food pack

Rubber grips stop items floating away.

Space food

Meals on the space shuttle are prepared from 70 different foods and 20 drinks. The meal tray is strapped down and the food eaten with the hand or cutlery. Liquids are sucked from cartons or tubes.

Space toilet

Astronauts outside the spacecraft "go to the toilet" in their spacesuit, where the waste materials are collected. Inside the craft, they use a space toilet, making sure they are firmly strapped to the seat. The waste is sucked away by the toilet and collected in a secure unit.

Rubber suction cups

Suction shoes

Staying in one place in a spacecraft can be a problem. Suction-cup shoes allow astronauts to get a better grip.

Working in space

Each member of a space crew has specific tasks. These may include flying the craft, releasing a satellite into orbit, or testing new equipment. The weightless conditions of space mean that astronauts can also perform experiments not possible on Earth.

Repair work

Once a satellite is in space it is left to work on its own. But occasionally one needs repairing. The cargo bay of the space shuttle is equipped with a robotic arm, which specially trained astronauts use to recover the satellite. They can then repair the satellite and release it back into orbit.

Experiments

Astronauts have carried out many experiments in space. These include observing how living things such as bees are affected by weightlessness.

An astronaut, anchored to a foot restraint, works on the *Syncom IV-3* satellite.

Endurance record

Most astronauts spend only a few days in space, but some stay for months. Russian cosmonaut Sergei Avdeyev holds the overall endurance record (748 days). Russian Valeri Poliakov holds the record for longest single stay (438 days).

Valeri Poliakov

Space animals

Humans are not the only space travellers; early ones included dogs, rats, and mice. Animals are no longer sent into space alone, but flies, frogs, and tadpoles occasionally accompany human astronauts.

Chimpanzee Ham returned safely from his 1961 flight.

FIND OUT MORE   EXPLORATION   GRAVITY   HEALTH AND FITNESS   MOON   ROCKETS   SPACE EXPLORATION

ASTRONOMY

ASTRONOMY IS THE STUDY OF SPACE and everything it contains. It is a subject that has been studied since ancient times when humans used their eyes to gaze out at the stars and planets. Today's astronomers use sophisticated equipment to collect information about space and how the Universe as a whole works.

Kitt Peak Observatory

The largest optical telescope at Kitt Peak is the 4-m (13-ft) Mayall.

Observatories

An astronomer's telescopic equipment is housed and used in an observatory. The atmosphere distorts light and other radiations from space, so many observatories are located at high altitudes.

Optical observatory
The world's biggest optical observatories are on mountaintops, away from city lights and where the atmosphere is clear and dry. The Kitt Peak National Observatory, which has 22 major telescopes, is on a 2,100-m (6,900-ft) mountain in Arizona, USA. Observatories sited in such inaccessible places need support services for the astronomers and their equipment, including accommodation, workshops, and transport.

Radio observatory
Radio waves are largely unaffected by the atmosphere, so radio telescopes can be sited virtually anywhere. The 305-m (1,000-ft) Arecibo radio dish (above) is in a natural hollow on the island of Puerto Rico. It is the world's largest single radio dish.

Astronomers' tools

Astronomers collect data from space by analysing a range of electromagnetic radiations; light and radio waves as well as other wavelengths such as X-ray, infrared, and ultraviolet. Astronomers use specialized telescopes with various attachments for collecting and studying the data.

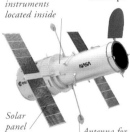

Telescope
The finest and most powerful telescopes use one or more mirrors to collect light from a distant object and form an image. Electronic devices or photographic plates rather than the eye collect the data. Other attachments, such as spectroscopes and photometers, help analyse light emitted by stars.

Space observatory
Telescopes in space collect data 24 hours a day and transmit it back to Earth. The Hubble Space Telescope, launched in 1990, orbits Earth, collecting data from optical and ultraviolet wavelengths.

Cameras and instruments located inside

Hubble Space Telescope

Antenna for sending data

Solar panel

Antenna for sending data

Lander under cover

Solar panel

Viking probe

Space probe
Objects in the Solar System have been studied at close hand by space probes. Instruments perform a host of investigations, including making detailed images of planets and their moons, and analysing what they are made of. Two identical Viking probes investigated Mars in 1976.

Astronomer at work

Most astronomers specialize in one area of research, such as planetary geology, interplanetary dust, stellar development, galaxy formation, or quasars. Whatever the subject, an astronomer can be found in one of two main locations: in universities and observatories.

Observation
Only a fraction of an astronomer's time is spent observing. Instead, most of the data comes from observations made and recorded by other astronomers on big telescopes, or from automatic equipment on space probes. The observations are used to help build theories or to confirm an established theory, such as how stars form.

Data collection
The CCD, an electronic chip that records data from space, can collect enough data in a few hours to keep an astronomer busy for years.

Charge-coupled device (CCD)

Fred Hoyle
The British astronomer Fred Hoyle (1915–2001) helped to solve some of the most baffling questions facing 20th-century astronomers. A major breakthrough was explaining nucleosynthesis – how chemical elements are produced from the hydrogen inside stars. He also wrote science fiction novels.

Analysis
Data can be collected directly on to a computer and then transferred to other computers for analysis. Computers can process images and handle large amounts of information much more quickly than an astronomer.

Timeline
1609 First use of the telescope for the systematic study of space.

1781 Discovery of Uranus doubled the diameter of the known Solar System.

1863 Analysis of starlight shows stars are made of the same elements as those on Earth.

Uranus

Quasar

1923 Astronomers observe galaxies other than the Milky Way.

1963 Quasar is discovered.

1987 Supernova 1987A explodes.

Supernova

1999 Hubble telescope sights 18 other galaxies up to 65 million years away.

FIND OUT MORE   ATMOSPHERE   GALAXIES   SPACE EXPLORATION   STARS   TELESCOPES   UNIVERSE

ATHLETICS

A

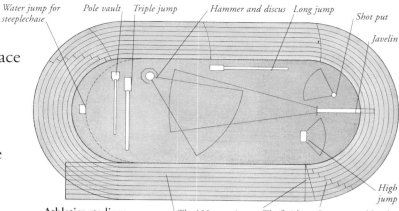

THIS POPULAR SPORT takes place mainly in a stadium where it is divided into two main categories: track and field. Track includes running and hurdling races; field includes jumping and throwing. Some athletics events involve more than one discipline – 10 in the decathlon for men; seven in the heptathlon for women. Other events are road and cross-country running. Major competitions are the Olympics and world and continental championships.

Water jump for steeplechase — *Pole vault* — *Triple jump* — *Hammer and discus* — *Long jump* — *Shot put* — *Javelin* — *High jump*

Athletics stadium
In an athletics stadium, there is a 400-m (437-yd) running track, usually marked with eight lanes. The field events take place in special areas on the grass area inside the track.

The 100-m sprint, 100-m hurdles, and 110-m hurdles are the only races run in a straight line.

The finish line is in the same place for all races.

Races around bends have a staggered start which means athletes do not start in a straight line.

Track events

Racing takes place on the flat and over hurdles. Competitors in events up to 400 m have to stay in their lane for the whole race. The 800 m is run in lanes until the end of the first bend. A photo-finish camera is used to determine final places, and runners are timed to 0.01 seconds.

Athlete stays in the air as short a time as possible.

Weights in the base of the stand keep the hurdle upright.

Carl Lewis

In 1984, American Carl Lewis (b. 1961) won Olympic golds in the 100 m, 200 m, 4-by-100-m relay, and the long jump. He won five more gold medals in later Olympics and retained his long-jump title three times (1988–96), becoming only the second athlete in history to win four golds in one event.

Hurdling
Athletes have to negotiate 10 hurdles in all the races – 100 m for women, 110 m for men, and 400 m for men and women. In the 3,000-m steeplechase, runners take four hurdles and the water jump on each full lap. They all use the same, fixed hurdles.

Running
Races on the track range from 100 m to the 25-lap 10,000 m. Runners use starting blocks for races from 100 m to 400 m. There are two standard relay races: 4 by 100 m and 4 by 400 m, with team members passing a baton.

Jumping events

There are four jumping events. In the high jump and pole vault, the bar is gradually raised. Competitors are eliminated if they have three consecutive failures. In the long jump and triple jump, competitors have a set number of attempts, the best one counting. The triple jump is a hop, step, and jump.

Pole vault
Poles, usually made of fibreglass, may be of any size. The vaulter plants the pole in a sunken box at the end of the run-up before taking off. The pole bends and then straightens as the vaulter tries to clear the bar feet first, releasing the pole.

Long jump
Competitors must take off before the end of a wooden take-off board sunk into the run-up. The jump is measured from the end of the board to the nearest part of the sand disturbed by the competitor with any part of the body, hands, or legs.

Throwing events

In the shot put, discus, and hammer, competitors throw from special circles. In the javelin, they throw from behind a curved line at the end of a run-up.

The marathon
This road race is 42.195 km (26.2 miles) long. Some major races start and finish in the stadium. It derives from the Battle of Marathon in 490 BC, when a messenger ran to Athens with news of the Athenian victory over the Persians.

Javelin distances are measured to where the tip first hits the ground. It does not have to stick.

Javelin

Shot is a metal sphere weighing 7.26 kg (16 lb) for men and 4 kg (8.8 lb) for women. It is "put" with one pushing action.

Shot

Hammer is a metal sphere fixed to a handle by steel wire. Most people turn three or four times before releasing the hammer.

Discus has a metal rim with a weight at the centre. Like the hammer, the discus is thrown from a cage for safety reasons.

Discus

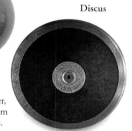

High jump
Most high jumpers use the Fosbury flop technique, which involves turning at take-off to pass head first and face up over the bar. Competitors are not allowed to take off from both feet together.

FIND OUT MORE

GREECE, ANCIENT   HEALTH AND FITNESS   HUMAN BODY   OLYMPIC GAMES   OWENS, JESSE   SPORT

ATLANTIC OCEAN

THE ATLANTIC IS THE WORLD'S second biggest ocean, covering about one-fifth of the Earth's surface. It separates the Americas in the west from Europe and Africa in the east. The Arctic Ocean lies to the north, and Antarctica to the south. There are several seas around the edges of the Atlantic, including the Baltic and the Mediterranean seas in the east, and the Caribbean Sea in the west. The Atlantic contains some of the world's richest fishing grounds, but is also the most polluted ocean because of the industry around its shores.

ATLANTIC OCEAN FACTS

AREA 82,442,000 sq km (31,831,000 sq miles)

AVERAGE DEPTH 3,660 m (12,000 ft)

GREATEST DEPTH 8,648 m (28,372 ft) Puerto Rico Trench

LENGTH 16,000 km (9,900 miles)

GREATEST WIDTH 8,000 km (4,900 miles)

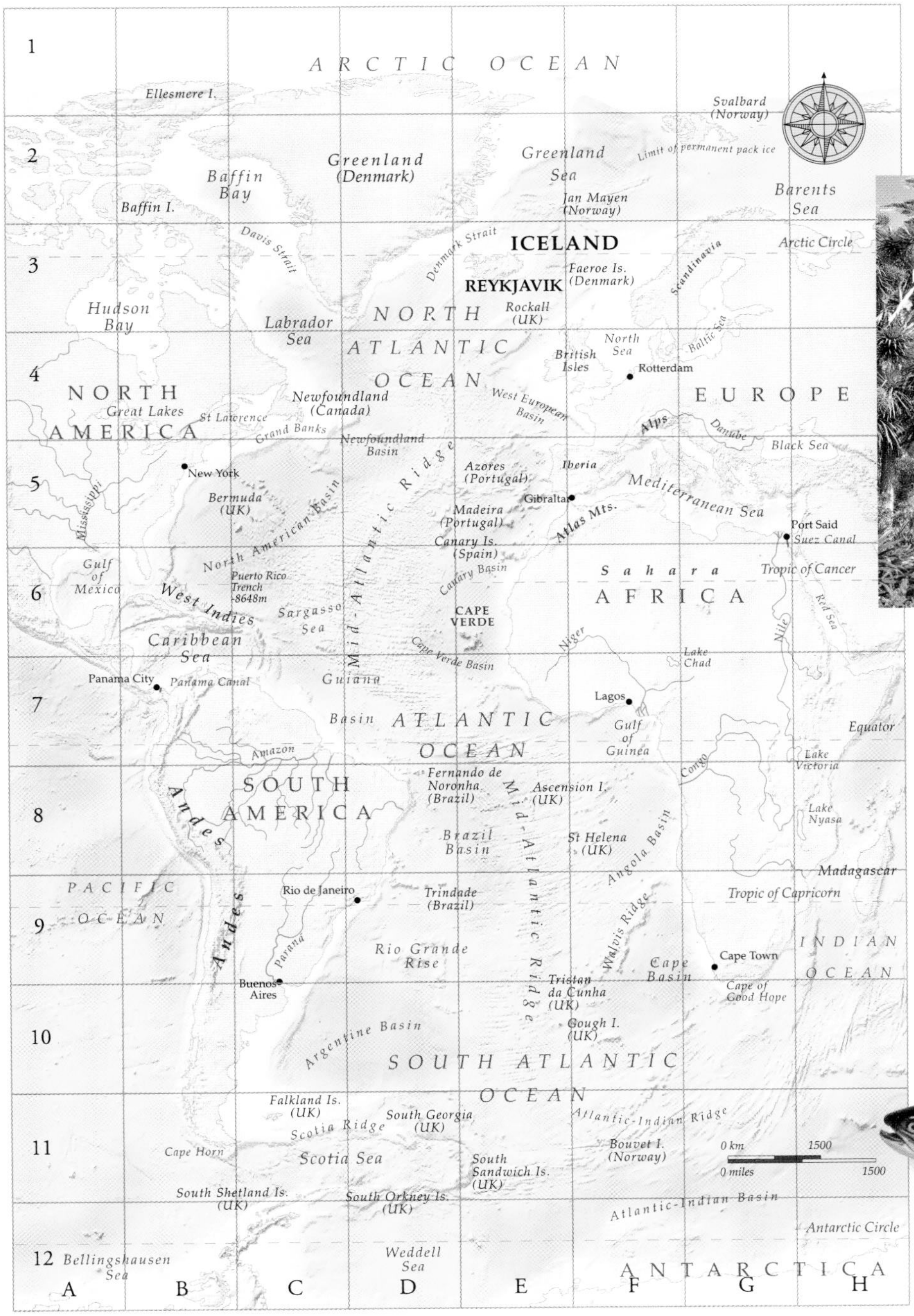

Physical features

The waters of the Atlantic are never still but move in huge belts of water or currents, such as the Gulf Stream, which affect the world's climate. The currents can be as warm as 30°C (86°F) or as cold as -2°C (30°F). Many of the islands in the Atlantic are volcanic and lie on the Mid-Atlantic Ridge. The largest islands are Greenland and Iceland, bordered by the Greenland Sea in the north Atlantic.

Gulf Stream
Although the Scilly Isles lie just off the coast of Britain, in the northern Atlantic, winters there are mild due to the influence of the Gulf Stream. This warm current, which flows at about 9 kmh (5.6 mph), starts in the Caribbean Sea, circles the Gulf of Mexico, and then heads north and east. Winds that blow over it pick up heat and raise the temperature of northern Europe, keeping ports free of ice in the winter.

Mid-Atlantic Ridge
An underwater mountain chain called the Mid-Atlantic Ridge runs down the middle of the Atlantic, where the ocean floor is splitting. Lava oozes up from the seabed and hardens, forming the mountain range. Many of the peaks surface as mid-ocean islands, such as Ascension Island. The ocean is growing wider at a rate of about 4 cm (1.5 in) a year.

Salmon

Fishing
Although Atlantic fish stocks have run low over the past 20 years because of overfishing, salmon fishing is a thriving industry, and salmon hatcheries are increasingly common.

89

Iceland

The island country of Iceland lies far north in the Atlantic, midway between Europe and North America, and is increasingly important for international communications. Its position on the Mid-Atlantic Ridge means it has many volcanoes and is prone to earthquakes. Iceland has been a republic since 1944.

Climate

Owing to the Gulf Stream, Iceland's southern lowlands are mild and breezy, and snow is rare. The north is colder, but less windy.

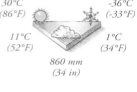

30°C (86°F)   -36°C (-33°F)
11°C (52°F)   1°C (34°F)
860 mm (34 in)

Built-up 1%
Barren 75%
Farmland 24%

Land use

The Icelandic people live in the more fertile coastal areas where 11 per cent are employed in farming, mainly raising sheep. Only about one per cent of the land is used for growing crops. No-one lives in the rocky centre.

Reykjavik

Heated by geothermal water from boreholes, Reykjavik is a clean, modern city, and home to about 100,000 people. It is a bustling hub of culture, industry, commerce, and government.

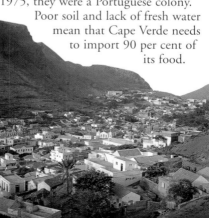
Brightly coloured houses in Reykjavik's old town

Physical features

Iceland is a land of fire and ice, where steaming hot volcanic springs bubble up through glaciers. The centre consists of uninhabitable plateaus and mountains. In the south are farmlands. There are many rivers, lakes, and spectacular waterfalls.

Volcanoes

The island of Little Surtsey is a volcano that rose from the sea close to Iceland in spring 1965, but disappeared again the following winter. Mainland Iceland has at least 20 active volcanoes that could erupt at any time.

Glaciers

Europe's largest ice-caps cover over one-tenth of Iceland. The biggest is Vatnajökull, which covers an area of 8,133 sq km (3,149 sq miles) in the southeast of the country.

Geothermal power

Every year, thousands of people visit the Blue Lagoon, to swim in this natural pool of healing, geothermal, mineral-rich sea water. Vast resources ensure that hydroelectric and geothermal power stations meet almost all of Iceland's electricity needs.

Fishing

Iceland relies on exporting fish to pay for all the necessities of modern living, which are imported from abroad. Fishing and fish processing are Iceland's leading industries and employ around 20 per cent of the labour force.

People

The first settlers in Iceland arrived from Norway in the 9th century. Today, Iceland boasts a classless society, and around 80 per cent of Icelanders own their own home. Most people live in towns where the standard of living is high, with extensive social security, health services, and free education.

3 per sq km (8 per sq mile)

91% Urban   9% Rural

ICELAND FACTS

CAPITAL CITY	Reykjavik
AREA	103,000 sq km (39,768 sq miles)
POPULATION	281,000
MAIN LANGUAGE	Icelandic
MAJOR RELIGION	Christian
CURRENCY	Icelandic króna
LIFE EXPECTANCY	79 years
PEOPLE PER DOCTOR	307
GOVERNMENT	Multi-party republic
ADULT LITERACY	99%

Cape Verde

The volcanic Cape Verde islands are divided into the Windward and Leeward islands. They lie in the Atlantic, off Africa's west coast. Until 1975, they were a Portuguese colony. Poor soil and lack of fresh water mean that Cape Verde needs to import 90 per cent of its food.

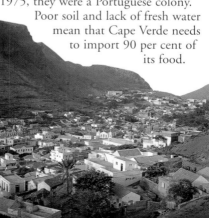

CAPE VERDE FACTS

CAPITAL CITY	Praia
AREA	4,033 sq km (1,557 sq miles)
POPULATION	437,000
MAIN LANGUAGES	Portuguese, Creole
MAJOR RELIGION	Christian
CURRENCY	Cape Verde escudo

São Nicolau

The island of São Nicolau in the Windward Islands has many Portuguese colonial-style buildings. Most of the people here are Portuguese-African Creole. Where they can, they grow bananas and sugar-cane.

Atlantic Islands

The Atlantic Ocean contains hundreds of islands. Some, such as the British Isles, are part of a continent. Others, like the Azores and the Canaries, are volcanic. Ascension, Bermuda, St Helena, and other small islands are the summits of undersea mountains and volcanic in origin.

Falkland Islands

The Falklands, with an area of 11,960 sq km (4,617 sq miles), are a British dependent territory off the coast of Argentina – which calls them Las Malvinas, and claims ownership. Until oil was found in their waters, most people were sheep farmers.

Canary Islands

The Canary Islands off northwest Africa are governed as two provinces of Spain. Popular with tourists, the seven islands and six islets have a total area of 7,270 sq km (2,807 sq miles), and a population of 1,630,000.

FIND OUT MORE   ARGENTINA, CHILE, AND URUGUAY   CLIMATE   CONTINENTS   ENERGY   FISHING INDUSTRY   GLACIATION   ISLANDS   OCEANS AND SEAS   TUNDRA   VOLCANOES

ATMOSPHERE

LIFE ON EARTH could not exist without Earth's atmosphere. The atmosphere is a colourless, tasteless, odourless blanket of gases that surrounds the Earth. It gives us air to breathe and water to drink. As well as keeping us warm by retaining the Sun's heat, it also shields us from the Sun's harmful rays. The atmosphere is approximately 700 km (440 miles) deep, but it has no distinct boundary. As it extends into space, it becomes thinner, eventually fading out. Human activity is upsetting the atmosphere's natural balance, with damaging results.

Layers of the atmosphere

The atmosphere is divided into five different layers. The composition of gases varies within these layers, as does the temperature which drops in the troposphere, the lowest layer, and rises in the stratosphere above.

Satellite

Exosphere is the outer layer of the atmosphere. Here lighter gases drift into space.

In the thermosphere, gases are very thin but they absorb ultraviolet light from the Sun, raising temperatures to 2,000°C (3,632°F). The ionosphere (layer within the thermosphere) is made of gases electrically charged or ionized by the Sun's light. Radio signals can be bounced off these ionized gases.

Aurora – lights in the night sky, possibly caused by charged particles from the Sun striking atoms.

Space shuttle

Meteorites

Stratopause is the boundary between stratosphere and mesosphere.

In the mesosphere, gases are so thin that temperatures drop rapidly with height to less than -110°C (-166°F), but the air is still thick enough to slow down meteorites.

Sonar balloon

Stratosphere contains 19 per cent of the atmosphere's gases, but little water vapour. It is very calm so airliners fly up here.

Tropopause borders troposphere and stratosphere.

Ozone layer shields the Earth from dangerous radiation.

Sea level

Troposphere extends about 12 km (7.5 miles) above the ground and is the only layer in which living things can survive naturally. It contains 75 per cent of the atmosphere's gases, water vapour, and clouds. Changes here create the weather.

Composition of the atmosphere

Earth's atmosphere is made mainly of two gases – nitrogen and oxygen. It also contains small amounts of argon and carbon dioxide, with tiny traces of other gases. The oxygen is made primarily by green plants, which maintain the balance of gases.

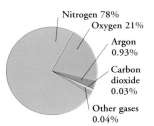

Nitrogen 78%
Oxygen 21%
Argon 0.93%
Carbon dioxide 0.03%
Other gases 0.04%

Pie chart showing the composition of the atmosphere.

Ozone layer

The thin layer of ozone gas within the stratosphere protects us by absorbing harmful ultraviolet rays from the Sun. But build-up of man-made gases called chlorofluorocarbons (CFCs) has depleted the ozone layer, and holes have started to appear in it every spring over the poles.

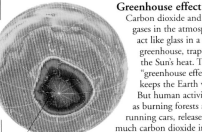

Ozone hole over Antarctica is shown as violet and pink

Greenhouse effect

Carbon dioxide and other gases in the atmosphere act like glass in a greenhouse, trapping the Sun's heat. This "greenhouse effect" keeps the Earth warm. But human activity, such as burning forests and running cars, releases too much carbon dioxide into the air and may cause global warming.

Some aerosol sprays use CFC gases.

Oxygen cycle

Gases continually circulate between the atmosphere and living things. Animals breathe in oxygen to help them release energy from food, and breathe out carbon dioxide. Green plants release oxygen back into the air and take in carbon dioxide as they absorb energy from the Sun. Oxygen is also used in the burning of fossil fuels.

Oxygen used in burning fossil fuels

Oxygen given off by marine plants

A large amount of oxygen is stored in the atmosphere.

Oxygen given off by plants and trees

Oxygen used up by marine animals

Oxygen used up by humans and animals

James Glaisher

English meteorologist James Glaisher (1809–1903) was one of the many balloonists who, during the 19th century, took great risks when they ascended to extraordinary heights to discover more about the atmosphere. Glaisher went up almost 12 km (7.5 miles) into the troposphere without oxygen or protective clothing. Such research led to the discovery that air becomes cooler with altitude.

FIND OUT MORE CLIMATE FORESTS GASES LUNGS AND BREATHING PLANETS POLLUTION SUN AND SOLAR SYSTEM WEATHER

ATOMS AND MOLECULES

A

TINY PARTICLES CALLED ATOMS are the basic building blocks that make up everything around us. Forces called bonds effectively "cement" the atoms together. A molecule is a cluster of atoms linked by bonds. There are just over a hundred different types of atom, which are themselves made up of even smaller "subatomic" particles, such as protons, neutrons, and electrons.

Electron shells and valency

Atoms can have up to seven shells of electrons. An atom with eight electrons in its outermost shell is very stable. Bonds form when atoms gain, lose, or share electrons in order to achieve this stable arrangement. An atom's valency is the number of bonds it can form with other atoms.

When sodium bonds, it loses an atom, leaving an outer shell of eight electrons.

Sodium
(3 shells, valency 1)

A carbon atom can form up to four bonds with other atoms.

Carbon
(2 shells, valency 4)

Ionic bonds

When an electron transfers from one atom to another, the atoms become charged particles called ions. The atom losing the electron becomes a positively charged ion, and the atom gaining the electron becomes a negatively charged ion. The force of attraction between the ions' opposite charges is called an ionic bond.

Sodium atom loses electron.

Electron transfers between atoms.

Chlorine atom gains electron.

Formation of ionic bonds in sodium chloride (NaCl)

Chemical formula
Scientists use a kind of code called a chemical formula to describe a substance. The formula uses letters and numbers to show which elements are present in the substance, and in what proportions. Methane, for example, has a chemical formula of CH_4, which shows that it contains carbon (C) and hydrogen (H), combined in the ratio of one carbon atom to every four hydrogen atoms.

Hydrogen atom

Methane molecule (CH_4)

Carbon atom

Linus Pauling
The American chemist Linus Pauling (1901–94) won the 1954 Nobel Prize for Chemistry for his work on chemical bonds and the structure of molecules. He calculated the energies needed to make bonds, the angles at which bonds form, and the distances between atoms. He also won the 1962 Nobel Peace Prize for his efforts to stop the testing of nuclear weapons.

Atomic structure
The centre, or nucleus, of an atom contains particles called protons, which carry a positive electric charge, and neutrons, which carry none. Arranged around the nucleus in layers called shells are negatively charged particles called electrons. The atom has no overall charge, because it contains equal numbers of electrons and protons, so the positive and negative charges are balanced.

Nucleus *Proton (red)* *Neutron (green)* *Electron shells*

Electrons move around the nucleus in paths called orbits.

Atom of carbon-12 cut in half

Nucleus of carbon-12 atom

Six protons *Six neutrons*

Isotopes
All the atoms of an element have the same number of protons in the nucleus, but some atoms, called isotopes, have different numbers of neutrons. For example, the carbon isotope carbon-12 has six protons and six neutrons, but the isotope carbon-14 has two extra neutrons.

Quarks
Both neutrons and protons consist of three smaller particles called quarks, stuck together by tiny particles called gluons. Quarks, in turn, may contain even smaller particles.

Quark *Gluons*

Inside a neutron

Covalent bonds
A covalent bond forms when two atoms link up by sharing electrons. Each atom supplies an electron, and the pair of electrons orbits the nuclei of both atoms, holding the atoms together as a molecule.

Covalent bonds in ammonia molecule (NH_3)

Hydrogen atom

Two shared electrons form covalent bond.

Nitrogen atom

Nitrogen bonds with three hydrogen atoms.

Double bonds
Sometimes atoms form covalent bonds by sharing two pairs of electrons. This is called a double bond. A triple covalent bond forms when atoms share three pairs of electrons.

Atoms share four electrons.

Oxygen molecule (O_2)

Double bond links two oxygen atoms.

Bonds between molecules
The molecules of covalent compounds are held together by weak bonds called Van der Waal's forces. Some hydrogen-containing compounds, such as water, have stronger forces called hydrogen bonds between their molecules. In water, these bonds form because each oxygen atom in a water molecule is attracted to hydrogen atoms in two nearby molecules.

Covalent bond *Hydrogen bond* *Oxygen atom* *Hydrogen atom*

Hydrogen bonds between water molecules

FIND OUT MORE ELEMENTS MIXTURES AND COMPOUNDS NUCLEAR POWER RADIOACTIVITY

AUSTRALASIA AND OCEANIA

AUSTRALIA, New Zealand, Papua New Guinea, and the nearby islands are collectively called Australasia. The wider area known as Oceania also includes the island groups of Melanesia, Micronesia, and Polynesia and spans a huge area in the South Pacific Ocean. Australia is the largest country and a continent in its own right. Although many Pacific islands were once European colonies, the region now has closer trade links with Asia.

Coral islands
Many of the thousands of tiny islands in Oceania are the peaks of undersea volcanic mountains that are just breaking the surface of the Pacific Ocean. Reefs of coral, teeming with tropical fish, often build up close to the islands' sandy shores.

Physical features

Australasia and Oceania include a wide range of landscapes, from tropical rainforest in northern areas to the arid desert of central Australia. Many islands are volcanic, with sandy beaches, high mountains, and a constant threat of earthquakes.

Geysers
These occur in New Zealand where hot rock heats water in an underground chamber. As the water boils, a fountain of scalding water and steam shoots 500 m (1,640 ft) into the air.

Pinnacles Desert
Tall pinnacles of limestone rise from the sand in parts of Australia's hot, dry Western Desert. These unusually shaped rocks have been sculpted by the eroding action of plant roots and harsh winds over the last 25,000 years.

Cross-section through Australasia

Australia is a largely flat continent, with low mountains in the southwest and a desert centre. The highest mountains are the Great Dividing Range in the east. The Pacific Ocean between Australia and New Zealand dips to 5,000 m (16,405 ft). The Southern Alps run down New Zealand's South Island.

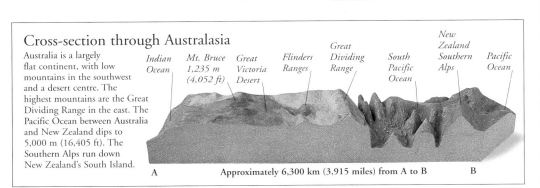

Indian Ocean — Mt. Bruce 1,235 m (4,052 ft) — Great Victoria Desert — Flinders Ranges — Great Dividing Range — South Pacific Ocean — New Zealand Southern Alps — Pacific Ocean

A — Approximately 6,300 km (3,915 miles) from A to B — B

AUSTRALASIA AND OCEANIA FACTS

AREA 8,508,238 sq km (3,285,048 sq miles)

POPULATION 29,700,000

NUMBER OF COUNTRIES 14

HIGHEST POINT Mt. Wilhelm (Papua New Guinea) 4,509 m (14,794 ft)

LONGEST RIVER Murray Darling (Australia) 3,750 km (2,330 miles)

BIGGEST LAKE Lake Eyre (Australia) 9,583 sq km (3,700 miles)

93

Climatic zones

With a wide range of landscapes and spanning such a vast area, Australasia and Oceania experience many different climates. Northern Australia and Papua New Guinea are always hot with wet and dry seasons, the east has hot summers and mild winters, and the centre is dry desert. New Zealand is mild and damp. The most westerly of the Pacific islands have a wet, tropical climate.

Wetland

Desert

Tropical rainforest

Deciduous woodland

Scrub *Grassland* *Mountain*

Small, stunted shrubs

Grassland

Australia contains vast areas of dry, open grassland, known as the "outback". The best grazing land for cattle and sheep is in Queensland and New South Wales. Scarce surface water is supplemented by underground water from artesian wells. Lush grassland covers the eastern side of New Zealand's South Island.

After rain, flowers burst into bloom.

Many species of insect and animal live in the canopy.

Tropical rainforest

Steamy tropical rainforest covers most of the Solomon Islands, the mountains of Papua New Guinea, and parts of northern Australia. Often shrouded in mist, these dense, lush forests are a haven for wildlife and contain more than 600 species of tree. As a measure to protect the environment, logging is controlled in Queensland.

Scrub

At the edges of the four major deserts that make up the interior of Australia are areas of arid brush where there is little, often unreliable, rainfall. These areas support coarse grass, scattered shrubs, and low trees.

Bushes are mostly stunted, evergreen, and spiny.

Eucalyptus woods

Many kinds of gum tree, also known as eucalyptus, grow in Australia. There is a species of gum tree for virtually every environment, from cold, damp mountain tops to hot, dry inland areas. Gum trees are evergreens, with leathery leaves.

Mountain gum leaves

Narrow leaves hang down to avoid drying out in the hot sun.

Sandstone is worn smooth and rounded by erosion.

Coastal climate

The coastal strip between Brisbane and Melbourne in southeast Australia is backed to the west by the peaks of the Great Dividing Range, including the Australian Alps. Warm breezes blow in from the Pacific Ocean, bringing rain to this green and fertile region. The long, sandy beaches and mild, pleasant climate make this the most populated region in Australia.

Powerful waves create long, sandy beaches. **Byron Bay, New South Wales**

Hot desert

The spectacular red Olgas rocks rise unexpectedly out of the arid flat expanse of Australia's scorching central desert. Situated near Uluru (Ayers Rock), this giant mass of boulders formed more than 570 million years ago and gradually eroded during the past 150 million years.

Deciduous woodland

The west coast of New Zealand's South Island is covered with deciduous woodland. Here, oak, beech, and hickory trees thrive in the mild, damp climate.

Beech forest in New Zealand's Fiordland National Park

People

The earliest inhabitants of Australasia were the Aboriginals of Australia, and the Polynesians and Melanesians from the Pacific islands. White Europeans began colonizing Australia and New Zealand in the late 1700s. Since the 1970s, Australia has allowed many other peoples to settle there, including Chinese, Cambodians, and Vietnamese.

Australian schoolchildren

Resources

Land is a major resource for Australia and New Zealand and is used extensively for grazing cattle and sheep, and for growing wheat. Australia is rich in minerals and leads the world in the production of bauxite (aluminium ore), diamonds, and lead ore. The main resources of the Pacific islands are fish and coconut products, such as copra, coir (rope), and matting.

Coconut

Sheep

Tuna

 FIND OUT MORE ABORIGINAL AUSTRALIANS · AUSTRALIAN WILDLIFE · CLIMATE · CORAL REEFS · DESERTS · EARTHQUAKES · FORESTS · ISLANDS · PACIFIC OCEAN · TREES · VOLCANOES

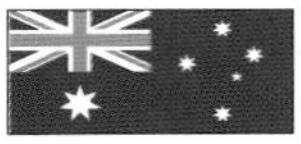

AUSTRALIA

A COUNTRY and at the same time a continent, Australia is an ancient land mass, and the smallest, flattest, and, after Antarctica, the driest continent. It is the world's sixth largest country yet only 18.9 million people live there, mostly along the coast as the centre of the country consists of desert or semi-desert – the outback. Australia consists of six states and two territories. It has strong trade links with Europe, the USA, and Asia and makes significant contributions to international affairs. The population consists of a wide range of ethnic groups, making Australia a truly multicultural society.

Physical features

The centre of Australia is covered by a vast, flat, arid plain called the outback – one of the hottest places on Earth. Around the coast are tropical rainforests, snow-capped mountains, and magnificent beaches.

A

Great Barrier Reef

Green Island forms part of the Great Barrier Reef, which stretches 2,000 km (1,243 miles) along the northeast coast of Australia. Its coral is formed by layer upon layer of tiny anemone-like creatures, making it the largest living thing on Earth. Thousands of tourists flock to see it each year, attracted by the clear, warm waters and more than 1,500 species of fish. Recent fears that divers and swimmers may be damaging the reef have led to it becoming a protected World Heritage Area.

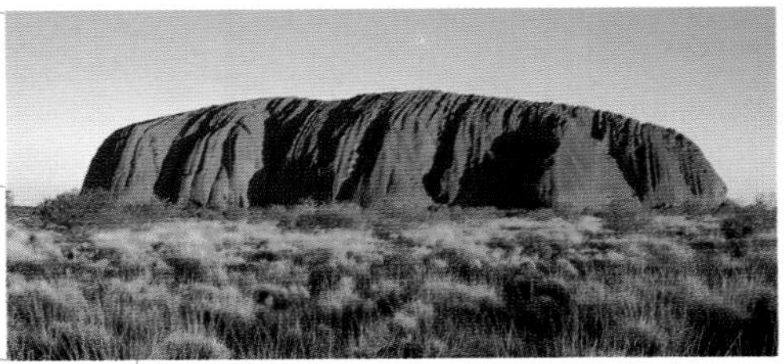

Uluru (Ayers Rock)

This giant block of red sandstone that rises from the desert is more than 2.4 km (1.5 miles) long. Once known as Ayers Rock, Uluru, meaning "great pebble", is the original name given to it by the Aboriginal people, who regard it as sacred.

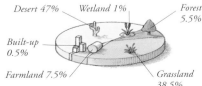

Great Dividing Range

The Great Dividing Range is a series of high plateaus and low mountains that extends down the east of Australia. It shields the arid interior of the country from the rain-bearing clouds that blow in from the Pacific Ocean. In winter, snow covers the higher peaks, and people can ski there.

Canberra

Founded in the early 20th century, Australia's capital, Canberra, is home to about 300,000 people. It is primarily a centre for government and has few industries. Official buildings include Parliament House, the Australian National University, the National Library, and the National Gallery.

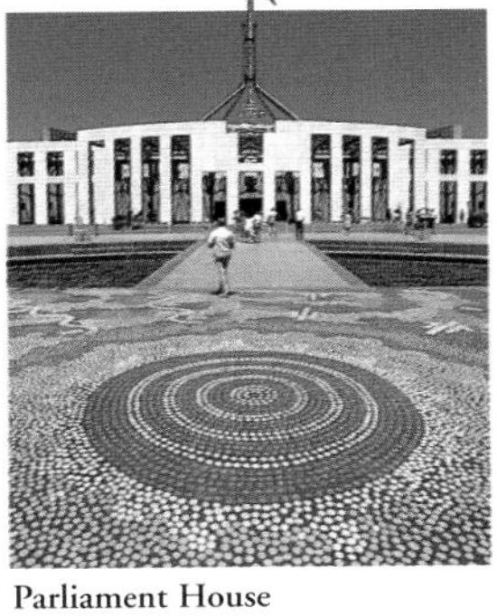

Parliament House

Climate

Most people live in the temperate zones that occur within 400 km (249 miles) of the coast in the east and southeast, and around Perth in the west. The interior, west, and south are arid. The north is hot, humid, and tropical.

52°C (126°F) -22°C (-8°F)

20°C (68°F) 6°C (42°F)

629 mm (25 in)

Desert 47% Wetland 1% Forest 5.5%

Built-up 0.5%

Farmland 7.5% Grassland 38.5%

Land use

Most of Australia's interior is inhospitable desert. Sheep and cattle are reared in the east and north of the country, and wheat is grown in the fertile southwest and southeast. Australia has rich mineral deposits, many of which are in the barren interior.

A

People

Aboriginal people, Australia's first inhabitants, make up only about four per cent of the population. The rest are of mainly European origin, descended either from British settlers, or from Europeans who emigrated to Australia after 1945. Recent years have also seen an influx of Asians.

Multicultural society
Australian society reflects the many different nationalities who have settled in the country. Aboriginal people, English, Irish, and Central and Eastern Europeans have all made their mark, and since immigration restrictions were lifted in 1972 the arrival of Chinese, Indo-Chinese, and Indonesians has added new influences. Diverse languages, customs, foods, and festivals combine to make Australia a varied and exciting society.

2 per sq km (5 per sq mile) | 85% Urban | 15% Rural

Leisure

Australians love the outdoors. Because most live near the coast, many people enjoy water sports such as swimming, skin-diving, surfing, and sailing. Cricket is a popular spectator sport, as are rugby and the unique Australian Football.

Surfing
The crashing waves of Australia's east coast attract thousands to try their luck at riding the surf. The aptly named Surfers' Paradise, in Queensland, is a favourite spot.

Australian Football
One of Australia's national winter sports is Australian Football. It was invented in the 1850s and is based on Gaelic Football. Besides Australia, the only other country where it is played is Papua New Guinea.

Farming

Less than five per cent of the labour force are farmers, yet over half the land is used for grazing cattle and sheep. Grapes and cereals are also grown.

Livestock
Beef cattle roam the Australian outback, grazing on dry grass and drinking water drawn from artesian wells. They are raised on vast cattle stations mainly for their meat. Australia has seven times more sheep than people. They produce around one-third of the world's wool.

Cereals
Although less than four per cent of the land is suitable for farming cereal crops, Australia grows barley, millet, oats, and rice, and ranks highly in world production of wheat. Other crops include sugar-cane, fruit, and vegetables.

Grapes
The gentle climate of parts of southern Australia is ideally suited to growing grapes for winemaking. The Australian wine industry has grown by leaps and bounds in recent years, now producing about 450,000 tonnes (495,000 tons) of wine a year. Much is exported.

Food

Traditionally, Australians are a nation of meat-eaters. They love plain foods, such as fried eggs and grilled steaks that are cooked on the barbecue. But the influx of people from mainland Europe and Asia has brought a wide range of cooking ideas from China, Greece, Indonesia, and Italy.

Barbecued lamb

Grilled pumpkin

Industry

Australia has a strong mining industry, and is a major exporter of coal, iron ore, bauxite, lead, gold, copper, and diamonds. About 16 per cent of the labour force works in manufacturing, and two-thirds are employed in services such as banks, tourism, and government.

Diamonds

Gold

Quartz

Gold and diamonds
Australia is one of the world's top gold producers and exports more diamonds than any other country. Most of the diamonds are not gem quality and are used to make industrial cutting tools.

Tourism
The spectacular scenery of the Hamersley Range in Western Australia is popular with tourists, mostly from Japan, New Zealand, and Southeast Asia. About five million visitors visit Australia every year, providing a welcome addition to the country's foreign earnings.

Transport

With such a huge territory, and the nearest countries so far away from major population centres, Australians rely heavily on air transport. Buses, cars, and trains are used for short distances in the cities. Trucks carry most intercity freight by road.

Road train
Heavy loads are often transported across the outback by road train. These huge trucks may pull five or six trailers over vast distances, on deserted roads.

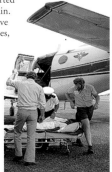

Flying Doctor
The Royal Flying Doctor Service was founded in 1928 to bring medical help to people living in lonely homesteads in the outback. Doctors are based at special stations where emergency callers can contact them by radio and receive treatment quickly.

FIND OUT MORE ABORIGINAL AUSTRALIANS | AUSTRALIA, HISTORY OF | CARS AND TRUCKS | CONTINENTS | CORAL REEFS | DESERTS | FARMING | ROCKS AND MINERALS | SPORTS

AUSTRALIA, HISTORY OF

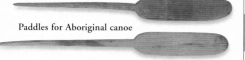

Paddles for Aboriginal canoe

FOR MOST OF THE LAST 40,000 years, Australia was inhabited only by Aboriginal peoples. The Aboriginals were Asian in origin and created a rich culture based on hunting and food gathering. Their peaceful existence was destroyed by the arrival of Europeans in the late 18th century. The first settlers were convicts sent from crowded British prisons, but later farmers and miners drawn by the wealth of the country joined them. In 1901, Australia became an independent nation, sending troops to fight in both world wars. Today, it is a multicultural country with a rich economy and close ties with Asia, America, and Europe.

First inhabitants

The first people to inhabit Australia were the ancestors of today's Aboriginals. They reached the country about 40,000 years ago after sailing across the shallow seas that then separated Australia from Asia. As sea-levels rose, they moved inland, using stone axes to clear trees to build shelters of wood and bark.

Outrigger canoe from Queensland

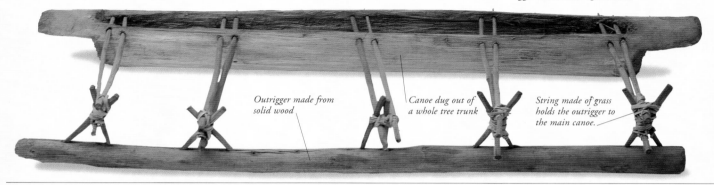

Outrigger made from solid wood

Canoe dug out of a whole tree trunk

String made of grass holds the outrigger to the main canoe.

Early sightings

In the 17th century, Spanish sailor Luis Vaez de Torres and Dutchman Willem Jansz explored the islands of Asia and the Pacific. Unplanned landings took place as ships were blown off course. In 1642–43 Dutchman Abel Tasman sailed round Australia without catching sight of it. He landed on an island he named Van Diemen's Land, now called Tasmania.

Early map of Australia

Botany Bay

In 1770, the British explorer Captain James Cook sailed into an inlet in southeastern Australia. He named the place Botany Bay and claimed the entire east coast of Australia for Britain. Joseph Banks, one of the ship's naturalists, sketched and collected hundreds of plants, that had never before been seen by Europeans.

Convict transportation

In 1787, the British decided to transport (ship out) convicts to Australia. The first fleet, containing 759 convicts, arrived in Botany Bay in 1788. A penal settlement was established at nearby Sydney Cove, in Port Jackson. Transportation finally came to an end in 1868.

Convicts were often used as servants.

The 19th century

Some 90 years after the arrival of Cook, the major settlements were all on the coast, and few people travelled inland. The first explorers mapped the Murray and Darling rivers in the south-east, while others tried to reach the heart of Australia.

Crossing the continent

The Royal Society of Victoria decided to send an expedition to cross the continent from south to north. Irishman Robert O'Hara Burke and Englishman William J Wills completed the trip in 1861, but died on the return journey. In July 1862 their rival, John Stuart, completed a similar journey, unaware that Burke and Wills had beaten him to it. He died in the attempt.

Surveyor's chain used to measure land, 1800s

Gold rush

The discovery of gold in 1851 brought a rush of fortune-hunters. By 1860, the population had grown from 200,000 in 1840 to 1.1 million, and Australian gold accounted for 39 per cent of the world's total output.

Prospectors' camp, Victoria

Growth

The colonies prospered in the last years of the 19th century. Industry grew quickly, especially in areas such as construction and manufacturing. Social policies were forward-thinking: for example, education for all was an early goal; trade unions were organized in many areas.

Banner for trade union

Ned Kelly

Throughout the 19th century, parts of Australia were lawless. One of the most notorious outlaws, or bushrangers, was Ned Kelly (1855–80), who led a gang of robbers. The gang killed three policemen in 1878 and robbed several banks before Kelly was caught and hanged in Melbourne in 1880. His fight against the authorities made Kelly a national folk hero.

A

Independent nation

In the early days, Australia consisted of six separate colonies. Each had its own administration but was subject to the sovereignty of Britain. As the agricultural and mining industries grew in strength, the six colonies began to work closely together. In 1901, Australia gained its independence from Britain, and a federal government for the entire country was established with its capital in Melbourne. Today, the federal capital is at Canberra.

Gallipoli

On 25 April, 1915, ANZAC forces landed at Gallipoli at the approaches to the Black Sea, Turkey. They hoped to take Constantinople (modern-day Istanbul) and force Germany's World War I ally, Turkey, out of the war. The men showed extraordinary courage and spirit, but the campaign was a disaster. No important gains were made and more than 11,400 ANZAC troops lost their lives.

Gallipoli memorial

Anzac Monument, Sydney

ANZAC forces

Australian and New Zealand forces fought for Britain in the Boer War (1899–1902) in South Africa and in both world wars. They fought together as the Australia and New Zealand Army Corps (ANZAC), making a contribution out of all proportion to their size. They suffered huge casualties, but the effort forged a strong sense of national identity.

Dominion status

When Australia became independent in 1901, it remained a Dominion of the British Empire and kept close links with its former ruler. But many people had few ties to the old "Mother Country". The threat of Japanese invasion during World War II led to closer links with the USA as the only power that could defend Australia.

The Federation Flag was based on the state flag of New South Wales.

Federation Flag

Immigration

In 1902, the government passed the Immigration Restriction Act to limit Chinese immigration. The act required settlers to speak a European language, and began a White Australia policy that lasted until the 1970s. Britons, Greeks, and Italians flooded into Australia in the 1950s and 1960s, but immigration from Asia later increased.

Scottish emigrants leave for Australia.

Modern Australia

After World War II, Australia continued its military alliance with the USA. The country sent troops to fight with the Americans in Korea during the 1950s and Vietnam in the 1960s. In recent years, those ties have weakened, and Australia has increasingly turned towards Asia, in particular Japan, for trade and investment. Today, Australia is an important trading partner with most of the powerful East Asian economies.

National symbol

Sydney Opera House, with its bold concrete roofs, has become the most widely recognized symbol of Australia.

Skyscraper, Sydney

Australian republic?

In 1992, the prime minister, Paul Keating, said he wanted the country be a republic by the year 2000, with an Australian as the head of state, instead of the British monarch. However, a referendum held in 1999 defeated any such proposals.

Chinese festival, Sydney

Multicultural Australia

Modern Australia is a multi-racial state with large Chinese and Greek populations. However, the Aboriginals are fighting a long campaign to be included in society and to secure their land rights and civil liberties.

Sailing in Sydney Harbour

Sports excellence

One way in which Australia has expressed its national identity is through sporting activities. There have been notable successes in sports as diverse as cricket and yachting. For example, in 1983 Australia overturned a century of US yachting dominance by winning the America's Cup. Sydney was chosen as the site of the Olympic Games in 2000.

Timeline

c.40,000 BC Aboriginals arrive in Australia.

1642–43 Tasman names Van Diemen's Land (Tasmania).

1770 Captain Cook lands at Botany Bay.

1788 First British convicts arrive.

Wallaby

1828 Charles Sturt begins to explore Murray and Darling rivers.

1851 Gold discovered in Victoria and New South Wales.

1860–61 Burke and Wills cross Australia from south to north.

1868 Britain abolishes the transportation of convicts.

Aboriginal digging sticks

1901 Australia becomes self-governing dominion in the British Empire.

1902 Immigration Restriction Act establishes the White Australia policy.

1914–18 60,000 Australians are killed fighting for Britain in World War I.

1927 Parliament meets for the first time in the new federal capital of Canberra.

1970s White Australia policy abolished.

1993 Aboriginal land rights recognized by law.

2000 Olympic Games held in Sydney.

2001 Fierce bush fires cause immense damage.

FIND OUT MORE ABORIGINAL AUSTRALIANS · CRIME AND PUNISHMENT · COOK, JAMES · EXPLORATION · OPERA · PREHISTORIC PEOPLE · WORLD WAR I · WORLD WAR II

AUSTRALIAN WILDLIFE

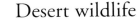

AUSTRALIA HAS BEEN ISOLATED by water for more than 30 million years, resulting in the evolution of many unique animals and plants. Half of all marsupials, such as the koala and kangaroo, live only in Australia, along with the platypus and echidna, the world's only egg-laying mammals, or monotremes. Much of Australia is desert or scrub. The animals and plants that live here are adapted to the hot, dry conditions. There are also areas of tropical and temperate forests, which contain the greatest diversity of life in Australia.

Desert wildlife

Australia's hot, dry, desert interior makes up half the continent. Drought-resistant vegetation, such as porcupine grass and acacias, grow here, providing a refuge for birds and insects. Many desert mammals rest in burrows by day to avoid the heat.

Emu
Emus are large flightless birds that can run at up to 50 kmh (30 mph), although they usually walk. They cover large distances in search of grasses, fruit, and flowers. They also eat insects. Males incubate the eggs and guard the young after they hatch.

Galah
The galah, or roseate cockatoo, is one of the most common parrots in Australia. Large flocks of these birds are found not only in dry areas but also in cities. Galahs eat seeds, leaf buds, and insects.

Strong bill is used to dig up insects.

Thorny devil
This lizard's scales are drawn out into long spines. When temperatures fall at night, valuable water condenses on the spines and runs down tiny grooves towards the mouth.

Spines protect against predators.

Porcupine grass
As its name suggests, porcupine grass is a spiny plant that grows in circular tussocks. It is adapted to dry desert conditions by having a thick outer covering (cuticle) to reduce water loss, and by having deep roots to reach water in the soil.

Mulgara
This carnivorous marsupial (pouched mammal) eats insects and small vertebrates, such as mice and lizards. It bites and shakes its prey to kill it. The mulgara digs burrows in sand, in which it shelters to escape the midday sun.

Mulgara eats prey head first.

Grass forms a refuge for insects, lizards, and birds.

Long, strong legs

Lizard searches for ants.

Scrub and grassland wildlife

Covering about a third of Australia, scrub and grassland are hot and dry in summer and cooler in winter. Occasional downpours of rain are exploited by plants that rapidly bloom and produce seeds, and animals, such as frogs, that emerge to reproduce.

Canopy provides shelter for animals from the midday heat.

Bottle tree
These large trees get their name from their bottle-shaped trunks. The swollen trunk stores water that helps the tree survive periods of drought. The tree also provides food for many animals, including insects, and shelter for some birds and mammals. Other vegetation common in scrubland includes dry grasses and dwarf eucalyptus.

Water is stored in bulbous trunk.

Short-beaked echidna
The short-beaked echidna is an egg-laying mammal found in Australia, Tasmania, and New Guinea. It uses its sticky tongue to extract ants and termites from their nests. If threatened, the echidna rolls into a ball, or digs down into the soil.

Mallee fowl
The male mallee fowl builds a mound of vegetation and soil in which the female lays her eggs. As the vegetation rots, it releases heat that incubates the eggs.

Male checks mound temperature with his beak, and by moving vegetation.

Water-holding frog
This frog survives drought by burrowing into the ground, and forming a thin layer of skin around itself to conserve water. It also stores water in its bladder.

Kultarr
This small, mouse-like marsupial is nocturnal. It has large eyes to help it see in the dark, and to catch insects and spiders. It moves by springing off its long hind feet and tail and landing on its front feet. During the day the kultarr shelters in logs, hollow stumps, and burrows.

Kultarr feeding on a spider.

Temperate forest wildlife

The temperate forests of south and east Australia are hot and dry in summer, and cooler and wetter in winter. They are home to birds, such as parrots and kookaburras, marsupials, including the koala, and a variety of reptiles and insects. Many trees found here, such as eucalyptus and mountain ash, are unique to Australia.

Silver wattle

The silver wattle, also known as mimosa, is a common plant in temperate forests. These trees, with their characteristic silver-grey leaves, can withstand dry periods as well as exploit the wet season.

Bright yellow flowers provide food for insects and other animals.

Kookaburra

The kookaburra is the largest member of the kingfisher family. It is rarely found near water, however, preferring open woodland. Kookaburras swoop down from a tree branch perch to pounce on insects, lizards, snakes, and small birds and mammals. They defend their territory by making loud cackling calls that sound like human laughter.

Male lyrebird sings a loud territorial song, mimicking other birds and animals.

Lyrebird

These ground-living birds use their large clawed feet to turn over stones and break open logs, in search of insects. The male lyrebird has a long tail shaped like a lyre, an ancient musical instrument. He performs courtship dances to attract females by vibrating his tail over his back.

Flattened tail helps platypus swim.

Heavy beak to kill reptiles and rodents.

Duck-billed platypus

This unusual-looking animal is an egg-laying mammal, or monotreme, that lives near rivers. The platypus feeds underwater on insect larvae and other food found by probing the stream bottom with its sensitive bill. It hunts mainly at night, spending most of the day in a burrow dug in the stream bank.

Long tail feathers

Koalas spend most of their time in eucalyptus trees, using their sharp claws and strong legs to climb through the branches.

Koala

Koalas are bear-like marsupials that feed on the leaves of eucalyptus trees. They eat mainly at night, spending most of the day resting or sleeping in the fork of a tree.

Tree kangaroo

The tree kangaroo is a marsupial adapted for life in the trees, by having rough paw pads and long claws for gripping. Its diet consists mainly of leaves and bark, but it sometimes descends to the ground to feed on shrubs and seedlings.

Tropical rainforest wildlife

Despite occupying only a tiny part of northeastern Australia, the rainforests contain one-third of Australia's frog and marsupial species, and two-thirds of its butterflies. The wide variety of ferns and trees, such as breadfruit trees, provide shelter and food for these animals, and many birds, bats, and insects.

Long tail for balancing in the trees.

Rainbow lorikeet

These brightly coloured parrots live in screeching flocks of up to 20 birds in the upper rainforest canopy. They feed on pollen, nectar, flowers, seeds, and fruit.

Trigger plant

When a bee lands on a trigger plant flower, the anther – the flower's male part – bends outwards to dust pollen on the bee's hairy back. When the bee visits another flower the pollen sticks to the stigma – the female part of the flower, thereby pollinating it.

Pink flowers attract bees.

Fangs are 1 cm (0.5 in) long so they can inject venom deep into their victims.

Queen Alexandra's birdwing

Found in New Guinea, this is the largest butterfly in the world. The female is larger than the male and has a wingspan of up to 28 cm (11 in). Queen Alexandra's birdwing flies in the sunlight of the upper canopy, where it feeds on flower nectar.

The male is brightly coloured.

Taipan

This forest snake is active in the early morning and evening, and feeds mainly on rats and other small mammals. The taipan is one of the world's most poisonous snakes; a bite from its long fangs is often fatal for humans. Taipans normally retreat and hide when people approach, but they will become aggressive if threatened.

Brown coloration provides camouflage for taipan.

| FIND OUT MORE | AUSTRALIA | BIRDS | BUTTERFLIES AND MOTHS | CAMOUFLAGE AND COLOUR | FLIGHTLESS BIRDS | FROGS AND TOADS | KANGAROOS AND OTHER MARSUPIALS | REPTILES | TREES |

AZTECS

A GREAT IMPERIAL power, the Aztecs came to dominate the Valley of Mexico in less than a hundred years. Egged on by bloodthirsty gods, they were a warlike people, outstanding for their military skill and well organized society. By the time the Spanish conquistador Hernán Cortés (1485–1547) arrived in 1519, the Aztecs and their allies were rulers of some 25 million people.

Rise of the Aztecs

The Aztecs were one of many tribes who invaded the Valley of Mexico soon after the collapse of the Toltecs in the late 12th century. They dominated the valley after 1438.

Human sacrifice
When they won a war, the Aztecs killed many prisoners as offerings to their gods. Aztecs believed that human sacrifices were necessary in order for the universe to continue.

Dish for human heart

Subject peoples
The Aztecs ruled over a network of city states. Subject peoples made regular payments to their Aztec overlords, in the form of maize, cacao, or cotton. As long as this "tribute" was paid, the peoples of the Valley of Mexico were left to govern themselves and to keep their customs.

Tenochtitlán

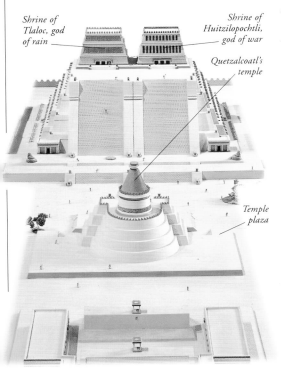

Shrine of Tlaloc, god of rain

Shrine of Huitzilopochtli, god of war

Quetzalcoatl's temple

Temple plaza

A city of canals and narrow streets, the Aztec capital was built on an island in Lake Texcoco. It was linked to the land by three narrow causeways. The city was home to 200,000 people – four or five times larger than any European city of the time. Most people lived in small houses in the narrow streets surrounding an area of temples – the Great Precinct.

Great Precinct
The centre of Tenochtitlán was dominated by the Great Precinct, surrounded by a wall decorated with huge serpent heads. Inside the enclosure were the temples of the leading gods. A skull rack displayed the heads of countless victims of human sacrifice.

Aztec society
Commoners lived in small mud houses and grew crops on the marshes. They dressed and ate simply. The nobles were warriors, tribute collectors, and judges; they were rewarded for their services with land.

Mother of new baby

Chief priest

Three boys call out baby's name.

Midwife

Customs
Aztec customs included an elaborate naming ceremony for newborn babies.

School teacher

Aztecs on the eve of conquest
By the early 16th century, the Aztec empire was showing signs of weakness. Shortly before the arrival of Cortés, priests and nobles were worried by a series of omens that seemed to forecast Aztec decline. These omens included the rumbling of the volcano Popocatépetl.

Quetzalcoatl, the feathered serpent

Quetzalcoatl
The Aztecs believed that the god Quetzalcoatl had been driven from his kingdom and would return to begin a golden age. When Cortés arrived, they thought he was the god. But the noise of Popocatépetl seemed to be an omen of defeat.

Popocatépetl

Montezuma II
The emperor Montezuma II (c.1466–1520) was unsure if Cortés was Quetzalcoatl, and did not repel the Spanish when they arrived. Cortés and his small army got as far as the capital, and Montezuma welcomed them there. But the Spanish seized the emperor and took him hostage. Montezuma died in prison, the last Aztec ruler.

Conquest of the Aztecs
In April 1519, Cortés founded Veracruz on the coast of the Gulf of Mexico, inside the Aztec empire. With his army of 600 men and 16 horses, he advanced towards Tenochtitlán, forging alliances with Aztec enemies. By August 1521, the Spanish had occupied Tenochtitlán, after laying siege with the help of many local soldiers.

Defeat by Tlaxcala
The growing thirst for human sacrifice led Aztecs to wage constant war on the neighbouring Tlaxcalans. Four years before the arrival of Cortés, the Tlaxcalans inflicted a heavy defeat on the Aztec armies, greatly weakening the empire.

FIND OUT MORE

CENTRAL AMERICA, HISTORY OF   MAYA   MESOAMERICANS   OLMECS

Aztec life
Everyday items

Water jar is made of glazed earthenware and has a narrow neck.

Bowl is decorated with bold abstract patterns in two colours.

Axe heads were often made of copper; they originally had wooden handles.

Adze was a woodworker's tool.

Chisel used by masons.

Flute made of bone could play simple tunes.

Ritual items

Flint knives

Obsidian hooked knife

Club with obsidian blades

Spear with obsidian blades

Tools had blades of flint or obsidian, often with wooden handles.

Mask may be made from skull of sacrificial victim.

Greenstone mask was left as an offering to the gods.

Flint knives may have been used to kill sacrificial victims.

Feathered cloak was worn by priest or warrior.

Ritual vessel was used in the temple.

Aztec people

Cleaner with broom

Boy carrying rushes

Boatman

Mother and babies

Carpenter

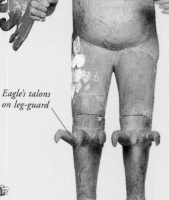

Mask in shape of eagle's beak

Sleeves in form of eagle's wings

Eagle's talons on leg-guard

Eagle warrior

Young woman

Weaver

Girl grinding maize

Painter

Boatman

Musician

Schoolmaster

Jeweller

Goldsmith

Featherworker

Messenger

BABYLONIAN EMPIRE

B

ON THE EUPHRATES RIVER, 4,000 years ago, an ancient settlement became the most magnificent city in the Near East. This city was Babylon, and when Hammurabi conquered Mesopotamia, he established his capital there. Over centuries, Babylonian fortunes rose and fell, as the city was invaded by the Hittites, Kassites, and Assyrians. The Assyrians destroyed Babylon in 689 BC. In 612 BC, the Babylonians retaliated by conquering the Assyrians, and again making their city the world's greatest. Babylonia's splendour continued after the Persian Empire absorbed it in 539 BC.

The first Babylonian Empire
By about 1770 BC, Hammurabi had conquered most of Mesopotamia. Babylon was established as the capital of the south for the duration of the Babylonian Empire.

King Hammurabi

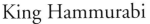

Mesopotamia's wisest king, Hammurabi (r.1792–1750 BC), followed ancient tradition by issuing laws to protect his subjects. Using cuneiform script, he had 282 laws carved on a black stone pillar. The empire he founded collapsed in 1595 BC, when Hittites from Anatolia looted it. The Kassites from the mountains to the east of Babylon then invaded and took over.

Kassites
Between 1600 and 1190 BC, people called the Kassites ruled Babylonia. They are best known for their boundary stones (kuddurus), which marked property divisions and recorded gifts of land. These were often decorated with divine symbols. After the end of Kassite rule, Babylonia fell into a long period of chaos.

Kudduru

Persian Empire
In 539 BC, the Persian king Cyrus II took over the Babylonian kingdom, and made Mesopotamia part of his empire. His son Cambyses was usurped by Darius I, also called "the Great", under whom the empire reached its greatest extent.

Darius I (522–486) introduced coinage.

Literature and art

The Babylonian Empire was world-famous for its great artistic and literary achievements. Literature such as the legendary epic of Gilgamesh, a Sumerian hero, was written on clay tablets in cuneiform. Artistic splendours included terracotta plaques, superb sculpture and glassware, and, above all, the lavish and decorative entrance to the city – the Ishtar Gate and Processional Way.

Science
Babylonia was famous as the home of scientists and scholars. Babylonian astrologers studied the movements of planets and stars, recorded their findings on clay tablets, and used these to predict the future. Many texts are so detailed that modern astronomers can date ancient events from them. Ancient Greeks and Romans used the Babylonian system for naming planets.

Venus tablet, Kish

Cuneiform script

Magical spirit

Religion
The Babylonians inherited their religion from the Sumerians. They believed that gods and spirits controlled every aspect of the world. These included Anu, the sky god, who gave birth to some of the most important deities, including Ishtar, goddess of love and war (represented by the planet Venus), and Ea, god of wisdom and fresh water. Ea was the father of Marduk, the god of Babylon, who created the world and made humans by mixing earth with divine blood.

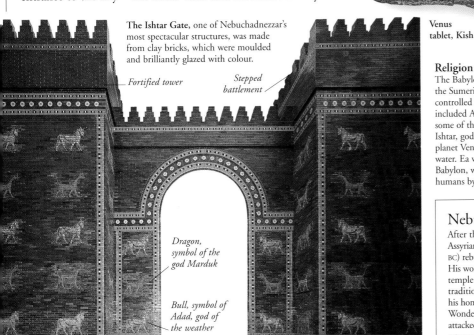

The Ishtar Gate, one of Nebuchadnezzar's most spectacular structures, was made from clay bricks, which were moulded and brilliantly glazed with colour.

Fortified tower

Stepped battlement

Dragon, symbol of the god Marduk

Bull, symbol of Adad, god of the weather

Nebuchadnezzar

After the Babylonian king Nabopolasser defeated the Assyrian enemy, his son Nebuchadnezzar (r.605–562 BC) rebuilt the devastated Babylon on a grand scale. His works included the fabulous Ishtar Gate, and a temple and ziggurat tower. According to Greek tradition, he also built the Hanging Gardens for his homesick wife, and these became one of the Seven Wonders of the World. In 596 BC, Nebuchadnezzar attacked the kingdom of Judah. Ten years later he returned, sacked Jerusalem, and took the Jews into exile in Babylon. They were not released until the reign of Cyrus II.

FIND OUT MORE   ARCHITECTURE   ASIA, HISTORY OF   ASSYRIAN EMPIRE   HITTITES   PERSIAN EMPIRES   SCIENCE, HISTORY OF   SEVEN WONDERS OF THE ANCIENT WORLD   SUMERIANS   WARFARE

BADGERS, OTTERS, AND SKUNKS

B

THESE THREE GROUPS OF ANIMALS are all members of the weasel family – Mustelidae. Their main characteristics are a long, low-slung body, short legs, and five toes on each foot. They are carnivores, although badgers have a mixed diet. The honey badger is especially fond of honey, as its name suggests. Most mustelids discharge a thick, oily, powerful-smelling fluid called a musk from their anal glands. They use this mostly to send scent messages to other members of the species, usually with their droppings.

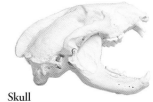

Skull
A badger eats meat and plants, and its large canines and broad molar teeth are ideal for this diet. Its jaw muscles are fixed to a rigid bone on the top of the skull, giving the animal a powerful bite.

Badgers

All badgers are thick set with very powerful legs which they use to forage for food and to dig their often extensive burrows. They are nocturnal animals, spending the day underground with others of their social group. There are eight species of true badger, plus the honey badger, which is classed in a sub-family of its own.

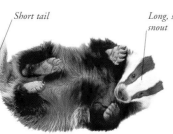
Short tail

Long, striped snout

Long coarse hairs over a dense underfur

Badgers have a good sense of smell.

Forepaw print   **Hind paw print**

Paws
A Eurasian badger's track is unmistakable. Each foot has five toes with a kidney-shaped pad behind. The front claws usually leave marks because they are long.

Eurasian badger
This is the largest badger and has the widest distribution. Females give birth to up to four cubs in February. These are weaned at 12 weeks, when they can forage for themselves.

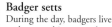

Badger setts
During the day, badgers live underground in a complex system of tunnels and chambers called a sett. A main badger sett is easily recognized by the entrances with piles of soil outside.

Otters

These semi-aquatic mustelids occur outside the polar regions in every continent except Australia. Some species are exclusively sea creatures, some use only fresh water, and others use both sea and fresh water. Most have sleeping dens, or holts, on land.

European river otter

Asian short-clawed otter

Paws
Although all otters swim, not all have webbed feet. For example, the European otter has a large amount of webbing. The Asian short-clawed otter has little webbing and uses its paws to find food by touch.

Fur
An otter's coat consists of two layers. A thick under-layer of fine hairs traps air for warmth, and longer, waterproof guard hairs keep the underfur dry.

Honey badger
The African honey badger, also known as the ratel, has a thick, loose skin. Predators can find it difficult to pierce its skin, and the badger can twist around inside its skin and bite back.

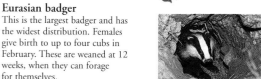

Movement
With their long back and heavy tail, otters can look clumsy on land. In the water they are graceful swimmers, propelling themselves forward by moving their hindquarters and tail up and down.

Spraints
Otters secrete a powerful scent. They mark their territory by leaving their droppings, called spraints, which smell of this scent, on high points such as rocks.

Skunks

There are 13 species of skunk, which all occur in the Americas. They are best known for their ability to squirt a foul-smelling fluid from their anal glands. They aim this fluid at the eyes of an enemy, and it can cause temporary blindness. Skunks search for insects and other small animals to eat, mainly at night.

Markings
Skunks have bold black and white coat markings. Like the yellow and black stripes of a wasp, these warn would-be predators of danger.

EURASIAN BADGER

SCIENTIFIC NAME *Meles meles*

ORDER Carnivora

FAMILY Mustelidae

DISTRIBUTION Europe and a wide band across Asia

HABITAT Mainly lowland farmland and woodland

DIET Worms, insects, birds, and other small animals, fruit, cereals, fungi

SIZE Length: 1 m (3.3 ft)

LIFESPAN About 7 years

FIND OUT MORE • ANIMAL BEHAVIOUR • LAKE AND RIVER WILDLIFE • NORTH AMERICAN WILDLIFE • POLLUTION • WEASELS AND MARTENS

Formerly known as **BALKAN STATES**

SOUTHEAST EUROPE

SLOVENIA, CROATIA, Bosnia
and Herzegovina, Serbia and
Montenegro, Macedonia, and
Albania all lie in Southeast Europe.
Ruled by Turkey for nearly 500 years, all the
countries, except Albania, were united as Yugoslavia
in 1918. It was, however, an uneasy peace, and, in
1991, Yugoslavia split up as a result of rival ethnic
and religious tensions. War broke out, lasting until
1995. Since then, fresh conflicts have occurred and
the region is still struggling to recover from war.

Physical features
The western region of Southeast Europe
is made up of limestone plateaus and steep
mountain ranges separated by forested
valleys. In the northwest of the region
are the flat plains of the River Danube.

23°C
(73°F)

1°C
(34°F)

870 mm (34 in)

Regional climate
The inland plains and the coastal strip have
a temperate continental climate, with hot
summers and cold winters. Snow falls in
the mountains in winter.

Mountains
Mixed forests of deciduous trees and
conifers cover the mountain slopes that
dominate the north of the region. The
Dinaric Alps are barren limestone ranges,
or *karst*, that rise to about 1,800 m
(5,905 ft) along the Adriatic Sea coast.

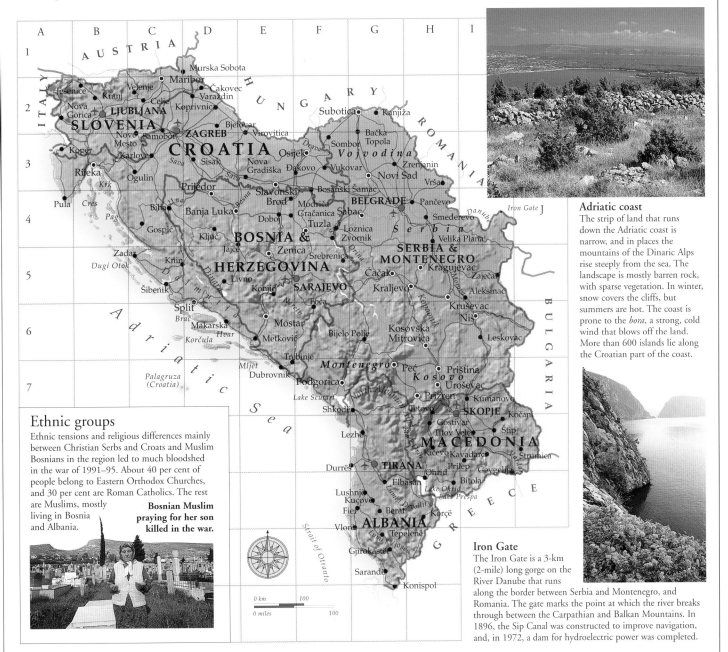

Adriatic coast
The strip of land that runs
down the Adriatic coast is
narrow, and in places the
mountains of the Dinaric Alps
rise steeply from the sea. The
landscape is mostly barren rock,
with sparse vegetation. In winter,
snow covers the cliffs, but
summers are hot. The coast is
prone to the *bora*, a strong, cold
wind that blows off the land.
More than 600 islands lie along
the Croatian part of the coast.

Ethnic groups
Ethnic tensions and religious differences mainly
between Christian Serbs and Croats and Muslim
Bosnians in the region led to much bloodshed
in the war of 1991–95. About 40 per cent of
people belong to Eastern Orthodox Churches,
and 30 per cent are Roman Catholics. The rest
are Muslims, mostly
living in Bosnia
and Albania.

**Bosnian Muslim
praying for her son
killed in the war.**

Iron Gate
The Iron Gate is a 3-km
(2-mile) long gorge on the
River Danube that runs
along the border between Serbia and Montenegro, and
Romania. The gate marks the point at which the river breaks
through between the Carpathian and Balkan Mountains. In
1896, the Sip Canal was constructed to improve navigation,
and, in 1972, a dam for hydroelectric power was completed.

B

Slovenia

Historically and geographically, Slovenia has more in common with Austria than with other neighbouring states. The country was ruled by Austria for almost a thousand years. Slovenia has many small farms and thriving businesses. Despite economic problems caused by the conflict in areas to the south, it is the region's wealthiest country.

SLOVENIA FACTS

CAPITAL CITY Ljubljana

AREA 20,253 sq km (7,820 sq miles)

POPULATION 2,000,000

MAIN LANGUAGE Slovene

MAJOR RELIGION Christian

CURRENCY Tolar

Resources
Slovenia mines mercury, lead, oil, and zinc for export. There are also deposits of brown coal and lignite, but they are poor quality and difficult to extract. One-third of the country's energy comes from a nuclear plant in Krsvo.

Mercury ore

People
About 90 per cent of the population are Slovenes who have kept their language and traditional culture despite centuries of Austrian domination. Wages are higher than in other Balkan states, and standards of education are high. One in seven Slovenes lives in the capital, Ljubljana, which has textile, electronics, chemical, and manufacturing industries.

Tourism
Slovenia is slowly rebuilding its tourist industry, which suffered as a result of the war in Bosnia. Skiing, spa resorts, and lakeside scenery attract many visitors to the Alps in the north of the region.

Lake Bled is a popular tourist destination.

Croatia

Ruled by Hungary for more than 800 years, Croatia became part of Yugoslavia in 1918, gaining independence in 1991. Croatia's economy was damaged by the war with neighbouring Bosnia, but it is fortunate in having important ports and rich resources, including oil, coal, and bauxite. The tourist industry is recovering.

Adriatic coast
Croatia's Adriatic coast has sandy beaches and hundreds of offshore islands that once attracted up to 12 million tourists every year. However, the outbreak of war in 1991 abruptly halted all tourism. The country still has a thriving fishing industry, with an annual catch of about 25,000 tonnes (27,500 tons).

CROATIA FACTS

CAPITAL CITY Zagreb

AREA 56,542 sq km (21,831 sq miles)

POPULATION 4,700,000

MAIN LANGUAGE Croatian

MAJOR RELIGIONS Christian

CURRENCY Kuna

Flax stalks

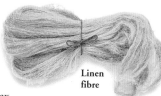

Linen fibre

Flax
Fields of flax are cultivated in the fertile river valleys of northern Croatia. Flax fibre, which is obtained by crushing the stalks of the plant, is woven into linen and canvas, and its seeds yield linseed oil. Apricots, grapes, and plums are also grown in northern Croatia.

Zagreb
The cultural and industrial capital of Croatia is Zagreb, which grew out of two medieval settlements on the River Sava. The city has museums, art galleries, 13th-century buildings, and cathedrals, such as St Mark's and St Stephen's. Most people travel around by tram and bus.

Bosnia and Herzegovina

In 1991, bitter fighting broke out in the twin states of Bosnia and Herzegovina between the Roman Catholic Croats, Muslim Bosnians, and Orthodox Serbs. In all, about 300,000 people were killed, more than 2,000,000 fled the country, and many historic cities were devastated. A delicate peace has prevailed since 1995.

BOSNIA AND HERZEGOVINA FACTS

CAPITAL CITY Sarajevo

AREA 51,129 sq km (19,741 sq miles)

POPULATION 4,100,000

MAIN LANGUAGE Serbo-Croat

MAJOR RELIGIONS Christian, Muslim

CURRENCY Marka

Muslims
During the war, Serbs from Bosnia forced Croats and Muslims out of areas they regarded as their own. Thousands were killed, and many Muslims fled abroad. In 1995, a peace agreement split the country into two provinces: Bosnian-Serb and Muslim-Croat.

Sarajevo
Straddling the River Miljacka, Sarajevo is the capital of Bosnia and Herzegovina. Under communist rule the city was transformed from a sleepy, Islamic town to a bustling, multicultural industrial centre. During the civil war, however, it was shattered by 2,000,000 shells, which killed tens of thousands of people. Serbs attacking the city were forced to withdraw in 1995.

Farming
Bosnia and Herzegovina's main farming region lies in the southwest. The area has fertile, well-watered soil and hot, dry summers. Crops include citrus fruit, grapes, maize, pomegranates, figs, olives, rice, and tobacco. Sheep are reared on the upland areas.

Figs

Pomegranates

Serbia and Montenegro

Two of the former Yugoslavia's states, Serbia and Montenegro, kept the name Yugoslavia in 1992. As a result of the part Serbia played in helping Serbs fight in Bosnia and Croatia, many countries imposed sanctions and refused to trade with the new Yugoslavia. Its disgraced former president Slobodan Milošević was called to a war crimes tribunal.

Razznjici

Cubes of grilled lamb | Skewer

People
The people of Serbia and Montenegro speak Serbo-Croat, which they write in the Russian-like Cyrillic alphabet. The largest minority group is Albanian (17 per cent). Most people belong to the Serbian Orthodox Church.

Food
A favourite Yugoslavian dish is *raznjici*, which is made of cubes of lamb grilled on skewers and served with yoghurt. *Djuvetsch*, meat with rice and vegetables, is also popular. The favourite national drink is *slivovitz*, plum brandy.

Sveti Stefan was once a popular tourist destination.

Tourism
Before the war, the beautiful beaches and historic towns and villages on Montenegro's coast attracted millions of tourists. However, many beauty spots have been devastated. Yugoslavia only received 150,000 visitors in 2001 and is trying to rebuild its shattered tourist industry.

SERBIA & MONTENEGRO	
CAPITAL CITY	Belgrade
AREA	102,350 sq km (39,517 sq miles)
POPULATION	10,500,000
MAIN LANGUAGE	Serbo-Croat
MAJOR RELIGIONS	Christian, Muslim
CURRENCY	Yugoslav dinar, Euro

Macedonia

The official name of the country is the Former Yugoslav Republic of Macedonia to appease the Greeks, who have a province called Macedonia. Land-locked, it is self-sufficient in energy, with efficient metal, chemical, textile, and food processing industries. Air pollution is a serious problem. Renewed ethnic conflicts broke out in 2001.

Lakes
Lake Ohrid and Lake Prespa in southwestern Macedonia are two of Europe's most beautiful lakes and, in peaceful times, they attract visitors for the scenery and the fishing. Ohrid is 294 m (964 ft) deep. Underground channels link the two lakes.

People
The largest group of people is made up of Eastern Orthodox (Christian) Slav Macedonians who account for two-thirds of the population. Many ethnic Albanian refugees arrived from Kosovo in 1999.

Skopje
Despite having been destroyed four times by earthquakes, most recently in 1963, Macedonia's capital, Skopje, is the hub of the country's communications and industry.

MACEDONIA FACTS	
CAPITAL CITY	Skopje
AREA	25,333 sq km (9,781 sq miles)
POPULATION	2,000,000
MAIN LANGUAGES	Macedonian, Serbo-Croat, Albanian
MAJOR RELIGIONS	Christian, Muslim
CURRENCY	Macedonian Denar

Albania

From 1944 to 1991, Albania was a one-party state with the most rigid communist regime in the world. It is now a democracy, but in 1997 there was a severe economic crisis. Tirana, the capital, was founded in the 17th century and has light industry as well as government buildings.

Grapes
Tomatoes
Potatoes
Watermelon

Farming
About 24 per cent of Albania is cultivated. Wheat, maize, potatoes and other vegetables, fruit, and sugar beet are the main crops. Sheep, goats, and cattle are reared for meat and milk, and donkeys are bred for transport.

People
As a way of making the population grow rapidly, the communist government encouraged men and women to have large families. Under communism, Albania was the only official atheist state and, even today, many people are non-believers.

Transport
Communications are difficult in this rugged land. There are only 440 km (273 miles) of rail lines, and 7,450 km (4,630 miles) of roads, 60 per cent of which are dirt tracks. There is only one car for every 50 people. Horses and carts are the main means of transport.

ALBANIA FACTS	
CAPITAL CITY	Tirana
AREA	28,748 sq km (11,100 sq miles)
POPULATION	3,100,000
MAIN LANGUAGE	Albanian
MAJOR RELIGIONS	Muslim, Christian
CURRENCY	Lek

FIND OUT MORE | CHRISTIANITY | EARTHQUAKES | EMPIRES | EUROPE, HISTORY OF | FARMING | FISHING INDUSTRY | ISLAM | LAKES | TEXTILES AND WEAVING | TRADE AND INDUSTRY

BALLET

ONE OF THE MOST beautiful of the arts, ballet is a combination of dance and mime performed to music. Many ballets tell a story; others are abstract and experiment with form and movement. Ballet began in Italy. It was taken to France in 1533 by Catherine de Médicis, a member of a famous Italian family, who married a French prince. In 1661, Louis XIV founded the first ballet school, L'Académie Royale de Danse. Today, children learn the basics in ballet schools around the world.

Arms open wide

Both arms held in front

One arm in front, the other out to the side

One arm up, the other out to the side

Both arms up

First position – heels together, feet turned out.

Second position – heels apart, feet turned out.

Third position – one foot crossed halfway in front of the other.

Fourth position (crossed) – one foot in front of the other.

Fifth position – Feet crossed and touching.

Ballet positions

Every step in ballet makes use of the basic positions. It was at L'Académie Royale de Danse that the five basic positions of the feet were established. To achieve them, the whole leg has to be turned out from the hips. The position of the arms is known as *port de bras*.

Benesh notation

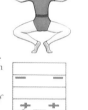

For ballets to survive, the steps must be written down, or notated. One of the most popular notation methods was devised by Rudolf and Joan Benesh in the late 1940s. Symbols represent the position of the hands and feet.

Each line represents a part of the body: top of head; shoulder; waist; knee; floor.

Romantic ballet

In the early 1800s, the Romantic Movement, with its fascination with the supernatural, affected all the arts. One of the most important men in 19th-century ballet was the choreographer August Bournonville. His ballets were influenced by his years in Paris where Romantic ballet began.

Marie Taglione

Taglione (1804–84) was an Italian ballerina who created the role of *La Sylphide*, She perfected the art of dancing on the tips of her toes, or *en pointe*.

Giselle

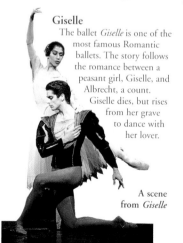

The ballet *Giselle* is one of the most famous Romantic ballets. The story follows the romance between a peasant girl, Giselle, and Albrecht, a count. Giselle dies, but rises from her grave to dance with her lover.

A scene from Giselle

Nijinsky

The Ballets Russes

Many Russian choreographers and dancers became bored with Classical ballet. Organized by Serge Diaghilev (1872–1929), they formed the Ballets Russes and toured Europe. The dancers included Vaslav Nijinsky (1890–1950), famous for his jumps.

Anna Pavlova

Russian ballerina Anna Pavlova (1881–1931) was the most famous dancer of her time. She danced with the Imperial Ballet, and also toured with the Ballets Russes. She formed her own company and toured all over the world.

Ballet in Russia

In 1847, French dancer Marius Petipa went to Russia to work with the tsar's Imperial Ballet in St Petersburg. With his assistant Lev Ivanov, he created Classical ballets – grand lavish ballets in three or four acts, designed to show off the brilliant techniques of the dancers.

Classical ballets all contain dazzling dances for the hero and heroine to perform together.

Partners have to trust each other.

Tchaikovsky

Russian composer Pëtr Tchaikovsky (1840–93) wrote probably the most famous ballet music of all. He worked with Marius Petipa and Lev Ivanov on the three great classical ballets, *Sleeping Beauty* (1890), *The Nutcracker* (1892), and *Swan Lake* (1895).

Moscow City Ballet in Sleeping Beauty

Ballet today

Almost every country has its own ballet company. The dancers perform Romantic and Classical ballets, ballets created by the Ballets Russes, and the works of more modern and contemporary choreographers.

Jumps require strength.

New York City Ballet

The New York City Ballet (left) was founded by the Russian choreographer George Balanchine (1904–83). This is his ballet *Apollo*.

The Royal Ballet

Britain's Royal Ballet started as the Vic-Wells Ballet in 1931. It often dances works by past artistic directors Frederick Ashton and Kenneth MacMillan.

A character from Ashton's Tales of Beatrix Potter

FIND OUT MORE

ART, HISTORY OF   DANCE   DRAMA   JAZZ   MUSIC   MUSICAL INSTRUMENTS   OPERA   STRAVINSKY, IGOR

BALL GAMES

A WIDE VARIETY OF BALL GAMES is played around the world with all shapes and sizes of ball; on pitches, courts, courses, and tables; by teams and by individuals. As well as various football games and racket games, there are bat-and-ball games such as cricket and baseball, stick-and-ball games such as hockey, hurling, shinty, and golf; and billiard-table games such as pool, snooker, and billiards. Other ball games include basketball, which involves throwing a ball up and into a small hoop, volleyball, in which the ball is hit over a high net, and bowls, in which balls are rolled along the ground.

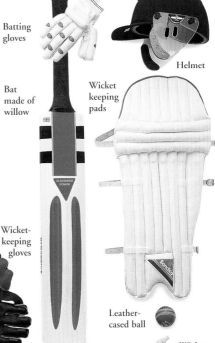

Batting gloves

Helmet

Bat made of willow

Wicket keeping pads

Wicket-keeping gloves

Leather-cased ball

Wicket

Cricket

This game is played between two teams of 11, one team bowling and fielding against two on the batting side. The batsmen score runs by running between the wickets or hitting the ball over the boundary. The fielding side may dismiss the batsmen in several ways, including bowling at and knocking over the wicket with the ball.

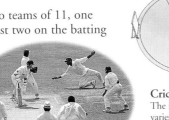

Sightscreen helps the batsman see the ball.

Pitch

Cricket field
The field is usually oval but its size varies. The boundary is marked by a rope or white line. The pitch, situated at or near the middle of the field, measures 20.12 m (22 yd) between wickets and 3.05 m (10 ft) across.

Cricket equipment
Cricket is played with a hard ball, and many players wear protective clothing. The wicket-keeper and batsmen wear special gloves and strapped-on leg-pads. Batsmen and close fielders may wear helmets with face-guards.

Catcher's glove with hard ball

Catcher's mask

Bat

Baseball

Baseball is played between two teams of nine which take turns to bat and field. A pitcher throws the ball and the batter attempts to hit it and score runs by progressing around four bases without being tagged or forced out by a fielder. The game has nine innings. An inning is over when six batters – three from each side – are out.

Baseball equipment
The catcher, who crouches behind the batter, wears a mask and body padding. Batters wear a helmet and fielders wear a catching mitt. The ball is made of cork wrapped in yarn and encased in leather.

Babe Ruth
The sensational hitting of American baseball player Babe Ruth (1895–1948), brought crowds to baseball in the 1920s. Originally a World Series-winning pitcher with the Boston Red Sox, he joined the New York Yankees in 1920 and slugged record after record, including 60 home runs in 1927 and a lifetime total of 714.

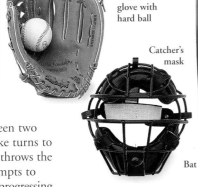

Outfield

Home plate

Infield

Baseball field
The field is made up of an infield, or "diamond", and an outfield. A pitcher throws from a mound at the centre of the infield, which has a base at each corner. A batter stands at home base, or plate.

Hockey

This is played between two teams of 11. Each player has a hooked stick, only the flat side of which can be used for playing the ball. The object of the game is to hit the ball into the opponents' goal. Goals may be scored only from inside a semi-circle called the striking, or shooting, circle.

Ball, traditionally white

Goalkeeper's helmet

Stick

Hockey equipment
Players wear guards under their socks to protect their shins and ankles. The goalkeeper wears a helmet with a face mask, shoulder and elbow pads, padded gauntlets, substantial leg guards, and "kickers" over the boots to protect the feet when kicking the ball away.

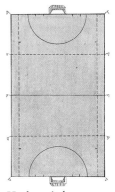

Hurling
This is a 15-a-side game played with wooden sticks called hurleys, which are used to strike or carry a small, hard ball. Goals are like soccer goals with extended posts. Points are scored for hitting the ball under the crossbar (three points) or over it (one point).

Hockey pitch
The pitch measures 91.4 m x 54.9 m (100 yd x 60 yd). Goals are 3.66 m (12 ft) wide and 2.13 m (7 ft) high. The shooting circles are joined quarter circles drawn from each post.

Basketball

A five-a-side game, basketball allows free substitution from as many as seven other players. The aim is to put the ball into the opposition's basket. Baskets, or field goals, are worth three points when scored from outside the three-point line, and two points when scored from inside the line.

The player holds the ball in both hands when preparing to shoot.

Players can pivot and jump with the ball, as when trying to score a "basket".

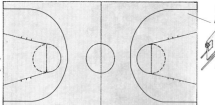
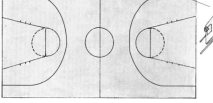

Three-point line

Basketball court
A basketball court is 28 m x 15 m (91.8 ft x 49.2 ft). The baskets stand 3.05 m (10 ft) above the ground.

Basketball

Ball is made of rubber, encased in leather, rubber, or synthetic material.

Basket

Basketball equipment
The main equipment needed for basketball is a ball and two baskets. Official time-keepers use clocks to keep track of the many time restrictions in the game, including the five-second limit on a player holding the ball.

Backboard

A moving player may take one stride with the ball.

High-sided boots are needed to support the ankles when turning and pivoting.

Netball
This seven-a-side game is played by women and girls only. The aim is to throw the ball into the opponents' net. Players must stay in certain areas of the court and may not move with the ball. They wear letters to show where they should be.

Volleyball
Teams of six players aim to score points by propelling the ball over a net into the opponents' court so that they cannot return it. Players can play the ball with their hands or any part of the body above the waist. A team is allowed three touches to hit the ball over the net.

Golf

The aim in golf is to take as few strokes as possible to hit a ball a certain distance into a cup set in the ground. Players have a choice of clubs with which to strike the ball. The standard course has 18 holes of various lengths with different hazards.

Following through after contact

Starting a swing to hit the ball

End of follow-through

Tees

Golf balls

Bowls and bowling

Flat-green bowls is played on a flat lawn, or indoors on a carpet. Players roll balls called woods, aiming to get them as close as possible to a smaller white ball called the jack. Tenpin bowling is played on indoor alleys. At each turn, bowlers have two goes to knock down as many pins as possible.

Cue-and-ball games

Games played on billiards and pool tables include snooker and pool. Players use a stick called a cue to propel a white ball on to coloured balls to knock them into a pocket, or pot them. Billiards is played with three balls – one white cue ball for each player and a red ball.

Snooker balls

Playing a hole
Holes range from about 90 m (100 yd) to 550 m (600 yd). The first shot is played from the teeing ground with either a wood, which is used for long shots, or an iron. Irons are used for the next shots until the putting green is reached, when the putter is used.

Wood

Iron

Putter

Golf equipment
Players are allowed up to 14 clubs, which they carry in a bag or trolley. Most players have three or four woods, nine or ten irons, and one putter. The ball is supported for the first stroke of each hole on a small stand, or tee. Players must wear studded shoes.

Flat-green wood

Indoor bowls

Jack

Bowling ball

Pool
Eight-ball is the most widely played variety of pool. To win, one player must pot balls 1 to 7 in any order and then the 8, or black ball. The other player tries to pot balls 9 to 15 and then 8. Players take turns, remaining at the table until they fail to pot a ball, or commit a foul.

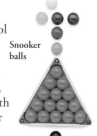

Snooker
Players pot a red for one point, and then any colour for two to seven points, depending on the colour. The colours are replaced until no reds remain and then potted in order of their value.

Pins

Equipment
Woods for bowls are weighted on one side so that they curve when rolled. Bowling balls have holes for the thumb and two fingers. The ten pins are cleared and reset automatically.

FIND OUT MORE   FOOTBALL   HEALTH AND FITNESS   OLYMPIC GAMES   SPORT   TENNIS AND OTHER RACKET SPORTS

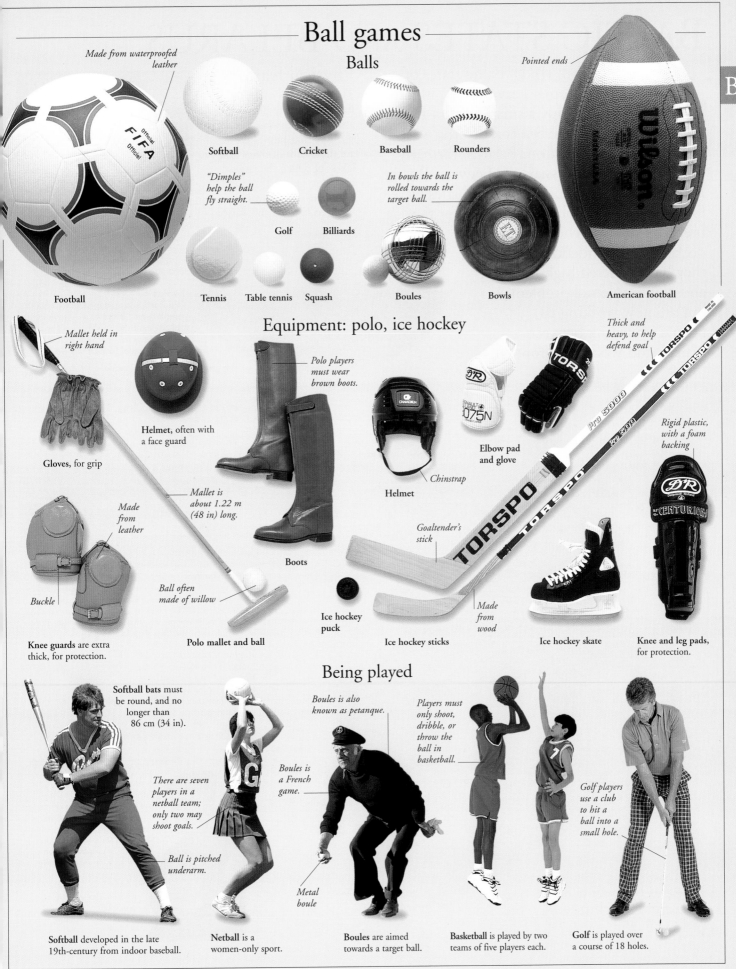

Ball games

Balls

Made from waterproofed leather

Pointed ends

Football

Softball

Cricket

Baseball

Rounders

"Dimples" help the ball fly straight.

Golf

Billiards

In bowls the ball is rolled towards the target ball.

Tennis

Table tennis

Squash

Boules

Bowls

American football

Equipment: polo, ice hockey

Mallet held in right hand

Gloves, for grip

Helmet, often with a face guard

Polo players must wear brown boots.

Thick and heavy, to help defend goal

Helmet

Chinstrap

Elbow pad and glove

Rigid plastic, with a foam backing

Made from leather

Buckle

Knee guards are extra thick, for protection.

Mallet is about 1.22 m (48 in) long.

Ball often made of willow

Boots

Polo mallet and ball

Goaltender's stick

Ice hockey puck

Ice hockey sticks

Made from wood

Ice hockey skate

Knee and leg pads, for protection.

Being played

Softball bats must be round, and no longer than 86 cm (34 in).

There are seven players in a netball team; only two may shoot goals.

Ball is pitched underarm.

Boules is also known as petanque.

Boules is a French game.

Metal boule

Players must only shoot, dribble, or throw the ball in basketball.

Golf players use a club to hit a ball into a small hole.

Softball developed in the late 19th-century from indoor baseball.

Netball is a women-only sport.

Boules are aimed towards a target ball.

Basketball is played by two teams of five players each.

Golf is played over a course of 18 holes.

B

BALTIC STATES AND BELARUS

B

THE THREE Baltic states of Estonia, Latvia, and Lithuania occupy a small area on the Baltic Sea coast to the west of the Russian Federation. Belarus, formerly known as "White Russia", sits between Russia, Poland, and Ukraine. All four countries were former Soviet republics; in 1991, after the break-up of the Soviet Union, they declared independence. Since then, they have suffered high inflation and environmental problems, but are now working to form a trade link between eastern and western Europe.

Physical features

The Baltic states have a flat landscape of plains and low hills, with forests and swampy marshes. There are thousands of rivers and lakes, of which the largest is Peipus, at 3,626 sq km (1,400 sq miles), shared between Estonia and Russia.

Baltic coast and islands
Estonia, Latvia, and Lithuania all have coasts and ports on the Baltic Sea, and ice covers much of the sea in winter. Estonia has the longest coastline, and the country includes more than 1,500 islands that form a barrier protecting the Gulf of Riga.

Forests
Dense deciduous and coniferous forests cover between 30 and 40 per cent of the Baltic region. Belarus is dominated by lakes and thick forests full of wildlife such as deer and mink. The east of Latvia is forested.

Forested Ganja River valley, Latvia

Pripet Marshes
Covering a vast area of southern Belarus, the Pripet Marshes are the biggest wetland area in Europe. They stretch for 40,000 sq km (15,000 sq miles), and are fed by several rivers including the Byerazino and Dnieper. The soils of the Pripet are clay or sandy, and large areas are waterlogged.

Regional climate
Estonia, Lithuania, Latvia, and Belarus have cold winters and cool, wet summers, because of their location on the Baltic Sea. Heavy snow falls during the winter throughout the region, particularly in Belarus.

17°C (63°F)   -5°C (23°F)
668 mm (26 in)

Cultural diversity
Estonia, Latvia, and Belarus have large Russian populations, who were resettled in the Baltic states under communist rule. This has caused some racial tension with ethnic peoples in Estonia and Latvia. In Belarus, where most people are Russian speakers, and Lithuania, where 80 per cent are ethnic Lithuanians, there is social harmony.

Folk dancer, Estonia

Estonia

The smallest and most northerly of the Baltic states, Estonia has a long coastline and beautiful scenery that attracts many tourists from Finland and Scandinavia. Under Soviet rule, its rural economy was transformed. It is now an industrial nation, and most people live in towns. Estonians are closely related to Finns and speak a similar language.

ESTONIA FACTS

CAPITAL CITY	Tallinn
AREA	45,226 sq km (17,462 sq miles)
POPULATION	1,400,000
MAIN LANGUAGES	Estonian, Russian
MAJOR RELIGION	Christian
CURRENCY	Kroon

Tourism
More than one million tourists visit Estonia every year. The medieval buildings of Tallinn, Estonia's capital, are a major attraction, with a wealth of historical monuments. Summer regattas and boating and yachting in the sheltered waters of the Gulf of Riga are also popular.

Flax stems are used to make linen fabric and ropes.

Flax
Textiles made from flax and cotton are among Estonia's leading exports. Flax is harvested at different times for various purposes: young green stems make fine cloth called linen; tougher fibres are used for ropes and mats.

Latvia

Sandwiched in a central position between Estonia and Lithuania, Latvia is a flat country with about 12,000 rivers. Manufacturing, encouraged under Soviet rule, is the basis of the economy. Like the other states in this region, Latvia suffered high inflation during the 1990s. Farming, fishing, and timber are valuable sources of income.

LATVIA FACTS

CAPITAL CITY	Riga
AREA	64,589 sq km (24,938 sq miles)
POPULATION	2,400,000
MAIN LANGUAGES	Latvian, Russian
MAJOR RELIGION	Christian
CURRENCY	Lats

Farming
Latvia has a larger area of fertile land than the other Baltic states. Since independence, the huge state farms introduced by the Russians have been dismantled and are now privately owned. Most are dairy farms.

People
About one-third of Latvians are of Russian origin and there are smaller numbers of Ukrainians and Belarussians. Just over half the population are ethnic Letts, or Latvians, who cling to their cultural heritage. They celebrate many traditional and religious festivals.

Women wear traditional costumes in Latvia's Rites of Spring Festival.

Lithuania

Once a powerful nation, ruling lands that extended to the Black Sea, Lithuania sits south of Latvia. Most people live in the interior of the country, working in industry or farming. The short coastline, fringed with sand dunes and pine forests, is famous for amber. Since 1991, there have been disputes with Latvia over Baltic Sea oil.

LITHUANIA FACTS

CAPITAL CITY	Vilnius
AREA	65,200 sq km (25,174 sq miles)
POPULATION	3,700,000
MAIN LANGUAGES	Lithuanian, Russian
MAJOR RELIGION	Christian
CURRENCY	Litas

Hill of Crosses, near Siauliai, a shrine to honour the dead.

Yellow amber

Amber
The Baltic states produce two-thirds of the world's amber, the fossilized sap of pine trees. Amber is used to make jewellery in shades of yellow, orange, and deep gold.

Religion
By contrast to Estonians and Latvians, who are mainly Protestants, Lithuanians are mostly Roman Catholics. They managed to keep their faith even under Soviet rule, which discouraged religion.

Belarus

Land-locked, and with few natural resources, Belarus suffers great poverty. In 1986, an accident at the Chernobyl nuclear reactor in the Ukraine severely contaminated farmland. Many areas remain unsafe. The shaky economy is based on the manufacture of machines, cars, chemicals, and a large farming sector. Unlike the other Baltic states, Belarus has maintained close political and economic ties with Russia and is taking steps to set up a union.

BELARUS FACTS

CAPITAL CITY	Minsk
AREA	207,600 sq km (80,154 sq miles)
POPULATION	10,100,000
MAIN LANGUAGES	Belarussian, Russian
MAJOR RELIGION	Christian
CURRENCY	Belarussian rouble

Ceramics
Belarus produces many beautifully crafted ceramic and porcelain items, such as vases and ornaments. The country is also known for its high-quality decorated glassware, made by heating sand with salt, limestone, and old glass, then moulding the molten liquid glass.

Food
The national dish of Belorussia is *draniki*, made from fried, grated potatoes, and served with sour cream and pickled berries or beetroot. Soup made from beetroot is also a popular dish.

Draniki   Sour cream

FIND OUT MORE   CHRISTIANITY   FARMING   FESTIVALS   FORESTS   FOSSILS   GLASS   LAKES   NUCLEAR POWER   RIVERS   SOVIET UNION   TEXTILES AND WEAVING

BANGLADESH AND NEPAL

NORTH OF THE BAY OF BENGAL, between India and Burma (Myanmar), is Bangladesh, a poor but fertile country whose low-lying land and repeated flooding has largely dictated its fortunes. Nepal and Bhutan are small Himalayan states, ruled by kings, but slowly adopting democratic ideas. All three countries have a subsistence farming economy, and the majority of the people, who are a mix of Muslims, Hindus, and Buddhists, live in small, rural villages. Manufacturing industries are being developed.

Himalayas
Nepal lies in the highest part of the Himalayas, a vast mountain range that stretches 2,400 km (1500 miles) between India and China. Mount Everest, the world's highest peak at 8,850 m (29,035 ft), is part of the range and several other peaks are more than 6,000 m (19,685 ft) high, including Ama Dablam in Nepal, at 6,856 m (22,493 ft).

Physical features

Bangladesh is dominated by a low-lying plain created by soil caught up and carried on the great Ganges River and its tributaries. Much of the land is less than 15 m (50 ft) above sea-level. By contrast, Nepal and Bhutan sit high in the mountains, with plunging forested valleys watered by many rapid streams.

23°C (73°F)   11°C (52°F)

1,901 mm (75 in)

Regional climate
Bangladesh has a hot tropical climate, and monsoon winds bring heavy floods to 67 per cent of the country. Southern Nepal and Bhutan are hot and wet, but the Himalayas are cold and harsh, with much snow.

Forests
About 70 per cent of Bhutan is forested. Deciduous forests, which include hardwoods such as teak, grow in the south, while thick pine forests cover the steep mountains of central Bhutan. Bangladesh's flat landscape rises in the north and southeast to form wooded hills.

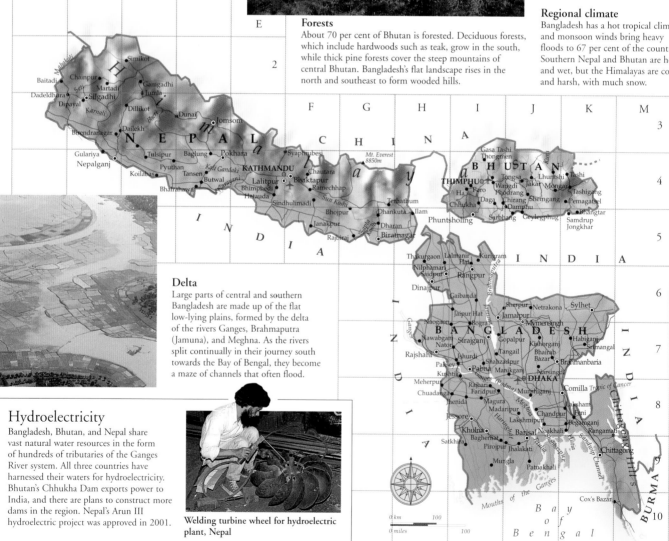

Delta
Large parts of central and southern Bangladesh are made up of the flat low-lying plains, formed by the delta of the rivers Ganges, Brahmaputra (Jamuna), and Meghna. As the rivers split continually in their journey south towards the Bay of Bengal, they become a maze of channels that often flood.

Hydroelectricity

Bangladesh, Bhutan, and Nepal share vast natural water resources in the form of hundreds of tributaries of the Ganges River system. All three countries have harnessed their waters for hydroelectricity. Bhutan's Chhukha Dam exports power to India, and there are plans to construct more dams in the region. Nepal's Arun III hydroelectric project was approved in 2001.

Welding turbine wheel for hydroelectric plant, Nepal

Bangladesh

Formed in 1971 when it became independent of Pakistan, Bangladesh has a troubled political history. Democracy was restored in 1991, after a period of military rule. Bangladesh has one of the world's highest population densities and half of its people live in poverty. The country's vast water resources provide good farming conditions, but floods and cyclones wreak seasonal havoc.

BANGLADESH FACTS

CAPITAL CITY	Dhaka
AREA	144,000 sq km (55,598 sq miles)
POPULATION	140,400,000
MAIN LANGUAGE	Bengali
MAJOR RELIGIONS	Muslim, Hindu
CURRENCY	Taka

Stilt houses
Many people live in houses that are built on stilts to protect them from the frequent floods. The country is overcrowded, and about 75 per cent of the people live in rural communities. Most grow just enough rice to live on, and fish in the Ganges.

Jute rope

Jute
Bangladesh is second only to India in the production of jute, a tough fibre used for sacking, rope, and carpeting. The country provides about 80 per cent of the world's jute fibre. Jute products make up 13 per cent of Bangladesh's exports.

Dhaka
The capital, Dhaka, lies on the Buriganga River, which links ports around the country. This has made it a centre of trade and commerce. The city contains more than eight million people, many of whom live in overcrowded slums.

Textiles
Many Bangladeshis work in the textile industry, with cotton and silk the country's leading fabrics. Ready-made garments are the main product, totalling 60 per cent of exports. Women are the backbone of the textile industry.

Silkworms spin a silky thread up to 1 km (0.6 miles) long.

Nepal

The Himalayas and their forested foothills cover most of this land-locked country. Nepal was an absolute monarchy until 1991, but now has a multi-party constitution. It is one of the world's poorest countries; the people are mostly farmers whose crops depend on the monsoon rains.

NEPAL FACTS

CAPITAL CITY	Kathmandu
AREA	140,800 sq km (54,363 sq miles)
POPULATION	23,600,000
MAIN LANGUAGE	Nepali
MAJOR RELIGIONS	Hindu, Buddhist, Muslim
CURRENCY	Nepalese rupee

People
There is a wide variety of peoples in Nepal, and most are of Indian or Tibetan descent. The Sherpas of the north are skilled, tough mountaineers. About 90 per cent of Nepalese people are Hindus, who combine their religion with Buddhism.

Hindu holy man

Farming
Nepal is dependent on farming, which, with forestry, employs 90 per cent of the work-force. Rice, maize, and sugar are grown on terraces cut into the mountainsides.

Kathmandu
Lying in a valley 1,370 m (4,500 ft) above sea-level, Nepal's capital, Kathmandu, is a city full of ornate temples and shrines. About 400,000 people live in the city, including the Newars of the valley who are famed for their wood carving.

Buddhist temple overlooking Katmandu.

Trekking
Mountain climbing and trekking in the Himalayas attract 450,000 visitors to Nepal each year. Tourism attracts much-needed income, but threatens the ecology.

Bhutan

A small, isolated country, Bhutan is covered in forests and snow-capped mountains. Ruled by a monarch, known as the Dragon King, it is an isolated state, though there are plans for modernization. Three-quarters of the people are of Tibetan descent; the rest are Nepalese or Hindus. Farming, fishing, forestry, and small-scale industry provide jobs.

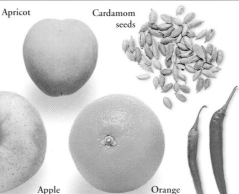

Apricot

Cardamom seeds

Apple

Orange

Chilli peppers

Crops
Less than ten per cent of Bhutan's land can be cultivated, but 90 per cent of the people make a living from farming. Rice, maize, and potatoes are the staple foods, and cash crops, such as apricots, apples, chillies, cardamom, and oranges, for export to other Asian countries, are being developed in the fertile central valleys.

BHUTAN FACTS

CAPITAL CITY	Thimphu
AREA	47,000 sq km (18,147 sq miles)
POPULATION	2,100,000
MAIN LANGUAGE	Dzongkha
MAJOR RELIGIONS	Buddhist, Hindu
CURRENCY	Ngultrum

FIND OUT MORE — ASIA, HISTORY OF · BUDDHISM · DAMS · ENERGY · FARMING · HINDUISM · INDIA · ISLAM · MOUNTAINS AND VALLEYS · RIVERS · TEXTILES AND WEAVING

BARBARIANS

To THE ANCIENT GREEKS, all foreigners or outsiders were known as barbarians, but from the 3rd century on, this term was increasingly applied to nomadic mounted tribespeople from Asia, eastern Europe, and parts of Germany, such as the Huns and Goths. Organized into fearsome cavalry armies, these so-called barbarians caused havoc in their search for land, and were finally responsible for the collapse of the western Roman Empire.

Who were the barbarians?
To most Europeans, barbarian tribes included Huns and Avars (from Asia), and Saxons, Vandals, and Goths (from Germany). Huns migrating from Asia into Europe caused fear among the resident Germanic tribes, who then poured in huge numbers across the Roman Empire's frontiers. In a short time, this migration led to the fall of the empire.

Huns

Huns made bows and arrows out of strips of bone.

Horse saddle

Hunting on the Steppes by Chen Chii-Chung (Sung dynasty)

The Huns were a nomadic Mongol people from the high plains, or steppes, of Central Asia who invaded southeastern Europe in c.370. Fierce in battle and famous for their skill on horseback, they conquered the Ostrogoths and drove the Vandals and other tribes westward.

Under the leadership of Attila they reached their zenith, ravaging the Byzantine Empire and invading Gaul (modern France). In the 5th and 6th centuries, the White Huns, a related people, raided Persia (Iran) and northern India.

Catalaunian Plains
The Huns were deadly in battle as mounted archers. They made short bows of bone, which were light and easy to use while on horseback. They also fought with sabres at close quarters. Under Attila, the Huns were victorious many times, but in 451, they were finally defeated by the Romans and their allies at the Catalaunian Plains, Gaul (now Chalons-sur-Marne, France).

Attila the Hun
Attila (c.406–453) became king of the Huns in 434 jointly with his brother Bleda, whom he murdered in 445. Attila united his people into a vast horde based in Hungary, then waged campaigns to win land and tribute from the Roman and Byzantine empires. Short and crafty, the so-called "Scourge of God" was cruel to his enemies but fair to his own people. He died – possibly of poison – on his wedding night.

Ostrogoths and Visigoths
The Ostrogoths were a Germanic tribe on the Black Sea who were related to the Visigoths from the Danube area. After the Roman Empire fell in 476, the Visigoths adopted Christianity, and translated the Bible from Latin into a "Gothic" script, which was used for centuries in German printing.

Gothic architecture
Many medieval churches and cathedrals were built in the Gothic style. The highly decorative details, such as gargoyles, were believed by Renaissance artists to be "barbarous" when compared with the simplicity of older Roman buildings. So the artists named them after the Gothic tribes that overran Rome.

Notre-Dame gargoyles, Paris, France

Saxons
"The barbarians drive us to the sea, and the sea drives us back to the barbarians; one way or another we die." So wrote a group of 5th-century Britons to their former masters in Rome. The seafaring barbarians threatening them were Saxons, Angles, and Jutes – Germanic tribes of skilled craftworkers and farmers who conquered and settled stretches of fertile Britain from c.500.

Saxon shoulder clasp

Gold and enamel

Gold and garnet

Saxon purse lid

Etched snake designs

Gold

Mosaic glass

Saxon buckle

Richborough Fort
The Romans built bases at Richborough and elsewhere on the southeastern English coast in the 3rd and 4th centuries. From these forts they could see and try to intercept Saxon raiders.

Walls were 1.2 m (4 ft) thick.

British ships destroying Chinese junks

Barbarians in the East
People beyond Europe also believed that outsiders were barbarians. The 18th-century Chinese looked down on "foreign devils", and insisted that all trade between China and the west took place only in the port of Canton. The Japanese actually stopped any foreigners from entering Japan for more than 200 years, until 1854.

FIND OUT MORE · ARCHITECTURE · ANGLO-SAXONS · ROMAN EMPIRE · WARFARE

BATS

WITH ALMOST 1,000 species, bats are the second largest order of mammals after the rodents. They are the only mammals that can truly fly. The name given to their order is Chiroptera, meaning "hand wings". When bats are resting, they hang upside-down. Most bats are nocturnal. They eat a variety of food, which they find either by scent and sight, as fruit bats do, or by using sound waves, a process called echolocation, as insect-eating bats do.

Wing is formed by a membrane stretched over the bones of the fingers and forelimb.

Bat features

A bat's wing consists of an elastic membrane of skin that is stretched between the elongated fingers of its front limb, and back to its hind limb. Bats have lightweight bodies and strong, clawed toes with which they cling to a suitable support.

Insect-eating bats have large ears, which are needed when the animal uses echolocation.

Bats have a clawed thumb on the edge of each wing.

Furred body

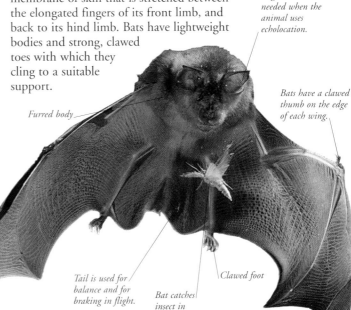

Tail is used for balance and for braking in flight.

Bat catches insect in midair.

Clawed foot

"Fingers"

Greater horseshoe bat

Types of bat

Bats are divided into two groups. These are the Megachiroptera, or megabats, which are the old world fruit bats, and the Microchiroptera, or microbats, sometimes called insect-eating bats.

Megabats

Fruit bats, or megabats, are also sometimes called flying foxes. They live in the tropical and subtropical parts of Africa, Asia, and Australasia. Most megabats eat fruit, but some also feed on flowers, nectar, and pollen.

Large eyes and nose

Epauletted fruit bat

Ears are almost as long as the bat's head and body combined.

Long-eared bat

Microbats

The term insect-eating bats is a misleading name for these bats. Many feed on fruit, meat, fish, pollen, and even blood, as well as insects. Microbats live in both temperate and tropical regions, but in cooler climates they hibernate or migrate for the winter.

Roosts

Bats need a variety of places to roost, or rest. At night they rest between bouts of feeding and often settle to eat large prey. During the day, they need somewhere to sleep and groom. Females choose a safe, warm place to give birth.

Tent bats

Cave habitats

In warm climates, caves provide daytime and nursery roosts, where females give birth and look after their young. Bracken Cave in Texas, USA, has the largest colony in the world with up to 20 million bats.

Free-tailed bats in Bracken Cave

Tree habitats

Microbats often roost in tree holes, such as old woodpecker nests, or cracks caused by storm damage. These Honduran white bats, also called tent bats, build a tent from large leaves.

Hibernation

Bats need to hibernate somewhere cold but where they will be protected from frost, which would kill them. The place where they roost, called a hibernaculum, also has to be damp so that the bats do not dry out. Suitable sites include caves, loft spaces, and tree holes.

Natterer's bat

Echolocation

To find objects in the dark, a microbat makes bursts of high-frequency sound. The sound bounces off objects, such as a moth, and the bat pinpoints the moth's position by listening to the returning echoes.

Insect prey

Returning echoes

Horseshoe bat

How a horseshoe bat catches prey

Horseshoe bats emit sounds through their noses.

1 The "horseshoe" on the bat's nose focuses the sound into a narrow beam. The bat sweeps its head from side to side as it flies along, scanning for insects.

Small eyes

Broad, rounded wings

2 The bat's large, mobile ears pick up vibrations made by the movement of an insect's wings. The bat can tell the size of an insect from the vibrations.

3 When the bat has located its prey, it scoops up the insect in its wings, often eating in midair.

The bat uses its wing membrane to put food in its mouth.

117

B

Feeding

Bats have a wide variety of food sources. Most bats eat insects and can consume huge amounts in one night. The smaller bats, such as pipistrelles, catch tiny gnats and mosquitoes. Larger bats, such as noctules and serotines, feed on cockchafers and dung beetles. Some bats pounce on prey that is on the ground, and pick insects off leaves. Fruit-eating bats live mostly in the tropics, where they have a year-round supply of food.

Bulldog bat

Fishing bats trail their long legs in the water to catch a fish.

False vampire bat

The bat finds its prey using echolocation.

Fishing bats

Some bats use echolocation to detect fish just below the water's surface. Fishing bats have long legs and they fly along the surface and catch the fish with long, sharp claws.

Meat-eating bats

Many larger microbats catch and eat mice, rats, frogs, and lizards. False vampire bats from Asia and America carry their catch to a suitable perch to devour it, using their thumbs and wing membranes to hold the heavy prey.

Vampire bats

True vampire bats feed on the blood of mammals or birds. Using their razor-like incisor teeth, they make a wound on an ear or ankle. As the blood flows, the vampire bat drinks it with a grooved tongue that acts like a drinking straw.

Bat drinking from a donkey.

Incisor teeth

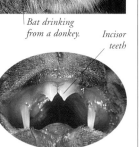

Bats will only eat the pulp of the fruit.

Some nectar-feeding bats hover above the flower.

Spectacled flying fox

Fruit bats

These bats squash ripe fruit against ridges on the roof of their mouth. They spit out the rind and large seeds that are difficult to digest. Fruit bats sometimes eat the fruit in the tree where they pick it, but they may carry it to a safe roost to eat.

Glossophagine bat

Nectar feeders

Trees that are pollinated by bats provide the animals with nectar and pollen as a reward for their services. The tongues of nectar-feeding bats have a brush-like tip which the bats use to lap up the nectar and pollen inside the flowers.

Nursery

Like all true mammals, a female bat carries her young inside her womb until she gives birth. Usually, only one bat is born at a time to minimize the extra weight a pregnant female has to carry in flight. Females gather, often in large numbers, to give birth in a nursery roost.

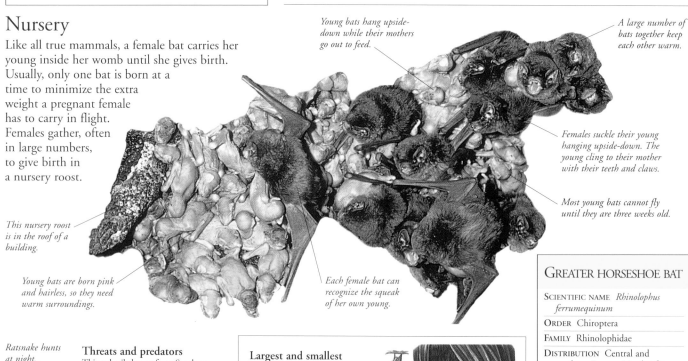

Young bats hang upside-down while their mothers go out to feed.

A large number of bats together keep each other warm.

Females suckle their young hanging upside-down. The young cling to their mother with their teeth and claws.

Most young bats cannot fly until they are three weeks old.

This nursery roost is in the roof of a building.

Young bats are born pink and hairless, so they need warm surroundings.

Each female bat can recognize the squeak of her own young.

Ratsnake hunts at night.

Threats and predators

This red-tailed racer from Southeast Asia, also known as a mangrove ratsnake, catches bats in the tops of mangrove trees. Other animals that prey on bats include bat hawks, owls, and cats. Some of the greatest threats to the survival of bats around the world are habitat destruction, pesticides, and human vandalism. Many species are in danger of extinction.

Largest and smallest

The largest bat is a Malaysian flying fox which can have a wingspan of up to 1.7 m (5.6 ft). The smallest bat is the bumblebee bat, also known as Kitti's hog-nosed bat. This tiny animal is only about 30 mm (1 in) long and weighs only 2 g (0.07 oz).

GREATER HORSESHOE BAT

SCIENTIFIC NAME	*Rhinolophus ferrumequinum*
ORDER	Chiroptera
FAMILY	Rhinolophidae
DISTRIBUTION	Central and southern Europe, North Africa across to Japan
HABITAT	Woodland, pasture, human settlements
DIET	Insects
SIZE	Length: 6–7cm (2.4–2.75 in)
LIFESPAN	Up to 30 years

FIND OUT MORE   CAVE WILDLIFE   CONSERVATION   HIBERNATION   MAMMALS   WHALES AND DOLPHINS

Bats

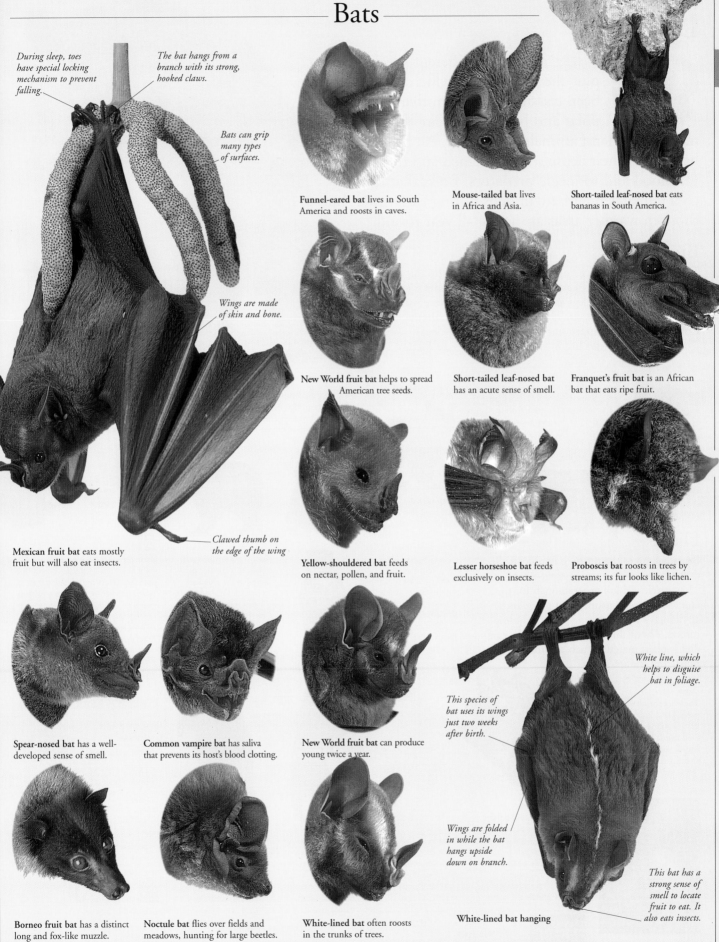

During sleep, toes have special locking mechanism to prevent falling.

The bat hangs from a branch with its strong, hooked claws.

Bats can grip many types of surfaces.

Wings are made of skin and bone.

Mexican fruit bat eats mostly fruit but will also eat insects.

Clawed thumb on the edge of the wing

Funnel-eared bat lives in South America and roosts in caves.

Mouse-tailed bat lives in Africa and Asia.

Short-tailed leaf-nosed bat eats bananas in South America.

New World fruit bat helps to spread American tree seeds.

Short-tailed leaf-nosed bat has an acute sense of smell.

Franquet's fruit bat is an African bat that eats ripe fruit.

Yellow-shouldered bat feeds on nectar, pollen, and fruit.

Lesser horseshoe bat feeds exclusively on insects.

Proboscis bat roosts in trees by streams; its fur looks like lichen.

Spear-nosed bat has a well-developed sense of smell.

Common vampire bat has saliva that prevents its host's blood clotting.

New World fruit bat can produce young twice a year.

This species of bat uses its wings just two weeks after birth.

White line, which helps to disguise bat in foliage.

Wings are folded in while the bat hangs upside down on branch.

This bat has a strong sense of smell to locate fruit to eat. It also eats insects.

Borneo fruit bat has a distinct long and fox-like muzzle.

Noctule bat flies over fields and meadows, hunting for large beetles.

White-lined bat often roosts in the trunks of trees.

White-lined bat hanging

BEARS

THERE ARE SEVEN different species of bear, plus the giant panda which has recently been classified as a primitive bear. The polar and brown bears are the largest meat-eating land animals alive today. All bears rely heavily on their acute senses of smell and hearing to find food and to locate predators. Bears that live in cool climates hibernate in dens during the winter, but those in warmer areas are active all year round.

Brown bears have a large hump of muscle and fat.

Brown bears

There are nine subspecies of brown bear. The largest is the Kodiak bear found on islands in Alaska. It may stand 3.5 m (12 ft) tall on its hind legs and is one of the most powerful animals in North America. The grizzly bear, also of North America, has white-tipped fur, giving it a "grizzled" look. The other brown bears live in Europe and temperate Asia.

North American brown bear

Fishing
Bears of North America have a rich source of salmon when the fish swim up rivers to spawn. The bears may stand in the water and catch fish in the air as they leap up a waterfall.

Large canine teeth and powerful jaws

Asian black bear feeding

Diet

Bears belong to the order of mammals called carnivores, meaning meat-eaters. They catch and kill other animals for food and eat carrion, but they will take almost any kind of food they can find, including insects. About three-quarters of most bears' diet is plant material, such as fruits, nuts, roots, and shoots.

Paws
There are five clawed toes on a bear's paws. The animals use their forepaws to gather food and manipulate small food items. They can kill another animal with one blow from a paw, or use their long claws to dig up roots, and open insects' nests.

Kermodes bear
Most American black bears are black, but some are brown, beige, or blue-black. Small isolated populations of white black bears, called Kermodes bears, live on the coast of British Columbia, Canada.

Types of bear

Brown bear This bear lives across the northern hemisphere, but in small populations only. It has disappeared from many areas.

Shaggy black fur

Sloth bear A long-coated bear from India and Sri Lanka, the sloth bear eats mainly termites, which it sucks up through its lips.

Spectacled bear The only South American bear, this rare animal lives on the wooded slopes of the Andes. It eats mostly plant material, especially fruit, but will eat meat if it is available.

Sun bear This bear from south-eastern Asia is the smallest bear. It has short, dense fur, with a yellow mark on its chest. It has a long tongue with which it licks up ants and termites.

A crescent of white fur accounts for this bear's other name of moon bear.

Polar bear This white-coated bear is the most carnivorous, eating mainly seals and fish. It lives on the Arctic coast.

Asian black bear An agile climber, this bear lives in woods of south-eastern Asia, from Afghanistan to China and Japan.

American black bear Found across North America, this bear will raid tents, cars, and dustbins for food.

Cubs' games are practice for adult conflicts.

Cubs
A female bear gives birth to her cubs in a den, where she stays with them for up to two or three months. Each litter usually contains one to three cubs, which are born helpless and weigh only a tiny percentage of their mother's weight. They develop quickly but will stay with their mother until nearly full-grown. This may be for as long as two or three years in the case of the larger bears. Female bears make good mothers and will defend their cubs ferociously.

GRIZZLY BEAR

SCIENTIFIC NAME *Ursos arctos horribilis*

ORDER Carnivora

FAMILY Ursidae

DISTRIBUTION Northwestern North America

HABITAT Mountains, forests, wilderness

DIET Almost anything, including berries, leaves, roots, small animals, fish, and carrion

SIZE Length: 1.8–2.8 m (6–9 ft) Weight: 160–230 kg (350–500 lb)

LIFESPAN 25–30 years

FIND OUT MORE

ASIAN WILDLIFE   HIBERNATION   NORTH AMERICAN WILDLIFE   PANDAS AND RACCOONS   POLAR WILDLIFE

BEATLES, THE

JOHN LENNON PLAYED rhythm guitar, Paul McCartney played bass, George Harrison played lead guitar, and Ringo Starr played the drums. Together they formed The Beatles – the most famous and influential group in the history of popular music. Their songs dominated the 1960s, when people believed that music could change the world, and the songwriting skills of Lennon and McCartney have ensured that their music lives on. Their songs still influence many musicians today.

Early life
All four Beatles were born in the English port of Liverpool and played in various rock and roll groups in the late 1950s. In 1960–61 John, Paul, George, and drummer Pete Best played at the Star Club in the German port of Hamburg, which taught them much about live performance. Back in England, The Beatles played regularly at Liverpool's Cavern Club. In 1962 their manager, Brian Epstein (1934–67), replaced Best with Ringo Starr as drummer.

Live performances
The Beatles began by playing live in clubs in and around Liverpool, UK. Their lively performances were an exciting contrast to the staid and solid players who dominated popular music at the time. The Beatles' reputation was based on the songwriting abilities of John Lennon and Paul McCartney. At first they both wrote traditional rock and roll songs about friendship and love, but as the pair developed, their subjects became more varied.

The Beatles play a football stadium in the USA

Beatlemania
In January 1964 , "I Want To Hold Your Hand" reached the top of the American music charts. A new word, "Beatlemania", entered the language as thousands of screaming fans mobbed the group wherever they went. Within months, The Beatles were the biggest music group in the world.

Recording
In 1966 The Beatles stopped performing live, and spent more time in the studio. There they experimented with different instruments, such as string orchestras and sitars, and with new recording techniques. Their masterpiece, *Sgt. Pepper's Lonely Hearts Club Band*, took many months to produce and made use of techniques such as tape-splicing and multi-track recording.

Plates with pictures of The Beatles

Memorabilia
The Beatles were one of the first bands to be featured on a host of souvenirs and memorabilia. The four were immortalized on everything from mugs and T-shirts to buttons, badges, posters, and other souvenirs. Many fans bought everything that featured their four favourite musicians.

Toy guitar with pictures of The Beatles

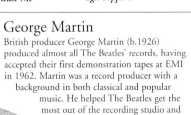
Please Please Me   *Sgt. Pepper's*

George Martin
British producer George Martin (b.1926) produced almost all The Beatles' records, having accepted their first demonstration tapes at EMI in 1962. Martin was a record producer with a background in both classical and popular music. He helped The Beatles get the most out of the recording studio and the wide range of instruments used in their records, translating many of their ideas into polished musical form.

The last albums
By 1969 the group was falling apart as conflicts grew between the four members and their musical interests took different directions. Their last albums to appear were *Abbey Road* (1969) and *Let It Be*, which was released in 1970 but recorded before *Abbey Road*. The Beatles disbanded later that year. All four continued their careers as solo musicians.

The Beatles recording tracks for *Let It Be*

THE BEATLES

1940 John Lennon and Richard Starkey (Ringo Starr) born.

1942 Paul McCartney born.

1943 George Harrison born.

1957 John and Paul form first group, The Quarrymen.

1962 First record with EMI; Ringo Starr joins as drummer.

1964 Beatles head charts in USA.

1967 *Sgt. Pepper's Lonely Hearts Club Band* released.

1970 *Let It Be* released; Beatles disband.

1980 John Lennon shot dead.

1997 Paul McCartney knighted.

2001 George Harrison dies.

FIND OUT MORE   MUSIC   ORCHESTRAS   ROCK AND POP   SOUND RECORDING

B

BEES AND WASPS

THEIR STINGS USUALLY bring these insects to our attention. However, by pollinating crops and killing pests, bees and wasps play vital roles in the world we live in. There are 115,000 species of bees and wasps. Most, such as carpenter bees, are solitary, but some, including the honeybee and common wasp, are social insects, living in complex colonies. People keep honeybees in hives for their honey and wax.

Features of bees and wasps

Bees and wasps are similar in appearance, with narrow waists between the thorax and abdomen. Most species have two pairs of wings and are excellent fliers. They have two compound eyes and three small eyes, giving them good eyesight. Bees are hairier than wasps, and are normally herbivores, while wasps are generally carnivores.

Two pairs of wings for rapid flight

Compound eye

Waist

Pointed abdomen

Claws **Common wasp** *Antenna*

Jointed legs with claws **Honeybee**

Stings

Only the females of most species of bees and wasps have stings. The sting evolved from the egg-laying tube. Wasps have unbarbed stings that they can use repeatedly for defence or to kill prey. Bees have barbed stings that cannot be extracted, causing the bee to die. Consequently, bees only sting if provoked.

Bee sting *Abdomen*

Poison sac

The sting may be painful and, in rare cases, fatal.

Queen

Social bees and wasps have a queen in their colonies which lays eggs and runs the colony. Honeybees have one queen per hive; if two appear at the same time they fight to the death. Queens produce queen substance, a chemical that stops full sexual development of the workers.

Worker

Queen is larger than workers.

Life cycle of a honeybee

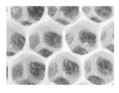

1 The queen bee spends most of her day checking cells and laying single eggs in them. She lays more than 2,000 eggs a day when there is a plentiful food supply. After 1–2 days, larvae hatch from the eggs.

2 Workers feed the larvae honey, pollen, and royal jelly. If fed extra royal jelly, larvae become queens. The larvae grow and moult, and on day 5 they spin a silk cocoon and pupate. Workers seal the cell with wax.

3 By about day 21 pupation is complete and the new adult bees have to chew their way out of the cell. Once the external skeleton has hardened and they are able to walk, the bees begin their tasks within the nest.

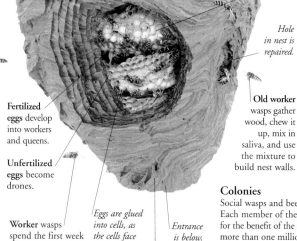

Protective layers of paper

Common wasp's nest

Pupae in cocoons

Hole in nest is repaired.

Fertilized eggs develop into workers and queens.

Unfertilized eggs become drones.

Old worker wasps gather wood, chew it up, mix in saliva, and use the mixture to build nest walls.

Worker wasps spend the first week of their adult life cleaning the nest. Once able to fly, they leave the nest and hunt for insects to feed to the grubs (larvae) in the nest.

Eggs are glued into cells, as the cells face downwards.

Entrance is below.

Nest walls are striped because the wood is collected from many sources.

Nests

Common wasps' nests have the texture of paper and are made of chewed-up wood, saliva, and water. They are usually built in hollow trees or below ground. Other wasps, such as oriental stenogaster wasps, build nests out of mud. Honeybee nests are made of wax produced from glands on the bees' abdomens. Wasp and bee nests usually contain combs – layers of six-sided cells in which the young grow.

Colonies

Social wasps and bees live in large groups called colonies. Each member of the colony has a specific duty and works for the benefit of the whole nest. Wasp colonies may contain more than one million individuals; bees' nests can exceed 70,000 in number, consisting of one queen, about 69,000 workers, and 300 drones. Both queen wasps and queen bees run their nests; drones are fertile males who mate with the queen and die soon after; workers perform many tasks from building the nest to foraging for food. Drones appear before swarming time. This is when new queens leave the nest, mate with the drones, and set up nests on their own.

Food supplies

Wasps eat fruit and insects, which they also feed to their young. Adult and larval bees feed on nectar and pollen that the adults collect. Bees do a dance to tell other bees the location of the flowers, and navigate there by using the Sun.

Pollen carried on legs

Pollen, nectar, and honey
Bees carry pollen on hairs on their legs and store nectar in their stomachs. At the nest, they regurgitate the nectar. Water evaporates, concentrating the nectar to form honey. Honey and royal jelly, a high-protein substance made by workers, are also fed to the larvae.

Types of bee and wasp

Parasitic bees
These solitary bees abandon their eggs in other bees' nests. The young then destroy the original eggs and wait to be fed by the host.

Hornets
Hornets are among the largest of the social wasps. They live in large colonies and defend their nests aggressively.

Hunting wasps
These solitary wasps paralyse other insects with a sting and lay their eggs on them. The young hatch and feed on the live host.

HONEYBEE	
SCIENTIFIC NAME	*Apis mellifera*
ORDER	Hymenoptera
FAMILY	Apidae
DISTRIBUTION	Worldwide
HABITAT	Nests are built in hollow trees in the wild; also cultivated in hives
DIET	Pollen and nectar from flowers
SIZE	Length: workers: 10–15 mm (0.4–0.6 in); queen: 15–20 mm (0.6–0.8 in)
LIFESPAN	Workers live for 2–3 months; queen lives for 3–5 years

FIND OUT MORE

ANIMAL BEHAVIOUR • ANTS AND TERMITES • ARTHROPODS • EGGS • FLIGHT, ANIMAL • FLOWERS • INSECTS • NESTS AND BURROWS • WOODLAND WILDLIFE

BEETHOVEN, LUDWIG VAN

FROM HIS BIRTH in Bonn in 1770 to his death in Vienna in 1827, Ludwig van Beethoven's lifetime spanned a period of revolution and transformation. Despite a tragically unhappy life, beset with family problems and deafness, he became the major composer of his time. His symphonies, sonatas, and chamber music expanded the Classical forms, introducing exciting new musical ideas that ushered in the fiery Romantic style. Unlike previous composers, Beethoven tried to remain independent, writing for himself rather than for a single rich patron. Independence allowed him to develop his own personal expressive musical style.

Beethoven's birthplace

Early life
Beethoven was born in Bonn, Germany. His childhood was not a happy one. His father, himself a musician, forced Ludwig to practise and perform in public at an early age, hoping he would become a child prodigy. When his mother died and his father lost his job, young Ludwig had to provide for the whole family.

Vienna

Beethoven's first visit to Vienna was cut short by his mother's illness, but he returned in 1792 to study with the composer Haydn. He soon established himself as a pianist and teacher, and settled there for the rest of his life. However, as his deafness worsened, he suffered from depressions and raging tempers, and withdrew from social life. He found consolation in composing music which expressed both his despair and his optimism and joy.

Performance
Until the onset of deafness, Beethoven earned his living as a teacher and performer. He was a superb pianist, whose emotional performances could move his audience to tears. Many of his piano compositions, especially the sonatas and concertos, explore the expressive capabilities of the instrument and are amongst his finest works.

Deafness
In his late twenties, Beethoven's hearing began to fail. By 1820, he was almost totally deaf. Unable to hear what he was playing, he could not earn a living from performing. Instead, he concentrated on composing.

Ear trumpets

Notebooks
We can get a good idea of how Beethoven worked by looking at his manuscripts and notebooks. They show how he revised his work until he was completely satisfied with it. He wrote quickly and furiously, often crossing out and rewriting whole sections of the music.

Beethoven's Broadwood grand piano

The symphonies

Symphonies before Beethoven's time were orchestral works that followed a fairly set pattern, but, in his nine symphonies, Beethoven developed the form into a large and expressive work. From the third symphony, the *Eroica*, on, these works became longer and more adventurous, using new instruments and even vocalists and a choir in the ninth symphony.

Manuscript of the *Pastoral* symphony

Chamber music
Much of Beethoven's music is for small groups, such as the string quartet. This chamber music was often written for amateur players, but Beethoven found it provided an ideal way of expressing his new musical ideas.

Pastoral symphony
This symphony is unusual because it describes a scene: the countryside around Vienna where Beethoven loved to walk. It is full of the sounds of the country, including imitations of birdsong and a thunderstorm.

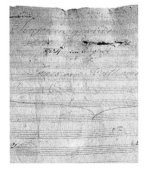

Eroica symphony
Beethoven originally dedicated this symphony to his hero Napoleon, but was disgusted when Napoleon proclaimed himself emperor. He scratched out the dedication, but kept the title *Eroica* (heroic).

LUDWIG VAN BEETHOVEN

1770 Born in Bonn, Germany

1792 Moves to Vienna, studies with Joseph Haydn

1796 Begins to go deaf

1802 Writes a letter, known as the "Heiligenstadt Testament", to his brothers, describing his unhappiness about his deafness

1803 *Eroica* symphony

1808 *Pastoral* symphony

1809 Piano Concerto No 5, "The Emperor"

1824 *Choral* symphony

1827 Dies in Vienna, Austria; some 10,000 people attend his funeral

FIND OUT MORE MOZART, WOLFGANG AMADEUS   MUSIC   MUSICAL INSTRUMENTS   NAPOLEON   ORCHESTRAS

BEETLES

THERE ARE AT LEAST 350,000 types of beetle. They make up 30 per cent of all animals and 40 per cent of all insects. They range in size from the 2 mm (0.08 in) long battle d'or beetle to the giant timber beetles, which grow up to 150 mm (6 in) long. Beetles live almost everywhere, from hot deserts to snowy mountain tops, but they are most numerous in the tropics. They eat a wide range of food, including crops, and are considered pests, but they perform a valuable role by breaking down dead animals and plants and returning the nutrients to the soil.

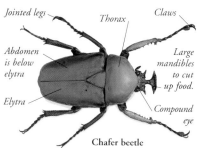

Jointed legs *Thorax* *Claws*
Abdomen is below elytra *Large mandibles to cut up food.*
Elytra *Compound eye*

Chafer beetle

Features of a beetle

Beetles have three body parts – the head, thorax, and abdomen. They have compound eyes, and antennae used for touch and smell. Their forewings have developed into hard wing cases, or elytra, which protect the hind wings. The wings, elytra, and six legs are fixed to the thorax.

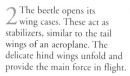

Feathery antennae spread to sense the air currents.

Beetle often opens and shuts elytra several times before taking off.

2 The beetle opens its wing cases. These act as stabilizers, similar to the tail wings of an aeroplane. The delicate hind wings unfold and provide the main force in flight.

Elytra raised

How a beetle flies

1 Large beetles, such as this cockchafer beetle, take a few seconds to get airborne. First the beetle pumps air into its body by expanding its abdomen.

Cockchafer beetle

Wings beat during flight.

Outstretched hind legs help streamline the beetle.

Wings unfurling, ready to beat.

3 The cockchafer beetle pushes off with its legs and starts to beat its hind wings. Within a few seconds the hind wings reach the 200 beats per second needed for take-off, and the wing cases help to provide lift. During flight, the beetle uses 100 times more oxygen than it does at rest.

Wood-boring beetles

Some beetles remain as larvae for many years. Jewel beetle larvae may live in wood for over 40 years. They eat the wood, making tunnels through it, leaving small holes.

Jewel beetle

Reproduction

Most beetles undergo complete metamorphosis. Larvae hatch from eggs laid by an adult female and are the main feeding stage in a beetle's development. Once the larvae have finished growing, they turn into pupae. Inside, they change, or metamorphose, into the adult beetle that will eventually emerge from the pupa.

Mealworm beetle larva
Inside – the larva's body breaks down and changes into the adult.
Pupa develops for about 6 weeks.
Adult beetle has emerged.

Giant mealworm beetle

Fighting

Male beetles often fight with each other over a possible mate. They use their mandibles (mouthparts) as weapons. Stag beetles have huge, but not very powerful mandibles, which they use mainly to impress rivals. Despite their size, the mandibles do little harm. In this way, fighting is more symbolic, and both beetles live to fight and mate again.

The beetle clasps his rival in his huge jaws and tries to throw it on its back.

Stag beetles fighting

Feeding

Beetles' feeding habits, like beetles themselves, are diverse. Many, including spider beetles, feed on decaying leaf litter; others consume both living and dead wood. Some beetles, such as tiger beetles, actively hunt for live food. Scavengers, such as hide beetles, feed on rotting vegetation, dead animals, and dung. Some beetles, for example, rove beetles, are even parasites, living on creatures such as bats.

Ladybird feeding on an aphid.

Ladybirds

Ladybirds are found worldwide. They prey on small insects, such as aphids and scale bugs. In this way they are helpful animals to have in the garden and can be used to control pests instead of using polluting chemicals.

Defence

Well-armoured external skeletons and camouflage protect many beetles from predators. The bombardier beetle has an ingenious method of defence. It ejects a hot mixture of potent chemicals from its rear with an audible pop.

Bombardier beetle

Water beetles

Many beetles live in water. Diving beetles use their oar-like legs to push themselves through the water after their prey. Whirligig beetles scavenge for food that floats on the water's surface. They have special eyes that are split in two. One half looks downwards for fish, while the top half scans the air for predatory birds.

Whirligig beetle

COCKCHAFER BEETLE

SCIENTIFIC NAME
Melolontha melolontha

ORDER Coleoptera

FAMILY Scarabaeidae

DISTRIBUTION Europe and western Asia

HABITAT Gardens and woods

DIET Adult feeds on sap and nectar; the larvae feed on the roots of plants, such as rose and oak

SIZE Larvae: 4 cm (1.6 in) in length; adults: 2–3 cm (0.8–1.2 in) long

LIFESPAN Larvae take about 2 years to become adults; adults live for about 2–3 months

FIND OUT MORE — ARTHROPODS • DESERT WILDLIFE • GRASSLAND WILDLIFE • INSECTS • WOODLAND WILDLIFE

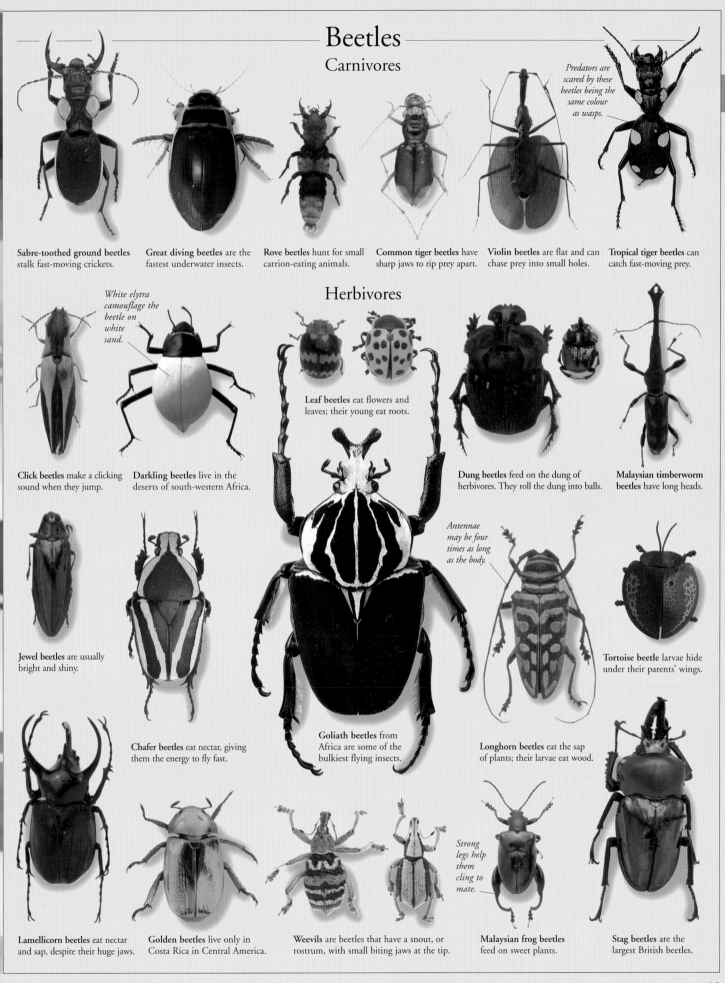

Beetles

Carnivores

Predators are scared by these beetles being the same colour as wasps.

Sabre-toothed ground beetles stalk fast-moving crickets.

Great diving beetles are the fastest underwater insects.

Rove beetles hunt for small carrion-eating animals.

Common tiger beetles have sharp jaws to rip prey apart.

Violin beetles are flat and can chase prey into small holes.

Tropical tiger beetles can catch fast-moving prey.

Herbivores

White elytra camouflage the beetle on white sand.

Leaf beetles eat flowers and leaves; their young eat roots.

Click beetles make a clicking sound when they jump.

Darkling beetles live in the deserts of south-western Africa.

Dung beetles feed on the dung of herbivores. They roll the dung into balls.

Malaysian timberworm beetles have long heads.

Antennae may be four times as long as the body.

Jewel beetles are usually bright and shiny.

Tortoise beetle larvae hide under their parents' wings.

Chafer beetles eat nectar, giving them the energy to fly fast.

Goliath beetles from Africa are some of the bulkiest flying insects.

Longhorn beetles eat the sap of plants; their larvae eat wood.

Strong legs help them cling to mate.

Lamellicorn beetles eat nectar and sap, despite their huge jaws.

Golden beetles live only in Costa Rica in Central America.

Weevils are beetles that have a snout, or rostrum, with small biting jaws at the tip.

Malaysian frog beetles feed on sweet plants.

Stag beetles are the largest British beetles.

BELGIUM

THIS SMALL, DENSELY POPULATED country in northwest Europe borders France, Germany, and the Netherlands. Its current borders were settled in 1919, after World War I (1914–18). Today, Belgium is a highly developed industrial nation with a thriving economy. As a founder member of the European Union since 1957, and of the Benelux alliance (with the Netherlands and Luxembourg), Belgium plays an important role in European and international affairs.

BELGIUM FACTS

CAPITAL CITY Brussels

AREA 30,510 sq km (11,780 sq miles)

POPULATION 10,300,000

MAIN LANGUAGES Dutch, French, German

MAJOR RELIGION Christian

CURRENCY Euro

LIFE EXPECTANCY 78 years

PEOPLE PER DOCTOR 263

GOVERNMENT Multi-party democracy

ADULT LITERACY 99%

Physical features

In the north of Belgium is a flat plain stretching from Flanders to the Dutch border. The central plateau is bounded to the south by the Meuse and Sambre rivers. The Ardennes Plateau extends into Luxembourg and France.

Ardennes Plateau
The Ardennes Plateau covers 10,000 sq km (3,860 sq miles) in southern Belgium, Luxembourg, and northern France. Crossed by deep river valleys such as the Semois and Meuse, this upland area is rocky and heavily wooded and has spectacular limestone caves.

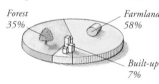

River Meuse
The Meuse flows slowly through gentle farmland and steep-sided valleys for 950 km (590 miles) from its source in France, west to east across Belgium, to the Dutch coast.

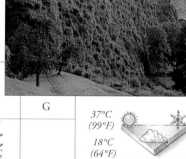

Map with grid references A–G, 1–6:
North Sea, Zeebrugge, Oostende, Brugge, Sint-Niklaas, Flanders, Roeselare, Gent, Aalst, Ieper, Kortrijk, Mouscron, Mechelen, Turnhout, Antwerpen, Genk, Hasselt, Leuven, Tienen, Tournai, La Louvière, Seraing, Liège, Verviers, Mons, Charleroi, Namur, Dinant, BRUSSELS, BELGIUM, FRANCE, NETHERLANDS, GERMANY, Ardennes, Meuse, Sambre, Ourthe, Bastogne, Vianden, Sûre, Diekirch, LUXEMBOURG, Arlon, Moselle, Esch-sur-Alzette

0 km 50 / 0 miles 50

Climate
The Belgian climate is generally mild, but the skies are often cloudy. Rainfall is plentiful, especially in the mountains of the Ardennes where winter snow lingers. Summers tend to be short.

37°C (99°F) / -18°C (0°F) / 18°C (64°F) / 2°C (36°F) / 825 mm (32 in)

Land use
Much of Belgium is built-up and densely populated. Farmers produce cereals, fruit, vegetables, and sugar beet and raise cattle, sheep, and horses. Belgium has few natural resources and uses over 60 per cent nuclear power.

Forest 35% / Farmland 58% / Built-up 7%

People
In southern Belgium people speak Walloon, a dialect of French. In the north people speak Dutch, formerly called Flemish. A few people in the east speak German.

311 per sq km (805 per sq mile) / 97% Urban / 3% Rural

Brussels
With about a million inhabitants, Belgium's capital, Brussels, is the centre of government and trade. With three languages – Dutch, French, and German – it is a truly international city and the administrative headquarters of the European Union.

Gothic buildings in Brussels' Grand Place

Industry
Belgium has highly developed business and service industries, such as banking and insurance. The once-thriving coal and steel industries on the rivers Meuse and Sambre are now in crisis and are being rapidly replaced by new industries producing pharmaceuticals, chemicals, electrical equipment, and textiles. Belgium is one of the world's largest exporters of chocolate, and produces fine beers.

Belgian chocolates

Luxembourg

This tiny country shares borders with Belgium, Germany, and France. Its people enjoy low unemployment and Europe's highest living standards. It is known as a banking centre.

Finance centre
Despite its tiny size, Luxembourg is a key member of the European Union. The headquarters of the European Parliament and the European Court of Justice are based in Luxembourg City.

LUXEMBOURG FACTS

CAPITAL CITY Luxembourg

AREA 2,585 sq km (998 sq miles)

POPULATION 442,000

MAIN LANGUAGES French, German, Letzeburgish

MAJOR RELIGION Christian

CURRENCY Euro

FIND OUT MORE — EUROPE | EUROPE, HISTORY OF | EUROPEAN UNION | FARMING | NETHERLANDS | TRADE AND INDUSTRY | WORLD WAR I

BENIN EMPIRE

ESTABLISHED IN THE 11TH CENTURY, Benin was a powerful West African kingdom which flourished in the forests west of the River Niger. The wealth of Benin was based on trading: trans-Saharan trade with African savannah kingdoms, which linked the Benin Empire with the Mediterranean and the Middle East, and, coastal trade with Europeans. Benin's obas, or kings, controlled the trade networks. Immensely powerful, they lived in the royal palace in the capital city of Benin. In 1897, the British conquered Benin and ended the empire.

Empire boundaries

The Benin Empire was in modern Nigeria, where Benin City now stands. Both it and the modern republic west of Nigeria take their name from the old empire.

Sahara Desert

• Benin City

Benin City

The empire of Benin was centred on the impressive capital, Benin City. A wide road ran through the centre, and a huge earthwork wall surrounded the city. The wall acted as a defence and would have taken some considerable time to build. Its size stood as a symbol of the influence held by Benin's oba. The city housed the oba's royal palace, and areas called wards where the craftspeople lived.

Engraving of Benin City

Craft guilds

Guilds of craftspeople, such as leather workers, blacksmiths, drummers, weavers, carpenters, ivory carvers, and brass casters lived in Benin City. The brass casters formed one of the most important guilds. They made the distinctive "bronze" heads and plaques for the royal palace.

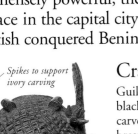

Spikes to support ivory carving

Only obas wore neck rings.

Bronze head

Benin "bronze" heads are actually made of brass. They commemorated dead obas and their family members, court ceremonies – even European traders. Carved ivory adorned the heads, which were kept in shrines in the royal palace.

Memorial head of an oba

Obas and courtiers wore ornamental weapons on ceremonial occasions.

Oba flanked by two courtiers

Brass plaques

Carved plaques decorated the wooden pillars that supported the oba's palace roof. They depicted court life and important events, such as the presentation of gifts from the oba to his courtiers.

Ivory carving

Ornately carved ivory tusks were among Benin's luxury goods. All trade in ivory was controlled by the oba. If elephant hunters killed an elephant, they had to give one tusk to the oba before they could sell the other.

Carved human figures

Carvings often told of the oba's wealth and military strength.

Carved elephant's tusk

Trade

For centuries, Benin traded with African kingdoms to the north, including the Songhai Empire. The arrival of the Europeans in the 1400s disrupted these traditional relationships and established new trading outlets.

Brass manilla

Brass manillas

In Benin, merchants used bracelet-shaped objects called manillas to buy expensive purchases, but they used tiny, white cowrie shells for smaller items.

Merchants

Travelling by sea, Portuguese traders bought slaves, peppers, cloth, gold, and ivory from Benin, and paid with manillas, cowrie shells, and guns.

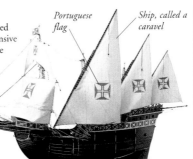

Portuguese flag

Ship, called a caravel

British conquest

In 1897, in revenge for an attack on a British party, the British burnt and looted Benin City, exiled the oba, and brought Benin under colonial rule.

Oba Ewuare the Great

The warrior-king Ewuare (r.1440–80) rebuilt Benin City and, under his rule, the surrounding territory reached its greatest extent. Ewuare also established a tradition of secure hereditary successsion.

Ewuare's leopard-shaped arm ornament

Timeline

11th century Benin Empire founded in the forests of Nigeria.

1450 Peak of Benin Empire.

1486 First European to visit Benin is Portuguese explorer, Afonso d'Aveiro; shortly afterward a Benin chief establishes a trading store for the Portuguese.

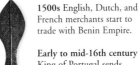

1500s English, Dutch, and French merchants start to trade with Benin Empire.

Early to mid-16th century King of Portugal sends Christian missionaries to Benin to convert Oba Esigie, and build churches.

Benin ornamental sword

1688 Dutchman Olfert Dapper writes a history of Benin.

1700s Empire weakened by succession struggles.

1897 Britain takes Benin City by force.

1960 Nigeria, including the old Benin Empire, gains independence.

FIND OUT MORE

AFRICA, HISTORY OF • EMPIRES • EXPLORATION • METALS • SONGHAI EMPIRE

BICYCLES AND MOTORCYCLES

B

FUN, AND ENVIRONMENTALLY friendly, the bicycle is the simplest form of mechanical transport. A bicycle, or bike, is a two-wheeled machine that converts human energy into propulsion; a motorcycle, or motorbike, is a bicycle with an engine. Modern motorcycles are complex, with engine sizes ranging from 50cc (cubic centimetres) to more than 1,000cc. In many countries, such as China, most people travel or transport goods by bicycle. Across the world, bicycles and motorcycles are used for sport and leisure.

Cannondale SH600, hybrid

Reducing drag
Drag is the resistance of air that can slow down a bicycle or motorcycle and its rider. It is reduced by creating a streamlined shape for the air to flow around – some competitive bicycle riders even shave their legs to achieve this streamlined effect.

Time-trial bike

Parts of a bicycle

From a mountain bike to a racing bike, or a hybrid (a cross between the two), all bicycles are built in a similar way. Designed to be easy to pedal and comfortable, the weight is also important, as it affects the speed at which the bike can be propelled.

Saddles are adjustable, moving up and down to accommodate different riders.

Gears, operated by levers, move the chain between different-sized gear wheels, to change the speed at which the wheels turn.

Handlebars may be dropped for riding crouched.

Brakes are controlled by pulling levers on handlebars, which force brake blocks against wheel rims to slow the bicycle down.

Seat post slides in and out of frame to adjust seat level.

Frame, made from metal tubes, to support the rider.

Brake cable

Chain wheel

Spokes are arranged to create a strong but lightweight wheel.

Pedals, attached to the chain wheel, are pushed to turn the wheel.

Wheel hub secures the wheel to frame.

Tyres fitted on a metal wheel rim give a smooth, quiet ride over small bumps; mountain bikes have fatter tyres to handle rough and rocky terrain.

Parts of a motorcycle

Like a bicycle, a motorcycle has a frame, a rear wheel that drives it along, a front wheel for steering, and controls on the handlebars. Like a car, it has an internal combustion engine and suspension. The suspension supports the motorcycle's body on the wheels, and stops it being affected by the bumping of the wheels on the road.

Two-stroke engine with one cylinder. Larger motorcycles have more cylinders.

Lightweight frame

Fuel tank

Speedometer

Ignition switch

Indicator and warning lights

Engine rev counter

Motorcycle instrument panel
Motorcycles have an instrument panel in the centre of the handlebars. Control switches for lights and indicators can be operated with hands on the handlebars.

Front suspension

1992 Yamaha FZR1000 Exup

Three-spoke alloy rear wheel, supported by suspension strut.

Motorcycle tyres grip the road even when the motorcycle leans over at corners. These are smooth, treadless, "slick" racing tyres.

Riding a motorcycle
A motorcycle rider changes speed by twisting the right-hand handlebar grip, and changes gear by flicking a foot lever up or down. The front brakes are operated by hand, and the rear brakes by foot. To go round a corner, the rider turns the handlebars and leans the motorcycle over.

Small engine for speed and economy

Open "step in" frame

SFX moped

Mopeds and scooters
Small motorcycles used for short journeys in towns and cities are called mopeds or scooters. They have small engines, so they cannot go very fast, but are very economical. Mopeds, restricted to a 50cc engine, have pedals which the rider can use on steep hills.

Timeline

1839 Kirkpatrick MacMillan, a Scot, invents a lever-driven bicycle.

1863 The French Michaux brothers build the first pedal-powered bike, a velocipede.

1868 The Michaux brothers add a steam engine to a bike, creating the first motorcycle.

1885 In England, James Starley makes modern-style bicycles.

1885 German Gottlieb Daimler builds an engine-powered tricycle (below).

1901 The 1901 Werner is the first practical road-going motorcycle.

1914–18 Motorcycles used extensively in World War I.

1963 Dutchman Van Wijnen designs what will become the Ecocar – covered pedal-powered transport.

| FIND OUT MORE | AIR | CARS AND TRUCKS | ENGINES AND MOTORS | ENERGY | FORCE AND MOTION | MACHINES, SIMPLE | MOTOR SPORTS | POLLUTION | SPORTS | TRANSPORT, HISTORY OF |

Bicycles

Criterium racer allows the rider to pedal round corners easily, especially in races.

5-speed Peugeot is a traditional "ladies" bike – without a crossbar.

Mountain bikes, ideal for off-road cycling, have rugged frames and fat tyres.

BMX (Bicycle Motocross) bikes are used for rough terrain and tricks, such as "wheelies".

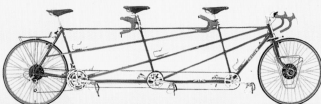

Triple tandems have three sets of pedals for three riders, linked by a chain to the back wheel.

Pedicabs are pedal-powered taxis. This one was made in 1980, in Bangladesh.

Tricycles have three wheels for additional balance.

Kingcycle Bean, 1990, is designed to reduce drag for extra speed.

French Velocar, 1933, is a recumbent, which allows the rider to sit back while pedalling.

Motorcycles

Harley Davidson, 1942, was adapted for military use, but was based on the civilian model.

Harley Davidson Knucklehead 61E, 1936, took the lead in American design; its engine resembled a clenched fist.

Harley Davidson Hydra Glide, 1951, has a classic chopper look with the machine stripped down to the bare essentials.

Heinkel Perle, 1956, has all the wires and cables running from the handlebars through the frame.

BMW R/60, 1956, has links to vary the angle between the "Steib" sidecar and the bike.

"Mod" scooters were popular in the 1960s: the more mirrors and lights, the more fashionable they were.

BMW R75/5, 1971, is a touring bike that combines reliability with comfort.

Honda GL1500/6 Gold Wing, 1991, has a 1500cc engine, an extra pair of cylinders, and luxuries such as a cassette player.

Husqvarna Motocross TC610, 1992, is a racing motorcyle, for driving through fields or mud.

BIG BANG

AN INCREDIBLE EXPLOSION called the Big Bang is believed to have created the Universe. Observations of galaxies and heat radiation from space have helped confirm this theory. Astronomers are now working to explain exactly what happened from the point of the Big Bang explosion which created everything in today's Universe – matter, energy, space, and time – to the present Universe with its galaxies, stars, planets, and us.

Steady State theory

In the late 1940s and the 1950s, the Steady State theory was as popular as the Big Bang theory. It proposed that the Universe looked the same at any place and at any time. Although expanding, it would stay unchanged and in perfect balance. Material was being continuously created to keep the density of the Universe constant. As scientists found proof for the Big Bang, the Steady State theory was largely abandoned.

A Steady-State universe now (left) and later in time (right). The galaxies have moved apart, but new ones (coded orange) have been created to take their place. The density stays the same.

Georges Lemaître

In 1931, Belgian cosmologist Georges Lemaître (1894–1966) was the first to put forward the theory that the Universe started from a dense, single unit of material in a big explosion. The name Big Bang followed in 1950, introduced by Fred Hoyle, a British astronomer and supporter of the Steady State theory.

Origin of the Universe

One of the most difficult problems facing scientists in the 20th century was to explain how the Universe was created. The Universe is changing, but from what and to what? The Steady State theory suggested that the Universe had no beginning or end. The alternative, and now generally accepted, theory is the Big Bang. It proposes that the Universe was created in an explosion 15 billion years ago. From very small and simple beginnings it has grown vast and complex.

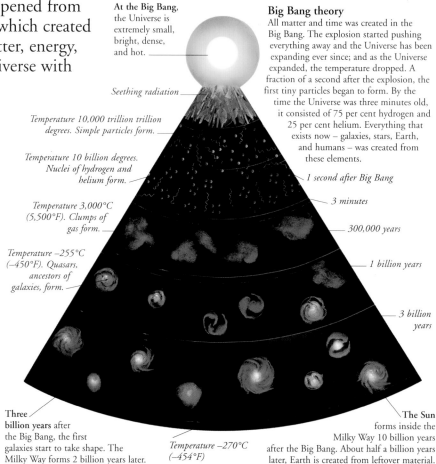

At the Big Bang, the Universe is extremely small, bright, dense, and hot.

Seething radiation

Temperature 10,000 trillion trillion degrees. Simple particles form.

Temperature 10 billion degrees. Nuclei of hydrogen and helium form.

Temperature 3,000°C (5,500°F). Clumps of gas form.

Temperature –255°C (–450°F). Quasars, ancestors of galaxies, form.

Three billion years after the Big Bang, the first galaxies start to take shape. The Milky Way forms 2 billion years later.

Temperature –270°C (–454°F)

Big Bang theory

All matter and time was created in the Big Bang. The explosion started pushing everything away and the Universe has been expanding ever since; and as the Universe expanded, the temperature dropped. A fraction of a second after the explosion, the first tiny particles began to form. By the time the Universe was three minutes old, it consisted of 75 per cent hydrogen and 25 per cent helium. Everything that exists now – galaxies, stars, Earth, and humans – was created from these elements.

1 second after Big Bang

3 minutes

300,000 years

1 billion years

3 billion years

The Sun forms inside the Milky Way 10 billion years after the Big Bang. About half a billion years later, Earth is created from leftover material.

Expanding Universe

In the 1920s, analysing starlight from galaxies showed that the galaxies are moving away from Earth. This is true of galaxies in every direction from Earth. Over time, the Universe is becoming larger and less dense. The idea that the Universe started in an explosion from a single point grew out of observations that the Universe is expanding.

Background radiation

The heat produced by the Big Bang has been cooling ever since. It now has a temperature of –270°C (–454°F), detected as microwave radiation from all over the sky. The false-colour map shows variations in the temperature 300,000 years after the Big Bang. The blue (cooler) patches are gas clouds, from which the galaxies formed.

Redshift: The faster a galaxy is moving away, the more the wavelength of its starlight is stretched, or redshifted.

The lines are shifted towards the red end of the spectrum.

Lines on the spectrum reveal a galaxy's speed.

More distant galaxies are speeding away faster than closer ones. Their light has a greater redshift.

Future of the Universe

Nobody knows for certain what is going to happen to the Universe. At present, it is getting larger and less dense. Most astronomers believe there will be a time when it stops expanding. But there is disagreement about what happens then: will the Universe live on for ever, wither and die, or start to contract?

Big Crunch

The Universe may end in a Big Crunch if it starts to contract until it is hot and dense once more. But even this may not mean the end of the Universe. The Big Crunch might be followed by another Big Bang explosion, and the whole process could start over again.

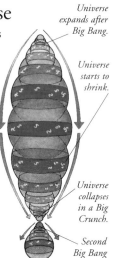

Universe expands after Big Bang.

Universe starts to shrink.

Universe collapses in a Big Crunch.

Second Big Bang

FIND OUT MORE · ASTRONOMY · BLACK HOLES · GALAXIES · GRAVITY · STARS · TIME · UNIVERSE

BIOLOGY

WHEN YOU LOOK at a running horse, you know immediately that it is alive; a beach pebble, by contrast, is non-living. What distinguishes the two is life, or the state of being alive. Biology is the study of life and living things, and it can be divided into two main fields: zoology and botany. People who study biology are known as biologists; the living organisms they study range from animals such as horses to micro-organisms such as green algae. All use energy obtained from food and released by respiration in order to fulfil their natural processes.

Classifying living things

There are around 2 million species of living organisms, and biologists classify them into groups. The largest and most general group is called a kingdom. There are five kingdoms: Monera (bacteria), Protista (protozoa and algae), Fungi, Plantae (plants), and Animalia (animals).

Number of lifeforms in the world

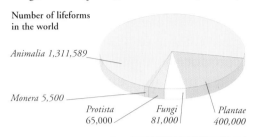

Animalia 1,311,589

Monera 5,500

Protista 65,000

Fungi 81,000

Plantae 400,000

Branches of biology

Biology covers a number of different studies. Ecology examines how living things interact and where they live. Physiology looks at how organisms work. Genetics is concerned with how characteristics inherited from one generation pass to the next. Other branches include anatomy, taxonomy, microbiology, and parasitology.

Bird skeleton

Anatomists study skeletons to understand how an organism functions.

Anatomy
Anatomy is the study of the structure of living organisms. Anatomists investigate the shape and form of the parts that make up organisms. This analysis allows them to work out things such as how bats and birds are able to fly.

Case displays butterflies and moths

Taxonomy
The science of classifying the millions of living things into groups of related organisms is called taxonomy. Scientists called taxonomists identify and name organisms, and then group them together according to the characteristics they share and their common ancestry.

Microbiology
Micro-organisms are living things that are too small to be seen without a microscope. Microbiology is the study of all aspects of the biology of these tiny organisms, which include bacteria, viruses, protists, and some types of fungi such as yeasts.

Compound microscope

Parasitology
Parasites live in or on another organism and exist at its expense; the study of parasites is called parasitology. Fleas are parasites that suck blood from their host. Tapeworms live in and feed in their host's intestine.

Magnified flea image

Flea uses needle-like mouth part to suck blood.

Zoology

Zoology is the branch of biology that is concerned with the study of animals. Animals are an amazingly diverse group of living organisms and encompass everything from sponges, spiders, and earthworms to lobsters, cats, and chimpanzees. Zoologists study the structure of animals, how their bodies function, and how they live and behave in their natural environment.

Lorenz

Ducklings imprinted on Lorenz instead of their mother.

Ethology
The study of animal behaviour is called ethology. Austrian zoologist Konrad Lorenz (1903–89) helped establish the science of ethology. He discovered imprinting, a rapid learning process that occurs early in life. Imprinting to food, surroundings, or mother, happens instinctively during a short, fixed timespan early in life.

Kew Gardens, London, England

Botany

Botany is the study of plants. Plants are diverse organisms, encompassing everything from mosses and ferns to trees, cacti, and flowers. They make their own food by a process called photosynthesis which transforms sunlight into energy. Botanists are concerned with all aspects of the structure, function, and ecology of plants.

Work of a biologist
Biologists are trained in all branches of biology, but usually focus on one specific area. Their research might involve observing animal behaviour, investigating plant photosynthesis, or studying ecosystems.

Petri dishes contain control samples.

Biologist at work in a laboratory

Rachel Carson
In 1962, the American marine biologist and writer Rachel Carson (1907–64) published a book called *The Silent Spring*. In it, she warned that the indiscriminate use of pesticides and weedkillers was poisoning the natural world. Her pioneering book was fundamental in starting the environmental movement and in making ecological information accessible to the public.

FIND OUT MORE — ANIMAL BEHAVIOUR • ANIMALS • ECOLOGY AND ECOSYSTEMS • GENETICS • MICROSCOPIC LIFE • PARASITES • PHOTOSYNTHESIS • PLANTS

BIRDS

IN THE LIVING WORLD, only birds, insects, and bats are capable of powered flight. Birds are the largest and fastest of these flying animals, and are the only ones that have feathers. There are about 9,000 species of bird, and they live in a huge range of different habitats – from deserts to the open oceans. They eat a variety of food, which they find mainly by sight. All birds reproduce by laying eggs. Most look after their young until they can fend for themselves.

Wings almost touch during the upstroke.

Fanned tail feathers act as a brake.

Flight feathers are spread out as the bird prepares to land.

Pigeon in flight

Feet are held against the body during flight.

Bird features

Birds have a lightweight skeleton and their feathers give them a smooth outline, which helps them move easily through the air. They do not have any teeth, but they have a hard beak instead. Birds use their beaks for eating, and also for many tasks that other animals carry out with their front legs and feet, such as grasping items, or tearing up food.

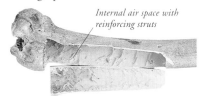

Internal air space with reinforcing struts

Legs and feet
A bird's feet and lower legs are usually covered with scales. Muscles that move them are close to the body. The feet are shaped according to their use.

Beak
A bird's beak is covered with keratin – the same substance that makes up human fingernails. The keratin keeps growing so that the edges of the beak do not wear away.

Bone structure
Most of the larger bones of a bird are hollow, which saves weight. They contain air spaces that connect to the special air sacs the bird uses when it breathes. Some diving birds have solid bones to make diving easier.

Skeleton
Birds have fewer bones than reptiles or mammals, and many of the bones are fused together. A large flap called the keel sticks out of the breastbone and anchors the muscles that power the wings.

Wings
The bones in a bird's wing are similar to those in a human arm. Most birds use their wings to fly. Strong muscles pull the wings downward when the bird flies; other muscles fold them up when not in use.

Feathers

Birds use their feathers to fly, and also to keep warm and dry. Each feather is made of fine strands called barbs that carry rows of smaller barbules. In some feathers, the barbules lock together with hooks to produce a smooth surface needed for flying through the air. In others, they stay partly or fully separate. These feathers are soft and fluffy for warmth.

Microscopic hooks lock barbules together.

Macaw flight feather

Curved tip with interlocking barbules

A hollow quill anchors the feather in the bird's skin.

Continuous curved surface

Central quill

Breeding colours
Male birds often have bright colours which attract mates. In some species, these colours disappear at the end of the breeding season when the birds moult and a new set of feathers grows. In other species, such as pheasants, the colours are permanent.

Down feathers
These short fluffy feathers do not have hooked barbs. They form an insulating layer next to a bird's skin. They trap air, which helps to stop heat from escaping from the bird's body.

Body feathers
The tips of these feathers overlap like tiles on a roof, giving the bird a smooth shape. The fluffy base of each feather is close to the body and helps to save heat.

Flight feathers
These feathers are strong but flexible. They provide lift when the bird is airborne. Birds have to preen them carefully to keep them in good condition.

Tail feathers
A bird uses its tail feathers for steering and braking. Some male birds have long or brightly coloured tail feathers. These play an important part in courtship.

B

Breeding

Birds lay their eggs either directly on the ground or in a nest. One parent – or both – keep the eggs warm by sitting on them, or incubating them. Young birds hatch from eggs at different stages of development. Some can look after themselves almost immediately; others rely on their parents for food and protection.

Eggs
Birds' eggs have a hard shell. Ground-nesting birds often lay eggs that match their background. Birds that nest in trees often lay plain eggs.

Helpless young
Tree-nesting birds usually produce poorly developed young without feathers. The young stay in the nest until they are ready to feed themselves.

Well-developed young
The young of most ground-nesting birds can feed within hours of hatching. They soon leave the nest and follow their mother.

Foster parents
Brood parasites are birds that trick others into raising their young. Here a reed warbler is feeding a cuckoo that hatched in its nest.

B

Senses

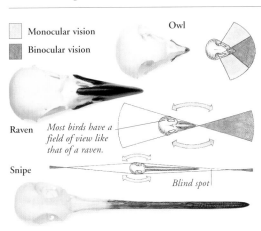

- ☐ Monocular vision
- ◼ Binocular vision

Owl

Raven

Most birds have a field of view like that of a raven.

Snipe

Blind spot

Vision
Birds that hunt, such as owls, have eyes at the front. This restricts their field of view, but they can judge distances accurately. Shorebirds, such as the snipe, have eyes at the side. They can spot danger in any direction, including behind.

For most birds, vision is by far the most important sense. It guides them to their food and helps them to avoid their many enemies. Hearing plays a part in helping birds to communicate, and is important to birds that hunt in the dark. The sense of smell is far less vital to birds than it is to many other animals, although some birds, such as the kiwi, use it to find food.

Crane
Like most birds, a crowned crane has keen eyesight. Its eyes are so big that they almost meet in the centre of the skull. Its ear openings are at the base of its crown, but they are hidden by short feathers. Its nostrils are in its beak.

Crown of spiky feathers

Crowned crane

Flight

This complex way of moving requires superb co-ordination. Some birds stay airborne almost entirely by flapping, but others hold their wings out and glide through the air, using the natural curve of their wings to provide lift. During flight, a bird adjusts the shape of its wings to alter its speed and height.

A pigeon's wings allow good manoeuvrability when extended, and fast flight when partly closed.

A kestrel's large wings provide lift as the bird flaps them non-stop while it hovers in the air.

A grouse's wings are shaped for load-bearing rather than speed. A grouse flies only in short bursts.

A peregrine falcon's slender wings partly fold up when it dives out of the sky on to its prey.

Wing shapes
Birds have evolved a variety of wing shapes that enable them to fly in different ways. Some wings provide lots of lift but do not work well at speed. Others create as little friction as possible when they cut through the air, allowing a bird to fly faster.

Flightless birds
During the course of evolution, some birds have given up being able to fly. Flightless birds do not need a light body, and although some are quite small, they include the biggest birds that have ever lived.

Largest and smallest
The world's heaviest bird is the ostrich. It weighs up to 125 kg (275 lb). This is about 80,000 times heavier than the rare bee hummingbird, the smallest bird. This tiny bird's eggs are the size of peas.

The flightless rhea comes from South America.

Feeding and diet

Birds spend much of the time looking for food. To be able to fly, birds need food that provides them with lots of energy. Many of them eat small animals, which they catch either on land, in the air, or in water. Others visit plants and eat fruits, seeds, nectar, and pollen. Some have a mixed diet. Unlike mammals, only a few birds eat grass or the leaves of other plants.

Fish eaters
The great blue heron catches fish by stabbing them with its beak. Other fish eaters snatch their prey with talons, dive-bomb them from above, or chase them through the water.

Seed eaters
Different birds eat different seeds. They usually crack open the seed's husk before eating the food inside. The goldfinch is a typical seed eater. It feeds on thistles.

Insect eaters
Insect-eating birds search for their food on the ground or on plants, or snap it up in mid-air. The goldcrest often feeds high up in trees. Like other small insect eaters, it is expert at spotting insects hidden on leaves or bark.

Meat eaters
Many birds eat small animals, but owls and birds of prey specialize in hunting larger animals, such as mammals, reptiles, and other birds. A hooked beak allows them to tear up their food before swallowing it.

FIND OUT MORE

| ANIMAL BEHAVIOUR | BIRDS OF PREY | EGGS | FLIGHT, ANIMAL | FLIGHTLESS BIRDS | NESTS AND BURROWS | OWLS AND NIGHTJARS | SKELETON | SONGBIRDS |

Birds

Fish and meat eaters

Large eyes

Black-crowned night heron hunts for fish mainly after dark.

Inca tern flutters in the air before diving down to snatch fish from the surface of the sea.

Spectacled owl has keen eyesight and hearing for catching small animals.

Harris's hawk uses its hooked beak to tear off meat before swallowing it.

Flamingo feeds with its head down, trailing its beak through the water.

Kookaburra is a member of the kingfisher family and feeds in woodland and forests.

Seed eaters

Scarlet eyestripe

African pygmy goose uses its broad beak to collect seeds floating on the water.

Patagonian conure lives in open grasslands of Argentina and Chile.

Mourning dove feeds on the ground in North America.

Eurasian goldfinch has a fine beak and extracts seeds from flowers.

Common waxbill is a common African finch that feeds in open grassland.

Sparrows have short, stout beaks that can crack the husks from small seeds.

Insect eaters

Bushy crest

Kentucky warbler has a narrow beak, ideally shaped for picking up small insects.

Ochre-bellied flycatcher chases after insects and catches them on the wing.

Flycatchers wait on a perch for insects to fly by that they can catch.

Didric cuckoo of Africa specializes in feeding on hairy caterpillars.

Striated yuhina of Asia picks insects off leaves, and often searches under the leaves.

Racquet-tailed roller often feeds on ants and termites from the ground.

Nectar eaters

Bright yellow throat

Blue-crowned hanging parrot has a brush-tipped tongue that helps it to collect nectar and pollen.

Duyvenbode's lory feeds on flowers of New Guinea forest trees, lapping up nectar with its tongue.

Yellow-fronted woodpecker feeds on fruit, probing deep into flowers to reach their nectar.

Rufous hummingbird pumps nectar into its mouth with its tongue.

Booted racquet-tail has quite a short beak, and feeds at flowers with spreading petals.

Fruit eaters

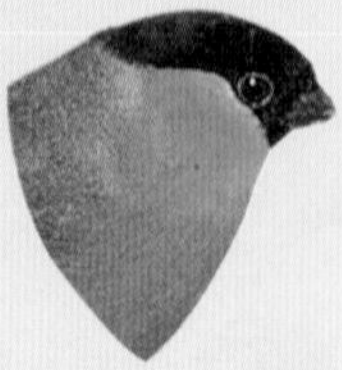

Bill has serrated edges.

Eurasian bullfinch feeds on buds as well as fruit, using its short powerful beak.

Bearded barbet feeds mainly on figs, and uses its heavy bill to dig nest holes in wood.

Chestnut-eared aracari uses its long bill to reach for fruit on the end of long branches.

Fire-tufted barbet of Malaysia eats insects as well as fruit.

Splendid glossy starling gathers in isolated trees that carry ripe fruits.

Long-tailed starling searches for fruit in trees along forest edges.

Mixed food eaters

Eurasian jay feeds on acorns in autumn and winter, but many foods during the rest of the year.

Alpine chough eats small animals and seeds, and also scavenges animal remains.

Blue magpie eats seeds and fruits, and small animals including lizards and snakes.

Swainson's thrush eats insects, spiders, and fruit, particularly in winter.

Red-capped manakin hovers in front of plants to eat the fruit, and also eats insects.

Red-throated ant tanager catches flying insects, and also eats fruit.

BIRDS OF PREY

MOST BIRDS OF PREY, INCLUDING EAGLES, hawks, and falcons, kill and eat live animals. They soar high above the ground or dart among trees, using their excellent eyesight to search for their prey. Once they spot a victim, they attack with their sharp talons, then tear up their food with their hooked beaks. Not all birds of prey feed in this way. A few species eat unusual foods, such as snails or nuts. Vultures eat carrion – animals that are already dead. They often wait for another animal to make a kill and then swoop down to the ground to feed on the remains of the carcass.

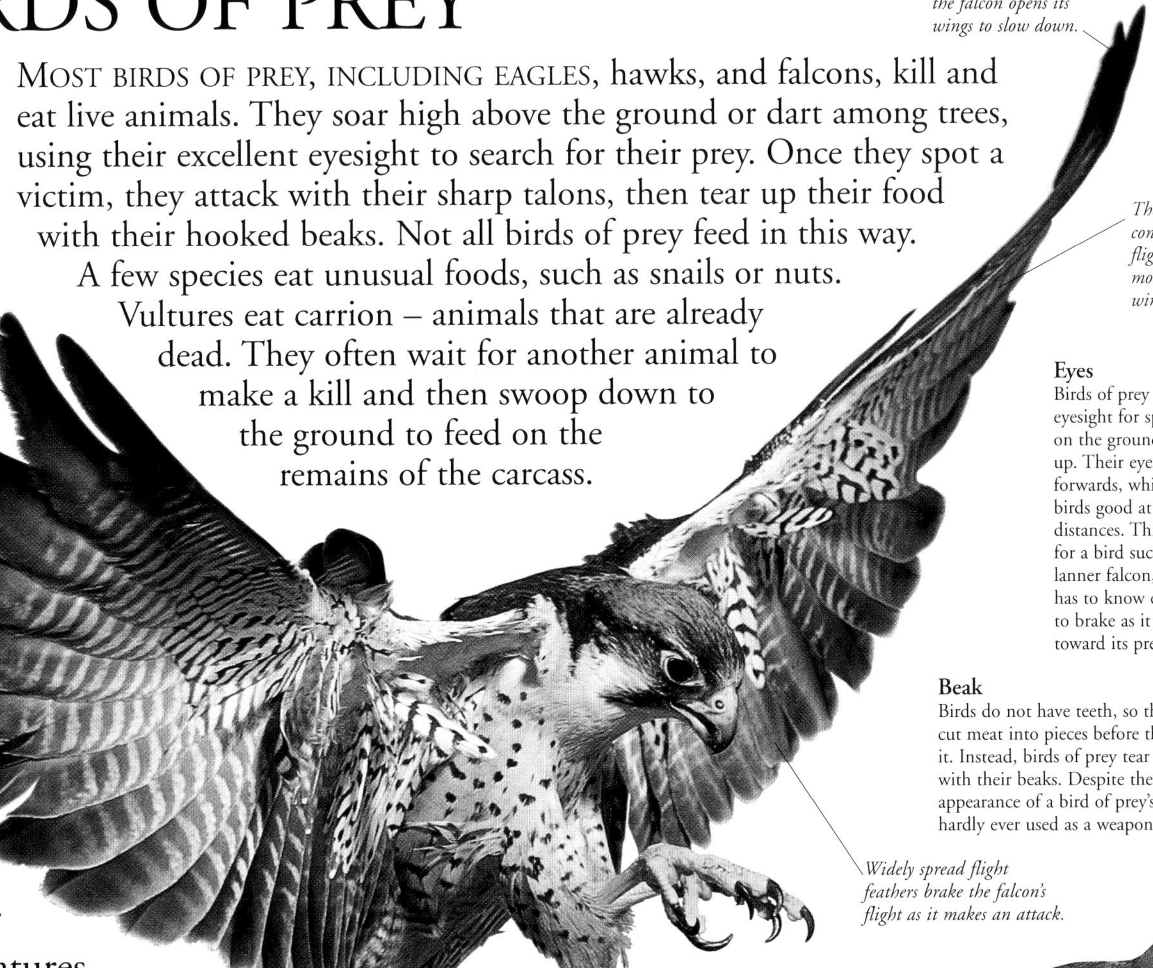

At the end of a dive, the falcon opens its wings to slow down.

The falcon controls its flight by moving its long wing feathers.

Long broad wings with finger-like tips

Eyes
Birds of prey have superb eyesight for spotting prey on the ground from high up. Their eyes face forwards, which makes the birds good at judging distances. This is essential for a bird such as the lanner falcon, because it has to know exactly when to brake as it hurtles toward its prey.

Beak
Birds do not have teeth, so they cannot cut meat into pieces before they swallow it. Instead, birds of prey tear up their food with their beaks. Despite the ferocious appearance of a bird of prey's beak, it is hardly ever used as a weapon.

Widely spread flight feathers brake the falcon's flight as it makes an attack.

Bird of prey features
With their forward-facing eyes, sharp claws, or talons, and hooked beak, birds of prey are perfectly adapted for hunting and feeding on meat. Most species have feathers covering the upper legs. These are for warmth and protection.

Lanner falcon
This falcon lives in desert and savannah areas of southern Europe, Africa, and the Middle East. Like other falcons, it catches prey by folding its wings back and falling on it in a steep dive. Falcons also attack birds in mid-air by diving on them from above.

Talons
Birds of prey have large feet with long toes. Each toe ends in a talon, which stays sharp by flaking into a point as it grows. The birds use their talons to kill food, and carry it away. Many species can lift more than half their own weight.

Tail feathers are used to steer in flight.

Chukar partridge is prey of the falcon.

Flying styles
Most large birds of prey, such as eagles, look for food while soaring on currents of rising air. This uses little energy, allowing the birds to fly long distances every day. Smaller species, such as hawks, usually fly in short bursts. Kestrels are unusual in being able to hover in the air.

Splayed feathers reduce air turbulence.

Flight path of kestrel

Kestrel can see small animals on the ground.

Long, narrow wings

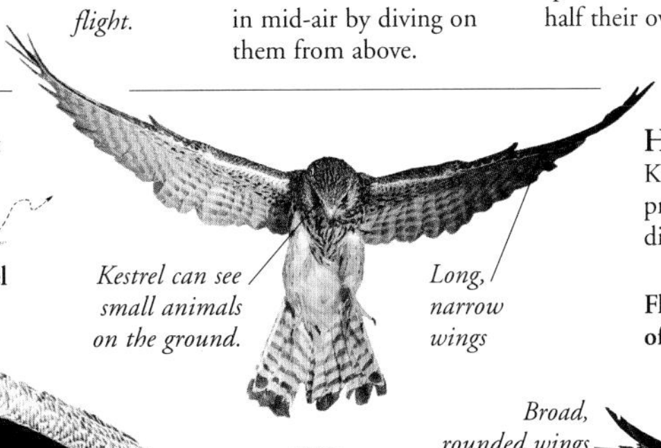

Hovering
Kestrels hover close to the ground while looking for prey. This uses a lot of energy, but the kestrels can dive quickly on anything that moves below them.

Flight path of goshawk

Broad, rounded wings

Long, broad wings

Soaring
Eagles, buzzards, and vultures soar by riding on currents of rising air. They spiral around slowly as they soar upwards, keeping their wings straight and steady.

Low-level flight
Hawks usually hunt by flying in short bursts. They are highly manoeuvrable, and can swerve between trees and over hedges, using surprise to catch small birds.

Flight path of eagle

Roosting
These turkey buzzards from North America have gathered in a tree to roost, or settle for the night. Many vultures roost high in trees or on rocky ledges, because this makes it easier for them to take off and become airborne when the day begins.

Vulture guards carrion while companion eats.

Long neck enables the vulture to reach into a carcass.

Vultures feeding on carrion

White-backed vulture
With a wingspan of more than 2.5 m (8 ft), this huge vulture soars high over open country in southern Europe, Asia, and Africa. Like most other vultures, it has a bare head and neck. If it had long feathers, they would become soaked with blood when it feeds, as it tears the meat from inside a carcass with its beak.

Bare head and neck for ease of cleaning

Carrion eaters

Instead of hunting live animals, vultures feed on the remains of ones that are already dead, carrion. Vultures live in open places, such as deserts, grasslands, and mountains, and find their food by soaring and looking for animal carcasses from the air. Vultures have large beaks, but their talons are weak.

Feeding
Vultures have keen eyesight. If one vulture spots a carcass, and drops down to feed, others quickly follow. Soon vultures arrive from all around. The largest and most dominant species feed first, leaving the smaller species to fight over the scraps.

Specialist eaters

During millions of years of evolution, some birds of prey have developed highly specialized diets as well as specific techniques to deal with their food. Most of these specialist feeders eat animal food, but a few are vegetarians. Some species of bird have learned to live alongside humans, particularly in urban environments, and they eat the variety of food scraps that people throw away.

Egyptian vulture
The Egyptian vulture is one of only a few birds that uses tools to obtain food. It eats ostrich eggs, which it breaks open by picking up stones and hurling them against the shell until it breaks. As well as in Egypt, it lives in other parts of Africa, Europe, and Asia.

Egyptian vulture

Secretary bird

Eyes face to the side instead of the front.

Slim, athletic build for hunting on the ground in open country

Feathery quills, like those once used for writing, give the secretary bird its name.

Lightly built with long wings

Long tail feathers provide balance.

Snail kite

Snail kite
The snail kite lives in marshy places from the southern USA to Argentina in South America. It feeds almost entirely on freshwater snails, which it snatches from the water with one of its feet. It then hooks out the snail's body with its long slender beak.

Palm-nut vulture
The diet of this African vulture is based mainly on the fruits of oil palms, but it eats some small animals. Unlike other vultures, it does not have to fly long distances in search of food, and spends most of its time in trees.

Secretary bird raises its crest of black feathers to attract a mate.

Brightly coloured face

Tough scales protect the legs from poisonous snake bites.

Secretary bird
This highly unusual bird of prey from Africa hunts on the ground. It has long strong legs, and kills animals by stamping them to death. The secretary bird often feeds on snakes, and when attacking uses its wings like a shield to protect itself.

Largest and smallest
The Andean condor is the largest bird of prey, with a wingspan of more than 3 m (10 ft). It is a carrion eater. The smallest birds of prey are pygmy falcons and falconets, which feed mainly on flying insects. Some are only 15 cm (6 in) long.

LANNER FALCON

SCIENTIFIC NAME	*Falco biarmicus*
ORDER	Falconiformes
FAMILY	Falconidae
DISTRIBUTION	Southern Europe, Africa, and the Middle East
HABITAT	Scrub and desert
DIET	Birds, small mammals, and lizards
SIZE	Length, including tail: male – 37 cm (14.5 in); female – 47 cm (18.5 in)
LIFESPAN	About 10 years

FIND OUT MORE

AFRICAN WILDLIFE   BIRDS   DESERT WILDLIFE   FLIGHT, ANIMAL   MOUNTAIN WILDLIFE   OWLS

Birds of prey
Eagles, hawks, and falcons

Large broad wings

Tail is fanned out to provide lift as the kestrel hovers.

Common kestrel hovers to find its prey, instead of chasing it like other falcons.

Tawny eagle is a scavenger, feeding on carcasses, and even human rubbish. It also steals from other birds of prey.

Goshawk hunts in forests and often catches birds in mid-air.

Black eagle is from southern Asia. It flies over forests and often snatches birds from their nests.

Feathers down to the toes as in all true eagles

American kestrel is a small falcon. It often feeds on insects.

Golden eagle lives in remote places throughout the northern hemisphere.

Harris's hawk sometimes hunts in groups, which is unusual for a bird of prey.

Imperial eagle is rare. It lives in Spain, eastern Europe, and Asia.

Caracara has long legs and toes that enable it to hunt on the ground.

Peregrine falcon is the fastest bird in the world.

Bataleur is almost tailless. This African eagle has an unusual zigzagging flight.

Vultures

Black vulture lives in the Americas. Like the turkey vulture, it has slender legs and toes.

Turkey vulture has an immense range, stretching from Canada to Tierra del Fuego at the tip of South America.

Collar of white feathers around the base of the neck

Huge flight feathers allow effortless soaring.

Worn feathers will be replaced when the vulture moults.

Andean condor is the largest bird of prey. As its name suggests, it lives in the Andes Mountains of South America.

Feet are too weak for catching food.

White-backed vulture has only a few feathers on its neck and a bare head like all vultures.

A bare neck is easy for the vulture to clean after feeding.

BLACK DEATH

IN THE 14TH CENTURY, a deadly epidemic swept the world. The Black Death, as it became known, was bubonic plague, a terrible disease that begins with fever, causes agonizing black swellings in the glands, and leads to death, usually within a few days of infection. Millions died. Terrified people fled infected areas and carried the plague with them. In towns the doors of plague carriers were marked with crosses to warn others to keep away. The dead were collected in carts and buried in mass graves. In Europe about one-third of the population died; a similar number probably died in Asia.

Progress of the plague

The plague reached the Black Sea from Asia in 1346. From there, it was carried by Italian traders to ports on the Mediterranean. It then spread up rivers and land routes into northern Europe. By 1350, most of Europe was affected.

Plague-free areas
Black Sea
Prague
Paris
Milan
Constantinople
Genoa Florence
Bordeaux

c.1351
Dec 1350
June 1350
Dec 1349
June 1349
Dec 1348
June 1348
Dec 1347

Plague-free areas
Some areas, such as modern-day Poland and Milan, escaped the plague, but the reason for this is still a mystery.

Disease carriers

Plague is caused by a bacterium that lives on rodents. The disease was caught by black rats in Asia, which then colonized ships to Europe and spread the disease among people there. An infected person could also pass the plague through the air, by coughing.

Plague bacterium
The bacterium is called *Yersinia pestis*, after the Swiss biologist Alexander Yersin, who discovered it. It is common in wild animals such as field mice, ground squirrels, and marmots.

Flea carriers
The plague bacterium lives in the digestive system of a flea, and causes a blockage there. When the flea feeds, the blockage makes it vomit the newly eaten blood back onto its host, along with plague bacteria, which then infect the host.

Animal carriers
The black rat lived in towns and on ships and scavenged in food stores and rubbish heaps. Rats carry fleas, and when plague-carrying rats died of the disease, their fleas searched for other hosts. If these new hosts were people, they, too, caught the plague.

Human carriers
The plague turned into an epidemic so rapidly because human travellers helped spread it. Mongol nomads and Asian merchants carried it across Asia. The traders of the great Italian cities, such as Genoa and Venice, carried it around Europe in their ships.

Effects of the plague

The disease was so widespread that many left their families and took to the road to try to escape death. Some thought the plague was God's punishment for the sins of people, and mercilessly whipped themselves in the streets to show repentance.

Labour force
By the end of the 14th century, the smaller population of Europe meant that life was better for those who had survived. Because there were fewer peasants, they got higher wages and there was more food to go around. But recurring peasant rebellions showed that they still had grievances.

Population decline
When Pope Clement VI asked how many people had died from the plague, he was told at least 20 million people in Europe, and 17 million in Asia. In comparison, around 8 million soldiers died in World War I.

20M

8M

= 2 million dead

Black Death
World War I

Tombs
During the plague, people faced death every day. Death is often realistically shown on 14th-century tombs, where images of skeletons and decaying corpses are common.

Chantries
People often left money for masses to be said for their souls. These masses were said in special chapels inside churches known as chantries. This chantry is at Winchester, England.

Dealing with the plague

Some people tried to fend off the plague by using herbal remedies, bleeding by leeches, fumigation, and even bathing in urine. A 14th-century poem, called the Dance of Death (which states that death comes for people of every rank) was often enacted and painted, to remind people that death – and the plague – could strike at any time.

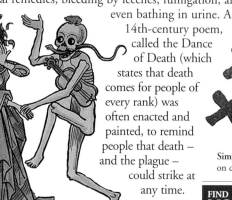

Lungwort   Mint   Rose

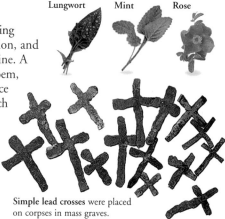

Simple lead crosses were placed on corpses in mass graves.

FIND OUT MORE   ASIA, HISTORY OF   DISEASES   EUROPE, HISTORY OF   MEDIEVAL EUROPE   MICROSCOPIC LIFE

BLACK HOLES

ASTRONOMERS HAVE SPENT much time analysing how stars form and how they develop. One problem was to explain what happened to a massive star at the end of its life. In 1967, the term "black hole" was used to describe one type of object that is left when a massive star dies. Four years later, Cygnus X-1 was found, the first candidate for a black hole.

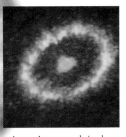

A massive star ends its days in an explosion, leaving a very dense core that then collapses.

Stellar collapse

Massive stars can end their lives in an explosion, called a supernova, that leaves behind a central core. If the core's mass is more than that of three Suns, it becomes a black hole. Gravity forces the core to collapse. As the core shrinks, its gravity increases. At a certain point it reaches a critical size, that of the event horizon.

Detecting a black hole

Black holes appear black because nothing, not even light, can escape from their powerful gravity. Astronomers cannot detect them directly, but can "see" them because of the effect their gravity has on everything around them, such as gas from a nearby star. The boundary of the black hole is called the event horizon. Material pulled in towards the hole is swirled around by the gravity, forming a disc, before crossing the horizon.

Event horizon

Gravity increases as the core of the dying star shrinks.

Anything trying to escape the gravity must travel almost at the speed of light, as the core approaches the size of the event horizon.

Once the core is smaller than the event horizon, not even light can escape.

The core continues collapsing until it takes up virtually no space. The star is a singularity, a point mass of infinitely high density inside a black hole.

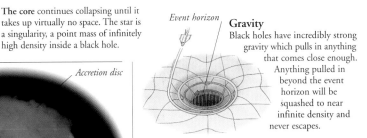

Event horizon

Gravity
Black holes have incredibly strong gravity which pulls in anything that comes close enough. Anything pulled in beyond the event horizon will be squashed to near infinite density and never escapes.

Gas is torn from a nearby star.

Close to the black hole, the gas glows with heat.

Black hole

Gravity pulls the gas towards the black hole.

Accretion disc

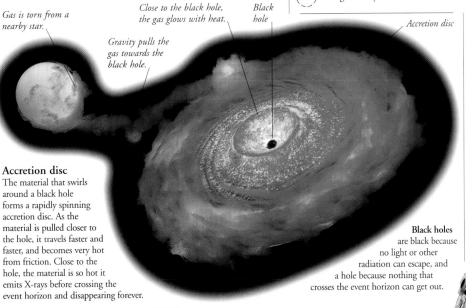

Accretion disc
The material that swirls around a black hole forms a rapidly spinning accretion disc. As the material is pulled closer to the hole, it travels faster and faster, and becomes very hot from friction. Close to the hole, the material is so hot it emits X-rays before crossing the event horizon and disappearing forever.

Black holes are black because no light or other radiation can escape, and a hole because nothing that crosses the event horizon can get out.

Entering a black hole

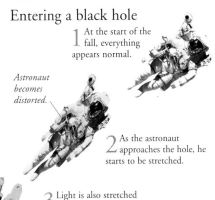

1 At the start of the fall, everything appears normal.

Astronaut becomes distorted.

2 As the astronaut approaches the hole, he starts to be stretched.

3 Light is also stretched to a longer wavelength so the astronaut appears redder.

Galaxy NGC 4261 in the constellation of Virgo has what appears to be a huge accretion disc – 30 million light years across – swirling around a huge black hole.

Supermassive holes

Some galaxies have very active centres that give out large amounts of energy. An object of powerful gravity, such as a supermassive black hole, could be the cause of the activity. Such a hole would be a hundred million times more massive than the Sun.

Inside a black hole

Space and time are highly distorted inside a black hole. Anyone unlucky enough to fall into one would be stretched to resemble spaghetti, as gravity pulled more on the feet than the head. An observer watching the person fall would also see time running slower as the person fell towards the event horizon.

4 Gravity stretches the astronaut. Close to the hole, he is torn apart.

Roger Penrose

The English mathematician Roger Penrose (b. 1931) theorizes on the nature of space and time. He has shown that a massive collapsing star inevitably becomes a black hole, and that all black holes have a singularity – a point, occupying virtually no space, that contains the entire mass of the dead star. Penrose believes the singularity is always hidden by an event horizon.

FIND OUT MORE   FRICTION   GALAXIES   GRAVITY   STARS   SUN AND SOLAR SYSTEM   UNIVERSE

B

BOLÍVAR, SIMÓN

SIMÓN BOLÍVAR WAS the brilliant and charismatic leader who led South America to independence from 400 years of foreign rule. Together with other generals, he overthrew the Spanish in just 12 years. As president of the federation of Gran Colombia, he wanted to rule the whole continent, but this dream came to nothing. To this day, he is still known as "The Liberator", and one of the South American nations, Bolivia, is named after him.

Early life

Bolívar was born into a rich family in Caracas, Venezuela, in 1783. His parents died when he was young, and he was educated by private tutors, such as Simón Rodríguez, a teacher who taught him about European ideas, such as liberty.

Fighting for independence

At the start of the 19th century, all of South America, except Brazil and Guiana, was under the rule of the Spanish king Ferdinand VII. Many South Americans resented this and wanted to govern themselves. In response, independence movements broke out all over South America. Bolívar, keen to work in the independence movement, returned to South America and fought the Spanish in Venezuela.

Bolívar's storms to victory at the Battle of Carabobo

Bolívar in Europe

In 1799, Bolívar was sent to Madrid to live with relatives and improve his education. While in Europe, Bolívar learned of an attempt in 1806 by Francisco de Miranda to liberate Venezuela from Spanish rule. The rebellion failed, but inspired Bolívar to fight for independence.

Ferdinand VII of Spain

First republic

In 1810, Francisco de Miranda returned from exile in Europe and was made president of the new republic of Venezuela. In 1811, it became the first South American country to declare independence from foreign rule. Bolívar joined the rebel army, but the republic collapsed. He carried on the struggle, going to Colombia to fight the Spanish there.

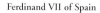

Francisco de Miranda in prison

The Liberator

From 1811 onwards, Bolívar was the focus of independence movements across South America. In 1813, he defeated the Spanish and entered Caracas, where he was given the title of "The Liberator". In 1819, he put together an army of 2,500 men and marched them across the continent to Boyacá, Colombia. He won the resulting battle, and Colombia gained its independence.

Angostura Congress

At a congress held at Angostura, now Ciudad Bolívar, Bolívar was elected president of Venezuela. The congress also proposed the formation of Gran Colombia, a federation that included present-day Venezuela, Colombia, Ecuador, and Panama. Between 1819 and 1822, Bolívar won a series of victories against Spain, confirming the independence of Colombia and Venezuela, and liberating Peru.

Bolívar and Sucre

Bolivia

In 1825, Bolívar dispatched Sucre to conquer Alto Perú, in west central South America, which was still under Spanish control. Once the Spanish were defeated, the newly independent country was named Bolivia in honour of the Liberator. By now, every South American state except Uruguay had won its independence.

Bolívar's statue at government buildings, La Paz, Bolivia

Ecuador and Peru

In 1822, one of Bolívar's most talented generals, Antonio José de Sucre, defeated the Spanish at Pichincha to win Ecuador's independence. Two years later, Bolívar made a deal with the Argentinian liberator José de San Martín, whose forces were active in Peru. As a result, Sucre defeated the Spanish at Ayacucho, bringing independence to Peru. As a result of Bolívar's influence, another large area of South America was liberated.

SIMÓN BOLÍVAR

1783	Born in Caracas, Venezuela.
1799	Sent to Europe.
1811	Venezuela declares its independence; Bolívar becomes a military leader.
1812	First republic is defeated.
1813	Bolívar enters Caracas as "The Liberator", but is soon defeated.
1819	Angostura Congress.
1819	Bolívar wins Battle of Boyacá to win Colombian independence.
1821	Bolívar wins Battle of Carabobo to win Venezuelan independence.
1822	Ecuador wins independence.
1825	Bolivia named in his honour.
1830	Dies of tuberculosis.

FIND OUT MORE CENTRAL AMERICA, HISTORY OF • NAPOLEON BONAPARTE • SOUTH AMERICA, HISTORY OF • SPAIN, HISTORY OF

BOLIVIA AND PARAGUAY

BOLIVIA AND PARAGUAY are the only land-locked countries in South America. They are also two of the poorest in the continent, reliant on their neighbours for access to the sea. In a bitter war (1932–35) between them over ownership of the Gran Chaco, Bolivia lost, but both countries suffered political turmoil. Under Spanish rule between the 1530s and 1820s, Bolivia and Paraguay still bear its legacy: Spanish is an official language, and more than 90 per cent of the region's population is Roman Catholic. Many people farm and, in Bolivia, some grow and sell coca for cocaine, a drug that the government has taken steps to banish.

Aymara
The Aymara are a group of native South Americans who have farmed on the Bolivian Altiplano for hundreds of years, strongly resisting cultural change. With the Quechua, another native group, they make up more than half of Bolivia's population, but suffer discrimination and do not contribute to politics or the economy. The state has successfully persuaded many Aymara to move into towns.

Aymara farmers, Altiplano, Bolivia

Physical features
The Altiplano dominates the west of Bolivia, while the east is covered by a lowland plain called the Oriente. Paraguay is divided north to south by the Paraguay River. In the west is the Gran Chaco, a region of grass and scrub; the east is covered in grassy plains and forests, and drained by the mighty Paraná River.

Altiplano
At about 3,800 m (12,467 ft) above sea-level, the Altiplano, a vast, windswept, almost treeless plateau, lies between two ranges of the Bolivian Andes. Despite its cold, arid climate, more than half of Bolivia's population lives here, growing a few crops and rearing animals such as llamas and alpacas.

Lake Titicaca
The clear blue waters of Lake Titicaca cover 8,288 sq km (3,200 sq miles) at a height of 3,810 m (12,500 ft) above sea-level, making it the highest navigable lake in the world. It is the last surviving stretch of an ancient inland sea known as Lago Ballivián.

Gran Chaco
The flat, dry plain that covers southeastern Bolivia and northwest Paraguay is called the Gran Chaco. Since so few people live in this region of coarse grass, thorny shrubs, and cactus, a wide range of plants and animals thrives here.

Regional climate
Bolivia's Altiplano has a cool, crisp, dry climate. The eastern part of the country is warm and humid, as is most of Paraguay. The Chaco is hot, with 50–100 cm (20–40 in) of rain a year, although it often has droughts in winter.

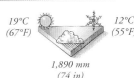

19°C (67°F)   12°C (55°F)

1,890 mm (74 in)

Bolivia

The highest and most isolated nation in South America, Bolivia is named after Simón Bolívar, who, in the 1800s, led wars of independence against the Spaniards. Despite rich natural resources, exporting is difficult because of Bolivia's position. About half the people are Native Americans; the rest are Spanish or of mixed blood.

La Paz
Although Sucre is Bolivia's official capital, the country is governed from La Paz, which also has capital status. At 3,631 m (11,913 ft) above sea-level, La Paz is the world's highest capital and Bolivia's largest city, with a population of about 2,515,000, of whom over half are Native Americans. La Paz has chemical and textile industries, but unemployment is generally high.

Chuqui

Pipes are made from a local reed. The longer the reed, the deeper the sound.

Music
Bolivian music has Incan, Amazonian, Spanish, and African influences. Rural Aymara orchestras are often composed entirely of panpipes, called *chuqui*. Other instruments include drums, flutes, and the *phututu*, made from a cow's horn.

Deforestation
Tropical rainforests in Bolivia are being cut down at the rate of 2,000 sq km (772 sq miles) a year, mostly for cattle ranching or growing coca for cocaine. Chemicals used in the manufacture of cocaine are discharged directly into the rivers of Amazonia, many of which have high pollution levels that damage plant and tree life.

Tin

Metal mining
Bolivia is rich in mineral deposits. Its tin mines lie high in the Andes mountains and it is the world's largest producer of tin. It is also a leading exporter of antimony and silver. Other mineral deposits include zinc, gold, and lead.

BOLIVIA FACTS

CAPITAL CITIES La Paz, Sucre

AREA 1,098,580 sq km (424,162 sq miles)

POPULATION 8,500,000

MAIN LANGUAGES Spanish, Quechua, Aymara

MAJOR RELIGION Christian

CURRENCY Boliviano

Potatoes

Maize

Barley

Crops
Bolivian farmers living on the Altiplano grow potatoes, soya beans, barley, and wheat for themselves and their families. Rice, maize, bananas, and plantains are grown in the lowlands. Cash crops include sugar-cane, cocoa beans, and coffee, although the profits from illegal coca crops greatly exceed all legal farming produce combined.

Paraguay

The Paraguay River, from which the country takes its name, divides the land in two. To the east lie the fertile hills and plains that are home to 90 per cent of the people. The vast majority are *mestizos,* people of mixed European and Native American ancestry; the rest are Guaraní or Europeans. To the northwest is the Gran Chaco, large areas of which Paraguay won from Bolivia in the 1930s. Only five per cent of the people live in the Chaco, including 10,000 Mennonites, farmers of German descent who retain their culture.

Macá bag

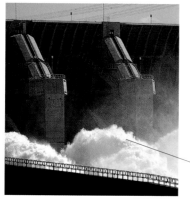

Macá
The Macá are a small ethnic group who follow a traditional lifestyle in the Gran Chaco. They make a living from farming. Macá women also weave bags and cloth for the tourist trade.

Beef
The main industry in Paraguay's Gran Chaco is cattle ranching. Herds of animals roam the flat grasslands, tended by skilled Paraguayan cowboys called *gauchos* who round the cattle up on horseback. The farms are called *estancias* and are some of the only buildings in this open landscape.

Itaipu Dam
With a reservoir 3,250 sq km (1,255 sq miles) and 220 m (722 ft) deep, the Itaipu Dam, on the Paraná River was undertaken as a joint project with Brazil. It provides water for the world's largest hydroelectric plant and generates enough electricity to make Paraguay self-sufficient in energy.

Dam generates 13,320 megawatts of electricity – enough to supply New York City.

PARAGUAY FACTS

CAPITAL CITY Asunción

AREA 406,750 sq km (157,046 sq miles)

POPULATION 5,600,000

MAIN LANGUAGES Spanish, Guaraní

MAJOR RELIGION Christian

CURRENCY Guaraní

Jesuits
In 1588, Spanish missionaries from the Jesuit order of the Roman Catholic Church arrived in Asunción. They converted the local Guaraní people to Christianity, and taught them trades such as weaving. The Jesuits built large stone churches.

Exports
Soya-bean flour and cotton make up around 50 per cent of Paraguay's exports. The country also sells timber from its forests, vegetable oils, and processed meat. Leading trading partners include Brazil, Argentina, and the Netherlands.

FIND OUT MORE BOLÍVAR, SIMÓN · CHRISTIANITY · DAMS · DRUGS · ENERGY · FARMING · MUSIC · NATIVE AMERICANS · ROCKS AND MINERALS · SOUTH AMERICA, HISTORY OF · TEXTILES AND WEAVING

BOOKS

FROM ENCYCLOPEDIAS TO NOVELS, books are a vital record of human life and achievement. They store the thoughts, beliefs, and experiences of individuals and societies, preserving them after the author's death. There are many kinds of books, from religious works, such as the Qur'an, and non-fiction, such as dictionaries and educational books, to fiction such as plays and stories. The Chinese invented printing in the 9th century; it arrived in Europe during the 15th century. Printing made it possible to mass-produce books, and knowledge was spread more widely. Today, publishing is a global industry.

Early Chinese book, made of fragile bamboo strips

Early books

The first books were not made of paper. Long before 3000 BC, the Sumerians wrote on clay tablets. Around 1300 BC, the Chinese began making books from bamboo strips bound together with cord.

Making books

Much preparation goes into making books and some take several years to produce. For example, making an encyclopedia will involve a team of people that includes authors, editors, designers, picture researchers, illustrators, photographers, and IT experts, as well as printers.

Artist's pencil roughs

Finished pieces of colour artwork

The colour proof before text is added to page

Transparencies are a high-quality image format.

Illustration
The designer draws a detailed plan, showing the position of each illustration. The artist makes rough sketches, which are checked, then paints each picture separately. The artwork is photographed, and carefully positioned on the page using a computer, until the design is perfect.

Author
The author is the first person to start work, researching and writing the contents of the book. The author advises the designer on suitable images for the book and works closely with the editorial team throughout the project.

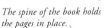

The printed colour matches the original artwork as closely as possible.

The editor checks the author's text for mistakes and adjusts length of text if necessary.

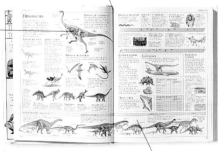

The spine of the book holds the pages in place.

Pictures and text are perfectly integrated.

Text
The text is edited on a computer screen, and then produced as a page called a proof. The proof is matched with the artwork to make sure that words and images fit exactly, before going to the printer.

Finished book
At last the book is finished, and fitted with a hard cover and a protective jacket. It is now ready to sell. An illustrated book may take several years to make, although new technology is speeding up this process.

Papyrus plants grow by the Nile.

Paper
The ancient Egyptians wrote on scrolls made from papyrus, which grew by the River Nile. Later civilizations in the Middle East wrote on parchment made from animal skin. Modern paper was probably invented in China around AD 150. It was made by pulping flax fibres, then flattening and drying them in the sun. The Chinese kept this process a secret for 500 years before they passed it on to the rest of the world.

CD Roms
There is a limit to how big any book can grow before it becomes too heavy and cumbersome to be practical. Now, modern technology is developing compact alternatives to traditional books. One CD Rom can contain as much text as a shelf of encyclopedias. Text and pictures from CD Roms can be read and transmitted by computer.

CD Rom

Paperbacks
A paperback book contains the same text as a hardback, but has a soft cover. The first modern paperback books were published in London by Penguin, in 1935, priced sixpence. They are far cheaper than hardbacks, and many more people can buy them.

Timeline
c. 285 BC Egyptian pharaoh Ptolemy I establishes a library at Alexandria, Egypt.

AD 300s Books with pages first invented.

Gutenberg Bible

c.1440 Johannes Gutenberg invents the metal type.

1789 French Revolutionaries proclaim the fundamental public right to print without fear of censorship.

1796 Lithography (a technique for printing illustrations) invented.

1811 First totally mechanized printing press invented, USA.

1935 First paperback books published for mass market by Penguin in UK.

1980s Electronic books for the computer published in CD Rom format.

1990s Books first published on the Internet.

FIND OUT MORE

CHILDREN'S LITERATURE | COMPUTERS | DRAMA | EGYPT, ANCIENT | LITERATURE | POETRY | PRINTING | WRITING

BRAIN AND NERVOUS SYSTEM

EVERY THOUGHT YOU HAVE, every emotion you feel, and every action you take is a reflection of the nervous system at work. At the core of the nervous system are the brain and spinal cord, known as the central nervous system (CNS). The most complex part of the CNS is the brain; this constantly receives information from the body, processes it, and sends out instructions telling the body what to do. The CNS communicates with every part of the body through an extensive network of nerves. The nerves and the CNS are both constructed from billions of nerve cells called neurons.

Brain is the body's control and co-ordination centre.

Cranial nerves

Cervical nerves

Brachial plexus

Spinal cord relays information to and from the brain and the rest of the body.

Thoracic nerves

Lumbar nerves

Sacral nerves

Nerves

Nerves form the "wiring" of the nervous system. Each nerve consists of a bundle of neurons (nerve cells) held together by a tough outer sheath. Nerves spread out from the brain and spinal cord and branch repeatedly to reach all parts of the body. Most nerves contain sensory neurons that carry nerve impulses towards the CNS, and motor neurons that carry nerve impulses away from the CNS.

Inside a nerve

Sensory neuron

Motor neuron

Bundle of neurons

Blood vessels

Outer sheath of the nerve

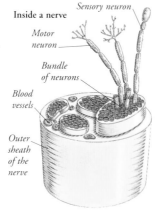

Radial nerve controls the muscles in the arm and hand.

Lumbar plexus

Sacral plexus

Nervous system

The nervous system is made up of the CNS and the peripheral nervous system, which consists of the nerves. The peripheral nervous system has two sections: the somatic system which controls voluntary actions, and the autonomic nervous system which controls automatic functions such as heart rate.

Sciatic nerve controls the muscles in the leg and foot.

Tibial nerve controls the muscles of the calf and foot.

Nerve endings

At the ends of sensory neurons there are nerve endings called sensory receptors. If you touch an object, a sensory receptor in the skin is stimulated, nerve impulses travel to the brain along the sensory neuron, and you feel the object. In this way, visually impaired people can "read" the Braille language with their fingertips.

Neurons

Neurons are long, thin cells adapted to carry electrical signals called nerve impulses. There are three types of neurons: sensory neurons, motor neurons, and association neurons. The most numerous are association neurons, which transmit signals from one neuron to another and are found only inside the CNS.

Nerve impulses

Nerve impulses are the "messages" that travel at high speed along neurons. Impulses are weak electrical signals that are generated and transmitted by neurons when they are stimulated. The stimulus may come from a sensory nerve ending, or from an adjacent neuron. Nerve impulses travel in one direction along the neuron.

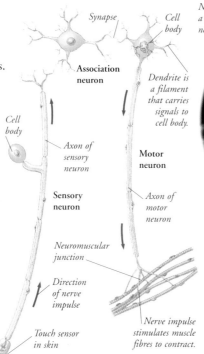

Synapse

Cell body

Association neuron

Dendrite is a filament that carries signals to cell body.

Cell body

Axon of sensory neuron

Motor neuron

Sensory neuron

Axon of motor neuron

Neuromuscular junction

Direction of nerve impulse

Touch sensor in skin

Nerve impulse stimulates muscle fibres to contract.

Neuromuscular junction is a synapse between a motor neuron and muscle fibre.

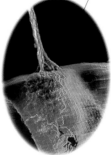

Synapses

A synapse is a junction between two neurons. At a synapse, neurons do not touch. Instead, there is a tiny gap. When a nerve impulse reaches a synapse it triggers the release of chemicals, which travel across the gap and stimulate the second neuron to generate a nerve impulse.

Reflex actions

If you touch something sharp, you automatically pull your hand away without thinking about it. This is a reflex action. A sensory neuron carries impulses to the spinal cord, where an association neuron transmits impulses to a motor neuron, and the arm muscle contracts.

Brain

Sensory receptors

Motor neuron

Muscle

Receptors in hand detect the prick of a pin and send signal to spinal cord.

Sensory neuron

Santiago Ramón y Cajal

Spanish anatomist Santiago Ramón y Cajal (1852–1934) pioneered the study of the cells that make up the brain and nerves. He developed methods for staining nerve cells so they could be seen clearly under the microscope. His work revolutionized the examination of brain tissue.

Brain

The brain is the body's control centre. Your brain enables you to think and to have a personality, and also regulates all your body processes. It has three main regions: the forebrain, the cerebellum, and the brain stem. The forebrain consists of the cerebrum (which is made up of two halves or hemispheres), the thalamus, hypothalamus, and the limbic system, which controls emotions and instinctive behaviour.

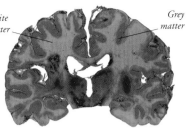

White matter

Grey matter

Section through brain tissue

Grey and white matter

Each cerebral hemisphere has two layers. The outer layer, the cerebral cortex, consists of grey matter containing cell bodies of neurons that form a communication network. The inner layer, or white matter, consists of nerve fibres that link the cerebral cortex to the other parts of the brain.

B

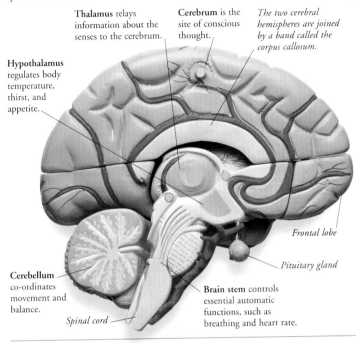

Thalamus relays information about the senses to the cerebrum.

Cerebrum is the site of conscious thought.

The two cerebral hemispheres are joined by a band called the corpus callosum.

Hypothalamus regulates body temperature, thirst, and appetite.

Frontal lobe

Pituitary gland

Cerebellum co-ordinates movement and balance.

Spinal cord

Brain stem controls essential automatic functions, such as breathing and heart rate.

Left and right brains

The left cerebral hemisphere controls the right side of the body, and the right cerebral hemisphere controls the left side of the body. Although both hemispheres are used for almost every activity, each hemisphere has its own specialist skills. In most people, the left hemisphere is involved in spoken and written language, mathematical ability, and reasoning, while the right hemisphere controls the appreciation of art and music, insight and imagination, and shape recognition.

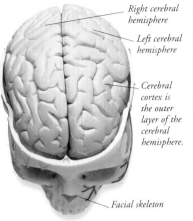

Right cerebral hemisphere

Left cerebral hemisphere

Cerebral cortex is the outer layer of the cerebral hemisphere.

Facial skeleton

Brain cells

The brain consists of hundreds of billions of nerve cells. Many of these are association neurons that are constantly receiving and transmitting nerve impulses. Any one of these neurons can have links to over 1,000 other neurons, producing a complex network. The brain also contains other nerve cells, called glial cells, which hold the neurons in place.

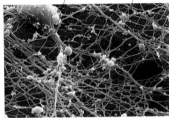

Association neuron in brain

Glial cell

Brain areas

Certain areas of the cerebrum are involved with particular body functions. These areas can be highlighted on a brain map. Motor areas of the brain, such as the speech and basic movement areas, send out instructions to control voluntary movement. Sensory areas, such as the hearing, taste, smell, touch, and vision areas, receive information from sensory receptors around the body. Association areas, such as the frontal lobe, deal with thoughts, personality, and emotions, analyse experiences, and give you consciousness and awareness.

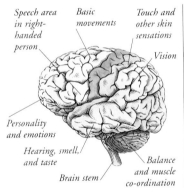

Speech area in right-handed person

Basic movements

Touch and other skin sensations

Vision

Personality and emotions

Hearing, smell, and taste

Brain stem

Balance and muscle co-ordination

Brain waves

The brain's neurons are constantly sending out and receiving nerve impulses. This process produces electrical signals that can be detected using a machine called an electroencephalograph (EEG). Electrodes linked to the EEG can be attached to a person's scalp in order to record the brain's electrical activities as a series of patterns called brain waves.

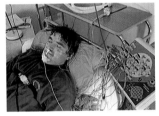

Sleep and dreams

As you sleep, you move repeatedly between phases of light REM (rapid eye movement) sleep and phases of deeper NREM sleep. These shifts can be detected using an EEG.

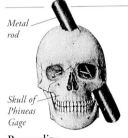

Metal rod

Skull of Phineas Gage

Personality

The frontal lobe of the brain plays a major role in deciding personality. This was shown by the case of an American worker called Phineas Gage. In 1848, an accident sent a metal rod through Gage's cheek and frontal lobe. He survived but his personality changed from being friendly to being aggressive.

Spinal cord

The spinal cord relays information between the brain and the rest of the body, and is involved in many reflex actions. It is a flattened cylinder of nervous tissue, about 43 cm (17 in) long and as thick as a finger. It runs from the base of the brain to the lower back, surrounded by the backbone.

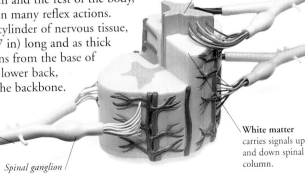

Section of spinal cord

Grey matter relays information between spinal cord and spinal nerves.

Spinal nerve relays nerve impulses to and from all parts of body.

Spinal ganglion

White matter carries signals up and down spinal column.

Pierre Paul Broca

French anatomist and surgeon Pierre Paul Broca (1824–80) demonstrated that a specific region of the brain controlled a particular body function. Broca found that a small area co-ordinated the muscles in the mouth and throat that produce speech. This area is now called Broca's area, or the speech area. Broca made his discovery when treating a patient who could not talk after damage to part of his brain.

FIND OUT MORE   CELLS   EYES AND SEEING   HORMONES AND ENDOCRINE SYSTEM   HUMAN BODY   MUSCLES AND MOVEMENT   SKIN, HAIR, AND NAILS   SMELL AND TASTE

BRAZIL

B

THE LARGEST COUNTRY in South America, Brazil is a land of opposites. Watered by the second longest river in the world, the Amazon, it has the world's largest rainforest, arid deserts in the northeast, and rolling grassland in the south. Crowded cities contrast with remote areas that have never been explored. The country has many well-developed industries and a huge, successful agricultural base, but many people live in poverty. Brazilian society is a vibrant, diverse mix of cultures.

Physical features

The Amazon Basin and its forests, some mountainous, occupy northern Brazil. The southeast is a region of plateaus that vary from sunburnt arid scrublands to rich fields and pastures.

BRAZIL FACTS

CAPITAL CITY	Brasília
AREA	8,511,965 sq km (3,286,470 sq miles)
POPULATION	172,600,000
MAIN LANGUAGE	Portuguese
MAJOR RELIGION	Christian
CURRENCY	Réal
LIFE EXPECTANCY	68 years
PEOPLE PER DOCTOR	769
GOVERNMENT	Multi-party democracy
ADULT LITERACY	85%

Highlands
The Brazilian Highlands extend from the Amazon Basin to the coast, rising to 3,000 m (10,000 ft). About 60 per cent of the country is dominated by the plateau, where landscape ranges from tropical forest to dry, rocky desert.

Amazonian rainforest
Around half of Brazil is cloaked in dense rainforest. The River Amazon, 6,448 km (4,007 miles) long, runs through the north of Brazil, giving life to more than 40,000 different species of plants and animals in the forests.

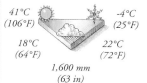

41°C (106°F) -4°C (25°F)
18°C (64°F) 22°C (72°F)
1,600 mm (63 in)

Climate
All except the extreme south of Brazil lies in the tropics, so temperatures are always high. The Amazonian rainforest receives about 4,000 mm (157 in) every year. By contrast, droughts are common in the northeast corner. Farther south, summers are hot and winters can be cold with frosts.

Brasília
Brazil's modern capital city, Brasília, lies on the extreme northern edge of the plateau region. Purpose-built in the 1950s on the site of a felled rainforest, the city replaced Rio de Janeiro as capital. Its inland position has helped to develop new areas away from the coast. There are many imaginative, futuristic buildings, including the spectacular cathedral.

Brasília Cathedral

Built-up 0.3% Farmland 10%
Desert 29.7%
Forests 59.5%
Wetland 0.5%

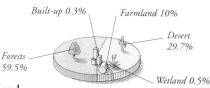

Land use
Thick forests cover the majority of the land, but are being cleared at an alarming rate to make way for farmland and roads. The fertile southeast, especially around São Paulo, is permanently farmed. Much of the land is desert.

People

The Brazilian people have a wide ethnic background, and there are large groups of African, European, and Asian origin. The original inhabitants of Brazil form only a tiny percentage of the population. Many families are tight knit, fiercely loyal, and strict Roman Catholics. The majority live in towns clustered along the southeastern coast.

Indian groups
Some native Brazilians still live in the rainforests, following traditional ways of life. However, about 14 groups now shelter in Xingu National Park, set up when their forest home was destroyed.

20 per sq km (52 per sq mile)

81% Urban   **19% Rural**

Leisure

The mainly Roman Catholic people of Brazil celebrate many religious festivals, such as the Rio and Bahía carnivals. Sports, including football, basketball, and water sports along the coast, are the chief leisure activities for millions of Brazilians. The samba, one of the world's most popular dances, originated in Brazil.

Rio Carnival
Known as one of the world's largest and most spectacular festivals, the Rio Carnival, in Rio de Janeiro, is held just before Lent every year. During the carnival, processions of brightly decorated floats, and a myriad of colourful singers, musicians, and dancers with imaginative costumes, fill the streets.

Football
Many Brazilians have a passion for football, either as players or spectators. The national team has won the World Cup more times than any other team. Its star player, Edson Arantes do Nascimento, known as Pelé, was the world's leading player in the 1960s and is regarded by fans as a living legend.

Farming

Brazil has immense natural resources. About 22 per cent of the labour force works on the land, growing all Brazil's own food, with a vast surplus for export. The best farmland is around Rio de Janeiro and São Paulo, where water is plentiful and the climate is frost-free. About 150 million cattle are reared on large ranches in this region.

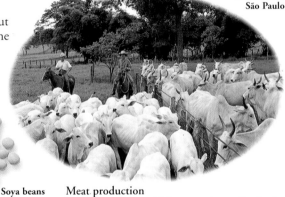

Cattle ranch, São Paulo

Orange

Coffee leaves and berries

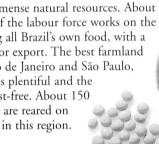

Soya beans
Each berry contains two beans, which are washed, dried, and roasted.

Meat production
Brazil is one of the world's largest producers of beef and veal. Cows graze on the rich, green pastures of central Brazil. Large areas of tropical rainforest are cleared to create new cattle ranches, but the soil is soon exhausted and more forest has to be felled.

Crops
Brazil is a leading producer of cocoa beans, coffee, oranges, and sugar-cane, and one of the world's largest growers of soya beans and bananas. About 22 per cent of the world's coffee comes from Brazil, and millions of oranges are picked every year. These crops grow successfully in the warm, fertile soils of central and southern Brazil.

Bananas

Forest products

The plants and trees of the Amazonian rainforest have long been used for food, housing, and medicine by the people who live there. Some of these, such as rubber and Brazil nuts, are now known world-wide. Other lesser-known plants are quinine, taken from chinchona bark and used to treat malaria; ipecacuanha, an ingredient of cough medicines; and curare, once part of an arrow poison, now a life-saving muscle relaxant used in operations.

Brazil nuts

Transport

A vast network links Brazil's main centres, but of the 1,660,352 km (1,031,693 miles) of roads, only nine per cent are paved. Brazil has one of the world's largest national air networks. Cities with rapid growth, such as São Paulo, are expanding their subways.

Industry

The manufacturing industry employs about 15 per cent of the Brazilian work-force. Machinery, textiles, cars, food products, industrial chemicals, and footwear are the main export products. Brazil has large mining, oil, and steel industries, but has suffered high inflation.

Mining
Brazil is a leading producer of gold, manganese, and tin ore. The country is noted for its precious stones, such as amethysts, diamonds, and topaz, but the quest for mineral wealth has led to much forest destruction.

Steel
South America's top steel maker, Brazil ranks highly in world production. This, and cheap labour, have attracted many car makers to invest in the country.

"Green" cars
About one-third of all Brazil's cars are run on so-called "green petrol", or ethanol, which is made from fermented sugar-cane. Because it produces less carbon monoxide than petrol when it is burned, it is less harmful to the environment and is reducing pollution.

 FIND OUT MORE   CHRISTIANITY   CRYSTALS AND GEMS   FARMING   FESTIVALS   FOOTBALL   FORESTS   NATIVE AMERICANS   RIVERS   ROCKS AND MINERALS   SOUTH AMERICA, HISTORY OF

BRIDGES

B

CURVING MAJESTICALLY across rivers and valleys, bridges are some of the most spectacular structures engineers have ever created. They are also some of the most useful, because bridges can speed up journeys by cutting out ferry crossings, long detours, steep hills, and busy junctions. The first bridges were probably tree trunks laid across streams. Wooden beam bridges and stone or brick arches were the main types of bridge from Roman times until the 18th century, when iron became available to engineers. Most modern bridges are made of steel and concrete, making them both strong and flexible.

Types of bridges

On a journey, you may see many different shapes and sizes of bridge, but there are really only a few main types: arch bridges, beam bridges, cantilever bridges, suspension bridges, and cable-stay bridges. The type of bridge used depends on the size of the gap it must span, the landscape, and traffic that will cross it.

Arch bridge
The arch is used to build bridges because it is a strong shape that can bear a lot of weight. To bridge a wide gap, several arches of stone or brick are linked together.

Beam bridge
In a beam bridge, the central span (or beam) is supported at both ends. Very long beams are impractical, because they would be liable to collapse under their own weight.

Cantilever bridge
A beam fixed at one end and stretching out over a gap is a cantilever. Balanced cantilever bridges have several supports, each with two beams that reach out from either side.

Suspension bridge
The deck of a suspension bridge hangs from cables slung over towers and anchored to the ground at each end of the bridge. Such bridges have spans of up to 1 km (0.62 miles).

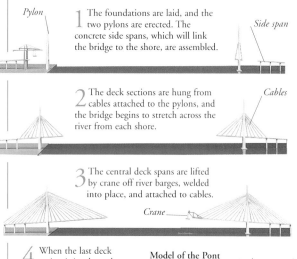

Pylon

1 The foundations are laid, and the two pylons are erected. The concrete side spans, which will link the bridge to the shore, are assembled.

Side span

2 The deck sections are hung from cables attached to the pylons, and the bridge begins to stretch across the river from each shore.

Cables

3 The central deck spans are lifted by crane off river barges, welded into place, and attached to cables.

Crane

4 When the last deck section is in place, the bridge is complete. The cables transfer the weight of the deck to the pylons.

Building a bridge

A cable-stay bridge is a type of suspension bridge with a deck hung from slanting cables that are fixed to pylons instead of the ground. Once the pylons are in place, the bridge is built outwards in both directions from each pylon. This ensures that the forces on the pylons balance, so that there is no danger of the pylons collapsing.

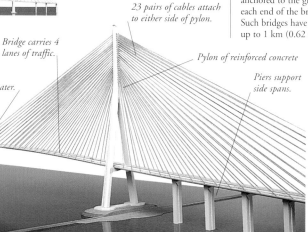

Model of the Pont de Normandie

Bridge carries 4 lanes of traffic.

23 pairs of cables attach to either side of pylon.

Pylon of reinforced concrete

Piers support side spans.

Deck is 52 m (170 ft) above water.

Steel cables are coated in plastic to prevent rusting.

Foundations of pylons extend 50–60 m (164–197 ft) below ground.

Isambard Kingdom Brunel
English engineer Isambard Kingdom Brunel (1806–59) was a genius of bridge design. Brunel designed and built two of the earliest suspension bridges. He also planned and built railways and several huge steamships.

Aqueducts
Not all bridges carry roads or railway tracks. An aqueduct is a bridge that carries water. The Romans built aqueducts to supply water to the baths and drinking fountains in their cities. More recent aqueducts carry canals over steep-sided valleys in order to keep the canal level. This avoids having to build long flights of locks.

Aqueduct on the River Dee, Wales

Timeline
200 BC Roman engineers build arch bridges of stone or wood, and aqueducts.

1779 The first bridge made of cast iron is built at Ironbridge, England.

1883 In the USA, New York's Brooklyn Bridge is the first bridge to be supported by steel suspension cables.

1930 Switzerland's Salginatobel Bridge is constructed of reinforced concrete (concrete strengthened with steel).

Sydney Harbour Bridge, Australia

1932 Australia's Sydney Harbour Bridge opens, carrying a road and rail tracks suspended from a huge steel arch.

1998 The Akashi Kaikyo suspension bridge over Japan's Akashi Strait has the longest main span in the world.

FIND OUT MORE

BUILDING AND CONSTRUCTION · IRON AND STEEL · RIVERS · ROADS · ROMAN EMPIRE · SHIPS AND BOATS · TRAINS AND RAILWAYS · TRANSPORT, HISTORY OF · TUNNELS

BRONTË SISTERS

THREE OF THE FINEST writers of the 19th century, Charlotte, Anne, and Emily Brontë, were brought up in solitude in a small town in northern England. In spite of many difficulties, including being far away from the world of publishing in London, they produced some of the most popular novels of the period. The books portrayed characters with a new frankness and showed how difficult life could be for women of that era. Their stories still enthral readers of today.

Haworth parsonage

The Brontë sisters were brought up in the small town of Haworth in Yorkshire, northern England. Their father was the curate (priest) at the local church, so they lived at the parsonage (clergyman's house). It was a grim stone building, with a view over the graveyard.

Brontë family
Charlotte, Emily, and Anne lived with their father, Patrick Brontë and their brother, Branwell. Their mother, Maria, died when the children were young and two other children died in infancy, so the sisters were brought up by their aunt. They had a lonely life. They mixed little with other children and had to make their own entertainment.

Education

Charlotte and Emily were sent away to Cowan Bridge school. The conditions were poor and made Charlotte ill. Lowood school, in *Jane Eyre*, is based on her time there. All three sisters later worked as teachers, or governesses – one of the few jobs then open to educated young women.

Cowan Bridge school

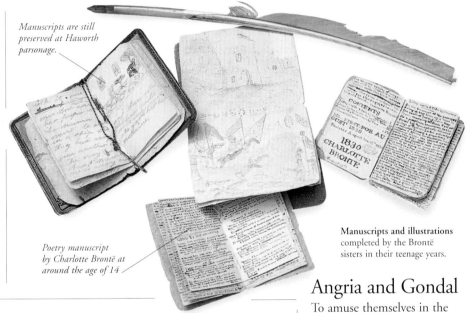

Manuscripts are still preserved at Haworth parsonage.

Poetry manuscript by Charlotte Brontë at around the age of 14

Manuscripts and illustrations completed by the Brontë sisters in their teenage years.

Angria and Gondal

To amuse themselves in the bleak moorland rectory, the Brontë children invented two imaginary lands, called Angria and Gondal. They wrote many stories and poems about these lands, which were peopled with heroes and heroines who lived exciting and tragic lives.

Novelists

In 1846, the Brontës started to get their works published. They began with a volume of poems, but only two copies were sold. In the following two years Emily's *Wuthering Heights*, Charlotte's *Jane Eyre*, and Anne's *Agnes Grey* were published. At the time it was not thought proper for the daughters of clergymen to write fiction, so the sisters used pseudonyms (false names), to keep their identities secret. Many people bought the books and wanted to know more about the authors.

Bell brothers
The Brontë sisters published their books under three male names – Acton, Currer, and Ellis Bell, the initials of which matched those of the sisters' own names. To begin with, even their publishers did not know who the "Bell brothers" really were.

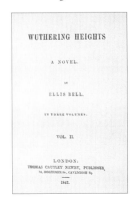

WUTHERING HEIGHTS

A NOVEL.

BY

ELLIS BELL.

IN THREE VOLUMES.

VOL. II.

LONDON:
THOMAS CAUTLEY NEWBY, PUBLISHER,
72, MORTIMER St., CAVENDISH Sq.
1847.

Jane Eyre
Charlotte Brontë's first novel tells the story of Jane Eyre and her struggle to be an independent woman in a hostile society. Working as a governess, she falls in love with her employer, Mr Rochester, only to discover terrible secrets in his past. The novel was considered radical in its time.

Wuthering Heights
Emily Brontë's novel follows a series of tragic relationships through different generations and is especially famous for its depiction of Catherine and Heathcliff. Set against the Yorkshire countryside, the novel deals with contemporary issues of social change and industrialization.

CHARLOTTE BRONTË

1816	Born Yorkshire, England.
1822–32	Educated at Cowan Bridge School and Miss Wooler's School, Roe Head, Yorkshire.
1846	Publishes her poems.
1847	Publishes *Jane Eyre*.
1849	Publishes *Shirley*.
1853	Publishes *Villette*.
1854	Marries Arthur Nicholls.
1855	Dies.

FIND OUT MORE BOOKS   CHRISTIANITY   DICKENS, CHARLES   FILM AND FILM-MAKING   LITERATURE   UNITED KINGDOM, HISTORY OF   WRITING

B

BRONZE AGE

IN ABOUT 3000 BC, prehistoric people began to use bronze – an alloy of copper and tin – instead of stone, to make weapons and ornaments. The dates for this development, which is known as the Bronze Age, vary from culture to culture, but the earliest bronze workers probably lived in Mesopotamia (modern Iraq). These people initially used pure gold and copper, which were easy to hammer into shape, before discovering how to make bronze. They were also responsible for developing the world's first civilizations. The Bronze Age was followed by a time when people learned to smelt and shape iron ore to produce stronger tools and weapons. This period is known as the Iron Age.

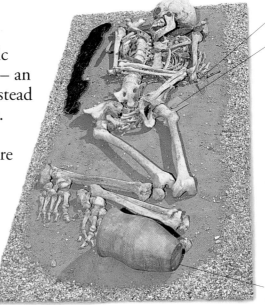

Stone wristguard with gold screws
Copper dagger blade
Pottery beaker for use in the afterlife

The Barnack grave, c.1800 BC

The first metalworkers

In the early days of the Bronze Age, metalworkers used gold, copper, and bronze for luxury items, or for high-status weapons, such as the dagger in the Barnack grave, England. People still made tools from stone, because stone was harder than bronze.

Making bronze

People learned how to extract metal from ores by heating the rock. The metal could then be used to make useful or decorative objects.

Ore
This common type of copper ore was fairly easy for people to spot on the ground.

Yellow chalcopyrite
Blue bornite

Smelting
To extract the metal, Bronze Age people heated the ore to a high temperature. When the metal in the ore reached melting point, they collected it in a round, stone crucible.

Trace of an ingot

Ingots
Early metalworkers discovered how to add molten tin to copper to make bronze. Liquid bronze was poured into round moulds and left to set. The blocks of bronze were called ingots.

Casting

Bronze Age people cast objects by pouring hot, molten bronze into a mould. When the metal had cooled and set, the mould was opened, revealing the finished item. Casting was used to produce decorative items.

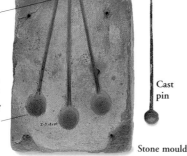

Molten metal was poured through holes.
The mould was carved to the shape of the item.
Cast pin
Stone mould

Mould
This is one half of a stone mould for casting pins. It was made in Switzerland, c.1000 BC. To use the mould, the two halves were fastened together, and metal poured in through the holes at the top.

Cast pin
Bronze pins like this were cast in the stone mould. The mould used to make this pin was carved to create the delicate pattern on the pin-head.

Prongs for lifting meat from a cauldron

Flesh hook

Copper
The royal family of the city of Ur in Mesopotamia used copper for jewellery, as well as for everyday items, such as this flesh hook. They used gold to make beautiful vessels for special occasions.

Ornate French sword

Bronze swords were sometimes cast, although they were stronger when the bronze was beaten into shape. This Danish sword is polished to show the original golden colour of bronze.

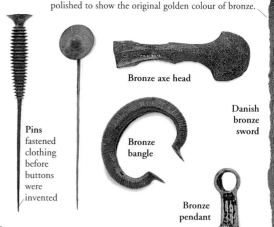

Bronze axe head

Danish bronze sword

Pins fastened clothing before buttons were invented

Bronze bangle

Bronze pendant

Bronzeware
Bronze was prized for its beauty. In Europe, the nobles liked to wear bronze jewellery, such as bangles and pendants, and bronze pins in their clothing. Bronze swords were high-status weapons.

Timeline
3800 BC The earliest known metal objects are produced by smelting. Copper is the main metal smelted in Tepe Yahya, Iran.

3000 BC Bronze objects are used throughout western Asia, where copper is being combined with tin.

2500 BC Bronze is used in the cities of Mohenjo-Daro and Harappa, Indus Valley.

2000 BC Bronze-working comes to the civilizations of the Minoans on Crete and the Myceneans in mainland Greece. These Aegean cultures trade in Europe for copper and tin.

1900 BC Iron Age starts in western Asian areas such as Turkey, Iran, and Iraq.

Shaft-tube axe, Hungary

1800 BC Bronze Age reaches European areas, such as modern Slovakia.

800 BC Early Iron Age starts in central Europe.

FIND OUT MORE   GREECE, ANCIENT   INDUS VALLEY CIVILIZATION   METALS   MINOANS   POTTERY AND CERAMICS   STONE AGE   SUMERIANS

B

BUDDHA

BUDDHISM IS A WORLD faith that has changed the lives of millions of people. It began in Sakya, a small kingdom in northeast India. The founder of Buddhism was a prince, called Siddhartha Gautama, but today he is known simply as the Buddha, a title meaning "the enlightened one". When he was a young man, Siddhartha began a search for an understanding of suffering. By the end of his life he had become the Buddha, founded the Buddhist faith and already had many followers.

Siddhartha, later called the Buddha

Maya, mother of the Buddha

Early life
According to tradition, Siddhartha was born while his mother, Maya, was on her way to visit her parents. She died soon afterwards. His father was told that the boy would become either a great ruler or a Buddha. The king was afraid that Siddhartha would leave the court to become a holy beggar, so confined him to the palace grounds. But eventually he left to search for the true meaning of suffering.

The Buddha meditating

Buddha sat under a holy fig or bo tree

Enlightenment
When Siddhartha left the palace, the suffering he saw around him made him decide to become a holy man. He spent six years depriving himself of food and sleep, and learning about spiritual matters. Eventually he realized that this made him too weak for deep reflection, so he meditated under a tree. Here he made the breakthrough to an understanding of the truth known as enlightenment.

Teaching
After experiencing enlightenment, the Buddha set out to teach others what he had learned. Many were converted, and the Buddha sent them away as wandering missionaries. Later, the Buddha returned to his father's court to teach his own people what he had learned. His father was among the first to be converted.

Sarnath
At Sarnath, near Varanasi, the Buddha preached his first sermon to five men who had previously sought enlightenment with him. He taught them that suffering is caused by desire, and to end suffering they must give up desire. Sarnath became the site of one of the greatest Buddhist shrines.

Mara, the demon

Buddha

Temptations
While Siddhartha was meditating, a demon named Mara sent his beautiful daughters to tempt him from his chosen path. Mara also whipped up a storm and hurled thunderbolts at Siddhartha. But the young man carried on meditating, unmoved. He meditated for a whole night before understanding the truth, which he called *dharma,* and reaching peace, or *nirvana,* in his heart.

Buddha

Bimbisara
Even during his own lifetime, the Buddha commanded so much respect that many people left their homes to follow him and form orders of monks and nuns. When King Bimbisara gave the Buddha a generous gift of land – "the gift of the bamboo grove" – Buddha's followers built the first Buddhist monastery there.

King Bimbisara

THE BUDDHA
Earliest records of Buddha's life were written more than 200 years after he died, so details are hard to verify. The following dates are accepted by most authorities.

563 BC Siddhartha Gautama, son of King Suddhodana of the Sakya, born in northeast India.

533 BC Siddhartha leaves his father's court to become a holy man.

527 BC Siddhartha attains enlightenment, and becomes the Buddha.

483 BC Buddha dies at Kusinagara, in Oudh, India.

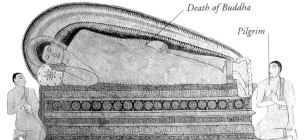

Death of Buddha

Pilgrim

Later life
When the Buddha was 80 years old, he ate some food that had been accidentally poisoned, and died at Kusinagara in India amongst his disciples. Many people came to pay homage to him. His body was cremated and the remaining bones were placed under stone mounds that have since became holy places of pilgrimage for Buddhists.

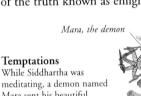

FIND OUT MORE   BUDDHISM   CHINA   INDIA, HISTORY OF   MAURYAN EMPIRE   MONASTERIES   SHRINES

BUDDHISM

THE BUDDHIST FAITH was founded by an Indian nobleman called Gautama Siddhartha in the 6th century BC. Gautama, who became known as the Buddha, or the "Awakened One", told people how to achieve fulfilment. He taught that fulfilment is reached by meditation, wisdom, and correct behaviour in all aspects of life. Buddhists also believe in reincarnation, in other words that a person can be reborn after death. The Buddha is revered by his followers, but not worshipped as a god. For this reason, Buddhism exists side-by-side with other religions in many countries. There are probably some 320 million Buddhists worldwide, although the majority are in Asia.

Rites and ceremonies

Ceremonies at Buddhist temples are usually simple. They involve reciting extracts from Buddhist scriptures and making offerings to the Buddha. A monk may give a sermon. Some Buddhist rituals also involve candle-lit processions and music-making. The Buddhist year is enlivened with festivals, most of which take place at full Moon. The most famous festival is Wesak, at New Year, which celebrates the birth, enlightenment, and death of the Buddha.

Hand gestures on a statue of the Buddha

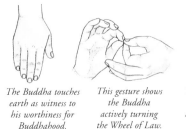

The Buddha touches earth as witness to his worthiness for Buddhahood.

This gesture shows the Buddha actively turning the Wheel of Law.

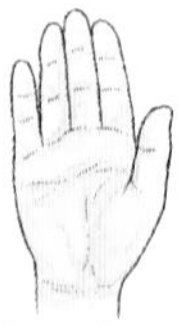

The Buddha reassures an approaching person.

The Buddha

Statues of the Buddha are kept in temples and homes to inspire Buddhists to live as he did. Buddhists bow before the statue to show their respect. They also carry out the ceremony called "Going for refuge", in which they recite texts that show their dedication to the Buddha, to his teaching (the Dharma), and to the community of Buddhists (the Sangha).

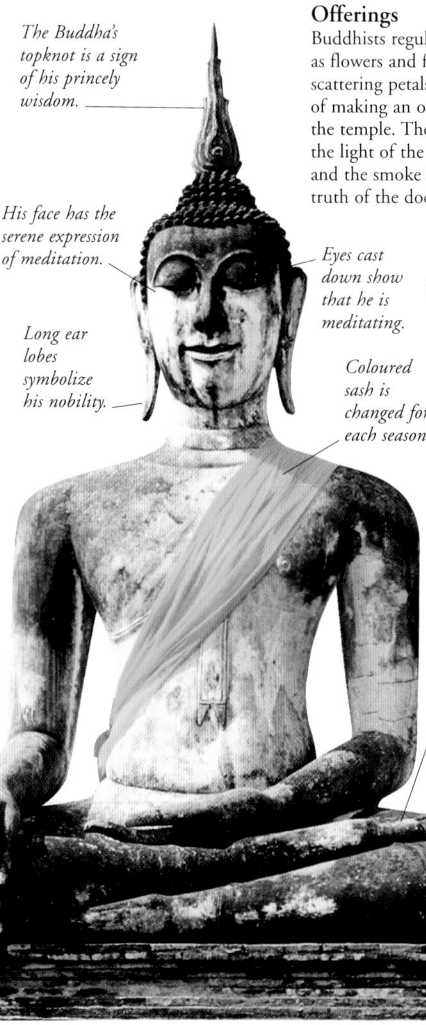

Teachings

The Buddha taught the Four Noble Truths, which explain the Buddhist attitude to suffering and how fulfilment can be achieved. The Truths say that suffering is always present in the world; that the human search for pleasure is the source of suffering; that it is possible to be free from these desires by achieving a state called nirvana; and that the way to nirvana is through the Eightfold Path.

Pictures in the inner circle reveal the six realms of existence.

In each realm, a Buddha-figure helps the beings there.

Three animals in the centre are symbols of ignorance.

Wheel of Life

Wheel of Law

The Eightfold Path

The Path teaches that the way Buddhists lead their lives should be correct in eight important aspects: understanding, thought, speech, action, means of livelihood (work), effort, recollection, and meditation. The eight-spoked Wheel of Law shown above represents each of the eight stages of the Path.

Karma

Buddhists believe in the law of karma. According to this law, good and bad actions result in fitting rewards and punishments, both in this life and in later rebirths. The Wheel of Life is a symbol of rebirth. When people die, they are reborn into one of its six realms of existence.

Offerings

Buddhists regularly make offerings to the Buddha, such as flowers and food. Burning incense or candles and scattering petals around the Buddha's statue are ways of making an offering that also beautifies the temple. The light of the candles is the light of the Buddha's great wisdom, and the smoke from incense wafts the truth of the doctrine towards the devotees.

Candles

Incense

Lotus flowers

The Buddha's topknot is a sign of his princely wisdom.

His face has the serene expression of meditation.

Long ear lobes symbolize his nobility.

Eyes cast down show that he is meditating.

Coloured sash is changed for each season.

Buddha's cross-legged position is called the lotus position.

Meditation

Buddhists meditate in order to purify their minds and free themselves from thoughts about material things. In this way they hope to achieve "perfect mindfulness", one of the stages in the Eightfold Path. One way in which they meditate is to concentrate on feeling their breath going in and out. This empties the mind of selfish thoughts, making the person calmer and the mind clearer.

Branches of Buddhism

From its beginnings in India, Buddhism spread around eastern and Southeast Asia, where the majority of the world's Buddhists still live. There are also Buddhist communities in other parts of Asia, and in the West. Buddhism has two main strands – Mahayana and Theravada – but other forms of Buddhism with distinctive features have also developed.

Theravada

This branch of Buddhism is closest to the teachings of the Buddha himself. It is dominant in Southeast Asia (Burma, Cambodia, Laos, Sri Lanka, and Thailand). Theravada Buddhists revere the Buddha and do not worship other figures. They aim to become "perfected saints" by following the Eightfold Path and tend to believe that people can reach the state of nirvana only through their own efforts.

Mahayana

This form of Buddhism prevails in China, Korea, Japan, Mongolia, Nepal, and Tibet. A follower's first aim is to become a Bodhisattva, an enlightened being who does not pass into nirvana but remains in this world in order to help others to enlightenment. Mahayana Buddhists therefore place a high value on charity.

Monks are given offerings of food by locals.

Almsgiving emphasizes the close relationship between monks and lay people.

Chinese Bodhisattva head

Zen

This form of Buddhism originated in China and spread to Japan in about the 13th century. Zen Buddhists aim to lead a simple life, close to nature, using everyday actions as a means of meditation. Zen Buddhists meditate in a way that tries to see beyond logical patterns of thought and preconceived ideas.

Tibetan Buddhism

A form of Mahayana Buddhism is found in Tibet. Here, special value is placed on the Buddhist virtues of meditation and wisdom. Tibetan Buddhists have their own rituals, such as repeating sacred sayings, or mantras. Since the Chinese invasion of Tibet in the 1950s, few Buddhist monasteries remain in Tibet.

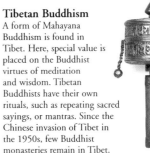

Mantra

Inside a prayer wheel is a mantra that the monk repeats while spinning the wheel.

A Zen monk tidies a garden.

Monasticism

Buddhist monasteries began when the Buddha's followers built permanent settlements to live in together during the rainy season. Today there are many monks (and some nuns) who devote their lives to explaining the Buddha's teachings and setting an example by the way they lead their lives.

Shaven head shows the monk has renounced worldly vanities.

The monk's meditative pose suggests peace and stability.

Sharpening stone

Alms bowl lid is also used as a plate.

Needle and thread   **Razor**   **Water strainer**

Alms bowl lid

Living as a monk

Monks live apart from their families and have few personal possessions. They rely on gifts for survival, carrying alms bowls into which people place food. They obey strict rules. They must avoid entertainments in which there is singing or dancing, give up decorative clothes, and eat only at set times.

Alms bowl   **Belt or girdle**

Sacred texts

Buddhism has sacred texts made up of sayings and sermons, many of them attributed to the Buddha. One of the most important books of writings is the Dharmapada, which forms part of the Pali Canon, the oldest collection of Buddhist scriptures.

In Tibetan-style libraries, manuscripts are wrapped in cloth and placed between boards.

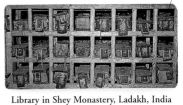

Library in Shey Monastery, Ladakh, India

Temples

The religious buildings of Buddhism vary widely in their shape and decoration, from Japanese pagodas to Thai wats. But all contain statues of the Buddha. The statues act as a focus for devotion and for offerings. People go to the temples to carry out acts of private worship and for special ceremonies.

Wat Benchamabophit, in Thailand's capital, Bangkok, is known as the marble temple.

Stepped roofs symbolize stages of spiritual development.

Devotees gather with their offerings in the grounds of the temple.

Dalai Lama

The Dalai Lama is the spiritual and political leader of Buddhists in Tibet, who believe that each Dalai Lama is a reincarnation of the previous one. The present Dalai Lama, Tenzin Gyatso, was born in 1935. In exile since 1959 following the Chinese takeover, he is still Tibet's most important leader.

FIND OUT MORE   ASIA, HISTORY OF   BUDDHA   CHINA, HISTORY OF   FESTIVALS   MAURYAN EMPIRE   RELIGIONS   SHRINES   SIGNS AND SYMBOLS   THAILAND AND BURMA

BUFFALO AND OTHER WILD CATTLE

THE FIVE SPECIES OF BUFFALO, and all other cattle, are members of the family Bovidae. They have split, or cloven, hooves, and both sexes have horns which they can use to defend themselves. The animals also gain some protection from living together in herds. Only the anoas are solitary animals. Cattle were among the earliest animals to be domesticated. The Asiatic buffalo, yak, banteng, and gaur all have a domesticated version. Loss of habitat, hunting, and diseases have drastically reduced the world's wild cattle. No fewer than nine of the eleven species are in danger of extinction.

Broad hooves support the weight of the buffalo.

Plains bison

Bison

Often wrongly called buffalo, there are two species of bison. The American bison is a grassland animal which appears in two forms – the plains bison and the woods bison. The European bison, or wisent, is a forest dweller. Bison are massive animals standing more than 1.5 m (5 ft) tall and weighing more than 910 kg (2,000 lb).

American bison
The head, neck, and forequarters of the American bison are covered with long hair, which, with the large hump, makes the forequarters appear much bigger than the hindquarters. The horns are short and curved, and are grown by both sexes.

European bison
The wisent lives in Poland's Bialowieza Forest. It is taller than the American bison and has a longer, less barrel-like body, and longer legs. Its hindquarters are also more powerfully built.

African buffalo

The buffalo is the only species of wild cattle found in Africa. Cape buffalo bulls are up to 1.5 m (5 ft) at the shoulder and weigh more than 816 kg (1,800 lb). Their horns have a span of up to 1.5 m (5 ft) and form a massive helmet, or boss, across the head. A smaller sub-species, the forest buffalo, lives in equatorial forests.

Asiatic buffalo
There are four species of Asiatic buffalo – the water buffalo (shown here), the lowland and mountain anoa, and the tamarau. The water buffalo occurs in a domestic and a wild form, but only a few wild herds survive. Its horns are semi-circular and sweep outward and backward.

Endangered tamarau
Confined to the highlands on the island of Mindoro in the Philippines, this dwarf buffalo has been relentlessly hunted. Only about 100 survive today.

Oxen

The group of wild cattle commonly called oxen contains four species – the yak, the banteng, the gaur, and the kouprey. Domestic cattle also belong to this group. Most breeds of domestic cattle are descended from the now-extinct aurochs, which at one time inhabited the plains and woodlands of Europe and Asia in great numbers.

Yak
Largest of the wild cattle, the wild yak lives in herds high up on the Tibetan Plateau in Central Asia. To protect them against the bitterly cold climate, yaks have long, shaggy black hair reaching almost to the ground, with a thick undercoat.

Banteng
Found in Southeast Asia, Java, and Borneo, the banteng is a shy animal. Females and young are a brick-red colour; adult males are black.

Largest and smallest
Wild cattle range in size from the wild yak, which is more than 2 m (6.5 ft) high at the shoulder, to the mountain anoa, which is no more than 76 cm (30 in) high.

Mountain anoa

Wild yak

CAPE BUFFALO

SCIENTIFIC NAME	*Syncerus caffer*
ORDER	Artiodactyla
FAMILY	Bovidae
DISTRIBUTION	Africa, south of the Sahara
HABITAT	Grassland and woodland savannahs, but seldom far from water
DIET	Mainly grass, occasionally supplemented with foliage
SIZE	1.5 m (5 ft) at the shoulder
LIFESPAN	About 20 years

FIND OUT MORE   DEER AND ANTELOPES   FARMING   NORTH AMERICAN WILDLIFE   SHEEP AND GOATS

BUGS

THE WORD BUG is often used to describe any crawling insect or a disease-causing germ. The true bugs are a group of insects that have long feeding tubes specially adapted for sucking fluids out of plants and animals. Bugs, such as shield bugs, are often brightly coloured, and, as a group, they are remarkably varied in shape. There are about 55,000 species of bug, including large solitary insects, such as giant water bugs and cicadas, and tiny creatures, such as scale insects, bedbugs, and aphids. It is the smaller bugs, such as greenfly and leaf hoppers, that create problems for farmers because of the severe damage they cause to crops.

Features of a bug

All bugs have specialized mouthparts with cutting implements for piercing, and needle-like sucking tubes held within a protective sheath. Some bugs, such as lantern bugs, have their membranous wings exposed when at rest; others have forewings that are partially thickened and used not for flight, but as a protective cover for the delicate hind wings.

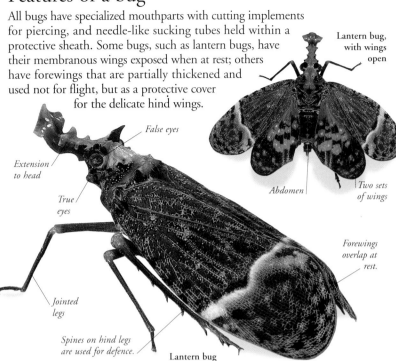

Lantern bug, with wings open

False eyes

Extension to head

True eyes

Abdomen

Two sets of wings

Forewings overlap at rest.

Jointed legs

Spines on hind legs are used for defence.

Lantern bug

Reproduction

Bugs attract a mate in many ways, such as giving off scent, or vibrating the surface of water. Male cicadas attract females with their loud song, produced by drum-like organs on the abdomen. During mating, male and female bugs are often attached for hours. Females usually lay hundreds of eggs. These hatch into nymphs – tiny versions of their parents – and moult many times before reaching adult size.

Parthenogenesis

Aphids such as greenfly and blackfly, multiply rapidly, because they can reproduce without mating. Females produce a succession of identical female offspring from unfertilized eggs, each of which later produces more of the same. This is called parthenogenesis.

Shield bugs

Shield bugs are found virtually worldwide. They are also called stink bugs, as they can give off a bad smell. Females protect their eggs and young from attack.

Young shield bug nymphs being guarded by their mother.

Feeding

Bugs use their mouthparts to cut a hole in their food and pierce the soft parts inside. They inject enzymes and digestive juices through a pair of tiny tubes to break down solids and suck up the resulting fluids. In this way, predatory bugs, such as assassin bugs, can suck their victims dry. Bedbugs are parasites that suck the blood of birds and mammals, including humans. Some bugs feed only on plant juices.

Assassin bugs

Assassin bugs are carnivores. Most prey on other invertebrates, such as millipedes. Some steal prey already caught in spiders' webs. Assassin bugs can squirt toxic saliva at would-be predators.

Feeding tube

Assassin bug feeding on a cockroach.

Leaf hoppers

Leaf hoppers are herbivores. They are often considered pests as they cut holes in the leaves of plants, such as cotton plants, to suck out the sap, thereby weakening the plants.

Defence

Small bugs face many enemies from ladybirds to birds. To deter would-be attackers, bugs have evolved a range of defences. Some bugs, such as tree hoppers, have developed elaborate camouflage; others, such as stink bugs, give off bad smells. The larvae of spittle bugs, also known as frog hoppers, hide within a frothy substance called cuckoo spit. Aphids employ ants to protect them by providing their guardians with a nutritious sugary secretion.

Tree hoppers

Tree hoppers camouflage themselves with projections of cuticle that resemble thorns.

Water bugs

Some bugs live in water. Pond skaters skim over water on their dainty legs, while water boatmen dart below the water using paddle-shaped limbs. Underwater bugs come to the surface to breathe, or carry around an air bubble.

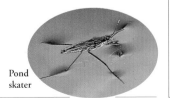

Pond skater

RED-BANDED LEAF HOPPER

SCIENTIFIC NAME	*Graphocephala coccinea*
ORDER	Homoptera
FAMILY	Cicadellidae
DISTRIBUTION	Eastern USA and eastern Canada
HABITAT	Meadows and gardens
DIET	Plant juices
SIZE	Length 8–11 mm (0.4–0.5 in); wingspan 12–16 mm (0.5–0.6 in)
LIFESPAN	Adults: up to 4 months

FIND OUT MORE · ARTHROPODS · CAMOUFLAGE AND COLOUR · FARMING · FLIGHT, ANIMAL · INSECTS · LAKE AND RIVER WILDLIFE · PARASITES · PLANTS, DEFENCE

BUILDING AND CONSTRUCTION

THE SIMPLEST BUILDING is a permanent structure with a roof and four walls. Buildings come in a huge variety of shapes, sizes, and appearances – from skyscrapers and factories to schools, hospitals, houses, and garden sheds. Despite these differences, all buildings have the same basic purpose – to provide a sheltered area in which people can live, work, or store belongings. The engineers, surveyors, and construction workers who plan and build these structures also work on other projects, such as roads, bridges, dams, and tunnels.

Ancient tower-house, Sana, Yemen

Early building
Since the beginning of history, people have built shelters to protect themselves from the weather, wild animals, and their enemies. The first buildings were simple, single-storey structures made of materials such as wood, stone, and dried grass and mud. The first large-scale stone constructions were temples for the worship of gods and goddesses, and palaces in which powerful leaders lived. About 6,000 years ago, people discovered how to bake clay bricks. In time, engineers developed new building methods that enabled them to build higher and lighter structures.

Walls are made from mud and bricks dried in the Sun's heat.

Anatomy of a building
Most buildings have certain features in common, such as walls, a roof, and floors. A large modern building, such as this airport terminal, also has a strong internal frame. Underneath this are the solid foundations on which the whole structure rests. The building is equipped with services, such as electricity and water supplies, as well as escalators, stairs, or elevators to give access to different storeys, and fire escapes that enable people to leave the building rapidly in the event of an emergency.

Roof
A roof is a protective covering over a building. Roofing materials include thatch, clay tiles, slate, glass, and steel. Roofs in wet climates are shaped to make rainwater run off; in cold countries, they slope steeply to stop snow from building up; and in dry climates, they are often flat. Sloping roofs are held up by supports called roof trusses.

Steel beams **Overhead cutaway of roof**

Roof trusses sit on frame. *Roof truss*

Kansai Airport, Japan

Glass wall lets in a lot of light.

Roof is clad with shiny steel panels.

Floor rests on columns, which are part of frame.

Foundations
A building's foundations spread its huge load evenly into the ground, stopping the building from sinking under its own weight. Pile foundations are columns that rest on hard rock; raft foundations are concrete platforms that rest on soft rock. The foundations form the base on which the building's frame is constructed.

Internal frame
The "skeleton" of a large building is its internal frame, which supports the roof, the walls, and the floors. Frames can be made of wood, steel, or reinforced-concrete columns and beams joined together.

Foundations extend underground.

Basement houses service machinery.

Walls and floors
In a house, the walls – which may be made of wood, stone, or brick – are strong enough to hold up the floors, ceilings, and roof trusses. In a larger structure, however, the frame supports the building's weight, and the walls simply hang from the frame. The floors in a large modern building are reinforced-concrete slabs.

Structural engineers
Long before the construction of a building is underway, structural engineers begin working on the design of the building with an architect. They calculate how strong the building's structure needs to be and draw up detailed plans, usually on a computer. When the building work commences, they make sure that everything happens safely, on time, and within the financial budget.

Structural engineer on a building site

Surveyors
Accuracy is extremely important in construction work if the completed building is to have vertical sides and level walls, and be structurally safe. Even small errors in the design or assembly can result in parts not fitting together properly. People called surveyors check the building at every stage of its construction, using special instruments, such as theodolites and spirit levels, to take accurate measurements.

Hard hat

Theodolite is an instrument that measures angles to find distances, lengths, and heights.

Surveyor using theodolite

Building sites

The different stages in the construction of a large building must always take place in a certain order, starting with the preparation of the site. Materials and machinery must arrive just when they are needed: if they are too early, the site may get too crowded; if they are too late, the building work may be delayed.

Site clearance and excavation
The building site must first be cleared, which may involve demolishing other buildings, removing vegetation, and levelling the site. Holes are excavated (dug) for the foundations and basement.

Foundation laying
The next stage is to build the foundations. This involves driving steel beams, called piles, into the ground, or pouring liquid concrete into a deep pit to form a solid base that will support the building.

Frame building
The building's frame soon rises from the foundations. The frame is built either by bolting together steel beams, or by pouring concrete into moulds crossed by steel rods. A shell of metal poles and wooden planks, called scaffolding, is temporarily erected around the building so that workers can reach all parts.

Completed building is ready for use.

Completion
With the frame in place, work starts on the floors, walls, and roof. Services such as water and waste pipes, heating and air-conditioning ducts, and electricity and telephone cables are installed on each storey. Finally, the windows are inserted, and the interior is decorated.

Equipment

Some of the tasks on a building site, such as plastering a wall or laying bricks, are done by tradespeople using hand tools. Other tasks, such as erecting the building's frame or lifting heavy objects, may require large, specialized machines. Together, these machines are known as construction plant.

Plumbline

Set square

Spirit level

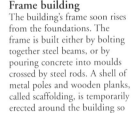

Trowel

Bricklayer's tools

Hand tools
Each tradesperson involved in building and construction uses special tools. A bricklayer, for example, uses a trowel to spread mortar on to bricks, a plumbline to ensure that a wall is vertical, and a spirit level and a set square to check that it is horizontal.

Construction plant
Powerful machines, such as cranes and cement mixers, can do jobs in a few minutes that would take manual workers hours or even days. Other machines include pile-drivers to hammer steel piles into the ground, bulldozers to level building sites, and excavating diggers.

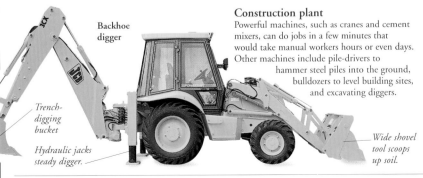

Backhoe digger

Trench-digging bucket

Hydraulic jacks steady digger.

Wide shovel tool scoops up soil.

Building materials

Some building materials, such as steel, concrete, and bricks, are structural – that is, they make up the basic structure of the building. Other materials, such as ceramics and glass, are mainly decorative. Traditional materials, such as stone and wood, have been used for many centuries and are often found locally.

Building site materials

Steel rods for reinforced concrete

Wooden planks for scaffolding

Steel girders for frame

Concrete and steel
Most modern buildings contain concrete, steel, or a combination of both. Concrete is a mixture of cement, water, and small stones (called aggregate) that hardens like rock when it sets. Steel is iron that contains a tiny amount of carbon. Concrete strengthened by steel rods is called reinforced concrete.

Types of concrete

Wood
Some houses have floors made of wooden planks and wooden beams for roof trusses. Scaffolding may have walkways of wooden planks.

Bricks
Blocks of hardened clay, called bricks, are laid in rows and joined together with mortar – a mixture of cement and sand.

Local materials
Many buildings throughout the world are built from materials that occur naturally in the surrounding area. These local materials may include straw, mud, stone, wood, and even animal dung. They can do just as good a job as modern manufactured materials, which are usually more expensive and have to be imported from elsewhere.

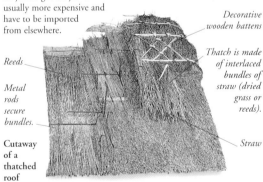

Decorative wooden battens

Reeds

Metal rods secure bundles.

Thatch is made of interlaced bundles of straw (dried grass or reeds).

Cutaway of a thatched roof

Straw

Construction workers
People from a wide range of trades with many different skills will work on a building before it is finished. These tradespeople include welders, bricklayers, electricians, carpenters, plasterers, and plumbers. For safety reasons, construction workers often wear hard hats and other protective clothing, such as goggles.

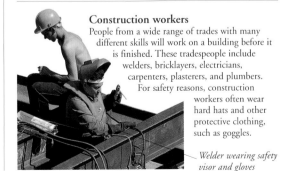

Welder wearing safety visor and gloves

FIND OUT MORE   ARCHITECTURE   BRIDGES   CHURCHES AND CATHEDRALS   DAMS   HOUSES AND HOMES   IRON AND STEEL   ROADS   TUNNELS

B

BUTTERFLIES AND MOTHS

SCALY WINGS AND A COILED feeding tube set butterflies and moths apart from other insects. Together, they form a single group of about 170,000 species, of which 90 per cent are moths. Both have four stages to their life cycle in which they change from a caterpillar to an adult with wings. They feed on plants, and rely on camouflage, irritating hairs or spines, or poisons in their body for protection against predators.

Scales overlap like the tiles on a roof.

Wing scales
Scales on the wings contain coloured pigments. Some scales produce colours by reflecting the light.

The front and back wings of a moth are hooked together.

Moth's bright colouring indicates it is poisonous

Zygaenid moth

Moths

Most moths fly at night. They tend to have drab colours, and have a fatter body and longer, narrower wings than butterflies. When resting, moths usually hold their wings open or fold them flat over their back.

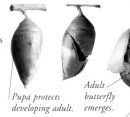

Swallowtail butterfly

Butterflies

In most cases, butterflies are more brightly coloured than moths and have a thinner body. Unlike moths, they hold their wings upright when resting. The front and back wings are loosely joined together by a lobe on the back wing that grips the front wing. Butterflies are usually active by day rather than by night.

Wings are made of a tough membrane supported by a network of rigid veins.

Proboscis is rolled up when not in use.

Moth antennae have a large surface area for picking up scents.

Feeding tube
Adult butterflies and moths suck up liquid food, such as flower nectar, through a tube called a proboscis. A few moths have no proboscis because they do not feed as adults.

Antennae
Insects use their antennae for smelling, touching, and tasting. Butterfly antennae are clubbed; moth antennae range from single strands to feathery branches.

Life cycle
Butterflies and moths start life as an egg, which hatches into a caterpillar. This feeds and grows until it turns into a pupa. The adult develops inside the pupa. This process of change is called metamorphosis.

Pupa protects developing adult.

Adult butterfly emerges.

Butterfly pumps blood into its wings to expand and stiffen them.

Adult Blue Morpho

Defence

To escape from predators, butterflies and moths often fly away or hide. Some have irritating hairs or spines, or are poisonous. Bright colours may warn predators that a butterfly or moth is poisonous. Poisons often build up in a caterpillar from the plant it eats. These then remain in the adult.

Camouflage
Many butterflies and moths blend in with their surroundings at some stage of their life cycle. Camouflaged like this, they may escape predators.

Eyespots
False eyes on the wings can startle predators or stop them from pecking the real eyes. A damaged wing is not as serious as an injury to the head.

Mimicry
Some butterflies and moths gain protection by looking like another species of butterfly or moth. The top butterfly shown here is poisonous; the bottom one is not.

Wing colour
When a butterfly is resting, only the underside of its wings shows. This is often coloured for camouflage. The colours of the upper side help to attract a mate.

SWALLOWTAIL BUTTERFLY

SCIENTIFIC NAME	*Papilio palinurus*
ORDER	Lepidoptera
FAMILY	Papilionidae
DISTRIBUTION	From Burma to the islands of Borneo and the Philippines in Southeast Asia
HABITAT	Tropical rainforest
DIET	Flower nectar
SIZE	Wing span: 9.5 cm (3.75 in)
LIFESPAN	Varies (The adults of most butterflies live for only a few weeks or months)

FIND OUT MORE

CAMOUFLAGE AND COLOUR   INSECTS   FLIGHT, ANIMAL

Butterflies

Owl
butterfly

Japanese emperor

Brown-veined white

Orange-barred
giant sulphur

Great spangled fritillary

Viceroy

Great orange tip

Common opal

Peacock

Common blue

Blue morpho

African
giant
swallowtail

Small copper

Chequered
skipper

Swallowtail

Cairns
birdwing

Hewitson's
blue hairstreak

Moths

African
moon moth

Goat moth

Buff-tip

Owl moth

Hornet moth

Magpie moth

Provence
burnet moth

Hoop pine moth

Garden tiger

Giant agrippa

Verdant
sphinx

Oak eggar

Madagascan
sunset moth

Pale tussock

Hieroglyphic moth

B

159

BYZANTINE EMPIRE

IN 395, THE GREAT ROMAN EMPIRE split into eastern and western sections. The western half – still called the Roman Empire – was centred on Rome. The eastern half became the Byzantine Empire with its centre at Constantinople. The Greek character – in language, customs, and dress – of Constantinople contrasted with Latin Rome. Despite efforts on the part of emperors to reunite the two halves of the old empire, the Byzantine Empire gradually grew away from Rome. The Roman Empire collapsed in 410, but the Byzantine Empire existed until 1453 when the Ottoman Turks captured it.

Extent of Byzantine Empire, c.565
Because of its fabulous wealth, superb shipbuilding facilities, and strategic position between Asia and Europe, the Byzantine Empire was under almost constant siege by its powerful neighbours – Persia, Arabia, Turkey, and some states of the Christian west.

Byzantium to Constantinople

Mosque

The ancient Greek port of Byzantium stood on the Golden Horn, a strip of land surrounded by sea on three sides. Constantine the Great (c.274–337) re-designed the city and re-named it Constantinople in 330 AD. Soon it was one of the world's most beautiful cities.

Bridge over the Bosporus Strait, linking Asia and Europe

Art and religion

Byzantine churches were famous for their interiors, which were lavishly decorated on a huge scale, with painted icons and intricate mosaic images of Christ, the Virgin, and saints.

Icons
In the 8th century, the empire was racked by arguments over whether it was idolatrous to worship beautiful religious statues and paintings, known as icons. Finally in 843, it was declared to be legitimate, and their production increased. Later, icons were portable, and collected by Renaissance artists.

East versus west

By the 9th century, the Byzantine form of Christianity was changing from the western, or Roman, form. Greek had replaced Latin as the official language, and the Roman pope and Byzantine patriarch argued over church ritual. However, they were united in their fear and hatred of the non-Christian Turks and Arabs.

Great Schism
In 1054, representatives of the Roman and Byzantine churches excommunicated each other. This religious split, or schism, destabilized political links between east and west, and caused mutual suspicion and hostility.

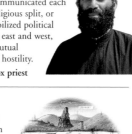

Orthodox priest

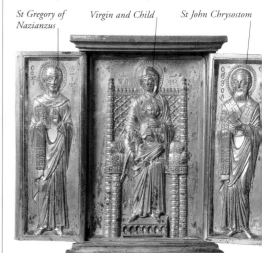

St Gregory of Nazianzus   Virgin and Child   St John Chrysostom

Triptych icon, 12th century   Gilt covering

Hagia Sophia
The biggest church in the eastern empire, Hagia Sophia was built in only five years (532–37). The Ottomans converted it into a mosque in the 16th century, and today it is a museum.

Fall of Constantinople
Constantinople was conquered twice: once by the west and once by the east. In 1204, it was ransacked by Christians on their way to the Holy Land. In 1453, Ottoman Turks overran it, and it became a Muslim stronghold.

Fall of Constantinople, 1453

Mosaics
Byzantine artists pressed cubes of tinted glass, marble, or precious stones into beeswax or lime plaster to make a mosaic. The artists often decorated the images with gold and silver leaf.

Christ Pantokrator, 11th century

Timeline

395 Roman Empire divided into west (Roman) and east (Byzantine).

867–1056 Empire reaches its peak.

The Good Shepherd mosaic, 5th century

529–34 Justinian I introduces his Roman Law Code.

976–1025 Basil II, known as "the Bulgar-slayer", gains more land than any emperor since Justinian I.

1054 Great Schism: Byzantine church breaks with the Roman church and forms the Eastern Orthodox church.

1096 First Crusade: European army joins Byzantine army at Constantinople.

1204 Fourth Crusaders sack Constantinople.

1453 Ottoman Turks capture Constantinople, ending the empire.

Emperor Justinian I
Justinian I (r.527–565), expanded the empire in the west by conquering North Africa, southern Spain, and Italy, while holding off the Persian threat in the east. In addition Justinian built Hagia Sophia, and his Codex Justinianus, or Roman Law Code, still forms the basis of the legal system in many European countries.

FIND OUT MORE
ART, HISTORY OF   CHRISTIANITY   OTTOMAN EMPIRE   PERSIAN EMPIRE   ROMAN EMPIRE

CAESAR, JULIUS

JULIUS CAESAR WAS A BRILLIANT general and ruler of the Roman world. He is one of the most famous, and controversial, figures in history. He transformed the Roman world, expanding Rome's territory into Gaul and suppressing many revolts. He was a fine administrator, reforming the Roman calendar and Roman law and bringing strong government to the republic. Caesar was also a great writer and orator. But he could be unscrupulous in pursuit of his own interests, and made many enemies during his career.

Early life
Caesar was born in Rome in about 100 BC. A member of a rich family, he had a successful military and political career, rising through various offices to become Pontifex Maximus, or high priest, in 64 BC. In 61 BC he became Governor of Further Spain, one of the most important jobs in the Roman republic.

Triumvirate

In the years leading up to 60 BC, rival politicians competed to gain power. Order was restored when Caesar, the financier Marcus Crassus, and the army commander Pompey set up a three-man committee, or triumvirate, to rule Rome. In 59 BC, the triumvirate allowed Caesar to be elected consul, one of the two magistrates who held supreme power. As consul, Caesar strengthened and reformed the government.

Pompey
Gnaeus Pompeius Magnus (106–48 BC), known in English as Pompey, was a Roman general who conquered Palestine and Syria, and did much to get rid of opposition to Roman rule in Spain and Sicily. Although he was a member of the triumvirate and he married Caesar's daughter, he was always Caesar's rival.

Pompey the Great

Gallic wars

From 58–50 BC, Caesar waged a series of wars which led to the incorporation of Gaul (modern France and Belgium) into the Roman republic. Caesar displayed great military ability in the Gallic Wars, and was ruthless with any tribes who tried to resist conquest. Caesar recorded his achievements in his famous memoirs of the campaign.

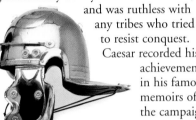

Roman legionary's helmet

Civil war

After the death of Crassus in 53 BC, rivalry between Caesar and Pompey reached new heights. Pompey became sole consul in 52 BC and, with the support of the Roman senate (parliament), declared Caesar an enemy of the people. In 49 BC, Caesar crossed the Rubicon, the river dividing Italy from Gaul, and marched on Rome in triumph. In 48 BC he defeated Pompey. By 45 BC, Caesar had removed all opposition, becoming master of the Roman world.

Roman catapult bolts

Roman cavalry spur

Cleopatra
Caesar followed Pompey to Egypt and remained in the country after Pompey's death. He befriended and lived with Cleopatra, queen of Egypt, and helped establish her firmly on the throne. When Caesar returned to Rome in 47 BC, Cleopatra came with him. After Caesar's death, the Egyptian queen had twin sons with the Roman soldier and politician Mark Antony (c.82–30 BC).

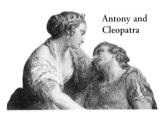

Antony and Cleopatra

Caesar as soldier

Caesar crosses the Rubicon.

Pharsalus
Caesar showed his military skills when, in 48 BC, he defeated the much larger army of Pompey near the Greek town of Pharsalus. Caesar's strategic sense and better location enabled his small force to overwhelm Pompey's army, which was routed. Pompey himself fled to Egypt, where he died.

Battle of Pharsalus

Dictator

In 45 BC, Caesar was appointed dictator for life. He reformed the living conditions of the Roman people by passing new agricultural laws and improving housing. He also made the republic more secure from its enemies.

Assassination
Despite his reforms, Caesar's dictatorial rule made him enemies in Rome. On 15 March 44 BC – the Ides of March – Caesar was stabbed to death in the senate house by rival senators, including Cassius and Brutus. But his work lived on in his great-nephew and adopted son, Octavian, who became emperor.

Assassination of Caesar

JULIUS CAESAR

c.100 BC	Born in Rome.
80 BC	First military service in Turkey.
60 BC	Forms triumvirate with Crassus and Pompey.
59 BC	Elected consul.
58–50 BC	Conquers Gaul.
50 BC	Roman senate declares him an enemy of the people.
49 BC	Starts civil war against Pompey.
48 BC	Defeats Pompey and follows him to Egypt.
44 BC	Assassinated in the senate in Rome by rival senators.

FIND OUT MORE

CAMELS

WELL-SUITED TO DESERT LIFE, camels can withstand extreme conditions. There are two main types: the one-humped dromedary, which lives in Africa and Arabia, and is usually domesticated; and the two-humped Asian Bactrian, some of which still roam wild in the Gobi Desert. Closely related to camels are four animals without humps – llamas, alpacas, guanacos, and vicuñas. All six species, called camelids, belong to the artiodactyls, a group of herbivorous, even-toed mammals that also includes cattle.

Features of a camel

Camels are the largest of the even-toed mammals, standing up to 2.4 m (8 ft) at the shoulder. They have long legs, and walk at an ambling pace. Camels have a split upper lip, which allows them to eat dry, spiky plants. Their lips and upright heads have given camels a reputation for arrogance. In reality this is nonsense. However, camels may spit at, or bite, humans if annoyed or frightened. During the mating season, male camels often fight, biting their rivals when competing for females.

Long eye lashes · *Slit-like nostrils* · *Split upper lip*

Head of dromedary camel

Hump
Contrary to popular belief, the camel's hump is not filled with water, but is a fat store that provides the camel with energy when food is scarce. Because fat is stored in the hump, there is less fat under the rest of the skin enabling the camel to lose heat more easily in hot conditions.

Thick fur keeps camel warm during cold desert nights, and helps prevent overheating in the day.

Feet
Camels' feet have two toes joined by a web of skin; underneath is a soft, flexible pad that splays out when the camel walks. The camel's feet are very wide, and this, together with the pad, prevents the camel from sinking into soft sand and enables it to walk over rough terrain.

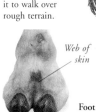

Web of skin

Foot of dromedary

Large, wide feet with soft pads allow camel to walk on sand.

Shaggy fur

Bactrian camel

Long legs help camel walk long distances.

Dromedary camel

Long, curved neck, allows camel to reach desert vegetation.

Eyes and nostrils
Camels have long eyelashes that protect their eyes from fierce sandstorms and enable them to see under difficult conditions. They can close their slit-like nostrils to reduce the amount of sand and dust blowing up the nose, and minimize moisture loss from the nasal cavity.

Ships of the desert

Camels are the only animals that can carry heavy loads long distances in extreme heat and with little water. Nomadic peoples survive in deserts by using camels as pack animals, as well as for meat, milk, and skins.

Salt-laden caravan, Taoudenni, Mali

Water loss

Camels can exist for long periods without water, but make up the loss quickly when water is available. Camels are also adapted to reduce water loss by producing dry faeces and small amounts of syrupy urine. In addition, their body temperature can rise to 40.5°C (104.9°F) during the day, reducing the need to keep cool by sweating, a process that also causes water loss.

During long periods without drinking, a camel can lose 40 per cent of its body mass as water.

Within 10 minutes, camels can drink sufficient water to make up huge losses.

Types of camelid

Related to camels are two species of domesticated camelid, the llama and alpaca, and two wild species, the vicuña and guanaco; all live in or near the Andes mountains in South America. Small herds of guanaco feed on grass and shrubs in shrubland and savannah up to heights of 4,250 m (13,900 ft), from southern Peru to southern Argentina.

Vicuñas are a protected species.

Alpacas' wool may be black, brown, or white.

The wool, milk, and meat of llamas are all used.

Vicuña
Vicuñas, the smallest of the camelids, live in family groups at high altitudes.

Alpaca
The highland peoples of Peru and Bolivia breed alpacas for their long, soft wool.

Llama
Llamas are used as pack animals to carry loads of up to 100 kg (220 lb), at altitudes of 5,000 m (16,400 ft) over long distances.

DROMEDARY CAMEL

SCIENTIFIC NAME *Camelus dromedarius*

ORDER Artiodactyla

FAMILY Camelidae

DISTRIBUTION Domesticated in North Africa, Middle East, southwestern Asia; feral populations in Australia

HABITAT Desert

DIET Any type of desert vegetation, including thorny twigs and salty plants that other animals avoid

SIZE Head and body length 3 m (10 ft); shoulder height 2 m (6.5 ft); weight up to 600 kg (1,320 lb)

LIFESPAN Up to 50 years

 FIND OUT MORE
ANIMALS • ASIAN WILDLIFE • DESERTS • DESERT WILDLIFE • MAMMALS • PIGS AND PECCARIES • SOUTH AMERICAN WILDLIFE

CAMERAS

A LIGHTPROOF BOX with a hole or lens at one end, and a strip of light-sensitive film at the other, is the basic component of a traditional camera. To take a photograph, the photographer points the camera at an object and presses a button. This button very briefly opens a shutter behind the lens. Light reflected from the object passes through the lens and on to traditional film or a digital chip to produce an image.

Shutter release button
Shutter and film speed dial
Self-timer lever
Lens
Lens release button

Shutter and film speed dial
Connection for flash
Film rewind knob
Shutter release button
Aperture scale
Distance scale
Lens

Parts of a camera

The quality of a photograph is controlled by adjusting the film and shutter speed dials, flash, and aperture scales. This is because the final image will depend on the type of film in the camera, the amount of light that enters the lens, and the length of time that the film is exposed to light.

35mm cameras
The most popular cameras are the 35mm, named after the width of the film they use. These cameras are small and easy to manage. They often have in-built features, which adjust automatically to variations in light and distance, to ensure that a clear photograph is taken every time.

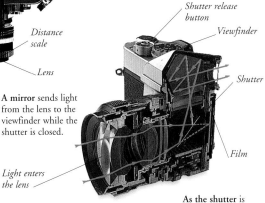

Shutter release button
Viewfinder
Shutter
Film

A mirror sends light from the lens to the viewfinder while the shutter is closed.

Light enters the lens

As the shutter is released, the mirror slips up allowing the light to reach the film (shown by the dotted line).

Digital cameras

Digital cameras contain no film. Instead, the image is captured on a photosensitive chip. Photos are displayed instantly on a screen on the camera and can be deleted if not liked. Images can be loaded into a computer and printed out.

Computer imaging
After an image has been stored on a digital camera, it can then be fed into a computer. From here it is printed out on photo paper or sent over the Internet. Special software allows the picture to be manipulated and gives the photographer a lot of control over the image.

Images are set to high or low quality.
Some cameras can also record tiny video clips.

Digital camera
Batteries inside supply power.

Movable flash head
Flash light sensor

Flashes
A flash provides the extra light needed for taking pictures after dark, or in dim conditions. The flash is electronically controlled to go off at the moment the shutter opens.

Single-lens reflex camera
Unlike other cameras, the view through a single-lens reflex (SLR) camera is that of the actual image that is recorded on the film. Mirrors in the viewfinder correct the upside-down image sent from the lens.

Lenses

Different lenses achieve different visual effects. A wide-angle lens allows more of the scene to appear in a photograph than a normal lens. A telephoto zoom lens can take a close-up shot of a distant object. The fisheye lens distorts images for dramatic effect. These lenses are detachable from the camera.

Normal lens

Wide-angle lens

Telephoto zoom lens

Fisheye lens

Film types
Today, plastic film comes in various sizes and speeds, in a colour or a black and white format, packaged as rolls or plates. The speed, given in ASA/ISO or DIN numbers, indicates how quickly the film reacts to light. A new device, the Electronic Film System, fits into a 35mm camera and holds up to 30 digital images which can be transferred to a computer.

110mm film
35mm film
Plate film

George Eastman
An American inventor, George Eastman (1854–1932), formed the Kodak company. In 1884, he produced the first roll film and in 1888 the first box camera, making photography an accessible hobby. In 1889, he used clear celluloid film on which the first movie pictures were taken.

Timeline
4th century BC The "camera obscura" is developed; it consists of a darkened room into which an image is projected.

1822 Frenchman Joseph Niepce takes the first photograph on a sheet of pewter, coated with bitumen.

1839 Niepce's colleague, Louis Daguerre, announces process for recording images on copper.

1839 William Fox Talbot, an Englishman, invents a process that allows photographs to be copied.

1895 The Lumière brothers of France patent their original camera/projector using celluloid film with sprocket holes at the edge.

1948 American inventor Edwin Land develops the first instant camera, which is marketed by the Polaroid Corporation.

1956 A camera that records onto reel-to-reel magnetic videotape, rather than plastic film, is invented.

1980s First digital cameras prototyped.

1986 Disposable camera launched.

1992 The jpeg, a compressed file format for storing digital images, is introduced.

FIND OUT MORE   COLOUR   FILMS AND FILM-MAKING   GLASS   INVENTIONS   LIGHT   PHOTOGRAPHY   PLASTICS AND RUBBER   TELEVISION   VIDEO

163

Stills cameras

Early cameras

Image projected upside down

Shutter operated by a cord

Box made camera sturdy

Upper lens is for viewing

Fox Talbot's camera of 1835 required exposure times of over an hour.

Daguerreotype camera of mid-1800s was the first model sold to the public.

Kodak Autographic Special of 1918 was an early roll-film camera.

Ensign of the 1930s, with a side viewfinder: was popular in sports photography.

Brownie Hawkeye of the 1940s reflected the new use of plastic in design.

1950s Duaflex was modelled on the superior twin-lens cameras of the time.

35mm cameras

Shutter and film speed dial

Shutter release button

Zoom controlled by motor

Image is seen here

Manual SLR camera needs to be focused and wound on manually.

Automatic SLR camera has an automatic film-loading and wind-on mechanism.

Basic compact camera has a fixed length lens and built-in flash.

Advanced compacts are often fitted with a zoom lens, giving extra flexibility.

Leica cameras were the first to use the small-format, 35mm film.

Waist-level viewer attachment allows photos to be taken from waist height.

Medium- and large-format cameras

6 x 4.5 cm camera is a small, light, medium-format camera.

6 x 6 cm camera produces a square image and is used by many professionals.

Direct vision camera has rangefinder focusing lenses, reducing size and weight.

6 x 7 cm camera produces a rectangular image ideal for landscape photography.

6 x 9 cm camera produces large images that make very clear enlargements.

Large-format camera uses individual sheets of film for each image.

Special cameras

Large viewfinder

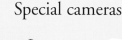

Moving bellows along track alters magnification

Film exit slot

Built in flash

Underwater camera has large easy-to-read dials for use deep underwater.

Panoramic camera rotates to take a view of up to 360° in one exposure.

Bellows camera allows for a very wide range of image magnifications.

Polaroid camera produces a finished photo seconds after taking the picture.

Disposable camera is simple and light, and is used only once.

Digital camera does not use film, but stores pictures digitally.

Movie cameras

Debro pavro was an early movie camera. The handle was turned to start filming.

Technicolor three-strip camera produces good, but expensive films.

Magazines hold three strips of film separately

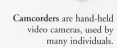

Cine 8 takes still photographs in rapid succession.

Images are recorded directly on video tape

Marey's rifle is a camera shaped like a rifle, with the lens in the barrel.

Trigger works like a shutter release

Matt-box keeps stray light out of the lens

Camcorders are hand-held video cameras, used by many individuals.

CAMOUFLAGE AND COLOUR

ANIMALS HAVE EVOLVED different colours, shapes, and patterns that help them survive. Some, such as birds-of-paradise, are brightly coloured to attract a mate; others, such as the fire salamander, use colour to advertise that they are poisonous to eat. Animals, such as lapwings and polar bears, are camouflaged – coloured or patterned – in such a way that they blend with their surroundings. Camouflage helps animals to hide from predators, but it can also help predators to creep up on their prey.

Bright colours of male make him stand out and attract females.

Types of coloration

Coloration falls into two main categories: cryptic and phaneric. Cryptic colours and patterns help an animal to remain concealed, thus helping protect it from enemies, or assisting in the capture of its prey. The factors that cryptic species suppress – colour, movement, and relief – are exaggerated in phaneric species. Phaneric coloration makes an animal stand out. It can include the conspicuous display of brilliant colours, shapes, and actions, as demonstrated by birds-of-paradise.

C

Newly hatched lapwings match colour of straw.

Young lapwings in nest

Cryptic coloration

Cryptic coloration is common among birds. The plumage of many desert species blends perfectly with the ground colour of their habitat. Birds of the forest canopy, such as parrots, are frequently green to match the dense foliage in which they live. Not all members of the same species are of cryptic colours. Sometimes the female or nestlings, which are generally in greater need of concealment, may be of cryptic colour, while the male is conspicuously coloured to attract a mate.

Red-headed gouldian finch

Phaneric coloration

Phaneric coloration used by animals such as macaws and mandrills makes them stand out and be noticed. It is used between male and female in courtship displays, between parent and young and members of a group for purposes of recognition, between rival males in threat displays, and between predators and prey as warning signals, bluff, or to deflect attack. Long ear- and head-plumes, fans, elongated tail feathers, wattles, and inflatable air sacs are all used to attract attention.

Camouflage

For concealment to be effective, the colour and pattern of an animal's coat or skin must relate closely to its background. A bird's colour often harmonizes with its nesting requirements; some ground-nesting birds choose a nest site with surroundings of similar colour to their eggs as an aid to concealment. Colour and posture can be a highly effective form of camouflage. The many types of concealment include disruptive coloration, disguise, and immobility.

Disruptive coloration

Irregular patches of contrasting colours and tones of an animal's coat divert attention away from the shape of the animal, making it harder to recognize. Tigers and giraffes show disruptive coloration.

Tiger camouflaged in long grass

Giant spiny stick insect

Disguise

Cryptic coloration aims to disguise rather than conceal. The combination of colour, form, and posture can produce an almost exact replica of a commonplace object associated with the habitat. Stick insects, for example, resemble small twigs, while nightjars, when lying down, look like stones or wood fragments.

Mimicry

Mimicry is an extreme form of concealment. It occurs when a relatively defenceless or edible species looks like an aggressive or dangerous species. The mimic not only takes on the appearance of the object it is mimicking, but also adopts its behaviour, assuming characteristics that are completely alien to it. For example, harmless milk snakes resemble poisonous coral snakes so that other animals will not attack them. The monarch, a poisonous butterfly, is mimicked by a non-poisonous species, *Hypolimnus*, which is indistinguishable from it.

Coral snake

Milk snake

Milk snakes have stripes of the same colour as coral snakes, but in a different order.

Immobility

Effective camouflage is possible only if an animal remains still. Many animals react to danger by freezing. For example, if confronted with danger, reedbuck crouch down with their necks outstretched, and by remaining motionless, become hard to distinguish from their surroundings. Some birds, particularly ground-nesting birds such as nightjars, squat down to reduce the shadow they make.

Reedbuck

Assassin bug

Many species of assassin bugs resemble the insects on which they feed. This enables them to get close to their prey without being detected, before seizing it and injecting a toxic fluid. One species of assassin bug, *Salyavata variegata*, lives in termite nests. It camouflages itself by covering its body in debris, including the bodies of termites, and then enters the nest, unnoticed, to feed on the inhabitants.

Assassin bug covered in debris by termites' nest

Termite

Social displays

Social displays take many different forms, from threat display to courtship and bonding. Both cuttlefish and octopuses can change colour; they darken and flash different colours to intimidate rivals or enemies. The male Uganda kob, a type of antelope, establishes territorial breeding grounds by displaying along the boundary of his territory. Lowering his head, he makes a mock attack with his horns. This warns rival males to keep out of his territory, while at the same time, induces other females to join his harem.

Ring-tailed lemurs signalling with raised tails

Signalling

Signs and signals help animals to maintain contact, preserve the social hierarchy, and intimidate rivals and enemies. The signals have to be conspicuous and unmistakable. The ring-tailed lemurs of Madagascar raise their long black-and-white tails to waft scent at their rivals, and to enable all members of a group to maintain contact. The black rings encircling the cheetah's white-tipped tail enable the cubs to follow their parent, which would otherwise be invisible in the long grass. The young of ringed plovers have a white neck-band which helps the parents keep the brood together.

Courtship

Many animals use courtship displays to attract a mate. The fiddler crab, for example, waves its outsize claw, the elephant seal inflates its nose, and the grouse spreads its tail and inflates its air sacs. Among the most impressive courtship displays are that of the male peacock, which spreads his brilliantly coloured tail plumage, and the elaborate rituals of birds-of-paradise and bowerbirds. These involve vibrating the body, fanning feathers, puffing out plumage, decorating nesting areas, and calling loudly.

Tail feathers overlap and rest on the ground when relaxed.

Peacock

Strong feathers at the rear, attached to muscles, are used to raise the long feathers.

Peacock with tail feathers raised

Peacock starting to erect tail plumage.

Male calls as he starts to display.

Warning signals

Animals use many methods to frighten off other animals. Warning colours make prey appear unpalatable to discourage predators. Many poisonous and venomous animals do not need to be camouflaged; they advertise themselves with bright coloured patterns of red, yellow, and black, which are recognized warning colours. Skunks' black and white coats warn they can squirt foul-smelling spray.

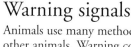

Red and black froghopper

Henry Walter Bates

The English naturalist and explorer, Henry Bates (1825–92) spent 11 years exploring the Amazon, returning with 8,000 species of previously unknown insects. In 1861, he published a paper on mimicry which made an important contribution to the theory of natural selection. He suggested that some harmless insects looked like harmful ones to discourage predators from attacking them.

False warning

Many animals employ bluff as a means of defence. In birds, this may take the form of fluffing up feathers, spreading wings, and clacking beaks. Many frogs and toads blow themselves up, to make them appear larger; the hawkmoth caterpillar looks like a snake to intimidate enemies; and the Australian frilled lizard erects its frill and hisses loudly to intimidate intruders.

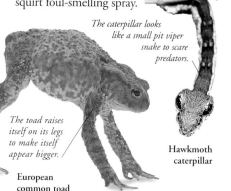

The toad raises itself on its legs to make itself appear bigger.

European common toad

The caterpillar looks like a small pit viper snake to scare predators.

Hawkmoth caterpillar

Seasonal change

Some Arctic animals, such as the polar bear and snowy owl, remain white throughout the year; others undergo a seasonal change. In far-northern latitudes, the stoat becomes completely white in winter, except for the tip of its tail, which remains black. In the warmer parts of its habitat, it can retain its russet coloration, become part-coloured, or change to white as needed. This ability to change colour provides the stoat with effective camouflage throughout the year.

Stoat with dark summer coat

Stoat with pale winter coat

FIND OUT MORE   BIRDS   BUGS   DEER AND ANTELOPES   FROGS AND TOADS   LIONS AND OTHER WILD CATS   MONKEYS AND OTHER PRIMATES   OWLS AND NIGHTJARS   POISONOUS ANIMALS   SNAKES

CAMPING AND HIKING

ONE OF THE MOST popular types of holiday, camping offers people the chance to enjoy the great outdoors at close quarters. For many people, their first experience of camping is as children, setting up a tent in their own back yard. But it is also a popular activity with adults, who enjoy getting away from cities to explore the countryside, and perhaps even learning survival skills in the wild. Camping offers the freedom to choose to stay at one campsite through a holiday, or to set up camp at a different site each night. Whatever the type of holiday, it is important to take the appropriate clothing, food, and equipment.

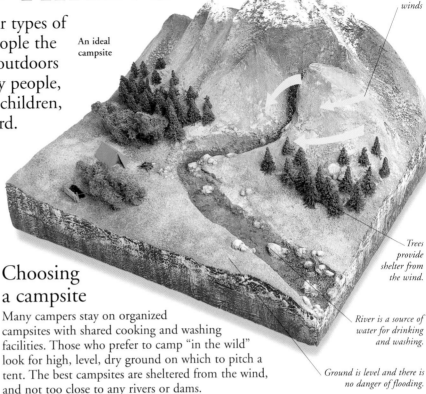

An ideal campsite

Prevailing winds

Trees provide shelter from the wind.

River is a source of water for drinking and washing.

Ground is level and there is no danger of flooding.

Choosing a campsite

Many campers stay on organized campsites with shared cooking and washing facilities. Those who prefer to camp "in the wild" look for high, level, dry ground on which to pitch a tent. The best campsites are sheltered from the wind, and not too close to any rivers or dams.

Making a teepee fire

Fires provide warmth and a means of cooking, but they can also be dangerous. Campers must make certain that a fire is permitted, safe, and will not harm their tent or the surroundings. They are especially careful if a strong wind is blowing.

Fire ingredients

Tinder

Kindling

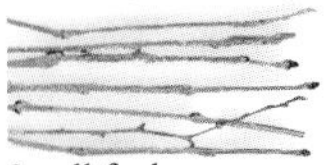

Small fuel

Main fuel

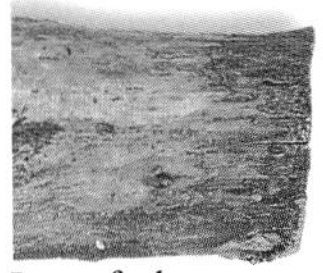

Large fuel

1 The camper gathers the fuel he or she needs (ranging in size from twigs to branches), cuts out a square of turf, and puts a layers of sticks in the hole.

Make sure the fuel is dry.

2 The camper then balances four sticks to meet at the top in a teepee shape, making sure the teepee has enough space for tinder inside the sticks.

3 Gradually, the camper adds more sticks, making the teepee as sturdy as possible, and puts some tinder, such as leaves and dry grass, inside.

Hole for putting in tinder

4 Having set light to the tinder, the camper gradually adds more tinder, then twigs and larger pieces of fuel. He or she takes care not to knock the teepee over. When the teepee burns, it will collapse and create embers that can be used for cooking.

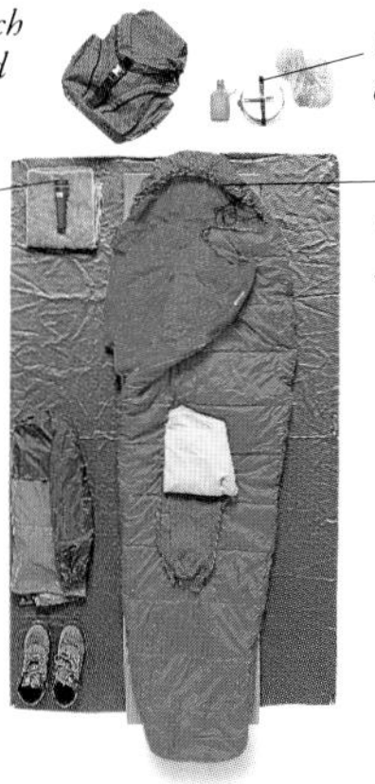

Keep a torch at the head of the sleeping bag.

Unpack things only as needed.

The head of a sleeping bag should face the door.

Living in your tent

There is very little room inside a tent, so campers need to be well organized, or they may lose things and be uncomfortable. To stop damp seeping in from the soil under a sleeping bag, campers put a waterproof sheet on the ground beneath the tent.

Things to take camping

It is better to take only the basic items of equipment camping. These include all the tools needed to set up a camp, as well as cooking and eating utensils. In addition, campers should take hard-wearing clothes to protect them against all types of weather.

First-aid kit

Survival kit

Binoculars

Torch

Swiss army knife

Sewing kit

Matches

Wash kit

Plastic Mug

Lip salve

Compass

Plastic plate and bowl

Cutlery

Food and water

For healthy eating, campers aim to maintain a balanced diet, including fruit and vegetables, bread, and food containing protein, such as fish and meat. If it is difficult or impossible for campers to buy food while they are away, they take tinned or freeze-dried foods, which will not perish. Campers should only drink water from approved sources. If necessary, they take water purifiers or a portable water filter.

Hot drink

Breakfast *Porridge*

Keep water containers spotlessly clean.

Water

Snacks

Chocolate and biscuits

Sugar

Tea

Herbs

Fruit and nuts

Hot soup

Soaked lentils

Lunch

Soup

Stew

Evening meal

Peach juice

Peaches

Meals for a day on the trail

When campers are going on a long hike, they plan their meals before they set out, sorting food into labelled plastic bags. They eats main meals at the start and end of the day, and nibble snacks during the day for energy.

Freeze-dried meal is dehydrated, leaving the texture of food intact.

Dried foods

Dried meals are useful for hikers. They are portable and are prepared simply by adding hot water. This saves time and fuel. If meals are prepared in their bags and resealed, hikers can eat them on the trail.

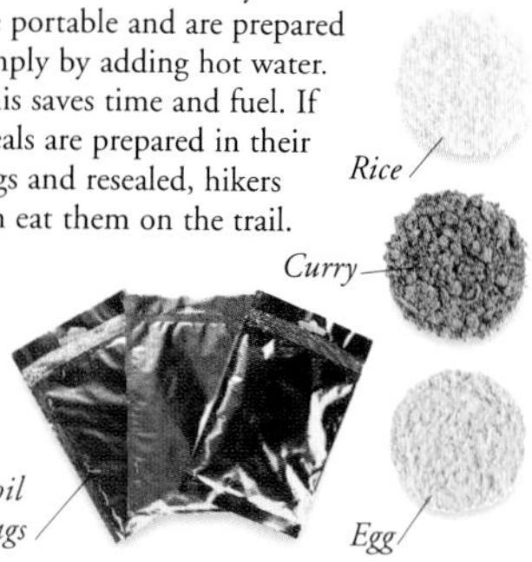

Rice

Curry

Foil bags

Egg

Food for travelling

Boiled sweets

Kidney beans

Gravy cubes

Portable foods

To keep their backpack easy to carry, experienced campers put as much of their food as possible into bags. When they do take tins, these are small enough for the camper to eat the contents in one go.

Salami   **Pasta meal**

Sardines

Frankfurters and baked beans

Canoe hiking

In some parts of the world, people can go hiking in canoes. They travel along rivers and spend the nights camping on the riverbank. Where the river is too dangerous for canoeing, they move to the land and carry their canoes. The canoes used are light and easy to carry.

Caravanning

A popular alternative to camping is caravanning. Caravans are small, compact homes on wheels, which can be towed by a car to a campsite. They are more comfortable to live in than tents. Most have stoves, beds, and toilets, and some may even have refrigerators and showers. Some campsites have permanent, fixed caravans that you can rent for a holiday if you do not have your own.

Using a compass

Hikers take a map and a compass when they go on a long walk, so that they can follow the route and not get lost. A protractor compass, shown here, is popular because it is light, reliable, and accurate.

Hiking

Walking through the countryside, for a few hours or for up to several weeks, is a form of exercise enjoyed by people of all ages. Hikers walk in groups, so that if an accident occurs, at least two can go for help together, and one can stay with the injured member of the party. Hikers should be fully equipped for the sort of journey they are making and should tell someone where they are going.

Shoulder straps can be adjusted to fit.

Ice pick

Windproof jacket with a hood.

Ice hammer

Backpacking

A comfortable way to carry belongings, backpacks range from light day packs to large packs that have space for everything needed for several days' hiking. They sit as high as possible on the shoulders, to distribute weight.

Mountain walking

The most difficult and dangerous form of hiking is mountain climbing. Mountain climbers enjoy testing their strength and skill on steep rock faces. They need to be particularly fit, and use special climbing equipment.

Crampon

Tent poles and pegs in the same bag

The pack is kept full so heavy items stay at the top.

Sleeping bag at the bottom.

How to pack a backpack

To keep the contents of a backpack dry, line it with a plastic bag and put everything in separate plastic bags. Pack the lighter, bulkier things at the bottom and the heavier things at the top. Spare clothes can be packed down the back to protect the spine.

FIND OUT MORE

ENERGY   **EXPLORATION**   **FIRE**   **FIRST AID**   **FOOD**   **HEALTH AND FITNESS**

CANADA

THE WORLD'S SECOND LARGEST country, Canada covers the northern part of the North American continent and is made up of ten provinces and three territories. Canada borders Alaska and the Pacific Ocean to the west, and the Atlantic Ocean to the east. Winters in the northern third of the country, much of which lies within the Arctic Circle, are so severe that very few people can live there. About 80 per cent of Canadians live within 320 km (200 miles) of the US border. Canada has huge forests, rich mineral resources, and open, fertile farmland.

CANADA FACTS

CAPITAL CITY	Ottawa
AREA	9,976,140 sq km (3,851,788 sq miles)
POPULATION	31,000,000
MAIN LANGUAGES	English, French, Chinese, Italian, Native American
MAJOR RELIGION	Christian
CURRENCY	Canadian dollar
LIFE EXPECTANCY	79 years
PEOPLE PER DOCTOR	476
GOVERNMENT	Multi-party democracy
ADULT LITERACY	99%

Ottawa

Canada's capital sits on the south bank of the Ottawa River, and has a population of 921,000. The city has clean, wide streets, many lined with parks. The Rideau Canal, part of a complex of lakes and canals linking Ottawa with Lake Ontario, freezes in winter, becoming the world's longest skating rink.

Skating on the Rideau Canal

Physical features

Covered in lakes, rivers, and forests, Canada has one-third of the world's fresh water. Frozen islands lie in the Arctic, high mountains in the west, and vast prairies in the south.

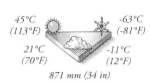

45°C (113°F)   -63°C (-81°F)
21°C (70°F)   -11°C (12°F)
871 mm (34 in)

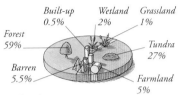

Built-up 0.5%   Wetland 2%   Grassland 1%
Forest 59%
Tundra 27%
Barren 5.5%
Farmland 5%

Climate

Most of Canada has a continental climate with long, bitterly cold winters and hot, humid summers. Coastal areas are generally mild, especially the Pacific west coast. The glaciers and ice-caps of the north are permanently frozen.

Land use

Canada's vast prairies are used for growing wheat. The forests support a thriving timber industry. Only five per cent of Canada's land area is cultivated.

Rocky Mountains

The snow-capped Rocky Mountains dominate western Canada, extending south into the USA. Canada's highest mountain is Logan, at 5,959 m (19,551 ft).

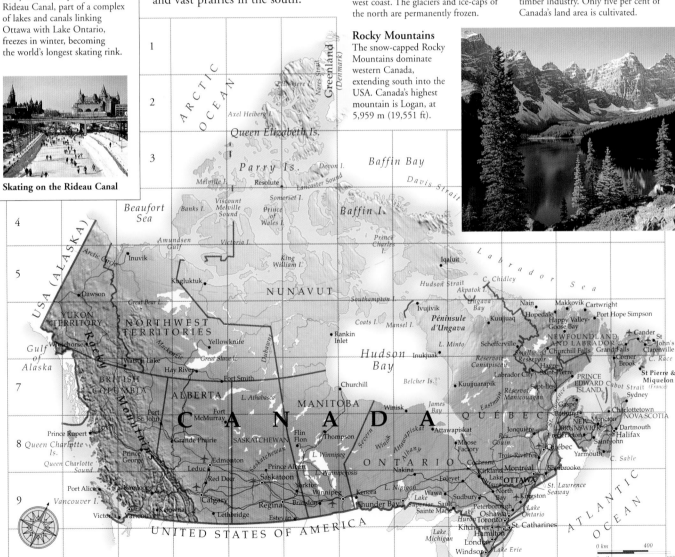

People

Most Canadians have European ancestors who emigrated to Canada from the UK, France, Germany, Scandinavia, and Italy. There are large numbers of Ukrainians, Indians, and Chinese. The indigenous peoples of Canada form about four per cent.

3 per sq km
(8 per sq mile)

77% **23%**
Urban **Rural**

Inuit
The Inuit are one of the country's indigenous groups, and almost 50,000 Inuits live in northern Canada. One-quarter are settled on Baffin Island, in the east Arctic, and speak their own language, *Inuktitut*. In 1999 the Inuit homeland of Nunavut was made a territory.

Leisure

Many Canadians enjoy outdoor activities. In the summer, people sail, raft, canoe, or simply enjoy one of Canada's many well-kept parks. The major spectator sports are hockey, baseball, and football.

Winter sports
Plentiful snow makes skiing and ice-skating popular with many Canadians. Ice hockey is played everywhere, from frozen backyards to national stadiums. Calgary hosted the 1988 Winter Olympics.

Calgary Stampede
One of the world's largest rodeos, the Calgary Stampede attracts one million visitors every year. Held in July, the 10-day rodeo is an exciting recreation of the Wild West. People dress up in cowboy outfits and try their luck at calf roping, chuck wagon racing, and bronco riding.

Hardwood stick

Tough rubber puck is hit into the goal.

Farming

Five per cent of Canada's land is arable, and the country is a top exporter of wheat, oats, maize, and barley. Forest products and fish are also key exports. Cattle and pigs are raised on the pastures of the southeast. Three per cent of the work-force are farmers.

Apple

Cranberries

Niagara Fruit Belt
The land between Lakes Ontario and Erie is called the "Niagara Fruit Belt" because the soil and climate are ideal for growing soft fruit, such as cherries and peaches. Apples and cranberries flourish in British Columbia. In the east, the maple tree, whose leaf is Canada's national emblem, yields rich syrup, a favourite served with sweet pancakes.

Maple leaves

Wheat
Canada's main cereal crop is wheat, and on the eastern prairies, around Saskatchewan, wheat farming is a way of life. About half of the 29,870,000 tonnes (32,930,000 tons) grown every year are exported.

Transport

The 8,000-km (5,000-mile) Trans-Canada Highway links the east and west coasts. The St Lawrence Seaway provides trade links for the eastern provinces. A vast air network, railways, rivers, and the lakes are also used for transport.

St Lawrence Seaway
Opened in 1959, the St Lawrence Seaway links the Great Lakes with the St Lawrence River and the Atlantic. Over 725 km (450 miles), a series of locks enables ocean-going ships, from all over the world, to sail inland.

Industry

The centre of Canada's industry is at the western end of Lake Ontario, a region known as "the Golden Horseshoe". Canadian factories process foods, assemble cars, and make steel, chemical products, and paper. The service industries are thriving, and tourism now employs one in ten Canadians.

Nickel

Zinc

Mining
Minerals have been one of the major factors in the growth of Canada's economy. The country is the world's largest producer of zinc ore and uranium, and second of nickel and asbestos.

Forestry
Canada's abundant forests have made it the world's second largest exporter of softwood (fir and pine) and wood pulp. Ten per cent of Canada's labour force work in the lumber industry, where timber is used as a raw material. British Columbia, Québec, and Ontario are the major timber-producing provinces.

Snowplough
Canada's long, cold winters bring heavy snow and ice to the country, making travelling by road difficult and dangerous. Snowploughs work through the day and night to keep roads clear. Most Canadian roads are wide to allow room for snow to be piled up on either side.

Québec

At the heart of French Canada, Québec City has many stone houses and 17th-century buildings, and its old town was declared a World Heritage Site in 1985. The province of Québec is home to nearly 7,500,000 people. More than three-quarters of the people are of French descent, and keep the French language and culture alive. There have been many attempts by the province to claim independence from Canada.

Château Frontenac, Québec old town

FIND OUT MORE CANADA, HISTORY OF FARMING FISHING INDUSTRY FORESTS LAKES NATIVE AMERICANS PORTS AND WATERWAYS ROCKS AND MINERALS TUNDRA WINTER SPORTS

CANADA, HISTORY OF

FOR MOST OF ITS history, Canada has been home to Native Americans and Inuits. They were descendants of the first people to settle there during the Ice Age, and built advanced cultures based on hunting and trapping fish and animals. In 1497, the first Europeans visited the country, establishing settlements in the early 1600s. In the 18th century, French and British armies fought for control of the entire country. The British won, but a sizeable French community has remained in Québec to this day.

First Canadians

The first inhabitants of Canada were peoples from northern Asia who crossed a land bridge from Siberia and moved south through America more than 20,000 years ago. The Inuits lived in the Arctic regions, while other Native American peoples occupied the plains and coastal areas. They all developed their own distinctive cultures. For example, the tribes of the northwest coast recorded their family history on totem poles, carving out representations of the family spirits on the trunks of cedar trees.

Jacques Cartier

The French sea captain Jacques Cartier (1491–1557) was hired by Francis I of France, to look for a northwest passage to China round the north of America. In 1534, he sailed into the Gulf of St Lawrence, and, in 1535, discovered the St Lawrence River. As he sailed up the river, he stopped at two Indian villages – Stadacona (modern Québec) and Hochelaga (Montreal). As a result, French immigrants began to settle by the St Lawrence River.

Fur trading

European settlers were attracted to Canada by the wealth to be made from furs and skins of animals trapped in the forests. The English-owned Hudson's Bay Company, established in 1670, and other trading companies set up fortified trading posts to trade furs and other goods with local Indian tribes. Québec (established 1608) and Montreal (1642) became important centres of the fur trade.

Traders travelled by canoe in order to reach the trading post.

Missionaries built churches to convert Native Americans.

Wigwams made of birch wood covered with skins or bark.

Trading post

Houses and walls were built of wood from the forests.

Capture of Québec

In 1759, British forces led by General James Wolfe attacked Québec, capital of the French colony of New France. Wolfe captured the city arriving from the Gulf of St. Lawrence with a flotilla of 168 ships that carried over 30,000 men. However, both he and the French commander, Louis, Marquis de Montcalm, were killed. All of French North America came under British control.

Wolfe's flotilla arrives in Québec.

Independence

In 1867, Canada became an independent dominion (nation) within the British Empire. At first, the new country consisted only of parts of Ontario, Quebec, and two provinces on the Atlantic coast. Gradually, the other provinces joined. By 1905, most of Canada had joined the Dominion.

Northwest Territories, 1870
Saskatchewan, 1905
Canadian provinces
Nunavut 1999
Ontario, 1867
Alaska
Québec, 1867
New Brunswick, 1867
Yukon Territory, 1898
Newfoundland 1949
British Columbia, 1871
Nova Scotia, 1867
Alberta, 1905
Manitoba, 1870

Immigration

At the end of the 19th century, Canada's economy expanded and two transcontinental railways improved communications. Canada became an attractive place for European emigrants, and between 1891 and 1914, over three million people came to Canada in search of work and a new life. Canada's government encouraged Europeans to emigrate, promising future citizens health and wealth in their new home.

Canadian government poster

Timeline

1497 John Cabot, an Italian sailor, claims Newfoundland for Britain.

1534–35 Jacques Cartier explores the Gulf of St. Lawrence for France; then discovers the St. Lawrence River.

1605 French establish the first European colony at Port Royal, Nova Scotia.

1754 French and Indian War between Britain and France. France forced to relinquish Québec to Britain.

1846 Oregon Treaty confirms present borders with USA

1949 Founder member of NATO

1968 Québec Party formed to demand independence for Québec.

1989 UK transfers all power relating to Canada in British law.

1998 Government apologises to Native Americans over land.

Canadian flag

Québec

Canada recognized both its English- and French-speakers as equal, but in the 1960s, many people in French-speaking Québec began to press for their province to become independent. In 1982, Québec was given the status of a "distinct society", but referendums seeking independence were defeated in 1980 and 1995.

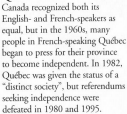

FIND OUT MORE   EXPLORATION   FRANCE, HISTORY OF   NATIVE AMERICANS   NORTH AMERICA, HISTORY OF   UNITED KINGDOM, HISTORY OF   UNITED STATES, HISTORY OF

CARIBBEAN

C

HUNDREDS OF ISLANDS lie in the Caribbean Sea, east of the USA and Central America, and stretching west into the Atlantic Ocean. These Caribbean islands, also known as the West Indies, take their name from the Caribs, the original inhabitants of the region, until the Spanish arrived in 1492. Most islanders today are descendents of African slaves brought to work in plantations between the 16th and 19th centuries. The islands have a tropical climate, turquoise waters, and fine beaches, and have developed a booming tourist industry. However, many people are poor and live by farming.

Volcanic islands

Many Caribbean islands are made of volcanic rocks that emerged from the ocean millions of years ago. Some, such as the St Lucian Gros Piton, 798 m (2,619 ft), and the Petit Piton, 750 m (2,461 ft), are the remains of ancient volcanoes that rise up from the sea on the west coast, near the town of Soufrière. One or two are still active, such as La Soufrière, at 1,219 m (4,000 ft) on St Vincent.

Physical features

Long, sandy beaches, tropical seas, and fine natural harbours have earned the Caribbean islands a reputation for beauty. Most of the islands are forested and mountainous. Some are volcanic in origin, others are founded on coral reefs. Hurricanes, earthquakes, and active volcanoes shake parts of the region from time to time.

Coral islands

The warm, tropical seas of the Caribbean provide ideal conditions for corals. Some of the Caribbean's volcanic islands, such as Barbados and the Cayman Islands, are fringed with coral reefs, which protect them against the lashing waves. The 700 islands and 2,300 islets of the Bahamas are entirely built up of coral, which can be viewed from the bridge that links Nassau with Paradise Island.

Hurricanes

Powerful tropical storms called hurricanes sweep the Caribbean between May and October every year, often causing great damage and economic hardship. They begin as thunderstorms that are whipped up by high winds and warm waters to form destructive stormclouds, swirling around a single centre at up to 360 kmh (220 mph). The violent winds and torrential rain can last for 18 hours.

Regional climate

The countries of the Caribbean all enjoy a warm, tropical climate. Mountainous islands, such as the Windwards, receive three times as much rainfall as lower areas. Most islands have a wet, hurricane-prone season between June and November. From January to March, it is generally dry and pleasant.

28°C (82°F)　23°C (73°F)

1,167 mm (46 in)

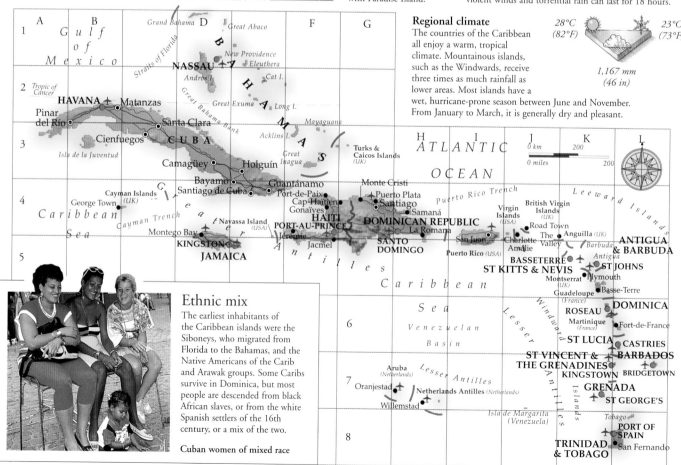

Ethnic mix

The earliest inhabitants of the Caribbean islands were the Siboneys, who migrated from Florida to the Bahamas, and the Native Americans of the Carib and Arawak groups. Some Caribs survive in Dominica, but most people are descended from black African slaves, or from the white Spanish settlers of the 16th century, or a mix of the two.

Cuban women of mixed race

Cuba

The largest island in the Caribbean, Cuba has fertile lowlands set between three large mountainous regions. Sugar, rice, tobacco, and coffee are grown on the lowlands, and chromium and nickel are mined. Formerly a Spanish colony, Cuba has been a communist state since 1959. Hostile politics caused the USA to impose a trade embargo, which has disabled Cuba's economy and kept it agricultural.

Sugar is extracted from the cane.

Sugar
With an annual production of 50,000,000 tonnes (55,000,000 tons), sugar-cane is Cuba's largest crop. It is grown around Havana and processed in the city's factories. Cuba is one of the world's largest producers but suffered a decline in the 1990s following the collapse of one of its main customers, the Soviet Union.

Communism
The only communist state in the Caribbean, Cuba is led by Fidel Castro (b. 1926), who led the revolution in 1959. Under Castro, and with Soviet help, Cuba made considerable social and economic progress, although living standards suffered with the breakup of Soviet communism in 1991. US policies remain hostile.

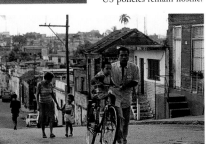

Havana
Situated in a natural harbour, Cuba's chief port and capital, Havana, was founded by the Spanish in 1515. Its old town has many ancient buildings and cobbled streets. There are no shanty towns here, unlike many capitals in the region, but of its 2,328,000 people, half live in sub-standard houses.

Cigars
Cuba's fertile soil and warm climate are ideal for growing high-quality tobacco. Havana cigars are popular all over the world and are made from a blend of at least five different types of tobacco. Cigars are still rolled by hand at long wooden tables.

CUBA FACTS

CAPITAL CITY	Havana
AREA	110,860 sq km (42,803 sq miles)
POPULATION	11,200,000
MAIN LANGUAGE	Spanish
MAJOR RELIGION	Christian
CURRENCY	Cuban Peso

C

Bahamas

Located to the northeast of Cuba, the Bahamas extend south for about 965 km (600 miles). Of the 3,000 coral islands and islets, only 30 are inhabited. Most of the people are black, but on Spanish Wells island, there are around 1,200 white descendants of Puritan settlers. Tourism, fishing, and financial services flourish on the islands.

Festival
Music and dancing are everywhere in the Caribbean, but especially so at the Junkanoo Festival on the Bahamas islands. Held at the end of every year, Junkanoo is a lively celebration with street dancing, music, and colourful parades where people wear wild costumes and blow whistles. The festival has roots in the celebrations of a slave leader called John Canoe, and slaves' days off at Christmas.

BAHAMAS FACTS

CAPITAL CITY	Nassau
AREA	13,940 sq km (5,382 sq miles)
POPULATION	308,000
MAIN LANGUAGE	English
MAJOR RELIGION	Christian
CURRENCY	Bahamian dollar

Jamaica

The third largest island of the Caribbean, Jamaica is a land of springs, rivers, waterfalls, and sandy beaches. A few wealthy families dominate the island, but the slum areas around Kingston are controlled by violent gangs. Many of the people of those areas are Rastafarians, worshippers of the former Emperor of Ethiopia. Jamaica is a prosperous country, with booming tourist, mining, and farming industries. Cricket is a popular game.

Reggae
Jamaica's distinctive form of popular music, reggae, began in the 1960s as an offshoot of rhythm and blues, with songs calling for social and political change. Bob Marley (1945–81), whose band won world fame in the 1970s, is a reggae icon, and his birthday is celebrated by all Jamaicans.

JAMAICA FACTS

CAPITAL CITY	Kingston
AREA	10,990 sq km (4,243 sq miles)
POPULATION	2,600,000
MAIN LANGUAGE	English
MAJOR RELIGIONS	Christian, Rastafarian
CURRENCY	Jamaican dollar

Women
The Caribbean women's rights movement began in Jamaica, and many Jamaican women hold senior posts in economic and political life. An increasing number of women prefer to be single mothers, especially those who have careers. Women also dominate the growing data-processing industry, largely because they work for lower wages than men.

Okra (Lady's fingers)

Breadfruit

Dasheen, or taro

Vegetables
Jamaicans grow a wide range of vegetables. *Dasheen*, or *taro*, is a staple vegetable whose root and leaves are eaten. There are more than 1,000 varieties of *dasheen*, and it is also used for medicinal purposes. Okra, or lady's fingers, are green pods that are used in "pepperpot stews". Breadfruit, with a creamy, pulpy texture, grow to 13 cm (5 in) wide, and are eaten baked or roasted.

Bauxite
Jamaica is the world's third largest producer of bauxite, the ore from which aluminium is made. Refineries produce alumina, the next stage in producing the metal, worth ten times as much as the ore. This provides about half of Jamaica's export income, and accounts for 10 per cent of global output.

Haiti

Occupying the western third of the island of Hispaniola, Haiti is one of the most mountainous countries in the Caribbean. It is also the poorest. About 95 per cent of its people are descendents of black slaves. The country is overcrowded, and has suffered deforestation, soil erosion, and desertification, as well as a turbulent political history.

Voodoo
A Haitian blend of West African religions and Christianity, voodoo uses drums, singing, and dance. Its followers believe that through worship of spirits, they can live in harmony with nature and their dead. Many celebrations coincide with Christmas and the Mexican Day of the Dead.

Voodooists on Gede, or All Saint's Day

HAITI FACTS
CAPITAL CITY Port-au-Prince
AREA 27,750 sq km (10,714 sq miles)
POPULATION 8,300,000
MAIN LANGUAGES French, French Creole
MAJOR RELIGIONS Christian, Voodoo
CURRENCY Gourde

Port-au-Prince
Smart modern hotels have lured many visitors to Haiti's capital, Port-au-Prince. The city has two cathedrals, a university, and many government buildings. However, it also has the worst slums in the Caribbean, most of which are found to the north of the centre. They have no water facilities and are overcrowded.

Puerto Rico
About 1,600 km (994 miles) southeast of Miami, the crowded island of Puerto Rico is a self-governing territory of the USA. It is home to more than 3.8 million people, of African and Spanish descent, of whom half live in the capital, San Juan. An old walled city, it has colonial buildings.

Balconies, old San Juan

Dominican Republic

Lying 966 km (600 miles) southeast of Florida, the Dominican Republic spreads across the eastern two-thirds of Hispaniola. It has the Caribbean's highest peak, Pico Duarte, 3,175 m (10,417 ft), and also its lowest point, crocodile-infested Lake Enriquillo, 44 m (144 ft) below sea-level. Nickel, amber, and gold mining are important industries, and holidaymakers flock to the island for its long, pearly beaches, modern hotels, and wildlife.

People
With a higher standard of living than neighbouring Haiti, the Dominican Republic provides good healthcare for its people. The mixed race middle classes form about 73 per cent of the population. The minority of blacks work as farmers, selling their produce at market.

Farming
About 24 per cent of the labour force work on farms, which are mostly in the north and east of the country, and in the San Juan valley. Sugar, tobacco, and cocoa are main crops, and, although the market has slowed, most are exported to the USA.

Tobacco leaves are hung upside down to dry and then made into cigars and cigarettes.

DOMINICAN REPUBLIC FACTS
CAPITAL CITY Santo Domingo
AREA 48,380 sq km (18,679 sq miles)
POPULATION 8,500,000
MAIN LANGUAGES Spanish, French Creole
MAJOR RELIGION Christian
CURRENCY Dominican Republic peso

Tourism
The Dominican Republic is the largest tourist destination in the Caribbean, attracting two million each year. The industry brings in half of the country's earnings and provides much-needed jobs.

St Kitts and Nevis

The two islands of St Kitts (or St Christopher) and Nevis sit in the northern part of the Leeward Islands. Both are mountainous, and their idyllic, palm-fringed beaches attract many tourists. Most people are descendents of black Africans, and nearly all work in farming or tourism.

ST KITTS AND NEVIS FACTS
CAPITAL CITY Basseterre
AREA 261 sq km (101 sq miles)
POPULATION 41,000
MAIN LANGUAGE English
MAJOR RELIGION Christian
CURRENCY Eastern Caribbean dollar

Sugar-cane
The main crop on St Kitts is sugar-cane, which accounts for 25 per cent of exports and provides 12 per cent of jobs. Low world prices and hurricane damage have created problems.

Antigua and Barbuda

The largest of the Leeward Islands, Antigua has two dependencies: Barbuda, a small, coral island bursting with wildlife, and Redonda, an uninhabited rock with its own king. The blue lagoons and corals that surround Antigua teem with tropical fish.

ANTIGUA AND BARBUDA FACTS
CAPITAL CITY St John's
AREA 442 sq km (170 sq miles)
POPULATION 66,400
MAIN LANGUAGE English
MAJOR RELIGION Christian
CURRENCY Eastern Caribbean dollar

Yachting
The harbour at St John's has an annual Sailing Week that attracts many visitors and rich yachtspeople. Cruise ships and luxury boats call at the 18th-century Nelson's Dockyard.

Dominica

The largest and most mountainous of the Windward Islands, Dominica has some of the finest scenery in the Caribbean, with rainforests containing 200 wildlife species. Bananas and coconuts are principal exports; prawn farming is proving successful.

Carib Reservation

In the 1900s, the British forced the Caribs to move to a reservation. Today, the Carib reservation, on the east coast of the island, is home to more than 2,000 Caribs, descendants of the original inhabitants. Within the reservation – a popular tourist attraction – Caribs follow traditional lifestyles although their language has died out. Many Carib craftspeople make a living selling bags made from banana leaves and grasses.

DOMINICA FACTS

CAPITAL CITY	Roseau
AREA	754 sq km (291 sq miles)
POPULATION	73,000
MAIN LANGUAGES	English, French
MAJOR RELIGION	Christian
CURRENCY	Eastern Caribbean dollar

St Lucia

The beautiful island of St Lucia has clear seas, sandy beaches, and striking volcanic mountains. Most people work in farming, tourism, or industry.

Each year, 150,000 tonnes (165,000 tons) of bananas are exported.

ST LUCIA FACTS

CAPITAL CITY	Castries
AREA	620 sq km (239 sq miles)
POPULATION	156,300
MAIN LANGUAGE	English
MAJOR RELIGION	Christian
CURRENCY	Eastern Caribbean dollar

Ecotourism

St Lucia's lush rainforests, boiling springs, and twin Piton peaks are attractions that lure visitors to the island. Aromatic tropical plants, trees, and flowers grow everywhere.

Barbados

Known as the "singular island", Barbados lies 160 km (100 miles) east of the Caribbean chain. Barbados retains a strong English influence, and many Britons retire to the island. The people of Barbados, called Bajans, enjoy some of the Caribbean's highest living standards.

BARBADOS FACTS

CAPITAL CITY	Bridgetown
AREA	430 sq km (166 sq miles)
POPULATION	268,000
MAIN LANGUAGE	English
MAJOR RELIGION	Christian
CURRENCY	Barbados dollar

Tourism

Barbados has one of the Caribbean's most well-developed and lucrative tourist industries. About 556,000 people visit the island every year.

St Vincent and the Grenadines

The quiet island of St Vincent is fertile and volcanic, while its 100 tiny sister islands of the Grenadines are flat coral reefs. Both are exclusive holiday resorts, and their waters are popular with yachtspeople. Bananas are the main export.

Arrowroot

St Vincent is the world's largest producer of arrowroot, a starchy liquid that is removed from the arrowroot plant. It is used as a thickening agent in foods, and more recently, as a fine finish for computer paper. Arrowroot is St Vincent's second largest export.

Arrowroot

Arrowroot powder

ST VINCENT AND THE GRENADINES FACTS

CAPITAL CITY	Kingstown
AREA	389 sq km (151 sq miles)
POPULATION	115,500
MAIN LANGUAGE	English
MAJOR RELIGION	Christian
CURRENCY	Eastern Caribbean dollar

Grenada

The most southerly of the Windwards, Grenada rises from a rugged coast to a high, forested interior. A former British colony, Grenada has built its economy on agriculture and tourism. Its people are of African or mixed origin.

Nutmeg

Ginger

Cinnamon

Spices

Grenada is described as the "spice island". It grows about two-thirds of the world's nutmeg, and, with Indonesia, dominates the market. Large quantities of cloves, mace, cinnamon, ginger, bay leaves, saffron, and pepper are also cultivated on the island.

GRENADA FACTS

CAPITAL CITY	St George's
AREA	340 sq km (131 sq miles)
POPULATION	98,000
MAIN LANGUAGE	English
MAJOR RELIGION	Christian
CURRENCY	Eastern Caribbean dollar

Trinidad and Tobago

The low-lying island of Trinidad and its smaller partner, Tobago, lie just off the coast of Venezuela. The islands have a vivid, cosmopolitan culture, home to people from every continent. Both have fertile farmland, fine beaches, and abundant wildlife.

Steel bands

Trinidad and Tobago are the home of steel bands, calypso, and limbo dancing. The first drums, or *pans*, began as empty oil containers. Today, drums are hand-decorated and tuned so that melodies can be played on them. They provide the beat for lively calypso songs.

TRINIDAD AND TOBAGO FACTS

CAPITAL CITY	Port-of-Spain
AREA	5,128 sq km (1,980 sq miles)
POPULATION	1,300,000
MAIN LANGUAGE	English
MAJOR RELIGIONS	Christian, Hindu, Muslim
CURRENCY	Trinidad and Tobago dollar

FIND OUT MORE

CARIBBEAN, HISTORY OF · CHRISTIANITY · FARMING · FESTIVALS · ISLANDS · MUSIC · RELIGIONS · ROCKS AND MINERALS · SLAVERY · VOLCANOES

CARIBBEAN, HISTORY OF

FOR CENTURIES, the Caribbean islands were home to the Carib and Arawak peoples. Their way of life was abruptly disturbed when Europeans arrived in the 1490s. Within 100 years, most had been wiped out by new European rulers who brought thousands of Africans into the Caribbean to work on sugar plantations. The sugar-based economy continued until its decline in the late 19th century. From the mid-1960s, the islands gradually gained independence from European control.

Original inhabitants
The Caribs were expert navigators, travelling great distances in wooden canoes. The Arawaks were skilled craftworkers, who produced baskets and furniture.

Arawak-style wooden seat from the Bahamas

Spanish conquest
The arrival of the Spanish-sponsored navigator Christopher Columbus in the Caribbean in 1492 transformed the region. Convoys of galleons laden with gold and other treasures from the Spanish empire in South America soon crossed the sea on their way back to Spain. Within a few years, Spanish armies had conquered and settled almost every island. Most of the Caribs were killed by the invaders.

Columbus's ship, the *Santa Maria*

European settlement
In the 16th century, with unofficial government backing, English, French, and Dutch pirates raided Spanish treasure ships. They also captured many of the smaller islands. Settlers from Europe arrived, and by 1750, most of the islands were under British, French, or Dutch rule.

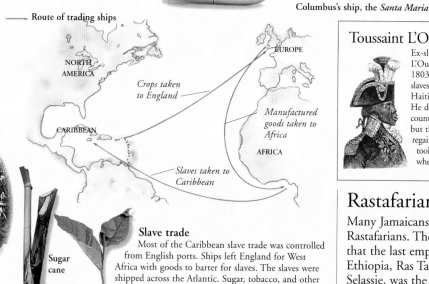

Route of trading ships

NORTH AMERICA

Crops taken to England

CARIBBEAN

EUROPE

Manufactured goods taken to Africa

AFRICA

Slaves taken to Caribbean

Plantations
Europeans set up plantations to satisfy demand for sugar and tobacco in Europe. African slaves worked on the plantations. By 1750, the Caribbean produced most of the world's sugar.

Sugar cane

Tobacco

Slave trade
Most of the Caribbean slave trade was controlled from English ports. Ships left England for West Africa with goods to barter for slaves. The slaves were shipped across the Atlantic. Sugar, tobacco, and other crops were then taken back to England for sale.

Toussaint L'Ouverture

Ex-slave Toussaint L'Ouverture (1743–1803) led a revolt of slaves in French-ruled Haiti in the 1790s. He declared the country a republic, but the French regained control and took him to France, where he died.

Rastafarians
Many Jamaicans are Rastafarians. They believe that the last emperor of Ethiopia, Ras Tafari, or Haile Selassie, was the new messiah who would lead his people back to Africa.

Cuban War
In 1895, following an earlier, unsuccessful uprising, the Cubans rose in revolt against their Spanish rulers. In 1898, the USA declared war on Spain, and freed Cuba.

Emigration
After World War II, many people left the Caribbean in search of work and a better standard of living in Europe. In 1948, the *Empire Windrush* took 492 emigrants from Kingston, Jamaica to London, UK. Over the next 20 years, thousands of Caribbean islanders emigrated to Britain.

Fidel Castro
In 1959, Fidel Castro (b.1927) became the President of Cuba and introduced many social reforms. The US government tried to depose him in 1961, and he turned to the USSR for help. When Soviet nuclear missiles were installed in Cuba in 1962, the world came close to nuclear war.

Timeline
1300s Caribs drive out Arawak people from the eastern Caribbean islands.

1492 Christopher Columbus lands in the Bahamas.

1500s The Spanish take control of the Caribbean.

1700s French, British, Dutch, and Danes capture many islands.

1804 Haiti becomes first Caribbean island to achieve independence from European rule.

1898–1902 Cuba under rule of USA.

1933 Fulgencio Batista becomes ruler of Cuba.

1948 *Empire Windrush* takes first emigrants to Britain.

Capturing a slave

1959 Cuban Revolution; Fidel Castro takes power.

1962 Cuban missile crisis brings the USA and the USSR to the brink of nuclear war.

1983 USA overthrows left-wing regime in Grenada.

1962 Jamaica becomes the first British Caribbean colony to win independence.

1962–83 Most British islands win independence; Dutch and French islands remain tied to Europeans.

1994 USA intervenes to secure democracy in Haiti, after years of dictatorship on the island.

Flag of Jamaica

FIND OUT MORE

AFRICA, EAST | COLUMBUS, CHRISTOPHER | EMPIRES | EXPLORATION | FRANCE, HISTORY OF | GOVERNMENTS AND POLITICS | SLAVERY | SPAIN, HISTORY OF

CARNIVOROUS PLANTS

PLANTS THAT catch and "eat" insects are called carnivorous plants. These plants fall into two groups. Some species, such as the Venus flytrap, have active traps with moving parts. Other species have passive traps, catching their victims on a sticky surface or drowning them in a pool of fluid. Carnivorous plants live in areas where the soil is poor in nitrates and other nutrients, such as bogs, peatlands, and swamps. They obtain extra nutrients by catching insects, which are digested by special juices.

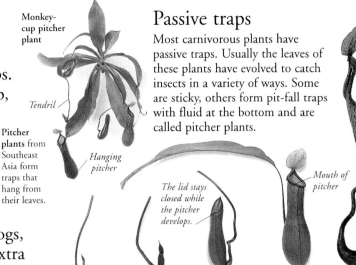

The lid and the smooth rim are often brightly coloured to attract insects.

Monkey-cup pitcher plant

Tendril

Pitcher plants from Southeast Asia form traps that hang from their leaves.

Hanging pitcher

Passive traps

Most carnivorous plants have passive traps. Usually the leaves of these plants have evolved to catch insects in a variety of ways. Some are sticky, others form pit-fall traps with fluid at the bottom and are called pitcher plants.

Rim of the pitcher contains nectar.

The lid stays closed while the pitcher develops.

Mouth of pitcher

Insects fall into the liquid and are digested.

Development of a pitcher plant

1 A young leaf tip extends into a tendril.

2 An upturned swelling appears at the end.

3 The swelling develops into a pitcher.

4 The lid opens when the pitcher is mature.

American pitcher plants
Although they catch their prey in the same way as other pitcher plants, American pitcher plants grow up from the ground rather than hanging from leaves. The inside of the pitcher is slippery and lined with downward pointing hairs which prevent the insects from escaping. The liquid below drowns and slowly digests them.

Pitcher plant

Pitcher is made of leaves joined at the edges.

Butterworts
These small plants have sticky leaves. Small flies are attracted to their smell and get stuck. The leaves slowly roll up, and the insects are digested by juices that ooze out of the leaf.

Common butterwort

Leaf

Sundew flowers develop at the end of a long stalk.

A fly stuck to the hairs on a sundew leaf

Cape sundew

Active traps

Any trap with moving parts is called an active trap. These include plants such as sundews and butterworts, and the Venus flytrap.

Sundews
The upper surface of a sundew leaf is covered with red hairs that secrete drops of clear, sticky liquid. Insects get stuck, then the edges of the leaf slowly roll inward enclosing the insect, and the plant secretes juices that digest it.

Sticky leaf

Venus flytrap
The most spectacular of all the carnivorous plants is the Venus flytrap. It is related to the sundews but has evolved a more elaborate trap. The Venus flytrap grows wild only in one small patch of marshy ground on the border of North and South Carolina, USA. Its trap springs closed when an insect touches the hairs on its surface.

Closed trap

Bladderworts
These are rootless water plants. Their leaves and stems bear tiny bladders with a lid covered in sensitive hairs. If a creature brushes the hairs, the lid of the bladder flips open. Water rushes in, carrying the victim with it.

Greater bladderwort

Venus flytrap

Stimulation of at least three trigger hairs sets off the mechanism that closes the trap.

Surface of the trap

Magnified view of a trigger hair

How a Venus flytrap works

1 An insect lands on a leaf, touching the sensitive trigger hairs.

2 The leaf closes, and the spines interlock, trapping the insect.

3 The trap is fully closed in 30 minutes, and digestion begins.

Trigger hair

Trap is fringed with long spines.

Insect is trapped in one-fifth of a second.

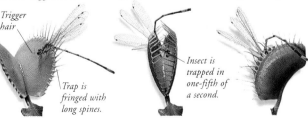

 FIND OUT MORE ASIAN WILDLIFE FLOWERS INSECTS NORTH AMERICAN WILDLIFE PLANTS PLANTS, ANATOMY PLANTS, DEFENCE PLANTS, REPRODUCTION SOUTH AMERICAN WILDLIFE

C

CARS AND TRUCKS

OF ALL THE DIFFERENT FORMS of transport, cars have the biggest effect on our lives. Cars give people the freedom to go where they like, when they like – with some types of car you don't even need a road. Trucks are used for long-distance haulage and for performing many specialized tasks, such as fire-fighting. In parts of the world where there are no railways, trucks offer the only way of transporting goods. But cars and trucks create pollution. Because there are now so many of them on the roads, the world's cities have become clogged with traffic, and the air that many of us breathe is poisoned with traffic fumes.

A Benz Motor Wagen of 1886

Early cars

Early cars were called "horseless carriages". They were made by manufacturers of horse-drawn carriages and coaches, and had the same large wheels, high driver's seat, and suspension. They were powered by a single-cylinder petrol engine, which could reach a top speed of 15 kmh (9 mph).

Modern cars

Efficiency, safety, and comfort are the most important features of a modern car, as well as minimal air pollution from exhaust fumes. To be efficient, cars need engines that use as little fuel as possible, and a streamlined shape to reduce air resistance. In some cars electronics help efficiency and safety. Modern cars are built with the help of computers and robots in high-tech, automated car plants.

Stiff bodyshell is made from thin sheets of steel pressed into shape and welded together. It is chemically treated and painted to protect against rusting.

Windscreen of toughened glass protects driver and passengers from wind and rain. If hit by a stone, the windscreen cracks but does not shatter.

Henry Ford

American engineer Henry Ford (1863–1947) formed the Ford Motor Company in 1903. In 1908, Ford launched the Model T. It was made cheaply on a factory assembly line and sold by the million.

Side windows can be lowered.

Padded seats

Engine burns fuel and uses the energy stored within the fuel to propel the car along.

Bonnet is raised to examine engine.

Radiator circulates water around the engine to cool it.

Luggage is stored in boot.

Rear bumper

Exhaust pipe carries waste gases away from the engine and expels them at the rear of the car.

Hub-cap covers the centre of the wheel.

Suspension spring allows the wheel to move up and down as the car travels over bumps in the road, protecting passengers against uncomfortable jolting.

Driveshaft (or prop shaft) connects the gearbox to the rear wheels, which are driven round by the engine.

Gearbox contains intermeshing gear wheels that change the amount of power going to a car's wheels.

Pneumatic (air-filled) tyres grip the road and help give a smooth ride.

Front bumper

Luggage is carried in the boot. **Family saloon**

Aerodynamic design enhances speed performance. **Sports car**

People carrier/MPV *Three rows of detachable seats*

Formula 1 racer *Wing* *Driver's cockpit*

Types of cars

The most popular car is the saloon, which has an enclosed passenger compartment and a separate rear space for luggage. Hatchbacks are saloons with a large rear door and a folding back seat for extra luggage space.

Sports cars

Sports cars are designed to be stylish, fast, and fun. Some sports cars are convertibles, which have a flexible roof that can be folded down so that passengers can enjoy driving in the open air. Luxury convertibles have roofs that open and close automatically.

People carrier

One of the latest types of car is the people carrier, or multi-purpose vehicle (MPV). This vehicle is a cross between a saloon car and a minibus. People carriers are very versatile, with at least six seats and plenty of space for luggage. They are perfect for outings or holidays.

Racing car

Some cars are purpose-built for racing. They have a very powerful engine, wide tyres, and a low, wide body for stability around fast corners. An aerodynamic "wing" on the back helps keep the car on the road at high speeds. Saloons can be converted into racing or rallying cars.

C

Trucks

Trucks are used for carrying cargo along roads. Their journeys can range from a few kilometres on local deliveries to thousands of kilometres across continents. The first trucks were built in the 1890s, and were driven by steam engines. Since then, trucks have grown ever larger. In Australia, trucks called road trains tow hundreds of tonnes of cargo across long distances in several full-sized trailers. Some trucks are "rigid", that is, built in one piece. Articulated lorries are built in two sections: a tractor unit and a semi-trailer, which is designed to carry specialized loads. Great skill is required to drive an articulated lorry.

Modern trucks

At the heart of most modern trucks is a powerful diesel engine, using diesel oil, a type of petroleum. Some diesel engines are turbocharged for extra power. The engine powers the truck, and operates any hydraulic parts, such as the lifting arms of a dumper. Some trucks, such as military vehicles, have chunky tyres and strong suspensions, to enable them to travel off-road in rough terrain.

Some trucks have up to 20 forward and 10 reverse gears.

A tractor unit and semi-trailer

Inside a truck cab

Long-distance truck drivers spend many hours in the cabs of their trucks. Cabs are designed for comfort, and some of the controls, such as the steering and brakes, are power-assisted to make them easy to use. Many cabs have a small rear room, with a bunk, washing facilities, and television. To help prevent accidents, some countries have introduced tachometers to record how many hours the truck is on the road. It is illegal for the driver to go beyond a certain number of hours.

Heating controls (temperature selector and fan speed selector) keep cab at a comfortable temperature in hot or cold weather.

Cassette, radio, and CB (citizens' band) radio provide entertainment on the road. Drivers may use CB to warn each other of traffic jams.

Adjustable nozzles allow fresh air into the cab.

Warning indicators light up if anything goes wrong with the truck.

Gauges, such as the speedometer, show speed, engine temperature, and the amount of fuel left.

Large diameter steering wheel is easy to turn with power assistance. This is known as power steering.

Gear selector   *Clutch pedal controls gears.*   *Brake pedal*   *Accelerator pedal*

Karl Benz

In 1886, German engineer Karl Benz (1844–1929) patented his first car, using an internal combustion engine. The car had electric ignition, three wheels, differential gears, and was water-cooled. In 1926, his company merged with Daimler to become one of the leading car and truck producers in the world.

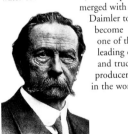

Research and development

Modern research aims at improving car economy, safety, and ecology. Because petroleum reserves are limited and its use is environmentally unsound, research is taking place into new fuels from sustainable sources, such as plant oils. Researchers are also experimenting with new materials for car parts, including plastics for car bodies. Car manufacturers are aware that making cars cleaner and safer is likely to improve sales.

Crash test dummy

Testing airbag inflation

Catalytic converter

Cars and trucks are gradually becoming "cleaner", which means they create less pollution. Most new cars have a catalytic converter, which removes carbon monoxide, nitrogen oxides, and other poisonous chemicals from the exhaust gases.

A catalytic converter from a car exhaust

Safety features

Manufacturers are constantly developing new safety features, such as airbags that inflate automatically in the event of an accident. They are also working on new ways of preventing accidents, such as anti-lock brakes.

Types of truck

Most trucks start life as a standard chassis and cab. Car manufacturers can then add the body, which determines the function of the truck. Common specialized trucks include rubbish trucks, flat trailers to transport large items, such as cars, tankers, fire engines, and vehicles modified to carry animals, such as horse boxes.

Rubbish truck

This truck has a closed container for rubbish and a rubbish-bin lift that empties a bin into the body through a protective shield.

Car transporter

A car transporter is used to convey cars to showrooms. There are ramps at the back which fold down at the rear so that the cars can be driven on and off. The trailer of a car transporter can carry up to 18 vehicles.

Storage space above the cab

Horse box

This truck carries horses to shows. The horse enters the truck via a door at the rear, which folds down to make a loading ramp.

FIND OUT MORE   BICYCLES AND MOTORBIKES   ENGINES AND MOTORS   FORCE AND MOTION   OIL   POLLUTION   ROADS   TRANSPORT, HISTORY OF   TRAVEL   UNITED STATES, HISTORY OF

Cars

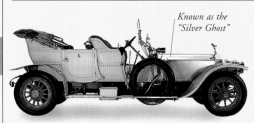

Known as the "Silver Ghost"

Rolls Royce 40/50, UK; launched 1907; top speed 88 kmh (55 mph)

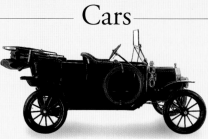

Model T Ford, USA; launched 1908; top speed 68 kmh (42 mph)

Introduced front wheel drive

Citroën Traction Avant, France; launched 1934; top speed 113 kmh (70 mph)

Best-selling car ever produced

Volkswagon Beetle, Germany; launched 1939; top speed 132 kmh (82 mph)

Jaguar XK120, UK; launched 1949; top speed 203 kmh (126 mph)

An icon of 1950s' America

Ford Thunderbird, USA; launched 1955; top speed 183 kmh (114 mph)

Famous "gullwing" doors

Mercedes-Benz 300SL, Germany; launched 1954; top speed 265 kmh (165 mph)

Fiat 500 D, Italy; launched 1957; top speed 95 kmh (59 mph)

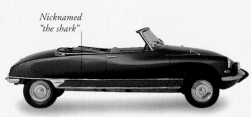

Nicknamed "the shark"

Citroën DS, France; launched 1960; top speed 187 kmh (116 mph)

Austin Mini Cooper, UK; launched 1963; top speed 161 kmh (100 mph)

A sporty, compact car

Ford Mustang, USA; launched 1964; top speed 204 kmh (127 mph)

Won the Le Mans 24-hour race four times in a row

Ford GT40, USA; launched 1964; top speed 322 kmh (200 mph)

Streamlined shape

Porsche Carrera 911 RS, Germany; launched 1972; top speed 243 kmh (150 mph)

Classed as a passenger van

Toyota Previa, Japan; launched 1990; top speed 180 kmh (111 mph)

Micro-car is ecologically designed and easy to park.

Smart car, France/Germany; launched 1998; top speed 139 kmh (87 mph)

Trucks

Pickup or utilities truck: useful for carrying small loads, these popular trucks have open, flat backs

So heavy and wide, it can use only major roads

Front, tractor section

18 wheels

Semitrailer: a monster truck suitable for a wide range of bulk or heavy goods

180

CARTOONS AND ANIMATION

CARTOONS, OR ANIMATED FILMS, are movies in which drawings or models seem to come to life. The effect is achieved by slight changes to the drawing or model between each frame of film. Animated films first appeared in the 1900s, and the art has developed alongside motion pictures; computer animation is now used to create amazing special effects in movies. Cartoons usually have a comic theme, although animation can also be a thought-provoking medium for a serious message.

Hanna-Barbera
The US animators Bill Hanna (1910–2001) and Joe Barbera (b.1911) created many of the most popular TV cartoon characters. Their first film, called *Puss Gets the Boot,* was released in 1940 and starred Tom and Jerry, the cat and mouse rivals. Other Hanna-Barbera characters include Yogi Bear and the Flintstones.

Direct animation
With this method the animator creates characters from clay or other media. The characters are slightly repositioned before the camera between each frame of film, creating the effect of movement.

Scene from *A Close Shave* (1995)

Clay model in an animated sequence

Step 1: figure starts out with his back to the camera.

Step 2: position is manually altered before next frame is shot.

Step 3: a sequence has been created which shows him turning around.

Wallace & Gromit
Wallace & Gromit are the creations of British animator Nick Park and have starred in several award-winning films. The plasticine puppets are less than 15 cm (6 in) high. It took a budget of £1.3 million and a crew of 25 animators, modelmakers, and camera operators to make *A Close Shave.*

Key shapes
Traditionally, one of the most difficult areas of direct animation has been to show a character talking. Specific mouth and lip positions, called "key shapes", must be created for every word spoken. Today, computers can aid this process.

Cel animation
In cel animation, animators produce at least 12 drawings for each second of action. The background, which usually does not move, is drawn on paper. The animator draws the moving characters on layers of cel (clear plastic film), so there is no need to redraw the parts that do not move between frames. The background shows through the clear areas of cel.

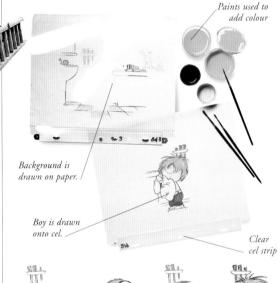

Paints used to add colour

Background is drawn on paper.

Boy is drawn onto cel.

Clear cel strip

Chuck Jones
US animator Chuck Jones (1912–2002) drew the rabbit Bugs Bunny and many other famous characters in Warner Brothers' "Looney Tunes" cartoons. He directed his first animated film in 1938 and made 300 films in his lifetime, winning three Academy Awards.

Computer animation
Animators use computers to draw the images between the start and end of an action, or to improve or alter hand-drawn images. Computers can now generate an entire film, as in *Toy Story* (1996), as well as breathtaking special effects.

Aladdin
Aladdin (1992) was one of Disney's first major computer-animated films. Although the characters were hand-drawn, three-dimensional software was used to create dramatic effects in lighting, texture, and movement, such as the lava sequence.

© Disney

The Simpsons
Matt Groening created *The Simpsons* while still at school, publishing them as a newspaper comic strip. The animated series made its debut on US television in 1989 and has since become one of the world's most popular shows. The quirky storylines centre on Bart and his family.

The Simpson family

Homer

Marg

Maggie

Lisa

Bart

MATT GROENING

| FIND OUT MORE | CAMERAS | DISNEY, WALT | FILMS AND FILM-MAKING | NEWSPAPERS AND MAGAZINES | PAINTING AND DRAWING |

CASTLES

IN MEDIEVAL EUROPE, castles acted as both home and military stronghold. They were occupied by a lord, his family, servants, and sometimes an army of professional soldiers. They provided refuge for local people in times of war. Local lords could control the surrounding land from their castles, hence they were a very important part of feudalism. Castles were built to be defended, with walls strong enough to keep out an enemy, while allowing the occupants to shoot at any attackers. Designs changed as builders invented better methods of defence, or adapted new ideas from castles in the Islamic world.

The Chapel
Every castle had its own chapel. It was usually in an upper room in one of the towers. This is the chancel of the chapel at Conwy. The altar would have been beneath the windows, and there would have been enough room for everyone in the castle to gather together.

North-west Tower

Outer Ward

The Great Hall was the centre of activity. There was a high table for the lord and lady, and lower tables for everyone else.

The Kitchen was where food for the whole castle was prepared. There were wood fires, oak tables, and alcoves.

The Stockhouse Tower got its name when stocks for prisoners were made here in the 1500s.

The Inner Ward was the last refuge in time of attack.

Machicolations, or overhanging parapets, allowed defenders to pour boiling water on their opponents.

Chapel Tower

The King's Tower
This room on the first floor, close to the royal apartments has a stone fireplace and a recessed window. The recess means a person looking out remains safe from any enemy fire. The original floors have been removed.

The Prison Tower had a deep, dark dungeon.

Bakehouse Tower

King's Tower

Conwy Castle, Wales, in the 13th century

The East Barbican was the first line of defence against attack by sea, and was also a good position from which to fire. Defenders could isolate the enemy in this area.

Lookout Tower

Chapel

King's Tower

Parts of a castle

Early castles had a keep, which contained the lord's rooms, hall, chapel, storerooms, and a well-defended gatehouse. Later castles abandoned the keep, and replaced it with a Great Hall, which was built against the castle walls. The lord's rooms were sometimes built into the gatehouse, but in Conwy they are in the Inner Ward, which was the heart of the castle, and most easily defended.

Timeline

1066 The Normans erect wooden motte-and-bailey castles during the conquest of England. These are quick to build, and the motte, or tower on top of a mound, is easy to defend. Most buildings are in the bailey, or courtyard.

Krak des Chevaliers, Syria

1142 Krak des Chevaliers built in Syria; one of the most easy-to-defend crusader castles, has concentric stone walls.

1127 Rochester Castle built: includes a great hall, chapel, and storerooms. The entrance is well protected, and defenders can shoot at attackers.

Great Tower, Rochester, England

1150 Many French lords build castles along the River Loire. Examples built (or extended) during this period include Loches, Chinon, and Montreuil-Bellay.

1200 The German lords of Liechtenstein build their castle on a high crag for extra defence.

Caerphilly, Wales

1238 The Muslim rulers of medieval Spain begin the castle-palace of the Alhambra.

1271 Concentric castles, like Caerphilly, become popular. They have rings of walls and sometimes water defences (moats).

How castles were built

Building a castle required many skilled workers. A master mason drew up plans and supervised the work, and less senior masons carried out the building. Carpenters did the woodwork, and metalworkers made hinges and door fasteners. In a large castle, some specialists stayed on permanently to do the maintenance work.

Wood and earthwork

The Normans chose a site where there was a water supply, built a mound and a wooden castle on top, and surrounded the structure with a wooden fence, or palisade. Most were replaced with stone constructions.

Motte-and-bailey

Stonework

Building a stone castle took decades, but the result was a strong castle that would withstand attack well. The important structures, such as the outer walls, mural towers, and keep, were all made of stone. Buildings in the castle courtyard were still made of timber and had thatched roofs.

Windows

Most castle windows were narrow or cross-shaped slits. They usually had a large alcove on the inside of the wall. This allowed an archer to stand to one side and avoid missiles while preparing to shoot.

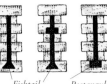

Fishtail bottoms *Rectangular opening* *Crosslet* *Round ended cross* *Gun loop*

Arrow slits developed that were large enough for a defender to shoot an arrow out, but too small for an attacker's missiles. Later, the gun loop developed with a circular hole to fit a gun barrel.

C

Edward I

In the early years of his reign, Edward I (r.1272–1307) conquered Wales, and built an "iron ring" of castles in strategic Welsh towns to keep the country under his control. Many of these Welsh castles, such as Harlech and Beaumaris, were built on the concentric plan, which meant they had both inner and outer walls for defence. Concentric castles were very difficult to attack successfully.

Asian and African castles

Castles have been built in many different places. There was a strong tradition of castle-building in the Islamic world, and medieval soldiers took Muslim ideas about fortification to western Europe when they returned from the crusades.

Himeji Castle, Japan

Seventeenth-century Japan had a feudal system similar to that of medieval Europe, and Japanese lords also lived in castles. Tall towers with pagoda-like roofs had narrow window openings through which soldiers could shoot. The towers were surrounded by courtyards and walls.

Fasilidas Castle, Ethiopia

The central stronghold shows many features in common with western castles, including thick walls of stone, round corner towers, and battlements. The remains of the outer curtain wall can be seen in the foreground to the right.

Van Castle, Turkey

Built on a rocky outcrop, Van Castle was begun in 750. It was later extended, and was occupied by the Seljuk and Ottoman Turks before being taken over by Armenian Christians.

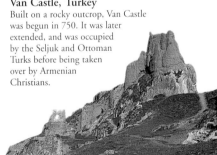

Attack and defence

Attackers could fire arrows, hurl missiles using catapults, break down doors or walls with battering rams, climb the walls using ladders, or try to demolish the walls by tunnelling under them (mining). As well as defence features, such as thick walls and doors, moats, and machicolations, a castle also needed plenty of storage space for food so that the stronghold could withstand a long siege.

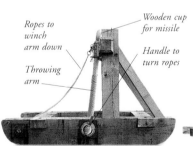

Arm

Sling pouch

Rope to pull arm down again

Hauling rope

Ropes to winch arm down

Throwing arm

Wooden cup for missile

Handle to turn ropes

Crossbow

Crossbows were powerful but slow to reload. Despite this they could be useful in defending castles, where they could be reloaded behind the safety of the stone walls.

Catapult

The soldiers used a handle attached to a rope (made from a skein of twisted rope) to winch the throwing arm down. They then released it, and the arm flew up, releasing its missile, usually a rock, from a wooden cup.

Traction trebuchet

This siege engine was like a giant catapult. When soldiers pulled down on the ropes, the end of the arm flew upward, and the sling opened to release a missile, which usually weighed about 45–90 kg (100–200 lb).

Pfalzgrafenstein, Germany

1338 Many German castles are built on the Rhine because of the river's importance as a trade route.

Bodiam, England

1385 Bodiam Castle has a curtain wall around a court-yard, which contains the hall and chapel.

Real de Manzanares, Spain

1416 By this time many French castles, such as Saumur on the River Loire, have conical towers, strong defensive walls, and luxurious rooms.

1435 The elaborate Real de Manzanares is built.

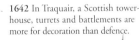

1642 In Traquair, a Scottish tower-house, turrets and battlements are more for decoration than defence.

Traquair House, Scotland

1600s Many castles were built by local lords in Japan, like Himeji.

FIND OUT MORE   ARCHITECTURE   EUROPE, HISTORY OF   FEUDALISM   MEDIEVAL EUROPE   NORMANS

CATS

DOMESTIC CATS are related to wild cats, such as lions and tigers, and they are able to fend well for themselves. They are excellent hunters, and their eyes, ears, nose, and whiskers are well adapted for their natural preference for hunting at night. Cats are affectionate and respond well to humans. They were domesticated about 4,000 years ago to keep people company and to destroy pests.

Kittens

Cats have an average of four or five kittens in a litter. Kittens love to stalk, chase, and pounce on things. This helps to make them strong, and develops the skills they will need as adults.

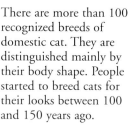

Domestic cats

There are more than 100 recognized breeds of domestic cat. They are distinguished mainly by their body shape. People started to breed cats for their looks between 100 and 150 years ago.

White · Lilac · Red · Blue · Chocolate

Siamese · British shorthair · Persian longhair · Devon Rex

Fur

Cats can be divided into long- and short-haired breeds. Fur is of various textures. Common coat colours are grey-blue, black, brown, white, red, and mixtures of these, such as silver and lilac.

Head shapes

Cat head shapes range from large and round, like that of the British shorthair, to wedge-shaped, like that of the Siamese. Some breeds have special characteristics, such as the Scottish fold, which has the tip of its ears bent forward.

Games enable kittens to practise hunting skills, such as stalking and catching.

1 If a cat suddenly falls, balance organs in its ears tell it which way is up.

Papillae

Grooming

Cats are very clean animals and spend at least an hour a day grooming, using their tongue as a "comb". The tongue has tiny hard spines, called papillae, on its surface. The licking helps to keep the fur clean and waterproof, and also spreads the cat's scent all over its body.

Loose-fitting skin gives freedom of movement.

2 The cat turns its head around first so that it can see where it is falling, and where it is going to land.

Flexible spine allows the cat to twist its body.

3 Then the cat turns the rest of its body. By the time it reaches the ground, it will be the right way round.

Balance

A cat's long flexible tail helps it to balance. Cats will almost always land on their feet, even when falling from a great height. They have very quick reflexes and can twist and turn their body the right way up in a fraction of a second.

Back paws are brought forward.

Senses

Cats can see well in low light and can focus on small objects a long way away. Their super-sensitive hearing picks up sounds that we cannot hear and can also take in two sounds at once, such as a mouse in a thunderstorm. Whiskers are sensitive to touch. Cats use them to feel their way in the dark, and to measure whether spaces are wide enough for them to go through.

Ears are funnel-shaped to draw sounds inside the ear.

Long, flexible ears can turn toward sounds.

4 The cat stretches out its front legs to absorb the impact of landing.

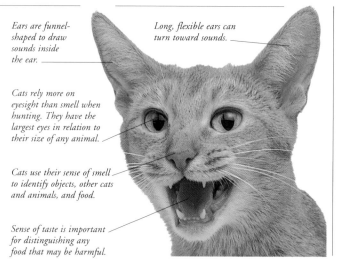

Cats rely more on eyesight than smell when hunting. They have the largest eyes in relation to their size of any animal.

Cats use their sense of smell to identify objects, other cats and animals, and food.

Sense of taste is important for distinguishing any food that may be harmful.

Claws

Cats use their claws to defend themselves and to climb. At other times, the claws are drawn in, or retracted, for protection. They are covered by a bony sheath that is an extension of the last bone of each toe and fit inside pockets in the skin.

Narrow pupils in the light

Large pupils in the dark

Changing pupils

A cat's pupils expand enormously in the dark to let in as much light as possible. A layer of cells at the back of the eyes, called the tapetum, reflects light back into the eye which helps cats see in the dark.

FIND OUT MORE

ANIMAL BEHAVIOUR · EYES AND SEEING · LIONS AND OTHER WILD CATS · MAMMALS · MOUNTAIN WILDLIFE

Cats

Long-haired

Turkish van (auburn) has a chalky white coat.

Long silky fur

Persian longhair (blue) has a short, bushy tail.

Flattish, round face

Birman (seal tabby point) has pure white paws.

M-shaped tabby marking

Somali (sorrel) was bred from the Abyssinian.

Ragdoll (blue mitted) goes limp when it is stroked.

Matching mittens

Turkish angora (blue-cream) has fine, silky fur.

Tufted ears

Balinese (blue tabby point) has a long, well-plumed tail.

Javanese (cinnamon) is graceful and lithe – a typical Oriental cat.

Somali (silver) has ticking (bands of colour) on each hair.

Longer fur forms a ruff.

Maine coon (brown classic tabby) is a large, hardy cat.

Colour pointed longhair (chocolate point) has thick fur.

Short-haired

American wirehair (brown mackerel tabby) is active.

Crimped coarse fur feels like lamb's wool.

Burmese (chocolate) has glossy fur with a satin feel.

Scottish fold (tortie and white) has folded ears.

Ears are folded forward and downward.

Exotic (blue) is playful and affectionate.

Massive round head on a thick neck

Manx (red classic tabby) is bred to have no tail.

Thick undercoat with longer top coat

American shorthair (silver classic tabby) has thick fur.

Widely spaced ears with rounded tips

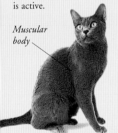

Korat (blue) is a playful cat. It has close-lying fur.

Muscular body

Japanese bobtail (red and white) is usually patterned.

10-cm- (4-in-) long inflexible tail

Egyptian mau (silver) has a spotted coat.

Dorsal stripe

Siamese (seal point) has an angular face and large ears.

Colour gets darker with age.

California spangled (gold) has well-defined spots.

Colour pointed British shorthair (cream point).

Small rounded ears and rounded head

Oriental shorthair (foreign red) is a sleek, slender cat with fine glossy fur.

British shorthair (chocolate) has a solid build with a round face and short nose.

Cornish rex (cinnamon silver) has a short wavy coat, patterned over the whole body.

Flat skull and large ears

Chartreux (blue-grey) is an old French breed. All Chartreux are this colour.

Tonkinese (cream) is a Burmese and Siamese cross. It is active and affectionate.

Abyssinian (usual) is an elegant cat, and looks similar to the cats of ancient Egypt.

Large pricked ears

Russian shorthair (blue) has a graceful, long body with thick, fine fur.

Coat has a silvery sheen.

Oriental shorthair (Havana) was developed from a chocolate point Siamese.

CAUCASUS REPUBLICS

THE COUNTRIES of Georgia, Armenia, and Azerbaijan lie just within Asia, on a narrow plateau sandwiched between the Greater and Lesser Caucasus mountains. They are often collectively called Transcaucasia or the Caucasus Republics. To the west of the region lies the Black Sea, and to the east, the land-locked Caspian Sea. All three countries were part of the former Soviet Union and only gained their independence in 1991. Since the end of communist rule, growing ethnic and religious tensions have caused civil unrest throughout much of the region.

Physical features

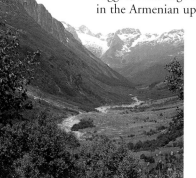

Much of the land is mountainous and rugged, with large expanses of semi-desert in the Armenian uplands. The Kura is the longest river, flowing 1,364 km (848 miles) from central Georgia, through the fertile lowlands of Azerbaijan to the Caspian Sea. The low Black Sea coastal area in western Georgia is lush and green. The area suffers earthquakes.

Regional climate

26°C (79°F)   0°C (32°F)

375 mm (15 in)

The varied landscape of this region gives rise to a wide range of climates. Georgia's Black Sea coast is warm and humid, while Armenia is generally dry with long, cold winters. The lowland areas of Azerbaijan have long, hot summers and cool winters. Winters in the mountains are bitterly cold.

Ararat Plains

Most of Armenia is a high plateau with large expanses of semi-desert. In the southwest, the land drops towards the River Aras, which forms the border with Turkey and drains most of Armenia. Known as the Ararat Plains, this fertile, sheltered strip is used for growing vegetables and vines.

Lake Sevan

Once valued for its pure waters and stunning setting, Armenia's Lake Sevan is at the centre of an ecological crisis. Tragically, irrigation and hydroelectric projects begun in the 1970s have caused the water level to drop by up to 16 m (52 ft).

Greater Caucasus Mountains

The Greater Caucasus range stretches for about 1,200 km (745 miles) from the Black Sea to the Caspian Sea, effectively separating Europe from Asia. Rich in copper, iron, and lead, the mountains also shelter the Caucasus Republics from the icy winds that blow down from Russia in the north. The highest mountain is Mount El'brus at 5,633 m (18,481 ft), just over the Russian border.

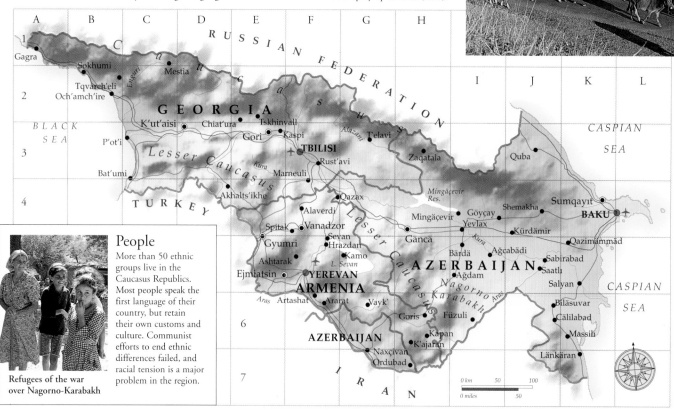

People

More than 50 ethnic groups live in the Caucasus Republics. Most people speak the first language of their country, but retain their own customs and culture. Communist efforts to end ethnic differences failed, and racial tension is a major problem in the region.

Refugees of the war over Nagorno-Karabakh

Georgia

Georgia is the westernmost of the three republics. About 70 per cent of the people are ethnic Georgians, most of whom belong to the Christian Georgian Orthodox Church. In recent years, the economy has suffered as a result of civil wars and ethnic disputes in the regions of Abkhazia and South Ossetia, which are trying to break away. This has damaged the Black Sea tourist industry.

Gold threads enhance bright patterns.

Textiles
Georgia produces fine silk cloth, and mulberry bushes, used to feed silkworms, grow well. Bright cotton fabrics are used to make the headscarves worn by so many of the Georgian women.

People
More Georgians claim to live for over 100 years than any other nationality in the world. Contributing factors are thought to be a healthy diet, regular exercise, a clean environment – and a genetic predisposition to longevity. Claims for ages over 120 have not so far been proved.

Tbilisi
Situated on the banks of the River Kura, Tbilisi, Georgia's capital since the 5th century, is a multicultural city of 1,200,000. Home to most of Georgia's Armenian minority, it has places of worship for many religions.

Tea and wine
More than 90 per cent of the tea sold in Russia is grown in Georgia, which produces about 250,000 tonnes each year. Georgia also has extensive vineyards and produces excellent red wines.

Armenia

Land-locked and isolated from its neighbours, Armenia is the smallest of the Caucasus Republics. The only way out of the country is by difficult road and rail links over the mountains to Georgia. The people, mostly ethnic Armenians, speak a unique language. The country exports fruit, brandy, and minerals such as copper.

Cubes of meat are separated by peppers and onions for flavour. *Metal skewer allows cooking meat to be turned.*

Food
Lamb is the main meat, often served as kebabs, with a variety of vegetables. Cooks use pine-nuts and almonds for flavouring. Local cheeses and rich desserts are specialities.

Azerbaijan

The largest of the Caucasus Republics, Azerbaijan also has the most extensive area of farmland. Around 93 per cent of the population are Muslims. Most other people are Christian Armenians and Russians. Naxçivan, a separate part of Azerbaijan, lies within Armenian territory.

Oil industry
Natural gas and oil are extracted from the Caspian Sea. Pipelines link Baku, which is the centre of the industry, with Iran, Russia, Kazakhstan, and Turkmenistan. Other oil-related industries include the manufacture of chemicals and oil-drilling equipment.

Yerevan
Armenia's capital, Yerevan, is also its largest city. Situated on the River Razdan, it is a major cultural and industrial centre. Market traders sell fruit, vegetables, and rich, colourful rugs woven locally from silk and wool.

Territorial conflict
Nagorno-Karabakh, an enclave in southern Azerbaijan, has been the subject of armed conflict with Armenia since 1988. Most of the people here are Armenians, and Armenia claims the territory. A ceasefire was negotiated in 1994, but dispute over the area continues today.

Soldiers on parade, Karabakh

Farming
Agriculture, mainly in the Aras river valley, employs 30 per cent of the workforce and is the country's main source of wealth. Crops include cereals and fruit such as apricots, grapes, olives, and peaches.

People
Communal drinking of hot, sweet tea from tiny glasses is a typically male ceremony. As in neighbouring Georgia, the Azerbaijanis have a reputation for longevity, and it is not uncommon for people to continue working into their eighties.

 FIND OUT MORE · ASIA, HISTORY OF · CHRISTIANITY · ENERGY · FARMING · ISLAM · MOUNTAINS AND VALLEYS · OIL · SOVIET UNION · TEXTILES AND WEAVING · TRADE AND INDUSTRY

CAVES

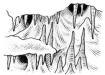

BENEATH THE GROUND, there is a network of large holes, or caves. Caves are naturally occurring chambers, formed out of rock. There are many different cave types, some housing hidden lakes and waterfalls; caverns are extensive networks of giant caves. Some caves are no bigger than a cupboard, but others are huge. The Sarawak Chamber in Malaysia is 700 m (2,296 ft) long and 50 m (164 ft) high; the world's biggest sports stadium, the Louisiana Superdome, could fit into it three times over. Damp and dark, caves have distinctive features, such as stalactites and stalagmites.

Types of cave

The biggest and most common cave systems are found in carbonate rocks, such as dolomite and limestone, but small caves form in all kinds of rock. Caves are found in many terrains, from the sea to glaciers, and can have different formations.

Sea cave
Small caves form in sea cliffs; waves force water into cracks, blasting the rock apart. The hole may emerge as a blow-hole on the cliff-top.

Fissure cave
The movement and force of an earthquake can create deep fissures, long, narrow openings, and caves.

Ice cave
Greeny-blue tunnel caves form under glaciers after spring meltwater carves out passages under the ice.

Lava cave
Tunnel-like caves form in lava – surface layers harden, and molten lava flows underneath.

Limestone cave
Most caves form in limestone. This rock has many joints and its calcium content is vulnerable to the acid in rainwater.

How a cave forms

Most of the world's biggest caves are formed by water trickling down through soluble rocks, such as limestone. The water widens joints or cracks by dissolving the rock. Rainwater is dilute carbonic acid and wears away the rock, creating a cave.

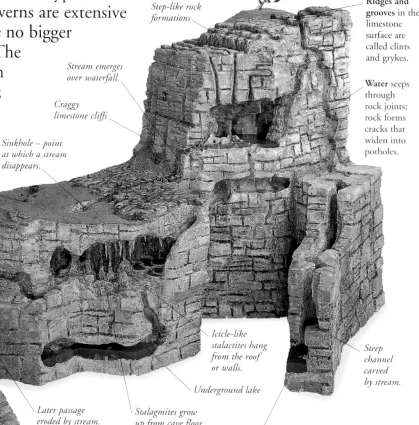

Step-like rock formations

Stream emerges over waterfall.

Craggy limestone cliffs

Sinkhole – point at which a stream disappears.

Sparse vegetation

Ridges and grooves in the limestone surface are called clints and grykes.

Water seeps through rock joints; rock forms cracks that widen into potholes.

Icicle-like stalactites hang from the roof or walls.

Steep channel carved by stream.

Underground lake

Later passage eroded by stream.

Stalagmites grow up from cave floor.

Stream exits via cave mouth and flows along the valley bottom.

Groundwater fills a previously dry cavern to the level of the water table, which can rise and fall over time.

Cave features

Formed over thousands of years, stalactites and stalagmites are found in caves. Droplets of water partially evaporate to form calcium deposits (calcite); drips create hanging stalactites on the roof, and upright stalagmites where they fall to the floor. Spiralling drips form twisted helictites. Flowstone is solidified calcite on the cave floor or walls.

Stalagmite

Stalagmites and stalactites
Stalactites can form in different ways – a long, thin curtain stalactite is formed when water runs along the cave roof. When stalactites and stalagmites meet in the middle, they form a column. The biggest stalactite, 10 m (33 ft) long, is in Pruta do Janelão, Minas Gerais, Brazil; the biggest stalagmite is over 32 m (105 ft) tall in the Krasnohorska Cave in Slovakia.

Merged stalactites

Stalactite

Stalactite with ring marks

Curtain stalactite

Potholing

Potholes are the vertical pipes that lead down to many extensive cave networks. Today, potholing is a popular but dangerous sport. Exploring and discovering caves can unearth historic treasures. The caves at Lascaux, France, for instance, which contain a wealth of prehistoric wall paintings and tools, were discovered by potholers.

FIND OUT MORE   CAVE WILDLIFE   COASTLINES   EARTHQUAKES   FOSSILS   PREHISTORIC PEOPLES   ROCKS AND MINERALS   SPORT

CAVE WILDLIFE

A DEEP CAVE is a world of its own, with conditions far removed from those outside. Deep within a cave there is no light at all. No day and night pass, and temperatures change little with the seasons. Without light plants cannot grow, yet animal life exists even here. Some creatures enter caves for shelter or to hunt for prey; others spend their entire lives in this dark, dank environment and have adapted to move about and sense food in the dark.

Caves

Caves occur in sea cliffs, around volcanoes, and under glaciers, but the most spectacular are those formed when rainwater hollows out fissures in limestone rock. Limestone caves contain various habitats for wildlife, including narrow tunnels, chambers, streams, pools, and the partly lit entrance. Some caves, especially those in the tropics, are teeming with life. Bat colonies live in the roof, and an army of invertebrates consumes their droppings on the floor below.

Limestone cave

Plants

No plants can grow deep in a cave due to lack of light. But the cave entrance is often framed by a fringe of plants, such as liverworts, mosses, ferns, and algae, that have adapted to damp, shady conditions. Many of these plants grow without soil, sending out small roots that grip the bare rock.

Moss

Fern

Invertebrates

Caves are often full of invertebrate life. Beetles, spiders, snails, worms, and crayfish survive in large numbers in caves. They feed on debris brought in by running water or dropped by animals that feed outside.

Touch-sensitive spikes

Long antennae

Cave cricket

Scavenging cave crickets use their long, wiry antennae to feel their way past objects in the dark and towards food on the cave floor. Alert for the merest brush against them, they try to out-manoeuvre prey such as cave centipedes. Cave crickets, like cockroaches and other invertebrates, feed on debris dropped by bats and cave birds. They also eat the fallen carcasses of these animals when they die.

New Zealand glow-worm

These glow-worms are gnat larvae that live at the entrances to caves. They have evolved an ingenious method of catching food. The larvae spin dangling sticky threads that they illuminate with a light produced from their own bodies. In the darkness of a cave, the glowing threads lure and ensnare small flying insects that the larvae haul up and devour.

Larvae hauling up an insect.

Trapped insect

Eyes

Transparent legs

Cave crab

Tropical caves are often home to some small species of crab that use their pincers to pick food debris from underground streams or the cave floor. Like many cave dwellers – among them millipedes, spiders, salamanders, and shrimps – cave crabs are ghostly pale in colour. In the total darkness of deep caves, skin pigmentaion is of no value. Some animals also lose their sight due to the lack of natural light.

Birds

Some birds, such as barn owls and swifts, make nests within caves. The oilbird of South America nests deep within caves and uses rapid tongue clicks to navigate by echolocation. Colonies of oilbirds fly outside the cave at night to feed on fruit in the surrounding forests. The birds' droppings litter the cave floor below the birds' roosting ledges, and bring nutrients into the cave from far and wide.

Oilbird

Mammals

Some mammals make temporary or permanent homes in caves. The American black bear sometimes shelters in caves during the winter months, as do some foxes. Many species of bat roost, rear their young, or hibernate in the security of caves, some forming colonies thousands strong. Hanging from the roof by their hind feet, the bats are out of reach of almost all predators.

Lesser horseshoe bat

The lesser horseshoe bat is found in large numbers in caves all over Europe, Asia, and northern Africa, where it hibernates during the winter months. Like other bats, it navigates in the dark by using echolocation. It emits high-pitched calls and listens for the echoes that bounce back from the cave walls, stalactites, and other obstructions.

Wings made of elastic skin supported by bones.

Fish

A number of fish species have adapted to living in subterranean streams that flow inside cave systems throughout the world. Most are sightless, with only remnants of eyes underneath their lids, because nothing can be seen underground.

Blind cave characin

Sightless cave animals compensate for their lack of vision with a highly refined sense of touch. Most fish have a lateral line along their sides – a row of sense organs containing nerve endings. The blind cave characin of Mexico has a very prominent lateral line with which it can sense vibrations from passing prey.

Row of dark scales is the lateral line.

| FIND OUT MORE | BATS | BIRDS | CAVES | CRABS AND OTHER CRUSTACEANS | FERNS | FLIES | FISH | GRASSHOPPERS AND CRICKETS | HIBERNATION | MOSSES AND LIVERWORTS |

CELLS

ALL LIVING ORGANISMS are made of self-contained units of life called cells. Some, such as the amoeba, consist of a single cell, while others, such as humans, are made up of billions of cells. Each cell has a nucleus that contains the genetic material DNA, which provides the instructions the cell needs to maintain itself. Surrounding the nucleus is the cytoplasm, which contains the matter that makes the cell function. Forming a layer around the cytoplasm is the cell membrane, which forms the cell's boundary.

Specialized cells

Nerve cell

Sperm cell

White blood cell

Muscle cell

Most plants and animals consist of many cell types, each specialized to perform a specific task. Neurones are long cells that carry nerve impulses around an animal's body; guard cells are rigid box-like structures filled with fluid. They open and close pores on the surface of plant leaves.

Palisade mesophyll cell

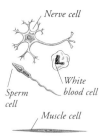

These cells are found in the upper layer of the middle part, or mesophyll, of plant leaves. They are packed with chloroplasts, which contain the green pigment chlorophyll that harnesses the energy in sunlight.

Palisade mesophyll cell

Liver cells

The human liver has over 500 functions related to controlling the chemical balance of the body. These functions are carried out by cells called hepatocytes. For instance, some liver cells remove poisons from blood.

Liver cell

Abnormal cells

When cells divide inside an organism they do so in a controlled way. Sometimes, cells become abnormal and start dividing uncontrollably, leading to the production of growths called tumours. The presence of these abnormal cells and tumours causes a number of different forms of a disease called cancer.

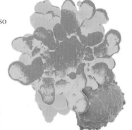

Cancer tumour cell (yellow) being attacked by a T-lymphocyte cell (green).

Marie-François Bichat

French pathologist Marie-François Bichat (1771–1802) showed that an organ, whether a leaf of a plant or a kidney of an animal, is made of different groups of cells. He called each group a tissue, and showed that the same tissues could appear in different organs. His research formed the basis of histology – the study of organs and tissues.

Cell structure

Most cells have similar structures. They consist of a fluid called cytoplasm, a surrounding cell membrane, and a nucleus. Cytoplasm contains structures known as organelles. Plant cells, unlike animal cells, have a tough outer wall and chloroplasts.

Model of an animal cell

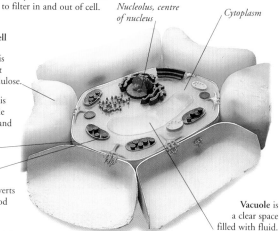

Endoplasmic reticulum is a maze-like network of membranes that make and store chemicals.

Golgi apparatus sorts and stores proteins.

Nucleus is the cell's control centre.

Vacuole is a small and temporary space where food and waste is stored.

Glycogen granules are food reserves or insoluble waste.

Pinocyte allows substances to filter in and out of cell.

Plasma membrane is the thin flexible layer surrounding the cytoplasm.

Mitochondrion generates energy from sugars and fatty acids.

Cytoplasm forms the bulk of the cell and gives it its shape.

Organelles are any structures that live in the cytoplasm and control special functions.

Model of a plant cell

Nucleolus, centre of nucleus

Cytoplasm

Cellulose cell wall is a tough outer jacket mainly made of cellulose.

Plasma membrane is selectively permeable or semi-permeable and is concerned with receiving stimuli.

Chloroplast is an organelle present in green plants; it converts light energy into food by photosynthesis.

Vacuole is a clear space filled with fluid.

Cell division

Cells reproduce by dividing. During cell division the nucleus divides first, followed by the cytoplasm. There are two kinds of cell division: mitosis and meiosis. Mitosis produces cells needed for growth and to replace dead cells. Meiosis produces sex cells for reproduction.

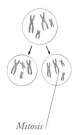

Mitosis
This produces two daughter cells that are identical to the parent cell. The cell's chromosomes (genetic material) make copies of themselves. These separate and move to opposite ends of the cell to form two new nuclei. The cytoplast splits and two new cells are formed.

Mitosis

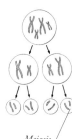

Meiosis
This takes place in sex organs and involves two cell divisions. It makes four sex cells that differ from the parent cells because they have half the normal number of chromosomes. These sex cells are called sperm in males and ova in females.

Meiosis

Studying cells

Cells are so small they need to be studied with a microscope. Both the light microscope and the electron microscope have revealed cells' external and internal structure. For this study cells must be carefully prepared to see their details clearly.

Chemical dyes used for staining cells

Staining cells

When cells are seen under a microscope they are often transparent, showing little detail. For that reason, they are coloured with chemical stains to pick out details such as the nucleus.

FIND OUT MORE   BIOLOGY   GENETICS   HUMAN BODY   MICROSCOPES   MICROSCOPIC LIFE   PHOTOSYNTHESIS   PLANTS, REPRODUCTION   REPRODUCTION

CELTS

PROUD WARRIORS AND SKILLED METALWORKERS, the Celts were among Europe's oldest peoples. The first tribes lived in central European hillforts, but by 400 BC, they also dominated the British Isles, Spain, Italy, and France, and even pushed on into western Asia. Unique and decorative Celtic arts spread with their mythology and religion via trade routes, but the Celts showed no interest in building an empire, or even unifying all their territories. By 50 BC, the mighty Romans and Germanic peoples had squeezed the Celts into Europe's fringes, where they converted to Christianity. Today, Celtic culture and languages survive in Ireland, Scotland, Wales, and parts of France and England.

Celtic world c.200 BC
The first phase of Celtic society probably developed around Hallstatt (now in Austria) between 1200 and 750 BC. From 500 to 50 BC there was a second phase known as La Tène, after its centre in modern France.

Celtic society

Celtic tribes were made up of three main classes: warriors, druids, and farmers. Warfare was an important part of life, so the warriors, armed with their sophisticated iron weaponry, formed an aristocracy. Druids were religious leaders, who often held the power of life and death over other tribe members. Farmers, who reared cattle and cultivated crops using iron tools, kept the economy going. Celts lived in fortified camps called hillforts. Though built for defence, hillforts were also places of trade and religious worship – some even grew into towns. Each pagan Celtic tribe had its own king, and maybe even its own gods. Skilled metalworkers probably had high status.

Thatched roof

Timber fence

Wooden frame supports roof.

Ditch

Souterrain, or underground passage, used for storage or defence

Earthen bank

Celtic hillfort

Celtic horse
The horse played a major part in early Celtic warfare and religion. A horse-goddess called Peon was worshipped first by the Celts, but then also by cavalrymen in the Roman army. There are several chalk figures cut into the rock in former Celtic areas. Some resemble the horse figures that appear on surviving Celtic coins.

Chalk bedrock

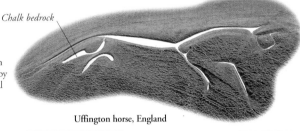

Uffington horse, England

Druids

The druids were holy men in pagan Celtic society. The earliest record of them was made by Julius Caesar, who reported that they acted as judges, led rituals in forest clearings, and used golden sickles to cut mistletoe from sacred oak trees. Druids were skilled in herbalism, and kept oral records of their tribe's history. Occasionally, they performed human and animal sacrifices. Those wanting to become druids had to study for up to 20 years.

Oak leaves

Ritual
The druids left no written records, so their rituals are shrouded in mystery. Celts worshipped many gods and spirits, particularly of trees, rocks, and mountains. One of the oldest gods, Cernunnos, is known as the lord of the beasts. He is often portrayed either wearing antlers or with horned animals, such as stags. He is also often shown wearing golden torcs, and seems to represent fertility and abundance.

Stags are often shown with Cernunnos.

Horned animals symbolize aggression and vitality.

Detail from Gundestrup Cauldron

A stone head with three faces is called a triple head.

Cult of the head
The human head was very important to the pagan Celts, as was the number "3". One custom was to cut the head off a dead enemy, hang it from a horse bridle, then put it on public display. This may have been because the druids believed that a person's soul was in his head, and had to be mastered.

Boudicca

Boudicca (d.61 AD) was queen of the Iceni, one of Britain's Celtic tribes. When the Romans conquered Britain after 43 AD, the Iceni joined forces with them to defeat a rival tribe. However, the Romans then seized Iceni lands and flogged Boudicca. She led a huge revolt, destroying the Roman settlements at St. Albans, Colchester, and London. The Romans finally defeated the rebels, and Queen Boudicca killed herself by taking poison rather than risk being captured.

C

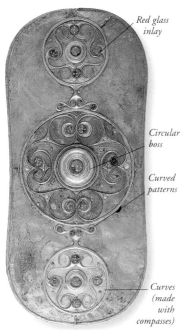

Red glass inlay

Circular boss

Curved patterns

Curves (made with compasses)

Battersea shield

Art and decoration

The Celts were a warlike people, but they were gifted craftworkers and artists too. Celtic metalworkers excelled at decorated weaponry, jewellery, vessels, and mirrors. After the conversion to Christianity, Celtic monks in the British Isles made illustrated holy books of awesome detail. The Lindisfarne Gospels (c.700) feature 45 different colours – all made from finely ground minerals or vegetable dyes.

Battersea shield
Many of the most beautiful bronze Celtic shields were too thin for use in battle, and were purely ornamental. The Battersea shield was probably used only for military parades. It was found in the River Thames, London, in 1857.

Torc
According to the ancient Greek writer, Strabo, Celts loved to dress in colourful clothes and wear jewellery in gold, silver, or electrum (an alloy of gold and silver): "They wear torcs around their necks, and bracelets on their arms and wrists," he wrote. Many gold, bronze, and silver torcs have been found in Celtic graves.

Electrum torc

Tara brooch
Brooches, such as the Tara, date from the 8th century – the early Christian era in Celtic Ireland. Only 9 cms (3.5 inches) in diameter, the Tara brooch is a magnificently detailed piece of jewellery, featuring filigree, gilt chip-carvings, enamelled glass, amber, and gold wire.

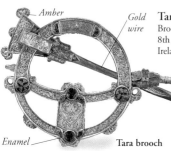

Amber

Gold wire

Enamel

Tara brooch

Sculpture
Animals and birds often figured in Celtic art and decoration, and certain animals were sacred, such as pigs or boars, which often appear in Celtic legend. The legendary King Arthur himself was known as "the Boar of Cornwall".

The boar was an important symbol for the Celts.

Bronze boar

Metalworking
As well as sophisticated iron weaponry and farming tools, skilled Celtic metalworkers produced high-status goods for chieftains, and elaborately decorated items for trade throughout Europe. In Gaul (modern France) the smiths even had their own god – a smith-god known as Sucellos.

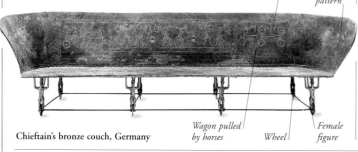

Sword and shield

Swirling abstract pattern

Chieftain's bronze couch, Germany

Wagon pulled by horses

Wheel

Female figure

Celtic cross

Christianity

During the Roman occupation, Christianity came to Britain – but failed to take deep root. However one convert, St Patrick, went on to convert pagan Celtic Ireland in the 5th century. After this, the Celts adopted the religion with gusto and Ireland became a Christian stronghold for the next three centuries.

Monks
Celtic Christianity was famous for the harshness of the monks' lives, and the enthusiam of their devotions. From c.500, monasteries ranged from simple cells for single monks to communities the size of towns.

Early Christian church, Ireland

Missionaries
After Irish Christians set up monasteries in Britain, France, and northern Italy, they started to convert the native peoples. The monks loved learning and helped to keep culture alive in Europe, during the chaos that followed the decline of the Roman Empire. Irish monks operating from the island of Iona, off western Scotland, produced the beautiful *Book of Kells*, c.800, with its extraordinary illuminated (decorated) lettering.

XRI is short for "Christ".

Greek letter X

Greek R

Greek I

Monogram page, Gospel of St Matthew, Book of Kells

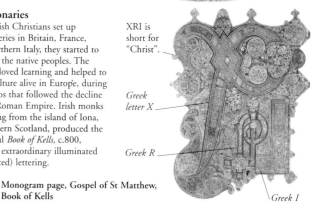

Myths

The pagan Celts had a rich oral tradition. Their stories included myths about mighty gods, such as the Welsh Bran the Blessed, and the Irish Dagda (Father of All); legends about fearless warrior-heroes, such as Cuchulain and King Arthur; and tales of the "shape-changers" – magical creatures from the Underworld. Since the Celts had no written language, monks later wrote down the stories for future generations.

Merlin
The first written legends of the Welsh wizard, Merlin, said that he was a Celtic boy whose father was the devil. At an early age, he found he could foretell the future. In later stories, he appeared as the wizard and mentor of King Arthur of England.

Engraving of the wizard Merlin

Languages
Two types of Celtic language continue to be spoken and written today: Brythonic (Breton, Welsh, Cornish) and Gaelic (Irish, Scots Gaelic, Manx). They may all be traced back to a common ancient Indo-European language.

Modern Irish

"Hill"

"Beach"

km 4 Ceann Tra
17 Dun Chaoin

FIND OUT MORE

BARBARIANS   CHRISTIANITY   EUROPE, HISTORY OF   IRELAND, HISTORY OF   METAL   MYTHS AND LEGENDS   RELIGIONS

CENTRAL AMERICA

SEVEN SMALL COUNTRIES make up Central America, a tapering neck of land that connects northern North America to South America. The Pacific Ocean lies to the west, and the Caribbean Sea, an arm of the Atlantic Ocean, lies to the east. The two oceans are connected by the Panama Canal, a short cut that saves ships months of sailing time. The original peoples of Central America were Native Americans, conquered by the Spaniards in the 1500s. Since gaining independence, these countries have had periods of turbulent politics and unstable economies.

Physical features

Central America has a backbone of rugged volcanic peaks and massive crater lakes that run from Guatemala down to Costa Rica. The Pacific coast is flat and fertile, and the eastern lowlands, stretching to the Caribbean Sea, are wild, empty swamps and rainforests, with little cultivation.

Tropical rainforest
The hot, tropical climate and high rainfall of Central America's Caribbean coast gives rise to vast areas of dense rainforest, particularly in Belize and Guatemala, and on Nicaragua's Mosquito Coast. Economic pressure is forcing people to cut and clear parts of the forest for crops.

Sierra Madre
The Sierra Madre is the highland region of Guatemala and El Salvador, and is a continuation of the Sierra Madre of Mexico. It includes Tajumulco, an extinct volcano, which, at 4,220 m (13,845 ft), is the highest peak in Central America. Most Guatemalans live in this cooler region.

Lake Nicaragua
Covering an area of 7,925 sq km (3,060 sq miles), Lake Nicaragua is the only freshwater lake in the world to contain sea fish, including sharks, which swim up the San Juan River from the Caribbean Sea. The lake is dotted with 310 islands, the largest of which is Ometepe.

Regional climate

Throughout Central America the climate is tropical and hot, with a distinct rainy season from May until November or December. Mountain and upland areas are cooler. Rainfall is higher along the Caribbean coast than on the Pacific side, and can be as high as 6,600 mm (260 in) per year.

25°C (77°F) 22°C (72°F) 1,615 mm (63 in)

Pan-American Highway

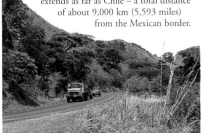

The Pan-American Highway runs the length of Central America, providing an important road link between North and South America. In the north, the road connects with the US highway network, and in the south, it extends as far as Chile – a total distance of about 9,000 km (5,593 miles) from the Mexican border.

Pan-American Highway, Costa Rica

193

Guatemala

Once the hub of the Mayan civilization, modern Guatemala is Central America's largest and most populated country, and has the biggest manufacturing sector. Guatemalan factories produce foods, textiles, paper, pharmaceuticals, and rubber goods. Plantations in the south grow coffee, bananas, cotton, and sugar-cane for export.

Farming

About half of Guatemala's people are of Mayan descent. Most live in the western highlands, growing crops and rearing animals, which they trade at local markets. People from distant hamlets use weekly markets as a chance to socialize and keep abreast of local news.

GUATEMALA FACTS

CAPITAL CITY Guatemala City

AREA 108,890 sq km (42,042 sq miles)

POPULATION 11,700,000

MAIN LANGUAGES Spanish, Quiché, Mam, Kekchí, Cakchiquel

MAJOR RELIGION Christian

CURRENCY Quetzal

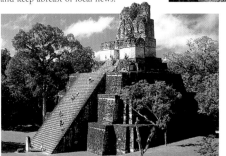

Tikal

Tourism is a growing industry in Guatemala, and each year about 500,000 people visit the country's Mayan ruins. Tikal, once a great Mayan city, was founded in about 600 BC and flourished until about AD 890, when it was suddenly deserted. The city once had about 40,000 inhabitants.

El Salvador

The smallest country in Central America, El Salvador has a rugged landscape that includes more than 20 volcanoes. A thick layer of volcanic ash and lava provide ideal conditions for growing coffee. Economically, El Salvador is still recovering from a civil war that raged between 1979 and 1992 and major earthquakes in 2001.

EL SALVADOR FACTS

CAPITAL CITY San Salvador

AREA 21,040 sq km (8,124 sq miles)

POPULATION 6,400,000

MAIN LANGUAGE Spanish

MAJOR RELIGION Christian

CURRENCY Colón and US dollar

People

El Salvador is Central America's most densely populated country. There are about 304 people per sq km (788 per sq mile) and the population is growing at about two-and-a-half per cent a year. Almost 90 per cent are *mestizos*, and three-quarters are Roman Catholics. More than one-third are farmers who scrape a living in the highlands.

Deforestation

Today, only about five per cent of El Salvador is still forested. Vast tracts of forest, including cedar, oak, and mahogany, have been felled for export and to clear land for farming cash crops such as coffee.

Honduras

A small, poor country, Honduras relied for many years on bananas and timber as its main sources of income. However, since the banana industry was devastated by Hurricane Mitch in 1998, coffee, flowers, and fruit now supply the country's income. Unemployment is high, and most people live in small villages.

HONDURAS FACTS

CAPITAL CITY Tegucigalpa

AREA 112,090 sq km (43,278 sq miles)

POPULATION 6,600,000

MAIN LANGUAGES Spanish, English Creole, Garifuna

MAJOR RELIGION Christian

CURRENCY Lempira

People

About 90 per cent of Hondurans are *mestizos*, of mixed European and Native American descent. Along the Caribbean coast are settlements of the Garifuna, descendants of black slaves who swam ashore more than 350 years ago when slave ships from Nigeria were shipwrecked off the Honduran coast.

Hurricane Mitch

The vast banana plantations in the northeast of the Honduras were wiped out by Hurricane Mitch in 1998. The storms caused £2 million ($3 billion) worth of damage and the deaths of 5,600 people. Bananas comprised 40 per cent of the country's exports, but have been replaced by coffee, shrimp, and melon.

Belize

As most of Belize is dense rainforest, most of its small population live along the Caribbean coast. The two largest groups are the *mestizos* and Creoles, who also have African blood, and are descended from black slaves who were marooned in Belize in the 17th century.

Barrier reef

Protecting Belize's swampy coastal plains from flooding is the world's second largest barrier reef, 290 km (190 miles) long. The reef supports a wide variety of colourful fish.

BELIZE FACTS

CAPITAL CITY Belmopan

AREA 22,966 sq km (8,867 sq miles)

POPULATION 200,000

MAIN LANGUAGES English, English Creole, Spanish, Maya, Garifuna

MAJOR RELIGION Christian

CURRENCY Belizean dollar

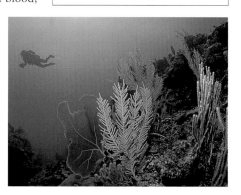

Belmopan

Belize City, the country's chief port, was the capital for many years. In 1960, a hurricane and tidal wave caused severe damage, so in 1970, a new capital, Belmopan, was built in the centre of the country, far from coastal storms. Its population is only 4,000, mostly civil servants.

Nicaragua

Occasionally called the land of lakes and volcanoes, Nicaragua lies at the heart of Central America. Volcanoes and earthquakes frequently shake the country, and Hurricane Mitch caused great damage in 1998. In 1978, Nicaragua experienced a civil war between the left-wing Sandinista government and right-wing "contras", backed by the USA. The war ended in 1990.

Delivery of sugar-cane

Farming
Agriculture employs about one-quarter of the work-force, growing cotton, coffee, sugar, bananas, and meat for export. The country has also developed related industries, such as sugar refineries and canning factories that process agricultural produce.

People
Mestizos make up 70 per cent of Nicaraguans. The rest are whites or blacks, descended from Africans who were taken to Nicaragua as plantation workers in the 18th century. Three-quarters of the population is below the age of 30. Families are tight-knit, and up to three generations may live together.

Chilli pepper
Garlic
Black pepper
Onion
Spring onion
Hot chilli sauce

Food
Nicaraguans enjoy maize roasted on the cob. Meat and bean dishes are spiced with pepper and garlic and scooped up in thin pancakes called tortillas, which are made from maize flour. Food is often topped with hot chilli sauce.

Costa Rica

Unlike its neighbours, Costa Rica is a stable and peaceful country with a democratically elected government. The army was abolished in 1949. Costa Ricans enjoy excellent schools and hospitals. Most people are *mestizos* of Spanish origin. In the Puerto Limón area on the east coast, one-third are English-speaking blacks, descended from plantation slaves.

Costa Rica has some 750 species of bird – more than the whole of the USA.

San José
Founded in 1737, San José became Costa Rica's capital in 1823. With many parks and a mix of traditional and modern Spanish architecture, San José is a commercial centre and has food-processing factories. It has rail links with Pacific and Caribbean ports and lies on the Pan-American Highway.

Tourism
More than 20 per cent of Costa Rica has been set aside to create a network of national parks, including volcanic peaks and undisturbed tropical forest rich in plant and animal species. Many ecotourists are attracted by the country's resident wildlife, such as jaguars, giant sea turtles, crocodiles, and armadillos.

Coffee
Costa Rican coffee is some of the world's finest, and fetches a high price. It grows in the rich black volcanic soils near the capital, San José. Costa Rica was the first Central American country to grow the beans. Bananas are the other leading cash crop.

Dark-roasted coffee beans have a deep, rich taste.

Panama

Occupying the southernmost and narrowest part of Central America, Panama is cut in two by the Panama Canal, which links the Atlantic and Pacific Oceans. A country of swamps, mountains, and grassy plains, Panama has some of Central America's wildest rainforest.

Some 14,000 ships pass through the canal every year, earning Panama valuable toll fees.

Financial centres
At opposite ends of the Panama Canal, Colón and Panama City are important business centres, providing banking, financial, and insurance services. A free trade zone in Colón enables goods to be imported and exported free of duty.

Panama Canal
Linking the Caribbean Sea with the Pacific Ocean, the Panama Canal was built by the USA, and opened in 1914. It is more than 65 km (40 miles) long, and passes through three sets of locks. The length, which is the distance between deep-water points of entry, is 82 km (51 miles).

Shrimps
Panama has a busy and important fishing fleet. The leading catch is shrimps, which form 11 per cent of the country's exports. Anchovetas, small fishes used for fish meal, make up three per cent of exports. Other catches include herrings and lobsters.

FIND OUT MORE — CENTRAL AMERICA, HISTORY OF · CORAL REEFS · EARTHQUAKES · FARMING · FISHING INDUSTRY · FORESTS · MAYA · NATIVE AMERICANS · PORTS AND WATERWAYS · TRAVEL

CENTRAL AMERICA, HISTORY OF

RICHLY ENDOWED WITH natural resources, Central America has had a violent history, with civil wars, revolutions, and terrible repression. The area was home to the great Maya civilization, but the Spanish arrived in the 16th century and began to conquer and settle Mexico and the lands to the southeast. As a Spanish colony, the area was called the Captaincy General of Guatemala and had its capital in Guatemala City. After gaining independence in the 1820s, the region split into separate nations ruled by a few rich families. During the 20th century, the United States often intervened in Central American politics with aid and arms.

Maya
Maya civilization was at its peak in the tropical forest lowland area of Guatemala from about AD 250 to 900. Here the Maya built cities, with step pyramids. Around AD 900, the Toltecs from the north conquered the Maya. The Maya revived around 1200, but were in decline by the time of the Spanish conquest.

Maya pottery bowl

Captaincy General
A small group of wealthy Spanish merchants born in Central America dominated the rich trade in indigo dye, and also the political life of the colony. The area was ruled by a Captain General of Guatemala and his council at Guatemala City.

Panama Canal
With military support from the USA, Panama separated from Colombia in 1903. US engineers built a great canal linking the Atlantic and the Pacific. The Panama Canal, which runs across the south of the country, opened in 1914. After this, the Panamanian economy came to depend almost entirely on the USA.

Independence
In 1821, following the example of Mexico, Central America declared independence. A federation of new states was proposed, but politicians disagreed over what form it should take. The disputes led to war and the break-up of the area into five self-governing republics in 1838.

Coffee
In the 1850s, there was a high world demand for coffee. Rich landowners began to grow coffee in large quantities, forcing local people off their land. Coffee export enabled Costa Rica and El Salvador to achieve some stability in the late 19th century, but changes in coffee prices brought problems later.

Coffee growing, El Salvador

Coffee beans

Modern Central America
Immense differences between rich and poor, combined with the strong economic, political, and cultural influence of the United States, made Central America a turbulent region in the 20th century. Many rulers were dictators and governments changed rapidly, giving little chance of political stability. There were many revolutions, which were often suppressed with huge loss of life.

US intervention
During the 20th century, the United States was closely involved in the affairs of Central America. In 1909, the US supported a right-wing revolution in Nicaragua, and US marines occupied the country until 1933 when, after a guerilla war, Augusto Sandino (1895–1934) forced them to withdraw. Later, the US intervened to stop left-wing revolutions and to prevent the spread of communism during the Cold War. More recently, the US supported the Contras (right-wing guerillas) in Nicaragua and, in 1989, invaded Panama to oust corrupt ruler General Manuel Noriega.

Students in El Salvador erect a statue of Augusto Sandino.

Somoza family
Anastasio Somoza and his sons ruled Nicaragua from 1937–79. The economy grew under their rule, but there was widespread corruption. In 1979, an uprising led by the Sandinistas (a left-wing group named after the former socialist leader Augusto Sandino), ousted the Somozas from power.

Daniel Ortega
Socialist politician Daniel Ortega (b.1945) became the Nicaraguan head of state in 1981 and won free elections in 1984. But he failed to free his country from the conflict between the right-wing politicians backed by the USA and his own left-wing allies.

Oscar Romero
Archbishop Oscar Romero (1917–80) was head of the Catholic church in El Salvador. His reading of the Bible led him to demand better conditions for the poor. Many Catholics began to get involved in social activism in the 1970s. This annoyed the government, which employed death squads to kill priests. When Romero declared that armed struggle was the only option left, he too was shot dead.

FIND OUT MORE
AZTECS   CENTRAL AMERICA   CHRISTIANITY   EXPLORATION   MAYA   RELIGIONS   SOUTH AMERICA, HISTORY OF   SPAIN, HISTORY OF   UNITED STATES, HISTORY OF

CHARLEMAGNE

ON CHRISTMAS DAY, 800, a remarkable emperor was crowned in Europe. His name was Charles, and he was known as Charles the Great, or Charlemagne. He was king of the Franks of northern France, and managed to create a large empire after the turmoil that followed the fall of Rome. Under Charlemagne, Europe enjoyed a period of peace and unity it had not had for 400 years. Yet the king was illiterate and brutal, and held his empire together only by force.

Early life
Charlemagne was born in Aachen in what is now Germany in about 742. He was the oldest son of Pepin, king of the Franks, and inherited his kingdom in 768, jointly with his brother, Carloman. When Carloman died in 771, Charlemagne became sole ruler of the Franks.

Carolingian Empire

In order to control his vast territory, Charlemagne installed bishops and counts in each district to run both the religious and the secular affairs of the empire. He supported an educational system based on the monasteries, and introduced a legal system that owed much to the Roman Empire.

Marches
In order to protect his vast empire, Charlemagne established marches, or buffer zones, along the southern border with Muslim Spain and the eastern border with the various Germanic tribes. Troops of armoured horsemen patrolled the marches to protect the empire against raids across its lengthy borders.

Extent of the empire
By the time of his death in 814, Charlemagne controlled an empire that stretched from Hamburg in northern Germany to south of Rome, and from the Atlantic Ocean to the River Danube. He converted the warlike Saxons to Christianity, and subdued the Lombard kingdom of northern Italy.

Charlemagne's realm

- Frankish lands, 714
- Adjoining territories
- — Empire of Charlemagne

Aachen
Trier
Paris
Aquileia
Ravenna
Rome

Charlemagne used cavalrymen to protect the borders of his empire.

Double-edged blade

Socket to attach shaft

Carolingian spearhead

A new Roman emperor

In the 8th century, the Pope's security as head of the Christian church was threatened by the Lombards from northern Italy. In 773, Charlemagne conquered Lombardy. To recognize his support, the Pope gave Charlemagne the title of Emperor of the Romans.

Coin of Charlemagne

Coronation
Charlemagne visited Rome in 800, and Pope Leo III crowned him and paid him homage. For the first time since the Roman Empire, Christian Europe was united, and the idea of a Holy Roman Empire was born.

Dark Ages

For centuries, historians talked of the time after the fall of the Roman Empire as the Dark Ages. But we now know that the period was a time of great achievement in scholarship and the arts. This activity reached its height under Charlemagne.

Aachen
At his capital of Aachen (Aix-la-Chapelle), Charlemagne created a brilliant court where art flourished. He built a vast palace and chapel which some visitors thought was like a "second Rome".

Scholarship
Scholars came from all over Europe to Aachen to work for Charlemagne. They rescued classical Latin learning from oblivion, and ensured that future generations could learn about the Roman Empire.

CHARLEMAGNE

- **c.742** Born in Aachen.
- **768** Succeeds to Frankish Empire with his brother Carloman.
- **771** Takes sole control of empire.
- **772** Begins conquest of Saxony in northern Germany.
- **773** Subdues Lombards in Italy.
- **778** Conquers Bavaria in southern Germany.
- **795** Establishes Spanish march to protect his kingdom from Muslim Spain.
- **800** Crowned emperor of the Romans by Pope Leo III.
- **814** Dies and is buried at Aachen.

FIND OUT MORE FEUDALISM • FRANCE, HISTORY OF • GERMANY, HISTORY OF • HOLY ROMAN EMPIRE • KNIGHTS AND HERALDRY • ROMAN EMPIRE • SPAIN, HISTORY OF • WRITING

CHAVÍN

FROM THE 10TH to the 1st centuries BC, a brilliant civilization flourished in Peru. It is known today as Chavín, after the important town of Chavín de Huántar in central Peru. Its people produced large temples, fine textiles, and created religious art in a distinctive style. They were also the first people to unify the flat coastal region of Peru with the high Andes Mountains beyond. By doing this, they prepared the way for other important Peruvian civilizations, such as the Incas.

- Chimú
- Huari
- Tiahuanaco
- Chimú and Huari

Civilizations
Other cultures, such as the Chimú, grew up in the Andes region after the Chavín declined.

Castillo
The people of Chavín de Huántar built stone temples at the centre of their city. The famous Old Temple or Castillo was a complex stone structure, containing many intricate passages. Some of these were probably drainage ducts, designed to channel away water from the temple. The adjoining rooms may have been storerooms for offerings and religious equipment.

Chavín de Huántar
The main city of the Chavín civilization was built at a natural transport interchange. It lay on the Mosna River next to two passes into the mountains. The city was therefore well placed for trade, with food such as chillies and salt coming down to the city through the mountain passes.

Art
Chavín art was highly elaborate. Chavín artists made carved stone reliefs, statuettes in precious metals, and beautiful textiles, some of which have survived. Their favourite subjects were gods and goddesses, and the priests, birds, and animals that attended them. Many works of art, such as the textiles and gold statuettes, were small and easily portable. They were traded far and wide in South America, and later cultures copied their styles.

Kennings
Chavín sculptors liked to use the kenning, a type of visual pun, to represent parts of the body. Instead of carving a person's face realistically, they made up their features using repeated elements such as eyes or snakes. Many Chavín carvings, like this stone relief of a god, are therefore intriguing but difficult to understand.

Jaguar vessel

Pottery vessel
Andean peoples, such as the Chavín, made highly decorated pottery vessels with tall, curved handles. This example, from Chavín de Huántar, has the face of a jaguar god with a gold nose ornament and large, dangling earrings.

Animal-figure bowl

Ornate bowl
This bowl in the shape of an animal is another example of the skill of the Chavín potters' art. It may have been used in a religious ceremony, or adorned the table of a wealthy member of the Chavín nobility.

God carries shield with cross design in his left hand.

God carries staff in his right hand.

Religion
The Chavín people had several gods, including a creature called El Lanzón, or "the smiling god". His statue was placed in a central room in the temple at Chavín de Huántar. Above the statue was a hole. A hidden person could speak through this hole, giving the impression that the god himself was speaking.

The staff god
Another important Chavín deity is known as the staff god. This figure is shown in carved reliefs waving a long staff. He was often shown with crops such as manioc, gourds, and peppers, and was thought to be the provider and protector of these valuable foodstuffs.

El Lanzón
This was probably the main god of the Old Temple. Its statue is found in one of the innermost rooms in the building. It was a human figure that had cat-like teeth, suggesting that it was part-human, part-jaguar, like many ancient gods of South and Central America.

After the Chavín
Several civilizations dominated the Andes after Chavín declined. Tiahuanaco, another highland culture, and their neighbours the Huari, flourished from AD 500 to 900. On the coast, the Chimú were the dominant people from the 10th to 15th centuries, until they were conquered by the Incas.

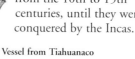

Vessel from Tiahuanaco

Tiahuanaco
This highland empire was a strong, centralized state based in a city on a high plain some 4,000 m (13,100 ft) above sea-level. Its monuments included the Gateway of the Sun, which was carved out of a single block of stone.

Face of Sun god

Carved lintel

Typical square-headed opening

Gateway of the Sun

FIND OUT MORE | GODS AND GODDESSES | INCAS | POTTERY AND CERAMICS | SOUTH AMERICA, HISTORY OF

CHEMISTRY

THERE IS MORE TO CHEMISTRY than messy experiments in laboratories – doctors use it to fight diseases, chefs use it to cook food, and farmers use it to increase the growth of their crops. Chemistry is the branch of science that studies the structure of different elements and compounds. It also investigates how they change and interact with each other during processes called chemical reactions.

Chemical change

When a pile of orange ammonium dichromate crystals is heated by a flame, a chemical reaction occurs. Heat, light, and gases are given off, and a mound of grey-green ash is left behind. The ash not only looks different from the crystals, but it also has a different chemical make-up – it has changed into the substance chromium oxide.

The reaction is so vigorous that a cloud of ash is hurled into the air.

Pile of crystals is lit by a flame.

Ash

Ammonium dichromate crystals

Antoine and Marie Lavoisier

The French chemist Antoine Lavoisier (1743–94) showed that burning is a chemical reaction, that air is a mixture of gases, and that water is a compound of hydrogen and oxygen. His wife, Marie (1758–1836), translated and illustrated many of his scientific works.

$$2H_2 \quad + \quad O_2 \quad \longrightarrow \quad 2H_2O$$

Chemical equations

Scientists write equations to describe what happens during reactions. The equation above shows how hydrogen (H_2) and oxygen (O_2) react in the ratio of 2 to 1 to make water (H_2O).

Rates of reaction

Reactions can be speeded up by making the reacting particles come into contact with each other more often. One way of doing this is by increasing a reactant's surface area. Sulphuric acid reacts more rapidly with powdered chalk than with chalk pieces, because the powder has a greater surface area.

There is a gentle fizzing as carbon dioxide gas is given off.

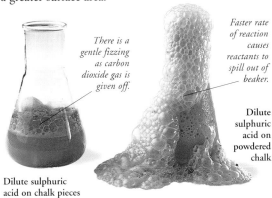

Faster rate of reaction causes reactants to spill out of beaker.

Dilute sulphuric acid on powdered chalk

Dilute sulphuric acid on chalk pieces

Catalysts

Compounds called catalysts speed up a chemical reaction by helping substances react together. The catalysts are left unchanged by the reaction. Many cars are fitted with a catalytic converter to remove polluting gases from engine fumes. The converter forces the gases into close contact with catalysts. The catalysts make the gases react rapidly with each other, producing less harmful gases that escape out of the exhaust.

Chemical reactions

During a chemical reaction, substances called reactants break apart and new substances called products form. Energy is taken in to break the bonds between the reactants' atoms. As the atoms link up again in different combinations to make the products, new bonds form and energy is given out.

Exothermic reactions

In an exothermic reaction, such as burning, more energy is given out than is taken in from the surroundings.

Endothermic reactions

Most of the reactions that occur in cooking are endothermic, which means that more energy is taken in than is given out.

Oxidation and reduction

When iron rusts, a reaction occurs between the iron and oxygen in the air. The iron gains oxygen, and an orange-brown compound called iron oxide forms. A reaction in which a substance gains oxygen is called oxidation. When oxidation occurs, there is a simultaneous reaction called reduction, in which a substance loses oxygen. When iron oxidizes, the air is reduced as it loses oxygen to the iron.

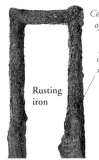

Coating of iron oxide forms on the metal.

Rusting iron

Reversible reactions

Many chemical reactions permanently change the reactants, but reversible reactions can go both forwards and backwards. For example, when nitrogen dioxide is heated, it breaks down into nitrogen monoxide and oxygen. Cooling this mixture makes the two gases react to form nitrogen dioxide again.

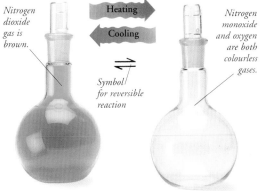

Nitrogen dioxide gas is brown.

Heating

Cooling

Symbol for reversible reaction

Nitrogen monoxide and oxygen are both colourless gases.

Nitrogen dioxide

Nitrogen monoxide and oxygen

Chemical industry

The chemical industry is one of the world's largest and most important industries. It involves taking raw materials – such as air, oil, water, coal, metal ores, limestone, and plants – and using chemical reactions to change them into useful products. These products include food, clothing, medicine, pesticides and fertilizers, paints and dyes, soaps and detergents, plastics, and glassware.

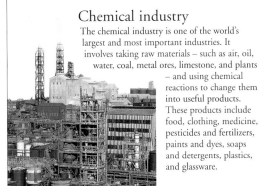

C

1 A container of full-cream milk is allowed to stand for a day or so. The curds are removed and then heated.

Organic chemistry

The study of carbon compounds is called organic chemistry, because all living organisms depend on carbon compounds for their existence. Today, chemists can also create synthetic carbon compounds. Natural and synthetic carbon compounds occur in a wide range of materials, such as food, fuel, paint, textiles, and plastics. This experiment shows how paint can be made from casein – an organic compound derived from milk.

Electrochemistry

The study of the relationship between electricity and chemical substances is called electrochemistry. Many compounds consist of electrically charged particles called ions, which form when atoms lose or gain electrons. A battery uses a chemical reaction to generate an electric current.

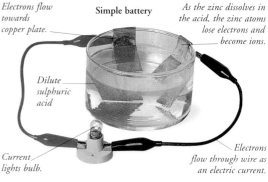

Electrons flow towards copper plate.

Simple battery

As the zinc dissolves in the acid, the zinc atoms lose electrons and become ions.

Dilute sulphuric acid

Current lights bulb.

Electrons flow through wire as an electric current.

Acetic acid

2 Acetic acid is added to the warm curds. This causes a white, rubbery material called casein to form in the liquid.

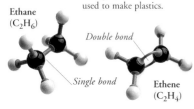

Casein forms in curds.

3 The casein is removed by straining the liquid, It is kneaded in warm water and then dried.

4 Casein can then be mixed with other materials to form paint. The casein is used to bind the pigment to the surface.

Casein hardens as it dries.

Casein-based paint

Aliphatics

Organic compounds containing a chain of carbon atoms linked by single, double, or triple bonds are called aliphatics. The aliphatic ethane occurs in natural gas, and ethene is used to make plastics.

Ethane (C_2H_6)

Double bond

Single bond

Ethene (C_2H_4)

Aromatics

The strong-smelling organic compounds called aromatics contain a ring of six carbon atoms. Benzene, the simplest aromatic, is a colourless liquid obtained from coal, natural gas, and petroleum. Aromatics are used to make vivid dyes called anilines.

Carbon atoms (black)

Benzene (C_6H_6)

Hydrogen atoms (white)

Electrolysis

The process of splitting up a compound by passing an electric current through it is known as electrolysis. Two metal or carbon rods called electrodes are placed in the compound and connected to a battery. As electricity flows through the compound, positive ions are attracted to the negative electrode (the cathode), and negative ions are attracted to the positive electrode (the anode), causing the compound to split apart.

Chlorine gas collects at top of tube.

Deposits of copper metal form as copper ions move to cathode.

Chlorine ions move to anode and form chlorine gas.

Electrolysis of copper chloride solution

Fats and oils

Liquid vegetable oil is an unsaturated fat – a type of fat in which some of the carbon atoms are linked by double bonds. When the oil reacts with hydrogen, the double bonds break and the carbon atoms link up with extra hydrogen atoms, forming a solid fat such as margarine. Solid fats contain only single bonds between their carbon atoms. These fats are said to be saturated because they cannot bond with more hydrogen atoms.

Liquid oil   Solid fat

Polymers

Polymers are giant molecules that consist of winding chains of thousands of small organic molecules called monomers. Fats, starches, and proteins are natural polymers; plastics and artificial fibres are made of synthetic polymers. Polythene contains polymers made of many ethene monomers joined together.

Plastics, such as polythene and PVC, are made up of polymers.

Plastic products

Research into respiration

Geochemist examining rocks

Biochemistry

The study of the chemistry of living organisms and the chemical processes, such as respiration, that take place within them is called biochemistry. The discoveries of biochemists are used in industry, medicine, and agriculture.

Geochemistry

The Earth's composition and the chemical structure of rocks are studied in geochemistry. The findings of geochemists give us a greater knowledge of the Earth's history and help us to find ores, minerals, and other resources.

Alfred Nobel

The Swedish chemist Alfred Nobel (1833–96) invented the explosives dynamite in 1867 and gelignite in 1875, which made him very rich. On his death, he left his vast wealth to pay for a series of annual awards – the Nobel Prizes – for achievements in science, art, and medicine.

Timeline

2 BC Egyptian alchemists try to change "base" metals, such as lead, into gold.

1661 Robert Boyle, an Irish scientist, realizes that chemical reactions can be explained by the existence of small particles.

1770s Antoine Lavoisier investigates compounds such as air and water.

1807 Englishman Humphry Davy uses electrolysis to discover the element sodium.

Davy's equipment

1808 English scientist John Dalton proposes that each element has its own unique type of atom.

1830s German chemists focus on studying carbon and its compounds.

1909 American Leo Baekeland makes the first fully synthetic plastic – Bakelite.

1939 Linus Pauling, an American chemist, explains the nature of chemical bonds between atoms and molecules.

Bakelite radio set

FIND OUT MORE

ACIDS AND ALKALIS   ATOMS AND MOLECULES   DYES AND PAINTS   ELECTRICITY   ELEMENTS   GLASS   MEDICINE   MIXTURES AND COMPOUNDS   PLASTICS AND RUBBER

CHESS AND OTHER BOARD GAMES

BOTH CHILDREN AND ADULTS enjoy games, whether for the challenge of perfecting a skill, the excitement of competition, or simply for fun. Board games, in which competing players move pieces on a special board following rules agreed in advance, are particularly popular. They have a long history, and exist in every culture. They range from demanding games of skill and strategy, such as the ancient game of chess, to more simple games of chance, like snakes and ladders, where a throw of the dice determines the winner.

Strategy games

Games of strategy are challenging, for superior skill, concentration, and tactics decide the winner. Chance plays no part. In most strategy games two players aim to cross the board, or to encircle or capture their opponent's pieces.

Go
Go, also known as *wei-ch'i*, is at least 4,300 years old. It is extremely popular in China, Japan, and Korea. Players capture areas of the board by surrounding them with their own pieces.

Chess

Chess is a war-game. Two players aim to capture, or take, the other's pieces, ultimately trapping the opponent's king. This situation, known as checkmate, occurs when the king cannot be protected by his own pieces, and cannot move without being taken. The word checkmate comes from the Persian *shah-mat* (the king is dead). Chess can be enjoyed at all levels: by beginners, or contested by grandmasters in international competition.

The board has 64 squares.

Each player starts with 16 pieces.

Kasparov plays the computer

Illumination from Persian treatise on chess, undated

History of chess
It is thought that chess originated in China or India more than 1,400 years ago. It spread to North Africa and was introduced to Europe after the Muslim conquest of Spain. Early pieces were based on an Asian army, with elephants, chariots, and footsoldiers.

Pieces
Chess pieces consist of eight pawns, two bishops, knights, and rooks (castles), a king, and a queen. Each piece has its distinctive moves: pawns, for instance, can only move one space forward, while the queen can move in any direction, as far as is needed.

Computer chess
Computers can be programmed to play chess against humans. In 1997, the chess world was shocked when a supercomputer beat the Russian world champion Gary Kasparov (b.1963) in a match. A vast memory for the tactics of past games gives computers an edge.

Race games

Many board games are races, where the winner is the first player to reach a certain part of the board or remove all their pieces. Some race games depend on luck, when a throw of the dice decides how quickly a player moves. This allows players of different ages or levels to compete fairly against each other.

Starting position for mancalah

Mancalah
There are many varieties of this ancient game of skill from Africa. Two or more players compete to clear their side of the board. Each takes turns to pick up a pile of pebbles, dropping them one by one in the hollows.

Pachisi
In India, pachisi is a popular game. Four players race counters around a cross-shaped board; they throw dice or shells to see how many spaces to move. Many other games, such as ludo, are based on pachisi.

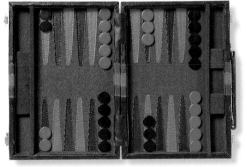

Starting position for backgammon

Men playing pachisi in India.

Backgammon
Invented 5,000 years ago in Asia, backgammon is a fast-paced game for two players. It draws on both skill and chance, and is most popular around the Mediterranean. The first player to remove all his or her "men" from the board wins.

Playing cards

Card games do not need a special board, but must be played on a flat surface. Generally, games are for two or four players. Some games, such as bridge, require concentration and skill, and are played at international competition level; games such as poker, which rely more on luck, are often played by gamblers for money.

A pack of cards contains 52 cards, divided into four groups, known as suits.

Hearts

Diamonds

Spades

Clubs

FIND OUT MORE — CHINA AND TAIWAN — COMPUTERS — INDIA AND SRI LANKA — JAPAN — SPAIN, HISTORY OF

Chess and other board games
Chess pieces

King moves one square at a time in any direction.

Bishop moves diagonally across the board.

Rook travels in straight lines but not diagonally.

Pawn moves forward one square at a time.

Knight can jump over other pieces to new position.

Queen can move in any direction, but cannot jump.

Board games

Game accessories

Draught piece

Draughts is a game of skill that was played in ancient Egypt.

Pieces move around board collecting pies.

Monopoly tokens

Trivial Pursuit, introduced in 1982, is available in a range of editions.

Monopoly, patented in 1935, can be adapted to show streets of any major city in the world.

Players build up words from letter blocks.

Harry Potter, launched in 2000, is based on JK Rowling's children's book series of the same title.

Each player chooses a character.

Marbles are used as pieces.

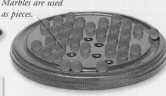

Scrabble, originally known as Criss-Cross, is a word game that was devised in 1931.

Scrabble letters

Solitare is game of skill that is played by only one person.

Cluedo, a detective game played around the world, was created in 1944.

Ludo, a game for two to four players, originated from an ancient Indian game called pachisi.

A compendium is a collection of different board games contained in one box.

Snakes and Ladders is a game of chance. Players move their pieces up ladders or down snakes.

CHILDREN'S LITERATURE

WRITTEN LITERATURE has existed for more than 3,000 years, but it is only in the last 300 years that literature has been created especially for children. Before then, children listened to oral fables and folk tales. Early children's books were educational, but in the 19th century many new forms, or genres, developed such as adventure and fantasy stories, and picture books.

Fables

A short story which illustrates a moral or lesson is called a fable. Fables usually feature animals with human characteristics, such as wisdom or carelessness, and have traditionally been read or told to children in order to encourage good behaviour. A fable may, therefore, end with a proverb such as "look before you leap".

Aesop's Fables

The most famous collection of fables are attributed to a Greek called Aesop who is thought to have lived in the 6th century BC. There are many stories about him; he is often described as a slave who gained freedom to become a royal adviser. The stories attributed to Aesop were first passed on orally, then written down in the 4th century BC.

The *Tortoise and the Hare* is one of Aesop's most famous fables.

Modern fables

Some modern children's stories have been strongly influenced by ancient fables. English author Beatrix Potter (1866–1943) wrote a story about a squirrel called Nutkin whose naughty behaviour ended in punishment.

Uncle Remus

The *Uncle Remus* stories by American author Joel Chandler Harris (1848–1908) are fables based on the stories of plantation slaves in the United States. Told in African-American dialect, the tales are narrated by a wise, genial black man to the son of a plantation owner, and feature characters such as the trickster Brer Rabbit.

Brer Rabbit and Brer Fox

James Thurber (1894–1961)

In *Fables for Our Time* (1940), American author James Thurber reworked traditional stories, such as fairy tales, into fables that were relevant to the 20th century. For example, in Thurber's reworking of the tale of *Little Red Riding Hood*, the girl recognizes the wolf and shoots him dead.

Books

Children's books are produced in more styles, shapes, and sizes than any other form of literature. They range from pop-up books to picture books and novels. Books for younger readers have large type, and use pictures to help explain the story. As readers get older, their books become longer and the stories more complex.

Finnish
French
German
Japanese
Russian
Swedish
Italian
Iranian

Folk and fairy tales

These are among the most popular types of stories, particularly for young children. All cultures have created their own stories about magical beings and events, and the same folk story may occur in many places. For instance, the tale of an orphaned girl with a wicked stepmother is found in most societies.

A scene from *Cinderella*, by the London City Ballet

Monkey King

The daring Monkey King is one of the best known folk heroes in Chinese literature. The Chinese writer Wu Cheng'en used many oral folk tales as source material in his novel about the Monkey King's adventures, *Journey to the West* (1500s).

Monkey battles with the White-Bone Demon

An illustration from Andersen's *The Snow Queen*

Hans Christian Andersen

Danish writer Hans Christian Andersen (1805–75) was one of the first authors to write new fairy tales. His first collection, *Fairy Tales*, was published in 1835. By the time of his death, he had published more than 160 stories; most of them, such as *The Ugly Duckling*, are still read today.

Charles Perrault

Frenchman Charles Perrault (1628–1703) was the first person to write down oral folk tales. His *Tales of Past Times* (1697) included *Cinderella*, but his version was less violent and bloody than the original.

Brothers Grimm

German brothers Jakob (1785–1863) and Wilhelm (1786–1859) Grimm were the editors of *Grimm's Fairy Tales*, which included *Snow White*, and *Hansel and Gretel*. Their scholarly approach to collecting folk tales from Europe means that their versions of these ancient tales are often seen as the definitive versions.

Wilhelm Grimm   Jakob Grimm

Fantasy stories

Until the mid-19th century, most of the stories written for children were concerned with the teaching of morals and good behaviour. However, the enormous success of Hans Christian Andersen's fairy tales encouraged many writers to produce wild fantastic stories which celebrated the imagination above all else.

Alice in Wonderland
Written in 1865, English author Lewis Carroll's (1832–98) fantasy revolutionized children's literature with its fantastic plot, bizarre characters, and absence of any moral. The half dream, half nightmare world that Alice encounters when she plunges down the rabbit hole shows the limitless possibilities of the fantasy story.

Tenniel illustration of the Mad Hatter

Peter Pan
English author JM Barrie (1860–1937) originally wrote *Peter Pan* as a play in 1904. Peter, a motherless half-magical boy, takes the Darling children to Never Land.

Wonderful Wizard of Oz
American author L Frank Baum (1856–1919) wrote this fantasy in 1900. Dorothy is carried by a whirlwind out of Kansas to the magical Land of Oz, where she befriends the Scarecrow, Tin Woodman, and Cowardly Lion. In 1938, it was made into a popular film, ensuring that people world-wide know the story, even if they have never read the book.

The Hobbit
JRR Tolkien (1892–1973) published the tale of the Hobbit, Bilbo Baggins, in 1937. The trilogy that followed it, *The Lord of the Rings,* is one of the most popular stories ever published.

Peter Pan

Still from the 1938 film of The Wizard of Oz

The Hobbit

Adventure stories

The 19th century saw the beginning of great adventure stories for children. The books celebrated bravery, daring, and excitement, although the heroes were often boys rather than girls. Some books, such as *Treasure Island*, described imaginary lands while others, such as *Huckleberry Finn*, were about adventures close to home.

Huck and Jim

Treasure Island
Scottish author Robert Louis Stevenson (1850–94) told a story of piracy. The tale is told by Jim Hawkins, who acquires a map showing hidden pirate gold. He has to defeat the pirates before he can claim the treasure.

Huckleberry Finn
American author Mark Twain (1835–1910) set his novel on the banks of the Mississippi River. One of its themes, black slavery, is illustrated by Huck's friendship with the runaway slave Jim.

A scene from the 1950 film of Treasure Island

School stories

School is part of children's experience, and often features in literature. The first and most famous school story was called *Tom Brown's Schooldays* (1857) by Thomas Hughes (1822–96). It was based on the author's own time at boarding school in England. Today's school stories usually reflect the experiences of most children.

Harry Potter
Author JK Rowling published the first in the Harry Potter series in 1997, *Harry Potter and the Philosopher's Stone*. The book won several literary awards and was followed by equally popular sequels. The stories centre on Harry, an orphan who is sent to live with his aunt and uncle and discovers the Hogwarts School of Witchcraft and Wizardry. By 2002 the series had sold 100 million books in 46 languages.

Daniel Radcliffe played Harry Potter on screen.

Roald Dahl
British author Roald Dahl (1916–90) is known for his fantasy stories, which include *James and the Giant Peach* (1961), *Charlie and the Chocolate Factory* (1964), *Matilda* (1988), and *The BFG* (1989). His popularity is partly due to his skill in describing adults' frightening peculiarities in such a way as to make them laughable.

Illustration from Tom Brown's Schooldays

Family stories

Children's literature often takes as its theme family life. Stories of family life date back to the 19th century; one of the first was *Little Women* (1869) by Louisa May Alcott. Today's family-based stories look at the difficulties that children may experience, such as divorced parents, bereavement, or abuse.

Little Women
Louisa May Alcott's (1832–88) novel about life in a small town in New England, was one of the first books that presented children in a realistic fashion. The story of the March family, Meg, Jo, Beth, Amy, and their mother, Marmee, was in part autobiographical. It inspired many other American writers to produce stories about family life. Alcott wrote several sequels to *Little Women* including *Little Men* and *Good Wives*.

A scene from the 1949 film of Little Women

Picture books

Children's picture books have a long history; from the *Orbis Pictus* in 1658 there have been picture books for children. Babies and young children can enjoy books in which pictures are just as important as words. The illustrations tell stories and help teach concepts such as colours, shapes, and the names of things. Many talented artists now make books for children.

Visible world

Even the earliest books included illustrations. However, the first picture book that was specially designed for children was called *Orbis Pictus*, or *Visible World* (1658), by John Amos Comenius. It used pictures in order to help the translation of German into Latin.

Merchandising

Successful children's books are now big business. Popular characters soon appear as toys, games, and even crockery. The image of the characters can be found printed on clothing and books.

Pierre Lapin

Beatrix Potter books are printed in many languages.

Beatrix Potter

The first master of the picture story book was Beatrix Potter (1866–1943). She was a lonely child who taught herself to draw and became skillful at painting animals. Her first book, *The Tale of Peter Rabbit*, was published in 1901. The books of Beatrix Potter are still popular throughout the world.

Cuddly Peter Rabbit toy

Beatrix Potter merchandise

Teapot

Jug

Mug

Board game

Where the Wild Things Are

When this book was published by the American writer Maurice Sendak (b.1928) in 1963, many people thought it was too scary for children. It tells the story of a boy called Max, who sails away to the land of the Wild Things, where after many adventures, he becomes their king.

Dr Seuss

The American artist Dr Seuss (Theodore Geisel 1904–90) created many classic picture books. Stories such as *The 500 Hats of Bartholomew Cubbins* (1938) are built around strange and improbable situations. Dr Seuss was one of the first authors to make rhyming storybooks that helped teach children to read. In *The Cat in the Hat* (1958), a cat visits two children and creates rhyming chaos while their mother is away.

Children's poetry

Verse for children dates back to the songs and ballads of the oral tradition, and children still memorize rhymes and songs and pass them on among themselves. Children's poetry has been written in every style imaginable, from humorous fantasies and nonsense limericks to powerful social commentary.

Nursery rhymes

Spoken rhymes are found all over the world, and many are ancient. Little Bo Peep is linked to a hide-and-seek game called Bo-Pepe, which is more than 600 years old. Ring A Ring O' Roses describes the symptoms of the plague, which left rose-like marks on its victims.

Limericks

The English artist Edward Lear (1812–88) wrote many nonsense rhymes. His limericks generally involve all sorts of people in very odd situations.

"There was an old man of Whitehaven, who danced a quadrille with a raven."

Prizes

Today, more children's books are being published than ever before. To encourage good writing and illustration, prizes are awarded for the best books. There are awards for everything from teenage fiction to picture books. Some prizes are nominated by children.

Newbery Medal

The American Library Association awards this prize for the year's best children's book. It is named after John Newbery (1713–67), who opened the world's first children's bookshop in 1745.

Carnegie Medal

This prize has been awarded by the British Library Association since 1936. It takes its name from American millionaire Andrew Carnegie (1835–1919), who founded libraries in Britain and the United States.

Timeline

15th century Chapbooks (crime and miracle stories) published. Courtesy books tell children how to behave.

1745 John Newbery sells *Little Goody Two-Shoes* in the first children's bookshop.

Little Goody Two-shoes

1877 English author Anna Sewell publishes *Black Beauty*.

1883 *Pinochio*, by Italian author Carlo Collodi (1826–1890) published.

1894 *The Jungle Book*, by Rudyard Kipling (1865–1936) published.

1908 Kenneth Grahame (1859–1932) publishes *The Wind in the Willows*.

1922 The first Newbery Medal for children's literature awarded.

1926 *Winnie-the-Pooh*, by AA Milne (1882–1956) published.

1929 *Emil and the Detectives* by German author Eric Kästner (1899–1974) published.

1931 French artist Jean de Brunhoff publishes *The Story of Babar*.

1952 EB White (1899–1985) publishes *Charlotte's Web*.

1968 *The Pigman* by Paul Zindel (b.1936) published.

1975 *Forever*, one of the first books for teenagers, by American author Judy Blume (b.1938) published.

1997 JK Rowling publishes the first book in the *Harry Potter* series.

FIND OUT MORE   BOOKS   DRAMA   EDUCATION   LITERATURE   MYTHS AND LEGENDS   POETRY   PRINTING   WRITING

C

CHINA AND TAIWAN

THE WORLD'S THIRD LARGEST COUNTRY, after Russia and Canada, China covers a vast area of eastern Asia. It has, by far, the largest population in the world and contains about 36 per cent of Asia's people. China has a long Pacific coastline to the southeast, but also borders 14 countries inland. Closely associated with China are Taiwan, an independent island, and the two former European colonies of Hong Kong and Macao. China is ruled by a communist government, which is working to continue the country's economic boom of the 1990s.

Great Wall

More than 2,200 years ago, about 300,000 slaves built the Great Wall of China to keep out invaders from the north. Stretching from Central Asia to the Yellow Sea, the wall's total length is 6,400 km (3,980 miles), and is the world's longest human-made structure.

Soldiers walking along the Great Wall

Physical features

China's vast land area includes rugged hills, subarctic regions, deserts, and tropical plains, and is watered by many river systems. High mountains, mainly in the north and west, dominate one-third of China's land.

Huang He
Two mighty rivers flow in eastern China, the Chang Jiang and the Huang He. At 5,464 km (3,395 miles), the Huang He is known in English as the Yellow River, or "China's Sorrow", after the yellow soil left behind by its devastating floods.

Guilin Hills
China's agricultural heartland lies in the south and centre of the country. The Li river is used to irrigate land that can be intensively farmed. Here at Guilin, the river supports fishermen and their families who make a living from its rich waters. The steep Guilin Hills rise up behind the river.

Climate
China has two main climates. More than half of the country is arid or semi-arid, and in the north and west, deserts and mountains experience extreme temperature variations. The winters are bitterly cold and summers are hot and dry. The summer monsoon brings rain from the Pacific to areas nearer the sea, particularly the south and east, where conditions are wet, warm, and often humid.

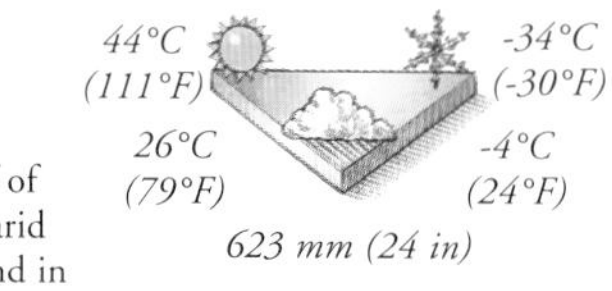

44°C (111°F)   -34°C (-30°F)
26°C (79°F)   -4°C (24°F)
623 mm (24 in)

206

China

Ruled by the Communist Party since 1949, China is divided into 22 provinces, five autonomous regions, and three special municipalities. Although technically governed from Beijing, many of these are becoming increasingly independent. About 93 per cent of China's people are Han Chinese, and around 60 per cent follow no religion, because the communist rulers discourage religious beliefs. Although fertile land is in short supply, farming is often intensive and employs two-thirds of the work-force. The Olympic Games will be held in Beijing in 2008.

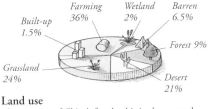

Land use
The majority of China's farmland is in the east and south of the country. Much of the desert and mountain regions is uninhabitable. China has large mining areas in the Shaanxi and Sichuan basins, and is the world's largest coal producer.

Built-up 1.5%
Farming 36%
Wetland 2%
Barren 6.5%
Forest 9%
Grassland 24%
Desert 21%

CHINA FACTS

CAPITAL CITY	Beijing
AREA	9,596,960 sq km (3,705,386 sq miles)
POPULATION	1,290,000,000
MAIN LANGUAGE	Mandarin Chinese
MAJOR RELIGIONS	Traditional beliefs, Buddhist
CURRENCY	Renminbi (known as yuan)
LIFE EXPECTANCY	71 years
PEOPLE PER DOCTOR	588
GOVERNMENT	One-party state
ADULT LITERACY	84%

Schoolchildren in Beijing

People

Around 80 per cent of Chinese live in less than half the country's land area, mostly in small villages. However, more than 30 of China's cities have more than one million inhabitants. China's population is growing by 15 million a year, so the government has asked families to have just one child, and fines those who have more. Known as "Little Emperors", single boy children are often spoiled.

137 per sq km (335 per sq mile)

Urban 32%   Rural 68%

Beijing

For more than 2,000 years, Beijing has been a capital city, either of all China or part of it. Built symmetrically within three rectangles, it is a bustling city of historical buildings, temples, and beautiful parks. The Forbidden City lies at its heart, home to the 15th-century emperor's Imperial Palace. Also from that period is the Temple of Heaven, designed in the Chinese pagoda style.

Temple of Heaven, Beijing

New Year
China's most important festival is the celebration of New Year, which begins in January or February, at the second new Moon of winter. People celebrate with colourful processions and dragon dances and close all shops and offices. Each year is named after an animal.

Leisure
City-dwellers, who have no gardens, are encouraged to take exercise in the well-kept parks. At weekends and on summer evenings, neighbours meet to play board games such as *mah jong*.

Food

Chinese food varies greatly from region to region. Rice is the basis of all dishes in the south, where it grows, whilst in the north, wheat noodles are the staple food. Both noodles and rice are usually served with stir-fried vegetables and meat. Cantonese food is reputed to be the most exotic in China, using rare meats such as snake and turtle. Fish and duck are also served frequently. The Chinese eat with chopsticks held in one hand.

Chopsticks

Dry-braised noodles

Xi'an bicycle factory, Shaanxi

Handle-bars

Industry
China has well-developed heavy industries such as iron and steel. Since the late 1970s, growth has been concentrated in Special Economic Zones in eastern China, where joint Chinese and foreign trade and enterprise are encouraged.

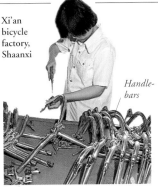

Rice farming
Many women work in flooded paddy fields in southern China. Rice is the main crop, and in a good year two yields can be harvested as well as one of vegetables. When the crop is ready for harvesting, it turns golden. The women cut and tie the stalks into bundles for threshing, which separates the grain and its protective husk from the stalk.

Tibet
The mountainous region of Tibet became a part of China in 1965. Most Tibetans are devout Buddhists, but under Chinese rule their religious and civil liberties were taken away. Opponents of the government were exiled, and some Han Chinese were resettled in the area, causing tension. The monks still practise their faith and carry out ceremonies, such as offering beer to Buddha in a *hosar*, or New Year, ritual.

Shanghai
A leading centre of trade and industry and a busy harbour, Shanghai is China's largest city and home to about 16,000,000 people. The city has traditional pagodas and glittering skyscrapers alongside the Chang Jiang River.

Tibetan monk pours Chang beer at hosar festival.

C

Hong Kong

Hong Kong is a special administrative region in southeast China, made up of 236 islands and a mainland area. It has a busy port and is a leading financial centre. More than six million people live there. A former British colony, Hong Kong was returned to China in 1997. It experienced economic setbacks after the transition, but is now recovering.

Gambling
Gambling is a popular activity in Hong Kong. Playing mahjong, a traditional game, with friends and family is a way of socializing. Horse racing is a big industry, with many people placing bets online.

Houseboats
Some Hong Kong fishing families live in houseboats called sampans, which are moored in the harbours. The fishermen are now facing increasing competition from more efficient deep-sea trawlers.

Macao

A tiny peninsula in southeast China, Macao became a Portuguese colony nearly 450 years ago and was returned to China in 1999. Situated about 64 km (40 miles) west of Hong Kong, Macao is a popular tourist destination, with fragrant woods, and a sandy coastline onto the South China Sea.

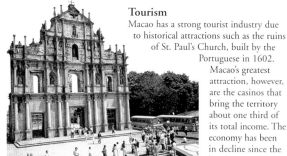

Tourism
Macao has a strong tourist industry due to historical attractions such as the ruins of St. Paul's Church, built by the Portuguese in 1602. Macao's greatest attraction, however, are the casinos that bring the territory about one third of its total income. The economy has been in decline since the handover to China.

Taiwan

Often referred to as a "Little Dragon", Taiwan has one of Asia's most rapidly expanding economies. However, it is not recognized by the UN and lies at the centre of a debate over ruling rights. China claims Taiwan to be a province of Beijing, although the Taiwanese have governed here since the communists gained control of China in 1949. Despite this tension, Taiwan has established global trading markets, and its people enjoy high living standards.

People
About 84 per cent of Taiwanese are Han Chinese, who moved to Taiwan when the communists took power in 1949. They live in extended family groups, following traditional customs. Taiwan's native peoples of Indonesian origin now make up only two per cent of the population. The Ami, of the eastern mountains, are the largest group. Expert potters and farmers, their women rule the household.

TAIWAN FACTS

CAPITAL CITY	Taipei
AREA	35,980 sq km (13,892 sq miles)
POPULATION	22,200,000
MAIN LANGUAGE	Mandarin Chinese
MAJOR RELIGIONS	Buddhist, traditional beliefs
CURRENCY	Taiwan dollar
LIFE EXPECTANCY	77 years
PEOPLE PER DOCTOR	894
GOVERNMENT	Multi-party democracy
ADULT LITERACY	94%

Opera
Traditional Chinese opera was brought to the island with settlers from China. The operas are based on traditional stories. Stage sets are basic, but the costumes are elaborate, made from richly coloured silks with delicate embroidery. Make-up is used to highlight emotions.

Fishermen unload their catch.

Sun Moon Lake
Taiwan's scenic Sun Moon Lake, known as *Jih-yüeh Tan,* is surrounded by the Central Mountains. The two parts of the lake, Sun Lake and Moon Lake, supply a hydroelectric plant that produces four per cent of the country's power. The tranquil, forested area is known for its ornate buildings, including the Buddhist Wen Wu Temple.

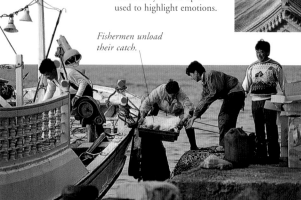

Fishing
Taiwan's fishermen land 1,171,000 tonnes (1,290,793 tons) of fish annually from the rich fishing grounds surrounding the island. Some Taiwanese fishermen have been accused of plundering Atlantic fishing grounds. Much of the catch goes to supply the huge Japanese market. Freshwater ponds are used for farming carp.

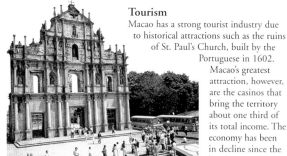

Taipei
The high-tech capital in the north of the island is the fastest growing city in Asia, having expanded to four times its original size. Many of the three million inhabitants ride to work on motor scooters, causing pollution and jams.

Industry
Few natural resources have forced Taiwan to develop a booming, highly specialized industry. Backed by an educated, ambitious work-force, the country exports electronic equipment, such as computers and television sets, machinery, textiles, sports equipment, toys, and watches. Profits are invested, or used to buy oil for energy. Farming and fishing ensure self-sufficiency in food.

FIND OUT MORE ASIA, HISTORY OF   BUDDHISM   CHESS AND OTHER BOARD GAMES   CHINA, HISTORY OF   FESTIVALS   FISHING INDUSTRY   GARDENS   OPERA   PORTS AND WATERWAYS   TRADE AND INDUSTRY

CHINA, HISTORY OF

CHINA IS THE WORLD'S oldest continuous civilization. For more than 2,000 years, from 221 BC to AD 1911, it was united as a single vast empire under a series of all-powerful rulers. During this period, borders changed, capitals shifted, and the country was invaded by fierce tribes, including the Mongols. However, for most of its history, China led the world in art and technology, with inventions including paper, porcelain, and gunpowder. Despite its huge size, a unique system of government and a strong sense of national identity have helped to maintain a united China.

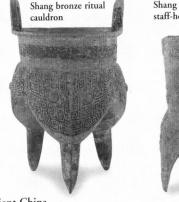

Shang bronze ritual cauldron

Shang bronze staff-head

Ancient China
The first known Chinese dynasty, the Shang, ruled from about 1500 to 1027 BC. The Shang rulers were believed to be semi-divine, and wre called the Sons of Heaven. It was their duty to maintain good relations between earth and the heavenly realm.

Qin Shi Huangdi

When Zheng (258–210 BC), the leader of the victorious Qin army, took control of China in 221 BC, he took the title of First Sovereign Qin Emperor, or Qin Shi Huangdi. The First Emperor treated his subjects harshly, and his dynasty was overthrown by a peasant rebellion in 207 BC. The name China comes from Qin.

Unification

By 400 BC, central government had broken down, and many small kingdoms fought among themselves. In 221 BC, the state of Qin emerged victorious, uniting all the rival kingdoms under the rule of the First Emperor. The Great Wall was built at this time, using slave labour.

Each soldier has a different face and is modelled on a real soldier.

Hollow body

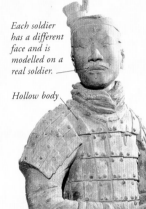

Han Dynasty

Chinese civil service exam paper

In 207 BC, a new dynasty took power. The Han emperors, who ruled until AD 220, set up a national civil service to run the country. Officials studied the teachings of the philosopher Confucius (551–479 BC), and were selected by a rigorous examination system. The structure of the civil service remained largely unchanged for 2,000 years. The Han reign marked a period of peace and prosperity.

Characters are read vertically.

Terracotta army
The First Emperor's tomb was guarded by thousands of life-sized terracotta warriors with horses and chariots, whose job was to protect the emperor in the afterlife. This terracotta army was found in 1974 by men digging a well. The tomb lies near to the modern-day city of Xian.

The soldiers once carried real weapons made of bronze, but these were stolen by grave robbers.

Solid legs

Great Wall

Qin Empire

First empire
Protected by the Great Wall, the Qin empire covered what is now northern and eastern China. The wall was built as a defence against hostile tribes from Central Asia.

Inventions

Throughout Chinese history, emperors encouraged the development of science and technology. Paper and printing, gunpowder, harnesses for animals, the magnetic compass and stern rudder, and the wheelbarrow were all invented in China.

15th-century gun

Shield protects soldier.

Multiple gun fires a hail of bullets.

Bronze "knife coins"

Paper money
The Chinese perfected paper-making in about AD 105, using pulped silk waste. In later years, hemp, bark, or bamboo were used. The development of printing followed, and paper money was first circulated in China in the 9th century. By this time, the Chinese were also printing books using carved wooden blocks.

Gunpowder
Chinese scientists first produced gunpowder in the 9th century, and soon adapted their technology to make fireworks and weapons. Early Chinese rockets, fuelled by gunpowder, were in use by the 13th century. The Chinese also invented the gun, the bomb, and the mine.

Chinese character, or symbol, which translates to mean "happiness and good fortune".

福

Three perfections
The Chinese call calligraphy, poetry, and painting "the three perfections". From the Song dynasty (960–1279) onwards, the combination of these three disciplines in a single work of art was considered to be the height of artistic expression, and to be skilled in them was seen as the greatest accomplishment of an educated person. Calligraphers spent many months practising the brushwork of just one or two characters.

C

Ming roof tile
decorated
with horse

Ming dynasty

In 1368, Hong Wu, a peasant who had led
revolts against China's Mongol rulers, managed
to drive the Mongols out and create a new
dynasty, the Ming. He built a new capital at Beijing
and established peace, prosperity, and good government.
To make society more equal, he abolished slavery, confiscated
big estates, gave land to the poor, and taxed the rich.

Admiral Zheng

As part of the policy of
restoring Chinese prestige,
the Ming emperors sent
Admiral Zheng He
(1371–1433) to visit foreign
rulers. Zheng made seven
voyages in Southeast
Asia and the Indian
Ocean, sailing as far west
as East Africa. He was
accompanied by a fleet
of 317 ocean-going junks.

Ocean-going junk

*Tile would have
decorated the ridge of a roof.*

Foot binding

The Chinese believed that tiny feet
were a vital part of female beauty.
Young girls from rich families had
their feet tightly bound to prevent
them from growing. This process
was very painful. Adult women
were also forced to wear platform
shoes. In 1902, the emperor issued
an order banning foot binding,
although it continued for many years.

*Platform shoes
made the wearer take tiny steps.*

Opium
pipe

Decline of the empire

During the last 250 years of the Chinese
empire, the throne was occupied by the
Manchus, a non-Chinese people from north of
the Great Wall. The first Manchus were
enlightened rulers, but later emperors
feared that change might lead to
rebellion and they clung to old
traditions. In 1911, the Chinese
overthrew the feeble Manchus,
and established a republic.

Opium wars

In 1839, the Chinese tried to stop the British
opium trade in Canton. The British went to
war, forcing the Chinese to open ports to
foreign trade and to cede Hong Kong to the
British. France, Russia, and later Japan, made
similar demands.

Boxer rebels

Boxer Rebellion

In 1900 a secret group called the Society of Harmonious Fists
(Boxers) rose up in protest at European involvement in China.
The rising was swiftly put down when an international force
captured Beijing, but it weakened China's government.

*Japanese
troops in
Manchuria*

Japanese invasion

Civil war and a communist uprising weakened the
new republican government. In 1931 the Japanese
took advantage of the chaos to invade the northern
province of Manchuria. Six years later they invaded
the rest of China, capturing cities and ports.

Communist China

In 1949, the communist party led by Mao
Zedong (1893–1976) finally took control of
China after years of civil war. The new
government nationalized industry and the
land, and began a series of five-year
plans to transform the country
into a major industrial power.

Red star, symbol from the Communist
Chinese flag

Modern China

After the death of Mao Zedong
in 1976, the Chinese began
to modernize their economy by
introducing western ideas and
technology. Central government
control over the economy
relaxed, and this led to an
economic boom as new
industries were established.

Tiananmen Square

In 1989, students took
to the streets of Beijing
demanding democratic
reform. Many students
occupied Tiananmen
Square, Beijing. On 4
June, the army entered
the square, killing more
than 3,000 people. After
the Tiananmen massacre
the pro-democracy
movement was
ruthlessly suppressed.

Troops in Tiananmen Square

Timeline

c.1650–1027 BC Shang dynasty rules
northern China; bronzeworking and
writing are developed.

221 BC First Emperor, Qin Shi
Huangdi, founds the Qin dynasty
and unites the country.

221 BC–AD 618 Great Wall of
China built.

589–618 Short-lived Sui dynasty
builds the Grand Canal linking
major rivers.

618–906 Tang dynasty brings
great prosperity to China; art
and trade flourish.

960–1279 Industrial revolution
occurs under the Song dynasty.

1279 Mongols under Kublai Khan
conquer China; trade with Europe
flourishes along the Silk Road.

1368–1644 Ming dynasty
establishes China as world power.

1644–1911 Manchu dynasty.

Mao Zedong

1911 Chinese republic declared.

1949 Communists declare the People's
Republic of China.

1966 Mao Zedong heads Cultural Revolution.

1997 Deng Xiaoping dies. Hong Kong
handed back to China by the UK.

1999 Portugal hands back Macao to China.

Shang bronze halberd (dagger)

FIND OUT MORE   ASIA, HISTORY OF   CHINESE REVOLUTION   GUNS   INVENTIONS   MONGOL EMPIRE   POTTERY AND CERAMICS   WRITING

Chinese arts and crafts

Jewellery and adornment

Belt and garment hooks, worn by men, could be beautifully decorated.

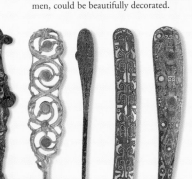

Belt and garment hooks were sometimes inlaid with turquoise and gold.

Gilded hair comb has prongs of silver; it was probably used by a high-ranking woman.

Silver and gilt belt plaque is decorated with a pattern of fruit.

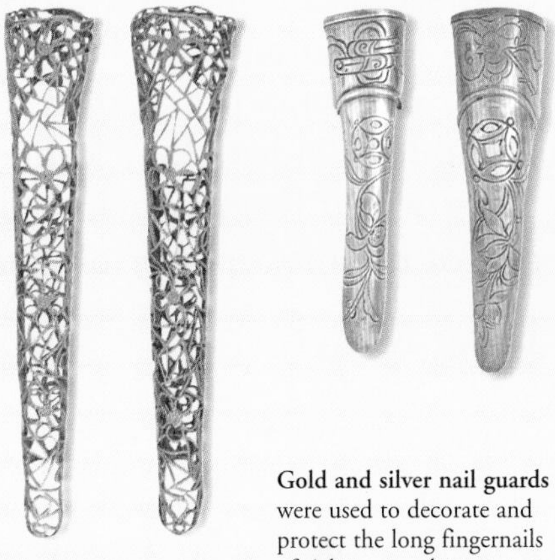

Gilded sleeve weight helped wide sleeves hang properly.

Gold buckle is decorated with carved patterns.

Gold and silver nail guards were used to decorate and protect the long fingernails of rich men and women.

Status artifacts

Jade buckle plaque with dragon design

Rich, gilded decoration

Fish is Buddhist symbol representing spiritual freedom.

Decoration made by pushing enamel paste into gaps between metal.

Box is made of lacquer, carved with leaves.

Cup carved from jade, a precious gemstone.

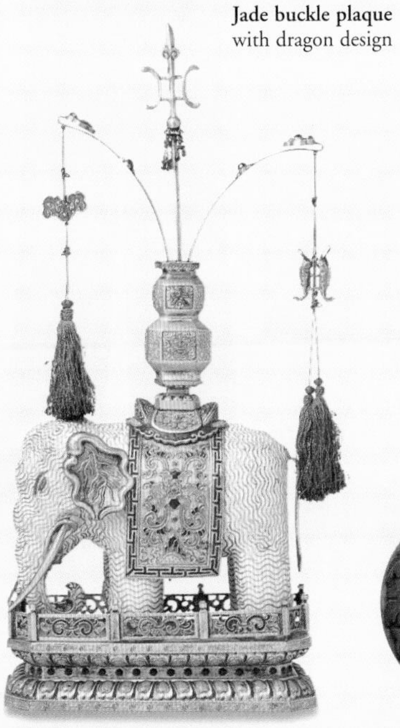

Jade pot was used for washing writing brushes.

Camel ornament is made of glazed earthenware.

Jade pot is adorned with carving of man and house.

Elephant ornament is made of gold and ivory, inlaid with gems.

Box is made of lacquer, carved with peony flowers.

Fish vase is decorated with enamel paste and gilded metal.

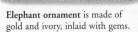

Inlaid lid for writing brush

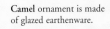

Writing brush has wolf-hair tip and is inlaid with mother-of-pearl.

Extremely detailed work

CHINESE REVOLUTION

THE CHINESE REVOLUTION refers to the bitter struggle for control of China between the Kuomintang, or Nationalists, led by Chiang Kai-shek, and the Communists, led by Mao Zedong. The struggle began in the 1920s, when the Nationalists expelled the Communists from their movement; it ended in 1949, when the Communist Party took power, and Chairman Mao proclaimed that China was a People's Republic. Under Mao's leadership, China was transformed from a backward peasant society into one of the most powerful nations in the world.

1911 Revolution
In 1911, a Nationalist revolution overthrew the Manchu dynasty, and created a republic in southern China. Sun Yat-sen (1866–1925) was elected provisional president of the republic, but the lives of the peasants did not improve, and real power remained with warlords (military leaders).

Kuomintang

In 1926, a Kuomintang general named Chiang Kai-shek (1887–1975) defeated the warlords, helped by the Communist Party. Chiang set up a government in Nanking but, once in power, he threw the Communists out of the government and massacred many Communist leaders.

Long March

In 1931 Mao and a small band of Communists set up China's first communist state in Jiangxi, southern China. The Kuomintang attacked them constantly, and in 1934 Mao was forced to withdraw. The following year he led 100,000 people, mostly peasants, over 9,000 km (6,000 miles) of some of the world's roughest terrain, to a new base in Shaanxi province in the north. The Long March crossed 18 mountain ranges, 24 rivers, and passed through 11 provinces and 62 cities.

Only 30,000 marchers out of the original 100,000 reached their destination.

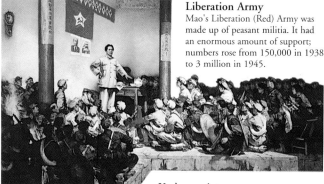

Mao Zedong addressing followers at the Yan'an soviet during the early days of the revolution.

Liberation Army
Mao's Liberation (Red) Army was made up of peasant militia. It had an enormous amount of support; numbers rose from 150,000 in 1938 to 3 million in 1945.

Yan'an soviet
In 1935, Mao set up new headquarters in northern China – his Yan'an soviet, or base. He and his followers lived in caves around the city of Yan'an, and went into the countryside where they recruited a huge following among the peasantry.

Cap featuring red star
Epaulettes show rank
Green wool trousers
Red Army uniform

• Yan'an
• Chengtu
Kunming
• Guilin
• Ruijin

Mao Zedong

The son of a peasant, Mao (1893–1976) followed the nationalist ideals of Sun Yat-sen. In 1921, he helped found the Chinese Communist Party. Convinced that revolution should come from the peasants, not the industrial workers, he built a huge following. After victory against Chiang Kai-shek, he became chairman of the new republic.

Little Red Book

Cultural Revolution

In 1966, in an attempt to introduce revolutionary zeal, Mao introduced a socialist cultural revolution to attack the four "olds": old ideas, old culture, old customs, and old habits. Those accused of "revisionism" (rejecting the revolution) were publicly humiliated in "struggle meetings". The Cultural Revolution ended in 1969, but its excesses nearly led to civil war.

Red Guard
Radical students, trained as Red Guards, were the main participants in the Cultural Revolution. Using the *Little Red Book*, containing the thoughts of Chairman Mao, the Red Guard attacked anyone they believed guilty of betraying the revolution.

Timeline
1911 Nationalist revolution ends rule of the Manchu dynasty. A republic is formed.

1921 Chinese Communist Party formed.

1926 Northern Expedition: Communists and Nationalists unite to fight warlords.

1927 Kuomintang under Chiang Kai-shek attacks and executes hundreds of Communists.

Chairman Mao

1931 Japan invades Manchuria.

1934–35 Long March. Communists march to Shaanxi.

1937–45 Japan invades China. Communist guerillas harass Japanese and liberate most of northern China by 1945.

1945–48 Civil war between Kuomintang and Communists after Japanese surrender in World War II. Mao's

Communists gain control, and set up government in Beijing (Peking). Nationalists and Chiang Kai-shek flee to Taiwan.

1 October 1949 People's Republic of China is declared.

FIND OUT MORE | CHINA, HISTORY OF | COLD WAR | GOVERNMENTS AND POLITICS | JAPAN, HISTORY OF | RUSSIAN REVOLUTION | SOVIET UNION

CHRISTIANITY

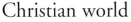

CHRISTIANS BELIEVE that Jesus of Nazareth was the son of God, who came to Earth as promised in the Old Testament, and through whose life, death, and resurrection believers are freed from their sinful state. Christianity began in the first century AD in the area now known as Israel and Palestine, which was then a part of the Roman empire. The faith was gradually spread around the Mediterranean by followers of Christ, such as Saint Paul.

Cross

Christ's death on the cross, and his resurrection, were the two key events in his life on Earth. The cross has therefore become the most important Christian symbol. Every church is marked by a cross, and crosses are placed on altars and in other prominent places inside. During worship, some Christians make the sign of the cross.

The cross symbolizes Christ's resurrection from the dead.

This elaborate gold cross is ornamented with precious stones.

Christian world

In the early years there were few Christians, and they were persecuted by the Romans because they refused to worship the Roman gods. But in AD 394, Christianity became the official religion of the Roman empire after the conversion of the emperor Constantine. The faith spread quickly through the empire. Today's Catholic Church is still based in Rome and claims to be the descendant of the early Church in the Mediterranean. There are now nearly 1.6 billion Christians worldwide.

Shading shows worldwide distribution of Christians.

Christianity is the largest world religion.

Stained glass window showing St Luke and St John teaching the gospel.

Spreading the word

Jesus preached the coming of God's kingdom, but his message was rejected and he was put to death. On the third day after Christ's death, God brought him back to life. Christ met his followers and told them to spread the word. Since then, Christianity has been spread by preachers and missionaries. From Europe, colonists took the faith with them to Africa, the Americas, and Australasia.

God the Father

The Holy Spirit is shown as a white dove, the symbol of peace.

Christ on the cross is a symbol of death and salvation.

Beneath Christ's feet is a globe representing the Earth.

Holy Trinity

Christians believe that God exists as three persons: God the Father is the creator; God the Son is Jesus Christ; and God the Holy Spirit is the presence of God on Earth. It is the Holy Spirit that inspires prophets and that acts as a means of divine revelation. Although there are three persons in the Holy Trinity, they exist as one substance, so Christians believe in one God.

Branches of Christianity

Two important groups have split from the Roman Catholic Church: the Protestant Churches, which broke away during the Reformation of the 16th century; and the Eastern Orthodox Church, which is strong in eastern Europe and western Asia.

Roman Catholicism

Catholics make up the largest Christian denomination. They stress the importance of the Church's role in interpreting the scriptures and the authority of the Pope as the leader of the Church. They believe in the doctrine of transubstantiation, in other words that the bread and wine used in the Mass are actually converted into the body and blood of Christ.

Medieval censer

In Catholic churches, incense is burnt to release scented smoke.

Charcoal is put into the censer and lit to heat the incense.

A Protestant service in London, UK

Bare walls without paintings or statues

Protestantism

There are many different Protestant Churches based around the world, but especially in North America. To a greater or lesser extent, they all stress the authority of scripture itself, rather than the clergy's interpretation of the text of the Bible. They do not believe in the doctrine of transubstantiation. Although there is great variation in their rituals, Protestants have simpler church buildings and less elaborate ceremonies than the Catholic and Orthodox Churches.

Orthodox Christians pray to icons, such as this image of St George.

Orthodoxy

Like the Roman Church, the Eastern Orthodox Church stresses the importance of the sacraments. Orthodox Christians do not recognize the authority of the Pope: the highest authority is the Church's Ecumenical Council.

Ceremonies

The most important Christian ceremonies are the sacred rites known as sacraments. The Roman Catholic and Orthodox Churches recognize seven sacraments: baptism (the rite of entry into the Church); confirmation (a further initiation ceremony); the Eucharist (Mass); penance (turning to God after sin); extreme unction (preparation for death); ordination (becoming a priest); and marriage. The Protestant Churches recognize baptism and the Eucharist.

Baptism

This ritual is an act of ceremonial cleansing before becoming a member of the Church. In some cases, holy water is splashed on the head of the infant. In other cases, an adult entering the Church is totally immersed in water.

Marriage

Christians believe that marriage symbolizes the relationship of Christ with his Church. It marks the beginning of a new family and a new generation.

Eucharist

At his last supper with his disciples, Christ identified the bread and wine as his body and blood. Christians remember this at the Eucharist (or Mass), at which a priest consecrates bread and wine and distributes it among the worshippers.

Head of saint

A priest blesses the wine in a chalice.

Sixteenth-century silver chalice

Festivals

The most important Christian festival is Easter, when believers commemorate Christ's crucifixion and resurrection. The celebration of Christ's birth, Christmas, is an important festival. Ancient pagan festivals merged with Christian festivals, so that old fertility rites are linked with Easter and winter festivals with Christmas.

An Amish couple in Pennsylvania travel in a horse-drawn carriage.

Amish

The Amish are a Protestant sect founded in the 17th century. Its followers live separately from the rest of society and believe that salvation can only be reached within the community. In the United States, Amish communities follow a simple lifestyle with strict rules. They reject modern technology and wear traditional dress, such as waistcoats and hats and bonnets and capes.

In the Middle Ages, saints' relics were kept in reliquaries.

Saints' days

Christians who have lived outstanding lives, or who were killed for their beliefs, are revered as saints. Each saint has his or her own special day, and these are often marked with processions, celebrations, and church services. Festivals on saints' days are particularly popular in Catholic countries.

Reliquary of St Eustace, an early Roman Christian martyr

The Adoration of the Magi by Botticelli (1444–1510)

Easter

The celebration of Easter can involve many moods, from the solemn prayers of Good Friday, when the crucifixion is remembered, to joy at the resurrection three days later. A spring festival, Easter is a time when new life is celebrated. Christ's resurrection is reflected in the new growth of plants and crops, and is celebrated in the giving of Easter eggs.

Christmas

Christ's nativity (birth) is traditionally celebrated in December. The Christmas story tells of his birth in a stable in Bethlehem. The many Christmas customs include giving presents, decorating trees, lighting candles, singing special hymns (or carols), and eating elaborate meals.

This nativity painting shows the worship of the Magi, the three Wise Men who came bearing gifts.

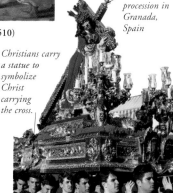

An Easter procession in Granada, Spain

Christians carry a statue to symbolize Christ carrying the cross.

Bible

The sacred text of the Christian religion is the Bible. Its first part is the Old Testament, a group of books inherited from the Jews, among whom Christianity originally grew up. Second comes the New Testament, which is made up of books dealing with the early history of Christianity. The New Testament includes the four Gospels, the Acts and Epistles (giving details of the spread of Christianity), and the Book of Revelation (containing prophecies for the future).

The Dead Sea Scrolls

Gospels

The first four books of the New Testament are called the Gospels, from a word meaning "good news". They tell the story of the life of Christ. Three of the four Gospels (those of Matthew, Mark, and Luke) are very similar and are known as the Synoptic Gospels. John's gospel is quite different from the others, and its author may not have known the other three texts.

Dead Sea Scrolls

These scrolls of parchment were discovered in caves near Qumran on the Dead Sea in the 1940s and 1950s. They contain writings which include texts of parts of the Old Testament in versions earlier than any previously discovered. They were hidden in AD 68.

St Paul

Originally opposed to Christianity, Paul (d. AD 64) converted when he had a vision of Christ. He began to preach Christianity and spread the faith on four arduous missionary journeys through Greece and Asia Minor. His role was central to the early development of the Church. He wrote several of the New Testament books in the form of letters to the Christian communities he visited.

FIND OUT MORE CHURCHES AND CATHEDRALS   CRUSADES   EUROPE, HISTORY OF   FESTIVALS   HOLY LAND, HISTORY OF   JESUS CHRIST   MONASTERIES   MOTHER TERESA   REFORMATION   RELIGIONS

CHURCHES AND CATHEDRALS

CHURCHES AND CATHEDRALS are Christian places of worship. Early churches were small, with only enough room for an altar and a small congregation. As Christianity spread, larger churches, with separate areas for the clergy and the followers, were built. A cathedral is a church in which a bishop presides; he organizes the day-to-day running of local parishes.

The first churches

Christianity began in the Mediterranean during the time of the Roman Empire. Early churches were modelled on the public buildings of ancient Rome, especially basilicas, where meetings and law courts were held. The congregation sat in an area called the nave, and the altar was housed in a smaller area, the sanctuary.

St Sabina, Rome
Founded in AD 422, this early church has a wide nave and small, semi-circular sanctuary.

Parts of a cathedral

Many cathedrals and churches are designed in the shape of a cross. The "arms" of the cross, the transepts, contain small chapels. The altar lies to the east to face the rising sun; the nave lies towards the west.

123-m (404-ft) spire

Columns and vaults
The interior has decorative stone ceilings, called ribbed vaults, supported on columns of local Purbeck marble. Each column is surrounded by four shafts (smaller columns), which create a light, delicate effect.

Bell towers have openings to allow the sound of the bells to escape.

The large nave can accommodate big congregations.

Salisbury Cathedral
This 13th-century Gothic cathedral has slender walls and pointed arches and windows. These features help make it elegant and delicate in spite of its huge size. The 14th-century spire is the tallest in England and can be seen from far away.

Lady chapel — *High altar*, *Sanctuary*
Eastern transept — *Sacristy*
— *Western transept*
North aisle — *Nave*
— *South aisle*
North porch — *West front*

Floor plan
The cross shape symbolizes the wooden cross on which Christ died.

Intricately carved west front

Western transept *Eastern transept*

Sanctuary

Pointed arches are a typical feature of Gothic architecture.

Lady chapel

Cathedral interior
The great nave, with its high, vaulted ceiling, is made to appear larger still by aisles on either side. Light comes in through stained-glass windows.

Main entrance

Buttresses (supports) help bear the weight of heavy vaults.

Church decoration

Many churches and cathedrals are richly decorated with symbols of the Christian religion, including images of Christ, angels, the saints, and crosses. Protestant churches tend to be less elaborately decorated than Roman Catholic and Eastern Orthodox churches.

Fan vaulting
This delicate fan vault can be found at Canterbury Cathedral, England.

Gargoyle
Devils and grotesques were carved on church exteriors during the Middle Ages to represent evil outside the church.

Triptych
The finest decoration of all is usually close to the altar, such as this triptych in St Peter's Basilica, Rome.

Statuary
Representations of the Madonna and Child are found in Roman Catholic churches. This Renaissance-style statue, which was finished in 1896, is in the church of the Sacré-Coeur, Paris.

Mosaic
Mosaics were an early form of decoration in Mediterranean churches. This 9th-century mosaic is in the Santi Nereo e Achilleo, Rome.

Stained-glass windows
Beautiful coloured windows that decorate churches often illustrate Bible stories told by Jesus and his disciples.

Churchyards

Churchyards separate a church from noisy streets and provide land to bury the dead. Burials also take place in purpose built cemeteries.

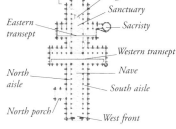

Celtic cross
This cross in Ireland combines two Christian symbols: the cross and the circle, a symbol of eternity.

Columbarium
A Columbarium houses the ashes of cremated people.

Tombs
Some tombs tell the lives of those buried inside. This tomb of much-imprisoned French revolutionary Raspail, is in the form of a prison.

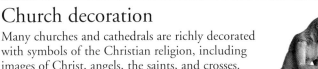

FIND OUT MORE   ARCHITECTURE   CHRISTIANITY   FESTIVALS   GLASS   MEDIEVAL EUROPE   RELIGIONS

CITIES

LESS THAN 200 YEARS AGO most people lived in villages. Today, around one-half of the world's population lives in cities. During the 19th century, towns and cities expanded as people moved away from rural areas to work in new industries. Cities have continued to grow, but haphazardly, in contrast to the carefully-planned cities of the ancient world.

Hole in roof instead of door

Walls made of mud

Çatal Hüyük

Early cities had no streets.

First cities

Settlements in western Asia, such as Jericho (Israel), Çatal Hüyük (Turkey), and Ur (Iraq), started to expand around 4000 BC. At this time, craftworkers began to trade goods outside their local areas, creating new wealth that was used to build palaces, large temples, and strong, defensive walls. These towns grew in importance and emerged as the first cities.

Modern cities

The world's cities have grown rapidly in modern times but inadequate planning has contributed to poor living conditions and poverty in many urban centres. Poor areas, wealthy neighbourhoods, and areas dominated by one particular ethnic group are all features of city life. Most cities offer many people a wide choice of jobs, houses, and recreational facilities.

Gardens, parks, and squares give people the chance to escape the bustle of city streets.

Entertainment is a feature of most cities. Cities are usually cultural centres with theatres, museums, galleries, and music venues, such as Sydney's striking Opera House.

Residential
There are different residential areas in cities. Older houses and flats are close to the city centre, while modern developments extend outwards, clustering around railway lines and major roads.

Sydney, Australia

Business is always located close to the heart of the city. Nowadays, the business area is usually dominated by tall office blocks.

Apartment building

Skyscraper

Converted loft

Brownstone

Underground

Services

New York
The city of New York in the USA contains some of the world's tallest skyscraper office blocks. It also has large apartment buildings, low-rise commercial sites (some of which have been converted into homes called lofts), tall, 19th-century brownstone (a type of sandstone) houses, and smaller, modern houses. Steps lead to underground trains and shops.

Roads, railways, boats, and airlines bring people into the city centre.

Manufacturing
Small factories and workshops were once at the heart of cities. Today, large industrial complexes are usually built further out, reducing pollution.

Villages

A traditional village is a small, rural settlement, often by a stream or river. In most parts of the world, people still live and work in villages, farming the surrounding countryside, and trading with nearby settlements.

Maasai village, Kenya
Many of the Maasai people live in groups of thatched, mud houses surrounding a central cattle enclosure.

Stilt village, Sumatra
In many Southeast Asian villages, houses are raised on stilts to keep out unwanted animals, like snakes.

Gold rush town
Towns grew around 19th century gold mines. Abandoned as the gold ran out, some still stand as "ghost towns".

Forbidden City
The Forbidden City in Beijing, China, was built in the 15th century. Only the emperor, his family, and his officials were allowed in.

Timeline

8000 BC Strong walls and a stone tower are built at Jericho.

3500 BC City-states such as Ur, develop in Mesopotamia (modern-day Iraq).

5th century BC Greeks plan and build the elegant city of Athens.

1st century BC The Roman Empire expands, and new European cities are built.

12th century AD Stone walls, such as those at Carcassonne, France, are built to protect medieval towns and cities.

1421 Construction starts on Forbidden City, Beijing, China.

15th century Renaissance architects lay out classical cities, such as Florence and Siena in Italy.

Siena, Italy

19th century Industrialization stimulates growth of towns and cities in Europe and America.

1950s Brasilia designed and constructed as new capital of Brazil.

1990s Skyscrapers dominate most city skylines.

FIND OUT MORE   ARCHAEOLOGY   ARCHITECTURE   BUILDING AND CONSTRUCTION   INDUSTRIAL REVOLUTION   IRON AND STEEL   RENAISSANCE   SOCIETIES, HUMAN   TRAINS AND RAILWAYS

CLIMATE

WEATHER CAN CHANGE from moment to moment. Over a long period of time, a region's characteristic weather – however changeable – is called its climate. Climates are generally warm near the Equator, the imaginary line around the middle of the Earth, and cool towards the poles. Other influences on the three broad climate types – warm tropical, cold polar, and mild temperate – include the distance from sea and the position within a continent. The climate determines a region's animal and plant life.

Polar
Mountain
Tundra
Temperate
Mediterranean
Dry grassland
Desert
Subtropical
Tropical

Climate zones
Close to the Equator, the Sun's warmth is strong – it climbs high in the sky at midday: closer to the poles, the Sun's warmth is weaker – it climbs less high. Climatic zones, which effect vegetation, can be further classified by physical features.

Polar bear

Annual rainfall / Temperature
Polar climate – Greenland

Polar climate

Towards the ice-capped poles, the Sun is always low in the sky, and in winter barely rises at all: summers are brief. Winter temperatures in the tundra regions around the North Pole are below -60°C (-76°F).

Tropical climate

Weather in a tropical climate, such as Brazil, is always warm, often with heavy rainfall. Some tropical climates, such as deserts, are hot and dry; others, such as rain-forests, are warm and moist.

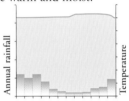
Parrots

Oak sprig

Annual rainfall / Temperature
Temperate climate – Seattle, USA

Temperate climate

In mid-latitude (imaginary lines parallel to the Equator) areas such as the USA, summers are warm, and winters cool, with regular rain. A Mediterranean climate with dry summers and warm, damp winters is a type of temperate climate.

Oceanic and continental climate zones

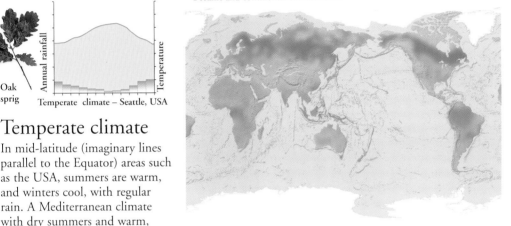

Annual rainfall / Temperature
Tropical climate – Brazil

Monsoons
These are warm, tropical climates with wet and dry seasons. In India, it is dry from October to May as the winds blow out to sea, and very wet from June to September as the monsoon winds blow inland.

Mountain climate
High altitude causes the air to cool, thus creating a cold climate. Exposed mountain tops also make mountain climates very wet and windy. Above a certain height called the snow-line, there is always snow.

Oceanic and continental climate

Coastal regions have wet, changeable weather. The summers are cooler and the winters are warmer, because the ocean heats up and cools down more slowly than the land. Places in the continental interior, such as Moscow, have cold winters.

Desert climate
Over a fifth of the world's land surface is desert, where there is typically an annual rainfall of less than 100 mm (4 in). In the tropics, desert temperatures frequently climb above 50°C (122°F).

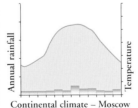

Annual rainfall / Temperature
Continental climate – Moscow

Each tree ring shows one year's growth: a wide ring means the weather was warm and the tree grew well.

Climate change

Over long periods of time, climate fluctuates. Signs of widespread glaciation, for instance, show that the world was once much colder. We now live in an interglacial period. Subtle changes in the climate's recent past are revealed by such things as variations in the sizes of tree rings.

Global warming
Pollution may be warming the world up. Certain gases trap the Sun's heat in the Earth's atmosphere. Rising levels of these "greenhouse gases", such as carbon dioxide, which come from burning oil or forest land, may trap so much heat that the Earth could warm up by 4°C (7.2°F) over the next 50 years.

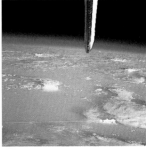

| FIND OUT MORE | DESERTS | MOUNTAINS AND VALLEYS | OCEANS AND SEAS | POLLUTION | RAIN | WEATHER | WEATHER FORECASTING | WINDS |

CLOTHES AND FASHION

PEOPLE HAVE ALWAYS WORN CLOTHES, either as protection from the weather or for modesty. Yet through history, people have also chosen clothes to impress or attract others, or to reflect their job, social status, or religious beliefs. Clothes send out signals about the wearer's lifestyle and the type of society they live in: for instance, during the 20th century, the emancipation of women was reflected in the kind of clothes they wore, such as practical trousers.

Sports cap is now casual everyday wear

Hats
In the early and mid-20th century, adults usually wore hats in public. The way people dress has become less formal since then, and the hat's importance as a smart accesssory has declined.

Clothing design

Designers choose the fabric, colour, and shape of a garment. Their decisions are influenced by the function of the item, and who will eventually wear it. A work shirt, for example, must be made from durable fabric; a high-fashion shirt can be made from less practical silk or linen.

Belt

Sample of fabric

Design
Some designers sketch their ideas for a new style onto paper. Others work directly with the fabric, draping it over a dressmaker's dummy, and pinning it until the right shape emerges.

Pattern
Once the design has been decided, it is translated into pattern pieces, made from paper or card. These are used as a guide for cutting out the fabric. The pattern pieces are made in different sizes, and sent to the cutting room.

Sketched design

Daily wear

The popular informal outfit of shirt, jeans, and trainers can be seen in many parts of the world, worn by both sexes of all ages. This casual outfit is an example of the changing attitudes to clothes seen in the 20th century. For the first time, everyday clothing crossed barriers of age, gender, and social class.

Sample pattern

Sleeve

Back section

Cutting instructions

Shirts
In medieval Europe, shirts were worn beneath a tunic. Over the years, more and more of the shirt was allowed to show, and now it is regarded as an outer garment. Everyday shirts need to be hard-wearing and easy to put on.

Jeans
Bavarian-born retailer Levi Strauss (1829–1902) sold the first blue jeans – Levis – to miners in the 1850s. They have been popular ever since, because they are hard-wearing, and easily adapted to changes in fashion.

Trainers
Trainers were originally made for tennis or basketball players – the rubber soles stopped them from slipping. They have since become fashionable "street" wear.

Rubber sole

Leather or fabric upper

Cotton

Computerized control panel

Clothing manufacture

The clothes manufacturing industry is massive, and employs millions of people worldwide. Some designs are exclusive, produced by the great fashion houses. Most clothes however are manufactured in standard sizes and, from cutting to pressing, are mass-produced in factories.

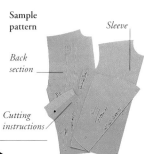

Cutting
Up to 150 layers of fabric are spread out on long tables. The pattern pieces are then laid on top and the material is cut, using either a mechanical knife or a laser.

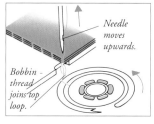

Needle

Sewing machine
To make a stitch, a sewing machine must loop one thread around another. The latest models are computerized: touching a panel changes the type of stitch. Domestic machines perform about 1,000 stitches a minute; industrial machines are ten times faster.

Sewing
The cut pieces are carried to the person whose job it is to match them up for the sewing machinist. Each machinist concentrates on a particular part of the garment, such as the sleeves.

Pressing
Once the clothes are sewn together, they are laid on large, flat tables to be pressed. Then a final inspection is held to check the quality of the finished garment, before it is sold to a wholesaler.

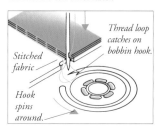

Thread loop catches on bobbin hook.

Stitched fabric

Hook spins around.

Needle moves upwards.

Bobbin thread joins top loop.

1 As the needle pierces the fabric, it makes a loop of thread, which is picked up by a bobbin hook beneath the needle plate.

2 The loop is pulled around thread drawn from within the bobbin, joining the top thread as a stitch. Both threads are then released.

Traditional clothing

The clothes worn in some parts of the world combine modern lifestyles and traditions thousands of years old. Traditional national costumes often reflect the dress of peasants, whose garments were suited to the local climate and the kind of work they performed.

Traditional jacket (parka) in modern fabric

Insulated boots

Canada
Inuit people dress to protect themselves against cold weather: in northern Canada, it snows from October to May.

Shaved head

Rubeka

Tanzania
The Maasai wear vivid pieces of cloth called *rubeka*. Young women who are old enough to marry wear special headdresses.

Silk jacket

Sports shoes (not traditional)

South Korea
This traditional silk costume is called *hanbok,* meaning "Korean clothing". It is worn on special occasions.

Headscarf

Embroidery

Hang pen

Vietnam
The traditional outfit of the Dao people, a hill tribe, is a *lamchu:* a scarf, skirt, jacket, and *hang pen* wound around the legs.

India
The most popular dress for Indian women is the *sari,* which is usually made from a length of silk or cotton.

Elegantly draped sari

Tying a sari
The sari is a length of material, between 5 and 9 metres long, and just over a metre wide. It is worn over a tight-fitting bodice, called a *choli,* and a long petticoat. When the weather gets hot, the sari can be adjusted to let in cool air.

Choli

Sari fabric

1 First, the material is wrapped round once, and tucked into the petticoat.

2 The sari fabric is pleated, then tucked into the petticoat again.

3 The spare fabric is draped over the shoulder.

Coco Chanel
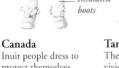
The French designer Gabrielle "Coco" Chanel (1883–1971) had a powerful influence on Parisian and world fashion for almost 60 years. Her designs stressed simplicity and comfort at a time when clothes tended to be restrictive and uncomfortable. Many of her innovations are now fashion classics, such as bell-bottomed trousers, bobbed hair, and the so-called "little black dress".

Body decoration

Every culture has practised some form of body decoration, ranging from scarring and tattooing, which are permanent, to make-up and body paint, which last for only a few hours. One of the oldest forms of body decoration is jewellery, worn to show wealth and status, for protection and healing, or for beauty. Examples include rings, necklaces, earrings, bracelets, and brooches.

Glass necklace

Dress clips

Bracelet

Jewellery
Beads, berries, feathers, shells, bone, glass, precious stones, and metals have all been used to make jewellery. Most fashion jewellery is made from cheap materials, such as plastic, because it is only worn for a short time.

Plastic brooch

Body painting
People paint their faces and bodies to mark a religious occasion, celebrate important events in their community, or ward off illness. Sikh brides, for example, paint ornate, beautiful patterns on their hands using dye from the henna plant.

Body paint in Papua New Guinea

High-fashion wedding dress

Fashion

Following fashion (the changing trends in clothing) was once so expensive that only the wealthy could afford it. Today, however, advances in manufacturing, and the invention of synthetic fabrics, allow more people to follow fashion. Styles have changed faster than ever before, and fashion has become big business. Shows by fashion houses such as Dior (France) or Ralph Lauren (USA) attract buyers from all over the world.

Hats and shoes

Through the ages, hats and shoes have come in many styles: hats have ranged from headdresses to berets, shoes from simple leather sandals to chunky platform boots.

Riding hat

Badge

Police officer's cap
Hats may stand for authority, as with the police officers' cap, which is part of their uniform.

Chin strap

Hard hat
People who are especially at risk of head injuries, such as riders or construction workers, wear hard hats to protect themselves.

Shoe
Shoes must suit people in different climates, as well as follow fashions. They are commonly made from durable leather, but rubber, plastic, silk, and canvas are also used.

Lining

Tongue

Thin upper encloses foot

Cross-section of shoe

Steel shank supports arch of foot

FIND OUT MORE
DYES AND PAINTS · GLASS · INDIA AND SRI LANKA · METALS · PLANT USES · TEXTILES AND WEAVING

Fashion in the 20th century

Corset pushes chest forward and hips back

Daywear, typical S-bend silhouette, 1900s

Daywear, narrow, tailored line, 1910s

Shirt collar is turned down, a recent development in fashion

Lounge suit, single-breasted, 1910s

Orange-blossom headdress

Wrapover skirt

Wedding dress, with new, shorter skirt, 1920s

Wide knicker-bockers, or "plus-twos"

Three-piece suit, for country wear, 1920s

"Modesty" skirts on both costumes

Wool bathing costumes (knitted one-piece), 1930s

Bias cut fabric clings to the body

Crepe evening dress, full-length, 1930s

Boxy style, economical with fabric

Felt trilby

Daywear from World War II, 1939–45

Tightly fitted bodice

Long, full skirt

Suit, in style of French designer Christian Dior, 1950s

Thigh-high hem

Mini dress, "Space Age" influence, 1960s

"Ethnic" styles influence fashion

Flared (wide-leg) trousers

"Hippy" fashion, 1970s

Trousers

Day wear, 1990s

Underwear, hats, and shoes

Cotton camisole with lace inserts, 1900s

Brassieres from the 1920s and 1930s

Corset, worn from the 1930s to the 1950s

Underwear in easy-care nylon, 1960s

One piece in polyester, 1980s

1920s "Long Johns"

Aertex cotton shorts, 1950s

Brief cotton pants, 1980s

Men's underwear

Boater, worn on the river and as informal wear, 1900s

Silk hat on wire-frame base, 1920s

Cloche, bell-shaped hat with small brim, 1920s

Bowler, worn horse-riding, 1920s

Felt hat, with shallow crown, 1930s

Silk hat, with glass berries, 1950s

Shoes with steel beading, early 1900s

Kid boots, possibly worn for cycling, early 1900s

Reptile-skin shoes, popular in the late 1920s

Lace-up shoes with a wedge sole, 1940

Boots with black and gold thread woven into fabric, 1960s

Platform soles, high fashion in the 1970s

CLOUDS

WHEN YOU LOOK UP at the sky, you may see clouds. In temperate or mild climates, there are usually at least a few clouds and, sometimes, cloud cover is total. Clouds are dense masses of water drops or ice crystals so light and small that they float on the air. Clouds form when rising air cools to a point where it can no longer contain its water vapour, and so the vapour condenses. There are three basic forms, or shapes, of cloud – puffy cumulus, layered stratus, and feathery cirrus – but each form can vary to make many different cloud types. The type of cloud depends on how high the air rises, and its temperature.

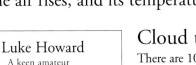

Cloud formation

Clouds form by the condensation or freezing of water vapour. The way they form depends on their height and on the speed of upward air movement. When pockets of warm air rise rapidly, clouds form in heaped shapes (cumulus). When air rises slowly and evenly over a large area, clouds form in layers (stratus).

Making a cumulus

The sun-warmed ground creates thermals – rising currents of warm air. The air cools as it rises. Eventually, it becomes so cool that water droplets condense and a cloud forms. The cloud continues to build up as long as the thermal continues to supply water vapour.

Formation of a cumulus cloud in three stages

Luke Howard

A keen amateur meteorologist, but a pharmacist by profession, British-born Luke Howard (1772–1864) kept detailed weather diaries. These provided valuable meteorological data, before official records were kept. Howard used Latin names to identify each cloud by shape. His classification of clouds is still used today.

Cloud types

There are 10 distinct types of cloud. Cirrus, cirrostratus, and cirrocumulus clouds form 5–11 km (3–7 miles) above sea-level. Altocumulus, altostratus, and nimbostratus clouds form 2–7 km (1–4 miles) above sea-level. Stratocumulus and stratus form at 2 km (1 mile) or under above sea-level. Cumulus and cumulonimbus clouds form over a wide range of heights.

Cirrus clouds form at high altitude where air is cold and strong.

Cirrostratus is a high level veil of cirrus cloud.

Altostratus is a thin watery sheet of cloud.

Cirrocumulus are clouds of ice crystals with a dappled appearance.

Cloud cover

The amount of sunlight reaching the ground depends on how much sky is covered by cloud. This is measured in "oktas" (eighths). One okta means one-eighth of the sky is covered in cloud; two oktas equals two-eighths of cloud cover in the sky, and so on.

Clear   1   2   3   4

5   6   7   8   Cloudy

Cumulonimbus is created by strong updraughts, bringing heavy thunder and rain.

Fog and mist

When water vapour in the air condenses near the ground it forms fog and mist. "Radiation" fog forms on cold, clear, calm nights, when the ground rapidly loses the heat it has absorbed during the day and cools the air above to its dew point. "Advection" fog forms when warm, moist air flows over a surface so cold that the water vapour in the air condenses.

Altocumulus are puffs or rolls of clouds at medium height.

Cumulus are fluffy white clouds, often short-lived.

A cloud plume floating around a mountain-top is called a banner cloud.

Sea mist

When warm moist air flows over cold water, water vapour in the air may condense to form a kind of advection fog called a sea mist. These mists are most common on early summer mornings, when the air is calm.

Beachy Head, Sussex, England

Nimbostratus are layers of dark rain clouds.   **Stratus** are cloud layers, often giving long periods of rain.

FIND OUT MORE   ATMOSPHERE   CLIMATE   RAIN   STORMS   WEATHER   WEATHER FORECASTING   WINDS

COAL

MORE THAN two hundred million years ago huge trees grew in the warm, humid swamps that covered vast regions of the world. They captured the Sun's energy to make their wood. When they died, their trunks became buried and gradually changed into coal. When we burn coal today, we release the energy the trees captured all those years ago. Because of its origin, coal is called a fossil fuel. It was the first fossil fuel to be used by people, and is still today second only to petroleum in importance for energy production worldwide.

Coal mining

Almost 5 billion tonnes of coal are mined a year. China and the United States mine the most coal, with annual outputs exceeding 1.6 billion tonnes. Coal deposits can be up to about 20 m (66 ft) thick, but they average less than 3 m (10 ft). Some deposits are found on the surface, but most lie underground, sandwiched between rock layers.

Piles of dead plant material accumulate in swampy regions

How coal is formed

Coal began to form in swampy forests about 350 million years ago, during the Carboniferous period. Decaying plants were buried under layers of mud. As heat and pressure increased, plant remains slowly converted into coal. Today, there are three main grades of coal – lignite, bituminous coal, and anthracite.

Peat represents an early stage in coal-formation. It is soft, fibrous, and moist, but still gives off heat when burned.

Lignite, or brown coal, is a low-grade fuel containing up to about 60 per cent carbon, along with plant remains and moisture. It is soft and crumbly.

Bituminous coal is a better quality fuel, comprising more than 80 per cent carbon. It is the most common solid fuel used in industry. It is hard, but dirty to the touch.

Anthracite is the highest grade coal, containing more than 90 per cent carbon. It is shiny black, clean to touch, and burns with little smoke.

Collecting coal at a strip mine

Strip mining

One method of surface, or opencast, mining is called strip mining. The coal is excavated in a series of long strips. Any soil above each strip is used to fill in the trench created when the coal has been removed from a previous strip.

Drilling coal in a shaft mine

Shaft mining

Coal seams deep below the surface are reached by a system of vertical shafts and horizontal tunnels. The coal is dug out by powered coal-cutters and hydraulic tools.

Coal products

Coal can be processed into valuable products, by a method called destructive distillation. Coal is heated in coke ovens at up to 1,300 °C (2,400 °F) without air. A mixture of liquid vapours and gases escapes and is then separated into coal gas, ammonia liquid, and coal tar. The solid left behind is called coke.

Coke

This solid, porous substance is, like coal, an excellent fuel, which contains more than 80 per cent carbon. It is widely used in industry, mostly in blast furnaces for making iron. In the furnace, it also acts as a chemical agent in the iron-extraction reaction.

Coal tar

Coal tar is a black oily liquid that is a rich source of mostly organic chemicals, such as benzene, phenol, and creosote. These can be processed into a variety of materials including dyes, paints, and drugs.

Coal tar soap

Mine safety

Mines are dangerous places because of the risk of rock falls and the build-up of explosive gases, such as methane. One safety device was invented by an English scientist, Humphry Davy, in 1815. His safety lamp was able to detect dangerous levels of poison gases.

Davy lamp

Power

About 25 per cent of the world's energy supply is generated from coal. In coal-fired power stations, the coal is first pulverized (powdered) and then burned in a furnace. The hot gases produced pass over tubes containing water and turn it into steam. The steam drives powerful turbogenerators, which produce electricity. The electricity is then transmitted through a national grid network.

Coal-fired power station, Germany

Domestic fuel

Until the mid 1900s, coal was the fuel most used in Western homes. Each room was heated by open coal fires, and cooking was usually done on a coal-burning stove. Today, few modern homes have coal fires, as people tend to use other forms of heating. Some cities and towns allow only smokeless fuels to be used for energy.

Burning smokeless fuels keeps pollution low

FIND OUT MORE   CHEMISTRY   DYES AND PAINTS   ELECTRICITY   ENERGY   FIRE   INDUSTRIAL REVOLUTION   IRON AND STEEL   OIL   PLASTICS AND RUBBER

COASTS

A COAST IS SIMPLY defined as the boundary between the land and sea – an area that may range from a rocky cliff to a sandy beach. This boundary is always shifting as the sea continues its relentless assault on the land – waves roll up and down, and tides ebb and flow. The action of the sea creates distinctive landforms, such as a cliff, created by eroding (wearing away) rock; a shore (an area between low tide levels and the highest storm waves); or a beach, built up by shore deposits. Wind and rain erosion also contribute to the changing aspect of coastlines.

Evolution of a coast

Waves crash against a shore with great force, wearing away rocks by pounding them with water, and hurling rocks and stones at them. On high coasts, the waves undercut the foot of the slope, creating a cliff. The model below shows the gradual effect of waves and seawater on the coast.

Beaches and sandbars

Material worn away from rocky coasts is pounded by waves into sand and shingle and deposited elsewhere as beaches and sandbars – an offshore strip of sand or shingle. A spit resembles a sandbar, with one end attached to the land; a tombolo is a spit that links an island to the mainland.

Sea erodes into the cliffs, sculpting patterns of rock, such as this arch.

Waves eat back inland, leaving a wave-cut platform which juts out beyond the cliff.

Eroded material accumulates at the shoreline, forming beaches.

Stack or lone pillar

Cliffs are attacked by storms; sea arch roof collapses, leaving a stack; another arch appears behind.

Cliff retreats further as rocks fall.

Rough seas continue to erode coastline, spurting through a blowhole, a crack in the cliff.

Storm waves eat away at cliff base.

Stack is worn down.

Cave mouth

Cliff face marked with crags and gulleys where boulders fall.

Coastline has moved backwards with erosion of cliffs.

Types of coasts

Coasts vary according to their composition and structure. Whether the coast is high or low, and made of soft or hard rock, affects whether it has been formed largely as a result of erosion or by deposition.

Bay-head beach
This is formed when material eroded from headlands (high land jutting into the sea) is washed into a bay, a coastal inlet between the headlands.

Wave direction

Drowned coast
Where the sea-level has risen or the land sunk, valleys are flooded to form narrow inlets, or rias. Where the valleys are glacial, the inlets are called fjords.

Wave direction

Highland coast
Where the sea meets a highland coast, it generally wears away the rocks, creating cliffs, small coves, and wave-cut rock platforms.

Raised beach

Lowland coast
Broad beaches, salt marshes, and estuaries are features of lowland coasts.

River slopes towards new sea level.

Waves

The wind whips the sea's surface into waves. Waves travel across the water, but the water in them circulates on the spot. When waves reach the shore, the bottom touches the beach and slows down; the top spills on, causing the wave to "break".

Wave formation

Top spills over; wave breaks.

Circular motion is upset as the wave hits the beach.

Waves grow steeper as they approach the shore.

Water circulates in the wave in orbital paths.

Coastal protection
When waves strike a beach, they wash sand or pebbles across the beach at an angle,. This repeated process is known as longshore drift. Fences or groynes may be built, to slow down such reshaping of the beach.

Coastal fences

Beach material

Fine sand and silt are usually found lower down a beach; bigger storm waves wash gravel and pebbles higher up. On some beaches, there is a ridge of pebbles, called a storm beach, which has been flung up beyond the high-tide mark by violent storms.

Pebbles and stones

Fine sand

Gritty sand

FIND OUT MORE CAVES CORAL REEFS GLACIATION MOUNTAINS AND VALLEYS OCEANS AND SEAS ROCKS AND MINERALS SEASHORE WILDLIFE

CODES AND CIPHERS

A CODE IS ANY SYSTEM of prearranged symbols, words, or numbers that is used in communication. For example, the flags that are used to send messages at sea are a naval code. We use codes to simplify, organize, and communicate complex information, for instance, in dialling and postal codes, or bar codes that describe goods in a way that machines can read. Not all codes have an everyday use. Ciphers (secret codes) hide the true meaning of a message. Banks use them to keep financial deals private, and spies or criminals to avoid capture.

Ciphers

In a cipher, each letter is represented by a different letter or symbol. For instance, it is easy to encipher a message by jumbling the alphabet, changing C into M and M to C. It is easy to break such a simple cipher, but computers can create ciphers that are impossible to read without the key (a long number that unlocks the meaning).

Spies

A spy is a secret agent, who collects information for a government or organization. A spy's work often involves stealing the secrets of rival governments. Spies use ciphers to scramble data when they send it to their employers.

Spy codesheet

Cipher discs

These devices create ciphers by replacing letters of the message on the outer ring with the letters alongside them on the inner ring.

Cipher disc

Cipher machines

The Enigma cipher machine was used during World War II. It had a typewriter keyboard with electrical connections that scrambled the letters. Each letter was coded separately, making the cipher hard to break.

Metal cover plate fits over rotor cylinders

Viewing window shows code letters

Rotor cylinder

Coding rotor

Keyboard

Plugboard setting is altered to change cipher

Filter to dim lights

German Enigma cipher machine, World War II

Smoke signals

Fire beacons and smoke codes were used to send signals by the people of ancient China, Egypt, and Greece. Native Americans, such as the Cheyenne, Comanche, and Sioux, communicated over distances using smoke signals, shaping smoke with an animal hide or blanket. There were a few generally understood signals – two puffs meant "all's well" – but each group also had secret codes which they shared only with people they wanted to read the messages.

Frederic Remington, *Smoke Signals*

Uses of code

Codes make messages quicker to send. They have been used for many reasons. Sailors, for example, used flag codes to communicate for more than 1,000 years. By flying the three flags standing for the letters NKA, a warship could send a message meaning "I have not sighted any vessels since leaving my last port". A code book carried on every ship translated the codes.

Computer codes

Special codes are used to program information inside computers, where letters and punctuation marks are represented by binary numbers. Ciphers can also be also used to protect e-mail (mail sent between computers), so that it can only be understood by the sender and the addressee.

E-mail can be encrypted so that only the addressee, who holds a secret "key" (a long number), can read it.

The alphabet in Morse code

A	•━	N	━•
B	━•••	O	━━━
C	━•━•	P	•━━•
D	━••	Q	━━•━
E	•	R	•━•
F	••━•	S	•••
G	━━•	T	━
H	••••	U	••━
I	••	V	•••━
J	•━━━	W	•━━
K	━•━	X	━••━
L	•━••	Y	━•━━
M	━━	Z	━━••

Morse code

The telegraph was invented in the 19th century; it used electricity to send messages quickly over long distances for the first time. The system could not transmit speech, so to communicate operators used an alphabetic code devised by US artist Samuel Morse (1791–1872). Letters were represented by dots and dashes (long and short pulses of power). Operators tapped a key to turn the electric current in the telegraph wires on and off. Morse code is still in use.

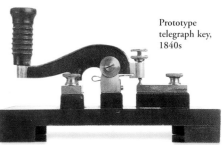

Prototype telegraph key, 1840s

William Friedman

Russian-born American William Friedman (1891–1969) decrypted secret messages for the US government in World Wars I and II. In 1940, William led the team that discovered the key to the Japanese Purple cipher. A message in this cipher warned of the Pearl Harbor attack.

FIND OUT MORE   FLAGS   INFORMATION TECHNOLOGY   LANGUAGES   NATIVE AMERICANS   SIGNS AND SYMBOLS   WORLD WAR II

COLD WAR

IN 1945, THE ALLIED FORCES of the USA, Britain, France, and the USSR – now known once again as Russia – gained victory over Germany in World War II. Within four years, the allies had become enemies, and a new war had broken out. This was not a military war, but a "cold" war – a political and diplomatic battle between communist Eastern Europe and capitalist Western Europe. The rival blocks expressed hostility by backing opposing sides in conflicts such as Korea and Vietnam. The Cold War ended in 1990, when Eastern Europe's communist governments fell.

Winston Churchill, FD Roosevelt, and Josef Stalin, Yalta Conference

Yalta Conference
In 1945, the British, American, and Soviet leaders Churchill, Roosevelt, and Stalin met in the Russian resort of Yalta to determine the shape of post-war Europe. The conference agreed Soviet control over Eastern Europe. This started the political division of Europe into east and west that was to last until 1990.

Iron Curtain
By 1949, there was a clear division in Europe between the communist states in the east that followed Russia, and the capitalist states in the west that followed the USA. Both east and west became secretive and hostile. In 1946, the British Prime Minister Winston Churchill famously described this polarization as "an iron curtain ... (descending) across the continent."

Iron Curtain

Austria was divided until 1955.

Switzerland was neutral during the war.

Capitalist   Communist

Mig-15 jet

Korean War
In 1945, Korea was divided between a communist north and an American-backed south. In 1950, North Korea invaded the south; the USA supported South Korea, while the USSR and China supported North Korea. War raged until an armistice was agreed in 1953. Korea remains divided to this day.

Red Scare
In the early 1950s, fear of Communism in the USA led to a witch-hunt against known Communist Party members and possible sympathizers. Senator Joe McCarthy led a government committee that created a "Red Scare" in the USA, and caused hundreds of innocent people to lose their jobs.

Spies
Technological information was very important during the Cold War. In order to find out what the other side was planning, both sides of the Iron Curtain employed spies. Spies worked undercover in civilian and defence jobs, passing vital military secrets back to their own governments.

Invisible powder stuck to a spy's body and was detectable under ultraviolet light.

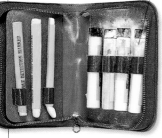

Chemical detection kit

Soviet ship returning to the USSR

Cuban missile crisis
In 1962 Soviet ships delivered nuclear weapons to the Cuban government. The US – only 90 miles (145 km) from Cuba – blockaded the island, which caused a crisis between the USA and the USSR. After several days of tension, the USSR withdrew its missiles.

Détente
In the 1960s, tension between east and west began to ease. In the 1970s, Willy Brandt, West Germany's leader, negotiated treaties with Poland and the USSR. In the late 1980s, Mikhail Gorbachev began to reform the USSR, which eventually led to the fall of communism in Eastern Europe.

Berlin Wall is dismantled, 1989

Anti-communist poster

Timeline
1945 Europe divides into eastern and western blocks.

1949 Western nations set up NATO (North Atlantic Treaty Organization).

1950–54 McCarthy era, USA.

1950–53 Korean War.

NATO symbol

1955 Warsaw Pact establishes military alliances between communist countries.

1961 Berlin Wall divides East from West Berlin (and East from West Germany).

1962 Cuban missile crisis marks the peak of the Cold War; its resolution slowly leads to détente.

1989 Fall of the Berlin Wall begins the fall of communist governments throughout Eastern Europe.

1990 Re-unification of East and West Germany.

1991 Gorbachev resigns; collapse of communism in USSR.

Mikhail Gorbachev
Gorbachev (b.1931) became leader of the USSR in 1985. He attempted to reform the USSR, and negotiated arms reduction agreements with US President Reagan. Despite his success, he failed to improve the living standards of the Soviet people, and resigned in 1991.

 FIND OUT MORE   EUROPE, HISTORY OF   RUSSIA, HISTORY OF   SOVIET UNION   UNITED STATES, HISTORY OF   WARFARE   WEAPONS   WORLD WAR II

COLOUR

A WORLD WITHOUT COLOUR would be dull and uninspiring. Colour is a form of light. Light is made up of electromagnetic waves of varying lengths. The human eye detects these different wavelengths and sees them as different colours. White light – like that from the Sun – is a mixture of all the different wavelengths. Objects look coloured because they give out or reflect only certain wavelengths of light.

White light spectrum

Passing white light through a transparent triangular block called a prism separates out the different wavelengths of light. The prism refracts (bends) each wavelength by a different amount, forming a band of colours called a white light spectrum, or a visible spectrum. The seven main colours are red, orange, yellow, green, blue, indigo, and violet. Red has the longest wavelength and violet the shortest. Here, a convex lens combines the colours back into white light.

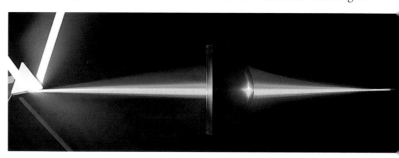

Rainbow

A rainbow at dawn

If it rains on a sunny day, you may well see a rainbow if you stand with your back to the Sun. A rainbow is a curved white light spectrum that forms when light is reflected and refracted by raindrops in the sky.

How a rainbow forms

When white sunlight passes through a raindrop, the raindrop acts like a tiny prism. The raindrop refracts the light and splits it up into its separate colours. The colours fan out and emerge as a spectrum. A rainbow is made up of spectra from millions of raindrops.

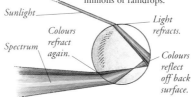

Sunlight

Colours refract again.

Spectrum

Light refracts.

Colours reflect off back surface.

Colour and temperature

Objects at room temperature emit (give out) electromagnetic waves, but these waves are too long for human eyes to see. Heating an object, such as this steel bar, gives the waves it emits more energy and makes them shorter. The waves eventually become short enough to be seen, and the bar begins to glow. As the bar's temperature rises, it glows with different colours.

Steel bar at 630°C (1,170°F)

Steel bar at 1,530°C (2,790°F)

Spectroscope

An instrument called a spectroscope is used to analyze the light given out by hot substances. Inside the spectroscope, a prism or diffraction grating (a glass slide scored with fine lines) splits light from a glowing substance into its component wavelengths.

Light source

Diffraction grating

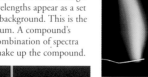

Emission spectrum

Each chemical element gives out a unique range of light wavelengths when heated. Seen through a spectroscope, these wavelengths appear as a set of bright lines on a dark background. This is the element's emission spectrum. A compound's emission spectrum is a combination of spectra from the elements that make up the compound.

Emission spectrum of a sodium flame

Sodium flame

Cone cells

At the back of the eye there are special cells called cones that enable humans to see colours. There are three types of cone, called red, green, and blue cones. Each type of cone is sensitive to a different range of light wavelengths. White light stimulates all three types of cone.

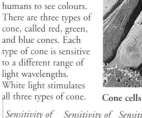

Cone cells

Sensitivity of red cones

Sensitivity of green cones

Sensitivity of blue cones

Visible spectrum

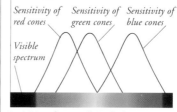

Sensitivity of cone cells in the human eye

Glowing white

Glowing red

Visible spectrum

Red hot and white hot

As the steel bar gets hotter, it emits more and more of the visible spectrum. At about 630°C (1,170°F), it is "red hot" and emits light from the red end of the spectrum. At about 1,530°C (2,790°F), the "white hot" bar emits the entire white light spectrum.

Hot stars

The colour of a star gives a clue to its age. To the naked eye, most stars look white, but their true colours can be seen using a telescope. Young stars are hot and glow with white light. Older stars are relatively cool and glow red or orange.

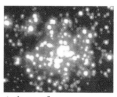

A cluster of young stars

Joseph von Fraunhofer

The German physicist Joseph von Fraunhofer (1787–1826) became interested in the nature of light while training as a mirror maker and lens polisher. His training enabled him to make spectroscopes of great precision. From 1814–17, he used them to make the first scientific study of the Sun's emission spectrum.

Munsell colour system

Describing colours exactly using words alone is not easy. To avoid confusion, manufacturing industries use standard colour-identification systems. The Munsell system is used to specify colours for dyes and pigments. It defines a colour by its value (brightness), its chroma (strength), and its hue (position in the spectrum).

Colour matching systems

Graphic designers use swatches of colour cards to match the colours in their work with those available from printers. The designer supplies the printer with the reference number of the colour, so the printer knows exactly what is wanted.

Each colour has a reference number.

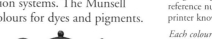

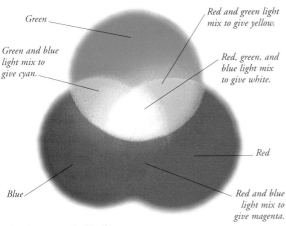

Green

Green and blue light mix to give cyan.

Blue

Red and green light mix to give yellow.

Red, green, and blue light mix to give white.

Red

Red and blue light mix to give magenta.

Coloured lights

Different amounts of red, green, and blue light can be mixed to form light of any other colour. This process is called colour addition. Unlike paints, red, green, and blue are the primary colours of light. Equal amounts of any two primary colours give a secondary colour (yellow, cyan, or magenta). When all three primaries are mixed in equal amounts, white light is produced.

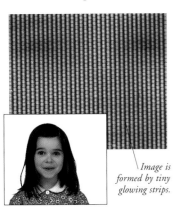

Colour television
The principle of adding coloured lights is used in colour television. The screen is covered with tiny strips that glow with red, green, or blue light. They are so small that, at a normal viewing distance, the human eye mixes the light coming from them. By adjusting the intensities of these three colours, the sensation of any other colour can be produced.

Image is formed by tiny glowing strips.

Painting with dots

"Pointillism" is a style of painting in which an artist uses thousands of tiny coloured dots to build up a picture. When viewed close up, the colours of the individual dots are clearly visible. Like the coloured strips on a television screen, the dots are too small to be seen from farther away. When viewed from a distance, the dots seem to merge, giving areas a single colour.

Pigments

A pigment is a chemical that absorbs only certain colours from white light. This process is called colour subtraction. Yellow, magenta, and cyan are primary pigments. Each absorbs one of the primary colours of light and reflects the other two. For example, a yellow pigment absorbs blue light but reflects green and red, which mix to give yellow. An equal mix of all three pigments absorbs all the colours from white light, giving black.

Colour printing

To print a full-colour picture, three single-colour images are printed on top of each other – one in cyan, one in magenta, and one in yellow. Each picture is made up of tiny coloured dots. The dots overlap and absorb the right wavelengths of light to give all the other colours required. A black image is then added to make the picture sharper.

Picture is made up of tiny ink dots.

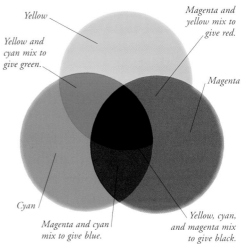

Yellow

Yellow and cyan mix to give green.

Cyan

Magenta and cyan mix to give blue.

Magenta and yellow mix to give red.

Magenta

Yellow, cyan, and magenta mix to give black.

Mixing paints

Paints are pigments mixed with water or oil. Any colour except white can be made by mixing the three primary pigments. Mixing paints has the effect of evenly mixing the pigments, and absorbing more of the white light spectrum.

Scattering and interference

Two other processes, called scattering and interference, can remove colours from the spectrum. Interference occurs when light from two sources meets and combines. In scattering, some parts of the spectrum are briefly absorbed by particles of matter and then radiated out again in all directions.

Blue sky
Sunlight includes all the colours of the spectrum. The sky appears blue during the day because air molecules in the atmosphere scatter light from the blue end of the spectrum in all directions.

Soap bubble

When white light strikes a soap bubble, it reflects off both the inner and outer surfaces of the bubble. The reflected light rays interfere, making some colours cancel each other out but others appear bright.

Interference creates a pattern of bright colours and dark bands.

Using interference

Stress is a force that can stretch or bend objects. Engineers shine light through plastic models of their designs to test their ability to withstand stress. The plastic molecules make the light rays split up and interfere. The interference patterns show the points of greatest stress.

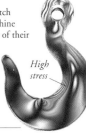

High stress

Thomas Young

The English doctor and physicist Thomas Young (1773–1829) carried out many experiments to prove that light travels as waves. He realized that colours are light waves of different lengths, and that interference colours occur where light waves meet and combine. Young also investigated colour vision. In 1801, he proposed that the human eye contains three types of colour sensor (now called cone cells), sensitive to blue, red, and green light.

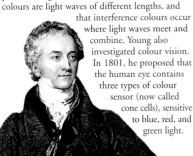

Reflecting colours

Objects have colour only when light falls upon them, because colours do not exist in total darkness. An object that appears one colour in white light may look different when illuminated by coloured light. The yellow pot in this sequence of pictures appears yellow only in white light.

White light
The yellow pot reflects the red and green parts of the white light spectrum, but absorbs the blue part.

Red light
The yellow pot reflects red light, and therefore appears red when illuminated by red light.

Green light
When illuminated by green light, the yellow pigment reflects the green light and so appears green.

Blue light
When only blue light is available, the yellow pot absorbs the blue light, making it look black.

FIND OUT MORE

DYES AND PAINTS   EYES AND SEEING   LIGHT   PHOTOGRAPHY   PRINTING   TELEVISION

COLUMBUS, CHRISTOPHER

CHRISTOPHER COLUMBUS was the first European since the Vikings to visit America. In the 1400s, Europeans did not know that America existed – they thought that Asia faced Europe across the Atlantic Ocean. In 1492, Columbus set sail from Spain across the Atlantic. He hoped to open up a trade route to Asia that would be quicker than the old land journey. He found some islands he believed were the East Indies, off what was presumed to be the Asian mainland. What he had really discovered was a continent soon to be known as America by the Europeans.

The port of Genoa in the 16th century

Early life
Columbus was born in the port of Genoa, Italy in 1451 and was named after St Christopher, the patron saint of travellers. His father was a weaver, and Christopher had little formal education. As a boy, he went to sea, and later worked in Lisbon, Portugal, where he drew sea charts for Portuguese sailors.

Crossing the Atlantic

While the Portuguese and other sailors were trying to find a sea route to Asia by sailing south and east round Africa, Columbus believed that, since the world was round, he could reach Asia from the opposite direction by sailing west across the Atlantic. In 1492, he persuaded the king and queen of Spain to finance his voyage, and set sail with three ships, the largest of which was the three-masted *Santa Maria*. At his first attempt, he landed in the Bahamas. Columbus, however, thought these islands were off the coast of Asia.

The *Santa Maria*

Royal flag of Spain

Main mast

Mizzen mast

Square-rigged sails

Columbus' four voyages
- — 1492
- → 1493
- — 1498
- — 1502

Four voyages
Columbus made four voyages across the Atlantic between 1492 and 1504. On the first, he reached Cuba, the Bahamas, and Hispaniola; on the second, he explored Jamaica; on the third he reached Trinidad and the South American coast. On his fourth voyage he actually set foot on the mainland of the "new" continent.

Navigation
Columbus had few instruments to help him navigate across the ocean. He used a crosstaff and astrolabe to calculate the ship's latitude, but had no way of knowing its longitude. Despite this lack of information, he managed to navigate successfully back home to Europe.

Astrolabe

Room for 40 crew below deck

Using the crosstaff

Crosstaff

Foremast

Because accommodation was so cramped, food was often cooked on deck.

West Indies

Columbus was amazed by the beauty and lush vegetation of the Caribbean islands, but he was disappointed that he had not found the rich trading cities of Asia. However, his discoveries encouraged other Europeans to visit the area in the coming centuries, founding colonies and opening up new trade links between Europe and the Caribbean.

Columbus arriving at the island of Hispaniola

New discoveries
While in the West Indies, Columbus and his crew tasted new foods, such as pineapple, potatoes, and sweetcorn. They saw people sleeping in hammocks, and observed the Arawak peoples of Cuba rolling up dried tobacco leaves and smoking them.

Later life
In 1493, Columbus was made governor-general of all the lands he discovered, but he was a poor administrator. In 1500, there were complaints about his rule of Hispaniola. As a result, Columbus was arrested and sent back to Spain in chains. He retired to Seville, where he died in 1506.

CHRISTOPHER COLUMBUS

1451	Born in Genoa, Italy
1476	Becomes a chartmaker in Lisbon, Portugal
1479	Marries Filipa de Perestrello e Moniz
1484	Becomes master mariner in Portuguese merchant service
1492	First voyage: sails across Atlantic Ocean in search of new route to Asia
1493–96	Second voyage
1493	Establishes European colony on Hispaniola
1498–1500	Third voyage
1502–04	Fourth and final voyage
1506	Dies in Seville, Spain

FIND OUT MORE   CENTRAL AMERICA, HISTORY OF   EXPLORATION   NAVIGATION   SHIPS AND BOATS   SOUTH AMERICA, HISTORY OF   SPAIN, HISTORY OF

COMBAT SPORTS

The judo suit, or "judogi", is a loose-fitting cotton jacket and trousers.

FIGHTING SPORTS, which had their origins in ancient Greece, developed in different ways. Judo and the other martial arts, such as karate, kung-fu, taekwondo, and aikido, evolved in the East, often as a way of life or connected with religion. Only since the 1950s have their secrets become known in the West and their popularity as sports spread. The chief Western combat sports are boxing, wrestling, and fencing. These have Eastern counterparts – kick boxing, sumo, and kendo respectively.

Players grip an opponent by the jacket.

Judo

Judo means "the gentle way", and players try to use their opponent's weight and strength against them. Players can use more than 40 recognized throws to put their opponent on their back. Or, in groundwork, they try to pin their opponent's back on the mat with a hold. In competition, a referee awards points for throws and holds.

The arm is used to absorb the impact of a throw.

The shoulder is pinned to the ground during groundwork.

Performing a hip throw

Scoring

A perfect throw or 30-second hold-down earns *ippon*, worth ten points, and wins the contest outright. Near-perfect throws or shorter hold-downs earn *waza-ari*, worth seven points, and two of these win a contest. If the contest goes its full length, other scores and penalties count.

Red
Black
Brown
Blue
Green
Orange
Yellow

Belts

The colour of the belt a player wears around the jacket indicates his or her grade. Judo grades range from *kyu*, meaning student, to the advanced *dan* grades when the player wears a black belt, or red for ninth or tenth dan.

Fencing

In fencing, points are scored by registering "hits" on the opponent's target areas. These vary according to the weapon used: the upper body including the arms for a sabre; the trunk only for a foil; and the whole body for an épée. A bout lasts until one player has scored the agreed number of hits or the time limit has been reached.

Scoring a hit

Weapons

A foil and sabre must not weigh more than 500 g (17.5 oz), an épée not more than 770 g (26.9 oz). The foil and épée have a 90-cm (35.4-in) blade and must strike the target with the point. The edges of a sabre's 88-cm (34.7-in) blade may be used for a hit.

Foil

Épée

Sabre

Wired-up over-jacket

Gauntlet   *Mask*

Fencing kit

Fencers wear protective clothing on the body, a mask of steel or plastic mesh, and a padded gauntlet on the sword hand. In competition, target areas may be electrically wired to register hits, signalled by lights.

Boxing

Boxers fight in a raised, square "ring" bounded by ropes. Amateur boxing is staged over three three-minute rounds. Professional fights last up to 12 rounds (15 in title fights). Fights may be won by a knock-out, by the referee stopping the fight, or on points.

High-sided boots

Amateur's headgear

Padded gloves

Muhammad Ali

Arguably the most colourful figure in sport, Muhammad Ali (b.1942) was the first boxer to regain the world heavyweight title three times. Born Cassius Clay, he won the Olympic light-heavyweight title in 1960, turned professional, then gained the world heavyweight crown with a shock win over Sonny Liston in 1964. He changed his name when he joined the Black Muslims.

Other combat sports

Like judo, most of the other Eastern combat sports come from Japan, including karate, sumo wrestling, and kendo.

Karate, meaning "empty hands", uses kicks and strikes by the hands, elbows, and head.

Sumo wrestling is steeped in the ritual of the Shinto religion. Each contestant tries to throw his opponent or push him out of the ring.

Kendo pays tribute to the samurai fighters of feudal times. "Swords" are bamboo sticks.

FIND OUT MORE

GREECE, ANCIENT   JAPAN, HISTORY OF   OLYMPIC GAMES   RELIGIONS   WEAPONS

C

COMETS AND ASTEROIDS

COMETS AND ASTEROIDS ARE LEFTOVERS from when the nine planets formed in the Solar System 4.6 billion years ago. Comets are fragile balls of snow and dust found at the edge of the Solar System in the Oort Cloud. Some leave the cloud and travel towards the Sun. The Sun's heat melts the snow and the comet appears to grow in size many times over. Asteroids are made of rock and are found mainly between the orbits of Mars and Jupiter.

For most of its orbit, a comet is a dirty snowball.

Tail develops as comet approaches Sun.

Tail is longest near Sun.

Tail shrinks as comet moves away from Sun.

Anatomy of a comet

At the centre of a comet is the nucleus – a dirty ball of snow and dust that is just a few kilometres across. If a comet is close to the Sun, the snow becomes gas, and gas and dust are released, forming a vast cloud of material – the coma – and one or two tails.

Thin, straight gas tail

Comet West passed Earth in 1976. It had two distinctive tails.

Broad dust tail

Nucleus

Coma

Periodic comets
When a comet leaves the Oort Cloud it can travel on an orbit which returns it again and again to the inner Solar System. This is a periodic comet. About 150 are short-period comets; they return to appear in Earth's sky in periods of less than 200 years. Halley's Comet passes Earth every 76 years.

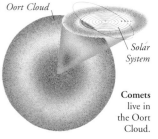
Oort Cloud
Solar System
Comets live in the Oort Cloud.

Halley's Comet
Halley's Comet is the only comet that has been seen up close. Five spacecraft went to investigate when it travelled through the inner Solar System in 1986. The space probe *Giotto* took this image of its dark, potato-shaped nucleus.

Edmond Halley
Comets are usually named after their discoverer, but one is named after the English scientist, Edmond Halley (1656–1742). He was the first person to show that comets can be periodic and follow orbits that return them again and again to Earth's sky.

Oort Cloud
Surrounding the Solar System is the Oort Cloud, made up of 10 trillion comets. Although the cloud is large, it is so distant that the comets cannot be seen. Comets only become visible when they travel within the inner Solar System. Astronomers have seen about 700 comets in Earth's sky.

Meteoroids

Tiny pieces of dust and chunks of rock travel through space. They are meteoroids and originate from two main sources: comets and asteroids. About 220,000 tonnes of such material enter Earth's atmosphere a year. The smallest meteoroids produce meteors. Larger pieces reach Earth and land on its surface. These are meteorites.

Meteors
Tiny meteoroids burn up as they travel through Earth's atmosphere, producing streaks of light known as meteors. When Earth travels through a concentration of meteoroids, a meteor shower is produced. The meteoroid material is left by comets as they pass close to the Sun.

Meteorites
More than 3,000 meteorites land on Earth every year. Most fall in the sea, but a handful are seen to fall on land. There are three main types of meteorites: stony, iron, or stony-iron.

Nakhla meteorite

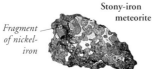
Fragment of nickel-iron
Stony-iron meteorite

Rock from Mars
Eight meteorites are known to have come to Earth from Mars. The Nakhla meteorite fell in Egypt in 1911. It is 13 million years old. Such meteorites tells us that Mars once had running water.

Impact crater
When a meteorite lands on Earth, it can create a crater. Earth was once bombarded by meteorites but its surface has since changed, removing the evidence. Today, about 150 impact craters can be identified, including Wolfe Crater in Australia.

Asteroid belt

Between the orbits of Mars and Jupiter is the asteroid belt – a doughnut-shaped ring made of millions of asteroids, pieces of rock, and metal. The smallest are specks of dust; the biggest, Ceres, is more than 900 km (550 miles) across.

Gaspra
About 5,000 asteroids have been identified, but only about 10 are spherical and larger than 250 km (150 miles) across. The smaller ones, such as the stony asteroid Gaspra, are irregular in shape.

Asteroid belt
Jupiter
Mars
Trojan asteroids

Asteroid groups
Not all asteroids are in the asteroid belt. About 10 per cent travel in groups away from the belt. The Trojans travel along Jupiter's orbit, one group in front and one group behind the planet. The Amor, Apollo, and Aten groups all follow orbits closer to Earth.

Wolfe Crater

FIND OUT MORE   ASTRONOMY   PLANETS   SPACE EXPLORATION   SUN AND SOLAR SYSTEM   UNIVERSE

COMPUTERS

WITH LIGHTNING SPEED, a computer carries out millions of calculations each second. Sets of instructions called programs tell the computer what to do. The hard-disk unit is the heart of a computer. It contains the central processing unit (CPU), which controls all of the operations of the computer. The hard-disk unit, monitor, keyboard, and other connected devices are called hardware. The programs that enable it to function and carry out specific tasks are known as software.

Personal computer

A personal computer (PC) is a compact computer that can be operated by only one person at a time. It consists of a hard-disk unit, to which hardware called peripherals is connected so that data can be either input or output. Keyboards and printers are examples of peripherals. Interfaces are electronic circuits that allow the hard-disk unit to communicate with each peripheral.

C

Personal computer (PC) with peripherals

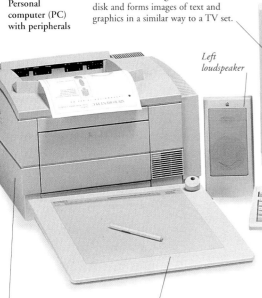

Monitor receives signals from the hard disk and forms images of text and graphics in a similar way to a TV set.

Left loudspeaker

Right loudspeaker with controls

Hard-disk unit contains the memory, the CPU, and the disk drives.

Mouse mat

Keyboard consists of numbers, letters, and special function keys that allow data to be typed directly into the computer.

Mouse controls pointer on screen; inside the mouse is a ball that rotates as the mouse moves, and the ball's movement sends signals to the computer.

Scanner copies an image and translates it into on-off pulses of electricity that are fed into the computer, so that the image can be displayed on the monitor screen.

Printer receives data from hard disk and produces print-out of documents and graphics.

Graphics tablet enables images to be "drawn" on the monitor screen, as a pen-like device moves over its surface.

Motherboard

A motherboard is a large circuit board in the hard-disk unit to which the computer's key electronic components are attached. These components are linked together by strips of metal called "buses" on the underside of the motherboard. Also attached to the motherboard are the interfaces that link the hard-disk unit to the peripherals, as well as expansion slots, to which other circuit boards can be added to improve the computer's performance or capabilities.

Memory
A computer's electronic memory allows it to "remember" how to function. There are two parts to the memory: the random access memory (RAM) and the read-only memory (ROM). Both consist of circuits called microprocessors, or silicon chips.

PC motherboard

Video card controls operation of monitor screen.

Expansion slots for extra circuit boards

Sockets called ports allow peripherals such as a modem or printer to connect to the hard disk.

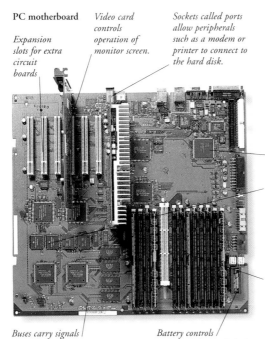

Buses carry signals around the computer.

Battery controls computer's internal clock.

Central processing unit (CPU)

ROM (read-only memory) chips store important programs, such as the disk-operating system, whose content cannot be changed.

RAM (random-access memory) chips store data fed into the computer on disks or via the keyboard, which can then be retrieved and changed as desired.

Charles Babbage
English mathematician Charles Babbage (1791–1871) built a mechanical computer called the Difference Engine that consisted of hundreds of gear wheels. It could do complicated sums more quickly than doing the same calculations by hand.

Monitor screen displays data.

RAM

CPU

Data input via a keyboard.

ROM

Central processing unit (CPU)
The CPU is a single microprocessor that holds a large number of circuits. The CPU receives data from the ROM, RAM, and keyboard. It sends data to the RAM for storage, and to output devices, such as the monitor.

Computer disks

Programs and data can be stored on computer disks. Magnetic disks record data as magnetic patterns in tiny iron particles that coat the disks' surfaces. A hard disk is a stack of magnetic disks inside a computer. Other types of disk include compact discs (CDs) and digital versatile discs (DVDs). A device called a disk drive is used to store data on disks and retrieve it.

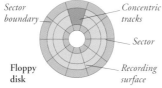

Sector boundary
Concentric tracks
Sector
Floppy disk
Recording surface

Types of computer disk

How a disk drive works

Disks arrange data into divisions called tracks and sectors. A disk drive has a magnetic read-write head that "reads" data from, or "writes" data to, a specific sector and track on the disk. In CD and optical disk drives, the read-write head is a laser beam.

Operating system allows this girl to use a program for learning Spanish.

 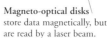 

Floppy disks are small magnetic disks.

Optical mini-disks are small magneto-optical disks.

SyQuest disks are large magnetic disks able to store more data than floppies.

Magneto-optical disks store data magnetically, but are read by a laser beam.

Compact discs (CDs) store data as tiny pits in the surface of the disk.

Operating system

Every computer has a program called an operating system (OS) that controls its basic functions. The OS is always at work "behind the scenes" when other applications are running. A graphical user interface (GUI) often forms part of a computer's OS. The GUI allows the computer operator to use a mouse to move information or to run programs.

Steve Jobs and Steve Wozniak

The Apple Computer company – one of the world's largest – was founded in 1976 by Steve Jobs (b. 1955) and Steve Wozniak (b. 1950), who wanted to make computers affordable to ordinary people. Their 1977 Apple II computer was the first PC made for the mass market. It was hugely successful, because users of the Apple II needed no prior knowledge of electronics or computing.

Types of computer

Most schools and many homes have personal computers, but there are many other types of computer, both larger and smaller than a PC. Some computers enable people to work while they are travelling; others are designed purely for entertainment. Large, powerful, high-speed computers are often used to process information for many people at once, or perform many tasks simultaneously.

Dedicated computer
While some computers can carry out many different tasks, others are "dedicated", meaning that they are designed for one specific purpose. A familiar example of a dedicated computer system is a games computer.

Laptop
Many business people take small, portable PCs called laptops with them when they travel. A laptop contains rechargeable batteries that allow it to function on trains, buses, outdoors – in fact, almost anywhere.

Mainframe
Most large organizations have a mainframe computer that can be used by many people at once, each working at a separate monitor, or terminal. A mainframe must be kept in a cold, dry environment.

Supercomputer
The most powerful computers are supercomputers. They are used to perform very complex tasks, such as forecasting future weather systems or analysing gravity and black holes in space. The first supercomputer was launched in 1976 by Cray.

Timeline

1642 Blaise Pascal invents the first mechanical adding machine.

1834 Charles Babbage designs a mechanical computer, which he calls the Difference Engine.

1939 John Atanasoff, an American, completes the first electronic computer.

Commodore personal computer, 1970

1945 ENIAC, the world's first automatic computer, is built in the USA.

1967 Keyboards are used for data entry.

1970 Floppy disks appear.

Late 1970s Mass-produced PCs are introduced.

1975 The first portable computer is introduced.

Late 1970s The Xerox Corporation invents the graphical user interface.

1983 The mouse is first used on an Apple computer.

1985 Computer CDs appear.

Assorted software programs

1980s Sales of PCs soar.

1990 IBM Pentium PC performs 112 million instructions per second.

2000 Mobile phones and other hand-held devices are designed to include computing facilities, software, and Internet.

FIND OUT MORE ATOMS AND MOLECULES ELECTRONICS INFORMATION TECHNOLOGY LASERS AND HOLOGRAMS MATHEMATICS NUMBERS SOUND RECORDING WEATHER FORECASTING

CONFUCIUS

TWO THOUSAND YEARS AGO, China was in a state of turmoil and warfare. Strong imperial government had collapsed, and civil order had broken down. One man learned the lessons of this disorder. Confucius devised a moral code based on respect, kindness, and the strength of the family. He believed people could be taught to behave themselves as members of a well-ordered community. This vision, although based on a traditional view of Chinese society, is still influential in China today.

Early life

Confucius was born in Lu province in northeast China in about 551 BC. His name was Kong Qiu. His father died when he was three, leaving his mother to bring him up. He became known as K'ung Fu-tse, or "great master kong". In the West he was called Confucius, the Latin form of this title.

Confucius' teaching

Confucius learned to develop his new moral outlook from his experience in government. He taught that a good ruler should set an example by dealing fairly with his subjects, using force only as a last resort. In return, subjects had a duty to respect and obey their ruler.

Ancestor worship

In all his teachings, Confucius encouraged ancestor worship because it strengthened family ties. As a result, the Chinese people came to see themselves as part of a great national family that included not only living people but also the dead and those people who were still to be born. Many of the traditional Chinese gods and goddesses were believed to be ancestors who once lived as ordinary people in China and who, after their death, could influence everyday life.

Chün-tzu

According to the writings of Confucius, the ideal gentleman, or Chün-tzu, was a person who was compassionate, self-controlled, respectful of superiors, and concerned for the welfare of others. As a result, he was against slavery and human or animal sacrifices. Under the influence of Confucius it became common to bury pottery figures in tombs, rather than living animals or slaves.

Bronze tomb model of a rhinoceros

Traditional goddess, Kuan Yin

Zhou dynasty

Between 1027–256 BC, most of northern China was ruled by the Zhou dynasty. The early Zhou emperors ruled well, but later, as a result of pressure from powerful local lords, China split into a number of warring states. Confucius looked on the early years of the Zhou as a golden age of social harmony.

Handle in the form of mythical beast

Ritual vessel, Zhou period

Political career

For some years, Confucius worked as an adviser to the Duke of Lu and other local rulers. He attempted to promote good government by advising respect for the existing social order and fostering political stability. But his severe lifestyle and strict views were not popular, and Confucius eventually left Lu province.

Analects

Most of what we know about the teachings of Confucius can be found in a book of his sayings, the *Lun Yü,* or Analects. These sayings were collected by the followers of Confucius after his death. Confucius is also said to have compiled or edited five classic books known as the *Wu Ching*. The most famous of these is the *I Ching,* or Book of Changes. The *I Ching* provides a method of revealing the future through the use of 64 patterns of broken and unbroken lines.

Chinese characters written by a later follower of Confucius

Mencius

After Confucius' death, a number of his followers carried on his work. The most famous was Mencius (c.371–c.288). He believed that people are basically good, and that it is the duty of the ruler to ensure the prosperity, education, and moral well-being of his subjects. His pupils wrote down his thoughts and sayings in *The Book of Mencius.*

Impact

Although Confucius did not found a religion, his teachings are still influential throughout the world, especially in China, where the traditional values of the family are still based heavily on his views. The moral code taught by Confucius fits well with such established religions as Buddhism, Taoism, and Shinto, while his writings and classic texts are still widely studied in the West.

Chinese family, 19th century

CONFUCIUS

1027 BC	Zhou dynasty takes control of northern China.
c.551 BC	Confucius born in Lu.
532 BC	Confucius marries.
531 BC	Confucius' son born.
517 BC	Confucius goes into exile for the first time.
501–496 BC	Holds important post in Lu province.
483 BC	Returns to Lu province after many years of wandering.
c.481–221 BC	China splits into seven warring states.
c.479 BC	Death of Confucius.

FIND OUT MORE   BOOKS   CHINA, HISTORY OF   PHILOSOPHY   RELIGIONS   SOCIETIES, HUMAN   WRITING

CONSERVATION

THE PRINCIPLE AIM of conservation is to ensure the survival of life in all its forms and variety, and to make certain that natural resources are not used beyond their capacity for renewal but continue for the benefit of future generations. Conservation requires an understanding of ecology – the interrelationships of the different plants and animals (including our own species) with each other, and with their environment. Concern for the health of the environment is steadily increasing, as can be seen from the growth of conservation organizations on almost every continent.

Why we need conservation

Ever increasing human populations lead to an increase in the demand for natural resources. This has many effects including deforestation, habitat loss, pollution of air and water, and extermination of species. Poaching of animals for meat, fur, and the medicine trade also reduces animal numbers. Conservation is an active means of slowing down or reversing these trends, in an attempt to safeguard the environment and all living things within it.

Endangered species
As human numbers increase, more land is needed to grow food, so forests are cut down and habitats destroyed. Without its habitat, wildlife cannot survive. Human pressure and hunting is causing many species, such as the white rhino, to become rare or endangered, some to the point of extinction. It is too late for animals such as the Tasmanian wolf, but others, such as the grey whale, have been saved from extinction.

Rhinos are hunted for their horns.

White rhino

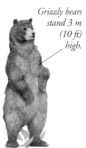

Grizzly bears stand 3 m (10 ft) high.

Grizzly bears are the largest and most powerful of the animals living in Yellowstone National Park.

Sage grouse are the most spectacular of the North American grouse. When displaying, the male struts around vibrating his wings and emits a booming sound.

When displaying, male lifts tail into a fan.

Wingspan may reach 9 cm (3.5 in).

Phoebus butterflies appear in the Rockies in mid-summer.

Males use antlers to fight.

Wapitis live in the forests of Yellowstone. They are larger than the red deer of Eurasia, but their behaviour is similar.

Conservation

Conservation means wise use of resources, thus recognizing that to use natural resources is perfectly acceptable, as long as they are not exploited beyond their capacity for renewal. Conservation is concerned with the survival of life in all its forms, and with maintaining organic life at the optimum rate of productivity.

Forests are home to wapitis.

Preservation
Preservation differs from conservation in that preservation means strict protection as an end in itself, without regard for the consequences. The first area of land to be preserved was Yellowstone National Park in the USA, where animals such as grizzly bears and wapitis thrive in this undisturbed environment. Over-protection can lead to a build-up of the animal numbers, causing habitat destruction and the starvation and decline of the animals. This can be avoided by good management and by culling excess numbers of animals.

Yellowstone National Park, USA

Environmental organizations
Hundreds of organizations are concerned with safeguarding the Earth's resources. The International Union for Conservation of Nature and Natural Resources (IUCN), and the Worldwide Fund for Nature (WWF), carry out conservation projects worldwide.

Park rangers, WWF, Tsavo National Park

Methods of conservation

The establishment of national parks and wildlife sanctuaries is a very effective method of conserving natural areas and their wildlife. Other methods include education, breeding programmes, using renewable energy such as solar, wind, and wave power, and legislation. Some developing countries have agreed to safeguard areas of natural habitat in return for a reduction in their foreign debt.

Legislation
The Convention on International Trade in Endangered Species (CITES) controls trade in rare species, such as tigers; other groups control fishing and pollution.

Tiger bones are used to make oriental medicines.

Siberian tiger remains

Education
The importance of educating young people about conservation and the effect it has on their lives cannot be overstated. The need for education is as vital in the west as in the developing world. For conservation to be effective, it must have the support of the local people.

Game ranger teaching children

Breeding programmes
The best chance of survival for some animals close to extinction lies in breeding them in captivity for eventual return to their natural habitat. In one of the earliest breeding programmes, the few remaining Arabian oryx were captured, bred in the USA, and later successfully re-introduced to Oman.

Pale fur helps conceal oryx in the desert.

Arabian oryx

FIND OUT MORE   BEARS   DEER AND ANTELOPES   ECOLOGY AND ECOSYSTEMS   ENERGY   LIONS AND OTHER WILD CATS   POLLUTION   RHINOCEROSES AND TAPIRS   ZOOS

Endangered animals

Dugongs live in tropical oceans, where they feed on sea grass.

Blue whales are the largest animals ever to have lived, reaching a length of 30 m (100 ft) or more.

Great white sharks are man-eating sharks, found in warm seas worldwide.

Cuvier's beaked whales are widely distributed, except in polar seas.

Giant pandas are bears that feed exclusively on bamboo.

Tigers are hunted for their fur and their bones, which are used in Chinese medicine.

Jaguars are endangered, due to habitat destruction and hunting for their fur.

These are among the world's largest butterflies.

Kakapos are preyed on by introduced rats and stoats.

Wingspan may reach 2.7 m (9 ft).

Queen Alexandra's birdwings live only in Papua New Guinea.

Daubenton's bats hunt for insects over ponds and rivers.

St Vincent parrots live on the island of St Vincent.

Kakapos are nocturnal, flightless birds from New Zealand.

Californian condors are among the largest living birds.

This weta is among the largest insects in the world.

Great crested newts are the largest of the European newts, at up to 15 cm (6 in) long.

Golden mantellas from Madagascar are threatened by habitat destruction.

Stephen's Island weta is confined to a small island off the coast of New Zealand.

Przewalski's horses are extinct in the wild, but captive bred animals have been re-introduced.

Gorillas are endangered, due to destruction of their rainforest habitat.

Père David's deer, extinct in its native China, has been bred in captivity.

White rhinos are scarce in Zaïre, but more abundant in South Africa.

Endangered plants

Insects are trapped when the two lobes of the leaf snap shut.

This plant is threatened by introduced goats.

Cactus shrinks back into the ground for part of the year.

Dawn redwoods were rediscovered in China.

Venus's flytraps feed on insects.

Silverswords live on the volcanic islands of Hawaii.

Knowlton cacti are among the world's rarest cacti.

New Zealand brush lilies are eaten by introduced possums.

Japanese sago palms are slow-growing evergreens.

CONTINENTS

THE WORLD'S SEVEN great land masses are known as continents. The seven continents are North America, South America, Africa, Europe, Asia, Antarctica, and Australia. Although you may not realize it, the continents are crunching together and drifting apart even as you read this page. This is because the Earth's outer shell, or crust, is made up of a number of vast, ever-moving slabs of rock called tectonic plates. The continents are embedded in these plates, which move very slowly – Europe and North America, for example, are drifting apart by just 4 cm (1.5 in) each year. Over millions of years, however, the continents have shifted this way and that across the globe, dramatically changing the face of the planet time and time again.

Continental drift

If you study a world map, you will notice that the east coast of South America looks as if it would fit neatly into Africa's west coast. This is because 220 million years ago Africa, South America, and all the other continents formed a single giant "supercontinent", now called Pangaea. Eventually, Pangaea split up into smaller land masses that drifted over the Earth's surface, giving the arrangement of continents that appears on your map today. Earth scientists call this theory continental drift.

200 million years ago: Pangaea, the single land mass, begins to break up.

Asia

135 million years ago: the South Atlantic opens up, pulling Africa and South America apart; India moves towards Asia.

Africa *India* *Europe* *Australia*

South America

South Atlantic *North Atlantic*

North America

10 million years ago: Antarctica and Australia drift apart; the North Atlantic opens up, moving North America away from Europe.

Antarctica

Tectonic plates

There are nine major tectonic plates and a number of smaller ones. They fit together like the pieces of a jigsaw, covering the whole of the Earth's surface. The continents are carried by continental plates, such as the Eurasian plate. Oceanic plates, such as the Pacific plate, form most of the seafloor; the rest is made up of the fringes of the continental plates, which lie underwater.

Glossopteris fossil

Fossilized *Lystrosaurus* skull

Evidence for continental drift
Identical fossils of land-based plants and animals, such as the fern *Glossopteris* and the mammal *Lystrosaurus*, have been found in continents now widely separated by the sea. The only plausible explanation is that the continents were once linked together.

Alfred Wegener

German meteorologist and geophysicist Alfred Wegener (1880–1930) devised the theory of continental drift. As evidence, he cited the continents' matching coastlines, similar rock strata in continents separated by huge oceans, and fossil discoveries. Although widely accepted now, his ideas were ridiculed at the time.

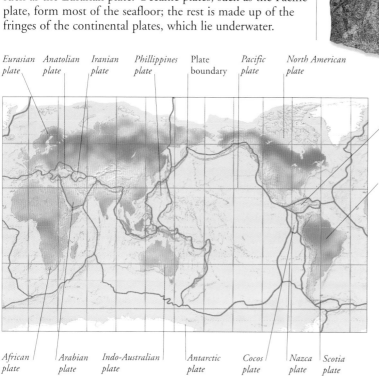

Eurasian plate / Anatolian plate / Iranian plate / Phillippines plate / Plate boundary / Pacific plate / North American plate

Caribbean plate

South American plate

African plate / Arabian plate / Indo-Australian plate / Antarctic plate / Cocos plate / Nazca plate / Scotia plate

The major plates of the Earth's crust

Triple junctions

At places called triple junctions, a column of magma – hot, molten rock from the Earth's interior – burns its way through a continental plate. This splits the plate three ways, producing huge rift valleys between the fragments of the plate. The Great Rift Valley in East Africa was formed in this way. The fragments of the plate are forced further apart over millions of years, creating new continental land masses. As the rift valleys widen, new oceans form between the pieces of the fragmented plate.

Satellite image of Africa's Great Rift Valley

236

Diverging plates

At some places beneath the world's great oceans, the tectonic plates that make up the Earth's surface are slowly diverging. These places are called constructive margins. As the plates pull apart, molten rock called magma wells up through the crack between the plates and emerges as lava. When the lava cools, it adds new material to the sea floor. This process is known as sea-floor spreading.

Mid-ocean ridge

As two plates pull apart, the lava emerging from the Earth's interior solidifies and builds a line of undersea mountains along the crack. This is called a mid-ocean ridge. There is such a ridge beneath each of the world's great oceans. In Iceland, the North Atlantic Ridge rises above sea level and can be seen as a long gash in the landscape.

North Atlantic Ridge, Thingvellir, Iceland

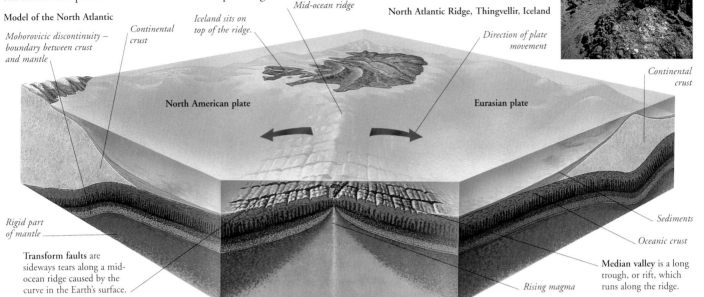

Model of the North Atlantic

Mohorovicic discontinuity – boundary between crust and mantle

Continental crust

Iceland sits on top of the ridge.

Mid-ocean ridge

Direction of plate movement

North American plate

Eurasian plate

Continental crust

Rigid part of mantle

Transform faults are sideways tears along a mid-ocean ridge caused by the curve in the Earth's surface.

Rising magma

Sediments

Oceanic crust

Median valley is a long trough, or rift, which runs along the ridge.

Converging plates

In many places the tectonic plates are converging, or moving against one another. In places known as destructive margins, oceanic plates are drawn underneath the continental plates. The oceanic plate is pulled down into the layer of the Earth's interior called the mantle, where it is destroyed by intense heat. This process is called subduction. In other places called collision zones, the edges of two continental plates may crumple as they collide. This process creates great mountain ranges such as the Alps and the Himalayas.

Transform

In some places where tectonic plates meet, the plates neither collide nor pull apart, but simply slide past each other in opposite directions. These places are called transforms, or conservative margins. Perhaps the most famous transform is the San Andreas Fault in California, USA, where the Pacific and North American plates grind slowly past one another. As the plates move, they often snag and judder, setting off violent earthquakes.

San Andreas Fault, California, USA

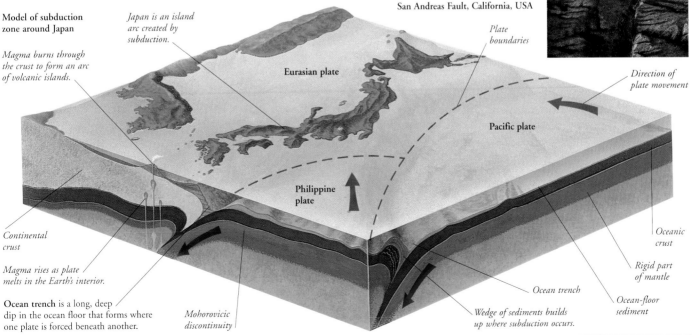

Model of subduction zone around Japan

Japan is an island arc created by subduction.

Magma burns through the crust to form an arc of volcanic islands.

Eurasian plate

Plate boundaries

Direction of plate movement

Pacific plate

Philippine plate

Continental crust

Magma rises as plate melts in the Earth's interior.

Ocean trench is a long, deep dip in the ocean floor that forms where one plate is forced beneath another.

Mohorovicic discontinuity

Wedge of sediments builds up where subduction occurs.

Ocean trench

Oceanic crust

Rigid part of mantle

Ocean-floor sediment

FIND OUT MORE   EARTH   EARTHQUAKES   FOSSILS   GEOLOGY   MAGNETISM   MOUNTAINS AND VALLEYS   OCEAN FLOOR   OCEANS AND SEAS   VOLCANOES

COOK, JAMES

UNTIL THE MID-18TH CENTURY, European
explorers were motivated by trade or plunder.
James Cook, a British naval captain, began a
new form of exploration – he was more interested
in scientific research. From 1768 to 1779, he made three
voyages to the South Pacific, applying scientific methods
to navigation for the first time, and making astronomical
observations that would help future sailors. He also carefully
recorded everything he saw, bringing back many specimens
and drawings of previously unknown flora and fauna.

Early life
James Cook was born in the town of
Marton-in-Cleveland near Whitby,
England in 1728. He went to sea as a
boy, sailing in the Baltic before joining
the British Royal Navy in 1755. Cook
rose quickly through the ranks and was
given command of his first ship in 1759,
during the Seven Years' War with France.

Port of Whitby, England

The Endeavour

During the 1760s, Cook mastered the skills of navigation.
These were put to good use when he was asked in 1768
to sail to Tahiti in the South Seas to observe the transit
of the planet Venus across the sky. His choice of ship
was unusual: the *Endeavour,* a converted collier
familiar to Cook, and known for its toughness
and ability to carry a heavy cargo.

The Endeavour / *Main mast* / *Mizzen mast* / *Cook's explorations* / *Fore mast*
Red ensign (British naval flag)

Large hold for supplies

Cook's sextant

Navigation
Navigation during Cook's
time was primitive but
effective. Cook used a
chronometer to determine
longitude (position east-
west) and a quadrant or
sextant to determine
latitude (position
north-south).

Diet
Cook was the first sea captain to
take measures against scurvy – a
disease caused by lack of vitamins
– and supplied his crew with
fresh fruit, meat, and vegetables
wherever possible.

Lemons and limes

Mapping the Pacific

Cook made three voyages around the Pacific, circumnavigating
New Zealand, mapping the east coast of Australia, and exploring
many islands. He guessed correctly that there was an area of
frozen land around the South Pole, and confirmed that Australia
was a large island and not part of any southern continent.

Joseph Banks
Cook took with him botanist
Joseph Banks, artist Sydney
Parkinson, and a team of
scientists. They discovered
many species, such as the
breadfruit and the kangaroo,
previously unknown to
Europeans. One area
yielded so many new
species that they
called it Botany Bay.
It is now a suburb
of Sydney, Australia.

Some of Parkinson's illustrations
Joseph Banks

Death of Cook
On his third voyage, which started in 1776, Cook
came across the Hawaiian Islands, which he
named the Sandwich Islands. He spent the winter
of 1778–79 in Hawaii, learning much about the
inhabitants, and he returned in the spring of
1779, after exploring the west coast of America.
This time, however, the local people were less
friendly, and after a quarrel broke out, Cook was
stabbed to death.

Cook is killed fighting the Hawaiian islanders.

Hawaiian clubs, used against Cook

JAMES COOK

1728 Born in Marton-in-Cleveland, Yorkshire, England

1755 Joins Royal Navy

1759 Takes command of his first ship

1768–71 Sails to the Pacific Ocean to observe the transit of Venus; explores Tahiti, New Zealand, and Australia

1772–75 Second voyage: maps many of the Pacific islands and sails south towards Antarctica

1776–79 Third voyage: sails into North Pacific; looks for inlet into Arctic Ocean

1779 Stabbed to death in Hawaii

FIND OUT MORE AUSTRALIA • AUSTRALIA, HISTORY OF • EXPLORATION • NAVIGATION • SHIPS AND BOATS

CORAL REEFS

TEEMING WITH WILDLIFE from shrimps to sharks, coral reefs are some of the most beautiful underwater structures. A coral reef takes thousands of years to form; it is composed of the living and dead skeletons of colonies of tiny animals called corals. Corals have flourished and built reefs in shallow, tropical seas for more than 440 million years. Corals are related to sea anemones and jellyfish, and belong to the group of animals called coelenterates. Australia's Great Barrier Reef is 2,000 km (1,240 miles) in length but is under serious threat from increased pollution.

Corals compete for light and food-bearing water currents.

Coral reefs

Coral reefs cover 619,000 sq km (239,015 sq miles) of the Earth's surface. Fringing reefs grow along coastlines, atolls are reefs that grow around extinct volcanoes, and cays are complete islands made of coral. Coral comes in all colours from red and yellow to blue and green, and grows in a variety of shapes and sizes including delicate fan corals, upright staghorn corals, and dome-shaped brain corals. Many animals hide in the holes and crevices within the reef.

Staghorn coral releasing eggs

Reproduction

Corals reproduce asexually to form colonies of genetically identical polyps. They also reproduce sexually, releasing eggs and sperm into the water. The fertilized eggs turn into larvae that join the plankton, which is carried on the currents, ensuring wide distribution.

Symbiotic algae live within corals and give them their bright colours.

Coral polyps open at night

Coral polyps close in the day

Coral polyp

Coral reefs are made up of many individual animals called coral polyps. They normally live in large colonies, but a few species are solitary. Soft corals have a rigid inner layer for support; hard corals secrete a cup-shaped chalky skeleton from their jelly-like bodies. A circle of tentacles, armed with stinging cells, immobilizes prey and pushes it through the mouth into the stomach. Coral polyps close up during the day, but at night the reef comes to life when the corals extend their tentacles into the water currents ready to trap prey.

Fish

Coral reefs are home to fish of all shapes and sizes, from solitary giant groupers and wrasse, at up to 1.8 m (6 ft) long, which lurk in reef caves and recesses, to shoals of tiny damselfish, which graze the fronds of seaweed on the top of the reef. Some, such as the moray eel, are vicious predators; others such as parrot fish, feed on coral.

Tubular mouth

Seahorses often hide within seaweed.

Prehensile tail grasps seaweed.

Seahorse

Seahorses are pipe fish with upright S-shaped bodies and prehensile tails. They eat small crustaceans, such as shrimps, and suck them into their tubular mouths. Females lay eggs in the males' brood pouches; the young develop and later emerge.

Spine can be raised.

Mandarin fish

The most poisonous fish of the reef are the various scorpion fish, such as the mandarin. Their bodies are protected by bony plates and poison-tipped spines. Mandarin fish swim slowly. They live near the seabed, waiting to pounce on their prey.

Black tip reefshark

The largest inhabitants of the reef are the black tip reefshark and its distant relative, the giant manta ray. They patrol the seaward drop-off flank of reefs, on the lookout for potential fish prey that stray too far from the protection of the reef. By contrast, mantas are filter feeders attracted to the reef by the upwelling of plankton.

Eyes close when eating.

Black tip of fin

Jaws contain sharp teeth.

Gills

Streamlined body for speed

Powerful tail

Reptiles

Sea turtles and sea snakes are reptilian inhabitants of reefs. Both need to surface to breathe air, but while turtles have to move onto land such as oceanic island reefs to breed, sea snakes can give birth to live young at sea. Some turtles prey on other animals, while others feed on grass. Sea snakes are good swimmers and are the most venomous snakes in the world. They prey on the abundant reef fish.

Flippers

Wide feet help it paddle in water.

Green turtle

Invertebrates

Reefs provide a variety of habitats for invertebrates such as sea slugs, sea cucumbers, and sea urchins. The reef protects delicate filter feeders, such as sponges, from the impact of the waves. Some bivalve molluscs nestle in crevices; others such as mussels, anchor themselves to the coral with root-like hairs. Many crustaceans, such as shrimps, scavenge amongst the corals.

Strong suckers help octopus grip rocks.

Common octopus

The reef is an ideal environment for the octopus to hide – its soft body slips easily into crevices. A stealthy hunter, it grabs prey with sucker-covered tentacles. When out in the open, its ability to change the texture and tone of its skin provides excellent camouflage.

Giant clam

This biggest living shellfish grows to 1 m (3 ft) long and, like corals, is inhabited by symbiotic algae. A clam opens its shell to feed on plankton and closes it if danger threatens. Giant clams remain stationary once they are adult.

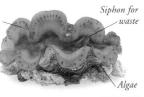

Shell is made of two halves.

Siphon for waste

Algae

FIND OUT MORE   AUSTRALIA   FISH   OCEAN WILDLIFE   OCTOPUSES AND SQUIDS   SHARKS AND RAYS   TURTLES AND TORTOISES

239

CRABS AND OTHER CRUSTACEANS

THERE ARE SOME 30,000 SPECIES in the crustacean class, including crabs, barnacles, copepods, krill, lobsters, prawns, shrimps, and woodlice. Crabs and other crustaceans share characteristics including two pairs of antennae, mandibles, and a shell. In size they can range from microscopic freshwater fleas to giant Japanese spider crabs, which have a claw-to-claw span of 3.6m (11 ft). Most crustaceans live in the sea, others prefer fresh water, and a few, such as the woodlouse, live on land. Some are parasitic – they live on or in other animals.

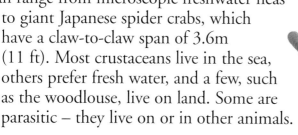

Smooth legs

Pincers

Bumps on front legs

Carapace, or hard shell

Spikes protecting carapace

Mouth and eyes under edge of carapace

Jointed legs

Walking legs

Spiny spider crab

Teeth

Defence

Apart from the protection they get from their shells, crabs can also defend themselves using their enlarged claws, or pincers, which often have a sharp serrated (toothed) edge. Some crabs, such as the decorator crabs, camouflage themselves by fixing seaweed to their shells, and blending into their surroundings. However, even with these methods of defence, crabs are still eaten by octopuses, fish such as bass, shore birds, and mammals.

Claw of Japanese spider crab

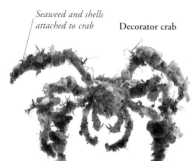

Seaweed and shells attached to crab

Decorator crab

Features of a crab

Crabs belong to the order Decopoda (10-legged). They have four pairs of jointed walking or swimming legs, plus an extra modified pair, called pincers. They have two pairs of antennae, gills, and a segmented, calcareous shell, or carapace. As they grow, crabs shed the carapace and grow a new one.

Feeding

Crabs, such as the hermit crab, are generally omnivorous, and can be either predators or scavengers. Hermit crabs catch their prey in their pincers. The crab then uses the pincers like a fork, to pass the food to its mandibles (specialized jaws). The crab chews its food, then uses two pairs of adapted limbs to push the food further into the mouth.

Fish **Hermit crab**

Breeding

After the male has fertilized the female's eggs, she may carry them in a brood pouch until ready to hatch, or release them into the sea. Some crustaceans hatch as tiny adults, but crabs go through a larval stage, and spend their early life as plankton.

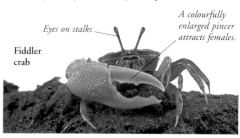

Eyes on stalks

A colourfully enlarged pincer attracts females.

Fiddler crab

How a crab moves

Crabs walk slowly forwards or backwards on their jointed legs when exploring their surroundings under water, but scuttle sideways across the ground when threatened. Some crabs, such as velvet crabs, are able to swim because their hind legs have been adapted into flattened paddles, also known as swimmerets.

Pincers

Crab crouching in defence.

Crab starts to turn to its left.

Shore crab turning. *Missing limb* *Small flap-like abdomen* *Fully turned crab can scuttle away.*

Barnacles

Young barnacles float in the sea until they find any stable surface, such as a rocky shore. They then attach themselves to a rock, and secrete a calcium-based substance that forms protective plates around them. They leave an opening for feeding, which closes when the animal is exposed to the air at low tide. Barnacles are hermaphrodites – that is, both sexes exist in one individual.

Goose barnacles attach themselves to driftwood with long stalks.

Goose barnacles

Feeding

Most barnacles feed themselves using their feet! When covered by water, these fine, feathery, curly limbs protrude from the barnacle's opening. The feet trap food as it floats past, filter it from the seawater, and transfer it into the barnacle's mouth. Goose barnacles do this while floating in the sea.

Woodlice

Woodlice are the only true land-living crustaceans. A woodlouse's "shell" consists of flat, waterproof plates that protect its back. Woodlice can dry out, so some species, such as the pill bug, have developed the ability to roll up and reduce water loss.

Waterproof plates

Lobsters

Lobsters, together with crabs, shrimps, prawns, and crayfish, are all known as crawlers, because of their movement. They live on the seashore, seabed, and in streams. Lobsters have large pincers for defence and feeding. The male's pincers are usually larger than the female's. The biggest species is the blue lobster, which weighs up to 25 kg (55 lb). Crayfish, close relatives of the lobster, live in freshwater and tend to be smaller.

Environments

Lobsters prefer an environment featuring many nooks and crannies. Their ideal hiding place is a sandy burrow under a rock.

Lobster backing into its burrow.

Large antennae sense food and danger.

Second pair of legs has claws.

When threatened, the lobster's large pincers open.

Defence

Lobsters can evade capture by discarding a limb. There is a special "breaking plane" near the base of the leg that, when twisted, causes the leg to snap off. The wound soon heals and a new limb starts growing immediately.

Small antennae *Eyes*

Common lobster adopting a defensive pose

Lobster march

In an extraordinary event known as the lobster march, hundreds of lobsters gather and walk one after the other for more than 100 km (60 miles) across the seabed. It is possible that they are looking for a suitable area to settle, with an adequate supply of food. The lobsters make sounds during their migration and it is thought that these are noises of communication that help co-ordinate the journey. This event has not been seen in any of the other larger crustacean groups.

Spiny lobsters

Water fleas

Water fleas, a group that includes brine and fairy shrimp, all breathe through leaf-shaped gills on their feet. Apart from brine shrimp (which live in saline pools), water fleas inhabit freshwater. Fairy shrimp live in temporary puddles. When these dry up, their eggs become airborne until they fall into another pool.

Daphnia water flea

Cleaner-shrimps

Brightly coloured and easily recognizable cleaner-shrimps remove external scale and gill parasites from passing fish, such as the goby – and even remove unswallowed food particles from within the fish's mouth. Both animals benefit from this association, which is known as "cleaner symbiosis". Other symbiotic relationships exist between shrimps and sponges, sea anemones, and corals.

Cleaner-shrimp

Shrimps

The world's seas are full of scavenging shrimps and prawns. They look similar but prawns have a pointed rostrum (a saw-like structure at the front of the body) and two pairs of pincers, while shrimps have only one pair. Krill, small shrimp-like animals that live in the Antarctic seas, form the main food of whales.

Growth of shrimps

Most crustaceans, including shrimps, are unable to increase in size because their exoskeleton (shell) is inflexible. Therefore, they moult their shells at regular intervals. The new soft exposed skin underneath hardens quickly to form another, larger shell.

Shrimps have flatter bodies than prawns.

Strawberry shrimp

Mussel shrimp

The tiny mussel or seed shrimp (so-called because its carapace is made up of two shells, like that of a mussel) produces the largest sperms in the animal kingdom. The 0.3-mm (0.01-in) long male of one species produces sperms 20 times its own length.

Copepods

These tiny creatures are an important part of plankton, which provides most of the world's fish with food. One species, *Calanus finmarchicus,* forms the staple diet of open-sea fishes, such as herring, sprat, and mackerel. Others, however, are parasitic and live in or on worms, molluscs, other crustaceans, fish, and whales.

Long fringed tentacles

Legs are extended for food gathering.

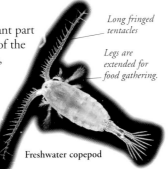

Freshwater copepod

Gribble

Able to digest wood, the gribble bores into the submerged wooden supports of jetties, wharfs, bridges, and pilings. It can turn these structures into a pulpy mass, causing them to collapse.

Segmented shell

SPINY SPIDER CRAB

SCIENTIFIC NAME	*Machrocheira kaempferi*
SUBCLASS	Malacostraca
ORDER	Decapoda
DISTRIBUTION	Seas around Japan
HABITAT	On the seabed
DIET	Scavenges anything edible from the seabed – an omnivore, it eats meat and plant matter
SIZE	Span claw-to-claw 3.6 m (11 ft)
LIFESPAN	Unknown, but lobsters, a relative, have lived up to 70 years in captivity

 FIND OUT MORE ARTHROPODS · CAVE WILDLIFE · CORAL REEFS · OCEAN LIFE · OCEANS AND SEAS · SEASHORE WILDLIFE

241

CRAFTS

BASKETMAKERS, WOODCARVERS, and stone masons are craftspeople; they handmake objects that are both useful and attractive. Unlike other art forms, crafts are concerned with function as well as beauty: they are made to be used. Before the Industrial Revolution, craftspeople made the furniture for the home and tools for the workplace. Today these items are mass-produced in factories, so hand-crafted objects are valued for their individuality, and because they often come from a tradition that is centuries old.

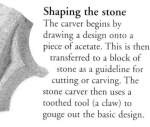
Goggles for protection

Stone carver at work

Carver taps chisel gently to cut stone to pattern.

Plaster-of-Paris holds stonework steady

Carpet to protect edges of stone

Banker, or workbench

Early craftspeople

Medieval craftspeople made their living from being skilled in one particular craft, such as coopering (barrel making), dyeing cloth, leather work, or goldsmithing. Each craft had its own guild, which was an association of the workers. The guilds fixed prices and standards of work, and supported members who fell on hard times.

Judging a masterpiece

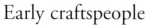
Dyers

Apprentices
Boys aged between 10 and 15, who wanted to learn a trade, would pay to start work as an apprentice to a craftsman. They spent between four and seven years learning every aspect of their craft from a master.

Masterpieces
At the end of his term as apprentice, each boy was required to produce an object that showed he had learned his craft. It was called a masterpiece, because it was judged by a master craftsman.

Mallet
Hammer-head chisel

Mallet-head chisels

Craft workshop

Many craftspeople have a workshop where they keep tools and materials. People who produce crafts objects for a living often sell goods from their workshop, so they can work when they are not helping customers.

Stonework
The craft of cutting and shaping stone for building is centuries old. Medieval masons prepared the stone to build churches, dams, and bridges; stone carvers, also known as banker masons, prepared ornamental finishes.

Stone, trimmed (cut) into a small block

Marked out design

Shaping the stone
The carver begins by drawing a design onto a piece of acetate. This is then transferred to a block of stone as a guideline for cutting or carving. The stone carver then uses a toothed tool (a claw) to gouge out the basic design.

Finished article
A variety of chisels and carving gouges further define the shape of the carving, removing the worst of the marks left by the claw in the process. Finally, a double-ended file, called a riffler, is used to smooth out the marks left by the chisels. It takes years to master ornamental carving.

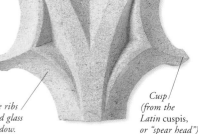

Cusp (from the Latin cuspis, or "spear head")

This piece links the ribs that support stained glass in a cathedral window.

Types of crafts

Almost any material can be used in craft, from wood, stone, and metal, to beads, reeds, and shells. A craftsperson may sell work to earn a living, but craft is also a popular leisure activity.

Traditional weaving technique

Finished baskets

Basketwork
From prehistoric times, basketmakers worldwide have woven materials, such as leaves, twigs, grass, and bark, to make unbreakable containers, to build boats and houses, and to make shoes and hats. Machines cannot yet match the fine technique displayed in a hand-woven basket.

Basketmaker, Spain

Silk thread used for wings

Gold thread used for outline

Embroidery
Embroidery, where designs are stitched onto fabric, decorates everyday clothing and furnishings, as well as garments for festive occasions. The embroiderer either draws the design onto the fabric before stitching into the cloth, or develops it while she or he is working on the embroidery.

Butterfly detail, embroidered sleeve, China

African beadwork

Beadwork
Beads, made from materials such as wood, bone, shell, seeds, plastic, and glass, have been used to decorate material for centuries. The geometrical designs of Native North American beadworkers feature on clothing, bags, and shoes. African beadwork decorates vessels, festive garments, and jewellery.

Papier-mâché items, such as this bowl, can be simple to make.

Papier-mâché
Some people take up a craft as a hobby. One popular example is papier-mâché. Named after the French word meaning "chewed paper", it involves building up layers of paper and paste over a mould. When the paste dries, the paper is firm and can be painted and varnished.

FIND OUT MORE

| INDUSTRIAL REVOLUTION | MEDIEVAL EUROPE | POTTERY AND CERAMICS | UNIONS, TRADE | TEXTILES AND WEAVING |

Crafts
Basketwork

Shopping basket, rope detail decoration, England

Sewing basket, bamboo handles, Canada

Basket, traditional design, Thailand

Sisal basket, Kenya

Willow potato basket, wire base, France

Stone and woodcarving

Mason's tools

Decorated vault, Italy

Roof decoration, carved fruit and leaves, Britain

Ballflowers decoration, Britain

Flowing tracery, medieval Britain

Wall ornament, medieval Britain

Carved panel, 16th-century Britain

Church roof detail, medieval Britain

Embroidery and beadwork

Tobacco pouch, North America

Beaded gourd, Africa

Necklace, South Africa

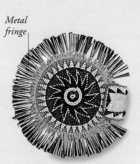

Metal fringe

Tobacco pouch, North America

Zulu beadwork, Africa

Flask, made from gourd fruit, Africa

Charm to ward off evil

Amulet, North America

Cradleboard, North America

Imported glass beads

Traditional design

Child's coat, North America

Colourful embroidery

Masquerade costume, Africa

Deerskin moccasin, North America

Colourful geometric pattern

Embroidered sandals, North Africa

CRIME AND PUNISHMENT

A CRIME IS A FORBIDDEN ACT, punished by law because it may harm a society or injure its members. The type of act that is considered a crime varies from culture to culture, changing as societies and attitudes develop. For example, in some parts of the Middle East, it is a crime to drink alcohol, but a man may have more than one wife. In the United States, alcohol is not illegal, but having more than one wife is against the law.

Bronze cat from ancient Egypt, dedicated to the cat goddess Bastet.

Killing cats
The ancient Egyptians honoured cats as sacred animals, depicting them in paintings and sculptures. As a result, killing a cat was seen as a serious crime. The punishment was usually instant execution.

Types of crimes
Some acts, such as murder and theft, have been crimes in all civilized societies for thousands of years, and are known as *malum in se* (the Latin phrase for "bad in themselves"). Other crimes, such as driving an unregistered or untaxed car, are known as *malum prohibitum* (bad because the law says so).

Murder

Crime against the person
When one person intentionally kills another, this is known as murder. It is a crime against the person, and does not respect the individual's right to live his or her life without fear of attack and violence. Assault, rape, and kidnapping are other such crimes. Killing someone in self-defence (to protect your own life), or killing an enemy of one's country in times of war, is not considered to be murder.

Crime against property
Laws exist to protect people's right to own property. It is a criminal act to take or damage the property of another against the owner's wishes. Examples of such crimes include theft, forgery, arson, and vandalism.

Silverware   Antiques   Jewellery   Electrical goods   Stolen property

Organized crime
Organized crime consists of large-scale activities by groups of gangsters, sometimes known as the underworld. They make much of their money by providing illegal goods, including drugs, and services, such as gambling or prostitution.

Al Capone

Crime syndicates
Secret criminal organizations exist across the world, such as the Mafia, which first originated centuries ago in Sicily. During the 1920s a powerful crime syndicate grew up in Chicago, USA, run by brutal gangsters, such as the notorious Al Capone (1899–1947).

Prison
Someone who commits a crime may be sent to prison for a length of time which reflects the seriousness of the offence. Prison is mainly a punishment, but it also offers criminals a chance to reform. It acts to deter other people from crime and keeps dangerous criminals away from the public.

High-security cell in a British prison

Barred window   *Window for keeping a watch on prisoners*

Prisoners can send only one letter a week.
Simply furnished
Inmates can bring only a few personal belongings to prison.

Men and women go to separate prisons. As inmates, they may spend as much as 23 hours a day locked in their cells, which they usually share with one or two others. They must wear prison uniforms.

Alcatraz
A maximum-security prison was built on the island of Alcatraz in San Francisco Bay, USA. It was in use from 1933 to 1963; in that time, not one prisoner escaped alive. Of the 23 that tried, five were shot dead, six drowned, and 12 were recaptured.

High-security cell
Criminals convicted of serious crimes are sent to high-security prisons. Inmates are only allowed to leave their cells to eat, work, or for study programmes. People who commit lesser crimes may be sent to open prisons, where they have more freedom.

Punishment
Theories about punishment have developed since the 18th century when even minor offences were harshly punished to deter others from committing crime. Around the world, law-breakers are punished in various ways: in the UK, for instance, criminals are usually fined, or sent to prison.

Cat-o'-nine tails whip
Each strand is knotted

Corporal punishment
In some countries, people are whipped for certain minor crimes. This is corporal punishment. It was once common, and beatings took place in public as a warning to deter others from crime.

Capital punishment
The ultimate penalty for a crime is death, or capital punishment. Hanging, gassing, and the electric chair are some of the methods that have been used. Many people now argue that mistakes can be made and that capital punishment is morally wrong. In the USA, this issue is hotly debated; many other Western nations have abolished the death penalty.

Electric chair

FIND OUT MORE   EGYPT, ANCIENT   HUMAN RIGHTS   LAW   POLICE   SOCIETIES, HUMAN

C

CROCODILES

SUBMERGED BELOW water, crocodiles lie in wait ready to attack almost any animal that strays too close. Crocodiles belong to the group of reptiles, called the crocodilians, which has remained largely unchanged for more than 140 million years. This group contains crocodiles, alligators, caimans, and gharials which are all very similar apart from small differences, such as snout shape and arrangement of teeth. All are effective freshwater predators and are well adapted to a semi-aquatic way of life.

Eyes

A crocodile's eyes protrude above its snout providing 25° overlapping vision to judge distance. A third eyelid slides across from the side to allow underwater vision. Special pupils allow more light to reach the retina in low light levels and protect the retina from bright light. The retina itself has a layer of night-seeing cells that glow red in torchlight.

Third eyelid moves across from side.

Transparent eyelid converts eye for underwater vision.

Crocodiles

Crocodiles are tropical reptiles found in freshwater habitats around the world. There are 14 species ranging from the 2 m (7 ft) long dwarf crocodiles of western Africa to the huge man-eating 7.5 m (25 ft) long Indo-Pacific crocodiles. The American, Nile, and Indo-Pacific crocodiles can live equally as well in the sea as in freshwater. The Cuban and Siamese crocodiles are endangered due to habitat destruction and hunting.

Nostrils and eyes are high on head so crocodile can breathe and see when almost submerged in water.

Huge cone-shaped teeth line the long jaw.

Nile crocodile

Snout shape

Alligators and caimans have broad, rounded snouts, while gharials have very narrow snouts. Crocodiles have broad or narrow snouts. They also have an externally visible fourth tooth. This distinguishes them from alligators in which this tooth is concealed.

Caiman

Alligator

Crocodile

Gharial

Breeding

Loud bellowing preceeds mating under water. One month later females lay up to 90 leathery-shelled eggs that they incubate for 2–3 months in nests. Some species lay eggs in several locations to avoid total loss by flooding or predation. High temperatures during incubation result in more males than females. A hatchling calls its mother with squeaks and breaks out of the eggshell by "pipping" with an egg tooth on the tip of its snout.

Mother carries young to a crèche where she will guard them until they become independent.

Baby crocodile pushing itself out of its egg.

Nile crocodile with eggs

Movement

On land crocodiles may slide along on their bellies, scooting with their feet. Sometimes they adopt the "high walk" and raise their bodies fully off the ground. The "gallop" is when crocodiles run with their tails in the air, usually when being chased. The "tail walk" is used to snatch prey from branches above the water. In water, crocodiles swim using powerful sweeps of their tails.

High walking

Dwarf crocodile

Tail walking involves pushing the body up using the tail.

Feeding

After lying hidden for hours, a crocodile suddenly seizes prey from riverbanks and drags it below water until it drowns. Crocodiles cannot chew, so prey is dismembered by shaking and spinning. The whole animal is eaten. Strong juices and pebbles in the stomach help break down the food.

Topi

The jaws close with tremendous force, splintering bone and crushing tissue.

Alligators

There are two true alligators. The American alligator from south-east United States is up to 5.5 m (18 ft) long. It is the only crocodilian that is not endangered. The Chinese alligator from the Yangtze River, eastern China, is smaller at up to 2 m (7 ft). Alligators are subtropical, and are more widely distributed than other crocodilians.

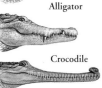

Regular-sized scales

American alligator

Thick muscular tail

Caimans

Caimans are South American alligators. There are six species ranging from the 1.5 m (5 ft) long dwarf caiman that lives in forest creeks to the 4.5 m (15 ft) long black caiman of larger rivers. The spectacled caiman has ridges around the eyes resembling spectacle frames.

Spectacled caiman

Stocky body

Gharials

There are two species of gharial, which have long narrow snouts. The Ganges gharial lives in India, Bangladesh, Pakistan, Nepal, and Burma. It reaches 7 m (23 ft) in length. Some males have a bulbous swelling on the end of their snout. The other species, the tomistoma, lives in Indonesia and Malaysia. It reaches a length of 4.7 m (15.5 ft).

Widely spaced teeth line the forcep-like jaw

Ganges gharial

NILE CROCODILE

SCIENTIFIC NAME *Crocodylus niloticus*

ORDER Crocodylia

FAMILY Crocodylidae

DISTRIBUTION Africa south of the Sahara, excluding the Kalahari; Madagascar. Now largely exterminated from the River Nile in Egypt

HABITAT River systems, lakes, marshes, estuaries, and mangrove habitats. Also able to swim out to sea

DIET Fish, frogs, reptiles, wading birds, and mammals up to the size of water buffalo. Humans are also sometimes victims

SIZE Length: 6 m (20 ft)

LIFESPAN 25–100 years

FIND OUT MORE

CONSERVATION   EGGS   LAKE AND RIVER WILDLIFE   MARSH AND SWAMP WILDLIFE   REPTILES   RIVERS

CROWS

CROWS AND THEIR RELATIVES are intelligent and noisy birds that are sometimes found in flocks. They are most widespread in the northern hemisphere and are often common in woods and farmland. Some species can be found in gardens and backyards. Birds in the crow family are not specialized for one particular way of life and this allows them to make the most of different kinds of food. Many of them will eat almost any kind of food that they come across, including young birds.

The crow family

There are about 113 species in the crow family. These include ravens, jays, magpies, rooks, and jackdaws. Most species are almost jet black, but many jays and magpies are brightly coloured. Members of the crow family are classified as songbirds, but they communicate mainly by harsh chattering calls or croaks.

Carrion crow
This widespread crow lives throughout Europe and much of Asia. Like most crows, it is a great opportunist, and often feeds on the remains of dead animals that have been run over on roads.

Glossy black plumage

Broad wings used for soaring high.

Powerful beak can tear open the bodies of dead animals.

Powerful legs covered with large scales.

Blue jay
Measuring 28 cm (11 in) long, this brightly coloured bird is one of the smallest species in the crow family. It lives in eastern North America.

Common raven
Ravens are the largest members of the crow family. They live in remote places, such as mountains and rocky coasts, and have a deep, croaking call.

Feeding

Crows have strong beaks, but compared to many birds they are not fussy about what they eat. They are fond of seeds, worms, and insects, and in spring they sometimes eat the eggs and nestlings of other birds. They are determined feeders. Farmers try to scare them off with scarecrows or shotguns; small birds have more difficulty keeping them away.

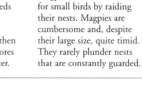

Seed eaters
Unlike most members of the crow family, some jays live mostly on the seeds of oaks, pines, and other trees. They collect seeds during the autumn, and then bury them. These seed stores provide food for the winter.

Nest robbers
Magpies make life difficult for small birds by raiding their nests. Magpies are cumbersome and, despite their large size, quite timid. They rarely plunder nests that are constantly guarded.

Carrion eaters
Ravens search for food by flying high over open ground, just like birds of prey. Instead of killing animals, they usually eat ones that are already dead.

Azure-winged magpie
This magpie lives in two different areas of the world: China and Japan, and Spain and Portugal. Some people think it was brought to Europe from Asia long ago. Others think it once lived all over Europe and Asia, but disappeared from many areas because of climate changes.

Long tail gives the magpie manoeuvrability in the air.

Jackdaw hierarchy
These small but boisterous crows come from Europe and western Asia. They live in groups in which there is a strict hierarchy. They are good at living near humans and often nest on buildings.

Rooks
These birds build their nests at the top of high trees, and they gather together as the sun begins to set. These nesting sites are called rookeries. The same name is used to describe breeding groups of many other animals, from penguins to seals.

Social groups

Ravens, jays, and magpies often live on their own or in pairs, but some members of the crow family spend their lives in large flocks. This way of living makes it easier for the birds to defend themselves against predators, and also increases their chances of finding food.

COMMON RAVEN

SCIENTIFIC NAME	*Corvus corax*
ORDER	Passeriformes
FAMILY	Corvidae
DISTRIBUTION	North America, Europe, northern and central Asia
HABITAT	Mountains, moorland, and rocky coasts
DIET	Seeds, small animals, and animal remains
SIZE	Length: 64 cm (25 in)

FIND OUT MORE   ANIMAL BEHAVIOUR   BIRDS   BIRDS OF PREY   FLIGHT, ANIMAL   PENGUINS   SEALS   SONGBIRDS

CRUSADES

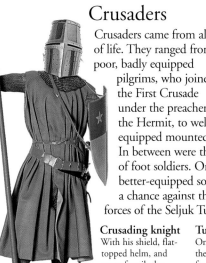

JERUSALEM HAD LONG been a place of pilgrimage for Christians from Europe, but by the 11th century the area was ruled by devoutly Muslim Turks, and pilgrims were often attacked. In 1095, Pope Urban II called for a crusade, or Holy War, to conquer Jerusalem for the Christians – the First Crusade. Over the next two centuries, a pattern emerged: Christians attacked and captured cities such as Jerusalem and Damascus, and the Muslims recaptured each one, until finally the crusaders lost all their territory and retreated from the Holy Land (Palestine) for the last time.

Crusaders

Crusaders came from all walks of life. They ranged from poor, badly equipped pilgrims, who joined the First Crusade under the preacher Peter the Hermit, to well-equipped mounted knights. In between were thousands of foot soldiers. Only the better-equipped soldiers stood a chance against the strong forces of the Seljuk Turks.

Crusading knight
With his shield, flat-topped helm, and coat of mail, the crusading knight was well protected against enemy swordsmen.

Turkish warrior
One dynasty of Turks, the Seljuks, were formidable defenders of Muslim lands, helped by expert marksmen.

Land and sea routes

The route from western Europe to Syria and Palestine was long and hazardous. Many travellers died from disease and hunger, and never saw the Holy Land. Sea travellers relied on trading cities, such as Venice and Genoa, to provide ships. The sea route was also far from safe – the Holy Roman Emperor Frederick I drowned while leading the Third Crusade.

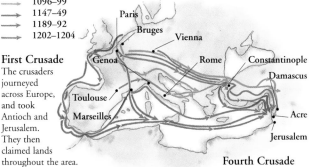

→ 1096–99
→ 1147–49
→ 1189–92
→ 1202–1204

Paris, Bruges, Vienna, Genoa, Rome, Constantinople, Damascus, Toulouse, Marseilles, Acre, Jerusalem

First Crusade
The crusaders journeyed across Europe, and took Antioch and Jerusalem. They then claimed lands throughout the area.

Second Crusade
After their earlier defeat, the united Muslims attacked Christians in the east. They captured Damascus, and routed the new French and German crusaders.

Third Crusade
In 1187, the great Saladin reconquered Jerusalem. Crusaders from England, France, and the Holy Roman Empire retaliated, but achieved only the capture of Acre.

Fourth Crusade
Sponsored by the pope, crusaders sailed to Constantinople, looted the city, and installed Baldwin of Flanders as emperor. They did not carry on to the Holy Land.

Children's Crusade
In 1212, thousands of children marched from the Rhineland to the Mediterranean. Most died of hunger or disease, and were caught and sold as slaves.

Military orders

The military orders were founded during the 12th century. They were monks who took religious vows but, unlike other monks, also bore arms and fought against Muslims. They included the Knights of St John, the Templars, and the Teutonic Knights (a German order).

Knights of St John
The Knights of St John, or the Hospitallers, used their medical skills to care for wounded crusaders and sick pilgrims. They eventually settled on Malta, where they continued to fight for the Christian cause.

The spread of knowledge

The crusades increased contact between East and West, and helped take Islamic science and technology to Europe. Western medicine and architecture improved, although this may also have been due to contact with Muslims living in Spain.

Windmills
Wind power was used in the eastern Mediterranean to provide power to grind corn, and crusaders may have taken the idea back to Europe with them. The first European windmills appeared in France in 1180.

Templars
Originally a group of knights who protected Christian pilgrims, these men were given a base in the Holy Land in 1118. They became a religious order and took their name from their base near the Temple of Jerusalem.

Islamic medicine
Islamic medicine was well developed, and the writings of the Arabian physician Avicenna, or Ibn Sina (980–1037), were influential. Herbs were used as medicines. Myrrh was used for various infections, while balm of Gilead was used for chest and throat diseases.

Balm of Gilead

Myrrh

Saladin
The brave Salah-ed-din (1138–1193) ruled Syria and part of northern Africa. He expelled the crusaders from Jerusalem in 1187, and ruled most of Palestine (modern Israel) from then on.

Richard I
King Richard I of England (the Lionheart) spent most of his reign (1187–1199) abroad. Despite victories on the Third Crusade, he never captured Jerusalem. After the Crusades, he was put in prison, ransomed, and spent his last years in France.

Timeline

1096–99
First Crusade:
The victorious armies establish first bases in the Holy Land.

1147–49 Second Crusade:
Muslims retake Damascus; crusaders fail to retrieve it.

1189–92 Third Crusade:
Christians take Acre, but Muslims keep Jerusalem.

1202–1204 Fourth Crusade: armies conquer Egypt, and loot Constantinople.

1218–21 Fifth Crusade: Crusaders capture land in Egypt, but fail to keep it.

1228–29 Muslims and Christians negotiate a truce which lasts 10 years.

1248–70 Seventh and Eighth Crusades.

1291 Muslims recapture the city of Acre, which is the last Christian stronghold in the Holy Land.

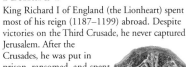

FIND OUT MORE

BYZANTINE EMPIRE | HOLY LAND, HISTORY OF | KNIGHTS AND HERALDRY | MEDICINE, HISTORY OF | MEDIEVAL EUROPE

C

247

CRYSTALS AND GEMS

THE WORLD AROUND US is made of tiny crystals. Much of the Earth's surface is made of rocks that contain minerals which are, in turn, formed from crystalline particles. A crystal is a solid substance that has grown in a regular, geometric form, with a smooth, plane surface, or face, and straight edges. Crystals have many different properties, and are used in industry, and for decoration. Most gemstones are crystals prized for their beauty; they are usually cut and polished to enhance their appearance.

Limescale crystals that form in a kettle

Crystal structure
Crystals are usually made from a single mineral. They are built up from a regular lattice, or framework, of atoms. Each atom has its own special position and is tied to others by bonding forces. The atoms of each mineral always bond together in the same way to form crystals of that mineral.

Cecil Rhodes
Known as the "King of Diamonds", British imperialist and businessman Cecil Rhodes (1853–1902) made his fortune after staking a claim in a diamond mine in Africa in 1871. By 1888 he had secured a virtual monopoly of the African diamond industry.

Cartoon of Rhodes as "King of Diamonds"

Crystal systems
Well-formed crystals have regular, symmetrical shapes. The geometrical shapes in which minerals crystallize are grouped into seven crystal systems. Within each of these systems many different forms are possible, but all the forms can be related to the symmetry of that system.

Cubic system contains cube-shaped crystals, and also includes 8- and 12-sided crystals.

Hexagonal and trigonal are two systems with similar symmetry.

Tetragonal systems are generally more elongated than the cube.

Triclinic is one of the least symmetrical of the crystal systems.

Orthorhombic system has prisms and flattened tabular forms as its most typical features.

Monoclinic has less symmetry than the cubic system.

Crystal habit
Crystals form as molten magma cools, or as a liquid evaporates from a solution containing a dissolved mineral. Crystals rarely form perfectly. The conditions under which crystals grow affect their shape. The general shape of crystals is called their habit.

Massive crystals grow in a mass in which individual crystals cannot be seen.

Prismatic crystals are prism-shaped.

Dendritic crystals have tree or plant shapes.

Acicular crystals have slender, fragile, needle-like masses.

Aggregates are groups of crystals. This is an aggregate of prismatic crystals.

Bladed crystals look like the blade of a knife.

Gems
Highly valued and used in jewellery, most gemstones are beautiful, rare, and durable inorganic crystals. A few gems are organic, such as amber, jet, and pearls. Others, called synthetics, are produced in laboratories. They have similar appearances and properties to natural gemstones, but are cheaper to buy.

Diamond in kimberlite

Diamonds
The world's hardest substance, diamonds are sought after not only for their unique lustre, but also for use in drill bits and glass cutters.

Geode
Many gemstones are found in geodes, round rock-hollows lined with crystals. These are formed from the bubbles of hot gas and mineral-rich fluids in magma. They are prized by collectors.

Amethyst crystals in geode

Gem cutting
Most rough crystals have to be cut and polished to remove surface imperfections and to reveal their true brilliance. Before this happens the lapidary, or cutter, studies the rough stone through a loupe (lens) to see if it is suitable for cutting.

Quartz
Quartz is "piezo-electric". This means that when an electric current passes through quartz, it resonates at such regular intervals that it can be used to keep time very accurately.

Quartz watch

1 The cutter identifies the natural grain and flaws, then marks where the diamond should be cut and ground.

2 The diamond is sawn in two to remove the top pyramid, then rounded by grinding it against another diamond.

3 The stone is mounted on a dop (stick) and several flat facets, or faces, are ground on a cast-iron wheel called a scaife.

4 Slanted side facets called bezels are ground between the table facet (the flat top) and the girdle (the rim).

5 The stone is turned over and faceted in the same way. It is then finished by a brillianteer who adds 40 small facets.

FIND OUT MORE | ATOMS AND MOLECULES | CLOTHES AND FASHION | ROCKS AND MINERALS | SOLIDS | TIME

Gems

Precious stones

Drop-shaped
morganite

Black
precious
opal

Sapphire

Brilliant cut
diamond

Pendeloque
emerald

Octagonal
aquamarine

Cushion
cut ruby

C

Morganite, which is coloured by manganese, is the pink form of beryl.

Opal is hardened silica gel. Precious opal is iridescent.

Sapphire is a precious form of corundum. It is usually blue.

Diamonds are made from carbon placed under extreme pressure.

Emerald is a green variety of beryl.

Aquamarines are a blue-green variety of beryl.

Ruby is the red, precious form of corundum.

Semi-precious stones

Crystallization progresses
towards centre
of cavity

Quartz crystals
are built-up
in layers.

Smoky quartz crystals joined together in a twisted group.

Amazonstone is a blue-green type of microline.

Amethyst is a purple form of quartz.

Rose quartz is best used for carvings and making into beads.

Calcite is the main component of limestone and marble.

Chalcedony is a massive variety of quartz made from tiny fibres, or grains, of silicon dioxide.

Rose quartz is usually found in great lumps – single crystals are very rare.

Turquoise is usually
intense blue
or green.

Some people believe crystals
have healing
properties.

Labradorite can be multi-coloured and has a sheen.

Rhodochrosite gets its colour from manganese.

Turquoise is sought after for its amazing colours.

Rock crystal is an almost colourless form of quartz.

Lapis lazuli contains several different minerals.

Carnelian is a red variety of chalcedony.

Organic gems

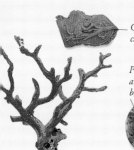
Coral
carving

Polished
amber
bead

Ivory
relief

Shell pill box

Cut and
polished jet

Jet
containing
fossils

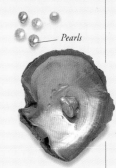
Pearls

Coral is the calcium carbonate skeleton of colony-living sea creatures. It is usually pink.

Amber is the fossilized resin, or sap, of trees. It is usually translucent.

Ivory comes from the teeth and tusks of mammals. The best ivory comes from the African elephant.

Mother-of-pearl lining of shells is prized for its iridescence.

Jet is a fine-grained black stone formed from very hard coal.

Pearls are tiny pellets of calcium carbonate that form inside some shellfish.

CURIE, MARIE

THE PHYSICIST MARIE CURIE was a pioneer in the science of radioactivity – the study of powerful rays emitted by certain rare materials. Her work changed physics and chemistry and formed a basis for later research in nuclear physics. She discovered two previously unknown elements and also founded an important research institute. In 1903, she shared the Nobel prize for physics with her husband Pierre, with whom she worked, and French scientist Henri Becquerel. In 1911, she was awarded the Nobel prize for chemistry. She died after suffering for years from an illness caused by exposure to radiation.

Early life
Marie Curie was born in Warsaw, Poland. After finishing school, she worked as a governess to save up money to go to university in Paris. In 1891, she left to study at the Sorbonne. She was top of her year there, in spite of being so hungry sometimes that she fainted during classes.

Poland
At the time that Marie was born, Poland was under the rule of neighbouring Russia, and the best jobs and education went to Russians. After she had finished her schooling, Marie began to go to secret meetings of the "Floating University", a group of Polish people who met to read books that the Russians banned in case they might stir up rebellious ideas.

Radioactivity

In 1895, the German physicist Wilhelm Röntgen discovered invisible "penetrating rays", which he called X-rays, coming from an electric tube in one of his experiments. The following year Becquerel discovered similar rays coming from the metal uranium. The Curies devoted the rest of their lives to studying these rays.

Equipment
For much of her life, Marie Curie worked under difficult conditions. Her laboratory was in an unheated shed and much equipment was home-made. Pierre helped her design and build some of her equipment, including a device called an electrometer, which measured the strength of radiation coming from uranium compounds.

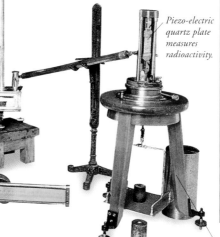

Electrometer measures electric current.

Piezo-electric quartz plate measures radioactivity.

Ionization chamber contains radioactive substance.

Tripod stand

Isolating radiation
The Curies noticed that pitchblende, the ore from which uranium is extracted, was many times more radioactive than uranium itself. They realized that pitchblende must contain other radioactive substances, so they processed tonnes of pitchblende to extract these other radioactive elements.

Pierre Curie
Born in Paris and educated by his father, Pierre Curie (1859–1906) began work as a laboratory assistant in Paris. He made several important discoveries before he met Marie in 1894. After they married he spent the rest of his life working with her. He made some of her equipment and worked beside her in the laboratory. He was killed in a street accident in 1906.

Pitchblende
The Curies spent about 12 years separating out the radioactive elements in pitchblende. They found there were two substances. One they named polonium, after Marie's home country, and the other they called radium.

X-rays
When World War I (1914–18) broke out, Marie Curie raised funds to set up mobile X-ray units to be used on the battle front. She supervised the conversion of around 200 vans for this purpose. These became known as "Little Curies".

Radium Institute

In 1912, the Sorbonne and the Pasteur Institute decided to found a Radium Institute in Paris, devoted to research into radiation and the medical uses of radioactivity. Marie became a director of the Institute and spent much of her time supporting scientists in their work and raising money for research.

The Joliots
Marie Curie's daughter, Irène, was also a scientist. She and her husband, Frédéric Joliot, worked together, much like Marie and Pierre. They discovered how to make non-radioactive substances radioactive, by bombarding them with radioactive rays. In 1935 they were awarded the Nobel prize for chemistry.

MARIE CURIE

1867	Born Manya Sklodowska in Warsaw, Poland
1891	Goes to the Sorbonne, Paris; changes first name to Marie
1895	Marries Pierre Curie
1898	Discovers the elements polonium and radium
1903	Awarded Nobel prize for physics
1910	After 12 years of work on pitchblende, she produces pure radium for the first time
1911	Awarded Nobel prize for chemistry
1918	Radium Institute opens after delay owing to World War I; Marie becomes research director
1934	Dies in France

FIND OUT MORE   CHEMISTRY   ELEMENTS   MEDICINE, HISTORY OF   PASTEUR, LOUIS   RADIOACTIVITY   WORLD WAR I   X RAYS AND THE ELECTROMAGNETIC SPECTRUM

CYCLING

CYCLE SPORTS are held on tracks, roads, and cross-country circuits. Races range from 1,000-m (1,094-yd) sprints on an indoor track to multi-stage events over hundreds of kilometres that last a week or more. Special courses are prepared for off-road racing, which includes cyclocross and mountain-bike racing. Racers ride specialized bikes for the different races. Some need to be be as light as possible; others need to be strong, and the top riders have bicycles made for them to their own specifications.

Track racing

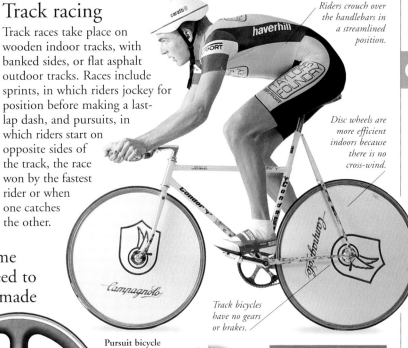

Track races take place on wooden indoor tracks, with banked sides, or flat asphalt outdoor tracks. Races include sprints, in which riders jockey for position before making a last-lap dash, and pursuits, in which riders start on opposite sides of the track, the race won by the fastest rider or when one catches the other.

Riders crouch over the handlebars in a streamlined position.

Disc wheels are more efficient indoors because there is no cross-wind.

Track bicycles have no gears or brakes.

Pursuit bicycle

Saddle is set high for more pedalling power.

Criterium bicycle

Road racing

Races take place on courses set along ordinary roads. There are single-stage races and multi-stage events such as the Tour de France, in which the total time determines placings. In individual and team time-trials on the road, the riders start at intervals. Criterium races are 40–100 km (25–62 miles) long. They take place over short courses with many laps, along city streets and through parks.

Types of wheel
The design and material of wheels are constantly being improved to suit particular uses. Weight and shape are the important factors. Using spokes saves weight, but increases drag.

Composite wheel

Spoked wheel

Team pursuit
In team pursuit, riders take turns to lead their group of four. The time of the third rider in each team determines the result. One rider usually makes an all-out effort near the finish before trailing off.

British cyclist Chris Boardman on his revolutionary Lotus bike

Time-trials
In time-trials, competitors ride as fast as possible, on their own, over a set distance or for a fixed time. Time-trials are some of the hardest races and require continuous effort.

Tour de France
The world's leading road race is the Tour de France which lasts about three weeks. The overall leader on total time wears the famous yellow jersey for the next stage.

Off-road racing

Bicycles for off-road races have chunky tyres for the rough terrain. Cyclocross is the original form of cross-country cycling, with world championships since 1950. Mountain biking is now the most popular form, with world championships since 1990 and Olympic recognition in 1996.

Cyclocross
In cyclocross, races take place over laps of a cross-country course. Riders often find it quicker to dismount and carry their bikes over obstacles such as fences, gates, and ditches, and may have to run up steep hills or wade through water with them.

For log hopping, the rider must learn to shift her weight.

Mountain biking
Mountain bikes are built to survive rough handling. Most have steel-alloy frames, straight handlebars, and flat knobbly tyres. Courses for races have many climbs and descents, with routes over fields and gravel pits.

Rider brings her weight over the front wheel.

Weight is kept over the front wheel until the hop has been completed.

Weight over the rear wheel

Miguel Indurain

Spanish road racer Miguel Indurain (b. 1964) became the first cyclist to win the Tour de France in five successive years (1991–95), equalling the record number of wins. In 1996, he took first place in the Olympic road time trial.

FIND OUT MORE

BICYCLES AND MOTORCYCLES   FRANCE   HEALTH AND FITNESS   MOTOR SPORTS   OLYMPIC GAMES   SPORT

DAMS

IN MANY AREAS of the world, people rely on dams for their water and electricity supplies. A dam is a barrier that holds back water. The dam itself and the surrounding hills form a bowl in which water collects to form an artificial lake called a reservoir. Most dams are built across a river valley to catch the river's flow, but some dams create reservoirs into which water is pumped for storage. How strong a dam needs to be depends on the depth of the water in the reservoir. Some dams are enormous: the Grand Coulee Dam in the USA weighs nearly 10 million tonnes.

Water from reservoir enters intake towers.

Arched concrete wall

Sides of river valley

Reservoir

Roadway across top of dam

Water flows through pipes in dam to hydroelectric power station.

Model of an arch dam

Types of dam

There are three main types of dam: arch dams, gravity dams, and buttress dams. The type of dam that engineers decide to build depends on the geography of the location. Factors affecting the decision include the width and depth of the river valley and the type of rock around the site.

Buttress dam
A buttress dam is a huge concrete wall that leans into a reservoir of water. The wall is made up of concrete slabs that are supported on the downstream side of the dam by concrete projections known as buttresses.

Arch dam
An arch dam is built across the entrance to a narrow valley, so that the height of the dam is greater than its width. The dam's curved shape holds back water because it transfers the push of the water to the rock of the valley sides.

Gravity dam
A gravity dam is a huge embankment of earth or rock. Leakage is prevented by a waterproof clay core or a concrete skin on the upstream side of the dam. The dam's immense weight prevents the water from pushing it over.

Anatomy of a dam

This model shows an arch dam that creates a reservoir for supplying water and electricity to nearby towns and cities. The dam is made of thin concrete strengthened by thousands of steel bars. Water flowing through pipes in the dam drives electricity generators in the hydroelectric power station at the foot of the dam.

Spillway lets excess water flow into river, so that dam does not overflow.

Flood control

On large rivers, dams help prevent flooding by holding back surges of flood water and releasing them downstream slowly. A flood barrier is a movable dam built across a tidal river. The barrier has gates that are usually open to allow the river to flow freely, but which can be closed when dangerously high tides threaten to surge upstream.

Hydraulic rockers turn the gate arm.

Circular gate arm opens and closes gate.

Model of Thames Flood Barrier, UK

Steel-plated roof

Water level

Environmental effects

A river dam and the reservoir it forms can harm the environment. Huge areas of countryside are drowned by the reservoir, and the dam disrupts the river's natural flow, affecting wildlife and irrigation downstream. A dam also prevents fish from moving freely up and down the river.

Tidal barrage

A barrage is a dam across a river estuary that generates hydroelectric power. The dam holds back the tide as it ebbs and flows. The water is forced through pipes inside the barrage, where it drives electricity generators.

La Rance barrage, France

Weir

A weir is a low river dam that controls the flow of water by creating a stretch of deeper water upstream. Deep water makes the river navigable for boats.

Weir in Middlesex, England

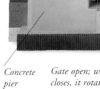

Concrete pier

Gate open; when gate closes, it rotates into its vertical position, blocking the flow of water.

Barrier gate is a hollow semi-circle plated with high-strength steel.

Steel piles sunk into riverbed.

FIND OUT MORE — BUILDING AND CONSTRUCTION • ELECTRICITY • ENERGY • FARMING • LAKES • RAIN • ROADS • OCEANS AND SEAS • RIVERS

252

DANCE

WHEN PEOPLE MOVE in time to music they are dancing. People have a natural urge to move in time to rhythms. Children jump up and down when they are excited; babies move naturally to rhythms they hear or feel. In dancing, these natural movements are organized into rhythmic and visual patterns. Different dances have developed all over the world, and are performed for different reasons. Dancing can be both an art form and recreation. It can express an emotion, tell a story, or set a mood.

Maasai dancers
The Maasai of East Africa move in straight lines as they dance, and include high jumps in their routines. As happens in all African dance, they are accompanied by rhythmic, exhilarating drumbeats.

African dance

Dancing is an essential part of life to many Africans, and important events, such as births, deaths, and initiation to adulthood, are all observed by dancing. African dances can last for many hours. The dances for men are usually very energetic, and include a lot of stamping and leaping. Women tend to do more gentle dances, clapping and swaying to the music or rhythm.

Origins

Dancing is one of the oldest art forms. The first dances may have evolved from spontaneous stamping steps. These steps were later given rhythms and shapes and accompanied by grunts and shouts.

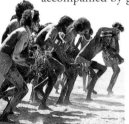

Australian Aboriginals performing the corroboree

Ceremonial dance
Early people found that rhythmic movements had a strong effect on the mind, and felt that dancing must have magical powers. They began to dance to ward off evil spirits, heal people, and ensure good crops.

Dance as entertainment
The ancient Egyptians were the first people known to use dancing simply as a form of entertainment. Professional dancing girls entertained the pharaoh and his guests at banquets, performing dances that included running, high kicks, and sensual hip movements.

Ancient Egyptian dancing girls

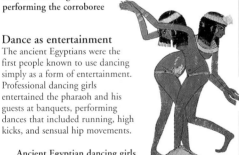

Chorus depicted on a Greek vase

Dance as theatre
The ancient Greeks made dance the basis of all their theatre. The chorus in a Greek play was a group of actors who danced and sang a commentary on the action.

Asian dancing

The main influence on dance styles in Asia comes from India. Many Asian dances make use of stylized hand movements, particularly those from countries such as India, Sri Lanka, Burma, Thailand, and Cambodia.

Head-dress

Bent-back fingers

Indian dances
Indian classical dancers mime out stories from Indian mythology, and include sequences of more abstract dance movements.

There are six styles of Indian classical dance.

Dragon
The mythical dragon is a very important symbol in Chinese culture. Dragon dances are performed to celebrate festivals such as the Chinese New Year.

Dancers wear a dragon costume.

Southeast Asian dances
Classical dance in Southeast Asia typically includes slow, controlled movements, with many graceful hand and arm gestures. Dance-dramas, performed by highly trained dancers, are particularly popular in Indonesia and Thailand. Throughout the region there is a wide variety of traditional folk dances.

Royal Thai classical dancer

European folk dancing

Every European country has its folk dances, which are now essentially social. Some of them have been taken to other countries by settlers. The dances are often performed in traditional costumes, and many of them involve people forming simple patterns, such as lines and circles.

Flamenco
Perhaps the most famous of all Spanish dances is the flamenco. This dance is a mixture of both the Spanish and Arab cultures. The men use complicated footwork, while the women weave patterns with their arms. The dancers are accompanied by fast, dramatic guitar music.

Flamenco dancers also use their voices.

Irish dancing
Irish jigs are usually performed either by pairs or by individuals, but large groups also perform Irish dances. The jig is based on simple steps, but the dancers can elaborate and perform complicated leaping steps. They hold their upper body still and their arms straight down at their sides or holding hands. The dances are usually accompanied by the fiddle or bagpipes.

South American dancing

The dances of Central and South America reflect the cultures not only of the native peoples who have long occupied the region, but also of the European colonists and their African slaves. Many dances that originated in this region, such as the tango and samba, have become popular all over the world.

Macumba
The Macumba dance was taken to Brazil by African slaves as a form of voodoo-worship in which the dancer is believed to be possessed by a god. Macumba dancers worship Yemannjah, a goddess of the sea. Like all voodoo dances it involves shaking of the head and shoulders.

Tango
This dance originated in Argentina about 200 years ago. It had to be "cleaned up" before it became fashionable in Europe in the 1900s, because it was considered too immodest for the dance halls.

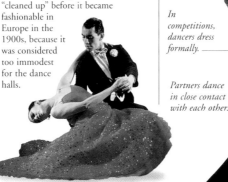

Contemporary dance
This style has no fixed technique. Dancers express their feelings in their movements. Contemporary dance began at the start of the 20th century, when US dancer Isadora Duncan broke away from ballet and developed her own style.

Samba
The samba was first danced in Brazil, especially at Carnival time, and became extremely popular in the United States and Europe in the early 1940s. It is danced by couples who perform simple backward and forward steps, swaying their bodies. In Brazil, there are many versions of the dance, each with a different rhythm, tempo, and mood.

Dancers adopt a flirtatious carnival mood.

There is no body contact in the samba.

Dancing the samba

Ballroom dancing

Developed in the courts of Europe, many ballroom dances, such as the waltz and samba, were adapted from folk dances. They were danced on flat, polished floors, which allowed for elegant gliding movements, rather than the jumping and stamping which folk dancers developed to cope with the rough floors or grass on which they danced.

Dancing the waltz

In competitions, dancers dress formally.

Partners dance in close contact with each other.

The couple progress around the dance floor in an anticlockwise direction.

Waltz
When the waltz first became popular with the aristocracy, in the 1700s, it caused a scandal because the couple was expected to dance close together. It was originally a simple Austrian peasant dance, but by the 19th century it was highly fashionable and composers such as Austrian Johann Strauss the younger (1825–99) specialized in writing waltz music.

Top-class dancers require strong ankles and a fit body.

A tilting pelvic action is required in many figures.

Dancers compete in the Rio de Janeiro Carnival every February.

Couples progress in an anti-clockwise direction.

Gene Kelly
American dancer Gene Kelly (1912–96) made film musicals popular with his athletic dance style. His best known films include *For Me and My Gal* (1942), *An American in Paris* (1951), and *Singin' in the Rain* (1952).

US dancer and actor Fred Astaire

Tap dance
In 19th-century America, black slaves combined African rhythms with the jigs of English and Irish settlers. Tap dance was thus created and became very popular.

Jazz dance
When jazz music became popular in the 1920s, an energetic, expressive form of dance developed with it. Today, jazz dancing is the main form of dancing in musicals and films.

Disco
Disco dancing became popular in the 1970s. The name comes from the clubs called discotheques, in which records were played for dancing. Couples usually dance facing, but not touching, each other, using simple repetitive movements.

FIND OUT MORE BALLET   DRAMA   FILMS AND FILM-MAKING   JAZZ   MUSIC   OPERA   ROCK AND POP

DARWIN, CHARLES

THE BRITISH NATURALIST Charles Darwin is best known as the man who developed the remarkable theory of evolution by natural selection. The theory, which describes how one species can develop or evolve into another, caused a revolution in biological science. Darwin was not the first person to suggest a theory of evolution, but was the first to present a solid body of evidence for the idea. He also wrote books about his travels, coral reefs, barnacles, the pollination of flowers, and insect-eating plants.

Early life
Darwin was born in 1809, in Shrewsbury, England. His grandfather, Erasmus Darwin, had put forward his own theory of evolution in the 1790s. At first, Charles Darwin did not believe in the idea of evolution. He trained as a priest before studying geology and biology.

D

Galápagos Islands
Darwin studied thousands of plants and animals all around the world on the *Beagle*'s journey. The most interesting part was the few weeks spent in the Galápagos Islands, about 1,000 km (600 miles) from the coast of South America. Darwin noticed that the species there were different from those elsewhere in the world.

Notebooks used by Darwin in Galápagos

List of species

Map pasted into notebook

Galápagos Islands

Notebooks
During his voyage on the *Beagle*, Darwin made careful, copious notes of everything he saw, gaining him the nickname "the old philosopher" from the ship's officers. The wealth of information he gathered helped him later, when he was developing his theory of evolution.

Darwin's finches
When he got home, Darwin realized that the finches on the Galápagos Islands had different beaks, depending on which island they inhabited. He decided that the birds had developed beaks that were best suited to the diet on their particular island.

The Beagle
At Cambridge, Darwin made friends with John Henslow, the professor of botany. Henslow suggested that Darwin would be a good choice as official naturalist on the naval survey ship HMS *Beagle*, which was about to sail around the world on a five-year scientific cruise. The trip lasted from 1831 to 1836.

Darwin's watch

Darwin's telescope

Fossil finds
When he landed in South America, Darwin found fossils of extinct animals, such as the giant sloth (now called *Mylodon darwini*), that closely resembled modern species. This suggested that animals had gradually changed to suit their environments.

Bones of Macrauchenia, a prehistoric mammal found by Darwin

Rock hammers

The Origin of Species
Darwin returned to England and wrote an account of his travels. He spent years studying the specimens he had collected and the notes he had made. Gradually, he developed his idea that species evolved as animals adapted to suit their environments. He published his findings in his book *On the Origin of Species by Means of Natural Selection*. The work caused an outcry among Christians because it challenged the creation story in the Bible.

Wallace
The British naturalist Alfred Russel Wallace (1823–1913) drew up a theory of evolution by natural selection quite independently of Darwin. He wrote to Darwin for advice, and the men wrote a paper about evolution together.

CHARLES DARWIN

1809 Born in Shrewsbury, England.

1831 Sets sail on the *Beagle*.

1836 Returns to England.

1858 Wallace writes to Darwin about his evolutionary theory; they produce a paper on evolution together.

1859 Darwin publishes his *Origin of Species*.

1871 Publishes *The Descent of Man*, on human evolution.

1875 Publishes *Insectivorous Plants*, which describes how the sundew traps insects.

1880 Publishes *The Power of Movement in Plants*, which shows how light influences the direction of plant growth.

1882 Dies at Downe, England.

The naturalist
After his voyage, Darwin spent the rest of his life studying specimens, doing experiments, and writing up his findings. He never left England again, and for much of the rest of his life he was too ill to leave his home. Illness did not stop him working on subjects ranging from earthworms to the pollination of plants.

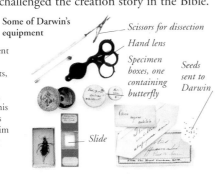

Some of Darwin's equipment

Scissors for dissection

Hand lens

Specimen boxes, one containing butterfly

Seeds sent to Darwin

Slide

Natural selection
Parents produce many offspring, all different from each other. Only those best suited to their environment will survive, passing on some of their features to their offspring.

Lesser black-backed gull

Herring gull has same ancestor as Lesser black-backed, but has evolved separately.

FIND OUT MORE

BIOLOGY • DINOSAURS • EVOLUTION • EXPLORATION • FOSSILS • GEOLOGY • HUMAN EVOLUTION • SCIENCE, HISTORY OF

DEER AND ANTELOPES

D

THE MOST noticeable difference between deer and antelopes is in their headgear. Deer have branched antlers that are shed, whereas antelopes have unbranched horns that are permanent. Both deer and antelopes are herbivorous hoofed mammals. They look similar to each other, but belong to different families. Deer are in a family of their own, while antelopes belong to the cattle family. They include gazelles, duikers, and spiral-horned antelopes.

Female red deer have no antlers.

Fringe-eared oryx
Oryx live in the arid grasslands of Tanzania and Kenya, in Africa. They obtain water from roots and tubers.

Red deer
This is the most widespread deer. It is found across Europe and Asia, and as far as Japan, the Himalayas, and Australia.

Stages of antler growth in a fallow deer
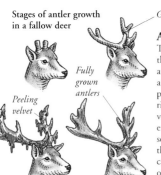
Growing antlers
Fully grown antlers
Peeling velvet

Antlers
The larger a stag's antlers, the more females it will attract. While the antlers are growing, they are protected by a velvety skin, richly supplied with blood vessels and nerves. At the end of the deer's breeding season, the blood supply to the antlers is cut off, causing the velvet to dry out and peel off in strips.

Deer

There are 38 species of deer spread over most of Europe, as well as Asia, North Africa, and the Americas. Some have been introduced into Australasia. Most species live in herds that split up in the breeding season. Most male deer, or stags, bear multi-branched antlers, which are shed and regrown every year.

Both sexes have long, straight horns.

Antelopes

Most of the 60 species of antelope live in Africa. Some, such as the blackbuck and the Tibetan antelope, are Asian. A few species have been introduced to other countries. Antelopes range in size from the giant Derby eland to the pygmy and royal antelopes, which are no bigger than hares.

Antelope horns

All male antelopes have horns, but only some females. The males use their horns to intimidate their rivals and to defend their territory.

Horns are hollow.

Front view of greater kudu horns

Front view of hartebeest horns

Browsing antelope

Grazing gazelles

Four-horned antelope
Males have two pairs of horns, making the deer a sought-after trophy for hunters. The front pair of horns is smaller than the back pair.

Nyala
The nyala, found in southeast African forests, has dark brown horns with a white tip. These can be up to 78 cm (31 in) long, with usually one open curve.

Hartebeest
Both male and female hartebeests have curved horns. Each has about 12 ridges but a smooth tip. Seen from the front, the horns are angular.

Greater kudu
The triple-spiralled horns of the male greater kudu are among the most imposing horns of any living animal. They grow up to 1.5 m (5 ft) long.

Roan antelope
Males and females have horns. About 55 cm (22 in) long, they are strongly ridged and curve gradually backward.

Browsers and grazers
The antelopes include both grazing and browsing species. In Africa, for example, some species, such as Thomson's gazelle, graze on grass. Other species, such as the gerenuk, browse the leaves and shoots of trees. Grant's and dorcas gazelles browse and graze, according to what is available.

Largest and smallest deer
The largest of all deer is the moose of North America, known as the elk in Europe. An adult male moose may stand 1.8 m (6 ft) at the shoulder and weigh 545 kg (1,200 lbs). The smallest deer is the South American pudu, which stands only about 40 cm (16 in) at the shoulder and weighs about 9 kg (20 lbs).

Père David's deer
This deer once lived wild in China. Then, for 3,000 years, it existed only in parks. In 1865, the missionary Père David saw the last surviving herd. This herd was later wiped out, but the Duke of Bedford established a herd in England. In recent years, deer bred in captivity have been sent to China and reintroduced into a special reserve.

Rutting

For most of the year, red deer stags remain apart from the females, or hinds, and their young. During the breeding season, known as the rut, males collect harems of hinds which they vigorously defend by roaring or, if necessary, by fighting.

Breeding

Most species of antelope and deer give birth when the weather is fine and food is abundant. Young caribou are born in early June when the herd is migrating. The calves can follow their mother within minutes of birth. The young of some species are left alone. Their mothers come to suckle and clean them several times a day, until they are strong enough to join the herd.

Caribou

The Eurasian reindeer and the North American caribou are the same species. They live in large herds and migrate long distances every year to find food. The reindeer has been semi-domesticated by, among others, the Lapps of north Europe.

Female reindeer are the only female deer that grow antlers.

Females in a herd give birth within two weeks of each other.

A calf can run with the herd when only an hour old.

A reindeer calf weighs about 4 kg (9 lb) at birth.

Reindeer with calf

Antelope habitats

Antelopes are found in most kinds of tropical and subtropical habitats. Most are creatures of the open plains and forests, but others have adapted to live in deserts, wetlands, and mountains. Grazing antelopes live where there is plenty of grass, whereas the browsers tend to inhabit woodlands and forests.

Woodland inhabitant

Also called the chousingha, the shy, solitary four-horned antelope lives in wooded, hilly country. Hunting has greatly reduced its numbers, but it still survives in several wildlife reserves in India, and one reserve in Nepal.

Sitatunga hoof

Swamp inhabitant

The sitatunga lives only in swamps and marshes. It has evolved long hooves that help it to walk on marshy ground. When danger threatens, it submerges itself in water leaving only its nostrils exposed.

Pointed antler

Muntjak head

Tusk-like teeth

Muntjak skull

Defence

Some deer and antelope, the larger species in particular, may sometimes use their antlers and horns to defend themselves, although generally antlers and horns are not strong enough for defence. Most deer and antelopes rely on their excellent eyesight and acute sense of hearing to detect potential enemies, and on speed to escape from any predators that attack.

Self-defence

If attacked, a muntjak's first defence is to run away. If this fails, males thrash with their antlers. These are mounted on "stalks" of bone as long as the antlers themselves. Males also have two tusk-like teeth used mainly in fighting rivals.

Camouflage

Some deer and antelope avoid predators because they blend into their surroundings. Kirk's dik-dik is an African antelope that lives in dry bush country, where the thorny thickets protect it.

Pronking

The springbok of Africa can run fast to escape a predator. Like most gazelles, it will often leap high into the air, with legs stiff, hooves close together, and back arched. Called pronking, or stotting, this action may confuse predators, raise the alarm, or simply give the gazelle a better view.

RED DEER

SCIENTIFIC NAME *Cervus elaphus*

ORDER Artiodactyla

FAMILY Cervidae

DISTRIBUTION Europe and Asia. Introduced into Australia, New Zealand, and South America

HABITAT Woodland and open country

DIET Grass, leaves, shoots, flowers (it both grazes and browses)

SIZE Height at the shoulder: 1.4 m (4 ft 6 in)

LIFESPAN 12–15 years

 FIND OUT MORE AFRICAN WILDLIFE BUFFALO AND OTHER WILD CATTLE GRASSLAND WILDLIFE

DENMARK

THE SMALLEST, flattest, and most southerly country in Scandinavia, Denmark occupies the Jylland peninsula, the islands of Sjaelland, Lolland, Falster, and Fyn, and more than 500 smaller islands. The Faeroe Islands and Greenland in the North Atlantic are self-governing Danish territories. A prosperous, environmentally conscious, and liberal nation, Denmark offers its people a high standard of living and was one of the first countries to set up a welfare system in the 1930s.

Physical features

Denmark's flat landscape is broken by low, rolling hills and gentle valleys with shady beech forests. There are also extensive areas of heathland, a beautiful lake district, and a coastline of cliffs, dunes, and broad sandy beaches.

Jylland (Jutland)

The Jylland peninsula makes up about 70 per cent of Denmark's land. Its west coast is edged with beaches and the southwest has a sandy plain. Strong winds sweeping across the land drive windmills for generating electricity.

Baltic islands

The steep, chalk cliffs on the Baltic island of Møn contrast with the gentle dunes on other islands. The Danish take great care of their environment and beaches.

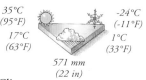

35°C (95°F) -24°C (-11°F)
17°C (63°F)   1°C (33°F)
571 mm (22 in)

Forest 11%   Farmland 87%

Built-up 2%

Climate

Denmark's usually mild and damp climate is dominated by stiff westerly winds. In many coastal areas, to prevent sand from the dunes from blowing over the land, the Danes have planted conifers as windbreaks.

Land use

Over four-fifths of Denmark is farmland, including lush pasture for grazing cattle and for raising pigs. Denmark's land yields few natural resources, although high winds are harnessed to produce power.

People

Only four per cent of the population is foreign – mainly Europeans. The only minority groups are Turks and Inuits from Greenland. The Danish have liberal policies on homosexuality and marriage, with a high divorce rate. Today, 47 per cent of all children are raised by unmarried couples or single parents. Three-quarters of all women work, and Denmark has the best child-support system in the world.

Danish pigs

125 per sq km (324 per sq mile)

85% Urban   15% Rural

Danish family visiting Legoland on Jylland

Farming and industry

Danish farming is efficient and often run by co-operatives. Only about four per cent of the work-force is employed in farming, mainly of dairy cattle and pigs, yet agriculture accounts for much of the country's export income. Denmark also has successful fishing, manufacturing, and food industries for processing bacon and dairy products. Service industries employ 79 per cent of workers.

Map of Denmark

(1) Skagen, Hirtshals, Hjørring, Løkken, Frederikshavn
Hanstholm, Fjerritslev, Brønderslev, Åbybro, Læsø
(2) Thisted, Alborg, Limfjorden
(3) Nissum Bredning, Mors, Lemvig, Skive, Hobro, Randers, Grenå
Struer, Viborg, Holstebro, Gudenå
Ringkøbing, Ikast, Silkeborg, Ebeltoft
Ringkøbing Fjord, Herning, Brande, Samsø
Skjern, Give, Horsens, Endelave, Sejerø
Varde, Grindsted, Vejle, Kalundborg, Nykøbing, Hillerød, Helsingør, Hørsholm
Esbjerg, Kolding, Fredericia, Otterup, Roskilde, COPENHAGEN, Tastrup
Ribe, Brørup, Middelfart, Arup, Odense, Slagelse, Køge, Ringsted
Haderslev, Toftlund, Ringe, Kvaerndrup, Korsør, Store Heddinge
Tønder, Abenrå, Fåborg, Svendborg, Naestved, Praestø, Vordingborg
Gråsten, Sønderborg, Troense, Nakskov, Sakskøbing, Møn
Maribo, Nykøbing, Lolland
Gedser
DENMARK, Alborg Bugt, North Sea
Rønne, Bornholm, Baltic Sea
Skagerrak, Jammerbugten
The Sound, Sjaelland, Fyn, Storebaelt, Lillebaelt, Langelands
Kiel Bay, Falster, Baltic Sea, Era
GERMANY

0 km 100
0 miles 100

Copenhagen

Denmark's capital is also its most important port and Scandinavia's largest city. Criss-crossed with a network of canals, quaint alleys, and cycle paths, Copenhagen has many historic buildings and churches. It also boasts the Tivoli Gardens, an amusement park that attracts millions every year.

Tourist boat on canal

FIND OUT MORE: ATLANTIC OCEAN · ENERGY · EUROPE · EUROPE, HISTORY OF · EUROPEAN UNION · FARMING · FOOD · SCANDINAVIA, HISTORY OF · TRADE AND INDUSTRY · VIKINGS

DESERTS

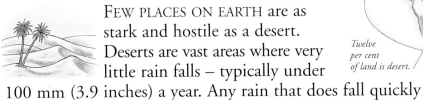

FEW PLACES ON EARTH are as stark and hostile as a desert. Deserts are vast areas where very little rain falls – typically under 100 mm (3.9 inches) a year. Any rain that does fall quickly evaporates. Few plants can survive, and soil cannot develop in such a dry and barren or arid environment. The landscape is bare sand, gravel, or rock. Clear skies and sparse vegetation leave the ground exposed to extremes of temperature. In the tropics, cloudless skies create hot deserts with daytime temperatures which are often over 50°C (122°F). Deserts at higher latitudes can be extremely cold.

Areas thought to be at risk of desertification (shown in orange)

Twelve per cent of land is desert.

Desert regions
The world's great deserts lie deep within continents far from the moisture of the oceans. They are also along the Tropics of Cancer and Capricorn, on either side of the Equator, where sinking air creates stable dry weather.

D

Desert landforms and dunes

Strong winds, sudden flash floods, and exposure to extreme temperatures create distinctive desert features. The wind piles sand up in dunes or sand-blasts rocks. Flash floods carve canyon-like valleys. The desert heat creates corrosive chemicals which sculpt rocks into bizarre shapes.

Wadi – gorge-like, generally dry valley

Mesa – isolated, flat-topped, steep-sided mountain

Parabolic dunes are also common on coasts.

Oasis
An oasis, such as the Azraq oasis in Jordan (above), is a fertile area within a desert that lies near an underground stream or a spring. Crops such as date palms can grow and desert dwellers can live supported by the land. Artificial oases can be created through irrigation.

Butte – eroded mesa

Seif dunes form where sand is sparse and wind comes from two directions.

Oasis is a pocket of water.

Zeugen rocks are produced by weathering.

Hamada is an area strewn with boulders and stones.

Eroded arch

Playa is a dry lake bed of salt.

Bolson is a drainage basin.

Barchan dune is shaped like a crescent and its tips usually point downwind.

Transverse dune – ridge lying across the wind

Bajada is a slope of sand deposited by rivers along mountain edges.

Mirage
Sometimes the desert heat is so intense that desert travellers believe that they can see water. This is an optical illusion (a trick of the eye), caused by the reflection of a faraway object, which may give the false appearance of a sheet of water.

Types of deserts

Climatic conditions create different types of deserts. In Africa, the Sahara has vast areas of erg (sand seas), hamada (stony plateaus), reg (pebble plains), rocky deserts, canyons, and cliff deserts. In the Antarctic there are ice deserts, while in the deserts of the western USA the heat evaporates rain so quickly that it leaves behind dissolved minerals in a hard, salty crust.

Sandy desert
In flat areas, vast sand seas, or ergs, develop. After a rainfall, water rushes along a wadi, a dry river bed. The sandstone cliffs on either side are gradually worn away by the heat, wind, and rain.

Rocky desert
Many of the world's deserts are strewn with boulders that have been washed there by flash flooding. These rocks are gradually broken down by the action of wind and weather.

Rocks brought to desert by flood water.

The shifting desert

As climatic conditions change, deserts shrink and expand. In the past, the Sahel, the southern margin of the Sahara, was watered by summer rains moving up from the south. In recent years, the lack of rain in the Sahel has caused drought and famine in places such as Sudan and Ethiopia.

Desertification
The effect of drought and heavy grazing by cattle, sheep, and goats destroys vegetation cover, turning the area permanently to desert. This process is known as desertification.

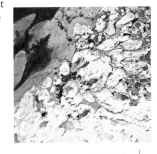

FIND OUT MORE   CLIMATE   DESERT WILDLIFE   ECOLOGY AND ECOSYSTEMS   ROCKS AND MINERALS   WEATHER

DESERT WILDLIFE

THE DRIEST PLACES ON EARTH are known as deserts. Food is scarce, and there is little shelter from the sun and wind. Deserts are among the most inhospitable of all places in which to live. In spite of this, many remarkable animals survive and even thrive in these hostile surroundings. Birds, mammals, insects, arachnids, amphibians, and reptiles are all represented, together with some equally remarkable plants.

Deserts

Many different types of desert exist in different parts of the world. Some are mountainous and rocky; others are pebbly or full of sand dunes. Some become baking hot by day; others have bitterly cold winters.

Sahara
Stretching across North Africa, the Sahara is the greatest of all deserts. It is a vast wilderness of sand and rock, with only scattered palms and bushes to offer shade from the searing daytime sun. Most of the animals that live there find shelter under rocks or in burrows.

Oases
Oases provide reliable sources of drinking water for wildlife in the desert. They form in the few places where springs bubble up from underground, or where rainwater from neighbouring mountains collects in hollows.

Birds

Though some desert-dwelling doves and finches forage for seeds, the most well-known birds of arid lands are predators. They probe vegetation and scour the ground for prey, obtaining all the moisture they need from the bodies of their victims.

Pale-coloured fur reflects heat.

Dwarf hamster
Only about 8.5 cm (3.3 in) long, this hamster lives in the deserts of Mongolia, Siberia, and China. It has thick fur, which helps to keep it warm in the bitterly cold winters.

Long, bushy tail can be curled around the body to keep it warm during the night.

Mammals

Desert mammals show a remarkable ability to cope with conditions that would be dangerously hot and dry for most animals. Some, such as camels, can tolerate steep rises in their body temperature and long periods of dehydration. Others have special means of securing shade, obtaining moisture, finding food, and avoiding danger in the wide-open terrain.

Large erect ears help the fox to hear the slightest sound of prey and tell from where it is coming.

Fennec fox
The fennec fox is small with large pointed ears. The large size of the ears helps the fox lose excess heat from its body during the heat of the day. The fox has dense fur, which keeps it warm on cold nights.

Gila woodpecker
The Gila woodpecker forages for insects in the deserts of Mexico and the USA. Typically, it hammers out nest-holes in the stems of large cacti.

Roadrunner
Roadrunners seldom fly, but they are extremely fast, agile runners. They often prey on desert snakes, which they subdue with a series of lethal stabs from their sharp beaks.

Falcons can spot prey from a great height.

Lanner falcon
This darting bird of prey nests among rocks and cliffs in the Sahara. It hunts small birds, which it chases and snatches in mid-air or on the ground. It also preys on smaller animals, such as gerbils, lizards, and locusts.

Red kangaroo
In Australian deserts, red kangaroos browse on bushes. They produce dry dung as a way of saving moisture, but still make regular trips to waterholes to replace moisture lost through sweating.

Kalahari ground squirrel
These burrowing rodents eat seeds and other plant material in the Kalahari Desert of Africa. During the day, they hold their bushy tails over their bodies for shade.

Bactrian camel
Camels are perfectly adapted for life in deserts. They can roam about for days without drinking or sweating. The two humps of the Bactrian camel act as fat reserves, off which the animal can live. The shaggy coat protects the camel during the cold winters in Asia's Gobi Desert.

Humps flop over when the fat is depleted.

Long fur covers the upper surface of the feet.

D

Reptiles and amphibians

Both snakes and lizards are tolerant of dry climates, and these reptiles are among the most common of desert animals. Amphibians are much more in danger of drying out, but a few species do appear on the desert surface, especially after rare bouts of rain.

Sand viper buries itself tail first.

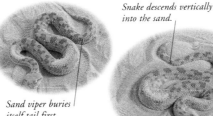

Snake descends vertically into the sand.

Sand viper
The sand viper has perfected an efficient way of disappearing on desert dunes. It wriggles down into the loose sand, becoming buried within seconds. It does this to escape danger and to be ready to attack prey.

D

Fringe-toed lizard
This lizard forages in sandy deserts. When the surface becomes too hot, it stands on two legs to help keep cool. Projections between its toes spread its weight and stop it from sinking into the sand.

Lizard can close its nostrils to prevent sand getting into its air passsages.

Water-holding frog
For months, this frog lies dormant underground in a waterproof cocoon. It emerges to feed and breed only after heavy rains, swelling its body with water before it returns into the soil.

Smooth scales

Sandfish
The sandfish is a lizard that makes its home on desert sand dunes. It is named after the way it moves across and through the sand, pushing sideways with its flattened toes as if it were swimming. Like other small lizards, it hunts mainly for insects.

Gila monster
The Gila monster is a fearsome lizard. Large, with a venomous bite, it leaves its burrow at dawn to hunt rodents and raid birds' nests. Fat stored in its thick tail provides nourishment when prey is scarce.

Yucca moth
The yucca moth of American deserts has evolved a close relationship with the yucca plant. The moth pollinates the plant; the yucca flowers give shelter to the moth larvae.

Desert cricket
An inhabitant of the deserts of India and Pakistan, the desert cricket can bury itself quickly in the sand. It digs a hole directly beneath itself with its star-shaped feet and sinks down.

Invertebrates

Few insects and other invertebrates can withstand the full force of the desert Sun. Those that can have an especially tough, waxy covering, or cuticle, that prevents them from drying out. Other invertebrates take shelter during the day.

White spots warn off predators.

Domino beetle
This domino beetle lives in the dry lands of northern Africa through to the Middle East. During the day, it hides under rocks and in holes made by other animals. At night, it emerges to hunt insects and other small prey.

Scorpion
Scorpions are among the hardiest of desert invertebrates, able to tolerate strong sunshine though they normally hunt at night. Armed with strong claws and a lethal sting, they ambush foraging insects such as locusts, as well as spiders and other scorpions.

The venom of this scorpion is strong enough to kill a person.

The scorpion holds its prey in its large claws.

Plants

Only the hardiest of drought-resistant plants can survive all year in the desert. Among these are cacti and yuccas. Seeds of more fragile plants lie dormant in the soil. After a rainburst, they sprout and flower before the moisture evaporates.

Desert holly
Some desert plants, such as the desert holly, have dusty-looking leaves. Salt secreted through leaf pores forms a fine whitish powder. This reflects some of the Sun's rays, helping to keep the leaves cool and preventing excessive evaporation of moisture.

Cacti
Many different kinds of cactus grow in American deserts. All store water in their green swollen stems. They do not have leaves, and this prevents excess moisture loss. Sharp spines deter animals from biting the succulent stems.

Seeds develop after the vine's flower has been pollinated by insects.

A welwitschia plant may live for 1,000 years or more.

Welwitschia
This plant has two ribbon-like leaves that trail across the sand. Each leaf has millions of pores that extract moisture from the sea fogs that sweep the Namib Desert in Africa.

Little snapdragon vine
Rains in the Mexican desert bring the seeds of snapdragon vines to life. The vines quickly grow, trailing over the soil and curling around other plants. They flower and set new seed before they die as the conditions get dry again.

Each leaf grows up to 2 m (6.5 ft) long.

Leaves usually split into several strips.

FIND OUT MORE | AFRICAN WILDLIFE | AMPHIBIANS | ASIAN WILDLIFE | BIRDS | BIRDS OF PREY | DESERTS | INSECTS | MAMMALS | PLANTS | REPTILES

DESIGN

ORIGINALLY A DESIGN was an artist's first sketch for a work of art; today, design plays a broader role in our lives. Before any object can be made, it must be designed. Most things around us have been designed to carry out a particular job. The design of objects is known as product design. There are also many other areas of design, such as fashion, garden, interior, and graphic design. Changing tastes can result in popular design movements, such as art nouveau and Bauhaus.

Product design

In order to design an object, the designer has several factors to consider. He or she must select a shape that suits the object's purpose but also consider other factors, such as the material to be used, the cost of manufacture, the safety and durability of the product, and how it will finally look. Product design usually aims to be both functional and stylish.

This bottle's shape is easily recognizable.

A can's ringpull opening is designed to open easily.

Classic design
Some product designs so successfully combine functionality with a strong sense of style that they are timeless. The distinctive shape of the Coca-Cola bottle, for example, is a classic design that has hardly changed since 1915.

Coca-Cola bottle

Headlamps and bumpers are chrome.

Large steering wheel

The MGB is compact but stylish.

EBW 45B

MGB Tourer

Classic cars
Some classic designs express certain ideals perfectly. The sleek lines of a sports-car's body, such as this MGB, are intended to suggest speed and freedom. Launched in 1962, the MGB became the best-selling single model sports car ever, with 512,000 owners worldwide.

The design process
The first stage in the design process is writing a design brief which details the functions and features to be achieved in the finished object. The designer then does a first sketch. This is translated into a rough model, or prototype, which is repeatedly tested and revised as needed. The design process of making numerous small amendments is called an iterative process. Finally, the actual product is made.

1 The designer does a first sketch on a drawing board or computer. This sketch shows a vacuum cleaner.

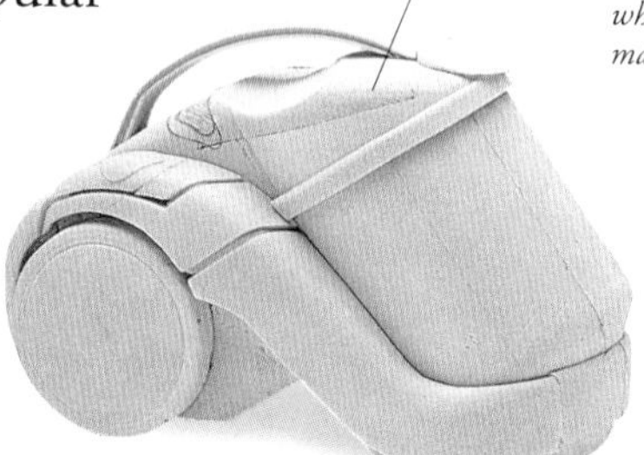

This prototype is shaped out of hard foam.

The plastic casing is very strong and light.

Dust collects in this area.

Large back wheels for manoeuvring

Long nozzle

Early prototype

Vacuum cleaner

2 A series of prototypes is made out of different materials to test aspects of the design. The final prototype is handmade and painted to look identical to the final product.

3 The final product is made to the revised design brief. Designs can be patented (protected by copyright law) to prevent someone copying an original design.

This vacuum cleaner uses a unique cyclone system to pick up dirt.

Graphic design

Graphic designers use words and images to communicate a strong visual message. We are surrounded by graphic design, in magazines and books, on posters, on street signs. Designers use letters in different sizes and typefaces, often with colours and patterns, to make an impact.

London Underground map
The London Underground map is a brilliant piece of design. By distorting the distances between stations, it is possible to see the entire London Underground at a glance.

Shell Oil logo

Logos
Logos are graphic designs that aim to communicate a message without words. Companies design logos to be easily recognized by the public. The simple shape and strong colours of the logo shown above advertise the Shell Oil Company worldwide.

Computer-aided design
Increasingly, much of the design process is carried out on computer. Using computer-aided design, the designer creates a three-dimensional model, such as a car, on screen which can then be rotated and viewed from all angles.

Art Nouveau
Design movements are trends in design, some of which have a lasting influence. Art Nouveau was a design movement beginning in Europe in the 1880s that aimed to make ordinary objects, such as buildings, furniture, and jewellery, beautiful.

This Art Nouveau window in Paris, France, shows typical decorative curves based on organic forms.

Walter Gropius
In 1919, the German architect Walter Gropius (1883–1969) founded the Bauhaus design school. It taught the importance of functional design and of using materials such as steel, glass, and concrete. Bauhaus influenced the development of the arts. Gropius (on right) is shown with the French architect, Le Corbusier (1887–1965).

FIND OUT MORE   ARCHITECTURE   ART, HISTORY OF   BUILDING AND CONSTRUCTION   CARS AND TRUCKS   CLOTHES AND FASHION   FURNITURE   GARDENS   PAINTING AND DRAWING   PRINTING   TRADE AND INDUSTRY

DICKENS, CHARLES

CHARLES DICKENS IS one of the greatest writers in the English language. He was a household name in his own lifetime. His lively descriptions of 19th-century Britain combine with a superb gift for depicting people and their eccentricities, a social conscience, and compassion for the problems faced by ordinary people. He brought to the English novel the ability to portray an entire society in one book. His novels are still loved by readers of all ages.

Early life

Charles Dickens was born in Portsmouth, England, in 1812. His father was a clerk in the Royal Navy pay office and worked for a time in the royal dockyards in Chatham, Kent, where Charles spent much of his childhood. When his father was imprisoned for debt in London's Marshalsea Prison, Charles, then aged 12, had to take a series of menial jobs in factories and offices. He later used these painful experiences in some of his novels.

"Boz"

As a young man, Dickens was a journalist, covering Parliament for the *Morning Chronicle*. In 1833 he began to write a series of articles, mostly about London life, using the pseudonym "Boz". These were collected together in *Sketches by Boz* in 1836. Following their success, he was commissioned to write some humorous sporting stories. These appeared in 1836–37 as *The Posthumous Papers of the Pickwick Club* and made Dickens the most famous writer of his day.

Scrooge meets the Ghost of Christmas Past

David Copperfield

David Copperfield

In 1849–50 Dickens wrote *David Copperfield*, a partly autobiographical novel in which he used his own experiences of an impoverished childhood and menial employment to great effect. Of all his books, it was Dickens' favourite. The novel features Mr Micawber, who is loosely based on Dickens' father. Always in debt, and always waiting for "something to turn up", Micawber is one of the great characters of English literature.

Household Words

From 1850, Dickens edited and contributed first to the magazine *Household Words*, and then, from 1859, to *All The Year Round*. He used these monthly magazines to publish his latest novel in instalments, reaching a far wider readership than he would have done by simply publishing a book. Both magazines featured works by other famous writers of the time, such as Elizabeth Gaskell and Wilkie Collins. Dickens also included articles about the social problems of his time, such as poor housing and factory accidents.

A Christmas Carol

Ebenezer Scrooge, who refused to celebrate Christmas, and his impoverished clerk Bob Cratchit make *A Christmas Carol* (published in 1843) one of Dickens's most popular novels. Scrooge changes his ways when he witnesses a series of visions, including his own death and the ghosts of Christmas Past, Present, and Future.

In a scene from *Oliver Twist*, Oliver asks for more porridge.

Oliver Twist

The story of Oliver tells of a pauper child of unknown parentage who was brought up in a workhouse and dared to ask for more food. *Oliver Twist* was first published as a book in 1838. The book was later made into a successful musical and film. The story was the first by Dickens to explore the dark side of London life in the 19th century, and the fact that thousands of children were living rough on the streets or in inhuman workhouses.

Dickensian London

In Dickens's time, London was a rich city at the centre of the biggest empire the world had ever seen. But many people lived in poverty, making a living from whatever work they could find. Dickens described their suffering, but he loved London – its sights, sounds, and smells feature in all his books.

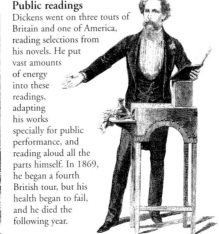

London street, 19th century

Public readings

Dickens went on three tours of Britain and one of America, reading selections from his novels. He put vast amounts of energy into these readings, adapting his works specially for public performance, and reading aloud all the parts himself. In 1869, he began a fourth British tour, but his health began to fail, and he died the following year.

Social reforms

Dickens often spoke in public about the plight of the poor, the need for educational reform, and the importance of good sanitation to remove the threat of disease. His speeches and novels helped to raise awareness of the need for radical reform, and led to many changes in the law.

CHARLES DICKENS

1812	Born in Portsmouth, England.
1824	Father imprisoned for debt.
1836	Marries Catherine Hogarth; publishes *Sketches by Boz*.
1836–7	*Pickwick Papers*
1838	*Oliver Twist*
1839	*Nicholas Nickleby*
1850	*David Copperfield*
1853	*Bleak House*
1857	*Little Dorrit*
1858	First reading tour
1859	*A Tale of Two Cities*
1861	*Great Expectations*
1864	*Our Mutual Friend*
1870	Dies and is buried in Westminster Abbey.

FIND OUT MORE

BOOKS   EMPIRES   INDUSTRIAL REVOLUTION   LITERATURE   UNITED KINGDOM, HISTORY OF   WRITING

DIGESTION

D

THE BODY NEEDS THE nutrients in food to grow, maintain its structure, and provide energy. But the food we eat cannot be used by the body until it is processed by the digestive system. This is essentially a long tube, running from mouth to anus. As food passes along the digestive system it is chewed, and crushed, and then broken down chemically by enzymes. As it passes along the small intestine, food resembles a thin soup, and simple food molecules can be absorbed into the body itself by way of the bloodstream.

Swallowing

Once food is chewed, the tongue pushes the ball of food, or bolus, to the back of the mouth. As it touches the throat, the bolus triggers a reflex action and passes into the oesophagus. A flap called the epiglottis closes the entrance to the trachea (windpipe) to stop food entering the lungs.

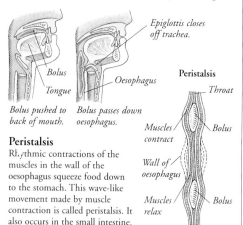

Epiglottis closes off trachea.

Bolus

Tongue

Oesophagus

Bolus pushed to back of mouth.

Bolus passes down oesophagus.

Peristalsis

Throat

Muscles contract

Bolus

Wall of oesophagus

Muscles relax

Bolus

Peristalsis

Rhythmic contractions of the muscles in the wall of the oesophagus squeeze food down to the stomach. This wave-like movement made by muscle contraction is called peristalsis. It also occurs in the small intestine.

Digestive process

The digestive process has four stages: ingestion, digestion, absorption, and egestion. Ingestion happens when you eat food and is followed by digestion. Absorption is the transfer of food molecules into the bloodstream and egestion is the removal of waste as faeces.

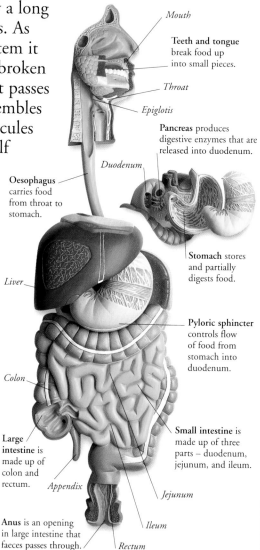

Mouth

Teeth and tongue break food up into small pieces.

Throat

Epiglotis

Pancreas produces digestive enzymes that are released into duodenum.

Duodenum

Oesophagus carries food from throat to stomach.

Liver

Stomach stores and partially digests food.

Pyloric sphincter controls flow of food from stomach into duodenum.

Colon

Large intestine is made up of colon and rectum.

Appendix

Small intestine is made up of three parts – duodenum, jejunum, and ileum.

Jejunum

Ileum

Anus is an opening in large intestine that faeces passes through.

Rectum

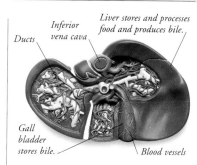

Inferior vena cava

Liver stores and processes food and produces bile.

Ducts

Gall bladder stores bile.

Blood vessels

Liver, pancreas, and gall bladder

These three organs take part in digestion even though, since they have other body functions, they are not part of the digestive system. The liver produces bile, which is stored in the gall bladder and helps digest fats. The pancreas produces digestive enzymes that are released into the small intestine.

Absorption

Simple food molecules are absorbed into the bloodstream across the wall of the small intestine. Tiny finger-like projections called villi (singular: villus) greatly increase the surface area over which food can be absorbed.

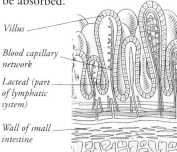

Villus

Blood capillary network

Lacteal (part of lymphatic system)

Wall of small intestine

Imaging the intestine

A special liquid is introduced into the large intestine to show clearly its position and internal shape. This type of X-ray enables doctors to detect signs of disease inside the large intestine without having to operate.

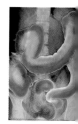

William Beaumont

The US Army surgeon William Beaumont (1785–1853) was the first to observe how food was digested in the stomach. In 1822, Beaumont treated a patient who had shot himself in the side and was left with an opening into his stomach. Through this opening, Beaumont was able to observe the stomach's movements during digestion and to record his findings.

Food and enzymes

Enzymes are biological catalysts that speed up the conversion of one substance into another. Digestive enzymes speed up the breakdown of the complex carbohydrates, fats, and proteins that make up most of our food.

Carbohydrates

The body's main fuel, carbohydrate, comes in the form of sugars and complex carbohydrates, which include starch. Enzymes break starchy foods down into sugars such as glucose.

Glucose molecules

Starch molecule chain

Fat droplets

Fatty acids

Protein

Amino acids

Fats

Fats provide the body with energy. Foods rich in fats include eggs and meat. Fats are broken down by enzymes in the small intestine to form fatty acids.

Proteins

Proteins are needed for growth and maintaining the body. Protein-rich foods are meat, fish, and nuts. Proteins are broken down into amino acids.

FIND OUT MORE

CHEMISTRY   FOOD   HORMONES AND ENDOCRINE SYSTEM   HUMAN BODY   IMMUNE AND LYMPHATIC SYSTEM   TEETH AND JAWS

DINOSAURS

FOR 150 MILLION YEARS, from the Triassic Period until the end of the Cretaceous Period, 65 million years ago, dinosaurs lived on Earth. Their remains have been discovered in every continent including Antarctica. They formed a varied group of land-living reptiles. People who study prehistoric life, called palaeontologists, divide them into two main groups – the Ornithischia and the Saurischia. There were meat-eating and plant-eating dinosaurs. Some dinosaurs, were huge; others were only the size of chickens.

Iguanodon skull

Iguanodon tooth

Iguanodon skull

Gideon Mantell, an English doctor, named *Iguanodon* in 1825, noting the similarity between its teeth and those of the modern iguana. *Iguanodon*'s teeth were shaped to fit tightly together. They wore down as the dinosaur chewed its food of tough vegetation with the help of a hinged jaw.

Iguanodon

This was one of the first dinosaurs to be discovered. Modern reconstructions give it an outstretched tail and forelimbs that can reach the ground.

Iguanodon

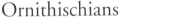

Iguanodon foot

Iguanodon

Iguanodon foot

The feet of *Iguanodon* had small hooves on the toes instead of claws, and would have made recognizable three-toed prints with rounded digits. *Iguanodon* probably walked on its toes, which, therefore, had to be strong to carry the animal's great weight.

Ornithischians

The Ornithischia, or bird-hipped dinosaurs, such as *Iguanodon*, were all herbivorous. They had a huge number of teeth – *Corythosaurus* had 2,000 – and a hinged upper jaw that allowed them to chew.

Tyrannosaurus

Saurischians

The Saurischia, or lizard-hipped dinosaurs, include the meat-eating theropods, which walked on two legs, such as *Tyrannosaurus*, and the plant-eating sauropods, which walked on four legs, such as *Diplodocus*. The sauropods were the largest ever land animals.

Tyrannosaurus tooth

Carnivorous dinosaurs had curved, pointed teeth. The sharp edges often had serrations, which helped the dinosaurs to slice through skin and meat. Palaeontologists still have to be careful when handling these teeth.

Tyrannosaurus tore off the flesh of its prey with its teeth and claws.

Pubis bone

Ischium bone

Tyrannosaurus skeleton

Tyrannosaurus may have hunted as well as scavenged on other dinosaurs. It had a massive skull with powerful jaws, supported by a short, flexible neck. This flexibility allowed the animal to twist its head around to wrench flesh from its prey.

Long, hollow tubular crest

Tail was used for balance.

Ischium bone

Pubis bone

Rounded, hoof-like claws

Skeleton of *Parasaurolophus*, an ornithischian

Toothless jaws

Pubis bone

Long foot bones suggests Gallimimus could run fast.

Skeleton of *Gallimimus*, a saurischian

Tyrannosaurus

Although not thought to be the largest of the carnivorous dinosaurs, *Tyrannosaurus* was still an extremely fearsome predator. It walked on its hind legs with its back level and head raised. It could run very fast, its tail balancing the weight of its huge heavy body.

Fossil dung

Preserved pieces of dung are called coprolites. They contain the remains of what dinosaurs ate, such as bone fragments, fish scales, or plant remains. Scientists can study these to find out about the diet of dinosaurs.

Hips

Dinosaurs fall into one of the two main groups, according to the structure of their hip bones. The bird-hipped dinosaurs (ornithischians), such as *Parasaurolophus*, had a pubis bone in their hip girdle that sloped backward, parallel to the ischium bone. The lizard-hipped dinosaurs (saurischians), such as *Gallimimus*, had a pubis bone that sloped forward away from the ischium.

Orodromeus *laid up to 24 eggs.*

The first dinosaurs

One of the earliest dinosaurs was *Eoraptor*, meaning "early plunderer". It was no bigger than a large dog and lived 225 million years ago (mya). As with all the early dinosaurs, it was a carnivore and walked on two legs.

Orodromeus nest

Eoraptor skull

Breeding

Dinosaurs laid hard-shelled eggs as some reptiles do today. Many dinosaurs laid a clutch of eggs in a hollowed-out nest in the ground. Several fossilized nests have been found close together, which suggests that some dinosaurs nested in colonies. The chicks developed rapidly and may have left the nest soon after hatching. Many were cared for by the parent dinosaur until they were able to look after themselves.

Richard Owen

Born in Lancaster, England, Richard Owen (1804–92) became the Hunterian Professor of the Royal College of Surgeons in 1836. As well as being an anatomist, he was a brilliant palaeontologist. He was the first to use the term "dinosaurs", which means "terrible lizards", in a report in 1842. He noted that these animals had pillar-like legs, rather than the sprawling legs of modern reptiles, and should be classified separately.

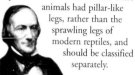

Defence

Dinosaurs protected themselves against attack from predators. Different dinosaurs developed a variety of powerful defences. For example, *Triceratops* had horns on its head, *Euoplocephalus* had a tail club, and *Tuojiangosaurus* had a spiky tail. Some of these adaptations may have had several functions, but one of them was likely to have been defence. Scientists cannot say exactly how these animals defended themselves, but it is easy to imagine.

Tuojiangosaurus

The flanks and belly of *Tuojiangosaurus* were vulnerable to attack. Near the tip of its tail were four bony spikes. These pointed up and outwards, producing a formidable defence when the dinosaur swung its tail. This animal was a type of bird-hipped dinosaur called a stegosaur. It lived in China 157-145 mya.

Tuojiangosaurus

All stegosaurs had a double row of plates running down their back.

Small narrow head with a walnut-sized brain

Short front limbs

Defensive spikes

Euoplocephalus had thick bone plates and spikes over its back, with a large shoulder spike for added protection.

Reconstruction of *Iguanodon* hand

Thumb spike

Raised nodules for protection

Iguanodon spike

When *Iguanodon* was first reconstructed, its large spike was placed on its beak. It is now known that the spike was on its thumb and may have been used as a defensive weapon against predators. The spike could have pierced the belly, throat, or eye of an attacker. The dinosaur may also have used it in fights for status with other *Iguanodons*, and even to help it feed.

Dinosaur skin

Occasionally, the skin, or skin impression, of dinosaurs is preserved. From these fossils we can tell that the skin of many dinosaurs was not smooth, but nodular and rough. This would have given some protection against the claws and teeth of predators. This is the skin of *Polacanthus*.

Euoplocephalus

Club was made out of several bones fused together.

Euoplocephalus

This armoured ornithischian had a large bony club at the tip of its muscular tail. It could have swung this with great force, disabling a predator.

Claw

Brow horn

Frill anchored the jaw muscles.

Nose horn

Triceratops

The ceratopsians, or horned dinosaurs, were ornithischians. Most of them had brow horns and nose horns. *Triceratops*, the largest ceratopsian, had two long horns on its brow, a short nose horn, and also a bony neck frill protecting its neck. Its head took up nearly one-third of its length. It probably used its horns to fend off predators, and males used them to deter rivals in the herd, mostly by display, but also by fighting.

Triceratops skull – side view

Triceratops skull – front view

Dinosaur discoveries

Removing dinosaur fossils from surrounding rock is tricky. Some need to be protected in a jacket made of plaster or polyurethane foam before they are taken to a laboratory. Fossils are found every year, and each discovery teaches us more about these extinct animals.

Finding dinosaur bones.

FIND OUT MORE   ANIMALS   ANIMAL BEHAVIOUR   EVOLUTION   FOSSILS   PREHISTORIC LIFE   REPTILES   SKELETON

Dinosaurs
Ornithischians

Six long spikes

Iguanodon could walk on two or four legs.

Styracosaurus was a short-frilled ceratopsian.

Heterodontosaurus was one of the first bird-hipped dinosaurs. It lived about 205 mya.

Corythosaurus had a tall crest on its head.

Scelidosaurus was the oldest-known armoured dinosaur.

Spiky tail for defence

Body built for speed

Long thigh compared to the rest of the leg.

Swinging tail club

Euoplocephalus had body armour and a tail club to protect it against attack.

Hypsilophodon was once thought to have lived in trees, but its limbs were not built for climbing.

Stegoceras was a pachycephalosaur, and had a thick-domed skull.

Stegosaurus was the largest stegosaur at 9 m (30 ft) long. It had large plates along its back.

Stiff tail helped with balance.

Saurischians

Deinonychus was a meat eater and may have hunted in packs.

Gallimimus was shaped like an ostrich and was one of the fastest running dinosaurs.

Toothless beak

Flat, crocodile-like jaws

Dilophosaurus had two high crests on top of its large head.

Long neck enabled Barosaurus to reach leaves at the top of trees.

Tail was used for balance at speed.

Hands could be used to grasp food.

Ankle joint

Long, clawed fingers

Baryonyx had a huge 30-cm (12-in)-long claw on each hand.

Whiplash tail used in defence.

Anchisaurus may have eaten both meat and plants.

Long foot bones increased the length of the leg.

Dagger-like teeth

Large hind legs were needed to bear the weight of the body.

Small arms with two-fingered hands

Body like Archaeopteryx, the first bird

Two clawed fingers on each hand

Compsognathus was small – only 74 cm (2.5 ft) long.

Herrerasaurus was a carnivore that lived in Argentina 228 mya.

Barosaurus resembled *Diplodocus*. It was about the same size with a shorter tail and longer neck.

Tyrannosaurus was one of the largest known land-living carnivores, weighing up to 6 tonnes.

DISEASES

JUST LIKE A MACHINE, the human body works smoothly and efficiently most of the time. However, it may occasionally stop operating normally. This may be due to an injury, such as a broken bone, but, more commonly, it is caused by a disease. Diseases occur because the body has been infected by a pathogen (germ), as in the case of influenza or food poisoning, or because of problems arising inside the body, such as heart disease or diabetes. Some diseases can be controlled and defeated by the body's immune system. More serious diseases may need drug treatment or surgery in order to cure them.

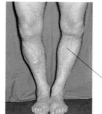
Epidemiologist tests samples in laboratory.

Epidemiology

Epidemiology is the study of diseases as they affect groups of people. Epidemiologists are concerned with why diseases occur in a population, and their control and prevention. They have discovered links between disease and diet, environmental factors, and lifestyle. Epidemiologists first discovered the link between smoking and lung cancer.

Non-infectious diseases

If a disease is non-infectious, it is not caused by a pathogen and cannot be passed from one person to another. Non-infectious diseases include circulatory system diseases, such as heart attacks, strokes, and cancer, and respiratory diseases, such as bronchitis and emphysema.

Nutritional diseases

Nutritional diseases are caused by a lack of a balanced diet, causing a deficiency of vitamins and minerals. A child not getting enough vitamin D may suffer from rickets, where the skeleton does not form properly.

Rickets may leave sufferer with bow-legs.

Miners may develop lung problems.

Industrial diseases

Work situations may affect a person's health. Industrial processes can create harmful environments or use chemicals that cause diseases. Some miners develop a lung disease called pneumoconiosis.

Infectious diseases

Infectious diseases are those, such as the common cold or pneumonia, that are caused by pathogens that invade the body. The most common pathogens are bacteria and viruses, although some diseases, such as thrush, are caused by fungi, and some, such as malaria, by tiny organisms called protists. They are normally destroyed by the body's immune system. Those that are not can often be dealt with by drugs.

Bacteria are in water, air, and soil, as well as many plant and animal tissues.

Bacteria

Bacteria are single-celled micro-organisms. Most bacteria are not harmful to humans. However, some multiply inside the body and produce toxins that cause disease. Bacterial diseases include typhoid and scarlet fever. Most can be treated with drugs called antibiotics.

Chickenpox causes an itchy rash that, when scratched, can leave scars.

Viruses

Viruses are tiny infective particles, not usually classed as living things. They take over a body cell's genetic material (DNA) and make copies of themselves that infect other cells. Human viral infections include colds, measles, and HIV.

Spreading infection

Most diseases are acquired from other people by skin-to-skin contact, breathing in droplets when someone sneezes or coughs, or by sexual contact without the use of condoms. Infection can also be spread through infected food, contaminated water, and insect bites. Drug users who share needles risk infections of the blood, such as hepatitis and HIV.

Sanitation

Human faeces contain bacteria and viruses that cause disease. If there is poor sanitation and human waste is discharged into rivers, people may catch diseases such as dysentery or cholera through contact with polluted water.

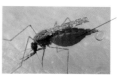

Some mosquitoes carry strains of malaria that are resistant to drugs.

Insects

Insects such as mosquitoes and fleas feed on human blood and can carry disease. A mosquito transmits the malaria micro-organism if it feeds on an infected person's blood.

Keeping rivers clean prevents diseases that can be caught if people drink, wash, or grow food in the water.

HIV and AIDS

HIV

The human immunodeficiency virus, or HIV, causes AIDS (Acquired Immune Deficiency Syndrome). HIV infects and destroys the cells that form part of the body's immune system – the body's defences against diseases. HIV is transmitted by some bodily fluids, such as blood and semen. The system becomes progressively weaker, and the person becomes infected with various diseases, known collectively as AIDS.

Preventing disease

Disease prevention is an important part of modern medicine. Diseases can be prevented by better sanitation, immunization, and improving food hygiene. Eating a balanced diet and exercising may also prevent disease.

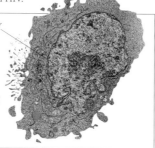

Syringes that are not properly sterilized after use can spread disease.

Pills contain measured amounts of drugs.

Bottled water is a way of assuring water is safe in certain countries.

FIND OUT MORE

BLACK DEATH   CELLS   CURIE, MARIE   DRUGS   HUMAN BODY   IMMUNE AND LYMPHATIC SYSTEM   PASTEUR, LOUIS

DISNEY, WALT

IN 1901, A MAN WAS BORN who would change the face of entertainment. Walt Disney became interested in animation as a schoolboy; by the time he was 20 he was making short animated films. But it was his later work that changed the history of the cinema. He created a string of cartoon characters which have been favourites ever since – Donald Duck, Goofy, and, above all, Mickey Mouse. Walt Disney also made the first feature-length animated film, *Snow White and the Seven Dwarfs* (1937), which was followed by many other screen successes.

Early life

In 1906, Disney's father Elias bought a farm at Marceline, Missouri. This was where young Walt first saw animals at close quarters. He also became interested in drawing. The first he ever sold was a drawing of the local doctor's stallion, for which the doctor paid Disney a nickel.

Early animation

Disney began to make animated films in 1920. These films featured characters which were made by cutting figures out of paper. The figures could be moved while they were photographed with a hand-cranked camera.

Disney with a hand-cranked camera

Hollywood

Disney moved to Hollywood in 1923. There were no animation studios, so he set up his own. He was soon in the forefront of technical innovation, pioneering the use of synchronized sound and the three-colour Technicolor process.

Mickey Mouse

Steamboat Willie, the first cartoon to feature Mickey Mouse, appeared in 1928. This was also the first cartoon with sound. Disney himself supplied Mickey's voice, and the film was an instant success. Mickey has since appeared in many other films. He has become the instantly recognizable Disney symbol and has appeared on countless Disney merchandise products.

Walt Disney with Mickey Mouse and Donald Duck

Snow White with the seven dwarfs

Snow White

In the 1920s, cartoons were normally shown before a full-length live-action film. But in 1935, Disney had the idea of producing a full-length cartoon, *Snow White and the Seven Dwarfs* (1937). Hundreds of animators worked on the film, which was followed by many other full-length animated features.

Mary Poppins

From the 1950s onwards, Disney produced many live-action films. Some of these, such as the musical fantasy *Mary Poppins* (1964), also included animated sequences.

Julie Andrews in a scene from Mary Poppins

The Disney Club

Disney was the first US major studio to create locally produced children's programming such as The Disney Club, and is the only studio to maintain a world-wide network of production offices. This network produces more than 40 weekly Disney programmes, which reach over 300 million viewers.

Disney Club logo

Disneyland

For many years, Walt Disney wanted to recreate the sets and characters of his films in a recreational park. The result, Disneyland, opened in 1955 in Anaheim, near Los Angeles, California. This theme park is one of the world's most popular attractions. Other parks have since opened: Walt Disney World in Florida and Disneyland ® Paris.

Disneyland

WALT DISNEY

1901	Born in Chicago, USA.
1919	Begins to make animated films.
1923	Moves to Hollywood.
1928	*Steamboat Willie*, featuring Mickey Mouse.
1937	*Snow White and the Seven Dwarfs*, the first feature-length animated film.
1940	*Pinocchio*.
1940	*Fantasia*.
1942	*Bambi*.
1955	Disneyland opens.
1964	*Mary Poppins*.
1966	Walt Disney dies.

FIND OUT MORE   CARTOONS AND ANIMATION   FILMS AND FILM-MAKING   TELEVISION

DOGS

DOGS HAVE LIVED with people for more than 12,000 years. They may have started to stay near humans for food and warmth. Then people began to train dogs to work for them. They bred certain types of dog for herding and guarding other domestic animals, then for hunting and for companionship. Gradually, different types of dog developed, but it was not until the end of the 19th century that specific breeds were classified. Today, there are about 200 dog breeds throughout the world. They are more varied in their appearance and behaviour than any other domestic animal.

Siberian husky

English setter

Shetland sheepdogs

Chihuahua

Scottish terriers

Bloodhound

Dog groups

The people of ancient Egypt and western Asia were the first to breed distinct types of dog for different purposes. By Roman times, dogs were kept for much the same reasons as they are today. There are six main groups – (from left to right) top row: working, sporting, herding; bottom row: companion, terriers, and hounds.

Domestic dogs

All breeds of domestic dog, from the Great Dane to the chihuahua, are descended from the wolf and have inherited the wolf's instincts. Like wolves, dogs are pack animals. They treat humans as part of their pack, and can be trained to accept their owner as the pack leader, and to follow his or her commands.

Borzois have sharp eyesight and hunt by sight.

Long, strong legs and a flexible body for speed

The borzoi was bred in Russia in the 13th century and used first to hunt wolves.

Dog features

The wolf is designed to chase, capture, kill, and eat its prey. It is agile, with strong legs for running long distances. Domestic dogs retain many of the features of a wolf, but through selective breeding now exist in many shapes, sizes, and colours.

Coats

There are three main types of dog coats – long, short, and wiry. Most breeds have an outer coat of guard hairs and an undercoat of shorter hairs. They moult, or shed their fur, changing their coat in spring and autumn.

Short hair   Long hair   Wire hair

Feet

Dogs walk on their toes rather than the soles of their feet. Their paw pads help with grip, as do their claws, which are non-retractable.

Senses

Dogs have highly developed senses of hearing and smell. They use these in communication and to track down their prey. The police use dogs to sniff out explosives, criminals, and drugs. The dogs can see well in the dark and are good at seeing movement in the distance.

Beagles were bred to hunt hares.

Reproduction

A female dog is pregnant for about nine weeks, then gives birth to several puppies known as a litter. At birth, puppies are blind and deaf. Their eyes open at about 10 to 12 days old and they are able to hear at 13 to 17 days old. Teeth start to grow between three and five weeks of age.

A young puppy is defenceless.

All puppies are born with short legs and a little tail.

Eyes are fully open.

1 At one week old, a puppy spends most of its time sleeping and feeding by suckling from its mother.

2 At two weeks old, the puppy takes its first wobbling steps and begins to explore. Its eyes are now open and it can hear.

3 At three weeks old, the puppy may start to eat solid food. At first, its mother will regurgitate meat for it.

4 At six weeks old, the puppy no longer feeds from its mother. It can soon be taken away from her to a new home.

FIND OUT MORE   ANIMALS   ANIMALS, BEHAVIOUR   CATS   GRASSLAND WILDLIFE   MAMMALS   POLICE   WOLVES AND WILD DOGS

Dogs

Working dogs

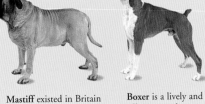

Great Dane makes an excellent family pet.

Mastiff existed in Britain in ancient Roman times.

Boxer is a lively and affectionate dog.

Up to 60 cm (24 in) tall

German shepherd dog is intelligent and enthusiastic.

Dalmatian, used to deter highwaymen in the 1800s.

St Bernard exists in wire- and smooth-haired forms.

Companion dogs

"Papillon" refers to the shape of the ears.

Large head

Papillon is named after the French for "butterfly".

Pekingese has a flattened face, with a broad nose.

Bulldog is a strong but affectionate dog.

Thick, harsh-textured coat

Miniature poodle, world's most popular dog in the 1950s.

Cavalier King Charles spaniel, bred in 1900s.

Pug has a soft coat and a curled tail.

Terriers

Coat comes in a variety of colours.

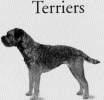

Airedale terrier is the largest terrier breed.

Border terrier was first bred for hunting rats.

Staffordshire bull terrier is loyal and devoted.

Tail carried upright

Boston terrier originated in Boston, USA, in the 1800s.

Smooth fox terrier is alert and tireless.

Parson Jack Russell terrier has a mostly white coat.

Long body for its height

Yorkshire terrier is a small but spirited guard dog.

Cairn terrier has a shaggy, water-resistant coat.

Australian terrier is capable of tackling a snake.

Hounds

Slightly curved tail

Long body and short legs

Strong back

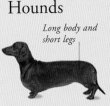

Basset hound is an agile and single-minded hunter

Dachshunds can be long-, smooth-, or wire-haired.

Whippet was bred in the 1800s for racing.

Muscular neck

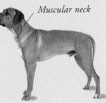

Rhodesian ridgeback has a ridge of hair on its back.

Afghan hound needs plenty of exercise.

Greyhound is built for speed.

Powerful hindquarters

71–90 cm (28–35 in) tall

Lurcher: individuals vary considerably within the breed.

Saluki, fast and agile, was once used to hunt gazelles.

Irish wolfhound is the tallest dog in the world.

Herding dogs

Deep muscular chest

Hair falls over the eyes

Australian cattle dog has great stamina.

Border collie is an outstanding sheepdog.

Old English sheepdog has a thick, shaggy coat.

Sporting dogs

Obvious stop on the muzzle

Water-resistant coat

Pointer is agile, athletic, and needs much exercise.

English springer spaniel is one of the largest spaniels.

Curly-coated retriever is one of the oldest breeds.

DRAMA

DRAMA HAS BEEN DELIGHTING people for at least 2,500 years. A Broadway musical, a play by Shakespeare, and a television soap opera are all different sorts of drama. What they have in common is the presence of actors, who perform a story (the play) in a theatrical setting, to entertain an audience and make them think. Dramatists (writers of drama) use their art to entertain and thrill their audience or, more seriously, to explore human character and raise questions about the nature and meaning of life.

Renaissance and 17th century

The traditions of ancient Greek drama were revived in Renaissance Italy and spread through Europe. Many plays were written in verse. Drama thrived in the 16th and 17th centuries, the age of English playwright William Shakespeare (1564–1616) and his contemporaries.

Lope de Vega

France
The French dramatist Jean Racine (1639–99) wrote plays that were heavily influenced by Greek tragedy and often based on Greek mythology. Unusually for the time, many featured women in the title role. Another great dramatist of the era, Molière (1622–73), developed French comedy with plays that mocked the middle classes.

Phèdre (1677), by Racine

Spain
The 17th century was the Golden Age of Spanish theatre. The Spanish dramatist Lope de Vega (1562–1635) wrote some 1,500 plays; his play *Fuenteovejuna* was one of the first to deal with ordinary working people. The other great Spanish dramatist of this time was Pedro Calderón de la Barca (1600–81), who produced many tragedies and historical plays.

Early drama

Western drama originated in ancient Greece, where plays were staged to honour the gods. The Greeks invented two of the most enduring dramatic forms, tragedy and comedy, which were later imitated by the Romans.

Classical Greek drama
The ancient Greeks held regular drama festivals, at which dramatists competed for prizes. Their tragedies were based on characters from Greek mythology. Their comedies ranged in style from uproarious satires to more realistic dramas.

Statuette of muse, holding a mask from Greek comedy

Medieval drama
Western drama went into a decline at the end of the Roman Empire, but revived in the 10th century, with the rise of Christian religious drama. Amateur players produced plays enacting stories from the Bible, performed over a number of days. The audience watched out of doors, in market-places and other public spaces.

Religious drama, York, England, 13th century

Realism and 20th century

From the mid-18th century onwards, drama became increasingly realistic, with playwrights portraying middle-class characters in familiar situations. Theatres were fitted with picture-frame stages and realistic sets. It was fashionable for plays to deliver a direct, moral message. During the 20th century, dramatists experimented with dialogue and plot structure, in order to challenge "realism" or give dramas a symbolic meaning.

A Doll's House (1879), by Ibsen

Realistic drama
Dramatists such as Norwegian Henrik Ibsen (1828–1906) and Swede August Strindberg (1849–1912) produced plays that attacked the narrow social attitudes of their time and sometimes shocked audiences with their frankness.

Bertolt Brecht
In his plays, the German writer Bertolt Brecht (1898–1956) put forward serious socialist messages. He constantly reminded his audience that they were watching a play, to make them think about the socialist ideas in his works, and look more closely at the world outside the theatre.

Types of drama

The many types of drama include tragedies (serious plays that deal with the downfall of a flawed but heroic individual) and light-hearted comedies (plays with happy endings). Other types include historical plays, thrillers, and musical theatre.

The stage is empty, except for a single tree.

Waiting for Godot (1955), by Irish writer Samuel Beckett (1906–89), is a type of modern drama known as the "Theatre of the Absurd": the plot seems to lead nowhere, suggesting life has no point.

Mother Courage (1941), by Brecht, is set during the Thirty Years' War.

The heroes wait for someone who does not arrive.

Broadway

A street in New York at the heart of the city's theatre-going district, Broadway is world famous, and synonymous with the commercial theatre in North America. Broadway productions need a big budget and guaranteed audiences, so more experimental plays often appear in theatres "off-Broadway" first, and transfer to a Broadway theatre if successful.

Broadcasting

Anyone with access to a television or radio can now enjoy drama every day. Sometimes these are productions of works originally written for the stage, and adapted. More common are dramas specially written for broadcasting. Many of these are run as series, so that every week, or even every day, people can watch or listen to another episode of their favourite drama. Some forms of television drama have proved especially popular, such as crime stories, adventure series, and soap operas.

O Maraja, *satirical Brazilian soap opera*

Soap operas
Immensely popular, these serialized television dramas usually deal with the lives and loves of "ordinary" people. Soap operas are so-called because they were at first sponsored by commercial companies such as soap manufacturers.

Actors

The skill of the actors is vital to the success of a drama. Using the right tone of voice, facial expression, or gesture, an actor creates the illusion that the audience is watching or listening to real people and events on stage or screen. Many actors study at drama school before becoming professionals, paid to appear on stage.

Drama festivals
Drama festivals are held around the world so that theatre-goers can celebrate the best in acting and writing. Plays range from traditional productions to experimental works from new writers. The Edinburgh International Festival, held annually, is world famous.

At a festival held each year in Salzburg, Austria, actors re-enact a medieval religious drama.

Chinese opera
Traditional Chinese, or Beijing, opera retells stories from historical events and Buddhist stories. The action comprises arias and recitations, mime, song, and dance, with music from an orchestra of traditional instruments, such as the lute, clappers, gongs, and drums.

Farewell My Concubine is a film about Chinese opera.

World drama

Many non-Western cultures have produced their own, distinct traditions of drama, which draw on local conditions and skills. In Asia, for example, drama draws on local mythology and tales of gods and goddesses. Such drama also uses local craft skills to produce striking costumes and masks, and may be accompanied with music played on traditional instruments.

Noh theatre

In traditional Japanese Noh drama, actors wear elaborate costumes and masks, but perform on a bare stage. They move slowly and make special, meaningful gestures. They chant their lines, accompanied by music. Plays are performed in groups, the whole programme lasting an entire day.

Noh masks represent five groups: male, female, old people, the gods, and monsters.

Ritual drama

In parts of Africa, Asia, and Melanesia, traditional drama forms an important part of religious ritual. A high priest or shaman puts on a mask and costume that completely disguises him and, as he dances to music, people believe that he actually becomes the spirit he is imitating.

Noh mask

Papua New Guinea Trobrianders: ritual religious drama.

Circuses

A circus is a form of entertainment that combines a number of different skills, such as juggling, acrobatics, clowning, and conjuring. Circuses date from the end of the 18th century. Animal acts once formed part of circus routines, but these are now less popular in the West.

Moscow State Circus

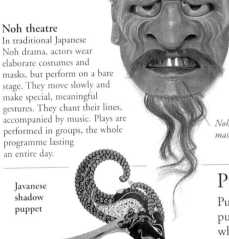
Javanese shadow puppet

In shadow plays, puppets are used to tell traditional stories.

Puppetry

Puppetry is a type of drama involving puppets, figures that seem to come to life when a human operator moves them. It is one of the oldest types of drama, dating from at least the 5th century BC. One example is shadow puppetry, which is popular in Southeast Asia. A light is used to cast a shadow from the puppet onto a translucent viewing screen. The puppet then acts out a play.

Robert Lepage

The Canadian playwright and director Robert Lepage (b. 1957) has achieved world status for his experimental work. Giving everyday objects symbolic meaning, and working closely with actors, he has taken risks that, while not always a critical success, push back the boundaries of drama.

Made from leather

The operator uses thin rods to move the puppet.

Timeline

5th century BC The Greeks pioneer tragedy and comedy.

11th to 15th centuries AD Religious drama becomes popular in Europe.

Statue of comic actor from Roman drama

1580–1642 In England, the Elizabethan and Jacobean dramatists revitalize English drama.

1600–80 The Golden Age of Spanish drama.

1782 Friedrich von Schiller (1759–1805) stages *The Robbers*, one of the plays that inspires the German Romantic movement in the 18th century.

c.1800 In Vietnam, Hat Boi theatre dramatizes tales of war and suffering.

Late 1800s "Realist" drama develops, exploring modern social issues.

1960s The "Theatre of the Absurd" subverts the conventions of the theatre.

1990s Musicals are the most popular type of play.

FIND OUT MORE FESTIVALS · FILMS AND FILM-MAKING · GREECE, ANCIENT · LITERATURE · MEDIEVAL EUROPE · OPERA · RENAISSANCE · SHAKESPEARE · THEATRES

DRUGS

A DRUG IS ANY SUBSTANCE that, when put into the body, alters its normal workings or body chemistry. Natural body hormones, such as insulin, can act as drugs when taken in concentrated form. Medical drugs have many uses. Some, such as cough suppressants, may relieve symptoms; others, such as analgesics, deaden pain; while others, including antibiotics, treat the cause of disease. Drugs may also be taken for non-medical reasons, such as steroids to enhance sports performance and body-building. The abuse of such drugs may be illegal, and can cause physical harm.

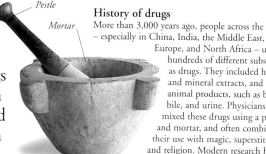

Pestle
Mortar

History of drugs
More than 3,000 years ago, people across the world – especially in China, India, the Middle East, Europe, and North Africa – used hundreds of different substances as drugs. They included herbal and mineral extracts, and animal products, such as blood, bile, and urine. Physicians mixed these drugs using a pestle and mortar, and often combined their use with magic, superstition, and religion. Modern research has discovered that some are effective.

Types of drugs
Drugs can be grouped by their medical uses or effects. For example, antibiotics kill bacteria, analgesics deaden pain, anti-inflammatories reduce swelling, anti-pyretics lower body temperature, and anti-coagulants help to prevent unwanted blood clots. Some drugs, such as aspirin, can be placed in more than one category.

Antibiotic
These drugs kill or disable germs (harmful microbes) known as bacteria. Most come from chemicals made either by fungi, or by other bacteria.

Antibiotic cream

Analgesic
Painkillers come in two types: narcotics, such as morphine, codeine, and other opiates originally from the opium poppy; and non-narcotics, such as paracetamol, which have a different origin.

Cytotoxic
The name means "cell-poisoners", but cytotoxic drugs are designed to affect only the out-of-control cells in tumours and malignancies (cancers), while leaving normal body cells unharmed. They are one type of anti-cancer drug. They are very powerful and their doses and uses must be carefully supervised.

Syringe containing cytotoxic drugs   Tablets and capsules

How drugs work
Drugs change the processes within the cells of the body. Their effectiveness depends on the dose (quantity), and method of administration (or route into the body). These routes include: absorption through the skin from a cream or a skin patch; injections into a muscle, vein, or under the skin; inhalation; eye or ear drops; or the oral route, where medication is swallowed as tablets, pills, capsules, or liquid.

Transdermal patches   Syrup

Pressurized inhaler

Chewing gum   Suppositories   Pills and tablets

Drugs from nature
Half of modern drugs originate from plants, fungi, animals, or microbes. In ancient times, people were unable to separate the actual drug – the active ingredient – from its source. As chemistry became more sophisticated, scientists identified and purified these ingredients making the drug safer. Some drugs extracted originally from nature are now made from genetically engineered microbes.

Fresh leaves

Witch hazel   *Resin*   *Dried parts*

Paul Ehrlich
The German scientist Paul Ehrlich (1854–1915) dreamed of finding a substance that would act as a "magic bullet", by destroying invading germs, while leaving healthy body cells unaffected. He pioneered synthetic drugs (chemical agents made in the laboratory, rather than extracted from natural sources). The first of these was Salvarsan, which was a laboratory-made drug containing arsenic; it was effective against syphilis and related infections.

Drug research
In the laboratory, scientists analyse potential new drugs. They perform tests on the drug to establish its chemistry, and how it affects the body's processes. Then they test it on tissues and cells in the laboratory, on animals, and finally on human volunteers in clinical trials.

Drug research laboratory

Aspirin

Brand name – the name by which manufacturers sell a drug, e.g. Aspro.

Generic name – the name by which the active ingredient is known, e.g. aspirin.

Common chemical name – showing the chemical subgroups, e.g. acetyl-salicylic acid.

Chemical formula – lists the atoms and their numbers in the drug, e.g. $C_9H_8O_4$.

Pharmacies

The science of drugs is known as pharmacology. Pharmacy refers to both the practice of preparing and dispensing drugs, and the place where this happens. A person qualified in pharmacology is called a pharmacist (or chemist). The dispensing chemist can advise on which drugs to use for minor ailments.

Pharmacist at work

Prescription

Some drugs, known as controlled substances, are only available with a doctor's permission. A prescription is a written and signed instruction from a doctor that authorizes a pharmacist to dispense a controlled substance. Prescriptions include the name and dosage of the drug, how often the patient must take it, and any other relevant instructions.

Hospital pharmacy

Over-the-counter drugs

Over-the-counter drugs are available without a prescription. They can be bought at supermarkets and pharmacies, and are usually less powerful than prescription drugs. They have fewer side-effects or contra-indications (health problems that warn against their use), but they are still open to misuse. Pharmacists are qualified to recommend certain drug preparations, although they cannot diagnose or prescribe treatment.

D

Non-medical drugs

Some drugs can be taken for their non-medicinal effects on the mind and body. These effects may include the stimulation or sedation of the mind, a temporary boost to physical performance in sport, or a feeling of emotional well-being.

Caffeine is found in coffee, tea, and cola.

Wine and brandy

Coffee

Sedatives

These drugs sedate (slow down) bodily functions, including physical activity and mental agility. Sedatives can make the user feel relaxed and peaceful for a short time. They include sleeping pills, antihistamines (which suppress allergic reactions), antidepressants, and alcohol, which is probably the most widely used non-medical drug in the world.

Stimulants

These drugs temporarily stimulate (speed up) bodily functions and mental processes. However, they can cause after-effects, such as depression. Stimulants include caffeine, nicotine (in tobacco), and cocaine.

Drug abuse

This is the improper non-medical use of legal or illegal drugs for physical or psychological reasons. The feelings and mental state experienced by the taker are often very different to that person's actual behaviour, seen by onlookers. After too much alcohol, a drinker may feel bright and witty, while onlookers see a slurring bore.

Customs official arresting a drug trafficker

Illegal drugs

Some drugs are so powerful and dangerous that they are illegal almost everywhere in the world. These include LSD and mescaline (known in some countires as Schedule I drugs), amphetamines, cocaine, and narcotics (Schedule II drugs). Supplying these illegal drugs to users has become a vast international business.

Tobacco shop

Legal drugs

The legality of drugs varies greatly all over the world. As well as the drug's strength and effects, legality often depends on tradition, religion, and availability. One of the most powerful and addictive drugs is alcohol. Alcohol is fully legalized in some countries, partly legalized (for people over 18 or 21) in others, and completely banned in others. Nicotine in the form of cigars, cigarettes, chewing tobacco, and snuff is also legal in most countries.

Group therapy session

Dependence and addiction

A person may come to depend on addictive drugs in order to function. Addiction – intense craving – is hard to control. If the user stops taking the drug, his or her body undergoes "withdrawal", which includes symptoms, such as headaches, sweating, hallucinations, and mood swings. People trying to stop using addictive drugs often find support groups are helpful.

Jonas Salk

Vaccines are substances that give the body resistance or immunity to certain infecting germs. In the 1950s, American microbiologist Jonas Salk (1914–95) developed the first effective vaccine against the crippling disease of polio (poliomyelitis). It spread into worldwide use from 1955 on. From 1960, an oral form of the vaccine, Sabin, gradually replaced the Salk injection.

Timeline

1840s Anaesthetics begin to be used during surgery.

1881 Artificial vaccine used against anthrax.

1910 Paul Ehrlich introduces chemo-therapeutic drugs.

Fresh witch hazel

1922 Frederick Banting and others treat diabetes using insulin, a natural body hormone.

1936 Treatment of infections improves with the advent of Prontosil, the first sulpha drug.

1940s Howard Florey and Ernst Chain make penicillin available as an antibiotic. It is used widely in World War II.

1956 Oral contraceptives (birth control pills) are introduced, using the natural female hormones, oestrogen and progestogen.

1967 Fertility drugs help couples conceive.

1983 Cyclosporin, an immuno-suppressant, helps prevent rejection of transplanted organs.

1990s AIDS drugs tested.

Tablets and capsules

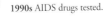
FIND OUT MORE   FIRST AID   HOSPITALS   MEDICINE   MEDICINE, HISTORY OF   PASTEUR, LOUIS   PLANT USES

DUCKS, GEESE, AND SWANS

MOST DUCKS, GEESE, AND SWANS spend their life on or near water. They belong to a family of birds called waterfowl and are closely related to each other. They have broad beaks and short legs with webbed feet. They are good swimmers and have waterproof plumage, which keeps them dry and also helps them to float. There are about 160 species of waterfowl in the wild. Some species of duck and goose have been domesticated and are often raised on farms.

Khaki Campbell – a domestic duck

Ducks

Ducks are the smallest and most varied waterfowl. Males are often brightly coloured and females are usually drab, which helps to camouflage them when they are sitting on their eggs. Some ducks live in coastal waters, but most live on rivers, lakes, and ponds.

Webs stretched open

Webs closed

Swimming

A duck's webbed feet work like paddles to push it through the water. When it pushes its feet backward, it spreads its toes to stretch out the webs between them. When it pulls its feet forward, it closes its toes to shut the webs, which then offer less water resistance.

Plumage

Ducks produce a waterproof oil from a gland near the base of their tail. When they preen their feathers, they spread the oil over them. This oil is so effective that a duck stays dry even when it dives beneath the surface.

Swans

The largest waterfowl are swans, with a wingspan of up to 2.3 m (7.5 ft). Most of the eight species are white, but the Australian black swan has a black body and white flight feathers. A swan spends a lot of its time on water. It uses its long neck to reach plants below the surface.

Mute swan has a black knob at the base of its beak.

With its wings held wide, the duckling jumps.

Big feet and stubby wings work like parachutes to slow the duckling's fall.

A Mandarin duckling leaves the nest in response to its mother's call.

A tree duckling must jump before it is a day old to find food.

Mute swan egg is an oval shape.

Swan egg

Young swans
Young swans, or cygnets, stay with their parents for a whole year, which is a long time for a bird. When they develop their adult plumage, their parents drive them away.

Nesting swans
Swans nest on the ground close to the water's edge. The female incubates the eggs for up to 38 days, and she hisses loudly at anything that comes too close. If her warnings are ignored, she attacks. Her powerful beak and wings make formidable weapons.

Tree-nesting ducks
Most ducks nest on the ground but a few lay their eggs in holes in trees. Soon after the young have hatched, their mother leaves the nest and calls to them to follow her. The ducklings are too young to fly, and instead they jump to the ground.

Swan takeoff
Swans can weigh up to 13 kg (28.5 lb), which makes them among the world's heaviest flying birds. Swans cannot take off from a standing start. Instead, they have to run across the water to gain enough speed for takeoff.

The duckling walks away on landing.

Geese

Unlike most waterfowl, geese usually feed on land. They eat grass, gripping it in their beaks and pulling it up with a tug. Many geese breed in the tundra of the far north. These white-fronted geese, seen here in western Scotland, fly north to Greenland after the winter.

MUTE SWAN

SCIENTIFIC NAME	*Cygnus olor*
ORDER	Anseriformes
FAMILY	Anatidae
DISTRIBUTION	Western Europe, parts of central Asia; also introduced into other parts of the world, including North America, Australia, and New Zealand
HABITAT	Lakes and rivers
DIET	Water plants
SIZE	Length: 152 cm (60 in)
LIFESPAN	About 20 years

FIND OUT MORE ANIMAL BEHAVIOUR · BIRDS · EGGS · FARMING · FLIGHT, ANIMALS · PENGUINS · SEABIRDS

DYES AND PAINTS

DYES AND PAINTS are substances that are used to stain or give colour to a range of objects, from textiles and paper to buildings and machinery. The substances that give colour to dyes are called dyestuffs, which, when dissolved in water, penetrate the fibres of fabrics by means of a chemical reaction. Pigments form the colour in paints. These are held in place using a varnish-like substance called a vehicle, or binder, which also binds the pigment to the surface being painted. Throughout history, people have created colour, first by means of natural dyes and pigments, and today by using synthetic ones.

Early pigments

The first materials used as pigments were probably coloured clays, which were mixed with water or animal oils to make paint. Dyes made from plants and animals were later used to colour textiles. Common plant dyes included woad, madder, saffron, and turmeric. Animal sources included cochineal (beetle) and the Murex sea snail.

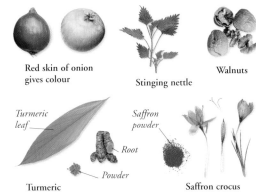

Red skin of onion gives colour

Stinging nettle

Walnuts

Turmeric leaf

Saffron powder

Root

Powder

Turmeric

Saffron crocus

Dyes

Some natural dyes still exist, but most used today are synthetic. These are organic chemicals produced by processing petroleum and coal-tar chemicals such as benzene. Most dyes are used in the textile industry, but are also used in the leather, paper, food, and cosmetics industries. The dyes can be applied to the fibre or fabric using either a direct or indirect process.

Fabrics can be coloured using a range of dyes

Wool can by dyed using a mordant dye, but this dye is now avoided in Western countries due to its use of potentially harmful chemicals.

Indirect dyeing

In some dyeing processes, a number of steps are needed to dye the fibre. In one process, a chemical called a mordant is first added to the fibre, which is then dyed. The mordant molecules fix the dye to the fabric.

Direct dyeing

In most industrial dyeing processes today, dyes can enter the fibre and colour it in one step, without the need of a mordant. The dye is dissolved in hot water, strained, and then added to the fabric. Sometimes the dye is mixed with salt to help fix the colour.

The T-shirt on the left shows how the dye has faded.

This T-shirt shows how the colour has remained fast.

Colour fastness

Two of the most important properties demanded of a dye by clothes manufacturers are its abilities to resist being washed out, and not to fade in the light. The colour fastness of a fabric also varies according to the dyeing process that is used and the type of material that is being dyed.

Paints

Paint comes in many colours and can be used as a coating on rigid structures such as houses, bridges, ships, and cars. Finer paints are used by artists to produce imaginative and colourful works of art. The pigments used to make the paints may be natural, such as rutile (titanium dioxide) or synthetic, such as phthalocyanine blue.

Oil paints usually come in tubes so that users can squeeze out the exact amount of paint needed.

Oil paints

Artists' paints

Artists use a variety of types of paint to achieve different effects, including watercolours, oils, and acrylics. The pigments in watercolour paints are mixed with a water solution of gum arabic, in oils they are mixed in a slow-drying oil, such as linseed oil, while in acrylics the pigments are mixed with a synthetic-resin vehicle.

Industrial paints

Industrial paints are custom-made for specific jobs. Some paints contain powdered metal and metal oxides, so that the paint can protect exposed structures, such as iron bridges. Paints such as those used on cars are designed to withstand rusting and high temperatures.

Paint-spraying car body

Domestic paints

Most decorating paints are made for easy application. Non-drip paints are jelly-like in the can, but flow easily when applied. Emulsion paint uses water as its vehicle, so splashes can be removed and brushes easily cleaned.

Can of non-drip paint and brush

William Henry Perkin

British chemist William Henry Perkin (1838–1907) accidentally produced the first synthetic dye, mauve, in 1856. He was attempting to make the drug quinine from coal-tar chemicals, but instead produced a purple liquid dye. This was the start of the synthetic dye industry.

FIND OUT MORE — ART, HISTORY OF · CHEMISTRY · CLOTHES AND FASHION · COAL · COLOUR · MIXTURES AND COMPOUNDS · MONET, CLAUDE · PAINTING AND DRAWING · TEXTILES AND WEAVING

EARS AND HEARING

WHEN A BEE BUZZES, a soprano sings, or a jumbo jet takes off, each generates invisible vibrations called sound waves that enter the ears, the body's organs of hearing. The sound waves travel deep inside the skull to the part of the ear that does the hearing. Here, sound waves are converted into nerve impulses that travel along nerves to the auditory, or hearing, area on each side of the brain. In the brain, the impulses are interpreted as sounds. The ears can pick up a wide range of sounds and, with the eyes, they help us to make sense of our surroundings.

Anatomy of the ear

Mostly concealed within the skull, the ear is divided into three parts. The outer ear consists of the pinna (ear flap) and the auditory canal. The middle ear is filled with air and contains three tiny bones called ossicles. The inner ear is fluid-filled and contains the cochlea and the semi-circular canals.

Temporal bone

Semicircular canal   *Inner ear*

Cochlea

Middle ear contains three bones called the ossicles: the malleus, incus, and stapes.

Eardrum

Auditory canal carries sound into ear and produces wax that keeps the ear dust and insect free.

Eustachian tube connects middle ear to throat to equalize air pressure inside and outside the ear.

Pinna

Hearing sounds

Sound waves channelled into the auditory canal cause the eardrum and the ossicles to vibrate. These vibrations travel through the fluid-filled cochlea. Inside the cochlea, sensory hair cells convert the vibrations into nerve impulses. These are carried by the cochlear nerve to the brain.

Eardrum

The eardrum, or tympanic membrane, is a taut piece of skin that separates the auditory canal from the middle ear. When sound waves hit the eardrum, it vibrates like a drum and transmits its vibrations to the ossicles of the middle ear.

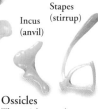

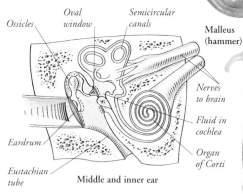

Ossicles   *Oval window*   *Semicircular canals*

Malleus (hammer)   **Incus (anvil)**   **Stapes (stirrup)**

Nerves to brain

Fluid in cochlea

Eardrum

Organ of Corti

Eustachian tube

Middle and inner ear

Ossicles

The ossicles are the three smallest bones in the body. The malleus, incus, and stapes connect the eardrum to the cochlea by way of the oval window.

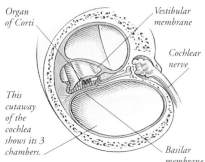

Organ of Corti   *Vestibular membrane*

Cochlear nerve

This cutaway of the cochlea shows its 3 chambers.

Basilar membrane

Cochlea

The cochlea is a long, coiled tube in the inner ear that is filled with fluid. It is divided by two membranes into three chambers that run lengthways. The middle of these three chambers, the cochlear chamber, contains the spiral organ of Corti, which consists of over 20,000 sensory hair cells that send nerve signals to the brain.

Bartolomeo Eustachio

Italian anatomist Bartolomeo Eustachio (1520–74) studied the detailed anatomy of the ear, as well as other body organs and systems, while he was a professor in Rome. He wrote the first full description of the ears in his book *The Examination of the Organ of Hearing*, published in 1562. Included in this was the first detailed description of the tube that links the middle ear with the throat. This was later named the Eustachian tube.

Air pressure

You hear most clearly when the air pressure inside the middle ear is the same as the air pressure outside your body. If the air pressure outside changes suddenly, you may not be able to hear properly. This can happen if you are a on a plane that is taking off or landing, or if you are travelling on a fast train.

Balance

Part of the inner ear helps you to balance. Sensors inside the three semicircular canals detect movements made by the head and the rest of the body. Sensors inside two adjoining chambers, the saccule and utricle, detect whether the body is upright, upside-down, or in between. Nerve impulses from the semicircular canals are analysed by the brain to assess the body's position.

Gymnast's outstretched arms help balance.

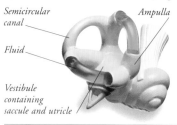

Semicircular canal   *Ampulla*

Fluid

Vestibule containing saccule and utricle

Semicircular canals

The three semicircular canals in each ear are filled with fluid. At the base of each canal is a bulge, called an ampulla, which contains sensory hair cells that send impulses to the brain. The three canals are set at 90° to each other, so they can detect movement in any direction.

Hearing ranges

The pitch of a sound depends on the frequency of the sound waves that produced it. High-pitched sounds have a high frequency, and low-pitched sounds have a low frequency. Frequency is measured in units called Hertz (Hz). Our hearing ability decreases as we get older, from 20,000 to 12,000 Hz.

Bats' ears can hear very high-pitched sound waves called ultrasound.

20–20,000 Hz   1,000–120,000 Hz

FIND OUT MORE   BRAIN AND NERVOUS SYSTEM   HUMAN BODY   MUSIC   SOUND

EARTH

WE LIVE ON A GIANT BALL OF ROCK spinning round the Sun, which we call the Earth. The Earth is one of nine planets in the Solar System and one of the four made of rock. However, the Earth is unique, because it is the only planet in the Solar System – and perhaps even in the Universe – that can support life. The distance of the Earth from the Sun makes it neither very hot like Venus, nor icy cold like Pluto, enabling liquid water to exist on its surface. The Earth also has an oxygen-rich atmosphere. These two substances – water and oxygen – are the key factors that allow life to flourish on the Earth.

Structure of the Earth

By recording the way vibrations from earthquakes reverberate through the Earth, scientists have discovered that the Earth has an egg-like structure. At its centre is a "yolk" of metal, surrounded by an "egg-white" of soft rock called the mantle, and an outer "shell" of hard rock called the crust.

The Earth's crust consists of a number of interlocking slabs of rock called tectonic plates.

Earth's ingredients

Although more than 80 elements (basic substances) occur naturally on the Earth, the bulk of the Earth is made of iron (35%), oxygen (28%), magnesium (17%), and silicon (13%). The following elements are present in significant, but small, amounts: nickel (2.7%), sulphur (2.7%), calcium (0.6%), and aluminium (0.6%). Tiny proportions of other elements make up the remainder (0.6%).

Solid iron

Molecule of oxygen gas

Magnesium ore (magnesite)

Investigating Earth's composition
By taking rock samples from the Earth's interior, geologists have been able to understand the Earth's chemical make-up. Analysis of meteorites – solid pieces from an exploded planet – has led some geologists to believe that the Earth may have formed from the same space debris of which meteorites are made.

Locket containing crystal of silicon

Nickel ore (nickeline)

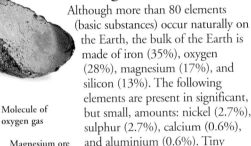

Chondrite meteorite

Sulphur crystals

Meteorites
Meteorites are natural objects that fall to the Earth from space. They are made of iron, stone, or a mixture of both. The two main types of meteorite are called chondrites and achondrites.

Calcium-rich chalk

Aluminium ore (bauxite)

Achondrite meteorite

The Earth's structure

Inner core, like the outer core, is made of iron and nickel, but although temperatures reach 3,700°C (6,690°F), the pressure is so great that the metal remains solid.

Atmosphere is a thin surrounding layer of gases about 640 km (400 miles) deep.

Crust, Earth's outer layer of rock varies in thickness: beneath the oceans, it is 6–11 km (4–7 miles) thick, but it stretches up to 70 km (43 miles) under mountain ranges.

Mohorovicic discontinuity, or Moho, is the boundary between the crust and the mantle.

Mantle is a partially molten layer beneath the crust, extending to a depth of about 2,900 km (1,800 miles) and made largely of a rock called peridotite.

Gutenberg discontinuity is the boundary between the mantle and the core.

Outer core reaches to a depth of about 4,900 km (3,050 miles) and is made of molten iron and nickel – magnetic metals that give the Earth its magnetic field.

Richard Oldham

By examining the seismographic recordings of earthquakes, the British geologist Richard Oldham (1858–1936) discovered that earthquakes produce two different kinds of vibration. He called them primary (P) waves and secondary (S) waves. Oldham's analysis revealed that P waves travel more slowly through the core of the Earth than through the mantle. He concluded that Earth's core must be liquid, which is partly true.

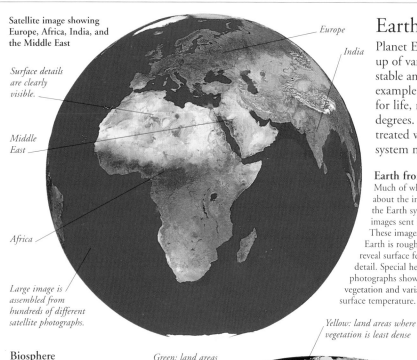

Satellite image showing Europe, Africa, India, and the Middle East

Europe

India

Surface details are clearly visible.

Middle East

Africa

Large image is assembled from hundreds of different satellite photographs.

Earth system

Planet Earth seems to operate like a vast, complex system made up of various interconnected processes that keep conditions stable and suitable for life. The atmosphere's unique make up, for example, ensures that the Earth stays at an ideal temperature for life, never heating up or cooling down by more than a few degrees. Scientists now realize that the environment must be treated with care, because a change to one part of this complex system may have unpredictable repercussions in other parts.

Earth from space
Much of what scientists know about the interrelated parts of the Earth system comes from images sent back by satellites. These images show us that the Earth is roughly spherical and reveal surface features in clear detail. Special heat-sensitive infrared photographs show the distribution of vegetation and variations in the Earth's surface temperature.

Energy regulation
The Earth system exchanges energy with its surroundings, but there is no overall gain or loss of energy. The Earth receives heat, light, and other forms of energy directly from the Sun. Some of this energy is reflected back by the clouds, oceans, land, and atmosphere; the rest is absorbed and then released back into space. The total energy the Earth gives out equals the total energy it receives from the Sun.

Biosphere
Between the atmosphere's lowest layers and the ocean floor is a rich diversity of life, from tiny ocean organisms called plankton to the largest trees and animals. Together, these organisms form the biosphere – the living part of the planet. Satellite images can help scientists understand the complicated links between living things and the Earth.

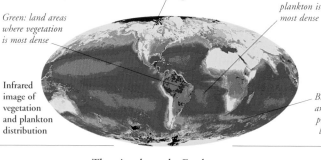

Yellow: land areas where vegetation is least dense

Green: land areas where vegetation is most dense

Red: ocean areas where plankton is most dense

Infrared image of vegetation and plankton distribution

Blue: ocean areas where plankton is least dense

Infrared image of temperature variations in the Atlantic Ocean off the USA's eastern coast

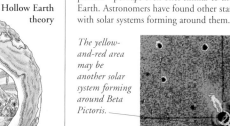

Locator map

Gaia theory

Greek statue of Gaia, 450 BC

British scientist James Lovelock (b. 1919) suggests that the Earth and all the lifeforms upon it function as if they were a single living organism. He calls this "organism" Gaia, after the Greek goddess of fertility. Like any other organism, he says, Gaia is self-regulating, meaning that it will naturally change its environment to maintain the right conditions for life – even if humans make the Earth unfit for themselves by polluting it and using up its limited resources.

Theories about the Earth
There have been many theories about the Earth that may seem strange to people today, but which were widely believed at the time. The ancient Egyptians, for example, thought that the Earth was a flat square under a pyramid-shaped sky, and people in medieval Europe believed that it was the Sun that revolved around the Earth, and not vice versa. Similarly, before technology enabled scientists to understand more about the interior of the Earth, people suggested that the Earth was hollow.

People assumed the Earth had a vast, empty core.

Hidden lands and oceans, complete with plants and animals and warmed by a subterranean Sun, were thought to lie within the centre of the Earth.

Hollow Earth theory

Search for another Earth
Astronomers have recently detected signs of the existence of planets beyond the Solar System. Wobbles in the movements of the stars 47 Ursae Majoris, 70 Virginis, and 51 Pegasi suggest that they may be orbited by planets – perhaps even ones similar to Earth. Astronomers have found other stars with solar systems forming around them.

The yellow-and-red area may be another solar system forming around Beta Pictoris.

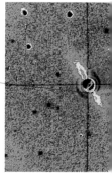

False-colour satellite image of the star Beta Pictoris, about 50 light years away

Timeline
c.4,600 mya The Earth and the other planets form as parts of a vast cloud of hot gas and dust circling the Sun begin to cluster together.

c.4,300 mya The Earth's crust forms.

c.4,200 mya As the Earth cools, gas bubbles and water vapour rise from the interior to form a cloudy atmosphere.

Gneiss rock

c.4,000 mya The crust and mantle separate; rain begins to fall; the atmosphere clears.

c.3,800 mya The first organisms are single-celled bacteria.

c.3,000 mya The atmosphere becomes oxygen-rich as ocean plants absorb sunlight and release oxygen into the air.

c.1,500 mya Protists, such as amoeba, are the first complex living cells; later, protists join up to form sponges – the first multi-celled organisms.

c.570 mya A huge variety of complex lifeforms develops in the Earth's seas and oceans.

Sponge

c.440–400 mya Land-based plants and animals become widespread.

c.220 mya There is a single, vast land mass, now known as Pangaea, which later breaks up into the smaller land masses we today call continents.

c.200–70 mya The era of the dinosaurs.

c.100,000 ya First modern humans appear.

FIND OUT MORE ATMOSPHERE   CONTINENTS   EARTH SCIENCES   ELEMENTS   FOSSILS   GEOLOGY   MAGNETISM   PREHISTORIC LIFE   PLANETS   SUN

EARTHQUAKES

FROM A GENTLE RIPPLE to terrifying and violent movements in the Earth, earthquakes literally rock the world. Earthquakes are tremors in the ground, created by the sudden movement of tectonic plates – huge slabs of rock that make up the Earth's crust. The majority of earthquakes are so gentle that no one notices them, but some are so violent they destroy whole cities. An earthquake's effect and intensity are measured on different scales. In earthquake-prone countries, planning minimizes the damage earthquakes cause.

Earthquake zones

Earthquake zones
Although earthquakes can occur anywhere, they are more frequent in earthquake zones. These zones, such as Japan and California, lie near the moving margins of the tectonic plates, called fault lines.

What is an earthquake?
Tectonic plates usually slide past each other, but sometimes they get stuck together. The stress on the rocks builds up until they fault (crack). The tectonic plates then jolt past each other, sending shock waves through the ground. These vibrations, known as seismic waves, cause the earth to quake.

The Mercalli scale rates an earthquake according to its effect on a scale of I–XII: a swinging light bulb measures I; extensive structural damage measures XII.

Epicentre
The point at which an earthquake occurs is known as the focus. Above the focus is the epicentre – the point on the Earth's surface where the effects of an earthquake are most devastating. The focus may be as much as 700 km (185 miles) below the epicentre. In 1985, an earthquake in Mexico City, with its epicentre in the Pacific Ocean, left 9,500 people dead. It measured 8.1 on the Richter scale.

Seismometer
Seismometers show seismic waves, and measure an earthquake's location and intensity on the Richter scale. The height of each line shows the wave's force.

Reading from Kobe, Japan

Destruction diminishes as shock waves travel away from the epicentre, recording less on the Richter scale.

Earthquake that causes small object to fall rates V on the Mercalli scale.

Folds form in the ground as the Earth moves.

Epicentre

Focus

Shock waves radiate outwards in circles from focus.

The Richter scale measures the force of an earthquake on a scale from 1–10, taken from seismograph readings of the seismic waves. Each figure represents a force 10 times greater than that of the next lowest figure.

Tsunami
These are huge waves precipitated when an earthquake or volcanic eruption shakes the sea floor. Tsunamis roll along the ocean floor as fast as a jet plane. When they reach shallow coastal waters, they rear up into water ridges about 30 m (100 ft) high. Many tsunamis occur in the Pacific Ocean, such as the one in Hawaii, 1964 (left).

Earthquake proofing
Technology cannot prevent earthquakes but it can help limit their damage, particularly in building design. Most loss of life is caused not by the shaking ground, but by the collapse of buildings and roads, and fires started by damage to electrical equipment.

Building design
Pyramid-shaped, curved, and fire-resistant buildings and structures, such as this staircase in California, USA, bend rather than break during an earthquake. Mounting foundations on rubber also helps absorb some of the earthquake shocks.

Timeline
1556 Reports of an earthquake in the region of Shaanxi, China. Almost a million deaths.

1755 Lisbon, Portugal, is destroyed by an earthquake and the subsequent flood.

1883 Krakatoa Island destroyed by earthquake and tsunami.

1906 Quake flattens San Francisco, USA.

1964 Alaska hit by a very severe earthquake, measuring 9.2 on the Richter scale.

1964 Earthquake in Alaska generates a tsunami, which causes damage as far away as California, USA.

1976 Earthquake in China kills 255,000.

1990 In Iran 40,000 people die in quake.

1995 Kobe, central Japan, is devastated by an earthquake.

1999 Turkish quake kills 20,000 and makes 200,000 homeless.

2001 Earthquake in Gujarat, India, leaves 30,000 people dead.

FIND OUT MORE   BUILDING AND CONSTRUCTION   CONTINENTS   EARTH   GEOLOGY   OCEAN FLOOR   RADAR AND SONAR

EARTH SCIENCES

FOSSILS PROVIDE CLUES to the ages of rocks; the atmosphere provides clues to tomorrow's weather. Amongst others, these elements are studied within the discipline of Earth sciences. This is the study of the planet's physical characteristics, from volcanoes to raindrops. The different branches of Earth sciences cover all of the Earth's dynamic systems, apart from life forms, which are studied within biology. Knowledge about the Earth's history and formation also informs us about its needs, which will help ensure the future survival of the planet.

Branches of Earth sciences

The term Earth sciences has been used since the 1970s. It covers the range of subjects that were previously bracketed under the term "physical geography". Although each of the Earth sciences is a distinct study focusing on one aspect of the Earth, each is also a key element of the inter-related study of Earth sciences.

Granite

Pebbles

Anthracite, a form of coal

Palaeontology
Fossils, the remains of once living organisms preserved in sedimentary rock, are studied within the branch of Earth science called palaeontology. From fossils, scientists can work out the ages of rocks and develop a picture of the history of plant and animal life on Earth over billions of years.

Fossil of a sea creature

Geology
The oldest branch of the Earth sciences, geology is the study of the Earth's history, structure, and make-up. Although it centres on rocks and the composition of the Earth's crust, geology also relates to the other Earth sciences, except for meteorology.

Earth sciences cover many different areas of study.

Volcanology
The study of volcanoes, and the reasons why they erupt, is known as volcanology. It may involve volcanologists working close to an erupting volcano. The scientists wear special clothing to protect them from gas, heat, and flying lava bombs.

Volcanic bombs

Geomorphology
The study of landforms and the processes that shape them is known as geomorphology. It includes landforms ranging from mountains and valleys to rivers and glaciers, and the effects of different shaping processes upon them, such as the erosion caused by weathering.

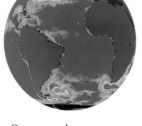

Oceanography
The study of the oceans is called oceanography. It covers ocean chemistry, the ocean bed and currents (shown above by satellite), and marine life.

Geography
This is the study of the Earth's surface. Human geography looks at world patterns of human activity; physical geography studies the Earth's physical environment.

Meteorology
The atmosphere is studied within the discipline of meteorology. This focuses on the processes that make the weather, and on weather forecasting. Climatology is the study of weather patterns.

Surveying the Earth

Earth scientists can learn very little about the Earth from laboratory studies. Instead, they must make observations, collect data, and test their theories in the outside world – this may mean climbing mountains or braving earthquakes. Satellite photography has provided a vast new source of data, but most information continues to come from field work.

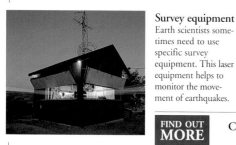

Survey equipment
Earth scientists sometimes need to use specific survey equipment. This laser equipment helps to monitor the movement of earthquakes.

Earth resources

The Earth provides all the materials we need for living, from the food we eat and the water we drink, to the bricks we use for building. Earth sciences help us to identify the location of these resources. They also show what damage we may be doing to them by exploiting them thoughtlessly.

Squid

Fruit

Air
We need air to breathe virtually every second of our lives. However, this vital resource is becoming increasingly damaged by human pollution.

Tourmaline gemstone

Minerals
From metal for cars to concrete for buildings, nearly everything we make comes from the minerals or chemicals taken from the Earth's crust. Gems are another of its rich resources.

Water
All forms of life are dependent on water. Patterns of human activity are controlled by the need to be near a source of clean water.

Food
Food is provided by things living on the Earth's surface. These depend on the mineral resources, water, and air provided by the Earth.

Energy
Ninety per cent of the energy we use comes from a finite supply of minerals – oil, coal, and gas – extracted from the Earth's crust.

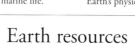

FIND OUT MORE

CLIMATE   EARTH   FOSSILS   GEOLOGY   OCEANS AND SEAS   ROCKS AND MINERALS   VOLCANOES   WEATHER

ECOLOGY AND ECOSYSTEMS

NO LIVING THING exists in isolation. It interacts with other living things and with its physical surroundings. The study of these relationships is called ecology. Ecologists consider all the organisms that live in one area as an inter-dependent community. All plants and animals rely on, and influence, vital factors in their environment, such as the supply of nutrients, food, and water. A community and its environment is called an ecosystem.

Communities
Wildlife communities exist almost everywhere you look, on land, in rivers, and in the oceans. A typical community contains a mixture of plants, various animals that feed on them or hunt one another, and organisms that burrow through the soil debris below.

Trees offer shelter for animals, and food in the form of leaves, berries, seeds, and blossom.

Insects feeding on flowers help to pollinate them.

Habitats
The habitat of a species is the surroundings in which it lives, including the rocks, soils, water, and plants. Different habitats are suitable for different species and have a certain type of community.

Mice eat seeds, and are hunted by bigger animals.

Dense undergrowth provides shelter for small animals.

Most of the tadpoles that hatch out from the frog spawn will be food for other animals.

Rotting wood is home to fungi and invertebrates.

Snails feed on the leaves of plants and are food for some birds such as thrushes.

As ferns grow, they take nutrients from the soil.

Frogs live in both land and water habitats.

Biomes
The biggest ecological units are biomes, such as deserts, rainforests, and lakes, across which similar climatic and other conditions create similar ecosystems. The plants and animals may differ across a biome, but they make up the same sort of communities with the same ecological features.

Seashores
Battered by waves and flooded by tides, seashores have few plants other than seaweeds. Animals include shellfish, rockpool fish, and wading birds.

Deserts
Cloud-free, dry climates create deserts. These are home only to plants and animals that are able to cope with extremes of aridity and temperature.

Grassland
Grassland is normal in places where there is a long dry season. It can support lots of grazing animals, some preyed on by swift-running predators. The savannah of East Africa is one of the best-known areas of grassland.

Rainforests
In hot, humid climates, dense forests develop that are home to a huge variety of animal life. Tropical rainforests cover only 10 per cent of the Earth's land surface, but contain more than half of all animal and plant species.

Ecosystems
An ecosystem contains several different wildlife communities and their habitat. Ecologists use the term to mean all the complicated interactions that take place among living and non-living things in an area. The various components of the ecosystem include sunshine, water, nutrients in the soil, bacteria, plants, and animals.

Fresh water
Lake- and river-dwelling communities include floating or submerged plants, freshwater plankton, and fish. Different species live in different parts of a river or lake, depending on the conditions that they tolerate. This is Bow Lake in the Canadian Rockies.

E

E

Ecological interactions

The components of an ecosystem interact with each other in lots of different ways. Rain, for example, provides water for plants. Plant growth and decay affect the form and content of soil. Soil provides a home for worms, and worms, as they move about, change the structure of the soil.

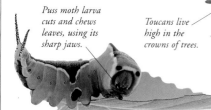

Puss moth larva cuts and chews leaves, using its sharp jaws.

Toucans live high in the crowns of trees.

Food

Perhaps the most obvious way in which living species affect one another's lives is by feeding. Most things are food for something else. For example, caterpillars eat leaves, but are themselves food for animals such as birds. The birds are food for other animals, and so on up the food chain.

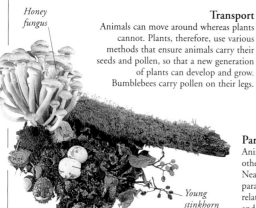

Honey fungus

Young stinkhorn fungus

Transport

Animals can move around whereas plants cannot. Plants, therefore, use various methods that ensure animals carry their seeds and pollen, so that a new generation of plants can develop and grow. Bumblebees carry pollen on their legs.

Pollen sac

Bumblebees collect nectar with their tongue.

Shelter

The cover and shelter that trees and vegetation provide offer much more security than bare, open ground. In a rainforest, the large trees provide toucans with shelter from the weather, a place where they can raise their young in relative safety, and protection from predators.

Parasitism

Animals, plants, and fungi that live off other living things are called parasites. Nearly all animals and plants are host to parasites of some kind. A parasitic relationship exists between a honey fungus and a tree. The fungus steals food from the tree, usually harming it in the process.

Symbiosis

When two species have a close relationship in which both benefit, it is called symbiotic. Symbiosis often involves giving shelter in return for protection or food, and it occurs among all kinds of organisms.

Clownfish

Clownfish find shelter among the stinging tentacles of sea anemones, which do not harm them. The fish may lure in other fish for the anemones to consume.

Clownfish stay where they are protected.

Adaptation

All plants and animals are specially suited to live in their particular habitat. How they become suited, or adapted, is the key to evolution. How and where a species lives, how it gets its food, what it eats, and how it interacts with others, is known as its ecological niche.

Cacti

A cactus has adapted in many ways to desert life. For example, its leaves have adapted into spines, to prevent water from evaporating too easily. When rain does fall, a cactus stores as much water as possible in its stem.

Spines protect the swollen stem.

Cycles in nature

Nature automatically recycles the substances that are vital for life. Oxygen, nitrogen, carbon, and water are constantly being exchanged between the air, the soil, the oceans, and living things. If substances were not continuously put back into the ecosystems to be used again, the supply for organisms would soon run out and life would stop.

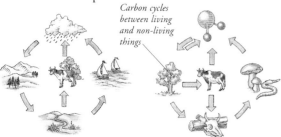

Carbon cycles between living and non-living things

Water cycle

Water lost by evaporation from plants, rivers, and seas, forms clouds in the atmosphere. This falls back as rain, runs into rivers and seas, and is soaked up from the soil by the roots of plants.

Carbon cycle

Organisms release carbon dioxide into the air. Carbon is also released when organisms decay, or when coal is burned. Plants absorb carbon from the air, which passes into animals that eat them.

Ecological change

Ecosystems do not always stay the same but may change over time. If an event changes the landscape, for example, high winds create a clearing in a wood, first grasses and herbs grow, then shrubs colonize the plot until trees take over once again.

The process of change from grassland to woodland is called succession.

Land erosion in Madagascar

Human impact

People's actions also change ecosystems and often the impact is so great that nature cannot repair the damage. For example, poor farming techniques sometimes cause so much soil to be eroded away from the land, that plants cannot get established and the vegetation can never recover.

FIND OUT MORE   ANIMAL BEHAVIOUR   EVOLUTION   FOOD WEBS AND CHAINS   POLLUTION   SOIL

ECUADOR AND PERU

TOGETHER ECUADOR AND PERU form the western side of equatorial South America, lying between Colombia to the north, Chile to the south, and Brazil and Bolivia to the east. The dominant influences in the west of the region were the Incas, who ruled until the 1500s, and the conquering Spaniards, who imposed their own culture and language. About 40 per cent of the population are *mestizos*, who are people of mixed blood resulting from intermarriage between Spaniards and Incas. Many Native Americans still live in remote Amazonian villages.

E

Physical features

Lying on South America's Pacific Coast, Ecuador and Peru are dominated by the jagged volcanic peaks of the Andes, whose eastern slopes descend to the hot, humid, tropical rainforest and wetlands of the Amazon Basin. To the west is the coastal strip. Peru's coast is largely arid desert, but Ecuador's coast is hot, swampy, or forested.

Mount Cotopaxi
A perfect cone capped with snow, Cotopaxi, 5,897 m (19,345 ft) is the world's highest active volcano and Ecuador's second highest peak. It lies in the Andes, which form the backbone of both Ecuador and Peru. Ecuador has 15 major volcanoes, ten of which are active. The whole region is shaken from time to time by earthquakes, which cause damage to cities.

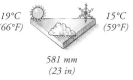

Amazon Basin
The steamy Amazon Basin occupies the eastern regions of Ecuador and Peru. The forest is not an uninterrupted mass of trees, but contains pockets of grassland and swamps. The headwaters of the Amazon originate in this region. Much of this area is disputed territory awarded to Peru in 1942.

Regional climate
19°C (66°F)   15°C (59°F)

Ecuador is hot and humid along the coast, cool and fresh in the Andes, and hot with heavy rainfall in the Amazon Basin. Peru

581 mm (23 in)

has a more mixed climate. The coastal region is dry, and kept cool by the cold waters of the Peru Current. The western part of the Peruvian Andes is fairly dry, but the eastern Andes and tropical Amazonia have heavy rainfall.

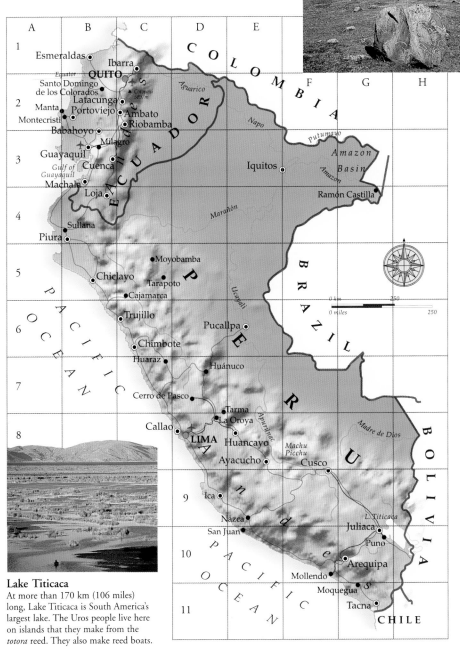

Lake Titicaca
At more than 170 km (106 miles) long, Lake Titicaca is South America's largest lake. The Uros people live here on islands that they make from the *totora* reed. They also make reed boats.

Coca

The Incas used to chew coca leaves to relieve fatigue and hunger. Today, in remote areas, coca is grown illegally to produce the powerful and dangerous drug cocaine for supply to the international drug trade. Governments are offering farmers money to destroy their coca crops and grow bananas, cocoa, or coffee instead.

Picking coca leaves, Quillabamba, Peru

E

Ecuador

The third smallest, most densely populated independent country in South America, Ecuador is also one of the most geographically varied and politically stable. Agriculture and oil dominate the economy. About 1,000 km (630 miles) off Ecuador's Pacific coast, the lonely Galápagos Islands, famous for their unique wildlife, are part of the country.

Quechua woman gathering gladioli for market

People
Native Americans make up 25 per cent and *mestizos* more than 50 per cent of the population. The rest of the people are white, black, or Asian. More than 93 per cent of the people are Roman Catholic, although some people blend Catholicism with traditional beliefs.

ECUADOR FACTS

CAPITAL CITY	Quito
AREA	283,560 sq km (109,483 sq miles)
POPULATION	12,900,000
MAIN LANGUAGES	Spanish, Quechua
MAJOR RELIGION	Christian
CURRENCY	US dollar

Oil
Since the 1970s, oil, piped from the eastern lowlands, has been the mainstay of Ecuador's economy and accounts for 40 per cent of exports. Other exports are balsa wood, shrimps, processed fish, and textiles. Most goods are exported via Guayaquil, Ecuador's main port and largest city.

Crops
Beans, maize, and potatoes are the main crops grown in the Andes. Bananas, cocoa beans, rice, coffee, oranges, and wheat are cultivated on the coast, mostly for export. Roses, carnations, gladioli, and statice (sea lavender) are grown for markets.

Bold rug designs, often with an animal theme, are woven from homespun wool fibre.

Otavalo market
The small town of Otavalo lies high in the Andes, north of the capital Quito. Local Indians weave brightly coloured ponchos and rugs to sell at the famous Otavalo market, which dates from pre-Inca times.

Panama hats
Originally made in the 1800s in Ecuador, to protect the heads of travellers, panama hats are constructed from the fibres of the toquilla plant. A panama can be rolled up for packing – a good one will pass through a finger ring.

Peru

Four hundred years ago, Peru was at the heart of the Inca Empire, ruins of which still survive high in the Andes. The country has great mineral resources, yet most Peruvians are poor farmers, growing potatoes, maize, rice, and cereals for their own use, and cotton and coffee for export. Political terrorism by the Maoist Shining Path group has forced military rule in some areas.

Railways
Peru has two unconnected railway networks – the Central and Southern Railroads – both of which go from the coast to the highlands. A branch of the Central Railroad linking Lima and Huancayo in the Andes reaches 4,818 m (15,806 ft) above sea-level, making it the highest standard-gauge line in the world.

Machu Picchu
Peru's greatest tourist attraction is the ruined Inca city of Machu Picchu in the Andes. The ruins, hidden by dense forest vegetation, were discovered in 1911, when American archaeologist Hiram Bingham stumbled upon them, almost by accident. The ruins are made of stone and were built without mortar.

People
About half of Peruvians are Native American, and one-third are *mestizo*. The most populated areas are the highlands and the coastal plain. Only five per cent of people live in the remote Amazon Basin areas, including 70 Native American groups.

Jivaro man

PERU FACTS

CAPITAL CITY	Lima
AREA	1,285,220 sq km (496,223 sq miles)
POPULATION	26,100,000
MAIN LANGUAGES	Spanish, Quechua, Aymara
MAJOR RELIGION	Christian
CURRENCY	Nuevo sol (new sol)

Sardines

Fishing
The cold waters of the Peru coastal current bring rich nutrients that attract large numbers of pilchards, sardines, tuna, and other fish, making fishing a major industry in Peru. However, every few years, the arrival of the El Niño current raises the temperature of the water driving away the fish and causing great hardship to the fishermen.

Mining
Peru is a leading producer of copper, lead, tungsten, silver, and zinc and has reserves of gold, iron ore, and oil. However, low world mineral prices and industrial problems have badly affected mining.

Opencast lead mine in the Andes

FIND OUT MORE FARMING FISHING INDUSTRY INCAS NATIVE AMERICANS OIL PACIFIC OCEAN ROCKS AND MINERALS SOUTH AMERICA, HISTORY OF TEXTILES AND WEAVING TRAINS AND RAILWAYS VOLCANOES

EDISON, THOMAS

ONE OF THE GREATEST INVENTORS of all time, Thomas Alva Edison produced a number of inventions that changed the world – electric lighting, sound recording, and an early form of moving pictures, among many others. He had little formal schooling, but he was fascinated by science. He worked extremely hard, and would spend days, months, or even years experimenting in order to make something work. He often slept fully clothed on one of his worktables, so that he could start work again first thing in the morning.

Early life
Edison was born in 1847 in a small town in Ohio, USA. His teachers thought he was stupid, so his mother taught him herself, inspiring his interest in science. In 1869, after moving to New York, he improved the "ticker", a machine for relaying information about the stock market. The machine earned him $40,000.

Menlo Park

In 1876, using the money from his stock "ticker", Edison built an "invention factory" at Menlo Park, 39 km (24 miles) from New York City. This barn-like two-storey building was the world's first research laboratory, where a staff of scientists helped Edison to develop his ideas into devices that actually worked. In the six years that Edison worked at Menlo Park, he patented more than 400 different inventions.

Research work
At Menlo Park, Edison would come up with rough ideas and sketches. These would be refined, built, and tested by his assistants. They often had to build inventions again and again to find out why they did not work. Edison, when asked about his success, stressed the importance of these setbacks. "I failed my way to success," he said.

Organ, for experiments on sound

Edison watches to see how strongly the bulb glows.

Bench contains chemicals and other scientific equipment.

Electric light

Perhaps Edison's most important invention was the electric lightbulb. He saw that a bulb with a glowing thread or filament would work, using little electricity. It took him thousands of experiments before he discovered that the best material for the filament was carbonized cotton thread. British scientist Joseph Swan (1828–1914) invented a lightbulb at the same time as Edison, and the two men later joined forces.

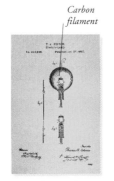

Carbon filament

Patent drawing for the lightbulb

Other inventions

Edison patented 1,093 inventions in his lifetime. He helped make the first successful typewriter, a dictating machine, and an improved telephone mouthpiece. He came close to inventing radio, and predicted the use of atomic power.

Recording cylinder

Mouthpiece

Edison's phonograph

Handle to turn cylinder

Phonograph
The phonograph, a device for recording and playing back sounds, was Edison's favourite invention. He sketched the machine and gave it to an assistant to build. It worked, but Edison did not realize this because he had poor hearing.

Recording the voice

Kinetoscope
In 1889, Edison invented the kinetoscope, a projector with a peepshow-type viewer to go with it. Kinetoscopes were installed in special viewing parlours in the USA, and customers paid to watch short films.

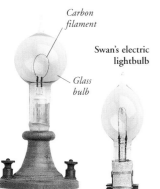

Carbon filament

Glass bulb

Swan's electric lightbulb

Edison's electric lightbulb

Lighting the city
Having developed the lightbulb, Edison went on to create a complete electric lighting system, powered by a central generator. His first power plant opened in 1882, serving 85 satisfied customers. Soon, whole cities were lit with electricity.

THOMAS EDISON

1847	Born, Milan, Ohio, USA.
1869	Improves the "ticker", for relaying prices on the stock market.
1876	Moves to Menlo Park.
1877	Creates the phonograph.
1877	Invents the carbon microphone, for use in telephone mouthpieces.
1879	Patents the electric lightbulb.
1882	Power switched on at the Pearl Street generating station, New York.
1883	Edison and Swan form an electric company.
1889	Invents the kinetoscope.
1931	Dies, aged 84.

FIND OUT MORE   ELECTRICITY   FILM AND FILM-MAKING   INVENTIONS   PHYSICS   SCIENCE, HISTORY OF   SOUND RECORDING   TECHNOLOGY

EDUCATION

FOR A SOCIETY TO SURVIVE and progress, each generation must pass its knowledge, skills, and values on to the next. This process is called education. Passing on knowledge is so vital that most countries have established formal systems of education for teaching children, by sending them to schools and colleges. Throughout our lives we are also educated informally, by parents, friends, or the media. Education provides society with doctors, teachers, and scientists; gives industry a capable workforce; and helps maintain law and order by instructing people in social values.

Early education

In prehistoric times, elders taught children the survival skills they needed, such as how to hunt or make fire. As civilizations developed and writing was invented, formal institutions of learning – schools – were created so that some people could learn to read and write.

The ancient world
As happens today, education in the ancient world reflected the state's needs and attitudes. In warlike Sparta, for example, education was geared towards producing good soldiers. Throughout the ancient world and medieval Europe, women and the poor did not have the same acccess to education enjoyed by the male, ruling classes.

Teacher and pupil, Romano-Germanic period

Theories of education

Some theories state that people learn by practice; others, that pupils must work things out themselves in order to learn; and some suggest that pupils learn by following their emotional needs and acquiring the skills and knowledge to fulfil them. Most people probably learn in all three ways.

Beads in number units

The child learns basic arithmetic skills by creative play with special, three-dimensional equipment.

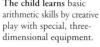

The Montessori system of education stresses that every child wants to learn. Children freely choose for themselves what and when to study.

Multiplication board

Types of education

Different types of education cater for different needs. The best-known example is the general education that schools and colleges provide, in subjects such as reading, writing, and arithmetic.

Vocational
Vocational education prepares people for specific jobs; it is available through courses at school, or training at specific colleges. Skills or crafts are also passed on informally, perhaps from parent to child, when a trade is passed on from one generation to the next.

Mother teaches sewing skills to children.

Adult education
Adult education is for those who, although not full-time students, choose to continue an aspect of their education, or learn something new. The courses keep adults up-to-date, improve job prospects, and bring new interests.

Learning computer skills

Special needs
Wealthy nations can afford to provide some schools where education is tailored to the special needs of certain children, such as the physically challenged, or the highly-gifted.

Disabled boy learns sailing skills.

Socialization

The first form of education a child receives starts from birth, by his or her immediate carers. Known as socialization, it includes not only learning such basic skills as speaking, but also teaches the child how society expects that he or she should behave. The child learns from instruction, and by imitating others. Socialization also takes place at school, and through cultural influences such as television.

Table manners are a learnt form of social behaviour.

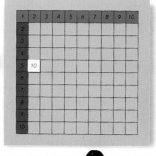

Maria Montessori

The Italian educationist Maria Montessori (1870–1952) developed teaching methods that encouraged children to work things out for themselves through practical activity, rather than simply obeying instructions. She developed her ideas while working with children with learning difficulties.

Timeline

c.3500 BC Sumerians invent writing.

3rd century BC Greek thinker Plato (427BC–347BC) proposes that education should be run by the state.

1524 German priest Martin Luther (1483–1546) advocates education be made available for all, so that everyone is able to read the Bible.

1762 French philosopher Jean Jacques Rousseau (1712–1778) argues education should prepare children to be adults.

1763 Prussians introduce compulsory schooling from the ages of 5 to 13.

1899 US educator John Dewey (1859–1952) publishes *School and Society*, an influential analysis of the social function of education.

1945 World War II ends: with the desire to build a better world, many countries reform school systems to make secondary education available to all.

1990s Education is fully recognized as vital to social and economic growth.

FIND OUT MORE   CRIME   SCHOOLS AND COLLEGES   SOCIETIES   TRADE AND INDUSTRY   WRITING

EGGS

MANY KINDS OF ANIMAL, from earthworms and insects to fish and birds, reproduce by laying eggs. An egg is a single living cell complete with a supply of food. After the egg is laid, the cell starts to divide, and gradually a young animal's body takes shape. When the animal is ready to start life in the world outside, it breaks out of the egg, or hatches. There is a great variety of eggs – large and small, with shells and without. Some animals lay just a few eggs each time and look after them carefully. Others lay thousands or millions of eggs and leave them to develop on their own.

Types of egg

Some eggs are so small that they can be seen only under a microscope; others are as big and heavy as a coconut. Animals that live in water usually lay jelly-like eggs. Animals that live on land, such as insects, reptiles, and birds, lay eggs with a hard or leathery shell. The shell helps to stop an egg drying out.

E

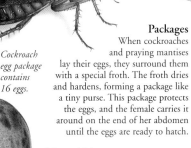

Cockroach egg package contains 16 eggs.

Packages
When cockroaches and praying mantises lay their eggs, they surround them with a special froth. The froth dries and hardens, forming a package like a tiny purse. This package protects the eggs, and the female carries it around on the end of her abdomen until the eggs are ready to hatch.

Mermaids' purses
Sharks lay some of the most unusual eggs. Instead of being round, their eggs can be flat, or even spiral. Dogfish, which are small sharks, lay eggs called "mermaids' purses". These have long tendrils with which the dogfish anchors the eggs to underwater plants.

Eggs without a shell
Frogs' eggs do not have a shell. Instead, they are surrounded by a layer of jelly. The jelly swells up when the eggs are laid, forming a floating mass that can be more than 30 cm (12 in) across.

Eggs in strings
The common toad lays eggs like those of frogs, but they are laid in strings up to 3 m (10 ft) long. As the female lays the eggs, she winds them around underwater plants. The tadpoles hatch after about two weeks.

Leopard gecko's egg

Leathery eggs
Lizards and many other reptiles have eggs with a leathery shell. Unlike amphibians, reptiles can lay their eggs in dry places, because the shell helps keep the inside of the egg moist.

American robin's egg

Chalky eggs
The shell around birds' eggs is reinforced with a substance like chalk. To hatch, most young birds peck open their shell, but some kick their way out.

Leatherhead's egg

Egg development

After an egg has been laid, a young animal starts to develop inside it. With some insects, such as the house-fly, this can take less than a day, but with birds it may take more than a month. Eggs develop more quickly if they are warm, and most birds keep their eggs warm by sitting on them. This is called incubation.

Mallee fowl
Instead of sitting on its eggs, the Australian mallee fowl buries them in a huge compost heap that it makes out of dead leaves. Heat from the giant heap keeps the eggs warm.

Development of a bird's egg
A bird's egg is divided into two main areas – the white and the yolk. The white is made of a substance called albumen. It stores water and cushions the developing chick from any sudden jolts. The yolk contains a store of food, which the chick uses up as it develops.

1 When the egg has just been laid, the part that will become the chick looks like a tiny pale spot. It lies on the upper surface of the yolk.

2 Within a day, cells in the spot start to divide to form an embryo. A network of blood vessels fans out over the yolk and supplies the embryo with food.

3 Three days after the egg was laid, the embryo is growing fast. Its eyes start to form, and tiny buds grow that will soon develop into wings and legs.

4 After seven days, the embryo has become a chick, and a special bag has formed to collect its waste. In three weeks, the chick's development will be complete.

Egg clutches

Some animals, such as queen termites, lay a steady stream of eggs, but most animals produce eggs in groups called clutches. The number of eggs in a clutch is closely linked to their size. For example, a wandering albatross has very big eggs, but it produces only one egg every two years. By contrast, a sunfish has tiny eggs, but it releases millions each time it breeds.

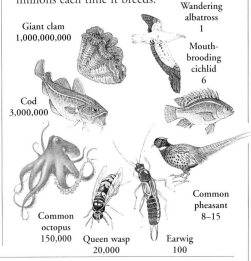

Giant clam 1,000,000,000

Wandering albatross 1

Mouth-brooding cichlid 6

Cod 3,000,000

Common octopus 150,000

Queen wasp 20,000

Earwig 100

Common pheasant 8–15

FIND OUT MORE | ANIMAL BEHAVIOUR | BIRDS | FISH | FROGS AND TOADS | INSECTS | MAMMALS | NESTS AND BURROWS | REPTILES | SHARKS AND RAYS

Eggs
Non-passerine birds

Glossy ibis eggs are not camouflaged.

Willow grouse eggs are laid on the ground where they are camouflaged.

Plains wanderer lays eggs in a grass-lined hollow.

Jamaican tody eggs are almost spherical and have an extremely thin shell.

Black shouldered kite eggs often have marks concentrated at one end.

Guira cuckoo eggs are, unusually for cuckoos, incubated by the parents.

Common guillemot eggs are sharply pointed.

Limpkin eggs are camouflaged to blend in with dead leaves of waterside plants.

Nacunda nightjar eggs have brown blotches.

Prairie chicken lays up to 16 eggs in each clutch.

Southern cassowary eggs have a grainy surface created by raised bumps.

Manila nightjar lays its eggs on bare ground.

Elegant tinamou eggs have a glossy sheen.

Passerine birds

Olive sunbird eggs have a distinctive ring of marks.

Yellow-streaked greenbul eggs have sparse markings formed just before the egg is laid.

Cetti's warbler eggs are reddish-brown.

Bokmakierie eggs are blue with red spots.

Cape crow eggs have a large amount of red spots or speckles on them.

Paradise riflebird eggs have dark streaks that look like brush marks.

Black-headed weaver eggs are laid inside a woven nest.

Scarlet minivet eggs have variable patterns.

Black-capped mockingthrush's eggs are mottled with red spots.

Black and yellow grosbeak's eggs have streaks that may help to break up the outline.

EGYPT, ANCIENT

ABOUT 5,000 YEARS ago, the great civilization of ancient Egypt grew up on the banks of the River Nile. It lasted virtually unchanged for 3,000 years. During this time the Egyptians built the first large stone buildings, invented one of the earliest forms of writing, and created a cult of the dead unlike anything known in any other culture. This cult involved preserving dead bodies, and burying them with their possessions. As a result, people today know a great deal about the ancient Egyptians.

River Nile

The River Nile was the lifeblood of the whole region. Every year the river flooded, depositing dark silt on the banks. This silt made the soil fertile and, because of this, most Egyptians lived by the river. When the Nile flooded and work in the fields was impossible, many people helped on the great royal building projects, such as the Great Pyramid at Giza.

3,000-year-old bread found in a tomb
Pomegranate
Grapes
Figs

Crops
The Egyptians cultivated wheat and barley, from which they made bread and brewed beer. The hot climate also allowed them to grow many different kinds of fruit, including figs, dates, pomegranates, and grapes.

Mediterranean Sea · Nile delta · Giza · Memphis · Saqqara · Thebes · River Nile · *Extent of floodplain*

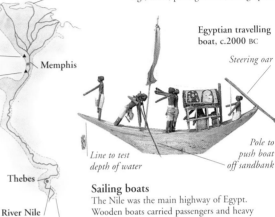
Egyptian travelling boat, c.2000 BC
Steering oar
Line to test depth of water
Pole to push boat off sandbank

Sailing boats
The Nile was the main highway of Egypt. Wooden boats carried passengers and heavy cargo up and down the river. Water transport was especially useful for heavy loads, such as stones for the pyramids. Egyptian boat-builders were among the first to attach sails to their craft.

Tilling the soil
Egyptian farmers used a lightweight plough pulled by oxen. The plough had a wooden blade and a handle so that the farmer could steer it, and was effective enough to cut a furrow in the light Egyptian soil.

Egyptian farmer, c.2000 BC

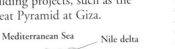
Models of everyday activities, such as tilling the soil, were often found in tombs.

Pharaohs

Ancient Egypt was ruled by kings called pharaohs. The pharaohs had absolute power, and the Egyptians believed that they joined the gods in the next world when they died. For this reason, the Egyptians took special care when burying their pharaohs, mummifying them and building splendid tombs.

Pharaoh's court
A pharaoh was surrounded by officials, high priests, and ambassadors, all of whom helped him run the kingdom. The court was also the home of entertainers and the women of the royal harem. The pharaoh and courtiers lived in great luxury. They took pride in their appearance, dressing in fine linen. The women used black eye make-up, and had elaborate hairstyles.

Rameses II
Rameses II (r.1304–1237 BC) was famous for his military campaigns and great building projects. He defended Egypt against the Hittites, signing a peace treaty with them. His many buildings included the mortuary complex at Thebes on the west bank of the Nile, and the Abu Simbel temple.

Gods

The Egyptians believed in many different gods. Some were local gods, who represented each district of Egypt. Others had more general powers, such as Thoth, the god of wisdom.

Anubis, the god of death

Amun-re, king of the gods

Osiris, the god of the underworld

Bast, the cat goddess

Temples
Karnak at Thebes was the greatest of the Egyptian temples. Temples were run by priests, who maintained the building and left offerings for the gods. The most important temples had large estates and rich treasuries, so high priests were very powerful.

Bronze mirror
Comb and hair pins
Wine jar made from faience (decorated and glazed earthenware)
Containers for eye paint

Timeline

3000 BC Ancient Egyptian civilization begins; early Dynastic Period. The two kingdoms of Upper and Lower Egypt are united under Narmer.

2650 BC Step Pyramid of Zoser is built at Saqqara. It is the first pyramid and the first large-scale stone structure.

2500s BC Largest of the pyramids is built for Khufu at Giza.

2100 BC Middle Kingdom begins. Funerary (funeral) customs spread from royalty to other classes.

Saqqara · Giza

Mummification

Ancient Egyptians believed in life after death. They thought that people had a spirit as well as a body, and that for the person to live in the next world, the spirit had to be reunited with the body. They therefore preserved the body of the dead person in the form of a mummy.

Mummy cases

The Egyptians placed the mummy inside a coffin or case, and put a cover on top. By the time of the Middle Kingdom (c.2100–1550 BC), they used two coffins to give added protection from tomb robbers and animals. The coffins were decorated with writing, images of the gods, and sacred amulets, or lucky charms.

Book of the Dead

This is a series of prayers, written on papyrus, that were meant to help the dead person travel to the next world.

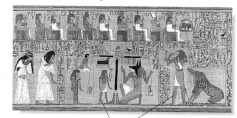

The Weighing of the Heart ceremony where the dead person is judged by the gods.

Thoth, the god of wisdom, writes details of the person's actions when alive.

Making a mummy

The Egyptians first removed the organs, and dried out the body with natron. They filled the body with sawdust or dry leaves, then wrapped the body in bandages.

Plate to cover the cut in the body

Embalming tools

Dish of natron, a natural salt used to dry out the body.

The body's organs were placed in containers called Canopic jars.

Unwrapped mummy, showing how well preserved the body is.

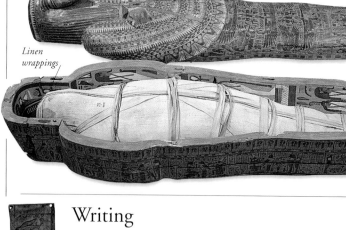

Red straps usually indicate a priest

Linen wrappings

Writing

Ancient Egyptians developed a complex system of writing, called hieroglyphics, in which simple pictures represented objects. Some pictures also stood for letters. Ideas that were too complicated to be shown by one picture were written as groups of hieroglyphs.

Royal door plate inscribed with the name of Amenhotep.

Hieroglyphs and hieratic script

Hieroglyphs were slow to write, so the Egyptians used them mainly for sacred texts and tomb carvings. They used another, faster script, called hieratic, for business and literary texts. Later, they invented a third script, called demotic.

Hieratic script

Hieroglyphs

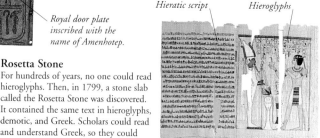

Rosetta Stone

For hundreds of years, no one could read hieroglyphs. Then, in 1799, a stone slab called the Rosetta Stone was discovered. It contained the same text in hieroglyphs, demotic, and Greek. Scholars could read and understand Greek, so they could work out the meaning of the hieroglyphs.

Daily life

For most Egyptians, life consisted of hard work in the fields, and on the great building projects. They ate mainly vegetables and bread, and drank beer. High officials and royal courtiers lived a much more leisurely life.

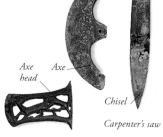

Axe head

Axe

Chisel

Carpenter's saw

Houses

Ancient Egyptians built houses of sun-dried mud-bricks. They covered the walls with smooth plaster. Small, high windows let in the breeze, but kept out the sun. The house pictured above belonged to a royal official, and had a garden with fruit trees.

Work

Most ancient Egyptians worked at producing their own food. Others were craft workers, making items for the home from wood, pottery, and metal. Their tools, such as saws and chisels, were very similar to the hand tools used by craftworkers today.

1550 BC New Kingdom founded. Height of Egyptian civilization.

1503–1482 BC Reign of Queen Hatshepsut. She sends expeditions to the mysterious land of Punt to buy incense.

1379–63 BC Reign of Akhenaten. This pharaoh, with his queen, Nefertiti, encourages realistic art, and changes Egyptian religion by banning all gods except the sun god.

Nefertiti

1363–52 BC Brief reign of Tutankhamun, who restored the old gods but is most famous for the riches discovered in his tomb.

Tutankhamun

Abu Simbel

1304–1237 BC Reign of Rameses II, who builds Abu Simbel.

30 BC Death of Cleopatra VII; the Romans take over.

FIND OUT MORE

| BUILDING AND CONSTRUCTION | FARMING, HISTORY OF | GODS AND GODDESSES | HITTITES | PYRAMIDS | WRITING |

Ancient Egyptian amulets

Funerary amulets

Set-square amulets

Steps amulet, symbolizing the stairs on Osiris's throne.

Cartouches, containing names of the dead.

Obsidian head-rest amulets, used by ancient Egyptians instead of pillows.

Rising sun amulet, made from cornelian.

Shen amulet, symbolizing eternity

Finger amulets were placed on cuts made in the body during embalming.

Winged-heart scarab, made from faïence.

Scarabs, sacred dung beetles that represented rebirth after death.

The Ankh, the ancient Egyptian symbol of life

Wedjat eyes, representing the eye of the god Horus, were placed on mummies to protect their health.

Girdles amulets, for protecting mummies

Papyrus columns

Sons of Horus amulets guarded the canopic jars, which held the vital organs removed from a mummy.

Soul-bird amulet

Djed pillars, amulets representing the backbone of Osiris, were thought to give the mummy strength after death.

Ushabti figures

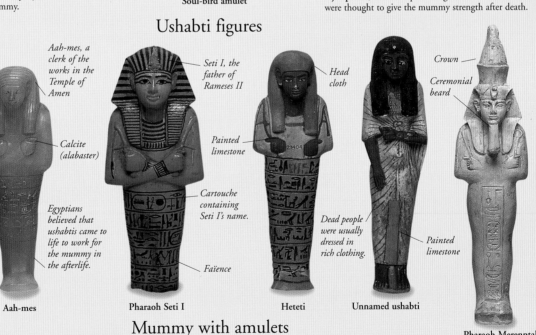

Painted wood

Aah-mes, a clerk of the works in the Temple of Amen

Seti I, the father of Rameses II

Head cloth

Crown

Ceremonial beard

Calcite (alabaster)

Painted limestone

Passage from the Book of the Dead

Egyptians believed that ushabtis came to life to work for the mummy in the afterlife.

Cartouche containing Seti I's name.

Dead people were usually dressed in rich clothing.

Painted limestone

This ushabti dates from c.1500 BC.

Faïence

Rensenb

Aah-mes

Pharaoh Seti I

Heteti

Unnamed ushabti

Pharaoh Merenptah

Mummy with amulets

Heart scarab

Ushabti figure

EINSTEIN, ALBERT

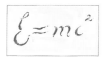

ALBERT EINSTEIN WAS a scientific genius who changed the way we view our universe. In 1905, he united space and time in one mathematical description. Ten years later he proposed a complete theory of gravity that explained how the universe works, relating mass and energy in the famous equation $E = mc^2$. Many people doubted his theories, but later investigation has since proved Einstein's theories to have been correct. As well as transforming the science of physics, Einstein's work paved the way for the creation of nuclear weapons.

Early life
Einstein was born in Ulm, Germany, and studied in Switzerland before graduating from Zurich's Institute of Technology in 1900. He did not fit in at school because he asked many difficult questions, and could get no work until he found a job in the Patent Office in Bern in 1902.

Special Theory of Relativity

In the early 1900s, Einstein developed the Special Theory of Relativity. This says that time is relative: it passes differently for individuals, depending on how fast or slowly they move. The faster anything travels, the slower time seems to pass. If one person travels into space close to the speed of light and another stays on Earth, time passes slower for the person in space. On their return, the person on Earth will be older.

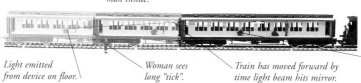

Light beam sent by device on floor.

Light bounces off mirror on ceiling.

Train acts as "light clock" – the time taken by light, moving at constant speed, to go along train, acts as one "tick" of the clock.

Train appears stationary to man inside.

Light beam detected.

Man observes short "tick".

Light emitted from device on floor.

Woman sees long "tick".

Train has moved forward by time light beam hits mirror.

Train has moved still further by time light beam hits detector on floor.

Moving clocks
According to the special theory, time measured by a moving clock will run slower than if measured by a stationary clock. This can be demonstrated by light beams carried on a train travelling at nearly the speed of light. A person on the train sees the light travel a short distance; an observer on the platform sees it travel further because of the train's movement.

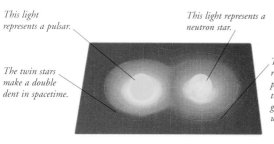

This light represents a pulsar.

This light represents a neutron star.

The twin stars make a double dent in spacetime.

These lines represent peaks and troughs in gravitional waves.

General Theory of Relativity

Einstein developed the General Theory of Relativity that explained gravity and the nature of space. He explained that as light travels the shortest path through space, when it bends space must be curved. Planets that travel round the Sun are thus following as straight a path as possible through curved space.

Making waves
Stars in a binary pulsar rotate round each other. As they move, they make waves in space. The waves carry energy from the stars, causing the stars to slow down as they lose energy. The rate that a pulsar slows in its orbit exactly matches Einstein's theory, though the first pulsar was not discovered until 1968.

Ripples in space
Einstein's theory predicted that objects jiggling around in space – such as two stars in a binary pulsar system – would make ripples in space. These ripples can be detected as gravitational waves. Subsequent experiments have proved Einstein's theory correct.

Stars rotate anti-clockwise.

Neutron star moves around pulsar.

Stars' positions change in relation to observer.

Stars continuously swap places.

Mileva Einstein
Einstein married his first wife Mileva, a mathematician and scientist in 1903. They had a daughter and two sons. Mileva worked closely with her husband and helped with his research, though to what degree she influenced his work is unknown. They were divorced in 1919.

Mileva and her son Hans Albert

Political life

In 1933, Einstein moved to America to avoid Nazi persecution as a Jew, and campaigned for a Jewish state. He realized that his theories made possible the creation of nuclear weapons, but campaigned against such weapons after World War II. In 1952, he was offered the presidency of Israel, but declined the offer.

The bomb
In the late 1930s, Einstein feared that Nazi Germany would use nuclear weapons in war, so he wrote to US president Franklin D. Roosevelt in 1939, urging the USA to begin constructing atomic weapons to counter this threat.

Explosion of atomic bomb

ALBERT EINSTEIN

1879	Born in Ulm, Germany.
1896–1900	Studies at Institute of Technology, Zurich, Switzerland.
1902–9	Works in Patent Office, Bern, Switzerland.
1905	Obtains doctorate; writes Special Theory of Relativity.
1914	Moves to Berlin.
1915	Writes General Theory of Relativity.
1921	Awarded Nobel Prize for Physics.
1933	Moves to the USA.
1952	Offered presidency of Israel.
1955	Dies in Princeton, USA.

FIND OUT MORE NUCLEAR POWER   PHYSICS   SCIENCE, HISTORY OF   WORLD WAR II

ELECTRICITY

A FLASH OF LIGHTNING is striking evidence of the invisible energy called electricity. This energy is produced by the movement of electrons – tiny particles found in atoms of matter. Every electron carries an identical negative electric "charge". When electric charge builds up in one place, it is called static electricity. If the charge flows from place to place, it is called current electricity.

Electric circuit

The path around which current electricity flows is called a circuit. In the circuit shown here, electricity from the battery lights the bulbs. Two bulbs connected one after the other are described as being "in series". Bulbs in separate branches of the circuit are said to be "in parallel".

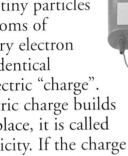

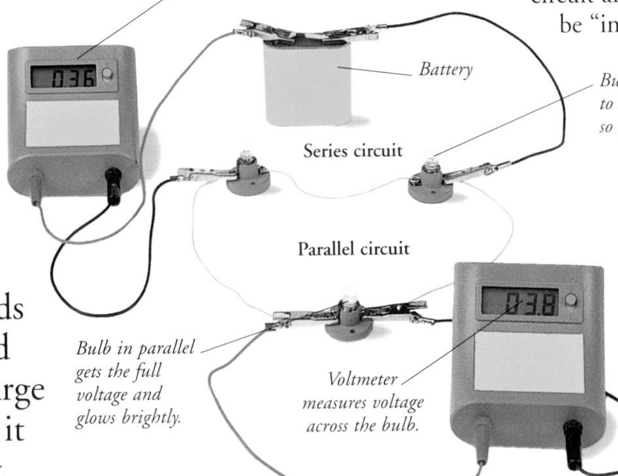

Ammeter measures current from battery.

Battery

Series circuit

Parallel circuit

Bulb in parallel gets the full voltage and glows brightly.

Voltmeter measures voltage across the bulb.

Bulbs in series have to share the voltage, so they glow dimly.

Electric current

Electrons pushed through the wires of a circuit form an electric current. The push on the electrons is called electromotive force (e.m.f). Voltage is a measure of e.m.f. The greater the voltage, the more current flows through the circuit.

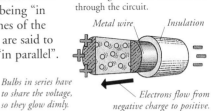

Metal wire   *Insulation*

Electrons flow from negative charge to positive.

Battery

A battery is a source of electric current. A chemical reaction between materials in the battery separates electrons from their atoms. The battery's e.m.f makes electrons flow out of the negative terminal, around a circuit, and back to the positive terminal.

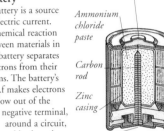

Positive terminal (+)

Ammonium chloride paste

Carbon rod

Zinc casing

Negative terminal (–)

Static electricity

Rubbing two materials together can transfer electrons from one material to the other. A material that loses electrons gains a positive charge of static electricity, and a material that gains electrons gets a negative charge.

Attracting and repelling

A positively charged balloon attracts electrons to the surface of nearby hairs, giving them a negative charge. Opposite charges attract, so the hairs are pulled towards the balloon. Charges of the same type repel (push each other away).

Lightning

A tremendous charge of static electricity builds up inside a storm cloud. A flash of lightning occurs when this charge is suddenly released as a powerful electric current.

Steel is a good conductor.

Conductors

Current can flow only through materials called conductors, whose electrons are bound loosely to their atoms and can be moved easily through the material.

Plastic blocks current.

Insulators

Current cannot flow through insulators. The electrons in an insulator are bound firmly to their atoms and cannot move through the material.

Generator

Most of the electricity used in homes and factories is produced by devices called generators. Inside a generator, coils of wire spin rapidly in a magnetic field. The magnetism moves electrons through the wire, creating an electric current. In this simple version, bar magnets produce the magnetic field.

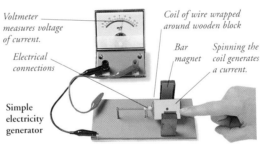

Voltmeter measures voltage of current.

Electrical connections

Simple electricity generator

Coil of wire wrapped around wooden block

Bar magnet

Spinning the coil generates a current.

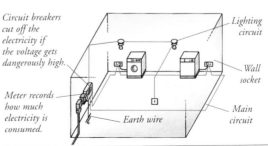

Circuit breakers cut off the electricity if the voltage gets dangerously high.

Meter records how much electricity is consumed.

Earth wire

Lighting circuit

Wall socket

Main circuit

Electricity supply

Electric current produced by generators in power stations reaches consumers via cables buried underground or carried by tall towers called pylons. The current alternates, which means that it changes direction many times each second. A battery produces direct current, which flows in one direction only.

Electricity in the home

Separate circuits in the home supply different voltages for different purposes. An electrical appliance takes power from the circuits through a plug that fits into a wall socket. The sockets are linked to the ground outside by an earth wire. If an electrical fault occurs, the current is diverted safely into the ground.

Michael Faraday

In 1831, the English scientist Michael Faraday (1791–1867) built the first generator after noticing that moving a magnet in and out of a wire coil made a current flow through the wire. Faraday also invented the electric motor and pioneered electrolysis (using electricity to break down substances).

Timeline

500s BC The ancient Greeks discover static electricity when they notice that amber (fossilized tree sap) attracts small objects if rubbed with wool.

Charged amber attracting feather

1752 American scientist and politician Benjamin Franklin proves that lightning is an electrical phenomenon.

1799 Italian physicist Alessandro Volta makes the first battery.

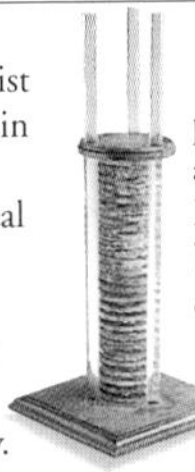

Volta's battery

1831 American physicist Joseph Henry and English Michael Faraday independently build "induction coils" – the first electricity generators.

1868 French chemist Georges Leclanché invents the Leclanché cell, the forerunner of modern zinc-carbon batteries.

1897 English physicist Joseph John Thomson discovers the electron.

FIND OUT MORE   ACIDS AND ALKALIS   ELECTROMAGNETISM   ENERGY   FRICTION   MAGNETISM   STORMS

E

ELECTROMAGNETISM

AT THE FLICK OF A SWITCH, an invisible force turns the drum of a washing machine 1,600 times every second. This force is called electromagnetism. It is a form of magnetism produced by electricity. When an electric current flows through a wire, it produces a magnetic field around the wire. Making the wire into a coil increases the strength of the magnetic effect. Winding the coil around an iron bar makes the magnetism even stronger. Any device that exerts electromagnetic forces is called an electromagnet.

Connections to battery

Coil

Compasses show magnetic field around coil.

Solenoid
A coil of current-carrying wire forms a type of electromagnet called a solenoid. The magnetic field around the coil is the same as that around an ordinary bar magnet. The field's strength depends on the number of turns in the coil and the amount of current flowing through the wire.

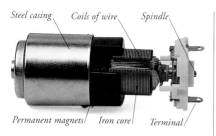

Steel casing *Coils of wire* *Spindle*

Permanent magnets *Iron core* *Terminal*

Electric motor
Inside an electric motor are wire coils surrounded by permanent magnets. Electricity flowing through the wire produces a magnetic field around each coil. The magnetism of the coils interacts with the magnetic fields of the permanent magnets. They push and pull on each other, making the coils rotate. This movement is used to drive machines such as electric drills.

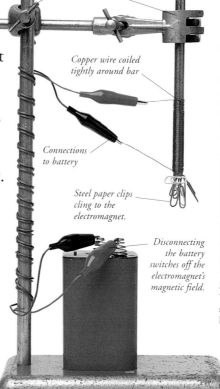

Clamp stand *Clamp holding iron bar*

Copper wire coiled tightly around bar

Connections to battery

Steel paper clips cling to the electromagnet.

Disconnecting the battery switches off the electromagnet's magnetic field.

Electromagnet
Most electromagnets consist of a coil of wire wrapped around an iron bar. When an electric current flows through the wire, a magnetic field forms around the electromagnet. The magnetism can be switched off by disconnecting the electricity supply.

Scrapyard electromagnet
Waste metal is moved around a scrapyard by a crane carrying a huge electromagnet. When the electromagnet is switched on, it picks up metal scraps containing iron. The metal is moved to a different place and then dropped by switching off the electromagnet.

Electric drill
An electric drill can quickly make a hole in wood, stone, and even some metals. Inside the body of the machine, gears harness the rotation of a powerful electric motor to drive the drill at high speed. A cooling fan prevents the drill from overheating.

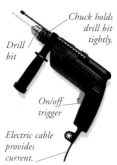

Chuck holds drill bit tightly.
Drill bit
On/off trigger
Electric cable provides current.

Uses of electromagnetism
Some electrical appliances contain electric motors that use electromagnetism to produce movement. But electromagnetism is also used in many other ways, such as to make sound or detect hidden objects.

Loudspeaker
A loudspeaker contains a paper or plastic cone that vibrates and creates sound waves in the air around it. The cone is attached to a wire coil surrounded by a permanent magnet. The magnetic fields of the coil and the magnet interact. This causes the coil to move rapidly to and fro, making the cone vibrate.

Cone vibrates as electricity flows through coil.

Metal detector
Inside the walk-through arch of an airport metal detector are large coils of wire carrying an electric current. Any person who walks under the arch passes through the magnetic field produced by the coils. A hidden metal object will affect the strength of the field and trigger an alarm.

Transformer *Portable radio*

Transformer
Many electrical devices use a transformer to alter the voltage of an electrical supply. Inside a transformer are two wire coils. When a varying current flows through one coil, it produces a varying magnetic field. This field causes an electric current to flow through the second coil, but at a different voltage.

Hans Christian Oersted
The Danish physicist Hans Christian Oersted (1777–1851) discovered electromagnetism in 1820. He placed a compass near a wire carrying an electric current and noticed that the compass needle was deflected and no longer pointed north. Oersted realized that the current had produced a magnetic field around the wire.

Timeline
1799 Italian physicist Alessandro Volta invents the battery, which allows scientists to experiment with electric currents.

1820 Oersted's discovery of electromagnetism opens the way for the development of the electric motor and the electromagnet.

Faraday's electric motor

1821 English scientist Michael Faraday makes an electric motor, in which a current-carrying wire rotates around the pole of a magnet. It has no practical use.

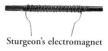
Sturgeon's electromagnet

1828 English scientist William Sturgeon builds the first electromagnet – a coil of wire around an insulated iron bar.

1883 Croatian-born physicist Nikola Tesla invents the "induction motor" – the first practical motor.

1885 American engineer William Stanley invents the transformer.

 FIND OUT MORE ELECTRICITY • ENGINES AND MOTORS • FORCE AND MOTION • MAGNETISM • MACHINES • SOUND

ELECTRONICS

THE ELECTRONICS REVOLUTION is rapidly changing our world: whether we are at home, at work, or out shopping, we are surrounded by electronic machines and equipment. Electronics involves using devices called components to control electric currents, which are flows of tiny, electrically charged particles of matter called electrons. An electronic circuit is an arrangement of linked components – such as transistors and diodes – that manipulates current in order to carry out a specific task, such as adding numbers in a calculator.

Light Emitting Diodes (LEDs) glow when current passes through them, and are used to indicate that a device's power supply is on.

Variable resistors allow the level of current flowing through a circuit to be adjusted.

Capacitors are components that store electric charge; electrolytic capacitors can store more charge than ceramic ones.

Electrolytic capacitors

Ceramic capacitors

Radio circuit board and components

Integrated circuits consist of a plastic case containing a complete circuit etched on to a tiny silicon chip.

Power cables

Circuit board

The components for an electronic device, such as a radio, are attached to a circuit board, which is a flat base with metal tracks running along its underside. The components are secured to the tracks using an alloy called solder. The tracks link the components to form a circuit.

Inductors are wire coils that produce magnetic fields when current passes through them, creating a resistance that restricts the flow of current.

Variable capacitors can be adjusted to store varying levels of charge; in radios, they are used to select radio stations.

Diodes allow electric current to pass through them in one direction only.

Transistors can be used to amplify electrical signals (make them stronger) or switch circuits rapidly on and off.

Resistors allow only a fixed amount of electric current to flow through a circuit.

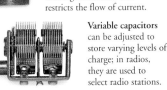

William Shockley
US physicist William Shockley (1910–89) was part of a three-man team that invented the transistor in 1947. The transistor made it possible to build tiny electronic circuits and so develop more compact electronic devices.

Remote control
Pressing a button on the remote-control of a TV – for example, to change channels – makes an LED flash pulses of infrared light to the TV set. The TV set decodes the pulses and obeys the instruction.

Semiconductors
The element silicon is a type of material called a semiconductor, because it conducts electricity only under certain conditions. The properties of a semiconductor can be altered by adding chemical impurities to it in a process called doping. Doped semiconductors are used to make diodes, transistors, and many other electronic components.

Silicon crystal

Pins connect to circuit board.

Silicon chip sealed under metal cover *Ceramic casing*

Microprocessors
Many electronic devices – including computers – are controlled by circuits called microprocessors, or "silicon chips". A microprocessor is made from a single slice of doped semiconductor. The circuit, which may contain thousands of components, can carry out many complex tasks.

Uses of electronics
Electronic circuits are either analogue or digital. Analogue circuits deal with continuously varying electric currents, such as television and radio signals. Digital circuits process information in the form of thousands of on-off pulses of electric current every second.

Pocket calculator

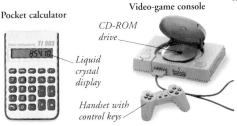

CD-ROM drive

Liquid crystal display

Handset with control keys

Video-game console

Calculator
A calculator's digital circuits split up a calculation into a series of simple steps, each of which is performed at high speed.

Video game console
Digital circuits inside the console control the play. The console sends an analogue signal to a TV screen, which displays a picture of the game.

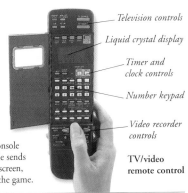

Television controls
Liquid crystal display
Timer and clock controls
Number keypad
Video recorder controls

TV/video remote control

FIND OUT MORE   COMPUTERS   ELECTRICITY   ELEMENTS   INFORMATION TECHNOLOGY   METALS   TELEPHONES   TELECOMMUNICATIONS   VIDEO

ELEMENTS

AN ELEMENT IS a substance composed of only one type of atom. Elements are the most basic substances in the Universe and cannot be split into anything simpler. There are 109 elements – 91 of which occur naturally, and 18 of which can be made artificially. All life on Earth is based on the element carbon, which is vital to the functioning of living cells. Oxygen is the most plentiful element on Earth. It occurs in air, water, and even rocks.

Elements in nature

Only a few of the naturally occurring elements can be found in their pure state. Most elements combine, or react, with other elements to form more complex substances called compounds. Pure gold can be mined directly from the ground because it is unreactive – that is, it does not readily form compounds.

Gold veins in quartz rock

Quartz rock is a compound of the elements silicon and oxygen.

Pure gold.

Groups of elements

Just as the members of a human family share the same characteristics, there are "families" of elements that have similar properties. An element's chemical properties are determined by the structure of its atoms. Elements in the same group have similar atomic structures.

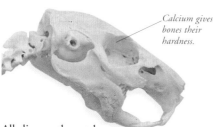

Calcium gives bones their hardness.

Alkaline-earth metals

Calcium and magnesium belong to the group of elements called the alkaline-earth metals. They are so named because they form alkaline solutions in water, and their compounds occur widely in nature. Calcium, for example, occurs in sea shells, bones, teeth, milk, and chalk. Magnesium occurs in the substance chlorophyll, which plants use to make food by photosynthesis.

Iodine   Bromine   Chlorine

Halogens

Swimming pools smell the way they do because the halogen chlorine is put in the water to kill germs. Compounds of fluorine, another halogen, are put in water and toothpaste to prevent tooth decay. The halogens, which also include iodine, bromine, and astatine, are all strong-smelling, highly reactive non-metals.

Alkali metals

Potassium (which is used in fertilizers) and sodium (which occurs in salt) are both alkali metals. All the elements in this group are soft, extremely reactive metals. They react violently or even explosively with water to form alkaline solutions.

Reaction of potassium in water

Iron compounds are often red, black, or brown.

Iron sulphide

Iron carbide

Iron oxide

Coloured compounds of iron

Transition metals

The transition metals are a large group of hard, dense elements that conduct electricity and heat well, form coloured compounds, and some of which (iron, cobalt, and nickel) are magnetic. Other transition metals include copper, gold, chromium, titanium, platinum, and tungsten.

Noble gases

Multi-coloured street signs often contain noble gases, because each of these gases glows a different colour when electricity flows through it. Neon, for example, glows red, helium yellow, and argon blue. The noble gases are unreactive non-metals that rarely form compounds.

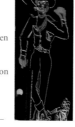

Allotropes

It may seem difficult to believe, but hard, sparkling diamond is made of the same types of atoms as soft, black graphite. Diamond and graphite are allotropes of carbon, meaning that they are different physical forms of the same element. Their atoms link up in different ways to make them look and behave differently.

Diamond consists of carbon atoms linked strongly to each other in a rigid framework.

Only weak bonds hold sheets together.

Graphite is made up of sheets of carbon atoms that can slide over each other easily.

Graphite pencil

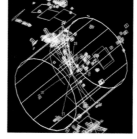

Artificial elements

New elements can be created by bombarding existing elements with high-speed subatomic particles in a device called a particle accelerator. Since 1937, scientists have made 18 new elements, some of which only exist for a few millionths of a second.

Computer image of a particle accelerator collision

Hydrogen

The element hydrogen makes up 90 per cent of all the matter in the Universe. It was the first element to form when the Universe was created in the explosion known as the Big Bang. Hydrogen is a tasteless, colourless, odourless, non-toxic gas. It is the simplest of all the elements, with atoms containing just one proton orbited by a single electron. Hydrogen gives acids their acidic properties.

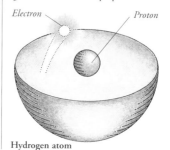

Electron

Proton

Hydrogen atom

Dmitri Mendeleyev

In 1869, the Russian chemist Dmitri Mendeleyev (1834–1907) devised a chart called the periodic table, which classified the 63 elements then known into different groups. He used the table to predict the existence of three new elements, all of which were discovered a few years later.

FIND OUT MORE   ACIDS AND ALKALIS   AIR   ATOMS AND MOLECULES   BIG BANG   MATTER   METALS   MIXTURES AND COMPOUNDS   SKELETON   TEETH AND JAWS

ELEPHANTS

THE AFRICAN AND ASIAN elephants are the only two living species of a once much larger family that was found on every continent. The African elephant is the largest land mammal, but despite its size and power it is a gentle creature. Elephants are highly intelligent, very sociable animals, that live in close family units. The African and Asian elephants are descended from different ancestors; the Asian elephant is more closely related to the mammoth than to the African elephant.

Teeth
The elephant has only four teeth, one in each quarter of the jaw. Each tooth is about 30 cm (12 in) long. As one wears down, another pushes in from behind. This can happen only six times, after which the supply of teeth is exhausted. Without teeth, the elephant can no longer eat, so dies of starvation.

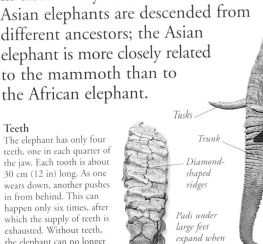

Large ears

Tusks

Trunk

Diamond-shaped ridges

Pads under large feet expand when trodden on.

Features of an elephant
Everything about an elephant is oversized. Its most conspicuous feature is the long flexible trunk – an elongation of the nose. The huge tusks are overgrown incisor teeth. Besides hearing, the large ears are used as a fan to cool the elephant. They also make the animal appear larger than it really is, and spreading the ears helps intimidate a rival or a potential enemy. Soft fatty cushions on the underside of the feet spread as the elephant walks.

Elephant using tusks to dig into ground.

Tusks
A tusk is a specialized type of tooth, growing from either side of the upper jaw. Tusks are used mainly as tools and weapons. The heaviest pair of tusks ever recorded weighed 102 kg (225 lb) and 109 kg (240 lb). The longest pair measured 3.35 m (11 ft) and 3.5 m (11 ft 5 in) in length.

Skin
The skin is very wrinkled. Deep crevices increase the surface area of the skin, and allow greater heat loss. The crevices also help to trap water which then takes longer to evaporate, and helps to keep the elephant cooler for longer.

Tail

E

Trunk
The elephant's trunk is highly flexible and serves much the same functions as a human arm and hand. It combines great strength with delicacy, and is so versatile that it can pluck a single leaf as easily as it can lift a heavy log. Because the elephant has a trunk it does not need to lower its head while feeding, thus allowing it to remain alert. The trunk also allows the elephant to reach high above its head to browse on leaves that are out of most other animals' reach.

The elephant uses its trunk to feed.

Fingers are used to hold objects.

Nostrils
Located at the tip of the trunk, the elephant's nostrils can be raised high above its head, like a periscope, and turned in any direction to pick up traces of scent carried on the wind. The elephant relies on its sense of smell more than its other senses. While swimming, the trunk may be lifted above the surface of the water, and used as a snorkel if the elephant gets out of its depth.

Picking up scent on the wind

Fingers
As well as the nostrils, the tip of the trunk has fleshy "fingers". The African species has two opposing fingers, but the Asian elephant has only one which it uses to grip against the wide underside of the trunk. Fingers enable the elephant to perform precise movements and pick up very small objects.

Upper finger

Lower finger

Fingers of the African elephant trunk

Ivory trade
The elephant's only enemy is humans, who kill them for their tusks. In recent years, the demand for ivory has led to killing on a vast scale. From 1979 to 1989, the number of elephants in Africa was reduced from 1.3 million to 609,000.

Ivory is made into carvings and trinkets.

Types of elephant

Asian elephant
The Asian elephant, found in forests in India and south-eastern Asia, has been domesticated for at least 2,500 years. It is used for ceremonial purposes and forestry work. Of the 34,000–56,000 elephants remaining in Asia, 10,000 are working animals.

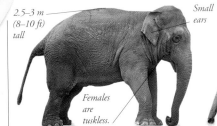

2.5–3 m (8–10 ft) tall

Small ears

Females are tuskless.

African bush elephant
The African bush elephant lives in open country and woodland in Africa south of the Sahara. It is larger, with much larger ears and a more concave back than the Asian elephant. Both males and females have tusks. Unlike the Asian elephant, it has never been domesticated.

Large ears

4 m (13 ft) tall

Elephant reaching up with its trunk.

Small rounded ears

African forest elephant
The forest elephant is a smaller subspecies of the African bush elephant, with smaller, more rounded ears. It does not need such large ears to help it keep cool, as it lives in the tropical rainforests of the Congo basin in equatorial Africa. Its tusks are slender and downward pointing.

Family group

The elephant's social organization is based upon a group of 10–12 females and their calves, led by a mature female. Harmonious relationships often develop between individual members of the group. Friendships can last for decades as elephants often live for up to 80 years. Elephants show great affection for their young, but discipline is strong, and any lapse of acceptable behaviour is dealt with firmly. Family groups often seek shade during the heat of the day, preferring to feed and drink in the cool of the evening. Elephants browse on leaves and shoots, but they also eat grass. They spend about 18 hours a day feeding, to satisfy their huge appetites.

Herd gathering

Separate family groups associate closely with each other. They often live only a few hundred metres apart, constantly coming together and drifting apart again. Occasionally, many family groups congregate in an exceptionally large herd of more than a thousand animals.

Young

Females normally conceive every four years and give birth to a single calf after 22 months' gestation. This is the longest gestation period of any animal. The newborn calf stands about 84 cm (33 in) high. Other calves from previous matings remain with their mother after the new calf is born. The older calves help to take care of their younger siblings.

Matriarch

Leadership of the family unit rests with the oldest and most experienced female, the matriarch, who is usually the mother or grandmother of the whole group. Each member of the group knows its position in the hierarchy and respects matriarchal authority without question.

Water holes

Elephants like to drink every day. They also enjoy bathing and spraying themselves with water. As the dry season advances, food and water become scarce, and they may have to walk up to 80 km (50 miles) between watering and feeding grounds. They also dig holes in some riverbeds to reach water below the surface, thereby providing water for other animals.

Secretion shows bull is in musth.

Bulls

Only immature bull calves are allowed in the family group; as soon as the bulls reach maturity they are expelled. They live alone or in small bachelor groups. Mature bulls briefly rejoin the herd when any of the cows are ready for mating.

Musth

By 25 years of age, bulls come into musth once a year. Musth is a period of aggressive behaviour where a bull picks fights with other bulls searching for a female ready to mate. A thick secretion from the temporal gland indicates he is in musth.

Fighting

Young bulls often have mock battles to test each other's strength. They are usually harmless affairs where they clash tusks and grapple with each other's trunks. Older bulls, especially those in musth, may sometimes fight in defence of territory or to establish dominance.

Young bulls sparring

Threat displays

Differences between elephants are generally resolved peacefully. Displeasure is indicated by means of a threat display. This involves head-shaking, ear-spreading, trunk-twirling, and foot-shuffling. If this fails to deter, the elephant may make a full-scale charge. This is a rare event where the elephant covers ground at rapid speed, with its trunk raised and ears outstretched, while trumpeting furiously. Threat charges are rarely carried through; the elephant usually halts or turns at the last moment.

Ears spread wide to intimidate an enemy

Communication

Touch is an important way of communicating in elephant society. When elephants meet, they greet each other by entwining trunks and touching each other's face and body. At rest, they often stand together, head to head. If a young calf misbehaves, its mother may actually use her trunk to smack it. When a calf is frightened, other elephants help to calm it by standing close, and caressing it with their trunks.

Elephants standing face to face and touching each others' heads and trunks.

Rumbling

Elephants maintain contact by means of rumbling sounds from the throat, back of the nose, and trunk. A sudden cessation of rumbling warns the herd of possible danger. Elephants are also capable of communicating over substantial distances, by low-frequency sounds which humans cannot hear.

AFRICAN ELEPHANT

SCIENTIFIC NAME	*Loxodonta africana*
ORDER	Proboscidea
FAMILY	Elephantidae
DISTRIBUTION	Africa south of the Sahara
HABITAT	Open savannahs and woodlands
DIET	Grasses, leaves, shoots, twigs, and other browse
SIZE	Height at shoulder: 4 m (13 ft); weight: 6.1 tonnes (6 tons)
LIFESPAN	70–80 years

FIND OUT MORE

AFRICAN WILDLIFE · ANIMAL BEHAVIOUR · ASIAN WILDLIFE · CONSERVATION · ECOLOGY AND ECOSYSTEMS · GRASSLAND WILDLIFE · MAMMALS · RAINFOREST WILDLIFE

ELIZABETH I

FOR 45 YEARS from 1558–1603, a truly remarkable woman governed England. By force of personality and political skill, Queen Elizabeth I united her divided country and presided over a glorious period in the arts and culture. Yet she had to struggle all her life: her mother died when she was only three, her half-sister, Mary, put her in prison and, as an adult, she was a single woman in a world dominated by men. But Elizabeth overcame every adversity, and when she died in 1603, she left England one of the most prosperous and powerful nations in Europe.

Elizabeth I's accession to the throne, at the age of 25

Early life
Elizabeth was the daughter of Henry VIII (r.1509–47) and his second wife, Anne Boleyn. She was born in Greenwich Palace on 7 September, 1533. Elizabeth's mother was executed for treason when Elizabeth was just three years old. The future queen was imprisoned briefly while her Catholic half-sister Mary was crowned queen. Elizabeth took the throne on 17 November, 1558, after Mary's death.

Church and State
Elizabeth's father Henry VIII broke with the Roman Catholic Church in 1534, establishing the Protestant Church of England. Her half-sister Mary I (r.1553–58) tried to return England to Catholicism, but Elizabeth introduced the Anglican faith, as a compromise between Catholicism and extreme Protestantism.

William Cecil
Cecil, later Lord Burghley, served Elizabeth first as her Chief Secretary of State and, after 1572, as Lord Treasurer. He introduced many reforms and was an able adviser to the queen. He died in 1598, and his son became chief minister.

Mary, Queen of Scots
Mary was Elizabeth's heir, but also a Catholic. She became the centre of plots against Elizabeth, notably one led by Mary's page Anthony Babington. Elizabeth reluctantly had Mary tried and executed for treason in 1587.

Spanish Armada
As leader of Catholic Europe, Philip II of Spain, husband of Elizabeth's half-sister Mary, was a threat to Protestant England and encouraged plots against the queen. After the execution of Mary, Queen of Scots, Philip decided to invade England. In 1588, he sent a huge Armada of 130 ships carrying 20,000 soldiers. Harried by English ships, attacked in the English Channel, and wrecked by severe storms, the Armada was forced to return, in defeat, to Spain.

English fire ships are sent to meet the Spanish fleet.

Spanish ships escape towards the North.

Francis Drake
Between 1577 and 1580, in his ship the *Golden Hind*, Francis Drake became the first Englishman to sail around the world. He delayed preparations for the Spanish Armada by attacking the fleet while it was at anchor in Cadiz Harbour in 1587, and played an important part in its defeat the following year. He continued to attack Spanish shipping until his death off the coast of Panama in 1596.

Phoenix emblem
Elizabeth created a strong public image of herself by adopting the phoenix as her emblem. The "Phoenix Jewel", dated around 1574, shows a bust of Elizabeth, with a reverse image of the mythical phoenix rising from flames.

The famous "Phoenix Jewel"

Virgin Queen
Elizabeth spent her life surrounded by suitors, yet she never married. Powerful foreign monarchs courted Elizabeth throughout her life, eager for a stake in her flourishing kingdom, but she played her suitors off against each other for political gains. Elizabeth gloried in her role as the Virgin Queen, using it to create a national self-confidence that fuelled a flowering of the arts, distinguished by William Shakespeare, the poet Edmund Spenser, and composers such as Thomas Tallis.

Elizabeth stands on a map of her kingdom.

ELIZABETH I

1533 Born in Greenwich Palace near London, England.

1536 Elizabeth's mother, Anne Boleyn, executed for treason.

1554 Elizabeth put under house arrest by half-sister, Mary.

1558 Succeeds to the throne; appoints William Cecil as Secretary of State and Matthew Parker as Archbishop of Canterbury.

1559 Act of Supremacy makes her head of Anglican Church.

1588 Spanish Armada defeated.

1603 Dies in Richmond Palace.

FIND OUT MORE

CHRISTIANITY   DRAMA   HOUSES AND HOMES   REFORMATION   SHAKESPEARE, WILLIAM   THEATRES   SPAIN, HISTORY OF   UNITED KINGDOM, HISTORY OF

EMPIRES

Ottoman sword and scabbard

A LARGE SUPER-STATE under a single ruler is called an empire. There have been many different empires through history, from the ancient Roman Empire to the great empire of the Incas in Peru. The largest ever was the British Empire. Most empires have an army, to conquer territory and suppress revolts, and a civil service to carry out the day-to-day running of the empire and collect taxes. No empire lasts for ever – though the effect on the host country may be permanent – and empires perish for many reasons, including internal rebellion, economic decline, or the sheer difficulty of uniting many peoples under one leader.

Growth of empires

Empires grow because ruling powers want extra income from trade or taxes, or they may have territorial ambitions. Sometimes they may want to spread a religion. Would-be empires always need a strong army.

Imperial cross

Ottoman Empire
The Ottoman Turks expanded their empire by military might. At their height in the 17th century, they dominated the Mediterranean coast from present-day Greece to Tunisia.

Holy Roman Empire
Based in Germany, the leaders of this empire saw themselves as heirs to the Roman emperors. The emperors wanted to wield religious power over all western Christians, and to exert political power over the other European rulers, such as the German and Italian princes.

British Empire

The largest empire the world has ever seen had its beginnings in the 18th and early 19th centuries, when Britain acquired Australia, Canada, and a range of territories from Honduras to Hong Kong. The "jewel in the crown" of the empire was India, which Britain dominated through the East India Company. Queen Victoria (r.1837–1901) took the title Empress of India in 1876. The British Empire had a lasting influence on its territories – for both good and bad. British-style administration provided a model for local civil servants when territories gained independence. On the other hand, the British exploited local labour forces on a massive scale.

British Empire, 1918

Extent of the empire
After winning the Napoleonic Wars, and the decline of the older empires of Spain, Portugal, and the Netherlands, Britain was clearly one of the world's strongest countries. As the 19th century wore on, the already vast British Empire added parts of Africa and South-east Asia. By 1918, the empire had reached its peak.

Victoria Station, Bombay, India

Gordon of Khartoum
In 1884, two years after Egypt became part of the empire, General Charles Gordon (1833–85) came to the Sudan to aid Egyptians defending their garrisons against a local revolt. Gordon was cut off in the city of Khartoum and withstood a 10-month siege, but was finally killed. There was an outcry that a relief force had not been sent quickly enough to save Gordon, and he became a hero of the empire.

Resources of the empire
Britain had limited resources but an expanding industry, so the British used their empire as a source of raw materials, and a market for goods. The far-flung empire provided raw materials, such as cotton, gemstones, and hard wood, and raw materials included tea, rubber, tin, copper, and wool.

Timber

Cotton   Emerald

Public works
The British made the major towns of the empire as similar to British cities as possible. They sent British engineers and architects all over the world to build government headquarters, churches, railway stations, art galleries, and public buildings. Former imperial cities, such as Bombay, still have Victorian-era administration and transport centres.

Timeline

509 BC–AD 476 Roman Empire dominates much of Europe, western Asia, and northern Africa.

221–206 BC Qin emperor unites China.

321–187 BC Mauryans rule much of India.

395–1453 Byzantine Empire established in the eastern territory of the Roman Empire.

962–1806 Holy Roman Empire dominates central Europe.

1206–1405 Mongols create an empire, including most of Asia.

1345–1521 Aztec emperors hold power in Mexico.

Conquistadore's helmet

1521–1825 Spain builds large empire in southern America.

1580–1931 British Empire increases in size.

1930s British Empire starts to decline. By the 1940s, territories are claiming independence.

Imperialism

The economic domination of Asia, North America, and Africa by Europe, the United States, and Russia from the 17th century is known as modern imperialism. Ancient imperialism peaked with the Roman Empire.

The bear, symbol of Russia, 1888

FIND OUT MORE   BYZANTINE EMPIRE   HOLY ROMAN EMPIRE   ISLAMIC EMPIRE   OTTOMAN EMPIRE   PERSIAN EMPIRES   ROMAN EMPIRE

ENERGY

WE RELY ON THE ENERGY stored in food to keep us alive and on the energy locked within fuels to drive our machines and industries. Energy is the ability to make things happen, whether it is moving something, heating it up, or changing it in some way. Energy exists in many different forms, including electricity, sound, heat, and light.

Weights gain potential energy.

When this woman lifts the weights, she is doing work.

Her power is how long it takes her to do the work.

Types of energy

All energy is either kinetic or potential. Kinetic energy is the energy of moving objects, while potential energy is energy that is stored, ready for use. Energy is measured in units called joules (J).

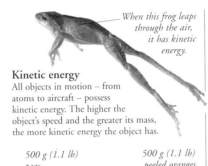

When this frog leaps through the air, it has kinetic energy.

Kinetic energy
All objects in motion – from atoms to aircraft – possess kinetic energy. The higher the object's speed and the greater its mass, the more kinetic energy the object has.

Potential energy
An object may gain potential energy if its position or condition alters. A bungee-jumper standing on top of a bridge has potential energy – that is, the potential to fall back to Earth. When he jumps, his bungee rope gains potential energy as it stretches, because it has the potential to pull him back up again.

The jumper's potential energy changes to kinetic energy as he falls.

500 g (1.1 lb) peas
90 g (3 oz) beef
50 g (1.8 oz) sugar
500 g (1.1 lb) peeled oranges
30 g (1 oz) butter
50 g (1.8 oz) cheese

Chemical energy
Foods and fuels contain energy stored within chemical compounds. This is a type of potential energy called chemical energy. Some foods store more energy than others. All the foods above contain the same amount of energy, but you would have to eat 500 g (1.1 lb) of peas to get as much energy as you would from just 30 g (1 oz) of butter.

Power
The rate at which work is done and energy changed from one form to another is called power. Power is measured in watts (W), and is calculated by dividing the work done by the time taken to do it.

100 W fan
1,000 W iron

Electrical power
Every electrical appliance is given a power rating. If a fan has a power rating of 100 W, it shows that the fan converts 100 J of electrical energy into kinetic energy each second. Similarly, a 1,000 W iron changes electricity into heat at the rate of 1,000 J per second.

Work
When a force moves an object, energy changes from one form to another and work is the result. This woman does work as she lifts weights. The force she applies converts the kinetic energy of her moving arms into the potential energy of the raised weights. Multiplying the force by the distance through which the object moves gives the amount of work done.

Both bulbs give out the same light.
60 W bulb (incandescent)
15 W bulb (fluorescent)
Fluorescent bulb uses less electricity.

Efficiency
Out of every 100 J of electrical energy used by a 60 W incandescent bulb, only 10 J are changed into light; the rest are lost as heat. The bulb has an efficiency of 10%. A 15 W fluorescent bulb is 40% efficient. It gives the same light using a quarter of the electricity.

Energy transfer

The Law of Conservation of Energy says that energy is always conserved – that is, it can be neither created nor destroyed. This law means that when objects gain or lose energy, the energy simply transfers from place to place, or changes into a different form.

Harvested wheat
Bread is made from wheat.
Friction occurs between brake and wheel.

1 Tremendous temperatures at the Sun's surface cause it to give out light and other forms of energy, some of which reach the Earth.

2 When sunlight falls on plants, some of the light energy transfers to the plants by a process called photosynthesis. It is stored as chemical energy.

3 Eating plant-based food, such as bread, enables you to break down the food. This releases the chemical energy and transfers it to your body.

4 Riding a bicycle changes the chemical energy into kinetic energy. If you brake, friction changes this energy into heat as you slow down.

James Joule

The unit of energy, the joule, is named after the English physicist James Joule (1818–89), who helped to develop the Law of Conservation of Energy. Joule noticed that if he rotated a set of paddles in water, the water soon became warm. He realized that the work of turning the paddles changed their kinetic energy into heat, proving that heat is a form of energy.

Timeline

1829 French physicist Gustave Coriolis introduces the term "kinetic energy".

1843 James Joule's experiments show how heat, work, and power are related.

1847 Joule and German physicists Hermann von Helmholtz and Julius Meyer independently state the Law of Conservation of Energy.

1853 Scottish scientist William Rankine devises the concept of "potential energy".

1881 The world's first electricity-generating power station opens in Surrey, UK.

1884 Irish engineer Charles Parsons invents the steam turbine.

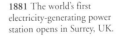

Parsons' turbine

1905 German physicist Albert Einstein suggests that matter is a form of energy, and vice versa.

1980s Declining fossil fuel reserves and pollution bring calls for machines and industries to be more energy efficient.

E

E

Power station

Most of the energy used in homes, offices, and factories is electricity produced by power stations. Inside a coal- or oil-fired power station, chemical energy stored within fuel turns into heat energy as the fuel burns in a furnace. The heat is used to boil water into steam, which drives turbines linked to electricity generators. The electricity reaches consumers via a network of cables called a grid.

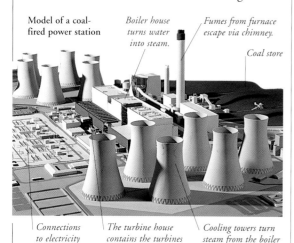

Model of a coal-fired power station

Boiler house turns water into steam.

Fumes from furnace escape via chimney.

Coal store

Connections to electricity grid

The turbine house contains the turbines and generators.

Cooling towers turn steam from the boiler back into water.

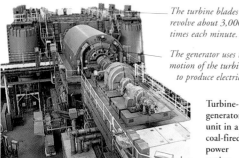

The turbine blades revolve about 3,000 times each minute.

The generator uses the motion of the turbine to produce electricity.

Turbine-generator unit in a coal-fired power station

Turbine

A turbine is a machine powered by the force of moving liquid or gas. It consists of a set of angled blades mounted on a shaft. In a power station, jets of high-pressure steam strike the turbine blades and make them revolve at high speed. The turbine shaft is connected to an electricity generator. As the shaft spins, it turns an electromagnet inside the generator, producing an electric current.

Renewable energy

Energy that is produced without permanently using up the Earth's limited resources is called renewable energy. Apart from biomass fuels, which produce smoke and other fumes when burned, renewable energy sources are pollution-free, because they harness the energy of natural phenomena such as winds and waves. As the Earth's fossil fuel reserves are gradually used up, people will have to rely much more on renewable energy sources.

Geothermal power

Below the Earth's surface, water is turned into steam by geothermal energy – that is, the energy of hot, molten rocks. By drilling a well, this steam can be harnessed to drive generators. Electricity produced in this way is called geothermal power.

Wind power

A wind turbine is a tall tower with propeller-like blades that converts the kinetic energy of the wind into electricity. As the wind blows, the turbine's blades rotate and drive a small generator. A group of wind turbines is called a wind farm.

Biomass fuels

Plant material is called biomass. Millions of people around the world burn peat, wood, animal dung, and other biomass fuels to heat and light their homes, and to cook food. Burning biomass fuels releases chemical energy stored within the plant material.

Hydroelectric power

A hydroelectric power station converts the kinetic energy of falling water into electricity. The power station sits under a dam at the end of a reservoir. Inside the power station, turbines and generators are driven by water rushing down with tremendous force from the reservoir above.

Wave power

Towers such as the one above stand in coastal waters and use the movement of the ocean's waves to produce electricity. As the waves rise and fall, they push a column of air inside the tower up and down. The to-and-fro motion of the air turns a turbine and drives a generator.

Tidal barrage

At high and low tides, huge amounts of water move up and down river estuaries. A tidal barrage is a dam across an estuary. As the tides come in and go out, some water is allowed to pass through tunnels in the dam. The tidal flow drives electricity generators built into the dam.

Solar power

Electricity produced from sunlight is called solar power. A "solar furnace" uses a vast bank of mirrors to focus sunlight on to water. The water boils into steam, which drives turbines and generators.

Fossil fuels

Coal, oil, and natural gas are called fossil fuels, because they formed underground over millions of years from the fossilized remains of plants and animals. The Earth has limited supplies of these fuels, which cannot be replenished once exhausted.

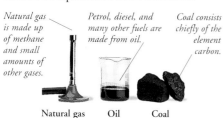

Natural gas is made up of methane and small amounts of other gases.

Petrol, diesel, and many other fuels are made from oil.

Coal consists chiefly of the element carbon.

Natural gas   Oil   Coal

Charles Parsons

The engineer Charles Parsons (1854–1931) was born in London, England, of Irish parents. He is best known for inventing the steam turbine in 1884. Power stations around the world still use steam turbines based on Parson's designs. In 1897, his boat Turbinia became the first to use a steam turbine to power its propellers.

World energy use

Around 90 per cent of all the energy used comes from fossil fuels, which give out a lot of energy when burned, but release polluting gases into the air. Nuclear power is an alternative to fossil fuels, but produces dangerous radioactive waste. Hydroelectric power is the only form of renewable energy that is used in any significant amount.

Oil 40%

Nuclear power 6%

Hydroelectric power 7%

Gas 22%   Coal 25%

FIND OUT MORE   COAL   ELECTRICITY   FOOD   HEAT AND TEMPERATURE   LIGHT   NUCLEAR POWER   OIL   SOUND   X-RAYS AND THE ELECTROMAGNETIC SPECTRUM

ENGINES AND MOTORS

EVERY MACHINE THAT MOVES OR HAS moving parts needs an engine or a motor to make it work. A motor is a machine that converts some form of energy, such as fuel or electricity, into motion. An engine is a form of motor. Engines and motors, both huge and tiny, are everywhere – in vehicles from motor cycles to airliners and railway locomotives, and in appliances around the house, in industrial machines, and in power stations.

Early engines

The first engines were developed in the middle of the 18th century, and were steam powered. During the 19th century, a new form of engine was developed: the internal combustion engine, which was lighter and had more practical uses than its predecessor.

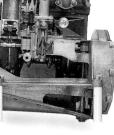

Early four-cylinder petrol engine

Modern engines

Fuel efficiency, plenty of power for its low weight, and little need for maintenance are the hallmarks of the modern car engine. Many engines have electronic components that increase their fuel efficiency further.

Internal combustion engine
Most cars are fitted with internal combustion engines – so-called because they combust, or burn, fuel inside a cylinder. The power this combustion produces is harnessed by pistons and used to power the engine.

Camshaft controls the opening and closing of the valves. There are separate camshafts for fuel inlet and exhaust valves.

Timing belt drives the camshaft.

Spark plug

Combustion chamber is where fuel burns to force the piston down.

Sectioned view of a petrol-fuelled internal combustion engine

Distributor feeds a spark of electricity to each cylinder at the right moment, to start the fuel burning.

Valves let fresh fuel into each cylinder, and spent gases out.

Valve assembly

Exhaust manifold channels waste gases and heat to exhaust pipe.

Cylinder and piston

The pistons slide up and down in the cylinders, providing the driving force that keeps the engine running. The number of cylinders in an engine varies; there are usually at least four, and sometimes more.

Oil filter

Sump reservoir for lubricating oil

Lubricating oil is pumped around the engine, continuously covering the moving parts with a thin film of oil that stops them rubbing together and wearing out.

Crankshaft turns the wheels via the clutch and gearbox. Connecting rods turn the up-and-down motion of the pistons into the circular motion of the crankshaft.

Water pump pulley

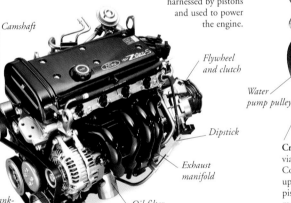

Exterior of internal combustion engine

Camshaft

Flywheel and clutch

Dipstick

Exhaust manifold

Crank-shaft

Oil filter

How engines work

This sequence of diagrams shows what happens in one cylinder of a petrol engine while the engine is running. During the sequence, the piston goes down, up, down, and up again. This is called a four-stroke cycle. The cycle is repeated over and over again – up to 50 times a second when the engine is turning at high speed. In an engine with more than one cylinder, the cylinders fire one after the other to provide continuous power.

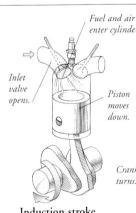

Fuel and air enter cylinder.

Inlet valve opens.

Piston moves down.

Crankshaft turns.

Induction stroke
The piston moves down, and the inlet valve opens. A mixture of fuel and air is sucked into the cylinder.

Valves closed

Piston moves up.

Compression stroke
The valve closes. The piston moves up again, squeezing the fuel and air into the top of the cylinder.

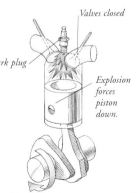

Valves closed

Spark plug

Explosion forces piston down.

Power stroke
The spark plug flares and ignites the fuel which explodes, pushing the piston back down.

Exhaust valve opens.

Piston moves up.

Exhaust stroke
The piston moves up, pushing waste gases out of the cylinder. The exhaust valve opens to let exhaust gases out.

E

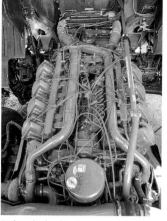
Eight-cylinder diesel truck engine

Diesel engine

A diesel engine is a four-stroke engine without spark plugs. The engine's cylinder has a piston, which rises and falls, squashing the fuel-and-air mixture in the cylinder into a tiny space. The mixture gets so hot, it explodes.

Using diesels
Diesel engines are very fuel-efficient. They are used for driving electricity generators, and in vehicles that need to keep going for long periods without refuelling, such as lorries, taxis, trains, ships, and boats. Many modern cars are also fitted with diesel engines.

Steam engine

The pistons of a steam engine are moved up and down in their cylinders by steam under high pressure. The pistons are connected to rods that turn the wheels. The steam is made outside the cylinders by heating water in a coal-fired boiler, which is why steam engines are called external combustion engines.

Using steam
Until the middle of the 1900s, most railway locomotives and ships were powered by steam engines. Steam also drove many early trucks and buses. The first steam engines were used for pumping flood water out of mines, and to work industrial machines.

Steam leaves train via a funnel.

Steam engine | Firebox | Pipes heat water, which turns into steam. | Steam is fed into the cylinder. | Piston

Solar power

Petroleum and coal are fossil fuels, formed from decayed prehistoric organisms. They are expensive to produce, and create harmful gases when they burn. Solar energy is energy from the Sun. It can be used to heat houses, run air conditioning, and to generate electricity to power lightweight vehicles.

Solar panels
Sunlight can be turned into electricity by solar panels. These are made from many photovoltaic cells. The bigger the area of photovoltaic cells, and the brighter the sunlight, the larger the electric current the solar panel will produce.

Solar-powered car

The heated air turns the turbine blades at rear.

Burning fuel heats the air in the combustion chamber.

Air is sucked in the front.

Gas turbine engines

In a gas turbine, burning fuel makes a stream of hot gas that spins a set of turbine blades very fast. A shaft attached to the turbine drives a compressor that sucks air into the engine so the fuel burns.

Turboshaft engine
Some turbine engines make ship or aircraft propellers spin. The spinning turbine turns a shaft connected to the propeller. Large hovercraft have turboshaft engines to create their air cushion and to drive their propellers. Large helicopters also have turboshaft engines to turn their rotors.

Jet engine
High-speed aircraft have a type of turbine called a turbojet or turbofan. The stream of hot air and gases created in the engine turns the turbine, then shoots out of the back of the engine, pushing the aircraft forwards.

SR.N4 ferry hovercraft

Electric motors

An electric motor produces movement from electricity. Inside it are electromagnets – wire coils that become magnets when an electric current flows through them. The electromagnets are turned on and off in sequence to pull a magnetic shaft around and around. Motors are used in household appliances.

Suck
A vacuum cleaner has a powerful electric motor that turns an air pump. The pump sucks air through the machine, where the dust is removed from it. The motor has to generate a lot of power, so it needs electricity from the mains to drive it.

Hairdryer

Blow
The electric motor in a hairdryer turns a fan to blow air that is heated by hot wire coils. A switch adjusts the speed of the motor. The larger the current it allows through, the stronger the magnets become, and the faster the motor spins.

Turn
Many kitchen gadgets, such as food processors, have an electric motor that moves their working parts. Gears slow the speed of the motor, so the parts turn slowly. The electricity comes either from the mains or from batteries.

Vacuum cleaner

Food processor

James Watt
British engineer James Watt (1736–1819) improved the design of steam engines, and produced the first effective one in 1765. In 1774, he and Matthew Boulton began building steam engines for pumping water from mines. The unit of power, the watt, is named after him.

Timeline
1st century AD Hero of Alexandria, a Greek inventor, makes a novelty toy that is turned by steam.

1698 Englishman Thomas Savery (c.1650–1715) builds the first machine to provide power by using steam.

1815 British engineer George Stephenson (1781–1848) builds the first steam-powered locomotive.

Gears

1876 In Germany, Nikolaus Otto (1832–91) develops the first four-stroke petrol engine. It is a great commercial success.

1892 The diesel engine, used for driving machines, is patented by German engineer Rudolph Diesel.

1894 The *Turbinia*, the first ship with a steam-turbine engine rather than a piston engine, is demonstrated in England.

1937 The first jet engine is demonstrated by the British jet-power pioneer Frank Whittle (b. 1907).

FIND OUT MORE   AIRCRAFT   CARS AND TRUCKS   ELECTRICITY   FORCE AND MOTION   INDUSTRIAL REVOLUTION

ETRUSCANS

A PIRATE PEOPLE OF MYSTERIOUS ORIGIN, the Etruscans dominated the Mediterranean world from the 8th to the 4th centuries BC and formed a league of 12 city-states in what is now modern Tuscany, Italy. Though many of these cities – possibly the first in the area – have been lost over the centuries, superb painting and statuary remain. Etruscan fortunes, based on trade and conquest, started to decline after c.500 BC when the Romans, who had lived under Etruscan rule for a century, began to absorb their former masters into their own expanding empire.

Expansion
From their base in Etruria, the Etruscans' influence spread between the northern Alps and Naples. From 616 BC, the Tarquins, an Etruscan dynasty, ruled Rome itself.

Art
Vivid wall paintings have survived in tombs at the ancient cities of Orvieto, Veii, and Tarquinia – some dating to c.600 BC. Scenes often show dancing, religious observances, or the underworld. Etruscan art was influenced by the Greeks in subject matter and style, but as the Etruscan civilization grew it developed its own bold, colourful, and naturalistic style.

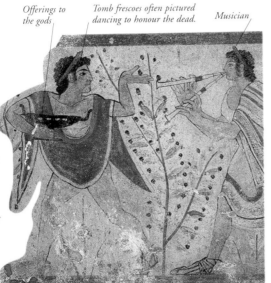

Offerings to the gods

Tomb frescoes often pictured dancing to honour the dead.

Musician

Wall painting, Tomb of the Leopard, Tarquinia

Cities of the dead
Rich Etruscans were buried in underground tombs, some of which were carved from the rock to resemble rooms. These cities of the dead contained frescoes, furniture, and lavish ornaments that tell us much about daily life.

Etruscan rock-cut tombs, Sovana

Bronze sculpture
The best sculptures were made in metal, especially bronze. Early sculptors made copies of imported Syrian or Phoenician objects, but then Greek styles became more popular.

Pan, the liveliest Greek god, in Etruscan style

Statuary
Etruscan craftworkers made statues of terracotta – a brownish-red, unglazed, fine pottery. The sculptors were particularly skilled at creating realistic human faces and figures, such as those at the precinct of Apollo in the city-state of Veii.

Pirates and traders
For centuries Etruscan ships dominated the area of the Mediterranean called the Tyrrhenian Sea. Feared at first as pirates, they later turned to legitimate and prosperous trade with the Phoenicians, Greeks, and Egyptians. This continued until they were eclipsed by Rome.

Etruscans adopted the letters of the Greek alphabet.

Bronze coin

Language
Though examples of Etruscan writing survive on coins and tablets, the language remains a mystery. All scholars know is that it was the last survivor of those languages spoken before Indo-European (from which all modern European languages descend) took over. The first six numbers were *mach, zal, thu, huth, ci, sa*, but no one can be certain which of them match the numbers 1, 2, 3, 4, 5, 6.

Fragment of marble statue

Sheep livers and cloud patterns were thought to reflect the will of the gods.

Relationship with Rome
The last Etruscan king was overthrown in 510 BC, as Rome took over the Etruscan cities one by one. Many practices, such as predicting the future by studying sheep entrails, lived on in the new Roman republic. Leading Roman families were proud of their Etruscan ancestry.

Trade
Etruscan agriculture, industry, and commerce all flourished in the period before the rise of Rome. Mineral deposits in the area were a great advantage to the Etruscans. Wealthy merchants traded metal products, such as jewellery and bronze figurines, as far away as Scandinavia and England.

Flowers

Fruit

Gold earrings

Etruscan jewellers
Etruscan jewellers were especially good goldsmiths, and surviving pieces show originality and artistry. Much gold jewellery was made for trade with Greece.

Semi-precious stones

Gold bead

Necklace

Naturalistic human features

Gold medallion

Gold wreath hair ornament

City people
No one can be sure exactly which 12 walled cities formed the original Etruscan league. Ancient walls still surround modern Tuscan hill-towns, such as Orvieto. The original cities were built haphazardly, and each was dominated by temples.

FIND OUT MORE

ART, HISTORY OF   ARCHITECTURE   GREECE, ANCIENT   ITALY, HISTORY OF   METAL AND METALWORKING   RELIGIONS   ROMAN EMPIRE   SCULPTURE

EUROPE

THE SECOND SMALLEST of all the continents, Europe nevertheless has the third largest population after Asia and Africa. Rich, fertile soils, a variable but hospitable climate, and abundant natural resources have made it easy for people to live in Europe for thousands of years, establishing more than 40 nations and much wealth. Shifting land borders and inhabitants of wide ethnic diversity have caused conflict, but Europe is politically stable and is a major world power.

Physical features

Europe's landscapes range from frozen tundra and coniferous forests in the north to the balmy Mediterranean coast and arid semi-desert of central Spain. The high mountains of the Pyrenees, Alps, Carpathians, and Urals give way to the low-lying North European Plain. Rivers provide communication and transport.

Ural Mountains
The Ural Mountains in Russia separate Europe from Asia. They stretch 2,400 km (1,500 miles) from the Arctic Ocean to the Caspian Sea. The highest mountain is Narodnaya at 1,894 m (6,214 ft).

North European Plain
The vast, rolling North European Plain extends from southern England, across France and Germany, and into Russia as far as the Urals. Rich in coal, oil, natural gas, and fertile farmland, this is Europe's most densely populated area.

Alps
The high Alps dominate western Europe. Stretching 1,500 km (932 miles) from southern France, through Switzerland, Germany, Italy, Austria, and Southeast Europe, this vast arc of mountains separates northern Europe from the warmer south. The highest point is Mont Blanc in France at 4,808 m (15,774 ft).

Cross-section through Europe

Fertile farmland on France's Atlantic coast rises to the plateau of the Massif Central and the Alps at more than 4,000 m (13,125 ft) above sea-level. It then drops down to the Hungarian plain before climbing upwards again to the Carpathians and down into the Black Sea.

Bay of Biscay · Massif Central · Mont Blanc · Alps · Plain of Hungary · Carpathian Mountains · Black Sea

A — Approximately 2,400 km (1,500 miles) from A to B — B

EUROPE FACTS

AREA 10,400,000 sq km (4,000,000 sq miles)

POPULATION 704,900,000

NUMBER OF COUNTRIES 43

BIGGEST COUNTRY Russian Federation

SMALLEST COUNTRY Vatican City

HIGHEST POINT Mt. El'brus 5,633 m (18,481 ft), Caucasus Mountains

LOWEST POINT Volga Delta 28 m (92 ft) below sea-level, Caspian Sea

LONGEST RIVER Volga

BIGGEST FRESHWATER LAKE Lake Ladoga

Climatic zones

Europe's position and varied landscape greatly affect its climate. Apart from the far north where it is always cold, European winters are generally cool, and summers warm or hot. Europe's west coast is milder because of the Gulf Stream, which brings warm waters northwards. Mountains, such as the Alps and Pyrenees, form a natural barrier, protecting the south from the rain and cold winds that blow from the north.

Polar
Coniferous forest
Tundra
Wetland
Deciduous woodland
Scrub
Mountain
Grassland
Desert

Only shallow-rooted plants can survive the cold.

Tundra

The extreme north of Europe lies inside the Arctic Circle and has a polar climate. The vegetation there is tundra – treeless plains where much of the subsoil is permanently frozen ground called permafrost. Only in summer does the topsoil thaw and plants flourish.

Deciduous woodland

Broad-leaved woods and forests are found in many parts of Europe. The trees, which lose their leaves in winter, include the quick-growing birch and ash, and the slower-growing, longer-lived beech, chestnut, maple, plane, and oak. Today, few ancient wild forests survive, and most forest trees have been planted.

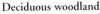

Oak leaves and acorns

Beech trees lose their dead leaves in spring when the new buds sprout.

Straight trunks provide timber for making paper, furniture, and boards.

Taiga

In Russian, the word taiga means a marshy forest. The trees in the forests of northern Europe are mainly conifers, such as fir, larch, and pine. They keep their needle-like leaves even during the cold winters when they may be covered with snow for many months.

Pine-needles and cone

Garrigue

The warm dry hillsides close to the Mediterranean Sea in countries such as Spain, Greece, and France are covered with thorny, often aromatic plants and low bushes. On limestone soils this vegetation is called *garrigue*, elsewhere it is *maquis*.

Many plants have small leathery leaves so they can conserve water in the summer heat.

Grasslands

Large areas of Europe, such as the central *meseta* region of Spain and the steppes of southern Russia and southeastern Ukraine, are covered in vast expanses of grassland. Much of this land is used for grazing animals and growing crops. Drought can be a problem in extreme summer temperatures.

During the spring the grass is lush and green, but becomes scorched as summer progresses.

Ice, rain, and wind make it impossible for plants to survive on the peaks.

Pyrenees

The Pyrenees form part of a vast arc of comparatively young mountains that stretch almost continuously across southern Europe and join with the Himalayas in Asia. Unlike the ancient mountains in Britain and Scandinavia, their shape is still changing because of plate movements beneath the Earth's crust. Mount Aneto is the highest peak at 3,404 m (12,962 ft).

People

Most Europeans live in densely populated towns and cities, many of which lie on the fertile North European Plain. Living standards are generally high compared with other parts of the world, and Europeans benefit from plentiful food and good healthcare. Many countries have sizeable ethnic minorities, usually from former colonies. The majority of Europeans are Christian.

Finnish girl   **Greek boy**   **French girl**

Resources

Europe is rich in natural resources. More than half the land is used for farming a wide variety of food crops, from cereals, such as wheat, barley, and oats, to grapes, olives, citrus fruits, and salad vegetables. Europe mines 40 per cent of the world's coal and around 33 per cent of its iron ore. There are also large reserves of oil and natural gas, and lead, zinc, and other metals. Many rivers supply hydroelectric power.

Grapes
Wheat
Coal

FIND OUT MORE   CLIMATE   CONTINENTS   EUROPE, HISTORY OF   EUROPEAN WILDLIFE   FARMING   FORESTS   MOUNTAINS AND VALLEYS   ROCKS AND MINERALS   TREES   TUNDRA

E

EUROPE, HISTORY OF

EUROPE HAS PLAYED a much more important role in world history than its small population or size would suggest. The Greeks and Romans colonized large parts of North Africa and western Asia, and from the 15th century onwards, European nations established trading empires that spanned the globe. The Industrial Revolution of the 18th century gave Europe an economic strength which allowed it to dominate world trade, and both World Wars began in Europe. Since 1945, Europe's global influence has declined, as wealth and military power has shifted to North America and Asia.

Prehistoric Europe
The first settlers in Europe were primitive hunters who moved around in search of food. By about 5000 BC, people learned to farm and settled in villages. Bronze-working, and later iron-working, spread across the continent.

Prehistoric "Venus" figurine from Lespugue, France

Civilizations of Europe

After 900 BC, four civilizations made their successive mark on Europe. The first were the Greeks, who created powerful city states. They were followed a century later by the Etruscans in Italy. By 200 BC the Celts had settled across Europe. Finally the vast and powerful Roman Empire spanned the continent, reaching its height in AD 117.

Greek Europe
The independent city states of ancient Greece got most of their wealth from trade. Their merchants sailed around the Mediterranean, and founded colonies from Spain to the Black Sea. The most powerful Greek cities were Athens and Sparta.

Ionic-style capital from ancient Greek temple

Christian Europe

In the 4th century, Christianity became the official religion of the Roman empire, and over the next 700 years the faith spread throughout Europe. With the break-up of the Roman empire by 476 and the lack of any strong political force after then, Christianity became the single unifying force across the continent and the church gained great power.

Papacy
As head of the Roman Catholic Church, the popes had enormous spiritual power. Vast landholdings also gave the popes much political power, which led to many conflicts between the papacy and the leading rulers of Europe.

Papal ring

East and west
Attempts by the pope in Rome to establish his jurisdiction over the entire Christian Church were resisted by the Orthodox Churches of eastern Europe, centred around the ancient city of Constantinople. In 1054, this schism (split) became final, leading to a religious division in Christian Europe that survives to this day.

College built around a central quadrangle

Merton College, one of Oxford's earliest colleges

Growth of education
The Church dominated education, at first through the monasteries and then the universities. The first university in Europe, specializing in medicine, was established at Salerno in southern Italy in the 9th century; others, such as Bologna, Paris, and Oxford, followed later.

Orthodox icon of the Archangel Gabriel

Latin inscription from a Roman tomb

Roman Europe
From its foundation in c.753 BC, the city of Rome gradually expanded its power until, by the first century AD, it controlled most of Europe. The Romans gave Europe a network of roads, a common language (Latin), and a legal system, all of which survived long after the fall of the empire in the 5th century.

Nation state

By the 16th century, centralized national governments had emerged right across Europe, from Spain in the west to Russia in the east. The Holy Roman Empire had began to break up, and in countries such as England power was concentrated in the hands of the monarch who ruled with the support of a parliament, composed of members of the aristocracy and church.

The royal coat of arms of Philip II of Spain decorates the cover of one of his books.

Henry IV of France was raised Protestant, but later converted to Catholicism.

Religious wars
The creation of new, Protestant Churches in the 16th century divided western Europe. Roman Catholic and Protestant states fought for supremacy in a series of bitter wars which lasted until the middle of the next century.

Basilica in Goa, India

Overseas empires
In the 15th century, European nations built up empires. Spain and Portugal colonized Central and South America; Britain, France, and the Netherlands colonized North America and the Far East.

E

World imperialism

The Industrial Revolution began in Britain in the mid-1700s, and it transformed world politics and economics. Within a century, European nations were strong and rich enough to set up colonies all around the world. Only the United States of America was able to resist European influence.

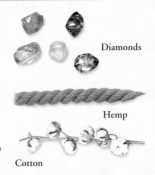

Diamonds

Hemp

Cotton

Global economy

During the 19th century, European steamships took raw materials from their colonies to factories in Europe, and shipped out finished goods to markets abroad. The huge industrial cities of Europe gained vast wealth, but at the expense of poor producers in African and Asian colonies.

Nationalism

During the 19th century, many of the peoples of Europe struggled to obtain their freedom from outside rulers. In one year, 1848, Italians, Germans, Hungarians, Poles, Irish, and others fought for independence or fairer forms of government.

Fighting at Catánia, Italy, 1848

World wars

Austrian officer's hat

Scottish private's cap

Soldiers' hats, 1914

Twice in the 20th century, European conflicts led to war on every continent. In 1914, national rivalries resulted in a four-year war that cost 22 million lives. Germany was defeated and dissatisfied with the peace treaty. Again, war broke out in 1939. By the end of that war, in 1945, Europe was exhausted. Two superpowers, the USA and the Soviet Union, now dominated international affairs.

End of empires

World War I led to the defeat of four great European empires – Germany, Austro-Hungary, Russia, and Turkey – and weakened both Britain and France. After World War II, Europe's overseas colonies fought successfully for independence, with only France retaining sizeable overseas possessions.

The double-headed eagle symbol of Germany

Flag of Nazi Germany

Rival ideologies

Communism was established in Russia after 1917 and in Eastern Europe after 1945, while Fascism and Nazism took hold in Italy, Germany, and Spain in the years up to 1945. By 1990, parliamentary democracy, at first weak in Europe, was the dominant form of government.

Iron Curtain

After World War II, Russian troops occupied much of Eastern Europe. A clear border, known as the Iron Curtain, emerged between the Russian-dominated east and American-dominated west. The border split Germany into two countries.

YOU ARE LEAVING
THE AMERICAN SECTOR
ВЫ ВЫЕЗЖАЕТЕ ИЗ
АМЕРИКАНСКОГО СЕКТОРА
VOUS SORTEZ
DU SECTEUR AMÉRICAIN
SIE VERLASSEN DEN AMERIKANISCHEN SEKTOR

Checkpoint between two sectors of the city of Berlin

Modern Europe

After World War II, French and German politicians worked together to overcome their old hostilities. Economic collaboration between the two countries developed into a formal European Union that grew to include many other western European countries. With the collapse of communism and the rise of market economies in Eastern Europe, many former communist countries lined up to join the EU.

Collapse of Communism

During the late 1980s, Russia withdrew its military and economic support from its communist allies in Eastern Europe. Popular protests then overthrew communism in every East European nation by 1990, but by the late 1990s, there was deep unrest in many East European countries.

Revolution on the streets of Romania

Willy Brandt

Willy Brandt (1913–92) was born in Lübeck, Germany, but lived in Norway during World War II, where he was active in the Resistance. As Chancellor of West Germany from 1969–74, Brandt worked to improve east-west relations and made treaties with Poland and the USSR. He was awarded the 1971 Nobel Peace Prize.

Timeline

Bronze statue of Roman legionary

C.1250 BC Mycenaean culture flourishes in Greece.

C.900 BC Greek city-states gain power.

C.753 BC Rome is founded.

C.200 BC Celts spread across Europe.

AD 117 Roman Empire is at its height.

1054 Christian Church splits into Orthodox east and Roman Catholic west.

1500s European nations use their navigation skills to explore and colonize large parts of the globe.

Mid-1700s Industrial Revolution begins to transform the European economy.

1871 The map of Europe is transformed as Germany and Italy become unified nations.

1914–18 World War I.

1939–45 World War II.

Flag of European Union

1940s–80s Europe gives up most of its colonies.

1957 EEC is set up.

1989–91 Communism falls.

1994 Outbreak of war in Southeast Europe.

2001 Euro is launched.

FIND OUT MORE | CELTS | COLD WAR | EMPIRES | GOVERNMENTS AND POLITICS | GREECE, ANCIENT | HOLY ROMAN EMPIRE | MEDIEVAL EUROPE | ROMAN EMPIRE | WORLD WAR I | WORLD WAR II

EUROPE, CENTRAL

LYING AT THE HEART of Europe on the North European Plain, central Europe consists of four countries: Poland, the Czech Republic, Slovakia, and Hungary. With poor defenses because of the flat terrain, this historically troubled region has often been invaded by neighbouring powers and its country borders redrawn. At one time or another, French, Germans, and Russians have all dominated the area. After World War II (1939–45), the countries of central Europe became communist states closely tied to the former Soviet Union. Since their independence in the late 1980s, many have struggled to compete on the world market.

Physical features

Most of central Europe lies on the vast North European Plain and is largely flat, rolling farmland, broken by the low Sudeten and Carpathian Mountains in the south. In the north, rivers flow into the Baltic; in the south, they flow into the Danube on its way to the Black Sea.

Tatra Mountains
The Tatra Mountains between Poland and Slovakia are the highest part of the Carpathian Range. Their breathtaking scenery makes them popular with walkers in summer, and in winter the snow-covered peaks attract skiers.

Forests
Poland's Bialowieza National Park is the largest area of woodland in northern Europe. Some woods have survived for thousands of years, but acid rain now threatens them. One quarter of central Europe is forested.

Roman Catholicism
In spite of repeated invasions of the area, and half a century of anti-religious communist rule, Roman Catholicism remains the dominant religion of central Europe. Throughout the region, colourful processions celebrate saints' days and other religious festivals.

Religious procession, Kraków, Poland

Danube River
The Danube is 1,775 miles (2,857 km) long and links Germany and the Rhine River to the Black Sea. It is Europe's greatest waterway and is used for carrying freight and generating hydroelectric power in Slovakia.

Regional climate
Central Europe has a temperate climate with hot summers and cold winters. Winters tend to be milder in the south, except in the Carpathian Mountains and other upland areas where heavy snow falls. The summer months are often the wettest.

20°C (68°F)   -2°C (13°F)

553 mm (22 in)

Poland

This country of medieval towns and scattered farms and villages has a history of invasion and occupation by foreign powers. From 1945 to 1989, Poland was a communist state. Since the collapse of communism, however, Poland has been experiencing massive economic, social, and political change. Poland has a strong strategic position between eastern and western Europe and joined NATO in 1999.

Warsaw

Poland's capital since the 1500s, Warsaw was almost completely destroyed during World War II (1939–45). Working from original plans, paintings, and photographs, the Poles have rebuilt the city, restoring its ancient landmarks and treasured buildings. Today, the reconstructed buildings line wide streets and squares.

Old Town Square

Root crops

Beet

Potato

Sugar beet

Poland is a major producer of rye, and also of root crops such as potatoes, sugar beets, and beets. Nearly half the land is used to grow crops or raise livestock, particularly pigs. State farms account for about 10 per cent of this land. Most privately owned farms are small, producing some crops to sell, and the rest to feed farmers' families. Farming employs a quarter of Poland's work-force.

People

Like the neighbouring Czechs and Slovaks, Poles originate from the Slavic peoples of Europe. Poland has few ethnic minorities, and more than 95 per cent of the people are Polish-speaking Roman Catholics. Many Poles have a traditional way of life; local folk arts and crafts flourish. These include wood carving and colourful embroidery.

Wheat

Poland's leading grain crop is wheat, although yields are poor. Two-thirds of the wheat is fed to livestock, some, with potatoes, is used to distil vodka, and with the rest, farmers bake bread.

Industry

About one-fifth of Poland's labour force works in industry, but production in the huge old Soviet-style factories is inefficient. In order to compete on the free market, the government is slowly privatizing industry. Shipbuilding is an important industry on the Baltic Coast, and the Gdansk shipyard is one of several. Poland has a thriving iron and steel industry, and big reserves of coal, lignite (brown coal), copper, lead, silver, and zinc.

Czech Republic

The Czech Republic consists of the two ancient states of Bohemia and Moravia, which once formed part of the Holy Roman Empire. From 1918, it was part of Czechoslovakia and only emerged as an independent country in 1993, when Czechoslovakia was partitioned. The Czech Republic is central Europe's most industrialized nation, and manufacturing employs 40 per cent of its work-force.

Prague

One of the most beautiful capital cities in Europe, Prague has remained virtually unchanged for centuries. Today, it plays host to an increasing number of visitors who come for both business and pleasure. However, air pollution caused by nearby factories poses a major problem.

St. Nicholas's Church

Farming

Only five per cent of the Czech work-force is employed in farming. Much of the land is controlled by large farms owned by the state or cooperatives. Czech farms have some of the highest grain yields in central Europe, but most is fed to livestock because the Republic specializes in meat and milk production.

Bohemian glass

Since the 1300s, the Bohemians of the south have made beautifully decorated glass from the fine sands found in this region. Bohemian glass is prized for its high quality, elegance, and delicacy.

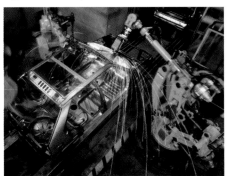

Beer

Czech beers are popular all over the world, and Budweiser, Budvar, and Pilsner are household names. Brewing traditions go back hundreds of years.

Industry

The break-up of the communist regime led to the privatization of many Czech companies. However, some of the very large factories, such as the Skoda works at Plzen, remain under state control. Czech factories are able to produce about 200,000 cars a year. As well as cars, Skoda produces locomotives, machine tools, and weapons. The Czechs also produce iron and steel, machinery, and transport equipment, although there is a trend to move away from heavy industry into consumer goods such as textiles.

E

Slovakia

Slovakia was the rural and poorer half of Czechoslovakia, and after its independence in 1993, the country suffered economically. Much of the land is mountainous and forested. About half is used for crops or grazing, but industry now employs a large number of workers. Most people are Slovaks, speaking their own language, but there are also some Roma and Czechs, as well as a nine per cent Hungarian minority.

SLOVAKIA FACTS

CAPITAL CITY	Bratislava
AREA	48,845 sq km (18,859 sq miles)
POPULATION	5,400,000
MAIN LANGUAGE	Slovak
MAJOR RELIGION	Christian
CURRENCY	Slovak Koruna

Bratislava

From 1536 to 1784, Bratislava was the capital of Hungary. Now it is the capital of an independent Slovakia. The city was founded in the 10th century, and has had a university since 1467. The new parliament buildings were once the home of an archbishop. Bratislava is a Danube river port and a rail centre. Its factories make chemicals and engineering goods.

Rural life

The Slovakian countryside is a mixture of mountain villages, ancient walled towns, and castles. There are still many large state-run farms, but about 20 per cent of the land is farmed by tiny, family-run concerns. The main crops are potatoes, sugar beet, and grains. Rural life is hard, and poverty is common, driving increasing numbers of young people to towns in search of work.

Folklore

Folk traditions are strong in Slovakia, where puppet shows are popular. The former Czechoslovakia is acknowledged as the original home of European puppetry. The Slovakian people enjoy folk festivals where they can dress in regional costumes and sing and dance to traditional music.

Wooden puppet

Hungary

Hungary was formed about a thousand years ago by the Magyars, an ethnic group from Russia that makes up 90 per cent of today's population. Hungary was communist from 1945 until 1990, and since then its industries have had to compete on the world market. The country's skilled scientists and engineers have succeeded in attracting foreign investment.

Thermal springs

Hungary has hundreds of hot thermal springs; their warm mineral waters are said to have medicinal properties. The country has more than 150 spring baths, which are open to the public.

HUNGARY FACTS

CAPITAL CITY	Budapest
AREA	93,030 sq km (35,919 sq miles)
POPULATION	9,900,000
DENSITY	107 per sq km (278 per sq mile)
MAIN LANGUAGE	Hungarian (Magyar)
MAJOR RELIGION	Christian
CURRENCY	Forint
LIFE EXPECTANCY	71 years
PEOPLE PER DOCTOR	313
GOVERNMENT	Multiparty democracy
ADULT LITERACY	99%

Goulash is a traditional Hungarian stew.

Wine

Hungary is a world-class wine producer and exports a wide range of high-quality red and white wines. The best known Hungarian wine is Tokay, pronounced tok-eye. It is a sweet, rich, golden wine, widely believed to be healthful. Another well-known Hungarian wine is Bull's Blood, so-called for its dark blood-red colour.

Paprika

Hungarians grow more than 40 per cent of the world's paprika, a sweet, bright-red pepper used in cooking. One town, Kalocsa in southern Hungary, even has a museum devoted entirely to this spice. Paprika originally came from Central America. Hungarian farmers also grow rye, corn, wheat, barley, sugar beets, and potatoes, as well as grapes, olives, and figs. Sunflowers are grown for their oil.

Goulash

Hungary's most famous dish is goulash, a stew of beef with vegetables, flavoured and coloured with paprika. A pork version is called *pörkölt*. Other traditional dishes with paprika include bacon and potato casserole, and chicken paprikash.

Budapest

Straddling the Danube, Budapest is two cities in one – Buda on the hilly right bank, and Pest on the low-lying left bank. Buda was the old royal capital of Hungary, and has fine old buildings and the remains of a Roman town. Pest is the country's administrative and industrial centre.

The Parliament buildings in Pest, viewed from Buda

Horse breeding

Hungary has a long tradition of horse breeding, located at the great stud farms at Mezőhegyes and Bábolna. The best-known Hungarian breeds are the Nonius and Furioso, which were developed at Mezőhegyes, and the Shagya Arab at Bábolna. Today, these stud farms develop horses for taking part in shows.

Hungary's oldest stud farm at Mezőhegyes

FIND OUT MORE

CHRISTIANITY · EMPIRES · EUROPE · EUROPE, HISTORY OF · FARMING · GOVERNMENTS AND POLITICS · HOLY ROMAN EMPIRE · HORSES · SOVIET UNION

EUROPEAN UNION

TWENTY-FIVE COUNTRIES have joined together to form the European Union (EU). But Europe was not always united. Between 1870 and 1945, France and Germany were at war three times. Determined to ensure that their two countries never fought again, the French and Germans decided to link their coal and steel industries so that their nations would be forced to work together. The creation of the European Coal and Steel Community (ECSC) in 1951 led to today's European Union.

The euro
On 1 January 2002, a single currency, the euro, was fully launched in 12 countries of the European Union (EU). The notes and coins of this new currency replaced the national currencies of those nations. The only EU countries to stay out of the monetary union were Britain, Denmark, and Sweden.

Uniting Europe

In 1957, the ECSC evolved into the wider European Economic Community (EEC). Ten years later this became the European Community (EC). In 1991, EC leaders signed the Maastricht Treaty, which started Europe towards full economic and monetary union. When the treaty came into force in 1993, the EC became the European Union (EU).

The growing union
The European Union has 25 members. A number of states have applied for membership, with more considering joining. Trade and cooperation agreements are already in place between the EU and many applicants. Switzerland has close trade links with the EU, but a national referendum in 2001 rejected joining.

1 Netherlands
2 Belgium
3 Luxembourg
4 Slovenia

More countries in central and eastern Europe are intending to apply.

Date of joining
- 1957
- 1973
- 1981
- 1986
- 1995
- 2004

Members of the EU, 2004

Structure of the EU

The EU has three main institutions: the Commission, based in Brussels, Belgium, is the civil service which runs the EU; the Parliament, in Strasbourg, France, and Brussels, provides control over the EU; the European Court of Justice, in Luxembourg, makes sure EU laws are applied properly.

European Parliament
Every five years, adults throughout the EU go to the polls to elect 732 Members of the European Parliament (MEPs) to represent their interests. Although it does not have the same powers as a national parliament, the European Parliament advises the Commission and supervises its work and annual budget.

Jean Monnet
Jean Monnet (1888–1979) was a French economist who convinced the French foreign minister, Robert Schuman (1886–1963), that the only way to avoid another war between France and Germany was to integrate their coal and steel industries. The ECSC was set up with Monnet as its first president. His vision led directly to the development of today's EU.

What the EU does

The European Union has many different roles covering economic, financial, commercial, political, industrial, agricultural, social, and cultural matters. Its two main achievements have been to establish free trade between the member states by abolishing customs duties, and to set up a common agricultural and fisheries policy.

The EU has sponsored a common European passport.

EU aid
The EU provides subsidies to the less well-off regions of Europe, for projects such as developing new industries. Much EU aid is targeted towards improving transport links in Europe, such as building roads and railways, so all regions can share in the benefits of the single market.

Agricultural policy
In order to guarantee food supplies and increase agricultural productivity, the EU runs a very complex Common Agricultural Policy (CAP). This has established free movement of farm produce throughout the EU.

Social policy
The EU tries to improve employment for unemployed workers and young people by investing in education and training in deprived regions. It has also established a common Social Chapter of Workers' Rights.

Timeline
1951 European Coal and Steel Community (ECSC) is set up.

1957 The ECSC nations sign the Treaty of Rome, setting up the European Economic Community (EEC);

1967 ECSC, EEC, and Euratom merge to form the European Community (EC).

1979 European Monetary System set up to link currencies.

1991 Maastricht Treaty sets out timetable for full economic union.

1993 EC becomes the European Union (EU).

2002 The euro replaces existing currencies in 12 EU countries.

2004 Ten additional countries become members of the EU.

FIND OUT MORE   EUROPE, HISTORY OF   FARMING   FISHING INDUSTRY   FOOD   MONEY   TRADE AND INDUSTRY   WORLD WAR II

EUROPEAN WILDLIFE

EUROPE IS A landmass that contains many different habitats, ranging from the Arctic tundra, through broad-leaved forests, and mountainous areas, to dry, hot regions around the Mediterranean. Only deserts and tropical forests are missing from the list. European wildlife is not as rich as it once was; human intervention in the form of agriculture and forest clearance, as well as the sheer size of the human population, has diminished the number of plants and animals. Yet in undisturbed forests and wetlands, a large diversity of wildlife remains.

Broad-leaved woodland wildlife

Broad-leaved woodlands extend across Europe. The trees within them, such as oaks and sycamores, are broad-leaved, or deciduous, trees, which means they lose their leaves in winter. In spring and summer, when the leaves reappear and plants bloom, woodlands support many insects, birds, and mammals, such as squirrels and mice.

Dappled coats help to camouflage deer as they graze on grass.

Oak tree
Commonly found in broad-leaved woodlands, oaks provide homes and food for many animals. Insects, for example, feed on leaves and other parts of the tree, while they themselves are food for larger animals, such as birds. Acorns, the fruits of the oak, appear in late summer.

Once acorns have fallen to the ground, they provide a nutritious meal for birds, squirrels, and mice.

Female nut weevil drilling into acorn with her mouthparts.

Rostrum

Nut weevil
This beetle lives on oak trees, feeding on buds and leaves. It has a snout-like rostrum, at the end of which are its jaws. In late summer, the female makes holes in the oak's acorns. In each hole she deposits an egg. The larva that hatches from the egg feeds on the acorn.

Red fox
Red foxes live on their own or in small family groups in underground dens. They are most active at night when they hunt for rabbits, rodents, and worms. They may also eat fish and fruit.

Females flick their large, bushy tails to warn cubs of danger.

Fallow deer
Woodland provides cover and food for fallow deer. Females and young live in small herds. Males have antlers, and are solitary or live in small groups. Males and females meet during the mating season in the autumn.

Wetland wildlife

Europe's wetlands are rich in wildlife. Reeds, bulrushes, and marsh plants provide food and shelter for wetland animals, such as voles and otters. Insects and other invertebrates are a food source for fish and frogs, which themselves are eaten by many water birds.

Bulrushes provide nesting sites for birds.

Flower head

Bulrushes
These tall grass-like plants grow at the fringes of lakes and ponds. Their roots are often in wet soil or submerged in water, while their stems and leaves extend above the water. Bulrushes have dark, compact, cylindrical flower heads.

European kingfisher
This small bird hunts for fish and other water animals from a perch along the banks of streams and lakes. Once prey is spotted, the kingfisher plunges into the water, grabs it with its long, pointed beak, and returns to the perch to eat its meal.

European otter
Otters are strong swimmers, adapted for rapid movement in water. An otter's body is long and streamlined, its dense, glossy fur is water-repellent, and it has webbed feet. Otters hunt underwater, catching prey such as fish, water birds, and frogs. They are equally agile on land, and catch water voles and other animals that live on riverbanks.

Water vole
Water voles are good swimmers. They build tunnels in banks next to lakes and slow-moving rivers. These tunnels have chambers for food storage and nesting, and entrances that open above and below the waterline.

Water voles feed on plants, roots, and bulbs.

Edible frog
Edible frogs live in marshes and lakes, sometimes emerging at night to feed on land. They catch insects with their long, sticky tongues. Larger prey, such as newts and small fish, are caught in the jaws and pushed into the mouth with the feet.

Alpine chough

In summer, choughs live in flocks above the tree line. They walk over rocky ground, probing under vegetation and in crevices for insects and snails. They glide on air currents, coping easily with the strong gusts of wind found at high altitude.

Mountain wildlife

The Alps and the Pyrenees are the major mountains of Europe. Vegetation changes with increasing altitude; each zone has its characteristic wildlife. Animals tend to move to lower altitudes during the cold winter months when food becomes scarce.

Mouflon

The mouflon is a wild sheep that lives in remote, mountainous regions. It feeds on grasses and other plants during the day, and rests at night. The mouflon is surefooted, moving easily over rough terrain. Males bang their heads and horns together when competing for mates.

Alpine meadow

Alpine meadows are found above the tree line and below the snow line. In summer, they are covered in a blanket of bright flowers and dwarf shrubs. These provide food for hordes of insects, which in turn are eaten by birds. Meadow vegetation is also eaten by grazing animals.

Bears eat rodents, deer, insects, salmon, carrion, tubers, and berries.

Cubs are born in dens in mid-winter.

Brown bear

These large bears live in remote forested areas of mountains and as far north as the tundra. They have no natural enemies apart from humans. In winter, brown bears usually retire to a den for a period of dormancy.

Coniferous forest wildlife

Coniferous forests of evergreen trees, such as spruce and pine, extend across northern Europe. They are dense and dark, with few ground plants. Summers are warm; winters are cold, with heavy snow falls. Many animals eat the leaves and seeds of conifers.

Norway spruce

Norway spruces have reddish trunks, dark green crowns, and grow up to 55 m (180 ft) in height. These seeds of the spruce, as well as the bark, buds, and needle-like leaves, provide food for forest animals.

Triangular outline prevents snow accumulating and snapping branches.

Pine marten

Pine martens hunt in the morning and evening, using their excellent hearing and sight to locate birds, squirrels, rabbits, and rats.

Pine martens climb trees, resting by day in tree hollows.

Common crossbill

The common or red crossbill lives in the forest canopy and is rarely seen on the ground, except when it lands to drink. Its crossed beak provides the bird with a strong "tool" for prising open the scales of pine and spruce cones. It then uses its tongue to extract the seeds.

Upper and lower parts of bill are crossed.

Arctic hare

The arctic hare lives in the coniferous forests and tundra of the far North. Its fur turns from brown in summer to white in winter, to conceal it from predators such as foxes.

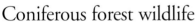

Bright yellow flowers are strongly scented.

Mediterranean wildlife

The Mediterranean region of Europe has hot, dry summers, and milder and wetter winters. Aromatic plants, such as thyme, and trees such as cedar grow here. Many animals survive by sheltering in midday heat; others migrate.

Black, bristly feathers give it its other name of bearded vulture.

Lammergeier

The lammergeier lives in mountainous areas. It eats carrion, including the bones, which it drops on to rocks from a height to smash them and expose the soft marrow.

Short antenna

Spanish festoon butterfly

This brightly patterned butterfly is found on the coasts of Spain, France, and Portugal. It can be seen from late winter, when temperatures start to rise, until early summer, when mating is complete.

Zig-zag wing pattern

Ear tufts are used to signal to other lynxes.

Common lizard

A common sight in southern Europe during the summer, this lizard sunbathes in the morning to increase its body temperature, making it more active when searching for insects.

Broom

This shrub can survive the hot, dry conditions of the Mediterranean summer. The seed pods produced by the flowers dry in the sun, and split open to scatter the tiny seeds.

Spanish lynx

This cat, once found all over Spain, is now restricted to the pine forests, scrub, and sand dunes of the Coto Doñana National Park in southwest Spain. Lynx feed on rabbits and hares, deer fawns, and ducks.

FIND OUT MORE   BIRDS OF PREY   FORESTS   LAKE AND RIVER WILDLIFE   MARSH AND SWAMP WILDLIFE

EVOLUTION

THE TERM EVOLUTION refers to the theory that existing animals and plants have evolved, or developed, through a process of continual change from previous life forms. Some scientists argue that by looking at fossil evidence we can find out more about the past. Fossils have shown that primitive life forms appeared more than 3.8 billion years ago, and that vertebrates existed at least 500 million years ago. Over generations, better-adapted organisms have developed.

How a species evolves

An organism may undergo change due to a number of processes, such as natural selection and adaptation, induced by the environment in which it lives. For example, selection may have promoted larger and faster horses adapted for living on open grassy plains. In some cases, a subspecies can change so much that it becomes very different from the rest of its species.

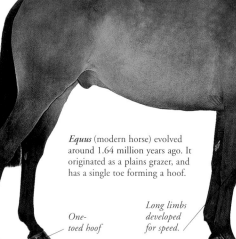

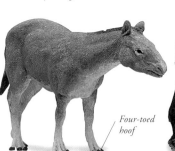

Hyracotherium, the first in a long line of horses, appeared approximately 55 million years ago.

Equus (modern horse) evolved around 1.64 million years ago. It originated as a plains grazer, and has a single toe forming a hoof.

Four-toed hoof

One-toed hoof

Long limbs developed for speed.

The third toe became larger until the side toes eventually disappeared.

Three-toed Hipparion appeared around 15 million years ago.

Third toe

Foot of early four-toed *Hyracotherium*

Foot of three-toed *Hipparion*

Hoof of modern horse, *Equus*

Natural selection

The theory of natural selection suggests that environmental factors may favour some members of a species over others, enabling the fittest to survive. Experiments with the carnivorous plant, sundew, backed this theory. Plants that were fed meat produced more flowers and seeds than plants which were not.

Plant fed meat produces flowers.

Unfed plant has fewer flowers.

Heredity

Heredity studies how characteristics of certain individuals are passed on from one generation to the next. This process often involves the expression of a parent's dominant gene, which may mask the effect of the recessive gene.

Variation

Variation refers to the differences within a species. Certain variations, such as shell colour, may give certain individuals advantages over others. These individuals will have a greater chance of surviving and reproducing.

Banded snails

Shell colours allow snail to adapt to local habitat.

Mutations

Occasionally during reproduction, the process of replicating genetic material (DNA) goes wrong and produces an accidental mutation. Normally, these mutants do not live but some survive as an important source of variation on which selection operates.

Fuller's mutant teasel has curved spines, allowing easier seed dispersal.

Teasel plant

Sexual selection

Some animals choose their mates by means of sexual selection. A male may have elaborate features, such as bright feathers, to attract a mate. Characteristics such as these, which may be beneficial to the species, are passed to the next generation.

Russian hamsters

Recessive albino gene

Dominant grey gene

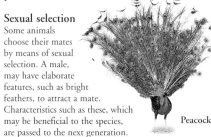

Peacock

Adaptation

The process of adaptation occurs when an organism evolves in a certain way to make it better suited to its environment. Some people believe that this can lead to a new species, and that an animal or a plant will adapt to its surroundings so that it has a better chance of survival.

Plant-feeding finch

Insect-feeding finch

Darwin's finches

While visiting the Galápagos Islands, English naturalist Charles Darwin (1809–82) noticed the variety of finches living there. Because they resembled finches of mainland South America, he argued that each finch species had evolved a differently shaped beak to meet the needs of its particular diet.

Monarch butterfly

Viceroy butterfly

Mimicry in butterflies

Mimicry is a form of adaptation where one species has developed a resemblance to another as a means of protection. Birds find the monarch butterfly distasteful, but also avoid the similarly coloured viceroy, even though it is palatable.

Intermediates

Intermediates are thought to be the "halfway" species that should exist if one group of organism has evolved from another. In 1861, discovery of the earliest fossil bird, *Archaeopteryx*, provided important support for this theory. The fossil clearly combines the reptile characteristics of a dinosaur in its skeleton, but at the same time has the uniquely bird-like feature of feathers.

Lungfish

Living intermediates
The lungfish can breathe oxygen directly from air and has paired fleshy fins for swimming. Lungfish arose about 380 million years ago when animals first stepped on land; it is thought that the first land-going tetrapods (four-footed animals) evolved from lungfish-like intermediates.

Human impact

For centuries humans have had an impact on animal and plant habitats. For example, some animals have had to adapt to new environments created by human settlement and industry. Also, by selective breeding, scientists have altered the genetic make-up of some plants and animals to create superior crops and meat for human consumption. Fruits, such as grapes and oranges, have been bred so that they no longer have seeds and are therefore easier to digest.

Tomatoes are bred to have a longer shelf life.

Seedless orange

Seedless grape

Artificial selection
Scientists can manipulate the genetic make-up of plants and animals by artificially selecting particular strains according to need. For instance, genetically altered products, such as tomatoes with enhanced flavour, are already on sale. Dog breeders, too, can alter the temperament, shape, size, and colour of dogs. The ability to alter genetic make-up raises many ethical questions.

Shar pei dog

Impact by pollution
It was discovered that during the Industrial Revolution, light coloured peppered moths, previously camouflaged from bird predators, became vulnerable on soot blackened trees. However, darker coloured peppered moths did survive and went on to breed more dark moths.

Peppered moths

Evidence

Much of the evidence for evolution is based on fossils. These show how life originated from simple forms in the sea and then evolved to occupy land, freshwater, and air. Study of the common characteristics of organisms suggest how they could be inter-related. Also, investigations into genetics and its molecular basis have led to a greater understanding of how evolution works.

Fossil evidence
Fossils of animals and plants show that there have been significant changes throughout geological time. Fossils show how the first land living plants appeared some 440 million years ago, but were not sufficiently well established to form forests until about 320 million years ago.

Fossil of fern plant

Molecular evidence
Often, if two new species evolve from a common ancestor, their DNA begins to change. For example, both the red and grey squirrel feed on acorns. However, the red squirrel lacks the digestive enzyme which breaks down chemicals in the acorn. This has led to a decline of red squirrels in the British Isles.

Grey squirrel population outnumbers that of the red squirrel in Britain

Creation theories
Evolutionists believe that life on Earth has evolved progressively over thousands of millions of years, originally from non-living materials. However, some people argue that all life forms on the Earth were created by design, in or close to the form in which they exist today. Although creationists as a group reject the theory of evolution, many accept that life forms on Earth can change. They believe that God created various kinds of creatures that have diversified within each kind until the present day.

19th-century caricature of Charles Darwin

Jean Baptiste de Lamarck
French naturalist Jean Baptiste de Lamarck (1744–1829) proposed a theory of evolution that broke the prevailing idea of the fixity of species. He claimed that by striving to fit into their natural surroundings, organisms changed in bodily form, and that such transformations were passed on to their offspring. According to his theory the giraffe developed a long neck by stretching to eat leaves from trees.

The sturdy armadillo limb is adapted for digging.

Armadillo forelimb

Finger digits

Wrist bone

The chimpanzee's arm is very similar to the basic vertebrate bone pattern.

Upper arm

Chimpanzee's arm

In bats, the hand and finger bones developed into supports for the membranes of the wing.

Bones of bat's wing

Comparative anatomy
French naturalist Georges Cuvier (1769–1832) demonstrated that the function of the vertebrate skeleton reflects the way in which the animal lived. Since vertebrates have a common ancestry, the structure of the skeleton has a similar plan. Armadillo limb bones may be directly compared with the arm bones of a chimpanzee, and those of a bat's wing.

FIND OUT MORE ANIMALS BIG BANG DARWIN, CHARLES DINOSAURS FOSSILS GENETICS HUMAN EVOLUTION PREHISTORIC LIFE PREHISTORIC PEOPLE

EXPLORATION

SINCE THE EARLIEST TIMES, people have been curious about the world in which they live. For more than 3,000 years, explorers have charted most of Earth's surface by land and sea. Often these brave pioneers went out into the unknown inspired by more than mere curiosity. Sometimes they went in search of riches, or to find new and less overcrowded places to live, or in a quest for scientific knowledge. In the course of mapping the world, explorers quashed many myths while bringing back true stories that could seem even stranger than fiction.

Ancient exploration

In ancient times, peoples such as the Phoenicians explored new regions in their quest for trading partners. The Greeks and Romans also discovered more about the world as their empires expanded. People began to read about far-flung places in books by classical geographers such as Strabo (c.63 BC–c.AD 21).

Xuan Zang

The Buddhist monk Xuan Zang (602–664) was one of the greatest travellers of ancient China. In 629 he set off alone on the famed Silk Road to visit India, Nepal, Sri Lanka, and Pakistan, making friends for China and studying as he went. He returned in 654 laden with the finest Asian artworks. After Xuan Zang's death, the Emperor Gaodong built the Xingjiao monastery outside Xi'an to honour him.

Exploration for trade

After the Ottomans captured Constantinople in 1453, European rulers paid sailors to find alternatives to the land route to Asia. It was soon proved quicker and cheaper to ship luxury goods such as spices and silks by sea.

Han dynasty (206 BC–220 AD) figurine

Chinese jade horse

Chinese dragon

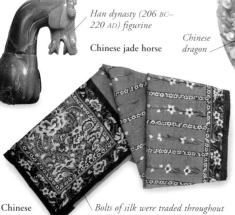

Ivory imperial seal

Silk Road

In ancient and medieval times, there was a 6,400-km (4,000-mile) overland trade route between China and Europe, known as the Silk Road. It fell into disuse when Asian and European traders adopted new east-to-west sea routes in the 15th and 16th centuries.

Chinese silk

Bolts of silk were traded throughout the Silk Road.

Marco Polo

The Venetian pioneer trader Marco Polo (c.1254–1324) travelled overland to China, and served the Emperor Kublai Khan as a diplomat for 17 years. Back in Europe, while in prison for debt (1296–98), he dictated a hugely popular book about life in the Far East. Centuries later it helped inspire Columbus to find a new westward sea route to the East.

Kublai Khan and Marco Polo

Mongol emperor Kublai Khan

Marco Polo

Clove tree

Spice Islands

Europeans knew that valuable spices, such as cloves, grew wild in the East, and some of the greatest explorations were efforts to find the Spice Islands, which are today known as the Moluccas. Portuguese, Spanish, Dutch, and British navigators all fought to control this valuable source of trade for their countries.

Vasco da Gama

Portuguese navigator Vasco da Gama (c.1469–1524) became the first European to sail to India when he landed at Calicut (Calcutta) in 1498. Da Gama returned twice: in 1502 to avenge the deaths of some Christian traders, and for the last time, in 1524, as Viceroy of India. He died shortly after this appointment.

Aztec sacrificial knife

New World

From 1492 Europeans aimed to reach India by sailing west. When they discovered that America was in their path, they hailed this continent as a "new world". But as they explored it, they brutally plundered and destroyed the rich empires of the Aztec, Inca, and Maya.

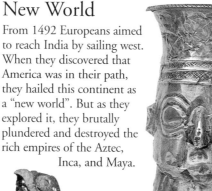

Aztec portrait beaker

Southern Continent

For centuries Europeans believed that there was a Terra Australis Incognita – or Unknown Southern Continent. In the 17th and 18th centuries Dutch and British seamen, such as James Cook (1728–79), began to explore it, and the great continent became known as Australia.

Robert O'Hara Burke and William J Wills

Early European settlement of Australia was coastal. Burke (1820–61) and Wills (1834–61) made the first journey from Melbourne across the continent's parched interior to the northern coast. On the way back, they died of starvation in the Outback.

Death at Cooper's Creek

Exploration tools

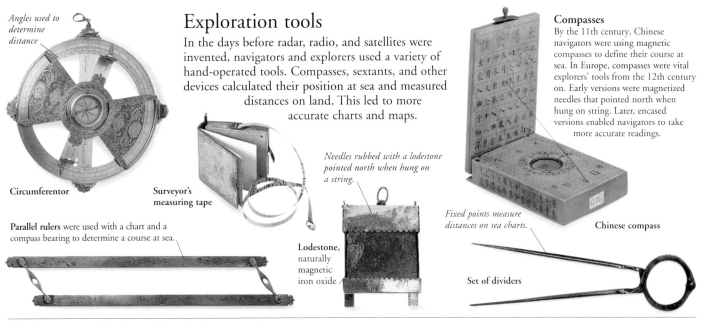

Angles used to determine distance

Circumferentor

Surveyor's measuring tape

In the days before radar, radio, and satellites were invented, navigators and explorers used a variety of hand-operated tools. Compasses, sextants, and other devices calculated their position at sea and measured distances on land. This led to more accurate charts and maps.

Needles rubbed with a lodestone pointed north when hung on a string.

Compasses
By the 11th century, Chinese navigators were using magnetic compasses to define their course at sea. In Europe, compasses were vital explorers' tools from the 12th century on. Early versions were magnetized needles that pointed north when hung on string. Later, encased versions enabled navigators to take more accurate readings.

Parallel rulers were used with a chart and a compass bearing to determine a course at sea.

Lodestone, naturally magnetic iron oxide

Fixed points measure distances on sea charts.

Chinese compass

Set of dividers

Pundits
In the 19th century, the British in India trained Indian surveyors, known as pundits, to make maps of the Central Asian territories of Karakoram, the Hindu Kush, and the Himalaya. In 1863, one of the earliest pundits, Muhammad-i-Hameed, made the first recorded trip over the Karakoram range to Chinese Turkestan. He died after spending six months in Yarkand, but his surveying equipment and notebook containing vital topographical information were taken back to India.

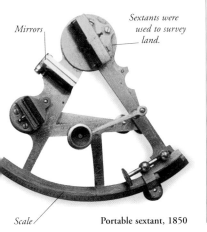

Mirrors

Sextants were used to survey land.

Scale   **Portable sextant, 1850**

Empire building

From the 15th century, the Spanish, Portuguese, Dutch, British, and French created huge empires outside Europe. After a nation's explorers, traders, and settlers had made links with an overseas territory, it might easily come under that nation's rule as a colony. Africa, Australia, parts of Asia, and the Americas were all colonized by Europeans at one time.

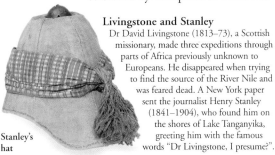

Livingstone and Stanley
Dr David Livingstone (1813–73), a Scottish missionary, made three expeditions through parts of Africa previously unknown to Europeans. He disappeared when trying to find the source of the River Nile and was feared dead. A New York paper sent the journalist Henry Stanley (1841–1904), who found him on the shores of Lake Tanganyika, greeting him with the famous words "Dr Livingstone, I presume?".

Stanley's hat

Charles Sturt
Despite the presence of two great rivers, the Murray and the Darling, Australian settlers could find no river mouths on the southeast coast, so explorers searched for an inland sea. In 1828–30, Sturt (1795–1869) mapped these river systems for 1600 km (994 miles). In 1844, he explored the Australian interior, or Outback, and finally proved there was no inland sea.

Final frontiers

In 1909 and 1911 the first-ever expeditions reached the North and South Poles. Since then there have been few places on Earth left to map but, with technological advances, scientists have been able to extend exploration to include investigations of the oceans and space. In 1969, explorers landed on the Moon for the first time.

Hubble Space Telescope
Astronomers can now explore time as well as space. The Hubble Space Telescope, launched in 1990, orbits Earth at a distance of 600 km (370 miles). From this distance it collects images travelling through space from millions of years ago.

Equipment box

Solar panel

Mary Kingsley
Few women took part in the first explorations of the world. It was generally believed that only men had the courage to venture into uncharted foreign lands. However, keen English naturalist, Mary Kingsley (1862–1900), proved that this was untrue when she travelled through West Africa in 1893 and 1894, collecting fish and beetle specimens for the British Museum and making a study of African religions. In 1900 she returned to Africa to nurse soldiers in the Boer War, and died there.

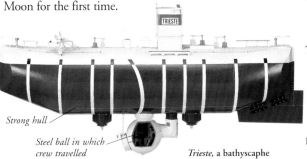

Strong hull

Steel ball in which crew travelled

Trieste, a bathyscaphe

Trieste submarine
The bathyscaphe, *Trieste* – a manned diving vessel designed to reach depths of up to 11 km (7 miles) in the ocean – was developed by the Swiss scientist Auguste Piccard (1884–1962). In 1960 it dived to a record 10,916 m (35,815 ft) in the Mariana Trench of the Pacific Ocean. On board were Piccard's son Jacques and Lieutenant Donald Walsh of the US Navy.

FIND OUT MORE   AUSTRALIA, HISTORY OF   ASIA, HISTORY OF   AFRICA, HISTORY OF   CENTRAL AMERICA, HISTORY OF   COOK, JAMES   EMPIRES   POLAR EXPLORATION   SOUTH AMERICA, HISTORY OF   SPACE EXPLORATION

EYES AND SEEING

YOUR EYES ENABLE you to see by stimulating the creation of images in your brain. Each of the two eyeballs is a sphere measuring 6.25 cm (2.5 inches) in diameter. Eyeballs contain sensory cells that, when stimulated by light, send messages to the brain that are interpreted as images. Reflex mechanisms control the amount of light entering the eye, and enable the eye to focus on objects whether they are near or distant. Much of the eyeball is hidden because it is protected within the orbit, a bony socket in the skull. The delicate outer surface of the eye is also protected by the eyelids.

Moving the eye
Your eyes move constantly, even when you are staring. Six muscles move each eyeball and hold it in place inside its skull socket. Each muscle pulls the eye in a different direction, enabling the eyeball to move up and down, from side to side, and diagonally. Your brain controls these movements to make sure that both eyes move together.

Eye-moving muscles

Eyeball

Seeing
The eyes gather light from whatever you look at. The cornea and lens focus this light on the retina to produce an upside-down image. Cells inside the retina, called rods and cones, respond to light by sending nerve impulses along the optic nerve to the brain. The brain interprets these impulses so you see the image the right way up.

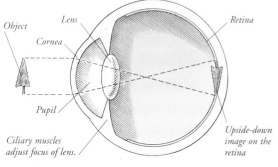

Object
Lens
Cornea
Retina
Pupil
Ciliary muscles adjust focus of lens.
Upside-down image on the retina

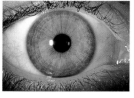

Iris and pupil
The iris controls the amount of light entering the eye. Muscles in the iris alter the size of the pupil, the opening that allows in light. In dim light, the pupil widens; in bright light, the pupil gets smaller.

Rods and cones
There are about 120 million rods and 7 million cones in the retina. Rods work best in dim light. Cones are responsible for colour vision and enable you to see things in detail.

Tears
Tears are released by lacrimal (tear) glands above the eye. When you blink, tears spread over the eye's surface. This keeps the cornea moist, washes away dust, and kills germs. After flowing over the eye, tears drain through two small openings at the side of the eye into the lacrimal duct, and then into the nose.

Inside the eye
The transparent cornea at the front of the eye helps to focus light as it enters. Behind the cornea are the iris, which controls the amount of light entering, and the lens, which fine focuses light on the retina. Two liquids, aqueous and vitreous humour, maintain the shape of the eyeball.

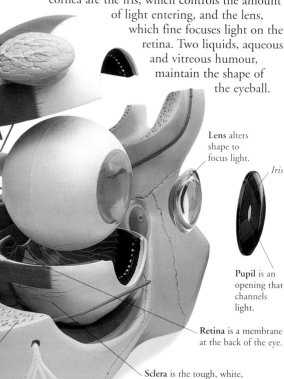

Tear gland moistens and protects eye.

Optic nerve sends messages from retina to brain.

Choroid supplies inside of eye with blood.

Eyeball lies within a protective bony socket.

Nerve

Lens alters shape to focus light.

Iris

Pupil is an opening that channels light.

Retina is a membrane at the back of the eye.

Sclera is the tough, white, outer coat of the eye.

Vision defects
The most common vision problems are long sight and short sight. In both cases the eye does not focus light properly on the retina. Some people, mainly males, have colour blindness and cannot distinguish between certain colours, most often red and green.

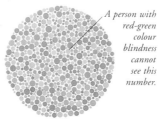

A person with red-green colour blindness cannot see this number.

Long sight
A long-sighted person sees distant objects clearly, but has a blurred view of close objects. This happens because light from near objects is focused behind the retina, rather than on it.

Short sight
A short-sighted person can see close objects clearly, but sees distant objects as a blur. Short sight is usually caused by the eyeball being longer than normal. This means that light entering the eye from distant objects is focused in front of the retina, rather than on it.

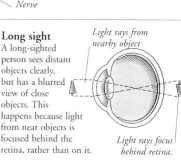

Light rays from nearby object
Light rays focus behind retina.

Light rays from distant object
Light rays focus in front of retina.

FIND OUT MORE
BRAIN AND NERVOUS SYSTEM
CAMERAS
CELLS
COLOUR
GENETICS
HUMAN BODY
LIGHT
MEDICINE, HISTORY OF

E

FARMING

BY CULTIVATING CROPS and raising animals, farms produce food and other products. Ten per cent of people in developed nations, and 60 per cent in developing countries, make their living from farming. In the West, technology makes the land highly productive, producing abundant, cheap food, and requiring fewer workers. In developing countries, farms have much lower yields because the soil or climate are often unsuitable for agriculture, and farmers, unable to afford new machines and chemicals, must rely on labour-intensive methods.

Crops

Ancient farmers bred crop plants by collecting and sowing the seed from the healthiest wild plants: the first cultivated crop was probably a kind of wheat. Today's major food crops are wheat, rice, maize (corn), and potatoes; major non-food crops include cotton and tobacco. The types and quantities of crops a farmer can grow are determined by soil and climate.

Cotton bolls (seed pods)

Cotton
The cotton crop provides fibres and oil. The main producers of the world's cotton are China and the USA.

Rice
Rice is a cereal, and the main food of half the world's people. Asia produces 90 per cent of the world's crop. Plants are grown in warm climates, usually on flooded "paddy" fields. Rice is a labour-intensive crop, which means most of the work is done by people, rather than machines.

Harvesting rice by hand

Terraced fields

Rice seedlings

2 days old *2–3 weeks* *4–5 weeks*

Paddy field, China

Plants are cut down, and left in bundles to dry out.

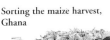
Sorting the maize harvest, Ghana

Types of farms

In the developed world, mixed farms were once common; farmers grew a few different crops and kept some livestock. Today's technology makes it advantageous for farms to specialize, raising just one kind of crop or animal with very high output. Such farming is big business. Some farmers, concerned by the possible effects on the environment, have changed to organic farming, where artificial fertilizers and pesticides are not used.

Shepherd shakes seed pods from a tree to feed sheep.

Subsistence farming
Subsistence farmers produce only enough to feed their household, with little or no surplus to sell. This is more common in developing nations where many farmers cannot afford the chemicals or machinery that would increase their yield, and rely on centuries-old farming methods.

Subsistence farming, Kenya

Commercial farming
Commercial farmers farm animals and crops intensively. They aim for a high yield and sell their produce for profit. In many countries, farmers produce too much food. When surplus crops and animals force food prices down, damaging the food industry, governments pay farmers to grow less.

Cattle fair, Argentina

Livestock

Farmers rear livestock (animals) for meat, milk, eggs, skins, and wool. In some cases, livestock is reared intensively, with many animals kept indoors in artificial conditions to encourage fast growth. By contrast "free-range" animals are reared outside; they live more like their wild counterparts, but their products are more costly.

Farmers kept goats and sheep for milk long before cattle.

Sheep's milk

Dairy farming
Dairy farming is the breeding of animals for their milk and milk products. Cows are the main dairy animals, producing 10 to 15 litres (2.6 to 4 US gallons) of milk a day on average. Sheep and goats are also raised for their milk.

Butter, from cow's milk

Cheese, from goat's milk

Sheep
The versatile sheep produces meat, wool, and milk. Sheep do not need such rich pasture as cattle: they can survive on poor quality land, and in dry or cold climates.

Sheep-shearing takes place in late spring.

Maize
Maize is a kind of grass. There are many varieties, which can be ground into flour, eaten as a vegetable, made into oil, or used as animal feed. Maize is a major crop in the United States, Brazil, southern Africa, and parts of Asia.

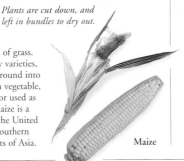
Maize

Farming technology

Ever since the Agricultural Revolution in the 18th century, scientific advances in agriculture have rapidly raised farms' productivity. Artificial fertilizers, pesticides, research into selective breeding, and genetic engineering keep the increasing Western populations fed. Selective breeding programmes improve crops and livestock by combining the strengths of each parent in their offspring. By modifying genes directly in the laboratory, scientists can achieve the same results as selective breeding in a fraction of the time.

Chemicals in farming

Fertilizers enrich the soil with the minerals essential for plant growth. Animal manure is an organic fertilizer; science has also developed inorganic (artificial) fertilizers. Pesticides are chemicals that control the pests which attack crops. While these chemicals improve productivity, some chemicals get into the water supply, possibly harming human health.

Cattle raised in zero-grazing pen

Vegetables can be bred to be regular in shape, and so more attractive to shoppers, even though there is no difference in taste.

Intensively farmed

Irregular shape

Intensive rearing

Intensive farming maximizes the production of crops and livestock with chemicals and machines. Shoppers prefer cheap food: to produce this, the cost of raising livestock must be kept to a minimum. Cattle, pigs, and other animals live in controlled conditions; for example, pigs live in units, and are fed a precise mix of nutrients that make them put on the most weight in the least time.

Machinery

During the 20th century, new machinery increased farm productivity in industrialized nations, while also cutting labour requirements. Tractors, motor vehicles that pull farm machinery, quickly replaced horses as the source of pulling power on the farm. The tractor's power allowed farmers to plant and harvest crops over vast areas.

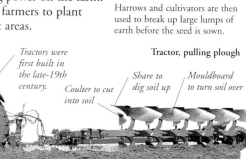

Tractors were first built in the late-19th century.

Tractor, pulling plough

Coulter to cut into soil

Share to dig soil up

Mouldboard to turn soil over

Because combine harvesters work so quickly, they reap a crop at its best.

Equipment

Milking machines have changed the face of dairy farms, with farmers now able to keep much larger herds of cattle. Farmers operate machines that milk cattle twice a day, although in the Netherlands robotic machines have been introduced that milk cows whenever the cows want it. The robots place vacuum cups on the cows' teats to draw out their milk. Each cow wears a radio collar which tells the robot where to look for the udder.

Preparing the land

To prepare the soil for sowing seed, farmers first plough the fields. The blade of a plough cuts a deep furrow in the soil and turns it over, burying weeds, which rot to enrich the soil. Harrows and cultivators are then used to break up large lumps of earth before the seed is sown.

Harvesters

Machines can speed the harvest. A combine harvester both cuts a crop of wheat and separates the grain from the stalk. In less than an hour, a machine with one driver can turn two hectares of wheat into grain. Sugar, potatoes, and peas are other crops harvested by machine.

Robotic milking parlour, the Netherlands

The farmer's year

The changing seasons set the pace of a farmer's work. On a livestock farm, for instance, spring is the time when lambs or calves are born. The arable (crop-growing) farm is busiest during the spring-to-autumn growing season. Apple growers must carry out different tasks through the year to produce the best crop.

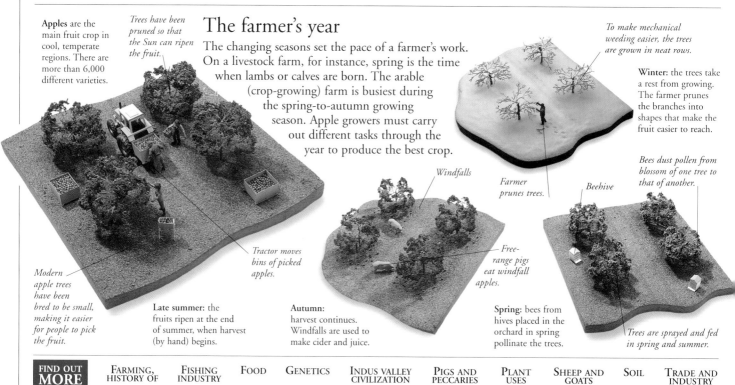

Apples are the main fruit crop in cool, temperate regions. There are more than 6,000 different varieties.

Trees have been pruned so that the Sun can ripen the fruit.

Modern apple trees have been bred to be small, making it easier for people to pick the fruit.

Late summer: the fruits ripen at the end of summer, when harvest (by hand) begins.

Tractor moves bins of picked apples.

Windfalls

Autumn: harvest continues. Windfalls are used to make cider and juice.

Farmer prunes trees.

Free-range pigs eat windfall apples.

To make mechanical weeding easier, the trees are grown in neat rows.

Winter: the trees take a rest from growing. The farmer prunes the branches into shapes that make the fruit easier to reach.

Bees dust pollen from blossom of one tree to that of another.

Beehive

Spring: bees from hives placed in the orchard in spring pollinate the trees.

Trees are sprayed and fed in spring and summer.

FIND OUT MORE — FARMING, HISTORY OF · FISHING INDUSTRY · FOOD · GENETICS · INDUS VALLEY CIVILIZATION · PIGS AND PECCARIES · PLANT USES · SHEEP AND GOATS · SOIL · TRADE AND INDUSTRY

Farming

Animals farmed for produce

Chickens are bred for eggs and meat.

Peacocks are bred for their exotic plumage.

Ducks are farmed for feathers, eggs, and meat.

Sheep are bred for milk, meat, skins, and wool.

Geese are kept for meat, down, and eggs.

Red deer are bred for their meat, called venison.

Jerseys are farmed for their very rich milk.

Angora goats have a coarse undercoat and a curly wool outer coat.

Cattle are the world's most numerous farm animals.

Cattle are farmed for milk and meat.

Herefords were first bred in Britain and are now farmed in 50 countries.

Goats are farmed for milk, meat, and wool.

Goats can feed on scrubby grass and thorny branches.

Now scarce in the wild

Almost every part of a pig can be eaten.

Udders

Pigs are versatile feeders.

Ostrich chick: farmed for meat and feathers.

Saanen goats are bred in Europe for their milk.

Chinchillas, rodents bred for their soft, delicate fur.

Pigs are farmed for pork, bacon, other meat products, skins, and bristles.

Animals bred to work

Long, erect ears

Well-muscled leg

Poitou donkeys are the world's largest.

Elephants pull heavier loads than any other animal.

Camels are used as pack animals, and also farmed for wool, milk, hides, and meat.

Heavy horses, used where a farmer has no tractor.

Donkeys carry large loads on little food or water.

Mules are interbred from horses and donkeys.

Elephants are used as draught (pulling) animals in southeast Asia.

F

325

FARMING, HISTORY OF

TEN THOUSAND YEARS AGO, the first farmers began to grow crops and breed animals for food. Before that, nomadic hunter-gatherers fed on berries, plants, and wild beasts they encountered on their travels. With the emergence of farming, however, people were able to produce a reliable food supply, and to settle permanently in one place, giving rise to the world's earliest civilizations in Mesopotamia, Egypt, India, and China. Farming methods continued to evolve slowly until, in the 18th century, a so-called Agricultural Revolution led to dramatic changes. Since then, farming has become more mechanized and feeds ever greater numbers of people.

Early farmers

The first farmers tamed wild animals, kept them in herds, and used them for meat, milk, skins, and wool. By contrast, nomadic herders moved their animals constantly in search of new pastures.

Flint sickle in wooden handle

Rice farming

Neolithic revolution
After the New Stone Age, c.8000 BC, (Neolithic) people in western Asia began to grow crops. This type of farming supported 10 times more people than hunting and gathering.

Irrigation
Early farmers needed water for their crops. Rivers and artificial canal systems played a vital role in the ancient agricultural civilizations of Egypt, the Indus Valley, and China.

Agricultural revolution

From about 1750, a series of major changes ushered in the era of modern farming. Key developments included large-scale farming, the intensive breeding of livestock, and the improvement of a number of agricultural techniques – such as four-course crop rotation – all of which were first developed in Britain.

Goat

Selective breeding
Robert Bakewell (1725–95), the fifth Duke of Bedford (1765–1802), and other British stock breeders during the Agricultural Revolution, used selective breeding on their farms and estates to develop larger, healthier animals, such as cattle, goats, sheep, and turkeys, with a higher milk or meat yield. Later breeders used the same system to develop animals for a particular purpose. For example, the Camargue bull which is bred only for fighting.

Camargue bull

Crop rotation
During the Agricultural Revolution, farmers found that if they grew certain crops, such as turnips, clover, barley, and wheat in successive years, they did not need to let the land lie fallow for a year. Root crops, such as turnips, improved the soil, and therefore the quality of the next harvest.

Turnips and wheat

New farm machinery
Machines, such as the thresher (formulated in 1786 by Scots inventor Andrew Meikle), eased workloads and improved productivity. Threshers, which separated the grain from the straw, became more effective after 1850 when farm workers attached steam engines to power them.

Medieval farming

Farmers in medieval Europe divided the land around their village into three fields. Each family had one 12-hectare strip of land in each field. Everyone followed the same three-year farming cycle: one field was left fallow (unused) each year to restore the soil's nutrients, and the other two grew barley, oats, rye, or wheat.

Enclosures
From the 1500s, English landowners enclosed common land with fences, ditches or hedges, to turn it into private property. As a result, the co-operative medieval system of farming gave way to a system of private ownership where land-owners made all the decisions about what to farm.

Book of Hours, 1416

Charles "Turnip" Townshend
A main forerunner of the Agricultural Revolution, Viscount Townshend (1674–1738) retired from a brilliant career in politics to concentrate on farming. He popularized a four-course rotation of crops, and pioneered "marling" (using limey clay as fertilizer). His widespread cultivation of the turnip – as a fodder crop to keep animals fed during the winter – earned him his nickname.

Green Revolution
In the 1960s, a Green Revolution took place. New "high-yield" crop varieties were developed to increase wheat and rice production, particularly in highly populated countries such as India, and China. Critics claimed this process damaged the environment through overuse of fertilizer and concentration on only a few species. Recently farmers have been rediscovering traditional farming methods and using organic fertilizers and insecticides.

Black Norfolk turkey

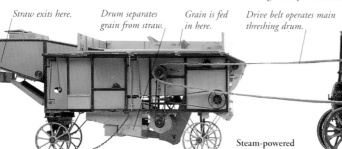
Straw exits here.   Drum separates grain from straw.   Grain is fed in here.   Drive belt operates main threshing drum.

Drive wheel rotates to turn drive belt.   Coal stored here.
Steam-powered threshing machine

Seaweed, an organic fertilizer

FIND OUT MORE
BRONZE AGE   CHINA, HISTORY OF   EGYPT, ANCIENT   EUROPE, MEDIEVAL   FARMING   INDUSTRIAL REVOLUTION   INVENTIONS   KHMER EMPIRE   STONE AGE   SUMERIANS

FERNS

THE MOST ADVANCED of all the non-flowering, spore-bearing plants are the ferns and their relatives, known as the Pteridophytes. There are about 12,000 species of Pteridophyte, of which about 10,400 are ferns. The others include horsetails and club mosses. Pteridophytes are vascular plants, that is, plants whose stems contain tissues that transport water and food around the plant internally. They flourish best in warm, damp environments, but also grow where it is cool or dry.

Ferns

A typical fern plant has underground stems, or rhizomes, from which grow roots, and leaves called fronds. Upright rhizomes produce a fern with a short radiating crown of fronds, while long horizontal rhizomes produce a spreading fern. Ferns grow in a variety of places, but all have a two-stage life-cycle. The gametophyte is a small, short-lived plantlet that produces sex cells. After fertilization, a female sex cell grows into a sporophyte, which is the fern plant.

Epiphytic ferns
An epiphytic fern grows on the bough or trunk of a tree. It takes no nourishment from its host, but obtains moisture and minerals from rain and debris that become trapped among its roots.

Fronds hang clear of the branch.

Tree ferns
Tree ferns have woody, fibrous trunks topped with a crown of fronds. They are found in all climates, most frequently in the tropics and sub-tropics. The tallest species reaches 20 m (65 ft).

Radiating fronds

Base of dead fronds

Water ferns
Some ferns are aquatic. They either root into mud in fresh water, or float free. This *Azolla* species floats. Its tiny roots dangle in the water below a mat of fronds.

Male fern
Ferns similar to this male fern, so-called because of its vigorous growth, are found in woods all around the world. This species has stiff, bright green fronds. Each blade is divided into "leaves" called pinnae (singular: pinna), each of which is further divided into pinnules.

A full-grown frond may reach as much as 150 cm (5 ft) long.

Pinna and pinnules

The frond continues to lengthen as the lower parts unfurl.

Young frond

A developing male fern plant

Stipe is the "stalk" of the fern.

Rhizome

Root

1 Frond buds develop on the rhizome. Each bud produces just one frond. It takes up to three years for a bud to develop and a frond to start growing.

2 A frond can grow rapidly because all the cells of the stalk and leaflets are fully formed, though very small. They just have to expand.

3 A male fern produces tall fronds, each on a scaly stipe. Fertile fronds are the last to unfurl, so that the spores are released in the summer.

Club mosses

These small plants grow on damp ground or on rainforest trees. Their creeping stems are covered with tiny leaves arranged in a spiral. Spores are carried in modified leaves on fertile stems.

Horsetails

The stiff upright stems of horsetails grow in dense patches from underground stems. Branches are arranged in whorls, although fertile stems often have no branches. Tiny brown leaves grow in rings around the stems and branches. Spores are borne in cone-like structures on the tip of fertile stems.

Sterile stem

Fertile stem

The life-cycle of a fern

Sori

Pinna

Sorus

Sporangia

Fertile fronds have sori (singular: sorus), usually on the lower surface of each pinna.

Within each sorus are clusters of sporangia, which contain the spores.

Dry weather causes the sporangium to burst at a weak spot.

Spores

Sixty-four spores develop inside each sporangium. The sporangium then bursts, releasing all the spores.

Sex organs are carried on the underside of the gametophyte.

Gametophyte is a thin green plantlet.

A spore landing on damp soil germinates into a gametophyte. This bears male and female sex organs.

Archegonium containing female sex cells

Antheridium containing male sex cells

Male sex cells swim in a film of soil moisture to the female sex cells and then fertilize them.

New fern plant – the sporophyte

The first female sex cell to be fertilized grows into a fern plant.

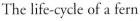

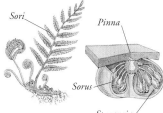

FIND OUT MORE | MOSSES AND LIVERWORTS | PLANTS | PLANTS, ANATOMY | PLANTS, REPRODUCTION | RAINFOREST WILDLIFE | TREES

F

FESTIVALS

ALL OVER THE WORLD, people set aside special days each year to enjoy themselves at festivals. These public celebrations are held for many reasons: they may be linked to a community's religious beliefs, mark the changing seasons, or honour important events in a country's history.

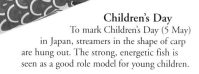

Streamers are hung from a pole.

Day of the Dead

On 1 November, Mexicans celebrate the Day of the Dead, to honour people who have died. Families have picnics by the graves of their relatives, decorate the streets with flowers and carved skeletons, and eat sweets shaped like skulls and coffins.

Papier-mâché skeleton

Calendar festivals

The majority of festivals are held at the same time each year. Many religions have adapted the celebrations of early peoples to their own ends: the Christian Christmas and the Hindu Diwali are held around the same time as ancient feasts marking the onset of winter.

Children's Day

To mark Children's Day (5 May) in Japan, streamers in the shape of carp are hung out. The strong, energetic fish is seen as a good role model for young children.

Harvest festivals

Ancient peoples thought that thanking the gods would ensure a good crop the next year, and people still celebrate festivals based on this idea. There are many festivals in Africa and Papua New Guinea that celebrate the yam crop, and the Oktoberfest beer festival in Germany began as thanks for the crop of hops.

Radishes

On Christmas Eve, townspeople in Oaxaca, Mexico, celebrate their radish crop by carving large, recently harvested radishes into elaborate shapes, which they use to decorate market stalls and restaurants. Food is served on chipped plates, which are saved for the occasion and smashed at the end of the night.

Corn

In England, people often used the last of the year's corn to make a figure called a corn dolly. The dolly kept the corn spirit alive through the winter, ensuring another good harvest the next year.

Traditional English corn dolly

Carnivals

Originally, carnivals were pagan festivals to celebrate the rebirth of nature in spring. Later, they became associated with the Roman Catholic festival of Lent. The start and duration of the carnival season varies from country to country.

Carnival in Venice

This famous Italian carnival first began in the 11th century. Traditionally, many revellers wear masks. They originally did this to hide their faces while they behaved outrageously.

Float pulled by tractor

Mardi Gras float

Caribbean carnival

Carnival in the Caribbean combines African and European traditions; dance, costume, and music are important parts of African religious beliefs.

Mardi Gras

In many Roman Catholic countries, carnival is by tradition a last chance for merry-making before the start of Lent, the weeks of fasting that come before Easter. Thousands of people enjoy the week-long Mardi Gras carnival in New Orleans, USA, which is named after the French for "Fat Tuesday". This refers to Shrove Tuesday, the day before Lent begins, when all the fats in the home must be used up. Another spectacular Mardi Gras carnival is held in Rio de Janeiro, Brazil.

Modern festivals

Most festivals set up today mark non-religious events. The Olympics celebrate excellence in sports; the Edinburgh festival in the UK promotes the performing arts.

Mime artist, Edinburgh Festival

Roskilde

Thousands of fans attend this summer rock music festival in Denmark.

Political festivals

Significant political dates are often the cause for regular celebration. Festivals mark the anniversary of a nation's independence or a great leader's birthday: in the USA, there is a holiday on George Washington's birthday.

May Day

Once a springtime fertility festival, May 1 is a now a public holiday to honour workers. In Russia, May Day is marked with trades union parades.

FIND OUT MORE CHRISTIANITY | FILM AND FILM-MAKING | FOOD | HINDUISM | SPORT | UNIONS, TRADE

FEUDALISM

IN PARTS OF MEDIEVAL ASIA and Europe, a system arose for organizing society known as feudalism. In the feudal system, the king gave land to powerful barons, who then gave land and protection to lesser lords, and so on through to the peasants. Each level was then expected to fight to protect its overlords whenever needed. European feudalism started in the late 9th century, and spread all over the continent. Outside Europe, the feudal system operated in Palestine during the Crusades, and also in Japan, where samurai gave military service to their overlords in return for land.

How feudalism began

The great emperor Charlemagne insisted that all his nobles swear loyalty to him. This bond between lord and warrior began the feudal system. Over the next two centuries, feudalism spread through France, Germany, northern Italy, the Slav countries, and finally the British Isles and Sicily.

Mounted warriors
Warriors riding horses to war became more common after 950. These warriors were the first knights. They had great prestige, and became an important part of the feudal system.

Lords and vassals

In the European feudal system, the only person who actually owned land was the king. When the king granted land to a baron, the baron knelt and pledged to be the king's vassal (servant). Lesser lords swore a similar oath to the barons and became their vassals, and peasants swore allegiance to the lords. Bishops were also the king's vassals, and held nearly as much power as the barons.

Derisive image of king with cat, not crown, on his head

King
Although the king owned the land, he could rarely afford to keep an army. He was often in conflict with the barons, on whom he relied for his warriors.

Barons
The most powerful of all the nobles, the barons got their lands directly from the king. Because they provided the royal army, they had great power and prestige.

The manor

Farmland and its ownership was the most important part of feudalism, and the manor was the administration centre of the system. The lands surrounding the manor house were divided into the demesne (for the lord's own use), the arable (granted in parcels to the peasants), and the meadow lands (used by everyone for livestock).

Feudal counsel
Kings and barons often asked for advice, or counsel, from their vassals when making any important decisions. This 14th-century French manuscript shows Philip VI of France judging Robert of Valois, helped by the bishops on his right hand and the barons on his left.

Local lords
Local knights got their land (or manor) from the barons. In return, they fought for the barons when needed. As time went on, local lords often paid a tax called scutage (shield money) instead of fighting, and the king used this money to hire professional soldiers. In peacetime, they farmed and kept order.

Ightham Mote, England

The manor house
Every manor house had a hall. This acted as the dining and living room for the family, and also a general reception room where the peasants paid their rent. The kitchen was at one end of the hall, beside a pantry and buttery (store room for drinks). Buildings in the courtyard outside included workshops and cattle-sheds. The whole complex was often surrounded by a moat for protection.

Feudal contract
The people owed their loyalty to the monarch. This "contract" meant that Philip VI could – and did – tax his subjects heavily to finance the Hundred Years War.

Peasants
The peasants, at the bottom of feudal society, got their plots of land from the local lord of the manor. He allowed them to farm this land; in return, they paid rent in produce and money. The peasants also contributed several days' labour on "public" projects such as road- and bridge-building.

The Hall, Ightham Mote

Domesday Book

For the feudal system to work well, the ruler needed detailed information about the land and who lived on it. William of Normandy, who introduced feudalism to Britain, had a complete record made of all land ownership in England in 1085–86. This became known as the Domesday Book.

The book is the most complete record of land-holding in medieval Europe.

William I
The illegitimate son of Duke Robert I of Normandy, William (c.1028–1087) conquered England in 1066. He introduced the feudal system to the island, and replaced Saxon nobles with Norman lords.

FIND OUT MORE   CHARLEMAGNE · HUNDRED YEARS WAR · KNIGHTS AND HERALDRY · MEDIEVAL EUROPE · NORMANS · SAMURAI AND SHOGUNS

FILMS AND FILM-MAKING

IN 1895, THE Lumière brothers held the first public film screening, in a room below a Parisian café. The black and white images flickered on a silent screen, yet the audience was enthralled. The magic of the movies has continued ever since. Technology developed rapidly: sound arrived in 1927, colour in the 1930s, and today's complex films often involve stunning special effects. Film production is now an international industry, generating great wealth and employing thousands worldwide.

Casting
It is vital to the success of a movie to cast (place) actors who suit their parts artistically. Audiences have their favourites, so the choice of a popular star can turn a promising film into a huge box-office success.

Pre-production
Film-making begins long before the cameras start to turn. After a studio (a film-making company) agrees to make a movie, a script is prepared, the budget drawn up, actors and skilled crew hired, and the entire production planned to the last detail.

The producer
A producer decides which film to make, finds the money to finance it (often millions of pounds), and brings together the stars, script, and director.

Storyboard
With one small picture for each shot, a storyboard is important in planning a film and gives an idea of what it will look like. Notes outline the action and dialogue.

Pictures represent each shot.

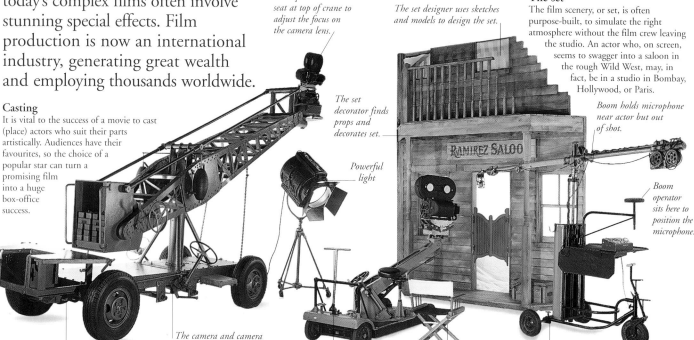

Focus puller has a seat at top of crane to adjust the focus on the camera lens.

The set designer uses sketches and models to design the set.

The set
The film scenery, or set, is often purpose-built, to simulate the right atmosphere without the film crew leaving the studio. An actor who, on screen, seems to swagger into a saloon in the rough Wild West, may, in fact, be in a studio in Bombay, Hollywood, or Paris.

The set decorator finds props and decorates set.

Powerful light

Boom holds microphone near actor but out of shot.

RAMIREZ SALOO

Boom operator sits here to position the microphone.

Crane raises the camera above the actors' heads.

The camera and camera equipment on set are moved by the grip.

The camera operator sits here to work the camera during shooting.

Director's folding chair next to camera

When the actors move, grips push the stand to move the microphone.

Production
When filming begins, a movie set is crowded with equipment, and each piece is the responsibility of a specific member of the crew. Between takes (sequences of filming), everyone works frantically to ensure that everything is adjusted exactly as the director wants. Off the set, props, wardrobe, and make-up have their own staff on hand.

The director
Responsible for the artistic side of the film-making process, the director is the most important person on set. Directors control the action and judge how well each take brings the script to life. They consult with experts in each department, such as the director of photography, who is responsible for the way the film looks.

Motion pictures
The continuous action on a movie screen is, in fact, an illusion. What we are watching are thousands of still photographs, taken rapidly one after the other. A film camera shoots 24 photographs (frames) every second, and when the images are projected at the same rate, our eyes merge the pictures together. Over 27 m (90 ft) of film is shot for just one minute of cinema.

Post-production
Separate scenes in a film are shot in whatever order suits the crew. Then the director chooses the best sections, and the film editor links them in the right sequence to tell the story. While working closely with the director and other technicians, the editor carefully aligns the sound track and pictures, and adds the special effects.

Screen to view the film

Loudspeaker plays back sound track

Editing table

Editing
The editor cuts up the disjointed sequences of film, cutting between frames, and splices them together. Cuts are viewed at an editing table.

Sound track
Music, the actors' speech, and any background sound effects are each recorded separately and then combined to make the sound track.

Types of films

From the simplest short cartoon film to a full-length feature with an all-star cast, films cover every subject. There have been notable films on many topics, but some of the most successful movies have been in areas where film can add an extra dimension, such as the vivid settings of fantasy and space adventures or western movies, the special effects of science-fiction and horror films, or the singing and dancing of American musicals.

Babe is a piglet who believes he is a sheepdog.

Babe, 1995

Comedy
The first films were silent, yet the comic antics of the actors made audiences roar with laughter. Today, comedies range from biting social commentaries to the gentle humour of an animal film such as *Babe*.

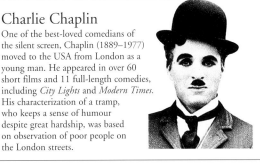

Charlie Chaplin
One of the best-loved comedians of the silent screen, Chaplin (1889–1977) moved to the USA from London as a young man. He appeared in over 60 short films and 11 full-length comedies, including *City Lights* and *Modern Times*. His characterization of a tramp, who keeps a sense of humour despite great hardship, was based on observation of poor people on the London streets.

Jean-Louis Barrault   Arletty

s Enfants du Paradis, 1944

Romance
Love stories are always popular. The romantic *Les Enfants du Paradis* was made in German-occupied France during World War II; in 1979, French critics voted it the best French film ever made.

Horror
German film makers were the first to realise that audiences like being frightened: directors were making horror movies in Germany by 1913. By the 1930s, horror had caught on in Hollywood, where it has been popular ever since. *Frankenstein* appeared in 1931. More than 100 films have been based on the same theme since.

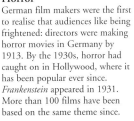
Boris Karloff as Frankenstein's monster

Going to the movies
By the 1930s, going to the cinema was popular entertainment, but in the 1950s television took over and the film industry declined. Recently, movie-going has grown popular again. Today, multiplex cinemas screen many films at the same time, offering audiences a wide choice of pictures.

Special effects
Anything can happen on film, thanks largely to the special effects department, a complex and skilled area of film-making. Effects may range from animals that seem to talk, to horrific dripping wounds, or people appearing to fly through the air.

Eyes, nose, and mouth operated by motors.

Dog, from The Storyteller

Motor

Le Grand Rex cinema, Paris, France

Dramatic lighting

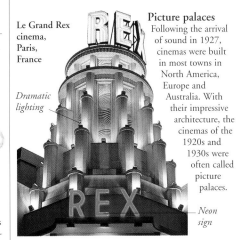

Picture palaces
Following the arrival of sound in 1927, cinemas were built in most towns in North America, Europe and Australia. With their impressive architecture, the cinemas of the 1920s and 1930s were often called picture palaces.

Neon sign

Make-up
Actors wear make-up to look natural under the bright film lights. Make-up also helps when an actor must look unnatural. A make-up artist can make an actor look much older, or use latex rubber and lining colours to add dreadful wounds. In horror and science-fiction films, make-up is used to turn people into aliens.

Movie models
Where it is too costly, dangerous, or impossible to use the real thing, film-makers may turn to models. Tiny models stand in for massive spacecraft in science-fiction films. A talking animal may be a puppet, or an actor in costume whose remote-controlled mask is operated by a puppeteer. This kind of puppetry is called animatronics.

Make-up in Terminator 2

Hype and merchandise
The cost of film production means it is vital to make the public eager to see a movie, so that the producers can earn back their investment and make a good profit. Publicists work hard to sell a film before it opens. They inform journalists, and arrange for the actors to appear on television talk shows. This process is known as hype. Selling items related to a movie, such as socks or a mug, is another way of making more money.

Batman logo

Blue screen
To create the illusion that a character is flying, an actor is filmed in front of a blue screen. Wind machines make his clothes flutter, as if air is moving past. An optical printer then combines the sequence with footage shot from a plane, or of a simulated space environment. The printer re-photographs images from each film onto a single frame, to blend the two films seamlessly.

Computers
Computers can manipulate images to create extraordinary special effects. Programs also allow operators to draw and animate characters on screen. Changes are much easier to make here than in animation which has been hand-drawn frame by frame.

Disney's Toy Story *is a computer-generated film.*

Actor held by wires

Batman merchandise
TM & © 1996 DC Comics

© Disney

Timeline

1895 The Lumière brothers open the first public cinema in Paris, France.

1913 By this date, Hollywood, Calif., is the centre of the US film industry.

Academy Award (Oscar)
© A.M.P.A.S. ®

1920s Russian director Sergei Eisenstein (1898–1948) introduces cross-cutting, showing bursts of action one after the other so they seem to happen simultaneously.

1927 The Academy of Motion Picture Arts and Sciences is set up; in 1929, it honours film-makers for the first time.

1927 *The Jazz Singer*, made in the US, is the first full-length film with sound.

1932 The "three-strip" process is introduced by the Technicolor company, and colour films, originally developed much earlier, begin to take off.

Technicolor three-strip camera

1941 US actor-director Orson Welles (1915–85) releases *Citizen Kane*; it explores new techniques in lighting, dialogue, and the use of camera lenses.

1952 The CinemaScope process introduces wide-screen cinema.

1960s *Nouvelle Vague* ("New Wave") film-makers in France introduce influential new techniques.

1980s The VCR allows people to see films at home.

1990s Special effects techniques are advanced.

FIND OUT MORE   CAMERAS   CARTOONS AND ANIMATION   EDISON, THOMAS   VIDEO

F

Film posters

United States

The Gold Rush (USA, 1925), a classic silent film, is touching yet very funny.

Raging Bull (USA, 1980) is one of the most influential films of the 1980s.

Blade Runner (USA, 1982) portrays a bleak Los Angeles in 2019.

Do the Right Thing (USA, 1989) develops from comedy to social comment.

Europe

Metropolis (Ger. 1926) is a disturbing vision of an "ideal" city in the year 2000.

Pelle the Conqueror (Den/Swe. 1987) won top international awards.

Oceania

Once Were Warriors (NZ, 1994): a great success critically and at the box-office.

Four Weddings and a Funeral (UK, 1994) is a light-hearted, appealing romance.

Women... (Spain, 1988) is a manic farce from talented director Pedro Almodóvar.

The Piano (Aust. 1993), directed and written by Jane Campion, won three Oscars.

The Battleship Potemkin (USSR, 1925), commissioned by Soviet leaders to put across a powerful political message, is still referred to as a masterpiece of cinema.

Africa

Yeelen (Mali, 1987) tells the story of the struggle between a father and son.

The Sixth Day (Egypt, 1986), directed by Youssef Chahine, starred actress Daleeda.

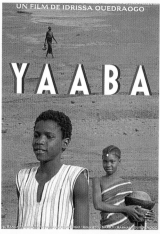

In **Yaaba** (Burkina, 1989), a friendship develops between a boy and an old woman cast out by other villagers.

Asia

Ran (Japan, 1985) is based on *King Lear* by Shakespeare; the battle scenes are superbly staged and shot.

Pather Panchali (India, 1956) brought its director, Satyajit Ray, world recognition.

Raise the Red Lantern (HK, 1991) looks at a woman's life in 1920s' China.

FINLAND

A LAND OF LAKES AND FORESTS, Finland is bordered by Russia to the east, the Baltic Sea to the south, and Sweden and Norway to the west and north. Finland shares government of Lapland, in the Arctic Circle, with Sweden and Norway. Finland was ruled by Russia until 1917, and, as a result, Finns have more in common culturally with the east than with their Scandinavian neighbours. A wealthy, liberal nation, Finland was the first European country to give women the vote.

F

FINLAND FACTS	
CAPITAL CITY	Helsinki
AREA	337,030 sq km (130,127 sq miles)
POPULATION	5,200,000
MAIN LANGUAGES	Finnish, Swedish
MAJOR RELIGION	Christian
CURRENCY	Euro
LIFE EXPECTANCY	78 years
PEOPLE PER DOCTOR	323
GOVERNMENT	Multi-party democracy
ADULT LITERACY	99%

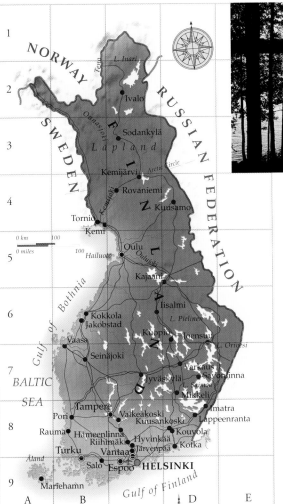

Physical features

From the air, Finland is a patchwork of lakes, peat bogs, and trees. Forests dominate the land, and water covers about ten per cent of the country. There are some 98,000 islands within the lakes, and 30,000 off the coast. The Arctic north, including part of Lapland, is a bleak area of rocky tundra.

Forests
Pine, spruce, and birch trees cover 80 per cent of Finland, making it the ninth most forested country in the world. The forest is most dense just south of the Arctic Circle and is often covered in snow.

Lakes and islands
Finland has more than 60,000 lakes, mainly in the southeast, carved out by glaciers in the last Ice Age. Many islands are scattered in the lakes and off the warm southwest coast, including 6,000 of the Åland Islands.

| 33°C (91°F) | -41°C (-42°F) |
| 17°C (62°F) | -6°C (21°F) |

618 mm (24 in)

Climate
Finland has short, bright summers and long, cold winters when lakes often freeze up to 1 m (3 ft 3 in) deep. The Arctic north sees midnight sun in its 73-day summer.

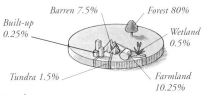

Barren 7.5% Forest 80%
Built-up 0.25% Wetland 0.5%
Tundra 1.5% Farmland 10.25%

Land use
Dense forests and a maze of lakes, rivers, and peat bogs mean only 11 per cent of Finland's land can be used for crops or grazing animals. Despite this, farmers produce all of the country's dairy foods. The forests support a valuable timber industry, and the waters are used for fishing and hydroelectric power.

People
Almost half of the population lives around Helsinki. Families are close-knit, and most homes have a sauna, or hot, steamy relaxation room. Women enjoy equal rights and about 50 per cent pursue a career.

Cooling off after the sauna

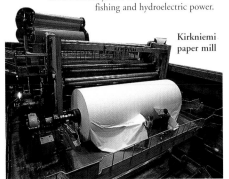

Kirkniemi paper mill

Farming and industry
Finland produces all of its own food. Most crops are grown in the southwest and on the sunny Åland Islands. The country is a world leader in the production of plywood, wood pulp, and paper, and these alone make up 30 per cent of the total exports. Furniture and high-tech manufacturing compete in world markets and, with the service sector, employ the majority of the work-force.

Helsinki

Standing on a peninsula and several islands in the Gulf of Finland, the vibrant capital of Helsinki has about 770,000 inhabitants. Tree-lined avenues and a colourful market back onto a busy harbour. Only half of the city's area has been developed, leaving parkland for the residents to enjoy.

The bustling Helsinki harbour

17 per sq km (44 per sq mile)

67% Urban 33% Rural

FIND OUT MORE — ARCTIC OCEAN · ENERGY · EUROPE, HISTORY OF · FISHING INDUSTRY · FORESTS · GLACIATION · LAKES · PAPER · SCANDINAVIA, HISTORY OF · TRADE AND INDUSTRY · WINTER SPORTS

FIRE

BURNING OUT OF CONTROL in forests or cities, a fire leaves a trail of destruction. Yet life without the benefits of fire is unimaginable. We use fire in power stations, car engines, and kitchens, to provide electricity and transport, or to cook food. Early humans realized the value of fire about half a million years ago – perhaps when lightning set a tree on fire. Learning to control and use the flames helped them hunt, clear land for farming, survive in colder climates, and eat foods that were inedible when raw. No wonder some religions still worship fire as a hungry god.

Flame is a glowing gas, produced in burning.

Combustion or burning
Fire is the heat and light produced when fuel burns. This process is known as combustion. The fuel can be any flammable material (one that can catch fire). The material must first be heated to a temperature called the ignition temperature; above this, it will burst into flame. As a fire gets hotter, more fuel catches alight, and the flames spread. Gases and vapours burn quickly; liquids and solids take longer to burn.

Using fire
To make fire do useful work, the supply of air or fuel must be controlled to keep the flames burning evenly. Furnaces, cooking stoves, and power plants use fire for the heat energy it produces. Heat is not always the main purpose of creating fire. In a car engine fuel burns explosively. Expanding gases drive the vehicle; the heat produced is wasted.

Welder at work

Welding
Many industrial processes rely on combustion. In the welder's torch, oxygen and acetylene gas mix and produce a flame hot enough to melt steel.

Fire-engine with hydraulic platform, used to reach awkward spaces.

Some booms are up to 62 m (203 ft) long.

Rescue platform

Arm, or boom

Built-in hose

Leg for support

Mouthpiece steadies drill
Wooden drill
String
Modern model of bow drill
Hearth

Bow drills
Rapidly turning the string of a bow drill causes friction at the tip, which starts flames.

Piston handle is pumped to compress air.

A fire piston works like a bicycle pump: compressing air in the tube raises the temperature until the tinder (flammable material) inside catches alight.

Making a fire
In the past, there were two main methods of starting a fire: raising the temperature until flames appeared, or striking sparks to set light to tinder. Cigarette lighters still start fires by using the spark of flint on steel.

Tinder stored in box
Lid with candle holder
Steel
Flint

A tinder box contains flint, which makes sparks when struck against metal (the steel).

Matches
Invented in 1827, these wooden splinters were tipped with chemicals. The chemicals were ignited by heat, generated by rubbing the tip against sandpaper. Safety matches burn only when rubbed against a specially coated strip on the matchbox.

Cooking
Many foods must be cooked before they can be eaten. When food is heated, chemical changes take place that improve its taste and make it easier to digest. Early people ate raw food until they discovered cooking, probably by accident.

Cooking with fire

Fighting fire
Fires feed on fuel, air, and heat; removing any one of these puts out the flames. Firefighters spray a blaze with water to remove heat and to create a blanket of steam that chokes off the air supply.

Myths about fire
The power and danger of fire made ancient peoples wonder about its origin. Myths that explain how people learned to tame flames occur in many separate cultures. Most fire myths involve a hero who brings fire to the world.

Prometheus
In Greek mythology, the chief god, Zeus, hid the secret of fire from mortals (humans) to punish them for a trick that a lesser god, Prometheus, had played on him. But Prometheus snatched a glowing ember from the Sun, and brought fire to the Earth.

Prometheus

FIND OUT MORE   FOOD   HEAT AND TEMPERATURE   INVENTIONS   LIGHT   PREHISTORIC PEOPLE

FIRST AID

FIRST AID RANGES from cleaning a small wound and covering it with sticking plaster, to dealing with serious injuries at a major disaster. But its main aims are the same: to save life, prevent the casualty's condition from worsening, promote healing and recovery, and arrange for expert help at the earliest opportunity. Recently, first aid has advanced greatly due to a better understanding of the body's needs in serious injury or disease, improved medical equipment, and mobile communications. It now plays an even more vital role in saving lives, and speeding a casualty's recovery.

Scene of a motorcycle accident

At the scene

Effective first aid – the temporary treatment of injury or illness while waiting for medical aid – relies on correctly assigning priorities. At an accident, one of the first priorities is to summon the emergency services.

Assessing conditions
Experienced first aiders know that noisy casualties are not necessarily the most hurt. At a multiple accident, they assess quickly the condition of all casualties, then concentrate available first aid on the most seriously injured. In hospitals, this assessment is known as triage.

Raising the alarm
A telephone call is usually the best way to get help. Special telephones are located in areas such as motorways, but calls to the emergency services are free on all telephones. Shouting, waving flags, or firing flares are all alternative methods.

Spanish public telephone

Further danger
First aiders should never place themselves or others in danger. Before treating the casualty, they should try to make the area safe. Fire, traffic, electricity, and unsafe structures are some of the hazards that may delay treatment.

Fire extinguisher

ABC of first aid

ABC stands for the body's three vital needs. "A" stands for airway: the airway needs to be open so that oxygen-containing air can enter the lungs. "B" stands for breathing, by which the body inhales fresh air and expels stale air. "C" stands for the circulation of the blood, which distributes oxygen around the body. When dealing with an unconscious casualty, the first aider must check that the casualty has a clear airway, is breathing, and has a pulse that indicates blood circulation.

Two fingers pressing lightly on a pulse point

Checking for a pulse
The heart pumps blood around the body, causing a pulse. A first aider can check the heart is still beating by feeling for this pulse in arteries located in the neck or wrist.

Airway
Inhaled foreign bodies or fluid can block the airway. By tipping the head back and straightening the airway, a first aider can look for blockages.

Breathing
If breathing stops, the first aider may blow air at regular intervals through the casualty's mouth into their lungs. This is called artificial ventilation.

Circulation
If a pulse is absent, the first aider may carry out heart massage (external chest compression) to try to stimulate the heart into action.

First-aid kit

In many countries, the law requires workplaces and schools to keep first-aid kits. The contents should be kept in a clean, marked container and be re-stocked regularly. Because there is a danger of misusing drugs, the contents of some kits are restricted to sterile wound dressings.

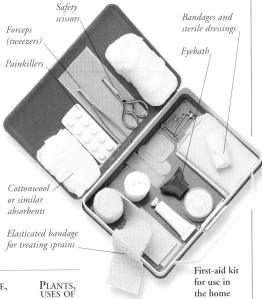

Safety scissors
Forceps (tweezers)
Painkillers
Bandages and sterile dressings
Eyebath
Cottonwool or similar absorbents
Elasticated bandage for treating sprains

First-aid kit for use in the home

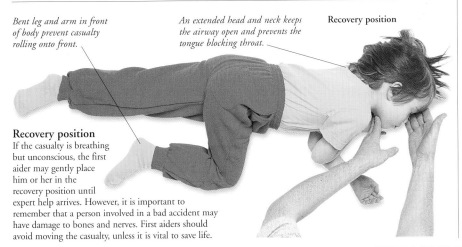

Bent leg and arm in front of body prevent casualty rolling onto front.

An extended head and neck keeps the airway open and prevents the tongue blocking throat.

Recovery position

Recovery position
If the casualty is breathing but unconscious, the first aider may gently place him or her in the recovery position until expert help arrives. However, it is important to remember that a person involved in a bad accident may have damage to bones and nerves. First aiders should avoid moving the casualty, unless it is vital to save life.

FIND OUT MORE   DRUGS   HOSPITALS   MEDICINE   MEDICINE, HISTORY OF   NIGHTINGALE, FLORENCE   PLANTS, USES OF

FISH

THE FIRST FISH appeared in the seas 470 million years ago. Today, more than 20,000 species have been described, ranging from the great whale shark to the pygmy goby. Fish live in freshwater streams, rivers, and lakes, and in saltwater seas and oceans. A few, including eels and salmon, migrate from salt to fresh water. Some fish are fierce predators, and because of this many others have evolved a range of methods of defence. Although most fish leave their eggs and young to look after themselves, some species protect their young.

Fins
Most fish have a dorsal fin, paired pectoral and pelvic fins, and a tail for movement. In some fish, fins have become specialized as lifting foils, walking legs, suckers for holding on, or poisoned spines for protection.

Scales
Most fish have a covering of backward-facing scales that help to streamline them. Bony fish have either flat, oval, or square overlapping scales, while sharks have tooth-like structures buried in the skin.

Dorsal fin

Caudal, or tail, fin

Operculum (gill cover)

Pectoral fin **European carp**

Anal fin

Pelvic fin

Gills
Almost all fish have gills for breathing. The sharks and rays have paired gills in the throat, with openings to the outside known as gill slits. Bony fish have paired gills at the back of the head, with one opening covered by a flap of skin known as the operculum.

Fish features

Fish have a number of features in common. They breathe through gills, and are generally streamlined in shape with paired body muscles along each side. They have a tail for propulsion, fins for steering, and scales for protection. Their heads contain paired eyes and an obvious mouth with teeth.

Swim bladder
Bony fish have a swim bladder containing air, and they are able to fill and empty it at will. In many bony fish the swim bladder controls buoyancy, allowing the fish to move up and down in the water.

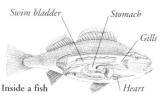

Swim bladder   *Stomach*

Gills

Inside a fish   *Heart*

Flatfish

Flatfish spend most of their lives lying on their sides, half buried and camouflaged in the sand on the seabed. Like most fish, the young develop in eggs. They hatch into normal larval fish that swim "the right way up" in the plankton.

10 days old

1 The larval fish has an eye on either side of its head.

17 days old

2 One eye gradually "migrates" to the other side of the head.

35 days old

3 An adult flatfish lies on one side. Its eyes are on top.

Fish groups

The fish are divided into three groups: jawless and primitive fish (cyclostomes), which include the lampreys and hagfish; cartilaginous fish (elasmobranchs), which include the sharks, rays, and ratfish; bony fish (teleosts), which include the more familiar fish, such as herring, cod, plaice, trout, eels, goldfish, sticklebacks, and guppies.

Caudal fin   *Dorsal fin*

Great white shark

Gill slits

Pectoral fin

Sharp teeth

Pike

Jawless fish
Hagfish and lampreys have funnel-shaped mouths. Lampreys attach themselves to other fish with their mouths and rasp away flesh with their teeth. Hagfish are scavengers.

Sea lamprey

Bony fish
These fish are divided into two groups – those with jointed bony fin rays, such as most fresh- and saltwater fish, and those with fleshy fin lobes, such as lungfish.

Cartilaginous fish
Sharks and rays have large mouths with many teeth in rows that are continually being replaced. Their skeletons are made of cartilage (gristle), instead of bones.

Where fish live

There are fish living wherever there is water. Some fish live in oceans, the largest numbers living in the shallow seas of the continental shelf. The most brightly coloured fish live on coral reefs. Other fish live on muddy, sandy, or rocky seashores, in estuaries, in rivers and streams, and even in temporary puddles.

On land
Inhabitants of Indo-Pacific mudflats and mangrove swamps, mudskippers are able to leave the water. They can stay on land for hours, absorbing oxygen through the mouth and pharynx. They have eyes on top of their heads for all-round vision.

Mudskipper

Red mullet

Rainbow trout

Oceans
The oceans provide a range of habitats for fish. Light-producing fish live in the deepest ocean trenches, while other fish live near hot volcanic vents. Some, such as sharks, roam the open oceans searching for smaller fish to eat.

Fresh water
Fish live in fast-flowing streams, slow-moving rivers, ponds, and lakes, and are suited to their habitat. Some have to be powerful swimmers or have suckers for holding on to stones. Others live in shoals or are camouflaged to avoid predators.

F

F

Protection

As well as scales, fish use colour, camouflage, or poisonous spines to protect themselves. The spiny puffer fish can take in water or air and swells up to more than twice its size. Some eels use an electric discharge, while other fish live in shoals, making it difficult for a predator to pick out any one individual.

Clown fish

Colour
Fish use colour to warn other fish that they are poisonous. Colour also helps some fish hide from predators. The fish's colour depends on its lifestyle. Cave fish have no colour; deep-sea fish are black; open-sea fish are a silvery colour.

Cutting blade
The surgeon fish has a formidable cutting blade that lies in a groove. This defensive structure is a developed scale and is as sharp as a surgeon's scalpel. If attacked, the fish erects the blade and slices its opponent with a blow from its tail.

Plaice

Camouflage
Some fish look like the plants among which they live. The triple tail looks like a mangrove leaf, and the leafy sea-dragon and sargassum fish look like seaweed. The plaice can change colour to match the surrounding seabed.

Cutting blade in a groove in the body

Blade extended

Weever fish

Poison
Several fish are poisonous. The weever fishes are extremely dangerous. They lie partly buried and camouflaged in sand, waiting for food. The spines on their gill covers and dorsal fin can inject poison into anyone who steps on one.

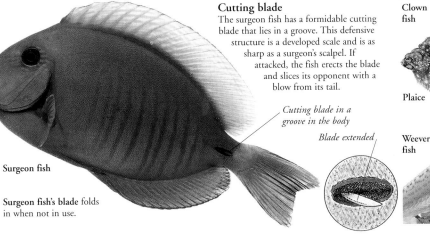

Surgeon fish

Surgeon fish's blade folds in when not in use.

Carnivorous red-bellied piranhas

Food

Many larger fish, including sharks, groupers, pikes, and barracudas, are predators and catch and eat their prey. Most smaller shoal fish feed on plankton, which floats around in the water. Some fish are bottom feeders, such as plaice, while others are grazers, such as the parrot fish, which rasps organisms from rocks.

Cleaner fish
Fish called cleaners, such as some wrasses, have "cleaning" stations where they wait for customers. The customers allow the cleaners to remove bits of food and parasites from their skin, gills, fins, and even right inside their mouths.

Cleaner wrasse at work

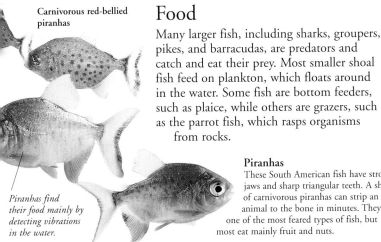

Piranhas find their food mainly by detecting vibrations in the water.

Piranhas
These South American fish have strong jaws and sharp triangular teeth. A shoal of carnivorous piranhas can strip an animal to the bone in minutes. They are one of the most feared types of fish, but most eat mainly fruit and nuts.

Angler fish with lure

Angler fish
Angler fish usually live in deep water. They have a dorsal fin ray modified into a fishing line, with a lure on the end to attract their prey. They can swallow fish much larger than themselves.

Reproduction

Most bony fish lay eggs in the water, and these are then fertilized by a male's sperm. The parents usually leave the eggs to their fate, but some species protect their young in their mouths, in pouches, or in nests. Some sharks, such as the dogfish, lay eggs in an egg case, while others bear live young.

Sticklebacks
Male sticklebacks make a nest and attract females by doing a zigzag dance. The female lays her eggs in the nest, and the male fertilizes them. He then protects the nest from any intruder until the young hatch and are ready to fend for themselves.

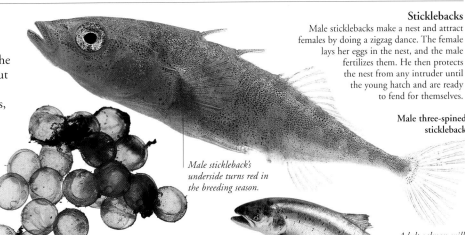

Male three-spined stickleback

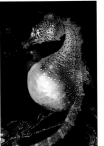

Seahorses
Within 10 seconds of mating, the female seahorse transfers 200 fertilized eggs into the brood-pouch of the male. The male carries them around with him for four weeks until they are ready to hatch. The male then "gives birth", and the young seahorses swim away.

Male stickleback's underside turns red in the breeding season.

Stickleback eggs

Salmon
The Atlantic salmon lays its eggs in upland streams. The young, called parr, live there for three years; then they are called smolt. The smolt swim down-river to the sea and travel across the Atlantic. At maturity, the salmon return to spawn in the same stream where they hatched.

Adult salmon will leap up waterfalls on their journey upstream to spawn.

FIND OUT MORE

| CAMOUFLAGE AND COLOUR | LAKE AND RIVER WILDLIFE | MARSH AND SWAMP WILDLIFE | MIGRATION | OCEAN WILDLIFE | POISONOUS ANIMALS | SHARKS AND RAYS |

Fish

Marine

Blenny lives in shallow water and often rests on the bottom.

Royal gramma fish identifies itself to a mate with dazzling colours.

Zebra pipe fish hides in eel-grass.

Large black spots look like spots on a panther.

Cuckoo wrasse is a colourful fish that lives in British waters.

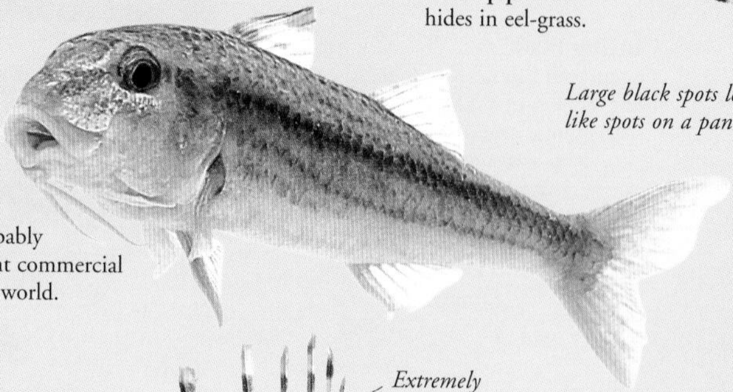

Red mullet is probably the most important commercial marine fish in the world.

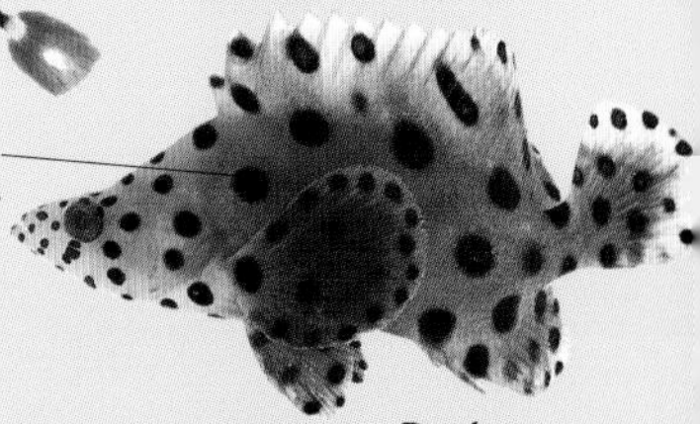

Panther grouper is a lethal predator like its namesake.

Extremely poisonous fin ray spines

Both eyes are on the upper surface.

Plaice is a flat fish and can change colour to merge with the seabed.

Juvenile lumpsucker

Clown triggerfish has a spiny dorsal fin that it can lock erect like a trigger.

Lumpsucker has sucker-like fins for clinging safely to stones and rocks in rough seas.

Lionfish is brightly coloured, which warns its enemies that it is deadly poisonous.

Large free dorsal fin rays

Spiny boxfish has a rigid body from which it gets its name.

Port Jackson shark produces an egg case, or "mermaid's purse", in which the young develop.

John Dory sucks up its food in a tube formed by extendable jaws.

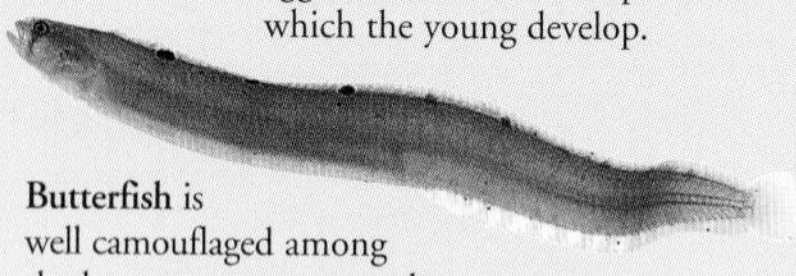

Butterfish is well camouflaged among the browny-green seaweed-covered rocks where it lives.

Angelfish are often brightly coloured.

Blue-ringed angelfish is flattened from side to side, making it difficult to see from the front.

Large sensitive eyes for seeing in the dark

Hatchetfish lives in the deep sea and has luminescent lights along its sides.

Freshwater

Bitterling lays its eggs in a freshwater mussel.

Large eyes for accurate shooting

Minnows live in shoals for protection.

Minnows are small silvery fish that live in clean, fast-flowing, freshwater streams.

Archerfish shoots a jet of water above the surface to capture its insect prey.

Uncoloured guppy, or toothcarp, bears its young alive, unlike most fish, which lay eggs.

Blue-ribbon eel is long and thin, allowing it to hide in narrow crevices.

Neon tetra is a very small, brightly coloured, tropical fish, often kept in aquaria.

FISHING INDUSTRY

LONG BEFORE FARMING BEGAN, people fed themselves by hunting fish and land animals. Today, the fishing industry continues this hunting tradition. Fishing vessels go to sea from every country with a coastline. Small boats, such as the stern trawler, have few crew members, and fish within a day's sailing of their home port. The biggest fishing ships can stay at sea for months, and freeze their catch on board.

Fishing with lines
To catch valuable tuna, fishing boats trail a line as long as 180 km (112 miles, 97 nautical miles). Branching off this line are 200 smaller lines, each ending in a baited hook. This arrangement is known as a drifting longline.

Sea fishing

Most sea fish live within 50 m (165 ft) of the surface. They are concentrated in the shallow waters around the coasts of continents. In the past, the supply of sea fish appeared limitless. However, intensive fishing in areas that were once rich in fish, such as the Grand Banks of North America, has driven cod and other popular species to the edge of extinction.

Deep-water fishing
To catch demersal fish (those that live near the ocean floor), fishing boats sink bag-shaped nets in the water. The fish are trapped by towing the net along the bottom (trawling) or drawing the neck of the net closed (seine fishing). The boat then hauls in the net to land the catch.

Seine fishing

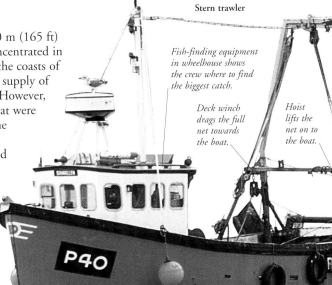

Stern trawler

Fish-finding equipment in wheelhouse shows the crew where to find the biggest catch.

Deck winch drags the full net towards the boat.

Hoist lifts the net on to the boat.

P40

Crew launch the trawl net over the boat's stern.

Lobster pot

Traps
Bait lures lobsters into this basket-like "pot", which rests on the seabed in shallow water. Its funnel-shaped entrance makes escape impossible. Fish traps take many different forms: the Mediterranean tuna trap, for example, is like a maze of net corridors anchored to the seabed. There are even special aerial traps for catching flying fish.

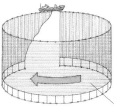

Net closes like a purse, entrapping fish.

Weighted net hangs down from floats.

Surface fishing
Many species of pelagic fish (those that live near the surface) swim together in large groups called shoals, and it is these shoals that fishing boats seek. They catch them by enclosing the shoal in a purse seine net, which is like a circular curtain. Pulling a line closes the bottom of the net, preventing the fish from escaping.

Freshwater fishing

Only 5 per cent of the world's fish catch comes from freshwater sources, such as rivers and lakes. However, in non-industrialized nations freshwater fishing with lines and nets is a vital industry, especially on great lakes such as those in East Africa's Rift Valley. In industrialized nations, anglers have to pay to fish on the few remaining stretches of unpolluted water.

Fur and feather make hook resemble an insect.

Freshwater rods

Barb

Point

Double hook   Treble hook   Fly-fishing bait   Weight

Ocean mammals
The oceans are also home to mammals. Fishing for whales, the world's largest mammals, has now almost ceased because their numbers fell so low. The fur of the seal makes it a target for hunters, and although few fishing vessels catch dolphins deliberately, many dolphins die because they become entangled in abandoned nets.

In the past, whaling crews made beautiful carvings out of the bones and teeth of sea mammals.

Fish farming
Just as farming produces meat more efficiently than hunting, farming fish is more efficient than catching them. Fish farms breed fish carefully to give good-quality stock, and protect the young fish in ponds or enclosures from predators. Carp and trout are the main freshwater farm fish.

Angling
Fishing for sport is known as angling, and is as ancient as fishing for food. Anglers fix a hook to a thin line and then cast it into the water using a long, flexible rod. To lure fish, anglers bait the hook with worms or insects. They may also use a "fly", which is a hook disguised as an insect.

FIND OUT MORE   FARMING   FISH   FOOD   SHIPS AND BOATS   SPORT   WHALES AND DOLPHINS

F

F

FLAGS

FOR HUNDREDS of years, people have used flags as emblems, signals, or rallying points. Among the earliest flags were those flown in battle, so that soldiers could identify their leader and tell each side apart. The flag has since developed as a means of communication, used to send rapid signals, or as a symbol representing a nation or group. Every country has its own flag, as do many states and most political organizations.

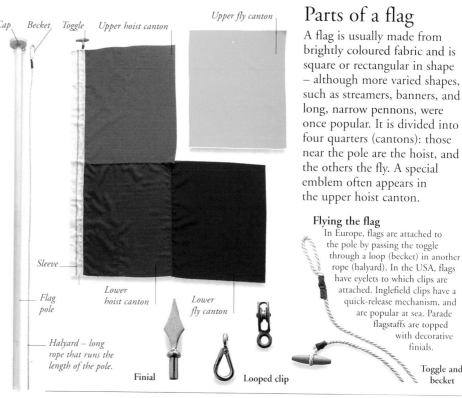

Cap Becket Toggle Upper hoist canton

Upper fly canton

Sleeve

Flag pole

Lower hoist canton

Lower fly canton

Halyard – long rope that runs the length of the pole.

Finial

Looped clip

Parts of a flag

A flag is usually made from brightly coloured fabric and is square or rectangular in shape – although more varied shapes, such as streamers, banners, and long, narrow pennons, were once popular. It is divided into four quarters (cantons): those near the pole are the hoist, and the others the fly. A special emblem often appears in the upper hoist canton.

Flying the flag
In Europe, flags are attached to the pole by passing the toggle through a loop (becket) in another rope (halyard). In the USA, flags have eyelets to which clips are attached. Inglefield clips have a quick-release mechanism, and are popular at sea. Parade flagstaffs are topped with decorative finials.

Toggle and becket

First flags

Many ancient armies carried standards, carved symbols on the end of a pole. The Roman standard first introduced cloth flags. These hung from horizontal poles, to make them easy to carry on horseback.

Homemade flag
The first flag was probably a piece of brightly coloured cloth tied to a stick. A plain red flag spelt danger to early peoples, just as it does today.

Cloth dyed with natural earth pigment

Finial on top of pole could show legion badge

Badge of legion

Name of legion

Pride of a legion
The Roman standard was awarded to a military unit only as a reward for special endeavour.

Uses of flags

Flags communicate across language barriers. At sea, the International Code of Signals is a system of signalling with flags: the meanings are the same in every language. In both sports and politics, flags also send messages that are understood universally.

Red Cross flag

Flag of the United Nations

The dove on the Greenpeace flag, a symbol of hope

Rallying cries
Modern flags may be developed to identify political movements, or for international medical or environmental groups. The emblems and colours represent the organization's ideals: for instance, a white background stands for peace, while olive branches symbolize reconciliation.

Soccer flags are raised to signal when the ball has gone out of play.

Sports flags
Flags are used in many sports for marking out the area of play or signalling to participants.

Golf flags are attached to slender pins to mark the holes on a course.

Plastic marker flags

Political symbols
A symbol on a national flag can sum up political ideals that would otherwise take many words. The former Soviet red flag with its hammer and sickle symbol represented the workers and farmers who took part in the Russian Revolution.

Semaphore
This method of signalling with just two flags is still used at sea. Signallers can spell out a message quickly, simply by changing the position of their arms. Red and yellow flags are chosen because they can be seen over long distances.

FIND OUT MORE

FOOTBALL   PEACE MOVEMENTS   ROMAN EMPIRE   SHIPS AND BOATS   SIGNS AND SYMBOLS   SOVIET UNION   UNITED NATIONS

International Code of Signals
Alphabet and single flag messages

A I have a diver down; keep well clear at slow speed.

B I am taking in, or discharging, or carrying dangerous goods.

C Yes.

D Keep clear of me; I am manoeuvring with difficulty.

E I am altering my course to starboard.

F I am disabled; communicate with me.

G I require a pilot (or, I am hauling nets).

H I have a pilot on board.

I I am altering my course to port.

J I am on fire and have dangerous cargo on board; keep well clear of me.

K I wish to communicate with you.

L You should stop your vessel instantly.

M My vessel is stopped and making no way through the water.

N No.

O Man overboard.

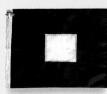

P All persons should report on board as vessel is about to proceed to sea.

Q My vessel is healthy and I require free pratique [permission to trade].

R [No single letter meaning]

S My engines are going astern.

T Keep clear of me; I am engaged in pair trawling.

U You are running into danger.

V I require assistance.

W I require medical assistance.

X Stop carrying out your intentions and watch my signals.

Y I am dragging my anchor.

Z I require a tug.

Two-flag messages

DX I am sinking.

NG You are in a dangerous position.

AC I am abandoning my vessel.

NH You are clear of all dangers.

Numerals

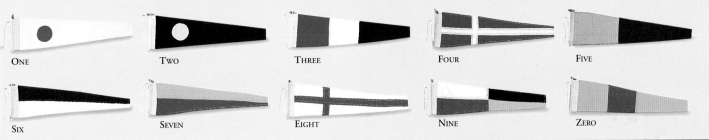

ONE   TWO   THREE   FOUR   FIVE

SIX   SEVEN   EIGHT   NINE   ZERO

FLIES

THEY MAY BE PESTS AT TIMES, but flies are remarkable insects. As their name suggests, they have mastered the power of flight. Fast and agile in the air, flies dart about, hover, and make lightning turns. There are about 90,000 different insects that we call flies. About 75,000 of these are true flies, which have only one pair of wings and belong to the insect group Diptera. The remainder form many other groups of insects with two pairs of wings. Unlike most other types of fly, the larvae of true flies are completely different from the adults. Often called maggots, they have simple bodies with no legs and are little more than eating machines.

Feeding

Fly larvae feed on foods such as microscopic organisms, living flesh, plants, and dung. The mouthparts of adult flies are adapted for a liquid diet. They have extendible tubes to draw fluids into their bodies. The feeding habits of flies cause many health problems worldwide, from stomach upsets to more serious illnesses such as cholera.

Abdomen swollen with blood

Bloodsuckers and predators
Bloodsuckers and flies that catch prey have piercing mouthparts that cut holes in their victims. They inject anti-clotting agents to keep blood flowing, or poison to kill the prey. Enzymes are also released to help break down the body contents.

Tsetse fly

Hoverfly

Nectar and waste feeders
Flies that feed on nectar or decaying matter have soft pads on the ends of their sucking mouthparts, that help soak up liquid food. On solid food, flies deposit saliva, then suck up the partly digested juice that results.

Features of a true fly

The body of an adult fly is clearly divided into three main parts: the head, thorax, and abdomen. The head bears the sucking mouthparts and a bulging pair of compound eyes, between which sprouts a pair of antennae. Attached to the thorax are the fly's six legs and its membranous wings. The abdomen contains most of the body organs.

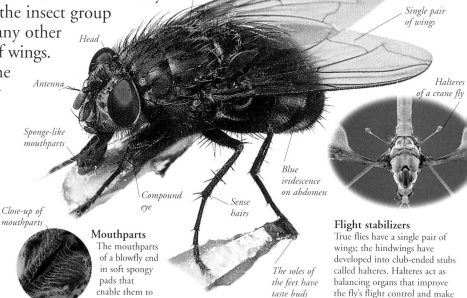

Long hairs on thorax

Single pair of wings

Head

Antenna

Haltere of a crane fly

Sponge-like mouthparts

Blue iridescence on abdomen

Close-up of mouthparts

Compound eye

Sense hairs

Mouthparts
The mouthparts of a blowfly end in soft spongy pads that enable them to suck up liquids.

The soles of the feet have taste buds on them.

Bluebottle feeding

Flight stabilizers
True flies have a single pair of wings; the hindwings have developed into club-ended stubs called halteres. Halteres act as balancing organs that improve the fly's flight control and make it easier to change direction.

Breeding

After mating, female flies lay hundreds of eggs on a suitable feeding site for the larvae, that develop from the eggs. These sites may be in dung, soil, or water, or on leaves, dead bodies, or living animals. The larvae eat voraciously, and grow into pupae within which they change into their adult shape and form.

Robber flies mating

Bluebottle larvae

Mating
Before mating, flies may go through elaborate courtship rituals. Fruit flies dance on leaves, and gnats dance in the air. After mating, female robber flies commonly eat their mates.

Larvae
Fly eggs often hatch out into larvae on dead animals, which they begin to eat. The larvae, also called maggots, may live longer than the adult flies into which they develop.

Aquatic larvae

Mosquitos and many other bloodsucking flies lay their eggs in water. The larvae that develop float upside-down on the surface. They breathe through a tube attached to the abdomen, that pokes above the water. After pupation, the adult emerges to fly away.

Tube takes in air.

Mosquito larva

Types of fly

In addition to true flies, many other kinds of fly exist that all have two pairs of wings, such as dragonflies and mayflies. The young that emerge from their eggs have a more complicated body structure than the larvae of true flies – some even look like wingless versions of the adults.

Dragonflies
Dragonflies are large predators. They dart around in seach of other insects that they catch in flight with their long legs. They lay their eggs in water.

Giant compound eyes

Caddis flies
Adult caddis flies always live near water. Their larvae live underwater, and carry with them a protective case made of plant debris or sand.

Long antenna

Mayflies
Young mayflies live below water. After growing wings, they leave the water and form swarms in the air. The adults mate, lay their eggs, then die a few hours later.

Long, thin legs

Lacewings
Lacewings often hibernate in houses over winter. The adults and larvae prey on other insects such as aphids. They are weak fliers.

Delicate wings

BLUEBOTTLE

SCIENTIFIC NAME *Calliphora erythrocephala*

ORDER Diptera

FAMILY Calliphoridae

DISTRIBUTION Europe

HABITAT Fields, meadows, houses, and buildings

DIET Rotting flesh, faeces, and other decomposing organic matter; adults also eat nectar

SIZE Length 10 mm (0.4 in)

LIFESPAN Larvae: 7 days; pupae: 8–10 days; adults: unknown

FIND OUT MORE   ARTHROPODS   DISEASES   EGGS   FLIGHT, ANIMAL   INSECTS   MARSH AND SWAMP WILDLIFE

FLIGHT, ANTL

THE ONLY ANIMALS CAPABLE of powered flight are birds, bats, and insects. Some other animals can glide for short distances. Flight is very useful. It helps the animals to find food, escape from predators, and migrate long distances. Flying animals need wings, powerful wing muscles, a streamlined shape, and a lightweight body. They also need to eat lots of food to give them the energy to flap their wings.

Minla in flight

Birds

A bird's wings are an aerofoil shape – curved on top and slightly hollow underneath. As the wings move through the air, a difference in air pressure is created above and below, which lifts the bird up into the air. A bird steers by changing the angle of one or both wings, twisting its wings, and spreading and twisting its tail.

Hovering
Hummingbirds are among the birds that hover. They beat their wings in a figure-of-eight pattern, producing lift on both the upstroke and downstroke. They can also fly sideways, straight up and down, backwards, and even upside-down.

Between flaps, the bird folds its wings and rests.

Tail used to steer and change direction

Red-tailed minlas have an up-and-down flight.

Forward flight
Most small birds, such as this minla of eastern Asia, fly by flapping their wings up and down. As the wings go down, they push air backwards, moving the bird forwards. As the wings go up, the feathers at the wingtips move apart to allow air to slip through.

Feathers closed for the downstroke

Swan taking off

Gliding albatross

Gliding
Some large birds rarely flap their wings. Albatrosses and other large seabirds glide on strong winds rising off the waves. Albatrosses can travel for hundreds of kilometres a day. Large land birds, such as vultures and eagles, float on columns of rising hot air called thermals.

Taking off
Small birds take off by jumping into the air and flapping their wings. They may take off straight from the ground or from a perch. A large, heavy bird, such as a swan, cannot do this. It needs to run along while flapping its wings to create enough lift for take-off.

Insects

A small insect, such as a mosquito, flaps its wings 1,000 times a second. Most insects flap about 520 times a second. Dragonflies are the fastest insect fliers, reaching nearly 300 km/h (190 mph). Some insects, such as flies, have one pair of wings. Others, such as bees, have two pairs.

Vertical muscle contracts, moving the wings up

Horizontal muscle contracts, moving the wings down.

Wing muscles
Insect wings developed from their hard body covering. They are not modified legs, like the wings of birds or bats. Insects do not have any muscles on the wings. Instead, their wing muscles are inside the thorax, the middle part of the body.

Cockchafer take-off
The cockchafer is a beetle with two pairs of wings. The front wings are hard wing cases, which are held out of the way during flight. They give the beetle some lift when it flies fast. The flexible back wings flap up and down to provide the power for flight.

Bats

The only mammals able to fly, bats are more acrobatic than birds. They have four large pairs of flight muscles and several smaller pairs, while birds have only two pairs. Each wing consists of skin stretched between four long fingers.

Wing is made of an elastic membrane covered with skin.

The bat flexes its arm bones up and down to flap its wings.

Long narrow wings are for fast flight in open areas.

Horseshoe bats find prey by echolocation.

Thumbs are used for clinging to surfaces.

Gliding animals

Some animals can glide slowly downwards. They have developed large fins, or webs or flaps of skin, which they spread out to slow their fall. They have to be able to judge speeds and distances accurately.

Flying squirrel

Flying squirrel
Flaps of skin allow a flying squirrel to glide up to 100 m (330 ft) between trees. The squirrel uses its tail as a rudder, and has sharp claws to grasp the surface on landing.

Flying fish
To escape predators, flying fish swim fast along the surface, then take off and glide for up to 50 m (160 ft), with their huge fins held out.

Flying gecko
The gecko (above) has flaps of skin along the sides of its body and tail. It spreads out the flaps to glide between trees. It has webbed feet to help with steering.

Flying fish

FIND OUT MORE AIRCRAFT ANIMALS BATS BIRDS FLIGHT, HISTORY OF INSECTS MIGRATION

FLIGHT, HISTORY OF

EVERY DAY, MILLIONS OF PEOPLE fly to destinations all over the world. Planes are a common sight in the skies, but, despite their widespread use, they were first developed only about 90 years ago. The urge to fly is ancient, but by the start of the 20th century, the only flying machines were hot-air balloons, airships, and gliders. World War I stimulated the development of aeroplanes and, by the end of World War II, advances had resulted in jets and rockets. Since then, flight technology has produced supersonic planes and space travel.

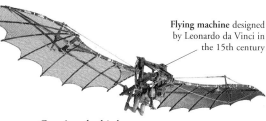
Flying machine designed by Leonardo da Vinci in the 15th century

Copying the birds
Wings are the part of an aircraft that provide the upwards lift needed to keep it in the air. Successful aeroplanes were impossible to build before people understood how wings worked. Early attempts at flight concentrated on copying the flapping action of birds, which proved to be impractical because a human's muscles are far too weak. Many "bird men" were killed trying to fly.

First controlled flight
The first controlled flight of a powered aeroplane took place on 17 December 1903 in Kitty Hawk, North Carolina, USA. The plane, *Flyer I*, flew 36 m (119 ft) in a flight that lasted under 12 seconds: it is nonetheless perhaps the most famous flight of all time. *Flyer I* was designed and built by the Wright brothers, Orville and Wilbur, after years of experiments with kites and gliders. It was powered by a petrol engine they built themselves.

Flyer I climbed to a height of 3 m (10 feet)

Wilbur Wright watches his brother Orville take off.

Warplanes
The military's interest in the potential of aeroplanes as weaponry was central to the advancement of flight technology. During World War I (1914–18), warplanes were transformed from being slow and vulnerable to being fast, easily manoeuvrable fighting machines. Huge bomber and fighter planes were made in this period.

Protective clothing worn by World War I pilots included flying helmet, goggles and gauntlets.

Biplane of 1917

Biplane
World War I pilots flew biplane (twin-winged) fighters. Built from wood and fabric, biplanes were sturdier than monoplanes, but flying them was little fun. The cockpit was open to the cold and wet, and to spits of oil from the engine. Larger fighters had a second cockpit for a navigator and gunner. Single-seaters had a machine gun that fired through the spinning propeller.

Airships
Airships are held aloft by a vast gas-filled envelope and driven forward by engines with propellers. Airships were an important form of passenger and military transport until long-distance aircraft were developed in the 1940s.

Modern age
The basis for the modern aeroplane first appeared in the 1920s. It was a monoplane (single-winged) aircraft. The wing was made of metal, as was the fuselage. All aircraft had piston engines and propellers until the late 1930s, when a new type of engine, the jet, was invented.

Boarding pass
Airline ticket

Amelia Earhart
American aviation pioneer Amelia Earhart (1898–1937) set several long-distance flight records. She was the first woman to fly solo across the Atlantic. In 1937, in a bid to fly round the world, she disappeared near New Guinea.

Harrier GR5 jet fighter

Jets
A turbojet engine allows aircraft to fly much faster and more quietly than a propeller engine. Jet aircraft were increasingly used after World War II and became standard for fighter aircraft and for long-distance passenger planes.

Passenger flight
Fast, comfortable, and affordable air travel had become accessible by the 1960s. Today, millions of passengers fly around the world in the Boeing 747, a so-called "jumbo jet" which has quiet, turbofan engines.

Ariane launch vehicle

Space flight
The first rockets powerful enough to reach space were built in the late 1950s. Today, modern launch vehicles and re-usable spacecraft, such as the Shuttle, make going into orbit almost an everyday event.

FIND OUT MORE   AIRCRAFT   AIRPORTS   AIRSHIPS AND BALLOONS   LEONARDO DA VINCI   SPACE EXPLORATION   TRANSPORT, HISTORY OF   TRAVEL   WARPLANES   WEAPONS

FLIGHTLESS BIRDS

FLYING IS A VERY USEFUL WAY of moving, but it does have drawbacks. It uses a lot of energy, and it is possible only for animals with a light body. During the course of evolution, some birds have given up flight and the problems it brings. Instead, they run, or, as is the case with penguins, they swim; some can move extremely fast. There are about 40 species of flightless birds alive today, including kiwis, emus, and the world's biggest bird, the ostrich. Many more flightless species, including some record-breaking giants, existed in the past, and some of today's species are also in danger of extinction.

Long neck with sparse feathers

Weak, fanlike wings used in courtship rituals.

Females are slightly smaller than males, with brown plumage instead of black.

Two large clawed toes on each foot

Ostrich crèche
Young ostriches are guarded by an adult male. Several families of chicks gather together, forming a group called a crèche.

Kiwis

These medium-sized birds are found only in the forests of New Zealand. Their wings are only about 5 cm (2 in) long, and their body is covered with a unique plumage that looks like hair. Kiwis are nocturnal and because they have poor eyesight, they find food mainly by smelling it.

Ostrich

The ostrich is the world's largest bird. It can run at up to 65 kmh (40 mph), and uses its speed and stamina to outdistance most of its enemies. An ostrich's feet have two toes, and each toe ends in a large claw. If an ostrich is cornered, it uses these claws as deadly weapons to defend itself.

Hatching
The shell of an ostrich egg is thicker than a china mug, but not as hard. The young ostrich breaks out by kicking and pecking at the shell.

1 The chick turns its body as it pecks and pushes at the shell.

2 Half the shell is in pieces, and the chick is almost free of the egg.

3 The chick tumbles out and will soon start to look for food.

Sensory, whisker-like feathers at the base of the beak

Small wings are hidden under the body plumage.

Hard "helmet," or casque

Rheas escape from danger by running away.

Cassowaries
These large, flightless birds live in dense forests in northern Australia and New Guinea. They use their claws as weapons and have been known to kill people.

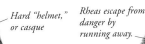

Rheas
There are two species of rheas, both of which live on the open plains in South America. Young rheas have bright stripes, but the adults are grayish-brown.

Strong legs with large feet

This egg is shown in proportion to the kiwi above.

Probing beak
The kiwi has nostrils at the tip of its long, curved beak, instead of near its head. It uses its beak to find food on the forest floor.

Kiwi egg
The kiwi's egg is 13 cm (5 in) long, and is a quarter of the female's weight. Relative to her body, the female kiwi lays the largest eggs of all birds.

Emus
Found only in Australia, emus are the second largest birds in the world, after the ostrich. Emus live in large flocks and wander long distances in search of food. They can cause problems on farms by raiding crops.

OSTRICH	
SCIENTIFIC NAME	*Struthio camelus*
ORDER	Struthioniformes
FAMILY	Struthionidae
DISTRIBUTION	Tropical western and eastern Africa, and southern Africa
HABITAT	Savannah and semi-desert
DIET	Fruit, seeds, leaves, small animals
SIZE	Height up to 2.4 m (8 ft); weight up to 154 kg (340 lb)
LIFESPAN	About 30 years

 FIND OUT MORE  AUSTRALIAN WILDLIFE   BIRDS   EGGS   FLIGHT   GRASSLAND WILDLIFE   PENGUINS   SOUTH AMERCIAN WILDLIFE

FLOWERS

THE FIRST flowering plants appeared about 120 million years ago. They are now the largest group of plants, and are widespread. Flowers are the advanced reproductive structures of plants. The majority of them are pollinated by the wind or by animals. Over millions of years, flowers and insects have co-evolved to produce some very complex and interesting relationships.

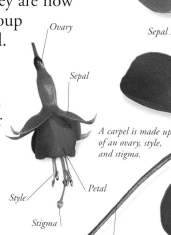

Fuchsia flower

Ovary

Sepal

Style

Petal

Stigma

Flower stalk

The flower is the structure that brings about sexual reproduction in the plant.

Petal

Anther

Filament

A stamen is made up of an anther and a filament.

Sepal

Ovary

A carpel is made up of an ovary, style, and stigma.

Stigma

Style

Anthers produce pollen grains.

Sepals enclose the flower when in bud.

Petal

Petals are brightly coloured to attract insects.

When the anthers are ripe, they split to release masses of pollen.

Parts of a flower

A plant's reproduction organs are inside the flowers. Stamens are male and produce pollen. The female organs are called carpels. These contain ovules, which develop into seeds. A ring of petals attracts pollinators, and sepals protect the flower when in bud.

Pollination

In order for seeds to develop, a flower has to be pollinated. Pollen from the stamens of a flower of the same species must stick to the plant's stigma. Cross-pollination occurs when pollen from one plant lands on the flowers of another. If a flower is pollinated by its own pollen, it is called self-pollination.

Bee at a *Narcissus* flower

Insect pollination
Flowers are mostly pollinated by insects. These are attracted to the flowers by their petals, a scent, and a supply of nectar or pollen to eat. The pollen sticks to a visiting insect and is carried to another flower.

Freesia

Tobacco plant

Scent and colour
The colour and scent of a flower attract insects or other animals. Drops of sugary nectar secreted at the base of the petals provide food for the insects, which are dusted with pollen while they drink. Flowers are often sweetly scented, but some smell unpleasant, especially those pollinated by flies.

Wattle

Water pollination
Aquatic plants may have aerial, submerged, or floating flowers. A few use the surface film of water to carry pollen. The flowers float in shallow dips. The pollen slides into these and pollinates the flowers.

Starwort

Wind pollination
Some plants rely on wind to waft their pollen from one flower to another. Their flowers may have no petals, or just tiny ones. They are often arranged in catkins with conspicuous stamens and stigmas.

Hazel catkins and pollen

Bird pollination
Many flowers that rely on birds to pollinate them are red or orange – colours that attract birds. The flowers tend to be tubular so that birds can dip their beaks in. Stamens dust the birds' heads with sticky pollen.

Hummingbird at a thistle flower

Mammal pollination
Important mammal pollinators include some species of tropical bat and many types of tiny Australian possum. They pollinate flowers as they feed on nectar and pollen.

Pygmy possum feeding on a *Banksia* flower

Insect mimics
Many orchids have such specialized partnerships that only one type of insect serves as a pollinator. Some orchids look and smell so like a female insect, that males of that species try to mate with them, picking up pollen as they do so.

Bee orchid

The bee orchid can be pollinated by a bee, but is often self-pollinated by the wind.

An orchid's pollen is produced in small clumps called pollinia.

Part of the flower looks and smells just like a bee.

FIND OUT MORE | CARNIVOROUS PLANTS | FRUITS AND SEEDS | INSECTS | PLANTS | PLANT ANATOMY | PLANT REPRODUCTION | PLANT USES | TREES | WINDS

Flowers

Insect-pollinated

Urn-shaped flowers

Brown lines on the petals guides insects to the nectar.

Each flower contains a drop of nectar.

Bramble pollinators include beetles and bees.

Bell heather is pollinated by short-tongued bees.

Primrose flowers appear in the spring.

Hollow-stemmed asphodel has hollow stems and leaves.

Red clover has a head of tubular flowers.

Greater periwinkle is pollinated by bees.

Domed hood

Mirror orchid has pollen in clumps called pollinia.

Anemone pavonina is pollinated by insects.

Magnolia flowers have thick, waxy petals.

Corn marigold flowerhead has many tiny flowers.

Fox and cubs has strap-shaped ray florets.

Bastard balm attracts bees with its large petal.

Dwarf elder has small flowers clustered together.

Early dog violet has dark veins, which guide insects.

Wild pansy is pollinated by long-tongued bees.

Insects crawl into the bell-shaped flowers.

Foxglove is pollinated by bumblebees.

Umbels of tiny yellow flowers

Thorow-wax has clusters of flowers called umbels.

Marsh cinquefoil has much larger sepals than petals.

Red valerian has tiny tubular flowers pollinated by moths and butterflies.

Carline thistle has yellow flowers surrounded by stiff, spiny bracts.

Honeysuckle has scented flowers which attract honeybees and hawk moths.

Cornflower has scented flowers and is pollinated by flies and bees.

Common rockrose is pollinated by insects, but can be self-pollinating.

Red campion is pollinated by long-tongued bees and also by hoverflies.

Bird- and mammal-pollinated

Petals bend back so that birds are dusted with pollen.

Stamens and stigmas on a long column

Fuchsia is pollinated mostly by birds.

Passionflower is pollinated by nectar-drinking birds.

Silver wattle flowers attract birds and possums.

Nasturtium flowers are pollinated by birds.

Hibiscus dusts hawk moths and birds with pollen.

Urn plant flowers are surrounded by spiny bracts.

Wind-pollinated

Spike of petal-less flowers

Anthers protrude from the tiny green flowers.

Long slender catkins

Female flowers

Broad-leaved pondweed has a dense spike of flowers.

Greater plantain has purple anthers.

Armenian oak has male flowers in yellow catkins.

Sand couch has flowers in stalkless spikelets.

Alder has male flowers in long, dangling catkins.

Stinging nettle has catkins of male or female flowers.

FOOD

WE ARE WHAT WE EAT: our bodies get the energy and nourishment they need from our daily diet. Not having enough of the right food, or eating too much of the wrong food, causes ill-health. Food and eating are important in other ways too. Many countries have a distinctive cuisine (cooking style), which reflects the eating habits of its people and the ingredients available locally. In many industrialized nations, cooking is a hobby as well as a necessary task. Today there is concern about levels of chemicals in food, and many people choose an organic diet.

Fast food is food that is mass-prepared and served quickly in takeaway outlets. The hamburger is a popular fast food in many western countries.

A delicacy in France

Popular in Japan

Made with pig's blood

Jews and Muslims do not eat pork.

Frog's legs   Seaweed   Black pudding   Snails   Pork sausages

What is food?

Anything humans can digest counts as food. Worldwide, diets vary widely: food habits are influenced by availability, climate, and religious, moral, or social factors. Ideally, a daily diet should include staple, energy-giving carbohydrates, such as rice or pasta, plus proteins, fats, vitamins, and minerals. In reality, poverty or warfare make this impossible in many places.

Processing and preserving

Even before they are cooked, most foods must be processed to make them ready for cooking: for example, wheat must be ground into flour before it can be baked as bread. Preserving food allows it to be stored for use later; this reduces the risk of shortages, and prolongs availability. A food industry has grown up to provide the food we eat, and process, preserve, and package it.

Preparing cassava

Cassava
Many foods are indigestible without processing but bitter cassava, the main food in many tropical areas, is actually poisonous. Grating, pressing, and heating the root removes the deadly cyanide it contains.

Preparing food

Although some foods, such as salad vegetables and fruit, are delicious when raw, many foods need to be cooked first. Cooking makes food tastier and easier to digest. Cooking root vegetables, for instance, makes their starch grains absorb water, swell, and burst, releasing essential nutrients.

Salad

Fennel

Orange

Cooking methods
There are many cooking methods, such as simmering food in water, which heats it to just under 100°C (212°F). Only a few foods, such as eggs, cook at temperatures lower than this. Grilling or frying in oil heats food to a much higher temperature, cooking it faster.

Steaming fish is a healthy way to cook it.

Food preservation: freezing peas

Viner

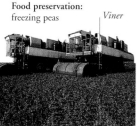

Frozen peas

1 Until frozen peas were invented, the only peas most people could eat were dried or tinned. A machine called a viner harvests the peas when they are sweet enough to be frozen. It tumbles them in a drum to remove the pods. These are ploughed back into the field as fertilizer.

2 Once at the factory, the peas are washed and blanched. They are then carried on a conveyor to the freezing chamber. On the way, jets of cold air prevent them sticking together. In the chamber, the peas are blast-frozen at a temperature of -18°C (-2°F).

3 Before packaging, the peas are assessed for quality and taste. Fresh vegetables begin to lose their nutrients as soon as they are picked. Because these peas have been frozen within two and a half hours, they are fresher than fresh peas in a shop.

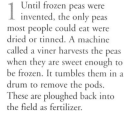

Cocoa beans

Chocolate
Chocolate is a food product derived from the cocoa bean. The Aztecs of Mexico enjoyed a chocolate drink, flavoured with chilli. When the Spanish conquered Mexico in the 16th century, they introduced the drink to Europe. People began to eat solid chocolate from about 1630, but chocolate bars were a luxury until the 20th century.

Frozen food
Freezing food to preserve it dates from prehistoric times in cold regions. Following the appearance of home electric refrigerators in 1913, frozen vegetables first went on sale in the USA in 1930.

Peas in the pod

Frozen vegetables

Hunger and famine

Each year, 800 million people cannot get enough food to lead healthy lives, despite food surpluses in other parts of the world. Children suffer most. Malnutrition in children severely damages their physical and mental development. Every year in the developing world, famine (widespread starvation) occurs when insects, plant diseases, drought, or warfare destroy crops, and a harvest fails.

FIND OUT MORE   DIGESTION   FARMING   HEALTH AND FITNESS   TRADE AND INDUSTRY

Food

Types of food

Uncooked rice

Puffed rice cakes

Grains of wheat

Bread made with wheat flour

Maize

Tortilla chips

Rice is a staple food for Southern Asia and parts of Africa.

Wheat is a staple in North America, Europe, Australia, and parts of Asia.

Maize (corn) is a staple food in some African, Asian, and American countries.

Potatoes

Lettuce

Soybeans

Coconut

Watermelon

Honeycomb

Starchy roots are a good source of carbohydrate.

Vegetables are an important source of vitamins.

Pulses (beans and peas) are rich in protein.

Nuts and seeds can be pressed to make oils.

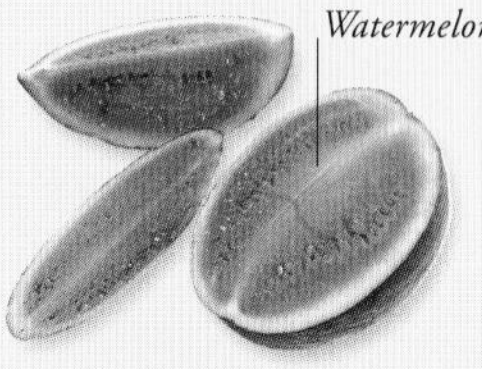

Fruits are an important source of vitamins.

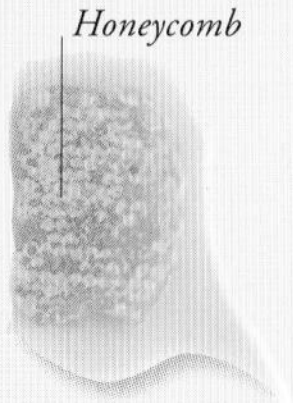

Sugars and honey sweeten food.

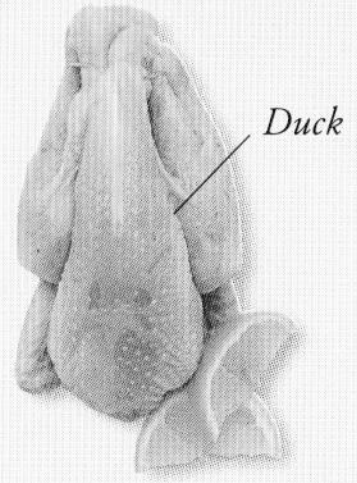

Duck

Lobster

Cheese

Olive oil

Chillis

Vanilla

Meat is a major protein source.

Fish and shellfish are a low-fat protein source.

Eggs are a valuable source of protein.

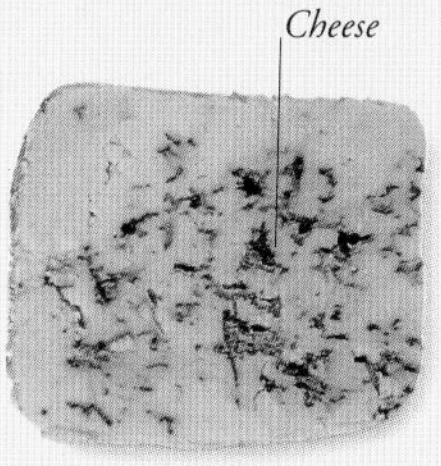

Milk and milk products provide protein and important minerals.

Fats and oils store energy.

Spices and herbs add flavour to a meal.

World cookery

Chicken

Mussels

Prawns

Salad

Raw salmon

Parmesan cheese

Yorkshire pudding

Australia: meats grilled out-of-doors on a barbecue

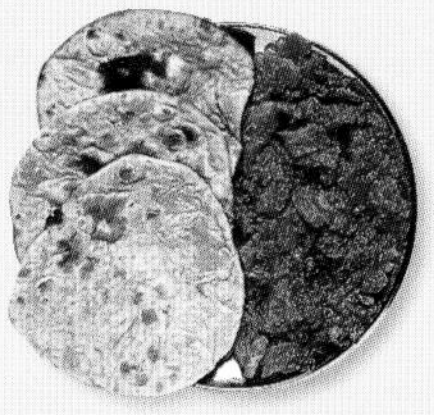

India: vegetable curry and *roti* (wheat bread)

France: *bouillabaisse,* fish soup, served with bread

Mexico: *buritto,* a pancake with chilli, meat, beans

Vietnam: spring rolls filled with pork, prawns, noodles

Morocco: chicken baked with spices

Spain: *paella,* rice simmered with chicken, seafood, and spices

United States: pork ribs with black-eyed peas

China: roast duck with an aromatic seasoning

Italy: *fettucini,* a kind of pasta, in a tomato sauce

Thailand: *pad thai,* Thai fried noodles

Japan: *sushi,* extremely fresh, raw fish, with rice and seaweed

United Kingdom: roast beef, gravy, and roast potatoes

Russia: *borscht* (beetroot soup) with *blinis* (pancakes)

FOOD WEBS AND CHAINS

THE LIVES OF DIFFERENT species in a wildlife community are linked together through the process of feeding. As plants and animals grow and are eaten by others, energy and food substances locked up in their body tissues pass on along a chain. These food chains interlink with one another, and the resulting network is called a food web. The number of different animals and plants in a community is naturally balanced. If the balance is upset it can affect the whole web.

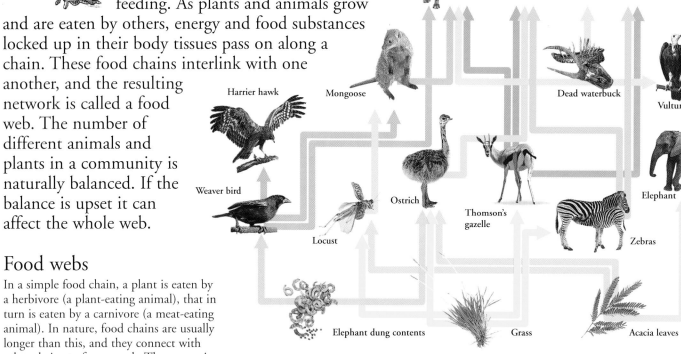

Hyena

Lion

African hunting dog

Harrier hawk

Mongoose

Dead waterbuck

Vulture

Weaver bird

Ostrich

Thomson's gazelle

Elephant

Zebras

Locust

Elephant dung contents

Grass

Acacia leaves

Food webs

In a simple food chain, a plant is eaten by a herbivore (a plant-eating animal), that in turn is eaten by a carnivore (a meat-eating animal). In nature, food chains are usually longer than this, and they connect with other chains to form a web. The arrows in this diagram show how different plant foods on a typical African savannah are eaten by a range of animals, that, in turn, provide food for various other animals.

Decomposers
Some animals, fungi, and bacteria feed on dead or waste plant and animal tissue. They turn it back into simple substances, which plants use to grow.

Producers
In ecology, plants are called producers. They start the food chain by using the sun's energy to produce food from simple substances.

Consumers
Animals are known as consumers because they get the biological material they need for life from the plants or other animals that they eat or consume.

Top predator

The tawny owl at the top of this food chain is known as the top predator. An owl needs to eat many weasels and rodents to meet its energy needs.

The number of animals or plants represents the amount of energy available to the next level.

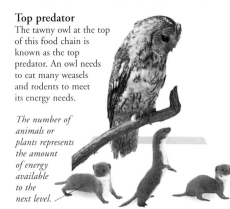

Trophic pyramids

Ecologists call each stage in a food chain a trophic level. These levels can be represented as a pyramid. Animals use much of the energy they gain from their food to grow. They also use energy to live, to move about, breed, feed, and avoid their enemies. This means that at each trophic level there is less energy available to the next level.

Secondary consumers
Weasels are secondary consumers because they get energy from the plants through other consumers. There are more weasels in a community than the owls that hunt them.

Primary consumers
Mice and voles get energy directly from plants. They use a lot of energy; many are needed to support the weasels.

Primary producers
Energy is stored in plants. It takes a large quantity to support the rodents.

Population cycles

A change in the population of one species affects the population of other species in the food chain. The lemming population in the tundra and Arctic rises and falls on roughly a four-year cycle. When there are lots of lemmings, Arctic foxes, which hunt them, breed more successfully, so their numbers increase too.

Arctic fox

Giant African land snail

Partula snail

Upsetting the balance
When the giant African land snail was taken to Pacific islands, the snails destroyed vegetation because there was nothing to prey on them. Another type of snail was released to eat their eggs, but these began to wipe out the native *Partula* snail instead.

FIND OUT MORE
ANIMALS · AFRICAN WILDLIFE · ECOLOGY AND ECOSYSTEMS · ENERGY · FOOD · GRASSLAND WILDLIFE · PHOTOSYNTHESIS · RAINFOREST WILDLIFE

FOOTBALL

THE VARIOUS FORMS OF FOOTBALL are among the most popular sports to play and watch. Association football, or soccer, is played in almost every country by men and women. Rugby games are less widespread, but the new professional rugby union is becoming increasingly international. American football, although watched worldwide on television, is played little outside the United States. Other "national" games include Australian football, played chiefly in the state of Victoria, and Gaelic football, an Irish game.

Soccer ball

Soccer

Soccer is a kicking game played 11-a-side. The goalkeeper is the only person allowed to handle the ball. The object is to propel the ball into the opposition's goal with a foot or the head. A game lasts 90 minutes, with a 15-minute interval plus, in some knock-out competitions, an extra 15 minutes each way.

Soccer pitch

Helmet

Face mask made from unbreakable plastic coated in rubber

Shoulder pads

Upper arm pad

Rib pads tie to shoulder pads.

Hip pad

Breeches

Thigh pad

American football

A handling game, American football is played 11-a-side with limitless substitution from 40 players or more. It is divided into short bursts of action as the attacking team advances in a series of "downs". Points are awarded chiefly for touchdowns and field goals.

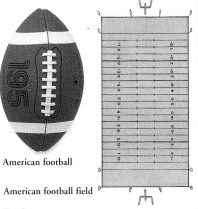

American football

American football field

Equipment
To withstand the crunching tackles and blocks, players wear extensive protective padding under their uniform, the amount and type depending on their role. Players wear a number from 1 to 99 to identify them.

World Cup
The soccer World Cup is as popular as the Olympics. About 170 countries enter competitions to qualify for the 32 places in the finals, which take place every four years.

Pelé
Brazilian soccer star Pelé (b. 1940) won universal acclaim when he inspired Brazil to win the World Cup for the first time in 1958. His performances in Brazil's 1970 triumph have gone down in soccer folklore. In a first-class career he scored 1,281 goals.

Women's soccer
In 1991, the first women's soccer World Cup was held, and women's soccer was accepted as an Olympic sport in 1996. In many countries, girls now begin playing soccer at school.

Australian football
Australian football is played 18-a-side on a huge oval field. Players kick, catch, and run with the ball which must be grounded every 10 m (33 ft). A goal, kicked between the inner posts, is worth six points; a behind, kicked inside the outer posts, scores one point.

Rugby

The rugby codes are rugby union and rugby league. They are handling games featuring running, hand-to-hand passing, tackling, and kicking. Points are scored for a try – touching the ball down over the opposition goal line, or a goal – kicking the ball over the cross bar and between the posts. The two codes have a slightly different ball and pitch.

Rugby union ball

Rugby union pitch

Rugby union
This is played 15-a-side with eight forwards, two halfbacks, four three-quarters, and one full-back. It features scrums (shown here), line-outs to restart play, and tactical kicking. Tries score five points and conversions two points.

Rugby league
Rugby league is played 13-a-side. A tackled player may rise and play the ball with his foot. After six successive tackles, a team must give up the ball to the other team. Tries score four points, goals one or two.

Gaelic football
This is played 15-a-side with a round ball. It is a cross between soccer and Australian football. The ball may be kicked, fisted, and passed hand-to-hand. Points are scored by kicking the ball between the posts, under the bar for three points, over for one point.

FIND OUT MORE

BALL GAMES   OLYMPIC GAMES   TENNIS AND OTHER RACKET SPORTS   SPORT

FORCE AND MOTION

THE WORLD IS NEVER STILL – traffic and pedestrians rush along busy streets, clouds race across the sky, and the Earth turns on its axis and whirls around the Sun. Forces make all this motion, or movement, possible. A force is a push or a pull that causes an object to start or stop moving, or to change its speed or direction. When forces combine, they can hold things still or make things balance. The study of the way objects move when forces act upon them is called dynamics.

Speed and acceleration

An object's speed is how far it moves in a period of time. Speed in a particular direction is called velocity. Acceleration is the rate at which an object's velocity changes.

A sprinter who runs 60 metres in 12 seconds has an average speed of 5 m/s.

The sprinter's feet push against the starting blocks.

The force exerted by the sprinter's feet propels him forward.

A sprinter's acceleration is greatest during the first few seconds of a race.

Combining forces

Equal forces acting on an object in opposite directions will have no effect. If the forces are not equal, or if they do not act in opposite directions, they will combine to give an overall force called the resultant.

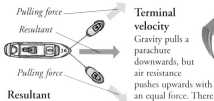

Pulling force

Resultant

Pulling force

Resultant

Two tugboats helping an ocean liner into port do not pull in the direction the ship needs to travel. They pull at an angle to each other so that the resultant force moves the ship straight ahead.

Terminal velocity

Gravity pulls a parachute downwards, but air resistance pushes upwards with an equal force. There is no resultant, because the forces cancel each other out. The parachute cannot accelerate, so it falls to the ground at a constant speed, known as terminal velocity.

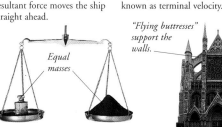

"Flying buttresses" support the walls.

Equilibrium

An object is in equilibrium when the forces acting upon it balance. This set of scales is in equilibrium when two equal masses are placed on the pans, because gravity pulls on each pan with the same force.

Equal masses

Statics

Statics is the study of forces acting on stationary objects in equilibrium. It is important in building design, because a building will collapse if the forces acting upon it do not balance.

Inertia

An object's mass makes it resist a force that tries to change its state of motion, whether it is moving or at rest. This resistance is called inertia. The greater an object's mass, the more inertia it has. For example, the same force will accelerate a small car more than a loaded truck, because the car has a smaller mass and less inertia.

Momentum

When a moving object collides with a stationary one, the result depends upon a quantity called momentum. An object's momentum is calculated by multiplying its mass by its velocity. For example, a heavy bowling ball has more momentum than a light plastic ball moving at the same velocity, because it has a greater mass.

The mass of the bowling ball gives it enough momentum to scatter the pins.

The lighter plastic ball has a smaller mass and simply bounces off the pins.

Archimedes

Archimedes (c.287–212 BC) was a Greek mathematician and inventor who studied forces and how they could be used by simple machines. He founded statics, discovered why objects float and sink, and worked out the principles behind levers and pulleys.

Newton's laws of motion

In 1687, English physicist Sir Isaac Newton devised three laws to summarize the principles of force and motion.

Force → Motion →

First law

An object continues in a state of rest or constant motion unless a force acts upon it. The inline skater in the picture will keep on rolling at the same speed until a force, such as friction, acts to stop him.

Second law

An object's acceleration is equal to the size of the force acting upon it divided by the object's mass. This inline skater's acceleration depends on how heavy he is and how hard he is pushed.

Third law

For every force there is an equal force acting in the opposite direction. Forces act in pairs, so when A pushes B, an equal and opposite force acts on A, making both inline skaters move apart.

A B

Circular motion

A free-moving object will naturally move in a straight line. Centripetal force is needed for the object to move in a circle. This is a force that pulls an object towards the centre of a circle, constantly changing its direction and stopping it from moving off in a straight line. A motorcycle uses centripetal force to travel around a bend.

Friction between the tyres and the road provides centripetal force.

FIND OUT MORE   FRICTION   GRAVITY   MACHINES   MAGNETISM   PRESSURE

FORESTS

A THIRD OF THE WORLD'S land surface consists of forest – areas of land covered by dense tree cover. Each forest is an ecosystem – a group of animals and plants interacting with the physical environment and one another. More plants and animals live in forests than in any other environment. Forests differ according to the climate – boreal, temperate, or tropical. They help maintain the Earth's natural balance; trees absorb and release gases which regulate the climate.

Tropical forest

Tropical forests, or rainforests, tend to thrive in warm and wet climates. The porous soil is generally rich in aluminium and iron. In one hectare there may be more than 200 species of trees, hundreds of birds, mammals, and reptiles, and thousands of insects.

Emergent trees rise up to 60 m (197 ft).

Canopy of trees 15 m (50 ft) above the ground

Plants twine around branches.

Understorey contains shrubs and young growth.

Tropical forest

Each forest has layers of vegetation. In a tropical forest emergent trees poke through the top. Below are the canopy, the understorey, and the forest floor.

Broad leaves of deciduous trees grow rapidly in summer, and are shed in winter.

Tropical forest
Temperate forest
Boreal coniferous forest

Temperate forest

Down-angled branches allow the trees to shed the weight of the snow in cold climates without breaking them.

Forest floor is dark with little plant growth, but vegetation decay enriches the soil.

Temperate forest

These forests are found in mild or temperate climates, where winters are cool and summers are warm. The majority of trees are deciduous, such as oak and beech. Many temperate forests have been cleared for farmland because the soil beneath is very fertile.

Boreal coniferous forest

In cool, northern, or boreal regions, such as North Asia, there are vast areas of boreal forests, sometimes known as taiga. These dense forests contain hardy coniferous or evergreen trees, such as spruce, pine, fir, and larch trees.

Soil beneath these trees is acid and infertile.

Boreal coniferous forest

Afforestation

More people are becoming aware of the value of forests. In Southeast Asia, new forest land is created with tree-planting programmes. Some forests are now conservation areas.

Deforestation

Each year, forest land the size of Washington State, USA is destroyed. Trees are cut down for farmland or timber. Deforestation can cause huge environmental problems, disturbing the soil and forest life. Fewer trees to absorb carbon dioxide may also disrupt the climate.

Cattle ranching
Huge areas of rainforest in Brazil are cut down for cattle-ranching, which exhausts the soil within a few years.

Slash and burn
Nomadic farmers slash and burn forests for farmland. After a few years, they move on to allow the soil to regenerate.

Overgrazing
A shortage of land forces nomadic farmers to stay in one place. The land is over-grazed, and the soil dries up.

FIND OUT MORE · CLIMATE · ECOLOGY AND ECOSYSTEMS · PLANT USES · POLLUTION · RAINFOREST WILDLIFE · SOIL · TREES · WOODLAND WILDLIFE

FOSSILS

THE REMAINS AND TRACES of past life forms are called fossils. All living organisms are potential fossils, but only a few are preserved. The most common fossils are those of hard parts of animals and plants. Only rarely is soft tissue fossilized. Sometimes, trace fossils, such as footprints, are found. The study of fossils, called palaeontology, is crucial to our understanding of life.

Graptolite

Conodont

Fossil dating
Some fossils, such as graptolites and conodonts, evolved and became extinct over geologically short periods of time. This makes them useful for dating the rocks in which they are found.

How a fossil is formed

In order for something to fossilize, it must be buried quickly by sediment, such as sand or mud, before it decomposes. Fossils form in a variety of ways, depending on the environment in which the animal or plant lived, and the conditions after it was buried.

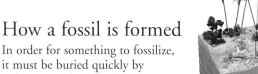

The skeleton may be broken up.

Water deposits sediment.

Erosion of the rock brings the fossils nearer the surface.

1 After death, the soft parts of a *Triceratops* decompose quickly, leaving just the hard skeleton and horns.

2 Through time, the bones are buried under thick layers of sediment and harden to form fossils.

3 The layers of sediment turn to rock. They may be pushed up or folded to form mountains.

4 Erosion exposes the bones. Palaeontologists can then collect and study the dinosaur remains.

Studying fossils

The study of the evolution of environments and natural communities is an important part of palaeontology. This limestone contains fossils of different animals, such as trilobites and corals. It shows a community that existed on the seafloor more than 400 million years ago.

Limestone from Much Wenlock, England

Coral
Fossil corals are common because they have a hard skeleton. Soft-bodied animals, such as sea anemones and jellyfish, would have lived in the same community, but are unlikely to have fossilized.

Trilobite
Trilobites were arthropods that lived in the sea. They shed their shells regularly, as modern arthropods do, and these shells are often found as fossils. They are divided into three distinct parts, or lobes, hence the name "trilobite". A few fossils of soft parts have been found.

Amber
The fossilized resin of trees, called amber, often contains trapped insects and other small animals and plants. The trapped fossils are often preserved with much detail.

Females were larger than males.

Ammonite shells replaced with iron pyrites, or "fools' gold".

Jurassic ammonite

Ammonites
These molluscs were abundant in the seas of the Mesozoic Era. Their shells were made of the mineral aragonite and were often replaced by other minerals during fossilization.

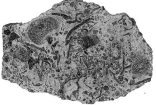

Volcanic ash
This child's body was buried by volcanic ash at Pompeii, Italy, in AD 79. Ash turns to rock quickly. A buried animal or plant may rot away to leave a hollow, which, if filled with plaster, forms a cast.

Trees
Fossilized trees, such as these *Lepidodendron* trunks and roots, can be preserved as internal moulds of the bark. The inside rots away and is replaced by sand.

Petrification
These monkey-puzzle cones have been turned to stone, or petrified. This happened when silica-rich waters crystallized within the cells of the cones.

Concretions
Hard lumps, or concretions, are often formed around fossils in sediments. This concretion reveals the fossil shell and mould of a clam.

Types of fossil

Fossils range from microscopic plants and animals to the huge bones of dinosaurs. They can be almost unchanged from the original or replaced by minerals.

Bones
Vertebrate fossils are made of many parts and are usually found as single pieces. If conditions are right, a skeleton can be preserved whole, as in this *Diplomystus*, an ancestor of the modern herring.

Georges Cuvier
A French zoologist, Georges Cuvier (1769–1832) realized that the parts of the body were interrelated. For example, an animal that has hooves is a herbivore, and must have herbivore's teeth. He identified a fossil as a marsupial from a jaw.

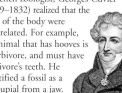

FIND OUT MORE　　ARTHROPODS　　DINOSAURS　　EVOLUTION　　GEOLOGY　　PREHISTORIC LIFE

Fossils

Invertebrates

Raphidonema is a sponge from the warm waters of the Cretaceous Period.

Didymograptus are Ordovician graptolites. They floated in oceans.

Trachyphyllia is a Miocene solitary coral.

Lonsdaleia lived as a colony during the Carboniferous Period.

Lovenia is a heart urchin with a flattened shell.

Archaeogeryon is a deep-water Miocene mud crab.

Mesolimulus is a horseshoe crab of the Jurassic and Cretaceous Periods. It has a horseshoe-shaped shell.

A stalk attached the brachiopod to the sea floor.

Viviparus is a freshwater snail.

Terebratula is a brachiopod, also known as a lamp shell.

Lingula is a brachiopod with a thin shell.

Stem made up of disc-like plates.

Dimerocrinites is a sea lily, or crinoid, from the Silurian and Devonian Periods.

Vertebrates

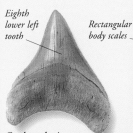

Eighth lower left tooth

Carcharocles is an extinct shark.

Rectangular body scales

Dapedium is a fish from the shallow seas of the late Triassic and Jurassic Periods.

Macrocranion from the Eocene Period resembles a living hedgehog without the spikes.

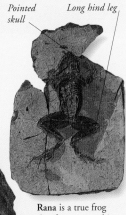

Pointed skull   *Long hind leg*

Rana is a true frog that first appeared in the Eocene Period.

Raphus is a huge, extinct, flightless pigeon, commonly known as the dodo.

Nostril

Ichthyosaurus is a sea reptile of the Jurassic Period.

Ring of bones around the eye

Nostril

Dagger-like teeth

Dimetrodon is a mammal-like carnivorous reptile of the Permian Period.

Eye socket

Plants

Collenia is an alga of the Precambrian and Cambrian Periods.

Stigmaria are the root-bearing branches of a Carboniferous club-moss.

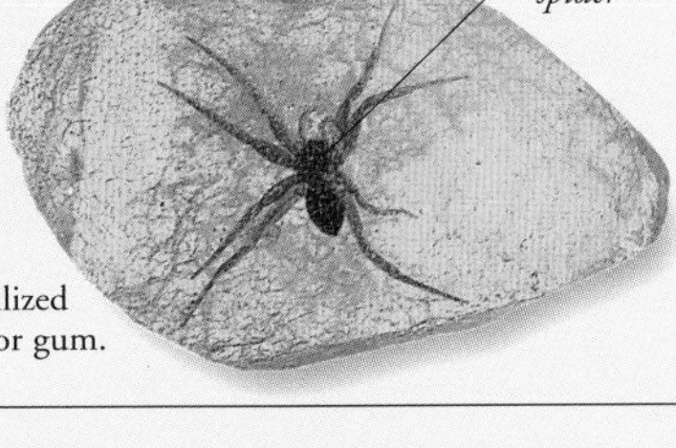

Amber is fossilized tree resin or gum.

Ficus is a fig which first appeared in the Eocene Period.

Porana is a Miocene flower.

Trapped spider

Populus is a poplar, almost identical to poplars today.

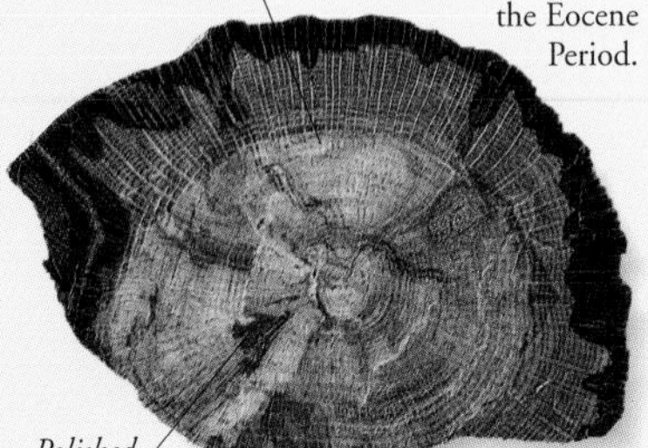

Jet is a type of fossilized wood.

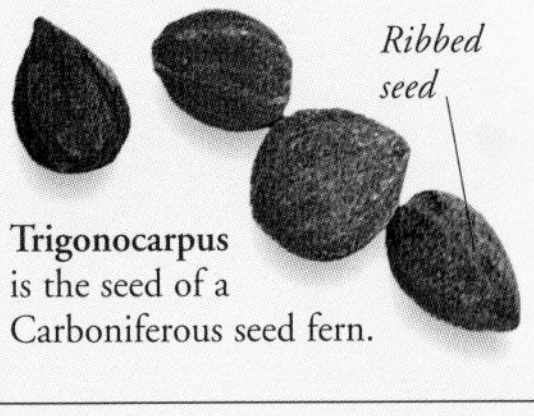

Growth rings

Quercus is oak. It first appeared in the Eocene Period.

Polished, petrified wood

Carved jet

Ribbed seed

Trigonocarpus is the seed of a Carboniferous seed fern.

FRANCE

THE LARGEST COUNTRY in western Europe, France stretches from the Pyrenees in the south to the English Channel in the north. A founder member of the European Economic Community (now European Union), France plays a key role in world affairs. It is a leading industrial nation, although some five per cent of the population works in farming. The first of the modern republics, France includes Corsica, Guyana, and various islands in the Caribbean and Pacific Ocean.

FRANCE FACTS

CAPITAL CITY	Paris
AREA	547,030 sq km (211,208 sq miles)
POPULATION	59,500,000
MAIN LANGUAGE	French
MAJOR RELIGION	Christian
CURRENCY	Euro
LIFE EXPECTANCY	79 years
PEOPLE PER DOCTOR	333
GOVERNMENT	Multi-party democracy
ADULT LITERACY	99%

River Seine
From its source in the east, the River Seine crosses Paris, before winding its way north to the Atlantic Ocean. France's river network, which also includes the Loire and the Rhône, is used for transport and for irrigating farmland.

The Seine in Normandy

Corsican *maquis*

Physical features
France's landscape varies from undulating fields in the north to sparse hills in the Massif Central, and mountains in the Alps and Pyrenees in the south.

Corsica
With an area of 8,630 sq km (3,350 sq miles), Corsica is the third largest Mediterranean island. Fragrant, thorny scrub called *maquis* covers the slopes of towering granite peaks, and rich fertile valleys are used to graze sheep and grow vines. The capital is Ajaccio.

Climate
Northwest France, particularly Brittany, is mild but damp. The east has hot summers and stormy winters. Summers in the south are dry and hot, and forest fires are common. In the Pyrenees and Alps, winter snowfalls are heavy, making these ideal areas for skiing.

39°C (102°F) -17°C (1°F)
18°C (64°F) 3°C (37°F)
584 mm (23 in)

Barren 1%   Farmland 60%
Forest 36%
Built-up 3%

Land use
France's fertile farmland includes gently rolling pastures and fields of wheat and sugar beet in the north, and vineyards and lavender fields in the south. Much of the Massif Central is pasture land for grazing sheep.

Paris
The Louvre Museum lies on the fashionable Right Bank of the River Seine, which divides the city. The Left Bank is traditionally home to students, artists, and the famous Eiffel Tower. One of the world's most beautiful and most visited capitals, Paris is the cultural and political centre of France.

The Louvre Museum

F

People

People of French descent make up about 94 per cent of the population. Among these are several groups who speak their own languages and have strong independence movements. These include the Bretons of Brittany in the north, about 500,000 Basques in the Pyrenees, and the Corsicans.

Ethnic groups
France's five million immigrants include mainly North African Muslims and economic migrants from South and Central Europe. Most live and work in the cities.

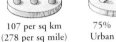

107 per sq km
(278 per sq mile)

75%
Urban

25%
Rural

Leisure

Football, rugby, cycling, and tennis are all popular sports in France, as are horseracing and Formula 1. The French Open is a major international tennis championship.

Tour de France
Each year, more than a hundred of the world's leading professional cyclists compete in this famous cycle race over a 3,400-km (2,113-mile) route in 24 one-day stages.

Boules
Throughout France, groups of people playing *boules* are a common sight in the town or village square. *Boules* is France's national game and involves rolling heavy balls at a smaller target ball.

Farming

The French grow a variety of crops, such as wheat, barley, sugar beet, and grapes for making wine. About a third of all the farmland is pasture for grazing cows and sheep, which are reared for milk to make dairy products, and for meat.

Cantal

Livarot

St.-Nectaire

Cheese
France produces more than 365 kinds of cheese, from cow, sheep, and goats' milk. These include St.-Nectaire, Cantal, and Livarot, and the famous Brie, Camembert, and Roquefort. Milk and butter are also important exports.

Cereals
France's main cereal crop is wheat, which grows on large farms in the north of France where the soil is good.

Wine
The wines of Bordeaux, Burgundy, Champagne, and the Rhône valley are sold worldwide. France is the leading producer and controls quality strictly.

Food

French cuisine is world famous, and words such as café, restaurant, paté, and quiche are common in many languages. Special French dishes include *bouillabaisse* (fish soup), *escargots* (snails), and *grenouilles* (frogs' legs).

Prawn

Slice of lemon

Whelk

Lobster / *Mussel*

Industry

France has strong chemical, steel, electronics, and manufacturing industries, and an active aerospace programme. Nuclear power provides three-quarters of the country's electricity. Perfume and fashion are also a major source of income.

Perfume
French perfumes, such as Chanel, are world famous. Many are made from the fragrant oils extracted from roses, jasmine, and lavender that grow in the southeast of the country.

Tourism
The fashionable resorts of the Côte d'Azur in southeast France attract thousands of tourists every summer. France is now the world's leading tourist destination, attracting 75 million visitors each year.

Car production
Most French drivers buy French cars, such as this Renault Espace. Other makes include Peugeot and Citroën. The French car industry ranks fourth in the world.

Transport

France boasts the world's fastest train, the TGV, which can travel at speeds of up to 300 kmh (186 mph). A direct service now runs to England via the Channel Tunnel.

Monaco

This tiny independent principality on the Côte d'Azur derives its income from tourism, banking, sales tax, and gambling. It has close ties with France.

Grand Casino
The people of Monaco pay very little tax and earn more per head than any other country in the world. The gaming rooms and roulette wheels of the Grand Casino in Monte Carlo are open to anyone with money to spend.

MONACO FACTS

CAPITAL CITY
Monaco

AREA 1.95 sq km
(0.75 sq miles)

POPULATION 31,700

MAIN LANGUAGE French

MAJOR RELIGION Christian

CURRENCY Euro

FIND OUT MORE   CARS AND TRUCKS   CLOTHES AND FASHION   CYCLING   EMPIRES   EUROPE, HISTORY OF   EUROPEAN UNION   FARMING   FRANCE, HISTORY OF   TRADE AND INDUSTRY   TRAINS AND RAILWAYS

FRANCE, HISTORY OF

THE LARGEST COUNTRY in western Europe, France has dominated European history ever since the Franks conquered the country in the 5th century. Its vast natural wealth and large population have enabled a succession of rulers, such as Charlemagne in the 9th century, Louis XIV in the 17th, and Napoleon in the 19th, to create powerful empires that spanned Europe. Despite three bitter wars with Germany between 1870 and 1945, France emerged as one of the world's superpowers. Today, France is a leading member of the European Union, and one of the wealthiest countries in the world.

Samian ware bowl

French potters made this type of ware in the Roman period.

Horses heads, carved c.10,000 BC

Prehistoric France
The first inhabitants of France were prolific artists. More than 20,000 years ago, they adorned caves at Lascaux and elsewhere with lifelike pictures of animals. They also carved likenesses of animal heads from bone, antler, and rock.

Roman France

Between 58 and 51 BC, a Roman army led by Julius Caesar conquered France. The new province of Gaul was one of the richest in the empire. Trade flourished, and the Romans built many roads and bridges. They also introduced growing grapes for wine.

Franks
In 486, the Franks from Germany routed the last Roman governor of Gaul and took control, giving France its name. At first the Franks continued with Roman customs, but their empire broke up in civil wars. The 8th-century kings Charles Martel, Pepin the Short, and Charlemagne restored order.

Charlemagne

Medieval France

In common with other European rulers, the power of the French kings was always limited by the strength of local nobles. Despite this weakness, France became one of the richest countries in Europe during the 11th century. Major trade fairs in the Champagne region attracted merchants from all over Europe, and trade and commerce flourished.

Angevin Empire
As a result of marriage and war, Henry II of England (r.1154–89) ruled much of western and northern France. His vast realm was called the Angevin Empire, after the county of Anjou. For years it was a threat to French unification.

Château Gaillard, an Angevin castle

Religious wars
The Reformation split France, with many Catholics becoming Huguenots (Protestants). In 1562, civil war broke out between the two sides; religious toleration was agreed by the Edict of Nantes in 1598, but tension remained high. In 1685, Louis XIV revoked the Edict, and many Huguenots fled to England and Holland.

Hand-painted figures

Gilded decoration

Sèvres porcelain vase

Renaissance France

Joan of Arc, who fought the English for independence, was burnt at the stake in 1431. During the 15th century, the French kings drove out the English, and united their country. They also crushed the power of the nobles. During the next century, the ideas of the Italian Renaissance entered France. New châteaux were built, and the arts flourished.

Golden age
The 17th and 18th centuries were a golden age of the arts. Royal support led to the founding of the Gobelins tapestry works in 1602 and the royal pottery at Sèvres in 1756. The nobility supported artists such as Watteau and Fragonard, dramatists such as Racine, Molière and Corneille, the writer Montaigne, creator of the essay, and the fable-writer La Fontaine.

Louis XIV
During the long reign of Louis XIV (r.1643–1715), the power of the French kings reached its height. Louis believed in the divine right of kings to rule, and governed without parliament. He reorganized the army and expanded French territory. But his lavish lifestyle left France almost bankrupt.

Bourbons

Under the Bourbon kings, France emerged as the major power in Europe during the 17th century. Habsburg-ruled Spain and Austria – enemies of France – were defeated, and all power was centralized under the king. Industry and commerce were supported, and France established colonies in North America and India.

Palace of Versailles
In order to increase his own power, and reduce that of the nobility, Louis XIV built this vast new palace outside Paris. Some 36,000 people worked on the building, decorating it with the best examples of French art and design. At the centre was the king's bed chamber, where Louis received guests.

F

Monarchy and empire

After the defeat of Napoleon in 1815, France had a series of short-lived, weak governments. The restored Bourbon monarchy was overthrown in 1830 and King Louis Philippe lost his throne in 1848. The resulting Second Republic collapsed when its president, Louis-Napoleon (r.1852–70), became emperor. In spite of these problems, France grew prosperous.

Revolution of 1848
In February 1848, Parisians rose up against their ineffectual king, Louis Philippe. A republic was set up, with Louis-Napoleon, a nephew of Bonaparte, as president. Radical reforms were promised, but in 1852 Napoleon became emperor.

Revolutionaries in Paris, 1848

French Revolution
Revolution broke out in 1789, sweeping away the king and nobility. A new National Assembly was set up, and swore the famous tennis court oath, that they would not disband until France had a proper constitution. Napoleon Bonaparte became Emperor in 1804, marking the end of the revolutionary period.

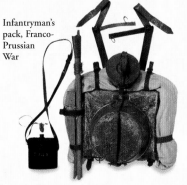

Infantryman's pack, Franco-Prussian War

Franco-Prussian War
Although successful at home, Napoleon III was no match for Bismarck, chancellor of Prussia. In 1870, rivalry between France and Prussia led to war, but the French armies were unprepared and were soon defeated. France lost the provinces of Alsace and Lorraine to Germany.

Third Republic
The Third Republic (1870–1940) was riven with internal disputes and conflicts between moderates, radicals, socialists, and royalists. Between 1918 and its collapse in 1940, there were 44 governments and 20 different prime ministers. Yet France stayed one of the leading states in Europe, with a worldwide empire and a strong economy.

J'Accuse, writer Emile Zola's pamphlet supporting Dreyfus

Dreyfus case
In October 1894, French army captain Alfred Dreyfus was court-martialled for treason, for passing military secrets to Germany. But a mistake had been made, and a campaign to free Dreyfus began. He was cleared in 1906, but the case split the nation between his supporters and those who refused to change the verdict.

Vichy France
In 1940, German forces invaded France. French general and right-wing politician Marshal Pétain set up a government in Vichy, central France. This government collaborated with the occupying forces; opposition was led from London by Charles de Gaulle, leader of the Free French. Vichy France was occupied by the Germans in 1942.

Cross of Lorraine | Flag of the Free French

Modern France
After the liberation of France from German occupation in 1944, a Fourth Republic was set up to govern the country. Like its predecessor, it was weak and was brought down by the unrest caused by the Algerian war in 1958. Charles de Gaulle then set up the Fifth Republic, aiming to restore French prestige and prosperity.

May 1968
In May 1968, students demanding more money for education demonstrated against high defence spending. Riots broke out in Paris and elsewhere, with fighting between police and students. A general strike ensued, and de Gaulle's government was weakened.

After the riots, Paris, May 1968

Charles de Gaulle
Charles de Gaulle (1890–1970) trained as a soldier, rising to command an armoured division. On the fall of France in 1940, he fled to Britain and called on French people to resist German occupation. As leader of the Free French, he did much to boost French morale during the war. In 1958 he became president, leading his country until he resigned in 1969.

Algerian war
In 1954, Algeria, one of several African countries colonized by France, demanded that it be granted its independence. This led to conflict with the many European settlers in the country. The French army supported the settlers in their wish to remain French and waged a vicious war against the Algerian rebels. Algeria finally won its independence in 1962.

Timeline

FIND OUT MORE | EUROPE, HISTORY OF | FRENCH REVOLUTION | GERMANY, HISTORY OF | MEDIEVAL EUROPE | NAPOLEON BONAPARTE | NAPOLEONIC WARS | ROMAN EMPIRE | WORLD WAR I | WORLD WAR II

FRANKLIN, BENJAMIN

INVENTOR, PRINTER, PUBLISHER, writer, scientist, politician, diplomat, and an author of both the US Declaration of Independence and the US Constitution – there was nothing Benjamin Franklin did not turn his hand to. He was born into a poor family, but had a fertile mind very receptive to new ideas. He invented items such as the lightning conductor and bifocal spectacles, but he is most respected for his contribution to the founding of the USA. He is sometimes known as the "wisest American".

Early life
Benjamin Franklin was born in 1706 in the American port of Boston. He was the son of a candle and soap maker, and left school at 10 to help in his father's business. Later he worked for his half-brother James, printer and publisher of a newspaper to which Benjamin contributed. After disagreements with James, he left Boston in 1723 to work as a printer in Philadelphia.

Printer
Franklin prospered as a printer. As publisher of the popular *Poor Richard's Almanac* between 1732–57, he introduced numerous common-sense sayings that have since become part of the American language. He also set up an academy that later became the University of Pennsylvania.

Scientist
In 1748, Franklin handed over his printing business to his foreman so that he could devote his life to science. He researched the nature of electricity, and this work led to him inventing the lightning rod, to protect tall buildings from lightning. He also worked out a theory of heat absorption and tracked the paths of storms across the sky.

Bend caused by lightning.

Lightning rod

Lightning
In 1752, Franklin flew a kite in a thunderstorm to prove that lightning is electrical. Electricity from the thunderclouds flowed down the string to a metal key tied on it near the ground. Sparks flew from the key, showing the presence of the electrical charge in the sky.

Franklin experimenting with a kite and lightning

Inventor
Franklin was a tireless inventor, using his scientific knowledge to devise a number of inventions that were designed to make human life safer and more comfortable. These ranged from bifocal spectacles – combining two lenses of different strength in one frame to correct both close and distant vision – to a musical glass "armonica". Among his useful inventions were the lightning rod and an energy-saving stove still made today.

The armonica was played by rubbing the fingers gently on the edges of the glasses.

Stove
Among Franklin's many inventions was a practical stove that made use of the heat that would otherwise have escaped up the chimney. Stoves like this were installed in many American houses.

Armonica
In the early 1760s, Franklin built a musical instrument made up of a series of glass bowls, graduated in size and fitted one inside another. By rotating a spindle, the edges of the bowls passed through a trough of water. Contact with the musician's fingertips produced a penetrating sound. Composers such as Mozart and Beethoven wrote music for this strange device.

Statesman
During the American Revolution, Franklin was a member of the committee that wrote the Declaration of Independence, which he signed in 1776. Later that year, he sailed to France to win diplomatic recognition for the new nation. When the war ended, he was one of the main US negotiators in the peace talks.

Constitution
In 1787, Franklin helped to write the new American constitution. Although his proposal for a single-chamber congress was rejected, he negotiated a compromise between the different authors which resulted in the constitution that survives today.

Franklin (left) talks to the French king and queen (seated, right) and members of their court

BENJAMIN FRANKLIN

1706	Born in Boston, USA
1723	Begins work as a printer
1732–57	Publishes *Poor Richard's Almanac*
1752	Conducts famous experiment with lightning
1776	Helps to draft Declaration of Independence
1781	Chosen as one of the US negotiators with Britain
1787	Member of group which draws up US constitution
1790	Dies in Philadelphia

 FIND OUT MORE · AMERICAN REVOLUTION · ELECTRICITY · EYES AND SEEING · GOVERNMENTS AND POLITICS · INVENTIONS · MUSICAL INSTRUMENTS · UNITED STATES, HISTORY OF

FRENCH REVOLUTION

National Assembly • Jacobin Club
Guillotine •
Place de la Révolution • • Tuileries Palace
Concièrgerie • • Bastille Prison

IN 1789, REVOLUTION BROKE OUT in France when people rose up against poverty and injustice. The French Revolution swept away the power of the monarchy and ended the traditional social order. When the revolution began, poverty was widespread, the king was unpopular, and people resented the clergy and nobility. Following the formation of the National Assembly, France was declared a republic, the king was executed, and, for a while, terror reigned. In 1799, Napoleon came to power, and the revolution ended.

Revolutionary Paris

The key events of the revolution occurred on the streets of Paris. Various political groups sprang up, such as the Jacobin Club, which relied on the Parisian *sans culottes* for support.

National Assembly

In 1788, France ran out of money, and King Louis XVI called the Estates General, representing clergy, nobility, and middle classes. The Third Estate formed a National Assembly, seized lands, and drew up a new constitution.

Rights of Man

The National Assembly issued the *Declaration of the Rights of Man and the Citizen,* stating that "Men are born and remain equal". Women's rights were not included, but the ideals of "liberty, equality, and fraternity" inspired everyone.

Storming of the Bastille

In 1789, angry demonstrators seized the Bastille, a prison that had been a symbol of oppression for many years. This act sparked a wave of rebellion. Outside Paris, peasants attacked the country houses of the nobility they hated.

Coarse working blouse

The bonnet rouge, or red bonnet, symbolized freedom. It looked like the cap worn by freed Roman slaves.

Reign of Terror

By 1792, the revolution was under threat. There were food shortages, royalist uprisings in the countryside, and a threat by Prussia to invade and restore the monarchy. Extremists, known as Jacobins, grew in power, declaring a republic and executing the king in 1793. They set up the Committee of Public Safety, and a reign of terror began. Anyone suspected of being an enemy of the revolution was arrested and guillotined. Thousands died. By 1794, the leaders of the Committee were themselves executed, and the terror was over.

Revolutionaries

The revolutionaries were men and women from all social classes: lawyers, peasants, workers. Street revolutionaries were known as *sans culottes* (without breeches) because they wore striped trousers. Two rival revolutionary groups emerged: the Girondins and the more radical Jacobins.

Guillotine

Named after a French doctor, the guillotine consisted of a wooden frame, with a sharp blade mounted on it, which sliced off the victims' heads. This killing machine was quicker than previous methods of execution, and was, therefore, thought to be more humane.

Sharpened blade fell on victims' necks.

Robespierre

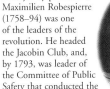

A lawyer by profession, Maximilien Robespierre (1758–94) was one of the leaders of the revolution. He headed the Jacobin Club, and, by 1793, was leader of the Committee of Public Safety that conducted the Reign of Terror. In 1794, he, too, went to the guillotine.

MARCHE DES MARSEILLOIS

Marseillaise

From 1792, revolution spread outside French borders. A soldier composed the *Marseillaise* as a revolutionary marching song. Today, it is France's national anthem.

White was the colour of the royal family.

Red and blue were the colours of Paris.

Striped trousers

Strong leather shoes

1788 France bankrupt. Louis XVI summons Estates General.

May 1789 Third Estate forms National Assembly,

Louis XVI

14 July, 1789 Paris mob storms the Bastille; French Revolution begins.

27 August, 1789 National Assembly issues *Rights of Man.*

October 1789 Women march to Versailles from Paris to demand bread.

1791 The French revolution inspires a slave rebellion in Haiti.

1792 National Assembly abolishes monarchy. France becomes a republic and goes to war with Austria and Prussia.

1793 Louis XVI executed. Counter-revolution breaks out. Revolutionary war spreads across Europe.

1793–4 Reign of Terror.

1795 The Directory, a more moderate board of governors, is formed and takes power.

1799 Napoleon overthrows Directory and takes power.

1798–99 Revolution inspires uprisings in Ireland.

FIND OUT **MORE** | AMERICAN REVOLUTION | EUROPE, HISTORY OF | FRANCE, HISTORY OF | GOVERNMENT AND POLITICS | NAPOLEONIC WARS

FREUD, SIGMUND

ONE HUNDRED YEARS AGO, people viewed the workings of the human mind as a great mystery. Sigmund Freud helped to make sense of that mystery. Because of his innovative ideas, he is often known as the father of psychiatry. Freud was an Austrian doctor who worked in Vienna almost all his life. He researched the meaning of dreams, how the unconscious mind works, and how events in our past influence the actions we take. In developing the science of psychoanalysis, he provided insights that have affected every aspect of modern life.

Early life

Freud was born into a Jewish family in 1856 in Freiburg (Pribor), in what is now the Czech Republic. In 1859 his family moved to Vienna. Freud was a brilliant student, coming top of his class in school for six years. In 1873 he began to study medicine at Vienna, and in 1881 he qualified as a doctor.

Freud's couch

Psychoanalysis

In 1886, Freud began to specialise in neuroses, or nervous diseases. To find out what was causing his patients' illnesses, he used first hypnotism and then free association – instructing his patients to say whatever came into their head in the belief that they would reveal the cause of their illness. Freud published his ideas in 1895 in *Studies on Hysteria*, the first-ever account of psychoanalysis – the interpretation and treatment of mental disorders.

Freud's spectacles

Notes on one of Freud's patients

Analyst's couch

Much of Freud's work consisted of listening to his patients as they talked about themselves. The patient lay on a couch in Freud's study, and Freud sat at his desk, surrounded by his collection of ancient Egyptian statues, listening and taking notes. This technique, devised by Freud, is still used widely today. Many of Freud's books are made up largely of case studies – reports of the psychoanalytic sessions and the conclusions Freud drew from them.

The Psychopathology of Everyday Life (1904)

The Interpretation of Dreams (1900)

Interpretation of dreams

Freud believed that beneath our conscious mind is a submerged unconscious that governs much of our behaviour. Dreams are the way in which the unconscious comes to the surface. He published this theory in *The Interpretation of Dreams* in 1900.

Chair is made in the shape of a person.

Freud's chair

Freudian slips

In his book *The Psychopathology of Everyday Life* (1904), Freud explained how slips of the tongue can reveal hidden, unconscious wishes. Freud made many connections between what we say and do and what we actually mean.

International Psychoanalytical Association

Early in his career, Freud attracted intense hostility to his work, but gradually his ideas were accepted. In 1902, he established a psychoanalytical society in Vienna, and in 1910 he set up the International Psychoanalytical Association (IPA) to promote his ideas. Regular IPA meetings and discussions helped Freud confirm his theories about the mind and spread them to a wider audience.

Carl Gustav Jung

The Swiss psychiatrist CG Jung (1875–1961) and Freud lectured together in the USA in 1909. Jung was the first president of the IPA, but resigned in 1914 because he disagreed with Freud about the origins of neurosis. He later created his own school of thought about the mind's workings.

Later life

In the 1920s, Freud developed a new theory that the mind is made up of three parts – the id, which contains impulses, the ego, which represents reasoning, and the superego, the self-critical area. He was developing this theory when he left Austria in 1938 because it was occupied by Nazi Germany.

Anna Freud

In 1938, Freud moved to London, where he died in exile the following year. His work was carried on by his youngest daughter, Anna (1895–1982). A qualified teacher, she specialized in child psychiatry. She founded and directed a world-famous clinic for child therapy in London and wrote several books.

SIGMUND FREUD

1856	Born in Freiburg, Moravia.
1859	Family moves to Vienna.
1886	Begins work as a specialist in nervous disease.
1900	*The Interpretation of Dreams.*
1910	Sets up International Psychoanalytical Association.
1923	Has his first operation for cancer of the jaw; publishes *The Ego and the Id.*
1938	Leaves Vienna for London; publishes *An Outline of Psychoanalysis.*
1939	Dies in London.

FIND OUT MORE
BRAIN AND NERVOUS SYSTEM · GERMANY, HISTORY OF · HOSPITALS · MEDICINE · MEDICINE, HISTORY OF

FRICTION

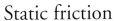

DRAGGING A HEAVY OBJECT across the floor is difficult because of friction, a force that opposes motion. Friction occurs between any two surfaces that are in contact, because even seemingly smooth surfaces have microscopic ridges and troughs that make them grip one another. Friction is greater between rough surfaces than smooth ones. Static friction stops surfaces at rest from moving. Dynamic friction slows down surfaces in motion.

Static friction

Friction acts between these two masses and the wooden slope. Static friction on the stationary block is great enough to prevent it from moving. The moving block has overcome static friction, but it then produces dynamic friction, which limits its speed.

Gravity makes the mass on the smooth surface overcome static friction and slide down the slope.

Smooth surface

Rough surface

The rougher surface increases the force of static friction and prevents the mass from sliding.

Using friction

Friction can be useful. Without friction, no one would be able to walk or run. Friction helps people's shoes grip the ground and stops their feet from sliding out from under them. In the same way, friction enables a vehicle's tyres to grip the road. Most brakes use friction to slow a vehicle down. Friction between surfaces always produces heat, and sometimes electricity.

The pattern on the soles of these shoes is designed to create friction to give maximum grip.

Balloon charged by friction

Disc brakes
When the rider of this motorcycle applies the brakes, a pad presses against the metal disc fixed to the wheel. The rubbing action of the pad against the moving disc produces friction and slows the wheel enough to stop the motorcycle.

Brake pad unit

Disc

The brakes glow as the racing car slows down.

Friction and electricity
Rubbing two objects together can produce a charge of static electricity. Friction between a T-shirt and a balloon will dislodge negatively charged electrons from the atoms of the shirt. The electrons transfer to atoms in the balloon and give it a negative charge, while the shirt becomes positively charged. Opposite charges attract, so the negatively charged balloon clings to the positively charged shirt.

Friction and heat
In cold weather people often rub their hands together to warm them. Friction between two surfaces always produces heat. When a racing car brakes at high speed, the brakes glow red as the energy of the car's movement is changed into heat.

Reducing friction

If two moving machine parts rub together, friction will eventually damage them. Friction in machines generates heat and wastes a great deal of energy. Most methods of reducing friction involve keeping the surfaces apart in some way.

1-kg (2-lb) mass

Mass moves smoothly over flat surface.

Steel roller

Rollers
The rollers under this 1-kg (2-lb) mass allow it to move smoothly over a flat surface. The mass and the surface are not in contact, so there is no friction between them. If the mass is pushed or pulled, the rollers will roll instead of dragging over the surface.

Axle passes through centre.

Outer ring attaches to wheel.

Ball bearing
A ball bearing is a device used to reduce friction between a wheel and its axle. As the wheel turns, the steel balls in the bearing roll around and prevent the wheel and axle from rubbing together.

Lubrication
Using a fluid such as oil to make machine parts move more smoothly and reduce wear is called lubrication. The oil coats the surfaces of the moving parts, preventing them from rubbing together.

Air resistance
Dynamic friction between the air and a moving object is called air resistance. Streamlining gives an object a smooth shape so that air flows more easily around it. Here, smoke trails blown over a streamlined car show how the air moves over its surface.

Hovercraft
A hovercraft overcomes the problem of friction by using high-pressure air as a lubricant. Fans pump air from the atmosphere into a flexible skirt around the craft's hull. This powerful downward jet of air allows the craft to hover over the water, reducing friction with the water's surface to a minimum. Large propellers on top of the craft move it quickly across the water.

Christopher Cockerell

In 1953, English engineer Christopher Cockerell (1910–99) began working on ways to reduce the friction between a ship's hull and the water. His solution was to lift the vessel above the water on a cushion of compressed air. In 1959, after making successful models, he produced the world's first practical hovercraft, called the SR-N1.

FIND OUT MORE   AIR   ATOMS AND MOLECULES   CARS AND TRUCKS   ELECTRICITY   FORCE AND MOTION   HEAT AND TEMPERATURE   MACHINES, SIMPLE   SHIPS AND BOATS

FROGS AND TOADS

THE CROAKING SOUNDS of frogs and toads are often heard in spring as they try to attract a mate. Frogs and toads are amphibians – cold-blooded animals that live both on land and in water. In Europe, they are easy to distinguish – frogs have slimy skins and live mainly in the water; toads have dry, warty skins and live mainly on land. In the tropics, they are more diverse and harder to tell apart. There are more than 2,600 species of frog and toad, living in most parts of the world where there is fresh water. Their habitats range from lakes and marshes, to rainforests, mountains, and deserts.

Features of frogs and toads

Frogs and toads have porous skin – water and air can pass through it – enabling them to breathe through their skin as well as their lungs. Most have sharp teeth, and can see and hear well. They have four legs, varying in length between species. Frogs range in size from a few centimetres long to the West African Goliath frog, which is 40 cm (16 in) in length. Some unusual species are the hairy frog – the male grows hair in the breeding season – and the Borneo flying frog that glides between trees.

Feeding
Most tadpoles are herbivorous, while adult frogs and toads are insectivorous or carnivorous. Prey includes insects, worms, spiders, fish, other frogs, or small reptiles, depending on species. Most species catch insects with their long sticky tongues. Larger frogs and toads rely on ambush. Giant horned toads and bullfrogs have powerful jaws and wide mouths and can even eat mice.

Sticky tongue is used to catch the worm.

Warty skin

Green toad

Short legs for hopping

Hind legs in full stretch

Feet push off from the ground.

Frog in a streamlined position in mid-flight

Back legs are long and very powerful.

Front legs are held back.

Northern leopard frog

Eyes closed for protection

Frogs swim by pulling their hind legs towards their bodies, then kicking them backwards, so pushing themselves forwards through the water.

Webbed feet

Frogs use their front legs like brakes when they enter the water.

Leaping and swimming
Long-legged frogs, such as this Northern leopard frog, can jump more than 30 times their own length in a single leap. When swimming, its long webbed toes help propel it through the water. Short-legged frogs walk, crawl, or do short hops. Some species, such as spade-foot frogs, have feet that can burrow into loose earth. Toads usually have short legs and can only hop weakly or walk. Some species, such as the natterjack toad, can run.

Reproduction

Most frogs and toads mate in water. The male fertilizes the eggs externally as the female lays them; a few species fertilize eggs internally. Some bear live young; others form "mating-balls" of a female and several males. The eggs develop into tadpoles that live in water and breathe through gills. The tadpoles change into air-breathing adults with lungs.

The dark dots develop into tadpoles.

The eggs stick together.

Tadpole uses its tail to swim.

Tiny buds from which front legs will grow.

Back legs

Tail eventually disappears.

Life-cycle of a common frog

1 Eggs stick together to form frogspawn. Each egg contains a dark centre that will become a tadpole. Many eggs are infertile and die, or are attacked by fungus or predators.

2 The newly hatched tadpole lives in the water and breathes through external gills. Most species at this stage are herbivorous and feed on plants.

3 By 6–9 weeks, the tadpole has grown considerably in size. The hind legs have developed. The tadpole now prepares to metamorphose, or change, into a froglet.

4 At 12 weeks, the tail has almost receded. The tadpole has become a froglet. It is now ready to leave the water to begin its adult life – partly on land.

Croaking
Frogs and toads croak to attract mates. Normally, it is the males that croak, using inflatable vocal sacs in the throat. Each species has its own distinctive croak so that the calls of the male only attract females of the same species. This avoids mating between different species in regions where there are many similar frogs and toads.

Painted reed frog

Vocal sac

Defence

Some frogs have poisonous skin that they advertise with bright colours. Others such as tree frogs may secrete bad-tasting sticky substances. Many toads, including cane toads, have poison-secreting glands. Large species, such as horned toads, give painful bites.

Poison dart frog
This South American frog is the most poisonous frog in the world. Its bright skin warns predators that it is poisonous to eat.

Skin is highly toxic.

Golden poison dart frog

Red belly

Fire-bellied toad
Fire-bellied toads in Europe have drab backs but bright red bellies. If threatened, the toad exposes its belly. This flash of colour frightens away predators.

Tree frogs
Tree frogs move with ease within trees. They have sticky discs on their toes and an opposing thumb enabling them to grip most objects, even smooth surfaces. Flying frogs are tree frogs with very large webbed feet that enable them to glide downwards from branch to branch.

Sticky pads on their toes enable them to grip branches.

Red-eyed tree frog

NORTHERN LEOPARD FROG

SCIENTIFIC NAME *Rana pipiens*

ORDER Anura

FAMILY Ranidae

DISTRIBUTION Northern and western USA and Canada, as far south as New Mexico

HABITAT Found in most habitats, even those far from water, which explains its other name of "meadow frog"

DIET Insects

SIZE Length 9–11 cm (3.5–4.5 in)

LIFESPAN Up to 6 years (in captivity)

FIND OUT MORE   AMPHIBIANS   CONSERVATION   EGGS   LAKE AND RIVER WILDLIFE   MARSH AND SWAMP WILDLIFE   POISONOUS ANIMALS   RAINFOREST WILDLIFE   URBAN WILDLIFE   WOODLAND WILDLIFE

Frogs

Colours help camouflage frog in earth and leaf litter.

Colour varies from deep red to pale orange.

Asian painted frogs are burrowers that emerge onto the surface at night and inflate themselves if touched.

Foam-nesting frogs lay eggs in self-made foam in trees above water, into which the tadpoles drop.

Tomato frogs from Madagascar live on land, but breed in slow-moving or stagnant water.

Eyespots look like eyes to confuse predators.

Large digital discs help it land after gliding.

Bright colours indicate it is poisonous to eat.

Long fingers and toes

A diet of tiny invertebrates makes skin poisonous.

Chilean four-eyed frogs have eyespots on their backs that deter predators.

Malayan flying frogs cannot fly, but glide downwards.

Yellow and black poison dart frogs live in cracks in riverside rocks.

Paradoxical frogs develop from tadpoles twice their length and shrink as they "grow".

Green and black poison dart frogs have toxic skin.

Very wide mouth

These toads can reach 20 cm (8 in) in length.

Smooth, slimy skin

Sticky pads below fingers

Golden mantellas are poisonous frogs from Madagascar. They feed on small invertebrates.

African bullfrogs are large, carnivorous frogs that feed on other frogs, reptiles, and even mice and rats.

Common frogs are becoming rarer, partly due to the loss of wetland areas.

White's tree frogs are large Australian frogs.

Toads

Smooth skin is unusual for a toad.

These toads run rather than hop.

Developing eggs

Fleshy horns project over eyes to enhance leaf-like appearance.

Asian tree toads have flat digital discs, enabling them to climb riverside trees.

Natterjack toads, also called running toads, are the rarest toads in Britain.

Male midwife toads carry their eggs on their backs until they hatch into the water.

Asian horned toads resemble dried leaves, to escape discovery on the forest floor.

Narrow fingers used for feeding.

Warty skin

Ornate horned toads may even eat others of the same species.

Cane toads were originally from South America.

Webbed feet

African clawed toads are totally aquatic.

Ornate horned toads from Argentina are large, aggressive toads with huge appetites.

Cane toads were introduced to Australia to control sugar cane pests, but have become pests themselves.

Mexican burrowing toads live in dry areas, rarely emerging onto the surface.

FRUITS AND SEEDS

CHERRIES, TOMATOES, and pea pods are all fruits. A fruit is the part of a plant that contains and protects the seeds. A fruit forms after a flower has been pollinated. First the petals wither and fall, then the part of the flower called the ovary swells. This becomes the fruit, containing one or several seeds, which are the plant's way of reproducing itself. Inside the fruit, the seeds are supplied with nutrients through tiny stalks connecting them to the fruit wall. As the seeds grow, the fruit ripens. Some fruits are sweet and juicy and may be edible; others are inedible, or even poisonous.

Parts of a fruit

In some fruits, the fruit wall, or pericarp, has three distinct layers – an outer epicarp, a middle mesocarp, and a hard, inner endocarp. These layers are easy to see in fleshy fruits, such as plums, but in other fruits the layers are not so clear. The fleshy part of an apple, for example, is actually formed from the receptacle – the swollen tip of the flower stem.

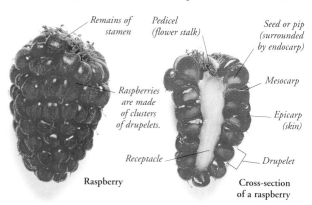

Remains of stamen

Raspberries are made of clusters of drupelets.

Receptacle

Pedicel (flower stalk)

Seed or pip (surrounded by endocarp)

Mesocarp

Epicarp (skin)

Drupelet

Raspberry

Cross-section of a raspberry

How a fruit develops

Once a flower has been pollinated and fertilization has taken place, its ovary becomes known as a fruit. This fruit and the tiny seeds within begin to develop and grow. Graduall y the fruit enlarges, and as it matures, its shape, colour, and texture also change. When a juicy, edible fruit such as this melon ripens, its flesh becomes very sweet and succulent.

The flower is brightly coloured and attracts insects that will pollinate it.

After pollination, the ovary starts to swell.

The flower is no longer needed, so it shrivels up and dies.

The fruit begins to form.

The fruit grows larger as it ripens.

The fruit has ripened and contains hundreds of seeds deep inside.

A melon is a kind of berry.

Parts of a seed

All seeds contain a tiny embryo and seed leaves called cotyledons, which are full of stored food. These are all enclosed in an outer seed coat, called a testa. The embryo has a minute root called a radicle and a tiny stem called a plumule. When the seed germinates, the food store provides nourishment for the tiny seedling.

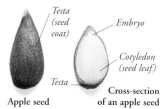

Testa (seed coat)

Embryo

Cotyledon (seed leaf)

Testa

Apple seed

Cross-section of an apple seed

Seed dispersal

Plants need to spread their seeds to increase their chance of survival. Seeds are dispersed by wind, water, and animals. In some plants, parts of the fruit wall or flowerhead also help to spread the seeds. As the fruit dries, the fruit wall splits open and the seeds are scattered.

Dispersal by burial

Seeds are a valuable source of food for mammals and birds. Squirrels and other rodents bury acorns and other nuts, then forget to dig them up. These grow into plants where they were left.

Squirrel burying nuts

Bird dispersal

Brightly coloured orange and red berries attract birds, which like to feed on them. The birds swallow the berries whole but digest only the fleshy part. The seeds pass out, unharmed, in the bird's droppings.

Redwing

Water dispersal

Some fruits and seeds float. Their fruit wall contains oil droplets or air to make them buoyant. Coconut palm fruits float in the sea until they are washed up on a beach.

Coconut growing on a beach

Wind dispersal

Light fruits and seeds are spread by the wind. The seeds of a columbine are scattered when the breeze shakes the seed head. Maple tree seeds have papery wings to carry them on the wind.

Columbine seed head

Animal dispersal

Some seeds are encased inside hooked fruits that can easily become trapped in the fur of mammals. They are carried along by the animals and drop off later in another place.

Bison with seeds trapped in fur

Types of fruit

Simple fruits have a single ovary; compound fruits have more than one. When ripe, some fruits remain succulent; others become woody and hard, or dry and papery, such as larkspur. False fruits develop from other flower parts in addition to the ovary.

Berries

Berries have a combined mesocarp and endocarp layer. They often have many seeds that each have a tough seed coat, or testa.

Grapes

False fruits

In most false fruits, the receptacle swells to enclose the true fruit. Tiny true fruits may also be fixed to the surface of the receptacle.

Pear

Drupes

Drupes, or stone fruits, have a thick, fleshy mesocarp and a woody endocarp – the stone. Fruits such as raspberries are made up of many tiny drupelets.

Plum

Dry fruits

Dry fruits often have lids or seams that open to release the ripe seeds. This capsule has round openings called pores.

Love-in-a-mist capsule

FIND OUT MORE   BIRDS   FLOWERS   FOOD   MAMMALS   PLANTS   PLANTS, ANATOMY   PLANTS, REPRODUCTION   PLANT USES   RATS AND OTHER RODENTS

Succulent fruits

Berries

Kiwanos have a spiky rind to prevent animals from eating them until the seeds are ripe.

Avocados have a single large seed and oily flesh.

Redcurrant seeds are spread by birds.

Persimmons are juicy berries with many seeds.

Grapes each have a tiny stalk and grow in large clusters.

Tomato seeds are covered in a jelly layer that protects them while inside an animal's gut.

Melons are a firm-walled kind of berry called a pepo.

Gooseberry seeds are embedded in juicy flesh.

Lemons are citrus fruits with flesh made of juice-filled hairs.

Lychees have a fleshy layer that grows from the seed stalk.

Rambutans have very hairy skin.

Kiwis have black seeds embedded in firm green flesh.

Drupes and drupelets

Peaches have juicy flesh and a single seed protected inside a woody stone.

Cherries have a single seed inside a hard stone.

Apricots are cultivated fruits that have a single seed inside a woody stone.

Blackberry fruits each consist of many single-seeded drupelets.

Nectarines are a cultivated variety of peach with a smoother skin.

Damsons are small plums. Their seeds are spread when animals eat the flesh.

Mangoes have a large, single seed and sweet flesh.

Greengages are a kind of plum with green or yellow flesh.

Loganberries are made up of many single-seeded drupelets.

Plums have juicy flesh and a single seed inside a stone.

Sago palm fruits have a corky layer that allows them to float.

Coconuts are the fruit of a palm tree.

False fruits

Rowan berries are the swollen tips of the flower stem. They enclose the real fruit.

Apple flesh is the swollen tip of the flower stem, and the pips are the seeds.

Fig fruits are tiny woody pips contained in a fleshy swollen flower stem.

Strawberries consist of a red fleshy receptacle covered in tiny fruits.

Quinces have hard flesh and a seed-filled core.

Breadfruits have many fruits in a large, fleshy flowerhead.

Dry fruits

Honesty has a papery fruit and flat seeds.

Dandelion fruits have hairs that help them float in a breeze.

Goosegrass fruits have hooks that cling to animals' fur.

Sycamore fruits have wings that carry them on the wind.

Larkspur fruits split open to release the seeds.

Hogweed fruits are papery and contain two seeds.

Laburnum pods split to release the hard seeds.

Poppy capsules contain masses of tiny seeds.

Burdock has a head of hooked fruits.

Acorns are nuts with a tough, woody fruit wall.

Sweet chestnuts are enclosed in a spiny case.

Beech nuts are arranged in threes inside a rough case.

FURNITURE

EVERY DAY, PEOPLE SIT on chairs, sleep in beds, and eat from tables. All these are items of furniture, the movable equipment of a home. At one time, furniture was handmade, so most homes contained only basic, functional pieces. A wide range of more affordable furniture became available when production was mechanized in the 19th century. Today, furniture design is largely determined by function, cost, size, and fashion.

The chairs in this Roman sculpture are similar to modern chairs.

Early furniture
Different cultures have produced very similar furniture. The ancient Egyptians had folding beds, and the Romans had armchairs. The earliest furniture to survive was sealed in Egyptian tombs.

Antique furniture
Antiques are objects made more than 100 years ago. Antique furniture was usually handcrafted, using fine materials, in many different styles. Antiques are frequently considered valuable and are highly prized by collectors today.

An 18th-century cabinet

Types of furniture

Furniture made for use in a home is designed to be as comfortable as possible. Choices of shape and fabric let the buyer express personal taste. Office furniture is usually plainer and more functional. Furniture is found outdoors in the form of litter bins, street lamps, and bus stops.

Domestic furniture
Most homes have a bed or a futon. Originally created in Japan for modern, urban life, the futon saves space by serving as a bed at night and a sofa during the day.

Office furniture
Modern office furniture, such as this Anglepoise lamp, is designed to be practical, sturdy, and long-lasting.

The lamp head is easily adjusted.

The heavy base provides balance.

Street furniture
Despite having similar functions, street furniture looks very different all over the world. This elaborate public drinking fountain is in Paris, France.

How an armchair is made

Most modern furniture is mass-produced by machine rather than handcrafted. Furniture such as sofas and armchairs have machine-made parts that are fitted together by hand and then upholstered. This armchair is made from materials that have been built up around a wooden frame.

Steel springs attached to the frame help spread a person's weight evenly.

Arms are cushioned with foam padding and a fleece layer.

Upholsterer fits the fabric covering securely into position.

Castors are small wheels beneath the chair that allow it to be moved easily.

Metal springs make the chair comfortable to sit on.

Upholstery
A layer of padding called upholstery covers the basic wooden frame of a chair. Upholstery also refers to the way in which fabric is fitted to the frame. The top layer of fabric is chosen from a range of colours, patterns, and textures.

Cushions are filled with foam or feathers.

Fabric covering is durable.

Layers of metal mesh and hessian hold the springs in place.

Interior design
In furnishing a room, people try to choose colours, pictures, fabrics, and furniture that go well together. This process is known as interior design. It began in Europe in the 16th century, when furniture makers were first given charge of entire rooms to decorate as a unified whole.

Soft furnishings are materials such as rugs, cushions, and curtains. These materials are chosen to make a room comfortable and to help create its overall look.

Cushions and wallpaper borders are coordinated.

William Morris

The British designer, artist, and socialist William Morris (1834–96) was active in many areas. He was influential in the design of furniture and fabrics, argued for a return to handcrafted furniture, and founded the Arts and Crafts Movement for design.

FIND OUT MORE

ARCHITECTURE   ART, HISTORY OF   CRAFTS   DESIGN   EGYPT, ANCIENT   HOUSES AND HOMES   MUSEUMS

English furniture

Lights

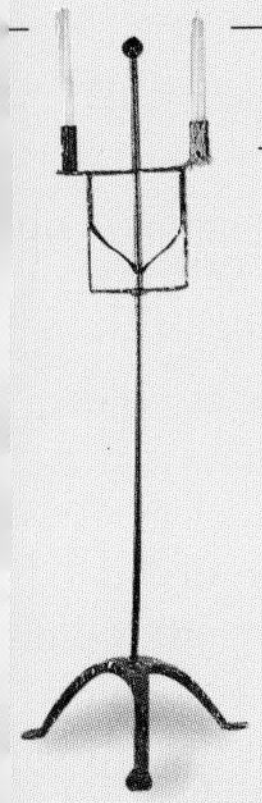

Iron candlestand,
late 17th century

Brass candlesticks,
early 18th century

Bronze storm lamp,
early 19th century

Gilt gaslight pendant,
mid 19th century

Glass electric pendant
with brass edgings, c.1900

Standard lamp,
1930–40

Chairs

Carved oak armchair,
c.1620

Walnut chair,
c.1680

Beech armchair with
caned seat, c.1815

Upholstered chair with beech
and walnut frame, c.1860

Ebonized beech
side-chair, c.1890

Birch veneered
plywood chair, 1989

Tables and cabinets

Pine and oak side-table gilded
in Chinese style, c.1690

Mahogany and walnut table
on a tripod stand, c.1760

Rosewood side-
table, c.1800

Combined games and
needlework table, c.1830

Mahogany table in
Moorish style, c.1895

Maple veneer side-
table, late 1930s

Queen Anne cabinet on chest,
walnut veneer on a pine frame, c.1700

Shelves projecting
from back panel

Open shelf

Cupboard
with painted
panel set
into door

Mahogany cabinet with inset painted panels and
decoration, designed by Lewis F Day in 1880

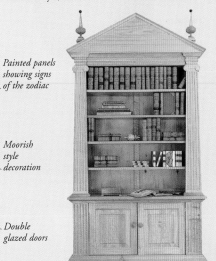

Painted panels
showing signs
of the zodiac

Moorish
style
decoration

Double
glazed doors

Oak bookcase with fluted columns,
handcrafted in a traditional style, 1993

F

GALAXIES

G

A HUNDRED billion galaxies exist in the Universe. Each consists of a vast collection of stars, gas, and dust. They started life thousands of million of years ago, slowly forming into distinctive shapes. Each galaxy can contain billions of stars. Gravity keeps the stars together and keeps the galaxies in clusters.

Milky Way

About 500 billion stars make up the spiral-shaped Milky Way. The arms contain young, hot, bright stars; older, dimmer stars make up the nucleus. A thin halo of old stars surrounds our Galaxy. The Sun is in one of the arms, about two-thirds of the way from the centre. It orbits the centre of the Galaxy once every 220 million years.

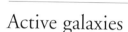

Spiral arm in profile *Central hub*

The Milky Way is about 100,000 light years wide and 13,000 light years across at the central hub.

Types of galaxies

Most galaxies have a central ball of stars, the nucleus, and many have a flattened disc coming out of this. Astronomers have classified galaxies into three main types based on these features. No one knows why galaxies become a particular shape. It may be to do with how fast a galaxy spins and how quickly stars form inside.

Elliptical

About 60 per cent of galaxies are ball-shaped collections of old stars. They range in shape from round to flattened ovals. Astronomers describe their shape with the letter *E* followed by a number between *0* and *7* – the higher the number, the flatter the galaxy.

Spiral

A hub of older stars is surrounded by a flattened disc with spiral arms containing younger stars. The shape of a spiral is described by the letter *S*, followed by a letter between *a* and *d* to indicate how tightly wound the arms are and the size of the hub.

E0   E3   E5   E7   Sa   Sb   Sc

SBa   SBb   SBc

Classification of galaxies by shape

Irregular

About 10 per cent of galaxies are irregular. They are collections of stars with no distinctive shape or structure, and do not fit into any of the classifications. They are smaller than the average galaxy and contain large amounts of gas and dust.

Barred spiral

These galaxies consist of a central bar of older stars with arms containing younger stars coming from the ends of the bar. Barred spirals are described as *SB* followed by a letter from *a* to *d* to indicate how tightly wound the arms are and the size of the hub.

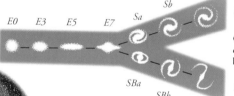

Active galaxies

Unusually large amounts of energy are emitted from some galaxies. This energy may come from an object that is visible, such as a quasar, or from an invisible object, such as the lobes of a radio galaxy. How the energy is created is uncertain, but evidence suggests it could be from a supermassive black hole at the centre of the galaxy.

Quasars

Quasars are the brightest, most distant, fastest moving, and youngest objects visible outside the Milky Way. Thousands are known, each emitting huge amounts of energy. They are found at the heart of large galaxies.

Radio galaxies

Powerful radio energy is emitted by radio galaxies. The energy comes from lobes at either side of the visible core, and is detectable with radio telescopes. Centaurus A is the nearest active galaxy: it is 16 million light years away.

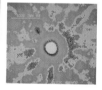

Core

Lobes

Centaurus A

Colliding galaxies

Galaxies can collide as they move through space, as is happening (left) with two galaxies in the constellation of Boötes. Such collisions will change the shape of a galaxy or result in a merger.

Edwin Hubble

In 1923, the American astronomer Edwin Hubble (1889–1953) proved that there are galaxies other than the Milky Way. The next year he classified galaxies according to their shape. He went on to show that galaxies are moving away from each other, and so provided proof that the Universe is expanding.

Galaxy clusters

Galaxies are grouped together in clusters. The Milky Way belongs to a cluster of about 30 galaxies called the Local Group. The Virgo Cluster (right) contains about 2,500 galaxies, mostly spirals.

Superclusters

Clusters of galaxies group together into superclusters that spread across many millions of light years. In turn, hundreds of superclusters group together to form huge walls and filaments, such as the Stick Man, which stretch for hundreds of millions of light years.

The Stick Man contains millions of galaxies.

FIND OUT MORE   ASTRONOMY   BIG BANG   BLACK HOLES   GRAVITY   STARS   UNIVERSE

GALILEO GALILEI

THE ITALIAN SCIENTIST Galileo Galilei was one of the greatest astronomers and physicists of all time. He was the first person to use a telescope to look at the heavens. He started a branch of physics called mechanics, showing that nature obeyed mathematical rules. His belief that science should be based on observation made him one of the first modern scientists. It also led him into trouble, because his views about the Solar System went against those held by the Roman Catholic Church.

Early life
Galileo was born in Pisa, Italy, in 1564. After school he went to the University of Pisa to study medicine. But Galileo was more interested in mathematics and physics, and left without a degree. By the time he was 25, he was back at the university – as professor of mathematics.

Telescope
In 1609, Galileo heard of the invention of the telescope and made one of his own. He used it to look at the heavens and made many astronomical discoveries. He noticed that the planet Venus has phases like the Moon. This gave support to the theory of Nicolaus Copernicus that the planets went round the Sun.

Replica of Galileo's telescope, 1609

Moving bodies
In the 16th century, people believed that the Sun moved around Earth. Galileo did not agree with this, and developed Copernicus's theory of Earth moving around the Sun.

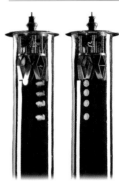

Falling feather

Coin falls at same speed

Gravity
Galileo showed that all objects fall at the same speed, no matter what their weight. Previously, people had believed that heavier objects fell faster. There is a story that Galileo proved his theory by dropping objects from the leaning tower of Pisa, but this is probably not true. He certainly did an experiment like this, in which objects of different weights were dropped in identical jars from which the air was pumped out.

Artist's impression of the Milky Way

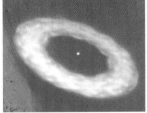

Milky Way
In 1610, Galileo built a telescope that could magnify 1,000 times. It enabled him to see thousands of stars that no human being had ever seen before. He trained his new telescope on the Milky Way and found that it was a vast collection of stars, clustered together in groups of various sizes.

Planet with two moons

Planet with ringlike formations

Galileo's drawings of Saturn

Planets and moons
Through his telescope, Galileo saw what he first thought were two small moons orbiting the planet Saturn. He drew these "moons" in his notebooks. Later observations by Christiaan Huygens identified these as Saturn's rings. Galileo also discovered the four moons that orbit the planet Jupiter, and was able to examine the craters on our own Moon.

The Starry Messenger
In March 1610, Galileo published many of his discoveries in his book, *The Starry Messenger*. The book also showed that Copernicus was right to say that the Earth moved around the Sun, and that the Roman Catholic Church's idea of an unmoving Earth at the centre of the Universe was wrong. *The Starry Messenger* infuriated many churchmen.

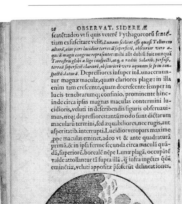

Crater on Moon

Illustrated pages from *The Starry Messenger*, 1610

Inquisition
Galileo's support for Copernicus's ideas outraged the Catholic Church because the priests thought that the Earth should be at the centre of the Universe. In 1633, the Church called Galileo to appear before its court, or inquisition, in Rome. The court ordered him to deny his beliefs under threat of torture. Galileo was forced to agree that Earth was the centre of the Universe, but was heard to mutter, "Yet it *does* move".

Trial of Galileo

GALILEO GALILEI

1564	Born, Pisa, Italy.
1589	Becomes Professor of Mathematics at Pisa University.
1609	Makes his first telescope.
1610	Publishes *The Starry Messenger*.
1632	Publishes *Dialogue*, explaining the two theories of the universe.
1633	Sentenced by the Inquisition.
1642	Dies under house arrest at Arcetri, Italy.

FIND OUT MORE

FORCE AND MOTION · PLANETS · SCIENCE, HISTORY OF · STARS · SUN AND SOLAR SYSTEM · TELESCOPES

GANDHI, MOHANDAS

WHEN THE VAST AND HEAVILY populated nation of India gained independence from Britain in August 1947, one man more than any other was responsible for that achievement. Mohandas Gandhi united the different communities of India and led them to independence. He believed in non-violent protest and despised the racial violence of his homeland. He became known as Mahatma, or "great soul". Although he did not live long enough to see the results of his work, Gandhi is remembered today as the instigator of three movements crucial in the 20th century: the campaigns against racism, colonialism, and violence.

Early life
Mohandas Kamarchand Gandhi was born in Porbandar, India, in 1869. Educated in India and Britain, he trained in law and became a barrister in 1889. In 1893 he moved to work in South Africa. While there, he edited a newspaper called *Indian Opinion* and campaigned against racial injustice, forcing the South African government to grant Indians rights of permanent citizenship in 1914.

Indian nationalism

The British had controlled India since the 18th century, but many Indians wanted to govern themselves. In 1915, Gandhi returned from South Africa and became one of the leaders of the independence movement. He led many peaceful campaigns against British rule, using the tactic of non-violent civil disobedience. He called this method Satyagraha ("holding to the truth"). It was copied by many civil-rights campaigners around the world.

Gandhi with Jawaharlal Nehru, leader of the socialist wing of Congress

Congress
The Indian National Congress Party was founded in 1885. Its members wanted to increase Indian participation in government and represent all religions and cultures. During the 1920s, under the leadership of Gandhi and Jawaharlal Nehru, Congress took the lead in campaigning for Indian independence.

Gandhi's spectacles

Gandhi's sandals

Gandhi lived a simple life, wearing plain clothes and keeping only a few possessions.

Gandhi's watch

Imprisonment
During his many campaigns, Gandhi was often imprisoned by the British for civil disobedience. But after each spell in prison, Gandhi emerged more powerful and more respected than before. His personal prestige was so high that people began to call him Mahatma, the "great soul". He alone seemed able to unite the diverse elements of the independence movement that represented the many different religions and cultures in the huge subcontinent of India.

Salt march
The British controlled the production of salt in India. This monopoly forced up prices and was very unpopular. In 1930, Gandhi led a 320-km (200-mile) march to the sea to get his own salt and thousands joined him on the way. Gandhi was imprisoned for civil disobedience, but the march showed the power of Satyagraha.

Social reforms

In 1937, the Indian provinces received a large measure of home rule. The Congress Party took control of seven of the 11 provinces and began to reform the country. Gandhi pushed for social, economic, and educational improvements designed to rebuild India. He encouraged crafts such as spinning cotton, because he believed that small cottage industries could help India's villages.

Gandhi spinning cotton

Independence

In 1947, India gained its independence. Hindus in the Congress Party wanted a united India, but Muslims wanted a country of their own. The country was, therefore, divided into India and Pakistan, a division Gandhi bitterly opposed.

Assassination
Gandhi took little part in the independence talks, but threatened to fast to death to protest against the violence between Hindus and Muslims. In January 1948, he was assassinated by a Hindu fanatic who resented his concern for the Muslims.

Monument at the place where Gandhi died

MOHANDAS GANDHI

1869 Born in Porbandar, India.

1889 Becomes a barrister in England.

1891–93 Works as a lawyer in India.

1893–1915 Works in South Africa.

1920s Takes control of Congress Party with Nehru.

1930 Leads salt march to the sea.

1942 Launches Quit India campaign during World War II, and is interned until 1944.

1945 New British government promises independence by 1947.

1947 India gains its independence.

1948 Gandhi is assassinated.

FIND OUT MORE EMPIRES HINDUISM HUMAN RIGHTS INDIA, HISTORY OF SOUTH AFRICA, HISTORY OF

GARBO, GRETA

SOPHISTICATED, SUPERIOR, scornful, and beautiful, Greta Garbo was everyone's idea of the perfect film star. The daughter of a poor labourer in Stockholm, Sweden, she conquered Hollywood in the 1920s and 1930s. Her audiences adored her, but at the height of her career she retired, becoming a recluse and never showing her face in public again. Yet this most celebrated actor received no Oscars, only a belated special award for her unforgettable films.

Early life
Greta Gustafson was born in the Swedish capital of Stockholm in 1905. Her family was poor, and she worked from an early age in a barber's shop and a department store. Her first film part was in *How Not to Dress*, a publicity film for the store.

Training
Early in her career, Garbo appeared as the female lead in a slapstick comedy, *Peter the Tramp*. She then applied for and won a scholarship to Sweden's Royal Dramatic Theatre training school, where she was soon playing small parts on stage.

Mauritz Stiller
While at training school, Garbo was spotted by the Swedish film director Mauritz Stiller. Stiller was best known for such films as the comedy *Love and Journalism,* and the sexually charged movie *Erotikon.* Stiller took a special interest in Garbo's career, gave her the surname Garbo, and made her into a star.

Garbo and Mauritz Stiller

First success
Garbo's first major film role was as the star of *The Atonement of Gösta Berling*. The film was a romantic tale of a priest set in the Swedish countryside. The premiere in Stockholm in 1924 attracted a huge audience and launched Garbo on her film career.

Still from *Gösta Berling*

Hollywood
In 1925, after the success of *Gösta Berling*, Garbo moved to Hollywood, the centre of the US film industry. She signed a contract with Metro-Goldwyn-Mayer (MGM) and began filming *The Torrent*. Her first major success was *Flesh and the Devil*, made in 1926 and directed by Clarence Brown. By 1927, she was earning $5,000 a week from MGM. In all, Garbo made 24 films in Hollywood, and became one of the most famous, and best-paid, film stars in the world.

Studio system
Film-making in Hollywood was dominated by a few large companies, such as MGM, Paramount, and Warner Bros. These and other studios kept actors and directors on tight contracts, so that they could not work for a rival company. As a result, Garbo was forced to star in films she did not like.

Anna Karenina
Garbo's reputation as a tragic heroine was established by *Anna Karenina* (1935), based on the novel by the great Russian writer Leo Tolstoy. The film won numerous awards and confirmed Garbo's reputation as the leading actress of her day.

"Garbo talks!"
In 1930, the first sound film starring Garbo appeared. The publicity slogan was "Garbo talks!". The film, *Anna Christie,* had a heroine with a Swedish accent. The producers thought this would be an ideal role for Garbo. They believed that audiences might not otherwise accept her heavily accented voice.

Garbo laughs
Garbo's reputation was as a serious, intense actress. In 1939, she astounded audiences with her relaxed performance in the romantic comedy *Ninotchka.* Publicity for the film made much of her laughter in this role.

A life apart
In 1941, Garbo announced her retirement from making films, having no wish to disappoint her admirers by growing old on screen. Despite her success in Europe, her popularity was declining in the USA. She became an American citizen in 1951 and led the life of a recluse, although she remained friends with many famous people.

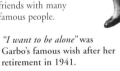

"I want to be alone" was Garbo's famous wish after her retirement in 1941.

GRETA GARBO

1905	Born in Stockholm, Sweden.
1924	Stars in *The Atonement of Gösta Berling,* her first major film.
1925	Moves to the USA and signs contract with MGM.
1930	Has her first talking role, in *Anna Christie.*
1935	*Anna Karenina.*
1938	Nominated for an Oscar for *Camille.*
1939	*Ninotchka.*
1941	Retires from film-making.
1954	Honoured at Academy Awards.
1990	Dies in New York.

FIND OUT MORE   CAMERAS   FILMS AND FILM-MAKING   LITERATURE

GARDENS

LIKE LANDSCAPES in miniature, gardens are set-aside areas of land where plants are grown to provide beauty and relaxation. Gardens have a practical purpose too. From ancient times, they have helped people nurture plants for food and medicine. They reduce noise and air pollution in cities, and create a refreshing environment in a hot climate. Glorious landscaped gardens can enhance the finest modern buildings, and botanic gardens are places of scientific study.

Tools

Gardeners use a variety of tools. Some have hardly changed in hundreds of years, such as forks. Mechanical aids such as the lawnmower, invented in 1832, are relatively new developments.

Shears, for cutting hedges

Thick blades

Used for digging soil

Spade and fork

Watering can

Trowel

Hand fork

Clipped shrubs

Development of gardens

Gardens have an ancient history. They were planted in Mesopotamia, China, Egypt, Persia, and Greece. The Romans spread knowledge of gardening to northern Europe during their rule of the Mediterranean lands. From the 4th century AD, when Roman power declined, monks continued the tradition of cultivating plants in monastery gardens. European gardens were enclosed by abbey or castle walls until the Renaissance.

China and Japan

Gardens in China and Japan often have a religious significance, where nature itself is honoured. This tradition is centuries old. For Zen Buddhists, landscaped gardens of raked gravel, where a rock may represent a mountain, are places of silent meditation.

Temple garden, Kyoto, Japan

Islamic gardens

North African Moors created shady courtyard gardens, with pools and fountains to reflect the sky and cool the air. When they conquered Spain in the 8th century, the Moors took the style to Europe, as seen in the Court of the Myrtles, the Alhambra, Spain.

Renaissance formality

During the Renaissance in the 14th century, architects planned gardens as settings for the grand houses they designed. Fashionable gardens were formal, open, and regular, reviving a style established by the Romans.

Villa Lante, Bagnaia, Lazio, Italy

This small Classical temple, in a wooded glade, is typical of the Jardin Anglais style.

18th-century naturalism

The Jardin Anglais (English garden) style spread through Europe during the 18th century. The trend was first set by the English architect William Kent (c.1685–1748), who planned less formal gardens than had been common previously. He used an open style, which he believed to look more natural, to set off the formality of his buildings.

Chiswick House, London, England

Botanic gardens

In botanic gardens, specimen plants are collected and cultivated for scientific study. They developed from the herb or physic gardens tended by medieval monks, where plants were grown for medicinal purposes.

Plant collectors

From the late 1600s, European explorers returned from their world expeditions with many new and exotic varieties of plant. Serious plant-collecting expeditions began in the 18th century, bringing back specimens for scientific study and to decorate gardens.

The peony, a native of China, was taken to Europe by plant collectors.

Roberto Burle Marx

Brazilian garden designer Roberto Burle Marx (1909–1994) created stunning gardens for modern buildings in Brazil, using only plants native to his country. He made Brazilians more aware of the amazing plants found in their countryside.

Wildlife gardens

In the 20th century, gardeners became more interested in the wild creatures that inhabited their plants, trees, and ponds. Instead of treating them as pests, they welcomed wildlife. Careful planting of a wildlife garden creates many different habitats, encouraging the widest possible range of animal visitors.

Gardeners plant flowers that attract insects.

FIND OUT MORE

ARCHITECTURE   BUDDHISM   ISLAMIC EMPIRE   MEDICINE, HISTORY OF   MONASTERIES   PLANT USES   RENAISSANCE

G

GASES

WHEN YOU CATCH an unpleasant smell given off by a chemistry experiment, your nose is detecting the presence of a gas released by a chemical reaction. A gas is a type of matter with no fixed shape or volume. Not all gases have a smell, and many are invisible, but all are made up of tiny, fast-moving particles that move rapidly and randomly.

G

Gas particles
The forces between the speeding particles of a gas are too weak to hold them in one place, so the gas spreads out.

Nitrogen dioxide gas soon escapes from the beaker and mingles with the air.

Copper and nitric acid react, releasing brown nitrogen dioxide gas.

Properties of gases
A gas quickly spreads out to fill any available space because its free-moving particles travel in all directions. The higher the temperature of a gas, the more energy its particles have and the faster they move. The pressure of a gas is linked to the number of collisions between the gas particles and the walls of its container: the more frequent the collisions are, the greater the pressure the gas exerts.

Amedeo Avogadro
In 1806, an Italian lawyer named Amedeo Avogadro (1776–1856) gave up his legal career to devote himself to the study of physics. In 1811, Avogadro proposed that equal volumes of all gases at the same temperature and pressure will contain the same number of particles. This is now called Avogadro's Law.

Condensation

Tiny droplets form on the inside of a cold window when water vapour in the air is cooled by the glass and turns into liquid water. The change of a gas to a liquid is called condensation. As a gas cools, its particles lose energy and slow down. The forces between the particles grow stronger and pull them together to form a liquid.

Vapour
A gas normally forms when a liquid boils. However, a type of gas called a vapour sometimes forms when a liquid is below its boiling point. Paint, for example, dries when liquid particles at its surface gain enough energy to escape into the air as a vapour.

Gas laws
The gas laws are a set of proven theories that allow scientists to predict how a gas will behave when there is a change in its volume, pressure, or temperature. The laws apply only when a gas is held in a sealed container.

Charles's Law
This law, formulated by French physicist Jacques Charles (1746–1823), states that the volume of a gas at a constant pressure is proportional to its temperature. Thus, when the temperature of the gas halves, so does its volume.

1 When a gas-filled balloon is cooled in liquid nitrogen at -196°C (-321°F), the gas particles slow down.

2 The particles strike the balloon walls less often, so the gas volume shrinks, and the balloon collapses.

3 As the gas warms again in the air, the gas particles speed up, the volume expands, and the balloon reflates.

The air molecules collide more often with the syringe walls, so the air pressure rises.

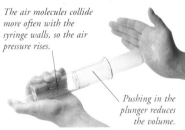

Pushing in the plunger reduces the volume.

Boyle's Law
Put your finger over the end of a syringe, push in the plunger, and you will feel the air pressure in the syringe rising. The air obeys Boyle's Law, formulated by the Irish physicist Robert Boyle (1627–91). The law states that when a gas is at a constant temperature, its pressure is inversely proportional to its volume. In other words, if the volume halves, the pressure doubles.

Pressure inside the can blows off the lid.

Pressure Law
Heating a sealed can raises the air pressure inside the can until it is so great that the lid blows off. The air obeys the Pressure Law, which states that when a gas's volume is constant, its pressure is proportional to its temperature. This means that if the gas's temperature doubles, so will its pressure.

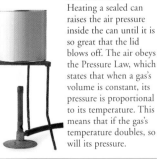

Brownian motion
Dust particles can often be seen dancing in shafts of sunlight. Their random, jittery path is caused by tiny, unseen air molecules that bombard the dust particles. This motion – called Brownian Motion after Robert Brown (1773–1858), a Scottish biologist – shows that gas particles are constantly moving.

Diffusion
When a jar of bromine gas and a jar of air are placed together, the gases quickly intermingle as their moving particles spread out to fill all the available space. This process is called diffusion. Food cooking in the kitchen is soon smelt throughout the house as gas particles released by the food rapidly diffuse in the air. Diffusion also occurs when solids and liquids dissolve to form solutions.

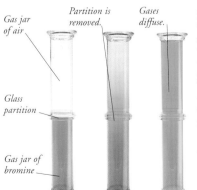

Gas jar of air

Partition is removed.

Gases diffuse.

Glass partition

Gas jar of bromine

FIND OUT MORE   AIR   ATOMS AND MOLECULES   HEAT   LIQUIDS   MATTER   PRESSURE   SOLIDS

GENETICS

EACH PERSON IS UNIQUE, but he or she also inherits some characteristics and even appearance from his or her parents. The study of how characteristics are passed on from parents to offspring is known as genetics, and it affects all forms of life. At the centre of the process is the deoxyribonucleic acid (DNA) molecule, which exists inside every living cell and contains a complex chemical "code" that controls the way in which life forms are put together and operate. DNA is composed of genes, and DNA, in turn, makes up chromosomes. All of these microscopic structures live in the nuclei of cells.

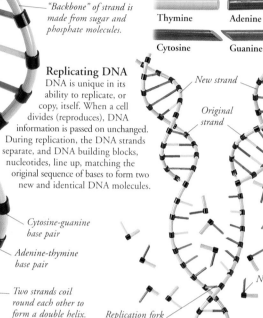

"Backbone" of strand is made from sugar and phosphate molecules.

Cytosine-guanine base pair

Adenine-thymine base pair

Two strands coil round each other to form a double helix.

A length of DNA molecule

DNA

A DNA molecule contains all the information required to make and operate a specific organism. DNA is found in the nucleus of a cell and is a long structure which consists of two strands twisted together to form a double helix. The strands are linked by four chemicals called bases: thymine, adenine, cytosine, and guanine.

Thymine	Adenine
Cytosine	Guanine

Replicating DNA
DNA is unique in its ability to replicate, or copy, itself. When a cell divides (reproduces), DNA information is passed on unchanged. During replication, the DNA strands separate, and DNA building blocks, nucleotides, line up, matching the original sequence of bases to form two new and identical DNA molecules.

New strand

Original strand

Nucleotide

Replication fork

DNA replication

Original double helix, or parent DNA molecule

Chromosomes

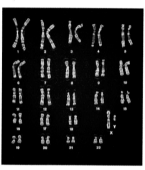

A chromosome is a thread-like structure found in the nucleus of a cell. Chromosomes store DNA and carry DNA molecules when a cell reproduces by dividing. Most human cells contain 46 chromosomes, divided into 23 pairs; 23 chromosomes are derived from each of the parents.

Chromosomes, stained and paired

Chromosome defects
A chromosome defect can result from the wrong number of chromosomes, a missing piece of chromosome, or an unnecessary extra piece. Alternatively, there may be a "mistake" in part of the DNA. Any of these can cause a genetic disorder before or after birth, or later in life.

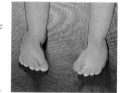

Genetic defect causes malformed feet.

An albino squirrel is a mutation.

Mutations
A mutation is an accidental change in the structure of part of a DNA molecule, or sometimes in the number or shape of chromosomes. Mutations may result in new or unusual characteristics.

Variations
While members of a species look similar, they are not identical, as we can see from people around us. Variation happens because each individual receives a unique combination of DNA from its parents during reproduction.

Variations in types of flowers

Genes

A gene is the basic unit of inheritance, a small segment of a DNA molecule. There are about 100,000 genes in the 46 human chromosomes. Genes contain the instructions to construct proteins, which control cell activities. Therefore, genes help to determine the characteristics of an organism.

Genotype and phenotype
The genotype is the overall genetic blueprint for an organism. The phenotype is what an organism actually looks like, based on genotype and environment.

Alleles
Each gene has two or more forms called alleles. They control the same characteristic (for example, eye colour) but different versions of it (for instance, blue or brown).

Franklin, Watson, and Crick
The discovery of the DNA molecule was a collaborative effort. Rosalind Franklin (1920–58) completed groundbreaking work, which was consolidated in 1953 by Francis Crick (b.1916), James Watson (b.1928), and Maurice Wilkins (b.1916). Watson, Crick, and Wilkins shared the 1962 Nobel Prize.

James Watson, American biologist

Rosalind Franklin, British biochemist

Francis Crick, British scientist

Grey-blue eye, round-shaped, with long eyelashes, and large eyelid

Dark brown eye, almond-shaped, with short eyelashes

Medium-brown eye with fine eyelashes, and small eyelid

Heredity

Heredity is the transmission of characteristics from one generation to the next. These inherited characteristics, such as size, shape, and colour, are determined by genes passed on by parents. When different forms of the same genetic characteristic meet (for example, blue and brown eye colour), some genes are dominant (effective) and some are recessive (ineffective).

Family inheritance

Children inherit genetic traits and characteristics from parents.

Each child is unique because it inherits a different mix of genes from its parents.

Each child resembles, but is not identical to, its parents.

Parent's genotype: two dominant alleles

Sex cell genotype

Sex cell genotype

Parent's genotype: two recessive alleles

Pink flower

Sex cell genotype

White flower

Sex cell genotype: parent genotype divides during reproduction

Frame containing four offspring of pink parent with white parent

Dominant genes

If two forms of the same gene, alleles, are present in the same cell, only the dominant gene exerts its effect. In this case, R, the gene that controls pink flower colour, is the dominant gene, so the colour white remains recessive.

Parent's genotype

Sex cell genotype

Sex cell genotype

Parent's genotype

Parent with one dominant gene and one recessive gene

Sex cell genotype

Parent with one dominant gene and one recessive gene

Sex cell genotype

White flower colour produced by two recessive genes

Recessive genes

A recessive gene is one of a pair of alleles that, if present in a cell with its dominant partner, does not exert its effect. If two recessive genes are in the cell, however, they prove effective. In this case, r, the gene that controls white flower colour, is recessive until it meets another recessive gene: together they are effective.

Diagrams show fertilization between two parent flowers, and how genes determine colour in offspring.

Sex chromosomes

Whether an animal is male or female is determined by one pair of chromosomes called the sex chromosomes. In humans and other mammals, a female's sex chromosomes are identical and are called XX. In males, one chromosome is smaller, and the pair is called XY.

Human X chromosome

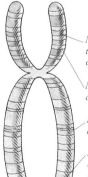

Mutation in gene in this area causes a form of muscular dystrophy.

Mutation in gene here causes an eye disease.

Mutation in gene here causes cleft palate.

Mutation in gene here causes haemophilia, a disease that affects blood clotting.

Sex determination
Sperm and eggs each carry one sex chromosome. Eggs carry an X chromosome, and sperm carry an X or a Y. When a sperm and an egg meet during fertilization, there is a 50:50 chance of producing a male (XY) or a female (XX), depending on which chromosome the sperm is carrying.

Most ginger cats are male.

Tortoise-shell cats are always female.

Sex-linked inheritance

Sex chromosomes also carry genes that determine other characteristics apart from an animal's sex. More of these sex-linked genes are found on X chromosomes than Y. So some characteristics are specific only to males or to females.

Genetic code

DNA contains the instructions to make the proteins that construct the cell and control its functions. Four chemical bases – adenine (A), cytosine (C), guanine (G), and thymine (T) – combine in pairs to form a sequence, or code. The cell then translates this code and produces a protein.

Human Genome Project

The genome is the complete set of genes found in the nucleus of every body cell. In the 1980s the Human Genome Project set out to identify all of those genes by working out the sequence of bases. In 2001 they announced the existence of some 30,000 genes.

Genetic codes are made up of bases (A, C, G, T).

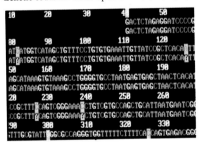

Genetic engineering

Genetic engineering involves taking genes from one cell and inserting them into another cell. This gives the cell new characteristics, which are determined by the transferred gene. In the future, genetic engineering may be used on human cells, so that genetic disorders can be eliminated.

Genetically modified (GM) food

Food products can also be altered by genetic modification or engineering. For example, scientists can genetically engineer certain fruits and vegetables, so that they do not rot so quickly. There is much debate about the safety of GM foods.

Genetically modified tomatoes

 FIND OUT MORE   BIOLOGY   CELLS   DISEASES   FOOD   HUMAN BODY   PLANTS, REPRODUCTION   REPRODUCTION

GEOLOGY

PEOPLE ONCE THOUGHT that the Earth was just a simple ball of rock. Recently geologists have shown that it is much more complex. Geology is the study of the Earth's history, structure, and composition. Originally only the study of rocks and rock structures, the scope of geological study broadened after the discovery in the 1960s that the Earth's crust is made up of giant, continually moving plates. These plates affect everything from the creation of continents to the eruption of volcanoes. The science of geology also helps us to locate mineral reserves, and to understand our environment.

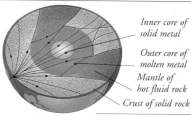

Inner core of solid metal
Outer core of molten metal
Mantle of hot fluid rock
Crust of solid rock

Structure of the Earth
Geophysicists and geochemists study the structure of the Earth. Geophysicists focus on its physical processes, such as the circulation of heat deep inside; geochemists study the Earth's chemical composition.

Seismographs
The seismic waves, earthquake vibrations, are picked up by seismographs. These can reveal to geologists the structure of the rock they have passed through.

Seismographs

Rock and field geology
Petrology is the study of rocks and minerals. Surveys and rock samples indicate the occurrence of different rocks beneath the landscape, their structure, and their history.

The rock strata
Many rocks were formed in strata (layers) of sediment deposited on the seabed. Stratigraphy is the study of these layers. A break in a sequence of rock layers is called an unconformity, shown as a red line on the models below.

James Hutton
Scottish–born James Hutton (1726–97) was the founder of modern geology. With his collection and analysis of rock formations, he proved that the Earth was more than just a few thousand years old, and that all its rocks and land-forms had been formed over millions of years.

Angular unconformity – the older rock strata below the unconformity are at a different angle to the new layers.

Parallel conformity – strata either side of unconformity dip at the same angle.

Limestone pavement

Evidence of old landscape shaped long before the rocks above were formed.

Disconformity – an irregular eroded surface between parallel strata.

Nonconformity – strata overlie eroded surface of igneous or metamorphic rock

Rock strata models

Key to strata:
- Shale
- Conglomerate
- Red Sandstone
- / Unconformity
- Igneous rock
- Mudstone
- Clay
- Sandstone

Geologist's hammers
Chisels
Goggles
Club hammer for use with chisels.

Tools
In order to examine the Earth's structure, geologists need some basic tools. These are goggles to protect their eyes from fly-ing rock chips, and a hammer and chisel for collecting rock samples.

Depth	Era	Period	Epoch	Mya
				0 Mya
	Cenozoic	Quaternary	Holocene	0.01
			Pleistocene	1.6
		Tertiary	Pliocene	6.3
20km (12 miles)			Miocene	23
			Oligocene	36.6
			Eocene	53
			Palaeocene	66
40km (25 miles)	Mesozoic	Cretaceous		135
		Jurassic		205
60 km (37 miles)		Triassic		250
		Permian		290
80 km (50 miles)	Palaeozoic	Carbon-iferous	Pennsylvanian (North America)	320
			Mississippian (North America)	355
100 km (62 miles)		Devonian		410
		Silurian		438
120 km (75 miles)		Ordovician		510
		Cambrian		570
140 km (87 miles)		Precambrian		4,600

Key:
- / Mud
- / Limestone
- / Sandstone
- / Shale
- / Metamorphic

Historical geology
The study of rocks of the Earth's crust is explored within historical geology. Just as the day is split into hours, minutes, and seconds, geological history is split into units called eras (lasting millions of years), periods, and epochs.

Geological rock column
If layers of rock remained undisturbed, a column cut down through the layers would reveal the sequence in which they formed. The rock types shown along the side of this visual representation of geological time, are the predominant rocks of each period.

Geologists locate rock structures likely to contain oil; drilling can confirm this.

Exploration and survey
Each mineral in the Earth's crust is linked to a different type of geological structure. After using satellite and aerial surveys to target a particular area, the geologist then uses specific instruments to pinpoint the mineral.

FIND OUT MORE EARTH • EARTHQUAKES • EARTH SCIENCES • FOSSILS • ROCKS AND MINERALS • VOLCANOES

GERMANY

THE FEDERAL REPUBLIC of Germany lies at the heart of Europe, bounded by nine other nations and the Baltic and North Seas. Since the country was reunified in 1990, it is, more than ever, a link between east and west for both trade and culture. Germany is one of the world's wealthiest nations and Europe's leading industrial power. It was a founder member of the European Union and plays a key role in international affairs. Germany has the second largest population in Europe after Russia.

Physical features

Germany has a varied landscape. It includes lakes, heaths, and islands in the north, fertile pastures and great forests in the centre and southwest, and great mountains, such as the Bavarian Alps, in the south.

G

River Rhine

The Rhine is one of Europe's most important rivers. It rises in the Swiss Alps and flows into the North Sea at Rotterdam in the Netherlands. The total length is about 1,320 km (820 miles), nearly half of which is in Germany. Long barges regularly carry freight such as coal, grain, and timber. Many tourists visit the southern part of the Rhine to see the scenery, vineyards, and castles that flank its sides.

Black Forest

Germany's Black Forest lies in the southwest of the country. The name comes from the dark conifers that clothe its mountain slopes and provide timber for the traditional wooden houses. Tourists flock to the region, attracted by the beauty of the scenery, spa resorts, such as Baden-Baden, and Lake Constance, which lies nearby.

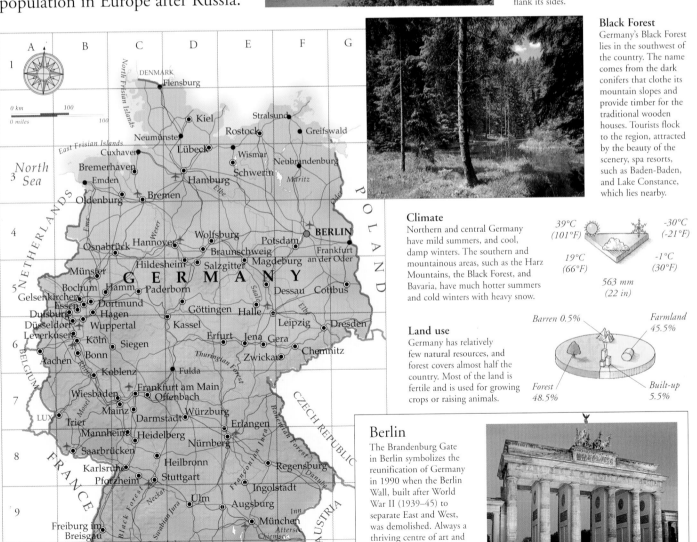

Climate

Northern and central Germany have mild summers, and cool, damp winters. The southern and mountainous areas, such as the Harz Mountains, the Black Forest, and Bavaria, have much hotter summers and cold winters with heavy snow.

39°C (101°F) -30°C (-21°F)

19°C (66°F) -1°C (30°F)

563 mm (22 in)

Land use

Germany has relatively few natural resources, and forest covers almost half the country. Most of the land is fertile and is used for growing crops or raising animals.

Barren 0.5% Farmland 45.5%

Forest 48.5% Built-up 5.5%

Berlin

The Brandenburg Gate in Berlin symbolizes the reunification of Germany in 1990 when the Berlin Wall, built after World War II (1939–45) to separate East and West, was demolished. Always a thriving centre of art and culture, there are plans to rebuild this grand capital, Germany's largest city.

Brandenburg Gate

G

People

About 92 per cent of the people are Germans. Turks make up the largest minority group of more than 2,000,000, having gone to Germany in the 1960s to boost the labour force. Since 1990, many immigrants have arrived from eastern Europe. Some racial discrimination has caused social tension.

235 per sq km (609 per sq mile)   87% Urban   13% Rural

Society
German society prides itself on equal opportunities and a comprehensive social welfare system, with free education and healthcare. Germans are environmentally aware, and the influence of the Green Party has led to strict anti-pollution policies.

Leisure

The Germans love sports and outdoor activities. Many enjoy hiking and cycling in the countryside, or canoeing and sailing on the lakes and rivers. In winter, skiing and skating are popular. Germans also excel at football, tennis, and motor-racing.

Skiing
Snow-covered slopes in the Bavarian Alps provide Germans with plenty of opportunities to practise their skiing. Children begin the sport early. Many people also travel to nearby French and Swiss ski resorts.

Football
The German national team has won the World Cup three times, as well as the Euro '96 cup against the Czech Republic. Association football, or soccer, is the most popular sport in Germany both for players and spectators, and there are many clubs.

Farming

Only three per cent of Germany's labour force work on the land, yet the country grows about two-thirds of all the food it needs. Crops include cereals, potatoes, and other vegetables. Pigs and cattle are reared.

Wheat

Grapes

Crops
Germany's chief cereal crops are barley, oats, rye, and wheat. Sugar beet for refining to produce sugar is also widely grown. Grapes grow best in the areas bordering the Rhine and Moselle rivers, and are used for producing Germany's world-famous white wines.

Sugar beet

Dairy
The lush green pastures of Germany's Allgäu valley, in the Alps, are ideal for grazing dairy cattle for milk, butter, and cheese.

Food

German people enjoy traditional smoked sausages, smoked meats and cheese, *sauerkraut* (pickled cabbage), and smoked and pickled fish, usually eaten with good, sourdough bread and a glass of cold beer. They also make tasty soups, sweet and savoury dumplings, and enjoy afternoon *Kaffee und Kuchen*, coffee with cakes.

Lid keeps flies out of beer.   *Gherkin*   *Salami*

Wurst

Smoked sausage

Beer stein   **Selection of meats**   *Bread*

Industry

Over the last 50 years, Germany has become one of the world's leading industrial nations, and is an important manufacturer of cars, trucks, electrical goods, ships, and chemicals. The heart of German industry lies in the Ruhr, once a major coal-producing region.

Cars
Germany is one of the world's largest car manufacturers. Volkswagen is an internationally renowned make. Other famous brands are BMW, Mercedes-Benz, and Porsche.

Transport

Germany has an excellent transport system with 14 international airports, major sea ports in Hamburg and Bremen, and a highly efficient rail and road network. Canals and rivers, such as the Rhine and Ruhr, carry as much freight as the roads.

Inland waterways
Many of Germany's rivers are linked by canals, like the Danube-Main canal, creating an extensive network that makes long-distance freight transport practical.

Shipbuilding
Hamburg, Germany's largest port on the mouth of the Elbe river, has a long tradition of shipbuilding, as has Bremen on the mouth of the River Weser. Germany leads the rest of Europe in shipbuilding, and ranks highly in the world.

Precision work
Electronic devices such as calculators, computers, and electrical equipment such as this drill, form a large part of Germany's industrial output. The country also produces precision optical equipment.

Autobahns
Germany has Europe's most elaborate motorway network stretching almost 11,400 km (7,084 miles), with no speed limit. The first *Autobahn* was built in the 1930s for military use.

FIND OUT MORE CARS AND TRUCKS   EUROPE   EUROPE, HISTORY OF   EUROPEAN UNION   FARMING   FOOTBALL   GERMANY, HISTORY OF   PORTS AND WATERWAYS   SHIPS AND BOATS

GERMANY, HISTORY OF

ALTHOUGH THERE HAVE ALWAYS been German speakers living in Europe, a single German country did not exist until 1871. For much of its history, Germany consisted of many small kingdoms, duchies, and other states, kept apart by rivalries. Unification was eventually achieved under the diplomatic and military leadership of the north German state of Prussia. German industrial strength allowed the new nation to dominate Europe, but defeat in two world wars left the country divided again. In 1990, Germany reunited, and once more became the major economic power of Europe.

German tribes
In about 370, Huns from Asia swept into Germany, forcing native German tribes to pour into the neighbouring Roman Empire. Within a century, Rome had collapsed, and Germanic tribes such as the Visigoths and Franks controlled much of western Europe.

Brooch made by Germanic Lombard tribe

Medieval Germany

In 962, Otto I of Saxony united the German kingdoms in the Holy Roman Empire. This empire was long-lasting but weak, as local rulers fought to protect and increase their own power. Despite this disunity, the country became increasingly rich. By the late 15th century, German cities such as Augsburg controlled European banking and finance.

Ulm cathedral

Seal of Hamburg

Hanseatic League
The cities of northern Germany worked together to support their trading interests. In 1241, Lübeck and Hamburg concluded a treaty that led to the growth of the Hanseatic League, a trading alliance that dominated commerce in northern Europe. At its height there were 160 cities in the League.

Coming of Christianity
From the 5th century onwards, individual Germans became Christian. Some churches, such as Ulm Cathedral, were founded in the early 7th century, but it was not until the mission of St Boniface in the early 8th century that most of the people converted to Christianity.

Isenheim Altarpiece, by Mathias Grünewald

German Renaissance
In the 15th century, the Renaissance spread to Germany. Artists such as Albrecht Dürer (1471–1528) perfected the technique of the woodcut, Hans Holbein (1498–1543), working mostly in Switzerland and England, produced superb portraits, and Mathias Grünewald (1480–1528) painted religious masterpieces.

Peasants' War

In the 16th century, there was much tension between Catholics and Protestants in Germany. In 1524, peasants in southern Germany exploited the confusion to rise up and demand social reforms. The revolt was crushed in 1526.

Peasant rebellion in southern Germany

Thirty Years' War

In 1618, a revolt broke out in the Protestant province of Bohemia against the rule of the Catholic Habsburgs. War spread through Germany as Protestant princes rebelled against the Habsburgs. Other nations, notably France and Sweden, entered the war on the Protestant side to end Habsburg domination of Europe.

Inscription says that the owner "Fights for God".

Treaties of Westphalia
When the treaties ended the Thirty Years' War in 1648, German agriculture and commerce were in ruins, and the population had been reduced by half. The Habsburgs were seriously weakened by the years of conflict and Germany was more disunited than ever before, split into no fewer than 234 states and 51 independent cities.

German rapier of the 1630s

Prussian by 1648 ☐
Prussian by 1772 ☐

Hamburg • Berlin • Cologne • Prague • Frankfurt Augsburg • Munich

Prussian lands in Europe

Rise of Prussia
Prussia was one of the few German states to emerge from the Thirty Years' War with increased power. Under successive rulers, Prussian territory expanded across most of northern Germany and, by 1795, also included western Poland.

Frederick the Great
Frederick, King of Prussia from 1740–86, laid the foundations of later Prussian greatness. An inspired military leader, his diplomacy enabled Prussia to expand by outwitting Austria and Russia. At his death, Prussia was Europe's foremost power.

German unification

After Napoleon's defeat in 1815, many Germans wanted to unite as one nation. A confederation of states was set up, but it was too weak to last. In 1861, Wilhelm I became king of Prussia. Prussia's strength grew, and the other German states agreed to unite with Prussia. At last, in 1871, Wilhelm was made emperor of a united Germany.

Prussian power

A strong army gave Prussia the power to defeat France in the Franco-Prussian War of 1870–71. Prussian strength also enabled the newly-united Germany to negotiate a powerful and advantageous alliance with Austria-Hungary and Russia in 1881. This gave Germany great influence throughout the Continent.

Prussian army officer's helmet

Otto von Bismarck

Otto von Bismarck (1815–98) became chief minister of Prussia in 1862. In a brilliant series of diplomatic and military campaigns he removed all foreign influence from Germany, making Prussia the leading German state. He was chancellor of Germany for 19 years.

Imperial Germany

Under Wilhelm I and Wilhelm II, Germany became the leading power in Europe. Germany sought its "place in the sun" by acquiring colonies in Africa, China, and the Pacific, but its aggressive foreign policy led to world war in 1914 and the collapse of its empire in 1918.

Factories, Ruhr Valley

Industrialization

Between 1870 and 1914, Germany's population rose from 33 to 65 million, and its industrial output quadrupled. The Ruhr Valley became the centre of large iron, coal, steel, and armaments industries. This industrial power helped Germany to become the most powerful state in Europe by 1914, and helped provide resources and finances for World War I.

Chair by Bauhaus designer Marcel Breuer

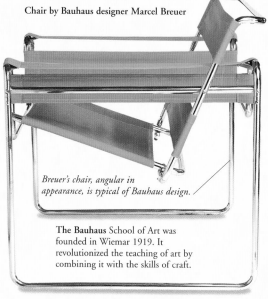

Breuer's chair, angular in appearance, is typical of Bauhaus design.

The Bauhaus School of Art was founded in Wiemar 1919. It revolutionized the teaching of art by combining it with the skills of craft.

Nazi swastika and eagle badge

Badge of the SS, the Nazi security force

Weimar Germany

In 1918, following its defeat in World War I, Germany became a republic. A new constitution was agreed in 1919 in the town of Weimar, where the National Assembly met until it moved back to Berlin in 1920. However, Germany was badly affected by economic problems in the 1920s. and by 1932, over 5 million people were unemployed.

The rise of the Nazis

The unfavourable terms of the peace settlement after World War I, together with the economic failures of the 1930s, saw Germany crippled by high unemployment and hyper-inflation, and led to a desire for change among the people. Support grew for the Nazis, an extreme nationalist party led by Adolf Hitler that took power in 1933. The Nazis promised to rebuild Germany's strength and power. It was Hitler's imperialist ambitions that were one of the causes of World War II.

Statuette of soldier

Modern Germany

After World War II, the country was occupied by French, British, US, and Russian troops. In 1949, Germany was divided in two, with a communist, Russian-backed state in the east and US-backed capitalist state in the west. Living conditions in West Germany were much better than in the east.

Housing complex, East Germany

Reunification

In the late 1980s, Russian control over East Germany weakened. The Berlin Wall, which divided the former capital, was taken down in 1989, and free access between the two countries was guaranteed for the first time. By October 1990, the two halves of Germany were politically united once more.

People flocked to Berlin to see The Wall come down.

Demolition of the Berlin Wall

Timeline

962 Otto I of Saxony establishes Holy Roman Empire.

1241 Hamburg and Lübeck combine to form Hanseatic League; German trade prospers.

1517 German monk Martin Luther begins Protestant Reformation.

The medieval castle of Pfalz

1618–48 Thirty Years' War devastates Germany.

1740–86 Frederick the Great rules Prussia.

1815–66 German Confederation tries to unite Germany.

1871 Wilhelm I is made German emperor.

1871–90 Bismarck governs as chancellor.

1914–18 Germany fights in World War I, is defeated, and empire collapses.

1919 Weimar Republic is established.

Banknote, 1931

1931 German economy crashes; prices rise, the currency becomes worthless, and many suffer unemployment.

1939–45 Germany fights in World War II.

1949 Germany divided into East and West.

1990 East and West Germany reunited as a single state.

FIND OUT MORE   ARMIES   BARBARIANS   COLD WAR   EUROPE, CENTRAL   EUROPE, HISTORY OF   FRANCE, HISTORY OF   HOLOCAUST   HOLY ROMAN EMPIRE   WORLD WAR I   WORLD WAR II

GERONIMO

A CENTURY AFTER the native people of North America fought the white settlers to stay on their land, one name is remembered above all others. As a fearless warrior, Geronimo had no equals. In his early 20s, he lost his entire family to Mexican raiders, and he determined to fight to the death to safeguard his Apache way of life. Only in old age, defeated by the superior arms of the US government, did he surrender, ending his days as a wealthy farmer, revered by people across the USA.

Early life

Geronimo was born in about 1829 in Arizona, southwest USA. He was a member of the Mimbreño Apache tribe, and his Apache name was Goyanthlay. Spaniards called him Geronimo.

Massacre

In 1858, a band of Mexican raiders killed Geronimo's mother, wife, and children. Geronimo was filled with a deep hatred of white people, and decided to spend the rest of his life fighting them.

Native American encampment

Apaches

The Apaches lived among the arid mountains and deserts of southwest USA. Because their land was unsuitable for farming, they earned a living hunting and raiding for food. This brought them into conflict with the many settlers who were moving into the area from Mexico and the eastern USA.

The young warrior

As a young warrior, Geronimo was trained to shoot, track enemies or wild animals across the land, map out a new and unfamiliar terrain, and survive for days away from camp. He also learned the skill of travelling through the countryside over vast distances without being observed. For recreation, he took part in Apache games such as the loop-and-pole game (left), arrow shooting, and wrestling.

Reservations

As European settlers pushed west, Native Americans were forced into special areas called reservations. The Native Americans were, therefore, excluded from their traditional lands and prevented from roaming over vast areas as they had done before. In response, many tribes broke out and raided neighbouring areas.

San Carlos reservation

In 1877 Geronimo and 16 of his warriors were captured by US forces and marched 400 miles to the San Carlos reservation in Arizona. The new reservation was brutal and corrupt, with suppliers making vast fortunes at the expense of the native inhabitants. Many resentful and half-starved Apaches left the reservation to go on raids.

Sharp metal blade

Bowl of pipe

Ornately carved wooden shaft

Warfare

Geronimo was a skilled warrior who many times had to fight for his life. With only a small group of followers, he managed to pose a threat to large numbers of US law enforcers. His ability to move quickly and quietly across the land, thus avoiding detection, created great fear among local settlers. If he was followed, he and his men would split up. Their understanding of the country enabled them to vanish into the bush.

Raiding

US officials tried to reform the San Carlos reservation, but Geronimo and his followers continued their raiding. Overwhelmed by the superior force of the US Army, Geronimo was forced to surrender in 1886.

Geronimo (far right) before his surrender

Apache tomahawk pipe

Fort Sill

After his surrender, Geronimo was sent first to Florida, then Alabama, and finally, in 1894, to Fort Sill, Oklahoma. He sold native American handicrafts, became a farmer, adopted Christianity, and appeared at the 1904 St Louis World's Fair and in President Theodore Roosevelt's inaugural parade in 1905. To the end of his life, he hoped to return to his native southwestern mountains.

GERONIMO

c.1829 Born in Arizona, USA.

early 1850s Raiders kill his family.

late 1850s Accepts Cochise, head of the Chiricahuas, as his leader, and marries a Chiricahua wife.

1876 Retreats into the Sierra Madre mountains and raids both sides of the US–Mexican border.

1877 Confined to the San Carlos reservation, but continues to raid the surrounding lands.

1886 Surrenders; exiled to Florida.

1894 Confined to Fort Sill.

1909 Dies at Fort Sill.

FIND OUT **MORE**   HUMAN RIGHTS   NATIVE AMERICANS   UNITED STATES, HISTORY OF

GIRAFFES

G

WITH ITS MASSIVE neck and long legs, the giraffe is the world's tallest animal. Despite its ungainly appearance, it is very graceful. Giraffes live in the savannahs of Africa – grasslands with a few trees and bushes. Their distribution closely follows that of the acacia trees on which they feed. They avoid open grassland because of their feeding habits, but also because their size makes them conspicuous in the open. There is only one species of giraffe, but eight subspecies, which differ mainly in the colour and pattern of their coats.

Thick rubbery lips and saliva protect a giraffe's tongue and mouth from thorns.

An adult male giraffe can stand 5.3 m (17.5 ft) high.

Short mane

The giraffe's long neck has the same number of vertebrae as other mammals, but they are larger.

Hoof

Reticulated giraffe

Reticulated giraffes have regular russet-coloured markings.

Browsing
The giraffe's great height is a specialized adaptation for browsing the upper branches of trees. Leaves and small twigs form the greater part of the giraffe's diet. It also eats shoots, flowers, fruit, seed pods, even bark, but never grass. Many acacias and other trees have vicious thorns to discourage browsing, but the giraffe's tongue is well equipped to get past such strong defences.

Drinking
For an animal as tall as the giraffe, drinking presents special problems. To lower its head the giraffe has either to bend its knees forward or to extend its forelegs out to either side. This awkward posture greatly reduces the animal's field of vision, leaving it vulnerable to attack.

Features of a giraffe
Massive shoulder blades carry the huge muscles that support the giraffe's head and long neck. Its hind legs are shorter than its forelegs, but the angle of the back makes them appear shorter than they really are. By breaking up its outline against its surroundings, a giraffe's coat markings help to camouflage it.

Herds
Giraffes usually live in small groups of up to about 12 females and their calves. Adult males live apart and visit the herd only for mating. Occasionally, giraffes gather together in large groups of up to 70 animals that stay together for a few days, or sometimes just a few hours.

Coat markings
Giraffe markings range from regular geometric patterns to irregular fuzzy-edged patterns. Old males darken with age and may become almost jet black.

Reticulated giraffe

Rothschild's giraffe

Masai giraffe

Giraffes have exceptionally good eyesight.

Standing still and staring towards a potential threat acts as a warning sign of danger.

Median horn

The horns are covered with hairy skin.

Horns grow on the crown of the head above the eyes.

Large nostrils

Horns
Giraffes of both sexes have a pair of short stubby horns, about 30 cm (12 in) in length in an adult male. Some giraffes, such as the reticulated giraffe, have a third (median) horn in the middle. Rothschild's giraffe also has a small pair of horns behind the ears, for which reason it is often known as the "five-horned giraffe".

Necking
Necking is a form of ritualized sparring that determines dominance within a group. It begins with one bull challenging another by advancing towards it with its head held high, legs rigid, and neck erect. After much preliminary jostling, one bull swings its head in a huge arc, in an attempt to strike its opponent's neck with its head.

Giraffe's neck is very flexible.

Okapi
The giraffe's only living relative, the okapi, is a much smaller animal, with shorter limbs and neck. While the giraffe lives in herds for mutual protection and is active by day, the forest-dwelling okapi is a solitary animal, active by night. It lives in the tropical rainforests of Zaire. The okapi's vision is poor, but its hearing and sense of smell are acute and more useful in the forests where visibility is limited.

Males have horns

Large ears

Deep chestnut-coloured coat

Creamy-white, or light grey, markings help camouflage the okapi.

Striped legs

RETICULATED GIRAFFE	
SCIENTIFIC NAME	*Giraffa camelopardalis reticulata*
ORDER	Artiodactyla
FAMILY	Giraffidae
DISTRIBUTION	Africa south of the Sahara
HABITAT	Savannahs
DIET	Leaves, shoots, small twigs, flowers, and fruit
SIZE	Height: males 5.3 m (17.5 ft); females 4.5 m (15 ft)
LIFESPAN	25 years

FIND OUT MORE

AFRICAN WILDLIFE • CAMOUFLAGE AND COLOUR • GRASSLAND WILDLIFE • MAMMALS • PLANT DEFENCE • RAINFOREST WILDLIFE

GLACIATION

THE SHAPING OF THE LANDSCAPE by ice is called glaciation. All over the world there are landscape features that were formed during past ice ages by glaciers, huge moving rivers of ice, and even bigger mounds of ice called ice sheets. In cold places, such as the polar regions, glaciers and ice sheets are still present, and glaciation still continues. The landscape created by ice is dramatic. Glaciers carve out deep, trough-like valleys, ice sheets pile up huge quantities of debris, and the icy conditions around can shatter rock into jagged peaks and knife-edge ridges.

How a glacier forms

Glaciers are created when layers of snow are compacted in icy mountain regions to form rivers of ice, which slowly creep downhill until they melt. The ice on the surface of the glacier cracks, forming deep crevasses, and both the surface and the underside of the glacier are covered with debris plucked away from the valley sides by the sheer weight of the passing ice.

Valley glaciers
In high mountain ranges, such as the Alps and the Himalayas, glaciers form in valleys as snow slides from the peaks of the mountains. These are called alpine glaciers. Where these emerge from the mountains, they may cause piedmont glaciers, so called because they spread out in the shape of a foot.

Cirque, the deep hollow where the glacier begins.

Frost shatters rocky summits into jagged "horn peaks".

Valley glacier, Norway

This glacially carved edge is called an arête.

Bergschrund, the deep crack at the head of a glacier

Frost-shattered ridges form knife-edges, or arêtes.

Glacial erosion
Glaciers have immense erosive power. In some places this works through abrasion; the moving ice acts like sandpaper, scraping away the rock with the huge amount of rock debris trapped in its base. Sometimes, it simply sweeps away loose rock shattered by the cold. Occasionally, it can freeze round rocks and literally picks them up.

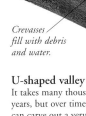

Ice fills the valley.

Debris is swept along beneath the glacier.

Crevasses fill with debris and water.

Frost-shattered rock falls on to the ice as lateral moraine along the side of the glacier.

U-shaped valley
It takes many thousands of years, but over time a glacier can carve out a very distinctive, deep, U-shaped trough of a valley. If this reaches the coast and fills with seawater, it is called a fjord.

Huge quantities of subglacial moraine are swept along underneath the glacier.

Ice fall, where the ice flows over a step in the valley floor.

Medial moraine – a band of moraine formed as two glaciers flow together.

Traces of glaciation
Glaciers carry huge quantities of debris, called moraine, which either fall on to the glacier from the mountains above or are swept away from the rock beneath. The moving ice pushes this debris into giant piles, or leaves it scattered over the landscape as the ice melts.

Lateral moraine forms terraces along the valley side.

Holes in the ice fill with debris, which is left behind when the ice melts.

Subglacial streams often leave winding ridges of debris called eskers.

Meltwater lakes fill up behind debris in front of the glacier.

Terminal moraine is the band of debris across the snout of a glacier

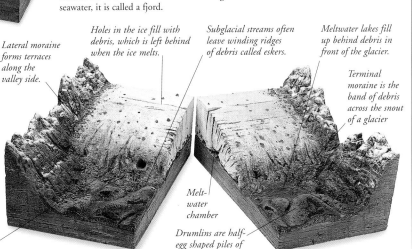

Lower end of the glacier

Meltwater chamber

Drumlins are half-egg shaped piles of subglacial moraine.

Fjords
Fjords are steep-sided, narrow coastal inlets, formed where glaciers have ground out deep valleys along existing riverbeds. When the ice melted, the valleys were flooded as the sea-level rose. The coast of Norway has many fjords.

G

Snow-line

Above a certain height, called the snow-line, the air is so cold that the snow never melts. In the tropics the snow-line is well over 5,000 m (16,000 ft), but comes down to 600 m (1,900 ft) in Greenland and is at sea-level at the North and South Poles.

Mount Kilimanjaro, Tanzania

Avalanches

The snow cover on steep slopes is often far from stable. If the layers are not well compacted, even a slight disturbance – a falling rock, a skier, or even a shout – can make an entire snowfield collapse in an avalanche.

A powder snow avalanche such as this can produce shock waves powerful enough to explode buildings.

Ice sheets and caps

Ice sheets are huge layers of ice, thousands of metres thick, that may cover not just a single valley but an entire continent. Ice caps are smaller dome-shaped sheets of ice that cover a mountain. The sheets of ice over Antarctica and Greenland are also called ice caps. The ice deep within the polar ice caps first fell as snow many millions of years ago.

Icebergs

Icebergs are huge chunks of ice that have broken off from the edge of an ice sheet or glacier to float in the sea. They are generally rounded or block-like in shape. Icebergs float because ice is less dense than water, but it is only a little less dense, so about one-eighth of the iceberg is visible above the surface

Formation of an ice cap

Ice caps form gradually by accumulation as snow falls, stays frozen, and is compacted by the addition of new snow. Some ice is lost by "ablation" (melting and evaporation), but if the ice is formed faster than it is lost, then the ice cap grows.

1 An ice cap forms when the snow covering a peak remains frozen all year.

2 Fresh snowfalls compact the snow beneath, turning it into dense crystals.

3 Eventually, the lower layers are compacted into solid opaque ice.

Ice sheets are thousands of metres thick, but vary in extent and depth between summer and winter, which effects the Earth's climate.

Isolated mountaintops jutting through the surface of an ice cap are called nunataks.

Glacier moves by sliding over melted ice.

Rocks under glacier are slowly eroded.

Ice fall – crevasses form where glacier flows over steep rock.

Around 10,000 icebergs a year break away from the glaciers in Greenland.

When Arctic glaciers reach the sea, the tides and waves heave the ice up and down, cracking bits off to float away as icebergs, a process known as calving.

Only about 12 per cent of an iceberg is visible above the surface of the ocean.

Icebergs may be broad and tabular (flat). They are often hundreds of kilometres long and may last for years before melting.

It is estimated that the average age of the ice in an iceberg is 5,000 years.

Titanic disaster

Because most of an iceberg is hidden below the surface, it can pose a real hazard to shipping if one drifts across sea lanes. In 1912, the luxury liner *Titanic* sank after a collision with an iceberg, resulting in the loss of about 1,500 lives.

Louis Agassiz

Swiss-American geologist Louis Agassiz (1807–73) realized that past ice ages had shaped the landscape. In 1836, he noted that glaciers are not static, but move, and found rocks that had been scoured by glaciers. He concluded much of northern Europe had at one time been covered by ice.

Shaded areas show the extent of the ice cover during the last ice age.

Ice Age

There is no doubt that ice ages have occurred several times in the Earth's past. Some geologists believe they are linked to the variations in the energy reaching Earth from the Sun as the Earth wobbles and tilts in its orbit. Others think there may be some other trigger for an ice age.

FIND OUT MORE ARCTIC   ANTARCTICA   GEOLOGY   POLAR EXPLORATION   POLAR WILDLIFE   RAIN   RIVERS   TUNDRA

GLASS

FEW MATERIALS have the same remarkable properties as glass. It is transparent, easy to shape and clean, does not rot, and resists attack by most chemicals. Glass is also cheap to produce because it is made from sand, one of the most common materials on Earth. When sand is heated with other materials, it turns into a liquid, which, when cooled, solidifies into glass. Although the glass looks crystalline, it still has the structure of a liquid, and is termed a "supercooled" liquid.

Ancient glass

Decorative glass objects have been found in ancient Egyptian tombs dating back to 2500 BC. After the invention of the blowpipe in about 100 BC, glass was made across the ancient world, particularly in Rome.

Roman glassware, dating from 1st century AD

Working glass

Glass is easy to work, but only when it is in a molten state. The most common method of shaping glass is blowing by craftworkers or machines. Other methods include pressing molten glass into a mould, a traditional technique still used today, and casting it into a mould to make lenses.

Sheet glass

Sheet glass was originally made by drawing a ribbon of molten glass vertically upwards. However, this caused distortion. Today, it is made by floating molten glass on a bath of molten tin. This float glass is of even thickness throughout and shows no distortion.

Glass building

Types of glass

Three main ingredients are used to make glass: pure silica sand, soda ash, and lime. These are heated in a furnace to about 1,400 °C (2,500 °F), to produce soda-lime glass. This is the ordinary glass we use to make bottles and windows.

Different kinds of glass can be made by adding other ingredients.

Lead crystal

Lead glass

Also called crystal glass, lead glass contains lead oxide, which makes it easy to cut. The cut glass exhibits a diamond-like sparkle.

Spectacles

Magnifying glass

Optical glass

Optical lenses are made from pure glass. A variety of substances, such as lead and titanium, are added to give glass its optical properties.

Heat-resistant glass jug

Heat-resistant glass

Boron oxide is sometimes added in the glassmaking process to produce heat-resistant borosilicate glass.

Fibreglass

Glass may sometimes take the form of fibres, which are used for loft insulation, reinforcement for plastics, and fibre-optic cables.

Fibreglass

Stained glass

Stained glass is normally used to create decorative windows, using pieces of coloured glass set in a lead framework. Medieval stained glass may seem richer to the eye because it is full of impurities.

Stained-glass window

Glassblowing

Most glassblowing is done mechanically, but traditional methods, shown in the following sequence, are still used for making special objects.

Molten glass

Iron rod

Strong shears

1 An iron rod is dipped into the furnace to pick up a gob (lump) of molten glass. The glassblower cuts off the correct quantity of glass needed using special glass shears, and drops it into a measuring mould.

Measuring mould

Shaping mould into which the shaped parison is fitted.

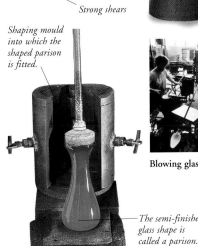

Blowing glass

The semi-finished glass shape is called a parison.

2 The glassblower picks up the molten glass from the measuring mould on a blowing-iron, then blows air through the iron, to shape the glass and form a parison.

Layers of steam protect and cushion the glass.

3 With further blowing, the glass expands and takes its final shape inside the mould. At the same time, the rod is spun to stop the object showing signs of joints from the mould.

The bottle shows no signs of the joint between the two halves of the mould.

4 The glassblower removes the final object from the mould, and smooths the mouth of the bottle by reheating it in the furnace and shaping it.

Bottles ready to be recycled

Recycling glass

Glass is an easy material to recycle because it melts readily. It is recycled, not for the purpose of conservation, but to save energy because the original glassmaking process requires such high temperatures. In Europe alone, about four million tonnes of glass are recycled each year.

FIND OUT MORE ARCHITECTURE CHURCHES CRYSTALS AND GEMS EYES AND SEEING PLASTICS AND RUBBER POLLUTION ROCKS AND MINERALS ROMAN EMPIRE

GODS AND GODDESSES

SINCE PREHISTORIC TIMES, humans have worshipped gods and goddesses – spirits that are believed to control nature and human destinies. The mythology that surrounds them attempts to explain the how and why of life, and account for forces that are beyond human control. The rituals associated with these supernatural beings, or deities, are a powerful force in binding societies together. The variety of gods and goddesses worshipped around the world reflects the diversity and power of human imagination.

Mother goddess

Every culture had a mother goddess, one of the earliest deities, who represented nature and fertility. In ancient Egypt, she was called Isis and may have been a model for the Christian Madonna.

Hades and Persephone

Persephone
In Greek mythology, Hades, god of the underworld, abducts Persephone. She returns to the world for six months every year, bringing spring and summer.

Durga
In Hinduism, Durga is the powerful warrior-goddess. She is often represented with a beautiful face and 10 arms, each one holding a weapon.

Venus figure, c.4000 BC

Gods

Much of what we know of gods and goddesses was passed down by men rather than women, so male gods – often gods of war – predominate in mythology. Many myths portray the struggle between good and evil. Some deities are kind and just, while others, such as the Norse god Loki, commit acts of evil and treachery on other gods or humans. Gods may be depicted either in human form, or as part-human and part-animal.

Thor
In Norse mythology, Thor was the god of the sky, rain, thunder, and farming. Thor's hammer, known as Mjollnir, made thunderbolts when the god threw it. Norse gods such as Thor and Odin were worshipped in parts of Scandinavia up until the 12th century.

Thor fighting frost giants

Mars was popular in Rome.

Mars
Mars, god of war, was said to be the father of Rome's founder. Many Roman gods were equivalent to earlier Greek versions: Mars was called Ares in Greek mythology, and Demeter, goddess of spring, was Persephone.

Sacrifices

A sacrifice is an offering of an animal, plant, possession, or even a human life, to please or pacify a deity. In ancient cultures, sacrifices were made to gods and goddesses on special days or at important ceremonies. Ancient Romans marked such occasions with a *suovetaurilia,* a special sacrifice involving a bull, a ram, and a pig – the most valuable items of Roman livestock.

Wicker man
Roman historians recorded that Celtic tribes in Gaul (France) placed human sacrifices inside wickerwork figures, then burnt them alive. Wicker figures are still burnt at festivals in Spain.

Mountain-top sacrifice
The Aztecs offered human sacrifices to the god of the Sun, Tezcatlipoca. This deity was the most feared of the Aztec gods and thousands, usually prisoners of war, were sacrificed in his name. The Aztecs carefully chose their victim, who was accorded great honours for one year. Then, on the day of the sacrifice, a priest cut open the victim's chest and offered his heart up to Tezcatlipoca.

Aztec warrior and his prisoner of war

Priests

In many societies, priests are the human links between the natural world and the supernatural world of the gods. They are thought to have special, often magical power, and may carry out sacred rites.

Priest in traditional costume

Priest's costume
Costumes convey authority and represent tradition. The priest's costume of the Nkimba people of the Congo, West Africa, includes an ornate carved wooden mask and a grass net decorated with feathers.

Shaman's mask
The shamans of Native American tribes wore masks representing a guardian spirit. This showed the connection between the human and spirit worlds.

Oracles

The term "oracle" describes a direct communication with a deity though the mouth of a priest. The most famous oracle was at Delphi in ancient Greece, at a temple to the god Apollo. In Greek mythology, the heroes Oedipus and Heracules consulted the oracle, whose replies to questions were always ambiguous.

Delphi Oracle, Greece

| FIND OUT MORE | AZTECS | CELTS | EGYPT, ANCIENT | GREECE, ANCIENT | MAYA | RELIGIONS | ROMAN EMPIRE | WITCHES AND WITCHCRAFT |

Mask "transforms" into eagle head.

Gods and Goddesses
Nature

Mayan rain god

Men is an Anatolian Moon god.

Luna drives a chariot across the night sky.

Luna is the Roman Moon goddess.

Syrian river god

Aztec agricultural god

Balls of thunder

Ceres is the Roman corn goddess.

Poseidon is the Greek god of the sea.

Silvanus is the god of uncultivated land.

Celtic god of rivers

Apollo is the Roman Sun god.

Hephaistos is the Greek god of fire.

Japanese god of thunder and lightning.

Love and Fertility

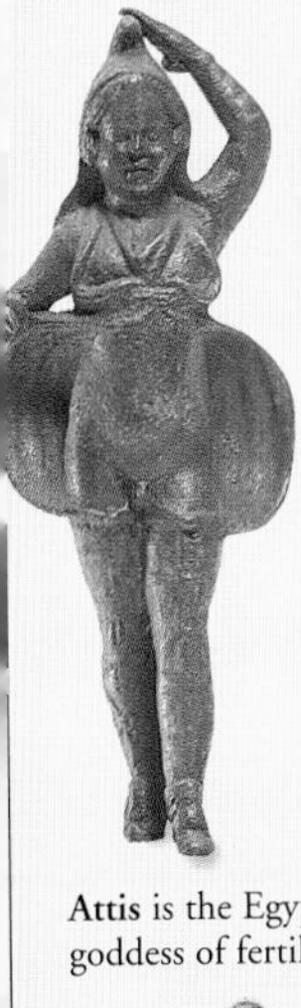

Artemis is the Greek goddess of fertility.

Cupid is the Roman god of love.

Aphrodite is the mother of Eros.

Eros is a god of love.

Priapus is the Roman god of fertility.

Attis is the Egyptian goddess of fertility.

Venus is the Roman goddess of love and beauty.

Aphrodite is the Greek goddess of love and beauty.

Juno is the Roman goddess of marriage and maternity.

War and Death

Cerberus is a dog that guards the underworld.

Hades is the Roman god of the underworld.

Proserpina is the Roman queen of the underworld.

Ares is the father of Eros.

Athena is the Roman goddess of war.

Ares is the Greek god of war.

Serapis is an Egyptian god of the dead.

Osiris is the Egyptian god of the underworld.

Antlered Celtic goddess

GOODALL, JANE

FROM 1960 TO 1995, Jane Goodall spent 35 remarkable years devoted to studying chimpanzees in the wild, and became one of the world's most respected and influential zoologists. She began her painstaking research alone in the middle of the tropical forest in Tanzania, East Africa, and steadily built up one of the foremost centres for field research on primates. Her observations and those of her colleagues revolutionized our knowledge of chimpanzee behaviour and shed light on our own human ancestry.

Early life
Jane Goodall was born in London, England, in 1934. As a teenager she dreamed of studying wildlife in Africa, and the ambition never faded. In 1957, with savings from a summer job as a waitress, she embarked on a trip to Kenya. There she approached the famous anthropologist Louis Leakey, and told him she wanted to work in Africa. Leakey gave her a job as a secretary.

Tool used to open bees' nests

Fishing stick

Wooden chisel

Research
In spite of Jane Goodall's lack of formal training, Louis Leakey decided to help her realize her dream. In 1960, he raised funds for her to begin a research programme at Gombe, Tanzania. She has been based there ever since. In the 1960s, most primatologists studied captive animals in zoos. Goodall's task was different – to gain the confidence of the chimps and study them at close quarters in their natural environment.

Goodall with one of the chimps at Gombe

Communication
Goodall was fascinated by the way the chimps used sounds, gestures, and expressions to communicate with each other. Every noise conveyed a different message, and gestures and body movements were also forms of communication.

Displays
Goodall saw how body movements act as visual displays of emotion and intent. Males issue threats to rivals by charging forward with their fur raised, often dragging branches or throwing stones. Early on, Goodall noted that groups of chimps would react to coming rainfall with an agitated "rain dance".

Charging display

Touch
Goodall observed that chimps would often pat, embrace, or kiss as a way of calming distressed individuals. She also saw them grooming each other's fur. This has a calming effect and strengthens social bonds.

In her lonely observation posts in the jungle, Goodall made careful drawings of the chimps' use of tools and other behaviour.

Two of Goodall's notebooks

Working methods
Goodall worked by spending day after day alone in the forest with the chimpanzees. Gradually, she won their confidence and they accepted her. She filled her notebooks with descriptions of the chimpanzees, and wrote freely of the emotions, personalities, and intelligence of the chimps.

Toolmaking
One of Goodall's most startling discoveries was that wild chimps are good toolmakers. They use objects as tools, modifying them to suit their purpose. She saw chimps stripping twigs to make probes for "fishing" termites from their nests, and chewing clumps of leaves to make sponges for getting water from shallow pools.

Conservation
Goodall championed the cause of chimpanzee conservation and campaigned for better conditions for captive chimps. In 1977, she launched the Jane Goodall Institute for Wildlife Research, Education, and Conservation in the USA. By the late 1990s, it had branches in the UK, Canada, and Tanzania.

Goodall campaigning for chimpanzees

FIND OUT MORE   AFRICAN WILDLIFE   CONSERVATION   LEAKEY FAMILY   MONKEYS, AND OTHER PRIMATES

JANE GOODALL
1934 Born in London, England.
1957 Travels to Kenya and meets Louis Leakey.
1960 Establishes research station at Gombe, Tanzania.
1965 Gains doctorate from Cambridge University.
1971 Publishes *In the Shadow of Man*, first of several influential books.
1977 Founds Jane Goodall Institute.
1991 Launches international youth environmental programme, "Roots and Shoots".
1995 Receives Hubbard Medal.

GOVERNMENTS AND POLITICS

A GOVERNMENT IS an institution which makes the political decisions about running a country. Governments and politics are individual to each country because they result from that country's unique history and culture. Yet despite those differences, the systems of government and the issues of political debate are similar everywhere, for they concern how to govern the country best for the benefit of the people.

The orb symbolizes a monarch's spiritual authority over his or her subjects.

German orb

The crown symbolizes sovereignty.

Russian Imperial crown

Prussian sceptre

The crown jewels (crown, orb, and sceptre symbolize the monarch's authority.

Types of government

There are almost as many types of government as there are countries in the world. The three main types of government are republican, monarchical, and dictatorial, although these have many variations. Anarchists believe that governments are not necessary.

Republic
Most countries in the world are republics, that is, where electors vote for their head of state as well as for their government. The power of the president ranges from holding real political power, as in the USA, to being a symbolic figurehead, as in India.

Monarchy
In a monarchy, the head of the royal family is head of state and is succeeded by his or her closest relative in hereditary succession. In most monarchies, such as Britain or Japan, the monarch has little real power, but in countries such as Morocco, Saudi Arabia, or Jordan, the king holds considerable political power.

Dictatorship
Many countries in the world have at one time or another been ruled by dictators, that is, single rulers with absolute power. Most dictators gain power either through a military take-over or by seizing leadership from an existing ruler, as Saddam Hussein did in Iraq in 1979. Dictators eliminate any opposition to their rule.

Democracy

In a democracy, electors vote for a government from a range of political parties. There are two main types of democracy: presidential, where voters elect the president who then runs the government and may choose the prime minister; and parliamentary, where voters directly elect the government of their choice.

Presidential
As the President of Ireland, Mary McAleese (b.1951), is the symbolic head of the nation. In France and Russia, the president chooses the prime minister.

Old Parliament House, Canberra, Australia

Parliamentary
Parliamentary systems exist in both republics and monarchies. Parliament is made up of politicians from different political parties. Electors vote for the party or individual of their choice, and the government is drawn from the largest political party in parliament. The leader of this party becomes head of government. Most nations in the world are parliamentary democracies.

How government works

Each country has its own system of government, usually consisting of four separate parts. The executive governs the country, the legislature makes the laws, the civil service carries out those laws, and the judiciary ensures the laws are applied fairly.

Judge calls court to order with a gavel.

Judiciary
The judiciary makes sure laws are carried out fairly. Judges sit in judgment in individual cases, and also review the operation of the law or suggest changes to improve it. The judiciary is independent from the executive and legislature to maintain its neutrality.

Legislature
The legislature is the place where laws are made and the executive is held to account for its actions in governing. The legislature is made up of elected representatives, and often consists of a lower house of parliament, where laws are made, and an upper house, which keeps a check on the lower house. The British upper house (the House of Lords) is unique in mainly consisting of hereditary, not elected, members.

Parliament House, New Delhi, India

Executive
The executive's role is to govern the country. In parliamentary democracies, the executive consists of senior ministers and the prime minister, who sit in the Houses of Parliament. In the USA, the executive, such as the Secretary of State, Colin Powell (b. 1937), is chosen by the president and is separate from the Houses of Congress.

Civil service
The role of the civil, or public, service is to administer the country. Once the executive has proposed a law, and the legislature has passed it, the civil service implements it. Civil servants are non-political and work for whichever government is in power. Their work ranges from local issues, such as street lighting, to national issues, such as defence.

Pentagon, USA

Elections

In a multi-party democracy, every three to five years voters go to the polls to elect their government, choosing the politicians who will represent them from a list of candidates. Elections are an opportunity for politicians to present their ideas for the government of the country, and for the electorate to debate and consider matters of interest and concern to them. In the past, elections were local, personal affairs, in which candidates for office tried to meet each elector in person. Today, most electioneering is carried out by advertising and television.

Voting

The electors vote in secret for the candidate of their choice by marking a ballot paper. The ballots are then counted and the winning candidate is elected. In many countries, electors rank candidates in order of preference. A system of proportional representation (PR) then ensures that the candidates with the most preferences are elected.

Political parties

Political parties are formed to represent particular political beliefs, such as the Socialist Party in France or the Christian Democratic Party in Germany, or to represent particular areas of a country, such as the Scottish Nationalists, who wish to see Scotland become independent from Britain. Political parties are active at local and national levels in getting their supporters out to vote and in attracting new voters to their cause.

Swedish Christian Democratic Party — French Socialist Party

Politicians

People become politicians for different reasons. Some people stand for election because they believe in serving the public, or have a particular skill that would be useful in government. Others stand to represent a particular political viewpoint. In the USA, the cost of a campaign restricts candidates to those with money.

US Democratic Convention, 1996

Politics

Politics is the organization of political debate and discussion in a country. That debate can take place in a formal setting as in parliament, or informally. Any subject can be discussed, from major issues such as the economy or international relations, to local issues such as the siting of a new road.

Chamber of the House of Commons, London, UK

Public pressure

Everyone can play a part in politics, from full-time politicians to individuals who are concerned about a particular issue or event. Apart from elections, individuals can bring pressure to bear on governments, both by participating in public protest, such as strikes and demonstrations, and by joining pressure groups that are set up to campaign for particular issues, such as protecting the environment or civil liberties.

Protest groups

In order to force an issue into the public view, it is sometimes necessary to take direct action. Recently, protest groups have achieved success against the siting of nuclear weapons and the proposed building of new roads.

Pressure groups

Pressure groups play an important part in focusing attention on issues of public concern. Environmental pressure groups, such as Greenpeace, raise public awareness on issues of pollution or environmental damage that cross national borders.

Dove bearing olive branch symbolizes hope.

Political beliefs

Different political beliefs play a large part in determining how a country is governed. Left-wing ideologies, such as communism and socialism, favour a large role for the state acting on behalf of its citizens, while right-wing ideologies, such as capitalism, favour individual action and responsibility by citizens.

Capitalism

Capitalism is the system in which wealth and profit in the hands of a few people drive the country's economy. Capitalism can lead to great differences in income between rich and poor.

Fascism

Fascism is the system of government under which total authority resides in the leader of the country, who pursues nationalist and militarist policies. Like other far-right ideologies, fascism glorifies the state for providing strong national leadership.

Socialism

Socialism is the system in which the economy is controlled by the state for the benefit of the whole community. Countries such as the Netherlands and Sweden aim for a more equal distribution of wealth.

Communism

Communism is the system in which land and property are owned by the whole community and each person is paid according to their needs and abilities. China and North Korea are examples of communist countries.

Machiavelli

Niccolò Machiavelli (1469–1527) was a civil servant in the Florentine Republic in Italy. He was a realist who observed the political chaos of his times and urged governments to pursue practical, realistic politics rather than lofty political ideals. In his book *The Prince* (1532), he described politics as the art of the possible and pointed out what a government can do rather than what it ought to do.

FIND OUT MORE — COLD WAR — EUROPE, HISTORY OF — EUROPEAN UNION — HUMAN RIGHTS — LAW — PEACE MOVEMENTS — UNIONS, TRADE — UNITED NATIONS — WARFARE — WOMEN'S MOVEMENT

GRASSES, RUSHES, AND SEDGES

THESE THREE GROUPS of plants are all monocotyledons – flowering plants whose seedlings possess a single cotyledon, or seed leaf. In common with many other monocotyledons, grasses, rushes, and sedges have long, narrow leaves with parallel veins. They are all wind-pollinated and, therefore, do not have showy blossoms to attract animals. Instead, they have tiny flowers grouped in spikes or clusters. These produce large amounts of dry pollen.

Flower stem, or culm

Flowerheads at the top of tall, leafy stems

Yorkshire fog

Cross-section of sedge flower stem

Grasses

There are about 9,000 species of grass, including cereal crops such as wheat and barley. They are the most widespread flowering plants. Grass plants often grow close together to make a turf. Each plant has a mass of fibrous roots, leafy shoots, and flowerheads borne on long stems.

Sedges

The sedge family includes true sedges, cottongrasses, club-rushes, and galingales, totalling about 4,000 species. Unlike grasses, sedges have leaves in tufts around the base of the stem. The flower stem is usually leafless and three-angled.

Cross-section of rush stem

Rushes

The 400 or so species of rush are small to medium-size plants. They are found mostly in the damper habitats of temperate and mountain regions. Rushes have green, white, or brown flowers that turn into dry fruits called capsules. Leaves may be flat like grass leaves, or cylindrical. The stems of all rushes are circular in cross-section.

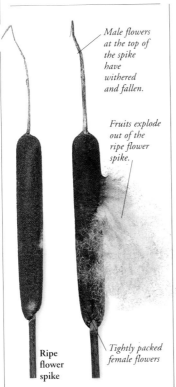

Male flowers at the top of the spike have withered and fallen.

Fruits explode out of the ripe flower spike.

When these leaves are cut off, new shoots grow from the base of the plant.

Ripe flower spike

Tightly packed female flowers

Reed mace
Often wrongly called bulrushes, these tall plants grow in shallow, slow-moving or still water. There are about 15 species in their own family. Each plant has a flower spike made up of densely packed flowers. This splits open when ripe, releasing a mass of single-seeded fruits.

Tillers
The reason grasses can tolerate the pressures of constant grazing or mowing is that new leafy shoots arise from buds at ground level. This kind of branching is called tillering.

Woody bamboo canes have many uses, from kitchen utensils to scaffold poles.

Soil particles are trapped and held by a network of rootlets.

Bamboo
About 830 tropical and sub-tropical species of grass have tough, woody stems. These are called bamboos. The tallest species reaches 35 m (115 ft) tall.

Soil binding
The roots of grass plants growing close together make a densely interwoven mat. This stabilizes loose, dry soils and prevents erosion of all kinds of soil.

FIND OUT MORE   ECOLOGY   FARMING   FLOWERS   PLANTS   PLANTS, ANATOMY   PLANTS, REPRODUCTION

Grasses

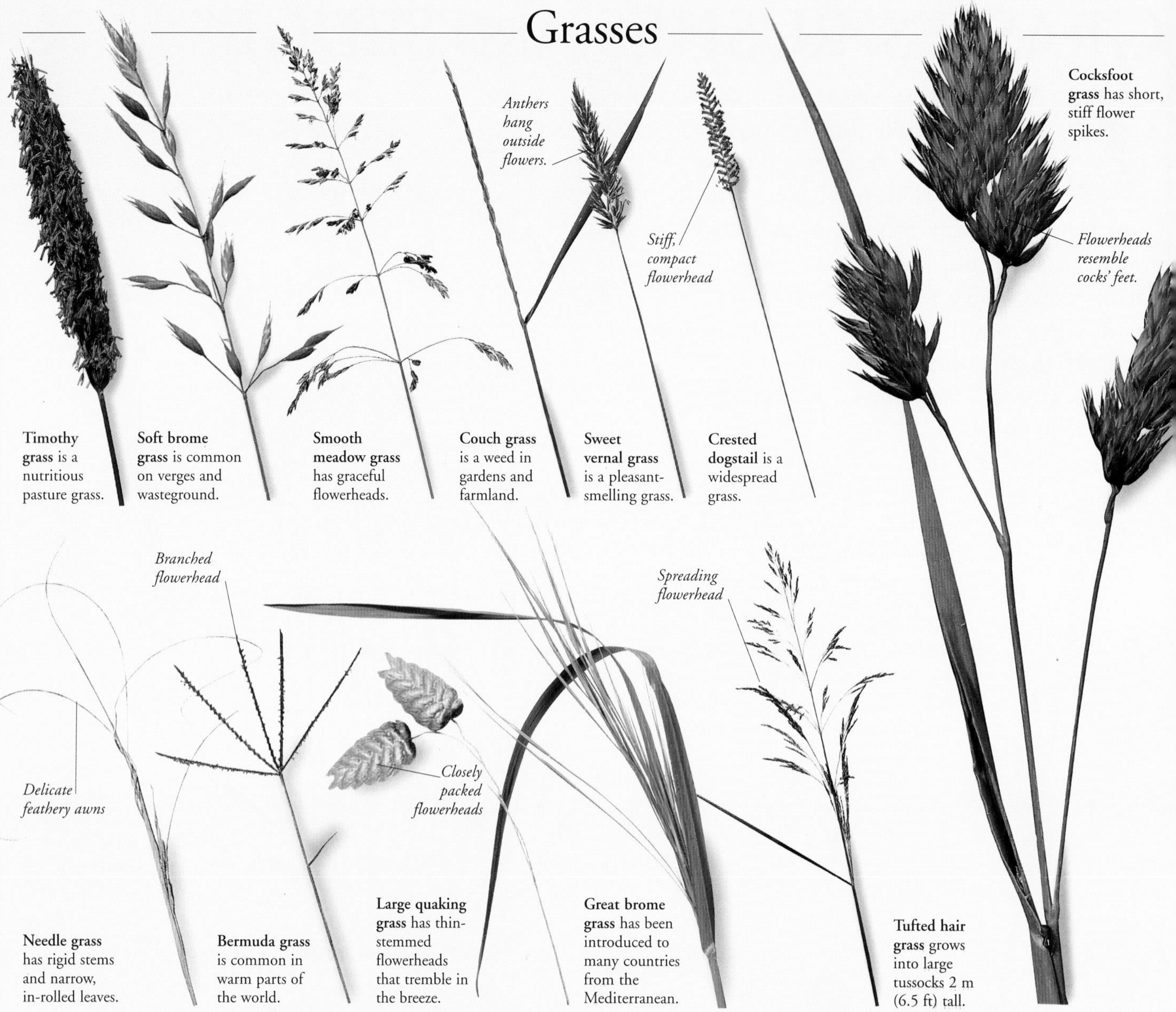

Anthers hang outside flowers.

Stiff, compact flowerhead

Cocksfoot grass has short, stiff flower spikes.

Flowerheads resemble cocks' feet.

Timothy grass is a nutritious pasture grass.

Soft brome grass is common on verges and wasteground.

Smooth meadow grass has graceful flowerheads.

Couch grass is a weed in gardens and farmland.

Sweet vernal grass is a pleasant-smelling grass.

Crested dogstail is a widespread grass.

Branched flowerhead

Spreading flowerhead

Delicate feathery awns

Closely packed flowerheads

Needle grass has rigid stems and narrow, in-rolled leaves.

Bermuda grass is common in warm parts of the world.

Large quaking grass has thin-stemmed flowerheads that tremble in the breeze.

Great brome grass has been introduced to many countries from the Mediterranean.

Tufted hair grass grows into large tussocks 2 m (6.5 ft) tall.

Rushes and sedges

Soft rush is a very common rush of bogs and marshes.

Common sedge spreads on creeping underground stems.

Hairy sedge has hairy leaves and fruits.

Clusters of flowers borne up the stem

Woodrush has fine hairs on the margins of its leaves.

Greater tussock sedge has stiff leaves with finely toothed edges.

False fox sedge has sharp-angled triangular stems.

Pendulous sedge has long drooping flower spikes.

Greater pond sedge grows beside rivers and ponds.

GRASSHOPPERS AND CRICKETS

FAMOUS FOR THEIR ATHLETIC LEAPS and chirping calls, grasshoppers and crickets are among the largest and most distinctive of insects. Most are weak fliers and prefer to move by walking or jumping. They live mainly in grasslands and rainforests, but some live in deserts and caves, and a few wingless species burrow underground. Grasshoppers tend to be active by day, but crickets are out and about after dark; in many parts of the world their constant chirps fill the night air.

G

Features of a grasshopper

Grasshoppers have long bodies, big heads, large eyes, and downward-pointing mouthparts. Their long, thickened forewings protect delicate hind wings, which they use mainly for flying. Grasshoppers use their powerful, long hind legs for leaping. Bumps on the hind legs rub against the forewings to make sounds.

Wings outstretched during flight, before it lands

Grasshopper gains height by holding its wings back.

Compound eye

Grasshoppers may jump up to 0.3 m (1 ft) before opening their wings.

Hind legs held out almost straight behind

Front legs outstretched over eyes, ready to touch down

Leaping

Propelled forward by snapping their hind legs straight, grasshoppers can out-jump all other insects. If danger threatens or if the grasshopper wants to move to another clump of vegetation, it springs into the air, opens and flutters its wings to prolong the leap, and drops down as much as 1 m (3.3 ft) ahead.

Long, strong back legs

Front legs

Grasshopper poised, ready to leap

Common field grasshopper

Crickets

Crickets are similar to grasshoppers but differ in some key features: their hearing organs are on their legs rather than abdomen; they have longer antennae, sometimes longer than their bodies; and they make sounds by rubbing their wings together.

Long antenna

Bush cricket

Eardrum on legs

Crickets have a swelling below the knee that consists of a drum-like membrane, called a tympanum, on either side of the leg. This is the cricket's ear and is sensitive to sound vibrations.

Cricket's leg showing eardrum

Locust swarms

Locusts are grasshoppers. After heavy rains, lush plant life grows, creating the right conditions for locusts to breed in large numbers. Swarms of up to 50 billion set out across the land. They devastate crops and plants, causing famine.

Swarm of locusts in Ethiopia

Reproduction

During mating a male grasshopper or cricket transfers tiny packets of sperm to the female to fertilize her eggs. She then uses a spike-like ovipositor to place batches of up to 100 eggs at a time into the soil or into plant stems and leaves. Tiny nymphs – miniature versions of the parents – hatch from the eggs. They moult and grow many times until they reach adult size.

Grasshopper rubs its legs rapidly against its wings to generate sounds.

Male has laid a sperm sac that is being taken up by the female.

Ovipositor

Bush cricket transferring sperm sac

Stridulation

The rapid rubbing sounds made by grasshoppers and crickets are known as stridulation. To amplify the sounds, crickets rub veins and ridges on both wings together; grasshoppers rub ridges on their legs against a tough vein on their wings. Breeding males produce stridulations to attract mates. Sounds are characteristic of each species and uttered at specific times of the day.

Feeding

Most grasshoppers feed on leaves, buds, and other parts of plants that they chew with their mouthparts. Crickets have a more varied diet. Many eat plants but also catch and devour other insects – in fact, some bush crickets are dedicated hunters. Crickets that live in houses and caves scavenge on dead and waste matter.

Bush cricket eating a grasshopper

Great green bush cricket

Defence

Many grasshoppers and crickets are brown or green so they are less visible to predators. Others have brightly coloured hind wings that they flash to warn off enemies. Some have elaborate camouflage, with body parts resembling leaves and plant stems.

Weta

Legs raised in warning posture

Bright colours confuse predators

Foaming grasshopper

Posture

Large crickets, called wetas, have spines on their hind legs. If disturbed, they raise their hind legs into a threatening posture to frighten predators.

Flash coloration

At rest, only the outer wings of this grasshopper are exposed. If disturbed, it flashes its lilac inner wings to confuse enemies, as the colour disappears when it settles.

Warning coloration

This grasshopper eats poisonous plants and stores the poisons in its body. Its bright stripes warn predators that it is unpleasant to eat.

COMMON FIELD GRASSHOPPER

SCIENTIFIC NAME	*Chorthippus brunneus*
ORDER	Orthoptera
FAMILY	Acrididae
DISTRIBUTION	Europe
HABITAT	Dry open areas with short grass
DIET	Grass and other low-lying plants
SIZE	Length: males up to 18 mm (0.7 in); females up to 23 mm (0.9 in)
LIFESPAN	6–7 months

FIND OUT MORE

ARTHROPODS • CAVE WILDLIFE • CAMOUFLAGE AND COLOUR • GRASSLAND WILDLIFE • INSECTS • NORTH AMERICAN WILDLIFE

GRASSLAND WILDLIFE

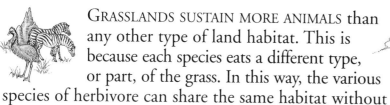

GRASSLANDS SUSTAIN MORE ANIMALS than any other type of land habitat. This is because each species eats a different type, or part, of the grass. In this way, the various species of herbivore can share the same habitat without competing for food. On the African plains, for example, zebras eat the tops of grasses, wildebeest prefer the middle layers, while Thomson's gazelles graze close to the ground. Tall grasses also provide shelter for myriad insects, and a refuge for small animals, such as birds and rodents, many of which live in burrows due to the lack of shelter from trees.

The world's major grasslands are shown, marked in green on the map below.

Prairies of North America

Eurasian steppe

Pampas of South America

Savannahs of Africa

Australian grasslands

Giraffes browse on trees.

Zebras and springboks graze on grass.

Giraffes, springboks, and zebras grazing on the African savannah

Grasslands

Grasslands cover 25 per cent of the Earth's land surface. The world's principal grasslands are the Eurasian steppe, the savannahs of Africa, the pampas of South America, the prairies of North America, and the Australian grasslands. Grasslands are areas where it is too dry for many trees to grow, but tough grasses grow in abundance. Grasses can withstand constant grazing by animals, and recover quickly from damage by fire, flood, or drought.

Mammals

Grasslands sustain a wide variety of mammals, mainly herbivores, often in large numbers. The herbivores support a population of carnivores, while scavengers, such as hyenas, jackals, and vultures, dispose of their remains. Typical grassland mammals include zebras in Africa; prairie dogs and coyotes in North America; maned wolves in South America; marmots in Eurasia; and kangaroos in Australia.

Patagonian hare
The Patagonian hare, or mara, looks like a hare but is closely related to the guinea pig. It lives in burrows in groups of 30–40, in the Argentinian pampas and the stony Patagonian desert.

Long, thin legs help hare run fast.

American bison
The most characteristic animal of the Great Plains of North America, the bison once numbered 50–60 million. By the 1880s, the huge herds had been almost destroyed by hunting. Only 500 remained, but given protection, numbers rose to 25,000. The bison now live in herds of up to 50 animals.

Blackbuck
Blackbucks are a type of antelope that once roamed the Indian grasslands in herds of up to 10,000. More recently, hunting has reduced their numbers, and there are now more blackbucks in Argentina and Texas, where they have been introduced, than in their original homeland.

Males have slender, spiralled horns.

Pairs of African wild dogs run down animals larger than themselves.

Huge ears and good sense of smell help to locate prey.

African wild dog
The wild dog lives in packs of up to 12 on the open savannahs of Africa. It employs a very effective method of communal hunting; having singled out an animal, such as a zebra or gazelle, from the herd, a pair of dogs chases it until they are tired, when a fresh pair takes over. Relays of dogs continue in this way until the prey is exhausted, and the pack closes in for the kill.

Invertebrates

Invertebrates are of great importance in tropical grasslands. They feed on dead vegetation, helping decompose it, and make nutrients available to plants. They also bring subsoil to the surface, helping to keep the soil healthy.

Dung beetle
Dung beetles roll dung into balls, which they lay eggs in, and push into holes. The larvae hatch and feed on the dung.

Ant lion
Ant lion larvae build pits in sandy soil and wait at the bottom for an ant or spider to dislodge grains of sand. Once alerted, the larva squirts sand at its victim, making it slide into the pit where the ant lion seizes it in its powerful jaws.

Termites
Tropical grasslands are dotted with termite nests, each containing several million of these insects. Termites are an important food source for many animals, especially echidnas, numbats, aardvarks, and pangolins.

Termite nest may be 6 m (20 ft) high.

Queen termites have huge, swollen bodies and can lay up to 30,000 eggs a day.

G

Reptiles

Many reptiles live in grasslands where they can tolerate the harsh conditions during the dry season. However, when the grass is short it provides little cover in which to hide, so reptiles need to be camouflaged. Many grassland snakes and lizards are dull coloured, with brown or grey mottled markings that blend into the surroundings.

Large claws help it to catch prey.

Strong jaws and sharp, curved teeth help it catch snakes, rabbits, and birds.

Perentie
Reaching a length of 2 m (7 ft), the perentie is the largest of the Australian monitor lizards. It lives in grasslands and among rocky outcrops in deserts. Like other monitors, the perentie is a carnivore with a voracious appetite. It also eats carrion. If threatened, it inflates its body, hisses, and lashes out with its tail.

The perentie can lash its huge tail from side-to-side in self-defence.

Grass snake
This small, non-venomous reptile lives in grasslands close to water. It is a strong swimmer, and catches much of its prey, such as fish, frogs, and newts, in water. If attacked, it releases a bad smell, or feigns death by lying on its back, with its tongue hanging out. Grass snakes hibernate in winter, usually in holes in the ground.

Grass snakes usually lay a clutch of up to 30–40 eggs in decaying vegetation.

Puff adder
Hidden within the grass stems of the African savannah lurks the slow-moving, dangerous puff adder. Camouflaged in the grass, it lies in wait for prey. It produces a powerful venom for immobilizing prey, such as rodents and frogs, and as a means of defence, against mongooses, secretary birds, and eagles.

Mottled markings break up outline against the grass.

Birds

Grasslands support many birds, among them bustards, guineafowl, francolins, long-legged seriemas, and the secretary bird. Many birds nest on the ground as there are few trees. The burrowing owl even goes underground and nests in burrows on the American prairies. Other birds, such as weaver birds, flock in droves to the same isolated tree to weave their basket-shaped nests.

Greater bustard
A turkey-sized, ground-dwelling bird with a wing span of up to 2.4 m (8 ft), the greater bustard lives in the open grasslands of Asia and southern Europe. It is famous for the male's spectacular courtship display. He inflates the air sac on his throat, and twists his back and tail feathers forwards, transforming himself from a drab grey colour into a shimmering white mass.

Long neck gives bustard a clear view over the grass.

Emu
The emu is the second largest bird in the world, after the ostrich. It is flightless and lives on the Australian grasslands, where it feeds on grasses, berries, fruit, and insects. Emus live in small, nomadic flocks, moving long distances in search of food and water. They are powerful runners, covering the ground in 2.7 m (9 ft) strides, reaching speeds of up to 50 kmh (30 mph) over short distances. Males incubate the eggs and look after the chicks.

Long, shaggy feathers

Bare skin on neck

Indian white-backed vulture
Vultures are a group of carrion-eating birds of prey. They perform a vital role of scavenging and keeping the environment clean by disposing of waste. Indian white-backed vultures hunt, by soaring on thermal currents from where they can spot a kill; once sighted, the vultures land to feed on the remains. The sight of vultures spiralling down draws other scavengers to the kill.

Long legs for running

Vulture feeding on a goat

Plants

Grasslands sustain numerous types of grass, among the best known are red oat grass in Africa and buffalo grass in America. Which species grow depends on altitude, temperature, soil type, and rainfall. Grassland trees often have deep roots to reach water supplies far below the ground, allowing them to survive during the dry season. Some trees can store water. The baobab tree can store about 9,000 l (2,400 gal) of water in its huge swollen trunk.

Acacia tree
The characteristic tree of Africa's arid and semi-arid grasslands is the flat-topped umbrella tree, *Acacia tortilis*. This tree is protected from grazing animals by sharp thorns, but these do not deter giraffes, which manage to pluck the leaves and blossoms. Acacias produce a mass of pods that fall to the ground providing food for many animals. Acacias also provide welcome shade for the animals of the savannah.

Fluffy, white seed heads

Pampas grass
The Argentine pampas extends from the foothills of the Andes to the Atlantic coast. Many of the grasses that grow there can be up to 2.5 m (8 ft) high.

Petals and bracts are covered with small hairs.

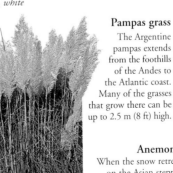

Anemones
When the snow retreats on the Asian steppes, many wild flowers, including anemones and peonies, grow amidst the sea of grass.

FIND OUT MORE · ANTS AND TERMITES · BIRDS OF PREY · BUFFALO AND OTHER WILD CATTLE · DEER AND ANTELOPES · GRASSES, RUSHES, AND SEDGES · PLANTS, DEFENCE · WOLVES AND WILD DOGS

GRAVITY

WITHOUT GRAVITY, we would fly off the spinning Earth and into space. Gravity is a force of attraction that acts between any two objects. The objects can be as large as galaxies or as small as subatomic particles. The strength of the gravity between two objects depends on their masses and the distance between them. Objects with large masses exert a strong force of gravity. Objects far apart attract each other weakly.

Centre of gravity

Centre of gravity is directly below the string, making the object very stable.

Every object consists of tiny particles of matter. Each of these particles has a small force of gravity acting upon it. Together, the forces act like a single force pulling downwards at just one point, called the centre of gravity. An object will balance when it is supported in line with its centre of gravity. Balancing is easiest if the object has a low centre of gravity.

Gravity in space

Gravity is a universal force, because it acts between any two objects, wherever they are in the Universe. The force that keeps our feet firmly on the ground is the same one that holds huge clusters of stars together as galaxies.

Galaxies
A typical galaxy is about 100,000 light-years across. The stars are so massive that gravity can still act over this huge distance, preventing the stars from drifting off into space.

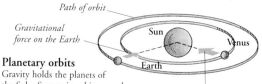

Path of orbit

Gravitational force on the Earth

Sun

Venus

Earth

Gravitational force on Venus

Planetary orbits
Gravity holds the planets of the Solar System in orbit around the Sun. Venus and the Earth have similar masses, but because Venus is closer to the Sun than the Earth, the force of gravity keeping it in orbit is greater.

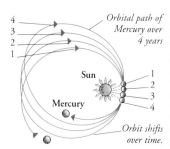

Orbital path of Mercury over 4 years

4
3
2
1

Sun

Mercury

1
2
3
4

Orbit shifts over time.

General Relativity
In 1915, German-born physicist Albert Einstein published his Theory of General Relativity. This theory sees gravity not as a force, but as a curvature of space caused by bodies of matter. In 1919, the theory was used successfully to explain why Mercury's orbit gradually varies over time.

Weight

The force of gravity acting on an object is called weight. Like all forces, weight is expressed in units called newtons (N). An object's weight is directly related to its mass. On Earth, 1 kg (2.2 lb) of matter weighs about 10 N.

Apple weighs about 1 N.

Newton meter measures weight and other forces.

Apple has a mass of 100 g (3.5 oz).

The force of gravity acting on the ball is constant.

Balls slow down as they are thrown upwards.

Balls speed up as they fall.

Gravity tries to pull the balls downwards.

Earth's gravity

Gravity always acts towards the centre of the Earth, defining the "downwards" direction at every point on the planet's surface. Gravity pulls a juggling ball towards the ground, slowing it as it rises, and speeding it up as it falls. The ball also pulls on the Earth, but the Earth is so massive that the ball's gravity has no noticeable effect.

Moon's gravity
The Moon is smaller and has less mass than the Earth, so the force of gravity is weaker on the Moon. A hammer on the Moon weighs one-sixth of its weight on the Earth. It takes 1.1 seconds for a hammer to fall 1 m (3.3 ft) on the Moon, but only 0.44 seconds on the Earth.

Earth   Moon

Aristotle

The Greek philosopher Aristotle (c.384–322 BC) believed that heavy objects fall faster than lighter ones. Aristotle's ideas were accepted until the Italian scientist Galileo Galilei (1564–1642) showed that gravity pulls all objects to Earth at the same speed.

Harbour at low tide

Tides
Twice each day, the waters of the ocean rise a little and then fall back. This movement is called a tide, and it is caused by the pull of the Moon's gravity. The Sun also influences tides. When the Earth, Sun, and Moon are in line, their combined gravity produces tides that are higher than normal, called spring tides.

Timeline

4th century BC Aristotle proposes that stones fall to the ground simply because they are heavy, and that smoke rises because it is light.

1604 Italian scientist Galileo Galilei investigates how objects fall to Earth.

17th century English physicist Isaac Newton publishes his Law of Gravitation, perhaps inspired by seeing an apple fall from a tree.

Model showing how space curves around a planet.

1915 Einstein's Theory of General Relativity describes gravity as a curvature of space.

1919 English astronomer Arthur Eddington (1882–1944) obtains proof of Einstein's theory by observing light, reaching Earth from a distant star, being bent by the Sun's gravity.

FIND OUT MORE   EINSTEIN, ALBERT   FORCE AND MOTION   MATTER   MOON   NEWTON, SIR ISAAC   OCEANS AND SEAS

GREAT DEPRESSION

ON 24 OCTOBER, 1929, the world's financial heart – the New York Stock Exchange – stopped beating. Share prices crashed, consumers stopped investing, banks failed, and millions of people lost their jobs. Within a year, a severe economic depression gripped the world, and governments struggled to cope with the crisis. Ill-thought-out economic policies led to social unrest and the rise of right-wing authoritarian governments in Europe. The Great Depression lasted for a decade; it ended when the threat of war resulted in the need for workers to produce armaments.

Roaring Twenties
Once western economies had recovered from World War I, they entered a period of rapid growth. High public confidence, low interest rates, and optimistic investments created a boom in the 1920s. Women enjoyed greater freedom, and most people spent more on leisure and entertainment than ever before.

A fashionable 1920s' "flapper"

US magazine front cover, 1926

Wall Street Crash

In 1929, after years of rising share prices, the Stock Exchange on New York's Wall Street saw a dramatic crash (fall) in prices. The crash bankrupted many companies and private citizens.

Bread line, New York, 1932

Soup kitchens
Many people lost their life savings after the Wall Street Crash, and bankrupt companies had to lay off their workers. With no work and no social security system, millions of American families faced poverty and hunger. Every town opened soup kitchens to provide at least one good meal a day.

Jarrow March
By the early 1930s, the effects of the Depression had spread to Britain, Germany, and the rest of the world. Poverty was rife. In 1936, 200 unemployed workers marched 444 km (276 miles) from Jarrow, northeast England, to the capital, London, demanding jobs. Almost 70 per cent of Jarrow's workers were out of work.

Jarrow marchers on their way to London

A family in the Texas Dust Bowl, 1938

Dust Bowl

In the United States, years of over-farming and drought caused dust storms throughout the mid-western states during the 1930s. Thousands of farmers, already hit hard by the Depression and suffering desperate poverty, were forced to abandon their land to seek work in the fruit farms of California. Few found it. Their plight was immortalized in John Steinbeck's classic novel, *The Grapes of Wrath* (1939).

Rearmament

From the 1930s, world leaders took action to combat unemployment: the USA's President Roosevelt started the New Deal to get people back to work. However, it was renewed war in Europe that ended the Depression. Armament factories producing aeroplanes and tanks created new jobs and revitalized the world economy.

New Deal
In 1932, FD Roosevelt won the US presidential election against President Hoover. He pledged "a new deal for the American people", establishing agencies to regulate business, start public works programmes, and build a series of huge hydroelectric power plants, such as the Hoover Dam, in order to provide employment.

Franklin D Roosevelt
Roosevelt (1882–1945) became Democratic senator for New York in 1910, and Assistant Secretary to the Navy from 1913–1920. In 1921 he developed polio and was paralysed, which confined him to a wheelchair for the rest of his life. He returned to public life in 1928 as governor of New York, and won the 1932 presidential election. He promised "direct, vigorous action" against the Depression, and won re-election three times. He led the USA to victory in World War II.

Hoover Dam, Nevada, USA

Timeline
1929 Wall Street Crash.

1930 World unemployment doubles.

1931 Britain forms national government to deal with crisis.

1932 More than 1 in 4 workers unemployed in USA; unemployment in Germany triples to 5.6 million.

1933 Hitler comes to power in Germany, with promises to get the country back to work through rearmament and national expansion.

1933 Slow recovery begins in USA and Europe.

1939 Outbreak of war in Europe ends Depression as workers are employed in armament factories.

Italy's Fascist leader Benito Mussolini taking the salute at a rally

Rise of Fascism
The Depression caused much tension. Socialists agitated for reform, but some countries looked to right-wing solutions. Italy had had a Fascist government since 1922; Germany got one in 1933, and Spain in 1936. Authoritarian governments across Europe quashed dissent from workers and left-wingers.

FIND OUT MORE   GERMANY, HISTORY OF   UNITED STATES, HISTORY OF   WORLD WAR II

GREAT ZIMBABWE

ONE OF AFRICA'S GREATEST archaeological mysteries is the walled city of Great Zimbabwe. This massive granite zimbabwe – a word literally meaning chief's court – was begun in the 13th century. By the 14th century, it had become the capital of a vast kingdom that stretched between the Zambezi and Limpopo rivers. The people of Great Zimbabwe were mainly farmers, but the city was also the main centre for trade and religion. However, by 1450, Great Zimbabwe had been abandoned for reasons that remain a mystery. Today its ruins stand in modern Zimbabwe, the southern African country named after this remarkable walled structure.

Rise of Great Zimbabwe
Great Zimbabwe's first city started as a farming settlement, possibly as early as the 2nd century. As well as rearing and selling cattle, its people mined for gold and copper on the Zimbabwe plateau. By the 12th century, long-distance trade based on gold and copper was passing through the city from the east coast of Africa. As Great Zimbabwe rose in importance and wealth, it was rebuilt in stone and increased in size.

Great Enclosure
Built of massive granite blocks, the Great Enclosure is a huge dry stone wall that surrounded the city, providing protection for Great Zimbabwe's people. Inside the enclosure, people lived in circular houses made from daga (a gravel-like clay) and roofed with thatch. There were also small oval enclosures – but, like the stone conical tower, their purpose remains a mystery. Near to the enclosure was a hill complex, which was used for religious rituals.

The conical tower was 9 m (27 ft) high, and made of solid stone.

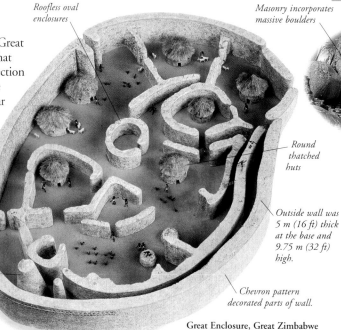

Roofless oval enclosures

Masonry incorporates massive boulders

Round thatched huts

Outside wall was 5 m (16 ft) thick at the base and 9.75 m (32 ft) high.

Chevron pattern decorated parts of wall.

Great Enclosure, Great Zimbabwe

Hill complex

Hill complex
The religious centre, where the ancestors' spirits were worshipped, was built on a hill near the Great Enclosure. At the front of the complex, there was a public space where the mambo (ruler) conducted sacred rites.

Conical tower
A massive and mysterious cone-shaped tower stands inside the Great Enclosure. Some archaeologists think it may be a monument celebrating the power and wealth of the rulers of Great Zimbabwe.

Farming
Great Zimbabwe at its height had 10,000 people living in and around it. Most people were farmers in the surrounding areas. They herded cattle and grew millet, sorghum, and vegetables, which they sold to the many traders visiting the walled city.

Zimbabwean cattle

Ancestor worship
The people of Great Zimbabwe worshipped the spirits of their dead rulers, known as ancestors. In sacrificial rites, they killed calves, and offered the meat to ancestor spirits on beautifully carved soapstone dishes. They placed the dishes in sacred places outside the hill complex.

Birds
Eight carved soapstone birds have been found at Great Zimbabwe. They stood in sacred places on 1-m (3-ft) high soapstone columns. Each of the birds may represent a royal ancestor, and one of them is now used as the symbol of the modern state of Zimbabwe.

Soapstone bird on column

Trade
The prosperous trading centre of Great Zimbabwe was situated on one of the trade routes that linked southern Africa to the east coast. Traders from Sofala and Kilwa (in modern Mozambique) obtained gold and copper from Great Zimbabwe to export to Arabia and Asia.

Metal exports
The people of Great Zimbabwe mined gold, copper, iron, and tin on the Zimbabwe plateau. Cross-shaped ingots were exchanged for trade goods from Asia, such as beads, glassware, and ceramics.

Copper ingot

Karl Mauch
A German self-taught geologist, Mauch (1837–75), travelled southern Africa from 1865 to 1872. During his nine months in Great Zimbabwe (1871) he drew diagrams of the ruins and sketched the carved stone and metal objects found there. Much of today's knowledge of the area is based on Mauch's diaries.

Timeline
c.900 Iron Age (Shona) people settle between the Zambezi and the Limpopo rivers in southern Africa.

1100s Trade passing through Great Zimbabwe to Africa's East Coast increases.

1200s Zimbabwean gold being exported to Asia.

1250 Building in stone begins at Great Zimbabwe.

Early 1400s Great Enclosure is completed; and Great Zimbabwe reaches its greatest extent.

1450 Great Zimbabwe is abandoned, probably because its people leave to look for new and better farmland.

FIND OUT MORE   AFRICA, HISTORY OF   METALS   MALI EMPIRE

GREECE, ANCIENT

MORE THAN 2,500 YEARS AGO one of the world's most influential civilizations flowered in mainland Greece. From the 8th until the 2nd centuries BC, Greek writers, thinkers, and artists made a huge contribution to western culture – especially in politics, drama, mythology, architecture, and literature. Greek civilization declined when, after defeating the Persians and peacefully colonizing much of Europe, they were absorbed into the Roman Empire.

Mycenaean civilization

The Mycenaeans formed the first great mainland Greek civilization (c.2700–1120 BC), and were the forerunners of classical Greece. These Bronze Age traders and warriors ranged all over the Mediterranean area from their settlement at Mycenae. The gold mask was once thought to be of Agamemnon, a leader in the legendary Trojan War.

G

Polis

Ancient Greece was made up of hundreds of separate city-states. Some were hardly bigger than villages, while others were based around great cities, such as Sparta or Athens. Each of these city-states was known as a polis (plural: poleis). Laws, festivals, and government systems varied, and there was often war between rival poleis, despite their common Greek background. The need for land led some poleis to colonize other parts of the Mediterranean between the 8th and 6th centuries BC, and in this way ancient Greece expanded.

The Parthenon

Red marble tiles covered the roof.

Coloured frieze

White marble columns

Reliefs decorated the exterior.

Temples were built on stepped platforms.

Ancient Greece, c.4th century BC

Sparta

Life in Sparta was disciplined and harsh. Spartans trained both girls and boys to excel at sports and feats of endurance. To strengthen military power, all the boys went on to become soldiers. After helping Athens defeat the Persians in 480 BC, Sparta conquered Athens in the Peloponnesian War (431–404 BC), and became master of Greece.

Spartan warrior

Athens

From the 6th century BC, Athens was governed by a form of democracy (rule by the people), in which all male citizens voted. In the 5th century BC, thanks to its powerful navy, Athens had a maritime empire in the Aegean Sea, and its 250,000-strong population enjoyed a golden age of art and culture. After their triumph against the Persians, the Athenians celebrated by building a massive "fortified citadel" – the Acropolis. The Parthenon (447 and 432 BC) was the most important temple in the Acropolis, and was dedicated to Athena.

Clash of the Titans

The Greeks believed that the world was originally inhabited by giants called Titans. Their ruler, Cronos, swallowed his children alive, so that they could not overthrow him. One son, Zeus, escaped this fate when his mother gave Cronos a clothed stone to swallow instead. Zeus grew up in secret, made Cronos vomit up his siblings, defeated the other Titans in battle, and made himself king of the gods.

Cronos eating his children

The Legend of Troy

Little of the ancient city of Troy (in modern Turkey) remains. Homer's *Iliad* says that a Greek army besieged Troy for 10 years in the late Mycenaean Age (c.1250 BC). This became known as the Trojan War. According to legend, Athena advised the Greeks to smuggle their soldiers into the city inside a huge wooden horse, and in this way they gained victory.

Model of Trojan Horse

Mount Olympus

Ancient Greeks believed that various deities (gods and goddesses) watched over ordinary mortals from a cloud-palace above the highest mountain in Greece – the snow-capped Mount Olympus. The deities who lived there were also known as Olympians. Each Olympian had specific responsibilities: Poseidon was in charge of the sea, Athena of wisdom and the arts, Apollo of music and poetry, and Demeter of crops. The supreme god was Zeus, lord of sky and earth. Greek cities regarded different deities as their special protectors. For example, Athens was devoted to the cult of Athena.

Oracle at Delphi

Ancient Greeks consulted the gods for advice or prophecies at holy places called oracles. The most famous oracle in Greece was at Delphi. People went there to ask questions at Apollo's shrine about religious or political matters. A high priestess went into a trance to give Apollo's answers. Most gods had their special shrine, but they competed with each other for the best ones. Legend has it that Athena won a competition against Poseidon over the Parthenon in Athens, the largest city in Greece, and he had to move his shrine to Attica.

Poseidon was Zeus's brother and god of the sea.

Part of a trident

Poseidon is usually shown holding a fish.

Poseidon, god of the sea

Homer

The Greek poet Homer probably lived in the 7th or 8th century BC. He is believed to be the author of two of the world's greatest epic poems: the *Iliad*, which is about the siege of Troy, and the *Odyssey*, which describes the wanderings of the hero Odysseus after the Trojan War. According to to later writers, Homer was blind.

Ceres, goddess of the harvest

Cloak

Chiton, or full tunic

Culture

Ancient Greek art and science was of the highest standard, and set the standard for European culture for centuries. "Greece, though conquered," wrote the Roman poet Horace, "brought the arts to the uncivilized Latin peoples" (Romans) – and through them to modern Europe.

Sculpture

Ancient Greek sculpture was famous for its naturalness, beauty, and perfect proportions. Statues related to all aspects of life, including religious worship and sport. Those of deities, such as Ceres, were popular among farmers, and were left at shrines to ensure a good harvest.

Drama and architecture

The ancient Greeks learned much from the Egyptians about using stone in their architecture – but their theatres were original. In the golden age of Athens (400s BC), dramatists, such as Aeschylus, Sophocles, and Euripides wrote tragedies that are still performed.

Epidaurus theatre

Amphora

Human figures at a banquet

Art

Red-figure painting replaced black-figure in c.530 BC. Most red-figure vases (amphorae) were made from Athenian clay. Subjects were usually male, and were often shown banqueting or engaged in athletics.

Pericles

From 443 BC, Pericles (c.495–429 BC) was the most important politician and general in Athens. A great public speaker and champion of democracy, he strengthened and expanded the Athenian empire after defeating the Persians. He also made Athens the most splendid city in Greece by arranging for the Parthenon and other buildings to be built on the Acropolis, a rocky hill overlooking the city.

Language and literature

Ancient Greek, like Latin, is known as a "classical" language. Many great works of Greek literature have survived by authors such as Hesiod and Appolonius (poets), Thucydides (a historian), and Plato (a philosopher).

Greek inscription of thanks to Asclepius, the god of medicine

ΑΣΚΛΗ
ΠΙΩ
ΚΑΙ
ΥΓΕΙΑ
ΤΥΧΗ
ΕΥΧΑΡΙΣ
ΤΗΡΙΟΝ

Alphabet

The word "alphabet" (used in many modern languages, including English) was formed by joining the first two letters of ancient Greek: alpha and beta. The Cyrillic alphabet of eastern Europe also grew out of the Greek alphabet.

Greek-Persian wars

After 545 BC, the mighty Persian Empire took over Greek cities in Ionia, the easternmost part of Greek territory. When Athens tried to lend support to the cities (499–494 BC), the Persians invaded mainland Greece, but were driven back at Marathon. Ten years later, an alliance between Athens, Sparta, and other Greek cities defeated another massive Persian expedition on land and sea at Salamis.

The Treasury, Delphi

Battle of Marathon

In 490 BC, a Persian force sailed across the Aegean Sea, and landed in Attica. On the plain of Marathon, against all odds, it was heavily defeated by an army of Athenians and their allies. The Athenians built a treasury at Delphi to mark this victory, filled it with Persian spoils, and dedicated it to Apollo, the god of war.

Battle of Salamis

In 480 BC, the Persian emperor Xerxes the Great led a huge force along the shores of the Aegean Sea. As central Greece fell, the Athenians evacuated their city. A smaller Greek fleet then lured the Persians into battle in the straits between the mainland and the island of Salamis – and defeated them decisively.

Philip of Macedon

Warrior-king Philip II ruled Macedon, a northern state in Greece, from 359 to 336 BC. A strong king and a great diplomat, Philip made Macedon the dominant power in the Greek world. He was murdered on the point of invading Persia, but by then had laid the foundations for his son, Alexander, to continue his military feats.

Jason and the Argonauts   *Poseidon*   *The Clashing Rocks*

Jason and the Argonauts

Even today, Greek myths are rewritten, and made into plays and films. Few tales are as dramatic as the quest by Jason and his ship, the *Argo*, to steal the Golden Fleece of the Sun from a watchful dragon. On their journey, Jason and his crew (including the hero Herakles) were helped and hindered by many gods, monsters, witches, and giants.

Timeline

c.2700–1120 BC Myceneaen civilization flourishes.

c.750–550 BC Greeks colonize areas in Italy and Africa.

560–510 BC Athenian influence spreads.

Detail from amphora

510 BC Cleisthenes, an Athenian statesman, introduces democracy to Athens.

c.510–366 BC Peloponnesian League forms, led by Sparta.

499–494 BC Revolt against Persia by Ionian Greeks.

490 BC Battle of Marathon.

480–479 BC Greeks repel Persian invaders at Salamis and Plataea.

477 BC Athens and Ionian Greeks form Delian League against Persia.

459 BC Sparta defeats Athens in first Peloponnesian War.

443–429 BC Pericles dominant in Athens.

431–404 BC Sparta wins second, or Great, Peloponnesian War.

378–371 BC Thebes overthrows Sparta as leading Greek power.

359–323 BC Reigns of Philip II and his son Alexander the Great of Macedon.

Hephaistos, god of fire

FIND OUT MORE   ART, HISTORY OF   ALEXANDER THE GREAT   CITIES   ETRUSCANS   EUROPE, HISTORY OF   GODS AND GODDESSES   MINOANS   PERSIAN EMPIRES   ROMAN EMPIRE   SOCRATES

GREECE AND BULGARIA

ALTHOUGH Greece and Bulgaria share a border, high mountains separate the two countries, making communication difficult. Greece and Bulgaria are quite different. Three-fifths of the Greek mainland is mountainous, and only one-third of the land is cultivated. By contrast, Bulgaria is much more fertile with a strong agricultural tradition. Greece has a strong history of democratic government, while Bulgaria is only just emerging from almost half a century of communist rule.

Physical features

Surrounded by sea on three sides, the country of Greece is made up of the mainland, the Peloponnese peninsula, and more than 2,000 islands. It is a mixture of high mountains, dry, dusty plains, and dramatic coastlines. Landlocked on three sides, Bulgaria has broad fertile valleys, separated by the Balkan and Rhodope mountains.

Regional climate

44°C (111°F)   -25°C (-13°F)
24°C (75°F)   6°C (43°F)
525 mm (20.5 in)

Greece has very hot, dry summers and cooler winters. The northern mountains have cold winters. Annual rainfall is low, and the country suffers from water shortages. Bulgaria, by contrast, has warm summers and cold, snowy winters, with a high rainfall – especially in the mountains.

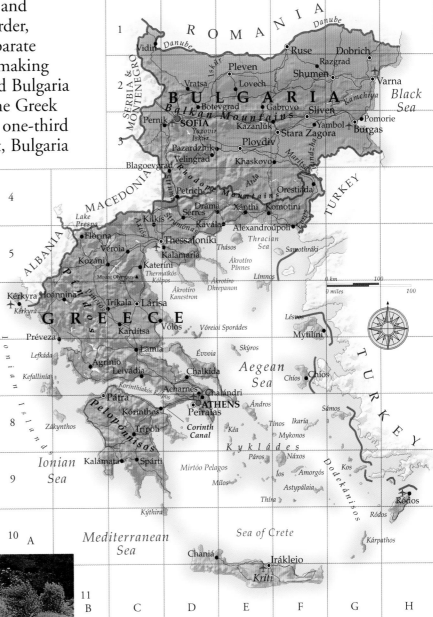

Danubian Plain

The mighty River Danube forms most of Bulgaria's northern border with Romania, flowing through the vast and fertile Danubian Plain that extends across the width of the country. This rolling farmland is used for grazing sheep, goats, and cattle, and for cultivating a variety of crops including sunflowers, which are grown for their oil.

Crete

The largest of the Greek islands at 8,380 sq km (3,235 sq miles), Crete lies 100 km (62 miles) southeast of the Greek mainland. More than 600,000 people live on the island, and one third of Cretans are farmers. Many people work in tourism.

Mount Olympus

Much of central and western Greece is made up of steep, rugged mountains, many of which are capped with snow for several months of the year. Mount Olympus is Greece's highest peak at 2,917 m (9,570 ft). Once thought to be the home of the gods, it is now a national park with busy ski resorts.

Orthodox Church

Greece is the only official Christian Orthodox country in the world. Priests are responsible community figures and play an important part in national events. Most Greeks and Bulgars belong to the Eastern Orthodox Church, which split from the Roman Catholic Church in 1054. Each country has its own branch of the Church, which also flourishes in other parts of eastern Europe, and Russia. Around one tenth of the world's Christians belong to the Orthodox Church.

Greek Orthodox priest

Greece

One of Europe's oldest nations, Greece gained independence from almost 500 years of Turkish rule in 1830. Although it is the poorest member of the European Union, the country has a thriving tourist industry and a large shipping fleet. The Greek people have a strong national unity, based on their deep-rooted Orthodox religion, and a language that has remained in use for 2,700 years.

Parsley

Tomato *Cucumber*

Olives *Aubergine*

Farming

High mountains and poor soils make farming difficult in Greece. However, agriculture employs about 23 per cent of the work-force, mainly on small, traditional farms. The main crops are olives, citrus fruits, salad vegetables, tomatoes, and grapes. Small herds of sheep and goats produce meat, and milk for cheese and yoghurt. Greece is the world's third largest producer of olive oil.

GREECE FACTS

CAPITAL CITY	Athens
AREA	131,940 sq km (50,942 sq miles)
POPULATION	10,600,000
DENSITY	81 per sq km (210 per sq mile)
MAIN LANGUAGE	Greek
MAJOR RELIGION	Christian
CURRENCY	Euro
LIFE EXPECTANCY	78 years
PEOPLE PER DOCTOR	244
GOVERNMENT	Multi-party democracy
ADULT LITERACY	97%

Food

The Greeks love to eat outdoors in the warm summer months. Meals are simple and tasty and consist mainly of tomatoes, salad, olives, feta cheese, lamb, some fish, and yoghurt made from sheep's milk. Retsina, a wine flavoured with pine resin, is often served with food.

Athens

Home to almost one-third of the Greek population, Athens is famous for its ancient buildings, such as the Acropolis and the 2,400-year-old ruins of the Parthenon temple. On certain days, cars are banned from the capital to protect the ruins. Nearby, pinewoods and mountains provide a retreat from the busy city.

Ruins of the Parthenon temple

Tourism

Each year, more than 12,000,000 tourists visit Greece, attracted by its warm climate, ancient monuments, and beautiful islands. Tourism is the mainstay of the economy and employs thousands of Greeks each summer.

Greek islander selling sponges to tourists

Shipping

Greece has the world's largest merchant fleet, and relies on ships to move goods between the many islands. The narrow Corinth Canal, built in 1893, links the Ionian and Aegean seas, providing important access to Athens.

Bulgaria

From 1944 to 1989, Bulgaria was part of the Russian communist bloc. Since gaining independence, Bulgaria is slowly adapting to a democratic government and a western-style economy. About 85 per cent of Bulgaria's population are Bulgars, with minorities of Turks, Macedonians, and Roma. The small groups have suffered discrimination, but are gaining power in parliament.

Tourism

Bulgaria's Black Sea coast is becoming increasingly popular as a holiday destination, in particular the towns of Varna and Burgas. New airports serve western tourists, whilst Russians cross the Black Sea by ferry. Many new resorts have been built, and the natural beauty of the coastline, with its sandy beaches, pine forests, and old fishing villages, is often spoiled by high-rise hotel developments.

Resort near Varna

BULGARIA FACTS

CAPITAL CITY	Sofia
AREA	110,910 sq km (42,822 sq miles)
POPULATION	7,900,000
DENSITY	71 per sq km (185 per sq mile)
MAIN LANGUAGE	Bulgarian
MAJOR RELIGIONS	Christian, Muslim
CURRENCY	Lev
LIFE EXPECTANCY	71 years
PEOPLE PER DOCTOR	286
GOVERNMENT	Multi-party democracy
ADULT LITERACY	98%

Sofia

Bulgaria's capital is also its largest city, with more than one million inhabitants. Founded by the Romans, it is now the cultural and economic centre, with one-fifth of the country's industry. The Alexander Nevsky Cathedral was built in the 1870s to celebrate liberation from Turkish rule.

Alexander Nevsky Cathedral

Energy

Twenty-five per cent of Bulgaria's electricity comes from the Kozloduy nuclear power station built by the former Soviet Union in an earthquake zone. Increased safety measures have been introduced since 1990. Bulgaria imports 70 per cent of its energy due to poor coal and oil resources, and has built a hydroelectric generator.

Farming

Near the town of Kazanlúk in the Balkan Mountains, vast fields of roses are grown. The petals, picked at dawn in midsummer, are used to produce attar, the essential oil of roses, which is used in perfume manufacture. Farther south, in the Maritsa valley, tobacco plants are grown and dried for cigarettes. Black grapes grown on the Danubian Plain are used for making high-quality red wine.

FIND OUT MORE CHRISTIANITY EUROPE, HISTORY OF EUROPEAN UNION FARMING GREECE, ANCIENT POLLUTION PORTS AND WATERWAYS SHIPS AND BOATS SOVIET UNION

GROWTH AND DEVELOPMENT

AS THE HUMAN BODY grows and develops, it follows a regular sequence of changes. After birth, a human being passes through infancy, childhood, puberty and adolescence, and into adulthood. The body grows at different rates at different times. Rapid growth, called a growth spurt, occurs during infancy and again at puberty, while growth is steady throughout childhood, but ceases in adulthood. In later life, the body ages as it becomes less efficient. Eventually, one or more of the body's systems stop working, and a person dies.

G

Changing proportions

Different parts of the body grow at different rates. Changing body proportions can be compared by fitting photographs of children and young adults into a panel that makes them appear the same height. The panel divides each body into eight equal parts. The head, for example, makes up one quarter of the height of a newborn baby, but only one eighth of the height of a 20-year-old.

2 months 55 cm (1 ft 10 in)	2 years 86 cm (2 ft 10 in)	4 years 110 cm (3 ft 8 in)	7 years 120 cm (4 ft)	12 years 145 cm (4 ft 10 in)	20 years 175 cm (5 ft 10 in)

From baby to child

During the first two years of life, a young human being grows and develops rapidly. A six-week-old baby is helpless and must have everything done for it, but by the age of two years, the baby can walk, talk, and feed itself. Growth and development is marked by a series of age milestones at which children have learned certain skills.

6 weeks
The baby sleeps when not being held or fed, and cries when distressed. She can follow objects with her eyes and listen to a person talking.

6 months
The baby can sit supported with her head up and back straight. She holds objects, squeals, and babbles.

8 months
The baby can sit up by herself, will try to crawl, and can stand if supported. She turns towards the sound of a familiar voice, and can imitate simple sounds.

10 months
The baby can crawl rapidly, pull herself up to a standing position, point to and pick up objects. She says her first words, usually "mama" and "dada".

Toddler can walk a few steps on her own.

Child needs help getting dressed but can put on own shoes and socks.

Child can dress and undress herself.

14 months
The child can stand alone and may walk without help. She speaks a few words, and tries to indicate what she wants.

2 years
She can run and jump, turn the pages of a book, identify pictures of familiar objects, and form a few short phrases.

4 years
The young girl now has good balance and can hop on one foot. She can draw simple pictures and copy some letters.

Developing bones

The skeleton is formed before birth from flexible cartilage. During childhood, this is replaced by bone, as revealed by X-rays. The skeleton continues to get larger and harder during the teenage years.

A newborn baby's skeleton is made of both bone and cartilage. Unlike bone, cartilage cannot be seen on an X-ray.

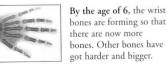

By the age of 6, the wrist bones are forming so that there are now more bones. Other bones have got harder and bigger.

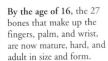

By the age of 16, the 27 bones that make up the fingers, palm, and wrist, are now mature, hard, and adult in size and form.

Adolescence and puberty

Adolescence is the whole process of growing up from a child to an adult. During adolescence, changes occur to a person's body and in the way they think and feel. Puberty is part of adolescence during which the body grows rapidly and changes shape, and boys and girls become sexually mature and able to reproduce.

Puberty in boys   Puberty in girls

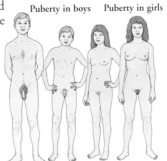

Changes during puberty
In girls, puberty begins between the ages of 10–14. The body becomes rounder, breasts grow, and periods begin. In boys, puberty begins between the ages of 12–16. The body becomes more muscular, the testes produce sperm, and the voice deepens.

Ageing

Growing old is a normal part of life. Humans age because the body's cells gradually become less efficient. Signs of ageing usually appear after 40 years of age. The body becomes less mobile, hair thins and turns grey, and the skin wrinkles. Bones become brittle and can break more easily. Exercise and a healthy diet can help to slow down the ageing process.

FIND OUT MORE   BRAIN AND NERVOUS SYSTEM   HORMONES AND ENDOCRINE SYSTEM   HUMAN BODY   MUSCLES AND MOVEMENT   REPRODUCTION   SKELETON

GULF STATES

SAUDI ARABIA, Yemen, Oman, Kuwait, United Arab Emirates, Qatar, and Bahrain – make up the Arabian Peninsula. Six of these countries – all except Yemen – have coastlines on the Gulf and are often called the Gulf States. As a result of the rich oil deposits in the region – about half the world's total – many of these countries are wealthy, and the region is politically very important. In the past 50 years, there has been great industrial and social change in what was an underdeveloped region. Even so, most of the land is uninhabited.

Physical features

Nearly all of the Arabian Peninsula is dry desert, sandy or rocky, with some rugged, bare mountains near the coast. There are small fertile areas along the coasts, in some mountain regions, and at oases. Most of the fresh water for cities and industry comes from large desalination plants that remove salt from and purify sea water from the Gulf.

Red Sea
The warm, salty waters of the narrow Red Sea, 2,000 km (1,243 miles) long, separate Africa from Asia. The Red Sea is connected to the Mediterranean Sea by the Suez Canal, which was built in 1869 to provide a route for ships between Europe and eastern Asia.

Yemeni Mountains
These rugged mountains in the west of Yemen reach a height of 3,760 m (12,336 ft). The western slopes are well watered by rain blowing in from the Red Sea and are extensively cultivated by terracing. The climate is ideal for growing coffee, grapes, and cotton.

96°C (36°F)   63°C (17°F)
118 mm (4.5 in)

Regional climate
Most of the region is very dry and hot all year, although winter temperatures in northern Saudi Arabia and Kuwait may drop below freezing. Only southwest Saudi Arabia and north Yemen receive rain. Some desert areas have no rain for years at a time.

Islam

For almost 1,500 years, Islam has been the dominant religion in the Gulf States. Muslims, the followers of Islam, believe in one god, Allah, and the prophet Muhammad, who was born in the Saudi Arabian town of Mecca. In many countries, life is interrupted five times a day while people pray.

Najd Desert
The Najd is a vast area of stony desert plateau at the heart of Saudi Arabia. Some Najdi people still live here, leading a semi-nomadic existence tending camels and sheep, although many are moving into towns. Saudi Arabia's largest desert is the uninhabited Rub' al Khali, in the south, known as the "Empty Quarter".

Worshippers outside the mosque, Dubai

Saudi Arabia

The largest and most important country in the Arabian Peninsula, Saudi Arabia is 95 per cent hot, dry, and inhospitable desert. The most populated areas lie along the Gulf and Red Sea coasts. Founded in 1922 by Ibn Saud, Saudi Arabia has grown wealthy as a result of its vast oil reserves, discovered in 1938. It has major refining and petrochemical industries and spends freely on farming, education, and agriculture.

Riyadh

Saudi Arabia's capital since 1932, Riyadh is a modern city of around two million people. Lying among oases of orchards and palm groves, it is the centre of Saudi Arabia's commerce and government. Buildings range from smart, modern skyscrapers, erected since 1950, to poor shacks.

Saudi-Cairo Bank

People

Most Saudi people are Muslim Arabs. They take their religion seriously and interpret the Qur'an, the Islamic holy book, strictly. Women must wear veils and may not drive cars. However, about 33 per cent of schoolchildren are girls, and women may take certain jobs, such as nursing and teaching.

Cardamom pods are added to flavour the coffee.

Bedouin

Nomadic Bedouin roam the vast desert, grazing their camels, sheep, and goats in oases. They live in portable tents, but the government is trying to persuade them to give up their wandering life to settle in cities.

Lentils   **Dates**

Mecca (Makkah)

Every year, two million Muslims visit the Ka'ba shrine in the Great Mosque at Mecca, birthplace of Muhammad and Islamic holy city. All Muslims should make a pilgrimage, or *hajj*, to Mecca at least once in their lives.

Farming

Massive irrigation projects using desalinated sea water to irrigate vast, circular fields now make it possible for Saudi farmers to cultivate wheat, fruit, and vegetables. Farming employs one-eighth of the work-force.

Tomato

G

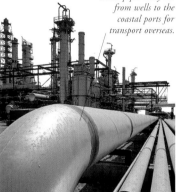

Giant pipes carry oil from wells to the coastal ports for transport overseas.

Oilfields

Saudi Arabia has the world's biggest oil and gas reserves – a quarter of the world's total – and is the world's leading oil exporter. Income from oil has improved living standards.

Yemen

Formerly two separate countries, Yemen was united in 1990. The north is mountainous, with a narrow, fertile coastal strip on the Red Sea coast, where cotton and grapes are grown. The arid Rub' al Khali desert, or "Empty Quarter" covers the northeast. Yemen's main source of income is oil, some of which is refined in the port of Aden.

Traditional coffee pot

Coffee

Yemen produces fine coffee beans, and coffee drinking is thought to have originated here. Mocha coffee is named after the port of Al-Makha from where it was exported. Yemenis chew *qat*, shoots of a narcotic shrub, with coffee.

Sana

Yemen's modern capital, Sana, sits in the centre of the country, 2,380 m (7,808 ft) above sea-level. With a population of about half a million, it is a modern commercial and industrial centre with historic buildings, markets (*souks*), and ornately decorated mosques.

Oman

Ruled by a sultan, the Sultanate of Oman is mostly desert, with a narrow fertile strip along the Gulf of Oman in the north, where most of the people live. Oil has brought the country great prosperity. About 75 per cent of the people belong to the Islamic Ibadi sect, which adopts a liberal attitude towards women. Pakistani Baluchis make up one-quarter of Omanis.

Sardines

Anchovy

Fishing

Omani fishermen catch 118,000 tonnes of fish a year in the rich waters of the Arabian Sea and Gulf of Oman. The main catches are anchovies, cod, cuttlefish, sardines, and tuna. The country exports dried fish and fish meal.

City of the sands

Archaeologists have discovered the remains of a city, believed to have been built in about 3000 BC, buried beneath the sands of southern Oman. They think it may be the remains of the legendary lost Arabian city of Ubar.

Kuwait

Oil has transformed Kuwait, a tiny desert country at the northern end of the Gulf, into one of the world's most prosperous nations. Iraq's invasion of Kuwait, in 1990, was quelled by a United Nations force after a brief war. Since its liberation, Kuwait has built a wall to separate its territory from Iraq.

Kuwait City

The country of Kuwait is named after its capital city, which was founded in the 18th century. Situated on the shores of a natural harbour, Kuwait City is modern, built on a grid pattern with many attractive houses. The country's affluence is reflected in its glittering skyscrapers.

KUWAIT FACTS

CAPITAL CITY	Kuwait City
AREA	17,820 sq km (6,880 sq miles)
POPULATION	2,000,000
MAIN LANGUAGES	Arabic, English
MAJOR RELIGION	Muslim
CURRENCY	Kuwaiti dinar

Oil

Kuwait has about ten per cent of the world's total oil reserves. The oil industry, which attracts large overseas investment, accounts for more than 80 per cent of the country's export earnings. Kuwait also has reserves of natural gas.

Free education

The revenue from the oil industry enables the Kuwaiti government to provide its children, both male and female, with free education, from nursery level to university. The Kuwaiti people have some of the world's highest salaries, pay no income tax, and receive free health care and social services.

United Arab Emirates

The United Arab Emirates (UAE) is a federation of seven small states: Abu Dhabi, Ajman, Dubai, Fujairah, Ras al Khaimah, Sharjah, and Umm al Quaiwan. Each ruled by its own independent emir, or sheik, they unite for international matters and to sell the oil that has made them rich.

Fishing

All the states bordering the Gulf have busy fishing fleets. In high summer they also send divers down to collect pearls from the pearl oysters. This industry has flourished for many hundreds of years.

Pearl develops from a grain of sand inside the shell.

UNITED ARAB EMIRATES FACTS

CAPITAL CITY	Abu Dhabi
AREA	82,880 sq km (32,000 sq miles)
POPULATION	2,700,000
MAIN LANGUAGES	Arabic, Farsi
MAJOR RELIGION	Muslim
CURRENCY	UAE dirham

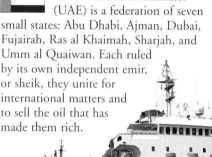

Mina' Jabal 'Ali port

The UAE is one the world's leading exporters of natural gas and oil, both of which leave the country via Mina' Jabal 'Ali port, the world's largest artificial harbour. Since less than three per cent of the UAE land can be cultivated, the port is also used to import food products.

Tourism

Hot sun, sandy beaches, and duty-free shopping make the UAE an attractive winter holiday resort for visitors from Europe and Japan (summer is too hot for tourism). The federation is gradually building up its tourism. Other attractions include trips into the desert, luxury hotels, and traditional markets.

Qatar

A small peninsula in the Persian Gulf, Qatar, like other Gulf States, depends on natural gas and oil for its wealth. Although most of the country is desert, Qatar grows most of its own food by tapping reserves of underground water. Qatari women are free to drive cars and not to wear veils.

QATAR FACTS

CAPITAL CITY	Doha
AREA	11,437 sq km (4,416 sq miles)
POPULATION	575,000
MAIN LANGUAGES	Arabic, Farsi
MAJOR RELIGION	Muslim
CURRENCY	Qatar riyal

Bahrain

Three inhabited islands and 30 smaller ones make up the small country of Bahrain. The oil reserves that made it rich are now running low, but the country has plenty of natural gas. Bahrain has a long history, and 4,000 years ago was a transit port for trade with India.

BAHRAIN FACTS

CAPITAL CITY	Manama
AREA	620 sq km (239 sq miles)
POPULATION	652,000
MAIN LANGUAGES	Arabic, English
MAJOR RELIGIONS	Muslim, Christian
CURRENCY	Bahrain dinar

Foreign workers

Only 20 per cent of the people are native-born Bedouin Qataris. The country has had to import workers from India, Asia, Iran, and other Arab countries to cope with the work produced by the oil industry. Almost 90 per cent of the population live in the capital, Doha.

Women's role

Bahrain is the most liberal of the Gulf States. Although the people are Muslim, women are not obliged to wear the veil. They have equal access to education and many follow careers.

FIND OUT MORE   ASIA, HISTORY OF   DESERTS   ENERGY   FARMING   FISHING INDUSTRY   ISLAM   ISLAMIC EMPIRE   MOSQUES   OIL   PORTS AND WATERWAYS

GUNS

FROM A BOOMING cannon to a pocket pistol, all firearms (guns) work on the same principle: a controlled explosion in one part of the gun propels a shell or bullet out of a tube or barrel. Firearms appeared in Europe in the early 14th century; although they were feeble at first, in time they changed warfare forever. Armour could not stop bullets, nor castle walls withstand cannon balls. Without guns, no nation could resist invasion for long; armed with them, European peoples colonized most of the world.

15th-century illustration of a battlefield shows cannons in action.

Origins of guns
The first guns were cannons, known to have been in use before 1326, when drawings of them appeared in a book. At first smiths built the barrels from strips of iron. Safer, cast cannons came into use a century later, when bell-founders began to make them by filling a mould with liquid metal.

Artillery

A gun is described in terms of calibre, which is the width of the hole through its barrel, or the weight of the shell it fires. The shells of artillery (heavy firearms) are big enough to destroy buildings. Artillery includes mortars, with a fairly short range, or longer-barrelled, long-range guns.

Howitzer in use

Muzzle (front)
Shield protects gun crews
Breech (back), where ammunition is loaded.

Mountain howitzer

Small arms
Soldiers carry small arms for individual use. These compact, lightweight weapons may have a stock for bracing the gun against the shoulder, or they may be fired from the hand. Most fire bullets rapidly from preloaded magazines. Some are very powerful: a modern rifle can fire a bullet more than 1,800 m (2,000 yards).

.45-calibre bullet

Automatic Colt 1911 A1 pistol

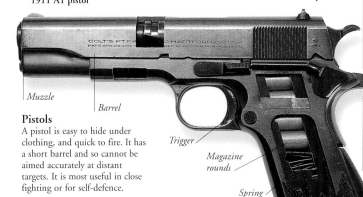

Muzzle *Barrel* *Trigger* *Magazine rounds* *Spring pushes bullets up.*

Pistols
A pistol is easy to hide under clothing, and quick to fire. It has a short barrel and so cannot be aimed accurately at distant targets. It is most useful in close fighting or for self-defence.

Plastic hand guard

Submachine gun
30-round magazine stored here. *Pistol grip*

Automatic weapons
Set to automatic, many small arms will continue to fire as long as the soldier holds back the trigger.

Hiram Maxim
American-born inventor Hiram Maxim (1840–1916) developed the first practical automatic machine gun in 1884. Maxim guns fired so quickly that by World War I (1914–1918) soldiers no longer fought on horseback, but tried to hide from the bullets in trenches.

Howitzers
A howitzer is a field gun, which may be towed or self-propelled to the battlefield. Its barrel and aim is midway between that of a mortar and a gun. Shells can be fired at a high angle, so that they fly above hills or other defences before reaching enemy targets.

Sniper's rifle *Barrel* *Stock*

Rifles
Rifling (spiral grooves) inside the barrel of a gun makes the bullet spin in flight, improving accuracy. Self-loading rifles use the energy from firing a bullet to expel the cartridge case, and load the next shot.

10-round magazine *Rifles are fired from the shoulder.*

Ammunition
The missile that a gun fires, the propellant (explosive charge), and the means of firing it, are known together as ammunition. The first guns fired round stones, propelling them from the barrel with loose gunpowder, lit with a hot wire. From the mid-19th century on, following the introduction of rifled gun barrels, shells were long and pointed in shape. Today, in all but the biggest guns, a metal cartridge holds the missile, propellent, and means of firing together.

Machine gun belt, World War I
250 rounds on the belt

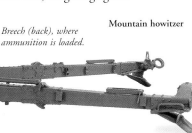

Armour-piercing shell, fired by anti-tank gun.

Used by 5.56-mm (.22-in) calibre gun

Rifle cartridge **Machine gun bullet**

Bullet, for .44 revolver

Gun control
A few civilians need to own guns for security, target shooting, pest control, and other uses. However, guns are dangerous, and most countries control ownership. Many people believe these controls should be stricter to stop criminals getting hold of and using guns, and to reduce the number of shooting accidents.

Gun safety poster, USA

FIND OUT MORE ARMS AND ARMOUR | WARFARE | WEAPONS | WORLD WAR I

GUPTA EMPIRE

AT THE BEGINNING of the fourth century, India was made up of a number of separate kingdoms. In 320, Chandragupta I, ruler of Magadha, who was named after the warlike Mauryan ruler, took over neighbouring kingdoms to found the Gupta Empire. Under his successors, the empire expanded to include much of India, and became the greatest Asian country of the time, lasting about 150 years. It was a golden age of Indian painting, architecture, sculpture, and literature.

Magadha

Gupta Empire

How the empire was run

The Guptas ran their empire as a group of small regions, or sub-kingdoms. Each sub-kingdom had its own ruler, but all were under the control of the emperor in Magadha. The first two Gupta emperors expanded the empire, while the later emperors had the task of holding the territory together.

Gupta coins had symbols, such as horses, on them instead of portraits.

Chandragupta I
In his short reign, the fierce Chandragupta I (320–330) expanded his territories by conquest, and by his marriage to Princess Kumara Devi of the Lichchavi tribe.

Samudragupta
Chandragupta I's son (r.330–376) extended the empire into Bengal, central India, and the valleys of the upper Yamuna and Ganges rivers.

Chandragupta II
Named after his grandfather, the third Gupta had a long and peaceful reign (376–415), during which Indian art and literature began to flourish.

Art and literature

During the Gupta period, Indian artists created some of their finest works. Magnificent palaces and temples contained the highest quality sculpture and paintings. Classical forms of music and dance, created under the Guptas, are still practised today all over Asia.

Exteriors of the Buddhist cave-shrines at Ajanta, western India

Padmapani, the "lotus-bearer"

Bodhisattva

Musician with lyre

Sculpture
Lifelike sculptures adorned Gupta shrines and palaces. The most popular subjects were people who had made donations to the shrine, the Buddha and scenes from his life, and people known as Bodhisattvas (those who have reached the Buddhist goal of enlightenment and help others to do likewise). Many sculptures, such as the seated musician, were made of terracotta.

Wall paintings
There are more than 30 Buddhist shrines and monasteries in the Ajanta hills. The walls of many of these were decorated with colourful frescoes, or wall paintings. This was a fashion that continued for hundreds of years. The paintings show scenes from the life of the Buddha, and other devotional subjects.

The figures are dressed in Gupta-period costumes.

A procession of elephants

Wall paintings are a good source of information about life in the empire.

Painting from the Jataka stories, Cave 17, Ajanta

The golden age of learning
Under the Guptas, universities expanded and became famous for philosophy, medicine, and logic. The Sanskrit language was also developed, and was used for major epic stories. One of the finest writers of the period was Kalidasa, who lived during the reigns of Chandragupta II and Kumaragupta. His works include comedies, poems, and heroic plays which are still performed.

Sanskrit inscription

Fa-Hsien
In 399, Fa-Hsien, a Chinese Buddhist, went to India to study the sacred writings of Buddhism. In the 10 years he was there, he wrote about life under the Gupta emperors. His writings form one of the most important sources for the history of this period.

Cave-shrines
Many of the Buddhist cave-shrines in western India were cut out of the cliffs – a task which must have taken years of labour with the simple tools the Guptas used. The cave-shrines are dark but beautifully decorated with sculptures and paintings. The Buddha in this example is making the gesture known as *abhaya mudra*, or "have no fear".

Timeline

320 Chandragupta I founds the Gupta Empire.

330–376 Samudragupta expands the empire from the Indus River to the Bay of Bengal, and up into the northern mountains.

Bodhisattva

376–415 Chandragupta II makes the empire secure, and encourages trade.

415–450 Kalidasa composes most of his poetry in the reign of Kumaragupta (415–455).

c.450 Empire begins to collapse under pressure from invading Huns.

554 The Gupta dynasty ends when the last emperor dies.

Silver Gupta horseman

FIND OUT MORE

BUDDHISM · HINDUISM · INDIA, HISTORY OF · MAURYAN EMPIRE · SHRINES

GYMNASTICS

THERE ARE TWO MAIN BRANCHES of gymnastics – artistic and rhythmic. In artistic gymnastics, the gymnasts perform on fixed apparatus, such as bars and beams. In rhythmic gymnastics, they perform routines with apparatus such as hoops and balls. Other gymnastic sports include sports acrobatics and trampolining. In major artistic gymnastic competitions, the apparatus is set out on a large platform, or podium, and several events take place together. The competitors are awarded marks out of 10 by a panel of judges.

Men

There are six events in men's competitions. They are the floor, pommel horse, vault, rings, parallel bars, and high bar. Boys and men usually wear a singlet with shorts or white trousers. Men's gymnastics calls for strength as well as balance and dynamic movement.

Pommel horse
The pommel horse needs arm and shoulder strength. The gymnast moves back and forth along the horse, swinging his legs up and over, supporting himself on his hands only.

Parallel bars
The bars are a good all-round test for men. There is a wide choice of movements that a gymnast can perform, including swings and balances, and support and strength moves.

Holding a position to show strength

Floor
Men's floor exercises last 50 to 70 seconds and feature balances as well as somersaults and handsprings. Gymnasts must not step off the square mat.

Rings
More strength is needed on the rings than on any other apparatus. Gymnasts must hold some positions for two seconds and must not swing on the ropes.

Vault
This is the shortest event. Boys and men perform only one vault. Until they are about 13, boys vault across the horse, but after that they vault along its length.

High bar
High bar routines contain continuous swinging moves. The gymnast circles around and around, with turns, twists, and changes of direction and grip.

Women

There are four women's events – the floor, beam, asymmetric (uneven) bars, and vault. In competitions there is also an overall championship. Women and girls usually wear one-piece leotards with short or long sleeves. Women's exercises call for balance and agility, and floor exercises include elements of dance.

Beam
The beam is 5 m (16.4 ft) long and only 10 cm (4 in) wide. Gymnasts must perform deliberate movements and graceful balances. The leading gymnasts can perform somersaults and backflips.

Springing into a flic flac

Gymnast looks for the floor.

One leg is brought over first.

Floor
The women's floor routine is performed to music. Women and girls have from 60 to 90 seconds. Gymnasts are expected to include dance steps in their routine, as well as spectacular running somersaults.

Women vault across the width of the horse.

Vault
Women and girls have two vaults in a competition, the better of the two marks counting. Different turns and somersaults are used, especially as the gymnast thrusts off the horse before landing neatly.

Asymmetric bars
This is possibly the most difficult of the women's appparatus. The gymnast must make full use of two bars 2.3 m (7.5 ft) and 1.5 m (5 ft) high, swinging and changing grip. The routine must have a flowing rhythm with no stops or hesitations.

Nadia Comaneci

Romanian gymnast Nadia Comaneci (b.1962) became the first person to score a maximum 10 points in Olympic competition, at the age of 14. She scored seven 10s in the 1976 Montreal Olympics, winning the overall gold medal as well as separate golds for the bars and beam.

The ribbon is attached to a wand.

Ribon

Ball

Clubs

Rope

Hoops

The ribbon is made of silk.

Rhythmic gymnastics
Performed only by women and girls, rhythmic gymnastics consists of five individual exercises – ribbon, clubs, ball, hoop, and rope. There are also group exercises performed by a team, usually with two different pieces of apparatus.

Trampolining
This is an excellent exercise routine for practising moves such as twists and somersaults, and it is also a sport in itself. There are solo competitions and synchronized pairs. Judges award marks for difficulty and how well a routine is performed.

Sports acrobatics
This type of gymnastics comprises tumbling, pairs, and group events. Tumbling is like the floor exercises, but performed on a straight, sprung track. The routines in pairs (men, women, or mixed), the trio (women), and fours (men) are like those of circus acrobats.

A mixed pair balance

FIND OUT MORE
OLYMPIC GAMES
ROMANIA, UKRAINE, AND MOLDAVIA
SPORT

Gymnastics
Sports acrobatics

Clasps hands firmly

The base rests much of his body on the floor.

Leg positions can be varied.

The top holds her body in a straight line.

The top keeps her body still.

The top lifts and straddles her legs.

The base carries his partner's weight on his legs.

Keeps her body tensed

Leans back

Counterbalance: gymnasts use their weight against each other.

Shoulder balance: a simple, stable position.

Simple balance: the base supports the top.

Stag balance: elegance contrasts with strength.

Straddle lever balance: an advanced position.

Rhythmic sequences

Gymnast performs to music.

Moves elegantly throughout the sequence.

Full side bend

The gymnast keeps her arm straight.

Graceful arm position

1 Swings hoop around the waist.

2 Lets a side of the hoop drop.

3 Jumps through the hoop.

4 Carries hoop to the side.

1 Carries the ball to one side.

2 Circles the ball out behind.

3 Spirals to the other side.

4 Rises into an arabesque.

Artistic, floor

This move is known as a Y-balance.

Legs held together and straight

Stretching his arms upwards helps the gymnast stand.

Keeps toes pointed

Gymnast presses legs together.

Gymnast tucks his body down into a roll.

Moves round in quarter turns

Gymnasts generally prefer to work barefoot.

The gymnast moves smoothly into each stage of the exercise.

Head tucked in

Spread fingers

1 Gymnast holds balance for two seconds.

2 Springs into a dive.

3 Upwards and forwards into a dive roll.

4 Lands on hands and rolls.

5 Rolls onto feet and comes up to stand.

6 Kicks up to a handstand, then turns round by moving his hands.

Artistic, beam

The beam, used only in women's gymnastics, is very difficult. For safety's sake, a gymnast must progress from floor skills, to a low beam, then a practise beam.

The gymnast learns to walk, turn, and sit on a beam first.

Head up, back straight

Looking ahead

In competition, judges deduct points for wobbly or faulty landings.

The gymnast tries to jump as high as possible.

She bends her knees as she lands.

Toes pointed

1 Gymnast mounts the side or end of the beam.

2 Performs low move, known as a V-sit.

3 The gymnast begins a W-jump.

4 With one step, takes off from both feet.

5 She points one leg forward and tucks the other behind.

6 Prepares to land.

7 She keeps a steady balance.

HEALTH AND FITNESS

IF A MACHINE is treated with care and given proper maintenance, it is more likely to function efficiently. Similarly, the human body is most likely to function to the best of its ability if it is kept fit and healthy. Health may be defined as the state of being well in body and mind. Fitness is an indication of how efficiently the body's muscles, heart, and lungs are working. If people are fit, they can deal with the requirements put upon their bodies by everyday activities, such as walking and lifting, but also with sudden demands, such as sprinting for a bus. Mental health – the mind's fitness – is also important for well-being.

What is health?

When someone is in good health it means their body is working to its full potential and is not impeded by physical or mental diseases. People's health may suffer as they become older, if they eat a poor diet, if they are poor, if they are exposed to pollution, or work in a harmful environment.

Outdoor play contributes to the healthy development of children.

Maintaining health

Many people in developed countries are overweight, take little exercise, and eat too much fatty food. This makes them unfit, and often unhealthy. Following a balanced diet with plenty of fresh fruit and vegetables and not too much fat, combined with regular exercise, aid better health.

Diet
A healthy diet consists of the right amounts of protein, carbohydrate, fat, vitamins, minerals, and fibre. The energy it provides should keep the body at its ideal weight.

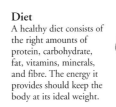

Fruit and vegetables are full of vitamins.

Fish provides energy, iron, and protein.

Dairy products provide protein and fat.

Meat is full of protein and vitamins.

Nuts and fungi contain protein and minerals.

Pulses, rice, and pasta provide carbohydrates.

Exercise
The human body requires exercise to improve fitness. Exercise makes the heart and lungs work more efficiently, and strengthens muscles and bones. This helps keep the body flexible.

Stretching side lateral muscles and abdomen

Clothing is loose and comfortable.

Body weight is put on right leg to stretch left thigh.

All major muscle groups are stretched.

Gentle stretching is a good way to start an exercise programme

Training shoes should be used.

Legs are stretched gently to prevent any strain.

Relaxation
Regular relaxation reduces stress and tension, increases a sense of well-being, and decreases the risk of disease. There are many ways to relax, including massage, yoga, and meditation.

Yoga lotus position

Mental health
Mental health is the fitness of the mind. Problems may be caused by heredity or emotional problems caused by relationships or lifestyle. Keeping fit, discussing problems, and seeking professional help can all improve a person's mental health. Some people are affected by mental illnesses that have been caused by brain disorders.

Doctors who look after mental health are called psychiatrists.

Public health

Public health is concerned with the effect environment has upon a population's health, and how the health of the community can be improved. Workers in this field are interested in, for example, good housing, effective sanitation, reducing air pollution, and the immunization of children and adults against infectious diseases.

Sanitation
Sanitation is the provision of clean drinking water, enclosed sewers, and drains. It stops food and water being contaminated by potentially fatal pathogens (germs) from human waste and helps stop the spread of disease.

Poor sanitation in slums in 19th-century England

Syringe

Immunization
Immunization protects people from disease. It involves injecting them with small amounts of pathogens of a certain disease. This stimulates the body to produce antibodies that fight the disease, producing protection.

Check-ups
A doctor carries out a check-up, or physical examination, to make sure that a person is healthy, and to look out for anything that may be wrong. During a check-up, the doctor will ask the patient how he or she feels, look at and feel the patient's body, use a stethoscope to listen to breathing and the heart, and measure blood pressure.

Doctor examines girl's throat

FIND OUT MORE | DISEASES | DRUGS | FOOD | HUMAN BODY | MEDICINE | SOCIETIES, HUMAN | SPORT

HEART AND CIRCULATORY SYSTEM

THE HEART IS A FIST-SIZED muscular pump that beats non-stop, 24 hours a day, sending blood around the body along a massive network of tubes called blood vessels. Together, they make up the circulatory system. The larger blood vessels divide repeatedly to form smaller vessels, which travel to every cell in the body, supplying them with oxygen from the lungs and nutrients from digested food, and carrying away waste. Blood helps defend the body against infection and also distributes heat around the body, helping to maintain its temperature.

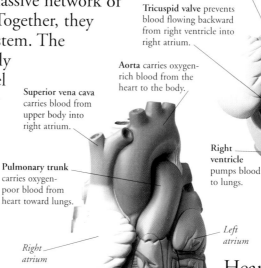

Right atrium receives oxygen-poor blood from body.

Left atrium receives oxygen-rich blood from lungs.

Tricuspid valve prevents blood flowing backward from right ventricle into right atrium.

Semilunar valve stops blood flowing back into right ventricle.

Aorta carries oxygen-rich blood from the heart to the body.

Superior vena cava carries blood from upper body into right atrium.

Left ventricle pumps blood to body.

Right ventricle pumps blood to lungs.

Pulmonary trunk carries oxygen-poor blood from heart toward lungs.

Left atrium

Septum is wall that separates ventricles.

Right atrium

Coronary artery supplies heart with blood.

Right ventricle

Left ventricle

How the heart beats

The wall of the heart is made of cardiac muscle that contracts automatically. The two halves of the heart beat together to pump blood around the body. Inside the heart, blood passes from the atria (upper chambers) to the ventricles (lower chambers). Valves ensure that blood cannot flow backwards through the heart. Each heartbeat is not a single contraction, but consists of three stages.

Heart

The heart consists of two muscular pumps, left and right, which lie side by side. Each pump is divided into a smaller upper chamber, or atrium, and a lower chamber, or ventricle. The left ventricle has a thicker wall because it has to pump blood around the body; the thinner-walled right ventricle pumps blood to the lungs.

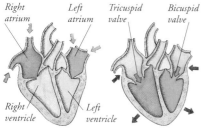

Right atrium

Left atrium

Tricuspid valve

Bicuspid valve

Aorta

Pulmonary artery

Right ventricle

Left ventricle

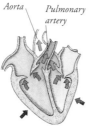

1 During the first stage (diastole) both the atria and the ventricles are relaxed. Blood flows into and fills both atria. The semilunar valves at the exit points of the ventricles are closed.

2 During the second stage (atrial systole) the tricuspid and bicuspid valves between the atria and the ventricles open. Both atria contract and squeeze blood into the ventricles below them.

3 During the third stage (ventricular systole) the ventricles contract to push blood out of the heart. The tricuspid and bicuspid valves close, while the semilunar valves open.

Monitoring heart rate during exercise.

Heart rate

The heart normally beats about 70 times per minute. This is your heart rate. It changes according to the oxygen demands of the body. If you exercise, heart rate increases to pump more oxygen-carrying blood to your muscles.

William Harvey

English doctor William Harvey (1578–1657) was the first person to show that blood circulated around the body. Before Harvey, it was thought that blood ebbed and flowed along blood vessels rather like the tide coming in and going out. Harvey concluded that blood travelled in one direction only, and that it was pumped by the heart.

Blood

Blood is a liquid transport system that travels to every cell in the body. It supplies body cells with oxygen and nutrients, and carries away waste products. Blood consists of billions of blood cells floating in a yellowish liquid called plasma. There are three types of blood cells: red blood cells, white blood cells, and platelets. Red blood cells make up 99 per cent of all blood cells. A soft tissue inside bones called red marrow produces blood cells.

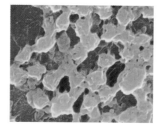

Platelets

Platelets are cell fragments that help stop blood leaking from injured blood vessels. If a blood vessel is damaged, platelets gather at the wound and stick to each other to form a plug.

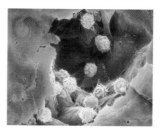

White blood cells

White blood cells defend the body against infection. There are three main types. Granulocytes and monocytes engulf invading germs; lymphocytes release chemicals that destroy germs.

Red blood cells

Red blood cells are packed with a red substance called haemoglobin. Haemoglobin picks up oxygen in the lungs and releases it as blood passes through other parts of the body.

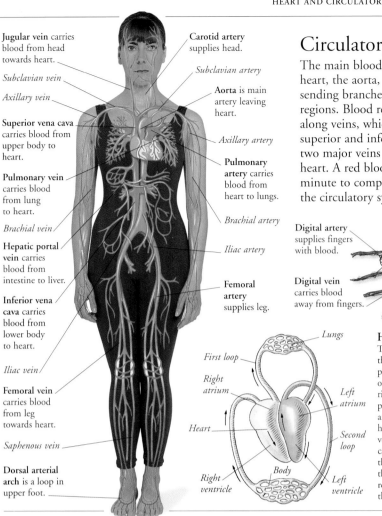

Jugular vein carries blood from head towards heart.

Subclavian vein

Axillary vein

Superior vena cava carries blood from upper body to heart.

Pulmonary vein carries blood from lung to heart.

Brachial vein

Hepatic portal vein carries blood from intestine to liver.

Inferior vena cava carries blood from lower body to heart.

Iliac vein

Femoral vein carries blood from leg towards heart.

Saphenous vein

Dorsal arterial arch is a loop in upper foot.

Carotid artery supplies head.

Subclavian artery

Aorta is main artery leaving heart.

Axillary artery

Pulmonary artery carries blood from heart to lungs.

Brachial artery

Iliac artery

Femoral artery supplies leg.

Circulatory system

The main blood vessel leaving the heart, the aorta, divides repeatedly, sending branches to major body regions. Blood returns to the heart along veins, which unite to form the superior and inferior venae cavae, the two major veins which re-enter the heart. A red blood cell takes just one minute to complete its journey around the circulatory system.

Digital artery supplies fingers with blood.

Digital vein carries blood away from fingers.

Circulation in the arm

The blood vessels of the arm show how the circulatory system works. The brachial artery divides into several branches, including the radial artery. Veins carrying blood from the hand and wrist unite to form the brachial vein leaving the arm.

Axillary vein carries blood towards heart.

Cephalic vein

Basilic vein

Radial vein

Ulnar artery

Ulna

Radius

Humerus

Brachial artery

Axiliary artery supplies arm with blood.

How blood circulates

There are, in fact, two parts to the circulatory system. The pulmonary circulation carries oxygen-poor blood from the right side of the heart along the pulmonary arteries to the lungs and back to the left side of the heart along the pulmonary veins. The systemic circulation carries oxygen-rich blood from the left side of the heart along the aorta to the body, and returns oxygen-poor blood to the right side of the heart.

Lungs

First loop

Right atrium

Heart

Left atrium

Second loop

Body

Right ventricle

Left ventricle

Flushing

Exercise can cause a reddening of the face and body known as flushing. This happens when, to cool the body down, blood vessels near the skin's surface widen as blood flow increases to lose heat from the skin. The increased blood flow makes the skin redden.

Blood clotting

When a blood vessel is damaged, clotting reduces the loss of blood. Platelets accumulate at the wound and stick together to form a plug. Red blood cells are trapped in threads of fibrin to form a clot. White blood cells prevent infection beneath a hard outer scab.

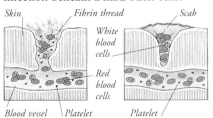

Skin

Fibrin thread

Scab

White blood cells

Red blood cells

Blood vessel

Platelet

Platelet

Fibrin

Chemicals in the blood and damaged cells trigger the production of the protein fibrin. This forms strands which trap red blood cells into a clot. A hard crust, called a scab, forms over the clot to protect the wound.

Blood vessels

There are three types of blood vessels: arteries, veins, and capillaries. Arteries divide into smaller vessels called arterioles, which themselves divide into a network of capillaries. Blood then passes to venules and veins.

Arteries

Arteries carry blood away from the heart. They have thick, muscular walls that can withstand the high pressure produced when the heart beats. Arteries usually carry blood that is rich in oxygen.

Arteriole

Artery

Capillary network

Venule

Valve

Vein

Thin wall of vein

Thick wall of artery

Veins

Veins carry blood towards the heart. They have thin walls because pressure inside them is low. They contain valves to prevent blood flowing backwards.

Capillaries

Capillaries are the tiny blood vessels that carry blood between arterioles and venules. They supply individual cells with food and oxygen and remove wastes.

Karl Landsteiner

Austrian/American Karl Landsteiner (1868–1943) discovered the existence of blood groups, and made safe blood transfusion a reality. In 1900, Landsteiner showed that red blood cells may clump together when blood from different people is mixed. He worked out the ABO blood group system, and was awarded a Nobel Prize.

Blood groups

People belong to different blood groups, depending on the antigens (chemicals) in their red blood cells. The ABO blood group system has two antigens, A and B. It has four blood groups: A (carries A antigen); B (carries B antigen); AB (carries both antigens); and O (carries neither).

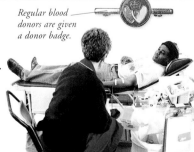

Regular blood donors are given a donor badge.

Blood compatibility

Blood transfusion is the donation of blood by one person to another. People who share the same blood groups can give or receive blood safely because their blood is compatible. In an emergency, however, people with type O blood can give blood to any other group.

FIND OUT MORE   CELLS   FIRST AID   HEALTH AND FITNESS   HORMONES AND ENDOCRINE SYSTEM   HUMAN BODY   IMMUNE AND LYMPHATIC SYSTEM   LUNGS AND BREATHING   MEDICINE   MUSCLES AND MOVEMENT

HEAT AND TEMPERATURE

IN GREEK MYTHOLOGY, Icarus flew too close to the Sun and plummeted to his death as the Sun's heat melted his waxen wings. Heat is a type of energy that can indeed melt wax, and many other substances. The temperature of a substance – how hot or cold it is – can be thought of as how much heat energy that substance contains. More precisely, temperature is a measure of the average energy possessed by the moving particles of matter inside the substance.

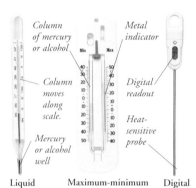

Column of mercury or alcohol

Column moves along scale.

Mercury or alcohol well

Liquid

Metal indicator

Digital readout

Heat-sensitive probe

Maximum-minimum   **Digital**

Thermometers
A device that measures temperature is called a thermometer. A liquid thermometer contains a column of mercury or alcohol that expands and contracts as the temperature changes, moving up and down a scale. A maximum and minimum thermometer records the highest and lowest temperatures over a certain period, using metal indicators that are moved by a liquid column. A digital thermometer contains a heat-sensitive electronic probe. The probe produces an electric current that varies with changes in temperature.

Temperature scale
Just as the scale on a ruler shows length in centimetres or inches, a temperature scale shows temperature in units called degrees Celsius (C), degrees Fahrenheit (F), or kelvin (K). Most temperature scales are defined by two "fixed points". The Celsius scale uses the melting and boiling points of water as its fixed points.

Absolute zero
There is no upper limit to temperature, but there is a lower limit, called absolute zero (-273°C, -459°F, 0K), at which atoms and molecules are stationary. Scientists have managed to achieve temperatures within a millionth of a degree of absolute zero. The study of how matter behaves at very low temperatures is known as cryogenics.

Cryogenics scientist at work

Thermal expansion
Heating a substance gives its particles more energy so that they move faster and farther. The particles take up more room and increase the volume of the substance. This is known as thermal expansion.

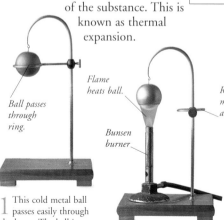

Ball passes through ring.

Flame heats ball.

Bunsen burner

1 This cold metal ball passes easily through the hoop. The ball is a solid object, composed of millions of tightly packed, vibrating particles.

2 A hot flame heats the ball, giving its particles more heat energy.

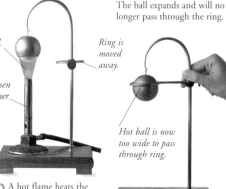

Ring is moved away.

Hot ball is now too wide to pass through ring.

3 The extra energy increases the size of the particles' vibrations, making them take up more space. The ball expands and will no longer pass through the ring.

100°C (212°F, 373K): water boils

58°C (136°F, 331K): highest recorded temperature on Earth

43.3°C (110.3°F, 316.3K): normal body temperature of a sparrow

37°C (98.4°F, 310K): normal human body temperature

28.1°C (82.6°F, 301.1K): normal body temperature of echidna (spiny anteater)

18°C (64°F, 291K): normal room temperature (water is in its liquid state)

0°C (32°F, 273K): freezing point of water

Celsius scale

Refrigerator
A refrigerator is a machine that is used to chill food, drinks, and other items. A liquid called a refrigerant flows through pipes inside the refrigerator. The liquid absorbs heat from the refrigerator's contents and evaporates. The vapour is compressed and pumped into a tube on the outside of the refrigerator. As the vapour passes through the tube, it loses heat to the surrounding air and condenses back to a liquid.

Producing heat
Heat can be produced in a number of ways, including by friction, through chemical reactions, and using an electric current.

Drilling machine

Heat from friction
The American scientist Benjamin Thompson (1753–1814) discovered that friction produces heat. At his weapons factory in Germany, he noticed that when a drilling machine bored into a gun barrel, friction between the two objects made the gun barrel extremely hot.

Heat and chemical reactions
Athletes often use a device called a hot pack to treat a sprained limb. The pack contains powdered iron that reacts with oxygen from the air when the pack is shaken. The heat from the chemical reaction warms the joint and eases the pain.

Heat and electricity
An electric current always produces heat. When current flows through an electric toaster, for example, the heat produced raises the temperature of the wire element so that it glows red-hot and toasts bread.

Element

Tube is called a condenser.

Refrigerant absorbs heat from inside refrigerator and loses it to air outside.

Insulated walls

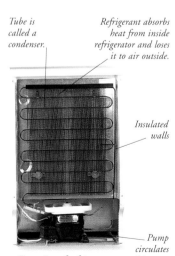

Pump circulates refrigerant.

Rear view of refrigerator

Water molecules gain heat from the hot pan and vibrate faster.

Bubbles appear as the water molecules use heat from the flame to break free from each other and form steam.

Latent heat

When a liquid is at its boiling point, an input of heat energy will not raise the liquid's temperature any further. Instead, the extra energy enables particles in the liquid to break free from each other and form a gas. This energy is called latent heat. The energy is released again if the gas condenses into a liquid. Latent heat is also absorbed when a solid melts, and released when a liquid freezes.

Thermal motion
All matter is made up of moving particles. This movement is called thermal motion. The temperature of an object is a measure of its thermal motion. Heating the object makes its particles vibrate faster and raises its temperature.

Radiation

All objects give out energy in the form of infrared rays, which are similar to X-rays. A hot object, such as a light bulb, gives out a lot of infrared rays. These rays will heat up any object that absorbs them. Dull surfaces absorb infrared rays well, but shiny surfaces reflect them. Infrared rays are invisible, but you can feel their effect. The closer you put your hand to a light bulb, the warmer it feels, because the radiation is more intense.

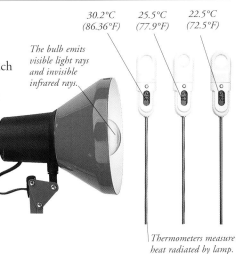

The bulb emits visible light rays and invisible infrared rays.

30.2°C (86.36°F)   25.5°C (77.9°F)   22.5°C (72.5°F)

Thermometers measure heat radiated by lamp.

Propagator
Seeds sprout and grow more rapidly in warm conditions, so they are often planted in a tiny greenhouse called a propagator. Sunlight passes through the propagator's plastic cover and warms the seeds and soil, which radiate the heat back out again as infrared rays. The rays cannot pass through plastic, so the heat is trapped inside and the temperature rises.

Convection

The way heat travels as moving currents through a gas or a liquid is called convection. If a tank of water is heated from below, the warm water at the bottom will rise as it expands and becomes less dense. The cooler, denser water above sinks to take its place. Soon, this cooler water also warms and starts to rise, creating a circulation of water called a convection current.

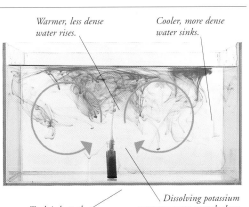

Warmer, less dense water rises.
Cooler, more dense water sinks.
Tank is heated from below.
Dissolving potassium permanganate crystals show the movement of the water.

Heat conduction

When a substance is heated, its vibrating particles knock against neighbouring particles and pass on some of their thermal motion, spreading heat throughout the substance. This is called conduction. Heat always conducts from a warm substance to a cooler one. The warm air in a room can lose heat through a window. Heat conducts from the warm air to the window, and then to the cooler air outside.

Temperature outside is 18.3°C (65°F).
Temperature inside is 21.7°C (71°F).

Thermometer records temperature difference across window.

Heat conductors
Some materials – called conductors – conduct heat better than others. If you press wax on to the ends of metal and plastic spoons in hot water, the wax on the metal spoon melts first. This is because metal is a better conductor.

Heat conducts up the spoons.
Wax melts and slides down the handle.
Metal conducts faster than plastic.

Hot or cold?
A marble tile feels colder than a carpet at room temperature. Marble is a better conductor than carpet. Marble takes heat rapidly away from the body, making the marble tile feel much colder to the touch than the carpet.

Marble tile   Carpet

Heat insulators

Poor conductors of heat, such as plastics, wood, cork, and air, are known as insulators. Using such materials to reduce heat loss from an object is called insulation. When these two jars are filled with water at 80°C (176°F) and left for 15 minutes, the jar covered in bubble wrap retains the most heat. Bubble wrap (plastic filled with pockets of air) is a good

27°C (80.6°F)   42.4°C (108°F)

Bubble wrap

Uninsulated jar   Insulated jar

Vacuum flask
A vacuum flask keeps drinks hot or cold by stopping the transfer of heat to or from the liquid. Conduction can only occur through matter, so the flask has two walls with a vacuum between them to prevent conduction. Shiny walls reflect heat radiation, while the flask is sealed with an airtight stopper made of a good insulator.

Airtight stopper
Hot or cold liquid
Vacuum between double walls of flask
Shiny walls reflect heat radiation.

FIND OUT MORE

ELECTRICITY   ENERGY   FRICTION   GASES   LIQUIDS   MATTER   METALS   SOLIDS   X-RAYS AND THE ELECTROMAGNETIC SPECTRUM

HEDGEHOGS AND OTHER INSECTIVORES

THE ORDER INSECTIVORA, which means insect-eating, contains more than 370 species, including hedgehogs, moles, shrews, and tenrecs. Most of these mammals, especially the shrews, are highly active and have to eat almost constantly to sustain themselves. They have poor eyesight, but a good sense of smell. They rely on smell to find their prey of worms and snails as well as insects. Insectivores have sharp teeth for preying on invertebrates. The hedgehogs and some tenrecs are protected from predators by spines.

The long snout bears many highly sensitive whiskers which the hedgehog uses to find its way around and also to locate food.

A female hedgehog usually has two litters of young each year.

Ordinary fur grows on the chest and belly.

Hedgehogs

Like most insectivores, hedgehogs are nocturnal, solitary animals that associate only to mate. Each adult animal needs its own territory in order to find enough to eat. Not all hedgehogs are spiny, but the European and desert hedgehogs have a thick covering of spines on the top of the head and body to protect them against predators such as foxes.

European hedgehogs build up a layer of fat during the summer to sustain them during the winter when they hibernate.

Young hedgehogs accompany their mother to find food.

Hedgehog spines
A European hedgehog has about 5,000 spines. These are hairs modified into sharp, stiff tubes. Hedgehogs are born with their first coat of pale spines flat under the skin, but these come through within a few hours. At two days old, the hedgehog's dark spines start to grow.

When threatened, a hedgehog raises its spines.

Each spine is controlled by muscles in the hedgehog's skin.

Spines normally lie flat over the hedgehog's body.

For extra protection, a hedgehog can roll into a prickly ball.

Young hedgehogs stay with their mother until they are about seven weeks old.

Moles

Moles live underground in a system of tunnels that they dig through the soil. They are well adapted for this existence, having a compact body, short legs, tiny eyes, and no protruding ears. They are active day and night, looking for food such as worms, insect larvae, and beetles.

Fur lies in no particular direction, so that the mole can push backward or forward through its tunnels.

Strong claws for loosening the soil.

Molehills
Mounds of soil, often called molehills, are the result of a mole's tunnelling activities. The mole pushes loose soil to the surface up short vertical tunnels.

A nest under the mound

Mole feet
The front paws are broad with large claws, and do the digging. The hind feet are narrower with sharp claws, and are used to push soil to the surface.

Shrews
These small mammals have a long snout and short legs. They are highly active and need a constant supply of food to keep them alive. Shrews are extremely aggressive and will attack one another if they meet. Many predators avoid shrews because of a foul-smelling secretion that they can produce from scent glands.

Shrews eat up to 130 per cent of their body weight every day.

Tenrecs
The 30 species of tenrec live only on the island of Madagascar. Some swim, some climb, and others live underground. Some have spines, others look more like shrews. They have many young. The common tenrec may have 34 in one litter.

EUROPEAN HEDGEHOG

SCIENTIFIC NAME *Erinaceus europaeus*

ORDER Insectivora

FAMILY Erinaceidae

DISTRIBUTION Europe, east into Russia. Introduced to New Zealand

HABITAT Farmland, suburbs, woodland, and mountains

DIET Beetles, worms, caterpillars, other invertebrates, small mammals, and carrion

SIZE Length: 25 cm (10 in)

LIFESPAN 4–7 years

FIND OUT MORE   ANIMALS   ANIMAL BEHAVIOUR   HIBERNATION

HERONS, STORKS AND FLAMINGOS

HERONS AND THEIR relatives are distinctive birds, with long, slender legs and a large beak. Most of them eat fish and other water animals, and can wade out into the water to look for food without getting their feathers wet. Herons hunt by stealth, and several species have developed remarkable fishing techniques. Flamingos catch their food by straining it through fibrous plates in their beak. Although storks have long legs, most of them do not wade, but catch their food on land. Many of these birds are sociable animals, living and nesting in large flocks or colonies. This gives them some protection from predators.

Neck is hunched at rest and in flight.

Herons often rest with one leg raised.

Herons

There are about 60 species of heron. They live all over the world, except Antarctica and the far north. Most live close to water, and they often nest in groups. They usually build their nests out of sticks and reeds in a tree or bush.

Cattle egret
This small heron lives near cattle and other grazers, and snaps up the small animals that they disturb. In recent years, cattle egret have become one of the world's most widespread birds.

Bittern
Bitterns live in dense reedbeds where they are perfectly camouflaged. When threatened, they point their beak skyward and sway gently. This makes them look like the reeds moving in the wind.

Juvenile goliath heron

Adult goliath heron

Long, straight legs

Black heron fishing
The African black heron strides into the water and raises its wings like an umbrella. This casts a shadow on the surface, which probably helps the heron to see any fish swimming below.

Fishing

Many herons, including the goliath heron, catch fish by wading into the water and then keeping absolutely still with their necks hunched. When a fish swims near, the heron crouches down toward the surface, then suddenly stretches out its neck and stabs the fish with its beak. Other herons have developed different fishing techniques.

Flamingo skull

Marabou stork

Flamingos

Many of the five species of flamingo live in shallow, salty lakes where little else survives. They feed with their head upside down, using their uniquely shaped beak to filter tiny animals and plants from the water.

Storks

There are 19 species of stork. Some feed by wading into water, but others live in quite dry places. The giant African marabou stork is a scavenger. It feeds on already dead animals, in the same way as vultures, but it will also eat live prey, such as insects, fish, rats, and small birds.

This stork has one of the largest wingspans of all birds.

Long legs and toes

Green heron
This heron usually hunts at night when many small animals are active. It often perches, legs bent, on a low branch, ready to pounce on its prey.

Fishing with bait
The North American green heron throws small twigs or pellets into the water. It waits for fish to be attracted by this bait and catches them when they come within range.

Colonies
Flocks of flamingos can contain more than 2 million birds. They build mound-like nests with mud that they scrape up with their beaks.

Nests
White storks migrate long distances and return to the same place in Europe every year to breed. They are traditionally encouraged to nest on houses because they are supposed to bring luck.

GOLIATH HERON	
SCIENTIFIC NAME	*Ardea goliath*
ORDER	Ciconiiformes
FAMILY	Ardeidae
DISTRIBUTION	Africa, Arabian peninsula, India
HABITAT	Coasts, lakes, rivers, marshy ground
DIET	Mainly fish
SIZE	Length: 150 cm (59 in)
LIFESPAN	About 25 years

FIND OUT MORE   BIRDS   BIRDS OF PREY   LAKE AND RIVER WILDLIFE   SHOREBIRDS

HIBERNATION

DURING WINTER, as temperatures drop and food becomes scarce, some animals hibernate to survive the harsh conditions. Hibernation is a resting state in which the animal's body temperature falls to just above that of its surroundings, and its metabolic rate (the rate at which it consumes energy) drops dramatically. The animal resumes its active lifestyle in the spring. Hibernation is triggered by shortening day length, a fall in temperature, or by the animal's internal biological clock. Some other animals rest, or remain dormant, to withstand adverse conditions.

Rodents
Rodents, such as dormice and woodchucks, form the largest group of hibernating mammals. Many smaller rodents living in the northern hemisphere hibernate in the winter months when the plant material and small animals they feed on are in short supply. Some construct nests in tree hollows or underground in which they curl up, to minimize heat loss, and go into a deep sleep. Many species wake periodically either to eat, drink, or urinate, to get rid of accumulated waste.

Hibernation
Rodents, bats, and insectivores are all mammals that hibernate. Their small size allows them to cool down and warm up quickly. Some animals eat more in early winter to build up fat stores to use while hibernating; others wake every few weeks to feed on food in their nest. A squirrel shows changes typical of a hibernating mammal; its metabolic rate drops to 1 per cent of normal, and its body temperature falls from 37°C (99°F) to 4°C (39°F). When it emerges its body weight will have fallen by 40 per cent.

Natterer's bat

Bats
Many temperate species of bat hibernate when their insect food disappears. They often hibernate in large numbers and cluster together to conserve warmth. The site where bats hibernate is called a hibernaculum; it may be a cave, mine, tree hollow, or a deserted building.

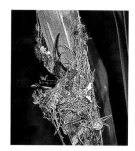
Hummingbird in nest

Birds
Most birds migrate to avoid cold winters; a few such as the North American poorwill enter a state of torpor and hibernate. Many hummingbirds show a form of daily hibernation. At night, their body temperature falls, enabling them to survive cooler conditions without consuming much energy.

Nest of straw and grass
Hibernating dormouse
Dormouse curled up in its nest

Dormancy
Some large mammals, such as bears and badgers, that live in northern parts of North America and Europe, go into a resting state, called dormancy, during winter. Dormancy differs from hibernation; the animal's body temperature does not drop significantly, and it can wake up quickly if danger threatens. However, this small fall in body temperature, combined with a lack of activity, produces significant energy savings for the animal.

European badger
Badgers live in forests where they dig extensive burrows called setts. In winter, badgers rarely leave their sett. They curl up in nesting material and go into a dormant state, living off fat reserves accumulated in summer and autumn. Dormancy can last for seven months in Siberia.

Bear feeds on berries to build up fat reserves.

Brown bear
The brown bear lives in Asia, North America, and Europe. In summer it builds up fat on which it lives in winter. In autumn, the bear excavates a den, lines it with vegetation, and goes into its winter "sleep". Its body temperature falls by 5°C (9°F), and its metabolic rate drops by 50 per cent. The bear emerges in spring weighing half what it did in the autumn.

Cabbage white butterfly pupa

Diapause
Diapause is the insects' equivalent of hibernation. Some insects enter diapause to survive adverse conditions, such as cold or lack of food. During diapause, growth and development are suspended, usually at the egg or pupa stage of the life cycle. For example, if the cabbage white butterfly lays her eggs in late summer, the pupal stage goes into diapause over winter, resuming development in spring.

Aestivation
Aestivation is a state of dormancy, shown by animals such as African lungfish, during hot, dry summers. Lungfish live in places that flood in the wet season and bake in the dry season. As river levels fall, the lungfish digs a burrow in the mud, ending in a chamber. The fish curls up in the chamber, secretes a protective mucus bag around itself, and remains there for up to six months until the rains come.

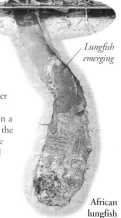
Lungfish emerging
African lungfish

FIND OUT MORE | ANIMAL BEHAVIOUR | BATS | BEARS | HEDGEHOGS AND OTHER INSECTIVORES | MAMMALS | MIGRATION | RATS AND OTHER RODENTS

HINDUISM

THE OLDEST OF THE GREAT world religions, Hinduism began in India at least 5,000 years ago. Hindus believe in one great power, or supreme god, called Brahman, that exists in everything. They believe in a cycle of death and rebirth – when we die, our souls live on in another person, animal, or plant. The goal of the Hindu is to live such a good life that the soul breaks this cycle and itself becomes part of Brahman. There are some 733 million Hindus, mostly living in Asia.

Vishnu

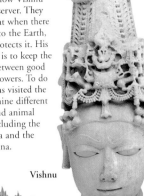

Hindus know Vishnu as the preserver. They believe that when there is danger to the Earth, Vishnu protects it. His main task is to keep the balance between good and evil powers. To do this, he has visited the Earth in nine different human and animal forms, including the lord Rama and the god Krishna.

Vishnu

Gods

Hindus worship many gods, each of which represents part of Brahman. Some of the gods can take different forms. Hindus can choose a favourite god; two of the most popular are Hanuman, the intelligent monkey-god, and Lakshmi, the goddess of beauty and wealth. But the most important of all is the holy trinity of Vishnu, Shiva, and Brahma. This group of three makes up Brahman, the supreme god.

H

Shiva

Hindus know this god as the destroyer. Shiva destroys things which are no longer needed, but also allows new things to be created, so he is said to control life and death. He is shown in many forms. As Lord of the Dance, he brings the dance of life to an end so the new cycle of life can begin.

Shiva beats a drum to summon up a new creation.

His left foot is a symbol of liberation.

Shiva bears a flame as a symbol of destruction.

The ring of flames represents the energy of the Universe.

Brahma

As the creator of the Universe, Brahma has four arms to symbolize the four points of the compass. He has four faces so he can look in all directions at the same time. These features also suggest that Brahma can be in all places at all times.

These figures represent holy scriptures.

Shiva dances on the defeated figure of the demon of ignorance.

Ganesha

Ganesha, the elephant-headed god of wisdom and strength, is the son of Shiva and Parvati. Hindus worship him at the beginning of journeys because he is thought to remove obstacles.

Sacred texts

Hinduism has many sacred books that explain the religion and instruct people how to lead their lives. The oldest texts are four books known as the *Vedas*. These contain hymns to the gods and texts telling priests how to carry out their duties. At the end of the *Vedas* are the *Upanishads*, which are philosophical discussions about religious belief. The *Puranas* are a series of books discussing and explaining the Vedas. The *Laws of Manu* provide teachings about everyday life.

Rig-Veda

The oldest and most sacred of the *Vedas* is the *Rig-Veda*. It contains some 1,000 hymns of praise to 33 of the most important of the gods. Like the other *Vedas*, it was originally composed in around 1200 BC, and passed on by word of mouth. The texts were written down in Sanskrit in around AD 1400.

Indra is the Vedic god of conquest. He is a warrior and a destroyer of demons.

In the Bhagavad-Gita, *Krishna drives the warrior Arjuna's chariot.*

The epics

Two great epic poems tell stories in which the gods come to Earth. The *Mahabharata* is probably the longest poem ever written. Its 100,000 verses tell of Vishnu visiting Earth as Krishna. It contains the text known as the *Bhagavad-Gita*, the Song of the Lord. The *Ramayana* tells a story in which Vishnu comes to Earth as lord Rama.

Blue houses in Jodhpur were for Brahmins.

Caste system

Hinduism divides people up into four separate groups, or varnas. The four groups are Brahmins (generally priests), Kshatriyas (soldiers and rulers), Vaishyas (traders and farmers), and Shudras (servants). These broad divisions are split into smaller groups called jatis, or castes. Traditionally, people would not have anything to do with castes lower than their own, but nowadays there is much more social flexibility.

Festivals

Throughout the Hindu year, festivals celebrate the gods in a variety of ways. At Janmashtami, Hindus commemorate Krishna's birthday with readings of the *Bhagavad-Gita* and gifts of sweets. Divali, the festival of lights, remembers the story of lord Rama's victory over his enemies and his lamp-lit procession home.

Pilgrims come to bathe in the River Ganges.

The sacred water is said to wash away one's sins.

Holi

The festival of Holi is held for two days in spring to celebrate the rescue of Krishna from the clutches of the demoness Holika, who was burnt to death by Vishnu. After worship a bonfire is lit to symbolise good overcoming evil. Dancing and processions take place.

Pilgrimages

Going on a pilgrimage to a holy place is important for many Hindus. They may go to a shrine or to a place where one of the gods is said to have appeared on Earth, believing that their prayers are more likely to be answered if said at such a place. A favourite goal for pilgrimage is a holy river, particularly the River Ganges, in north-western India. Varanasi on the Ganges is India's most sacred city.

On the second day of Holi, people of all castes cover each other with coloured powders.

Sacred cows

The white cow is a Hindu symbol of the soul, and cows are sacred in Hinduism. They are allowed to rove freely, and there are penalties for killing a cow. Hindus may drink milk and use cow dung as fuel, but must not kill cows for food. The cow's status is part of a wider respect for life and many Hindus are vegetarians.

Daily traffic in the city of Delhi skirts around seated cows.

Worship

Since Hindus believe that god is in everything, any human activity, done well, can become an act of worship. But Hindus also perform special acts of worship at least once a day. They may worship in a temple, but the most common place for worship is in the home, in front of a shrine to a favourite god. Rituals include meditation and reciting sacred texts and prayers. Hindus light candles, make offerings to the gods, and waft incense around the shrine.

Vishnu is the main image.

Shesha the serpent protects Vishnu.

Krishna and his half-brother Balarama are shown with Vishnu.

Shrines

The household shrine is the focus of daily worship. It may contain an image of one of the principal gods, plus pictures of other deities. It may also have a container full of water from the sacred River Ganges. Although some shrines are elaborately decorated, others may be as simple as a shelf or holy picture in the corner of a room.

Puja

Before puja (worship) takes place, the image of the god is washed, dried, and anointed with turmeric or sandalwood powder. Offerings such as flowers, fruit, and cooked food are made to the god. The worshipper stands or sits in front of the shrine, reciting holy texts.

Incense burner

Burning incense welcomes the god to his shrine.

Kamal

This scent-shaker is shaped like the lotus flower, the symbol of creation.

Yoga

All Hindus strive to break the cycle of rebirth (samsara) and merge with Brahman. They believe that one way of achieving this state is through following the physical and mental disciplines of yoga. There are different types of yoga, but all aim to attain ultimate spiritual enlightenment.

A Hindu carrying out yoga exercises.

The temple's tall towers symbolize mountains that are sacred dwelling places of the gods.

The very fabric of the temple is sacred.

The shrine room is in the inner sanctum.

Temples

Hindus attend temples on holy days and festivals, and at other times to perform private acts of worship. A temple is itself an object of worship because it is believed to be the earthly dwelling place of the gods. At the heart of the temple is the shrine room, which contains the sacred image of the god. Around this are rooms in which the priests live. Entrance halls are used for religious dancing and music.

Images of gods and mythological figures may adorn the temple walls.

Windows represent the ears of the divine body.

FIND OUT MORE FESTIVALS · GODS AND GODDESSES · INDIA, HISTORY OF · INDUS VALLEY CIVILIZATION · LITERATURE · RELIGIONS · SHRINES · SIGNS AND SYMBOLS · WRITING

HIPPOPOTAMUSES

SPENDING THE DAY submerged in water, hippopotamuses emerge at dusk to feed on nearby grasslands. Well-used pathways lead to their feeding grounds. There are two species of hippo – the common hippo and the pygmy hippo – both of which live in the equatorial regions of Africa. The common hippo is the third largest land animal after the elephant and the white rhino. Common hippos have a huge appetite and can consume vast quantities of grass. In places where they are numerous, they may destroy the vegetation for a considerable distance from the river or lake in which they live, sometimes causing serious soil erosion.

Common hippopotamus

The common hippo is a very large and aggressive animal. It is the second heaviest land animal after the elephant. Despite its huge size and legs that seem too short for its enormous barrel-like body, it can move at surprising speed. Anything coming between it and the water is liable to be attacked. Hippos make a variety of noises from bellowing to snorting.

Skin

Hippo skin is smooth and almost hairless except for a few bristles on the nose, in the ears, and on the tail. Underneath the skin is a thick layer of fat. Pores on the skin exude drops of a thick pink fluid that acts as a sunscreen and a lubricant. The fluid is also thought to disinfect wounds sustained by males during fights.

Scars are usually the result of sparring between adult males.

Small ears

Hippos feed on grass.

School of hippos

The common hippo lives in groups of 20–100 animals called schools. A school spends the day partly submerged in water or wallowing in mud pools. Hippos establish a territory with males around the edge, and females and young in the centre. Males are excluded from the female area except in the breeding season. Any male approaching too close will be attacked by the females.

Young

Thirty-four weeks after mating, the female gives birth to a single young. Birth normally takes place on land, but occasionally in water. The newborn hippo can swim, walk, and run within a few minutes of being born. If a female temporarily leaves the territory, she puts her calf in the care of another female.

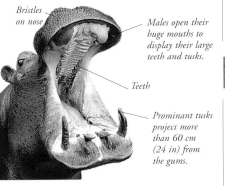

Bristles on nose

Males open their huge mouths to display their large teeth and tusks.

Teeth

Prominant tusks project more than 60 cm (24 in) from the gums.

Threat displays

Males challenge each other by opening their mouths to maximum gape. If this fails to deter a rival, they may rise up out of the water and try to slash each other with their tusks. Ferocious fights often develop between rival males and may lead to serious injury.

Eyes, ears, and nostrils appear above the water surface.

Hippos spend up to 18 hours a day submerged in water.

Hippo underwater

The common hippo, whose name means "river horse", is more at home in water than on land. When submerged it can hold its breath and seal its nostrils and ears. Normally, it stays underwater for 3–5 minutes before having to surface to breathe, but, if necessary, it can remain submerged for considerably longer. It swims easily and may walk along the bottom of the riverbed.

Hippo walking on the bottom of a riverbed.

Pygmy hippopotamus

The pygmy hippo is about one-fifth the size of the common hippo. It swims well, but is less aquatic than the common hippo. It lives in marshland and swamp forest where it makes tunnel-like tracks through the undergrowth. If alarmed it seeks refuge in dense undergrowth. The pygmy hippo is a shy, nocturnal animal living alone or in pairs. It spends most of the day resting and feeds during darkness on swamp plants, fruit, and leaves.

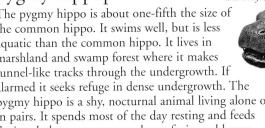

Round head and body

Thick skin

COMMON HIPPOPOTAMUS

SCIENTIFIC NAME	*Hippopotamus amphibius*
ORDER	Artiodactyla
FAMILY	Hippopotamidae
DISTRIBUTION	Tropical Africa
HABITAT	Rivers, lakes, and estuaries
DIET	Grass and aquatic vegetation – up to 45 kg (100 lb) per day
SIZE	Height: 1.52 m (5 ft); weight: 4.06 tonnes (4 tons)
LIFESPAN	50 years

FIND OUT MORE

AFRICAN WILDLIFE CONSERVATION LAKE AND RIVER WILDLIFE MAMMALS MARSH AND SWAMP WILDLIFE

HISTORY

THE STUDY OF HISTORY is an attempt by people today to understand the lives of people in the past. Historians – the people who study history – look at primary sources – those writings and artefacts that have survived – and try to piece together a realistic picture of life in previous years. But not every piece of historical evidence survives to the present day, and that which does survive can sometimes be interpreted in many different ways. As a result, history is a complex and sometimes controversial subject that excites considerable debate among historians and non-historians alike.

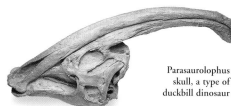

Parasaurolophus skull, a type of duckbill dinosaur

Prehistory
Writing has existed for around 5,500 years. The period before written records is called prehistory. Archaeologists study material evidence, such as bones, fossils, and artefacts, to help them understand prehistoric periods, such as the Stone Age.

Records of history

All primary sources, whether photographic or written, need careful study, because they may be biased, that is, illustrate a subjective (personal) viewpoint.

Meroë pyramid, Sudan

Sources of history

What we know of history is based on material evidence, such as buildings, roads, tools, artworks, and clothes; written evidence, such as books; and oral evidence handed down through generations. All these sources provide valuable information about past societies and the people who created them.

Material evidence
By piecing together material evidence, historians can discover much about the people of the time. The Bayeux Tapestry is the record of a known historical event – the Norman invasion of England (1066). But when historians study it more closely, they discover a wealth of information, not just about the event the tapestry is relating, but about life of the time generally – and even about the women who made the tapestry.

English soldiers   *Norman knights*

Normans attack the English, Bayeux Tapestry

Chinese letter, written on a scroll

The larger the document, the more useful it is to a historian.

Written evidence
Books, diaries, poems, letters, account books, receipts, state documents, and newspapers are all written evidence and help historians in their work. But written evidence needs careful study, because it is often personal, and has to be balanced against other accounts or other types of evidence to gain a more rounded picture of past events.

Propaganda
Historical evidence may be altered to serve political needs. The Soviet Union saw a power struggle between Josef Stalin (1879–1953) and Leon Trotsky (1879–1940) after the death of Lenin. When Stalin became leader, he had Trotsky removed from all official photographs.

Lenin

Trotsky appeared in the original of this photograph.

Dark Ages
Historians often label historical periods, though people of the time may not have agreed with the label. The chaotic period in Europe after the Roman Empire fell (c.500) is often called the Dark Ages, yet in places it was a time of culture and learning.

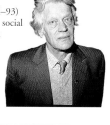

The Book of Durrow, c.800

EP Thompson
Edward Thompson (1924–93) was an important English social historian. His best-known work, *The Making of the English Working Class* (1965) studied the politics and protests of ordinary people as opposed to the history of political leaders.

Oral history
Many societies know their own history, even though they have not written it down. In West Africa, storytellers known as *griots* record the history of their tribes through lengthy narrative stories set to music. In the 1960s and 1970s, there was a move towards sociological history, whereby historians recorded the stories of people previously left out of historical record-making, such as women and the working classes.

Warrior's mother, Kenya

Timeline
c.400s BC Herodotus writes history of the Greek–Persian wars.

c.800 Monks begin the Anglo-Saxon Chronicle.

1380s Arab historian Ibn Khaldun writes *Kitab al-Ibar*, to explain why civilizations rise and fall.

1800s History established as an academic subject, with the emphasis on primary sources, rather than interpretation.

1860s Karl Marx (1818–83) argues a view of history in which economic factors determine events.

Ammonite, prehistoric material evidence

1930s French historians of the Annales school concentrate on social history.

1960s Historians focus on people previously ignored in accounts of history, such as women.

1992 US historian Francis Fukuyama argues that the fall of communism "ended" history.

FIND OUT MORE   ARCHAEOLOGY   MARX, KARL   RUSSIAN REVOLUTION   SEVEN WONDERS OF THE ANCIENT WORLD

HITTITES

A WARLIKE PEOPLE, known as the Hittites, flourished from 1600 to 1200 BC, when they had one of the most powerful armies of the ancient world. They settled in Anatolia (central Turkey) around 2000 BC, then established control over the area from their great fortified capital at Hattusas. Gradually, the Hittite kingdom expanded into Syria, where they clashed with Egypt, and the growing might of Assyria. Despite their fearsome reputation, the Hittites were astute politicians, and preferred diplomacy to armed conflict where possible. Eventually, attacks from outside forces, combined with famine, put an end to their empire.

The Hittite Empire covered most of Turkey and Anatolia at its height, c.1300 BC.

Teshub was often portrayed holding a weapon.

A three-pronged lightning fork

Chariot warfare
From 2000 BC the introduction of horses, the development of the bit, and strong, spoked wheels transformed the chariot from a humble cart pulled by asses, into a dangerous weapon which changed warfare in the Near East. The Hittites were masters of this weapon.

Battle of Kadesh
The world's earliest battle that can be reconstructed was between the chariots of the Hittite king, Muwatallis, and the Egyptian Rameses II at Kadesh in c.1290 BC. Chariots continued to be important to ancient armies for over 2000 years.

Diplomacy
The Hittites favoured diplomatic marriages to secure peace, especially with Egypt. For instance, after the Battle of Kadesh, a Hittite princess was married to a pharaoh. On another occasion, an Egyptian queen, possibly Tutankhamun's widow, wrote to the Hittite king asking to marry one of his sons.

Rameses II

Politics

Hittite rulers were supreme commanders of the army (and chief judges and high priests). The greatest king was Suppiluliumas I (r.1380–1346 BC), who conquered all Syria, between the Euphrates and the sea. Though he took this territory through military might, he kept it by bribing his Egyptian rivals with gold. Many Syrian gods were accepted by the Hittites as leading deities, including Teshub, who symbolized storms and the destruction of war.

Ugarit
A wealthy trading city on the Mediterranean coast, Ugarit was a main area of conflict between the Hittites and the Egyptians because of its location. It was abandoned in the turmoil that destroyed the Hittite Empire. Archaeologists have unearthed one of the world's earliest cuneiform alphabets here.

Teshub, the Hittite storm god

Head-dress, indicating high status

Art and literature

Hittite myths emphasize divine warfare, and many feature Teshub defeating evil outside forces. In the remains of their hilltop capital at Hattusas (modern Boghazkoy, Turkey), stone reliefs in the city wall show helmeted warriors, and some of the many Hittite gods. Tiny figures, crafted in gold, have been found. These depict kings and gods, and wear the distinctive upturned boots of a mountain people.

Hittite wall relief

Neo-Hittites
The Syrian city-states belonging to the empire adopted Hittite hieroglyphics and art. After the collapse of the empire, this influence continued, and the cities became known as the Neo-Hittite states.

Food and drink
The main crops were barley and wheat, which were used for making bread and brewing beer. The Hittites also grew fruits, such as apples, figs, and apricots, and they made wine from grapes. Bees produced honey, and farmers raised sheep, oxen, and cattle.

Apple   Figs   Apricots

Short-sleeved tunic

Upturned boots

Gold figurine, possibly of a Hittite king

Timeline

Hittite warhorse

1600–1400 BC
The first Hittite kingdom is established in Anatolia.

1595 BC King Mursili I sacks Babylon, but does not remain.

1550 BC The fortified Hittite capital is established at Hattusas.

c.1460 BC Tudhaliyas II begins conquests that establish last phase of empire.

1380–1346 BC Suppiluliumas commands a vast empire stretching from present-day western Turkey to north Syria. Hattusas (modern Boghazkoy) is the main cultural influence in the area.

c.1290 BC One of the earliest known battles takes place, between Hittite and Egyptian forces, at Kadesh.

1283 BC Peace treaties are signed between Hittites and Egyptians.

1200 BC The growth of the Assyrian Empire, forces invading from the north and west, and famine combine to destroy the Hittite Empire.

| FIND OUT MORE | ASIA, HISTORY OF | ASSYRIAN EMPIRE | BABYLONIAN EMPIRE | EGYPT, ANCIENT | PERSIAN EMPIRES | SUMERIANS |

HOLOCAUST

BETWEEN 1939 AND 1945, six million European Jews were systematically murdered by the German Nazi regime. Some were killed in their own towns, but most died in concentration camps. This mass murder of Jews is known as the Holocaust, after a Biblical term meaning "slaughter by fire". It was a deliberate national policy established by Adolf Hitler and his Nazi followers to wipe out all traces of Jewish life and culture. Jews have been persecuted throughout history, but the Holocaust, which slaughtered nearly 70% of Europe's Jews, is history's worst example of anti-Semitism. Today, people still ask how such an atrocity was allowed to happen.

Warsaw Ghetto

Star of David
From 1933, the Nazis began to segregate (separate) German Jews from the rest of the population. Jews had to wear the yellow Star of David to identify them, and they were banned from public places. Nazi propaganda encouraged hatred, and people attacked Jewish shops and homes.

Warsaw Ghetto

In 1939, Germany invaded Poland. The capital, Warsaw, was home to half a million Jews, who were rounded up, forced to live in a ghetto (part of the city cut off from the rest), and given starvation rations. In 1943, the Jews made a brave and desperate attempt to fight back, but this uprising was mercilessly crushed. By the time Soviet troops liberated Warsaw in 1945, only 200 Jews remained alive.

Concentration camps

Special concentration camps were built by the Nazis to detain people considered "undesirable", particularly Jews. From 1941, many camps were set up throughout eastern Europe, including Chelmno, Treblinka, and Auschwitz. These were literally death camps, built to achieve Hitler's "final solution" of exterminating all European Jews. Thousands of men, women, and children were led into chambers where they were killed with a cyanide compound, Zyklon B, introduced through vents in the walls. Non-Jews were also killed, including gypsies and the disabled.

Entrance to Auschwitz

Auschwitz
One of the most feared death camps was Auschwitz (Oswiecim) in Poland, where some 12,000 victims a day were gassed and their bodies cremated. It was this burning in the death camps that gave the Holocaust its name.

Death camps were in eastern Europe

Main death camps

France

Greece

Deportation
European Jews from France to Greece were rounded up, loaded onto trains, in cattle cars, and deported to death camps. local people hostile to Jews often helped the Nazis to do this. Up to a thousand people were forced into each train, and deprived of food and water. On arrival, survivors were sent to the gas chambers.

Jewish resistance
Despite the power of the Nazis, the Jews did resist oppression. During the war, there were revolts by Jews in ghettoes, such as Warsaw, and even in the concentration camps, such as Sobibor. Elsewhere, small bands of Jews formed partisan groups that fought heroically in enemy territory, attacking Germans, and destroying military stores and railway tracks.

Liberation
From 1942, news of the death camps began to reach the West. It was only in 1945, however, that the full story emerged. When the Allied forces liberated the camps, they found, to their horror, huge mounds of skeletal people either dead or dying.

Timeline

1925 Adolf Hitler publishes *Mein Kampf* (My Struggle). In it, he states his anti-Semitism (hatred of Jews).

1933 Hitler becomes Chancellor and begins the persecution of German Jews. First camp is built at Dachau.

1935 Nuremberg Laws declare Jews to be second-class German citizens.

9–10 Nov 1938 "Kristallnacht" (Night of Broken Glass), Germany. People attack more than 7000 Jewish shops and homes, and 30,000 Jews are sent to concentration camps.

1941 Hitler, Eichmann, and other leading Nazis announce their "final solution". Death camps are set up throughout Europe for mass slaughter.

1943 Warsaw Ghetto Uprising. Nazis kill or deport more than 56,000 Jews in four weeks.

1945 Allied forces liberate concentration camp in Eastern Europe.

1962 First tree is planted in Israel's Avenue of the Righteous, which commemorates non-Jews who saved Jewish life during World War II.

Anne Frank
Born in Frankfurt, Anne Frank (1929–45) was a German Jew. In 1933, she and her family fled to Amsterdam, Holland, to escape persecution. In 1941, the Nazis invaded Holland, and from July 1942, Anne and her family were hidden by friends. While in hiding, she wrote a diary that is now world famous. In August 1944, the family was betrayed and sent to the concentration camps. Anne died in Bergen Belsen camp at the age of 16.

FIND OUT MORE

COLD WAR   EUROPE, HISTORY OF   GERMANY, HISTORY OF   JUDAISM   WORLD WAR II

HOLY LAND, HISTORY OF

OVER THE CENTURIES, THIS VARIED region of mountains, deserts, and marshes has had shifting borders, various conquerors, and many names, including Canaan, Zion, Israel, Judah, and Palestine. The area is holy to three world religions: Judaism, Christianity, and Islam. Jews believe it is the Promised Land God gave them, and that Abraham, father of the Jews, settled there in about 1900 BC. The land is holy for Christians because Jesus Christ lived there; and for Muslims, Jerusalem is sacred as the site of many of Muhammad's activities. The Bible records mainly Jewish history in this region.

The Holy Land

This crossroads between Europe, Africa, and Asia has been conquered by Babylonians, Persians, Greeks, Romans, Arabs, Byzantines, Ottomans, and British in turn. Today it includes Israel, and parts of Jordan and Syria.

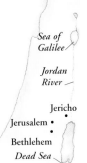

Sea of Galilee

Jordan River

Jericho

Jerusalem •

Bethlehem

Dead Sea

Jericho
Excavations show that the walled city of Jericho may be the oldest settlement in the world. According to the Bible, it was destroyed many times in its history – once by Joshua, who led the Israelites after the death of Moses.

Jerusalem

Over the centuries Jews, Christians, and Muslims have all fought for access to holy shrines, such as Solomon's Temple. This has caused many wars in one of the world's holiest cities.

Solomon's Temple
This temple, completed by Phoenician craftsmen in 957 BC, housed the Ark of the Covenant, and was the first permanent Jewish religious centre. In 587 BC, the Babylonians destroyed the first temple. It was rebuilt in 37 BC but destroyed by the Romans in AD 70. All that remains today is the so-called Wailing Wall on the west side.

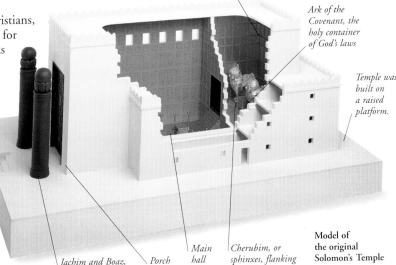

Holy of holies, inlaid with gold

Ark of the Covenant, the holy container of God's laws

Temple was built on a raised platform.

Jachim and Boaz, the bronze columns

Porch

Main hall

Cherubim, or sphinxes, flanking the Ark

Model of the original Solomon's Temple

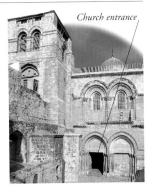

Church entrance

Holy Sepulchre Church
In the 12th century, Crusaders rebuilt a Christian church on Mount Calvary, Jerusalem, where Jesus Christ was crucified. The church contains Greek Orthodox, Roman Catholic, and Armenian chapels. In a grotto underneath is the empty tomb of Jesus.

Dome of the Rock
This massive rock is sacred to Muslims because Muhammad is said to have risen to heaven from this spot. It is sacred to Jews because Abraham is said to have prepared his son Isaac for sacrifice here.

Philistines

The Philistines were part of a group of warriors also known as the Sea Peoples. In about 1100 BC, the Philistines threatened the Israelites, who had settled the southern coast of Palestine (in modern Israel). The Israelites lived subject to the Philistines for 200 years until the Israelite King David (r.1013–973 BC) managed to subdue them.

Slingshots.

David and Goliath
Goliath, a huge Philistine champion, challenged the Israelites to present a man for single combat. No one dared respond until David, a young shepherd, volunteered. Against all the odds, he knocked Goliath out with one slingshot, and cut off his head. David went on to become Israel's greatest king, and made Jerusalem a great political and religious centre.

Timeline

Holy Sepulchre Church

c.8000 BC Evidence of human settlement, Jericho.

c.1900 BC The patriarch Abraham settles in Canaan.

c.1200s BC The Exodus: Moses leads the Israelites out of slavery in Egypt.

1033–1013 BC Reign of Saul, first king of Israel.

1013–933 BC Reigns of David and Solomon.

587 BC Babylonians destroy first Jewish temple, Jerusalem.

AD 33 Romans crucify Jesus Christ in Jerusalem.

AD 70 Romans destroy the second Jewish temple at Jerusalem.

636 Muslim rule begins.

1096–1291 European Crusaders fight to control the territory.

1948 Declaration of the state of Israel.

King Solomon

The son of King David and his wife Bathsheba, Solomon (r.973–930 BC) built the first temple at Jerusalem, and a number of cities. He was famous in ancient Israel for making profitable foreign alliances, and, during his reign, Israel reached its greatest extent of territory. Myths present Solomon as very wise, but he was actually a rather harsh and despotic ruler.

FIND OUT MORE   ARCHITECTURE   CHRISTIANITY   CRUSADES   ISLAM   ISRAEL   MYTHS AND LEGENDS

HOLY ROMAN EMPIRE

FOR MORE THAN 800 years, most of central Europe was loosely tied together in the Holy Roman Empire, an attempt to revive the old Roman empire, with backing from the Christian Church. It was founded in 962. After 1273, the Habsburg family of Austria won the throne and dominated the empire from then on. The emperors were elected by seven German princes and crowned by the Pope in Rome. The emperor had little power, but the title made him political leader of Europe.

Jewelled cross

Crown is set with enamel plaques.

10th-century imperial crown

Otto's German lands

The empire in 987

Emperors were also kings of Italy

The empire

From its foundation in 962 until the mid-13th century, the Holy Roman Empire included much of Germany, the Low Countries, Switzerland, Austria, and northern Italy. Over the next centuries, it shrank, but it remained dominant in Germany.

Otto I: the birth of empire

In 936, Otto, a descendant of Charlemagne, became king of Germany. He defeated the Magyar invaders at the battle of Lech in 955 and went on to conquer northern Italy. In 962, the Pope crowned him Holy Roman Emperor.

Habsburgs

The Habsburgs took their name from a castle in Switzerland and held vast estates in Switzerland, Austria, and southern Germany. In 1273, a member of the Habsburg family became Rudolf I of Germany and then the Holy Roman Emperor. With a few short breaks, the Habsburgs ran the empire until its end in 1806. Under their rule, the interests of the empire were secondary to those of increasing Habsburg family power.

Maximilian I married Mary of Burgundy in 1477 and acquired Burgundy.

Philip I, son of Maximilian, married Juana of Castile and Aragon in 1496.

Mary of Burgundy

Charles's brother, Ferdinand I, married Anna and inherited Bohemia and Hungary.

Charles V, son of Philip, inherited Spain through his mother, Juana and the Habsburg lands from his grandfather Maximilian.

Struggle for power

The emperor was the supreme secular (worldly) ruler of Christian Europe; the Pope was its supreme spiritual ruler. The two often clashed. In 1076, Pope Gregory VII deposed Emperor Henry IV. The conflict led to a decline in the power of the emperors over the next few centuries.

Charles V

Habsburg power in Europe reached its peak in 1519, when Charles V (1500–58) became emperor. He acquired vast lands from each of his grandparents, including Spain and its empire in America. Charles kept this empire together until 1556, when he gave up the throne and divided his empire between his brother Ferdinand, who became emperor on Charles's death in 1558, and his son Philip, who ruled Spain, Italy, and the Low Countries.

Ornate Renaissance decoration

Imperial Vienna

The Habsburg capital was the Austrian city of Vienna. It was one of the leading cities in Europe, with fine churches, palaces, and other civic buildings. The centre of Habsburg power was the Hofburg Palace, a vast complex including imperial apartments and government offices.

The Schweizertor, a gate to the Hofburg

Maria Theresa

In 1740, Emperor Charles VI died, leaving his daughter Maria Theresa on the throne. Prussia and France disputed her right to inherit the throne and declared war. Maria was an inspired leader and managed to keep her empire together, making Austria into a powerful, centralized state.

Timeline

800 Charlemagne crowned.

962 Otto, king of Germany, becomes first Holy Roman Emperor.

1076 Pope overthrows emperor Henry IV and establishes papal power over emperor.

1273 Rudolf I becomes first emperor from the Habsburg family.

Imperial knight

1517 Reformation under Martin Luther results in a divide between German Protestant princes and the Catholic emperor.

1519 Charles V is crowned emperor and becomes most powerful man in Europe.

1556 Charles splits his empire between brother Ferdinand and son Philip; Habsburg Austria dominates the Holy Roman empire.

1806 Francis II abolishes the Holy Roman empire.

FIND OUT MORE CHARLEMAGNE CHRISTIANITY GERMANY, HISTORY OF REFORMATION ROMAN EMPIRE

HORMONES AND THE ENDOCRINE SYSTEM

THE ENDOCRINE SYSTEM is one of the body's control systems. It consists of endocrine glands that produce chemicals called hormones, and release them into the bloodstream. The hormones act as chemical messengers and instruct specific areas of the body to carry out certain actions. Hormones usually work slowly and have a long-lasting action, regulating processes such as growth and reproduction.

Hypothalamus is part of the brain that controls the pituitary gland.

Pineal gland regulates body's internal clock.

Pituitary gland

Thyroid gland controls body's metabolic rate.

Thymus gland stimulates development of immune system.

Brain

Parathyroid gland regulates calcium levels in blood.

Lung

Adrenal gland helps deal with stress.

Kidney

Pancreas releases hormones that control blood glucose levels.

Testes release male sex hormones.

Ovary releases female sex hormones.

How a hormone works

The blood carries hormones throughout the body, but they only affect certain target cells within target tissues. The hormone attaches itself to a site on the surface of a target cell. This locking-on causes changes inside the target cells, which produce the required action. For example, the pancreas releases the hormone insulin in order to reduce levels of glucose molecules in the blood. Insulin does this by stimulating the body cells to take in glucose.

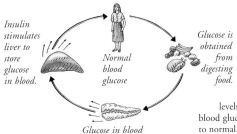

Insulin stimulates liver to store glucose in blood.

Normal blood glucose

Glucose is obtained from digesting food.

Glucose in blood stimulates pancreas to release insulin.

Hormone levels

Hormone levels in the blood are controlled by a feedback mechanism. For example, insulin is released from the pancreas in response to increased levels of glucose. Higher levels of insulin will then cause blood glucose levels to return back to normal. The lowered glucose levels "feed back" to the pancreas, which produces less insulin.

Endocrine system

The endocrine system consists of many glands scattered throughout the body. Glands are the same in men and women, except for the reproductive glands. The pea-sized pituitary controls many other glands. Some organs are linked to the endocrine system because, as well as having other functions, they also release hormones. The pancreas, for example, produces digestive enzymes and releases hormones.

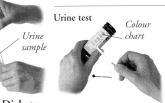

Urine test

Urine sample

Colour chart

Diabetes

Diabetes is a condition that occurs when blood glucose levels become very high because the pancreas cannot produce enough insulin. Doctors can monitor blood glucose levels by measuring the amount of glucose in a urine sample.

Pituitary gland

The pituitary gland releases at least eight hormones. Some affect body functions directly, while the remainder stimulate other endocrine glands to produce hormones of their own. The pituitary gland has two parts, or lobes. The anterior lobe produces and sends hormones around the body; the posterior lobe releases hormones produced in the hypothalamus.

Hypothalamus

Nerves carry hormones from hypothalamus to posterior lobe.

Blood vessels carry hormones around body.

Tissues release hormones received from hypothalamus.

Posterior lobe

Anterior lobe

Jokichi Takamine

Japanese chemist Jokichi Takamine (1854–1922) was the first person to isolate a pure sample of a hormone.

Using extracts of adrenal glands, he prepared crystals of a substance that increased blood pressure in animals. This substance was later called adrenaline.

Prolactin

Prolactin is a hormone that is produced by the anterior lobe. It stimulates the production of milk when a woman breastfeeds her baby. When the baby sucks on the nipple, prolactin is immediately released from the mother's pituitary gland.

Growth hormone

The anterior lobe produces growth hormone, which encourages the body to grow. It works by stimulating the body's cells to divide. Although growth hormone affects all tissues, its main targets are bones and skeletal muscles. Growth hormone is most active in childhood and adolescence.

Adrenaline

If you have ever been frightened and felt your heart pounding, you have experienced the effects of adrenaline. It is a hormone that helps the body react to danger. When the adrenal glands release adrenaline, your breathing and heart rate speed up, and blood flows to your muscles so you can run from danger.

FIND OUT MORE

BRAIN AND NERVOUS SYSTEM   DIGESTION   GROWTH AND DEVELOPMENT   HUMAN BODY   REPRODUCTION

HORSE RIDING

PEOPLE RIDE HORSES for leisure and in competitions, which are often described as equestrian (from *equus*, meaning horse). These include show jumping, eventing, and dressage, all of which test the horse's ability to jump or perform special movements, and each of which appears in the Olympic programme. Equestrian events also include racing events – flat racing, steeplechasing, and hurdling – where jockeys ride specially bred horses called thoroughbreds. Other riding sports include polo, in which teams of riders compete to score goals.

Riding
Riders learn how to start, stop, steer and control the speed of a horse using their hands, legs, and body-weight. The natural gaits of a horse are the walk, trot, canter, and gallop.

Hard hat is essential.

Bridle

Reins

Stirrup

Saddle

Horse breaks into a canter from a trot.

Show jumping

This involves riders taking their horses around a set course of jumps which may include artificial gates, a wall, and a water jump. Competitors receive faults if their horse refuses or knocks down a jump, or exceeds the specified time. The competitor with the fewest faults wins.

Rider keeps looking ahead.

Rider's hands move up the reins to allow the horse to use his head and neck.

Rider leans forward from the hips.

Landing

Jumping a single pole

Horse draws up his hind legs and stretches to clear the jump.

Horse tucks up his forelegs.

Taking off

Puissance
This show jumping competition tests the ability of a horse to jump high fences. From four to six fences are jumped, the number being reduced and the height raised for each round.

Racing

Racing can be flat or over jumps. Some events such as the English Grand National – a steeplechase – are world famous and attract thousands of spectators and involve heavy betting on different runners. Horses may have to carry extra weights under the saddle, as well as the jockey (rider).

Polo
This game is played four-a-side on a large field. Players mounted on polo ponies use mallets to strike a ball into their opponents' goal. A game consists of up to eight seven-minute periods called chukkers. Riders usually change ponies after every chukker.

Dressage

In dressage, each competitor guides his or her horse through paces, figures, manoeuvres, and halts (stops). Judges award points for the quality of the performance. Dressage is a formal sport and riders wear top hat and tails or military uniform; it needs a high degree of discipline and schooling.

English Derby

Jumping
The main types of jumping races are hurdling, for three-year-old horses upwards, and steeplechasing for four-year-olds upwards. Hurdles are low and may be knocked over; steeplechase fences are larger and include ditches and water jumps.

Flat racing
Horses are raced over distances from 5 furlongs (1 km) to 2 miles (3 km) or more. Many countries follow the English tradition of Classic races for three-year-olds, which include a Derby, and for fillies (young female horses), an Oaks, over 1.5 miles (2.4 km).

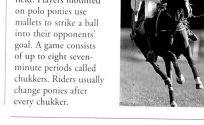

Grand National

Eventing

In three-day eventing, riders take their horses through a different discipline each day to test all aspects of the horse's abilities. Dressage tests a horse's obedience and show jumping its powers of recovery. There is also a four-phase endurance test which includes a steeplechase.

Cross-country
The cross-country phase may cover 7 km (4.3 miles) with about 30 fixed obstacles of all kinds. The course has to be completed in a set time to avoid time penalties. The jumps are often spectacular and include water, slippery grass banks, steps, solid walls, and drops.

Mark Todd
A New Zealand eventer, Mark Todd (b. 1956) won the individual three-day event gold medal at the 1984 and 1988 Olympics on the horse Charisma. He was deprived of a third successive gold when his mount broke down on the second day after scoring well in the dressage.

FIND OUT MORE   EVOLUTION   HORSES   MAMMALS   MONGOL EMPIRE   OLYMPIC GAMES   SPORT

HORSES

ALL MEMBERS OF THE HORSE family, which includes zebras and asses, are social animals. In the wild, they live in family groups which join to form a herd. People first tamed horses about 6,000 years ago, and today there are more than 300 breeds of domestic horse. They can be divided into three groups: heavy horses, light horses, and ponies, which are less than 14.2 hands high (1.47 m or 4.8 ft).

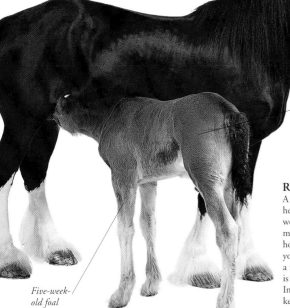

A foal will drink its mother's milk until it is about one year old.

Five-week-old foal

The horse

Naturally grazing animals, horses in the wild eat grasses and shrubs. In each jaw, they have six incisor teeth for cutting and 12 molars for chewing. They rely on their sharp senses to survive, using taste and smell to check their food, and hearing and sight to detect danger. If they face possible danger, their first defence is to run away.

Ear positions
Horses can move their ears separately to pick up sounds, and the position of their ears is a good indication of their mood. Ears forward show interest; one ear forward and one back means the horse is not sure; ears back show aggression or fear.

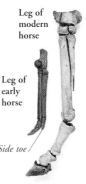

Leg of modern horse

Leg of early horse

Side toe

Reproduction
A female horse carries her young in her womb for about 11 months. Within an hour of its birth, a young horse, called a foal, will get up and is soon able to run. In the wild, it has to keep up with the herd.

Hooves and feet
Modern horses have one toe on each foot, protected by a hoof. It has taken 50 million years for them to evolve. The first horses, which were the size of small dogs, had a pad with four toes on the forefeet and three on the hind.

Dapple grey

Dun

Skewbald

Light bay

Colours
Originally, the colour of a horse's coat may have provided camouflage. Today, horses are bred in several colours. In some, the legs, mane, and tail are a different colour from the rest of the body. Some horses have white markings on the face and legs.

Movement
Horses can travel using four main patterns of leg movements, called gaits. These are the walk, trot, canter, and gallop. The gallop is the fastest, but a horse can gallop only short distances. Humans have bred horses to perform other artificial gaits, such as the paso done by the Peruvian paso, and the tölt done by the Icelandic pony.

The walk is a four-beat gait. The horse moves its legs in turn.

The trot is two-beat. Opposite fore and hind legs move together.

The canter has three beats.

In the canter, one leg moves, then a diagonal pair, then the last leg.

All feet are off the ground together.

The gallop is like the canter, but paired feet go down separately.

Horse family

The horse belongs to the family of mammals called the *Equidae*. Also in this family are donkeys, zebras, the wild asses of Africa and Asia, Przewalski's wild horse of Mongolia, and the recently discovered Riwoche wild horse of Tibet.

Zebras
There are three species of zebra, each with a different pattern of stripes. Herds of all species live wild in tropical Africa.

Wild asses
The three species of wild ass are the African wild ass, and the onager and kiang of Asia. This kulan is a type of onager.

Donkey
Descended from the African wild ass, donkeys have great strength and stamina.

Przewalski's
An ancient breed of horse, it has been reintroduced into the wild.

Herds

Members of a herd are close friends. They communicate using a variety of sounds, smells, and body language. For example, if a horse is startled, it will raise its head and tail, arch its neck, and flare its nostrils. This alerts the others, which prepare to run.

Zebra

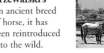

Feral herds
These wild horses in Australia, called brumbies, are described as feral. They are domesticated horses now running wild.

FIND OUT MORE | EVOLUTION | FARMING | GRASSLAND WILDLIFE | HORSE RIDING | TRANSPORT, HISTORY OF

Horses
Light horses

Strong build

Strong arched neck

Irish draught was originally used for work on small Irish farms.

Saddlebred is an American horse with a high action. It is a brilliant show horse.

Australian stock horse is an all-rounder, with great endurance and stamina.

Pinto is also called the paint horse. It comes in a variety of types and sizes.

Camargue horses live in semi-wild herds in the Rhône delta, France.

Welsh cob is a bold horse. It is extremely hardy and easy to keep.

Compact body

Long tail and mane

Big joints

Hackney horse is often used in showring harness competitions.

Lipizzaner is used in the Spanish Riding School of Vienna, Austria.

Morgan descends from one stallion. named Justin Morgan after his owner.

Andalucian is a Spanish breed from which the Lipizzaners derive.

Tennessee walking horse is good-tempered. It has three smooth gaits.

Hanoverian is popular in Germany for show-jumping and dressage.

Appaloosa as a breed was first bred by the Nez Percé Indians of North America.

Quarter horse is claimed to be the most popular horse in the world.

Arab is the oldest breed and is accepted as the original source of all breeds.

Orlov trotter is a tall lightly built horse. It was first bred in Russia.

Thoroughbred is the fastest horse breed, with almost perfect proportions.

Barb comes from Morocco in North Africa. It is one of the oldest horse breeds.

Ponies

Good sloping shoulders

Compact body with depth through the girth

Dartmoor is noted for its long, low action.

Connemara is fast and a brilliant jumper.

Exmoor lives on Exmoor in southwest England.

American Shetland is used mostly as a harness pony.

Australian pony has an excellent temperament.

Welsh mountain pony is hardy as well as beautiful.

Tail set low

Shetland is up to 102 cm (40 in) high, but is strong enough to carry a man.

Highland is sure-footed, strong, and docile. It is known to be long-lived.

Icelandic horse can carry heavy weights, at speed, over long distances.

New Forest pony is a friendly, comfortable riding pony.

Fjord comes from Norway and is descended from Przewalski's horse.

Falabella is a miniature horse. standing up to only 7 hh (70 cm/28 in).

Heavy horses

Deep, strong neck

High withers

Short back

Large, rounded quarters

Suffolk punch is very powerful. It was used as an all-round farm horse.

Clydesdale originated in the Clyde Valley, Scotland, in the 18th century.

Shire is the heaviest of the draught breeds. It is gentle and easy to handle.

Percheron is a French breed containing a great deal of Arab blood.

Ardennais falls into two types – a lively, light draught, and a heavy type.

Belgian draught is also known as the Brabant. It is a very old breed.

HOSPITALS

ANCIENT ROME HAD special places where sick people could receive medical treatment – the world's earliest hospitals. Today, hospitals have more responsibilities: patient care, health education, and medical research. Whether general or specialist, most hospitals have wards for in-patients, clinics for out-patients, operating theatres for surgery, and pharmacies for dispensing drugs. Trained staff, such as doctors and nurses, care for patients using complex equipment, while non-medical staff, such as cooks, porters, cleaners, and engineers, are crucial in making the hospital function. In some poorer countries, there may be only one hospital for every million people.

Specialist hospitals

Some specialist hospitals focus on groups of patients, such as women or children. Others concentrate on groups of diseases, such as eye problems, psychiatric disorders, or neurological (nerve-and-brain) diseases. Teaching hospitals train nurses, doctors, and other medical staff.

Children's hospital

Hospitals specializing in the care of sick children use scaled-down equipment, such as surgical instruments, bandages, beds, and chairs. Wards are bright and cheerful for the small patients, and there are toys and games. Parents are able to stay in nearby hospital rooms.

Child's teddy

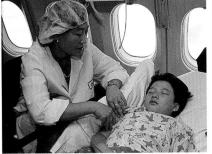
Flying eye clinic, China

Eye clinics

Ophthalmology – the branch of medicine concerned with eye and sight problems – requires exceptionally detailed and precise equipment, and specialist facilities for patients who may be temporarily unable to see. Some large countries with remote regions, such as China or Australia, can provide these facilities in a mobile form – usually a small plane.

General hospital

A general hospital provides medical facilities for a large area. Its wards cater for patients with common health problems. More complex cases are referred to a specialist hospital. General hospitals also arrange community services, such as visits by nurses.

Chart Hospital beds in a ward

Wards

In-patients usually stay in dormitory-type wards. They are separated into medical and surgical groups of children, men, women, and the elderly. Patients with infectious diseases usually stay in isolation rooms.

Ambulance, New York, USA

Accident and emergency

The A&E department receives medical emergencies, such as accident or heart-attack victims. The patient's problem is identified and stabilized, after which he or she may be sent home, or transferred to a suitable general ward.

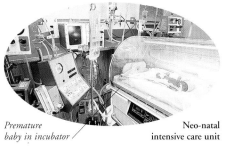
Premature baby in incubator Neo-natal intensive care unit

Intensive care unit

In intensive care, expert staff attend gravely ill patients round the clock. Electronic equipment continually monitors their vital processes, such as heartbeat and breathing.

Waiting room

Out-patients

Out-patients attend the hospital to undergo screening tests or have minor surgery. They do not stay overnight.

Staff

Doctors usually work in different hospital departments for several years, to gain general training, before choosing a speciality. Nursing staff may also specialize, for example, in paediatrics (children), psychiatry, or intensive care. A hospital's staff usually includes radio-graphers, laboratory technicians, physio-therapists, and anaesthetists.

Nurses

Nurses attend to patients' comfort and daily needs, such as feeding and washing. They also carry out medical tasks, such as taking and recording pulse rate and body temperature, and giving edications.

General nurse

Equipment

Modern equipment – especially that modified to be mobile – is crucial in hospitals. In an emergency, some of the most useful pieces include breathing apparatus (face masks or tubing), long syringes to administer fast-acting drugs, such as heart stimulants, and fluid products for intravenous infusions (drips).

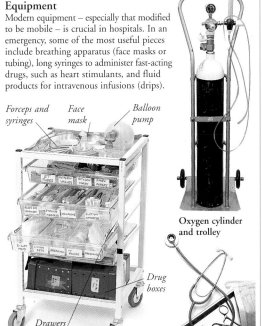
Forceps and syringes *Face mask* *Balloon pump*

Drug boxes

Drawers

Emergency trolley

Oxygen cylinder and trolley

Stethoscope

FIND OUT MORE   DRUGS   FIRST AID   MEDICINE

HOUSES AND HOMES

EVERYONE NEEDS A HOME, to provide comfort and shelter from the weather. It usually takes the form of a permanent house, although some people live in temporary structures, such as tents. Houses differ greatly around the world. They vary in what they are made of, because builders usually use local materials; in their structure, because their features must cope with local weather; and their plan. But they all provide a place for the inhabitants to sleep, eat, and cook.

Brick from local mud

Straw woven into matting

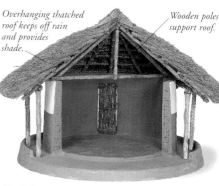

Overhanging thatched roof keeps off rain and provides shade.

Wooden poles support roof.

Early houses
From the earliest times, people built their houses out of materials that were available locally. Houses such as this African example have been made for thousands of years and are still built today. A wall of mud bricks is covered by a thatched roof supported on wooden pillars.

Inside a house

A modern house includes many parts that are normally hidden from view. Many of these are to do with the services – such as running water, drainage, heating, and electricity – that are provided for the occupants. Water tanks are concealed in the roof space, pipes and wiring are hidden behind plaster, and drains are dug below ground level.

Water tanks in the attic store cold water piped in from the water mains.

Wooden roof truss

Wooden floor

Inner leaf of concrete blocks

Outer leaf of bricks

Window, framed with wood or PVC

Wooden front door with porch

Box containing electricity meter

Construction
Modern houses in Europe and North America are most commonly made of brick, timber, and concrete. A popular building method is to construct an inner wall or "leaf" of concrete blocks, which are faced with an outer leaf of more attractive bricks. Wood is used for floors, doors, and roofing supports.

Solar panel

Roof covered with concrete tiles

Drainpipes take rainwater from gutter.

Wooden joists support floor.

Central-heating boiler

Rainwater cylinder

Pipe carries all waste to mains drain.

Concrete foundations

Central-heating radiator

Insulation cavity between wall leaves

Japanese house
Traditional Japanese houses have a timber framework. The gaps between the timber uprights are filled with wooden panels or sheets of paper to let through some sunlight. The rooms are designed to be covered by a set number of standard-sized straw mats called tatami mats.

Flats and apartments

In towns and cities, where space is limited and many people want to live near the centre, the answer is often to build upward, creating blocks of flats. This type of home became common in the 19th century, when cities began to expand quickly, and new devices such as steam cranes made it easier to lift building materials high up.

Roman apartments
The ancient Romans were the first to build blocks of apartments. In cities such as Rome and Ostia, rising ground rents and growing populations encouraged the trend, and many brick-and-concrete five- or six-storey apartment blocks were built.

In Ostia, the ancient Romans built flats above street-level shops.

Modern flats made of concrete and steel, in France

Modern apartments
From Paris to New York, apartment blocks are common in cities. Each apartment is linked to the ground by metal fire escapes to prevent residents from being trapped if there is a fire.

FIND OUT MORE | AFRICA, HISTORY OF | ARCHITECTURE | BUILDING AND CONSTRUCTION | CITIES | CRAFTS | FURNITURE | INDUSTRIAL REVOLUTION | JAPAN | ROMAN EMPIRE

Houses and homes

Permanent homes

Troglodyte houses hollowed out of rock, eastern Turkey

Stilts protect occupants from vermin and floods.

Wooden stilt-house with thatched roof, Malaysia

Adobe house built from sun-dried clay bricks, New Mexico, USA

Thick walls and few windows keep house cool.

Decorated mud house, Saudi Arabia

Turf provides insulation.

Farmhouse covered with turf and built into hillside, Iceland

Stone-built palace

Small windows help to conserve heat.

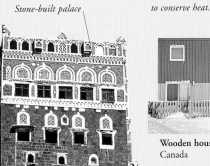

Wooden house on stilts, Canada

Sloping roof to shed snow.

Wooden log house, Switzerland

Wooden log cabin with overhanging roof, Wyoming, USA

Stone cottage with thatched roof, Donegal, Ireland

Large roof space for storage.

Wooden cross-braces add strength.

Wood-framed house with brick panels, Germany

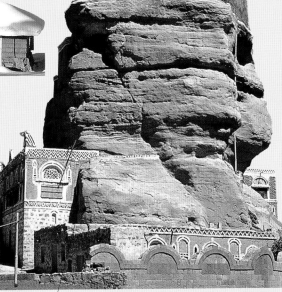

Tall outcrop of sandstone

Summer Palace, Wadi Dahr, Yemen

Dormer windows provide extra space on upper floor.

Wooden panels give extra protection against weather.

Wooden house with clapboard panels, USA

Temporary and movable homes

Gypsy horse-drawn caravan, UK

Dome of compressed snow

Tunnel entrance

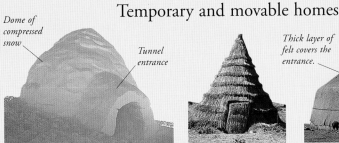

Inuit igloo built from blocks of snow and ice, Canada

Thick layer of felt covers the entrance.

Shepherd's cabin woven from bundles of straw, Spain

Yurt made from layers of felt lashed to a circular frame, Mongolia

Wooden poles bound at top into a cone shape.

Circular entrance

Tepee made of buffalo hides over poles, Arizona, USA

HUMAN BODY

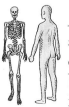

ALTHOUGH WE ALL LOOK different, we are identical in the way our bodies are constructed and function. Each human body is built up from 12 major systems, including the digestive system, skeletal system, and muscular system. These systems interact to produce co-ordinated, active, intelligent humans. The study of the body's structure is called anatomy. Externally, the only consistent anatomical differences between humans are between males and females.

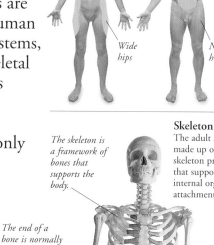

Female
Narrower shoulders

Male
Wider shoulders

Breasts

Wide hips

Narrow hips

Anatomy

The human body is divided into the head and neck, the trunk (consisting of the chest, abdomen, and pelvic region), and the arms and the legs. Men and women differ in their external genitals and in the places where fat accumulates (shown in green).

From cells to systems

The body's billions of cells are organized into tissues. Each tissue consists of similar types of cell. One or more types of tissue work together inside an organ, such as a bone or a lung. Organs are linked together to form a system that has one or more major roles. Together the systems are collected together to form the body.

Skeleton
The adult skeletal system is made up of 206 bones. The skeleton provides a framework that supports the body, protects internal organs, and provides attachment points for muscles.

The skeleton is a framework of bones that supports the body.

The body is made up from hundreds of billions of cells.

The end of a bone is normally covered by cartilage.

Ligaments are strips of tissue that hold bones together at joints.

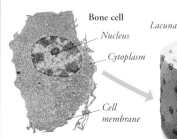

Bone cell
Nucleus
Cytoplasm
Cell membrane

Lacuna

Compact bone
Haversian canal
Circular layers of compact bone

Compact bone

Thigh bone

Spongy bone

Movable joints between bones make the skeleton flexible.

Cell
Osteocytes, or bone cells, are spider-shaped cells that make up the tissues that form a bone. Osteocytes are found in spaces called lacunae that are scattered about the hard matrix (material) found in bone tissue. Their job is to maintain the hard matrix.

Tissue
Compact bone is one of the tissues that makes up a bone. It consists of layers of hard bone around a central tube called the Haversian canal. This carries blood vessels which supply the osteocytes with food and oxygen.

Organ
Each bone consists of different tissues. Compact bone is a bone's hard outer covering. Spongy bone and bone marrow are tissues found inside bones. Cartilage is the slippery tissue found in joints.

Body
The skeleton and the other major body systems form the living human body. The body's systems do not work in isolation, however. For example, the skeleton is supplied with blood vessels, lymph vessels, and nerves, and requires muscles to move it.

Body systems

Each body system contributes to the body's normal functioning. Together, the body's systems are controlled by the nervous and endocrine systems. They enable us to move, talk, and perceive the world, while our internal processes run automatically.

Muscular
The muscular system moves and supports the body. It consists of over 620 skeletal muscles attached to bones.

Nervous
The nervous system controls the body's activities. It consists of the brain and spinal cord, and a network of nerves.

Circulatory
The circulatory system transports material around the body. It consists of the heart, a network of blood vessels, and the blood.

Digestive
The digestive system supplies the body with food. It consists of the mouth, oesophagus, stomach, and intestines.

Integumentary
The integumentary system is the body's outer, protective covering and consists of skin, hair, and nails.

Respiratory
The respiratory system supplies the body with oxygen. It consists of the nose, throat, trachea, and lungs.

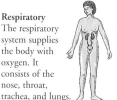

Urinary
The urinary system removes waste. It consists of the two kidneys, the ureters, the bladder, and the urethra.

Endocrine
The endocrine system regulates many body processes. It consists of glands that make hormones.

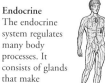

Lymphatic
The lymphatic system protects the body against disease. It consists of a network of lymph vessels.

Reproductive
The reproductive system enables us to produce children. Male and female systems are different.

FIND OUT MORE

BRAIN AND NERVOUS SYSTEM   CELLS   GROWTH AND DEVELOPMENT   HEART AND CIRCULATORY SYSTEM   HUMAN EVOLUTION   MUSCLES AND MOVEMENT   REPRODUCTION   SKELETON   SKIN, HAIR, AND NAILS

HUMAN EVOLUTION

MUCH DEBATE HAS SURROUNDED the evolution of humans. However, most scientists are now agreed that modern humans, *Homo sapiens*, are the sole survivors of a number of human species that evolved from the common ancestor of humans and apes some six million years ago. Climatic changes forced our earliest ancestors out of the tropical forests and into open woodlands and grasslands. The challenge of these new habitats resulted in important changes, such as the ability to walk upright and an increase in brain size.

Evolutionary tree

The evolutionary sequence from the earliest human ancestors is not a straight line, but is instead a "tree" with many dead ends. Because the fossil evidence is limited, scientists disagree about how many human species have existed and which were ancestors of others. This evolutionary tree provides a simple guide to relationships but does not necessarily indicate ancestry.

Common ancestors

Paranthropus
3–1 mya

Australopithecus
5–2 mya

Homo habilis
2–1.5 mya

Homo erectus
1.7 mya – 250,000 years ago

Homo neanderthalensis
200,000– 35,000 years ago

Homo sapiens
100,000 years ago

Proconsul climbed trees and mostly walked on all fours.

Proconsul
Proconsul is the earliest known member of the hominoids, the group to which apes and humans belong. It lived in the tropical rainforests of East Africa between 24 and 18 million years ago. Compared to its ancestors, *Proconsul* had a large brain.

Australopithecines

The Australopithecines are thought to be the earliest hominids (human-like people). Although ape-like, with a small brain and projecting jaws, *Australopithecus* stood upright and walked on two feet. This is known from its leg bones and backbone, and from 3.7 million–year–old footprints found at Laetoli in Tanzania.

Lucy
"Lucy" is the name given to the most complete Australopithecine skeleton yet discovered, found in Ethiopia in 1974. It was an adult female, 3.18 million years old. Lucy was about 1.1 m (3 ft 6 in) tall.

Projecting jaw and low forehead

Long arms and short legs

Chimpanzees
The chimpanzee is our closest living relative. Chimpanzees and humans share over 98 per cent of their DNA (genetic material). Chimpanzees and gorillas are known collectively as the African apes. About six million years ago, humans and African apes split from their common ancestor to evolve separately.

Paranthropines had small brains and flattened faces.

Paranthropines

The Paranthropines were strongly built "man-apes" that lived in southern and eastern Africa between three and one million years ago. They were probably descended from the Australopithecines, but were not part of the evolutionary pathway that led to modern humans.

A male Paranthropus was about 1.35 m (4 ft 4 in) in height.

Homo

Homo is the genus, or group of species, to which modern humans belong. It probably evolved from the Australopithecines between three and two million years ago, although there is no direct evidence for this. Early members of the genus showed increasing brain size and the ability to make tools.

Homo habilis
"Handy man" is the earliest known species of *Homo*. It lived in the woodlands and savannahs of Africa. *Homo habilis* had a brain size of 650 to 800 ml. It made and used simple stone tools, and was a successful forager and scavenger.

Flat face and slender jaw

Reconstruction of Homo habilis

Homo erectus
Homo erectus was the first human to leave Africa and move to Europe and Asia. It had a sloping forehead, flattish face, and a brain size between 850 and 1100 ml. These humans exploited more habitats than their ancestors, and were the first to use fire.

Neanderthals
Neanderthals were the first humans to have adapted to life in the cold climates of Europe and Asia. They had strong physiques and large brains. They wore clothes, made a range of tools, and used fire to keep warm. They were the first humans to bury their dead.

Homo erectus skull

Neanderthal reconstruction

Homo sapiens
Modern humans first evolved in Africa. *Homo sapiens* has a large brain, considerable intelligence, and the ability to use language. Humans increasingly took control of their surroundings as they developed agriculture, societies, and technology.

A modern human has an average brain size of 1400 ml.

Prominent brow

Face is straight rather than forward-jutting.

FIND OUT MORE — ARCHAEOLOGY · BRONZE AGE · DARWIN, CHARLES · EVOLUTION · FOSSILS · GENETICS · HUMAN BODY · LEAKEY FAMILY · PREHISTORIC PEOPLE · SKELETON · STONE AGE

HUMAN RIGHTS

MOST OF US BELIEVE that as human beings we have certain rights – to say what we want, to be treated fairly, and not be discriminated against because of our gender, colour, age, religion, sexual orientation, or ethnic group. These and other rights are human rights we carry with us wherever we live. In many countries, these rights are written into national law, but in others they are denied. Recently, world attention has focused on countries that deny their citizens basic human rights. Despite this, abuses of human rights are still common.

Justice is often symbolized as a blindfolded figure, holding a pair of scales.

A fair trial is a basic human right.

Clean water

What are human rights?
Human rights are those rights and privileges which people possess, regardless of the country they live in. Basic human rights include the right to freedom of speech, political liberty, and religious freedom. Some people believe that the right to the necessities of life, such as food and clean water, should also be viewed as basic human rights. These are often lacking in areas of severe poverty.

Bills of Rights

Many countries have incorporated a declaration of human rights into their constitutions. In France, for example, the Declaration of the Rights of Man and of the Citizen, written in 1789, today forms part of the constitution of the French Republic.

The US Bill of Rights
The first ten amendments to the US Constitution constitute the US Bill of Rights. It includes the right to freedom of worship, the right to bear arms, and the Fifth Amendment (the right to remain silent to avoid self-incrimination); witnesses took this in the 1950s to protect themselves against investigations into "un-American activities".

Taking the Fifth Amendment, 1950s

Modern human rights

The horrors of world war and countless atrocities in the 20th century have led people to believe that the only way to protect human rights is by setting an international standard to which all countries agree. Since 1945, many international agreements have been signed to protect the rights of oppressed people around the world.

Universal Declaration
In 1948, the United Nations passed a Universal Declaration of Human Rights to serve as "a common standard of achievement for all peoples and all nations". American Eleanor Roosevelt (1884–1962), chair of the UN Commission on Human Rights and widow of a former US president, was the person most responsible for getting the Declaration approved.

Eleanor Roosevelt

Amnesty International
Set up in 1961, Amnesty International is a global pressure group, which campaigns for the release of people "detained anywhere for their beliefs, colour, sex, ethnic origin, language, or religion".

Amnesty symbol

The European Court ruled against corporal punishment in schools.

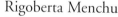

European Court of Human Rights
The European Court, which meets in Strasbourg, France, exists to hear human rights cases from the whole of Europe. Individuals can bring cases against their government if they believe their human rights are threatened.

Civil rights

Civil rights are those rights that people enjoy in individual countries and that are protected by law. Civil rights include basic human rights, as well as political rights such as the freedom to join a trade union. Where civil rights are denied, popular movements may be formed, committed to repair the injustice.

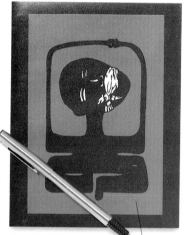

© Amnesty International

Amnesty leaflet against censorship

Freedom of expression
The right to express your views without fear of censorship or persecution, for example, in speaking against a government, is a fundamental human right. But it is denied in some countries, where newspapers and television are heavily censored, and people are not allowed to demonstrate or express their views in public.

Minority rights
The law is often used unfairly against certain groups of people whose culture has minority status within their society. Ethnic, religious, and other minorities have all had to protest in order to receive the rights already enjoyed by the majority of the population.

As a minority, homosexuals have had to campaign for equal civil rights in many countries.

Rigoberta Menchu
Guatemalan human rights activist Rigoberta Menchu (b.1959) has campaigned since she was a teenager to secure and protect the rights of the native people in her country, who have been oppressed by Guatemala's military rulers. Menchu's own parents and brother were killed by the security forces. She was awarded the Nobel Peace Prize in 1992 for her work.

FIND OUT MORE   FRENCH REVOLUTION   PEACE MOVEMENTS   SLAVERY   SOCIETIES, HUMAN   UNITED NATIONS   UNITED STATES, HISTORY OF   WOMEN'S MOVEMENT

HUNDRED YEARS' WAR

IN 1337, EDWARD III of England (r.1327–77) began a bitter war with France that was to last for over 100 years. Edward and his successors felt they had a claim to the French throne, but they also wanted to protect their inherited lands in south-western France. In the beginning, under Edward III and his great-grandson Henry V, England seemed to be winning. Then, as the independent duchy of Burgundy abandoned the English and joined forces with the French army, fortunes changed, and France began to win. In the end, the French drove the English from their country, leaving Calais as the only English possession on the European mainland.

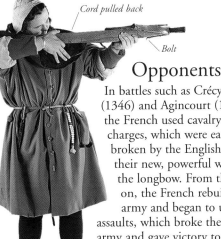

Cord pulled back

Bolt

French crossbowman

Yew wood stave

Hemp string

English longbowman

Ash wood arrow shaft

H

Opponents

In battles such as Crécy (1346) and Agincourt (1415), the French used cavalry charges, which were easily broken by the English using their new, powerful weapon, the longbow. From the 1420s on, the French rebuilt their army and began to use rapid assaults, which broke the English army and gave victory to the French.

French crossbows
The crossbow was a slow but powerful weapon. After each shot, a lever or winder mechanism pulled back the string for the next shot. This took 30 seconds, during which time the bowman was open to attack.

English longbows
The longbow was quicker to reload than the crossbow. An archer could shoot up to 12 arrows per minute. One arrow could pierce armour from as far away as 180 m (600 ft) – but they were not as accurate as the crossbow bolts.

Early phases of the war

Helped by their Burgundian allies, the English had many successes until 1429, when the French, under the brilliant leadership of Joan of Arc, defeated them at Orléans. The French-Burgundian alliance of 1435 proved too strong for England, which steadily lost its French lands.

1340–1360
The English inherited Aquitaine, and, in 1347, captured Calais. In 1359, they attempted to invade French territory. The French held them off, and the Treaty of Brétigny followed in 1360.

1360–1429
Although the English had lost Aquitaine by 1429, they had gained territory in northern France, including Normandy. Within 30 years they lost everything until, by 1453, their only possession in France was Calais.

Leaders of the war

The personalities and military skills of Joan of Arc and Henry V of England inspired their followers with courage and trust. The dukes of Burgundy were crucial for a different reason: they held the balance of power between England and France.

The Black Prince
Named because he wore black armour, Edward (1330–76) was the eldest son of Edward III. He fought at Crécy and Poitiers, and ruled Aquitaine in the 1360s.

Charles VII of France
Charles VII (r.1422–61) was not crowned King of France until 1429, after the victory at Orléans. He was then able to organize an army against the English.

Philip the Good
Philip (1396–1467), duke of Burgundy, was an English ally at first, but then changed sides and helped France to victory. He built his dukedom into one of the most powerful in Europe.

Henry V

Henry V (r.1413–1422) of England captured major cities, such as Rouen, and led his men to many victories. Through his marriage to Catherine of Valois, he would have inherited the French throne from his father-in-law, King Charles VI of France, but he died before Charles. Shakespeare's play *Henry V* describes Henry's achievements.

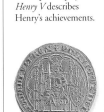

Joan of Arc

Joan of Arc (1412–31) heard voices telling her to free France. At 17, she led the French to victory against the English. Later, she was captured and sold to the English, who burnt her at the stake as a heretic. In 1920, she was declared a saint.

Timeline

1346 Battle of Crécy: England builds up strength in France.

1360 Peace of Brétigny: Edward III acquires Aquitaine and gives up other French claims.

1415 English victory at Agincourt; Henry V controls Normandy.

1420 Henry V named heir to French throne.

1422 Charles VI and Henry V die.

1429 Joan of Arc liberates Orléans and escorts Charles VII to Reims to be anointed as king of France.

1431 Joan of Arc is burnt at the stake as a heretic.

1435 Council of Arras: Burgundy joins forces with the French army.

1453 French victory at Castillon: England loses all her French lands, except Calais.

FIND OUT MORE   ARMS AND ARMOUR   EUROPE, HISTORY OF   FEUDALISM   FRANCE, HISTORY OF   MEDIEVAL EUROPE

HYENAS

THE EERIE CACKLING LAUGH of the spotted hyena is one of the characteristic sounds of the open grasslands of Africa. There are three main types of hyena – spotted, striped, and brown. The spotted hyena is the largest; all three have large, broad heads and powerful jaws. Their front legs and shoulders are larger and more powerful than their weaker hindquarters. Although hyenas look rather like dogs, they are in fact more closely related to the cat family.

Spotted hyena

The spotted hyena is the most aggressive and most numerous member of its family. It is usually found in open country, but sometimes also on the forest fringes. Spotted hyenas' furtive movements and liking for carrion have given them a reputation for cowardice and dependence on the kills of other animals, but they are in fact predators in their own right. They have an important ecological role in keeping herds of hoofed animals moving. By forcing these animals to move to fresh grazing grounds, hyenas help to conserve the habitat.

Large, broad head with very powerful jaws

Sloping shoulders

Red-brown coat with dark spots

Forelegs are longer than hind legs.

Large sharp canine teeth

Powerful heavy jaws

Clan

Spotted hyenas live in clans of between 10–100 animals. They scavenge by day and hunt by night. Members of the clan work together and are capable of driving lions off their kill, and may even kill an old solitary lion. Females are larger than males and the most dominant female presides over the clan.

Jaws

Bones and marrow form an important part of the spotted hyena's diet. Unlike any other carnivores, it will even eat hard tusks and horns. To cope with this diet, the spotted hyena's jaws and teeth are immensely powerful, and capable of crushing the heaviest of bones.

Feeding

Spotted hyenas scavenge the remains of other animals' kills, but also kill their own prey, frequently taking young gazelles, wildebeest calves, and zebras. They may hunt singly but are more effective in packs. The pack size varies according to the availability of prey in their territory.

A pack of hyenas feeding on a carcass.

Young

Normally, two to three cubs are born in an underground burrow. They can see immediately. Several females often establish a nursery where they and their young live together communally. One female remains in the burrow to guard the cubs while the others go in search of food. The cubs are not fully weaned until they are 18 months old.

Cubs play together but may also fight fiercely, to establish who will become the most dominant.

Female hyenas nurse the young cubs.

Types of hyena

The hyena family consists of four species: the spotted, striped, and brown hyenas, and the aardwolf, which is sometimes placed in a separate family. The spotted and striped hyenas live in Africa and Asia; the brown hyena and the aardwolf are confined to southern Africa.

Striped hyena

A much smaller animal than its spotted cousin, the striped hyena inhabits an area from India to the Middle East and southwards to Tanzania. It is less predatory and less aggressive than the spotted hyena and tends to be more solitary by nature. It lives in rock clefts, caves, or burrows.

Long wispy mane

Striped body and legs

Brown hyena

Essentially a desert species, the brown hyena is unaggressive, shy, and so secretive that it is seldom seen. At night it searches for the remains of other animals' kills. It lives in southern Africa, mainly in Namibia and Botswana.

Wispy brown coat

Aardwolf

A timid animal, the aardwolf spends the day underground, often in another animal's abandoned den. It has weak jaws, small, widely spaced teeth, and a long flexible tongue – adaptations to the termites and other insects on which it feeds. To deter predators it emits an evil smell from an anal gland.

Small head

Striped coat

SPOTTED HYENA

SCIENTIFIC NAME *Crocuta crocuta*

ORDER Carnivora

FAMILY Hyaenidae

DISTRIBUTION Northern and eastern Africa and southern Asia

HABITAT Open grassland

DIET Mainly carrion, but is also an opportunist predator and will kill large animals, such as zebras, antelopes, and gazelles

SIZE Height at shoulder: 79 cm (31 in); weight: 80 kg (175 lb)

LIFESPAN 20 years

FIND OUT MORE AFRICAN WILDLIFE   ASIAN WILDLIFE   CATS   DESERT WILDLIFE   GRASSLAND WILDLIFE   MAMMALS

IMMUNE AND LYMPHATIC SYSTEMS

EVERY DAY THE BODY IS INVADED by disease-causing micro-organisms called pathogens, or germs. The immune and lymphatic systems are the body's defence against these pathogens. The immune system is a collection of cells that keep detailed records of invading pathogens so, if they reappear, they can be destroyed, making you immune to that disease. The lymphatic system drains fluid called lymph from tissues, filters out any pathogens, and returns the lymph to the bloodstream.

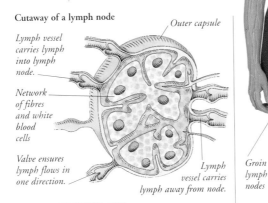

Tonsils guard throat against infections.

Neck lymph nodes

Thoracic duct empties lymph into a main vein.

Heart

Spleen is a lymph organ that also stores blood.

Lymph node removes pathogens from lymph.

Groin lymph nodes

Network of lymph vessels

Knee lymph node

Lymphatic system

The lymphatic system consists of a network of tubes called lymph vessels that reach all parts of the body, and several lymphatic organs. Lymph is carried by the vessels to the main lymph ducts which empty into the bloodstream.

Lymph nodes

Lymph constantly leaves the bloodstream and flows through the spaces surrounding cells. It passes through lymph nodes, which are small swellings of the lymph vessels that clean and filter the lymph. Inside each lymph node is a network of fibres which supports large numbers of two types of immune system cells, lymphocytes and macrophages.

Cutaway of a lymph node

Outer capsule

Lymph vessel carries lymph into lymph node.

Network of fibres and white blood cells

Valve ensures lymph flows in one direction.

Lymph vessel carries lymph away from node.

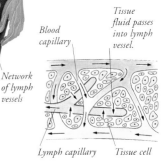

Blood capillary

Tissue fluid passes into lymph vessel.

Lymph capillary　*Tissue cell*

Lymph vessels

The smallest lymph vessels are capillaries. Excess fluid drains through the walls of lymph capillaries from the surrounding tissue. Lymph capillaries join to form larger lymph trunks.

Lymphocytes
Lymphocytes, found in the lymph nodes recognize and destroy specific pathogens using chemicals that are called antibodies. Lymphocytes are also to be found circulating within the bloodstream.

Macrophages
Macrophages are cells with voracious appetites that detect, engulf, and destroy viruses, bacteria, cancer cells, and any other foreign material in the lymph that passes through the lymph node.

Immunization

Immunization gives a person protection against a specific disease. There are two types of immunization. In active immunization, a vaccine containing some dead pathogens is injected into the body to stimulate the immune system to make antibodies. Passive immunization involves injecting antibodies and gives short-term protection.

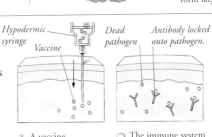

Hypodermic syringe　*Vaccine*　*Dead pathogen*　*Antibody locked onto pathogen.*　*Real pathogen*　*Antibody*

1 A vaccine containing dead or weakened pathogens is injected into the body.

2 The immune system produces antibodies and keeps a "memory" of the pathogen.

3 If the real pathogens enter the body, large numbers of antibodies are released.

Quilt for AIDS charity

AIDS
Acquired Immune Deficiency Syndrome (AIDS) is caused by the Human Immunodeficiency Virus (HIV). A person with AIDS becomes infected with diseases that the body would normally fight off. This is because HIV attacks and destroys immune system cells. In time, the immune system weakens and the person becomes unable to fight infections and eventually dies.

Lady Mary Wortley Montagu

Lady Mary Wortley Montagu (1689–1762) was an English author who introduced an early form of immunization against smallpox to England. In Turkey, she had seen people scratching pus from small-pox blisters into the skin of healthy people to protect them from catching smallpox. She had her children "vaccinated" and publicized the method.

Allergies

If you have an allergy, it means that your immune system has wrongly identified a harmless substance, called an allergen, as being harmful. The body's reaction to these allergens produces symptoms such as sneezes and rashes. Common allergens include pollen, fur, dust, shellfish, and strawberries.

Strawberry

A skin patch test is used to identify possible allergens.

FIND OUT MORE | CELLS | HEALTH AND FITNESS | HEART AND CIRCULATORY SYSTEM | HUMAN BODY | MEDICINE | MEDICINE, HISTORY OF | PASTEUR, LOUIS

441

INCAS

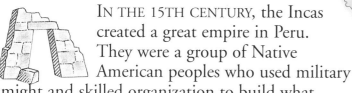

IN THE 15TH CENTURY, the Incas created a great empire in Peru. They were a group of Native American peoples who used military might and skilled organization to build what was then one of the world's biggest nations. Their empire took in most of the great mountain range of the Andes and huge areas of desert and rainforest. In 1532, Spanish adventurers conquered the Incas.

Inca Empire

Machu Picchu

Cuzco

Peru

Farming terraces

Machu Picchu

The Incas built their cities using great blocks of rock so finely cut that they fitted together without cement. Machu Picchu, high in the Andes Mountains, is the most spectacular remaining example of Inca architecture. Its stone buildings clinging to the mountain could accommodate thousands of people.

Cuzco

The Inca capital was called Cuzco, from the Inca word meaning "centre". It is 3,400 m (11,000 ft) up in the mountains. Cuzco was an awe-inspiring city, made great by the emperor Pachacuti Inca. At the centre of the city was the Temple of the Sun. Many Inca remains survive in the modern city.

Central plaza (square)

Palace

Temple of the Sun

Machu Picchu

Inca industry

The state collected manufactured goods, such as food, wool, and clothing, which were kept in storehouses. Every town had at least two storehouses: one for the ruler, one for the rest of the people. Goods were transported by llamas along a large network of paved roads.

Quipus

The Incas had no system of writing, but they kept records by knotting different coloured strings on to a stick or cord known as a quipu. They could record figures such as the numbers of wool bales or the amount of births in a year using this method.

Agriculture

The Incas introduced terraced farming, which enabled crops to be grown on steep slopes. Bird droppings and fish heads were used as fertilizer. Most of the work was done collectively, and most of the land was owned in common by the local community.

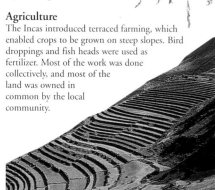

Inca society

At the top of society were the Inca ruler and his relatives. They could be identified because they were allowed to enlarge their ears with huge ornaments. Some of the nobles left their palaces in Cuzco to rule outposts of the empire. Ordinary people were organized into groups of villages called ayllus. Each ayllu was governed by an elected council of elders. Sometimes the emperors moved groups of people around the empire, so that they could place loyal people in areas that were otherwise difficult to govern.

Workers

Inca workers produced some goods for themselves, and some for the emperor and nobles. These provided the state with the resources for public works and other royal projects.

Cup with emperor's portrait

Emperors

The Incas believed their rulers were descended from the Sun god, so they were worshipped as holy beings. This portrait of an Inca emperor decorates a cup used in religious rituals.

Religion

Sun god

Chief of the gods was the creator Viracocha, who was worshipped by the Inca priesthood and nobility. Next in importance was the Sun god, Inti, claimed by royal Incas as their ancestor. Other Inca deities included gods of the Moon and stars. The earth god was also central, because the Incas relied on farming for wealth and food.

Pachacuti

Pachacuti Inca was crowned in 1438. With his son, Topa Inca, Pachacuti enlarged the territory of the Inca state. He came to dominate many provinces, was a great organizer, and an effective administrator.

Spanish conquest

Shortly before the Spanish ships reached Peru's coast, civil war broke out among the Incas. The Spaniards, led by Francisco Pizarro (c.1475–1541), took advantage of this division and captured the Inca Empire for the King of Spain.

Spanish coins

 FIND OUT MORE

FARMING, HISTORY OF   GODS AND GODDESSES   SOUTH AMERICA   SOUTH AMERICA, HISTORY OF   SPAIN, HISTORY OF

Inca arts and crafts
Gold items

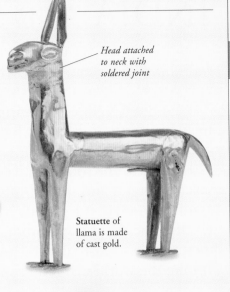

Gold figurines of gods were often left as offerings in the tombs of prominent Incas.

Small tomb figure was made of cast gold.

Belt ornaments were made of gold cut and hammered into shape.

Head attached to neck with soldered joint

Statuette of llama is made of cast gold.

Everyday items

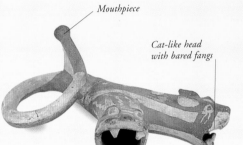

Mouthpiece

Cat-like head with bared fangs

Clay trumpet has twin cat-like heads, which may have represented a god.

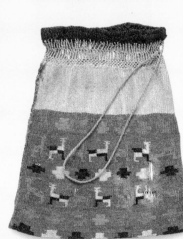

Drawstring bag is decorated with tapestry bearing design showing Peruvian llamas.

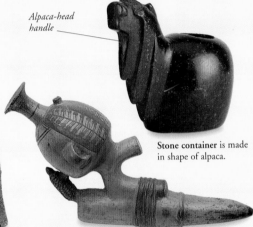

Alpaca-head handle

Stone container is made in shape of alpaca.

Pottery vessel has elaborate base; its exact use is unknown.

Pipes are made from quills.

Panpipes have different-length tubes for each note of the scale.

Flat-sided vessel could be hung on the back of a llama.

Stone bowl is decorated with a religious procession.

Jug is painted with simple geometric design.

Wooden beaker was made for Spanish conqueror Pizarro.

Copper chisels may have been used for woodcarving.

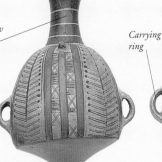

Tall, narrow neck

Carrying ring

Inca pots were often made in standard shapes; a common design had a conical base, long, flaring neck, and twin carrying handles; this type of pot was used for carrying water and beer.

Beaker decorated with Inca royal figures

443

INDIA AND SRI LANKA

SEPARATED FROM other Asian countries by the Himalayas in the north, India forms part of a subcontinent that also includes Pakistan, Bhutan, Bangladesh, Nepal, and the island of Sri Lanka, which lies 32 km (20 miles) to the south. India is the world's seventh largest and second most populated country. Poverty is a serious problem, but India is self-sufficient in food production and increasingly industrialized, counting among the world's largest economies.

Physical features

The Himalayan peaks form a natural border in northeastern India. The Indo-Gangetic Plain is drained by the Ganges and Indus rivers and stretches from Pakistan to Bangladesh. The Thar Desert is on the Pakistan border. The peninsula land slopes west from the Western Ghats across the Deccan Plateau to the Bay of Bengal.

Western Ghats
The Western Ghats mountains stretch along India's west coast, rising to a height of 2,695 m (8,842 ft). Forests of tropical palms cover the lowlands west of the mountains, and lush, evergreen rainforest, home to tigers and elephants, cloaks the slopes. To the east is dry, deciduous forest.

Ganges
At 2,700 km (1,678 miles) the Ganges is the biggest river in India, flowing through a vast, highly populated plain. Its source is 4,200 m (13,779 ft) above sea-level in an ice cave in the Himalayas. It ends in a huge delta that is mostly in Bangladesh. For Hindus, the Ganges is a sacred river.

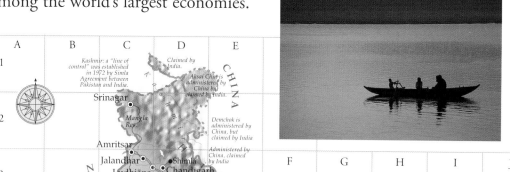

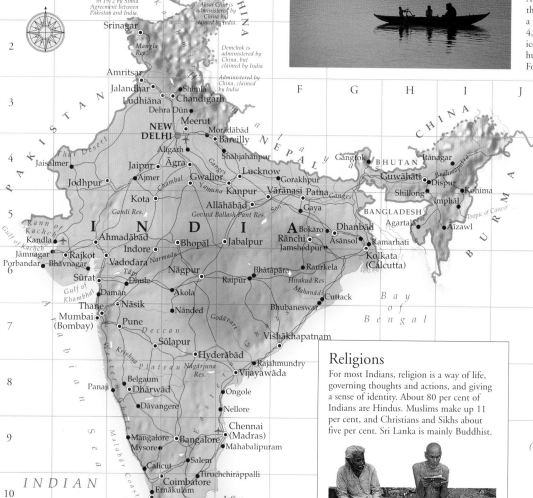

Kashmir: a "line of control" was established in 1972 by Simla Agreement between Pakistan and India.

Claimed by India.

Aksai Chin is administered by China but claimed by India.

Demchok is administered by China, but claimed by India

Administered by China, claimed by India

Sri Lanka
Just off the southeastern tip of India lies the island of Sri Lanka, which is a country in its own right. At the centre of the island are high mountains surrounded by a low coastal plain. Like southern India, Sri Lanka has a tropical climate with two monsoon seasons each year. However, the southwest has no dry season and is humid all year, while the northeast is drier, with open forest and grassland.

Religions
For most Indians, religion is a way of life, governing thoughts and actions, and giving a sense of identity. About 80 per cent of Indians are Hindus. Muslims make up 11 per cent, and Christians and Sikhs about five per cent. Sri Lanka is mainly Buddhist.

Hindu priest

46°C (115°F)
31°C (88°F)
-14°C (7°F)
14°C (57°F)
640 mm (25 in)

Climate
Heavy and persistent monsoon rains soak India and Sri Lanka between June and September. The coolest season is from November to March. Winter temperatures rarely fall below 20°C (68°F) except in the high Himalayas, and may top 50°C (122°F) on northern plains in summer.

India

With more than 450 million voters, India is the world's largest democracy. In 1947, the country became independent of Britain, and was left with a vast rail network, international ports, and working farms and factories, all of which have contributed to its industrial success. Today, India has many industries and large modern cities, although millions of people still live in extreme poverty. India has rich mineral resources, including oil, iron, bauxite, coal, and manganese.

People

Most Indians live according to the caste system, which indicates their role in society, who they can marry, and the work they can do. However, the caste system is now more flexible than in the past. Women have equal rights by law, but rarely in practice. Several measures to reduce India's rising population have been initiated by the state, but have remained largely unsuccessful.

341 per sq km (883 per sq mile)

28% Urban   72% Rural

Indian family

New Delhi

Jama Masjid, Delhi

Purpose-built by the British as India's capital, New Delhi has a population of 301,000 and lies 5 km (3 miles) from the old city of Delhi, with 16,000,000 people. Compared with Delhi's winding streets, temples, mosques, and bazaars, New Delhi has tree-lined boulevards and spacious parks.

Farming

About two-thirds of Indians are involved in agriculture. Many are poor farmers who grow just enough food to feed their families. Others work on plantations producing cash crops, such as tea, rubber, coffee, sugar, bananas, mangoes, cotton, and tobacco. India exports timber, including teak, sandalwood, and rosewood. Cattle are reared for butter and ghee, but not for beef, forbidden by the Hindu religion.

Bananas

Mango

Sesame seeds

Industry

The country's economy is still based on small, cottage industries. But, aided by a large, cheap work-force, India's industry is growing rapidly. In the south, Bangalore is now a centre for electronics, and many international companies have factories there. India also exports machinery, cut diamonds, textiles, clothing, and chemicals.

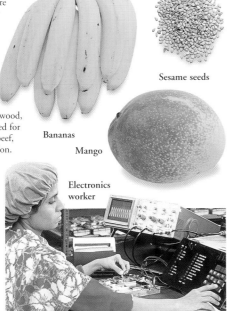

Electronics worker

Land use

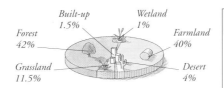

Built-up 1.5%   Wetland 1%

Forest 42%

Farmland 40%

Grassland 11.5%   Desert 4%

Most of India's farmland is used for growing fruit and cereals, and the country is largely self-sufficient in food. With such a large population to feed, demand for farmland is high, and many Indian forests have been felled to make way for crops. Some of the land is used for mining.

Films are often packed with stars, dancing, action, and romance.

Film-making

India has a highly successful film industry and makes more films than any other country including the USA. The centre of the film industry is "Bollywood" – India's Hollywood – in Bombay.

Music

India has a long and varied musical tradition. There are two classical forms of music: *Hindustani* and *Carnatic*. Both are based on the *raga*, a mixture of melody and scales. Typical classical instruments include the *sitar* and the *sarod* (which are both lutes), flutes, drums, and the European violin. Folk music varies from region to region and is played on at least 500 different kinds of instruments.

Sitar

Kashmir

In 1947, Pakistan and India separated. Since then, they have disputed ownership of the former princely state of Kashmir. Part of Kashmir lies in the Indian state of Jammu and Kashmir. The rest is ruled by Pakistan, which claims it all because most of the people who live there are Muslims. Fighting breaks out from time to time.

INDIA FACTS

CAPITAL CITY	New Delhi
AREA	3,287,590 sq km (1,269,338 sq miles)
POPULATION	1,030,000,000
MAIN LANGUAGES	Hindi, English
MAJOR RELIGIONS	Hindu, Muslim
CURRENCY	Indian Rupee
LIFE EXPECTANCY	63 years
PEOPLE PER DOCTOR	2,500
GOVERNMENT	Multi-party democracy
ADULT LITERACY	57%

I

Food

The traditional Indian food is curry, a sauce flavoured with a subtle blend of spices, such as turmeric, cardamom, ginger, coriander, nutmeg, and poppy seed, eaten with meat or vegetables. Meat dishes, mainly lamb and chicken, are savoured in the north. In southern India, vegetables and pulses such as *dhal* (lentils), coconut, and fresh sea food are enjoyed with curry. Rice and unleavened breads, such as *chapatis*, *parathas*, and *poori*, are eaten with meals.

Vegetables in a spicy curry sauce

Boiled rice

Transport

Railways in India total 62,810 km (39,030 miles). Every year they carry two-thirds of all freight and three billion passengers. India has 2,160,000 km (1,342,000 miles) of roads, only half of which are paved. Only one person in 300 owns a car, but buses are widely used and very crowded. In rural areas, ox carts are common, and in cities, people ride bicycles, scooters, or travel by taxi and rickshaws.

Kashmiri winters are cold.

Sri Lanka

 Known as Ceylon since 1796, Sri Lanka adopted a new name and constitution in 1972. It is separated from India by the Palk Strait, and is made up of one large island and the several coral islets of Adam's Bridge. In 1960, Sri Lanka became the world's first nation to choose a woman as prime minister, Sirimavo Bandaranaike. Since 1983, civil war has raged between the Sinhalese, who rule the government, and the Tamils, who are fighting for independence.

Tamils

The Tamils, a mainly Hindu minority ethnic group, have been campaigning for an independent state in the northern peninsula of Jaffna since the 1980s. They object to the control of the government by the majority Sinhalese, most of whom are Buddhist. The Tamil Tigers, a ruthless guerrilla group, have fought many fierce battles in which up to 50,000 people have been killed.

Tamil man

SRI LANKA FACTS

CAPITAL CITY Colombo

AREA 65,610 sq km (25,332 sq miles)

POPULATION 19,100,000

MAIN LANGUAGES Sinhala, Tamil, English

MAJOR RELIGIONS Buddhist, Hindu

CURRENCY Sri Lankan rupee

Procession of decorated elephants in Kandy's Perahera Festival

Colombo

Sri Lanka's capital and chief port, Colombo, was developed by the Portuguese after 1507. The commercial capital is at Fort, so-called as it was a military garrison during Portuguese and Dutch occupation from the 16th to the 18th centuries. Today's city has a population of 2,241,000. It is a blend of old and modern buildings, with a busy bazaar area known as the Pettah. There are also Buddhist and Hindu temples and mosques.

The Sacred Tooth

At the heart of Sri Lanka is the Buddhist holy city of Kandy, with a population of more than 100,000. There, in a gold casket inside the Dalada Maligawa (Temple of the Tooth), is a tooth that is said to have come from Buddha's funeral pyre (fire) in 486 BC. Every August, in the grand Perahera procession, the tooth casket is paraded on the back of a sumptuously decorated elephant.

The Fort

Education

At 92 per cent, Sri Lanka has one of the highest Asian literacy rates. It has nearly 19,000 schools and 12 universities, including an Open University. Begun in 1980, it was modelled on the British Open University, a self-instructional learning scheme, aided by television, recordings, and mailed course materials.

Cloves – pungent

Chicory – bitter

Lemon – sour

Rock salts – salty

Sage leaves – astringent

Sweet potato – sweet

Ayurvedic medicine

The traditional Hindu form of medicine called Ayurvedic medicine is practised throughout Sri Lanka. Its name comes from the Ayurveda, an ancient treatise on healing that divides foods into six tastes. A healthy diet combines all of these. Ill-health can be cured by adjusting their intake. Sri Lanka also has an extensive national health service.

Farming

Most Sri Lankans live in the humid southeast of the island. About 38 per cent are poor farmers growing rice, sugar-cane, cassava, and sweet potatoes for their own consumption, or working on plantations producing tea, rubber, and coconuts for export. Nearly 30 per cent of the land is used for crops, and almost seven per cent for grazing cattle, buffaloes, and goats.

Coconut

Rice

Buddha figure carved from sapphire.

Gemstones

Sri Lanka produces brilliant gemstones, which are found near Ratnapura, the "City of Gems", which lies southeast of Colombo. It is especially noted for its sapphires. Other gems include deep yellow topazes, large rubies, and amethysts. Many are made into jewellery.

Tea

Sri Lanka is the world's largest tea exporter. The tea is still marketed abroad as Ceylon tea. There are more than 2,000 tea estates. Their teas are described as high-grown, medium-grown, or low-grown, according to their height above sea-level. The best quality comes from the cooler climate of the central highlands. The tea is hand picked, mostly by women, to preserve the delicate leaves. The pickers are paid by the basketful.

Dried tea leaves

Tea leaves

Tourism

Despite the civil war, Sri Lanka's tourist industry is beginning to flourish. Increasing numbers of Europeans in search of winter sun visit the island's beautiful palm-shaded sandy beaches and coral reefs. Buddhists from all over the world make pilgrimages to the sacred Buddhist city of Kandy.

FIND OUT MORE

ASIA, HISTORY OF   BUDDHA   BUDDHISM   CRYSTALS AND GEMS   FARMING   FILMS AND FILM-MAKING   HINDUISM   INDIA, HISTORY OF   MEDICINE   MUSIC

INDIA, HISTORY OF

THE SUBCONTINENT OF INDIA has been home to some of the world's great civilizations. Dynasties such as the Buddhist Mauryans, the Hindu Guptas, and the Muslim Mughals spread their cultures and religions across India. As a result, India has remained dominated by a host of different cultures, a fact that has made it difficult to unify under one ruler. The Mughal Empire declined in the 18th century, and Britain added India to its empire, imposing strong rule from outside. India became independent in 1947, when the Muslim state of Pakistan was also created.

Buddhist and Hindu empires

In 324 BC, Chandragupta Maurya, king of Magadha, eastern India, began to conquer northern India. He founded the Buddhist Mauryan Empire, the first to unite the subcontinent. His dynasty was followed by the Guptas, a family of Hindu rulers who controlled India from c. AD 320 to c.700.

Ancient India

People have lived on the Indian subcontinent for about 400,000 years. Some came to India from western Asia; others probably sailed on primitive boats from eastern Africa. By 2500 BC, the subcontinent's first civilization was developing on the banks of the Indus River.

Steatite seal from Indus Valley, 2500–2000 BC

Indus civilization
This culture flourished from c.2500–1600 BC. It was based in large, well-planned cities near the Indus River (in what is now Pakistan). The people grew corn, wove cotton, and wrote a script we are unable to read.

Aryan culture
Around 1600 BC, hordes of nomads moved out of the area between the Black and Caspian Seas. Some of them moved into the area around the Indus. Ancient religious texts called the Vedas describe their life, their gods, and their system of social castes or classes, which later spread to the rest of India.

Statue of Surya, a god of the Aryans

Nalanda University, founded during the Gupta period

Gupta Empire
India flourished under the Guptas. They promoted education, founding some of the earliest universities, and encouraged the arts of architecture, painting, sculpture, dancing, and music. The writers of the period produced books in the Sanskrit language that are still read today.

Coming of Islam

Between the 8th and 12th centuries, many Muslim invaders from Arabia and western Asia attacked India. By 1206, a Muslim sultan, based in Delhi, ruled the whole of the northern Indian plain. Under the Delhi sultans and the later Mughal emperors, large areas of India were under Islamic rule. India's Muslim rulers built fine cities, but some were intolerant of other religious faiths.

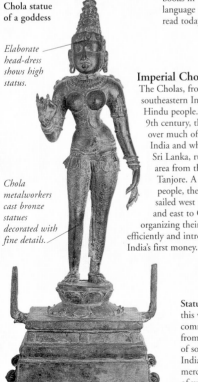

Chola statue of a goddess

Elaborate head-dress shows high status.

Chola metalworkers cast bronze statues decorated with fine details.

Imperial Cholas
The Cholas, from southeastern India, were a Hindu people. In the late 9th century, they took over much of southern India and what is now Sri Lanka, ruling the area from the city of Tanjore. A seafaring people, their merchants sailed west to Arabia and east to China, organizing their trade efficiently and introducing India's first money.

Statues such as this were often commissioned from the artists of southern India by Chola merchants, many of whom were very wealthy.

Mughal dagger

Sharp steel blade

Complex engraved decoration

Mughal Empire
The Mughals ruled India from 1526. Under their greatest emperor, Akbar, they brought prosperity to India, but after 1700, their power was weakened by opposition from Hindu southern India. Mughal emperors remained on the throne until 1858, but they had little power.

Tomb of the Muslim emperor, Tughluq Shah, near Delhi.

Delhi Sultanate
In the 13th and 14th centuries, the sultans of Delhi ruled much of northern India, from the Punjab in the west to Bihar in the east. But this empire was unstable. The sultans always had to fight opposition from Hindu states in southern India, and from the Mongols, who conquered Delhi in 1398.

Aurangzeb
The last great Mughal ruler, Aurangzeb (1618–1707), became emperor in 1658. In 1678, there was a Hindu revolt against his rule and Aurangzeb began a series of costly wars against the Hindus. He expanded the empire, but bankrupted it with his wars, and it began to break up on his death.

I

East India companies

In 1600, European countries founded East India companies to trade in India. England's company set up forts at Madras, Bombay, and Calcutta and began to trade in textiles. The English used the company to rule India, making alliances with local princes and driving out French colonists. Portugal also set up an Indian colony at Goa.

Figure is finely carved and painted.

Gilt

Statue of Portuguese East India Officer

British India

In the late 1700s, the British East India Company defeated rival European colonists and established an empire based on the three "presidencies" of Bombay, Madras, and Bengal. By 1850, the company ruled some three-fifths of India, with the rest run by local princes who were subject to the British.

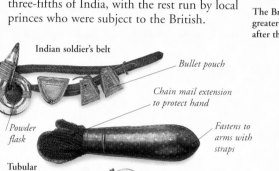

Indian soldier's belt

Bullet pouch

Chain mail extension to protect hand

Powder flask

Fastens to arms with straps

Tubular arm guard

Double-edged blade

Handle made of steel

Recurved dagger

Indian mutiny

In 1857–58, there was a mutiny of Indian troops in the British army, arising from British insensitivity to Indian customs and religions. The rebels took large areas of India, but the British soon regained the territory, restoring order by July 1858, after much bloodshed.

The British parliament took a greater part in Indian government after the mutiny.

British rule

After the Indian mutiny, the British disbanded the East India Company. The British adopted a more positive attitude towards the Indian people. A new government department was formed and an official called a Viceroy ruled on behalf of the crown. However, the Indian people remained far poorer than the British.

Building the railway system in India

Rise of industry

During the 19th century, India became an industrialized country. The British built Asia's largest rail network in India, and developed steamship and telegraph services. India exported raw materials to British factories, but also built its own steel and textile mills.

Independence

In 1885, the Indian National Congress was founded to campaign for Indian rights. By the 1920s, under the leadership of Mohandas Gandhi, it was demanding Indian independence. A long campaign of resistance to British rule followed, but it was not until the end of World War II, in 1945, that Britain agreed to make India an independent state.

Lahore

India

Pakistan

Delhi

Dhaka

Modern Bangladesh

Indian Ocean

Indian Ocean

Sri Lanka

Pakistan

During World War II, the Muslim League, led by Muhammad Jinnah, demanded a separate independent Muslim state in the Indian subcontinent. In 1947, the Muslim country of Pakistan was created, originally in two parts. In 1971, after a war between the two parts, East Pakistan became the independent state of Bangladesh.

Nehru

Jawaharlal Nehru (1889–1964) was one of the leaders of the Indian National Congress and was imprisoned nine times for his political activities. In 1947, after India's independence, he became India's first prime minister. He funded industry and developed India's role as a superpower. Nehru's daughter, Indira Gandhi, became prime minister in 1966.

Regional superpower

Under Nehru, India avoided alliances with major states. This policy of non-alignment gave India great power in its own right, power which increased when India supported East Pakistan in its civil war with West Pakistan in 1971.

Chemical works, India

First Indian National Congress

Congress Party

The Indian National Congress had led India's independence movement. After 1947, it became the Congress Party. It controlled India for much of the period after independence, under the leadership largely of members of Nehru's family: Nehru himself (prime minister 1947–64), his daughter Indira Gandhi (1966–77; 1980–84), and her son Rajiv (1984–89).

Timeline

c.2500 BC Rise of the Indus Valley civilization.

c.1600 BC Aryan nomads invade western India.

326 BC Alexander the Great invades the Punjab.

324–320 BC Mauryan dynasty.

320–c.700 Gupta Empire.

711 First Muslim invasions of India.

1206–1526 Sultans of Delhi rule northern India.

Terracotta Mother Goddess figure from Mohenjo-Daro, Indus Valley civilization.

1526–1707 The Mughal Empire is established and reaches its peak.

1600 British East India Company is founded.

1746 War between British and French colonists in India.

1858 Indian mutiny defeated; British impose direct rule.

Mohandas Gandhi, campaigner for independence

1917–44 Mohandas Gandhi leads campaign of resistance to British rule.

1947 India and Pakistan become independent.

1971 New state of Bangladesh formed.

1990s Efficient agricultural methods provide India with a healthier economy.

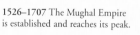

FIND OUT MORE   ALEXANDER THE GREAT   EMPIRES   GANDHI, MOHANDAS   GUPTA EMPIRE   INDUS VALLEY CIVILIZATION   MAURYAN EMPIRE   MUGHAL EMPIRE   UNITED KINGDOM, HISTORY OF

INDIAN OCEAN

BOUNDED BY AFRICA to the west, Australia and Indonesia to the east, and Asia to the north, the Indian Ocean is the world's third largest ocean. In the south it merges with the Southern Ocean that extends right around the globe. Unlike the Atlantic and Pacific, it has no natural outlet to the north, although the Suez Canal at the northern tip of the Red Sea links it with the Mediterranean Sea. Monsoon winds bring flooding to the Indian subcontinent and Southeast Asia.

Physical features

The currents of the Indian Ocean change direction spectacularly according to the monsoon winds. Between February and March, a strong current flows southwest along the coast of Somalia, changing direction completely between August and September. In the Bay of Bengal, the current flows clockwise in February, and counter-clockwise in August.

Ocean islands
There are estimated to be more than 5,000 islands in the Indian Ocean. Many, such as the Seychelles and the Maldives, are coral atolls, where attractive beaches and a warm climate attract increasing numbers of tourists.

Monsoon
During the northern winter, cool, dry winds blow over the ocean from the northeast. However, in summer, the wind direction changes and southwesterly winds blow north from the ocean bringing heavy monsoon rains to coastal areas. Although farmers depend on these rains, they often cause serious flooding.

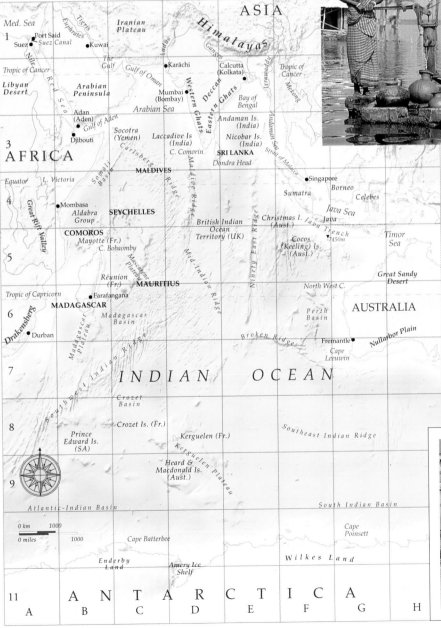

Strait of Malacca
Lying between the Indonesian island of Sumatra and the Malay Peninsula, the shallow Strait of Malacca is one of the main trade routes at the eastern end of the Indian Ocean, effectively providing a link with the Pacific Ocean. Melaka in Malaysia and Singapore are the two leading ports.

Salt
Around the shores of the Indian Ocean, particularly in India and the Middle East, people extract salt from the sea water. They channel water into shallow enclosures called pans and allow it to evaporate in sunshine, leaving crystals of pure salt that can be collected, packaged, and sold. Oceans are salty because minerals dissolved from rocks by rivers are washed into them.

Salt panning, Karachi, Pakistan

Maldives

The Maldives is a tiny Asian republic in the Indian Ocean, just southwest of Sri Lanka. It consists of 1,190 small coral islands, only 202 of which are inhabited. People have lived here for 2,300 years. Today, the islanders live from fishing and growing coconuts. However, tourism is the principal source of income on the bigger islands.

MALDIVES FACTS

CAPITAL CITY Male

AREA 300 sq km (116 sq miles)

POPULATION 300,000

MAIN LANGUAGES Dhivehi, Sinhala, Tamil

MAJOR RELIGION Muslim

CURRENCY Rufiyaa

Reef protection
Many of the coral islands in the Indian Ocean have an average height of just 1.8 m (6 ft), and are at risk of suffering serious storm damage, especially during the monsoon season, when waves can break right over them. To help give some protection, many islanders build a stout sea wall around their island to act as a barrier against the water.

Stone and concrete walls

Tourism
Maldivians prefer to keep tourists away from the villages where they live, and many of the main luxury hotels have been built on some of the uninhabited islands. The islands are popular with divers, who like to explore the coral reefs and their shoals of brightly coloured tropical fish.

Seychelles

The Seychelles is an independent African country that sprawls over 400,000 sq km (150,000 sq miles) of the Indian Ocean northeast of Madagascar. Of the 115 islands, 32 of them, where the majority of the population live, are formed of granite rock, and the rest are low, isolated outcrops of coral.

SEYCHELLES FACTS

CAPITAL CITY Victoria

AREA 455 sq km (176 sq miles)

POPULATION 79,300

MAIN LANGUAGES Creole, English, French

MAJOR RELIGION Christian

CURRENCY Seychelles Rupee

Wildlife
The isolated position of the Seychelles has permitted the evolution of many unique species of plants and animals, including the coco-de-mer palm, which produces the world's heaviest seed pods, and unique varieties of orchid, giant tortoise, gecko, chameleon, and "flying fox" – a type of fruitbat. Several reserves have been set up to protect this natural heritage.

Tea picking in Victoria

People
Most Seychellois are of mixed African and European origin. About 90 per cent of them live on the island of Mahé. The people enjoy some of the highest living standards in Africa. Tea, copra, and fish are the main exports. However, 90 per cent of foreign earnings now come from tourism.

Mauritius

Dominated by the peaks of former volcanoes, the African country of Mauritius lies 2,000 km (1,200 miles) off the southeast coast of Africa. It consists of Mauritius Island itself and a few smaller islands several hundred kilometres to the north. Mauritius is densely populated. More than half the people are Hindu Indians; most of the rest are Creoles and Chinese.

MAURITIUS FACTS

CAPITAL CITY Port Louis

AREA 1,860 sq km (718 sq miles)

POPULATION 1,200,000

MAIN LANGUAGES English, French, Creole, Hindi, Bhojpuri, Chinese

MAJOR RELIGIONS Hindu, Christian, Muslim

CURRENCY Mauritian Rupee

Sugar
The main cash crops are tea and cane sugar, which makes up 30 per cent of the country's exports. Textiles and tourism are also thriving industries. Mauritius belongs to the Indian Ocean Commission, which seeks to promote trade.

Molasses

Sugar-cane   *Raw cane juice*

Education
Mauritius has a well-educated work-force, which raises hopes that it may become an independent financial centre. The University of Mauritius, founded in 1965, has about 1,800 students. It specializes in research on agriculture and sugar technology.

Other islands

Most other islands in the Indian Ocean are very small. Of special note are the atolls of the Aldabra group, where giant tortoises still roam in the wild. Christmas Island, an Australian territory near Java, is so-called because a British seaman sighted it on Christmas Day in 1643.

Réunion
The island of Réunion is a self-governing overseas department of France. It has an area of 2,510 sq km (969 sq miles). Most of the 728,400 people are French Creoles. The mountains get heavy rainfall.

Mayotte
The French island of Mayotte forms part of the Comoros Islands. It covers an area of 374 sq km (144 sq miles) and has a population of about 142,000. People grow ylang-ylang and vanilla for export.

Fishing
Although the fishing industry is not as developed in the Indian Ocean as it is in the Atlantic and North Pacific oceans, the total annual catch is about 3,360,000 tonnes (3,703,728 tons). Most of the fish are caught by shore-based fishermen. There are few areas of shallow seas where fish may breed.

Fishermen on the Maldives

FIND OUT MORE   CORAL REEFS   FARMING   FISHING INDUSTRY   ISLANDS   OCEANS AND SEAS   PORTS AND WATERWAYS   TRADE AND INDUSTRY   VOLCANOES   WINDS

450

INDONESIA

THE LARGEST archipelago in the world, spread over 8,000,000 sq km (3,000,000 sq miles) of ocean, Indonesia is made up of 13,670 islands. The country was a Dutch colony from the 1700s to independence in 1949. Military rule dominated for more than 30 years until public protests forced an end to the General Suharto regime in 1998, leading to democratic elections. In 1999 East Timor, a former Portuguese colony annexed by Indonesia in 1975, voted for independence. The ensuing transitional process has been very turbulent.

Physical features

Lying between the Pacific and Indian Oceans, the Indonesian islands are mountainous, volcanic, and forested. There are five main islands: Sumatra, Java, Kalimantan, Sulawesi, and Irian Jaya, part of New Guinea.

Krakatoa

Indonesia's position on the join of two of the Earth's plates means it is prone to earthquakes and volcanic eruptions. Indonesia has 400 volcanoes; 100 are active. Krakatoa, a volcanic island near Java, had a major eruption in 1883, blowing the island apart.

Islands

As well as the five main islands there are thousands of smaller ones, and about half are uninhabited. Rich in marine life, the coral reefs that surround the islands are popular with divers. Tourists are drawn to the palm-fringed beaches, rainforests, and striking volcanoes.

Tropical rainforest

Lush tropical rainforests cover nearly two-thirds of Indonesia's land. Tigers and elephants live in the forests of Sumatra, as well as rare animals such as the Komodo Dragon, a carnivorous lizard. As many as 100 different tree species can be found in one hectare. Logging has destroyed large areas of rainforest. In 1997 smog from forest fires created a regional health hazard.

26°C (78°F)   26°C (78°F)

1,775 mm (70 in)

Regional climate

Tropical monsoons between December and March bring humidity and heavy rains to Indonesia. Java and the Sunda Islands have a dry season between June and September. Mountains are cool.

Land use

Although much of Indonesia's land is mountainous and forested, rice is grown on terraces cut into the hillsides. Animals graze on the pastures of Irian Jaya. Forestry and logging are important businesses.

Forest 62% Wetland 3.5% Farmland 26%
Built-up 2% Grassland 6.5%

Jakarta

The modern metropolis of Jakarta is Indonesia's capital and the largest city in Southeast Asia, with a population of 10,800,000. A trading centre for 2,000 years, it was used by the Dutch as a hub for the spice trade. Colonial buildings are overshadowed by tall skyscrapers, a sign of the growing economy.

Jakarta's glittering skyscrapers tower over the residential area.

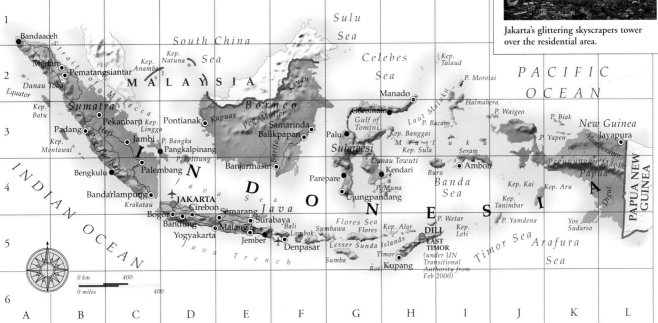

People

Indonesia has the world's fourth largest population. About 60 per cent of Indonesians live on the crowded main island of Java. The majority are Muslims descended from the first Malay settlers, but society is diverse, with about 360 ethnic groups speaking more than 250 different languages.

118 per sq km (306 per sq mile)

40% Urban

60% Rural

Minangkabau
The Minangkabau live in the hills of central Sumatra. They are Muslims, but, unusually, the Minangkabau are matriarchal – property and family names descend through the mother's line, and women have authority.

Leisure

The Indonesians retain many traditions of music, dance, painting, wood- and stone-carving, and textile crafts. Elaborate puppet theatres are popular in Java. Badminton is the main international sport.

Gong-chimes are struck with a padded hammer.

Gamelan
A common form of music in Indonesia is the *gamelan*, which contains bowed and wind instruments with gongs, gong-chimes, drums, and rattles. The orchestra has up to 40 players.

Dancing
Elaborate dance routines, accompanied by large *gamelans*, are a feature of life in Java and Bali, and are popular tourist attractions. Colourful dance dramas often tell stories derived from Hindu mythology. The Ramayana ballet is performed by moonlight outside the 9th-century Hindu Ramayana Temple at Yogyakarta.

Farming

About 46 per cent of Indonesia's labour force works in farming, which is the main economic activity. As well as rice, farmers grow cassava, palm nuts, maize, sugar-cane, and potatoes on the fertile volcanic soils. Cash crops include coffee, rubber, and tea.

Whole dried nutmeg

Nutmeg on plant

Grated nutmeg

Spices
The islands of Maluku, formerly known as the Moluccas, are Indonesia's famed "Spice Islands". Nutmeg is the principal cash crop, and cardamom, chillies, cumin, cinnamon, coriander, star anise, and ginger are grown.

Rice
Indonesia ranks third in world rice production. The country has been self-sufficient since 1984, mainly due to an intensive rice-planting programme. Farmers are encouraged to grow many varieties of high-quality rice in irrigated fields or on hillside terraces, some of which are about 2,000 years old.

Food

Rice and the many unique Indonesian spices form the basis of all meals. Fiery hot chillies, nuts, and coconut milk are used freely in cooking, and are often used to make a sauce, served with meat or fish dishes. Fried rice is a popular dish, easily adapted to contain meat, fish, or vegetables.

Fried rice

Communications

Spanning four time zones and separated by vast expanses of sea, the Indonesian islands need good communications. A state shipping company links the islands, several of which are also served by air.

Industry

Indonesia has vast mineral reserves and ranks highly in gold and tin production worldwide. Manufacturing is being encouraged to diversify the country's economy.

Oil and gas
The country's economic backbone since the 1870s, oil and gas make up one-quarter of export and domestic earnings. Huge gas supplies are exported in liquid form. Oil output is declining.

Satellite telephones
Indonesia was one of the first countries in the world to install satellite communications. Because of the difficulties involved in linking so many islands with cables, a satellite telephone system was installed. This enables messages to be relayed via orbiting satellites.

Batik printing block

Batik-decorated cloth

Tourism
More than five million tourists flock to Bali, Sumatra, and Java every year. The Balinese have worked hard to promote their island, and enjoy high numbers of visitors, who come for the beautiful scenery, colourful street life, and golden beaches.

Batik
First developed in Java more than 1,000 years ago, *batik* is a technique of dyeing cloth. A design is drawn on cotton and painted over with a dye-proof substance, such as hot wax or rice paste. When the cloth is dipped in dye, the waxed parts remain white. *Batik* textiles are made into scarves and wrap-around garments called *sarongs*.

Shipping
Indonesia owns more than 2,300 ships, many of which are used for transporting timber, oil, and gas. Ports are being expanded to improve trade links.

FIND OUT MORE ASIA, HISTORY OF · CORAL REEFS DANCE FARMING ISLAM MUSIC OIL SHIPS AND BOATS TELECOMMUNICATIONS TEXTILES AND WEAVING VOLCANOES

INDUSTRIAL REVOLUTION

MORE THAN 200 YEARS AGO, changes took place in industry that transformed society, and altered the way goods were made. The changes, which began in Britain in about 1760, are known as the Industrial Revolution. They included the use of water and steam power, the invention of new machinery, increased coal and iron production, the introduction of factories, the growth of towns, and a revolution in transport. Industrialization also created new types of work and new social groups. By 1850, the Industrial Revolution was spreading to the rest of the world.

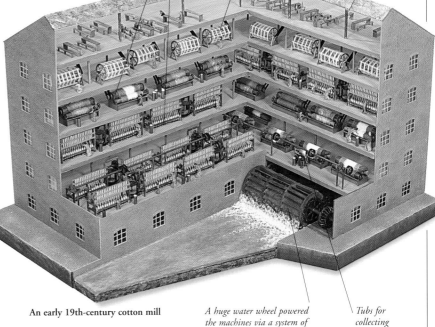

Carding machines separated out cotton fibres.

Water-driven spinning frames produced cotton thread.

Reeling and winding machines wound the cotton onto bobbins.

A drive shaft took power from the water wheel to machines in the factory.

An early 19th-century cotton mill

A huge water wheel powered the machines via a system of unguarded cogs and wheels.

Tubs for collecting cotton.

New technology

The textile industry was the first to be mechanized. In the 1700s, new water- or steam-driven machines replaced the old spinning wheels. This change meant that cloth, particularly cotton, could be produced faster than ever before.

The spinning jenny
James Hargreaves, an English weaver, invented the spinning jenny in 1764–1767. Worked by one person, it consisted of a frame and a number of spindles that spun several threads at once.

The water frame
As the name suggests, the water frame was a spinning frame powered by water. It replaced the spinning jenny, and was used in the first factories.

Factories

People used to make goods in their homes, but the invention of new machinery took manufacturing into factories. The first factories were cotton mills powered by water wheels, and the factory owners employed huge numbers of people to operate the machines. Most employees worked 16 hours a day, six days a week, and were subjected to harsh discipline. The work was hard and sometimes dangerous, but, for the first time, workers received regular wages.

Child labour
Factory owners employed children in mills and mines because they could enter cramped spaces, and their small hands could operate delicate machinery. Dangerous conditions meant that many children died.

Transport

A revolution in transport was stimulated by the need to move raw materials and finished goods cheaply and quickly. From 1760, a network of canals was built to carry coal, iron, and steel to and from the new industrial centres. However, by the 1840s, one of the greatest achievements of the industrial age had appeared – the railways.

Ironbridge
In 1779, the world's first iron bridge was built across the River Severn, England.

Severn Gorge

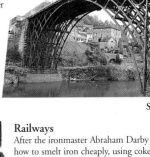

"Puffing Billy"

Railways
After the ironmaster Abraham Darby discovered how to smelt iron cheaply, using coke rather than charcoal, the way was clear for the mass production of iron. The world's first public railway opened in 1825, linking the coal mines of Darlington with the port of Stockton, England. By the 1870s, there were 25,000 km (15,000 miles) of railway track in Britain alone.

New industrial towns

As industrialism increased, new towns sprang up around coal mines and factories. Many people arrived from the countryside in search of work. Living conditions in the new towns were dreadful, with poverty, overcrowding, poor sanitation, and illness. After the 1850s, urban conditions began to improve.

Social change

The Industrial Revolution transformed society. It created a new social group, the industrial, waged, working class. A new army of industrial workers sprang up, including railway workers, dockers, textile workers, engineers, and factory girls. Industrialization also produced a new, wealthier middle class. The separation of work from home had profound effects. For the first time, and for the middle classes only, the home became a place of peace and leisure.

New products

As mass production increased in factories, new goods became available. Cheap cotton clothing was the first product to be made completely by machinery. Soaps, dyes, and iron goods became widespread. However, many of the industrial processes were harmful to the workers' health.

Iron goods
Developments in the iron industry meant that cast iron could be moulded into any shape, from pots and pans to iron bedsteads and machine parts.

Soap
The growing textile industry stimulated a demand for soap and bleach. When a process was invented that turned table salt into baking soda, soap could be mass produced.

Matches
The first friction matches were produced in the 1830s. To make the matches, women dipped splinters of wood into white phosphorus, an inflammable chemical. As the phosphorus ate away the skin of their faces, many suffered "phossy jaw".

Gas lighting
Coal provided steam for new machinery, and heated coal produced a combustible (burnable) gas. By 1850, gas lamps were common in the streets of most towns and cities.

Middle classes
The middle classes included merchants and industrialists. Middle-class men worked as managers and owners in industry, middle-class women remained at home, living lives of enforced idleness. Some of these women, irritated by boredom, worked with the poor and needy, or began to fight for women's rights.

Satin- and lace-trimmed hat

Mother-of-pearl buttons

Silk parasol

Silk bow and a lace collar

A middle-class girl's dress was usually made of delicate material, such as silk, or had a lot of handiwork on it, such as a lace collar.

Kid leather high-heeled boots

Working classes
Most working people lived lives of relentless drudgery in the early years of the Industrial Revolution. Men worked long hours in the new industries, and women had a double burden of work both inside the home, and outside in the mills and factories.

Cotton mob-cap

Two woollen shawls for warmth

Thick woollen shirt

Thick calico skirt

A factory girl's clothing had to be warm and hard wearing. It was often made of cheap material, such as wool or cotton.

Hobnailed leather boots

Popular protest

The early years of the Industrial Revolution were hard for the workers. Social unrest increased as different groups fought for improvements in working conditions. Some, such as the Luddites, attacked the new machines that were taking away their jobs and skills. Trade unions, which emerged after 1824, sought better working conditions and workers' rights.

Co-operative movement
The followers of this early political and social movement challenged the competitiveness of the new industrial society. They argued instead for co-operation, and a form of socialism, or common ownership. In 1844, the movement established the first co-operative shop in Rochdale, Lancashire.

Timeline

Traditional spinning, c.1900

1709 Abraham Darby uses coke to smelt iron ore.

1733 John Kay develops the flying shuttle, which speeds up weaving.

1764–1767 Spinning jenny invented.

1761 Bridgewater canal links coal mines to Manchester.

1768 Richard Arkwright develops a water-driven spinning frame.

1769 James Watt improves the steam engine.

1789 Steam-powered loom introduced in Britain.

1830s Industrial Revolution in Belgium and USA under way.

1833 Factory Act bans children under nine from working in cotton mills, to allow time for school.

1842 Coal Mines Act bans women and children from mines in England.

Robert Owen

Born in Wales, Robert Owen (1771–1858) was an early socialist. His book *A New View of Society* (1813) argued for co-operation instead of competition in all levels of society. His ideas led to the first co-operative shop in England, which sold fresh, cheap food, on a non-profit basis. He also set up one of the first trade unions, and created model working communities in Lanark, Scotland, and New Harmony, USA.

FIND OUT MORE CITIES   CLOTHES AND FASHION   EUROPE, HISTORY OF   UNIONS, TRADE   UNITED KINGDOM, HISTORY OF

INDUS VALLEY CIVILIZATION

ON THE BANKS of the Indus River in modern-day Pakistan, one of the world's earliest civilizations grew and flourished between c.2700 and 1750 BC. It was centred on the cities of Mohenjo-Daro and Harappa, each of which contained up to 40,000 people. Large public buildings, built of mud bricks, show that the civilization was prosperous. We know little about the day-to-day life of Indus Valley citizens, except that they traded with Sumeria and may have practised an early form of Hinduism. Their civilization mysteriously collapsed after 1750 BC; this may have been due to invasions, or the River Indus changing its course.

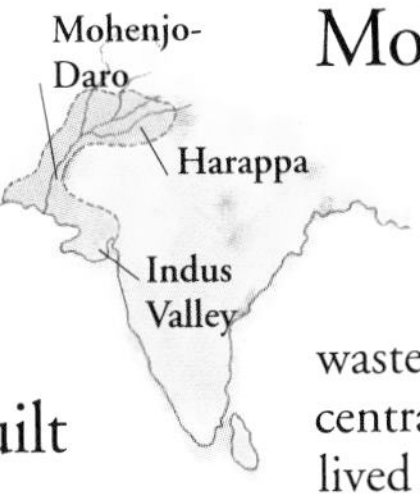

Mohenjo-Daro

Harappa

Indus Valley

Mohenjo-Daro

Indus Valley cities were planned and built on a grid pattern. They had broad main roads and narrow lanes. Drains carried away the household waste. All the houses were built around central courtyards. During the day, people lived and worked in these courtyards.

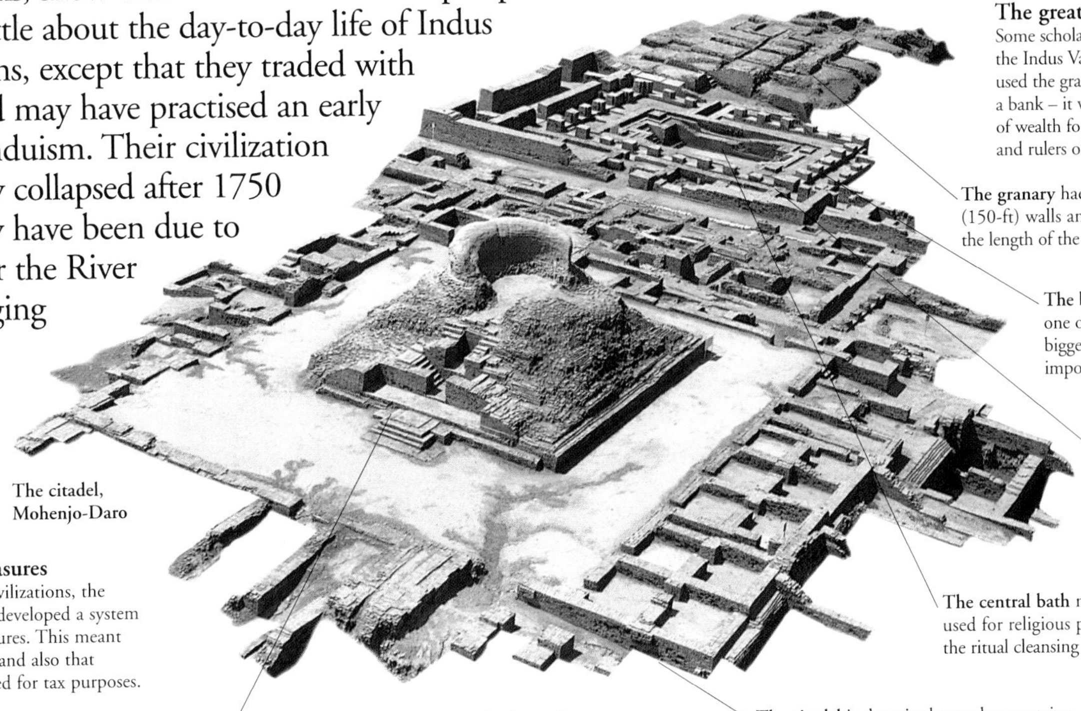

The great granary
Some scholars think that the Indus Valley people used the granary rather like a bank – it was a secure store of wealth for the merchants and rulers of the city.

The granary had wooden 46-m (150-ft) walls and roofs running the length of the building.

The bath-house was one of Mohenjo-Daro's biggest and most important buildings.

Small baths are in buildings near the bath-house.

The citadel, Mohenjo-Daro

Weights and measures
Like most ancient civilizations, the Indus Valley people developed a system of weights and measures. This meant trade became easier, and also that goods could be valued for tax purposes.

The central bath may have been used for religious purposes, such as the ritual cleansing before ceremonies.

A stupa, or Buddhist shrine, was built much more recently than the ancient city of Mohenjo-Daro. The original main temple of the Indus Valley people may be hidden beneath the stupa's mound.

The citadel is the raised area that contains the important public buildings, such as the bathhouse and the great granary. The higher ground makes the area easier to defend.

Ancient script

Archaeologists have found stone seals in a script unlike any other ancient form of writing. When long texts are found, scholars can often decipher them – but the Indus Valley inscriptions are very short, so their meaning remains a mystery.

Unicorn   *Indus script*

Seals
The Indus people used seals to show ownership. Each seal is carved with the image of an animal, such as a unicorn, and an inscription.

Religion

Little is known about the Indus religion. The importance of water, shown by the existence of the bath-house, has led some scholars to link it with later Hinduism. Various statues have been found that may represent gods and goddesses.

Head-dress

Goddess figures
Most of the statuettes found in the Indus cities have headdresses and jewellery, showing they were probably goddess figures.

Priests
This steatite (soapstone) statue is the most famous object found at Mohenjo-Daro. It has a serene expression that suggests it might be a statue of a priest or one of the Indus Valley gods.

Crafts

Indus people were skilled potters and metalworkers. They made fine painted vessels, terracotta statues, and beautiful gold jewellery. They also learned how to blend copper and tin to produce bronze.

Terracotta animals, Mohenjo-Daro

Bull

Pig

Gold jewellery, Harappa

INFORMATION TECHNOLOGY

THANKS TO information technology, you can enjoy the fantasy world of a virtual reality game and make friends with people on the other side of the world via the Internet. Information technology (IT) is the use of computers to handle, store, process, and transmit information. The key to information technology is software: sets of instructions called programs that tell computers what to do. Software can be used to design magazines and forecast the weather, and may even one day enable computers to think like humans.

Programs enable processing of information.

Computer languages

A computer can process information only when it is in the form of binary numbers, which are made up of the digits 0 and 1. It is difficult to write a computer program in this form, so programmers write their instructions in special codes called computer languages. The computer then translates the instructions into binary numbers, which it can understand.

A spreadsheet shows a grid of columns and rows on the screen.

Illustrator can change the colours in the photograph.

Programs

Computers cannot work without programs. A program is a sequence of simple instructions that tells a computer how to perform a specific task, such as adding up a list of numbers or printing a document. The programs that make a computer work are called software.

Alan Turing

British mathematician Alan Turing (1912–54) made important advances in the theory of computers. He was the first to propose that computers might one day be able to "think" – that is, perform a task in an identical way to a human.

Software applications

The software that controls a computer's essential functions is called its operating system. All other software programs are called applications. They include word processing, which helps you to write letters and documents, and multimedia, which combines text, pictures, video, music, and animation into one.

Spreadsheet

A spreadsheet is a software application that performs calculations on a table of numbers, such as sums of money or dates. Businesses use spreadsheets to display financial accounts, forecast sales figures, and plan work schedules.

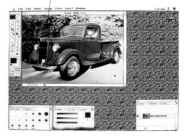

Computer graphics

Illustrators can use software to produce computerized images called graphics. Graphics software enables an illustrator to create entirely new images on-screen, or to alter images fed into the computer with a scanner.

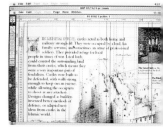

Desktop publishing (DTP)

Designers of books, newspapers, and magazines arrange the pictures and text on each page, using software called desktop publishing. DTP also allows editors to correct the text on-screen.

Computer simulation

Given the correct information and programs, powerful modern computers can simulate real-life situations, such as flying an aircraft, manoeuvring the space shuttle, or exploring the ocean depths. Computer simulation is used for research, education, training, and entertainment.

Hand-held control unit

Virtual reality

One form of computer simulation is called virtual reality. A computer creates 3-D images and sounds that seem almost real. Using a headset and a hand-held unit, the user can move around in and interact with this "virtual" world, created by the computer.

Virtual reality game

Headset makes player feel part of computer-generated scene.

Virtual reality kit

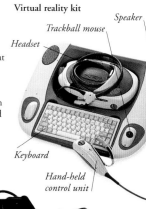

Trackball mouse

Speaker

Headset

Keyboard

Hand-held control unit

Computer modelling

Meteorologists use simulations called computer models to forecast changes in the weather. Using information gathered by weather stations, a computer creates a realistic model of a complex weather pattern, such as a hurricane, and then predicts how it will develop. Many scientists use computer modelling to test their theories.

Tracking sensor detects horizontal and vertical movement and sends this data to the controlling computer.

Earphones supply stereo sound.

Virtual reality headset

Small screen in front of each eye gives a sense of depth and realism.

Information superhighway

The information superhighway is a planned communications network that will use the optical fibres of the telephone line to bring a huge choice of services to people's homes. Using the latest multimedia software, a special terminal – like a combined television and computer – will allow users to access the Internet, watch interactive television and movies, play games, listen to music, and even do their shopping from their own homes.

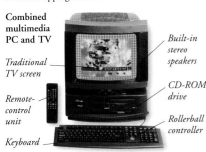

Combined multimedia PC and TV

Traditional TV screen

Remote-control unit

Keyboard

Built-in stereo speakers

CD-ROM drive

Rollerball controller

Artificial intelligence

The ability of a computer to think for itself is called Artificial Intelligence (AI). Some computers can already assess their own performance and work out ways to improve it. However, many people believe that computers can never be truly intelligent, because they can only follow instructions. AI research has so far produced neural networks and speech synthesizers.

Braille keyboard and special software for visually-impaired user

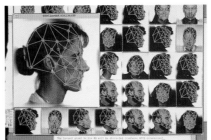

Face-recognition programme

Neural networks
One area of research into artificial intelligence uses circuits that work in a similar way to the nerves (neurons) in the brain. These circuits, called neural networks, can learn to do simple tasks, such as recognizing human faces.

AI for disability
Some people with disabilities use computers to help them communicate. Computers called speech synthesizers can recognize spoken words or produce speech from text typed in. Braille keyboards, voice recognition, and special software are all used by visually-impaired people.

Internet

The Internet is a global network of computers linked together by the telephone system. Once your computer is connected to the Internet, you can send and receive electronic mail (e-mail), exchange views in newsgroups (groups of Internet users with shared interests), and browse information on the World Wide Web – a collection of information "pages" held by museums, governments, businesses, colleges, universities, and individuals.

Internet communication
Text, pictures, sound, and other information is sent across the Internet from computer to computer in the form of binary digits, or bits. The bits are coded in a type of computer language called a protocol, and sent as tiny "packets" of data.

Packets are addressed and sent to the correct destination via the Internet.

Binary digits

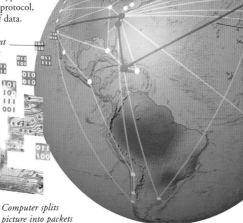

Receiving computer reassembles the packets.

If the route is busy, the packets find another way to reach their address.

World Wide Web
Information is stored on the Internet at linked sites called pages. The pages can be thought of as a web of information that spans the globe. Web pages are viewed with software called a browser. By clicking on a certain part of a page with a mouse, the user can visit other pages holding related information.

E-mail
Letters typed on a computer can be sent quickly, easily, and cheaply across the Internet using e-mail. Each Internet user has a unique e-mail "address", so that they can receive mail from other users. Mail is sent and received through a large computer called a server.

Personal computer (PC)

Computer splits picture into packets of data.

E-mail message typed into PC is sent as binary data to the modem.

PC modem

Receiving

Sending

Telephone line carries modem signal.

Modem
A modem is a device that converts binary computer data into a varying electrical signal and sends it along the telephone line.

Server modem

Receiving

Sending

Server's modem converts signal back into binary data.

Server

Server
A server is a powerful computer that routes out-going e-mail to the correct Internet address, and holds incoming messages in a "mail box" until the user wishes to open it.

John Von Neumann

The Hungarian-born mathematician John Von Neumann (1903–57) was the first to suggest that the program needed to operate a computer should be stored in its memory. He also devised a way of making a computer create random numbers – a vital function in many modern software applications.

Timeline

1960s The US military links up all its large computers, forming a network known as ARPANET.

Late 1970s Users can now interact with computer data by clicking on icons and windows on the screen with a mouse.

1981 The first IBM personal computers using MS-DOS become available.

Microsoft's Bill Gates

1980s ARPANET becomes the Internet, as the US military withdraws from the network, and it is used increasingly by universities and colleges.

1984 Apple Macintosh computers, using software produced by American Bill Gates' Microsoft company, become increasingly popular.

1985 First CD-ROMs appear.

1990s Use of Internet and email becomes widespread.

1994 RISC (reduced instruction set computing) allows for faster microchips.

2001 A web server the size of a match-head is produced.

FIND OUT MORE   **BRAIN AND NERVOUS SYSTEM**   **COMPUTERS**   **ELECTRONICS**   **NUMBERS**   **TECHNOLOGY**   **TELECOMMUNICATIONS**   **TELEPHONES**

INSECTS

FOR THEIR ABUNDANCE and diversity, no animals can match the insects. There may be a million species across the world. Insects are invertebrates and belong to the group called arthropods. They are the only arthropods that can fly. Many have a complex life cycle. Wherever they exist, they have a huge ecological impact as herbivores, hunters, decomposers, plant pollinators, and disease carriers. They are in turn food for predators, against which they have evolved some remarkable defences.

Field digger wasp
This parasitic wasp paralyzes its prey, such as a fly, and takes it back to its nest for its grubs to eat. Its paralyzing sting is borne on the tip of its long abdomen.

The thorax is in three segments and bears the legs and wings.

The head carries feeding apparatus and sense organs.

Fly
The exoskeleton, or cuticle, of flies, like that of all insects, is fragile and lightweight. This gives the flies flexibility, but also makes it easier for predators to pierce them with a bite or sting.

The abdomen contains most of the internal organs.

Breeding

Insects normally reproduce by mating, attracting one another first with scents, displays, vibrations, or other signals. The male's sperm is transferred into reproductive organs containing eggs in the female's abdomen. The female lays the fertilized eggs, often burying them in soil, or attaching them to a surface such as a leaf.

Adult mayfly

Mayflies
Breeding is all a mayfly does during the last stage of its life. As soon as it turns into an adult, it has just a few hours to find a mate and reproduce before it dies.

Parent bugs
Most adult insects leave their young to fend for themselves. Some bugs and earwigs look after their young offspring and try to protect them.

Parent bug with young

Insect features

Adult insects have a head, a thorax, and an abdomen, each composed of segments. They also have six jointed legs modified for walking, jumping, digging, or swimming. All parts are enclosed in an exoskeleton.

Hard wings form a protective case for the other pair.

Cardinal beetle

Eyes
The huge eyes of this dragonfly, like those of most insects, contain hundreds of units, each with its own lens. Together, the units make up a composite image.

Antennae
Reaching their maximum length in longhorn beetles, the antennae of insects are used to sense the shape and texture of objects and to detect scents and tastes.

Mouthparts
An insect's mouthparts include mandibles (hard jaws), maxillae (secondary jaws), and a labium (lower lip) for sucking fluids. This lacewing has large mandibles for biting.

Wings
The wings of flying insects are delicate membranes supported by veins. Most insects have two pairs of wings, and in beetles one pair is hard.

Life cycles

Different stages exist in the life of an insect between hatching and adulthood. Some insects undergo a dramatic change called complete metamorphosis. Other insects start out as wingless nymphs, then grow in steps, moulting their old cuticles before becoming mature adults.

Incomplete metamorphosis
Though it lives underwater after hatching, a young damselfly, or nymph, resembles the adult, which flies. After several "steps", the final nymph surfaces, breaks out of its cuticle, and unfurls its new wings.

Complete metamorphosis
Young butterflies, bees, flies, and beetles are totally different from their parents. Eggs hatch into larvae. Later, the larvae pupate, when their tissues reform into the shape of an adult.

1 A female butterfly, in this case a swallowtail butterfly, lays an egg on the leaf of a suitable food plant.

2 A larva, called a caterpillar, hatches out of the egg and starts to feed on the plant immediately.

3 The caterpillar grows and develops, moulting its skin several times as it does so.

4 At last it stops eating and turns into a chrysalis, or pupa. It may secure itself to a plant.

5 Inside the pupal cuticle, the insect transforms into an adult butterfly and then emerges.

A nymph crawls up a stem out of the water.

The cuticle splits along the back.

The adult damselfly gradually breaks free.

Blood is pumped into the wings.

The adult reaches its full size.

This adult damselfly is about 4.5 cm (1.75 in) long.

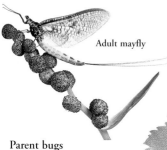

Habitats

Insects abound in most of the world's habitats, even the seemingly inhospitable. Though they reach their greatest diversity in the humid tropics, teeming numbers of them also exist in grassland and woodland, both among the vegetation and hidden away under the soil. Land and air are their true domains, but some species live in water for all or part of their life.

Tropical caves
Among the extreme environments occupied by insects are deep tropical caves. In the darkness, hordes of specialized scavengers, among them beetles and cockroaches, sift through bat droppings on the cave floor.

Scarab beetle

Deserts
Securing food and water in deserts and other dry places requires special effort. Scarab beetles dig underground shelters for their larvae, which they supply with ample food – balls of dung rolled from camel or buffalo droppings.

Water
A few insects, such as diving beetles and water boatmen, spend all their life in fresh water. Many more live there as nymphs or larvae, crawling along the bottom or in plants. Caddis fly larvae carry their own covering of debris for protection against enemies.

This covering is made of leaves stuck together with silk.

Nests
Many insects make homes from objects in their environment. The most accomplished builders are social insects such as wasps, bees, ants, and termites, which build communal nests. Wasp colonies create beautiful "paper" nests of chewed wood pulp.

The queen wasp lays one egg at the bottom of each cell.

The small entrance controls the temperature and humidity.

Caddis fly larva

As the larva grows, it makes its case longer.

Paper wasp's nest

Cross-section of a paper wasp's nest

A species of gryloblattid

Snowfields
Tiny wingless insects live in the intense cold and harsh winds of mountain peaks. Gryloblattids live on minute fragments of food blown up on the ice from lower altitudes. Anti-freezing substances in their body fluids stop them seizing up in the freezing conditions.

Feeding

Between them, insects eat virtually all types of organic matter. Few plants are safe from attack by larvae or adults, and insects play a major ecological role in breaking down plant and animal remains. Some insects are specialist feeders, such as many weevils that attack human foodstuffs; others, such as cockroaches and bush crickets, eat anything.

Nectar feeders
The energy-rich nectar of flowers lures pollinating insects such as butterflies, bees, flies, and beetles. As they feed, the insects get dusted with pollen, which they transfer from flower to flower.

Hunters
Some insects are fierce hunters. They have strong jaws for biting or piercing their prey with poison-filled probes. Some, such as mantids, use stealth to snatch passing prey; others actively seek out and chase their victims.

Mantid grasps a fly with its front legs.

Furniture beetle

Wood borers
The larvae of insects such as the furniture beetle gnaw tunnels through timber. They need to eat a large amount to get enough nourishment, because wood is very indigestible.

Parasites
Parasitic insects eat the living tissue and body fluids of larger animals. They live either on or in their host or, as in this bloodsucking fly, land on the skin to feed. As well as damaging their host directly, they also pass on diseases such as malaria and sleeping sickness.

Piercing, sucking mouthparts

Weta raises its spiny legs.

Defence

Both adult insects and their young are food for a host of predators, including other insects, spiders, lizards, birds, and mammals. They are not without their own means of defence and escape. Some actively threaten or counter attack the enemy; others are designed to avoid being detected in the first place.

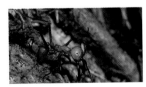

Attack
Some insects drive off enemies with squirts of poison, blows, bites, or stings. Among the most formidable weapons are the jaws of soldier ants like this one from Venezuela. Squadrons of ants attack intruders and often fatally injure them.

Stripes like those of a wasp

Mimicry
The hoverfly is one of a number of insects that avoid attack because they look like more aggressive species. Because of its similarity to a wasp, the hoverfly fools many predators into leaving it alone.

Leaf insect

Camouflage
A blend of shape and colour can make an insect extremely difficult to spot in its natural habitat. Amid dense foliage, the leaf insects of tropical forests have almost perfect camouflage.

Threat
Aggressive postures and alarming noises can be enough to ward off enemies. The wetas – large cricket-like insects of New Zealand – raise their spiny hindlegs and drop them with a crackling sound.

FIND OUT MORE ANIMALS CAMOUFLAGE AND COLOUR ECOLOGY AND ECOSYSTEMS EVOLUTION FLIGHT, ANIMAL FLOWERS NESTS AND BURROWS

Insects

Beetles, wasps, ants, and bees

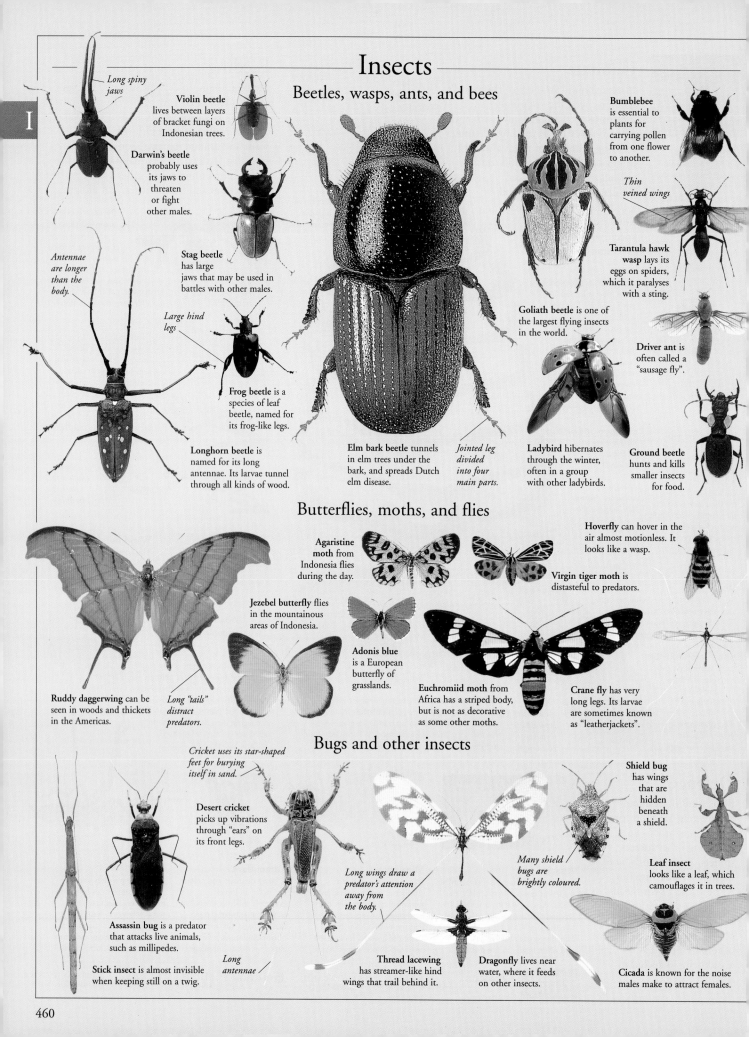

Long spiny jaws

Violin beetle lives between layers of bracket fungi on Indonesian trees.

Darwin's beetle probably uses its jaws to threaten or fight other males.

Stag beetle has large jaws that may be used in battles with other males.

Antennae are longer than the body.

Large hind legs

Frog beetle is a species of leaf beetle, named for its frog-like legs.

Longhorn beetle is named for its long antennae. Its larvae tunnel through all kinds of wood.

Elm bark beetle tunnels in elm trees under the bark, and spreads Dutch elm disease.

Jointed leg divided into four main parts.

Bumblebee is essential to plants for carrying pollen from one flower to another.

Thin veined wings

Tarantula hawk wasp lays its eggs on spiders, which it paralyses with a sting.

Goliath beetle is one of the largest flying insects in the world.

Driver ant is often called a "sausage fly".

Ladybird hibernates through the winter, often in a group with other ladybirds.

Ground beetle hunts and kills smaller insects for food.

Butterflies, moths, and flies

Agaristine moth from Indonesia flies during the day.

Hoverfly can hover in the air almost motionless. It looks like a wasp.

Jezebel butterfly flies in the mountainous areas of Indonesia.

Virgin tiger moth is distasteful to predators.

Adonis blue is a European butterfly of grasslands.

Ruddy daggerwing can be seen in woods and thickets in the Americas.

Long "tails" distract predators.

Euchromiid moth from Africa has a striped body, but is not as decorative as some other moths.

Crane fly has very long legs. Its larvae are sometimes known as "leatherjackets".

Bugs and other insects

Cricket uses its star-shaped feet for burying itself in sand.

Shield bug has wings that are hidden beneath a shield.

Desert cricket picks up vibrations through "ears" on its front legs.

Long wings draw a predator's attention away from the body.

Many shield bugs are brightly coloured.

Leaf insect looks like a leaf, which camouflages it in trees.

Assassin bug is a predator that attacks live animals, such as millipedes.

Stick insect is almost invisible when keeping still on a twig.

Long antennae

Thread lacewing has streamer-like hind wings that trail behind it.

Dragonfly lives near water, where it feeds on other insects.

Cicada is known for the noise males make to attract females.

INVENTIONS

AN INVENTION is something created by human effort that did not exist before. Most are useful to society or industry, and simplify the way things are done. Inventions range from the simple, such as the safety pin, to the complex, such as the television. An invention can come from the work of an individual or the work of a team. Human civilization is founded on a host of inventions, from the stone tools of prehistoric people to the robots of today.

Making life easier

Most people's lives have been improved by inventions, particularly during the 20th century. For example, the development of computers has led to global communications via the Internet, jet engines have provided a faster means of transport across the world, and the tractor has transformed agriculture. In the home, inventions such as the refrigerator have made preserving food easier, while the microwave oven has proved invaluable to those with busy lifestyles.

Industry
The steam engine and spinning jenny were two key inventions that set in motion the Industrial Revolution in the 18th century. Factories improved their productivity following Henry Ford's introduction in 1913 of the moving assembly line. By the late 1960s, the development of the microprocessor ushered in the modern electronics industry.

Home
Many inventions have improved life in the home. For example, the invention of electrical appliances provided cheap, clean lighting and the power to run devices which make cleaning, cooking, and washing easier. Less housework meant women could work outside the home for the first time.

The wheel
The wheel is probably the most important invention of all time. Today wheels are found in almost all machines. The first wheel was used by potters to help shape clay in Mesopotamia, more than 5,000 years ago. Wheels were then fitted to carts, revolutionizing transport.

Archimedes' screw
In about 200 BC, Greek scientist and mathematician, Archimedes (c.287–212 BC) invented a water-lifting machine incorporating a screw-like mechanism. This device is still used in irrigation schemes in some countries, and is the basis of drill bits and kitchen mixers.

Early inventions

The use of stone tools and weapons, such as bows and arrows, in prehistoric times gave people greater mastery over their environment. When they settled as farmers, the plough (c.3000 BC) greatly improved crop production. Around the same time, the wheel revolutionized transport. The alphabet (c.1500 BC) was also a milestone in civilization, becoming the basis of the written language.

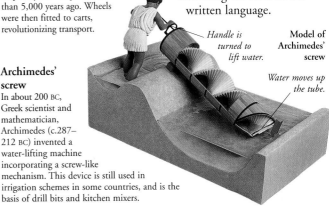

Handle is turned to lift water.

Model of Archimedes' screw

Water moves up the tube.

The cathode screen is coated with powder that glows when struck by cathode rays.

Anode hole creates beam of electrons.

Metal plates repel and attract beam.

Cathode emits rays.

Cathode-ray tube

Scanning coil sweeps electron beams across screen.

Electron guns emit beams that strike red, green, and blue phosphorous on to screen to give colour picture.

Colour television tube

Science
Many scientific inventions provide the foundations of the technologically based society we live in today. For example, electronics took off after the forerunner of the modern TV receiver tube, the cathode-ray tube, was invented in 1892. Also, medical inventions have helped to improve diagnosis and treatment.

Kellogg brothers

Today's flourishing cereal industry has its origins in the inventive mind of US physician John Harvey Kellogg (1852–1943), and the business skills of his brother William Keith (1860–1951). John Harvey developed cereals such as cornflakes as part of a vegetarian diet for his patients. His brother founded the Kellogg company in 1906 to sell John's inventions.

W. K. Kellogg

J. H. Kellogg

Inventors

Some people invent when there is a need for something, prompting the saying "necessity is the mother of invention". Others invent when they have a sudden flash of inspiration, and to make money. Today, more inventions are the result of organized research by a team, rather than by one person.

Patents
To prevent other people copying and profiting by their inventions, inventors must register a patent. This gives the inventor the sole right to make and sell the invention. The patent also details why the invention is new and original. Inventors have to register patents in as many countries as they can afford.

Patent for zip fastener

FIND OUT MORE   EDISON, THOMAS   ELECTRONICS   FOOD AND FOOD INDUSTRY   INDUSTRIAL REVOLUTION   INFORMATION TECHNOLOGY   MEDICINE, HISTORY OF   TECHNOLOGY   TRANSPORT, HISTORY OF

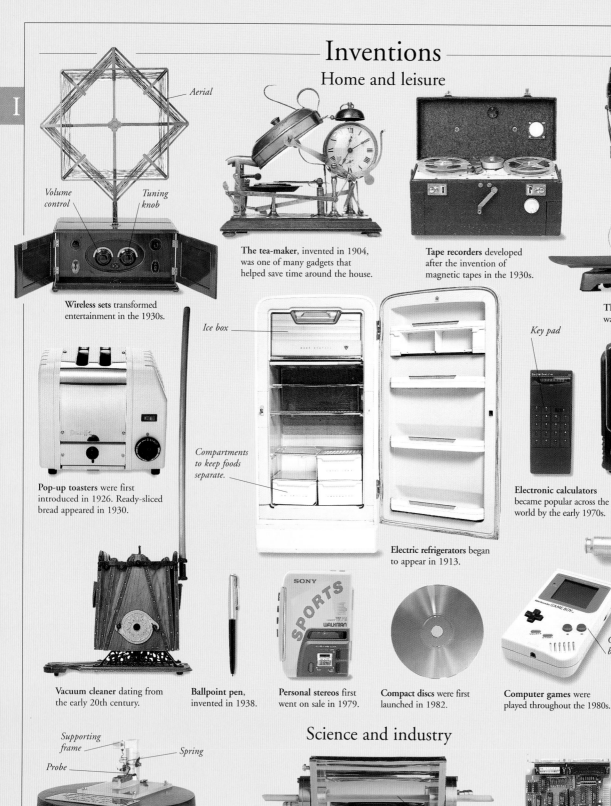

Inventions
Home and leisure

Aerial

Volume control   *Tuning knob*

Wireless sets transformed entertainment in the 1930s.

The tea-maker, invented in 1904, was one of many gadgets that helped save time around the house.

Tape recorders developed after the invention of magnetic tapes in the 1930s.

This food mixer from 1918, was driven by an electric motor.

Ice box

Compartments to keep foods separate.

Pop-up toasters were first introduced in 1926. Ready-sliced bread appeared in 1930.

Electric refrigerators began to appear in 1913.

Key pad

Electronic calculators became popular across the world by the early 1970s.

1950s television; the first TV was invented by John Logie Baird in 1926.

Vacuum cleaner dating from the early 20th century.

Ballpoint pen, invented in 1938.

Personal stereos first went on sale in 1979.

Compact discs were first launched in 1982.

Control buttons

Computer games were played throughout the 1980s.

Hair dryers were first sold for personal use in 1920.

Science and industry

Supporting frame   *Spring*

Probe

Transistors, invented in 1947, are still used in electronic devices.

Filament

Ruby crystal

Printed circuit boards were patented in 1943.

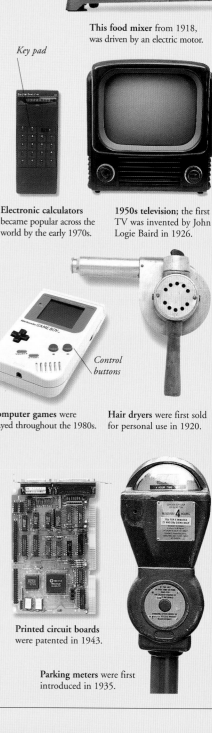

Pacemakers, invented in the 1960s, control heartbeats.

Audion valves, invented in 1906, amplified radio signals.

Lasers were developed in the 1960s for a variety of electronic uses.

Parking meters were first introduced in 1935.

IRAN AND IRAQ

A REGION OF inhospitable, rugged mountains and barren, rocky desert, Iran and Iraq both lie within the area known as the Middle East in southwest Asia. Border disputes and rivalries between these strongly Muslim countries resulted in a damaging war between 1980 and 1988. As with many other Middle Eastern countries, oil has brought great wealth to Iran and Iraq, enabling them to provide higher living standards for their people. However, a US-led war in Iraq deposed the Iraqi dictator, Saddam Hussein, in 2003, and the country faces many difficult changes.

Physical features

Mountains dominate the north, west, and south of Iran and the east of Iraq. Much of the rest of the region is vast, uninhabited desert. Iran's Caspian Sea coast is green and fertile, and southern Iraq has marshland.

32°C (90°F)   6°C (-43°F)

193 mm (8 in)

Regional climate
Iran and Iraq have very hot, dry summers, but winters are much colder and harsher in Iran than in Iraq. The region's annual rainfall is low, and fresh water is scarce.

Elburz Mountains
In northern Iran, the Elburz Mountains rise from the Caspian Sea. Winds blowing south from the Russian Federation bring rain to the northern slopes, which are covered in forest and farmland. Sheltered from the rain-bearing winds, the southern side of the mountains is arid and infertile. The highest point is Mount Damävand at 5,671 m (18,605 ft). Snow is common, and there are ski resorts east of Tehran.

Kurds
There are about 25 million Kurdish people. They live in Kurdistan, a mountainous region that straddles the borders of Turkey, Syria, Iraq, and Iran. Their fight for self-government has been put down repeatedly with much bloodshed. Forced to leave Iraq after the Gulf War, many Kurds became refugees.

Iranian Kurds cooking food

Iranian plateau
Closed in by the Zagros and Elburz Mountains to the west and north, Iran's vast central plateau consists of two great deserts, the Dasht-e Kavir and the Dasht-e Lut. Lying at about 900 m (2,950 ft) above sea-level, these barren, rocky deserts are uninhabited because of the almost total lack of water.

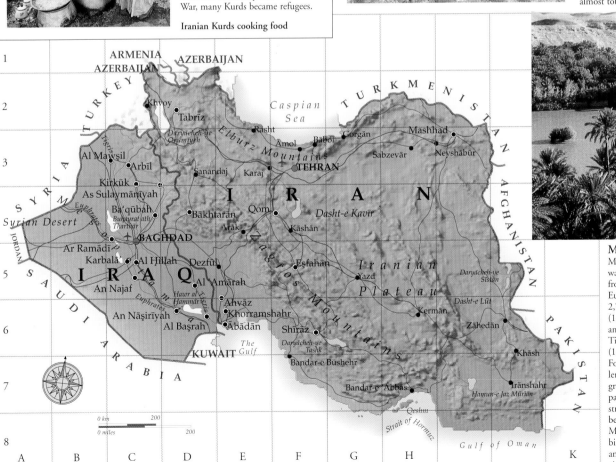

Mesopotamia
Most of Iraq's water comes from the River Euphrates, 2,753 km (1,700 miles) long and the River Tigris, 1,850 km (1,150 miles) long. For much of their length, these two great rivers run parallel. The fertile strip of land between them is Mesopotamia, birthplace of the ancient Sumerian civilization.

Iran

Bordered by Afghanistan to the east, Iraq to the west, and former Soviet republics to the north, Iran was called Persia until 1935. For years the country was ruled by shahs, or kings, but, in 1979, when Ayatollah Khomeini (1900–89) deposed the last shah, the country became an Islamic republic. The modern Iranian government rules according to strict Islamic laws.

Mosques

All mosques (Muslim places of worship), have a tower, (minaret), from which the faithful are called to prayer five times a day. Mosques are also often ornately decorated with abstract designs and inscriptions from the Qur'an, the holy book of Islam.

14th-century Friday mosque, Kerman

IRAN FACTS

CAPITAL CITY	Tehran
AREA	1,648,000 sq km (636,293 sq miles)
POPULATION	71,400,000
MAIN LANGUAGE	Farsi
MAJOR RELIGION	Muslim
CURRENCY	Iranian Rial
LIFE EXPECTANCY	69 years
PEOPLE PER DOCTOR	1,111
GOVERNMENT	Islamic republic
ADULT LITERACY	77%

Tehran

Iran's capital lies in the foothills of the Elburz Mountains. Tehran contains parks, art galleries, and museums, as well as one of the world's largest bazaars. Tehran was modernized by the last shah, and the Shahyad Monument commemorates 2,500 years of shah rule.

Shahyad Monument, built in 1971

Carpet woven from Iranian wool

Persian carpets

Iran has been famous for its handwoven rugs and carpets since the 13th century. With rich, dark colours and traditional patterns, they are the country's second largest export.

Tehran carpet traders

Farming

Although farming employs about 33 per cent of the Iranian work-force, the lack of water means that only 11 per cent of the land can be cultivated. Underground irrigation channels called *qanats* are used to transport water to farming areas. Wheat, barley, and rice are the main crops. Sheep are raised for wool and meat.

Wind separates the wheat grain from the chaff.

Iraq

Iraq was a strong military power in the Middle East. Between 1979 and 2003, under Saddam Hussein (b.1937), it attempted to dominate its neighbours, but a stalemate in the war with Iran, the foiled annexation of Kuwait (1990–91), and the war against the USA (2003) has ended this. It is now attempting to rebuild its shattered economy and adopt democracy. Iraq is a strongly Islamic country.

Oil

Iraq has huge reserves of oil and gas. Before the Gulf War, oil accounted for more than 95 per cent of the country's export earnings. However, following the United Nations' ban on the sale of Iraqi oil to member states and a second war, Iraq now has a poor economic situation and is faced with the task of rebuilding its oil industry.

IRAQ FACTS

CAPITAL CITY	Baghdad
AREA	437,072 sq km (168,753 sq miles)
POPULATION	23,600,000
MAIN LANGUAGE	Arabic
MAJOR RELIGION	Muslim
CURRENCY	Iraqi Dinar
LIFE EXPECTANCY	61 years
PEOPLE PER DOCTOR	2,000
GOVERNMENT	Transitional
ADULT LITERACY	56%

Baghdad street trader selling bread

Food

People in Iraq eat lamb, chicken, or fish with vegetables and chick peas, served with rice and *khubz* (pitta bread). Popular dishes are stuffed vine leaves called *dolma* and *quozi,* grilled lamb stuffed with rice and spices.

Farming and industry

Agriculture employs about 12 per cent of the work-force, but does not produce enough crops to supply the country's needs. Trade bans imposed after the Gulf War limited imports, leading to food shortages. Only about eight per cent of Iraq's workers are engaged in manufacturing, mainly in food processing.

View of mosque with a decorative minaret

Baghdad

Iraq's capital on the banks of the River Tigris has been an important Arab city since AD 752. An industrial and cultural centre, its old, narrow streets and bustling markets contrast sharply with modern buildings. There are many mosques, and monuments to President Saddam Hussein.

Marsh Arabs

The Tigris and Euphrates join to form the Shatt-al-Arab, which is surrounded by marshland. This area is home to the Marsh Arabs, who live in reed houses built on artificial islands made of reeds and mud. They are threatened by plans to drain the marshes.

FIND OUT MORE   ASIA, HISTORY OF   DESERTS   FARMING   ISLAM   ISLAMIC EMPIRE   LAW   MOSQUES   OIL   PERSIAN EMPIRES   SUMERIANS   TEXTILES AND WEAVING

IRELAND

THE IRISH REPUBLIC occupies two-thirds of the island of Ireland in the Atlantic Ocean off the west coast of the United Kingdom. The rest of the island, the six counties of Northern Ireland, chose to remain part of the United Kingdom when, in 1922, the Republic voted for independence. The Republic is a member of the European Union and has efficient farming and food-processing industries. Electronic goods account for 25 percent of all exports. The 1998 Good Friday Agreement made steps towards resolving conflicts in the area.

Physical features

Central Ireland consists of a fertile plain, punctuated by lakes, peat bogs, and undulating hills. Low mountains rise to the south, west, and southeast. The west coast has deep inlets and bays. The Shannon is the longest river in the British Isles.

Connemara

Hundreds of beautiful lakes and peat bogs are typical of the wild scenery of Connemara in western Ireland. The spectacular peaks of the Twelve Bens mountain range were carved out by glaciers in the last Ice Age.

Emerald Isle

Ireland's high rainfall results in fresh green fields, giving it the nickname of the "Emerald Isle". The land is used for grazing dairy cattle and growing crops. Ireland is famous for its butter and cheese, and for horses and horseracing.

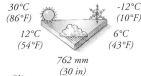

30°C (86°F)   -12°C (10°F)
12°C (54°F)   6°C (43°F)
762 mm (30 in)

Climate

The warm waters of the Gulf Stream account for Ireland's mild, damp climate. Ocean winds bring the country plenty of rain, especially along the west coast.

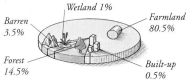

Wetland 1%
Barren 3.5%
Farmland 80.5%
Forest 14.5%
Built-up 0.5%

Land use

Ireland's most important natural resources are its fertile farmland and peat, used for fuel and gardening. There are oil reserves off the coast.

Farming and industry

Ireland has one of the fastest-growing economies in Europe. Traditional industries such as hand-cutting peat compete alongside a rapidly expanding high-tech sector. A historical trend of emigration has now been reversed due to a strong economy. Only eight per cent of the work-force are farmers.

Dublin

Dublin is a lively centre of commerce, social activity, and cultural heritage. Christchurch Cathedral was restored in the 1870s and is one of Dublin's finest landmarks alongside Trinity College, Dublin Castle, and the Custom House.

Christchurch Cathedral

People

Ninety-five per cent of the population of Ireland are Irish and 93 per cent are Roman Catholics. The church plays a key role in society, although the younger Irish question its strict policies on birth control, divorce, and abortion. Long-standing, bitter, conflict exists between Catholics in southern Ireland and Protestants of Northern Ireland.

People crossing Dublin's Ha'penny Bridge

54 per sq km (139 per sq mile)

59% Urban   41% Rural

Stacking peat to dry in County Galway

FIND OUT MORE   CHRISTIANITY   COAL   ENERGY   EUROPE   EUROPE, HISTORY OF   EUROPEAN UNION   FARMING   GLACIATION   IRELAND, HISTORY OF   TRADE AND INDUSTRY

IRELAND, HISTORY OF

THE RICH CELTIC culture of Ireland distinguishes it from its neighbour, England, but its history has been dominated by struggle with that country. The English invaded Ireland in 1171. At first, their rule was weak, but, by the 17th century, English control was complete. However, the religious differences between the Protestant English and Roman Catholic Irish led to long-lasting tensions. In 1921, the island was divided: the Catholic counties of the south, west, and east were given self-government; the northern, mainly Protestant counties remained part of the United Kingdom.

The Celts excelled at metalwork.

Celtic gold boat

Celtic Ireland
Around 600 BC, Celtic people from central Europe settled Ireland. Celtic craft and design – especially metalwork – have influenced Irish art ever since.

St Patrick

In 432, a missionary named Patrick landed in Ireland. By 631, Patrick had converted the whole country to Christianity. For the next 300 years, Ireland enjoyed a golden age of arts and scholarship, which was centred on the monasteries. Irish missionaries set out to convert other parts of Europe.

Book of Kells
One of Ireland's most famous monasteries was built by the brilliant missionary, St Columba, at Kells. It housed an outstanding 8th-century illuminated manuscript of the Latin Gospels.

Illuminated initial from the *Book of Kells*

Brian Boru
Ireland lacked strong government, and in the 8th century, Viking invaders started to settle along the coast. In 1002, Brian Boru, king of Munster, made himself High King of all Ireland. In 1014, he defeated the Vikings at Clontarf. Brian lost his life in the battle, but ended the Viking threat to Ireland.

English rule

In 1155, Pope Adrian IV gave the lordship of Ireland to his English ally Henry II. Henry's invasion in 1171 marked the start of eight centuries of English rule, though initially this was restricted to a small area. From the 1600s, religious differences and the ascendancy of the wealthy Protestant English over the Catholic Irish worsened Anglo-Irish relations.

Battle of the Boyne
In 1690, the Protestant William of Orange took the throne of the Catholic James II of England after defeating him in battle. Northern Irish Protestants still celebrate this victory with a march on 12th July – Orangeman's Day.

Great Famine
In 1845, the potato crop – the main food of the Irish peasantry – failed. Over the next four years, one million people died of starvation, and more than 1,600,000 emigrated to the USA. Meanwhile, landlords were still demanding their starving tenants pay rent on their lands.

Potatoes were blighted by an airborne fungus.

Modern Ireland

In 1921, Ireland was divided into two parts: six Protestant counties in the north and 26 Catholic counties in the rest of the country. In 1922, the 26 counties formed a free state within the British Empire. The Free State achieved independence in 1937 and changed its name to Eire.

General Post Office, Dublin, a symbol of the Easter Rising

Easter Rising
On Easter Monday, 1916, militant republicans staged an uprising in Dublin and occupied the General Post Office. One of the leaders, Patrick Pearse, proclaimed Ireland an independent republic from the GPO's steps. The British soon crushed the rebellion, and executed 14 of its leaders. This caused a wave of sympathy among the people, and resistance to British rule increased.

Northern Ireland
In 1921, British and Irish political leaders signed the Anglo-Irish Treaty in which six counties in Ulster remained within the United Kingdom. Ulster's Protestant local government practised anti-Catholic policies, which led to civil-rights protests and violence in 1968. The British government posted troops to Northern Ireland to keep order. They have remained to the present day.

Mural in Belfast, Northern Ireland

Mary Robinson
In early 1991, Mary Robinson (b.1944) became the first-ever woman president of the Republic of Ireland. As a lawyer, Robinson had campaigned for civil and women's rights. As president, she spoke up for the disadvantaged in Irish society. In 1997 she went on to become the UN High Commissioner for Human Rights.

Timeline

c.461 Death of St Patrick. Ireland's conversion is complete.

795 Vikings first sail to Ireland.

1171 Henry II of England invades Ireland.

1607–41 Scottish and English Protestants colonize province of Ulster.

1690 William of Orange defeats James II. Protestant Ascendancy begins.

1801 Act of Union unites Ireland and England.

1845–48 The Great Famine.

1916 Easter Rising.

1921 Partition; Northern Ireland is formed.

1922 Irish Free State formed; war between supporters and opponents of Partition.

1973 Ireland joins European Union.

FIND OUT MORE   CELTS   CHRISTIANITY   EUROPE, HISTORY OF   MONASTERIES   UNITED KINGDOM, HISTORY OF

IRON AND STEEL

OUT OF THE 70 or so metals that exist on Earth, iron is the most important. It is used more than all the other metals put together – some 600 million tonnes every year. It is used to build many things from bridges, skyscrapers, and ships to cars, bikes, and tools. However, iron is not generally used in its pure state, but in the form of its alloy, steel. The presence of traces of carbon in this alloy makes it hard, strong, and tough. Steel also contains smaller amounts of other metals, producing a range of alloy steels with different properties.

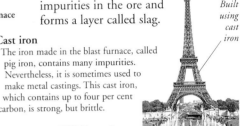

Iron ore
The main raw material for iron-making is iron ore. There are two main iron-ore minerals: haematite and magnetite. Haematite is named after its blood-red colour; magnetite is so-called because it is naturally magnetic.

Haematite

Iron smelting

Iron is produced when the ore is heated with coke and limestone in a blast furnace. The coke acts both as fuel and as a chemical agent to remove oxygen from the ore, leaving the metal. The limestone absorbs impurities in the ore and forms a layer called slag.

Adding iron ore to furnace

Built using cast iron

Cast iron
The iron made in the blast furnace, called pig iron, contains many impurities. Nevertheless, it is sometimes used to make metal castings. This cast iron, which contains up to four per cent carbon, is strong, but brittle.

Traces of carbon in cast iron

Iron cross-section

Eiffel Tower, France

Steel refining

Most pig iron produced is sent for further processing, or refining. Refining removes many of the impurities from the iron, especially the carbon. The result is steel. The most common refining method is called the basic-oxygen process. A high speed jet of oxygen is blasted into molten pig iron and burns out the impurities.

Steel is poured into ingot moulds and taken to be shaped.

Ladle containing molten steel

Scrap iron is tipped into the converter.

Molten pig iron is poured into the ladle ready for transfer to converter.

Manufacturing steel

The converter is filled with molten pig iron, scrap, and additives. Oxygen is blown in, causing a violent chemical reaction.

Containers holding molten pig iron from the blast furnace

Shaping steel
Once refined, steel is usually cast into huge ingots, which are then shaped further. This is done using a variety of methods such as rolling and forging. In rolling, the reheated ingot is passed between heavy rollers. In forging, the ingot is hammered or squeezed by powerful machines.

Steel cross-section showing small traces of carbon

Henry Bessemer

In 1856, English engineer Henry Bessemer (1813–98) invented the first process for producing steel cheaply. His method involved blowing air through molten pig iron in a converter. The air blast burned out carbon and other impurities in the iron.

Types of steel

There are basically two main types of steel – carbon steel and alloy steel. The properties of carbon steel depend on the percentage of carbon it contains, while the properties of alloy steel are based on the nature of the other alloying metals added during its manufacture.

Stainless steel products   Steel chain

Carbon steel
The most common steel, mild steel, is a carbon steel containing up to about 0.25 per cent carbon. Other carbon steels, with carbon contents up to 1.5 per cent, are stronger and harder, but more brittle.

Mild steel car body

Stainless steel
This is one of the most widely used of all alloy steels. It contains about 18 per cent chromium and 8 per cent nickel. Both of these metals resist rusting and staining, and impart this property to steel.

Rust

When iron or steel is exposed to damp air, it soon becomes covered with a reddish-brown film called rust. Rust is a hydrated iron oxide, formed when iron is attacked by oxygen and moisture in the air. Protective paints applied on some surfaces can prevent rust from forming.

Rust on an abandoned car

FIND OUT MORE   BRONZE AGE   BUILDING AND CONSTRUCTION   CARS AND TRUCKS   CHEMISTRY   COAL   INDUSTRIAL REVOLUTION   METALS   SHIPS AND BOATS

ISLAM

IN THE 7TH CENTURY AD a new faith appeared in the world. This faith was revealed to the prophet Muhammad and its name is Islam, which is an Arabic word meaning "submission to the will of God". Believers in Islam are called Muslims. They believe in one God, whom they call Allah, who is eternal and created the universe. They also believe that Allah sent a series of prophets to explain his wishes and to tell people how to live their lives. The most important prophet was Muhammad.

The Qur'an

The sacred book of Islam is called the Qur'an. Muslims believe that the Angel Gabriel, acting as Allah's messenger, dictated it to Muhammad, and it was later written down by the Prophet's followers. The Qur'an reveals Allah's will for humankind. All Muslims study the Qur'an, and its text is often copied out using beautiful calligraphy.

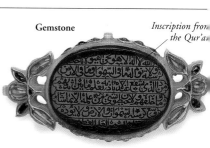
Gemstone
Inscription from the Qur'an

Shading shows worldwide distribution of Muslims. Islam is the second largest world religion.

The Islamic world

The centre of the Islamic world is Mecca, in the Arabian peninsula. From here, in the 7th and 8th centuries, the faith spread quickly, until much of the area from Spain in the west to the Indus River in the east was converted. Islam has continued to expand, and there are now probably about 750 million Muslims in the world.

Pillars of Islam

There are five duties that every Muslim must obey. These are known as the five Pillars of Islam. The first is Shahadah, the sincere delaration of faith that there is "no other God but Allah and that Muhammad is his prophet". The second, Salat, means that Muslims should pray five times a day. The third pillar, Zakah, is the gift of money to the poor. The fourth, Sawm, is to fast during Ramadan. The final pillar, Hajj, is the duty to make the pilgrimmage to Mecca.

The Ka'bah is the holy shrine in the Great Mosque at Mecca.

Hajj

Every Muslim who can afford it and who is well enough has an obligation to make the pilgrimmage to Mecca, in Saudi Arabia, the birthplace of Muhammad. Each year, during the twelfth month of the Muslim year, more than two million Muslims visit Mecca. Many save up for years to make the journey, which is the most important event in their lives.

Muslims walk seven times anti-clockwise around the Ka'bah.

Salat

Five times each day Muslims stop whatever they are doing, face the direction of Mecca, and pray. Men go to prayers at the mosque at midday on Fridays, but at other times may pray in any clean place; women usually pray at home. Before following the sequence of prayer positions, a Muslim must carry out a washing ritual.

An imam (priest) begins his prayer by raising his hands to his ears and making a declaration of faith.

The imam bows down from the waist, hands on knees, reciting a prayer.

This prayer mat has a built-in compass showing the direction of Mecca.

Jihad

The Qur'an says that Muslims should oppose anyone who rejects the faith, if necessary by means of armed struggle. The term "jihad" (the Arabic word for struggle) means striving to spread the Islamic way of life, sometimes through a "holy war". Jihad can also take other forms, such as learning, good works, and self-control.

Medieval conquests spread the Islamic faith.

This is known as the Sujud position.

He prostrates himself with his forehead, nose, palms of hands, knees, and toes touching the ground.

After a few moments sitting up on his knees, the imam returns to the Sujud position.

At the end of the set of prayers, the imam turns his face to the left and then to the right.

Muslims may pray kneeling on a woven carpet, straw mat, or clean ground.

Festivals

Muslims celebrate several important events in Muhammad's life. These include the prophet's birthday (Mawlid al-Nabi) and the Night of Power (Laylat al Qadr), which commemorates the night when Muhammad received the Qur'an from the Angel Gabriel. The Night of the Journey (Laylat al-Mi'raj) celebrates the night when Muhammad was taken up to heaven. The two most important festivals are Id al-Fitr and Id al-Adha.

Celebrations for Id al-Fitr include music and dancing for these Muslims in Cameroon, Central Africa.

Id al-Adha
This festival takes place during the twelfth Muslim month, which is the pilgrimage month of Dhul-Hijjah. It marks the sacrifice of Abraham, who was prepared to sacrifice his son Isaac to God, but at the last minute God told him to give a ram instead. Muslims traditionally sacrifice a sheep or goat and give one-third of the meat to the poor.

Id al-Fitr
The ninth month of the Islamic year is Ramadan, the month of fasting. The end of Ramadan is celebrated by Id al-Fitr. This festival begins with a light meal and a meeting at the mosque for prayers, at which thanks are given for a successful fast. After prayers there are parties, at which people eat special cakes and sweets, and exchange presents and cards. Before the festival, people give money to the poor so that everyone can join in the celebrations.

Whirling dervishes
Dervishes are members of mystical Islamic sects called Sufi that developed during the 12th century. There are various orders of dervishes, but they are best known for a prayer ritual in which they perform an ecstatic whirling dance, aiming to induce a trance and a direct experience of God.

Daily life

Islam affects the whole of a Muslim's life – everyday conduct, art, ethics, laws, and government. The Qur'an gives guidelines for all aspects of life and stresses the importance of the family. Family members are expected to care for one another, and the elderly are regarded as head of the family. Marriages are usually arranged. It is traditional for women to stay at home to look after the house, but increasingly Muslim women go out to work. Women often cover their head out of doors.

Verses from the Qur'an

Arabic script

Ornamental border decorates verses

Halal food
According to the Qur'an, food that Muslims are allowed to eat is called halal. Products which come from animals that eat other animals are forbidden, as is meat from pigs. Other meats are halal, when they are slaughtered correctly. All fish, fruit, grains, and vegetables are halal too.

Education
Every Muslim must understand the text of the Qur'an because its teachings are part of everyday life. Education is therefore very important in Islam. Mosques traditionally contain a school where pupils learn to read the Qur'an in its original Arabic.

Islamic fundamentalists at a protest in Iran, carrying posters of Ayatollah Khomeini.

Islamic fundamentalism
Some Muslims have turned their backs on the influence of modern western society in favour of traditional Islamic values. They are known as Islamic fundamentalists.

Branches of Islam

Islam has two main branches: Sunni and Shi'ah. After the death of Muhammad, his followers chose Abu Bakr as their leader. Umar, Uthman, and Ali (Muhammad's son-in-law) were chosen in turn after Abu Bakr. But one group of Muslims thought they should be led by Muhammad's descendants.

They broke away, choosing the descendants of Ali as leaders. This break-away group is known as the Shi'ahs, and the group that remained are Sunni Muslims.

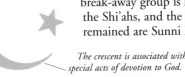

The crescent is associated with special acts of devotion to God.

This Shi'ah standard bears the names of God, Muhammad, and Ali.

Sunni and Shi'ah
Sunnis make up the larger of the two groups of Muslims. Their name derives from an Arabic word meaning "authority". The Shi'ah Muslims, who make up about 10 per cent of the Islamic population, live mainly in Iran and Iraq. Their leaders are known as ayatollahs. The two groups have separate theologies, legal systems, and ways of performing their rituals.

FIND OUT MORE   CRUSADES   FESTIVALS   HOLY LAND, HISTORY OF   ISLAMIC EMPIRE   MOSQUES   MUHAMMAD   OTTOMAN EMPIRE   RELIGIONS   SIGNS AND SYMBOLS   WRITING

ISLAMIC EMPIRE

IN THE 8TH CENTURY, Arabian conquerors ruled a massive empire that stretched from Spain to China's borders. The Arab rulers had a mission to spread Islam, a religion whose powerful message was of equality, and whose followers are called Muslims. Under Muslim rule, people from many different lands worshipped one God, used a common tongue, and had one holy book. It was a time of great wealth and learning: palaces, mosques, and universities were built in superb Islamic cities, and within them knowledge was pursued by the world's best scientists.

Spread of the empire, c.750
The Arab conquest was speedy. Within a century of Muhammad's death, Arabs had defeated the Persian and much of the Byzantine empires. There were many converts to Islam, but the conquerors also tolerated other religions.

Conquered before 632

Conquered between 632 and 750

Early dynasties

Religious leaders, known as caliphs, ruled the empire. During the reign of the fourth caliph, two rival branches of Islam formed – the Sunni and Shi'ah. After the Umayyad and Abbasid (Sunni) dynasties fell, the Fatimid (Shi'ah) dynasty took over, and used separate local rulers to keep order. This ended the idea of one supreme caliph ruling a single empire.

Umayyads and Abbasids
The aristocratic Umayyad caliphs had a luxurious lifestyle. The Abbasid dynasty resented this, and eventually seized power. Their best-known caliph, Harun al-Rashid (766–809), featured in the famous *A Thousand and One Nights.*

Royal escape, *A Thousand and One Nights,* **1898 edition**

Capital cities

Muslim cities always have a central mosque and bazaars (covered markets). The first Muslim capital was Mecca, Muhammad's birthplace and Islam's holiest city. In 752, the Abbasids founded Baghdad, which, within 50 years, had become the largest city in the world.

Damascus
Before the Abbasid dynasty built Baghdad, the Islamic capital was at the ancient city of Damascus. The Umayyads built a Great Mosque in marble, and decorated it with mosaics.

Umayyad mosque, Damascus

Science

Islamic science brought together many branches of knowledge. At the college in Baghdad, scholars translated books from ancient Greece, Persia, and India into Arabic. Scientists observed and measured the natural world. Mathematicians invented algebra (from the Arabic *al-jabr*), and the Arabic system of numbers is used worldwide today.

Astronomers hung their astrolabes from their belts.

Star map and zodiacal circle

Astronomy
Muslims led the world in astronomy – they built many observatories and perfected the use of the astrolabe. Arabian nomads used the stars to navigate through the desert.

Alidade (movable pointer) is at the centre.

Persian astrolabe

Circumference is marked off in degrees.

Ginger

Coriander

Cardamom

Medicine
Islamic doctors absorbed and followed ancient Greek theories, but also formulated many of their own. They knew, for example, long before Europeans, that blood circulates around the body. They stressed the importance of a healthy diet, and understood the healing power of herbs and plants.

Ibn Sina
The Islamic Empire's greatest philosopher and scientist, Ibn Sina (980–1037), was born in Bukhara in modern Uzbekistan. He was an exceptionally good doctor who was known to Europeans as Avicenna. His *Canon of Medicine* is one of the most famous books in medical history.

Canon of Medicine, **1400s**

Timeline

632 Muhammad dies. Four of his close companions succeed him in turn as caliph. Islamic Empire begins.

634–650 Muslims conquer Middle East.

650 Qur'an is written.

661–750 Umayyad caliphate (dynasty) rules. They make Damascus their new capital.

670–708 Muslims attack and then conquer North Africa.

Cinnamon

711–721 Muslims conquer Spain.

732 Muslim advance turned back in France.

750–880 The Abbasid dynasty rules the Islamic empire.

909 The (Shi'ah) Fatimid dynasty captures North Africa. Muslim territories split up and are ruled under separate leaders for the first time.

1055 Seljuk Turks begin to control the Islamic Empire.

FIND OUT MORE | ARCHITECTURE | ASIA, HISTORY OF | EMPIRES | ISLAM | MEDICINE, HISTORY OF | MUHAMMAD | PERSIAN EMPIRE | SAFAVID EMPIRE | SCIENCE, HISTORY OF

ISLANDS

DOTTED OVER THE OCEANS OF THE WORLD are millions of islands. Some islands are no bigger than rocks, but others are vast land masses – Greenland, for example, covers 2.2 million square kilometres (0.85 million square miles). An island is an area of land smaller than a continent that is surrounded by water. Islands may be created when the sea rises or the land sinks, drowning valleys to leave only the highest ground above sea level. Islands may also form when ocean-floor volcanoes, built up by the lava from successive eruptions, emerge above water.

How a coral island forms

Coral polyps are tiny sea creatures that live in colonies in tropical oceans. A coral reef is an underwater ridge formed from the remains of dead coral. A reef may form around the exposed summit of an underwater volcano. If the volcano sinks, it may leave behind a ring-shaped island called an atoll.

Over time, volcanic eruptions may build an ocean-floor volcano up so high that its summit emerges above the surface of the water, forming an island. In warm tropical waters, a fringing reef of coral may begin to grow along the shoreline.

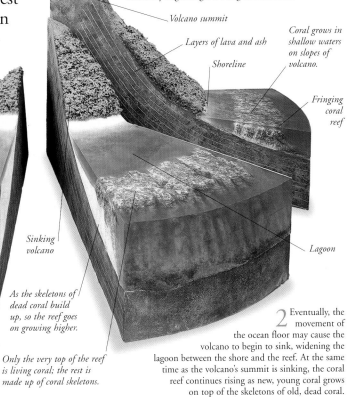

Volcano summit

Layers of lava and ash

Shoreline

Coral grows in shallow waters on slopes of volcano.

Fringing coral reef

Reef-top becomes colonized by vegetation.

Only tip of volcano is visible.

4 Eventually, the volcano's summit is completely submerged, leaving only the coral reef. The reef begins to form a ring-shaped island called an atoll as it is covered first by sand and then by vegetation.

Lagoon gradually fills with sand.

Sinking volcano

Lagoon

As the skeletons of dead coral build up, so the reef goes on growing higher.

3 The volcano goes on sinking, and the coral continues to grow. As the lagoon expands even more, small outcrops of new coral appear within the lagoon. In places where the coral is growing particularly rapidly, the tops of the reef begin to dry out.

Growing reef stays above the water as the volcano sinks.

Only the very top of the reef is living coral; the rest is made up of coral skeletons.

2 Eventually, the movement of the ocean floor may cause the volcano to begin to sink, widening the lagoon between the shore and the reef. At the same time as the volcano's summit is sinking, the coral reef continues rising as new, young coral grows on top of the skeletons of old, dead coral.

Volcanic islands

The Hawaiian Islands are a chain of volcanoes formed above a "hot spot" – that is, a place where hot, molten rock burns through the Earth's crust. The Hawaiian chain is slowly growing longer as the movement of the ocean floor shifts each volcano along, and a new volcano erupts over the hot spot.

Island arcs
Where two pieces, or plates, of the Earth's crust collide, molten rock escapes and creates a long arc of volcanic islands. Java, Bali, the Philippines, and Japan are all part of the same giant island arc.

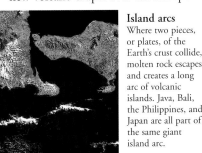

The islands of Java and Bali

Drowned lands

Many large islands form when the movement of the Earth's crust causes the land to sink. This is how Britain became an island, and how the Isle of Wight was separated from mainland Britain.

Satellite image of Isle of Wight, Britain

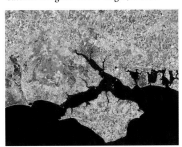

Eyot
Where a large river flows over broad, flat flood plains, the river channel may split up into several smaller channels. If the river carries a lot of sediment, such as sand or mud, it may deposit the sediment as sand bars or mudbanks between the channels. Small islands called eyots (or aits) form as the sand bars and mudbanks dry out.

Eyot in the River Seine, France

Cyclades Islands form an archipelago

Archipelago
Sea levels rise locally as land sinks, or globally as an era of warmer climates melts the polar ice caps and increases the amount of water in the oceans. When this happens, low-lying coastal lands are drowned. A new coastline is formed, fringed with tiny islands that are the summits of former hills and mountains. These island clusters are known as archipelagos.

FIND OUT MORE COASTS · CONTINENTS · CORAL REEFS · EARTH · ISLAND WILDLIFE · OCEAN FLOOR · ROCKS AND MINERALS · VOLCANOES

471

ISLAND WILDLIFE

ISOLATED LOCATIONS and the lack of large predators, competitors, and disease has allowed the evolution of a unique range of wildlife on many islands. Island habitats vary greatly, from the ice and rock of Greenland to the tropical rainforests of Borneo. Island floras and faunas are fragile ecosystems, easily upset by foreign invaders and freak weather conditions. Some islands possess unique species found nowhere else (endemics); other remote islands are inhabited by species from otherwise extinct groups (relics).

Islands

Continental islands, such as Borneo, became separated from larger land masses. Their wildlife is similar to that of the mainland. Oceanic islands, such as Fiji, are more remote and are either coral reefs or volcanic in origin. Their flora and fauna are often very varied. Sulawesi, for example, has wildlife of Asian and Australasian origin, as well as an animal unique to the island – the babirusa.

Colonization

In 1883, a volcanic eruption destroyed all life on the island of Krakatoa. Since then the process of recolonization – the establishment of plants and animals in a new environment – has been studied. Colonizers crossed 40 km (25 miles) of water. First came ferns and algae. Then after 40 years there were forests, 29 bird species, two geckos, one python, one monitor lizard, insects, bats, and rats.

Dense vegetation cover provides homes for many animals.

Mammals

Large carnivorous mammals are found only on large islands that have a large population of prey. Many isolated islands have large herbivorous mammals, that are often unique to that island. Madagascar is home to lemurs, such as the aye-aye, that live nowhere else in the world, and the anoa dwarf cow lives only on Sulawesi. On very remote islands bats are often the only mammals, because they arrived by flying.

Long toe to get bugs out of bark.

Aye-aye

Moorea, French Polynesia

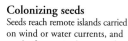

Seeds are spear-shaped and stick in ground where they land.

Red mangrove

Plants

The fertile volcanic soil of oceanic islands provides ideal growing conditions for plants. Some plants, such as coconut palms, are widely distributed around many islands, others are unique to specific islands. For example, the Canaries are home to 500 species of endemic plants, including ancient dragon trees; Madagascar has seven species of baobab tree, whereas the African mainland has only one.

Baobab tree

Coconut

Colonizing seeds

Seeds reach remote islands carried on wind or water currents, and on the feet, or in the guts, of birds. The coconut has a tough outer shell which protects the inner kernel during long ocean journeys. The first plant to become established on oceanic islands is often the red mangrove. Its seeds start to germinate before they drop from the parent plant and are ready to take root where they land.

Giant tortoise

Reptiles

Most reptiles are good swimmers and easily colonize close islands or float on driftwood to more distant ones. Fijian iguanas are related to those in America; their ancestors are believed to have rafted on vegetation across the Pacific. Tuataras live on islands off the New Zealand coast; they resemble lizards, but they are actually relicts from the far distant past. Relicts are ancient animals that survive on isolated islands long after their relatives are extinct elsewhere.

Giants and dwarves

Different conditions on islands compared with the mainland can affect the size of animals. Giant tortoises grow large because of the lack of large predators in the Galápagos Islands. On Chappell Island, near Australia, black tiger snakes also grow larger than normal. They feed on mutton bird chicks that exist for a brief period only. The snakes get big as they eat many chicks at once to build up reserves for the rest of the year. Island dwarves also exist where food or other resources are limited.

Tuatara

Strong legs help when excavating burrows.

Invertebrates

Invertebrates have colonized many islands. They arrived by rafting on vegetation, by flying, or by being carried on the wind. Larger species such as the Pacific robber crab cannot migrate. However, its larvae hatch from eggs laid in the sea and drift on the ocean currents to colonize islands thousands of miles away.

Large claws used to climb palms and sever coconuts.

Robber crab

Birds

Many islands are rich in bird life because flight enables birds to colonize islands easily. Strong fliers, such as frigate birds, are often the first birds to arrive. But with no natural predators, many island birds, such as the New Guinea cassowary, became flightless. Introduced species pose a threat to these birds which lack a means of defence or escape. For example, feral dogs often kill New Zealand kiwis.

Frigate bird

FIND OUT MORE   CONTINENTS   CRABS AND OTHER CRUSTACEANS   FLIGHTLESS BIRDS   FRUITS AND SEEDS   ISLANDS   MONKEYS AND OTHER PRIMATES   PIGS AND PECCARIES   REPTILES

ISRAEL

ISRAEL IS A LONG, NARROW COUNTRY, lying between the River Jordan and the Mediterranean Sea. Although it is a new nation, founded in 1948 as a homeland for the world's Jews, Israel is also a very old country. Previously called Palestine, it was a home for Arabs for about 1,400 years, before which it was a Jewish land for about 1,700 years. Since 1948, Israel has fought several wars with its Arab neighbours. Despite peace talks begun in 1993, relations in Israel are still very tense between Jews and Palestinians with renewed outbursts of war.

ISRAEL FACTS

CAPITAL CITY	Jerusalem
AREA	20,770 sq km (8,019 sq miles)
POPULATION	6,200,000
MAIN LANGUAGES	Hebrew, Arabic
MAJOR RELIGIONS	Jewish, Muslim, Christian
CURRENCY	Shekel
LIFE EXPECTANCY	79 years
PEOPLE PER DOCTOR	256
GOVERNMENT	Multi-party democracy
ADULT LITERACY	96%

Physical features

Israel stretches south through the Negev Desert to Elat on the Red Sea. The green Plain of Sharon runs along the coast, while inland, parallel to the coast, is a range of hills and uplands with fertile valleys to the west and desert to the east.

Negev Desert
In Hebrew, the word Negev means "arid land". Like many other deserts, the Negev is not completely lacking in life. Much of it is covered by scrub; when rain comes, it springs into life with a carpet of wild flowers. Large areas are now being irrigated for farming.

Dead Sea
The Dead Sea lies between Israel and its eastern neighbour, Jordan. It is a vast lake 74 km (46 miles) long and 16 km (10 miles) wide. At 400 m (1,300 ft) below sea-level, it is also the lowest point in the world. It is so salty that nothing can live in it – and even non-swimmers cannot sink. The water contains useful minerals, such as sodium and potassium.

Coast
The Mediterranean coastal plain is nowhere more than 32 km (20 miles) wide. Several rivers flow through the region, fertilizing the soil. It contains fine sandy beaches, popular with holidaymakers. In the north are cliffs with beautiful caves and grottoes.

54°C (129°F)   -13°C (9°F)
23°C (73°F)   9°C (48°F)
528 mm (21 in)

Climate
Israel has hot, dry summers, and mild winters when most of the rain occurs. Rainfall varies from 25 mm (1 in) per year in the southern Negev to 1,088 mm (43 in) in parts of Galilee.

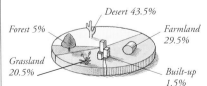

Forest 5%
Desert 43.5%
Farmland 29.5%
Grassland 20.5%
Built-up 1.5%

Land use
Almost half of Israel is desert, but irrigation has enabled large areas to be reclaimed as farmland. The country has valuable mineral resources in the Dead Sea area, and reserves of copper ore and gold.

Jerusalem
Dating back more than 3,000 years, Israel's capital, Jerusalem, is a cultural and religious centre for Jews, Muslims, and Christians. The Western wall of Herod's Temple is sacred to Jews, the Dome of the Rock is a Muslim holy place, and the Church of the Holy Sepulchre marks the site of Jesus's crucifixion. The modern city is home to half a million people.

The Dome of the Rock

People

More than 80 per cent of Israelis live in high-rise apartment blocks. The majority of people are Jewish, but there are about 800,000 Palestinians, who are Muslim. Most Israelis work a six-day week.

Jewish people
Some Jews have always lived in Israel, but the majority moved to the country after World War II (1939–45). Sephardic Jews from the Middle East and the Mediterranean are in the majority, but Ashkenazi Jews, from Central Europe, dominate politics and business. Women enjoy equal opportunities and serve in the army. Orthodox Jews keep the Sabbath, from Friday night to sunset on Saturday.

305 per sq km (790 per sq mile) | **91% Urban** | **9% Rural**

Leisure

Israelis enjoy sports such as football, tennis, basketball, and badminton. On the coast, Israelis swim, surf, sail, and water ski. Aqualung diving is popular in Elat. People like to listen to jazz, rock, and pop music, and attend folk festivals.

Dead Sea mud
Many of the minerals in mud extracted from the Dead Sea have medical properties. Special soaps and creams are sold world-wide to treat skin complaints and arthritis.

Dead Sea mud cosmetics

Jewish festivals
There are many Jewish festivals, when families spend time together. The annual Israel Festival is a three-week cultural extravaganza, including circus and theatre shows.

Farming

Only about 30 per cent of Israel's land can be used for growing crops. Lack of water is a constant problem, and irrigation is a necessity. Most of the crops are grown on the fertile coastal plain, where vineyards and citrus groves are plentiful.

Sprinklers water the crops.

Roses are grown for cut flowers.

Crops
Farming accounts for about five per cent of exports. Almost half of Israel's food is grown on *kibbutzim*, places where several families live and work together, sharing everyday tasks such as cooking and cleaning. Cash crops include citrus fruit, pomegranates, grapes, roses, and carnations.

Irrigation
Israeli farmers rely heavily on efficient irrigation to water their crops, which would otherwise die in the heat. Computerized irrigation has enabled parts of the desert to be cultivated, supporting specialized agriculture.

Pomegranate

Citrus fruits

Food

Kosher food, prepared according to Jewish religious dietary laws, is eaten by Orthodox Jews, but many Israeli restaurants serve a variety of foods including eastern European, Russian, Austrian, and German dishes. *Falafel* is a well-known Israeli food – balls made from chick peas, herbs, and spices, and fried in oil, served with *tahini*, a paste of sesame seeds, and pitta bread.

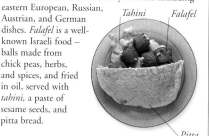

Tahini | *Falafel*

Pitta

Industry

Israel has a diverse manufacturing economy. Tel Aviv-Yafo is the centre of the country's industry, which is concentrated in electronics, engineering, plastics, chemicals, textiles, and food processing. Tourism is growing steadily.

Diamonds
Cutting and polishing diamonds is a major Israeli industry. The uncut stones account for 16 per cent of total imports. Cut stones make up about 22 per cent of exports. The only other major diamond-cutting countries are India and the Netherlands.

Mining
Copper, gypsum, limestone, and a small amount of oil and gas are mined, especially in the Negev. Factories like these around the Dead Sea extract potash, magnesium, and bromine, used for photography, and making dyes and anaesthetics.

Transport

Israel has good road links. Bus services are efficient and the railways are being extended. Freight travels by rail or boat, from the ports of Hefa and Ashdod on the Mediterranean, and Elat in the Gulf of Aqaba. Tel-Aviv-Yafo is the main airport.

Hefa port

Palestinians

In 1948, when Israel was created, many Palestinian Arabs left the country, leading to a conflict between Jews and Palestinians that would last many years. About 800,000 Palestinians remained in Israel. In 1967, Israel occupied the Palestinian territory of the Gaza Strip. Land negotiations continue over Gaza, Jericho, and the West Bank.

Tensions still exist between Jews and Muslims.

FIND OUT MORE | ASIA, HISTORY OF | CHRISTIANITY | CRYSTALS AND GEMS | DESERTS | FARMING | HOLY LAND, HISTORY OF | ISLAM | JUDAISM | ROCKS AND MINERALS

ITALY

BOUNDED BY THE ALPS in the north, the boot-shaped peninsula of mainland Italy stretches about 800 km (500 miles) into the Mediterranean Sea. An agricultural society for centuries, Italy has recently emerged as a leading industrial power. The country's wealth, best farmland, and industry are concentrated in the north. By contrast, the south is arid, and farming and industry are on a smaller scale. Italy also includes the islands of Sicily and Sardinia.

Physical features

Mountains dominate the Italian landscape, from the valleys and lakes of the Alps and Dolomites in the north, to the Apennines that run down the southern peninsula. South of the Alps is the green, fertile valley of the River Po. Italy is prone to earthquakes and has active volcanoes, such as Vesuvius, Stromboli, and Etna.

Apennines
Extending for about 1,400 km (860 miles) from northwest to southwest Italy and across the sea into Sicily, the Apennine mountains form the backbone of the country. The highest point is Mount Corno at 2,914 m (9,560 ft).

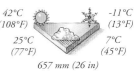

Sicily
The largest island in the Mediterranean Sea, Sicily is mainly mountainous. The highest point is Mount Etna at 3,332 m (10,930 ft), an active volcano, which towers over the town of Catania. Farming and tourism are the main sources of income. Sicily's warm climate, beautiful beaches, and ancient ruins attract increasing numbers of visitors each year.

42°C (108°F)   -11°C (13°F)
25°C (77°F)   7°C (45°F)
657 mm (26 in)

Climate
Southern Italy has hot, dry summers and mild winters. In the north, the summers are cooler, especially in the hills and mountains, and the winters colder and wetter. The Po Valley tends to be foggy in winter, and snow covers the Alps. The Adriatic coast suffers from strong, cold winds, such as the bora.

Barren 1.5%   Farmland 68.5%
Forest 27.5%   Built-up 2.5%

Land use
Most of Italy is cultivated or used as pasture for grazing sheep on grassy mountain slopes. The most fertile area is the broad, flat Po Valley in the north of the country. Italy has very few mineral resources and imports most of its oil products.

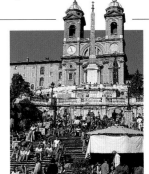

Rome
Founded about 2,500 years ago on seven hills near the River Tiber (Tevere), Rome is one of the finest cities in the world. Tourists flock to enjoy the ancient Roman ruins that sit alongside modern offices, fashionable shops, and Renaissance palaces, all of which are part of daily life for the three million inhabitants. Rome is also the home of Italy's democratic government.

People

Most Italians are Roman Catholics. Italy has few ethnic minorities and few racial tensions, but there is conflict between the wealthy north and poorer south. In the 1950s and 1960s, a weak economy forced many Italians to find work abroad.

195 per sq km (905 per sq mile)   67% Urban   33% Rural

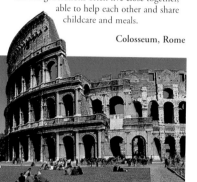

Family life
Most Italians live at home before marriage, and life revolves around the extended family. Several generations often live close together, able to help each other and share childcare and meals.

Colosseum, Rome

Industry

Italy has few natural resources, but its skilled work-force transforms imported raw materials into sophisticated manufactured goods. Major exports include cars, electronic and electrical goods, clothing, shoes, and textiles. Italy is famous for the style and innovation of its product design.

Tourism
Italy's magnificent towns, varied and scenic countryside, ancient Roman ruins, buildings, paintings, and sculptures lure millions of tourists each year. Tourism plays a vital role in the country's economy.

Design
The Italians' flair for design is particularly obvious in their cars and clothes. The fashion houses of Milan, Rome, and Florence rival those of Paris, and designer names such as Benetton, Gucci, and Armani are world famous. Italian clothes and shoes are widely exported.

Shoes made by Gucci

Leisure

Italy's three great passions are football, fast cars, and opera. Italians also enjoy skiing, sailing, and volley-ball. Horse-racing is a popular spectator sport.

Carnevale
Every spring most Italian towns and villages celebrate *carnevale,* a festival in which people dress in bright costumes and wear masks. The most famous *carnevale* is held in Venice.

La passeggiata
In the early evening many Italians like to take a stroll – *passeggiata* – in the square, or *piazza,* or through the streets, talking to friends and stopping for a cup of coffee or a glass of wine. Covered footpaths called colonnades make a stroll possible even if the weather is bad.

Farming

Italy's countryside is dotted with small family-run farms producing a variety of crops, such as cereals, fruit, vegetables, and vines. Italy is a leading producer of olives and olive oil, as well as oranges and lemons.

Grapes
Italy is the world's largest wine producer. Grapes grow everywhere, but the best wine, such as Chianti, comes from the north. Sicily produces Marsala, a dessert wine.

Food and drink

The two traditional Italian foods are pizza, with a variety of toppings, and pasta, a type of dough made with flour and water and served with a sauce, often as a first course. In the north, where rice and maize are grown, people also eat a rice dish called risotto, and polenta, a savoury maize porridge. Meals are eaten with wine or, in the north, beer.

Anchovies · Tomato sauce · Mozzarella cheese · Pizza napoletana

Vatican City State

The Vatican City in the centre of Rome is the world's smallest independent state. It is the world centre of the Roman Catholic religion, and the Pope is the head of state.

St. Peter's Basilica
Over 50,000 people can worship in St. Peter's, which is the largest and most important Christian church in the world.

VATICAN CITY STATE FACTS

CAPITAL CITY	Vatican City
AREA	0.44 sq km (0.17 sq miles)
POPULATION	524
MAIN LANGUAGES	Italian, Latin
MAJOR RELIGION	Christian
CURRENCY	Euro

San Marino

Perched in the northern Apennines, San Marino was founded in the 4th century AD and is the world's oldest republic. Each year San Marino has a famous Grand Prix.

Tourism
San Marino's main source of income comes from the two-and-a-half million tourists who visit the country each year.

SAN MARINO FACTS

CAPITAL CITY	San Marino
AREA	61 sq km (23.6 sq miles)
POPULATION	26,900
MAIN LANGUAGE	Italian
MAJOR RELIGION	Christian
CURRENCY	Euro

Malta

Lying midway between Europe and Africa, the islands of the Maltese archipelago were ruled by foreign powers until independence in 1964. The main income is tourism.

Grand Harbour
Valletta's Grand Harbour is a busy modern port. It developed due to its position on the trade route between Africa and Europe.

MALTA FACTS

CAPITAL CITY	Valletta
AREA	316 sq km (122 sq miles)
POPULATION	392,000
MAIN LANGUAGES	Maltese, English
MAJOR RELIGION	Christian
CURRENCY	Maltese lira

FIND OUT MORE   CHRISTIANITY   DESIGN   EUROPE   EUROPE, HISTORY OF   EUROPEAN UNION   FARMING   FESTIVALS   ITALY, HISTORY OF   ROMAN EMPIRE   VOLCANOES

ITALY, HISTORY OF

ONCE THE CENTRE of the great Roman empire, Italy has been disunited and divided for most of its history. Most of the Italian cities were independent of each other, and foreign powers ruled large parts of the country. Some of the cities, such as Venice, Florence, and Bologna, became powerful in their own right. Because of their wealth, Spanish, German, and French armies fought for control of Italy's great cities for centuries. It was not until 1861 that Italy became a single, united country, free of foreign control. Today, Italy is at the forefront of the European Union.

Cosimo d'Medici

End of the Roman empire

In the 5th century, Germanic tribes overran the Roman empire. Italy was taken over by the Ostrogoths, many of whom soon converted to Christianity and adopted Roman customs.

Mausoleum of Theodoric, Ostrogoth ruler of 6th-century Italy, Ravenna

Italian city states

While other European countries, such as Spain and France, were gradually united during the 14th and 15th centuries, Italy remained a patchwork of small warring states. The south of the country was ruled by Spain, the centre by the Pope in Rome, and the north consisted of various rich republics and monarchies.

Medici family
This family took over the Republic of Florence in 1434 and ruled it for almost 300 years. Florence became one of Europe's richest cities, and the Medici family grew very powerful.

Venice
This coastal city made its wealth from seaborne trade. Its galleys carried much of the eastern Mediterranean trade, while its merchants traded as far afield as China.

Ruler's palace, Venice

United Italy

In 1860–61, the previously disunited states of Italy came together to form a united country under King Victor Emmanuel II of Piedmont. In 1866, the Austrians were thrown out of Venice, and in 1870 the Pope lost control of his lands around Rome. For the first time in centuries, Italy was free of foreign control.

Cavour
Count Cavour (1810–61), prime minister of Piedmont from 1852, was a strong believer in Italian unification. Through clever diplomacy, he overcame all the potential enemies of unification, and proclaimed a united Italy in March 1861.

Unification of Italy map labels: Piedmont, Venetia, Tuscany, Rome, Papal States, Sardinia, Kingdom of the Two Sicilies. Legend: Sardinia / United 1860 / United 1870

Garibaldi

In May 1860, the Italian patriot Giuseppe Garibaldi (1807–82) sailed from Genoa with 1,000 volunteer soldiers called red shirts. His plan was to overthrow the kingdom of Naples and Sicily, and to unite it with the rest of Italy. He then tried to invade Rome, but was prevented from entering the city. He is remembered as one of the founders of modern Italy.

Modern Italy

In 1946, Italy voted to become a republic. Despite frequent changes in government and a weak political leadership, Italy has become one of the leading industrial powers in Europe. The country is a world leader in fashion and design, producing a range of high-quality goods from household items to sports cars. In 1957, Italy helped establish the European Economic Community – now known as the European Union – by organizing the Treaty of Rome. Italy remains a prominent member of the Union.

Ferrari sports car

Fascism

In 1922, Benito Mussolini became prime minister of Italy. He was leader of the Fascist Party, an anti-socialist group believing in strong government and national pride. The Fascists encouraged the arts, but led Italy unprepared into World War II.

The Flight of the Swallows by Giacomo Balla

Timeline

410 Visigoths under their leader Alaric destroy Rome.

476 Invading Goths depose the last Roman emperor.

1271 Merchant Marco Polo leaves Venice for China.

Towers of Bologna

1434 Medicis rule Florence and employ Renaissance artists.

1494–1559 France and Spain fight for control of Italy.

1796 Napoleon Bonaparte invades Italy.

1852 Count Cavour becomes prime minister of Piedmont.

1860–61 Italy united under the leadership of Piedmont.

1870 Rome joins the rest of Italy and becomes the capital.

1914–18 Italy fights with Allies in World War I.

Benito Mussolini, 1883–1945

1922 Mussolini takes power.

1940 Italy sides with Germany in World War II.

1943 Italy surrenders.

1945 Mussolini is executed.

1957 Italy becomes founder member of European Union.

FIND OUT MORE

EUROPE, HISTORY OF · EUROPEAN UNION · GOVERNMENTS AND POLITICS · HOLY ROMAN EMPIRE · MEDIEVAL EUROPE · RENAISSANCE · ROMAN EMPIRE · WORLD WAR I · WORLD WAR II

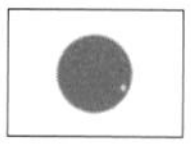

JAPAN

FOUR PRINCIPAL ISLANDS, Hokkaido, Honshu, Kyushu, and Shikoku, and more than 3,000 smaller ones off the east coast of Asia make up Japan. They stretch about 1,900 km (1,200 miles) into the Pacific Ocean and its "ring of fire" where the Earth's plates collide, making the country vulnerable to earthquakes and erupting volcanoes. Most Japanese live on Honshu, the largest island, and enjoy high living standards. Japan's booming economy is a global phenomenon, and its future lies in new technology for the 21st century.

JAPAN FACTS

CAPITAL CITY Tokyo

AREA 377,835 sq km
(145,882 sq miles)

POPULATION 127,300,000

MAIN LANGUAGE Japanese

MAJOR RELIGIONS Shinto, Buddhist

CURRENCY Yen

LIFE EXPECTANCY 81 years

PEOPLE PER DOCTOR 526

GOVERNMENT Multi-party democracy

ADULT LITERACY 99%

Physical features

Japan's main islands are mountainous, and about 90 per cent of the land is covered in forest. There are 26,505 km (16,566 miles) of coastline, breaking into fertile plains inland. On Honshu, the volcanic Japanese Alps separate the snowy west coast from the warmer east.

Ryukyu Islands
Okinawa forms part of the Ryukyu chain of over 100 islands. Their coral reefs and beaches attract many visitors, and more than one million people have settled in the area.

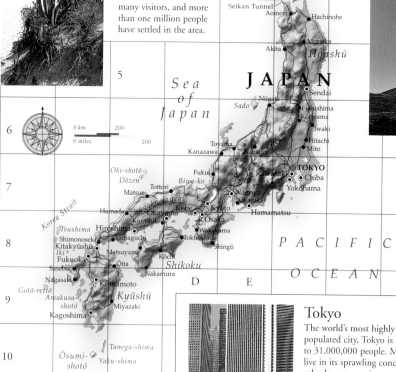

Hokkaido
Japan's second largest island, at 78,485 sq km (30,303 sq miles), Hokkaido is a rural, forested area where wild bears roam. Winters are long and snowy. Only about five per cent of Japanese people live on this northerly island, including the Ainu, who were the first people to settle in Japan. Fewer than 20,000 survive today, keeping their own culture, language, and religion.

Mount Fuji
Known as Fuji-san in Japan, Mount Fuji is the country's highest peak at 3,776 m (12,388 ft). Located near the Pacific coast of central Honshu, the perfectly symmetrical volcanic cone can be seen from a great distance. Mount Fuji is regarded as a sacred symbol of Japan, and thousands of pilgrims climb up to its crater every year.

Climate
Japan's climate varies from north to south. Hokkaido is covered in snow for four months of the year, while the southern islands enjoy a tropical climate. Honshu has humid summers and cold winters with snow; Kyushu and Shikoku have long, hot summers and mild winters. Rainfall is high.

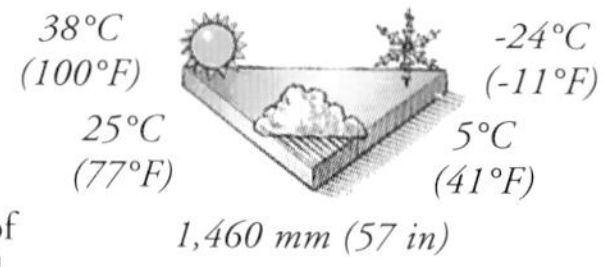

38°C (100°F) 25°C (77°F) −24°C (−11°F) 5°C (41°F) 1,460 mm (57 in)

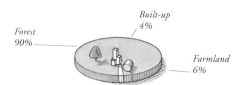

Forest 90% Built-up 4% Farmland 6%

Land use
Flat land for growing crops or raising livestock is scarce in Japan. Forested mountains cover some of Hokkaido, but more than half of Japan's cereals are grown on the island's fertile plains. Lack of space has required buildings to be built very close together, especially in cities.

Tokyo
The world's most highly populated city, Tokyo is home to 31,000,000 people. Most live in its sprawling concrete suburbs, commuting to the crowded centre on the extensive train networks. All Japan's major companies have headquarters in Marunouchi, the central state-of-the-art district that leads the world in business and banking. Here, shiny modern office blocks stand side by side.

Tokyo's skyscrapers

People

Ethnic Japanese make up 99 per cent of the population. More than three-quarters of the people live in overcrowded urban areas. Most families are wealthy in terms of consumer goods. Japan has a low birth rate, and around one fifth of its population is elderly.

337 per sq km (872 per sq mile)   79% Urban   21% Rural

Children
Japanese children have long school days that include a half-day on Saturdays and sometimes extra evening classes. They are expected to work hard and respect their elders. Young people are cherished and have a special Children's Day.

Leisure

The Japanese spend many hours at work but are encouraged to relax. There are many traditional activities and festivals throughout the year, including colourful religious street processions, the tea ceremony, and spring blossom-picking.

Sports
People enjoy traditional Japanese sports, such as karate and judo. Baseball is the most popular player and spectator sport, and work stops during the All Japan Schools tournament. Business executives often play golf or tennis.

Bonsai
The Japanese love nature and many are skilled in the art of bonsai, growing miniature trees. Junipers, pines, and maples are grown to 60 cm (2 ft) tall and survive for years.

Farming

The average Japanese farm is just 1.2 hectares (3.3 acres), but Japan grows much of what it needs to support its large population. Half the farmland is devoted to rice cultivation. Sheep graze on mountain slopes.

Tuna fish

Fishing
Japan has one of the world's largest fishing fleets and its annual fish catch accounts for 15 per cent of the global total. About 15,000 people work at Tokyo's fish auction, where restaurateurs use sign language to bid for over 100 varieties. Fish are processed on board ship.

Rice
Despite the shortage of arable land, Japan ranks highly in world rice production, with 13,225,000 tonnes (14,578,000 tons) each year. Fertilizers and modern machinery help farmers grow good-quality rice and use every piece of land. Most paddies lie in the south.

Food

Rice and fish form the basis of most Japanese cooking. On average, each person eats 30 kg (66 lb) of fish a year. People use chopsticks to eat their meals, which are attractively presented on black lacquer dishes with attention to colour and detail. Raw fish, called *sashimi*, is eaten with vinegared rice, called *sushi*.

Chopsticks

Rice

Marinated raw fish

Transport

Trains and planes are the main means of transport in Japan. Crowded streets, expensive road tolls, and lack of parking hamper the use of cars in the cities. Bicycles are popular for short journeys.

Industry

Japan has become an industrial giant, over the past 50 years, manufacturing high-quality goods ranging from huge oil tankers to tiny electronic components. Traditional industries, such as coal-mining, steel, and fine arts, are profitable, but their importance has decreased with the success of the export-led economy.

Work ethic
The Japanese have a long working week, and much time is spent entertaining clients after work. Very often, people are employed by the same company for all their working lives. In return, employers look after their staff, providing housing and healthcare. Most workplaces begin the day with physical exercise and loyalty declarations.

Bullet Train
Travelling at speeds of 210 kmh (130 mph) or more, Japan's *Shinkansen*, or "Bullet Train", is one of the world's fastest trains. The rail network covers the entire country, and tunnels and bridges link the country's main islands, providing access to remote areas.

Electronics
Japan is a world leader in the production of high-tech electronic consumer goods, such as personal stereos, televisions, computers, cameras, and computer games machines. More than 50 per cent of the world's robots are made in Japan.

Motor industry
Cars, motorcycles, and lorries are Japan's largest exports. Toyota, Nissan, and Honda are household names throughout the world. Japan is the leading motorcycle manufacturer.

Honda motorcycle has a top speed of 190 kmh (120 mph).

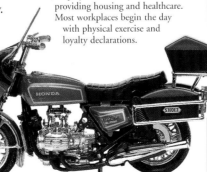

Air traffic
Japan's air route between Tokyo and Chitose, on Hokkaido, is one of the busiest in the world. Tokyo has two large airports. Environmental protests delayed the opening of Narita City airport, 66 km (41 miles) north of the capital, for 20 years. It finally opened in 1978.

FIND OUT MORE   AIRPORTS   BALL GAMES   CARS AND TRUCKS   EARTHQUAKES   ELECTRONICS   FARMING   FISHING INDUSTRY   JAPAN, HISTORY OF   MOUNTAINS AND VALLEYS   TRAINS AND RAILWAYS

JAPAN, HISTORY OF

THE ISLAND NATION OF JAPAN has a long history of imperial rule, which began in the 4th century when many small kingdoms unified. In the 6th century, Japanese emperors adopted the Chinese imperial system of government. However, their rule weakened until, in the 12th century, warrior leaders, called shoguns, seized power and made the emperors mere figureheads. In 1868, the patriotic samurai abolished the shogunate and reinstated the imperial family. Over the next 50 years Japan opened up to western influences. It modernized, expanded, and was then all but destroyed in World War II. However, Japan has recovered to become an economic superpower.

Ainu people
The Ainu are racially different from Japanese, who over centuries forced them to the northern island of Hokkaido. Most now live by fishing and farming.

Chinese influence

China influenced the history of Japan. By the 7th century, Japanese society had adopted Buddhism, Chinese script, Confucianism, a new calendar, a new legal system, and many architectural and artistic techniques from T'ang China.

Nara
Japanese emperors built their first capital at Nara (Heijo-kyo), and based its design on the Chinese capital, Chang'an. As Japan's religious and political centre from 710 to 794, Nara had splendid architecture, particularly visible today in its Buddhist temples.

Great Buddha, Todaiji, Nara

Kyoto

In 794, Kyoto (Heian-Kyo) replaced Nara as Japan's capital. Japan was moving away from Chinese influences, and Kyoto became the centre of purely Japanese artistic and cultural developments. Kyoto declined as a political and cultural force in 1185 when the rule of the shoguns (military dictators) began. From 1338, the Ashikaga shoguns based their court there and revived Kyoto as a cultural centre. Their elegant temples and villas survive today.

Court culture
Kyoto's court was a place of artistic merit. Courtiers excelled at poetry-writing and painting. One noblewoman, Murasaki Shikibu, wrote *The Tale of Genji* (11th century), one of the world's first novels.

Prince Genji visiting ladies

Kiyomizu Temple
(meaning pure water) was built close to mountain streams.

Kondo, or main hall

Stilted platform commands a view over the city.

Kiyomizu Temple, established in 798

Tokugawa period
In this period (1603–1868), centuries of civil unrest ended. The Tokugawa shoguns made strict laws that ensured peace. Swords became less functional and more lavishly decorated. In 1641, the shogun closed Japan to the outside world to prevent foreign influences destabilizing the country.

Tokugawa-period court sword

Warrior centuries

By 1300 the weak Ashikaga shogunate was losing control over the provinces. The fall of Kamakura was followed by anarchy in the late 1400s to 1603, which was known as the Era of the Nation at War. During the unrest, the missionary, St Francis Xavier (1506–52), arrived in Japan, and converted 100,000 Japanese to Christianity. Fearful of a takeover, Toyotomi Hideyoshi (1536–98) expelled all missionaries, and in 1596 he ordered the crucifixion of 26 Christians.

Civil war
In the Era of the Nation at War, feudal lords seized control of vast tracts of land. In the late 1500s, the first of Japan's three greatest military leaders – Oda Nobunaga (1534–82) – restored order. Oda was followed by his general, Hideyoshi, who reunified Japan. Tokugawa Ieyasu (1542–1616), who followed Hideyoshi, founded the dynasty that was to last into the modern age.

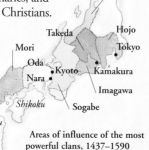

Hokkaido

Honshu

Uesugi

Takeda   Hojo

Mori
Oda   Tokyo
Nara   Kyoto   Kamakura

Imagawa
Shikoku   Sogabe

Kyushu

Areas of influence of the most powerful clans, 1437–1590

Japanese art

As Chinese influence waned, Japanese art developed a unique style. In the Momoyama period (1573–1616), artists preferred extravagant displays of craftwork and colour. Subject matter included court life, the seasons, and the military.

Decorated 17th-century fan

Lacquerware
China and India developed the art of lacquer. From China, lacquering travelled to Korea, and thence to Japan. Once in Japan, lacquer artists invented a stunning lacquering technique using gold powder.

Dragon design

Lacquer screen

Commodore Perry's expedition, 1853

Meiji Restoration

In 1853, Commodore Perry of the US Navy sailed into Tokyo Bay. Western powers then forced the shogun to open up the country. In 1868, afraid of Japan's loss of independence, rebel samurai defeated the shogun's army, restored Emperor Meiji as the figurehead of a new government, and moved the capital to Tokyo.

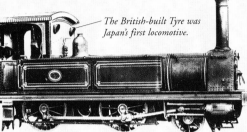
The British-built Tyre was Japan's first locomotive.

Industry
After 1868, Japan experienced rapid industrialization. The Meiji government developed modern industries, such as shipbuilding. The building of new railways was particularly important – they unified Japan and helped trade and industry grow.

Tyre locomotive, 1870

Expansion

Japan competed with China and Russia to gain territory. This rivalry led to the Sino-Japanese war (1894–95) and the Russo-Japanese war (1904–5). Japan won both conflicts, and gradually expanded into China and the Pacific area.

Russian warship   Japanese torpedo boat

Battle of Tsushima, 1905

China and Russia wars
After their speedy victory over China, Japan took over Taiwan as a colony. Ten years later, after the Japanese victory over the Russians at Tsushima, Japan gained recognition as a world power, and took control of valuable Russian ports in Manchuria (China). In 1911 Japan finally annexed Korea.

J

World War II

By the spring of 1942, Japan had conquered Malaya, Thailand, Burma, Hong Kong, the Philippines, the Dutch East Indies, and parts of China. But by 1945, Japan was losing ground, and suicide missions flew against American ships in a desperate attempt to avoid defeat. Japan surrendered after the atomic bombing of Hiroshima and Nagasaki.

Kamikaze means "Divine Wind".

Hiroshima
On 6 August 1945, an American B-29 plane dropped an atomic bomb on Hiroshima. About 200,000 people died, either outright or from the bomb's effects. Three days later a second atomic bomb destroyed most of Nagasaki and killed an estimated 140,000 people.

Hiroshima, August 1945

Kamikaze, or suicide pilots

Pollution
Industrial development brought problems. During the 1960s, air, water, and soil pollution caused deaths and painful illnesses. Firms responsible were forced to pay compensation to victims, and new laws improved the environment. Nuclear waste is still transported worldwide by Japanese ships.

Waste carrier *Akatsu Maru* leaving for Europe

Modern Japan

Japan's industry suffered during World War II, but since 1945 it has made a remarkable recovery and developed new products and markets. Car manufacturing has expanded, and high-tech consumer goods are exported worldwide.

Wealth and leisure
As Japan has become wealthier, leisure industries have expanded rapidly. By 1989, leisure accounted for 28.8 per cent of private spending. Sports – including golf, aerobics, skiing, and baseball – have become increasingly popular, as have cultural activities, such as concerts. Travel is now common, and more Japanese visit foreign countries than ever before.

Golf driving range

Economic prosperity
The Japanese economy grew so rapidly in the 1950s and 1960s that people often spoke of an economic miracle. This "miracle" was, in fact, produced by good industrial relations, high education levels, and the development and use of modern equipment.

Datsun 240 Z

Hand-held computer plugs into mobile phone to access Internet.

Mobile Internet

Timeline

Emperor Hirohito

Hirohito (r.1926–1989), known since his death as the Showa ("enlightened peace") emperor, ruled through World War II and in the years of rapid change afterwards. His reign was turbulent and his political power was limited, but Hirohito helped to unite the nation during years of war and peace.

FIND OUT MORE

ARCHITECTURE   ASIA, HISTORY OF   KUBLAI KHAN   SAMURAI AND SHOGUNS   WORLD WAR II

JAZZ

JAZZ IS ONE OF THE GREATEST, most exciting musical developments of the 20th century. It began in the southern United States, where musicians blended elements from ragtime, blues, and spirituals with West African rhythms. Its earliest form, Dixieland, was played by small groups; by the 1930s, big bands were playing rearranged orchestrations called swing. Later developments marked a return to smaller groups of players, and experiments in combining jazz with classical and rock music.

Minstrel shows were part of the early New Orleans music scene.

New Orleans
Jazz had its roots in New Orleans, USA, during the 1900s. It was first performed by black musicians, but because of racism it became widely popular only when played by white musicians, when it spread to cities such as Chicago, Kansas, and New York. Riverboats, which carried bands for entertainment, and the development of commercial sound recording, helped spread jazz.

Modern jazz quartet

Jazz band
The main features of jazz are strong rhythm, improvised melodies, and syncopation. It can be played by single performers or by large bands or orchestras. Small groups of musicians are common: three, four, or five players, usually but not always including a rhythm section (drums, bass, and/or piano), and a trumpet, saxophone, or singer as the lead.

Improvisation
Jazz players improvise, or vary, melodies so that each performance sounds different, though based on the same musical structure.

Syncopation
Rhythm is a key part of jazz music – players may shift the beat of a melody unexpectedly (a technique called syncopation) and use the beat as the driving force of the music.

The roots of jazz
Jazz developed from a combination of many musical styles. An important element was the African traditions that slaves took to America and kept alive in their work songs, such as strong rhythm and melodies that singers could vary with each performance. Slaves who converted to Christianity mixed Christian songs with their own harmonies. Ragtime and the blues were also key elements.

Scott Joplin

Ragtime
In about 1900 ragtime music sprang up in New Orleans, St. Louis, and Memphis, USA. It was played on the piano, with a steady bass beat and a syncopated melody. The best known composer was Scott Joplin (1868–1917).

Blues musician, 1902

Blues
Black musicians invented the blues, a mournful, mainly vocal style. Most early musicians knew hundreds of songs, which they accompanied on the banjo, guitar, or mouth organ.

Types of jazz
There are many varieties of jazz, including boogie-woogie, swing, bebop (a fast style, with interesting harmonies), and cool, a more relaxed style typified by the trumpeter Miles Davis (1926–91). Jazz has also influenced classical composers and rock and pop musicians, who use blues harmonies in their work.

High-kicking move

Swing
Big bands appeared in the 1920s. Their leaders, such as "Duke" Ellington (1899–1974), composed, arranged, and wrote down their music, which was known as swing. Tightly syncopated rhythms gave swing a typically bouncy character.

Free jazz
In the 1960s saxophonist John Coltrane (1926–67) broke away from the conventions of jazz, and formed a quartet to explore new sounds and techniques. For example, he experimented with ways to achieve harmonic richness.

John Coltrane

Jazz dance is sometimes fast and showy.

Jazz dancer

Jazz dance
Exuberant dance styles go hand-in-hand with the rhythms and lively melodies of much jazz music, especially swing or bebop. Jazz dance moves have influenced other modern dance forms.

Ella Fitzgerald
American Ella Fitzgerald (1918–96) was one of the all-time great jazz singers. She was celebrated for her rich, deep voice and the elegant, relaxed style with which she sang with big bands. She was also a great "scat" singer – a style in which the vocalist improvises meaningless words to a tune.

FIND OUT MORE

DANCE   MUSIC   MUSICAL INSTRUMENTS   ROCK AND POP   SLAVERY

JELLYFISH, SEA ANEMONES AND SPONGES

THESE PRIMITIVE ANIMALS have lived in the oceans for more than 550 million years. They are all invertebrates – animals without backbones. Jellyfish and sea anemones belong to a group of animals called the Coelenterata, which also includes corals. Most have tentacles and poison-loaded stinging cells, which they use to kill their prey. Sponges belong to a group of animals called the Porifera. They live in all waters from the ocean depths to shallow freshwaters. There are soft sponges, such as natural bath sponges, and hard ones with silica skeletons.

Translucent dome, or bell, of jellyfish

Thick tentacles

Mouth lies below centre of bell.

Tentacle of Portuguese man-of-war releases stinging cells.

Upside-down mangrove jellyfish

Stinging tentacles
Jellyfish tentacles contain special cells. Each cell has a projecting hair and contains a coiled poisonous thread, called a nematocyst. If an animal touches the hair, this triggers the explosive release of the nematocyst, so injecting the prey with paralysing toxins. Other types of nematocyst release sticky threads or coil around prey.

Jellyfish
Two cell layers separated by firm jelly-like material make up the body of a jellyfish. The body is dome-shaped, like a delicate gelatinous umbrella, and is called a medusa. Its beauty, however, is deceptive; an array of trailing tentacles hides a battery of stinging cells that can capture and immobilize prey. The tentacles feed the prey through the mouth into the digestive cavity.

Life-cycle of a jellyfish
Common larger jellyfish produce both sperm and eggs. The eggs are fertilized in the female medusa. These turn into larvae that escape and settle on rocks. Each larva turns into a polyp that multiplies by producing a stack of smaller polyps. One by one the polyps separate into new free-swimming medusae.

Polyps break away to form new medusae.

Polyp multiplies to form a stack of small saucer-shaped polyps.

Polyp of jellyfish

Movement
A jellyfish swims by lifting the sides of its bell to suck up water below. Then, by contracting the bell, water is squirted backwards, which pushes the jellyfish forwards. If the bell stops opening and closing, the jellyfish will sink.

Jellyfish with bell contracted

Moon jellyfish

Sponge
Sponges are among the most simple multi-celled animals known. They are like vase-shaped sieves, with porous body walls, supported by a "skeleton" of hard minerals or protein fibres. Water enters the sponge through the body wall and passes out through a central opening.

Central opening

Tube sponge

Feeding
Most sponges are filter feeders. Their cells have projections that beat and draw water through their body walls. Special cells lining the walls filter out small food particles suspended in the water.

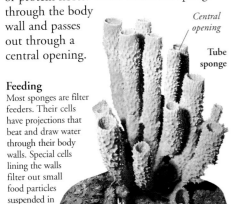

Sponge releasing sperm

Reproduction
A sponge reproduces sexually by sperm from other sponges entering its body in water currents to fertilize its eggs. These turn into larvae, settle on rocks, and grow into new sponges. Asexual reproduction involves growth and budding.

Sea anemone
Sea anemones have soft bodies consisting of a stout, muscular column ending in a basal disc. The disc produces a sticky cement-like substance that secures the anemone to the seabed or rock. Stinging tentacles form a circle around a central mouth, that opens into the digestive cavity. The sea anemone uses its tentacles for defence and to catch prey. Although often beautiful in colour and shape, some anemones are aggressive predators and even cannibals. They escape attack by floating, burrowing, or taking off from the seabed.

Basal disc

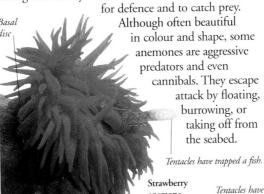

Tentacles have trapped a fish.

Strawberry anemone

Body column

Tentacles have pulled fish inside to be eaten.

Feeding
Sea anemone tentacles are armed with stinging cells that fire on contact to paralyse their prey. Even small fish are caught and pushed through the mouth into the stomach. Inside, enveloped by sheets of tissue that release enzymes, the flesh of the prey is broken down and digested by cells lining the stomach.

Symbiosis
Sea anemones have a range of mutually beneficial, or symbiotic, relationships with other animals. Clown fish are covered in mucus for protection against the tentacles of anemones in which they hide. The anemones in turn, are protected by the fish. Cloak anemones hitch a ride on the shell of a snail, occupied by a hermit crab. The anemone protects the crab in exchange for food.

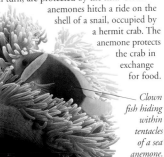

Clown fish hiding within tentacles of a sea anemone.

MANGROVE JELLYFISH

SCIENTIFIC NAME	*Cassiopeia sp.*
PHYLUM	Coelenterata
CLASS	Scyphozoa
ORDER	Rhizostomeae
DISTRIBUTION	Marine Caribbean
HABITAT	Shallow, tropical mangrove bays
DIET	Small organisms
SIZE	Length: up to 30 cm (12 in)
LIFESPAN	Several years

FIND OUT MORE

ANIMALS　　CORAL REEFS　　FISH　　MARSH AND SWAMP WILDLIFE　　OCEAN WILDLIFE　　POISONOUS ANIMALS　　SEASHORE WILDLIFE

JESUS CHRIST

J

IN ABOUT AD 30, a young Jewish man began to preach in Palestine that he was the son of God, the Messiah, or anointed one, that the Jews had been expecting. Many people accepted his message and his following grew rapidly. The Jewish authorities resented his work, and he was arrested and crucified by the Roman governor of Palestine in about AD 33. Within a century, his message had spread throughout Asia Minor and into Europe, becoming tolerated throughout the mighty Roman Empire in 313. Today, Christianity, the religion he founded, is one of the world's great religious faiths.

Early life
Jesus was born in Bethlehem in what is now the Israeli-occupied West Bank. He trained as a carpenter. The Bible says that his mother, Mary, was a virgin when she gave birth. In his early 30s, he gave up work and devoted his time to preaching and healing.

Jesus' work
For three years, Jesus preached his message in Palestine. He gathered 12 local men to support him; they became known as the Apostles, from a Greek word meaning a person sent or chosen. Jesus declared the need for people to repent of their sins and to believe and follow him. Within three years, his preaching, and his ability to heal the sick, brought him a considerable following throughout Palestine. His wider group of followers became known as disciples.

Apostles
The 12 apostles of Jesus were local men who did ordinary jobs, such as fishing and farming.

Miracles
According to the Bible, Jesus used miracles to prove that he could conquer adversity and suffering. On one famous occasion, he is said to have provided enough food for a gathering of 5,000 people, although only a few loaves and fishes were available.

Five loaves and two fishes were all that Jesus had to feed the five thousand.

Parables
In order to get his message understood, Jesus often used parables, or stories with a meaning. One of the most famous was the parable of the sower, in which Jesus compared his words to the seeds cast by a man sowing corn. Some seed falls on stony ground and withers away; some falls on good soil, where it flourishes.

Seed was sowed by throwing it on to the land.

Sower's bag and seed

John the Baptist
At the time of Jesus' birth, many Jews, including John the Baptist, Jesus' cousin, were expecting the coming of the Messiah. John prepared the way for Jesus, prophesying his coming and baptizing him in the River Jordan.

Sermon on the Mount
Throughout his ministry, Jesus preached sermons to his disciples and the many people who followed him. The most famous was the Sermon on the Mount, in which Jesus summed up the main beliefs of the Christian religion and told his followers how people should lead their lives.

Mary Magdalene
Mary was one of the most famous of Christ's followers. Jesus cured her of "demons" (probably a physical illness), and she accompanied him and helped him in Galilee. Mary witnessed Christ's crucifixion and burial. Three days later, Christ appeared to Mary, and told her that he was ascending to heaven.

Death
After three years preaching, Jesus was arrested by the Roman authorities who governed Palestine at that time. He was tried by the Roman governor Pontius Pilate, tortured, and crucified.

Last Supper
Just before he was arrested, Jesus ate supper with his disciples. He broke bread and drank wine with them, asking them to remember him and to continue his work. Christians still celebrate the Last Supper in the ceremony of the Mass, or Eucharist, when they share bread and wine, believing it to represent Jesus' body and blood.

Crucifixion
Jesus was put to death by crucifixion – being nailed to a wooden cross – a common form of punishment in the Roman Empire. His followers believe that three days later he rose from the dead.

JESUS CHRIST
- **c.4 BC** Born to poor parents in Bethlehem.
- **c.AD 30** Begins ministry, preaching and healing the sick.
- **33** Arrested, tried, and crucified by Roman authorities in Jerusalem.
- **33** St Paul and other followers of Jesus begin to spread the Christian message; Christians are persecuted in the Roman Empire.
- **65–75** St Mark writes his Gospel, the earliest surviving record of the life of Jesus.
- **313** Christianity receives official tolerance in the Roman Empire.

 FIND OUT MORE   CHRISTIANITY   CHURCHES AND CATHEDRALS   MONASTERIES   RELIGIONS   ROMAN EMPIRE

JOHNSON, AMY

ONE OF THE GREAT pioneers of aviation, Amy Johnson showed that women could succeed in a man's world. When she learned to fly in June 1929, Amy Johnson became one of the world's first women pilots. Her flying instructor said she would only be taken seriously as a pilot if she did something remarkable, like fly to Australia. And so, in April 1930, she took off on a 19-day flight half-way round the world. In spite of bad weather, breakdowns, and crash landings, she arrived in Australia. She also landed in the record books: for this and other flights she is remembered as one of the great aviators.

Early life
Amy Johnson was born in 1903 in the English port of Hull, where her parents worked in the fishing industry. She went to university and then took a secretarial course. But she did not want one of the office jobs that were open to women in the 1920s.

Learning to fly
Johnson overcame a great deal of prejudice to learn to fly. Flying was a male occupation and there were few flying clubs that accepted women. But she persevered, and first flew solo in June 1929. At the end of the year, she had gained an aeronautical engineer's licence.

Flight to Australia
Amy Johnson covered the 16,000 km from London to Australia in 19 days, landing in Darwin on 24 April 1930. On the way she coped with jungle landings, sandstorms, and damage to the aircraft.

Equipment
As a solo pilot, Johnson had to take equipment to cover every eventuality. She took a flying suit and helmet, but wore khaki shorts for most of the flight. To defend herself, she took a gun. Her first-aid kit doubled as a repair kit for the aircraft!

Protective goggles

Amy Johnson's flying helmet

Chin strap

Amy Johnson's flying suit

The route
Johnson's plan was to avoid flying over open sea, where her chances of survival would be much less if she crashed. She therefore flew southeast over mainland Europe and Asia before turning south to fly down the Malay peninsula and hop from island to island along Indonesia. The final stretch of the flight was the most hazardous, because it involved flying across the exposed Timor Sea.

Gypsy Moth
The aeroplane Johnson chose for her flight was a second-hand Gypsy Moth, one of the most popular small aircraft of the day. She had it fitted with extra-large fuel tanks for long-distance flying. Its canvas wings got damaged en route and she mended them with sticking plaster.

Overnight bag containing first-aid and repair equipment

Landing at Darwin
When Johnson took off from London's Croydon Airport she was unknown. As her flight progressed, newspapers and radio began to report on her epic flight. By the time she climbed down from her plane in Darwin, she was an international heroine.

Later life
The great flight made Amy Johnson world-famous. The British *Daily Mail* newspaper gave her £10,000 to go on a publicity tour, and she made many speeches and media appearances around the world. Songs were written about her and her amazing flight. However, Johnson found all this publicity very strenuous and suffered a nervous breakdown as a result.

Marriage
Johnson married a fellow pilot, James Mollison, and this seemed an ideal match. They made several long-distance flights together. But the couple were not suited. Their marriage soon broke up and Johnson went back to her solo flying career.

Disappearance
In 1940, Amy Johnson began work flying planes from factories in Scotland to air force bases in the south of England. In January 1941, a plane she was piloting from Prestwick, near Glasgow, crashed into the Thames Estuary. Her body was never found.

AMY JOHNSON
1903 Born in Hull, England.

1929 Learns to fly at the London Aeroplane Club; makes first solo flight and gains engineer's licence.

1930 First woman to fly solo from England to Australia.

1933 Flies east to west across the Atlantic with James Mollison.

1936 Sets new record on return flight from Cape Town to London.

1940 Joins war effort, piloting planes from factories to air force bases.

1941 Dies when plane crashes in Thames Estuary.

FIND OUT **MORE** **AIRCRAFT** **AIRPORTS** **EXPLORATION** **FLIGHT, HISTORY OF** **WOMEN'S MOVEMENT** **WORLD WAR II**

JUDAISM

THE FIRST OF THE GREAT WORLD RELIGIONS to teach belief in one God, Judaism emerged in about the 13th century BC. Its followers are called Jews. At the core of Judaism is the Torah, the sacred text that God, or Yahweh, revealed to the prophet Moses and the ancient Israelites. Because they were chosen to receive this revelation, the Jews look upon themselves as God's chosen people, with the responsibility of bringing God's message to the rest of humanity. Jews also look forward to the time when God will send his Messiah, who will usher in an age when all Jews will be united in Israel and God's rule on Earth will begin.

Branches of Judaism
Orthodox Jews follow closely the traditional Jewish way of life. They include groups such as Hasidic Jews (above), who wear traditional clothes and study only religious subjects. Non-Orthodox, or Progressive, Jews have become part of wider society and adopted western dress, while still observing Jewish law.

Origins
The ancient leaders Abraham, Isaac, and Jacob were the first to worship one true God, and are the founding fathers of Judaism. The Bible tells how their descendants, the Israelites, were conquered by the Egyptians and made to work as slaves in Egypt. Moses led the Israelites to freedom, and received the Torah, or written law, from God.

The Ten Commandments
On Mount Sinai, God gave Moses the Ten Commandments. This is celebrated today in the festival of Shavuot (Pentecost), when the story of Moses is read in the synagogue and Jews stay up at night reading the Torah, to show they are ready to receive the word of God again.

Jews around the world
Today, there are some 14.5 million Jews worldwide. Most can trace their ancestry to one of two main ethnic groups. Ashkenazi Jews have their origin in central and eastern Europe. Their traditional everyday language is Yiddish. The majority of Jews in the USA are Ashkenazi Jews. The other group is the Sephardic Jews, who came originally from Spain and Portugal.

Jerusalem, the capital of Israel, was the centre of the ancient Jewish kingdom.

Shading shows worldwide distribution of Jews. Judaism is the sixth largest world religion.

Israel
The Jews have a long history of living in many different countries and suffering persecution. In 1948, the modern state of Israel was established as a permanent homeland. Supporters of Israel, who are known as Zionists, hoped that Jews would be able to live and worship there peacefully.

Sacred texts
The Jewish Bible is called the Tenakh. It contains 24 books, written by different authors, which were collected together in the 10th century. The first five books make up the Torah. There are also books of the Prophets and texts such as the Psalms and the Proverbs. A body of writing containing teachings, commentaries on the Bible, and learned debates is called the Talmud.

The ark of the covenant
The Torah scrolls are kept in the ark of the covenant. This is a cabinet that sits behind a curtain in the synagogue wall that faces towards Jerusalem. The original ark of the covenant held the Ten Commandments while the people of Israel journeyed from Egypt towards the Promised Land.

Embroidered mantle

The crown symbolizes the Torah as the crowning glory of Jewish life.

Handles support the Torah scroll because it is too sacred to touch.

The lion is a Jewish symbol associated with the tribe of Judah.

The scrolls of the Torah

A ribbon binds the scrolls.

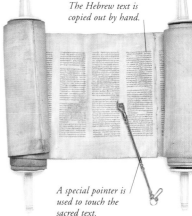

The Hebrew text is copied out by hand.

A special pointer is used to touch the sacred text.

The Torah
This collection of books is at the core of Judaism. It contains a series of 613 commandments which are God's instructions to the people of Israel. For religious Jews, these instructions are binding. The Torah scrolls are kept covered by an embroidered mantle or in a rigid container.

Guidance of God
In the Torah, God has revealed teaching about himself, his purposes, and how he wishes his people to obey him in every part of their lives. An important part of worship is reading the Torah aloud in the synagogue. At Simchat Torah, the yearly cycle of readings from the Torah comes to an end and is begun again.

Holy days and festivals

The Jewish year begins in autumn with the New Year Festival. Ten days later comes the Day of Atonement, or Yom Kippur. This is the most solemn event in the Jewish calendar; Jews spend the day praying, fasting, and seeking God's forgiveness. Other festivals occur during the year. Many commemorate events in Jewish history, such as the Israelites' escape from Egypt, the giving of the Ten Commandments to Moses, and the destruction of the first and second temples in Jerusalem.

Pesach

The spring festival of Passover, or Pesach, commemorates the time when the Jews left their captivity in Egypt and returned to Israel. Jews believe that God punished the Egyptians by killing their firstborn sons, but he passed over the houses of the Israelites. This gives its name to Passover; on that day Jews eat a ritual meal called Seder.

Lettuce for the food eaten in slavery.

Egg symbolizes new life

Seder plate

Shankbone of lamb recalls lambs killed at the first Passover.

"Pesach" is the Hebrew word for Passover.

Herbs represent spring

Nut and fruit paste

Bitter horseradish represents the misery of slavery.

Jews drink salt water to remind them of the tears of slavery.

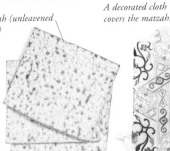

Matzah (unleavened bread)

A decorated cloth covers the matzah.

Succoth

The harvest festival of Succoth commemorates the way God provided for the Jews as they wandered in the wilderness on their way to the Promised Land. Jews weave palm leaves into a lulav and may build festive huts to symbolize the tents that gave them shelter. Work is restricted and the festival ends with a time of joy called Rejoicing of the Torah, or Simchat Torah.

Lulav made of woven palm leaves

At Succoth, a lulav and an etrog are carried around the temple seven times.

A citrus fruit called an etrog is a symbol of the heart.

Hanukkah

The festival of lights, Hanukkah is an eight-day long midwinter festival that is marked by the lighting of candles. It celebrates the rededication of the temple of Jerusalem after it was recaptured from an enemy army in 164 BC. Like several other festivals in the Jewish religious year, Hanukkah reminds Jews of God's faithfulness to his people in the past.

Daily life

The home and the family are important in Judaism, and there are many rules to guide behaviour. For Orthodox Jews in particular, these rules affect every aspect of daily life, from getting up in the morning, when the hands are ritually washed, to going to bed at night, when benedictions are said. Other rules concern food and dress.

Menorah, nine-branched candlestick

On Friday, the woman of the household lights the Sabbath candles.

Kosher food

Jews must eat food that is kosher, or fit to eat. Animals that do not have cloven hoofs and chew the cud are forbidden, as are birds of prey and sea creatures without fins and scales. Animals that Jews eat must have been slaughtered according to specific rules.

Sabbath

The weekly day of rest – from dusk on Friday to after dark on Saturday – commemorates the way God rested after the creation. On the Sabbath, Jews dress in their best clothes, and do not cook, work, or use transport. They light the Sabbath candles and attend the synagogue.

Worship

The synagogue is the place for community prayers, readings from the Torah, and for learning about the faith. On weekdays there are prayers for morning, afternoon, and evening; on the Sabbath and on festivals there are longer services. When a Jewish boy reaches 13, a ceremony in the synagogue called Bar Mitzvah marks his coming of age.

Jewish men wear skull caps at prayer.

A tefillin contains prayers.

Rabbis

Rabbis were originally teachers and they devoted themselves to studying the Torah. Today, rabbis play a leading role in worship and take spiritual care of their community, like the leaders of other religious faiths.

Anti-semitism

For centuries, the Jews existed without their own state and were often treated as second-class citizens. In some cities, Jews were forced to live in cramped areas known as ghettos. Pogroms – organized campaigns of persecution or killing – are a feature of Jewish history. The worst example is the Holocaust.

A mob assaults a Jew in front of soldiers in Russia, 1881.

KANGAROOS AND OTHER MARSUPIALS

K

IN AUSTRALIA, NEW GUINEA, and the Americas, there is a group of mammals that is not found anywhere else in the world. These are the 266 species of marsupials, or pouched mammals. Marsupials include the familiar kangaroos and koala, as well as numbats, bandicoots, wombats, possums, and wallabies from Australia, and the American opossums. In contrast to other mammals, marsupial young undergo little development in their mother's uterus before being born. Instead, female marsupials have a marsupium, or pouch, into which the young crawl and complete their development.

Ears swivel to hear sounds in all directions.

Strong tail aids balance when leaping and standing.

Red kangaroo

Claws

Reproduction

Marsupials differ from other mammals in the way they reproduce. After a male and female mate, the fertilized egg develops in the female's uterus for about 30 days. The young is then born, but is tiny at birth; for example, a red kangaroo weighing about 27 kg (60 lb) gives birth to a single young weighing just 800 mg (0.03 oz). The newborn has a mouth and well-developed forelimbs, but is otherwise like an embryo. It continues to develop in its mother's pouch for 6–11 months, feeding on her milk.

Red kangaroo

The red kangaroo is the largest of all marsupials. Males are reddish-brown in colour, and may be twice the size of females, which are bluish-grey. They have powerful back legs and long feet adapted for hopping. Like many other marsupials red kangaroos are largely nocturnal, resting by day under the shade of trees, but they are also active on cooler winter days. They graze mainly on grass, but also feed on the foliage of low-growing shrubs, by leaning forwards on their forelimbs and balancing on their tail.

Mob of eastern grey kangaroos feeding

Mobs

Red and grey kangaroos, and wallabies, live in groups called mobs. A mob is a social grouping of 10 or more individuals, including a mature male, a few younger males, females, and their young. Sometimes, a larger mob containing hundreds of kangaroos may form at a good feeding site.

Females can be pregnant, with a joey in the pouch and one out, at the same time.

Eastern grey kangaroo with joey

Boxing

Within a mob a male kangaroo may gain control over one or more females so he can mate with them. Sometimes other males challenge for access to these females. The competing males stand upright on their hind legs and link forearms in an attempt to push each other to the ground. If this does not resolve the battle for supremacy, they box, hitting each other violently with their forepaws, and kicking out with their hind feet, until one of them submits.

Thick stomach skin prevents excessive damage during boxing.

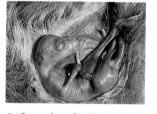

Life-cycle of a kangaroo

1 After birth, the blind, naked kangaroo struggles through the fur on its mother's abdomen to reach her pouch, and attach itself to her teat.

2 The baby kangaroo, or joey, is now about five months old. No longer attached to the teat, the joey can stick its head out of the pouch, but still depends on its mother for milk.

3 After a year, the joey will have left the pouch and be feeding mainly on vegetation. It still occasionally sticks its head in the pouch to suckle, and some joeys return to the pouch if threatened.

Leaps and bounds

Kangaroos and small wallabies move in a distinctive manner, using their powerful hind legs and large feet like springs, to hop from one feeding area to another. The long tail helps them balance. A kangaroo covers 1–2 m (3–6 ft) with each leap when moving slowly; this increases to 9 m (30 ft) when travelling at high speed. Kangaroos are incapable of moving their back legs separately so cannot walk.

Kangaroos may travel at speeds of up 50 kmh (31 mph) when leaping.

Kangaroo pushes off ground with large back feet.

Tail is raised to act as a counterbalance when leaping.

Back legs are extended forwards ready to touch down.

Eastern grey kangaroo hopping

Doria's tree kangaroo

Curved claws

Tree kangaroo

Close relatives of kangaroos and wallabies, tree kangaroos live in the tropical forests of NE Australia and New Guinea. They have long, strong forelegs, shortened hind feet, and a long tail. They are good climbers, using their claws to grip and tail to balance. They feed on leaves and fruit, and can travel rapidly from tree to tree in search of food.

Tasmanian devils

The largest carnivorous marsupial, the Tasmanian devil resembles a stocky terrier-sized dog. It is found only on the island of Tasmania, off the coast of Australia. It was probably given the name "devil" because of the eerie whine it makes. The Tasmanian devil shelters by day in wombat holes or hollow logs, coming out at night to hunt for food. It catches prey such as snakes, lizards, and small mammals, but most of its diet consists of carrion.

Keen sense of smell is used to hunt for food.

Powerful jaws and sharp teeth are used to eat meat, fur, skin, and bones.

Koalas

Koalas live in the tops of trees in eucalyptus woods in eastern Australia. They feed, breed, and sleep in the trees, rarely descending to the ground. They spend up to 18 hours each day resting and sleeping in the forks of trees, apparently to save energy. Koalas have an opposable thumb and toe that help them to grip tree trunks. They climb by grasping the trunk with their sharp front claws, bringing up their back legs in a series of jumps. Females have a single young that leaves its mother's pouch after seven months.

Eucalyptus leaves provide all the food and water that a koala needs, so it rarely has to drink.

Young are carried on mother's back for a few months after they leave the pouch.

Virginia opossum

Opossums are American marsupials that live mainly in South and Central America. The cat-sized Virginia opossum is the largest of the 75 species, and is the only one in North America. It has litters of 10 or more young, up to three times a year in warmer regions. When threatened, the Virginia opossum pretends to be dead ("playing possum") in order to avoid attack.

They forage in trees and on the ground for fruit, insects, eggs, and small vertebrates.

A prehensile tail and grasping hands and feet enable them to climb well.

Numbat

The numbat lives in the forests of western Australia; it is the only Australian marsupial fully active in the day. It feeds on ants and termites, turning over old logs in search of their nests. The numbat rips open the nest with its front legs, and extracts the insects with its long, sticky tongue.

It uses its long snout and foreclaws to root around in the soil for food.

Long-nosed bandicoot

Mostly rabbit-sized or smaller, bandicoots are very active, night-time foragers that move in a galloping fashion. Like other bandicoots, the long-nosed bandicoot uses its strong, clawed forelegs to dig for insects, other invertebrates, seeds, fungi, and juicy plant roots in the soil. Bandicoots breed throughout the year. Females have a litter of 2–5 young, which develop in their mother's pouch for about 50 days.

Feeding

Koalas have a very specialized diet, eating the leaves of only 12 out of 100 species of eucalyptus tree. An adult koala eats about 1.1 kg (2.5 lb) of leaves each day, and can store them in its cheek pouches. Koalas are adapted to extract the most out of the leaves, which are not very nutritious, by having a very long intestine in which the leaves can be fully digested.

Common wombats

Common wombats are shy, burrowing marsupials from southeast Australia. They emerge from their burrows at night, covering up to 3 km (2 miles) in search of roots, grasses, and fungi. Wombats lead a solitary life except when they mate. Females give birth to a single young, which stays in the pouch for six months. The pouch opens at the rear to prevent it filling with earth as the wombat burrows.

Burrows are rarely shared, but often form part of a large network.

Wombats have sharp, strong incisors, for gnawing through tough vegetation.

Burrows

Wombats are rapid, powerful diggers. They use their strong front legs and large claws to dig networks of burrows up to 30 m (100 ft) in length. By resting in their burrows during the day, wombats keep cool in summer and warm in winter. They sometimes emerge to sunbathe in small hollows that they scrape out near the burrow.

RED KANGAROO

SCIENTIFIC NAME *Macropus rufus*

ORDER Marsupialia

FAMILY Macropodidae

DISTRIBUTION Throughout inland Australia, excluding the extreme north, extreme southwest, and east coast

HABITAT Dry grassland and scrub, often near dense vegetation that can provide shelter; semi-desert regions

DIET Grasses and other short plants

SIZE Males: height, up to 2 m (6 ft 6 in); weight 82 kg (180 lb)

LIFESPAN 12–18 years

FIND OUT MORE | ANIMALS | AUSTRALIAN WILDLIFE | GRASSLAND WILDLIFE | MAMMALS | NESTS AND BURROWS | NOCTURNAL ANIMALS | RAINFOREST WILDLIFE

KHMER EMPIRE

ONE OF THE MOST important civilizations in Southeast Asia, the Khmer Empire was ruled from the 9th to the 15th centuries by god-like kings. They glorified themselves and their people by their magnificent building projects. Angkor, the royal capital of the Khmers, was founded in 802 by Jayavarman II. People flocked to the city from all over the region. In the 12th century, Angkor's masterpiece, Angkor Wat, was built. Shortly afterwards both city and temple were sacked by the Chams, but they were rebuilt by Jayavarman VII within 50 years.

Extent of the empire

Angkor, the capital of Khmer culture, was in present-day Cambodia. At the peak of its power, the empire stretched from the South China Sea to the Gulf of Siam (modern Thailand), and included all of what is today Cambodia, eastern Thailand, Vietnam, and Laos.

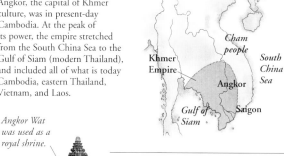

Angkor Wat was used as a royal shrine.

The five towers represent Mount Meru – the home of the Hindu gods.

Grassy areas were once moats.

Outer walls represented mountains at edge of the world.

Religion

Most Khmer kings were Hindu, therefore many of Angkor Wat's sculptures are monuments to Hindu gods. Some of the kings were actually thought to be god-kings. The Hindu Suryavarman II believed himself to be an incarnation of the Hindu god Vishnu, while his Buddhist son, Jayavarman VII, believed himself to be a reincarnation of the Buddha.

Buddhist head, Angkor Thom

Elephants

The Khmers, believing that elephants had great religious significance, captured them and trained them for war service and parades. One famous regiment included around 200,000 elephants.

Angkor Wat

Angkor Wat is the greatest Khmer temple and was the largest religious building in the world for centuries. Built of stone – materials reserved for the gods – it took about 50,000 workers just over 40 years to complete in the reign of Suryavarman II (1113–50). Legend has it that the temple was not built by humans but by the Hindu god Indra, who came to Earth to create it. Reliefs include scenes of Hindu gods, the Khmer people at war, and royal processions.

Elephants support the Khmer infantry.

Bayon

Historical events, life at court, and parades are carved around the walls of the Bayon, the last great Khmer temple built at Angkor. Suryavarman II's son, Jayavarman VII, built the Bayon in c.1200 to commemorate a resounding victory over the neighbouring Cham people, who had destroyed Angkor in 1177.

Farming and foodstuffs

The Khmers' success was due to their agricultural sophistication. An advanced system was needed to support the large populations within the temple-palaces. Engineers built networks of channels, which – apart from containing fish – also irrigated rice fields and fruit trees in the dry season, so they produced abundant harvests. Because of this, the empire became the richest in Southeast Asia.

Rice

Mango

Carp

Decline

The neighbouring Siamese (Thai) people attacked Angkor in 1431. This, combined with the cost of maintaining the monuments, led to the great city's decline, and Angkor was abandoned shortly afterwards. Over centuries, jungle vegetation covered the temple, and Angkor became known as the "Lost Capital". In 1861, it was rediscovered by French naturalist Henri Mouhot.

Temples were carved with dancers, animals, and birds.

Engraving of the central tower, Angkor Wat, 1875

Jayavarman VII

The heroic Jayavarman (1181–1219) was leader of the Khmers. After the destruction of Angkor by the Cham people, Jayavarman led a successful counter-attack, and encouraged his people to rebuild Angkor. During his long life he constructed a new temple, the Bayon, to commemorate his triumphs. The massive stone faces carved on the outside walls of the temples represent Jayavarman and are also meant to resemble the Buddha. Jayavarman changed the state religion from Hinduism to Buddhism.

FIND OUT MORE   ARCHITECTURE   ASIA, HISTORY OF   BUDDHISM   HINDUISM   FARMING, HISTORY OF

KING, MARTIN LUTHER

IN THE LONG FIGHT of black Americans for equal rights, one man stands out for his great commitment to racial equality. Martin Luther King was a Baptist Church minister whose Christian faith informed all his work. He believed in non-violent protest as a way of obtaining change, and led many sit-ins, marches, and voter registration campaigns. King was an inspired speaker, whose words gave hope to millions. His assassination in 1968 dashed many of those hopes.

Early life

Martin Luther King Jr was born in Atlanta, Georgia, in the southern USA, on 15 January 1929. King's father was a prominent Baptist minister, inspiring his son to follow him into the church to study theology. King received his doctorate of theology in 1955.

Little Rock
In 1957, the governor of Arkansas refused to admit nine black children to the all-white Little Rock Central High School. President Eisenhower sent 1,000 paratroopers and 10,000 national guardsmen to protect the children as they went to school.

Civil rights movement

Black Americans were given equal rights under the US Constitution, but were still treated as second-class citizens in many southern states. Local state laws denied black Americans the right to vote or go to multiracial schools. Black and white people were segregated (kept apart) and even had to sit in different seats on buses. Black protests led to a growing civil rights movement in the 1950s and 1960s. King emerged as the charismatic leader of this movement.

Bus boycott
On 1 December 1955, Rosa Parks, a black woman, refused to give up her seat on a bus to a white man in Montgomery, Alabama, and was arrested for violating the city's segregation law. Black residents, led by King and Rev Ralph Abernathy, encouraged a boycott of the city's buses that led to their desegregation.

Sit-ins
A favoured tactic of civil rights campaigners was to stage sit-in demonstrations in segregated restaurants and other public places. In 1960 King was arrested at a segregated lunch counter in an Atlanta department store. He was sent to prison, and was only released after the intervention of the Democratic presidential candidate, John F. Kennedy.

"I have a dream"
On 28 August 1963, King led the historic March on Washington to demand civil rights reform. More than 200,000 marchers heard his words: "I have a dream that one day this nation will rise up and live out the true meaning of its creed: 'We hold these truths to be self-evident, that all men are created equal'".

Birmingham Jail
King went to jail many times for his beliefs. During a period in jail in Birmingham, Alabama, in Spring 1963, he wrote an eloquent letter outlining his philosophy of non-violent protest. He was inspired in this policy by the Indian leader Mohandas K. Gandhi's non-violence campaign against British rule in India, the movement known as satyagraha (devotion to truth).

Malcolm X
Many black people disagreed with King's aim of full integration of black and white, preferring to aim for black separatism. Their leader was Malcolm X, who was a member of the Black Muslim movement led by Elijah Muhammad. He later converted to orthodox Islam, and took up the cause of racial unity. He was assassinated in February 1965.

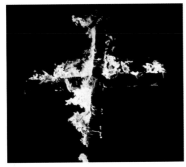

Freedom rides
In 1961, black and white civil rights protesters defied state segregation laws by travelling together on segregated buses. The government sent in national guardsmen to protect the riders. This led to increased racial tension and activity by the racist Ku Klux Klan, who carried flaming crosses in marches in southern USA.

Assassination
The last years of King's life were marked by increasing disputes with more radical black leaders who disagreed with his non-violent approach. In April 1968, he visited Memphis, Tennessee to offer support to striking city sanitation workers; he was assassinated at the motel where he was staying on 4 April. Protest riots broke out in most major US cities.

MARTIN LUTHER KING

1929	Born in Atlanta, Georgia.
1951	Receives Bachelor of Divinity degree.
1954	Becomes pastor of Baptist Church in Montgomery, Alabama.
1960	President of the Southern Christian Leadership Conference; sent to prison for his part in a sit-in in Atlanta.
1963	Spells out his doctrine of non-violent protest; leads march on Washington.
1964	Awarded Nobel Peace Prize.
1968	Assassinated in Memphis, Tennessee.

FIND OUT MORE   HUMAN RIGHTS   SLAVERY   SOCIETIES, HUMAN   UNITED STATES, HISTORY OF

KINGFISHERS AND HORNBILLS

THE KINGFISHER FAMILY includes some of the world's most brightly coloured birds. Many kingfishers feed on fish, but forest kingfishers, which include the kookaburra, live in dry places and eat insects, snakes, and even small birds. Kingfishers hunt by watching for small animals from a convenient perch, or by hovering over water until they see food, then diving down to catch it. Hornbills are bigger and more powerful than kingfishers. Some feed entirely in the treetops on fruit, but others spend a lot of time on the ground, feeding on anything edible they can find.

Belted kingfisher
This is one of the only two species of kingfisher that live in North America. It makes a loud rattling call often when it is flying. It breeds as far north as Alaska, and winters further south, some birds as far south as Panama.

Kingfishers

There are about 90 species of kingfisher. A few live in Europe and the Americas, but they are most common in Africa, Asia, and Australia. Kingfishers are fast fliers, and they are often seen speeding low over the water from one perch to another. All kingfishers nest in holes. Those that live near water peck burrows in riverbanks, while forest kingfishers nest in tree-holes.

The kingfisher carries its prey to a perch and strikes it on a branch before swallowing it.

The kingfisher uses its wings to flap its way out of the water.

Clear membrane covers the eyes underwater.

Sharp-edged beak holds slippery prey.

Grooves in the face give good forward vision.

Water runs off the kingfisher's waterproof plumage.

Kookaburra
This Australian bird is the world's largest kingfisher. It is more than 40 cm (16 in) long from beak to tail. It lives in forests and scrub, and is famous for its loud call, which sounds like crazy laughter.

Fishing
About two-thirds of kingfishers, including this common kingfisher, live near water and feed on fish and other water animals. They catch their food by diving straight in, or by hovering and then making an attack. Once they have caught something in their beak, they carry the prey to a perch or to their burrow.

Protecting the young
Hornbills nest in tree cavities, and they protect their young in a remarkable way. When the female is about to lay her eggs, she enters the nest and the male makes a mud wall to seal her in. He passes food through a small hole in the wall.

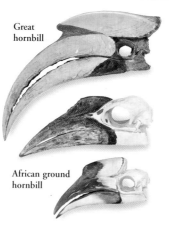

Great hornbill

African ground hornbill

White-billed pied hornbill

Hornbill beaks
A hornbill's beak is not as heavy as it looks because it contains lots of air spaces that reduce its weight. The shield, or casque, above it is also hollow. The main function of the casque is probably as an ornament during courtship.

Hard shield, or casque, covers the top of the beak.

Partly joined front toes

Trumpeter hornbill
This medium-sized hornbill lives in southern Africa. Like most other hornbills, it has a long tail, strong feet, and a patch of bare skin around its eyes. It also has a loud call that sounds like a mixture between a crying baby and a badly tuned trumpet.

Long, rounded tail with banded feathers.

Hornbills

There are nearly 50 species of hornbill, and the largest are more than 1.2 m (4 ft) long. These birds get their name from their huge downcurved beaks. They live in the forests of Africa and Asia. When they fly, their wings make a loud whooshing sound, which can be heard a long way away.

COMMON KINGFISHER

SCIENTIFIC NAME	*Alcedo atthis*
ORDER	Coraciiformes
FAMILY	Alcedinidae
DISTRIBUTION	Europe, North Africa, Asia, and Indonesia
HABITAT	Rivers, streams, canals, and drainage ditches
DIET	Small fish
SIZE	Length: 16 cm (6.5 in)
LIFESPAN	About 5 years

FIND OUT MORE · AUSTRALIAN WILDLIFE · ANIMAL BEHAVIOUR · BIRDS · NESTS AND BURROWS · SEABIRDS · WOODPECKERS AND TOUCANS

KITES

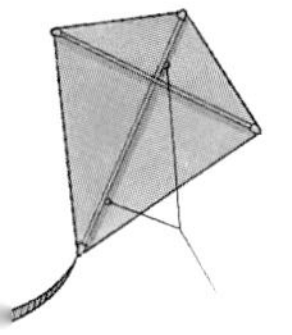

THE FIRST FLYING MACHINE was a kite, flown about 3,000 years before people took to the air. A basic kite consists of a frame and covering material. Launched and held in the air by the upward push of the wind currents on its underside, a kite is controlled from the ground by a flying line. Kites have had many uses: the Chinese used them to estimate the position of the enemy in war; in 1752, American scientist Benjamin Franklin hung metal from a kite to prove the electrical nature of lightning. Today, kite flying is both a popular pastime and a competitive sport.

History of kite flying

The Chinese were flying kites long before the first recorded reference to a wooden bird kite, in 500 BC. Gradually, kites became popular in other Asian countries, such as India, where often they had religious significance. By the time kite flying spread to Medieval Europe, the Chinese were building kites big enough to carry people into the air.

An 18th-century Indian painting of kite flying

Types of kites

There are several basic kite shapes, but for each shape there are hundreds of different designs. Most kites can be made cheaply from sticks and paper. Some need a tail to help them fly in a stable position, but tails, ribbons, and colour are used mostly for decoration.

Flat kites
Simple, flat kites are the oldest design. They are made from a framework of thin sticks tied together, covered with paper or fabric.

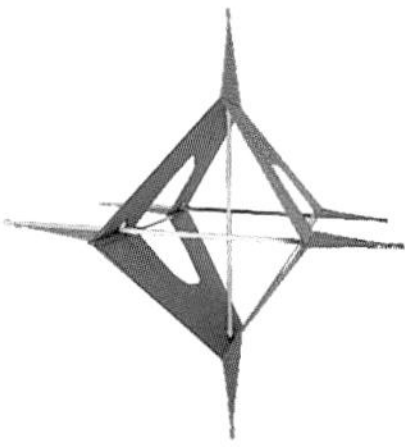

Box kites
Made of a frame containing squares or triangles of paper or fabric, box kites are stable fliers. They have been used to carry weather forecasting instruments.

Delta kites
The wings of a delta are supported by spars or rods. The wingspan makes it fast and easy to manoeuvre, ideal for stunt or fighter kites.

Aerofoil kites
Made of fabric, an aerofoil kite is inflated by the wind, giving it shape. Wing-shaped inflatable kites have a different name – parafoils.

Stunt kites
Stunt kites are used for displays. They can be flown singly or stacked together on the same flying lines to create a spectacular kite train.

Making kites

Kites can be simple structures made from paper and sticks. They are frequently more complex, made from silk or other light materials. Bright colourful designs are often used to adorn kites.

How to fly a kite

Before launching a kite, search for an open space where there is an even breeze, preferably a gently sloping hillside where the wind blows upward. Avoid buildings and trees (which disturb the wind), roads, electricity pylons, and cables. Attach a flying line to the kite, then launch the kite as shown here.

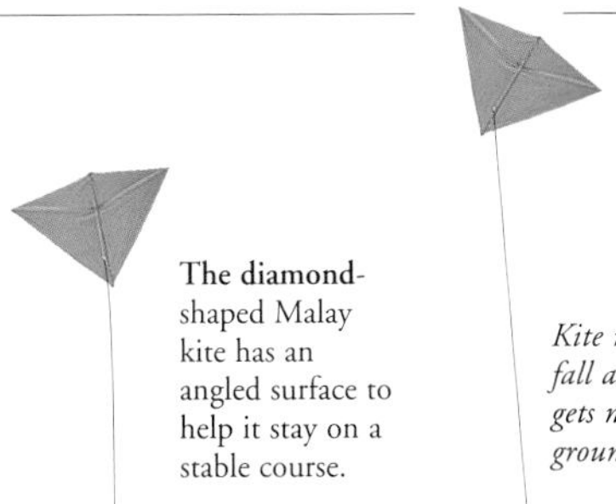

The diamond-shaped Malay kite has an angled surface to help it stay on a stable course.

Kite may fall as it gets near ground.

Equipment

In addition to the actual kite, you need a flying line and a reel to store it on. Flying lines must be strong enough to hold the kite, but light enough to let it fly, such as nylon fishing line. Reels can be simple, or handle shaped to make them easier to hold. Stunt kites require strong hand grips.

Reel

Hand grip

Handle

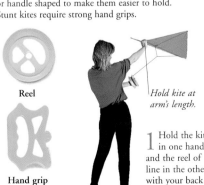

In light winds give gentle tugs on the line.

Hold kite at arm's length.

Twist reel to let line out.

Hold reel sideways to pay out line quickly.

Pull in line with free hand.

Keep reel upright.

1 Hold the kite in one hand and the reel of line in the other, with your back to the wind.

2 As the kite catches the wind, release it. Gradually allow out more line to let the kite rise.

3 If the kite veers left or right, let out more line to stabilize it. Add a tail to a very unstable kite.

4 Retrieve the kite by winding in the line. In stronger winds, walk towards the kite.

Kite festivals

In many Asian countries kite festivals are popular. There is also a serious competitive sport in which fighting kites compete for air space.

FIND OUT MORE • AIR • ELECTRICITY • FESTIVALS • FLIGHT, ANIMAL • FLIGHT, HISTORY OF • FRANKLIN, BENJAMIN • WINDS

K

Kites
Traditional kites

Thai Pakpao is made from paper and bamboo.

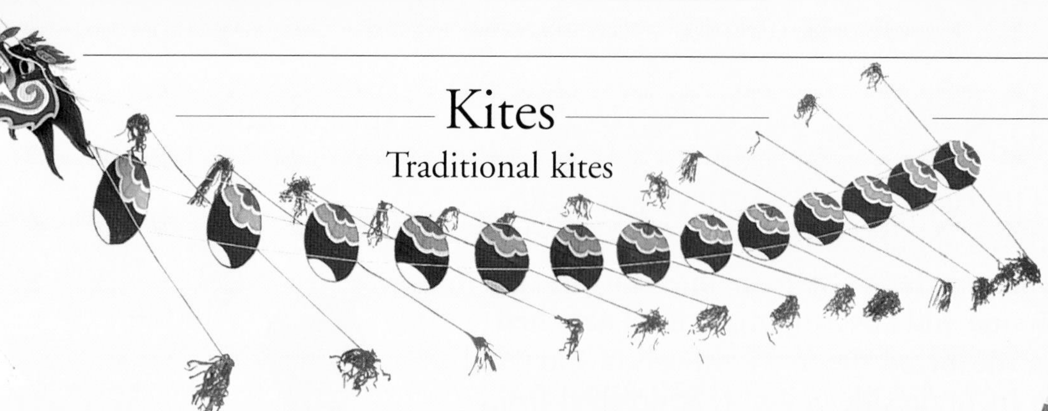

Chinese centipede is a traditional Chinese kite, consisting of circular kites, joined together in a train led by a dragon's head.

Japanese Edo has a classic Japanese design.

Simple kites

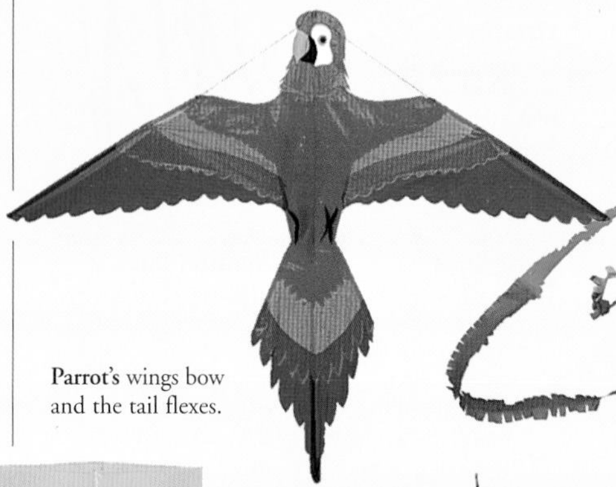

Parrot's wings bow and the tail flexes.

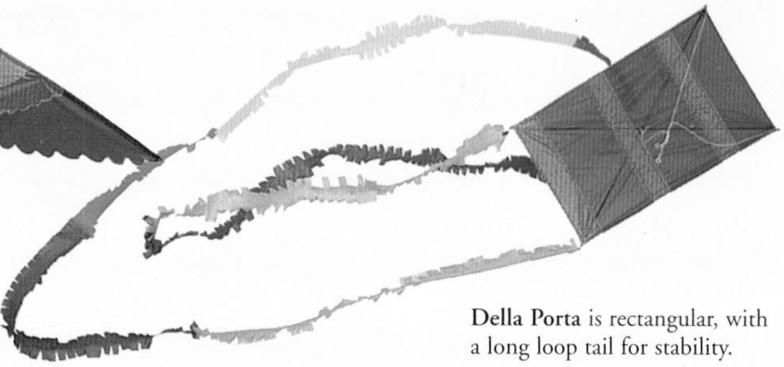

Della Porta is rectangular, with a long loop tail for stability.

Cat is a variation on the hexagonal-shaped kite.

Box kites

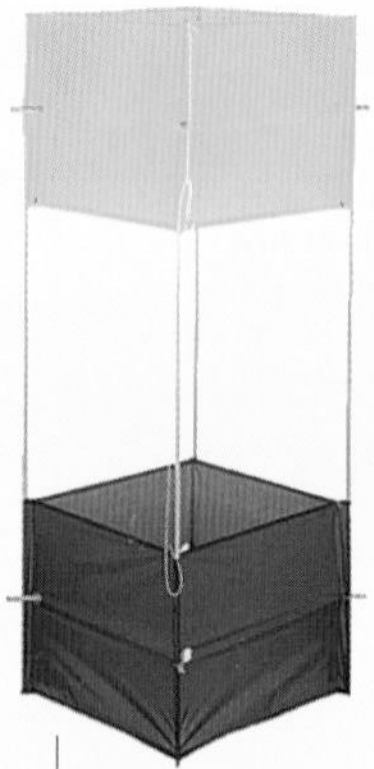

Classic box kite is made up of two square cells.

Professor Waldorf is an early multi-cellular kite.

Nova lacks the stability of a two-celled box, but manoeuvres well.

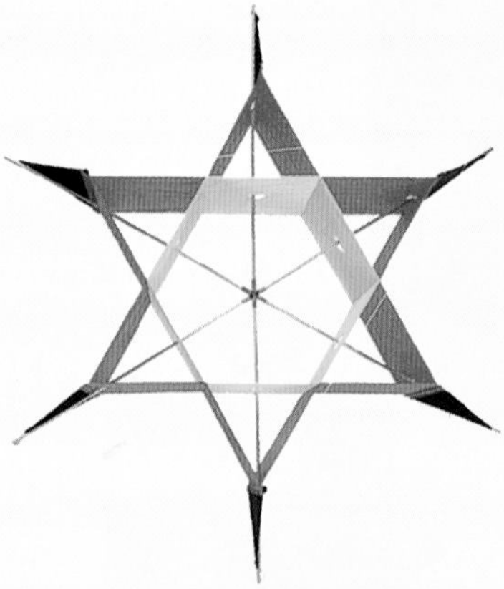

Star is a two-celled structure, supported by three spars.

Single-celled kite

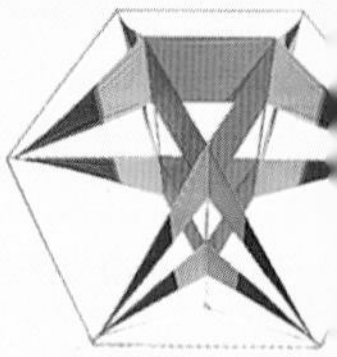

Tri-star has two triangular sections.

Fighters and stunt kites

Grandmaster is a modern version of the traditional Indian fighter.

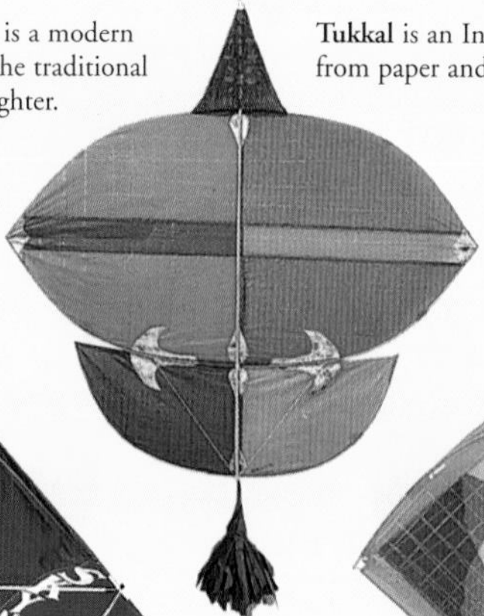

Tukkal is an Indian fighter, made from paper and bamboo.

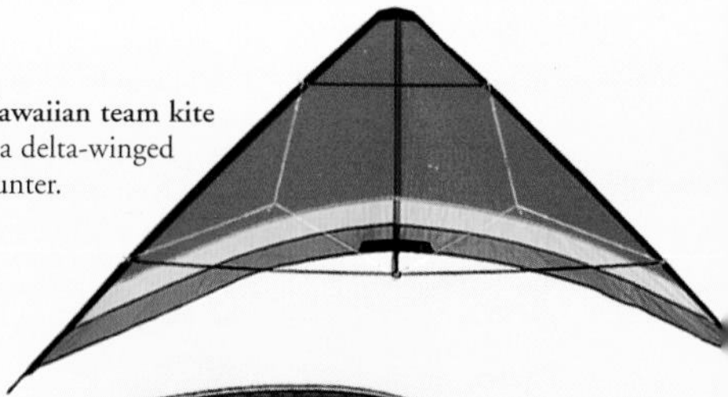

Hawaiian team kite is a delta-winged stunter.

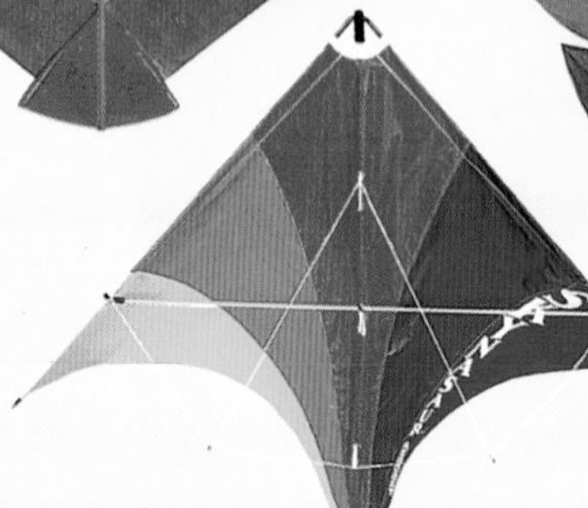

Bamboo spine held in place by gold foil.

Skynasaur aerobat flies in a range of winds without turning fast.

Traditional Indian fighter has appliquéd coloured tissue paper.

Flexifoil uses the wind to give it shape during flight.

KNIGHTS AND HERALDRY

KNIGHTS WERE HORSEBACK WARRIORS whose heyday lasted from the 11th to the 15th century in Europe. In wartime they formed the nucleus of any ruler's army, and in peace they helped to keep local order. During the medieval period, knights rose in status and wealth to form part of an European ruling class. Each knight was expected to lead a Christian life and to obey the Code of Chivalry. They developed a great sense of their own importance, which was reflected in an obsession with heraldry: the formation of distinguishing coats of arms. After 1500, the introduction of new weapons, such as the cannon, and new military methods meant that the knights' importance waned.

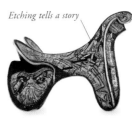

Prick or goad

Miniature spur

Iron stirrup

Specialist warriors

Rulers paid knights for their services with valuable gifts of land. The people on the land worked for the knights in return for protection. The first knights were sometimes men of humble origin, but in time they became a group of warrior-governors.

Etching tells a story

Horseback advances
Spurs helped mounted knights control their horses in battle. Stirrups and high-backed saddles – used to stop knights being thrown – also came into use between the 8th and 11th centuries. During this period the knights' importance increased.

Wooden etched saddle

Code of Chivalry
Medieval knights followed the ideals of the Code of Chivalry, and demonstrated prowess (bravery, strength, and skill), largesse (generosity), loyalty, piety, and courtesy. This code attempted to civilize what was really a primitive activity – fighting.

Courtly love
Minstrels' tales, or romances, helped to shape the Code of Chivalry, and many knights believed that romantic love inspired great deeds – as in the French *Roman de la Rose*, and the many stories surrounding Britain's King Arthur.

Christian knight
Churchmen encouraged new knights to fight non-Christians, but never to harm Church property or unarmed people.

Scene from *Roman de la Rose*, 1487

Knights
The knight's prime duty was to fight. After 1300, his armour became increasingly elaborate, expensive – and heavy. A suit could weigh as much as 25 kgs (55 lbs) and fitted snugly. One medieval poet called the knight "a terrible worm in an iron cocoon".

Falling plates allowed more air to reach the face.

Lance rest

Small plates on gauntlet gave freedom of movement to the hand.

Plates above and below the knee allowed movement without exposing the hose beneath.

The sole was left exposed so shoe did not skid.

Tournaments
Originally, knights used practice battles to help them train. These turned into a dazzling medieval spectator sport – the tournament – with teams of opposing knights. Single combat between champions was called a joust, and was fought using various war weapons. Victory often resulted in fame and riches.

Tournament, 15th century

Heraldry
Tournament crowds identified their heroes by their coats of arms, a personal combination of patterns (devices) displayed on surcoats, shields, and horse-draperies. In live battle, the coat-of-arms helped knights tell friend from foe, and enabled the official observers, known as heralds, to record any great feats.

Art of blazonry
From around 1140, heralds were experts in blazonry (the recording and regulating of the devices used in coats of arms). One rule in blazonry is that where there are two coats of arms, they can be "quartered". From 1250, French and English heralds kept records, called rolls. The rolls are used to check the family history.

Jar with two coats of arms, quartered

Squires
Squires were young men who served apprenticeships to become knights. The word comes from the French *escuyer*, meaning "shield-carrier". A squire might enter a knight's service at 14, where he would learn arts of combat and chivalry, and become a knight at around 21. As a "knight bachelor", he would look for a heiress to marry, to finance his career in arms.

Pel

Squire at the pel, or practice post

FIND OUT MORE   ARMS AND ARMOUR   EUROPE, HISTORY OF   MEDIEVAL EUROPE   NORMANS   SAMURAI AND SHOGUNS   WARFARE

Heraldry collection
Personal

Pope Sixtus V's coat of arms, Rome

Servants often wore a livery badge.

Arm badge worn by the servant of a knight, François de Lorraine

Keys symbolize entrance to the Kingdom of Heaven.

Pope Urban VIII's coat of arms, St Peter's, Rome

Stemmata belonged to important citizens.

Stemmata, or stone-carved coats of arms, are often seen on public buildings in Tuscany, Italy.

Pope Pius II's coat of arms, Tuscany, Italy

Pope Clement X's coat of arms, Rome

Crown indicates a royal person.

Arms of Maximillian I (r.1493–1519) of Austria

Coat of arms of the Medici family, art patrons, Florence

Organizations

Crest

Supporters are heraldic animals.

Metropolitan Police Force, London, UK

Scales of justice

Magistrates' Association coat of arms, UK

Shield, or escutcheon, the most important part of any coat of arms

British Broadcasting Company coat of arms, UK

Royal Society for the Prevention of Cruelty to Animals coat of arms, UK

Motto

Crest is the sun.

Supporters are hawks.

Worshipful Company of Spectacle Makers, England, 1629

Geographical

Swedish "lesser" coat of arms is not as ornate as the "greater" coat of arms, but it is still used as the symbol of Sweden's royal family.

Spanish dish showing arms of Castile and Léon

Symbol of the city of Paris

Bohemia

Moldavia

Silesia

Coat of arms of the modern Czech Republic

The inscription reads "truth victorious".

One of the 17 *contrada* (district) symbols, Siena, Italy

Shields and weapons often featured arms. This 15th-century wooden shield has the city of Prague arms on it.

KOREA, SOUTH AND NORTH

SOUTH AND NORTH KOREA together form a peninsula between the Yellow Sea and the Sea of Japan in East Asia. They were one single country until 1948, when South Korea separated from communist North Korea. In 1950, North Korea invaded the south, leading to the Korean War, which devastated South Korea's economy. In the following years, however, South Korea bounced back. In 2000, leaders from the two nations met for the first time since 1953.

K

South Korea

At the southern tip of the Korean peninsula, South Korea is one of the most successful of the Pacific Rim "tiger" economies. The country has strong trade links with Japan, the USA, and, more recently, China.

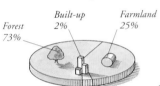

Forest 73%
Built-up 2%
Farmland 25%

Land use
Most of South Korea's farmland lies in the west and south and is under permanent cultivation. There is only a small amount of pasture land, mainly on mountain slopes.

People
More than 99 per cent of the people are Koreans whose ancestors settled in Korea thousands of years ago. Family life is central to Korean society. Women play a traditional role, and it is not respectable for married women to work.

474 per sq km
(1,228 per sq mile)

80% Urban
20% Rural

Economy
Once a mainly rural society, in the great reconstruction that followed the Korean War, South Korea has become highly industrialized. It is one of the world's leading shipbuilders and a major producer of cars and electronics.

Seoul
South Korea's capital since 1394, Seoul was devastated during the war, but has been rebuilt and expanded. It is now home to 11,100,000 people – nearly one-quarter of the total population. The 1988 Olympic Games were held in Seoul.

Seoul's public transport all runs to one timetable.

Forest in Soraksan National Park

Forests
More than two-thirds of South Korea is covered in thick, temperate forest, much of which cloaks the mountain slopes in the east and south. The stunning scenery and blaze of autumn colour attract many tourists to the country's national parks.

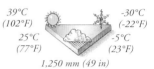

Mountains
Two ranges of mountains dominate South Korea. The T'aebaek-Sanmaek range runs down the east coast, while the Sobaek-Sanmaek lies in the south.

T'aebaek-Sanmaek Mountains

39°C (102°F)
25°C (77°F)
-30°C (-22°F)
-5°C (23°F)
1,250 mm (49 in)

Climate
Seasons are distinct. Winters are very cold and dry while summers are humid with heavy rains. The island of Cheju has a warm climate.

North Korea

Communist North Korea is isolated from the outside world, both politically and financially. North Korea has rich mineral resources, but lacks the money needed to exploit them. The economy is currently weak, leading to food shortages.

Collective farming
Agriculture is carried out mainly by collective farms, each run by about 300 families. Floods wrecked harvests between 1995 and 1996.

Map labels

1 Onsŏng, Kyŏnghŭng, RUS. FED.
2 Tumen, Komusan, Najin, Ch'ŏngjin
3 Hyesan, Manp'o, Kanggye, Myŏngch'ŏn, Kilchu, Kimch'aek, Tanch'ŏn, Iwŏn
NORTH KOREA, Sakchu, Hŭich'ŏn, Pukch'ŏng, Sinŭiju, Kusŏng, Kujang, Ora, Hamhŭng, Pakch'ŏn
4 Korea Bay, Chŏngju, Sukch'on, Hŭngnam, Sunch'ŏn, Munch'ŏn, Wŏnsan, PYONGYANG, Yangdŏk, Kuŭm, Kosŏng
5 Namp'o, Songnim, Kosan, Sea of Japan, Chaeryŏng, Sariwŏn, P'an-mo, Sokch'o, Changyŏn, Haeju, Kŭmch'ŏn, Kaesŏng, Kangnŭng, Ongjin, Ŭijŏngbu, Ch'inch'ŏn, Tonghae
6 Kyŏnggi-man, Inch'ŏn, Anyang, Wŏnju, Han, SEOUL, Suwŏn, Chech'ŏn, Yŏngju
7 Yellow Sea, Sŏsan, Ch'ŏngju, Yŏngju, Andong, SOUTH KOREA, Taejŏn, Kumi, P'ohang, Kunsan, Iri, Kimch'ŏn, Kimje, Chŏnju, Taegu, Kŭmho, Kyŏngju, Ulsan, Chŏngju, Sobaek-Sanmaek, Miryang
8 Kwangju, Sŏmjin, Chinju, Ch'angwŏn, Chinhae, Kŭmsong, Masan, Pusan, Sunch'ŏn, Ch'ungmu, Koje-do, Mokp'o, Kohŭng, Yŏsu, Korea Strait
9 Cheju Strait, Cheju, Cheju-do

Korea Bay
Sea of Japan
Yellow Sea
Hamgyŏng-sanmaek
Tongjosŏn-man

0 km 100
0 miles 100

FIND OUT MORE

ASIA, HISTORY OF | CITIES | FARMING | FORESTS | GOVERNMENTS AND POLITICS | MOUNTAINS AND VALLEYS | PACIFIC OCEAN | SHIPS AND BOATS | TRADE AND INDUSTRY

KUBLAI KHAN

KUBLAI KHAN WAS one of the most powerful emperors the world has known. As leader of the great Mongol Empire, he overthrew the powerful Song dynasty of southern China, placing China under foreign rule for the first time. Under Kublai's rule, China prospered and he developed trade with Europe and the rest of Asia. By the time of his death in 1294, Kublai Khan had truly earned the title of Great Khan, the greatest of the Mongol chieftains.

Early life
Kublai Khan, the grandson of Mongol leader Genghis Khan, was born in 1215. He was educated by Confucian scholars, and established himself as a war leader when a young man. In 1248, his older brother, Mongo, became Khan. Mongo died in 1259, and a fight to succeed him broke out between Kublai and a cousin. Kublai won, and in 1260 became Great Khan.

Kublai Khan's army, Indonesian carved relief

Conquests

Kublai Khan's greatest achievement was the conquest of China. When he became Great Khan in 1260, the Mongols controlled only the part of China north of the Yellow River. After almost two decades of warfare, Kublai conquered the Song Empire in the south, taking control of the entire country by 1279. The Mongols ruled China until they were driven out in 1368.

Xanadu •
Cambaluc (Beijing)

Empire of Kublai Khan

Kamikaze
Kublai Khan made two unsuccessful attempts to invade Japan. The first, in 1274, was called off after a storm forced the Mongols back to port in Korea. The second, in 1281, ended in disaster when a typhoon, known to the Japanese as the kamikaze, or divine wind, destroyed the Mongol fleet.

Southeast Asia
In five separate incursions between 1257–92, Mongol forces under Kublai Khan moved south from China into Burma, northern Thailand, and Annam (now northern Vietnam). An expeditionary force of the Mongol navy even visited the Indonesian island of Java in 1292–93. Although the Mongols did not actually conquer Southeast Asia, the area was under their firm control for more than a century.

Yüan dynasty

The Mongols were foreigners, but their rule was accepted by most of China. Kublai founded a new ruling dynasty – the Yüans – and encouraged trade by removing restraints on merchants, formerly subject to heavy taxation. He did much to improve the administration of the country, and, importantly, built a new imperial capital at Cambaluc, now known as Beijing.

Communications
Kublai Khan encouraged economic prosperity, and improved communications in his vast empire by building or improving canals, and by creating roads. He also established regular postal stations for mail. The Mongols controlled the ancient silk route (Silk Road) between Europe and China, and enabled traders from Europe to travel safely to China.

Early Chinese paper banknote

Social changes
Kublai Khan made many changes to Chinese society. He reintroduced a proper civil service based on merit to govern the country, recruiting scholars from many different nations as his staff, but excluding Chinese. Many members of the old Chinese civil service retired. Kublai also prepared a standardized code of law, built up the Chinese education system, and developed the use of paper currency.

Covering of mats

Single oar propels boat.

Eye for boat to "see"

19th-century model of a Chinese river boat

Marco Polo

The Venetian merchant Marco Polo (1254–1324) went to China in the 1270s. He stayed for 17 years, serving as an official in the civil service. On his return to Europe in 1295, he wrote his *Travels*, giving Europeans their first glimpse of the Mongol Empire.

Arts
Arts and culture prospered under the Yüan dynasty. The writing of fiction flourished, as did the theatre, where many new plays were produced. Craftworkers made distinctive blue and white porcelain, a skill which was perfected by the potters of the Ming dynasty.

Porcelain vase with dragon motif

Xanadu
Kublai Khan built a luxurious palace at Xanadu (modern Shantou). The 18th-century English poet, Samuel Coleridge, immortalized the palace in a poem.

Manuscript of Coleridge's poem, *Kubla Khan*

KUBLAI KHAN

1215	Birth of Kublai Khan.
1257	First Mongol incursion into Annam (northern Vietnam).
1260	Kublai becomes Great Khan.
1274	First attempt to invade Japan.
1275–95	Marco Polo works for Chinese government.
1279	Kublai completes conquest of Song China.
1281	Kamikaze destroys Mongol invasion fleet in Japan.
1292–93	Mongol fleet visits Java.
1294	Death of Kublai Khan.

FIND OUT MORE   ASIA, HISTORY OF   CHINA, HISTORY OF   EMPIRES   EXPLORATION   MONGOL EMPIRE   POTTERY AND CERAMICS

LAKE AND RIVER WILDLIFE

THE FRESHWATER habitats on land may be tiny in volume compared with the oceans, but the many lakes, ponds, and rivers are home to a huge variety of wildlife. Plants take root in the soft soil and provide food and shelter for many different animals. These include air-breathing animals that enter the water from the surroundings as well as truly aquatic creatures, which spend all their time in the water. Together, they show all manner of adaptations to underwater life, including ways of making shelters and of coping with fast currents or murky conditions.

Lake contains cold, clear water from mountain streams.

L

Lakes and rivers

Along the course of a typical river, there is a variety of freshwater habitats. Different water conditions in lakes and rivers – for example, flow rate, depth, turbulence, clarity, and temperature – suit different wildlife species.

Wonder Lake near Mount McKinley, Alaska

Hippos stay in the water to keep cool in the hot African sun.

Mammals

Only a few species of mammal, such as river dolphins, spend their whole life in fresh water. Many others enter the water to feed, and are excellent swimmers. The steep banks alongside rivers make good burrow sites for rodents such as water voles.

The otter uses its muscular tail for moving and steering through water.

Otters
Sleek-bodied river otters dive in search of fish. They propel themselves with their tails and webbed hind feet. Otters have dense waterproof fur and can close their nostrils and ears when swimming.

Beavers
Beavers use rivers and lakes for refuge rather than feeding. They build "lodges" for themselves in the water from piles of timber that they cut from waterside bushes.

Hippopotamus
A hippopotamus typically spends the daytime resting in a lake or river. It emerges at dusk to graze on the land. Weighing up to 3 tonnes, this heavy animal can dive and swim with ease.

Birds

Many species of bird are closely associated with lakes and rivers. Some are able to dive underwater; others paddle over the surface, wade through the shallows, flit about at the water's edge, or fly close to the water to snatch fish.

Flamingos
Long legs enable flamingos to wade through the margins of lakes, sifting the water for small food items. Some African lakes are home to more than a million birds.

Grebe
Skilful swimmers, grebes paddle over the surface of lakes. In a flash they will twist and disappear, barely making a ripple as they dive to catch a fish.

The wagtail bobs its tail as it forages for insects.

Grey wagtail
The grey wagtail often nests along the banks of fast-running upland streams. It perches on rocks to snatch waterside insects.

Reptiles and amphibians

Though few species spend their entire time in water, a great many reptiles and amphibians never stray far from rivers and lakes. Turtles, crocodiles, frogs, and newts are all closely associated with water. Many snakes, lizards, and toads also readily enter rivers to feed, take shelter, or deposit their eggs.

Newt tadpole swims from its egg.

Tadpoles
The larvae of newts and other amphibians are fully aquatic. The tadpoles have gills for extracting oxygen from the water and large tails to help them swim.

Anaconda
The most massive of all the snakes, the South American anaconda hunts its prey in rivers and pools, and snatches animals at the water's edge. It kills large prey by crushing it in its coils.

Nile crocodile
Like the hippopotamuses, which sometimes share their habitats, Nile crocodiles lurk in the water with only their nostrils and eyes exposed. They seize unsuspecting mammals that come down to the river to have a drink.

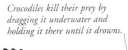

Crocodiles kill their prey by dragging it underwater and holding it there until it drowns.

Sharp teeth are replaced continuously.

Strong claws

Fish

Rivers and lakes all over the world are, above all, the domain of fish. Totally adapted to an aquatic life, fish have internal gills for taking in oxygen from the water, and a series of fins with which to propel themselves about. They abound in all types of freshwater habitat.

Trout

The trout represents the typical strong-swimming freshwater fish. With its streamlined body and powerful fins, it can hold its own in the fastest river currents. It also thrives in the calm waters of lakes. Trout often rise to the surface to feed on insects.

Black spots on the trout's back help it to blend in with the riverbed.

This freshwater catfish is from South America.

A piranha's short, broad jaws are very powerful.

Piranhas

These deep-bodied fish live in South American rivers. Some feed on plant matter, but a few, such as these red-bellied piranhas, have razor-sharp teeth for cutting flesh. Hunting in schools, they may attack and devour animals much bigger than themselves. Even these carnivorous piranhas eat meat only when their normal food of fruit and nuts is in short supply.

Catfish

These fish live at the bottom of rivers and lakes, where they avoid mid-stream currents but are surrounded by sediment-laden water. They probe the riverbed for food, using their long, sensitive feelers.

Cichlid

Cichlids are a large group of often colourful fish. They live mostly in tropical lakes and rivers. Unusually for fish, many look after their eggs and fry (young). Some let the fry shelter in their mouths when danger threatens.

Invertebrates

A host of invertebrate animals inhabit lakes and rivers. Among them are insects and their larvae, shellfish, shrimps, and crayfish. A great many invertebrates simply float in the water or crawl around on the riverbed, but some have elegant adaptations which help them swim.

Water boatman

The water boatman uses its long hind legs as paddles. It spends all its life in water, swimming upside-down in a hunt for crustaceans, tadpoles, fish fry, and the larvae of other insects.

Great pond snail

Although it resembles a land snail, this plant-eating pond dweller cannot survive for long out of water. It lays jelly-like eggs, often on the underside of water-lily leaves.

Leeches

Leeches are parasitic, worm-like creatures. They attach themselves to fish and other animals that enter the water, and feed on their blood.

Plants

Without vegetation to provide food and shelter, the diversity of animal life in lakes and rivers would be far poorer. Many plant species grow only in and around water, either rooted in the waterlogged sediment and soil or floating on the surface.

Water-lily

Sprouting up from the bed of a pond or slow-flowing river, water-lilies unfurl their round leaves flat on the surface of the water, where they make convenient floating platforms for frogs and other wildlife. The flowers poke into the air, attracting flying insects to feed on, and pollinate them.

Stiff stalks keep the flowerheads above water.

Leaves have a waxy surface, so water runs off them easily.

After flowering, each flower becomes a fruit that develops underwater.

Alder tree roots take in water.

Stalks are soft and flexible so they bend in the water.

Plants

Some plants rooted to the riverbed remain wholly underwater, their leaves, stems, and roots providing shelter for invertebrates and fish. The long, branched roots of alder trees keep the soil of the riverbank together, stopping it from being washed away.

Reeds

The shallow edges of lakes and rivers often have a dense green fringe of plants, such as reeds, growing out of the water. The roots of the plants are submerged, but the stems and flowers may rise more than a metre into the air.

Algae

Simple plants called algae are an important source of food for the wildlife of most lakes and rivers. Floating clumps of algae can form on still or slow-flowing water.

FIND OUT MORE   AMPHIBIANS   BIRDS   FISH   INSECTS   LAKES   MAMMALS   PLANTS   RATS AND OTHER RODENTS   REPTILES   RIVERS

LAKES

A FIFTH OF THE WORLD'S fresh water is contained in lakes – large bodies of inland water. A small amount of this water comes from rainfall but most lakes are fed by rivers. Lakes usually lose water through a river outlet, but some lakes, such as Lake Eyre in Australia, lose water by evaporation, leaving the lake salty. Lakes are geologically temporary features, lasting at most a few hundred thousand years. Lake Baikal in Siberia is one of the few exceptions, as it is already 25 million years old. Lakes are useful for drinking water supplies, generating electricity, and field irrigation.

The life of a lake

A few lakes have lasted many millions of years, but most lakes last just a few thousand years. They eventually clog up with sediment dumped by rivers, or dry up as rainfall dwindles. Marshes, bogs, and swamps are often the remnants of old lakes, clogged with vegetation and silt.

Young lake gradually begins to fill up as rivers dump their load of mud and gravel.

Delta (a low-lying area of dry land at the mouth of a river) may build up where the river flows into the lake.

Lake gets shallower; reeds grow in the shallows turning the lake margins into swamps.

Unique range of flora and fauna thrive in the surrounding area.

River dumps more sediment and the delta grows.

The vegetation makes water move sluggishly through the lake, so the river deposits even more sediment.

Eventually, the lake is completely filled in; plants take over the whole wetland.

Stages showing the formation and destruction of a lake.

The world's greatest lakes

The biggest lake in the world is so big it is called a sea – the Caspian Sea in Asia. It covers an area of 370,980 sq km (143,236 sq miles). The deepest lake is Lake Baikal in Siberia, at a depth of 1.7 km (1.06 miles).

Salt-water lakes

In dry areas, many rivers drain into enclosed lakes. The intense water evaporation under the desert sun concentrates inflowing salts, making the water salty. Such lakes – the Great Salt Lake, USA or the Dead Sea, Middle East – eventually dry out into salt pans or playas.

Jerusalem

Dead Sea evaporates.

Types of lakes

The shape of a lake usually depends on how and where it forms. The biggest lakes tend to be those created by glaciation, such as the Great Lakes of North America, or by earth movements, such as Lake Baikal, Siberia.

Artificial lakes

Artificial lakes, or reservoirs, are created to control a river, store water, or provide water pressure for hydroelectric power. Lake Nasser, behind the Aswan High Dam on the River Nile, is the largest in the world.

Artificial lake

Glacial erosion lakes

Glaciers scoop out U-shaped valleys and ice-eroded hollows that may be dammed by moraine (glacial deposits) when the ice retreats. Long "ribbon" lakes may fill the valley floor while small, circular lakes, or tarns, may fill the hollows. Ice sheets may also leave behind huge hollows that later fill with water, like the lakes of Kuopio, Finland.

Ribbon lake

Circular tarn lake

Glacial deposition lakes

Ice sheets leave behind moraines (glacial deposits) that can dam smaller lakes. Glaciers may also leave behind ice, or flowtill, which later melts to form little hollows; these fill with water to form lakes known as "kettles".

Glacial till lake

Volcanic lakes

Lakes may form as rainwater collects in the crater of an extinct or dormant volcano, such as Crater Lake in Oregon, USA. A lake may also form when the lava flow from a volcano dams a river, such as the Sea of Galilee in the Middle East.

Crater lake

Lava-dammed lake

Tectonic lakes

The movement of the Earth's crust can create large lakes. A downfold in the Earth's crust can create a giant basin. A rift valley (a block of land sinking between tectonic plates) can make a trough-like lake, such as Lake Nyasa in Africa. Landslides, too, can dam a river to create a lake.

Rift valley lake

Landslip lake

River and marine lakes

When a river erodes through the neck of a meander – a curve in the course of a river – and cuts it off, it may form a lake, called an oxbow lake, in the old bend. A lake may also be formed when the ocean builds up a bar of sand on the coast that dams in a lagoon.

Cut-off river meander

River

Oxbow lake

FIND OUT MORE   CONTINENTS   DAMS   ELECTRICITY   FOSSILS   GLACIATION   LAKE AND RIVER WILDLIFE   OCEANS AND SEAS   RIVERS   VOLCANOES

LANGUAGES

WHETHER TALKING OR writing, we communicate with each other by using language: a system where sounds or signs convey objects, actions, and ideas. Language is one of the things that made the growth of civilization possible. Because people could speak, they were able to pass on knowledge. Having developed over thousands of years, languages adapt constantly to reflect the changing needs of their users: new words, such as "internet", enter the vocabulary all the time, and grammar, the rules that govern the use of language, also changes.

The world's languages
There are at least 4,000 speech communities (people who speak the same language) around the world. About 90 per cent are in danger of dying out. On the North American continent alone, 100 languages have fewer than 300 speakers each.

About 750 languages are spoken in Papua New Guinea.

Families

By identifying similar words or structures that occur in different languages, we can see that many languages are related, and probably developed from the same ancestor. For instance, Russian is similar to many languages in Europe and Central Asia. People in these areas perhaps adopted the language of nomads who migrated from southern Russia 6,000 years ago. Scholars also group languages into families, by comparing the languages as they are used today.

The languages spoken in Africa reflect that it was once heavily colonized.

The major languages
Almost half the world's people speak the 10 most widespread languages. Many of these languages originated in Europe, but spread around the world as Europeans colonized other countries. For example, the Portuguese spread their language to Brazil.

Key: millions of speakers

Arabic: 170m	Portuguese: 160m
Chinese: 1,000m	Russian: 270m
English: 1,400m	Spanish: 280m
French: 220m	Hindi: 400m
	Others

Noam Chomsky

Influential US linguist Noam Chomsky (b.1928) argued that we are born with the ability to speak a language. He suggested that some very general aspects of grammar are built into every human mind, no matter what the nationality.

Speech

Nobody knows how human speech evolved from animal grunts. Although humans can make a vast range of sounds, most languages use fewer than 40. Usually, sounds are only meaningful when joined as words. Even then, a listener may not understand a word without hearing the whole sentence.

Dialects
A dialect is a variation on the pronunciation of a spoken language. Sometimes a dialect becomes a language in its own right: Spanish, Italian, and French were once all dialects of Latin.

Gypsies around the world speak a dialect which mixes a local language with Romany, the gypsy language.

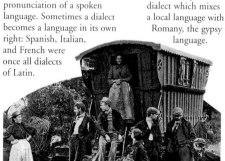

Sign and body languages

There are other forms of language as well as speech and writing. Gestures can also communicate, and emphasize the spoken word. Banging the table with an angry fist is a crude example; much more subtly, a conductor uses a baton to control a whole symphony orchestra.

Arms folded, a barrier to ideas

Body language
Even when we are trying hard to control what we say, our bodies may communicate our inner feelings. In this picture, the woman who has folded her arms is signalling that she does not want to hear what she is being told.

Sign languages
People who have hearing or speech difficulties may communicate with others by a variety of sign languages that use hand gestures or finger spelling.

US manual alphabet

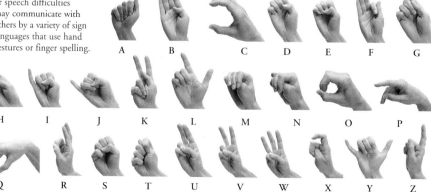

A B C D E F G
H I J K L M N O P
Q R S T U V W X Y Z

FIND OUT MORE CODES AND CIPHERS · EDUCATION · GENETICS · SIGNS AND SYMBOLS · SOCIETIES, HUMAN · WRITING

LASERS AND HOLOGRAMS

Microchips etched by NdYAG laser

A LASER BEAM CAN CUT through steel as easily as a knife cuts through butter. A laser is a device that produces a powerful beam of light. The word laser stands for **L**ight **A**mplification by **S**timulated **E**mission of **R**adiation. All lasers produce coherent light. Coherent light is very pure, which means that all the light waves have the same wavelength, they are all "in step" with one another, and they are all travelling in exactly the same direction. Laser light can be used to create three-dimensional photographs called holograms.

Laser beam rapidly etches letters and numbers into surface of chip.

How a laser works

The heart of a laser is a material called a lasing medium. The lasing medium is given energy, usually by an electric current or by light from a device called a flash tube. The atoms of the lasing medium absorb the energy and then give it out again as waves of coherent light. The light reflects back and forth between two mirrors, becoming more and more intense, until it emerges from one of the mirrors (which is only partly reflective) as a laser beam.

Theodore Maiman

In 1953, US physicist Charles Townes (b. 1915) invented a device called a maser, which produced microwaves. In 1960, his fellow US physicist Theodore Maiman (b. 1927) used the principles of Townes' device to build a laser. Maiman's laser used a ruby crystal as the lasing medium.

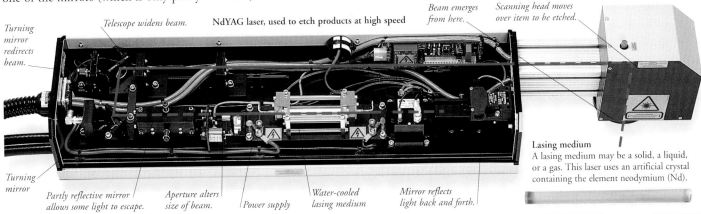

Turning mirror redirects beam.

Telescope widens beam.

NdYAG laser, used to etch products at high speed

Beam emerges from here.

Scanning head moves over item to be etched.

Turning mirror

Partly reflective mirror allows some light to escape.

Aperture alters size of beam.

Power supply

Water-cooled lasing medium

Mirror reflects light back and forth.

Lasing medium
A lasing medium may be a solid, a liquid, or a gas. This laser uses an artificial crystal containing the element neodymium (Nd).

Applications of lasers

Lasers have many uses, because they produce a powerful beam of uniform light that will not spread out over long distances and that can be directed very precisely. Lasers are used to read supermarket bar codes, play compact discs, guide weapons, and send signals along optical fibres.

Metal cutting
A powerful infrared laser beam can generate enough heat to cut through metals or to weld (join) them together by melting them.

Laser surgery
Surgeons can control lasers with great precision to burn away cancer cells or delicately trim the lens of an eye to improve a person's sight.

Light show
Laser beams always follow a straight line, so they can be used to produce stunning visual effects at rock concerts and other special events.

Holograms

Holograms are photographs that appear three-dimensional (3-D). This effect is produced by taking a photograph using two different sets of light waves from a laser beam. Holograms have many uses because they allow people to see an object from different angles.

Hologram of radar dish

Making holograms
To make a hologram, a laser beam is split into two parts, one called an object beam and the other a reference beam. Only the object beam reflects off the object that is to be photographed. Both beams strike a plate of photographic film, where they interfere (combine) and create a 3-D-looking image.

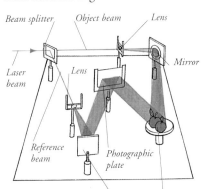

Beam splitter *Object beam* *Lens*

Laser beam *Lens* *Mirror*

Reference beam *Photographic plate*

Hologram photography *Mirror* *Object*

FIND OUT MORE

ELECTRONICS ENERGY LIGHT METALS PHOTOGRAPHY SOUND RECORDING WEAPONS X-RAYS AND THE ELECTROMAGNETIC SPECTRUM

LAW

THE LAW can be defined as the rules and standards that administer all aspects of society. They regulate the government of the state, the relationship between the government and individuals, and the conduct of individuals towards each other. The police and the courts are usually responsible for enforcing the law. Throughout history, in different parts of the world, laws have been codified in many different ways, but the law is a fundamental element of all societies.

Law-maker, Hammurabi

Hammurabi code
The earliest surviving law code was drawn up by Mesopotamian ruler Hammurabi (1792–1750 BC). It contains 282 laws, with headings such as Family, Labour, Personal Property, and Trade. His codes were engraved on a stone pillar.

Early law
Every society's code of law has been gathered over several centuries, often incorporating many elements of law codes of earlier societies. Most Western societies have inherited legal principles from Imperial Rome. Emperor Justinian (c. 483–565) codified more than 1,000 years of Roman law. His code was written in Latin, which is still the language of law in the western world.

Justice
Courts aim to administer the law according to generally accepted principles that are seen as fair and just. In English law, for example, it is accepted that a person is innocent until proven guilty, and that he or she has a right to legal representation.

Scales of Justice show that justice weighs opposing evidence

The US Capitol is the site of the Senate and House of Representatives. The Supreme Court is nearby.

Legislation
In democratic societies, new laws are formulated and passed by governments. Legislation, or law-making, is a complex process. Firstly, legal advisers are responsible for drafting the wording of the law. Provisional laws are scrutinized and debated by the legislative assembly and, as a result, may be amended and altered. When they are finally accepted, they are known as statute laws.

Capitol, Washington DC, US's law-making centre

Types of law
Many people are familiar with criminal law; famous cases are highly publicized, and courtroom dramas on film and television are very popular. However, the law deals with every aspect of life, from traffic offences to mass murder. Governments are ruled by constitutional and international laws. The actions of individuals are regulated by criminal law, family law, and civil law. Civil law embraces specialist areas such as taxation, property, inheritance, and medical law. Some legal firms only work in business law.

Sinking of Greenpeace's *Rainbow Warrior* by France led to legal proceedings

International law
These laws govern the relationship between states, as well as regulating international organizations and multinational corporations. The United Nations has the power to use international law against a nation or individuals who are committing acts of aggression. International law is also used to resolve disputes between nations and international organizations.

Constitutional law
A nation's constitution is a set of political principles by which a state is governed, and constitutional law is a body of rules and practices that are laid down, based on these principles. In some countries, such as Great Britain and France, the constitution is unwritten, but the United States of America has a written constitution. It was signed in 1787, at the end of the War of Independence. Its first Ten Amendments guarantee certain basic rights, for example, the right of the individual to bear arms and to enjoy freedom of religion and freedom of speech. These rights are the foundation of US law.

The Declaration of Independence laid the foundation for the American constitution.

Criminal law
Criminal laws impose obligations on all members of society not to do certain things that are considered an offence against both society and an individual. Acts of violence, such as assault and murder, and crimes against a person's property, such as theft, are the most obvious examples. However, criminal law also deals with minor misdemeanours such as failure to pay parking fines, traffic offences, and public disorder.

Suspect with crime number

`123456/97X`

Civil law
This branch of the law deals with claims by individuals that another has injured their property, person, or reputation, or failed to carry out a legal obligation (contract). These claims can range from minor disputes between neighbours to complex cases involving international corporations. Civil law also covers day to day events such as buying or selling a house.

Some people may choose to take legal advice when buying or selling a property.

Family law
Relationships between couples, parents and children, and within families are all governed by family law. The most common areas of dispute resolved by family lawyers are divorce settlements, and the question of custody of, and access to, children. Family law can also safeguard the rights of children against violent or neglectful parents.

Lawyers often consider the needs of a couple's children as a high priority in divorce cases.

Law and society

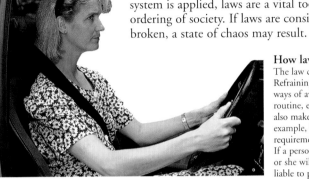

This British car driver obeys the law by wearing a seat belt.

Every society has evolved a system of rules and regulations, but their legal systems are not always the same worldwide. For example, in parts of the Islamic world the law is based on religious principles, while in some tribal societies the right to judge offenders is hereditary, passing from chief to chief. Whatever system is applied, laws are a vital tool in the regulation and ordering of society. If laws are consistently disregarded and broken, a state of chaos may result.

Sultan Hasan Mosque, Cairo, Egypt

How law affects us

The law can affect many aspects of daily life. Refraining from violence and theft are obvious ways of avoiding breaking the law. Many routine, everyday actions, such as driving a car, also make legal demands on individuals. For example, in many countries it is a legal requirement to wear a seat belt while driving. If a person chooses to disregard these laws, he or she will be breaking the law and, if caught, liable to prosecution.

Religious law

Some Islamic countries are governed by the Sharia ("The Path"), a system of Islamic law which was formulated in medieval times. The law code is taken directly from the teachings of the Qur'an and the prophet Muhammad. Like western law, Sharia regulates the individual's relations with family, neighbours, and the state, and it also rules each person's relationship with Allah (God). Many Islamic countries adopted western law codes in the 19th century, and confined the use of Sharia to family law.

Courtroom

In most cases, the application of the law involves verbal discussion and argument between trained and qualified lawyers. This normally takes place in a courtroom. English-speaking nations use the "adversarial" system whereby the prosecution puts forward arguments against the accused, which are resisted by the defence. An impartial third party – a judge, and sometimes a jury – reviews the arguments and makes a final decision as to guilt or innocence. Hearings are normally conducted in public.

The judge is an official who controls the court proceedings and has the authority to hear cases in court, and pass sentence.

A clerk of the court is a legally qualified assistant to the judge, responsible for the administration of the courtroom, for legal research, and for advising the judge on points of law.

Evidence
Legal trials normally involve the examination of evidence. This may be spoken evidence, given by witnesses, who are then cross-examined by lawyers. It can be written evidence, which is the most common in civil cases. In some criminal trials, the evidence might be an actual object, such as a murder weapon, or scientific data, for example blood samples.

Witness box

Judge's bench

The recorder records, and later transcribes, everything that is said in court. Recorders may use a stenograph (a machine that types in shorthand) or a tape recorder.

The jury is a body of randomly selected men and women (usually 12), chosen to attend the trial, review the evidence, and make a judgment. In the UK, most people between the ages of 18 and 70 are liable for jury service.

The defence team represents the accused in criminal trials. They must rebut the arguments of the prosecution, and defend the innocence of their client. In many courts the accused will sit with their lawyers, unless called to the witness box.

The prosecution represents the State, which brings the case against the accused in criminal trials. The prosecution is responsible for proving guilt.

Law reports

Members of the public are allowed into the courtroom in most criminal trials. The family of the accused and representatives of the press are given priority.

Legal teams assist lawyers by carrying out research and interviewing witnesses before the trial.

FIND OUT MORE

AMERICAN REVOLUTION   BABYLONIAN EMPIRE   CRIME   GOVERNMENTS AND POLITICS   HUMAN RIGHTS   ISLAM   POLICE   RELIGION   UNITED NATIONS

LEAKEY FAMILY

ONE FAMILY HAS DONE more than any other to unravel the early development of the human race and the history of our fossil relatives, the hominids. Working in Africa, the husband-and-wife team of Louis and Mary Leakey, and their son Richard, found fascinating evidence of human ancestors, showing that the continent was home to three different stages of human ancestry. There is still controversy about how these ancestors were related, but without the Leakeys, that debate could not have taken place.

Mary Leakey

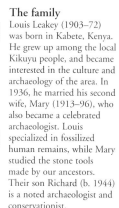

Louis Leakey

Richard Leakey

The family
Louis Leakey (1903–72) was born in Kabete, Kenya. He grew up among the local Kikuyu people, and became interested in the culture and archaeology of the area. In 1936, he married his second wife, Mary (1913–96), who also became a celebrated archaeologist. Louis specialized in fossilized human remains, while Mary studied the stone tools made by our ancestors. Their son Richard (b. 1944) is a noted archaeologist and conservationist.

Olduvai Gorge

Louis and Mary Leakey spent more than 20 years excavating the Olduvai Gorge, south of the Serengeti Plain in Kenya. It yielded some remarkable finds. They found many animal bones, together with stone tools made by hominids who lived millions of years ago. Both Mary and Richard discovered hominid bones of immense importance in the gorge, establishing the area as one of the most important archaeological sites in the world.

Homo habilis
In 1961, Louis Leakey discovered some hominid remains. These were of a species which was later named *Homo habilis* (or "handy man"), so-called because he used primitive tools. *Homo habilis* is two million years old. Louis and Richard Leakey both argued that *Homo habilis* is an ancestor of modern humans, or *Homo sapiens.*

Skull of *Homo habilis*

Laetoli

In 1978, Mary Leakey made a dramatic discovery: the fossilized footprints of three hominids, preserved in volcanic ash at Laetoli, southwest of Olduvai. The footprints proved that *Australopithecus* walked upright at least 3.6 million years ago, earlier than scientists had previously suspected.

Footprints, found at Laetoli.

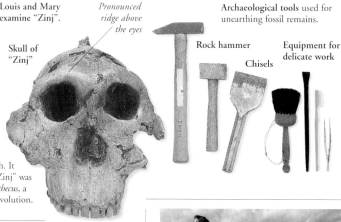

Louis and Mary examine "Zinj".

Pronounced ridge above the eyes

Skull of "Zinj"

Archaeological tools used for unearthing fossil remains.

Rock hammer

Chisels

Equipment for delicate work

Zinjanthropus
In 1959, Mary discovered the remains of a human skull. She named the creature *Zinjanthropus.* "Zinj" turned out to be 1.75 million years old, thus tripling the time it was known that hominids had lived on Earth. It was some time before it became clear that "Zinj" was not a direct human ancestor, but an *Australopithecus*, a pre-human hominid from a parallel line of evolution.

Lake Turkana

Richard Leakey carried on his parents' work, making important discoveries at Lake Turkana, Kenya, and other sites in East Africa and Ethopia. He has found remains of *Homo habilis* dating from 1.88 million years ago.

Turkana boy
In 1984 Richard made one of his most important discoveries: the almost complete skeleton of a young male *Homo erectus* (upright man), a close ancestor of modern humans.

Kenyan affairs
In 1989, Richard Leakey became Kenyan National Parks director of wildlife management. He fought against the poaching of elephant and rhinoceros for their tusks, and tried to reform the corrupt management of the parks. This brought him into direct conflict with the government of President Moi. Richard formally entered politics in 1997, serving in government until 2001.

LEAKEY FAMILY

1903	Louis Leakey born in Kabete, Kenya.
1913	Mary Nicol born in London.
1936	Louis's first marriage ends and he marries Mary.
1944	Richard Leakey born.
1959	Mary discovers "Zinj" at Olduvai Gorge.
1961	Louis discovers *Homo habilis* at Olduvai Gorge.
1972	Richard discovers *Homo habilis* at Lake Turkana.
1972	Louis Leakey dies.
1978	Mary discovers Laetoli footprints.
1996	Mary Leakey dies.

FIND OUT MORE   ARCHAEOLOGY   EVOLUTION   FOSSILS   HUMAN EVOLUTION   PREHISTORIC PEOPLE

LEONARDO DA VINCI

PAINTER, DRAFTSMAN, SCULPTOR, inventor, scientist, anatomist, architect: Leonardo da Vinci had many skills. He was born in 1452 during the golden age of the Italian Renaissance in art and architecture, and made his name as a painter, producing a series of masterpieces for rich patrons in Italy and later France. His restless mind led him to enquire into every area of scientific and artistic research, recording in his notebooks many inventions that show him to be outstanding in the scope of his knowledge.

Early life
Leonardo was born in Vinci, a hill village near the Italian city of Florence, in 1452. His father, Piero, was a legal clerk and his mother was a peasant. In 1466 he moved to Florence and became apprenticed to Andrea del Verrocchio, a prominent Florentine artist. He was soon undertaking artistic work of his own.

The artist
Leonardo was a uniquely gifted artist who produced paintings of unequalled beauty and complexity. Yet, as the Renaissance art historian Giorgio Vasari relates, he "envisaged such subtle, marvellous, and difficult problems that his hands, while extremely skilful, were incapable of ever realizing them". As a result, few of his paintings were ever completed. Those that were finished are often in a poor state today, because Leonardo constantly experimented with new pigments and materials, and many of these have failed to stand the test of time.

The Virgin and Child
Before he began to paint a picture, Leonardo would draw a detailed sketch, known as a cartoon, so that he could lay out the composition in advance. The finished picture of *The Virgin and Child with St John the Baptist and St Anne*, if it was ever completed, has never been found, but the cartoon gives a good idea of what it might have looked like.

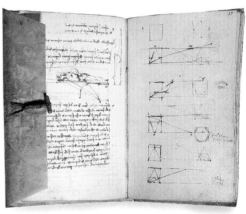

Perspective sketches
Throughout his life, Leonardo made detailed notes on the art of painting. These writings are collected together in his book, *Treatise on Painting*. In 1492 he wrote a lengthy piece on perspective, investigating the way space and distance are perceived by the eye. On the pages shown above, he illustrates his method for transferring a figure on to the sides of a curved vault, a revolutionary technique that formed the basis of the later device called *trompe l'oeil* (paintings which "deceive the eye").

Mona Lisa

In about 1503, Leonardo began to paint a portrait of a local Florentine woman, believed to be Lisa Gherardini, the wife of a wealthy merchant. The portrait, known as the *Mona Lisa*, now hangs in the Louvre gallery in Paris. Its subject's enigmatic smile made it one of the world's most famous paintings.

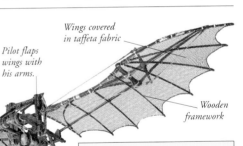

Wings covered in taffeta fabric

Pilot flaps wings with his arms.

Wooden framework

The inventor
Leonardo was a skilled scientist and inventor. Throughout his life, he drew designs for flying machines, weapons, mathematical puzzles, and musical instruments. He invented a centrifugal pump and a diving suit. He designed buildings and fortifications, and built military canals and collapsible bridges for use in wartime.

Flight
Using his observations of birds in flight, Leonardo designed a flying machine powered by human muscles. Although the wood-and-canvas machine was technically clever, it would never have flown because of the weight of materials needed to build it.

War and warfare
Although he considered war a "beastly madness", Leonardo devised several war machines. He drew designs for a scythed chariot and for an early tank, with guns around its rim. He also claimed to have invented a machine that fired lethal missiles which, as they exploded, showered the enemy with deadly fire.

Anatomy
Leonardo was fascinated by the workings of the human body, which he saw as a machine. He dissected more than 30 bodies, studying them in order to solve mechanical problems.

LEONARDO DA VINCI

1452 Born in Vinci, near Florence.

1466–72 Apprenticed to Andrea del Verrocchio in Florence.

c.1482 Moves to Milan and works for the Duke of Milan.

c.1485–88 Draws design for a tank.

1492 Investigates linear perspective.

c.1497 Paints *The Last Supper* at a monastery in Milan.

1498–99 Draws cartoon of *The Virgin and Child*.

1500 Returns to Florence.

c.1503–06 Paints the *Mona Lisa*.

c.1515 Accepts invitation from King Francis I to settle in France.

1519 Dies in France.

FIND OUT MORE   ART, HISTORY OF   FLIGHT, HISTORY OF   INVENTIONS   PAINTING AND DRAWING   RENAISSANCE

L

LIGHT

WITHOUT LIGHT, you would not be able to read this page, because it is light that enables us to see the world around us. Light is a form of energy called electromagnetic radiation, which travels as invisible waves. Our most important source of light is the Sun, but light can also be produced artificially using electricity or fire. Lenses and mirrors enable us to use light to form images and to see tiny or distant objects.

Incandescence

Glowing flame

The production of light by hot objects, such as a bulb's filament, a burning candle, or the Sun's surface, is called incandescence. Luminescence is the collective name for all the other ways in which light can be produced.

The temperature at the Sun's surface is 5,500°C (9,900°F).

Bioluminescence
Fireflies have special chemicals inside their bodies that react together and produce light. This process is called bioluminescence.

Fluorescence
In a type of luminescence called fluorescence, substances absorb light energy briefly and give it out again. Some washing powders contain fluorescent chemicals to make clothes look brighter.

Fluorescent washing powder

Electroluminescence
Street lights make light by electroluminescence. Electricity is passed through a gas in a tube. The electrical energy causes the gas atoms to emit light.

Street light's discharge tube

Light source

Any object or substance that emits light is called a light source. The light source in a torch is a thin metal wire in the bulb called a filament. When you switch on the torch, an electric current makes the filament glow white-hot. A curved mirror behind the bulb directs the light out of the front of the torch as a bright beam.

Atoms of filament vibrate faster.

Vibrating atoms emit rays of light.

Filament
A light-bulb filament is usually a coil of tungsten wire. When the bulb is switched on, the filament heats up to around 2,000°C (3,600°F). Atoms of all substances vibrate. As the filament heats up, the atoms gain extra energy and vibrate more vigorously. Eventually, they give out this extra energy as light.

Bulb filament glows white-hot.

Light bounces off mirrored surface.

Polarized light

The rays of light from a source, such as a bulb, vibrate in many different planes (directions). Some materials, called polarizing filters, allow rays vibrating in one plane only to pass through them. Light in which all the rays vibrate in the same plane is called polarized light.

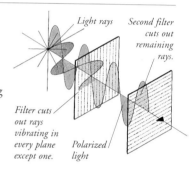

Light rays

Second filter cuts out remaining rays.

Filter cuts out rays vibrating in every plane except one.

Polarized light

"Lenses" are polarizing filters.

Sunglasses
On a sunny day, the bright glare from the sea and other reflective surfaces makes you squint. Sunglasses use polarizing filters adjusted to the correct angle to cut out the rays causing the unpleasant glare, but allow other rays to pass through.

Liquid crystal display (LCD)
In a calculator's LCD, strips of a substance called liquid crystal are held between two polarizing filters. Pressing the calculator's keys makes the liquid crystal change the direction in which light rays passing through the display vibrate. The filters block the light in some places, but not in others, forming numbers on the display.

Augustin Fresnel

The French physicist Augustin Fresnel (1788–1827) carried out experiments to prove that light travels as waves and investigated polarized light. He also invented a type of lens in which the surface is cut into a series of concentric ringed steps. This type of lens (now called a Fresnel lens) is especially good for concentrating light into a strong beam. Fresnel lenses are used in lighthouses, searchlights, and car headlights.

Rays of light in the early morning

Speed of light

Light travels through space at a speed of 299,792.5 km/s (186,287.5 miles/s). This is the ultimate speed limit, because nothing can travel faster. Light travels more slowly in different substances: in water, for example, it travels at about 225,000 km/s (140,000 miles/s), and in glass at about 200,000 km/s (124,000 miles/s). Light always travels in straight lines called rays, but its direction can be deflected by objects in its path.

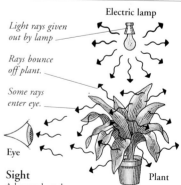

Electric lamp

Light rays given out by lamp

Rays bounce off plant.

Some rays enter eye.

Eye

Sight
A houseplant does not produce light, and is only visible to us because light rays from another source – such as the Sun or an electric lamp – bounce off the plant and into the eye. Inside the eye is a lens that forms an image similar to the image formed in a camera. Cells at the back of the eye sense the image and pass information to the brain.

Plant

Matter and light

A material's appearance depends on the way the particles of matter inside it respond to light. A clear or milky material allows light to pass through it, and is said to be either transparent or translucent. An opaque material will absorb or reflect light, making it dull or shiny. When light hits an opaque object, it casts a shadow, which is an area where light does not reach.

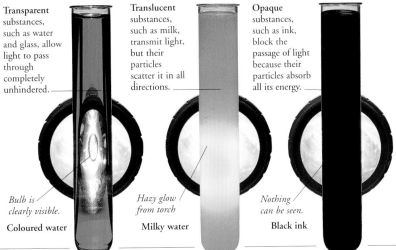

Transparent substances, such as water and glass, allow light to pass through completely unhindered.

Translucent substances, such as milk, transmit light, but their particles scatter it in all directions.

Opaque substances, such as ink, block the passage of light because their particles absorb all its energy.

Bulb is clearly visible.

Coloured water

Hazy glow from torch

Milky water

Nothing can be seen.

Black ink

Hero of Alexandria

The first comprehensive study of the reflection and refraction of light was *Catoptrics*, written by Hero (1st century AD), a Greek inventor and mathematician who lived in Alexandria, Egypt. Hero also invented various pneumatic (air-powered) machines, and a steam-powered engine. In geometry, he devised a formula (still known as Hero's formula) for calculating the area of a triangle.

Refraction and reflection

If you rest a pen in a glass of water, the part of the pen below the surface appears to bend. This is caused by refraction – a process in which light entering a transparent material at an angle bends, or refracts. When light strikes a shiny material, however, it simply bounces off the surface. This process is called reflection. Mirrors and lenses work by reflection and refraction.

Light refracts as it passes through water, glass, and air.

Plastic pen

Pen appears to bend.

Pen looks as though it is split in two.

Lenses

A lens, such as a magnifying glass, is a curved piece of transparent material that changes the direction of light rays passing through it by refraction. Lenses can be used to form images of objects. They occur in cameras, spectacles, telescopes, microscopes, and projectors.

Convex lens makes stamp look larger.

Magnifying glass

Convex lens

A convex lens curves outwards. Parallel light rays passing through a convex lens will converge (come together) at a point called the focus. Convex lenses can make an object look larger or smaller, depending on the distance of the object from the lens. They are used in spectacles to correct long sight.

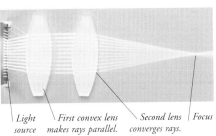

Light source

First convex lens makes rays parallel.

Second lens converges rays.

Focus

Concave lens

A concave lens is bowl-shaped and curves inwards. When parallel light rays pass through a concave lens, they diverge (spread out). Concave lenses make objects look smaller than they really are. This type of lens is used in spectacles to correct the vision disorder known as short sight.

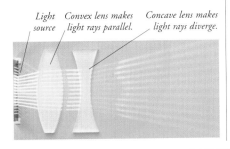

Light source

Convex lens makes light rays parallel.

Concave lens makes light rays diverge.

Mirrors

A mirror is a shiny surface. Parallel light rays striking a plane (flat) mirror will reflect off it at the same angle. Like lenses, curved mirrors cause light either to come together at a focus or to spread out. Convex and concave mirrors may form images and are used in many devices, including huge telescopes.

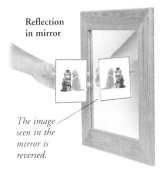

Reflection in mirror

The image seen in the mirror is reversed.

Concave mirror

A concave mirror, such as a shaving mirror, curves inwards. Parallel light rays striking a concave mirror converge to a focus. A concave mirror can make an object look larger or smaller, depending on its distance from the mirror.

Concave mirror

Convex mirror

Convex mirror

Parallel light rays diverge when they strike an outward-curving convex mirror. A convex mirror can make an object look smaller. A car's rear-view mirror gives a wide view, but makes other vehicles look farther away than they really are.

Total internal reflection

If a light ray enters a material at a shallow enough angle, it may be refracted so much that it does not emerge from the material, but is reflected inside it. Such total internal reflection is the reason light can travel along the length of a narrow glass bar. This principle is used in optical fibres, which are thin glass threads that carry laser light in telecommunications links.

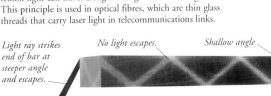

Light ray

Prism focuses light.

Light ray strikes end of bar at steeper angle and escapes.

No light escapes.

Shallow angle

Glass bar

Timeline

c.500,000 BC Fire used as lighting in cave dwellings.

1792 William Murdoch invents gas lighting.

c.1815 Augustin Fresnel, a French physicist, shows that light travels as waves.

1849 Fizeau shows that speed of light is 315,000,000 m/s.

1864 James Clerk Maxwell proves light is electro-magnetic radiation.

1879 Edison and Swan invent the light bulb.

1905 Einstein shows that light consists of particles.

1939 Fluorescent lamps first demonstrated

1999 New bulbs invented to last for 100,000 hours.

2000 Princeton scientists break the light barrier.

Edison's bulb

FIND OUT MORE   COLOUR   EINSTEIN, ALBERT   ENERGY   EYES AND SEEING   LASERS AND HOLOGRAMS   MICROSCOPES   TELESCOPES   X-RAYS AND THE ELECTROMAGNETIC SPECTRUM

LINNAEUS, CAROLUS

CAROLUS LINNAEUS, ALSO KNOWN as Carl von Linné, was a Swedish botanist, naturalist, and doctor, who was one of the first people to try to catalogue the immense variety of life in an organized way. To do this, he devised a system of scientific names using Latin, which was at the time the international language of science and learning. His system proved so simple and effective that it is still in use today.

Early life
Linnaeus was brought up in southern Sweden. He was fascinated by plants from a very early age, and was encouraged to study medicine by a local doctor who shared his interest in medicinal herbs. After receiving his degree, he became a university lecturer in botany.

Linnaeus as a young man

Travelling scientist

European travel played an important part in Linnaeus' achievements as a scientist, because it enabled him to see plants and animals from many different habitats. From 1732, he travelled throughout much of Europe, including the Arctic, but he also made a point of visiting the botanical gardens in Europe's great cities, where plants from far-off places were grown for scientific study. This gave him a broad insight into the variety of life on Earth.

Flora Lapponica

Lapland journey
In 1732, Linnaeus went on a three-month expedition to Lapland. This was one of the most important events in his life. Despite the difficult conditions during his explorations, he made detailed records of everything he found, and published them in a book called *Flora Lapponica* (The Plants of Lapland). This book established his reputation as a botanist, and paved the way for important works that were to follow.

Working abroad
In 1735, Linnaeus went to university in Holland to further his medical career. There he met a rich merchant, George Clifford, who owned a garden of exotic plants. Linnaeus identified and classified these plants. He also travelled to England and visited the Physic Garden at Chelsea, London, where medicinal plants are grown.

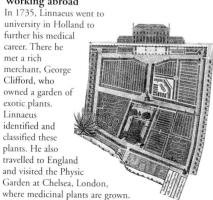

Botanist

Linnaeus was interested in almost every aspect of the living world, but botany, the study of plants, was his great love. In the early 1740s, after his stay in Holland, he returned to Sweden, where he became a professor of medicine, then of botany. In 1753, his book *Species Plantarum* (Species of Plants) appeared. It is still the most important book on plants ever published.

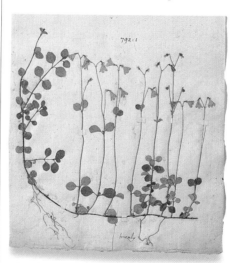

Classification
Linnaeus' greatest contribution to science was his system of two-part Latin names, or binomials. He devised them to simplify the confusing jumble of plant names that existed in his time, but their coverage slowly grew to include all living things. Today, they are an essential part of biological classification.

Later life
By the time he had reached his fifties, Linnaeus was one of the most respected scientists in the world. In 1761, he was given the Swedish rank of nobleman, and by the time he died in 1778, he had written nearly 200 scientific books. After his death, in 1778, Linnaeus' influence continued. His way of identifying living things has proved invaluable in showing how different species are related.

Hand lens

Linnaeus' dissecting equipment

Classifying plants
Linnaeus devised a new way of classifying plants. He called it his *Methodus sexualis*, or sexual method, because it was based largely on dissecting flowers to determine their male and female parts. Today, botanists no longer use this system, but it was an important first step in classifying plants in a logical way.

Genera Plantarum, with Linnaeus' own notes

Catalogues of life
In 1737, Linnaeus published *Genera Plantarum* (Types of Plants), one of his first great works of classification. This and his other books classified everything from plants and animals to types of rocks. His huge work *Systema naturae* (The System of Nature) was the largest of these books. It was constantly growing, and many editions were published.

CAROLUS LINNAEUS

1707	Born at Råshult, southern Sweden.
1727	Enters University of Lund.
1732	Expedition to Lapland.
1735	First edition of *Systema Naturae*.
1736	Visits England.
1741	Appointed Professor of Medicine at Uppsala.
1742	Appointed Professor of Botany at Uppsala.
1753	*Species Plantarum* published.
1778	Dies in Uppsala.

FIND OUT MORE   BIOLOGY   PLANTS   SCIENCE, HISTORY OF

LIONS AND OTHER WILD CATS

WILD CATS ARE SPECIALIST predators. They usually stalk their prey, dash from close range, and kill by biting the neck or head. There are 36 species of wild cat, ranging from the black-footed cat, weighing 2.2 kg (5 lb), to the tiger, weighing up to 280 kg (620 lb). Lions, tigers, jaguars, leopards, and snow leopards are called big cats and can roar; smaller cats can only purr. Many wild cats have been hunted almost to the point of extinction, some for their fur, others for preying on farmers' cattle.

Teeth

Wild cats have sharp teeth and powerful jaws, which equip them to eat flesh. The small, pointed incisors grip prey; large, curved canine teeth tear flesh, and sharp-edged cheek teeth (carnassials) cut through hide and muscle.

Broad head

Flexible back

Sandy-coloured coat

Claws (except those of the cheetah) can be retracted into protective sheaths, to protect them from unnecessary wear.

Strong, muscular body

Lioness

Large paws

Features of a wild cat

Wild cats have powerful bodies, and long tails to aid balance. They have sharp, curved claws that are used both to seize and hold prey and for defence. They have quick reflexes and excellent eyesight and hearing. Although they spend most of their time on the ground, wild cats are good climbers. Most wild cats are solitary creatures.

Long tail to aid balance.

Lioness grips buffalo around neck and bites throat.

Lions

Lions are the most powerful of all carnivores. They live mainly in Africa, but a small number survive in India. The males are about a third larger than females, which are known as lionesses. Males have manes that darken with age from a sandy colour to black. Manes help males look larger to impress females and intimidate rival males.

Shaggy mane

Roaring

The roar of the lion is one of the most characteristic sounds of the African night. It is heard at dawn and dusk, rarely during the day. Roaring is a means of marking out territory, and serves as a warning to other lions to keep away. All the big cats can roar.

African lion

Hunting

Lions live in grasslands where zebras and other animals on which they prey live in large numbers. Lionesses do most of the hunting, usually at dusk, and stalk their prey before launching an attack from close range. They leap on the animal, drag it to the ground, and bite its neck to kill it. Hunting is often communal, with one group of lionesses driving the prey towards another group lying in ambush. Male lions move in on the lionesses' kill and eat first.

Pride of lions

Lions are social animals and live in prides – family groups of several females and their young in loose association with a male. The females give the pride stability and strength. The male is lazy and regards the pride as a means of satisfying his needs, with the least exertion to himself. He mates with all the females, who give birth every two years to 2–6 cubs after 110 days' gestation. The cubs are reared communally by the females.

Lion

Cub

Lionesses rear cubs for 18 months and teach them how to hunt.

Flehmen

Flehmen forms part of a courtship display in which a male lion licks the female's urine, raises his head, and pulls back his upper lips to expose his teeth. He then draws air over a taste and smell organ in his mouth that enables him to identify females ready to mate. Flehmen is also linked to territorial behaviour.

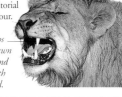

The lips are drawn back and the teeth exposed.

Tigers

There are eight types of tiger. They live in an area ranging from India through Southeast Asia to Siberia, Manchuria, and Indonesia. The Siberian tiger is the largest wild cat; males stand up to 110 cm (43 in) at the shoulder and weigh up to 280 kg (620 lb). Loss of habitat and reduction of its natural prey have seriously reduced tiger populations.

Reproduction

Tigresses mate every few years from about 3 years of age. The female comes on heat for 3–7 days and a pair mate many times during this period. After about 3½ months' gestation, 2–6 cubs are born; they are blind for the first 10 days. The mother suckles them for 8 weeks. Only 1–2 cubs in each litter survive.

Sumatran tiger with cubs

Indian tiger in undergrowth

Cubs stay with mother for 2–3 years.

Camouflage

The striking pattern of dark stripes on the contrasting tawny base colour acts as effective camouflage, and helps conceal the tiger in forest and grassland surroundings.

Territory

Tigers have individual territories, varying in size according to the terrain and quantity of prey. They mark out their territories by shredding tree bark and spraying urine. Female territories are small at 26 sq km (10 sq miles); male territories are larger and incorporate those of several females. A tiger may have several dens within its territory.

Sumatran tiger scratching tree

Leopards

Leopards live in much of Africa, southern Asia, and the Middle East; in fact they are more widely distributed than any other wild cat. Most leopards live in forests, but some live on grassland and woodland savannahs. They are excellent climbers, their long tails helping them to balance. They sleep, rest, and watch for prey from the branches of trees. Their coat varies from pale yellow to black and is covered in spots, providing effective camouflage against the light and shade of their surroundings.

Leopard roars to deter scavengers.

Leopard keeps a firm hold of the impala with its large paws and claws.

The impala is wedged into the fork of the tree to prevent hyenas, jackals, and other scavengers from eating it.

Female leopard with cub

Hunting

Leopards normally hunt at dusk or dawn and prey on many animals, including deer, medium-sized antelopes, baboons, and warthogs. They stalk their prey or lie in ambush, maybe on a branch overhanging a game trail. Leopards kill their prey by biting the throat or the back of the head. They are strong, agile animals and can easily carry prey of their own weight into a tree.

Reproduction

Leopards reach sexual maturity by 2½–3 years. The male is attracted by the smell of the female's urine when she is in season. They mate and stay together for a week. After a 3½-month gestation period, the female gives birth to 2–3 cubs in a rock crevice or dense thicket. The cubs are weaned by 3 months and independent by 2 years.

Cheetahs

With their long legs, small heads, and light build, cheetahs are the fastest animals on land. They can run at speeds of up to 100 kmh (62 mph). Female leopards usually live alone. Males often live in groups of 4–5 animals, typically brothers, that may stay together for life. In Africa, only 9,000–12,000 cheetahs remain due to their intolerance of disturbance and to their susceptibility to certain viral diseases transmitted by domestic animals.

Small head

Cheetah running at full speed

Male cheetahs often hunt together in small groups.

Long legs

Hunting

Cheetahs hunt by day when other predators are resting. They prey on small antelopes and gazelles, relying on their superior speed to run them down. They can only maintain high speed for short distances, and give up when they tire.

Habitat

Most wild cats live in forests, but they have adapted to live in habitats as diverse as deserts, wetlands, grasslands, and mountains. The sand cat, for example, lives in deserts and can get all the water it needs from its prey. It has thick pads on its feet so it can move fast over soft sand. The fishing cat lives in wetlands and has learnt to hunt by flipping fish out of the water.

Forest cats

Forest cats often have coats of stripes and spots that help them blend in with the light and shade of the forest. The margay and clouded leopard can hang upside down from branches, and run down trunks headfirst.

Jaguar in the rainforest

Mountain cats

Thick coats and dense underfur help wild cats to withstand cold mountain conditions. Camouflage is also important, especially for cats active by day. The snow leopard's coloration, for example, blends well with the grey rocks and snow of the mountains of central Asia.

Snow leopard in the snow

Small wild cats

Serval

Servals are agile creatures, with narrow heads and long legs. They live in well-defined territories in lightly wooded areas and the savannahs of sub-Saharan Africa. They hunt mainly at dusk, listening for the movement of lizards and rodents, such as the mole rat.

Large, erect ears

Very long legs

European wild cat

The European wild cat is believed to be the ancestor of the domestic cat. It lives in habitats ranging from forest to open grassland over most of Africa, western Europe, and Asia. It hunts on its own or in pairs, preying chiefly on rodents and birds.

Striped fur

Caracal

Caracals, also called desert lynxes, live in the semi-desert areas of Africa and India. They prey on animals such as birds, rodents, and small antelopes. They are good at leaping, and catch birds nesting in low branches; they may even leap into the air to seize birds on the wing. They can turn their ear tufts to communicate with rivals or mates.

Black ear tufts

Bobcat

The bobcat, or bay lynx, from North America, has adapted to live in high mountains, marshlands, forests, and deserts. At night it preys on rabbits, hares, and rodents. Males defend vast territories of up to 100 sq km (39 sq miles), and females an area half this size.

Short, stumpy tail

LION

SCIENTIFIC NAME *Panthera leo*

ORDER Carnivora

FAMILY Felidae

DISTRIBUTION Africa south of the Sahara, and the Gir Forest in India

HABITAT Open grasslands and lightly wooded savannahs

DIET Carnivorous, preying on animals such as wildebeest, zebras, antelopes, and gazelles. A group of lionesses will even tackle a buffalo. If very hungry, lions will also attack rhino calves

SIZE Height at shoulder 0.8 m (2 ft 6 in); weight 204 kg (450 lb)

LIFESPAN 15–16 years

FIND OUT MORE AFRICAN WILDLIFE ASIAN WILDLIFE CAMOUFLAGE AND COLOUR CATS CONSERVATION MOUNTAIN WILDLIFE NORTH AMERICAN WILDLIFE RAINFOREST WILDLIFE

Wild cats

Grassland cats

Shaggy mane makes male appear much larger than he really is.

Pumas also live in the mountains. They are powerful and may cover 7 m (23 ft) in a single leap.

Forest cats

Leopards' coat markings camouflage them very well, both in trees and on the ground.

Black panthers are a melanistic, or all black, version of the leopard.

Lions are the largest and most powerful of the grassland predators.

European wild cats are now quite rare in Europe. In Britain, they live only in Scotland.

Lynxes use their ear tufts to communicate, as their tails are too short for this purpose.

Servals can leap up to 3 m (10 ft) into the air to catch birds on the wing.

Cheetahs rely on their tremendous speed to run down their prey.

Jaguars, the largest and stockiest of the South American cats, are good tree climbers.

Tigers, the largest members of the cat family, are poor climbers, but good swimmers.

Mountain cats

The snow leopard's coat gets paler in winter which makes it less conspicuous.

Geoffroy's cats live at high altitude in the Andes.

Snow leopards live in the mountains of central Asia at heights of up to 5,500 m (18,000 ft).

Leopard cats live in the forests of Southeast Asia, and prey on small mammals and birds.

Bobcats get their name from their short, "bobbed" tails.

Ocelots have been hunted extensively for their beautiful coats.

Margays spend most of their time in trees, and hunt at night for nesting birds.

Ocelots hunt on the forest floor, but may also pounce from branches.

Wetland cats

Fishing cats scoop fish from the water with their paws.

Jungle cats live in reedbeds and among dense riverside vegetation.

Desert cats

Ear tufts

Sand cats live in the Sahara and the deserts of western Asia. They sleep by day in burrows.

Caracals can kill rodents and even small antelopes.

LIQUIDS

WHEN YOU SPILL A DRINK, it spreads out into an irregular puddle. None of the drink is lost, it simply takes on a different shape. This is because the drink is a liquid – a form of matter with a definite volume but no fixed shape. A liquid is made up of tiny vibrating particles of matter, such as atoms and molecules, held together by forces called chemical bonds. Water is by far the most common liquid on Earth.

When a liquid flows, its particles tend to cluster together as drops.

Properties of liquids

A liquid forms random shapes when it is allowed to flow freely. It also takes the shape of any container it is placed in. It is difficult to compress a liquid, because the forces between its particles prevent them from coming too close together.

A flowing liquid has no regular shape.

Liquid particles
A liquid's particles are able to move past one another, which is why a liquid can flow.

Surface tension

The attraction between a liquid's particles produces a force, or tension, across the liquid's surface that causes it to behave like a stretched "skin". Surface tension pulls drops and bubbles into spheres. Mercury has much stronger forces between its particles than water, so it has greater surface tension and forms more rounded droplets.

Water Droplet

Mercury droplet

Water   Mercury

Meniscus
A liquid's surface forms a curve called a meniscus where it meets the walls of its container. Liquids with weak bonds between their particles, such as water, cling to the walls and curve upwards. Those with strong bonds, such as mercury, pull away from the walls and curve downwards.

Viscosity
A liquid's viscosity is a measure of its ability to resist flowing. It results from friction between the liquid molecules as they try to slide past one another. Thick, viscous liquids, such as black treacle, have a lot of friction between their molecules; runny liquids, such as clear honey, have less friction and a lower viscosity.

Treacle   Syrup   Honey

Boiling point

Heating a liquid gives more energy to its particles and makes them vibrate faster. At a certain temperature, called the boiling point, all the particles have enough energy to break free of their bonds and bubbles of gas form rapidly throughout the liquid. Each liquid has its own specific boiling point.

Evaporation
Below its boiling point, a liquid may slowly change to a gas by evaporation. At the liquid's surface, a few particles at a time gain sufficient energy to escape into the air as a gas. Water evaporates from laundry on a clothes line because its molecules gain extra energy from the Sun and the wind.

Freezing
As a liquid cools, its particles lose energy and the bonds between them get stronger. At a temperature called its freezing point, the liquid becomes a solid. Impurities can lower the freezing point. For example, sea water, which contains salt, freezes at a much lower temperature than pure water.

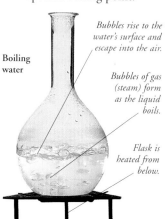
Boiling water

Bubbles rise to the water's surface and escape into the air.

Bubbles of gas (steam) form as the liquid boils.

Flask is heated from below.

Water

Each water molecule contains two hydrogen atoms linked to one oxygen atom. Above its boiling point (100°C, 212°F), water takes the form of a gas called steam. Below its freezing point (0°C, 32°F), water becomes a solid called ice. Water dissolves many substances, such as salt and sugar, to form solutions.

Hydrogen

Water molecule (H_2O)

Hydrogen

Oxygen

Hydrometer
A liquid's density is often given relative to the density of water. This "relative density" is measured with a device called a hydrometer. The higher the hydrometer floats in the liquid, the more dense it is. Glycerine has a relative density of 1.3, meaning that it is 1.3 times more dense than water. White spirit has a relative density of 0.7.

The relative density of water is 1.

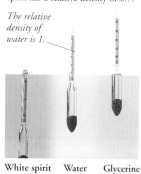
White spirit   Water   Glycerine

Ice
Most substances contract when they freeze, because their particles grow closer together. Water, however, expands as it freezes into ice, because its molecules spread out. This is why a drink sometimes rises out of the bottle as it freezes.

Frozen juice

Orange juice is mostly water.

Osmosis

When two solutions of different concentration are separated by a semi-permeable membrane (a porous barrier), liquid will flow from the weaker solution to the more concentrated one. This process is called osmosis. When you soak dried fruit, the fruit swells up as it absorbs water by osmosis through the walls of the fruit cells.

Dried fruit

Dried fruit after soaking in water

FIND OUT MORE ATOMS AND MOLECULES   FRICTION   GASES   MATTER   OCEANS AND SEAS   SOLIDS

LITERATURE

LITERATURE IS A WORK of art in words. It is writing that carries strong and lasting value through beauty or emotional power. At its heart, literature offers the reader important insights into the nature of human feelings and desires. The oldest form of literature is oral poetry, which was handed down by word of mouth and only later put into writing. Other forms include plays, novels, and short stories. Letters, journalism, speeches, and diaries can also be literature if they are especially well written.

What is literature?
Literature expresses the writer's thoughts, hopes, and fears. But not everything that is written is literature. Writing becomes literature only if it is well written and of lasting interest to people of many societies and different generations. Sometimes writers try to use literature to change the world in which they live, by protesting against injustice and influencing the opinions of people or governments.

Most modern literature is printed in bound books.

Oral literature
Long before written literature, people recorded their myths and stories in poems, told down the generations. Each storyteller added new details so the tales grew richer with every telling.

Costume design for Scheherazade

One Thousand and One Nights
This is a collection of folk tales that were once told by storytellers in Middle Eastern bazaars. In medieval Europe, the tales were written down and linked by the story of Scheherazade, a queen whose husband threatens to kill her. She enchants him by telling him stories for 1,001 nights until he spares her life.

Greek helmet

Iliad
The *Iliad* is an ancient Greek poem, one of the most famous ever written. It was probably composed orally before 800 BC. It tells of the war fought by Greece and Troy over Helen, the most beautiful woman in the world.

Epics and sagas
Epics are long poems telling the stories of legendary heroes, their adventures, and great deeds. They often record a culture's most precious traditions and beliefs. Sagas are prose epics written about the lives of famous men and women in medieval Iceland.

Beowulf
The Old English epic *Beowulf* was written c.700. It tells of the hero Beowulf, who kills two monsters, Grendel and Grendel's mother, but is finally slain by a dragon.

Themes of literature
Writers use their work to explore key themes that concern them and their readers. Throughout history and in every language, some themes are always present: love, death, morality, religious truth, and human loyalty. They can be explored through high-spirited comedy or bleak tragedy. Often, writers pick up themes, subjects, or styles from other writers and develop them further.

Pilgrim from the Tales

Chaucer
Geoffrey Chaucer (c.1343–1400) was one of the great figures of English literature. His most famous work, *The Canterbury Tales* (1387–1400), is a set of intertwined stories told by a group of pilgrims travelling to Canterbury. Chaucer borrows themes from European literature and English folk tales and turns them into a richly varied series of poems. Some are comic, others serious. They have remained popular for 600 years.

Illuminated page, *The Canterbury Tales*

Scenes from the story of Faust

Faust is confronted by the Devil.

Goethe
Johann Wolfgang von Goethe (1749–1832) is a central figure of German literature. He wrote poems, novels, and plays. His most famous literary work is a poetic drama, *Faust*, which is based on the medieval legend of a magician who sells his soul to the devil. Goethe uses the story to explore themes of sin, redemption, and the nature of art.

Dante
The Italian poet Dante Alighieri (1265–1321) was born in Florence. His masterpiece, *The Divine Comedy*, depicts the poet visiting Hell, Purgatory, and Paradise in a dream. The poem discusses the philosophical and religious questions of the day.

Book of Kings
For 1,000 years, the *Book of Kings (Shah-nameh)* has been the central achievement of Persian literature. The work of Firdausi (c.935–c.1020), it tells the story of the kings of Persia from mythical times. The many battles and fights against monsters it describes have made it a favourite source for modern Iranians.

Book of Kings

Rise of the novel

Novels are prose narratives presented in book form. Since the 18th century, they have become the most important literary form in the western world. Their popularity derives from their amazing variety. Novels can be minutely detailed pictures of ordinary life, or outrageous fantasies. They can explore realistic characters who reflect human problems, or tell simple exhilarating tales.

Windmills at La Mancha

Still from the film, *Sense and Sensibility*, 1995

Jane Austen
One of the first novelists to focus closely on the lives of ordinary people was the English writer Jane Austen (1775–1817). In novels such as *Sense and Sensibility* (1811), she wittily portrays the behaviour of men and women searching for happiness in love and marriage.

Miguel de Cervantes
The Spanish writer Miguel de Cervantes (1547–1616) published *Don Quixote* from 1605–15. The confused hero thinks he is a knight. In his madness, he attacks windmills, aided by his squire Sancho Panza. The book's popularity enabled Cervantes to write professionally.

Leo Tolstoy
The novels of Count Leo Tolstoy (1828–1910) include *War and Peace* (1863–69), set during the Napoleonic Wars, and *Anna Karenina* (1873–77), in which a married woman falls in love with a dashing soldier. The novels combine studies of Russian life with perceptive analyses of the characters' motives.

A samovar (tea urn) is part of Russian domestic life.

John Steinbeck
John Steinbeck (1902–1968) wrote about the hard life of the rural American poor. His most famous novel, *The Grapes of Wrath* (1939), follows a family who leaves the barren lands of Oklahoma to start a new life on the richer soil of California. Steinbeck won the Nobel Prize for Literature in 1962.

Still from the film *The Grapes of Wrath*, 1940

Short stories
The most successful short stories are very tightly plotted and carefully written. Often they hinge upon a single powerful event. In *The Metamorphosis* (1916), by the Czech writer Franz Kafka (1883–1924), a man wakes to find he has become a giant cockroach. Short stories often have a shocking ending. In 1841, the American writer Edgar Allen Poe (1809–49) published *The Murders in the Rue Morgue*, in which the killer turns out to be an orang-utan.

Orang-utan

Non-fiction

Not all literature is fictional. Many books have been written about real events, in the form of biographies, histories, and personal memoirs. Some of the most fascinating are diaries, such as that of Samuel Pepys (1633–1703), who lived through the Great Fire of London (1666). The diary of Anne Frank (1929–1945), which gives a moving account of her persecution by the Nazis during World War II, has been read by millions.

Jung Chang

Wild Swans
This book by Jung Chang (b.1952) recounts China's troubled recent history, as seen through the eyes of three generations of the author's family. It was published in 1991.

Popular culture

Many books do not try to explore deep truths about life, but satisfy the reader's desire to escape reality into a world of high adventure, fantasy, horror, or romance. Part of the writer's craft lies in giving a new twist to a familiar theme, such as crime-detection or espionage.

Boris Karloff

Magnifying glass

Red roses symbolize romance.

Horror
Since the 19th century, horror novels such as *Frankenstein*, published in 1818 by English author Mary Shelley (1797–1851), have exploited people's fear of monsters, ghosts, and the supernatural.

Crime
Ever since Arthur Conan Doyle (1859–1930) wrote about Sherlock Holmes, stories of crime and detection, or "whodunnits", have been hugely popular. Readers can try to solve the crimes for themselves, and marvel as the detective unravels the truth.

Romance
People often dream about finding perfect love, and popular romances show that dream coming true. The hero or heroine must overcome many obstacles and misunderstandings, before finally winning the heart of their loved one.

Timeline

From the film *Mahabharata*

Before 400 BC The epic poem *Mahabharata* is written in India. It is the longest poem ever composed.

c. 1000 AD The world's first novel is *The Tale of Genji* by Lady Murasaki, of the Imperial Court in Japan.

1100s The *Rubaiyat* is written by the Persian poet Omar Khayyám.

1580–1612 William Shakespeare (1564–1616), greatest ever British dramatist, writes his plays.

1719 Daniel Defoe (1660–1731) writes *Robinson Crusoe*, the first successful natural-style novel.

1852 *Uncle Tom's Cabin* by American Harriet Beecher Stowe (1811–96) features slavery.

1864 First science fiction story, *Journey to the Centre of the Earth* by Frenchman Jules Verne (1828–1905), is published.

1958 Nigerian writer Chinua Achebe (b.1930) publishes *Things*

Fall Apart, which charts Africa's journey from tradition to modernity.

1993 US writer Toni Morrison (b.1931), is the first black woman to win the Nobel Prize for Literature.

Toni Morrison

FIND OUT MORE   BOOKS   CHILDREN'S LITERATURE   DRAMA   LANGUAGE   PAPER   POETRY   PRINTING   WRITING

LIZARDS

BASKING IN THE SUN allows lizards to absorb its rays. Many lizards do this because they are cold-blooded reptiles and need heat to activate their bodies. There are more than 3,000 species of lizard and they live in most parts of the world. They vary in size from tiny chameleons, which can sit on a match head, to huge Komodo dragons. Not all lizards are sun-lovers; many have adopted nocturnal rainforest lifestyles or have adapted to live in caves.

Features of a lizard

Lizards belong to the same group of scaled reptiles as snakes. Unlike snakes most lizards have legs, moveable eyelids, ears, and a notched rather than a forked tongue, but there are exceptions. Some lizards, such as glass lizards, have small legs or none at all, and are thought to be more highly evolved than lizards with legs. Some small skinks, such as coconut skinks, have a clear spectacle over their eyes instead of eyelids. Monitor lizards have forked tongues and the Borneo earless monitor lizard lacks ears. Many lizards have a third, or pineal eye, used to monitor radiation levels when basking in the Sun.

L

Folds of scaled skin

Five toes with sharp claws

Eyed lizard

Worm lizards

There are about 100 types of worm lizard. They are related to true lizards, but belong to a different group of animals called the Amphisbaenia. They have ringed bodies and either no legs or just a front pair. They burrow in sand or leaf litter and feed on invertebrates. The largest worm lizard also eats carrion and small reptiles. They live in the tropics, except for one species that lives in Greece.

Black and white worm lizard

Adaptation to habitat

Lizards live in most environments from seashores to mountains, and from deserts to rainforests. Forest lizards such as chameleons can camouflage themselves and some have prehensile tails for climbing. Geckos have special toes to climb smooth surfaces. Marine iguanas have glands to excrete excess salt, and many mountain lizards are black to maximize heat absorption.

Rainforest lizards

Lizards live in all parts of the rainforest from the canopy down to the leaf litter. Rainforest lizards are agile climbers with long toes and claws. Most are green or brown for camouflage. "Flying geckos" and "flying lizards" do not actually fly, but have evolved a means of gliding downwards from high trees.

Sulawesi flying lizard

Desert lizards

Desert lizards obtain all their water from food and the early morning dew. They usually have flattened bodies and are pale brown in colour. Many are unusual in appearance, such as Australian frilled lizards, bearded dragons, thorny-backed molochs, and American horned toads, which are lizards despite their name.

Spikes on skin

Claws

Bearded dragon

Feeding

Lizard jaws and teeth are strong and can crush hard prey such as snails. Some eat insects, some eat larger animals and carrion, and others eat only plants. Many insectivorous lizards, such as some geckos, ambush their prey at night when they are attracted to lights; others, including chameleons, stalk and capture their prey with their long, sticky tongues.

Fly has just been captured.

Chameleon shoots out tongue at high speed.

Turret eyes can swivel in any direction.

Flap-necked chameleon

Movement

Lizards' legs join the body at the side so they have a twisting motion when they run. Some legless lizards move in jumps by flicking their tail. "Flying lizards" glide downwards using flaps of skin on their sides, legs, and tails that slow and aim their descent. Basilisks, also called "Jesus lizards", have long toes that enable them to run over the surface of water. Gecko feet are covered in tiny lamellae that help them grip smooth surfaces.

Tokay gecko

Reproduction

Some lizards lay leathery-shelled eggs in leaf litter or sandy holes. The eggs are left to incubate, and the young break out by using a special egg tooth. Other lizards are live bearers giving birth to fully formed infants in membranous sacs. A few species are parthenogenetic and exist only as females, producing offspring without a mate.

Soft-shelled eggs

Sand lizards with clutch of eggs

Defence

Lizards have evolved many ways of defending themselves. Horned lizards squirt blood from their eyes, crocodile skinks make loud screeching noises, and blue-tongued skinks stick out their bright blue tongues. Many lizards can shed their tails voluntarily; tensing the muscles suddenly breaks off the tail, which is left wiggling to confuse predators. Chameleons change colour to camouflage themselves, and many geckos are secretive by nature.

Australian frilled lizard

These lizards are found thoughout northern Australia and southern New Guinea. If threatened, they try to scare off attackers by erecting a large fan of skin supported by bones. The frill is also used in territorial disputes between rival males.

Frill of skin

EYED LIZARD

SCIENTIFIC NAME	*Lacerta lepida*
ORDER	Squamata
FAMILY	Lacertidae
DISTRIBUTION	Spain, Portugal, southern France, northwestern Italy, and North Africa
HABITAT	Dry scrubland, vineyards, and olive groves
DIET	Insects, smaller lizards, nestling birds, small mammals, and fruit
SIZE	Length 0.8 m (2 ft 7 in)
LIFESPAN	Up to 14 years (in captivity)

| FIND OUT MORE | CAMOUFLAGE AND COLOUR | DESERT WILDLIFE | EGGS | ISLAND WILDLIFE | RAINFOREST WILDLIFE | REPTILES | SEASHORE WILDLIFE |

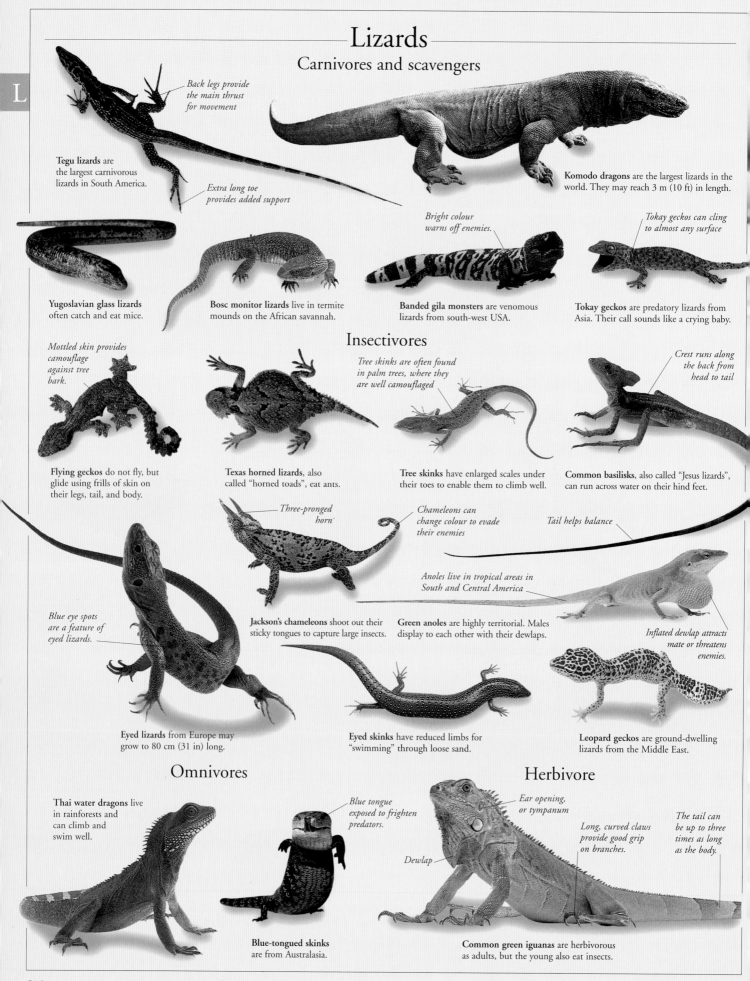

Lizards
Carnivores and scavengers

Back legs provide the main thrust for movement

Tegu lizards are the largest carnivorous lizards in South America.

Extra long toe provides added support

Komodo dragons are the largest lizards in the world. They may reach 3 m (10 ft) in length.

Bright colour warns off enemies.

Tokay geckos can cling to almost any surface

Yugoslavian glass lizards often catch and eat mice.

Bosc monitor lizards live in termite mounds on the African savannah.

Banded gila monsters are venomous lizards from south-west USA.

Tokay geckos are predatory lizards from Asia. Their call sounds like a crying baby.

Insectivores

Mottled skin provides camouflage against tree bark.

Tree skinks are often found in palm trees, where they are well camouflaged

Crest runs along the back from head to tail

Flying geckos do not fly, but glide using frills of skin on their legs, tail, and body.

Texas horned lizards, also called "horned toads", eat ants.

Tree skinks have enlarged scales under their toes to enable them to climb well.

Common basilisks, also called "Jesus lizards", can run across water on their hind feet.

Three-pronged horn

Chameleons can change colour to evade their enemies

Tail helps balance

Anoles live in tropical areas in South and Central America

Blue eye spots are a feature of eyed lizards.

Jackson's chameleons shoot out their sticky tongues to capture large insects.

Green anoles are highly territorial. Males display to each other with their dewlaps.

Inflated dewlap attracts mate or threatens enemies.

Eyed lizards from Europe may grow to 80 cm (31 in) long.

Eyed skinks have reduced limbs for "swimming" through loose sand.

Leopard geckos are ground-dwelling lizards from the Middle East.

Omnivores

Thai water dragons live in rainforests and can climb and swim well.

Blue tongue exposed to frighten predators.

Blue-tongued skinks are from Australasia.

Herbivore

Ear opening, or tympanum

Long, curved claws provide good grip on branches.

The tail can be up to three times as long as the body.

Dewlap

Common green iguanas are herbivorous as adults, but the young also eat insects.

LUNGS AND BREATHING

EVERY ONE OF THE BODY'S CELLS needs oxygen in order to release energy from food. The release of energy, known as aerobic respiration, produces a waste product called carbon dioxide that is expelled during exhalation. Breathing pumps air in and out of the lungs. Inside the lungs, an exchange takes place: oxygen moves from the air into the blood and carbon dioxide from the blood into the air. The lungs, and air passages linking the lungs to the outside of the body, make up the respiratory system.

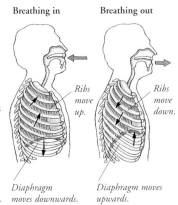

Breathing in **Breathing out**

Breathing
Although the lungs do not have muscles of their own, our breathing is nevertheless controlled by muscles. Air is pumped in and out of the lungs by the action of the intercostal muscles situated between the ribs and by the diaphragm between the chest and abdomen.

Ribs move up. *Ribs move down.*

Diaphragm moves downwards. *Diaphragm moves upwards.*

Lungs
The two lungs are spongy, pink organs lying in the chest, protected by the ribcage. Below the lungs is a sheet of muscle called the diaphragm. An airway called the bronchus enters each lung and branches repeatedly to form smaller bronchi, which themselves branch into very fine airways called bronchioles.

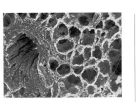

Alveoli
The bronchioles end as tiny air sacs called alveoli. It is through the alveoli that oxygen enters, and carbon dioxide leaves, the blood. There are over 600 million alveoli in the lungs.

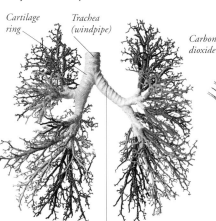

Cartilage ring
Trachea (windpipe)

Bronchiole is the smallest branch of a bronchi. It ends in alveoli.

Bronchus is one of two main branches of the trachea; it divides into smaller bronchi.

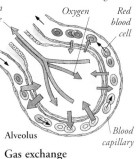

Carbon dioxide *Oxygen* *Red blood cell*

Alveolus

Gas exchange
Each alveolus is surrounded by a network of blood capillaries. Oxygen from the air dissolves in the moisture lining the alveolus and passes into the blood. Carbon dioxide passes from the blood into the alveolus.

Blood capillary

Vocal cords

Larynx (voice box)

Cartilage ring helps keep trachea open during breathing.

Trachea carries air to and from lungs.

Right lung

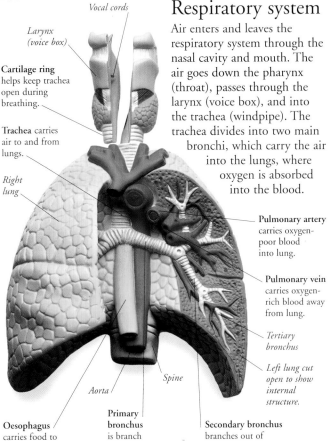

Respiratory system
Air enters and leaves the respiratory system through the nasal cavity and mouth. The air goes down the pharynx (throat), passes through the larynx (voice box), and into the trachea (windpipe). The trachea divides into two main bronchi, which carry the air into the lungs, where oxygen is absorbed into the blood.

Pulmonary artery carries oxygen-poor blood into lung.

Pulmonary vein carries oxygen-rich blood away from lung.

Tertiary bronchus

Left lung cut open to show internal structure.

Aorta *Spine*

Oesophagus carries food to stomach.

Primary bronchus is branch of trachea.

Secondary bronchus branches out of primary bronchus.

Larynx
The larynx links the throat to the trachea. It is made of pieces of cartilage, one of which you can feel as a triangular lump called the Adam's apple in the front of your neck. The upper piece of cartilage forms a flap called the epiglottis, which blocks the entrance to the larynx when you swallow food. Stretched between the pieces of cartilage at the base of the larynx are the vocal cords.

Coughing and sneezing
Coughing clears mucus and dirt from the trachea, and sneezing clears the nose. For both actions, you take a deep breath and muscles squeeze your lungs. Your vocal cords suddenly open and air rushes upwards dislodging particles.

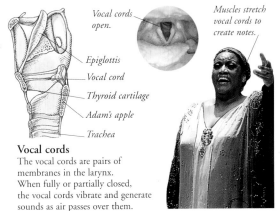

Vocal cords open.

Epiglottis
Vocal cord
Thyroid cartilage
Adam's apple
Trachea

Vocal cords
The vocal cords are pairs of membranes in the larynx. When fully or partially closed, the vocal cords vibrate and generate sounds as air passes over them.

Muscles stretch vocal cords to create notes.

People yawn when resting or tired.

Yawning
When you yawn, you breathe in deeply with your mouth wide open. This ventilates the lungs, flushing out "stale" air and replacing it with fresh air.

FIND OUT MORE | DIGESTION | FIRST AID | GASES | HEALTH AND FITNESS | HEART AND CIRCULATORY SYSTEM | HUMAN BODY | MUSCLES AND MOVEMENT | SKELETON

M

MACHINES, SIMPLE

A MACHINE IS A DEVICE that makes a job easier to do. Most of the machines in our daily lives are complex devices made up of a combination of simpler machines such as pulleys, levers, and gears. Machines that magnify a force, or "effort", applied to them are said to give a mechanical advantage. Other machines change the size, direction, or speed of a movement.

Inclined plane

A slope that reduces the effort needed to lift a load forms a simple machine called an inclined plane. A shallow slope reduces the effort more than a steep one, but the slope is longer, so the load must travel farther.

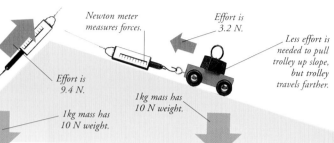

Newton meter measures forces.

Effort is 9.4 N.

1kg mass has 10 N weight.

Effort is 3.2 N.

Less effort is needed to pull trolley up slope, but trolley travels farther.

1kg mass has 10 N weight.

Inclined planes

Lever

A rod that moves about a pivot, or fulcrum, is called a lever. A force (the effort) applied to one part of a lever moves another part with a larger or smaller force (the load), and through a different distance. This mechanical digger uses levers to move soil from place to place.

Dipper is a lever that moves the bucket in and out.

Boom is a lever that raises and lowers the dipper.

Bucket is a lever that scoops up material.

Effort

Fulcrum

Load

Class one levers are levers in which the fulcrum lies between the effort and the load. Pliers consist of two identical class one levers with the same fulcrum.

Class two levers have a load between the fulcrum and the effort. A nutcracker is a pair of class two levers. The load is the force required to crack the nut.

Class three levers are produced when the force is applied between the fulcrum and the load. Kitchen tongs consist of two class three levers joined at the fulcrum.

Fulcrum

Effort

Load

Effort

Fulcrum

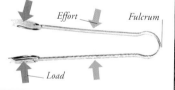

Load

Effort and load

On an inclined plane, the effort is the force needed to pull an object up the slope. The load is the weight of the object being lifted. These forces are measured in units called newtons (N).

Screw

A screw is a shaft with a spiralling inclined plane, called a thread, wrapped around it. Turning the screw makes it move forward with a greater force than the effort used to turn it. As the screw turns, objects are pushed away or pulled up the thread. This clamp uses a screw to hold an object tightly onto a work surface.

Screw thread

Christopher Polhem

Swedish inventor Christopher Polhem (1661–1751) contributed much to our understanding of machines. He wrote over 20,000 articles on engineering and many other subjects, and was one of the first to see the potential of using machines to replace human labour.

Mechanical advantage

A machine's mechanical advantage is calculated by dividing the load by the effort. The shallow slope above gives an advantage of 3.13 ($10 \div 3.2$), while the steep slope gives only 1.06 ($10 \div 9.4$).

Spiral staircase

A staircase is a type of inclined plane that makes it easier to lift your body to the top of a building. Wrapping the stairs around a shaft to form a spiral staircase saves space. The steeper the stairs, the fewer turns it takes to climb them, but the more force you need to apply on each step.

Machine elements

Inside most complex machines, a number of simple machines and other mechanical parts link together to control, transmit, or change force and motion, so that the larger machine can perform a specific task.

Flywheel is a heavy disc that rotates at a constant speed and ensures that a machine runs smoothly.

Crank is a rod linked to a rotating shaft that changes circular motion into to and fro motion.

Cam-follower

Worm gear

Cam is an irregularly shaped wheel that moves a rod called a cam-follower to and fro as it rotates.

Bevel gear

Spur gear

Gears are toothed wheels that alter the size of a force, or the speed or direction of motion.

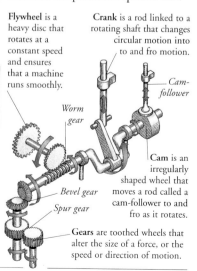

Block and tackle

A block and tackle is a device for lifting heavy loads. It consists of a rope (the tackle) passing over a pulley wheel (the block), and changes the direction of pull on the rope.

Multiple pulley arrangements

A rope looped around a number of pulleys becomes a force magnifier. When the rope is pulled, the load moves a shorter distance than the rope, reducing the effort needed to lift it. The more loops of rope there are, the more the effort is reduced.

Wheel and axle

A wheel fixed to a central shaft forms a machine called a wheel and axle. When the axle turns, the wheel rim turns with less force, but travels a greater distance. Turning the wheel rim moves the axle a shorter distance, but with more force.

Engine turns axle, rotating wheel and moving vehicle.

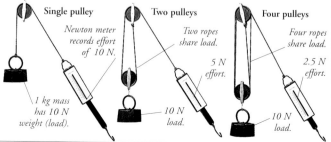

Single pulley

Newton meter records effort of 10 N.

1 kg mass has 10 N weight (load).

Two pulleys

Two ropes share load.

5 N effort.

10 N load.

Four pulleys

Four ropes share load.

2.5 N effort.

10 N load.

FIND OUT MORE ENGINES AND MOTORS FORCE AND MOTION FRICTION TECHNOLOGY

MAGELLAN, FERDINAND

FERDINAND MAGELLAN, A PORTUGUESE sailor employed by Spain, was the first person to sail westwards across the Atlantic and Pacific Oceans. He did this because the Spanish wanted to find a route to the rich Spice Islands (now the Moluccas) in southeastern Asia, which were unclaimed by any foreign power. Although it was not Magellan's original intention, one of his ships continued the voyage westwards, eventually arriving back in Europe. By completing this remarkable voyage, its crew became the first people to sail all the way around the world.

Early life
Magellan was born into a noble Portuguese family in about 1480. He served as a page in a royal household and then worked in India for Francisco de Almeida, the first Portuguese viceroy (governor) in India. In 1513–14, he worked for the Portuguese in Morocco, but was accused of financial irregularities and lost the favour of the king of Portugal. The king rejected Magellan's proposal to reach the Spice Islands by sailing a westerly course across the Atlantic Ocean.

M

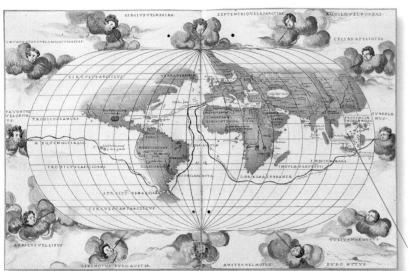

Map of the *Vittoria*'s route

Circumnavigation
In 1517, Magellan took his plan for a journey to the Spice Islands to Charles V of Spain, who provided him with five ships and about 265 men. In September 1519, Magellan set sail from Seville. In November 1520, he entered the Pacific and sailed west towards Asia. He reached the Philippines in 1521, where he was killed. Some of his men got back to Spain in 1522.

The Moluccas in southeast Asia were Magellan's goal when he set off on his westward voyage around the world

Mutiny
While Magellan was spending the winter of 1520 at San Julian at the tip of South America, some of his crew tried to mutiny. One ship was wrecked and two more were lost. Later, one ship deserted Magellan and returned to Spain.

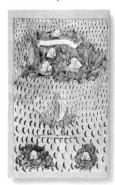

East Indies
In 1494, Pope Alexander VI divided the then unclaimed world of America and Asia between Spain and Portugal. West of the dividing line was land claimed by Spain, east was territory claimed by Portugal. But the Moluccas in the East Indies, with their rich spice crops, remained unclaimed. To reach these islands, Magellan had to sail west across the Pacific. Magellan named this ocean the Pacific (peaceful), because its waters were so calm after the turbulent Atlantic.

Cinnamon

Nutmeg

Ginger

Strait of Magellan
In October 1520, the two lost ships reappeared, reporting that they had found a channel between the mainland and the island of Tierra del Fuego. Magellan set sail with his three remaining ships and, on 21 October, entered the channel, now called the Strait of Magellan. By 28 November they had become the first Europeans to sail into the Pacific.

Death of Magellan
On 6 March 1521, Magellan reached the Mariana Islands. Ten days later, he made landfall in the Philippines. At Mactan, on the island of Cebu in the Philippines, Magellan intervened in a local war, but was killed in a skirmish on 27 April. His crew decided to continue on towards Europe without him.

Vittoria
In April 1521, after Magellan's death, his lieutenant, Sebastián del Cano, took command, setting sail with just two ships. One ship, the *Trinidad,* then sailed across the Pacific to Panama, leaving the other, the *Vittoria,* to sail on around the world. In September 1522, the *Vittoria* returned to Spain.

FERDINAND MAGELLAN	
c.1480	Born in Portugal.
1505–12	Serves in India.
1513–14	Serves in Morocco but loses the favour of Portugal's king.
1517	Approaches the king of Spain with proposal to sail to the Spice Islands.
1519	Sets sail from Seville.
1520	Sails into the Pacific Ocean.
1521	Killed in the Philippines.
1521	Under the command of del Cano, the remaining two ships load with spices in the Moluccas.
1522	The *Vittoria* returns to Spain.

FIND OUT MORE	MAPS AND MAPPING	EXPLORATION	SPAIN, HISTORY OF

MAGNETISM

SAILORS USED MAGNETIC compasses to find their way on the world's oceans at least 1,000 years ago, but the true nature of magnetism puzzled people for many centuries. Magnetism is an invisible force that comes from objects called magnets. The region around a magnet in which its magnetism acts is called a magnetic field.

Magnet

A magnet has two points, called a north pole and a south pole, where its magnetism is strongest. Lines of magnetic force loop around the magnet from pole to pole.

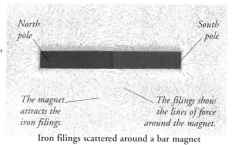

North pole

South pole

The magnet attracts the iron filings.

The filings show the lines of force around the magnet.

Iron filings scattered around a bar magnet

Magnetic forces

When two magnets are placed pole to pole, a force acts between them. Different poles (a north and a south) pull each other together. This is attraction. Similar poles (two north or two south) push each other apart. This is repulsion.

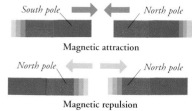

South pole   *North pole*

Magnetic attraction

North pole   *North pole*

Magnetic repulsion

Magnetic Earth

The Earth itself acts like a giant bar magnet, with a magnetic field and two magnetic poles. These poles are found near the Earth's geographical North and South poles. The Earth's magnetism is probably caused by the movement of molten iron at the Earth's core.

Compasses line up with the Earth's magnetic field.

Magnetite

The rocky mineral magnetite, which contains iron, is naturally magnetic. Early sailors used a piece of this rock suspended from a string as a magnetic compass. Magnetite is also called lodestone, which means "guiding stone".

Compass

A compass is a navigational device containing a small, free-moving magnet called a "needle". The needle is attracted by the Earth's magnetism. It swivels round on a pivot until one end points to the Earth's magnetic north pole and the other end points to the magnetic south pole.

Maglev train

A maglev (magnetic levitation) train hovers above the track, supported by a strong force of repulsion between magnets on the train and the track. Other magnets pull the train along the track.

Magnetism in space

The Earth's magnetic field stretches more than 60,000 km (37,000 miles) out into space. In addition to affecting objects on the planet's surface, the Earth's magnetism also affects electrically charged particles such as electrons and protons emitted by the Sun. The other planets in the Solar System also have magnetic fields, as does the Sun itself.

Geographic North
Magnetic north

Earth's magnetic field

Magnetic south
Geographic South
Lines of force

Magnetic materials

When placed within a magnet's force field, some materials turn into magnets themselves – either briefly or permanently. These materials are said to be magnetic.

Magnets will attract iron and some other metals.

Domains in a magnetic material   **Domains in a magnet**

Non-magnetic materials, such as plastic and cloth, cannot be picked up by magnets.

Magnetic domains

Inside a magnetic material are tiny regions of magnetism called domains, all pointing in different directions. Their effects cancel out, so there is no overall magnetism. In a magnet, the domains all point the same way. Their effects combine to give a strong magnetism.

This steel rod is magnetized by stroking it with a bar magnet.

Magnetic induction

Placing a magnet near a magnetic material causes the material's domains to line up and point in the same direction, turning it into a magnet. This is magnetic induction. The effect is usually temporary, but some materials, such as steel, stay permanently magnetized.

William Gilbert

The study of magnetism was pioneered by William Gilbert (1544–1603), an English doctor and physicist. He suggested that the Earth's magnetism is best understood by thinking of the Earth as a huge bar magnet. Gilbert was also the first to use the term "magnetic pole".

Aurora

The Earth's magnetic poles pull electrically charged particles from the Sun into the atmosphere. As the particles strike atoms or molecules in the air, coloured light is emitted in a dazzling display called an aurora.

Solar prominence

Occasionally, disturbances in the Sun's magnetic field allow huge streams of hot gas to erupt from the Sun's surface. Such eruptions are called solar prominences, and they can be up to 100,000 km (62,000 miles) high.

FIND OUT MORE   EARTH   ELECTRICITY   ELECTROMAGNETISM   FORCE AND MOTION   X-RAYS AND THE ELECTROMAGNETIC SPECTRUM

MALAYSIA AND SINGAPORE

THE 13 STATES of Malaysia are split into two distinct parts. Most people live in Malaya, a long peninsula of mainland Southeast Asia containing 11 states, which has the island of Singapore at its southernmost tip. The two remaining Malaysian states of Sarawak and Sabah occupy the northern part of the island of Borneo. Sandwiched between them is Brunei, one of the richest countries in the world. Malaysia, Singapore, and Brunei are all former British territories; Malaysia and Singapore gained independence in the 1960s, and Brunei in 1984. Since then, their economies, particularly Malaysia's, have developed at a dramatic rate.

Plural societies

Like other Southeast Asian countries, Malaysia, Singapore, and Brunei are plural societies. The term describes peoples who live together, but keep their own culture, language, and way of life. Kuala Lumpur is home to a cosmopolitan mix of people, including Malays, Chinese, Indians, and various indigenous groups.

People waiting at a bus stop, Kuala Lumpur

Mountains and forests
Large areas of Sabah and Sarawak are dominated by mountains that are covered with forest and jungle. In some places the vegetation is so dense that the terrain is virtually impenetrable. The Rajang river loops through Sarawak, interrupted by spectacular waterfalls.

Cameron Highlands
Located in Penang state on the Malay Peninsula, the Cameron Highlands rise about 1,200 m (4,000 ft) above sea-level. The fresh, cool air and magnificent views have made them one of the best-known resorts in Asia. The soil is rich, and the Highlands have become the centre of Malaysia's tea-growing industry.

Regional climate
Malaysia, Singapore, and Brunei have a hot and humid tropical climate all the year round. They are vulnerable to seasonal monsoon winds, which can cause dramatic differences in the distribution of rainfall. The coolest areas are the mountains and high ground, and where breezes sweep in from the sea.

27°C (81°F)   27°C (81°F)

2,403 mm (95 in)

Physical features
A central mountain chain in the Malay Peninsula divides fertile plains in the west from a narrow coastal belt in the east. Singapore is largely flat and is built-up, making it almost a single city-state. Sabah and Sarawak have swampy coastal plains and are separated from the Indonesian part of Borneo by rugged, heavily forested mountains. The interior of Brunei is covered with humid tropical rainforest.

Sarawak Chamber
Lubang Nasib Bagus, also known as the Sarawak Chamber, is the world's largest single cave. The chamber forms part of a large cave system in Gunung Mulu National Park, and measures about 700 m (2,300 ft) long, 300 m (980 ft wide), and more than 70 m (230 ft) high.

Malaysia

One of the most dynamic countries in Southeast Asia, Malaysia has experienced tremendous economic growth in recent years. While the timber, oil, rubber, and tin industries are still predominant, Malaysia has encouraged manufacturing, which now accounts for over two-thirds of exports. As a result, urban areas are rapidly expanding, although 43 per cent of the population still lives in rural areas, mostly in the Malay Peninsula. Only about 19 per cent live in Sabah and Sarawak. Malaysia's 13 states are ruled by sultans and governors, from which a new king is chosen every five years.

People

Malays and other indigenous people form about 60 per cent of Malaysia's population. Chinese traders settled in the country from the 1400s onward, and later, during the British colonial period, many Indian and Chinese people were brought in as workers. These Perenakan (Malaya-born) Chinese formed their own society, a mixture of Chinese and Malay cultures, and now make up 30 per cent of the population. They control much of Malaysia's business and are richer than the Malays, causing some tension.

Wealthy Perenakan women

Kuala Lumpur

Malaysia's capital city began as a mining camp at the junction of two rivers. Its Malay name literally means "muddy meeting place". It is a bustling city, with modern high-rise buildings and traditional temples. One of the most elaborate buildings is the railway station. The city is home to 1,500,000 people. However, a new capital city is being planned at the high-tech development of Putrajaya.

Railway station

Sepak raga

Among Malaysia's traditional sports is *sepak raga*, which is played with a *raga*, or ball woven from strips of rattan. Rattan comes from the reedy stems of certain species of palm trees that are extensively grown in the country. In the game, players try to pass the ball by kicking or heading it, but must not use their hands. The player who lets the ball touch the ground is the loser. Another popular game is *main gasing*, played with spinning tops made from hardwood and carefully placed lead weights.

Kite-flying

Malaysia's national pastime is kite flying, known as *wau*, which was introduced from China. An international festival is held in Kelantan every June, in which the object is to keep one's kite flying as high and for as long as possible.

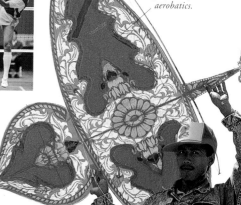

Experienced kite-flyers can make their huge, brightly coloured kites perform spectacular aerobatics.

Tea

A tea shoot, or flush

Malaysia's hot, humid climate is ideal for growing tea, and about 6,000 tonnes (6,613 tons) are produced every year. Most tea grows in plantations, particularly around the Cameron Highlands. Tea-pickers, usually women, collect the young, tender shoots, called flushes, in large baskets, which they carry on their backs. New shoots appear every few days and must be dried quickly for the best flavour.

Dried tea leaves

Palm oil

Malaysia leads the world in the production of palm oil, which comes from the fruit of the oil palm tree. The oil is mainly used for cooking and is exported around the world for use in the manufacture of margarine, ice cream, and soap. This industry has reduced Malaysia's dependence on rubber.

Rubber

Malaysia is the world's second largest producer of natural rubber. Rubber trees were introduced from Brazil in 1876 and are now grown in large plantations on the slopes of the Malay Peninsula. Workers collect latex in a cup or halved coconut as it oozes from cuts made in the trees' bark. The latex is then sent to a local factory where it is mixed with water and acid to make rubber sheets, which are hung out to dry.

Electronics

The electronics industry, developed since the 1970s to broaden Malaysia's economic base, is now its most profitable. Malaysia is one of the world's major producers of disk drives for computers, and one of the leading manufacturers of integrated circuits. Japan is a key trading partner, often exchanging finished products for raw materials, such as oil and gas.

Proton cars

More than 150,000 Proton cars are produced every year. First made in 1985, they are the most popular cars in Malaysia and are exported to Indonesia, Singapore, and the UK. Such is the Proton's success, that a second model was launched in 2000.

Singapore

In 1819, Sir Stamford Raffles (1781–1826) set up a British trading post in Singapore, formerly known as Temasek, which enabled the island to be a free trade centre for the East Indies. Now, it boasts a successful export-led economy and tourist trade. One of the world's most densely populated countries, Singapore has a myriad of traditional cultures and buildings alongside towering skyscrapers and space-age shops.

Chinatown
Nearly 78 per cent of the population are Chinese. Chinatown, in Singapore City, is a colourful, busy area where traditional cultures flourish. The district is a popular tourist attraction, offering authentic Chinese foods, ancient crafts, and ornate temples.

Laws
Singapore's government keeps strict control over the media, and dropping litter, chewing gum, eating on trains, and smoking in public are forbidden in urban areas. As punishments are severe, Singapore enjoys a very low crime rate.

Golf
Singapore is known for its high density of golf courses, and now offers specialized golfing holidays. The facilities are enjoyed both by people on business and local golfers. It is usual for games to go on well into the evening.

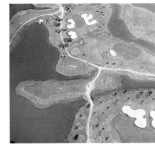

Financial centre
Since the 1960s, Singapore has become one of the leading financial centres of eastern Asia. It has secured huge foreign investment in establishing manufacturing and electronics industries. The many banks and the stock exchange generate about one-quarter of the country's wealth alone. Singapore's economic future is predicted to be in the high-tech skilled field.

Orchids
Land for farming is scarce in Singapore, but the country has several orchid nurseries. At the Mandai Garden, the largest commercial orchid nursery in Singapore, exotic and rare flowers are cultivated intensively for export using the latest technology. The orchids are prized for their beauty and colour and are flown to Japan, Australia, Europe, and the USA.

The orchid is Singapore's national flower.

SINGAPORE FACTS

CAPITAL CITY	Singapore
AREA	648 sq km (250 sq miles)
POPULATION	4,100,000
MAIN LANGUAGES	Malay, Mandarin, Tamil, English
MAJOR RELIGIONS	Buddhist/Taoist, Muslim
CURRENCY	Singapore dollar

Singapore harbour
Over 25,000 ships dock at Singapore harbour every year, making it one of the busiest ports in the world. Tankers bring crude oil from the Gulf States to be refined and shipped out to neighbouring east Asian countries. Most of Malaysia's export trade flows through the port.

Transport system
About 800,000 passengers a day travel on the Mass Rapid Transport System, a highly efficient train that runs partly underground. It was created as part of a policy to relieve congested roads. Car drivers must bid at auction for the right to buy new cars, and must pay to enter the city during rush hour. Singapore also has rail links with Malaysia.

Brunei

The tiny state of Brunei is an Islamic monarchy. Massive offshore reserves of oil and natural gas have made it extremely wealthy. As a result, the small population enjoys free education, healthcare, and pensions, and pays no income tax. Only about 15 per cent of the land is farmed, since Brunei is mostly rainforest. Rice, tropical fruit, and cassava are the main crops.

Sultans
Brunei is a monarchy, ruled since 1967 by the sultan Hassaal Bolkiah. He is one of the world's richest men, believed to be worth US$25 billion. Recently, the sultan built a lavish royal palace in the capital, Bandar Seri Begawan. The city also houses Southeast Asia's largest mosque, named after Bolkiah's predecessor, Omar Ali Saifuddien. A popular tourist site, it has its own lagoon.

BRUNEI FACTS

CAPITAL CITY	Bandar Seri Begawan
AREA	5,770 sq km (2,228 sq miles)
POPULATION	335,000
MAIN LANGUAGES	Malay, English
MAJOR RELIGION	Muslim
CURRENCY	Brunei dollar

Mineral wealth
Huge offshore oil reserves were discovered in Brunei in 1929. Recent estimates say there are at least 40 years' worth of natural gas and 25 years of oil reserves left. Much of Brunei's mineral income is invested.

FIND OUT MORE ASIA, HISTORY OF · CARS AND TRUCKS · ELECTRONICS · EMPIRES · FLOWERS · ISLAM · KITES · MONEY · OIL · PORTS AND WATERWAYS · TRAINS AND RAILWAYS

MALI EMPIRE

M

ONE OF THE WEALTHIEST medieval African kingdoms was that of the Mali. Founded in c.1235 in West Africa by a great warrior-king, Sundiata, the empire reached its peak in the 14th century under Sundiata's descendent, Mansa Musa. Mali wealth came from gold mines and trans-Saharan trade, and helped the empire dominate surrounding peoples, such as the Songhai. In the 1400s the Songhai began to attack the overgrown Mali Empire and eventually conquered it.

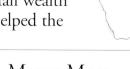

Mansas

Mansa, or "king of kings", was the title used by all Mali's rulers. Sundiata (r.1235–55), the first mansa, was a member of a tribe ruled by ancient Ghana. Sundiata overthrew Ghana (which was 800 km, or 500 miles, northwest of modern Ghana), established his empire there, and converted to Islam.

Mansa Musa

Mansa Musa

Kankan Musa, better known as Mansa Musa (r.1312–37), was Mali's greatest ruler, as famous for his piety as for his military successes. After conquering Tombouctou, Gao, and Walata, he established new schools, colleges, and libraries in Tombouctou, and made it a centre for Islamic learning.

Charles V's Catalan map, 1375, depicting the Mali Empire

Extent of empire

At its height in the 14th century, the Mali Empire covered a large part of what is now Senegal, Gambia, Guinea, and the Republic of Mali. The city of Djénné, and the Songhai cities of Tombouctou and Gao on the River Niger, became major trading centres. Tombouctou was particularly famous for its trade in gold. The gold was mined in the Niger and Senegal river valleys and exported to North Africa across the Sahara Desert.

Pilgrimage to Mecca

In 1324–25, Mansa Musa made a pilgrimage to Mecca. This pilgrimage was so lavish it made Mali famous throughout the world. When he passed through Egypt, Mansa Musa distributed so much gold – possibly as much as 1.5 tonnes – that he devalued the metal and depressed the local gold market for years afterwards.

Architecture

The 14th-century Great Mosque in Djénné is the world's largest surviving dried-mud building. Every year, after the rainy season, local people gather together to replaster it by hand. While on pilgrimage in the 14th century, Mansa Musa met the Spanish scholar and architect As-Saheli and persuaded him to go to Mali. When As-Saheli arrived at the important trading town of Tombouctou, he introduced "burnt" bricks as a new building material for important buildings, such as mosques and palaces.

Spires decorated with ostrich eggs, the symbol of fertility and fortune • *Protruding beams*

Great Mosque at Djénné

Trade

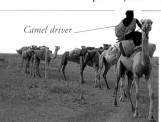
Camel driver

Caravans
Camel caravans of up to 10,000, transported Mali's goods across the Sahara. They could cover 350 km (200 miles) of desert in a week.

As well as spreading Islam, Arab traders also developed caravan routes across the Sahara. These routes linked north African towns, such as Fez and Cairo, with west African towns, such as Djénné. The wealth of sub-Saharan empires depended on controlling these trade routes, which Mali did between 1235 and c.1400.

Djenné
Traders transported goods along the River Niger to and from Djénné. The town was also on a caravan route going south. Therefore, it became a market place for northern African goods going to southern forest kingdoms, such as Benin.

Modern market day, Djénné, Mali

Ibn Battuta
In 1325, the Moroccan writer, jurist, and diplomat Ibn Battuta (1304–77) went on pilgrimage to Mecca. Over 29 years he covered 120,000 km (75,000 miles) in 44 countries. His last journey was to the Mali Empire where he visited the court of Mansa Sulayman, praised Mali piety, but saw little of the famous Mali gold.

Timeline
1235–55 Sundiata rules Mali, after subjugating Ghana Empire.

1255 Sundiata's eldest son, Mansa Oulin, seizes power. Decades of struggle over the succession follow.

1298 Sundiata's general, Sakura (1285–1300), seizes power.

1300 Saharan robbers murder Sakura.

African figs

1312–37 Mansa Musa rules.

1324–25 Mansa Musa's pilgrimage to Mecca.

c.1320–40 Mali Empire reaches its peak.

1336–58 Reign of Mansa Sulayman (Mansa Musa's grandson).

1352 The Arab traveller, Ibn Battuta, stays in the old Mali capital of Niani for nine months.

c.1400 Gao rebels against Mali overlords; empire begins to decline.

1468 Songhai Empire takes over Mali Empire.

FIND OUT MORE AFRICA, HISTORY OF • BENIN EMPIRE • ISLAMIC EMPIRE • ISLAM • SONGHAI EMPIRE

MAMMALS

MAMMALS ARE a very complex and diverse group of animals, which includes the largest creatures on Earth. They are remarkably flexible and through adaptations they are able to live in all regions of the world apart from the Antarctic continent. Mammals are characterized by having hair, a backbone, mammary glands with which they feed their young, and a particular articulation of the lower jaw. They are warm blooded, which means they have a constant internal body temperature, rather than adjusting to the temperature of their immediate surroundings.

Skeleton

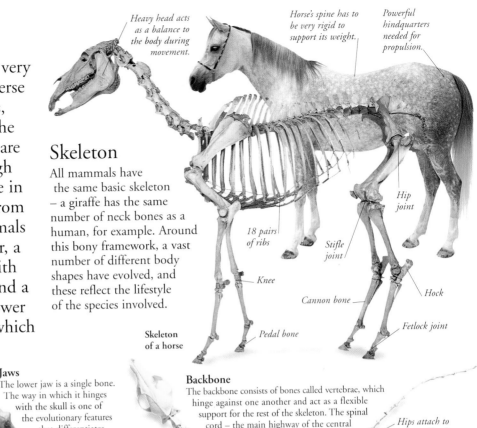

Heavy head acts as a balance to the body during movement.

Horse's spine has to be very rigid to support its weight.

Powerful hindquarters needed for propulsion.

All mammals have the same basic skeleton – a giraffe has the same number of neck bones as a human, for example. Around this bony framework, a vast number of different body shapes have evolved, and these reflect the lifestyle of the species involved.

18 pairs of ribs

Hip joint

Stifle joint

Knee

Hock

Cannon bone

Pedal bone

Fetlock joint

Skeleton of a horse

Jaws
The lower jaw is a single bone. The way in which it hinges with the skull is one of the evolutionary features that differentiates mammals from reptiles. The upper jaw does not move.

Chimpanzee skull

Backbone
The backbone consists of bones called vertebrae, which hinge against one another and act as a flexible support for the rest of the skeleton. The spinal cord – the main highway of the central nervous system – runs through the backbone.

Shoulder blades attach here.

Hips attach to sacrum (fused vertebrae).

Backbone of a red fox

Teeth

Most mammals have four different types of teeth: incisors, canines, premolars, and molars. The way in which these develop differs depending on diet and lifestyle. The skull, small at birth, grows quickly, and, in order to have teeth that fit the fully grown jaws, mammals typically have two sets – milk and adult.

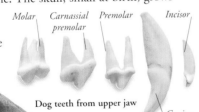

Molar *Carnassial premolar* *Premolar* *Incisor*

Dog teeth from upper jaw

Canine

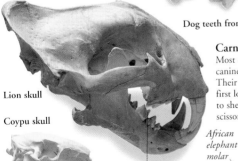

Lion skull

Coypu skull

Carnassials

Carnivore teeth
Most carnivores have large canines to catch and grip prey. Their last upper premolar and first lower molar are arranged to shear against one another like scissors and are called carnassials.

Rodent teeth
Rodents' incisors keep growing and have hard enamel only on the front. The teeth wear down behind, keeping them sharp. Rodents have a gap between their incisors and premolars. They can seal off their mouths while gnawing inedible substances.

Elephant teeth
Elephants eat coarse food and their teeth wear down very quickly. They have three premolars and three molars in each quarter, but use only one at a time. As one becomes worn out, the next one slides into place.

African elephant molar

Asian elephant molar

Hair

This is one of the key features that sets mammals apart from other animals. Some mammals, such as the musk ox, are obviously hairy while others appear to have no hair at all. Elephants have only a sparse covering while whales have just tiny whiskers when they are young. Most of the hair of armadillos and pangolins has been replaced by scales.

Hedgehog unrolling

Protective hair
Most of a hedgehog's hairs have become thickened and stiffened to form spines. These are pointed at the outer end and form a rounded bulb under the skin. If threatened, a hedgehog will roll into a tight ball, erecting its prickly spines, which point in all directions.

Asian short-clawed otters

Waterproof hair
Otters have thick underfur that is kept dry by the dense guard hairs of their outer coats. Otters have to groom regularly, and sea-going species often have to wash the salt from their coats in fresh water.

Long, stiff whiskers

Sensitive hairs
A cat's whiskers are stiff hairs that project mainly from its face around the mouth, eyes, and cheeks. They are highly sensitive, and a cat can use them to avoid objects and judge the size of openings in total darkness.

M

Temperature control

Some mammal species keep their temperatures at the same level. Others allow their temperatures to vary considerably, and save energy by hibernating in the winter or by going into a state of torpor when at rest. Their temperature may fall almost to freezing point and their metabolic rate slows down.

Keeping cool

Elephants have a high volume in relation to their surface area and can become too hot. To lose heat, they flap their large ears, which have prominent veins at the back. The blood leaving the ears is 19° C (66.2° F) cooler than the blood entering.

Large blood vessels

Elephant's ear

Heat loss

Many small bats have difficulty in keeping warm, because their wings consist of a large area of uninsulated skin from which they lose heat. When at rest, they save energy by allowing their body temperature to fall to that of their surroundings.

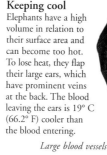

Sweat glands

Primates, such as monkeys and apes, have sweat glands all over their skin. The sweat evaporates and this process cools the animals. Dogs have sweat glands only on the soles of their feet. To help keep cool, they pant to allow their saliva to evaporate.

Red fox

Size

Arctic foxes live in the cold far north. They are smaller than other foxes, such as the red fox, which live in temperate climates, and therefore need to eat less. In winter, when it is really cold, red foxes can forage less often and stay curled up in their warm dens instead.

Arctic fox

Surface area

Polar bears have a low surface-to-volume ratio. (The larger the animal the smaller its surface area in relation to its volume.) This means they are able to conserve heat better than the smaller brown bears, which live in warmer climates.

Brown bear

Polar bear

Scent glands

Most mammals live in a world dominated by smell, and scent is very important for transmitting various items of information. Scent glands can be found in many different places on mammals – on the cheeks of cats, under the tails of badgers, under the chins of rabbits, and on the heels of deer. Scent can also be deposited in many different ways.

Communication

Some mammals, such as hyenas, leave traces of scent to pass on information to others of their species. They paste scent on stems of grasses, from which it may be possible to tell their sex, sexual status, and diet.

Identification

A badger uses a gland under its tail to deposit scent on the other members of its social group. The rest of the social group do the same and a composite scent is built up. This is a sort of family smell, and strangers can be readily recognized.

Establishing dominance

Dwarf mongooses use scent from glands in their cheeks to pass on information about their social status to other members of their pack. This helps them to establish dominance.

Reproduction

The most common form of mammalian reproduction is placental reproduction. After a successful mating, the embryo is attached to the mother's uterus via a placenta through which it absorbs nutrients from its mother and expels waste products. It is this placenta that forms the main part of the afterbirth, which is expelled immediately after the birth of the baby mammal.

Cat giving birth

Kittens are born deaf and blind.

Domestic cats usually have four or five kittens in a litter.

1 After nine weeks' gestation, the kittens are pushed down the birth canal and expelled into the outside world.

2 The mother licks the membrane away from the kitten, which stimulates it to take its first breath.

3 The mother then eats the placenta that was expelled with the kitten. In the wild, it would attract predators if left.

4 The mother licks and dries all her kittens repeatedly. They will begin to suckle from her within an hour of birth.

Parental care

Female mammals feed their young on milk excreted from their mammary glands, but parental care does not stop there. For some species, such as gorillas, parental guidance, teaching, and protection can go on for many years.

Delayed implantation

Grey seals come on land to give birth and mate once a year. Their gestation period is less than 12 months, so the embryo floats, unattached to the mother, for some months after mating.

Monotremes

Monotremes, such as the platypus, lay eggs. The platypus incubates the eggs in a nest, and after they hatch, feeds the young on milk that runs from mammary glands on to the mother's fur.

Marsupials

While in the mother's uterus, a marsupial embryo lives mainly on a yolk-sac. It is born premature after about 12 days and follows a trail of saliva left by the mother, crawling through her fur to her pouch, where it starts to drink milk from a nipple.

Wallaby and young

FIND OUT MORE | ANIMALS | ANIMAL BEHAVIOUR | KANGAROOS AND OTHER MARSUPIALS | MONKEYS AND OTHER PRIMATES | RATS AND OTHER RODENTS | REPRODUCTION | SKELETON | SKIN, HAIR, AND NAILS

Mammals

Rusty-coloured patch gives this wallaby its name.

Red-necked wallaby is a marsupial, and carries its young in its pouch.

Koala is an Australian marsupial that lives on eucalyptus leaves and spends much of its time asleep.

Spotted hyena is the second largest carnivore in Africa.

African elephant is the largest land mammal. Its nose and top lip form a trunk.

Defensive spines

Sumatran rhinoceros is the smallest rhino and is very rare. It lives in Southeast Asia.

Huge paws

Stripes camouflage the tiger in long grass and forests.

Indian tiger is on the verge of extinction in the wild.

European mole is adapted to an underground lifestyle and is a capable digger.

Short-beaked echidna from Australia is a mammal that lays eggs.

Common raccoon has dextrous front paws with which it feels for food in water.

European rabbit is a lagomorph that lives in large social groups.

Common weasel is one of the smallest carnivores, but can single-handedly catch and kill prey larger than itself.

Camel can survive for long periods using the fat stored in its hump.

Antlers are shed and regrown every year.

Reindeer is the only deer to have a furry nose, which allows it to forage comfortably in the snows of the Arctic.

Hollow hairs contain air, which traps body heat.

Zebra's stripes may confuse predators.

Dromedary lives in the desert areas of North Africa and southwest Asia.

Broad feet prevent the camel sinking into the sand in the desert.

Long legs keep the dromedary's body high off the ground in the cooler air.

Ring-tailed lemur evolved on the island of Madagascar and occurs nowhere else.

Western lowland gorilla is one of three gorilla sub-species – the largest living primates.

Common zebra lives in family groups led by a stallion.

Polar bear is the largest land carnivore and one of seven species in the bear family.

Manatee is a herbivorous sea mammal related to elephants.

Meerkat belongs to the mongoose family. It lives in social groups in the Kalahari Desert.

Gorillas sleep in trees and bushes.

MANDELA, NELSON

IN THE STRUGGLE by black South Africans to get rid of the policy of apartheid, Nelson Mandela stands out above all others. His work with the African National Congress and his constant campaigning for the rights of black people eventually led to his imprisonment. For 27 years Mandela was kept in prison, refusing offers for his release except on his own terms. The South African government finally set him free in 1990. In 1993 he won the Nobel Peace Prize with white leader F W de Klerk for their work in bringing peace and reconciliation to their country. The following year, he was elected president of the country that had imprisoned him.

Early life

Nelson Mandela was born the son of a Xhosa chief in Mvezo, Transkei, in 1918. He went to local schools, and then to Healdtown, the top school for black children. He then studied at the University College, Fort Hare, before reading law at Witwatersrand University. Once qualified, he practised law in Johannesburg.

African National Congress

The African National Congress (ANC) was founded in 1912 to protect and advance the interests of black people in South Africa. As a young man in Johannesburg, Mandela met civil-rights activist Walter Sisulu, who introduced him to the ANC and was to become a lifelong friend. Mandela became active in the ANC's Youth League and joined the ANC executive in 1950. Mandela travelled widely in South Africa for the ANC, championing its ideal of a free, multiracial, democratic government.

Mandela and Sisulu

Mandela burns his pass book

Sharpeville

On 21 March 1960, in one of the worst civilian massacres in South Africa, police opened fire on a demonstration against the pass laws in the township of Sharpeville, southwest of Johannesburg. Sixty-nine Africans were killed and nearly 400 wounded. The demonstration was part of a campaign of civil disobedience, organized to force the government to change the laws. A state of emergency was then declared across South Africa, which faced widespread international criticism for the shootings.

Burning his pass

Every black African was required by the law to carry a pass book at all times that restricted access to white-only areas. Along with many others, Mandela refused to carry his pass, joined protests against these unjust, racist apartheid laws, and demonstrated publicly by burning his own pass.

Imprisonment

In 1961 the ANC was banned and its leaders arrested. At first Mandela evaded capture, but he was finally caught and jailed for five years. While in prison, he was charged under the Suppression of Communism Act for organizing sabotage and trying to cause revolution. In June 1964, he was sentenced to life imprisonment. He spent much of the time in a maximum security prison on Robben Island, but was moved in 1985 to a Cape Town hospital and then to a less secure prison.

Winnie Mandela

In 1961, Mandela married Winnie Mdikizela, his second wife. While he was in prison, she campaigned tirelessly for his release and for the ANC. However, some of her own political activities attracted considerable controversy, and after his release from prison in 1990, the couple separated and later divorced in 1996.

Boycotts

Around the world, anti-apartheid campaigners boycotted South African produce, such as fruit and wine, in protest against apartheid and Mandela's imprisonment. The boycotts, which included a complete ban on sporting links, did much to persuade the apartheid government to release Mandela and negotiate with him.

Fruit from South Africa

Freedom

On 2 February, 1990, South African president F W de Klerk lifted the ban on the ANC. Nine days later Nelson Mandela walked out of Victor Verster prison, near Cape Town, after 27 years behind bars. His release was greeted by celebrations all over the world.

President

After his release from prison, Mandela began negotiations with the South African government to abolish apartheid and introduce multiracial government. Free elections were held in April, 1994, resulting in an overwhelming victory for the ANC. The following month, Mandela became the first black president of South Africa. The new government began the long and difficult task of modernizing and stabilizing the country.

Mandela and de Klerk

NELSON MANDELA

1918 Born, son of a chief of the Xhosa people, Transkei province.

1944 Joins the Youth League of the ANC.

1950 Becomes part of the ANC's executive.

1961 Imprisoned for his leadership of the ANC.

1964 Sentenced to life imprisonment for trying to cause revolution.

1990 Released from prison.

1994 Becomes South Africa's first black president.

FIND OUT MORE

AFRICA, HISTORY OF   GOVERNMENTS AND POLITICS   HUMAN RIGHTS   SOCIETIES, HUMAN   SOUTH AFRICA   SOUTH AFRICA, HISTORY OF

MAORIS AND POLYNESIANS

FROM ABOUT 1300 BC, peoples from Southeast Asia began an epic journey across the uncharted waters of the Pacific, settling the scattered island archipelagos. They took seeds and livestock with them and soon established small farming communities. From about the 9th century AD, groups of settlers began to reach the large islands of New Zealand, where over several centuries they evolved the unique Maori culture.

Map showing settlement of the Pacific

Settlement of the Pacific

Peoples from New Guinea reached the island of Fiji in about 1300 BC. They then made their way, via Samoa and Tonga, into Polynesia. They reached the Marquesas Islands in about 200 BC, and from there travelled vast distances to Hawaii, Easter Island, and New Zealand.

Polynesians

The Polynesians lived by farming tropical fruits such as yams, breadfruit, and taro, and raising pigs and chickens. They supplemented their diet with fish. Until Europeans arrived in the 18th century, the Polynesians had no knowledge of metal, but they were expert craftworkers in wood, stone, bone, and shell. Today, many islanders continue the traditional farming way of life.

Wood carving of Polynesian god

Religion

Polynesians worshipped many deities in elaborate temple complexes, or *marae*. Their lives were ruled by the idea of "taboo": certain practices, people, or things were considered to be sacred, and any crimes against them were punished. Their religious and everyday rulers, or chiefs, were protected by the rules of taboo, and were therefore extremely powerful.

Navigation

The Polynesians sailed the Pacific in canoes, navigating by the position of the Sun and stars. Stick charts, which used cowrie shells to indicate the positions of the islands and sticks to represent the currents, were used as maritime maps.

Easter Island statues

On Easter Island, at the eastern edge of Polynesia, the peoples carved massive statues, which stood on raised platforms called *ahu*. It is not known why these statues were made, but they are thought to have religious significance. The statues, many as high as 12 m (40 ft), were actually carved in stone quarries. Once finished they were transported using a combination of sledges, trestles, ropes, and sheer strength, and then levered up to their final position.

Measuring a statue on Easter Island

Maoris

The warlike Maoris of New Zealand lived by fishing, farming, and hunting. They decorated their bodies with tattoo designs to enhance their appearance, and to provide camouflage in times of war. The Maoris resisted the British colonization of their island in the 19th century, and a series of bloody wars followed. Peace was reached by 1880.

Rafters lead down to figures of other ancestors around the walls.

The poutokomanwa supports the ridge pole.

The Koruru represents the head of the ancestor.

Meeting house

The focus of Maori life is the meeting house, a large wooden building, elaborately carved with curved shapes and spirals. It often symbolizes the body of a specific ancestor: the ridge pole is the ancestor's spine, while the rafters represent the ribs. The meeting house is a place for official business, communal decisions, weddings, funerals, and other rituals. The square, or *marae*, in front of the meeting house is sometimes used for open-air debates.

Maihi represents the ancestor's arms.

Raparapa are the ancestor's fingers.

Tatau *(door)*   Whakamahau *(porch)*   Matapihi *(window)*

Maoris today

Today, Maoris account for about 10 per cent of the population of New Zealand. There is still a great deal of resentment between the Maoris and the government. For many years the Maoris felt that the 19th-century peace treaties signed with the British had not been honoured, and fought for ancestral lands that had been taken by colonists. In 1995 the British crown apologised to the Maoris, and the 1998 Waitangi Tribunal ordered a return of lands. The Maoris continue to protect their language and culture.

Maori society

Maori society was divided into many tribes, and warfare between them was common. Many still uphold these tribal traditions. The All Blacks rugby team's *haka* dance, performed on rugby fields across the world, is a legacy of the Maori war dance, and is a gesture of aggression and defiance.

FIND OUT MORE | ART, HISTORY OF | COOK, JAMES | HOUSES AND HOMES | MYTHS AND LEGENDS | NAVIGATION | NEW ZEALAND | NEW ZEALAND, HISTORY OF | POLYNESIA | SOCIETIES, HUMAN

MAPS AND MAPPING

THROUGHOUT HISTORY, maps have been used to survey and record territory, plot routes, and reflect our knowledge of the world's geography. Many of the principles used in modern mapping were laid out by classical Greek geographers, such as Ptolemy. Over time, new discoveries in mathematics, astronomy, and space technology have transformed mapmaking.

Map by Italian Enrico Martello, c.1470 showing area around Mediterranean.

Map of Iberia, Western Europe

Early maps

The first map was made in Babylon in about 2500 BC. Mapmaking was revolutionized in the 15th century by explorers, who increased their knowledge of the size and geography of the globe.

Map projections

Cartographers (mapmakers) use different projections to show the spherical surface of the Earth on a flat piece of paper. All projections involve some distortion of the globe. Cartographers must, therefore, choose projections that best suit the purpose of the map.

Key/Legend

- ● Capital city
- ◉ City
- ● Town
- — Road
- — Railway
- — Lakes and rivers
- ⌇ Country boundary
- ✈ Airport

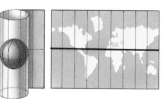

Compass point indicates magnetic North.

Relief represents the height of the land. Different techniques, such as contour lines or colours, are used to give accurate height readings.

The scale bar shows the relationship between distance on a map and the corresponding distance on the Earth's surface.

Lines of latitude are a series of horizontal lines which represent distances north and south from the Equator.

Lines of longitude are grids of vertical lines that join the poles at each end of the Earth's axis, to show east-west distances.

Cylindrical

In this projection, the Earth's sphere is "unwrapped" from a cylinder onto a flat surface to make a rectangular shape. The lines of longitude and latitude are shown as a regular grid of straight lines. Visually, the Earth's surface becomes more distorted towards the poles. The most common world map is Gerardus Mercator's projection, which was devised in 1569.

Conical

This projection may be used for making regional maps. The globe is projected on to a cone which, when opened, forms the map. The lines of longitude converge towards the apex of the cone, often above one of the poles.

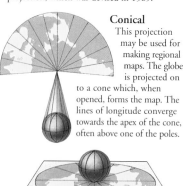

Azimuthal

In this projection, the image gives the impression of looking at the Earth from space. The surface of the globe is projected onto a flat sheet, which touches the globe at the point that lies at the centre of the map. Because distortion increases as you move away from the centre of the map, this projection is often used for mapping polar regions.

Parts of a map

Most maps use a similar range of symbols, known as conventions, which are instantly recognizable. The main conventions used – colours, different kinds of type, and symbols – are explained in the key or legend.

Types of maps

Maps are used for different reasons, and their style varies according to their purpose. Some are used to find a route, others record settlements and land division. Satellite maps record landscape features of parts of the Earth's surface.

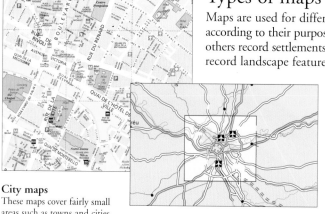

City maps

These maps cover fairly small areas such as towns and cities. Most people use these maps to find individual streets, railway stations, and hospitals, as well as particular places of interest such as parks, museums, and churches.

Road maps

One of the most frequently used categories of route maps is the road map. Different classes of road are represented by colour and width of line, so it is possible to differentiate instantly between a motorway and a minor road.

Satellite maps

Satellites orbiting the globe are used to observe and record the Earth's surface. By using remote sensing equipment, they can pick up energy from human settlements, rocks, water, and vegetation, and translate it into images. Satellite images are used to create highly accurate maps.

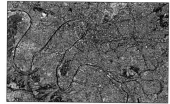

FIND OUT MORE

ASTRONOMY · COLUMBUS, CHRISTOPHER · EXPLORATION · MAGNESTISM · NAVIGATION · SATELLITES · SPACE EXPLORATION · TRAVEL

MARSH AND SWAMP WILDLIFE

THE SALT AND FRESHWATER wetlands of the world provide some of nature's finest havens for wildlife. These areas where shallow, still, or slow-moving water mingles with emergent vegetation are commonly called marshes and swamps, and act as a crossroads between land and aquatic habitats. The animals that live here are adapted to exploit food opportunities, avoid danger, move around easily in their habitat, and cope with changes in water levels. Saltwater wetlands undergo daily changes in water level with the ebb and flow of the tides, whereas freshwater wetlands undergo changes throughout the year as water levels rise and fall, and some even dry out completely.

Marshes and swamps

Wetlands often develop on coastal flats, alongside rivers, lakes, and estuaries, and in inland depressions where water cannot quickly drain away. Wetlands vary according to terrain, water conditions, and climate. Marshes are areas of poorly drained land; swamps are areas of permanently waterlogged ground that are usually overgrown. Other types of wetland include mossy upland peat bogs, low-lying flood meadows, mangrove swamps, saltmarshes lining river mouths, and dense reedbeds.

M

Reeds often grow at the water's edge.

Water lilies provide perches for some animals.

Many animals lurk below the water's surface.

Okavango delta, Botswana

Mammals

Mammals that live in marshes and swamps swim or wallow regularly, or can move over flimsy vegetation and soft mud without sinking. They range in size from tiny harvest mice that cling to reed stems, to hefty giants such as hippos and rhinos. Wetlands are important havens for mammals such as tigers, jaguars, and otters, threatened elsewhere, as human hunters have difficulty in this terrain.

Large nose, or proboscis, of male may reach 7.5 cm (3 in) in length.

Proboscis monkey
Saltwater flooding and the changing tides make a mangrove swamp a hostile environment for most ground-based mammals, whereas tree-dwelling monkeys can climb among the branches of the mangroves, well above the rising water. The strange-looking proboscis monkey feeds mainly on mangrove leaves around the coast of Borneo.

Sitatunga antelope
The sitatunga of tropical Africa is more at home in wetland habitats than any other antelope. It can swim well, even in deep water, and easily copes with walking over treacherously swampy surfaces. Flexible joints in its feet mean the antelope can splay out its long hooves, and so spread its weight on soft ground.

Webbed toes make movement in water easier.

Capybara
The wetlands of South America are the home of the capybara – the largest of the world's rodents. Family groups of capybara spend most of the time in and around water. They are good swimmers, and submerge themselves in water to avoid enemies, leaving just their eyes and nostrils poking above the surface.

Birds

Large beak

Very sensitive eyes allow kingfisher to see when it dives below water.

Marshes and swamps are ideal habitats for birds. The mixture of open water, muddy shallows, and emergent vegetation provides feeding opportunities for many birds, including waterfowl, waders such as redshanks, and aerial predators. The dense vegetation also provides a safe place for birds, such as reed warblers, to roost. Many birds fly from other habitats into marshy areas, but few dry-land predators will tread through water to follow them.

Malachite kingfisher
This is a common waterside bird across most of tropical Africa. It perches on reeds, mangroves, and other swampland plants to scan the water below for signs of prey. On sighting a small fish or dragonfly larva near the surface, the kingfisher dives down to snatch the unwary victim in its bill.

Bittern is well camouflaged in the reeds.

European bittern
Reedy European marshes are the home of the bittern, a wading bird, whose narrow-striped plumage provides excellent camouflage against surrounding reed stems. When the bird senses danger, it raises its long, sharp bill upwards, to accentuate its camouflage and make it almost impossible to detect.

Amphibians

Both tropical and temperate freshwater wetlands are ideal habitats for amphibians. Frogs, toads, salamanders, and newts relish the part-land, part-water environment. Few amphibians can tolerate saltwater habitats because of their permeable skin.

American bullfrog
Well known for its deep, loud croaks, the American bullfrog is suited to life in wetlands. Webbed feet help it swim, and eyes on the top of its head allow it to see when submerged in water. It spends its time in and out of the water, and eats various prey, including smaller frogs.

Large ear drum enables bullfrog to hear well.

Long legs for leaping

Reptiles

Marshes and swamps are some of the best places to see reptiles in tropical regions. Crocodiles and turtles often bask in the sunshine at the water's edge, and freshwater and saltwater wetlands also harbour lizards, such as green iguanas. Venomous and non-venomous snakes are common predators in swamps where they slither through the vegetation or swim across the shallow water.

The mangrove snake spends most of its time in mangrove trees.

Caiman can lie hidden below water while still able to see and breathe.

Strong teeth to seize and chew prey.

Spectacled caiman

Although smaller than crocodiles and alligators, the caimans of South America can still grow to nearly 3 m (10 ft) in length and are large enough to carry off a full-grown capybara in their many-toothed jaws. In the vast wetlands of the Brazilian Pantanal, the spectacled caiman is still the most common large predator, despite its population having been severely reduced by hunters.

Snapping turtle

Lurking unseen on the swamp bed among aquatic vegetation, the snapping turtle of North and South America is a patient, but fearsome predator. As soon as any suitably sized prey such as fish, frogs, waterbirds, or rodents draw too close, the turtle shoots its head forwards with lightning speed and clamps its jaws shut around its victim.

Mangrove snake

The beautifully patterned mangrove snake patrols the mangrove swamps of Southeast Asia. It spends most of the day draped over a branch of a mangrove tree. Later in the day it descends to hunt among the branches and foliage for birds and their nests, which it raids for their young. It bites its prey and injects venom through grooved fangs. Sometimes it moves right down to the mud to snatch other prey.

Invertebrates

Wetlands are home to a huge diversity of invertebrates. Insects and spiders live on plants, crustaceans and the larvae of insects, such as mosquitoes, live in water, and worms and shellfish remain buried in mud. They feed on plants, debris, or hunt each other. They themselves provide food for many larger marsh and swamp animals.

Great raft spider

This large spider – females may be more than 2 cm (0.8 in) long – lives in marshy areas of Britain. It hunts from vegetation at the water's surface. It lures small fish by tapping the water with its front legs, then lunges to attack them with its fangs.

Emperor dragonfly

This large dragonfly lives in wetlands in Britain. Males are normally bright blue and females green. On summer days adults hunt back and forth over pools, chasing other flying insects. If their homes dry up during a drought, emperor dragonflies migrate long distances to search for new breeding sites.

Its normally bright colour has faded after preservation.

Fish

The dense vegetation, fluctuating water levels, and often oxygen-poor water of marshes and swamps have created many adaptations in the fish that live there. For example, freshwater angelfish have flattened bodies to slip easily among the stems of underwater plants. Lungfish bury themselves in mud when pools dry up, while Siamese fighting fish can breathe air from the surface if the water becomes stagnant.

Fish aims jets of water at insects to knock them off leaves.

Archer fish

In the mangrove swamps of Southeast Asia, archer fish may pick up insects from the surface of the water. Even insects resting on leaves are not safe. The archer fish can spit a precisely aimed jet of water up to 1 m (3.3 ft) high, to bring unsuspecting prey down into its jaws.

Mudskippers

Mudskippers live in mangrove swamps. When the tide retreats, they do not need to travel with it. Stiff front fins act like legs and enable them to skip about on the mud. As long as their skin remains moist, they are comfortable out of water.

Front fin

Mottled skin for camouflage

Fiddler crab

Holes dotted across the bed of a mangrove swamp are the burrows of fiddler crabs. When the seawater retreats, the crabs emerge to scoop edible morsels from the mud. Males use only their smaller claw for feeding. The other claw, hugely enlarged and vividly coloured, is mainly for show. The male waves it at females to attract them to mate and brandishes it to ward off other males from his patch of mud, using it as a weapon if a rival does not back down.

Huge right pincer of male

Plants

Plants that thrive best in marshes and swamps are those adapted to growing in waterlogged soil and capable of efficiently channelling air from the leaves to the oxygen-starved, submerged roots. Most wetland plants are non-woody, such as low-growing herbs and mosses and tall, narrow-stemmed reeds and papyrus. Some large woody plants do grow in wetlands, including willows, swamp cypress, and mangroves.

Pitcher plants contain enzymes to digest their prey.

Pitcher traps insects

Pitcher plant

Carnivorous plants

These meat-eating plants obtain nutrients from insects' bodies, in addition to making food by photosynthesis. They are common in bogs and marshes where it is hard to extract nutrients from soil. Pitcher plants, sundews, and flytraps have special devices to trap or ensnare their prey.

Reeds

Tall, thin-stemmed reeds grow closely together in shallow water to form dense reedbeds at the edges of lowland lakes. As old plants decay and trap sediment, the base of the reedbed builds up until it rises above the water level. Eventually, the bed dries out, and new plants colonize the former marsh.

Mangroves

Tropical shores are often lined with mangrove swamps. Mangroves can tolerate being submerged in saltwater up to their stems. The leaves secrete excess salt, and parts of the roots project above the swamp mud to absorb oxygen directly from the air when the tide is out.

FIND OUT MORE   AMPHIBIANS   CARNIVOROUS PLANTS   CROCODILES   FISH   GRASSES, RUSHES AND SEDGES   HERONS, STORKS AND FLAMINGOES   PHOTOSYNTHESIS   REPTILES   SNAKES

MARX, KARL

ACROSS EUROPE, the Industrial Revolution created huge differences in wealth between capitalists, who owned the factories and took the profit, and workers, who produced the wealth. The German philosopher Karl Marx created a radical new plan to end this system. With the rallying cry of "Working men of all countries, unite!", he set out a theory of history that made economics the driving force of every event. He believed that a class struggle would break out between capitalists and workers, and that workers would one day construct a classless, communist society. Marx's ideas were ignored during his lifetime, but had an enormous impact on the history of the 20th century.

Early life
Marx was born into a German-Jewish family in the Rhineland town of Trier in 1818. He studied at Bonn and then Berlin, where he read law but was more interested in history and philosophy. Marx became strongly critical of religion and the luxurious life of the upper classes.

M

The Communist Manifesto
In 1848, Marx and Engels wrote The Communist Manifesto. Opening with the words: "The history of all hitherto existing society is the history of class struggles", the book describes communism and urges workers to overthrow the bourgeoisie – those who possess capital and property – and take power themselves. The manifesto was hugely influential in the development of communism.

Das Kapital
Marx's life-time work was a study "to lay bare the laws of motion of capitalist society". The first volume of *Das Kapital* was published in 1867; two more volumes appeared after his death. In *Das Kapital*, Marx set out to explain why working people are exploited in capitalist societies. He predicted that capitalism would fail, giving way to a classless communist society.

Title page of *Das Kapital*

1848 revolutions
In 1848, revolutions broke out in many European countries. They occurred independently of each other, but had much in common, as discontent against rulers erupted onto the streets. The revolutions were quickly crushed, but they gave Marx hope that a full-scale communist revolution would soon break out.

Revolutionaries fighting on the streets of Vienna.

Friedrich Engels
Engels (1820–95) was born in Germany but spent much of his life working in his father's textile business in Manchester, England. There he became interested in the conditions of working people, and used his considerable wealth to support Marx in his writing and research. After Marx's death, he edited and had published the final two volumes of *Das Kapital*.

Marx in London
Marx lived in Germany in 1848, but was charged with high treason and fled, eventually, to London. There he spent the rest of his life in poverty, supported by money from Engels and income from journalism. He devoted his life to studying capitalism.

19th-century London street

The First International
The First International Working Men's Association was established by Marx in 1864 to further his ideas and to co-ordinate revolutionary activities around the world. After a series of rows between Marx, who favoured strong central control, and the anarchist Mikhail Bakunin, who favoured local power, the First International dissolved itself in 1876.

The Paris Commune
After the defeat of France in the war with Prussia in 1871, the citizens of Paris refused to accept the entry of German troops into the city. They rose in revolt and set up a government, or Commune, based on France's revolutionary government of 1792. They were put down with great severity. Many of the Communards were influenced by Marx's ideals, and the defeat of the Commune was a bitter blow to communists everywhere.

Death of Marx
Tired, dispirited, and plagued by ill-health, Marx wrote a steady stream of books and articles in his later life. He died in March 1883; his much-loved wife and daughter both died before him. Marx was buried in Highgate Cemetary in North London.

Memorial to Marx

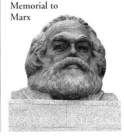

KARL MARX

1818 Born in Trier, Rhineland.

1835–41 Studies in Bonn and Berlin.

1842 Works as a newspaper editor in Cologne.

1843 Marries Jenny von Westphalen.

1848 Writes *The Communist Manifesto* with Friedrich Engels.

1849 Flees to London, where he spends most of the remaining years of his life.

1864 Forms the International Working Men's Association know as the "First International".

1867 Publishes the first volume of *Das Kapital*.

1883 Dies in London.

FIND OUT MORE

COLD WAR | EUROPE, HISTORY OF | GOVERNMENTS AND POLITICS | INDUSTRIAL REVOLUTION | RUSSIAN REVOLUTION | SOCIETIES, HUMAN | SOVIET UNION | TRADE AND INDUSTRY

MATHEMATICS

M

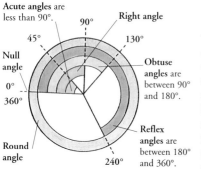

WE ARE ALL MATHEMATICIANS, because we all use numbers in our daily lives. The study of numbers, shapes, and quantities is called mathematics. People invented mathematics long ago to help them count and measure things, survey land, and construct buildings. Mathematics is an essential tool for understanding the world around us. Today, scientists use it to test their theories, engineers use it to design new machines and structures, and businesses use it to monitor their sales and income. There are many different branches of mathematics, including geometry and statistics.

Pyramid

2-D shapes around the home

Polygons, such as squares and triangles, are flat shapes with three or more straight sides.

Squares

Triangle

Hexagon

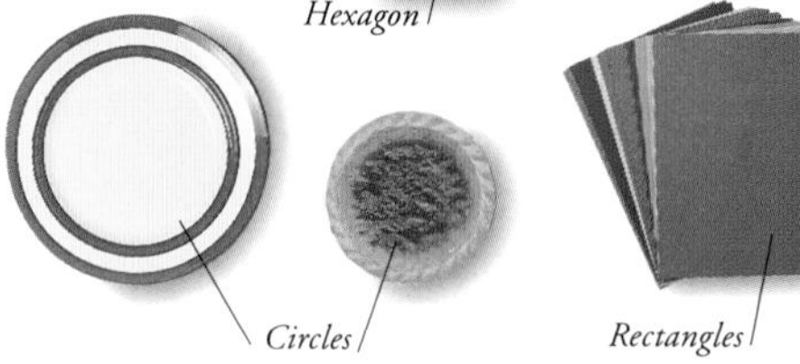

Circles

Rectangles

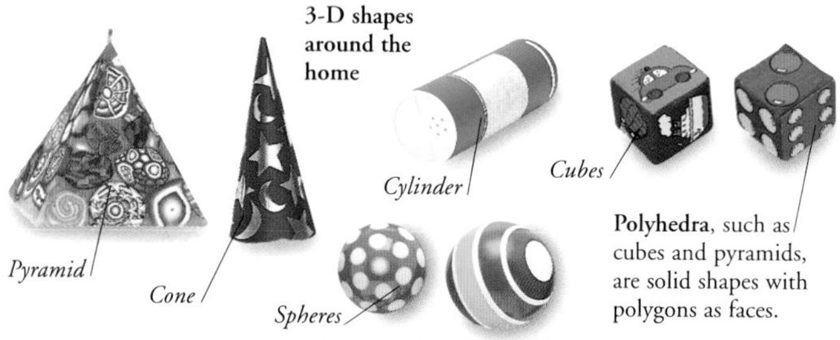

3-D shapes around the home

Cone

Cylinder

Cubes

Spheres

Polyhedra, such as cubes and pyramids, are solid shapes with polygons as faces.

Geometry

The branch of mathematics that studies the properties of shapes, points, lines, curves, surfaces, and angles – and the relationships between them – is called geometry. Geometry classifies shapes into two main groups: flat shapes, such as squares and circles, and solid shapes, such as cubes and spheres.

Flat shapes
Shapes that have length and width but no depth are said to be two-dimensional (2-D). They have an area but no volume. They may have straight sides, such as squares and triangles, or curved sides, such as circles.

Solid shapes
Spheres and cubes are solid shapes, because they have depth as well as length and width. Solid shapes are said to be three-dimensional (3-D). Solid shapes take up space, so they have a volume. They also have a surface area.

Angles

An angle is a measure of how much an object turns, or the amount of rotation between two lines that meet. A clock's hands, for example, move through various angles as time passes. The minute hand makes one complete turn every hour, and the hour hand makes one turn every 12 hours.

Acute angles are less than 90°.

Right angle

Null angle

Obtuse angles are between 90° and 180°.

Reflex angles are between 180° and 360°.

Round angle

90°
45°
130°
0°
360°
240°

Types of angle
Angles are measured in units called degrees (°). An angle of 0° is a null or zero angle. The angle between the lines that meet at a corner of a square is 90°, and is called a right angle. One complete turn of 360° forms a round angle.

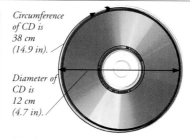

Circumference of CD is 38 cm (14.9 in).

Diameter of CD is 12 cm (4.7 in).

Pi (π)
If you divide the circumference of any circle by the circle's diameter, the result of the calculation will always be about 3.14. This number expresses the ratio of the circumference of a circle to its diameter, The ratio is exactly the same for every circle. It is called pi, after one of the letters of the Greek alphabet, and is normally written as the symbol π.

Symmetry
A line drawn down the middle of your face divides your face into two halves that look like mirror images of each other. Shapes with this property are symmetrical. The dividing line is called a line of symmetry – some shapes have two or more lines of symmetry.

Symmetrical numbers

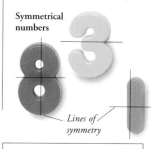

Lines of symmetry

Right-angled triangles

A right-angled triangle is a triangle in which two of the sides meet at an angle of 90°. Engineers, mathematicians, and scientists use such triangles to find heights or lengths. There are two ways of doing this. Knowing the lengths of two sides of a right-angled triangle, you can find the length of the third using Pythagoras' theorem, named after the Greek philosopher Pythagoras (c.580–c.500 BC). Trigonometry uses the angles of a triangle to find the lengths of its sides.

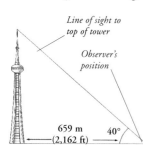

Line of sight to top of tower

Observer's position

659 m (2,162 ft)   40°

Trigonometry
A right-angled triangle's angles are directly related to the lengths of its sides by three special ratios called the tangent, sine, and cosine. A person 659 m (2,162 ft) from a tower and looking up at an angle of 40° to see its top can use trigonometry to find its height. The distance multiplied by the tangent of 40° (0.839) gives a height of 553 m (1,814 ft).

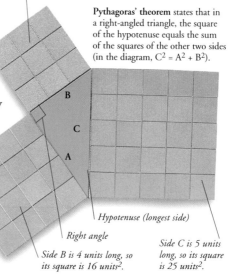

Side B is 3 units long, so its square is 9 units².

Pythagoras' theorem states that in a right-angled triangle, the square of the hypotenuse equals the sum of the squares of the other two sides (in the diagram, $C^2 = A^2 + B^2$).

B

C

A

Hypotenuse (longest side)

Right angle

Side B is 4 units long, so its square is 16 units².

Side C is 5 units long, so its square is 25 units².

Euclid
Euclid (c.300 BC), a Greek mathematician, was one of the founders of geometry. His 13-volume book *Elements* studied the geometries of all the major shapes and outlined the key mathematical theories of the time. It was used as a school text until the 20th century.

Algebra

Substituting letters or symbols for unknown numbers, and using equations (statements that two things are equal) is called algebra. In this equation, a banana represents an unknown number. The banana's value is clearly 4. Algebraic equations involve variables (numbers that can change their values) and constants (those that stay the same).

$+ 2 = 6$

What is the value of the banana?

Functions

A function is an equation that relates two or more variables. In the function $C = (F - 32) \times 5 \div 9$, the variables C and F represent temperatures on the Celsius and Fahrenheit scales. The function makes it easy to calculate that 80°F is equivalent to just under 27°C ($C = [80 - 32] \times 5 \div 9$).

All the bricks that are not red and not cubes are outside the sets.

Venn diagram

Modern mathematics

Mathematics is about more than just numbers and shapes. Much of modern mathematics studies the relationships between groups of items called sets. Other important areas include logic, which is used to test new mathematical ideas, and chaos, which studies the behaviour of unpredictable systems.

Sets

The items in a set may be numbers, objects, or even ideas. The relationships between the members of different sets can be shown on a Venn diagram, named after John Venn (1834–1923), a British mathematician. This simple Venn diagram of different-shaped coloured bricks shows a set of red bricks and a set of cube-shaped bricks. Bricks that are red cubes are found where the sets intersect, or overlap.

Chaos

A small disturbance in wind or temperature can alter the way the weather develops a few days later, making it almost impossible to make accurate long-term weather forecasts. In principle, even the flapping of a butterfly's wings could affect the weather. The sensitivity of "chaotic" systems, such as the weather, is often called the butterfly effect.

Can a flapping butterfly change the weather?

Set containing all the bricks that are cubes

Where the sets overlap, all the bricks are red cubes.

Set containing all the red bricks

Statistics

The word statistics has two meanings: it refers not only to collections of numbers called data, but also to the the science of analysing data. The study of statistics enables mathematicians to calculate trends in collections of data. Graphs display the data visually, making the trends easier to understand. Data can also be split into different categories and shown on a bar chart or a pie chart.

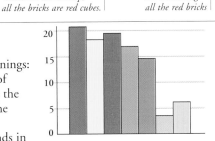

Bar chart

A bar chart displays collections of data or different quantities as columns against a vertical scale. The height of the columns shows the size of the quantities. Without the scale, the chart would be meaningless.

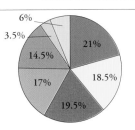

Pie chart

On a pie chart, different quantities are represented by different angles within a circle. The larger the quantity, the larger the angle, and the greater the area of the circle it occupies.

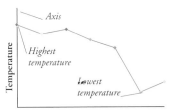

Axis

Highest temperature

Lowest temperature

Temperature

Time

Line graph

The change of a variable quantity over a period of time can be shown as a line graph. This graph records temperature on the vertical axis, while time runs left to right along the horizontal axis.

Probability

When you toss a coin, there is an equal chance of throwing heads or tails. Probability is the study of the chances of events occurring. The chance of throwing a head is said to be a probability of one-half (0.5). Using probability, statisticians can take data gathered from a small sample of items and make guesses about a much larger number of similar items.

Tossing a coin

Timeline

30,000 BC "Tally marks" are made on bones to represent numbers.

c.2300 BC The first proper number system is devised in Mesopotamia.

c.500 BC Geometry is used in mathematical proofs in Greece, India, and China.

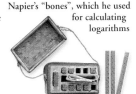

Napier's "bones", which he used for calculating logarithms

c. AD 1000 Arab mathematicians use algebra as well as geometry.

1614 Scottish mathematician John Napier invents logarithms.

1660s Englishman Isaac Newton and Konrad Liebniz, a German, publish key works on mathematics.

1980s US mathematicians develop chaos theory.

FIND OUT MORE

BUTTERFLIES AND MOTHS   HEAT AND TEMPERATURE   MONEY   NEWTON, SIR ISAAC   NUMBERS   PHYSICS   WEATHER   WEIGHTS AND MEASURES

M

MATTER

EVERY OBJECT AND SUBSTANCE that exists in the Universe is made up of matter – including the air we breathe, the water we drink, the ground we walk on, and even our own bodies. Scientists define matter as anything that occupies a space. All matter is made up of tiny particles, such as atoms and molecules. Forces called chemical bonds link the particles together in a variety of ways to form many different types of matter.

The air is made up of a mixture of gases, such as oxygen and nitrogen.

Gas
The bonds between the widely spaced particles of a gas are very weak, or non-existent. This means that a gas will spread out to fill any available space.

The water cascading down the cliff is a liquid.

Liquid
Liquid particles have more energy and are spaced a little farther apart than solid particles. The flexible bonds between them enable the liquid to flow.

The rocks that make up the cliff are solids.

Solid
The particles of a solid are packed tightly together. The bonds between the solid particles are stronger and more rigid than those between liquid particles.

Mass and density
The mass of an object is the amount of matter it contains. Mass is measured in units called kilograms (kg). An object's density shows how concentrated the matter is. Density is calculated by dividing the object's mass by its volume. A wooden block has a greater volume than a lead block of the same mass, because lead is more dense, with particles packed more closely together.

Lead is 11 times more dense than wood.

The two blocks have the same mass, so the pans balance.

Lead · Wood

States of matter
Most substances can exist as a solid, a liquid, or a gas – together, these are known as the three states of matter. The state of a substance depends upon the way its particles are arranged, how much energy they have, and the strength of the bonds between them.

Changing state
A substance may change its state if its temperature rises or falls sufficiently. When heated, solids change to liquids by melting, and liquids change to gases by evaporation. When cooled, gases change to liquids by condensation, and liquids change to solids by freezing. The change of a solid directly into a gas (and vice versa) is called sublimation.

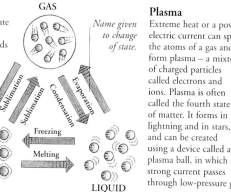

GAS

Name given to change of state.

Sublimation · Sublimation · Condensation · Evaporation

Freezing · Melting

SOLID · LIQUID

Plasma
Extreme heat or a powerful electric current can split up the atoms of a gas and form plasma – a mixture of charged particles called electrons and ions. Plasma is often called the fourth state of matter. It forms in lightning and in stars, and can be created using a device called a plasma ball, in which a strong current passes through low-pressure gases.

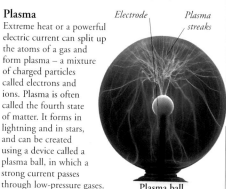

Electrode · *Plasma streaks*

Plasma ball

Conservation of matter
Matter is always conserved during a chemical reaction, which means that the atoms of the reacting materials (the reactants) are not destroyed, but rearranged to form new materials (the products). The combined masses of the reactants are the same as the combined masses of the products.

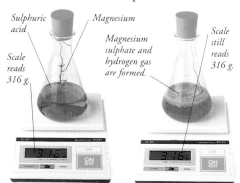

Sulphuric acid · *Magnesium*

Magnesium sulphate and hydrogen gas are formed.

Scale reads 316 g.

Scale still reads 316 g.

Before the reaction · After the reaction

Matter and energy
Scientists have discovered that when the nucleus, or centre, of an atom splits into two smaller nuclei during a nuclear reaction, there is a tiny loss of mass. The scales in the picture show that mass is lost when a uranium nucleus splits to form nuclei of barium and krypton. According to the German physicist Albert Einstein (1879–1955), the missing mass is converted into energy. Einstein showed that mass and energy are effectively the same thing, which is why scientists today prefer to use the term "mass-energy".

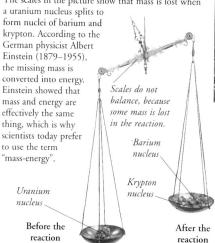

Scales do not balance, because some mass is lost in the reaction.

Barium nucleus

Krypton nucleus

Uranium nucleus

Before the reaction · After the reaction

Living matter
Animals and plants are often referred to as living matter. Like rocks, air, and water, living organisms are made up of atoms, but they are different from non-living forms of matter because they can grow, move, reproduce, and react to their environment.

Toucan

Vacuum
A total absence of matter is called a vacuum. It is impossible to obtain a perfect vacuum. Pumping air out of a container produces a near vacuum, but some air molecules will always remain inside. When scientists refer to a vacuum, they usually mean a space with very few atoms in it. The closest thing to a true vacuum is the space between stars.

FIND OUT MORE

ATOMS AND MOLECULES · EINSTEIN, ALBERT · GASES · LIQUIDS · NUCLEAR POWER · SOLIDS

MAURYAN EMPIRE

IN c.322 BC, a young nobleman and great warrior, called Chandragupta Maurya, overthrew the foreign governors installed in western India by Alexander the Great. Chandragupta and his successors then formed the Mauryan Empire, by uniting almost the whole of India, Afghanistan, and what is now Pakistan, as one great nation for the first time. The empire reached its height under its greatest ruler – Chandragupta's grandson, Asoka, who introduced Buddhism to India.

Origins of the empire

When Alexander and a battle-weary army took over what is now the Punjab, his conquest lasted only a few years. From a base in Pataliputra, Chandragupta seized the neighbouring kingdom of Magadha, and pushed westward through Alexander's lands in the Punjab.

Alexander the Great

The pillar at Sarnath showing the four lions, India's emblem.

Asoka

In 261 BC, Asoka conquered the southern state of Kalinga. Thousands of people were killed during the battle, and this slaughter so shocked Asoka that it turned him against violence for ever. He converted to Buddhism, and devoted his life to governing peacefully. The empire reached its peak under Asoka's rule.

Fragment of the sixth pillar of edict

Edicts of Asoka

Asoka had many of his edicts (sayings) inscribed on rocks, in caves, and on pillars that were specially built all over India. These inscriptions advise a life of toleration, non-violence, simplicity, and vegetarianism. They describe the emperor, who once wrote that "All men are my children", as striving for the well-being of his subjects.

Governing the empire

The Mauryan government was well organized. A civil service dealt with births and deaths, immigration, manufacturing, industrial arts, trade, and tax collection. A justice system prescribed severe punishments for lawbreakers. Governors administered each region. The two emperors that came before Asoka held the system together with an army of 700,000 men and a secret police force, that sent spies all over the empire.

Religious tolerance

Asoka used an idea called "dharma" (the principles of right thinking), instead of conquest, to hold his empire together. He encouraged a policy of religious tolerance among his nobles and civil servants, and this policy helped him to unite an empire that contained people of different religious beliefs.

Part of stupa gateway

A yaksi, or female nature spirit

The yaksi guards treasure hidden under tree roots.

Buddhism in the Mauryan Empire

Buddhism became a major religion during the Mauryan period, and many craftworkers began to create beautiful religious items, particularly from steatite. These include reliquaries (containers for sacred relics), and symbols that were central to Buddhist ideas, such as the Wheel of Law. The spokes of the wheel symbolize rays of light, or enlightenment, shining from the Buddha.

Wheel of Law

Steatite reliquary

Steatite casket

Steatite is a type of soapstone.

Casket contains crystal reliquaries and coins.

Stupas

Asoka sponsored the building of many Buddhist shrines, or stupas. These were places of pilgrimage for Buddhists, and the carvings inside them inspired prayer and meditation. Most have been rebuilt, but the entrance gates of the Great Stupa at Sanchi are from the Mauryan period.

Timeline

322 BC Chandragupta Maurya founds the Mauryan Empire.

c.301–269 BC Reign of Bindusara, Chandragupta's son. He conquers parts of the Deccan, southern India.

269–232 BC The Mauryan Empire reaches its height under Asoka, Chandragupta's grandson.

261 BC Asoka conquers the kingdom of Kalinga.

Carving of the Buddha

Crystal reliquary

184 BC The empire collapses when Brihadnatha, the last emperor, is killed by a rival dynasty.

c.250 BC Asoka builds Buddhist stupas and erects pillars bearing inscriptions.

FIND OUT MORE   ALEXANDER THE GREAT   BUDDHISM   BUDDHA   GUPTA EMPIRE   INDIA, HISTORY OF

MAYA

SOME 2,000 YEARS AGO, the Mayan culture began to emerge in Central America. The peak of this culture – its Classic period – was between 300 and 900. The Maya were a sophisticated people and had skilled astronomers and mathematicians. They developed a writing system, and built spectacular cities, such as Palenque and Tikal, whose ruins still tower over the rainforest today. The Maya traded with the Mesoamericans of central Mexico, worshipped a large group of gods, and performed religious rituals based on their calendar. They survived in the region until the Spaniards arrived in the 1500s.

Palenque • Tikal

Temples

Mayan cities always had a ceremonial centre, where the people built stepped pyramids, and placed sacred temples on the top of them. This was a way of getting closer to the gods, who were often connected with the sky. At the same time, it moved the rituals away from the eyes of ordinary people.

Palenque
This lowland city grew in influence in the 7th century under its greatest leader, Pacal. The king adorned the city with a large palace and several pyramid temples. He extended his power over the surrounding area by military raids and marriage alliances.

Rituals

The Maya conducted special rituals on particular dates in the calendar, and many of these involved the king. Blood-letting, or human and animal sacrifice, were common in the rituals because the Maya believed that sacrificial blood nourished their gods. The victims were often prisoners of war, or orphans.

Blood-letting
This stone lintel from Yaxchilan temple shows the lord, Shield Jaguar, and his wife, Lady Xoc, carrying out a royal blood-letting ritual. Mayan rulers thought their own blood was of the highest status, so shedding royal blood, as Lady Xoc is doing by threading a thorny cord through her tongue, was a way to satisfy the gods, and prove royal lineage.

This glyph says "He is letting blood".

Shrunken head on the king's headdress

Beaded necklace with image of Sun God

This glyph says "She is letting blood".

The name of "Lady Xoc"

Jaguar-pelt sandals

The name of "Shield Jaguar"

The torch shows that this ritual probably took place at night.

Traditional headdress

Scrolls on Lady Xoc's cheeks and lips represent the blood she sheds to feed the gods.

Thorn-lined rope that Lady Xoc pulls through her tongue

Blood-spotted paper in a woven basket

Glyphs

The Maya developed a system of writing using signs, called glyphs. Glyphs were used for recording the many dates and festivals of the complex Mayan calendar, which was based on the movement of the sun. Glyphs were also used to write the names and dates of the Mayan rulers. Many of the glyphs were pictorial – they were pictures used to represent ideas. For example, a glyph of a shield and a club together meant "war".

People

At the top of Mayan society there was a lord or king. Below him there were nobles, who were high-ranking farmers, merchants, and priests. Below them were commoners, who were farm workers, hunters, or craft-workers. Lowest of all were slaves – men and women who had been taken prisoner in war and who did the hardest work, such as building.

Mayan lord

Cloth given as tribute

Lords
This vase, from c.700, shows a Mayan lord with tributes, or gifts, given to him by subject (conquered) peoples.

Hunter

Deer

Hunting
Mayan men hunted game in the Yucatan Peninsula to supplement their diet of vegetables. Hunters called this area the "land of turkey and deer" for this reason.

Food basket

Terracotta figure

Farming
Peasant women, such as the one represented in this figure, grew most of the food on terraced hillside farms or forest clearings. Their main crops were maize, squash, beans, and chillies.

Flint carvings
These carvings were highly prized, and were often buried with the dead. They were made by flaking away the flint to leave a silhouette. Typical subjects were human faces, figures of the gods, and mythical creatures.

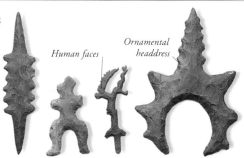

Human faces

Ornamental headdress

Timeline

2000 BC–AD 300 This period begins with a rural economy and ends with the rise of the Mayan cities.

300–550 Early Classic period: city-states develop in the Mexican lowlands.

550–900 The Late Classic period: art and architecture flourish in the Mayan cities. The population rises, and agriculture becomes more intensive to support the population.

Terracotta frog pot

900 onward Mayan cities decline, and other Mesoamerican peoples, such as the Toltecs and later the Aztecs, begin to dominate the area.

FIND OUT MORE   AZTECS   CENTRAL AMERICA, HISTORY OF   INCAS   MESOAMERICANS   PYRAMIDS

MEDICINE

MEDICINE IS A SCIENCE that aims to prevent or treat the disorders that affect the human body. These range widely, from minor injuries, such as a sprained ankle, to life-threatening conditions, such as heart disease. The skill and knowledge of doctors and nurses, as well as major advances in modern diagnostic techniques, surgery, and drugs, have made medicine highly effective. Today, more people live in good health, for longer than ever before.

Diagnosis

Identifying the cause of an illness and prescribing the appropriate treatment is called diagnosis. It requires great skill from the doctor, and involves a number of stages. After listening to a description of the symptoms, the doctor examines the patient, for example, checking heart beat or blood pressure. Samples may be sent for testing, before a doctor finally decides on a course of treatment, or refers the patient to a specialist at a local hospital.

Patients are not always able to describe the symptoms of their illness.

Symptoms and signs
Symptoms are the indications of an illness noticed by a patient and described to the doctor. Symptoms include pain, bleeding, or a rash. The doctor considers these factors with any signs of disease that he or she notices, to formulate a diagnosis.

Tests
Doctors use a range of diagnostic tests to help them make an accurate diagnosis. They may take samples of blood, urine, mucus, faeces, vomit, or pus. The samples are put in labelled tubes and sent for testing at a laboratory.

Blood sample
Disposable specimen bottles
Brush and wooden spatula

Diagnostic kit
Tongue depressor
Nasal speculum
Mirror
Laryngeal mirror
Ophthalmoscope
Laryngoscope head
Otoscope head examines inside ear.

Medical instruments
Doctors use a range of medical instruments to help them diagnose a patient's illness. Ophthalmoscopes are used for looking into the eyes. Otoscopes are for looking into the ear canal to detect infections. With a laryngeal mirror and laryngoscope, doctors examine the throat and trachea.

Doctors
By law, a medical doctor must complete a period of training before he or she is qualified to diagnose and treat patients. This involves at the very least three years of study, followed by work as a trainee in a hospital. In most countries, a national register lists those doctors who are qualified to practice; doctors can be struck off the register for malpractice.

Branches of medicine
Medicine has many branches, and no one doctor could be an expert in all of them. Some doctors are general practitioners (GPs); the first contact for most patients, they have a broad understanding of most conditions. When necessary, a GP refers patients to specialists in a wide range of fields, from orthopaedics to psychiatry.

M

Orthopaedics
Orthopaedics deals with diseases and injuries of bones, joints, muscles, ligaments, and tendons. Orthopaedic surgeons treat a range of conditions, including broken bones.

Broken leg in plaster

Paediatrics
The study of the growth and development of babies and children, and the treatment of diseases experienced in childhood, is called paediatrics.

Psychiatry
The diagnosis and treatment of emotional and behavioural problems, and mental illness, is called psychiatry. Psychiatrists use counselling, drugs, and in some cases electroconvulsive therapy, also known as ECT, to help patients. **ECT**

Dermatology
This is the study of the skin, hair, and nails, including treatment of conditions such as skin cancer, acne, warts, and eczema.

Eczema

Gynaecology
Gynaecology is concerned with the woman's reproductive system. It deals with pregnancy and childbirth, and also disorders such as menstrual problems or infertility.

Pregnant woman

Neurology
Neurologists treat disorders of the brain and nervous system – conditions such as muscular dystrophy and Parkinson's disease. **Brain**

Dr Christiaan Barnard
South African surgeon Dr Christiaan Barnard (1923–2001) performed the world's first heart transplant operation at Groote Schuur Hospital, Cape Town, in 1967. The patient survived for just 18 days, but Barnard's operation introduced a pioneering procedure that is now carried out routinely in hospitals around the world.

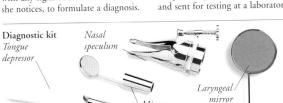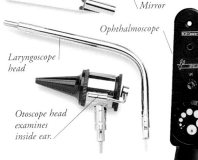

Surgery

Surgery is a branch of medicine that involves cutting into the body to treat a disease or an injury. Surgeons carry out procedures, called operations, in operating theatres. An operation may be minor, such as the removal of a skin blemish, or major, such as a heart by-pass operation that takes many hours.

Surgical instruments

Forceps

Scalpel

Retractor

Suture scissors

Artery forceps

Metzenbaum scissors

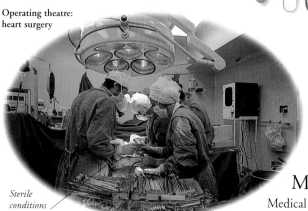

Operating theatre: heart surgery

Sterile conditions

Surgical instruments
These are the instruments used during operations. They include scissors for cutting tissue and trimming stitches; scalpels, used for cutting; retractors, which hold tissue apart; and artery forceps, used to clamp blood vessels.

Anaesthetics
Anaesthetics are drugs used to relieve a patient's pain during surgery. The drugs can be injected or inhaled. Local anaesthetics numb only the affected part of the body; general anaesthetics render the patient unconscious.

Oxygen cylinder on trolley

Patrick Steptoe and Robert Edwards

British gynaecologist Patrick Steptoe (1913–88) and physiologist Robert Edwards (b.1925) developed the technique of *in vitro* fertilization (IVF), which helps infertile women have babies. IVF involves removing an egg from the mother, then fertilizing it with sperm and returning the fertilized egg to the mother's uterus. The first baby conceived by IVF was Louise Brown, born on 25 July 1978 in England.

Patrick Steptoe

Robert Edwards

Medical technology

Medical technology advanced rapidly during the 20th century. Imaging techniques, such as X-rays and PET scans, allow a disease to be diagnosed without having to cut open the patient. With sophisticated surgical equipment, doctors carry out increasingly complex treatments, curing more diseases and keeping more patients alive.

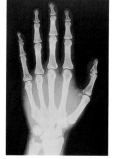

X-ray of bones in hand

X-rays
An X-ray is radiation used to take photographs of bones and teeth. As X-rays pass through a patient's body, they are absorbed by bone but not by softer tissues. Detected by photographic film, this produces a shadowy image of the inside of the body.

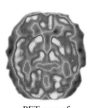

PET scan of healthy brain

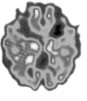

PET scan of brain with Alzheimer's disease

PET scan
PET (positron emission tomography) scanners investigate activity in the brain. They detect radiation given off by the brain and produce an image. They are used to locate tumours and diagnose epilepsy.

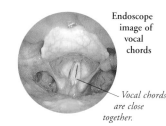

Endoscope image of vocal chords

Vocal chords are close together.

Endoscope
Doctors look inside the body using an endoscope – a long, flexible tube of optical fibres. Some fibres carry light into the body; others carry an image back to the doctor on a video screen.

Alternative medicine

Alternative medicine is the collective term for therapies that take a different approach to curing illness from orthodox medicine. Some, such as acupuncture, are ancient; others, such as homeopathy, date from the 19th century. Some therapies are now used instead of, or alongside, conventional medicine.

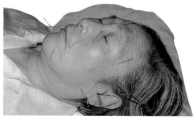

Acupuncture
This ancient Chinese therapy involves treating disease by sticking needles in the skin at particular points, called meridians. Insertion of the needles controls the flow of Qi (vital energy) along meridians, restoring good health.

Patient undergoes acupuncture for facial paralysis.

Homeopathy
Homeopaths give patients dilute forms of natural substances that, if undiluted, would produce symptoms of the disease in healthy people. This is believed to boost the body's natural defence system and its healing abilities.

Homeopathic remedies

Big toe is connected with top of head and brain.

Region of foot that governs diaphragm and solar plexus.

Part of the foot thought to be responsible for base of spine.

Reflexology
Reflexology is based on the theory that each part of the foot is linked to a specific area of the body. By massaging and manipulating the foot, reflexologists aim to stimulate the body into healing itself or relieving pain.

Reflexology

Part of the foot thought to be connected with the heart.

Area thought to be linked with bladder.

FIND OUT MORE   DISEASES   DRUGS   FIRST AID   HEALTH AND FITNESS   HEART AND CIRCULATORY SYSTEM   HOSPITALS   HUMAN BODY   MEDICINE, HISTORY OF   PLANT USES

MEDICINE, HISTORY OF

RECORDS OF PHYSICIANS treating the sick stretch back more than 4,500 years. However, for most of this time doctors had little real knowledge, and relied mainly on superstition and herbal cures. Medical science as we know it began 300 years ago, when a flowering of knowledge helped doctors understand how the body works; later, innovations, such as immunization, helped cure its ills. Today medical advances save more lives than ever before, but it can be expensive – and many of the world's poorest people cannot afford it.

Prehistoric medicine

Buried skeletons provide hints about prehistoric medical treatment. In a procedure called trepanning, early surgeons drilled their patients' skulls, perhaps thinking this would let diseases escape. Archaeologists have found skulls that show partial healing, so not all patients died after the operation.

Trepanned skull, 2000 BC

Egyptian cures

Ancient Egyptians founded the first medical school 2500 years ago. Our knowledge of Egyptian medicine comes from the Ebers Papyrus, a scroll containing 700 remedies – some of which are still used.

Qing-dynasty needles

Ancient Egyptians thought that raw garlic cured tapeworm.

Garlic

Acupuncture

Chinese physicians began using acupuncture around 2,500 BC. Acupuncturists aim to ease pain and cure disease by pushing tiny needles into the body. Today, western scientists accept that acupuncture stops pain, but they cannot explain why.

Acupuncture needles and mahogany case

Ancient Greece and Rome

Greek doctors learned surgery by treating war wounds, but blamed the gods for any failures. Ancient Romans improved public health with clean water supplies and sewer systems.

Hygieia *Asclepius*

Asclepius and Hygieia

The Greek god of medicine, Asclepius, may have actually been a real physician 3,200 years ago. The Romans worshipped both him (as Aesculapius), and his daughter, Hygieia, whose name gives us the word "hygiene".

Greek sculpture

Melancholy

Blood

Four humours

A Greek surgeon named Galen (129–199) believed incorrectly that human beings were in good health only when they had a perfect balance of their bodily fluids – their "four humours". The humours (blood, phlegm, choler, and melancholy) corresponded to physical build and certain ailments. This idea dominated medicine for 1,400 years.

Choler *Phlegm*

Four humours

Hippocrates

Greek physician Hippocrates (c.460–370 BC) separated medicine from magic. His treatments included diets, purgatives, baths, and fresh air. He was one of the first to realize that a poor environment can cause bad health. Today, trainee doctors still pledge their dedication to patients by repeating an oath once said to be written by Hippocrates.

Medieval medicine

For 1000 years in medieval Europe, doctors trusted religion, astrology, and Galen's teachings. Even during the Renaissance there was wide-spread ignorance about illness and its treatment.

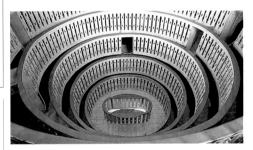

Anatomy theatre, Padua University

Medical schools

There were few medical schools in medieval and Renaissance Europe. The 16th-century medical faculty at Padua University, Italy, has a steeply tiered anatomy lecture theatre, so that students could see the corpse being dissected.

Islamic medicine

Religion was a powerful force in the Arab world. The holy books of Islam contain rules about hygiene and diet. Galen's ideas about the four humours strongly influenced early Islamic medicine, but in the 13th century, the Arabs advanced medical knowledge when the physician Ibn-an-Nafis (1210–88) made important discoveries about the circulation of the blood.

Wise women

For most people the only source of medical help was a "wise woman". These neighbourhood healers cured illnesses using traditional herbal remedies, such as coltsfoot. However, when universities began to educate doctors, most excluded women, despite their knowledge.

Coltsfoot, used to treat coughs

Modern Turkish baths, Istanbul, Turkey

Islamic medicine recognized that cleanliness was an important part of maintaining good health.

M

Scientific Revolution

Smellie's short forceps c.1746

From the 17th century, medicine benefited from a new spirit of investigation and observation that revolutionized all sciences. This is known as the Scientific Revolution. One of the most important breakthroughs was the discovery, by the English physician William Harvey (1578–1657), that the heart pumps blood continuously around the body.

Immunization
By infecting a boy with a mild disease (cowpox) in 1796, English physician Edward Jenner (1749–1823) gave him immunity (protection) from the deadly smallpox. Developments of Jenner's method now keep us safe from many previously fatal diseases.

Jenner performs the first vaccination.

Childbirth
Until the 1700s, pregnancy often ended in death for mother and baby. Hungarian Ignaz Semmelweis (1818–65) showed that lack of cleanliness killed the mothers – and improved hygiene saved eight out of 10 lives. To help save babies' lives during a long delivery, a Scottish doctor named William Smellie (1679–1763) developed special forceps.

Pain control
Before anaesthetics were invented, surgery was a painful ordeal. American dentist William Morton (1819–68) showed that patients who inhaled ether vapour became unconscious and did not feel the surgery.

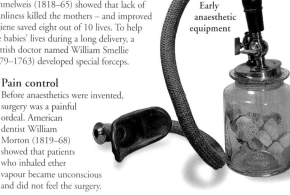

Early anaesthetic equipment

Mental illness

Strait-jacket

Treatment of mentally ill people used to consist of chaining them up in cells to control their "madness". In the 1700s, hospitals abolished cells and chains. Psychotherapy started more than a century later, when the Austrian doctor Sigmund Freud (1856–1939) began talking to patients about their disturbing thoughts.

Straps were less cruel than chains when restraining violent patients.

Straitjacketed patient, c.1818

Joseph Lister
English surgeon Lister (1827–1912) learned of germs from Louis Pasteur (1822–95). In 1865, Lister realized that he could prevent wound infection by killing germs in operating theatres, so he developed antiseptic (rot-preventing) surgery. His idea reduced the death rate following operations by two-thirds.

Modern medicine

In the 20th century, medical knowledge developed more quickly than ever before. The control of infectious diseases meant that children in the developed world born in the late 1990s can now expect to see 25 more birthdays than children born in 1900. Through a better understanding of how our bodies work, scientists devised new drugs, new ways of detecting illness, and new treatments, which now make our lives healthier as well as longer.

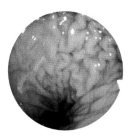

Endoscope view of stomach

Drug treatment
Originally drugs, such as penicillin, came from a natural source, such as a mould. Modern scientists can now produce a wide range of artificial (synthetic) drugs, including antibiotics.

Medical imaging
The discovery of X-rays in 1895 allowed doctors to get a clear picture of a patient's bones without surgery. In the 1950s, doctors perfected the first flexible endoscope (an instrument for examining the inside of the body without using a scalpel). Doctors developed an early version of this instrument – a tube and a candle – in the 18th century.

Medical research
Research has led to the invention of many diagnostic and imaging tools. One of the most useful modern research tools is the CAT (computerized axial tomography) scan. This machine allows doctors to view the body in sections, which makes diagnosing brain disease or damage much easier and treatment quicker.

CAT (computerized axial tomography scan)

Eye drop dispenser

Tablets and capsules

Rediscovery of traditional cures
Initially, 20th-century medicine rejected all ancient herbal remedies. However, the medical establishment has re-assessed this view, and traditional cures are now sometimes used with modern medicines. One American company has even tried to patent (own) the turmeric poultices used in India for minor wounds.

Turmeric powder, traditionally used in poultices

Timeline

1st century The Roman Aulus Celsus (25 BC–AD 50) writes one of the first medical textbooks.

12th century In Europe, monastery hospitals improve medical treatment.

1163 Church forbids monks to practise surgery; for the next 600 years barbers act as surgeons.

1543 Flemish anatomist Andreas Vesalius (1514–64) publishes the first accurate pictures of the human body.

Pain-killing morphine drug comes from poppies.

Poppy seeds

1849 Elizabeth Blackwell is first US woman to gain medical degree.

1854 John Snow (1813–58) links clean water and good health.

1860s Pasteur discovers germs.

1921 Insulin treatment is developed for fatal diabetes.

Syringe

1928 Bacteriologist Alexander Fleming discovers penicillin.

1953 John Gibbon Jr performs cardiac surgery with his heart-lung machine.

1960 John Charnley (1911–82) invents replacement hip joint.

1979 Mass immunization frees the world of smallpox.

1986 "Keyhole surgery" invented.

2001 Important breakthroughs in treatments for incurable illnesses such as cancer and HIV.

FIND OUT MORE   DRUGS   FREUD, SIGMUND   GALILEO GALILEI   HEART AND CIRCULATORY SYSTEM   ISLAMIC EMPIRE   MEDICINE   PASTEUR, LOUIS   SCIENCE, HISTORY OF   VESALIUS, ANDREAS   WITCHES AND WITCHCRAFT

Early medicine
Ancient drugs

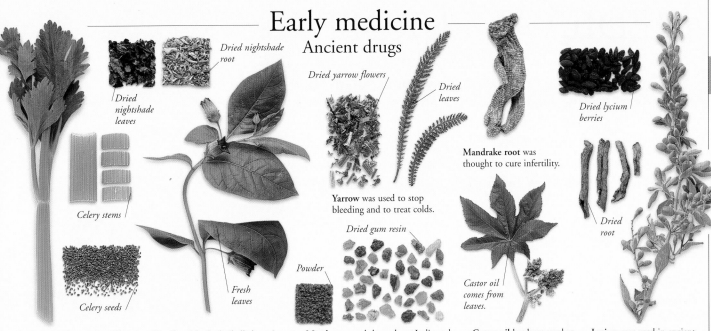

Dried nightshade leaves

Dried nightshade root

Dried yarrow flowers

Dried leaves

Dried lycium berries

Mandrake root was thought to cure infertility.

Celery stems

Yarrow was used to stop bleeding and to treat colds.

Dried gum resin

Dried root

Powder

Fresh leaves

Celery seeds

Castor oil comes from leaves.

Celery was used in ancient China and Egypt to relieve arthritis.

Deadly nightshade (belladonna) was a traditional European anaesthetic.

Myrrh was used throughout India and the Middle East as an antiseptic.

Castor oil has been used as a laxative for 4,000 years.

Lycium was used in ancient China as a blood tonic.

Instruments

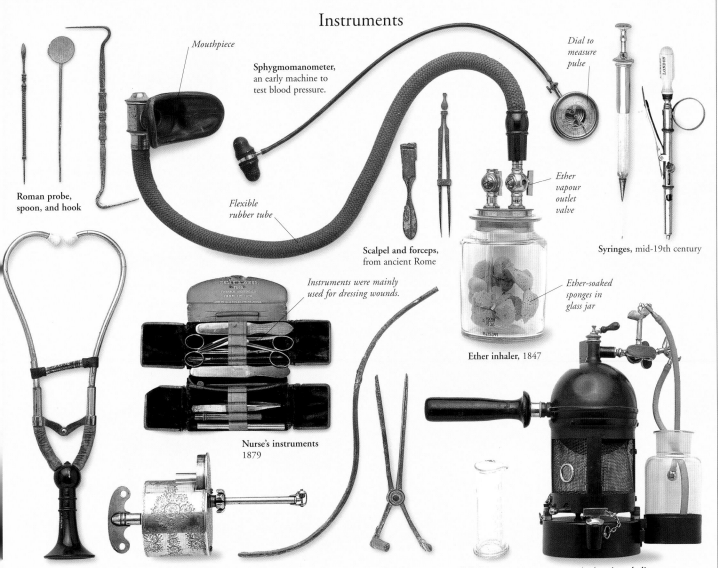

Mouthpiece

Sphygmomanometer, an early machine to test blood pressure.

Dial to measure pulse

Roman probe, spoon, and hook

Flexible rubber tube

Ether vapour outlet valve

Scalpel and forceps, from ancient Rome

Syringes, mid-19th century

Instruments were mainly used for dressing wounds.

Ether-soaked sponges in glass jar

Ether inhaler, 1847

Nurse's instruments 1879

Laënnec's stethoscope, 1855.

Dental drill was run by clockwork, 1864.

Ancient Roman catheter and speculum have a similar design to the modern instruments.

Minim measure, to measure medicine

Antiseptic carbolic steam spray, designed by Lister

MEDIEVAL EUROPE

THE MEDIEVAL PERIOD IN EUROPE, also known as the Middle Ages, lasted roughly from 1000 to 1500. It was the time between the obscurity of the Dark Ages, and the intellectual flowering of the Renaissance. There was an expansion of trade during this period, and a population explosion, followed by the formation of many towns. People were still governed by kings, but the powerful Catholic Church dominated Europe's culture. Medieval Europe was a time and place of contrasts: the finest religious art was being created, while most people lived lives of desperate poverty.

Sovereigns and the State

In most medieval countries, the sovereign – usually a man – owned all the land. He also tried to control the Church, claiming that he got his power directly from God. This often brought Church and State into conflict.

Frederick II
A gifted lawgiver and soldier, the Holy Roman Emperor Frederick II (1194–1250) was also a religious sceptic. He quarrelled with the Pope, who excommunicated him for refusing to go to the Holy Land on a crusade. When Frederick finally arrived in the Holy Land in 1228, he claimed Jerusalem by diplomacy, and without any bloodshed.

St Louis
Louis IX (r.1226–70) of France was a pious king who governed his fellow Christians peacefully, but was intolerant of non-Christians. His first crusade to the Holy Land was unsuccessful, and he returned to follow peaceful policies at home. In 1270, he began a crusade against the Muslims in northern Africa. He died of the plague at Tunis.

Eleanor of Aquitaine
Wife of two kings – Louis VII of France and Henry II of England – and mother of two others, Eleanor (1122–1204) was one of the most powerful women of her time. She went on a crusade in 1147, and gave Henry II extensive French lands when they married. She played a key role in English government during the reign of her son, Richard I.

Bishops and the Church

One of the strongest forces in Europe, the Church was ruled by a network of archbishops and bishops, headed by a pope. These educated men believed that they were responsible for the souls of the people and that they could supervise all human affairs – even those of kings.

Monasteries
Monks and nuns lived a life apart, giving up their personal possessions and leading lives of chastity. But they still played a vital part in medieval society, providing many services today run by the government – such as education, healing, and care of the poor and needy.

Becket is carried to Heaven by angels.

Becket is killed by one of King Henry II's knights in Canterbury Cathedral.

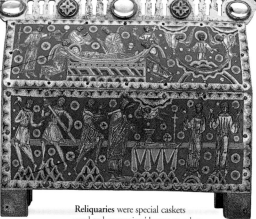

Reliquaries were special caskets used to house saints' bones or other relics. This 12th-century example depicts the murder of St Thomas Becket, the English Archbishop of Canterbury (1118–70).

Churchmen
In medieval Europe, the eldest son of a rich family inherited all his father's property. The younger sons often "took holy orders" and made careers in the Church. Many became bishops, gaining considerable power. Rulers often appointed churchmen to positions of power in the state. These appointments gave the Church a chance to influence state affairs.

Peasants' revolts

Europe's population fell dramatically after the Black Death. Peasants had to work harder, but were not paid higher wages. This caused peasant uprisings in France (1358) and in England (1381), both of which were ruthlessly crushed.

Wat Tyler is attacked. *Richard II*

Wat Tyler and the Peasant's Revolt
Tyler and the peasants marched to London to ask Richard II to lift the poll tax. Tyler's first meeting with the king was successful – the king promised to lift the tax – but at their second meeting, a scuffle broke out and Tyler was killed.

How people lived

Most people lived in the countryside and worked on the land. They gave a share of their produce to a local lord in return for protection and a home. Life expectancy was much shorter than it is today. Because of frequent and unpredictable Black Death epidemics, death was seen as a malicious joker ready to take anyone at any time.

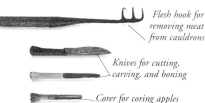
Flesh hook for removing meat from cauldrons
Knives for cutting, carving, and boning
Corer for coring apples

At home
Ordinary families lived in small huts, which often had just two rooms: one for animals, and another for people. Food was prepared in cauldrons using simple utensils. Times were hard in the winter, since food could not be preserved. A bad harvest meant that people starved the following winter.

Billhook for maintaining hedges
Sickle for cutting crops
Trowel

On the land
People worked hard on the land. The horse-drawn plough prepared the ground for cultivation, but there were no other labour-saving machines. Everything from digging to cutting crops and shearing sheep, was done by hand.

M

Towns and trade

Towns, mainly based around markets or ports, flourished because of an increased interest in trade and a growth in population. By the 14th century, some 70 towns in northern Europe had formed the Hanseatic League to monopolize trade in the area.

Money
Coins became common in medieval Europe because there was so much trade. Gold coins were issued for the first time since the 7th century. Merchants used small balances like this to weigh the coins, to make sure the precious metal they contained had not been removed.

Town walls
High stone walls and strong gatehouses fortified most medieval towns. These kept out bandits in peacetime and enemy soldiers in war. Carcassonne, France, still has its medieval walls.

Medieval science

Medieval European science relied on the writings of the ancient Greeks and Romans. Europeans had not yet developed the necessary approach to make new discoveries, as was happening in the Islamic world. There were advances in some areas, however: medieval engineers developed and built grand structures, such as the great Gothic cathedrals.

Blakene astrolabe

Book of Hours

Man

Woman

Zodiac signs

The astrolabe was an Arab invention developed to measure the altitude of the Sun, Moon, and stars. It came to Europe via trade routes and helped astronomers navigate at sea.

Parts of the body were thought to be ruled by the signs of the zodiac, as this 14th-century manuscript shows.

Medicinal herbs
Medieval physicians relied on herbs to make medicines, ointments, and poultices. Modern scientists have analysed the plants and found that they contain healing substances. Sage, for example, contains acids that are effective against colds; lavender contains an oil that is effective against burns and stings.

Rosemary Mint Fennel Dill Myrtle Feverfew Lungwort

Medieval art

Most medieval art was commissioned by the Church to decorate cathedrals and monasteries. Many of the buildings were in a style called "Gothic" – marked by dramatic, pointed arches. Within the buildings, Gothic painters used vivid, lifelike colours, but were not realistic.

Old Testament figures

Sculpture
Cathedrals were decorated with statues of the Holy Family, Bible scenes, saints, and bishops. Large-scale figures, such as these at Chartres, became the hallmark of the Gothic style.

Architecture
Medieval masons built fine stone houses as well as churches. This one was built in Lincoln, England, for a 12th-century Jewish merchant. The rounded doorway arch shows it is in the "Romanesque" style, that was popular before the Gothic style.

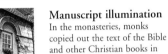

Manuscript illumination
In the monasteries, monks copied out the text of the Bible and other Christian books in longhand. They adorned the text with beautiful illustrations, and illuminated important letters (that is, painted them with bright colours and gold leaf).

Stained-glass windows
Scenes from the Bible were brought to life in the vivid stained-glass windows in churches and cathedrals. The pictures were created with small pieces of coloured glass, joined together using strips of lead. These examples come from the superb Chartres Cathedral in France – one of the wonders of the medieval age.

The Blue Virgin Window shows Christ turning water into wine.

The South Rose Window

The Redemption Window illustrates the Passion and Death of Christ on the cross.

Tree of Jesse shows Christ's family tree.

Clothing

Peasants wore simple clothes made of wool – loose smocks for the body and hose stockings for the legs. Richer materials, such as linen, velvet, and finer wool fabrics, were available to merchants and the nobility. Boots and shoes were made out of leather as were accessories, such as belts and bags.

Felt hat

Straw hat

Laces, or "points"

Short woollen jacket

Linen shirt

Leather flask, or "costrel"

Leather working boots

Woollen "split" hose

Labourer

Bailiff

Peaked felt hat

Doublet

Pewter buttons

Linen lining

Stirrups

Leather boots

Long woollen jacket

Merchant

"Borrelais" hat

Woollen coat

Eating knife

Mid-calf leather boots

"Joined" hose

Linen head wrap

Townswoman

Linen shift

Prayer beads

Woollen stockings with leather garters

Over sleeves

Wooden clogs, or "pattens"

FIND OUT MORE BLACK DEATH CHURCHES AND CATHEDRALS CRUSADES EUROPE, HISTORY OF FEUDALISM FRANCE, HISTORY OF HOLY ROMAN EMPIRE MEDICINE, HISTORY OF NORMANS

MEITNER, LISE

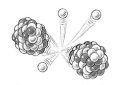

SOME OF THE MOST important discoveries in nuclear physics were made by Lise Meitner, a woman who often had to struggle to get the research facilities she needed. In spite of facing prejudice as a woman and a Jew, she published more than 130 scientific papers in a long career in Austria, Germany, and Sweden. Many of her discoveries were made with her colleague, physicist Otto Hahn (1879–1968). These included nuclear fission, the process that forms the basis of nuclear power and atomic weapons. She gained many awards for her work including the Ferni Award in 1966.

Early life
Lise Meitner was born in 1878 in Vienna, Austria. While she was growing up, her heroines were the British nurse Florence Nightingale and the French physicist Marie Curie. As a young woman, she persuaded her father to pay for a private tutor to prepare her for university. She went to the University of Vienna, and received her doctorate in 1906.

Radioactivity
In 1896, French physicist Henri Becquerel (1852–1908) discovered radioactivity (the rays that are emitted from certain substances). Meitner's work made a huge contribution to the understanding of radioactivity. During her time in the laboratory, she was often unwell, as she frequently came into contact with dangerously radioactive substances and mercury vapour.

Woman physicist
In the early 20th century, it was unusual for a woman to become a physicist, and Meitner endured a great deal of prejudice. At Berlin University, where she was a professor from 1926 to 1933, she worked in an old workshop, because women were not allowed in the main building. Male colleagues tended to ignore her and discuss work with Hahn only.

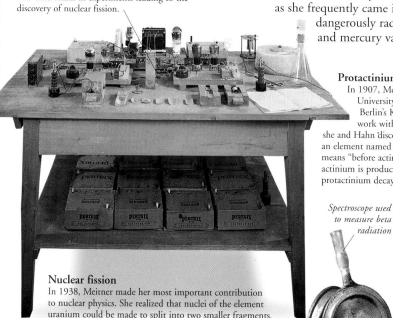

Worktable and equipment used by Lise Meitner and Otto Hahn in experiments leading to the discovery of nuclear fission.

Lise Meitner and Otto Hahn worked as equals, but Meitner was subjected to much prejudice.

Protactinium
In 1907, Meitner went to work at Berlin University. In 1917, she moved to Berlin's Kaiser Wilhelm Institute to work with Otto Hahn. The next year, she and Hahn discovered an important form of an element named protactinium. The name means "before actinium", because the element actinium is produced when the atoms of protactinium decay radioactively.

Spectroscope used to measure beta radiation

Letter announcing the discovery of protactinium

Nuclear fission
In 1938, Meitner made her most important contribution to nuclear physics. She realized that nuclei of the element uranium could be made to split into two smaller fragments. The process, which she called "fission", released a great deal of energy. This energy has been used in nuclear power stations and nuclear weapons. Meitner refused to be involved in the creation of nuclear weapons.

Exile in Sweden
In 1938, Meitner, a Jew, was forced to flee Nazi Germany to avoid persecution. Another great scientist, Danish physicist Neils Bohr, helped her escape and find research facilities at the University of Stockholm, Sweden. She continued her research with her nephew, Otto Frisch, who was also in exile in Sweden.

Interpreting fission
While Meitner was in Sweden, Hahn continued their work in Germany, bombarding atoms of uranium with particles called neutrons. Hahn found traces of the element barium in the experiments, but did not know why they were there. Meitner found the answer. She realized that each uranium atom had split in two fragments, one of which was barium.

Notes on fission by Lise Meitner

Hahn-Meitner Institute
In 1959, a research institute was founded in Berlin in honour of Meitner and Hahn. Its original aim was to carry out research into nuclear physics, chemistry, and mathematics. Scientists there have also done research on materials science and the future of solar power.

LISE MEITNER

1878	Born in Vienna, Austria.
1906	Receives doctorate from the University of Vienna.
1907	Travels to Berlin to attend a lecture, and ends up staying for more than 30 years.
1918	With Otto Hahn, discovers a form of the element protactinium.
1926	Becomes a professor at the University of Berlin.
1938	Flees Nazi Germany and moves to Stockholm, Sweden.
1939	With Otto Frisch, publishes a paper explaining nuclear fission.
1949	Becomes Swedish citizen.
1968	Dies in Cambridge, England.

FIND OUT MORE · CURIE, MARIE · NIGHTINGALE, FLORENCE · NUCLEAR POWER · PHYSICS

MESOAMERICANS

WONDERFULLY RICH CULTURES flourished in ancient Mesoamerica – the middle part of the Americas, today known as Mexico, Belize, Guatemala, and Honduras. The Toltecs, Mixtecs, and Huaxtecs were separate groups, but with many things in common. They all worshipped the same group of gods, practised human sacrifice, developed writing, and played a similar ball game. Their finest achievements are their stone temple-pyramids, and superb sculpture and pottery, but they never developed the wheel, and did not use bronze or iron. They were at their peak from 900, but perished when Spanish invaders arrived in Mexico in the early 1500s.

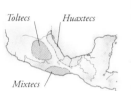

Toltecs Huaxtecs

Mixtecs

Ball game

This "game" had great religious and political significance to the Mesoamericans, and losers were often sacrificed to the gods. Players had to hit a small rubber ball through a high opening on the side of a court, by using hips, elbows, and knees – but no hands or feet.

M

Ball player

Players were usually noblemen. They dressed in special protective garments to play, all of which were padded – including the thick leather belt. The padding cushioned the player from the impact of the hard rubber ball, which often travelled at high speed.

Ball court, Chichen Itza

Ball court

The Mesoamericans built large ball courts in many of their city centres. The playing area was widened at either end, making a shape like a capital "I".

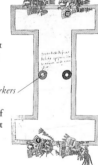

Circular stone markers

Codex illustration of a ball court

Hacha

When the ball players started a game, they hung ceremonial heads from their belts, which were known as "hachas", or axes. The Mesoamericans used a stone head, such as this, to mould the hacha.

Belt mould

Mesoamerican craft-workers used greenstone moulds to make protective belts for the ball players. They wrapped a strip of wet leather around the mould and left it to dry. When they removed the leather, the workers stuffed it with a padding material similar to cotton, called kapok.

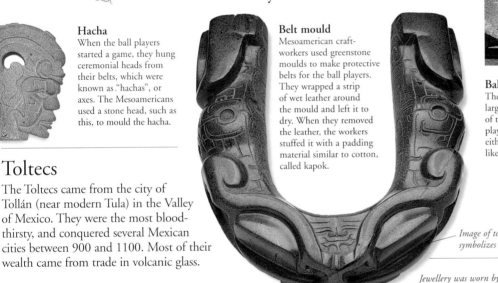

Image of toad on the belt symbolizes Earth.

Toltecs

The Toltecs came from the city of Tollán (near modern Tula) in the Valley of Mexico. They were the most blood-thirsty, and conquered several Mexican cities between 900 and 1100. Most of their wealth came from trade in volcanic glass.

Tollán

The great Toltec capital had a central precinct, which contained a market and a temple-pyramid. Most Toltec art was military in style. For example, the pyramid columns are in the form of soldiers.

Warriors

Some pottery figures have a butterfly breastplate, which helps identify them as warriors.

Funerary urn

Tripod vase

Crafts

Skilled Toltec potters decorated their work in relief with painted designs, as on this funerary urn. The tripod vase features images of Quetzalcoatl, the feathered serpent god also worshipped by the Aztecs.

Jewellery was worn by the upper classes.

Mixtecs

The Mixtecs were based in the northern Oaxaca mountains in c.1200, and were famous for their metalwork. They were also warlike, conquering nearby cities, and resisted the mighty Aztecs in the 15th century.

Gold ring

Gold pendant

Huaxtecs

The Huaxtecs were trading people, who reached the peak of their civilization between 900 and 1450. Their traders travelled all around the Gulf of Mexico and up into the Central Highlands. Their craftsmen were excellent sculptors in stone.

Headdress shows this figure has high status.

Hands over the womb shows this deity may be a fertility goddess.

Huaxtec deity in stone

 FIND OUT MORE   AZTECS   CENTRAL AMERICA, HISTORY OF   EXPLORATION   OLMECS

METALS

M

SINCE EARLY TIMES, metals have played a key role in shaping human civilization, and the extraction and working of metals is still a vital industry in the modern world. All metals are elements. Metals provide us with strong, long-lasting materials for use in construction, engineering, transportation, and manufacturing.

Shaping iron on an anvil

Metalworking

One of the reasons why metals are so useful is that they are relatively easy to shape, whether they are cold, hot, or molten. They can be hammered over an anvil, rolled out into sheets, or stretched out into tubes and wires. Other techniques include casting (pouring molten metal into a mould) and forging (pressing a hot metal into shape using a huge metal block).

Welding

Metal parts can be joined by welding. The edges of two metal pieces are melted with a gas flame or a powerful spark of electricity called an electric arc. The molten metals fuse together and form a strong joint as they cool.

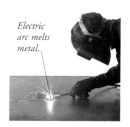
Electric arc melts metal.

Metallic bonds

Metal atoms are held together by forces called metallic bonds. All atoms contain negatively charged particles called electrons. In metals, some of the electrons break free from their atoms to form a common pool of electrons called an electron gas. The free-moving electron gas binds the metal atoms firmly together in a strong metallic bond.

Electrons move freely between atoms.

Pouring molten iron into a mould.

Casting iron

Properties of metals

Most metals are hard and dense, and conduct heat and electricity well. Metallic elements are solid at room temperature (20°C, 68°F), and generally have much higher melting and boiling points than non-metal elements. Iron, for example, melts at 1,535°C (2,795°F), while the non-metal nitrogen has a melting point of -210°C (-346°F).

Top of nail is exposed to air.

Rust flakes off surface of nail.

Rust forms as iron reacts with oxygen in air and water.

Iron nail in water

Semimetals

Some elements, such as germanium and silicon, are called semimetals because they have some of the properties of metals and some of non-metals. They are also known as semiconductors, which means that they conduct electricity only under certain conditions. They are ideal for use in electronic components, such as microchips, in which electric current has to be carefully controlled.

Silicon chip

Microchip

Mercury

Mercury is the only metal that is liquid at room temperature. Its silvery colour and the fact that it flows easily earned mercury the name quicksilver. It is used in thermometers, barometers, and batteries.

Rust

If iron is exposed to air and water, its surface will corrode and form a flaky material called rust. Most metals corrode in air and water. Corrosion can be prevented by giving the metal a protective coating.

Ores

Only a few metals occur naturally in their pure state. Most are locked up within rocks and minerals called ores. A metal can be extracted from its ore by heating the ore or passing a powerful electric current through it.

Copper ore (chalcopyrite)

Types of metal

Some metals are highly valued for their appearance, while others are valued for their usefulness. However, most of the "metal" objects that we encounter in our daily lives are actually metal mixtures called alloys.

Brass ship's bell

Bronze Roman helmet

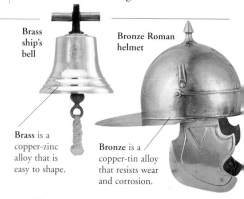

Brass is a copper-zinc alloy that is easy to shape.

Bronze is a copper-tin alloy that resists wear and corrosion.

Silver

Gold

Tin

Lead pellets

Platinum

Precious metals

Gold, silver, and platinum are often used in jewellery. They are known as precious metals because their rarity, beauty, and durability make them more expensive than base metals, such as iron, which are commonly available.

Poor metals

Some metals, such as aluminium, tin, and lead, are known as poor metals because they are weaker than most metals and melt more easily. Despite their name, they are very useful, and they are widely used in alloys. Lead and tin, for example, form the alloy solder, which is used to link electronic components.

Alloys

An alloy is a mixture of two or more metals. Alloys have different properties from the pure metals they contain. Copper and tin are weak metals, but when mixed together they form the strong alloy bronze. Some alloys contain non-metals: steel, for example, is mixture of iron (metal) and carbon (non-metal).

FIND OUT MORE | ATOMS AND MOLECULES | BRONZE AGE | ELECTRONICS | ELEMENTS | IRON AND STEEL | MIXTURES AND COMPOUNDS | ROCKS AND MINERALS | ROMAN EMPIRE

MEXICO

A LINK BETWEEN the USA and the Spanish-speaking countries of Central America, Mexico lies within the continent of North America. Before Spanish conquerors arrived in the Americas in the 1500s, Mexico had several thriving civilizations of its own, including the Mayan and Aztec empires. Spectacular ruins of their buildings still survive and many Mexicans have Aztec and Mayan ancestors. Mexico has great mineral wealth, but, because it has one of the world's fastest growing populations, unemployment is high, its economy is shaky, and millions live in poverty.

MEXICO FACTS	
CAPITAL CITY	Mexico City
AREA	1,972,550 sq km (761,602 sq miles)
POPULATION	100,400,000
MAIN LANGUAGE	Spanish
MAJOR RELIGION	Christian
CURRENCY	Mexican Peso
LIFE EXPECTANCY	73 years
PEOPLE PER DOCTOR	588
GOVERNMENT	Multi-party democracy
ADULT LITERACY	91%

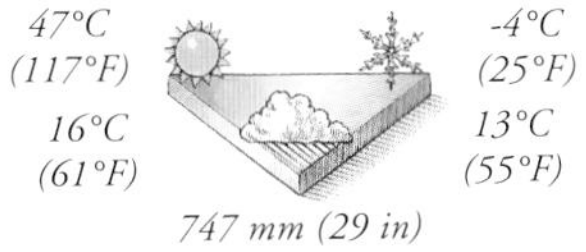

M

47°C (117°F)   -4°C (25°F)
16°C (61°F)   13°C (55°F)
747 mm (29 in)

Physical features

Mexico's varied landscape includes deserts, grasslands, tropical forests, swamps, and snow-capped volcanic peaks. Two parallel mountain chains, the Sierra Madre Occidental and Oriental, dominate the country. The most fertile land is found on the central plateau between them.

Climate
The climate varies according to height. The north is mostly arid, but can be bitterly cold in the mountains. The south and coasts are hot and humid with the most rainfall.

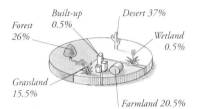

Built-up 0.5%
Forest 26%
Desert 37%
Wetland 0.5%
Grassland 15.5%
Farmland 20.5%

Land use
About 40 per cent of Mexico's land is so arid that few people live there, and it cannot be farmed. The once abundant rainforests have been cleared to make way for urban growth.

Sierra Madre
The two chains of the Sierra Madre, or mother range, form barriers in the east and west of Mexico. The western range has dormant, smoking volcanoes, notably Popocatépetl. Mexico's tallest peak is Citlatépetl, at 5,700 m (18,700 ft).

Sonoran Desert
Straddling the border between Mexico and the USA, the dry Sonoran Desert, at 310,000 sq km (120,000 sq miles), is one of the largest in the world. Here, at Pinacate National Park, west of Nogales, the desert is littered with some of the world's largest cacti, the giant saguaro, which can grow up to 18 m (60 ft) tall.

Mexico City

The world's second most populated city, Mexico's capital has 20,899,000 residents. The city lies on the site of the old Aztec capital, built in the 1300s. Mexico City sits below two high volcanoes, a position resulting in earthquakes, and air pollution from trapped urban smog.

Presidential palace

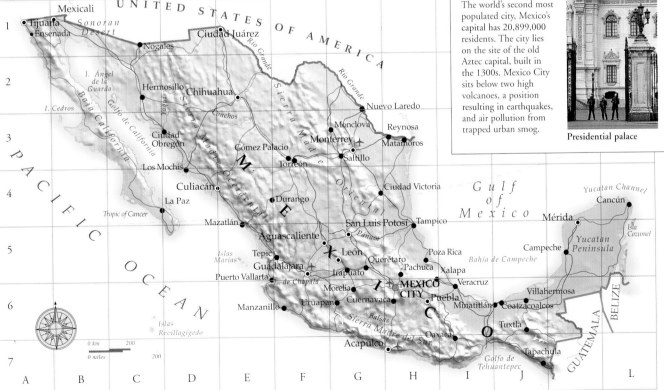

M

People

Mexico's population is set to increase by more than half by 2050. More than one-third of the people are under the age of 14. Poverty is a problem for many Mexicans, and several generations of one family often live together. Most people are *mestizos*, of mixed European and Native American descent.

52 per sq km
(134 per sq mile)

75% Urban   25% Rural

Native Americans
About 20 per cent of Mexico's people are Native Americans. Tarahumara Indians live in the Sierra Madre region of Chihuahua. They are known for their brightly coloured textiles, which are made and taken to market by the women.

Leisure

Sport and festivals are the favourite leisure activities for Mexicans. Spanish sports such as bullfighting are popular, as are rodeo events called *charreadas*. Football matches draw huge crowds.

Day of the Dead
At the beginning of November, Mexicans celebrate the Day of the Dead. During this festival, influenced by ancient Aztec traditions, death is not mourned, but celebrated. On the Day of the Dead, the streets are decorated with flowers, and skeletons made from papier mâché are everywhere.

Papier mâché skeleton

Festivals
Mexicans celebrate more than 120 fêtes and festivals every year, many of which are religious Roman Catholic celebrations. Some are national holidays. The Guélaquetza annual dance in Oaxaca is a colourful event that dates back to pre-Columbian times.

Farming

More than one-fifth of Mexicans work in agriculture, but only one-fifth of the land is used for growing crops. Water is scarce and, in some areas, all irrigation is artificial. Some farmers work under the *ejido* system, by which government-owned land is allocated to them; they work it and keep the profits.

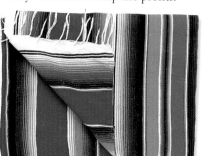

Corn

Avocado

Chilli peppers

Green pepper

Textiles
Monterrey, Mexico's ninth largest city, is a centre for textile weaving. Cotton is grown as a cash crop on the farms around the city. Traditional brightly coloured patterns are still chosen, but now most garments are machine-made.

Crops
Coffee, tomatoes, fruit, and vegetables are grown for export, whilst sugar-cane, corn, and wheat feed the Mexican farmers' families. Avocados, green peppers, and chillies are also home-grown foods. Citrus fruit grow well in Mexico's warm climate.

Food

Mexico has introduced many foods to the world, including avocados, chocolate, corn, tomatoes, and vanilla. *Tortillas*, or corn pancakes, are eaten like bread or made into snacks called *tacos* and filled with *guacamole*, a thick, spicy sauce made from onions, tomatoes, red peppers, and avocados.

Guacamole

Beer

Tortillas

Industry

Oil and silver production are Mexico's largest industries, but the service sector, including tourism, employs the most people. Car assembly, steel, textiles, food products, and breweries are important businesses.

Shrine for making sacrifices.

Tourism
Fine beaches and spectacular ruins lure nearly 20,000,000 visitors to Mexico every year. Impressive Mayan temple-pyramids such as Chichén Itzá were built strategically on the Yucatan Peninsula, and are now World Heritage archaeological sites.

Silver brooch

Silver
Mexico is one of the world's largest producers of silver. The metal is mined at Durango, in the centre of the country, where it was discovered by Spanish settlers in the 16th century. Mexico also has reserves of gold, lead, and tin.

Oil
Mexico ranks highly in world production of oil, which accounts for one-quarter of the country's total export earnings. Most of the oil is drilled from offshore wells in the Gulf of Mexico and along the Atlantic coast. Oil revenues have been used partly to finance an extensive industrialization programme to boost Mexican business. Fluctuations in oil prices caused economic problems in the 1990s.

Maquilladoras
Many US companies have set up assembly plants in northern Mexico around the Rio Grande. Known as *maquilladoras*, they have attracted US investment because labour costs are less than in the USA.

FIND OUT MORE AZTECS CENTRAL AMERICA, HISTORY OF DESERTS FARMING FESTIVALS MAYA NATIVE AMERICANS OIL ROCKS AND MINERALS TEXTILES AND WEAVING VOLCANOES

MICROSCOPES

MILLIONS OF TINY PARTICLES which play vital roles in the processes of life would go undetected without the help of microscopes. A microscope magnifies small objects to reveal details invisible to the naked eye. The simple microscope uses one lens, capable of magnifications of between 70 and 250 times. Compound microscopes use a combination of two lenses and can produce magnifications of up to 2,000 times the size of the object being viewed. Electron microscopes use beams of electrons instead of light; they can magnify by hundreds of thousands of times.

Compound microscopes

The compound microscope uses two lenses (an objective lens and an eye piece). This gives it a much greater power of magnification than the simple microscope. It was the use of the compound lens that led to the discovery of cells.

Robert Hooke

English scientist Robert Hooke (1635–1703) was responsible for improving the early compound microscope, and also introduced the term "cell" to biology. He was a versatile scientist, who devised a spring for watches and an early telegraph system, as well as discovering how elastic objects stretch. Following the fire of London in 1666, he also designed several of London's most prominent buildings.

How a compound microscope works

The lens closest to the object (objective lens) creates a magnified image inside the microscope. The larger eyepiece lens uses this image as its object and acts as a simple microscope, further magnifying the image. The total magnification is the combined power of the eyepiece and the objective lens.

Simple microscopes

Dutch scientist Antoni van Leeuwenhoek's (1632–1723) simple microscope consisted of a single convex lens held between two metal plates. The eye had to be placed close to the lens to see the object placed on a pin. Using different lenses produced different magnifications.

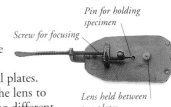

Pin for holding specimen
Screw for focusing
Lens held between two plates

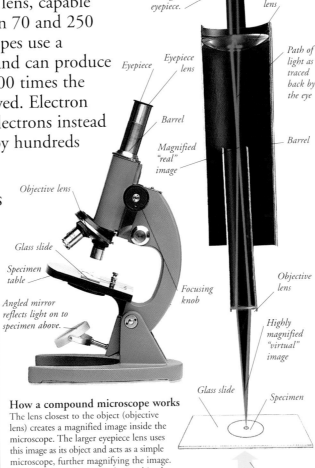

Observer looks through eyepiece.
Eyepiece lens
Path of light as traced back by the eye
Eyepiece
Eyepiece lens
Barrel
Magnified "real" image
Barrel
Objective lens
Objective lens
Glass slide
Specimen table
Focusing knob
Angled mirror reflects light on to specimen above.
Highly magnified "virtual" image
Glass slide
Specimen
Light source

How a simple microscope works

A simple microscope, such as a magnifying glass, consists of one convex lens which bulges outwards and bends light inwards. Seen through the convex lens, the object is shown as a magnified and upright image.

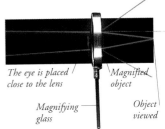

The eye is placed close to the lens
Magnified object
Magnifying glass
Object viewed

Magnified images

Forms of life such as the dust mite, which surround us, but which the human eye cannot see, are made visible by the use of a microscope. Under a microscope, a shaft of hair can be matched to an individual, identified by the DNA present in the hair.

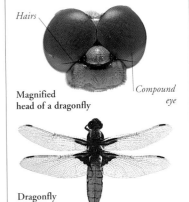

Hairs
Magnified head of a dragonfly
Compound eye
Dragonfly

Petrograph microscopes

A petrograph microscope is used to study the make-up of rocks (petrology is the study of the composition of rocks). It uses polarized light to identify the minerals in thin sections of rocks.

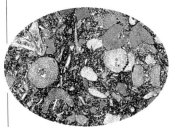

Black marble seen through petroscope

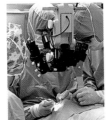

Microscopic surgery

One of the latest developments in surgery is microscopic surgery. An endoscope (optical fibre) is inserted into the patient. The surgeon can see the operation through the fibre optic and microscope.

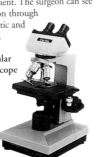

Binocular microscope

Binocular microscopes

Using two eyes provides a depth to the images perceived. Binocular microscopes, with two separate instruments fastened together, provide microscopic vision for both eyes. This allows for detailed study of an image.

Electron scanning microscopes

Electron scanning microscopes can magnify extensively without losing the clarity of the image. The electrons are reflected off the surface of the specimen, producing a fluorescent image on a screen. This is photographed showing the surface in great detail.

Electron scanning microscope image of pollen

Electron scanning microscope

FIND OUT MORE — ATOMS AND MOLECULES · CELLS · FLOWERS · GLASS · LIGHT · INVENTIONS · MEDICINE · SCIENCE, HISTORY OF · TELESCOPES

M

MICROSCOPIC LIFE

A MICRO-ORGANISM is a life-form that is too small for the human eye to see clearly. This usually means that it is less than 1 mm (0.04 in) in size.

Micro-organisms include protozoa, bacteria, fungi, algae, and viruses. The two main groups into which micro-organisms are divided are the protist and moneran groups. Some protists, such as the brown algae called kelp, can grow to more than 50 m (164 ft) in length, but most are microscopic, with the smallest measuring only 0.00000001 mm³ in volume.

Protists

Protozoa, algae, and microscopic fungi are all protists – they belong to the Protista kingdom of organisms. Most protists are uni-cellular organisms, and their cell structure is similar to that of plants and animals. Some protists are multi-cellular, but their structure is simpler than that of higher organisms. There are up to 120,000 species of protist.

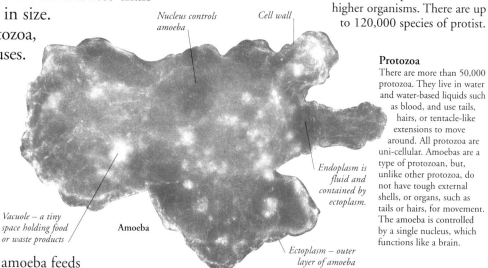

Nucleus controls amoeba

Cell wall

Endoplasm is fluid and contained by ectoplasm.

Vacuole – a tiny space holding food or waste products

Amoeba

Ectoplasm – outer layer of amoeba

Protozoa

There are more than 50,000 protozoa. They live in water and water-based liquids such as blood, and use tails, hairs, or tentacle-like extensions to move around. All protozoa are uni-cellular. Amoebas are a type of protozoan, but, unlike other protozoa, do not have tough external shells, or organs, such as tails or hairs, for movement. The amoeba is controlled by a single nucleus, which functions like a brain.

How an amoeba feeds

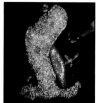

1 Amoebas move by pushing the more rigid part of their body, the ectoplasm, against the more fluid part, the endoplasm.

2 When an amoeba meets a possible food item, such as another protist, it slowly envelops the prey with its entire body, and sucks inwards.

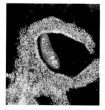

3 The food is then drawn towards the centre of the cell, where the nutrients are dissolved. Any waste products are expelled.

Single-cell algae

Algae are plant-like organisms that generally obtain their food through photosynthesis. Most are made up of a single cell, but some are multi-cellular and look very much like true plants. A highly diverse group of micro-organisms, the most plant-like are green algae, and it is from these that plants are thought to have evolved.

Diatoms, single-cell algae

Microscopic fungi

Although mushrooms and toadstools are often large, many other types of fungi are microscopic. Fungi do not obtain their food from photosynthesis, as plants do. Instead, they produce minute, thread-like structures called hyphae. The fungi use the hyphae to absorb food from the surface on which they are growing.

Microscopic fungi grown by termites in their nest

Slime moulds

Although similar to fungi, slime moulds are categorized separately. Many slime moulds acquire a fan-like shape as they flow over the surface on which they grow, such as damp, decaying logs. As the slime mould expands, it absorbs other micro-organisms and bits of decaying plant material. Like fungi, slime moulds reproduce by producing spores.

Slime mould

Plankton

Billions of tiny plants and animals float in sea- and freshwater; together, they make up plankton. The smallest plankton, phytoplankton, are microscopic algae and bacteria. Phytoplankton forms the first link of the food chain in water and is eaten by predatory protists and zooplankton, which is composed of the young of marine animals, such as crabs and shrimps.

Marine zooplankton

Monerans

The kingdom Monera includes organisms such as bacteria, which live in the air, on land, and in water. Most monerans are uni-cellular, but some are multi-cellular and resemble fungi. Monerans are divided into two groups: bacteria and blue-green bacteria; many are parasites.

Bacteria

Bacteria are often classified by their shape. Some, such as *Bacillus subtilis*, are rod-shaped; others are spherical or curved. In some species, individual cells are joined together to form long chains.

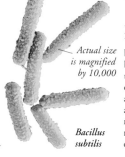

Actual size is magnified by 10,000

Bacillus subtilis

Reproduction

Bacteria usually reproduce by splitting in two. This process is called binary fission. The two new bacteria are called daughters. Bacteria, such as *Klebsiella*, reproduce this way; it allows a massive increase in population.

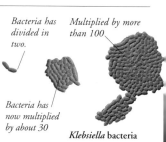

Bacteria has divided in two.

Multiplied by more than 100

Bacteria has now multiplied by about 30

Klebsiella bacteria

Blue-green bacteria

Until recently, blue-green bacteria were thought to be a type of algae. Now they are classified as a type of bacteria. They occur in a wide range of habitats, and when conditions are right they can multiply rapidly, causing "blooms" on lakes and in the sea.

"Bloom" forms green surface on lake

Viruses

Viruses, such as rubella which causes German measles, belong to a group of disease-producing organisms. Each virus is made from a length of nucleic acid surrounded by a protein coat. Viruses are inactive chemicals that show no sign of life until they invade a host. Once they have infected their host, they can reproduce in great numbers. Viruses can cause allergic reactions in the host cell, as well as causing it physical damage when they burst free from it.

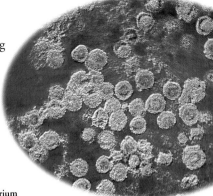

Rubella viruses

Rubella viruses erupting from cell

Reproduction

Viruses reproduce by inserting their nucleic acid, or genetic material, into that of a host cell and forcing the cell to produce more viruses. Almost every species of bacterium is parasitized by one or more viruses. These viruses are also known as bacteriophages.

Reproduction of a virus

Virus invading a bacterium

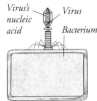

Virus's nucleic acid · Virus · Bacterium

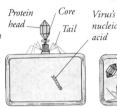

Protein head · Core · Tail

Virus's nucleic acid

New viruses are formed inside the bacterium.

New virus breaking free

1 The virus's nucleic acid is stored in a head made out of protein. The head sits on a core with a tail. When a bacterium is found, the virus imbeds its tail in the cell wall.

2 The tail of the virus contracts, pulling the core downwards. All of the nucleic acid contained in the virus's head is injected into the bacterium.

3 The nucleic acid from the virus joins with the bacterium's nucleic acid and forces it to produce more viral nucleic acid. The cell is then forced to make protective proteins for the virus's survival.

4 After about half an hour, the bacterium bursts open, releasing another generation of viruses. By this time, the virus has been replicated 300 times, and the host cell has been damaged.

Antony van Leeuwenhoek

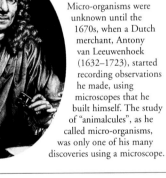

Micro-organisms were unknown until the 1670s, when a Dutch merchant, Antony van Leeuwenhoek (1632–1723), started recording observations he made, using microscopes that he built himself. The study of "animalcules", as he called micro-organisms, was only one of his many discoveries using a microscope.

Microbial diseases

Like most other organisms, humans are prone to attack by micro-organisms, such as protists and viruses. These microbes, as they are called, can cause the host to become sick or can even kill it. Microbes injure their host in a number of ways. Some bacteria produce poisons, while protists can cause an allergic reaction in the host.

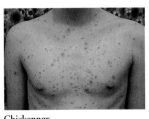

Salmonella causes food poisoning in humans.

These bacteria can occur in milk, meat, and eggs.

Salmonella enteridis

Protozoan diseases

Worldwide, more people have died from protozoan attacks than have died in war. In Africa, the protozoan *Trypanosoma brucei* causes sleeping sickness, which can weaken the human immune system and result in death.

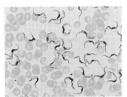

Trypanosomes in human blood

Fungal diseases

Only a few fungi infect humans. *Trichophyton soudanese* causes ringworm. Fungal infections are called *tinea* and are named after the part of the body they infect. For example, athlete's foot is called *tinea pedis*.

Trichophyton soudanese

Bacterial diseases

Many species of bacteria live in the digestive tracts of animals. Most bacteria are harmless, but some, such as those that cause cholera, typhoid, and *Salmonella* infections, can be fatal.

Viral diseases

Every year, thousands of people die from the results of viral infections, such as influenza, rabies, HIV, and yellow fever. Vaccines are available for many of the more common viruses, such as chickenpox, smallpox, and polio.

Chickenpox

Symbiotic micro-organisms

Some micro-organisms are essential to the life of their host: the two have a symbiotic relationship. For example, algae called zooxanthellae, live inside corals. They can photosynthesize and convert sunlight into carbohydrates on which the coral feeds. Other micro-organisms live in the guts of animals, including humans, and aid the digestion of food.

Zooxanthellae algae (yellow in colour) live inside the coral polyps.

Coral packed with zooxanthellae algae

Micro-organisms in food

The bacterium commonly called yeast (made up of single-celled organisms) is central to the fermentation process needed to make bread, beer, and wine. Other useful bacteria are used to refine crude oil or to preserve foods, such as milk and butter. Even the holes in the Swiss cheese Emmental are caused by carbon dioxide-releasing bacteria.

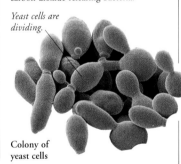

Yeast cells are dividing.

Colony of yeast cells

AMOEBA

SCIENTIFIC NAME *Amoeba proteus*

ORDER Amoebida

FAMILY Gymnamoebidae

DISTRIBUTION These single-cell protists are found throughout the world wherever there is water

HABITAT Amoebas need to live in water. This can be in ponds, puddles, or even in the digestive systems of animals

DIET Minute particles of organic matter and other micro-organisms

SIZE 0.1–2 mm (0.004–0.08 in)

LIFESPAN Maximum of 1 month

FIND OUT MORE CELLS CORAL REEFS DISEASES GENETICS MICROSCOPES MUSHROOMS AND OTHER FUNGI OCEAN WILDLIFE PARASITES PHOTOSYNTHESIS

M

MIGRATION, ANIMAL

SEVERAL HUNDRED BILLION animals are on the move at any one time, making journeys from one place to another called migrations. Migrating animals include insects, fish, amphibians, reptiles, birds, and mammals, including humans. They find their way using inherited knowledge, familiar landmarks, the Earth's magnetic field, or the position of the Sun, Moon, and stars. An animal's migration is usually connected with food, overcrowding, or finding places to breed. Some migrations take place regularly every year; others take several years to complete.

To reproduce

An important reason for migration is to find a place where there is enough space, food, and suitable weather to raise a family. In the oceans, mammals such as whales and seals may migrate to warm water to have their young. Some species of fish also migrate between feeding and breeding grounds.

Gray whale
Many large whales feed in cold polar waters, where there is plenty of food, but migrate to warmer areas in the tropics to breed. The gray whale travels from the Arctic to the coast of California, USA.

Salmon have strong muscles and are powerful swimmers.

Elvers

Salmon
Young salmon hatch out in rivers and streams and spend some years there before swimming to the ocean. After feeding and growing for several more years, they follow chemical clues in the water to find their way back to the river where they were born. They often have to leap up waterfalls as they fight their way upstream. After laying their eggs, they die.

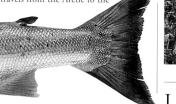

Eels
Born in the Sargasso Sea, southeast of Bermuda, eels migrate to rivers in North America and Europe to feed and grow. The young eels, called elvers, may wriggle overland to reach their feeding grounds.

Escaping the weather

Animals may migrate to escape freezing winters or hot summers. They return when the weather is more favourable. If animals stayed in one place, there would be too much competition for food, space, and places to breed. Seasonal migrations can be short, such as up and down a mountain.

Each bird flies in the slipstream of the bird in front to save energy.

Spiny lobster
As many as 100,000 spiny lobsters may migrate each autumn, walking along the seabed in single files of up to 60 individuals. The lobsters stay in contact by touching each other with their antennae.

Snow goose
Snow geese breed in the Arctic summer, but migrate south in winter to the Gulf of Mexico. They fly in a "V" formation as this helps to save energy for the long journey.

Bogong moth
These moths migrate up the Australian Alps for the hot summers. They sleep in cracks in the rock until it is cooler.

Looking for food

If the food supply in a location changes regularly every year, animals make regular annual migrations to tap new supplies. When conditions vary from year to year, migrational patterns are irregular.

Locusts
Migratory swarms of locusts occur where suitable habitats are scarce and there is overcrowding. The locusts gather in large groups and grow longer wings and wider shoulders. They migrate up to 3,200 km (1,980 miles) a year.

Wildebeest
On the plains of East Africa, wildebeest migrate to find fresh grass and water. They can sense water up to 100 km (60 miles) away and follow the seasonal movement of the rains. The herds are under constant danger of attack from predators, such as lions and hyenas.

Long-distance travellers

The distances travelled by animals on migration often run into several thousand kilometres each year. These long journeys use up huge amounts of energy, and birds may double their weight before setting off.

Arctic tern
This bird migrates further than any other bird. It flies from one end of the globe to the other and back again each year – a round trip of more than 50,000 km (31,000 miles).

Monarch butterfly
These butterflies migrate up to 4,000 km (2,500 miles) every autumn, from Canada to Mexico and California, to hibernate in mountain forests. They, or their offspring, then make the return trip.

Northern fur seal
Female northern fur seals migrate some 5,000 km (3,100 miles) from their breeding grounds in the north to spend the winter in warmer water. They return in the spring.

FIND OUT MORE AFRICAN WILDLIFE ANIMAL BEHAVIOUR HIBERNATION POLAR WILDLIFE TRAVEL WHALES AND DOLPHINS

MINOANS

ON THE ISLAND OF CRETE in the Aegean Sea, an advanced and fabulously rich civilization emerged in around 2500 BC – Europe's first empire. These people, who were traders, became known as the Minoans, after the legend of the wealthy King Minos of Crete. The Minoans built gorgeously decorated palaces on Crete, and we know a lot about them from the paintings, buildings, and luxury items found there. However, scholars have only deciphered part of their writing. In 1450, the Minoans were overrun by the warlike Mycenaeans from Greece.

M

Spread of the Minoan Empire
From their homeland on Crete, the Minoans dominated the Aegean Sea from 2000 to 1450 BC. The settlements were mainly coastal, and the most important – Knossos, Mallia, Phaistos, and Zakros – were built around large palaces.

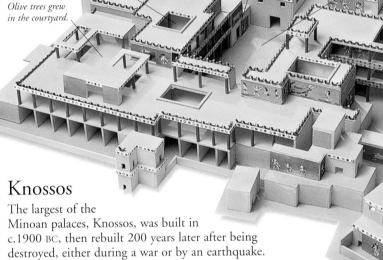

Light well allowing light into the palace

Throne room

Bull leaping may have taken place in the central courtyard.

Olive trees grew in the courtyard.

Wooden pillars were painted red and blue.

Bull jumping
In this sport, which possibly had a religious significance, young men and women took turns to somersault over the back of a bull.

Pottery
The storerooms at Knossos were full of earthenware jars, (pithoi), some 2 m (6 ft) tall. These stored oil and wine.

Knossos
The largest of the Minoan palaces, Knossos, was built in c.1900 BC, then rebuilt 200 years later after being destroyed, either during a war or by an earthquake. The huge, richly decorated complex may have been a religious centre and a base for trading, as well as home for the local ruler. The palace is arranged around a central courtyard and contains rooms for many different purposes – royal apartments, ceremonial chambers, such as the throne room, shrines, workshops, and dozens of storerooms.

Religion

Bird

Snake

Flounced skirt

Many hilltops and all the palaces contained shrines, where the Minoans made offerings of food and drink to the gods. Several different deities were worshipped, including a god of animals and the hunt. Bulls were also believed to be sacred. The most important deity was a goddess of the Earth and fertility.

Snake maiden
Archaeologists have found many images of this goddess, wearing the typical costume of a Minoan woman. She sometimes carries snakes in her hands, and sometimes has them twined around her body. Minoans probably saw her as a guardian of the home, and also as a deity who would encourage fertility and promote good harvests in the fields.

Trade

Grapes

Olives

The Minoans traded using a circular route around the Mediterranean, from Crete to Egypt, on to Palestine, and back to Crete via Cyprus. They exported pottery, metalwork, and food. They took back raw materials, such as copper and precious stones.

Thera
A volcanic eruption on nearby Thera in 1470 BC was once thought to have caused the end of the Minoan Empire. Research now shows that invaders from mainland Greece, known as the Mycenaeans, wiped out the Minoans.

Timeline
2500 BC Trading Settlements begin to expand on the island of Crete.

1900 BC First Cretan palaces are built; Minoans begin to trade and build up overseas links.

1800 BC Writing begins on Crete, as Minoan scribes develop the Linear A script.

1700 BC Cretan palaces are destroyed by fire, possibly during warfare between different Cretan states. The palaces are rebuilt.

1550 BC Cretan civilization at peak.

1500 BC Linear B script (a way of writing an ancient form of Greek) starts to be used.

1470 BC Eruption on island of Thera.

1400 BC Knossos falls, after Crete is overrun by invaders from the Greek mainland, the Mycenaeans. At the same time, the mainland Mycenaean palace civilization expands, as does Mycenaean trade in the Mediterranean.

FIND OUT MORE

EUROPE, HISTORY OF

GODS AND GODDESSES

GREECE, ANCIENT

WRITING

MIXTURES AND COMPOUNDS

WE CANNOT SEE THE SALT in the ocean, but we know it is there because the water tastes salty. The salt and water form a mixture called a solution. Salt and water themselves are compounds – substances that contain elements bound strongly together by a chemical reaction. In science, a mixture is a combination of elements or compounds mingled loosely together. Mixtures are much easier to separate into their component parts than compounds.

The crystals break up into tiny particles that spread throughout the liquid.

After a few seconds, the crystals have dissolved completely in the water.

Solutions

Potassium permanganate crystals dissolve rapidly when they are dropped into water. The two substances are soon indistinguishable because they form a uniform mixture called a solution. In a solution, particles of a solid (the solute) are completely intermingled with the particles of a liquid (the solvent). A solution is said to be concentrated if it contains a large amount of solute, and dilute if it contains only a small amount.

Crystals of potassium permanganate

Suspensions and colloids

When muddy water is left to stand, the mud settles and the water becomes clearer. Muddy water is a suspension – a mixture of solid particles hanging in a liquid. The mixture eventually separates because gravity makes the particles sink to the bottom. A colloid is a mixture of tiny particles of matter dispersed evenly throughout a solid, liquid, or gas. The particles are too small to be separated by gravity and too large to dissolve, so they stay suspended in the main substance.

The two substances are evenly mixed.

Eventually, the solid lead iodide particles settle out.

Suspension of lead iodide in potassium iodide

Types of colloid
The particles in a colloid can be gas bubbles, droplets of liquid, or tiny solid pieces. Colloids include aerosols, gels, emulsions, and foams. Fog, for example, is an aerosol of water particles in air. Colloids are also known as dispersions.

Aerosols are solid or liquid particles suspended in a gas.

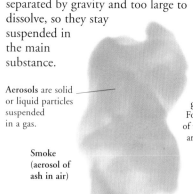

Smoke (aerosol of ash in air)

Gels consist of solid particles suspended in a liquid.

Shaving foam (air in liquid soap)

Foams are colloids of gas particles dispersed evenly throughout a liquid or solid.

Emulsions are mixtures of liquid particles suspended in another liquid.

Hair gel (solid fat in water)

Emulsion paint (liquid pigment in oil)

Separating mixtures

Pouring coffee through a filter is a familiar way of separating a mixture: the filter separates the coffee grounds from the liquid coffee, making it more drinkable. Other separation methods include decanting, centrifuging, distillation, and evaporation. Decanting, the simplest method, involves pouring a liquid off from a denser liquid or solid sediment.

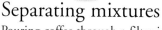

Decanting oil from vinegar

Oil is less dense than vinegar.

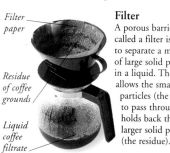

Filter paper

Residue of coffee grounds

Liquid coffee filtrate

Filter
A porous barrier called a filter is used to separate a mixture of large solid particles in a liquid. The filter allows the small liquid particles (the filtrate) to pass through, but holds back the larger solid particles (the residue).

Centrifuge
A centrifuge is a machine that separates mixtures by spinning them round very fast in test tubes. Denser substances sink to the bottom and separate out. Centrifuges are used to extract dense blood cells from blood plasma.

Mixture is held in test tubes.

Overhead view of centrifuge

Distillation
A process called distillation can be used to separate a liquid from a mixture. The mixture is heated until the liquid boils and turns into a gas. The gas is then led into a tube called a condenser, where it cools to form a pure liquid.

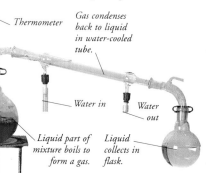

Thermometer

Gas condenses back to liquid in water-cooled tube.

Water in

Water out

Liquid part of mixture boils to form a gas.

Liquid collects in flask.

Evaporation
Heat can separate a liquid from a mixture by evaporation. In hot climates, this method is often used to obtain salt from seawater. Shallow pools called salt pans are dug out on the coast and filled with seawater. The water evaporates in the warm sun, leaving salt crystals behind.

M

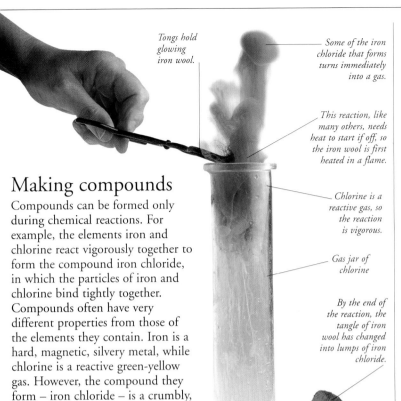

Tongs hold glowing iron wool.

Some of the iron chloride that forms turns immediately into a gas.

This reaction, like many others, needs heat to start if off, so the iron wool is first heated in a flame.

Chlorine is a reactive gas, so the reaction is vigorous.

Gas jar of chlorine

By the end of the reaction, the tangle of iron wool has changed into lumps of iron chloride.

Making compounds

Compounds can be formed only during chemical reactions. For example, the elements iron and chlorine react vigorously together to form the compound iron chloride, in which the particles of iron and chlorine bind tightly together. Compounds often have very different properties from those of the elements they contain. Iron is a hard, magnetic, silvery metal, while chlorine is a reactive green-yellow gas. However, the compound they form – iron chloride – is a crumbly, orange-brown solid that is non-magnetic and fairly unreactive.

Sampling molten iron in a blast furnace

Separating compounds

Compounds can only be broken apart by chemical reactions. Most metals have to be extracted from naturally occurring compounds called ores. In a blast furnace, the metal ore iron oxide (a compound of iron and oxygen) is heated with coke, which contains carbon. The heat of the furnace causes a chemical reaction in which the carbon removes the oxygen from the iron ore, leaving behind molten iron metal.

Structure of compounds

Inside a compound, the particles of different elements are bound together by forces called bonds, which form during chemical reactions. Covalent compounds contain atoms linked together into groups called molecules. In ionic compounds, electrically charged particles called ions link up to form a structure called a lattice.

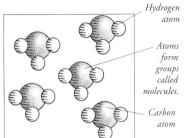

Hydrogen atom

Atoms form groups called molecules.

Carbon atom

Methane

Covalent compounds

At normal temperatures, covalent compounds, such as methane, form liquids, gases, or soft solids. They are poor conductors of electricity. There are only weak bonds between the molecules of covalent compounds, which is why they have low boiling and melting points.

Ionic compounds

Inside ionic compounds, such as sodium chloride (common salt), strong bonds hold the ions of the different elements firmly together. Ionic compounds form hard, brittle solids. They have high boiling and melting points, and are good conductors of electricity when molten or in solution.

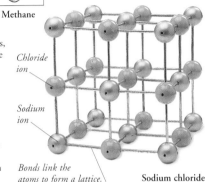

Chloride ion

Sodium ion

Bonds link the atoms to form a lattice.

Sodium chloride

Justus von Liebig

The German chemist Justus von Liebig (1803–73) made many advances in the study of carbon-based compounds. He established a teaching laboratory in 1839, and devised standard procedures such as distillation for separating and analysing mixtures and compounds. He was one of the discoverers of chloroform, and also pioneered the development of artificial fertilizers.

Chemical analysis

There are many ways of analysing a mixture or compound to find out what it is made of and how much of each ingredient it contains. These techniques are used to check food and medicine for purity, test air and water samples for pollution, and examine blood and urine for signs of disease.

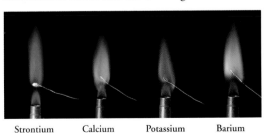

| Strontium | Calcium | Potassium | Barium |

Flame tests

If a metallic element is present in a substance, it can be identified with a flame test. A clean wire is dipped into a powder of the substance and then put into a flame. Different metals burn with flames of different colours, so the flame's colour identifies the metal. Fireworks use metal compounds to produce coloured sparks.

Dyes separate out into coloured rings.

Filter paper

Chromatography

The technique known as chromatography uses an absorbent material to identify the ingredients of a solution. When a drop of black ink (a mixture of different dyes) is placed in the centre of a filter paper, the ink spreads out to form rings of different colours. The dyes in the ink are absorbed by the paper at different rates, depending on the size and shape of their molecules.

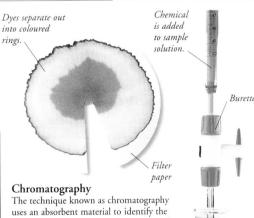

Chemical is added to sample solution.

Burette

Chemical reaction changes colour of sample solution.

Mass spectrometry

The ions of each element have a different mass. A mass spectrometer uses this fact to analyze unknown substances. It changes the atoms of an unknown substance into ions, and separates them according to their mass. It then produces a graph called a mass spectrum, which shows the proportions of each element present.

Titration

The concentration of a solution can be found by titration. The sample reacts with a chemical whose concentration is known. When the reaction is complete, a colour change occurs. The amount of the chemical needed to bring about this colour change enables chemists to calculate the concentration of the sample.

FIND OUT MORE | ATOMS AND MOLECULES | CHEMISTRY | COLOUR | ELEMENTS | GASES | LIQUIDS | MATTER | OCEANS AND SEAS | ROCKS AND MINERALS | SOLIDS

MONASTERIES

A MONASTERY IS HOME to monks, people who have chosen to live apart from society, devoting their lives to religion. Most organized religions have monasteries, especially the Christian and Buddhist traditions. As well as being a church or temple, a monastery is where monks live and work. Nuns, women who choose to follow a religious life, normally live in convents.

The nave, at the western end of the church, is where lay people worship.

The choir, at the eastern end of the church, is where monks worship.

The cloister is a covered walkway within the monastery.

The cloister garth is a courtyard used for rest and relaxation.

Gatehouse

Storeroom

Parts of a Christian monastery

At the heart of a Christian monastery is the church, where the monks or nuns gather for worship at set times every day. It also contains the buildings in which the monks or nuns live – including rooms for eating, washing, sleeping, and studying. Some monasteries also have accommodation for guests.

Monks spend many hours of each day in the monastery church, attending eight services from midnight to early evening before bed. The words of many services are chanted, not sung. This music is called plainsong.

The chapter house is where the monks meet to discuss the business of the monastery. The monks eat together in the refectory, while one of them reads from a religious book.

Refectory

The garden provides produce for the monks' table. Monasteries also often had outlying farms where livestock was raised.

Rosemary

Bay leaves

Life in a monastery

Prayer dominates monastery life. In Medieval Europe, monasteries also provided education, and monks wrote books, composed music, or healed the sick. Today, monks and nuns still teach, or help the poor or homeless.

Produce

In the Middle Ages, a monastery was self-sufficient, producing all its own food. Monks became skilled farmers and gardeners. Today, they make all sorts of produce for sale.

Honey made to raise money for monastery.

The dorter, or dormitory, is where monks sleep. In some orders, there is more privacy, with a small area partitioned off for each person.

The infirmary, or hospital, is housed in a separate building, to reduce the risk of spreading infection.

Herb gardening

Many different herbs were grown in the gardens of medieval monasteries. Aromatic plants, such as bay, rosemary, and garlic, were used to flavour the monastery's food and to make medicines and ointments for healing the sick.

Monks and nuns

Life in a monastery or convent follows strict rules. Monks and nuns vow to obey their spiritual leader, and to give up personal property and relations with the opposite sex.

Novices

In their first years of monastery life, monks and nuns are called novices. During this training period, they make sure they can live by their religious vows.

Buddhist monk

Roman Catholic nuns often wear austere habits (gowns).

Eastern monasteries

Monasteries play a large part in many eastern religions. In Buddhist countries, young men often spend a short time as a monk as part of their normal education. The Hindu, Taoist, and Jain faiths all have strong monastic traditions.

Monastic caves

Monks and nuns deny themselves comforts they would have as lay people. Few led a harsher life than the monks of St Antoine, Lebanon, who lived in caves in cliffs.

Caves of the order of St Antoine

FIND OUT MORE   BUDDHISM   CHRISTIANITY   CHURCHES AND CATHEDRALS   HINDUISM   MEDICINE, HISTORY OF   MEDIEVAL EUROPE   RELIGIONS

MONET, CLAUDE

IN 1874, A PAINTING WAS exhibited which gave its name to a revolutionary movement in art. The painting was *Impression: Sunrise* and the artist, Monet, became the most famous Impressionist painter. Monet found new ways of painting what he saw. Instead of working in a studio, he liked to take his easel into the open air. He, and artists such as Renoir and Degas, developed a loose, rapid style of painting, which was completely unlike the smooth, highly finished style then fashionable among artists. Painting was never the same again.

Impressionism

Monet and his friends did not like the pictures that were shown at the Salon, France's yearly painting exhibition. So in 1874, Monet and a group of 29 other artists put on their own exhibition. Many of the paintings were small canvases painted in the open air. The artists used loose brushstrokes and many dabs of pure colour – hallmarks of what is now called the Impressionist style. At first, people thought the pictures looked "unfinished", but they are now among the most popular paintings in the world.

Two paintings of Rouen Cathedral

Impression: Sunrise, 1872
Monet included this view of the French port of Le Havre in the exhibition of 1874. A critic named Louis Leroy wrote an article attacking the painting, which he thought too sketchy to be shown as a finished work. Leroy called his article "Exhibition of the Impressionists", meaning the term as an insult. But the name stuck, and it is now used to describe the work of Monet and his friends.

Changing light
Monet was fascinated by light. He painted several groups of pictures of the same subject, showing how the colours varied with the changing light. In 1892–93, he painted a series of pictures of Rouen Cathedral, France. He worked quickly, on as many as 14 different paintings in one day, building up heavy layers of paint which seemed to imitate the thickness of the stone itself.

Canopy shelters the deck.

Monet's floating studio

Giverny
In 1883, Monet moved to Giverny, northwestern France. He created a beautiful garden around his house, and built a pond in which he planted water-lilies. For the next 25 years, this garden was his favourite subject, and he painted the lily pond again and again. He was fascinated by the colours of the flowers, the effects of light on the foliage, and the reflections in the water in the pond. Many of the water-lily paintings were huge, so Monet built a special studio in which to work.

Water-lilies

Monet at Giverny

Early life
Claude Monet was born in Paris in 1840, but his family moved to the town of Le Havre in Normandy when he was five. There he learned to paint, producing pictures of his family and local scenes, and portraits of the people of Le Havre.

From Normandy to Paris
As a young man in Le Havre, Monet met the landscape painter Eugène Boudin (1824–98). Boudin painted in the open air, and he persuaded Monet to do the same. Monet enjoyed this experience and realized that he wanted to be an artist. In 1859, he went to study art in Paris, where he met the painter Camille Pissarro (1830–1903) and other artists who became his friends.

Berthe Morisot
Berthe Morisot (1841–95) was the first female member of the Impressionist group. She was born into a rich French family and had private lessons in painting and drawing. But she rejected the conventional style of her teachers and decided to paint in an Impressionist style. Morisot specialized in gentle paintings of family life and seascapes painted in delicate brushstrokes.

Monet's palette

Painting outdoors
In the early 19th century, artists usually sketched out of doors, but painted their finished pictures in the studio. Monet was one of the first to paint entire, finished canvases in the open air. He took his easel everywhere – the beach, fields, railway stations – and had a boat made into a floating studio so that he could paint along the River Seine.

Windows all around cabin

CLAUDE MONET

1840	Born in Paris.
1845	Moves to Le Havre.
1859	Returns to Paris to study.
1874	Exhibits in First Impressionist Exhibition.
1876–78	Paints at Gare St Lazare railway station, Paris.
1883	Retires from Paris to Giverny.
1892	Begins series of paintings of Rouen Cathedral.
1900	Paints by the River Thames in London.
1908	Works on water-lily paintings; starts to lose his eyesight.
1926	Dies at Giverny.

FIND OUT MORE   ART, HISTORY OF   COLOUR   CHURCHES AND CATHEDRALS   FRANCE   LIGHT   PAINTING AND DRAWING   PICASSO, PABLO

MONEY

YOU CANNOT EAT MONEY, WEAR IT, or live in it, but people need it to feed, clothe, and house themselves. People use money to pay for the things they want to buy – it is a means of exchange that works as long as the buyer and the seller both agree on the value of the paper, metal, or plastic used to pay. Money works as a standard of value, allowing one to see how much goods are worth. It also provides a store of wealth more convenient than other things of value, such as property. Before money was invented, people bartered, swapping one item for another.

Gold standard
Each country has its own money, or currency. So governments need a standard way of judging how much a nation's currency is worth, to work out exchange rates from one currency into another. In the 20th century, many Western governments measured the value of a currency according to the value of gold and a nation's gold reserves. Various systems existed, which all related the value of a banknote to a precise weight of gold. The gold standard system ended in the 1970s; now the value of currency depends on the market.

17th-century banknote, Sweden

Serial number

Australian dollars

Credit card

Banknotes
They may be only pieces of paper, but banknotes are accepted as valuable because of the sum they represent. Banknotes first appeared in China in the 11th century, and in Europe six centuries later.

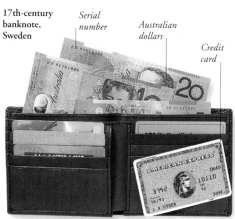

Credit card
With a credit card, a person can buy something and pay for it later. The cards are issued by banks, credit companies, and large stores, and can be used in most shops. Each month the company sends a total bill to the cardholder. Cardholders must repay the debt promptly, or will owe interest (extra money) on the balance.

Tiny computer

Smart cards can now make and record payments

Types of money
The most familiar forms of money are coins and banknotes, also known as cash. Much of the money stored in a bank exists not as piles of notes, but as data stored in computers. To spend it, people use cheques and plastic cards.

Cheque

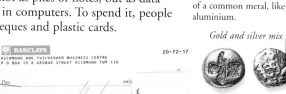

Payee's name written here

Ten pence

One penny

Two pence

Twenty pence

Five pence

Fifty pence

Pound coin

Modern British coins

Cheque guarantee card

Coins
The first coins were made in Lydia, Turkey, c.600 BC. Early coins were made of precious metal. Today, they are more likely to be made of a common metal, like aluminium.

Gold and silver mix

The lion's head, an emblem of the Lydian kings.

Lydian coins

Cheque
A cheque is a written instruction to a bank to pay money to someone. For security reasons, cheques are often unusable without identification, such as a cheque guarantee card.

The origins of money
The earliest records of money being used come from ancient Mesopotamia (modern Iraq) some 4,500 years ago. Payments were made with weighed amounts of silver. Since then, weighed amounts of metal have been used as money in many places worldwide.

Weight
Weighing the precious metal showed how much a person had and what it was worth.

Mesopotamian weight

Price list
This clay tablet contains a price list written in Mesopotamia in the 19th century BC. It expresses prices in terms of shekels and minas, the standard weights of the time. One shekel of silver would buy twelve mina of wool, ten mina of bronze, three measures of barley, or three measures of sesame oil.

First designs show the main pictures and words that appear on the note.

Design for the lines, shades, and colours, meant to discourage forgers

Anti-forgery elements, such as security thread, are often added to the paper used to make the banknotes.

Printing inks are mixed specially, giving the exact colours required for the note. This is another process that makes forgery difficult.

Printing inks

Making banknotes
To reduce the chance of forgery, the process of making banknotes is shrouded in secrecy and production is made as complicated as possible. This is why the design includes so many fine details hardly noticeable at first glance, and why special inks and papers, not used in ordinary printing, are involved.

Burnisher smooths the flat surfaces

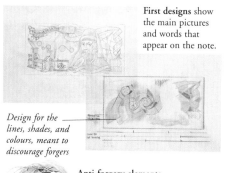

Burin used to cut design into intaglio plate

Printing
Three printing processes are used: one for the background, one for the main design, and another for the serial number. One process, intaglio, makes the ink stand slightly raised up from the paper – another indication that the note is genuine.

Finished specimen note

Banks

Most people store their money with a bank, which keeps an account of how much money each customer deposits. People gain access to their money through cash machines, counter transactions, or by writing cheques. Banks may provide interest when a certain amount of money is kept in the account, but will charge customers who borrow money. Banks also provide financial services, such as pensions and insurance policies.

Italian bankers

Early banks

Banks were set up about 3,000 to 4,000 years ago in Babylon as a secure place for customers' money. By 600 BC, there were banks in China; later, in ancient Rome, banks offered investment and foreign exchange services. Banking declined in medieval Europe because the Church disapproved of money-lending for profit. But in the 15th and 16th centuries, important banks were set up in Italy, providing financial services all over the Mediterranean.

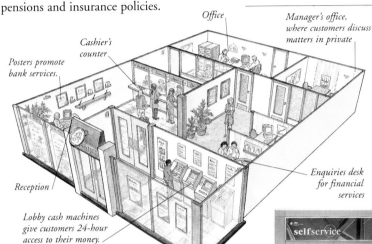

Office

Cashier's counter

Posters promote bank services.

Manager's office, where customers discuss matters in private

Reception

Lobby cash machines give customers 24-hour access to their money.

Enquiries desk for financial services

How a high street bank works
High street banks have branches in main towns. Cashiers serve customers through toughened glass panels. They can cash cheques, using money kept in tills beneath the counter, and inform customers about their accounts, using a terminal connected to the bank's central computer. Customers can also buy foreign currency for trips overseas. Most of the money is kept in vaults with massive steel doors.

Card inserted here

Panel for keying in PIN

Cash machines
Cash-dispensing machines allow customers to take money from their accounts 24 hours a day, even while the bank is shut. Customers insert a plastic card and key in a personal identification number (PIN). The machine is connected to a computer, which contains information about the amount of money held in each person's account, and records any transactions.

Security
A security van delivers banknotes to a bank, where they are stored in vaults for safekeeping. These are strongrooms, built for maximum security, and are usually equipped with time locks. At the end of a working day, all the cash at the counter tills is counted and returned to the vaults.

Bank vault

Reinforced door

Security guards

Deposit box

Safety deposit boxes
Banks keep their cash in strongrooms. For a fee, they also keep a customer's valuables, such as share certificates, in strong boxes in the strongroom.

Stock markets

People who want to invest in a company buy shares. Stock is the money raised by the company as a result of selling its shares. Major centres of financial trading, such as London, New York, and Tokyo, have stock markets where shares in companies are bought and sold.

How the exchange works
Rather than buy shares directly from a company, investors deal with brokers who are based at the stock market. Dealers work out the share prices by balancing the shares on offer with the current demand. Investors hope to buy shares before they rise in value and to sell them when the price is at its height, but it is usually difficult to predict exactly when this will be. Increasingly, brokers rely on computers to keep in touch with prices worldwide.

Screens show up-to-date share prices

Broker at work on the hectic floor

New York Stock Exchange

Fort Knox
The greatest gold reserves in the world are held at the US Depository in Fort Knox, Kentucky. Since 1936, the bulk of the United States' gold has been stored there. The gold is kept in steel and concrete vaults, enclosed in a large, bomb-proof building with massive walls. Electronic alarm systems, closed-circuit television, and armed guards provide extra protection.

Company	Price	Weekly change +/-
Gordon Properties	44	-2
JCP Interiors	69	-1
O'Neill Group	162	+7
Shaw Associates	121	+5
Thomson PLC	46	+2

Stocks and shares
The value of shares goes up and down. Prices are published regularly in the press so that people can see the value of their investments. The current price is printed along with the amount gained or lost in the share's value during the day.

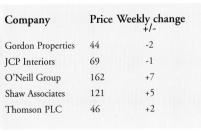

Inflation
When prices rise, and people must spend more money to buy the same amount of goods, this is known as inflation. For example, if inflation in the US is running at 10 per cent per year, then a basket of shopping which cost $30 in year one will cost $33 in year two. Governments try to control inflation; if it gets out of control, money becomes worthless.

FIND OUT MORE

GOVERNMENTS AND POLITICS | GREAT DEPRESSION | SOCIETIES, HUMAN | TRADE AND INDUSTRY | UNITED STATES

World banknotes

Captions identify denominations of currency and year issued

Africa and Europe

Austria, Belgium, Finland, France, Germany, Greece, Ireland, Italy,
Luxembourg, Netherlands, Portugal, Spain
5, 10, 20, 50, 100 euros (2002)

Denmark
100 kroner (2001),
200 kroner (1992)

Poland
50, 200 zlotych (1994)

Switzerland
10 francs (1995),
20, 50 francs (1994)

Kenya
100 shillings (2001),
200 shillings (2000)

Zimbabwe
5, 10 dollars (1994)

South Africa
10 rands (1993),
50 rands (1992)

Gambia
5, 25 dalasis (2001)

Egypt
5, 100 pounds (2001)

The Americas

Venezuela
10,000 bolívares (2000),
20,000 bolívares (1999)

Chile
1,000 pesos (1994),
10,000 pesos (1992)

Asia and Australia

Japan
1,000, 5,000 yen (1993)

Indonesia
10,000 rupiahs (1992),
20,000 rupiahs (1995)

Mexico
100, 200 pesos (2000)

Colombia
5,000 pesos (1995),
10,000 pesos (1994)

Australia
10 dollars (1993), 20 dollars (1994)

India
500, 1,000 rupees (2000)

Canada
5 dollars (1986), 10 dollars (1989),
20 dollars (1991)

United States
5, 10 dollars (2000), 20 dollars (1998)

Singapore
2 dollars (2000), 50, 100 dollars (1999)

North Korea
1, 5, 50 won (2000)

MONGOL EMPIRE

FOR CENTURIES, the Mongols lived a nomadic life on the steppes, or grasslands, of Asia. Suddenly, during the 13th century, they erupted onto the world stage. Led by Genghis Khan, the Mongols carved out a vast empire that stretched across Europe and Asia. They were ruthless soldiers, reducing every city they conquered to ashes. Yet they gave their empire a century of peace. Trade flourished along the Silk Road between China and Europe, and China was united after years of division. Their empire was short-lived, and broke up with the death of Kublai Khan in 1294.

Mongol archer carried a bow and about 30 arrows.

Mongol shield made of wood and leather.

Foundation of the empire

In 1206, a kuriltai (assembly) of Mongol tribes met and proclaimed Temujin, leader of the Mangkhol tribe, supreme ruler "of all who dwell in tents of felt". They gave him the name Genghis Khan, "prince of all that lies between the oceans". By 1279, they ruled an empire that stretched from central Europe along the ancient Silk Road to the Pacific Ocean.

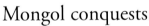
Genghis' empire

M

Yurts
The Mongols lived in yurts, or gers (tents). They were made of skins and handwoven cloth stretched over a wooden frame, and easy to dismantle.

Mongol warriors

The Mongols were skilled and agile horsemen, able to cover more than 160 km (100 miles) a day. They rode small horses chosen for their ability to withstand the intense cold and capable of short bursts of great speed. Their mounted archers were only lightly armed. They used bows and arrows that could pierce an enemy's armour.

Fighting
The Mongols were devious and clever in battle, stampeding riderless horses into the enemy lines to confuse them, and tying stuffed sacks onto horses to make their armies look bigger than they were. A favourite tactic was to pretend to withdraw, luring the enemy into an ambush.

Genghis Khan
Genghis Khan, or Temujin as he was then known, was born in Mongolia in about 1167. As a young man he became a fearsome chief. After his election as supreme leader of the Mongols, he led his armies to victory across Asia. He died in China in 1227, but his death was kept secret until his son could succeed him.

Mongol knife set

Ivory chopstick

Steel-bladed knife

Leather sheath

Mongol warrior's boots
Leather stitched to uppers for decoration and extra strength.

Tough leather uppers

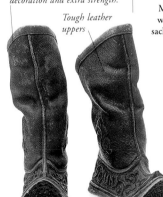

Mongol conquests

At first, the Mongol armies overran northern China, capturing Beijing in 1215. They then conquered most of central Asia and Persia. Later campaigns took them west into Hungary and Poland, south into Egypt and India, and east towards Java and Japan.

Mongol warriors sack Kiev.

Sacking of Kiev
In 1240, Mongol armies reached the great Russian city of Kiev. They burned the city to the ground, and killed or mutilated every person. Six years later, a Papal envoy on his way to see the Mongol leaders reported that only 200 of Kiev's houses were left.

Tamerlane
In the early 14th century, Mongol power decreased. But in 1369, Timur "Leng" (the lame), known as Tamerlane (1336–1405), made himself ruler of Samarkand in Central Asia and began to recreate the Mongol Empire. He conquered most of Central Asia, but died before he could invade China.

Timeline
1206 Temujin proclaimed Genghis Khan at a Mongol tribal assembly.

1211 Mongols begin invasion of northern China.

1229 Ogodei, son of Genghis, is elected Great Khan.

Genghis Khan, ruler of the Mongols 1206–1270

1240 Mongols overrun Russia and advance into Hungary and Poland.

1241 Death of Ogodei halts Mongol invasion of Europe.

1258 Mongols capture Baghdad.

1260 Egyptians defeat Mongols at Ain Jalut; Kublai Kahn becomes fifth and last Great Khan.

1279 Kublai Khan finally conquers southern China and founds Yuan Dynasty.

FIND OUT MORE

| ARMS AND ARMOUR | ARMIES | ASIA, HISTORY OF | CHINA, HISTORY OF | WARFARE |

MONGOLIA

THE RULERS of Mongolia once dominated China, Central Asia, and eastern Europe. Today, this land-locked country, north of China, is a remote, sparsely populated place, with a mainly agricultural economy that is steadily becoming more industrialized. Mongolia has mineral reserves, and manufacturing is growing. Dominated by China for many years, Mongolia became an independent communist state in 1924. It is now a multi-party democracy.

Physical features

Mongolia is a high plateau, ringed by mountains to the north and west, and by the cold semi-desert and desert of the Gobi in the south. Much of the eastern side of the plateau is dry, open grassland. There are lakes and forests in the northwest.

MONGOLIA FACTS

CAPITAL CITY Ulan Bator

AREA 1,565,000 sq km (604,247 sq miles)

POPULATION 2,600,000

MAIN LANGUAGE Khalkha Mongolian

MAJOR RELIGION Buddhist

CURRENCY Tugrik (Tögrög)

LIFE EXPECTANCY 63 years

PEOPLE PER DOCTOR 417

GOVERNMENT Multi-party democracy

ADULT LITERACY 99%

Ulan Bator

Once a small country town called Urghat, Mongolia's capital, now called Ulan Bator, was transformed into a major city by its communist rulers. It is the country's political, cultural, and industrial centre, producing processed foods and textiles.

Choghin Temple in the Buddhist Gandan Monastery, Ulan Bator

Gobi Desert

The Gobi Desert covers about one-third of the country and has an area of 1,040,000 sq km (401,500 sq miles), making it the world's fourth largest desert. The Gobi is sand or rock and is the site of a discovery of fossil bones and dinosaur eggs.

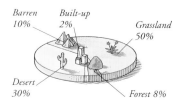

Barren 10% Built-up 2% Grassland 50% Desert 30% Forest 8%

Land use

Much of the Gobi is barren, surrounded by steppe (dry grassland), where animals can graze. In wetter areas, farmers grow cereals, such as millet, oats, and wheat.

Altai Mountains

The eastern arm of the Altai Mountains separates Mongolia from Russia in the north and China in the southwest. The average height ranges from 2,000–3,000 m (6,600–1,000 ft); the Altai's highest peak in Mongolia is Najramdal Uur at 4,374 m (14,350 ft).

Climate

Mongolia is dry and windy with short, mild summers and long, severe winters when temperatures plummet. The country is prone to violent earthquakes.

22°C (72°F) -30°C (-22°F)
17°C (63°F) -26°C (-15°F)
208 mm (8 in)

2 per sq km (4 per sq mile)   59% Urban   41% Rural

People

Khalkha Mongols form the largest ethnic group. Mongolians are traditionally nomads, but their numbers are steadily declining as people give up their *yurts* (tents) and move to houses in the towns. Mongols are skilled horse riders. Many people are Buddhists.

Farming and industry

Many Mongolians still work as animal herders, although there are large state-run farms that produce grain. Harsh winters ravaged livestock in 2000–01. Industry is concentrated around Ulan Bator and is dominated by wool, food processing, and animal hides. Coal is mined in Darhan and Choybalsan.

FIND OUT MORE | ASIA | ASIA, HISTORY OF | BUDDHISM | CHINA, HISTORY OF | DESERTS | FARMING | GOVERNMENTS AND POLITICS | MONGOL EMPIRE | MOUNTAINS AND VALLEYS

MONGOOSES AND CIVETS

RENOWNED FOR ITS ability to kill snakes, the Indian mongoose will tackle a full-grown cobra. It is one of 38 species of mongoose, belonging to a group of carnivorous mammals that also includes civets, genets, the fossa, and binturong (or bear-cat). Mongooses live in southern Europe, southern Asia, and much of Africa. They range in size from the Indian mongoose, measuring 1.22 m (4 ft) in overall length, including the tail, to the dwarf mongoose, which is only 30 cm (12 in) long. Meerkats, or suricates, are a type of mongoose living on the dry, open plains of Africa.

Bands of dark fur

Thick, coarse hair

Long, bushy tail

Short legs

Long claws

Narrow snout

Banded mongoose

M

Features of a mongoose
Mongooses have slender bodies, long, coarse hair, bushy tails, short legs, and claws that cannot be retracted. Most mongooses are grey, grey-brown, or lightly speckled; the banded mongoose is distinguished by dark stripes across its body. Mongooses spend most of their time on the ground, but are very agile and can climb and swim quite well. Most species reach sexual maturity by 18–24 months, and the females give birth to 2–8 young.

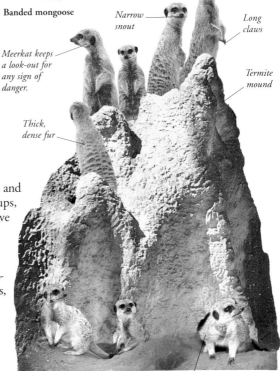

Narrow snout

Long claws

Termite mound

Meerkat keeps a look-out for any sign of danger.

Thick, dense fur

Feeding

Mongooses eat small mammals, birds, lizards, insects, fruit, tubers, and bulbs. The crab-eating and marsh mongooses live close to water and feed on crustaceans, frogs, and fish. The marsh and banded mongooses also feed on birds' and crocodiles' eggs; they smash them on the ground and lap up the contents.

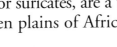

Banded mongoose with egg

Mongooses and snakes
The larger mongooses, such as the Indian grey mongoose, often kill snakes. They are no more immune to snake bites than other animals, but rely on their quick reactions and agility to avoid being bitten. They sieze the snake behind the head and hang on until it dies.

Indian mongoose attacking a cobra

Family groups

The banded and dwarf mongooses and the meerkat all live in family groups, and are very sociable. Meerkats live in groups of up to 30 animals. Each animal has specific duties to enable the group to work together harmoniously. Sentries keep a look-out from a high point for predators, and bark a warning to the rest of the group if danger threatens. Females remain close to the nest and look after the young, while hunters go in search of food.

Burrows
The banded and dwarf mongooses and the meerkat live in burrows, which they dig themselves, or take over from other animals, such as termites. At first light they emerge from their burrow to sun themselves. Sentinels are posted to warn of impending danger. They usually stay near their burrows so they can dive to safety if danger threatens. Birds of prey are among mongooses' chief enemies; if one of a group is attacked, the others leap to its defence.

A disused termite mound taken over by meerkats

Meerkat emerges from hole in termite mound.

Solitary mongooses
Most mongooses, such as the white-tailed, Indian, and marsh mongooses, are solitary, nocturnal animals. The marsh mongoose lives among reeds or long grass bordering swamps and rivers. It is a good swimmer, and preys on waterfowl, small mammals, frogs, fish, and insects.

Marsh mongoose

Civets

Civets are weasel-like in appearance. They are solitary, nocturnal creatures, mostly living in forests. The African civet favours more open country, hiding by day, often in an abandoned aardvark or porcupine burrow, and emerging at night to hunt. It has good senses of hearing, sight, and smell. Civets are omnivores, preying on rodents, small mammals, birds, lizards, frogs, and locusts, as well as eating eggs, berries, fruit, and even carrion.

Coarse hair

Back legs are longer than front legs.

Patterned coat helps camouflage the civet in the forest.

African civet

Musk
Civets secrete a strong-smelling, oily fluid, called musk, from well-developed scent glands under the tail. Musk is in demand for the perfume industry. In parts of Africa – for example, Ethiopia and Zanzibar – civets are kept in captivity, and the musk removed several times each week.

BANDED MONGOOSE

SCIENTIFIC NAME	*Mungos mungo*
ORDER	Carnivora
FAMILY	Viverridae
DISTRIBUTION	Africa south of the Sahara
HABITAT	Savannahs close to water
DIET	Lizards, snakes, frogs, birds' eggs; will also break open elephants' droppings to obtain dung beetles
SIZE	Length of body: up to 45 cm (18 in); tail: up to 30 cm (12 in) long
LIFESPAN	Up to 11 years

FIND OUT MORE

AFRICAN WILDLIFE   ANIMALS   ANTS AND TERMITES   GRASSLAND WILDLIFE   MAMMALS   NESTS AND BURROWS   NOCTURNAL ANIMALS   SNAKES

MONKEYS AND OTHER PRIMATES

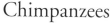

MONKEYS BELONG TO a group of animals called primates. Most primates live in trees, but some live on the ground. They have grasping fingers, long arms, and forward-looking eyes. Monkeys have tails, but apes are tailless and include gibbons, orangutans, gorillas, and chimpanzees. There are two main groups of primates. The higher primates, or anthropoids – monkeys, apes, and humans – all have large brains and a high level of intelligence. The lower primates, or prosimians, are less intelligent and include the lorises, tarsiers, lemurs, bushbabies, and pottos.

Features of a monkey

Monkeys and other primates have large brains and are quick to learn. They have forward-looking eyes and strong fingers. Their fingers and toes usually have flat nails. Most primates have an opposable thumb that can be pressed against the fingers to grasp and manipulate objects; some also have a similar big toe. Some primates have a prehensile tail that can be wrapped around a branch; it acts as an extra limb.

Fur-covered body

Large eyes

Long arms

Five long, grasping fingers

Capuchin monkey

Prehensile tail acts as a fifth limb and aids balance.

Chimpanzees

Our closest relative, the chimpanzee, occupies the forests and savannahs of central Africa. Chimps are highly intelligent and sociable and live in groups of up to about 60 animals with a complex, ever-changing hierarchy. They spend most of the time on the ground, but each night they build a nest to sleep in, up to 30 m (100 ft) above the ground.

Social grooming

Chimps comb each other's fur with their fingers to pick out lice and dirt. Grooming is an important social activity and helps strengthen family ties and friendships.

Grooming sessions often last for about an hour.

Upper lip covers teeth in a happy playful face.

Playing

Young chimps spend much of their time playing together. They wrestle, chase each other about, and swing through the trees. Play is important as it helps teach young chimps about chimp society and how to survive in the forest. Chimps stay with their mothers until reaching full maturity at about 13 years of age. The older offspring help to look after their younger siblings.

Chimp using a twig to "fish" for termites.

Feeding

Chimps eat mainly plant food, including leaves, flowers, and fruits such as wild figs. They also prey on other animals, including small antelopes and bush pigs. Some even kill other primates, such as the red colobus monkey. Several chimps chase the prey towards others that are waiting to block its escape.

Chimps climb trees to search for food.

Tool-making

Next to humans, chimpanzees are considered the most intelligent of the primates. They can learn to understand simple sign language and are adept at using "tools". They use long twigs to extract termites from their mounds, a wad of leaves as a sponge to obtain water from tree hollows, and rocks to break open nuts. They have even learned to use sticks and stones as weapons against rivals and enemies.

Communication

Chimps have developed a body language with a large range of facial expressions, which, together with sounds, helps them to communicate a range of emotions.

Curiosity, apprehension, or sullenness (if accompanied by a puzzled expression) are shown by protruding lips.

Anger is shown by baring the teeth; if combined with certain postures and calls, it acts as a warning to rivals.

Dian Fossey

American zoologist, Dr. Dian Fossey (1932–1985), devoted her life to studying the mountain gorilla, of which only a few hundred survive. She learned to imitate the sounds and gestures that gorillas make and was able to communicate with them in their own "language".

Gorillas

The mountain gorilla lives in the highlands of Rwanda. It forages on the ground for wild celery, berries, and bamboo shoots. The lowland gorilla lives in the rainforests of equatorial Africa. It is the largest of all the primates; a mature male may weigh up to 150 kg (330 lb) and reach 1.7 m (5 ft 6 in) tall, when standing upright. Despite their massive size and strength, gorillas are seldom aggressive. They live in family groups of 10–20 animals, led by a dominant male.

Silverbacks are mature male gorillas whose backs have turned a silvery-grey colour with age. The dominant male of the family group is always a silverback.

Chest-beating

A male gorilla intimidates rivals with a display of chest-beating. This starts with a loud roar followed by a series of hoots. He then waves handfuls of leaves or uproots bushes and hurls them into the air. Finally, he rises to his full height and beats his chest with the cupped palms of his hands.

M

Orangutans

Orangutans are solitary apes that live in the rainforests of Borneo and Sumatra. They live in the forest canopy and, except for the adult males, rarely descend to the ground. Their short legs contrast with their very long arms, which may span 2.1 m (7 ft). Males are larger than females, with longer hair and large cheek pouches. Females give birth once every four years to a single young with whom they develop a strong bond.

Mothers suckle their young for up to five years.

Durian fruit

The fruit is rich in protein and carbohydrate.

Mangosteens

Sleeping

Female orangutans and their young make a nest each night in which to sleep. The nests are made by the orangutan pulling vegetation around herself and weaving it together for support and padding. Adult males are too heavy for a nest and sleep on the ground.

Long, thick hair

Feeding

Orangutans feed mainly on plant matter, such as leaves and nuts, but they also eat insects and their eggs. Their favourite food is fruit, particularly the fruit of the durian for which they search far and wide. They use their strong hands and large front teeth to open tough-skinned fruits, such as mangosteens.

Red howler monkey

Howler monkeys, such as the red howler, have exceptionally loud calls that carry over a long distance. At dawn and dusk, the forest echoes to the male's loud booming call. He may be joined by other members of the group. Howlers live in troops of up to 30, in the forest canopy. They have a prehensile tail that they can wrap around a branch and use as an extra limb. They can hang upside down by their tails.

Baboons

Baboons generally live on open savannahs, in large bands of up to 100 animals. They forage for almost anything they can find from insects to lizards and other small animals. Given the opportunity, baboons will also kill larger animals, such as hares and young gazelles. The mandrill, the most brightly coloured of all the primates, lives in the forests of West Africa.

Huge canine teeth can inflict a severe wound.

Olive baboon

Threat display

Baboons have long, dagger-like canine teeth that can deliver a vicious bite. They bare their teeth to warn off opponents and intimidate rivals and enemies.

Black and white colobus monkey

The leaf-eating colobus monkeys live in the canopy and upper levels of African rainforests, rarely descending to the ground. Colobus live in small family troops and follow a regular route through the trees from their sleeping area to their feeding place. The male's distinctive call, echoed by the other members of the troop, is a feature of the African rainforests.

Coat of black-and-white hair fans out when they leap.

Golden lion tamarin

This tiny monkey, found only in the Atlantic coastal forest of southeast Brazil, is one of the most brightly coloured of all primates. Females normally give birth to twins, which the male and older offspring help look after. They feed on fruit, flowers, nectar, tree sap, and small vertebrates. Destruction of the rainforest has brought the golden lion tamarin close to extinction. A captive breeding programme was started in 1970 to breed animals for subsequent release into the wild.

Golden mane

Tamarins differ from most primates in not having opposable thumbs.

Long tail helps balance.

Gibbons

Gibbons live in family groups, consisting of a mated pair and their young. They are highly territorial. They call to each other, large sacs in their throats amplifying the sounds. With their long arms, fingers, and toes, and their light build, gibbons move swiftly through the trees, swinging hand over hand, a method of movement known as brachiation. In this way, gibbons can swing over gaps of up to 7 m (23 ft) wide. There are nine species of gibbon; the largest is the siamang.

Gibbon grasps branch with its left hand.

Gibbon twists its body around so it can then change its grip to its right hand.

Gibbon grasps branch with right hand, lets go with left hand, and continues along in this way.

Right arm has been lifted up to branch.

Throat sac

Ring-tailed lemur

Lemurs are primitive primates found only on the island of Madagascar. There are 21 species. Ring-tailed lemurs live in the forest but spend a lot of time on the ground. They live in groups of 5–30 animals, presided over by a dominant female. Males mark their territories by impregnating their tails with scent from special glands and raise them high in the air to waft the scent towards rivals.

Tail is longer than body

Right arm of gibbon hangs by its side, but will be raised to grip branch when changing hands.

Siamang

CHIMPANZEE

SCIENTIFIC NAME *Pan troglodytes*

ORDER Primates

FAMILY Pongidæ

DISTRIBUTION Africa, from Sierra Leone to western Uganda and Lake Tanganyika at heights up to 2,800 m (9,200 ft)

HABITAT Woodland and savannah

DIET Mainly vegetation, but also termites, larvae, and other small mammals, sometimes including other primates, such as young baboons and colobus monkeys

SIZE Height of male standing: 120–170 cm (47–67 in); weight: up to 55 kg (120 lb)

LIFESPAN Up to 50 years (in captivity)

FIND OUT MORE   ANIMAL BEHAVIOUR   CONSERVATION   GOODALL, JANE   GRASSLAND WILDLIFE   HUMAN EVOLUTION   RAINFOREST WILDLIFE

Higher primates

Mona monkeys live in troops of up to 20 animals.

Red howler monkeys have large mouths to amplify their loud calls.

Bright nose of male

De Brazza's monkeys are shy and live in the forests of Zaïre and Uganda.

Very long tail for balance

Long legs help this monkey to sprint fast.

Crest of black hair

New-born baby

Semi-prehensile tail

Rufous patas monkeys are also called military monkeys, because of their distinguished appearance.

Mandrills are baboons. Mature males have brightly coloured noses and buttocks.

Sulawesi crested macaques live in groups with a complex hierarchy.

Black-capped capuchins spend most of their time in the rainforest canopy.

Thick, strong prehensile tail

Large eyes for night vision

Long, white crest

Young are carried on father's back.

Flexible tail curls around branch for support.

Douroucoulis are the world's only nocturnal monkeys.

Cotton-top tamarins spend much time grooming each other.

Silvery marmoset young are cared for by their fathers.

Crab-eating macaques live in mangrove swamps.

Squirrel monkeys from South America are agile and acrobatic.

Humboldt's woolly monkeys eat mainly leaves and fruit.

Very long fur

Very long arms

Large hands help orangutan grip branches.

Silver back of mature male

Hamadryas baboons live on the ground in open grasslands.

This orangutan is a 5-year-old male.

Lar gibbons live in family groups of two parents and up to four offspring.

Lowland gorillas often need to walk long distances to find food, as there are few nutritious plants on the rainforest floor.

Gorillas walk on their knuckles.

Chimpanzees are the most intelligent of the great apes.

Orangutans are shy, solitary animals. Only close relatives play with, and groom each other.

Lower primates

Indris call loudly each morning.

Slender lorises feed on birds, lizards, and insects.

Long hind legs help it leap from branch to branch.

Head turns through 180°.

These lemurs have an acute sense of smell.

Coquerel's sifakas live in the forests of NW Madagascar.

Indris, from Madagascar, are the largest of the lemurs.

Slender lorises feed on birds, lizards, and insects.

Eastern tarsiers are nocturnal. Large eyes help them see at night.

Black-and-white ruffed lemurs are superb climbers.

Greater bushbabies live in African rainforests.

MOON

A GREY, DRY, AIRLESS, and lifeless ball of rock – the Moon – is Earth's closest neighbour in space. The Moon is about a quarter of Earth's size and its only natural satellite. It orbits the planet as they travel together round the Sun. It is the only celestial body, apart from Earth, that humans have stood on.

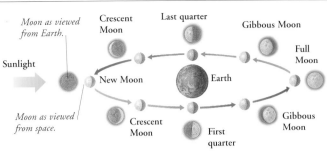

Moon as viewed from Earth.

Crescent Moon · Last quarter · Gibbous Moon · Full Moon

Sunlight · New Moon · Earth · Crescent Moon · First quarter · Gibbous Moon

Moon as viewed from space.

Phases of the Moon
The Moon is lit by the Sun. At any one time, half of the Moon is in daylight and half in darkness. As the Moon orbits Earth, different amounts of the sunlit side are visible. These are known as the phases of the Moon and range from a thin crescent to a full face. Each cycle lasts for 29.5 days, beginning at the "New Moon" when the sunlit side of the Moon is not visible from Earth at all.

Lunar surface
Every part of the Moon's surface is made of rock and dust. It is also covered with craters. Most of these craters were formed about three billion years ago when space rocks bombarded the Moon. Material thrown out from these impact craters formed mountain ranges, and volcanic lava filled many of the larger craters. The lunar surface has remained virtually unchanged for millions of years.

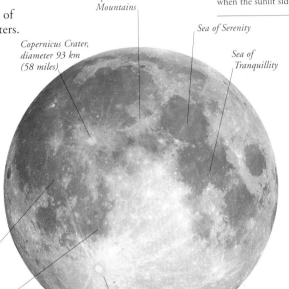

Apennine Mountains

Copernicus Crater, diameter 93 km (58 miles)

Sea of Serenity

Sea of Tranquillity

Ocean of Storms

Tycho Crater

Moon rock
About 2,000 samples of rock and dust have been brought to Earth from the Moon by American astronauts and Russian robotic spacecraft.

Mare
Early observers thought the lava-filled craters were oceans of water and called them mare, which is the Latin for "sea" (plural maria). The name has stuck even though there is no water on the lunar surface.

Eclipse of the Moon
As the Moon orbits around Earth, it is at times farther from the Sun than Earth. Sunlight still reaches it because the Earth is not in perfect alignment between the Sun and Moon. Two or three times a year, the three are aligned directly and the Moon is in Earth's shadow. It is eclipsed; no sunlight reaches the Moon, and it disappears from Earth's view.

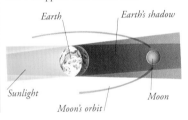

Earth · *Earth's shadow*

Sunlight · *Moon*

Moon's orbit

Craters
When a space rock collides with the Moon it creates a crater. The bigger the impact, the bigger the crater. A rock 1 km (0.6 mile) across travelling at 100,000 kmh (60,000 mph) would produce a crater about 18 km (11 miles) across. The largest on this picture is 80 km (50 miles) across.

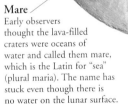

Terminator
The Moon keeps the same side facing Earth because as it orbits Earth it also spins on its axis. From Earth, it is possible to see light areas, which are highland, and darker areas of lowland. More detail can be seen along the terminator, the line separating the sunlit and dark sides of the Moon.

Lunar origins
It is not known for certain where the Moon came from. It may have been captured by Earth's gravity or formed from material left over when Earth was formed. The most popular theory is that an object the size of Mars crashed into the young Earth and dislodged material, which came together to form the Moon.

Neil Armstrong
In July 1969, American astronaut Neil Armstrong (b.1930) was at the centre of one of the most important events in human history. He was the first person to walk on the Moon and became instantly famous. He spent 2 hrs 35 mins on its surface.

Moon landings
Twelve men landed on the Moon between 1969 and 1972, spending almost 80 hours on its surface. They explored 90 km (55 miles) of it on foot or by "moon-buggy", collected rock, set up experiments, and played golf before returning to Earth.

Footprints
When the astronauts left the Moon, they left behind some equipment and their footprints. There is no water, air, or life to erode the footprints, so they could stay for millions of years unless an impacting space rock wipes them out.

 FIND OUT MORE · BIG BANG · COMETS AND ASTEROIDS · EARTH · PLANETS · SPACE EXPLORATION · SUN AND SOLAR SYSTEM · VOLCANOES

MOSQUES

AT THE HEART OF EVERY MUSLIM community is a mosque, the Islamic place of worship. When Muhammad moved to Medina in 622, his house became the model for all subsequent mosques. Devout Muslims pray five times a day, and a mosque's main purpose is to provide a place for prayers. Mosques range from simple places serving the local community or large, beautifully decorated buildings in big cities.

Parts of a mosque

The most important part of a mosque is the prayer hall, where the congregation meets to pray, and to listen to sermons and readings from the Muslim holy book, the Qur'an. Mosques also usually have a courtyard and a tower called a minaret. Larger mosques may have many more rooms, which are used as schools, hospices, and kitchens to provide food for the poor.

Islamic arch

The horseshoe-shaped arch of this mosque doorway is typical of Islamic architecture. The arch is repeated many times inside the building. Above the door is a richly tiled decoration in abstract patterns. A heavy curtain covers the entrance.

Courtyard

People coming to prayers wash at one of the fountains in the courtyard, then they leave their shoes by the door before entering the prayer hall. There is little furniture inside the hall because Muslims kneel to pray. Separate areas inside the mosque are reserved for men and women.

A mihrab is a niche, often beautifully decorated, that shows the direction of Mecca. Next to it is a mimbar, or pulpit.

Prayer hall

Plain walls with few windows show that this is an inward-looking building, in which people are encouraged to concentrate on their prayers. The minaret and the colourful tiles at the door are the only signs that the austere exterior conceals a sacred place of worship

Minaret, from where a muezzin calls the faithful to prayer

Mosque decoration

The Islamic religion forbids figurative art, on the grounds that the artist must not try to imitate God's creation. Mosques are, therefore, decorated with abstract patterns and beautiful inscriptions. Decoration is often concentrated around doorways and the mihrab.

Tiled decoration

Tiles are used widely in mosques. They lend themselves to pattern-making, can be made with beautiful, subtle colours, and can create a cool atmosphere, an advantage in the hot Arabic countries where Islam has its roots.

Blue often used in tiling

Tile decorated with sacred text

Tiles designed to form wall panels.

Tiles from a Tunisian mosque

Calligraphy

Quotations from the Qur'an often adorn mosque interiors. These texts are meant to inspire people by their beauty, while also reminding them of the words of Allah.

Islamic architecture

There are two common styles of mosque design. In one, the roof of the prayer hall is supported by numerous decorated columns. In the other, the roof is a large dome.

Great Mosque, Córdoba

This vast Spanish mosque, also known as *La Mesquita*, was begun in 786. Elegant proportions, fine carved decoration, and contrasting use of stone and brick in dozens of arches combine to give the interior a striking appearance.

Córdoba mosque, now a Christian cathedral

Sinan

Sinan (c.1491–1588) was the greatest architect of Ottoman Turkey. He was born into a Greek Orthodox Christian family, but was taken into the Sultan's service and became a Muslim. He trained as a military engineer and in 1538 Sultan Süleyman I made him chief imperial architect. He designed many buildings, including 79 mosques (among them the famous Süleymaniye Mosque in Istanbul built between 1550–57), and 34 palaces.

FIND OUT MORE   ARCHITECTURE   ISLAM   ISLAMIC EMPIRE   MUHAMMAD   OTTOMAN EMPIRE   PERSIAN EMPIRE   RELIGIONS

MOSSES AND LIVERWORTS

THERE ARE ABOUT 25,000 species of moss and liverwort, which are together known as the Bryophytes. They are small, flowerless, low-growing plants that reproduce by means of spores. Bryophytes have a distinctly two-stage life-cycle. The plant body, or thallus, of a green moss or liverwort produces male and female sex organs. A long-stalked capsule grows from a fertilized female cell. This produces masses of minute spores, each of which can grow into a new moss or liverwort.

Capsule containing spores

Stalk

Tiny leaves

Mosses cling to the ground, rocks, trees, or walls by means of short, root-like rhizoids.

A common moss
(*Bryon* species)

Types of moss

Mosses are small plants with very tiny leaves. Different species grow in different ways, and their characteristic growth forms help to distinguish one from another.

Moss plants growing into a soft, cushion-like clump

Branched stems

As older parts of the stem die, the tips keep growing into new moss plants.

Cushion-forming mosses
Hundreds of tiny moss plants growing very close together make a compact, dome-shaped cushion. Sometimes, the whole cushion will come loose from the ground.

Branched mosses
Some kinds of moss have stems that branch and spread out over the surface of the ground. They form a loose mass of intertwined leafy stems, or a dense mat.

Tufted mosses
Many of the largest mosses grow as loose tufts of plants that may be branched or unbranched. The largest is an Australasian species that reaches 70 cm (27 in) long.

Sphagnum
Acid-loving sphagnum mosses live in wet, boggy places. They are slow-growing plants that, in cold, wet climates, help to form a thick layer that eventually turns into peat. Sphagnum holds an amazing amount of water. This helps to keep the surface of a bog moist, even in summer.

Mosses

There are three groups of mosses: the true mosses, the small group of mountain mosses, and the sphagnum mosses. Mosses are most abundant in damp habitats, but they flourish everywhere except in the sea or in deserts. They can absorb moisture and dissolved minerals all over their surface.

Waxy surface has pores for vital gas exchange.

A thallose liverwort

Liverworts

There are two kinds of liverwort – leafy liverworts and thallose liverworts. They both grow in moist or wet environments, anchored to the ground by means of root-like cells called rhizoids. The thallose liverworts are plate- or ribbon-like. The leafy liverworts grow in tufts, or form a mat of stems.

Leaves are often cupped to hold water.

Leafy liverworts
These delicate liverworts have tiny thin leaves that grow in two or three rows along the stem. The two side rows are easy to see, but the third row of smaller leaves grows underneath the stem.

Ripening moss capsule

Capsule turns brown as it dries.

The capsule is held above the plant.

Peristome teeth

Open teeth

1 A stemmed capsule called a sporophyte grows. The foot of the stem is embedded in the moss plant.

2 As the capsule ripens, the hood, called the calyptra, falls off, revealing peristome teeth at the tip.

3 Inside each capsule, thousands of minute, dust-like spores are produced. The capsule begins to dry out in fine weather.

4 When the peristome teeth are dry, they flick open to release the spores. These are shaken out and spread over a wide area by air currents.

Gemmae
Some thallose liverworts reproduce vegetatively by means of bud-like growths called gemmae. These develop in small cups on the surface of the liverwort and are splashed out by rain. Each gemma can grow into a new plant.

Gemmae

FIND OUT MORE MARSH AND SWAMP WILDLIFE   PLANTS   PLANTS, ANATOMY   PLANTS, REPRODUCTION

MOTHER TERESA

IN ONE OF THE POOREST cities in the world – Calcutta, India – a European woman devoted her life to helping the poor and needy. Mother Teresa, a Macedonia-born nun, led the Missionaries of Charity, an international order of nuns dedicated to helping those most in need. When the order was first given the backing of the Catholic Church in 1950, the Missionaries had few resources of their own. But now, thanks to the work of Mother Teresa and her order, money flows in from donors all over the world and is used to alleviate the suffering and poverty of those unable to help themselves.

Early life
Agnes Gonxha Bojaxhiu was born in 1910 into a prosperous family of Albanian descent. Her father, a businessman, died when Agnes was nine, and suddenly she and her family were poor. This first-hand experience of poverty left her with the conviction that she should become a nun and help the poor in India.

Education
At the age of 18, Agnes joined a Roman Catholic order of nuns, the Sisters of Loreto in India. She served nine years as a novice. On taking her vows in 1937, she took the name Teresa, after St Teresa of Lisieux, and remained in India.

Missionaries of charity
Other nuns came to help Teresa in her work with the poor. She formed the Missionaries of Charity to concentrate on this work, and became known as Mother Teresa.

Sisters of Loreto
Teresa became the Mother Superior of the convent at Entally, Calcutta. She worked there for 11 years, surrounded by poverty. In 1948, she received permission to work outside the convent, setting up a school for poor children and helping to care for the sick.

Entally Convent, Calcutta

The poor
As she walked through Calcutta, Mother Teresa saw poverty all around her. The poor and sick often had no homes, and lay in squalor in the streets. Teresa helped them with food and clothes, and took unwanted children into her mission to look after them.

The sick
Mother Teresa tried to relieve sick people's pain and, when the end came, helped them die in dignity. She also taught people how to recognize the early signs of diseases such as leprosy, so that they could be cured.

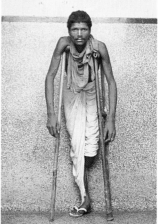

Expansion
Gradually, the Missionaries grew in number and strength. The organization expanded across India, and in 1963 began to admit men. In 1965, the first overseas mission was opened, in Venezuela. Today, there are more than 4,000 nuns and 40,000 lay people working for the Missionaries of Charity around the world. The Missionaries even have their own newspaper, *Ek dil* (One Heart), which publicizes their work.

Mobile clinic
In order to take their work to those most in need, the Missionaries of Charity established mobile clinics that toured India to help the poor and heal the sick. These clinics gave hope to many poor people in remote areas. They have also done much to spread the word about the Missionaries, and increase their recognition for doing good works among the poor.

Prizes
In recent years, Mother Teresa received many international awards and prizes. In 1979, she was awarded the Nobel Peace Prize. She used the prize money to expand her work for the world's poor and needy.

Mother Teresa with her Nobel Prize

MOTHER TERESA

1910	Born in Skopje, Macedonia.
1928	She enters a Convent of the Sisters of Loreto in Skopje.
1928–37	Serves as novice in India.
1937	Becomes head of convent at Entally, Calcutta.
1948	Works outside the convent.
1950	Catholic Church officially backs Missionaries of Charity.
1965	Opens first mission outside India.
1979	Awarded Nobel Peace Prize.
1997	Steps down as head of Missionaries of Charity.
August 1997	Dies in Calcutta

FIND OUT MORE　　CHRISTIANITY　　HOSPITALS　　INDIA　　INDIA, HISTORY OF　　MEDICINE　　MONASTERIES　　RELIGIONS

MOTOR SPORTS

THERE ARE MANY VARIETIES of motor sport, featuring four- or two-wheeled vehicles and taking place on special circuits, regular roads, or rough country tracks. Motor sport on four wheels ranges from Formula One grand prix racing and Indy car racing to karting, which is the sport in which many top drivers first experience motor racing. In between, there are various other types of racing including dragster, sports car, and stock car racing, as well as rally driving. The two-wheeled sports range from powerful grand prix motorcycle racing to motocross and speedway. Cars and motorcycles are constantly modified to make them faster and more reliable.

Formula One

Manufacturers and their drivers compete for world championships throughout the season. There are 16 races run on different grands prix circuits around the world. Races are preceded by practice sessions in which the cars' best times determine their positions on the starting grid. Points awarded to the first six cars to finish are 10, 6, 4, 3, 2, and 1.

M

Start of a Brazilian Grand Prix

Aerofoil pushes the car down.

Williams 1990 car

Powerful 10-cylinder engine

Slick tyres used in dry weather.

Streamlined engine cover

Flags

End of race — Danger — Return to pits

Oil on course — Service car on track — All cars to stop in pits

Officials use coloured flags to signal to drivers during the race, mostly to warn them of danger or to give them instructions. Drivers want to be the first to see the chequered flag, which signals the end of the race.

Formula One car

Cars race under categories called formulas to ensure that similar machines are matched against each other. There are rules governing bodywork as well as engines. Formula One cars are light, single-seater vehicles with a body that fits over a one-piece, or monocoque, chassis.

Formula Three race

Other formulas

Before Formula One cars, drivers usually race less powerful models. Formulas have varied, but among the most popular have been Two, Three, Ford, and 3,000. Some have grand prix and national and continental championships.

John Surtees

A British motorcyclist who became a racing driver, John Surtees (b. 1934) was world champion at both sports. From 1956 to 1960, he won seven motorcycle world titles at 350 cc and 500 cc. In 1964, he won the World Drivers' Championship.

Pit stops

The pit is an area just off the track where mechanics can work on the cars during a race. Pit stops are important in grand prix racing. The speed with which teams refuel their cars and change tyres can make the difference between winning and losing a race.

Indy car racing

This takes place on large oval tracks and twisting road circuits, and competitions run mostly in the United States. The cars are similar to Formula One models, and annual championships are decided on the number of points acquired over a number of races. The sport gets its name from the Indianapolis 500, the classic event in American motor car racing.

Indianapolis 500

The oval Indianapolis track is known as the Brickyard because the surface is made of 3.2 million bricks. Its four turns are banked at 9°, and its total length is 4.025 km (2.5 miles). The Indy 500 is raced over 200 laps – 805 km (500 miles).

A top-fueller

Drag racing

In drag racing, pairs of dragsters race side by side along a straight 400-m (quarter-mile) track in a series of elimination races. There are several classes of design, engine, and fuel. The fastest – lightweight supercharged top-fuellers – run on rocket fuel and can complete the course in less than six seconds.

Karting

Karting is a sport enjoyed by people of all ages. The simplest karts have a 60 cc or 100 cc engine and no gearbox, and can be driven by boys and girls from about the age of eight. Karts have a low chassis, and the driver sits no more than 3 cm above the ground.

Kart racing

The 250 cc karts are like racing cars in miniature, and reach speeds of 240 km/h (150 mph). In long-circuit racing, which takes place on wide tracks, as many as 60 karts can compete. In short-circuit racing, about 20 karts can compete. Karting has its own world championships.

250 cc karts have sponsors, just like Formula One cars.

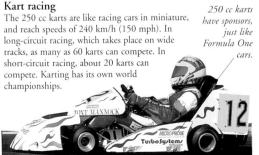

Rally driving

These are long-distance events over regular roads, with special stages over country roads and tracks. They may be held on one day, or last several days or weeks. Rallies are not strictly races. Drivers aided by navigators set out at intervals in "souped-up" saloons. They lose points for exceeding the time limits between control points.

Monte Carlo Rally

This event made rallying famous. It was established in 1911 to encourage tourists to visit the Principality of Monaco in winter. Motorists set out from all parts of Europe and the final stages centre on Monte Carlo.

Stock cars

Stock car racing takes different forms on opposite sides of the Atlantic. In Europe, it is mostly racing on small oval circuits, and cars are driven into each other. In the United States, it features high-speed racing of modified saloons and is a major sport in the south, where it takes place on huge, banked oval circuits.

Land speed record

A land speed record must be the average time of a two-way run over one straight kilometre or mile. The British driver Richard Noble achieved a record 1,019.5 km/h (633.5 mph) in 1983 in his jet-powered *Thrust 2*. He sped along the hard surface of the Black Rock Desert in Nevada, USA.

Speedway

Most speedway races are contested by four riders over four laps of the track. Racing takes place on an oval cinder track. The bikes have no brakes or gears so the riders slide around bends, trailing a leg in the cinders, in a move called broadsiding. Three points are awarded for first place, two for second, and one for third. Competitions include team matches and individual events.

Ice speedway

Speedway racing on ice is popular in some northern parts of Europe and the United States. The bikes have special tyres with spikes to provide grip on the smooth ice track. There are individual and team world championships.

Le Mans 24-hour race

This famous sports car race is held annually on the 13.6-km (8.5-mile) Le Mans circuit near Paris, France. A team of two or three drivers takes turns at the wheel, driving non-stop through the day and night. The event has become a national institution in France, with shops, funfairs, and restaurants opening for the huge crowds that turn up to watch.

Motorcycle racing

Motorcycle racing takes place on special circuits. At the top level, manufacturers and drivers compete in 12 or more grands prix each season for world championships in various classes: 500 cc, 250 cc, 125 cc, and sidecar. Points are awarded for the first 15 home in each grand prix, 25 for first, 20 for second, down to one point for 15th.

Riders lean right over at an angle when cornering.

500 cc racing motorcyle

Motorcycle and sidecar moulded together as one unit.

Rider and machine are covered in sponsors' logos.

Passenger leans out to balance the machine when cornering.

Racing sidecar

Trials

Best-known as six-day events, trials feature slow sections over difficult natural terrain, including water, mud, loose rock, and steep hills. Riders are penalized for stopping or putting a foot on the ground. The bikes are specially low-geared to allow riders to progress very slowly over the rough course.

Off-road racing

Off-road bikes have chunky tyres to provide grip on loose materials and in mud. The engines are fixed higher to avoid damage.

Motocross

Also known as scrambling, motocross takes place over rough country. In big events, as many as 40 riders race over several laps of a winding, muddy, hilly course. World championships are held annually in several categories.

FIND OUT MORE

BICYCLES AND MOTORBIKES   CARS AND TRUCKS   CYCLING   ENGINES AND MOTORS   TRANSPORT, HISTORY OF

MOUNTAINS AND VALLEYS

THE EARTH'S surface is not flat. In some places, movements of the Earth create gentle hills and sheer, towering mountains. In other places, valleys and gorges are carved into the landscape. Mountains are steep-sided rocks, raised over 600 m (2,000 ft) high by the huge force of the tectonic plates that shift the Earth's crust and make volcanoes erupt. Valleys are elongated depressions eroded slowly from the landscape by rivers, weather conditions, and glaciers (large rivers of slowly moving ice). A few mountains are isolated summits, but most occur in huge mountain ranges, such as the Himalayas in Asia.

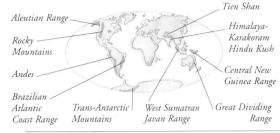

Aleutian Range
Rocky Mountains
Andes
Brazilian Atlantic Coast Range
Trans-Antarctic Mountains
West Sumatran Javan Range
Central New Guinea Range
Great Dividing Range
Tien Shan
Himalaya-Karakoram Hindu Kush

Mountain systems
Most of the world's mountains are grouped into ranges, like the Jura in Europe. Ranges are often linked together into long chains, or cordilleras. Huge mountain systems, such as the Himalayas, include several chains and many ranges.

M

Mountain building

Mountains are formed in three main ways. A few are isolated volcanoes, built up by successive eruptions. Some are huge blocks thrust upwards as the Earth's crust cracks. But most mountains are folds, created by the crunching together of huge tectonic plates that make up the Earth's surface.

Stages in fold mountain creations
Layers of sand represent layers of crustal rock.

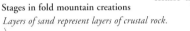

First Z-shaped fold forms.

Second Z-shaped fold forms.

New folds begin to form and the first fold becomes more deformed.

Nappe – a completely overturned fold

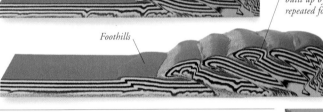

Foothills

Fold mountains built up by repeated folding.

Fold mountains
When two tectonic plates collide, the Earth's crust buckles, throwing up huge ranges of fold mountains. Mountains are usually created in short mountain-building phases. Most of today's major ranges are less than 50 million years old. Some, such as the Himalayas, are still growing.

Layers of lava build up into a mountain.

One slab of rock is thrust above another.

Volcanic mountain
Isolated mountain peaks are generally volcanoes built up after eruption. But volcanic peaks can also occur within fold mountain ranges, creating some of the world's highest mountains, such as Aconcagua in Argentina.

Reverse fault
Some mountains are created not by the crumpling of the rock, but rather where faults, or cracks, appear in the Earth's surface. In a reverse fault, plate movements squeeze one block of rock up over another, so that one overhangs the other.

Valleys

From rivers and glaciers to heavy rainfall, forces of erosion eat away at the landscape, forming valleys. Mountains are assaulted by the weather as soon as they are raised. Rivers carve out steep, narrow valleys that become broader and gentler as the river and its tributaries wear away the rock. The different formation of a valley determines its type.

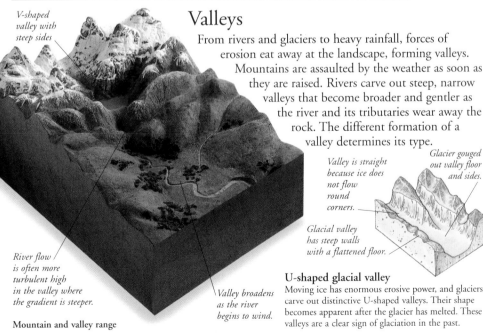

V-shaped valley with steep sides

River flow is often more turbulent high in the valley where the gradient is steeper.

Valley broadens as the river begins to wind.

Mountain and valley range

Valley is straight because ice does not flow round corners.

Glacier gouged out valley floor and sides.

Glacial valley has steep walls with a flattened floor.

U-shaped glacial valley
Moving ice has enormous erosive power, and glaciers carve out distinctive U-shaped valleys. Their shape becomes apparent after the glacier has melted. These valleys are a clear sign of glaciation in the past.

Wadi
In deserts, rainfall is rare. But when it does arrive, it can create huge floods that wash out steep gorges in the dry, crumbly landscape. When the water drains away, it leaves deep, dry channels, known as wadis.

Rift valley
When tectonic plates move apart, the stress can create long faults. This allows a belt of land to drop between them, creating a "rift" valley, such as Pingvellir in Iceland where ravines and cliffs mark the line of the Atlantic Fault.

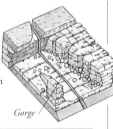

Gorge
In places where there is little surface water – in deserts and in limestone landscapes – valley sides may stay almost cliff-like as a river carves down through the landscape. The result is a deep gorge, like the Grand Canyon in the USA.

Gorge

FIND OUT MORE ASIA CONTINENTS EARTH GLACIATION MOUNTAIN WILDLIFE OCEAN FLOOR RIVERS ROCKS AND MINERALS VOLCANOES

MOUNTAIN WILDLIFE

THE GREAT MOUNTAIN CHAINS of the world are very beautiful but they offer testing conditions for wildlife. The animals that live there, such as the alpine ibex, are either exceptionally hardy to cope with steep and rocky terrain or, like the Andean condor, specially adapted to high winds and cold nights in the thin air. In temperate and cold climates, winter is very harsh in the mountains, bringing gale-force winds and deep snow that drive many animals down towards shelter. By contrast, in summer, the strong sunshine of high altitudes gives a real boost to life, bringing the buzz of insects and the songs of nesting birds to mountain slopes.

Mountains

Mountains are areas of high land where physical conditions become harsher with increasing altitude. Typical mountainside shows a succession of different wildlife habitats from bottom to top. Forest on the lower slopes – rainforest in the tropics or deciduous woodland in temperate regions – gradually gives way to a band of stunted "cloud" forest or to hardy conifers. Higher still, trees give way to bogs and meadows before plant life dwindles to leave just bare rocks and, on the highest summits, permanent caps of ice and snow.

High, exposed rocky crags

Snow on higher slopes

Treeline – above this level it is too cold and harsh for trees to grow.

Dense tree cover and other vegetation on lower slopes

Barren mountains and lush lowlands

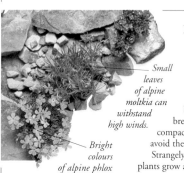

Plants
On high slopes above the treeline most plants are small and low-growing. Some plants, such as the alpine lily, have supple stems that allow them to bend in the wind without breaking. Cushion plants are compact and ground hugging, to avoid the wind and retain warmth. Strangely, in some areas, very large plants grow above the treeline, such as the 5 m (16 ft) tall giant lobelia of Africa.

Small leaves of alpine moltkia can withstand high winds.

Bright colours of alpine phlox attract pollinating insects.

Birds

Birds cope admirably with the hardships of life in the mountains. Well insulated from the cold by their feathers and unaffected by steep terrain, they can search far and wide for food in a habitat where food is scarce. Large, powerful birds such as eagles can ride on the mountain winds with little effort. Many birds migrate to avoid the winter, but some resident mountain species remain, such as seed-eating finches, insectivorous chats, and scavenging vultures.

The Andean condor is the largest flying bird in the world.

Thick feathers for warmth

Mountain dusky salamander
The mountain dusky salamander lives in cool moist areas such as woodland springs in the mountains of northeastern USA. It is lungless and may grow to up to 11 cm (4.5 in) long. It hunts for insect larvae, worms, and other invertebrates on which to feed.

Wallcreeper
The wallcreeper inhabits cliffs and crags in the Alps. It uses its curved beak to probe inside rock crevices to catch insects. Strongly gripping claws enable it to scurry up and down vertical cliff faces with ease. In winter, the wallcreeper flies to sheltered and warmer valleys where food is in better supply.

Andean condor
The Andean condor's huge 3 m (10 ft) wingspan enables it to soar effortlessly in the gales that howl around its nesting crags. When searching for carrion to scavenge, a condor can glide long distances across windswept valleys without a single beat of its wings.

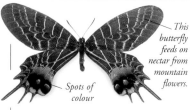

This butterfly feeds on nectar from mountain flowers.

Spots of colour

Bhutan glory
The Bhutan glory lives in the mountain meadows of Central Asia. It flies close to the ground to avoid being swept away by strong winds. Other invertebrates such as spiders and worms also live in the mountains, providing vital food for birds. Some, such as grylloblattid insects, have anti-freezing agents in their bodies for protection against the cold.

Mammals

Fewer mammals live on the open heights of mountains than in the forests below – those that do have thick fur to protect them from the cold. Rodents and other small mammals vulnerable to the cold, shelter at night in burrows and hibernate over winter. Larger mammals such as goats retreat downhill to wooded shelter in winter.

Huge horns

Alpine ibex
Ibex have ridges on their hooves that provide them with a remarkably firm grip, even on icy rocks. They can climb steep crags easily and jump between narrow rock ledges. Their thick coats protect them from the cold winter temperatures.

Snow leopard
This rare, beautiful creature hunts for mountain goats, sheep, rodents, and birds at heights of up to 5,000 m (16,500 ft) in the mountain ranges of Central Asia. Its thick, pale-coloured coat keeps out the cold and provides excellent camouflage against the snow and the grey, rocky landscape. In winter, the snow leopard follows its hoofed prey downhill to wooded shelter below the treeline.

MOZART, WOLFGANG AMADEUS

M

THE WORLD'S MOST FAMOUS child prodigy, and the finest composer and performer of his time, Wolfgang Amadeus Mozart was born in Salzburg, Austria, in 1756. He wrote his first compositions when he was five, and went on to compose the greatest operas, symphonies, concertos, and chamber music of the Classical period. He produced some of his finest works in Vienna, where he lived from 1781, but although these were very popular, he never became a rich man. Tragically, illness dogged him throughout his short life, and he died in 1791, just before his thirty-sixth birthday.

Early life
At a very early age, Mozart showed signs of musical genius. His elder sister, Maria Anna, was also a gifted performer, and their father, Leopold, a professional musician, was keen to show off their abilities. The family toured Europe from 1762, giving concerts to appreciative audiences, but it was young Wolfgang's amazing talent that stole the show. During this tour, Mozart wrote his first symphonies.

Mozart played both chamber music and concertos on this violin.

Mozart's violin

Flute of Mozart's time

The composer
Mozart had a steady job as concert-master to the Archbishop of Salzburg, but he gave this up to make his way by teaching, playing, and publishing his music. Before he left his job, much of his music was rather conventional, but after 1781 he began to write operas and works for orchestra that were soon recognized as masterpieces. He reached the height of his fame in Vienna in the 1780s, both as a composer and performer of his own music.

Concertos
Mozart was a brilliant pianist and violinist, and wrote many concertos in which he played the solo part himself. He composed concertos for other instruments, written for friends of his such as the horn player Ignaz Leutgeb and the clarinettist Anton Stadler. He also wrote several flute concertos for a rich patron, although he did not like the sound of the instrument.

Horn of Mozart's time

Voice and orchestra
Theatre was Mozart's passion. His first great opera, *Idomeneo*, was an immediate success, and the three comic operas he wrote to words by the librettist Lorenzo da Ponte (*The Marriage of Figaro, Don Giovanni* and *Così fan tutte*) are still very popular. He also wrote much orchestral music, from dances to symphonies.

Score of Symphony No. 41, the "Jupiter"

Symphonies
Mozart wrote 41 symphonies, developing his skill in writing for the orchestra throughout his life. In 1788, he composed his last three symphonies. These works are very dramatic and expressive, unlike the symphonies by other composers of the time.

Magic flute
Mozart's finest opera was *The Magic Flute*, written in the last year of his life. The opera, a fairy story, tells of an Egyptian Prince, Tamino, who sets out to rescue Pamina, daughter of the Queen of the Night, with a magic flute and a bird-catcher, Papageno. The opera was instantly popular.

Papageno

Stage setting for *The Magic Flute*

Mozart's death
In November 1791, Mozart caught an undiagnosed and terrible fever, and on 5 December he died. After a simple funeral, he was buried in an unmarked grave.

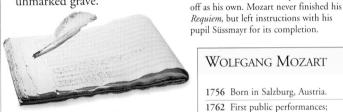
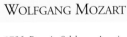

Manuscript of Mozart's *Requiem*

Antonio Salieri
One of the rumours about Mozart's death is that the composer Antonio Salieri (1750–1825), jealous of Mozart's fame and musical ability, poisoned him. Salieri was in fact well respected during his lifetime, and there was no plot to kill Mozart. But the story persists and forms the basis of a modern play, *Amadeus*, by the British writer Peter Shaffer.

Requiem
A few months before he died, Mozart accepted an anonymous commission to write a requiem, or a mass for the dead. A stranger dressed in black came with the request for the work, and Mozart thought this was an ill omen. The caller was a servant of Count Franz von Walsegg, a nobleman who wanted to pass the work off as his own. Mozart never finished his *Requiem*, but left instructions with his pupil Süssmayr for its completion.

WOLFGANG MOZART

1756	Born in Salzburg, Austria.
1762	First public performances; starts European tour.
1769	Appointed concert master to the Archbishop of Salzburg.
1781	Resigns from his Salzburg post after an argument with the Archbishop; settles in Vienna.
1786	*The Marriage of Figaro* performed in Vienna.
1788	Composes symphonies Nos. 39, 40, and 41 (the "Jupiter").
1790	*Così fan tutte* performed in Vienna.
1791	*The Magic Flute* performed; Mozart dies in Vienna.

FIND OUT MORE

BEETHOVEN, LUDWIG VAN · DRAMA · MUSIC · MUSICAL INSTRUMENTS · OPERA · THEATRES

MUGHAL EMPIRE

DURING THE 16TH CENTURY, a new ruling dynasty – the Mughals – came to power in India, bringing a rich, Islamic civilization and uniting the subcontinent for the first time in over 1,500 years.
The first Mughal ruler, Babur, came from Persia and was related to the Mongol emperors. He and the later Mughals built an empire that, by 1700, included all of India except its southern tip. The Mughals encouraged the arts, and helped spread Islam across India. In the 18th and 19th centuries, the empire gradually declined as a result of British colonization.

Akbar and his army cross the Ganges

India under the Mughals

Early Mughals

In 1526, Babur defeated the Sultan of Delhi and took over central northern India. But Babur was a poor administrator and the empire began to break up when he died in 1530. By 1600, the emperor Akbar (r.1556–1605) had pulled the empire together and extended it southward.

Rule of Akbar

Akbar (1542–1605) was the greatest of the Mughal rulers. The grandson of Babur, he became emperor in 1556, defeating an Afghan claimant to the throne in the same year and so securing his hold on power. During his long reign, he enlarged the Mughal Empire, patronized the arts, and encouraged religious toleration.

Akbar and the Hindus

Akbar knew that to unite India he would need the help of local Hindu chiefs. So he gave many of these men jobs in his civil service and tried to promote Hindu interests. He introduced a fairer tax system, abolishing the higher taxes that had been levied on Hindus.

Capital cities

At first, Akbar ruled from Agra in north-central India, where he built the famous Red Fort. Later he moved the capital to his new city, Fatehpur Sikri. Here he reorganized the civil service, sent out governors to the provinces, and reformed the coinage and weights and measures.

Red Fort at Agra

Later Mughals

In 1605, Akbar's son, Jahangir, became emperor. He was succeeded by his son, Shah Jahan, who extended the empire southward, and built many great cities and palaces. He and his son, Aurangzeb, showed far less religious tolerance than Akbar, and Aurangzeb destroyed many Hindu temples. After his rule, the empire began to break up.

Indian Mughal battle scene, from a 15th-century miniature

Akbar receives two black-robed Jesuits in the House of Worship

Religious tolerance

In the 16th century, India was a country of many religions. Akbar saw that the route to peace was to tolerate all faiths. He built the Ibadat Khana, or House of Worship, as a place where people of different faiths could come to discuss their religious ideas. Muslims, Hindus, Sikhs, and even Christians from Europe were made welcome.

Carvings and murals cover many of the buildings.

Sheikh Salim's tomb, Fatehpur Sikri

Fatehpur Sikri

In 1569, Akbar built the city of Fatehpur Sikri in north-central India. Built to honour the Muslim saint Sheikh Salim, who had foretold the birth of his son and heir Jahangir, the city became Akbar's capital until 1584.

Taj Mahal

One of the greatest Mughal achievements was the magnificent Taj Mahal. It was built as a tomb for Mumtaz Mahal, the beloved wife of Shah Jahan, who died in 1631. The construction took 17 years, and involved hundreds of workers from all over India.

Taj Mahal

Timeline

1504 Babur rules Kabul.

1526 Babur defeats the Sultan of Delhi at the Battle of Panipat.

1530 Babur's son Humayun comes to the throne; the empire starts to split up.

1556–1605 The reign of Akbar: the empire expands and there is a golden age of culture and religious tolerance.

1605 Akbar's son Jahangir comes to the throne; a lover of luxury and heavy drinker, he is a poor ruler.

Breastplate from Mughal suit of armour

1628–57 The rule of Shah Jahan, builder of the Delhi Palace, the Pearl Mosque, and the Taj Mahal.

1658 Aurangzeb seizes power from his brother Shah Shuja. The empire begins to disintegrate.

FIND OUT MORE   ARCHITECTURE   EMPIRES   GUPTA EMPIRE   INDIA, HISTORY OF   ISLAM   MONGOL EMPIRE

MUHAMMAD

MUHAMMAD, A MERCHANT from Medina in Arabia, became the prophet of a new religion, Islam, in the 620s. Followers of Islam believe that Muhammad was selected by God as his prophet.
He attracted many followers, and the faith spread rapidly. By the time of Muhammad's death in 632, Islam had been adopted throughout the entire Arabian peninsula. A century later, the Islamic faith was practised from the Atlantic Ocean in the west to the borders of India in the east, and Islam has affected the lives of millions.

The angel Gabriel appears to Muhammad.

Early life
Muhammad was born in the western Arabian city of Mecca in about 570 AD. He was orphaned soon after birth, and was brought up first by his grandfather and then his uncle, Abu Tâlib, who was head of the Hashim clan. At the age of about 25, Muhammad got a job working for Khadija, a wealthy widow. Shortly afterwards he married her. Muhammad became a merchant, and travelled widely throughout the Arabian peninsula. This gave him the chance to study the different religions of the local people.

Birth of Muhammad

The mission
In his dream, Muhammad was instructed by the Angel Gabriel to preach a faith centred on the one true God, Allah. The central beliefs of the faith were dictated to Muhammad in a series of visions throughout his life. He began to convert his family and friends in Mecca.

The Revelation
In about 610, Muhammad gave up his daily work as a merchant and went into the local mountains north of Mecca to meditate. In a cave on Mount Hira, he had a dream in which he was told that he had been selected by God to be the prophet of the true religion.

The Hegira
In Mecca, Muhammad made few converts and many enemies. In 622, he and some 70 followers fled Mecca and moved north to the more welcoming city of Medina. This journey is known as the Hegira (flight).

Medina
Muhammad's reception in Medina was very different from the one he received in Mecca. He attracted many supporters in the city, and established and built up the first Muslim community there. He also built mosques, in which his followers worshipped.

Facing Mecca
In about 624, Muslims in Medina began to face Mecca during prayer. This practice is still followed by Muslims. Niches called mihrabs in mosques show the direction of Mecca, so people know where to face.

The Qur'an
Muhammad wrote down the message dictated to him in his visions in a book, the Qur'an (Koran). Muslims believe it contains the direct word of Allah as revealed to his prophet, Muhammad. The Qur'an is one of the most widely read books in the world. Its text is treated with great reverence, and is often written out in beautiful calligraphy. Muslims read it in the original Arabic, and most learn to read Arabic by studying the Qur'an.

Copy of the Qur'an, made in Turkey | *Flap to protect book* | *Arabic text written in Naski script*

Mosque

Mihrab in mosque

The struggle
While in Medina, Muhammad and his followers regularly ambushed caravans of traders travelling to and from Mecca. In 624, a pitched battle between Muhammad and an armed force from Mecca resulted in victory for Muhammad, giving his new religion great prestige throughout the Arabian world.

The surrender of Mecca
In 629, Muhammad went on a pilgrimage to Mecca and made many converts to Islam. By this time, Muslim missionaries were active throughout the Middle East as far afield as Iran and Ethiopia. Muhammad was now strong enough to capture Mecca, which fell without a fight. The entire Arabian peninsula was now ruled by Muhammad and his Muslim followers.

Death of Muhammad
After a final pilgrimage to the city of Mecca, Muhammad died on 8 June, 632 in Medina, where he was buried. He was succeeded as leader of the Islamic people by his father-in-law, Abu Bekr, who took the title caliph (successor, or ruler).

MUHAMMAD

c.570	Born in Mecca, modern Saudi Arabia
594	Marries Khadija, a wealthy widow
610	Has a vision, in which he is told to preach the new faith
622	Leaves Mecca and travels to Medina
624	His followers defeat the army of Mecca at Battle of Badr
625	Indecisive Battle of Uhud against the Meccan army
630	Returns to Mecca and conquers the city
632	Dies in Medina

FIND OUT MORE   AFRICA, HISTORY OF   ASIA, HISTORY OF   IRAN AND IRAQ   ISLAM   ISLAMIC EMPIRE   MOSQUES   RELIGIONS   SPAIN, HISTORY OF   WRITING

MUSCLES AND MOVEMENT

ALL OUR ACTIONS depend on muscles. Muscles are tissues that actively contract, or get shorter, in order to move parts of the body. They use the energy released from the food we eat and convert it into movement. There are three types of muscle: skeletal, cardiac, and smooth. Skeletal muscles move the skeleton under the conscious control of the brain. The other types of muscle work automatically. Cardiac muscle keeps the heart beating. Smooth muscle, or involuntary muscle, is found in the walls of hollow organs such as the intestine and the bladder.

Inside a muscle

Muscles are made up of bundles of long cells called muscle fibres. Each muscle fibre contains many tiny strands called myofibrils that run the length of the fibre. Each myofibril contains two types of protein filament, called actin and myosin, which cause muscle contractions.

Skeletal muscle
The fibres of a skeletal muscle lie parallel to each other. Its actin and myosin filaments are arranged into regular blocks called sarcomeres, that are repeated along the length of the fibre.

How muscles work
In the relaxed muscle fibre, the myosin and actin filaments overlap a little. If the muscle fibre receives a nerve impulse, the actin and myosin filaments slide over each other. The myofibril shortens, and the muscle contracts.

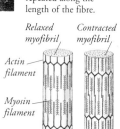

Relaxed myofibril   *Contracted myofibril*

Actin filament

Myosin filament

Myofibrils inside muscle

Von Szent-Györgyi
Albert von Szent-Györgyi (1893–1986) was an American biochemist, born in Hungary, who carried out important research into the way that muscles contracted. He discovered the protein actin that forms part of the contraction mechanism in muscles. He was also the first to isolate vitamin C (ascorbic acid), for which he was awarded the Nobel Prize in 1937.

Muscular system
The skeletal muscular system consists of about 620 muscles that make up over 40 per cent of body weight. Muscles are attached to the skeleton by tendons. Most muscles are attached at one end to a bone that does not move, and at the other end to a bone that does move. When a muscle contracts, it pulls part of the skeleton in that direction.

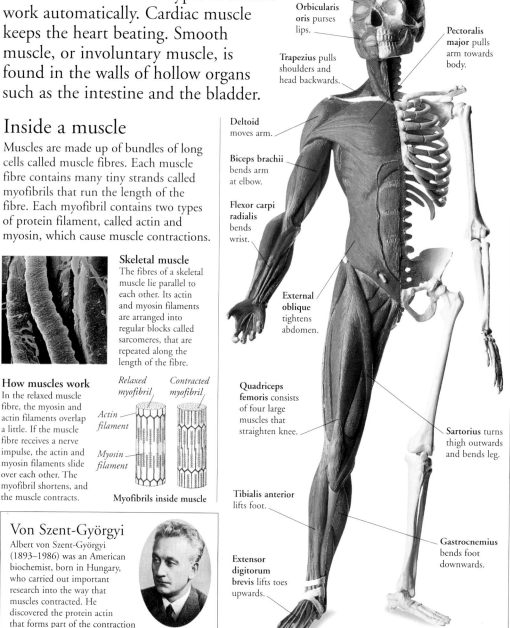

Orbicularis oculi closes eye.

Orbicularis oris purses lips.

Trapezius pulls shoulders and head backwards.

Frontalis raises eyebrows and wrinkles forehead.

Pectoralis major pulls arm towards body.

Deltoid moves arm.

Biceps brachii bends arm at elbow.

Flexor carpi radialis bends wrist.

External oblique tightens abdomen.

Quadriceps femoris consists of four large muscles that straighten knee.

Sartorius turns thigh outwards and bends leg.

Tibialis anterior lifts foot.

Gastrocnemius bends foot downwards.

Extensor digitorum brevis lifts toes upwards.

Smiling and frowning
Facial expressions, such as smiling and frowning, are produced by over 30 small facial muscles. These muscles are unusual in that when they contract they pull the skin of the face, rather than a bone.

Smiling

Frowning needs more than twice as many muscles as smiling.

Frowning

Movement
Muscles move the body by pulling, not pushing. This explains why many movements are caused by pairs of muscles that produce opposite pulling forces. Each member of the pair is arranged across one side of a joint between bones. When one muscle in a pair contracts, the other relaxes.

Forearm extended
The biceps and triceps are the pair of muscles involved in extending (straightening) and flexing (bending) the forearm. When the forearm is extended, the biceps is relaxed and the triceps is contracted.

Biceps relaxed

Triceps contracted

Forearm half raised
To raise the forearm, the brain sends nerve impulses to the biceps, which stimulate it to contract. As the biceps contracts, the triceps starts to relax and lengthen.

Upper arm

Forearm

Forearm flexed
When the forearm is flexed, the biceps is fully contracted and at its minimum length, while the triceps is relaxed and at its maximum length. Other muscles help steady the shoulder and forearm, while the arm bends.

Biceps contracted

Elbow bends

Body builders
Body builders are men or women who greatly increase the bulk of their skeletal muscles. They build up their muscle mass by lifting weights regularly over long periods, using heavy weights that target specific muscle groups.

FIND OUT MORE
BRAIN AND NERVOUS SYSTEM HEALTH AND FITNESS HEART AND CIRCULATORY SYSTEM HUMAN BODY SKELETON SPORTS

MUSEUMS

THE FIRST MUSEUMS originated in ancient Greece, where offerings to gods or goddesses were displayed in temples. Today, a museum or gallery exhibits works of art or other objects to the public. Museums can cover a vast range of subjects from wide-ranging natural history displays to smaller private collections. Some museums, such as the Guggenheim in New York, are distinctive landmarks that have been specially built for their purpose.

Inside a museum

National museums exhibiting objects bought with public money were set up in the 18th and 19th centuries. In these, the exhibits were simply labelled and displayed inside glass cabinets, safely protected from visitors.

Medieval plate

Interactive museums

Modern museums try to make their exhibits more accessible to the public. They use the latest technology, such as computers and CD audio guides, to provide information. Many now have interactive exhibits so visitors can enjoy a hands-on experience.

At this interactive science museum in Wales, visitors carry out their own experiments on the exhibits.

A museum's role

A museum has four main purposes. First, the staff are responsible for acquiring works of art or other artefacts. Second, they need to study the collection and, third, ensure it is displayed informatively. The other main purpose of a museum or art gallery is to look after and restore its collection.

Conservation of paintings

Works of art are often very fragile and have to be looked after carefully. Curators need to monitor levels of humidity and light to ensure they do not damage the paintings.

This painting has been restored to its original quality.

Adam and Eve Expelled from Paradise by the Italian artist Masaccio (1401–28)

Restoration of paintings

The restorer removes dirty varnish and fills in areas where the original paint has been lost with paint that matches closely, trying to keep as true as possible to the artist's intentions.

Private collections

Some small private collections reflect the particular interests of their founder. A museum may be set up in a private home, such as this collection of over 1,000 bells. Some large national museum collections, such as the Prado in Spain, began as private collections and were later bequeathed to the public.

Art galleries

Museums that collect and display works of art are known as art galleries. Some galleries, such as the Van Gogh Museum in Amsterdam, the Netherlands, display the work of just one artist. Others, such as the Louvre in Paris, France, which has over five million visitors a year, show a vast range of art by a variety of artists.

Guggenheim Museum, New York, USA

This art gallery was designed by the American architect Frank Lloyd Wright (1869–1959).

The main part of the gallery is the Great Rotunda, where special exhibitions are held.

Natural light enters through the skylight.

Visitors walk down a gentle slope lined with works of art.

Visitors get a lift to the top and walk down.

Sculpture is displayed outdoors in a sculpture garden.

Exhibitions in the Small Rotunda show work by 19th- and 20th-century artists.

Main entrance

ARCHITECTURE | ART, HISTORY OF | DYES AND PAINTS | EDUCATION | GODS AND GODDESSES | GREECE, ANCIENT | PAINTING AND DRAWING | SCULPTURE

MUSHROOMS AND OTHER FUNGI

NEITHER PLANT NOR ANIMAL, mushrooms and other types of fungi form a unique group of organisms of more than 80,000 species. Unlike plants, fungi lack the green food-making compound – chlorophyll – so cannot make their own food. Instead, they release enzymes that decompose living, dead, or dying organisms and absorb the nutrients and minerals released. Fungi range from dull grey mushrooms to brightly coloured toadstools (a name usually given to more colourful and poisonous fungi).

M

Features of a mushroom

Mushrooms are the part of a fungus, called the fruiting body, that grows above ground. They contain spores, which enable fungi to reproduce. Spores are produced on the underside of a mushroom and released from flaps called gills, or hollows called pores. Below the fruiting body lies the mycelium, a network of fine threads called hyphae, that are usually hidden within a plant, animal, or soil.

Mushroom shrivels and spores are released in inky liquid

Shaggy ink-cap mushroom

Fruiting body

Cap of mushroom

Stem ring – remnants of veil

Gills are located beneath the cap.

The stem of the mushroom lifts the cap into the air to improve the dispersal of the spores.

Life-cycle of a mushroom

Mushrooms release spores from their gills or pores. These germinate and produce hyphae that divide to form the mycelium. This may lie hidden in wood, plants, or animals for many years. Gradually, the hyphae spread through the wood and absorb nutrients. When conditions are right, normally in the autumn, mushrooms appear on the surface and release more spores.

Spore

Hyphae

Emerging fruiting body

1 Spores are released from mushrooms. They contain small food reserves. Only a few spores find the right conditions to germinate.

2 On germination a single fungal thread, or hypha, grows from the spore. It divides to form the mycelium.

3 As the fungal mycelium expands into its surroundings, it absorbs water and nutrients to build up energy to form the fruiting body.

4 After rain the fruiting body enlarges with the rapid uptake of water and becomes a recognizable mushroom, in this case a shaggy ink-cap mushroom.

5 The shaggy ink-cap has the characteristics typical of a mushroom: a stem or stipe, gills on the underside of a cap, and a veil that protects the gills as it pushes up through the soil.

6 Most fungal fruiting bodies release their spores into the air for distribution, but as the ink-cap matures, its cap breaks down to produce a black liquid in which the spores float away.

Spore dispersal

Fungal fruiting bodies are diverse in shape and colour, but are all designed to disperse spores. Many release their spores directly into the air from gills, spines, or pores; other fungi, including stinkhorns, are eaten by animals, such as pigs and flies, which disperse the spores in their faeces. A few types of fungi, such as the cramp ball, shoot their spores away; puffballs puff out a cloud of spores when hit by a raindrop.

Puffball exploding

Common stinkhorn
Stinkhorn spores are distributed by insects. The fruiting body develops below ground in an egg-like structure. When mature, the stem grows rapidly carrying the cap upwards. The cap is covered in a slimy, smelly mass of green spores. Carrion-feeders, such as flies and beetles, are attracted by the putrid smell. They eat the slime and disperse the spores in their faeces.

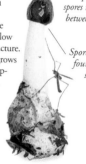

The spaces between spores mirror those between the gills.

Spores are found in slime.

Spore print
A spore print is the pattern that spores make when the cap of a mushroom is placed gill-side down on paper. Spores are used to help identify fungi.

Types of fungi

There are many types of fungi. The spores and mycelium of most species are similar in appearance. The main differences occur between the fruiting bodies which come in many sizes, shapes, and colours. They vary depending on how they reproduce. On this basis, fungi are divided into five groups.

Common morel

Chicken-of--the-woods

Pin mould

Athlete's foot

Potato blight

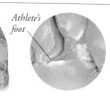

Sac fungi
Sac fungi, including morels, cup fungi, and truffles, produce spores in a special sac, or ascus.

Club fungi
Club fungi, such as chicken-of-the-woods and puffballs, produce spores on club-shaped fertile cells.

Blights
Blights, such as potato blight and mildew, produce oospores. Many blights live in water.

Moulds
Moulds have woolly growth and produce zygospores. Pin mould often grows on bread.

Imperfect fungi
Imperfect fungi, such as athlete's foot, ringworm, and thrush, have no sexual stage to their life-cycle.

Where fungi live

Fungi grow wherever other living, dying, or dead organisms are found on Earth, mainly in warm, damp conditions. They live in the sea, in rivers, hedgerows, and lakes, on mountains, and in caves – in fact, in all habitats. They can grow on fruit, bread, cheese, leather, rotting wood, and garden refuse. Warm weather after rainfall offers the perfect conditions for mycelium to produce a crop of fruiting bodies.

These mushrooms grow in woods, parks, and hedgerows.

Shaggy parasols

Woods
Many fungi live in woods and forests, both on the forest floor and directly on the trees. Different types of fungi grow in coniferous forests compared to those found in deciduous forests.

Meadows
Undisturbed grassy meadows are home to many autumn mushrooms. Fairy rings are circles of mushrooms created when hyphae spread out in all directions and sprout a circle of mushrooms above.

Fairy ring fungi

Luminous fungi
The lamp mushroom of Australia and the Jack O'Lantern of North America both have luminous caps. The purpose of the luminescence is still unknown, but their green lights, glowing on the forest floor at night, may attract animals, which help to disperse their spores.

Feeding

The majority of fungi live on dead organic matter, breaking it down into a form that they, and other living things, can absorb. These fungi, called saprophytes, play a vital role in recycling nutrients in the environment. Some fungi live on animal dung; others are predatory and trap soil worms. Some fungi even obtain nutrients from paints, petrol, and plastics. There are also parasitic fungi that live on a live host, and symbiotic fungi that live in harmony with their partners.

Parasitic fungi
Parasitic fungi feed on live animals, plants, or fungi. For example, honey fungus is often found growing on apple trees. Some fungi, such as blights and rusts, harm their plant hosts, but Dutch Elm disease and oak wilt kill theirs. Aspergillus, a fungal lung disease, attacks birds, and ringworm attacks humans.

Honey fungus on apple tree

Symbiotic fungi
Many fungi are found in association with certain plants, such as fly agaric and birch trees. The hyphae penetrate the plant roots to form a partnership, or mycorrhiza, between the plant and fungus; the fungus saps nutrients from the plant, but helps the plant collect water and minerals from the soil. Lichens are fungi that live with algae; the fungi provide protection while the algae provide the nutrients.

Fly agaric fungus by decaying birch tree

Problem fungi

Many fungi cause problems; some are poisonous if eaten, some cause disease, and others may cause structural damage to houses. In the 19th century, many people died in France from the disease called St. Anthony's fire after eating bread infected with ergot fungus. Blue moulds, brown rots, and scab cause fruit, such as apples, to rot, while the honey fungus is the most destructive tree parasite, capable of killing whole orchards.

Caps reach 15 cm (6 in) in width.

Stem is white or grey-green.

Death cap

Poisonous fungi
Some fungi are poisonous if eaten. The death cap looks harmless enough, but 28 g (1 oz) can kill a person in just a few hours. Other fungi, such as magic mushrooms, cause hallucinatory effects.

Dry rot
Dry rot fungus lives on damp wood in houses and churches. The mycelium rapidly covers vast areas of timber and damp brickwork. It causes catastrophic decay and weakens the beams, which may eventually collapse.

Ringworm
Ringworm is a fungus that attacks the skin, especially children's scalps. It often causes hair to fall out. A ringworm epidemic occurred in the 1940s in Britain, causing a serious public health problem.

Useful fungi

Many edible forms of fungi are commonly used in cooking, baking, and brewing. Quorn, a fungal meat substitute, is one of the most recent additions to vegetarians' larders. The chemical industry also uses fungi to produce many products, including citric, gluconic, and oxalic acids, enzymes for washing powders, and colourful dyes.

Yeast
Yeast is a type of fungus used in baking to make bread rise, and in brewing to turn sugar to alcohol. It is also used to make blood plasma substitutes, extracts high in vitamin B12, and anticoagulants.

Perigord truffle

Edible fungi
Many types of fungi are low in food value but are eaten for their flavour. Commonly eaten fungi include chanterelles, oyster mushrooms, and morels. Truffles grow underground and are considered a delicacy.

Penicillium
Penicillium moulds grow on many damp substances. They are often used to flavour cheese. These fungi also produce antibiotics, such as penicillin, which are used to combat bacterial infections.

SHAGGY INK-CAP

SCIENTIFIC NAME	*Coprinus comatus*
CLASS	Homobasidiomycetes
FAMILY	Coprinaceae
DISTRIBUTION	Australasia, South Africa, Europe, North America, Venezuela
HABITAT	Fields, wasteland, lawns, paths
DIET	Dead organic material in the soil
SIZE	10–35 cm (4–14 in) high
LIFESPAN	Fruiting body present for a few days from April to November

---

FIND OUT MORE   DISEASES   ECOLOGY AND ECOSYSTEMS   FOOD   MEDICINE, HISTORY OF   MICROSCOPIC LIFE   WOODLAND WILDLIFE

Mushrooms and other fungi
Club fungi

Common Puffballs grow in clusters, mainly in woodland.

Horn of Plenty fruits in clusters in leaf litter or moss.

Fluted Bird's Nests disperse their spores when rain falls.

Barometer Earthstar curls up its rays in dry weather.

Yellow Spindles grow in moss-rich meadows.

Woolly Milk Caps produce hot-tasting milk when cut.

Dryad's Saddle grows out of half-dead trees and stumps.

Amethyst Deceivers grow on soil among leaf litter.

Fairy-ring Champignons grow in circles on lawns.

Razor-strop Fungus fruits all year on old birch trunks.

Devil's Finger was introduced to Europe from Australasia.

Yellow Brain Fungus is parasitic and grows on hardwood trees.

Sulphur Tufts are common in temperate woodlands.

Many-zoned Brackets fruit in tiers on the sides of tree stumps.

Meadow Coral Fungus grows in grasslands and woodlands.

Chicken-of-the-Woods often grows high up in trees.

Beefsteak Fungus grows on tree trunks. It can make oaks hollow.

Fly Agaric toadstools are highly poisonous.

Fine-scaly Honey Fungus is a deadly tree parasite.

Common Hedgehog has short spines on the underside.

Cinnabar Brackets grow in sunny sites on tree trunks.

Sac fungi

Orange Peel Fungus grows on dirt roads, lawns, and between paving.

Candle-snuff Fungus fruits on tree stumps all year round.

Summer Truffles fruit below ground among tree roots.

Curly-haired Elf Cups grow on moss-covered wood.

Scaly Earth-tongue grows in grass or moss.

Beech Jelly-discs live on the bark of fallen trees.

Jelly Babies have a rubbery texture.

Cramp Balls forcibly eject their spores.

Orange Caterpillar Fungus parasitizes moth larvae or pupae.

Green Stain produces a stain inside the wood on which it grows.

Common White Saddles grow on woodland soil.

☠ Do not pick wild fungi as many are poisonous.

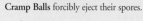
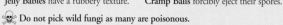
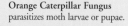

MUSIC

THE URGE TO MAKE MUSIC is ancient, and it is an essential part of all cultures. Music is thought to be the oldest form humankind has found for expressing its feelings. It can affect emotions, making people dance or cry, or make repetitive work easier to bear. Music is played whenever there is a celebration, from a harvest to a wedding. Essentially, all music is made from sounds called notes organized into patterns of melody, rhythm, and harmony.

Melody

The basis of any song is its tune, or melody, which consists of a series of single notes. Because most wind and stringed musical instruments normally play one note at a time, the music they play is essentially melodic.

18th-century Japanese musician

The sitar has an exotic, shimmering sound.

Indian classical musicians

Mridangam

The musician sits on the floor to play.

Asian melody
Melody is important in the traditional music of Asia, such as the elegant sounds of Japanese woodwind and string players. The complex chiming sounds of the gamelan, a traditional Indonesian orchestra, are made by a huge variety of gongs, bells, and xylophones, playing variations on a simple melody.

Ragas and talas
Indian classical music is based on sets of notes called ragas and rhythmic patterns called talas. There are about 130 ragas in common use. Each is associated with a different time of day, and has its own distinctive mood, such as happy, sad, or peaceful. The performer, a vocalist or sitar player, chooses a raga and tala and improvises with them. The performer is accompanied by drums.

Ancient music

Music in ancient civilizations was passed on by listening and repetition; there was no accurate system of writing it down. Some ancient instruments have been found and, together with pictures and descriptions of different periods, they give us an idea of the kinds of music that people played.

Greece
The ancient Greeks were very concerned with the arts, especially poetry, dance, and music. The philosopher Pythagoras (c.580–500 BC) analysed music mathematically, explaining the relationships between musical notes and naming the notes with letters of the alphabet.

Lyre player

China
Music and philosophy were linked in ancient China, and philosophers wrote documents on music's place in society. Confucius, a philosopher in the 5th century BC, recognized the power of music and recommended it should be under state control. As a result, *yayue* (elegant music), the music of the ancient style, dominated until the revolution of 1911.

Lute

Model musician, T'ang dynasty

The Middle East
Music was an important part of the cultures of the ancient Middle East. Lyres, harps, flutes, and tambourines were played in Mesopotamian rituals in about 2000 BC. Similar instruments appeared in Egypt 500 years later. Musicians played them in state and religious ceremonies and for entertainment.

Egyptian tomb painting, c.1400 BC

Rhythm

Underlying each piece of music is the beat, a pattern that divides music into units of time. The rhythm of a piece of music is determined by how the composer has grouped beats together, by the length of each note, and how notes are accented.

African drum

African traditions
Complex, exciting rhythms are central to the many styles of traditional African music. Generally, music is for group performance. Tuned and untuned drums, rattles, and handclaps maintain the rhythm. The call-and-response style of solo singer and chorus is important as well. This was taken by African slaves to America, and developed from a simple "field holler" into jazz and the blues.

African musicians

Harmony

The sound produced when two or more notes are played simultaneously is called harmony. Harmonies accompany the instruments playing the melody and can change the mood of a piece.

Polyphony
Most Western classical music is based on polyphony. Developed by medieval musicians, this is a harmonic style that combines separate melodies. Italian composer Giovanni Palestrina (c.1525–1594) wrote some of the finest polyphonic music.

Giovanni Palestrina

Gospel music
The rich harmonies and inspirational performances of American gospel choirs have become popular outside the church, too. Gospel music has its roots in a mixture of black American and Protestant evangelical styles.

Gospel choir

Folk music

Traditional music played by non-professional musicians, especially in rural communities, is known as folk music. Each country has its own folk traditions. There is a huge variety of styles, often using instruments with a strong local association, such as the Scottish bagpipes, or the Russian balalaika. Some professional musicians have taken an interest in folk music, writing down and recording examples for posterity.

Notation

Composers use notation (signs and symbols giving musicians precise instructions as to what they should play) to write down the music they create. Monks in the 9th century AD were the first to use notation, and it was fully developed by 1200. It was the basis of Western art music, as it provided a permanent record of a composer's intentions.

Scale

The position of a note on the horizontal staff lines indicates its pitch (how high or low the note is). Notes are given letter names from A to G. They can be arranged in ascending and descending sequences called scales. These are either major, with a bright sound, or minor, with a darker, more serious sound.

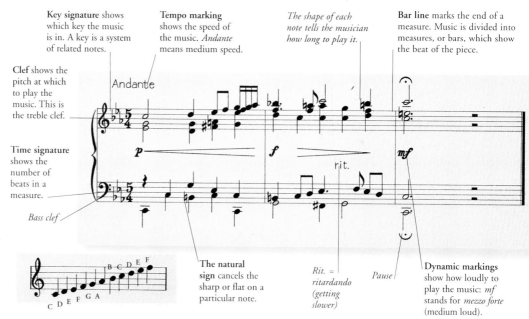

Key signature shows which key the music is in. A key is a system of related notes.

Clef shows the pitch at which to play the music. This is the treble clef.

Time signature shows the number of beats in a measure.

Bass clef

Tempo marking shows the speed of the music. *Andante* means medium speed.

The shape of each note tells the musician how long to play it.

Bar line marks the end of a measure. Music is divided into measures, or bars, which show the beat of the piece.

The natural sign cancels the sharp or flat on a particular note.

Rit. = ritardando (getting slower)

Pause

Dynamic markings show how loudly to play the music: *mf* stands for *mezzo forte* (medium loud).

Medieval music

Until the late 11th century, music mainly took the form of simple melodies. Church music was sung in unison (everybody singing the same notes); other music took the form of simple songs. When notation developed, composers could write more complex vocal music in several parts. Meanwhile, early European instrumental music was developing, in dances such as the estampie.

Gregorian Chant

Monasteries were early centres of music-making. The melodies sung by monks during the reign of Pope Gregory (r.AD 590–604) are often called Gregorian Chant, or plainsong. Later, other parts were added to these chants, providing the first examples of harmony. By the 14th century, European composers were writing sophisticated pieces for choirs with several different voices.

Troubadours

In medieval Europe, travelling singers entertained at the aristocratic courts. They sang songs of love, accompanied by stringed instruments such as viols and harps. The trend began in France, where the singers, or troubadours, were highly respected as poets and musicians.

J. S. Bach

The German composer J. S. Bach (1685–1750) was a very religious man, who wrote choral Church music as well as some of the finest instrumental music of the Baroque period. His major works include the *Brandenburg Concertos*.

Baroque music

Western music between 1600 and 1750 was ornate, often using several melodies together in a style called counterpoint. The system of tonality (where music shifts from one key to another) evolved, allowing composers to write work that explored the moods of major and minor keys.

Concerts

Public music-making increased in the 17th century. The first operas appeared around 1600, and orchestras played the first truly public concerts. George Frideric Handel's (1685–1759) *Music for the Royal Fireworks* had a spectacular performance.

Renaissance music

In about 1471 in Italy, music printing appeared for the first time. Its arrival helped to spread new musical styles through Europe, and encouraged a surge in non-religious music in particular.

Musicians and courtiers in Renaissance France

Madrigal, arranged so that the parts can be read and sung by four people seated around a table.

Madrigals

Madrigals are pieces of music for several unaccompanied singers. They developed in 14th-century Italy, but became popular through Europe in the 16th century. Generally about love, madrigals were the first choral music to be written for performance in the home.

Court of Burgundy

During the 14th and 15th centuries, Burgundy in eastern France became an influential centre for all the arts, including music. The composers Guillaume Dufay (c.1400–1474) and Josquin des Prez (1440–1521) taught there, among others. Josquin is known for music that expressed emotions more directly than earlier styles.

St. Mark's, Venice

Venice, Italy was at the heart of Renaissance thinking, a mixture of the Church and secular society. Andrea Gabrieli (c.1510–1586) and his nephew Giovanni (c.1557–1612) wrote exciting new music to be performed in the cathedral of St. Mark. Their compositions explored the contrasting sounds made by different groups of musicians or singers.

Interior of St. Mark's, Venice

Classical music

Late in the 18th century, composers reacted against the complex style of Baroque music and developed a simpler style. This is known as Classical music, although the term "classical" is often used loosely for any serious or art music. Composers include the Austrians Haydn (1732–1809) and Mozart (1756–1791), and the German Beethoven (1770–1827). Music was written in forms such as the symphony, and sonatas for the newly invented piano.

Esterháza palace

Beethoven composition

The symphony was the main form of Classical orchestral music.

Patronage
During this period, rich nobles often became patrons to composers. Prince Paul Esterházy employed Haydn as director of music at his palace in Hungary; the composer wrote much of his music here.

Symphony
A symphony is a work usually in four sections, or movements. Each movement is different in character, and the music changes from one key to another within the movements, changing the mood.

Nationalism
Romantic music was largely created by composers from Germany and Austria. Its traditions did not always suit composers elsewhere who wanted to express their own national character. Nationalist composers, such as the Norwegian Edvard Grieg (1843–1907) used folk tunes in their music to produce works that summed up the nature of their own countries.

Norwegian fjord

Romantic music

This dramatic style of music emerged during the 19th century. Although composers continued to use Classical forms, such as the symphony and sonata, the mood of Romantic music was more intense, emotional, and individual. Composers also wrote programme music, which depicted scenes and stories, using the increased range of sounds available from the new instruments in the orchestra.

The waltz
This romantic dance first gained popularity in the 19th century. When it first appeared it was considered shocking, because the dancers stood so close together.

Franz Liszt
Recitals of piano music were popular entertainment in the Romantic era. The Hungarian composer and pianist Franz Liszt (1811–86) gained practically superstar status for his dazzling recitals of his own music, such as the *Hungarian Rhapsodies*. Liszt was an innovative and brilliant composer. He invented the form of the symphonic poem, which tells a story through music.

Twentieth century

By 1900, tonality (the use of keys) was stretched to its limits. Revolutionary new styles appeared that moved away from traditional melody and harmony. Russian composer Igor Stravinsky (1882–1971) used jagged rhythms that shocked the musical establishment. Some composers, such as John Cage, introduced random elements into their music.

Arnold Schoenberg

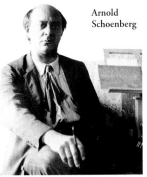

Debussy and Schoenberg
Among the pioneers of early 20th-century music were the composers Claude Debussy (1862–1918) and Arnold Schoenberg (1874–1951). Debussy experimented with unusual sounds and harmonies in his impressionist pieces, such as *Prélude à l'après-midi d'un faune*. Schoenberg wrote music that was atonal, with no feeling of key, as in the *Five Piano Pieces*.

New notation
Much late-20th century music, especially for electronic instruments, cannot be written down in the traditional way. Some composers have developed forms of graphic notation to represent these new sounds.

John Cage
The immensely influential US composer John Cage (1912–1992) wrote music that experimented with noise and chance events, making the listener think again about what music really is. In his highly innovative works, Cage suggested that all sounds, musical or non-musical, are of equal interest. For instance, the famous piece *Imaginary Landscape No. 4* was written for 12 radios, tuned at random.

Broadcasting
The invention of the radio and gramophone brought professional music into the home for the first time. Sales of recordings helped finance musicians, and broadcasting companies often commissioned new works for their orchestras to perform.

Transistor radio, 1940s

Tape part

Guitar part

Graphic score for electric guitar and tape

Extract, "Caressing Eternity" © Natasha Barrett 1994

Timeline

Medieval stone carving of musician

c.1200 The French monks Léonin and Péotin compose the first properly polyphonic music, based on traditional plainsong melodies.

c.1450 Guillaume Dufay writes the mass *Se la face ay pale*, which includes elements of both the medieval and the new Renaissance styles.

c.1600 The first concertos, using contrasting groups of musicians, are published in Italy.

1741 Handel completes *The Messiah*, a setting to music of religious texts known as oratorio.

1824 Beethoven's *Ninth Symphony* marks the end of the Classical period, developing the symphony form so that it expresses intense human emotions.

1912 Schoenberg composes a set of songs, *Pierrot Lunaire*, in which he abandons all sense of tonality

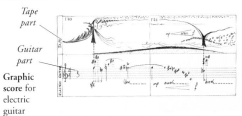
20th-century recording

1952 John Cage composes *4'33"*, four minutes and 33 seconds of silence.

1993 French composer Pierre Boulez (b.1925) explores computers in art music with a piece called ... *explosante fixe*.

FIND OUT MORE | BEETHOVEN, LUDWIG VAN | DANCE | JAZZ | MOZART, WOLFGANG AMADEUS | MUSICAL INSTRUMENTS | OPERA | ORCHESTRA | ROCK AND POP | SOUND

M

MUSICAL INSTRUMENTS

BY PRODUCING THE SOUNDS we call notes, musical instruments make music to enrich our lives. There are many different instruments throughout the world. Most of them can be grouped into four main families, depending on how they make sound: percussion, wind (including brass and woodwind), strings, and keyboard. Until the relatively recent development of electronic music, all musical instruments were based on these types.

Brass instruments

Brass instruments are long tubes with a mouthpiece, bent into coils to make them easier to handle. Most have valves which can be pressed down to open up more of the tube, producing different notes. With their loud, triumphant sound, brass instruments are well suited to outdoor events and grand occasions.

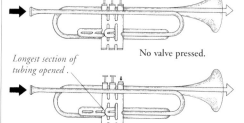

Trumpet player

Percussion

Percussion instruments are played by being shaken or struck. The first percussion were probably sticks and bones, banged together to accompany people while they sang. Today the huge variety of instruments ranges from drums to rattles or the triangle. Some, such as the xylophone, can be tuned to produce a definite musical note; others emphasize a rhythm.

Crash cymbal

Tom-tom drum

Ride cymbal

Snare drum

Floor tom

Bass drum

Drums
Drums are found worldwide. They are especially important in traditional African music, which is rhythmically complex and exciting.

Wooden percussion
The short, dry sound of wooden percussion, a feature of South American dance music, is produced by the claves, castanets, maracas, and wood blocks.

Seeds inside hollow shell

Wooden maracas

Gong and bells
Metal percussion instruments produce long, sustained sounds. These vary from crashing cymbals to the exquisite sound of gongs and bells produced by Indonesian *gamelans*.

How they work
Brass players produce sound by making their closed lips vibrate in the instrument's mouthpiece. By altering the tension of the lips, the player makes different notes, and can use the valves to produce a complete scale.

Pressing a valve opens side-sections of tubing, and increases the length of the whole tube.

No valve pressed.

Longest section of tubing opened.

Third valve pressed.

Woodwind instruments

Any woodwind instrument is basically a hollow tube, with an arrangement of holes and keys. Blowing into the tube makes a column of air inside vibrate, and so give out a sound. The musician uses the keys or holes to make the column of air longer or shorter, changing the pitch of the note. The woodwind family includes the flute, pipe, whistle, recorder, clarinet, saxophone, oboe, and bassoon.

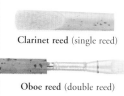

Clarinet player

The sheng, a sort of mouth organ, has been played in China for about 3,000 years.

Early brass
The first brass instruments were made from conch shells and animal horns. During the Renaissance, the sackbut (an early trombone), the cornett (a wooden trumpet), and the serpent (a bass cornett) appeared. Apart from the trombone, these instruments disappeared in the early 1800s, but have been revived.

Serpent

Shofar
The shofar is an unusual instrument made from a ram's horn; it produces drawn-out, sobbing sounds. It is played on important Jewish public and religious occasions, such as Yom Kippur, the Day of Atonement.

Clarinet reed (single reed)

Oboe reed (double reed)

Bassoon reed

How they work
Blowing across a bottletop makes a note in the same way as the panpipes and flute are played. Some woodwinds, such as the clarinet or oboe, have a mouthpiece with a reed (a thin piece of cane). This vibrates when the player blows into it; the tube of the instrument modifies the sound produced.

Early woodwind
Once, all woodwind instruments were made of wood, but today they are often made from metal or plastic. The sounds produced by early woodwind include the loud shawm, the buzzing crumhorn, and the low notes of the racket.

Stringed instruments

The huge family of stringed instruments can be divided into two main groups by the way they are normally played. Most stringed instruments, including the guitar, harp, lute, and sitar, are plucked with the fingers or a plectrum. Instruments such as the violin and its relatives are usually played by drawing a horsehair bow over the strings to make them vibrate. Many cultures have their own versions of both plucked and bowed instruments.

Plucked strings
In ancient Egypt and Greece, musicians played the lyre to accompany songs and poetry. Today, plucked instruments are still played as accompaniment. The harp and zither evolved from the lyre. The Arabic 'ud, which dates back 4,000 years, developed into the guitar.

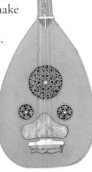
Moroccan 'ud

The player's chin and shoulder support the instrument.

Violin player

Bowed strings
Bowed stringed instruments originated in Arabia, but now are found all over the world. In a modern orchestra, the string section is made up of the members of the violin family – violins, violas, cellos, and double basses. These evolved in Italy during the Renaissance.

How they work
When a string is made to vibrate, the sound is amplified by the body of the instrument. The length, thickness, and tension of the string all affect the pitch of the notes produced.

1 Moving a finger up the string shortens the length that vibrates, making the note higher.

2 Strings differ in thickness – thicker, heavier strings produce lower notes.

3 A tightened string vibrates more quickly, so the note it produces is higher.

Antonio Stradivari
Italian Antonio Stradivari (1644–1737) is perhaps the best-known and greatest violin-maker of all time. He learnt his craft in Italy, placing his own label on a violin for the first time in 1666. The violins and cellos he made between 1700 and 1715 are considered the finest in the world, and some are still being played.

Instrument-making

In the history of music, the instrument-makers are as important as the performers and composers. Instrument-making takes years to master and combines art, craft, and science. Makers continually improve the sound of instruments, while Bartolomeo Cristofori (1655–1731), who invented the piano, and Adolphe Sax (1814–94), inventor of the saxophone, added new sounds to music.

Carving the body

Keyboard instruments

The keyboards are the most versatile of instruments, because they are capable of playing many notes at the same time. Pressing a key activates a mechanism inside the instrument. In the harpsichord, this plucks a string; in the piano, a felt-covered hammer strikes the string. In an organ, the keyboard action sends air passing through sets of pipes.

Harpsichord
The harpsichord and similar instruments, such as the spinet and virginal, were popular from the 15th to the 18th centuries, when musicians began to favour the newly-invented piano.

Spinet, 1550s

Organ
The organ is the largest musical instrument of all, and produces a wider range of sounds than any other instrument. It is mainly associated with church music, but is sometimes included in orchestral pieces.

Hundreds of pipes

Piano
This instrument is very expressive, producing a wide range of sound: players are able to draw notes out, cut them short, or make each note loud or soft. As a result, a great deal of solo music has been written for the piano. The grand piano has a rich, powerful tone and is used for concerts. Upright pianos are more convenient for most homes.

Metal frame, on which strings are stretched.

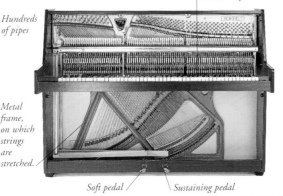
88-note keyboard

Soft pedal   *Sustaining pedal*

Making a violin
Months of effort go into shaping, finishing, and assembling a violin. Most of the work is by hand.

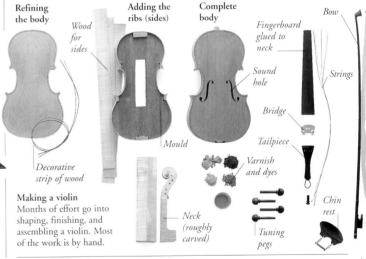

Refining the body

Wood for sides

Adding the ribs (sides)

Complete body

Mould

Decorative strip of wood

Neck (roughly carved)

Sound hole

Varnish and dyes

Fingerboard glued to neck

Bow

Strings

Bridge

Tailpiece

Tuning pegs

Chin rest

Electrical and electronic instruments
The first electronic instrument, the Ondes Martenot, had a keyboard, but could not play chords. More recent electronic keyboard instruments, such as the Hammond organ or the synthesizer, are more versatile, producing all kinds of unusual sounds. They often play alongside electrically amplified instruments, like the electric guitar.

Display panel

Synthesizer

FIND OUT MORE   BEETHOVEN, LUDWIG VAN   JAZZ   MOZART, WOLFGANG   MUSIC   OPERA   ORCHESTRA   RADIO   ROCK AND POP   SOUND

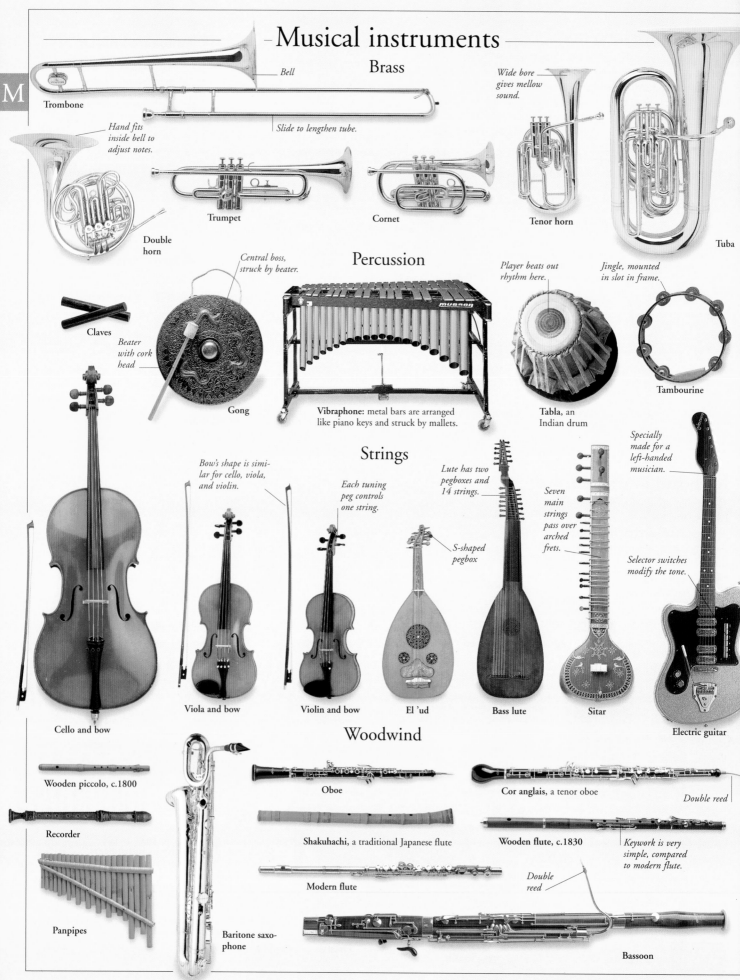

Musical instruments

Brass

Trombone

Bell

Slide to lengthen tube.

Hand fits inside bell to adjust notes.

Double horn

Trumpet

Cornet

Wide bore gives mellow sound.

Tenor horn

Tuba

Percussion

Claves

Central boss, struck by beater.

Beater with cork head

Gong

Vibraphone: metal bars are arranged like piano keys and struck by mallets.

Player beats out rhythm here.

Tabla, an Indian drum

Jingle, mounted in slot in frame.

Tambourine

Strings

Bow's shape is similar for cello, viola, and violin.

Each tuning peg controls one string.

S-shaped pegbox

Lute has two pegboxes and 14 strings.

Seven main strings pass over arched frets.

Specially made for a left-handed musician.

Selector switches modify the tone.

Cello and bow

Viola and bow

Violin and bow

El 'ud

Bass lute

Sitar

Electric guitar

Woodwind

Wooden piccolo, c.1800

Recorder

Panpipes

Baritone saxophone

Oboe

Shakuhachi, a traditional Japanese flute

Modern flute

Cor anglais, a tenor oboe

Wooden flute, c.1830

Double reed

Double reed

Keywork is very simple, compared to modern flute.

Bassoon

MYTHS AND LEGENDS

WHEREVER PEOPLE have lived together they have told stories to explain the mysteries of the universe: of creation and destruction, of how people and animals first came to be, of the characters of the gods and goddesses they worshipped. These tales are called myths, and, with their cast of heroes and monsters, explain how life works. Legends, too, are tales of adventure, but, unlike myths, are thought to have some basis in historical fact. Myths and legends are a record of how past peoples saw the world.

Navajo blanket

King Arthur

A scene from the film *Excalibur*

The legend of Arthur, king of the Britons, has endured for centuries. Films and books retell the story of the knights of the Round Table at Arthur's court in Camelot. The real Arthur was probably a Romano-British chief who fought against the Saxon invasion in the 6th century.

Navajo creation
In Navajo mythology, the maize (corn) plant often symbolizes a creation goddess. Many Navajo blankets, based on the design of sandpaintings, depict healing ceremonies involving the sacred plant.

Ra
The sun god Ra, or Re, was the creator god of ancient Egypt. Ra created all the other gods, and when he cried, his tears became humans. In ancient Egyptian mythology, Ra's granddaughter, the sky goddess Nut, swallows Ra every night, and gives birth to him each morning, creating a new day. During the night, Ra fights the evil serpent Apep. Ancient Egyptians believed that if Apep succeeded in devouring Ra, the world would end.

Beginnings

In every culture from Asia to the Americas, creation myths exist to explain how the world began, and how the first people came to exist. In Norse mythology, the creator god Odin made the earth from a giant's flesh, and the sky from his skull. One of the Aztec creator gods, Quetzalcoatl, also known as the plumed serpent god, made heaven and earth from the body of a serpent.

Yang

Yin-Yang symbol

Yin

P'an-ku
A Chinese myth tells of a cosmic egg formed at the start of time. When the egg hatched, P'an-ku emerged as the first being. He filled the space between the two opposing forces of Yin, which represents the heavens, and Yang, which represents the earth. When P'an-ku died, his eyes became the sun and the moon, his tears became seas, and his fleas became humans.

Legendary animals and plants

Animals and plants play a major role in world legend. Mythical animals include the dragon, the unicorn, and the phoenix, all endowed with special powers. The phoenix, for example, was believed to bring prosperity whenever it appeared, and bad luck whenever it departed.

14th-century imperial seal

Dragon
The Chinese dragon represented wisdom and goodness, and is still a symbol of good fortune today.

Yeti
For centuries, people have searched for the yeti – an ape-man believed to dwell in the Himalayas.

Amaterasu
When Amaterasu, the Japanese sun goddess, was frightened by her brother, Susanowo, the storm god, she hid in a cave. Consequently, heaven and earth were plunged into darkness, and the crops died. The other gods placed a mirror by the cave entrance and lured Amaterasu out with her own reflection, restoring light to the world.

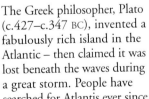

Fairies
Between 1917 and 1920, two English schoolgirls in Cottingley, England, took a series of photographs, which they claimed were of fairies. Experts believed that the photographs were genuine for many years, until, in later life, the girls confessed that the images were faked.

Mandrake
In medieval times, mandrake was attributed with magical powers. Its roots were thought to resemble human legs, and it was said to scream when uprooted; those people who heard it went insane.

Atlantis

The Greek philosopher, Plato (c.427–c.347 BC), invented a fabulously rich island in the Atlantic – then claimed it was lost beneath the waves during a great storm. People have searched for Atlantis ever since.

Urban myths and legends

In 1935, the *New York Times* reported that an alligator had been found in the city's sewers. Since then, rumours have spread of a colony of giant white alligators living under New York. The tale of the Vanishing Hitch-hiker, told throughout Europe and America, is an example of an old legend adapted to suit modern times. The 19th-century version tells of a traveller who mysteriously disappears during a journey in a horse-drawn carriage; in the modern version, the traveller is a hitch-hiker, and the vehicle is a car.

FIND OUT MORE • EGYPT, ANCIENT • GODS AND GODDESSES • LITERATURE • RELIGIONS • WITCHES AND WITCHCRAFT

NAPOLEON BONAPARTE

BETWEEN 1799 AND 1815, one man dominated Europe. Napoleon Bonaparte was a brilliant military leader who led the French armies to a string of victories over every major European power. As emperor of France, he was also a fine administrator, transforming the government of France and setting up a legal system that survives in Europe to this day. However, he was a controversial figure, because he overturned many of the gains of the French Revolution and ruled his empire with as much authority and power as did the kings of France, whose rule the revolution had ended.

Early life
Napoleon was born in 1769 on the island of Corsica. He had a military education, joined the army in 1785, and won acclaim when he seized the port of Toulon from the British in 1793.

Napoleon's army in Egypt

Bonaparte in Egypt
Napoleon was promoted for his role at Toulon. He defeated the Austrians in Italy in 1797 and the following year set out for Egypt, on the way to invade India and crush the British empire. He was fascinated by Egypt and took scholars with him to study its ancient civilization.

Emperor
In 1804, Napoleon extended his power by crowning himself Emperor of the French in front of the Pope. As ruler of France, he introduced many reforms. He centralized the state's administration, set up a national school curriculum, and in 1801 made peace with the Roman Catholic Church, which had opposed his rule.

The Napoleonic Code
Napoleon introduced a new legal code in 1804 which was based on the principles of the French Revolution. The code protected property rights, established the equality of all people before the law, and allowed freedom of worship. It was carried throughout Europe by French armies, and remains the basis of many European legal systems today.

Court scene from the time of Napoleon

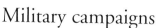

18 Brumaire
Napoleon's rise to power came in several stages. In a coup on 9 November, 1799, known by its revolutionary calendar date of 18 Brumaire, the ineffectual Directoire, or committee, governing France was overthrown. Napoleon was one of the three Consuls who were appointed in its place to govern the country. In 1802, he was made First Consul for life.

Military campaigns
Napoleon was one of the most brilliant military commanders of all time. He could march his armies speedily across Europe and defeat much larger forces. He had notable victories over Austria, Germany, and Spain, but he was defeated in Russia, because of the strength of Russian resistance and the hard Russian winter.

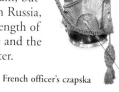

French officer's czapska   *Napoleon's monogram*

Napoleon at the head of his Great Army

Invasion of Britain
France ruled mainland Europe, but the British navy ruled the seas. In 1803, Napoleon built up his army to invade Britain, but he needed control of the sea. In 1805, a British fleet led by Nelson defeated a Franco-Spanish fleet at Trafalgar, ending all invasion plans.

Napoleon hoped to invade England in balloons.

Joséphine
Napoleon married Joséphine de Beauharnais (1763–1814) in 1796, captivated by her beauty and wit. Her previous marriage had ended in 1794 when her husband was beheaded during the revolution. She already had two children, but when she failed to produce an heir for Napoleon, the emperor divorced her in 1809. Josephine died in retirement.

Napoleon in exile
After his defeat in Russia in 1812, Napoleon gradually lost control of his empire. In 1814, he abdicated the throne and retired to the Mediterranean island of Elba. But he soon left Elba, leading the French army to final defeat at Waterloo in June 1815. He was then exiled to the South Atlantic island of St. Helena, where he died in 1821.

NAPOLEON BONAPARTE

1769 Born in Ajaccio, Corsica.

1785 Joins the army.

1795 Becomes commander of the army of the interior.

1796 Marries Joséphine.

1799 Overthrows the Directoire and becomes First Consul.

1802 Made First Consul for life.

1804 Crowns himself emperor; introduces Napoleonic Code.

1809 Divorces Josephine.

1814 Abdicates and retires to Elba.

1815 Defeated at Waterloo; exiled to St. Helena.

1821 Dies on St. Helena.

FIND OUT MORE FRANCE, HISTORY OF   FRENCH REVOLUTION   HOLY ROMAN EMPIRE   NAPOLEONIC WARS

NAPOLEONIC WARS

BETWEEN 1797 AND 1815, a series of wars engulfed Europe. Known as the Napoleonic Wars, after Napoleon Bonaparte, they involved France on one side, and the old kingdoms of Austria, Prussia, Britain, and Russia on the other. France had been at war since 1792, when its armies fought in support of the Revolution. However, wars of defence became wars of conquest as Napoleon extended the boundaries of France to create an empire. By 1808, Napoleon's armies controlled most of western Europe and seemed unbeatable. British supremacy at sea, Napoleon's disastrous Russian campaign, and a general European uprising turned the tide, and, by 1815, combined European forces had finally defeated Napoleon.

Battles and campaigns
After his major victories against the Austrians (in 1800 and 1805), the Prussians (in 1806), and the Russians (in 1807), Napoleon's empire was the largest in Europe since the fall of Rome.

Trafalgar
The victory of Lord Nelson's navy over Napoleon's fleet at Trafalgar (1805) ensured British supremacy at sea. Napoleon was unable to blockade British goods, so supplies reached allied forces in occupied areas.

Napoleon's armies
The French armies were the largest and most powerful in Europe. Most of the soldiers were conscripts (young men forced to fight), either from France or from occupied countries. Between 1803 and 1815, some two million men were conscripted, and Napoleon regularly commanded forces of 250,000. Napoleon's army was divided into semi-independent corps. Soldiers moved fast and, in battle, fought in massed ranks that broke the enemy lines.

Weapons
Soldiers were constantly drilled, or trained, in the use of their weapons. Drills helped combat nerves, avoid accidents, and taught the men to load and fire very quickly. Speedy reloading often made the difference between winning or losing a battle. The most common gun in the French infantry was the musket, and movable muzzle-loader (front-loading cannon) were used by both sides.

Medicine and food
Napoleon's soldiers lived off the land, finding or stealing whatever food they needed. Medical treatment was primitive; casualties were high. In the Battle of Borodino (1812), Napoleon lost some 30,000 men.

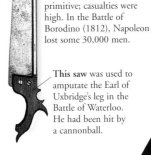

This saw was used to amputate the Earl of Uxbridge's leg in the Battle of Waterloo. He had been hit by a cannonball.

1777-pattern Charleville musket

Muzzle-loader

French corporal's uniform

Shako plate with imperial eagle and regiment number

Chevron for five years of good conduct

Corporal's stripes

Loose-fitting trousers over close-fitting knee breeches

Short sword

Brass buckles

Studs helped shoes last longer.

Russian campaign of 1812
When Napoleon and 500,000 men invaded Russia, the Russians drew them deeper into the country by retreating, burning food and shelter as they went. The French reached Moscow, but, far from supplies in the harsh winter, thousands starved or froze to death.

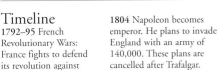

Battle of Waterloo
The last major battle of the war took place in 1815 at Waterloo, Belgium. Combined Prussian forces under Blücher, and British forces under Wellington, defeated Napoleon for the last time. This victory led to a period of stability in Europe.

Timeline
1792–95 French Revolutionary Wars: France fights to defend its revolution against the hostility of other European nations.

1800 Battle of Marengo results in victory for the French.

1804 Napoleon becomes emperor. He plans to invade England with an army of 140,000. These plans are cancelled after Trafalgar.

1805–9 Napoleon's victories include Auerstädt, Austerlitz, Friedland, Jena, and Wagram. He now controls most of Europe.

1808–14 Peninsular War. British forces combine with Spanish guerillas to fight against France in Spain and Portugal, finally driving the French forces out of Spain.

1813–14 Wars of Liberation. Austria, Prussia, and Russia defeat France at the "Battle of Nations" in Leipzig.

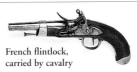

French flintlock, carried by cavalry

1814 Allied forces enter France. Napoleon exiled to Elba.

1815 Napoleon returns briefly, but is defeated at Waterloo.

Uniforms
Morale and efficiency were crucial for success in war. Stylish uniforms made both French and English soldiers proud to be in the army, and taking care of them properly taught the men discipline and obedience. This training helped the soldier to carry out orders instinctively in the heat of battle.

| FIND OUT MORE | ARMIES | FRANCE, HISTORY OF | FRENCH REVOLUTION | NAPOLEON BONAPARTE | WARFARE |

NATIVE AMERICANS

PEOPLE FIRST ARRIVED in North America more than 30,000 years ago, when they crossed an Ice Age land bridge that joined Siberia and Alaska. They lived a peaceful existence until Europeans arrived. These new settlers gradually displaced the Native Americans from their homelands and confined them to reservations, where some still live today, upholding their traditions.

Tribes of North America

The climate and local resources shaped the way Native Americans lived. When the Europeans arrived in the 17th century many tribes lived in the northeast, along the Atlantic coast and fertile shores of the Great Lakes. In the arid southwest, farmers lived in villages, or pueblos. The tribes of the Great Plains were nomadic until Spanish settlers arrived.

Southwest
California
Mississipian
Great Basin
Plains
Northeast
Iroquois
Plateau
Northwest coast
Arctic
Subarctic

Cultural areas of Native Americans

Homes

Native American homes were designed to provide shelter from a range of climates, from the frozen Arctic to the hot and arid southwest. The homes were often built by women, and made from locally available materials such as ice, snow, wood, grasses, and animal hides. Some buildings accommodated only one family. Others were built for large groups.

Longhouse

The Iroquois built impressive longhouses of timber and bark, which could reach up to 60m (200 ft) in length. They accommodated up to 20 families, who lived in separate compartments along the sides. Shared cooking fires were placed in the central aisle.

Elm-bark covering

Maize (corn) is left to dry on storage racks in the roof rafters.

Frame made from wooden poles.

Families shared cooking fires set at intervals along the length of the longhouse. Smoke escaped through the roof.

Igloos

Blocks of snow compressed into ice.

Between October and May, the Inuit of the central Arctic lived in igloos. These could be built in a few hours, and were made of blocks of compressed snow, cut with antler or bone knives, and built up in a dome-shaped spiral. A fire was kept alight inside for cooking, and keeping warm.

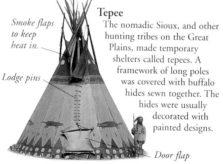

Smoke flaps to keep heat in.

Tepee

The nomadic Sioux, and other hunting tribes on the Great Plains, made temporary shelters called tepees. A framework of long poles was covered with buffalo hides sewn together. The hides were usually decorated with painted designs.

Lodge pins

Door flap

Crazy Horse

Crazy Horse (c.1842–77) was the Sioux chief of the Oglala tribe. He fought against settlers' invasion of the Great Plains, and led his people against US government plans to build roads through their territories in Montana. He waged constant warfare on the US army until he finally surrendered in 1877. He was imprisoned, and was killed trying to escape.

Domestic life

Most American tribes lived in small villages, securely defended by a wooden fence. They grew crops such as corn, squash, pumpkins, and tobacco in well-kept gardens.

Axe

Arrows

Hunting weapons

Native Americans revered the animals they hunted, and there were many rituals associated with the hunt. As well as meat, animals provided hide, hair, horns, and bone, which were used for clothing, ornaments, utensils, and weapons.

Women

In most tribes women worked much harder than men. They made the clothes and looked after the children and the home. They also prepared food, tended crops, or – if they belonged to hunting tribes – butchered meat.

Bow   *Spear-thrower*

Modern Native Americans

As Europeans moved west during the 19th century, tribes were forced into reservations. Between 1860 and 1890, resistance to resettlement led to the Indian Wars, but the new settlers overwhelmed the native people. Recently Native American culture, language, and history, long suppressed by the government, have been undergoing a revival.

City life

Between 1950 and 1970, the US government tried to relocate Native American Indians into cities, but many found it difficult to adjust. In the 1980s, the Native Americans opened gambling casinos, creating new jobs.

Reservation life

From the 19th century, the US government tried to enforce a pass system that kept Native Americans confined to reservations. In the 1970s, legal groups helped Indians regain their lost lands, and today about 1.5 million Indians live on reservations that they govern themselves.

FIND OUT MORE   CANADA   CANADA, HISTORY OF   COLUMBUS, CHRISTOPHER   GERONIMO   HOUSES AND HOMES   INCAS   NORTH AMERICA, HISTORY OF   SOCIETIES, HUMAN   WEAPONS

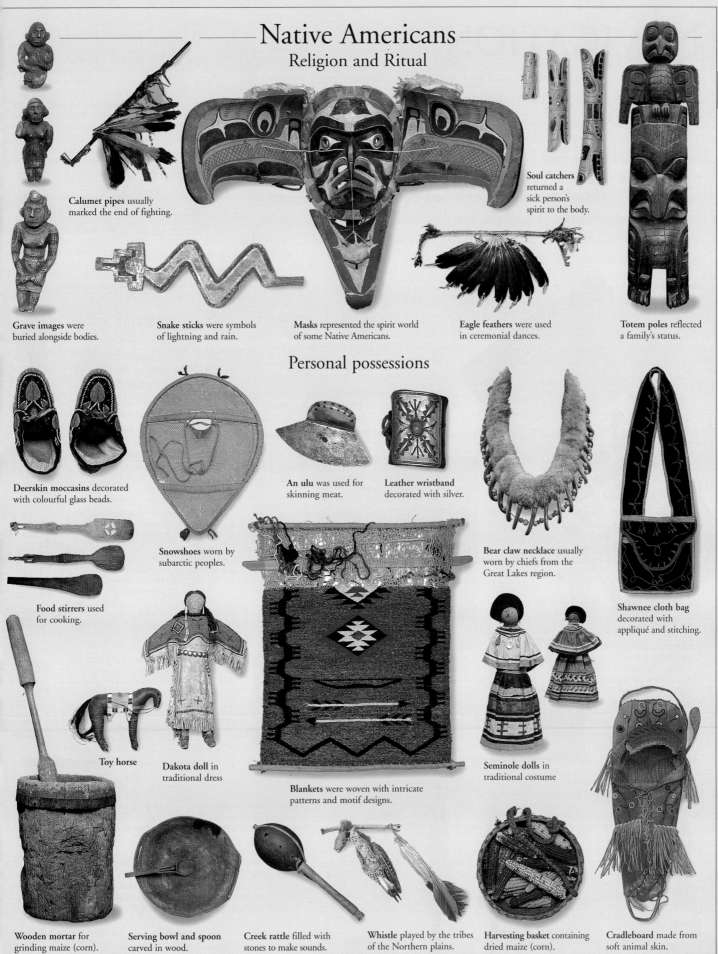

Native Americans

Religion and Ritual

Calumet pipes usually marked the end of fighting.

Soul catchers returned a sick person's spirit to the body.

Grave images were buried alongside bodies.

Snake sticks were symbols of lightning and rain.

Masks represented the spirit world of some Native Americans.

Eagle feathers were used in ceremonial dances.

Totem poles reflected a family's status.

Personal possessions

Deerskin moccasins decorated with colourful glass beads.

An ulu was used for skinning meat.

Leather wristband decorated with silver.

Snowshoes worn by subarctic peoples.

Bear claw necklace usually worn by chiefs from the Great Lakes region.

Shawnee cloth bag decorated with appliqué and stitching.

Food stirrers used for cooking.

Toy horse

Dakota doll in traditional dress

Blankets were woven with intricate patterns and motif designs.

Seminole dolls in traditional costume

Wooden mortar for grinding maize (corn).

Serving bowl and spoon carved in wood.

Creek rattle filled with stones to make sounds.

Whistle played by the tribes of the Northern plains.

Harvesting basket containing dried maize (corn).

Cradleboard made from soft animal skin.

NAVIGATION

WHEN YOU WALK, CYCLE, OR DRIVE from one place to another, you plan your route first, and keep checking you are on course until you arrive at your destination. This process is called navigation. Unless you know the way, you will also need navigational aids, such as maps and a compass. Accurate navigation is especially important at sea or in the air when no landmarks are visible. The first, simple navigational aids, such as lighthouses, allowed early mariners to leave inland waters and navigate their way safely across the oceans.

Lines of longitude

Lines of latitude

Latitude and longitude
Maps and charts often show lines of latitude and longitude, imaginary lines criss-crossing the Earth's surface. Navigators use them to help locate their position and to chart their route. Latitude is a north-south division, drawn parallel to the Equator: longitude is an east-west division, drawn from pole to pole.

Maps and charts
A map is like a picture of the ground, drawn from above. It shows features on the ground, such as buildings and hills. To navigate, these can be matched up with the features on the ground; positions are checked using the lines of latitude and longitude. Charts are more detailed maps, specifically for navigating at sea or in the air.

Map showing landscape detail

Electronic navigation

Modern navigational aids use complex electronics and are very accurate. They detect radio signals sent from fixed radio beacons, and use them to work out the receiver's position. The most common and effective equipment is the Global Positioning System (GPS). This detects signals from a network of satellites or space craft rather than from Earth-bound beacons.

Rotating antennae picks up satellite signals.

Display screen

Different channels

GPS receiver calculates the distance between the satellite and receiver to provide the location of the receiver.

Global Positioning System receiver

The air traffic control radar scan at Heathrow Airport, UK, shows the position of all the aircraft in the area.

Navigational aids

For centuries, travellers have used navigational aids. The sextant, which measures the angle between two objects in the sky, such as stars or the Sun, is still used by modern navigators.

Modern sextant

Sight

Magnetic compasses
Because the Earth acts like a huge magnet, a pivotal magnetized compass needle will line up with the Earth's magnetic north and south poles.

Objects are lined up with the "sight" on a hand-bearing compass.

Gyrocompasses
A gyroscope is a device which remains stable while spinning. The gyrocompass needle stays steady, even if it is tilted, making it ideal for accurate navigation.

Gyrocompass

Automatic navigation
Many aircraft have an automatic, computerized navigation system. It consists of a GPS receiver and computerized maps. The aircraft's steering is automatically adjusted to maintain the craft on the correct course. Ships operate with similar systems.

Radar and sonar
Distant objects are located with radar (radio detection and ranging) and sonar (sound navigation ranging). Radar bounces radio waves off objects and detects the reflected waves. Sonar locates underwater objects with sound and echo waves.

LOWRANCE

Sonar fish finder

Log line

Logs
A log consists of an under-water propeller, or rotator, which spins faster as the ship increases speed. A register counts the number of spins, giving the distance travelled.

The govenor transmits spins to log line.

Register

Rotator

Lights and buoys

At sea, a system of visual aids helps vessels navigate safely. Lighthouses and lightships send out a unique pattern of flashing signals. Buoys are floating markers. Their shape and colour indicate different hazards, such as the edge of a shipping lane or sandbanks.

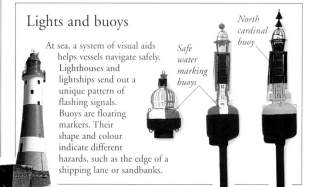

North cardinal buoy

Safe water marking buoys

Timeline

11th century Chinese mariners use simple compasses.

14th century The Portuguese develop the astrolabe. Using the Sun and stars, it helps locate a position on Earth.

1569 Flemish geographer Gerardus Mercator (1512–94) publishes the first world map. Mariners use it to navigate.

1762 British inventor John Harrison (1693–1776) wins a prize for building a chronometer, a mariner's clock. This accurately calculates longitude for the first time.

1930s Scottish scientist Robert Watson-Watt (1892–1973) develops the first practical radar system. Radar is used extensively in World War II.

1934 In England, Percy Shaw (1890–1976) nearly drives his car off the road in foggy conditions. He invents cat's eyes – reflecting lights placed in the road to help motorists navigate safely in poor visibility.

FIND OUT MORE ASTRONOMY MAGNETISM MAPS AND MAPPING RADAR AND SONAR

NESTS AND BURROWS

SOME ANIMALS SPEND ALL THEIR LIFE in the open and are always on the move. Others are more like humans. They build homes and use them to shelter from bad weather, and also to bring up their young. Animals make two main types of home – nests or burrows. Most birds collect building materials and then carefully shape them into a nest. Some fish behave in a similar way. Mammals and insects also make nests, but many of them burrow into the ground instead. A burrow keeps them warm and safe from most of their enemies.

Pied wagtail's nest

Birds' nests

The smallest bird nests can fit into an egg-cup; the biggest weigh more than a tonne. Many birds use twigs, sticks, and leaves for the frame of their nests, but some use mud mixed with saliva. This mixture is soft when wet, but turns hard when it dries.

Social weaver nest
Unlike other birds, social weavers from Africa join together to make giant communal nests. The nests are made of grass and can house several hundred pairs of breeding birds. The nests sometimes get so heavy that they bring down trees.

Each pair of social weavers has its own compartment in the nest.

Mud   Seed heads   Horsehair

Leaves   Twigs   Feathers

    Wool   Cattle hair

String   Metal foil   Moss

Baler twine   Paper   Lichen

Grass

Nest materials
This pied wagtail's nest contains several different kinds of material. Leaves and twigs help to create its shape; feathers, wool, and cattle hair keep it warm; moss and lichen help to disguise it from predators.

Fish homes

Most fish release their eggs directly into the water and do not play any part in raising their young. A few are more careful, and make nests to hold their eggs. Some adult fish make themselves a temporary "home" every night to help keep enemies at bay.

Streambed nest
Small freshwater fish called sticklebacks are skilled builders. The male builds a tunnel-shaped nest from the leaves and roots of water plants, and the female lays eggs inside. The male fertilizes the eggs, then guards the nest.

Nest of foam
A male paradise fish, from southern Asia, blows bubbles near the water's surface to make a floating nest of foam. The female releases her eggs below the foam so that they float upwards into the nest. The male guards the nest until the eggs hatch.

Overnight shelter
As night falls, a tropical parrot-fish hides away in a crevice in a coral reef and surrounds itself with a bag of transparent mucus. This slimy cocoon makes it more difficult for predators to attack the fish. In the morning, the fish wriggles out of the mucus.

Fish carries bits of water plant in its mouth.

Fish prods weeds into place with its snout.

Nest is sited beneath a small boulder.

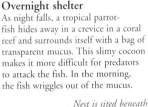

1 The male three-spined stickleback looks for a gravel-covered area of the streambed near waterplants. He excavates a shallow pit by fanning his fins and by sucking up pieces of grit in his mouth. He then starts to collect the building materials.

2 Leaves, roots, algae, and pieces of twig all help to make up the nest. The male collects them in his mouth and piles them up to form a small heap on the gravel base. When he has collected enough nesting material, he sets about gluing it together.

3 The male cements the nest material together using a sticky substance made by his kidneys. Once the nest is firm, he pushes his snout through it to make a tunnel. When the male has completed the nest, the female swims into the tunnel to lay her eggs.

Types of nest

The nests of some large birds, such as eagles and herons, are untidy piles of sticks. By contrast, the nests of many other birds are often carefully crafted.

Bag nest
This Baltimore oriole nest is made of cattle hair interwoven with string. The bird wound some string around a twig for support.

Basket nest
A reed warbler's nest is slung between the stems of reed plants.

Cup nest
The songthrush's nest has an outer cup of twigs and grass and a mud lining. It will last, even in rain, for many months.

Insect homes

In the insect world, females often work on their own to build nests for their young. Social insects, which include bees, wasps, ants, and termites, are different because they work together in family groups. Some social insect nests are like miniature cities, complete with their own ventilation systems and stores of food.

Stenogaster *wasp nest*

Working alone

Stenogaster wasps, from Southeast Asia, make nests out of mud. Each nest is built by a single female and contains just enough room for two or three wasp grubs. The female brings food to the grubs and seals up the nest when they are ready to pupate.

Leaf miners

Some moth caterpillars are so small that they can live inside a leaf. As a caterpillar munches its way through a leaf, it leaves a crooked transparent trail called a leaf mine. The mine gets steadily wider as the caterpillar grows bigger.

Leaf miner's trail in a blackberry leaf

Mammal nests and burrows

Some mammals make nests above ground; others dig burrows beneath the surface. The burrows often contain special nursery and sleeping quarters, which are lined with dry grass and leaves. Most burrowing mammals come to the surface to feed, but some find everything they need underground.

Earth mound indicates burrow

Naked mole rat's burrow

This African rodent lives in family groups containing about 40 members. The queen produces young, while the others dig tunnels with their front teeth to find food.

Drey is in the fork of a tree.

Mole burrow

Moles spend almost all their life underground. They sleep and give birth in a special chamber, and collect food in hunting tunnels that run parallel to the surface. Insect grubs and earthworms drop into these tunnels from the soil, and the moles find them by smell and touch.

Squirrel drey

Small mammals, such as the grey squirrel, lose heat easily, and they often build nests in which to shelter from the worst of the winter weather. A squirrel's nest, or drey, looks like a ball of sticks wedged in high branches. A lining of leaves keeps out the wind.

Dormouse's winter nest made of dry bracken and grass

Dormouse burrow

In summer, the common dormouse builds a small nest out of grass. In autumn, it makes a bigger nest with thicker walls for hibernating. When the nest is ready, the dormouse climbs in, rolls into a ball, and begins its long winter sleep.

Woodmouse burrow

A woodmouse's burrow is less than 2 cm (0.75 in) across. It is small enough to keep out most predators, but it is not totally safe: one predator – the least weasel – can slip inside.

Working together

1 Common wasps build their nests with a kind of paper made from wood fibres. The queen begins the nest. She builds walls around a group of cells containing one egg each.

Common wasp starting her nest

2 When the grubs hatch, the queen brings back food for them. Meanwhile, she starts to expand the nest by adding more layers, in this case made of white wood fibres.

Queen chews wood fibres and mixes them with saliva to make the paper.

New layers are built down and around older layers

3 The nest is now surrounded by several layers of paper. Paper is a good insulator, so the interior of the nest is warmer than the air outside. This helps the grubs to develop.

Small entrance hole helps to keep the nest warm.

4 When the first batch of grubs have become adult wasps, they join in the building work. They tear down the old inside walls and add new ones on the outside. The queen lays more eggs.

Worker dismantles inner walls.

5 By midsummer, the nest may be as big as a football and home to hundreds of wasps. The workers all die in late autumn, but young queens survive to make new nests the following spring.

Multi-coloured walls produced by different kinds of wood

Worker ants return with pieces of leaf.

Fungus gardens

Leafcutter ants

In Central and South America, leafcutter ants work together to make a nest underground. A large nest may be several metres across. The ants slice pieces off leaves and carry them back to the nest. In the nest, they chop up the leaves into small fragments and use them to grow a special fungus that they eat. These ants have made a nest in a glass tank so the fungus can be seen.

FIND OUT MORE   ANIMAL BEHAVIOUR   ANTS AND TERMITES   BEES AND WASPS   BIRDS   FISH   HEDGEHOGS AND OTHER INSECTIVORES   HOUSES AND HOMES   INSECTS

NETHERLANDS

ALSO CALLED HOLLAND, the Netherlands straddles the deltas of five major rivers in northwest Europe. The Dutch people say they created their own country because they have reclaimed about one-third of the land from sea or marshland by enclosing the area with earth barriers, or dikes, and draining the water from it. Despite being one of the most densely populated countries in the world, the Netherlands enjoys high living standards. Amsterdam is the official capital, although the government is based at The Hague.

N

Physical features

The Netherlands is mainly flat, with 27 per cent of the land below sea level, and protected from the sea by natural sand dunes along the coast, and by artificial dikes. Wide sandy plains cover most of the rest of the country, falling into a few, low hills in the eastern and southern parts of the country.

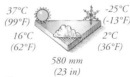

Canals
The Netherlands is a land of canals, which drain the land and serve as waterways for the movement of people and freight. Amsterdam alone has more than 100 canals.

Windmills
For centuries the Dutch landscape was dotted with 10,000 windmills, which powered pumps to drain water from the land. Electric pumps now do this work in the battle to keep the sea back.

37°C (99°F)   -25°C (-13°F)
16°C (62°F)   2°C (36°F)
580 mm (23 in)

Climate
The Netherlands has mild, rainy winters and cool summers. In winter northerly gales lash the coast, damaging dikes and threatening floods. Frosts sometimes freeze canals.

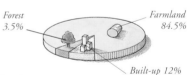

Forest 3.5%   Farmland 84.5%
Built-up 12%

Land use
Almost one-third of the land has been reclaimed from the sea. These areas are known as polders and are extremely fertile. The country has large natural gas reserves in the north, and there is some offshore oil drilling in the North Sea.

Amsterdam
The Dutch capital is built on 70 islands, linked by about 500 bridges, which span its many canals. The best way to get around is by bicycle, and around 750,000 people cycle to school or work each day. Today, Amsterdam is a busy centre for tourism and diamond trading.

One of Amsterdam's many canals

People
The Dutch see their society as the most tolerant in Europe, with relaxed laws on sexuality, drugs, and euthanasia. The country has a long history of welcoming immigrants, often from former Dutch colonies. Most of these people are now assimilated as Dutch citizens. However, members of the small Turkish community, which makes up just one per cent of the population, do not enjoy full citizenship.

Street scene, Amsterdam

466 per sq km (1,206 per sq mile)

89% Urban   11% Rural

Farming and industry
The Dutch economy is one of the most successful in Europe. Most imports and exports travel through Rotterdam, the world's biggest port. In addition to high-tech sectors such as electronics, telecommunications, and chemicals, the Netherlands has a successful agricultural industry. Productivity is high, and products such as vegetables, cheese, meat, and cut flowers are significant export earners.

Dutch tulips

FIND OUT MORE   DAMS   EMPIRES   EUROPE   EUROPE, HISTORY OF   EUROPEAN UNION   FARMING   NETHERLANDS, HISTORY OF   PORTS AND WATERWAYS

NETHERLANDS, HISTORY OF

THROUGHOUT THEIR HISTORY, the Dutch have been influenced by the sea. At first, they had to reclaim their low-lying land from beneath the North Sea and protect it from flooding. Then they used their maritime skills to create a rich, worldwide trading empire. In the 16th and 17th centuries, cities such as Amsterdam and Rotterdam prospered on the spice trade with the East, and merchants patronized the arts and sciences. Despite a decline during the 18th century, the Netherlands has kept its close relationship with the sea to this day.

Windmill on reclaimed land

Sea

Dutch water engineering
During the 13th century, the Dutch began to reclaim land from the North Sea by building a series of dykes and drainage canals. Dutch engineers became so good at designing drainage schemes that their skills were in demand throughout Europe.

William the Silent
Prince William (1533–84) came from Orange, in southern France, but was a major landowner in the Netherlands and resented Spanish rule. In 1576, he became leader of the Dutch United Provinces and proved to be a superb general. He was assassinated before the Dutch won their independence.

William of Orange leading the revolt

Revolt against Spain

In 1556, the Netherlands became part of the Spanish branch of the Habsburg Empire. The Protestant Dutch resented being ruled by Catholic Spain. A revolt broke out and in 1581 the seven northern provinces declared independence from Spain. After a long and bloody war, a truce was announced in 1609. Independence from Spain was finally agreed in 1648.

Detail from The Night Watch, *by Rembrandt*

Golden Age

Freed from Spanish rule, the Dutch state became wealthy. Merchants grew rich on overseas trade, while skilled Jewish and Protestant refugees flooded in, fleeing persecution in Catholic Europe. The openness of Dutch society encouraged a free exchange of ideas. Science flourished and painters such as Vermeer and Rembrandt produced masterpieces for the rich middle classes.

Dutch wars
As the leading maritime trading nation in Europe, the Dutch had to fight to protect their wealth. Commercial rivalry, first with England and then France in the late 17th century, led to wars, that weakened Dutch power.

Tomb of Michiel de Ruyter, admiral killed in French wars

Wealth of empire
The Dutch merchants grew rich on the trade with the East. Although some were based in the capital of the Dutch eastern empire, Batavia (now Jakarta, Indonesia), most built large houses for themselves in Amsterdam. These houses had to be lightweight in construction, because they were sited on unstable, reclaimed land next to the city's canals. They were, therefore, built of light materials such as brick or sandstone, with large windows.

Dutch empire

In the late 1500s, Dutch merchants sailed into the Indian Ocean in search of spices from Asia. In 1602, the Dutch East India Company was set up to exploit this trade. Trading posts were set up in India, China, Japan, and what is now Indonesia. By 1650, the Dutch ruled a vast empire in eastern Asia.

Spice trade
Spices such as pepper, cloves, and nutmeg fetched huge prices in the 16th and 17th centuries. The Dutch defeated the Portuguese and the British to control the spice trade with Europe. They set up an empire in southeast Asia, where they also grew crops such as coffee.

Nutmeg

Fresh peppers

Dried pepper

20th century
The Netherlands was neutral in World War I but was invaded and occupied by Germany from 1940–45. Since World War II, the Dutch have created one of the most successful economies in Europe. During the government of the Social Democratic Party, a welfare state was introduced. The Netherlands is a keen supporter of closer integration within the European Union.

Timeline
1300–1400s Netherlands is part of Burgundy.

1477 Netherlands becomes part of the Habsburg empire.

1555 In the partition of the empire, Netherlands is ruled by Spain.

1568 Revolt against Spanish rule begins.

1579 Seven northern provinces unite in the Union of Utrecht.

1581 The United Provinces declare their independence from their Spanish rulers.

1648 The Treaty of Westphalia recognizes Dutch independence from Spain.

1830 Belgium, its Catholic citizens resenting Protestant rule, at last gains its independence from the northern Netherlands.

1940–45 Netherlands occupied by Germany.

1949 Dutch colony of Indonesia obtains its independence.

1957 Netherlands is a founder member of the European Community (now known as Union).

FIND OUT MORE

ART, HISTORY OF   ASIA, HISTORY OF   EUROPE, HISTORY OF   HOLY ROMAN EMPIRE   SPAIN, HISTORY OF   WORLD WAR II

NEWSPAPERS AND MAGAZINES

NEWSPAPERS PROVIDE PEOPLE with important sources of information on local and international affairs. They cover events in great detail, and are vital in shaping public opinion. They contain up-to-date articles on politics, current affairs, lifestyle, and sport, together with advertising and comic strips. Magazines come out less frequently, and are less concerned with the latest news. They cost more than newspapers, and often use colourful designs.

Early writings
In ancient Rome, news sheets called *Acta Diurna* (Daily Events) were regularly posted up to give people news about gladiatorial contests and military successes. Another early newspaper was the *Dibao*, which was distributed to civil servants in Beijing, China, between 618 and 1911.

Types of newspapers
There are many kinds of newspapers. Some support political parties, while others try to remain independent. Some cover world news, while others report local news and events. Still others specialize in areas such as finance or sport. Newspapers can be daily or weekly publications.

Sports section

Finance section

Separate book review section

Tabloid size to vary the newspaper's style and format

Colour supplement magazine

Broadsheet size

Masthead

Leading photograph

Byline (journalist's name)

Columns for easy reading

Banner headline

Tabloids
Tabloids cover news events in brief, sensational, and often lurid detail. They attract their readers' interest by printing simple headlines in large type.

Broadsheets
Broadsheets cover important new topics and issues in far more extensive detail than the tabloids, and present a more sophisticated analysis.

Features of a paper
Modern newspapers cover many areas of public interest. Their front section is always devoted to the most important national and international current events, but they may also have separate sections on culture, sport, and finance. Sometimes they also include separate supplementary magazines.

New York Times
Founded in 1851 by Henry J Raymond, *The New York Times* is one of the world's most famous daily newspapers, and is sold globally. Renowned for the quality of its writing, and directed at a sophisticated audience, it covers a wide range of national and international interests in its separate sections.

William Randolph Hearst
William Hearst (1863–1951) was one of the most powerful press owners in the USA. He used sensational reporting, brash publicity, and aggressive headlines to achieve record sales. At one point, he owned 28 newspapers and lived in a castle in California.

Making a paper
Putting together a newspaper requires great efficiency. Reporters and photographers send in their copy (stories) and pictures. A sub-editor then fits them together accurately on the page. Advertising copy, a major source of revenue, is also placed. The pages are then printed and delivered to outlets by morning.

Paparazzi in action

Paparazzi
Pictures sell newspapers, and editors pay vast sums for controversial photographs. Some photographers, often known as paparazzi, go to any lengths to get exclusive photographs of famous people.

Newsroom
News comes into the newsroom from reporters and news agencies all over the world. Editors must quickly choose the most interesting or important stories for the paper to feature, and allocate staff to write and research them.

Inside a newsroom

Page layout on screen

Working on screen
Since the 1980s, editors and designers have assembled newspapers by adjusting text and pictures on computer screens. The pages are automatically sent to the printing presses.

Distribution
Newspapers need large circulations, so an efficient distribution system is required to sell copies. Often printing is carried out in several places at once to make it easier to transport the paper quickly to newsagents across the country.

News kiosk

N

Early magazines

Magazines are descended from cheap pamphlets, which were printed in the 1600s to publicize political or religious views. Magazines covering many kinds of interest became popular in the 1700s. Competition was fierce. In 1821, the editor of *The London Magazine*, a literary periodical, was killed by a rival in a duel.

Turn-of-the-century French magazine

Jazz magazine

Car magazine

Readership for this magazine is fairly specialized.

Magazines

The word magazine also means a storehouse, and all magazines are stores or collections of articles, published at regular intervals. Often a magazine's content does not date as quickly as that of newspapers. Also, magazines are generally printed on better paper. Modern magazines cover every imaginable subject and range from the most specialized scientific and trade journals, to more general lifestyle and fashion magazines that are read by millions.

Computer magazine

Women's lifestyle magazine

House-decorating magazine

Scientific magazine

Features

Features are the staple of many magazines. They vary greatly according to the type of magazine they are published in, but are usually articles that look at particular subjects in depth, often accompanied by photographs and illustrations. In a current affairs magazine, this may mean an analysis of an issue that is making news, or in a homes magazine it may look at how to use a particular colour or technique when decorating.

Article features colour blue for a strong image on page.

Design makes the subject matter attractive.

Feature has seasonal theme of Easter.

Special photography is commissioned to complement text.

Comics

Comic strips are a series of pictures that tell a story. They may be funny, exciting, or satirical. They first became popular in the 1890s, when American press owners put them in newspapers to attract readers. More than one-third of the world's population reads comics.

Superhero comics

Ever since the 1930s, one of the most popular and enduring forms of American comic has been the superhero strip. Superheroes have amazing powers and fight against threats to humanity. Batman was invented by Bob Kane in 1939, and the adventures have since been transferred to both film and television.

Early Batman comic

Advertising

Newspapers and magazines rely on advertising for income and to keep the publication's cost down. The higher the readership, the more a publication can charge for advertising. Specialist titles with small readerships are useful for targeting specific groups of people. Advertising ranges from the straightforward to subtle messages, using humour or strong visuals.

Advertisement page selling cars uses images and descriptions to sell its products.

Timeline

59 BC Handwritten newspapers first produced in Rome.

1615 First printed newspapers published in Germany.

1766 Sweden becomes the first country to guarantee freedom of the press.

American World War II magazine

1815 In Britain, *The Times* prints 5,000 copies daily.

1842 *The Illustrated London News* is the first publication to use extensive illustrations.

1854 First war reports on Crimean War for *The Times*.

1939 Batman cartoon published.

Arab newspaper

1989 The Tokyo *Yomiuri Shimbun* newspaper has a circulation of almost 15 million copies a day.

1990s Newspapers begin to publish online.

NEWTON, SIR ISAAC

THE BRITISH SCIENTIST and mathematician Isaac Newton was one of the greatest scientists of all time. A leader of scientific thought in England, he worked out how the universe was held together, discovered the secrets of light and colour, and invented calculus. Newton did most of this work on his own, without any help from assistants or colleagues. However, the great man had his weaknesses. His work was often affected by his furious temper and his inability to take criticism from other scientists. He also spent much of his time dabbling in alchemy (the attempt to turn base metals into gold), and it is thought that his poor health in later life was due to his testing substances by tasting them.

Early life

Isaac Newton was born in 1643 at Woolsthorpe, England. At school he was more interested in making mechanical devices than studying.

Newton's mathematics

At 18, Newton went to Cambridge, but, when the university was closed because of the plague, he went home to study. When he was in his late twenties, Newton invented a method of calculation which studied the rates at which quantities changed. He called this "fluxions"; today, it is known as calculus. The equations Newton developed are still used by mathematicians. As a result of this work, he was made Lucasian Professor of Mathematics at Cambridge when he was only 26.

One of Newton's mathematical manuscripts

Newton's optics

Newton studying the Sun's rays coming into the room through a hole in a screen

In 1665, Newton began to study the nature of light. After a series of experiments he was able to prove that white was made up of a rainbow-like spectrum of colours. He also tried to make a telescope, so that he could study the stars. He found that if he used two lenses, the images he saw through the telescope had coloured edges. To avoid this, he invented the reflecting telescope – a telescope that used a lens together with a curved mirror.

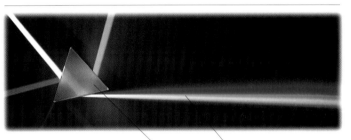

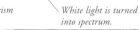

Prism   *White light is turned into spectrum.*

White light

Newton shone a beam of sunlight onto a prism. The light split into a spectrum of colours, which Newton projected onto a board. He then drilled a hole in the board where the red light fell, to make a red beam. When he placed another prism in the path of the red beam, the light changed direction but did not make a spectrum. Newton concluded that white light was made up of different colours.

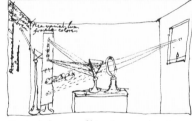

Newton's drawing of his prism experiment

Newton and gravity

Newton realized that every star and planet in the Universe exerts an attracting force – gravity – which pulls neighbouring bodies towards it. He saw that this force keeps the Moon in its orbit around the Earth, and that only the Moon's own movement prevented it from crashing into the Earth. The power of gravity is determined by the amount of matter that makes up the two bodies and the distance between them.

Principia Mathematica

In 1687, Newton published one of the most important science books ever written: *Philosophiae Naturalis Principia Mathematica* (The Mathematical Principles of Natural Philosophy). The book contains Newton's work on the laws of motion, theory of tides, and theory of gravitation. It was also the first book to contain a unified system explaining what happens on Earth and in the heavens.

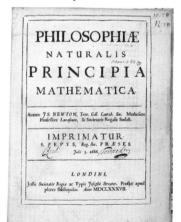

Title page of Newton's *Principia*

The Royal Society

In 1671, London's Royal Society asked to see the telescope that Newton had invented. They were so impressed that they elected him a fellow of the Society. He became president in 1703, and held this office until his death. In 1696, he became Warden of the Mint, and made various changes to British coins.

The original Royal Society building

ISAAC NEWTON

1643 Born in Woolsthorpe, England.

1661 Goes to Cambridge University.

1665 Returns home when the university is closed due to plague.

1665–66 Formulates his three Laws of Motion.

1687 *Principia Mathematica* published.

1672 Newton is elected a Fellow of the Royal Society.

1696 Becomes Warden of the Royal Mint, London.

1703 Becomes President of the Royal Society.

1704 Publishes *Opticks*.

1705 Newton is knighted.

1727 Dies in London.

FIND OUT MORE   GRAVITY   LIGHT   MATHEMATICS   MOON   PHYSICS   SCIENCE, HISTORY OF   SUN AND SOLAR SYSTEM   TELESCOPES

NEW ZEALAND

LYING MIDWAY between the South Pole and the Equator, and 1,600 km (990 miles) east of Australia, New Zealand consists of two main islands and a number of smaller islands. As a South Pacific nation, it has developed special ties with Australia, its closest neighbour, and has rapidly expanding trade links with other countries around the Pacific Rim. It is a member of the Commonwealth and the United Nations and was the first country to give women the vote.

Physical features

Both North and South Island have mountains, hills, fertile farmland, forests, and short, swift-flowing rivers that provide a valuable source of hydroelectric power. North Island is volcanically active.

South Island

The Southern Alps form a ridge along South Island. Amongst them is Aoraki (Mount Cook), New Zealand's highest point, at 3,754 m (12,316 ft). To the east are the fertile Canterbury Plains and rolling farmland. The southwest has lakes and glaciers and spectacular fjords.

North Island

New Zealand's North Island is a mixture of green meadows, forest, hot springs, and active volcanoes, such as Mount Ngauruhoe. Geothermal power is generated in this region. The northern peninsula has long, sandy beaches to the west, and islands and inlets to the east.

Climate

The climate in most of New Zealand is generally damp and temperate. However, summers in the far north are warm and subtropical, and winter can bring heavy snow to the Southern Alps. The weather is often changeable.

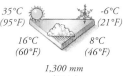

35°C (95°F)   -6°C (21°F)
16°C (60°F)   8°C (46°F)

1,300 mm (51 in)

Land use

New Zealand's rich pasture is its key resource, and sheep, wool, and dairy products are an important source of income. Energy resources are plentiful, and the country has reserves of coal, oil, gas, gold, and iron.

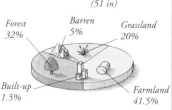

Forest 32%
Barren 5%
Grassland 20%
Built-up 1.5%
Farmland 41.5%

People

The people of New Zealand are ethnically and culturally mixed. About 77 per cent are of European origin, and Maoris, the original inhabitants, number about 12 per cent. In recent years there has also been an influx of non-Maori Polynesians and Melanesians. About three-quarters of the population live on North Island.

15 per sq km (38 per sq mile)
87% Urban   13% Rural

Young Maori woman from North Island

D   E   F   G
1   North Cape
Kaitaia
2   Whangarei   PACIFIC
                         OCEAN
Auckland   Coromandel
3   Bay of Plenty
Hamilton   Tauranga   East
                  Rotorua   Cape
A   B   C   North Island
4   Taupo
NEW   New Plymouth   Gisborne
ZEALAND   L. Taupo   Napier
5   Wanganui   Hastings
Tasman   Cook
Sea   Strait   Palmerston North
                 Nelson   Masterton
                                 WELLINGTON
Westport   Blenheim
6   PACIFIC
Greymouth   Kaikoura   OCEAN
South Island
                 Aoraki
7   (Mt. Cook)   Christchurch
                 3744m   Canterbury
                 Ashburton   Plains
                 Timaru   Canterbury Bight
Milford Sound
8   Queenstown   Hampden
     Lumsden
     Invercargill   Dunedin
     Foveaux Strait
9   Stewart I.

0 km   200
0 miles   200

Wellington

One of New Zealand's largest cities, Wellington has a population of about 346,500. It is a leading port, and lies at the heart of a manufacturing region. Notable buildings include Parliament House, known as the Beehive because of its shape, and St. Paul's Cathedral, which is built of timber.

The Beehive

Farming and industry

New Zealand is the world's largest exporter of coarse wool and butter, and also a chief producer of cheese and meat. The country has more than 50 million sheep, and its Canterbury lamb, named after the Canterbury Plains of South Island, is world famous. Cattle are also raised for their meat, hides, and milk. New Zealand's manufacturing industry has grown to include wool products, such as carpets and clothing, as well as electronic equipment. Apples, wine, and kiwi fruit are exported worldwide.

Herding sheep

FIND OUT MORE | AUSTRALASIA AND OCEANIA | EARTHQUAKES | MAORIS AND POLYNESIANS | NEW ZEALAND, HISTORY OF | PACIFIC OCEAN | POLYNESIA | UNITED NATIONS | VOLCANOES

NEW ZEALAND, HISTORY OF

IN ABOUT 1350, a fleet of Polynesians sailed across a huge expanse of ocean to settle in New Zealand, one of the last places on earth to be inhabited. They developed a warlike culture that was to remain undisturbed until European settlers arrived in the country in the 19th century. Within a few years, Europeans had taken over the islands, leaving the Maoris to fight for their lives and their land. New Zealand maintained close ties with Britain, but recently the nation has looked more to its Pacific island neighbours and to Asia for its trade and prosperity.

First inhabitants

The first people to settle in New Zealand were Polynesians, who crossed the Pacific Ocean in their wooden dug-out canoes in about AD 1000. They took with them sweet potatoes and other island crops, and added fish, game birds, and edible ferns to their diet after they arrived.

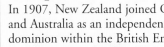

Maori chief's staff
Eyes made of haliotis shell
Decoration of parrot's feathers
Wooden shaft

Hollowed-out scoop for water

Carved wooden boat bailer

European settlement

After James Cook claimed New Zealand as a British colony in 1769, European traders and whalers regularly visited the islands. In 1840, the first permanent European settlement was founded at Wellington, North Island. All the settlers were colonists sent out from Britain by the New Zealand Company. Within a few years, British settlers outnumbered the Maoris.

Maori battle axe

Axe is made of green basalt stone.

Whalebone, the usual material for clubs

Abel Tasman

The first European to see New Zealand was the Dutch navigator Abel Tasman (1603–59), who sighted the North Island of New Zealand in 1642. He named the land after Zeeland, a province of the Netherlands.

Maori clubs

Carved wooden decoration

Signing the Treaty of Waitangi

Maori wars

After the Treaty of Waitangi between the British and the Maoris, there was growing Maori opposition to the increasing number of European settlers on their land. In 1860, conflict broke out between Maoris and settlers; it lasted until an uneasy peace was restored in 1870.

Treaty of Waitangi

On 6 February, 1840, the Maoris signed a treaty with the British government. The British agreed to protect Maori lands in return for the Maoris recognizing British sovereignty over their country. Today, 6 February is a national holiday in New Zealand.

Independent nation

In 1907, New Zealand joined Canada and Australia as an independent dominion within the British Empire. Britain continued to handle most of New Zealand's foreign affairs until 1947. Ties with Britain remained very close, and New Zealand troops fought on the Allied side in both world wars.

Welfare state

After a long period of economic depression, a Liberal government was elected in 1890. It created the world's first welfare state, introducing old-age pensions and other reforms. In 1893, New Zealand became the first country in the world to grant women the vote.

Modern New Zealand

Despite a history of economic hardship, reforms since 1984 have boosted the economy. In 1986 New Zealand signed the Treaty of Rarotonga, forming a nuclear-free area in the South Pacific. The 1998 Waitangi Tribunal ordered the return of confiscated ancestral homelands to the Maoris.

Apirana Ngata

Apirana Ngata (1874–1950) was a Maori lawyer who fought for Maori rights all his life. As secretary of the Young Maori political party, he tried to revive Maori society by introducing a public health service and modern farming methods. Ngata was an MP for nearly 40 years, and worked hard to improve the Maoris' standard of living.

Timeline

AD 1000 First Maoris settle in New Zealand.

1642 Dutch navigator Abel Tasman is first European to visit New Zealand.

1769 James Cook claims New Zealand for Britain.

1840 First permanent European settlement established in Wellington, North Island.

1840 Treaty of Waitangi establishes full British sovereignty over the country.

1852–56 New Zealand becomes self-governing.

1893 Women get the vote; other social reforms are introduced.

1907 New Zealand gains the status of an independent dominion.

1914–18 and 1939–45 New Zealand fights with the Allies in both world wars.

1995 The British crown apologizes for historical exploitation of Maori lands and signs Waikato Raupatu Claims Act.

FIND OUT MORE

AUSTRALIA, HISTORY OF

ECOLOGY AND ECOSYSTEMS

EXPLORATION

POLYNESIA

NIGHTINGALE, FLORENCE

N

IN THE 19TH CENTURY, nursing was not thought to be a respectable career for women. Most nurses were untrained and worked in appalling conditions. Attitudes were changed by the efforts of one woman – Florence Nightingale. As a nurse in the Crimean War, she experienced the terrible conditions suffered by injured soldiers, and dedicated her life to improving those conditions. She campaigned for better training for nurses, and better hospitals. By the time of her death in 1910, the status of nurses had improved and hospital conditions had changed beyond recognition.

Early life
Florence Nightingale was born in Florence, Italy, in 1820 to rich English parents. She seemed destined for the leisured life of an English country lady but wanted to do something more worthwhile. She decided to become a nurse. This was unacceptable for a woman of her status, but she insisted, did her training, and took a job in a women's hospital.

Crimean War

In 1853, on the Crimean peninsula by the Black Sea, war broke out over the future of the Ottoman Empire. Nightingale persuaded the British Secretary of State for War to allow her to go to the Crimea as a nurse. She left Britain in October 1854, with 37 other nurses, and stayed in the Crimea until war ended in 1856.

Medical knowledge
Medical knowledge was still crude in Florence Nightingale's time. Antibiotics were unknown and surgery primitive, and few patients survived a lengthy stay in hospital. While in the Crimea, Nightingale worked hard to improve conditions for the sick and injured, travelling with her personal supply of medicines, and setting new standards for nursing care.

Laudanum for relieving pain

Disinfectant for killing germs

Quinine to treat malaria

Glass measuring beaker

Tonic pills

Stout wooden box

Florence Nightingale's travelling medicine chest

Scutari Military Hospital
In the Crimea, Nightingale worked in the Scutari Military Hospital. The conditions in the wards were almost as bad as on the battlefield itself, with no proper medical or nursing care for the injured soldiers. Nightingale cleaned up the hospital, provided basic supplies such as beds and medical equipment, improved the food, made sure proper nursing was available, and even provided a place where soldiers could convalesce before returning to the fight.

Lady with the lamp
Florence Nightingale took a personal interest in her patients, touring the wards at night with a lamp to see that all the injured men in the wards were comfortable and free of pain. On her return to Britain, the nurse was celebrated as a hero, and the image of the lady with the lamp caring for her patients stayed with her for the rest of her life.

Mary Seacole

Mary Seacole was the daughter of a Jamaican mother and a Scottish father. She trained as a nurse in Jamaica but when she offered to work for Florence Nightingale in the Crimea, she was refused. Ignoring this, she volunteered to nurse soldiers at Balaclava, throwing all her energy and resources into her work. After the war, she returned to Britain in poverty, and wrote a book about her adventurous life.

Mary Seacole tends a wounded soldier

Training the nurses

After the war, Nightingale used her new fame to campaign for better training for nurses. She set up a fund to establish the Nightingale Training Centre at St Thomas' Hospital, London, where nurses could receive proper instruction. She also fought for better conditions for British troops overseas.

FLORENCE NIGHTINGALE

1820 Born in Florence, Italy.

1853 Finishes training as a nurse and takes a job as superintendent of the Institution for the Care of Sick Gentlewomen, a hospital for women.

1854 Goes to the Crimea and nurses soldiers at the Scutari Military Hospital.

1856 Returns to Britain a hero, where she begins to campaign for better standards in nursing.

1860 Establishes a school for training nurses in London.

1907 Awarded the Order of Merit, the highest civilian award in Britain.

1910 Dies aged 90.

FIND OUT MORE ARMIES   DRUGS   HOSPITALS   MEDICINE, HISTORY OF   OTTOMAN EMPIRE   PASTEUR, LOUIS   WOMEN'S MOVEMENT

NOCTURNAL ANIMALS

AS NIGHT FALLS in the world's forests, grasslands, and gardens, many animals become active. These nocturnal animals sleep or rest by day and emerge at night to hunt and feed. Having a nocturnal lifestyle avoids competing for food and other resources with animals active during the day. Darkness also allows some animals to seek invisibility and avoid their predators. Many animals from hot deserts are nocturnal because it is too hot to emerge during the day. Nocturnal animals are adapted to navigate, find food, avoid predators, and attract mates in the dark.

Large eyes for seeing at night.

Large ears to locate insect prey.

Night eyes

Owls, small primates including bushbabies, aye-ayes, and lorises, and other mammals, such as cats, have large eyes in relation to their body size. The larger the eyes, the more efficient they are at gathering light, helping the animal make sense of its surroundings at night. Most nocturnal animals have pupils that can open very widely at night, to allow the maximum amount of available light to enter the eye. They also have a special layer in their eyes, called the tapetum, which helps them see in the dark.

Cat's eyes shining at night

Bushbaby
Huge eyes allow the bushbaby to see in the night-time darkness of the African forests. Its eyes are also forward-facing, enabling the bushbaby to judge distances accurately, so it can leap in darkness from branch to branch, in search of food.

Tapetum
This mirror-like layer in the eye reflects light and makes the eyes more sensitive to dim light. Cats' eyes, for example, are six times more sensitive to dim light than humans' eyes are.

Sensitive ears

Some nocturnal animals use their acute sense of hearing to hunt for prey, or to avoid being eaten by predators themselves. The bat-eared fox swivels its large ears to pick up the faint sounds and location of the insects and scorpions that form most of its diet. Cats use their ears in a similar way, to listen out for the rustling sounds made by mice and other prey.

Large hind legs enable the kangaroo rat to hop over large areas each night in search of seeds.

Kangaroo rat
Many desert-dwelling animals are nocturnal. The kangaroo rat, for example, rests in an underground burrow to avoid the daytime heat and emerges at night to feed. It has large eardrums and other modifications inside the ear that make its hearing very sensitive. In most other environments, such acute hearing would deafen the animal, but in the silence of the desert this extra sensitivity is invaluable. The kangaroo rat can even hear the sound of wind against an owl's wings and the rustlings of a rattlesnake's scales moving over sand in time to escape these enemies.

Large ears to pick up echoes.

Navigation at night
Nocturnal animals must be able to find their way at night without bumping into objects. Most bats navigate by echolocation. A bat sends out high-pitched sounds through its mouth. The sounds bounce off objects, and the echoes are picked up by the bat's ears and converted by its brain into a "sound picture". Cats navigate with their eyes and whiskers. Whiskers detect slight changes in air pressure when they pass close to an object.

Long-eared bat

Rattlesnake
Snakes have poor eyesight but detect their prey by tasting the air with their tongue, or by picking up vibrations made as the prey moves. Rattlesnakes and their relatives have an additional sense – an organ called a heat-sensitive pit on each side of the head between the eye and nostril. The pit is sensitive to infra-red radiation and enables the snake to detect heat given off by prey. Even in total darkness, the snake can locate prey and strike accurately.

This is the infra-red image of a rat that a rattlesnake can "see" at night.

Acute sense of smell

Some nocturnal animals find food by sensing odours. For example, the grey wolf follows the scent trails of its prey up to 2.5 km (1.5 miles) from their source. Insects can also track smells. Female mosquitoes detect the smells and heat released by warm-blooded animals on whose blood they feed.

Moths
Moths are usually nocturnal so have difficulty finding a mate. Many male moths have feathery antennae to detect attractive smelling chemicals, called pheromones, released by female moths. Moths also avoid capture by bats, by detecting the high-pitched squeaks that the bats make.

Antennae of North American robin moth

Patterned skin for camouflage

| **FIND OUT MORE** | ANIMAL BEHAVIOUR | BATS | CORAL REEFS | DESERT WILDLIFE | MONKEYS AND OTHER PRIMATES | OWLS AND NIGHTJARS | RATS AND OTHER RODENTS | SNAKES | URBAN WILDLIFE |

NORMANS

IN 911, THE FRANKISH KING Charles III (879–929) allowed a group of Vikings to settle on land in France. These settlers were called Normans, because they came from the north, and their new homeland became known as Normandy. They adopted French language and customs, but they were fearsome warriors, and in the 11th century they conquered Sicily, and then England. The Normans made a great contribution to the culture of France, England, and Italy, leaving behind original and beautiful architecture in their castles and cathedrals, a legal system and civil service, and fine French and English literature.

Territorial control

The Normans built and occupied castles and cathedrals in all their lands. This made the territories stable, so culture could flourish – as on the island of Sicily, which became an important scientific centre during the 12th century.

Falaise Castle
This castle in Normandy was Duke William's birthplace, and where he made plans to invade England. Many other castles survive in Normandy.

Cefalù Cathedral
The buildings the Normans left behind include this beautiful cathedral in Sicily, founded by Roger II.

White Tower
Norman castles always contained large, stone towers for the lord, like this one at the Tower of London.

Conquests

Norman brothers Robert Guiscard and Roger I conquered Sicily between 1060 and 1091. The island became a base for further conquests in the Mediterranean. Meanwhile, in 1066, Duke William II of Normandy sailed to England, defeated the Anglo-Saxon King Harold II at the Battle of Hastings, and became King William I of England.

Fleet
Like their Viking ancestors, the Normans were skilled boat-builders. They could ship large numbers of soldiers, weapons, and even materials for castle-building to the places, which they conquered.

Soldiers
Normans soldiers wore pointed helmets and carried kite-shaped shields. Though Vikings fought on foot, Normans copied the use of knights, or mounted warriors, from the French.

Roger II of Sicily
Roger II (1095–1154) was crowned in 1130. He united earlier Norman conquests on Sicily, gained control of parts of southern Italy, and made conquests on the North African coast. He governed wisely, and founded the Sicilian civil service. He believed in religious tolerance, and his court had many links with the Arab world.

Architecture

The Normans loved bold carved details in their buildings, and their masons invented the pointed "Gothic" style, replacing rounded windows and arches. Although Norman walls looked very thick, sometimes they were made of rubble covered by outer "skins" of stone.

Abbey of St Etienne
Before conquering England, Duke William and his wife Matilda founded twin monasteries in Caen – one for monks, one for nuns. St Etienne was the abbey for monks. It was completed in 1115, long after William's death.

St Etienne, Caen, France

Durham Cathedral
This beautiful cathedral is one of England's finest Norman buildings. The Normans had two favourite patterns for carving on columns: the zig-zag, known as the chevron, and the diamond-shaped lozenge. The Gothic ribbed vault with its pointed arches was a major contribution to architecture, and was used for the first time in Durham.

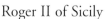

Church and state

There was rivalry between monarchs and senior churchmen, because both sides wanted ultimate power over the population.

Henry II   Richard I

King John   Henry III

Control of the Church
The Church was central to people's lives – to control it was to control the people. Rulers of the 13th century, such as those above, did this by founding cathedrals.

St Anselm (c.1033–1109)
Anselm, Archbishop of Canterbury, disagreed with William II and, later, Henry I, over whether kings or popes had the most power within the Church.

Timeline
911 Rollo the Viking and the Frankish king, Charles the Simple, agree that Vikings can settle in northern France.

1061 Normans conquer Messina, Sicily.

Coin of William I

1066 Battle of Hastings: Normans conquer England.

1086 Domesday Book written.

1087 William I dies. Sons William Rufus and Robert rule England and Normandy.

Seal of William II (Rufus)

1100 Henry I, son of William I, inherits England, and seizes Normandy (1106).

1130 Roger II unites Sicily, Calabria, and Apulia.

FIND OUT MORE

CASTLES   FEUDALISM   FRANCE, HISTORY OF   MEDIEVAL EUROPE   UNITED KINGDOM, HISTORY OF

NORTH AMERICA

NORTH AMERICA includes the countries of Canada, the USA, and Mexico, as well as Greenland (the world's largest island), the Caribbean islands, and the narrow isthmus of Central America that joins the continent with South America. Most of the population and industry are concentrated in the northeast, which has a temperate climate. The hotter south and drier west are thinly populated, and few people live in the far north. The USA and Canada are powerful, wealthy countries, while Mexico and Central America have weak economies.

Physical features

Northern North America has two main mountain ranges: the Rocky Mountains, which form a huge barrier in the west, and the older, wooded Appalachians in the east. Between them lie the fertile Great Plains, crossed by the River Mississippi. Northern Canada lies within the Arctic Circle, and most of Mexico is in the tropics. Between Canada and the USA are the Great Lakes.

Great Lakes
Lying between Canada and the USA, the five Great Lakes cover a total of 246,300 sq km (95,096 sq miles) and contain one-fifth of the world's fresh water. Lake Superior is the world's largest freshwater lake; the others are Huron, Michigan, Erie, and Ontario. They are linked to the Atlantic Ocean by the St Lawrence Seaway, which enables ocean-going ships to use inland ports.

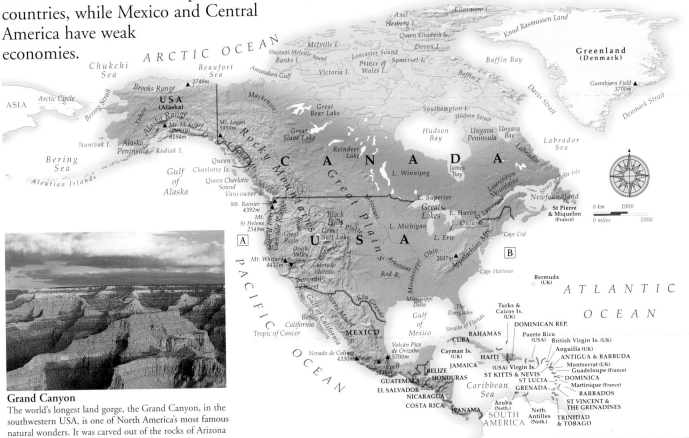

Grand Canyon
The world's longest land gorge, the Grand Canyon, in the southwestern USA, is one of North America's most famous natural wonders. It was carved out of the rocks of Arizona over millions of years by the River Colorado and its tributaries. In places it is 1.8 km (1 mile 240 yds) deep.

Cross-section through North America

Travelling from California to the Atlantic coast, the land rises to low coastal mountains and then up to the craggy Rockies. East of the Rockies are the flat, open grasslands of the Great Plains, broken by the Great Lakes. Just before the east coast are the gentle Appalachian Mountains.

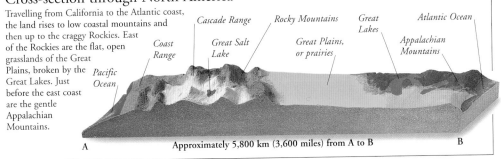

Approximately 5,800 km (3,600 miles) from A to B

NORTH AMERICA FACTS

AREA 24,235,583 sq km (9,357,359 sq miles)

POPULATION 465,000,000

NUMBER OF COUNTRIES 23

BIGGEST COUNTRY Canada

SMALLEST COUNTRY St Kitts and Nevis

HIGHEST POINT Denali/Mt. McKinley (Alaska) 6,194 m (20,322 ft)

LOWEST POINT Death Valley (California) 86 m (282 ft) below sea-level

LONGEST RIVER Mississippi

BIGGEST FRESHWATER LAKE Lake Superior

Climatic zones

North American climates vary according to latitude, altitude, and distance from the east or west coast. A permanent ice sheet covers Greenland, and cold tundra and taiga extend over the far north. The lush grasslands of the Great Plains enjoy a warm, semi-arid climate. In the southwest, the climate turns from snowy mountains to desert.

Tundra
Polar
Mountain
Grassland
Scrubland
Desert
Needleleaf forest
Deciduous forest
Wetland
Tropical rainforest

Tundra
The northern parts of Alaska and Canada lie within the Arctic Circle. In the cool, short summers, the land thaws enough to allow flowers to shoot up. Winters are long and bitter, with temperatures dropping below -60°C (-76°F).

Mountain ranges
The Rockies, a comparatively new mountain range, run down the west of the continent from Alaska to Mexico, where they continue as the Sierra Madre. West of the Rockies are the Coast Ranges. The older Appalachians run parallel to the east coast.

The Rockies rise up to 6,187 m (20,300 ft).

Needles

Douglas Fir

Cone

Rivers often provide the only access to the forest.

Canadian Rockies

Needleleaf forest
Vast forests of fir, larch, pine, and spruce trees extend over much of Canada and Alaska, broken only by lakes and rivers. Coniferous forests also cover the slopes of the Rockies. The biggest conifers are the huge redwoods of the US Pacific coast.

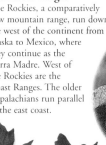

Oregon maple leaves

The autumn colours of the Canadian forest are a brilliant display.

Cacti in the Sonoran Desert can survive drought.

Deciduous forest
Extensive deciduous (broadleaf) forests cover the area south of the Great Lakes, and both sides of the Appalachians in Canada and the USA. Tropical rainforests cloak parts of Central America.

Long grasses of the Prairies

Great Plains
The Great Plains, or prairies, of central Canada and the midwestern USA are often called the bread basket, because much of the world's wheat is grown there.

Wetland
Covering 7,112 sq km (2,745 sq miles), the Everglades in Florida, USA, are the world's largest wetlands. Between Georgia and Florida, the Okefenokee Swamp covers 1,555 sq km (600 sq miles).

Deserts
Semi-desert and desert regions cover northern Mexico and southwestern USA, experiencing searing temperatures and very low rainfall. They include the Great Basin near the Rocky Mountains, the Mohave Desert, Death Valley, and the Sonoran Desert, which straddles Mexico's border with the USA.

People
Most North and Central Americans are descendants of European settlers. About 12 per cent descend from black African slaves. Few Native American peoples survive. In recent years, many Asians and Hispanics have settled in North America, increasing its variety of cultures.

North America has a multiracial population.

Resources
North America is rich in resources. It has nearly every important mineral, fertile soil suited to agriculture, huge forests of timber, and access to some fine fishing grounds, although these are in danger of being overfished. Crops include cereals, fruit, and vegetables.

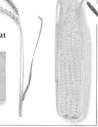

Maize

Wheat

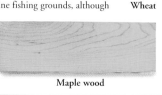

Maple wood

FIND OUT MORE CLIMATE CONTINENTS DESERTS FORESTS GRASSLAND WILDLIFE LAKES MOUNTAINS AND VALLEYS NATIVE AMERICANS NORTH AMERICAN WILDLIFE TREES TUNDRA

NORTH AMERICA, HISTORY OF

FOR THOUSANDS OF YEARS, the peoples of North America developed a series of advanced civilizations that traded and fought with each other over the vast plains and river valleys of the North American continent. Some of these peoples constructed complex buildings and developed farming techniques, others moved around in search of food and shelter. Yet within a short period of 350 years, European settlers overthrew them all, conquering the entire North American continent from coast to coast and setting up two new independent nations: the United States of America and Canada.

First people

Until about 15,000 years ago, North America was in the grip of an Ice Age. Because so much water was frozen, sea levels had dropped by about 90 m (300 ft), creating a land bridge to Asia. Before the Bering Strait opened, hunter-gatherers from Asia crossed the land bridge to North America.

Inuit knife, made of walrus tusk

Pueblo Bonito

As the first inhabitants of North America moved south and became more established in their new land, they began to build permanent settlements. One of the most impressive of these was at Pueblo Bonito in the Chaco Canyon area of what is now the southwest United States. It was built by the Anasazi people, who lived there between AD 950 and 1300. At its height, more than 1,200 people lived in the mud-brick-walled pueblo (large walled village), farming on the cliff tops above the canyon. The dwellings in the pueblo were built one above the other in a structure that rose to four storeys in some places. The pueblo was the largest apartment building in North America until the late 19th century.

Ceremonial dress of the Anasazi people

Rear wall rose to four storeys.

Flat roofs used as open balconies to work on.

Round rooms were for religious ceremonies.

Lower rooms were probably used for storage.

Native American food

The plains and river valleys held abundant food supplies. Fruit and vegetables were plentiful, the land teemed with buffalo and other animals, and the rivers were full of fish.

Squashes
Pumpkins, marrows, and other squashes were eaten fresh or dried for eating in the winter.

Corn
Corn, or maize, was dried and made into porridge, or lightly roasted and eaten with honey, maple sugar, or fat.

Beans
Rich in proteins and vitamins, beans formed an essential part of the daily diet.

Adena people

The Adena lived by the Ohio River between 1000 BC and AD 200. They hunted and gathered, but also grew some of their own crops. They were the first North American people to build large burial mounds. The Adena mound, near Chillicothe, Ohio, gives the people their name.

Hopewells

Items such as this copper bird were specially made as burial goods.

The Hopewell people were farmers who lived along the banks of the upper Mississippi River from about 300 BC to AD 700. They buried their rulers in large mounds, some 30 of which survive. The mounds were filled with goods made from raw materials gathered from all over North America.

Clay statuette　　**Copper bird**

Timeline

c.20,000 BC Hunter-gatherers from Asia cross the Bering Straits land bridge and begin to move south across the continent in search of food and shelter.

c.9000 BC Hunter-gatherers begin to hunt bison on the Great Plains.

John Cabot

c.5000 BC The first farmers grow wheat and other crops in southwestern USA.

AD 500 Hopewell people build burial mounds along the Mississippi and Ohio Rivers.

700 First pueblos built in the southwestern region.

c.1000 Vikings land on the east coast.

1497 John Cabot, an Italian sailor paid by English merchants, sights Newfoundland and claims it for England.

1534–35 French navigator Jacques Cartier sails up the St Lawrence River and claims Canada for France.

N

European arrival

After the discovery of land across the Atlantic, many Europeans sailed west. The French sailed up the St Lawrence River into the interior; the English tried to find a route to Asia round the northern coast; the Spanish moved north from their empire in Mexico.

☐ French territory

☐ Spanish territory

☐ Russian territory

☐ British territory

Hernando de Soto

In 1539 Hernando de Soto (1496–1542), Spanish governor of Cuba, set out to explore and conquer North America. He landed on the Florida coast and went northwards in search of gold, silver, and jewels, which he failed to find. In 1541, he was the first European to see the Mississippi River, but died before he could return home.

De Soto in Florida

French-style houses

French Canada

After the voyage of the French navigator Jacques Cartier up the St Lawrence River in 1534–35, French settlers tried but failed to found a colony at Montreal in 1541. Only in 1608 was the first successful French colony in North America founded by Samuel de Champlain at Quebec. In 1663, Quebec became the capital of New France, as the growing French empire in North America was then known.

Lure of the New World

Religious persecution and poverty at home, the lure of exploring and conquering new lands, wealth to be made trading furs and other goods, and the hope of discovering gold and silver, led Europeans to settle in what they called the "New World". By 1750 there were English, French, Dutch, and German colonies in the north and east; the Spanish had settled on the west coast.

Religious persecution

During the 17th and 18th centuries, many religious dissenters fled from persecution in Europe to create their own religious communities in the New World. Puritans, Quakers, Presbyterians, Catholics, and others all established colonies where they could practice their own religion in peace.

Exploration

In 1682, the French trader Robert Cavelier de La Salle (1643–87) sailed down the Mississippi River, naming the land Louisiana after the French king Louis XIV. After Louisiana became part of the USA in 1803, the government sent William Clark and Meriwether Lewis to explore it.

Backstaff was used to work out latitude.

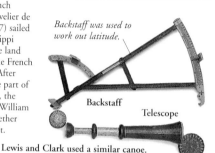

Backstaff

Telescope

Lewis and Clark used a similar canoe.

Gold

The discovery of gold in California in 1848 started a rush of prospectors across the continent in search of wealth. New cities, such as San Francisco, sprung up to house the new arrivals.

Prospecting for gold, USA

Fur cap

Gun for hunting and self-defence.

Warm, fur-lined clothing

Snowshoes

Fur trapper

Native American hunters were happy to exchange the pelts of wild animals such as foxes, bears, seals, and beavers with the colonists in return for guns, beads, blankets, and alcohol. English fur traders set up the Hudson's Bay Company to exploit this lucrative trade. In Canada, French settlers also traded furs from towns such as Montreal and Quebec.

Otter

Bear

Mink

Cabot and Cartier

While the Spanish and Portuguese explored and colonized Central and South America, England and France explored the North. The Italian navigator John Cabot (c.1450–c.1499) was hired by the English king Henry VII to find a new route to Asia. He was the first European to land in North America, claiming the island of Newfoundland for England. The French navigator Jacques Cartier (1491–1557) sailed up the St Lawrence River in 1534–35, visiting two Huron villages that later became Quebec and Montreal. The Huron word for village, *kanata*, gave the French the name Canada.

Timeline

1607 Jamestown, Virginia, the first permanent European colony in North America, is founded.

1608 French navigator Samuel de Champlain explores Canada and founds the first French colony at Quebec.

The *Mayflower*

1620 The Pilgrims sail from England in the *Mayflower* to establish a colony at Plymouth, Massachusetts.

1625 The Dutch found New Amsterdam (now New York).

1739 The War of Jenkins' Ear: Spain and Britain fight for control of the waters around North America and the Caribbean.

1759 British capture Quebec.

1763 British take complete control of French Canada.

1776 The 13 British colonies on the east coast declare independence.

1803 The Louisiana Purchase: the USA acquires vast tracts of land in the midwest from France.

1867 British colonies in Canada unite to create the independent Dominion of Canada.

FIND OUT MORE   AMERICAN CIVIL WAR   AMERICAN REVOLUTION   CANADA, HISTORY OF   CARIBBEAN, HISTORY OF   EUROPE, HISTORY OF   EXPLORATION   NATIVE AMERICANS   UNITED STATES, HISTORY OF

NORTH AMERICAN WILDLIFE

THE LARGE VARIETY of habitats found in the huge continent of North America (extending from the Arctic to Mexico, between the Pacific and Atlantic oceans), gives rise to an enormous variety of plant and animal life. This is despite the pressures imposed by growing human population, larger cities, and habitat destruction. The habitats of North America range from the cold tundra of the north, through large mountain ranges, the northern coniferous forests, the eastern deciduous forests, the prairies, and the wetlands, to the deserts of the southwest.

Tundra wildlife

This harsh region in the far north of North America has long, cold winters and brief summers. Sedges, grasses, mosses, and lichens survive in the thin layer that covers the frozen soil. In summer, plants flower, insects emerge, and mammals and birds become more active.

Caribou
Caribou (called reindeer in Europe) live in large herds in the tundra. They migrate north in summer to feed on grasses and sedges, and south in winter to feed on mosses and lichens. Their broad hooves enable them to walk easily in snowy conditions.

Caribou have thick, warm, waterproof coats.

Arctic fox
The Arctic fox has very dense fur enabling it to survive the subzero winds of the tundra winter. The fox is so resilient that it does not begin to shiver until temperatures drop to -70°C (-94°F). It eats almost anything, including berries, birds, rodents, and the carrion left by polar bears.

White fur provides camouflage in winter.

Snowy owl
The thick white plumage of the snowy owl, which extends to cover its toes, keeps the bird warm and acts as good winter camouflage. Snowy owls live in the tundra, but they may migrate south if food is scarce. They hunt by day or night for lemmings, hares, ducks, and gulls. They nest on the ground in the spring.

Sharp talons

Wetland wildlife

North American wetlands include lakes, rivers, marshes, subtropical wetlands such as the Everglades, swamps, and bogs. Wetlands provide homes for waterbirds, semi-aquatic mammals such as beavers and muskrats, frogs, fish, and insects.

American beaver
Beavers are North America's largest rodent. They live by streams and lakes and use their powerful, gnawing incisor teeth to cut down trees and branches for food, and to construct dams. In the ponds created by the dams, they build homes, called lodges, with underwater entrances.

American alligator
Alligators live in the subtropical wetlands of the southeastern USA. They spend much of the day basking on the muddy shores of swamps and lakes, but forage for food on land or in water, by day or night. Alligators eat birds, amphibians, fish, other reptiles, and mammals.

Green tree frog
Green tree frogs live in trees in or near springs, creeks, ditches, lakes, and swamps. Their green colour camouflages the frogs among the green of the leaves. They hunt at night, feeding mainly on insects and spiders. In spring, the frogs leave the trees to breed in water.

Body is streamlined when leaping.

Beavers have a streamlined body, flat tail, and webbed feet for swimming.

Saguaro cactus
This giant cactus survives the conditions of the Sonoran Desert by storing water, absorbed by shallow roots, in its ribbed stems. Its flowers, fruits, and seeds provide food for animals; woodpeckers and owls live in holes in its stems.

Saguaros reach up to 20 m (65 ft) in height.

Desert wildlife

Hot, dry deserts, including the Sonoran Desert, are found in southwestern North America. Plants such as cacti are often succulents, with water-storing stems, and small or absent leaves to reduce water loss. Many desert animals shelter from the daytime heat, emerging at night to feed.

Black-tailed jackrabbit
Jackrabbits are desert hares. They are active at night, feeding on grasses, cacti, and the bark and buds of shrubs. During the day, they shelter from the Sun's heat.

Long ears aid heat loss.

Long hind legs enable it to run up to 56 kmh (35 mph).

Roadrunner
The roadrunner rarely flies, but runs with head and tail extended at speeds of 20 kmh (12 mph) to catch prey or avoid enemies.

Desert tortoise
This tortoise shelters from the sun and potential enemies in its long burrow, emerging at dawn and dusk to feed on succulents.

Strong legs to dig into dry ground.

N

Mountain wildlife

The Rocky Mountains are one of North America's major mountain ranges. As altitude increases, vegetation changes from coniferous forest and grassland, to tundra and meadow, and higher still, bare rocky crags. Animals found at different levels vary depending on what they eat, and with the seasons.

Mountain bluebird

Mountain bluebirds live in western North America. During the summer these small birds live in meadows above 1,500 m (5,000 ft) where they feed on insects caught in flight, or on the ground. In winter, flocks of bluebirds avoid the harsh conditions by moving to lower altitudes. Females have duller plumage than males.

Males are bright blue.

Whitebark pine

Whitebark pine, a type of conifer growing on the slopes of the Rocky Mountains, is found up to 4,000 m (13,000 ft). It provides a home and food, including bark, seeds, and leaves, to many animals.

Cougar

Also called the mountain lion or puma, the cougar thrives in the wilderness of the mountains of western North America at altitudes of up to 4,500 m (15,000 ft). Cougars are powerful, expert hunters; they prey on many mammals, particularly deer.

Mountain goat

Mountain goats are sure-footed animals that move easily over rocky crags. In the morning and evening, small flocks may descend from the crags to feed on vegetation in the meadows above the treeline.

Hooves provide good grip.

Temperate forest wildlife

The temperate forests of the USA are home to insects, birds, and mammals, especially when summer vegetation carpets the floor. Over 150 species of tree grow here, such as oaks and maples.

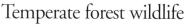

Yellow-bellied sapsucker

This species of woodpecker uses its beak to drill holes in the bark of trees such as maples and birches. The sapsucker then flies away, returning later to feed on the sugary sap that has oozed out of the hole. The same holes are returned to, and reopened, year after year.

Monarch butterfly

These butterflies migrate twice-yearly. In summer, they breed in the forests of northern USA. In autumn, a new generation of butterflies migrates to Mexico, to overwinter in large groups, returning north in spring.

Coniferous forest wildlife

North America's coniferous forest covers a very large area. Summers are warm; winters are cold and snowy. Forest animals include porcupines and hares, which feed on vegetation, and predators such as lynxes and wolves.

Hooves spread apart on wet ground.

Males use huge antlers to fight in the mating season.

American porcupine

Good climbers, porcupines feed on conifer needles and bark in winter, adding buds, roots, and berries in summer. Their quills can be used for defence.

Spiky quills

Moose

These large deer live in and near coniferous forests and feed on leaves and shrubs. They also stand in water, to feed on aquatic plants in streams, lakes, and bogs.

Burrowing owl

This small owl has adapted to a habitat with few trees, by living in a hole in the ground. It shelters and nests in the breeding season in abandoned burrows of rodents such as prairie dogs.

Prairie wildlife

The prairie is a grassland area which used to cover much of central North America. As the area was colonized, pronghorn and bison were almost wiped out. However, areas of prairie still survive and are home to animals such as ground squirrels and coyotes.

Buffalo grass

Buffalo grass is the dominant grass of the short grass prairie. This is the region of semi-arid plains of the western prairie, where the grasses are adapted to survive drier conditions. Prairie grasses provide food for rodents, insects, and grazing animals, including cattle.

Pronghorn

Small herds of pronghorns graze on the wide range of grasses and other prairie vegetation. Pronghorns can move fast, at speeds of up to 96 kmh (60 mph) to escape predators. Hunting once drove the pronghorn to near-extinction, but protected herds survive today, in and around parks and reserves.

Males have hooked horns.

Lubber grasshopper

These large, robust grasshoppers are found mainly in the western prairies. Lubber grasshoppers live among grasses and other prairie plants and eat their leaves. They are active in the summer and early autumn.

Yellow for camouflage in grass

Sharp claws to catch snakes, rodents, and insects.

| **FIND OUT MORE** | CROCODILES | DEER AND ANTELOPES | GRASSES, RUSHES, AND SEDGES | GRASSHOPPERS AND CRICKETS | LIONS AND OTHER WILD CATS | OWLS AND NIGHTJARS | RATS AND OTHER RODENTS | TREES |

NORWAY

A LONG, NARROW COUNTRY forming the western part of the Scandinavian peninsula, Norway shares its eastern borders with Sweden, Finland, and Russia. Its north coast is washed by the icy Arctic Ocean, and to the west are the Norwegian and North seas, rich with fish, oil, and natural gas. The small population enjoys equal rights and high living standards. The education system is well developed, and unemployment is consistently low.

NORWAY FACTS

CAPITAL CITY	Oslo
AREA	324,220 sq km (125,181 sq miles)
POPULATION	4,500,000
MAIN LANGUAGE	Norwegian
MAJOR RELIGION	Christian
CURRENCY	Norwegian krone
LIFE EXPECTANCY	79 years
PEOPLE PER DOCTOR	357
GOVERNMENT	Multi-party democracy
ADULT LITERACY	99%

Physical features

Norway has high, rugged mountains and steep river valleys. Its 21,900 km (13,600 miles) of coastline is one of the world's longest, and is indented with fjords (narrow sea inlets), and 150,000 rocky islands. The fast-flowing rivers have spectacular waterfalls.

Jostedal Glacier
The largest ice-field in western Europe, the Jostedal Glacier in southern Norway covers 487 sq km (188 sq miles). Snow covers the ground for three months of the year, but in spring it melts into the Utigard waterfall, the third highest in the world at 800 m (2,625 ft).

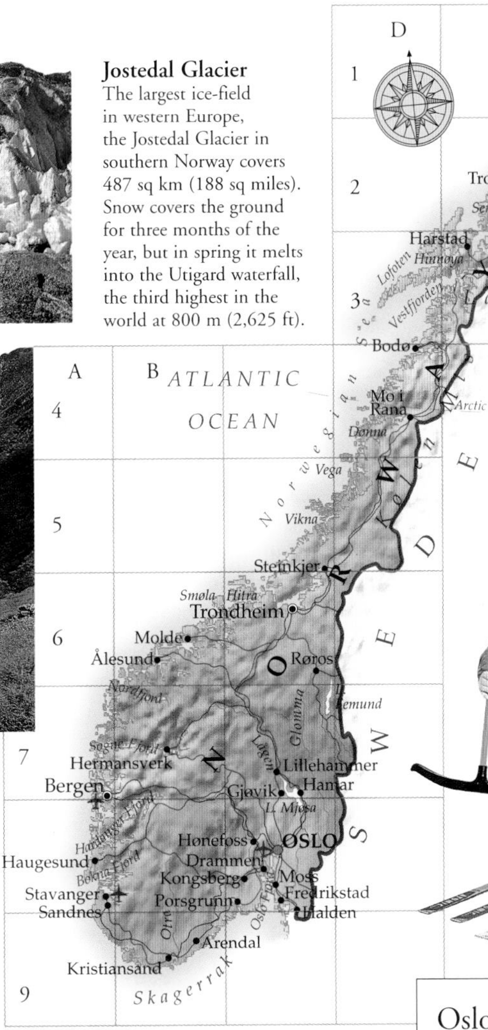

People
Ninety five per cent of the people are ethnic Norwegians. Their ancestors invented skiing for cross-country travel, and now it is the national sport. About 75 per cent of Norwegians live in towns. In the Arctic north, the Sami, or Lapps, herd reindeer and keep their own language and culture.

15 per sq km (38 per sq mile)

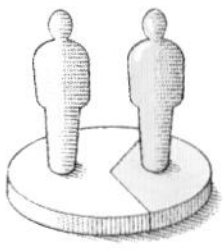

Taking a ski lift

75% Urban   25% Rural

Fjords
During the Ice Age, glaciers carved steep-sided valleys in the rocks along Norway's west coast. As the ice melted, the North Sea flowed in, creating spectacular fjords. The longest fjord in the country, Sognefjorden, can carry large ships more than 200 km (124 miles) deep inland.

Climate
The warm waters of the Gulf Stream keep Norway's climate mild, and most harbours remain ice-free, even on the Arctic Sea coast. Far north, in Norway's more extreme Land of the Midnight Sun, the sun shines all night at midsummer, but hardly rises at all in the depths of winter.

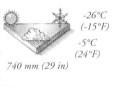

34°C (94°F)   -26°C (-15°F)

17°C (63°F)   -5°C (24°F)

740 mm (29 in)

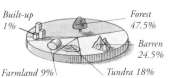

Built-up 1%
Forest 47.5%
Barren 24.5%
Farmland 9%
Tundra 18%

Land use
As only nine per cent of Norway's land can be farmed, livestock farmers combine it with forestry. Like its neighbour Finland, the nation uses its rivers for hydroelectricity.

Oil rig, Stavanger

Industry
Norway still depends largely on its abundance of natural resources. North Sea oil and gas are exported globally, and 99 per cent of its own electricity needs are met by hydroelectricity. Despite being the world's largest salmon supplier, Norway has to import much of its food. Shipbuilding is important and there is a large merchant fleet.

Oslo
A busy seaport and industrial centre, Oslo is Norway's largest city, as well as its capital. It was founded at the head of a fjord in 1050 and blends historic buildings with towering modern blocks. Over 500,000 people live in the suburbs, surrounded by forests and lakes.

Aker Port and City Hall

FIND OUT MORE: COASTS • DAMS • ENERGY • EUROPE, HISTORY OF • FISHING INDUSTRY • GLACIATION • MOUNTAINS AND VALLEYS • OIL • SCANDINAVIA, HISTORY OF • WINTER SPORTS

NUCLEAR POWER

N

AT THE CENTRE OF EVERY ATOM is a tiny powerhouse called a nucleus. Strong forces hold particles called protons and neutrons together inside the nucleus. In nuclear reactions, atomic nuclei split apart (fission) or join together (fusion), rearranging the forces between the particles and releasing huge amounts of energy called nuclear power. A nuclear power station harnesses the energy from controlled nuclear reactions in a reactor to generate electricity.

Fission reactor

The heart of a fission reactor is a tough steel container called a core. A continuous series of nuclear fission reactions, called a chain reaction, occurs inside the core and produces intense heat. A circulating fluid called a coolant takes heat from the core to steam generators. The steam generators use the heat to convert water into jets of high-pressure steam. The steam jets drive turbine engines linked to electricity generators.

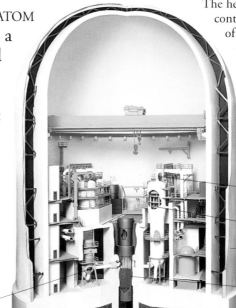

Pipes carry high-pressure steam to turbines outside the reactor.

Steam generators boil water into steam.

Two walls of reinforced concrete stop radioactive material from escaping.

The core contains about 4,000 rods of uranium fuel.

Pumps circulate coolant around the core.

Fusion reaction

The joining together of two atomic nuclei is called nuclear fusion. Only light elements – those with few protons and neutrons in their nuclei – can take part in nuclear fusion reactions. At very high temperatures, two hydrogen nuclei smash together and form a heavier helium nucleus, releasing energy and expelling a neutron. Fusion reactions occur in the Sun and other stars.

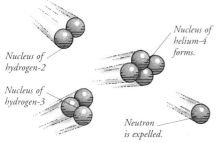

Nucleus of hydrogen-2

Nucleus of hydrogen-3

Nucleus of helium-4 forms.

Neutron is expelled.

Fusion reactor
Scientists have not yet made a practical fusion reactor. This ring-shaped experimental reactor is called a torus. It heats hydrogen gas to millions of degrees so that atomic nuclei can fuse together.

Experimental fusion reactor

Fission reaction

When the nucleus of an atom splits apart it is called nuclear fission. Some heavy elements have unstable nuclei that can be made to split by bombarding them with neutrons. As the nuclei split, they release energy and more neutrons, which may strike other nuclei and start a chain reaction.

Nuclear fuel rods
Most fuel rods consist of pellets or bars of the isotope uranium-235 held in an alloy casing. Uranium-235 has 235 protons and neutrons in the nuclei of its atoms.

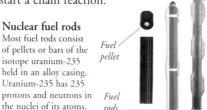
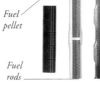

Fuel pellet

Fuel rods

The nucleus becomes unstable when struck by the neutron.

The nucleus splits, releasing energy and neutrons.

Neutron

Uranium-235 nucleus

Two lighter nuclei form.

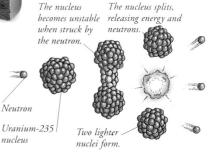

Fast breeder
A reactor that makes, or "breeds", fuel for itself is called a fast breeder. During the chain reaction, some of the uranium changes into plutonium, which can also be used as a nuclear fuel.

Nuclear hazards

The waste from nuclear fuel is dangerously radioactive, so it must be dumped at sea or buried safely underground. Nuclear weapons tests and accidents at reactors can cause long-term health hazards by releasing radioactive material into the air.

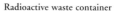

Radioactive waste container

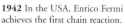

Nuclear weapons test

Enrico Fermi

The Italian-born nuclear physicist Enrico Fermi (1901–1954) left Italy in 1938 to live and work in the USA. In 1942, he built the first nuclear reactor in a disused squash court at the University of Chicago. Using this reactor, Fermi achieved the first nuclear fission chain reaction.

Timeline

1911 Ernest Rutherford, a New Zealand-born physicist, proposes that each atom contains a small, dense core called a nucleus.

1938 German chemist Otto Hahn and Austrian physicist Lise Meitner discover nuclear fission.

1939 German-born physicist Hans Bethe discovers that nuclear fusion powers the Sun.

1942 In the USA, Enrico Fermi achieves the first chain reaction.

1945 Nuclear bombs destroy Japanese cities of Hiroshima and Nagasaki.

1954 Russia's Obninsk reactor is the first to generate electricity.

1986 An explosion at the reactor in Chernobyl, Russia, releases clouds of radioactive material.

1991 In England, the JET (Joint European Torus) project achieves the first controlled fusion reaction.

FIND OUT MORE   ATOMS AND MOLECULES   EINSTEIN, ALBERT   ENERGY   MATTER   MEITNER, LISE   RADIOACTIVITY

NUMBERS

"FIVE, FOUR, THREE, two, one ... lift off!" is the countdown we hear before a rocket launch. It is natural for people to count, and we use numbers to do so. The simplest way to represent a number is as a series of marks, or tallies, with each tally representing one item. However, it is difficult to write down or read a very large number if it is represented as a collection of tallies. Our own number system, which represents numbers using the digits 0 to 9, enables us to write, read, and manipulate large numbers easily. Arithmetic is the use of numbers in calculations.

Turnstiles in the Paris Metro

Counting

Using numbers to find out how many items there are in a certain place is called counting. The turnstiles at a train station, for example, count the passengers using the trains. The numbers we use to count (1, 2, 3, 4, and so on) are called counting, or natural, numbers.

Types of numbers

We usually use whole numbers to count items such as cakes. However, if only a part of a cake is present, we must use a part of a whole number, called a fraction, to count it. Other types of number prove equally useful in different situations.

Fractions are amounts expressed as one number divided by another. The fraction $^3/_4$, for example, is equal to 3 divided by 4 (three-quarters).

Powers show how many times a number is multiplied by itself. For example, 10 multiplied by itself 3 times is 10 to the power of 3, or 10^3.

Logarithms (logs) show the power to which a number must be raised to obtain another number. For example, the log of raising 10 to 1,000 is 3, because 10 x 10 x 10 = 1,000.

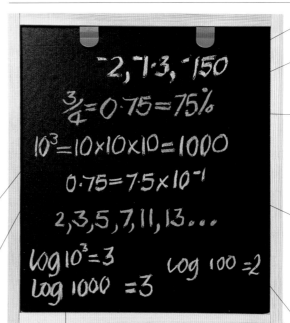

Chalkboard showing different types of numbers

Negative numbers are less than zero.

Percentages are fractions of 100, so 75 per cent (%) is the same as $^{75}/_{100}$.

Decimal numbers show values less than whole numbers as digits to the right of a decimal point: 0.75, for example, is seven-tenths-and-five-hundredths.

Scientific notation is a way of writing very large or small numbers using powers of 10. In scientific notation, 0.75 is written as 7.5×10^{-1}.

Prime numbers are whole numbers that can be divided exactly only by 1 and by themselves.

The tablet records figures for crop yields.

Babylonian clay tablet, 2900 BC

Number systems

In a place-value number system, the value of a digit in a written number depends on its position. In the number 22, the 2 on the left is worth ten times more than the 2 on the right. We use a system based on the number 10, but any number can be used as the base for a place-value system. The ancient Babylonians, for example, used a system based on the number 60.

1 x 8   1 x 4   0 x 2   1 x 1

These light bulbs represent the binary number we know as 13. In binary form, the number 13 becomes 1101 (8 + 4 + 0 + 1).

Car odometer

Binary system
The binary system is a place-value number system based on the number 2. The positions of the digits in a binary number represent, from right to left, 1s, 2s, 4s, 8s, 16s, and so on. All binary numbers are made up of the digits 0 and 1.

Denary system
The denary (base 10) system, or decimal system, became common because we first learn to count using our ten fingers and thumbs. Digits in denary numbers represent, from right to left, 1s, 10s, 100s, 1,000s, and so on. A car's odometer records the distance a car travels using a denary counter.

Each wheel turns 10 times faster than the wheel to its left.

Both sides of the equation have the value 6.

Equals sign separates the two quantities.

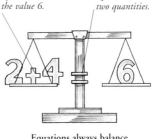

Equations always balance

Equations

An equation is two groups of symbols and numbers separated by an equals sign (=). The numbers and symbols on either side of the sign must be equal in value, just as the weights in the pans of a balance must be equal for the pans to balance. This means that if you add a number to one side of an equation, you must add the same number to the other side.

Arithemetical symbols
The symbols + (add/plus), - (subtract/minus), x (multiply), and ÷ (divide) represent the four main ways in which numbers can be used in calculations. These symbols are used in equations. For example, the equation 2 + 3 = 15 ÷ 3 is read as: "Two plus three equals fifteen divided by three".

Add means to find the sum of two numbers.

Multiply means to make something a number of times larger.

Subtract means to take one number away from another.

Divide means to find out how many times one number goes into another.

John Napier

John Napier (1550-1617), a Scottish mathematician, made many important discoveries about numbers. Napier is most famous for inventing logarithms, which make complex calculations much simpler. Many mathematicians and scientists have used logarithms to solve problems and to devise new theories.

FIND OUT MORE — COMPUTERS · INFORMATION TECHNOLOGY · MATHEMATICS · SCIENCE · WEIGHTS AND MEASURES

OCEAN FLOOR

FAR BENEATH the waves are the mountains, canyons, plains, and valleys that make up the ocean floor. This underwater landscape, which is home to as fantastic a diversity of wild creatures as any continent, covers more than 60 per cent of the Earth's surface. New features are continually being added to the ocean floor as molten rock wells up from the Earth's hot interior through gaps in the Earth's crust. Once formed, these features change very little, because they soon become covered by protective layers made up of the remains of dead sea creatures that sink to the ocean bottom.

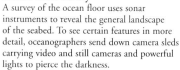

The world's ocean floor
Arctic Ocean
Pacific Ocean
Indian Ocean
Atlantic Ocean
Southern Ocean

Sonar mapping

Scientists known as oceanographers make maps of the ocean floor using sonar (SOund Navigation And Ranging) instruments, which send out pulses of sound that bounce off the seabed and return as echoes. The echoes are used to produce a picture of the ocean floor.

Ocean floor survey

A survey of the ocean floor uses sonar instruments to reveal the general landscape of the seabed. To see certain features in more detail, oceanographers send down camera sleds carrying video and still cameras and powerful lights to pierce the darkness.

Sonar image of mud flows on seabed

Submarine landscape

The ocean floor is really the entire seabed below the low-tide mark, but when people refer to the ocean floor, they usually mean the ocean-basin floor. This is the part of the seabed that lies beyond the continental shelf. Most of the ocean-basin floor is more than 2,000 m (6,500 ft) under the water. It is largely flat, but dotted with huge mountains called seamounts.

Features of the ocean floor

Continental shelf is the gently sloping area between the edge of a continent and the deep ocean.

Submarine canyon

Course of mud river

Continental rise

Guyot (flat-topped mountain)

Seamount

Mid-ocean ridge (gap in ocean floor)

Deep ocean trench, formed where one section of the seabed dips beneath another

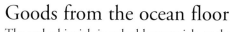

Continental crust

Volcanic rock

Abyssal plain – the smooth sea floor covered with a thick slime called ooze, largely the remains of sea creatures

Rising magma (molten rock)

Oceanic crust

Hydrothermal vents

Down on the ocean floor are strange, chimney-like structures that gush dark clouds of sulphur-rich hot water from the Earth's interior. These structures are called hydrothermal vents, or "black smokers". The warm water around these vents provides a home for huge quantities of marine life.

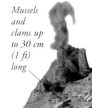

Poisonous jets of sulphurous water

Mound of solidified minerals

Smoker chimneys fused into an arch

Mussels and clams up to 30 cm (1 ft) long

Tube-worm tentacles up to 3 m (10 ft) long

Goods from the ocean floor

The seabed is rich in valuable materials, and many people are trying to find ways of extracting them. Already 20 per cent of the world's oil comes from beneath the seabed, extracted by oil rigs floating on the surface. The rocks of the ocean floor also contain important deposits of diamonds, tin, gold, and billions of tonnes of manganese nodules (rocky lumps rich in metals). Even the mud on the ocean floor contains silver, copper, and zinc.

Unpolished diamond crystals

Oil

Marie Tharp

American oceanographer Marie Tharp (b.1920) collated the results of a large number of surveys to build up a complete picture of the world's ocean floor. Her painstaking work revealed the existence of long chains of undersea mountains, now known as mid-ocean ridges.

FIND OUT MORE   CONTINENTS   EARTH   OCEANS AND SEAS   RADAR AND SONAR   ROCKS AND MINERALS   VOLCANOES

O

OCEANS AND SEAS

FROM SPACE, PLANET EARTH appears blue because the majority of its surface is covered by oceans and seas. There are five great oceans: the Pacific, Atlantic, and Indian Oceans, which all merge into the Southern Ocean around Antarctica, and the Arctic Ocean. Seas, such as the Mediterranean, Baltic, and Red Seas, are smaller expanses of water, often surrounded by land and connected to the oceans by narrow straits. The waters of the seas and oceans are constantly on the move, driven by the wind and the tides, and by powerful currents coursing through the ocean depths.

Ocean depths

The deepest places on Earth are ocean trenches, where the ocean floor plunges so steeply that the waters above could easily swallow Mount Everest. The first vessel to explore the deep ocean was a cast-iron sphere built in 1930 by the American Otis Barton. The Frenchman Jacques Cousteau made great advances in the 1960s with his "diving saucer" submersibles.

Deep-diving landmarks

JIM *diving suit Mark II*

Barton's bathysphere: 915 m (3,000 ft)

Cousteau diving saucer: 915 m (3,000 ft)

Barton's benthoscope: 1,370 m (4,500 ft)

Deep Submergence Rescue Vehicle: 1,520 m (5,000 ft)

Cousteau diving saucer Cyanea: 3,350 m (11,000 ft)

Argo *ROV (remote-operated vehicle) with Jason, a small robot equipped with TV cameras and lights .*

Alvin submarine: 3,810 m (12,500 ft)

Nautile submersible (France):. 6,000 m (19,690 ft)

Mir *submersible (Russia): 6,000 m (19,690 ft)*

Shinkai *submersible (Japan): 6,500 m (21,300 ft)*

The US Navy's bathyscape Trieste *holds the world record for the deepest dive: in 1960 it reached a depth of 10,911 m (35,797ft).*

At the bottom of the deepest oceans, the pressure can be equal to more than 10,000 kg pressing on each square centimetre (140,000 lb per sq in).

Mariana Trench (11,022 m (36,161 ft) in the Pacific Ocean, is the world's deepest place.

[Map]

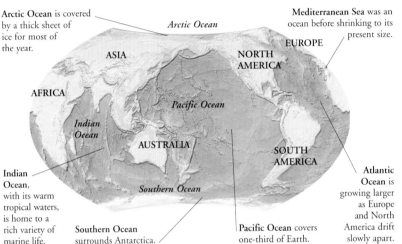

Arctic Ocean is covered by a thick sheet of ice for most of the year.

Arctic Ocean

Mediterranean Sea was an ocean before shrinking to its present size.

EUROPE

NORTH AMERICA

ASIA

AFRICA

Pacific Ocean

Indian Ocean

AUSTRALIA

SOUTH AMERICA

Southern Ocean

Indian Ocean, with its warm tropical waters, is home to a rich variety of marine life.

Southern Ocean surrounds Antarctica.

Pacific Ocean covers one-third of Earth.

Atlantic Ocean is growing larger as Europe and North America drift slowly apart.

Oceans and ocean currents

All the world's great oceans are interlinked, forming a continuous expanse of water. Prevailing winds disturb this water and cause surface currents – large flows of water that travel thousands of kilometres. At a deeper level, differences in the water's temperature and salinity cause vast deep-water currents to circulate.

Sea water

Sea "water" is only 96.5 per cent of water; most of the rest is dissolved mineral salts. The salt content, or salinity, of oceans and seas is highest in shallow tropical waters, where water quickly evaporates, and lowest in polar regions, where melting ice dilutes the concentration of salts.

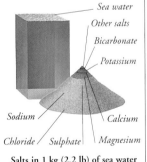

Sea water
Other salts
Bicarbonate
Potassium
Calcium
Magnesium
Sulphate
Chloride
Sodium

Salts in 1 kg (2.2 lb) of sea water

Ocean zones

Scientists divide the waters of the oceans into different zones, according to their depth beneath the surface. The relatively light, warm sublittoral zone is where most fish live. Few creatures live in the bleak abyssal zone above the deep ocean floor because it is always icy cold and pitch black, and the water pressure is intense.

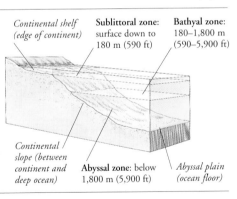

Continental shelf (edge of continent)

Sublittoral zone: surface down to 180 m (590 ft)

Bathyal zone: 180–1,800 m (590–5,900 ft)

Continental slope (between continent and deep ocean)

Abyssal zone: below 1,800 m (5,900 ft)

Abyssal plain (ocean floor)

Tides

The sea rises and floods on to the shore twice each day, and then ebbs away again. These daily changes in sea-level are called high and low tides. The strong gravitational pull between the Earth, Moon, and Sun stretches the Earth into an oval, making the oceans bulge up on either side of the Earth. As the Earth rotates, these bulges move across the globe, causing tides.

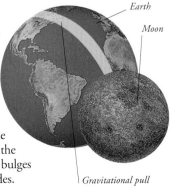

Earth
Moon
Gravitational pull

Tidal range

The difference between the water's height at high and low tide is called the tidal range. This is usually between 2–3 m (7–10 ft) at places on the open coast. In some river mouths and bays, the tidal range may be as great as 17 m (56 ft).

River mouth at high and low tide

 FIND OUT MORE   CONTINENTS   EARTH SCIENCES   ENERGY   ISLANDS   MOON   OCEAN FLOOR   OCEAN LIFE   STORMS   WINDS

OCEAN WILDLIFE

THE OCEAN COVERS two-thirds of the Earth's surface. This vast body of water is home to a great variety of plants and animals. On the ocean floor, there are underwater mountain ranges, plains covered with clays and mud-like oozes, deep trenches, and submerged mountains called sea mounts. Animals live in all of these regions and in all depths of the ocean. Generally, food is scarce in the deep sea because there is no light for photosynthesis, which enables plant growth. Plants are restricted to the sunlit waters near the surface, where they either drift in the sea or float, anchored to the seabed. Ocean wildlife is at its richest in the warm, shallow waters of coral reefs.

Oceans

The ocean can be divided into zones. The surface is a hard place to live, being exposed to the Sun and the waves. The sunlit waters just below the surface are where life is most abundant. Below that light begins to fade until, by 1,000 m (3,280 ft), there is no light at all.

A rich variety of marine animals live on coral reefs, from giant clams to brightly coloured fish.

Reptiles such as turtles have to come to the surface to breathe air.

Most ocean animals, such as fish, breathe by absorbing oxygen from the water.

Plants

The largest plants in the oceans are the seaweeds and sea grasses. The most abundant ocean plantlife are the microscopic organisms, such as diatoms, which drift in the sea. These are called phytoplankton. Phytoplankton get their food through photosynthesis and form the basis of the ocean food chain.

Sargassum weed
This seaweed is not anchored to the seabed. It floats free in tangled mats in the calm waters of the Sargasso Sea in the northwestern Atlantic. Animals like this sargassum crab live among the seaweed.

Sea grasses
Sea grasses grow in shallow coastal waters. They are among only a few flowering plants that live in sea water. They have proper roots that absorb nutrients and help anchor them to the seabed.

Plankton
Tiny animals that drift in the sea are known as zooplankton. These animals feed on the phytoplankton. Some of the animals spend all their lives as plankton; others are the young stages of animals such as crabs.

Mammals

Several groups of mammals have colonized the ocean. The most well-adapted to ocean life are the whales and dolphins, which have lost their hind limbs and use their tails to swim instead. Whales and dolphins give birth at sea, unlike seals and walruses, which breed on shore.

Nostrils on the upper part of the snout

Whiskers are sensitive to touch and vibrations in the water.

Large eyes adjust to seeing both in air and water.

Skin goes red when the walrus is hot.

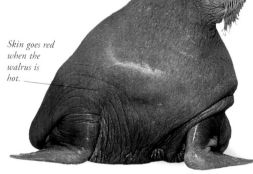

Sea lions
These superb swimmers use mainly their front flippers to "row" through the water. They can also walk on land. Male sea lions are much larger than females. In the breeding season, males have a territory where they keep guard over a group of females.

Walrus
Walruses live in the icy waters of the far north, where they feed mostly on shellfish on the seabed. They haul out on ice floes and along the coast. Walruses have thick blubber to keep them warm. Both males and females have tusks.

Humpback whale
Humpbacks often break through the surface of the water, called breaching. This may be a signal to other humpbacks, and perhaps a method of stunning shoals of fish. It may also dislodge irritating skin parasites.

Sperm whale
The deepest diver of all mammals, the sperm whale can go down even deeper than 1,000 m (3,280 ft). In its head is the spermaceti organ – a huge mass of oily, waxy tissues – which may help to regulate the whale's buoyancy.

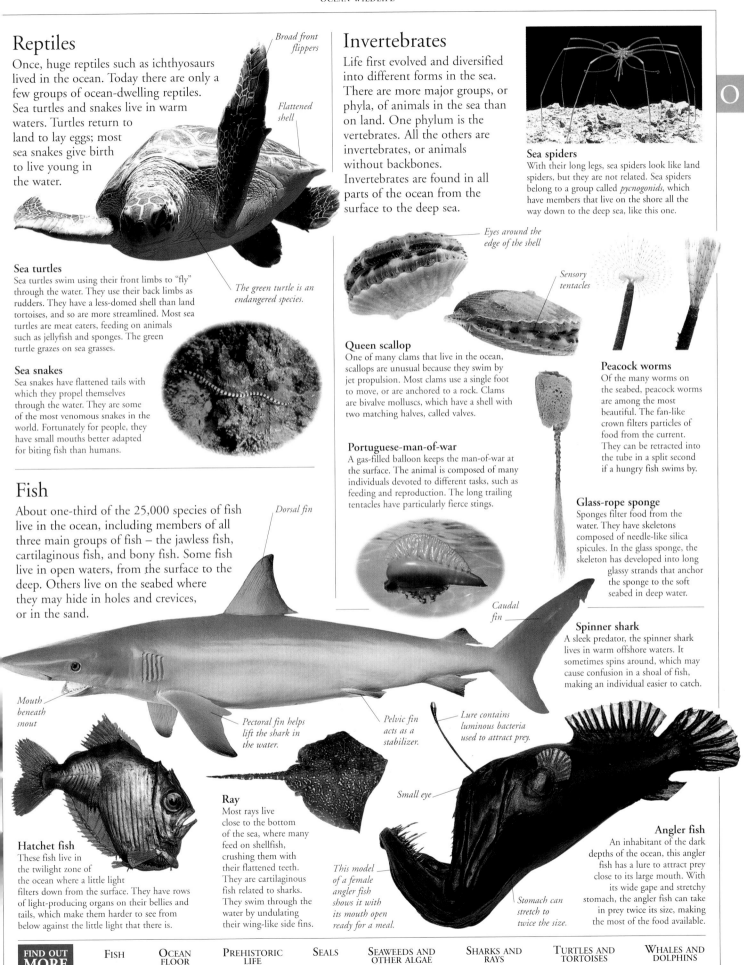

Reptiles

Once, huge reptiles such as ichthyosaurs lived in the ocean. Today there are only a few groups of ocean-dwelling reptiles. Sea turtles and snakes live in warm waters. Turtles return to land to lay eggs; most sea snakes give birth to live young in the water.

Broad front flippers

Flattened shell

The green turtle is an endangered species.

Sea turtles
Sea turtles swim using their front limbs to "fly" through the water. They use their back limbs as rudders. They have a less-domed shell than land tortoises, and so are more streamlined. Most sea turtles are meat eaters, feeding on animals such as jellyfish and sponges. The green turtle grazes on sea grasses.

Sea snakes
Sea snakes have flattened tails with which they propel themselves through the water. They are some of the most venomous snakes in the world. Fortunately for people, they have small mouths better adapted for biting fish than humans.

Invertebrates

Life first evolved and diversified into different forms in the sea. There are more major groups, or phyla, of animals in the sea than on land. One phylum is the vertebrates. All the others are invertebrates, or animals without backbones. Invertebrates are found in all parts of the ocean from the surface to the deep sea.

Sea spiders
With their long legs, sea spiders look like land spiders, but they are not related. Sea spiders belong to a group called *pycnogonids*, which have members that live on the shore all the way down to the deep sea, like this one.

Eyes around the edge of the shell

Sensory tentacles

Queen scallop
One of many clams that live in the ocean, scallops are unusual because they swim by jet propulsion. Most clams use a single foot to move, or are anchored to a rock. Clams are bivalve molluscs, which have a shell with two matching halves, called valves.

Portuguese-man-of-war
A gas-filled balloon keeps the man-of-war at the surface. The animal is composed of many individuals devoted to different tasks, such as feeding and reproduction. The long trailing tentacles have particularly fierce stings.

Peacock worms
Of the many worms on the seabed, peacock worms are among the most beautiful. The fan-like crown filters particles of food from the current. They can be retracted into the tube in a split second if a hungry fish swims by.

Glass-rope sponge
Sponges filter food from the water. They have skeletons composed of needle-like silica spicules. In the glass sponge, the skeleton has developed into long glassy strands that anchor the sponge to the soft seabed in deep water.

Fish

About one-third of the 25,000 species of fish live in the ocean, including members of all three main groups of fish – the jawless fish, cartilaginous fish, and bony fish. Some fish live in open waters, from the surface to the deep. Others live on the seabed where they may hide in holes and crevices, or in the sand.

Dorsal fin

Caudal fin

Spinner shark
A sleek predator, the spinner shark lives in warm offshore waters. It sometimes spins around, which may cause confusion in a shoal of fish, making an individual easier to catch.

Mouth beneath snout

Pectoral fin helps lift the shark in the water.

Pelvic fin acts as a stabilizer.

Lure contains luminous bacteria used to attract prey.

Small eye

Hatchet fish
These fish live in the twilight zone of the ocean where a little light filters down from the surface. They have rows of light-producing organs on their bellies and tails, which make them harder to see from below against the little light that there is.

Ray
Most rays live close to the bottom of the sea, where many feed on shellfish, crushing them with their flattened teeth. They are cartilaginous fish related to sharks. They swim through the water by undulating their wing-like side fins.

This model of a female angler fish shows it with its mouth open ready for a meal.

Stomach can stretch to twice the size.

Angler fish
An inhabitant of the dark depths of the ocean, this angler fish has a lure to attract prey close to its large mouth. With its wide gape and stretchy stomach, the angler fish can take in prey twice its size, making the most of the food available.

| FIND OUT MORE | FISH | OCEAN FLOOR | PREHISTORIC LIFE | SEALS | SEAWEEDS AND OTHER ALGAE | SHARKS AND RAYS | TURTLES AND TORTOISES | WHALES AND DOLPHINS |

OCTOPUSES AND SQUIDS

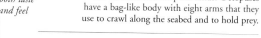
Streamlined, torpedo-shaped body

TOGETHER WITH cuttlefishes and nautiluses, octopuses and squids belong to a group of molluscs called cephalopods. They live in the sea, floating or moving through the water by jet propulsion, or crawling along the seabed. Cephalopods have a well-developed nervous system and brain. Many can change colour rapidly for camouflage, to confuse predators, or to attract a mate.

Cephalopod features

Cephalopod means "head-footed ones": all have a head surrounded by tentacles. The eyes are prominent and often complex. Cephalopods breathe through gills. They have beak-like jaws and a ribbon-like, toothed tongue called a radula.

Squids
As well as eight arms, squids have two retractile tentacles. These have suckers, often with horny rings for gripping prey. Squids have a horny shell inside the body, called a pen. They have two side fins that they use as stabilizers.

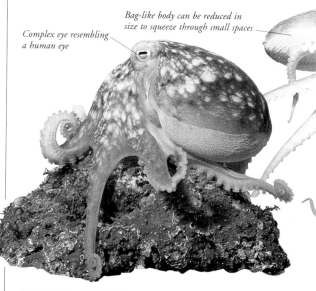

Complex eye resembling a human eye

Bag-like body can be reduced in size to squeeze through small spaces

Tentacles are the equivalent to the foot of other molluscs

Suckers can both taste and feel

Arms can be regenerated if torn off

Live nautilus

Octopuses
The most familiar octopuses live in shallow water among rocks and coral reefs, but there are also deep sea kinds. Octopuses have a bag-like body with eight arms that they use to crawl along the seabed and to hold prey.

Movement
Octopuses use their arms to crawl. To make a quick escape, they squirt water through a funnel and jet off with their arms trailing behind. Squids use jet propulsion more, to dart back and forth. Over short distances, squids are among the fastest sea creatures, reaching up to 32 km/h (20 mph).

Cross-section of nautilus shell

Cuttlefishes spend much of the time resting

Defence

The soft-bodied cepahalopods are vulnerable to attack. Many octopuses hide away in holes during the day, coming out only at night to find food. Squids often rise to the surface water at night, when there is less chance of being attacked by daytime predators, such as seabirds.

Decoys
Squirting ink out of its funnel, ★ this cuttlefish may confuse an attacker. Cuttlefishes, squids, and octopuses all produce ink from sacs inside their body. Some deep-sea squids produce luminous ink.

Buoyancy control
As a chambered nautilus grows, it adds a chamber to its shell. The new chamber is filled with fluid that is gradually absorbed and replaced by gas. The chambers keep the nautilus centrally buoyant, so it does not have to expend energy swimming to stop itself sinking.

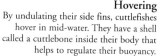

Hovering
By undulating their side fins, cuttlefishes hover in mid-water. They have a shell called a cuttlebone inside their body that helps to regulate their buoyancy.

Colour change
Like octopuses, cuttlefishes can turn lighter or darker to match the background by contracting or expanding bags of pigment in their skin. Some cephalopods turn vivid colours when irritated or when threatening an attacker.

Cuttlefish becomes lighter

Bites
Cephalopods use their beak-like jaws to bite their prey and to defend themselves. After taking a bite, some inject toxic saliva to subdue their prey. The saliva of the blue-ringed octopus can be strong enough to kill a person.

Jet propulsion
All cephalopods can move by jet propulsion. Squids usually jet off backward. They take water into the body cavity and expel it through a funnel near their head. They move the position of the funnel to change direction.

COMMON OCTOPUS

SCIENTIFIC NAME	*Octopus vulgaris*
ORDER	Octopoda
FAMILY	Octopodidae
DISTRIBUTION	Atlantic Ocean, Mediterranean and Caribbean seas
HABITAT	Rocky seabed in coastal waters
DIET	Shellfish, such as crabs, and fish
SIZE	Arm span on average 60–90 cm (23–35 in) long
LIFESPAN	Males up to 15 years

FIND OUT MORE

ANIMAL BEHAVIOUR   CAMOUFLAGE   SNAILS AND OTHER MOLLUSCS

OIL

DEEP DOWN IN THE EARTH, trapped by layers of rock, lie pools of the thick, black liquid called oil. It is a fossil fuel, produced from decayed animal and plant life that lived in the seas millions of years ago. Properly termed petroleum, oil has become a vital commodity in the world. Once refined, it is the source of petrol, kerosene, and diesel fuels. It also yields petrochemicals that are used to make a variety of products, including perfumes and plastics. Close to oil reserves there are often deposits of natural gas, which are also produced by the bacterial breakdown of ancient marine life.

Oil reservoirs
Most oil is found underground, but some may seep to the surface, sometimes creating huge lakes. Examples are Guanoco Lake in Venezuela and Pitch Lake in Trinidad. The liquid in these lakes is thick because light substances in the oil have evaporated.

An oil reservoir

Oil exploration
Oil prospectors search for areas that may contain oil and take measurements with instruments such as gravity meters and magnetometers (to measure local magnetism). They carry out seismic surveys that reveal the underground rock structure. If they locate possible rock formations with deposits of oil, they then drill an exploratory well.

Seismic surveying
Oil geologists often search for oil reserves by carrying out a seismic survey. This involves sending shock waves into the ground and recording their echoes which may locate likely reserves. Some geologists also use remote-sensing satellites that can spot details of rock formations in the ground.

Geologists conduct a seismic survey on a glacier in Spitsbergen, Norway.

Drilling
Oil is extracted through boreholes drilled into the ground. Drilling takes place from a rig, notable for its tall tower called a derrick. Beneath the derrick a rotary table turns the drill pipes, which are added one by one as the hole deepens. A toothed drill bit at the end of the bottom pipe cuts through the rock as it rotates.

Oil production well

Land wells
When oil is struck, the original borehole must be developed into a working well. If the oil flows naturally to the surface under pressure, the borehole steel casing is capped and fitted with valves. If not, pumps are installed to force the oil to the surface.

Sea wells
When oil is struck offshore, the borehole is temporarily capped and the production rig moves in. A production platform is installed from which more boreholes are drilled close to the original strike. Finally machinery is fitted, ready to extract oil from the seabed.

Oil rig at sea

Transporting oil
Two main methods are used to transport oil from the oil fields to the refineries. Oil is usually carried across land by means of a pipeline – for example, the United States has about 300,000 km (200,000 miles) of oil pipelines. Tankers are used to carry oil cargoes across the oceans.

Tankers
Tankers are among the biggest ships afloat, and may carry more than 500,000 tonnes of oil. For safety, the crude oil cargo is carried in a series of separate tanks to prevent it surging, which would otherwise capsize the ship.

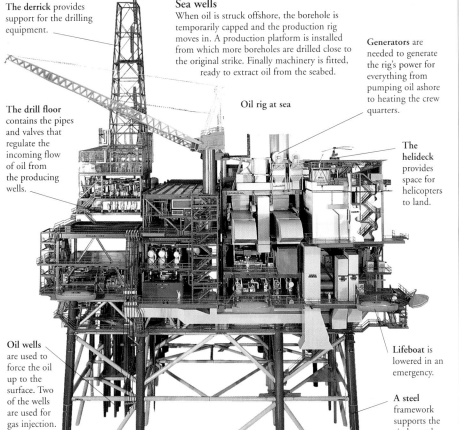

The derrick provides support for the drilling equipment.

The drill floor contains the pipes and valves that regulate the incoming flow of oil from the producing wells.

Oil wells are used to force the oil up to the surface. Two of the wells are used for gas injection.

Generators are needed to generate the rig's power for everything from pumping oil ashore to heating the crew quarters.

The helideck provides space for helicopters to land.

Lifeboat is lowered in an emergency.

A steel framework supports the rig beneath the sea.

Pollution
Oil can cause damage to the environment. Oil pipelines may burst and pollute the land, and tankers may collide with other vessels or run aground, spilling their cargo into the sea. Beaches become dirty, and wildlife is threatened.

Burning oil releases poisonous fumes

Refining

Crude oil is a complex mixture of hydrocarbons and in this form it is of limited use. However, oil is easily processed, or refined, into a host of useful products. The major process in an oil refinery is distillation, which splits up the oil into different sets, called fractions, of hydrocarbons.

Oil refinery at Antwerp, Belgium

Cracking

After distillation, cracking is the most important refining process. This chemical reaction breaks down heavy oil fractions into lighter compounds, to make useful products such as petrol. Another product of cracking is ethene, the starting point for many plastics and solvents.

Vacuum unit at a catalytic cracking plant

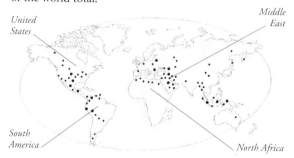

Oil products

The initial distillation process in an oil refinery produces the most familiar oil products, such as kerosene and diesel oil. Cracking and polymerization (building up light fractions) yield a variety of chemicals, called petrochemicals. These have become the lifeblood of the chemical industry, and are the main compounds used for making products such as as plastics and ethanol.

Collection of perfumes

Ethanol

This is the intoxicating substance found in alcoholic drinks such as beer, wines, and spirits. In industry ethanol is used as a solvent, or dissolving substance, in the manufacture of products such as paints, perfumes, and dyes.

Ski boots   Raincoat

Personal stereo

Plastics

Plastics are used throughout the modern world. They are used in a variety of products from clothing to household items. Three of the most important are polythene, polyvinyl chloride (both derived from ethene), and nylon.

Kerosene

Kerosene is an oil fraction which contains heavier hydrocarbons than petrol. It has a higher boiling point and so vaporizes less readily. Its main use is as fuel for aircraft jet engines. In the home, kerosene is used in portable heaters, and was once used in oil lamps. In industry, it is a valuable solvent for paints.

Kerosene lamp

Petrol

Of all oil products, petrol is the most valuable, because it powers most car engines. Petrol is a mixture of light hydrocarbons which turn easily to vapour. It contains additives to make it burn evenly, including, in leaded petrol, lead tetraethyl.

Petrol is also used for making some plastics.

Petrol pump

Oil nations

Oil deposits are not distributed evenly around the world. The largest deposits are found in the Middle East, the United States, and the countries of the former Soviet Union. Saudi Arabia is the biggest oil producer, with an output of about 8 million barrels a day, about a fifth of the world total.

United States

Middle East

South America

North Africa

• Principal oil reserves   • Other oil reserves

OPEC

Twelve oil nations from the Middle East, South America, and Africa belong to the Organization of Petroleum Exporting Countries (OPEC). It was set up in 1960 to safeguard members' interests against what they saw as exploitation by Western countries.

Natural gas

Natural gas formed millions of years ago beneath the sea. It is called natural gas to distinguish it from manufactured gases such as coal gas. Like oil, natural gas is a mixture of hydrocarbons. It contains methane, butane, propane, and ethane. Major gas-producing countries include Russia, the United States, Canada, and Indonesia.

Gas distribution works, Buenos Aires, Argentina

Liquid gas

The butane and propane found in natural gas can be liquified easily under pressure. In this form it is sold as bottled gas, such as that found in camping stoves and cigarette lighters. Natural gas is often liquified by refrigeration in order to transport it in tankers. In this form the gas takes up less space.

Camping stove fuelled by liquid gas

Gas impurities

Traces of other gases are found in natural gas as well as hydrocarbons. These include carbon dioxide, sulphur compounds, and helium. These gases may be present in sufficient quantities for industrial use. For example, sulphur can be used to make sulphuric acid, while helium is used to fill balloons and airships.

Balloons filled with helium gas

FIND OUT MORE | AIRSHIPS AND BALLOONS | COAL | CARS AND TRUCKS | CHEMISTRY | GASES | GEOLOGY | GULF STATES | PLASTICS AND RUBBER | ROCKS AND MINERALS | SOVIET UNION

OLMECS

AROUND 1300 BC, in the swampy lowlands of the Gulf of Mexico, one people began to stand out from the rest: the Olmecs. Because they lived mainly from farming, not hunting, they started to live a settled lifestyle. This enabled them to build towns and create a new kind of civilization. In their major towns, they built ceremonial centres with public buildings, temples, and massive stone sculptures of their rulers. Because of these achievements, Olmec culture is considered one of the first great civilizations of America. They worshipped a jaguar god, and so were known as the "People of the Jaguar".

Olmec centres

The Olmec ceremonial centres were sacred places, with pyramid temples, vast stone heads, and decorated monuments. The biggest ceremonial centres included those at San Lorenzo and La Venta.

Stone relief showing Olmec ruler.

Mexico
San Lorenzo • La Venta
Olmec empire

La Venta
This was the largest Olmec centre, in the modern Mexican state of Veracruz. It was built on a small island in coastal mangrove swamps. At its heart were pyramids, altars, long circular mounds, rows of stone columns, and tombs.

Head is 1.5 m (5 ft) tall and weighs over 20 tonnes.
Distinctive royal headdress
Colossal head known as "El Rey", the king

Colossal heads
The most famous of all Olmec monuments are colossal sculptured heads made of basalt, a dark volcanic rock. These heads represented actual people, probably Olmec rulers. Each head bears a head-dress with its own distinctive emblem, a symbol which identified the person's rank and family line.

Worship

Many early American societies believed that when the world was created, a race of part-human, part-jaguar beings was born. In Olmec civilization, these beings were identified with the priest-leaders. The spirit of the jaguar god was thought to live in the priests, giving them strength and agility, and making them Masters of People, just as the jaguar was Master of Animals. There were other gods, including a rattlesnake.

Stone figures
This group of jade and granite figures and tall ceremonial axes was left as an offering in an Olmec temple. It probably represented a group of leaders or priests.

Jaguar spirit
This ceremonial stone axe was carried by an Olmec priest in religious ceremonies. It is carved with the image of the spirit of the jaguar god.

Art

The first Olmec artists produced small statues in clay. The Olmecs were well known for their human figures, often with the faces of newborn babies. Later they mastered stone carving. They produced a wide range of work, from massive stone heads and carved reliefs to small sculptures and jewellery, using materials such as jade, serpentine (a green or brown mineral), and basalt.

Mask made of jade.
Jade necklace
Decorative jade mask

Jade masks
The Olmecs were fascinated by the human face and many of their sculptures are stone masks. Sometimes these masks were portraits of real people, such as ball game players, rulers, or nobles. Other masks showed the faces of figures from the stories in Olmec mythology.

Jade necklace
Green stones were valued more than any other in ancient Central America. Jade in particular was favoured by the rich as a material for jewellery. This necklace, with its central human head, would have been prized by a member of the Olmec nobility.

Food

The staple food of the Olmecs was maize, which they used to make porridge, or baked into pancakes. Olmec farmers also cultivated vegetables such as beans and squashes, and the tomato was popular. To vary this diet of vegetables, the Olmecs ate the meat of deer and rabbits.

Maize

Squash

Tomato

Jade fish
Fish were popular in coastal regions and near rivers. They could be caught with nets, hooks, or harpoons.

FIND OUT MORE
AZTECS | CENTRAL AMERICA, HISTORY OF | GODS AND GODDESSES | MAYA

OLYMPIC GAMES

THE MODERN OLYMPIC GAMES, held every four years, are the world's greatest festival of sporting competition. First held in 1896, they were inspired by the ancient Greek Olympics, which lasted for 1,000 years. Thousands of athletes, representing most countries in the world, assemble in a selected city to compete in more than 20 different sports. There are separate Winter Olympics for sports on ice and snow, and Paralympics for the disabled. These games are also held every four years.

Atlanta opening ceremony, 1996

The flame
Before every Games, a flame is lit from the rays of the Sun at the site of the ancient Olympics in Greece. The flame is transferred by a torch relay to the Olympic Stadium, where it burns for the duration of the Games. In 1996, the boxer Muhammad Ali was the final torch bearer.

Olympic sports

Athletics has always been the major Olympic attraction, but other sports, such as swimming, gymnastics, and show jumping, also have huge television audiences. Team games, such as soccer and hockey, are also popular. The Games were originally for amateurs only, but professionals are now allowed to participate.

Opening ceremony
At the opening ceremony, each country's athletes march into the stadium in turn, some teams with hundreds of competitors, others with only one or two. The host city puts on a spectacular show.

Medals
Gold medals are awarded for first place, silver for second, and bronze for third. All members of successful teams receive a medal provided they have taken part in at least one match or heat.

Olympic venues

Date	Venue
1896	Athens, Greece
1900	Paris, France
1904	St Louis, USA
1908	London, England
1912	Stockholm, Sweden
1920	Antwerp, Belgium
1924	Paris, France
1928	Amsterdam, Holland
1932	Los Angeles, USA
1936	Berlin, Germany
1948	London, England
1952	Helsinki, Finland
1956	Melbourne, Australia
1960	Rome, Italy
1964	Tokyo, Japan
1968	Mexico City, Mexico
1972	Munich, West Germany
1976	Montreal, Canada
1980	Moscow, USSR
1984	Los Angeles, USA
1988	Seoul, South Korea
1992	Barcelona, Spain
1996	Atlanta, USA
2000	Sydney, Australia
2004	Athens, Greece

Pierre de Coubertin
French scholar Pierre de Coubertin (1863–1937) pioneered the modern Olympics. Inspired in the 1870s by the excavation of ancient Olympia, he founded the International Olympic Committee, the governing body of the Games, in 1894.

1996 gold medal

1996 silver medal

1996 bronze medal

In some sports, both losing semi-finalists receive a bronze medal.

Gold medals are made of silver with a gold coating.

The Olympic rings
Five interlinking rings are the symbol of the Olympic Games. They appear on the Olympic flag on a white background and were designed to represent the coming together of the five "parts of the world" involved in the Olympic Movement when the flag was adopted in 1914.

Winter Olympics

The first separate Winter Olympics were staged in 1924 at Chamonix in France. Figure skating had been included in the summer schedule in 1908 and ice hockey was included in 1920. The Winter Olympics were held in the same year as the main Olympics until 1992 but, as from 1994, in Lillehammer, Norway, they are now held midway between the summer Games.

Winter events
The ice sports are figure and speed skating, and ice hockey. On snow, there is downhill and cross-country skiing and ski-jumping. Freestyle skiing events have recently been added. Sled sports are bobsleigh and tobogganing.

The start of a downhill race

Paralympics

Immediately after the main Olympics, a parallel set of games called the Paralympics is staged for people who have physical disabilities. The events take place at the the same venues as the Olympics. They have been held every four years since 1960. Sport for the disabled was pioneered by Dr Ludwig Guttman, who used it in the treatment of soldiers who had been disabled during World War II.

Paralympic events
There are events in the Paralympics for competitors in wheelchairs, for the blind or partially sighted, for amputees, and for those with cerebral palsy. Seventeen sports are staged, including athletics, swimming, archery, basketball, and tennis.

Tanni Grey, winner of gold in 1992 and 1996

FIND OUT MORE · ATHLETICS · COMBAT SPORTS · GYMNASTICS · HORSE RIDING · SPORT · SWIMMING AND DIVING · WINTER SPORTS

OPERA

AN OPERA IS A MUSICAL DRAMA in which singers act out a story, accompanied by an orchestra. Typically, an opera includes passages of sung dialogue, known as recitative, which move the plot along; solo songs called arias, that allow major characters to express their feelings; and scenes that feature a rousing chorus. The earliest operas appeared in Italy and were based on stories from classical mythology. Later, operas also dealt with political and historical subjects.

Jenny Lind

Major singers
Operatic soloists can become internationally famous. Jenny Lind (1820–87) was known as the Swedish Nightingale. The Italian tenor Luciano Pavarotti (b.1935) and the New Zealand soprano Kiri Te Kanawa (b.1944) are stars worldwide.

A scene from *The Marriage of Figaro*

Voices

In an opera company the leading female soloist, or prima donna, is usually a soprano, the highest female voice; the leading man often has a high tenor voice. Singers with lower voices, such as the female contralto or the bass (male), may also appear as soloists.

Libretto for *Cosi Fan Tutti*, by Mozart

Recitative

Libretto
The text of an opera is called the libretto. It may be adapted from a play or novel, or written specially for the composer. Only occasionally does the composer write both libretto and music.

Types of opera

There are many different forms of opera. In 18th-century Italy, operas were in the style of *opera seria* (serious opera) or *opera buffa* (comic opera). Composers worked within or around the traditions of these different styles to arrive at new forms – for example, the serious operas of German composer Richard Wagner (1813–83) are called music dramas.

Grand opera
Grand opera, featuring large choruses, elaborate scores, and spectacular sets, first developed in 19th-century France.

Musicals
Light, small-scale operas developed into the musicals of Jerome Kern (1885–1945) and others in the 1920s, weaving songs and dance around a modern story.

William Tell: grand operas are lavishly staged.

West Side Story: in 1961, a film was made of this 1950s' musical.

Staging an opera

It takes an enormous number of people to stage an opera and make it an exciting musical and dramatic spectacle. In addition to the singers and orchestra, designers and backstage staff are needed to take care of the spectacular sets, costumes, and lighting. A director works closely with the conductor to match the drama with the music.

Ornate interior of opera house

Boxes

The audience sits in the stalls.

Orchestra is positioned in front of the stage.

Bayreuth Festival Theatre, Germany: built to house Wagner's operas.

Famous opera houses
Early operas were staged in theatres, but soon buildings were made specifically for opera. Now, most major cities have opera houses which can put on the most lavish productions. Among the best known are Covent Garden, London; La Scala, Milan; and The Metropolitan, New York.

Giuseppe Verdi
The Italian composer Giuseppe Verdi (1813–1901) wrote 27 operas. However, an early opera failed so badly that he almost gave up! Instead, he went on to write *La Traviata, Aïda,* and his masterpiece *Otello,* written when he was over 70.

Timeline

1607 *La Farola d'Orfeo,* by Claudio Monteverdi (1567–1643), one of the first real operas, is performed in Italy.

1637 In Italy, public opera house opens.

1791 Wolfgang Amadeus Mozart's *The Magic Flute* is first performed.

1876 Richard Wagner finishes the major series of operas known as *The Ring of the Nibelung,* and sets up the Bayreuth Festival for his work.

1935 *Porgy and Bess,* by US composer George Gershwin (1898–1937), with music influenced by jazz elements, opens in Boston, USA.

1937 *Lulu,* by Alban Berg (1885–1935), is performed. Written in an experimental, harsh-sounding style, the music suits the violent, tragic story.

FIND OUT MORE   DRAMA   FILMS AND FILM-MAKING   JAZZ   MOZART, WOLFGANG AMADEUS   MUSIC   MUSICAL INSTRUMENTS   ORCHESTRA   SOUND   THEATRES

ORCHESTRAS

THE GLORIOUS SOUND of an orchestra in concert is one of the great thrills of classical music. An orchestra is a group of musicians playing together under the direction of a conductor. The players perform specially composed music that combines specific instruments to achieve a balanced, total sound. The stringed instruments (violin, viola, cello, and double bass) are the basis of every orchestra, but orchestral music often includes wind and percussion instruments also.

18th-century orchestra

Beginnings
Classical orchestras first appeared in Europe during the 17th century. They consisted of about 25 string players, usually with a harpsichord accompaniment. By the mid-18th century, wind instruments and kettledrums were also included. Through the 19th century, orchestras grew very rapidly: composers were able to write symphonies for more than a hundred players. This gave a wider range of different sounds.

Sections
The orchestra is divided into four sections by type of instrument: strings, woodwind, brass, and percussion.

Symphony orchestra
The number and type of instruments in an orchestra depends on the style of music being played. Symphonies are written for a full range of musical instruments. Many new instruments have appeared since the first orchestras, particularly in the wind and percussion sections; modern orchestras include most of them. Louder instruments are placed to the back; quieter instruments are in front.

Layout of modern symphony orchestra

Conductor's stand

An orchestra usually contains about 90 musicians.

Concerto
Many concerts include a piece called a concerto, featuring a solo musician accompanied by the orchestra. Concertos for piano, violin, and cello are most popular, but they have been written for almost every instrument.

Leader
The principal violinist, known as the leader, sits nearest the conductor. In the first orchestras, there was no conductor, and the leader beat time. Today the leader is a deputy conductor who helps with the management of the orchestra, and sometimes plays solo parts in concerts.

Chamber orchestra
Some pieces need an orchestra of only about 25 players. Such a group is known as a chamber orchestra. There are only a few performers for each part. They often play early music on authentic instruments.

Chamber music
Classical music written for very small groups of instruments is called chamber music. Such pieces are usually written for between three and eight musicians, with one player for each part; a popular combination is the string quartet, which has two violins, a viola, and a cello.

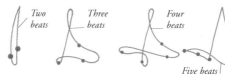

String quartet

Conductor
The conductor's role is to draw the best possible performance of a piece of music from the orchestra. Standing on a raised platform, he or she beats time, and interprets the mood of the music with gestures and facial expressions.

Conductor's expression tells the violinists to play with delicacy.

Beating time
The conductor's baton traces patterns through the air, indicating the tempo of the music to the orchestra.

Two beats

Three beats

Four beats

Five beats

Beats per bar: baton movements

Thomas Beecham
Sir Thomas Beecham (1879–1961) was a British orchestral and operatic conductor. He was a popular figure who used his own fortune to promote music, by financing performances of new works, and founding orchestras and opera companies.

Band
A group of musicians that play wind and percussion instruments only, without a strings section, is normally known as a band. Military and marching brass bands are suited to playing outdoors at sports events and ceremonies; dance bands have been popular since the Renaissance. Rock and pop groups are also sometimes called bands.

FIND OUT MORE — BALLET · BEETHOVEN, LUDWIG VAN · JAZZ · MOZART, WOLFGANG AMADEUS · MUSIC · MUSICAL INSTRUMENTS · OPERA · ROCK AND POP · THEATRES

OTTOMAN EMPIRE

THE OTTOMAN TURKS were originally a nomadic tribe of Asiatic horsemen with a fearsome reputation. From the 14th to the 17th centuries, these devout Muslim warriors carved out an empire spanning Greece, the Balkans, North Africa, western Asia, and the Middle East. The empire's great success was largely due to its custom of rewarding its people for their talent rather than their noble birth. After 1600, the empire went into a decline, due in part to corruption at the sultan's court. Even so, it staggered on, known as the Sick Man of Europe, until treaties after World War I dismantled it. The sultanate was abolished in 1922.

Expansion of empire
The Ottoman Empire evolved in several stages from a small base in Anatolia (in modern Turkey). In the 14th century, Ottomans expanded into the Balkans; after 1453, their fleet was dominant in the eastern Mediterranean; by the 16th century, with the conquest of Syria, Egypt, and Hungary, the Ottoman Empire was poised to take over the western world.

State and religion

A fierce religious fervour drove Ottoman expansion. The sultans, inspired by their Muslim faith, felt they had a duty to convert their neighbours to Islam, and therefore expanded the empire through conquest. Gazis, or frontier-fighters, called themselves "the instrument of God's religion".

House of Islam
To the Ottomans, the world was split between the House of Islam, where there was Muslim government and law, and the House of War, which was inhabited by infidels (non-Muslims). According to Muslim holy law, the Jihad (struggle) between the two Houses had to continue until the House of Islam finally triumphed.

Sultanate
The Ottoman sovereigns and religious leaders were known as sultans. Many of the earlier sultans were men of humble origins, who gained power through ability rather than noble birth. This policy was one of the empire's great strengths, until the sultanate became hereditary, and some sultans proved lazy and corrupt.

Few portraits exist because Islamic holy law does not encourage artists to depict people.

Sultan Ahmed I as a young man

Steel blade inlaid with verse by the Ottoman poet Nejati

Semi-precious stones

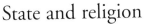

Ottoman court dagger, 16th century

Warfare

During the 16th and 17th centuries, the Ottoman Empire was constantly at war. As the cavalry (Sipahis) and infantry (Janissaries) conquered each new stretch of land, the sultan shared it between them. This system encouraged the soldiers to extend the frontiers.

Janissaries and dervishes
Janissaries were the crack infantrymen of the Ottoman armies. They usually started life as non-Turkish Christian boys from southeastern Europe. Dervishes – Ottoman holy men – recruited them and sent them to Istanbul for training, where they converted to Islam. If they showed talent in battle, they were well rewarded. This system of meritocracy, or rewarding talent, meant that the sultan could rely on the Janissaries' total loyalty.

Janissary, 16th century

Battle of Lepanto
By 1550, a vulnerable western Europe was torn between warring Protestants and Catholics, and open to sea attack from the Ottomans. However, in 1571, a rare Christian coalition between Spain, Venice, Genoa, and the Papacy drove off the Ottoman advance at a battle in the Mediterranean. This ended Ottoman expansion.

Topkapi Palace

In 1453, Sultan Muhammad II (1451–81) renamed Constantinople Istanbul. He built the magnificent Topkapi Palace, whose gracious courtyards and arcades can still be seen today.

Royal salon, Topkapi Palace

Timeline

1363 Early Ottoman conquests in Europe.

1453 Capture of Constantinople marks end of Byzantine Empire. The city is renamed Istanbul.

1463 Ottomans defeat Viennese.

1516–17 Ottomans conquer Egypt and Syria.

1526 Battle of Mohács leads to conquest of most of Hungary.

1529 Failed siege of Vienna.

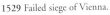

Sixteenth-century Janissaries

1571 Ottoman defeat at Lepanto.

1600 Empire begins decline.

1683 Another failed siege of Vienna.

1909 The last traditional sultan, Abdul-Hamid II, is overthrown and replaced by Muhammed V.

1922 Sultanate is abolished, preparing the way for a new Turkish republic.

Suleiman the Magnificent

The greatest sultan of all was Suleiman I (r.1520–66), called the Lawgiver by his 14 million subjects. Suleiman was also a poet and a patron of the arts. Under Suleiman's rule, the empire's lands reached their greatest extent, and his advance into Europe was halted only by the failure of a siege of Vienna in 1529. The Ottomans continued as a major sea power for another 50 years.

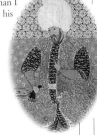

FIND OUT MORE   ARCHITECTURE   FEUDALISM   ISLAM   ISLAMIC EMPIRE   PERSIAN EMPIRES   WARFARE

OWENS, JESSE

OF ALL THE ATHLETES who have performed at the Olympics over the years, few have made more of an impression than Jesse Owens, the young, black American who won four gold medals at the 1936 games in Berlin. Nazi leader Adolf Hitler wanted to use the games to demonstrate his theories about the supremacy of the Aryan race, but Owens showed that such ideas are nonsense. The crowd adored him, for he was a true athlete, whose speed and agility won him admirers wherever he raced.

Early life
Jesse Owens was born in 1913 on a farm in Oakville, in the southern state of Alabama, USA. His grandparents were slaves, his parents sharecroppers (tenant farmers). Like many poor black families at this time, his parents were forced to leave the land to find work in the northern cities of the USA. The Owens family settled in Cleveland, Ohio. It was at his high school in Cleveland that Jesse Owens' remarkable talent for athletics was first discovered.

Athletics
At his high school in Cleveland, Ohio, Jesse distinguished himself in both track and field events. He won major events at the National Amateur Athletic Union meetings in 1934 and 1935, and then broke five world records while competing for the Ohio State University team at Ann Arbor, Michigan, on 25 May, 1935.

Owens wins the 100 yards at Ann Arbor, Michigan

Training and jumping
When he was a young man, Jesse Owens trained with coach Charles Riley, who was one of the first to recognize his athletic ability. Riley helped Owens improve his running style. He also trained Jesse for the long jump. One of the most outstanding records of Owens' career was his long jump at Ann Arbor in 1935, which he made after breaking no fewer than four track records. He made only one attempt at the jump, clearing 8.13 m (26 ft 8 1/4 ins) and setting a world record that was to stand for 25 years.

Berlin Olympics
In August 1936, the four-yearly Olympic Games were held in Berlin, the German capital. The German leader Adolf Hitler used the games as propaganda for his Nazi regime. He spent lavishly on training the German athletes, and hoped to glorify his racial myth of a superior "Aryan race", the white, northern Europeans. However, Owens' achievements smashed these hopes.

Owens takes the baton in the final leg of the 4 x 100 m relay.

Owens wins the long jump.

Lutz Long
The long jump final in the Olympics turned into a close contest between Owens and the German athlete Lutz Long. Owens eventually won with a new world record of 8.07 m (26 ft 5 3/8 ins), but such was the respect the two athletes had for each other, that they embraced at the end. This gesture annoyed Hitler. He congratulated Lutz Long, but completely ignored Owens.

Owens with Lutz Long

Track and field
Owens was the star of the 1936 Olympics, making 12 appearances and winning every heat and event he entered. Although Owens won four gold medals – for the 100 m, 200 m, long jump, and 4 x 100 m relay – and broke two world records, Hitler refused to meet him or shake his hand, as he did white American athletes.

One of Owens' four Olympic gold medals

Spikes on part of sole that touches ground

Whole shoe is made of leather.

Running shoe, worn by Owens

The professional
After the games, Owens had to take part in race meetings in Europe to raise money for the American team. Too tired to compete, he pulled out, and was suspended by the American Amateur Athletic Union. Later, he entered exhibition races to raise money for his family and for charity, most famously running a race against a horse.

Later life
Owens was secretary of the Illinois Athletics Commission until 1955, and was later active in youth work in the state. As a special envoy for President Eisenhower, he attended the 1956 Olympics in Melbourne, Australia. He also helped to publicize the Munich Olympic Games in 1972.

JESSE OWENS	
1913	Born in Alabama, USA
1933–34	After his family moves to Cleveland, Ohio, wins major athletics events
1935	Breaks world records (100-yard/91.4-m, and 220-yard/201-m sprints; 220-yard/201-m low hurdles; long jump)
1936	Wins four gold medals at the Berlin Olympics (100-m, 200-m, long jump, and 4 x 100 m relay)
1956	Acts as President's special envoy to Melbourne Olympics
1980	Dies at age 67

FIND OUT MORE

GERMANY, HISTORY OF   OLYMPIC GAMES   SPORTS

OWLS AND NIGHTJARS

MOST BIRDS ARE ACTIVE during the day and rest after dark. Owls and nightjars usually live the other way around. Both groups of birds come to life at sunset, just when the animals they eat are also on the move, but they feed in quite different ways. Owls snatch up small animals from the ground, using their sharp claws, or talons. They have very good eyesight and even better hearing. Some of them can find prey using their ears alone. Nightjars feed in the air. They also have good eyesight, but instead of using their claws to catch their food, they scoop up moths and other insects in their large beaks.

The owl spreads its wing feathers to control the speed of its approach.

White underparts show when the owl is in flight.

Forward-facing eyes help the owl to judge distances.

Feather-covered legs and feet

Barn owl
This silent hunter patrols fields and open ground on slowly flapping wings. If it sees or hears prey, it drops on it silently with talons outstretched. Barn owls can be recognized by their heart-shaped face, which channels sounds to the ears.

The barn owl usually flies just a few metres above the ground.

Soft-edged feathers keep flight silent.

A noise or movement attracts its attention, it prepares to pounce.

The owl's legs swing down, ready to attack.

Nightjars
Also known as nighthawks, there are about 80 species of these nocturnal insect-eaters. They have sharply pointed wings, a slim body, and plumage that camouflages them when they rest on the ground.

Camouflage
Nightjars roost and breed on the ground, or sometimes on a flat roof. They keep very still and their superb camouflage hides them from predators. This European nightjar looks just like a piece of wood.

Poorwill
In places with cold winters, most nightjars migrate to warmer regions. The North American poorwill avoids the cold in an unusual way for a bird. It crawls into a rock crevice and hibernates.

Oilbird
The oilbird of northern South America is a fruit-eating relative of the nightjars. It nests deep inside caves, and, like bats, uses sound to find its way through the darkness.

Barn owl feather

Feathers
An owl's flight feathers have a soft fringe on their front edge. These fringes soften the sounds that feathers normally make when they move through the air.

Fur and bones matted together in a whole pellet.

Fur

Skulls

Hip bones

Shoulder blades

Owls
There are 133 species of owl, and they live in almost every land habitat from tropical rainforest to Arctic tundra. Most species hunt after dark, but a few fly by day. Owls' eyes widen inside their heads, and the birds cannot swivel them in the socket. To look around, they twist their necks instead.

Pellets
Owls swallow their food whole. After digesting a meal, they cough up the bones, fur, and feathers in a compact lump called a pellet. This tawny owl's pellet has been pulled apart to show some of its contents. The owl that produced this pellet had been feeding mainly on voles.

Buffy fish owl
Fish owls live in Africa and Asia. The bottom of their toes is covered with sharp spines for gripping fish. Unlike other owls, they do not have fringed feathers.

Elf owl
Only 14 cm (5.5 in) long, this is the smallest owl. It lives in North American deserts, and nests in holes in trees or cacti.

BARN OWL

SCIENTIFIC NAME *Tyto alba*

ORDER Strigiformes

FAMILY Tytonidae

DISTRIBUTION World-wide, although absent from many islands and cold places

HABITAT Woodland edges, grassland, farmland, often near buildings

DIET Mostly small mammals, but occasionally insects, small birds, and amphibians

SIZE Length including tail: 34 cm (13 in); males slightly smaller than females

LIFESPAN About 15 years

FIND OUT MORE   BIRDS   BIRDS OF PREY   CAMOUFLAGE AND COLOUR   FLIGHT, ANIMAL   MIGRATION, ANIMAL   POLAR WILDLIFE

PACIFIC OCEAN

TWICE AS LARGE as its nearest rival, the Atlantic, the Pacific is the world's largest ocean, and covers one-third of the Earth's surface. It stretches from the Arctic in the north to the Antarctic in the south, and almost halfway around the globe from the Americas to Australia and Asia. The Pacific is dotted with more than 20,000 volcanic and coral islands, and ringed by active volcanoes. It is also the deepest ocean and drops to 11,033 m (36,197 ft) in the Mariana Trench. Important trade routes cross the Pacific, and some of the world's richest countries lie on its shores.

Physical features
"Pacific" means peaceful, yet the Pacific Ocean has many strong currents that affect climate and weather. These circulate clockwise in the north and anticlockwise in the south.

PACIFIC OCEAN FACTS

AREA 165,241,000 sq km (63,800,000 sq miles)

AVERAGE DEPTH 4,200 m (13,800 ft)

GREATEST DEPTH 11,033 m (36,197 ft) Mariana Trench

NUMBER OF ISLANDS 20,000–30,000

HIGHEST MOUNTAIN Mauna Kea, Hawaii, 10,205 m (27,605 ft) of which over half is below the ocean's surface

El Niño
Normally, a cold current flows from the western coast of South America. However, every few years, in December, a warm current called El Niño flows east towards Peru, causing worldwide weather changes, including severe droughts in Australia.

Ring of Fire
The Pacific is surrounded by deep ocean trenches where the Earth's tectonic plates are pulled downwards. Earthquakes are frequent in these areas, and the many volcanoes form a "Ring of Fire" around the ocean. The Pavlof Volcano on the Alaskan Peninsula is part of this ring.

International Date Line
The world's time zones are based on Greenwich Observatory, England, which is taken as 0° longitude. Halfway around the world at 180° longitude, an imaginary line down the middle of the Pacific Ocean marks one day from the next. So, when it is Monday in New Zealand, it is Sunday in Samoa. In some places the date line has to be moved to avoid dividing countries – it would be odd if it was Monday in the west of the archipelago of Fiji and Sunday in the east.

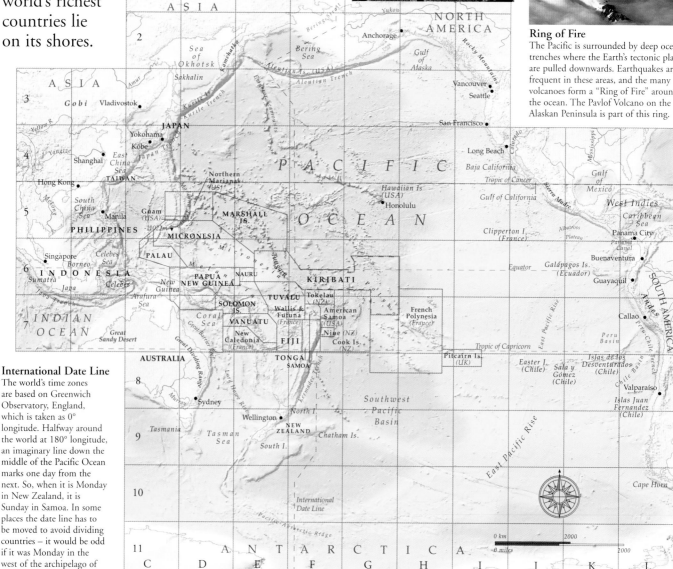

634

Islands

The thousands of islands in the Pacific are scattered over a vast area. They are home to about five million people, whose one great shared resource is the sea. Some islands are mountainous and volcanic in origin, while the lower islands are mostly coral atolls. Most islands are clustered in the southwest Pacific. Others, such as Easter Island and Hawaii, are more isolated – thousands of kilometres from their neighbours.

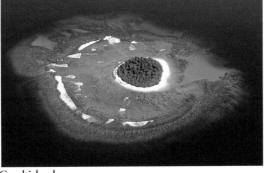

Coral islands
The warm waters of the southern Pacific provide ideal conditions for corals, which flourish there. Thousands of the Pacific islands are atolls, coral reefs sitting on the rims of the sunken craters of old volcanoes. Most of the Pacific's coral islands are tiny.

Hawaii
The islands of the US state of Hawaii are not part of the "Ring of Fire", but hot spot volcanoes that form where magma wells up through weak points in the seabed. As the Earth's tectonic plates move, these volcanoes form new islands. Hawaii's two active volcanoes constantly erupt, causing fountains of lava to shoot into the air.

Military bases
Several Pacific islands are used as military bases, especially by the USA. American bases include Midway, a naval base north of Hawaii, Guam, a naval base in the western Pacific, Wake, an air base, and Johnston atoll, once used for nuclear tests and now a dump for toxic gases and other chemical weapons.

US naval base on Guam

Bird sanctuaries
Many thousands of Pacific islands, such as the US territories of Baker, Howland, and Jarvis islands, are uninhabited by people, but are sanctuaries for millions of seabirds. Birds such as the Greater Frigate Bird return to the same islands every year to rear their young.

Tropical storms

Trade winds constantly blow across the Pacific, from northeast and southeast of the Equator. The trade winds are responsible for the violent tropical storms called either willy-willies in Australia or typhoons, from *tai fung*, which means "great wind" in Chinese.

Pacific trade

Nearly half the world's major shipping routes cross the Pacific. Large container ships transport cargoes between the countries of the Pacific Rim, which is the name given to the countries on the shores of the ocean.

Shipping
Huge supertankers and giant bulk carriers carry oil and other raw materials, such as iron ore and copper, from as far north as Alaska to countries of the Pacific Rim, such as Japan, North America, Australia, and countries of eastern Asia.

Container ports
Like many Pacific ports, the harbour at Hong Kong has been specially designed to load and unload large numbers of huge container ships that arrive every day from all over the world.

Resources

The Pacific's greatest resource is its stock of fish and other seafood. Parts of the seabed are covered in small black lumps called manganese nodules that contain many minerals and can be used to make paints, batteries, and steel.

Fish farming
Farming fish, often called aquaculture, has been practised in the Pacific for centuries. China and Korea farm seaweed as well as fish, oysters, and mussels. The endangered giant clam, which grows up to 1 m (3.3 ft), is now bred in the southern Pacific.

Fishing
Nearly half the world's fish are caught in Pacific waters. Most of the fish live close to land, particularly along the Asian coasts. During an El Niño, weather changes make them desert the South American coast.

Giant clam

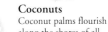

Husk　Coconuts

Flesh

Coconuts
Coconut palms flourish along the shores of all the tropical islands of the Pacific. The milky liquid in a coconut is an important drink; its flesh can be eaten fresh or dried as copra, which yields oil. The tough outer fibre can be woven to make ropes and matting for floors.

Skipjack tuna

Tourism

The tourist trade is developing slowly in the Pacific, because of the long distances to travel and the shortage of modern hotels. Fiji, Tahiti, American Samoa, and Hawaii are the fastest-growing centres. Islands such as the Galápagos Islands fear tourism will damage the environment.

Tourists on Santa Cruz in the Galápagos

FIND OUT MORE | CONTINENTS | CORAL REEFS | FISHING INDUSTRY | ISLANDS | OCEANS AND SEAS | PACIFIC, SOUTHWEST | POLYNESIA | SHIPS AND BOATS | VOLCANOES | WINDS

PACIFIC, SOUTHWEST

THE ISLANDS of the southwest Pacific are divided into Micronesia and Melanesia, which includes the eastern part of the island of New Guinea called Papua New Guinea. There are few large towns on the small islands. Most people live in villages and practise subsistence farming, which means they grow just enough food to support themselves. The chief exports are coconut products, bananas, cocoa beans, and cane sugar.

Physical features

Some southwest Pacific islands are low-lying and easily flooded in stormy weather, while others are volcanic. Several islands have volcanic, black sand. Papua New Guinea is highly mountainous and covered in tropical forest.

Volcanoes

Many of the mountainous islands of Micronesia and Melanesia are volcanic. Some island countries, like Vanuatu, have active volcanoes, likely to erupt at any time. Others are the rims of extinct volcanic craters, ringed with coral atolls. The combination of volcanic ash and coral results in poor soils.

Coconuts

Even where soils are poor, coconut palms manage to survive and are one of the most successful kinds of tree on the Pacific islands. Washed up on the shore, they succeed in sprouting even in salt water and can thrive in areas with very little fresh water. The Pacific islanders dry the coconut meat to make copra, which they can eat. The husk is used to make matting.

Regional climate

Melanesia and Micronesia have warm weather all year round. Rainfall varies, but the islands all have a wet and a dry season.

27°C (64°F)   27°C (64°F)

1,819 mm (72 in)

Languages

More than one-third of the world's languages are spoken in the southwest Pacific. Most are spoken in Melanesia, some 750 of them in Papua New Guinea, home to 1,000 different tribes. Micronesians have around 13 main languages, and there are several dialects.

Boys from Papua New Guinea in traditional dress

Papua New Guinea

Papua New Guinea consists of the eastern half of New Guinea island, plus over 600 islands of the Bismarck Archipelago and surrounding waters. The mainland consists of high mountains, divided by swampy river valleys, and is cloaked with tropical forest.

People and languages

Cut off from each other and from the outside world, each of the groups living in Papua's mountain villages has developed very different customs and languages. Great tensions exist between highland peoples who live by hunter-gathering. By contrast, the people in the lowland, coastal areas have frequent contact with the rest of the world.

Mining

Papua New Guinea ranks highly in world gold production and also has natural gas reserves. In recent years, copper mining has led to ecological problems including pollution and landslides.

PAPUA NEW GUINEA FACTS

CAPITAL CITY Port Moresby

AREA 462,840 sq km (178,703 sq miles)

POPULATION 5,200,000

MAIN LANGUAGES English, Pidgin English, Motu, Papuan, 750 native languages

MAJOR RELIGIONS Christian, traditional beliefs

CURRENCY Kina

Map labels

Northern Mariana Is (USA)
Guam (USA)
Hagåtña
MARSHALL ISLANDS
Mariana Trench
Yap
Caroline Islands
Chuuk Is.
Ratak Chain
Ralik Chain
MAJURO
KOROR
Pohnpei I.
PALIKIR
MICRONESIA
Micronesia
Kosrae
PALAU
PACIFIC OCEAN
Equator
PAPUA NEW GUINEA
NAURU
Bismarck Archipelago
New Ireland
INDONESIA
New Guinea
Madang
Bougainville I.
Mendi
Lae
New Britain
PORT MORESBY
Solomon Sea
Melanesia
Santa Isabel
HONIARA
SOLOMON ISLANDS
Santa Cruz Is.
VANUATU
Banks Is.
Coral Sea
FIJI
Vanua Levu
PORT-VILA
Viti Levu
SUVA
New Caledonia (France)
Îles Loyauté
Nouméa

0 km 400
0 miles 400

Micronesia

The Federated States of Micronesia consist of more than 600 islands stretching over 2,900 km (1,800 miles) of ocean. They are a mixture of hilly, thickly forested volcanic islands and low-lying coral atolls. Most islanders live without electricity or running water. The main source of income is copra and fishing.

MICRONESIA FACTS

CAPITAL CITY Palikir

AREA 702 sq km (271 sq miles)

POPULATION 133,000

MAIN LANGUAGES English, Trukese, Pohnpeian

MAJOR RELIGION Christian

CURRENCY US dollar

Traditional dancers
Although mainly Christian, the Micronesians follow a traditional way of life, celebrating important occasions with singing and dancing. Women play an important role in the society, and the title of chief is passed on through the female line. Although independent, Micronesians rely on US aid for funding.

Marshall Islands

Independent since 1990, this country, consists of five islands, 29 atolls, and 1,150 small islets. People live by selling fish and coconut oil.

Ebeye Island
Most of Ebeye's population were forced to move from Kwajalein in 1947 to make way for a US missile base.

MARSHALL ISLANDS FACTS

CAPITAL CITY Majuro

AREA 181 sq km (70 sq miles)

POPULATION 68,100

MAIN LANGUAGES English, Marshallese

MAJOR RELIGIONS Christian

CURRENCY US dollar

P

Nauru

This tiny island, independent from Britain since 1968, has grown rich through its phosphate deposits.

Phosphate mining
Over the last 100 years, the mining of the mineral phosphate for fertilizer, has left 80 per cent of the island unusable. As supplies run out, Nauru's future lies in investment.

NAURU FACTS

CAPITAL CITY None

AREA 21.2 sq km (8.2 sq miles)

POPULATION 11,800

MAIN LANGUAGES Nauruan, English

MAJOR RELIGION Christian

CURRENCY Australian dollar

Vanuatu

An archipelago of 82 volcanic, mountainous islands, Vanuatu forms a chain 1,300 km (800 miles) long. Many islands have coral reefs and dense rainforest. The people, who mostly live on the 16 largest islands, speak 105 languages.

VANUATU FACTS

CAPITAL CITY Port-Vila

AREA 12,190 sq km (4,707 sq miles)

POPULATION 200,000

MAIN LANGUAGES Bislama, English

MAJOR RELIGIONS Christian, traditional beliefs

CURRENCY Vatu

Carved wood figures
The people of Vanuatu are among the most traditional in the Pacific, and customs are important. They carve unusual wooden figures, similar in style to those on Easter Island, Polynesia.

Solomon Islands

The scene of fierce fighting in World War II (1939–45), the Solomon Islands were a British colony until 1978. There are six large islands and hundreds of islets and coral reefs.

SOLOMON ISLANDS FACTS

CAPITAL CITY Honiara

AREA 28,450 sq km (10,985 sq miles)

POPULATION 463,000

MAIN LANGUAGE English

MAJOR RELIGION Christian

CURRENCY Solomon Islands dollar

Saving trees
In 1998 a new forest policy was introduced to plant new trees to replace the thousands felled as timber for export.

Palau

The Palau archipelago in the western Pacific consists of more than 300 islands, only nine of which are inhabited. The society is unusual in that the clan chiefs are chosen by the women.

PALAU FACTS

CAPITAL CITY Koror

AREA 458 sq km (177 sq miles)

POPULATION 19,100

MAIN LANGUAGES Palauan, English

MAJOR RELIGIONS Christian, traditional beliefs

CURRENCY US dollar

Rock islands
These strange island mountains, viewed from the air, are thickly forested. Palau's island reefs contain 1,500 species of fish and about 700 types of coral.

Fiji

Fiji lies at the eastern edge of Melanesia. It consists of two large islands, which are mountainous and volcanic in origin, and more than 800 islets and coral atolls.

FIJI FACTS

CAPITAL CITY Suva

AREA 18,270 sq km (7,054 sq miles)

POPULATION 825,000

MAIN LANGUAGES English, Fijian

MAJOR RELIGIONS Christian, Hindu, Muslim

CURRENCY Fijian dollar

Fijian village
Most Fijians live off the land in rural villages. Many people work on sugar plantations. Cane sugar makes up around one-third of Fiji's exports.

FIND OUT MORE   AUSTRALASIA AND OCEANIA   CORAL REEFS   EMPIRES   FARMING   PACIFIC OCEAN   POLLUTION   RAINFOREST WILDLIFE   SCULPTURE   SHIPS AND BOATS   WORLD WAR II

PAINTING AND DRAWING

P

EARLY PEOPLE painted hunting scenes on cave walls using natural pigments. In 16th-century Europe, art schools were set up to teach drawing and painting skills. Today, we draw and paint with a variety of materials for a range of different purposes – from the creation of great works of art through to complex and practical architectural drawings and swiftly sketched design plans.

An artist mixes colours to find the right tone.

An artist's tools
Artists use crayons, paints, brushes, and palettes. These tools have hardly changed over centuries. Paints are made from pigments, which may come from sources such as bark and earth, or from metals.

Charcoal

Watercolours made of water and pigments.

Pigments

Pastels

Watercolour paint

Palette
The palette has a central thumb hole so the artist can hold it with one hand and paint with the other.

Drawing

Artists draw with pencils, inks, and crayons. Originally, drawings were done as preparatory sketches for a finished work, such as a painting or sculpture. In the early 16th century, however, artists began creating drawings as finished works of art, as many artists still do today.

Sketches
A quick, rough drawing that captures the impression of a subject is known as a sketch. This black chalk sketch of an elephant is by the Dutch artist Rembrandt van Rijn (1606–69).

Technical drawing
Engineers, architects, and designers do very accurate drawings based on precise mathematical calculations to show how to construct objects such as bridges and houses. This skill is known as technical drawing.

Looking at paintings

Paintings can be enjoyed in many ways: for the cleverness of their design; the quality of the light; or the beauty of the colour. But it can also take time to unravel exactly what is going on.

Artist's model

This detail shows the artist's model dressed as the Muse of history. In Greek mythology, each of the arts and sciences was represented by one of the nine Muses.

The Artist's Studio by Jan Vermeer (1632–75)

The drawn curtain suggests that we are almost spying on a private scene.

Light pours in from the top left of the painting.

In the curtain, Vermeer paints highlights with tiny beads of bright white.

An empty chair placed in the foreground invites the viewer into the scene as an onlooker.

The many straight lines in the painting, such as the roof beams, give the picture its sense of stability.

The large map shows Holland and Flanders because Vermeer was Dutch.

Jan Vermeer shows himself at work painting details of the model's costume.

The diagonal lines of the floor tiles and the table's edge lead the eye into the painting.

Ways of painting

Art is becoming increasingly experimental as artists try out new ideas, such as imaginative ways of applying paint to a canvas. Painting and drawing may be combined with other techniques such as collage, printing, and paper-making. This combining of techniques is known as mixed media.

The French painter Henri Matisse (1869–1954) combined paper cut-outs with paint.

Textures
Paint has texture as well as colour. In this painting, the artist emphasizes texture by painting different colours on to patches of material of contrasting textures.

Collage
Materials are cut and then arranged to create a collage. In this collage, vibrant colours and curved shapes are combined to create a sense of dynamism.

Paper
Artists control the colour and texture of the surface they paint on. This may be a flat canvas or it can be uneven handmade paper, as in this painting.

FIND OUT MORE

ARCHITECTURE | ART, HISTORY OF | DESIGN | DYES AND PAINTS | LEONARDO DA VINCI | MONET, CLAUDE | MUSEUMS | PICASSO, PABLO | RENAISSANCE | SCULPTURE

PAKISTAN

THE COUNTRY OF PAKISTAN was established in 1947 as an independent state for Indian Muslims. The country originally incorporated East Pakistan, formerly Bengal, which broke away in 1971 and became a separate nation called Bangladesh. Pakistan is home to four main ethnic groups. Punjabis make up more than half the population. The rest are Sindhis, Pathans, and Baluch. A military coup in 1999 led to the suspension of democratic elections. Pakistan played a key role in the 2001 US bombing of Afghanistan. Pakistan and India dispute ownership of the largely Muslim state of Kashmir.

PAKISTAN FACTS

CAPITAL CITY	Islamabad
AREA	803,940 sq km (310,401 sq miles)
POPULATION	145,000,000
MAIN LANGUAGE	Urdu
MAJOR RELIGION	Islam
CURRENCY	Pakistani rupee
LIFE EXPECTANCY	60 years
PEOPLE PER DOCTOR	1,667
GOVERNMENT	Military rule
ADULT LITERACY	46%

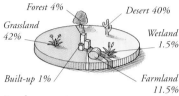

Forest 4%   Desert 40%
Grassland 42%   Wetland 1.5%
Built-up 1%   Farmland 11.5%

Land use
Much of the grassland is used as pasture for sheep. Huge irrigation projects in the Indus Valley enable crops to be cultivated. Opium is grown in the western mountains.

Physical features
The Karakoram and Hindu Kush mountain ranges, dominate the northwest of Pakistan. The Punjab and Sind contain fertile river plains. In the southwest is the dry, rocky Baluchistan plateau, while in the southeast, the Thar Desert extends into India.

Karakoram Mountains
The Karakoram Range lies along Pakistan's northern border with China. It includes K2, the world's second highest peak at 8,611 m (28,253 ft). The Hindu Kush range lies on the Afghan border.

River Indus
From its source in the Himalayas, the Indus flows 3,180 km (1,976 miles) through Pakistan, irrigating the fertile plains of the Punjab and Sind. The ancient Indus Valley civilization thrived here 4,500 years ago.

203 per sq km (526 per sq mile)   36% Urban   64% Rural

People
Nearly 97 per cent of Pakistanis follow Islam, a religion that unites the main groups. A class system exists, and the gap between rich and poor is overt. Overpopulation is a problem.

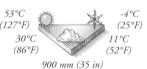

53°C (127°F)   -4°C (25°F)
30°C (86°F)   11°C (52°F)
900 mm (35 in)

Climate
Pakistan has three seasons. Winter (November to March) is warm and cooled by sea breezes on the coast. Summer (April to July) is hot. The monsoon season (July to September) brings heavy rain to hills and mountains.

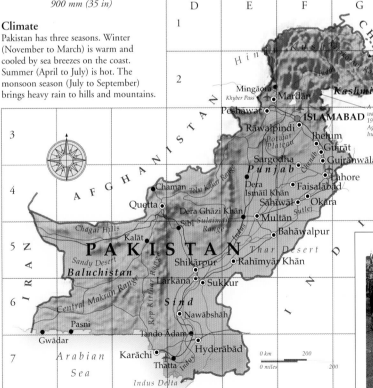

Fluffy cotton bolls are picked, then spun into thread to make cloth.

Ripe cotton flowers

Cotton
Pakistan is one of the world's largest producers of raw cotton, and cotton textiles and garments are the country's leading exports. The cotton is grown in the fertile Indus flood plains. Farming employs 44 per cent of Pakistan's work-force. Wheat is one of the chief crops, and rice and sugar-cane are also grown.

A "line of control" was established in 1972 by Simla Agreement between India and Pakistan

Islamabad
Built in the 1960s to replace Karachi as Pakistan's capital, Islamabad is home to 529,180 people. It is a spacious city with interesting modern buildings and has four areas: business, administrative, diplomatic, and residential. Islamabad also has the world's largest mosque. Karachi, with 9,200,000 people, is the country's largest city and chief port.

Street scene in Islamabad

FIND OUT MORE

ASIA, HISTORY OF   BANGLADESH AND NEPAL   DRUGS   FARMING   INDIA, HISTORY OF   INDUS VALLEY CIVILIZATION   ISLAM   MOUNTAINS AND VALLEYS   RIVERS   TEXTILES AND WEAVING

PANDAS AND RACCOONS

IT IS ONLY RECENTLY that zoologists have sorted out the relationship between pandas and raccoons. Modern scientific techniques now show that the raccoon family is divided into two subfamilies, one including raccoons, coatis, and the kinkajou, the other containing the red panda. The giant panda is related to bears. Apart from the red panda, all members of the raccoon family live in the Americas. The pandas are found only in Asia.

Pandas

The giant panda and the red panda have a number of similar characteristics, such as a false "thumb", so they were once considered to be closely related. It is now thought that the pandas' shared features probably developed as they evolved to survive in similar habitats.

Giant panda
About 1.5 m (5 ft) long, the giant panda lives only in the mountainous forests of southwestern China. Its main food is bamboo. This woody grass is low in nutrients, so pandas must eat about 38 kg (84 lb) of it every day to survive.

Paws
Both giant pandas and red pandas have five toes on each foot. They also have a false "thumb" on their forepaws. This has developed from the wrist bone and the pandas use it to grip bamboo stems.

False thumb

A raccoon often looks for food in streams, feeling underwater for prey with its sensitive paws.

Young raccoons

Raccoons

There are seven species of raccoon. The best-known is the common raccoon, with its black mask and ringed tail. This inquisitive animal eats most things, including fish, frogs, insects, small mammals, and fruit. It has adapted well to living near people and will rifle through dustbins, picking out food with its forepaws.

Red panda
An agile animal, the red panda is about 1 m (3.3 ft) long, including its tail. It lives on the slopes of the southern Himalayas and in parts of China, spending much of the day asleep in a tree. At night, it looks for food on the ground. Bamboo is just part of its diet. Other food includes birds' eggs, chicks, and berries.

Female and young giant panda

Red panda cub

Coatis
These forest animals are at home on the ground and in the trees. Females and young form groups and forage together during the day for food such as insects, lizards, and tubers. They use their forepaws and long flexible snout to hunt in crevices and on the forest floor.

Kinkajou
The nocturnal kinkajou lives in the forests of tropical Central and South America. It spends almost all its time in the trees and is the only American carnivore to have a prehensile tail, which means it can grasp things with it. The kinkajou uses its tail to cling to branches while it feeds – mainly on fruit and nectar. Its back teeth have lost the sharp edges that carnivores have for slicing meat. Instead their teeth are blunt and used for crushing fruit.

Young pandas
Giant pandas often give birth to twins but usually only one cub survives. A newborn cub is hairless and weighs only 90-100 g (3-3.5 oz). The female cradles it constantly for the first three weeks and carries it around for four to five months. Red pandas have up to four cubs; they can walk at about three days old.

GIANT PANDA

SCIENTIFIC NAME	*Ailuropoda melanoleuca*
ORDER	Carnivora
FAMILY	Ursidae
DISTRIBUTION	Southwestern China
HABITAT	Forests with bamboo
DIET	Bamboo, other plants, and meat.
SIZE	Length: Up to 1.7 m (5.5 ft)
LIFESPAN	Over 20 years (in captivity)

FIND OUT MORE

ANIMALS • ASIAN WILDLIFE • BEARS • SOUTH AMERICAN WILDLIFE • URBAN WILDLIFE

PANKHURST FAMILY

WHEN EMMELINE PANKHURST was born in 1858, women had few rights in Britain and were not allowed to vote to change the law. Emmeline and her two daughters devoted their lives to obtaining the vote for women so that they could influence decisions about their lives. They developed new strategies, organizing their supporters into a pressure group, going on protest marches, even chaining themselves to the railings of public buildings to get publicity for their cause. They also produced all kinds of merchandise to gain publicity and raise money. In 1918, after a long, bitter campaign, women aged 30 and over were given the vote in Britain .

The Pankhursts

Emmeline Goulden (1858–1928) was born in Manchester, England, and went to a womens' college in Paris. She married a lawyer, Richard Pankhurst, and had two daughters, Christabel (1880–1958) and Sylvia (1882–1960). Emmeline, a charismatic figure, inspired the WSPU, while Christabel was its leader.

Emmeline Pankhurst

Christabel Pankhurst

Sylvia Pankhurst
A socialist and a feminist, Sylvia built up a mass movement for suffrage among the poor of London's East End and was a pacifist during World War I. In later life, she championed the cause of Ethiopian independence.

WSPU

Emmeline was a member of the Independent Labour Party, but left it because of its resistance to women's suffrage (voting rights). In 1903, she formed the Women's Social and Political Union (WSPU) in Manchester. The WSPU led the campaign for women's suffrage, adopting more militant tactics after the Liberal prime minister refused to support suffrage in 1906.

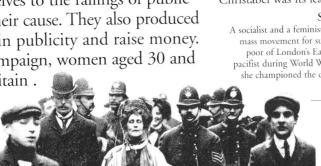

Votes for women
The Pankhursts were highly skilled at attracting publicity. They set up the Women's Press and produced a regular newspaper, *Votes for Women*, for sale on street corners and at meetings. They were also among the first to use manufactured items for publicity, producing a range of suffrage-related goods to fund and publicize the cause.

Suffragettes
Women of all classes and ages joined the women's suffrage movement. Those who favoured militant tactics were nicknamed suffragettes. Some risked great personal danger for their cause. In June 1913, Emily Davison threw herself in front of the king's horse at the Derby and was killed. Others risked arrest and imprisonment.

Demonstrations
Women organized demonstrations in Britain's big cities to further the cause of women's suffrage. In June 1908, more than 200,000 people gathered in Hyde Park, London, in the greatest demonstration of all. In addition, individual women performed acts of bravery by heckling and disrupting meetings, attacking prominent politicians, and damaging buildings. Many of these activities led to arrests.

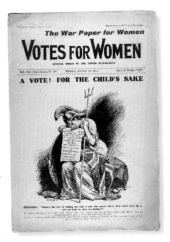

Hannah Mitchell
Hannah Mitchell (1871–1956) was born in poverty in rural England. She ran away from home aged 14 and worked as a maid and a seamstress. An active suffragette, Hannah Mitchell became a councillor and a magistrate in Manchester. Her autobiography, *The Hard Way Up*, is a classic account of a woman's rebellion against the unfair circumstances of her life.

Imprisonment

Many suffragettes spent time in prison for their beliefs. They were classed as criminals, and subjected to harsh conditions. In protest at not being treated as political prisoners, many suffragettes went on hunger strike, and were painfully force-fed.

Prison terms
The Pankhurst family were all jailed many times. In 1913, Emmeline was jailed and released 12 times under the "Cat and Mouse Act".

Emmeline and Christabel in prison clothes, 1908

The "Cat and Mouse Act"
In 1913, the British Parliament passed a law under which hunger strikers could be released from prison, but would be returned when they regained their health.

PANKHURST FAMILY

1858	Emmeline Goulden born
1880	Birth of Christabel
1882	Birth of Sylvia
1903	Women's Social and Political Union founded
1913	Emmeline sentenced to three years in prison for arson
1918	Christabel stands unsuccessfully for parliament
1918	UK Women aged 30 and over given the vote (compared with age 21 and over for men)
1928	Full voting equality obtained when UK women get vote at 21

FIND OUT MORE

CRIME AND PUNISHMENT · EDUCATION · GOVERNMENT AND POLITICS · HUMAN RIGHTS · LAW · WOMEN'S MOVEMENT

PAPER

PAPER TAKES ITS name from "papyrus" – a reedlike plant that the ancient Egyptians used to make the first ever writing material. Today most paper is made from the pulped wood of trees. Paper has played an influential role in spreading knowledge over the ages, and even in today's computer-based electronic age more paper is being consumed than ever before. A forest region covering about 450,000 sq km (174,000 sq miles), equivalent to the size of Sweden, needs to be felled each year to support the world's consumption of paper.

What is paper?
Paper is made up of a mass of short, very thin fibres of wood cellulose pressed tightly together. It may also contain certain additives to give colour and extra smoothness. If you tear a sheet of paper, you can see the cellulose fibres stuck together.

Cellulose fibres matted together

How paper is made

Paper can be made by hand or mechanically. Softwood logs are chopped into pieces and treated with chemicals which convert the wood to a mass of fibres. This "wood pulp" is mixed with water to make paper.

Making paper by hand

1 To make fine hand-made paper the raw material must first be broken down into wood chips and sawdust, which are then beaten to a pulp.

2 A mould and deckle are lowered into the liquid pulp. A layer of pulp covers the mould, its edges contained by the deckle. The mould is then lifted out and tilted to remove excess water.

Deckle

Mould

3 When drained, the thin layer of paper from the mould is laid on absorbent material. Successive layers are laid on top of each other and pressed. After two hours the sheets are separated and left to dry.

Layers of paper and absorbent material

Finished paper

Uses of paper

One of the biggest uses of paper is for printing newspapers. This relatively cheap paper is called newsprint. Coated papers that use a clay-like material to give a smooth effect are used for magazines. High quality writing papers are made from rag and wood pulp. Other paper products are made from different fibrous materials, such as hemp, used in manila envelopes, and straw, which can be used to make cardboard packaging.

Watermarked paper

Watermarked paper
When some types of paper are held up to the light, a translucent pattern or wording may be seen. This watermark signifies quality paper. The mark is pressed into the paper by a wire roller on the papermaking machine.

Cartridge paper

Tracing paper

Textured paper

Dyes are added to give a range of different colours.

Cardboard

Reinforced envelope

Bleached envelope

Collection of paper

Paper consumption

In the Western world a person may use – and throw away – up to about 200 kg (440 lb) of paper each year in its may different forms, from toilet paper to cardboard. Vast areas of forest are cleared to provide raw materials for making paper. This can destroy the landscape and deprive wildlife of precious habitats.

Recycling paper
Paper was the first material to be recycled on a large scale. Recycling helps save resources by reducing the number of trees that are felled each year, and some of the chemicals needed in papermaking.

Paper tip at recycling plant

Renewable resource
To maintain future timber supplies for papermaking, trees must be treated as a renewable resource. Over a given period, as many trees need to be planted as are cut down. Some countries, such as Norway and Sweden, already practise sustainable forestry.

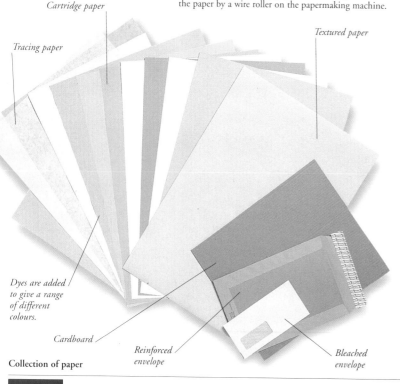

Tree plantation, a source of paper

| FIND OUT MORE | BOOKS | DYES AND PAINTS | EGYPT, ANCIENT | POLLUTION | PRINTING | NEWSPAPERS AND MAGAZINES | TREES | WRITING |

PARASITES

AN ORGANISM THAT LIVES inside, or on, another organism (the host), using it as a source of food, is called a parasite. In a parasitic relationship the host gets no benefit and is usually harmed in some way by the parasite. In contrast, the parasite gains not only a constant source of food, but also shelter by hiding inside the host or among its fur or scales. Many parasites have hooks, suckers, or claws, which they use to keep a firm hold on their host.

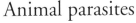

Shaft of hair

Eyes

Claw helps louse grip hair.

Human head louse

Animal parasites

Few animals manage to avoid parasites. Some parasites, such as lice and ticks, live on the outside of their hosts, clinging to their skin or fur, and are called ectoparasites; those that live inside their host's body, such as liver flukes and tapeworms, are called endoparasites. Few parasites are deadly because it is not in their best interest to kill their host; once the host is dead, the parasite will not have long to live either. Many human diseases, such as malaria and elephantiasis, are parasitic in origin.

Fleas and ticks

Many organisms feed on the blood of others, and can spread disease to their host. Fleas are insects that feed on blood once they are adults; their larvae feed on any scraps of organic matter, including the adult fleas' droppings. Ticks, on the other hand, feed from their host throughout their development.

Helmet-shaped head to cut through cat fur.

Cat flea

Reproduction

Parasites often have complex life cycles, involving more than one host at different stages. Because they need to ensure that their eggs reach a suitable host, many parasites produce huge quantities of eggs. For example, the broad tapeworm releases up to 13 million eggs every day within body segments that break off from its rear end.

Tapeworm can reach 10 m (33 ft) in length.

Broad tapeworm

Head hooks

Egg

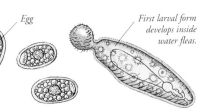

First larval form develops inside water fleas.

Secondary larvae develop inside fish.

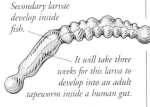

It will take three weeks for this larva to develop into an adult tapeworm inside a human gut.

Life cycle of a tapeworm

1 Tapeworms live in human guts, entering the body through infected fish. They attach themselves to the gut wall with head hooks.

2 Tapeworm eggs are released in human faeces. The eggs enter water, and hatch into embryos that are eaten by water fleas.

3 Inside the water flea, the embryo develops into its first larval form. Water fleas are often eaten by fish.

4 The larvae penetrate the tissues of the fish to form secondary larvae. If a human eats raw, infected fish, the larvae enter the intestines.

Flatworm

The flatworm *Leucochloridium macrostomum* is a parasite that develops in some snails. The parasite must also get into the guts of birds to complete its life cycle. To do this it enters the snail's eyestalks where it swells and develops bright bands of colour. These attract birds, which mistake the pulsating eyestalks for tasty caterpillars.

Mutualism

Mutualism is a relationship between two organisms in which both benefit, for example, between buffalos and oxpeckers. Buffalos are parasitized by ticks that can make the animal ill. The oxpecker scampers over the buffalo picking off the ticks. In this way, the bird gets a good feed and the buffalo is cleaned.

Red-billed oxpecker on buffalo's nose

Oxpecker feeds on parasitic ticks on the buffalo.

Plant parasites

Like animals, plants also have parasites. Usually, the parasitic plant attaches its root system to its host and draws off nourishing fluids; others use their host as a means of support. For example, the strangler fig climbs up a tree for support and to get to the light. Eventually, the fig kills the tree, but by this time, its own stem will be strong enough to support it.

Useful parasites

Most parasites are harmful, but a few are beneficial to people. In microsurgery the medicinal leech is still used to reduce the amount of damage that small blood clots can cause. Many crops are now sprayed with tiny nematode worms which are parasites on certain agricultural pests.

Mistletoe

Mistletoe is a parasitic plant that grows on trees. Birds eat its sticky seeds and deposit some on the bark of trees. The mistletoe grows roots that penetrate the bark and extract water and nutrients.

Dodder

The dodder cannot photosynthesize or produce its own food, so parasitizes heath plants such as gorse and heather. It grows long tendrils that swamp the host plant and absorb food.

Leech sucks blood from human.

Medicinal leech

HUMAN HEAD LOUSE

SCIENTIFIC NAME	*Pediculus humanus capitis*
ORDER	Phthiraptera
FAMILY	Pediculidae
DISTRIBUTION	World-wide, wherever there are humans
HABITAT	Attached to hair on head. Larvae live in hair at back of neck
DIET	Human blood
SIZE	1.5–3 mm (0.06–0.12 in)
LIFESPAN	Adults live for 1–2 months

FIND OUT MORE

DISEASES • MEDICINE • MEDICINE, HISTORY OF • MICROSCOPIC LIFE • PHOTOSYNTHESIS • SNAILS AND OTHER MOLLUSCS • WORMS

PARROTS

WITH THEIR NOISY CALLS and bright colours, parrots are among the most conspicuous of all the world's birds. There are about 330 species, many of which are now threatened by extinction. Most parrots live in forests and woodlands in warm parts of the world. They fly through the trees, or use their feet and their hooked beaks to clamber among the branches. Many live in pairs or flocks, and search together for their food of fruits, seeds, nuts, and flowers.

Parrots can hold things with their toes.

The area of bare skin on the face, is called the cere.

Features

Most parrots are sociable, thickset birds with short necks and large beaks. They have small eyes that are often surrounded by a patch of bare skin. Their feet are short but strong, with four fleshy, clawed toes. Parrots use their toes to grasp branches and to pick up food.

Sulphur-crested cockatoo

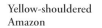

Yellow-shouldered Amazon
This medium-size parrot lives in forests along the northern coast of South America and on nearby islands.

Two toes pointing forward and two pointing backward

Crests
Types of parrot called cockatoos have feathery crests, which males raise and lower in courtship. They bob and swing their heads at the same time, this makes the crests more obvious and aims to attract the attentions of a watching female.

Scarlet macaw
Macaws are the world's largest parrots and live in the forests of Central and South America. They eat fruits, seeds, and nuts, which they crack open with their large beaks.

Powerful jaw muscles for cracking open nuts and seeds.

Diet

Parrots are almost entirely vegetarian. Their beaks are similar, but their tongues are shaped to suit different kinds of plant food. Most parrots find their food in trees, but some, such as kakapos and budgerigars, feed mainly on the ground.

Ground feeders
Wild budgerigars live in the dry grasslands of Australia. They often gather in huge flocks of several thousand birds, as they wander the outback searching for seeds to eat and water to drink.

Fruit feeders
The eclectus parrot is a fruit-eating parrot and has a fleshy tongue. The tongue helps the bird to hold the fruit or nut in the top part of its beak, so that it can use the lower part to break up the food.

Flower feeders
Lories and lorikeets, such as this Duyvenbode's lory, have slender tongues with brush-like tips. Though the parrots have short beaks they can use their tongues to lap up nectar and pollen from flowers.

Scavengers
The kea of New Zealand is one of the few parrots that eats meat from dead animals. It has a long pointed beak, which it uses to rip up meat and to probe for insects and grubs.

Parrots in danger

About a quarter of the world's parrot species are endangered. Some have suffered because they are caught and sold as pets. Others are in decline because their forest home is disappearing. Many are having to face predatory animals introduced by humans.

Long tapering tail

Beak
The upper part of a parrot's beak is much bigger than the lower part and has a hooked tip. When a parrot opens its beak, both parts hinge against its skull, allowing the bird to bite into large objects.

Trapping
Trading in wild parrots has been banned in many places but it still continues. These macaws will be sold as pets. Many will not survive.

Kakapo
This nocturnal parrot comes from New Zealand. It lives on the ground as it is too heavy to fly. Sadly its habitat has been invaded by predatory animals brought into the country from outside, and it is now nearly extinct.

SCARLET MACAW

SCIENTIFIC NAME Ara macao

ORDER Psittaciformes

FAMILY Psittacidae

DISTRIBUTION Mexico to Brazil and Bolivia

HABITAT Open forest and forest edges

DIET Fruit, nuts, and seeds

SIZE Length: 85 cm (34 in)

LIFESPAN About 40 years

FIND OUT MORE   BIRDS   CONSERVATION   RAINFOREST WILDLIFE

PASTEUR, LOUIS

LOUIS PASTEUR WAS one of the greatest scientists of the 19th century. He founded the science of microbiology – the study of organisms not visible to the naked eye. Pasteur believed that science should have practical uses, and that scientists and business people should not live in separate worlds. Much of his work was done in response to requests for help from businessmen. His solutions to problems in the wine and silk industries, and his work in combating life-threatening diseases, such as rabies, made him a hero. Pasteur's method of heating foods to kill harmful bacteria is still used in milk production.

Early life
Louis Pasteur was born in France and brought up in the village of Arbois. At first he did not seem to be a clever student, but his life changed when he went to classes given by a brilliant chemistry teacher. He got into the famous Ecole Normale Supérieure in Paris, and at 32 became Dean of the Faculty of Science at the University of Lille.

P

Bacteria

Pasteur's greatest discovery was that fermentation and decay were caused by microscopic living organisms – bacteria or germs. People had noticed the tiny organisms in decaying matter, but they thought that the organisms had appeared out of nowhere. Pasteur proved that living things could not simply appear spontaneously without living parent organisms.

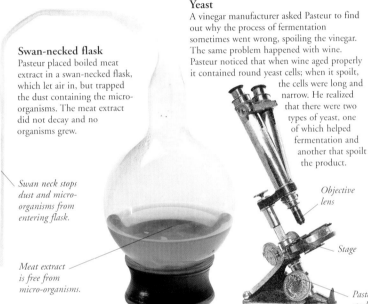

Swan-necked flask
Pasteur placed boiled meat extract in a swan-necked flask, which let air in, but trapped the dust containing the micro-organisms. The meat extract did not decay and no organisms grew.

Swan neck stops dust and micro-organisms from entering flask.

Meat extract is free from micro-organisms.

Yeast
A vinegar manufacturer asked Pasteur to find out why the process of fermentation sometimes went wrong, spoiling the vinegar. The same problem happened with wine. Pasteur noticed that when wine aged properly it contained round yeast cells; when it spoilt, the cells were long and narrow. He realized that there were two types of yeast, one of which helped fermentation and another that spoilt the product.

Objective lens

Stage

Pasteur used this microscope to study yeast cells.

Pasteurization
Pasteur discovered that heating wine to about 60°C (140°F) killed off the unwanted yeast. This method of gentle heating was soon applied to other stored liquids, especially milk. The process became known as "pasteurization", after its inventor. Pasteurization is still used widely today to kill harmful bacteria and help make food and drink safe for human consumption. One of the most familiar uses of the process is in milk production. Before it is sold in the shops, milk is heated for 30 minutes to kill bacteria which could cause tuberculosis in humans. The protein in the milk is unaffected.

Causes of disease

Pasteur proved that many diseases are caused by bacteria. Vaccination – breeding bacteria in a weak form and placing them in an animal's body – can help the animal develop immunity to the bacteria. Building on the work of British doctor Edward Jenner (1749–1823), Pasteur vaccinated sheep against anthrax.

Cocoon of silkworm

Silkworms
In 1865, Pasteur applied his theory of germs to diseased silkworms. He showed that a parasite was infecting the silkworms and the leaves they fed on. Destroying all the infested worms and leaves wiped out the disease.

Rabies
In 1881, Pasteur began to work on a cure for rabies, a disease which affected both animals and humans, and which killed hundreds of people in Europe every year. He found that brain tissue from animals with rabies (below) could be made into a vaccine against the disease. In 1885, he tried out the vaccine on Joseph Meister, a boy who had been bitten by a rabid dog. The boy recovered from the disease.

Pasteur Institute
Pasteur's discovery of a vaccination for rabies made him a hero, and a movement began to collect funds for an institute that would honour him and carry on his scientific work. People from all over the world, including the Tsar of Russia and the Emperor of Brazil, sent in contributions. The Institute was built in 1895; Pasteur died in the same year and was buried in the Institute.

Pasteur Institute, France

LOUIS PASTEUR

1822 Born, Dôle, France.

1843 Begins his studies at the Ecole Normale Supérieure, Paris.

1849 Marries Marie Laurent.

1854 Becomes Dean of the Faculty of Science at the University of Lille.

1857–65 Studies the fermentation process.

1865–70 Studies pebrine, a disease of the silkworm.

1881 Begins work on rabies disease.

1882 Proves the effectivenesss of the anthrax vaccine.

1885 Vaccinates Joseph Meister against rabies.

1888 Becomes director of the Pasteur Institute.

1895 Dies; Pasteur Institute building completed.

FIND OUT MORE   BIOLOGY   DISEASES   FOOD   MEDICINE, HISTORY OF   MICROSCOPES   MICROSCOPIC LIFE   SCIENCE, HISTORY OF

PEACE MOVEMENTS

THROUGHOUT HISTORY, people have engaged in warfare. And every time a war has been fought, some people have joined a peace movement to protest against it. Peace movements contain a wide variety of people: some oppose war for religious reasons or as a matter of individual conscience; others may oppose a particular war for political reasons. Huge demonstrations of thousands of people, and individual acts of courageous protest, contribute to effective campaigns for peace.

The dove is a traditional symbol of peace.

Pacifism

The belief that violence of any kind is wrong is known as pacifism. Pacifists have a principled objection to war and refuse to take part in any behaviour that might lead them directly or indirectly to threaten another human life. Pacifists conduct anti-war protests in non-violent ways (other people use direct action that may harm people and property).

Popular protest

Throughout history, popular protest against war or the threat of war has taken many forms. Individuals have refused to fight or work in war-related industries; groups of people have demonstrated, organized public protests and peace camps, or tried to disrupt war preparations.

White poppy, symbol of Peace Pledge Union

Worn to remember all those who have suffered in war

Objectors in prison, World War I

Conscientious objectors
During World Wars I and II, people on both sides refused to fight on principle. Some took no part at all in war activity; others worked in non-combat areas, such as the medical professions. Many suffered personal abuse, or were imprisoned.

Peace Pledge Union
The Peace Pledge Union is a pacifist organization that works for peace. It was set up in 1934, and by 1936, more than 100,000 people had signed the pledge to renounce war as a way of settling disputes between nations.

Anti-nuclear protest
From the late 1950s, popular peace movements have pressurized governments to cut their store of nuclear weapons. Leading groups include SANE and the Nuclear Freeze in the USA and the Campaign for Nuclear Disarmament (CND) in the UK.

Greenham Common
There is a long history of women playing a specific part in peace movements. In 1982, a permanent women-only peace camp was set up at the US air force base at Greenham Common, England, to protest at the siting of US nuclear missiles on British soil.

The CND symbol is a well-known symbol of anti-nuclear protest.

Greenham Common

Government action

Governments are the main cause of war, but can contribute to peace by maintaining friendly relations with other nations and also by attempting to reconcile international differences through negotiation or diplomacy. Countries prosper in peacetime, because they can trade safely with other nations. However, they also earn money through the export of weapons.

Since 1945, governments and individuals alike have campaigned for nuclear weapons to be banned.

Begin (left) and Sadat (right)

Camp David Accords
To end the historic enmity between their countries, Egyptian President Anwar Sadat (1918–81) and Israeli Prime Minister Menachem Begin (1913–92) signed this peace treaty in 1978. As a result, Sadat was assassinated in 1981.

Disarmament conferences
The first conference to reduce the world stockpile of weapons took place from 1932 to 1934. The talks failed, but since then international negotiations have reduced the nuclear stockpile.

Nobel Peace Prize
Since 1901, the Nobel Peace Prize has been awarded annually to people whose work has promoted peace between nations. The Swedish inventor of dynamite, Alfred Nobel (1833–96), left money in his will to fund the prize.

Timeline

1864 Geneva Convention protects the neutrality of non-combatants and medical staff during war.

1901 First Nobel Peace Prize awarded.

The founder of the International Red Cross was awarded the Nobel Peace Prize in 1901.

1915 International Congress of Women meets at the Hague, Holland, with proposals to end World War I. Envoys visit heads of state in 14 countries.

1932–34 World Disarmament Conference meets in Geneva, Switzerland.

1963 USA, USSR, and Britain sign the Partial Test Ban Treaty, banning the testing of nuclear weapons in the atmosphere.

1968 Nonproliferation Treaty forbids the export of nuclear weapons.

Polaris nuclear warhead

1972 USA and USSR agree to reduce their total number of nuclear weapons in the Strategic Arms Limitation Talks (SALT).

1980s Anti-nuclear demonstrations throughout Europe at the siting of US missiles on European soil.

1988 USA and USSR agreed to dismantle all short- and medium-range nuclear weapons.

FIND OUT MORE   COLD WAR   GANDHI, MOHANDAS   UNITED NATIONS   WARFARE   WEAPONS   WOMEN'S MOVEMENT   WORLD WAR I   WORLD WAR II

P

PENGUINS

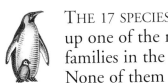

THE 17 SPECIES of penguin make up one of the most remarkable families in the entire bird world. None of them can fly, but their torpedo-shaped bodies are superbly adapted for swimming. They usually stand upright on land and move by walking or hopping, but on ice they sometimes lie flat and slide along like toboggans. They are well adapted for coping with the cold. Penguins are found only in the southern hemisphere, although one species, the Galápagos penguin, lives on the Equator.

Dense waterproof plumage

Sleek new plumage

Old feathers ready to moult.

Broad feet with stubby claws

Wings covered with short, hard feathers.

Moulting
Every year, penguins moult their old feathers. Unlike other birds, penguins' old feathers do not come out until the new ones have grown. This means the bird is always insulated against the cold.

King penguin
Only the emperor penguin is larger than the king penguin. Male and female king penguins look almost identical and they pair up for life. They breed on windswept islands, raising an average of just one chick every two years.

Types of penguin

Macaroni
This penguin breeds on islands around Antarctica. It has long, bright yellow feathers above its eyes.

Humboldt
This species feeds in the cool water of the Humboldt current, on the west coast of South America.

Adélie
The most common and widespread penguin of Antarctica, the small Adélie nests in huge colonies.

Galápagos
This rare bird lives on the Galápagos Islands. These are on the Equator, but the water around them is cold.

Penguin features
Penguins have a large pointed beak, a streamlined body, and short stiff wings, which they cannot fold up. Their legs are short, set far back on the body. When standing, they often use their tail as a prop. The birds have short, waterproof feathers all over that keep them streamlined. Under their skin is a layer of fat. This keeps them warm in icy water, and also acts as a store of food.

Penguin skeleton
Unlike flying birds, penguins have solid bones which make them almost as dense as seawater. This allows them to dive easily. Penguins have flexible shoulder joints but their wing bones are firmly locked together, so keep their wings stiff.

Skeleton of Rockhopper

Rockhopper penguin

Wings used like flippers.

Feet act as rudders.

Strong chest muscles pull down the wings.

Penguin rises through the water to break through the surface.

Swimming
Some penguins can swim at more than 40 kmh (25 mph). They propel themselves forward with their wings, and steer with their feet and tail. Many penguins burst through the surface of the water as they swim. This is called porpoising. It gives the penguins' feathers a coating of air bubbles, which helps to reduce friction between the penguins and the water.

Breeding
Most species of penguin build nests on the ground or in holes, but the king and the emperor penguin incubate a single egg on their feet under a flap of skin. Emperor penguins breed on Antarctic ice. The female lays one egg in the autumn, then heads out to sea. The male incubates the egg through the winter, when temperatures can drop to below -45°C (-50°F).

Birds take it in turns to get out of the wind.

Huddling reduces heat loss.

Adult emperor penguins carry small chicks around on their feet.

KING PENGUIN

SCIENTIFIC NAME	*Aptenodytes patagonica*
ORDER	Sphenisciformes
FAMILY	Spheniscidae
DISTRIBUTION	Islands and ocean north of Antarctica
HABITAT	Coasts and open sea
DIET	Fish and squid
SIZE	Length, including tail 95 cm (37.5 in)
LIFESPAN	About 20 years

FIND OUT MORE   ANTARTICA   BIRDS   FLIGHTLESS BIRDS   ISLAND WILDLIFE   POLAR WILDLIFE

PERSIAN EMPIRES

P

FOR ALMOST A THOUSAND YEARS, immensely powerful Persian rulers controlled three vast empires. The first "King of Kings", as they were known, was Cyrus the Great, who founded the Achaemenid dynasty. This empire was followed by nearly 100 years of Greek rule, which in turn was followed by the long-lived Parthian and Sassanian dynasties. Persian governments employed provincial rulers, or satraps, to keep order and collect taxes. A network of trade routes connected Europe, Arabia, and western Asia with India, Mongolia, and China. In the centre of all this, Persia absorbed influences from ancient civilizations, and influenced later ones.

Persian dynasties
The Achaemenid Empire (559–331 BC) was conquered by Alexander the Great in 333 BC. After a period of Greek rule, the Persians regained control, establishing the formidable Parthian dynasty. The final Persian dynasty was the Sassanian (227–651), which glorified its warrior kings in legend and fabulous art.

Persepolis

Darius the Great (r.521–486 BC) founded a complex of palaces at Persepolis, which was completed by his son, Xerxes I. Set in lush gardens, its vast audience hall and monumental staircases were designed for magnificent public ceremonies, most importantly the New Year festival on the first day of spring. In 330 BC, Alexander the Great burnt down Persepolis, possibly in revenge for the razing of the Acropolis in 479 BC by Xerxes.

Staircase to the Tripylon, Persepolis

Square towers

Slender columns

Rosette detail

Carvings of tribute bearers

Back-to-back bulls often decorated column tops, or capitals.

The king's bodyguards, known as the 10,000 Immortals

Lion attacking a bull

Rosette

Stone capital with two bulls, Susa

Wall carvings
Large portraits of kings, courtiers, and attendants were carved on the stone walls. The stairway walls depicted the New Year ceremony. People from all nations of the empire marched past, bringing the king jewellery and tributes. Gifts included live animals, such as bulls.

Shallow staircases were wide enough for eight horsemen abreast.

Darius III being defeated by Alexander the Great at the Battle of Issus, 333 BC

Battle of Gaugamela-Arbela
In 333 BC, Alexander defeated Darius III at the Battle of Issus in Syria. Darius fled. Two years later Alexander beat Darius again at the Battle of Gaugamela-Arbela, further to the east. This defeat signalled the end of the dynasty and, therefore, the Achaemenid Empire. Darius III, the last of the Achaemenid kings, fled east from Gaugamela-Arbela and was eventually killed by his own cousin. Alexander went on to conquer the great city of Babylon, and parts of India.

Trade and tribute

Kings received taxes and tribute from subjects all over the empire, and encouraged trade through busy ports on the Persian Gulf. During the Achaemenid dynasty, camels were used to carry goods for the first time, and a Royal Road stretched 2,500 km (1,600 miles) from Susa (Iran) to Sardis (Turkey). Its purpose was to move goods to and from the Mediterranean coast, and it had more than 100 rest stops for travellers.

Arabian camel

Sheep with young

Ivory

Greek influence

To consolidate his control of the area, Alexander the Great arranged for his soldiers to marry local Persian women. At the ancient capital of Susa, hundreds of couples were married in one day. After Alexander's death his general, Seleucus, founded the Seleucid dynasty. The dynasty built Greek-style cities and kept Greek culture alive. In Persian folklore, Alexander became a legendary hero called Iskander.

Cyrus the Great

Founder of the Achaemenid Empire, Cyrus II (r.559–530 BC), also known as "the Great", was a just and merciful ruler. After conquering Lydia and Media, Cyrus captured the city of Babylon without a battle in 539 BC, and ordered his men not to damage it. One of his first actions was to free the Jews who had been held captive there since 586 BC.

Gold

Honey

Government

The Achaemenids set up a basic system of government that continued for over 1,000 years. The king had a council of nobles who represented people from all over the empire. About 20 large provinces, called satrapies, were governed separately. The government spent tax money on public services, such as roads, drainage, and irrigation.

Impression of seal

Sassanian seals were used as symbols of authority.

Satrapies
Retired generals or local princes, known as satraps, controlled the satrapies. The satraps were tolerant: they allowed their subjects to follow their own customs and practise their own religions, so long as they paid tribute to the King of Kings.

Zoroastrianism

Two important prophets came from the Persian Empire: Zoroaster and Mani. Zoroaster (c.620– 551 BC) taught that life was a battle between good and evil, and that a supreme god named Ahura Mazda was the champion of goodness. Each Persian king believed Ahura Mazda chose him to rule others, and that he was, therefore, protected by the god. Zoroastrianism was the Persian state religion, but following the conquest of the Sassanian Empire by Arab Muslims, most Persians converted to Islam. The Zoroastrians fled to India where they still practise their religion and are called Parsi (from "Persian").

Modern Parsi priest, India

P

The magi
In Persia, a class of high priests, called magi (singular: magus) performed religious ceremonies involving sacrificial fire. Zoroaster may have been a magus, since the magi accepted his teachings, became leaders in the new religion, and made fire worship a part of it. Magi are often shown holding barsom – twigs used to feed sacred flames. Magi were also expert astrologers, and were revered and consulted by the people.

Arts and crafts

Persian artists, particularly the Sassanians, worked skilfully in stone, metal, clay, and textiles. Sassanian kings had valley rock-faces carved with enormous images of their royal glory, often using old Achaemenid palace sites. The great care lavished on stone carving was perfectly reproduced in metal-work objects, such as the gold and silver temple hoard, that were pulled from the Oxus River in Afghanistan.

Gold Achaemenid drinking horn

The death of Mani

Manichaeism
The Persian prophet Mani (216–276) founded a new religion, which comprised elements of many faiths. The magi objected and persuaded King Bahram I (r.273–276) to have him tortured and executed. Today, although the religion itself is dead, the influence of Manichaeism can be seen in Christianity and Chinese Taoism.

Figure holding barsom

Metalwork
The Persians were fascinated with animals. Gold, silver, and bronze vessels shaped as lions, eagles, and mythical horned beasts all had symbolic meaning. Sassanian metalwork was particularly highly prized, and huge numbers of valuable cups and serving bowls were used for lavish banquets. Merchants exported silverware along the trade routes to China, and Chinese craftsmen copied Sassanian designs.

The crown indicates that the figure is possibly a king.

Gilded lotus buds

Griffin

Gold figurine

Silver gilt drinking horn

Embossed design

Gold bowl, Oxus treasure

Griffin (mythical horned beast)

Inlaid precious stones

Gold armlet, Oxus treasure

Figures of ibexes

Gold boss

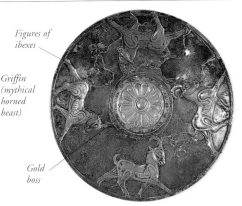

A circular silver shield with gold design

Darius the Great
Under Darius I (521–486 BC), the Persian Empire reached its height. Darius was an energetic military leader and a gifted ruler, with an efficient government at Susa, where he built an elaborate palace before founding Persepolis. Archaeologists have found gold, silver, and stone inscriptions describing Darius's achievements.

Timeline

c.620 BC Birth of the important prophet Zoroaster.

559 BC Cyrus II becomes king of Persia.

550 BC Cyrus defeats the Medes, founding the Achaemenid Empire.

539 BC Cyrus II conquers Babylon.

521–486 BC Darius I (the Great) reigns.

333 BC Battle of Issus.

Griffin from gold armlet

331 BC Battle of Gaugamela-Arbela ends Achaemenid Empire.

321 BC Greek Seleucid Empire is founded.

239 BC Beginning of Parthian Empire.

216 AD Birth of the prophet Mani.

227 Beginning of Sassanian Empire.

651 Sassanian Empire falls to the Arabs.

FIND OUT MORE

ALEXANDER THE GREAT BABYLONIAN EMPIRE METAL RELIGIONS SAFAVID EMPIRE

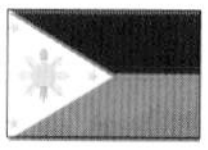

PHILIPPINES

ACROSS THE CHINA SEA from Southeast Asia are about 7,107 islands of the Philippines, of which only 900 are inhabited. The world's second largest island group, or archipelago, the Philippines lie on the "ring of fire", an arc of volcanoes that circles the Pacific Ocean. Spanish colonization in 1565, and American occupation from 1898 to 1946 have greatly influenced Philippine language and society. The islands are rich in natural resources, but half the population lives in poverty.

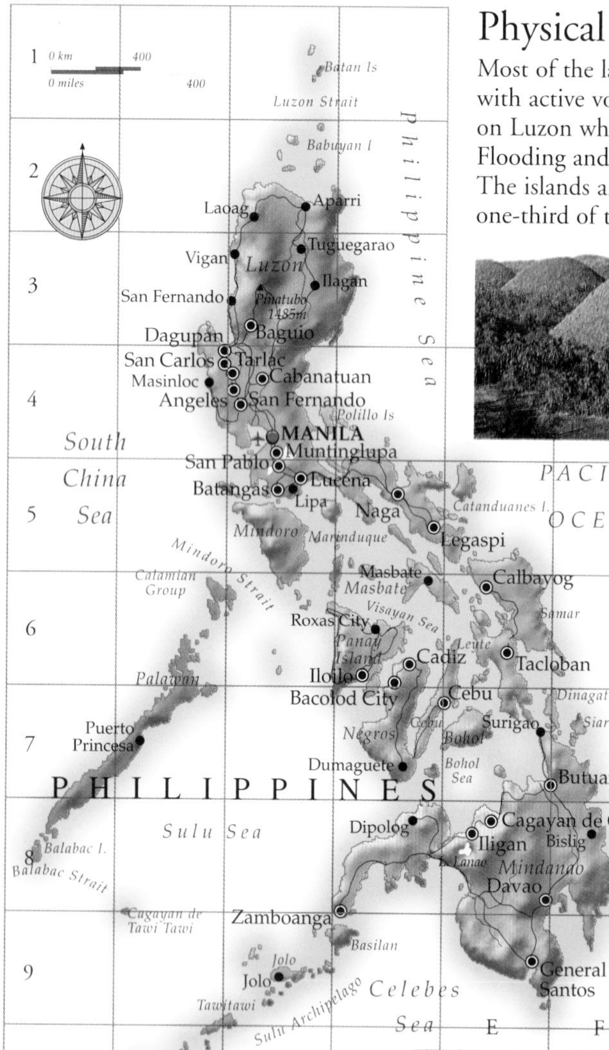

Physical features

Most of the large islands are mountainous, with active volcanoes, such as Mount Pinatubo on Luzon which erupted violently in 1991. Flooding and earthquakes are also common. The islands are thickly forested, and about one-third of the land is used for agriculture.

Terraces
The stunning Banaue rice terraces in northern Luzon are steps cut into the mountain on which large amounts of rice are grown. An ancient water system is used to keep each level moist and limit erosion of the soil. The terraces were built by hand, using stone walls, approximately 2,000 years ago and are now the subject of international research into rice plant breeding and harvesting.

Chocolate Hills
Bohol Island has a central plateau of more than 1,000 mounds, known as the Chocolate Hills, up to 120 m (394 ft) high.

Climate
The climate is hot and humid all year. The rainy season lasts from June to October. About five tropical storms strike the eastern coasts of the islands every year between June and December.

38°C (100°F)   20°C (68°F)
28°C (82°F)   25°C (77°F)
2,083 mm (82 in)

People
The Philippines is the only Christian state in Asia. Around 85 per cent of Filipinos are Roman Catholics, as a result of the Spanish colonization, and the Church plays an important role in social and cultural life. In the annual 36-hour Moriones festival, held from Good Friday to Easter Sunday, Jesus's crucifixion and resurrection are acted out.

Mock crucifixion during annual Moriones Festival

Workers must wear hard hats to protect their heads.

235 per sq km (609 per sq mile)

54% Urban   46% Rural

Manila
The capital Manila is a thriving centre for trade and industry, and home to more than ten million people. As a result of population growth and cuts in transport spending, traffic jams are among the worst in the world. Ex US-army jeeps, called jeepneys, left behind after World War II (1939–45) provide one of the main means of transport.

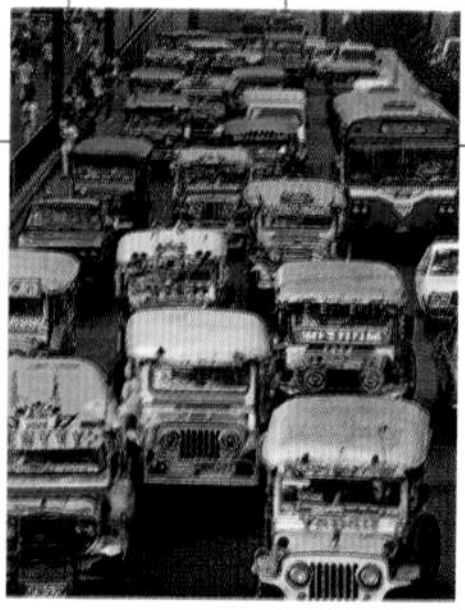

Traffic jam of jeepneys

Electricity plant of a cement works

Farming and industry
Most factories use electricity, around 40 per cent of which is provided by geothermal power from beneath the Earth's crust. Agriculture employs 39 per cent of the labour force, although many Filipinos work abroad. Food-processing factories export tropical fruits, sugar, coconuts, and tobacco. The islands are rich in minerals, and the waters around them teem with fish, which are the basis of Filipino cuisine.

FIND OUT MORE   ASIA   ASIA, HISTORY OF   CHRISTIANITY   EARTHQUAKES   EMPIRES   ENERGY   FARMING   ISLANDS   STORMS   VOLCANOES

PHILOSOPHY

PHILOSOPHERS AIM TO make sense of the world and of human experiences within it. They seek to understand abstract concepts, such as truth, beauty, right, or wrong, and look for deeper reasons for why we think the way we do. They examine ideas that we might otherwise accept without question. Western philosophy began in ancient Greece, and the word comes from the Greek meaning "love of wisdom". Then, philosophers considered the areas of science, knowledge, and enquiry. Modern philosophers are more likely to examine the nature of language itself, for example, questioning the meaning of words.

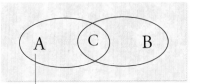

Epistemology
This is the study of the theory of knowledge. It asks what knowledge is, how we come to know things, how we can feel sure we know anything for certain, and whether our knowledge is based on reason or experience.

Branches of philosophy
Philosophy is divided into different categories, such as epistemology, logic, metaphysics, and ethics. Philosophers also study areas such as religion, language and the meanings of words, and the methods of science. They examine other fields of thought, such as politics and psychology, and question the methods by which political thinkers and psychologists arrive at their conclusions.

Venn diagrams are a visual way of representing the points of an argument.

Logic
When we discuss or argue, we usually follow basic rules in order to persuade others to agree with us. Logic is the study of these underlying rules: what they are, and why they are important.

René Descartes
French philosopher René Descartes (1596–1650) asked how we can be certain of what we know. He based all knowledge on a central truth: "I think, therefore I am". By this he meant that we cannot doubt the existence of our own thoughts, therefore we must exist.

Metaphysics considers the nature of the Universe.

Metaphysics
Metaphysical problems include the difficulty of explaining how our minds influence our bodies (and vice versa), what it is for something to exist (in reality, in imagination, in the past, present, and future), and how one event relates to another.

Ethics
We believe that certain acts, such as murder, are wrong, and that others, such as kindness, are right. In ethics, philosophers ask what these moral beliefs have in common, and what really makes a particular act right or wrong.

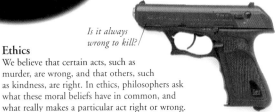

Is it always wrong to kill?

The work of a philosopher
Philosophers do not have any specific methods for proving their theories. They rely on reason and argument to explore ideas. To test statements that other people might think are self-evident, they propose made-up situations and examine them from different angles.

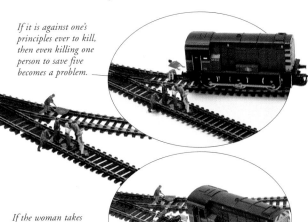

If it is against one's principles ever to kill, then even killing one person to save five becomes a problem.

A runaway train presents a difficult dilemma.

If the woman takes no action, five people will die. Does the absence of action make her responsible for these deaths?

Principles or consequences?
Philosophers examine hypothetical (made-up) situations to explore profound questions. The example shown here was suggested by the British philosopher Phillipa Foot. A woman sees a runaway train approaching a fork in the track. The train is heading for a branch with five people working on it, but the onlooker can divert it to kill one person instead. What is the right course of action to take? There are no easy answers.

The mind
Philosophers discuss the human mind. They ask whether the mind and the soul are the same, or whether the mind is just the sum of millions of electrical signals in the brain. Scientists know that parts of the brain are important for senses and skills, but have yet to explain things such as intention or desire.

Consciousness
Being aware of ourselves and the world around us is called consciousness. It is a central feature of the human mind. Some philosophers ask where this awareness comes from. For example, when I remember a scene, it is as if I project an image onto a screen. If I cannot explain where I am looking at this screen *from*, I cannot explain consciousness.

FIND OUT MORE   BRAIN AND NERVOUS SYSTEM   CRIME AND PUNISHMENT   GREECE, ANCIENT   LANGUAGES   LAW   MATHEMATICS   RELIGIONS   SOCRATES

PHOENICIANS

SOME 3,000 YEARS AGO, expert sailors and merchants known as the Phoenicians controlled trade throughout the Mediterranean. They originated in Phoenicia, a coastal strip at the eastern end of the Mediterranean Sea, often known as the Levant, and now part of Lebanon, Syria, and Israel. The Phoenicians sailed far and wide, and at their peak in the 1100s BC established trading posts and colonies in Sicily, Malta, Sardinia, and Tunisia, and along the coasts of Spain and North Africa. In 332 BC, Alexander the Great conquered Phoenicia and brought to an end one of the ancient world's greatest trading empires.

Seafaring empire

The Phoenician empire was based on trade. From their ports, fleets of ships laden with trade goods stopped at coastal colonies to exchange luxury items for raw materials. At home in Phoenicia, craftworkers made more goods for trade from the imported materials.

Carthage

According to legend, the African coastal city of Carthage (in modern Tunisia) was founded in 814 BC by a group of Phoenician aristocrats from Tyre, led by Queen Dido. Carthage – meaning "new city" – was built from scratch by the colonists. It became Phoenicia's most prosperous trading port, linking the African interior with the Mediterranean world. By c.600 BC Carthage, the largest African coastal city west of Egypt, gained independence from Phoenicia.

Phoenician dedication, Cyprus, 391 BC

Alphabet

Western scripts are all derived from the Phoenician alphabet. This was used by the ancient Greeks and the Etruscans, whose early civilizations existed at the same time as the peak of the Phoenicians.

Warships

Phoenician warships sailed ahead of the cargo ships to patrol trade routes and protect the cargo from pirates. Warships used both oars and sails and were three times faster than the bulky trading vessels. They were famous throughout the Mediterranean for a revolutionary new weapon – a bronze-tipped ram for piercing the hulls of enemy vessels.

A 4th-century silver shekel from Tyre

Trade goods

The Phoenicians traded carvings, glassware, and purple-dyed cloth in return for raw ivory, gold, and precious stones and metals. Trading ports included Tyre, Berytus (modern Beirut), and Carthage.

Ivory carvings

The craftspeople of Tyre used elephant tusks to make beautiful ivory carvings, often decorated with gold leaf and jewels. These carvings were then inlaid in furniture produced by Phoenician carpenters. Carthage was a main trading port for ivory goods.

Gilded ivory furniture panel

Pigments added to the glass created vivid colours.

Bottle for incense, 3rd–1st century BC

Glassware

The Phoenicians learned glass-making techniques from the ancient Egyptians, but Phoenician glass was clearer than Egyptian glass because the Phoenicians used a large amount of quartz in the sand. They sold glass-bead necklaces, glass bottles, and glass bowls throughout the Mediterranean world.

Glass beads

Pendant

Glass necklace, 7th–6th century BC

Purple dye

Only the Phoenicians knew the secret of how to extract purple dye from murex shells, and the word "Phoenicia" comes from the Greek for "purple". For the later Romans and Greeks, purple cloth was a status symbol.

Murex seashell

Queen Dido

Roman legend says that when Dido, the King of Tyre's daughter, landed in North Africa, she asked a hostile local ruler for some land. He said that she could have only as much land as one ox-hide would cover. Quick-witted Dido had the hide cut into thin strips and laid end to end, thus marking off a large area of land upon which to build the city of Carthage.

Timeline

1500 BC Phoenicians found cities along eastern Mediterranean.

1140 BC Phoenicians found their first North African colony at Utica (present-day Utique, Tunisia).

c.1000 BC Trade conflicts between the Phoenicians and the early Greek civilization; and between the Phoenicians and Rome.

c.1000 BC Phoenicians develop an alphabet. This alphabet is used later as the model for the Greek alphabet on which all western alphabets are based.

957 BC Phoenician carpenters and stonemasons complete the first Temple of Solomon in Jerusalem.

Ivory sphinx, 9th century BC

814 BC Phoenicians found the new colony of Carthage on North Africa's coast.

600 BC Carthage breaks away from Phoenician control.

332 BC Alexander the Great conquers Phoenicia. As Greek people move to Phoenician cities, Phoenician culture gradually dies out.

FIND OUT MORE
| ALEXANDER THE GREAT | GLASS | GREECE, ANCIENT | ROMAN EMPIRE | SHIPS AND BOATS | WRITING |

P

PHOTOGRAPHY

A PHOTOGRAPH CAN CAPTURE an instant of happiness or record an athlete's record-breaking sprint; it can show the cruelty of war or the beauty of the Earth from Space. Yet there is more to photography than pictures in a magazine. Although photography is less than 180 years old, it now influences every part of our lives. X-ray photography can reveal faulty welds in a gas pipeline, or faulty valves in your heart. A process called photolithography is used to etch microscopic circuits onto computer chips.

Daguerre's photograph of Paris rooftops

Early photographs
Although French inventor Joseph Niepce (1765–1833) experimented with photography, it was Louis Daguerre (1789–1851) who perfected the process in 1839. Early cameras could only take pictures of perfectly still objects.

Types of photography
Modern cameras have made photography easier, but different types of photography still demand different skills. Great news photographers can anticipate where historic events are about to unfold, while landscape photographers need patience and an artist's skill with composition.

Landscapes
Outdoor scenes offer the photographer infinite variety because the mood of every place alters with changing light, weather, and seasons. Skilful photographs capture atmosphere.

Action pictures
A camera can reveal actions that are too quick to see with the naked eye, splitting a second into 4,000 parts or more. To take good action pictures, a photographer must learn when to trigger the shutter to capture just the right one of those instants.

The people of Berlin pull down the wall that divided their city.

Close-ups
Our eyes cannot focus clearly on objects that are closer than a hand's width away. Photography magnifies tiny details so we can look much closer, filling the picture with a flower, or bringing us face-to-face with an insect.

News photography
Television broadcasts show news events as they happen, but photographs in a newspaper can have a more lasting impact. Today, powerful photographs have helped draw attention to the horrors of war and famine.

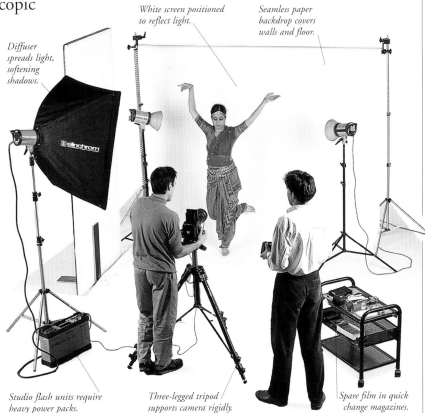

White screen positioned to reflect light.

Seamless paper backdrop covers walls and floor.

Diffuser spreads light, softening shadows.

Studio flash units require heavy power packs.

Three-legged tripod supports camera rigidly.

Spare film in quick change magazines.

A photographer at work
Photography is possible almost anywhere, but taking high-quality pictures is easiest in a specially equipped photographic studio. There, the photographer has complete control over the background, and can quickly change the direction, intensity, and colour of the lighting.

Image manipulation
Altering and manipulating photographs has always been possible, but computers now make it especially easy. Merging different images is called photocomposition.

A city backdrop is added on computer.

Photographic teamwork
Studio photography is complex and needs contributions from many specialists. Besides the model and the assistant, the photographer may also need the help of a hairdresser, make-up artist, and stylist.

Eve Arnold
When American Eve Arnold (b. 1913) began her career, most news photographers were male. She photographed scenes where men were excluded, such as the enclosed world of Arab women. She also photographed famous people, but she is best known for her extraordinary pictures of ordinary men and women.

FIND OUT MORE   CAMERAS   CARTOONS AND ANIMATION   COMPUTERS   FILM AND FILM MAKING   INVENTIONS   PRINTING   TELEVISION

PHOTOSYNTHESIS

PLANTS USE SUNLIGHT to make sugars from water and carbon dioxide. This process is called photosynthesis. It takes place mostly in the leaves, which contain the green pigment, chlorophyll. This pigment traps some of the energy in sunlight, using it to drive a sequence of chemical reactions that results in the production of glucose and water. Oxygen is produced as a waste product.

Light energy

Sunlight is a mixture of coloured light with different wavelengths. The most important wavelength for photosynthesis is that of red light. This is absorbed by the pigment chlorophyll in the plant. The other wavelengths are reflected, making the plant look green.

Sunlight is made up of red, orange, yellow, green, blue, indigo, and violet light.

Energy in sunlight is trapped by chlorophyll in the leaf.

Chloroplasts

Leaf cell

Chlorophyll

1 The pigment chlorophyll is found inside tiny structures called chloroplasts, which are found in most of a leaf's cells. Each leaf contains millions of chloroplasts. Inside each one, there are stacks of membranes that hold the chlorophyll molecules.

Carbon dioxide

2 About 0.03 per cent of the air is the gas carbon dioxide. It is breathed out by animals and also released when fossil fuels are burnt. For photosynthesis to occur, carbon dioxide enters a leaf through tiny pores called stomata. These are mostly on the underside of the leaf.

Carbon dioxide molecules

Stomata

Oxygen

5 This gas is a by-product of photosynthesis. It passes out of the leaves through the stomata and into the air. Plants produce all the oxygen that animals and plants need for respiration. The plants themselves use only a fraction of the oxygen they make.

Oxygen molecules

Water

3 For photosynthesis to proceed, a plant needs a constant supply of water. It takes the water up from the soil through its roots. The water then travels up the xylem tissue in the stem to the leaves. During photosynthesis, water molecules within the chloroplasts are split apart. This produces hydrogen ions (groups of atoms) and oxygen molecules.

Glucose molecule

Water molecules

Glucose

4 The glucose produced by photosynthesis is a simple sugar. It contains all the energy that the plant needs to grow and reproduce. A plant also uses glucose, together with essential minerals drawn up with water, to produce all the compounds in its make-up. These include starch, which acts as an energy store, and cellulose, which builds the plant's cell walls.

Transpiration

Much of the water reaching the leaves is lost through the stomata and evaporates. This process is known as transpiration. A plant replaces the water by taking up more through its roots. It also controls the amount transpired by closing its stomata.

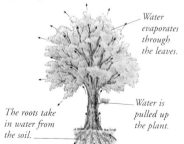

Water evaporates through the leaves.

The roots take in water from the soil.

Water is pulled up the plant.

Xylem and phloem

Water and dissolved minerals pass up the roots, stems, or trunk of a plant in tubes called xylem. These are made of non-living cells with reinforced walls. Sugars formed in the leaves are dissolved in cell sap and are carried to all parts of the plant in living cells called phloem.

Xylem transports water and dissolved minerals.

Phloem transports dissolved sugars.

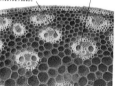

Jan Ingenhousz

The Dutchman Jan Ingenhousz (1730–99) studied physics, chemistry, and medicine. He was one of the first people to study photosynthesis. He followed up the discovery by Joseph Priestley (1733–1804) that plants give off oxygen, and later published a work on gas exchange in plants. He showed that the green part of plants take in carbon dioxide and release oxygen when sunlight falls on them. He also showed that the opposite happens in the dark.

FIND OUT MORE   AIR   ENERGY   FOOD WEBS AND CHAINS   GASES   LIGHT   PLANTS   PLANTS, ANATOMY   PLANTS, REPRODUCTION

PHYSICS

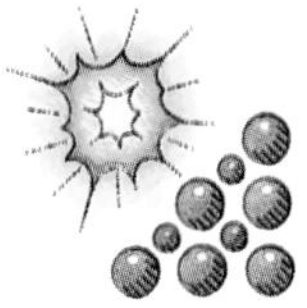

FROM THE SMALLEST SUBATOMIC particles to the largest galaxies in the night sky – these extremes illustrate the broad scope of physics, which is the study of matter and energy. Physics is really a central or general science, because it tries to discover the basic laws that govern how the Universe works. It can be used to explain concepts in chemistry, astronomy, biology, or any other science. One of the main tools of the physicist is mathematics. Using mathematics, a physicist can analyse the results of an experiment to prove or disprove a theory.

Classical physics

Before the 20th century, physics was limited to the study of electricity and magnetism, force and motion, and light and waves. The accurate theories of that time are today collectively called classical physics. Classical physics began in the 16th century with the study of the flight paths of cannonballs.

Modern physics

Electromagnetic radiation, nuclear reactions, chaos, and relativity are all studied in modern physics. Chaos tries to understand complex systems, such as the weather, where behaviour seems to be unpredictable. Chaos can be used to generate complex computerized images called fractals.

Computer-generated fractal

Experimental physics

A physicist who tests theories in a laboratory is called an experimental physicist. For example, a physicist investigating force and motion might carry out the experiment shown here to test a theory that a trolley moving down a slope accelerates at a constant rate. The results may or may not support the theory.

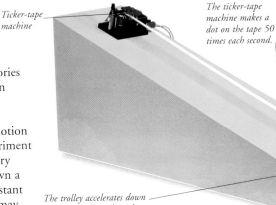

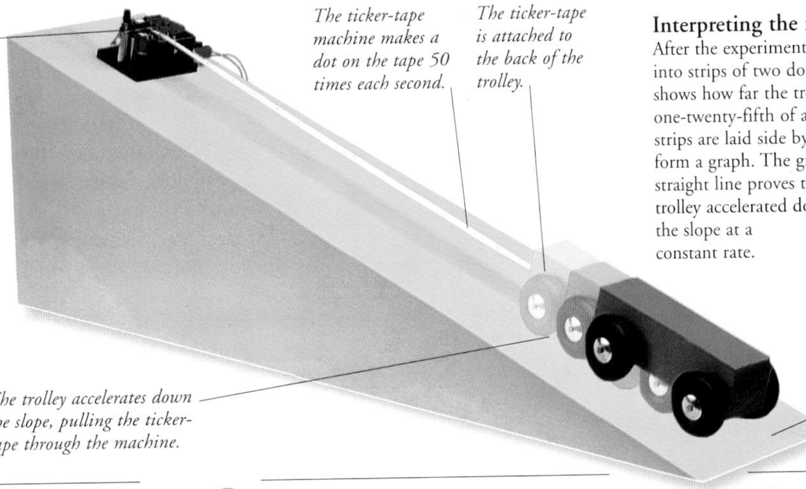

Ticker-tape machine

The ticker-tape machine makes a dot on the tape 50 times each second.

The ticker-tape is attached to the back of the trolley.

Interpreting the results

After the experiment, the tape is cut into strips of two dots. Each strip shows how far the trolley moved in one-twenty-fifth of a second. The strips are laid side by side to form a graph. The graph's straight line proves that the trolley accelerated down the slope at a constant rate.

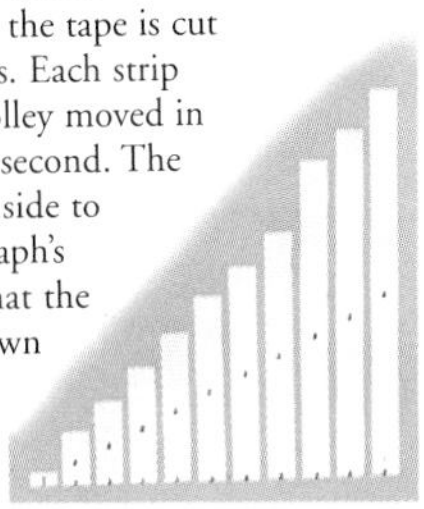

Graph of results

The trolley accelerates down the slope, pulling the ticker-tape through the machine.

The steeper the slope, the greater the trolley's acceleration.

Branches of physics

Physics examines the behaviour of matter and energy, which, together with empty space, make up the entire Universe. For this reason, the theories and methods of physics can be used in any area of scientific study.

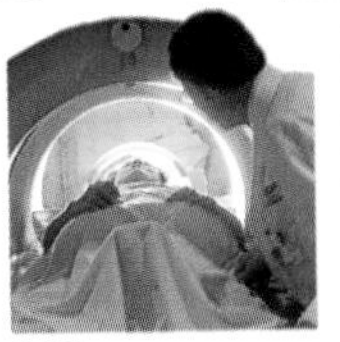

Dust mite seen in electron microscope

Biophysics

A biophysicist studies the physical processes and changes that occur in living things and the way they respond to stimuli such as heat and light. Electron microscopes allow biophysicists to see objects too tiny for even optical telescopes to detect.

Medical physics

Using the methods of physics to help diagnose and treat illness is called medical physics. One of the best known tools of the medical physicist is the CAT scanner, which uses X-rays to give 3-D images of body organs and tissues.

CAT scanner

Particle physics

Matter is made up of more than 200 different types of particle, including electrons, protons, and quarks. Machines called bubble chambers and particle accelerators allow physicists to study these tiny particles and discover new ones.

Particle tracks in a bubble chamber

Earthquake trace on a seismograph

Geophysics

A geophysicist studies the physical processes that take place on and within the Earth, including rock formation, the Earth's magnetism, and volcanoes. Devices called seismographs help geophysicists to record and predict earthquakes.

Observatory dome with telescope

Astrophysics

The study of the planets, stars, and galaxies that make up the Universe is called astrophysics. It makes use of data collected by telescopes. Cosmology is the part of astrophysics that attempts to explain how the Universe began.

Physical change

Matter may undergo a physical change if it gains or loses energy. An ice lolly melts in the sun because it gains heat energy. Physical changes are reversible. The ice lolly can be cooled in a freezer, until it re-freezes.

Timeline

c.400 BC Greek philosopher Democritus teaches that all matter is made up of tiny particles called atoms.

4th century BC Greek philosophers, such as Aristotle, state that the world must be explained by logical reasoning.

1600 English philosopher Francis Bacon argues that scientific theories must be proven by experiment. This is known as scientific method.

1680–1710 Englishman Isaac Newton lays the foundations of physics with his work on gravity, light, and mathematics.

1843 James Joule, an English physicist, explains the nature of energy.

1895 Modern physics is born when German physicist Wilhelm Röntgen discovers X-rays. Classical physics cannot explain Röntgen's discovery, so scientists start to work on new theories.

1905 German physicist Albert Einstein publishes his Special Theory of Relativity, which states that matter can be changed into energy.

1990s and beyond Physicists look for a single "Unified Theory" that will link all the existing theories and thus explain the whole Universe.

FIND OUT MORE   ATOMS AND MOLECULES   EINSTEIN, ALBERT   ENERGY   MATTER   MATHEMATICS   NEWTON, SIR ISAAC

PICASSO, PABLO

UNCHALLENGED AS THE GREATEST painter of the twentieth century, Pablo Picasso is also known for his sculpture, drawings, and graphics. In all, he produced some 20,000 works. He was one of the inventors of the Cubist style of art, and often shocked the public with his strange, powerful pictures. His work entirely changed our ideas about art. For Picasso, what he saw with his eyes was often only a starting point from which he began to paint. His works can be seen in galleries all over the world, and are widely reproduced.

Early life
Born in Málaga, Spain, in 1881, Picasso learned to draw before he could speak. He hated school, and never learned to write well. He often helped his father, a painter, in his studio. When Pablo was 13, his father gave up painting and gave his brushes to Pablo to continue the tradition.

Colours
Soon after Picasso arrived in Paris in 1901, he began to paint entirely in shades of blue, a colour he used to depict human misery. In this "Blue" period, he painted mainly beggars and other social outcasts. Later, in his "Rose" period, he portrayed circus performers.

Picasso's palette

Cubism

After his Blue and Rose periods, Picasso invented Cubism. He created images out of shapes such as cubes and cones. He showed objects as if seen from many different angles, so that he could show many aspects of the same object at once.

Les Demoiselles d'Avignon
The painting *Les Demoiselles d'Avignon* is seen by many as the starting point of many forms of modern art, including Cubism. Picasso worked on it for months before he would show it to his friends. Almost all of them were horrified by the distorted lines of the figures and the angular features of the women's faces. Picasso refused to sell the painting and kept it hidden from public view for many years.

The Blind Man's Meal, 1903, detail, (Blue period)   *Les Demoiselles d'Avignon*, 1907

Ballets Russes

Between 1917 and 1924, Picasso worked for the Ballets Russes, the Russian ballet company based in Paris and run by Sergei Diaghilev (1872–1929). The Ballets Russes dominated ballet in the early 20th century, and used the greatest talents of the age as choreographers, dancers, and designers. Composers such as Igor Stravinsky (1882–1971) and Erik Satie (1866–1925) provided the music. Picasso designed stunning sets for ballets such as *Parade*, *Le Tricorne,* and *Pulcinella*.

Parade
The ballet *Parade* was first performed in 1917. The music by Satie included the sounds of typewriters. The first-night audience hissed the ballet, but applauded Picasso's curtain. He also designed Cubist-style backdrops and costumes for the ballet.

Curtain for the ballet *Parade,* designed by Picasso

Guernica

In 1936, the Spanish Civil War broke out. The following year, Picasso painted *Guernica*. It shows the artist's horror at the bombing of the defenceless town by Fascists. It uses the image of the bullfight to depict the horror of war.

Guernica, 1937   *Mother with dead child*   *Horse, usually a symbol of power, here symbolizes terror.*   *Absence of colour suits the stark theme.*

Later work

Picasso experienced great hardship during the 1940s; his art became harsh and sombre, often depicting monsters. He also repainted old master paintings in his own style.

Scene from the film *Mystére Picasso*

PABLO PICASSO

1881	Born, Málaga, Spain
1900	Arrives in Paris, where he meets many of the most important modern artists
1901–04	Blue period
1906–07	Rose period
1907	Completes *Les Demoiselles d'Avignon;* the Cubist movement is born
1917	Begins to work as designer for the Ballets Russes
1930s	Produces his most important sculptures
1937	Paints *Guernica*
1940s	Experiments with different types of prints
1973	Dies in Mougins, France

FIND OUT MORE   ART, HISTORY OF   BALLET   MUSIC   PAINTING AND DRAWING   POTTERY AND CERAMICS   SCULPTURE   SPAIN, HISTORY OF

PIGS AND PECCARIES

A LONG, MUSCULAR SNOUT ending in a round, flat disc is the pig's most distinctive feature. It is used to root around in the soil for food. Other features include tusks which are used as weapons. The males of some species have large tusks, sometimes of a strange shape. There are 14 species of pig, ranging in size from the pygmy hog to the giant forest hog. Peccaries are related to pigs but are found only in South and Central America.

Breeding

Pigs produce lots of young, which is one of the reasons they were domesticated. Male wild boars mate after the age of about 4 years; females mate from the age of 18 months onwards. Males join the herd for mating during the winter months. Despite their thick skin, males are often injured during fights to determine who will mate with a female. After 115 days' gestation, a litter of 4–8, but sometimes up to 12 piglets, is born.

Feeding

Wild boars, like all other pigs, use their long muscular snouts and their strong sense of smell to root in the ground for food. They are most active at dawn or dusk when they may be heard grunting as they forage. Wild boars are omnivores, and will feed on almost anything including roots, fungi, leaves, fruit, and even small animals. They are particularly fond of wild garlic.

Wild boars

The wild boar – the direct ancestor of the domestic pig is more widely distributed than any other land mammal. It lives on every continent except Antarctica. The wild boar is a powerful animal with a heavy body, short legs, and thick skin that enable it to crash through thick undergrowth. Its straight tail is used to swat flies and also gives an indication of its mood.

Herds

Female wild boars live with their young in herds up to 50 strong. They all share feeding, resting, and wallowing sites. They wallow in mud pools to cool down and for protection from insects. Males live alone except in the mating season.

Coarse, bristly coat

Long snout

Piglets have striped coats for six months.

Kneeling on front legs to feed.

Types of wild pig

Babirusa
Restricted to Sulawesi and other Indonesian islands, the babirusa lives in rainforests along the banks of rivers and lakes. It is a strong swimmer and feeds on water plants. The male has antler-like tusks.

Almost hairless skin

Giant forest hog
The giant forest hog is the largest member of the pig family. It has very coarse black-brown hair and a large swelling beneath each eye. It lives in Africa, making its home within dense vegetation close to water.

Coarse hair

Pygmy hog
About the size of a hare, the pygmy hog is nocturnal and very shy. It was believed to be extinct until it was rediscovered in 1972, on a tea plantation in Assam, India. It lives in a belt of swampy jungle at the foot of the Himalayas.

Round body

Red river hog
The red river hog of West Africa is the most strikingly coloured of all pigs. It has a rusty-orange body, black and white markings on its face, long ear tassles, and a white crest running along its spine.

White crest along back

Eyes set high on large head

Broad snout

Curved semi-circular tusks

Protruberances, or "warts", on face protect eyes from injury.

Warthogs

Warthogs live on African savannahs south of the Sahara, where they feed on grass, leaves, fruit, and roots. They have poor eyesight but a good sense of smell and hearing, and sharp tusks that can cause serious injury. Warthogs live in family groups of a male, female, and their young. Old males may live alone. Warthogs move distinctively – trotting with their tails carried stiffly erect.

Den

Warthogs live in underground dens that they take over from other animals, usually aardvarks. When alarmed, they enter their dens, invariably entering backwards, to present their tusks to any intruder.

Warthog outside den

Peccaries

There are three types of peccaries: the collared, white-lipped, and Chacoan. All have a small tail and upper tusks that grow down instead of up. The white-lipped and Chacoan peccaries live in large herds. If danger threatens they stand together to present a row of gnashing tusks. The collared peccary lives in small herds and feeds on fruit, tubers, berries, and small vertebrates.

Collared peccary

WILD BOAR	
SCIENTIFIC NAME	Sus scrofa
ORDER	Artiodactyla
FAMILY	Suidae
DISTRIBUTION	Continental Europe, North Africa, and much of Asia, eastwards as far as Japan, Sumatra, and Java. Introduced to North America and New Zealand
HABITAT	Woodland and forest
DIET	Short succulent grasses, roots, fruit, fungi, and other plant material
SIZE	Height at shoulder: 100 cm (40 in); weight: up to 180 kg (400 lb)
LIFESPAN	Up to 18 years

FIND OUT MORE   AFRICAN WILDLIFE   ASIAN WILDLIFE   EUROPEAN WILDLIFE   FARMING   GRASSLAND WILDLIFE   MAMMALS   NORTH AMERICAN WILDLIFE   SOUTH AMERICAN WILDLIFE   WOODLAND WILDLIFE

PILGRIM FATHERS

ON 21 NOVEMBER 1620, a small ship anchored in the sheltered bay behind Cape Cod, on the east coast of America. The ship, the *Mayflower*, contained 35 religious dissenters who wished to start a new life in America so that they could worship the way they pleased. Sailing with them were 67 other emigrants. Together the voyagers are known as the Pilgrim Fathers. It was their pilgrimage across the ocean that created the first successful European colony in North America. They called their settlement Plymouth, in what is now Massachusetts.

The voyage of the Mayflower

The Pilgrims set sail from Plymouth, England on 16 September 1620. After a stormy crossing of the Atlantic, they sighted Cape Cod on 19 November. They then spent several weeks looking for a suitable place on the coast to land and settle. On 16 December they finally entered Plymouth Harbour. They began to build their first house on Christmas Day.

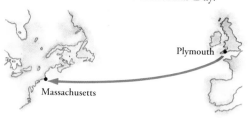

Plymouth

Massachusetts

Separatists and Puritans

A third of the passengers of the *Mayflower* were Separatists. They rejected the pomp and ceremony of the Church of England and wished to practise their own, simpler form of worship. They dressed in plain clothes and disapproved of frivolity and idleness. Later, Puritans (members of the Church of England who wanted to simplify its worship) also came to New England.

New England and the Wampanoag

The area that the Pilgrims first settled became known as "New England". Members of the Wampanoag tribe already lived here. Fortunately, one of them spoke English and, with him acting as a translator, the Wampanoags helped the colonists plant crops and hunt for food. Without their aid the Pilgrims would not have survived their first year in the new land.

Wampanoag people

Mayflower

The 180-tonne *Mayflower* was originally built to carry wine and other cargoes, not people, and was cramped and uncomfortable. Living quarters for each of the 102 passengers were no bigger than a single bed. Many of the Pilgrims were unprepared for their new life, taking plenty of books and pairs of shoes but no fishing lines or ploughs. Neither did they take any livestock, such as cows or sheep, to provide food and clothing for their new life. One passenger died and a baby was born on the voyage. However, many did not survive the first winter in America.

Pilgrim settlement

The first houses that the Pilgrims constructed were built of roughly cut planks of wood from the local forest. The roofs were coated with bark to keep the rain and snow out. Every Pilgrim had to work hard to help clear the site and plant the crops necessary for their survival. Religious services were held in the open until a church was constructed.

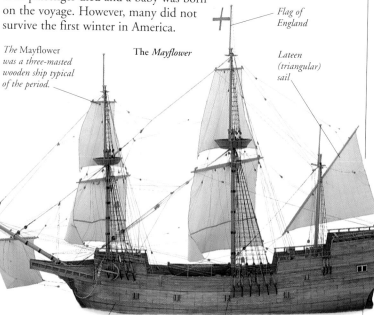

The Mayflower *was a three-masted wooden ship typical of the period.*

The *Mayflower*

Flag of England

Lateen (triangular) sail

The Mayflower *was about 30 m (90 ft) long.*

Cramped living accommodation below deck

Hold was originally used for carrying wine.

Thanksgiving

After a year in America, the Pilgrims celebrated their first successful harvest with a thanksgiving feast. Among the guests were 100 members of the Wampanoag tribe. The celebrations went on for several days. Among the foods the Pilgrims probably ate were pumpkin pie, pecan and apple pies, and roast wild turkey. The first national Thanksgiving Day was proclaimed in 1789. It became a national holiday in 1863.

Pumpkin pie

Roast turkey

Apple pie

Harvard University

The oldest university in America was founded by the colonists in 1636. It was named after John Harvard, a Puritan who emigrated to America and left his fortune to the university.

Timeline

September 1620 The Pilgrims set out from Plymouth, England.

November 1620 The Pilgrims draw up the Mayflower Compact, an agreement about how they will govern themselves.

December 1620 The Pilgrims land and establish a settlement at Plymouth, Massachusetts.

1621 Colonists sign peace treaty with local Wampanoag tribe; the peace lasts for 50 years.

1629–40 20,000 Puritans flee religious persecution in England; they settle in Massachusetts and the surrounding areas.

1691 Plymouth becomes part of Massachusetts Bay Colony.

FIND OUT MORE

EUROPE, HISTORY OF   FESTIVALS   GOVERNMENTS   NORTH AMERICA, HISTORY OF   RELIGIONS   SCHOOLS AND COLLEGES   UNITED STATES, HISTORY OF   WASHINGTON, GEORGE

P

PIRATES

ON THE WORLD'S OCEANS, robbers have a special name: pirates. Piracy began soon after mariners first sailed the world's waters, and pirates have threatened shipping ever since. In the days of sailing ships, these dangerous criminals piloted the fastest vessels. They swooped on defenceless ships, stealing their valuable cargo. Some pirate gangs sank the ship and killed the crew to hide their crimes. The most famous pirates attacked ships in the Caribbean three centuries ago. Story writers glamorized their exciting lives in tales and legends, but overlooked their savagery and greed.

Jolly Roger
To scare their victims into surrender, 18th-century pirate ships flew flags that carried symbols of death. The skull and crossbones design, called the Jolly Roger, is the best known, but many pirate captains designed their own emblems. This flag belonged to the English pirate captain, Jack Rackham (d.1720).

Pirate hunting grounds
Pirates lurked in places where they could be sure of finding vessels with rich cargoes: on traditional shipping lanes, or where straits and narrows forced ships to sail close to the shore. Pirates considered charts, maps, and surveys – especially of the areas around the Caribbean – to be valuable booty.

Mediterranean
Caribbean
South China Sea
Indian Ocean

The name came from the figure "8" on the coin.

Spanish Main
The Caribbean was one of the richest-ever pirate hunting grounds. In the 1500s, tales of Spanish treasure vessels loaded with gold lured generations of pirates, or buccaneers as they were known, to make their fortune.

Pieces of eight and gold doubloons

Mediterranean
The Mediterranean Sea has a long history of piracy. Pirates were attacking rich Greek and Roman ships 2,500 years ago. In the 16th century, Maltese corsairs (Christian pirates) clashed with Barbary corsairs (Muslim pirates) from North Africa.

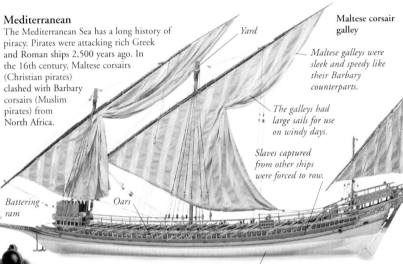

Yard

Maltese corsair galley

Maltese galleys were sleek and speedy like their Barbary counterparts.

The galleys had large sails for use on windy days.

Slaves captured from other ships were forced to row.

Battering ram

Oars

Slaves waxed the hull to maximize speed.

Gold seal ring

Garnet fan holder

Rose sapphire

Jewel necklace

Treasure
After raiding the ship's hold, pirates robbed the passengers. There were especially rich pickings on ships plying the Indian Ocean because all merchant vessels bound for India or China used this route. However, since pirates were often starving or sick, many valued food, medicine, and clothes more than riches.

Blackbeard
The English pirate Edward Teach (d.1718), better known as Blackbeard, plundered shipping off America's coast in the 18th century. Heavily armed and with long, thin candles smoking in his hair and beard, he terrified many crews into submission without even firing a shot. Though his piratical career lasted barely two years, Blackbeard earned a frightening reputation on the shores of Virginia and Carolina. According to legend he left fabulous buried treasure but it remains undiscovered to this day.

Women pirates
In a ship's crew, women had an independence that society denied them on land, and some became pirates. Irish pirate Anne Bonney (d.1720) plundered Caribbean ships, in the 18th century, and became famous for her courage and fighting skill.

Anne Bonney

Privateers
From the 1500s to the 1700s, warring nations relied on legal and licensed pirates, known as privateers, to supplement their navies. Their job was to plunder enemy shipping.

Sir Francis Drake
English admiral Drake (c.1540–96) became a national hero fighting Spain as a privateer. His drum, it is claimed, still beats when England is in danger.

Drake's drum, 1596

Modern piracy
Most modern piracy takes place in the South China Sea. The pirates usually attack merchant vessels, but in the 1980s refugees fleeing Vietnam with a few possessions became the targets of brutal piracy.

Vietnamese refugees

FIND OUT MORE
ARMS AND ARMOUR • EXPLORATION • FLAGS • MONEY • SHIPS AND BOATS • UNITED KINGDOM, HISTORY OF

PLANETS

THE NINE PLANETS of the Solar System have much in common. Each follows an elliptical orbit around the Sun and each was created from gas and dust left over after the Sun was formed. But the planets range enormously in size and structure. The four inner ones, including Earth, are spheres of rock. They are tiny compared with the four gas giants. These planets appear to be spheres of gas but solids and liquids lurk below their thick atmospheres. The most distant planet, Pluto, is a tiny sphere of rock.

Rocky planets

The four inner planets, in increasing order from the Sun, are Mercury, Venus, Earth, and Mars. Each is a ball of rock but each has a unique surface. Only two of them, Earth and Mars, have moons. The smallest and most distant of all the Solar System planets is Pluto. It is also a ball of rock but, because of its great distance from the Sun, it is an icy world. It is very unlike its neighbours, the gas giants, and something of a mystery.

Mercury

Closest to the Sun, second smallest, and the fastest moving planet is Mercury – it zips around the Sun in 88 days. It is a lifeless and dry world covered with craters. Deep below the surface is a large core of iron. The planet's gravity is too weak to hold on to an atmosphere and so heat is lost at night. Differences between day and night temperatures can be 600°C (1,080°F).

Only a third of Mercury's surface has been mapped from space, by *Mariner 10* in 1974–75.

Cratered world
Most of Mercury's craters were formed 3.5 billion years ago when meteorites bombarded the planet. The craters range in size from 1 m (3.3 ft) to more than 1,000 km (600 miles) in diameter. Here a younger crater (centre), about 12 km (7.5 miles) across, sits inside an older one.

Venus

Sunlight on the cloud tops makes Venus shine brightly in Earth's sky. As it moves it appears to go through phases similar to those of the Moon. The dense clouds trap the Sun's heat to make it the hottest of the planets. The acid clouds and unbearable pressure make it doubly inhospitable. Beneath the clouds are volcanic plains of hot desert covering about two-thirds of the planet.

Radar images were used to create this global view of Venus's surface.

Maat Mons

Surface temperature 465°C (870°F)

Beneath the clouds
Radar equipment on board spacecraft have "seen" through Venus's clouds. The most successful craft, *Magellan*, mapped 98 per cent of its surface in the 1990s. About two days of mapping were used to produce this picture of Maat Mons, the largest shield volcano on Venus.

Earth

Largest of the four inner planets, Earth is the only Solar System planet to support life and to have water in abundance. Earth has changed enormously since it was created 4.6 billion years ago. It has developed an atmosphere and gone through climatic and structural change. Internal heat currents push the land masses by up to 7 cm (3 in) a year.

Continent of Africa

Indian Ocean

Water vapour as clouds

Water covers more than 70 per cent of Earth's surface.

Antarctica

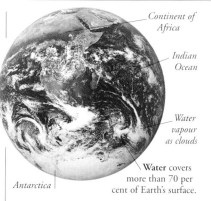

Mars

The most Earth-like of the planets, Mars is a little over half Earth's size and has polar ice caps. Its red colour comes from the iron-rich rock and dust which covers much of the planet. About 40 per cent of the surface is rock desert. Its most dramatic feature is the enormous canyons. Valles Marineris is 4,500 km (2,800 miles) long and up to 7 km (4.5 miles) deep.

Tharsis region

Valles Marineris

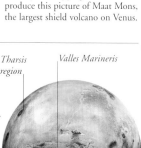

Mars is a cold, lifeless planet with a very thin atmosphere.

Argyre Planitia

Olympus Mons
Volcanic activity has changed Mars's surface in the past. There are two main volcanic areas: the Elysium Planitia and the Tharsis Region which includes Olympus Mons, the biggest volcano in the Solar System. At 26.4 km (16.4 miles), it is three times higher than Earth's tallest mountain, Mount Everest.

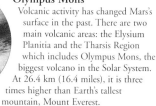

Pluto

This rock and ice planet is a dark and freezing world, more like a moon than a planet. Some astronomers believe it is a large asteroid. No spacecraft have visited Pluto, but astronomers have built up a picture of it from observations. The clearest image of Pluto and its moon was taken by the Hubble Space Telescope in 1990.

HST image of Pluto

Charon, Pluto's only moon

Pluto

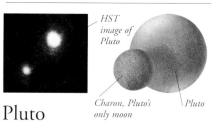

Clyde Tombaugh

The American Clyde Tombaugh (1906–97) was part of a team at the Lowell Observatory in Arizona, searching for a planet believed to be disturbing the orbital motions of Uranus and Neptune. On 18 February 1930 he discovered Pluto but it was too small to affect the orbit of Uranus. Tombaugh spent eight years looking for another planet, but none was found.

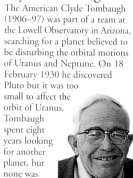

Gas planets

There are four gas planets. From the Sun, and in order of size, they are Jupiter, Saturn, Uranus, and Neptune. They are the biggest planets, the giants of the Solar System. All that is visible is their gas exterior. They each have a deep and dense atmosphere which is why they are called gas planets, but that is only part of the story. Immediately below the gas layer is liquid and at each of their hearts is a rocky core. All four have rings and many moons.

Jupiter

Sometimes called the king of the planets, Jupiter is the biggest and most massive planet and has 61 moons. It has a rocky core 10–20 times as massive as Earth. Above this is metallic and then liquid hydrogen, topped by about 1,000 km (600 miles) of atmosphere, 86 per cent of which is hydrogen and 14 per cent helium. Jupiter's narrow ring system, discovered in 1979, consists of three rings of dust particles. If it had been 50 times more massive, its core would have been hot enough to fuse hydrogen, and Jupiter would have developed into a star.

Galilean moons
Jupiter's four largest moons are named after the Italian astronomer who discovered them, Galileo Galilei. They are, in order of size, Ganymede, Callisto, Io, and Europa. Ganymede is the largest moon in the Solar System and is bigger than the planets Pluto and Mercury. Jupiter's other 57 moons are tiny in comparison, most are only tens of kilometres across.

Ganymede is the brightest of the moons. Its icy crust has craters and long parallel grooves.

Io has a brilliant orange and red surface caused by sulphur compounds ejected by its active volcanoes.

Callisto, with its surface layer of dirty ice, is the faintest of the moons. It is heavily cratered.

Europa has an icy crust with no mountains and few craters. Streaks and cracks crisscross the surface.

North Polar Region

North Temperate Belt

North Tropical Zone

North Equatorial Belt

South Equatorial Belt

Great Red Spot

Trace amounts of phosphorus in the atmosphere give the clouds their red colour.

South Polar Region

Belts and zones
Jupiter's fast spin produces powerful wind systems which divide the atmosphere into bands. The bands are made up of belts and zones running parallel to the equator. The red-brown belts are gases descending and the white-yellow zones are gases rising. The spots, ovals, and streaks in the cloud tops are weather disturbances produced where belts and zones meet.

Great Red Spot
One storm in Jupiter's upper clouds, the Great Red Spot, has been observed for well over 300 years. Over time it has changed colour and size. At its biggest, it was about three times Earth's diameter. It is an area of high pressure, above and colder than the surrounding atmosphere. This gigantic storm rotates above the atmosphere, completing one anticlockwise turn every few days.

Saturn

The second largest and sixth planet from the Sun is Saturn. Like Jupiter, it is made chiefly of hydrogen surrounding a rocky core. Its bands are less obvious and contain fewer features, apart from white spots caused by weather storms. Its mass is so spread out that it has the lowest density of all the planets. Saturn has an extensive ring system and 33 moons.

Faint bands in Saturn's atmosphere

The equator bulges because of the planet's rapid rotation.

Cassini division

A Ring

B Ring

C Ring

D Ring

F Ring

The ring system is up to 2 km (1.25 miles) thick

Saturn's rings

Galileo described the rings as Saturn's "ears" when he first observed them in 1610. Their ring-like nature was not explained until 1656.

Titan

More than half of Saturn's moons are small and irregular in shape. The largest by far is Titan which is just bigger than Mercury. It is one of three Solar System moons with atmospheres. Titan is a sphere of rock and ice surrounded by a thick mantle of nitrogen.

Giovanni Cassini
There are several gaps in Saturn's rings. The largest is the Cassini division, named after its discoverer, the French astronomer Giovanni Cassini (1625–1712). He was a skilful observer, and discovered four of Saturn's moons. His observations of Mars also helped establish the distances in the Solar System.

Ring system
Surrounding Saturn are thousands of ringlets made of billions of ice-covered rock and dust particles. Together they make seven main rings. The particles range in size from a few thousandths of a centimetre to a few metres across. This enhanced image taken by the *Voyager 2* probe reveals many of the individual ringlets in the system.

Uranus

This planet was discovered in 1781. Twice as far from the Sun as Saturn, it is difficult to observe from Earth. The first close-up views came in 1986 from the probe *Voyager 2*. The atmosphere is predominantly hydrogen but methane in the upper clouds gives Uranus its distinctive blue-green colour. It has a ring system and 26 moons.

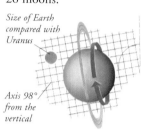

Size of Earth compared with Uranus

Axis 98° from the vertical

Clouds of frozen methane ice are the only features visible on Uranus.

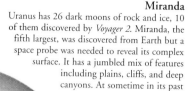

Miranda

Uranus has 26 dark moons of rock and ice, 10 of them discovered by *Voyager 2*. Miranda, the fifth largest, was discovered from Earth but a space probe was needed to reveal its complex surface. It has a jumbled mix of features including plains, cliffs, and deep canyons. At sometime in its past Miranda may have been knocked apart and then reassembled itself.

Rings of Uranus

The Uranian ring system was discovered in 1977 from Earth. When Uranus moved in front of a star, the star disappeared and then reappeared as each ring blocked the star's light. There are 11 rings, each one dark and narrow and made of lumps of rock roughly 1 m (3.3 ft) in size.

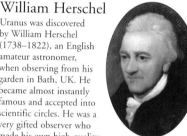

Sideways planet

Uranus is tilted on its axis as it orbits the Sun. This tilt makes the planet appear to be on its side with its moons and rings circling the top and bottom of the planet. No one knows why the Uranian system is like this – perhaps it is the result of a collision.

Uranus is far from the Sun and a cold planet. The temperature at the cloud tops is -210°C (-378°F).

William Herschel

Uranus was discovered by William Herschel (1738–1822), an English amateur astronomer, when observing from his garden in Bath, UK. He became almost instantly famous and accepted into scientific circles. He was a very gifted observer who made his own high-quality telescopes. His later work on double stars, clusters, and nebulae made him one of the most influential astronomers of his time.

Voyager fly-bys

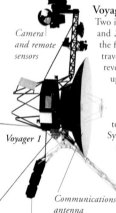

Camera and remote sensors

Voyager 1

Communications antenna

Radioactive power source

Magnetic sensor on extendible boom

Two identical probes, *Voyagers 1* and *2*, were launched in 1977 to the four gas giants. They both travelled to Jupiter and Saturn, revealing new tiny moons, close-ups of the planets and their larger moons, and the complexity of Saturn's rings. *Voyager 1* then moved off toward the edge of the Solar System, but *Voyager 2* travelled to Uranus in 1986 and Neptune in 1989. At these two planets it discovered new rings and a total of 16 moons.

Neptune

Like Uranus, Neptune is a cold and distant world. It is similar in size and is also blue-green because of methane gas in its hydrogen-rich atmosphere. Belts and zones are just visible in its cloud-top surface. Other visible features are white clouds and a dark spot. Neptune was discovered in 1846, but its dark rings – two broad and two narrow – and six of its 13 moons were discovered by *Voyager 2* in 1989.

Great Dark Spot

Great Dark Spot

Neptune is the windiest place in the Solar System. Wind speeds of up to 2,200 kmh (1,370 mph) have been recorded. The winds whiz around the planet in a westerly direction – the opposite direction to the planet's spin. The Great Dark Spot is a huge storm with ferocious winds. It is an oval area of high pressure measuring about 12,000 km (7,500 miles) across.

White clouds of methane ice

Great Dark Spot

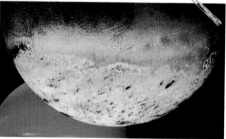

Triton

Neptune's largest moon is Triton, the coldest place in the Solar System at an icy –235°C (–391°F). Triton has a thin atmosphere, mainly of nitrogen, and is one of only three moons known to have an atmosphere. The surface changes as volcanoes throw out nitrogen and black dust which streaks the cracked and wrinkled surface.

Neptune is made of ice and liquid below the thick atmosphere. In the centre lies a rocky core.

The Scooter

Neptune looks blue because methane in the upper atmosphere absorbs red light and reflects blue.

Small Dark Spot, an anticyclone storm

FIND OUT MORE   ATMOSPHERE   COMETS AND ASTEROIDS   EARTH   EARTHQUAKES   GALILEO GALILEI   MOON   NEWTON, SIR ISAAC   SPACE EXPLORATION   SUN AND SOLAR SYSTEM   VOLCANOES

PLANTS

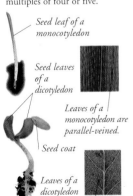

THERE ARE ABOUT 500,000 species of plant, divided into spore-bearing plants and seed-bearing plants. They are food for many animals and are fundamental for life on Earth. Plants vary in size from microscopic algae, to huge sequoia trees more than 8 m (26 ft) across their trunk. Most plants contain a green pigment called chlorophyll, which traps the energy in sunlight. The plants use this energy to make their own food in a process called photosynthesis. Plants struggle to survive in places where it is very cold, very dry, or very dark

Spore-bearing plants

Algae, mosses, ferns, and their relatives all reproduce by means of spores. These are tiny and are produced inside the sporangia in enormous quantities that look like fine dust. Each spore contains a minute amount of essential genetic material in a tough coat.

Spore-producing sporangia on the underside of a fern frond

Frond

Green seaweed

Spore capsule

Moss (*Bryum* species)

Leaf

Pinna (leaflet)

Frond of male fern

Algae
The simplest plants are algae. They do not have leaves, stems, or roots. Algae thrive in a moist or wet environment. Many are tiny, single-celled plants, but some seaweeds can be huge.

Mosses and liverworts
Mosses and most liverworts have simple stems and small, thin leaves. Some liverworts are flat and look like seaweed. They live mostly in mild, damp regions, but some survive in the world's coldest places.

Ferns
These are the most-advanced spore-bearing plants. Water and nutrients are carried around the plant. Many ferns grow well in cool, dry places, but the largest ones are found in the hot, damp tropics.

Seed-bearing plants

Conifers, or gymnosperms, and flowering plants, or angiosperms, reproduce by seeds. Each seed contains an embryo and a food supply, and is encased by a seed coat. A germinating seed is nourished by the food reserves until it can start to make its own food.

Angiosperms
Angiosperms are the flowering plants. They have seeds that develop inside a ripened ovary, called a fruit. There are at least 250,000 kinds of angiosperm, including most of our food plants.

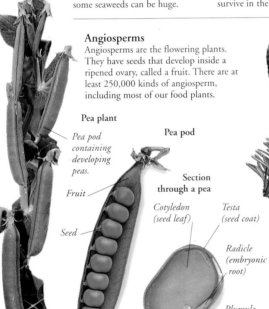

Pea plant

Pea pod containing developing peas.

Fruit

Pea pod

Seed

Section through a pea

Cotyledon (seed leaf)

Testa (seed coat)

Radicle (embryonic root)

Plumule (embryonic shoot)

Delavy's silver fir

Seeds develop on scales inside cones.

Gymnosperms
Gymnosperms are plants that have cones instead of flowers. Their seeds develop inside female cones. Most gymnosperms are trees or shrubs. The cones are not as varied as flowers, but they can be brightly coloured and attractive.

Cotyledons
Flowering plants have either one or two cotyledons (seed leaves). Monocotyledons (one seed leaf) have floral parts in multiples of three. Dicotyledons (two seed leaves) have floral parts usually in multiples of four or five.

Seed leaf of a monocotyledon

Seed leaves of a dicotyledon

Leaves of a monocotyledon are parallel-veined.

Seed coat

Leaves of a dicotyledon are net-veined.

Oldest plant
Bristlecone pines in Utah, Nevada, and Colorado, USA, are the oldest living plants. Some of these trees are more than 5,000 years old. Scientists study the width of growth rings in the wood of dead trees to see how the world's climate has changed.

Plant lifespans
Plants with non-woody stems (herbaceous plants) have a short life-cycle. Some grow from seed to mature plant in a few weeks, dying when their seeds are shed. Woody plants grow more slowly. Trees may be more than 20 years old before they have seeds, but they may produce them for hundreds of years.

Annuals germinate, grow, have flowers and seeds, and die within one year.

Corn marigold

Biennials produce only foliage in the first year. They then flower, fruit, and die in the second year.

Honesty

Perennials live longer than two years. Some die down in autumn and re-grow from a living rootstock the following spring.

Purple monkshood

FIND OUT MORE   FERNS   FLOWERS   FRUITS AND SEEDS   MOSSES AND LIVERWORTS   PHOTOSYNTHESIS   PLANTS, ANATOMY   PLANTS, REPRODUCTION   SEAWEEDS AND OTHER ALGAE   TREES

Plants

Dicotyledons

Prickly pear is a cactus with leaves modified to spines.

Swollen green stem

Poppy is an annual that springs up in disturbed ground.

Water-lily is an aquatic perennial with floating leaves and flowers.

Flowers open at dusk.

Common evening primrose grows in disturbed soil.

Honesty has flowers that turn into papery fruits.

Michaelmas daisy is a tall, stiff perennial with clusters of flowers.

Hottentot fig is a trailing perennial with fleshy leaves.

Himalayan balsam has fruits that explode when ripe.

Hairy leaves and stems

Common mallow is a sturdy perennial of meadows, roadsides, and hedgebanks.

Marsh marigold grows by ponds and in marshes.

Slightly fleshy leaves

Sea pea is a spreading plant that grows high on shingly beaches.

Spring gentian is a perennial often seen in mountain meadows.

Petals are cut into four narrow lobes.

Ragged robin grows in wet grassland and hedgerows.

Wild pansy is a small plant that is often a garden weed.

Bogbean is an aquatic plant that emerges above the water.

Meadow cranesbill is a hairy perennial with deeply lobed leaves and large mauve flowers.

All parts of the plant are poisonous.

Monk's hood is a perennial found in damp woodlands.

Flowers turn into red berries.

Bittersweet is a scrambling plant of ditches and hedgerows.

Sea kale is a coastal plant with thick, grey-green, waxy leaves.

Bell heather is a low-growing evergreen shrub that grows on dry heaths and moors.

Monocotyledons

Star-shaped flowers

Star-of-Bethlehem has leaves that appear before the flower spike.

Waxy flowers

Orchid: this is a rainforest orchid with fragrant flowers.

Stiff spiny leaves

Urn plant has small flowers surrounded by spiny bracts.

Flowering rush roots in mud at the bottom of ponds.

Large yellow flowers open in early summer.

Yellow flag grows in large dense clumps in wet ground.

PLANTS, ANATOMY

THE ANATOMY OF most plants consists of roots, stems, leaves, and reproductive organs, which, in flowering plants, are in the flowers. Some plants have a woody stem which lets them grow taller. Shrubs have woody stems that branch at ground level. Trees have one woody stem called a trunk. Herbaceous plants, such as wild flowers, have a non-woody stem. They die at the end of the growing season. Some plants die back, but store food, which they use to sprout again next year.

Flowers

A flower is made up of sepals, petals, stamens, and carpels. These are arranged in whorls on the tip of the flower stalk. Flowers contain the reproductive organs of the plant.

The stalk is called the petiole.

Each small leaf is a leaflet.

Compound leaf

The large vein running along the centre of the leaf is called a midrib.

Network of finer veins

Simple leaf

Leaves

A plant makes most food in its green leaves. Leaves are usually thin and flat, so they expose a large surface area to the Sun to collect energy. A network of veins supports the leaf and carries water, sugars, and dissolved minerals.

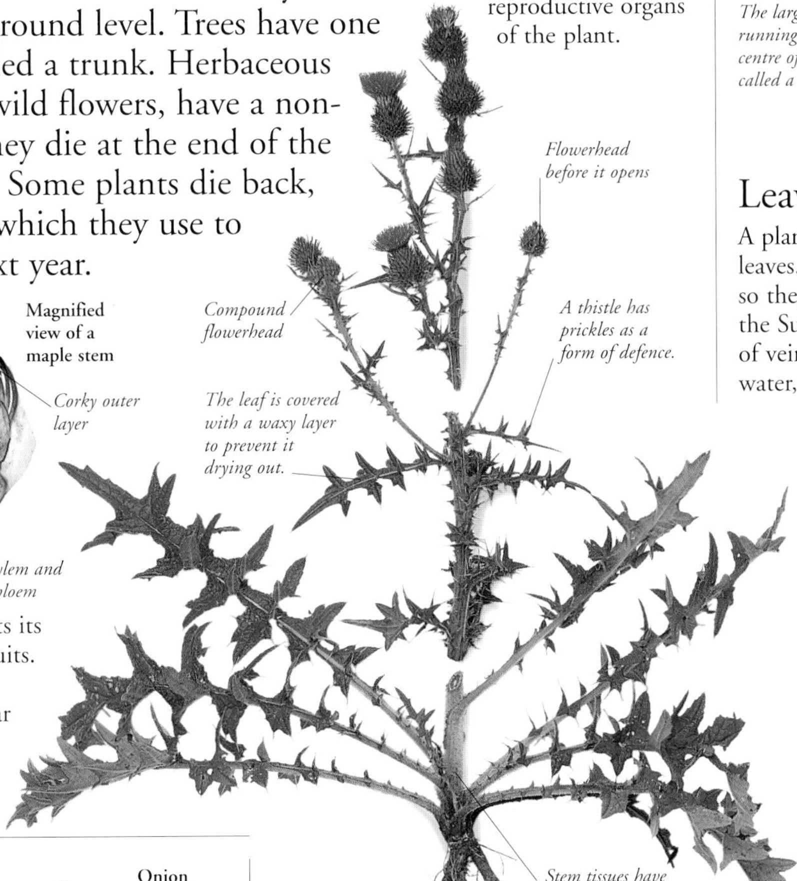

Flowerhead before it opens

Compound flowerhead

A thistle has prickles as a form of defence.

Magnified view of a maple stem

The leaf is covered with a waxy layer to prevent it drying out.

Corky outer layer

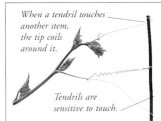

When a tendril touches another stem, the tip coils around it.

Tendrils are sensitive to touch.

Tendrils

Weak-stemmed plants, such as this gourd plant, often have modified leaves called tendrils, which twine around other plants for support.

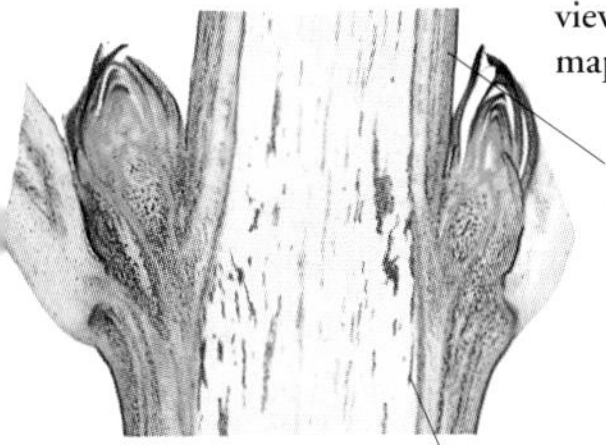

Stems

A plant's stem supports its leaves, flowers, and fruits. It contains xylem and phloem, called vascular tissues, which carry water and sugars around the plant.

Xylem and phloem

Roots

A plant is anchored in the ground by its roots. Older roots are thick and woody, with a waterproof, corky outer layer. The youngest roots take up water and dissolved minerals from the soil. These enter the root through fine root hairs found just behind each root tip.

Food stores

Some parts of a plant are swollen with reserves of starches or sugars. This stored food is used the next growing season by sprouting shoots.

Onion bulb

Bulbs

An onion bulb is a swollen bud. It is made up of layers of fleshy scales which contain the stored food.

Roots spread out to hold the plant in the ground.

Stem tissues have reinforced cell walls that give strength and rigidity, but allow the plant to bend.

Spear thistle

Ginger rhizome

Sweet potato tuber

Rhizomes

The ginger rhizome is a swollen underground stem that grows horizontally.

Tubers

Stem tubers, such as sweet potatoes, are the swollen tips of underground stems.

Breathing roots

All parts of a plant need to breathe, including the roots. Trees that grow in swamps, such as mangroves, have roots that are exposed above the water. These are called pneumatophores. The roots have lenticels (large pores) through which oxygen from the air can enter.

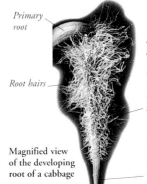

Primary root

The root is part of the plant's transport system and contains xylem and phloem tissues.

Root hairs

Root tip, where the root grows longer

Magnified view of the developing root of a cabbage

FIND OUT MORE | CARNIVOROUS PLANTS | CELLS | DESERT WILDLIFE | FERNS | FLOWERS | FRUITS AND SEEDS | MOSSES AND LIVERWORTS | PHOTOSYNTHESIS | SOIL | TREES

P

Plant leaves

Dicotyledons

Leaves can have a blunt or pointed tip.

Asarabacca has a simple, kidney-shaped (reniform) leaf.

(Black bindweed)

Black bindweed has a simple, arrow-shaped (sagittate) leaf.

Lesser spearwort has a simple, spear-shaped (lanceolate) leaf.

Chicory has a simple, spatula-shaped, or spathulate, leaf.

Common lungwort has a simple, oval leaf with white blotches.

Toothed leaflets

Hemlock has a compound leaf with many tiny leaflets.

Leaves grow in whorls of 3 to 5.

Himalayan balsam has a simple, elliptical leaf with a finely toothed margin.

Balm has a simple, ovate leaf with rounded teeth, described as crenate.

Dusky cranesbill has a simple leaf with spreading lobes, described as palmate.

Leaf is white underneath, with cottony hairs.

Slender thistle has a simple, elliptical leaf with spiny-edged lobes.

Chequer bloom has a simple leaf with lobes spread out like a hand.

Croton has a simple leaf. Its shape is described as panduriform.

Green hellebore has a palmately compound leaf with five to seven segments.

Field scabious has a simple leaf deeply divided into pinnate lobes.

Goat's rue has a pinnate, compound leaf with four to eight pairs of leaflets.

Leaflets often have a white crescent.

Red clover has a compound leaf in three parts, described as trifoliate.

Garden lupin has a compound leaf with 9 to 16 spear-shaped leaflets.

Branched tendrils

Broad-leaved everlasting pea has a compound leaf with branched tendrils.

Common holly has a simple, oval leaf with a prickly margin.

Astrophytum cactus is leafless. Its leaves have become protective spines.

Crassula has a simple, oval leaf that is fleshy and can store water.

Spurge-laurel has a simple, oblong leaf that is deep green and glossy.

White poplar has a simple leaf with a thick coat of white hairs underneath.

Kentucky coffee has a large, compound leaf with many ovate leaflets.

Monocotyledons

Leaves have a long stalk.

Frogbit grows in ponds and lakes. It has a simple kidney-shaped leaf.

Leaves all grow from the base of the plant.

Grape hyacinth has a long, thin leaf, described as linear.

Swiss cheese plant has a large, oval, pinnately lobed leaf.

Lady orchid has a glossy, elliptical leaf with parallel veins and a fleshy feel.

Lords and ladies has a simple, arrow-shaped leaf, often with a wavy edge.

Leaves have between three and nine curving veins.

Black bryony has a simple, shiny, heart-shaped leaf.

PLANTS, DEFENCE

THE ROOTS, TRUNKS, STEMS, leaves, flowers, fruits, and seeds of a plant are under constant attack. Herbivorous animals of all types feed on them. An extensive attack seriously damages the health and reproductive success of a plant. Many plants have evolved strategies that stop animals eating them. Some have sharp spines, prickles, or stings that make them painful to eat. Others contain poisonous substances that taste horrid and can make the animal become ill or even die.

Insects
Some acacias are protected by ants. The ants live in the hollow base of the tree's long, sharp thorns. When another insect or a mammal starts to eat the leaves, the ants rush out and attack them.

Ants on a thorn of an acacia tree

Acacia trees grow in hot, dry parts of the world.

On the African savannah, acacias are browsed by giraffes.

Chemicals
Acacias grow on the hot African savannah where there are few other trees. When an animal starts to eat the leaves of an acacia tree, the tree releases unpleasant chemicals. It also gives off a substance called ethylene. This stimulates nearby acacia trees to produce the chemicals too.

Spines
Cactuses and many other plants survive in arid areas by storing moisture in their stems. Their leaves have become modified into long, hard, sharp spines. These protect the succulent stems and their vital store of moisture from browsing animals. Some plants develop sharp prickles all around their leaf margins to stop animals from eating them.

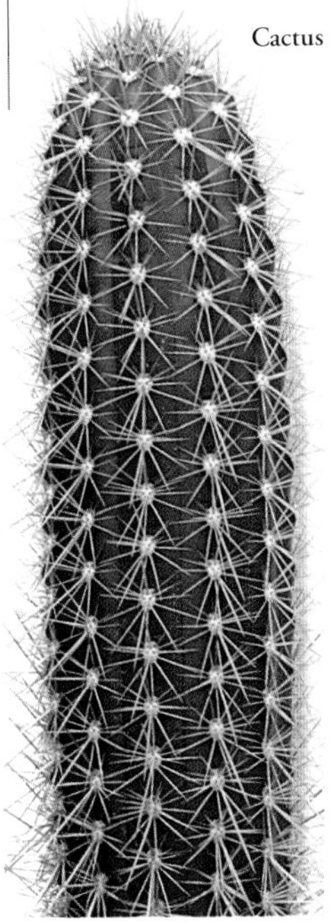

Cactus

Holly (*Ilex* sp.) **leaves**

Stings
Nettles have sharp hairs that can penetrate skin, even through fur, and inject chemicals called histamines. These "stings" are very painful, and animals soon learn not to touch a stinging nettle.

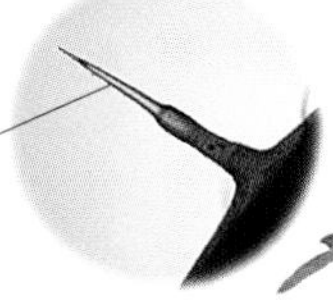

Hairs are borne on the leaves and stem.

Magnified nettle hair

Stinging nettle

Gums
Sticky substances secreted by some plants, such as the horse chestnut, gum up an insect's mouthparts and feet, and may even trap them.

Horse chestnut

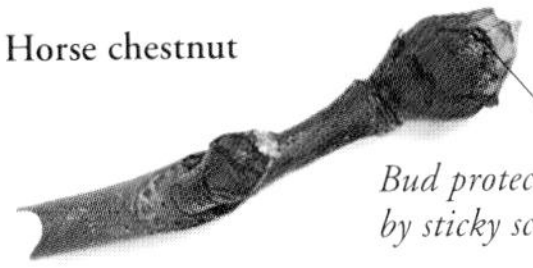

Bud protected by sticky scales.

Plant mimicry
Passion flower vines of tropical America contain poisons that deter most creatures from eating their leaves. Postman caterpillars can eat the leaves and the poison builds up in them and makes them poisonous. The butterflies lay eggs only on plants with no other postman eggs. The plant produces false "eggs" on its young leaves and tendrils. These deceive the female butterfly.

Passion flower leaf with false "eggs"

Poisonous plants

Foxglove is poisonous, but drugs prepared from the plant are used to treat humans for some heart conditions.

Poison ivy causes painful blistering and burning of the skin of anyone who brushes against it.

Dumb cane sap causes severe swelling of the mouth and throat.

Castor-oil seeds contain deadly ricin. A tiny amount will kill a human.

Deadly nightshade berries contain the poisonous substance atropine.

Useful drugs are made from a substance in foxglove leaves.

The strong poison is in the sap.

Dumb cane leaves

Poisonous berry

FIND OUT MORE   AFRICAN WILDLIFE   DESERT WILDLIFE   DRUGS   PLANTS   PLANT USES

PLANTS, REPRODUCTION

PLANTS, LIKE OTHER living things, reproduce to ensure the continued existence of the species. They propagate by means of seeds, spores, or plantlets, often in large numbers. Seeds and spores are formed by sexual reproduction involving male and female gametes (sex cells) from different plants. Plantlets are formed by asexual, or vegetative, reproduction, in which a plant produces new plants on its own.

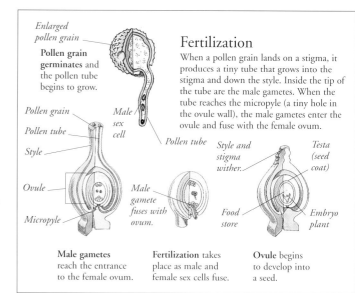

Fertilization

When a pollen grain lands on a stigma, it produces a tiny tube that grows into the stigma and down the style. Inside the tip of the tube are the male gametes. When the tube reaches the micropyle (a tiny hole in the ovule wall), the male gametes enter the ovule and fuse with the female ovum.

Enlarged pollen grain

Pollen grain germinates and the pollen tube begins to grow.

Pollen grain
Pollen tube
Style
Ovule
Micropyle
Male sex cell
Pollen tube
Male gamete fuses with ovum.
Style and stigma wither.
Testa (seed coat)
Food store
Embryo plant

Male gametes reach the entrance to the female ovum.

Fertilization takes place as male and female sex cells fuse.

Ovule begins to develop into a seed.

Sexual reproduction

Seeds are formed by sexual reproduction. This process ensures the mixing of genetic material from different plants. It keeps the species strong and more able to adapt to changes in conditions. If a female sex cell is fertilized by a male one, a seed develops.

Fertile disc of small flowers, or florets

Sterile ray floret for attracting pollinating insects.

Petals are no longer needed.

1 The flowerhead of a sunflower is made up of many small flowers. The large yellow head attracts insects to come to feed on the nectar inside the flowers. These insects bring pollen from another sunflower.

2 When the flowers have been fertilized, the bright yellow petals die away.

Developing fruits holding seeds.

3 Each fertile ovule develops into a seed. It will be dormant until conditions are right for growth.

4 A seed takes up moisture and begins to grow. This is called germination.

Seeds fall to the ground.

Radicle (first small root)

Developing flowerhead

Stem grows thicker and longer.

True leaf

Seed leaf

5 The plant uses food from its seed leaves to grow true leaves.

6 Gradually, the plant puts down roots, develops new leaves, and grows taller. The flowers form, eventually producing new seeds.

Asexual reproduction

Some plants reproduce without the fusion of sex cells. This vegetative reproduction produces plantlets that are all genetically identical to the parent plant. These plantlets are known as clones. Sometimes, the vegetative descendants of one plant cover a large area.

Adventitious buds

The Mexican hat plant develops small adventitious buds around the edge of its leaves. Each bud is a miniature plant with rootlets. The plantlets start to grow as soon as they fall to the ground.

Adventitious bud
Plantlet
Leaf

Runners

Strawberries produce new plantlets on creeping stems called runners. Each runner grows along the ground producing several new plants. The stem dies once the plantlets have grown their own leaves and roots.

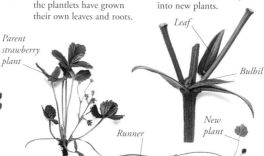

Parent strawberry plant
Runner

Bulbils

Some plants, such as this orange lily, produce tiny bulbils on their stems. These fall to the ground where, in the right conditions, they will grow into new plants.

Leaf
Bulbil
New plant

How plants grow

Plants contain hormones that control the way in which they grow. Some hormones make the shoots grow toward the light. Others make the roots grow away from the light into the ground. The movement of parts of a plant toward and away from light is called phototropism.

Stems grow toward the light.
Leaves and stems are positively phototropic.
Roots are negatively phototropic.

FIND OUT MORE   FLOWERS   FERNS   FRUITS AND SEEDS   GENETICS   MOSSES AND LIVERWORTS   PHOTOSYNTHESIS   PLANTS   PLANTS, ANATOMY

PLANT USES

ALL HUMAN SOCIETIES are dependent on plants and the products made from them. The use of vegetables and fruit as food is common to all cultures, but plants have a wide variety of other uses too. Starchy and spicy roots are used for food and flavourings, plant fibres are woven into textiles and ropes, and trees not only give us timber, but also rubbery latexes, cork, and pulp for paper. Perfume, tea, cooking oils, medical drugs, cosmetics, chocolate, and even chewing gum are all everyday items that we obtain from plants.

Wood

Every year, we use almost 3,000 million cubic metres (106,000 million cu ft) of wood worldwide. The unique properties of wood – its strength, durability, resilience, and appearance – make it ideal for the construction of boats, buildings, furniture, and smaller items such as musical instruments and toys. Resin that oozes from cut conifer trunks provides turpentine and rosin, and is used to make varnishes.

This trunk has been sawn so the boards keep their shape and have a decorative grain.

Bark is cut at an angle.

Latex is collected by making slits, or punctures, in the bark of the rubber tree.

Cork

Cork oak trees have a thick layer of cork below their bark, that is stripped from the trees every 8–10 years. This does no harm as the trees soon grow a new cork layer. Cork has many uses, as it is waterproof and has good sound and heat-insulating properties.

Untreated cork

Cork tile

Bottle corks

Rubber

Below the bark of rubber trees is a sticky sap, or latex, that oozes out when the bark is cut. As it dries, the latex becomes stretchy. It is treated to turn it into rubber. Rubber is used to make footwear and tyres, and is incorporated into many items where stretch and elasticity are needed.

Paper

Books, tissues, and printed items such as newspapers are a few examples of the kinds of paper that we use daily. Paper is made from wood pulp. Some natural forests are still being felled to provide pulp, but now much of the wood needed is grown on plantations of fast-growing trees, such as eucalyptus and poplar.

Cardboard packaging

Tissues

Tea bag

Paper napkin

Food and drink

Starchy plants, such as grains, potatoes, yams, and some grasses, form the basis of most diets. Plants provide tea, coffee, and cocoa, and refreshing, vitamin-rich juices can be squeezed from fruits. Food and drinks are often sweetened with sugar prepared from sugar cane or sugar beet. Wine is made from fermented grapes, and beers from fermented grains.

Spices and flavourings

The aromatic seeds, roots, and bark of some plants are dried to make spices and added to food to enhance its flavour. The nutmeg tree provides nutmeg from its seed, and mace from the flesh around the seed. Other spices include cinnamon and ginger.

Wheat is used to make flour for bread and pasta.

Oats are used in breakfast cereals.

Rice is eaten as a grain and is made into cereals.

Rye is used to make flour.

Barley is used to brew beer.

Millet is ground into flour to make bread and is used in porridge.

Fibres

Fibres from the leaves and stems of flax, hemp, raffia, and other plants can be spun into yarns. Some fibres such as cotton and kapok come from the seed heads. The finer, softer yarns are used to make clothes. Cloth of many colours and patterns is made by weaving threads together on a hand or machine loom. Coarser fibres from plants such as agave and sisal are woven into mats, ropes, and baskets.

Raffia cloth made from fibres of the raffia palm.

Vats of natural dyes in Morocco

Dyes

Before artificial dyes were invented, most yarns were coloured with natural plant dyes. These are made by pounding plants and mixing them with liquid. The colour is fixed with chemicals. The colours are quite subtle, but many people prefer them to artificial dyes.

Cosmetics

Plants are an important ingredient in cosmetics. Herbal extracts and fragrant oils, such as jasmine and lavender, are used to scent many cosmetics. Aloe vera and cocoa butter are used in moisturizing lotions, and alginates from seaweeds are used as gelling and stabilizing agents.

Henna plant yields long-lasting hair and skin dyes.

Indian bride's hand painted with henna

Henna powder

Fuel

Coal, oil, and natural gas are all derived from plants that lived long ago. Half the wood felled each year is also burnt for fuel. In some countries such as Ireland, peat – the compressed remains of mosses and sedges – is still dug from the ground and used as fuel.

Medicine

Some plants produce chemicals, that if eaten or touched, can have dramatic effects. These plants may be poisonous if taken in large doses, but in small amounts they often have valuable medicinal properties. Cinchona tree bark is used to make quinine to treat malaria. Digitalin extracted from foxgloves is used as a heart stimulant, and morphine and codeine from the opium poppy are used as painkillers.

Cinchona trees grow in South America.

Cinchona bark is used to make quinine.

Quinine tablets

PLASTICS AND RUBBER

PLASTICS HAVE BECOME one of the most used materials in the world. They come in many forms but have two things in common – their molecules are made up of long chains of atoms and they are easily shaped by heating. Most plastics are synthetic, made from chemicals that are usually extracted from petroleum. Common plastics range from polystyrene and polythene, used to make items such as plastic bags, to polyvinyl chloride (PVC) and nylon, used in clothing. Rubber, a gum extracted from trees, is a natural kind of plastic. Synthetic rubber, like plastic, is made using petrochemicals.

Polymers

Polymers are substances that are made up of very long molecules, which consist of a chain of repeated chemical units. Most plastics are polymers, and their chain molecules are built up from smaller molecules (monomers) in a chemical process called polymerization.

Polymers make up PVC used in raincoats

Moulding plastic

Plastics are most commonly shaped by moulding, a process in which molten plastic is injected or blown into a shaped mould. Other methods include extrusion, in which molten plastic is forced through the hole in a die (a shaped block), and vacuum forming, in which a plastic sheet is sucked into a mould by a vacuum.

Impression of channel through which plastic is fed.

Injection moulding ensures that related parts fit together.

Moulded electrical components

Types of plastics

There are a number of plastics in use today, but they all fall into two different classes according to the way they react to heat. Thermoplastics soften and melt each time they are heated, and harden, keeping their shape when the temperature falls. Thermosetting plastics will not soften again once they have been heated and set.

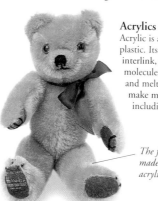

Acrylics

Acrylic is an example of a thermoplastic. Its long molecules do not interlink, so when heated the molecules slide over one another and melt. Acrylic is used to make many products, including textiles.

The fur is made from an acrylic fabric.

Cycle helmet

Epoxies

Epoxies are thermosetting plastics, which have long molecules that cross-link and form rigid structures. An epoxy resin is the resinous material used for moulding. A curing agent is then added and the mixture sets into a three-dimensional structure.

Fibreglass is set into a plastic matrix that gives a smooth shiny surface.

Chair

Carbon fibre frame

Tennis racket

Marbled Bakelite

Bakelite hair-dryer (c.1930s)

Bakelite

Named after its inventor Leo Baekeland (1863–1944), Bakelite was the first synthetic plastic. Baekeland first produced this material in 1909, by polymerizing phenol and formaldehyde. A thermoset, Bakelite is still used today for its heat and electrical resistance.

Composites

Some plastics are given added strength by reinforcing them with fibres, making a composite. The most common composite is fibreglass plastic. Carbon fibre composites are also used as reinforcements, as they are light as well as tough.

Rubber

Rubber may be natural or synthetic. Natural rubber comes from rubber trees cultivated in plantations, particularly in southeast Asia. It is made by processing the sap, or latex, that is collected from the trees when they are cut. Synthetic rubber is made by polymerization in much the same way as other plastics.

Tapping rubber from a tree plantation, Malaysia

Uses of rubber

Rubber is used for soles of shoes and motor tyres, because its resilience and elasticity make it a good shock absorber. It is also flexible and waterproof, and therefore is used in protective clothing, such as rubber gloves and rainwear.

Motor tyre

Rubber dummy

Properties of rubber

When first made from latex, rubber has little elasticity and deteriorates quickly in air. It becomes elastic and hardens when treated with sulphur, a process called vulcanization. A pigment called carbon black is added to make the rubber durable.

Recycling

Since most plastics are made from petroleum chemicals that cannot be replaced, there is a need for recycling. Thermoplastics, such as polythene, are easy to recycle because they can be re-melted. Thermosets, such as Bakelite, pose a problem as they cannot readily be broken down.

Plastic ready for recycling

FIND OUT MORE   ATOMS AND MOLECULES   CHEMISTRY   COAL   OIL   POLLUTION   TECHNOLOGY   TEXTILES AND WEAVING

POETRY

AN INTENSE FORM OF LITERATURE, poetry appeals directly to the emotions. In poetry, meaning is condensed to produce strong images, and words are arranged according to the pattern of their sounds. This pattern is like music. It is picked up by the listening ear, and reinforces the thoughts and feelings expressed by the words. Many people are attracted to the rhythms of poetry from infancy, when they learn children's nursery rhymes. All societies preserve great examples of the art, because it can articulate the deepest experiences of life.

Types of poetry

There are three main types of poetry. The oldest is epic poetry, which consists of long narratives with a heroic or profound subject. Dramatic poetry is written in the voices of its characters, and can be acted on stage. The third, and most widespread type, is lyric poetry. Lyric poems are the closest to song. They are usually short, colourful, and express the poet's feelings deeply and intensely.

Kipling's desk

Kipling's stories were set all over the world.

Rudyard Kipling's study

Gilgamesh

The world's oldest written poem is The *Epic of Gilgamesh.* Discovered in Persia (Iran), it is at least 4,000 years old. The poem tells the Babylonian legend of Gilgamesh, the great king of Uruk in Mesopotamia, who is half-god, half-man. Together with his friend Enkidu the wild man, he slays monsters sent to destroy him. But in the end, Enkidu dies, and Gilgamesh searches for and fails to find a way to live forever. The *Epic of Gilgamesh* is the first example of epic poetry.

William Blake

English poet and artist William Blake (1757–1827) enjoyed neither critical nor commercial success in his lifetime, although he is now regarded as one of the greatest figures of Romanticism. Many of Blake's poems are written from a child's point of view. One of his most famous works is *The Tyger* (1794).

Statue of Gilgamesh

Illustration by Blake

Rudyard Kipling

British writer Rudyard Kipling (1865–1936) is now best known for *The Jungle Books* and *Kim,* but during his lifetime he was much more popular for his poems about British soldiers, which were published in *Barrack-Room Ballads* (1892).

Goethe

The German writer Johann Wolfgang von Goethe (1749–1832) published his dramatic poem *Faust* in two parts (1808 and 1832), and it is still regarded as one of the greatest poetic and philosophical works of literature. *Faust* tells the story of a man tempted by the devil.

Poster for the film of *Faust*

World poetry

The narrative poem exists in almost every culture. It has various subjects, such as nature, religion, and legend. These are recited on important occasions, as poets were often regarded as divinely inspired. Today, many cultures still use the narrative poem. Others have evolved complex forms, such as the Japanese *haiku,* which is a poem containing 17 syllables.

Omar Khayyám

One of the most famous of Persian poets, Omar Khayyám (1048–1131) was also an architect and astronomer. He wrote many *rubaiyat* – verses in four lines that ponder eternal mysteries, and at the same time celebrate the simple pleasures that life has to offer.

Rubaiyat illustration by Rene Bull

African praise poetry

Praise poems are sung in African communities in celebration of many things, including people, animals, and weapons. In Nigeria, the Yoruba people dress in masks and costumes to recite important poems. The poems are handed down by oral tradition, but a praise poet can also choose to add lines of his own.

Pair of Yoruba tribal masks, Nigeria

War poetry

A new development in the 20th century was war poetry. First associated with World War I (1914–18), war poetry describes the horrors of war. One of the most famous poets was British soldier Wilfred Owen (1893–1918), whose poetry about the suffering of soldiers in the trenches was published after his death.

Sylvia Plath

American poet and novelist Sylvia Plath (1932–63) was little known at the time of her death by suicide, but she is now considered an important writer of the 20th century. From childhood she was dedicated to perfecting her art as a poet. Her work shows great skill and poise. Many of her later poems are preoccupied with death.

FIND OUT MORE
BABYLONIAN EMPIRE · BOOKS · DRAMA · LANGUAGES · LITERATURE · WRITING · WORLD WAR I

POISONOUS ANIMALS

POISONOUS AND VENOMOUS animals are often confused with each other. Venomous animals, such as snakes and scorpions, defend themselves by biting or stinging, and injecting venom, whereas poisonous animals are those that cause ill effects when eaten or handled. Many venomous and poisonous animals have no need to be camouflaged and advertise themselves with bright-coloured patterns including combinations of yellow, black, and red, which are recognized warning colours. Some harmless species mimic the colours of venomous or poisonous species for protection. For example, harmless milksnakes are similar in appearance to deadly coral snakes.

Pitahui bird

Birds used to be absent from the list of poisonous animals. But recently it was discovered that some species of pitahui bird of New Guinea, such as the black-hooded pitahui bird, have poisonous feathers and flesh. The poison is only mild, causing localized tingling and discomfort when eaten, but this may be sufficient to deter enemies.

Black-hooded
pitahui bird

Pufferfish

If eaten, pufferfish cause lung paralysis and even death, due to the poison tetrodotoxin. In Japan pufferfish meat is considered a delicacy. It is prepared so the diner receives just enough toxin for a tingling sensation; even so it causes 50 deaths each year.

Poisonous animals

Poisonous animals – those that cause ill effects if eaten or touched – are poisonous to deter enemies and avoid being eaten. Poisonous skin secretions that make a predator sick or cause its mouth to burn, teach it to avoid such prey in future. The European toad secretes a toxin from parotid glands on its head if molested; the cane toad secretes similar, but far more toxic secretions, that can even kill a dog.

Poison dart frog

South American poison dart frogs are poisonous to eat, so have few enemies. Their diet of insects makes them poisonous. Amerindians use blow-pipe darts tipped with poison from the most toxic species to hunt for monkeys.

Bright-coloured stripes indicate that it is poisonous to eat.

Black and red poison dart frog

Scorpion fish

Scorpion fish and lionfish are widespread in tropical waters. Their enlarged dorsal spines are highly venomous and can give a serious sting. Other venomous fish include freshwater stingrays, the lesser weaver fish of British coastlines, and the ugly stonefish of Australia, which is probably the most venomous fish in the world. Barefoot bathers are sometimes stung when they accidentally step on weaver fish or stonefish.

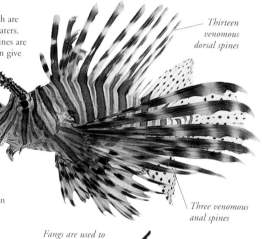

Thirteen venomous dorsal spines

Three venomous anal spines

Venomous animals

Venomous animals release toxins in various ways. Some snakes and spiders bite their victims, releasing toxins through fangs, an Amazonian caterpillar has venomous hairs, swarms of killer bees sting and kill people and animals, and beaded lizards chew toxins into their victims. Many venomous animals live in the sea. Cone shells release venomous harpoons, stonefish erect poison-filled spines, and box jellyfish ensnare and sting swimmers with their tentacles.

Antivenom

Antivenoms are drugs used to save victims of venomous bites or stings. Most snakebite antivenoms are made by giving horses a dose of snake venom. The horses produce antibodies to the venom; blood serum is taken from the horses and used to make antivenom. Some people are allergic to horse serum, and scientists are trying to raise antivenoms on sheep.

Snake is milked for its venom.

Fangs are used to bite victim and inject venom.

If alarmed, the blue spots enlarge.

Sensitive bill

Duck-billed platypus

Mammals are not normally considered venomous but three kinds are known. The male duck-billed platypus has large venomous spurs on its hind legs and the spiny echidna has small spurs, used mainly for defence. Insectivorous shrews subdue earthworms with a venomous bite.

Sydney funnel-web spider

The most dangerous spider to humans is the Sydney funnel-web. The male's bite causes muscle spasms and death. The black widow of Europe and USA, and the Australian red-back are also deadly.

Blue-ringed octopus

The blue-ringed octopus lives in rock pools in Australia. It is the most lethal octopus in the world. If handled, it bites and injects tetrodotoxin, the same poison as found in the puffer fish, which causes respiratory paralysis and, without treatment, death in two hours.

The coils make a warning sound as viper moves.

Carpet viper

Carpet vipers are small snakes common in highly populated areas of Africa and Asia. Their venom is dangerous and may cause kidney failure. Despite their small size, they can easily kill an adult human.

FIND OUT MORE	AUSTRALIAN WILDLIFE	CAMOUFLAGE AND COLOUR	FISH	FROGS AND TOADS	JELLYFISH AND SEA ANEMONES	OCTOPUSES AND SQUIDS	SNAKES	SPIDERS AND SCORPIONS

POLAR EXPLORATION

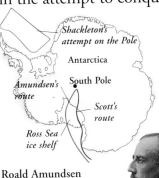

WHEN EXPLORERS FINALLY REACHED the North and South Poles in the early 20th century, their journeys were the last heroic voyages of discovery. Although navigators had always known about the location of the Arctic, the existence of the Antarctic land mass was not proven until 1820. Icy deserts covering both Poles make these mysterious places the harshest environments on Earth. Conditions include raging winds, sub-zero temperatures, and a lack of food. Polar explorers needed incredible stamina, resourcefulness, and courage – many died in the attempt to conquer the world's last frontiers.

Arctic

Native North Americans and Greenlanders have lived on the Arctic's fringes for 5,000 years. European navigators first explored the ice-cap 400 years ago, searching for sea routes to the riches of Asia.

Peary and Henson

American explorer Robert Peary (1856–1920) and his servant Matthew Henson (1866–1955) are thought to have been the first to reach the North Pole. In 1909, they left Greenland with 29 Eskimos and 133 dogs. Some people think that they did not reach it, but the latest research suggests they did.

Robert Peary

Northeast Passage

In the 1500s, Dutchman Willem Barents tried to reach Asia by sailing northeast from Europe. In 1878–79, Swedish geologist Nils Nordenskjöld (1832–1901) was the first to succeed.

Willem Barents (1550–97) seeks the Northeast Passage

Northwest passage

English explorer John Franklin (1786–1847) died searching for the elusive route to Asia along Canada's coast, known as the Northwest Passage. His expedition found the entrance, but the Norwegian explorer Roald Amundsen was the first to actually navigate it in 1906.

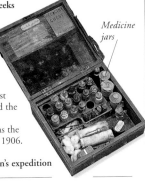

Medicine jars

Medicine chest from Franklin's expedition

Race to the South Pole

After the first reliable sighting of the Antarctic in 1820, expeditions from France, the USA, and Britain mapped the coastline. Interior exploration did not begin until 1900, but by 1906 a race was on between Britain's Captain Scott (1868–1912) and Norway's Amundsen to be the first to reach the South Pole.

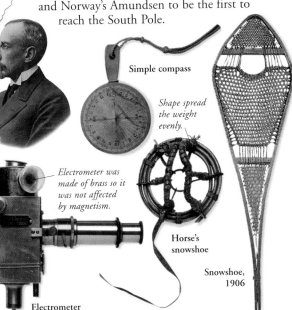

Roald Amundsen

Amundsen (1872–1928) and his four companions were the first to arrive at the South Pole on 14th December, 1911, a month before Scott and his team. Amundsen returned to his Ross Sea base safely but Scott's team died on the return journey.

Simple compass

Shape spread the weight evenly.

Early equipment

The first explorers took equipment such as simple compasses and electrometers, on polar expeditions. The Sun's position and the compass together determined a north-south direction. The electrometer measured changes in the atmosphere's electricity near the Poles.

Electrometer was made of brass so it was not affected by magnetism.

Horse's snowshoe

Snowshoe, 1906

Electrometer

Cross-country skis, 1901

Wooden skis

2.5 m (8 ft) long

Modern research

Although the polar regions have now been explored and mapped, multinational stations still conduct scientific research, particularly in the Antarctic.

Scott-Amundsen base

Overwintering stations

Today Antarctica has around 40 permanent and 100 temporary research stations that investigate wildlife, fossils, and minerals. Hundreds of scientists work in the summer at the American Amundsen-Scott base.

Ernest Shackleton

Irish explorer Shackleton (1874–1922) first went to the Antarctic in 1901. During an expedition in 1914, Shackleton made a heroic 1,300-km (800-mile) journey in an open boat to get help for his stranded team. His bravery earned him a place in history.

Timeline

1611 English navigator Henry Hudson set adrift to die by mutineers in the northern Canada bay named after him.

1733 Russian expedition explores Arctic land fringes.

1820 US sealer Nat Palmer sights the Antarctic.

Scott's matchbox

1901–1904 Scott's *Discovery* expedition penetrates Antarctic.

December 1911 Amundsen reaches the South Pole.

January 1912 Scott and his team reach the South Pole.

1929 First flight over South Pole by Richard E Byrd (1888–1957).

1937 Soviets create Arctic research stations.

1957–58 International Geophysical Year: 12 nations set up about 50 Antarctic bases.

FIND OUT MORE   ARCTIC OCEAN   EXPLORATION   INVENTIONS   NATIVE AMERICANS   NAVIGATION   SCANDINAVIA, HISTORY OF

673

POLAR WILDLIFE

SUB-ZERO TEMPERATURES, six months of darkness, hurricane-force winds, and desert conditions make the polar regions some of the most difficult places for wildlife. Only animals and plants specially adapted to the severe conditions can hope to survive. Every animal from the furry nosed reindeer to the thickly blubbered whale is particularly suited to its environment. All wildlife has to be able to breed or flower in the extremely short polar summer. For many animals, the sea, which is rich in plankton and krill, is the key to survival. Most mammals and birds, especially in the south, depend on it for their food.

Emperor penguins in the Antarctic

Polar regions

The Arctic and Antarctic Circles are defined as those parts of the planet that experience 24 hours of daylight and 24 hours of darkness for at least one day in the year. The Arctic and Antarctic are totally different from each other. The Arctic is a frozen sea surrounded by land; the Antarctic is an ice-covered continent surrounded by sea.

Mammals

The Arctic is warmer than the Antarctic and therefore has more vegetation. Some herbivorous land mammals can survive here; other mammals depend on the sea for their food, either directly or indirectly. The Antarctic mammals are all aquatic. Any carnivorous land mammals would create havoc among the millions of penguins that live there.

Polar bear
The polar bear has black skin to absorb heat, and hollow hairs for added insulation. It also has a thick layer of fat beneath its skin and is able to go for long periods without feeding by living on this fat.

Arctic fox
Smaller than the red fox, the Arctic fox changes colour from white to grey-brown in the summer. It has a very thick coat and is extremely tolerant of the cold. Its diet is very varied and includes birds' eggs, birds, lemmings, and carrion.

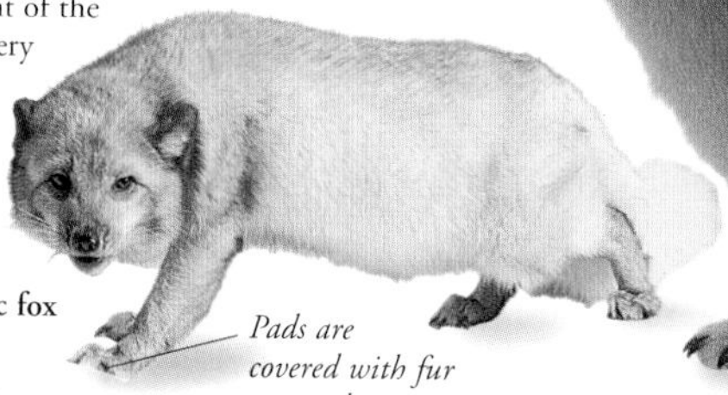

Arctic fox

Pads are covered with fur to save heat.

Strong, partly webbed front paws for swimming.

Polar bear

White fur blends with the snow.

Weddell seal

Seals
Seals are adapted to life in the sea and spend much of their time in the water, often under the ice. They haul out to rest and breed. In the Arctic, seals are hunted by polar bears. Antarctic seals are prey for leopard seals and killer whales.

Arctic hare
The Arctic hare matches its surroundings by changing colour from white in winter to brown in summer and is then more difficult for predators to spot. Unusually for hares, it digs burrows and these are often used by its young for shelter.

Musk oxen
These are not oxen but members of the goat antelope family. They have long black fur which absorbs heat. They are known for forming defensive circles when danger threatens, so that predators are faced with a barrier of horns.

Musk oxen

Whales
The polar regions provide whales with very rich sources of food. The largest whales are the baleen whales, which strain sea water through a series of bony plates and sieve out huge quantities of plankton. The toothed whales hunt fish, seals, and other sea life.

Colonies of barnacles and lice live on the whale's skin.

Scratches are from encounters with other whales, sharks, and boats.

Grey whale

Lemmings
These small vole-like creatures are common in the cold north. In good years their populations can explode, forcing them to migrate. When they come to an obstacle, such as water, large numbers may gather and be drowned.

Siberian lemmings

P

Birds

Antarctic birds fall into two main categories. They are either flightless like penguins, or magnificent fliers like albatrosses. The Arctic tends to have greater variety among its birds, which include a large number of migrants. Many wildfowl and waders fly there every year to breed during the short Arctic summer. Some birds of prey live in the Arctic, including snowy owls and gyrfalcons. They feed on small animals such as lemmings and birds.

Arctic tern
These remarkable fliers travel more than 31,000 km (20,000 miles) a year. They migrate from their Arctic breeding grounds to the Antarctic and back again, enjoying almost continuous summer-time throughout their lives.

Little auk
One of the smallest sea birds, the little auk nests in large colonies on the Arctic cliffs. Like other auks, it has narrow wings and feet set well back on its body. It specializes in diving for its food.

Forward-facing eyes for finding prey.

White feathers for winter camouflage

Feathers on legs and feet help keep owl warm

Snowy owl
This large white owl is solitary and active mainly by day. It chases other birds and also takes prey as large as Arctic hares and eider ducks. It perches on low branches to rest or preen, but nests on the ground.

Krill sieve food from the water.

Luminescent organs shimmer in the dark.

Krill are only 5 cm (2 in) long.

Krill can occur in such vast numbers that they turn the ocean red.

Krill
These small shrimp-like animals are found in the sea around the Antarctic and are the staple food of many species, including some whales. Penguin numbers have increased in recent years, probably because the slaughter of whales has left a surplus of krill for the birds.

Plants

It is a real struggle for plants to survive in such extreme climates. There are only two species of flowering plant in Antarctica, although the more maritime climate of the Arctic encourages more plant species. All tend to be low-growing as this gives them shelter from the strong winds. Mosses and lichens are the hardiest plants in polar regions.

Emperor penguin and chick

Penguins
Several species of these flightless birds breed in their millions in the Antarctic. They are kept warm by their dense plumage and by a layer of fat under their skin. They go without food for long periods while incubating eggs and protecting their young.

Gulls
The only gull that lives and breeds in the Antarctic is the kelp gull, which feeds mostly on limpets and krill. A number of other gull species breed in the Arctic in colonies on the tundra or on the sea cliffs. These fly south to live in warmer climates for most of the year.

Purple saxifrage
This creeping plant is generally found sheltering among rocks in the Arctic. Its beautiful purple flowers bloom almost as soon as the snow has melted, to make the most of the short spring and summer. They add a splash of colour to an often drab landscape.

Arctic willow
This is a low-growing shrub that grows in tundra swamps and wet ground. It sends out long woody stems along the ground. In the northern spring, it has small catkins that appear out of scale with the rest of the plant. Arctic willow and its close relative Alaska willow are favourite foods of moose.

Hairgrass
This and Antarctic pearlwort are the only two flowering plants found in the Antarctic. Hairgrass grows in low mats and is found only in those areas near the coast from which the snow recedes in spring and where the temperature is sufficiently high.

Lichens
Many species of these hardy plants grow in both the north and south polar regions, where they can thrive in the unpolluted air. Often colourful, they generally occur as encrustations on the rocks. They may be fertilized by droppings from nesting birds.

FIND OUT MORE   ANTARCTICA   ARCTIC   MIGRATION   OCEAN WILDLIFE   PENGUINS   PLANTS   SEABIRDS   SEALS   TUNDRA   WHALES AND DOLPHINS

POLICE

IN EVERY COMMUNITY, LAWS exist to regulate society. Within society, it is usually the police who ensure that these laws are enforced. The police prevent or solve crime, capture criminals and hand them over for trial, and protect and aid the public. In the course of these duties, the police may undertake many different tasks, such as directing traffic, controlling riots, or investigating murder and other serious crimes. In times of emergency, they may be asked to find shelter and protection for victims of fires, floods, or other disasters.

Bow Street Runner, 18th century

Early police
The first police force was set up in Egypt in about 1340 BC, to protect merchants on the river Nile from pirates. In Britain, the Bow Street Runners were set up in 1750 to capture criminals all over the country; they were replaced in 1829 by the Metropolitan Police, the world's oldest existing police force. In the USA, forces similar to the Metropolitan Police were set up from the 1840s on.

Police divisions

In order for the police to carry out their duties effectively, specially trained and equipped divisions exist to deal with specific tasks. Within a police force, a uniformed division patrols the streets, preventing crime or arresting people who are breaking the law. Detective divisions investigate crime; others deal with juvenile crime, drug dealing, or fraud.

Around the world

There is at least one police force in every country, but how they are run and who controls them differ widely. For example, in France the government directly controls a national police force which investigates major crimes, while local forces deal with minor matters. In other countries, such as Australia, separate forces cover different areas.

Hand signals tell drivers to stop or move along.

Police officer on duty, Hong Kong

In summer, the traffic police in Rome change to white uniforms.

Police officers wear uniforms so that the public can recognize them.

Crime prevention
Surveillance work is an important part of crime prevention. Police officers usually work in shifts, patrolling certain areas, and watching people, places of business, and traffic.

Traffic control
Specially trained officers are needed for traffic control, to prevent accidents on congested city streets or motorways. Traffic officers promote safety by directing traffic, assisting at motor accidents, and enforcing parking, speed, and traffic laws, such as seat belt regulations.

Police officer directs traffic, Rome, Italy

FBI emblem

US law enforcement
In the USA, police forces are organized at town, county, city, and state level. A national agency, the Federal Bureau of Investigation (FBI), investigates interstate crime, and runs a computerized information system on criminals and stolen property, which is accessible to all US police forces.

Interpol
To fight international crime, such as smuggling, police from more than 140 countries assist each other through the International Criminal Police Organization, known as Interpol.

Interpol HQ, outside Paris, France

Detection and investigation

Police officers who specialize in investigating crime are called detectives. Through collecting evidence (proof), interviewing witnesses, and interrogating suspects, detectives aim to discover who committed a crime. Once they believe that they have the right person, the police must present a convincing case so that the alleged culprit can be brought to trial by a law court, convicted, and punished.

The Bolshevik secret police were known as the Cheka.

Identification for Russian secret police officer, 1918

Secret police
Some governments run a secret police force to make sure that people do not speak or act against them. Such forces have a long history; during the 20th century they were used in the Soviet Union and Romania, among other countries.

At a murder scene, officers in the UK wear disposable suits, to avoid contaminating any evidence.

Fingerprinting kit

Forensic science
At the scene of a crime, specialist police officers search for clues that will lead them to the criminal and prove in court that he or she is guilty. Finding and interpreting such clues is known as forensic detection. Officers search for fingerprints, fibres, footprints, and even tiny amounts of skin, hair, and blood; all of these can be used to identify people.

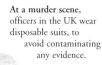

1 Lifting fingerprints takes care and skill. Aluminium powder is dusted on an object, to reveal any print marks.

2 If the prints are clear enough to be useful, sticky tape is used to lift them from the vase.

3 The fingerprint tape is mounted on a clear plastic sheet, and flattened out by a roller.

4 The print is put in a tamperproof evidence bag and sent to a police laboratory to be identified.

FIND OUT MORE | CRIME AND PUNISHMENT | DRUGS | GENETICS | HUMAN RIGHTS | LAW | SOCIETIES, HUMAN | SOVIET UNION

POLLUTION

EVERY DAY, HARMFUL MATERIALS are released into the environment as a result of human activities. This is pollution. Many different types of pollution – arising from farming, industry, transport, and energy use – enter the air, the soil, fresh water, and the oceans. Pollution's effects can be small-scale or global, gradual or dramatic, and include threats to wildlife and health problems for people. Pollution is a pressing environmental issue – one that we can all help to tackle.

Farmers use tractors and aircraft to spray pesticide chemicals on their crops. Some of these chemicals enter the soil or are washed into streams.

Smoke and invisible gases released high into the air from power stations and factories, can spread far and wide.

Coal-dust particles will be carried into the air.

Plant- and tree-life is reduced in urban and industrial areas.

Harmful waste chemicals from industrial processes, such as mercury compounds used in paper mills, are sometimes discharged into rivers.

Sewage plant

Most of the sewage from our homes is removed from the water at treatment plants, but the leftover waste may be dumped at sea.

Pollution hazards

Some types of pollution pose grave dangers to life. Animals may be directly poisoned or injured by pollutants, or they may suffer indirect ecological effects. These include the reduction of the oxygen supply in polluted water, the killing of food sources or vegetation cover, and the alteration of the climate because of atmospheric pollution.

Acid rain damages trees by disrupting the chemical balance in the soil around the roots. The first sign of attack is when foliage starts to die back.

Air and streams are cleanest in mountains.

Acid rain
Certain air pollutants, especially sulphur dioxide and nitrogen oxides from vehicle and factory fumes, can mix with water in the atmosphere and fall back to Earth in the rain. This acid rain seeps into the soil and contaminates fresh water, damaging trees and killing aquatic animals, such as frogs and fish.

Rubbish is often dumped into holes in the ground called land fill sites. Plastic and metal litter can trap and injure animals looking for food and poisonous liquids can leak out. Buried rubbish may get hot and catch fire. Gases are produced which may explode.

Chemicals from detergents and other household cleaning products pass from homes into the water system.

The fuel burned in motor vehicle engines gives off many harmful exhaust gases, which can cause severe air pollution along city streets.

Pollution types

Pollution enters the environment in many different forms, from different sorts of activity. Gases and smoke from industry and vehicles drift into the air. Household sewage, agricultural sprays, and other liquids are released on to land and into the oceans and rivers. Solids, too, such as refuse and mining waste, are dumped on the ground and into the sea.

Oil spilled or washed from the holds of tankers rides on the surface of the sea, harming ocean life and contaminating surrounding beaches.

Marine pollution is also caused by tourists when rubbish and debris from beaches and tourist resorts are washed into the sea.

Old, rusting, wrecked ships may steadily release pollutants into the sea from their cargo holds.

When plantlife at the bottom of the marine food chain is wiped out by pollution, other species in the food chain are affected.

Severe pollution hazards are caused when highly dangerous industrial wastes start to leak from containers buried on land or dumped in the sea.

P

Atmospheric pollution

Each year, millions of tonnes of pollutant gases are sent into Earth's atmosphere. Some remain at low-level, fouling the air and causing illness. Some accumulate in the upper atmosphere. They alter the way the Sun's heat energy and rays pass to and from Earth.

High   1979

Units of ozone

Low   1984

Ozone "hole"

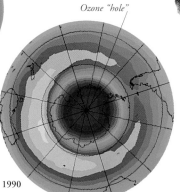

1990

Ozone holes
A natural layer of ozone gas, high in the atmosphere, shields us from harmful rays. Certain pollutant gases, including CFCs (chlorofluorocarbons) and methane, are destroying the ozone. Since 1979, "holes" have appeared in the ozone layer, first near the South Pole and now over the North. These are getting bigger, as can be seen by these satellite pictures of Antarctica. The colours represent different measures of ozone.

Greenhouse effect
Gases naturally present in the atmosphere help to keep Earth warm by trapping heat from the Sun that would otherwise radiate back out into space. The burning of fuel, such as oil in motor vehicles, and coal and wood in factories and homes, produces carbon dioxide and other "greenhouse gases". These are increasing the "greenhouse effect", leading to global warming. The air pollution can be seen easily in this road in Bangkok, Thailand.

Effects on wildlife

Most plants and animals suffer the effects of pollution, but not all to the same degree. Pollution-sensitive species have severely declined in the wild because their habitat has been contaminated. More resistant species have maintained their populations. A few have even increased.

Otters
Pollution has played a large part in the disappearance of otters from many rivers. Industrial waste and pesticides washed into the rivers contaminate the fish on which otters prey. The more fish an otter eats, the more poisons build up in its body, eventually killing it.

Peppered moths
The normally light-coloured peppered moth also has a dark form. This became more numerous in Britain after the Industrial Revolution of the 18th century. The increase in factories and smoke caused trees in some areas to be coated in soot. The dark peppered moths were well camouflaged against this and able to avoid more predators. They lived to produce more dark young.

Major incidents

Dramatic pollution incidents make news headlines. They can be the result of a gradual release of pollutants, or of a disastrous event. During the 1990–91 Gulf War, 850 burning oil wells blackened the sky with soot, and an oil slick ruined 460 km (285 miles) of coast.

An oil fire and slick in Kuwait, 1991

Oil slicks
Oil spilled at sea can form an oil slick on the water. Animals such as seals and seabirds have their fur or plumage clogged up when they touch the oil. Some are poisoned by swallowing the oil accidentally. A large oil slick, such as the one formed in the Gulf War, or one caused when an oil tanker is holed, can devastate wildlife and ruin the local fishing industry.

Organic farming
Some farmers have returned to organic methods of cultivating crops, such as vegetables, which do not rely on the heavy use of chemical pesticides and fertilizers. This reduces the amount of pollution from farms, with benefits for land and freshwater wildlife, as well as for people who eat the crops.

Cleaner cities
Efforts to reduce the pollution effects of fuels have included promoting unleaded petrol to avoid the release of lead from car exhaust fumes. The use of electrically powered transport, such as trams, is a further advance, but cyclists use the cleanest energy source of all – muscle power. This car-free shopping street is in Freiburg, Germany.

Reducing pollution

As "green" societies campaign against pollution, people are being made more aware of the harm they are doing. Fortunately, there is much that can be done to reduce the rate at which we are polluting the Earth, but it must be done now. Governments can pass laws to curb some of the worst polluting activities: contaminated habitats can be cleaned up; we can choose to buy products that are less polluting; and we can switch to less-polluting lifestyles.

Using public transport and cycling help reduce traffic pollution.

FIND OUT MORE   ATMOSPHERE   COAL   CLIMATE   ECOLOGY AND ECOSYSTEMS   FARMING   OIL

POLYNESIA

THE "MANY ISLANDS" that give Polynesia its name are scattered over a vast area of the central Pacific Ocean. Nobody knows how many of these islands there are. Some are just rocks in the sea, but others are inhabited by peoples whose ancestors colonized them thousands of years ago. Today, they include the countries of Kiribati, Samoa, Tuvalu, and Tonga as well as many dependencies. New Zealand also forms part of Polynesia. Many islands remain remote as such vast distances make travel difficult.

People

The Polynesian peoples include Samoans, Maori, Tongans, Tahitians, and Hawaiians. Between them, they speak about 20 native languages, all of which are closely related. Most Polynesians live off the fish they can catch and by cultivating their own food, such as cassava and coconuts. Nearly all of them are Christians.

Native girl wearing flowers, Polynesia

Physical features

The islands of Polynesia are the heads of old volcanoes that rise straight from the deep ocean floor. Many of them are topped with coral, forming atolls. The atolls contain sheltered lagoons formed by the volcanic craters, and are fringed by coral reefs. Dense tropical rainforest cloaks the mountains of the larger islands, and coconuts grow all over the islands.

27°C (81°F)   26°C (79°F)

2,815 mm (111 in)

Regional climate

Polynesia lies in the tropics and subtropics so its islands enjoy a warm climate all year round, with plenty of rain. However, on many of the islands vegetation is scant due to the poor quality of the soil, which consists largely of volcanic and coral debris.

Coconuts

Palm-lined beaches set against dramatic mountains are a common sight on some of the larger Polynesian islands, such as Bora Bora in French Polynesia. Many of the trees have sprouted from coconuts that have floated across the sea and been washed ashore. The Polynesians use all parts of the coconut – the "meat", milk, and husk.

Canoes

The Polynesians are seafaring people. They live off the fish they catch from their small, one-person canoes. They make their canoes by hollowing out a single log to which they attach a balance or outrigger. Their simple craft are very similar to those used by the first Polynesians who arrived from Southeast Asia thousands of years ago.

Outrigger balances craft in waves.

Canoe is made from a hollowed-out log.

Outrigger canoe

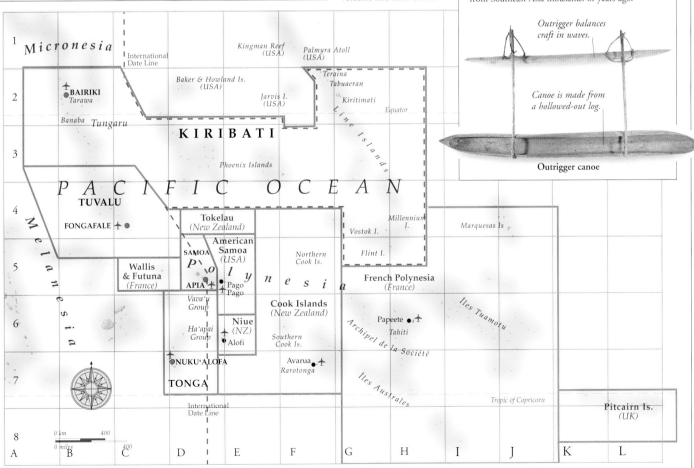

Kiribati

 Kiribati, pronounced Kiribass, consists of more than 30 islands. Kiribati is the local way of saying Gilbert, the name given to the islands by the British, who ruled them until 1979. Coconuts, copra, and fish are exported.

KIRIBATI FACTS

CAPITAL CITY Bairiki

AREA 717 sq km (277 sq miles)

POPULATION 92,000

MAIN LANGUAGES English, Kiribati

MAJOR RELIGION Christian

CURRENCY Australian dollar

Fishing

Like most Pacific islanders, the people of Kiribati depend on fish as a source of food and income. This fisherman is setting off with his nets for a day's work in his canoe. His house is thatched with leaves from the pandanus tree.

Samoa

 The western half of the Samoan island chain was ruled by New Zealand until 1962. Its nine volcanic islands are forested, and only four are inhabited.

SAMOA FACTS

CAPITAL CITY Apia

AREA 2,860 sq km (1,104 sq miles)

POPULATION 159,000

MAIN LANGUAGES Samoan, English

MAJOR RELIGION Christian

CURRENCY Tala

Fa'a Samoa

The "fa'a Samoa" is the Samoan way of life, and is based on the extended family, where many generations live together. Each family is headed by a *matai*, or elected chief. People live in timber-framed houses with roofs but no walls, except screens in wet weather. Clothing is simple.

Tuvalu

 Tuvalu is the world's fourth smallest state. This tiny, isolated state in the centre of the Pacific was a British colony until independence in 1978. The country is rapidly losing land to rising sea levels caused by global warming and is in danger of vanishing.

TUVALU FACTS

CAPITAL CITY Fongafale

AREA 26 sq km (10 sq miles)

POPULATION 10,800

MAIN LANGUAGES Tuvaluan, English

MAJOR RELIGION Christian

CURRENCY Australian and Tuvaluan dollar

Stamps

Copra from coconuts is Tuvalu's main export, but these tiny islands gain some revenue from their colourful postage stamps. Without foreign aid, however, they would be unable to survive.

Tonga

 People live on only 45 of Tonga's 170 islands. The easterly islands are low and fertile, while those in the west are volcanic. The Tongans live off the land, and grow cassava, coconuts, and passion fruit for export. Tonga is the only Polynesian nation to be ruled by a king.

TONGA FACTS

CAPITAL CITY Nuku'alofa

AREA 748 sq km (289 sq miles)

POPULATION 102,200

MAIN LANGUAGES Tongan, English

MAJOR RELIGION Christian

CURRENCY Pa'anga (Tonga dollar)

Tourism

Tropical beaches, a warm climate, and Tonga's friendly reputation attract more than 35,000 tourists every year, mostly from New Zealand and the USA. Tongans are anxious that visitors may undermine the island culture. These elaborate wooden figures have been carved by Tongan people to sell to visiting tourists.

Dependencies

Although many countries in the Pacific have become independent since World War II (1939–45), many people still live under the umbrella of Australia, the UK, France, New Zealand, and the USA.

Pitcairn (UK)
This tiny, remote volcanic island of 5 sq km (2 sq miles) has high cliffs and one small bay. It has only about 43 inhabitants.

French Polynesia (Fr)
This group of about 130 islands and atolls covers an area of 4,000 sq km (1,500 sq miles). Most of the people live on Tahiti.

Tokelau (NZ)
These three coral atolls cover an area of 10 sq km (4 sq miles) and have a population of 1,487. Copra and tuna fish are produced.

Niue (NZ)
With an area of 259 sq km (100 sq miles), Niue is the world's largest coral island. Three-quarters of Niueans live in New Zealand.

American Samoa (USA)
This tropical US territory consists of the seven small islands of eastern Samoa and has a total land area of 199 sq km (77 sq miles). The capital is Pago Pago.

Midway (USA)
Midway is a US territory. About 453 people live on its two large coral islands and several smaller ones. It is used as a naval air base and wildlife refuge.

Wallis and Futuna (Fr)
Two groups of islands form Wallis and Futuna, an area of 274 sq km (106 sq miles). The 14,600 people live off the land. Fishing licences are sold to Japan.

Cook Islands (NZ)
These 24 small islands lie 3,500 km (2,175 miles) northeast of New Zealand with which they have close ties. The population of nearly 12,900 live from clam and pearl fishing, tourism, and banking.

Nuclear testing
Since November 1952, Britain, France, and the USA have used the Pacific for testing nuclear weapons. In 1995, France carried out a series of underground nuclear explosions on Mururoa Atoll in French Polynesia, causing a storm of protest among the normally peaceful people who live on these islands.

Anti-nuclear protesters

 FIND OUT MORE AUSTRALASIA AND OCEANIA　CHRISTIANITY　CORAL REEFS　EMPIRES　FARMING　ISLANDS　PACIFIC OCEAN　RAINFOREST WILDLIFE　SHIPS AND BOATS　WEAPONS

PORTS AND WATERWAYS

SHIPS NEED PLACES to load and unload their cargos. Ports are places on rivers and coasts that provide special facilities for boats to berth and manage passengers and goods. The first ports were natural harbours – places that were sheltered from the wind with water deep enough for ships to sail right up to the shore. Today, large, modern ports can deal with many types of vessel, and have cranes and warehouses for goods, and dry docks for repairing ships. Waterways are rivers and canals. They are used to ship goods inland, or as a link between two seas.

Port of Roman London

Ancient ports
Many great cities of the ancient world first prospered because they were on or near natural harbours, such as bays and river estuaries. This made them good sites for trade and settlement. Breakwaters of wood or stone could be built out to sea to provide extra shelter.

Harbour facilities

The variety of modern cargoes means that all sorts of facilities are needed in a port. Some ports have special pumps and conveyor belts for handling bulk dry cargoes, such as sand, gravel, and grain. Oil terminals are designed to handle oil and related products, and are usually built near very deep water because oil tankers are huge ships. Many ports are designed to handle containers: large, standard-size boxes that can be loaded straight off ships and onto lorries or trains.

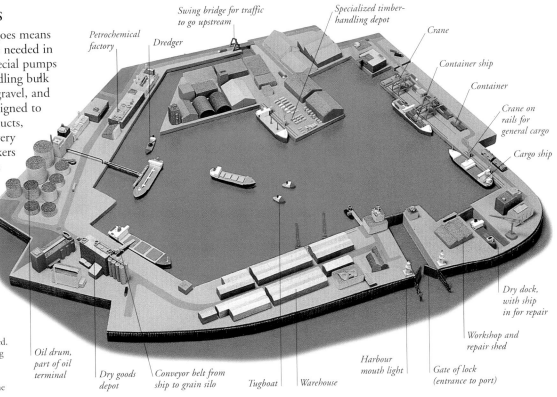

Swing bridge for traffic to go upstream

Specialized timber-handling depot

Petrochemical factory

Dredger

Crane

Container ship

Container

Crane on rails for general cargo

Cargo ship

Dry dock, with ship in for repair

Workshop and repair shed

Harbour mouth light

Gate of lock (entrance to port)

Warehouse

Tugboat

Conveyor belt from ship to grain silo

Dry goods depot

Oil drum, part of oil terminal

Docking
Every port has places where ships can berth to be loaded and unloaded. Built along the shoreline are loading platforms, called quays or wharves. In addition, there may be piers – structures built at right-angles to the shore where ships can tie up.

Aqueducts
Canals can cross deep valleys on aqueducts – water-carrying bridges that span the valley with tall arches of stone, brick, or metal. Not all aqueducts are navigable; some are used solely to carry water from a river to a town without an adequate water supply.

Canals

A canal is an artificial waterway. Most are built to transport cargo inland; others take water to dry land. Some, such as the Panama Canal in Central America, were built to make ocean journeys shorter.

Holiday barges travel through a lock.

Locks
A lock allows a canal boat to travel up or down hills. It consists of a section of water with gates at either end. Water is allowed to run in or out of the gates, so that the water-level inside can be raised or lowered to the level of the next stretch of canal.

Barges
Transporting cargo by canal is a cheap way of moving goods from place to place. Goods are carried by barge – a narrow, flat-bottomed boat with the capacity to carry a large cargo. Barges were orginally pulled by people or horses, but now generally have their own engines.

Powered barge

FIND OUT MORE | DAMS | INDUSTRIAL REVOLUTION | OIL | PHOENICIANS | RIVERS | ROMAN EMPIRE | SHIPS AND BOATS | TRADE AND INDUSTRY | TRANSPORT, HISTORY OF

P

PORTUGAL

WITH ITS LONG Atlantic coastline, Portugal occupies the southwest corner of the Iberian Peninsula. It is the westernmost country on the European mainland. The Azores and Madeira, two self-governing island groups in the Atlantic, are part of Portugal. The country joined the European Union in 1986. It is one of the poorest countries in western Europe, but a stable government and foreign investment are helping to improve the situation.

Physical features

Northern Portugal consists of a series of ridges and wide river valleys that cross the country from east to west. The north is mountainous, and the centre, south of the River Tagus, gently undulating. The south, the Algarve, is cut off by mountains.

PORTUGAL FACTS

CAPITAL CITY Lisbon

AREA 92,391 sq km (35,672 sq miles)

POPULATION 10,000,000

MAIN LANGUAGE Portuguese

MAJOR RELIGION Christian

CURRENCY Euro

LIFE EXPECTANCY 76 years

PEOPLE PER DOCTOR 313

GOVERNMENT Multi-party democracy

ADULT LITERACY 92%

Rio Douro
The Rio Douro, which means "river of gold" in Portuguese, slices across the width of Portugal for 200 km (125 miles) from the Spanish border to Porto on the coast. The mountain terraces that flank the stony sides of the valley are ribbed with vineyards producing grapes for making port. Lower down the valley, near Porto, *vinho verde*, a white wine, is made.

Algarve
The sandy beaches and pretty villages of the Algarve coast, attract thousands of holidaymakers every year. Many travel there from cooler northern European countries to take advantage of the mild winters and beautiful scenery. Other popular coastal resorts are Figueira da Foz and Estoril, near Lisbon, on what is called the Portuguese Riviera.

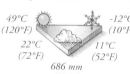

49°C (120°F)   -12°C (10°F)
22°C (72°F)   11°C (52°F)
686 mm (27 in)

Climate
The north of Portugal is cooler and wetter than the south, which is generally dry and sunny all year round. Temperatures tend to rise away from the coast towards the border with Spain. Like Spain, Portugal suffers from frequent periods of prolonged drought.

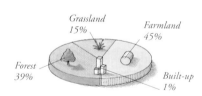

Grassland 15%   Farmland 45%   Forest 39%   Built-up 1%

Land use
Portugal has very few natural resources, and most of the land is used for rearing livestock or for growing crops such as olives, grapes, cork oaks, or eucalyptus. As the country does not produce its own gas, there are plans to pipe gas into northern Portugal from Algeria, via Morocco and Spain.

Lisbon
Surrounded by hills, Portugal's capital, Lisbon, lies at the mouth of the River Tagus. During the 15th century, it was a major port trading gold and spices. In 1755, a severe earthquake destroyed much of the centre, which was later rebuilt on a grid system. The old town, or Baixa, in the east of the city still has many craftworkers, such as silversmiths and shoemakers.

View over the rooftops of the Baixa

Map labels: SPAIN, Minho, Viana do Castelo, Braga, Chaves, Bragança, Póvoa de Varzim, Guimarães, Matosinhos, Porto, Vila Real, Vila Nova de Gaia, Douro, ATLANTIC OCEAN, Aveiro, Viseu, Serra da Estrela, Coimbra, Figueira da Foz, Covilhã, PORTUGAL, Castelo Branco, Caldas da Rainha, Tagus, Santarém, Portalegre, Barragem do Maranhão, Sintra, Rio Sorraia, Cascais, LISBON, Serra d'Ossa, Setúbal, Évora, Alcácer do Sal, Sines, Beja, Mira, Guadiana, Barragem da Bravura, Lagos, Algarve, Cabo de São Vicente, Faro, Olhão

P

People

About 99 per cent of the people are ethnic Portuguese. The remaining one per cent are immigrants mainly from Portugal's ex-colonies in Africa, such as Angola. In recent years, lack of opportunity has led about three million Portuguese to go abroad to find work.

107 per sq km
(277 per sq mile)

66% Urban   34% Rural

Rural communities
About one-third of all Portuguese live in rural areas, although more and more are being drawn to the big cities in search of work. Most Portuguese are Roman Catholics and family life is very important.

Golf
Many Portuguese enjoy a relaxing game of golf. The Algarve has some of Europe's finest golf courses, many of which are set against stunning backdrops of sea and sky.

Leisure

The Portuguese love watching and playing football and have many clubs such as Sporting Lisbon. They also enjoy tennis, golf, motor racing, and a wide range of watersports. Bullfights are a part of traditional life, as are bright, colourful fiestas with singing and dancing, usually to celebrate a local saint's day.

Bullfighting
The centre of Portuguese bullfighting is the province of Ribatejo where the bulls are bred. Fights take place from April to October, mainly on Sundays. The bull is not killed in the ring, but put down later.

Farming

About ten per cent of Portugal's labour force is employed in agriculture. Farms tend to be small and rely on traditional farming methods. Crops include olives and figs, wine, cork, and tomatoes. Drought often causes low yields.

Sheep
Much of Portugal is hilly or mountainous, providing ideal upland pasture for sheep, which are bred for their wool, meat, and milk. Most sheep farms are small and family-run. The Portuguese also breed pigs for meat.

Eucalyptus
Portugal and Spain are the only countries in Europe to cultivate eucalyptus, which is grown for its gum, resin, oil, and wood. Eucalyptus trees grow throughout Portugal.

Cork
Portugal is the world's leading producer of cork, the thick, spongy bark of the cork oak, used for making wine stoppers and floor tiles. Every nine or ten years, the bark is stripped off, steamed, and pressed into sheets for use.

Men grading quality of cork

Wine cork

Cork floor tile

Port
Portugal's most famous wine is port, a fortified drink named after the city of Porto, where much of it is shipped for export. The grapes grow in the Douro Valley.

Industry

Portuguese industry suffers from a lack of natural resources and nearly all gas and oil is imported. Tourism, banking, and textiles are the major sources of income, as well as shoemaking, food, wine, cork, and sardines.

Fishing
Local fishermen mending their nets on the quay are a common sight all along Portugal's coastline. Every day, small boats set out from coastal ports in search of sardines and oysters. Portugal has become a major exporter of canned sardines and pilchards, and has several large fish-processing plants.

Oysters

Sardines

Pottery
Portuguese street markets sell local handicrafts to the thousands of tourists who flock to Portugal throughout the year. Specialities include brightly painted pottery, glassware, silver filigree, porcelain, and embroidery.

Transport

Road transport has developed on a large scale since the 1960s. A main highway links Lisbon with Porto, but there are still few road links with Spain. Portugal also has a small, but efficient rail network.

Coastal shipping
Being such a narrow country, with a long coastline, Portugal relies on coastal shipping to carry much of its freight. However, many of the rivers leading to the interior are blocked by sandbars at their mouths.

FIND OUT MORE   ATLANTIC OCEAN   CHRISTIANITY   EMPIRES   EUROPE   EUROPE, HISTORY OF   EUROPEAN UNION   FARMING   FISHING INDUSTRY   MOTOR SPORTS   SPORTS

PORTUGAL, HISTORY OF

THROUGHOUT ITS LONG HISTORY, Portugal has always looked west to the Atlantic Ocean rather than east to Spain and the rest of continental Europe. Generations of fishermen have made their living from the sea, while explorers and traders created a vast empire during the 15th and 16th centuries. After a period of Spanish rule ending in 1640, Portugal declined, so that by the 20th century it was one of the poorest countries of Europe and slid into a military dictatorship. Today, it has shed its colonial and military past and is a thriving democracy.

Roman Portugal
The Romans ruled all of Portugal by the time of Augustus (r.27 BC–AD 14). The country thrived, adopting the Roman lifestyle and Latin language.

Roman bridge at Chaves

Independent Portugal

After the Roman period, the Germanic Visigoth tribe ruled Portugal until 711, when Moors (Muslims) from North Africa conquered the country. In 1143, Alfonso, a local lord, defeated the Moors in battle. Alfonso was then crowned the first king of independent, Christian Portugal.

Lisbon cathedral, built in the reign of Alfonso I

Exploration and empire

In the 15th century the Portuguese began a period of maritime exploration. Their sailors travelled south along the west coast of Africa, rounding the Cape of Good Hope in 1488. Soon their trading empire included parts of Africa, Brazil in South America, Goa in India, and Macao on the Chinese coast.

Portuguese empire

Church built by Portuguese settlers in Brazil

Henry the Navigator
Prince Henry the Navigator (1394–1460) encouraged Portuguese exploration of Africa. He set up a navigation school at Sagres and staffed it with the best astronomers and navigators. By the time of his death, Portuguese sailors had explored the entire west African coast.

Lisbon earthquake
On 1 November 1755 Lisbon was struck by a massive earthquake. Two-thirds of the city was destroyed and around 50,000 people were buried in the ruins. Sebastião de Carvalho, later to become Marquês de Pombal, chief minister of Portugal, rebuilt the city, giving it wide boulevards and elegant, classical lines.

Portuguese revolt in 1640
In 1580, Philip II of Spain claimed the vacant Portuguese throne. Portugal was weakened, and other nations seized many of her colonies. In 1640, a revolt led by John of Braganza brought Portugal independence once more.

Brazil
In 1493 Pope Alexander VI proclaimed that the world was divided between Spain and Portugal, giving Spain the west (and therefore all America). However, in 1494, the line was moved westward, giving Brazil to Portugal.

Modern Portugal

In 1910, a revolution overthrew the monarchy and made Portugal a republic. The country was neutral during the two World Wars, but became increasingly poor as it devoted its resources to its colonies in Africa. In the 1970s and 1980s, conditions improved, and in 1986 Portugal joined the European Union.

The 1974 revolution
Opposition to Portuguese rule in its African colonies led the armed forces to overthrow the dictatorship of Marcello Caetano in April 1974. There was turmoil until a failed left-wing coup allowed the Socialist, Mário Soares, to take control of the country. Free elections were held in 1976.

Left-wing protesters, Lisbon

Antonio Salazar
Economist Antonio Salazar (1889–1970) became finance minister in 1928. In 1932 he became prime minister, ruling as a dictator until 1968 and fighting colonial wars in Africa. In spite of his efforts to improve Portugal's economy, the country became poorer and living conditions worsened under his rule.

Dr Antonio Salazar

Timeline
1st cent BC–5th cent AD Romans rule Iberian peninsula including Portugal.

711 North African Moors invade Portugal.

1143 Alfonso I defeats Moors.

1498 Portuguese explorer Vasco da Gama reaches the Indian coast.

1500 Portugal claims Brazil. Portuguese empire founded.

1580–1640 Spain rules Portugal.

1755 Earthquake devastates much of Lisbon.

1822 Under Dom Pedro I Brazil declares itself independent from Portugal.

1910 Portuguese republic established.

1932 Antonio Salazar becomes prime minister; he changes the constitution to make himself dictator.

1974 Military coup overthrows the ruling dictatorship.

1986 Portugal joins European Union.

FIND OUT MORE

AFRICA, HISTORY OF • ARMIES • EARTHQUAKES • EMPIRES • EXPLORATION • ISLAMIC EMPIRE • ROMAN EMPIRE • SOUTH AMERICA, HISTORY OF • SPAIN, HISTORY OF

POTTERY AND CERAMICS

CERAMICS ARE OBJECTS which have been shaped from clay or another mineral, then baked hard at a high heat. This basic technique has been used for thousands of years to produce functional and often beautiful items, such as pottery, tiles, and bricks. Today, ceramics are also used to produce ceramic insulators, spark plugs for car engines, and heat-resistant materials for lining the insides of furnaces. Modern scientists have devised methods of making ceramic materials which are as strong as steel.

Bowl from the Ukraine, 3700–3000 BC

Early potters
People first made pots at least 9,000 years ago. Potters shaped clay with their hands, or built up lengths of clay in coils to make larger pots. Baked clay is such an enduring material that shards of pottery are now among the most common archaeological discoveries.

P

The potter at work
Clay can be moulded or pressed into shape, but perhaps the most popular way to shape pottery is on a potter's wheel. The wheel was invented in China in about 3000 BC and later, probably independently, in southern Africa. The potter uses both hands to draw clay into a perfectly round shape while the wheel spins. It takes many years to master this skill.

Apron protects clothes.

Prepared clay

Pressure of potter's hands guides the shape of the jug.

Potter keeps clay centred on the wheel.

Preparing the clay
The potter begins by kneading the clay to make it soft and smooth, and to eliminate air bubbles, which may cause the pot to crack during firing.

Tool helps to shape jug.

Shaping
The potter throws the ball of clay on to the middle of the wheel, and makes the wheel spin. He pushes his fingers into the centre of the clay, forming a pot with low, thick sides. Then he shapes the sides by pressing one hand on the inside and one on the outside of the pot. Once the pot is shaped, into a jug for instance, the potter trims off excess clay, removing the pot from the wheel with a knife or wire.

Bowl of water keeps the potter's hands wet.

Potter presses pedal to operate wheel.

Types of pottery
Pottery is usually earthenware, stoneware, or porcelain, depending on the type of clay and the temperature at which it is fired. Earthenware is fired at a fairly low heat. Stoneware is fired at higher temperatures; the heat damages the more colourful glazes, but makes the pottery strong and waterproof.

Porcelain
Porcelain is a white clay mixture used to make pottery that is valued for its strength and beauty. It is often called china, because it was first made in that country. Porcelain made during the Ming dynasty (1368–1644) is regarded by collectors as artistic treasure.

Earthenware
This type of pottery fires below 1,100°C (2,000°F). When left unglazed, it is porous (not waterproof).

Stoneware
This type of pottery is fired above 1,200°C (2,200°F). It is stronger than earthenware, and is waterproof.

Factories
Mass-produced mugs are made in pottery factories by pouring liquid clay (slip) into moulds made from plaster of Paris. The plaster absorbs water from the slip, leaving a clay coating inside the mould. The rest of the slip is poured away. Once the moulded clay is firm, the mug is taken out and the handle added. Then the pottery is fired and decorated.

Mechanized factory kiln, Holland

Firing
The dried pot is baked, or fired, in a large oven called a kiln. The temperature must be controlled carefully and will depend on the type of pottery being made, but it must be above 700°C (1,300°F).

Glazing
To decorate the fired pot and make it waterproof, it is coated with glaze, a glasslike covering. The pot is refired, melting the glaze on to it. A wide range of glaze colours are produced at different kiln temperatures.

Decorating
The methods of decorating a pot include scratching or pressing designs into it, adding underglaze colours, painting on to the unfired glaze, or applying details in liquid clay or enamel.

Ceramic washbasin

Bathrooms
Bathroom fixtures are often made of glazed ceramics, as the glaze makes them waterproof and easy to clean.

Qualities of ceramics
Ceramics are heat-resistant and do not conduct electricity. Unlike metals, they do not rust. This makes them ideal for use in home and industry.

Space shuttle
The nose of a space shuttle is covered with ceramic tiles capable of resisting the intense heat and pressure caused by re-entering the Earth's atmosphere.

Space shuttle

FIND OUT MORE   CRAFTS   GLASS   ROCKS AND MINERALS   SPACE EXPLORATION

Chinese porcelain

Fine white

Moulded design shows dragons.

Dish, for ritual use, Yuan dynasty, 14th century

Fish-shaped handle

Ewer, Liao dynasty, 10th or 11th century

Incised with dragons and floral decoration.

Cai Shen, god of wealth, Ming dynasty, 17th century

Copying a design from a silver bottle.

Bottle, Tang dynasty, 10th or 11th century

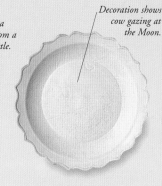

Decoration shows cow gazing at the Moon.

Dish, Jin dynasty, 12th century

Lion handle

Ewer, Liao dynasty, 10th century

Bottle, Liao dynasty, 10th century

Dish, Northern Song dynasty, 11th century

Base of dish, left, is only 20 per cent as wide as mouth

Handle

Jug, with handles to attach cover, 15th century

Water dropper, probably Liao, 10th century

Iron or copper glaze

Underglaze painted design

Vase, Yuan dynasty, 14th century

Anhua (hidden) dragon design

Bowl, Ming dynasty, 14th century

Pale brown iron glaze

Dish, Ming dynasty, 15th century

Plain copper glaze

Dish, Ming dynasty, early 15th century

Bowl, Ming dynasty, 15th century

Bowl, Ming dynasty, late 14th century

Cobalt underglaze

Dragon motif

Plate, Yüan dynasty, 14th century

Dish, Yüan dynasty, 14th century

Popular phoenix motif

Metal mount adds to status of porcelain.

Jar, Yüan dynasty, 14th century

Dish, Ming dynasty, early 15th century

Bowl, Ming dynasty, 15th century

Lychee design

Flask, Ming dynasty, early 15th century

Enamels

Trinket box, Ming dynasty, 15th century

Covered jar, Ming dynasty, 15th century

Ring handle

Altar vase with ring handles, Yüan dynasty, 14th century

P

PREHISTORIC LIFE

MORE THAN 3,800 MILLION YEARS AGO (mya) as
Earth cooled, liquid water produced oceans in
which small single-celled organisms evolved.
Many believe that this marked the first ever signs
of life. These early beginnings are called "prehistory", because
they happened before recorded history. Much of our
evidence of early life comes from fossils.
Using this evidence, palaeontologists
divided Earth's prehistory into time
spans called eras, and eras into periods.

In the beginning
Fossil prokaryotes (simple
single cells) have been found
in 3,400- to 3,300-million-
year-old rocks in Australia
and South Africa. Some of
these, such as the blue-green
bacteria, formed strings of
cells and produced layered
mounds called stromatolites.

Fossilized stromatolite

P

Paleozoic era

In the early part of the Paleozoic, the
Cambrian period (570 to 510 mya), life
was mostly confined to the oceans. By the
Carboniferous period (360 to 290 mya)
there were large forests of tree-ferns, and
club mosses such as *Lepidodendron*. By the
Permian period (290 to 245 mya), much
of the land was covered by desert.

*Continent distribution,
570 to 245 mya*

*Phacops rana,
a shelled
trilobite*

*Lepidodendron,
a Carboniferous
club moss*

Fossil of *Cephalaspis pagei,*
an armoured fish

First plants
Until the end of the
Silurian period (439
to 408 mya), most
plants lived in water.
The oldest known
plant, *Cooksonia,*
developed a rigid stem
for carrying water from
roots, allowing it to
thrive on land.

First shelled animals
The apparent explosion of
life at the beginning of the
Cambrian period may have
been due to environmental
changes. These changes
allowed shelled skeletons to be
preserved in the fossil record.

First fish
The first vertebrates were the
jawless fish, which appeared
about 470 million years ago.
Some of these fish developed
heavily armoured body plates
and lived in shallow marine
waters, rivers, and lakes.

Invasion of the land

As plants moved on to land,
invertebrate animals followed, evolving to
take advantage of the higher oxygen levels
and drier conditions. The first were the
arthropods. Some, such as *Acantherpestes,*
probably survived the same way millipedes
do today, by feeding on decomposing plants.
Amphibians and reptiles followed
the arthropods.

Modern
millipede

Acantherpestes

Mesozoic era

During the Mesozoic era (245 to 60 mya),
the supercontinent known as Pangaea moved
northward and split into the major continents
we know today. A major extinction at the
end of the Permian period allowed reptiles
to evolve on land, in the air, and in the sea.
The end of the era, the Cretaceous period,
saw the mass extinction of the dinosaurs.

*Continent distribution,
245 to 65 mya*

Reptiles
The earliest known reptile is *Westlothiana
lizziae,* which dates from 330 million years
ago. A reptile such as this gave rise to the
giant reptiles and dinosaurs which dominated
the Earth during the Mesozoic era. Some
adapted entirely to life on land; they were
able to stand upright and could easily
move around. Some, such as the
plesiosaurs, returned to the sea;
others, such as pterosaurs,
became capable of flight.

*Hair cover kept in
Megazostrodon's
body heat.*

First mammals
The first mammals to
appear developed from
the cynodonts, a group of
mammal-like reptiles. Some
survived the major extinction
at the end of the Permian period,
and developed mammalian
characteristics. *Megazostrodon*
was one of the first mammals
of the late Triassic period
(245 to 208 mya).

Model of
Megazostrodon

Modern bird's feather

Early birds
Birds with feathers developed early in
the evolution of dinosaurs, to which
they are closely related. Early birds,
such as the Jurassic bird *Archaeopteryx,*
may have used their feathers for
insulation or display, as well as flight.

Fossil feather

The pterosaur Criorhynchus,
late Cretaceous period

First flowers
Angiosperms (flowering plants) appeared in
the Cretaceous period (144 to 65 mya). Before
flowering plants, *Ginkgo* (maidenhair tree) was a
common leafy tree. This remarkable plant still
exists and is cultivated as a decorative tree.

*Westlothiana's
body was about
30 cm (1 ft) long.*

Model of *Westlothiana*

Ginkgo, tree
from Jurassic period

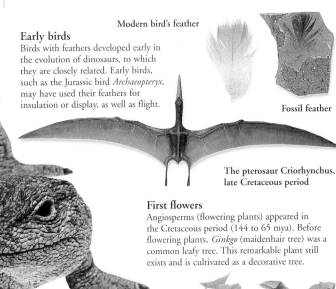

P

Cretaceous period

During the Cretaceous period (144 to 65 mya), dinosaurs continued to be the dominant large animals on land. The continents continued to drift apart, and what is now India moved north towards Asia. It is thought that the Cretaceous period probably ended with quite an impact.

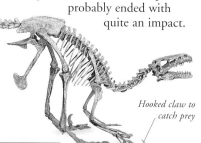

Skeleton of the dinosaur *Dromaeosaurus*, c.85 to 70 mya

Tail held rigid by bony rods.

Death of dinosaurs

Dinosaurs became extinct at the end of the Cretaceous period. A popular theory to explain this mass extinction is that an asteroid or a comet hit the Earth about 65 million years ago, throwing large amounts of dust into the atmosphere. This dust is thought to have blocked the sunlight for many months or more, killing off a variety of animals and plants.

Hooked claw to catch prey

Cenozoic era

During the Cenozoic era (65 mya to present), mammals gradually took over from the dinosaurs. Some reptiles, such as turtles, snakes, crocodiles, and lizards, survived the extinction and still exist today. Birds also survived to become more diverse than either mammals or reptiles today. India eventually collided with Asia, forming the Himalayan mountain range.

Continent distribution, c.65 mya

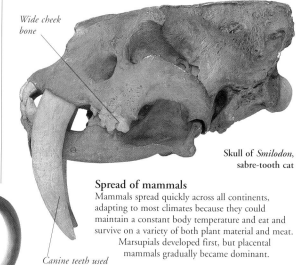

Wide cheek bone

Skull of *Smilodon*, sabre-tooth cat

Spread of mammals

Mammals spread quickly across all continents, adapting to most climates because they could maintain a constant body temperature and eat and survive on a variety of both plant material and meat. Marsupials developed first, but placental mammals gradually became dominant.

Canine teeth used to tear animal flesh.

Ice ages

Alternating periods of cold and warmth characterize the last 2,000 million years of Earth's climate. During cold periods much of Earth's water was locked up in ice sheets. Animals, such as the mammoth, adapted by growing thick woolly coats. Today, Earth is in an interglacial, warm period.

Thick woolly coat

Hair covered trunk to keep warm.

Model of *Mammuthus primigenius*, c.1.64 mya

Flying mammals

As birds gradually evolved to take the place of pterosaurs, mammals, such as the bat *Palaeochiropteryx*, also developed flight. This bat was only 7cm (3 inches) long, and one specimen that was found had remains of moths in its stomach. Bats are mainly nocturnal, using reflected sound to detect their prey.

Palaeochiropteryx, fossil bat

Extinction

Animals and plants evolving and becoming extinct is a pattern of life on Earth. Mass extinction occurs when many organisms become extinct at the same time. Several such events have occurred throughout Earth's prehistory their cause is not always known.

Dodo

The dodo from Mauritius died out in the late 1700s due to human impact. Today, other plants and animals, such as the African black rhinoceros and the South China tiger, are on the brink of extinction.

Reconstruction of a dodo

First humans

Our first ancestors may have been *Australopithecus afarensis*, a human-like creature that appeared in Africa about 4 million years ago. The earliest true human, *Homo habilis*, probably made and used tools more than 2.5 million years ago. *Homo sapiens* (modern humans) appeared about 100,000 years ago.

Cranium of *Homo habilis*, found in Africa

Timeline

3,800 mya Single-celled photosynthesizing organisms evolve.

550 mya Emergence of hard shells.

c.500 mya Primitive jawless fish appear.

Model of *Ichthyostega*

c.440 mya Plants and animals invade land.

c.395 mya Arthropods feed on decomposing plants and other arthropods.

360 mya First tetrapods, such as the amphibian *Ichthyostega*, appear.

Fossil of Jurassic dragonfly

c.210 mya Dinosaurs start to evolve.

65 mya Mammals take over after demise of dinosaurs.

100,000 years ago *Homo sapiens* appears.

FIND OUT MORE   COAL   DINOSAURS   EARTH   EVOLUTION   FOSSILS   GEOLOGY   HUMAN EVOLUTION   MAMMALS   PREHISTORIC PEOPLE   STONE AGE

PREHISTORIC PEOPLE

OUR EARLIEST ANCESTORS, the hominids, lived in Africa. As they evolved into an upright posture and learned to make tools, around 100,000 years ago, they became known as "modern people", or *Homo sapiens sapiens*. These people are sometimes called prehistoric, because they lived long before recorded history. From fossil evidence, we know they found food by gathering and hunting, made simple clothes, and built shelters out of local materials. People lived like this for many thousands of years. Around 9000 BC, for the first time, people in western Asia started to produce their food by farming.

Food supply

If early people could not find food in one area, they moved to another. They often followed the seasons, travelling to warmer areas in the winter months. In most societies the women gathered plant material – leaves, fruits, and roots – while the men hunted for meat and fish with weapons such as bows and arrows, clubs, and spears.

Arrow heads of bone were stuck to shafts with glue made from birch resin.

The flight was made of feathers and helped arrows fly over distance.

Hunting
Meat was an important food source when green vegetables were scarce. Hunting required co-operation – several men hunted together to track and bring down large animals, such as deer or mammoth.

Fishing
People who lived near the sea, a lake, or a river got most of their nutrition from fish, which they caught using small simple hooks.

As this stone relief shows, people hunted larger fish with bone or antler harpoons.

Gathering
Early people built up their knowledge about which plants were good to eat and which were poisonous. They ate mainly raw leaves, berries, and roots.

A digger was used to dig up roots and grubs.

Quartzite pebble acts as a weight.

Wedge

Food through the seasons
In spring, green plant material, such as dandelion leaves, was plentiful.

In summer, grapes and other fruits added variety and nutrients to the diet.

In winter, hunters brought home meat, to cook and eat with nuts and roots.

In the autumn, nuts and berries were gathered and stored for the winter.

Clothes

During the last ice age, about 18,000 years ago, people learned to skin animals and wear the pelts to keep warm.

Animal skin clothes

Raw wool

Spindle

Prehistoric people spun wool taken directly from the backs of sheep.

Religion

The existence of ceremonial sites, such as stone circles, and careful burials show that our earliest ancestors had religious rituals and believed in an afterlife.

Cult figures
Archaeologists have found many figurines in modern-day Greece and the Cycladic Islands. They are thought to represent the gods and goddesses of the prehistoric people who lived there.

Simple marble figurine, c.25,000 to 15,000 BC.

Burial of the dead
Prehistoric people were often buried in a curled up, or foetal, position. They were usually surrounded by personal items for use in the afterlife (grave goods).

Stonehenge
Stonehenge, a stone circle in southern England, was probably built for religious purposes at least 4,000 years ago. On Midsummer Day, the sun rises directly over Stonehenge's Heel Stone.

Carnac
Carnac, in France, has the world's largest stone alignment. It contains about 1,100 stones in 11 rows, and stands from east-to-west, suggesting that its creators followed a religion based on the sun.

Shelters

Caves made good homes – our early human ancestors were living in caves in Israel at least 100,000 years ago. If there was no natural shelter, prehistoric people made homes from nearby materials, such as wood, stone, or turf.

Sleeping platform

Thatched roof

Mud wall

Entrance

Cave shelters
Some caves, such as Silozwane Cave, Zimbabwe, were occupied permanently. Other caves were used as temporary shelters for hunters, or as bases for fishing expeditions.

Temporary shelters
About 18,000 to 12,000 years ago in Central Europe, prehistoric people built shelters from mammoth bones and skins. A fire kept in a clay and stone hearth heated the shelter.

Permanent shelters
Some early people of North America lived in well-built, permanent houses. They erected a frame made of poles, built a low mud wall, and then covered each house with a tall, thatched roof.

Timeline

35 million years ago First true humans, *Homo sapiens*, evolve from primate ancestors in Africa.	**2–2.5 million years ago** Hominids emerge in Africa. **100,000 BC** Modern humans, *Homo sapiens sapiens*, evolve.	**50,000 BC** First humans arrive in Australia and America. **11,000 BC** Humans domesticate animals in western Asia.	**10,500 BC** Pottery is produced in Japan. **9000 BC** Wheat and barley are cultivated in Asia. **6500 BC** The first towns start to develop in western Asia.

FIND OUT MORE   BRONZE AGE   FOSSILS   HUMAN EVOLUTION   STONE AGE

PRESSURE

A STILETTO HEEL can make dents in a hard wooden floor, while a hiking boot worn by the same person may leave it unmarked. This is because the stiletto heel exerts more pressure than the heavy boot. Pressure is a measure of how concentrated a force is. The stiletto heel concentrates the force of the person's weight on to a smaller area than the boot. Fluids – liquids and gases – can also exert pressure.

Blowing over the paper reduces the air pressure above it.

Higher pressure below the sheet pushes paper up.

Moving fluids

Hold a sheet of paper by the edge, and it hangs down limply; blow over the top of it, and it rises up. The pressure of a fluid, such as air, is lower when the fluid is moving than when it is still, so the moving air above the paper has a lower pressure than the static air below it. This difference in pressure lifts the paper.

Blaise Pascal

In 1646, the French physicist and mathematician Blaise Pascal (1623–62) showed that air pressure decreases with altitude by taking a barometer to the top of a mountain. Pascal was also the first to realize that the pressure exerted by a liquid acts in all directions.

Pressure machines

Fluids in a confined space exert pressure that can be used to power machinery and tools. Hydraulic machines are powered by high-pressure liquids, while pneumatic machines rely on pressurized gases.

Hydraulic brakes

Applying the brake lever of this bicycle squeezes fluid inside the brake cable. The fluid transmits the pressure to the brake pads, which grip the wheel and slow it down.

Pneumatic drill

High-pressure air is pumped into a cylinder inside this drill, where it pushes a piston up and down with great force. The piston hammers the drill into the surface of the hard rock.

Upthrust

A liquid exerts pressure on any object immersed in it. If you push a table tennis ball under water, you will feel the water pushing back. This pushing is an upwards force called upthrust, and it is caused by the pressure of the water on the ball. The upthrust is equal to the weight of the water pushed aside, or displaced, as the object is immersed.

Floating and sinking

If the upthrust on an immersed object is equal to the object's weight, then the object floats. In the experiment below, four balls of different weights are placed in a tank of water. Three of the balls sink until they displace enough water to produce an upthrust equal to their weight. The weight of the golf ball is greater than the upthrust from the water, so it sinks to the bottom of the tank.

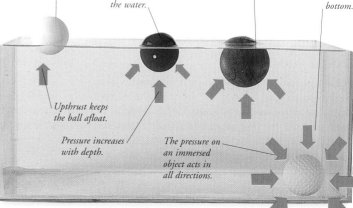

The light plastic table tennis ball floats on water's surface.

The rubber squash ball is heavier than the table tennis ball, and floats lower in the water.

Heavier still, the hardwood ball sinks until it is nearly underwater.

The golf ball weighs the most, and sinks to the bottom.

Upthrust keeps the ball afloat.

Pressure increases with depth.

The pressure on an immersed object acts in all directions.

High and low pressure

In some situations, solids, liquids, and gases exert a higher or lower pressure than normal. People have found many ways of using such pressure variations to their advantage, but our bodies can withstand only a limited range of pressures. The extreme pressure of the deep ocean can kill a person, while low air pressure at high altitudes makes breathing difficult.

Power cable

Observation window *Thruster*

Spacesuit

In space there is no air, so there is no air pressure. This would cause human lungs to collapse, so astronauts who leave their spacecraft wear pressurized suits to protect them. They breathe a supply of oxygen at normal Earth pressure.

Safety line connects to spacecraft.

Suit's airtight seams can withstand vacuum.

Submersible

At the bottom of the world's seas and oceans, the weight of the water above creates tremendous pressure. Deep-sea explorers travel to the seabed in small vessels called submersibles, which are strong enough to withstand such intense pressure.

Melted ice lubricates blade and reduces friction.

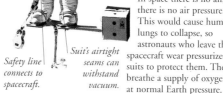

Ice skate

An ice skate's narrow blade concentrates a person's weight on to a small area. The high pressure under the blade melts the ice, reducing friction so that the skater glides over the ice.

Snow-shoe

Snow-shoes have long, broad bases that spread a person's weight over a wide area. They reduce the pressure exerted by the feet, so that the wearer can walk on soft snow without sinking.

Pressure cooker

A liquid's boiling point can be raised or lowered by increasing or decreasing the pressure acting upon it. Inside a pressure cooker, high pressure raises water's boiling point from 100°C (212°F) to 120°C (248°F). At this temperature, water cooks food more quickly.

High altitude

Lowering the pressure acting on a liquid reduces its boiling point. At high altitudes, it is difficult to make hot drinks or cook with boiling water. The air pressure is much lower, and this reduces the boiling point of water to as low as 60°C (140°F).

FIND OUT MORE — AIR · AIRCRAFT · FORCE AND MOTION · FRICTION · GASES · LIQUIDS · MACHINES · SHIPS AND BOATS · SPACE EXPLORATION · SUBMARINES

PRINTING

BEFORE THE 15TH CENTURY, books were copied out and illustrated by hand. The development, in the 1450s, of a printing press capable of using movable type led to an information revolution. Large numbers of books and leaflets could be copied mechanically, quickly and cheaply, allowing learning to spread rapidly. Today we are surrounded by printed material, from magazines, packaging, and posters produced in their thousands, to the smaller number of prints made by artists.

Colour separations

When a book is printed in colour, this usually means the paper is inked four times, in black, cyan, magenta, and yellow, to create a complete colour image. Each ink is laid on the paper from a printing surface, or plate, made from a separate film, called a colour separation. To make the separations, a device called a scanner, linked to a computer, analyses the original colour image to produce files in the four separate printing colours.

Colour film
The computer files are converted into four coloured images on clear film. The film is then used to make printing plates.

Black   Cyan   Magenta   Yellow

The printing process

Printing plates are made by shining light through the colour separations, recording their details onto a light-sensitive coating on the plate. Each plate is chemically treated to bring out the print images, then fitted onto a cylinder in the printing press. The inked image on the plate is transferred (offset) on to another cylinder (the blanket cylinder), and from there on to the paper.

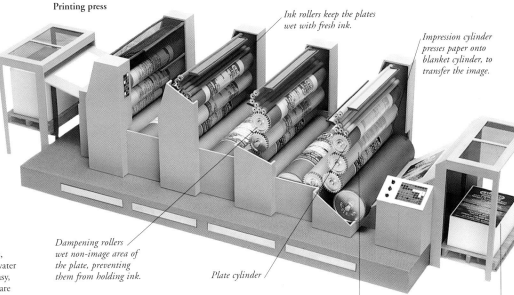

Printing press

Ink rollers keep the plates wet with fresh ink.

Impression cylinder presses paper onto blanket cylinder, to transfer the image.

Dampening rollers wet non-image area of the plate, preventing them from holding ink.

Plate cylinder

Blanket cylinder transfers image to paper.

Four-colour posters emerge at the end.

The printing press

There are many types of printing press. This modern press uses the offset lithography process, which works because grease attracts ink, while water repels it. The printing image on the plate is greasy, so ink is attracted to it. The non-printing parts are wet, so they do not get inked.

Coloured inks are added one after another to build up the full colour poster.

Johannes Gutenburg

In the mid-1400s, Gutenberg (c.1398–1468), a German goldsmith, devised a system of producing metal type in the form of individual letters. These could be arranged to form pages of text and then be printed in a press. After printing, the type could be reused to print another page. Soon presses were set up all over Europe with reusable metal type.

Gutenberg and his press

Typography

The design and use of letters printed on a page is called typography. Thousands of type styles, or typefaces, have been designed, from simple types for text to more elaborate ones for use in newspaper headlines or in advertisements.

ABCDEFGHIJKLMNO PQRSTUVWXYZ   Times

ABCDEFGHIJKLMNO PQRSTUVWXYZ   Helvetica

roman
italic
bold

Typefaces
Typefaces may be roman, italic, or bold. The last two styles are used for emphasis.

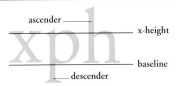

ascender

x-height

baseline

descender

ipsum dolor consectetuer adipiscing ipsum dolor consectetuer adipiscing ipsum dolor
9pt type on 9pt leading

ipsum dolor consectetuer adipiscing ipsum dolor consectetuer
9pt type on 14pt leading

The space between lines of type is called leading.

serif

Serif typeface
The main strokes in some typefaces end in small lines (serifs).

Sans serif typeface
Faces without lines are called "sans (without) serif".

691

Printing methods

The four main types of printing methods are screen printing, relief printing, the intaglio process, and lithography. These may be used by a commercial printing press to make thousands of copies, or on a smaller scale by an artist, to make a very few copies of an original image.

Monoprint

This simple method is so-called because it produces just one print. Paper is placed on an inked plate. A design is drawn or scraped onto the paper, which is then lifted off. The print is a mirror image of the original design.

Screen printing

In this type of printing, a stencil is attached to a mesh screen. The screen is then laid on the surface to be printed and ink is pushed through the mesh, leaving an image. Screen printing is widely used in business for printing posters and packaging. Prints can be made on many different surfaces, including paper, wood, metal, and fabrics.

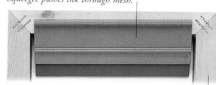
Squeegee pushes ink through mesh.
Wooden frame

Patrick Hughes, **Sea Change**

Fine art screen printing
The fresh, direct quality of the prints make screen printing a popular method with artists. The vividly coloured screen print portraits of Marilyn Monroe, by the American artist Andy Warhol, are a well-known example.

Relief printing

With this method, the non-printing areas of a plate are cut away, leaving a raised design, ready to be inked and printed. Letterpress printing, once used to print newspapers, is a type of relief printing.

Wood engraving
Until the 20th century, a popular method of printing illustrations for books was to engrave the design into a block of wood.

End grain wood block

Inked-up block, engraved design

Wood engraving print

Textiles
When fabric printing began in the 18th century, patterns were printed by hand with wood blocks. For mass-produced printed textiles, a process involving engraved copper rollers was developed in the late 18th century and is still used today. Screen printing is widely used for smaller quantities of textiles.

Printing block

Print

Hand-printed textile

Printed image — **Etching press** — *Rollers force paper and plate together*
Handle to operate rollers.
Inked-up copper plate

Intaglio process

In this process, a reversed design is engraved or etched into a metal plate. The plate is inked and wiped, so that only the grooves are filled with ink. Damp paper is laid on the plate, and both are passed through the rollers of an etching press. The paper is forced into the grooves to take up the ink, printing the design the right way round.

The intaglio process reproduces fine lines and details accurately.

Jock McFadyen, **Annie with a Sun Hat**

Lithography

This printing process works because oil and water do not mix. The printing image on the plate is not raised or engraved, but retains ink because it is greasy. The ink is washed off the non-greasy, non-printing wet areas. When the plate is inked and put into a press, the design prints on to a sheet of paper. Limestone is the traditional material for lithography plates but nowadays metal is usually used.

Image drawn on stone
Mandy Bonnell, **Crown Gateway 2**

Timeline

868 In China, wood blocks are used to produce books such as the *Diamond Sutra*, a Buddhist prayer text.

Early composing stick

c.1455 In Germany, Johannes Gutenberg prints about 160 copies of a Latin Bible, the first book printed using movable metal type, oil-based ink, and a wooden hand press.

1796 German printer Alois Senefelder invents the process called lithography.

1800 Charles, 3rd Earl Stanhope, British scientist and politician, develops the all-metal printing press.

1880s The linotype and monotype typesetting systems are introduced and streamline the typesetting process.

1890s Halftone printing is used to print posters and images in colour.

1904 US printer Ira W. Rubel develops the offset lithography process, a method which was first patented in England in 1853. The image from a lithographic plate is transferred to a long-lasting rubber cylinder before printing on paper or other materials. This quick, economical method becomes the most popular printing process.

Colour bar

1980s Computers are widely used in printing, in a range of applications,

Computer disk

such as importing text, altering images, and arranging the position of text and images on a page.

FIND OUT MORE
ART, HISTORY OF   BOOKS   CHINA, HISTORY OF   COLOUR   COMPUTERS   NEWSPAPERS AND MAGAZINES

P

PYRAMIDS

BUILT AS TOMBS for the pharaohs of ancient Egypt, the true pyramid was square at the base and rose steeply to a point, or apex. The triangular outline, as seen in the Great Pyramid of Giza, was significant to the Egyptians – it represented the mound upon which the sun god stood when he created the other gods. Thousands of years later, Central American peoples, such as the Maya, also built pyramid-like structures. These were made of stone blocks, and featured straight, steep staircases. They were often topped with a temple.

Egyptian pyramids

The Egyptians built their pyramids out of local limestone. The royal burial chamber had granite doors. Passages connected the burial chamber with the outside, and there were often false passages as well, which helped guard against robbers.

Saqqara
The Step Pyramid of the pharaoh Zoser was built in c.2950 BC, and is the oldest known pyramid. It takes its name from the series of six steps rising from the base.

Meidum
This 95 m (305 ft) high structure started as a step pyramid, and was later encased in stone to create a true pyramid. It was built under Snefru (c.2920 BC).

Dashur
This pyramid, also built for Snefru, looks "bent" because it started off steep, and then had to be levelled off by builders as cracks began to appear.

Giza
The Great Pyramid is 146 m (450 ft) high, and each side is 230 m (756 ft) at the base – the largest of all the Egyptian pyramids. It dates from c.2567 BC.

Inside the Great Pyramid

Made of 2.3 million limestone blocks, and taking 20 years to build, the Great Pyramid was the oldest of the Seven Wonders of the Ancient World. The uppermost burial chamber contained Khufu's coffin; but the other chambers may be false. Pyramids like this were usually in a large complex.

Roman pyramid
This striking, steep-sided pyramid is the tomb of Caius Cestius, a wealthy Roman magistrate who died in 12 BC. It took 330 days to build, and is faced in white marble. It was the only European pyramid for centuries.

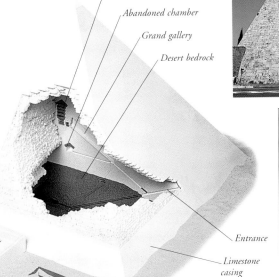

Pharaoh's chamber
Abandoned chamber
Grand gallery
Desert bedrock
Entrance
Limestone casing
Funerary boat buried in pit
Small pyramids for Khufu's three chief wives
Mortuary temple

Imhotep

The first known architect, Imhotep, designed the Step Pyramid at Saqqara. He trained as a scribe and became an adviser at the court of Zoser. He was also famous as a healer. His creative talents so impressed the Egyptians that, after his death, they turned him into a god. He was known as the son of Ptah, the Egyptian creator-god.

How an Egyptian pyramid was built

Pyramids were built using massive blocks of limestone – most of the blocks in the Great Pyramid weigh 2.5 tonnes or more. The Egyptians probably used some form of ramp to raise these blocks into position.

Labourers pull up stone using a simple winch.

Worker uses a sled to drag stone up a ramp.

Transporting the stone
The simplest way to transport the stone was by boat, along the River Nile. Limestone came from nearby quarries, but granite for chamber roofs, doorways, and other features came from Aswan.

On site
Workers dragged blocks on wooden sleds up ramps that were probably made of soil and rubble, and topped by wooden boards. Teams of workers could also haul stones up using a simple winch device consisting of a rope running over a wooden framework.

Central American pyramids

Pyramid-building in Central America reached its height between 300 and 1542. The Maya, Toltec, and Olmec peoples favoured step pyramids with staircases. They built temples at the top, which sometimes contained tombs.

Temple of the Inscriptions
This temple at Palenque contains writings that compare the Mayan Lord Pacal, who was buried here in 683, with the gods.

El Castillo
The Mayans built this pyramid at Chichen Itza around a Toltec temple. Its four staircases have 365 steps – to match the number of days in the year.

FIND OUT MORE

BUILDING AND CONSTRUCTION EGYPT, ANCIENT GODS AND GODDESSES MAYA MESOAMERICANS SEVEN WONDERS OF THE ANCIENT WORLD

RABBITS AND HARES

RABBITS AND HARES are found almost all over the world. They are not native to Australia and New Zealand, but the European rabbit was introduced there. The 40 or so species of rabbits and hares belong to the order of animals called Lagomorpha, which also includes 14 species of pika. These ground-dwelling mammals are herbivores – their diet includes grasses, flowers, roots, and the bark of young trees. The European rabbit lives in large groups, but hares and cottontails are mostly solitary animals, usually seen together only in the breeding season.

Prominent bulging eyes give all-round vision.

Rabbits and hares have large ears that help give them an acute sense of hearing.

Strong hind legs are kicked out when the rabbit is attacked.

Mountain hare

Rabbits have a good sense of smell.

European rabbit

Hares

Unlike rabbits, hares do not dig burrows, but rest in hollows in long grass called forms. They can run at 70 kmh (45 mph) and will zigzag and leap to escape from a predator. Young hares, called leverets, are able to run within minutes of being born.

Rabbits

Generally, rabbits are smaller than hares, with smaller ears and shorter hind legs. To warn of danger, they thump the ground with a hind leg, then rely on speed to escape. Rabbits produce a large number of young, which are helpless at birth.

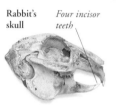

Rabbit's skull

Four incisor teeth

Teeth

All lagomorphs have large incisor teeth that grow continuously. They use these to cut their food, and they can graze very close to the ground. They use their cheek teeth to grind food.

Cottontails

Rabbits are sometimes called cottontails because of the white fur under their tail. This shows clearly when they run, signalling danger to others.

Desert cottontail

The short tail is called a scut.

Rabbit warrens

European rabbits live in large colonies. Each colony inhabits a system of underground burrows called a warren. There is a strict social hierarchy, with the dominant rabbits occupying the best parts of the warren.

Rabbits stand on their hind legs to get a better view of their territory.

Members of the colony graze close to their warren.

A rabbit can relax if another is watching for possible danger.

Main entrance leads to tunnels only 15 cm (6 in) wide.

A female builds a nest in a side chamber.

A nest is made of grass and fur.

Most tunnels are wide enough for only one rabbit, but passing places are built in some tunnels.

Boxing hares

In the breeding season, hares may be seen "boxing" each other. Male hares, or bucks, gather in the vicinity of a female, or doe, and fights may occur. Females "box" males whose advances are unwelcome. Long chases also occur at this time.

Rivals use their front paws in a fight.

Hares stand on their hind legs to box.

Large ears also aid hearing.

Jackrabbits

Blue-tailed and antelope jackrabbits live in the warmer climates in North America. They have enormous ears that help them to keep cool. Close to the surface of the skin of the ears, front and back, is a network of tiny blood vessels. As blood flows through these it loses heat to the air moving past the ears. The cooled blood then flows back into the body.

Arctic hare

In winter, hares that live in the Arctic and tundra regions grow a white coat instead of their summer brown coat. This fur is thick and keeps them warm and also camouflages them on the snow-covered ground. Hares that live on high mountain slopes also grow a white coat in winter for the same reasons. These hardy animals are active all through the year.

Pikas

Unlike rabbits and hares, pikas have short rounded ears, a rounded body, and no tail. Most live in mountainous areas of northwest North America, and central and northeast Asia, where they burrow under rocks. In summer, many pikas hoard grasses and seeds to provide them with food for winter.

EUROPEAN RABBIT

SCIENTIFIC NAME *Oryctolagus cuniculus*

ORDER Lagomorpha

FAMILY Leporidae

DISTRIBUTION Spain, northwest Africa; introduced elsewhere including Europe and Australia

HABITAT Grassland, pastures, sand dunes, woodland edges

DIET Grass, leaves, bark

SIZE Length: 35–45 cm (14–18 in)

LIFESPAN 3–6 years

FIND OUT MORE • ANIMAL BEHAVIOUR • CAMOUFLAGE AND COLOUR • NESTS AND BURROWS • POLAR WILDLIFE • RATS AND OTHER RODENTS

RADAR AND SONAR

THE HUGE ROTATING DISHES that you can see at any airport are radar antennas. They can detect aircraft hundreds of kilometres away, even at night and in the worst weather conditions. The word radar stands for RAdio Detection And Ranging. Radar is a type of echolocation, which is a way of finding the position of an object by bouncing a signal off it and then listening for the echo. Sonar is another form of echolocation used by ships and boats to locate underwater objects. The word sonar stands for SOund Navigation And Ranging.

How radar works

A radar dish, or antenna, sends out pulses of radio waves or microwaves. These waves bounce off any object in their path, and return to the dish, which detects them. The time it takes for the reflected waves to return to the dish enables a computer to calculate how far away the object is.

Approaching aircraft

Antenna sends out radio waves.

Antenna spins slowly, scanning the skies for aircraft coming in different directions.

Aircraft reflects radio waves back to antenna.

Radar antenna

R

Uses of radar

Radar is a useful detection-aid that helps aircraft and ships navigate safely, and police spot motorists driving too fast. Military forces use radar to aim missiles and locate enemy forces, weather forecasters use it to track rainfall, and astronomers use radar to map the surfaces of distant planets.

Air traffic control
In the busy skies over major airports, air traffic controllers use radar monitors to help them guide aircraft to a safe take-off or landing.

Navigation at sea
Ships use radar to find their way at sea, especially at night or in fog, when rocks, land, and other vessels may be hidden from view.

Speed trap
Police officers can measure the speed of cars with a hand-held radar scanner that fires pulses of microwaves at approaching vehicles.

Robert Watson-Watt
Although research into radar was undertaken in many countries, it was the Scottish physicist Robert Watson-Watt (1892–1973) who developed the first practical radar system in the mid-1930s. In World War II (1939–45), this system was used to give early warning of bombing raids by aircraft.

How sonar works

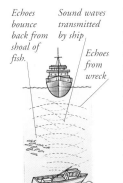

Echoes bounce back from shoal of fish.
Sound waves transmitted by ship
Echoes from wreck

Beneath a ship's hull, a device called a transponder sends out pulses of high-frequency sound, and records the echoes of the pulses as they bounce off the seabed or submerged objects. The time it takes for the echoes to return to the transponder indicates the object's depth and distance from the ship.

Sonar monitor showing ocean floor

Sonar monitor
The transponder detects the echoes returning to the ship and displays them as "blips" or shapes on a monitor screen. By looking at the monitor, the sonar operator can tell how deep the water is and identify underwater objects, such as shoals of fish, submarines, and even shipwrecks.

Echolocation

Dolphin

A few species of animal can use echolocation to help them find food or to build up a picture of their surroundings. Dolphins, for example, send out high-pitched squeaks that bounce off anything in their path and return as echoes. The dolphin's brain then analyzes the echoes to form an image.

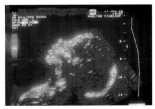
Ultrasound scan of a baby in its mother's womb

Ultrasound scan
Sound with a pitch above the range of human hearing is called ultrasound. Hospitals examine unborn babies with an ultrasound scanner, which sends ultrasonic waves into the mother's womb and then displays the returning echoes as a picture on a screen.

Timeline
1915 Following *Titanic* tragedy, French physicist Paul Langevin pioneers echolocation to detect submarines and icebergs.

1920s British Navy develops early sonar: the Asdic system.

1922 Italian Guglielmo Marconi suggests idea of radar.

1936 Ships begin to use radar for navigation.

1939–45 Radar used to detect enemy aircraft during World War II.

World War II mobile radar

1958 First ultrasound scans of unborn babies.

1970s and 1980s Radar maps surfaces of Venus and Mars.

2000 Sonar readings of Arctic ice thickness give key evidence about global warming.

FIND OUT MORE AIRPORTS • BATS • GLACIATION • NAVIGATION • PLANETS • POLICE • SHIPS AND BOATS • SOUND • WHALES AND DOLPHINS

RADIO

WHENEVER YOU TUNE IN to your radio, you are listening to sounds produced from invisible waves, travelling through space at the speed of light. At any one time, thousands of radio signals are moving through the atmosphere, and from these the radio receiver picks out the station you want. Before the 1890s, when radio waves were first used to send messages, information took weeks to travel around the world. Now it travels the same distance in a fraction of a second. This ability to transmit and receive information instantly has transformed the world.

1930s' radio set

Early radio
Early radio sets were inconvenient to use. Large, fragile glass valves amplified the sound: these had to heat up and did not last long. The choice of programmes was limited too. Nonetheless, radio provided people in the early 20th century with the first home news and entertainment system, and listening to the radio became the centre of a family's evening.

How radio works
Radio works by turning sound into electrical signals. The signals are themselves turned into radio waves, which travel through the atmosphere. This is done by a transmitter, using a device called a modulator. The modulator varies a steady radio signal according to the sound content of the broadcast. A radio receiver performs these operations in reverse, changing the signals back into sound.

Uses of radio

Handset

Radios are mainly used to bring information and entertainment into homes. Radio waves carry many different kinds of information, including television pictures and sound, and the signals sent by mobile telephones. In the form of in-car radio receivers and transmitters, radio also allows the emergency services to communicate while on the move. Even smaller radio sets, known as walkie-talkies, are used by contractors on large building sites.

Presenter in radio studio

Studios
The microphone in a radio studio turns the sound of a presenter's voice into sound signals. Other equipment turns the music on CDs and tapes into sound signals. All the signals are mixed together by an engineer, at a mixing desk in an adjoining control room; then the sound signals are sent to a transmitter.

Transmitters
Radio stations broadcast radio waves from a transmitter. This produces a high-frequency signal that varies according to the content of the sound fed into it from the studio. This varying signal is sent to the transmitter's aerial, which sends the signal into the atmosphere as radio waves.

Radio transmitter

Radio receiver
A radio receiver has its own aerial to pick up radio waves from the transmitter. It contains a tuner, to select the station, and a circuit that turns the radio waves into electrical signals. These signals are then amplified (made louder) and fed to a loudspeaker, which produces sounds that can be heard.

Radio in wartime
Soldiers use portable radios to stay in touch. They radio details of their own and enemy positions back to base, saving time on the battlefield. Radio can save lives in wartime, because details of casualties can be sent quickly, giving medical staff and ambulance crews exact information about the location of the injured.

Hand-held radio set, US military, 1990s

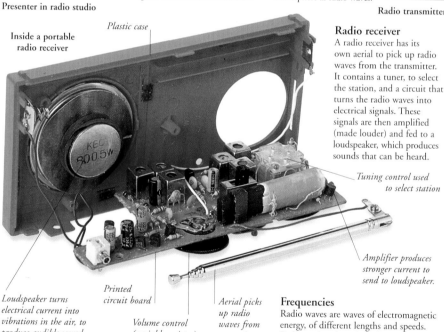

Plastic case

Inside a portable radio receiver

Tuning control used to select station

Amplifier produces stronger current to send to loudspeaker.

Loudspeaker turns electrical current into vibrations in the air, to produce audible sound.

Printed circuit board

Volume control (variable resistor) adjusts sound level.

Aerial picks up radio waves from transmitter.

Frequencies
Radio waves are waves of electromagnetic energy, of different lengths and speeds. Radio stations broadcast their programmes on a particular wavelength, or frequency.

Guglielmo Marconi

Italian engineer Guglielmo Marconi (1874–1937) was the first person to patent a method of sending signals by radio, in 1896. Marconi began experimenting with radio waves in his parent's attic while he was a teenager in Italy. By 1901 he sent the first radio signal across the Atlantic Ocean, using Morse code.

Timeline
1888 The German physicist Heinrich Hertz (1857–94) demonstrates radio waves for the first time.

1896 Marconi patents the first practical wireless telegraphy system.

1901 Marconi sends first transatlantic radio signal.

1906 USA: world's first public radio broadcast made.

1954 Transistor radio develops, replacing valves; radio receivers become much smaller.

1960 The first stereophonic (stereo) broadcasts are made.

1995 Clockwork radio broadcasts to places without electricity and batteries.

late-1990s Digital and Internet radio introduced.

Radio runs on self-generated power.

Clockwork radio

FIND OUT MORE   ELECTRONICS   ELECTROMAGNETISM   SOUND   SOUND RECORDING   TELEVISION

RADIOACTIVITY

ATOMS MAY BE TINY, but they can also be deadly! Some atoms, called radioisotopes, have unstable nuclei. This means that the nuclei are liable to decay, or break up, and give out high energy rays in a process known as radioactivity. Large doses of these rays can kill living cells, but radioactivity can also be used in many positive ways.

Radioactive glow

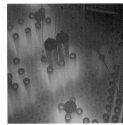

Radioactive objects – such as the fuel rods of a nuclear reactor – are often stored under water, because water absorbs radiation. As the radioactive particles travel through the water, they cause it to glow with blue light.

Antoine Becquerel

The French physicist Antoine Becquerel (1852–1908) discovered radioactivity in 1896. While investigating X-rays, he found that uranium salts fogged a photographic plate wrapped in dark paper. He realized that rays emitted by the uranium had penetrated the paper.

Geiger-Müller counter

Radiation can be detected with a Geiger-Müller counter, which consists of a tube filled with low-pressure gas connected to a meter. If radiation enters the tube, the gas splits into charged particles called ions and causes a pulse of electricity to flow. The more pulses there are, the stronger the radiation is.

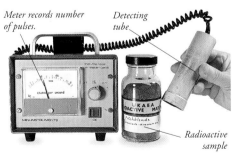

Meter records number of pulses.

Detecting tube.

Radioactive sample

Film badge

Workers in nuclear power stations wear special badges to record how much radiation they are being exposed to. When the radiation-sensitive film inside the badge is developed, it reveals the radiation levels experienced by the wearer over the previous month.

Types of radiation

The rays emitted by decaying nuclei are called radiation. There are three types of radiation – alpha, beta, and gamma rays. Gamma rays may accompany the emission of alpha or beta rays, and are sometimes given out on their own. Each type of radiation can penetrate different thicknesses of different materials, although all three types can be dangerous if absorbed by living tissue.

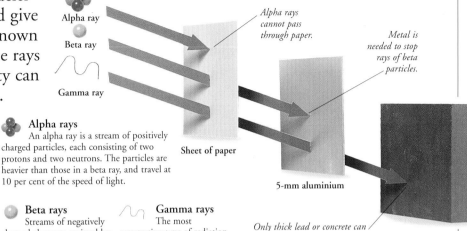

Alpha ray

Beta ray

Gamma ray

Alpha rays cannot pass through paper.

Metal is needed to stop rays of beta particles.

Sheet of paper

5-mm aluminium

Only thick lead or concrete can stop the powerful gamma rays.

Thick lead

Alpha rays

An alpha ray is a stream of positively charged particles, each consisting of two protons and two neutrons. The particles are heavier than those in a beta ray, and travel at 10 per cent of the speed of light.

Beta rays

Streams of negatively charged electrons emitted by a nucleus are called beta rays. These particles have hardly any mass and travel at 50 per cent of the speed of light.

Gamma rays

The most penetrating type of radiation is gamma rays – waves of electromagnetic radiation that travel at the speed of light. They have no mass.

Half-life

The time taken for half of the nuclei in a radioisotope to decay is called its half-life. If you make a pile of coffee beans and remove half the beans every 10 minutes, you will get some idea of how half-life works: over successive half-life periods, the radioactivity falls first to a half, then to a quarter, and so on. Each radioisotope has a different half-life. Uranium-238, for example, has a half-life of 4,500 million years, but radon-221's is just 30 seconds.

Coffee beans

After 10 minutes

Pile is now half the size of the original.

After 20 minutes

Only a quarter of the beans are left.

Carbon dating

Living things contain the radioisotope carbon-14, which has a 5,730-year half-life. The carbon-14 decays after an organism dies. Scientists can date the remains of dead organisms by measuring the amount of carbon-14 that has decayed. This technique is known as carbon dating.

Carbon dating bones

Uses of radiation

Radiation is used in many branches of medicine for treatment of diseased tissue, for tracing the passage of chemicals through the body, and for sterilizing equipment. It is also to used kill bacteria in food, to check pipes for leakages, and to detect wear on machine parts.

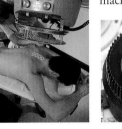

Radiotherapy

Patients suffering from cancer are often treated with radiotherapy. This involves focusing gamma rays from a radioisotope on to the cancer cells to kill them and stop the cancer from spreading.

Smoke detector

In some smoke alarms, a weak radioisotope emits radiation that causes a small electric current to flow. Any smoke entering the device interferes with the flow of current and sets off a warning alarm.

Timeline

1896 Becquerel discovers radioactivity in uranium.

1898 Polish-born chemist Marie Curie and her husband, French physicist Pierre Curie, discover the radioactive elements radium and polonium.

Marie Curie's flask

1911 New Zealand-born physicist Ernest Rutherford announces that atoms have a dense centre called a nucleus.

1908–28 German physicists Hans Geiger and Walther Müller develop a gauge (now called a Geiger-Müller counter) for measuring radioactivity.

Early Geiger-Müller counter

1934 French physicists Irène and Frédéric Joliot-Curie demonstrate that radioactivity can be produced artificially.

1968 Scientists pioneer radiation treatment as a way of preserving food.

FIND OUT MORE ATOMS AND MOLECULES CURIE, MARIE MEITNER, LISE NUCLEAR POWER X-RAYS AND THE ELECTROMAGNETIC SPECTRUM

R

RAIN

THE FRESH WATER that makes rivers flow, fills lakes, keeps plants alive, and provides water for us to drink, comes from rain. Like snow, rain is a type of precipitation – moisture falling from the atmosphere to the earth. Raindrops or ice-crystals form in a cloud and fall to the ground, when they become so heavy that the air can no longer hold them up. Depending on the cloud type and temperature, precipitation may also fall as drizzle (tiny droplets of rain), sleet, or hail, all of which are different sizes. Too much or too little rain can have a serious effect on plant and animal life.

Mountains force moist air upwards.

Air warms and dries as it descends.

Rain falls as moist air is cooled and condenses.

Orographic rain

Types of rain

Rain forms when warm air is swept high in a cloud, cooling the air, and condensing water vapour. Different clouds produce different rain types. Convectional rain is warm, rising air from cumulonimbus clouds. Orographic rain occurs as air is forced up into a cloud over a mountain. Frontal rain is from air rising at weather fronts.

Raindrops

In the warm tropics, clouds are generally warm too. Raindrops form when droplets of water come together and grow so big that they fall. Outside the tropics, raindrops usually start as ice-crystals. High in the clouds, the air is so cold that water turns to ice; ice-crystals grow and form snowflakes, which melt to rain as they fall.

Precipitation of raindrops

Small droplets of water in the cloud collide to form larger drops.

Large drops break up as they fall.

Freezing level

Small droplets collide again to form large droplets.

Strong air currents carry moisture up through the cloud.

Cumulonimbus cloud

Ice-crystals form.

Ice-crystals grow as they attract water.

Ice-crystals now form snowflakes or soft hail pellets.

Snowflakes and hail pellets melt into raindrops as they fall into warm air.

Warm rain: collision   Cold rain: ice-crystal

Snow

Ice-crystals fall from clouds as snow. Moisture freezes on to the crystals, which join together as snowflakes. Large snowflakes, formed when the temperature is above freezing, fall as wet snow. Crystals do not stick together well in extreme cold, and fall as dry, powdery snow.

Magnified snow crystals

Hailstones

Large pellets of ice fall from a thundercloud as hailstones, more than 5 mm (0.2 in) across. These can form when ice-crystals are whirled up and down inside the cloud, acquiring new layers, or when a crystal falls slowly, attracting water that freezes on in layers.

Hailstone

Monsoon

Torrential rain hits many tropical areas, such as the southern countries of Asia, for periods of up to six months. Formed by warm air rising over land and drawing in cool, moist air from the sea, monsoon rain can be so fierce that it causes major floods.

Snowflakes

Each snowflake is a collection of ice-crystals, which are usually hexagonal but may also be needle-shaped or columnar. No two crystals are identical. If snowflakes fall into air that is just above freezing point, they may melt to form sleet.

Hexagonal crystals form in clouds at 3-0°C (37.4-32°F).

Blizzard

When very heavy snow combines with a strong wind, the result is a blizzard. In a blizzard, visibility drops to almost nil, and the ground is quickly buried in thick snow, which may be blown by the wind into huge drifts that can engulf a house.

Frost

When moisture in the air freezes, it may coat the ground and other surfaces with a layer of sparkling white frost. Spiky needles of hoar-frost form when damp air blows over very cold surfaces. Rime (thick, clear ice) forms when icy air touches a surface. Fern frost (feathery ice-trails) forms on cold glass when dew-drops freeze.

Hoar-frost on car

Cloud seeding

In drought areas, aircraft are sometimes used to stimulate rain artificially by seeding thunderclouds with small chemical crystals. These cause the clouds to release rain.

FIND OUT MORE   ATMOSPHERE   CLIMATE   CLOUDS   DESERTS   FORESTS   POLLUTION   STORMS   WEATHER

RAINFOREST WILDLIFE

THE SCREECHING OF MONKEYS, the buzzing of insects, and the bright colour of a bird's wings are common sights and sounds in the world's richest ecosystem, the tropical rainforest. Rainforests provide a home for over half of all plant and animal species. An area of 100 sq km (39 sq miles) can contain 750 types of tree, 400 species of bird, 100 reptile species, and many thousands of insect species. The wildlife is not a random collection of animals and plants, but a complex community in which competition for resources is intense.

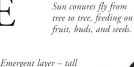
Emergent layer – tall trees rise high above the rest to gain the most light.

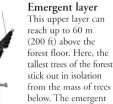
Sun conures fly from tree to tree, feeding on fruit, buds, and seeds.

Emergent layer
This upper layer can reach up to 60 m (200 ft) above the forest floor. Here, the tallest trees of the forest stick out in isolation from the mass of trees below. The emergent layer is home to bats, predatory birds, and fruit eaters, such as the sun conure.

Canopy – thick layer of treetops

Canopy
Between 30–45 m (100–150 ft) above ground level is the canopy. This dense layer of branches and leaves contains the greatest variety of animal life in the forest. Lianas – woody creepers – reach up to the sunlight of the upper canopy.

Understorey
Shrubs grow in the understorey layer wherever light penetrates through the canopy. Lizards, such as the common iguana, live here, climbing up tree trunks and feeding on insects and vegetation.

Understorey

Rainforests

Rainforests grow around the equator. The hot, steamy conditions are perfect for plants. In fact, rainforests contain the largest diversity of plant and animal life on Earth; many species are still unidentified. Rainforests form distinct layers, providing homes for animals at all levels.

Liana wound around trunk

Buttress roots

Ground layer

Ground layer
There are few plants on the dark forest floor, but many small animals, such as insects, feed on and recycle material that falls from above. Leaf-cutter ants use leaves as a compost to grow a fungus they feed on.

Harpy eagle

This huge eagle is the major bird of prey of the Central and South American rainforests. It soars over the canopy, watching for prey such as monkeys, sloths, opossums, and snakes. Once it spots them, the harpy eagle swoops through the treetops, snatching the animals from the branches with its razor-sharp talons.

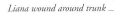
Eagle is up to 100 cm (40 in) in length.

Birds

Rainforests contain the richest variety of the world's birds. From the emergent layer, fast-flying predators, such as eagles and hawks, descend on forest animals. The canopy is home to birds such as hornbills, parrots, and toucans, which feed on fruit and small animals. On the forest floor, ground-dwelling birds scratch at the soil for insects and plant roots.

Leaves have a waxy layer to reduce evaporation and channel water down to a mat of roots.

This plant absorbs water from the air through scales on the leaves.

Epiphytic plants

Plants

Many rainforest trees are tall, with straight trunks, few branches, and are supported by buttress roots. Other plants include epiphytes, such as bromeliads and orchids. Epiphytes use other plants as a support, attaching themselves to branches by their roots to reach the light. They trap water and obtain nutrients from plant material that falls on them. Bromeliads have spiky leaves that channel water, leaves, and fruit into a pool in the centre; these rot to provide the bromeliad with nutrients.

Bromeliad

Red jungle fowl

Relatives of domestic chickens, Southeast Asian jungle fowl live in small groups on the forest floor, where they nest in grass-lined hollows. They scratch at the ground to unearth invertebrates and plant roots on which they feed.

Cuvier's toucan

Cuvier's toucan lives in the canopy of South American rainforests. It uses its long beak to reach for fruit and small animals at the ends of branches too thin to bear its weight.

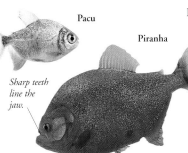
Pacu

Piranha

Sharp teeth line the jaw.

Fish

The streams and rivers that flow through rainforests are teeming with fish. Some, such as the pacus from South America, feed on fruit and seeds that fall into the water from overhanging branches; others, such as piranhas, are fierce predators that hunt in packs. They use their sharp teeth and powerful jaws to kill other fish and strip the flesh from larger animals that stray into the water. The electric eel can generate electric shocks to stun its fish prey. It also uses electric fields to detect prey, deter enemies, and navigate in murky water.

Strangler fig

These tall trees have an unusual life cycle. The seeds, deposited in bird droppings in the canopy branches, grow into plants that send roots down to the ground. The roots thicken, and surround the host tree in a lattice-like casing. The fig's leaves shade the host tree from the sun. As a result, the "strangled" host tree dies and rots, leaving a free-standing strangler fig, its hollow trunk formed by a network of roots.

R

Reptiles

Many lizards and snakes live in rainforests. Lizards, such as iguanas and geckos, have long toes and claws adapted for gripping trees; some also have prehensile (grasping) tails. Many forest lizards eat insects; some also feed on vegetation. Rainforest snakes include the boa constrictor and the venomous gaboon viper, which feed on insects, lizards, birds, and mammals.

Brown colour camouflages the snake, concealing it as it lies in wait for prey, coiled around a branch.

Tree boa
This South American snake spends most of its life moving between the branches of the understorey and canopy of the rainforest, seldom descending to the ground. If small mammals, birds, or lizards come close, the boa strikes and seizes the prey with its fangs. Like other boas, it then constricts, or squeezes, the prey to death, using its strong, muscular coils.

Parson's chameleon
This Madagascan lizard is well adapted for life in the trees. It grips branches and twigs with its toes, aided by its prehensile tail, and will lie in wait for hours for insect prey to come into range. When this happens, the chameleon shoots out its long, sticky tongue to catch the insect. Chameleons have the remarkable ability to change colour according to their mood, or to blend with their surroundings.

Dark stripes and spots

Skin is now very dark.

Changing colour

1 This Parson's chameleon starts to darken in colour to warn off a rival male who has entered his territory.

2 The chameleon darkens further, and dark purple stripes and spots appear. He becomes more aggressive and puffs up his body to make himself look bigger.

3 His tail has straightened and his colour has intensified. The colour is caused by dark pigments being released into the skin, triggered by hormones.

Invertebrates

Rainforests contain a huge diversity of invertebrates; many have yet to be identified. On the forest floor, worms, millipedes, beetles, and ants feed on vegetation and dead animals, that fall from the canopy. Spiders also hunt there and in trees for insects, small frogs, and birds. In the understorey and canopy, a multitude of insects such as bugs and wasps feed on the prey of other insects or vegetation, while in the canopy colourful, nectar-eating butterflies are common.

Blue morpho
This butterfly from South America has a wingspan of up to 18 cm (7 in). Invisible to us, and its predators, are beacon-like flashes produced when the wings open and close. These can only be seen by animals, like other morphos, that can detect ultraviolet light. They are used to attract a mate.

Flat body

Leaf insect
This leaf mimic, complete with veins and midrib, lives in Australia and Southeast Asia. To escape detection from birds, its camouflage is enhanced by side-to-side movements making it resemble a leaf in a breeze.

Long antenna

Poisonous fangs are below head.

Giant tiger centipede
This centipede from South America may be up to 20 cm (8 in) long. It eats insects, and even small reptiles and mammals. It senses prey with its antennae, then captures and paralyses it with the poisonous fangs below its head.

Amphibians

The warm, moist conditions of rainforests provide ideal conditions for frogs and toads. They defend themselves from larger animals by being camouflaged or distasteful to predators. Some frogs and toads live on the forest floor; others live in trees, and have grasping toes that help them climb.

Poison dart frog
The bright colours of these South American frogs warn predators, such as snakes, that they are poisonous to eat. Male frogs also use their skin colour to deter rivals from entering their territory during courtship.

Ridges look like leaf ribs and veins.

Asian horned toad
This toad's flat body and horns that project over its eyes and snout make it look like a leaf. The effect is enhanced by its colour which matches the dead leaves on the floor where it lives. This camouflage enables it to escape detection by predators and prey alike.

Mammals

Mammals are found at all levels of the rainforest. Numerous insect, plant, and seed-eaters live on the forest floor, many emerging at night to avoid predators. Larger forest floor herbivores include tapirs, capybaras, and deer. These mammals are prey for carnivores such as tigers and jaguars. Tree-dwellers of the understorey include opossums and civets, while in the heights of the canopy live bats, monkeys, and gliding mammals, including flying lemurs that feed on fruit and leaves.

Jaguars may climb trees to lie in wait for prey.

Jaguar
Jaguars are the only large cats found in the Americas. They hunt animals such as deer and peccaries, which they usually stalk through the forest. Their spotted coat provides perfect camouflage in the dappled light of the forest floor, enabling them to get very close to prey before pouncing on it.

Black spider monkey
This highly agile and active monkey lives in the canopy and emergent layer of the South American rainforest. Black spider monkeys move at speed through the branches, making leaps of up to 10 m (33 ft). They live in groups of up to 20 animals that move from tree to tree in search of fruit, rarely, if ever, descending to the forest floor.

Prehensile tail is used to grasp trunks, as an extra hand or foot.

FIND OUT MORE
| CAMOUFLAGE AND COLOUR | ECOLOGY AND ECOSYSTEMS | FORESTS | FROGS AND TOADS | INSECTS | LIONS AND OTHER WILD CATS | MONKEYS AND OTHER PRIMATES | REPTILES | TREES |

700

RATS AND OTHER RODENTS

RODENTS ARE the most numerous and widespread of all the world's mammals. A huge variety of species exist – more than 1,700 in all. The three main types are the mouse-like rodents, the cavy-like rodents, and the squirrel-like rodents. They are found all over the world, from the Arctic to Australia, and occupy all kinds of habitat from underground tunnels to trees. Between them, rodents lead many different lifestyles but most eat plant food and are nocturnal creatures. Rodents are usually small and compact and have sharp gnawing teeth.

The black rat is a skilful climber.

Rats and mice

A typical rodent, the black rat belongs to the mouse-like group of rodents, together with mice, voles, hamsters, and gerbils. It has short legs, a long tail, a pointed snout, large eyes and ears, and sensitive whiskers. Agile, alert, and quick to learn, it has adapted so well to living with humans and feeding off their food stores, that it has spread all over the world from its native Asia. It was first transported from Asia on board the ships of early explorers.

Food

Rodents worldwide eat a huge amount of plant food of all kinds, including underground roots, grass stems, seeds gathered from the ground, and nuts harvested in the treetops. Many also eat worms and insects, and some rodents tackle small mammals and birds. The fish-eating rat, as its name suggests, finds almost all its food in rivers, lakes, and ponds.

Empty cheek pouches

Extending pouches

Pouches full of nuts

Cavies
The cavy-like rodents are rather large and plump in build, compared with rats and mice. They include porcupines, guinea pigs, pacas, chinchillas, and the largest rodent – the capybara. Most are found in South America, although some porcupines live in North America, and the coypu is now found in Europe after escaping from fur farms.

Squirrels
Squirrel-like rodents, such as the grey squirrel, are usually larger than rats and mice, and many of them are more active by day than by night. They include tree-dwelling squirrels and chipmunks, burrowers such as marmots and prairie dogs, and water-loving beavers.

Eye socket

Paca skull

Incisor teeth

Rodent teeth
Rodents are equipped with an impressive set of front teeth. These large, sharp incisors enable the animals to gnaw through tough materials, such as nut cases, seed pods, and roots, which would be more than a match for normal teeth. The incisors grow all the time as they get worn down by continuous use.

Storing food
If they find a good supply of food, many rodents gather more than their immediate needs and store some for later. Hamsters are well known for carrying surplus food in their cheek pouches. It takes this food back to its burrow to use as winter supplies.

Hamster uses its paws to get the nuts out.

Breeding

Rodents breed fast. Some have large litters – hamsters regularly bear 12 young at a time. Others breed several times a year – voles often have four litters per season. These numbers are balanced out because so many are killed by predators or the effects of bad weather. Rodents go to great lengths to protect their young, building special burrow chambers, or nests from grass, leaves, and sticks.

1 At birth, baby mice weigh barely 1 g (a fraction of an ounce). They are born naked, blind, and unable to move much.

2 At six days old, the young mice are still rather helpless and vulnerable to predators. Their fur has begun to grow.

3 At 10 days old, most members of the litter have a full coat of fur. Their eyes are open and they can hear, but they still cannot leave the nest.

4 At two weeks old, the young mice start to explore. They are almost weaned. They will soon make their own way in the world and begin to breed.

R

Beaver lodges

Beavers are famous for the amazing homes, called lodges, that they build in rivers. A family of beavers begins its work by constructing a dam of sticks, mud, and stones across a river. This stops the river, and in the middle of the still water behind the dam, the beavers build a large conical mound.

The family's living quarters are above the water line.

The mound is entered by an underwater tunnel.

Beavers
Found in Europe and North America, beavers can be recognized by their broad, flat, scaly tail. They use their tail as a rudder while swimming, and when danger is near, they slap it on the water to warn their companions.

Habitats

Rodents occupy a tremendous variety of habitats: from the Arctic tundra to sweltering rainforests; from the driest deserts to waterlogged marshes. Their environment influences both their physical adaptations and the ways they go about finding food and shelter. Some, like the beavers, go to remarkable lengths to make their own shelters.

Mountains
Chinchillas live so high in the Andes Mountains of South America that they have to tolerate bitter cold at night. To help them survive the chill, they have extremely thick fur, and they take shelter in rock crevices.

A dust bath cleans the fur by dislodging dirt and parasites.

Defence

Rodents are food for many predators. The dangers they face explain why they are nervous creatures, preferring to keep under cover and dashing back there at the slightest threat. Many rodents have evolved defences to deter attackers or avoid detection.

Buildings
The house mouse, like the black rat, has colonized human homes and learnt to eat food we provide by mistake. It does most of its feeding in the quiet of night, and finds shelter during the day under floorboards and similar out-of-the-way places.

Mole rats have very poor vision.

Large ears and eyes for detecting predators.

Deserts
Desert rodents, such as some species of spiny mouse, have to cope not just with a scarcity of water, but also with a poor food supply. They are good at conserving moisture, and breed more freely when rain brings vegetation to life.

Underground
The hairless mole rat is one of several species of rodent that lives underground. They tunnel through the soil, gnawing roots and other food. Since they rarely come to the surface, many species have tiny eyes or are blind.

Camouflage
Meadow voles live in grassland and woods. They feed on the ground where their brown colouring helps to hide them. If danger threatens, they may "freeze", making them difficult to spot.

Spines
The fearsome spines of porcupines ward off most enemies. If attacked, a porcupine will run into the attacker, leaving spines in its skin. The attacker may die from its wounds.

Largest and smallest

The capybara is the largest rodent. It wallows in pools and swamps in South America. At up to 50 kg (110 lb) in weight, it is 10,000 times heavier than the smallest rodent, the pygmy mouse. This tiny mouse scurries through the grass in dry areas of Mexico.

Grooming

Rodents keep their coat in good condition with regular cleaning and grooming to remove dirt, food debris, and parasites. A brown rat may live among rubbish, or in sewers, but it meticulously combs through the fur all over its body, using its teeth and paws.

Claws scratch off lice.

The rat cleans its underparts with its mouth and front paws.

BLACK RAT

SCIENTIFIC NAME	*Rattus rattus*
ORDER	Rodentia
FAMILY	Muridae
DISTRIBUTION	Worldwide
HABITAT	Around human habitations and buildings, especially near docks and ships
DIET	Varied, but especially cereals and grains
SIZE	Body length 20–26 cm (8–10 in)
LIFESPAN	1–2 years

FIND OUT MORE   ANIMAL BEHAVIOUR   ANIMALS   DESERT WILDLIFE   MAMMALS   MOUNTAIN WILDLIFE   RABBITS AND HARES

Rodents
Rats and mice

Dwarf hamsters grow to only 8.4 cm (3.3 in) long.

Fieldmice can produce up to eight litters per year.

Hamsters groom frequently – their fur traps body heat and keeps them warm.

Voles resemble mice, but have rounder faces.

Voles defend themselves by speed and camouflage.

All gerbils have strong back legs and a long tail.

Gerbils make popular pets; they are gentle and easy to care for.

Chinese hamsters live in grasslands and deserts in Mongolia, China, Siberia, and Korea.

Pallid gerbils can leap about 0.5 m (1.6 ft) from a standing position. They live in dry, sandy areas, such as the Egyptian desert.

Egyptian spiny mice have stiff hairs in their fur, which stand on end when they are threatened.

Woodmice are usually nocturnal.

Yellow-necked woodmice feed on plant matter (grain, shoots, and leaves) and animal matter (insects).

Contrary to popular opinion, rats are very clean mammals.

Black-headed rats are less common than brown or black rats.

Tails can be shed in danger.

Black rats carried the fleas that caused bubonic plague epidemics.

Long tails help rats keep balance while climbing.

Squirrels and cavies

Loosely attached spines, or quills, may have barbs attached to their ends.

Cheek pouches

Guinea pigs were raised for food by the Incas of South America.

Frequent dust baths help maintain fur.

Porcupines, found in Europe and America, have evolved spines as a defence.

Chinchillas have luxuriant grey fur, which protects them from the harsh climate of the Andes Mountains of South America.

Chipmunks can manipulate their food with their hand-like forepaws.

Capybaras are the largest members of the rodent family. They live in Central and South America and can grow up to 1.2 m (4 ft) long.

Grey squirrels live in special tree nests, or dreys, in woodland.

REFORMATION

IN THE 16TH CENTURY, Europe's Christians relied on the Roman Catholic Church to guide them through their lives on Earth, and show them the way to reach Heaven. However many Catholic officials had become rich and corrupt, while ordinary priests were often poor and ignorant. Scholars began to demand reforms that would restore the Church's old purity. The authorities, however, were slow to respond, so the protesting scholars – backed by certain kings and princes – made their own Reformation by creating an alternative Protestant Church, which has existed ever since.

Protestant areas shown in green.

Catholic areas shown in cream.

Catholic and Protestant shown striped.

Christendom, c.1560
When a country's ruler became Protestant, the population usually followed suit. However, in France and the Netherlands, many ordinary people turned Protestant of their own accord, and were then persecuted by Catholic rulers.

Early protests

Forerunners of the Reformation included the English scholar, John Wyclif (c.1329–84) and the Bohemian (Czech) priest Jan Hus (c.1369–1415). Wyclif accused the Catholic Church of incompetence and corruption. After his death, many of his followers, known as the Lollards, were put to death for continuing to support his beliefs.

Coin commemorating Hus

Hussites

Hus supported Wyclif's views, called for reform, and was burnt at the stake as a heretic. His followers, the Hussites, proclaimed him a martyr and started an armed struggle against the Church. The Hussites were defeated, and Bohemia was forced back to Catholicism.

Hus was burnt at the stake

Martin Luther

German university teacher and priest Martin Luther (1483–1546) started the Reformation. From 1517, he challenged aspects of the Catholic Church's teaching and behaviour. He wanted people to find their own personal faith in God by individual Bible study. Luther was protected by sympathetic German princes, and his message was spread by the advent of printing.

Protestant division

The Protestant Church had divisions within itself as people in different countries followed the teachings of reformers, such as Ulrich Zwingli (1484–1531) and John Calvin (1509–64). Calvin greatly influenced the Swiss, Dutch, French, Scottish, and Polish Reformations.

Puritans

English followers of Calvin were called Puritans, after their desire for a "pure" form of worship. Some Puritans wielded great political power and were persecuted; others crossed the Atlantic to establish "godly" colonies in America.

Six Protestant martyrs

Protestantism

Protestants wanted to reform the Catholic Church, which, they believed, had slipped away from the Christian ideals set down in the Bible. Their reforms included a return to simple ceremonies, with less emphasis on priestly intervention and more on each worshipper's quest to find God. They also wanted services in the local language, rather than Latin, and an educated, uncorrupted clergy.

Dissolution of the monasteries

In the 1530s, the Reformation reached England. Monastic life had no place in Protestantism, so between 1536 and 1539, King Henry VIII dissolved (shut down) all England's monasteries and took their lands for himself.

Fountains Abbey, Yorkshire, England

Protestant allegory, by Cranach the Younger

Good wine growers represent Protestants.

Martin Luther

Drunk priest

Bad wine growers represent the Catholic Church.

St Bartholomew's Day Massacre

Huguenots

France's Catholic authorities tried to quash the Huguenots (French followers of Calvin). In August 1572, Catholic mobs in Paris killed 3,000 Huguenots, an event that became known as the St Bartholomew's Day Massacre. In 1789, the Huguenots won the right to worship freely.

Counter-Reformation

St Ignatius Loyola

During the 1500s, the Counter-Reformation set out to reclaim Protestant Europe for the Church. The Society of Jesus, a major part of this movement, was formed by Ignatius Loyola (1491–1556) in 1534. The Jesuits, as they were called, became famous for foreign missionary work and education.

FIND OUT MORE   CHRISTIANITY   GERMANY, HISTORY OF   HOLY ROMAN EMPIRE   NETHERLANDS, HISTORY OF   RELIGIONS   RENAISSANCE

RELIGIONS

IN ALL SOCIETIES throughout history people have felt the need for religion. A religion is a set of beliefs that relies on spiritual faith in its followers. Most religions have a god or gods and provide answers to questions such as how the world was created and what happens after death. Religions often have special rituals that act as ways of communicating with the gods or marking major events in a person's life. Finally, religions usually involve an ethical code, a set of rules that believers try to live by.

World religions

There are six major organized world religions – Christianity, Islam, Hinduism, Buddhism, Judaism, and Sikhism – and many smaller religions. For many people, religion provides moral guidance, a sense that life has a meaning, and a feeling of shared values and community. Yet in some places, religious conflict has led to war.

Sikhism
The fifth largest world religion, Sikhism was founded in northern India in the 16th century by Guru Nanak. It has one sacred scripture, the *Adi Granth*.

Shinto
The ancient religion of Japan, Shinto, involves beliefs in nature spirits called *kami*, ancestor worship, reverence for certain places and traditions, and respect for military virtues, such as chivalry. It was the state religion of Japan until 1945.

Jainism
Founded in the 6th century BC, Jainism is an Indian religion. Like Hindus, followers of Jainism believe that when people die they are reborn as another being. Nuns may cover their mouths to avoid the risk of harming living things.

Zoroastrians believe that fire is sacred and a flame is always kept burning in temples.

Zoroastrianism
This religion was founded in Asia in the 500s BC. It still survives in parts of Iran and India. Zoroastrians believe that life is a struggle between two forces: good, represented by the god Ahura Mazda, and evil, in the spirit Ahriman. They believe that good will eventually triumph, and Ahura Mazda will establish paradise here on Earth.

Traditional religions

The aboriginal peoples of North America, Australia, and Africa all follow different types of traditional religions. These religions have no written texts – ceremonies and beliefs are handed down from one generation to the next by word of mouth. Many traditional religions involve worship of ancestors or reverence for the forces of nature.

The Asante women of Africa carry this ritual figure to make their babies beautiful.

This Australian bark painting shows an Aboriginal ancestral group.

The Asante believe wood has magical powers because it is a living material.

Ancestor worship
Most traditional religions have a belief in some sort of afterlife, and the dead person's spirit is often thought to live on amongst the surviving people. Ancestors may be worshipped through objects that symbolize them, such as the carved totem poles in northwestern North America.

Animism
The belief that spirits inhabit all objects is called animism. These spirits control not only the object itself, but also the lives of people and the natural world. Animism is one of the earliest forms of religion and still exists among people living traditional lifestyles all over the world.

Communicating with the gods

All religions involve rituals, and an important purpose of these ceremonies is to communicate with the gods. At its simplest, talking to a god is a matter of saying a prayer, but more elaborate rituals are also used. Music, dance, readings from sacred books, ceremonies, and meditating are found in different religions to bring the faithful into closer contact with the world of the spirits.

Rosary beads

People pray using rosary beads.

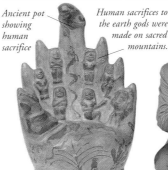

Ancient pot showing human sacrifice

Human sacrifices to the earth gods were made on sacred mountains.

Rastafarians play drums in worship.

Crucifix shows Christ on the cross.

Offerings
In many religions, believers make offerings such as money or food to the gods. In some religions, offerings included human sacrifices.

Music
Musics provides a common way of talking to a god. People are brought together in worship by singing hymns or chanting.

FIND OUT MORE BUDDHISM CHRISTIANITY FESTIVALS GODS AND GODDESSES HINDUISM ISLAM JUDAISM MUSIC SHRINES SIGNS AND SYMBOLS

705

Religions

Holy objects

Jewish baby cloth, worn after baby is circumcised

Hebrew text celebrating the Torah

Head-dress worn by a Tibetan monk

Mitre, or head-dress, worn by a bishop

Sikh kirpan, or sword

Peruvian figure used to guard tombs

Guardian figure used in ancestor worship

Charm necklace used by African healers

Screen showing ancestor spirits, Nigeria

Fertility dolls, Africa

Doll made from stick, beeswax, beads, and hide

Animist wood carving, Polynesia

Shinto god

Jain shrine

Christian Bible

Islamic lamp

Jain Tirthankara, or guide

Tibetan monk's bell

Holy places

Cathedral window, Britain

Christian church

Islamic window

Zoroastrian temple

Islamic mosque, Jerusalem

Decorative tiles on octagonal base

Christian chapel doorway, France

Dome above grey sandstone octagonal base.

Islamic mausoleum, or tomb, India

Minaret on an Islamic mosque

706

RENAISSANCE

FROM THE 15TH CENTURY, Europe experienced a remarkable flowering of the arts and sciences. This was known as the Renaissance, which in French means "rebirth". From its birthplace in Italy, the Renaissance spread to embrace most of western Europe, and deeply affected the way educated people looked at the world and its purpose. Inspired by the study of ancient Greek and Roman society, Renaissance scholars, thinkers, and artists abandoned medieval pessimism and constructed humanism – a new, optimistic outlook for the future, in which men and women played a central role and created a civilized environment. Some of the world's finest art and literature dates from this period.

Copy of an ancient Greek bronze

Renaissance origins

The Renaissance began in Italy when the poets Dante, Petrarch, and Boccaccio revived an interest in ancient Greek and Roman civilizations. They believed these societies had experienced a Golden Age of art and literature in the 2nd and 1st centuries BC, and wished to recreate it.

Francesco Petrarcha

Petrarch
The poet Petrarch (1304–1374) was a brilliant scholar of Latin. He studied the ancient authors Plato, Virgil, and Cicero. The work of these scholars became known as the "Classics" because of the elegance of their writing. Eventually this term included Greek and Roman architecture and art, as well as literature.

New order

Medieval thinkers argued that earthly life was less important than the afterlife. In contrast, the Renaissance view was that the mortal world, with all its human achievements, was the most significant part of God's Creation. This inspired explorers, inventors, and astronomers to expand human knowledge.

Age of exploration
Fired by the new spirit of enquiry, the Portuguese sailors Bartolomeu Diaz and Vasco da Gama discovered the sea route to India. Ferdinand Magellan set out to sail around the world, though he did not live to complete the trip.

Mappa Mundi, early 1400s

Planisphaerium Copernicum, c.1543

Stars and planets
The astronomer Copernicus was the first to realize that the Universe did not revolve around Earth. Instead Earth revolved around the Sun. Later astronomers, such as Galileo, supported this theory, and went on to form new ones, using the same system of planetary observation that Copernicus had pioneered.

New ideas
Major Renaissance figures believed that humankind could achieve anything it wanted; enough confidence, education, and faith in God would create a new Golden Age and a better Christian society. One true genius, the artist, engineer, and scientist Leonardo da Vinci (1452–1519), let his imagination run free and produced plans for flying machines about 400 years before they were actually invented.

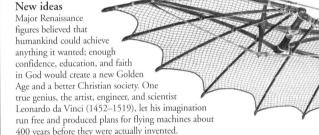

Thick struts supported the skeleton structure.

Crank and pulley mechanism

Wing span was 11 m (36 ft).

Foot pedals to operate the machine

Flying machine by Leonardo da Vinci

Human body

Medieval artists viewed the human form as "a withered fruit stinking in the nostrils of the Lord". The Renaissance overturned this view, and artists such as Michelangelo, Raphael, and Titian portrayed the human figure with beauty and grace. Michelangelo's sculpture the *Pieta* idealizes the human forms to represent their spiritual purity.

A study by Leonardo da Vinci

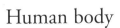

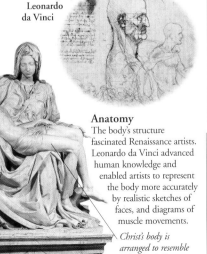

Anatomy
The body's structure fascinated Renaissance artists. Leonardo da Vinci advanced human knowledge and enabled artists to represent the body more accurately by realistic sketches of faces, and diagrams of muscle movements.

Christ's body is arranged to resemble a sleeping baby.

Pieta by Michelangelo

Michelangelo

Michelangelo Buonarroti (1475–1564) from Caprese, Tuscany, Italy, was one of the greatest artistic creators of all time. A sculptor, painter, draughtsman, poet, and architect, he was deeply fascinated by the human body and its representation. Sculpture was the art form he loved best. When he sculpted, he believed that he was "releasing" the figures trapped in the stone. His greatest painting was on the ceiling of the Sistine Chapel in the Vatican, Rome.

Hunt in the Forest by Paolo Uccello (1396–1475)

Perspective in painting
The greatest innovation in Renaissance art was the development of perspective. Artists, keen to represent the natural world accurately, learned how to put space and distance in their paintings. This had been missing in the flatter, two-dimensional works of the medieval period.

The Catholic Church

By 1400, the Church had become wealthy, worldly – and corrupt. The Renaissance directly challenged what was left of Church authority, because it emphasized the importance of enquiry. Churchmen ignored any suggestion of reform as, for the first time, cartoons circulated that made fun of the Church and its inability to cope with new ideas.

Interior of San Lorenzo Cathedral, Tuscany, Italy

Spread of learning

For centuries, the Church controlled art and learning in Europe. When the Renaissance started, there was an explosion of new ideas and inventions – one of which was printing. For the first time in history, printed books spread the ideas of thinkers and scholars from Italy to people all over Europe. Wealthy rulers such as Lorenzo de' Medici built fabulous libraries – some of which were in cathedrals – to house these books.

Cartoon of the Church, 1497

Humanism

As the Renaissance spread, northern European scholars developed humanism, a philosophy that greatly valued human dignity and moral values. The first humanists were passionate Christians. They studied the classics (ancient Latin, Greek, and Hebrew texts) and revolutionized education by teaching the humanities (moral philosophy, grammar, history, rhetoric, and poetry) instead of just learning the Bible by heart.

Desiderius Erasmus

The humanist movement in Europe affected Germany, Holland, and England. Erasmus (c.1468–1536) was a brilliant Dutch humanist, who led the revival of learning. He became famous through his religious translations and writings, in which he gently and humorously called for peaceful reform in the Church.

Erasmus by Holbein

Sir Thomas More

England's leading scholar Sir Thomas More (1477–1535) was a humanist. His book, *Utopia*, argued that all political and social evils would be cured by the common ownership of land, the education of both women and men, and religious tolerance. King Henry VIII had More executed for refusing to recognize him as head of the reformed English Church.

Thomas More's *Utopia*, 1516

Education

Humanists felt that people shaped their own destiny, and that Greek and Roman texts illustrated this. Therefore English humanist educators, such as Sir John Cheke (1514–57) and Nicholas Udall (1505–56), encouraged children to study the classics so they learned how to serve their society for the common good.

Humanists believed in education for women and men.

La scuola di Signor Buonoventura

The Field of the Cloth of Gold, 1520

Henry VIII

Joust and trials of strength

All tents were embossed with gold and velvet.

Henry VIII built a temporary palace.

Renaissance princes

As the Renaissance progressed, rulers became more sophisticated and ruthless. The political writer Niccolò Machiavelli (1469–1527) described the art of statecraft (methods used by a successful ruler to stay in power) in his book, *The Prince* (1532). He formed many of his theories by comparing his own Italian society with that of ancient Rome.

Francis I

King Francis I of France (r.1515–47) regarded himself as a perfect Renaissance prince. An able, quick-witted man, he loved art and learning and was the patron of geniuses such as Leonardo da Vinci and Benvenuto Cellini (1500–91). In June 1520, he vied with the era's other great Renaissance prince, Henry VIII of England, at a magnificent summit meeting at the Field of the Cloth of Gold near Calais, France.

Patronage

As artists' status rose during the Renaissance, rich rulers and noble families were glad to act as their patrons, giving them financial security while they produced their great works. The Florentine Medici family were the patrons of great artists such as Michelangelo.

Artemisia Gentileschi

The Medici of Florence

The Medici banking family rose to power in the early Renaissance and contributed much to the flowering of the arts. They made Florence an artistic and cultural centre – all of the great artists went there. Even those who were not patronized by the Medici, such as the Tuscan portraitist Artemisia Gentileschi (c.1590–1642), went to Florence to make contacts and improve their skills.

Albrecht Dürer

Dürer (1471–1528) from Germany was one of the greatest Renaissance artists. One of 18 children, Dürer was apprenticed to a painter and book illustrator at 15 years old. After four years Dürer began to travel around Europe, and picked up new ideas from other artists, including Bellini and Raphael. A true Renaissance man who mastered many subjects from Latin to mathematics, he is mainly remembered for his exquisite engravings and wood block prints.

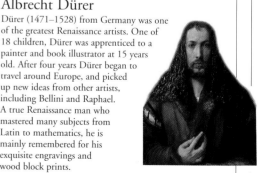

FIND OUT MORE

ART, HISTORY OF · GALILEO · GREECE, ANCIENT · EXPLORATION · LEONARDO DA VINCI · PHILOSOPHY · PRINTING · ROMAN EMPIRE · SCIENCE, HISTORY OF

REPRODUCTION

LIKE ALL LIVING THINGS, humans have to reproduce to ensure the survival of the species. Reproduction is the job of the reproductive system. The female reproductive system lies mainly within the body, while much of the male reproductive system is outside the body. Both systems produce special cells called sex cells. Male and female sex cells are brought together following sexual intercourse. If male and female sex cells meet, they fuse during fertilization into a single cell, which develops into a new human being made up of billions of cells.

Female reproductive system

- Ovary produces ova.
- Fallopian tube carries ova towards uterus.
- Urethra
- Labia minora
- Clitoris
- Labia majora
- Spine
- Uterus is the organ in which baby develops.
- Uterine muscle can expand.
- Cervix is the opening to uterus.
- Vagina leads from uterus to the outside.
- Vaginal opening

Male reproductive system

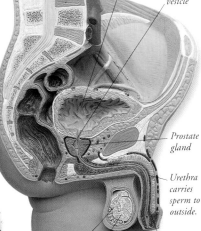

- Bladder
- Seminal vesicle
- Prostate gland
- Urethra carries sperm to outside.
- Epididymis is a coiled tube in which sperm matures.
- Testis is site of sperm production.
- Penis becomes erect during sexual intercourse.

Sperm

Sperm, or spermatozoa, are the male sex cells. Each sperm is about 0.05 mm (0.002 in) long and consists of an oval head containing a nucleus, a midpiece, and a tail. Sperm are produced in the testes of adult men. On average, a man produces about 300 million sperm every day.

- Head
- Tail propels sperm forwards.

Ova

Ova, or eggs, are the female sex cells. Each ovum is a rounded cell, with a nucleus, about 0.1 mm (0.004 in) in diameter. After puberty, an ovum matures each month and is released from an ovary. This is called ovulation.

An ovum emerging from an ovary

Reproductive systems

In a man, sperm are produced in the testes, nurtured by semen produced in the prostate gland and seminal vesicles, and released from the penis during sexual intercourse. In a woman, ova are released singly from the ovary, travel along the fallopian tube to the uterus, and, if fertilized, develop into a baby.

Menstrual cycle

The menstrual cycle is a series of changes that takes place in a woman's reproductive system each month. The menstrual cycle lasts about 28 days, and ovulation (part of the ovarian cycle) takes place around day 14. If the ovum is not fertilized, the uterus lining is shed through the vagina. This is called a period.

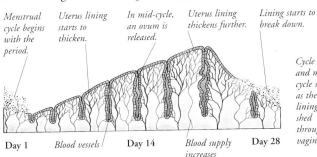

- Menstrual cycle begins with the period.
- Uterus lining starts to thicken.
- In mid-cycle, an ovum is released.
- Uterus lining thickens further.
- Lining starts to break down.
- Cycle ends and new cycle starts as the uterus lining is shed through the vagina.
- Day 1
- Blood vessels
- Day 14
- Blood supply increases
- Day 28

Contraception

Contraception, or birth control, means preventing pregnancy. Types of contraceptive include barrier methods, such as the condom and diaphragm, that prevent sperm from reaching an egg; and hormonal methods, such as the contraceptive pill, that prevent ovulation occurring.

- Contraceptive pills
- Contraceptive pessaries are used with a diaphram.
- A diaphragm is inserted into the vagina.
- Condom

Sexual intercourse

During sexual intercourse, a man pushes his erect penis into his partner's vagina. When he ejaculates, semen carrying millions of sperm spurts into the vagina. The sperm swim into the uterus and to the fallopian tubes, where fertilization may take place. The period from fertilization to implantation is conception.

Fertilization

Fertilization is the joining together of a sperm and an ovum. If an ovum is in the fallopian tube, thousands of sperm cluster around it, trying to break through its outer covering. One sperm succeeds.

Fertilization and implantation

2 Forty-eight hours after fertilization, the fertilized egg has divided into four. From now on, the cells divide about twice a day.

3 Seventy-two hours after fertilization, the egg has become a ball of 64 cells.

4 On about the sixth day, the ball of cells implants in the uterus.

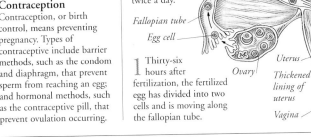

- Fallopian tube
- Egg cell

1 Thirty-six hours after fertilization, the fertilized egg has divided into two cells and is moving along the fallopian tube.

- Ovary
- Uterus
- Thickened lining of uterus
- Vagina

Implantation

The fertilized ovum develops into a hollow ball of cells called a blastocyst. At this stage it is ready to burrow into the lining of the uterus and become an embryo. The embryo will develop into a foetus and then into a baby.

Pregnancy

Pregnancy is the time taken for a baby to develop inside a woman's uterus. It begins with conception and ends with birth. On average, pregnancy lasts for 40 weeks. The woman's abdomen gradually swells as the foetus grows inside it. The foetus receives nutrition and oxygen from the mother via the placenta, a flat organ attached to the uterus lining. It floats protected in a liquid called amniotic fluid, linked to the placenta by the umbilical cord.

Infertility

Infertility means the inability in a man or a woman to have a baby. It can be treated in many cases. One treatment is in vitro fertilization (IVF). This involves removing eggs from a woman's ovaries, fertilizing them outside her body with sperm, and returning them to the uterus to develop.

Donated semen is stored in a laboratory.

Margaret Sanger

American Margaret Sanger (1883–1966) was a pioneer of contraception. She believed birth control was vitally important to improve the poor's living standards. In 1916, she opened a birth information centre and was arrested. After her release, she continued to campaign.

Fertilized egg

The fertilized ovum, or egg, divides rapidly as it travels along the fallopian tube towards the uterus, where it will implant.

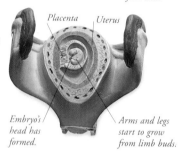

Egg has divided twice, producing four cells.

Embryo at 6 weeks

The embryo is now just 6 mm (0.25 in) long. Its digestive, blood, and nervous systems are developing, and the heart has started to beat. The beginnings of the ears, eyes, and mouth appear, as do the limb buds from which arms and legs will grow.

Placenta *Uterus*

Embryo's head has formed.

Arms and legs start to grow from limb buds.

Twins

There are two types of twins, identical twins and non-identical twins. Non-identical twins result when two eggs are released at the same time and are then fertilized by two different sperm. Identical twins develop from just one egg and are much rarer. Having more than two babies is rarer still.

Identical twins

Identical twins are produced when a fertilized egg divides into two separate cells, each of which develops into a foetus. Both foetuses share the same placenta. Because they develop from a single fertilized egg, identical twins share exactly the same genes and are always the same sex.

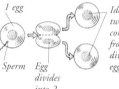

1 egg
Identical twins come from 1 divided egg.
Sperm *Egg divides into 2.*

Foetus at 12 weeks

At 12 weeks, the developing baby, now known as a foetus, is about 7.5 cm (3 in) long. It resembles a human being. Fingers and toes have formed, and the mouth opens and closes and can suck. The ears and eyelids are present. The external genitals have formed, and the foetus passes urine into the amniotic fluid.

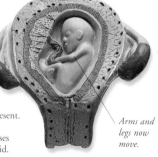

Uterus enlarges as baby grows during pregnancy.

Arms and legs now move.

Muscles of uterus will contract to push baby out.

Amniotic sac is filled with amniotic fluid.

Lining of uterus

Placenta

Blood vessels

Umbilical cord connects baby to placenta.

Labour

The sequence of events by which the baby is pushed out of the uterus is known as labour. It has three stages. Changes in the mother's hormone levels start labour. In the first stage, the uterus starts to contract and the cervix widens. In the second stage, the baby is born. Finally, the placenta is pushed out.

Foetus at 16 weeks

At 16 weeks, the foetus is about 15 cm (6 in) long. The foetus is now fully formed with all its organs in place, and it starts to grow and mature rapidly. The bones are starting to develop, and the muscles are getting stronger.

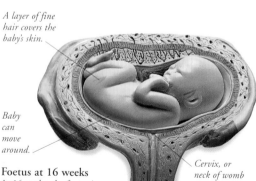

A layer of fine hair covers the baby's skin.

Baby can move around.

Cervix, or neck of womb

Baby's brain is well developed.

Foetus at 28 weeks

The foetus is about 37 cm (14.5 in) long, and almost fully mature. During the remaining weeks of pregnancy the foetus will grow plumper as fat builds up. If born prematurely at this stage, the baby could survive in an incubator.

Baby usually settles into an upside-down position, ready to be born headfirst.

Mucus plug blocks cervix during pregnancy.

Birth

During birth, the muscles in the wall of the uterus contract very strongly. The baby is pushed through the open cervix and into the vagina from which it emerges, normally headfirst. Once outside the body, the baby takes its first breaths. The doctor or midwife cuts the umbilical cord.

FIND OUT MORE   BIOLOGY   GENETICS   GROWTH AND DEVELOPMENT   HORMONES AND ENDOCRINE SYSTEM   HUMAN BODY   MEDICINE   MUSCLES AND MOVEMENT   PLANTS, REPRODUCTION

R

REPTILES

THE RULING AGE OF THE REPTILES was the dinosaur age, about 200 million years ago, but most modern reptiles evolved much more recently. Dinosaurs and other early reptiles evolved from amphibians that moved onto land and did not need water to breed. There are more than 6,000 species of reptile today. They have dry skin covered with scales or shields that prevent water loss. They reproduce with internal fertilization, and lay eggs from which the young hatch looking like their parents.

Crest makes the water dragon more imposing.

Large eyes provide excellent vision.

Tip of the tail has regrown after it was lost, maybe to a predator.

Tail is used for balance when running, as a rudder when swimming, and as a weapon for defence.

Powerful legs for running and climbing

Thai water dragon
The water dragon is a type of lizard from Thailand. It lives mainly in trees near water. When on the ground, it may stand up on its hind legs and run along upright for short distances to escape predators. It then climbs a tree or jumps in water and swims.

Thai water dragon

What is a reptile?
Reptiles are cold-blooded vertebrates (animals with a backbone). They are creatures that crawl, their name coming from the Latin *repto*, meaning "to crawl". They breathe using lungs, and are found in most habitats in the world except cold regions and high mountains. In temperate regions they survive winter by hibernating.

Reptile groups

There are four groups of reptiles – tortoises and turtles, snakes and lizards, crocodilians, and tuataras. Experts disagree about how closely related they are. Some think turtles and tortoises are far removed from other orders, and that crocodilians are more closely related to birds than other reptiles.

Tortoise skeleton cut in half.

Leopard tortoise

Tortoises and turtles
There are more than 270 species of these hard-shelled reptiles, which have existed, almost unchanged, for about 200 million years. Tortoises live on land, while turtles live in fresh water or oceans. The hard shell is growing bone attached to the animal's backbone and ribs. It is covered with shields made of keratin.

Marine iguana

Python skeleton

Burmese rock python

Tuataras
The two species of tuatara are the last survivors of the beak-headed reptiles, most of which became extinct 200 million years ago. The tuataras live on remote rocky islands off the coast of New Zealand. They are active mostly at night, feeding on insects.

Crocodilians cool off by submerging in water.

Spectacled caiman

Crocodilians
This group contains more than 20 species – crocodiles, alligators, caimans, the gharial, and the false gharial. They are survivors from the Jurassic Age of the dinosaurs.

Reptiles at sea
Ocean-going reptiles – sea turtles, the saltwater crocodile, sea snakes, and the marine iguana – are adapted to marine life. They have glands that excrete excess salt, and a powerful heart that maintains circulation during deep, rapid dives.

Snakes and lizards
The largest group of reptiles is divided into three suborders: snakes, lizards, and worm lizards. They have scales as opposed to the shields of turtles and leathery skin of crocodiles, and are the most recently evolved reptiles.

Skin and scales

The type of skin provides clues to a reptile's life. Tiny geckoes have thin, papery skin; skinks and other lizards and snakes have overlapping scales that allow easy movement through leaf-litter or up trees. Tortoises have warty skin on the head, tail, and legs – the parts that protrude from the shell. Crocodilians have leathery skin.

Caiman
The skin is thick and leathery. There may be extra toughened areas under the skin.

Chameleon
The texture of the skin is rough and granular. It can change colour.

Skink
Small smooth scales help skinks to burrow easily into sand or leaf-litter.

Plated lizard
The scales are large, plate-like, and protective. They allow flexibility.

Python
This snake has small scales on top, and large overlapping belly scales.

Growing new parts

Like insects, reptiles shed, or slough, their skin as they grow. Some reptiles also have the ability to lose parts of the body voluntarily to escape predators. For example, some lizards lose their tails. The lost part will regrow in a process known as regeneration.

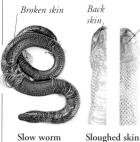

Broken skin

Back skin

Belly skin

Most recent links are nearest the body.

Slow worm sloughing

Sloughed skin of a rat snake

New skin

As snakes and lizards grow, the external layer of their skin gets too small. When a new layer has developed underneath, they slough the old skin, which comes off inside-out. A large meal that causes sudden growth or scar damage will also promote skin sloughing.

New rattles

When a rattlesnake sloughs its skin, the bit at the tip of the tail remains and adds a link to the rattle. Since rattles get damaged, and sloughing is not regular, the number of links does not indicate a snake's age.

New tail built on cartilage rather than bone.

New tail

Many lizards lose their tails on purpose to avoid predators. The lizard tenses its tail muscles, and the tail fractures and breaks off. The piece of tail often wiggles to attract the predator away from the escaping lizard.

1 This skink voluntarily sheds its tail to avoid being eaten and so save its life. The blood vessels in the tail stump have healed to prevent the lizard from losing blood. A new tail will begin to regenerate soon.

2 The new tail is simple. It lacks the complex scales of the original, and its colour and patterning will be more basic. Inside, the bony vertebrae have been replaced by a tube of cartilage.

Simple new tail regenerating from the old stump.

New tail is fully developed but lacks original colour and pattern.

3 The tail has grown to its original length. The ability for tail regeneration will diminish as the lizard gets older.

Breeding

Most reptiles lay eggs. The developing young inside absorb moisture and oxygen through the shell and feed on the yolk. The shells are usually soft and flexible, although some eggs have a hard shell. Some lizards and snakes give birth to fully formed "live" young.

Incubation

Female cornsnakes lay about 12 soft-shelled eggs. They play no part in their incubation, which takes about two months. Female pythons, on the other hand, incubate their eggs in their coils. King cobras build and guard a nest.

Hatchling is alert to danger.

Hatchling cornsnake has a different pattern from adults.

1 A cornsnake is ready to hatch. It makes a slit in the eggshell with a tooth called an egg tooth at the front of its upper jaw.

2 The head emerges, and the hatchling takes its first breath of air. The tiny snake rests frequently and is wary of danger.

3 The hatchling emerges slowly and flicks its sensitive tongue to taste its surroundings. Any movement, and it will retreat into the shell.

4 Following a disturbance, this hatchling retreated inside the egg for almost 24 hours. It eventually emerged through a new slit in the shell. Hatchlings may make several slits in the shell before leaving the egg.

5 Once free of the egg, the hatchling cornsnake is on its own. It will be sustained for 10 days by the egg yolk it absorbed in the shell, and will shed its skin before hunting lizards and baby mice.

Live young

Boas, such as this boa constrictor, and many vipers are born live. The young are born in a membranous sac that breaks soon after birth. This method of reproduction is ideal for reptiles in colder climates, where eggs would not survive.

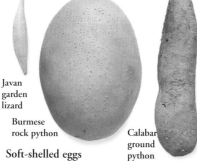

Javan garden lizard

Burmese rock python

Calabar ground python

Soft-shelled eggs

Snakes and many lizards have soft-shelled eggs. These reptiles have soft mouth parts that could not break a hard eggshell. Soft-shelled eggs vary in shape but are often oval or elongated, and may be pockmarked or discoloured.

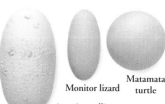

Monitor lizard

Matamata turtle

American alligator

Hard-shelled eggs

Tortoises, turtles, crocodilians, and some lizards have hard-shelled eggs. They survive dry conditions better than soft-shelled eggs but are more fragile. They are laid in a nest or underground for protection.

Reptiles in danger

Many reptiles are threatened with extinction because of trade in their body parts. Snake, lizard, and crocodile skins are used for bags, shoes, and belts; turtle shells become ornaments or combs; turtle meat is used for soup; snake gall or blood is used in Oriental medicine.

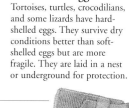

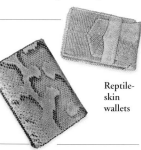

Reptile-skin wallets

FIND OUT MORE   AMPHIBIANS   CONSERVATION   CROCODILES   DINOSAURS   EGGS   LIZARDS   SNAKES   TURTLES AND TORTOISES

R

RHINOCEROSES AND TAPIRS

RHINOS' HUGE HORNS and massive bulk make them intimidating animals. There are five species of rhino: two from Africa and three from Asia. All have poor eyesight but rely on their good sense of smell and acute hearing to detect danger. Other animals help warn of danger – the oxpecker, a bird that feeds on ticks on a rhino's skin, will screech if danger threatens. Rhinos enjoy wallowing in mud pools. This covers their skin in mud to keep them cool and protects them from tormenting insects. Tapirs are related to rhinos. They are good swimmers and spend much of their time in water.

Feeding
The great Indian and white rhinos graze on grass but the Sumatran, Javan, and black rhinos browse on twigs and leaves. The black rhino uses its prehensile lip to grasp branches and strip them of their leaves and shoots.

Black rhinoceros
The black, or hook-lipped, rhino from Africa is a large, aggressive animal that will readily charge anything that invades its territory. It has very thick, tough, hairless skin and two large horns made of the substance keratin. It uses its prehensile (grasping) upper lip to feed on twigs.

Horn

Nostril

Prehensile lip grasps hold of branch.

Thick, stocky legs

Hooves

Thick, grey skin

Rhino horns
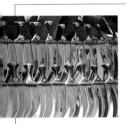
Rhinos have been heavily hunted for their horns and all but the white rhino are endangered. The horns are believed to have magical or medical properties. They are also carved into items such as dagger handles.

Types of rhino

Great Indian rhino
This quiet animal lives in India and Nepal. It has deep skin folds that look like armour plating. Both sexes have a single horn.

Large, single horn

Javan rhino
The Javan rhino is a very rare animal. The few survivors live in a reserve in Java. It has a prehensile upper lip. The males have a single small horn; females are hornless.

Small head

Sumatran rhino
This is the smallest rhino and is very rare. It lives in the forests of Southeast Asia and feeds on twigs and leaves. It differs from all other rhinos by having a hairy coat when young.

Fold in skin   Two horns

Large shoulder hump

White rhino
The white, or square-lipped, rhino from Africa is the largest of the rhinos. It has a long head and two horns. It is slightly paler than the black rhino.

Wide jaw

Reproduction
Female black rhinos are ready to breed at 3½–4 years old, and males at 6 years. After a 15-month gestation period, a single calf is born, weighing about 22 kg (48 lb). Within a few minutes of birth, it struggles to its feet to hunt for its mother's teats and takes its first drink. The calf is weaned at one year, but remains close to its mother for at least another year.

Young rhino suckling

Tufts on ears

Dried mud from a mud wallow

Large nostrils

Tapirs
There are four species of tapir, three of which live in the rainforests of South and Central America; the fourth lives in Southeast Asia. Tapirs are shy, solitary animals who prefer to come out at night. The snout is elongated into a flexible proboscis that they use for feeding on shoots, twigs, leaves, and water plants.

Thin coat of short hairs

Long, flexible snout

Hooves

Brazilian tapir

Territory
The black rhino lives in a restricted area, or "home range", of several square kilometres. The home range overlaps with that of other rhinos; they all share the same feeding grounds, watering places, tracks, and wallows, but otherwise live independently. The black rhino's way of life, behaviour, and habits are adapted to remaining in one place. Even in a severe drought it will not leave its home to find water elsewhere. To warn off other bulls, rhinos may mark out their territory by squirting showers of urine.

Black rhino scent marking.

BLACK RHINOCEROS

SCIENTIFIC NAME	*Diceros bicornis*
ORDER	Perissodactyla
FAMILY	Rhinocerotidae
DISTRIBUTION	Africa south of the Sahara
HABITAT	Thorn scrub and grassland savannahs
DIET	Leaves, buds, twigs, and small branches from various shrubs and trees
SIZE	Height at shoulder: 1.7 m (5.6 ft); weight: up to 1,300 kg (2,870 lb); maximum recorded horn length: 1.36 m (4.5 ft)
LIFESPAN	Up to 40 years

FIND OUT MORE

AFRICAN WILDLIFE   ASIAN WILDLIFE   GRASSLAND WILDLIFE   CONSERVATION   MAMMALS   RAINFOREST WILDLIFE   SOUTH AMERICAN WILDLIFE

RIVERS

WHEREVER THERE IS ENOUGH RAIN rivers form, flowing down from the mountains to the sea or lakes. A river is a natural channel in which water flows downhill. Typically, it begins as a trickle high up in the hills. As it runs downhill, rainwater flows in from the surrounding landscape and the water swells, first into a stream and then into a broad river. Aided by sand, boulders, and other debris carried in the water, a channel is carved out from the rock. The river eventually forms a valley and finally, as it nears the sea, a broad plain. A river often winds across this plain in a chain of elaborate loops, which are called meanders.

River types

Rivers may be permanent geographical features or seasonal, dependent upon rains to keep them flowing. In wet seasons or after snow melts, a river may rise so much that it floods the land.

Ephemeral
In deserts and their margins, or on porous rock, a river flows ephemerally, or intermittently. It dries up when there is no rain, leaving behind a gulch, or wadi.

Perennial
In wet areas, rivers are usually perennial – that is, they run throughout the year. A steady flow of groundwater lets the river flow between rainstorms.

River features

In its upper level, a river is small and often tumbles down over rapids and waterfalls. Further downstream, it becomes wider as tributaries bring in more water and silt. Typically, as it nears the sea, it flows across a broad plain formed by silt that is spread across the land in times of flood. It may split into branches, forming a delta, or flow into a wide estuary.

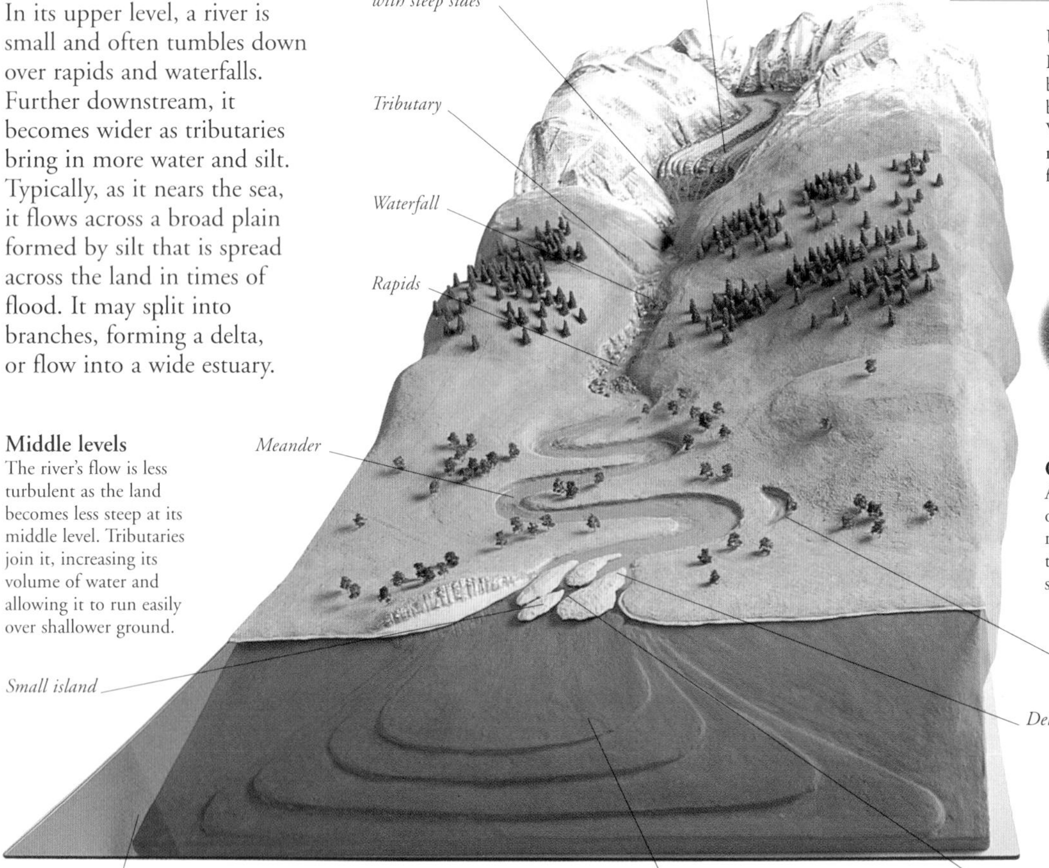

V-shaped valley with steep sides

Glacier

Tributary

Waterfall

Rapids

Meander

Small island

Sea

Deposited sediment

Upper levels
In its upper reaches, a river may wind between a series of hills. Valleys formed by the river are narrow and steep-sided. Water is often slowed by the rough riverbed, though there may be fast flowing rapids and waterfalls.

Oxbow lake
As a river wears away the outside bend of a meander, it makes the meander's neck narrower. Eventually it breaks through the neck, cutting the meander off and stranding the water in an oxbow lake.

Oxbow lake

Delta

Distributary

Middle levels
The river's flow is less turbulent as the land becomes less steep at its middle level. Tributaries join it, increasing its volume of water and allowing it to run easily over shallower ground.

Lower levels
By the time it reaches its lower levels, the river has widened enormously. The steeper valleys of its upper and middle sections give way to wider floodplains, often finishing in an estuary or delta.

Deltas
As a river meets the sea, its flow abruptly slows down. As a result, it may drop its load of sediment in a huge fan of deposits called a delta, and split into many branches or distributaries. Arcuate deltas have a curved arc-shaped coastline. Bird's foot deltas have a ragged coast, shaped a little like a bird's foot.

Chickahominy River, USA

Estuaries
As a river flows into the sea, it often widens, forming a broad inlet called an estuary. Water from the river may become muddy, as salt water from the sea causes small particles of clay in the fresh river water to clump together. This material sinks to the riverbed, causing sediment build-up, and aids the formation of deltas.

Blackwater estuary, UK

Waterfalls

On its course, a river will sometimes wear away soft rock on the riverbed, leaving a sill of hard rock above it. Water falls off this shelf to the soft rock below, forming a waterfall. Rocks and boulders swirl at the base of the waterfall, carving out a deep trough known as a plunge pool.

Rapids

In its upper realms, a river often tumbles over rocky sections that are strewn with boulders. The rocks at this point may be so hard that they are worn away slowly by the river. The slope of the river may be so steep that the river rushes down very quickly and forms rapids.

Hard rock is worn away slowly.

Flow of river is turbulent.

Rapids

Plunge pool

Soft rock is being worn away quickly.

Rocky riverbed

Loads

The material carried by a river is called its load. There are three main types of load. The bedload is stones and other large particles that wash along the riverbed. The suspended load is small particles that float in the water. The solute load is fine material that has dissolved in the water.

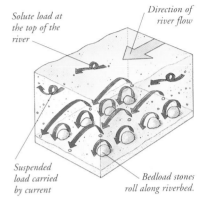

Solute load at the top of the river

Direction of river flow

Suspended load carried by current

Bedload stones roll along riverbed.

Stream erosion

Rivers wear away their channels in several ways. Hydraulic action is wear caused by the pressure of moving water; this loosens parts of the riverbed and bank. However, most of the wear is caused by abrasion; this is wear caused by boulders and pebbles grinding away the riverbed.

River water sources

All water flowing in rivers comes from snow and rain, but it reaches a river in a variety of ways. Some comes directly from over the ground, but most emerges from underground springs after it has been filtered through the ground. In mountain regions, rivers may emerge from glaciers.

Spring

Like a wet sponge, rock is saturated up to a certain level, called the water table. Where the water table meets the surface, water bubbles out of the ground, forming a spring.

Meltwater

In cold regions, rainwater is frozen up in snow and glaciers for months, years, or even centuries. When conditions warm, the water melts, filling rivers with water.

Mountain spring

Glacier with stream

Water on the land

When rain falls on the land, most soaks into the ground or runs off over the surface; the rest evaporates or is taken up by plants. Water that runs off the surface, called overland flow, gathers into rivulets and eventually into streams. When the rain is heavy, the overland flow may flood across the land, forming a sheet of water called sheetwash.

Catchment area

Scientists divide the landscape into different areas, according to where the water runs. The area that supplies a river with water is called a catchment area. A drainage basin is a region where several rivers flow into one river.

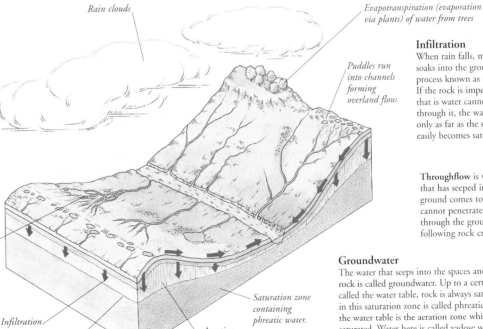

Rain clouds

Evapotranspiration (evaporation via plants) of water from trees

Puddles run into channels forming overland flow.

Sheetwash

Infiltration

Water table

Saturation zone containing phreatic water.

Aeration zone

Infiltration

When rain falls, most of it soaks into the ground – a process known as infiltration. If the rock is impermeable, that is water cannot pass through it, the water infiltrates only as far as the soil, which easily becomes saturated.

Throughflow is when water that has seeped into the ground comes to a layer it cannot penetrate and flows through the ground, following rock cracks.

Groundwater

The water that seeps into the spaces and cracks in rock is called groundwater. Up to a certain level, called the water table, rock is always saturated. Water in this saturation zone is called phreatic water. Above the water table is the aeration zone which is rarely saturated. Water here is called vadose water and is always seeping up or down.

FIND OUT MORE

CLOUDS   COASTS   DESERTS   LAKES   RAIN   ROCKS AND MINERALS   SHIPS AND BOATS   SOIL

R

ROADS

WITHOUT ROADS, it would be difficult to move people and goods around towns and cities, or from one part of the country to another. There have been roads since ancient times, but modern surfaced roads began to be built in the 18th century to speed up horse-drawn carriages carrying mail and passengers. With the invention of the motor car at the end of the 19th century, road building increased rapidly. Today, more roads are built to keep the ever-increasing numbers of cars moving. Environmentalists want road building to stop and more people to use public transport instead of their cars.

Ancient roads

Stone-paved paths and roads were built by many ancient civilizations, including the Chinese and the Mesopotamians. In Europe, the Romans developed a huge road network to speed up the movement of troops through their vast empire. By AD 200, people could travel from Spain to the Far East on roads.

Ancient road at Knossos, Crete

Road network

A road network enables people to get from place to place easily and efficiently. It consists of several different types of road, from urban streets and country lanes to motorways and by-passes (which carry traffic around the edge of a city, avoiding the city centre). Systems of one-way streets help the traffic to flow smoothly during busy periods.

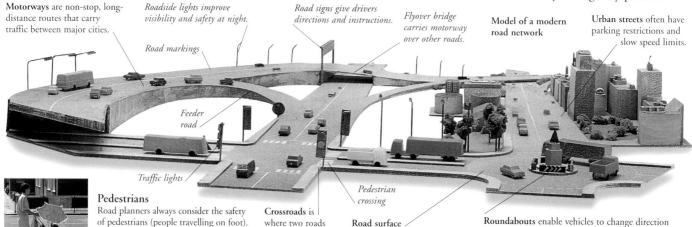

Motorways are non-stop, long-distance routes that carry traffic between major cities.

Roadside lights improve visibility and safety at night.

Road markings

Road signs give drivers directions and instructions.

Flyover bridge carries motorway over other roads.

Model of a modern road network

Urban streets often have parking restrictions and slow speed limits.

Feeder road

Traffic lights

Pedestrian crossing

Pedestrians

Road planners always consider the safety of pedestrians (people travelling on foot). Footpaths, pedestrian crossings, and subways (tunnels under roads) all help pedestrians move around busy streets. Traffic is banned from some city centres.

Crossroads is where two roads meet: the vehicles on one road have to give way to traffic on the other.

Road surface is asphalt or concrete over layers of crushed stone and compressed soil.

Roundabouts enable vehicles to change direction without crossing over other lines of traffic.

Traffic

The vehicles that use roads – such as motorcycles, cars, bicycles, buses, trucks, and even wagons and carts – are together known as traffic. Vehicles usually drive on the right-hand side of the road, but in some countries, such as the UK, Japan, and Australia, they drive on the left.

Road-building machinery in action

Road building

Building a main road is a complex task. It involves creating embankments and cuttings, and levelling the site with bulldozers. Then paving machines lay the road surface, and rollers compress the surface to make it smooth. Other machines may be used to build bridges and tunnels.

Traffic controls

In busy streets, surveillance cameras monitor the flow of traffic. Road markings and signs help to control traffic by directing vehicles into the correct lanes, showing how fast they may travel, and warning of hazards ahead. Traffic lights at crossroads tell drivers when to stop and go.

Traffic jams

The number of vehicles on the world's roads is rising rapidly. In every major city, traffic jams form in the rush hours as people travel to and from work. Such congestion wastes time and creates pollution as cars stand with their engines running.

Services

At regular intervals on major roads there are service areas where travellers can eat and rest during long journeys. Every service area has a petrol station, so that drivers can buy fuel and check the oil in their engines or the air pressure in their tyres.

Unsurfaced roads

Tarmac or concrete road surfaces allow rainwater to run off the road quickly, preventing erosion and damage. However, some dirt roads have no such protective surface. They are fine when it is dry, but during wet weather they become rutted and may even be washed away completely.

Unsurfaced dirt road, Mbuji-Mayi, Zaïre

FIND OUT MORE   BRIDGES   CARS AND TRUCKS   CITIES   POLLUTION   ROMAN EMPIRE   TRANSPORT, HISTORY OF   TRAVEL   TUNNELS

ROBOTS

ROBOTS PLAY AN EVER-INCREASING role in our world. Many people tend to think of robots as the walking, talking, human-like creations portrayed in science-fiction movies. However, a robot is in fact a mute, automatic machine, with electronic brains programmed to carry out specific tasks. Most robots are used in industry. For example, nuclear scientists use robots to handle radioactive materials. In the 1980s, scientists also began to research the use of robots in routine medical surgery.

Science-fiction robots
The first science-fiction robot was introduced in the play *Rossum's Universal Robots*, written by Czech playwright Karel Capek in 1921. The theme of human-like robots was developed in the 1926 film *Metropolis*, which featured the divine Maria. More recent film-goers would probably recognize the comedy couple C3PO and R2D2 from the *Star Wars* films. C3PO was an android, while R2D2 was more functionally built – its job was to carry out repairs on spacecraft.

Human-like Maria from film *Metropolis*

Uses of robots

Robots are most often used in difficult or dangerous situations to carry out tasks people wish to avoid. Many factories use robots on the production line, because they are unaffected by noise, heat, and fumes in the workplace. Robots are also used by security forces in bomb disposal operations and in handling dangerous materials. Space probes are robots used to explore other planets.

Bomb disposal
A mobile robot like this is used by bomb disposal experts to check suspect objects. It is radio-controlled and moves on crawler tracks. It has TV-camera eyes and an adjustable arm with a grab attached for gripping.

Industrial robots
The car industry is a major user of robots for welding car components (right), and spraying paint. The robot is programmed to carry out its tasks quickly and accurately.

Robot explorers
Space is a hostile place for humans to explore, but it suits robots involved in exploration. In 1976, American scientists sent two Viking probes to carry out a study of the planet Mars, and search for signs of life.

The gripper acts like a human hand to grip tools and objects.

The arm can pivot up and down and also extend telescopically in and out.

Elbow joint

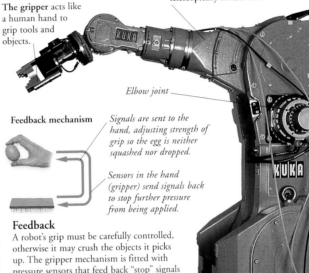

Feedback mechanism

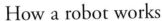

Signals are sent to the hand, adjusting strength of grip so the egg is neither squashed nor dropped.

Sensors in the hand (gripper) send signals back to stop further pressure from being applied.

Air lines feed compressed air to motors that move the joints.

Feedback
A robot's grip must be carefully controlled, otherwise it may crush the objects it picks up. The gripper mechanism is fitted with pressure sensors that feed back "stop" signals to the control centre when the required pressure is reached.

Swivel joints allow the robot to rotate in a circle.

How a robot works

A typical industrial robot is a one-armed machine with flexible joints equivalent to the human shoulder, elbow, and wrist. It has a gripping mechanism that works as a hand. The robotic arm swivels on its supporting base, and may be moved electrically or pneumatically, by using compressed air. All movements are controlled by the robot's computer brain.

Isaac Asimov
Science fiction writer Isaac Asimov (1920–96) proposed three laws of robotics to allay fears that one day robots could "take over". These are as follows: a robot must not harm people, or allow them to come to any harm; robots must obey their orders, unless this conflicts with the first law; and a robot must protect itself, unless this conflicts with the other laws.

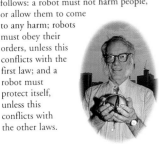

The future

As research into robotics continues, more versatile and user-friendly robots are being developed. Three-dimensional vision and increased sensitivity enable industrial robots to carry out more routine jobs, while advances in artificial intelligence will give robots more independence to solve problems as they arise.

Experimenting with human nerve cells on surface of silicon chip

Artificial intelligence
The aim of artificial intelligence (AI) is to develop machines that can think and learn, and interact with humans without having to be pre-programmed.

Robots in the home
Robots are good at performing simple, repetitive tasks that people find boring, such as washing-up and cleaning. However, such household jobs are actually quite complicated when broken down. Research is being carried out to make more sophisticated robots that have independent movement and careful co-ordination of "mind", "eyes", and "hands".

FIND OUT MORE

CARS AND TRUCKS · COMPUTERS · FILMS AND FILM-MAKING · INFORMATION TECHNOLOGY · SPACE EXPLORATION · TECHNOLOGY

ROCK AND POP

DURING THE 1950S, a new kind of popular music – rock and roll – developed in the United States. It was loud, raucous, and exciting, and soon became popular around the world. Rock, as it is now called, developed from various sources and has influenced most subsequent popular music. Pop music, once just an abbreviated term for all popular music, is now also a recognized musical style. Rock and pop music have been closely linked with the rise of youth culture. They are also big business: record companies make great profits from successful bands.

Early influences
Popular music in the early 20th century included the blues, jazz, and ballads associated with Tin Pan Alley in New York, USA, where music publishers worked. Modern music inherited elements of these styles. The blues influenced rock and roll; the songwriting traditions of Tin Pan Alley continue in many of today's melodic pop songs.

Blues performer Leadbelly

Rock and roll in the 1950s

In the early 1950s, blues musicians in the USA discovered the powerful sounds of the new, electrically amplified instruments. These led to the growth of a new kind of music – rhythm-and-blues.

Rhythm-and-blues
Unlike the traditional blues, rhythm-and-blues was fast-paced and exciting, stressing the rhythm of the music. Performed by black musicians, it soon became popular dance music. Its greatest performers were the Americans Muddy Waters (1915–83), Howlin' Wolf (1910–76), and Chuck Berry (b. 1926).

Muddy Waters

Teenagers
During the 1950s, teenagers on both sides of the Atlantic began to create their own culture. Rock and roll, with its rebellious image, was their music. Record companies exploited this market, promoting songs about first love, trouble with parents, or tragically early death.

Rock and roll dance was exuberant.

Bill Haley

Rock and roll
When US record companies saw the popularity of rhythm-and-blues, which had begun with black musicians, they brought in white players to sell the music across white America. The music, known as rock and roll, combined rhythm-and-blues with white country music traditions. Bill Haley and His Comets had the first rock and roll hit with *Rock around the Clock*, released in 1955.

Rock and roll dancers, 1956

Elvis Presley
The American singer Elvis Presley (1935–77) was the greatest rock and roll star of all, selling millions of records. His rich, clear voice and moody good looks made the blues harmonies of his music acceptable to white American audiences.

Sounds of the 1960s

During the 1960s, many young people identified with music that expressed their political opinions, as well as their musical tastes. In the USA, for example, some songs protested against the Vietnam war.

Soul music
Soul music is a development of rhythm-and-blues, which grew during the 1960s. Performed mainly by black musicians, it combines the passion of gospel music with a strong beat. Great soul artists include the American singer Aretha Franklin (b.1942).

Tamla Motown
The influential US record company Tamla Motown scored world-wide success during the 1960s and 1970s by promoting black rhythm-and-blues and soul music. Performers on the label included The Supremes, Stevie Wonder (b.1950), and Ray Charles (b.1930).

Beatles fans, 1964

The Beatles
During the 1960s, rock and roll became known as rock. British bands The Beatles and the Rolling Stones became famous around the world with earthy music that brought an exciting new sound to the rock scene. The Beatles especially attracted hysterical devotion from their young fans.

Reggae
Reggae music developed in Jamaica during the 1960s. It combines elements of US soul with Jamaican and African folk music. It is generally played with an emphasis on the second and fourth beats of the bar, at a relaxed pace. It is closely linked with the Rastafarian religion.

Jamaican musician Bob Marley (1945–81) was a leading reggae artist. While making political protests with his lyrics, he helped make reggae popular around the world.

Diana Ross (b.1944), later a successful solo star

The Supremes: from 1964 to 1969, this all-girl group had 16 top ten hit records in the USA.

Bob Dylan, influential singer and songwriter from the 1960s on

Folk rock
Rock and folk borrowed heavily from each other in the 1960s. The protest songs of Americans Bob Dylan (b. 1941) and Joan Baez (b. 1941) expressed the anti-war feelings of many young people.

R

Disco

In the 1970s disco, a dance music with a thumping beat, became the major force in pop music. It was played on records and tapes, rather than by live performers, in crowded nightclubs called discotheques. Leading disco artists included the British group The Bee Gees and US singer Donna Summer (b.1948).

Saturday Night Fever, a movie about the disco lifestyle made in 1977, featured a score by The Bee Gees.

Trends of the 1970s

Concerts during the 1970s were elaborate events, involving large-scale props and light shows. "Glam rock" took this to its limits, with outlandish stage shows by performers such as the British band T-Rex. Fashions reflected musicians' styles; people wore flared trousers and grew their hair long. The main movements of the 1970s, however, were disco, funk, and punk.

Punks

James Brown

Lyrics in funk music reflected the strengthening black civil rights movement in America.

Funk

In the late 1960s and early 1970s, the US singer James Brown (b.1933) took soul music in a new, aggressively rhythmic direction. The lyrics of the new style, which was called funk, made strong social comments. Other influential funk innovators included the US group Sly and the Family Stone.

Punk

In 1976, punk music appeared in Britain with The Sex Pistols. Punk was loud and distorted: musicians deliberately played their instruments badly, and their lyrics were offensive. Punks wore ripped, dirty clothes to show that they rejected conventional social attitudes.

1980s and on

Pop music in the 1980s was dominated by catchy melodies, simple harmonies, and unchallenging lyrics. Increasingly since the 1980s, bands have used electronically produced sounds in their music; new styles, such as rap, house, and techno, have emerged. In rap, performers speak over music in rapid rhymes, often with a social comment. In house and techno, artists use samples of sounds, beats, and melodies from other records to create a new dance music.

The band De La Soul mix other musicians' work in their recordings.

Vinyl record

Vinyl records and CDs

During the 1980s, sales of compact discs (CDs) overtook sales of vinyl records, because CDs are longer-lasting, easier to keep in good condition, and give a clearer, purer sound.

New technology

Electronic samplers, drum machines, and synthesizers made it possible for dance musicians to isolate and change any tone, beat, or noise, including vocals, from other records, as well as to create their own artificial and unusual sounds, and allowed them to structure their music in surprising new ways.

Electronic music

Much of today's music is made by electronic instruments. When the electronic drum pad, above, is hit with a stick, it produces an electric sound signal that gives an electronic drum sound.

With new computer technology, a musician can arrange many different tracks to achieve an original sound.

Mixing desk, to combine different musical tracks

Music industry

Rock and pop music provides a multi-million pound global market. Performers can make a fortune with just a few chart-topping hits. Music is sold on compact disc, cassette, vinyl, and video. Organizing the marketing and sales of these products is complex and costly. A few major companies dominate the music industry.

Bjork, an Icelandic singer with the One Little Indian label.

Record companies

When a performer has a contract with a record company, the company will promote his or her music, obtain radio airtime, and distribute the records around the world, as well as organize tours and provide recording studios and equipment.

Videos

Videos, short, creative films promoting a record, became widespread in the 1980s. Videos, released at the same time as the song, reach huge television audiences. Good video promotion vastly increases the sales of music.

Concerts

For most bands, live performances are a central part of their music. Famous bands take over vast stadiums to play to tens of thousands of fans. The massive Live Aid concert (1985), in aid of African famine relief, featured many of the best-known singers and bands in the world.

Madonna

By the late 1990s, the US pop singer and songwriter Madonna Ciccone (b.1958) was the biggest-selling female recording artist in the world. She sustained her popularity by constantly developing her image and musical style, and with spectacular, controversial tours.

FIND OUT MORE | BEATLES, THE | CLOTHES AND FASHION | DANCE | JAZZ | MUSIC | MUSICAL INSTRUMENTS | ORCHESTRAS | SOUND | SOUND RECORDING

ROCKETS

GRAVITY KEEPS EARTH'S inhabitants on the planet's surface. A powerful rocket is needed to escape this gravity and to take astronauts, satellites, probes, and other equipment into space. The first rockets were made about a thousand years ago in China, but the first to reach space was the German V2 which, in 1942, achieved a height of 160 km (100 miles). There are two main types of rockets; tall, thin ones which are used only once, and others which return to Earth to be used again. Both are launched pointing up at space and discard their fuel tanks, which fall back to Earth.

Escape velocity

Earth's gravity pulls on a rocket at the launch pad and keeps it on the ground. The rocket needs to move very fast to get away from this pull. When the rocket reaches a velocity of 40,000 kmh (25,000 mph) it can escape the effects of Earth's gravity and enter space. If it fails to reach this velocity, it will be pulled back to Earth.

Rocket's thrust

Earth's gravity

Rocket power

The payload of astronauts or equipment takes up only a small part of the rocket. Most of it contains the fuel needed to launch the rocket into space. Most rockets use liquid fuel with solid fuel for some of its stages.

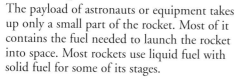

Oxygen tank

Fuel tank

Ignition system

Liquid fuel
The main thrust comes from a mixture of liquid oxygen and fuel (such as liquid hydrogen). The two are stored in separate tanks and ignite when put together. Hot gases are produced which are ejected at high speed, propelling the rocket up and away from the ground.

Solid fuel
Boosters of solid fuel are sometimes used to give extra thrust at liftoff. The fuel burns like a firework starting at one end and working its way up, or from the centre out. The boosters' thrust is short-lived but essential to get the rocket off the ground.

Solid fuel block

Thrust provided by hot exhaust gases escaping through nozzle.

Liquid oxygen and fuel combine in combustion chamber.

Solid fuel starts to burn, releasing exhaust gases into central cavity.

Exhaust gases escape through nozzle to provide thrust.

Ariane-5

The European Space Agency (ESA) launches satellites and probes into space with the *Ariane* series of rockets. The first was launched in 1979: since then, about 90 *Arianes* have been launched from the Guiana Space Centre in Kourou, South America. The latest and most powerful in the series is *Ariane-5*, designed to carry the new generation of heavy satellites into space and also to launch spacecraft with crew aboard. If *Ariane-5* carries crew, Europe will join the Americans and Russians in having rockets that can launch astronauts.

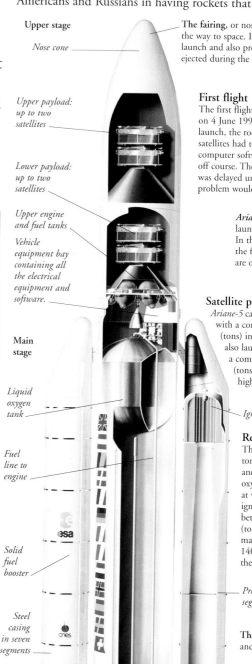

Upper stage

Nose cone

Upper payload: up to two satellites

Lower payload: up to two satellites

Upper engine and fuel tanks

Vehicle equipment bay containing all the electrical equipment and software.

Main stage

Liquid oxygen tank

Fuel line to engine

Solid fuel booster

Steel casing in seven segments

Liquid helium

Vulcain engine

Exhaust duct

The fairing, or nose, of the rocket points the way to space. It has the best shape for launch and also protects the payload. It is ejected during the flight.

First flight
The first flight of *Ariane-5* should have been on 4 June 1996. Less than a minute after launch, the rocket and its payload of four satellites had to be destroyed because a computer software problem sent the rocket off course. The launch of the next *Ariane-5* was delayed until ESA could be sure the problem would not recur.

Ariane-5 is moved to its launchpad 9 hours before liftoff. In the 6 minutes before launch, the final checks and countdown are operated automatically.

Satellite payload
Ariane-5 can launch up to four satellites with a combined weight of 20 tonnes (tons) into orbit close to Earth. It can also launch up to three satellites with a combined weight of 6.8 tonnes (tons) into geosynchronous orbit high above Earth.

Igniter

Rocket main stage
The main stage consists of 25 tonnes (tons) of liquid hydrogen and 130 tonnes (tons) of liquid oxygen stored in separate tanks at very low temperature. Once ignited, they provide thrust of between 114 and 120 tonnes (tons) for 570 seconds. The main stage is jettisoned at about 140 km (90 miles) above the ground.

Propellant-filled segment

The Vulcain engine is ignited and checked before liftoff.

Rocket boosters
At either side of the main body are solid-fuel rocket boosters. Each stands 26.5 m (87 ft) high by 3 m (10 ft) across, and uses 237 tonnes (tons) of fuel to provide 540 tonnes (tons) of thrust for 130 seconds. They are jettisoned 60 km (40 miles) above the ground, but are recovered and used again.

Launch

The countdown for a rocket launch begins long before the engines are ignited. The rocket undergoes a final thorough testing in the hours before launch. Once everything is ready, the engines are ignited. The rocket leaves the ground when the engines have produced enough thrust, and it gathers speed as it moves skyward. The next few minutes are vital. The rocket has to reach escape velocity. Only when the rocket has reached its target orbit can the launch be regarded as successful.

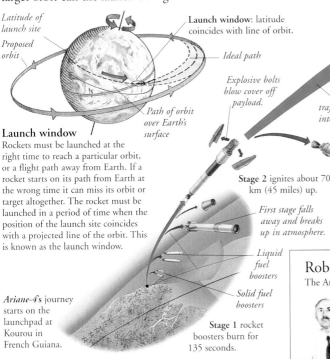

Latitude of launch site

Proposed orbit

Launch window: latitude coincides with line of orbit.

Ideal path

Path of orbit over Earth's surface

Explosive bolts blow cover off payload.

Launch trajectory into space

Launch window
Rockets must be launched at the right time to reach a particular orbit, or a flight path away from Earth. If a rocket starts on its path from Earth at the wrong time it can miss its orbit or target altogether. The rocket must be launched in a period of time when the position of the launch site coincides with a projected line of the orbit. This is known as the launch window.

Stage 2 ignites about 70 km (45 miles) up.

First stage falls away and breaks up in atmosphere.

Second stage falls to Earth. Ariane-4 is now 135 km (85 miles) high and travelling at 5.4 km/sec (3.4 miles/sec).

Liquid fuel boosters

Solid fuel boosters

Ariane-4's journey starts on the launchpad at Kourou in French Guiana.

Stage 1 rocket boosters burn for 135 seconds.

Rocket stages
A rocket can be made of a varying number of stages. Each stage is like a separate rocket with its own fuel and engine. As a rocket moves away from the ground, it rapidly consumes fuel. As the fuel in one stage is used up, its tank is discarded and the fuel in the next stage ignites, carrying the lighter and lighter rocket on its course. The final stage takes the payload to its orbit. Once the satellite or space probe is launched, the rocket's job is over.

Payload

Cylinder contains a second satellite to be launched later.

Satellite ready to be released.

Stage 3 engines ignite and burn for about 12 minutes until *Ariane-4* reaches target orbit.

Protective interstage falls away.

Space shuttle

Since the early 1980s, the US has used a reusable launcher to carry astronauts and equipment into space. It is called the space transportation system, or space shuttle. It has three main parts: the orbiter space plane, two large solid-fuel rocket boosters, and a liquid-fuel tank. The boosters are discarded and fall to Earth where they are collected and used again. When the space shuttle returns to Earth, it glides onto a runway like a plane. After the *Columbia* disaster, the space shuttle program was grounded. It will return in the near future.

Robert Goddard
The American rocket pioneer Robert Goddard (1882–1945) was the first person to launch a liquid-fuel rocket. It was launched on 16 March, 1926 and reached a height of 12.5 m (41 ft). The flight lasted 2.5 seconds.

Ground control

A rocket launch is controlled from Earth. A ground control centre monitors the spacecraft and any equipment launched until the mission is complete. Radio signals from the spacecraft let the control centre know if everything is going to plan. Tracking stations around the world relay the messages to the centre.

Control centre
The Mission Control Center at Houston, USA, monitors all American space shuttle missions. The mission is supported from the moment of rocket ignition until the shuttle is at rest back on Earth.

Launchpad
Some countries have more than one launch site. Other countries have joined together to share a site. By the late 1990s, nine nations had launched rockets into space from their own launch sites. The launch sites are scattered around the globe. As the Earth spins in an anticlockwise direction it can give an extra push to a rocket being launched. Many sites are close to the Equator where this effect is greatest.

Vandenburg — *Plesetsk* — *Kapustin Yar* — *Baikonur* — *Taiyuan* — *Wallops Island* — *Negev* — *Juiquan* — *Xichang* — *Tane-ga-Shima* — *Cape Canaveral* — *Al-Anbar* — *Kagoshima* — *Kourou* — *Equator* — *Hainan* — *San Marco platform* — *Sriharikota*

Timeline

1903 Russian schoolmaster, Konstantin Tsiolkovsky, proposes a liquid-fuel rocket for space.

1926 Robert Goddard launches a liquid-fuel rocket.

1942 *V2* is launched, the first mass-produced long-range rocket.

V2 rocket, 1945

1961 Soviet *Vostok* rocket carries first person into space.

Vostok

1961 *Mercury 3* launches the first American, Alan Shepard, into space.

1968 *Apollo 7* is launched – first time the US *Saturn V* carries a crew.

1970 Japan launches a satellite and becomes the fourth nation with a space rocket.

1981 First reusable spacecraft, the American space shuttle, is launched.

1988 Most powerful rocket ever, *Energia*, carries *Buran* – first Soviet space shuttle – into Earth orbit.

1999 First shuttle reaches International Space Station.

Space shuttle, 1981

FIND OUT MORE — ASTRONAUTS — ATMOSPHERE — FORCE AND MOTION — GRAVITY — MOON — NEWTON, SIR ISAAC — PLANETS — SATELLITES — SPACE EXPLORATION

ROCKS AND MINERALS

ALTHOUGH IT IS OFTEN HIDDEN under vegetation, soil, and water, every centimetre of the Earth's surface is made up of rock. Rocks have formed throughout the Earth's history – the oldest rocks date back 3.9 billion years, almost to the beginning of the Earth – and there are still new rocks forming every day. Rocks come in many sizes, shapes, and colours, but they all have a grainy texture because they are made from crystals of naturally occurring chemicals called minerals. The appearance and properties of each type of rock depend on the minerals it contains.

Formation of rocks

Igneous rocks form as magma – molten rock from the Earth's interior – cools and solidifies. Sedimentary rocks form when thin layers of debris on the seabed are compressed over millions of years. Metamorphic rocks form when old rock is crushed by the movement of the Earth's crust or seared by the heat of magma.

Schist

Metamorphic rocks
A metamorphic rock, such as schist, forms when heat and pressure deep below ground alter the mineral content of an existing rock. This change occurs while the rock is still in its solid state.

Gabbro

Igneous rocks
There are two main kinds of igneous rocks. Intrusive igneous rocks, such as gabbro, form when magma cools under the Earth's surface. Extrusive igneous rocks, such as obsidian, form from magma thrown out of erupting volcanoes in the form of lava.

The rock cycle

Eroded rock particles are carried by wind and deposited to form sand dunes.

River erodes valley floor, carrying rock particles downstream to ocean.

Waterfall erodes (wears away) rock of mountainside.

Glacier erodes rocks and carries rock particles to river.

Magma emerges as lava flows, which solidify to form igneous rock.

Volcano

Rising magma

Light rock particles settle on ocean floor as sediment.

Sandstone

Sedimentary rocks
Most sedimentary rocks, including sandstone, are clastic – that is, made from fragments of eroded rock washed into the sea. Limestone and some other sedimentary rocks are biogenic, which means they are made largely from plant and animal remains.

Compressed sediment layers become cemented together to form sedimentary rock.

Extreme pressure crushes and folds sedimentary rock into new metamorphic rock.

Intense heat of magma transforms the surrounding rock into metamorphic rock.

Mohs' scale of hardness
On this scale, a mineral scratches any mineral with a lower rating (everyday equivalents in brackets).

Magnified rock surface with tiny mineral crystals

Minerals

Some rocks are made of just one mineral; others are a combination of several minerals, perhaps as many as a dozen. About 98 per cent of the rocks in the Earth's crust are made up of silicate minerals, which contain the elements oxygen and silica. Geologists classify minerals into two main groups: silicates and non-silicates.

Identifying minerals
A mineral can be identified by its colour, cleavage and fracture (the way it breaks), lustre (how it reflects light), streak (the colour of the mark it leaves on a white tile), density, hardness, and how it reacts with acids. Mohs' scale compares the hardness of different minerals.

Silicates
There are more than 500 different types of silicate, including garnet, mica, feldspar, olivine, and the gem beryl. Silicates tend to be hard, transparent or translucent, and insoluble in acids.

Beryl

Non-silicates
The largest group of non-silicates are the sulphides. Many important metal ores are sulphides, such as galena (lead ore), sphalerite (zinc ore), and pyrite (iron ore). Other key non-silicate groups include carbonates, oxides, and sulphates.

Garnet

1 Talc: very soft

2 Gypsum (fingernail)

3 Calcite (bronze coin)

4 Fluorite (iron nail)

5 Apatite (glass)

6 Feldspar (penknife)

7 Quartz (steel knife)

8 Topaz (sandpaper)

9 Corundum

10 Diamond: very hard

Charles Lyell
The Scottish geologist Charles Lyell (1797–1875) is known as the founder of modern geology. His book *Principles of Geology*, published in 1830, led to the general acceptance of the idea that the Earth is very old and is constantly being shaped by gradual, everyday processes.

FIND OUT MORE   CAVES   CRYSTALS AND GEMS   EARTH   EARTHQUAKES   EARTH SCIENCES   FOSSILS   MOUNTAINS AND VALLEYS   VOLCANOES

Rocks

Igneous rocks

Basalt – a dark, extrusive, fine-grained rock – forms from quick-cooling lava.

Andesite is a fine-grained extrusive rock rich in silicon.

Tuff is a rock formed from fragments of hardened volcanic ash.

Rhyolite, fine-grained and intrusive, contains mainly quartz and feldspar.

Diorite is a light-coloured, coarse-grained, intrusive rock.

Dolerite has medium-sized grains and a mottled look.

Gabbro is an intrusive rock that forms deep underground.

Granite is intrusive and made of quartz, feldspar, and mica.

Syenite may resemble granite, but contains very little quartz.

Trachyte is extrusive, fine-grained, and rich in feldspar.

Peridotite is heavy, dark, intrusive, and coarse.

Sedimentary rocks

Siltstone is a smooth rock with very fine, angular grains.

Sandstone forms when grains of sand become cemented together.

Clay is fine-grained and may become malleable when wet.

Tufa forms when cool, calcite-rich springs evaporate.

Conglomerate contains rounded beach pebbles and other small stones.

Greywacke is a medium-grained rock that forms from ocean sediments.

Shale is a rock that forms from hardened particles of clay.

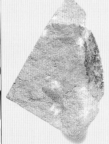

Limestone's main ingredient is calcite (calcium carbonate).

Chalk is a very pure, white limestone with a powdery texture.

Breccia is composed of fragments weathered and eroded from other rocks.

Arkose usually forms from granite fragments.

Gypsum forms from sediments left behind when salt water evaporates.

Mudstone is made up of hardened grains of mud.

Carboniferous limestone formed around 360 million years ago.

Metamorphic rocks

Marble is metamorophosed (transformed) limestone that occurs in a variety of colours.

Hornfels forms when hot lava recrystallizes the minerals in mudstone or shale.

Slate forms when mudstone or shale is crushed and baked during mountain building.

Schist forms in a similar way to slate, but at much higher temperatures.

Gneiss has coarser grains than schist; its minerals often separate into distinct bands.

Metaquartzite forms from loose-grained quartz-rich sandstone.

ROMAN EMPIRE

ONE OF THE GREATEST EMPIRES that ever existed, the Roman Empire in its heyday stretched over most of the known world. According to legend, the city of Rome was ruled by kings until 510 BC, when it became a republic. In 27 BC, the first of its emperors, Augustus, took over the republic and created an empire. Emperors ruled for the next 500 years. For much of this period, the empire was peaceful and prosperous, with one legal system, one language, remarkable engineering and building achievements, and a strong army. The western half of the empire, of which Rome was the capital, fell to the barbarians in 476. The eastern half of the empire survived as the Byzantine Empire until 1453.

Expansion
The Roman Empire peaked in the reign of Emperor Trajan (AD 98–117), when it stretched from Asia Minor to Portugal, and from North Africa to Scotland.

Roman lands

After a military conquest, the Romans organized the conquered peoples into provinces. Soldiers and civilians built a "mother city", and then Romanized the surrounding area, usually by example rather than by force. The Romans encouraged a standard way of life, and offered people Roman citizenship. A network of paved roads connected every province to Rome.

Top level showing soldiers from Dacia (modern Romania)

Roman legionaries attacking Dacians

Military camp

Roman standard

Emperor Trajan addressing his troops

Roman guard

Dacian campaign, Trajan's Column

Emperors
All rulers chose relatives to succeed them until 98 AD when Emperor Nerva chose his successor on ability. Eventually, after many succession problems, the eastern and western sections of the empire split. The last ruler of a unified empire was Theodosius (379–395).

Emperor Theodosius

Pax Romana
In the 1st and 2nd centuries, a Pax Romana (Roman peace) was maintained. This was a system where each province governed itself, but was still subject to taxation and military control from Rome. The system, which stretched from Persia to North Africa, made much of Europe stable, and meant that travel and trade were safe.

The family of Augustus, Altar of Peace, Rome

Divide and rule
Any revolts against Roman rule, such as the Palestine uprising (66–73 AD), were mercilessly crushed. Different tribes rarely helped each other during rebellions. This lack of unity was encouraged by Romans, and always aided their victory.

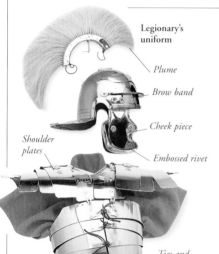

Legionary's uniform

Plume

Brow band

Cheek piece

Embossed rivet

Shoulder plates

Short tunic

Ties and tie hooks held the armour together.

Army

The efficiency, flexibility, and speed of the army was largely responsible for the Roman Empire's success. Professional footsoldiers were organized into some 30 units, called legions. Each legion had a name and number, and consisted of about 5,500 men. When veteran soldiers retired, they were often given land in colonies throughout the empire.

Hadrian's Wall
In 120, Emperor Hadrian (r.117–138) ordered a massive wall to be built across Britain "to separate the barbarians and the Romans". This 117-km (73-mile) wall became the empire's northernmost frontier. The army built defensive ditches, fortress bases, and signal towers along it. Often damaged by marauding tribesmen, it was abandoned in 383, as the empire started to decline, but parts of it can still be seen today.

Roman law

Effective and just, Roman law forms the basis of many of today's European law codes. The first collection of Roman laws was the Twelve Tables of c.450 BC, and the last was Emperor Justinian's *Codex Constitutionum* in 529 AD.

The Senate
Rome's ruling council was the Senate. It consisted of rich landowners (patricians). The lower classes (plebeians) had their own representatives called tribunes. The Senate advised the emperor, who controlled the government. The law was upheld by magistrates, who all came from the Senate. In public, magistrates were accompanied by servants carrying a symbol of authority – the *fasces*, an axe in a bundle of rods.

A lictor, or magistrate's servant, carrying the *fasces*.

Claudius

Claudius (r.41–54 AD) was an able ruler who added Britain and parts of North Africa to the empire. However, there was a lot of murder, madness, and betrayal in his family, and he was poisoned by his fourth wife, Agrippina.

Building

The Romans excelled at ambitious public buildings, such as the Colosseum, and were also ingenious town planners. Towns were usually divided by straight streets into a series of regular blocks – a grid. Within the grid, were luxurious villas, grand tombs, and triumphal arches to commemorate the brave.

Gallery

Entrances

Arena

Cells under the arena housed the animals.

Colosseum had three floors.

Statues

The Colosseum, Rome

Bath-houses

Public bath-houses in most towns had hot and cold pools where citizens could wash – and meet friends at the same time. Roman engineers also supplied water to wealthy private homes using lead, wood, or pottery pipes.

Pont du Gard aqueduct

Roman engineers were at their best when a practical end was in view. This aqueduct (canal-carrying bridge) was a superb system that carried fresh water to Nîmes, France, for over 500 years.

Gods

The Romans inherited many of their gods from the earlier Greek family of gods. Jupiter, Juno, and Mercury were Roman versions of the Greek gods Zeus, Hera, and Hermes. Many of the older beliefs lived on, even after Christianity became the official religion of the empire. One favourite was Castor, known as the horse-tamer, a great warrior who symbolized loyalty. At home, people kept shrines to household spirits, who were known as *lares*.

Castor and Pollux, twin brothers, were favourites with soldiers because they were believed to help the Romans in battle.

Castor, the horse-tamer

God-emperor Augustus

The first Roman emperor, Augustus (r.27 BC–14 AD), was deified (declared a god) after his death. After this, the more popular emperors were always deified, and Romans built temples to honour them. People worshipped the emperors as gods – those who refused to do so, such as the Jews and Christians, were persecuted.

Latin

Latin, the language of the Romans, was spoken in the western part of the empire (while Greek was spoken in the east). Latin forms the basis of many modern European languages, for example, Italian, French, and Spanish. Classic Latin literature, such as Cicero's speeches and Virgil's poetry, is still taught and enjoyed today.

Engraved metal plaque

The "X" shows that this silver coin was worth 10 copper coins.

Roman numerals

The numerals I, II, III, IV, V, VI, VII, VIII, IX, and X were used in everyday life in Europe for centuries. Roman numerals were eventually replaced by Arabic numerals 1, 2, 3, 4, 5, 6, 7, 8, 9, and 10.

Silver denarius

Roman capitals

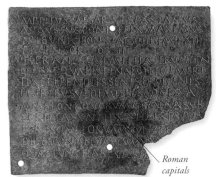

Constantine the Great

Constantine (c.280–337) succeeded his father, Constantius I, as Emperor of the West in 306. By 324 he reunited the Roman empire and made himself sole ruler. He built a new capital at Byzantium on the Bosporus, and named it Constantinople. In 313, his Edict of Milan stopped the persecution of Christians, and Christianity then became the empire's official religion.

Bronze gladiator

Bust of Hercules

Twist key to lock face guard.

Gladiator's bronze helmet

Games

Roman citizens expected lavish entertainments. Crowds of up to 50,000 watched combat sports in Rome's great amphitheatre, the Colosseum, built in 72–80 AD. In arenas all over the empire, gladiators were trained to fight wild animals – or each other – to provide a compelling and bloody spectacle. If they were very lucky, gladiators occasionally survived to win their freedom.

Timeline

753 BC Traditional founding of Rome by Romulus, the first king, and his twin Remus.

509 BC Romans drive Etruscans from Rome; Republic founded.

27 BC Augustus becomes the first emperor.

Hobnailed military sandals

AD 43 Claudius begins Roman invasion of Britain.

66 Jewish Revolt begins.

98–117 Trajan extends Roman citizenship in his reign.

212 All non-slaves in empire granted Roman citizenship.

285 Diocletian reorganizes empire into two halves.

330 Constantine moves the empire's capital to Constantinople.

395 After a century of compromise, the empire splits permanently into eastern and western sections.

Roman glassware

404 Jerome completes a Latin version of Christian Bible.

410 Visigoths sack Rome.

476 Western Roman Empire falls; eastern empire continues.

1453 Byzantine (eastern) Empire falls to Ottoman Turks.

FIND OUT MORE ARMS AND ARMOUR   ARCHITECTURE   BARBARIANS   BYZANTINE EMPIRE   CAESAR, JULIUS   ETRUSCANS   GOVERNMENTS AND POLITICS   GODS AND GODDESSES   ITALY, HISTORY OF   SCULPTURE

Roman empire

Everyday objects

Weighing scales

Bronze inkpot

Pottery inkpot

Faïence inkpot

Reed

Bronze

Pens

Glass table jug

Sewing needles

Sacrifice to Athena

Baking tin

Bronze toga figure

Terracotta cloak

Lace-up boot scent bottle

Lekane (bowl)

Bronze food strainer

Cheese grater

Bone pin

Medical objects

Folding knife

Bone saw

Probe

Spatula

Medical instruments

Sport and entertainment

Bronze sistrum, or rattle

Marble

Bone

Crystal

Agate

Dice

Greenstone

Bronze flutes

Glass marbles

Bronze cymbals

Military objects

Slingshot pellets

Catapult bolts

Ivory sword hilt

Religious objects

Bronze sacrificial jug

Winged goddess of victory

Terracotta tablet showing the sacrifice of a bull

Sacrifice to Hermes

Crater (pot) showing a sacrifice

Bronze libation bowl

Sacrificial altar knife

726

ROMANIA, UKRAINE AND MOLDOVA

Steppes
The steppes are vast, undulating, grassy plains that extend over much of Ukraine and Moldova. Because of their rich, fertile soils, more than half of the area is devoted to growing barley, maize, oats, and wheat. The rest is used mainly as pasture.

ROMANIA, UKRAINE, AND MOLDOVA lie in Eastern Europe, southwest of the Russian Federation. Ukraine and Moldova were both members of the former Soviet Union, whereas Romania, which was also communist, remained independent but was closely allied to the Soviet Union. Since the end of communist rule in Romania in 1989, and the break-up of the Soviet Union in 1991, all three countries have struggled to modernize their industries and compete in world economics.

Carpathians
The Carpathian Mountains form a huge arc from northwest to southwest Romania, enclosing the plateau of Transylvania. The highest peak is Moldoveanu at 2,543 m (8,343 ft). Bears and wolves roam through the dense forests that cover the slopes. The Carpathians are rich in mineral deposits.

Orthodox religion
Most people in the region are Christians and members of the Eastern Orthodox Church, but each country has its own variation. In this way, the different ethnic groups can maintain their own identity.

Eastern Orthodox memorial ceremony in Romania

Physical features
Most of Ukraine consists of a broad grassy plain. Bordered in the south by the Danube River, Romania is mountainous with a central plateau. Moldova has gentle hills and valleys.

Regional climate
Romania has a continental climate, but winters can be bitterly cold. Ukraine and Moldova have a similar climate, with warm summers and mild winters. Ukraine's Crimea has mild winters and hot summers.

22°C (101°F)   −4°C (25°F)

597 mm (24 in)

Crimea
The Crimea is a peninsula in Ukraine that juts into the Black Sea. Many of its resorts, once popular with communist officials, now cater for western tourists, especially Germans. Local vineyards produce high-quality wines.

Romania

R

Long dominated by the Ottoman, Russian, and Habsburg Empires, Romania became an independent country in 1878. In 1947, it became a communist dictatorship allied to the Soviet Union, and from 1965 was damaged by the harsh rule of Nicolae Ceausescu. Since 1989, when Ceausescu was executed, Romania has been struggling to modernize and rebuild its economy.

People

Nearly 90 per cent of the people are ethnic Romanians. The rest of the population is made up of Hungarians and Gypsies, also called Romanies, who make up nearly two per cent. Most Gypsies no longer have a travelling lifestyle, but live close to towns. Today, Romania's population is decreasing, as many people emigrate in search of work.

Young Gypsy girls

Bucharest

Home to more than two million people, Bucharest has been Romania's capital since 1861. Modelled on Paris, it is the country's cultural and commercial centre, as well as the seat of government. Many people live in huge apartment blocks.

Palace of the People

Bran Castle, home of Vlad the Impaler

Transylvania

The rich folklore of the Transylvanian plateau attracts tourists. The story of the bloodsucking Count Dracula is based on a real-life villain, Prince Vlad the Impaler, whose cruelties in the 1400s made his name feared.

ROMANIA FACTS

CAPITAL CITY	Bucharest
AREA	237,500 sq km (91,699 sq miles)
POPULATION	21,700,000
DENSITY	94 per sq km (244 per sq mile)
MAIN LANGUAGE	Romanian
MAJOR RELIGION	Christian
CURRENCY	Romanian Leu
LIFE EXPECTANCY	70 years
PEOPLE PER DOCTOR	556
GOVERNMENT	Multi-party democracy
ADULT LITERACY	98%

Ukraine

The second largest country in Europe, Ukraine broke away from the Soviet Union in 1991. About 70 per cent of the people are Ukrainians and 20 per cent are Russian, living mostly in the east. Ukrainian nationalist feelings have created longstanding tension between the two groups. Farming employs 24 per cent of the work-force.

St George's Church by the River Dnieper

Kiev

Ukraine's capital, Kiev, lies at the meeting point of the rivers Dnieper and Desna. About a thousand years ago, the Orthodox faith spread from here through Eastern Europe. With beautiful parks and churches, Kiev is a centre for culture, industry, and commerce.

Borscht with sour cream

Piroshki

Black bread

Food

Borscht is a traditional Ukrainian soup made from meat stock and beetroot. It is served with sour cream and *piroshki*, savoury patties. Other popular dishes are *varenniki*, dough filled with meat, cheese, or fruit, and *holubtsi*, stuffed cabbage rolls. Food is often accompanied by Crimean wines.

Industry

The Donets'k Basin in eastern Ukraine is rich in coal, iron ore, manganese, zinc, and mercury. Ukraine holds five per cent of global mineral reserves. Its factories produce ships, machinery, aircraft, cars, chemicals, processed foods, and consumer goods.

UKRAINE FACTS

CAPITAL CITY	Kiev
AREA	603,700 sq km (223,089 sq miles)
POPULATION	48,400,000
DENSITY	80 per sq km (208 per sq mile)
MAIN LANGUAGES	Ukrainian, Russian
MAJOR RELIGION	Christian
CURRENCY	Hryvna
LIFE EXPECTANCY	68 years
PEOPLE PER DOCTOR	333
GOVERNMENT	Multi-party democracy
ADULT LITERACY	99%

Moldova

Once a part of Romania, in 1940, the small, rural country of Moldova became a Soviet state. It is the most densely populated of the former Soviet republics, and tension exists between the ethnic Moldovan majority and the Ukrainians and Russians who want independence. Food and leather processing and farming are the main industries.

Wine

Moldova's warm climate is suited to growing vines. The country produces some excellent wines, which are stored in large underground vaults, tunnelled into rocky hillsides. Here the temperature remains cool and constant.

Farming

More than half of Moldova's population lives in the country in small, rural communities. About 65 per cent of the land is used to grow cereals, fruit, tobacco, beetroot, and grapes. Pigs, cattle, and sheep are reared for meat.

MOLDOVA FACTS

CAPITAL CITY	Chisinau
AREA	33,843 sq km (13,067 sq miles)
POPULATION	4,300,000
MAIN LANGUAGES	Romanian, Moldovan
MAJOR RELIGION	Christian
CURRENCY	Moldovan Leu

FIND OUT MORE CHRISTIANITY · EMPIRES · EUROPE, HISTORY OF · FARMING · GOVERNMENTS AND POLITICS · GRASSLAND WILDLIFE · ROCKS AND MINERALS · RUSSIA, HISTORY OF · SOVIET UNION · TRADE AND INDUSTRY

RUSSIAN FEDERATION AND KAZAKHSTAN

STRETCHING HALFWAY ACROSS the globe and straddling the continents of Europe and Asia, the Russian Federation, usually known as Russia, is the world's largest country. Most people live in the more fertile and industrialized European third of the country to the west of the Ural Mountains. East of the Urals is Asian Russia, called Siberia, which has a harsh climate and is sparsely populated. Kazakhstan, to the southwest of Russia, is a smaller country in Asia. Both countries were part of the former Soviet Union, a world superpower in which Russia played a dominant role.

Siberia
Stretching from the Urals to the Pacific Ocean, Siberia covers more than 4,900,000 sq miles (12,800,000 sq km). It contains vast stretches of forest and has around a million lakes, 53,000 rivers, and rich natural resources.

Women

More than 50 percent of all Russian workers are women. Many do physical jobs, such as working on construction sites or driving heavy vehicles, but increasing numbers of women now train in professions such as medicine and teaching. Working women benefit from good health- and childcare provisions.

Russian woman construction worker, Moscow

Physical features

From north to south, the region is made up of bleak, frozen tundra, the vast forests of the taiga, grassy steppes, and cold desert. Mountains cover much of eastern Russia.

102°F (39°C)   -90°F (-68°C)
66°F (19°C)   16°F (-9°C)

22 in (575 mm)

Climate
Russia has warm summers, bitterly cold winters, and short springs and autumns, with low rainfall. Temperatures in northern Siberia may drop as low as -90°F (-68°C).

Volga River
At 2,190 miles (3,530 km), the Volga is European Russia's longest river. From Moscow to the Caspian Sea, it has been transformed from a fast-flowing waterway to a series of dammed lakes, used for farming, power, and transportation.

Steppes
The steppes are flat grassy plains that extend across the Russian Federation and Kazakhstan. A large part is treeless and used for grazing, but vast expanses are also cultivated. To the south the steppes gradually give way to semidesert lowlands and mountains.

Russian Federation

R

Once part of a great empire, Russia is a federation of numerous regions, republics, and territories, many of which are autonomous and self-governing. The dominant element in the former Soviet Union, since the collapse of communism, Russia is today finding its role in the world. It has suffered great damage to the economy and much ethnic tension; most recently fighting broke out with the southwestern republic of Chechnya.

Forest 50% Grassland 2% Wetland 13% Tundra 18.5%
Built-up 0.5% Barren 6% Farmland 10%

Land use
Most of Russia's crops are grown in the "fertile triangle" that stretches between St Petersburg, the Caspian Sea, and Omsk in southern Siberia. Forest provides timber, and coal, oil, and natural gas are mined in Siberia.

RUSSIAN FEDERATION FACTS

CAPITAL CITY Moscow

AREA 17,075,200 sq km (6,592,735 sq miles)

POPULATION 144,700,000

MAIN LANGUAGE Russian

MAJOR RELIGION Christian

CURRENCY Russian Rouble

LIFE EXPECTANCY 66 years

PEOPLE PER DOCTOR 238

GOVERNMENT Multi-party democracy

ADULT LITERACY 99%

People
Most Russians live in small apartments in towns where living standards are low. Since the collapse of communism, crime rates have risen sharply, especially in the cities. Many people are disillusioned by food shortages, and the loss of job security, long-term employment, and guaranteed housing.

9 per sq km (23 per sq mile)   77% Urban   23% Rural

Queuing for food in winter

Ballet
Russia is renowned for its ballet, and Moscow's Bolshoi Ballet and the Kirov Ballet from St Petersburg are world famous. Ballet first arrived in Russia in the 18th century via Paris to St Petersburg, then a cultural centre of Europe. During the 19th century, Russian ballet developed its own individual style.

Ceramic chess set

Food
Cereals, potatoes, oil, and sugar form the basis of the Russian diet. Famous dishes are *borscht* (hot beetroot soup served with sour cream), beef *stroganov*, *blinis*, caviar (sturgeon-fish eggs), stuffed cabbage leaves, and *shchi*, a kind of cabbage soup. Russians drink large amounts of *chai*, or tea, served without milk, and vodka often flavoured with herbs and spices.

Blinis are small pancakes filled with caviar and served with sour cream.

Blinis   **Vodka**

Moscow
With a population of almost nine million, the capital, Moscow, is Russia's biggest city and is linked to the River Volga by the Moscow Canal. The seat of government is the Kremlin, a palace fortress that once belonged to the tsars (emperors). It is separated from the old town by the world-famous Red Square. Moscow has fine buildings, theatres, and universities, and a majestic underground railway opened in 1935.

May Day celebrations in Moscow

Chess
The ancient game of chess was introduced into Russia more than 1,000 years ago by travellers on the Baltic Sea trade routes. It was quickly adopted as a stimulating way of occupying dark winter evenings. Today, chess is often played outdoors in summer. International competitions are popular.

Russian Orthodox Church
The communist rulers of the Soviet Union discouraged religion, but since the late 1980s, many followers of the Russian Orthodox Church have recovered their church buildings from the state and opened new meeting places. Christmas Day (January 7 in the Orthodox calendar) is now a national holiday.

Russian Orthodox icon of the Madonna and child

Timber is sawn into many differently shaped sections, each used for a different purpose.

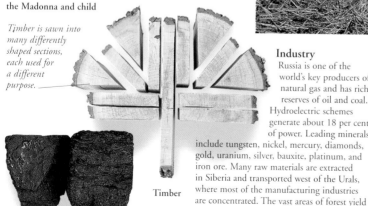

Farming
Only one-tenth of the land, mostly in European Russia, is suited to growing crops, yet Russia is a leading world producer of potatoes, oats, and rye. It also ranks highly in milk, butter, and wheat production. Men and women work the fields, often forced by lack of cash to rely on traditional farming methods. Farmers also raise cattle, sheep, and poultry for food.

Industry
Russia is one of the world's key producers of natural gas and has rich reserves of oil and coal. Hydroelectric schemes generate about 18 per cent of power. Leading minerals include tungsten, nickel, mercury, diamonds, gold, uranium, silver, bauxite, platinum, and iron ore. Many raw materials are extracted in Siberia and transported west of the Urals, where most of the manufacturing industries are concentrated. The vast areas of forest yield an almost endless supply of timber.

Timber

Coal

Trans-Siberian Express
The Trans-Siberian Railway links European Russia with the Pacific coast across Siberia. It is the world's longest continuous rail line, starting in Moscow and ending 9,297 km (5,777 miles) away in the Pacific port of Vladivostok. The journey takes eight days, and crosses eight time zones. Only one passenger train runs each way daily, but freight trains run every five minutes day and night.

Kazakhstan

Stretching almost 2,400 km (1,490 miles) from the Caspian Sea in the west to the Altai Mountains in the east, Kazakhstan is the second largest of the former Soviet republics of the USSR. Made up of dry, windswept steppes and mountainous plateaus, it is one of the world's most underpopulated countries. Its rich mineral resources give it great potential for wealth. The need to import most consumer goods has led the government to develop domestic manufacturing industries.

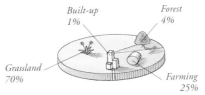

Land use

Much of Kazakhstan's grassland is used for grazing animals, mainly sheep, goats, and cattle. With the help of irrigation, large areas of steppe are cultivated, producing mainly wheat and rice.

Built-up 1%
Forest 4%
Grassland 70%
Farming 25%

KAZAKHSTAN FACTS

CAPITAL CITY Astana

AREA 2,717,300 sq km (1,049,150 sq miles)

POPULATION 16,100,000

MAIN LANGUAGES Kazakh, Russian

MAJOR RELIGIONS Muslim, Christian

CURRENCY Tenge

LIFE EXPECTANCY 65 years

PEOPLE PER DOCTOR 286

GOVERNMENT Multiparty elections

ADULT LITERACY 99%

People

As a result of the forced settlement of mainly Russians, Ukrainians, and Germans under communist rule, ethnic Kazakhs form only 53 per cent of the population. Increasing numbers of Kazakhs are now returning home from neighbouring states. Most people live in towns, and only a few Kazakh families still follow a traditional nomadic lifestyle roaming the steppes.

Nomadic Kazakhs live in tents called yurts.

6 per sq km (17 per sq mile)

56% Urban

44% Rural

Caviar

The tiny black eggs of the *beluga* sturgeon, a kind of fish, are salted and eaten as caviar, which is regarded as a delicacy. Some of the world's best caviar comes from fish caught in the Caspian Sea off the coast of Kazakhstan. The people in the region serve caviar as a sign of friendship.

Golden sterlet eggs

Black beluga eggs

Caviar served on toast

Almaty

The former capital, Almaty, enjoys a beautiful location between mountains and plains. It is a city of modern architecture, wide streets, cool fountains, parks, squares, and stunning mountain views. A major attraction is Zenkov Cathedral, one of the world's tallest wooden buildings.

Zenkov Cathedral

Religion

Islam is the main religion of the ethnic Kazakh people, and it has continued to grow in popularity since the end of the communist regime. Among the other ethnic groups there is a strong Christian element, largely belonging to the Russian Orthodox Church.

Farming

Irrigation projects set up under communism transformed the dry steppes of Kazakhstan into farmland. The country is now almost self-sufficient in food crops and is a major producer of grain, wool, meat, and fish from more than 48,000 lakes.

Many boats were stranded as the water dried up.

Aral Sea

In 1960, the Aral Sea was the fourth largest lake in the world. Now it is less than half its former size because so much water has been diverted for irrigation from the two main rivers that feed it: the Syr Daria in Kazakhstan and the Amu Darya in Uzbekistan. Unless drastic measures are taken, it will be completely dry in a few years.

Mining

Kazakhstan has plentiful reserves of copper, iron ore, lead, nickel, and uranium, and mining is the country's most important industry. Some of the world's largest oil deposits are located near the Caspian Sea, attracting foreign investment. Gold is a major export, and Kazakhstan is a world leader in chromium production. It is also a major producer of tungsten, zinc, and manganese.

Crude oil

Oil drill bit

Diamond tips enable drill to cut through rock.

Gold

Space centre

The former Soviet Union's space programme was run from the Baikonur Cosmodrome in the centre of Kazakhstan. The world's first artificial satellite and the first person in space were launched from here. The site is still used for Russian space launches.

FIND OUT MORE
ASIA, HISTORY OF
BALLET
CHESS AND OTHER BOARD GAMES
FARMING
OIL
RIVERS
ROCKS AND MINERALS
RUSSIA, HISTORY OF
SOVIET UNION
SPACE EXPLORATION
TRAINS AND RAILWAYS

RUSSIA, HISTORY OF

OCCUPYING THE VAST, empty expanses of northern Europe and Asia, Russia has remained on the fringes of both continents for most of its history. Landlocked, and impoverished by its harsh climate, Russia only gained access to the seas to the west in 1721, when it began to play a major part in European history. Over the next two centuries, the country slowly and painfully modernized itself, deposing its Tsar, and emerging under the Union of Soviet Socialist Republics (USSR) as one of the world's major superpowers. After the break-up of the Soviet Union in 1991, modern Russia has struggled to redefine its role on the world stage.

Early Russia

Before about 850, few people lived in what is now Russia. But in the 9th century, Viking raiders from Sweden pushed south in search of trade and plunder. They established their capital at Kyyiv (now Kiev in Ukraine), creating a trading empire in the surrounding area. Small, scattered tribes of farmers and hunters occupied the rest of Russia.

Rus
Russia's Viking settlers were known as the Rus. Their empire, based on trade routes between the Baltic and Black Seas, became the basis of the first Russian state.

Coming of Christianity
At the end of the 10th century, Christian missionaries from the Byzantine Empire arrived in Kyyiv. They converted the people to Greek Orthodoxy and introduced Cyrillic script, both of which survive to this day.

Rise of Muscovy

During the 1330s, the small state of Muscovy, centred on the city of Moscow on the northern edge of the Mongol Khanate, began to assert its independence. The Muscovites defeated the Mongols in 1380 and declared their independence a century later. By 1550, Muscovy was the leading state in Russia, expanding its territory into Poland in the west and Siberia to the east.

Ivan IV

Ivan IV (1530–84) became tsar in 1533 and ruled until he died 51 years later. He expanded the size of the state and broke the power of the nobility. Ivan was a ruthless ruler, killing many opponents, and gaining the nickname "Ivan the Terrible".

Peter the Great

Under Peter the Great (1672–1725), Russia became a major European power. Peter travelled in western Europe, returning with new ideas that helped him to modernize his country. He reorganized the government and encouraged education.

Hermitage, St Petersburg

St Petersburg
To symbolize his new country, Peter built a new capital at St Petersburg. He brought in architects and craftworkers from western Europe to create its streets and palaces. More than 150,000 workers died constructing the city, which was built to rival the palace at Versailles, France.

Kremlin

Every Russian city had a fortified area, known as a kremlin, to protect its civil and religious buildings. The Moscow Kremlin, beside the Movska River in the centre of the city, covered many hectares and contained fine churches and palaces.

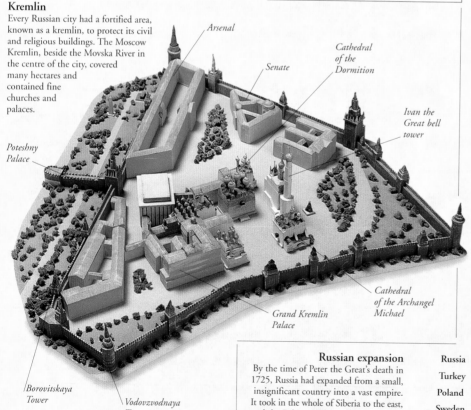

Arsenal

Senate

Cathedral of the Dormition

Ivan the Great bell tower

Poteshny Palace

Cathedral of the Archangel Michael

Grand Kremlin Palace

Borovitskaya Tower

Vodovzvodnaya Tower

Model of the Kremlin

Territory gained from Sweden 1700–1743

Russian expansion 1667–1795

St Petersburg

Territory gained from Turkey 1768–1792

Moscow

Territory gained from Poland 1767–1795

Kiev

Prague

Border shows extent of Russian territory by 1795

Russian expansion

By the time of Peter the Great's death in 1725, Russia had expanded from a small, insignificant country into a vast empire. It took in the whole of Siberia to the east, and the Baltic coastline to the west, thus gaining a "window on the west". Over the next century, further land was gained on Russia's western and southern borders.

Russia	
Turkey	
Poland	
Sweden	
Austria	
Prussia	

Imperial Russia

The Romanov dynasty ruled Russia from 1613 until 1917. The royal family kept power firmly in their own hands, resisting change, and the serfs, or peasants, remained tied to the land. Agricultural techniques were primitive, and most people lived in conditions of extreme poverty, causing discontent to develop.

Jewelled decoration

Design inspired by the French jewellers to the court of Louis XVI of France

Egg made by Carl Fabergé, goldsmith to the Russian emperors

Emancipation of the serfs

In 1861, long after the rest of Europe, Tsar Alexander II liberated the Russian peasants from serfdom (ownership by their landlords). They were allotted land, which they had to pay for – a new source of discontent.

Troops beat rebellious serfs.

Catherine the Great

In 1762, Catherine (1729–96) became empress after deposing her husband Peter III. She was an intelligent ruler who encouraged artists from all over Europe to work in Russia. She continued the work of Peter the Great in making Russia into a powerful state.

R

1905 revolution

In January 1905, troops in St Petersburg fired on workers who were demonstrating for higher wages and shorter hours. This outrage caused strikes and army mutinies across Russia. Tsar Nicholas II granted a constitution and summoned a Russian duma, or parliament, but the reforms were limited and short-lived.

Guns on the streets of St Petersburg

Duma

The Russian duma met on various occasions after 1905, but Nicholas II granted it only limited power. When the members disagreed with the tsar, the duma was usually dissolved. Later dumas achieved some limited reforms.

Early meeting of the duma

Soviet flag

Soviet Russia

In 1917, two revolutions swept away the old imperial government and introduced the world's first communist state. It developed into a major world power and played a pivotal role in defeating Germany in World War II. The state followed the collective principles laid down by Marx and Engels and took over all private land and property.

Modern Russia

In 1991, the Soviet Union collapsed and Russia re-emerged as an independent state. Under President Boris Yeltsin, Russia struggled to establish democracy and reform its economy and society along western lines, but it faced huge industrial and environmental problems.

Break-up of the Soviet Union

Mikhail Gorbachev, leader of the USSR from 1985, tried to reform the country. But he was forced to resign after an attempted coup in 1991. Most of the USSR's republics declared their independence, leading to the break-up of the USSR later that year.

Moscow

Key

Russia

Former Soviet states

Soviet legacy

The years of Soviet control left a terrible legacy for Russia. Industry was old-fashioned and inefficient, farms were unable to produce enough food, nuclear waste threatened people's health, and much land was polluted.

Decaying Soviet battleships

Market economy

The Russian economy was reformed along market lines. This led to food shortages in the cities and rising prices, but many people still demanded the kinds of good and facilities found in capitalist societies.

McDonald's, Moscow

Timeline

800s Viking raiders establish new state in the Ukraine, centred at Kyyiv (modern Kiev).

900s Greek missionaries convert Russians to Orthodox Christianity.

1380 Prince Dimitri of Moscow defeats the Mongols; Muscovy's power begins to increase.

St Basil's Cathedral, Moscow

1480 Ivan III of Moscow declares himself Tsar of all the Russias.

1533–84 Reign of Ivan IV (Ivan the Terrible).

1682–1725 Reign of Peter the Great.

1721 Russia defeats Sweden and gains access to the Baltic.

1762–96 Reign of Catherine the Great.

1861 Emancipation of serfs.

1905 Russia defeated in war by Japan; attempted revolution in St Petersburg.

1914 Russia enters World War I on the side of the Allies. More than a million Russians are killed.

Current Russian flag

1917 Revolutionaries overthrow Tsar Nicholas II, and set up world's first communist state.

1985 Mikhail Gorbachev begins to reform the Soviet Union.

1991 Soviet Union collapses; Russia emerges as independent nation.

 FIND OUT MORE — ASIA, HISTORY OF · COLD WAR · EUROPE, HISTORY OF · GOVERNMENTS AND POLITICS · MARX, KARL · MONGOL EMPIRE · RUSSIAN REVOLUTION · SOVIET UNION

RUSSIAN REVOLUTION

IN 1917, A REVOLUTION in Russia forced Tsar Nicholas II, a Romanov, whose family had ruled for over 300 years, to abdicate. As the first revolution to take power in the name of workers and peasants, and because it also inspired later revolutions in China and Cuba, the Russian Revolution is one of the most important events of the 20th century. The revolution began in March 1917, with the formation of a provisional government. This government, not considered radical enough by the people, was overthrown in November, when the Bolsheviks seized power and turned Russia into the world's first Communist state.

Causes of the revolution

By 1917, after years of difficulties, Russia was in crisis. Most Russians – peasants and industrial workers – lived in dire poverty. They were short of food and resented the tyrannical rule of Tsar Nicholas II. Russia was also suffering terrible losses against Germany in World War I. Unrest grew as all social groups demanded change.

1917 revolutions

There were two main revolutions in 1917, usually known as the February and October Revolutions. Russia's old-style calendar was 13 days behind the rest of Europe, so that the revolutions actually occurred in March and November. Many key events occurred in St Petersburg (formerly Petrograd), but the revolution affected the whole of Russia, as it moved from a series of small democratic changes, to national social upheaval.

Lenin sweeping away capitalism

February Revolution
Troops sent to quell food riots in Petrograd disobeyed their orders and joined the workers. Realising he had lost control, Nicholas II (r.1894–1918) abdicated, and a provisional government was formed.

July Days
Soviets (elected councils of workers and soldiers) sprang up all over Russia; they supported the radical Bolsheviks against the provisional government. During the July Days, armed workers and soldiers, calling for "power to the soviets", attempted to seize power. The government brutally suppressed them, and Lenin fled Russia.

October Revolution
Lenin's Bolsheviks stormed the Winter Palace, arrested the leaders of the provisional government, and seized power. Lenin immediately gave control of the factories to the workers, and redistributed land to the peasants. In 1918, the revolutionaries executed the Tsar and his family, and Lenin took Russia out of the war.

Lenin

Vladimir Ilyich Ulyanov (1870–1924), better known as Lenin, was the architect of the revolution. Born in Simbirsk on the Volga River, he became a revolutionary when his brother was hanged in 1887 for trying to assassinate the Tsar. Lenin studied the works of Karl Marx, and became leader of the revolutionary Social Democrats, later the Bolsheviks. He lived mainly in exile until 1917. Following the Bolshevik victory, he ruled the country until his death.

Civil war

In 1918, a bitter civil war broke out between the so-called Whites, who were opposed to the revolution, and the Reds, or Bolsheviks. The fighting was bloody, but after three years the Red Army led by Leon Trotsky (1879–1940) was finally victorious.

New Economic Policy

By the end of the civil war in 1921, famine was widespread, and much of the peasant classes had turned against Lenin. In response to this, Lenin introduced a New Economic Policy (NEP) that allowed limited private enterprise, (also known as free trade).

Famine victims

Timeline

1905 Workers' revolution leads to October Manifesto. Tsar Nicholas II agrees to a national assembly (duma), but refuses to allow any real changes.

1914 Russia enters World War I. Over three years, some 8 million Russians die or are wounded. Demonstrations against the war break out.

March 1917 (February in old-style calendar). International Women's Day turns into a bread riot in Petrograd. The revolution begins. Nicholas II is ousted from the throne.

Black bread

7 November 1917 (October in old-style calendar). Lenin and the Bolsheviks overthrow provisional government.

1918 Tsar Nicholas II and family are executed.

1918–21 Civil war

1921 Famine in Russia. Sailors mutiny in Kronstadt. Lenin introduces New Economic Policy (NEP), which, by 1925, had improved production levels.

1922 Russia's name changes to the Union of Soviet Socialist Republics (USSR), or Soviet Union.

FIND OUT MORE — CHINESE REVOLUTION · COLD WAR · GOVERNMENTS AND POLITICS · MARX, KARL · RUSSIA, HISTORY OF · SOVIET UNION

SAFAVID EMPIRE

AFTER THE DOWNFALL of its last empire in 651, Persia was under Arab domination for nearly 1,000 years. Then in 1502, a Persian warrior called Ismail founded the Safavid Empire. For more than 200 years, the Safavids ruled an independent land with a distinct national character. Shi'ism, a minority form of Islam, became the empire's official state religion. This set Persia against its Muslim neighbours, in particular the Ottoman Turks, but contacts with Europe developed, and Persia grew rich through trade. The Safavids, who loved beauty and impressive buildings, created world-famous art and architecture.

Extent of empire
After a series of swift victories against the Arabs, Ismail conquered what is now Iran and parts of Iraq. The Safavids replaced Arabic with Persian as the language of government. Tabriz was their first capital.

Ismail I
The founder of the Safavid Empire, Ismail I (1501–24), was a charismatic religious leader and brave soldier. He named the dynasty after his ancestor, the saint Safi ud-Din. Ismail was aged only 14 when he conquered Tabriz in modern Iran, and declared himself shah, or king.

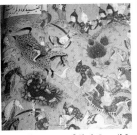

1541 illustation of Shah Ismail I fighting his rival, Alvand

Shi'ism
When Ismail conquered Persia, most people were Sunni Muslims. He invited Arab teachers to spread Shi'ism, and made it the state religion. Ismail's promotion of Shi'ism was seen as an affront to other Muslim countries.

Muslim prayers

Ottoman Turks
The Ottomans were the Safavids' main territorial rivals. As Sunni Muslims, they were also bitter religious enemies. In the 1500s, the great Ottoman ruler Suleiman I waged bloody war against the Safavids.

Sultan Suleiman I's dagger

Muharram
When Muhammad's grandson, Hossein, died in 681, early Shi'ite Muslims felt they had lost the rightful caliph of the Islamic empire. In the 16th century, Safavids began to mark the anniversary of his death with a mass outpouring of grief in the month of Muharram.

Colourful tiles, typical of the Persian style

Madresseh Chehar Bagh Vestibule, Isfahan

Isfahan
In 1598, Abbas I built a stunning new capital at Isfahan. He had all royal buildings and mosques decorated with dazzling tiles, and the city became a showcase of the Persian architectural style at its very best. This style greatly influenced other Islamic cities.

Abbas the Great

Abbas I (r.1587–1629) expanded the empire and founded an administration. Afraid his sons might steal his throne, he killed one and had two others blinded. But this left him without a successor.

The Prophet Muhammad's Ascent to Heaven

Angels

Gold paint

Prophet Muhammad

Buraq, a mythical winged beast

Chinese-style clouds

Decorative Persian writing

Miniatures
Decorated leather-bound books were a major expression of Safavid artistry. Court artists copied classic Persian poetry in elaborate handwriting, and added page-sized, colourful illustrations, known as miniatures. Artists used fine brushes and real gold to give a sumptuous effect.

Ascent of the Prophet
Traditional stories, love poems, and legends of ancient Persian kings (the *Book of Kings*) were popular subjects for miniatures. Religious topics were relatively rare, but one 16th-century artist, Aqa Mirak, illustrated the works of the great Persian poet Nezami (1141–1209).

Timeline
651 The last ancient Persian (Sassanid) Empire falls to the aarabs.

1502 Ismail conquers Tabriz and declares himself Shah.

1524–76 Reign of Shah Tahmasp I; Safavid art peaks, but empire weakens.

1603 Abbas I forces Turks out of all Persian territories. Empire at peak.

1722 Shah Hossein abdicates. Empire begins decline.

1736 Afghan general Nader Qoli Beg deposes Tahmasp III (a child), ending the Safavid dynasty. He declares himself shah.

Pierced metalwork standard

FIND OUT MORE | ARCHITECTURE | ISLAM | ISLAMIC EMPIRES | OTTOMAN EMPIRE | PERSIAN EMPIRES

SAILING AND OTHER WATER SPORTS

BOATS OF ALL KINDS can be found on rivers, lakes, canals, and the sea, both for leisure and in competition. Individuals and teams row, paddle, and sail in canoes, dinghies, and yachts. They ride on boards, ski across water, and drive powerful motor boats. Racing competitions range from 200-m canoe sprints that last less than a minute to round-the-world yacht races that take months to complete. Sailing, rowing, canoeing, whitewater canoeing, and windsurfing have all been included in the Olympic Games.

Sailing

Sailing boats use the power of the wind to drive them through the water. Vessels range from one-person dinghies to ocean-going yachts that have a crew of 12 or more. Boats can sail directly downwind or across the wind, but have to take a zigzag course, called tacking, to sail into the wind.

Mast

Mainsail

The side of the boat furthest away from the wind (this side) is called leeward; the side nearest the wind is called windward.

Yacht racing

Yachts race on inshore and offshore courses. Inshore races are held just off the coast, on courses marked out with buoys. Offshore races go across the seas. Some races are for yachts of the same design, and other competitions, called handicap races, are for boats of different designs.

Sailing dinghy

Hull

Rudder for steering

Boom

Ropes are called sheets.

Double boom, or wishbone

Canoeing

The two main types of canoe racing are over calm water and over rough water. There are two types of canoe – kayaks and Canadian canoes. In a kayak, the canoeist sits inside the boat with legs stretched out under the deck and uses a paddle with a blade at each end. In a Canadian canoe, the canoeist sits or kneels and uses a one-bladed paddle.

Canadian canoes

Flat-water racing

There are sprint and long-distance races for singles, doubles, and fours, for both kayaks and Canadian canoes. In long river races, obstacles such as locks and rapids are negotiated by portage; the canoeists have to carry their boats along the riverbank.

Kayaks

Whitewater racing

In slalom races, competitors set out one at a time. They have to negotiate a number of "gates" made from hanging poles and they incur penalties for mistakes. In whitewater, competitors are timed over a course that includes obstacles such as rocks and rapids.

Windsurfing

In windsurfing, the sailor stands on a board and steers by means of the sail, controlling it and supporting the rig with a double boom. There are several kinds of competition, including racing around buoys, slalom races, and performing tricks.

America's Cup

The America's Cup is contested by two yachts from different countries. The multi-crew vessels compete in a best-of-seven series. An international knock-out competition decides which two countries will contest the Cup. The race is named after the US schooner *America,* which beat the best British yachts in 1851.

Rowing and sculling

Racing boats carry one, two, four, or eight oarsmen or women, all on sliding seats, plus sometimes a cox to steer. Rowers operate a single oar each in a boat of two, four, or eight; scullers use two oars each and race as singles, doubles, or quadruples. The standard course on non-flowing, or flat, water is 2 km (1.24 miles).

Rowing

Sculling

Steven Redgrave

British oarsman Steven Redgrave (b. 1962) is the first rower to win gold medals in five consecutive Olympics, a feat achieved by only three others in any sport. His medals came in the Games of 1984, 1988, 1992, 1996, and 2000. His career total of 14 gold medals in world championships and Olympics is also a rowing record. He had decided to retire in 1996 due to health problems, but later changed his mind.

Surfing

Surfers paddle out to sea on lightweight boards and ride the waves back to shore. In competition, their moves and routines are judged for style and grace, and the difficulty of the waves they select to ride. Most competition boards have three fins on the tail.

Water-skiing

Water-skiers are towed behind a motorboat on one or two skis. Competitions have three sections. In slalom, water-skiers negotiate a series of six buoys over increasingly difficult runs. In jumping, they take off from a ramp. In tricks, points are awarded for special manoeuvres.

FIND OUT MORE

OLYMPIC GAMES   RIVERS   SHIPS AND BOATS   SPORT   SWIMMING AND DIVING

S

SALAMANDERS AND NEWTS

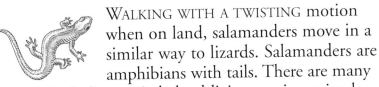

WALKING WITH A TWISTING motion when on land, salamanders move in a similar way to lizards. Salamanders are amphibians with tails. There are many types, including entirely land-living species, animals such as newts that return to water to breed, and species that live permanently in water. Most species live in the temperate northern hemisphere. Land-living salamanders prefer damp, dark, cool habitats – some live in caves. To avoid the cold of winter, they hibernate in mud or under stones. Species from hot regions live on mountains, or in rotten logs in forests, and remain dormant during hot, dry periods.

Smooth, streamlined head and body

Features of salamanders and newts

Salamanders and newts retain their tails from the larval stage into adulthood. Their skin is permeable to air and water and must be kept moist to avoid drying out. They can breathe through their skin as well as their lungs. Most species have four legs, but these may be very small as in congo eels. Sirens are similar to salamanders, but have front legs only and external gills for breathing.

Crest grows on male's back in breeding season.

Great crested newt

Four toes on front legs

Five toes on back legs

Tail frill

Newt
Newts are salamanders that return to water in the breeding season. They develop filamentous frills on the upper and lower edges of their tails that help them swim. Most newts live in cool water and are found in Europe, Asia, and North America.

Salamander
Most salamanders are small, with long bodies and short limbs, but some are huge – the Chinese and Japanese salamanders may grow to 1.8 m (6 ft) long. Salamanders live and breed on land. They usually live in damp areas, near streams. However, some live far from water, on mountains, or in woods. There are even cave dwellers such as the European olm.

Spotted salamander

Neoteny
Some salamanders and newts, such as the European cave olm, Mexican axolotl, and American mudpuppy, do not develop fully into adults. They retain their gills and remain in the water-dwelling larval form despite being sexually mature and able to breed. This condition is called neoteny.

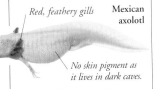

Red, feathery gills

Mexican axolotl

No skin pigment as it lives in dark caves.

Feeding
Larvae that develop in water have horny teeth and feed on invertebrates, smaller newt larvae, or young fish. Land-living adults have sharp teeth to catch prey such as insects and worms. Some salamanders feed on other smaller salamanders. The giant Japanese and Chinese salamanders also feed on animal faeces, and some climbing species nibble fungi on tree trunks.

Warts on skin

Mandarin salamander

Salamander grips earthworm in its teeth.

Reproduction

Most male salamanders lay a sperm sac, or spermatophore, on land that the female takes up into her body through an opening called the cloaca. The eggs are fertilized internally and laid on land. Some species lay eggs that hatch directly into small versions of the adults; others, such as the European fire salamander, bear live young. Newts mate in water; they either lay a single egg, or groups of eggs, on plants in the water.

Newly laid egg will be wrapped inside the leaf.

Long, feathery gills

Internal organs

Three pairs of external gills

Small back legs

Long, thin legs

Development of a great crested newt

1 The female newt lays her eggs singly on underwater vegetation. She folds a leaf around the egg with her feet to protect it inside a sticky envelope. The egg hatches after 3 weeks.

2 The larva is now 5 weeks old. It breathes with external gills. The membranes on the tail and back help it swim in short bursts. It feeds mainly on invertebrates.

3 By 8 weeks, the larva is bigger and stronger. It is now a voracious aquatic predator. By 2–3 months, the gills and tail filaments recede and the legs become stronger. It moves on to land and breathes using lungs. It keeps its tail.

Defence

Bright colours indicate it is poisonous.

European fire salamander
Fire salamanders have brightly patterned poisonous skin that is powerful enough to kill small mammals that may eat them.

Poison gland

Many salamanders and newts hide from their enemies or camouflage themselves. Some are bright in colour and have toxic skin that causes skin irritation and stomach cramps if eaten. Some salamanders, such as American sirens, give a nasty bite; others shed their tails to escape predators. The Pyrenean newt feigns death by lying on its back.

Spines

Iberian ribbed newt
This newt has spines down its side formed by the protruding tips of its ribs. These help to deter predators.

GREAT CRESTED NEWT

SCIENTIFIC NAME	*Triturus cristatus*
ORDER	Caudata
FAMILY	Salamandridae
DISTRIBUTION	Europe to central and southern Russia and northern Turkey and Iran in lowlands below 1,000 m (3,300 ft)
HABITAT	Deep water ponds
DIET	Aquatic invertebrates as a larvae; insects, worms, and slugs as an adult
SIZE	Length 15–16 cm (6–6.5 in); tail is 7 cm (2.75 in) of this length
LIFESPAN	25 years (in captivity)

FIND OUT MORE AMPHIBIANS • CAVE WILDLIFE • HIBERNATION • LAKE AND RIVER WILDLIFE • MARSH AND SWAMP WILDLIFE • MOUNTAIN WILDLIFE • POISONOUS ANIMALS • WOODLAND WILDLIFE

SAMURAI AND SHOGUNS

JAPANESE MILITARY DICTATORS, known as shoguns, seized control of all Japan from 1192 to 1868. Although they ruled in the emperor's name, the shoguns' power was lifelong and hereditary, and the emperors were mere puppets. Through local landowners called daimyos, the shoguns controlled an aristocratic warrior class known as the samurai, which means "one who serves". Over 700 years these samurai became famous for their bravery and military skill. In their code – Bushido, or "way of the warrior" – loyalty and honour were the highest virtues, and failure was unforgivable. People regarded the samurai as nobles, though many lived harsh and austere lives.

Origins of the samurai
Samurai first appeared in the early 10th century. Originally samurai formed bands with family members. Later, a feudal system came into effect: mounted samurai fought to the death for their local daimyo, and gained land if successful.

Kamakura shoguns

When Minamoto Yoritimo (1147–99) seized power and established a warrior government at Kamakura, he and his descendants became known as the Kamakura shoguns. After Yoritimo's death his wife's family, the Hojo, became regents – caretakers of the shoguns – who held more power than the shoguns themselves. In 1274 and 1281, the Hojo's samurai repelled Mongol invaders, but these campaigns weakened the Kamakura shogunate, which collapsed in 1333.

Minamoto family
The clan's first great chief was Minamoto Yoshiie (1039–1106). He built up the family fortunes to such an extent that the Minamoto could make a bid for power. In 1185, Yoshiie's descendent, Yoritimo, established his court at Kamakura; in 1192, he made himself the first shogun. From then on all shoguns were chosen from different branches of the Minamoto family.

Minamoto Yoshiie

Samurai armour
Over 700 years, the 23 pieces in a suit of armour became highly decorative – with gold detail, and coloured silk ties – but the basic style remained virtually unchanged.

- Kabuto (helmet)
- Menpo (face guard)
- Sode (shoulder guard)
- Mune-ate (breastplate)
- Do (cuirass)
- Chain mail kote (arm guard)
- Tekko (hand guard)
- Kusazuri (upper thigh guard)
- Haidate (lower thigh guard)
- Coloured ties
- Suneate (greave or leg guard)

Ashikaga shoguns

Ashikaga Takauji defeated the Kamakura shoguns in 1333 on behalf of the emperor, but then made himself shogun in 1338. He established his government in Muromachi, Kyoto. Ashikaga shoguns became interested in the arts, such as the tea ceremony and Noh drama, rather than in warfare. In 1573, a minor chieftain called Oda Nobunaga (1534–82) deposed the last Ashikaga shogun.

Lacquered bamboo

Rough and rustic crockery · *Irregular shape*

Tea ceremony
In the 12th century, a Buddhist priest introduced the formal drinking of tea from China. Three hundred years later the Ashikaga shogun Yoshimasa (1436–90) constructed a special room in his villa for the tea ceremony – Japan's first tea house. The 16th-century tea master, Sen no Rikyu, refined and simplified the ceremony. For shoguns and samurai alike, the tea ceremony was a quiet, spiritually refreshing cultural pursuit.

Tea ceremony tray and bowls

Tokugawa shoguns

Tokugawa Ieyasu, a military genius, started as a minor daimyo but, in 1603, he became shogun. He and his successors made strict political and economic rules that ensured peace for more than two centuries. In 1868, due to pressure at home and abroad, the last of the Tokugawa shoguns was forced to resign, and the emperor took over. This ended 700 years of shogun and samurai rule.

Tokugawa Ieyasu (1543–1616)

Bushido code
The samurai code of service – loyalty, honour, and bravery – extended to ritual suicide (hara-kiri or seppuku) when there was any threat of dishonour. In 1703, 47 ronin (masterless samurai) avenged the death of their lord, Asano, by killing his murderer, then committing hara-kiri to keep their honour.

Lithograph showing hara-kiri, or ritual suicide

Samurai armour of the 19th century

Modern samurai
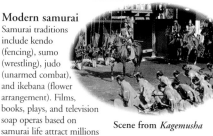
Samurai traditions include kendo (fencing), sumo (wrestling), judo (unarmed combat), and ikebana (flower arrangement). Films, books, plays, and television soap operas based on samurai life attract millions of Japanese. Classic Japanese films, such as *Kagemusha* and *The Seven Samurai*, celebrate samurai traditions.

Scene from *Kagemusha*

FIND OUT MORE | ARMS AND ARMOUR | ASIA, HISTORY OF | BUDDHISM | FEUDALISM | JAPAN, HISTORY OF | WARFARE

SATELLITES

CIRCLING THE EARTH, high above our heads, satellites are messengers and observers in the sky. They relay telephone calls, watch the weather, guide ships and aircraft, and carry out tasks that are impossible on the ground. They travel 10 to 30 times faster than an airliner. A satellite's speed prevents it from falling to the Earth and throws it outward. The inward pull of gravity balances this outward force and traps the satellite in an endless path around Earth.

Sputnik could broadcast clear signals even when it was spinning.

Two-thirds of *Sputnik's* weight consisted of batteries.

Sputnik 1
In 1957, Soviet scientists launched the first satellite, *Sputnik 1*. It was simple, and measured the temperature of the atmosphere, broadcasting the readings as it orbited.

ECS1 – European Communications Satellite 1

Solar panels turn the Sun's light into electrical power.

Solar panels unfold to catch sunlight.

Gold foil protects satellite from heat of the Sun.

Dish antenna

Transponders inside the satellite receive and transmit signals.

Anatomy of a satellite

The main structure is made of aluminium or plastic reinforced with carbon fibre. The satellite must be strong enough to withstand the force of being launched, yet as light as possible because the launch requires enormous amounts of power. There are two or three versions of every system on board so that a failure does not disable the satellite.

Ground station broadcasts signals from dishes pointed at the satellite.

Receiving antenna

Types of satellites

Once satellites were used mainly for spying or to detect the launch of nuclear missiles. Today, different kinds of satellites are used for more peaceful purposes.

Communications
These satellites carry telephone calls and television channels from one continent to another.

Weather
These satellites provide weather forecasters with pictures of cloud formations.

Observation
These satellites can "see" infrared light, so they can monitor vegetation, bare soil and rock, snow and ice, water, and urban areas.

Astronomical
Telescopes above the atmosphere can give astronomers a much clearer view of the Universe.

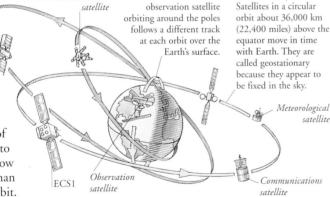

Elliptical orbit: Most satellites fly in elliptical orbits like flattened circles.

Soviet communications satellite

Astronomical satellite

Polar orbit: An observation satellite orbiting around the poles follows a different track at each orbit over the Earth's surface.

Geostationary orbit: Satellites in a circular orbit about 36,000 km (22,400 miles) above the equator move in time with Earth. They are called geostationary because they appear to be fixed in the sky.

Meteorological satellite

Orbits

A satellite's orbit is the curved path it follows around Earth. The pull of gravity is stronger closer to Earth, so a satellite in a low orbit must travel faster than one in a geostationary orbit.

ECS1

Observation satellite

Communications satellite

Space debris
Since *Sputnik* was launched, eight nations have launched an average of 100 satellites a year. Early launches created tiny pieces of debris, each of which can destroy a satellite. There are more than 7,000 large objects orbiting the Earth.

Konstantin Tsiolkovskii

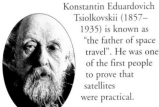

A Russian mathematicsbteacher Konstantin Eduardovich Tsiolkovskii (1857–1935) is known as "the father of space travel". He was one of the first people to prove that satellites were practical.

Timeline

1687 Isaac Newton describes how to launch an artificial satellite with a cannon.

1945 Arthur C. Clarke proposes a geostationary satellite.

1957 Soviets launch *Sputnik 1*, the first artificial satellite.

1958 USA launches first satellite, *Explorer 1*.

Telstar

1962 USA launches *Telstar*, the first communications satellite.

1963 USA sends *Syncom 2*, the first geostationary satellite, into orbit.

1972 USA launches *Landsat 1*, first Earth resources satellite.

1990 *Hubble Space Telescope* launched with a faulty mirror. This is corrected by astronauts in 1994

1992 USA satellite *COBE* captures temperature data from the afterglow of the Big Bang.

2000 Failed iridium telephone satellite network turned off.

FIND OUT MORE   ASTRONOMY   EARTH   ROCKETS   SPACE EXPLORATION   TELECOMMUNICATIONS   TELESCOPES

S

SCANDINAVIA, HISTORY OF

DESPITE ITS SMALL population, Scandinavia has had a huge impact on European history. The Vikings of Denmark and Sweden raided most European nations in the 9th and 10th centuries, leaving their mark wherever they landed. During the 16th century, Sweden emerged as one of Europe's most powerful nations, creating an empire that lasted for 200 years. In the 20th century, Scandinavian nations led the way in establishing welfare states to support their people, and Norway was the first European nation to give women the vote.

Empire of Canute

In 1016, the throne of England fell vacant. It was seized by Canute, brother of the Danish king. Within a few years, Canute added Denmark, Norway, and southern Sweden to his empire, ruling with great skill until his death in 1035.

Coin of Canute

Coming of Christianity
The nations of Scandinavia became Christian during the 9th to 11th centuries, although remote regions kept their traditional beliefs until much later. In Norway, the first churches were built of wood.

Union of Kalmar
In 1397, in Kalmar, Sweden, Margaret of Denmark persuaded Norway and Sweden to unite. Kingship was elected in all these countries, so the union could not be maintained. It collapsed in 1523, when Gustavus I became king of Sweden.

Margaret of Denmark (1353–1412)

Stave church, Gol, Norway

Church is built of vertical lengths of wood called staves.

Sweden

During the 16th and 17th centuries, Sweden took over Norwegian cities such as Trondheim and rose to become one of the most powerful states in Europe. The country adopted the Lutheran faith, and championed the Protestant cause. A succession of able kings carved out a vast empire that surrounded the Baltic Sea and included Finland and parts of Russia and northern Germany.

Swedish Empire

Trondheim

Stockholm

Great Northern War
In 1700, Sweden's neighbours joined together to break its stranglehold on the Baltic and its trade. When peace finally came in 1721, Sweden lost its supremacy in the region, and Russia achieved its "window on Europe" by gaining access to the Baltic.

Russia defeated Sweden at the Battle of Hango, 1714.

Gustavus II Adolphus
Gustavus Adolphus (1594–1632) became king of Sweden in 1611. Aided by his chancellor Axel Oxenstjerna, he improved the economy and extended the Swedish empire in northern Poland. In 1630, he entered the Thirty Years' War on the side of the German Protestants fighting against Catholic Habsburg domination. In a few months he won a series of battles that transformed the map of Europe.

Modern Scandinavia

Norway broke free from Swedish rule in 1905; Finland won independence from Russia in 1917. Later, the Scandinavian nations worked together, setting up the Nordic Council in 1952 to improve relations between them. Denmark, Sweden, and Finland have joined the European Union.

Modern public housing

Welfare states
The Scandinavian states were among the first to introduce a strong welfare system. Good child care and facilities for the sick and elderly were provided, and unemployment has been kept low. High taxes were needed to pay for these benefits.

Scandinavia in World War II
Denmark and Norway were occupied by Germany from 1940–45; Finland was occupied by the Russians. Sweden stayed neutral. Most people defied the occupying forces – King Christian X and other Danes helped Jews to escape to Sweden – but a collaborationist government was set up by fascist politician Vidkun Quisling (1887–1945) in Norway.

Christian X of Denmark (r.1912–47)

Timeline
700s Vikings raid Europe's coastline.

1016 Canute rules Denmark, Norway and England.

1397 Kalmar Union between Denmark, Sweden, and Norway.

1523 Sweden leaves union and gains independence.

1658 Swedish Empire reaches its greatest extent in Europe.

1700–21 Great Northern War: Sweden fends off an attempted takeover from neighbouring countries.

1814 Norway is transferred from Denmark to Sweden.

1905 Norway gains independence.

1917 Finland gains independence from Russia.

1940–45 Germany occupies Denmark and Norway; Russia occupies Finland.

1967 Denmark joins European Union.

1995 Sweden and Finland join European Union.

FIND OUT MORE   ANGLO-SAXONS   EUROPE, HISTORY OF   HOLY ROMAN EMPIRE   NORMANS   RUSSIA, HISTORY OF   UNITED KINGDOM, HISTORY OF   VIKINGS   WORLD WAR II

SCHOOLS AND COLLEGES

AS YOUNG CHILDREN, most of us first learn how to read and write at school. This is the place where we begin our formal education, which may continue up to college or university level. At school, skilled teachers pass on their learning to others and equip them to take their place in society. Until the 1800s, only a privileged few went to school. It is only recently, and in the industrialized nations, that education has become available to all.

Learning to write in ancient Greece.

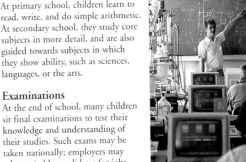

Early schooling
Schools were first created by the Sumerians c.3,500 BC, after the invention of writing. Teachers in the ancient world were often temple priests. Young boys were taught reading and writing, practising on pieces of flat stone or broken bits of pottery.

Geography work book, France

Maori school book, New Zealand

Dinosaur, drawn by 10 year old Japanese boy

Stages of schooling
In the industrialized world, schooling is divided into stages, which differ from country to country. In the UK, children up to five years attend nursery schools, where they learn through play. From age six to 11 years, children receive a basic education at primary school; at secondary schools, 12- to 18-year-olds study more specialized subjects. In the developing world, less money is available to provide education for all: schooling often ends at age 11.

Subjects
At primary school, children learn to read, write, and do simple arithmetic. At secondary school, they study core subjects in more detail, and are also guided towards subjects in which they show ability, such as sciences, languages, or the arts.

0	sifuri	5	tano
1	moja	6	sita
2	mbili	7	saba
3	tatu	8	nane
4	nne	9	tisa

School book, Kenya

Writing equipment

Natural science and maths books, Korea

Examinations
At the end of school, many children sit final examinations to test their knowledge and understanding of their studies. Such exams may be taken nationally; employers may select suitable candidates for jobs based on the results pupils achieve.

Science in secondary school

Higher institutes
Pupils who wish to continue their studies beyond school, or train for a career, may go on to college or university. Both are centres of learning: colleges tend to deal with a specific field, while universities offer a range of subjects and research opportunities.

Graduation gown

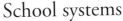

First universities
In Europe, the first modern universities were set up in medieval Italy (Bologna, 11th century), France (Paris, 12th century), and England (Oxford, 12th century).

Seal, University of Paris

Graduation
When a student successfully completes a period of study, the university or college awards a qualification, or degree: this is known as graduation.

School systems
Most countries provide some free education, although systems vary greatly. Schooling is generally compulsory for a number of years. In some places, education is centrally controlled by the government; in others, different regions run their own policies. Schools may be for children of mixed ability, or streamed, so that children study with others of a similar level.

China
All education in China is under the control of the government, and students are taught Communist ideas as well as other school subjects. Students who achieve the highest results in national examinations are sent to the schools with the best facilities.

Teaching
The chief means of passing knowledge from one generation to the next is teaching, the process by which a person helps others learn. In most countries, people who want to become school teachers must first attend college or university. There they learn about the principles of teaching and education, as well as studying one or two school subjects in depth.

Teacher and child in classroom

Timeline
1088 The first modern style university is established at Bologna in Italy.

1618 Parts of the Netherlands introduce free village schools.

1697 First Sunday schools started by Congregationalists in Wales.

1837 In Germany, pioneering educator Friedrich Froebel (1782–1852) opens his first kindergarten, to help young children learn in a creative way.

1854 First co-educational school opens in London, England.

1945 World War II ends; ambitious to create a better world, industrialized nations extend the opportunities for secondary education.

FIND OUT MORE CHINA AND TAIWAN EDUCATION MEDIEVAL EUROPE SOCIETIES, HUMAN WRITING

SCIENCE

"EUREKA!" shouted the ancient Greek mathematician and scientist Archimedes when he discovered the principle that explains why objects float in water. The word eureka means "I have found it", and the purpose of science is to find explanations for the things that happen in the world around us. Scientists test their ideas very carefully. If the ideas prove to be wrong, they develop new ones and test those as well. Scientists exchange ideas and the results of their experiments at conferences, through scientific societies, and in articles published in journals or on the Internet.

Scientific method

To find out why a particular event happens, scientists first suggest an explanation called a hypothesis. The hypothesis is tested by conducting an experiment so that the results either support or refute (disprove) the hypothesis. If the results support the hypothesis, the scientists can then develop it into a more detailed explanation called a theory.

Experiment | Control

Cylinder rotates so that light reaches plant from all directions.

Control plant is straight.

Plant from first cylinder is bent.

Leaves need light for growth.

Light reaches plant from one direction only.

Three weeks later

Hypothesis
A houseplant placed near a window will not grow straight upwards. The hypothesis that plants always grow towards the light could explain this, but it must first be tested by an experiment.

Experiment
In the experiment, a young plant receives light from one direction only. To check that no other factors are influencing the plant's growth, a "control" is set up, in which an identical plant receives light from all sides.

Observation
After several weeks, the plants are examined. The control plant has grown straight upwards, while the plant illuminated from one side only has bent in that direction.

Theory
From the results, the theory is devised that the plants contain a growth-promoting chemical that occurs on the side of a stem or leaf facing away from a light source.

Science and society

When English physicist John Cockcroft and his Irish colleague Ernest Walton first split the atom in 1932, few people realized that this achievement could lead to the building of devastating nuclear weapons. Because we often cannot predict how scientific discoveries will shape our future, it is important to analyze the role of scientists in the world and even sometimes to question the way in which they work.

John Cockcroft (1897–1967) and Ernest Walton (1903–96)

Science in practice

Scientists usually work together in groups and communicate with other groups of scientists who share an interest in the same type of research. They write up their work in publications called scientific journals, so that other scientists (their "peers") may check their work. This checking process is known as "peer review".

Laboratory
We often think of a laboratory as a room filled with bottles of chemicals and strange machines. A laboratory can be like that, but any space devoted to experimentation is a laboratory. In fact, laboratories have been set up in tents, aeroplanes, and even spacecraft.

Working in a biochemistry laboratory

Fieldwork
In some sciences, such as geology, it is vital to go out of the laboratory, to collect samples or data (information), or to make observations. This is called fieldwork. Data and samples collected during fieldwork are taken back to the laboratory and analyzed.

Geologist examining rock samples

Science and technology
The application of science to industry and trade is called technology. In the 20th century, technological developments enabled factories to mass-produce goods cheaply and quickly, and businesses to computerize the records of all their transactions.

Mass-production in a modern factory

NOVA
ATLANTIS
PER
FRANCISCUM BACONUM,
Baronem de Verulamio,
Vice-Comitem S. Albani.

VLTRAIECTI.
Apud Ioannem à VVaesberge,
Anno cIɔ Iɔ c XLIII.

Title page of Bacon's *Nova Atlantis*

Science fiction
In his book *Nova Atlantis*, the English politician and scientist Francis Bacon (1561–1626) foresaw many new technologies, including lasers, telephones, and genetic engineering. The book, like many science fiction novels, made predictions about the future based on the scientific ideas of the time.

Karl Popper

Austrian Karl Popper (1902–94) thought that true science must be able to be tested, so there is always a chance it may be found to be false. This means, for example, that the Big Bang theory of how the Universe began is not part of science, as it can never be tested.

FIND OUT MORE
ASTRONOMY   BIOLOGY   CHEMISTRY   EINSTEIN, ALBERT   GENETICS   GEOLOGY   MEDICINE   PHYSICS   TECHNOLOGY

SCIENCE, HISTORY OF

FROM THE TINIEST SUBATOMIC PARTICLE, through all living things, to the Universe itself, the scope of pure science is vast. Science is a quest for true explanations of how the world works. All the scientific knowledge we have today is the result of centuries of careful questioning, research, and observation – known as the scientific method – together with the inspiration of many brilliant minds. Before the scientific method was developed, people made discoveries about the world and developed technologies mainly through guesswork. Over the last four centuries scientific progress has become more rapid, and science has been able to create a more accurate picture of how the world works.

Technological advances

Before science

There were technological advances in very early civilizations, but no real science. After c.3800 BC, people in western Asia learned how to make metal, and this led to a decline in the use of stone tools.

Astronomy
Early people charted the heavens, but believed their gods were responsible for all that they observed. Many civilizations built observatories – huge stone circles – such as Stonehenge in England.

Fire

Earth

Air

Water

Natural philosophy

The ancient Greeks were perhaps the first to use reasoned argument when looking at the natural world. For the first time, people developed competing theories to explain familiar phenomena. Some of these theories, though untested at the time, are remarkably close to modern ideas. For example, the atomic theory, the idea that all matter is made up of tiny particles, or atoms, was first conceived by Democritus in c.400 BC.

Platonic solids
According to the ancient Greeks, four differently shaped types of atom made up the four elements – fire, earth, air, water – from which everything else in the world was made. The word "atom" comes from the Greek "atomein", meaning "indivisible". We now know that many kinds of atoms exist, and that they can be divided.

Medieval science

In medieval Europe, ancient theories prevailed – especially Aristotle's idea that all phenomena had a divine cause. Monks kept their love of learning alive by copying ancient scientific texts. The Islamic world, however, constantly added to the body of knowledge by developing new ideas in mathematics, astronomy, and medicine.

Alchemists at work

Crucible

The alembic was used to distil liquids.

Alchemy
Medieval alchemists, in their quest to make gold and discover the secret of eternal life, discovered much about the properties of metals and other substances. They developed many of the techniques we use today in chemistry laboratories.

Long metal tongs were used to lift the crucible out of the flames.

Renaissance science

By the 15th century, the ideas of the ancient Greeks, along with those of the church, had become dogma (regarded as truth) throughout Europe. During the Renaissance (which means "rebirth"), people began to question this dogma, and experiment in a truly scientific fashion. This new approach took nothing for granted, and used observation, experiments, and argument to develop theories to explain why things happen. Great scientists, such as Galileo and Newton, date from this period.

Scientific instruments
The use of scientific instruments, such as the telescope, made new observations of the Universe possible. Many of these observations challenged the accepted – but untested – ideas of the time. Physical models, such as the armillary sphere, helped to visualize and test the new theories, which now began to replace the old ideas.

This armillary sphere was used to help explain the complex movements of the heavens.

Principia Mathematica
After the printing press was invented, influential works, such as *Principia Mathematica* by Newton (published 1687), became available in great numbers, and helped spread the new scientific method. This book sets out the laws of motion and Newton's theory of gravity.

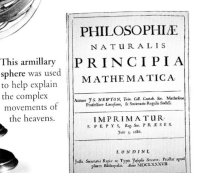

Francis Bacon

The English philosopher and statesman Francis Bacon (1561–1626) was the first person to formulate the scientific method. Before this approach became common, explanations of phenomena were accepted without question, but Bacon believed that any ideas about the natural world should be tested thoroughly for truth. In 1605, he published the *Advancement of Learning*, in which he urged people to classify facts about the world using the scientific method. In *The New Atlantis*, published after his death, he suggested the government should employ teams of scientists to conduct research.

743

S

Scientific societies

The new enthusiasm for scientific enquiry during the Renaissance gave rise to societies, where scientists shared ideas and promoted the study of particular scientific theories. The Royal Society for the Promotion of Natural Knowledge, founded in London, England, in 1660, was one of the first of these organizations. Members met regularly to discuss their experiments – but only in Europe, which still considered itself the centre of the world.

The Academy of Science and Fine Art, France

Desaguliers' steam engine, 1740

Mechanical principles

Industry and physical science were firmly linked during the Industrial Revolution. The invention of the steam engine resulted from a growing understanding of what steam was, how it worked – and how it could be harnessed. Steam engines were used to pump water from flooded mines, to drive machines in factories, and eventually to power the first trains.

Nineteenth-century science

Understanding in all the sciences – from the physical to the life sciences – dramatically advanced in the 19th century, thanks to better communications and scientific instruments, and the possibility of financial reward. Science became less religious, and scientists started to look at the world and everything in it as part of a huge machine, a view that helped them make some of the most important and unifying discoveries in the history of science.

Evolution

The theory of evolution – that species develop according to favourable characteristics – was proposed in the work of English biologist Charles Darwin. His observations led to the conclusion – controversial at the time – that human beings are related to apes and to the rest of the living world.

Handles turn paddles.

Water's movement generates heat, which is measured.

Paddles swirl water.

Forces of Nature

Up until the 19th century, the forces of nature – such as heat, light, electricity, and magnetism – were seen as being completely unrelated. In fact, heat is a form of motion, and the proof of this, along with the discovery of electromagnetism (magnetism produced by electricity), led to the development of the idea of energy during the 1840s. This concept was first recognized by the English physicist James Joule, who gave his name to the "joule" (unit of energy). This paddle wheel apparatus was used in one of his key experiments.

Modern science

By the end of the 1800s, many scientists believed their existing theories could explain everything in the world. Around 1900, however, scientists discovered that our galaxy is just one of millions of similar galaxies that make up the Universe. This and other events caused "classical" physics to give way to "modern" physics, causing new theories to arise. The best-known theories of modern physics are the theory of relativity (developed by the scientist Einstein) and the theory of quantum physics. These two theories have influenced the whole scientific world.

Cosmology

Einstein's theories of relativity, along with increasing knowledge of the Universe, started to give possible answers to the question of how time and space actually began. Most cosmologists now agree that they came into being in a massive explosion called the Big Bang.

Radio map of hydrogen gas, Andromeda Galaxy

Genetics

In the 1850s and 1860s, an Austrian monk, Gregor Mendel, worked out the basic laws of genetics – the study of inherited characteristics. In 1953, scientists finally worked out the structure of the DNA (deoxyribonucleic acid) molecule, a chemical that governs genetics, and that is found in every cell of every living thing.

DNA molecule

Carbon

Phosphorus

Oxygen

Nitrogen

Computer science

Advances in many fields of study, such as electronics and mathematics, contributed to the development of the electronic computer. Today, not only is computer science an established area of scientific study in its own right, but computers are essential tools for nearly all scientists.

Scientist using a computer

Modern medicine

The development of X-ray photography is just one of the techniques that has advanced modern medicine. Body scanning techniques, such as CAT (computer-aided tomography), along with knowledge from other scientific disciplines, have brought about better understanding of the body and have paved the way for new types of surgery.

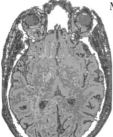
Brain scan showing left and right hemispheres.

Subatomic physics

In 1897, the electron became the first known particle smaller than the atom (subatomic particle). Hundreds of other sub-atomic particles have been discovered during collisions in huge particle accelerators, including protons and neutrons. Such discoveries are fundamental to understanding what matter is, because atomic particles are its building blocks.

Proton-photon collision

Alfred Nobel

Every year, outstanding achievers in physics, chemistry, physiology, and medicine are honoured by receiving a Nobel Prize, first awarded in 1901. The prizes are named after Swedish chemist, Alfred Nobel (1833–96). Nobel (who invented dynamite in 1867 and gelignite in 1875) left most of his fortune to recognize those whose achievements benefit mankind. In addition to the prizes for scientific achievement, Nobel Prizes are given for literature, peace, and economics.

FIND OUT MORE ATOMS AND MOLECULES COMPUTERS DARWIN, CHARLES EINSTEIN, ALBERT GENETICS INDUSTRIAL REVOLUTION MEDICINE NEWTON, SIR ISAAC SCIENCE

SCULPTURE

SCULPTURES ARE works of art created in three dimensions. They can be free-standing statues or bas-reliefs, which are like raised pictures on a background. Sculptors have traditionally worked in wood, metal, or stone, using the two main techniques of carving and casting. Carved sculptures are created by gradually taking material away, whereas cast sculptures are made by building material up.

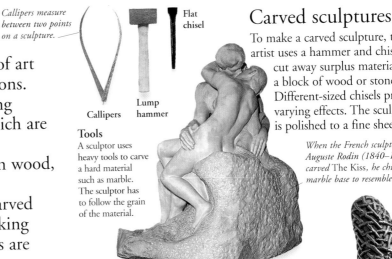

Calipers measure between two points on a sculpture.

Flat chisel

Lump hammer

Callipers

Tools
A sculptor uses heavy tools to carve a hard material such as marble. The sculptor has to follow the grain of the material.

Carved sculptures

To make a carved sculpture, the artist uses a hammer and chisel to cut away surplus material from a block of wood or stone. Different-sized chisels produce varying effects. The sculpture is polished to a fine sheen.

When the French sculptor Auguste Rodin (1840–1917) carved The Kiss, *he chiselled the marble base to resemble rock.*

Aeroplane **by Christopher Dobrowolski**

The wings are made of newspaper.

The engine is a real car engine from the 1940s.

Wooden tea chests form the plane's body.

A wooden garden shed is the base.

New materials
A number of contemporary sculptors have experimented with a variety of new materials, such as plastics, concrete, and even junk. Some sculptors have also set out to challenge conventional attitudes towards art by using everyday objects to create their work. The sculpture above, for example, is made from everyday objects that are instantly recognizable.

Cast sculptures

Cast sculptures are usually made of bronze. They are almost always hollow, and are therefore light. Bronze casting is a very ancient technique, and the earliest examples date from around 5,000 years ago. The sequence here shows the lost-wax process of casting a bronze head from Benin, west Africa.

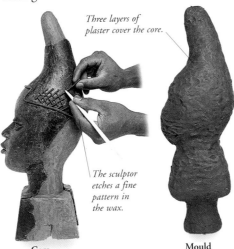

Three layers of plaster cover the core.

The sculptor etches a fine pattern in the wax.

Core

1 The core of the sculpture is roughly built up out of clay, made from soil and water. It is covered with a thin layer of wax, which the sculptor carves to add detail.

Mould

2 The wax-covered core is covered with a tough, heat-resistant plaster to form a mould. Holes are left at the top and bottom of the mould. It is ready to fire.

The bronze is heated until it is orange-hot, which is hotter than red-hot.

3 Molten metal is poured into the top of the mould. The heat of the metal melts the wax covering and the liquid wax drains out of the bottom, leaving a layer of metal which cools and hardens between the core and the mould.

4 When the metal has cooled, the sculptor breaks open the mould to reveal the sculpture. Its surface is polished to create shine and depth.

The finished replica head of the Queen Mother of Benin

Barbara Hepworth

The British sculptor Barbara Hepworth (1903–75) was one of a group of influential European artists who sculpted traditional materials in a new way. Their aim was to allow the natural properties of a material to dictate the sculpture's final form. Hepworth's works were carved out of wood or stone or cast in bronze, and were normally abstract sculptures.

Modern sculpture

In widening the range of materials they work with, sculptors have moved away from the traditional processes. Modern sculptors are now able to focus more on expressing their artistic ideas than on the technical skills of making a sculpture.

Abstract sculptures
Sculptures which do not represent things realistically are abstracts. This abstract sculpture *Pixel Lunch* is made from plastic lunchboxes.

Figures
This sculpture of two figures rising up out of the grass represents growth and the forces of nature. It is made from concrete and is displayed outside where, over time, weather will age it.

Two Standing Figures **by Federico Assler**

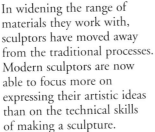

| **FIND OUT MORE** | AFRICA, HISTORY OF | ARCHITECTURE | ART, HISTORY OF | BENIN EMPIRE | CHURCHES AND CATHEDRALS | MUSEUMS | PAINTING AND DRAWING | POTTERY AND CERAMICS | RENAISSANCE |

Sculpture
Cast sculpture

Egyptian cat goddess, cast in bronze c.600 BC

Bronze equestrian statue of English king William III

Benin bronze cast of king's head, Africa

Viking 10th-century silver figure of a horseman

Bronze bust of a pug dog, France

Dancer, by Edgar Degas (1834–1917)

Carved sculpture

Nigerian wood carving of a European missionary

Native North American wooden totem pole

Carved wooden angel, from a medieval church, UK

Nigerian soapstone carving of ancestor figures

Native North American carved clay figurine

These figures are associated with healing.

Sierra Leone figures, carved in wood

Central American seated figure of a jaguar deity

Stone dragon, 19th century, London, UK

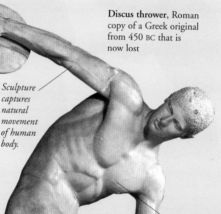
Discus thrower, Roman copy of a Greek original from 450 BC that is now lost

Sculpture captures natural movement of human body.

Carving of athlete's muscles and torso looks realistic.

David, by Michelangelo, 1504

Stone lion, London, UK, 1837

Demon and a Lady of Rank, 13th century, from a cathedral, France

Three Graces, by Antonio Canova, 1813

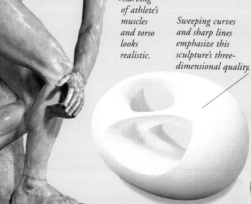
Sweeping curves and sharp lines emphasize this sculpture's three-dimensional quality.

Plaster cast sculpture, by Barbara Hepworth, 1943

Mother and Child, in marble, by Henry Moore, 1932

S

SEABIRDS

BIRDS THAT SPEND A LARGE part of their lives out to sea are called seabirds. There are about 300 species, belonging to 20 different families. They vary in size and shape and also in the way they catch their food. Some seabirds feed by flying close to the surface of the water and snatching their prey. Others plunge beneath the waves and use their wings or feet to swim. Seabirds sometimes wander huge distances over the open ocean, but all have to return to land to breed.

Northern gannet
This powerfully built seabird lives in the North Atlantic. It catches fish, such as herrings and mackerel, by diving head first into the water and scooping up a fish in its beak. Its head, beak, and body are streamlined to reduce the impact as the bird slams into the water from a height of up to 30 m (100 ft).

Gannets are strong fliers, alternately flapping and gliding.

Wings are folded back when the gannet plunges into the sea.

Feathers
Like other water birds, seabirds cover their feathers with a special oil to keep them waterproof. This oil is made by a gland near the base of the tail.

Salt glands
Seawater is salty, and a seabird's food contains lots of salt. This is disposed of through glands in the beak. The glands produce salty water that trickles out through the tip of the beak.

It takes five annual moults before young gannets grow the all-white adult plumage.

Seabird features

Front-facing eyes pinpoint fish from above.

Feet
All seabirds have webs of skin between their toes. This enables them to paddle through the water. The gannet uses its webbed feet to help it take off after a dive.

Seabirds share many features that help them to cope with life near salt-water. These include waterproof feathers, webbed feet, and glands that get rid of surplus salt in the body. Most seabirds are good swimmers, but many species rarely settle on the surface of the water.

Feeding

Seabirds live on a wide variety of food, from fish, squid, and jellyfish, to small scraps floating on the surface of the water. They use a range of feeding techniques according to the food they are catching. Some rarely catch their own food, but steal it from other birds.

The brown pelican is one of the biggest aerial divers.

Gulls have a long hooked beak.

Surface feeders
Albatrosses, gulls, and storm-petrels are surface feeders. Albatrosses and gulls usually snatch food out of the water while flying, but storm petrels patter over the water on their feet.

Aerial divers
Pelicans, gannets, and terns plunge into the water from the air. They have a buoyant body and do not dive deep, but quickly bob up to the surface.

Webbed feet

Cormorant drying
The cormorant does not have fully waterproof feathers so they absorb water. This reduces buoyancy, allowing the bird to dive deeply for fish. After feeding, it has to spread its wings out to dry.

Surface divers
Guillemots, puffins, and cormorants swim on the surface, but dive under to pursue their food. Guillemots swim underwater using their wings.

Food thieves
Frigate birds soar over the sea on their long narrow wings, but hardly ever land on the water. They chase other birds and force them to drop their food.

Largest and smallest

The wandering albatross is the largest seabird. It is about 1.35 m (53 in) long with a wingspan of up to 3.3 m (11 ft). The smallest seabird is the least storm petrel which is about 15 cm (6 in) long.

Nesting

Land can be a strange and unfamiliar place to many seabirds. Some spend several years at sea before they visit land to breed. To protect their eggs and chicks, most seabirds nest in large groups in places that land-based predators cannot reach. Some nest in burrows, but many others lay their eggs high up on cliff ledges.

Ground-nesters
Puffins dig cliff-top burrows. The females lay a single egg and the chicks spend more than six weeks underground.

Cliff-nesters
Kittiwakes nest in huge colonies on cliffs. Each pair makes a nest out of seaweed and raises two to three young.

Ledge-nesters
Guillemots lay their eggs on bare ledges. The eggs are pointed at one end so that they roll in a circle and not off the ledge.

NORTHERN GANNET

SCIENTIFIC NAME	*Sula bassana*
ORDER	Pelecaniformes
FAMILY	Sulidae
DISTRIBUTION	North Atlantic
HABITAT	Inshore waters and the open sea
DIET	Fish
SIZE	Length, including tail: 91cm (36 in)
LIFESPAN	About 20 years

FIND OUT MORE   BIRDS   EGGS   FLIGHT, ANIMAL   OCEAN WILDLIFE   PENGUINS   SHOREBIRDS

SEALS

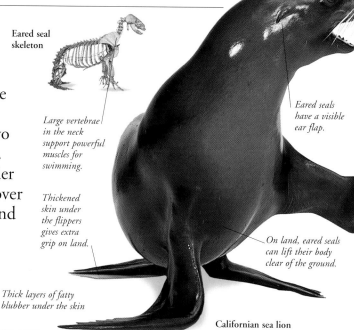

Eared seal skeleton

WITH A STREAMLINED body and four flippers, seals are suited to life in the water. They come on land to rest, mate, and give birth. There are two main groups of seals – true seals and eared seals. Together with the walrus they belong to the order Pinnipedia, meaning "wing foot". Seals live all over the world but are most common in the Arctic and Antarctic where there is plenty of food. They have been hunted for their fur and blubber for hundreds of years, and are now threatened by pollution of the oceans.

Large vertebrae in the neck support powerful muscles for swimming.

Thickened skin under the flippers gives extra grip on land.

Eared seals have a visible ear flap.

On land, eared seals can lift their body clear of the ground.

Californian sea lion

Thick layers of fatty blubber under the skin

True seal skeleton

Grey seal

Nails grip the ground.

Eared seals

The two groups of eared seals – sea lions and fur seals – are more agile on land than the true seals. They can bring their back flippers forward and turn their front flippers outward to walk. The main difference between the two groups is that fur seals have a thick underfur.

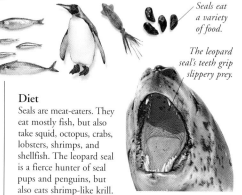

Seals eat a variety of food.

The leopard seal's teeth grip slippery prey.

Diet
Seals are meat-eaters. They eat mostly fish, but also take squid, octopus, crabs, lobsters, shrimps, and shellfish. The leopard seal is a fierce hunter of seal pups and penguins, but also eats shrimp-like krill.

True seals

The front limbs of a true seal are smaller than the back limbs and cannot support the seal's weight. True seals move awkwardly on land but are perfectly adapted for life in the water. Before diving deeply for food, they empty their lungs, and can stay underwater for more than 30 minutes.

True seal swimming
True seals use their back flippers to push themselves through the water. They press their front flippers against their sides to keep their body streamlined.

Eared seal swimming
An eared seal swims rather like a penguin, using its front flippers to move through the water. Sea lions are more powerful swimmers than fur seals, and dive deeper.

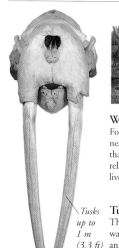

Walrus
Found in the Arctic Ocean, near land, walruses are larger than seals, and most closely related to eared seals. They live in groups all year round.

Tusks up to 1 m (3.3 ft) long

Tusks
The upper canine teeth of walruses are long tusks. The animals use these for display, fighting, and hauling themselves out of the water.

Elephant seals
Male elephant seals are much larger than females. They make loud calls through their trunk-like noses to defend their own group, or harem, of females.

Breeding

Seals choose isolated sites, such as rocky islands, to breed because they cannot escape easily from predators. Safe places to breed are rare, so space is often limited.

Seal colony
Fur seals gather to breed. Males fight for territory, then the females arrive to give birth. Males then mate with females in their territory.

GREY SEAL

SCIENTIFIC NAME *Halichoerus grypus*

ORDER Pinnipedia

FAMILY Phocidae

SUB-FAMILY Monachinae

DISTRIBUTION Western North Atlantic, Eastern North Atlantic, and Baltic Sea

HABITAT Ocean, coming on land to mate and give birth

DIET Mainly fish, some sandeels, octopuses, and lobsters

SIZE Length, up to 3 m (10 ft); males are larger than females

LIFESPAN Males 31 years; females 46 years

FIND OUT **MORE**   MAMMALS   MIGRATION   OCEAN WILDLIFE   POLAR WILDLIFE   WHALES AND DOLPHINS

S

SEASHORE WILDLIFE

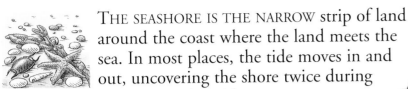

THE SEASHORE IS THE NARROW strip of land around the coast where the land meets the sea. In most places, the tide moves in and out, uncovering the shore twice during every 24 hours. During spring tides, at new and full moon, the tides reach furthest up the shore and lowest down the shore. Various animals and plants live at different levels on the shore, called zones, according to how well they tolerate being exposed to air or covered by sea water.

Storm waves can pound the seashore, dislodging animals and ripping away seaweeds.

Seashores

Zonation is most clear on rocky shores, where plants and animals live on the surface. Animals cling to rocks or are attached, like barnacles. Seaweeds are anchored by holdfasts. On exposed coasts, zonation is less distinct because spray extends higher up the shore.

The line of washed-up debris is called the strand line.

Rock pools low on the shore are regularly replenished by the tide and contain a rich variety of seashore life.

Rock pools high on the shore have less life because they suffer greater variation in temperature and salinity.

Sandy shore
There are few clues that animals live on sandy shores because they stay buried in the sand until the tide comes in. Often, the remains of animals, such as shells and the skeletons, or tests, of sea urchins, are washed up.

Plants

A variety of plants that can tolerate salt spray grow in the splash zone – the area that gets sprayed by the waves but does not get covered by the tide. Seaweeds grow from the upper shore to the lower shore, and into deeper water where there is enough light. In some parts of the world, sea grasses also grow on the lower shore.

Molluscs

All molluscs have a soft body surrounded by tissue called the mantle. This secretes the shell of molluscs that have one. Many kinds of mollusc live on the seashore. Most of those on rocky shores crawl around. Most molluscs on sandy shores stay buried in the sand.

Dog whelk
Common inhabitants of the middle shore, dog whelks are predators that feed mainly on barnacles and mussels. They drill a hole in the shell to get at the flesh. If the rock surface dries out, they lose their grip and roll down to damper parts of the shore.

Single foot of limpet, seen from underneath the shell

Tellins
These clams live buried in the sand on the middle shore and in shallow water. They feed when the tide is in by extending one of a pair of tube-like siphons over the surface to vacuum up debris.

Mussels
Mussels anchor their shells to rocks with strong strands called byssus threads. Tiny mussels can move around on their one foot, but they soon attach themselves to other mussel shells.

Limpets
A limpet's large muscular foot allows it to cling tightly to the rocks, both to avoid being washed away and to deter predators. When covered by the tide, limpets crawl around grazing algae from the rock.

Sea slugs
This sea slug gets its name of sea lemon because it looks rather like a lemon. Lacking a shell, sea slugs are delicate creatures that usually live below low tide. The sea lemon comes on to rocky shores in the summer to lay its eggs.

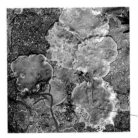

Encrusting algae
Some red seaweeds have chalky tissues. They grow as a crust in rock pools, on boulders, and even on shells, such as limpets.

Red lithothamnion seaweed

Seaweed
The largest seaweeds are the brown ones like wracks and kelps. This channelled wrack grows on the upper shore. Red and green seaweeds are smaller and more delicate, often growing in rock pools and on the lower shore.

Lichens
Orange, grey, and black patches on the rocks on the upper shore are lichens. These are made up of algal cells growing in a network of fungal tissue. Lichens are tolerant to both salt spray and dry conditions.

Crustaceans

There is a great variety of crustaceans, most of which live in the sea. They have a hard outer skeleton, jointed limbs, and two pairs of antennae in front of the mouth. Many crawl, and some swim, while barnacles spend their adult life stuck to surfaces such as rocks.

Narrow pincer for slicing flesh.

Barnacle cemented to lobster's shell

Hermit crabs
Most hermit crabs use a sea snail's shell to protect their soft abdomen. This colourful hermit crab lives on coral reefs. It is found at low tide hunting among the corals and in rocky crevices for food.

Heavy pincer for crushing shellfish.

First two pairs of legs end in pincers.

Second two pairs of legs end in claws.

Sea slaters
These relatives of woodlice live in damp places on the upper shore, where there is enough moisture for them to breathe through their gills. They come out from crevices at night to feed on rotting seaweed.

Lobsters
Occasionally, lobsters are found in rock pools on the lower shore. This one has become a home for barnacles, another type of crustacean. Most barnacles settle on rocks but space is limited so some settle on shells. These ones will lose their home when the lobster moults.

Echinoderms

This group of spiny-skinned sea creatures includes starfish and sea urchins, some of which live on the lower shore under rocks and seaweeds, and in rock pools. Most echinoderms have a five-rayed body plan. They all have tiny tube-feet filled with sea water and connected to canals inside their body.

Sand dollars
Sand dollars are sea urchins that are flattened in shape. When alive, they are covered in tiny spines. They live on the surface of the sand, often in warm waters. Bare shells are sometimes washed up on the beach.

Sea potato
The sea potato is a sea urchin. It uses the broader, flatter spines on its lower surface to dig itself down into the sand. It takes in sand, feeding on the film of nutritious material coating the grains.

Purple sunstar   **Spiny starfish**   **Bloody Henry starfish**

Starfish
These starfish live on the lower part of rocky shores and in deeper water. They have a double row of tube-feet on the underside of each arm. The tube-feet are tipped with suckers so the starfish can cling to the rocks.

Sea urchins
Like all sea urchins, the common sea urchin has a mouth on its underside. It has five strong teeth with which it scrapes off seaweeds and animals, such as sea mats, from rocks and the long stems of kelps.

Tube-feet   *Spines*

Worms

With their long wriggly bodies, worms look similar to each other, but there are many different groups, which are not all closely related. Among the worm groups that live on the seashore are the peanut worms that do not have body segments, and the bristleworms that do have body segments and bristles.

The body has more than 100 segments.

Ragworms
These bristleworms live under rocks and clumps of seaweed. They crawl using their paddle-like legs, and swim by passing wave-like motions toward the head.

Coarse bristles help the worm to move along.

Sea mouse
With its big flat body, this bristleworm does not look much like a worm. The sea mouse lives below low tide but can be washed ashore. The bristles protect it from predators as it crawls through the sand feeding on dead animals.

Worm inside its papery tube

Parchment worm
This bizarre bristleworm lives in a papery burrow it constructs in muddy sand on the lower shore and in deeper water. It beats its fan-shaped paddles back and forth to draw water into the burrow from which it takes in oxygen. Food particles in the water are trapped in a mucus net that the worm then eats.

Peanut worms
Some peanut worms look like peanut seeds when the front part of the body is retracted into the thicker trunk. The mouth is surrounded by a ring of tentacles. Peanut worms burrow in sand or mud, from the shore to the deep sea.

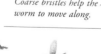

Beadlet anemones
These anemones unfurl their stinging tentacles when covered by water. The anemones use their tentacles to catch small prey and push it into their mouths.

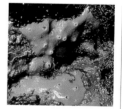

Breadcrumb sponge
Most sponges live in the sea from the shore to the deep sea. This sponge grows under rocks on the lower shore. Sponges are simple animals that usually grow attached to surfaces.

Sea turtle
Female turtles come ashore at night to lay eggs in the sand. Green turtles usually return to the beach where they hatched. They lay about 100 eggs at a time, laying up to five times during the breeding season.

 FIND OUT MORE   CRABS AND CRUSTACEANS   JELLYFISH, SEA ANEMONES, AND SPONGES   OCEAN WILDLIFE   SNAILS AND OTHER MOLLUSCS   STARFISH AND SEA URCHINS   TURTLES AND TORTOISES

SEAWEEDS AND OTHER ALGAE

ALGAE ARE THE SIMPLEST of all the plants. They they live in water or moist places. Algae range in size from minute, single-celled species to seaweeds that can be several metres long. In common with more advanced plants, all algae contain the green pigment chlorophyll. They also contain other pigments that mask the chlorophyll, so algae can be red, purple, or brown, as well as green.

Selection of green, red, and brown seaweeds

Seaweeds

Marine algae are better known as seaweeds. Like other photosynthetic plants, seaweeds need sunlight. Little sunlight penetrates depths greater than 15 m (50 ft), so most seaweeds grow in shallow waters around shores or reefs. Seaweeds provide food for tiny creatures, most of which filter dead particles from the water.

Wrack

Channelled wrack

Brown seaweeds

These seaweeds include the kelps, gulfweed, and wracks. They are tough, slippery plants. Many of them can survive for long periods out of water.

Green seaweeds

Less than 10 per cent of the green algae are seaweeds. Green seaweeds are small- to medium-sized plants, often with very thin, delicate fronds. Some, such as the sea lettuce, are used as food in some parts of the world.

Green seaweed

Red seaweeds

The seaweeds in this group get their red colour from a pigment called phycoerythrin. Red seaweeds are small- to medium-sized plants. Some of them are made rigid by a chalky secretion.

Maerl seaweed

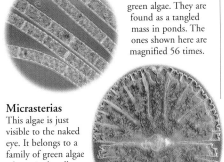

Spirogyra

These are thread-like green algae. They are found as a tangled mass in ponds. The ones shown here are magnified 56 times.

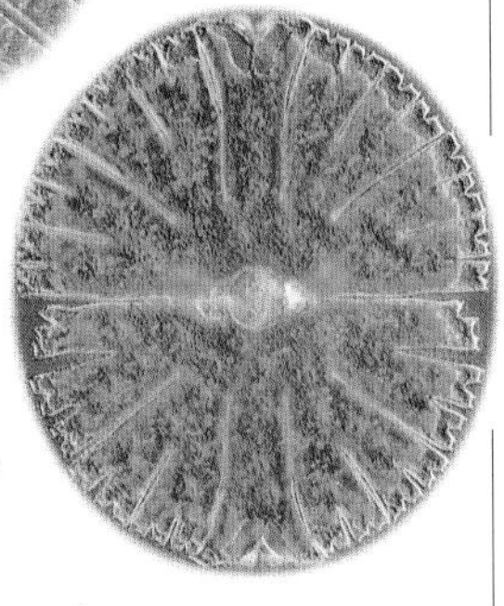

Micrasterias

This algae is just visible to the naked eye. It belongs to a family of green algae whose single cells are almost divided in two by a "waist". It is found among damp, waterside mosses.

Freshwater algae

Many freshwater algae can be seen clearly only under a microscope. They consist of just one or a few cells, or a long, thin line of cells.

Floats

Some species of wrack and kelp have fronds with conspicuous air bladders. These ensure that the fronds stay at the surface of the sea, where the light is brightest, even when the sea is rough.

Holdfast

The holdfast is frequently a many-branched structure that does just what its name suggests – it clings to rocks no matter how much it is pounded by the waves.

Parts of a seaweed

Seaweeds have no roots, leaves, flowers, or seeds. The seaweed plant body is called a thallus. It is divided into a holdfast (hapteron), a stalk (stipe), and a frond. The stalk may be very short – just a few millimetres long – or, occasionally, many metres long. In the sea, seaweeds float gracefully, but they cannot support themselves if taken out of the water.

Giant kelp

This seaweed lives in much deeper water than other seaweeds and can grow to more than 60 m (197 ft) long. Attached to the seabed, each plant produces a long stipe that can grow more than a metre in one day to reach light. Sea otters love to float among the fronds.

Lifecycle of a brown seaweed

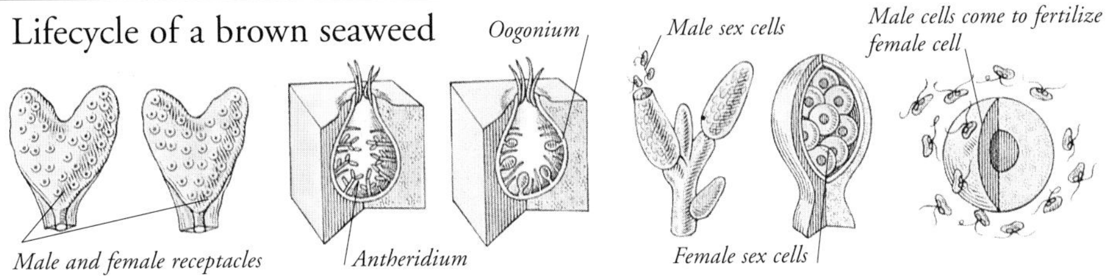

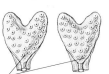

Male and female receptacles

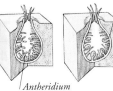

Oogonium

Antheridium

Male sex cells

Female sex cells

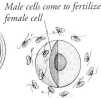

Male cells come to fertilize female cell

1 Separate male and female reproductive patches, called receptacles, develop at the tip of fronds.

2 Embedded in receptacles are conceptacles, which contain the sex organs – antheridia (male) and oogonia (female).

3 The oogonia split to release female sex cells. Male sex cells swim into the water through pores.

4 Male sex cells are attracted to a female cell to fertilize it by means of chemicals.

FIND OUT MORE

LAKE AND RIVER WILDLIFE

OCEAN WILDLIFE

PHOTOSYNTHESIS

PLANTS

SEASHORE WILDLIFE

S

SEVEN WONDERS OF THE ANCIENT WORLD

IN ANCIENT GREEK AND ROMAN TIMES, 2,500 years ago, as people became more interested in the world outside their villages, writers began to celebrate the greatest technological achievements of the age. These writers included the Greeks Herodotus and Antipater, and the buildings and statues they wrote about became known as the Seven Wonders of the World. The wonders ranged from the Pyramids of Giza in Egypt to the Colossus, a statue that towered over the harbour at Rhodes. They showed what the stonemasons, architects, sculptors, metalworkers, and engineers of the ancient world could achieve with the simple tools at their disposal.

The wonders were located around the Mediterranean Sea.

Pharos of Alexandria

This great lighthouse was planned in the reign of Ptolemy I of Egypt and completed by c.280 BC, on the island of Pharos just outside Alexandria in Egypt. The light from its fire was visible up to 50 km (30 miles) away. It was so famous that it became the model for many later lighthouses. In 796, the Pharos was damaged by an earthquake, but the foundations can still be seen.

Statue of Zeus

Pharos tower was 105 m (344 ft) high.

Constantly burning fire of wood or oil

Metal mirrors to reflect flames

The middle section was octagonal (eight-sided).

The bottom section was square.

Statue of Zeus
In 456 BC, the sculptor Phidias built a 13-m (43-ft) ivory-and-gold statue of Zeus, holding a figure of the goddess of victory. A temple was built around the statue at Olympia, Greece, home of the original Olympic Games. In AD 394, the statue was moved to Constantinople (Istanbul), but later destroyed.

Temple of Artemis
This temple was originally built in c.560 BC, in the Greek city of Ephesus (Turkey), as a sanctuary for Artemis, goddess of hunting, chastity, and childbirth. The temple was destroyed by the Ostrogoths in AD 263.

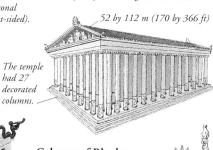

52 by 112 m (170 by 366 ft)

The temple had 27 decorated columns.

Mausoleum at Halicarnassus
The tomb of the Persian governor Mausolos was built in Halicarnassus, in present-day Turkey, in the 4th century BC. It was famous for its size and lavish carved decoration. The Mausoleum was damaged in an earthquake in the 13th century and was later demolished.

Hanging Gardens
The Babylonian king Nebuchadnezzar II, built these shady, lush gardens in the 7th century BC to remind his queen, Amytis, of her native home, Persia. It was a masterpiece of engineering, with small streams flowing along the terraces, bringing water to the plants and trees that grew there.

A statue crowned the top level.

The base was 38 by 32 m (126 by 105 ft).

Rooms for fuel storage and accommodation

Colossus of Rhodes
This huge statue of the Greek sun-god Helios stood near the harbour on the island of Rhodes, Greece. Standing at 33 m (110 ft), and made of cast bronze sections supported on an iron framework, it was the largest statue of its time. Sadly, an earthquake toppled the Colossus in c.225 BC – only 65 years after it was built to commemorate the end of a seven-year siege.

Great Pyramid
The Pyramids of Giza in Egypt are the only survivors of the Seven Wonders of the World, and are also the oldest. There are three: the Great Pyramid was built as his tomb by Pharaoh Khufu in c.2560 BC. The others were built for two of his successors, Khafre and Menkaure, and are smaller.

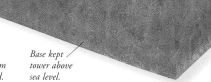

Ancient Egyptians built their pyramids from the centre outward.

Base kept tower above sea level.

Each side measured 230 m (755 ft) at the base.

Herodotus
Known as the Father of History, the Greek writer Herodotus (c.484– 425 BC) was born in Halicarnassus, western Asia. He described several of the wonders, particularly the pyramids, in his book, *The Histories*. He also wrote about the Walls of Babylon, which some lists included, instead of the Pharos of Alexandria.

FIND OUT MORE   ALEXANDER THE GREAT   BABYLONIAN EMPIRE   GREECE, ANCIENT   HOLY LAND, HISTORY OF   PYRAMIDS

SHAKESPEARE, WILLIAM

THE ENGLISH WRITER William Shakespeare was probably the greatest playwright who has ever lived. In spite of this, few facts are known about his life. Contemporaries who wrote about him described him as a good-looking man who liked a quiet life. Thirty-seven of his plays have survived, although he may have written more that have been lost. He wrote mostly in unrhymed verse, though he also used prose. He was a very successful playwright and actor, and was eventually able to buy a large house in his English home town, Stratford-upon-Avon. He retired there for the very last few years of his life, and died in 1616.

Shakespeare's birthplace

Early life
Shakespeare was born in 1564 at Stratford-upon-Avon, England. His father was a local businessman. Shakespeare probably went to the town grammar school, where he would have had a strict schooling.

Globe Theatre

From 1592, Shakespeare worked as an actor and writer in London. He joined a company called the Lord Chamberlain's Men. In 1599, he and six associates became owners of the Globe Theatre near the River Thames. This became the company's base, and many of his plays were produced there.

The Globe no longer survives; this is one possible reconstruction.

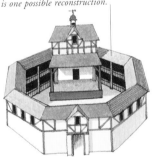

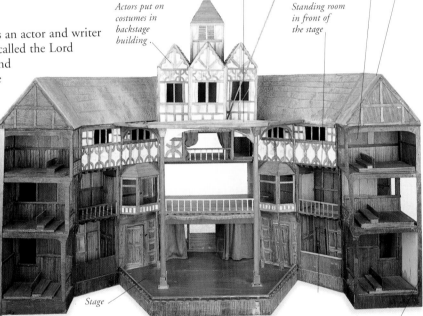

Wooden canopy over stage

Galleries with seats

Thatched roof

Actors put on costumes in backstage building

Standing room in front of the stage

Stage

Structure of oak beams

First Folio
Shakespeare did not publish his plays – he wanted to keep the scripts for his company. After his death, his friends John Hemminges and Henry Condell collected the plays and published them in 1623 in a book known as the *First Folio*.

Portrait of Shakespeare on title page of First Folio

Shakespeare's works

William Shakespeare wrote his plays with the actors of his company in mind. As well as comedies (featuring famous comic actor Will Kempe) and tragedies (for leading tragedian Richard Burbage), he wrote a whole series of plays, such as *Henry V* and *Richard III*, about English history. He was one of the most versatile writers of his time.

Richard III

Tragedies
Shakespeare's most famous plays are probably his tragedies. These plays, with their serious themes and sad endings, often centre on a heroic, if flawed hero, such as in *Othello, King Lear, Macbeth,* and *Hamlet.*

Othello

Comedies
Shakespeare's comedies are love stories with amusing twists. They are still among his most popular works. They include *A Midsummer Night's Dream, Twelfth Night,* and *As You Like It.*

A Midsummer Night's Dream

Sonnets
Shakespeare wrote 154 fourteen-line poems called sonnets. Some of these are addressed to a young man, others to a woman with dark hair, now known as the "dark lady" of the sonnets. It is not known for certain who these two people actually were.

SHAKE-SPEARES

SONNETS.

Neuer before Imprinted.

AT LONDON
By G. Eld for T. T. and are

Title page of the first edition of the sonnets

WILLIAM SHAKESPEARE

1564	Born, Stratford-upon-Avon.
1582	Marries Anne Hathaway.
1592	Writes his first plays in London for the Lord Chamberlain's Men.
1593–94	Plague epidemic forces theatres to close; Shakespeare writes poems such as *Venus and Adonis.*
1594–99	Writes comedies and histories.
1599	Globe Theatre built.
1603	Lord Chamberlain's Men gain the support of King James I; they become the King's Men.
1600–08	Produces many of the great tragedies.
1616	Dies in Stratford-upon-Avon.

FIND OUT MORE   DRAMA   ELIZABETH I   POETRY   THEATRES   UNITED KINGDOM, HISTORY OF

SHARKS AND RAYS

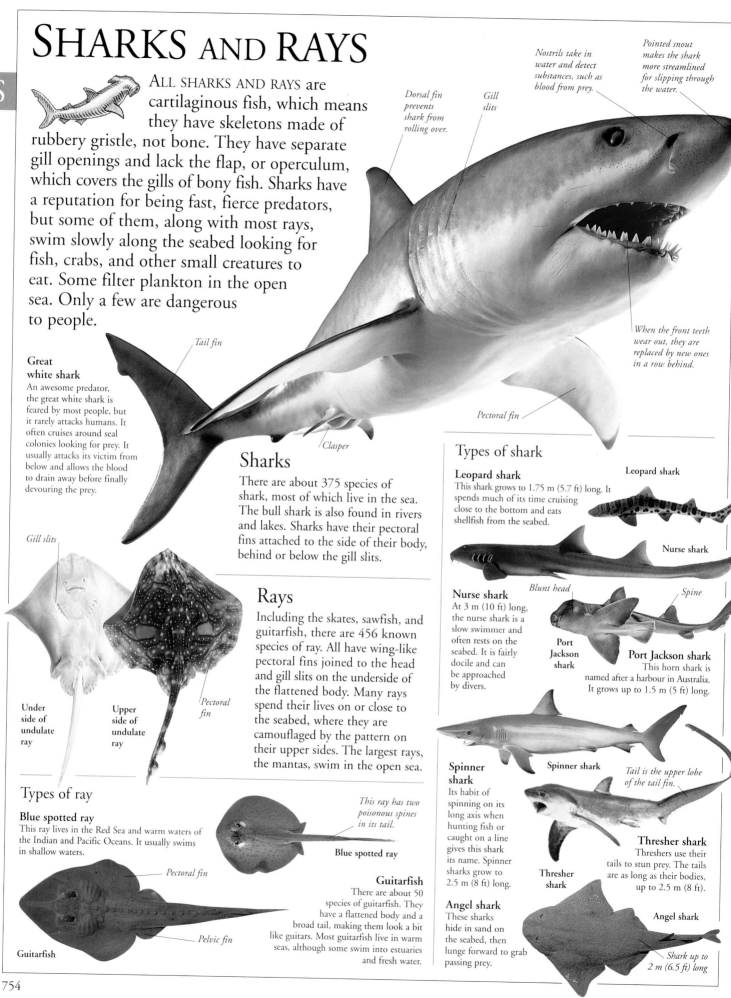

ALL SHARKS AND RAYS are cartilaginous fish, which means they have skeletons made of rubbery gristle, not bone. They have separate gill openings and lack the flap, or operculum, which covers the gills of bony fish. Sharks have a reputation for being fast, fierce predators, but some of them, along with most rays, swim slowly along the seabed looking for fish, crabs, and other small creatures to eat. Some filter plankton in the open sea. Only a few are dangerous to people.

Dorsal fin prevents shark from rolling over.

Gill slits

Nostrils take in water and detect substances, such as blood from prey.

Pointed snout makes the shark more streamlined for slipping through the water.

Tail fin

Pectoral fin

When the front teeth wear out, they are replaced by new ones in a row behind.

Clasper

Great white shark

An awesome predator, the great white shark is feared by most people, but it rarely attacks humans. It often cruises around seal colonies looking for prey. It usually attacks its victim from below and allows the blood to drain away before finally devouring the prey.

Sharks

There are about 375 species of shark, most of which live in the sea. The bull shark is also found in rivers and lakes. Sharks have their pectoral fins attached to the side of their body, behind or below the gill slits.

Gill slits

Pectoral fin

Under side of undulate ray

Upper side of undulate ray

Rays

Including the skates, sawfish, and guitarfish, there are 456 known species of ray. All have wing-like pectoral fins joined to the head and gill slits on the underside of the flattened body. Many rays spend their lives on or close to the seabed, where they are camouflaged by the pattern on their upper sides. The largest rays, the mantas, swim in the open sea.

Types of shark

Leopard shark
This shark grows to 1.75 m (5.7 ft) long. It spends much of its time cruising close to the bottom and eats shellfish from the seabed.

Leopard shark

Nurse shark

Nurse shark
At 3 m (10 ft) long, the nurse shark is a slow swimmer and often rests on the seabed. It is fairly docile and can be approached by divers.

Blunt head

Spine

Port Jackson shark

Port Jackson shark
This horn shark is named after a harbour in Australia. It grows up to 1.5 m (5 ft) long.

Spinner shark
Its habit of spinning on its long axis when hunting fish or caught on a line gives this shark its name. Spinner sharks grow to 2.5 m (8 ft) long.

Spinner shark

Tail is the upper lobe of the tail fin.

Thresher shark
Threshers use their tails to stun prey. The tails are as long as their bodies, up to 2.5 m (8 ft).

Thresher shark

Angel shark
These sharks hide in sand on the seabed, then lunge forward to grab passing prey.

Angel shark

Shark up to 2 m (6.5 ft) long

Types of ray

Blue spotted ray
This ray lives in the Red Sea and warm waters of the Indian and Pacific Oceans. It usually swims in shallow waters.

This ray has two poisonous spines in its tail.

Blue spotted ray

Pectoral fin

Guitarfish
There are about 50 species of guitarfish. They have a flattened body and a broad tail, making them look a bit like guitars. Most guitarfish live in warm seas, although some swim into estuaries and fresh water.

Guitarfish

Pelvic fin

S

Swimming

Sharks and rays do not have swim-bladders for buoyancy, as do bony fish. Some sharks have a large oil-rich liver which makes them more buoyant, but most have to keep swimming to avoid sinking. Sharks swim by beating their tail from side to side, while most rays propel themselves with their pectoral fins.

Leopard shark belongs to the smooth dogfish shark family.

Dogfish
As a dogfish swims, an S-shaped wave passes down its body towards its tail which then provides most of the forward propulsion. Water flowing over the stiff pectoral fins generates lift.

Electric ray

Electric current is discharged from organ at base of pectoral fin.

Spotted ray
This ray swims by undulating its pectoral fins. Waves pass along from the front to the back of the fins. The ray's tail is too thin to provide much propulsion.

Spotted ray

Electric ray
The electric ray propels itself forward by sweeping its broad tail from side to side. Undulations passing in waves along the edges of its pectoral fins also help it to swim. All electric rays produce electricity and can discharge over 300 volts.

Feeding

All sharks and rays are predators. The fastest sharks, such as makos and the great white, chase and kill fish and other prey. The sluggish sharks, such as nurse sharks and swell sharks, lie in wait for victims on the seabed or feed on slow-moving prey, such as clams. Most rays eat shellfish buried in the sand or mud, but manta rays eat plankton, which they filter out of the water.

Port Jackson shark's jaws, with pointed front teeth and crushing back teeth

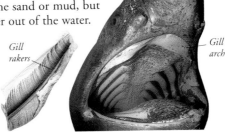

Gill rakers

Gill arch

Tiger shark tooth has a sharp point and a serrated cutting edge.

Teeth
The shape of a shark's teeth gives a clue as to what it eats. Sharp curved teeth grip fish; serrated teeth cut flesh; a fused row of flattened teeth crush shellfish.

Electrosense
Sharks can detect small amounts of electricity generated by their prey. They pick up signals via pores on their snout. They also appear to navigate by detecting changes in their electric field in relation to the Earth's magnetic field.

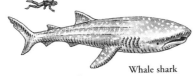

Whale shark

Largest and smallest
The largest shark, also the largest fish, is the whale shark, which reaches lengths of at least 12 m (39 ft). Like other ocean giants, it strains food out of the water using gill rakers, however, it also eats quite large fish. The lantern sharks are the smallest sharks. They grow to less then 20 cm (8 in) long.

Lantern shark

Gill rakers
Inside the basking shark's huge mouth are gill arches lined with rows of bristles called gill rakers. The rakers create a sieve through which water is strained before it flows out through the gill slits. Tiny animals called plankton, drifting in the water, are caught in the rakers and then swallowed.

Sawfish "saw"
Sawfish are types of ray that have a row of teeth on each side of a long snout. The sawfish uses its "saw" to probe the mud for prey, such as molluscs and crustaceans. It may also use its saw to kill fish by slashing at them with it as it swims through a shoal.

Reproduction

In both sharks and rays, the male passes sperm directly into the female with an organ called a clasper, so the eggs are fertilized inside her. Most sharks and rays give birth to live young, but some, such as dogfish, lay eggs with horny cases. Compared to bony fish, some of which lay millions of eggs at a time, sharks and rays produce relatively few eggs or young at a time – from one to 300.

Dogfish hatching

1 A dogfish embryo takes about nine months to develop before it is ready to hatch.

2 When the young dogfish breaks out of its egg case, it looks like a small version of its parents.

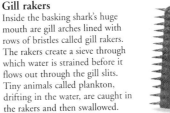

Tendrils anchor the egg to seaweed

Live birth
A lemon shark pup is born tail-first. Inside its mother, it was nourished by blood passing through a placenta, like a human baby. This is unusual. Most pups develop from large yolky eggs inside the mother.

3 The dogfish swims free and must fend for itself immediately. It will soon start to feed on small prey.

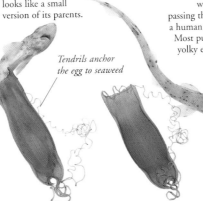

GREAT WHITE SHARK

SCIENTIFIC NAME	*Carcharodon carcharias*
ORDER	Lamniformes
SUBCLASS	Elasmobranchii
CLASS	Chondrichthyes
DISTRIBUTION	All oceans
DIET	Fish, seals, dolphins, and whale carcasses
SIZE	Up to 6 m (19.5 ft) long

FIND OUT MORE	EGGS	FISH	OCEAN WILDLIFE	POLAR WILDLIFE	REPRODUCTION	WHALES AND DOLPHINS

SHEEP AND GOATS

WITH THEIR THICK COATS and the ability to tackle rough terrain, sheep and goats can survive under harsh conditions, ranging from mountain cold to desert heat. Sheep and goats are closely related and belong to a group of mammals that also includes antelopes and cattle. There are many types of sheep and goat. They live in western North America, northern Africa, Europe, and Asia, spending the summer at high altitude, descending to the foothills and valleys in winter.

Corkscrew horns

Goats' foreheads curve outward

Hairy coat

Beard

Markhor
Markhors live in the Hindu Kush and nearby mountains in Afghanistan. Males and females have beards and manes that run along the chest, throat, neck, and back. The male's corkscrew horns may reach a length of 1.65 m (5 ft 5 in) along the curve.

Features of sheep and goats

Sheep and goats are agile creatures whose cloven, or split, hooves allow them to scramble over the craggiest of rocks. They have keen eyesight, good hearing, and coats of wool or hair. All rams (males) have horns. Goats have beards, and the males give off a pungent smell; sheep are beardless. Sheep graze on grass; goats browse mainly on shrubs. Both animals regurgitate their food and chew the cud.

Bighorn sheep
Bighorns live in the Rocky Mountains of North America. They take their name from the large horns of the rams. The horns grow backwards, then curve around to point forwards to eye level in the older animals.

Rams' horns can reach 91 cm (36 in) in length.

Sheep's foreheads curve inward

Woolly coat

Cloven hooves

Types of horn
The males of all wild sheep and goats have curved horns. Females of some species, such as barbary sheep and ibex, also have horns.

Himalayan ibex of both sexes have large, heavy, gnarled horns.

Mouflon, Europe's only wild sheep, have spiral horns with tips pointing inwards.

Argali, the largest of all sheep, may have horns up to 1.83 m (6 ft) long.

Bharal, or blue sheep, from central Asia, have horns that curve backwards and inwards.

Reproduction

Female sheep and goats mature by 2 years; males by 3–4 years. Mature males live apart from the females, but rejoin the herd in the rutting season to find a mate. In spring, after 5–7 months' gestation, females give birth to one kid, or sometimes twins. The young can walk almost at once and follow their mother, who protects them.

Chamois live in herds of up to 30 animals.

Family group of chamois

Female watches for danger.

Family groups
Most sheep and goats live in small herds of females and young. Old rams are solitary and live apart for most of the year. Young rams form separate bachelor groups. Sheep and goats feed in the early morning and evening and rest among rocks during the heat of the day. The herds are extremely wary; several females act as guards and either stamp or give a warning whistle if danger threatens.

Huge horns

Ram rears and will charge head on.

Alpine ibex fighting

Fighting
During the breeding season, males frequently fight to establish dominance. They kick and paw with their forelegs, then charge head on. They often rise up on their hind legs, lowering their heads at the last moment to meet with a skull-splitting crash, that can leave them dazed. Rams may also strike each other from the side.

Adaptation to habitat

Most sheep and goats are exceptionally hardy and live in highland regions. Agile species, such as the chamois, have special hooves that grip rock and cushion the shock of heavy landings, enabling them to move easily over sheer rock faces. Rocky Mountain goats can negotiate the steepest of inclines with ease, and can jump down vertical rock walls onto narrow ledges. The ability to thrive in harsh conditions makes sheep and goats suitable for domestication.

Dense white fur for warmth in the mountains

Rocky Mountain goats

BIGHORN SHEEP

SCIENTIFIC NAME *Ovis canadensis*

ORDER Artiodactyla

FAMILY Bovidae

DISTRIBUTION North America, from British Columbia to Mexico

HABITAT Craggy, often precipitous slopes extending above the timber line

DIET Primarily grazes on grass, but also eats berries, lichen, and bark in winter, and shoots and spruce in summer

SIZE Male – height at shoulder: 1.06 m (3.5 ft); weight: up to 136 kg (300 lb)

LIFESPAN Up to 15 years

FIND OUT MORE   ANIMALS   DEER AND ANTELOPES   EUROPEAN WILDLIFE   FARMING   MAMMALS   MOUNTAIN WILDLIFE   NORTH AMERICAN WILDLIFE

SHIPS AND BOATS

THROUGHOUT HISTORY ships and boats have provided an important means of transport. Early boats were simple, made from hollowed-out logs or bundles of reeds, but over the years the design of ships and boats improved as nations began to trade and fight for supremacy at sea. Although there are similarities between a boat and a ship, a boat is in fact much smaller and lighter. It is usually a single-decked craft propelled by either a sail, a pair of oars, or an outboard motor. A ship, however, is a large ocean-going vessel, powered by many engines. Unlike a boat, it can carry large cargoes and passengers across the seas.

Types of ships and boats

There are many different types of ships and boats. Most are designed to carry out a specific function, such as fishing, carrying goods and people, fighting, or leisure. As a result, there are differences in the shape of the hull, the size of the engine, and the equipment that is carried on board.

Sport and leisure boats
Boats used for pleasure are designed for a variety of purposes, such as racing and cruising. They range in size from lightweight jet skis to large luxury motor cruisers and yachts.

Fishing boats
Fishing boats are sturdy vessels designed to withstand rough seas. Various types of boats are used to catch different sorts of fish. A trawler, for example, is equipped to catch deep-sea fish. Today, most fishing boats are motorized.

Service vessels
Working boats have a variety of uses. For example, a tug tows larger ships in and out of harbours. In Arctic countries, icebreakers are used to crush through the ice and clear a path for other ships.

Warships
Warships are operated by the world's navies to patrol the seas and oceans. The largest is the aircraft carrier. Frigates protect aircraft carriers and search for enemy submarines.

Cruise liners

Cruise liners are large ships that carry travellers around the world. A liner is similar to a luxury hotel on water, and is a popular form of travel with many holidaymakers. Before long-distance air travel became common in the 1960s, passenger liners, such as the *Queen Mary*, were the only way for most people to travel between the continents.

How ships float
A ship's hull pushes through water, and the water pushes back on the ship with a force called upthrust. The upthrust balances the weight of the ship and keeps it afloat.

Upthrust from water pushing upwards

Sections of a liner
The inside of a liner is divided into decks, separating the sleeping areas from the rest of the ship. All outdoor activities take place on the upper decks, while entertainment rooms and cabins are located on the lower decks.

Captain
The captain of a ship is responsible for the safety of the passengers and crew on board. From the control room, the captain maintains contact with other ships in the surrounding waters and with onshore control centres.

Sun deck *Entertainment deck*

Passenger cabins *Medical quarters* *Crew's quarters*

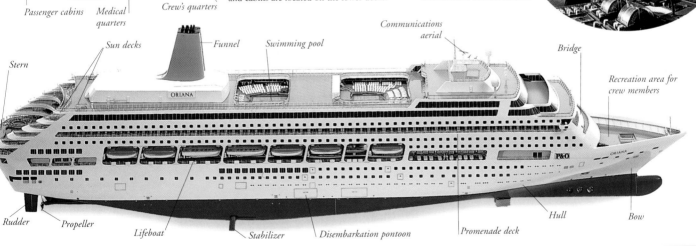

Sun decks *Funnel* *Swimming pool* *Communications aerial* *Bridge*

Stern

Recreation area for crew members

Rudder *Propeller* *Lifeboat* *Stabilizer* *Disembarkation pontoon* *Promenade deck* *Hull* *Bow*

Hull shapes

Ships and boats have different hulls that make the vessel more efficient at moving through the water and carrying cargo. The shape also determines how far the vessel sinks into the water, or how stable it is against rolling.

Keeled yacht
A yacht has a rounded hull to help control the boat in strong winds. The keel is filled with a heavy ballast, such as concrete, to stop the yacht tipping over too far.

Keel

Cargo ship
In the middle of a cargo ship, the hull is as large as possible so that it can contain heavy loads. The hull is more V-shaped towards the bow, and rounder at the stern.

Central hull

Speedboat
The shape of a speedboat's hull helps keep air between the boat and the water. As the boat speeds up, the hull starts to skim across the water, instead of cutting through it.

Flat V-shape

Catamaran
A catamaran has two separate hulls, joined together with strong crossbeams. This shape is very stable because it is so wide.

Crossbeam

S

Engines

Engines provide the power to push a ship or boat through the water. They normally turn one or more propellers under the stern of the vessel. The propellers bite into the water, forcing the ship along. Most ships burn diesel to produce gas or steam to turn the turbine engines. Some ships use nuclear energy. An outboard motor usually powers leisure boats.

Ship engineer checking machinery

Engine room
Situated on the lower decks of a ship, the engine room houses all the engines and electricity generators needed to make the ship function. Regular maintenance checks ensure that all the equipment is in order and safe to use. Many engine rooms on large ships are controlled by computers.

Outboard motor engine
Small boats are often powered by an outboard engine attached to the stern. A throttle is used to start up the engine, and the boat is steered using the tiller.

Throttle

On the bridge
The main control room of a ship is called a bridge. Located on the upper deck, towards the front of the vessel, it has large windows to give good all-round visibility. It houses the ship's steering and navigational instruments, such as radar, as well as controls for the engine room.

Radar

Compass

Engine controls

Throttle

Wheel to control rudder

Shipbuilding

Building a large ship is a major engineering project, requiring hundreds of expert workers. Although the basic structure of ships has not changed since the first wooden ships were built, materials such as steel and plastic are now used. Today, many ships are built in sections, which are then fastened together.

1 The first part of a ship to be built is the the keel, followed by the stern and hull. Scaffolding is used to support the hull and keel so they will not tip over. The ship is usually built on a metal slipway.

2 Once the structure of the ship is complete, the upper decks of the hull start to take shape. Skilled workers start to work on the rest of the ship. The ship is then launched as an empty shell, where it is equipped for a lifetime at sea.

Sailing yacht

Sailing yachts use wind for propulsion. They do not have to have the wind behind them – they can travel in almost any direction by adjusting the position of their sails. Most modern sailing boats have two sails, arranged in a "Bermuda" rig. Most yachts also have an engine, in addition to the sails.

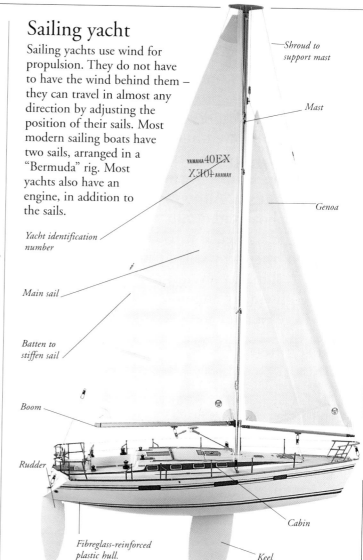

Shroud to support mast

Mast

Genoa

Yacht identification number

Main sail

Batten to stiffen sail

Boom

Rudder

Cabin

Fibreglass-reinforced plastic hull.

Keel

Passenger services

Despite the growth of airlines, ships still carry thousands of passengers to their chosen destinations. Modern passenger ships include ferries, hovercrafts, and hydrofoils. New designs mean that ships are faster, safer, more economical to maintain, and more environmentally friendly.

Hovercraft
A hovercraft reduces water resistance by riding just above the surface on a cushion of air. The cushion is made by large fans blowing air under the hovercraft. The air is held in place by a flexible "skirt". The hovercraft is pushed along by propellers in the air. Hovercraft can travel on to land for loading and unloading.

Hydrofoil
All boats are slowed down by the resistance of the water on their hulls. Hydrofoils have wing-like foils under the hull. As the boat speeds up, the foils lift the hull completely out of the water, and the boat skims across the surface. This allows the hydrofoil to travel much faster than other boats.

FIND OUT MORE   ENGINES & MOTORS   FISHING INDUSTRY   IRON AND STEEL   PLASTICS AND RUBBER   PORTS & WATERWAYS   RADAR   SAILING   SUBMARINES   TRANSPORT HISTORY OF

Ships and boats

Merchant ships

Tramp steamers are cargo-vessels with no fixed route.

Oil tankers are specially constructed to carry vast quantities of oil.

Liberty ships were mass-produced steel cargo ships. They were made by the USA during World War II.

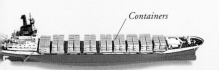

Containers

Container ships are designed to stow and transport large goods containers efficiently.

Cruise liners do not take goods vehicles, and are equipped with passenger entertainments and facilities.

Large goods vehicles park on deck.

Roll-on-roll-off ferries allow lorries and passenger cars to drive straight on and off without unloading.

Fighting ships

Torpedo tube

Torpedo boats are swift, small warships that carry torpedoes and other weapons.

Ship is controlled from bridge.

Flight deck

Aircraft carriers are huge warships with large landing platforms to allow aircraft to take off and land.

Minesweepers drag the water to remove undersea mines.

Utility craft and fishing vessels

Dredgers clear shipping channels, keeping them free from silt.

Life rafts are launched in emergencies.

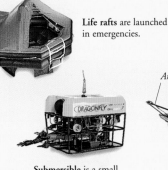

Mast

Trawlers are often diesel powered

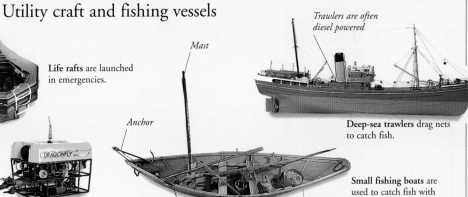

Deep-sea trawlers drag nets to catch fish.

Anchor

Police riverboats patrol waterways, sometimes in search of smugglers.

Submersible is a small underwater craft.

Small fishing boats are used to catch fish with rod and line.

Oar

Grapnel

Pleasure craft

Sailing yachts are used for pleasure cruising and racing.

Deck house

Speedboat is a small motor-boat with a powerful engine.

Sailing dingy is used to teach young people to sail.

Sprit

Mainsail

Mast made of lightweight alloy

Motor yacht has large, powerful engines for long-distance cruising.

Boom

Mast

Hull

Wooden rudder

Daggerboard

SHOPS

BUILDINGS DEVOTED TO BUYING and selling, shops allow customers to buy small amounts of what they need. They are the end of a chain that sees products travel from a manufacturer to a consumer, and shopping is a vital part of any national economy. Historically, shops such as butchers and bakers stocked only one sort of product. Today, shopping is big business; global chain stores sell a variety of goods. Customers can also buy from 'online shops' on the Internet and have the goods delivered.

Butcher's shop in ancient Rome

Early shops
Early nomadic peoples traded goods wherever they wandered. Shops began when people first settled in towns and were common by 3000 BC. They did not replace outdoor trading at fairs and in markets. The huge 16th-century market at Tlaltelolco, Mexico astonished Spaniards who came to conquer the Aztec empire.

Shopping centres

Increasingly, many different goods are sold under one roof. Department stores are large shops, each department specializing in a different kind of good. The first opened in Paris, France, in 1865. Shopping malls began in 19th-century Europe as arcades linking city-centre streets. The first modern-style mall opened in Kansas, USA, in the 1920s.

Harrods' merchandise

Supermarkets

A supermarket is a self-service food store. The first was opened in 1916 in Memphis, Tennessee, USA. The invention of the shopping trolley in 1937 allowed shoppers to buy more than they could carry, and ensured the success of the supermarket. By the 1950s, supermarkets were widely popular in the USA, and had spread throughout Europe.

Breakfast cereal packaging

Packaging
Food in supermarkets is generally pre-packaged, for speed and convenience, to keep food fresh, and to identify ingredients.

1950s' shopping trolley

Department stores
Some department stores are renowned around the world for the variety of luxurious goods they offer, and have become tourist attractions. They include Bloomingdales in New York, USA; GUM in Moscow, Russia; Au Bon Marché, in Paris, France; and Harrods in London, UK.

Malls
As well as shops, a mall may contain banks, cinemas, offices, and restaurants. The covered streets of a mall are traffic-free. They are often built in out-of-town sites, accessible only by car, so that builders must include adequate parking spaces.

F. W. Woolworth
US tycoon Frank Winfield Woolworth (1852–1919) made his fortune from discount shops that priced everything at either 5¢ or 10¢. The company he set up in 1879 now has 9,000 branches around the world.

Bar codes
A bar code identifies the contents of a package. A computer at the check-out scans the code, adds the item's price to the bill, and orders more product from the manufacturer when stock is low.

ISBN 0-7513-6034-1

9 780751 360349

Bar code

Markets

Malls may offer economy and convenience, but they lack the character of traditional markets everywhere in the world, where people gather to buy and sell goods.

Fresh vegetables

Selling spices in a Moroccan souk

Souks and bazaars
The roof of a souk (Arab market place) shades shoppers from the burning sun. Some are vast: the Grand Bazaar in Istanbul covers an area the size of 700 tennis courts.

Floating market
In Venice, Italy, where rivers are the quickest transport routes, water-borne shops are as convenient as malls are to the car driver.

Shopping from home in the 1930s

Mail order and online shopping
Catalogue shopping is especially useful for disabled people, and those in remote areas. The British Army and Navy Cooperative Society printed the first catalogue in 1872, and the Sears Roebuck catalogue began in the United States in 1894. TV shopping channels and buying over the Internet offer a more versatile and modern version of the mail order catalogue.

FIND OUT MORE | ADVERTISING AND MARKETING | MONEY | TRADE AND INDUSTRY

SHOREBIRDS

ALSO KNOWN as waders, shorebirds belong to 12 closely related families. There are about 200 species, all with long legs and slender beaks with which they probe for food in wet sand, soft ground, or mud. Some use their beaks to hammer open shells; others pull up worms or catch swimming animals. Many waders live on the shore, but others are found in a wide range of damp places, from riverbanks and woods to waterlogged hillsides.

Shorebird features

Shorebirds have specialized beaks for reaching a particular food. Some swim to find food, but most wade through water or walk over the ground on their long legs. They have good eyesight for watching out for danger.

Side-facing eyes for all-round vision

Strong beak is used to smash open shells.

Eurasian Oystercatcher

Oystercatchers
Like most shorebirds, an oystercatcher lays camouflaged eggs directly on the ground. If a predator approaches, a parent bird tries to lure it away from the eggs.

Feeding

Shorebirds eat a wide range of animals, from clams and snails to worms and shrimps. Many shorebirds live on creatures that are normally hidden in mud or cloudy water. The birds can catch these without being able to see them, because they can feel for them with the sensitive tip of their beaks.

American avocet

Oystercatcher hammers shells with the blunt end of its beak.

Slender, upturned beak

An avocet holds its beak open while looking for food.

Curlew

A curlew's beak is up to 19 cm (7.5 in) long.

Hammering beak
Some oystercatchers have a blade-like tip to their beaks, which they use to hammer open shells or prise them apart. Others have a pointed beak and eat worms.

Sweeping beak
An avocet sweeps its unique upturned beak from side to side, just below the water's surface. When the beak touches suitable prey, the avocet snaps it shut, trapping the animal inside.

Probing beak
The curlew uses its curved beak to probe deep into mud and damp grass. It can collect worms and molluscs that are beyond the reach of other birds.

Jacanas are also called lily-trotters.

Shield above the base of the beak

Jacanas
These waders live mainly in the tropics, on ponds and lakes with floating plants. Their weight is spread over their huge toes, allowing them to walk on plants without sinking.

Long legs

Slender toes with long claws

Grey phalarope
In most bird species, the males are more brightly coloured than the females. In waders called phalaropes, things are the other way around. The females are brighter, and the males raise the young.

Inland waders

Waders are found in many places inland. They live where the ground is damp enough for them to search for food, and where there are safe places for them to nest and raise their chicks.

Woodland waders
Woodcocks are shy woodland birds. They feed mainly after dark, when they probe the ground for worms. Their plumage provides them with superb camouflage.

Marshland waders
Northern lapwings are common in marshes and grassland in Asia and Europe. They are acrobatic fliers, and the males do aerial displays in the breeding season.

Riverbank waders
The blacksmith plover lives in southern Africa, and usually stays close to water. It gets its name from its alarm call, which sounds like a blacksmith hammering a piece of metal.

OYSTERCATCHER

SCIENTIFIC NAME	*Haematopus ostralegus*
ORDER	Charadriiformes
FAMILY	Haematopodidae
DISTRIBUTION	Europe, Asia, Africa
HABITAT	Rocky and muddy coasts
DIET	Molluscs, worms
SIZE	Length: 43 cm (17 in)
LIFESPAN	About 5 years

FIND OUT MORE   BIRDS   DUCKS, GEESE AND SWANS   HERONS, STORKS AND FLAMINGOS   MARSH AND SWAMP WILDLIFE   SEABIRDS

SHRINES

A SHRINE IS A SACRED PLACE dedicated to the memory of a person or event, or to a spirit god. Shrines range from tiny roadside structures housing pictures or statues to huge, richly decorated churches or temples. Sometimes special rocks, trees, or springs are also venerated as shrines. People visit shrines to pray and give offerings, hoping for good health or fertility.

Prayer flags flutter in the wind at a Buddhist shrine in Tibet.

Buddhist shrines
The Buddhist faith has many shrines and places of pilgrimage. These range from large and elaborate temples, adorned with statues of the Buddha, to simple hilltop sites. Some shrines are linked to the Buddha; others are associated with Bodhisattvas, outstanding people who help others along the Buddhist path of enlightenment. Flags often fly at Buddhist shrines. A prayer is written on each flag, so that the words can waft towards heaven as the flag flutters in the wind.

Spirits of nature
Many traditional religions worship nature spirits, which reside in sacred trees, springs, or rocks. When a shaman (priest) performs holy rituals at these shrines, his followers believe he actually becomes the nature spirit.

Well dressing
In some parts of England, ancient wells are decorated once a year with Christian designs of seeds, flowers, and other natural materials. They are often dressed at midsummer, indicating that the custom has survived from pagan times.

Decoration shows Jesus calling his disciples

Follow Me

1982

A well in Derbyshire, England, with traditional decoration

Many of the standing stones in Brittany, France are aligned in long avenues.

Fertility stones
Ancient standing stones of northern Europe are often placed so the Sun rises over them on Midsummer's Day. They were probably erected by people who wanted the Sun to ripen their crops. Women still visit the stones, hoping the stones will help them conceive.

Pilgrimages

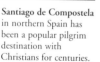

Santiago de Compostela is dedicated to St James.

Making a pilgrimage, a journey to a shrine, is important in many religions. Pilgrims hope their journey will bring them closer to God.

Cockle shell, symbol of St James

Santiago de Compostela in northern Spain has been a popular pilgrim destination with Christians for centuries.

Small shrines
In many countries people build small shrines wherever they want to pray or feel close to God at a spot with a beautiful view, beside the road, and in the home. Such shrines are treated with great reverence, and decorated with pictures and flowers.

Roadside shrines
Small shrines by the side of the road are common throughout Greece; they often commemorate the life of a local person, or mark a spot where someone died. They sometimes contain a statue or picture.

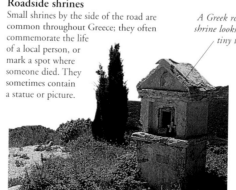

A Greek roadside shrine looks like a tiny temple.

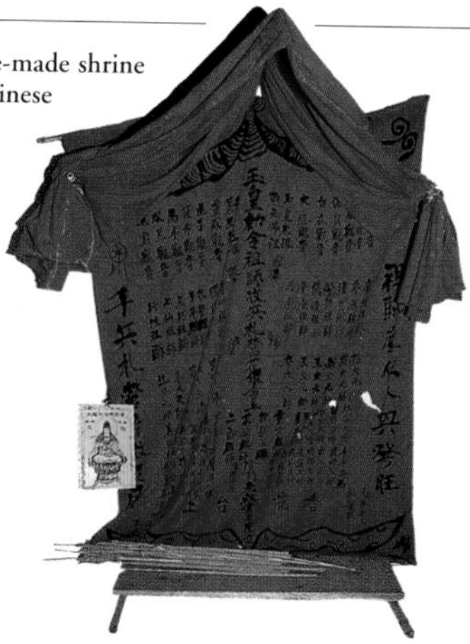

A home-made shrine in a Chinese kitchen

Household shrines
Many Chinese houses contain a small home-made shrine dedicated to one of the traditional Chinese gods or to the family's ancestors. The shrine may be made of wood and decorated with coloured cloth and beads. It opens to reveal a little statue of the deity. The family prays and makes offerings to their household shrine, especially when they have problems or are making important decisions about their lives.

FIND OUT MORE

ART, HISTORY OF   BUDDHISM   CHRISTIANITY   HINDUISM   ISLAM   PREHISTORIC PEOPLE   RELIGIONS   SCULPTURE

S

SIGNS AND SYMBOLS

LOOK UP FROM THIS BOOK, and you will probably see a sign or a symbol nearby. Both are means of communication, but in different ways. A sign is an object, gesture, or idea that points to something else, giving information clearly and quickly. A road sign, for example, advises drivers of conditions ahead; a trade mark guides shoppers to a product. A symbol is less direct; it usually represents something other than its image, to convey a hidden, deeper meaning.

Luck
Some people believe that certain symbols bring good luck. The eye is a common example. Portuguese fishermen paint eyes on their boats for luck; Chinese sailors believe a ship will lose its way without eyes to see. In the Mediterranean, people carry glass magic eye charms to turn away the intentions of evil-wishers.

Magic eye charm

Information signs

Signs must be concise and easy to understand, even for people who do not read or speak the language. For immediate impact, the most important information signs avoid words. An exclamation mark in a triangle spells "Danger!" in any language.

Picture signs help overcome language barriers in an international airport.

"Lifts to car park"

"Aeroplane departures"

"Men's, women's, disabled toilets"

"This way"

"Left luggage"

"Airport hotel"

Arrows
Signs work only when everybody agrees on their meaning. To most people, the sharp end of the arrow sign points the direction, just as a real arrow fired from a bow leads to its target.

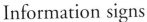

Trade marks

Manufacturers may mark the products they make with symbols called trade marks. A trade mark links a company's reputation to a product. The trade mark may be the main difference between competing products, so companies protect trade marks fiercely.

Brandnames
The best known brand in the world is probably Coca-Cola. Its distinctive symbol has become as much a symbol of American culture as of the drink itself. The trademark was created by a bookkeeper who worked for the Pemberton Chemical Company, which invented Coca-Cola.

Hallmarks
Hallmarks are tiny signs and symbols, stamped into gold and silver items to show the purity of the metal. In some countries, they are required by law. In the USA the symbols are not used: instead, the words "coin" or "sterling" are stamped into silver.

Officially tested in London

Year of testing (1986)

Some hallmarks and their meanings

Maker's mark

Made in UK

22-carat gold

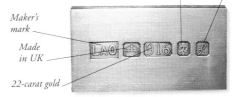

Seals and belonging

Signs and symbols act as a focus to unite people who belong to the same country, family, or organization, or who share the same beliefs. Some symbols have had the same meaning for centuries; others are modern, reflecting changes in society.

Seals and badges
Seals are raised images, pressed into wax, which governments once fixed to documents to prove they were genuine. The image represented an aspect of the organization. Modern seals and badges often continue this tradition.

Space shuttle crew members designed this badge.

AIDS ribbon
The folded, pinned red ribbon represents the fight against the disease AIDS. The wearer shows support for sufferers, and for research to find a cure for the disease.

The red ribbon, a symbol of the fight against AIDS since 1991

Religious symbols
A symbol may act as a focus for religious rituals. The symbol may stand for god, or may itself be holy. The Sikh religious community has five outward symbols.

State seal of Florida, USA

Space camp badge

Shopboards
Until street numbers began in the 18th century, shops hung out signs so customers could find them. Roman taverns, for example, hung out a bush to signal they sold wine. Some British public houses are still called the Bush, continuing the ancient tradition.

Symbolism
Artists, writers, and musicians use symbolism to subtly introduce a theme or an idea in their work, without actually showing it. For instance, western authors sometimes use bats to symbolize darkness, chaos, or impending doom. However, symbolic meanings are not necessarily the same worldwide. In China, the bat symbol represents good luck and happiness.

Kangha (comb) **Kara** (steel bangle)

Kirpan (sword)

The bat may symbolize death.

Three of the five Sikh symbols

FIND OUT MORE   ADVERTISING AND MARKETING   CODES AND CIPHERS   FLAGS   LANGUAGE   SHOPS

Signs and symbols
Religious signs and symbols

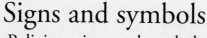

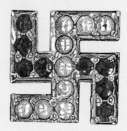

Om, a sacred syllable in the Hindu faith

Swastika, an emblem of the Hindu deity Vishnu

Star of David, the main symbol of Judaism

The sacred lamb, a Christian symbol for Jesus Christ

Animal symbols

The octopus is sometimes a symbol of fickleness.

Crocodile tears are a sign of hypocrisy.

The frog is associated with healing and wealth in China.

The camel, which kneels to receive a load, symbolizes humility.

The bald eagle is a national US symbol.

The whale is a symbol of death and rebirth.

Warning and prohibitive signs

A line through a red circle indicates that a certain action is not allowed.

Flammable

Radioactive
A triangle is a warning sign.

Toxic/poisonous

No cycling

Not suitable for drinking
A red circle is a warning sign.

No smoking

General information

Post office

Tourist information

Disabled access

Telephone

Women's toilets

Men's toilets

Weather symbols
International symbols used by meteorologists

Astronomical symbols

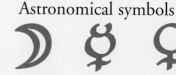

Wind calm

Fog

Drizzle

Rain

Snow

Showers

Sun

Moon

Mercury

Venus

Mars

Thunderstorm

Rainbow

Hail

Windspeed 18–22 knots

Cumulonimbus cloud, anvil top

Jupiter

Saturn

Uranus

Neptune

Pluto

SKELETON

THE BODY IS SHAPED and supported by a framework of bones called the skeleton. An adult skeleton consists of 206 bones, which protect internal organs, such as the brain and lungs, and provide an anchorage for the muscles. The skeleton can be divided into two main parts. The axial skeleton forms the axis of the body and consists of the skull, vertebral column (backbone), and ribcage. The appendicular skeleton consists of the bones of the arms and legs and the shoulder and hip girdles.

Ancient bones

If a person dies and is buried, the body tissues gradually break down and then disappear. However, the hard mineral salts that make up the bones remain and can retain their original shape for several thousands of years. The existence of ancient skeletons enables archaeologists to gather information about early people.

Movement

The skeleton is a flexible framework because bones meet at joints where they can move in relation to one another. Muscles are attached to the bones across joints so that when a muscle contracts, movement occurs. The body can perform a wide range of movements.

Arm movements help the body balance and move faster during running.

Leg bends at knee, before pushing down and back for next stride.

Leg straightens at knee, as the foot pushes against ground to propel body forwards.

Flexion is a movement that reduces the angle of a joint. This skeleton flexes, or bends, the left leg and the right arm.

Extension is a movement that increases the angle of a joint. This skeleton extends, or straightens, the right leg and the left arm.

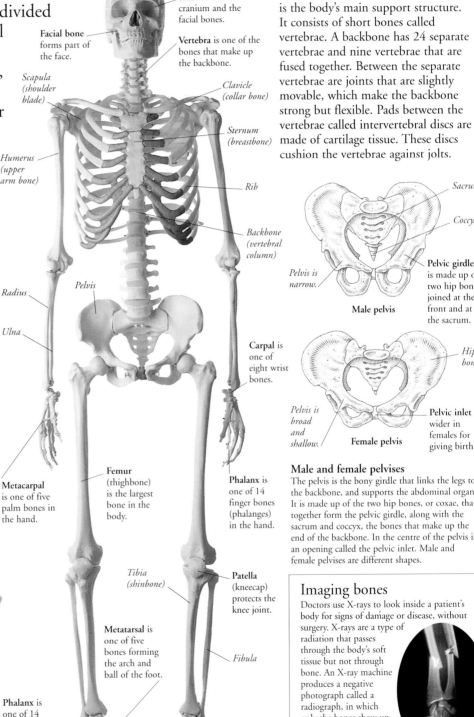

Cranium surrounds and protects the skull.

Skull consists of the cranium and the facial bones.

Facial bone forms part of the face.

Scapula (shoulder blade)

Vertebra is one of the bones that make up the backbone.

Clavicle (collar bone)

Sternum (breastbone)

Humerus (upper arm bone)

Rib

Backbone (vertebral column)

Radius

Ulna

Pelvis

Carpal is one of eight wrist bones.

Metacarpal is one of five palm bones in the hand.

Femur (thighbone) is the largest bone in the body.

Phalanx is one of 14 finger bones (phalanges) in the hand.

Tibia (shinbone)

Patella (kneecap) protects the knee joint.

Metatarsal is one of five bones forming the arch and ball of the foot.

Fibula

Phalanx is one of 14 toe bones (phalanges) in the foot.

Tarsal is one of seven ankle bones.

Backbone

The backbone, or vertebral column, is the body's main support structure. It consists of short bones called vertebrae. A backbone has 24 separate vertebrae and nine vertebrae that are fused together. Between the separate vertebrae are joints that are slightly movable, which make the backbone strong but flexible. Pads between the vertebrae called intervertebral discs are made of cartilage tissue. These discs cushion the vertebrae against jolts.

Sacrum

Coccyx

Pelvis is narrow.

Male pelvis

Pelvic girdle is made up of two hip bones joined at the front and at the sacrum.

Hip bone

Pelvis is broad and shallow.

Female pelvis

Pelvic inlet is wider in females for giving birth.

Male and female pelvises

The pelvis is the bony girdle that links the legs to the backbone, and supports the abdominal organs. It is made up of the two hip bones, or coxae, that together form the pelvic girdle, along with the sacrum and coccyx, the bones that make up the end of the backbone. In the centre of the pelvis is an opening called the pelvic inlet. Male and female pelvises are different shapes.

Imaging bones

Doctors use X-rays to look inside a patient's body for signs of damage or disease, without surgery. X-rays are a type of radiation that passes through the body's soft tissue but not through bone. An X-ray machine produces a negative photograph called a radiograph, in which only the bones show up.

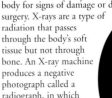

False-colour radiograph of a broken arm bone

S

Bones

Bones are made of a hard, living, self-repairing tissue that is supplied with blood vessels and nerves. Bone consists of widely spaced osteocytes (bone cells) and the matrix that lies between them. The matrix is made up of fibres of collagen, which give bone its flexibility, and mineral salts, mainly calcium phosphate, which give bone its strength. Surrounding all bone is a layer of hard, compact bone. Within the compact bone is a layer of lighter spongy bone. The spaces within spongy bone are frequently filled with red marrow.

Structure of compact bone

Haversian canal is a space that runs down the centre of the osteon, carrying blood vessels and nerves.

Blood vessel supplies bone cells with oxygen and food.

Lamella is one of the tubes of bone surrounding a Haversian canal.

Lacuna is a space that contains an osteocyte (bone cell).

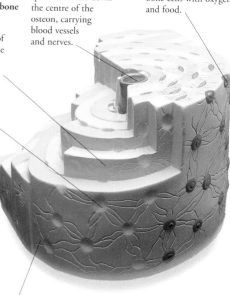

Red marrow is the site of red and white cell production.

Struts link to form a framework.

Each osteon consists of layers of lamellae.

An osteon is a small piece of compact bone made up of tiny bony tubes called lamellae arranged in circular layers around a central Haversian canal.

Bone marrow
Bone marrow is a jelly-like material found inside bones. Red bone marrow inside the hip, skull, collar bones, sternum, and backbones is the site of blood cell production.

Spongy bone
Spongy bone is a "honeycomb" layer that lies beneath compact bone. It forms a light but strong framework that reduces the bone's weight but not its strength.

Compact bone
Compact bone forms the outer part of bone. After teeth enamel, compact bone is the hardest material in the body. It is made up of parallel cylinders called osteons.

Joints

Joints occur where bones meet. The majority of joints move freely, and are known as synovial joints. They make the skeleton flexible, so that when muscles pull on bones, a part of the body moves. There are several different types of synovial joint, each of which allows a different range of movements. These include ball and socket, saddle, and hinge joints.

Femur (thighbone)

Knee joint is a hinge joint between tibia and femur.

Ball and socket
This joint consists of a ball-shaped head that fits into a cup-shaped socket. It is the most flexible type of joint and allows movement in most directions. It occurs in the hip joint and in the shoulder joint.

Movement in many directions

Saddle
In a saddle joint, the end of each bone is saddle-shaped. This allows movement forwards and backwards, from side to side, and, in a limited way, round and round. There is a saddle joint at the base of the thumb.

Movement in two planes

Hinge
In a hinge joint, the cylindrical surface of one bone fits into the curved surface of the other, so the bones can only be moved up and down. Hinge joints are found in the elbow and knee.

Joint allows movement in one plane.

Fibula

Tibia (shinbone)

Ligament is a tough strap that holds the joint together.

Frontal bone

Parietal bone

Edge of frontal bone forms suture with edge of parietal bone.

Skull
The skull is made up of 22 bones, 21 of which are held together by immovable joints called sutures. Only the mandible (lower jaw) is freely movable. In a suture, the edges of bones fit tightly together and are prevented from moving, as this would damage the brain.

Skull is "exploded" to show component parts.

Giovanni Ingrassias

Giovanni Ingrassias (1510–80) was one of the first doctors to study in detail the structure of bones. He was a physician and anatomy professor in Naples until 1563, when he returned to Palermo in his native Sicily. Among his achievements, Ingrassias discovered the stapes (stirrup), the innermost of the tiny ossicles in the ear and the smallest bone in the body.

Bone fractures

A fracture, or break, happens when a bone is exposed to a sudden force that it cannot withstand. There are two types of fracture. In simple or closed fractures, the broken bone ends remain below the skin; whereas in compound or open fractures, they stick out through the skin and often cause damage to surrounding tissues. Fractured bones mend themselves.

Casts
A cast is used to immobilize a limb so that the broken ends of a bone are lined up in the right position. A cast is applied by wrapping wet bandages impregnated with plaster of Paris or plastic around a limb. When dry, the plaster hardens.

1 A blood clot forms where bone is broken.

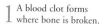

2 Spongy bone forms between broken ends.

3 Fracture has healed and bone returns to its original shape.

FIND OUT MORE   FOSSILS   GROWTH AND DEVELOPMENT   HUMAN BODY   HUMAN EVOLUTION   MEDICINE   MEDICINE, HISTORY OF   MUSCLES AND MOVEMENT   TEETH AND JAWS   X-RAYS AND THE ELECTROMAGNETIC SPECTRUM

SKIN, HAIR, AND NAILS

COVERING THE OUTSIDE of your body is a protective layer that consists of your skin, hair, and nails. Skin is the body's largest organ and it has several functions. It waterproofs the body and forms a barrier against bacteria, viruses, and the harmful effects of sunlight. Skin also contains sensors that detect pressure, pain, heat, and cold, enabling you to feel your surroundings. Nails and hair are extensions of the skin.

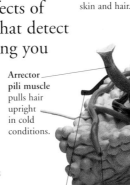

Dead cells flake from the top layer of epidermis.

Hair follicle

Hair shaft

Basal cell layer is at base of epidermis.

Epidermis is the outer part of the skin, which protects the dermis.

Sebaceous gland produces an oil called sebum, which lubricates skin and hair.

Dermis is the inner part of the skin which contains blood vessels and nerve endings.

Arrector pili muscle pulls hair upright in cold conditions.

Sweat duct carries sweat to the skin's surface.

Blood vessels supply skin with oxygen and food.

Artery   Vein   Sensory receptor detects pressure and vibrations.

Fat layer helps to insulate the body and keep it warm.

Sweat gland produces sweat.

Hair root

Skin

Skin consists of two layers: the epidermis and the dermis. The epidermis is the thin, but tough, outer protective part of the skin. It has a number of layers. The inner, thicker dermis contains sensory nerve endings, blood vessels, hair follicles, and sweat glands.

Pigmentation
Cells in the epidermis make a pigment called melanin, which protects the body against damage by strong sunlight. People with darker skin produce more melanin than those with lighter skin.

Temperature control
Skin helps the body maintain an even temperature of about 37°C (98.6°F). If your body gets too hot, glands release sweat and blood vessels widen to give off heat. To cool the body, blood vessels get narrower.

Sweat pore releases sweat on the skin's surface.

Epidermis
The upper layer of epidermis consists of dead cells packed with a tough protein called keratin, that are constantly being worn away and replaced. Cells in the lower epidermis divide and push new cells towards the surface to replace the lost ones. As they move upwards, these cells fill with keratin.

Nails

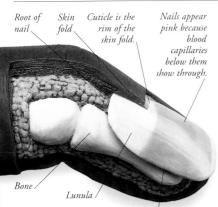

Root of nail   Skin fold   Cuticle is the rim of the skin fold.   Nails appear pink because blood capillaries below them show through.

Bone   Lunula   Nail protects sensitive skin.

Nail structure
Nails are made of the tough protein, keratin. The nails are colourless but appear pink because they rest on a bed served by blood vessels. They grow from active skin cells under skin folds at their base and sides. An opaque crescent called the lunula at the base of each nail contains many of these active cells.

Nails are hard coverings that protect the ends of fingers and toes. Cells in the root of the nail divide constantly, pushing the nail forward over the nail bed. Finger-nails grow at a rate of about 5 mm (0.2 inches) each month, but toenails grow more slowly.

No two people, not even identical twins, share the same fingerprints.

Fingerprints
The undersides of your fingers are covered with tiny epidermal ridges that, together with a sticky film of sweat and natural oils, help you to grip objects. When you touch an object, some of the film sticks to the object so that you leave behind a fingerprint.

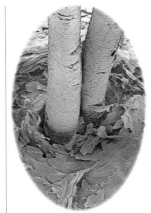

Hair structure
The shaft of a hair consists of three layers. The cuticle forms overlapping scales on the surface of the hair. Below the cuticle, the cortex forms the main part of the shaft and the medulla is the tough core. Cells in the follicle divide and push upwards to form the shaft of the hair.

Hair

Millions of hairs cover your body. There are two types of hair. Fine vellus hair grows over most of the body. Thicker terminal hair grows on the scalp, and makes up the eyebrows and eyelashes. Hairs grow out of pits in the skin called follicles. Hairs on your head grow about 1 cm (0.4 inch) a month.

Dense curly hair   Straight hair   Wavy hair

Types of hair
Whether the hairs on your head are straight, wavy, or curly depends on the shape of the hair follicles they grow from. Round follicles produce straight hair; oval follicles produce curly hair; and curved follicles produce wavy hair.

FIND OUT MORE   CELLS   CRIME AND PUNISHMENT   DISEASES   GENETICS   GROWTH AND DEVELOPMENT   HEAT   HUMAN BODY   HUMAN EVOLUTION   MUSCLES AND MOVEMENT   SKELETON

SLAVERY

THE PRACTICE OF SLAVERY, the ownership of one person by another, goes back to ancient times, when the Sumerians, Egyptians, Romans, and Greeks kept slaves. From the 15th century a huge slave trade developed, when Europeans began selling captured Africans for profit, and shipping them across the sea to work in European colonies. This trade in humans lasted until the 19th century, and greatly affected African and American cultures. Today, slavery is illegal, although it still exists in some parts of the world.

Ancient world
Slavery in ancient times reached its height in the Greek world and Roman Empire. Slaves made most of the goods, and worked in the home and on farms. They had few rights, but some gained freedom, and even high social status.

Slave trade

The Portuguese began the Afro-European slave trade in about 1440, but it reached its height under the English, who shipped vast numbers of Africans across the Atlantic to work as slaves on cotton and tobacco plantations in their American colonies.

More than 7 million Africans were transported from Africa to lives of misery in the Americas. The trade brought huge profits to European and African traders, and devastated some African kingdoms. It also changed the population of the Americas; by 1800, half of Brazil's population was African in origin.

Traders
Traders sailed to West Africa from English ports and exchanged goods for Africans who had been captured and marched to the coast. Slaves were branded like cattle, and shipped to the Americas.

Slave ships
Between 1701 and 1810, more than a million Africans died from suffocation, disease, or starvation on the journey across the Atlantic, which could take up to 10 weeks. Slaves were chained to prevent them from jumping overboard, because the loss of a slave meant a loss of profit.

Branding iron

Markets
In the Americas, traders auctioned Africans to plantation owners at slave markets. To traders and buyers, Africans were no longer people, only property. Families were usually separated forever.

Ankle fetter

Model of the English slave ship *Brookes*

Women's area

Men's area

Slaves survived on rice, maize, yams, pulses, and cassava.

Men and boys were kept at the front of the boat, and girls at the back; most slaves were between 16 and 45 years old.

Plantation slavery

Slaves worked long hours on cotton plantations in the southern United States, or they worked indoors cooking and cleaning. They lived in huts, and slept on floor mats. The black people had no rights; they were the property of the plantation owners. Because of this oppression, more than 250 slave revolts took place.

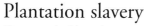

Abolitionists
From the late 18th century, there were English and American movements to abolish slavery. *Uncle Tom's Cabin* (1851) by the writer Harriet Beecher Stowe was an anti-slavery novel. In 1833, Britain ended its slave trade, but slavery continued in the United States, particularly in the south, until after the Civil War in 1865.

Timeline
73–71 BC Spartacus leads revolt of slaves in the Roman Empire. After the defeat of the slave revolt, 6,000 are crucified.

1100s Arab traders send West African slaves to Asia and Arabia.

1619 First shipload of African slaves arrives in Virginia.

1780–86 Some US states pass manumission (freedom from slavery) acts.

1831 Nat Turner leads slave uprising, Virginia, USA. All involved are hanged. Slave codes prohibit literacy.

1833 British abolish their slave trade.

1857 Dred Scott case: Supreme Court in the USA rules that African-Americans are not citizens.

1863 Emancipation Proclamation frees slaves in southern states of the USA.

1948 Declaration of Human Rights from the United Nations prohibits slavery and trade in slaves.

Harriet Tubman

Born into slavery in Maryland, USA, Harriet Tubman (c.1820–1913) escaped in 1849. She then helped some 300 slaves to freedom on a secret escape route from the South to the North, known as the Underground Railway. During the Civil War, Tubman worked for the North as a nurse and spy.

FIND OUT MORE   AFRICA, HISTORY OF   AMERICAN CIVIL WAR   CARIBBEAN, HISTORY OF   EGYPT, ANCIENT   GREECE, ANCIENT   HUMAN RIGHTS   ROMAN EMPIRE

SMELL AND TASTE

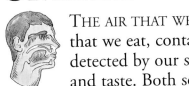

THE AIR THAT WE BREATHE IN, and the food that we eat, contain chemicals that can be detected by our senses of smell and taste. Both senses depend on chemoreceptors, which are sensors that react to the presence of certain chemicals by sending nerve impulses to the brain. Chemoreceptors in the nose detect smells, or odours, while those on the tongue detect tastes. Smell and taste work together. Your sense of smell is about 20,000 times more sensitive than your sense of taste.

Nose and mouth

The smelling part of the nose is the nasal cavity, which is divided into two halves, each served by one nostril. Smell receptors are found in the upper part of each nasal cavity. Taste receptors are found inside the mouth, on the surface of the tongue, and in the lining of the mouth cavity.

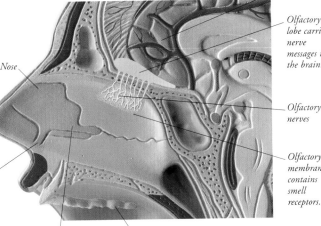

Brain

Olfactory lobe carries nerve messages to the brain.

Nose

Olfactory nerves

Olfactory membrane contains smell receptors.

Nostril is one of two openings to the nasal cavity.

Nasal cavity

Mouth

Smell

Your sense of smell operates when you breathe in through your nose. Chemicals carried by the air dissolve in the layer of mucus covering the olfactory membrane. The dissolved chemicals cause the olfactory cells to send nerve impulses to the olfactory lobes. From here, the nerve impulses are carried to the brain, where they are interpreted as smells.

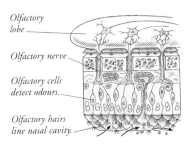

Olfactory lobe

Olfactory nerve

Olfactory cells detect odours.

Olfactory hairs line nasal cavity.

Olfactory membrane
The moist olfactory membrane covers an area the size of a postage stamp in the upper part of each nasal cavity. The membrane contains chemoreceptors called olfactory cells which detect odours.

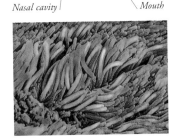

Smell receptors
Smells are detected by tiny hair-like projections called cilia located at the end of the olfactory cells. There are about 20 million olfactory cells in the nose and about 20 cilia project from each cell. Smell receptors on the cilia react to specific chemicals. This mechanism enables you to distinguish between thousands of different odours.

Taste

Your tongue can detect only four basic tastes: sweet, salt, sour, and bitter. The tongue is divided into different taste areas, each containing taste buds that are sensitive to one of these tastes. There are over 10,000 microscopic taste buds on the tongue, and these are located on or between tiny projections called papillae.

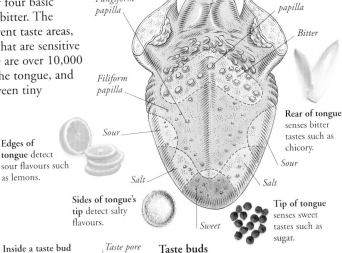

Tongue

Epiglottis

Fungiform papilla

Circumvallate papilla

Bitter

Filiform papilla

Rear of tongue senses bitter tastes such as chicory.

Sour

Sour

Edges of tongue detect sour flavours such as lemons.

Salt

Salt

Sweet

Sides of tongue's tip detect salty flavours.

Tip of tongue senses sweet tastes such as sugar.

Tongue papillae
Your tongue is not smooth. Its upper surface is covered by papillae which make the tongue rough so it can grip and move food during chewing. Papillae also allow you to lick food such as ice cream. Taste buds are found in pores on and between some of the papillae.

Inside a taste bud

Taste pore

Taste hairs

Taste cell

Nerve fibre

Taste buds
Each taste bud contains a cluster of chemoreceptors (taste cells). When food is chewed, chemicals dissolve in saliva, and pass into the taste bud through the taste pore. The chemicals stimulate taste hairs on the chemoreceptor cells. These send impulses along nerve fibres to the brain's taste area where the impulses are interpreted as salt, sour, sweet, or bitter tastes.

Sense of smell
Our sense of smell is poor compared to that of some other animals. Dogs, for example, have an olfactory membrane ten times more extensive than a human's. This enables them to detect much weaker smells, and a wider range of odours, than humans can. Dogs can be trained to sniff out drugs or explosives.

Detecting flavours

Your senses of smell and taste work together to enable you to detect many flavours. For example, when you eat food, information from the chemoreceptors in your nose and mouth is processed by your brain so that you can sense the flavour of the food. Some people use their very good senses of smell and taste to make a living as, for example, wine tasters and perfume blenders.

The durian is a very unusual fruit. It has a revolting smell but a delicious taste.

FIND OUT MORE | BRAIN AND NERVOUS SYSTEM | CHEMISTRY | DIGESTION | DOGS | FOOD | FRUITS AND SEEDS | HUMAN BODY | TEETH AND JAWS

769

SNAILS AND OTHER MOLLUSCS

THESE SOFT-BODIED animals all have a single muscular "foot", a gut, and a mantle cavity. Most produce a protective calcium-based shell, but in some species this has been reduced or lost altogether. The 80,000 or so living snails and mollusc species are divided up into bivalve, cephalopod, chiton, gastropod, and tusk shell groups which have colonized almost all areas of the world.

Gastropods

Snails and slugs belong to a group called gastropods. All gastropods move on a flat, muscular foot, and are equipped with tentacles and a rasping mouthpart called a radula. Most have a protective shell. Marine snails have gills. Many freshwater and land snails have adapted their gills to form lungs.

Snail

Shells protect snails from enemies and drying out, and are coloured to blend in with their environment. Snails have a mouth with a radula (tongue), and two pairs of tentacles, the longer of which has simple eyes. They are hermaphrodite (that is, they contain both male and female reproductive organs). They lay large eggs in warm, damp soil that hatch into young snails.

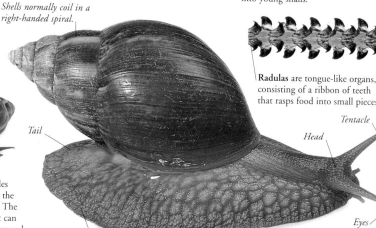

Shells normally coil in a right-handed spiral.

Tail

Foot produces slime.

Radulas are tongue-like organs, consisting of a ribbon of teeth that rasps food into small pieces.

Tentacle

Head

Eyes

Giant African snail

Emerging from shell

1 The snail's body is curled up inside the shell, sealed with a layer of mucus for protection.

2 In a special kind of twisting known as torsion, the snail's head emerges first from the shell, followed by the tail.

3 The long tentacles emerge last, and the eyes become visible. The snail's muscular foot can now lie flat on the ground.

Cone shell

Cone shell
The beautiful but deadly cones are well adapted for catching and killing their food. They attack their prey – usually small fish – with a single poison-filled tooth. Fish are swallowed whole; humans usually survive – though in 1960 an adult male died within two hours.

Slug
Slugs are snails with no shell, or a very tiny one. Without the protection that a shell can offer, slugs rely on their slime, which is sticky and offensive to predators. Some snails are carnivorous, but most land-living slugs are herbivores.

Head

Foot

Bivalves

Bivalves (meaning two-shelled) include clams, mussels, and cockles. Bivalves that dive underwater have gills for breathing and a foot, like the gastropods. Some bivalves cement themselves to rocks using thin threads called byssus strands. Most bivalves have two tubes, or siphons. One takes in water and food, and the other expels waste. Bivalves such as the giant Pacific clam can grow to more than 1.2 m (4 ft) across.

Queen scallop

Black-lipped oyster

Scallop
The beautifully coloured scallop swims by rapidly opening and closing its hinged valves. Scallops have a fringe of tentacles round the edge of the shell. This is interspersed with tiny light-sensitive eyes that can detect moving objects. Its main predator is the starfish.

Oyster
The oyster is one of the best-known bivalves. An oyster lays up to 50 million eggs in a single spawning season, but in its natural environment only a few reach adulthood. A popular foodstuff, oysters are cultivated commercially in marine oyster beds in America, Australia, Asia, and Europe.

Chiton
Chitons, also known as coat-of-mail shells, are small molluscs with eight flattened shell plates held together by a protective leathery girdle. A chiton's internal structures are simple, and it lives off algae. Chitons range in size from 2 mm (0.1 in) to 30 cms (12 in), and live on rocky shores.

Jointed shell plates

Girdle

Cephalopods

Cephalopods are also molluscs, but their "foot" has evolved into a set of tentacles on the animal's head. Cephalopods swim by pushing jets of water through a funnel under the body. Some produce a cloud of ink as a protective device. The largest-ever recorded cephalopod was a 20-metre (65-ft) squid.

Eye

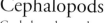

Tentacles on head

Cloud of ink

Cuttlefish releasing ink

Tusk shells
The marine bivalves known as tusks are so-called because they look like elephant's tusks. The broad end of the tusk is buried in sandy mud, and contains the head and foot of the animal. The narrow end, where respiration takes place, projects into the water. Tusks search for food with slender retractable tentacles, and some live at great depths.

GIANT AFRICAN SNAIL

SCIENTIFIC NAME	*Achatina achatina*
ORDER	Sigmurethra
SUPERFAMILY	Achatinacea
DISTRIBUTION	Africa, America, and Asia
HABITAT	Forests, gardens, and cultivation
DIET	Plants
SIZE	Shell can grow up to 15 cm (5.9 in) long
LIFESPAN	25 years (in captivity)

FIND OUT MORE

OCEAN LIFE

SEASHORE WILDLIFE

URBAN WILDLIFE

Snails and other molluscs

Gastropods

Land snails' colour and banding depends on whether their habitat is woodland or grassland.

Shells normally coil in a right-hand spiral.

Snails grow by adding new material to the open end of the shell.

Partula snails are close to extinction.

Posterior tentacle

Anterior tentacle

Brown-lipped snails live mainly on chalk downland.

Garden snails need to remain moist to survive. In dry conditions they seal themselves inside their shells to hibernate.

Apple snails are used in aquariums to keep the glass clean.

Thin shell

Whelks are sea snails that live just below the tideline.

Bubble shells appear to "fly" through the water.

Pond snails can live in very stagnant water.

Spine used to lever apart barnacle plates

Dog whelks are carnivorous and live on barnacles.

Gills absorb oxygen from sea water.

Common periwinkles move on a muscular "foot" like the land snail.

Lettuce slugs are brightly coloured and taste unpleasant.

Sea slugs, or nudibranchs as they are also known, live in rock pools.

Slugs are molluscs without shells. They tend to be more drab in colour than sea slugs.

Bivalves

Mantle

Shell halves are called valves.

Hinge

Giant clams live on coral reefs and have soft, colourful mantles. Barnacles often grow on the shells.

Spiny oysters are also known as chrysanthemum shells because they resemble the flower.

Queen scallops have two perfectly matched shell halves, that are connected by a hinge.

Oysters live in the sea, buried in sand or attached to rocks.

Green mussels use tough threads called byssus to attach themselves to rocks.

Cephalopods and other molluscs

To swim, an octopus takes water into its body cavity and forces it out through a funnel.

Eye is similar to a human eye.

Tentacles grasp food as it floats by.

The beak-like jaw has a poisonous bite.

Squid have a tube-like internal shell.

Squid, among the most common animals in the ocean, swim in shoals. Sperm whales feed on them.

Suckers

Octopuses feed mainly on shellfish. Their name comes from their eight tentacles.

Chambers contain gases that help the nautilus float.

Nautiluses live in the deep waters of the South Pacific.

Cuttlefish have a hard internal shell instead of an external shell.

SNAKES

SNAKES ARE LONG, scaly, legless reptiles. There are about 3,000 species of snake, 600 of which are venomous. Snakes are found on all continents except Antarctica, and also in the Pacific and Indian Oceans. They are believed to have evolved from lizards that lost the use of their legs. Snakes are successful predators – some, such as mambas, kill their victims with a venomous bite; others, like pythons, suffocate their prey to death. Snakes are feared around the world as they cause up to 100,000 human deaths every year.

Features of a snake

Snakes are legless reptiles, but boas and pythons have remnants of hind legs called spurs. Snakes are covered in an outer skin that they shed as they grow, often in one piece. They have no eyelids, but a spectacle called a brille, covers the eyes. They lack ears and are deaf, but can sense vibrations.

Forked tongue

The snake's tongue is a highly sensitive organ of taste, smell, and touch. It is used to find prey or a mate, to detect a threat, and to follow trails. The tongue collects scent particles that are analysed in the roof of the mouth in a structure called the Jacobson's organ.

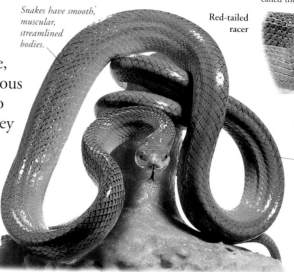

Snakes have smooth, muscular, streamlined bodies.

Red-tailed racer

Nostril

Forked tongue flicks in and out to test the air.

Scales are thickenings of skin made mainly of the substance keratin. The number and arrangement of scales vary between species.

Wagler's temple pitviper

Special pit detects heat from other animals.

Heat sensitive pits

Boas, pythons, and pitvipers have thermo-sensory receptors to locate warm-blooded prey. In pythons and boas they form a series of slits in the lip scales but pitvipers have a single large pit between the nostril and the eye. These receptors are very sensitive and enable tree boas to capture bats on the wing.

Movement

Most snakes move on land or in water using a twisting motion, but heavy snakes such as large anacondas move in straight lines. Some desert vipers move diagonally across loose sand by moving sideways, or "sidewinding", leaving J-shaped tracks marking the points of contact.

Sidewinding viper

Feeding

No snakes are herbivores; some kill their prey by biting and injecting venom, while many non-venomous snakes kill their prey by constriction. Most snakes feed on frogs, lizards, small mammals, and birds. Some also eat termites, crabs, and birds' eggs. King cobras eat mainly other snakes.

Fangs and venom

When a snake, such as a rattlesnake, bites its prey, venom is injected through hollow teeth called fangs. Venom kills prey by affecting the nervous system, muscles, heart, or blood. It also starts off the process of digestion. Spitting cobras primarily use venom for defence, causing intense pain or blindness.

Fangs of a rattlesnake

Boa constrictor eating a rat

Prey is eaten headfirst.

Coils squeeze the prey to make it easier to swallow whole.

Tail of the rat

Killing by constriction

1 The boa constrictor uses its sharp teeth to grasp its prey, in this case, a rat. Once the rat is secure within its mouth, the boa wraps its powerful coils around the victim's body.

2 The coils tighten until the prey cannot breath and it suffocates. When the prey is dead, the boa starts to devour its meal. The two halves of the lower jaw are not connected so they can articulate (expand) to swallow prey much wider than the the boa's head.

3 The boa's skin stretches as it swallows its prey. A muscular windpipe enables a snake to breathe during swallowing. Huge meals such as pigs or deer, eaten by large pythons, last for many months.

Reproduction

Most snakes, such as cobras and pythons, lay eggs. They normally bury the eggs in rotting vegetation or soil and leave them to incubate. King cobras build a nest that they guard; pythons coil around and incubate their eggs. A few snakes, such as boas, give birth to live young.

Green tree python guarding eggs

Habitat

Snakes live in most habitats, including deserts, rainforests, temperate forests, swamps, savannahs, cultivated land, estuaries, rivers, and even oceans. They do not live in areas of high altitude or latitude, where it is too cold. Most snakes live on land. They range from snakes such as desert vipers, with rough scales that help them grip and move along the ground, to burrowing blindsnakes with smooth scales that allow them to slip easily through the earth.

Slender body coils around branch.

Prehensile tail grasps branch.

Sea krait

Water snakes

Sea snakes and sea kraits have flattened tails for swimming huge distances. Sea kraits can move onto land and even climb cliffs; sea snakes are helpless on land.

Ornate flying snake

Tree snakes

Prehensile tails and ridged belly scales give tree snakes extra grip when climbing trees. Strong vertebrae allow them to bridge wide gaps.

RED-TAILED RACER

SCIENTIFIC NAME	*Gonyosoma oxycephalum*
ORDER	Squamata
FAMILY	Colubridae
DISTRIBUTION	Southeast Asia, from Thailand to Indonesia and the Philippines
HABITAT	Rainforests
DIET	Rodents and birds
SIZE	Length 1.75 m (5 ft)

FIND OUT MORE   DESERT WILDLIFE   EGGS   LIZARDS   MONGOOSES AND CIVETS   POISONOUS ANIMALS   RAINFOREST WILDLIFE   REPTILES   WOODLAND WILDLIFE

Snakes

Invertebrate eaters

This snake hunts for its prey at night.

Small head and smooth scales help this snake to burrow.

These snakes can burrow into leaf litter or forest topsoil.

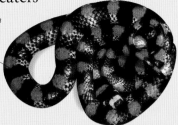

This snake is almost invisible in the bushes.

Ringed snail-eating snakes live in trees. They are experts at pulling snails out of their shells.

Ground snakes have tiny mouths and feed mainly on earthworms and insect larvae.

Black-banded snakes are mildly venomous. They are thought to eat only tropical centipedes.

Smooth green snakes from North America feed on insects and spiders.

Vertebrate eaters

Powerful bodies allow anacondas to suffocate their prey by constriction.

Milk snakes are often confused with deadly coral snakes as they have the same colour bands.

The snake must writhe around to crack the eggshell.

African egg-eating snakes have no teeth. They swallow bird eggs whole and cough up the shell.

This snake has an upturned snout for burrowing in leaf litter for food.

Green anacondas, the largest, heaviest, and strongest snakes in the world, feed on waterbirds, caimans, and sometimes humans.

Common milk snakes from North and Central America feed on small mammals, lizards, and other snakes.

Giant Madagascan hognose snakes are robust snakes capable of killing large rodents.

Bones in the neck spread out to form the hood.

Brown saddles (wide irregular markings) act as camouflage in woodlands.

This snake has patterns that vary from bands to saddles.

Mottled skin for camouflage

Gaboon vipers from Africa are huge and can capture rats from ambush.

Monocled cobras are from Thailand. They are highly venomous and eat rats.

Copperheads live in woodlands in North America. They use their heat-sensitive pits to locate mice.

Grey-banded king snakes from the deserts of Western Texas, USA, hunt for lizards at night.

If threatened, this snake can ooze blood-stained liquid from its cloaca.

Thick, muscular body allows python to squeeze and suffocate large animals to death.

Jaws can expand to swallow prey three times wider than the head.

Cornsnakes are common around houses in southeastern USA, where they hunt for mice.

Western long-nosed snakes of North America feed on lizards and their eggs.

This snake is banded, but others have stripes along their bodies.

Californian king snakes eat small mammals and other snakes, including rattlesnakes.

Burmese rock pythons are powerful snakes capable of killing large animals, such as deer and pigs, by constriction.

SOCIETIES, HUMAN

SINCE PREHISTORY, and in every culture, humans have organized themselves into groups, or communities, and have established "rules" of living. A society is the name we give to the customs and organization of such a community. Certain things are found in every society, such as the family, kinship, the division of work by gender or age, marriage, the sharing of food, and the idea of ownership. But the customs that govern behaviour at work, in the home, and in other social institutions and organizations vary greatly worldwide.

Families

The family is a basic social unit and exists in every culture. Most of us are born into one and first learn about the wider world through it. Later, we may start a family of our own. Nuclear and extended families are perhaps the two best-known family types, but family structures vary widely between, and within, societies as they are affected by such things as increasing divorce and changing social attitudes.

As well as their parents, aunts, uncles, and grandparents care for young children.

Adult children live with their parents.

Extended families
Families share out responsibilities, such as bringing up children, providing food, and performing domestic tasks. Many societies have a wide concept of the family group, with duties extending over several generations, who all live together. This type of family is often found in small, traditional communities, where shared property and kinship ties form a common bond.

Extended family of four generations

The study of people
Both anthropology and sociology are social sciences that study the origins and development of human societies and customs. They have revealed universal features of human societies and explained the emergence of important differences.

Sociologists collect data to study social behaviour, whether in crowded cities or rural communities.

Anthropology
Anthropologists examine humanity in terms of evolution and development. They also study the customs, religions, and laws of a specific people at a given time, and consider the differences between cultures.

Sociology
Sociology is concerned with how human beings behave in groups: how they organize themselves, and how one group relates to another. Sociologists may try to develop solutions to social problems, such as crime.

Nuclear families
The term "nuclear family" usually refers to a core family of just two parents and their children. It is the most widespread family type in industrialized nations, although today, single-parent families are also becoming more common.

People are now more financially independent than before and can choose to live alone.

Single-person household

One type of family structure

Nuclear family

Households
A household refers to the people who live under one roof. Single-person households are becoming more common as individuals either choose to live alone, or find themselves on their own.

Sister gives brother a raksha of coloured threads.

Kinship
Kinship is the recognition of blood or family ties between individuals. It is the binding force in families, clans, or tribes; some societies have strict rules governing kin relations.

In India, the Raksha Bandan festival celebrates the kinship between sister and brother.

Where people live
The jobs and available resources determine where people live. In early societies, people lived in hunter-gatherer communities of 80 to 150 people. As work patterns changed and populations grew, societies adapted in different ways.

Bedouin tent in the desert

Nomads
Where food, water, and grazing were scarce, people could not build fixed settlements, but moved their animals between grazing areas. Peoples who still live this nomadic lifestyle include the Bedouin in North Africa and the Mongols of the Asian Steppes.

Cities
Half the world's people live in cities, and this proportion is increasing. These large, crowded settlements offer the most job opportunites. Although the rise of cities has brought benefits, it has also created health problems, overcrowding, and pollution.

Shortage of housing is a problem in cities; high-rise blocks are one solution to lack of space.

Block of high-rise flats in Moscow, Russia

Social stratification

Sociologists have shown that all societies are stratified: they are divided into different strata, or layers. Stratification may be based on various factors, such as caste, class, gender, race, or even age. As a result of the layering, some people will have greater advantages or status than others, and this often leads to divisions in society.

Brahmans (priests) are the highest Hindu caste and have great social prestige.

Privileged pupils at a fee-paying school

Caste
This is an ancient social hierarchy which still exists among Hindus in India. It is inherited and fixed. There are four main levels, with the Brahmans supreme, and 36 lower levels, members of which are seen as inferior.

Class
People are said to belong to a social class depending on the property they own or their occupation. There may be some movement between classes; education helps people improve their class status.

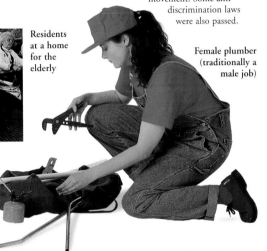

Residents at a home for the elderly

Age roles
Depending on their age, society gives people different status. Youth is generally seen as an advantage; old people may be discriminated against or venerated, depending on the culture in which they live.

Black woman worker

Race and gender
Within a society, a person's status may be affected by the ethnic group they belong to, or whether they are a man or a woman. They may earn less, and not be able to own property, or even do certain jobs. During the 20th century, racism and sexism were challenged – for example, by civil rights groups and the women's movement. Some anti-discrimination laws were also passed.

Female plumber (traditionally a male job)

Ceremonies and rites

In every society, people come together to mark or celebrate certain occasions or events that are meaningful to the larger community. Such ceremonies are shared events, which may involve traditional words, music, or dance, or include special ritual actions or costumes. The ceremonies linked to birth, marriage, and death often have a symbolic meaning: they mark the different phases in an individual's status in society.

Some people receive a key on their 21st birthday, a symbol of their entry into adulthood.

Gifts are given in celebration.

Hindu wedding ceremony

Marriage
When a man and woman marry, they make a formal commitment to spend their lives together; they agree to share their property and set up a new household; and their families are also linked to each other. This great change in social status is celebrated in wedding ceremonies worldwide, often of a religious nature.

Birth
Birth, when a new member arrives in a community, is marked in different ways. In Christian ceremonies, a baby's head is dipped in, or touched with, water. Male Jewish infants are circumcised eight days after birth. In western countries, an individual's 18th or 21st birthday is celebrated as a time when he or she becomes an adult, or "comes of age".

Margaret Mead
Pioneering and outspoken US anthropologist Margaret Mead (1901–78) studied social behaviour in Samoa, New Guinea, and Bali, writing on rites of passage and child-rearing. She also analysed US society and was an early advocate of women's rights.

Work
People spend most of their lives working, producing goods or services to support themselves and their families and to create wealth for their community. People also work for social status, intellectual satisfaction, or company.

Leisure
In western societies, work tends to happen in a certain place, for a set amount of time. Time away from work is sometimes known as leisure time. During this time, people may choose enjoyable activities, such as sport. In some countries, leisure is big business. In less wealthy societies, less time may be available for leisure.

Mourners wear veils made of rough hessian

Death
Death, when a loved and valued member leaves a community forever, is marked by rituals in most societies. In China, for example, Taoist mourners at funerals traditionally cover themselves to show their respect for the dead.

Taoist mourners

FIND OUT MORE   CRIME   EDUCATION   FESTIVALS   GOVERNMENTS   HUMAN RIGHTS   LAW   PHILOSOPHY   POLICE   RELIGION   WOMEN'S MOVEMENT

SOCRATES

THE GREEK THINKER Socrates, who lived 2,400 years ago, was one of the most important people in the history of philosophy. He wrote no books, and we know little about the events of his life, but Socrates still has a strong influence on western thought. He believed strongly that philosophy should concern itself with the conduct of everyday life, not with abstract ideas. He valued human intelligence, reason, and open discussion, and, through his teachings, showed people how to live a good and virtuous life.

Early life

Socrates was born in Athens, Greece, in 469 BC. Very little is known about his background, but it is thought that his mother was a midwife and his father, Sophroniscus, was a stonemason and sculptor. As a young man, Socrates probably followed his father's trade. He later served in the Athenian army as a *hoplite* (foot soldier), before turning to philosophy during his middle years.

Later life of Socrates

In his middle age, Socrates studied the teachings of other great thinkers, developed a philosophy of his own, and debated regularly with other philosophers. Most of what we know about his philosophy comes from the writings of two of his pupils, the philosopher Plato and the historian Xenophon.

Plato's dialogues

Plato (c.428–347 BC) wrote a series of books called dialogues, in which he sets out the arguments of Socrates in the form of conversations with other thinkers. Plato records that the oracle of Delphi considered Socrates to be the wisest man in Greece. Socrates was puzzled by this acclaim, until he realized that, while other people claimed to be intelligent without acknowledging their ignorance, he at least recognized his own ignorance.

Xenophon

Unlike Plato, who describes the philosophy of Socrates, Xenophon (c.430–354 BC), in books such as his *Memoirs* and *Anabasis*, draws a more practical picture. In his book *Oeconomicus*, for example, Xenophon describes a discussion between Socrates and another man about managing a household and a farm.

Philosophy of Socrates

Socrates believed that philosophy should be applied to the events of daily life. To lead a good life, we must, therefore, understand what virtue means. According to Socrates, "virtue is knowledge". He, therefore, stressed the importance of self-knowledge, and told his pupils to question every statement to test its truth.

Raphael's painting *The School of Athens*

Greek philosophers assemble for discussions.

"Know thyself"

Socrates believed that a full understanding of himself and his own beliefs was essential to help him comment on the outside world, and find a way of living that was best for others. The importance of self-questioning in philosophy began with Socrates.

Socratic method

Socrates' philosophical method was known as dialectic. When Greek philosophers gathered for discussions, Socrates pretended ignorance of the subject under discussion. He then asked a series of questions about each statement to find out if it was true. By questioning every assumption made in a statement, Socrates believed it was possible to arrive at the truth.

SOCRATES

469 BC Born in Athens, Greece.

c.420 BC Socrates marries Xanthippe.

399 BC Put on trial and sentenced to death in Athens.

387 BC Plato founds the Academy – the world's first formal philosophical school – to carry on Socrates' work.

NOTE Little is known of the life of Socrates, although the development of his philosophy was well described by his pupils, particularly Plato and Xenophon.

Trial of Socrates

During his life, Socrates made enemies because of his teaching. In 399 BC, he was brought to trial on a charge of "introducing strange gods" – in other words subversion – and for corrupting the young. He was found guilty and sentenced to death by drinking hemlock, a deadly poison. His death is recorded in Plato's dialogue, *Phaedo*, and in a painting, *Death of Socrates*, by the 18th-century French artist Jacques-Louis David.

Socrates

FIND OUT MORE

GREECE, ANCIENT   PHILOSOPHY   RELIGIONS   SOCIETIES, HUMAN   WRITING

SOIL

MUCH OF THE world's land surface is covered in decaying matter – soil. Soil is a layer of weathered rock fragments, rotting plants, and animals that coats the ground everywhere, except for deserts, polar regions, steep slopes, and artificial environments. Although soil is made from decaying material, it is far from dead; it is a living, ever-changing system. Tiny gaps in the soil are filled with water or air, in which live myriad bacteria, algae, and fungi. These micro-organisms speed up the process of decay, making the soil a good home for plant roots, insects, worms, and other creatures.

Soil type

A soil's texture, or average grain size, varies with the nature of the bedrock beneath. Soils are divided into three main types, according to their texture – clay, sandy, and loamy. However, there are many other soil types, which depend on climate, vegetation, and landscape. Soils are also classified by their acidity, or pH. They need to have the right pH to be fertile.

Clay

Sand

Chalk

Clay soils
In clay soil, most grains are fine clay or silt (medium-sized grains). Fine grains often stick together in clumps. When dry, the soil is hard and likely to crack. When wet, it is sticky and waterlogged.

Sandy soils
Sandy soils contain coarse sand-sized grains. Sandy soils are well-aerated, warm, and are easy to work or dig. However, they can be very dry, and their nutrients are quickly washed out.

Chalky soils
Chalky soils are thin and stony, and drain water quickly. Their high pH content makes them very alkaline and therefore not very fertile.

Loam

Peat

Loam
Loams are the best soils for plant growth. Loams are a mixture of clay, silt, and sand, which make them fertile and easy to work.

Peat
All soils contain rotting organic matter, but peat is made of nothing else. Its dark brown mass consists of rotten plants. Gardeners may add peat to other soils to boost their organic content.

The soil provides nutrients for plant and shrub growth.

Humus

A horizon

B horizon

C horizon

D horizon

Soil profile

Soils develop from a layer of loose weathered rock fragments, called a regolith. Chemicals released by rotting organic matter – anything derived from plants or animals – slowly transform the regolith into soil. As this happens, the soil forms distinct horizons, or layers.

Humus
The top coat is a thin dark layer of humus – rotting organic matter. Humus is crucial to maintaining the balance of minerals and nutrients needed for plant growth.

Topsoil
The topsoil, or A horizon, is the uppermost layer of soil. This is where plants grow and creatures burrow. It is usually rich in both humus and minerals.

Subsoil
The subsoil, or B horizon, contains more weathered rock fragments than organic matter. It is poor in humus but rich in minerals, leached (washed down) from above.

C horizon
Weathered rock fragments with little or no organic content make up the C horizon.

Bedrock
Beneath the soil is the D horizon. This is usually solid, weathered "parent" rock. It can also be the loose material deposited in huge quantities by rivers, glaciers, and wind.

Life in the soil
The soil provides the conditions for giving life to plants but is itself teeming with life, from ants and termites to earthworms and rodents. Earthworms play a vital role in improving the soil's texture by passing it through their digestive tracts and excreting it as worm casts.

Plants thrive in fertile soils.

Slugs and snails burrow in the soil.

Earthworms improve soil fertility: their burrowing mixes and aerates the soil.

Erosion

Damaged soil is infertile and unable to support plant or animal life. Erosion, a natural weathering process in which rain and wind erode soil from the land, can cause such damage. Human activity, such as over-farming, can also cause soil damage.

Salinization
In hot, dry places, dissolved mineral salts leave a salty crust, as water evaporates from the surface of the soil.

Leaching
In some places, water washes soil minerals down through the soil, depleting the topsoil of nutrients.

Lessivage
In wet areas, clay particles may be washed through the soil, coating the grains beneath and dampening the soil.

Soil creep
On steep slopes, soil often creeps slowly downhill over the years. Hill-side trees show the soil's movement.

FIND OUT MORE

FORESTS   MICROSCOPIC LIFE   PLANTS   ROCKS AND MINERALS   WORMS

SOLIDS

THE PHRASE "SOLID AS A ROCK" makes us think of something that is very hard and rigid. But rock is only one example of a solid, and some solids are weaker or more flexible than others. A solid is any piece of matter that has a definite shape and volume, and does not flow like a liquid or a gas. When a solid gets hot, it may turn into a liquid: the heat of a volcano can turn even the hardest rock into liquid lava.

Solid structure

Inside a solid, tiny particles of matter called atoms or molecules are packed together in orderly patterns, like bricks in a wall. The particles are "cemented" firmly in place by forces called chemical bonds.

Solid particles
Although solid particles are held close to their neighbours and cannot move away, they vibrate around fixed positions.

A certain amount of force is needed to break or change the shape of a solid.

Strong forces bind the particles together in granite, making it a very hard rock.

Melting

When heated, a bar of chocolate turns into a runny liquid. The change of a solid to a liquid is called melting. Heating a solid gives its particles energy and makes them vibrate more vigorously. At a temperature called the melting point, the particles are able to break free from their fixed positions, and the substance flows as a liquid.

Melting chocolate

Plumes of iodine gas rise up as the crystals sublime.

Iodine crystals are heated from below.

Sublimation
When heated, most solid substances will first melt to form a liquid, and then boil to form a gas. However, a few solids, such as iodine crystals and dry ice (frozen carbon dioxide), transform directly from a solid to a gas as they get warmer. This change is called sublimation.

Crystalline solids
Many solids, especially rocks, minerals, and metals, have crystalline structures. This means that they are made up of crystals, which are geometrically shaped pieces of solid matter with smooth surfaces, straight edges, and symmetrical corners. The atoms in a crystal are arranged in a regular, repeating pattern. It is this pattern that determines the shape of the crystal.

Sulphur crystals

William Henry Bragg
The English physicist William Henry Bragg (1862–1942) and his son William Lawrence Bragg (1890–1971) discovered that if a beam of X-rays passes through a crystal, it makes a pattern of dots on photographic film. This pattern shows how the atoms are arranged inside the crystal.

Properties of solids

Solid materials are often described in terms of their strength, elasticity, and hardness, and how easily they can be shaped. Such properties help scientists, engineers, architects, and designers decide how best to use the materials, and choose the most suitable material for a particular task.

A scratch test determines the hardness of two materials.

Nail scratches slate.

Hardness
Dragging a nail across a slate makes scratch marks on the surface of the slate, but leaves the nail unmarked. This is because the nail is harder than the slate. The ability of a material to resist scratching is called hardness. The particles in the iron nail are bound together more rigidly and tightly than those in the slate.

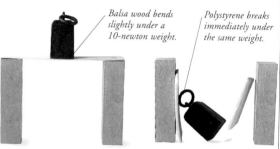

Balsa wood bends slightly under a 10-newton weight.

Polystyrene breaks immediately under the same weight.

Strength
A strip of polystyrene breaks more easily than a similar strip of balsa wood because the balsa wood is a stronger material. The strength of a material is its ability to resist forces that act upon it. The more powerful the forces between the particles in the material, the greater is its strength. Steel and concrete are extremely strong materials, which is why they are widely used in building and construction.

Elasticity
When you pull a spring and then let it go, it leaps back to its original size. Elasticity is the ability of a material to regain its size and shape after being stretched or squeezed. Most materials are elastic only up to a certain point, called the elastic limit. If too much force is applied, the material reaches its elastic limit and will not regain its shape.

Steel spring

Spring is stretched by weights.

Aluminium is a malleable metal.

Modelling clay is plastic and easy to shape.

Heavier weights stretch the spring to its elastic limit.

Copper is very ductile.

Plasticity
Modelling clay will not return to its original shape once it has been squeezed. A material that can be reshaped permanently when force is applied to it is said to be plastic. Most metals are plastic, but considerable force is needed to reshape them. A ductile metal is one that can be drawn out into fine wire. A metal that can be beaten or rolled out into thin sheets is said to be malleable.

FIND OUT MORE ATOMS AND MOLECULES · BUILDING AND CONSTRUCTION · CRYSTALS AND GEMS · GASES · LIQUIDS · MATTER · METALS · ROCKS AND MINERALS · VOLCANOES

SONGBIRDS

ALMOST HALF THE WORLD'S bird species are songbirds – a name given to the passerines, or perching birds. There are more than 4,000 species and they are found all over the world. The males of most species sing loudly during their courtship season, although some can only croak harshly. Females usually do not sing. Songbirds feed on insects or seeds according to the shape of their beak. Most are blind and helpless when they hatch.

Small head with a powerful beak

Female has a paler chest than the male.

Hind toe is larger and stronger than front toes.

Lungs

Trachea

Syrinx

Lungs

Songbird features

Songbirds are very varied, but most are quite small with a compact body and a small beak. They have small feet with four slender toes on each. Their toes lock around twigs or branches which enables the birds to perch, even when they are asleep. The male and female of a species sometimes look identical.

Gouldian finches
These brilliantly coloured seed-eaters from northern Australia are typical songbirds. They spend most of their time in tall grasses or bushes, but come to the ground to drink.

Perching feet
A songbird's feet have three toes pointing forward, and one pointing backward. When the bird rests its weight on its feet, its toes automatically close.

Syrinx
The syrinx is a songbird's voice-box. It is located at the base of its windpipe, or trachea. It has thin walls that vibrate to make complex sounds.

Seed-eaters
Seed-eaters, such as bullfinches, crossbills, and goldfinches, specialize in feeding at different types of plant. They have beaks shaped to extract the seeds and crack them open. Many of these birds also eat berries and buds, and occasionally insects.

Bullfinch

Buds

The bullfinch eats buds in spring and seeds in summer.

Thick beak for removing buds.

Cones

Crossbill

Cross-tipped beak extracts seeds from cones.

Teasels

The spotted flycatcher darts out from a perch to catch passing insects.

Spotted flycatcher

Goldfinch

Slender beak can reach into teasel flowerheads to extract the seeds.

Nectar-eaters
Only a few songbirds feed on nectar, but their beaks are specially adapted for reaching inside flowers. Sunbirds, which live in Africa and southern Asia, have slender beaks with a downward curve. They suck up the liquid food using their tongue like a straw.

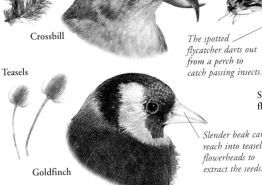

Sunbird

Beaks and diet

The shape of a songbird's beak provides important clues to what it eats. For example, those with short, stubby beaks usually feed on seeds. Those with long, narrow beaks feed on insects, or on a range of food. Insect-eating songbirds often migrate to warm places when winter approaches because insects are hard to find in cold weather.

Insect-eaters
Insect-eaters usually feed on their own. They use their beaks either to probe into crevices for hidden insects, or to catch flying insects in midair. Some eat their food on the wing, but others take it back to a perch.

Starling

A starling's sharp, straight beak probes grass-covered ground.

General feeders
Starlings, thrushes, and crows are all songbirds that have a varied diet. They feed on a mixture of seeds, worms, and insects, and sometimes on the remains of dead animals.

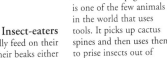

Using tools
The woodpecker finch from the Galápagos Islands is one of the few animals in the world that uses tools. It picks up cactus spines and then uses them to prise insects out of cracks in the bark of trees.

Feeding underwater
One of the few songbirds that ventures into water is the dipper. It jumps into fast-flowing streams and walks or swims beneath the surface, picking up insect grubs in its beak from the riverbed.

779

Courtship

During the breeding season, many male songbirds claim a small patch of land called a territory. They keep other males out of their territory, but encourage females to enter so that they can mate and raise a family. A male's song announces that he has a territory and will defend it against his rivals.

Attracting a mate
When a male robin has drawn a female into his territory, he often gives her presents of food. This is called courtship feeding. By doing this, the male encourages the female to mate and lay eggs.

Establishing territories
Territories change every year as male birds fight for space in which to feed and breed. If food is abundant, robin territories are small. If food is scarce, or if there are few males, each one claims a larger area.

Robin territories in consecutive years

Each colour represents a particular robin.

Song thrush

Warning call
A songbird's song is particular to the species. It is recognized by members of the species, but ignored by other birds. The song thrush's song is made up of clear phrases that are repeated.

Raising young

Most songbirds are expert nest-builders. They make their nests above the ground, usually in trees or dense vegetation. During the breeding season, the adults are kept extremely busy building nests and feeding the young. Once their first nestlings are ready to look after themselves, many female songbirds lay another clutch of eggs. Some species may raise up to five families a year.

Nest-building
Songbirds usually make cup-shaped nests. They collect twigs, leaves, and other materials and press them into shape with their breasts. Some species finish their nests with a smooth lining of mud.

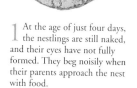

Feeding a family
Most songbird nestlings are completely helpless when they hatch. They rely on their parents to feed them and to keep them warm until they develop feathers. In most species, the male and female share the task of finding food and bringing it to the chicks in the nest.

Hatching
The blue tit is a typical small songbird. It lays between six and 12 eggs, and the female starts to incubate the eggs immediately after the last one has been laid. The eggs hatch after about two weeks, and during the following two weeks, the nestlings grow and develop their feathers, or fledge.

Feather tract on the back

Flight feathers on the wings

Flight feathers almost fully formed

1 At the age of just four days, the nestlings are still naked, and their eyes have not fully formed. They beg noisily when their parents approach the nest with food.

2 By six days, the nestlings' feathers are beginning to grow. They form in special patches called feather tracts. Some of these are on the body, and some along the wings.

3 At nine days, the nestlings' flight feathers are starting to emerge from their tube-like sheaths. Shorter feathers are beginning to cover the rest of the nestlings' bodies.

4 At 13 days, the nestlings are almost fully fledged. They will leave the nest in another four or five days, and will follow their parents as they learn how to feed.

Types of songbird

House sparrows are originally from Africa and Asia. This small songbird now lives all over the world.

Blue-faced honeyeater has a harsh call. This large Australian bird feeds on insects, fruit, and nectar.

Nightingales are known for their song, which can be heard during the day and night.

Golden-crowned kinglet

Northern oriole is a common North American bird. It belongs to a family of songbirds with sharply pointed beaks.

Kinglets are among the smallest songbirds. The Golden-crowned kinglet is 9 cm (3.5 in) long.

Scarlet tanager

Tanagers usually live in the American tropics and subtropics, but the Scarlet tanager lives as far north as Canada.

Red-billed queleas
These small African songbirds are probably the world's most abundant birds. They eat mainly seeds, and feed in flocks that are sometimes more than one million strong. In the whole of Africa there are at least one and a half billion of these birds.

GOULDIAN FINCH

SCIENTIFIC NAME *Chloebia gouldiae*

ORDER Passeriformes

FAMILY Estrildidae

DISTRIBUTION Tropical northern Australia

HABITAT Open woodland, grassland, and scrub

DIET Seeds of grasses and other plants

SIZE Length from the tip of the beak to the end of the tail: 13 cm (5 in)

LIFESPAN About 5 years

MIGRATION Non-migrant

PLUMAGE Females are slightly paler

NEST Dome of grass, usually in a hollow in the ground

FIND OUT MORE

ANIMAL BEHAVIOUR   BIRDS   EGGS   NESTS AND BURROWS

SONGHAI EMPIRE

ONE OF THE LARGEST empires of 16th-century West Africa was that of the Songhai. Tradition has it that the Songhai kingdom was founded in the 7th century by al-Yaman, a Christian, but in the 11th century, its rulers converted to Islam. In the 14th century, the Mali Empire ruled the Songhai kingdom, but in 1464 a warrior-king named Sonni Ali rose up and conquered the Mali capital of Tombouctou, making Songhai independent once more. The Songhai Empire then continued to grow in wealth and power until internal divisions coupled with a Moroccan invasion brought the empire to an end in 1591.

Boundaries of the empire
The Songhai Empire, which flourished from 1464 to 1591, initially occupied the same area as the previous West African empire of the Mali. Gao was the capital of the Songhai, and from here they expanded further eastwards, invading the territories of the Hausa states in modern northern Nigeria.

Songhai rulers
The two greatest Songhai rulers were Sonni Ali (1464–1492) and the statesman Askia Muhammad (1493–1528). After Sonni Ali founded the Songhai Empire by a series of conquests, Muhammad consolidated and expanded it.

Gilded tent

Mythical Songhai ruler

Askia Muhammad
When Sonni Ali died in 1492, his son, Sonni Baare, succeeded him. However Baare was a weak ruler and Askia Muhammad, a former general in Sonni Ali's army, overthrew him in 1493. Muhammad expanded the empire to its greatest extent by controlling trade routes to North Africa. He founded an efficient administration and protected all he had gained with a standing army and a fleet of war canoes.

Trans-Saharan trade
From trade centres in the Songhai Empire, such as the oasis town of Walata, goods travelled across the Sahara Desert in camel trains to countries in North Africa, especially Morocco, Algeria, and Libya. From there, they could go by ship to Europe, Arabia, and China.

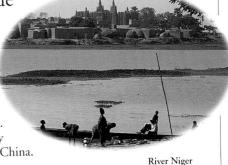

River Niger

Trade goods
Africa has always been rich in natural resources, such as copper, salt, and gold. The Songhai based their empire on their gold trade with Arabia and Europe. Songhai merchants also traded other home-grown goods, such as figs, dates, kola nuts (a stimulant), and ivory. In return they bought ceramics, silk, beads, and cowrie shells.

River Niger
The River Niger crossed the Songhai Empire from east to west. It was crucial to the success of the empire, as it had been in the 12th to 15th centuries when the Mali Empire was dominant. Merchants had fleets of canoes to transport goods between different trading centres along the River Niger, such as Djenné, Tombouctou, and Gao.

Dried figs   Copper   Salt   Kola nut

Dates   Gold   Ivory

Trade goods

Religion and education
Songhai boasted great scholars, including Ahmad Baba (b.1556), who wrote more than 50 books on Islamic tradition and a huge dictionary. The empire's most important religious and educational centre was Tombouctou.

Tombouctou
Known as the "holy town" of the Sudan, Tombouctou had three great mosques: the Jingereber, the Sidi Yahya, and the Sankore, which contained many superb copies of the Qur'an. It also had a university and 180 schools.

Islamic writing

Page from a 16th-century Qur'an

Decline of empire
Moroccans wanted to control the source of West African gold. In 1591, Ahmad al-Mansur (1578–1603), the Sultan of Morocco, sent a powerful army to conquer the Songhai Empire. The Moroccans conquered Tombouctou, which they ruled for more than 100 years. Shortly afterwards, Morocco absorbed the rest of the empire.

Moroccan coins

Timeline

1464 Sonni Ali conquers Tombouctou, the former centre of the Mali Empire.

1473 Sonni Ali conquers the trading town of Djenné.

1492 Sonni Baare, Sonni Ali's son, refuses to convert to Islam.

1493 Civil war; Sonni Baare is overthrown by the Muslim Askia Muhammad.

1496 Askia Muhammad's Mecca pilgrimage.

1528 Askia Muhammad is deposed by his eldest son Musa.

1588 Civil war erupts as Askia's descendants fight over the succession.

1591 The Moroccan army defeat the Songhai army at the Battle of Tondibi, near Gao.

Cowrie shells

FIND OUT MORE   AFRICA, HISTORY OF   MALI EMPIRE   MONEY   TRADE AND INDUSTRY

SOUND

FROM THE ROAR of city traffic to the quiet rustle of the wind in the trees, the world is full of sounds. A sound is a form of energy produced by vibrating objects, such as a person's vocal cords or a drum. When sound travels through a material such as air, molecules in the material vibrate and bump into other molecules, passing on their energy. Sound cannot travel in a vacuum.

Echoes

Sound can reflect off hard surfaces and return to its source as an echo. If you stand some distance away from a wall and shout or clap, you may hear an echo a short while later. The farther from the wall you stand, the longer the echo takes to reach you. Most of the sounds we hear are a mixture of the original sound and echoes from nearby objects.

Frequency and pitch

The pitch of a sound (whether it is high or low) depends on its frequency. Frequency is measured in hertz (Hz) – 1 Hz is one vibration per second. The lowest-pitched sound audible by most people has a frequency of about 40 Hz, and the highest has a frequency of around 20,000 Hz.

Fundamental

First harmonic

Second harmonic

Harmonics

Most sounds are made by objects that vibrate at several different frequencies at once. The sound consists of one main frequency, called the fundamental, mixed with several higher frequencies called harmonics.

Display

Sonic tape measure

Beams emerge from here.

Ultrasound

Sound with a frequency above the range of human hearing is called ultrasound. This sonic tape measure sends out beams of ultrasound that bounce off an object and return to the device. The time the sound takes to return reveals the distance to the object.

Speed of sound

Sound travels at about 330 m/s (1,080 ft/s) through air. This is far slower than the speed of light, which is why lightning is seen before thunder is heard. The time lapse between a lightning flash and a thunderclap tells you how far away a storm is – that is, about 1 km (0.6 mile) away for every 3 seconds that pass.

Sound waves

Our ears detect sound travelling through the air as vibrations called sound waves. As this tuning fork vibrates, its prongs move outwards and squeeze the air around them, creating high-pressure areas called compressions. As the prongs move back, the air expands and creates low-pressure areas called rarefactions. These pressure vibrations spread out from their source as sound waves.

Compressions
The air molecules are squeezed close together, so the air density and pressure increase.

Rarefactions
The air molecules spread apart, giving the air a lower density and pressure than normal.

Electrical signal is sent to oscilloscope.

Tuning fork

Microphone changes sound into electrical signal.

Oscilloscope displays waveform on screen.

Waveforms

The shape of a sound wave as displayed on the screen of an oscilloscope is called its waveform. The peaks and troughs of the waveform correspond to the areas of high pressure and low pressure in the sound wave. Sounds are defined by their frequency and amplitude. The frequency of a sound wave travelling through the air is the number of pressure changes per second. The amplitude is the size of the pressure changes.

Oscilloscope

A sound wave cannot be seen, but a device called an oscilloscope can be used to give a visual representation of the sound wave. The sound wave's pressure changes are displayed as a wavy line on the oscilloscope's screen.

Soft sounds have a small amplitude and waveforms showing little difference between areas of high and low pressure.

Loud sounds have a large amplitude, and their waveforms show a greater difference between high- and low-pressure areas.

Low-pitched sounds have a low frequency, which means that there are fewer sound waves per second and they are farther apart.

High-pitched sounds have a high frequency, so there are more sound waves per second and they are closer together.

Loudness

The louder a sound is, the more energy its sound waves carry. Loudness is measured in decibels (dB). Sounds of 0 dB are just audible to the human ear, while sounds of 130 dB or more cause pain. Listening to loud music on a personal stereo for too long can damage your hearing. Although the stereo is not very powerful, almost all the sound goes directly into the ears, creating high levels of sound energy inside the ear.

Headset

Christian Doppler

The pitch of a sound from a moving source, such as the siren of a speeding fire engine, changes from high to low as the object passes you. The Austrian physicist Christian Doppler (1803–53) explained this effect in 1842. He showed that it is caused by the way sound waves bunch up ahead of the moving object and spread out behind it, changing the frequency of the sound. This effect is now known as the Doppler effect.

FIND OUT MORE

EARS AND HEARING   ENERGY   MUSICAL INSTRUMENTS   SOUND RECORDING

SOUND RECORDING

COMPACT DISCS (CDs) enable us to listen to the past. The information stored on the disc allows a CD-player to recreate sounds made at another time and in another place. Sound consists of vibrations that travel as waves of varying air pressure. A microphone makes a copy of these vibrations as an electrical sound signal, which can be stored in a number of different ways, including on CDs, magnetic tape, and vinyl records. The stored signal may be a direct representation of the original sound (analogue recording), or it may be translated into electronic pulses (digital recording).

Recording studio

Sound recordings are often made in a recording studio, which normally consists of two adjoining rooms. In one room, people make music, sing, or speak. The sounds of the different voices and instruments are converted to electrical signals by microphones, and each is recorded separately. The separate signals are then added together again in the control room.

Recording studio

Performers speak or sing into microphone in soundproof booth.

Mixer takes the signals from the tape and the microphones and "mixes" them together to produce the desired sound.

Digital editing and recording system

Sound engineer controls the quality and "mix" of the sound.

TV screen for matching sound to screen actions.

Loudspeakers allow engineer to hear the sound from the booth.

Reel-to-reel tape machine can record sound from booth or add backing sound to new recordings.

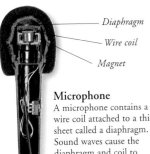

Diaphragm
Wire coil
Magnet

Microphone

A microphone contains a wire coil attached to a thin sheet called a diaphragm. Sound waves cause the diaphragm and coil to vibrate within the force field of a magnet. This movement produces a fluctuating electric current, called an analogue sound signal, that copies the vibrations in the sound waves.

Digital sound

In digital recording, the analogue sound signal produced by a microphone is measured, or "sampled", thousands of times every second. These measurements, which are in the form of numbers, are then converted into binary code – that is, into a series of on-off pulses of electricity. This is known as a digital sound signal.

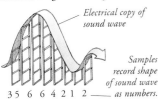

Electrical copy of sound wave

Samples record shape of sound wave as numbers.

3 5 6 6 4 2 1 2

Recording formats

Analogue formats store sound as wavy grooves or varying magnetic patterns that copy the changes in the analogue sound signal. Digital formats store the binary-code information of a digital sound signal as magnetic patterns or a series of tiny holes.

Vinyl records (analogue) record the vibrations of sound waves as undulations in a spiral groove cut into a vinyl disk.

Compact discs, or CDs, (digital) are metal and plastic disks that store sound as tiny pits on a spiral track.

Magnetic tape (analogue) records sound as changing patterns in magnetic particles on a plastic tape.

Digital audio tape, or DAT, works like magnetic tape, but stores sound information digitally.

Minidiscs (digital) store sound signals as a spiral pattern on a magnetic disk.

MP3 player

The MP3 was launched in the 1990s as a high quality digital file format for storing music. MP3 files, created on a computer, are very small and can be transferred over the Internet or saved onto a portable music device, called an MP3 player. The MP3 player can hold several hours' worth of music that can be updated regularly.

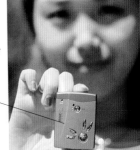

With headphones this device works like a personal stereo.

Portable MP3 player

Emile Berliner

German-born Emile Berliner (1851–1929) invented the gramophone, which could replay sound recorded on flat discs. He also devised a method of reproducing hundreds of these discs from a single master copy.

Timeline

1876 The microphone is invented by Scottish-born Alexander Graham Bell, who uses it in the first telephone.

1877 Thomas Edison, an American inventor, makes the first sound recording – the words "Mary had a little lamb" – on to tin foil.

1887 Berliner invents the gramophone.

1898 Danish inventor Valdemar Poulsen makes magnetic recordings of sound on to steel piano wire.

1887 Magnetic tape is used to record sound.

Poulsen's telegraphone

1948 The first vinyl disks are produced.

1964 The cassette tape becomes available.

1980s Compact discs become the main medium for sound recording.

1992 The Sony Corporation of Japan introduces the minidisc.

2001 Internet site Napster is banned from swapping MP3 files for free because it infringes artists' copyright.

FIND OUT MORE   EDISON, THOMAS   ELECTROMAGNETISM   LASERS AND HOLOGRAMS   MUSIC   SOUND   TELECOMMUNICATIONS   TELEPHONES   VIDEO

783

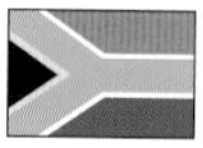

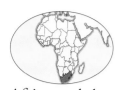

SOUTH AFRICA

LYING AT THE SOUTHERN TIP of the African continent, South Africa is bordered by both the Atlantic and Indian Oceans. Two small, independent countries, Lesotho and Swaziland, are enclaves within South Africa and depend on it heavily. Racism dominated politics for many years, and from 1948, the white minority ruled the land and enforced apartheid, a system of racial segregation. In 1994, the country held its first multiracial elections and, with the end of apartheid, Nelson Mandela became South Africa's first black president, ruling until 1999.

SOUTH AFRICA FACTS

CAPITAL CITIES	Pretoria, Cape Town, Bloemfontein
AREA	1,219,912 sq km (471,008 sq miles)
POPULATION	43,800,000
MAIN LANGUAGES	Afrikaans, English, Ndebele, North Sotho, South Sotho, Swazi, Tsonga, Tswana, Venda, Xhosa, Zulu
MAJOR RELIGION	Christian
CURRENCY	Rand
LIFE EXPECTANCY	52 years
PEOPLE PER DOCTOR	1,667
GOVERNMENT	Multi-party democracy
ADULT LITERACY	85%

Physical features

South Africa is a land of contrasts. The steep cliffs of the Great Escarpment separate the flat-topped plateau hills from the low-lying, sandy coastal regions. The arid Namib and Kalahari deserts to the northwest contrast with the lush forests of the northeast.

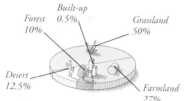

Built-up 0.5%
Forest 10%
Grassland 50%
Desert 12.5%
Farmland 27%

Land use
Although much of the country is high ground, the majority is used for grazing livestock and growing crops, including sugar, maize, and cereals. South Africa has vast mineral resources, such as gold and coal.

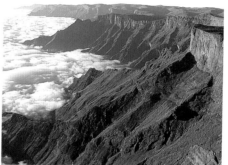

Drakensberg
The dramatic Drakensberg, or Dragon Mountains, are a vast range located in the southeast of South Africa and Lesotho. They rise out of the eastern rim of the high plateau land to form a steep escarpment. The highest peak measures 3,482 m (11,424 ft) above sea-level, at Thabana Ntlenyana, formerly known as Champagne Castle.

Climate
Generally, South Africa's climate is warm, sunny, and dry. The east receives about three times as much rain as the north and western desert regions. Winters are short, between June and August, and mild, although the Drakensberg and Cape mountains often have snow. The Cape Province has hot, dry summers from October to April.

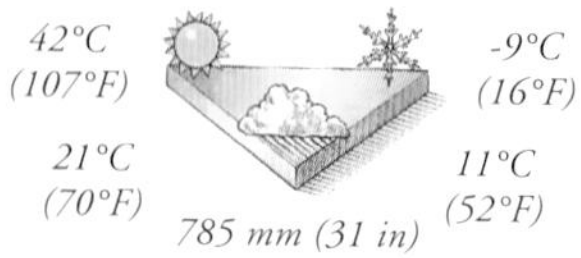

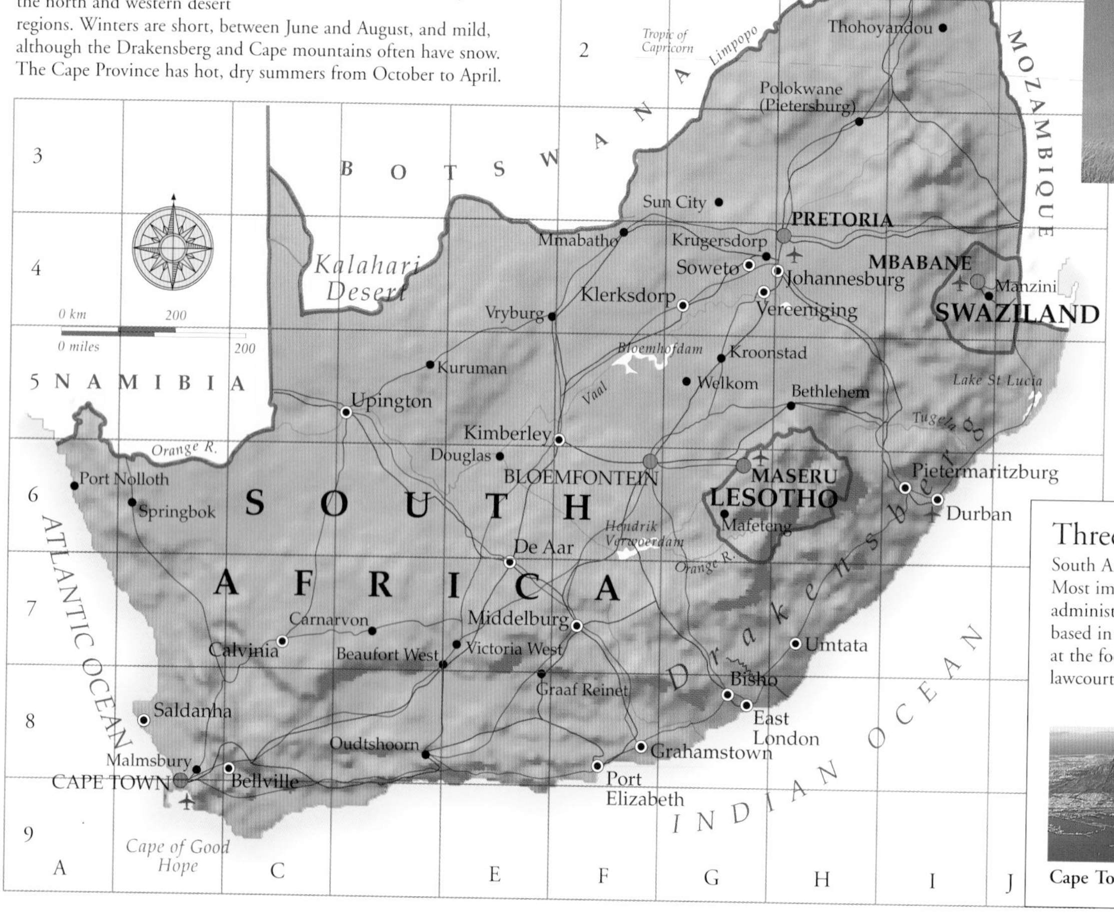

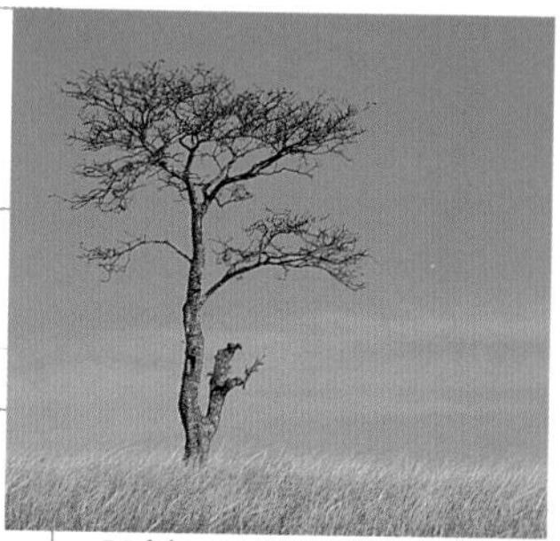

42°C (107°F)
21°C (70°F)
-9°C (16°F)
11°C (52°F)
785 mm (31 in)

ZIMBABWE
MOZAMBIQUE
BOTSWANA
NAMIBIA
SOUTH AFRICA
LESOTHO
SWAZILAND
ATLANTIC OCEAN
INDIAN OCEAN
Kalahari Desert
Tropic of Capricorn
Limpopo
Thohoyandou
Polokwane (Pietersburg)
Sun City
PRETORIA
Mmabatho
Krugersdorp
Soweto
Johannesburg
MBABANE
Manzini
Klerksdorp
Vryburg
Vereeniging
Bloemhofdam
Kroonstad
Kuruman
Welkom
Bethlehem
Lake St Lucia
Upington
Vaal
Tugela
Kimberley
Douglas
Orange R.
BLOEMFONTEIN
MASERU
Pietermaritzburg
Port Nolloth
Springbok
Mafeteng
Durban
Hendrik Verwoerdam
De Aar
Orange R.
Drakensberg
Carnarvon
Middelburg
Calvinia
Beaufort West
Victoria West
Umtata
Graaf Reinet
Bisho
Saldanha
East London
Oudtshoorn
Grahamstown
Malmsbury
CAPE TOWN
Bellville
Port Elizabeth
Cape of Good Hope
0 km 200
0 miles 200
1
2
3
4
5
6
7
8
9
A
C
E
F
G
H
I
J

Veld
The grassy plateau, or tableland, that covers most of South Africa is known as the *veld*. In many places it is more than 1,200 m (3,900 ft) above sea-level. The central plateau is dry savannah, with scattered trees. Rolling grassland and subtropical woods with a wide variety of flora and fauna make up the northeastern *Lowveld*, while sheep and cattle graze on the western *veld*.

Three capital cities

South Africa has three capital cities. Most important is Pretoria, the centre of administration. The government is based in Cape Town, which is situated at the foot of Table Mountain, and the lawcourts are in Bloemfontein.

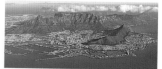

Cape Town and Table Mountain

S

People

Most South Africans are black and belong to the Zulu or Xhosa groups. About ten per cent are Coloureds, of mixed race, and the remainder are whites, of British origin, or Afrikaners of Dutch origin. Efforts are being made to create harmony between the races.

36 per sq km
(93 per sq mile)

55% Urban
45% Rural

Townships
Under apartheid, black South Africans had to live in purpose-built townships, and most still live there. Soweto, near Johannesburg, is a complex of 29 towns with a total estimated population of two million. Houses range from luxury to shacks, and many people queue for water.

Farming

A warm climate and fertile soils mean that South Africa can grow nearly all its food, as well as a surplus for export. Farming accounts for seven per cent of the country's economic activity. Maize, wheat, fruit, and tobacco are leading crops.

Lime
Orange
Lemon

Citrus fruits
Lemons, limes, and oranges grow well in tropical regions of South Africa, as do apples and pears, grown for export in the Cape area. A successful fruit juice industry has grown up in South Africa.

Vineyards
South African wines, made in the western and southern Cape, have been made in the region since 1662, and are known world-wide for their quality and flavour. Stellenbosch is a major wine-making centre.

Leisure

Many South Africans are sports lovers, especially of outdoor games such as cricket, rugby, and football. Since the end of apartheid, the country has rejoined international events.

Rugby
South Africa's national sport, Rugby Union football, is widely played and watched. In 1995, South Africa hosted its first Rugby World Cup, won by its own international team, the Springboks.

Housepainting
Ndebele women of the Transvaal are known for their brightly decorated homes. Every spring, women renew the paint, passing on their skills to younger girls. Older wall patterns are geometric, but modern symbols such as aeroplanes and cars are now portrayed in the designs.

Mining
One of South Africa's main employers, the mining industry forms the backbone of the country's economy. There are vast reserves of diamonds, manganese, chromium, and lead.

Diamond mines sprawl over large areas.

Industry

The South African economy is founded on its mineral wealth. The iron and steel industries are important, but manufacturing, mainly in Durban, Johannesburg, Cape Town, and Pretoria, now forms the largest sector in the economy.

Gold
South Africa leads the world in the production of gold. Its Johannesburg mines provide about 30 per cent of the world total, and most is used in jewellery and electronics.

Krugerrand

Lesotho

Lesotho is a tiny, mountainous monarchy surrounded by South Africa, on which it depends for work. Farming animals is the main activity for 86 per cent of the people. A new hydroelectric project is being developed, which will create energy.

Women dig a road by hand.

LESOTHO FACTS
CAPITAL CITY Maseru

AREA 30,355 sq km (11,720 sq miles)

POPULATION 2,100,000

MAIN LANGUAGES English, Sesotho

MAJOR RELIGION Christian

CURRENCY Loti

Women
Many women endure hardship and undertake labour in the community, because three-quarters of the men leave their homes to work in South African mines. Women in Lesotho have Africa's highest literacy rate.

Swaziland

Bordered by South Africa and Mozambique, Swaziland is a small kingdom perched on a series of plateaus. The country's mineral resources include bauxite and diamonds. Farming employs 40 per cent of the work-force. Citrus fruit and pineapples are grown in plantations, and sugar-cane is the main export crop.

SWAZILAND FACTS
CAPITAL CITY Mbabane

AREA 17,363 sq km (6,704 sq miles)

POPULATION 938,000

MAIN LANGUAGES Siswati, English

MAJOR RELIGIONS Christian, traditional beliefs

CURRENCY Lilangeni

Swazis
Most of the people are Swazis, who follow a traditional clan lifestyle. The clans settle in rural, scattered homesteads, run by a chief and his mother. Swazis have a rich history of poetry and folk-tales.

FIND OUT MORE

BALL GAMES   CRYSTALS AND GEMS   DESERTS   FARMING   GRASSLAND WILDLIFE   MANDELA, NELSON   MOUNTAINS AND VALLEYS   ROCKS AND MINERALS   SOUTH AFRICA, HISTORY OF

SOUTH AFRICA, HISTORY OF

FROM C.100, SOUTH AFRICA was increasingly populated by Bantu-speaking farmers. In the 1600s, Dutch settlers founded farms in Cape Colony, forcing African farmers off the land. British settlers followed the Dutch, and both groups clashed with the black majority, particularly the Zulus. By the 1800s, the British and the Dutch – now called Boers – were competing with each other to control South African wealth. By 1950, an all-white government was in power, which deprived black South Africans of the vote. In 1991 this policy was reversed, and democratic elections took place in 1994.

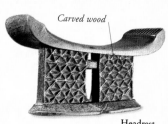

Carved wood

Headrest

Bantu
Two thousand years ago, Iron-Age Bantu-speaking farmers from the northeast settled South Africa's east coast and the savannah areas of the Transvaal. They were the ancestors of most of South Africa's black population. Today, most people speak some form of Bantu dialect.

European settlers

In 1651, Dutch farmers founded settlements in the Cape Colony. The settlers were called Boers (from the Dutch for "farmers"), and their descendents today are called Afrikaners. From 1795, as Dutch power faded, the British started to control more South African land.

Great Trek
In 1806, British settlers seized the Cape Colony from the Boers. To escape British control, the Boers migrated inland in large numbers. This became known as the Great Trek (1836–45). The Boers then formed two independent republics – the Orange Free State and the Transvaal.

Rest stop for a Boer family

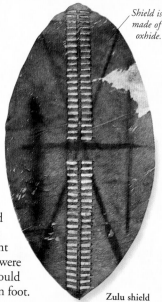

Shield is made of oxhide.

Anglo-Boer Wars
From 1880, the British attempted to take control of the Boer republics. They failed in the first Boer War (1880) but, after the discovery of gold and diamonds in the Transvaal in 1886, they redoubled their efforts. A second bloody war in 1899 finally led to a Boer surrender in 1902.

Boer War commemorative fan

Zulus

By 1818, a Zulu chief named Chaka (d.1828) had formed an empire called Zululand in northeastern Natal. His well-organized *impis* (warriors) fought both the Boers and the British. *Impis* were fierce and strictly disciplined: they could travel up to 64 km (40 miles) a day on foot.

Zulu shield

Union of South Africa

In 1910, British and Boer minorities formed the Union of South Africa, with the British in charge. There followed decades of repression of South Africa's non-whites.

Apartheid
Under the Apartheid (separateness) Policy of 1948, all South Africans were classified according to race. Black South Africans lost the right to vote, own land, travel, or work without permits. Asian and "coloured" South Africans were allowed to vote, but not to use the same facilities as white South Africans. Whites reserved for themselves the best housing, jobs, and schools.

Non-whites' post office entrance

ANC flag

African National Congress
The African National Congress, or ANC (founded in 1912), was the only political party that represented the interests of black South Africans. Its main aim was the abolition of apartheid. South Africa's government outlawed the ANC, but finally accepted its legality in 1990, just before Nelson Mandela's release.

New South Africa
In 1990, after spending 28 years in prison, one of the ANC's leaders, Nelson Mandela, was released. He immediately met President FW de Klerk to discuss political change in South Africa. Following their talks, apartheid was abolished and the first free, multiracial elections took place. For the first time, "Asians", "Blacks", and "Coloureds" gained full voting rights. The country elected Nelson Mandela president of a new, democratic South Africa.

Election queue, Katlehong

Steve Biko

Biko (1946–77) was an opponent of apartheid who founded South Africa's Students Organisation (SASO) and co-founded Black Consciousness. In 1977, he was arrested and beaten unconscious by police. Six days later he died; his death caused international outcry. No one was charged with his murder, but investigations into it were re-opened in 1997.

Timeline

1852 Boers create their independent republics.

1910 Union of South Africa formed, including Cape Province, Natal, Orange Free State, and Transvaal.

1931 South Africa gains independence.

Goatskin apron

1948 National Party (NP) is elected to government and passes Apartheid Policy. It establishes poor residential areas called Homelands for black majority.

1976 Police fire on a student march in Soweto; widespread protest demonstrations follow.

1970s World community imposes economic sanctions on South Africa.

1990 ANC deputy Nelson Mandela released from prison.

1991 Apartheid is abolished.

1994 First non-racial general election is held.

FIND OUT MORE   AFRICA, HISTORY OF   EMPIRES   EXPLORATION   GOVERNMENT AND POLITICS   MANDELA, NELSON

SOUTH AMERICA

THE FOURTH LARGEST CONTINENT, South America ranks only fifth in population. Its 12 independent countries were once colonies of European powers, particularly Spain and Portugal, whose languages, culture, and religion have greatly influenced the region. Many South Americans are farmers who grow their own food. Three-quarters of the continent's population live in large, overcrowded cities, often in squalid conditions. Many countries suffer huge foreign debts.

Physical features

Landscapes in South America range from the volcanic peaks of the Andes to the lush, tropical forests of the Amazon Basin in the east and centre. Further south are the rolling grasslands of the Chaco and Pampas. In the west is the hot, dry Atacama Desert; the cold Patagonian desert lies in the extreme south.

S

Map labels

Caribbean Sea
B
CENTRAL AMERICA
5800m
VENEZUELA
Apure
Orinoco
Angel Falls 980m
GUYANA
SURINAM
French Guiana (France)
Ruiz 5400m
COLOMBIA
Guiana Highlands
2810m
3035m
Equator
ECUADOR
Caquetá
Rio Negro
Amazon
Amazon Delta
Ilha de Marajó
Chimborazo 6301m
Marañón
Amazon Basin
Juruá
Madeira
Tapajós
Xingu
BRAZIL
Cabo de São Roque
Huascarán 6768m
Represa de Tucuruí
Araguaia
Tocantins
São Francisco
Represa de Sobradinho
Lake Titicaca
BOLIVIA
Mato Grosso
Brazilian Highlands
2033m
Sajama 6520m
Guallatiri 6060m
Lago Poopó
Gran Chaco
Paraguay
Pantanal
PARAGUAY
Tropic of Capricorn
A
2787m
Serra do Mar
Ojos del Salado 6880m
Atacama Desert
Cerro Bonete 6872m
Salinas Grandes
Paraná
Uruguay
1889m
Mercedario 6770m
Aconcagua 6960m
Salado
Laguna Mar Chiquita
Lagoa dos Patos
PACIFIC OCEAN
ATLANTIC OCEAN
CHILE
Villarrica 2840m
Pampas
Colorado
Río de la Plata
URUGUAY
ARGENTINA
Isla de Chiloé
Golfo San Matías
Salinas Grandes -40m
Península Valdés
Archipiélago de los Chonos
Chubut
Golfo San Jorge
Lago Buenos Aires 370m
Deseado
Patagonia
Isla Wellington
Bahía Grande
Falkland Is. (UK)
Lago Argentino
Strait of Magellan
Tierra del Fuego
Cape Horn

0 km — 1000
0 miles — 1000

Andes

Stretching 8,000 km (4,970 miles) down South America's Pacific coast from Venezuela to Chile, the Andes form the longest mountain chain in the world. The peaks are volcanic and subject to earthquakes. The highest point is Aconcagua in Argentina at 6,960 m (22,835 ft).

Amazon

The world's longest river, the Amazon stretches 6,500 km (4,040 miles); ships can navigate approximately 3,700 km (2,300 miles). The mouth of the Amazon, where it joins the Atlantic Ocean, is 150 km (90 miles) wide. It is estimated that about 95,000 litres (20,900 gallons) of water flow out each second.

Patagonia

Constant gales sweep the bleak southern plateau of Patagonia. With no more than 25 cm (10 in) of rain a year, much of Patagonia is cold desert, or semi-desert with scant, grey vegetation of scrub and tussock grass. A few sheep are reared in the north.

SOUTH AMERICA FACTS

AREA	18,589,118 sq km (7,177,259 sq miles)
POPULATION	385,000,000
NUMBER OF INDEPENDENT COUNTRIES	12
BIGGEST COUNTRY	Brazil
SMALLEST COUNTRY	Surinam
HIGHEST POINT	Aconcagua (Chile) 6,960 m (22,835 ft)
LOWEST POINT	Salinas Grandes (Argentina) 40 m (131 ft) below sea-level
LONGEST RIVER	Amazon (Peru/Colombia/Brazil)
BIGGEST FRESHWATER LAKE	Lake Titicaca (Bolivia/Peru) 8,288 sq km (3,200 sq miles)

Cross-section through South America

From the Pacific coast, the land rises steeply to the Andes, which separate into two parallel chains divided by a dry, grassy plateau called the Altiplano. East of the Andes is the steamy, forested Amazon Basin. In the east, the plateau of the Guiana Highlands rises, then drops to the Atlantic.

Andes Mountains
Lake Titicaca
Amazon Basin – source of the Amazon River
Guiana Highlands, a plateau of extensive savannah
Atlantic Ocean
Caribbean islands
Peru-Chile Trench (Pacific Ocean)
A
Approximately 3,637 km (2,260 miles) from A to B
B

Climatic zones

The tropical rainforest that occupies the Amazon river basin is intensely hot, humid, and wet all year. It has an average temperature of 21°C (70°F) and an annual rainfall of more than 2,000 mm (79 in). Much of the south of the continent has hot summers and cool winters, and there are wide grasslands with some semi-arid areas. In the Andes, the climate becomes cooler and drier towards the peaks, which are snow-capped all the time.

Tropical rainforest

Mountain

Desert

Grassland

Scrubland

Wetland

La Gran Sabana, Venezuela

Grassland

Temperate grassland covers vast areas of South America, such as the Pampas of Argentina and the Gran Chaco of Paraguay and Bolivia. In the north, close to the Equator, tropical grassland, or *llanos*, covers Venezuela's La Gran Sabana in the Guiana Highlands, the Brazilian Highlands, and the Mato Grosso plateau.

Large expanses of tropical grassland can be used for grazing.

Waxy leaves

Ulmo

Flowers appear in spring.

This tree's other name is monkey puzzle because of its twisted branches.

Cone

Chilean pine

Tropical rainforest

Dense, impenetrable rainforest crossed only by rivers covers the vast Amazon Basin in northern South America. This region contains about 30 per cent of the world's remaining forest and holds 20 per cent of the world's fresh water. The Amazon and its many tributaries drain 40 per cent of South America – an area of 7,000,000 sq km (2,702,700 sq miles).

Beneath the canopy are climbing plants called lianas and epiphytes, which attach themselves to the branches.

Dry woodland

In northeastern Brazil, down into Paraguay, central Chile, and northern Argentina, there are large areas of dry, open woodland and savannah. The vegetation here includes trees such as the Chilean pine and shrubs such as ulmo, whose evergreen leaves thrive during long periods without water.

Columns of eroded rock stick up from the bare Atacama desert. Very few plants can live here.

The forest in southern Brazil extends down to the Atlantic coast.

Small cacti grow in the hot sun along the coastlines.

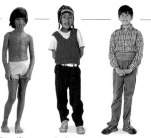

Hot and cold deserts

South America has two deserts – the cold Patagonian desert in Argentina, and the hot Atacama Desert, the world's driest, in northern Chile. The Atacama runs for about 965 km (600 miles) along the coast. Rain has not fallen on some parts of the Atacama for hundreds of years.

Deciduous rainforest

Parts of southern Brazil and northern Uruguay are covered in deciduous rainforest. Unlike the equatorial Amazonian rainforest, where rain falls almost all year round, these forests have a distinct dry season when many of the trees lose their leaves. There are fewer species of trees here than in the tropical forests.

Mediterranean scrubland

Chile's Central Valley has a warm, Mediterranean-type climate with hot, dry summers and mild, damp winters. Small, thorny shrubs, stunted trees, cacti, and tough grass cover coastal cliffs. This region is famous for its fine wines, produced from grapes grown on the rich, fertile soils, watered by the melting snows of the Andes.

People

Only two per cent of the population are descended from the Native Americans who settled in South America thousands of years before Europeans arrived. The majority are *mestizos* – of mixed American and European descent, and South Americans, who descend from Africans who either escaped from slave ships in the Caribbean, or worked plantations on the mainland.

Brazilian girl

Bolivian boy

Argentinian boy

Resources

Rich volcanic soil provides some of the best farmland in the world, yielding wheat, maize, fruit, coffee, and tomatoes and potatoes, which originated in South America. The rainforests are a treasure trove of medicinal and other valuable plants. The continent is rich in minerals, especially oil, natural gas, gold, copper, tin, and precious stones.

Coffee beans

Orange

Emerald

FIND OUT MORE   CONTINENTS   DESERTS   DESERT WILDLIFE   GRASSLAND WILDLIFE   MOUNTAINS AND VALLEYS   NATIVE AMERICANS   RAINFOREST WILDLIFE   RIVERS   SOUTH AMERICAN WILDLIFE

SOUTH AMERICA, HISTORY OF

SOUTH AMERICA was the home of many Native American civilizations until the first Europeans arrived in the 1520s. From that time on, Spanish and Portuguese conquerors took over, claiming the entire continent and its people, and ruling there for 300 years. In the early 19th century, the area won its independence, but the new South American countries were poor and unstable. Today, the nations of South America have a vibrant culture that includes local, European, and African elements.

Early civilizations

The Native Americans were ancient peoples, whose civilizations flourished for thousands of years, particularly in the Andes Mountains. At the time of the European conquest, much of South America formed part of the most important of these civilizations – the Inca Empire of Peru.

Inca pot in the shape of a human face

Spanish rule

After the conquests of Francisco Pizarro (1475–1541) and other Spanish *conquistadores*, much of South America was ruled from Spain. Later, the Spanish kings sent officials called viceroys to govern the area, raise taxes, and run the courts. In the 18th century, the Viceroyalty of New Granada ruled what are now Colombia, Ecuador, Panama, and Venezuela.

El Dorado

Rumours were rife among the early Spanish explorers that beyond the Andes lived a people so rich in gold that the king covered himself in gold dust every year. This Man of Gold – "El Dorado" – was never found, but the legend spurred on many Spanish adventurers in their quest for gold.

Quest for silver

In 1545, the world's largest silver deposits were discovered at Potosí, Bolivia. Silver was carried in great quantities to Seville, Spain, and it fuelled both European and transatlantic trade. However, conditions in the mines were terrible: four out of five Native American workers died in the first year of mining.

Silver mine, Potosí

Bolivian silver

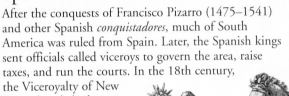

Francisco Pizarro

Native peoples

The native peoples of South America suffered terribly from the conquest. They had very poor resistance to the diseases introduced from Europe, and were badly treated by the conquerors. The population of South America dropped from 16 million to about 4 million in the hundred years after the conquerors arrived in the 16th century.

Bartolomé de las Casas

Dominican friar Bartolomé de las Casas (1474–1566) argued that the Spanish conquest was illegal, and that Native Americans were free. He campaigned against their mistreatment by Spanish settlers, and laws were enacted to protect the native peoples. But the laws were often not observed, and came too late for many.

Catholic church

Native temples and religious statues were nearly all destroyed during the Conquest. Most people were converted to Roman Catholicism, although many continued to hold on to traditional beliefs. Churches were built in the Spanish style, but were often adorned with native-style works of art.

Jesuit missions

The Roman Catholic order known as the Society of Jesus, or the Jesuits, founded missions in Paraguay among the Guaraní and Tapes peoples. By the mid-18th century, there were 30 missions. They were farming villages in which the land and animals were owned by the people as a whole. In the 1770s, the Jesuits were expelled from Spanish and Portuguese territories, and thousands of Native Americans were enslaved or killed.

Scene from the film, *The Mission*

Jesuit missionary

Local villagers

Churches

In order to protect the Native Americans from exploitation by Portuguese settlers, the Jesuits built their missions, with their Baroque-style churches, in the jungle, thus isolating themselves from the outside world.

Many of these Jesuit churches were simple stone buildings.

Independence

In the early 1800s, the French invaded Spain and replaced the king, Charles IV, with Joseph Bonaparte (1768–1844), brother of the emperor Napoleon. At first, the colonies remained loyal to Charles IV, but soon independence movements began in South America. The campaign for independence was led by "creoles", Spaniards born in South America, the most important of whom was Simón Bolívar. He hope for a united continent, but the different populations could not agree, and South America divided into many different nations.

Spanish colonies

British, Dutch, and French colonies

Portuguese colony

Lima

Santiago
San Fernando

Bernardo O'Higgins

O'Higgins (1778–1842) was the son of an Irishman who was governor of Chile. He became governor himself in 1814, but was removed by the Spaniards for his republican beliefs. He fought for Chile's independence and, in 1817, became the country's first head of state.

Red, white, and blue feathers symbolize liberty.

Bernardo O'Higgins

José de San Martín

José de San Martín

General José de San Martín (1778–1850) was born in Argentina, where he led the movement that brought independence from Spain to the colony in 1816. He then marched to Chile, where he defeated the Spanish and restored the patriot leader Bernardo O'Higgins. In 1821, he went to Peru, took Lima, and declared Peru independent.

Brazil

During the Napoleonic Wars, the king of Portugal, John VI, fled to Brazil and ruled from there. The country became rich, but the threat of revolution took the king back to Portugal. His son, Dom Pedro, declared Brazil independent in 1822.

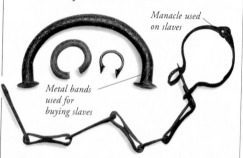

Manacle used on slaves

Metal bands used for buying slaves

Slavery

There were no large settled native populations in Brazil, so the Portuguese colonists brought slaves from West Africa to work on plantations and in mines. Runaway slaves formed settlements known as quilombos: the most famous was at Palmares, where several thousand runaway slaves lived in towns and villages.

Eva Perón

Born in poverty, Eva ("Evita") Duarte (1919–52) was a radio actress. She married politician Juan Perón, who became Argentine president in 1946. Adored by the poor of her country, she ensured Perón's re-election in 1952, but died of cancer in the same year.

Modern South America

In the 19th century, the new nations of South America relied on income from growing crops such as coffee. In the world depression of the 1930s, there was a sudden drop in demand for these products. Factories were set up, and thousands of people came to the cities to work there. Most South Americans still live in cities today.

The twin towers of Brasília's Congress Building

Brasília

In 1960, the capital of Brazil was moved from Rio de Janeiro to the new city of Brasília, with its purpose-built government offices, national museum, and university.

Chile

In 1970, Salvador Allende (1908–73) was elected president of Chile. He was a Marxist and pursued socialist policies. He died in a military coup, led by Augusto Pinochet (b.1915) who became head of state.

Salvador Allende

Rubber

The rubber tree grows naturally in South America. There was an increasing demand for rubber in the 19th and early 20th centuries, and plantations were set up in Brazil. In 1900–14 there was a "rubber boom", when many plantation owners made large fortunes. Demand slackened in the 1930s.

Latex (sap) is tapped from the trees and left to harden.

British troops arriving in the Falklands

Falklands War

In 1833, British settlers occupied a group of islands in the South Atlantic named the "Falkland Islands". Argentina disputed British sovereignty and invaded the islands in 1982. Britain sent troops to recover the islands, and Argentina surrendered, but the disagreement continued into the 1990s.

Timeline

900–1476 Chancay culture develops on the west coast of South America.

1438–1532 The powerful Inca civilization flourishes in Peru and the surrounding area.

Chancay figurine

1530s Portuguese settlers arrive in Brazil.

1530s–1560 Spain completes the conquest of most of South America.

1532 The Spaniards, under Pizarro, conquer the Incas.

1717 Spain sets up the Viceroyalty of New Granada to govern most of South America, except for the Portuguese colony of Brazil.

1767 Spanish king Charles III expels the Jesuits from Spain and its colonies.

1808 South American colonies begin to mount campaigns for independence.

Opera House, Manaus, Brazil

1825 The struggle for independence ends with the creation of the new state of Bolivia.

1900–14 Rubber boom in Brazil.

1955 Military coup in Argentina ousts Juan Perón.

1976–82 Thousands of Argentinians disappear, probable victims of the military rulers' death squads.

1982 Britain and Argentina at war after Argentina invades the Falkland Islands.

FIND OUT MORE   BOLÍVAR, SIMÓN   CENTRAL AMERICA, HISTORY OF   CHAVÍN   EXPLORATION   INCAS   MAYA   PORTUGAL, HISTORY OF   RELIGIONS   SPAIN, HISTORY OF

SOUTH AMERICA, NORTHERN

NORTHERN SOUTH AMERICA is made up of the four countries of Colombia, Venezuela, Guyana, and Surinam, and one colony – French Guiana. The people in the region are ethnically mixed. Most are *mestizos*, of Native American and European origin. Along the coast are small settlements of black Africans, descendants of slaves who were brought in by colonial masters to work the plantations of sugar-cane and coffee. Polarization of rich and poor, overcrowded cities, and trade in illegal drugs are a problem in most of the countries, many of which have a reputation for violence.

Physical features

The Andes dominate western Colombia and Venezuela. Lush lowlands surround Lake Maracaibo and the plain of the River Orinoco. Dense tropical rainforests cover much of the interior of Surinam and Guyana, both of which have a marshy coastal strip.

Northern Andes
The northern Andes are divided into three ranges by the valleys of the rivers Cauca and Magdalena. Most Colombians and many Venezuelans live on the lower slopes of the mountains.

Angel Falls
The spectacular Angel Falls on the River Churún in eastern Venezuela are the world's highest at 980 m (3,215 ft). The longest unbroken drop is 807 m (2,648 ft). Thousands of tourists visit the falls each year.

Shanty towns
Many South American countries have young, rapidly growing populations, with most people living in the towns and cities of the north. Unable to find adequate housing, many end up living in rough *barrios* (shanty towns), around modern city centres. Services such as running water and sanitation are poor.

Housing for poor people in the Pro Patria district of Caracas

20°C (68°F)   21°C (70°F)

7,090 mm (279 in)

Regional climate
Lowlands in northern South America are mostly hot and humid, but the Maracaibo coast is hot and dry. Temperatures in the Andes are much lower.

Rainforest
Dense tropical rainforests cover the southern regions of Colombia and Venezuela and most of Surinam, Guyana, and French Guiana. Untouched by modern life, isolated groups of Native Americans still live in some of the most inaccessible areas.

S

Colombia

Divided from north to south by the Andes, Colombia has coastlines on both the Caribbean and the Pacific. The country is economically one of the strongest in South America, but trade in illegal drugs poses a serious problem. With help from the USA, the government is waging a constant war against the "drug barons".

Colombian folk dancing

Cumbia

The *cumbia* is the most popular dance along Colombia's Caribbean coast. It is a blend of the region's Spanish, Native American, and African influences. Men in white, and women with long skirts, dance to flute music and drums.

41 per sq km
(105 per sq mile)

74% Urban   26% Rural

COLOMBIA FACTS

CAPITAL CITY Bogotá

AREA 1,138,910 sq km (439,733 sq miles)

POPULATION 42,800,000

MAIN LANGUAGES Spanish, Native American languages, English Creole

MAJOR RELIGION Christian

CURRENCY Columbian Peso

LIFE EXPECTANCY 71 years

PEOPLE PER DOCTOR 833

GOVERNMENT Multi-party democracy

ADULT LITERACY 92%

Bogotá

Founded by the Spanish in 1538, Colombia's capital and largest city, Bogotá, lies 2,610 m (8,560 ft) up in the Andes. Home to 6,700,000 people, it is the country's industrial, financial, and commercial centre.

Modern buildings in Bogotá

Barren 1%   Grassland 16%
Forest 48.5%   Wetland 1%
Built-up 0.5%   Farmland 33%

Mineral resources

Colombia produces about 60 per cent of the world's emeralds. It also has large reserves of gold and coal. The recent discovery of oil allows Colombia to be self-sufficient in energy.

Land use

Colombia's lush fertile lowlands enable a wide range of crops to be grown all year round. Rainforest covers the east.

Emerald
Calcite

Farming

Colombia is one of the world's largest producers of coffee, which is grown on thousands of small farms. Other leading crops include sugar-cane, rice, maize, plantains, bananas, sorghum, cotton, and cut flowers. Farmers raise cattle, vicuñas, pigs, and sheep. Farming accounts for more than half of the country's export earnings.

Venezuela

Drained by the River Orinoco, Venezuela's vast central plain is grazed by five million cattle. Despite its oil wealth and fertile lands, the country has been plagued by corruption, which led to crisis in the late 1990s, and a large devaluation of currency. Venezuelans in urban areas have suffered as a result.

Oil and minerals

Venezuela ranks highly in world oil production, which provides 80 per cent of export earnings. The richest reserves are to be found along the River Orinoco. Emphasis on the oil industry, however, has held back the development of the rest of the economy. Venezuela also has large reserves of coal, diamonds, bauxite, gold, and iron ore.

VENEZUELA FACTS

CAPITAL CITY Caracas

AREA 912,050 sq km (352,143 sq miles)

POPULATION 24,600,000

MAIN LANGUAGE Spanish

MAJOR RELIGION Christian

CURRENCY Bolívar

Guyana

Apart from a narrow coastal strip, where most people live, Guyana is covered by rainforest. Its economy is based on bauxite, gold, rice, and sugar. Half the population descends from Asians and 38 per cent from African slaves, both of whom the British brought to work the sugar plantations.

St George's Cathedral

Georgetown

The Dutch were the first Europeans to settle in Guyana, and the capital, Georgetown, still has old wooden Dutch buildings. The city sits on the bank of the River Demerara. It has wide streets, botanical gardens, and a university.

GUYANA FACTS

CAPITAL CITY Georgetown

AREA 214,790 sq km (83,000 sq miles)

POPULATION 763,000

MAIN LANGUAGE English

MAJOR RELIGIONS Christian, Hindu, Muslim

CURRENCY Guyana dollar

Surinam

Bauxite and aluminium, produced with hydroelectric power, are Surinam's main exports. In recent years, civil unrest has damaged the economy and about one-third of the people of this former Dutch colony have moved, in search of work, to the Netherlands.

Fishing

Sea fish, particularly shrimps, are among Surinam's chief exports. They are caught in the coastal waters of the Atlantic Ocean, which washes the Surinam coast.

SURINAM FACTS

CAPITAL CITY Paramaribo

AREA 163,270 sq km (63,039 sq miles)

POPULATION 419,000

MAIN LANGUAGE Dutch

MAJOR RELIGIONS Christian, Hindu, Muslim

CURRENCY Guilder

French Guiana

South America's only remaining colony, French Guiana has been an overseas department of France since 1946. It covers 91,000 sq km (35,000 sq miles), and has a population of about 172,605. The European Space Agency has its rocket-launching site there.

Ariane rocket

FIND OUT MORE   CRYSTALS AND GEMS   DANCE   EMPIRES   FARMING   FISHING INDUSTRY   NATIVE AMERICANS   OIL   SOUTH AMERICA, HISTORY OF   SPACE EXPLORATION

SOUTH AMERICAN WILDLIFE

SOUTH AMERICA'S habitats include tropical forests of the north, grasslands of the centre and south, tributaries of the River Amazon, the Andes mountains in the west, deserts fringing the west coast, and the wetlands of Brazil. South America is rich in wildlife, much of it found in the rainforests. The distinctive animals of South America, including anteaters, sloths, opossums, and New World monkeys, evolved when South America was separate from North America and isolated from the rest of the world.

Rainforest wildlife

South America's rainforests, including that of the Amazon basin (the largest rainforest in the world), contain a huge diversity of wildlife; many species are yet to be classified. The humid climate encourages rapid plant growth. Trees provide homes and food for insects, amphibians, reptiles, birds, and mammals.

Hoatzin
Relatives of cuckoos, these birds live in small flocks in trees bordering streams and swamps. Hoatzins are poor fliers that glide from tree to tree, then clamber up by using two hooked claws on each wing. Young hoatzins leave the nest soon after hatching and climb through the branches using their wings.

Two-toed sloth
The sloth spends most of its life upside-down in the trees, descending to the ground occasionally to defecate. It moves slowly along branches to find leaves to feed on.

Sloth feeds on leaves.

Sloths hang from branches by their long, curved claws.

Margay
These small cats are perfectly adapted for life in the trees. They grip onto branches with their claws and, unlike other cats, can run down tree trunks head first. Margays are solitary hunters that stalk prey such as tree frogs, lizards, birds, and small monkeys. The margay's coat provides camouflage in the dim forest light.

Hard-walled fruits contain nuts.

Margays spend most of their time in trees.

Brazil nut tree
The brazil nut tree is one of many species of tree found in the Amazon tropical forest. The tree reaches a height of more than 45 m (150 ft). It produces hard-shelled fruits that fall to the ground and break open to reveal 8–24 hard shelled nuts, or seeds, arranged like the segments of an orange. The canopy of the brazil nut, and neighbouring trees is home for many species of insects, birds, and mammals.

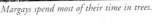
Pectoral fins

Hatchet fish
These small fish are one of many species of fish that live in the rivers that flow through the rainforest. The hatchet fish leaps from the river and beats its long pectoral fins noisily like wings, to "fly" for short distances above the water. It catches insects and crustaceans on, or above, the river's surface.

Very deep body

Wetland wildlife

There are two major areas of wetland in South America. Many streams flow into the huge River Amazon and flood the tropical forest floor. The streams are rich in animals, which feed on forest products that fall into the water. The Pantanal in southern Brazil is the world's largest wetland. It is an important habitat for water birds such as spoonbills.

Surinam toad
This toad lives in slow-moving tropical streams. It forages in mud for invertebrates, which it senses through touch organs on its fingers. The female lays eggs which the male presses into the skin on the female's back. The eggs hatch into tadpoles and develop under the skin, protected from predators. Later the pouch opens and the young emerge.

Streamlined body, flat tail, and webbed feet help the otter swim.

Eggs are covered in skin pockets on female's back.

Roseate spoonbill
Roseate spoonbills live in marshes, lagoons, coastal waters, and mangrove creeks. They find food while wading, by sweeping their spoon-shaped bills from side to side through the water, and grasping any small crustaceans, fish, or plants they come into contact with. Spoonbills nest in small colonies in trees or reeds.

Spoon-shaped bill

Webbed feet used for swimming

Giant otter
This large, powerful otter lives in tropical lagoons and shallow creeks. It catches catfish and other fish, which it clasps in its front paws and eats head first. It also eats mammals and water birds, and animals caught on land.

Yacare caiman
Caimans are related to alligators. They live in swamps, or on the banks of slow-moving rivers and backwaters with muddy bottoms. Caimans are strong swimmers and feed on fish, crustaceans, and other animals caught in the water. They also catch water birds and small mammals, pulling them under water to drown them, before eating them. Female caiman lay their eggs in nests, which they build and guard themselves.

Caiman has sharp teeth for crushing prey.

Wood stork
These large, long-legged wading birds live in flocks in wooded marshes and swamps, near pools. They rest and nest together in trees. Wood storks feed by standing in water, sometimes up to the belly, and moving their large, open bill from side to side. When they encounter prey, such as fish, frogs, or crustaceans, they snap their bills tightly shut.

Very long legs for wading in water.

S

Mountain wildlife

The Andes form a spine that runs down the western side of South America. The western side of the Andes has low rainfall and little wildlife; the eastern slopes have humid forests and a greater diversity of species. Mountain animals, such as the vicuña, are adapted for life at high altitudes.

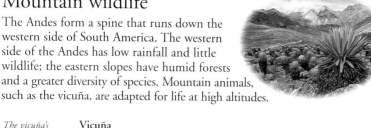

Andean condor

The Andean condor is the world's largest bird of prey with a wingspan of more than 3 m (10 ft). Condors feed mainly on carrion, but also attack animals that are old or wounded, and take eggs from sea bird colonies on the Peruvian coast.

Condors soar for hours at high altitude, above mountain summits searching for food.

Dense fur for warmth in the mountains.

Vicuña

The vicuña is the smallest member of the camel family. Small herds of vicuña graze on grasses in the high altitude grasslands of the central Andes between 3,800–5,000 m (12,500–16,500 ft). Once hunted to near extinction for its wool and meat, the vicuña is now protected in national parks.

The vicuña's moveable toe pads help it walk easily over all types of terrain.

Vicuñas have very fine, soft wool.

Spectacled bear

The spectacled bear is the only species of bear found in South America. It lives in the humid forests and grasslands of the northern Andes. The spectacled bear gets its name from the pale circles of fur around some of the individuals' eyes. An adult male weighs up to 180 kg (286 lb); females are about half this size. It is a good climber, and will climb trees in search of fruit and other vegetation. It also eats insects and carrion, and sometimes deer and vicuña.

Lesser rhea

This large flightless bird feeds among the tall grasses and shrubs on roots, plant seeds, insects, and other small animals. It nests in a hollow in the ground; the eggs, laid by several females, are incubated and guarded by just one male.

Rheas can run at speeds of up to 50 kmh (30 mph).

Giant anteater

Living in grasslands and open woodlands, the giant anteater feeds almost exclusively on ants and termites. It has a long, flexible snout and an acute sense of smell for detecting food. It uses its powerful front legs and large claws to open a termite or ant nest, then flicks its 60 cm (2 ft) long sticky tongue into the nest about 150 times per minute, to extract its food.

Long snout and tongue

Grassland wildlife

Grassland and scrub cover much of central, eastern, and southern South America. The best known area is the pampas of Argentina and Uruguay, now used for farming. Plants that grow there include grasses, sedges, and shrubs. In the west, the grasslands are hot and dry; in the east, they are wetter.

Hooked beak

Long legs for running through long grass.

Crested caracara

This ground-dwelling member of the falcon family uses its long toes and claws to turn over stones and scratch the ground, in search of prey, as well as for grasping prey. The crested caracara catches insects, frogs, lizards, snakes, young birds, and small mammals. It also flies low over grasslands in search of carrion.

Long legs for walking through the long grass.

Maned wolf

Maned wolves hunt at night by stalking prey and then pouncing on it. Their prey includes rabbits, rodents, armadillos, reptiles, and insects, as well as eggs and fruit.

Desert wildlife

South America's main deserts are the Patagonian Desert in Argentina, and the Atacama in Peru and Chile. The Atacama is the driest desert on Earth, but sea mists from the Pacific provide some moisture within a "fog zone", allowing some wildlife such as cacti, lizards, and rodents to survive.

Cardon

The cardon is a cactus found in Monte, a region of desert east of the Andes mountains in Argentina. Cacti are flowering plants adapted for surviving in hot, dry areas. The cardon has an extensive shallow root system which gathers water rapidly whenever it rains. Scarce water is stored within the ribbed, expandable stem. The cactus provides food and shelter for desert animals.

Chilean racer

This snake is found on the southern fringes of the Atacama Desert, southwards into the drier parts of Chile, from sea-level up to 1,500 m (5,000 ft) into the Andes. The Chilean racer hunts for prey by day, feeding mainly on lizards. It may climb into scrub when looking for its prey.

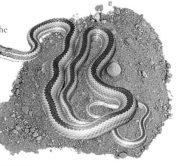

Spotted monitor tegu

This is one of several species of lizard found in the fog zone of the Atacama Desert and in dry regions on the western slopes of the Andes. It forages for prey, including insects and smaller lizards, during the day, and stores food reserves, in the form of fat, in its tail. It grows to 50 cm (20 in) in length.

Spotted skin camouflages lizard against the rocks.

Water is stored in expandable stems.

FIND OUT MORE — ANTEATERS, SLOTHS AND ARMADILLOS · BEARS · BIRDS OF PREY · CAMELS · CROCODILES · FLIGHTLESS BIRDS · LIZARDS · SNAKES · WOLVES AND OTHER WILD DOGS

SOVIET UNION

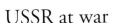

BORN OUT OF the chaos of the 1917 Russian Revolution, the Union of the Soviet Socialist Republics (USSR), or Soviet Union, was the world's first communist country. During its 75-year history, the Soviet Union became one of the world's most powerful states, playing a leading role in world politics and achieving huge technological advances. But the Soviet Union failed to deliver prosperity or liberty to its subjects. Efforts to reform the communist system failed, and the republics finally split up in 1991.

Propaganda poster showing Soviet workers

Five-Year Plans
During the 1920s and 1930s, Soviet leader Joseph Stalin produced a series of long-term plans to steer the country's economy. Known as Five-Year Plans, they covered areas such as heavy industry, agriculture, manufactured goods, defence, and arms production.

Soviet state

The Soviet Union was made up of several republics, which were governed by councils or soviets. Every aspect of Soviet life was rigorously controlled by the state. Industry and agriculture were taken over by the state, the press was censored, and cultural life was directed towards the glorification of the communist system. A vast secret police force (known as the KGB) kept control of the population and removed all dissent.

Joseph Stalin

Stalin (1879–1953) was born in the Russian state of Georgia. A communist from an early age, he seized control of the party in 1923, and took over the Soviet Union in 1924. He held absolute power, torturing and killing opponents and dissidents. This type of ruthless dictatorship is now known as "Stalinism".

USSR at war

On 22 June 1941, 79 German divisions invaded the Soviet Union, to bring it into the war on the same side as Britain and, later, the USA. Although the Germans soon occupied huge tracts of western Soviet Union, they failed to capture Moscow before winter set in and were heavily defeated at Stalingrad in January 1943.

Siege of Leningrad
In September 1941, German forces surrounded Leningrad. The city held out for 900 days, until supplies finally arrived in January 1944. Bombardment, hunger, and cold caused the deaths of thousands of citizens.

Consequences of war
Much of the western half of the country was destroyed in the war and more than 20 million people lost their lives. To stop this happening again, Soviet troops occupied much of Eastern Europe after 1945, setting up a buffer zone of communist governments.

Show trial of Stalin's opponents, Moscow

Show trials
In the 1930s, Stalin removed opposition to his rule in a series of show trials. Dissident leaders were shot or imprisoned, and hundreds of thousands of Soviet citizens were condemned to forced labour in Siberia or the Arctic lands.

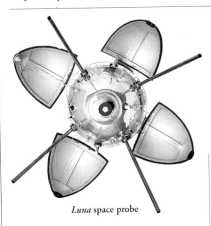

Luna space probe

Space race
In 1957, the USSR became the first nation to launch an artificial satellite into space, and sent the first astronaut – Yuri Gagarin – into space in 1961. Soviet space successes promoted a massive space race with the USA.

Superpower

The USSR emerged from World War II as a superpower. It competed with the USA in scientific and military affairs, using its first nuclear weapon in 1949. Direct armed conflict between the two sides did not break out in the so-called Cold War, but the Soviets supported nations such as Vietnam, in conflicts with the USA.

Perestroika

In 1985, Mikhail Gorbachev became leader of the USSR. He began to reform the communist system through perestroika (restructuring) and introduced glasnost (openness). Gorbachev resigned in 1991 after an attempted coup.

Mikhail Gorbachev

Timeline

1917 Russan Revolution, under leaders such as Trotsky, establishes communism.

1918–20 Russian Red Army wins civil war.

1924 Stalin takes over after revolutionary leader Vladimir I Lenin dies.

1928 First Five-Year Plan.

1941–45 USSR fights in World War II, sustaining horrendous losses.

1945 Russian troops occupy much of Eastern Europe.

1953 Death of Stalin.

Revolutionary leader Leon Trotsky (1879–1940)

1956 New leader Nikita Khrushchev denounces excesses of Stalin's rule.

1964 Khrushchev replaced by Leonid Brezhnev.

1985 Mikhail Gorbachev becomes leader and begins reforms.

1991 Gorbachev resigns and the USSR breaks up.

FIND OUT MORE   COLD WAR   EUROPE, HISTORY OF   MARX, KARL   GOVERNMENTS AND POLITICS   RUSSIA, HISTORY OF   RUSSIAN REVOLUTION   WORLD WAR II

SPACE EXPLORATION

THE SPACE AGE BEGAN IN 1957 with the launch of the first satellite. Since then astronauts and robots have journeyed from Earth to explore space at first hand. Twelve astronauts have landed on the Moon. Many more have studied space while orbiting Earth. Spacecraft equipped with robotic equipment have visited all the planets except Pluto, many moons, two comets, and two asteroids.

Galileo's **journey:** 1989 launched from space shuttle *Atlantis*; 1989–1992 circled Earth and Venus to gain momentum; 1995 reached Jupiter.

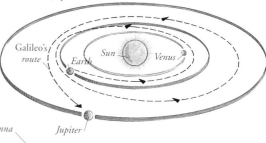

Galileo's route — Earth — Sun — Venus — Jupiter

Space probes

Robotic spacecraft have been used since 1959 to make long-distance journeys to the planets and their moons. The first flew by their targets; orbiters and landers came later. The real work starts when the craft reaches its target. Equipment switches on and collects data, which is transmitted to Earth for analysis.

Radioactive power source

Antenna

Jupiter

Galileo space probe

Main antenna

Attitude control thrusters inside protective shields

Sensing instruments

Low-gain antenna

Atmosphere probe

Heatshield protects the atmosphere probe.

Radioactive power source

Gravity assist
A space probe can fly by a planet to reach its target planet. It uses the planet's gravity field to change direction and speed. The *Galileo* probe used this technique to reach Jupiter: it passed by Earth twice and Venus once to gain speed, before heading toward Jupiter.

Galileo probe
This was the last great space probe of the 20th century, and the first to investigate the atmosphere of a giant planet by sending a mini-probe into it. As *Galileo* approached Jupiter in July 1995, a smaller probe separated from the main craft, or orbiter. Both reached Jupiter in December 1995. The small probe descended into the planet's thick atmosphere of hydrogen, helium, and other gases. It collected data for 57 minutes before it stopped working.

The *Galileo* orbiter was designed to orbit Jupiter and its moons 11 times and send data back to Earth for about two years.

Fly-by probes

Some probes simply fly by a planet. At a preplanned distance, the instruments switch on and start to record data. Once the probe has passed the planet, they switch off again.

Mariner 10
The only space probe to visit Mercury, *Mariner 10* was also the first to go to more than one planet. Between 1974 and 1975, it flew by Venus once and Mercury three times.

Mariner 10

Cameras

Sensor

Solar panel

Giotto
Ten instruments on *Giotto* investigated Halley's Comet in 1986. The probe flew within 600 km (400 miles) of the nucleus.

Orbiters

When some space probes reach their target, they follow a preset route which puts them into orbit around the planet. The orbiter may stay in orbit forever. It will transmit data back to Earth until it is shut down or stops working.

Magellan probe
In 1990, the *Magellan* space probe entered into orbit about Venus. Its radar equipment "saw" through the planets' clouds to produce detailed maps of the surface. *Magellan* completed six surveys before being destroyed as it plunged into the planet's atmosphere.

Magellan

Dish emits radar signals that bounce off the surface.

Radio signals show height.

Reflected radar signals

Venus's surface
Magellan mapped almost 99 per cent of Venus's surface. Impact craters, canyons, lava flows, and volcanoes were revealed. This *Magellan* image shows the highland area called Ishtar Terra.

Landers

Probes put into orbit round a planet may release a smaller probe to land on the planet. Landers have touched down on Venus, Mars, and the Moon. The data they collect is transmitted to the orbiter and from there to Earth.

Mars landers
Two *Viking* probes were the first to land on Mars in 1976. In 1997, a robotic rover explored the surface, sending back spectacular pictures. Two mobile robots, *Opportunity* and *Spirit*, landed in 2004 to conduct new experiments on the planet.

Viking lander

Antenna

Cameras

Atmosphere sensors

Robot arm to take soil samples.

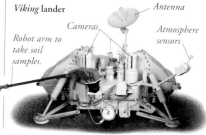

Wernher von Braun

Born in Germany, Wernher von Braun (1912–77) developed the *V2* rocket in 1942. He later became an American citizen, and developed rockets for the USA. His *Saturn V* rocket took astronauts to the Moon in the 1960s. In the early 1970s, he was in charge of planning NASA's future in space.

Space stations

A permanent spacecraft in orbit round Earth can act as a base for astronauts to live and work in, and as a station for beginning journeys into space. Russia and the USA have both launched space stations. A team of about 18 nations is working together to build *Alpha*, a space station for the 21st century.

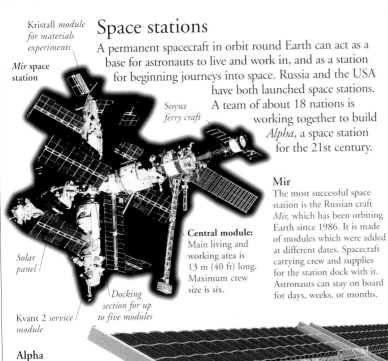

Kristall module for materials experiments

Mir space station

Soyuz ferry craft

Solar panel

Docking section for up to five modules

Kvant 2 *service module*

Central module: Main living and working area is 13 m (40 ft) long. Maximum crew size is six.

Mir
The most successful space station is the Russian craft *Mir*, which has been orbiting Earth since 1986. It is made of modules which were added at different dates. Spacecraft carrying crew and supplies for the station dock with it. Astronauts can stay on board for days, weeks, or months.

Alpha
Space station *Alpha* is roughly the size of a football pitch. Different countries are responsible for different parts. Russia is providing the core module, and the other parts will be added, piece by piece, in space. The American space shuttle, or its replacement *VentureStar*, will ferry people and supplies between Earth and *Alpha*. The goal is to make the station as self-supporting as possible. There will be living, work, service, and transport areas.

Solar array (USA)

Alpha space station

Science power platform (international)

Mobile servicing system (Canada)

Energy block (Russia)

Service module, including life support and utilities (Russia)

Storage and equipment module (USA)

Crew transfer vehicle (USA)

Laboratory (USA)

USA

Skylab

The only American space station, *Skylab*, was used by three teams of visiting astronauts between May 1973 and February 1974. They carried out experiments in the laboratory and used it as an observatory for looking out to space and down to Earth. In 1979, it burned up in Earth's atmosphere.

Aleksei Leonov
In 1965, the Russian cosmonaut Aleksei Leonov (b.1934) became the first person to "walk" in space. On his second space trip, in 1975, his *Soyuz* spacecraft docked with an American *Apollo* craft to make the first ever international space dock.

On the Moon

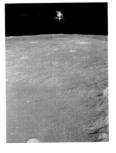

Twelve American astronauts landed at six sites on the Moon between 1969 and 1972. The first crews explored on foot, the later ones in a Lunar Roving Vehicle. They set up and carried out experiments and brought back about 380 kg (840 lb) of Moon rock and dust.

Lunokhod
The Russians landed the *Lunokhod 1* and *2* robotic explorers on the Moon in 1970 and 1973. They travelled over the lunar surface taking photographs and carrying out experiments.

Lunar module
The *Apollo 12* capsule carried two astronauts to the Moon's surface on 19 November 1969. They walked to the *Surveyor 3* spacecraft which had landed in 1967 and retrieved material from the craft for analysis.

Space missions

Space journeys are planned years in advance. An international team works to produce a probe to carry out agreed tasks. Some are part of a series, such as the *Apollo* lunar missions. Others, such as *Cassini*, are single missions.

Cassini
When the *Cassini* probe, scheduled for launch in 1997, reaches Saturn in 2004, it will make 23 fly-bys in a four-year study of the planet, its atmosphere, rings, and some of its moons. A smaller probe, *Huygens*, will separate from the main craft and head for the largest moon, Titan. It will make a three-hour descent through the thick atmosphere to Titan's surface.

Earth's messages
Space probes carry messages from Earth in case aliens ever find them. Plaques and discs on board the probes identify Earth and its life forms with maps, pictures, and, in more recent craft, sounds.

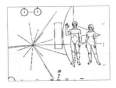

The plaque on *Pioneers 10* and *11* that identified Earth and its inhabitants.

Timeline

1962 *Mariner 2* flies by Venus, the first spacecraft to visit another planet.

Venus

1966 *Luna 9* makes the first successful landing of a craft on the Moon.

1971 *Salyut 1*, the first space station, is launched.

1973 *Pioneer 10* flies by Jupiter, the first craft to cross the asteroid belt and reach one of the giant planets.

1986 *Giotto* takes the first images of the nucleus of a comet.

1987 Astronauts on *Mir* start the first permanent manned space station.

1989 *Voyager 2* flies by Neptune, three years after it flies by Uranus.

1993 *Hubble Space Telescope* is repaired. First detailed images of outer space objects sent back to Earth.

1998 *Lunar Prospector* discovers ice on the surface of the Moon.

FIND OUT MORE | ASTRONAUTS | COMETS AND ASTEROIDS | EXPLORATION | MOON | PLANETS | ROCKETS | SATELLITES | SUN AND SOLAR SYSTEM | TELESCOPES | UNIVERSE

S

797

SPAIN

SEPARATED FROM the rest of Europe by the Pyrenees in the north, and from Africa by the Strait of Gibraltar to the south, Spain shares the Iberian peninsula with Portugal. Spain is the fourth largest country in Europe and, on average, also one of the highest. Once reliant on farming and fishing for its income, Spain has experienced rapid economic growth since becoming a member of the European Union in 1986. Today, it is a major industrial nation with a large agricultural sector and a booming tourist trade.

Physical features

Spain is a land of contrasts with mountains in the north, centre, and south, an arid plateau, the *meseta*, at the centre, green valleys in the northwest, and warm plains on the Mediterranean coast.

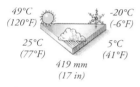

49°C (120°F)
-20°C (-6°F)
25°C (77°F)
5°C (41°F)
419 mm (17 in)

Climate

The *meseta* has hot, arid summers, but in winter snow blizzards are common. The coast and Balearic Islands have periods of drought in summer, and mild, damp winters.

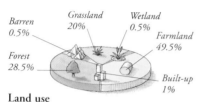

Grassland 20%
Wetland 0.5%
Barren 0.5%
Farmland 49.5%
Forest 28.5%
Built-up 1%

Land use

Spain has very few natural resources, including water. With the help of irrigation, half of the land is used for growing crops, such as cereals, olives, citrus fruits, and grapes. About one-fifth is pasture for grazing animals, mainly sheep.

Balearic Islands

Majorca, Minorca, and Ibiza are the largest of the Balearic Islands. They lie to the east in the Mediterranean, and have a total area of 5,011 sq km (1,935 sq miles); 700,000 people live there. The islands, which are governed by Spain, are famous for wine, fishing, and tourism. Thousands of holidaymakers visit each year.

Pyrenees

Separating Spain from France are the imposing Pyrenees. This mountain range runs from the Mediterranean to the Atlantic coast and contains many peaks more than 3,000 m (9,842 ft) high. It is a wild area, where bears and wolves still roam.

Meseta

The vast, dry plateau known as the *meseta* covers most of central Spain. Hills and low mountains break into the plateau, which is crossed by rivers, many of which dry up in the summer heat. There is little rain, and farmers rely on irrigation to water crops.

Madrid

King Philip II made Madrid the capital of Spain in 1561 because he liked the climate and location in the centre of the country. Home to around five million people, it has many fine buildings including the Prado, one of Europe's leading art galleries. The city is a centre for finance, government, and industry.

Gran Via

People

The Spanish are divided into regional groups, each with their own language and culture. About 16 per cent are Catalan, Galicians make up seven per cent, and just two per cent are Basques. Most of the rest are Castilian Spanish, which is the official dialect taught in schools.

79 per sq km
(205 per sq mile)

78%
Urban

22%
Rural

Urban life
Over three-quarters of Spaniards live in cities, where young people move in search of work. Madrid, home to about four million people, is Spain's centre of finance and government. Most people who live in rural areas are elderly. The status of women is rising quickly.

Leisure

Many Spaniards enjoy watching or playing soccer, and the teams of Real Madrid, FC Barcelona, and Valencia are well known internationally. The warm climate makes eating out of doors both practical and relaxing.

Fiestas
Most Spaniards are Roman Catholic, and fiestas, often to celebrate a local saint's day, include a procession of people in traditional costume, music, and dancing. Over 3,000 fiestas take place each year in Spain.

Flamenco
This traditional Spanish dance was developed by the gypsies of Andalucía in the 15th century. Men in black and women in bright dresses dance to flamenco music played on a guitar.

Industry

Spain's major industries are textiles, fishing, metals, shipbuilding, cars, and tourism. Since the 1980s, many new electronics and high-tech industries have been set up. Although Spain has few mineral resources, it is a major world producer of mercury.

Sherry
Spain is famous for producing sherry, a fortified wine made by adding alcohol to wine during fermentation. It is named after the town of Jerez de la Frontera where it is produced. Demand for the drink, which is popular as an aperitif, has made sherry production a major industry.

Olives
The warm climate and terraced slopes of the mountains, particularly in the south and east, are ideal for cultivating olives. Spain is second only to Italy's olive production. Some of the fruit is processed for eating, but most of the crop is made into olive oil.

Olives are often eaten as an appetizer.

Farming

Poor soil and lack of water make agriculture difficult, but farmers use every available bit of land. They grow barley, maize, sorghum, and wheat. Sheep are the main animals raised. People also keep many pigs, and smaller numbers of cattle and goats.

Oranges and lemons
The climate of the Mediterranean coast is ideal for growing citrus fruit. Spain is a major producer of oranges and lemons. The bitter oranges grown in the area around the city of Sevilla are the best for making marmalade.

Food
One of Spain's best-known dishes is *paella*, a tasty mixture of chicken, pork, shellfish, beans, tomatoes, peas, and rice. Food is often eaten with wine, such as Rioja from the north, or sangria, a blend of red wine, citrus fruit, lemonade, and brandy.

Prawn

Mussel *Chicken* *Rice*

Tourism
Sandy beaches, beautiful cities, and guaranteed sun attract about 48 million visitors a year. Tourism employs ten per cent of the work-force, and is a major source of income. The Costa Blanca on the southwest coast is popular with British and German holidaymakers.

Car manufacturing
Spain ranks highly in world car production. However, following the demise of once-famous national makes such as the Hispano-Suiza and the Pegaso, it is restricted to manufacturing foreign cars under licence. This Seat is being produced in Spain for the Italian company Fiat.

Andorra

Lying high in the Pyrenees, Andorra is a tiny country between France and Spain, which share in its government. Tourism is the main source of income and it has few resources. Divorce is illegal.

Landscape
Andorra is a country of mountains and valleys that attract large numbers of visitors to ski and sightsee. Duty-free goods draw summer shoppers.

ANDORRA FACTS

CAPITAL CITY
Andorra la Vella

AREA 468 sq km
(181 sq miles)

POPULATION 66,800

MAIN LANGUAGES
Catalan, Spanish

MAJOR RELIGION
Christian

CURRENCY Euro

ADULT LITERACY 99%

FIND OUT MORE | CARS AND TRUCKS | CHRISTIANITY | DANCE | EUROPE | EUROPE, HISTORY OF | EUROPEAN UNION | FARMING | FESTIVALS | FOOTBALL | SPAIN HISTORY OF

SPAIN, HISTORY OF

FOR MUCH OF ITS HISTORY, Spain has been ruled by foreign powers. Greeks, Romans, Visigoths, and Moors all left their mark on the country. In 1492, Spain was finally united. It became powerful, and acquired a vast empire in the Americas. However, the effort of holding this huge empire together weakened Spain – by 1700, the country was exhausted. The ailing monarchy was finally overthrown in 1931, and, after a vicious civil war, a Fascist government under General Franco took power. The monarchy was restored in 1975.

Roman Spain

In 133 BC, the Romans conquered Spain. They united the country and brought peace, prosperity, and, later, Christianity. Roman rule lasted for more than 500 years until Germanic invaders overran the country in the 5th century.

Roman carving

Moorish Spain

In 711, Moors (Muslims from north Africa) invaded Spain, driving the Christian rulers into the mountains of the north. For 700 years, the Moors ruled much of Spain. They introduced Islam, but allowed Jews and Christians to worship freely. They were known for their scholarship and fine buildings.

Ceiling at the Moorish palace of the Alhambra, Granada

Queen Isabella of Castile

King Ferdinand of Aragon

Ferdinand and Isabella

In 1479, the two main Christian kingdoms of Spain were united when Ferdinand of Aragon married Isabella of Castile. By 1492, the Moors were expelled from Spain, and the Christian "reconquest" was complete. Spain was a single country for the first time since the Romans.

Ferdinand and Isabella and their army

Cleansing of the Temple by El Greco

Golden Age

In the 16th and early 17th centuries, Spain was one of the most powerful countries in Europe, controlling much of Italy and the Netherlands, as well as a vast American empire. Gold and silver from mines of the Americas flooded into the country, creating huge wealth. Artists such as El Greco, Murillo, and Velásquez made Spain one of the artistic centres of Europe.

Civil War 1936–39

In 1936, civil war began between the Nationalists, whose leaders included army officers and who supported Fascist political policies, and the Republicans, who wanted to curb army power and to return a socialist government. Fascist Italy and Nazi Germany backed the Nationalists, and after three years of fighting and one million deaths, Nationalist leader Francisco Franco seized power.

Basques

The Basques of northern Spain are a distinct people with their own language and culture. In 1936, they sided with the Republicans. In response, German bombers supporting Franco attacked the town of Guernica, killing many.

Republican soldiers

EXPO 92

Juan Carlos

Franco died in 1975 and power passed to Juan Carlos (b.1938), grandson of the last Spanish king. Under his rule, Spain became a multi-party democracy, reaching world prominence with events, such as Expo 92.

Philip II

Philip II (1527–98) ruled Spain, southern Italy, and the Netherlands from 1556. Son of Charles V, Holy Roman Emperor, he continued his father's war against France, and drew England into the conflict. A revolt by the Dutch after 1568 weakened his rule and led him to send an ill-fated armada to invade England in 1588. His chief success was the conquest of Portugal in 1580.

Timeline

201–133 BC Romans rule Spain.

AD 300 Spain becomes Christian.

711 Moors invade Spain and establish Islamic rule.

1479 Kingdoms of Aragon and Castile are united.

1492 Moors expelled; Columbus sails the Atlantic, beginning Spain's American empire.

1556–98 Reign of Philip II.

1808–14 Napoleon's armies seize Spain.

1816–28 Spain loses empire in South and Central America.

General Franco

1936–39 Civil War leads to a Fascist dictatorship by General Franco.

1975 Franco dies and is succeeded by King Juan Carlos.

1986 Spain joins European Union.

FIND OUT MORE

CENTRAL AMERICA, HISTORY OF   COLUMBUS, CHRISTOPHER   HOLY ROMAN EMPIRE   SOUTH AMERICA, HISTORY OF

SPIDERS AND SCORPIONS

WITH THEIR LONG LEGS and silent movements, spiders can approach prey without warning. Likewise, scorpions give little notice before they sting. However, only a few species of spider and scorpion are dangerous to humans. Spiders and scorpions are arachnids – a group of mainly solitary, carnivorous, land-living invertebrates. Included in the group are 30,500 species of mites and ticks, and 4,500 species of harvestmen, or daddy-longlegs.

Fangs
Between the pedipalps of all spiders lie hollow fangs called chelicerae. They are connected to a venom gland that pumps venom into prey, when the spider bites its victim.

Irritant hairs may be kicked at predators.

Opisthosoma

Cephalothorax

Chelicera

1st leg

Pedipalp

2nd leg

3rd leg

4th leg

Red-kneed tarantula

Features of a spider
There are 40,000 species of spider. All have four pairs of legs, their span ranging from 2 mm (0.8 in) in tiny money spiders to 30 cm (12 in) in huge goliath spiders. They lack antennae, but frontal appendages called pedipalps are used as sense organs, and, in males, to transfer sperm. Spiders' bodies are made up of the fused head and thorax, or cephalothorax, and the abdomen, or opisthosoma. Most spiders have 4, 6, or 8 eyes.

Spinnerets
Three pairs of tiny organs called spinnerets lie at the base of the opisthosoma. They produce silk for making webs and cocoons. The silk is made from protein. It is very elastic, and stronger than steel wire of the same thickness.

Spinnerets

Silk and webs
Spiders spin silken webs to catch their prey. Each strand of a web may be made of several strands of silk. Some spiders make messy webs called cobwebs. Trap-door spiders lay silk trip lines near their burrows and strike if prey touches one. Silk is also used to make cocoons, or spun into nets to drop on prey, and wrap up food. Money spiders use silk as a parachute.

Spinning a web

1 The spider makes a Y-shaped structure of silk, then spins the radii, or spokes, of the web.

2 The spider has now spun a spiral of non-sticky web. It uses this spiral as a platform to spin the sticky spirals.

3 The spider now spins dense concentric spirals of special sticky silk, which it will use to trap prey.

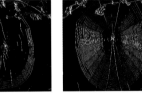

4 Having finished spinning, the spider now waits in the middle of its web to catch its first meal.

Feeding
Spiders are carnivores and kill prey such as insects. Most trap their victims in webs; some, such as wolf spiders, hunt for prey. Spiders cannot eat solid food. They inject venom to paralyse the prey, and enzymes to dissolve its internal organs. Once prey is liquefied, the spider sucks the fluids from its victim, leaving a crumpled external skeleton, in the case of an insect.

Wolf spider eating a fly

Reproduction
A female spider may mistake a male for prey as he approaches her to mate. To prevent this, male orb-web spiders pluck at the edge of the web in a specific way; other spiders present the female with gifts of food, or tie her up with silk while mating. Despite taking precautions, the male is still often eaten by the female after mating has taken place.

Black widow with cocoons

Cocoons
Many spiders, such as black widows, wrap their eggs in silk cocoons to protect them while they develop. This keeps the eggs together and prevents them drying out. The spiderlings hatch out of the eggs and cut their way out of the cocoons.

Defence
Spiders have a range of defences: many hide to avoid enemies; others disguise themselves as ants. Some tarantulas flick irritant hairs at attackers to blind them. Australian red-backs have bright colours to warn that they are venomous – but if attacked they, and funnel-webs, inject venom into their enemies.

Sydney funnel-web spider

Raised legs in defence posture.

Fangs

Scorpions
Most scorpions live in warm regions, hiding in crevices or below rocks by day. They are carnivorous and emerge at night to hunt their mainly insect prey. Scorpions use their pincers and the venomous sting in their tail, both to kill prey and for defence. Some, including fat-tailed scorpions, can kill humans. There are 2,100 species of scorpion; the largest is 18 cm (7 in) long.

Reproduction
Scorpions mate with care because of their stings and pincers. They grasp each other's claws and perform a ritual, called the scorpion dance. The male pulls the female forwards to guide her over a packet of sperm until it slots into her genital pore.

Sting

Pincer

Young sit on mother for two weeks.

Imperial scorpion

RED-KNEED TARANTULA

SCIENTIFIC NAME	*Brachypelma smithii*
ORDER	Araneae
FAMILY	Theraphosidae
DISTRIBUTION	Mexico
HABITAT	Dry srubland and woodland, especially in areas of rocky ground covered by thick vegetation
DIET	Large insects, other spiders, small reptiles, and occasionally small mammals
SIZE	Legspan: up to 16 cm (6.3 in)
LIFESPAN	Males live for 7–8 years; females live for 20–30 years

FIND OUT MORE   ARTHROPODS   CAVE WILDLIFE   DESERT WILDLIFE   MARSH AND SWAMP WILDLIFE   POISONOUS ANIMALS

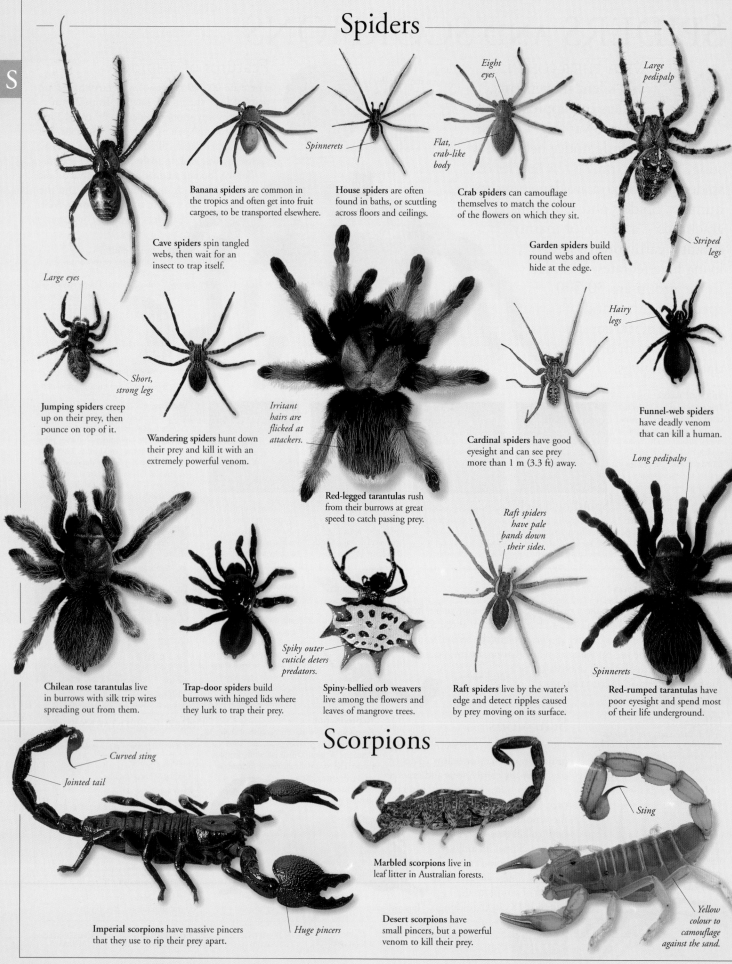

Spiders

Banana spiders are common in the tropics and often get into fruit cargoes, to be transported elsewhere.

House spiders are often found in baths, or scuttling across floors and ceilings.

Spinnerets

Eight eyes

Flat, crab-like body

Crab spiders can camouflage themselves to match the colour of the flowers on which they sit.

Large pedipalp

Cave spiders spin tangled webs, then wait for an insect to trap itself.

Garden spiders build round webs and often hide at the edge.

Striped legs

Large eyes

Short, strong legs

Jumping spiders creep up on their prey, then pounce on top of it.

Wandering spiders hunt down their prey and kill it with an extremely powerful venom.

Irritant hairs are flicked at attackers.

Hairy legs

Cardinal spiders have good eyesight and can see prey more than 1 m (3.3 ft) away.

Funnel-web spiders have deadly venom that can kill a human.

Red-legged tarantulas rush from their burrows at great speed to catch passing prey.

Raft spiders have pale bands down their sides.

Long pedipalps

Chilean rose tarantulas live in burrows with silk trip wires spreading out from them.

Trap-door spiders build burrows with hinged lids where they lurk to trap their prey.

Spiky outer cuticle deters predators.

Spiny-bellied orb weavers live among the flowers and leaves of mangrove trees.

Raft spiders live by the water's edge and detect ripples caused by prey moving on its surface.

Spinnerets

Red-rumped tarantulas have poor eyesight and spend most of their life underground.

Scorpions

Curved sting

Jointed tail

Sting

Marbled scorpions live in leaf litter in Australian forests.

Imperial scorpions have massive pincers that they use to rip their prey apart.

Huge pincers

Desert scorpions have small pincers, but a powerful venom to kill their prey.

Yellow colour to camouflage against the sand.

SPORT

SINCE ANCIENT TIMES, people have taken part in sport, either for recreation or for the thrill of competition. In ancient Greece, for example, men regularly visited gymnasiums to relax and to keep fit; some also participated in the more formal ancient Olympics. Today, there is an impressive range of sports to choose from, including activities as diverse as athletics, archery, and horse riding. Sports can be enjoyed for their own sake, as leisure or health pursuits, or at a competitive level.

Sport today

Sport is a thriving industry, with billions of pounds poured into it every year by television companies, sponsors, and the public. People pay to watch major events, and also buy sports equipment for their own use. There is now a growing concern for health and fitness and new trends in sport are always emerging.

Types of sport

Most sports can be classified under one or more of the following categories: air, athletic, ball, combat, equestrian, racket, target, water, wheel, and winter sports. These categories can be further divided into individual and/or team sports, and contact or non-contact sports.

Mountain biking   Inline skating

Cycling

Cycling is very popular around the world. It is a great way to keep fit, as well as a cheap and non-polluting means of transport. "Mountain bikes", first designed for offroad cycling, are now common in cities too.

Athletics

Athletics is probably one of the most popular groups of sport. It includes running, hurdling, jumping, and throwing. Running may range from jogging for health and fitness to more gruelling cross-country events.

Running for fun

Winter sports

Although many sports are played in winter, those known specifically as winter sports are performed on ice and snow, such as skiing, snowboarding, or ice hockey. Skating can be enjoyed all year on indoor ice-rinks.

Inline skating

Inline skating evolved from rollerskating during the 1980s. Inline skates allow high speeds and complex tricks. Although this sport is also called "rollerblading" that is in fact the trademarked name of just one manufacturer of inline skates.

Snowboarding

Gymnastics

Young people can excel at the highest level in this sport. It combines agility, grace, and physical discipline. Rhythmic gymnastics combines elegance with entertaining juggling skills.

Rhythmic gymnastics

Professionalism

Top sports stars, such as US tennis player Venus Williams, can earn a huge amount of money. With so much money in sport, even the main stronghold of amateurism – the Olympics – now allows professionals to take part.

Thousands of people watch events such as this international in Hong Kong, China.

Sponsorship

Companies sponsor teams, individuals, and competitions. They pay to promote their products on clothing and around stadiums at key matches.

International soccer match

Racing kart

Motor sports

People can take part in motor racing sports at various levels. In grand prix racing, sponsors' money and a large back-up team are needed to support the competitors.

Racket sports

Sports played with rackets need hand-eye co-ordination. Many people play tennis, badminton, squash, and table tennis for recreation. At the highest level, the games require great skill, fitness, and stamina.

Tennis

Horse riding

Riding can be an exhilarating pastime, enhanced by the necessary understanding between horse and rider. Young people enjoy competing in gymkhanas, and top-class show jumping and eventing are thrilling spectator sports.

Tacking up for riding

Wind surfing

Soccer

Water sports

Water provides the means for gentle activity or vigorous exercise. People enjoy sailing and rowing in boats, and swimming, which is enjoyed in indoor pools as well as outdoors.

Ball games

Controlling a ball with a hand, foot, stick, or bat is a satisfying experience. Ball games include team sports, such as soccer and basketball, and individual sports, such as golf.

Combat sports

Many of today's combat sports evolved from fight-to-the-death contests in ancient times, but the rules of sports such as judo, karate, and wrestling are designed to prevent injury and reward skill. Boxing is controversial because its aim is to inflict damage on the opponent.

Judo

FIND OUT MORE · ATHLETICS · BALL GAMES · COMBAT SPORTS · CYCLING · GYMNASTICS · HORSE RIDING · MOTOR SPORTS · SWIMMING AND DIVING · TENNIS AND OTHER RACKET SPORTS · WINTER SPORTS

STAMPS AND POSTAL SERVICES

EVERY DAY, MILLIONS OF PEOPLE send and receive mail. The sender fixes a postage stamp to the envelope or package to show that he or she has prepaid the cost of postage, then mails the item at the post office or a post box, confident that it will reach its final destination. Every country operates a postal service. It remains a vital means of national and international communication, despite the growth of electronic systems, such as e-mail and the fax machine.

Postal services

Services to collect and deliver mail have existed since ancient times. A major reform came with postage stamps, used regularly around the world from 1840. Previously, the recipient had paid on delivery for his or her mail; from then on, the sender paid in advance for postage by attaching a stamp. Today, the cost of postage is determined by the weight, destination, and priority of a letter. Mail is first collected from a post box, and taken to a central sorting office.

Philately

Philately (stamp collecting) began in the 1840s. As there were very few stamps in existence, early philatelists collected many of the same sort, and stuck them on walls or furniture for decoration. Today, a stamp album may include different stamps from every nation of the world. Because governments often use stamp designs to mark special political events, or to honour individuals, stamp collections can be interesting documents of social history, reflecting social attitudes and priorities in different nations.

Starter pack

Stamps from different countries

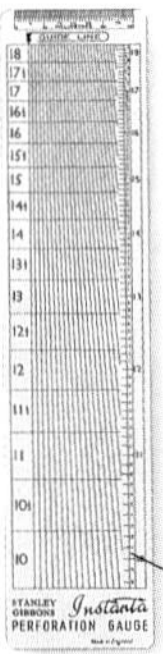

Collectors mount stamps in specially designed albums.

Perforation gauge

Protective sheet keeps stamp collection clean

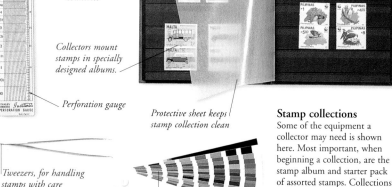

Sorting office

Sorting
At the sorting office a worker marks mail with phosphor dots, according to the postcode on the address. The dots are read by an automatic sorting machine, which sorts post into priority and non-priority mail, before cancelling every stamp so that it cannot be reused.

Delivery
Mail is transported by road, rail, or air, as quickly as possible. To speed the process, some rail carriages are also sorting offices. The mailsacks are then taken to the sorting office near their destination, sorted according to area, and delivered.

Transporting airmail

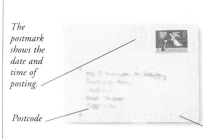

The postmark shows the date and time of posting.

Postcode

Phosphor dots are read by the sorting machine; such machines sort mail eight times faster than by hand.

Phosphor dots

The name of the issuing country appears on every postage stamp, apart from those issued in the UK.

Queen Victoria

Airmail stationery is made from lightweight paper.

Stamp collections
Some of the equipment a collector may need is shown here. Most important, when beginning a collection, are the stamp album and starter pack of assorted stamps. Collections can be organized in many ways: by country, shape, or theme. Stamps need not be rare or expensive, just interesting to the person collecting them.

Tweezers, for handling stamps with care

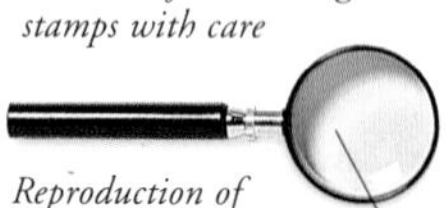

Reproduction of rare stamp appears on modern stamp

Magnifying glass

Colour key, to match against stamp shades

British Guiana One Cent appears on stamp from 1967

Valuable stamps
The world's rarest stamp is the 1856 British Guiana One Cent, because only one copy exists. It was found by a schoolboy in British Guiana in 1873. In 1980, a US millionaire bought it for $850,000.

Timeline
500 BC Cyrus the Great, Emperor of Persia, sets up mail route. Messengers on horseback carry royal commands across his empire.

1840 In Britain, the Penny Post introduces the first regular use of postage stamps, with the issue of the Penny Black and Twopence Blue. The sender pays the cost of postage.

Penny Black

1874 The Universal Postal Union is set up by international agreement to provide a uniform system for the exchange of mail between nations.

1919 First regular international air mail service begins.

1977 USA introduces Express Mail, for overnight delivery of priority post.

FIND OUT MORE · CODES AND CIPHERS · INFORMATION TECHNOLOGY · PERSIAN EMPIRE · TELECOMMUNICATIONS · TRADE AND INDUSTRY

Stamps and postal services

Stamp collections: the living world

Orchids,
Algeria

Orchids,
Belize

Giant anteater,
Guyana

Dahlia,
Japan

Shell duck,
Soviet Union

Red deer,
Belarus

Love birds,
USA

Transport and sport

Naval frigate,
Chile

Commemorates a European soccer tournament

Soccer,
Albania

Space shuttle,
USA

Yachting,
Japan

Ferrari

Racing car,
Belgium

Celebrates the Olympic Games

Javelin throwing,
Monaco

Golf,
Kenya

Rare or unusual

Marks the centenary of the Universal Postal Union

Island-shaped stamp,
Norfolk Island

Bananas are an important crop in Tonga.

Banana-shaped,
Tonga

Printed in 1913

Rare stamp with no watermark, Japan

Circular,
Singapore

Valuable for its unusually good condition

1861 3 cent,
USA

Printed on metallic paper

Kidney-shaped,
Bahamas

Cricket is a popular sport on the island.

Triangular,
Sri Lanka

Notable people

Hungarian activist
Flora Martos
(1897–1938)

Italian astronomer
Galileo Galilei
(1564–1642)

US film star
James Dean
(1931–55)

US president Richard
Nixon (1913–94)

US film star
Grace Kelly
(1929–82)

Chilean poet
Pablo Neruda
(1904–73)

Chilean leader
Salvador Allende
(1908–73)

Post boxes

France

Initials of reigning monarch at time post box was put up.

United Kingdom

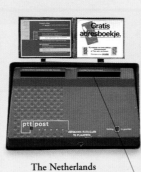

The Netherlands

Standard delivery post box

Box has one slot for local post and one for all other destinations.

United States

Italy

Express post box, guarantees next day delivery.

United States

STARFISH AND SEA URCHINS

ON THE SEABED lurk many spiny-skinned animals, including starfish and sea urchins. They, along with sea lilies, feather stars, brittlestars, and sea cucumbers, belong to a group of invertebrate animals – the echinoderms. The 6,000 species of echinoderm all live in the sea, moving slowly along the seabed by extending their tube feet. They have chalky plates, radially symmetrical bodies, and a water pumping system used for movement.

Anus is on upperside of central area.

One of five flexible arms

Tube feet

Small spines and pincers cover the starfish's upper surface.

Starfish

A starfish's body consists of five "arms" that radiate from a central area that contains the mouth on the underside and the anus on the upperside. The arms will often grow again if bitten off by predators. The underside of the body is covered in rows of sucker-like tube feet that enable the starfish to move and hold on to surfaces; chalky plates embedded in the spiny skin protect the upperside.

Feeding

Many starfish are active predators. They feed on shellfish, which try to clam up, but the starfish wraps its arms around the shell and pulls until the shellfish can resist no longer. Once the shell is open, the starfish pushes its stomach through its mouth to digest the flesh of the shellfish.

Common starfish feeding on mussels

Movement

Rows of tube feet line the underside of a starfish's arms and form part of the hydraulic vascular system common to all echinoderms. These tiny, water-filled tubes are elastic and have a bulb-shaped swelling at the base and a sucker-like disc for attachment at the end. Muscles squeeze the bulbs, pushing water through the tubes and extending them. This propels the starfish forwards.

Tube feet tipped with suction pads.

Tube feet of a common starfish

The starfish has started to turn itself back over.

Three arms reach out to find a surface to grip.

Two lower arms are attached to the seabed.

The starfish is now the correct way up.

How a starfish turns over

1 Starfish are often overturned by waves and water currents and are then vulnerable to attack with their soft undersides exposed.

2 Two arms stiffen and fix themselves to the seabed. The body rises and the tube feet on the other three arms feel for a surface to grip.

3 The three arms in the air are lowered to the seabed where the tube feet gain a purchase. Some species of starfish may take an hour to turn right over.

4 The whole body is now the right way up. A variation on the basic somersault method involves arching the body, and then toppling over.

Sea urchins

Most sea urchins are about 8 cm (3 in) in diameter and live in shallow seas on the seabed. They are like starfish with the arms folded up to make a ball. Their outer skeleton is covered in spines and tube feet, used for movement. Some species, such as the sand dollar, are flat in shape and have special spines for burrowing into sand; others can tunnel into rock.

Anus and genital openings on upper side

Spines

Tube feet

Mouth is on the lower side.

Defence

Slow-moving sea urchins need good protection. Spines, varying from long, sharp needles to short, stout clubs, cover their bodies. Muscles allow the spines to move during locomotion and for protection. Some sea urchins have poison-tipped spines; others have pincers that secrete a poison and are used to paralyse small animals.

Feeding

Most sea urchins eat algae and dead animal matter. Their tube feet push food into the mouth, where teeth chop it up before it enters the long gut. The teeth are set within a frame of chalky plates connected by muscles – a structure called Aristotle's lantern.

Aristotle's lantern

Feeding tentacles

Sea cucumbers

These soft-bodied creatures look like large slugs with feeding tentacles around the mouth. They live on the seabed in deep water where they move along on rows of tube feet. Some sea cucumbers can also burrow; others can swim.

Brittlestars

Brittlestars, so called because their arms easily snap off, are the most numerous echinoderms, with over 2,000 species. They are covered with chalky plates and spines and have long slender, occasionally branched arms clearly distinct from the body. The arms are used both for movement and feeding. Most brittlestars are filter feeders, but some are scavengers.

Common brittle star

Feather stars

Feather stars and sea lilies have flexible arms for filter feeding. Sea lilies grow on stems attached to solid surfaces. Feather stars use root-like arms to swim or hold on to surfaces.

Yellow feather star

COMMON STARFISH

SCIENTIFIC NAME *Asterias rubens*

ORDER Forcipulata

FAMILY Asteriidae

DISTRIBUTION At depths of 1–200 m (3–650 ft) in the Atlantic ocean and the NW European continental shelf

HABITAT Rock surfaces and stony sand sediment surfaces on seabeds

DIET Shellfish; a serious pest on oyster and scallop beds

SIZE Diameter: up to 30 cm (12 in)

LIFESPAN 2–4 years

FIND OUT MORE

ANIMALS　　CORAL REEFS　　OCEAN WILDLIFE　　POISONOUS ANIMALS　　SEASHORE WILDLIFE

STARS

THERE ARE MORE STARS than any other object in the Universe. Each is a spinning ball of hot, luminous gas. Most stars are made mainly of hydrogen and helium. As these gases are converted to heavier elements, energy is produced. A star has a life cycle of billions of years that takes it through many changes. The mass of the star, however, dictates how it will develop and die.

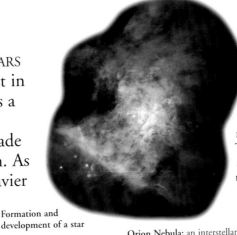

Orion Nebula: an interstellar cloud of gas and dust producing new stars. Left of centre are four young and bright stars known as the Trapezium.

Star birth

Stars are created from clouds of gas and dust. The cloud spins, and the material inside condenses and splits to form smaller clouds. These in turn spin and condense. Each is a protostar, a star in the making. Once material in the core of a protostar has reached a critical density and temperature, nuclear reactions start and energy is produced. The star is born. As the energy reaches the surface the star shines. The stars created from the original large cloud make a star cluster.

Double stars
About half the stars are in a double-star system. Both were created together from the same cloud of material, and the force of each other's gravity keeps them together.

Nucleosynthesis
Chemical elements are created inside stars by nuclear reactions. The process, called nucleosynthesis, starts by converting hydrogen to helium. A sequence of reactions at higher and higher temperatures produces heavier and heavier elements. The heaviest produced is iron. Most stars complete only part of the process in their lifetime.

Four hydrogen nuclei (called protons) are smashed together. Two positive particles escape, converting the two protons into neutrons.

Positively charged proton

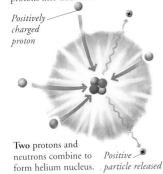

Two protons and neutrons combine to form helium nucleus. *Positive particle released*

Formation and development of a star

A protostar condenses, nuclear reactions start, and energy is produced.

Hydrogen is turned to helium in the star's core. The star has entered the main sequence of stellar development.

The Sun is halfway through its main sequence period of 10 billion years.

Stars expand as the hydrogen is used up. Their surfaces cool and redden.

Stars become red giants and leave the main sequence of stellar development.

The outer layers of a red giant become unstable. Most stars shed these layers and become white dwarfs.

Star clusters
Groups of stars living together are called clusters. A group may contain anything between a few or many thousands of stars, all created from the same cloud of gas and dust. The stars will be roughly the same age, but each develops in its own way.

Pleiades cluster

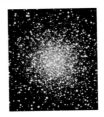

Globular cluster
Older stars are densely packed in globular clusters which are spherical in shape. The Hercules globular cluster contains several hundred thousand stars.

Hercules cluster

Open cluster
Young stars are loosely bound in open clusters and will disperse eventually. The stars in the Pleiades cluster are still surrounded by cloud material left over from their formation.

Star death

After billions of years, a star uses up its gases in the nuclear reactions taking place at its core. The star is starting to die, but death can still be millions of years away. The mass of a star dictates how it dies. A star like the Sun gradually sheds material from its outer layers. One with eight times the Sun's mass can end its life in a gigantic explosion, called a supernova because the explosion looks like a bright new star.

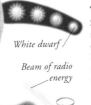

White dwarf

Beam of radio energy

Pulsar

White dwarf
Stars with less than eight solar masses end their lives as white dwarfs. Some of their material has been cast off; the rest condenses to form a compact star about twice the size of Earth.

A matchbox of material from a white dwarf would weigh as much as an elephant.

Neutron stars and pulsars
After a massive star explodes as a supernova, gravity forces the core to collapse with incredible force. The material is so densely packed that it is compressed into neutrons. The result is a neutron star, perhaps only 10-15 km (8-12 miles) across. Pulsars are neutron stars that spin rapidly, sending out beams of radio energy.

A pinhead of pulsar material would weigh more than the biggest supertanker.

Neutron star

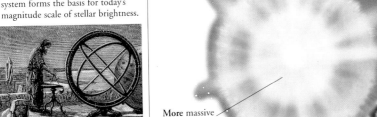

More massive stars explode as supernovas.

Brightness

A star's luminosity is the amount of light it produces – the true brightness. If all stars were the same distance from Earth their luminosity could be compared easily. But a star may appear bright because it is close rather than because it is truly bright. Astronomers use two scales – apparent and absolute magnitude – to measure the brightness of stars. Each allocates a number to indicate brightness: the higher the number, the fainter the star.

Apparent and absolute magnitude

The apparent scale describes how bright a star is when viewed from Earth. Stars up to 6 are visible with the naked eye. Stars of 7 and above need an optical aid to be seen. The absolute scale describes the true brightness of stars by comparing how bright they would appear if viewed at a standard distance of 32.6 light years (ly) from Earth. On both scales, each step in magnitude means a star is 2.5 times brighter or fainter than its neighbour.

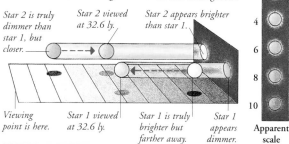

Star 2 is truly dimmer than star 1, but closer.

Star 2 viewed at 32.6 ly.

Star 2 appears brighter than star 1.

Viewing point is here.

Star 1 viewed at 32.6 ly.

Star 1 is truly brighter but farther away.

Star 1 appears dimmer.

Apparent scale

−2, 0, 2, 4, 6, 8, 10

Constellations

The sky is divided into 88 areas, or constellations, based on the patterns of stars that early astronomers used. Many are named after animals and figures from Greek mythology. Twelve constellations, known as the zodiac, form the backdrop against which the Sun and planets move.

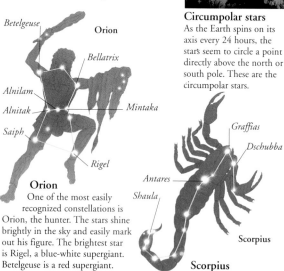

Circumpolar stars

As the Earth spins on its axis every 24 hours, the stars seem to circle a point directly above the north or south pole. These are the circumpolar stars.

Orion

Betelgeuse, *Bellatrix*, *Alnilam*, *Alnitak*, *Mintaka*, *Saiph*, *Rigel*

One of the most easily recognized constellations is Orion, the hunter. The stars shine brightly in the sky and easily mark out his figure. The brightest star is Rigel, a blue-white supergiant. Betelgeuse is a red supergiant.

Star names: Astronomers identify the prominent stars by a Greek-alphabet letter and the constellation name. Many of these stars also have their own name.

Scorpius

Graffias, *Dschubba*, *Antares*, *Shaula*, *Scorpius*

A red supergiant star, Antares, marks the centre of the scorpion's body and dimmer stars outline his tail. He is said to be the creature that stung Orion to death.

Star types

Stars are classified into groups according to the characteristics of their spectrums. A spectrum provides information on a star's colour, temperature, and chemical composition. There are seven main types of stars, each assigned a letter. They are, from hottest to coolest: O, B, A, F, G, K, and M.

Stellar spectrum

Light from star

Star

Prism splits light into spectrum.

Absorption lines

The light collected from a star is split to produce a spectrum. Dark "absorption" lines indicate the presence of particular atoms and molecules in the star. The strength of the lines indicates the temperature of the star. Blue-white stars classified A, for example, have hydrogen lines dominant, yellow G stars such as the Sun have ionized calcium dominant.

Star spectrum

Astronomers can deduce the colour of a star from its temperature, or vice versa. Blue stars, at left, are the hottest and red stars, at right, are the coolest.

The hottest stars are to the left, and the coolest to the right.

Blue supergiants

Red supergiants

°C	50,000	30,000	10,000	6,000	5,000	4,000	3,000°C
°F	90,000	55,000	18,000	11,000	9,000	7,000	5,500°F

Surface temperature

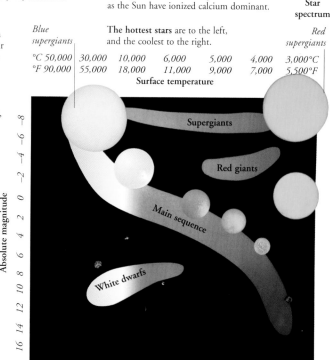

Supergiants

Red giants

Main sequence

White dwarfs

Absolute magnitude

−8, −6, −4, −2, 0, 2, 4, 6, 8, 10, 12, 14, 16

The brightest stars are at the top, and the dimmest are near the bottom.

Main sequence stars are those that are converting hydrogen to helium.

Star type: O, B, A, F, G, K, M

The Sun is a type G star in the main sequence group of stars. From here, it will move to the red giants and then to the white dwarfs.

Hertzsprung-Russell diagram

If the absolute magnitudes of stars are plotted on a graph against their temperatures, the stars form groups that represent the stages in a star's life. Most stars fall within a narrow band, the main sequence, which runs from top left to bottom right. The star moves from one position to another on the graph as it develops. As the hydrogen is used up, the star dims and then moves off the main sequence. Giant stars are found above the main sequence and dwarf stars below. Astronomers have used the graph, called a Hertzsprung-Russell diagram, since 1913 to help them understand stars, the relationship of their properties, and how a star changes. It is named after the two astronomers who created it.

Cecilia Payne-Gaposchkin

A British-American astronomer, Cecilia Payne-Gaposchkin (1900–79) spent her working life studying stars. When she started, one of the main problems taxing astronomers was the composition and structure of stars. She established the surface temperatures for each of the different types of star, and that the main sequence stars are made mainly of hydrogen and helium gas. She also found that the cycle time of a Cepheid star is related to its brightness.

Variable stars

The properties of some stars, such as brightness, vary in regular intervals that can last for minutes or years. In some stars, the dimming and brightening may be caused by a second star regularly eclipsing it. In other stars, the brightness varies because the star is pulsating: its outer layers alternately expand and contract, and the star dims and brightens.

Cepheid stars are yellow supergiants that change physically in size and temperature. As they alternately expand and contract, their brightness varies. They take between one and about 50 days to complete one cycle of change.

FIND OUT MORE

ASTRONOMY   BIG BANG   BLACK HOLES   GALAXIES   SUN AND SOLAR SYSTEM   TELESCOPES   UNIVERSE   X-RAYS AND ELECTRO-MAGNETIC SPECTRUM

STONE AGE

ABOUT TWO AND A HALF million years ago, human ancestors, or hominids, started to make and use basic stone tools, such as handaxes, for cutting and slicing. A million years later, hominids with larger brains, known as *Homo erectus* (upright people) made more complicated stone tools, such as arrowheads and small blades. This period is known as the Old Stone Age, or Palaeolithic Age. With these sharp tools, hominids carved bone and antlers, made clothes from animal skins, and chopped wood for fire and shelter. Later, in the Neolithic, or New Stone Age, humans created beautiful painting and sculpture. In Europe, the period between the Old and New Stone Ages was called the Mesolithic, or Middle Stone Age.

Types of stone and bone tools

When ancient flintworkers realized they could predict the size and shape of flint chips coming off a flint core, they began to use the chips, or microliths, as blades, and then as arrowheads. This way of working has become known as the Levallois Technique. Tools became more specialized and people began to make stone knives and scrapers. They began to make tools of other materials – hammers, needles, and harpoons were made of antler or bone.

Handaxe
The sharp points and twin edges of handaxes made them useful for all sorts of chopping and cutting jobs, from butchering meat and making clothes, to cutting down branches for shelter.

Harpoon
Ancient people mounted bone harpoon heads on wooden shafts and used them to spear fish.

Rounded head of hammer

Antler hammer
An antler or bone hammer was used for hitting flint rocks and detaching small flakes, which could then be used as blades.

Scraper
Flint tools with one curved sharp edge could be used to prepare animal skins for clothing. People probably used this example more than 35,000 years ago.

Arrowhead
Hunters tied finely worked flint arrowheads to wooden shafts, to make useful weapons.

Handaxe

Point for boring holes
Sharp edge for cutting

Burin
This type of pointed tool could have been used for making engravings on cave walls. This burin is more than 35,000 years old.

Art and sculpture

Humans produced some superb paintings and sculptures in the Stone Age. Often, these works were made in deep, dark caves. Archaeologists think that they were decorations for special ceremonial centres or secret religious shrines used by Stone Age priests.

Portable art
An artist in France carved this stylized mammoth from an animal's shoulder blade more than 10,000 years ago. Artists often portrayed the quarry of the local hunters, hoping that this would bring them good luck when hunting. Mammoth meat was popular food.

In-situ sculpture
Sometimes sculptures were "built-in" to caves. These clay bison form the centrepiece of a small, low chamber in a cave at Tuc d'Audoubert, France.

Cave and rock painting
Some of the finest Stone Age paintings have been found in the caves of Europe and the rock shelters of Australia. This painting of hunters or warriors comes from Valltorta in Spain, and may be 10,000 years old.

Making a handaxe

Simple pebbles were the very first tools, but then Stone Age people learned to make better tools by striking one piece of stone against another, a process known as flint-knapping. They could then turn a core tool, like the one below, into a handaxe.

Core tool
Flintworkers first trimmed a suitable piece of flint into a core tool by striking it with a stone hammer, such as a quartzite pebble. The tool was then roughly the right shape to be worked into a handaxe.

Flake tool
The flintworkers learned to predict how the stone would break when sharply hit with the stone hammer. They then sliced off long flakes from the underside of the core tool. This gave the axe a sharp, strong edge.

Underside

Pressure flaking
The flintworker finished the axe by hitting its edge with a bone or antler hammer to remove small flakes of stone. This made it very sharp.

Crafts

People used clay, reeds, and wood to produce cooking and carrying utensils. Few wooden objects have survived, though a plank at least 50,000 years old has been discovered in Japan.

Pottery
The first pots were made in Japan 12,500 years ago by rolling clay into a long sausage shape and coiling it in a spiral. The sides of the vessel were then smoothed down.

Bowl

Basket-making
Stone Age people wove twigs, reeds, grass, and canes to make containers. Impressions of basketwork in ancient mud floors in western Asia show that baskets date back 10,000 years.

Basket

Timeline

2–2.5 million years BC Hominids start to use crude pebble tools.

1.3 million years BC Handaxes are developed, followed by finely shaped tools in Africa.

460,000 BC First evidence of hominids using fire, Zhoukoudian, China.

100,000 BC Modern humans evolve.

60,000 BC Flint-knapping spreads to Europe.

9000–8500 BC Neolithic Age begins in western Asia.

6500 BC Neolithic Age begins in Europe.

Microliths

3000 BC Metal weapons and tools start to replace stone.

FIND OUT MORE

| ART, HISTORY OF | BRONZE AGE | CRAFTS | HUMAN EVOLUTION | PREHISTORIC PEOPLE |

S

STORMS

TORRENTIAL RAIN, THUNDER, lightning, and gales can bring turmoil and devastation. To most of us, a storm is a spell of severe weather, with strong winds and heavy rain. Meteorologists – people who study the weather – define a storm as a wind blowing persistently at over 103–117 kmh (64–72.7 mph). Storms form in areas of low pressure, where air is warm and less dense than the surrounding air. In certain conditions, more powerful storms can develop. These are known as typhoons, cyclones, hurricanes, or Willy-Willy in different parts of the world.

Hurricanes

These huge storms can measure about 650 km (400 miles) in diameter. Hurricanes develop as clusters of thunderstorms over warm tropical seas. They tighten into a spiral, with a calm central ring of low pressure, called the eye. They sweep westward with heavy rain and winds up to 350 kmh (220 mph). As they pass over cool water or land, their intensity lessens.

Slice through a hurricane

Ice-crystals form on the top of the clouds.

Air billowing from the top of the storm causes the clouds to spread out.

The strongest winds are found beneath the eye wall, immediately outside the eye.

Eye wall

Hurricane damage
Violent winds cause the most hurricane damage, flattening whole buildings and uprooting trees. There may also be a sudden rise in sea-level, called a storm surge. This can bring widespread flooding. Hurricane Andrew in Florida, USA (above) killed 15 people and left over 50,000 homeless in 1992.

Air descends into the calm eye, leaving it free of cloud. Winds are less than 25 kmh (16 mph).

Winds in excess of 160 kmh (100mph) occur beneath the storm.

Warm, moist air spirals up around the eye inside the hurricane.

Spiral rain band

The heat contained by the warm sea provides the energy needed to drive the storm.

Tornadoes

Small but ferocious, tornadoes are whirling masses of wind spiralling beneath a thunder-cloud. They roar past in minutes, bringing winds of up to 400 kmh (250 mph) that leave a trail of destruction. Air pressure at the centre is so low that air rushes in at enormous speed, sucking up people, cars, and even whole trains.

Thunderstorms

Created from huge cumulonimbus clouds, thunderstorms bring heavy rain, thunder, and lightning. They are made by strong updraughts along a cold front or over ground warmed by summer sun. Air expanding quickly causes thunder, the rumbling that follows lightning.

Lightning
Air currents in a thunder-cloud hurl water drops together so violently that the cloud bristles with electrical charge, which is then unleashed in a dramatic flash of lightning.

Waterspouts
When a tornado passes over water, it sucks water up into a column called a waterspout. These usually develop over shallow water in summer. Waterspouts tend to last longer than tornadoes, but their wind speed is often less than 80 kmh (50 mph).

Dust devils
In deserts, there is so much loose, light, dusty material that tornadoes create columns of dust – dust devils. These are caused by columns of hot air whirling up, carrying debris from the ground.

Clement Wragge
Popular myth has it that the idea of naming hurricanes came from Australian Clement Wragge (1852–1922). It is said that he decided to give hurricanes the names of women he particularly disliked. Today, hurricanes are named according to an alphabetic list, created each year, of alternating men's and women's names.

FIND OUT MORE | AIR | CLIMATE | CLOUDS | DESERTS | FRANKLIN, BENJAMIN | OCEANS AND SEAS | RAIN | WEATHER | WEATHER FORECASTING | WINDS

STRAVINSKY, IGOR

IGOR STRAVINSKY WAS probably the greatest composer of the 20th century. He was born in Russia in 1882, but later lived in Paris and the USA. He first found fame with *The Firebird*, a ballet based on old Russian stories. Much of his work had its roots in Russian traditional music, but it evolved throughout the composer's life as he changed his style to produce exciting and sometimes shocking musical effects.

Early life

Stravinsky was born near St. Petersburg, where his father was a singer. As a young man he trained as a lawyer, but, in 1902, he met the composer Rimsky-Korsakov and decided to devote his life to music. He studied with Rimsky-Korsakov, and the influence of the great Russian composers can be heard in his early music.

Firebird

Stravinsky's first score for the Ballets Russes, *The Firebird*, was first performed in 1910. The Russian story suited Stravinsky's colourful orchestral style. Although he lived in Western Europe, Stravinsky still wrote music on Russian themes.

Ballets Russes

Stravinsky wrote three of his best-known works – *The Firebird*, *Petrushka*, and *The Rite of Spring* – for this ballet company, run by Russian impresario Diaghilev. Stravinsky was still a young man when he wrote these nationalistic Russian ballets, and they took Paris by storm. The success of *The Firebird* made Stravinsky famous all over the world.

Sergei Diaghilev

Diaghilev

Sergei Diaghilev (1872–1929) was an active promoter of the arts in his native Russia before moving to Paris in 1908. The following year he founded the Ballets Russes, which commissioned music by the young Stravinsky and other notable composers to accompany the dancers.

Characters from The Rite of Spring

The Rite of Spring

This ballet tells the story of a sacrificial maiden dancing herself to death. Its jagged rhythms and violent harmonies were too much for some of the audience at the first performance. Fights broke out between those for and against the music, and the ballet ended in chaos. The piece launched modernism in music.

Brightly coloured costumes were a hallmark of the Ballets Russes.

Costume design for The Firebird

Neoclassicism

Soon after World War I, Stravinsky's style began to change. He rediscovered the music of 18th-century Europe, and adapted it to create the new, clear-sounding style now known as neoclassicism.

The Soldier's Tale

One of Stravinsky's most popular pieces is *The Soldier's Tale* (1918), a fairy tale for musicians, narrators, and a dancer. This piece of "music theatre" also shows the influence of popular musical forms, such as ragtime.

Performance

Stravinsky was a highly respected conductor as well as composer, famous for his very precise conducting style. He gave numerous concerts, particularly of his own works, and made many recordings of his music. These discs, still available, give us a clear idea of how he intended his music to be played.

Robert Craft

Later in life, Stravinsky took on an assistant, the American musician Robert Craft (b.1923), to help when ill health prevented him from conducting. Together, they also wrote several books about music, and Craft has written about their collaboration.

Stravinsky with Robert Craft

Date on which Stravinsky completed the composition.

Stravinsky's manuscript score of The Rite of Spring

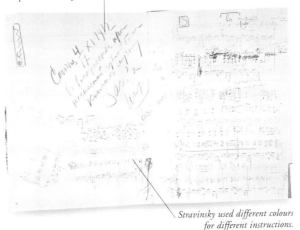

Stravinsky used different colours for different instructions.

Manuscript scores

Stravinsky's beautifully hand-written scores show how meticulous he was. He worked very precisely and carefully to achieve just the right effect, giving little room for a performer's or a conductor's own interpretation.

IGOR STRAVINSKY

1882	Born near St. Petersburg, Russia.
1910	*The Firebird* first performed.
1913	*The Rite of Spring* first performed, provoking a riot.
1920	Moves to Paris; neoclassical ballet *Pulchinella* first performed.
1926	Rejoins Orthodox church.
1930	Completes *Symphony of Psalms*.
1939	Moves to USA.
1951	Completes the opera *The Rake's Progress*.
1957	Completes *Agon*, ballet score using twelve-tone technique.
1971	Dies in New York.

FIND OUT MORE BALLET   DANCE   MUSIC   OPERA   ORCHESTRAS

SUBMARINES

THE ABILITY TO STAY hidden deep under the waves makes the submarine a powerful and effective warship. To travel underwater, a submarine needs a strong hull to resist high water pressure, and engines for both surface and underwater use. Submarines were used effectively as deadly weapons for the first time in World War I. Today, there are two main types of military submarines in operation. A patrol submarine searches for and attacks enemy vessels. A missile submarine carries long-range nuclear missiles.

Anatomy of a submarine

A submarine is encased in a strong steel hull. On top is a conning tower that stands above the water when the submarine is on the surface. Inside the submarine, rooms are arranged on two or three decks. Bulkheads separate the submarine into several sections that can be shut off from each other in case of leaks in the hull.

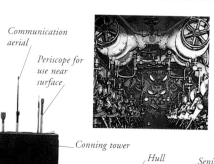

Engines
Submarines have engines that run on nuclear power or on a combination of electric and diesel motors. The engines drive a propeller that pushes the submarine through the water.

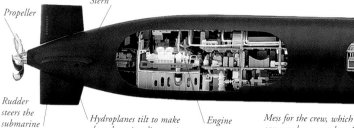

Communication aerial · Periscope for use near surface · Conning tower · Hull · Senior officers' mess (living quarters) · Torpedo tube · Bow · Propeller · Stern · Rudder steers the submarine · Hydroplanes tilt to make the submarine dive or rise. · Engine room · Mess for the crew, which can number more than 150. · Wireless office · Galley · Torpedo compartment · **Nuclear submarine**

Diving and surfacing

On the surface, a submarine floats like a normal ship. To dive, valves let water fill the large ballast tanks on either side of the hull. The extra weight causes the ship to descend. When submerged, the submarine moves up or down using its rudder-like hydroplanes. To surface, the water is blown out of the tanks.

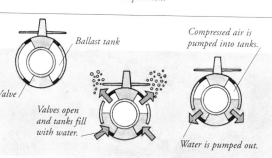

Ballast tank · Compressed air is pumped into tanks. · Valve · Valves open and tanks fill with water. · Water is pumped out. · Submarine floats. · Submarine dives. · Submarine surfaces.

Submersibles

Civil (non-military) submarines are called submersibles. They are smaller than military submarines and are used for carrying out specialized tasks deep underwater, from maintaining ocean pipelines to carrying out salvage operations, or marine research. Submersibles normally dive for only a few hours.

Deepest dives
Most military submarines can dive to depths of about 750 m (2,500 ft). The deepest dive was by a US Navy submarine that achieved a depth of 6.2 km (3.7 miles).

Nuclear submarines
The most powerful submarines are those that carry nuclear missiles, and are driven by nuclear engines. Each missile can destroy a large city, killing thousands of people. Nuclear engines allow a submarine to stay submerged for much longer than other submarines, which have to return to the surface to recharge their batteries.

Torpedoes
Military submarines carry underwater missiles called torpedoes. They are launched from tubes in the submarine's bow or stern. Homing systems, or signals from the submarine, guide modern torpedoes to their targets.

Timeline

1776 David Bushnell's *Turtle* is a waterproof wooden barrel, operated by hand and foot pedals.

The Turtle

1864 The human-powered, iron submarine *Hunley* is the first submarine to sink a ship. Its explosive charge is carried on a long pole.

1901 *Holland VI* is the first submarine with both petrol and electric engines.

1939–45 German submarines (U-boats) hunt Allied shipping in packs, sinking ships with torpedoes.

1954 The first nuclear-powered submarine is the US *Nautilus*.

1986 Crew on the US *Alvin* photographs wreckage of *Titanic*.

2000 The "unsinkable" Russian *Kursk* sinks.

FIND OUT MORE · ENGINES AND MOTORS · NUCLEAR POWER · PRESSURE · WARSHIPS · WORLD WAR I · WORLD WAR II

SUMERIANS

IN ABOUT 5000 BC, the Sumerians settled Mesopotamia, the fertile land between the Tigris and Euphrates rivers. They founded farming settlements, which, by 3200 BC, had grown into the world's first cities. As these cities flourished, the Sumerians developed the first known writing system. The Sumerian cities, linked by waterways, developed into a civilization based on a shared language, religious beliefs, art forms, and building styles. The cities traded with each other, but also fought for dominance. In c.2000 BC, eastern desert tribes in search of fertile land moved into the region, and the Sumerian civilization collapsed.

Fertile Crescent
Mediterranean Sea
Uruk
Ur

S

Shrine or temple

Ziggurats were pyramidal structures built with two to seven tiers of mud bricks.

Square bottom tier

The triple staircase at Ur was the first of its kind.

City life

Sumerian cities consisted of mud-brick houses, palaces, and temples enclosed by a large wall. Every day, people left home to farm the surrounding land or fish the rivers. Many worked for the king or the temple. As food production increased, more people were free to work with stone or metal, produce textiles, or make the thousands of mud bricks necessary to build ziggurats and temples.

The city of Ur
This ziggurat dominated the city of Ur, which was dedicated to the moon god Nanna. There were hundreds of gods in the Sumerian religion, and each city had its own special patron.

War
Competition between cities for farmland and materials led to almost endless warfare. The Standard of Ur, a gorgeously decorated wooden box, shows the ruler leading his soldiers against an enemy. The soldiers are equipped with copper helmets, felt cloaks, spears, and axes.

Gold necklace

Gold helmet

Gold bull on a lyre

Art objects
Sumerian artists were highly skilled. They decorated palace and temple walls with shell and stone inlays. Their craftworkers used imported stone to make statues of humans, animals, and gods. Metalworkers made exquisite jewellery of gold, silver, and rare stones, such as blue lapis lazuli and red cornelian, which they shaped into delicate animals and flowers.

Cuneiform script

The Sumerians invented writing, using a cut reed to draw signs on damp clay. The signs, representing sounds, were combined to form words. The impressions gradually became more cuneiform (wedge-like).

Farming and fishing
Farming communities developed in Mesopotamia between 6000 and 5000 BC. Food was easy to grow in the fertile soil of the marshes. Outside the marshes, the settlers gradually banded together, and built canals to irrigate the land. They cultivated the soil, and kept sheep, cattle, and pigs. Today, the Marsh Arabs of Iraq farm in a similar way to that of their predecessors, the Sumerians.

Marsh soil produced wheat and barley, and date palms.

Sargon

Legend tells how the baby Sargon was left in a basket on the Euphrates, and the goddess Ishtar gave him an empire. In fact, Sargon of Akkad (2000s BC) was the first conqueror of Sumer and most of Mesopotamia, and the first ruler to unify these territories into an empire.

Symbol for day three *Symbol for a commodity* *Symbol for 10 units*

Timeline

5000 BC Farmers and fishermen settle the Fertile Crescent of southern Mesopotamia.

3200 BC Large cities develop, such as Uruk.

3100 BC Sumerians invent writing.

2700 BC Kings, such as the legendary Gilgamesh of Uruk, rule independent cities.

2600 BC Sumerians trade their produce for luxury items, such as metal and precious stones.

c.2350 BC Sargon of Akkad unites Sumerian cities into an empire.

c.2300–2100 BC Sargon's empire fades. Political power shifts from city to city.

c.2100 BC Ur-Nammu of Ur controls the whole of Sumer, helped by his civil service.

Lapis lazuli
Goat statue, Ur

c.2000 BC Amorites from the Syrian desert invade the region, and Sumerian slowly ceases to be spoken. However, people continue to use Sumerian cuneiform script for monumental and religious inscriptions.

FIND OUT MORE	ASSYRIAN EMPIRE	BABYLONIAN EMPIRE	CITIES	FARMING, HISTORY OF	HITTITES	WARFARE	WRITING

SUN AND SOLAR SYSTEM

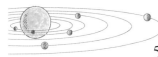

THE SUN IS A STAR – a huge ball of spinning gas – that is about 5 billion years old. It is important to us because it is the most massive and influential member of the Solar System. Its gravity keeps Earth and eight other planets, more than 60 moons, and millions of comets and asteroids orbiting around it. Together they make up a disc-shaped system which is billions of kilometres across. They share a past and a future dependent on the Sun.

Inside the Sun

The Sun is an incredibly hot sphere of gas that is generating energy. Its core is particularly hot and dense. Here nuclei of hydrogen collide and fuse to form helium. This reaction produces energy which, among other things, lights and heats the Solar System. The energy passes through the radiation and convection zones to the surface (photosphere), then through the Sun's atmosphere (chromosphere) into space.

Core 15 million°C (27 million°F)

Photosphere 5,500°C (9,900°F)

Chromosphere 50,000°C (90,000°F)

Life of the Sun
The Sun is a middle-aged star. As it ages, its appearance will change. In about 5 billion years, the hydrogen in its core will have been converted into helium and the outer layers will swell. It will expand to more than 150 times its present size, becoming a red giant. Mercury will be engulfed and life on Earth will cease. Eventually, the outer layers will drift off, and the remains will shrink to become a white dwarf.

Solar movement

The Sun spins on its axis. Different parts of it take different lengths of time to complete one turn. The equatorial regions move the fastest, taking about 25 days to complete a turn. The polar regions take 35 days.

Arthur Eddington
Present knowledge of the nature of stars owes much to an English astronomer, Arthur Eddington (1882–1944). His understanding of the internal structure of stars became the basis of future stellar work. He also produced the first proof for general relativity.

Ecliptic
The position of the Sun does not alter within the Solar System but it appears to move across Earth's sky. As the Earth spins, the Sun rises at the start and sets at the end of each day. The Sun's path, called the ecliptic, is measured against the more distant background stars. From Earth, the other planets and the Moon are seen to cross the sky close to the ecliptic.

North Celestial Pole

The ecliptic is the Sun's path through the sky.

Celestial equator

Ecliptic

Ecliptic

The Moon and planets cross the sky close to the ecliptic.

South Celestial Pole

The Sun's face

Earth is 149.6 million km (93 million miles) from the Sun, but still close enough for observers to make out surface features. Energy generated in the core takes millions of years to reach the surface, the photosphere, where some of it breaks through as sunspots, flares, and prominences.

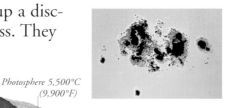

Sunspots
Disturbances in the Sun's magnetic field produce dark, cooler patches – sunspots – in the photosphere. Sunspots follow an 11-year cycle: they first appear at high latitudes and then increase in number, forming nearer and nearer the Equator during the cycle.

Sunspots are purple and black in this false-colour picture.

A solar prominence forms a loop.

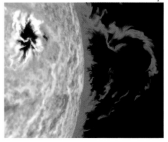

Flares and prominences
An explosive release of energy from the Sun is a flare. A jet of material shoots out from the photosphere, is brilliant for a few minutes, and fades in about an hour. Longer-lived jets are prominences. They may last several months and be 200,000 km (125,000 miles) long. Some shorter-lived prominences form a loop where ejected material is returned to the Sun.

Solar corona
Beyond the photosphere are the chromosphere and the corona – the Sun's inner and outer atmospheres. They are only visible during a solar eclipse when the Sun's face is obscured by the Moon. The corona extends for more than 1 million km (600,000 miles) beyond the photosphere.

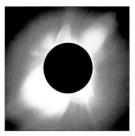

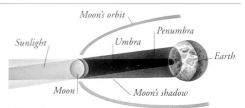

Moon's orbit

Penumbra

Sunlight

Umbra

Earth

Moon

Moon's shadow

Solar eclipse
When the Moon is directly between the Sun and the Earth, it covers the Sun's face. The Sun is eclipsed. From the part of Earth covered by the umbra (the darker, inner shadow), the Sun appears totally eclipsed. For those people in the penumbra (the outer shadow), the Sun is only partially eclipsed. The eclipse is possible because the Sun and Moon appear to be the same size in the Earth's sky. The Moon is 400 times smaller than the Sun, but it is 400 times closer.

S

 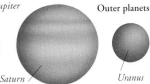

The Sun, the nearest star to Earth, is a sphere of gas. About 70 per cent of its mass is hydrogen and 28 per cent helium.

Inner planets
Venus *Mars* *Mercury* *Earth* *Jupiter*

Outer planets
Neptune *Saturn* *Uranus* *Pluto*

The planets
Nine planets orbit the Sun. The four inner ones are made of rock. The four largest, known as the gas planets, consist of large amounts of gas. The most distant, Pluto, is icy rock.

Solar System

Almost 99 per cent of the mass of the Solar System is in the Sun. It is not only the most massive but the largest object – 109 Earths could fit across its face; next is Jupiter, 11 Earths across. The smallest objects are tiny specks of dust. Each one of these objects spins on its axis and follows an orbit around the central Sun. The Sun was created about 5 billion years ago, followed by the planets and smaller bodies.

Sun's gravity

The mass of the Sun gives it the most gravitational pull. This keeps the planets and other objects orbiting it. They move fast to prevent being pulled into the Sun. The closest planets orbit the fastest. The more distant planets, where the gravitational pull is weaker, move more slowly.

Biggest planet

Jupiter is the most massive planet. It is made of the most material – 318 times the amount of material that makes Earth. It is also the biggest: it would take 1,330 Earths to fill Jupiter's space.

The axis of Venus is tilted by 178°.

Venus spins backwards, and takes 243 days to turn once.

Backward spinner

Each planet spins on its axis as it orbits the Sun. The planets are not upright – their axes are not at right angles to their orbital path. Earth is tipped by 23.5° and spins anti-clockwise as viewed from above the North Pole. Venus, Uranus, and Pluto are tipped over so far they spin on their axes in the opposite direction.

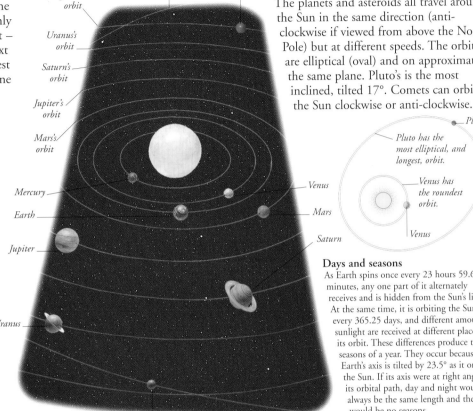

Pluto's orbit *Neptune* *Neptune's orbit* *Uranus's orbit* *Saturn's orbit* *Jupiter's orbit* *Mars's orbit* *Mercury* *Earth* *Jupiter* *Uranus* *Venus* *Mars* *Saturn* *Pluto*

Orbits

The planets and asteroids all travel around the Sun in the same direction (anti-clockwise if viewed from above the North Pole) but at different speeds. The orbits are elliptical (oval) and on approximately the same plane. Pluto's is the most inclined, tilted 17°. Comets can orbit the Sun clockwise or anti-clockwise.

Pluto — *Pluto has the most elliptical, and longest, orbit.* — *Venus has the roundest orbit.* — *Venus*

Days and seasons

As Earth spins once every 23 hours 59.6 minutes, any one part of it alternately receives and is hidden from the Sun's light. At the same time, it is orbiting the Sun once every 365.25 days, and different amounts of sunlight are received at different places on its orbit. These differences produce the seasons of a year. They occur because the Earth's axis is tilted by 23.5° as it orbits the Sun. If its axis were at right angles to its orbital path, day and night would always be the same length and there would be no seasons.

The seasons

June: North Pole faces the Sun – longest day in the north and shortest in the south.

September: Southern spring, Northern autumn – days and nights are equal length.

Sun *Earth's orbit*

March: Northern spring, southern autumn – day and night are equal length.

December: South Pole faces the Sun – shortest day in the northern hemisphere and longest in the south.

Origins

The Sun and all the objects orbiting it came from the same cloud of gas and dust. The spinning cloud condensed to form the young Sun surrounded by a disc of leftover material. Mercury, Venus, Earth, and Mars formed from the dust nearest the Sun. Farther out, where it was colder, snow and gas joined with dust to form Jupiter, Saturn, Uranus, and Neptune.

Asteroid belt

Smaller bodies in the Solar System, including Pluto and the planetary moons, were formed from material not swept up into the planets. Between Mars and Jupiter is the asteroid belt, made of millions of rocky pieces. The gravity of Jupiter prevented this material from staying together and forming one planetary object.

Johannes Kepler

The first accurate model of the Solar System was produced by the German astronomer Johannes Kepler (1571–1630). He developed three laws to describe the relative distances, speeds, and shapes of the planets' orbits. From then on, it was universally accepted by astronomers that the planets follow elliptical orbits around the Sun.

FIND OUT MORE   BIG BANG   COMETS AND ASTEROIDS   EARTH   GALAXIES   GALILEO GALILEI   GRAVITY   MOON   PLANETS   ROCKS AND MINERALS   STARS   TIME

SWEDEN

THE FIFTH LARGEST COUNTRY in Europe, Sweden occupies the eastern half of the Scandinavian peninsula, which it shares with Norway. The Gulf of Bothnia separates most of Sweden from Finland, and the Baltic Sea surrounds the jagged southeastern coastline. About 25 per cent of the country lies in Lapland, in the Arctic Circle. Sweden is a prosperous, environmentally conscious country, boasting one of the world's most efficient welfare systems to support its small population.

SWEDEN FACTS

CAPITAL CITY Stockholm

AREA 449,964 sq km (173,731 sq miles)

POPULATION 8,800,000

MAIN LANGUAGE Swedish

MAJOR RELIGION Christian

CURRENCY Swedish krona

LIFE EXPECTANCY 80 years

PEOPLE PER DOCTOR 323

GOVERNMENT Multi-party democracy

ADULT LITERACY 99%

Physical features

About half of Sweden is covered by the Inner Norrland, a region of gentle hills, dense forests of spruce and pine, and more than 100,000 lakes. The bitterly cold, mountainous north includes part of Lapland, shared with Finland, which makes up one-quarter of Sweden's land area.

Lakes, rivers, and waterfalls
This peaceful scene epitomizes Arctic Sweden's vast wilderness. Its long rivers rise on the Norwegian border and flow through many lakes to the Baltic Sea, generating hydroelectricity along the way. Sweden's largest lake is Vänern, at 5,584 sq km (2,156 sq miles).

Sarek National Park
Conservation is a key issue in Sweden, and there is much concern about forest damage from acid rain. Sarek, Europe's first national park, was set up in 1909 and forms part of its largest protected area.

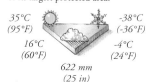

35°C (95°F)   -38°C (-36°F)
16°C (60°F)   -4°C (24°F)
622 mm (25 in)

Climate
Northern winters are bitterly cold, with six months of snow and only a few hours of sunlight. The south has a much milder climate, with only two snowy winter months.

People
Most of Sweden's small population live in the south, enjoying a comfortable lifestyle and equal rights for all. Women constitute half of the work-force, and men share childcare. Swedes have Europe's highest life expectancy because of their good diet and healthcare.

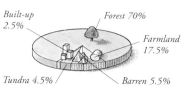

Built-up 2.5%   Forest 70%
                       Farmland 17.5%
Tundra 4.5%   Barren 5.5%

Land use
Less than nine per cent of the land is available for farming, but small areas of the fertile south are co-operatively used for crops and animals. Sweden is 70 per cent forest, and paper and wood products account for 16 per cent of exports. The country ranks highly in world softwood production.

Swedish family in local costume for midsummer festival, Dalarna

22 per sq km (56 per sq mile)   84% Urban   16% Rural

Volvo car

Farming and industry
Milk, beef, and pork are the main products of the small farming sector. Much larger are the growing technology industries, including Volvo and Ericsson, which have earned Sweden a reputation for design and reliability.

(Map of Sweden showing: Finland, Norway, Muonio, Torneträsk, Kiruna, Lapland, Lule, Torne, Gällivare, Jokkmokk, Pite, Arctic Circle, Uddjaur, Vindel, Luleå, Arvidsjaur, Piteå, Storuman, Skellefteå, Ume, Storsjön, Ångerman, Örnsköldsvik, Östersund, Umeå, Hjungan, Härnösand, Sundsvall, Ljusnan, Hudiksvall, BALTIC SEA, Mora, Falun, Gävle, Borlänge, Sandviken, Gulf of Bothnia, Uppsala, Karlstad, Västerås, Norrtälje, STOCKHOLM, Vänern, Örebro, Huddinge, Mariestad, Motala, Nyköping, Skövde, Norrköping, Uddevalla, Vättern, Linköping, Trollhättan, Borås, Jönköping, Fårö, Göteborg, Västervik, Visby, Kattegat, Varberg, Gotland, Halmstad, Oskarshamn, Växjö, Öland, Helsingborg, Hässleholm, Kalmar, Karlskrona, Malmö, Kristianstad, Ystad)

Stockholm
Sweden's capital is a harbour city, built partly on 14 islands, which are linked by 50 bridges. At the heart is Gamla Stan, the Old Town, founded in 1250. Its narrow, cobbled streets are lined with traditional craft and antique shops. The city also has more than 50 museums.

Central Stockholm

FIND OUT MORE — ARCTIC OCEAN · CARS AND TRUCKS · CONSERVATION · DAMS · DESIGN · ENERGY · EUROPE, HISTORY OF · FORESTS · PAPER · PORTS AND WATERWAYS · SCANDINAVIA, HISTORY OF

SWIFTS AND HUMMINGBIRDS

JET-BLACK SWIFTS AND JEWEL-LIKE hummingbirds belong to the same group of birds. They both have tiny feet and scythe-like wings and are agile fliers. Swifts eat insects, which they catch in mid-air, often twisting and turning after their prey with amazing speed. They hardly ever set foot on the ground, and make their nests in attics and chimneys, or in caves. The main food of hummingbirds is sugary nectar from flowers. They dart from plant to plant, and hover in front of flowers while they drink. Despite being small, hummingbirds are noisy and fearless. They often fight over the best places to feed.

Swifts

There are 92 species of swift, some of which spend most of their life in the air. Swifts often feed, mate, and even sleep on the wing. Many land only to breed. Swifts are found in many parts of the world, but they often migrate to warmer countries in winter when the supply of flying insects dries up.

Hummingbirds

There are about 300 species of hummingbird, and they are found only in the Americas. Hummingbirds are the most agile fliers in the bird world. As well as flying normally, they can hover in one place, to feed at a flower, and can even fly backwards.

Male

Brilliant metallic colours change as the bird moves.

Feather "boots"

Female

Booted racket-tail
In most hummingbird species, the male is much more striking than the female, but he takes almost no part in raising the young. This male racket-tail has two long tail feathers. They create an impressive display as he tries to attract a mate.

Flight
Swifts can beat each wing at a different speed. This unusual ability makes them very agile, and they can twist and turn in the air at high speed.

Narrow wings reduce friction at high speed.

The sword-billed hummingbird's beak is longer than its body.

Hummingbird beaks
The shape of a hummingbird's beak varies according to the flower it feeds at. The sword-billed hummingbird feeds at deep flowers, and its beak is straight. Some hummingbirds have curved beaks, and feed at curved flowers.

This hummingbird is 25 cm (10 in) long, including its beak.

Swift nests

Swifts do not land to collect nesting material. Instead, they make their nests out of saliva and material that they snatch up in the beak or break off with their claws.

Cave swiftlet nests

Chimney swift
This North American swift makes its nest from saliva and tiny twigs. It often glues it to the inside of a tall chimney or ventilation shaft.

How hummingbirds hover

Wings can beat at up to 90 times a second.

Joints inside the wing stay straight.

Wing muscles make up one-third of the hummingbird's weight.

1 The bird sweeps its wings backwards until they touch. This creates a downdraught that pushes the bird upwards.

2 The wings rotate on very flexible shoulder joints as the bird starts to bring them forward again.

3 The forward stroke also creates a downdraught. The moving air again pushes the bird upwards.

4 The wings swing backwards for the next stroke. The movement is usually too fast to be seen.

COMMON SWIFT

SCIENTIFIC NAME	*Apus apus*
FAMILY	Apodidae
ORDER	Apodiformes
DISTRIBUTION	Europe and Asia (summer); Africa (winter)
HABITAT	Open air, often above towns and cities
DIET	Flying insects
SIZE	Length, including tail: 18cm (7 in)
LIFESPAN	About 15-20 years

FIND OUT MORE   BIRDS   FLIGHT, ANIMAL   FLOWERS   MIGRATION   NESTS AND BURROWS   SONGBIRDS

SWIMMING AND DIVING

SWIMMING IS BOTH a popular recreation and an important competitive sport. It involves using legs and arms against the water to propel the body along. It is an excellent form of exercise, and a good way to learn to swim is to use buoyancy aids, such as water-wings, when practising strokes. Diving, in which a person enters the water head first, is fun too, although at competitive levels it calls for great agility. In competition, divers perfom about 10 dives from a choice of more than 80 dives recognized by the governing body.

Types of stroke

The four competitive strokes are freestyle (invariably front crawl), backstroke, breaststroke, and butterfly.

Knees begin to bend and part slightly.

Arms stretch out in front.

Breaststroke

This is the slowest stroke. Arms and legs move symmetrically underwater, the legs providing most of the thrust. The arms circle from an outstretched position, pulling through the water, around, and under the chin. At the same time, the legs move with a frog-like kick.

Preparing for the powerful arm stroke.

Butterfly

Purely a competitive stroke, butterfly was invented when swimmers began to bend the breaststroke rules. The arms move symmetrically from above the water with an explosive pull. The legs kick up and down together.

Backstroke

Swimmers lie on their backs in backstroke. The stroke requires alternate arm pulls, windmill style, and a flutter kick, in which the legs move up and down in the water.

Gertrude Ederle

First woman to swim the Channel in 1926

Cross-Channel swimming

Of all the long-distance sea swims, the Channel between England and France – 34 km (21 miles) minimum – has always provided the greatest challenge.

Front crawl

This is the fastest stroke, so it is used in freestyle races, but it may also be performed slowly. It is a popular recreational stroke and is used in long-distance swimming. The swimmer lies face down in the water. Both arms and legs move alternately – the arms pull down through the water from an outstretched position, and the legs move up and down.

Legs move up and down from the hips.

Arm pulls through the water.

The body rolls from side to side.

Arm comes out near the thigh.

Mark Spitz

American swimmer Mark Spitz (b. 1950) set an an unprecedented record when he won seven gold medals at one Olympic Games. At Munich in 1972, he won the 100- and 200-m freestyle and butterfly, and swam in three winning US relay teams, with world records in all events.

Swimming

Swimming is a major Olympic sport. Before going on to championship meetings, children can compete in their own age groups in swimming galas. Other aquatic sports involving swimming include water polo and synchronized swimming. The former is a seven-a-side ball game; the latter is a kind of underwater ballet.

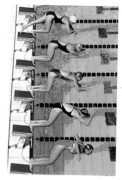

Racing

Races are started from blocks, and electronic touch-pads at the end of the pool enable major events to be timed to one-thousandth of a second. Olympic-size pools are 50 m (164 ft) long.

Diving

There are two standard diving events – the springboard, 3 m (10 ft) above the water, and the fixed platform, or highboard, 10 m (33 ft) high. The diver performs aerial manoeuvres such as twists and somersaults before entering the water. Points are awarded for technique and style.

Cliff diving

Cliff diving is a popular show for tourists in some Hawaiian and Mexican resorts, such as Acapulco, shown here. Divers plunge 35 m (115 ft) or more into water perhaps only 4 m (13 ft) deep, avoiding projecting rocks as they do so.

Types of dive

There are six main types of dive: forward, backward, twist, inward, reverse, and handstand.

Handstand dive
Handstand, or armstand, dives are performed from the highboard. The diver goes into a steady handstand on the edge of the board before proceeding with the dive.

Backward dive
In the starting position for a backward dive, the diver must keep a straight body, with head up. The arms are swung upward just before take-off from the platform or springboard.

Forward dive
Forward dives may be performed with a run-up as well as from a standing position. As with all dives, the body should enter the water straight, with legs, arms, and hands extended.

FIND OUT MORE   HEALTH AND FITNESS   MEXICO   OLYMPIC GAMES   SAILING AND OTHER WATER SPORTS   SPORT

S

SWITZERLAND AND AUSTRIA

MOUNTAINOUS AND LAND-LOCKED, Switzerland and Austria sit in the heart of Western Europe, with the tiny principality of Liechtenstein tucked in between them. This central position, and some of Europe's longest rivers, have enabled the three countries to take advantage of trading routes between east and west, and north and south. Switzerland's lack of raw materials has led to the development of specialized high-tech industries, which have made the country rich. Austria's mineral resources supplement its income from farming, and the picturesque lakes and mountains of all three countries attract millions of tourists.

Communications
Treacherous mountain passes were the only routes through the Alps until tunnels and high bridges were engineered. Switzerland's St. Gotthard traffic tunnel is the world's longest road tunnel, and stretches for 16 km (10 miles). Rivers have provided links for centuries. The river port of Basel on the Rhine connects Switzerland to the North Sea, while the mighty Danube joins Austria to the Black Sea.

Train on a high mountain bridge, Switzerland

Physical features
The highest mountains in Europe, the Alps, cover 70 per cent of Switzerland, 75 per cent of Austria, and much of Liechtenstein. Dense coniferous forest dominates Switzerland and is scattered around Austria and Liechtenstein. Two great rivers, the Rhine and the Danube, provide access to the north and south.

Alps
Forming a vast, rocky barrier between northern and southern Europe, the Alps are some of the most impressive mountains in the world. They range across western Europe and are at their most dramatic on the Swiss-Italian border, where the icy Matterhorn rises to 4,478 m (14,691 ft). The Alps are fragile, and tourism is controlled.

Matterhorn

Regional climate
19°C (66°F)   -1°C (30°F)

813 mm (32 in)

In Switzerland, Austria, and Liechtenstein, alpine regions are cooler and wetter than the valleys, and have a lot of snow. Switzerland's climate varies, and south-facing mountains are much warmer than northern slopes. On the plateau, summers are warm, and dry winds often bring high winter temperatures. Austria has a high rainfall in the west.

Austrian plains
Broad, fertile plains surrounding the River Danube and its tributaries cover part of northeastern Austria. The small, privately owned farms ensure Austria is self-sufficient in potatoes, sugar beet, and cereals. Surplus crops are exported. Cattle graze on mountain slopes.

Swiss lakes
Switzerland has some of the most scenic and famous lakes on the European continent, including the two largest lakes in Western Europe, Geneva and Constance. Pollution is affecting some of the more popular lakes, such as this tranquil area of Lake Silser, near St. Moritz.

Switzerland

Switzerland is a land of isolated valleys, divided into 26 provinces. A united confederation since 1291, Switzerland has a strong central government. The country has a long history of neutrality in war, and now many international organizations have their headquarters in Geneva. Successful banking and high-tech industries have made Switzerland the world's wealthiest country.

Bern

Home to more than 130,000 people, Switzerland's ancient capital, Bern, dates from the 11th century. Its streets mix historic medieval buildings with modern factories and offices. The bear is a city symbol and its namesake market is a colourful scene.

A panoramic view of Bern

People

Swiss people are the richest in the world, but their costs of living are high. The most multilingual of all European countries, Switzerland has three main languages, with German most used. The Swiss people vote on all major political issues, but two conservative cantons did not grant women the vote until 1989.

Dairy farming

Arable land is scarce in Switzerland, but mountain cattle-grazing has turned the country into a leading exporter of dairy products. Milk from the cows is used to make a wide range of cheese, and chocolate, invented by Henri Nestlé (1814–90).

Industry

About 35 per cent of the labour force work in manufacturing, one of the highest levels in Europe. The Swiss have a world-wide reputation for their precision engineering, especially for making clocks and watches. In 1968, they invented the quartz watch. Other important industries include making optical instruments and the growing chemical and pharmaceutical sector, which employs about ten per cent of the work-force.

Tag Heuer watch

Drug capsules

Banking

Financial stability, political neutrality, and strict secrecy laws combine to make Switzerland a major banking centre. Foreign investors are attracted by low taxes, and freedom from investigation by tax officials.

SWITZERLAND FACTS

CAPITAL CITY	Bern
AREA	41,290 sq km (15,942 sq miles)
POPULATION	7,200,000
MAIN LANGUAGES	German, French, Italian, Romansch
MAJOR RELIGION	Christian
CURRENCY	Swiss franc
LIFE EXPECTANCY	79 years
PEOPLE PER DOCTOR	294
GOVERNMENT	Multi-party democracy
ADULT LITERACY	99%

Austria

Once the centre of the Austro-Hungarian Empire and a major European power, Austria today is a small, industrialized republic. It has close ties with Switzerland and its powerful northern neighbour, Germany, with which it shares many aspects of language and culture. Nearly 94 per cent of the people are ethnic Austrians.

Music

Many great composers were Austrian, including the Strauss family, who composed the Viennese waltz. Spring's Festival of Vienna hosts concerts, balls, operas, and theatre performances.

AUSTRIA FACTS

CAPITAL CITY	Vienna
AREA	83,858 sq km (32,378 sq miles)
POPULATION	8,100,000
MAIN LANGUAGE	German
MAJOR RELIGION	Christian
CURRENCY	Euro
LIFE EXPECTANCY	78 years
PEOPLE PER DOCTOR	333
GOVERNMENT	Multi-party democracy
ADULT LITERACY	99%

Vienna

One of the most beautiful cities in Europe, Vienna was once the capital of the Holy Roman Empire. Many of its historic buildings, including St. Stephen's Cathedral, survived the bombs of World War II (1939–45). Others, such as the Opera House, were rebuilt.

St. Stephen's Cathedral

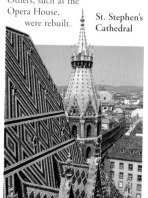

Skiing

Austria's winter sports bring in one-third of the country's tourist income, and more than 10 million people holiday in the Alps every year. Skiers flock to premier alpine resorts, such as St Anton, attracted by heavy snow, breathtaking views, and modern facilities.

Hydroelectric power

With limited fossil fuels, Austria has to rely on its fast mountain streams to provide power for its steel and manufacturing industries. The Danube has also been harnessed to provide 40 per cent of power used.

Liechtenstein

Nestling between the Rhine and the Alps, this tiny principality has close economic ties with Switzerland. A busy financial centre, its economy is highly industrialized. The people of Liechtenstein enjoy a high standard of living and traditional family life.

Lifestyle

Liechtenstein is known for its vineyards, forested nature reserves, and postage stamps. Most people are ethnic Liechtensteiners, but about 35 per cent are Swiss and German. Most disagree with equal rights for women, who only got the vote in 1984.

LIECHTENSTEIN FACTS

CAPITAL CITY	Vaduz
AREA	160 sq km (62 sq miles)
POPULATION	32,200
MAIN LANGUAGE	German
MAJOR RELIGION	Christian
CURRENCY	Swiss franc

FIND OUT MORE CHURCHES AND CATHEDRALS   DAMS   EMPIRES   EUROPE, HISTORY OF   EUROPEAN UNION   FARMING   HOLY ROMAN EMPIRE   MONEY   MOUNTAINS AND VALLEYS   MUSIC   WINTER SPORTS

SYRIA AND JORDAN

SYRIA, JORDAN, AND LEBANON together form part of a region called the Middle East that lies between Europe, Africa, and the rest of Asia. The majority of people are Muslim, sharing a common environment and culture. By contrast, the nearby island of Cyprus has strong ties with Europe and its people are mostly Christian. Politics in the region are volatile. The three mainland countries lie on important ancient trade routes, and Syria and Jordan have modern trade links in the form of pipelines that carry oil from countries farther east for shipment to Europe and beyond.

Physical features

The mainland countries of this region are dominated by dry deserts, with strips of fertile land along the Mediterranean coast and in the Jordan Valley. The River Jordan flows 320 km (200 miles) from its source on the border between Syria and Lebanon down to the Dead Sea. Cyprus has fertile plains, mountains, and sandy beaches.

Wadi Rum

In southern Jordan, the towering sandstone mountains of the Wadi Rum – an ancient watercourse that is now dry – rise sharply out of the sand to create one of the world's most spectacular desert landscapes. Now a national park, Wadi Rum is home to several Bedouin tribes who live in scattered camps throughout the area.

Troodos Mountains

The Troodos Mountains run for 113 km (70 miles) from east to west in southern Cyprus. The highest peak is Mount Olympus at 1,953 m (6,406 ft). Forests and vines cover the mountains, which contain mineral deposits, including asbestos, gold, and silver.

27°C (80°F)   10°C (50°F)

444 mm (17.5 in)

Regional climate

Summers throughout the whole region are hot and dry and winters cool, with moderate rainfall. Below sea-level, the Jordan Valley has warm winters and scorching summers. In the mountains of Lebanon and Cyprus, winters are colder and wetter with frequent snow.

Bedouins

Nomadic Bedouin peoples and their animals have roamed the deserts of the Middle East for centuries. Living in tents, family groups move around exploiting the limited water and grazing their animals on a seasonal basis. Some Bedouin are camel herders; others keep sheep and goats. Today, their way of life is under threat as governments urge people to settle in towns and cities.

Bedouin people in tent, Jordan

Jebel Liban Mountains

Almost half of Lebanon lies more than 900 m (3,000 ft) above sea-level. Two mountain chains run from north to south down the length of the country. The Jebel Liban run for about 160 km (100 miles) along the west coast, and in the east are the lower Jebel esh Sharqi, or Anti-Lebanon Mountains. The fertile Bekaa Valley lies between the two ranges.

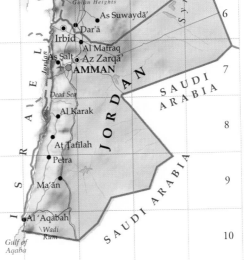

Map

TURKEY

CYPRUS
Rizokarpasso
Kyrenia
Akanthou
Polis
NICOSIA
Famagusta
Troodos Mountains
Larnaca
Paphos
Limassol

Al Qamishlí
A'zâz
Al Tall al Abyad
Al Hasakah
Halab
L. Assad
Ar Raqqah
Al Jazirah
Afrin
Orontes
Al Ládhiqíyah
Hamah
Dayr az Zawr
Euphrates
Tartûs
S Y R I A
Hims
Tudmur
Abū Kamāl
I R A Q
Syrian Desert

Tripoli
LEBANON
BEIRUT
Baalbek
Baabda
Zahlé
Saïda
DAMASCUS
Soûr
Al Qunaytirah
Golan Heights
As Suwaydā'
Dar'a
Irbid
Al Mafraq
As Salt
Az Zarqā'
AMMAN
SAUDI ARABIA
Dead Sea
Al Karak
JORDAN
At Tafilah
Petra
Ma'an
Al 'Aqabah
Wadi Rum
Gulf of Aqaba
SAUDI ARABIA
ISRAEL
Jordan
Jebel Liban
Jebel esh Sharqi

Mediterranean Sea

0 km   100
0 miles   100

S

Syria

Inhabited for tens of thousands of years, Syria has a rich cultural history. Only one-third of the land is cultivated and oil is the main source of income. About 20 per cent of Syria is desert, some of which can be grazed. Most Syrians are Muslim Arabs, with a small Kurdish minority who live in the north. The leading political force is the ruling Ba'ath Party.

SYRIA FACTS

CAPITAL CITY Damascus

AREA 184,180 sq km (71,498 sq miles)

POPULATION 16,600,000

MAIN LANGUAGE Arabic

MAJOR RELIGION Muslim

CURRENCY Syrian pound

Cotton

Syria's main cash crop is cotton, grown mainly in the north of the country on land watered by the Euphrates and Orontes rivers. Wheat, barley, fruit, and vegetables are also grown. Sheep and goats are raised for meat and milk.

Sacks of cotton ready for processing

Damascus

Syria's capital, built about 5,000 years ago on the River Barada, is the world's oldest inhabited city. The most important building is the 7th-century Umayyad Mosque, which contains parts of a former Christian church. Nearby, the booths of the Al-Hamidiyah bazaar sell all kinds of craftwork. Small shops sell fresh fruits grown in the orchards outside the city.

Lebanon

This small country on the Mediterranean coast was home to Phoenician traders around 1200 BC. From 1975 until 1991, Lebanon was shattered by civil war between Christians and Muslims. One-third of the land is cultivated, yet farming employs one in five Lebanese workers. The country produces fine wines.

LEBANON FACTS

CAPITAL CITY Beirut

AREA 10,400 sq km (4,015 sq miles)

POPULATION 3,600,000

MAIN LANGUAGE Arabic

MAJOR RELIGIONS Muslim, Christian

CURRENCY Lebanese pound

Beirut

Lebanon's ancient capital, Beirut, lies at the meeting point of three continents. The city is home to more than one million people and is a centre of culture, trade, and tourism. It is now being rebuilt after war damage.

Pickled chillies

Pickled swede

Kibbeh

Pastry

Lebanese food

The national food of Lebanon is *kibbeh*, made of lamb or fish pounded to a fine paste with *burghol* (cracked wheat) and served raw or baked in flat trays or rolled into balls and fried. The Lebanese also love pastries filled with nuts and dates and covered with honey.

Jordan

Apart from a short strip of coast on the Gulf of Aqaba, Jordan is land-locked. Since Eastern Jordan is desert, most people live in the more fertile northwest, close to the River Jordan – the main source of water. At 400 m (1,312 ft) below sea-level, the Dead Sea is the world's lowest point on land. Most Jordanians are Muslim and speak Arabic. Jordan plays a peacekeeping role between Israel and its Arab neighbours.

JORDAN FACTS

CAPITAL CITY Amman

AREA 92,300 sq km (35,637 sq miles)

POPULATION 5,100,000

MAIN LANGUAGE Arabic

MAJOR RELIGION Muslim

CURRENCY Jordanian Dinar

Minaret for calling Muslims to prayer

Mosque overlooking Amman

Farming and industry

Jordan receives most of its income from phosphate mining, light industry, and, increasingly, tourism. Although water is in short supply, Jordan grows tomatoes, cucumbers, aubergines, citrus fruit, and wheat.

Amman

Although Amman has been Jordan's capital since only 1921, the city dates back to biblical times when it was built on seven hills. Today, Amman is a mix of old and new buildings, including museums and art galleries. The central *souk* (market) is a lively and colourful reminder of the city's ancient origins. Amman has about one-third of Jordan's population.

Petra

The city of Petra was built 2,000 years ago by Nabatean Arabs who cut tombs, dwellings, and temples into the solid rock. Set in a valley surrounded by red stone cliffs, Petra is reached through the *Siq*, a narrow entrance. Petra is now a great tourist attraction.

Cyprus

Cyprus is the largest island in the eastern Mediterranean. Following Turkish and British rule it became independent in 1959. The majority of Cypriots is Greek- or Turkish-speaking. In 1974, increasing hostilities led to a split between the Greek south and Turkish north.

CYPRUS FACTS

CAPITAL CITY Nicosia (Lefkosia)

AREA 9,250 sq km (3,571 sq miles)

POPULATION 790,000

MAIN LANGUAGES Greek, Turkish

MAJOR RELIGIONS Christian, Muslim

CURRENCY Cyprus pound, Turkish lira

Tourism

Sun, sand, spectacular mountain scenery, and ancient Greek and Roman ruins lure around two million tourists to Cyprus each year. Tourism in the southern part of the island increased greatly in the 1980s.

FIND OUT MORE

ASIA, HISTORY OF   CRUSADES   DESERTS   FARMING   IRAN AND IRAQ   ISLAM   ISLAMIC EMPIRE   MOSQUES   OIL   PHOENICIANS   WARFARE

TECHNOLOGY

THE SCIENCE OF PUTTING inventions and discoveries into practical use is known as technology. A scientist discovers scientific principles, properties, and processes, while engineers use that knowledge to build machines and structures. Technology began in prehistoric times, but did not have a major impact until the 18th and 19th centuries. Then a host of new technologies sprang up, spawning a revolution in industry and at home. Today, it is information technology that is bringing about another major revolution.

Early technology

Prehistoric people pioneered technology when they made the first tools. They smashed pebbles to produce sharp cutting pieces, then later shaped flints into specialist tools such as hand axes, knife blades, and weapons. Tools continued to be made from stone until about 5000 BC, when copper was first smelted and used in the Middle East. In about 3500 BC, metal technology spread with the discovery of bronze. The Bronze Age was then followed by an Iron Age from about 1500 BC.

Stone-Age flint hand axe carefully worked to produce a sharp cutting edge.

Modern technology

The foundations of modern technology were laid in the 1700s, at the beginning of the Industrial Revolution. Inventions transformed traditional craft-based industries into factory-based ones. Key inventions, such as the spinning jenny (1764) and Watt's steam engine (1775), provided the materials, machines, and power necessary for technology to develop.

Quorn is a meat substitute made from mycoprotein – a protein derived from fungi.

Freeze-dried food is light, but still retains nutrients. This type of food is used by astronauts in space.

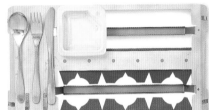

Tray to hold space foods

Food technology

One of the most important aspects of food technology is preservation. Methods such as salting meat have been practised for thousands of years to stop food spoiling, while canning and refrigeration are more recent. Modern methods include freeze drying, which helps preserve food structure better, and the use of additives. Food technology also includes the manufacture of synthetic substitutes such as TVP (textured vegetable protein).

Materials technology

A range of materials is used for manufacturing goods, machines, and structures. Plastics, for example, are popular because they are cheap and easy to shape. They are used in solid form, as synthetic fibres for textiles, film for packaging, and in composites such as fibreglass. Metals such as iron and aluminium are strong and continue to be important for building machines and structures. Concrete, usually reinforced, or strengthened, is the prime material for building massive structures such as dams, bridges, and skyscrapers.

Reinforced concrete

Information technology

Information technology, or IT, encompasses the revolution in communications and the exchange of information brought about by the widespread use of computers. One aspect of IT is the creation of the Internet, a global network that provides access to "sites" containing a range of information, and allows communication between network "surfers" (users).

Portable, or laptop, computers allow users to work anywhere.

Laptop computer

Engineering

Engineers make technology work. They design and mend machinery and electrical equipment, as well as build a range of structures, mines, and chemical plants. The five main categories of engineering are mechanical, civil, mining, chemical, and electrical engineering.

Glen Canyon dam, Arizona, USA

Civil engineering

Civil engineers are involved in construction engineering projects, which provide a range of structures that are beneficial to the public. These include roads, bridges, dams, tunnels, and skyscrapers. One of the most impressive engineering structures is the 50-km (31-mile) long Channel Tunnel under the English Channel, connecting France with the UK.

Appropriate technology

An appropriate technology can be defined as one which serves local needs, using local resources. Many developing countries cannot afford to develop large projects, so they tend to upgrade and manage existing technologies on a community level. They might make small water turbines to generate power, build irrigation schemes, or produce renewable energy sources, such as wind and solar power.

Irrigation pumps on wheat field

Research biochemist experiments in a sterile environment

Chemical engineering

Chemical engineers build and operate chemical manufacturing plants, such as those used in the petrochemical industry. They develop large-scale processes that research chemists have produced on a small scale in a laboratory. Their approach is to break down the manufacturing operation into a series of steps.

Service engineer

Design and maintenance

A team of engineers is responsible for developing a new product. Design engineers decide how to make it, and what materials to use. Detailed plans are then passed to production engineers who devise its manufacture. After sale, service engineers are on call to carry out maintenance and repairs.

FIND OUT MORE

BRIDGES • BUILDING AND CONSTRUCTION • DAMS • DESIGN • FOOD • INDUSTRIAL REVOLUTION • INFORMATION TECHNOLOGY • INVENTIONS • PLASTICS AND RUBBER

TEETH AND JAWS

BEFORE FOOD CAN BE SWALLOWED, it must be cut up into small pieces so it can travel down the oesophagus and into the stomach. The job of cutting and grinding is carried out by the teeth. These are small, hard structures embedded in the upper and lower jaw bones that grip, bite, slice, and crush food into a paste ready for swallowing. Different types of teeth are adapted to perform particular functions. As a child grows, his or her jaw bones increase in size, until by the end of adolescence they can accommodate a set of 32 adult teeth.

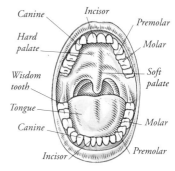

Canine · Incisor · Premolar · Molar · Hard palate · Wisdom tooth · Soft palate · Tongue · Molar · Canine · Premolar · Incisor

Types of teeth
Each adult jaw contains 16 teeth: four incisors, two canines, four premolars, and six molars. Incisors, at the front of each jaw, are cutting teeth that slide past each other to slice up food. Canines grip and tear food. Premolars and molars have flattened crowns to crush and grind food.

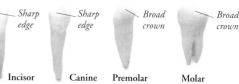

Sharp edge · Sharp edge · Broad crown · Broad crown

Incisor · Canine · Premolar · Molar

Growth of teeth and jaws

We have two sets of teeth during our lifetime. The first set are called primary, or milk, teeth and they gradually appear in babies until a set of 20 is in place. At about the age of six, the roots of some milk teeth loosen and they start to be pushed out and replaced by the permanent or adult teeth.

Milk teeth in gums · Maxilla (upper jaw) · Mandible (lower jaw)

A newborn baby has no visible teeth. Within the upper jaw and lower jaw, however, the milk teeth are developing. These start to erupt at around the age of six months.

Jaw bone grows · Permanent teeth · Milk teeth

A 5-year-old child has a full set of 20 milk teeth, consisting of four incisors, two canines, and four molars in each jaw. The permanent teeth are developing and will push out.

First permanent molars · Permanent incisors · Milk teeth still in place

A 9-year-old child has a combination of permanent and milk teeth. While most of the teeth are milk teeth, the first permanent molars and incisors have already erupted. By age 12, a child's teeth are all permanent teeth.

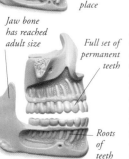

Jaw bone has reached adult size · Full set of permanent teeth · Roots of teeth

A 20-year-old's jaws are fully grown and contain a full set of adult teeth. Some people's wisdom teeth (the molars at the back of the jaw) do not erupt until their twenties. If there is not enough room for them the wisdom teeth are extracted.

Crown is the upper visible part of the tooth.

Gum is soft tissue covering jaw bone.

Blood vessels

Root anchors tooth in jaw bone.

Root canal contains pulp.

Blood capillary supplies tooth with food and oxygen.

Enamel is a very hard material that covers the crown.

Dentine is a living, bone-like material inside the tooth.

Pulp cavity contains pulp.

Cement and peridontal ligament hold root in socket.

Nerve ligament

Jaw bone

Structure of a tooth

Every tooth is made up of three basic layers. Enamel forms a hard cap that protects the tooth. Dentine forms the bulk of the tooth and extends into the root along the root canal. The pulp contains blood vessels and nerves, which allow you to detect pressure when chewing.

Brushing your teeth regularly helps get rid of plaque.

You brush the plaque away from your gums.

Tooth decay
Food leaves behind a sticky residue on your teeth called plaque. Bacteria in plaque release acids that eat away at the enamel. This can expose the inner parts of the tooth, causing tooth decay.

Chewing and biting

The first stage in digestion is chewing, which breaks food up into small particles ready for swallowing. Chewing is controlled by three pairs of muscles that move the lower jaw. The temporalis and masseter muscles pull the lower jaw upwards to crush food. The pterygoid muscles move the lower jaw from side to side, and slide it forwards, to grind food.

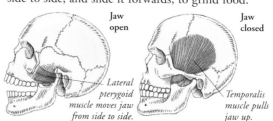

Jaw open

Jaw closed

Lateral pterygoid muscle moves jaw from side to side.

Temporalis muscle pulls jaw up.

Dentistry
In the past, a decaying tooth would have been extracted, but dentists now treat tooth decay by removing affected parts of a tooth, and filling the cavities with hard materials. Artificial crowns can be screwed into a tooth to replace the real thing. Dentists are also concerned with the prevention of tooth and gum disease.

FIND OUT MORE — DIGESTION · FOOD · GROWTH AND DEVELOPMENT · HUMAN BODY · HUMAN EVOLUTION · MEDICINE · MUSCLES AND MOVEMENT · SKELETON · SMELL AND TASTE

TELECOMMUNICATIONS

THE WORLD SEEMS TO BE shrinking thanks to modern telecommunications, which enables us to send messages across the globe in an instant. Telecommunications is the use of technology to send and receive information – such as speech, music, pictures, and documents – over long distances. The devices that make this possible include telephones, radios, satellites, televisions, and computers. The forerunner of modern telecommunications was the telegraph, which sent messages by electrical wires.

Network

Telecommunications devices send information across a network of links that create a pathway between the sender and receiver. The information travels as electrical pulses along copper cables, as flashes of light along optical fibres (thin strands of glass), or as radio or microwave signals between dishes on towers, buildings, and satellites.

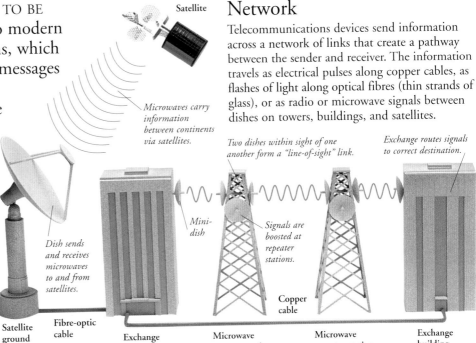

Satellite

Microwaves carry information between continents via satellites.

Two dishes within sight of one another form a "line-of-sight" link.

Exchange routes signals to correct destination.

Dish sends and receives microwaves to and from satellites.

Mini-dish

Signals are boosted at repeater stations.

Copper cable

Satellite ground station

Fibre-optic cable

Exchange building

Microwave repeater station

Microwave repeater station

Exchange building

Samuel Morse

American Samuel Morse (1791–1872) devised a telegraph system that used a type of modulation called Morse code. Letters and numbers represented by dots and dashes were sent along wires as long and short pulses of electricity.

Messaging technology

Until recently, a fax machine was the best way to send a written message quickly. However, e-mailing from a computer now allows all kinds of information to be sent instantly around the world, including large computer files. Text messaging via mobile phones is another new technology that is rapidly evolving.

Screen used to read and manage e-mail account

Control panel

Keypad for dialling numbers

Telephone handset

Telephone/e-mail machine

E-mail

E-mail works by sending images and words down a telephone line over the Internet. Most people e-mail from a computer, but e-mail is also becoming available on other devices, including telephone/e-mail machines, such as the one pictured, mobile phones, and even televisions with a digital connection and a keyboard.

Mini keyboard for typing

Modulation

Telecommunications information must be modulated (coded) in some way before it is sent across a network. Radio and television programmes are broadcast by coding the information into a "carrier" radio wave that is sent through the air to a receiving aerial. The aerial sends an electrical signal to a radio or television set, where it is demodulated.

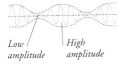

AM carrier wave

Low amplitude *High amplitude*

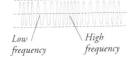

FM carrier wave

Low frequency *High frequency*

Amplitude modulation

In amplitude modulation (AM), the information is carried by changes in the amplitude, or size, of the carrier wave.

Frequency modulation

In frequency modulation (FM), information is represented by changes in the carrier wave's frequency (the number of waves per second).

Fax machine

A fax machine sends and receives facsimiles, or copies, of documents and pictures via the telephone line. The machine scans a document and sends the information down the line as electrical signals. The receiving fax machine decodes the signals and prints a copy of the original document.

Keypad for dialling numbers.

A document is sent down an ordinary telephone line.

Telephone handset

Liquid crystal display

Documents to be sent are fed in here.

Heat-sensitive paper prints documents received from other fax machines.

Telephone/fax machine

Timeline

1793 Frenchman Claude Chappe invents the semaphore, which sends messages using moving arms on towers.

1844 In the USA, Samuel Morse builds the world's first telegraph line.

Early Bell telephone

1876 Scottish-born Alexander Graham Bell invents the telephone.

1878 First telephone exchange opens in New Haven, USA.

1901 Italian inventor Guglielmo Marconi astounds the world by transmitting a radio signal across the Atlantic Ocean, from England to Canada.

1956 Undersea telephone cable installed in Atlantic.

1962 Satellite is first used to make telephone calls.

1977 Optical fibres are used for telephone calls.

1990s E-mail gains mass appeal around the world.

TELEPHONES

"I'LL GIVE YOU A CALL", we often say to our friends, but we rarely wonder how it is that, only a few seconds after entering a number on a keypad, we can be speaking to a friend many kilometres away – even on the other side of the world. A telephone is a device that transforms a person's voice into an electrical signal made up of varying electric currents. This signal travels along copper cables to reach its destination. Sometimes, it is changed into pulses of light and sent along thin glass strands called optical fibres. The signal can also be transmitted as radio waves or microwaves.

Mobile phone

Mobile phones allow the freedom to make calls from almost anywhere because they are not physically connected to the telephone network. They send and receive calls as radio wave signals. Mobile phone technology is fast evolving so that the hand-held devices can now also send text messages, emails and video images, as well as connect to the Internet.

Aerial inside receives radio waves from mobile phone exchange.

Designs have become more compact over the years.

Mobile phone

Text messaging
Mobile phones allow users to send instant text messages to other mobile phones. Pressing specific combinations of buttons converts the numeric keypad into a text keypad for spelling out words.

Videophone
Videophones are telephones that allow users to see each other. A tiny camera captures the image of the caller as a signal. The signal is sent to the receiving phone, where it is decoded to display the caller's face. A videophone can be either a mobile phone or a fixed-line telephone.

Receiving a text message

Alexander Graham Bell
In 1875, the Scottish-born inventor Alexander Graham Bell (1847–1922) made the first successful transmission of the human voice along an electrical wire. The first words he spoke were to his colleague, Thomas Watson. Bell patented the telephone the following year, beating his American rival Elisha Gray (1835–1901) by just two hours.

How telephones work

Once two telephones are linked via the telephone network, the sounds of the speakers' voices are picked up by microphones in the handsets. Loudspeakers reproduce and amplify (boost) these sounds, so that each caller can hear what the other is saying.

Switch hook opens line circuit when handset is down.

Circuit boards contain electronic components.

Keypad

Caller speaks into the mouthpiece.

Handset

Keypad
To make a telephone call, the caller picks up the handset, which switches on an electrical circuit. Pressing the keys on the handset sends a sequence of electrical pulses or different tones to an exchange. Each telephone number has a different sequence, so the exchange can easily route the call to the right number.

Earpiece

Earpiece
The earpiece contains a loudspeaker. When the telephone receives an electrical signal from the network, it causes a diaphragm in the loudspeaker to vibrate and recreate the sound of the person's voice at the other end.

Mouthpiece
Inside the mouthpiece is a microphone that contains a thin plastic disk called a diaphragm. The sound of the caller's voice causes the diaphragm to vibrate. As it vibrates, it generates an electrical signal that passes down the telephone line to the receiving telephone.

Telephone network

Every call reaches its destination via a network of communications links. A local exchange can make connections with any telephone in the caller's area. Long-distance connections are made via national or international exchanges, or even satellites. Cellular exchanges handle the radio signals that carry calls to and from mobile phones.

Telephone network

Satellites provide links between continents.

National or international exchange selects best route for call.

Caller dials number by pressing keypad.

Receiving phone rings when call is connected.

Cellular exchange can connect to mobile phones.

Local exchange can connect call to local numbers or send call to larger exchange.

Exchange
An exchange is a building containing equipment that recognizes dialled pulses and tones. It sends calls to the correct destination, represented by a unique telephone number. This process is called switching and is controlled by powerful computers inside the exchange.

Communications satellites
Long-distance telephone calls are often sent as microwave signals via satellites orbiting above the Earth. The satellite strengthens the signal and sends it back to Earth.

FIND OUT MORE   ELECTRICITY   ELECTROMAGNETISM   ELECTRONICS   LIGHT   SOUND   SOUND RECORDING   TELECOMMUNICATIONS   VIDEO

Telephones

Dials
Development of the telephone
Dials

Metal dial, pre-World War I (1914–18)

Coloured plastic dial from the 1930s

Black dial from 1920s Swiss-designed phone

Speaking and listening cone

Alexander Graham Bell's box telephone, 1876

Lightweight plastic dial, 1963

Alphanumeric dial, 1960s, with both letters and numbers

Phone engineer's dial, 1960s

Mobile phones

Hand-portable phone, mid-1980s: like all mobile phones, it contains a built-in radio transmitter and receiver.

Picking up the earpiece connected caller to the operator.

Hook for second earpiece if hard of hearing.

Early car phone, mid-1980s

Handset

Candlestick phone, 1905: users asked the exchange operator to dial the number they wanted to call.

Caller speaks in here.

Crank handle

Crank handle telephone, 1890s: user turned the crank to contact the operator in order to make a call, and again to tell the operator that the call was finished.

Mobile phones

Dial

Candlestick phone with dial, 1930s, allowed user to call without going through operator.

Flip-phone, late 1980s: this phone's mouthpiece flips down to reveal the keypad.

Hinged mouthpiece

Aerial

Compact mobile phone, mid-1990s

Liquid crystal display

Walnut-effect phone, 1920s, moulded in Bakelite plastic to look like wood.

Coloured phone, 1930s: new plastics allowed different coloured phones.

Compact table phone, 1967, designed for use in the home.

Memory keys

Self-contained keypad phone, 1970s: early models had a separate box for the keypad.

Modern phone, mid-1990s: this phone stores frequently called numbers in its electronic memory.

Novelty telephones

Mickey Mouse phone, 1980, based on the popular Walt Disney character.

Trim phone, 1960s, had a luminous dial and electronic ringer.

Bell housing

Separate-bell telephone, 1977: the long cord allowed the caller to move around while talking.

Earpiece

Bells

Transparent phone, 1950s, showed the internal workings of the phone.

Marble phone, 1984

Mouthpiece

One-piece desk phone, 1970s

Leather-bound phone, 1980s

Snoopy phone, 1980, features the character from the cartoon "Peanuts".

TELESCOPES

THE TINIEST OBJECT in the sky can become clearly visible when viewed through a telescope. An optical telescope forms a magnified image of a distant object by altering the path of light rays using lenses and mirrors. There are two main types of telescope. A refracting telescope forms an image by bending, or refracting, light rays using lenses. A reflecting telescope bounces, or reflects, light rays off mirrors so that they form an image. Powerful telescopes allow astronomers to see incredible distances into space. Radio telescopes form images from radio waves emitted by distant stars and galaxies.

Naked eye image   Telescope image

Bringing things closer
Seen with the naked eye, the Moon looks very small, because it is far away. A telescope can magnify (enlarge) this image, making the Moon seem larger and much closer. A telescope's magnifying power is shown by the symbol "x". A telescope with a magnification of 100x, for example, makes objects seem 100 times larger.

Reflecting telescope

A concave (inward-curving) mirror collects light rays from an object and reflects them on to a flat, angled mirror, which forms an image of the object. A lens (the eyepiece) then magnifies the image for the viewer. Using more than one mirror increases the power of the telescope.

Cutaway of a reflecting telescope

Viewing aperture

Eyepiece lens

Image forms here.

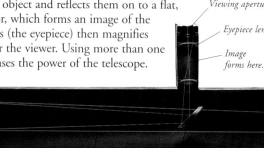

Concave mirror   *Reflected light*   *Flat mirror*   *Light enters here.*

Refracting telescope

As light rays from an object enter the telescope, a convex lens (the objective) bends them to form an upside-down image of the object. A second lens (the eyepiece) bends the rays again, magnifying the image.

Cutaway of a refracting telescope

Viewing aperture   *Eyepiece lens*   *Laser shows path of rays.*   *Objective lens*

Chromatic aberration
Light consists of many different colours. When light from an object passes through a lens, each colour bends at a different angle, creating a spectrum of colours around any image that forms. This is called "chromatic aberration". It can be eliminated by adding another lens.

Galileo's telescope
The Italian scientist Galileo Galilei (1564–1642) was the first to use a telescope to systematically study the night sky. He made many important discoveries about the planets and stars.

Sliding tube for focusing   *Objective lens*

Eyepiece lens   **Galileo's telescope (replica)**

Binoculars
A pair of binoculars consists of two compact refracting telescopes joined together. Each telescope uses two prisms to reflect light rays from the objective lens to the eyepiece lens. The image is focused by adjusting the position of the eyepiece lenses.

Eyepiece lens   *Focusing mechanism*

Prisms "fold up" the path of the light rays, enabling each telescope to be very compact.

Objective lens

Keck telescope
Many large telescopes are built on mountain tops, where the sky is clear and cloudless. The largest optical telescope, the Keck, is on Mauna Kea volcano in Hawaii. Its collecting mirror consists of 36 hexagonal mirrors, totalling 10 m² (108 ft²).

Sliding doors   *Incoming starlight*

Secondary mirror

Third mirror directs light to viewer.

Light reflects between mirrors.

Viewing position

Collecting mirror

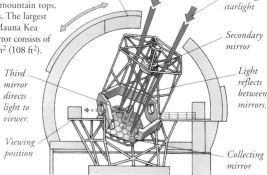

Radio telescope

A radio telescope detects radio waves emitted by stars, galaxies, nebulae, and other astronomical objects. It uses a large dish to focus the waves on to an aerial. The aerial changes the waves into electrical signals, from which a computer generates an image of the object.

Arecibo radio telescope, Puerto Rico

Timeline

10th century The Chinese discover that light rays can be bent by curved pieces of glass.

1608 Dutchman Hans Lippershey invents the telescope.

1673 Englishman Sir Isaac Newton makes a reflecting telescope.

William Herschel's telescope

1789 British astronomer William Herschel designs one of the first large telescopes.

1880 The prism binoculars are invented.

1917 The Mount Wilson telescope is erected in California, USA.

1931 American engineer Karl Jansky discovers that radio waves reach Earth from space.

1937 Grote Reber, an amateur US astronomer, builds the first radio telescope.

1948 The huge Hale reflecting telescope on Mount Palomar, California, USA, is completed.

Hubble Space Telescope

1970 The Very Large Array of radio telescopes is set up in New Mexico, USA.

1990 Launch of the Hubble Space Telescope, an optical telescope orbiting 500 km (310 miles) above the Earth.

2002 Giant telescope with 64 radio dishes planned in Chile.

FIND OUT MORE   ASTRONOMY   GALAXIES   GALILEO GALILEI   LIGHT   MOON   NEWTON, SIR ISAAC   STARS   X-RAYS AND THE ELECTROMAGNETIC SPECTRUM

TELEVISION

TELEVISION WAS ONE OF THE most significant inventions of the 20th century; it completely transformed society. Television (TV) works by converting pictures and sound into signals, and sending them out by transmitters, satellites, or underground cables. Television was first developed in the 1920s; it spread rapidly and by the 1980s, almost every American home had a TV set. By bringing information and entertainment directly into the home, television altered daily life. Today, new advances in television technology, including digital and broadband access, mean that TV can also provide interactive choices such as email, shopping, and information services.

Early television
The first television service began in the UK in 1936. By the 1950s, many families had TV sets, especially in the USA. People who could afford an expensive early receiver wanted to stay at home to be entertained. They were impressed by the up-to-date news coverage and the fact that they could see celebrities in their own homes.

Early TV screens were tiny, and the pictures were black-and-white.

Inside television

A television receiver (TV set) picks up the signals broadcast by a TV station and turns them into images, using a picture tube (known as a cathode-ray tube). The tube produces a series of black-and-white or colour images in rapid succession, creating the illusion that the picture is moving. The set also contains electronic circuits which enable viewers to tune into the channel of their choice.

Widescreen television

Electron guns
The television screen is just one part of the picture tube. Behind the screen, an electron gun fires three beams of electrons (parts of atoms) at the screen. These beams correspond to the three colours used in television – red, blue, and green. Mixed together, they produce full-colour images.

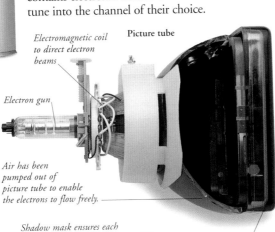

Electromagnetic coil to direct electron beams

Picture tube

Electron gun

Air has been pumped out of picture tube to enable the electrons to flow freely.

Shadow mask ensures each electron beam only strikes one colour of phosphor.

TV screen coated in tiny phosphor dots

Early electron gun

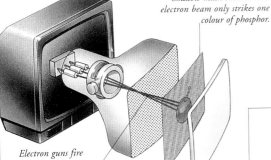

Electron guns fire streams of electrons towards the screen.

Producing a colour picture
The screen is coated with thousands of tiny dots of phosphor. When the electrons hit these dots, they cause them to glow and produce a red, green, or blue image, depending on the kind of phosphor. The strength of each electron beam varies according to the intensity of colour needed. Because 25 to 30 images are produced on screen every second, TV pictures appear to move.

Uses of television

Television broadcasts cover every area, from drama to documentary. TV informs, educates, and entertains us, depending on what we choose to watch. And, with audiences in the millions, information is spread further than ever before.

Millions watch the soccer World Cup live on TV.

Sponsorship
To raise awareness of their products, some companies sponsor television programmes or advertise during commerical breaks. Many TV programmes and events are underpinned by sponsorship money. Popular sports such as football have gained, with some benefits passed on to sports fans, such as funds for safer stadiums.

Current affairs
Thanks to television, we can now watch history as it is made, anywhere in the world, and are better informed than ever before. Satellites beam television signals around the world in seconds. Viewers can watch news events as they happen.

The revolution that overthrew Romanian dictator Nicolae Ceauçescu (1918–89) was shown live on television.

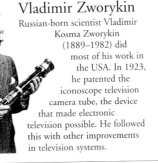

Ernie

Bert

Educational television
Television provides educational programmes for children and adults. Programmes are part of correspondance learning up to university level, being accessible to people in remote areas, or to those with limited time.

Sesame Street is an American programme that helps children learn to read.

Vladimir Zworykin
Russian-born scientist Vladimir Kosma Zworykin (1889–1982) did most of his work in the USA. In 1923, he patented the iconoscope television camera tube, the device that made electronic television possible. He followed this with other improvements in television systems.

Making a news programme

Before a programme appears on your screen, it is carefully produced (planned and put together). News programmes are planned only hours before screening. The news team meets to decide which of the day's stories to include; these are researched and a script is prepared. A news broadcast may also include location reports – stories filmed outside the studio.

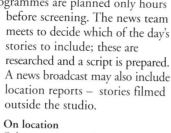

Light, portable video camera

Houses of Parliament, London, UK

Reporter

On location

Only one person is needed to work a video camera, so a reporter and camera operator can easily produce a simple news report on location. The operator is careful to include an identifiable scene in the background.

Original tape

New tape to be broadcast

Editing equipment

Editing suite

An editor gathers together the camera operator's original video tapes and copies the best sections from each on to another tape in the order in which they will be broadcast. This is done in an editing suite, where video recorders, monitor screens, and vision mixers are linked together with a computer.

In the studio

The live news programme *Newsround* is made for younger viewers by the BBC in the UK, and is broadcast five days a week. As with most programmes, it is made inside a TV studio. The presenter stands in front of a highly graphic, brightly lit set, reading the day's news stories from the autocue.

Autocue

The autocue enables the presenter to see the script while looking directly at the camera. A small computer screen just below the camera lens displays the words and reflects them up on to a diagonally-mounted sheet of glass in front of the camera. Although the news reader can see the words, they are invisible to both camera and viewer.

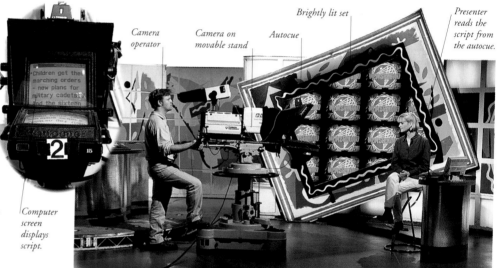

Camera operator

Camera on movable stand

Autocue

Brightly lit set

Presenter reads the script from the autocue.

Computer screen displays script.

The gallery

The gallery (control room) is where the material to make the news broadcast is coordinated during transmission. This includes sequences from the studio cameras, outside broadcasts, music, and graphics. Monitors (video screens) display the different material.

Clock, to check the timing of each part of the programme

Mixing desk, where video, sound, and graphics are mixed together

The rows of buttons on a mixing desk are known as buses and banks.

Mixing desk

Different shots are prepared for transmission by a vision mixer, seated at a computerized mixing desk. The vision mixer combines the different elements, fading, jump-cutting, or blending from one sequence to another.

The team in the studio and gallery talk to each other via microphones.

TV staff

The director and vision mixer sit in the gallery during the live broadcast. The director decides what image should appear on the screen, and for how long. He or she instructs the vision mixer. The producer has overall control.

Timeline

1923 Vladimir Zworykin begins to develop electronic camera tube.

1926 Scottish inventor John Logie Baird (1888–1946) demonstrates his mechanical television system.

1929 Experimental television transmissions begin in England, using Baird's TV system.

1936 World's first regular TV broadcasts begin in England, using electronic system.

1951 First colour broadcasts in US.

1960 Japanese firm Sony introduces all-transistor TV receivers.

1962 Telstar satellite relays television signals across the Atlantic.

1979 Flat-screen pocket television.

1990s Digital and broadband TV.

FIND OUT MORE   ADVERTISING AND MARKETING   CARTOONS AND ANIMATION   DRAMA   ELECTRONICS   INFORMATION TECHNOLOGY   INVENTIONS   RADIO   TELECOMMUNICATIONS

TENNIS AND OTHER RACKET SPORTS

LAWN TENNIS is the most popular and widely played of the racket sports – those in which rackets are used to strike balls of various shapes and sizes across a net or against a wall. Other racket sports are: squash, played in a walled court; badminton, played across a high net; and table tennis, played on a table. Real tennis is an ancient game still played in a few places, and the relatively new sport of racquetball is popular in some parts of the United States.

Server stands sideways on to the net with feet slightly apart.

Racket arm is bent behind the neck as the ball is thrown up.

Eyes on the ball

Racket arm is fully outstretched when hitting the ball.

Server puts power into the serve, using the leg muscles

Serving the ball to start a point

Lawn tennis

In tennis, players hit a ball over a net into the opponent's court so that it cannot be returned. When they win a point they score 15, then 30, 40, and game. A player with six games, two ahead of the opponent, wins a set. Tennis is played as singles with two opponents, or doubles, with opposing pairs.

Real tennis
Real, or royal, tennis was played by French and English royalty in the Middle Ages. The few courts around the world are bounded by open windows and doors and sloping roofs.

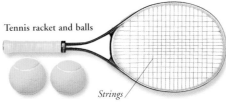

Tennis racket and balls

Strings

Tennis balls
White or yellow, tennis balls are 6.5 cm (2.5 in) across. They weigh about 57 g (2 oz) and must conform to a specific standard. In major tournaments, the balls are changed every nine games.

Tennis racket
The frame of a racket is made of wood, metal, or other material, such as carbon graphite, and must be evenly strung. The racket must be no longer than 81.3 cm (32 in) or wider than 31.75 cm (12.5 in) .

Tennis court

Tennis court
Tennis is played on a court 23.77 m (78 ft) long. It is 10.97 m (36 ft) wide for doubles, and 8.23 m (27 ft) wide for singles.

Andre Agassi
US tennis star Andre Agassi (b.1970) is one of the few players to have won six Grand Slam titles in his career. He also won an Olympic gold medal in 1996. The player has a reputation as a rebel on court due to his loud dress sense.

Squash

Mainly a singles game, squash is played in an enclosed court with four walls. The players use the same floor space. The object is to hit the ball against one or more walls, provided one is the front wall, so that the opponent cannot return it before it has bounced twice on the floor.

Taking a low ball

Squash ball and court
Squash is played with a small hollow ball which becomes more bouncy as the air inside gets warm and expands. The ball must land below the out-of-court line marked all around the court, and must not hit the board at the base of the front wall.

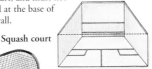

Squash court

Racquetball racket and ball

Racquetball
This game was invented in 1950 in the USA, where it has overtaken squash in popularity. The ceiling is used as well as the walls. As in squash, the ball must always hit the front wall and may bounce only once on the floor.

Badminton

The aim of this game is to hit a feathered shuttlecock over a high net into the opponent's court. The shuttle must be returned before it touches the ground. Matches are usually the best of three games, with a game being won by the first player to reach 11 or 15 points, two ahead of the opponent.

Badminton racket

Shuttlecocks

Badminton equipment
Shuttlecocks may be plastic, but most players prefer to play with shuttles made of a "skirt" of goose feathers fixed in a cork base. Rackets, made mostly of metal or carbon fibre, are extremely light.

Badminton court

Table tennis

Players aim to hit a ball over a net so that the opponent cannot return it. The ball must bounce before being hit. For service, it must bounce on the server's side first. The first player to score 11 points, wins.

Ball

Bat

Table

Table tennis
The small ball is made of light plastic. The blade of the wooden bat may be covered in pimpled rubber on both sides. The net is 15.25 cm (6 in) high. The table measures 2.74 x 1.52 m (9 x 5 ft) and is 76 cm (30 in) high.

FIND OUT MORE

BALL GAMES

HEALTH AND FITNESS

MEDIEVAL EUROPE

OLYMPIC GAMES

SPORT

TEXTILES AND WEAVING

A TEXTILE IS ANY MATERIAL that has been made from fibres, linked together. For thousands of years, all textiles were made from natural fibres, obtained from either animal or plant sources. From the 20th century, chemical processes have produced synthetic (artificial) fibres as well. Most textiles are made by weaving (textile comes from the Latin *texere*, meaning to weave), but they can also be made by knitting, or binding together in various ways. Finished textiles are made into a huge variety of goods, including clothing, furnishings such as curtains and carpets, string, rope, and parachutes.

Jacket, made from oil: mixture of nylon and Pertex® artificial fibres, designed to keep the wearer dry and not too hot.

Nylon rucksack: durable and waterproof

T-shirt: a mix of natural cotton and synthetic polyester fibres; polyester helps the t-shirt keep its shape.

Wool

Wool comes from the fleece of sheep, goats, camels, and llamas. It is popular for making clothes, carpets, and upholstery, as it is warm, strong, stretches, and is absorbent.

Fibres

Natural fibres include wool and silk from animals, and cotton, flax, and hemp from plants. Synthetic fibres, such as polyesters and acrylics, are made from wood, coal, or oil. Each fibre has different qualities; manufacturers may combine two or three kinds, to produce an "ideal" fabric.

Undyed fleece

Spun wool

Woven rug

Main wool producers are Australia, New Zealand, South Africa, and Argentina.

Denim, a tough fabric, is made from woven cotton.

Waterproofed textiles, such as those used in these trainers, have been coated with a thin layer of resin.

Spinneret and cooling nylon filaments

Crude oil

Nylon

Nylon, a synthetic fibre, is made from chemicals found in crude oil. When the chemicals are heated, they form a liquid, which is forced through a spinneret and cooled to form filaments. These are then spun into a yarn.

Making yarn

Before a fibre is made into cloth, it must be spun into yarn (thread). Most natural fibres are very short and must be spun into longer, stronger yarn. Artificial fibres are produced as a continous thread and are spun to make them stronger, rather than longer, or are spun to combine them with natural fibres.

Spinning cotton

Cotton can be spun by hand or by vast factory machines. The machines first squeeze the cleaned fibres together between rollers, into a mat. This is then divided and twisted together into finer and finer threads.

A cotton boll (a clump of fibres) may comprise 500,000 short, white fibres.

Spinning cotton by hand in India

Weaving

Once produced, yarn can be made into cloth. One of the most common means of making cloth is weaving. This is an ancient craft; the earliest evidence of weaving dates from 5000 BC. Most weaving is carried out on a frame called a loom; these can be either massive, machine-powered factory looms, or hand looms.

Mechanized looms in a textile factory

Weaving a rug by hand

Warp threads must be very strong.

Shuttle

Hand loom

The loom

A set of parallel threads, called the warp, are stretched lengthways on the loom. The threads that run widthways are called the weft. The weft is carried over and under the warp by a device called a shuttle. This process interlaces the weft and warp to make fabric.

Textile industry

Until the 18th century, weaving was a craft practised in the home on a small scale. The advances in technology made during the Industrial Revolution massively increased the amount a weaver could produce. Mechanical looms now produce thousands of metres of fabric in a day.

FIND OUT MORE   AUSTRALIA   CHEMISTRY   CLOTHES AND FASHION   DYES AND PAINTS   FARMING   FURNITURE   INDUSTRIAL REVOLUTION   OIL   SHEEP AND GOATS   TRADE AND INDUSTRY

THAILAND AND BURMA

LYING SIDE BY SIDE in the west of mainland Southeast Asia, Thailand and Burma (also known as Myanmar) resemble each other in many ways. Both countries have mountains and forests in the north, fertile river valleys, similar mineral resources, and a shared religion – Buddhism. However, their governments and economies differ greatly. Thailand is a wealthy, democratic monarchy; Burma is isolated and undeveloped, with a poor human rights record.

Physical features

The densely forested mountains in the north of Thailand and Burma give rise to many rivers, such as the Chao Phraya and the Irrawaddy, that cut through the fertile countryside on their way to the coast. The western coast on the Andaman Sea is dotted with many islands.

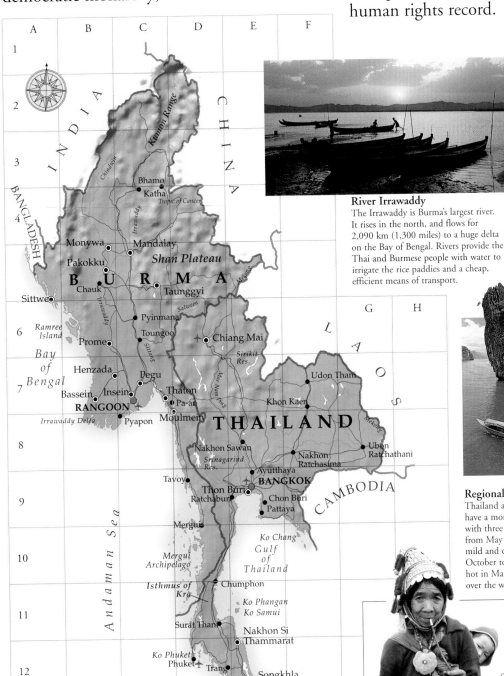

River Irrawaddy
The Irrawaddy is Burma's largest river. It rises in the north, and flows for 2,090 km (1,300 miles) to a huge delta on the Bay of Bengal. Rivers provide the Thai and Burmese people with water to irrigate the rice paddies and a cheap, efficient means of transport.

Monsoon rainforest
The border between Burma and Thailand is covered in thick, impenetrable monsoon rainforest. In the 1980s, the destruction of large areas of forest to provide timber, especially teak, for export led to serious flooding. As a result, in 1989, the Thai government banned logging.

Andaman Sea
To the west of the narrow strip of Burmese land at the top of the Malay Peninsula lies the Andaman Sea, which is part of the Indian Ocean. It is bordered by mangrove swamps, which help to prevent coastline erosion. Dotted with hundreds of tiny, remote islands, this area is a growing tourist attraction.

Regional climate
Thailand and Burma have a monsoon climate with three seasons: rainy from May to September, mild and dry from October to February, and hot in March and April. In the south, rainfall is spread over the whole year. The average temperatures are high.

27°C (80°F)   25°C (77°F)

2,008 mm (79 in)

Hill tribes

The mountainous and largely forested region where Thailand, Burma, and Laos meet is known as the Golden Triangle. Here, poor hill tribes live in villages, farming small plots of land, that have been cleared of trees using the "slash-and-burn" technique. They also cultivate opium poppies, which are used to make heroin and other drugs for the illegal drug trade.

Akha tribeswoman with opium pipe

Thailand

Bordered by Burma, Laos, Cambodia, and Malaysia, the kingdom of Thailand, once called Siam, was established in the 13th century, and the country has remained independent for much of its history. It was the only country in mainland Southeast Asia never to be colonized. Its name in the Thai language is Muang Thai, meaning "land of the free". Modern Thailand has one of the world's fastest growing economies, although there is still great poverty in rural areas, where 80 per cent of the people live. Bangkok, the capital and only big city, is very overcrowded.

Ethnic Thais
Most Thais are descended from people who began migrating south from China nearly 2,000 years ago. As a nation, they are traditional Buddhists. About 12 per cent of the population are ethnic Chinese.

King of Thailand
Thailand's ninth king, Bhumibol Adulyadej, came to the throne in 1946. His family, the Chakris, have ruled Thailand since 1782. The king has immense personal prestige and criticism of him is frowned upon.

Rice
About a quarter of Thailand is used for farming, mostly for growing rice in the fertile river valleys. Every year, 19,440,000 tonnes (21,488906 tons) are produced. Rice is the basis of all main meals, usually accompanied by at least five other dishes, flavoured with fish sauce and coriander.

Industry
Although only 15 per cent of Thai workers are employed in industry, manufacturing is increasingly important. In recent years, American and Japanese companies have set up factories in Thailand, which is now a leading producer of electronic goods. Other manufactures include rubber and jute products. Thai mines produce tin, other metals, and precious stones.

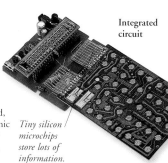
Integrated circuit
Tiny silicon microchips store lots of information.

Tourism
Thailand's ornate Buddhist temples and cultural heritage draw thousands of tourists every year. New golf courses are being built to attract Japanese visitors, and the northern hill villages, island resorts, and unspoilt beaches are also popular with holidaymakers.

Crops
More than half of Thailand's workers are employed in farming. Important crops include cassava, which is the source of tapioca, sugar-cane, and pineapples. Thailand is the world's biggest exporter of canned pineapple, and a leading producer of natural rubber. Thais also grow bananas, coconuts, jute, and cotton.

Pineapple
Cassava

Sugar-cane

Bangkok
Thailand's capital was originally built on a network of canals many of which are still used for transporting goods. For a city of over six million people, Bangkok has relatively few major roads and limited public transport, giving it the world's worst traffic jams. Many commuters equip their cars as offices, with phone and fax, so they can work on the move.

Floating market on a Bangkok canal

Burma

When Burma became independent in 1948, it adopted a policy of political and economic isolation that reduced this once wealthy nation to one of the poorest on Earth. Revolts by hill peoples, and a military government have kept out foreign influences.

Fishing
Fish served with vegetables form an important part of the Burmese diet. Shrimps and saltwater fish are caught off the coast. To harvest the freshwater fish that abound in the rivers, people build fishing huts on stilts over the water.

Teak logging
In 1990, Burma had about 70 per cent of the total world reserves of teak. Selective logging of teak using elephants is now seldom practised, and today vast areas are cleared by machine. Deforestation has caused erosion, and replanting is rare.

Rubies
The rubies mined in the northeast of Burma are considered to be the world's finest, prized for their glowing, deep red colour. Burma is also rich in silver, copper, jade, lead, zinc, and tin, and has extensive reserves of natural gas and oil.

 FIND OUT MORE — ASIA, HISTORY OF · BUDDHISM · CONSERVATION · CRYSTALS AND GEMS · GOVERNMENTS AND POLITICS · RAINFOREST WILDLIFE · ROCKS AND MINERALS · TRADE AND INDUSTRY · WINDS

THEATRES

THROUGHOUT THE AGES, theatres have provided two essentials: somewhere for performers to act, and a place for an audience to watch them. A theatre may be a purpose-built environment, such as the Paris Opera House, or it may be as simple as an open-air stage. Either way, theatres provide the setting for performances of all kinds, from plays to opera, and from puppet shows to dance. Most modern theatres have a huge pool of workers including craft workers, prop-makers, set designers, scene painters, make-up artists, and costumiers, as well as the actors themselves.

Roman amphitheatre

History of theatres

The earliest surviving theatres were ancient Greek open-air amphitheatres, in which audiences sat in a semicircle around a pillared stage. The Romans copied the Greek design, but from then until the Renaissance, theatres tended to be a temporary wooden stage.

The rich sat in the galleries; the poor stood in the courtyard.

Theatres through the ages

During the Renaisssance, theatres were once again permanent structures, but with simple interiors. The playwright Shakespeare's theatre, the Globe in London, had three enclosed galleries, but retained an open-air courtyard.

Modern theatres

During the 19th century, theatres became very ornate, but they simplified in design during the 20th century. Today, theatres, such as the National in London, are often housed in complexes, which also contain venues, such as cinemas.

Globe Theatre, UK

National Theatre, UK

Features

In the 1800s, drama became more realistic, with elaborate scene changes. Theatre structure reflected its functions. There were four main features in every theatre: stage, backstage, front of house, and auditorium.

Lighting grid

Central dome is supported by iron girders.

Auditorium has five tiers and seats 2,000 people.

Stage and orchestra pit

The Paris Opera House (built 1862–75) covers 1.2 hectares (3 acres) and was designed by Charles Garnier. The stage is 53 m (175 ft) wide and 26 m (85 ft) deep. It slopes upwards towards the back to let the audience see the action more clearly. The orchestra pit, where the musicians play, is located beneath the front of the stage.

Backstage area contains the "green room" where performers wait for their cue.

Grand foyer features a mosaic ceiling.

Garnier Opera House, Paris, France

Fly tower, with pulley system, hoists heavy pieces of scenery.

Below-stage scenery store

Stage at the Paris Opera House can hold up to 400 people.

Grand staircase

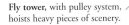

Front of house

The audience enters through an area known as front of house. This provides a space for people to meet before going into the performance, and also houses the box office where tickets are sold. The front of house of the Paris Opera House is one of the world's grandest. It includes a staircase (usual in theatres because seating is on different levels) and balconies, where 19th-century society's opera-goers could be seen arriving, as was the fashion.

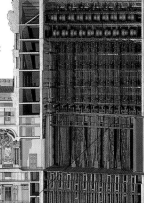

Grand staircase, Paris Opera House, France

Auditorium

The auditorium, such as that at London's Theatre Royal Haymarket, contains seating on different levels: stalls, tiered "circles" of seats, and private boxes. The stalls have the best view of the stage; they and the private boxes contain the most expensive seats. The dress circle above the stalls, and the upper circle above that, have cheaper seats. The upper circle (sometimes known as "the gods") has the poorest view.

Theatre Royal, Haymarket, London, UK

Production

Bill Alexander,
theatre director

Many people are involved in the production of a play – director, actors, designers, make-up, stage managers, lighting, and sound engineers. Rehearsals (meetings held to work out the production) may run over weeks, and end in a full dress rehearsal before the play is performed.

Director

The director interprets the play and "directs" the action. He or she works with the actors to decide how they should play the characters and speak the lines. The actors read through the script and learn the words. They write notes on their copies concerning movements, cues, and props.

Make-up

Under bright theatre lights, unmade-up faces look pale and flat. Make-up is therefore an essential part of theatre. It defines the performers' facial features, and brings characters to life.

Transformation

Theatrical make-up can be used to change the appearance of a face, for example, making actors look older than they really are. Another use of make-up is to produce an obviously unrealistic effect, such as the white face traditionally worn by clowns.

Black and white make-up and red-rimmed eyes give the actor a haggard look.

A stick-on grey beard immediately makes the actor appear older.

Final touches ensure that the make-up stays on under the hot lights.

Kabuki

Kabuki is a traditional theatrical form in Japan. In Kabuki, the all-male cast wears make-up according to 17th century rules, which have remained virtually unchanged. Each character has mask-like make-up, which identifies them to the audience.

Kabuki actor, Uzaemo Ichimura

Orson Welles

The American actor, director, and filmmaker Orson Welles (1915–85) is best known for his classic film *Citizen Kane* (1941). However, his theatre career established him as the leading director of his day. One of his first productions was a version of *Macbeth* (1936), which used an entirely black cast – the first time ever this was done.

Props

Articles used on stage, which are not costume or scenery, are known as properties or "props". Props may be varied, and are the responsibility of the stage manager, who looks after them between performances and makes sure they are left out – often on tables – backstage, where the performers can find them quickly when they are needed.

Audiences cannot see wear and tear.

Papier maché crown

Original 1920s telephone

Simple fastening

Plastic jam

Iron ball and chain

Jam dish

Lighting

Direct lighting creates dramatic shadows and builds atmosphere; spotlights pick out individuals. Multiple lighting produces a "natural" effect and allows parts of the stage to be dimmed or lit more brightly if necessary. There are special technical rehearsals for lighting.

Spotlight highlights individual performers.

Bank of lights

Production of *Jesus Christ, Superstar*

Costumes and sets

Most theatre productions need historical costumes and stage sets. Theatres usually employ a person in wardrobe. He or she takes care of the costumes and helps the performers change between acts.

Ruff, a 16th-century fashion

Velvet hat

Hat with feathers

Bright colours

Braiding

Leather shoes

Elizabethan man's costume

Original handmade shoes

1940s woman's costume

Stage model, *Dream King*

Set designers

Set designers design and create the stage set. First they construct a model. When this is approved, they work with scene painters and carpenters to make the set.

FIND OUT **MORE**

DRAMA · ELIZABETH I · FILM · GREECE, ANCIENT · JAPAN, HISTORY OF · OPERA · RENAISSANCE · ROMAN EMPIRE · SHAKESPEARE, WILLIAM

TIME

TIME IS LIKE A flowing river, carrying us steadily from the past, which we know, towards the future, which we cannot know. Although we are unable to control time, we can record its passing using measuring devices such as clocks and watches, and calendars that help us to organize and plan our lives. However, time is not constant, and in certain situations it can even slow down. Some scientists think that time may even come to a stop inside black holes in deepest space.

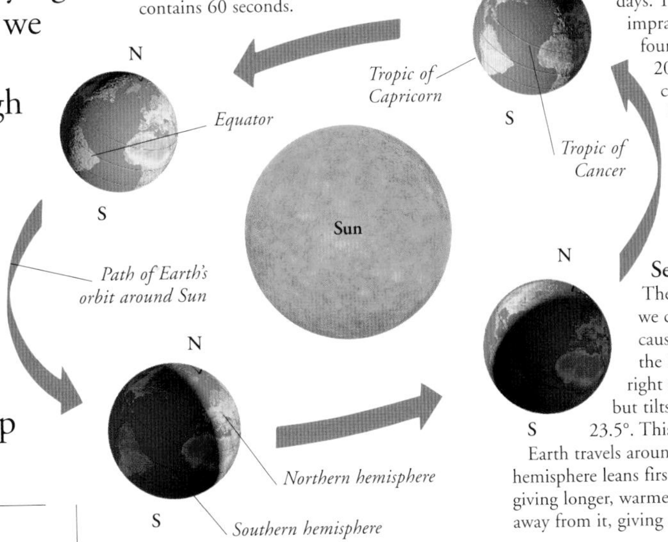

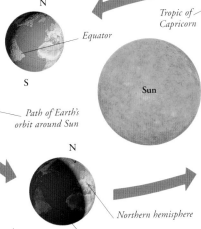

Day
One full day is the time it takes for the Earth to spin once on its axis. Each day contains 24 hours, each hour is made up of 60 minutes, and each minute contains 60 seconds.

Equator

Tropic of Capricorn

Tropic of Cancer

Sun

Path of Earth's orbit around Sun

Northern hemisphere

Southern hemisphere

Earth's axis

Year
A year is 365 days long. This is based on the time it takes for the Earth to orbit the Sun, which is 365 1/4 days. The 1/4 day is impractical, so every four years – except 2000 and other century years – the 1/4 days are added together to make up one extra day, giving a "leap" year of 366 days.

Seasons
The phases of weather we call seasons are caused by the fact that the Earth's axis is not at right angles to the Sun, but tilts at an angle of 23.5°. This means that, as the Earth travels around the Sun, each hemisphere leans first towards the Sun, giving longer, warmer days, and then away from it, giving shorter, colder days.

Time in modern physics

Scientists had to revise their ideas about the nature of time when the German physicist Albert Einstein (1879–1955) published his theories of relativity. The theories showed that time slows down for objects travelling close to the speed of light. Research has shown that this is true even for slower-moving objects: astronauts who spend a year in orbit age by one-hundredth of a second less than people on Earth.

Astronauts in space

Glass shatters into tiny fragments.

Time's arrow
How can we be sure that time does not go backwards? The proof lies in the increasing disorder of the Universe. For example, when a glass smashes, its orderly arrangement breaks into disordered fragments. Broken glass never reassembles itself, proving that time can move only forwards, from the present to the future.

Time on Earth

The passage of time on Earth is measured in terms of the motion of the Earth and the Moon. The rotating Earth turns us towards the Sun, giving day, and then away from the Sun, giving night. Day and night are of equal length during the equinoxes – the two occasions in the year when the Sun is directly overhead at the equator. At the two solstices, when the Sun is directly overhead at one of the tropics, one hemisphere has its longest day, while the other has its longest night.

Moon

Earth

Months
There are 12 months in a year. Months last between 28 and 31 days. They were originally based on the time it takes for the Moon to go through all its phases as it orbits the Earth, which is 29½ days.

Calendars
The Western world uses the 365-day Gregorian calendar. This is based on the Earth's orbit of the Sun, so the Sun appears in the same place in the sky on the same date each year. Many other calendars have been devised throughout history. The traditional Hindu, Chinese, Muslim, and Jewish calendars are based on the Moon's cycles. The Chinese calendar has 12 months and is 354 days long. The ancient Aztec calendar was solar, like the Gregorian calendar, but consisted of 18 months of 20 days, and five extra days that were considered unlucky.

Each year is named after an animal.

Chinese calendar

Aztec calendar

At the centre of the calendar is the Aztec Sun god.

Time and speed

To understand how fast an object moves, we need to know how far it travels and how long it takes to travel that distance. The graph below shows the relationship between distance and time for a car journey: the steeper the graph's slope, the faster the car is moving.

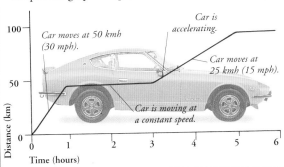

Car moves at 50 kmh (30 mph).
Car is accelerating.
Car moves at 25 kmh (15 mph).
Car is moving at a constant speed.

Distance (km) / Time (hours)

Time zones

The world is divided into 24 regions called time zones, each of which is about 15° of longitude wide. These time zones ensure that wherever you are in the world, when the Sun is directly overhead it will be 12 noon. The coloured areas and numbers on this map show how many hours each time zone is ahead or behind Greenwich Mean Time (GMT).

Early time measurement

To tell the time, ancient peoples used the changing shadows cast by the Sun as it moved across the sky during the day, and the movement of stars at night. Later, time-keeping devices, such as sundials, sand clocks, clock candles, and star dials, were developed. The invention of mechanical clocks made these methods redundant.

Sundials
As the day progressed, a shadow cast by the Sun moved slowly around a dial marked with hours.

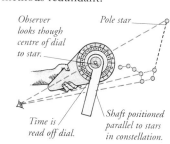

Observer looks though centre of dial to star.
Pole star
Time is read off dial.
Shaft positioned parallel to stars in constellation.

Clock candle
A candle ringed with notches recorded the passing of the hours as it burned down.

Star dial
A device called a star dial was used to find the time from the position of familiar stars and constellations in the night sky.

Sand clock
Sand flowed from the top of the glass to the bottom in a fixed amount of time.

Quartz watch

Most modern clocks and watches are controlled by a thin slice of quartz crystal. Electricity supplied by a small battery makes the crystal vibrate and give out pulses of current at a precise rate, or frequency. A microchip then reduces this rate to one pulse per second. This control signal goes to an electric motor that turns the hands or changes the numbers on the digital display. Most quartz clocks and watches are accurate to within about 15 seconds per year.

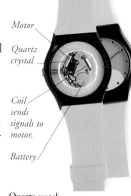

Motor
Quartz crystal
Coil sends signals to motor.
Battery

Quartz watch

Clock weighs about 30 kg (66 lb).

Caesium clock

Atomic clock
The most accurate of all clocks are atomic clocks, which will lose or gain just one second every 300,000 years. Atomic clocks measure time by recording the natural vibrations of atoms, usually of the element caesium. The second – the basic scientific unit of time – is defined as the time it takes for a caesium atom to vibrate 9,192,770 times.

Mechanical clocks and watches

Early all-mechanical clocks were made in European monasteries and cathedrals in the 13th century. They were powered by falling weights linked to a mechanism called an escapement. Clocks became more accurate when pendulums were used to regulate the escapement. The invention of the mainspring made smaller clocks possible and led to the development of the watch. Early watches were worn around the neck on a chain. Later designs were small enough to fit into a pocket or be worn around the wrist on a strap.

Hour hand
Hours in Roman numerals
Minute hand

Clock face
There are 12 hours marked on a clock face. This means that the hour hand moves around the clock face twice each day. The minute hand revolves once every hour. Many clocks also have a second hand that circles the clock face once every minute.

Falling weight drives the clock mechanism.

This weight acts as a counter-balance.

Anchor
Escape wheel
Pendulum
Weight

Pendulum
A pendulum is a weight that swings back and forth on a fixed string, rod, or wire. Each back-and-forth movement takes the same amount of time, and it is this regular motion that makes it useful for time-keeping. In a clock, a pendulum controls the escapement.

Each to-and-fro swing is called a period.

Escapement
Many pendulum clocks are driven by a falling weight linked to an escape wheel. As the pendulum swings, it rocks a lever called the anchor, causing it to grip and release the escape wheel with a regular motion. One tooth of the wheel escapes with each swing, moving the clock's hands on a little.

Mainspring
In the 16th century, springs began to replace falling weights as the energy source for clocks. The energy stored by winding the spring up with a key is then slowly released by the escapement to drive the hands.

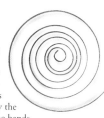

Twenty-four-hour clock
Transport timetables give arrival and departure times using the twenty-four-hour clock. In this system, midnight is 0000 and noon is 1200. Times after noon are given as numbers greater than 1200. For example, 4:00 pm is 1600.

Christiaan Huygens

Dutch physicist Christiaan Huygens (1629–95) built the first practical pendulum clock in 1657, and also found the mathematical rule that links the duration of a pendulum's swing to its length: the longer the pendulum, the longer its swing. Huygens gave an accurate description of Saturn's rings and was first to suggest that light travels as waves.

Timeline

c.2600 BC The Chinese develop a primitive form of sundial.

c.1400 BC The Egyptians use water clocks, which measure time by the flow of water through a vessel with a hole in it.

c.890 Clock candles appear in England.

c.1300 Mechanical clocks are built in Italian and English monasteries.

1581 Italian scientist Galileo Galilei observes the regularity of a pendulum's swing.

Chinese water clock

Pendulum clock designed by Galileo

1657 Huygens builds the first pendulum clock.

1759 Englishman John Harrison makes a marine timekeeper, or chronometer, that has less than one minute of error after five months at sea.

Harrison's chronometer

1884 The time at Greenwich, London, UK, is adopted as the standard time for the whole world.

1905 Einstein's Special Theory of Relativity gives a new understanding of the concept of time.

1929 Warren Morrison, an American, invents the quartz clock.

1948 The atomic clock is developed in the USA.

1965 US physicists Arno Penzias and Robert Wilson provide evidence that time began with the Big Bang.

 FIND OUT MORE   ATOMS AND MOLECULES   AZTECS   BLACK HOLES   CHINA, HISTORY OF   CRYSTALS AND GEMS   EINSTEIN, ALBERT   FORCE AND MOTION   GALILEO GALILEI   PHYSICS   SUN AND SOLAR SYSTEM

Time

Early time pieces

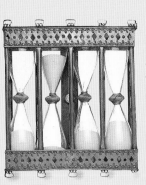

Sandglass marks time by sand flowing between two glass bulbs.

Gnomon (pointer)

Weights fall at regular intervals.

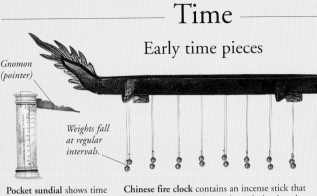

Pocket sundial shows time by gnomon's shadow.

Chinese fire clock contains an incense stick that releases weights as it burns through the threads.

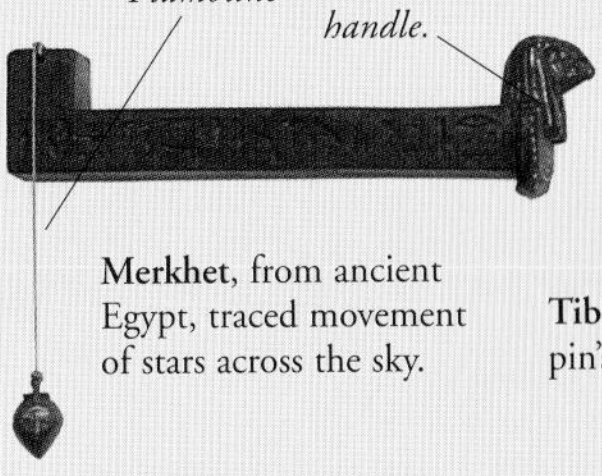

Plumbline

Ornamental handle.

Holes for pin

Position of pin was changed according to time of year.

Merkhet, from ancient Egypt, traced movement of stars across the sky.

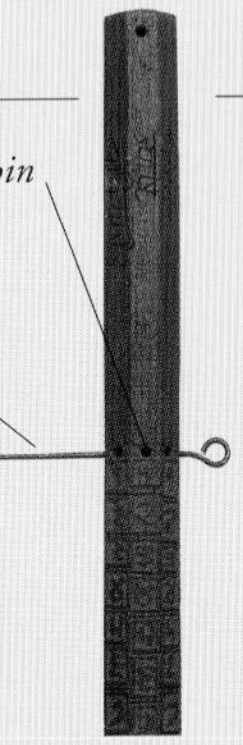

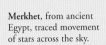

Tibetan timestick used pin's shadow to tell time.

Historical clocks and watches

Carrying handle

Watch could be hung from a chain attached to a button-hole.

Dials regulate mechanism and striking of the hour.

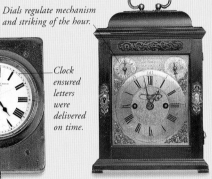

Clock ensured letters were delivered on time.

Carriage clocks were portable clocks used by travellers.

Pocket watch, 18th century

Mail clock, 19th century, for keeping time on mail trains.

Bracket clock, 17th century, stood on table or mantlepiece.

Swinging pendulum bob

Falling weight drives hands.

Bird emerges with cry of "cuckoo!" every hour.

Wooden case gave clock a loud "tick-tock" sound.

Clock regulated by moving small weights along a bar.

Outer dial shows minutes.

Verge watch, driven by a coiled spring

Pendulum clocks were controlled by the swing of a suspended weight.

Cuckoo clocks were invented in Germany around 1730.

Grandfather clocks housed pendulum in a long case.

Lantern clocks were named after their lantern-like shape.

Japanese ornamental clock, made out of the gemstone turquoise.

Modern clocks and watches

Braille watch used by people who are blind or partially sighted.

Dial shows diver's time under water.

Friendly panda

Talking watch speaks the time to the wearer.

Start/stop control

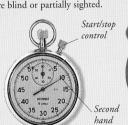

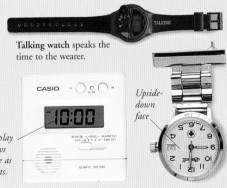

Second hand

Rubber strap

Display shows time as digits.

Upside-down face

Stopwatch can measure time in fractions of a second.

Mechanical alarm clock rings bells at pre-set time.

Waterproof watch for use by divers

Child's clock has large hands and clear numbers.

Digital alarm clock controlled by a tiny quartz crystal

Nurse's watch hangs from nurse's uniform.

TRADE AND INDUSTRY

ANY SORT OF ACTIVITY that is done to create wealth is known as industry. The term also describes a group of businesses that produce a similar service or provide a similar product. Trade is the process of buying and selling such products. The thousands of different industries do many things, such as mining, advertising, construction, farming, and broadcasting. Many industries change raw materials into products. Others provide services, from haircuts to health care.

Coal is an important fuel in industry; most of the world's supply is mined in Asia.

Primary industry
Coal, oil, stone, cereal crops, and timber are among the products of primary industry, which is concerned with extracting raw materials from the Earth. Such products may be used just as they are, or processed by the manufacturing industries into something else.

Service industries include restaurants, shops, and tourist businesses.

Types of industry
When most people talk about industry, they are thinking of the factories and assembly lines involved in manufacturing. In fact, there are three basic types of industry: primary, manufacturing, and service industries. In the developing countries, most people work in primary industry. Any country where most people work in the manufacturing and service industries is known as an industrialized nation.

Car manufacture

Manufacturing
The manufacturing, or secondary, industries make products either from raw materials or from other manufactured goods. Much modern manufacturing is heavily automated: machines carry out the heavy, repetitive tasks.

Service
The service, or tertiary, industries do not produce anything, but offer a service, such as banking. In some highly industrialized countries, more people work in service industries than in either of the other industries.

Restaurant in Paris

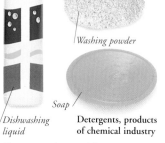

Washing powder

Soap

Dishwashing liquid

Detergents, products of chemical industry

What industry needs
In order for an industry to produce anything, it must have certain basic assets: money, machinery, labour, and raw materials. The aim of any industry is to make a profit. If the basic assets are abundant and inexpensive, then the industry produces a more profitable product or service. An industry also needs a market: if nobody wants to buy a product, the money and effort spent in making it is wasted.

Violin maker

Cottage industry
Cottage industry is where workers produce goods on a small scale, generally in the home or a small workshop. The workers may sell the goods themselves, or to an employer who pays per finished piece. The system may be abused by unscrupulous employers, who pay low rates for long hours.

Energy and materials
Both the primary and manufacturing industries must have materials to work with, and fuels and energy to power machines. In some countries, large industrialized regions, such as the Ruhr in Germany, develop near areas of raw materials, such as coal or iron ore.

Coal mines

Oil

Steel

Timber

Raw materials and fuels

The service industries depend most heavily on labour.

Stages in production
In the manufacturing industry, most products go through basic stages before they can be sold to the public. Once the product is designed, the design is checked to ensure that the product works and is affordable. The product is made from raw materials; finally, it is tested, to make sure there are no faults.

Product designs

Factory

Factory premises

Capital
Capital means money, which industries need to buy machinery, pay staff, and build or rent a factory or other premises. It also means the equipment that will help to manufacture a product over a period of time. Machines are regarded as capital, but the raw materials from which products are made are not.

Labour
Many industries are set up close to cities, so they can have a ready supply of workers, or labour. The labour supply must include management, accountants, and research and development staff among others, plus manual workers.

Communications
Good communications are vital for the growth of industry. Efficient road systems, railways, air and sea routes, and global telecommunications allow some industries to make their goods in parts of the world where property prices and wages are lower.

Trade

The process of exchanging the goods or services produced by industry is known as trade. It is a vital part of modern life. Even the richest nations do not have the resources to produce everything their people need or want; by trading surplus goods with others, countries earn the money to buy the things they need. Trade between different countries is called foreign trade. So-called domestic trade takes place within the boundaries of a country.

Market traders, 15th century

History of trade
Trade has an ancient history. From about 3000 BC, the Phoenicians traded metals, cloth, and animals with Mediterranean peoples. From 300 BC, traders travelled the Silk Road from China to Europe, a famous early trade route. Trade between different peoples led to the exchange of ideas and culture, as well as goods. Trade between different countries grew steadily from medieval times on, when merchants travelled the globe with goods.

Distribution

The movement of goods or services from the manufacturer to the consumer (the person who wants to buy them) is known as distribution. Distribution between producer, wholesaler, and retailer relies on efficient, economical transport systems. International trade has grown steadily, partly thanks to advances in transportation – for example, the arrival of the railways, air freight, and refrigerated cargo ships.

Refrigerated warehouse

Wholesalers
Many small shops rely on wholesalers to deliver products to them when needed. A wholesaler is a business that buys large quantities of goods directly from the manufacturers. It stores them in huge warehouses, ready to sell in smaller amounts at higher prices to retail outlets, or shops. Warehouses are found near major roads or railways, to ensure rapid, economical transport of the products.

Retailers
Retailers are businesses that buy products from wholesalers and sell them at a higher price. Most high-street shops are part of the retail trade – a place where consumers can buy the goods they want. As such, shops are the end of a long chain of trading.

Buying jeans from a shop

Imports and exports

The goods or services one country buys from another are called imports; the goods a country sells to others are called exports. To earn the money to pay for imports, a country must export its own produce.

Imports
Exports
Goods coming in
Goods going out

Balance of payments
The payments a country makes to others for imported goods, and the payments it receives from other countries for exports within the same period of time, are together known as the balance of payments. If a country does not export enough goods, it must borrow money to pay for imports.

Tariffs and customs

Some countries tax imported goods. This tax is known as a customs duty, or tariff. Such duties are a way of making money for the government, or of protecting the country's industries by raising the price of imported goods, which might otherwise be cheaper than those produced locally.

World Trade Organization building

World trade
International trade is regulated by the World Trade Organization, set up in 1995. It works to reduce trade barriers and tariffs between nations. It succeeded the General Agreement on Tariffs and Trade (GATT), set up in 1948 under the auspices of the United Nations.

Factory chimneys

Industrial pollution

Industry provides us with clothing, food, shelter, labour-saving devices, and medicines. But it has harmful side effects. Many industrial processes cause pollution in the form of smoke from factories, and waste products dumped in the sea, rivers, and lakes. The rapid growth of industry threatens to exhaust the world's supplies of oil and natural gas.

Werner von Siemens

German engineer Werner von Siemens (1816–92) helped the growth of the communications industry, by his improvements to the telegraph. The electrical manufacturer AG Siemens, which trades in more than 125 countries, evolved from a company originally established by the Siemens family.

Timeline

c.3000 BC Phoenicians trade with other countries around the Mediterranean.

c.1500 Commercial Revolution begins; merchants start trading around the globe.

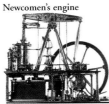
Newcomen's engine

1705 English inventor Thomas Newcomen (1663–1729) builds a simple steam engine that contributes to the 18th-century Industrial Revolution in Great Britain.

1871 Trade Union Act makes trade unions legal in Britain.

1913 US industrialist Henry Ford (1863–1947) introduces assembly-line procedures to produce his Model-T cars, stimulating mass-production.

20th century Transport and communications developments spur growth of foreign trade.

Model-T

1968 The European Economic Community (EEC) abandons trade tariffs between member nations, establishing a "Common Market".

1990s USA, Japan, and European nations are the world's major traders.

FIND OUT MORE
ADVERTISING AND MARKETING · FARMING · FISHING INDUSTRY · INDUSTRIAL REVOLUTION · MONEY · POLLUTION · PORTS AND WATERWAYS · SHOPS · TRANSPORT, HISTORY OF · UNIONS, TRADE

TRAINS AND RAILWAYS

WHEN YOU SEE a sleek express train whizzing by, you may find it hard to believe that the first railways were iron tracks with wooden wagons pulled by horses. The first steam railways were opened in the 1820s, allowing people and goods to travel at undreamed-of speeds. The new form of transport spread rapidly across the world. Today's trains are a very efficient method of transport – they use less fuel and produce less pollution than cars and trucks, and carry much larger cargos. Many people believe trains are the best form of transport for the future.

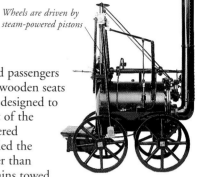

Wheels are driven by steam-powered pistons

"Catch Me Who Can", built in 1808

Early trains

The first train provided passengers with a bumpy ride on wooden seats in open goods wagons designed to carry coal. At the front of the train was a steam-powered locomotive, which pulled the wagons not much faster than walking pace. Some trains towed wagons onto which the passengers attached their own carriages.

Modern trains

Electricity and engines powered by diesel make modern trains move. In an electric locomotive, electric motors turn the wheels. The electricity comes from the track or from overhead cables. In a diesel-electric locomotive, a powerful diesel engine turns an electric generator. This creates electricity, which in turn drives electric motors. Modern carriages give a smooth, comfortable ride and are air-conditioned. They have automatic locking doors for the safety of their passengers.

Bullet train

Japanese Shinkansen, or "bullet" trains, travel along specially built high-speed tracks. They average speeds up to 225 kmh (140 mph). Other countries have also opened new lines designed for high-speed electric trains, including France, where the TGV train holds the world speed record of more than 500 kmh (310 mph).

Electric locomotive gets its electricity via a catenary (overhead cable system).

Bullet trains first ran in 1965.

Tracks

Overhead cables for electric locomotives

Gantries support cables and signals.

Points are intersections in the rails that move trains onto a new section of track.

Railway tracks have two parallel steel rails supported on wood or concrete sleepers which spread the weight of passing trains into the ground. Rails are often welded into a continuous track to allow trains to run smoothly. Points direct trains left or right on to diverging tracks. Most railways have different tracks for opposite directions.

Signals keep trains a safe distance apart.

George Stephenson

British railway engineer George Stephenson (1781–1848) established his locomotive works in 1823 and built the very first public railway, from Stockton to Darlington, England, in 1825. He also built many steam locomotives, working with his son Robert.

Trams

Many cities, especially in Europe, have a tram system. Trams run on railway tracks laid in the streets. They are usually powered by electricity from overhead wires.

Hong Kong trams

Double-decker trams have been running through the streets of Hong Kong for many decades. They provide a clean form of transport that is needed in a crowded city. Trams were taken out of some cities in the mid-20th century, but efficient new tram systems are now being built in their place.

Types of train

A train consists of locomotives and rolling stock (carriages and goods wagons for freight). Commuter trains and local trains, which make many stops and starts, often have combined locomotives and carriages, called multiple units. Sleeper trains travel long distances and have bunk beds for passengers.

Passenger express

Express trains usually have a separate locomotive at the front. The rolling stock often includes a buffet car for snacks and drinks and a dining car, as well as normal carriages with seats. Some high-speed trains have a locomotive at each end.

Goods train

A long goods train can have hundreds of trucks, and sometimes more than one locomotive. Some trucks are designed to hold specific cargoes, such as oil tankers.

FIND OUT MORE

CARS AND TRUCKS   ENERGY   ENGINES AND MOTORS   FORCE AND MOTION   INDUSTRIAL REVOLUTION   TRANSPORT, HISTORY OF   TRAVEL

TRANSPORT, HISTORY OF

FROM SIMPLE, PREHISTORIC rafts to the arrival of supersonic passenger flight, transport has a long history. For centuries, the only way to move around on land was to walk or to use animals as beasts of burden. The invention of the wheel around 3500 BC, and the ensuing development of wheeled vehicles, revolutionized transport. Also important was the arrival of powered vehicles, with the development of steam engines in the 18th century, and the internal combustion engine in the late 19th century.

Cast-iron spokes with wooden rim

Wheels
The most important invention in transport history was the wheel. Draught animals could pull wheeled vehicles with heavy loads for far longer than they could drag or carry the same load. Wheels were solid wood until spokes were developed in about 2,000 BC. Tyres were originally made from iron. Pneumatic tyres, filled with air and made of rubber to cushion the ride, appeared in the 1890s.

Wire spoked wheel

Strong and light metal alloy wheel

Carts and carriages
People travelled on early roads in two-wheeled carts and four-wheeled wagons or carriages. These were pulled by horses or oxen. "Horseless carriages" – carriages powered by steam engines – were first made in the 18th century.

Road transport

Roads began as footpaths that often meandered around the contours of the countryside. Then 2,000 years ago, Roman engineers built a vast network of straight roads that allowed people, goods, and troops to move quickly across their empire. Few new roads were built until the 18th century, when they were needed for mail coaches. In the 20th century, roads carrying several lanes of traffic crisscrossed the landscape as car ownership became widespread.

Chimney

Boiler

Carriage body

Driver's seat

Steam pipe

Iron tyre

Wooden spoke

A Bordino steam-powered carriage of 1854

Cars
Experimental motor cars were built soon after the invention of the internal combustion engine, which was compact enough to be carried around, in 1876. In 1886, the first practical motor car was demonstrated to the public. Today, the car is the most common form of transport in many countries.

The Toyota 2000GT Japan; launched 1966; top speed 206 kmh (128 mph); a classic small sports car.

Trucks
The first trucks appeared in the 1890s. Powered by steam engines, they began to replace heavy, horse-drawn carts for road haulage. Most modern trucks have powerful diesel engines. There are many specialized trucks for carrying different types of cargo, such as cars, liquids, or refrigerated foods.

Modern articulated truck

Kiichiro Toyoda
Japanese engineer Kiichiro Toyoda (1894–1952), established the Toyota Motor Corporation in 1937. He devoted much of his life to producing affordable passenger cars, and to building up a vast manufacturing company.

Rail transport

An important development in transport history came in 1804, when the first steam locomotive was built to run on rails. Passenger railways opened in the 1820s – the first fast form of land travel. Steam power lasted until the mid-20th century, when it was replaced by electric motors or diesel engines.

Modern trains
Electric current to power trains comes from the tracks or overhead cables. High-speed, long-distance trains are sleek and give a smooth, comfortable ride in air-conditioned carriages: an example is the Eurostar, which travels from London, England to Paris, France in a few hours. Local commuter trains carry thousands of people into and out of towns and cities every day.

Bicycles
The first type of bicycle was the Draisine of 1817. It had no pedals, but was pushed along by the rider's feet. Pedals attached to the front wheel appeared in 1839 and were improved upon in 1865. The modern-style bicycle, where the pedals drive the back wheel with a chain, was developed in the 1880s. Bicycles are a popular form of transport, especially on flat land, but in many countries they are now used mainly for leisure. In some parts of the world, such as China, most people still travel by bike.

Modern mountain bike

Early trains
Passengers on early trains travelled in uncomfortable open wagons pulled by slow, puffing steam locomotives. Steam engines gradually became more powerful and rolling stock more comfortable. By the end of the 1800s, steam locomotives were pulling express trains at more than 150 kmh (93 mph).

An electric-powered Eurostar express train waiting to leave its London terminus

Water transport

Travelling on water is one of the oldest forms of transport. The earliest craft were simple rafts made of logs lashed together. In the ancient civilizations of Egypt and Mesopotamia, people built boats from bundled reeds to travel up and down river. They also built wooden sea-going ships and used them for trading. Until the advent of the railways in the 1800s, boats and ships were the only way of transporting heavy goods over long distances. Today, there are various types of boats and ships made from many materials, from bark and animal skins to plastic, fibreglass, iron, and steel.

Queen Elizabeth II ocean liner

Steam and iron

In the 1800s, steam power began to replace sail. This freed ships from relying on the wind. At the same time, shipbuilders began to use huge plates of iron riveted together to construct hulls. This allowed them to build much bigger ships than was possible with wood. Huge luxurious passenger liners were built, which rivalled the best hotels on land.

Ferdinand de Lesseps

French entrepeneur Ferdinand de Lesseps (1805–94) was a great canal builder. His major achievement was the Suez Canal, opened in 1869, to link the Mediterranean and Red Seas.

Sail

The first sailing ships, built in about 3500 BC, had simple square sails. These were well suited for sailing with the wind behind, but oars were needed to go against the wind. From the 1600s, ships had both square and triangular sails. The triangular sail, or lateen, could be used for tacking – sailing in a zig-zag pattern to make headway into the wind. The sailing ship ushered in an age of worldwide exploration and trade.

Wooden masts support sails

Cloth sails stiffened with thin wooden spars

Traditional bargeware is still to be seen on today's pleasure barges.

Chinese junk with lateen sails

Hull of wooden planking

Sternpost rudder for steering

Decorated bargeware used on canal boats in the 19th century

Canals

Before the development of trains and trucks, heavy goods were transported from place to place via networks of purpose-built waterways, called canals. Cargoes were carried by flat-bottomed boats, called barges. Some shipping canals, such as Suez and Panama, were built to shorten sea routes by cutting across narrow strips of land. Today, though barges are still used for transporting goods, they are also popular for leisure trips.

Air transport

The first powered aeroplane flight was made in 1903. Airmail and passenger services began after World War I. Air travel has since developed into an everyday form of transport for passengers and goods.

Passenger travel

The first airliners were converted World War I bombers. Long-distance air travel really took off in the 1920s and 1930s with the development of all-metal airliners and huge flying boats driven by piston engines. Jet-powered airliners, such as the Boeing 707, were put into service in the 1950s, making air travel faster, quieter, and cheaper. The introduction of the wide-bodied jet in 1970 makes international jet travel commonplace.

Balloons and airships

The first manned flight was made in a hot-air balloon; but balloons are blown by the wind, and cannot be steered. By the 1920s, airships powered by engines carried passengers across the Atlantic. Filled with hydrogen, they were at terrible risk from fire.

Helicopters

Developed by many aircraft engineers through the 20th century, helicopters were first produced in large numbers in the 1940s. Unlike most other aircraft, they do not need a runway for take-off and landing, and can hover over the same spot. This makes them invaluable for fast transport to inaccessible places, and for rescue, police, and military work.

The helicopter's rotors are powered by a turbo-shaft jet engine.

Timeline

1804 Richard Trevithick builds first steam-powered railway locomotive.

1825 Stockton to Darlington Railway in England is the first public railway to start operations.

The Ordinary bicycle, nicknamed the "penny farthing"

1838 The steamship *Great Western* begins a regular transatlantic passenger service.

1874 In Britain, the Ordinary bicycle is invented. It has a massive front wheel, to make it as fast as possible, and a small rear wheel for balance.

1886 In Germany, the first petrol-engined car – a three-wheeled vehicle – makes its first public run.

Henry Ford's Model T

1903 In the USA, the Wright brothers make the first successful aeroplane flight in their *Flyer*.

1908 Introduction of the Model T Ford, the first small economy car to be mass produced.

1952 Jet-powered passenger services begin in the De Havilland Comet operated by British airline BOAC.

FIND OUT MORE   AIRCRAFT   AIRSHIPS AND BALLOONS   BICYCLES AND MOTORCYCLES   CARS AND TRUCKS   EXPLORATION   FLIGHT, HISTORY OF   PORTS AND WATERWAYS   SHIPS AND BOATS   TRAINS AND RAILWAYS

TRAVEL

PEOPLE HAVE BEEN on the move since prehistoric times: initially to find food or territory, and then for trade, exploration, and pleasure. Some have travelled great distances to escape danger or oppression. However, it is only since the 19th century, with the advent of new, efficient methods of transport, that mass travel has become widely available. In 1990, there were 425 million tourists worldwide.

Early travel
The ancient Romans visited thermal spas for their health, medieval pilgrims travelled great distances to reach religious shrines, and in 18th-century Europe young aristocrats made the "Grand Tour", visiting sites of classical antiquity. Before the advent of modern transport, travel was a gruelling experience. People covered vast distances on foot, often across lonely, wild landscapes, and at risk from bandits and wild animals. Only the rich could afford to travel in comfort.

Thermal bath, England

Tourism

Tourism has become the world's biggest industry as more and more people travel away from home for short periods of time. Although most people go to see family and friends, or to explore a new country, others may take short breaks to health spas, or take part in study tours. People also travel to attend business meetings.

Seaside holidays
In 18th-century England, trips to the seaside were a pastime taken up by the wealthy. By the 1840s, better social conditions marked the start of affordable holidays for the working class, who flocked to the seaside by train. Today, Europeans and North Americans take the most holidays to seaside resorts around the world.

Travel agents
The first travel agency opened in the 1850s. Since then, a large industry has developed devoted to organizing tours, booking tickets and hotels, and insuring holidaymakers.

Thomas Cook
Baptist missionary, Thomas Cook (1808–92) started a career in tourism in 1841, when he set up a train service for a party of missionaries. By 1855 he was organizing trips to the Paris Exposition, running the "Grand Tour" of Europe, and establishing the world's first travel agency.

Migration

Over the centuries people have been leaving their country of origin, searching for a better life, escaping famine, warfare, or hardship. Between 1892 and 1954, the United States saw the greatest wave of migration ever, when nearly 17 million people arrived in New York before settling in other parts of the country. Other popular destinations for people seeking a new life include Australia.

Statue of Liberty welcoming new arrivals to New York

Refugees
Famine, war, and conflict have displaced millions of people, driving them from their homes. They are forced to find asylum, or refuge, in other countries, and if they fail to do so, may remain stateless. Often refugees have to leave their homes quickly and only take the personal possessions they can carry on their backs. During the 1980s, the plight of refugees was highlighted by the Vietnamese boat people who fled their country in fear of persecution.

Tourists visiting pyramids in Egypt

Ecotourism
Regions that have interesting wildlife, such as Antarctica, have become holiday destinations for nature-lovers. Specialized travel companies provide organized tours to these remote parts of the world, little seen by other tourists. However, this kind of tourism can have a terrible impact on fragile ecosystems. The 1990s have seen a move towards responsible ecotourism, protecting the rare environments on which it depends.

Holidays today

Package holidays, which offer flights and hotels at bargain rates, are extremely popular. Increasingly, people are looking to remote corners of the globe to find undiscovered holiday destinations, while tour operators compete to meet this demand.

A rucksack can hold everything a backpacker needs, such as a sleeping bag and camping equipment.

Backpacking
Many people prefer independent travel to organized tourism, especially young people travelling on a tight budget for long periods of time. Backpackers like to take very little luggage, and they travel cheaply by using local transport, camping, and buying food in local stores. In this way, it is possible to explore remote and exotic regions that have not been reached by other tourists.

| **FIND OUT MORE** | AIRPORTS | CAMPING AND OUTDOOR PURSUITS | ECOLOGY AND ECOSYSTEMS | EXPLORATION | SEVEN WONDERS OF THE ANCIENT WORLD | TRANSPORT, HISTORY OF | UNITED NATIONS |

TREES

FOR MORE THAN 210 million years, trees have flourished on Earth. The earliest trees were giant, woody, spore-producing plants that were the ancestors of ferns and clubmosses. Today's trees are large seed-producing plants with a single upright woody stem called a trunk. Trees help to balance the atmosphere, stabilize the soil, supply all kinds of creatures with food, and produce wood for people to use. They fall into three groups: conifers, broad-leaved trees, and palms. Trees can live for a very long time; many species survive for 200 years, and the bristlecone pine can live for 4,000 years.

The top of a tree is called the crown.

How a tree grows

Each year the tree's crown grows a little taller and broader. The twigs and side shoots grow longer only from their tips. The branches and trunk become thicker as the layer of cells called the cambium divides. This process is called secondary thickening. A ring of growth called an annual ring is formed each year.

Tree trunks

Most of the tree trunk consists of wood, which is a very tough, durable material. Wood is rigid and strong, yet so flexible that the tree trunk can support the weight of the crown and sway in the wind without snapping.

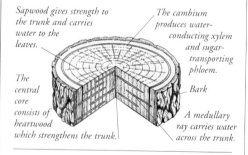

Sapwood gives strength to the trunk and carries water to the leaves.

The central core consists of heartwood which strengthens the trunk.

The cambium produces water-conducting xylem and sugar-transporting phloem.

Bark

A medullary ray carries water across the trunk.

Bark

Covering the trunk and branches is a layer of corky, waterproof bark. Beneath this is the layer called the phloem. The bark helps to protect the living phloem from hot and cold temperature extremes, and it also helps to stop insect and fungal pests from damaging the tree.

Poplar bark is cracked into vertical ridges.

River birch bark peels off the trunk in uneven flakes.

Himalayan birch peels in long, horizontal strips.

Parts of a tree

A tree consists of a trunk that supports a crown of branches, and roots that anchor the tree into the ground and absorb water and minerals from the soil. Water passes up the trunk from the roots, and sugars are carried to the roots from the leaves. The branches bear leaves, flowers, fruits, or cones.

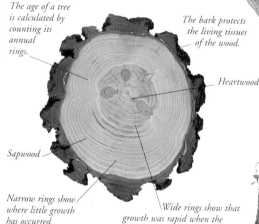

The age of a tree is calculated by counting its annual rings.

The bark protects the living tissues of the wood.

Heartwood

Sapwood

Narrow rings show where little growth has occurred.

Wide rings show that growth was rapid when the conditions were good.

Tallest trees

The tallest living coniferous tree in the world is the "National Geographic Society" coast redwood in North America, which has reached more than 111 m (364 ft) high. The tallest broad-leaved species of tree is the Australian mountain ash. This has been known to grow up to 113 m (370 ft) high.

Each spring, twigs, leaves, and flowers develop from buds.

As a tree grows taller, many twigs are shed, and only a few grow into branches.

Higher up the tree, the bark is often smooth and pale in colour.

The bark is thicker and darker near the base of the trunk, and is cracked into ridges, called plates.

The tangled network of roots spreads out horizontally as well as down into the soil.

Profile of an oak tree

Coniferous trees

All conifers are either tall trees or woody shrubs, and they are almost all evergreen. They belong to a group of flowerless plants called gymnosperms. The seeds of conifers are not enclosed inside fruits. Instead, they either develop between the woody scales of cones, or they are embedded in a fleshy cup or scale.

Cones open in warm weather to release their seeds.

Cones

Female pine cones are woody, and some are extremely hard, with sharp prickles at the tip of each scale. Male cones produce large amounts of pollen, then fall from the tree. The pollen is carried to the female cones by the wind.

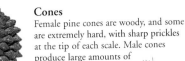

Cone shapes

Cones may be round, ovoid, or cylindrical. They range in size from the 1 cm (0.4 in) cones of some cypresses to the 60 cm (24 in)-long cone of the sugar pine. The heavy cones of the big cone pine tree may weigh up to 2.27 kg (5 lb).

Norway spruce cone

Douglas fir cone   Redwood cone

Pine trees

There are about 80 species of pine tree. All except one grow in the northern hemisphere. Pine trees are typical conifers. Their seeds develop inside hard pine cones. Pine leaves are narrow needles that grow in clusters and give off a pleasant, distinctive smell.

Pine tree

Needles

Pine trees have long, narrow, spiky needles that stay on the tree for at least two years. These needles are arranged in bunches of two, three, or five.

Conifers in winter

Evergreen conifers keep their needles all winter. A thick, waxy outer layer on the needles prevents frost from harming them. The branches of conifers curve downwards so that snow slides easily off their crowns.

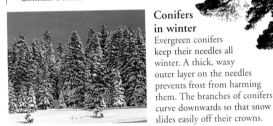

Resin

The roots, leaves, and trunk of conifers ooze sticky resins when the tree is cut or damaged. This resin helps to seal the wound, keeping out harmful insects and fungal spores. Resin can be tapped and used to make turpentine.

Tree shapes

Each type of tree has a certain shape. Broad-leaved trees usually have a spreading crown, whereas conifers often have a spire shape. Palms usually have a tuft of large, feathery leaves.

Broad-leaved tree   Conifer   Palm

Broad-leaved trees

This is the largest group of living trees, with more than 10,000 different species. Broad-leaved trees have thin, flat leaves on a spreading crown of irregular branches. Many broad-leaved trees are deciduous, shedding their leaves each autumn.

Each acorn sits in a little cup.

Acorns

The fruit of an oak tree is a one-seeded nut called an acorn. A large oak may produce thousands of acorns in a single season. Only a small amount germinate, and even fewer survive to grow into trees.

Oak trees

Oaks are typical broad-leaved trees. There are about 800 species. Oak wood is very hard and durable, so many types of oak tree are commercially important, providing valuable timber for building and furniture making.

Buds

Tightly folded inside each bud are the soft leaves of the next season's growth. Tough scales protect these buds and are shed as soon as the bud starts to open.

Leaves are grouped in clusters at the tips of the twigs.

Leaves

Broad, flat leaves have a large surface area, which makes them efficient at producing food for the tree. They are also easily damaged by wind and insects because they are thin. To deter insects, these leaves often contain unpleasant tasting substances, such as the bitter tannins in oaks.

Oak tree

How trees lose their leaves

1 Chlorophyll in the leaf starts to break down, and the tree reabsorbs nutrients.

2 Waste products enter the dying leaf, which provides a useful disposal system for the tree.

3 These chemical changes make the leaf change colour, creating the brilliant reds and golds of autumn.

4 Before a leaf is shed, a corky layer forms across the base of the leaf stalk. The leaf snaps off at this point, leaving a scar.

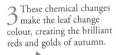

Bud

Leaf scar

Palm trees

Most palm trees grow in tropical or sub-tropical regions. Many have a tall, woody trunk without branches. The large leaves, called fronds, grow in a fan-like tuft on the upper part of the trunk.

The sago palm tree has a seed that is enclosed in a corky fruit covered with overlapping scales.

FIND OUT MORE · FORESTS · FRUITS AND SEEDS · FURNITURE · PHOTOSYNTHESIS · PLANTS · PLANTS, ANATOMY · PLANT USES · RAINFOREST WILDLIFE · WOODLAND WILDLIFE

Trees
Conifers

Male cone

Leaves have two white bands on the underside.

Cone consists of six overlapping scales.

Scalelike leaves

Monkey puzzle has stiff, sharp, triangular leaves. It grows naturally on the slopes of the Andes in South America.

Plum-fruited yew is a South American tree, not related to true yews. Its seeds are encased in an edible fleshy scale.

Incense cedar is a tall, narrow tree from North America. Its wood has a pleasant smell.

Egg-shaped upright cone

Giant fir is a 164 ft (150 m) tall tree of the damp coastal forests of the Pacific Northwest.

Stone pine grows all around the Mediterranean region. It has large, heavy cones full of edible seeds.

Japanese larch is one of the few deciduous conifers. It is an important tree for the timber industry.

Broad-leaved trees

A single brown nut is enclosed inside the fruit.

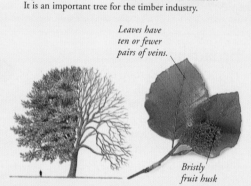

Leaves have ten or fewer pairs of veins.

Bristly fruit husk

Black walnut has large edible seeds and provides one of the most highly valued timbers in the world.

Silver birch is a graceful, white-barked tree. It quickly grows in open spaces. Flowers are borne in catkins.

Common beech is a valuable timber tree, with dense foliage that provides thick shade.

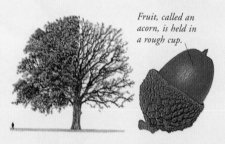

Fruit, called an acorn, is held in a rough cup.

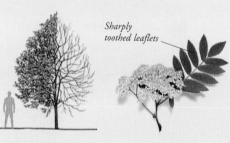

Sharply toothed leaflets

Leaves turn yellow to orange or red in fall.

White oak has large, lobed leaves that turn a brilliant purplish red in fall. It grows in eastern North America.

Mountain ash has clusters of small flowers followed by orange-red berries much loved by birds.

Sugar maple is also known as rock maple. It is tapped for its sap, which is then refined into maple syrup.

Cider gum is one of about 600 different kinds of eucalyptus trees from Australia.

Indian bean tree grows in moist places in the southeastern US. It has long narrow seedpods.

White poplar has foliage so thickly covered with cottony down when it is young that the leaves look white.

TRUTH, SOJOURNER

IN THE 19TH CENTURY, most black people in America were slaves, and black women had no rights at all. One remarkable woman dedicated her life to changing this situation. Sojourner Truth was born a slave, but was freed and spent her free life campaigning against slavery and fighting for women's rights. Her speeches and actions gave heart to all those who fought to abolish slavery, and inspired many early feminists.

Early life
Isabella Baumfree was born the daughter of two slaves in New York State, USA, in about 1797 – her owner did not record the year. Her parents died in 1809 and she was bought and sold several times. In 1826 she escaped from her owners, and was freed from slavery on 4 July 1827, when all slaves in New York State who had been born before 4 July 1799 were freed. Isabella took the name Sojourner Truth in 1843.

Campaigns

As soon as she gained her freedom in 1827, Isabella (as she was then known) began to fight against slavery. She gave support to the anti-slavery Union side in the US Civil War, especially to the black soldiers who fought in the war. She also cared for freed slaves, nursing them when they were ill, and helping to educate them. Throughout her life she travelled around the country, preaching the word of God, campaigning against the evils of slavery, and speaking in support of women's rights. She set an example that has been followed by black activists to the present day.

Speaking and preaching
Truth spent much of her life as a travelling preacher, paying her way by doing domestic work for the people who came to hear her speak. Although she could neither read nor write, she knew much of the Bible by heart. She was an electrifying platform performer and became a household name in the USA.

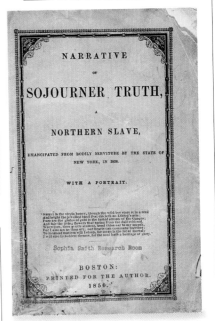

Narrative

In 1850, Sojourner Truth published her autobiography, *Narrative of Sojourner Truth*. This was a rare accomplishment for a black woman at that time, especially since Truth had never learned to read or write. She had to dictate the book to a friend. The book was successful and sold many copies, giving Sojourner Truth an income which she used to travel around the country on her campaigns against slavery.

Women's rights
As a black woman, Sojourner Truth had to face extreme prejudice on account of both her race and her sex. But this only reinforced her conviction that she was the equal of any man, and she, therefore, campaigned for women to be given equal status in American society. Although there were numerous campaigns for women's rights in the USA in the 19th century, most of them were organized by white women, some of whom did not accept Sojourner Truth, a black ex-slave, as their equal.

Poster for lecture

Meeting of women's rights campaigners

The war effort
During the American Civil War of 1861–65, Sojourner Truth made a tour of the midwestern states to get support for the anti-slavery Union cause. She met with great hostility in some of the places she visited. In one town an anti-war group threatened to burn down the hall where she was speaking. The threat did not deter Sojourner Truth. She retorted to the protesters: "Then I will speak upon its ashes".

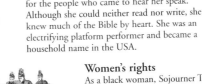

Cavalry officer / *Foot soldiers of the 58th regiment*

Memorial to black Civil War Regiment

Truth and Lincoln
Sojourner Truth was afraid of no one, even visiting the White House in 1864 to meet President Lincoln to persuade him to support her various causes. When she said that she had not heard of him before he was president, he replied that he had heard of her years ago.

Truth with Lincoln

SOJOURNER TRUTH

c.1797	Born in Hurley, New York State, USA.
1809	Parents Betsy and James die.
1826	Escapes from her owners.
1827	Granted her freedom on Freedom Day.
1843	Takes the name Sojourner Truth.
1850	*Narrative of Sojourner Truth* published.
1862	Supports anti-slavery side in US Civil War.
1883	Dies at Battle Creek, Michigan.

FIND OUT MORE

| AMERICAN CIVIL WAR | HUMAN RIGHTS | KING, MARTIN LUTHER | SLAVERY | SOCIETIES, HUMAN | UNITED STATES, HISTORY OF | WOMEN'S MOVEMENT |

TUNDRA

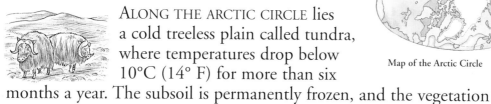

ALONG THE ARCTIC CIRCLE lies a cold treeless plain called tundra, where temperatures drop below 10°C (14° F) for more than six months a year. The subsoil is permanently frozen, and the vegetation is restricted to mosses, lichen, sedges, and rushes, with occasional flowers and small deciduous shrubs, such as hazel and alder. Animals include the Arctic fox and snowshoe rabbit. Worn flat by the vast ice sheets of the past, the tundra is now an open landscape of shallow lakes, bare rock outcrops, and small hummocks.

Map of the Arctic Circle

Tundra

Tundra regions

Tundra exists mostly within the Arctic Circle. There are also tundra regions in the far north of Alaska, Canada, Scandinavia, and Siberia. It is widest in North Siberia, on the Kara Sea, and reaches as far south as the Kamchatka peninsula.

Tundra landscape

Frequently covered in snow and ice, the ground in the tundra landscape is so cold that in many places it is permanently frozen. This is called permafrost. The occasional melting of the ice in the ground above the permafrost level causes "cryoturbation", a stirring up of the ground that creates a unique range of landforms.

Periglacial activity

The landscapes bordering ice sheets are periglacial (near glacial). The bitterly cold conditions produce a distinctive environment. All tundra is periglacial, as are nunataks and hills in ice sheets. In winter, the temperature never rises above freezing, and often drops to -50°C (-58°F). Short, mild summers allow the ice to melt.

Periglacial landscape

Stone stripes

In periglacial areas, water freezing in between stones in the ground heaves the stones upwards in places, creating stone patterns – stone stripes and rings called stone polygons.

Sparse vegetation

Lake

Frozen ground often cracks. Meltwater fills these cracks, and expands to create ice wedges.

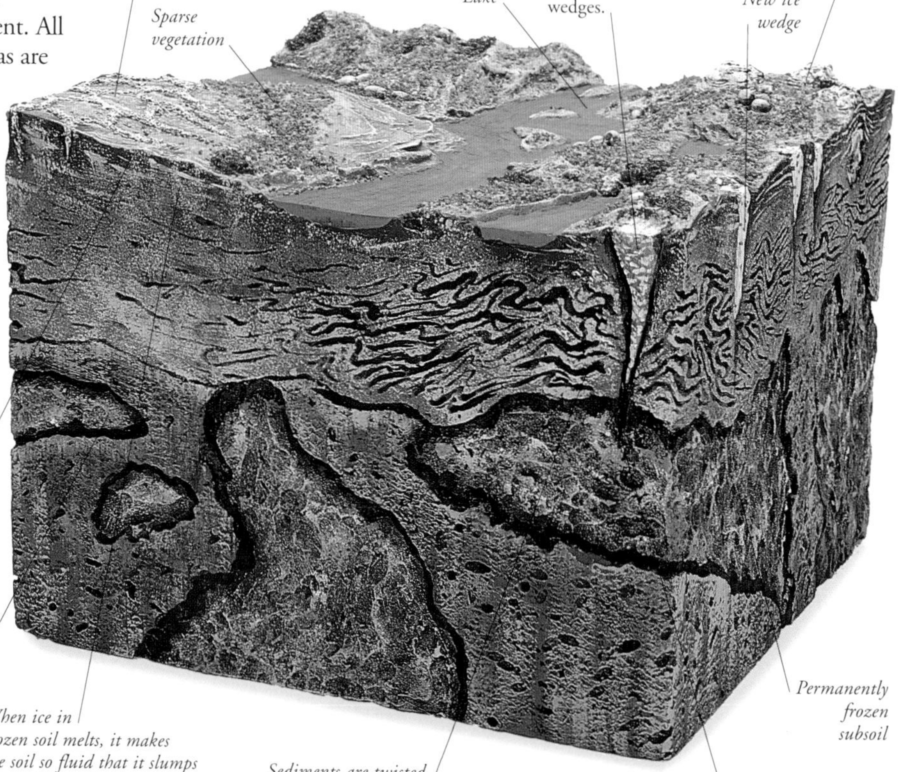

Ice beneath the ground creates pingos

New ice wedge

Topsoil defrosts during short summer months.

Mother rock

When ice in frozen soil melts, it makes the soil so fluid that it slumps down the gentlest of slopes.

Sediments are twisted by cryoturbation into buckled layers called involutions.

Permanently frozen subsoil

Ice wedge filled with gravel

Nunataks

Conditions and landforms on nunataks, upland areas protruding above the ice sheet, are very similar to those in the tundra. However, nunataks are cut off by vast seas of ice, so they are often completely bare of vegetation and animal life, and the ground is unprotected.

Mammoth

Permafrost has been frozen for thousands of years. It sometimes contains the perfectly preserved remains of long extinct animals, including complete carcasses of mammoths that died out over 10,000 years ago. This mammoth was found frozen in Siberia.

Pingos

These are mounds up to 50 m (160 ft) high which have been raised by the freezing and expansion of their ice core. The ice core may once have been a shallow lake that filled up with sediment, or it may be frozen groundwater. As the core melts, the pingo collapses.

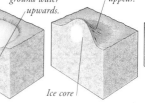
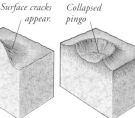

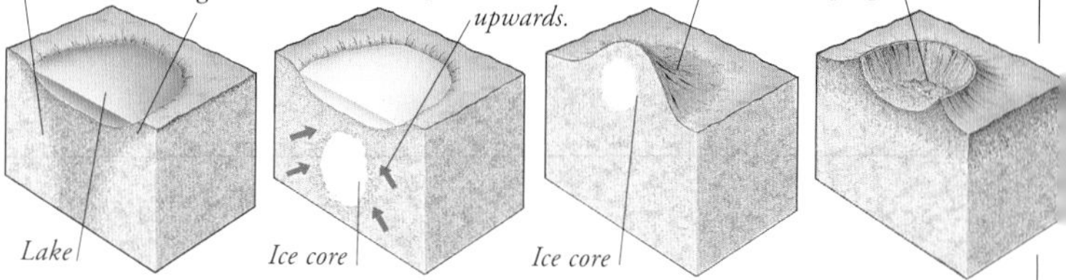

Permafrost *Unfrozen ground* *Permafrost forces ground water upwards.* *Surface cracks appear.* *Collapsed pingo*

Lake *Ice core* *Ice core*

FIND OUT MORE   ARCTIC   CLIMATE   GLACIATION   LAKES   MOUNTAINS   SOIL   WEATHER

TUNNELS

HIDDEN AWAY UNDER STREETS, hills, mountains, rivers, and seas are many thousands of kilometres of tunnels. Some carry roads, railways, canals, and pedestrian subways, making transport quicker and safer. Others carry services, such as water supplies, sewage, or communications cables. Using only hand tools, the ancient Greeks and Romans built the first tunnels to supply water to their cities. Modern tunnels are dug by special machines or blasted with explosives. Most tunnels are close to the surface, but mountain tunnels may be hundreds of metres underground.

Cut and cover
The simplest tunnel-building method is cut and cover, which is used for tunnels just below the surface, such as subways. Engineers dig a trench, build the tunnel inside it, and then cover it over.

Building tunnels
The method used to build a tunnel depends on the type of rock (either hard or soft) through which the tunnel will pass, and how deep under the ground the tunnel needs to go. In deep tunnels, the digging takes place at the tunnel face. The waste rock is removed along the tunnel.

Rock blasting
Tunnels are blasted through hard rock by placing high explosives in holes drilled into the rock face. Most hard-rock tunnels are strong enough to support themselves.

Pit props
Narrow tunnels are dug ro reach layers of coal or mineral ore far below the surface. The roof of each tunnel is held up by steel or wooden supports, called pit props.

Conveyor belts move lining segments to the tunnel face.

Concrete tunnel-lining segments

Model of tunnel boring machine (TBM)

Gripper shoes hold rock and thrust TBM forwards.

Control cabin

Rotating head cuts through rock.

Tunnel boring
A tunnel boring machine, or TBM, digs through the soft rock (such as chalk) underneath rivers and seas. The TBM creeps slowly forwards as its spinning cutting-head digs away the rock. The TBM lines the tunnel with concrete as it moves along.

Parts of a tunnel

A tunnel usually consists of a concrete, steel, or brick lining that supports the roof and makes the tunnel waterproof. Many "tunnels" – such as the Channel Tunnel, which runs under the English Channel and links Britain and France – are actually tunnel systems made up of several separate tunnels running parallel with each other. The tunnels are linked by cross passages.

Cross-section of the Channel Tunnel

Fire-fighting equipment

Relief duct stops air pressure building up in tunnels.

Drainage pipes

Communication cables carry train signals, telephone messages, and computer data.

Cooling pipes carry chilled water to absorb heat given off by the trains.

Electricity cables supply power to the trains, and to lighting, signalling, and ventilation equipment.

Service tunnel is used by engineers and emergency services.

Cross passages link tunnels.

Running tunnels, lined with tough concrete, carry high-speed trains travelling in each direction.

Tunnel safety
Modern tunnels are equipped with safety devices to warn of fire, flooding, and other dangers. In the past, miners and tunnel diggers took caged canaries underground. If a canary collapsed, it was a sign that there were poisonous or explosive gases in the air.

Canary

Ventilation
Road and railway tunnels must be well ventilated to provide passengers with fresh air. In long tunnels, particularly where cars emit toxic exhaust gases, there are ventilation shafts leading to the surface, or huge ventilation fans that create a flow of fresh air through the tunnel.

Timeline
1st century AD Roman engineers build an aqueduct that travels through 25 km (19 miles) of tunnels dug with pick axes and shovels.

1818 British engineer Marc Isambard Brunel invents the tunnelling shield – a device that makes underwater tunnelling safer.

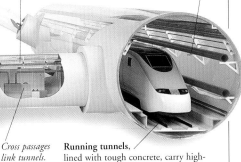

Pick axe

1867 Rock tunnelling becomes easier when Swedish chemist Alfred Nobel invents the explosive dynamite.

1871 The Mont Cenis (or Fréjus) tunnel beneath the Alps is the first to be built using compressed-air drills.

1988 Japan's underwater Seikan Tunnel opens – at 54 km (34 miles), it is the world's longest tunnel.

1994 The Channel Tunnel opens between Britain and France.

FIND OUT MORE   BIRDS   BRIDGES   COAL   PRESSURE   ROADS   ROMAN EMPIRE   TRAINS AND RAILWAYS   TRANSPORT, HISTORY OF   WEAPONS

TURKEY

SPLIT BETWEEN Europe and Asia, Turkey has a strategic influence over the Black Sea, Mediterranean, Middle East, and Central Asia, and is divided into two by a huge plateau. The European part has adopted western cultures and boasts steady industry and cosmopolitan cities. Asian Turkey is the country's rustic heartland, steeped in Islamic tradition, and home to farmers and nomads. Following the collapse of the Ottoman Empire in 1913, Turkey underwent a policy of modernization.

Physical features

European Turkey joins the tip of the Balkan Peninsula. In Asian Turkey, coastal plains border the Anatolian plateau, which is enclosed by the Pontic and Taurus Mountain ranges. The mountains converge in a vast region, where the Euphrates and Tigris rivers rise.

TURKEY FACTS

CAPITAL CITY Ankara

AREA 780,580 sq km (301,382 sq miles)

POPULATION 67,600,000

MAIN LANGUAGE Turkish

MAJOR RELIGION Muslim

CURRENCY Turkish lira

LIFE EXPECTANCY 70 years

PEOPLE PER DOCTOR 833

GOVERNMENT Multi-party democracy

ADULT LITERACY 85%

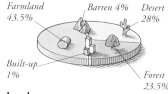

Farmland 43.5%   Barren 4%   Desert 28%
Built-up 1%   Forest 23.5%

Land use

Anatolia's western plateau is used mainly for grazing animals, while the broad, fertile valleys of the Aegean and Mediterranean coasts form the main farming region. About one-third of the land is isolated desert or rocky mountain.

Coastal regions

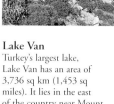

Turkey is bordered on three sides by long coastlines. The sandy beaches and turquoise seas of the Aegean and Mediterranean coasts give way to fertile plains inland. The unspoilt Black Sea coast also has long, sandy beaches but is more rugged, with mountainous forests and a changeable climate.

Anatolian plateau

Nearly 97 per cent of Turkey is raised, flat-topped land known as Anatolia. The western plateau is dry with few river valleys, while the smaller eastern plateau is rugged, with ochre-red plains, fertile valleys, and rocky caves. Central Anatolia has low mountains and grassy plains.

Ankara

Purpose-built in central Anatolia on an ancient site, Ankara replaced Istanbul as capital in 1923. The city is dominated by the Mausoleum of Atatürk, the nationalist who liberalized Turkey in the 1920s and 1930s. Giant stone monuments cover more than 1 km (0.6 miles) in area.

Atatürk's Mausoleum

Lake Van

Turkey's largest lake, Lake Van has an area of 3,736 sq km (1,453 sq miles). It lies in the east of the country near Mount Ararat, and is 1,650 m (5,400 ft) above sea-level.

Tenth-century Armenian church on Akdamar Island, Lake Van

43°C (109°F)   -36°C (-33°F)
23°C (73°F)   0°C (32°F)
367 mm (14 in)

Climate

The Aegean and Mediterranean coastal regions have hot summers and mild winters. The Anatolian plateau and the mountains have mild or warm summers and cold, snowy winters.

T

People

Seventy per cent of the people are ethnic Turks. About 20 per cent are Kurds, who live in the extreme east, and there are also Armenians, Arabs, Greeks, and refugees from former Soviet states.

87 per sq km (224 per sq mile)

74% Urban

26% Rural

People
Most Turks live in western Turkey. Many have moved from poor countryside areas to cities to try and make a living on the bustling market stalls, or bazaars. Almost all Turks are united by their shared religion, Islam, which plays a key role in history and culture.

Leisure

Most Turkish leisure pursuits are not considered appropriate for women, though as mothers they may attend family outings. Football and greased wrestling are both popular games for men and draw huge crowds.

Turkish coffee pot

Coffee houses
Turkish men meet regularly in coffee houses, or *kiraathanes*, to drink Turkish coffee, which is thick, strong, and sweet. While drinking, men play backgammon and smoke pipes.

Turkish delight – rose- or lemon-flavoured jellies.

Wrestling
Greased wrestling is the national sport of Turkey. Men smear their bodies with olive oil to resist the grip of their opponents. An annual wrestling feast called *kirkpinar* is held every spring.

Farming

About 38 per cent of Turkey's labour force works in farming. The country's varied climate allows a wide range of crops to be grown. Cotton, which supports a thriving textile industry, and tobacco, grown on the central plateau, are the main export crops.

Sheep and goats
On the pastures of eastern and western Turkey, sheep and goats graze. Goats provide angora wool, named after Turkey's capital, Ankara, originally called Angora.

Hazelnuts

Figs

Peach

Crops
Turkey is self-sufficient in food, and grows cereals as well as specialized crops such as aubergines, grapes, and dates. Hazelnuts and tea are cultivated along the Black Sea coast. Peaches, melons, and figs, of which Turkey is the world's largest producer, flourish on the warm coasts.

Food

Rice and yoghurt are the base of many Turkish dishes. Lamb or mutton are commonly served, most frequently in *shish kebab*, in which cubes of meat are grilled on a skewer with onion, peppers, and tomatoes. Fish such as swordfish, shrimps, and mussels, caught off the 8,300 km (5,160 miles) of coastline, are a speciality. *Baklava*, a sweet pastry stuffed with honey and nuts, is a treat.

Rice pilaf

Roasted pieces of lamb

Yoghurt sauce

Transport
Bordering the sea on three sides, Turkey has many fine harbours and a merchant fleet of nearly 900 ships. Ferries and two bridges link the Asian and European parts of the country. Turkey also has a railway network, 12,000 km (1,072 miles) in length, which joins its principal cities.

Industry

Turkey has more than 30,000 factories, mainly in the west of the country, which produce processed food, textiles, iron and steel, chemicals, machinery, and vehicles. Mining is concentrated in the east. Turkey has a rapidly expanding tourist industry.

Kilims
Knotted-pile carpets, called *kilims*, are made throughout Turkey. Every year, the country makes about 44,000,000 sq m (474,000,000 sq ft) of carpet. Each region has its own individual designs and colours, and the *kilims* are sold at street markets in every town.

Tourism
More than nine million tourists flock to Turkey every year, attracted by its wealth of historic sites, pleasant climate, and fine beaches. The Aegean coast is dotted with the remains of Greek and Roman cities. Pamukkale, a popular resort since Roman times, draws locals and visitors to its cascading, mineral-rich thermal pools, set on a chalky hillside.

At Pamukkale, calcium deposits form remarkable shapes.

Istanbul

The world's only city to be split between continents, Istanbul lies partly in Europe, partly in Asia. Once called Constantinople, it was Turkey's capital from AD 330–1923. Today, it is Turkey's largest city, home to about 8,000,000 people. It has a mix of colourful bazaars, elaborate mosques, and modern shops.

Sunset over Istanbul

FIND OUT MORE

ASIA, HISTORY OF   COASTS   EUROPE, HISTORY OF   FARMING   ISLAM   OTTOMAN EMPIRE   ROMAN EMPIRE   SEVEN WONDERS OF THE ANCIENT WORLD   SHIPS AND BOATS   TEXTILES AND WEAVING

TURTLES AND TORTOISES

APPROXIMATELY 250 SPECIES of turtle and tortoise exist today. They are reptiles with hard shells and can be found from the tropics to temperate regions. Those that live in water are called turtles; those that live on land are called tortoises. They lack teeth but have sharp horny lip shields. All reproduce by laying eggs, females laying from one to more than 100 eggs in loose soil or sand. Many tortoises and sea turtles are endangered, the result of trade in their shells or meat, and theft of their eggs.

Carapace covers the back.

Plastron covers the belly, and protects against stones and twigs.

Sea turtles

There are seven species of sea turtle. The largest is the leatherback, which grows to 1.8 m (6 ft) long and weighs 680 kg (1,500 lb). Other species include the hawksbill and the loggerhead turtle. Turtles migrate long distances from their feeding grounds to mate near traditional nesting beaches. The females lay up to 160 eggs in pits that they dig in the sand.

Shells

A tortoise or turtle shell comprises many small plate-like bones, and is part of the skeleton. The flat underneath is called the plastron; the domed upper part is called the carapace. The shell is covered by either hard horny plates or leathery skin, and provides protection when the animal withdraws inside.

Tortoises

Most tortoises have stumpy legs and a high rounded upper shell, although the crevice-dwelling pancake tortoise has a flattened upper shell, hence its name. The largest tortoises are the giant Galápagos and Aldabra tortoises of the Pacific and Indian Oceans. Both these species can weigh more than 250 kg (550 lb) and live for more than 150 years.

Hinge-back tortoises

There are three species of hinge-back tortoise, living in Africa and Madagascar. They can close the hind section of their carapace to give added protection to their legs and tail from predators. The plates on this part of the carapace gradually get worn.

Starred tortoise

Adult starred tortoises have a pattern of pale lines radiating over a darker background. This pattern may be indistinguishble on older ones. Young may be entirely yellow with black markings only between the shell plates.

Hinge allows back of shell to bend downwards for added protection.

Head, legs, and tail are pulled into shell.

Swimming

Sea turtles have flipper-like limbs for swimming. They can dive to considerable depths and hold their breath underwater for long periods.

Back pair of flippers used as rudders to steer turtle along.

Turtle shell is streamlined for gliding through water.

Powerful flippers propel the turtle through the water.

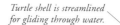

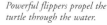

Green turtle swimming

Head and neck are about 14 cm (5.5 in) long.

Snake-necked turtle

With its long neck, this carnivorous Australasian turtle can snorkel for air from deep water, forage for food in deep holes, and defend any part of its body with a vicious bite. It must turn its head sideways to withdraw it under the carapace.

Freshwater turtles

Sometimes called terrapins, river- and swamp-dwelling turtles are found all over the world. Mostly small, like the 28 cm (11 in) red-eared slider, freshwater turtles also include giant Amazon river turtles, leathery soft-shelled turtles, and snapping turtles such as the 80 cm (31 in) alligator snapping turtle from the southeastern USA.

Legs rather than flippers allow the turtle to walk on land.

Turtles have a flatter carapace than tortoises.

Leopard tortoise hatching

1 The hatchling tortoise begins to crack the egg with a projection on its lip.

2 The egg shell fragments as the baby tortoise moves around inside.

3 The hatchling learns to use its lungs to breathe for the first time.

4 When the yolk has been absorbed, the hatchling leaves the egg.

STARRED TORTOISE	
SCIENTIFIC NAME	*Geochelene elegans*
ORDER	Testudines
FAMILY	Testudinidae
DISTRIBUTION	Central and southern India and Sri Lanka
HABITAT	Dry and wet forests
DIET	Vegetation
SIZE	Length 25 cm (10 in)

FIND OUT MORE CONSERVATION EGGS MARSH AND SWAMP WILDLIFE MIGRATION, ANIMAL OCEAN WILDLIFE REPTILES

Tortoises

Starred tortoise from India and Sri Lanka has a star pattern on its carapace.

Leopard tortoise is from dry parts of Africa. It has a spotted pattern.

Red-legged tortoise from South America has large red scales on its front legs.

Characteristic red scales

Stumpy front feet with short toes for walking

Hinged rear section of carapace

Hinge-back tortoise from Africa has a flexible section of carapace that hinges downwards to protect its rear quarters.

Herman's tortoise lives in areas in south and southeastern Europe where summers are hot. It hibernates in winter.

Pattern of radiating lines

Radiated tortoise from Madagascar has been known to live for at least 137 years.

Turtles

Red stripe easily identifies this species.

Leathery carapace lacks the characteristic hard scutes of other turtles.

Yellow-bellied slider is a close relative of the red-eared slider. This one is a newly hatched juvenile.

Spiny soft-shelled turtle lies buried in the sand of lake- or riverbeds in North America, ready to ambush passing prey.

Male red-eared sliders have long front toenails, used in courting females.

Red-eared slider of North America is commonly kept as a pet.

Large head with a strong beak cannot be retracted fully into the shell.

Shell colour is often hidden by growths of algae.

Mississippi mud turtle is known as a sawback when young because of the ridge down its shell.

Common snapping turtle is a voracious American turtle with a powerful bite.

Big-headed turtle from Southeast Asia is a poor swimmer, but a good climber.

Painted turtle has a brightly patterned carapace.

Neck as long as or longer than the body

Smooth, dark-coloured carapace

Snake-necked turtle from Australia actively hunts for aquatic animals. It sleeps with its long neck tucked sideways under the carapace.

Shell is used for tortoiseshell products.

White-lipped mud turtle has a double-hinged plastron that allows it to close up like a box.

European pond terrapin is the most widespread European turtle.

Big-headed mud turtle has a large head and powerful jaws. It is known locally in Belize as "toe-biter".

Green sea turtle is endangered because it is the source of turtle soup. It also drowns in fishing nets.

Alligator snapping turtle is the largest American freshwater turtle.

Razor-sharp lips

TWAIN, MARK

MILLIONS OF READERS, young and old, have enjoyed *The Adventures of Huckleberry Finn*, the story of an unconventional boy and a runaway slave as they travel down the Mississippi River on a raft. But behind the book is the amazing story of its author, Mark Twain. Born in 1835, Twain lost his father when he was 12. He worked as a printer, publisher, and river-boat pilot, using his experiences of life on the mid-west frontier of the USA in a series of books that changed American literature through their humour and use of everyday speech.

Samuel Clemens

Mark Twain was born Samuel Langhorne Clemens in 1835 in Missouri, mid-western USA. After the death of his father in 1847, Clemens was apprenticed to a printer in Hannibal, on the banks of the Mississippi River. Here he began his writing career, working on a newspaper owned by his brother.

Lecturer

When the American Civil War broke out in 1861, most traffic on the river stopped and Twain lost his job. He began writing for the *Virginia City Examiner* and later joined a newspaper in San Francisco. He began to publish humorous stories under the name Mark Twain and travelled widely, lecturing about his exploits to appreciative audiences.

Innocents abroad

After his return from a trip to the Mediterranean and Holy Land in 1869, Twain wrote of his journey in a book, *The Innocents Abroad*. The success of the book established Twain as an author, as well as beginning an American literary obsession with the "Old World".

Mississippi steamer

Steamboat pilot

In 1857, Clemens travelled south to New Orleans to seek his fortune in South America. But he never left the city, becoming instead a river-boat pilot on the Mississippi. While working on the river, he adopted the pseudonym Mark Twain. "Mark Twain" is the pilot's call, marking two fathoms' depth of water. Many of the sights he saw and people he met in his journeys along the river appear in Twain's later novels and short stories.

Clemens' pilot's licence

Charles Webster and Co

In the 1870s, Twain set up his own publishing company to print and publish his own novels and stories. He wrote a stream of books, including *A Tramp Abroad* (1880), inspired by a walking tour in Germany; *The Prince and the Pauper* (1882), a historical fantasy set in England; and *Life on the Mississippi* (1883), an autobiography of Twain's time as a river-boat pilot. By this time, Twain had become one of America's most celebrated authors.

Connecticut Yankee

Twain's *A Connecticut Yankee in King Arthur's Court*, published in 1889, is a disturbing satire, mixing historical and present-day characters. Twain contrasts the common sense of the American character with the superstition of the British court, to say something about the vast differences between the societies.

The Connecticut Yankee

Fine binding decorated with gold leaf

Huckleberry Finn

Tom Sawyer and Huckleberry Finn

Two books by Twain have made him one of the best-loved authors of all time – *The Adventures of Tom Sawyer* (1876) and its sequel, *The Adventures of Huckleberry Finn* (1885). Both books draw on Twain's childhood in Hannibal, and paint an unforgettable picture of frontier life on the Mississippi River. Although full of humour, both of these books make profound moral comments on American life, in particular, the institution of slavery.

Bankruptcy

In 1894, most of Twain's business ventures had failed and he was deeply in debt. To pay off his debts, he embarked on lengthy lecture tours and wrote books and stories designed to cash in on his famous name.

Later life

In his later years, Twain toured the world giving lectures. He was awarded honorary degrees by universities all over the world, including Oxford, England. His last years were marked by tragedy. By 1904, two of his three daughters had died, followed, after a lengthy illness, by his wife. In 1906, his own death was reported while he was still alive, forcing him to cable the Associated Press agency stating that "the report of my death was an exaggeration".

Twain's Oxford gown

MARK TWAIN

1835	Born in Florida, Missouri.
1857–61	Works as river-boat pilot.
1867	*The Celebrated Jumping Frog of Calaveras County*, a collection of short stories and sketches.
1869	*The Innocents Abroad*
1876	*The Adventures of Tom Sawyer*
1883	*Life on the Mississippi*
1885	*The Adventures of Huckleberry Finn*
1895–96	Series of lecture tours.
1910	Dies in Connecticut.

FIND OUT MORE   BOOKS   LITERATURE   UNITED STATES, HISTORY OF   WRITING

UNIONS, TRADE

AROUND THE WORLD, the response of working people to poor conditions or low pay has been to organize themselves into trade unions. Trade unions are formed and run by their members to represent their interests, and may sometimes conflict with employers or governments. In Britain, Australia, and the USA, unions are organized by craft, with unions of miners and engineers, while in the rest of Europe they are organized by industry, with unions of workers in the car or chemical industries.

Tolpuddle Martyrs
In 1834, six English farm workers from the village of Tolpuddle in Dorset, England, were deported to Australia for seven years for daring to organize a trade union. After a big campaign, they were pardoned in 1836.

Inside trade unions

A trade union is run by and for its members. The members elect the leading officers, who run the union's administration, and meet regularly to decide union policy and debate issues of common concern. Because of their large size, most unions are organized on a local factory or workplace basis, co-ordinated regionally and nationally.

Membership badges

Membership papers

Membership
Traditionally, trade unions have recruited male manual, or "blue-collar", workers. Today, many clerical and professional people, known as "white-collar" workers, as well as many more women, are union members. White-collar workers include civil servants, teachers, and journalists.

Workers in a car factory in Germany, where trade unions are organized by industry.

Services
Trade unions offer a wide range of services to their members, in addition to their work of negotiating employment conditions. Banking, insurance, pensions, credit cards, loans, and many other financial and personal services are all provided to support existing members and to encourage new members to join.

International unionism

Two international organizations exist to support trade unions around the world: the Communist-led World Federation of Trade Unions, set up in 1945, and the International Confederation of Free Trade Unions, established in 1949.

What unions do

Trade unions exist to support their members at work. They campaign for better pay and improved conditions, negotiate pay rises and other benefits, and represent individual members at tribunals and on health and safety issues.

Hard hat

Ear protectors

Strike
The ultimate weapon of any trade union is to call its members out on strike – that is, to refuse to work. Although strikes can be an effective weapon in achieving what unions want for their members, they can cause considerable hardship as workers lose their pay and possibly their jobs.

Collective bargaining
Trade unions bargain with the management to improve their members' working conditions. The two sides negotiate until they reach a deal that gives them both what they want. Without a trade union, individual workers must do this for themselves.

Industrial boards
In Sweden and some other European countries, trade unions sit on the management boards of companies and work with government and employers to help tackle national industrial and economic problems.

Lech Walesa
The Polish trade unionist Lech Walesa (b. 1943) was sacked from the Gdansk shipyards in 1976 for leading a strike. Walesa then set up a trade union called Solidarity, in opposition to the government unions. It was formally recognized in 1980. After Communism's fall, he became President of Poland in 1990.

Timeline

Early 1800s Industrial Revolution and the growth of factories leads to the formation of the first trade unions in Europe and the USA.

1850s Trade unions are formed in most European countries.

1868 First meeting of the Trades Union Congress (TUC) held in Manchester, UK.

1881 American Federation of Labor (AFL) set up.

1919 International Labour Organization (ILO) set up and affiliated to the League of Nations.

1926 General Strike causes state of paralysis in Britain.

1946 ILO affiliates with the UN, to improve workers' conditions through international agreement.

1955 AFL merges with the more militant Congress of Industrial Organizations (CIO).

FIND OUT MORE | EUROPE, HISTORY OF | GOVERNMENTS AND POLITICS | INDUSTRIAL REVOLUTION | MONEY | TRADE AND INDUSTRY | UNITED NATIONS

UNITED KINGDOM

THE UNITED KINGDOM consists of England, Wales, and Scotland, which make up the island of Great Britain, Northern Ireland, and hundreds of smaller islands. Great Britain is separated from mainland Europe by the English Channel and the North Sea. Highly urbanized and densely populated, the UK is one of the world's leading industrial economies and one of its oldest monarchies. The Isle of Man and the Channel Islands are self-governing Crown dependencies: the UK government handles their international affairs.

UNITED KINGDOM FACTS

CAPITAL CITY	London
AREA	244,820 sq km (94,525 sq miles)
POPULATION	59,500,000
MAIN LANGUAGE	English
MAJOR RELIGIONS	Christian, Muslim, Hindu, Sikh, Jewish
CURRENCY	Pound sterling
LIFE EXPECTANCY	78 years
PEOPLE PER DOCTOR	556
GOVERNMENT	Multi-party democracy
ADULT LITERACY	99%

Physical features

The rolling green fields of southern England contrast with the flat, marshy Fens in the east. Scotland, Wales, and northern England have craggy mountains and windswept moors and fells. Northern Ireland has undulating pasture and low coastal mountains.

Coastline

The UK has more than 5,000 km (3,000 miles) of coast. The rocky inlets and cliffs of the Cornish coast in southwest England contrast with the broad, sandy beaches in the southeast. The English Channel coast is characterized by the distinctive chalky "white cliffs of Dover".

Countryside

Viewed from the air, the English countryside forms a neat patchwork of colour that reflects generations of farming and cultivation. The pattern is broken only by farms, villages, and country roads. Fields are traditionally separated by hedgerows, many of which mark ancient boundaries. The hedges also provide a valuable refuge for wildlife.

Climate

The UK has a generally mild climate, but the weather is changeable. Rainfall is highest in the north and west, and lowest in the extreme southeast. Winter snow is common in northern and mountainous areas.

34°C (93°F) -17°C (1°F)
18°C (64°F) 5°C (41°F)
600 mm (24 in)

Land use

More than two-thirds of the UK is used for cultivating crops and rearing livestock. The most built-up region is southeast England. Scotland is five times less densely populated than the rest of the UK.

Farmland 71%
Barren 4%
Built-up 11%
Forest 14%

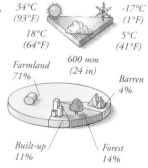

London

Capital of the UK, the largest city in Europe and home to about seven million people, London is the hub of British business and government. Founded by the Romans as a centre for trade with the rest of Europe, London is an exciting, bustling city. Every year, thousands of tourists visit its historic buildings, museums, galleries, and shops, and ride on traditional double-decker buses.

Big Ben and the House of Commons

U

People

The English, Scottish, Welsh, and Irish each have their own customs, traditions, and even languages. British society is still divided by a class system based on heredity and wealth. The standard of living is good, but poverty exists in some inner-city areas.

89% **Urban**   11% **Rural**   240 per sq km (622 per sq mile)

Multicultural society
Since the 1950s, thousands of people have settled in the UK from former colonies in Asia, Africa, and the Caribbean. The result is a multicultural society with a wide range of food, art, music, religions, and festivals, such as London's colourful Notting Hill Carnival.

Leisure

The British are great sports fans and enjoy playing and watching soccer, rugby, cricket, golf, snooker, and tennis. Fishing, walking, and cycling are popular outdoor pursuits. Many people, however, prefer to go to the theatre or cinema, or relax at home with the TV or a good newspaper.

Gardening
The British are avid gardeners and spend many hours out of doors creating colourful seasonal displays. Thousands of people flock to flower shows and open days, and garden centres selling a variety of plants, books, and equipment are big business.

Cricket
A summer cricket match on the village green is a traditional English scene. The English invented the game in the 1300s, and it is now played in many counties.

Farming

British farming is highly mechanized and produces 66 per cent of the UK's food, but only one per cent of the labour force works on the land. Most farms are small and are often run on a part-time basis, employing only one or two workers. Farming of both animals and crops is common.

Dartmoor sheep

Hereford bull

Crops
Wheat, barley, sugar beet, and potatoes are Britain's most widely grown crops. Kent, in the southeast, is famous for its hops for making beer. Large farms in eastern England produce cereals and vegetables such as peas and beans.

Livestock
Beef and dairy cattle are reared in areas of lush pasture. Sheep are reared in hilly, more rugged areas. Chicken and pigs are raised intensively in sheds, as well as free-range in the open.

Food

The British are best known for their cooked breakfasts, roast dinners, and afternoon teas. Fast food and takeaways probably started here, with fish and chips, the sandwich – a British invention – and Cornish pasties. The UK also produces a wide range of cheeses such as Cheddar and Stilton. The national drinks are tea, beer, and Scotch whisky.

A typical cooked English breakfast

Transport

Large container lorries transport nearly all Britain's freight over an extensive network of roads and motorways. The British drive on the left. Intercity trains are generally fast, comfortable, and efficient. Britain is also an international gateway for air and sea traffic.

Industry

Until recently, Britain had thriving coal, iron, and steel industries. Today, oil and natural gas from the North Sea have replaced coal, and light engineering and financial and service industries have become the mainstay of the economy. Reduced fish stocks have caused a decline in the fishing industry.

Banking
Dominated by glossy office buildings such as the Lloyds Building, the City of London is one of the world's leading financial centres. Situated strategically between Tokyo and New York City, more currency changes hands here than in any other city.

The Lloyds Building by Sir Richard Rogers

Cars
Britain ranks highly in world car production and produces about 1,300,000 vehicles a year. The industry has attracted investment from US, German, and Japanese manufacturers.
Vehicles make up ten per cent of exports. Famous makes include Rolls Royce, Vauxhall, and Rover.

Tourism
More than 25 million tourists visit Britain every year. Many are drawn by the history and culture of cities such as London and Edinburgh, while others are attracted by the wild scenery of Scotland, Wales, and the Lake District.

Channel Tunnel
The Channel Tunnel, Britain's first rail link with continental Europe, opened in 1994. High-speed Eurostar trains make the journey from London to Paris and Brussels in three hours. The tunnel is 50 km (31 miles) long, and 75 per cent runs under the sea.

Heathrow Airport
Situated within easy reach of the city, Heathrow is the largest of London's airports. It handles about 62,000,000 passengers and 480,000 flights annually. Plans for a new terminal, the fifth, are under way.

 FIND OUT MORE   AIRPORTS   BALL GAMES   EMPIRES   EUROPE, HISTORY OF   EUROPEAN UNION   FARMING   FESTIVALS   GARDENS   MONEY   TUNNELS   UNITED KINGDOM, HISTORY OF

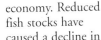

UNITED KINGDOM, HISTORY OF

THROUGHOUT THEIR HISTORY, the British Isles have been subject to frequent invasions. In turn, Celts, Romans, Anglo-Saxons, and Vikings invaded the islands and established their rule. In 1066, the Normans invaded and subjugated England. Thereafter, England emerged as the strongest nation, conquering first Ireland, and then Wales, before joining with Scotland in 1603. The United Kingdom thus formed the leading industrial and colonial power in the world, maintaining a supremacy that was to last into the present century.

Ancient British harness mount

Ancient Britain
The earliest inhabitants of Britain were nomadic hunter-gatherers, who moved from place to place in search of food. In about 4000 BC, people began to settle in villages, farm the land, and raise animals.

Roman Britain
Julius Caesar invaded Britain in 55 and 54 BC to stop local Celtic tribes helping the Gauls in France to undermine the Roman Empire. In AD 43, England and Wales were conquered and made part of the empire. The Romans built many towns and roads, and encouraged trade.

Roman towns
The Romans built a network of towns as centres of trade and local government. Among these were Londinium (London) on the River Thames, and Aquae Sulis (Bath) in the west of England.

Roman baths in the city of Bath

Anglo-Saxon invasions
After the Romans left in 410, Germanic Anglo-Saxons from northern Europe began to invade Britain. By 613, the Anglo-Saxons had conquered all of England, dividing it into seven kingdoms.

Christ is offered a sponge soaked in vinegar, to quench his thirst.

Anglo-Saxon relief of the crucifixion, Daglingworth, England

St Augustine
Under Roman rule, most of Britain was Christian, but the Anglo-Saxons had their own gods. Christian missionary St Augustine came to Canterbury in 597 and began to convert the area to Christianity.

Vikings and Cnut
In 787, Viking sailors made their first raid on the English coast, and soon controlled the north and east of the country. In 1013, they seized the entire kingdom; under King Cnut, England was part of a Viking empire called the Danelaw that included much of Scandinavia.

King Cnut

Norman England
In 1066, William Duke of Normandy invaded England to claim the throne. Near Hastings, he defeated the English army led by King Harold, and conquered the country. The Normans built castles to enforce their rule, and provided England with strong central government.

Magna Carta
Under Norman rule, arguments frequently occurred between the king and his most powerful lords. In 1215, at Runnymede in Surrey, King John signed the Magna Carta with his royal seal. This document, drawn up by senior lords, laid down the responsibilities and rights of citizens and the Church in relation to the crown. The Magna Carta is still one of the major constitutional documents of English government.

Magna Carta

Royal seal of King John

Bayeaux tapestry, showing the Norman victory

William I
William I (c.1027–87) was a descendant of Vikings who had settled in Normandy in northern France. As king of England, he was a strong ruler who brought stability to the country. He died after falling from his horse at Nantes, France.

Modern Houses of Parliament

Parliament
In 1265, Henry III called representatives of the towns, lords, and clergy, to the first parliament in London to advise the government. Within a century, parliament had the right to make laws and levy taxes.

Wales
England tried to rule Wales from Saxon times, but the Welsh princes resisted. In 1282, Edward I conquered the country, and built many castles to keep the Welsh subdued. An Act of Union in 1536 formally joined Wales to England. The Welsh language was suppressed for centuries afterwards.

Dolbadarn Castle, Wales

Tudors and Stuarts

Henry VII, the first Tudor king, seized power in 1485. He curbed the power of the lords, restored royal finances, and ruled strongly. The Tudors ruled until 1603. They were followed by the Stuarts, under whom England tried to keep its leading role in Europe, in spite of a bitter civil war.

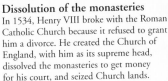

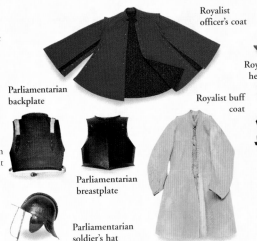

Royalist officer's coat

Parliamentarian backplate

Royalist helmet

Royalist buff coat

Royalist armour

Royalist backplate

Dissolution of the monasteries
In 1534, Henry VIII broke with the Roman Catholic Church because it refused to grant him a divorce. He created the Church of England, with him as its supreme head, dissolved the monasteries to get money for his court, and seized Church lands.

Henry VIII, the second Tudor king, painted by Hans Holbein

Parliamentarian breastplate

Parliamentarian soldier's hat

English Civil War
Conflicts between parliament and Charles I over the government of the country broke out into open war in 1642. The king was defeated and was executed in 1649. England became a republic until 1660.

Scotland
Scotland first became a kingdom in 843, and remained independent for centuries despite constant invasions by England. In 1603, the Scottish king, James VI, inherited the English throne from the Tudor queen Elizabeth I; in 1707, the two countries were formally united.

Crown of Scotland

Industrial England

In the 18th century, Britain became the world's first industrialized country. Millions of people moved from the countryside to the towns to work in new factories and workshops. Canals and railways moved raw materials and finished goods around the country. By 1850, Britain was the "workshop of the world".

Chartist demonstration

Victorian England
During the reign of Queen Victoria (1837–1901), Britain became the world's richest country, with an empire that covered one-quarter of the globe. Despite this wealth, living conditions were poor for many people in the cities.

Crystal Palace, site of the Great Exhibition of 1851

Chartists
In the early 19th century, demands grew for better representation of working people in government. In the 1830s and 1840s, groups such as the Chartists campaigned for reform. They were named after the People's Charter, drafted by William Lovett in 1838. Reforms were only granted much later.

Modern Britain

During the 20th century, Britain underwent many changes. It granted much of its empire independence, lost control of most of Ireland, and struggled to cope with economic decline. In the late 20th century, Britain became a more multi-cultural society, as many immigrants arrived from the country's former colonies in Africa, Asia, and the Caribbean.

Welfare state
In the early 20th century, Britain introduced national pensions and insurance schemes to protect workers against poverty, ill health, and unemployment. In 1948, a national health service established free medical treatment.

Free school milk

Items provided by the welfare state

Entry into Europe
After a referendum of the adult population, Britain joined the European Community (now called the European Union) in 1973. Membership brought many benefits, but the role of Britain in Europe has remained one of the most controversial issues for British political parties.

Wartime Britain
In 1940, Britain stood alone in the fight against Nazi Germany. British fighter pilots fought off a planned German invasion during the Battle of Britain, but British cities were heavily bombed throughout World War II.

Londoners shelter in the underground during air raids.

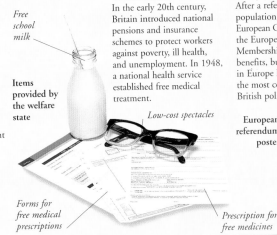

Low-cost spectacles

European referendum poster

Forms for free medical prescriptions

Prescription for free medicines

Timeline
54 BC Julius Caesar leads exploratory invasion of England.

AD 43–410 England and Wales are part of the Roman Empire.

613 Anglo-Saxons complete their invasion of England.

787 Vikings begin to raid coastline.

1016–35 Cnut rules England as part of large Scandinavian Empire.

1066 Battle of Hastings: Normans rule England under William.

1455–85 War of the Roses: the Houses of York and Lancaster, represented by a white and a red rose respectively, fight for the English throne.

Domesday Book, the Normans' complete survey of England

1603 James I (James VI of Scotland), the first Stuart king, comes to the English throne, uniting the English and Scottish thrones.

1707 The Act of Union between England and Scotland creates the United Kingdom of Great Britain.

1800 Union between Great Britain and Ireland.

1837–1901 Reign of Queen Victoria. British Empire at its height.

1922 Most of Ireland gains its independence from Britain and is called the Irish Free State.

1973 United Kingdom joins European Community, later called the European Union.

FIND OUT MORE | ANGLO-SAXONS | ELIZABETH I | EMPIRES | EUROPE, HISTORY OF | EUROPEAN UNION | INDUSTRIAL REVOLUTION | IRELAND, HISTORY OF | VIKINGS | WORLD WAR I | WORLD WAR II

UNITED NATIONS

AT THE HEIGHT OF WORLD WAR II, the 26 Allied countries fighting Germany, Italy, and Japan, pledged as the "United Nations" not to make a separate peace with the enemy. From this declaration grew the UN, a new international organization that aimed to keep world peace and bring warring nations closer together. Today, the UN includes almost every state in the world as a member. Its main success has been to act as an international forum where issues can be discussed and often resolved.

The League of Nations
Set up in 1919 after World War I, the League of Nations was designed to preserve peace and settle disputes by arbitration. However, the League had no armies of its own to enforce its decisions and relied instead on sanctions against offending nations. The absence of the USA and other important nations weakened the League, which collapsed during World War II. It was replaced by the UN.

General Assembly

The main forum in the UN is the General Assembly. Every member state sends one delegate to the Assembly, which meets for four months a year. Decisions are made by a simple majority vote, unless they are so important that they require a two-thirds majority. The Assembly has few powers, but it does serve as an international parliament in which member states can discuss issues of mutual concern.

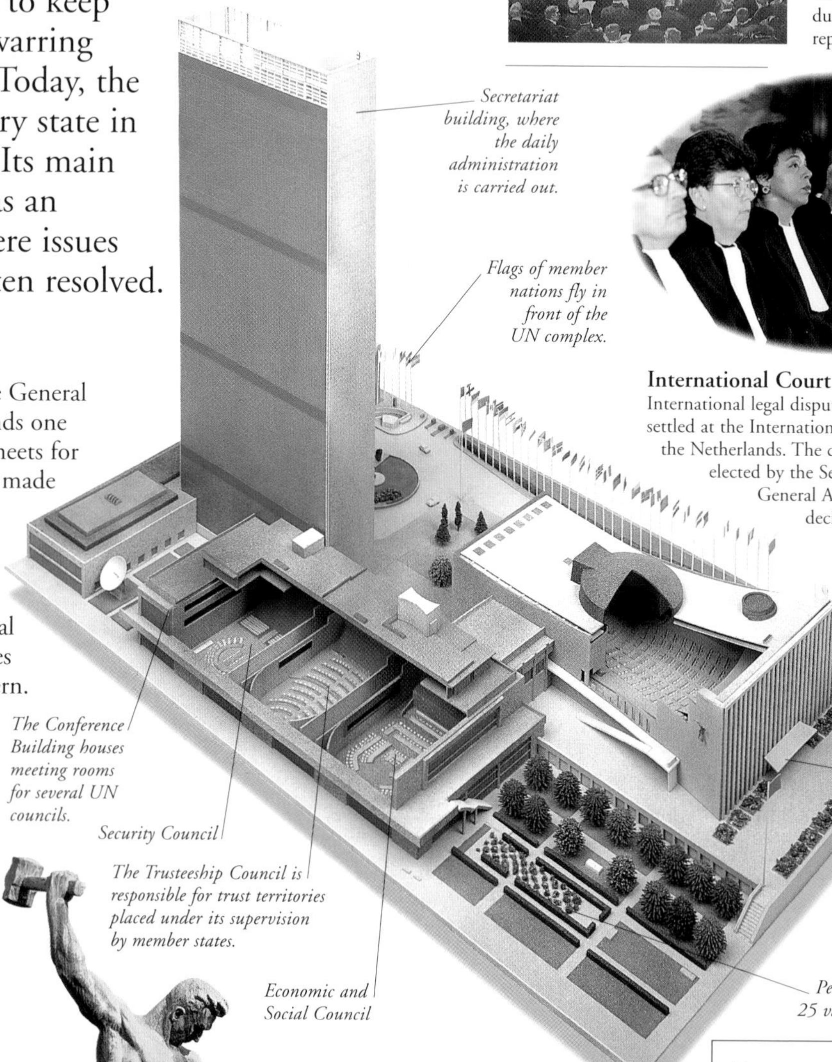

Secretariat building, where the daily administration is carried out.

Flags of member nations fly in front of the UN complex.

International Court of Justice
International legal disputes between nations are settled at the International Court at The Hague in the Netherlands. The court consists of 15 judges elected by the Security Council and the General Assembly and makes its decisions by a majority vote.

Visitors' entrance

The Conference Building houses meeting rooms for several UN councils.

Security Council

The Trusteeship Council is responsible for trust territories placed under its supervision by member states.

Economic and Social Council

The UN headquarters is in New York, USA. This site is an international zone and has its own stamps and post office.

Peace garden has 25 varieties of rose.

Security Council
The most powerful part of the UN is the Security Council. The council has a membership of 15, comprising five permanent members – USA, Russia, China, UK, and France – and 10 members elected for two-year terms by the General Assembly. The Council can meet at any time and can call on the armies of member states to enforce its decisions.

Economic and Social Council
The 54 members of the Economic and Social Council monitor the economic, social, cultural, health, and educational affairs of member states and work to ensure human rights throughout the world. The Council reports to the General Assembly.

Peacekeeping statue outside UN headquarters

Let Us Beat Swords Into Plowshares

Secretariat
The day-to-day administration of the UN is in the hands of the Secretariat. The staff of the Secretariat comes from every nation and works both in the headquarters of the UN in New York and in any country in the world where the UN is active.

Secretary-General

The most powerful person in the UN is the Secretary-General, who is elected for a five-year term by the General Assembly. Boutros Boutros-Ghali (b. 1922), shown here, was UN Secretary-General from 1992–96. As Secretary-General, he mediated in international disputes, and played a role in international diplomacy. However, the Secretary-General can only act if the Security Council members reach a joint agreement on policy.

U

Specialized agencies

Much of the detailed work of the UN is carried out by 15 specialized agencies affiliated with the UN. Some of the agencies, such as the International Labour Organization (ILO), were set up before the UN was founded; others are more recent. The organizations cover such areas as international aviation control, trade union and labour affairs, maritime law, and aid and development.

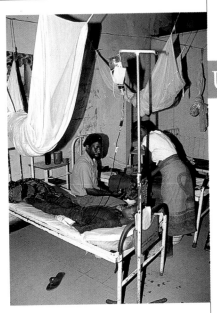

UNICEF
The United Nations Children's Emergency Fund (UNICEF) works for children around the world. It provides health care and health education in many developing countries and plays a vital role in looking after children orphaned or injured by war.

UNESCO
The United Nations Educational, Scientific, and Cultural Organization (UNESCO) was set up in 1946 to promote international cultural collaboration. Its broad range of activities includes restoring sites of cultural value, such as the Angkor Wat temple in Cambodia.

IMF

The International Monetary Fund (IMF) was set up in 1944 to promote international monetary co-operation and stability, and the expansion of world trade. The IMF advises member nations on their economic and financial policies.

WHO
The World Health Organization (WHO) works to improve standards of health and combat disease. Its most important achievement was the complete eradication of smallpox from the world by 1980. Other successful campaigns have been waged against polio and leprosy.

The work of the UN

The UN and its agencies are active in almost every country of the world, paying most attention to the poorer, less-developed nations and to areas of the world affected by war, civil strife, drought, or famine. The UN can offer its own technical assistance and advice, but relies on the support of member nations to provide the necessary funds, personnel, and, in case of war, army troops.

Peacekeeping sculpture outside UN headquarters

Peacekeeping
The UN tries to keep the peace between warring nations or sides in a civil war. The famous blue berets of UN troops have been in operation in most of the world's trouble spots, including the Middle East and former Yugoslavia. At the start of 2002, UN peacekeeping missions operated in 15 nations, deploying 47,000 troops.

Humanitarian aid
The UN plays an important role in providing humanitarian aid to people in distress. The UN High Commissioner for Refugees, based in Geneva, Switzerland, provides food and shelter for refugees fleeing war, famine, or drought, while other UN agencies work to improve water supplies or local health and education provision.

Environmental role
The UN has taken a major role in environmental issues as concern rises about threats to the world's ecology. In 1992, it convened a major conference in Rio de Janeiro, Brazil, on the environment and development. The conference, known as the Earth Summit, committed world nations to reduce pollution in order to prevent global warming.

A UN conference in 1996 votes to ban all nuclear testing.

Dag Hammarskjöld
The Swedish politician Dag Hammarskjöld (1905–61) became UN Secretary-General in 1953. He was a skilled diplomat who raised the prestige of the UN through his impartial handling of international crises, such as the invasion of Suez in 1956. In 1961, Hammarskjöld was killed in a plane crash. He was awarded the 1961 Nobel Peace Prize after his death.

Timeline
1945 San Francisco Conference drafts the UN Charter, which is ratified at the first meeting of the UN in London in October.

1946 Trygve Lie of Norway becomes the first UN Secretary-General.

Permanent members of the Security Council

1950–53 UN sends troops to South Korea to repel invasion by North Korea.

1953 Dag Hammarskjöld becomes Secretary-General.

1960–64 UN intervenes in civil war in the Congo (Zaïre).

1961 U Thant from Burma becomes Secretary-General.

1964 UN sends troops to keep the peace in Cyprus.

1971 Taiwan expelled from UN and its place taken by China.

1972 Kurt Waldheim of Austria becomes Secretary-General.

1982 Javier Pérez de Cuéllar of Peru becomes Secretary-General.

1992 UN troops are deployed in Bosnia after civil war erupts in the states of the former Yugoslavia.

1992 Boutros Boutros-Ghali of Egypt becomes Secretary-General.

1997 Kofi Annan of Ghana becomes Secretary-General.

FIND OUT MORE ARMIES COLD WAR ECOLOGY AND ECOSYSTEMS EUROPE, HISTORY OF GOVERNMENTS AND POLITICS MEDICINE MONEY PEACE MOVEMENTS POLLUTION WARFARE

UNITED STATES OF AMERICA

THE WORLD'S WEALTHIEST COUNTRY, the United States of America (USA) is also the fourth largest and the third most populated. It is made up of 50 states, 48 of which occupy the central part of North America. Alaska, the 49th state, lies in the northwest of North America and Hawaii, the 50th state, is a chain of Pacific islands. The USA is a major industrial and economic force; since 1945, it has also played a leading role in world affairs.

UNITED STATES OF AMERICA FACTS

CAPITAL CITY	Washington DC
AREA	9,626,091 sq km (3,717,792 sq miles)
POPULATION	281,400,000
MAIN LANGUAGES	English, Spanish
MAJOR RELIGION	Christian
CURRENCY	US dollar
LIFE EXPECTANCY	77 years
PEOPLE PER DOCTOR	370
GOVERNMENT	Multi-party democracy
ADULT LITERACY	99%

Climate

Summers are hot and humid; subtropical in Florida and tropical in Hawaii. Winters are snowy, and notably bitter in Alaska and the mountains. Storms, hurricanes, floods, and droughts are frequent.

57°C (135°F) -62°C (-80°F)
25°C (77°F) 1°C (34°F)
1,064 mm (42 in)

Physical features

A vast flat plain lies between the high Rocky Mountains in the west and the weathered Appalachians of eastern USA. The Mississippi River flows south across the plain. Thick forests grow in the northwest.

Monument Valley

In the arid desert of Arizona is Monument Valley, where giant rocks up to 300 m (1,000 ft) have eroded from red sandstone. The Mittens, so-called because they look like hands, are a striking feature.

Washington DC

Named after the first US president, the capital, Washington, lies between Virginia and Maryland. Home to 572,000, it is the centre of government and has many green parks and majestic marble buildings.

The Capitol Building

Built-up 0.5%
Forest 37.5%
Wetland 2.5%
Barren 3.5%
Desert 12%
Farmland 29.5%
Grassland 9.5%
Tundra 5%

Land use

The USA has huge forests, which serve a large timber and wood-pulp industry. On the vast fertile plains, or prairies, farmers cultivate wheat and half of the world's maize.

31 per sq km (80 per sq mile)

77% Urban 23% Rural

People

The USA has a diverse, multiracial population. Throughout its history, waves of immigrants have arrived from Europe, Africa, Asia, and South America.

Northeastern states

One of the first regions to be settled by European immigrants, the northeastern states have a rich historical and cultural heritage, and are a melting pot of peoples and cultures. Thanks to rich mineral resources, and many good harbours and rivers, this area has become the most industrialized and heavily populated part of the USA. Busy cities, such as Boston, New York City, Pittsburgh, and Philadelphia, contrast with the unspoiled rural farmsteads of New England.

At the end of October, city markets sell giant pumpkins for Halloween.

New York City

Covering an area of 780 sq km (301 sq miles), New York City is the largest city in the USA and a leader in the arts, business, and finance. Wall Street's Stock Exchange is the world's biggest, while Broadway is the heart of theatre land. More than 19 million people live and work in the New York metropolitan area, which stretches into New Jersey and Connecticut, enjoying its rich social and cultural mix and vibrant customs and festivals.

Fishing

The North Atlantic coastal waters are rich in fish such as cod, herring, and clams. Maine alone has 3,840 km (2400 miles) of coast, and the state is famous for its lobsters.

Cranberry farming

On meticulously cultivated water fields, cranberries are grown in large quantities. The scarlet berries are made into a sauce that is served with turkey at Thanksgiving, juiced, or used as a filling in pancakes.

Tourism

More than 50 million people visit the USA every year, and many come to the northeastern states, attracted by the rolling countryside and rich autumn colours of New England, as the maple leaves turn bright red and gold. Tourists flock to New York City and Niagara Falls, on the border with Canada. Fishing, rafting, hiking, and skiing are popular in this region.

Newspapers

More than 1,700 daily and 7,500 weekly newspapers are produced in the USA. Most newpapers are local, with the exception of the *Wall Street Journal*, which has a national circulation of 2,200,000, *USA Today*, which covers the diversity of life across the USA, and the *New York Times*. The newsprint media is facing increasing competition from satellite and cable television and the Internet.

Great Lakes states

The six states of Minnesota, Wisconsin, Illinois, Indiana, Michigan, and Ohio lie on the shores of the Great Lakes. Ocean ships serve lake ports, which are linked to the Mississippi River, whose trade routes to the Gulf of Mexico have boosted the region's agricultural and manufacturing industries. Vast natural resources, such as coal, iron, copper, and wood, and the fertile land of the prairies have brought this area much prosperity.

Motown records

Motown records

The USA has produced some of the most important popular music forms. In 1959, record producer Berry Gordy founded the Tamla Motown record label in Detroit, known as the "Motor Town". He promoted many black singers, including Stevie Wonder and Diana Ross.

Car industry

Detroit is the centre of the USA's car industry and, together, General Motors, Chrysler, and Ford employ about ten per cent of the city's work-force. More than five million cars are produced annually.

Chicago

America's third largest city, with a population of 2,900,000, Chicago is often called the "Windy City" because of the breezes that sweep in from Lake Michigan. Chicago is a centre of bold architectural innovation and a city of competing skyscrapers. The 110-storey Sears Tower, rising to 520 m (1,707 ft), was built in 1973.

Hamburgers

The USA is a giant in the production and consumption of fast food – 200 burgers are eaten every second in the USA. The hamburger originated in Hamburg, Germany and was brought across the Atlantic by German immigrants. Now, burgers are enjoyed worldwide.

Hamburger

Sailing

The five Great Lakes of North America form the world's largest area of fresh water, and attract millions of visitors each year. Marinas line their shores, and behind them are hundreds of holiday homes.

Sears Tower, world's second tallest habitable building

Chicago has 43 km (27 miles) of beaches.

Central and mountain states

The ten central and mountain states run from Montana, on the Canadian border, down to Oklahoma in the south. In this region of contrasts, the vast, open fields of the Great Plains, watered by the Mississippi and its tributaries, meet the steep Rocky Mountains. Tornadoes are common in the spring. Most of the people who live here are employed in the booming farming and mining industries.

Yellowstone National Park

Opened in 1872, Yellowstone, in northern Wyoming, was the first American national park. Covering 8,991 sq km (3,471 sq miles), the park's natural habitat is home to black and grizzly bears, and many species of animal and bird. It has hot springs and more than 200 geysers, including Old Faithful, which erupts, on average, every 73 minutes.

Cereals

The large farms of the Midwest are highly mechanized and efficient. Iowa is often called "the corn state", because it grows 20 per cent of America's maize, and its cereal factory at Cedar Rapids is the world's largest.

Cowboys

Modern American cowboys tend beef cattle on luxury family-run ranches on the plains. Increasingly, they are abandoning their traditional horseback lifestyle and keeping watch on the herd with the use of helicopters and pick-up trucks.

Traditional high-crowned Stetson

Western saddle

Carved heads of presidents Washington, Lincoln, Jefferson, and Roosevelt

Mount Rushmore

It took more than 14 years to create the faces of four US presidents in the granite cliffs of Mount Rushmore, South Dakota. Carved by Gutzon Borglum, whose son finished them in 1941, the heads stand 18 m (60 ft) tall and attract thousands of tourists.

Gold

Since gold was discovered in South Dakota in 1874, its Homestake Mine, the USA's largest, has been one of the world's main gold producers. About 300 tonnes (295 tons) of gold are mined every year.

Southern states

Three regions characterize the 14 southern states: the Appalachian Mountains in the centre, the fertile plains of the south and west, and the tropical Gulf of Mexico. The states' mixed fortunes were established in the 19th century by cotton plantations worked by African slaves. Now, the region has a prosperous and varied economy that runs on farming, oil, coal, manufacturing, and tourism. Many people are devout Christians.

Mouthpiece with single reed

Jazz

Originating in New Orleans around the beginning of the 20th century, jazz music developed from the ragtime style played by black musicians at funerals and street parades. It gradually spread north to Chicago and New York City. The "Original Dixieland Jazz Band", a group of white musicians, were the first band to make jazz recordings.

Jazz saxophone is accompanied by drums, piano, and double bass.

New Orleans

Founded by the French in 1718, New Orleans is a major port and one of the largest metropolitan areas in the south, home to more than 500,000 people. Half are African Americans, but French influences remain, notably in the vibrant Mardi Gras (Shrove Tuesday) Festival.

Cotton

The USA is the world's second largest producer of cotton, most of which grows in the south. Founded in the days of slavery, the cotton industry is now highly mechanized and large-scale. The cotton fabric is used to make towels, sheets, and clothes. Denim is woven to make jeans.

Denim jeans

Disney World

One of America's top attractions, with more than 20,000,000 visitors a year, Walt Disney World opened in Orlando, Florida in 1971. The fantasy complex based on cartoon characters is a myriad of colour and music in a world of hotels and restaurants. The nearby Epcot Center exhibits future technology.

Farming

The southern states grow soya beans, tobacco, and half the country's supply of peanuts, much of which is used to make peanut butter. Florida is the world's second largest orange grower, and produces 75 per cent of the nation's supply.

Peanut butter

Peanuts

Southwestern states

Made wealthy by the discovery of oil, the six southwestern states share an arid landscape including part of the Rockies. Close links with Latin America have given this area the largest concentration of Native Americans in the USA, as well as many people of Spanish and *mestizo* descent. Houston, in Texas, is America's fourth largest city, and is the centre of the US space programme.

Navajo people
About 150,000 Navajos live in Arizona, Utah, and New Mexico on America's largest Native American reservation, which covers 70,000 sq km (24,000 sq miles). Formerly a nomadic people, Navajos are farmers, growing maize, beans, and squashes. They are skilled potters, weavers, and silversmiths.

Distinctive Navajo geometric design.

Navajo rug

Beef
Cattle ranching began in the mid-19th century to meet the food demands of growing cities on the east coast. Today, it is still a successful business, and cattle are raised on the vast plains throughout Texas, New Mexico, and eastern Colorado.

Oil workers use a horizontal drilling method.

Las Vegas
Filled with glittering neon signs that lure people into nightclubs and casinos, Las Vegas is an opulent urban creation devoted to gambling. Situated near the Grand Canyon, in the middle of Nevada's desert, Las Vegas attracts about 30 million visitors every year.

Oil industry
Since the discovery of oil in 1901, Texas has become America's top oil producer, alongside Alaska. One of the country's wealthiest cities, Houston is the heart of the industry, with its vast refineries.

Pacific states

The three states of Washington, Oregon, and California have a long Pacific coastline. The scenery varies from the mountains, volcanoes, and forests of the north, to the arid desert and Sierra Nevada range of California. All three states enjoy thriving economies. California is the most populated and attracts many tourists.

Logging
One-third of America's softwood comes from the vast cedar and fir forests of Oregon and Washington. Most is used to make paper. The world's tallest living trees are California's coast redwoods, growing up to 111 m (363 ft).

Hollywood
Home to many famous film stars, and a major centre of production, Hollywood, a suburb of Los Angeles, nestles in pretty, natural scenery. From the 1920s onwards, many major studios were established, and the area gained its glamourous reputation during the cinema heyday of the 1940s and 1950s. Many studios have now moved, but Hollywood remains the film capital of the world.

Three-strip Technicolor camera

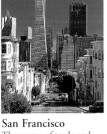

San Francisco
The centre of trade and shipping for the west coast, San Francisco lies on a natural bay. The hilly, green city endures frequent earthquakes, but its skyscrapers are built to withstand them. About six million people have made San Francisco and its suburbs their home.

CD

Silicon Valley
The Santa Clara Valley, south of San Francisco, has been dubbed "Silicon Valley", because more than 3,000 computer and other electronic firms are based there. It is a centre of high-tech innovation and thrives on the development of new ideas, often working in partnership with nearby Stanford University.

Avocado   Grapes   Almonds

Peach

Farming
Fertile soils and a warm climate enable California to produce about half of all America's fruit and vegetables, including avocados, peaches, and almonds. One-third of the country's apples are grown in Washington, but the main crop is grapes.

Alaska
Lying beyond Canada in northwestern North America, Alaska was bought from Russia in 1867. It is the largest of the states, and much of it is forest or snowy tundra with long, dark winter days. The oil discovery in 1968 made it one of the USA's greatest assets, and oil drilling, fishing, and forestry are the main activities. The population is sparse, but many Inuit still live there.

Hawaii
This chain of eight volcanic islands and 124 islets in the Pacific Ocean became the USA's 50th state in 1959. Palmed beaches have earned Hawaii a reputation as a tropical paradise, and tourism, with income from farming and US military bases, is the main earner. Most Hawaiians descend from Polynesian, European, American, Chinese, and Japanese immigrants.

FIND OUT MORE   DISNEY, WALT   EARTHQUAKES   FARMING   FILMS AND FILM-MAKING   FORESTS   JAZZ   LAKES   NATIVE AMERICANS   NEWSPAPERS AND MAGAZINES   NORTH AMERICA, HISTORY OF   OIL

UNITED STATES, HISTORY OF

JUST OVER 200 YEARS AGO, the British colonies on the east coast of America became the first colonies in the world to achieve independence from European rule. Within 100 years, they had created a nation that spanned the continent. Many Americans trekked westwards to settle on the prairies; others headed for California in search of gold. Millions of people came to America from Europe to escape poverty and persecution and begin a new life. Today, the United States is the world's richest nation, its people drawn from all over the globe.

Birth of a nation

The 13 British colonies on the east coast of America resented paying high taxes without being represented in the British parliament. In 1775, colonists rose up against Britain. The next year the 13 colonies declared their independence. After five years of fighting, they forced the British to surrender in 1781.

Declaration of Independence, 1776

US Constitution

In 1787, representatives of the American states drew up a constitution. They set up a federal system, sharing power between the states and central government.

Wagon trails

In 1862, the US government passed the Homestead Act, which gave farmers 65 hectares (160 acres) of land west of the Mississippi after they had cultivated it for five years. People headed for the plains in covered wagons. Some took the Oregon Trail over the Rockies to the northwest; others went south to California.

Waterproof canvas held up by iron hoops

Wooden wheel with iron rim

Wagon contained everything a family needed.

Expanding nation

Within 65 years of independence, the 13 original states on the east coast had expanded the territory of the USA across the whole continent.

	1776
	1783
	1803
	1845
	1846
	1848

Expansion of the United States

Wooden frame houses

Shanty towns

In order to exploit the mineral wealth of the country, workers lived in shanty towns around the mines. In 1848, gold was discovered in California, and many thousands of prospectors arrived in the area.

Coast to coast

Until the 1860s, most of the railways were in the eastern part of the country, and the only way to travel west was on horseback or by covered wagon. On 10 July 1869, the first transcontinental railway was completed, linking the two coasts together for the first time. Six further transcontinental railways were completed by 1909.

Immigration

Irish fleeing famine, Jews fleeing persecution, Italians and others fleeing poverty – all made their way across the Atlantic Ocean to start a new life in the USA. In one decade – the 1890s – the total population rose by 13 million to 76 million people. By 1907, more than 1 million people were arriving in the country each year from Europe. The USA became a melting pot of different languages and cultures.

Immigrants arrive in New York

Gettysburg

In 1861, civil war broke out between the northern and southern states over the issue of slavery. Fighting lasted for four years. One of the turning points was the Battle of Gettysburg in July 1863. At Gettysburg, the northward advance of the southern army was finally halted in a battle in which thousands lost their lives. The north eventually won the war, ensuring the abolition of slavery.

North and South clash at Gettysburg

Timeline

1783 United States of America is founded.

1787 Constitution of the USA is drawn up.

1789 George Washington is elected first president of the USA.

1861-65 Civil war between southern and northern states.

1890s USA becomes major industrialised power.

1903 President Roosevelt acquires right to build Panama Canal.

Theodore Roosevelt

U

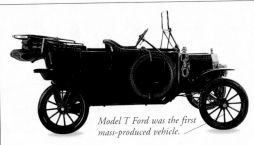

Model T Ford was the first mass-produced vehicle.

Industrialization

Between 1870 and 1914, industrial output in the USA trebled, making it a powerful economy. In 1912, Henry Ford introduced mass production into the car industry.

Pearl Harbor

When war broke out in Europe in 1939, the USA stayed neutral. But on 7 December 1941, Japanese aircraft bombed the US fleet at anchor in Pearl Harbor, Hawaii. The USA joined the war against Germany, Italy, and Japan, fighting on many continents until victory in 1945.

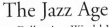

The Jazz Age

Following World War I, the American economy boomed. The 1920s became known as the Jazz Age, after the music of the time. In 1920, the American government introduced Prohibition – a ban on alcohol. Crime rose as gangsters fought for control of the alcohol trade.

Women's fashion of the early 1930s

JF Kennedy

Born in Massachusetts, John F. Kennedy (1917–63) was the 35th US President. He took office at the age of 43 – the youngest man to do so. His youth and vigour attracted many people, but he faced enormous problems. At home, he tried to tackle racial discrimination, as black Americans demanded the same rights as whites. Abroad he faced the threat of Soviet nuclear missiles in Cuba, which were removed after a tense period of negotiations in October 1962. Before completing his reforms, Kennedy was assassinated in Dallas, Texas.

Great Depression

In 1929, the New York Stock Exchange collapsed, causing a massive economic depression. By 1932, over 12 million Americans were out of work; soup kitchens were set up to feed the hungry.

Vietnam War

Between 1965 and 1973, Americans fought in South Vietnam in an attempt to prevent the unification of the country under communist North Vietnamese control.

Postwar society

Between 1945 and 1970, American science and industry flourished. The US economy quadrupled, and the real income of the average family doubled. Today, the nation is still a major power politically and economically, and is a world leader in technology and space research. However, this success does not extend to the whole population. Many cities suffer from mass unemployment and sub-standard housing, and many millions of Americans live in conditions of near poverty.

The 1950s

The 1950s were a period of rising wealth. Car ownership became common, and most families could afford to equip their homes with new electric appliances, such as washing machines.

Consumerism

In the 1950s, shopping malls opened across the country as rising prosperity allowed people to spend more on consumer goods. Many Americans were also able to take holidays abroad for the first time.

Woodstock

In the 1960s a new youth culture grew up based on rock music and, later, peaceful protests against the Vietnam War. More than 300,000 people, known as "hippies", went to the Woodstock music festival in 1969, one of the most successful music events of all time.

Wall Street

During the 1980s, the USA continued to prosper, and many people became wealthy by investing on Wall Street. But in 1987, the stock market crashed, wiping $500 billion off share values in a single day. Irresponsible trading was blamed for the disaster.

September 11, 2001

On September 11, 2001, the worst terrorist attack in history took place in the USA. Terrorists flew two hijacked passenger planes into the World Trade Center in New York City, resulting in explosions that demolished its twin towers and killed almost 3,000 people. Other synchronized attacks on the day included a plane flown into the Pentagon in Washington, D.C. The USA retaliated with the bombing of Afghanistan, believed to harbour the key perpetrators of the crime, including the head of al-Qaida, Osama bin Laden.

Firemen battled bravely to find survivors.

1917 The USA enters World War I allied with Britain and France.

1920–33 Prohibition laws ban the sale and making of alcohol in the US.

1929 Wall Street Stock Exchange crashes in New York.

1929–39 Great Depression causes mass poverty

News of Wall St crash

1933 President FD Roosevelt promises a "New Deal" to get the USA out of the economic slump.

1945 The USA drops atomic bombs on Japan, ending World War II.

1945–89 "Cold War" between USA and Soviet Union.

1954 Supreme Court prohibits racial segregation in schools.

1965–73 Over 50,000 US troops killed in Vietnam.

1960s and 1970s Black people fight for equal rights.

1969 American Neil Armstrong is the first person on the Moon.

Ronald Reagan and Mikhail Gorbachev

1987 Presidents Reagan and Gorbachev sign the Nuclear Forces Treaty.

1991 Operation Desert Storm is launched against Iraq in the Gulf War.

2001 Terrorist attacks in the USA lead to the bombing of Afghanistan.

2003 US-led coalition deposes Saddam Hussein's regime in Iraq.

FIND OUT MORE   AMERICAN CIVIL WAR   AMERICAN REVOLUTION   COLD WAR   GREAT DEPRESSION   KING, MARTIN LUTHER   NORTH AMERICA, HISTORY OF   PILGRIM FATHERS   TRADE AND INDUSTRY

UNIVERSE

EVERYTHING THAT EXISTS makes up the Universe, from the smallest particles to the biggest structures, whether on Earth or in space. It includes everything that is visible, much that is invisible, everything that is known, and more that is unknown. Over time, humans have had different ideas of what the Universe is and how it works, how it started, and what its future is. Today, scientists know more than ever before, but there is much still to be learnt.

Structure of the Universe

The most common object in the Universe is the star. There are billions and billions of them. At least one of these, the Sun, has planets. One of these planets, Earth, has life. On the face of it stars, planets, and humans are very different, but they do have things in common. They are all made of the same chemical elements, or compounds of them, and they are all affected by the laws of science, such as gravity and the electromagnetic force. By studying the constituents of the Universe and understanding the laws, scientists can build up a picture of the Universe, and discover its past and predict its future.

Interstellar material
Gas and dust are found in the vast spaces between stars and make up about 10 per cent of the Universe. In places, the gas and dust is so thinly spread that it is like a vacuum; in other places, they make enormous clouds. Gas and dust can form new stars and be replenished by material from dying stars. Gas and dust are also found between the galaxies.

Great Wall
The largest structures in the Universe are long thread-like filaments made of thousands of galaxies. They surround huge, empty voids. Here a computer simulation shows the view from an imaginary spacecraft travelling above one such filament, known as the Great Wall.

A large star dies as a supernova.

Galaxies contain billions of stars.

The Sun, an ordinary middle-aged star

Clusters of stars

The Universe was created 15 billion years ago in the Big Bang. Since then, matter has come together to form stars, galaxies, planets, and life.

Comet

Planets – balls of rock, gas, or ice

Cloud of gas and dust

Apparent position of star

Real position of star

Path of light rays

Ptolemy
Once the Earth was thought to be the centre of the Universe with the other celestial objects moving around it. This idea is the Ptolemaic view, named after Claudius Ptolemy, an Egyptian. In the 2nd century AD, he brought together the astronomical ideas of the ancient Greek world in his work, the *Almagest*.

Dark matter
Scientists have calculated how much material the Universe contains: the answer is about 90 per cent more than has been detected. This gas cloud, with a cluster of galaxies embedded in it, may contain some of the missing material.

Gravity
A star's gas is held together by gravity. Everything in the Universe is affected by gravity. Earth's gravity keep things on its surface, the Sun's gravity keeps the Solar System together, and the stars in the Milky Way are held together by gravity. In general, the more massive a body is, the more gravitational pull it has.

General relativity
Early in the 20th century, gravity was shown to affect not only objects but space itself. Massive objects, which have immense gravitational pull, curve space. This pull is seen when the light from a star, instead of following a straight path through space, falls into the curved space created by the Sun. This law is called the general theory of relativity.

Looking at the Universe

Everything known about the Universe has been learnt from Earth or close to it. Telescopes collect information by picking up electro-magnetic radiation, transmitted in a range of wavelengths, by every object in the Universe. By analysing different wavelengths, it is possible to build up a picture of the Universe.

Infrared
Andromeda Galaxy as recorded at infrared wavelengths. Infrared images can help astronomers locate cooler objects and regions not visible at optical wavelengths.

Visible light
The Andromeda Galaxy at optical wavelengths. It is the largest of the galaxies close to the Milky Way. It has two smaller companion galaxies, also visible in this image.

X-rays
An X-ray image of the Andromeda Galaxy. X-rays are short wavelengths with high energy. They pinpoint "hot spots" or areas of intense activity in space.

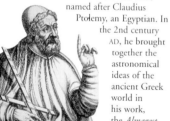

Edge of the Universe
As telescopes have improved, astronomers have been able to see farther and farther. With present instruments, they can see almost to the edge of the Universe, 15 billion light years away. This quasar, one of the most distant objects visible, is 12 billion light years away.

Each wavelength gives different information about an object.

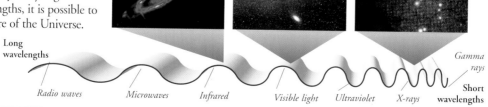

Long wavelengths

Radio waves   Microwaves   Infrared   Visible light   Ultraviolet   X-rays   *Gamma rays*   **Short wavelengths**

Scale of the Universe

Earth is tiny compared with other objects in space and the overall Universe. Distances on Earth are measured in kilometres or miles, but distances in space are so great that these measuring units become unwieldy. Astronomers use astronomical units (au) in the Solar System and light years (ly) outside it. The distances are always changing because the Universe itself is getting bigger. It has been expanding ever since it was created by the Big Bang.

Earth to the Sun

Earth does not stay a constant distance from the Sun, but moves closer and farther away as it orbits the Sun. The average distance is 149.6 million km (93 million miles), or 1 au. Light from the Sun takes 8.3 light minutes to reach Earth.

Earth to Sun:
1 astronomical unit (au)

Sun to nearest stars:
270,000 astronomical units

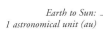

Sun to nearest star

The nearest star to the Sun is Proxima Centauri, 4.2 ly away. A light year is the distance light travels in one year (9.46 million km/5.88 million miles). Less than 10 stars are within 10 ly.

Sun to nearest stars: 10 ly

Milky Way: 100,000 ly wide

Distance across Galaxy

The Milky Way Galaxy is about 100,000 ly across, and is made up of billions of stars. On average, the stars are 4 ly apart. The Solar System is about 27,700 ly from the centre.

Milky Way: 100,000 ly wide

Milky Way to nearest galaxies: 2.25 million ly

Milky Way to Andromeda Galaxy

The largest of the nearby galaxies is the Andromeda Galaxy at 2.25 million ly away. The Milky Way and Andromeda Galaxy are part of the Local Group cluster, which consists of about 30 galaxies.

Distance across the Universe

By measuring the distance to the most distant galaxies, astronomers can calculate the size of the Universe. The radius is believed to be 15 billion ly.

Measuring the Universe

The nearest celestial objects to Earth are the Moon and the planets. Their distance is measured by radar. The closest stars, those up to about 1,600 ly away, are measured by parallax. The distance to more remote stars and galaxies is calculated by analysing the object's light or by comparing it with an object of known distance.

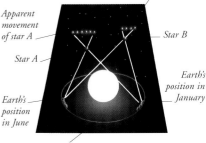

Apparent movement of star B

Apparent movement of star A

Star B

Star A

Earth's position in June

Earth's position in January

Earth orbits the Sun.

Redshift

Light from stars and galaxies travels as a wave, and can tell us if an object is moving away from, or towards, Earth. The light is split to produce a spectrum. If the object is moving away, the wavelength will be stretched towards the red end of the spectrum – a redshift. If the object is moving towards Earth, waves are squashed, and shift towards the blue end of the spectrum.

Both galaxies are moving away. But the redder the shift, the faster the galaxy is moving.

The fastest moving galaxies are the most distant.

Parallax

The parallax method requires a star to be observed twice, six months apart. In this time, the star appears to have shifted against the background of distant stars. The angle of shift – the parallax of the star – indicates the distance. The greater the angle, the nearer the star.

Universe through history

People have always tried to make sense of their surroundings, and different ideas of the Universe evolved as people discovered more. First, they struggled to explain the mechanics of the Solar System. Then, as they discovered more distant objects, the size of the Universe grew. Discoveries of new types of objects brought new questions to be answered.

Babylonian

Gods played an important part in the Babylonian view of the Universe 3,500 years ago. They had placed the Sun, Moon, planets, and stars in heaven and Earth was a large, round, hollow mountain resting on water, and supporting the domed sky.

Ptolemaic

The ancient Greeks saw Earth as the centre of the Universe. The Sun, Moon, and the five known planets moved around it. The sphere of fixed stars lay beyond.

Copernican

Devised in the 16th century, this system is the basis of today's understanding of the Universe. Earth rotates on its axis once a day, and orbits the Sun in one year. Earth is no longer at the centre; it is just one of the planets.

Copernicus

The work of the Polish astronomer Nicolaus Copernicus (1473–1543) marks a change in the understanding of the Universe. He proposed that the Sun, and not the Earth, was at the centre of the Universe. His theories were not generally accepted until the mid-17th century, when astronomers provided the proof that Earth and the other planets orbited the Sun.

Today

Astronomers in the 20th century learnt much about the structure, scale, and history of the Universe. The Milky Way is not the only galaxy: there are millions of them. The Universe is believed to have been created in a giant explosion, the Big Bang, 15 billion years ago. It has been evolving and expanding ever since.

 FIND OUT MORE · ASTRONOMY · BABYLONIANS · BIG BANG · BLACK HOLES · FORCE AND MOTION · GALAXIES · GRAVITY · GREECE, ANCIENT · STARS · TELESCOPES · X-RAYS

URBAN WILDLIFE

THE MAN-MADE LANDSCAPES of our towns and cities may seem an odd setting for wildlife, but a remarkable variety of animals, from foxes to cockroaches, have made their homes there. Some animals live among the greenery of forgotten corners that re-create wild habitats; others have colonized truly artificial places – even the most sterile concrete structures harbour life. For species such as rats, adaptable enough to try new foods, explore new places for shelter, and tolerate disturbance, the urban environment can be an attractive habitat free of many predators, but full of opportunities.

Types of urban habitat

The typical city offers wildlife an amazing assortment of habitats, from the concrete and tarmac of city centres to the ornamental greenery of parks and suburban gardens. Office blocks harbour insects, monkeys often linger around African market squares, and rubbish tips in North America may be visited by animals as large as polar bears. Railside verges, playing fields, waste ground, and reservoirs alike all have their typical animal residents.

Railway lines
Undisturbed land alongside railways provides a refuge that runs right through the heart of cities for wild plants and wild animals, such as foxes.

Houses and buildings
Many creatures live below floorboards, in attics, and on roofs. Some share our shelter; others raid our food supplies.

Raccoons often tip over dustbins to make their search for food easier.

This raccoon is foraging through the litter in search of food.

Raccoons are found scavenging from dustbins in towns in the USA.

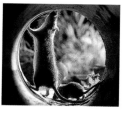

Life underground
Burrowing animals, such as brown rats, live in sewerage systems where they can shelter, devour waste matter, and breed free from disturbance.

Ultimate adapters

Cockroaches colonized Britain after being carried accidentally in imported food from the warmth of the tropics. They now thrive wherever there is artificial heating and food to plunder. They are common in bakeries and restaurants, as well as many houses.

Flat bodies help them fit through narrow gaps.

Cockroach

Source of food

Urban habitats offer rich pickings for scavengers of refuse, waste matter, and the food stored in kitchens, shops, and warehouses. City residents even encourage animals into their gardens by putting spare food out deliberately for pigeons, songbirds, and possums. Gardens, parks, and wastelands also provide plentiful food for non-scavenging animals. Insects feed on the nectar from flowers, birds eat berries, and weasels feed on nestling birds and mice.

Hedgehogs often visit people's gardens where food may be left out for them deliberately.

Re-created habitats

Many of the habitats that exist in urban areas re-create the types of habitat found in the wild. A garden pond, for example, serves as a miniature wetland, while a well-weathered wall resembles a rugged rockface. Buildings are often cliff like on the outside, while their unlit cavities within are similar to caves. It is little wonder that animals used to such habitats have moved in.

House martins used to nest mainly on cliffs and crags under overhanging rocks. Many now build their mud nests below the eaves of houses.

Neatly made mud nest

Frogs and toads have found refuge in garden ponds, as wetland habitats have declined in the countryside.

Many frogs now live in garden ponds.

City warmth

The heating of buildings and the heat generated by machines, motors, and ovens all create extra warmth that has been exploited by urban wildlife. Some birds, such as pigeons and starlings, roost in city centres on winter nights because it is normally a few degrees warmer there than the outskirts. Artificial heating has also enabled tropical insects to colonize buildings in cold climates.

Starlings roosting on ledges of a cathedral

FIND OUT MORE   CITIES   GARDENS   INSECTS   PANDAS AND RACCOONS   RATS AND OTHER RODENTS

URINARY SYSTEM

URINATING IS SOMETHING we do daily without really thinking about it. Urine is a waste liquid produced by the urinary system, which consists of the kidneys, ureters, bladder, and urethra. The two kidneys regulate water levels inside your body and filter waste substances from the blood. As blood passes through the kidneys, waste materials are extracted from it to make urine. Two long tubes called the ureters carry the urine to the bladder, and it is then passed out of the body through the urethra.

How the kidney works

Each kidney is divided into an outer cortex and a middle medulla where urine is produced. Each cortex and medulla contain about one million tiny filtration units called nephrons. Nephrons filter fluid from blood as it passes through the kidney, and then process it. Useful substances pass back into the bloodstream and unwanted substances form urine.

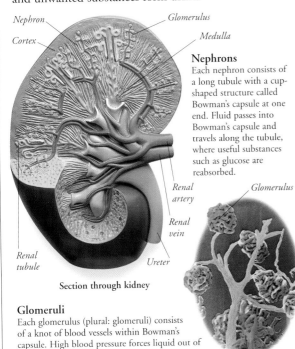

Nephron
Glomerulus
Cortex
Medulla

Nephrons
Each nephron consists of a long tubule with a cup-shaped structure called Bowman's capsule at one end. Fluid passes into Bowman's capsule and travels along the tubule, where useful substances such as glucose are reabsorbed.

Renal artery
Renal vein
Glomerulus
Renal tubule
Ureter

Section through kidney

Blood vessels leading to glomeruli

Glomeruli
Each glomerulus (plural: glomeruli) consists of a knot of blood vessels within Bowman's capsule. High blood pressure forces liquid out of the blood passing through the glomerulus and into Bowman's capsule. The walls of the glomerulus act as a filter. Water, salts, and other small molecules can pass into the tubules of the nephron, while blood cells cannot.

Carl Ludwig
The German physiologist Carl Ludwig (1816–95) fully explained the workings of the kidney. He determined that, once inside the kidney, blood was filtered through the glomeruli into Bowman's capsule before being concentrated in the long tubules of the nephron to form urine, which was then expelled from the body.

Kidneys and bladder

The two kidneys are reddish-brown, bean-shaped organs, each about 12.5 cm (5 in) long, attached to the back wall of the abdomen. The ureters gently squeeze urine from the kidneys to the bladder where it is stored. The bladder opens to the outside of the body through the urethra.

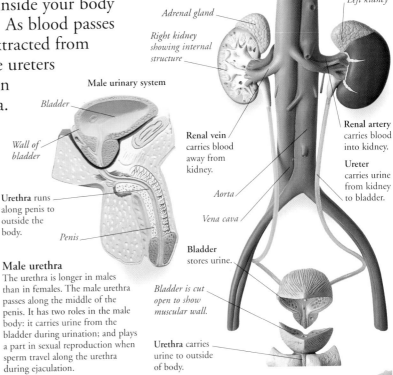

Female urinary system
Adrenal gland
Left kidney
Right kidney showing internal structure
Male urinary system
Bladder
Wall of bladder
Renal vein carries blood away from kidney.
Renal artery carries blood into kidney.
Aorta
Ureter carries urine from kidney to bladder.
Vena cava
Urethra runs along penis to outside the body.
Penis
Bladder stores urine.
Bladder is cut open to show muscular wall.
Urethra carries urine to outside of body.

Male urethra
The urethra is longer in males than in females. The male urethra passes along the middle of the penis. It has two roles in the male body: it carries urine from the bladder during urination; and plays a part in sexual reproduction when sperm travel along the urethra during ejaculation.

Bladder

Urine is produced continuously by the kidneys. The bladder stores urine until it is convenient to release it. At the base of the bladder, guarding the exit to the urethra, there are two rings of muscles called sphincters. As the bladder fills, the sphincters contract to prevent any leakage.

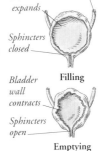

Bladder expands
Ureter
Sphincters closed
Filling

Bladder wall contracts
Sphincters open
Emptying

Controlling bladder
You can decide when you want to urinate. One of the sphincter muscles only relaxes when you tell it to. We learn to control our bladders in childhood.

Renal dialysis
If someone's kidneys stop working properly, poisonous waste products can build up in the blood making that person very ill. Kidney failure can be treated by renal dialysis; this uses an artificial kidney or kidney machine to "clean" the blood.

Water balance

Over half of your body is water. In order to work properly, your body must keep its water content at a constant level. However, water is constantly being lost from the body as urine and in other ways (see right). To balance these daily losses, we must take in more water by drinking regularly.

Sweat 200ml
Faeces 200 ml
Skin 400 ml
Lungs 400 ml
Urine 1,200 ml

FIND OUT MORE   DIGESTION   HUMAN BODY   LIQUIDS   MEDICINE   MUSCLES AND MOVEMENT

V

VESALIUS, ANDREAS

DURING THE 16TH CENTURY, physicians followed the methods laid down by ancient Greek doctors more than 1,500 years before. One Flemish doctor, Andreas Vesalius, challenged these teachings. He dissected human corpses to discover how the body worked, and then published his findings in a book, giving physicians the first reliable guide to human anatomy. By basing his conclusions only on research, Vesalius set new standards for medicine that have survived until today.

Early life
Andreas Vesalius was born in 1514 in the Flemish city of Brussels. His father was a pharmacist and encouraged his son to study medicine. Andreas began his studies in Paris. Vesalius learned about anatomy from the books of the Greek writer Galen. He later moved to Louvain near Brussels and then to Padua, Italy, where he took his medical degree at the university in 1537. The authorities at Padua recognized his talent and made him a professor of anatomy.

Early work

Vesalius was fascinated by anatomy, but was frustrated at the primitive knowledge of most anatomists. In the 16th century, it was almost unheard of for a doctor to dissect a human corpse to find out how the body worked. Vesalius wanted to do this, but he knew he would face opposition from the Roman Catholic Church, whose priests thought that cutting up a dead body was wrong.

Galen
Galen of Pergamum (129–199) was a Greek medical scientist. He experimented on animals, such as pigs and apes, to find out about their anatomy. Galen and his followers assumed that the inner organs of humans were similar to those of pigs and apes. Galen also established the importance of diagnosis and observation in treating disease.

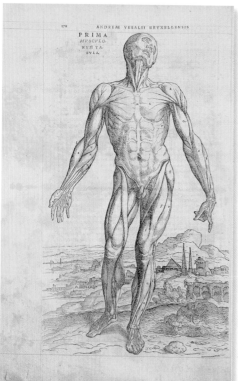

Structure of the human body
In 1543, Vesalius published *De Humani Corporis Fabrica (On the Structure of the Human Body).* The book contained many woodcut illustrations by the German artist John Stephen, depicting the results of the dissections that Vesalius had carried out. Vesalius challenged many earlier teachings, recognizing that Galen's beliefs rested on a knowledge of animals rather than humans. For the first time, an accurate guide to the human body was available.

Dissection

In spite of the objections of other doctors backed by the Church, Vesalius continued dissecting corpses. As he worked, he made careful drawings of the different functional systems of the body – such as the blood vessels, muscles, and digestive system. These detailed, first-hand studies put him in the forefront of medical science.

Arteries
In his book, Vesalius made a detailed study of the blood vessels, showing how the veins and arteries linked together in the body. With this work, he prepared the way for William Harvey, the 17th-century English scientist who correctly proposed that blood is pumped around the body by the heart, and not produced by the liver, as Galen had thought.

Woodcut of Vesalius's dissection of a human body

Human arteries

Shows bloodflow of the body

Vesalius's dissecting tools

Controversy

After his book was published, Vesalius continued to dissect corpses, and he published a revised version of the work in 1555. But his work attracted such controversy from other doctors that he resigned his post at Padua and became personal physician to the emperor Charles V and later to Charles's son Philip II of Spain.

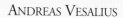

Holy Roman Emperor Charles V

ANDREAS VESALIUS

1514	Born in Brussels.
1530s	Studies in Paris and Louvain.
1537	Gains his medical degree from Padua University, where he becomes a professor.
1453	Publishes *De Humani Corporis Fabrica.*
1550s	Works as physician to Charles V and then Philip II of Spain.
1555	Publishes revised edition of *Fabrica.*
1563	Goes on pilgrimage to Jerusalem.
1564	Dies in Greece on his way back from Jerusalem.

FIND OUT MORE

MEDICINE, HISTORY OF

SCIENCE, HISTORY OF

VIDEO

ALL THE EXCITEMENT of a sports event or the happy memories of a birthday party can be captured using video. Video is the recording and playing back of television (TV) signals. A television signal is an electric current or digital transmission produced by a television camera. The signal carries both picture (video) and sound (audio) information that can be used to recreate a moving scene on a TV screen or computer. Video cassette recorders can record TV signals on to magnetic tape, and then play them back on a television screen. Nowadays, much video technology is digital.

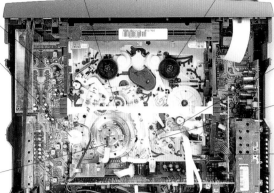

Video cassette recorder with top removed

Loading pole engages tape.

Tape cassette is inserted here.

Capstans rotate to feed tape through machine.

Circuitry

Erase head wipes off any previous recording from tape.

Guide roller ensures that tape runs smoothly through the machine.

Audio record/play-back head

Electric motor

Signals from TV aerial enter here.

Video-head drum spins 50 times every second.

Camcorder

A camcorder is a combined video camera and recorder in a hand-held unit. Until recently, most camcorders were analogue, which means that the image signal is captured electrically on tape. Today, digital camcorders are more popular because they have the advantage of producing a high-quality image that can be replayed over time without deteriorating. The digital image signal is recorded on tape using a binary computer code.

Compact design

Digital zoom

Lens

Camera also takes digital photos.

Playback monitor

LCD screen can be adjusted to any angle.

Digital camcorder

Rechargeable battery

Video cassette recorder (VCR)

A video cassette contains a reel of magnetic tape that stores a TV signal as changing patterns of magnetism. Inside a VCR, the tape moves past a video-head drum, which converts the patterns back into a video signal. The audio signal is picked up by a separate audio head. The signals are then sent to a TV set, which recreates the sounds and pictures. The audio and video heads can also record signals fed into the VCR via an aerial.

Diagonal scanning
The VCR records the information in the video signal as a series of diagonal tracks across the magnetic tape. To read the tracks, the video-head drum is set at an angle, so that it scans the tape diagonally. The audio information is recorded along the edge of the tape.

Using a camcorder
A camcorder is very simple to use: just point it at the scene you want to capture and press the "record" button. You can zoom in for a close-up or zoom out for a wider view, and use the controls to get the best lighting conditions. A playback screen allows you to view what you have recorded.

Digital video types
The two types of digital video format are Digital8 and the smaller MiniDV. Both produce crystal-clear images that can be edited easily on a home computer.

Plastic cards hold data in binary code.

Digital memory cards

Digital memory card
Some analogue camcorders can be partially upgraded to digital quality by recording the signal on to a plastic card instead of a tape. The card stores the signal digitally, as binary numbers made up of the digits 0 and 1. This produces better quality sound and pictures overall.

Uses of video

Video recording brings us news from around the world in an instant. The VCR makes it possible to record TV shows when we are doing something else, and watch films at home after release at theatres. Video cameras in shops and banks also help deter criminals.

Home entertainment
Most towns have shops where people can rent or buy video cassettes or digital video discs (DVDs). DVDs have superb image quality that does not fade.

Broadcasting
All the different elements of a TV show are pieced together and recorded on to video tape. The tape is then played back to viewers over the TV network.

Security
Shops, banks, and many other buildings install video cameras to catch thieves. The pictures the cameras produce can be used in court to help identify criminals.

News gathering
Reporters send video pictures of world events back to TV stations by cable or by radio waves, bringing news to the viewers almost as it happens.

FIND OUT MORE   CAMERAS   ELECTRONICS   FILMS AND FILM-MAKING   LIGHT   PHOTOGRAPHY   SOUND RECORDING   TELEPHONES   TELEVISION

VIETNAM, CAMBODIA, AND LAOS

THE COUNTRIES OF VIETNAM, Cambodia, and Laos form the eastern half of the Southeast Asian peninsula and for many years were known as Indochina. People from China migrated there about 2,000 years ago. The French colonized the area during the 1800s as French Indochina. Japan occupied Indochina in World War II (1939–45), and urged the people to seek independence. The French resisted this move, but were defeated in a war that raged from 1946 to 1954, when all three countries gained their independence.

Physical features

The region is a mixture of rugged, forested uplands and fertile river valleys. The only large lake is the Tonlé Sap in Cambodia. For seven months of the year it feeds the Mekong River, but in the monsoon the Mekong feeds water into the lake, making it ten times larger.

Ha Long Bay
A legend says that the fantastic limestone rocks and thousands of islands and caves of Ha Long Bay on Vietnam's Red River Delta were formed when a dragon smashed up the coast.

Mekong River
The world's tenth longest river, the Mekong rises in Tibet and flows for 4,180 km (2,600 miles) through China, Burma, Laos, and Cambodia, ending in a vast delta in south Vietnam. Many people live in riverside towns and villages and use the water to cultivate rice and other crops.

Forests
Dense rainforest covers much of the region, particularly the upland areas. These forests are home to scattered groups of hill peoples who clear small areas for farming. Hardwoods, such as teak and rosewood, are a significant resource in both Cambodia and Laos.

Regional climate
Cambodia, Laos, and southern Vietnam have a tropical climate with high temperatures all year round. The dry season ends in May with the arrival of the monsoon rains, which last until October. Northern Vietnam and Laos have cooler, more humid winters.

28°C (83°F)   21°C (70°F)

1,618 mm (61 in)

Rice
Rice is the staple food of Southeast Asia, where the warm, humid weather and plentiful water make it easy to grow. Vietnam is the world's fifth largest producer of rice, and one of the largest exporters. The most important growing areas lie in the deltas of the Mekong and Red rivers.

Rice picker, Phnom Penh, Cambodia

Vietnam

For 18 years, Vietnam was torn by a vicious war between the communist north and US-backed south, which devastated the economy. In 1975, the north won the war, and the country was unified. Today, Vietnam is slowly re-establishing its industrial strength and has close trade links with Japan, Eastern Europe, and Southeast Asia.

Boat people
After the end of the war, about a million Vietnamese set sail for Hong Kong, Singapore, and Malaysia, hoping to find refuge in the West. Crowded into tiny boats in appalling conditions, thousands died on the journey. Most were sent home, but some still live in Hong Kong.

Transport
Few Vietnamese can afford cars, and people rely on scooters, motorbikes and, more commonly, bicycles for travelling to work, to school, or to the shops. Rush hour is dominated by thousands of cyclists ringing their bells and shouting warnings. Heavy freight is transported mostly on the rivers.

Fishing
Seafood and fish are an important part of Vietnamese cooking. Thousands of people earn their living by fishing off the long coastline and in the river deltas. They catch more than a million tonnes of lobsters, fish, squid, and shrimps every year.

V

Cambodia

Once at the centre of the Khmer Empire, Cambodia was ravaged by war during the 20th century. From 1975 to 1979, the country was terrorized by the communist Khmer Rouge led by Pol Pot. More than a million people were killed, many of whom were intellectuals. Today, a democratic government is slowly rebuilding the shattered economy.

Minefields
More than three million active mines were left in the ground after the wars in Cambodia. As a result, thousands of people have been maimed or disabled.

Classical dance
The highly stylized classical dance of Cambodia is based on religious dances originally performed in the 12th-century temple complex of Angkor Wat. The dancers spend years perfecting the graceful movements, and wear costumes that are so tight they must be sewn on before each performance.

Khmers
Around 90 per cent of Cambodians are Khmers, an ancient people who had a flourishing kingdom two thousand years ago. Most live in small rural villages, where houses are often built on stilts to avoid flooding during the monsoon rains.

Laos

Surrounded by land on all sides, Laos has rich reserves of tin, lead, and zinc as well as iron, coal, and timber, yet it remains one of the world's least developed nations. About 80 per cent of the people work on the land, growing just enough food for themselves. Since 1975, Laos has been under communist rule.

Buddhism
More than half of the people in Laos are Theravada Buddhists, a branch of Buddhism that originated in Sri Lanka. Theravada means the "way of the Elders" and encourages followers to reduce suffering in the world.

Friendship Bridge
The Mekong River forms a natural border between Laos and neighbouring Thailand. Since 1988, there has been increased trade between the two countries, and in 1994, with Australian finance, a "Friendship Bridge" was built over the river's lower reaches. It connects Vientiane with the Thai town of Nong Khai, and gives Laos access to Thai ports.

Hill tribeswoman

Kha peoples
The Kha, the many hill peoples of Laos, were the country's first inhabitants. For centuries the Lao have treated them like slaves. The Kha live in scattered villages, and speak many different languages. They use traditional slash-and-burn farming methods to grow crops, and opium poppies for the drugs trade.

FIND OUT MORE

ASIA · ASIA, HISTORY OF · BRIDGES · BUDDHISM · DANCE · EMPIRES · FARMING · GOVERNMENTS AND POLITICS · KHMER EMPIRE · UNITED STATES, HISTORY OF

VIKINGS

FROM THE 8TH to the 11th centuries, the powerful Vikings emerged from their homelands in Norway, Sweden, and Denmark, and swept across Europe. They were superb ship-builders and navigators, and they used these skills to travel as far afield as the eastern coast of North America, and the eastern Mediterranean. Vikings had a reputation for raiding wherever they landed, and many of their leaders grew wealthy from plunder. However, they were not all raiders – some established peaceful colonies.

Greenland • Homelands • River routes • Iceland • Vinland • Constantinople

Exploration

Travelling by sea from Scandinavia, the Vikings raided and settled along the coasts of Europe, and crossed the Atlantic to Iceland, Greenland, and Newfoundland. They also sailed the rivers of Europe to Russia and Constantinople.

Mast
Square sail
Single square sail
Ropes, known as shrouds
Room for cargo
Shallow in depth, these ships could sail up-river

A knarr, or full-bellied ship, took settlers to Greenland.

Prow carved in the shape of a snake's head
Steering oar, which could be detached in shallow water
Oars could row the ship when there was no wind

Longships were streamlined and fast-moving so they were used for battle and long-distance travel.

Ships

All Viking ships had a keel, matching prow and stern, and were built with overlapping planks. Long, fast ships were used for raiding trips, while fatter vessels, with a large capacity, were used for carrying cargo.

Raiders

In 793 a group of Vikings raided the monastery of Lindisfarne, northern England. The attack was the first of many raids along the coasts and up the rivers of Europe. Houses and churches were plundered, people were taken as slaves, and the Vikings demanded money before they would leave.

Warriors
Each warrior provided his own armour. Some could afford strong mail armour, others made do with a leather tunic. But most wore pointed iron helmets and carried a round wooden shield.

Double-edged blade

Weaponry
Most Viking warriors fought with swords or axes, although spears and bows were also used. Iron swords were the most important weapons.

Conquests
The Vikings defeated some of the most powerful people in Europe, such as King Edmund of East Anglia, who was tortured and killed when he refused to give up Christianity.

Traders

Viking traders brought to Britain and the Mediterranean items such as furs, whalebone, walrus ivory, and timber. They brought back wheat and cloth from Britain, and pots and wine from the Mediterranean.

Furs
The Vikings traded animal products that could only be found in the north. Walrus hide could be turned into ropes and leather. The fur of animals such as brown bears and wolves made warm clothes.

Weights
The Vikings developed a system of weights and measures. These five pieces would have been used to weigh small items, such as jewellery made from precious metals. The largest weighs around 40 g (1.4 oz).

Arts and jewellery

Rich people wore brooches, arm-bands, rings, and gold or silver pendants. Poorer people wore bronze or pewter jewellery.

Gripping beast brooch

Silver spiral arm-ring

Coins

Most Viking traders worked by barter – exchanging goods from their homeland for items they wanted. Then coins came into use and, by the end of the 10th century, they were being widely used.

Brown bear
Grey wolf
Seal

Iron weights

Leif Ericsson

In about the year 1000 Leif Ericsson (born c.970) sailed to North America, and explored the coast, spending the winter in a place he named Vinland (wine land) after the grapes he found there. He was following up the accidental discovery of North America in 986 by a fellow Viking, Bjarni Herjolfsson, who was blown off-course on a voyage from Iceland to Greenland.

FIND OUT MORE · ARCHAEOLOGY · EXPLORATION · NAVIGATION · SCANDINAVIA, HISTORY OF · SHIPS AND BOATS

Vikings
Everyday objects

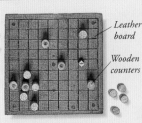

Glass counters *Wooden counters*

Leather board

Wooden counters

Wooden board

Hnefetafl was a popular Viking board game.

Nine men's morris is still played today in some places.

Glassware was used only by the richest Vikings because it was so difficult to get. Many jugs and cups were found in graves in Sweden.

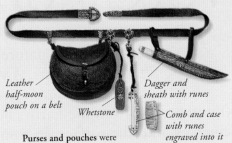

Leather half-moon pouch on a belt

Whetstone

Dagger and sheath with runes

Comb and case with runes engraved into it

Purses and pouches were an everyday necessity.

V

Weapons and body armor

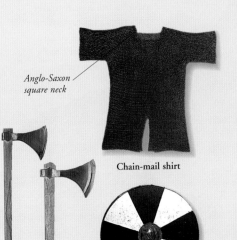

Anglo-Saxon square neck

Chain-mail shirt

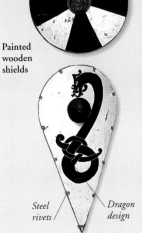

Painted wooden shields

Steel rivets

Dragon design

Dane axes

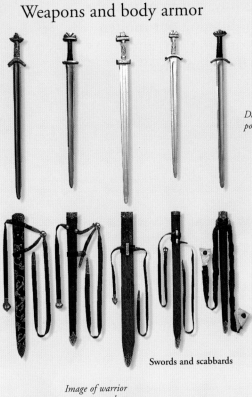

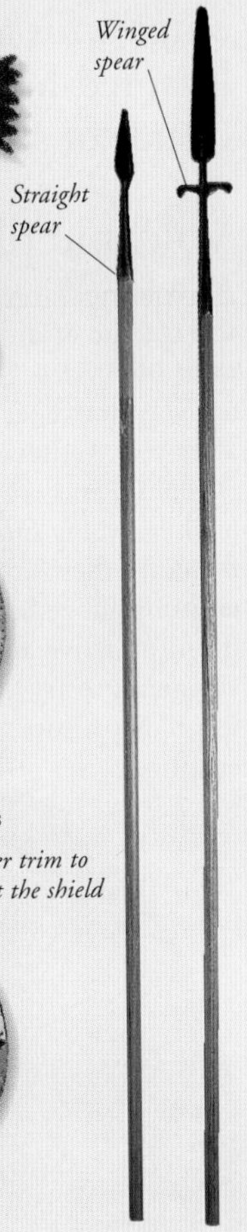

Winged spear

Straight spear

Dagger points

Chain-mail shirt

Swords and scabbards

Painted wooden shields

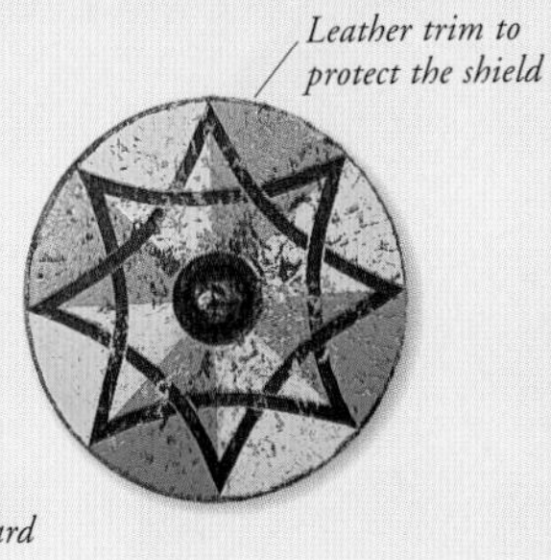

Leather trim to protect the shield

Image of warrior on nose guard

Nose guard

Helmets

Spears

Jewelry

Gripping beast brooch

Trefoil brooch

Swedish disk brooch

Oval brooch

Brooches were mainly used to fasten cloaks.

Disk pendant

Comb pendant

Cross pendant

Dwarf pendant

Pendants were often made of gold and silver for the rich, and bronze and pewter for the poor.

Thor's hammers

Amber and glass beads

Boar's tusks

Men's jewelry, such as this necklace, was often highly decorative.

Penannular brooch

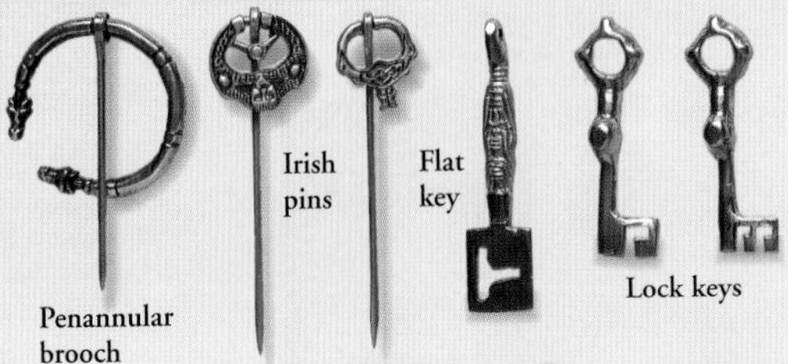

Irish pins

Flat key

Lock keys

Birka man   **Odin's head**

Valkyrie   **Birka crucifix**

Pendants could show pagan symbols, such as Odin's head or the Valkyrie, or Christian, such as the crucifix.

VOLCANOES

THE ERUPTION OF A volcano can be one of nature's most terrifying events. A volcano is a vent or fissure where magma (molten rock) from the Earth's hot interior emerges onto the surface. In some places, the molten rock, called lava once it has emerged on to the surface, oozes out slowly and gently. But in others, the eruption is a violent explosion, flinging out molten lava, red-hot lumps of rock, scorching ash, and clouds of steam which spread for kilometres.

Volcanic phases

All volcanoes, on land and under the sea, are at different stages in their life cycles. Some volcanoes are very active, erupting year after year. Others are dormant (sleeping) and erupt only once in a while. Many more are extinct – meaning they have stopped erupting altogether. Vulcanologists monitor active and dormant volcanoes to try to predict future eruptions.

Extinct
Once a volcano is extinct, it will begin to be eroded by wind and weather. All that remains of this extinct volcano in Le Puy, France, is the hard plug of material that once clogged the volcano's vent.

Active
Some volcanoes erupt almost continuously, while others erupt very violently but only at infrequent intervals. Each year there are about 25 major volcanic eruptions on land and thousands of minor ones.

Clouds of ash, steam, and rock fragments are hurled into the air.

Vent often becomes blocked by congealed magma.

Lava flow

Thick, slow-moving lava, called andesite, solidifies quickly to form the volcano's steep sides.

Magma is forced up the main vent and branch pipes.

Magma collecting in the magma chamber underground, increases the pressure on the clogged vent.

Magma chamber

Cone built up by successive layers of lava and ash.

Explosive volcanoes fling out large amounts of volcanic material during eruptions, which cools to form their distinctive cone shapes.

Volcanic eruptions

Volcanoes erupt violently when the build-up of magma in the magma chamber below creates enough pressure to blast through the clogged vent. This sudden release of pressure causes a rapid expansion of bubbles of carbon dioxide gas that remains dissolved in the magma while it is under pressure. This expansion creates fountains of lava that stream from the volcano's vent.

Types of volcano

Volcanoes are of different shapes and sizes, depending on the thickness of their lava and the shape of their vents.

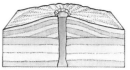

Shield volcanoes are broad, shallow cones made of very runny lava that flows easily.

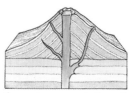

Composite cones are built up of alternate layers of lava and ash. Cones can be made of ash alone.

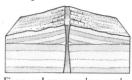

Fissure volcanoes are long cracks in the ground through which the magma oozes up gently.

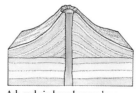

Ash and cinder volcanoes have concave-shaped cones made of the solid fragments ejected by eruptions.

Katia and Maurice Krafft

French vulcanologists Maurice Krafft (1946–91) and Katia Krafft (1947–91) were legendary for working consistently closer to erupting volcanoes than any other vulcanologists. They obtained unique data, amazing film footage, and close-up photographs of eruptions. Sadly, their bravery led to their deaths. In 1991 they were engulfed by a Japanese volcano. Their bodies were never found.

Types of lava

Lava is the molten rock thrown out by a volcano. The most common forms of lava are basalt, which is thin and runny, and cools to a heavy, black rock, and rhyolite, a thick, pale, biscuit-coloured lava. How a volcano erupts depends on the lava's thickness.

Acidic

Very viscous lava flows such as this one are usually linked to acidic magma, which contains a high proportion of the mineral silica.

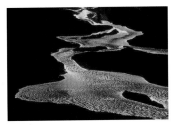

Aa

In Hawaii, where Mauna Loa is erupting almost all the time, lava that solidifies into sharp jagged chunks is known as aa, or block lava. Lava in this part of the world is basic, which means it is non-acidic.

Pahoehoe

Lava may cool quickly to form a skin tough enough to walk over. If lava continues to flow underneath, the surface wrinkles into rope-like coils. In Hawaii this is called pahoehoe, or corded lava.

Pyroclastic debris

When an explosive volcano blasts out the plug of volcanic material in its vent, the plug is shattered into an array of fragments. These fragments are known as pyroclasts, which means "fire-broken".

Ashfalls

Big volcanic eruptions can fling vast clouds of ash and dust high into the sky. These can often fall like snow, covering the ground for far around in a thick grey blanket.

Bubbles of air caught in the stone.

Tephra

Tephra are chunks of pyroclastic rock that are thrown high into the air during an eruption and rattle down on the slopes below.

Volcanic bombs

Pyroclastic fragments over 32 mm (1.26 in) across are known as volcanic bombs. They take various forms including "breadcrust bombs" (above).

Lapilli

Lapilli are smaller chunks of tephra. Sometimes they are foam-like magma fragments; sometimes they are more solid lithic (rock) pieces.

Pele's hair

Lava in Hawaii is so fluid that it forms long strands as it is flung out. This is known as Pele's hair, after the Hawaiian goddess of volcanoes.

Volcanic landscape

In volcanic areas, underground heat may create other effects on the surface as well as volcanoes. Hot gases may billow out through fissures, for instance, while the heat of rocks underground may be enough to boil groundwater, creating jets of water or bubbling mud pools.

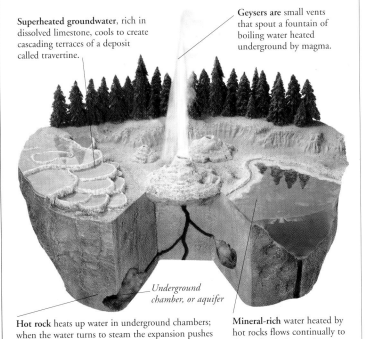

Superheated groundwater, rich in dissolved limestone, cools to create cascading terraces of a deposit called travertine.

Geysers are small vents that spout a fountain of boiling water heated underground by magma.

Underground chamber, or aquifer

Hot rock heats up water in underground chambers; when the water turns to steam the expansion pushes water above up through vents in the ground.

Mineral-rich water heated by hot rocks flows continually to the surface in hot springs.

Volcanic features

Volcanoes and volcanic activity leave behind all kinds of distinctive features in the landscape to bear witness to their ferocity and heat – sometimes relics of the outpouring of lava, sometimes relics of their effect on landscape features.

Calderas

Calderas are saucer-like craters at the tops of volcanic cones, created by the collapse of the cone during a huge explosion. Smaller calderas can occur when the top of a volcano is blown off by an eruption.

Giant's Causeway

The extraordinary hexagonal, basaltic columns that make up the Giant's Causeway in Co. Antrim, Northern Ireland, are formed of cooled lava from ancient volcanic activity.

Cones

The most distinctive volcanic relic is a cone-shaped mountain built up as lava which poured out from the vent and is then covered by ash. This process continues in successive eruptions.

FIND OUT MORE | CONTINENTS | EARTH | EARTHQUAKES | FOSSILS | MOUNTAINS AND VALLEYS | ROCKS AND MINERALS | ROMAN EMPIRE

WARFARE

WHEN PEOPLE DISAGREE about land, property, religion, or politics, one person may end the argument with violence. When nations cannot agree, the violence takes the form of warfare. If one nation is very strong, warfare can seem like an easy way of winning land or resources. But battles kill so many people, and cost so much, that nations usually start fighting only when diplomacy has failed. Peacekeeping organizations, such as the United Nations, aim to keep diplomacy working and stop wars before they begin.

Ancient warfare

Battles are part of every country's history. Some past civilizations glorified war as a means to make their nation strong. However, ancient wars were often smaller and less destructive; without modern industry and transport, it was more difficult to supply a huge army with weapons and food.

Stirrups

Technology decided the winner in ancient wars, as it does today. From at least the 4th century AD, Chinese horsemen were equipped with stirrups. Well-balanced in the saddle, they easily defeated enemies without stirrups.

Tomb figure of warrior

Modern warfare

As science and industry flourished and farms grew more food in the 19th century, European nations devised more awful forms of war. Inventions such as the machine gun could kill more soldiers; with better transport, armies could fight in more distant regions, and food surpluses meant troops rarely starved. In this "total war", everyone who could either fought or supplied troops.

World war

During the 20th centuy, warfare became truly global for the first time. World Wars I and II involved almost every nation. Countries taking part made military service compulsory, and poured all their resources into the conflicts. As well as using armies and navies, each side waged war against civilians and economic targets in order to break down the will to fight on.

Allied bombs devastated Dresden, Germany, in February 1945.

The ancient city was of no military value.

Civil war

In a civil war, groups within the same state fight each other. They battle for racial or religious reasons, or to control the government. Since the end of World War II in 1945, most wars that have broken out have been civil wars.

Civil war in El Salvador killed more than 70,000 people.

Guerilla organization flag, Cameroon

Guerilla war

Troops who occupy enemy lands may face guerilla (little war) soldiers. Guerillas often succeed, despite poor equipment and little training, because they know the countryside and have the support of local people.

US soldiers in Vietnam

Limited war

Some modern wars, such as the Vietnam War (1957–75) or the Iran-Iraq conflict (1980–88), are confined to a small region. These limited wars may not spread, because allies of the warring nations have little to gain by joining in, and much to lose.

Where war happens

A military leader must choose the battlefield with care. Each side's weapons, communications, and logistics (their ability to keep fighters fed, clothed, and armed) decide what makes a favourable battlefield for them, and a bad one for the enemy.

Infantry soldiers

On land

A major goal in war is to occupy the territory of a neighbour, so most wars are fought partly on land. However, because of the power of modern aircraft, armies must now control the skies before they can advance on the ground.

Stealth bomber

Karl von Clausewitz

Von Clausewitz (1780–1831) was a Prussian general. His influential book On War set out his theories on the nature of war and the tactics needed to win. It defined war as "an act of violence intended to compel our opponent to fulfil our will".

At sea

When all long-distance transport was by ship, warring nations battled to control the seas. Air transport has now made naval battles less important. Battleships and aircraft carriers are easy targets for missiles, so navies hide much of their power beneath the waves, in submarines.

German U-boat shells a merchant vessel, World War II.

In the air

War first spread to the air in World War I (1914–1918). Radar and missile systems now provide defences against bombers and fighter planes, but methods of attack have also improved: the "stealth" bomber cannot be detected by radar.

The rules of war

Formal rules to protect ordinary soldiers and civilians during war were first attempted in 1863, when the German-American scholar Francis Lieber (1800–1872) wrote *Code for the Government of Armies in the Field*. His work recognized the need to ban weapons that caused unnecessary suffering, and to protect the wounded and prisoners of war; it influenced later international agreements about the conduct of warfare.

International Red Cross logo

Geneva Convention

Henri Dunant (1828–1910), a Swiss citizen, founded the Red Cross to relieve the suffering of war wounded. In 1864, a Convention protecting them and those treating them was signed in Geneva by European nations; later treaties have extended its protection.

Nürnberg

After World War II, Nazi leaders were tried at a special court at Nürnberg, Germany, for the murder of more than six million people (mostly Jews). The court convicted 22 Nazis of breaking international treaties and the rules of war, and of crimes against humanity.

Prisoners of war

In the past, prisoners of war (POWs) became slaves, or bought their freedom, but the Geneva Convention now protects them. An army that captures uniformed enemy soldiers must move them away from the battlefield and imprison them in reasonable conditions until the war ends.

Boer women as prisoners of war

The cost of war

In war each side fears defeat so much that no price seems too high to pay for victory. Though the defeated side generally suffers more, the cost of winning can also be disabling. War costs are measured not just financially, but also in the loss of natural resources and human lives. During the 20th century, more than 100 million soldiers and non-combatants have been killed in wars.

The Unknown Soldier

Burying the body of an unidentified soldier in a special Tomb of the Unknown Soldier created a memorial to all the nameless war dead.

Refugees

When wars drive civilians across borders to seek asylum (a place of safety) they become refugees. They have no rights, and often no money or possessions. For food, water, shelter and medical care many depend on the country sheltering them, or on organizations such as the United Nations.

In the 1990s, war forced 4.5 million Sudanese to leave their homes.

Environmental damage

Wildlife and the natural environment always suffer in and around a battle zone. Sometimes, nations may use environmental damage as a weapon: in the Vietnam War, US forces deliberately killed crops and jungle to deny their enemy food and cover. Weapons testing, and the pressure that refugees put on the land as they try to survive, also severely damage the environment.

Bomb damage

War dead

War kills and injures huge numbers of servicemen and women; during World War I about 8.5 million servicemen died. But the changing nature of warfare meant that by World War II more civilians were killed than soldiers. In war today, bombs and bullets kill some; hunger and disease kill many more.

World War I graves in France

Government war bonds promise interest on loans.

Paying for war

War consumes a huge share of a nation's wealth: in 1944, for example, the British government spent 60 percent of its people's earnings on World War II. Governments may pay for war with borrowed money, which later generations repay.

Timeline

1096–9 European Christian knights win control of Palestine, the Holy Land, in the first, and most successful, Crusade (holy war) against the Arab world.

1240 Mongol warriors from central Asia capture Kiyyev (Kiev), Ukraine, in one of a series of wars that give them control of much of Asia and eastern Europe.

Mongol quiver

1861–5 In a bloody Civil War, northern and southern American states fight with modern weapons and supplies. The north wins; more than 600,000 people die.

1914–18 Thirty countries fight for control of Europe. Millions die in World War I.

1939–45 In World War II, more fighters die than in all previous wars put together.

1957–75 US fights a damaging war in Vietnam.

1967 The Six-Day War is fought between Israel and Arab forces. Israel wins.

The Nazis forced Jews to wear yellow stars as identity badges.

1990–91 A US-led alliance defeats Iraq in the Gulf War.

2001–02 September 11 terrorism leads to US-led war on Afghanistan.

2001–02 US-led coalition deposes Saddam Hussein's regime in Iraq.

FIND OUT MORE   ARMS AND ARMOUR   COLD WAR   GUNS   HOLOCAUST   PEACE MOVEMENTS   UNITED NATIONS   WARPLANES   WARSHIPS   WEAPONS   WORLD WAR I   WORLD WAR II

WARPLANES

AEROPLANES WERE first used in warfare during World War I (1914–18). They have been vital elements of armed combat ever since. Warplanes range from fast, nimble, jet-powered fighters to battlefield helicopters and tankers for in-flight refuelling. Between them, they find and destroy enemy aircraft and targets on the ground. Warplanes also help transport troops and equipment to and from the battlefield. In peacetime, military transport aircraft often help with emergencies and famine relief.

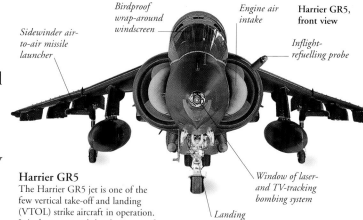

Sidewinder air-to-air missile launcher

Birdproof wrap-around windscreen

Engine air intake

Harrier GR5, front view

Inflight-refuelling probe

Window of laser- and TV-tracking bombing system

Landing light

Harrier GR5
The Harrier GR5 jet is one of the few vertical take-off and landing (VTOL) strike aircraft in operation. It is thrust upwards by the power of jet nozzles which point downwards. It does not need a runway, so can be hidden near to the battlefront.

Parts of a warplane
Fighters and fighter-bombers are highly sophisticated aircraft. On-board computers help the pilot fly and navigate the aircraft and operate the weapons. Warplanes carry air-to-air weapons (guns and missiles) for attacking other aircraft, and air-to-ground weapons (missiles and bombs) for attacking targets on the ground and at sea. They also have self-defence systems, including electronic beams and flares for confusing missiles fired at them.

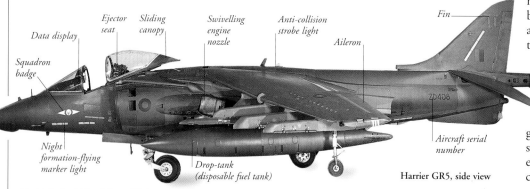

Data display

Squadron badge

Ejector seat

Sliding canopy

Swivelling engine nozzle

Anti-collision strobe light

Aileron

Fin

ZD408

Night formation-flying marker light

Drop-tank (disposable fuel tank)

Aircraft serial number

Harrier GR5, side view

Types of warplane
Warplanes are either combat aircraft or non-combat aircraft, which support other military forces. Combat aircraft include fighters (also called interceptors), which win superiority in the air, enabling other aircraft to operate over a battlezone, bombers, and fighter-bombers. Non-combat aircraft carry out reconnaissance, or carry troops and equipment rapidly to a battle zone.

Rockwell B-1B

Heavy bombers
Heavy bombers are large aircraft, often as big as passenger airliners. They fly high above the battlefield and release bombs, which fall to the ground. Several crew members are needed to operate the aircraft.

Air forces
An air force is much more than just a collection of aircraft and their crews. There are thousands of ground staff too, including the engineers who service the aircraft. Most air forces are divided into sections called squadrons. The first organized air force was the British Royal Air Force (RAF), formed in 1918.

Flying helmet

Oxygen mask

Life-jacket

Personal Equipment Connector

Anti-G trousers

Attack helicopters
A cross between helicopters and fighter aircraft, these destroy enemy targets on the battlefield with a cannon, rockets, and missiles.

Heavy-lift aircraft
Heavy-lift aircraft (right) carry hundreds of fully-equipped military personnel from home bases to a war zone.

Cobra Venom AH-1W

Lockheed C5 Galaxy

Reconnaissance aircraft
Keeping track of enemy positions is the job of reconnaissance aircraft (left). Some fly low and fast, taking photographs. Others fly high, using powerful radar to detect other aircraft.

Boeing E3A

Inflatable collar

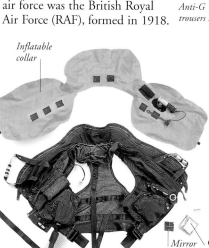

Uniform, jet crew member, British RAF

Jet crew wear life-jackets with survival aids, in case they need to eject from a plane.

Mirror

Code booklet

| FIND OUT MORE | AIRCRAFT | AIRSHIPS AND BALLOONS | ARMIES | ENGINES | FLIGHT, HISTORY OF | WARFARE | WEAPONS | WORLD WAR I | WORLD WAR II |

WARSHIPS

SEVERAL DIFFERENT TYPES OF SHIP are involved in modern warfare, from small, fast patrol boats to massive aircraft carriers. Each type carries out a particular job, such as protecting merchant ships from attack or searching for enemy ships and submarines. A modern warship is crammed with sophisticated navigation and weapon systems. Warships normally operate together in groups called fleets. They are supported by naval auxiliary ships, which deliver supplies such as fuel and food.

Parts of a warship

Warships are designed to be fast and easy to manoeuvre. They have lightweight aluminium hulls and powerful gas-turbine engines. Inside, each ship is divided into watertight sections that can be sealed off if the hull is holed during an attack. Here are the crew's quarters, store rooms, and control rooms. Above the deck are weapons and communication equipment. Warships carry several different types of weapons, including guns, missiles, and torpedoes.

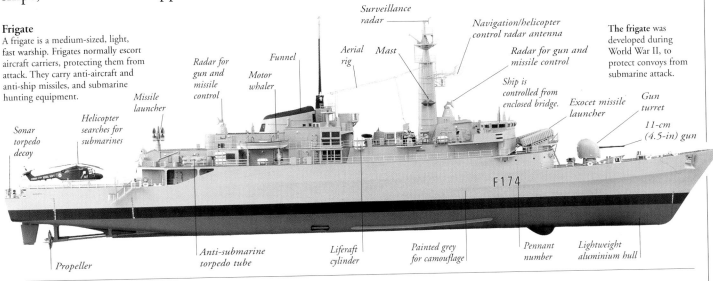

Frigate
A frigate is a medium-sized, light, fast warship. Frigates normally escort aircraft carriers, protecting them from attack. They carry anti-aircraft and anti-ship missiles, and submarine hunting equipment.

Surveillance radar

Navigation/helicopter control radar antenna

The frigate was developed during World War II, to protect convoys from submarine attack.

Radar for gun and missile control

Funnel

Aerial rig

Mast

Radar for gun and missile control

Motor whaler

Ship is controlled from enclosed bridge.

Exocet missile launcher

Gun turret

Missile launcher

11-cm (4.5-in) gun

Helicopter searches for submarines

Sonar torpedo decoy

F174

Propeller

Anti-submarine torpedo tube

Liferaft cylinder

Painted grey for camouflage

Pennant number

Lightweight aluminium hull

Types of warship

Warships are either surface warships or submarines. The most important surface warship is the aircraft carrier. Other types of surface ships defend carriers and attack enemy ships. Submarines are either hunter-killers, which search for and destroy enemy ships, or ballistic missile submarines, which stay hidden in the oceans for months.

German Navy minesweeper

Mine warfare vessels
Minehunters search for mines (explosive charges) sunk beneath the sea; minesweepers have special equipment to locate and destroy surface mines. These warships have wood or plastic hulls, because magnetic mines are set off when a steel hull comes near them.

US Navy aircraft carrier

Aircraft carriers
The aircraft carrier is the largest of all warships. It is a floating air base: as well as runways for take-offs and landings, it has hangars where planes are serviced, and a control tower to communicate with pilots. The largest aircraft carriers carry up to 100 airplanes and a crew of more than 2,000 sailors, plus a flying crew of more than 1,000.

Helicopter cruisers
Cruisers are large warships, armed with guns, missiles, and torpedoes. A helicopter cruiser has a deck at the rear where helicopters land, and hangers where helicopters are stored.

US Navy helicopter cruiser

Navies

In wartime, a navy's job is to keep a nation's sea lanes open, protect merchant and other ships at sea, hunt and destroy enemy ships, and support armies and air forces. In time of peace, they help with disaster relief and rescue work, and make visits to foreign countries to promote goodwill.

Uniforms
This uniform from the Soviet Navy is in a traditional style. Many nations have a similar uniform.

Sailor's badge

Trade badge

Jumper, shirt, collar

Boots

Trousers

Cap

FIND OUT MORE   ARMIES   RADAR AND SONAR   SAILING   SHIPS AND BOATS   SUBMARINES   TRANSPORT, HISTORY OF   WARFARE   WEAPONS   WORLD WAR II

WASHINGTON, GEORGE

AS LEADER OF THE AMERICAN forces that won the Revolutionary War against the British and as the first president of the new nation, George Washington is known as the "Father of his Country". He learned his military skills fighting for the British in the 1750s, and used those skills to good effect against them 20 years later. A fine politician and administrator, he worked hard to unite his new country and to reconcile conflicting interests. His honesty and moderation made him a symbol of his nation.

Early life
Washington was born in 1732 into a landed family in Virginia. When he was 11, his father died, and he went to live with his half-brother Lawrence. George wanted to go to sea, but was persuaded to train as a surveyor. A practical man, he succeeded despite his limited education.

Musket from the French-Indian War

French-Indian War
In 1753, French armies from Canada occupied the Ohio River Valley. George Washington fought for the British against the Frenchand their native American allies. He was promoted quickly for his military and organizational skills.

Mount Vernon

When his half-brother Lawrence died in 1752, George inherited the family's large estate of Mount Vernon, Virginia. He made many changes there and experimented with new crops. In 1759, he married Martha Custis, a wealthy widow, and entered Virginia politics. Throughout Washington's life, Mount Vernon was a welcome retreat, and he retired there at the end of his life.

Delegates at the Continental Congress

Continental Congress
Washington was an early champion of American independence. In 1774 and 1775, he served as a delegate from Virginia to the Continental Congresses held to organize the 13 colonies' struggle against the British. When the Revolutionary War broke out in 1775, the Congress appointed Washington commander-in-chief of the colonial army.

Washington Crossing The Delaware by Emanuel Leutze

Commander-in-chief

When war broke out in 1775, Washington took over a disorganized, ill-equipped army incapable of beating the professional, well-equipped British. Despite interference from Congress, he turned the colonial troops into an efficient force, able to outwit and defeat the British in 1781.

Trenton
In the first two years of the war, American troops were outmanoeuvred by the British. On 25 December 1776, Washington and his troops crossed the ice-bound Delaware River near Trenton, New Jersey. They captured the surprised British army the next day at the Battle of Trenton.

Valley Forge
The American army spent the winter of 1777–78 in Valley Forge, Pennsylvania. The winter was severe and food and clothing were scarce, but despite desertions and the threat of mutiny, Washington showed his grit and determination, holding his army together. In the spring, the army emerged well-prepared for battle.

President of the United States

After American independence was assured in 1783, Washington withdrew from politics. But conflicts between the states led to him taking a leading role. In 1787, he presided over the convention which drafted the constitution, and in 1789 was unanimously elected president of the new country. He served two four-year terms before retiring in 1797.

Thomas Jefferson

The author of the American Constitution, Thomas Jefferson (1743–1826) became secretary of state under Washington and led the Democratic-Republicans, who favoured individual and state rights. Washington tried to keep aloof from party politics but favoured the Federalists, who wanted a stronger national state. Party conflicts caused many problems during Washington's presidency.

Whiskey Rebellion
In 1794, rioting broke out against the imposition of a national tax on alcoholic drink. The American government tried to enforce the law, but in the end Washington was forced to use troops. This, and other troubles, meant that Washington decided against running for a third term as president.

GEORGE WASHINGTON

1732	Born in Virginia.
1743	On the death of his father, goes to live with his brother Lawrence.
1754–59	Fights in the British Army against the French.
1759	Enters Virginia politics.
1774–75	Delegate at two Continental Congresses.
1775	Appointed commander-in-chief of Colonial forces.
1783	USA wins independence from Britain.
1789–97	Serves two terms as President of the USA.
1799	Dies at Mount Vernon.

FIND OUT MORE — AMERICAN REVOLUTION · GOVERNMENTS AND POLITICS · LAW · UNITED STATES, HISTORY OF

WEAPONS

STRENGTH AND SKILL decide the winner in a fight without weapons, but in armed combat, the fighter with the better killing tool may win. Ever since people began to compete for land or food, warriors have sought weapons of increasing power. Changing technology supplied them: metals were used to make swords; nuclear power was first used in bombs. This arms race has now led to weapons so powerful that a nation that used them might win the war, but would destroy everything in the conquered lands.

Early weapons

Early warriors fought with clubs and short blades. Lances and spears kept the enemy farther away; missiles such as the boomerang allowed warriors to attack anyone within throwing distance. To launch missiles further still, fighters used slingshots or bows.

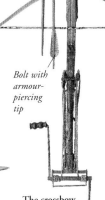

Bolt with armour-piercing tip

Blade could be stone, bronze, or iron.

The dagger, used in hand-to-hand fighting, was one of the first weapons.

The crossbow, a powerful weapon used in medieval warfare.

W

Gunpowder

Gunpowder

The most far-reaching development in weapons technology came in the 14th century, with the invention of firearms. These weapons were powered by gunpowder, an explosive. Although feeble at first, firearms were soon capable of firing missiles great distances. Battles could be fought at long range, instead of face-to-face.

Booby traps

Seemingly harmless objects or areas can be unexpectedly deadly. Guerilla fighters may capture or wound enemies with trip wires or spike-filled holes. Most modern traps rely on explosives. Buried anti-tank mines explode when vehicles crush them; smaller anti-personnel (AP) mines blast people treading on them. Aircraft can drop huge numbers of AP mines very quickly.

How an AP mine works

When someone treads on an AP mine, the pressure sets off a process that detonates an explosive charge. The force of the explosion travels upwards, causing terrible injuries. Such mines are designed to maim rather than kill, as a wounded person needs more care than a dead one, draining enemy resources.

Nikolaus von Dreyse

German gunsmith Dreyse (1787–1867) designed a more effective weapon for the battlefield: a rifle that fired twice as fast as earlier guns. Troops loaded bullets near the trigger so they could shoot lying down, safe from enemy fire. The Prussian army began using the gun in 1840.

Explosive material stored here.

Metal fragments to cause severe harm.

Pin

Box, 15 cm (6 in) long

Mine victims, Kurdistan, 1993

AP mine, World War II

Bombs and missiles

A bomb is a container filled with explosive material and a detonator to make it explode. The explosion causes a lethal blast, scattering deadly bits of the bomb casing far and wide. Missiles are weapons that are propelled towards a target; they allow a warring nation to destroy an enemy nation without risking the life of a single soldier.

Aerial bombing in World War I: bombs were originally dropped by hand.

Gravity bombs

Dropped from aircraft, gravity bombs contain high exlosive. Most explode when they hit the ground. Modern types may divide into many "bomblets" to blast a wider area.

Smart bomb approaches target.

Smart bombs

"Smart" bombs are missiles in which a warhead is guided directly to its target by a laser-aiming device or on-board computer map. Some contain video cameras in their noses.

Mass destruction

The most powerful weapons can destroy a city or poison the land of a whole nation. These weapons are so dangerous that there are international treaties which aim to outlaw their use in war, or at least reduce their numbers.

Respirator protects the lungs.

Special suit to protect the skin from gas.

Nuclear weapons testing, 1995

Nuclear weapons

In an atomic bomb, a sugar-cube-size piece of uranium has the same destructive power as a block of conventional explosive as big as a house.

Chemical weapons

Chemical and biological weapons spread poisons or epidemic diseases, so they kill or injure the enemy without damaging property. Casualties die slowly, overwhelming an enemy's medical facilities.

FIND OUT MORE   ARMS AND ARMOUR   GUNS   HUNDRED YEARS WAR   NUCLEAR POWER   PEACE MOVEMENTS   WARFARE   WORLD WAR I   WORLD WAR II

Weapons
Without gunpowder

Pick pierces armour

Head to stun the enemy

Flint

Arrowheads, c.2700–1800 BC

Double-edged, curved blade

Dagger (jambiya), of Arab origin

Fighting boomerangs

Japanese swords are the finest ever made.

Samurai sword and scabbard

Iron blade

Made by Europeans to trade with Native Americans

Tomahawk

Can be attached to a gun and used for attack or defence

Sword bayonet

War hammer

Bow was about as tall as the archer.

English longbow and arrow

Bow could shoot arrow 270 m (890 feet).

Metal mace, for attacking armour

Firearms

Storage space for cloth patches, to ensure that bullets fit snugly.

Rifle, effective at 275 m (900 ft), early 19th century

Silencer

Silenced Sten submachine gun, World War II

Switch for automatic or semi-automatic firing

Revolving wheel struck sparks to ignite gunpowder.

Early pistol, muzzle-loading

Telescopic sight made aim more accurate

6.5 mm type-97 rifle, used by snipers

Butt

Carrying handle

Foresight

Extendible butt

Colt Commando Carbine, a short, light rifle

Barrel of grenade launcher

Assault rifle, with grenade launcher

Grenade launcher trigger

Rifle trigger

Pistol grip

Nuclear warhead

Colt Peacemaker revolver

Ivory stock

Colt pocket pistol

Enlarged trigger guard for gloved finger

Taisho automatic pistol, modified for use in Arctic

Trigger guard

Liberator pistol, World War II

Slide

Heckler and Koch automatic pistol

Tanks, bombs, and missiles

Bomb powered by pulse-jet engine

Warhead

V1 flying bomb, a missile used in World War II.

Gun

Travels at 25 km/h (15 mph)

Infantry tank, World War II

Fin

Cap

Fuse set before firing

Mortar bomb, NATO practice ammunition

Weighs 25 tonnes

Polaris A3 missile, fired from a submarine to destroy land targets.

Warhead

Torpedo, a submarine weapon

WEASELS AND MARTENS

SMALL AND SLENDER mammals, weasels and martens are some of the most efficient hunters. They have a fierce reputation and, on their own, can kill prey much larger than themselves. With their excellent senses of smell, hearing, and sight, they track down their prey, then pounce, and kill it with a lethal bite. Different species occupy habitats from the polar regions to the tropics. Some live in trees, others in burrows or among rocks or tree roots.

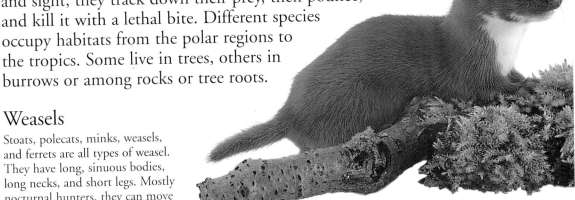

Young weasels
Weasels breed in the spring, producing litters of up to eight young. The baby weasels stay in the safety of the den in the first weeks of life, and are looked after by the female alone. After about two months, the young begin to hunt for themselves.

Common weasel
One of the most widespread weasels is the common weasel. It weaves through the undergrowth searching for small rodents, such as mice and voles, and is small and lithe enough to pursue them into their burrows. Males may be twice as big as females so they chase larger prey down larger burrows. Each weasel has its own territory, which may cover several hectares.

Weasels
Stoats, polecats, minks, weasels, and ferrets are all types of weasel. They have long, sinuous bodies, long necks, and short legs. Mostly nocturnal hunters, they can move extremely fast and run, climb, and swim after their prey.

Weasels have a flexible spine and strong back muscles.

Weasels are particularly good at hearing high-pitched sounds, such as a mouse squeaking.

Short legs allow the weasel to manoeuvre in small burrows.

All weasels stand up on their back legs to look around.

Stoat
The stoat, seen here tracking its prey by scent, looks similar to the common weasel, but it has a black tip to its tail and is a little bigger than the weasel. It can tackle prey as large as a hare. In the northern, colder parts of its range, the stoat's coat turns white in winter to camouflage it against the snow. It is then known as ermine.

Least weasel skull
The least weasel is the smallest carnivore in the world, only 17.5 cm (6.8 in long). Its strong jaws and sharp stabbing teeth are typical of all weasels.

Polecats are solitary animals, as are all weasels.

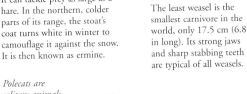

Polecats
Like most weasels, polecats are versatile hunters, eating rodents, rabbits, frogs, birds, and lizards. They patrol their territory at night, marking it with their scent.

Minks
These weasels are good swimmers, helped by their partly webbed feet. They usually live by rivers, lakes, and marshes, taking their prey of fish, frogs, and birds from the water.

Minks have thick, oily, waterproof fur.

Martens
There are eight species of marten inhabiting forests in Europe, Asia, Canada, and Alaska. They are larger than weasels, and their slightly longer limbs make them better climbers. They readily catch prey in trees, though they also hunt on the ground, taking squirrels, birds, eggs, insects, and plant food such as berries.

Pine marten
An extremely agile climber, the pine marten is able to run and leap along branches. It has a bushy tail that helps with balance, and long claws and large paws that grip the bark. It is the largest Eurasian marten.

Fisher
Despite its name, the fisher feeds largely on the flesh of birds and small mammals such as rabbits. It is known for its ability to kill porcupines, whose spines it avoids by attacking the unprotected face and belly.

Wolverine
A giant among weasels and martens, the wolverine weighs up to 25 kg (55 lb). It is powerful enough to kill and eat a reindeer. It catches its prey not by stalking, but by pouncing in ambush, often from a tree.

Zorilla
Widespread in Africa, the zorilla's vivid stripes act as a warning to larger predators not to attack. If the warning is ignored, the zorilla will raise its tail and spray a noxious fluid at the attacker.

COMMON WEASEL

SCIENTIFIC NAME	*Mustela nivalis*
ORDER	Carnivora
FAMILY	Mustelidae
DISTRIBUTION	Europe, most of Asia, northwest Africa
DIET	Rodents, moles, rabbits, birds
SIZE	Length 21–29 cm (8–11.5 in)

FIND OUT MORE   ANIMAL BEHAVIOUR   BADGERS, OTTERS, AND SKUNKS   FOOD WEBS AND CHAINS   MAMMALS

WEATHER

WIND, RAIN, SNOW, fog, frost, and sunshine are all signs of the constant shifting of the lowest level of the atmosphere. This continual change is what we call the weather. The weather changes in four main ways: its movement, which can bring winds; its temperature, which can cause anything from frosts to heat waves; its moisture content, which can bring rain and fog; and its pressure, which can cause anything from cloudless days to fierce storms. The average weather in one particular area is known as the climate.

Highs
These are caused by blocks of denser air in the upper atmosphere. The density of the air makes it heavy, which creates a high pressure region. With very little water vapour in it, a high creates a clear and cloudless day.

Depressions and fronts

The atmosphere often forms into blocks of air, or air masses, over an area where conditions are similar. A front is the boundary between two air masses. Where a warm and cold air mass meet, lighter air rises up over the cold, creating a low pressure zone, or depression. This brings storms as it develops and drifts eastwards.

High-level cirrus clouds precede the warm front.

Clouds form as the rising moist, warm air condenses.

Rain falls from nimbostratus clouds.

Altostratus cloud

Cold air sinks under the warm air mass.

Warm front

The mass of cold air dips sharply beneath the warm air.

Some of the moisture in the cloud-tops turns to ice.

High-level winds blow the cloud-tops into wedge shapes.

After the heaviest part of the storm, light showers may still occur.

Rising warm air

Cold front

Advancing front

Strong winds and heavy clouds occur along the cold front.

Warm front
In a depression, the front often breaks into two – a warm front and a cold front. As the depression passes, the warm front is usually ahead of the cold. The warm air slides gently up over the cold, bringing gentle, steady rain.

Cold front
After the warm front has passed, there is generally a brief pause. The cold air then drives sharply under the warm, forcing it upwards and creating huge clouds that bring heavy rain and thunderstorms.

Formation of a depression

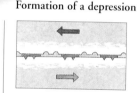

1 A polar front is where warm, tropical air meets cold, polar air.

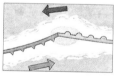

2 A depression begins to form, where warm air bulges over the cold air.

3 Cold air chases under the warm air and the front splits into two – warm and cold fronts.

4 The cold front may lift the warm front off the ground, to form an occluded front.

Air pressure

The force of molecules (groups of atoms) moving in the air creates air pressure. The more molecules are in motion, the greater the pressure. Warm air expands, making it less dense and reducing pressure. Cold air contracts, raising pressure. Pressure variations cause changes in the weather.

Barometer
Barometers measure air pressure and show changes in pressure on a dial. A dramatic fall in pressure usually means that a storm is on its way.

Aneroid barometer

Isobars
Air pressure is measured in millibars and is shown on weather maps by isobars (lines). Each isobar links points of equal pressure. The closer together the isobars are, the sharper the difference in air pressure.

Weather map showing isobars

Air temperature

Air temperature largely depends on the Sun's heat. Air temperatures are highest in the tropics, where the Sun is strongest. Meteorologists place thermometers in the shade, when measuring air temperatures, to get an overall picture.

Double-ended thermometer records the daily maximum and minimum temperatures.

Humidity

Humidity is the moisture content of clouds. Moisture is present as vapour in the air almost all of the time, but is invisible. When the air gets cold, however, the vapour condenses to water drops, forming clouds, fog, or even rain.

Wet and dry hygrometer uses a scale to show humidity.

FIND OUT MORE

AIR   ATMOSPHERE   CLIMATE   CLOUDS   RAIN   STORMS   TIME   WEATHER FORECASTING

WEATHER FORECASTING

FROM FARMERS TO ICE-CREAM makers, different communities, businesses, and individuals want to know what the weather is likely to be. Weather forecasting is the prediction of weather conditions over an area, either for days (short-range) or for months (long-range). Every three hours, 10,000 weather stations world-wide simultaneously record observations of weather conditions. These data, called synoptic values, feed huge computers in the 13 main weather centres of the World Meteorological Organization. Meteorologists – people who study the weather – produce weather forecasts based on the computers' calculations plus satellite and radar images.

Weather stations

Ships at sea, city roofs, and mountain-tops all provide sites for the world's weather stations. Most stations are equipped with thermometers and hygrometers to show temperature and humidity, anemometers to record wind speed, rain gauges to collect rainfall, and mercury barometers to monitor changes in air pressure.

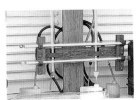

Stevenson screen
Air temperature readings are taken in the shade. A white box, called a Stevenson screen, shields thermometers from direct sunlight. Ventilation slats keep air flowing freely.

Radiosondes are filled with helium.

Weather balloon
Every day around the world, at noon and midnight GMT (Greenwich Mean Time), balloons, known as radiosondes, are launched into the atmosphere to measure conditions such as air pressure, temperature, and humidity at heights up to 20 km (12 miles).

Weather planes
These provide detailed information about conditions high in the atmosphere, especially around storms. Weather planes are equipped with a range of monitoring devices to record anything from the ice content of clouds to the presence of gases.

Weather charts

Some of the first weather forecasts were printed in the London *Daily News* in 1848. These reports were crude and very short-term compared to today's sophisticated predictions. Technology now enables satellite images of the weather to be taken from high above the Earth. A computer applies different colours to the map to indicate variations in temperature, humidity, clouds, and atmospheric pressure.

Colour spectrum shows temperatures, with red denoting the hottest and violet the coolest.

Orange and red tinting indicates very hot weather.

Swirl of cloud indicates a severe storm over the British Isles.

Images are taken from hundreds of miles above ground level.

Dark grey cloud shows heavy rain.

Colours show that it is generally warmer inland than on the coast.

Patchy cloud cover

Ocean is dark blue to reflect cool temperature.

Satellite image of Europe and North Africa taken in 1997

Weather satellites
The first weather satellite, launched by the USA in 1960, orbited 850 km (531 miles) above the North and South poles. In the 1970s, geostationary satellites were made to travel up to 40,000 km (25,000 miles) away.

A depression over the United Kingdom

Radar
Radar (which stands for Radio Detection And Ranging) signals reflect off water present in the air, such as snow and rain. Radar can be used to generate computer images of depressions and other systems to give a clear indication of where rain is falling, and how much.

Lewis Richardson

British mathematician Lewis Richardson (1881–1953) devised a system called numerical forecasting. This system forecast the weather, by feeding millions of simultaneous measurements of atmospheric conditions into giant computers.

Natural weather forecasters

Natural signs are still used to help forecast the weather. Many plants and animals react to moisture changes in the air, and so may indicate that rain is coming.

Closed pine cone scales warn of rain.

Wool shrinks and curls up in dry air.

Seaweed becomes limp in moist air.

FIND OUT MORE   AIRSHIPS AND BALLOONS   ATMOSPHERE   COMPUTERS   RADAR AND SONAR   SATELLITES   TREES   WEATHER

WEIGHTS AND MEASURES

IN ANCIENT EGYPT, the cubit was the main unit used to measure length. It was based on the distance from a person's elbow to his or her fingertips. Because different people have arms of different size, it eventually became necessary for the Egyptians to define a standard length for the cubit, so that the cubit was the same throughout the country. In the same way, our modern systems of measurement, such as the metric and imperial or customary systems, are based on standard units. The quantities we measure include length, area, volume, weight, and mass.

Measuring space

When we measure length, area, or volume, we are measuring space. Length is the amount of linear space between two points. Area is a measurement of the two-dimensional space of a surface such as a wall. Volume is the amount of three-dimensional space occupied by a solid object or an amount of liquid or gas.

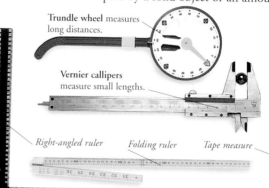

Trundle wheel measures long distances.

Vernier callipers measure small lengths.

Right-angled ruler   Folding ruler   Tape measure

Metal metre rule

Retractable steel rule

Length and distance

All devices designed to measure length or distance measure space along a line. The word length is used when measuring how long an object is; distance refers to the space between two places. Units of length or distance include the foot (ft), metre (m), mile (mi), and kilometre (km).

Measuring weight

We usually describe an object's "weight" in grams and kilograms, or pounds and ounces. However, these are really units of mass – that is, the amount of matter in an object. In science, weight refers to the force of gravity pulling an object downwards. Scientists measure weight in different units, such as newtons and poundals.

Digital scales

Scales and balances

To weigh things accurately, we must use scales or a balance. Digital scales use electronic components to find the weight of an object. A balance consists of two linked pans. The object to be weighed is placed in one pan, and standard weights are added to the other. The two pans will balance when they are carrying the same weight.

Flour   Simple balance   Weights

Area

To ensure you buy enough paint to cover a wall, it is important to know the area of the wall you are gong to paint. Area is measured in square units, such as square metres (m²) or square feet (ft²). Land areas are usually measured in different units, such as hectares (ha) or acres (ac).

The combined volume of the bricks equals the volume of the water.

0.64 l of water

Ten bricks, each 64 cm³ volume

Volume

Solid volume is measured in cubic units, such as cubic centimetres (cm³) or cubic inches (in³). Capacity units, such as litres (l) or pints (pt), measure liquid volume. Gas volume is measured in either cubic units or capacity units.

Standard units

Today, there are two major systems of standard units. The metric system, which is decimal, is the most common and is used by scientists world-wide. Some countries, such as the USA, use the older imperial or customary system. In other countries, such as the UK, people use the metric and imperial systems side by side.

Metric system

Units in the metric system include the centimetre (cm), metre (m), gram (g), kilogram (kg), litre (l), and hectare (ha). Prefixes such as milli- and kilo- denote smaller or larger units. For example, one-thousandth of a metre is a millimetre (mm), and 1,000 metres is one kilometre (km).

Imperial system

The inch (in), foot (ft), ounce (oz), pound (lb), pint (pt), and acre (ac) are all imperial units. Unlike metric units, which are all based on the number 10, imperial units do not all have the same number base: a foot is divided into 12 inches, but a pound contains 16 ounces.

Non-standard units

Parts of the body were once used as measuring units. The hand, for example, was used to find the height of horses. Such units were non-standard, because people's bodies are never the same. A horse could be 18 hands high to one person, but only 16 to another. The hand has now been standardized to a length of exactly 10 cm (3.94 in).

Thread (length): 8 m; 26 ft

Ribbon (length): 25 cm; 10 in

Oil (volume): 1 l; 1.76 pt

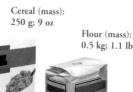
Cereal (mass): 250 g; 9 oz

Flour (mass): 0.5 kg; 1.1 lb

Grapes (mass): 200 g; 7 oz

Rug (area) 6 m²; 64 ft²

A hand was 4 fingers wide.

FIND OUT MORE   DYES AND PAINTS   EGYPT, ANCIENT   FOOD   GRAVITY   HORSES   MATHEMATICS   MATTER   NUMBERS   SCIENCE

WHALES AND DOLPHINS

Of all marine mammals, the best adapted to life in the sea are the whales. Underneath their thick smooth skin is a layer of blubber, which insulates them against the cold. Like all mammals, they are warm-blooded, air-breathing animals, and give birth to live young. Whales, including dolphins and porpoises, form the order Cetacea, and most probably evolved from four-legged land mammals. They are separated into two groups – the toothed whales, of which there are about 80 species, and the baleen, or whalebone, whales, of which there are about 12 species. The only other entirely aquatic mammals are the Sirenians.

Whale's body encrusted with barnacles

Gray Whale

Baleen whales

The baleen, or whalebone, whales are the giants of the ocean. They feed by swimming through a shoal of shrimp-like krill with their mouths wide open. When they close their mouths, the water is forced out through the baleen plates suspended from their upper jaws, leaving the krill trapped on the inside. Adult blue whales can swallow a huge quantity of krill in a single mouthful.

Teeth
A whale's teeth are all the same shape. A killer whale has stout, conical teeth that curve backwards.

Powerful jaws

Baleen
Plates of baleen are made from keratin. This is the same material that makes up human hair.

Toothed whales

Dolphins, porpoises, sperm whales, beaked whales, and the killer whale are all species of toothed whale. The unusual narwhal and beluga also belong to this group. The toothed whales have as many as 260 teeth or as few as a single pair. The whales use their teeth to catch and hold, but not to chew, their prey which includes fish and squid. Instead, they swallow their food whole.

Aerial view of a whale "blowing"

Blowholes
In the course of evolution, the nostrils of almost all the whales have moved to the top of the head. This makes it possible for the animals to breathe without having to expose their body above the surface of the water. Toothed whales have one blowhole; baleen whales have two. When a whale surfaces, it "spouts" by blowing moist air out through its blowhole. Then it breathes in, closes its blowhole, and submerges again.

Gray whale
A baleen whale, the gray whale feeds on crustaceans living on the seabed. It uses its snout to stir up sediment which it strains through short baleen plates. Each year, the California gray whale migrates from its feeding grounds in the Arctic Ocean to its calving lagoons in southern California and Mexico.

The baleen of right whales grows longer than that of other whales.

A narwhal's tusk is a greatly enlarged left upper incisor tooth.

A tusk can grow to 2.75 m (9 ft) long.

Until 17th century tusk was thought to be unicorn horn

Killer whale
A powerful and ruthless predator, the killer whale eats mainly fish, penguins, and seals. It is particularly efficient when hunting for food as a pack. Even a large whale stands little chance against a pack of killer whales.

Narwhal skull and tusk

Narwhal
Male narwhals have a long spiral-shaped tusk growing from the upper jaw. The narwhal's only other tooth rarely grows beyond the gums. Narwhals are found only in Arctic waters, where they live in herds of about 12 individuals.

The entire body comes out of the water.

Porpoising
Dolphins are renowned for their ability to make spectacular leaps out of the water. This is called porpoising, but, strangely enough, porpoises do not leap.

Common dolphin
Found in warm and temperate seas, the common dolphin sometimes gathers in schools of several hundred. It feeds on fish and is itself often caught in nets. As a result, its numbers have declined.

Dolphin enters the water headfirst.

Dolphin rises at high speed.

Dolphins and porpoises

Both dolphins and porpoises are toothed whales. They eat fish, cuttlefish, and squid. Most dolphins are larger than porpoises, which have rounder bodies and foreheads.

893

Fluking

A whale's tail is horizontal and flattened. It provides the whale with its means of propulsion and generates enormous power. Before beginning a deep dive, some whales lift their tail flukes into the air to help them get into position for a steep descent. This is called fluking. The way a whale flukes helps in its identification. Some, such as this sperm whale, bring their tails high into the air so that the underside can be seen. Others keep the flukes turned down.

Threats

The great whales have few natural enemies other than the killer whale. Smaller whales are at risk from sharks. Whales are still hunted by humans, and many species are on the verge of extinction. Even dolphins and porpoises are killed. A great number of whales are caught in fishing nets and drown.

Beaching

These pilot whales have become stranded on a beach in Tasmania, Australia. No one is sure why whales do this. One theory is that they rely on the Earth's magnetic field to orientate themselves, and sometimes become confused, as, for example, during a magnetic storm. Some people think pollution of the seas weakens the whales' resistance to disease.

Toothed whales use echolocation to find prey.

Echolocation

Toothed whales have developed an extremely sophisticated sense of hearing. Like bats, whales use a system of echolocation to detect other things in the water. They emit an almost non-stop stream of "clicks" that cannot be detected by the human ear. The clicks are reflected off nearby objects and picked up by the whales' receiving apparatus.

Whiskers are used to find food on the riverbed.

Manatees can weigh up to 1.6 tonnes.

West Indian manatee

Sirenians

The four species of Sirenians – three manatee and one dugong – are, like the whales, aquatic mammals. Often called sea cows, they are all herbivorous, feeding mainly on sea grasses. Manatees live in tropical coastal waters on either side of the Atlantic, entering large rivers and estuaries and rarely venturing into the open sea. The dugong lives around the edges of the Indian and western Pacific oceans.

Schools

Most whales live in communities. They associate in groups, called schools when referring to dolphins, or pods when referring to larger toothed whales such as these killer whales. The groups vary in size from a male, several females, and their calves, to thousands as sometimes happens with pilot whales.

Mother and calf stay close to each other.

Flukes are up to a quarter of the body length.

Largest and smallest

The blue whale is the largest of the Cetaceans. The smallest is the vaquita, also called the Gulf of California harbour porpoise. An adult is about 1.2-1.5 m (4-5 ft) long. Large numbers have been caught in fishing nets, but it is seldom seen in the wild and is believed to be rare.

A newborn blue whale weighs 2 tonnes and is more than 7 m (23 ft) long.

Throat grooves allow the mouth to expand.

Blue whale

By far the largest animal the world has ever seen, the blue whale grows up to 32 m (105 ft) long and weighs up to 160 tonnes. Its tongue alone weighs 4 tonnes – almost as much as a full-grown elephant. It can grow this size only becaue its huge bulk is supported by water. Blue whales live mainly in cold waters and open seas, distributed patchily worldwide.

Breeding

Whales usually give birth to one calf after a gestation period of 10-12 months. When the calf is born, the female guides it to the surface so that it can take its first breath. A mother whale takes great care of her calf, which may suckle from her for several years.

GRAY WHALE

SCIENTIFIC NAME	*Eschrichtius robustus*
ORDER	Cetacea
FAMILY	Eschrichtiidae
DISTRIBUTION	Pacific coasts of North America and Asia
HABITAT	Shallow coastal waters
DIET	Crustaceans

FIND OUT MORE

BATS MAMMALS MIGRATION OCEAN WILDLIFE POLAR WILDLIFE SEALS SHARKS AND RAYS

Whales and dolphins
Toothed

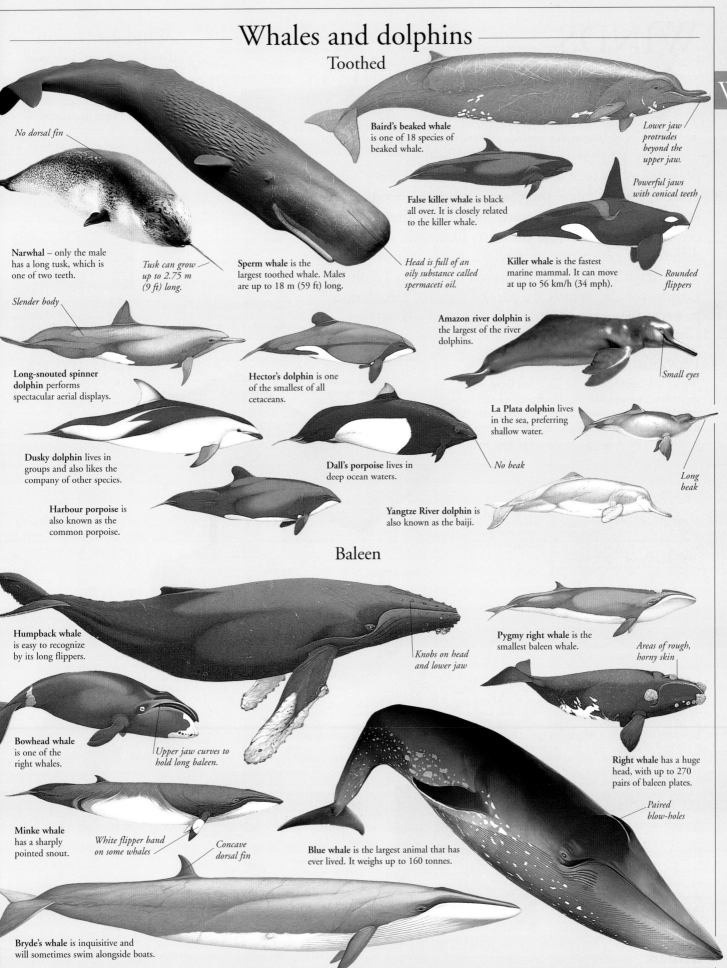

No dorsal fin

Narwhal – only the male
has a long tusk, which is
one of two teeth.

*Tusk can grow
up to 2.75 m
(9 ft) long.*

Sperm whale is the
largest toothed whale. Males
are up to 18 m (59 ft) long.

*Head is full of an
oily substance called
spermaceti oil.*

Baird's beaked whale
is one of 18 species of
beaked whale.

False killer whale is black
all over. It is closely related
to the killer whale.

*Lower jaw
protrudes
beyond the
upper jaw.*

*Powerful jaws
with conical teeth*

Killer whale is the fastest
marine mammal. It can move
at up to 56 km/h (34 mph).

*Rounded
flippers*

Slender body

**Long-snouted spinner
dolphin** performs
spectacular aerial displays.

Dusky dolphin lives in
groups and also likes the
company of other species.

Harbour porpoise is
also known as the
common porpoise.

Hector's dolphin is one
of the smallest of all
cetaceans.

Dall's porpoise lives in
deep ocean waters.

Yangtze River dolphin is
also known as the baiji.

Amazon river dolphin is
the largest of the river
dolphins.

Small eyes

La Plata dolphin lives
in the sea, preferring
shallow water.

No beak

*Long
beak*

Baleen

Humpback whale
is easy to recognize
by its long flippers.

*Knobs on head
and lower jaw*

Bowhead whale
is one of the
right whales.

*Upper jaw curves to
hold long baleen.*

Minke whale
has a sharply
pointed snout.

*White flipper band
on some whales*

*Concave
dorsal fin*

Blue whale is the largest animal that has
ever lived. It weighs up to 160 tonnes.

Pygmy right whale is the
smallest baleen whale.

*Areas of rough,
horny skin*

Right whale has a huge
head, with up to 270
pairs of baleen plates.

*Paired
blow-holes*

Bryde's whale is inquisitive and
will sometimes swim alongside boats.

895

WINDS

THE AIR AROUND us is rarely still. When air moves in a continuous stream, it becomes wind. Winds are caused by air moving from areas of high pressure to areas of low pressure. Rising air does not exert great force, thereby creating an area of low pressure. Sinking air exerts more force, thereby creating an area of high pressure. Dramatic pressure differences generate strong winds, such as hurricanes. The strength of winds is measured from 0 to 12 on the Beaufort scale. Winds are part of a global circulation pattern, that keeps temperature patterns in balance.

Cold air sinks over forests.

Air rising over warm areas creates a return air flow at high altitude to complete the air circuit.

Warm air rises over cities.

Air sinks over cool sea.

Area of low pressure as air is warmed by reflection of the Sun.

Cold air under high pressure moves to an area of lower pressure.

Local winds
Some winds only blow in certain places and at particular times, such as North America's Chinook. Cattlemen in the Rocky Mountains like the Chinook as this warm, dry wind rapidly removes snow cover.

Approach of strong winds

Wind generation
Low pressure areas are created where the Sun warms the Earth's surface. High pressure areas are created where the air is cooler. The extra pressure in these zones, (anticyclones, or highs) pushes air towards low pressure zones (depressions, or lows). At ground level, low-level winds blow from high to low; higher up, winds spread out above low pressure areas.

Prevailing winds
Winds are described by the direction from which they blow. A wind blowing from west to east is called a westerly, or west wind. In most places, the wind usually blows from one direction most of the time. This is known as the prevailing wind.

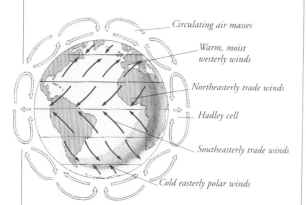

Circulating air masses

Warm, moist westerly winds

Northeasterly trade winds

Hadley cell

Southeasterly trade winds

Cold easterly polar winds

Hadley cells
Prevailing winds are the ground-level part of huge cells of circulating air. For every wind at ground level, there is a turning high-level wind. The cell in the tropics is called a Hadley cell, after English meteorologist George Hadley (1685–1768).

Coriolis effect
The Earth's rotation stops winds from blowing straight from high to low pressure areas. Instead, it deflects winds sideways. This is known as the Coriolis effect. In the northern hemisphere, winds are deflected to the right, and in the southern to the left.

Night land breeze

Air sinks over cool land, and is drawn seawards.

Air rises over warm sea.

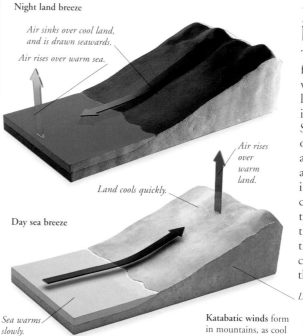

Land cools quickly.

Day sea breeze

Air rises over warm land.

Sea warms slowly.

Mountain winds
Mountains often generate their own local winds. At night, cool air flows down into valleys, creating katabatic winds. In the day, sun-warmed air rises out of the valleys, creating anabatic winds.

Down-valley wind

Land and sea breezes
The land heats up faster than the sea, so warm air rises over the land during the day as it is warmed by the Sun. At certain times of year, this can create a sea breeze, which is a gentle breeze blowing in to the land off the cold sea. At night, the land cools faster than the sea, reversing the air flow. This creates a land breeze, that blows out to sea.

Land warms quickly.

Katabatic winds form in mountains, as cool air sinks at night.

Anabatic winds form in valleys, as warm air rises during the day.

Up-valley wind

Jet streams
At high altitudes, there are narrow rivers of air that roar steadily around the world at speeds of 370 kmh (230 mph) or more. This photograph shows a jet stream high over the Sahara in Egypt.

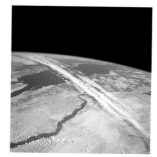

Rossby wave
Between the westerly winds and the polar easterlies, a jet stream runs eastwards. It meanders around the world in four to six giant waves, called Rossby waves, that form cyclonic storms below.

1 A Rossby wave develops as a major bend forms in the polar front of the stream.

Warm air

Cold air

2 The Coriolis effect makes the wave deeper and more pronounced.

Wave deepens

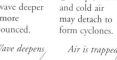

3 Caught in the loops, warm and cold air may detach to form cyclones.

Air is trapped

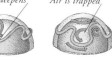

FIND OUT MORE AIR ATMOSPHERE COASTLINES ENERGY KITES MOUNTAINS AND VALLEYS OCEANS AND SEAS SAILING AND OTHER WATERSPORTS SHIPS AND BOATS WEATHER

WINTER SPORTS

THE TERM WINTER SPORTS refers to sports that take place on snow and ice. Keen competition has grown up around them, and the Winter Olympics are held every four years. There are two main types of skiing: Alpine skiing, which features downhill and slalom racing; and Nordic skiing, which is a cross-country sport that also includes ski jumping. A new type of skiing, freestyle, is about performance rather than speed. In sled racing, riders hurtle down special runs. Skating includes figures, ice hockey, and racing.

Mittens

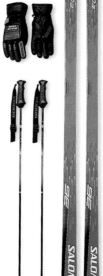

Alpine boot

Bindings automatically release the boot in the event of a fall.

Ski bindings

Skiing

Alpine racing is about speed and technique; Nordic more about stamina. The two disciplines use . different equipment. Alpine skis are wider and heavier than Nordic skis, and the boots are attached to the skis with safety bindings. Nordic boots are like trainers, and the heel lifts free with each stride.

Ski jumping
In ski jumping, competitors take off from the end of a chute on a ski tower. They aim to fly gracefully, perfectly balanced and still in the air, before landing smoothly. Judges award points for style as well as distance jumped.

Nordic racing
Cross-country courses have no steep slopes or sharp turns. Races range from 5 to 50 km (3 to 30 miles), with skiers starting at 30-second intervals. Placings are decided on time. There are relays, combined events, and the biathlon, which includes shooting at targets.

Ski poles

Skis

Alpine racing
In downhill racing, skiers take the fastest line down a set route, taking off into the air where necessary. In slaloms, skiers weave in and out of pairs of flags, or "gates". Both are decided on time.

Downhill racer

Sled racing

Any snowy slope is a site for sled racing, but for major competitions, special steep, twisty runs are made from ice and snow. The art is to shift the bodyweight to make the sled go the fastest way down, letting gravity do the work. Riders go one at a a time, and the winner is the one with the lowest total time from up to four runs.

Luge
The luge is a one- or two-person toboggan with no brakes or steering. The riders, or sliders, use their legs and shoulders to guide the vehicle. The luge is ridden face up, in a sitting or lying position.

Bobsleigh
Two- or four-man bobs have metal runners, steering, and brakes. In a four, the two middle men help to guide the bob by shifting their weight on turns. A brake man uses the brakes only for correcting skids or for stopping.

Skating

Figure skating takes place on an indoor ice rink. There are four events – men's and women's singles, mixed pairs, and ice dancing. Long-track speed skating usually takes place outdoors, and skaters race against the clock. Short-track is held indoors, with elimination heats. Ice hockey, on indoor ice rinks, is a major sport in North America and parts of Europe.

Speed skating
Long-track racing is held on a 400-m (436-yd) track with two skaters in separate lanes. There are no lanes in short-track racing, and four to six skaters jockey for position around a tight oval track.

Short-track racer

Arm held out for balance.

Skater is allowed to touch the ice with a hand.

Racers lean right over on the tight turns.

Toboggan
The skeleton toboggan is so-called because it has no structure above the runners. The rider lies face down, uses toe pieces for braking, and steers by shifting weight. The only major competitions are on the Cresta Run at St Moritz in Switzerland.

Sonja Henie

A Norwegian figure skater, Sonja Henie (1912–69) turned professional in 1936, after winning three Olympic gold medals and 10 world championships. With her theatrical performances and short skirts, she revolutionized the sport. She toured the USA with her own ice show, became an American citizen, and made several films.

Figure skating
Skaters perform set routines and free programmes to music, featuring spins, jumps, and, in pairs, lifts. Judges award marks out of six for artistic impression and for technical merit. Ice dancing is less athletic, with more emphasis placed on interpretation of the music.

Ice hockey
Ice hockey is played six-a-side with substitutes allowed at any time. The object is to propel a hard disc, the puck, into the opposition's goal. There are three 20-minute periods. Players serve time penalties for foul play.

Referee drops the puck to restart the game.

FIND OUT MORE

BALL GAMES   HEALTH AND FITNESS   MOTOR SPORTS   OLYMPIC GAMES   SPORT

WITCHES AND WITCHCRAFT

THE BELIEF IN WITCHES – people with supernatural powers – is ancient and universal. No one knows whether witches do actually have special powers, but from the earliest times, people in all cultures have believed that some men and women can use rituals, spells, and other magical means to influence events for good or evil. Definitions of witchcraft vary, but it is always associated with magic. Uniquely, however, in Europe from the 15th to the 18th centuries, witchcraft was associated with devil worship, and was punishable by death.

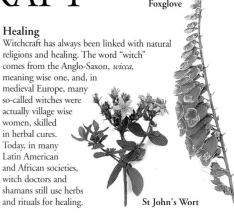
Foxglove

Healing
Witchcraft has always been linked with natural religions and healing. The word "witch" comes from the Anglo-Saxon, *wicca,* meaning wise one, and, in medieval Europe, many so-called witches were actually village wise women, skilled in herbal cures. Today, in many Latin American and African societies, witch doctors and shamans still use herbs and rituals for healing.

St John's Wort

Magic

Magic, or sorcery, is the attempt to use supernatural or natural forces to influence events. Belief in magic has a long history – evidence of magic spells has been found in prehistoric cave paintings – and it continues today in many cultures, either as a superstition or as a religion. In some cultures, magic is considered to be sacred and is practised by specially skilled people.

Carving of African shaman

Familiars

Identifying witches was difficult, because they looked exactly the same as any member of society. However, medieval people believed that true witches could fly – usually on a broomstick – and were accompanied by a "familiar", such as a cat, which was really a demon in disguise.

Torture
Suspected witches were savagely tortured in order to make them confess and also to name accomplices. Methods of torture included whipping, branding with red-hot irons, stretching on the rack, thumbscrews, and the gouging out of eyes. Most people confessed to almost anything just to stop the torture.

Eye gouger

Thumbscrews

Witch trials
Persecution of supposed witches reached its height between 1580 and 1660, when trials occurred throughout western Europe. As hysteria mounted, thousands were brought before Church and civil courts. Anyone old, alone, or eccentric could be accused, including elderly women, village midwives, and herbalists. Their persecution was fuelled by gossip and rumours, which were used as evidence in court.

European witch hunts

In early medieval Europe, belief in witches was a natural part of everyday life. However, from the 12th century, the Christian church redefined witchcraft as heresy, or treason against God. Witches were described as evil devil-worshippers, and the Church set up massive witch hunts in which anyone suspected of witchcraft was rounded up, tried, and often executed. The witch hunts lasted some 300 years, and at least 300,000 innocent people, mostly women, were put to death. Historians have put forward various reasons for the witch hunts. These included a general persecution of women, and the rise of medical science.

Witch burning

Proving witchcraft was a difficult matter, and various tests were devised. One of these was throwing a bound person into water. If she was guilty, she floated; if innocent, she sank. Death was the usual penalty for witchcraft, particularly burning at the stake, on the grounds that this punishment mirrored the fires of hell. Many thousands were put to death this way, including Joan of Arc, the French heroine who was accused of being a witch by the English and burned at the stake in 1431.

Malleus Maleficarum
In 1486, two Dominican monks, Heinrich Krämer and Jacob Sprenger, published the *Malleus Maleficarum* (Hammer of the Witches). This book included the pope's definition of witches as "anti-Christian", and set out rules for identifying, prosecuting, and punishing witches. The book quickly spread throughout Europe, and was used as the essential witch-hunter's reference.

Salem trials

The earliest English settlers took their fear of witches to the American colonies. In 1692, a series of notorious witch trials took place in Salem, Massachusetts. In all, 27 people were tried and convicted; of these, 19 were hanged, and one man was pressed to death with stones. The trials were later condemned, and the convictions overturned.

Halloween
Originally a Celtic festival for the dead, Halloween falls on 31 October. It was once believed that on this night, witches and warlocks flew abroad, and bonfires were lit to keep spirits away. Trick-or-treating has replaced witches' pranks today.

FIND OUT MORE

CRIME AND PUNISHMENT | EUROPE, HISTORY OF | HUNDRED YEARS WAR | MEDICINE, HISTORY OF | RELIGIONS

WOLVES AND WILD DOGS

THE FAMILY CANIDAE, the dog family, contains about 34 species, which can be divided into three main groups. The lupine (meaning wolf-like) group contains wolves, jackals, the coyote, wild dogs, and domestic dogs, many of which hunt in packs. The second group contains the vulpine (meaning fox-like) foxes. The third group contains the south American foxes, or zorros. Canids are mainly carnivorous. Alert, hardy mammals, they are able to catch and kill animals as large as, or larger than, themselves. They can travel long distances without tiring, keeping up a steady trot on long legs and large paws.

Foxes are lightly built for better agility.

The fox catches a small animal by pouncing on it like a cat and pinning it to the ground with its front paws.

Foxes

There are about nine species of vulpine fox, of which the red fox is the largest and most widespread. This agile animal owes its success to its intelligence and adaptability. It is able to thrive equally well in towns and in rural areas. Foxes do not form packs, but live alone or in small family groups.

Wolves

There are two species of wolf – the grey wolf and the red wolf. The red wolf is an endangered species and the grey wolf is nearly extinct in much of its former range. Wolves are social animals that live in packs led by a top male and female. The pack mark the boundary of their territory with urine and howl to tell other packs they are there.

Thick short underfur and long outer "guard" hairs insulate the wolf against freezing temperatures.

The wolf has excellent hearing, eyesight, and sense of smell.

Wolves have pale underparts, with darker fur on the body, ears, and tail to match their habitat.

Long legs with four toes on the hind feet and five on the front feet.

Most of the adults in a pack go on hunting trips.

In the snow, each wolf walks in the leader's tracks.

Raccoon dog with a white coat

Member of the fox species

Carnassials

Jackal skull

Jackals form pairs for life.

Mottled coloration gives African hunting dogs an effective camouflage.

Hunting

The most specialized pack hunters are the African hunting dogs. They hunt as an organized team, but they often lose a kill to stronger predators. Human persecution and introduced diseases have reduced their numbers drastically.

Red fox cubs do not forage with the adults until they are about 12 weeks old.

Wild dogs

The African wild dog, the dhole, and the dingo are known as wild dogs, often hunting in packs over huge areas. The maned wolf, the bush dog, and the raccoon dog are distantly related canids. The raccoon dog is a timid, solitary creature that lives in dense undergrowth feeding on fruit, insects, and small animals. It stays underground in harsh winter weather.

Jackals

The four species of jackal are closely related to wolves. As with most canids, they have two sharp carnassial teeth used for cutting meat. These are situated where the jaws exert greatest force. Their long pointed canine teeth are for gripping and killing prey.

Learning skills

Cubs will not survive into adulthood unless they learn to kill and defend themselves. They learn these skills through playing, chasing, and pouncing upon each other. Social canids may learn hunting skills from the adults in their pack.

RED FOX

SCIENTIFIC NAME	*Vulpes vulpes*
ORDER	Carnivora
FAMILY	Canidae
DISTRIBUTION	North America, Eurasia, North Africa, Australia
HABITAT	Everywhere except deserts
DIET	Meat, insects, and fruit
SIZE	Length: about 110 cm (42 in)
LIFESPAN	3 years in wild

FIND OUT MORE · ANIMAL BEHAVIOUR · AFRICAN WILDLIFE · DESERT WILDLIFE · DOGS · HYENAS · MAMMALS · POLAR WILDLIFE · URBAN WILDLIFE

Wolves and wild dogs

W

Bush dog is a strong swimmer and hunts other aquatic animals.

Raccoon dog has a varied diet, and has large cheek teeth for grinding up fruits and seeds.

Golden jackal shares parental duties with its mate.

An adult wolf needs to eat up to 6 kg (13 lb) of food every day.

A maned wolf is about 80 cm (31 in) tall.

Grey wolf is the largest wild dog. Although once widespread, it is now extinct or nearly extinct in many parts of its range.

Rounded ears

African hunting dog has a pattern of brown, dun, and white on its body, with a white-tipped tail.

Dingo is a wild dog from Australia. It was probably introduced there about 7,000 years ago.

Indian dhole has a coat that ranges from sandy brown to orange-red.

Maned wolf needs a large grassland territory. It lives in eastern South America.

Large ears can pick up the sounds of insects.

Fennec fox is the smallest member of the family.

Bat-eared fox feeds on beetles and other invertebrates.

Ruppell's sand fox lives in North Africa and the Middle East.

Like all dogs, foxes have an acute sense of smell.

Erect ears help the fox tell from which direction a sound is coming.

Paws are well furred to save heat.

Red fox has adapted to live in suburbs and towns.

Grey fox is a good climber and will make its den in large trees up to 9 m (30 ft) above the ground.

Arctic fox has a pale winter coat and a dark summer coat.

900

WOMEN'S MOVEMENT

FOR THE LAST 200 YEARS, women have fought for their rights. Their struggle is sometimes called the women's movement, although the term includes different campaigns. The first wave of organized feminism – the fight for women's rights – appeared during the 1800s, and was concerned with legal rights, and the right to vote. During the 1960s, a new wave of protest – the women's liberation movement – appeared that made women's rights a global issue. By the 1990s, the women's movement had gained many victories and changed society.

Early stirrings

In the 18th century, women had no rights – they were the property of their husbands or fathers. Inspired by the French Revolution, women began to challenge this situation.

W

Mary Wollstonecraft

In 1792 an Englishwoman, Mary Wollstonecraft (1759–97), wrote *Vindication of the Rights of Women*. She deplored the fact that married women were kept at home "confined in cages, like the feathered race", and called for an end to their oppression.

Mary Wollstonecraft

First Wave

During the 1800s, middle-class women, such as Madame Bodichon (formerly Barbara Leigh Smith) campaigned for a married woman's right to keep her own property, and for the right to education and meaningful work.

Madame Bodichon (1827–90)

Women's liberation movement

In the late 1960s, the women's liberation movement exploded on to the political scene. Increasing numbers of women around the world challenged oppression and traditional female roles. They demanded an end to all forms of sexual discrimination, and campaigned around issues such as equal pay, job opportunities, healthcare, childcare, abortion, sexuality, violence towards women, and racism.

National Union of Women's Suffrage Societies (NUWSS) banner

Votes for Women poster

Fight for the vote

From the 1840s, American and British women focused on fighting for the vote, because they believed that only by voting could they improve their situation. The Cause, as it became known, was a long struggle involving hundreds of thousands of women.

Miss World contest, 1970

Women on strike, 1977

Demonstrations

In 1970, feminists demonstrated at the Miss World beauty contest, protesting that it degraded women. The contest continued on a stage covered in flour and other debris thrown by the protesters. After this event, which was televised worldwide, more women began to meet in groups to discuss how sexism affected their lives, and to plan changes.

Equal rights

During the 1970s, the women's liberation movement was a major political influence in many countries. It forced the introduction of legislation that ensured equal rights for women by banning sex discrimination at work and in education. However, though this legislation established women's rights to equal opportunities, inequalities still existed.

International Women's Day

In 1908, socialists in the USA set aside one day for women's suffrage demonstrations. In the 1970s, feminists revived the idea, and today women worldwide celebrate 8 March.

Silver wattle, the Women's Day emblem

Timeline

1830s Anti-slavery campaign stimulates growth of women's movement, USA.

1848 First-ever women's rights convention, Seneca Falls, USA.

1869 Susan B Anthony and Elizabeth Cady Stanton form National Woman Suffrage Association, USA.

WSPU enamel badge

1893 New Zealand women are the first to gain the vote.

1968 Women workers at Ford, UK, strike for equal pay.

1970 Australian Germaine Greer writes *The Female Eunuch;* it calls for women's liberation.

1975 Equal rights laws passed, UK.

Simone de Beauvoir

French philosopher, Simone de Beauvoir (1908–86), was a major figure in modern feminism. In 1949, she wrote *Le Deuxième Sexe (The Second Sex),* in which she drew on history, art, literature, and psychology to show how men had consistently denied women's identity. Her book was very influential, and de Beauvoir herself campaigned actively for women's rights.

FIND OUT MORE   FRENCH REVOLUTION   HISTORY   HUMAN RIGHTS   PANKHURST FAMILY   TRUTH, SOJOURNER

WOODLAND WILDLIFE

IN TEMPERATE REGIONS, wherever rain often falls, woodland is the natural form of vegetation. In some areas, just a single species of tree occurs. Elsewhere, there is a mixture of needle-leaved conifers, broad-leaved trees, evergreens that keep their leaves all year, and deciduous trees that shed leaves in winter. Some woods are quite open to the sky; in others, tree crowns mingle to create a closed canopy. All woodlands are rich habitats for wildlife – there are few large animals, such as boars, but there are insects galore, and the birds that feed on them fill the habitat with their song.

Layers of the woodland

Woods are usually described as having five layers, each with its own characteristic vegetation and wildlife. A natural woodland, therefore, offers a rich mix of living spaces for wildlife, both across the habitat within clearings and streams, and in the layers that exist from the treetops down to the ground.

Canopy

Shrub layer

Field layer

Leaf litter

Canopy
The canopy consists of the crowns of the tallest trees. Branches and twigs sprout a luxuriant layer of greenery that traps most of the incoming sunlight. Here, well above ground level, the canopy provides protection from most predators for insects, birds, and tree-climbing mammals, such as squirrels.

Shrub layer
Beneath the canopy grow woody plants, including shrubs and bushes that never reach great height, such as hazel and hawthorn, and young trees yet to grow to maturity. They form an often densely foliaged layer, which provides nest sites for birds and plentiful insect food.

Field layer

Wildflowers, ferns, mosses, and other low-growing vegetation grow on the ground and are called the field layer. They can tolerate shade because so much sunlight is trapped by the trees above. These plants provide food for insects and snails and cover for small animals, such as rodents and weasels.

Leaf litter
The slow decay of fallen leaves creates a layer of leaf litter on the ground. Mixed with fallen twigs, nuts, and berries, the litter harbours its own wildlife community. Millipedes and beetles live here and supply food for foraging mammals, ground birds, and lizards.

Soil
Plants take root in soil that is richly supplied with nutrients from decaying leaf litter above. Moles tunnel through soil, and other mammals make their burrows here. Soil also provides food for beetle larvae and earthworms.

Earthworm

Mammals

Seldom seen because of their secretive or nocturnal habits, woodland mammals betray their presence in various ways – in the rustle of leaves made by a mouse in the undergrowth, in the fresh earth around the entrance to a fox's burrow, or in a track of hoof prints made by deer across fresh snow. Many mammals forage or hunt on the woodland floor; others climb into the trees to find food and shelter.

Chipmunk feeding

Eastern chipmunk
This chipmunk from North America moves easily through the layers of a woodland. It climbs among the branches, forages for seeds and nuts on the woodland floor, and makes its home in a burrow in the soil.

Roe deer
Foliage from the field layer up to the lower shrub layer provides food for the shy roe deer, which lives either alone or in small groups. Unable to climb or burrow, deer rely on their keen senses, inconspicuous colouring, and speed to avoid danger. When alarmed, the white hairs on the roe deer's rump fluff out.

Roe deer within deep foliage

Badger at entrance to burrow

European badger
Extensive family burrows, or "setts", dug out with strong claws, are the hallmark of European badgers. Each sett has a series of underground chambers, a network of tunnels, and several entrances from the woodland floor. Badgers emerge at night to rifle through leaf litter in search of worms, grubs, fruit, and nuts.

Birds

Woodland birdlife is wonderfully diverse. There are ground foragers, such as pheasants, berry-eaters of the shrub layer, such as blackbirds, songsters in the treetops, and menacing birds of prey that twist and turn among the branches as they swoop for the kill. Summer is the busiest time; when autumn comes, leaves fall, woodland life is at a low ebb, and many birds migrate to warmer climates far away.

Dappled brown feathers help conceal the owl by day.

Well-camouflaged nightjar

Tawny owl
The tawny owl hunts at night. It rests in the canopy and scans the ground for prey – its huge eyes and sensitive ears alert for the slightest movement from a shrew or rodent. Then, with a silent, agile swoop, the owl pounces on its victim.

Green woodpecker

Woodpeckers are famous for hammering rapidly into tree trunks with their sharp beaks to excavate nests. The green woodpecker climbs trunks to dig insect larvae out of the bark, but it also forages on the ground where it breaks into ants' nests to feast on the occupants.

Common nightjar
The common nightjar visits temperate woodlands to breed in summer, but migrates to Africa in winter. It lives at the edge of forests, and in more open woods where it darts through the air at night chasing moths. By day, it rests on branches or on the ground, camouflaged by its mottled plumage.

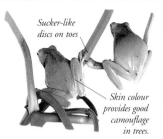

W

Reptiles

Most woodlands are inhabited by lizards and snakes. Many of them make their home on the ground, among the leaf litter beneath logs and rocks, or in hollow tree trunks; others climb into the shrubs above to hunt for insects and birds. The world's most northern woods are too cold for all but a few species of reptile that spend the winter in hibernation.

To escape from predators, the tail can break off.

Lizard can change the colour of its skin.

Anole lizard
With their long toe pads for gripping branches, anoles are among the most adept tree-climbers of all lizards. The green anole of North America hunts for insects and spiders among foliage, where its body colour provides effective camouflage. When the lizard scurries down a trunk or crosses the woodland floor, however, it changes to a brown colour within seconds.

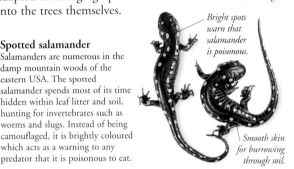

Rat snake
Living in the woodlands of North America, the rat snake preys on small mammals, birds, and lizards. In many areas, the cold winter weather forces the snake into hibernation. Concealing itself deep in leaf litter or in a hollow log, the snake enters a state of dormancy that can last several months.

The rat snake can grow up to 2.5 m (8 ft) in length.

Tongue

Amphibians

Although amphibians usually live in or near water, many species find the humid conditions they need in woodlands – both near streams and in the cool shade beneath a mature canopy. Toads and salamanders spend much of their lives crawling through damp leaf litter and undergrowth, snatching invertebrates to feed on. A few species of frog are adapted for foraging up into the trees themselves.

Sucker-like discs on toes

Skin colour provides good camouflage in trees.

North American tree frog
Tree frogs live in warmer areas of woodland across the world, where they snap up insects and spiders among the leaves of trees. They have loose belly skin and sucker-like toe discs enabling them to climb vertical surfaces. Tree frogs camouflage themselves by changing their skin colour to match their surroundings.

Spotted salamander
Salamanders are numerous in the damp mountain woods of the eastern USA. The spotted salamander spends most of its time hidden within leaf litter and soil, hunting for invertebrates such as worms and slugs. Instead of being camouflaged, it is brightly coloured which acts as a warning to any predator that it is poisonous to eat.

Bright spots warn that salamander is poisonous.

Smooth skin for burrowing through soil.

Insects

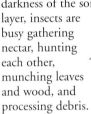

Worker ants foraging for food.

Antennae can detect chemicals produced by other ants.

During spring, when eggs have hatched and any overwintering larvae or adults have emerged from dormancy, a woodland is alive with insects. From the sunlit canopy to the perpetual darkness of the soil layer, insects are busy gathering nectar, hunting each other, munching leaves and wood, and processing debris.

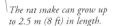

Antenna

Huge jaws used when fighting

Dark wings help conceal the moth on trees.

Wood ant
Wood ants live in huge colonies on the ground where they build domed nests of twigs and leaves, or pine needles. The queen ant produces batch after batch of young, while worker ants go out in search of food for the colony.

Cardinal beetle
The grubs of this brightly coloured beetle are among many beetle larvae that bore their way under tree bark. Here they remain safe from most predators, but they may still be plucked from hiding by woodpeckers.

Tree wasp
Tree wasps live in large colonies. They make nests of paper-like material that they suspend from the branches of trees and shrubs. Workers make the paper by scraping off and chewing fragments of wood from trees with their strong jaws, and mixing it with saliva.

Stag beetle
The stag beetle lays its eggs in rotting wood on the woodland floor. Male stag beetles use their impressive jaws not for feeding, but to brandish at rival males. During a fight, two rivals use their jaws like antlers to grapple and wrestle with one another. Stag beetles are the largest British beetle and may reach 7 cm (2.8 in) in length.

Old lady moth
Adults of the old lady moth appear only in high summer, flying at night, but hiding during the day in hollow trees. The larvae, or caterpillars, relish the leaves of some woodland shrubs. The larvae live longer than the adults, first emerging from eggs in late summer and spending the winter in hibernation.

Plants and fungi

Tall trees dominate woodlands, but many other types of vegetation exist with them, such as shrubs, creepers, mosses, and ferns. Wildflowers often bloom early in spring, taking advantage of the light available before new leaves on trees have grown. Most of these plants are adapted to grow in shade, and can extract the energy they need for growth from the sunlight that filters down to their leaves. Fungi and some orchids do not need light but obtain their energy directly from other plants.

Pine cone seeds

Ferns
Ferns are simple plants that produce spores instead of flowers. They are common in the humid shade of woodlands, where carpets of ferns can dominate the field layer. In warm climates, ferns grow so big that they form part of the shrub layer.

Ferns unfurl as they grow.

Oak galls
Galls are abnormal growths caused by gall wasps, which lay their eggs in the leaves of oak trees. When the grubs hatch, they cause the plant tissue to grow in a protective, food-rich ball around them.

Oak gall

Bracket fungus
Many types of fungi live near the shady woodland floor. Bracket fungus often sprouts from old tree trunks. Using fine root-like structures, fungi draw energy and nutrients from the plant matter on which they grow.

Pine cone
The needle leaves of pine trees offer little sustenance to animals, but their seed cones are full of nutritious food for many creatures. Squirrels and jays break into new cones to extract the seeds, while other animals wait for the cones to open and shed their contents.

FIND OUT MORE AMPHIBIANS BEETLES CAMOUFLAGE AND COLOUR FORESTS HIBERNATION INSECTS MUSHROOMS AND OTHER FUNGI PLANTS REPTILES SOIL TREES

WOODPECKERS AND TOUCANS

THEY LOOK DIFFERENT, and also feed in different ways, yet woodpeckers and toucans are close relatives. They live in forests and woodlands, and most of them spend nearly all their time in trees, making their nests in holes in the trunks. Woodpeckers usually feed by chiselling their way into wood to reach burrowing insects. Toucans clamber about among the treetops and use their huge colourful beaks to collect food.

Woodpeckers

There are about 200 species of woodpecker, and they live in every continent except Australasia and Antarctica. Instead of perching on branches, woodpeckers cling to tree trunks with their sharp claws. They use their strong beaks to bore holes in trees for nesting. They also use them to communicate with each other by hammering on dead wood.

Flight
When a woodpecker flies, it flaps its wings a few times, then keeps them closed for a few seconds. This makes the bird rise and fall.

Tail
The woodpecker uses its short tail to brace itself against tree trunks. Each of its tail feathers ends in a stiff point.

Claws
Woodpeckers have short but powerful legs, and feet that work like clamps. They lock themselves into position with their claws before they start to feed.

Acorn woodpecker
In western North America, the acorn woodpecker uses trees as larders. It pecks hundreds of holes in them and stores an acorn in each one as a future food supply.

Green woodpecker
This bird lives in trees, where it is well camouflaged, but it usually flies down to the ground to feed. It has a harsh laughing call that can be heard from a long way away.

Toucans

There are 33 species of toucan, found only in South and Central America. The family includes toucans, toucanets, and aracaris. Most have a large beak – up to two-thirds as long as their body. When feeding, a toucan juggles its food in its bill and then tosses its head back before swallowing.

The beak contains lots of air-filled spaces, which make it lighter than it looks.

Toucan beaks
Toucan beaks are often brightly coloured, this may help birds to identify their own species. The size and colour might also be to frighten away other birds.

Slender tongue

Glossy black beak

Beak much larger than the head

Chestnut-eared aracari
This bird's beak is long and narrow, and gently curved. Both parts have a distinctly serrated edge.

Ariel toucan
Found in the southern part of the Amazon rainforest, this toucan feeds on small animals, as well as fruit.

Toco toucan
This toucan has one of the largest beaks. It can use it to reach fruit on twigs that cannot take its weight.

Red-billed toucan

Red-billed toucan
The Red-billed toucan eats fruit, insects, spiders, and other animals, such as lizards and small birds. It lives in northern South America in the high branches of the rainforest. It usually occurs singly or in pairs.

Toucan nests
Toucans nest in tree trunks. They use either a natural hole where the wood has rotted away, or a hole that has been made by a woodpecker. Some species line the hole with leaves, but most leave it bare. Female toucans lay two to four shiny, white eggs. Both parents take it in turns to incubate the eggs and to bring food to the young chicks. After about three weeks the naked chicks will open their eyes, and by about six weeks they will be able to begin to survive on their own.

Tongue curled around skull

Tongue
A woodpecker's tongue can be three or four times as long as its beak, and it has a sticky or spiny tip. The woodpecker flicks it out and uses it to probe for insects. When not in use, the tongue curves right around the back of the skull, just beneath the skin.

GREEN WOODPECKER

SCIENTIFIC NAME	*Picus viridis*
ORDER	Piciformes
FAMILY	Picidae
DISTRIBUTION	Europe and western Asia
HABITAT	Woodland and grassy places
DIET	Ants and other insects
SIZE	Length, including tail: 30 cm (12 in)
LIFESPAN	About 7 years

FIND OUT MORE   BIRDS   EGGS   FLIGHT, ANIMAL   KINGFISHERS AND HORNBILLS   NESTS AND BURROWS   WOODLAND WILDLIFE

WORLD WAR I

FOR MORE THAN FOUR years, the world was engaged in a war of a ferocity and scale never seen before. The conflict, known then as the Great War and today as World War I, arose out of the economic, colonial, and military rivalry of the European empires. The assassination in 1914 of the heir to one of those empires – Austria-Hungary – was the spark that set the rivalries alight. Within months, fighting had broken out in Europe, Africa, and Asia. By the time the war ended in 1918, the old empires were in ruins, their place taken by a new world power – the USA.

- Neutral states
- Central powers Austria-Hungary
- Central powers Turkish empire
- Allies (1914 on)
- Allies (1915 on)

Western Front

The German plan was to sweep through Belgium and northern France to capture Paris and knock the French out of the war within weeks. This plan was thwarted by the French army at the River Marne. Both sides then dug lines of defensive trenches, which stretched from the English Channel to the Swiss border, to protect their positions.

Trenches at the Somme

The Somme
On 1 July 1916, Allied troops (those on the British and French side) tried to break through German lines near the River Somme, France. By the end of the four-month battle, the Allies had advanced 8 km (5 miles). One million men were killed.

Troops submerged in mud at Passchendaele

The Battle of Passchendaele

Passchendaele
In July 1917, the Allies tried again to get through German lines, this time near the village of Passchendaele, Belgium. Bad weather turned the area into a sea of mud, over 300,000 Allied troops lost their lives, and hardly any advance was made.

Outbreak of war
On 28 June 1914, the heir to the Austrian throne was killed in Serbia. Austria invaded Serbia, Russia came to Serbia's aid, and Germany supported Austria. Fearing war on two fronts, Germany invaded Belgium and France. Britain then declared war on Germany.

Recruitment
At first, regular troops were reinforced by thousands of volunteers. But as casualty rates soared, governments had to bring in conscription (compulsory military service) to keep up the strength of their armies.

South African recruitment poster

Eastern Fronts

The war in eastern Europe, between Germany and Austria-Hungary on one side, and Russia on the other, was more fluid than in the west. Most battles were held in open country, across what is now Poland and in the eastern Mediterranean. The war expanded into Asia when Turkey attacked Russia at the end of 1914 and the Allies launched the ill-fated Gallipoli campaign. Turkey also posed a threat in Syria and Palestine and so Allied troops were sent from Egypt to defend the region.

British troops in Palestine

Uniform of British Private, Scottish Battalion was khaki-coloured to blend with the mud.

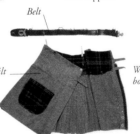

Sporran

Cap

Belt

Kilt

Doublet

French infantryman's equipment included spare ammunition and food supplies.

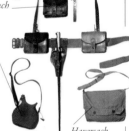

Cartridge pouch

Water bottle

Haversack

Manfred von Richthofen
The most famous pilot of the war was the German airman Manfred von Richthofen (1892–1918). He is said to have destroyed 80 Allied aircraft before he was killed when his aircraft was shot down over France. He was known as the Red Baron because of his bright red Fokker triplane.

Timeline
June 1914 Archduke Franz Ferdinand, heir to the throne of Austria-Hungary, is assassinated; Serbia is blamed.

July 1914 Austria-Hungary invades Serbia in retaliation; France, Germany, and Russia mobilize their armies in preparation for war.

August 1914 Germany declares war on Russia and France and invades Belgium; this brings Britain into the war; Germany pushes back Britain at Mons, Belgium; Germany defeats Russia at Tannenberg.

September 1914 German advance halted by the British and French at the River Marne.

German infantryman

October 1914 Turkey enters the war on the German side; in France a line of defensive trenches is dug, stretching along the Western Front.

April 1915 Germans use poison gas for first time at Ypres, Belgium; Allies try to force Turkey out of war by invading Gallipoli peninsula.

May 1915 Italy joins the war on the Allied side.

The civilian war

The huge armies of World War I needed a massive force of back-up workers to provide them with weapons, food, and other supplies. The entire civilian workforce was directed towards war work, producing arms and ammunition, growing food, and keeping industry and commerce going at home while millions of soldiers fought at the front.

British Mark V Tank

Canadian Ross .303 in MK III sniper's rifle

Gas mask

Women ambulance drivers at the front

Women at war

Before 1914, women traditionally worked in jobs men did not want. During the war, women were required to do jobs normally done by the men fighting at the front. Across Europe, women worked in factories and offices, drove buses and trams, dug fields, and even joined the police forces.

Propaganda

To stiffen morale and weaken the enemy's resistance, both sides used propaganda. People were made to believe the worst of the other side, with leaflets, posters, and radio broadcasts all used for propaganda. Those who refused to fight were given white feathers, a sign of "cowardice".

White feathers

World war

World War I was the first truly international war in history. People from every continent took part in the fighting. In Africa and Asia, the Turkish Empire and former German colonies were overrun by British Empire troops. There was also fighting in the Middle East and in the Pacific. The entry of the USA into the war in 1917 marked the end of European dominance of world affairs.

New weapons

The main weapons used in the war were the rifle (with its bayonet), the machine gun, and the artillery shell. In April 1915 the German army introduced a new weapon – gas – which both sides later used to deadly effect. The British first used tanks at the Somme in September 1916, and both sides made more and more use of aircraft – at first for reconnaissance, later for bombing.

End of the war

In mid-1918, fresh US troops arrived to fight on the Allied side, and there was increasing hunger and discontent among the German soldiers. The Allies broke through the German lines in August 1918. Austria-Hungary and Turkey collapsed in October, and the Allies finally forced Germany to make peace on 11 November 1918.

War art

The horrors of the war inspired painters and poets on both sides. The old romantic idea of war as a great cause was replaced by the realization of its cruelty and destructive force. Many young artists and writers fought at the front; some, such as the British poet Wilfred Owen (1893–1918) were killed in the fighting.

The Treaty of Versailles

The peace treaty was signed on 28 June 1919 in the palace of Versailles, France. Germany lost territory, and had to limit the size of its army, as well as pay compensation to the Allies. Subsequent treaties redrew the map of eastern Europe.

Signing of the treaty

War Landscape by British artist Paul Nash

The cost of war

No one knows how many people died in the war. About 9 million soldiers and possibly 13 million civilians were killed. A further 20 million died in the influenza epidemic that swept Europe during 1918–19. Poppies, which grew on the fields of France, became the symbol of those killed in the war.

Poppies

February 1916 German forces try to capture French fortress of Verdun in a 10-month battle.

May 1916 British and German fleets fight inconclusive Battle of Jutland, off Denmark.

French infantryman, 26th Regiment

July–November 1916 Battle of the Somme; tanks used for first time.

April 1917 USA enters war on Allied side.

July–November 1917 Battle of Passchendaele.

March 1918 Germany and Russia make peace at Brest-Litovsk.

March 1918 German forces make massive advances on the Western Front.

July 1918 German advance halted.

August 1918 With the help of American forces, Allied troops make the decisive break through German lines.

Hand-painted camouflage coat

October 1918 Italy defeats Austria-Hungary; both Austria-Hungary and Turkey ask for peace.

November 1918 Armistice signed between Germany and the Allies.

June 1919 Peace treaty signed at Versailles, France. The conditions imposed on Germany were later to become a major cause of World War II.

FIND OUT MORE   AFRICA, HISTORY OF   ARMIES   EMPIRES   EUROPE, HISTORY OF   FRANCE, HISTORY OF   GERMANY, HISTORY OF   UNITED KINGDOM, HISTORY OF   WORLD WAR II

WORLD WAR II

WORLD WAR II WAS the most devastating war in history. For the first time ever in warfare, more civilians than soldiers lost their lives. In total, more than 50 million people were killed, including 20 million Russians, 6 million Poles, and 6 million Jews. The war, which lasted from 1939–45, involved every continent, and few countries or people remained untouched by the carnage. In Europe, the strength of the Russian and American armies was required to defeat Germany. In Asia, atomic warfare was used for the first time to defeat Japan.

How war began

Adolf Hitler took power in Germany in 1933 and set out to restore German power in Europe. He built a strong army and air force, and began to expand German territory in central and eastern Europe. On 1 September, 1939, German troops invaded Poland. In response, Britain and France declared war on Germany.

German Messerschmitt Bf 109E fighter

British Hawker Hurricane Mark 1 fighter

Blitzkrieg
The German army moved tanks quickly into enemy territory, supporting them by aerial bombardment. This strategy, called Blitzkrieg, (lightning war), was successful in 1939–40.

Battle of Britain
For four months in 1940, British aircraft fought against the German air force. After heavy casualties, Germany cancelled its plans to invade Britain.

World war

In June 1941, German troops invaded Russia. Six months later, Japanese aircraft bombed the US naval base at Pearl Harbor, bringing the USA into the war. By the end of 1941, an international alliance of the USA, Russia, and Britain confronted the Axis powers of Germany, Italy, and Japan.

War in Europe

Norway, Sweden, Britain, Soviet Union, Atlantic Ocean, France, Germany, Ukraine, Spain, Italy, Bulgaria, Greece, Turkey, Algeria, Mediterranean Sea, Jordan, Libya

War in the Pacific

Korea, Japan, China, Hong Kong, Pacific Ocean, Philippines, Singapore, Australia, Japanese-controlled area by 1942

- Axis states
- Areas controlled by Axis
- Allied states
- Areas controlled by Allies
- Neutral states
- Extent of German military occupation
- Extent of Japanese occupation

Pearl Harbor
On 7 December, 1941, Japanese planes launched a surprise attack on the American Pacific Fleet stationed at Pearl Harbor in Hawaii, and also invaded the Philippines, Hong Kong, and Malaya. The USA then declared war on both Japan and Germany.

Bombing of the American fleet at Pearl Harbor

German tank, 1941

Operation Barbarossa
On 22 June, 1941, 79 German divisions invaded Russia in the biggest military operation in history. At first they made good progress, but Russian resistance ensured that they failed to capture Moscow and Leningrad.

Turning point

By mid-1942, the Germans occupied most of Europe and northern Africa, and the Japanese controlled most of the Pacific. Three battles turned the tide: Midway, where the USA stopped the Japanese; El Alamein in North Africa; and Stalingrad, where the Russians began to push back the occupying forces.

Cap

Breeches

Field service tunic

Leather boots

Items from a German officer's uniform

Adolf Hitler

Hitler (1889–1945) became German Chancellor in 1933. He quickly took dictatorial powers and ruled until his death in 1945. His spellbinding oratory convinced many people that he could restore German pride and greatness lost after World War I.

El Alamein
In 1942, German and Italian troops led by Field Marshal Rommel advanced across North Africa towards Egypt and the Suez Canal. In a lengthy battle, the British 8th Army led by General Bernard Montgomery, or "Monty" defeated Rommel at El Alamein, Egypt.

Rommel in North Africa

Timeline
March 1936 Germany begins to expand her territory by sending troops into the Rhineland.

October 1936 Germany and Italy make an alliance – the Rome-Berlin Axis.

November 1936 Germany becomes allied with Japan.

March 1939 German troops invade Czechoslovakia.

Major General, German army

September 1939 Germany and Russia invade Poland; Britain and France declare war on Germany.

April 1940 German troops overrun Denmark and Norway.

May 1940 Germany occupies the Netherlands, Belgium, and France, forcing the British to retreat.

July–October 1940 British air force defeats Germany in the Battle of Britain; preventing Germany's invasion.

Occupied Europe

Life in German-occupied Europe was hard. Food was rationed, newspapers and radio were censored, and everyone was put to work producing supplies for the German war effort. Jews lived in fear of their lives, as more and more of them were rounded up and sent to their deaths in concentration camps, such as Auschwitz and Treblinka.

Resistance

Across Europe, individual people fought to rid their countries of German occupation. In the Netherlands and Denmark, families sheltered Jews in their houses, while in France and Yugoslavia, armed fighters fought a spirited war against the occupying armies.

French resistance fighters

Incendiary bombs

Civilians at war

For the first time, war was brought into the homes of people far away from the battlefield. Bombing of towns and cities meant that civilians became the targets of enemy action and often had to take refuge in shelters. At sea, submarine warfare stopped ships bringing in food and other supplies, causing severe shortages.

Rationing

Shortages all over Europe led to many types of food being rationed. Everyone was given a ration card stating what food they were able to buy each week. People with gardens grew their own food.

Weekly food ration, British adult, 1941

Bacon: 113 g (4 oz)

Meat: 10p worth

Tea: 56.5 g (2 oz)

Margarine: 113 g (4 oz)

Butter: 56.5 g (2 oz)

Lard: 56.5 g (2 oz)

Cheese: 28 g (1 oz)

1 egg

Sugar: 226 g (8 oz)

Dresden, after the 1945 air-raid

Air-raids

During 1940–41, the German air force bombed many British cities, and many civilians lost their lives. As the war progressed in favour of the Allies, German cities came under attack. In February 1945, the Allied forces bombed Dresden, and more than 50,000 people were killed.

Winston Churchill

Churchill (1874–1965) became prime minister of Britain in May 1940. A fine orator whose speeches boosted British morale during the Battle of Britain and the rest of the war, Churchill led Britain to victory in 1945, but lost power in July 1945. He was elected prime minister in 1951–55.

Labour camps

In Germany, millions of Jews, gypsies, and prisoners of war were incarcerated in camps. Some camps held slave labourers, who produced munitions and other supplies; others were concentration camps to exterminate Jews and other "undesirables". Conditions were inhumane, and many died of ill-treatment and starvation. Prisoners of war (right) were also often kept in appalling conditions.

End of the war

By 1944, the war had turned in the Allies' favour. Italy had surrendered, and the Russians were making slow progress towards Berlin. In June 1944, the Allies invaded France, opening up a new western front. The Russians entered Berlin in April 1945, and Germany surrendered in May 1945.

D-Day

On 6 June 1944, more than 100,000 Allied troops, supported by thousands of ships and aircraft, crossed the English Channel and landed on the beaches of France. At first they met fierce German resistance, but by 25 August the Allies had liberated Paris. By the end of the year, they had retaken the whole of France.

Troops landing on D-Day

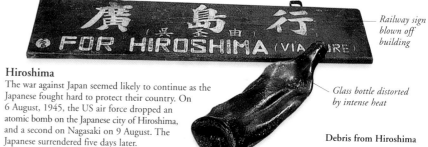

Railway sign blown off building

Hiroshima

The war against Japan seemed likely to continue as the Japanese fought hard to protect their country. On 6 August, 1945, the US air force dropped an atomic bomb on the Japanese city of Hiroshima, and a second on Nagasaki on 9 August. The Japanese surrendered five days later.

Glass bottle distorted by intense heat

Debris from Hiroshima

December 1941 Japan bombs US Pacific Fleet, leading to US entry into the war.

US serviceman's novel

1942 US fleet stops Japanese advance across the Pacific at the Battle of Coral Sea and the Battle of Midway.

November 1942 British defeat German forces at El Alamein in North Africa.

January 1943 German siege of Stalingrad (Volgograd) broken.

June 1943 Allies invade Italy.

July 1943 Italian fascist dictator Mussolini resigns.

June 1944 D-Day landings: the Allies invade France.

June–August 1944 Russian armies reach Warsaw, Poland, and eastern Prussia.

US serviceman's ration kit

April 1945 Adolf Hitler commits suicide, as the Russian army reaches Berlin.

May 1945 Germany surrenders.

August 1945 Atomic bombs are dropped on the Japanese cities of Hiroshima and Nagasaki; Japan surrenders.

FIND OUT MORE   ARMIES   ASIA, HISTORY OF   EUROPE, HISTORY OF   FRANCE, HISTORY OF   GERMANY, HISTORY OF   HOLOCAUST   UNITED KINGDOM, HISTORY OF   UNITED STATES, HISTORY OF

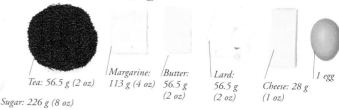

WORMS

WORMS ARE ANIMALS that have an elongated, tube-like body, and no legs. The body of a worm can be cylindrical, flattened, or leaf-like in shape. Worms vary enormously in size and can grow up to 30 metres (100 ft); they include segmented, ribbon, round-worms, and flatworms. We tend to think of these animals as the English naturalist Charles Darwin did – "little ploughmen" worming their way through the soil. However, worms also live in the sea, in fresh water, and as parasites of plants and animals.

Short antennae help the worm find food.

Tentacles

Flat body can squeeze into cracks.

Segmented worms

There are three groups of segmented worms. The first group includes the ragworm. The second group includes earthworms and bloodworms (small red freshwater worms living in polluted waters worldwide). The third group includes leeches, which survive by sucking blood from an animal host.

Ragworm

The omnivorous ragworm is a scavenger and a predator, and lives in shallow seashore burrows. Its clearly defined head has tentacles (which grow back if they are cut off), eyes, and a mouth with strong, pincer-like jaws. Bristled paddle-like flaps along each side give it the appearance of a tattered strip of rag. The ragworm moves by swimming or wriggling over surfaces. It is unisexual and usually dies shortly after mating.

King ragworm

Earthworms

The earthworm lives below ground in a burrow. By moving through the soil, eating as it goes, an earthworm allows air and water in, and distributes plant nutrients. When breeding, it produces a cocoon that protects its eggs until they hatch into tiny worms. One cubic metre (35 cubic ft) of grassland may contain 500 worms.

Cocoons, or egg capsules, have up to 20 eggs inside, but usually only one worm develops fully, and emerges.

Peacock worms

These worms live on the shoreline, in tubes made of mud or sand. They have a fan of feathery tentacles around their heads, which withdraw into the tube when they are threatened. One group of peacock worms can create reefs with their sandy tubes.

Gills for breathing and catching food

Mouth is in centre of gills.

How an earthworm moves

1 The earthworm has a set of circular muscles around its body. It contracts (squeezes) these, which propels the front half of the worm forwards.

2 Muscles running lengthways down the worm's body drag the worm's tail after its head. A mucus covering aids this movement.

Saddle

Tail end

Earthworm

Roundworms

Roundworms are unsegmented, spindle-shaped, and usually microscopic. Some roundworms live in the earth – the top 7.5 cms (3 in) of a hectare (2.5 acres) of soil contains up to 7,500 million round-worms. Other round-worms are parasitic, such as the filariasis worm. A single female roundworm can produce up to 200,000 eggs a day.

Filariasis worm

Elephantiasis

The roundworm *Wuchereria* causes the filariasis group of diseases. One of these diseases causes grossly enlarged human tissues, and is known as elephantiasis. Elephantiasis occurs when mosquitos infested with the *Wuchereria* larvae bite humans, infecting them with the larvae. The larvae then grow to adult worms within the body. They produce tiny young that they release into the lymph fluid. The larvae block the lymph vessels, and this causes the swelling.

Leg affected with disease

Ribbon worms

Some parasitic forms of worm such as ribbon, bootlace, or horsehair worms lay their eggs in fresh water. When the eggs hatch, the larvae find and infect an insect host. They will then feed on the host until eventually it dies.

Ribbon worm, foraging for food

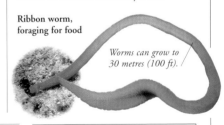

Worms can grow to 30 metres (100 ft).

Flatworms

There are three groups of flatworm: planarians, flukes, and tapeworms. The primitive planarians grow into new worms when cut into pieces. The best-known member of the second group is the liver fluke, which infests mammals, snails, and other vertebrates. The third group – tapeworms – includes the human gut tapeworm which can grow to 18 metres (60 ft).

Suckers attach worm to the gut wall.

Rosette of hooks

Sucker

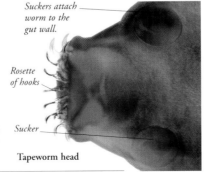

Human gut tapeworm   *Sections of tapeworm*   *Head*

Tapeworm head

FIND OUT MORE   COASTS   DARWIN, CHARLES   DISEASES   OCEAN WILDLIFE   PARASITES   SEASHORE WILDLIFE

WRITING

COMMUNICATING BY USING MARKS on a surface to represent spoken language is called writing. Its vital importance lies in its power to preserve thoughts and ideas that would otherwise be lost. Thousands of scripts have been invented, each expressing a different language or adapted to a particular surface, be it clay, wood, stone, or paper. Writing not only conveys meaning – it can also be beautiful in itself. The art of fine script is called calligraphy.

Chinese passage skillfully written on silk

Writing implements

Throughout history, writers have used many different kinds of tools, each one suited to the most commonly available writing surface. The kind of mark each tool makes profoundly affects the nature of the script.

Stick and clay
The first writing was devised by the Sumerians 5,000 years ago. They used sticks called styluses to make triangular marks in soft clay, which was then baked hard.

Stylus

Pen and ink
For centuries, people wrote on paper, using pens repeatedly dipped in ink. Early pens were trimmed goose quills. Later pens had metal nibs.

Early pens

Ballpoint pens
A ballpoint is a disposable pen that has a small ballbearing as a writing point, and an internal ink supply. One of the world's most-used ballpoint pens is the biro, patented in 1943.

Biros

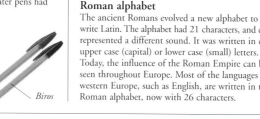
Monumental inscription in Latin

Roman alphabet
The ancient Romans evolved a new alphabet to write Latin. The alphabet had 21 characters, and each represented a different sound. It was written in either upper case (capital) or lower case (small) letters. Today, the influence of the Roman Empire can be seen throughout Europe. Most of the languages of western Europe, such as English, are written in the Roman alphabet, now with 26 characters.

Scripts

All writing consists of a series of marks, or characters, which make up a script. In some scripts, such as Chinese, each character carries the meaning of a spoken word. In alphabetic scripts, such as Latin or English, each character represents a sound, and must be fitted with others to make a word.

Chinese
Chinese has the longest history of all current writing systems, stretching back to at least 1500 BC. Each character represents a different word, so many thousands must be learned before even simple passages can be read. Traditional Chinese is written with brush and ink on paper.

The fluent lines of Arabic give beauty to each word.

Arabic
Arabic has 17 basic characters, written from right to left. Dots are added to create the 28 letters of the Arabic alphabet. The letters are joined with curved strokes, and there are further bold strokes at the end of each word. This gives Arabic an urgent sense of movement from right to left. The Qur'an, the holy book of Islam, teaches that writing is a gift from God. As well as using writing practically, to provide information, it is also used as decoration (like Chinese, Arabic calligraphy is a prized art form). Texts from the Qur'an are inscribed on mosque walls.

Unknown scripts

There are many ancient scripts that are no longer understood. Language experts work for years trying to decipher them. No one could read Egyptian hieroglyphics until the Frenchman Jean-François Champollion (1790–1832) deciphered them in 1824.

Mayan glyphs carved in stone *Rounded, stylized symbols*

Mayan glyphs
Between AD 300 and 1500, the Mayans of Central America produced thousands of carved stone inscriptions. Many of the 850 characters, or glyphs, clearly represent animals and objects, but others are abstract symbols. Very little Mayan writing was deciphered until the 1960s, when the life histories of Mayan rulers were first translated. About 85 per cent of gylphs can now be understood.

Shorthand
Words are spoken much faster than they can be written, and for people such as reporters it is useful to learn a quick way of jotting them down quickly and accurately. Shorthand systems replace words and phrases with brief marks, that can be read and understood later. Today, shorthand has largely been superceded by tape recorders and dictaphones.

Timeline

3100 BC Sumerians develop first writing system using pictograms (picture symbols of people, animals, and objects).

Pictograms

3000 BC Egyptians develop hieroglyphics.

1800 BC Chinese characters, similar to those in use today, are written on tortoise shells.

c. 1000 BC Greeks invent the first alphabetic script, where each character (letter) represents a sound, and letters combine to form words.

c.63 BC A Latin form of shorthand (a kind of speedwriting) is invented: it is used for 1,000 years.

1905 After 5,000 years, linguists produce the first modern translation of the Sumerian writing system.

FIND OUT MORE EGYPT, ANCIENT   LANGUAGES   MAYA   ROMAN EMPIRE   SIGNS AND SYMBOLS

X-RAYS AND THE ELECTROMAGNETIC SPECTRUM

INVISIBLE WAVES OF ENERGY called X-rays allow doctors to see through the soft tissues of the human body, enabling them to diagnose disease and injury without resorting to surgery. X-rays are a type of wave energy called electromagnetic radiation. They form just one part of a whole range of electromagnetic radiation called the electromagnetic spectrum, which also includes radio waves and light.

Electromagnetic radiation

The true nature of electromagnetic radiation still puzzles scientists, because it travels as waves of energy but also seems to be made up of tiny energy particles. This energy can travel through many types of matter, and also through a vacuum.

Photons
Scientists think that the energy carried by electromagnetic waves is split up into particle-like units called photons. They are often described as "wave packets". An electromagnetic wave probably consists of a stream of photons.

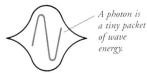

A photon is a tiny packet of wave energy.

Photon of red light

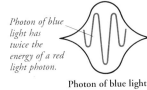

Photon of blue light has twice the energy of a red light photon.

Photon of blue light

Electromagnetic waves
A wave of electromagnetic radiation is made up of vibrating electric and magnetic fields. Electromagnetic waves spread outwards from a source, like ripples on a pond. They travel through space at 299,792.5 km/s (186,287.5 miles/s) – faster than anything else in the Universe.

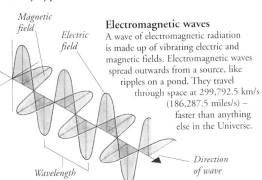

Magnetic field
Electric field
Wavelength
Direction of wave

James Clerk Maxwell
The Scottish physicist James Clerk Maxwell (1831–79) was the first to realize that light is a form of electromagnetic radiation. In 1864, he used mathematical equations to prove the existence of the electromagnetic spectrum. Maxwell also studied colour and colour blindness.

Solar radiation
The Sun gives out a wide range of electromagnetic radiation that travels through space and reaches the Earth. Most of this radiation is absorbed by gases in the Earth's atmosphere, but radio waves, the visible spectrum, and some infrared and ultraviolet are able to pass through.

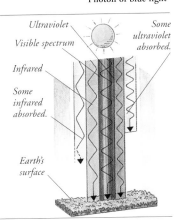

Ultraviolet
Visible spectrum
Infrared
Some infrared absorbed.
Some ultraviolet absorbed.
Earth's surface

Electromagnetic spectrum

Each type of electromagnetic radiation has a different wavelength and frequency (number of waves per second). Waves with the shortest wavelengths and the highest frequencies have the most energy.

Gamma rays
The nuclei (centres) of radioactive atoms give out gamma rays during nuclear reactions and explosions. These high-energy rays are very penetrating and can damage human cells as they pass through the body.

Nuclear bomb explosion

X-rays
An X-ray photograph shows the denser parts of the human body as light areas on a dark background. X-rays can pass through flesh, but are blocked by teeth, bones, and some organs.

X-ray photograph

Ultraviolet
A substance that absorbs the energy of ultraviolet waves and immediately releases it again as visible light is said to be fluorescent. A fluorescent rock glows in the dark when exposed to ultraviolet waves.

Fluorescent rock

Visible spectrum
Light is the only type of electromagnetic radiation visible to human eyes. Light includes all the colours of the rainbow, which together are called the visible spectrum.

Human eye

Infrared
All warm objects give out infrared rays. Photographs called thermographs record these rays and show the warm and cool parts of an object as different colours, from yellow (hottest) to blue (coldest).

Infrared photograph

Microwaves
Microwaves are actually short-wavelength radio waves. A microwave oven uses microwaves to cook food that contains water. The water molecules absorb the energy of the microwaves and vibrate faster, heating up the food.

Microwave oven

Radio waves
Electromagnetic waves with the lowest energy are called radio waves. They can have wavelengths of thousands of kilometres. These waves are easy to produce using an electrical device called an oscillator. Radio waves are used to transmit radio and television programmes.

Radio masts

Wavelength (in metres)

10^{-14}
10^{-12}
10^{-10}
10^{-8}
10^{-6}
10^{-4}
10^{-2}
1
10^2
10^4

Timeline

1667 English scientist Isaac Newton splits white light into the visible spectrum.

1800 William Herschel, a German-born astronomer, discovers infrared rays.

1801 German physicist Johann Ritter discovers ultraviolet radiation.

1864 Maxwell proves that the electromagnetic spectrum exists, and that electromagnetic radiation is caused by the link between electricity and magnetism.

1887 German physicist Heinrich Hertz makes radio waves artificially.

1895 German physicist Wilhelm Röntgen discovers X-rays.

1896 First medical X-ray taken by American scientist Michael Pupin.

1900 French physicist Paul Villard is the first to detect gamma rays.

1901 Italian inventor Guglielmo Marconi sends the first radio signal across the Atlantic.

1947 Microwave ovens on sale in the USA.

FIND OUT MORE   COLOUR   ELECTRICITY   ELECTROMAGNETISM   ENERGY   HEAT   LIGHT   MAGNETISM   RADIOACTIVITY

ZOOS

HUMANS HAVE ALWAYS been fascinated by animals, and their lifestyles. Since ancient times, animals have been kept in captivity. Today, many cities have a zoo, or zoological garden, where animals are kept for exhibition. In recent years, zoos have been criticized by those who believe it is wrong to keep animals in captivity. However, others argue that zoos can play a part in conservation.

Zoo history

Humans have kept animals for at least 25,000 years. Possibly the first animals kept purely out of curiosity were pigeons in Iraq over 6,500 years ago. The first animal collection was probably that of the ancient Egyptians over 4,000 years ago. It contained 100 elephants, 70 big cats, and thousands of other mammals. Rulers in China also established a huge zoo, called the Gardens of Intelligence, about 3,000 years ago. In the past, animals were often taught to perform for visitors; this rarely happens today.

London Zoo
In 1828, a small corner of Regent's Park was set aside for the use of the Zoological Society of London. The society's aim was to "interest and amuse the public". However, the zoo soon took on more serious scientific work concerned with living animals.

The role of a zoo

Zoos have three main aims: education, conservation, and research. Least important, is entertainment for the public. In this way, zoos help to protect animals instead of exploiting them. Organizations such as Zoo Check, in the UK, make sure the animals are given proper care, monitoring the animals' diet, enclosures, and physical and mental health.

Children watching rabbits from "rabbit hole".

Snow leopard under anaesthetic before surgery.

Penguin wearing tracking device to monitor its movements in Antarctica.

Education
As our access to the wild decreases, so does our contact with animals. For many people zoos are the only place where they can experience contact with animals. Zoos educate children to appreciate animals and the threats they face.

Animal welfare
The health of zoo animals is very important. Animals are encouraged to behave as they would in the wild. For example, chimps are given logs containing crickets for them to extract. Without this stimulation, animals get bored and start behaving abnormally.

Conservation
Due to habitat destruction, the only chance for many animals of avoiding extinction is to be kept and bred in captivity. Many species from rhinos to crickets have been bred in zoos and successfully returned to the wild.

Research
Zoos carry out research involved in developing pregnancy test kits for rhinos, treating illnesses, artificially inseminating animals, and tracking animals in the wild.

Greenhouse for growing food for locusts and other invertebrates.
These rainforest trees are normally found in the animal's natural habitat.
Glass sides for all round visibility
Breeding units for endangered species
Layered walkways allow animals to be observed at all levels of the trees.
Twilight world – dark cave setting for nocturnal invertebrates

Model of proposed new invertebrate house for London Zoo

Zoo of the future

With changing attitudes to animals kept in captivity and advances in technology, zoos are becoming more sophisticated. New enclosures are planned that simulate conditions in the animals' natural habitat. This is done both for the animals' welfare and so visitors can see animals in conditions similar to those in the wild. The combination of species, type of vegetation, temperature, and humidity are all considered. Food is hidden to encourage animals to forage, as they would in the wild.

Wildlife parks

Many people disagree with keeping animals behind bars. Most city zoos do not have enough space to keep animals in more natural settings; as a result, wildlife parks were developed. One of the first was Whipsnade Park Zoo, in the UK. With over 230 ha (567 acres), large animals can roam around in herds in more natural settings. Animals from the same country are often put together, making them feel more at home and giving the visitor a better idea of what they look like in the wild.

Giraffes in safari park

Sea-life centres

Aquatic animals need very specialist care so specially designed sea-life centres, or aquariums, have been built. In many of these centres the public get the opportunity to touch certain marine animals, something that is almost impossible in the wild. Sea-life centres primarily concentrate on displaying marine animals local to the area in which they are situated. However, some also have more exotic animals. Many people are unhappy about keeping large marine animals, such as dolphins and the orca, in captivity.

Killer whale in aquarium

FIND OUT MORE ANIMALS ANIMAL BEHAVIOUR CONSERVATION ELEPHANTS GIRAFFES PENGUINS RHINOCEROSES AND TAPIRS WHALES AND DOLPHINS

REFERENCE
SECTION

CLASSIFYING LIVING THINGS

BIOLOGISTS CLASSIFY LIVING things into large groups, called kingdoms. Each kingdom is then subdivided into several smaller groups. The classification chart on these pages shows the five kingdoms, together with most of the smaller groups that make up the living world.

Scientific names

Every species has a two-part scientific name that is the same worldwide. The first part of the name gives the genus; the second part the species. All numbers of species are approximate, as many more species still await discovery.

Classifying a species

Living things are classified according to the features they have in common. Kingdoms are the largest groups in the classification system, and species are the smallest groups. Each species contains a group of living things that can breed together. The chart below shows how biologists would classify one species – the tiger – in the animal kingdom.

Kingdom Animals (Animalia)
A kingdom is the largest grouping in the classification of living things.

Phylum Chordates (Chordata)
A phylum is a major group within a kingdom. It is sometimes called a division in the classification of plants.

Class Mammals (Mammalia)
A class is a major part of a phylum or sub-phylum. A sub-class is a large group within a class.

Order Carnivores (Carnivora)
An order is part of a class or sub-class.

Family Cats (Felidae)
A family is a large collection of species that have several features in common.

Genus Big cats (*Panthera*)
A genus is a small collection of similar species.

Species Tiger (*Panthera tigris*)

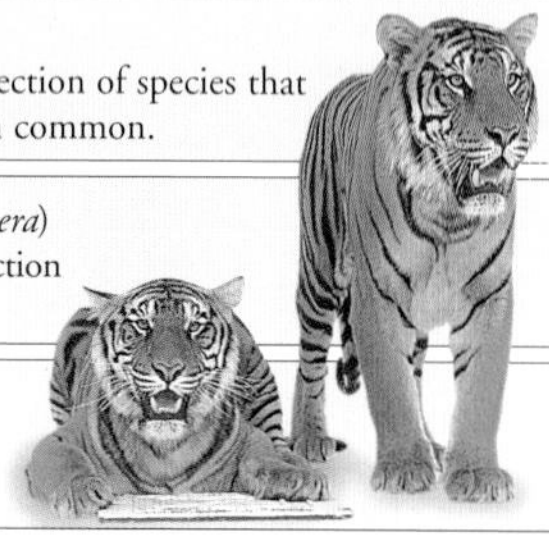

Protists

This kingdom contains simple organisms that mostly have a single cell. There are at least 65,000 species.

PROTISTS (PROTISTA)

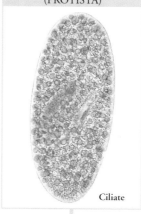

Ciliate

AMOEBAS (Sarcodina) 20,000 species

FLAGELLATES (Zoomastigina) 15,000 species

CILIATES (Ciliophora) 8,000 species

SPOROZOANS (Sporozoa) 5,000 species

ALGAE (Several phyla) 20,000 species

MONERANS (MONERA)

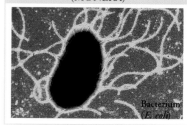

Bacterium (*E. coli*)

Monerans

This kingdom includes the single-celled organisms, such as bacteria. Monerans were the first life forms, and there are now over 5,000 species. It also covers blue-green algae.

PRIMITIVE BACTERIA (Archaebacteria) 500 species

TYPICAL BACTERIA (Eubacteria) 5,000 species

Plants

Plants cannot move; they reproduce by making spores or seeds. The kingdom contains more than 400,000 species.

PLANTS (PLANTAE)

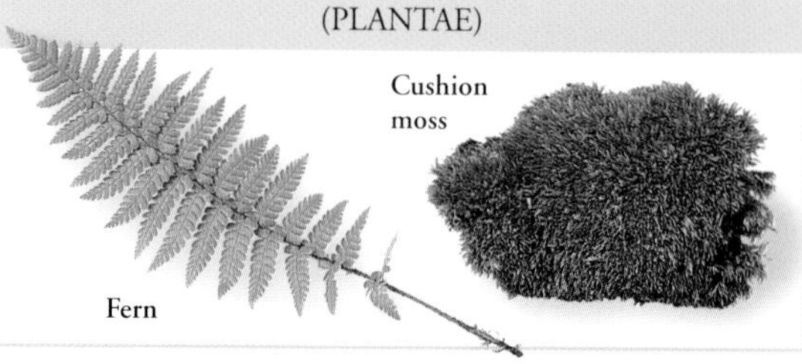

Cushion moss

Fern

FLOWERING PLANTS (Angiospermophyta)

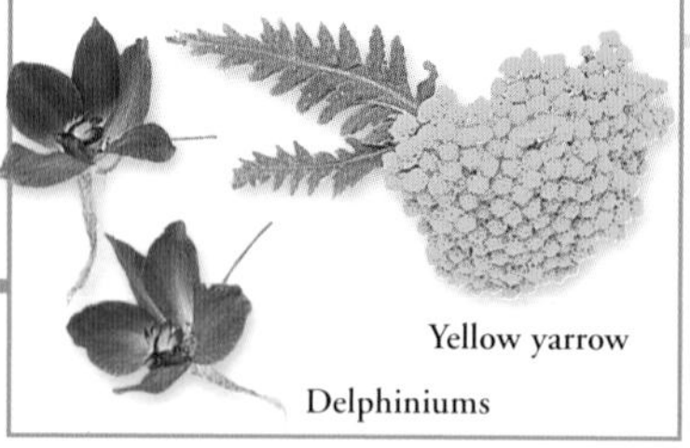

Yellow yarrow

Delphiniums

MOSSES AND LIVERWORTS (Bryophyta) 15,000 species

CLUB MOSSES (Lycopodophyta) 1,000 species

HORSETAILS (Sphenophyta) 15 species

FERNS (Pteridophyta) 12,000 species

CONIFERS (Coniferopsida) 500 species

CYCADS (Cycadopsida) 100 species

JOINT PINES (Gnetopsida) 70 species

GYMNOSPERMS (Gymnospermophyta) about 1,000 species

MONOCOTYLEDONS 80,000 species

DICOTYLEDONS 170,000 species

FUNGI (FUNGI)

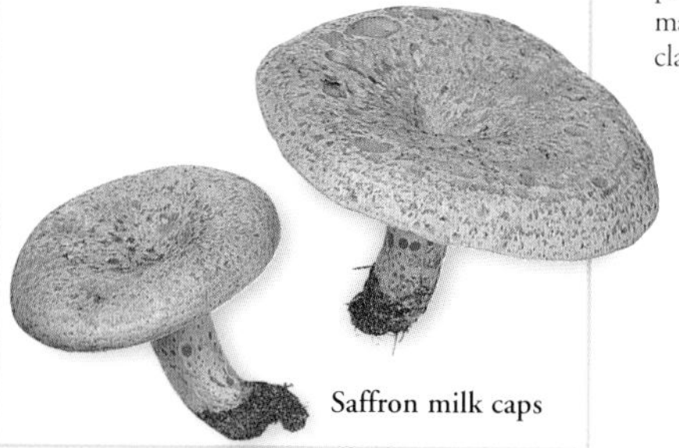

Saffron milk caps

Fungi

Fungi absorb food made by plants and animals. There are many thousands of species, classified into several phyla.

FUNGI IMPERFECTI (Deuteromycota) 25,000 species

CLUB FUNGI (Basidiomycota) 25,000 species

MOULDS (Zygomycota) 750 species

WATER MOULDS (Oomycota) 600 species

SAC FUNGI (Ascomycota) 30,000 species

ANIMALS (ANIMALIA)

| ROTIFERS (Rotifera) 2,000 species | MOLLUSCS (Mollusca) 110,000 species |

Animals

The animal kingdom contains organisms that cannot make their own food. Most animals can move around, but some spend their adult lives in one place.

| MOSS ANIMALS (Bryozoa) 4,000 species |

| c.13 OTHER SMALL PHYLA c.2,000 species |

OCTOPUSES, SQUIDS (Cephalopoda) 600 species

Octopus

ECHINODERMS (Echinodermata) 6,000 species

| SEA SPIDERS (Pycnogonida) 1,000 species | CENTIPEDES (Chilopoda) 2,500 species | ARTHROPODS (Arthropoda) at least 1,000,000 species |

| MILLIPEDES (Diplopoda) 10,000 species | HORSESHOE CRABS (Merostomata) 4 species |

| VELVETWORMS (Onychophora) 100 species |

SEA URCHINS (Echinoidea) 950 species

ARACHNIDS (Arachnida) 73,000 species

DEEP-SEA LIMPETS (Monoplacophora) 10 species

STARFISH (Asteroidea) 1,500 species

Camel spiders
Harvestmen
Micro-whip scorpions
Mites and ticks
Pseudoscorpions

Scorpion

Scorpions
Spiders
Tail-less whip scorpions
Tick spiders
Whip scorpions

| SPONGES (Porifera) 9,000 species |

SOLENOGASTERS (Aplacophora) 250 species

TUSK SHELLS (Scaphopoda) 350 species

BRITTLE STARS (Ophiuroidea) 2,000 species

INSECTS (Insecta) at least 1,000,000 species

| COMB JELLIES (Ctenophora) 90 species |

MUSSELS, CLAMS (Bivalvia) 15,000 species

SNAILS (Gastropoda) 35,000 species

CHITONS (Polyplacophora) 500 species

SEA CUCUMBERS (Holothuroidea) 900 species

Ants, bees, wasps
Beetles
Booklice
Bristletails
Bugs
Butterflies and moths
Caddis flies
Cockroaches
Diplurans
Dragonflies
Earwigs

Fleas
Flies
Grasshoppers, crickets
Grylloblattids
Lacewings and antlions
Lice
Mayflies
Praying mantids
Scorpion flies
Silverfish

Springtails
Stick and leaf insects
Stoneflies
Stylopids
Termites
Thrips
Webspinners
Zorapterans

| WORMS, LEECHES (Annelida) 18,600 species | ROUNDWORMS (Nematoda) 20,000 species | HORSEHAIR WORMS (Nematomorpha) 250 species | WATERBEARS (Tardigrada) 600 species | LAMPSHELLS (Brachiopoda) 300 species |

| FLATWORMS, FLUKES, TAPEWORMS (Platyhelminthes) 15,000 species | SEA ANEMONES, HYDRAS, CORALS, JELLYFISH (Cnidaria) 9,500 species | SPINY-HEADED WORMS (Acanthocephala) 1,500 species |

Morpho butterfly

BIRDS (Aves) 9,000 species

CHORDATES (Chordata) 45,000 species

CRUSTACEANS (Crustacea) 40,000 species

| AMPHIBIANS (Amphibia) 4,200 species | Caecilians Frogs and toads Newts and salamanders |

MAMMALS (Mammalia) 4,600 species

BRANCHIOPODS (Branchiopoda) 1,000 species

| REPTILES (Reptilia) 6,000 species | Crocodilians Lizards and snakes Tuatara Turtles, tortoises, and terrapins |

Red-tailed racer

Albatrosses, petrels, shearwaters, fulmars
Cassowaries, emus
Cranes, rails, coots, bustards
Cuckoos, roadrunners
Divers or loons
Ducks, geese, swans
Eagles, hawks, vultures, falcons, kites, buzzards
Grebes
Herons, storks, ibises, flamingos
Kingfishers, bee-eaters, rollers
Kiwis
Mousebirds
Nightjars, frogmouths
Ostriches
Owls
Parrots
Passerines
Pelicans, gannets, cormorants, frigate birds, darters
Penguins
Pheasants, partridges, grouse, turkeys
Pigeons, doves
Rheas
Sandgrouse
Swifts, hummingbirds
Tinamous
Trogons
Turacos
Wading birds, gulls, terns, auks
Woodpeckers, toucans, barbets, honeyguides, puffbirds, jacamars

Orange weaver

BARNACLES (Cirripedia) 1,220 species

Aardvarks
Bats
Carnivores
Edentates (anteaters, armadillos, sloths)
Elephants
Elephant shrews
Even-toed hoofed mammals
Flying lemurs
Hares, rabbits, pikas
Hyraxes
Insectivores
Marsupials (pouched mammals)
Monotremes (egg-laying mammals)
Odd-toed hoofed mammals
Pangolins
Primates
Rodents
Seals, sea lions, walruses
Sea cows
Tree shrews
Whales and dolphins

More than 20 orders including:
Carp
Catfish
Eels
Flying fish
Herrings, anchovies
Perch, marlins, swordfish, tunas
Salmon, trout

Clown fish

SPINY SAND SHRIMPS (Branchiura) 125 species

SAND SHRIMPS (Cephalocarida) 9 species

MYSTACOCARIDEANS (Mystacocarida) 10 species

| BONY FISH (Osteichthyes) 20,000 species |

| JAWLESS FISH (Agnatha) 75 species |

CRABS, LOBSTERS, AND SHRIMPS (Malacostraca) 20,000 species

| SEA SQUIRTS (Ascidiacea) 2,500 species |

Silverback gorilla

Crab

| SHARKS AND RAYS (Chondrichthyes) 800 species | Sharks, dolphins Skates, rays |

MUSSEL SHRIMPS (Ostracoda) 2,000 species

COPEPODS (Copepoda) 7,500 species

HOW LIVING THINGS WORK

ALL LIVING THINGS have characteristics in common: they grow, feed, reproduce, use energy, and respond to the outside world. Most living things have developed senses and patterns of behaviour that ensure the survival of their species.

REPRODUCTION RATES

Some animals can reproduce extremely rapidly, but only a few of their offspring survive to become adults.

SPECIES	BREEDING AGE	OFFSPRING PER YEAR
Fruit fly	10–14 days	Up to 900
Mouse	6 weeks	50–70
Rabbit	8 months	10–30
Northern gannet	5–6 years	1
Nile crocodile	15 years	50

Fourteen-day-old mice

ANIMAL SPEEDS

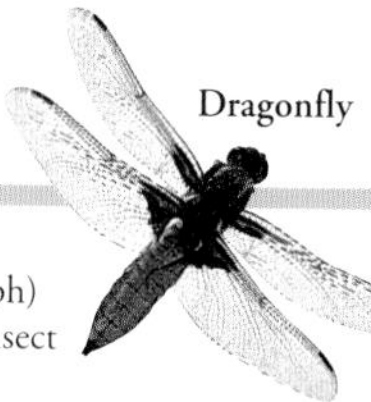

Dragonfly

AIR

Dragonfly
58 kmh (36 mph)
Fastest-flying insect

Frigate bird
153 kmh
(95 mph)

Spine-tailed swift
170 kmh (106 mph)
Fastest-flying bird

Peregrine falcon

Peregrine falcon
200 kmh (124 mph)
Fastest bird in a dive

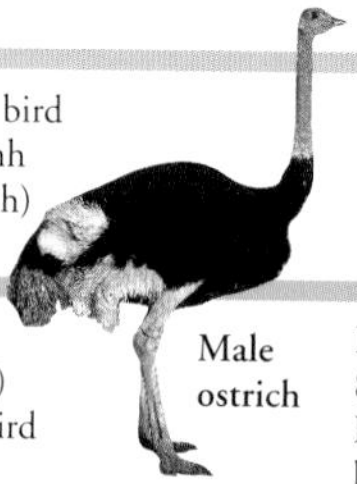

LAND

American cockroach
5 kmh (3 mph)
Fastest-running insect

Ostrich
72 kmh (45 mph)
Fastest-running bird

Male ostrich

Pronghorn antelope
86 kmh (53 mph)
Fastest mammal over
long distances

Cheetah
96.5 kmh (60 mph) Fastest
mammal over short distances

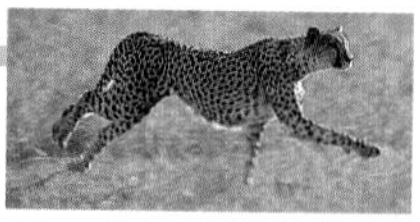

Cheetah

SEA

Gentoo penguin
35 kmh (22 mph)
Fastest-swimming bird

Killer whale
55 kmh (34.5 mph)
Fastest-swimming
mammal

Marlin
80 kmh
(50 mph)

Sailfish
109 kmh (68 mph)

Gentoo penguin

Black marlin

PLANT AND ANIMAL LIFESPANS

The chart below shows how long different animals and plants live. The ages given are the maximum average lifespans.

BACTERIA — 20 mins — Bacteria

PROTISTS — Several days

Honey fungus

Yew tree

FUNGI — Fairy ring mushroom (5 days) — Hyphae of honey fungus (10 years)

Bamboo

CONIFERS — Cedar of Lebanon (500 years) — Yew (3,500 years)

Foxglove

FLOWERING PLANTS — Foxglove (2 years) — Bamboo (30–60 years) — Saguaro cactus (150 years) — English oak (1,500 years)

ARTHROPODS — Housefly (17–30 days) — Housefly — Queen ant (15 years)

Toad

FISH — Goldfish (10–25 years) — Lake sturgeon (50–80 years)

English oak

AMPHIBIANS — Smooth newt (15 years) — Common toad (40 years) — Fire salamander (20 years) — Fire salamander

Giant tortoise

REPTILES — Boa constrictor (40 years) — American alligator (60 years) — Tuatara (101 years) — Giant tortoise (150 years)

BIRDS — Starling (1 year) — Wandering albatross (60 years) — Andean condor (70 years)

MAMMALS — Red fox — Red fox (8 years) — Giraffe (20 years) — African elephant (70 years) — Killer whale (90 years)

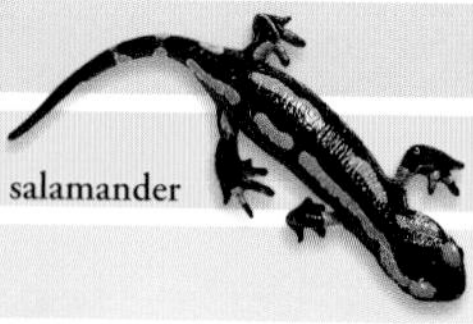

African elephant

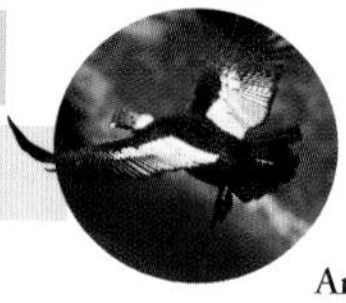

Andean condor

LIFESPAN FACTS

• The shrew has the shortest lifespan of all mammals. Shrews normally live for only 12–18 months in the wild.

• Humans are the longest-living mammals. The oldest elephant on record lived to the age of 82 in Sri Lanka.

Shrew

• Giant tortoises are the longest-living reptiles. The oldest tortoise ever recorded came from the Seychelles. It lived to the age of 152.

• The giant marine clam (Tridacna) is the longest-living animal in the world. It can live to be more than 200 years old.

Giant clam

BODY TEMPERATURES

The chart below shows the average body temperatures of exothermic ("cold-blooded") and endothermic ("warm-blooded") animals.

EXOTHERMIC ("COLD-BLOODED") ANIMALS

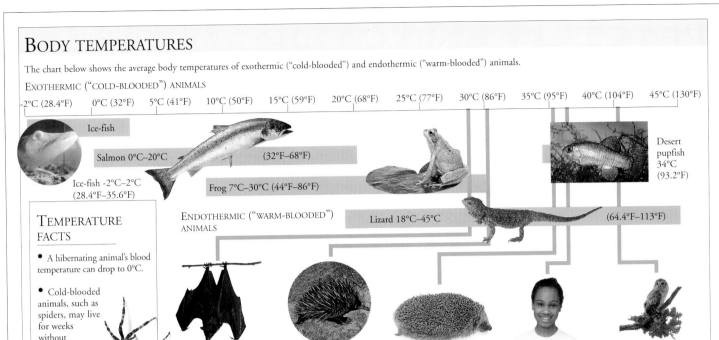

-2°C (28.4°F) 0°C (32°F) 5°C (41°F) 10°C (50°F) 15°C (59°F) 20°C (68°F) 25°C (77°F) 30°C (86°F) 35°C (95°F) 40°C (104°F) 45°C (130°F)

Ice-fish

Salmon 0°C–20°C (32°F–68°F)

Ice-fish -2°C–2°C
(28.4°F–35.6°F)

Frog 7°C–30°C (44°F–86°F)

Desert pupfish 34°C (93.2°F)

Lizard 18°C–45°C (64.4°F–113°F)

ENDOTHERMIC ("WARM-BLOODED") ANIMALS

TEMPERATURE FACTS

- A hibernating animal's blood temperature can drop to 0°C.

- Cold-blooded animals, such as spiders, may live for weeks without food.

Bat 28°C (82.4°F) Spiny anteater 30°C (86°F) Hedgehog 35°C (95°F) Human 37°C (98.6°F) Bird 40°C (104°F)

GESTATION PERIODS

The gestation period is the amount of time young take to develop inside the mother. Large mammals usually have long gestation periods, although kangaroos have gestation periods of only 33 days.

Longest gestation periods

MAMMAL	AVERAGE GESTATION (DAYS)
African elephant	660
Asian elephant	660
Baird's beaked whale	520
White rhinoceros	490
Walrus	480
Giraffe	460
Tapir	400

Giraffes

Shortest gestation periods

MAMMAL	AVERAGE GESTATION (DAYS)
Short-nosed bandicoot	12
Opossum	13
Shrew	14
Golden hamster	15
Lemming	16
Mouse	20

Opossum

GESTATION FACT

- The 480-day gestation of the walrus includes a delay of up to five months so that the young can be delivered at the most favourable time of the year.

Walruses

ANIMAL ENERGY NEEDS

The chart below shows how many kilojoules (kJ) different animal species need per day for a moderate amount of activity.

ANIMAL	kJ REQUIRED
House mouse	45.4
European robin	89.9
Grey squirrel	386
Domestic cat	1,554
Female human	10,080
Male human	13,713
Llama	16,128
Tiger	33,600
Giraffe	152,754
Walrus	159,852
Asian elephant	256,872

ENERGY FACT

- A flea can jump more than 100 times its own height using energy stored in pads in its leg joints.

Flea jumping

HEARING RANGES OF SELECTED ANIMALS

Sound is measured by its pitch in units called Hertz (Hz). A higher number means a higher pitch – a lower number, a lower pitch.

SPECIES	HEARING RANGES IN HZ
Elephant	1–20,000
Dog	10–35,000
Human	20–20,000
Bat	100–100,000
Frog	100–2,500

HEARING FACTS

- Crickets have "ears" on their knees made from a taut membrane that is sensitive to sound vibrations.

- Owls' left and right ears are often at different levels in the skull. This helps them to track their prey more effectively.

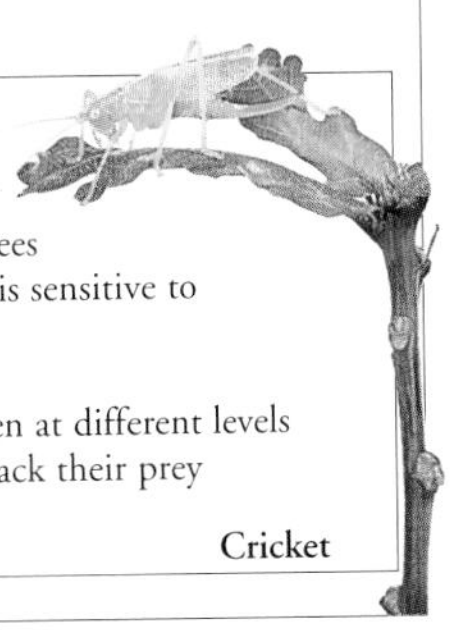

Cricket

ANIMAL HEART RATES

Animals with small bodies have much faster heartbeats than animals with larger bodies.

ANIMAL	BEATS PER MINUTE
Grey whale	9
Harbour seal (diving)	10
Elephant	25
Human	70
Sparrow	500
Shrew	600
Hummingbird (hovering)	1,200

Hummingbird

SLEEP REQUIREMENTS

This list excludes periods of hibernation, which can last up to several months.

ANIMAL	AVERAGE HOURS OF SLEEP PER DAY
Koala	22
Sloth	20
Opossum	19
Cat	15
Squirrel	14

Domestic cat

SLEEPING FACTS

- Big cats, such as leopards, sleep for about 12–14 hours a day. Since they have no natural enemies, they can sleep unprotected in the open air.

- Sloths are among the world's sleepiest animals. They hang upside down and sleep for up to 20 hours per day. Some species of sloth leave their trees only once a week.

PLANT AND ANIMAL RECORDS

THE PLANT AND ANIMAL kingdoms are the two largest groups of living things. These pages list the world's record breakers from the smallest and most poisonous frogs to the tallest and heaviest trees. Living things of the same species vary in size, so all measurements are approximate.

TREES

TALLEST SPECIES: Eucalyptus. These trees can grow to more than 130 m (427 ft) in height.

HEAVIEST SPECIES: Giant sequoia. Also known as wellingtonias, these conifers weigh up to 2,000 tonnes (tons).

OLDEST SPECIES: Ginkgo. This ancient species first appeared about 160 million years ago in China.

Coast redwood

OLDEST LIVING TREE: Bristlecone pine. Native to Arizona and Nevada, USA, this species can live for more than 5,000 years.

MOST DROUGHT-RESISTANT TREE: Baobab. This African tree can store up to 136,000 litres (29,920 UK gallons) of water in its trunk.

WORLD'S TALLEST LIVING TREE: A coast redwood in Montgomery State Reserve, California, USA. It stands 112.01 m (368 ft) tall.

WORLD'S BIGGEST LIVING TREE: The General Sherman giant sequoia in Sequoia National Park, California, USA. It is 84 m (276 ft) tall and its base is approximately 10 m (33 ft) wide.

Bristlecone pine

FLOWERING PLANTS

LARGEST FLOWER: Giant rafflesia. This foul-smelling flower can grow up to 1.05 m (3.5 ft) across and weigh as much as 7 kg (15.4 lb).

SMALLEST FLOWER: Australian duckweed. The flowers of this floating plant measure only 0.61 mm (0.024 in) across.

SMALLEST LAND PLANT: Dwarf snow willow. This miniscule plant grows only a few centimetres long.

LONGEST SEAWEED: Pacific giant kelp seaweed. The fronds of this seaweed can grow as long as 60 m (197 ft).

FASTEST-GROWING PLANT: Bamboo. This is the tallest and fastest-growing grass. Some species can grow to 30 m (98.4 ft) at a rate of 1 m (3.2 ft) a day.

Dioon edule. This evergreen shrub grows at a rate of only 0.76 mm (0.29 in) per year.

Bamboo

Snow willow

LEAVES

LARGEST LEAF: Raffia palm. Its leaves grow up to 20 m (66 ft) long.

SMALLEST LEAF: Floating duckweed. The leaves of this tiny plant are only 0.6 mm (0.02 in) long and 0.3 mm (0.01 in) wide.

Duckweed

FUNGI

Fungi used to be classified as plants, but, since 1969, botanists have classified them as a separate kingdom.

BIGGEST FUNGUS: Bracket fungus. This huge species measures several metres across.

MOST POISONOUS FUNGUS: Death cap. If eaten, this deadly mushroom can cause death within 15 hours.

Death cap mushrooms

SEEDS

LARGEST SEED: Coco-de-mer palm. Each seed can weigh up to 20 kg (44 lb) and take ten years to develop.

SMALLEST SEED: A species of orchid. A billion seeds weigh as little as 1 g (0.035 oz).

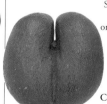

Coco-de-mer seed

Orchids

MOST POISONOUS ANIMALS

REPTILE: *Hydrophis belcheri.* This sea snake is far more poisonous than any land snake. The Australian taipan is the deadliest land snake. Its bite is fatal without an antitoxin that counteracts the venom.

FISH: Death puffer. This harmless looking fish keeps poison in its blood and organs. If eaten, it can kill a person.

ARACHNID: Brazilian wandering spider. This aggressive spider bites if disturbed.

MOLLUSC: Blue-ringed octopus. The painful bite of this Australian octopus can kill in minutes.

AMPHIBIAN: Golden-yellow poison-dart frog. The colourful poison-dart frogs from South and Central America and the Madagascan mantellas have highly poisonous chemicals in their skins.

Golden mantella

MAMMALS

LARGEST MAMMAL: Blue whale. The world's heaviest and longest animal, it can grow up to 35 m (115 ft) long and weigh up to 190 tonnes (tons).

LARGEST LAND MAMMAL: African elephant. The average male elephant is 3 m (9.8 ft) tall and weighs about 5 tonnes (tons).

TALLEST MAMMAL: Giraffe. The adult male giraffe can grow up to 5.9 m (19.4 ft) tall.

SMALLEST MAMMAL: Kitti's hog-nosed bat. Sometimes known as bumblebee bats, these tiny creatures have an average length of 3.3 cm (1.3 in) and weigh no more than 2 g (0.07 oz).

SMALLEST LAND MAMMAL: African pygmy shrew. From head to tail, it is only 70 mm (2.7 in) long and weighs between 1.5–2.5 g (0.05–0.08 oz).

HEAVIEST PRIMATE: Gorilla. The male gorilla can weigh as much as 220 kg (485 lb).

LARGEST FLYING MAMMAL: A flying fox (fruit bat of tropical Africa and Asia) can grow to the size of a small dog and have a wingspan of 2 m (6 ft).

Blue whale

REPTILES AND AMPHIBIANS

LARGEST LIZARD: Komodo dragon lizard. This Indonesian reptile grows up to 3 m (10 ft) long and weighs up to 166 kg (365 lb).

SMALLEST LIZARD: British Virgin Island gecko. This tiny lizard is only 18 mm (0.7 in) long.

LONGEST REPTILE: Saltwater crocodile. This is the longest animal on land, growing up to 6 m (20 ft) long.

LARGEST AMPHIBIAN: Giant salamander. The average length of the Chinese giant salamander is 1.5 m (5 ft).

SMALLEST AMPHIBIAN: Sminthillus limbatus. This tiny frog from Cuba is only 1 cm (0.5 in) long.

LARGEST TURTLE: Leatherback turtle. This turtle can grow more than 2 m (6.6 ft) long and weigh up to 450 kg (1,000 lb).

Saltwater crocodile

SNAKES

LONGEST SNAKE: Anaconda. The average length of the South American anaconda is 5.5 m (18 ft).

SHORTEST SNAKE: Thread snake. This tiny snake from the West Indies is less than 11 cm (4.4 in) long.

LONGEST FANGS: Gaboon viper. Its fangs can be as long as 5 cm (2 in).

FASTEST SNAKE: Black mamba. This African snake can travel at speeds of up to 19 kmh (12 mph).

Anaconda

SPIDERS AND INSECTS

LARGEST SPIDER: Goliath bird-eating spider. The largest specimen on record had a legspan of 28 cm (11 in).

LARGEST WEB: Orb-web spider. Tropical orb-web spiders can spin webs of up to 1.5 m (5 ft) in circumference.

LARGEST BUTTERFLY: Queen Alexandra's birdwing. It is the largest and heaviest butterfly with a wingspan of up to 28 cm (11 in).

LARGEST PREHISTORIC INSECT: Dragonfly. This huge insect had a wingspan of 75 cm (29.5 in).

LONGEST INSECT: Giant stick insect. This insect from New Guinea has an average length of 45 cm (17.7 in).

LARGEST WINGSPAN: Owlet moth. Its wingspan can measure up to 30 cm (12 in).

HEAVIEST INSECT: Goliath beetle. This huge African beetle weighs up to 100 g (3.5 oz).

SMALLEST INSECT: Fairyfly wasp. These tiny wasps grow only 0.2 mm (0.007 in) long.

Goliath beetle

Fairyfly wasp

MARINE ANIMALS

LARGEST FISH: Whale shark. Found in the Atlantic, Pacific, and Indian oceans, these huge fish can grow up to 12.65 m (41.5 ft) long.

SMALLEST FISH: Dwarf goby. The average length of a male fish is only 6 mm (0.3 in).

LARGEST MOLLUSC: Giant Atlantic squid. The largest specimens grow up to 17 m (55.7 ft) long.

LARGEST BIVALVE MOLLUSC: Giant clam. It can weigh as much as 300 kg (661 lb) and grow to 1.15 m (3.7 ft).

LARGEST CRUSTACEAN: Japanese spider crab. This huge crab has a legspan of 4 m (13 ft) and can weigh as much as 18.6 kg (41 lb).

SMALLEST CRUSTACEAN: Alonella water flea. This tiny crustacean grows only 0.25 mm (0.1 in) long.

Whale shark

BIRDS

LARGEST FLYING BIRD: Great bustard. A male bird can weigh up to 19 kg (42 lb).

LARGEST FLIGHTLESS BIRD: Ostrich. The African ostrich weighs 130 kg (280 lb) and grows to a height of 2.7 m (8.9 ft).

LARGEST PREHISTORIC BIRD: Elephant bird. This massive flightless bird from Madagascar weighed around 438 kg (966 lb) and stood 3 m (10 ft) tall.

SMALLEST BIRD: Bee hummingbird. This Cuban bird measures only 5.7 cm (2.2 in) and weighs just 1.6 g (0.05 oz).

FARTHEST MIGRATION: Arctic tern. Every year, this bird flies from the Arctic to the Antarctic and back again – a round trip of about 40,000 km (25,000 miles).

LARGEST WINGSPAN: Wandering albatross. The wingspan of this huge seabird can stretch up to 3.6 m (12 ft) across.

LARGEST EGG: Ostrich egg. The largest specimens can weigh up to 1.65 kg (3.64 lb) and measure up to 20 cm (8 in) long.

SMALLEST EGG: Bee hummingbird egg. These eggs weigh only 0.25 g (0.009 oz).

Albatross

Ostrich egg

WILDLIFE IN DANGER

Atlantic Empress disaster, 1979

SINCE LIFE BEGAN on Earth, many species of plants and animals have died out – mostly because of human interference. The main threats to wildlife today are habitat destruction, hunting and collecting, and pollution. Many plants and animals are now protected by law.

ENVIRONMENTAL DISASTERS

In 1989, the *Exxon Valdez* oil tanker ran aground in Alaska. It spilled more than 35,000 tonnes of oil into the Pacific, causing the deaths of thousands of seabirds. The table below lists the world's worst oil spills.

TANKER (LOCATION OF DISASTER)	DATE	OIL SPILLAGE IN TONNES
Atlantic Empress and *Aegean Captain* (Trinidad)	July 1979	300,000
Castillio de Bellver (Cape Town, South Africa)	August 1983	255,000
Olympic Bravery (Ushant, France)	January 1976	250,000
Showa-Maru (Malacca, Malaysia)	June 1975	237,000
Amoco Cadiz (Finistère, France)	March 1978	223,000
Odyssey (Atlantic Ocean, Canada)	November 1988	140,000
Torrey Canyon (Scilly Isles, UK)	March 1967	120,000
Sea Star (Gulf of Oman)	December 1972	115,000
Irenes Serenada (Pílos, Greece)	February 1980	102,000
Urquiola (Corunna, Spain)	May 1976	101,000

ENVIRONMENT FACTS

• It is estimated that over the next 20 years almost half a million species of plants and animals will become extinct.

• The ivory-billed woodpecker used to live in forest swamps. It is one of the world's rarest birds and is endangered.

• All species of rhinoceros are now protected by law. Many rhinoceroses were killed for their horns, which are reputed to have medicinal qualities.

• The population of the Komodo dragon, the largest-living lizard, is at a dangerously low level because of over-hunting by collectors.

• Turtles are often hunted for their shell, eggs, and meat. Several species of marine turtles are under threat.

Green turtle

DWINDLING FORESTS

Humans have destroyed almost half of the world's tropical rainforests. This table shows how many forests are being cut down annually for timber or building projects.

COUNTRY	ANNUAL LOSS IN KM2 (MILES2)
Brazil	17,658 (6,818)
Venezuela	9,240 (3,568)
Indonesia	8,440 (3,259)
Zaire	7,344 (2,836)
Bolivia	5,916 (2,284)
Mexico	5,161 (1,993)
Colombia	3,717 (1,435)
Peru	2,968 (1,146)
Burma	2,392 (924)
Malaysia	1,860 (718)

South American rainforest

ENDANGERED PLANTS

Habitat destruction, wetland drainage, urban growth, and modern farming methods threaten many plant species. Those most at risk are listed below.

COMMON NAME (LOCATION)	SCIENTIFIC NAME
Wild sago (USA)	Zania floridans
Chiapas slipper orchid (Mexico)	Phragmipedium exstaminodium
Sea bindweed (Europe)	Calystegia soldanella
Green pitcher plant (USA)	Sarracenia oreophila
Big-leaf palm (Madagascar)	Marojejya darianii
Socotran pomegranate (Yemen)	Punica protopunica
African violet (East Africa)	Saintpaulia ionantha
Green daffodil (Mediterranean)	Narcissus viridiflorus
Blue vanda (India/Thailand)	Vanda coerulea
Drago, or Canadian dragon, tree (Canary Islands/Madeira)	Dracaena draco
Caoba (Ecuador)	Persea theobromifolia

Sea bindweed

ENDANGERED ANIMALS

Endangered species all around the world are monitored by animal welfare organizations. The animals below are at risk of becoming extinct in the near future.

COMMON NAME (LOCATION)	SCIENTIFIC NAME
Blue whale (Antarctic Ocean)	*Balaenoptera musculus*
Black-footed ferret (North America)	*Mustela nigripes*
Giant panda (China)	*Ailuropoda melanoleuca*
Kemp's Ridley sea turtle (Mexico)	*Lepidochelys kempii*
Javan rhinoceros (Southeast Asia)	*Rhinoceros sondaicus*
Woolly spider monkey (Brazil)	*Bracyteles arachnoides*
Queen Alexandra's birdwing butterfly (Papua New Guinea)	*Ornithoptera alexandrae*
Mediterranean monk seal (Mediterranean coasts)	*Monachus monachus*
Yangtze river dolphin (China)	*Lipotes vexillifer*
Magpie robin (Seychelles)	*Copsychus sechellarun*
Californian condor (California, USA)	*Gymnogyps californianus*
Florida manatee (Atlantic Ocean)	*Trichechus manatus*

Blue whale

ENVIRONMENTAL ORGANIZATIONS

These environmental organizations are dedicated to helping plants and animals in danger and finding solutions to worldwide ecological problems.

Greenpeace
Canonbury Villas
London N1 2PN
www.greenpeace.org

FRIENDS *of the*
earth

Friends of the Earth
26–28 Underwood Street
London N1 7JQ
www.foei.org

IFAW

International Fund for
Animal Welfare
87–90 Albert Embankment
London SE1 7UD
www.ifaw.org

WWF

World Wildlife Fund
Panda House
Weyside Park
Godalming
Surrey GU7 1XR
www.wwf.org

UNIVERSE

THE KNOWN UNIVERSE contains countless millions of galaxies and stars. From Earth, the stars seem to form patterns in the sky. These patterns are known as constellations. We see different star patterns from month to month as Earth orbits the Sun.

Spiral galaxy

SUN DATA

- Age: About 5 billion years
- Diameter: 1,392,000 km (865,000 miles)
- Distance from the Earth: 149.6 million km (92.9 million miles)
- Time taken to orbit galaxy: 240 million years
- Surface temperature: 5,500°C (9,900°F)
- Life expectancy: 10 billion years
- Mass (Earth = 1): 332,946

MOON DATA

- Age: 4.6 billion years
- Diameter: 3,476 km (2,160 miles)
- Distance from the Earth: 384,000 km (238,000 miles)
- Surface temperature: −173 to 105°C (−279 to 221°F)
- Mass (Earth = 1): 0.012
- Gravity (Earth = 1): 0.16
- Rotation period: 27.3 days
- The pull of the Moon's gravity is largely responsible for the rise and fall of tides on Earth.

CONSTELLATIONS OF THE NORTHERN HEMISPHERE

Vega will be the Pole star in AD 14,000.

Betelgeuse is 400 times larger than the Sun.

Stars appear to revolve around the centre star, Polaris.

Clusters of stars form groups known as constellations.

1 Pisces
2 Pegasus 3 Delphinus 4 Aquila
5 Sagitta 6 Cygnus 7 Andromeda
8 Triangulum 9 Aries 10 Cetus
11 Taurus 12 Perseus 13 Cassiopeia
14 Cepheus 15 Lyra 16 Ophiuchus
17 Serpens Caput 18 Corona Borealis
19 Hercules 20 Draco 21 Ursa Minor 22 Polaris (North Star) 23 Auriga 24 Orion 25 Gemini 26 Monoceros 27 Canis Minor 28 Hydra 29 Cancer 30 Ursa Major 31 Leo Minor 32 Leo 33 Canes Venatici 34 Virgo 35 Boötes

CONSTELLATIONS OF THE SOUTHERN HEMISPHERE

Stars near the edge become visible month by month throughout the year.

Sirius is the brightest star in the night sky.

The edge of the map marks the celestial equator.

1 Cetus
2 Eridanus
3 Orion
4 Monoceros
5 Canis Major
6 Lepus 7 Columba
8 Caelum 9 Horologium
10 Fornax 11 Phoenix 12 Sculptor 13 Aquarius
14 Piscis Austrinus 15 Capricornus
16 Microscorpium 17 Grus 18 Indus 19 Tucana
20 Pavo 21 Apus 22 Hydrus 23 Reticulum
24 Mensa 25 Chameleon 26 Dorado 27 Pictor
28 Volans
29 Carinar
30 Puppis
31 Vela 32 Musca
33 Crux 34 Antlia
35 Hydra 36 Sextans
37 Crater 38 Corvus 39 Virgo
40 Libra 41 Centaurus 42 Lupus
43 Norma 44 Triangulum Australe
45 Ara 46 Sagittarius 47 Aquila
48 Corona Australis
49 Ophiuchus 50 Scorpius

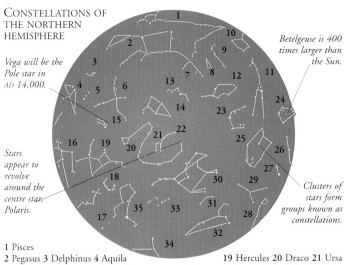

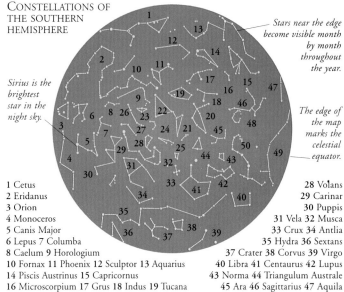

INNER PLANETS / OUTER PLANETS

PLANETS The nine planets in our solar system divide into two groups: the dense, rocky inner planets and the gaseous, icy outer planets.	MERCURY	VENUS	EARTH	MARS	JUPITER	SATURN	URANUS	NEPTUNE	PLUTO
DISTANCE FROM THE SUN IN MILLIONS OF KM (MILES)	57.9 (36)	108.2 (67.2)	149.6 (93)	227.9 (141.6)	778.3 (483.6)	1,427 (886.7)	2,871 (1,784)	4,497 (2,794)	5,914 (3,675)
DIAMETER IN KM (MILES)	4,878 (3,031)	12,103 (7,520)	12,756 (7,926)	6,786 (4,217)	142,984 (88,850)	120,536 (74,901)	51,118 (31,764)	49,528 (30,775)	2,284 (1,419)
TIME TAKEN TO ORBIT THE SUN	87.97 days	224.7 days	365.26 days	686.98 days	11.86 years	29.46 years	84.01 years	164.79 years	248.54 years
TIME TAKEN TO TURN ON AXIS	58 days, 16 hours	243 days, 14 hours	23 hours, 56 mins	24 hours, 37 mins	9 hours, 55 mins	10 hours, 40 mins	17 hours, 14 mins	16 hours, 7 mins	6 days, 9 hours
SURFACE TEMPERATURE	−180 to 430°C (−292 to 806°F)	500°C (900°F)	−70 to 55°C (−94 to 131°F)	−120 to 25°C (−184 to 77°F)	−150°C (−238°F) At cloud tops	−180°C (−292°F) At cloud tops	−210°C (−346°F) At cloud tops	−210°C (−346°F)	−220°C (−364°F)
NUMBER OF MOONS	0	0	1	2	61	31	27	13	1
MASS (EARTH = 1)	0.055	0.81	1	0.107	318	95.18	14.5	17.14	0.0022
DENSITY (WATER = 1)	5.43	5.25	5.52	3.95	1.33	0.69	1.29	2.1	2.03

EARTH

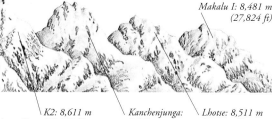

MORE THAN SEVENTY per cent of the Earth's surface is covered by water. Above sea level, Earth's land surface is made up of seven vast land masses called continents. The Earth is in a constant state of change, both above and below the surface. Most volcanoes and earthquakes are caused by the movements of huge rocky plates in the Earth's crust.

DESERTS

LARGEST DESERTS	AREA IN KM²	AREA IN MILES²
Sahara (Africa)	9,065,000	3,500,000
Arabian (Asia)	1,300,000	502,000
Gobi (Asia)	1,040,000	402,000
Kalahari (Africa)	580,000	224,000
Great Sandy (Australia)	414,000	160,000
Chihuahua (USA)	370,000	143,000
Takla Makan (Asia)	320,000	198,848
Kara Kum (Asia)	310,000	120,000
Namib (Africa)	310,000	120,000
Thar (Asia)	260,000	100,000

Sahara Desert

HIGHEST AND LOWEST POINTS IN THE WORLD

CONTINENT	HIGHEST POINT ABOVE SEA LEVEL	HEIGHT IN METRES (FEET)	LOWEST POINT BELOW SEA LEVEL	DEPTH IN METRES (FEET)
Asia	Mt. Everest	8,848 (29,030)	Dead Sea	−400 (−1,312)
Africa	Kilimanjaro	5,895 (19,341)	Qattâra Depression	−133 (−436)
North America	Denali (Mt. McKinley)	6,194 (20,323)	Death Valley	−86 (−282)
South America	Aconcagua	6,960 (22,834)	Peninsular Valdez	−40 (−131)
Antarctica	Vinson Massif	5,140 (16,864)	Bentley Subglacial Trench	−2,538 (−8,327)
Europe	Elbrus	5,633 (18,481)	Caspian Sea	−28 (−92)
Australia	Mt. Kosciusko	2,228 (7,310)	Lake Eyre	−16 (−52)

Everest: 8,848 m (29,028 ft)

Makalu I: 8,481 m (27,824 ft)

Highest mountains
The ten highest mountains in the world are all in the Himalayas, which lie between Tibet, China, and the Indian subcontinent.

K2: 8,611 m (28,250 ft)

Kanchenjunga: 8,598 m (28,208 ft)

Lhotse: 8,511 m (27,923 ft)

OCEANS AND SEAS

The table below lists the world's largest oceans and seas.

NAME	AREA IN KM²	AREA IN MILES²
Pacific Ocean	165,241,000	63,800,000
Atlantic Ocean	81,500,000	31,500,000
Indian Ocean	73,452,000	28,360,000
Arctic Ocean	14,089,600	5,440,000
Arabian Sea	3,864,000	1,492,000
South China Sea	3,447,000	1,331,000
Caribbean Sea	2,753,000	1,063,000
Mediterranean Sea	2,505,000	967,000
Bering Sea	2,269,000	876,000

LARGEST LAKES AND INLAND SEAS

LAKE	LOCATION	AREA IN KM²	AREA IN MILES²
Caspian Sea	Asia	370,980	143,236
Lake Superior	Canada/USA	82,098	31,698
Lake Victoria	Africa	68,880	26,595
Lake Huron	Canada/USA	59,566	22,999
Lake Michigan	USA	57,754	22,999
Lake Tanganyika	Africa	32,891	12,699
Lake Baikal	Siberia	31,498	12,161
Aral Sea	Asia	31,080	12,000

Caspian Sea

LONGEST RIVERS

NAME (LOCATION)	LENGTH IN KM (MILES)
Nile (Africa)	6,695 (4,160)
Amazon (USA)	6,500 (4,040)
Yangtze (Asia)	6,300 (3,915)
Mississippi– Missouri– Red Rock (USA)	6,020 (3,741)
Yenisey–Angara– Selenga (Asia)	5,540 (3,442)

Greatest waterfalls
The world's highest waterfalls are the Angel Falls in Venezuela. They were discovered by US pilot James Angel in 1935.

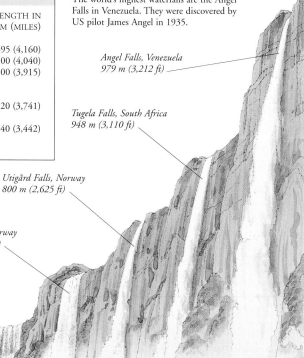

Angel Falls, Venezuela 979 m (3,212 ft)

Tugela Falls, South Africa 948 m (3,110 ft)

Utigård Falls, Norway 800 m (2,625 ft)

Mongefossen, Norway 774 m (2,540 ft)

Yosemite Falls, USA 739 m (2,425 ft)

EARTH FACTS

- Diameter: 12,756 km (7,926 miles) at equator; 12,713 km (7,899 miles) at poles
- Age: 4.6 billion years old
- Distance from Sun: 150 million km (93 million miles)
- Mass: 5,854 billion billion tonnes
- Area: 29.2% land, 70.8% water
- Orbiting time: 365.26 days
- Orbiting speed: 29.8 km/sec (18.5 miles/sec)

EARTHQUAKES

There are two different scales for measuring earthquakes: the Richter scale and the modified Mercalli scale.

Early Chinese seismoscope

Richter scale

The Richter scale was devised by American seismologist Charles F. Richter in 1935. It measures magnitude (the size of the shock wave and the energy it produces). Each number in the scale represents a shock ten times that of the previous one.

MAGNITUDE	PROBABLE EFFECTS
1	Detectable by instruments.
2–2.5	Can be felt by people.
4–5	May cause slight damage.
6	Fairly destructive.
7	A major earthquake.
8–9	A very destructive earthquake.

Modified Mercalli scale

The modified Mercalli scale measures how much an earthquake shakes the ground at a particular place. The original scale was devised by Italian Giuseppe Mercalli (1850–1914) in 1902. On Mercalli's scale, earthquakes are graded from one to ten.

INTENSITY	PROBABLE EFFECTS
1	Not felt by people, but recorded by instruments.
2	Felt by people resting.
3	Detected indoors. Hanging objects swing.
4	Doors rattle. Trees shake.
5	Felt outdoors by most people. Objects move.
6	Felt by everyone. Windows break.
7	Difficult for people to stand. Bricks and tiles fall.
8	Major damage to buildings. Tree branches break.
9	Damage to foundations. Some buildings collapse.
10	Large landslides. Many buildings are destroyed.
11	Major ground disturbances. Railway lines buckle.
12	Total destruction. River courses altered.

EARTHQUAKE FACTS

Earthquake damage, San Francisco, USA, 1989

- The first instrument for recording earthquakes was the seismoscope, invented in China in AD 132.

- The worst earthquake in the 20th century was the Tangshan earthquake in China in 1976. It measured 7.8 on the Richter scale and approximately 242,000 people were killed.

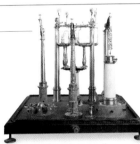

Italian seismograph

EXTREME WEATHER

Norilsk, Russia

LOWEST TEMPERATURE: –89.2°C (-128.6°F) at Vostok, Antarctica in 1983.

HIGHEST TEMPERATURE in shade: 57.7°C (136°F) at Al 'Aziziyah, Libya in 1922.

HIGHEST ANNUAL RAINFALL: 26,461 mm (1,041.7 in) during a 12-month period at Cherrapunji, India.

MOST RAINY DAYS: Mt. wai-ale-ale, Hawaii, which has on average 335 rainy days each year.

SUNNIEST PLACE: Yuma, Arizona, USA averages 4,127 hours of sunshine each year.

DRIEST PLACE: Atacama Desert, Chile has virtually no rain throughout the year.

HOTTEST PLACE: Dallol, Ethiopia has an average annual temperature of 34°C (90°F).

SNOWIEST PLACE: Mt. Rainier, USA, where 31,102 mm (1,224.5 in) of snow fell over a 12-month period in 1972–73.

Atacama Desert, Chile

COLDEST INHABITED PLACE: Norilsk, Russia has an average annual temperature of 10.9°C (12.4°F).

HIGHEST WIND SPEED: 372km/h (231mph) at Mt. Washington, USA on 12 April 1934.

WORST HAILSTORM: Moradabad, Uttar Pradesh, India, where 246 people were killed in 1888.

BEAUFORT SCALE

The Beaufort scale measures wind speed. It is used worldwide in weather reports and shipping forecasts. It was devised in 1805 by British Admiral Sir Francis Beaufort (1774–1857).

FORCE	DESCRIPTION	AVERAGE SPEED KM/H	MPH
0	Calm	1	1
1	Light air	3	2
2	Light breeze	9	5
3	Gentle breeze	15	10
4	Moderate breeze	25	15
5	Fresh breeze	35	21
6	Strong breeze	45	28
7	Moderate gale	56	35
8	Fresh gale	68	43
9	Strong gale	81	50
10	Whole gale	94	59
11	Storm	110	69
12	Hurricane	118	74

VOLCANOES

Volcanic glass

Worst volcanic eruptions

LOCATION	DATE	FATALITIES
Vesuvius, Italy	ad 79	20,000
Mt. Etna, Italy	1169	15,000
Vesuvius, Italy	1631	18,000
Mt. Etna, Italy	1669	20,000
Laki, Iceland	1783	20,000
Miyi-Yama, Java	1793	53,000
Tambora, Indonesia	1815	92,000
Krakatoa, Sumatra/Java	1883	36,380
Mont Pelée, Martinique	1902	40,000
Nevado del Ruiz, Colombia	1985	22,940

Major active volcanoes

NAME	HEIGHT IN METRES (FT)	LAST ERUPTED
Mt. St Helens, USA	2,549 (8,362)	1998
Ruapehu, New Zealand	2,796 (9,173)	1999
Kliuchevskoi, Siberia	4,850 (15,912)	2001
Nyamuragira, D.R. Congo	3,053 (10,016)	2001
Tungurahua, Ecuador	5,023 (16,475)	2002
Fuego, Guatemala	3,763 (12,342)	2002
Semeru, Indonesia	3,676 (12,057)	2002
Nyiragongo, D.R. Congo	3,465 (11,365)	2002
Mt. Etna, Sicily, Italy	3,350 (10,991)	2002
Soufriere, Montserrat	915 (3,002)	2002

Mt. Ruapehu, New Zealand

923

PERIODIC TABLE

THE PERIODIC TABLE CLASSIFIES chemical elements according to their atomic number and chemical properties. This chart arranges elements into vertical columns, called groups, and horizontal columns, called periods. Elements with similar chemical properties lie in the same vertical group.

TYPES OF ELEMENT KEY

- Alkali metals
- Alkaline-earth metals
- Transition metals
- Lanthanides
- Actinides
- Poor metals
- Semimetals
- Non-metals
- Noble gases

Non-metals

Non-metals include elements that are gases at room temperature (20°C/68°F), such as hydrogen and oxygen. Solid non-metals, such as sulphur and phosphorus, usually break very easily and are poor conductors of heat and electricty.

Sulphur

Poor metals

The poor metals are aluminium, gallium, indium, thallium, tin, lead, bismuth, and polonium. They are softer and weaker than other metals and melt more easily.

Aluminium

Alkali and alkaline-earth metals

At the beginning of the periodic table are two groups of highly reactive metals: the alkali and the alkaline-earth metals. Alkali metals, such as potassium, caesium, and rubidium, all react violently with water.

Like all alkali metals, sodium is soft enough to cut with a knife.

The atomic number is the number of protons in the nuclei of the element's atoms.

The atomic mass is the mass of one atom of the element compared to one-twelfth of the mass of an atom of the element carbon.

Chemical symbol Each atom has a chemical symbol. It is used for identification in chemical equations.

58	140
Ce	
Cerium	

Name of element

There are two alternative number systems for grouping the elements: Group 1–18 and Group 1–0.

1

1   1.01
H
Hydrogen

2

3 6.94	4 9.01
Li	**Be**
Lithium	Beryllium

11 22.99	12 24.31
Na	**Mg**
Sodium	Magnesium

3 | **4** | **5** | **6** | **7** | **8** | **9**

19 39.1	20 40.08	21 44.96	22 47.88	23 50.94	24 51.1	25 54.94	26 55.85	27 58.93
K	**Ca**	**Sc**	**Ti**	**V**	**Cr**	**Mn**	**Fe**	**Co**
Potassium	Calcium	Scandium	Titanium	Vanadium	Chromium	Manganese	Iron	Cobalt

37 85.47	38 87.62	39 88.91	40 91.22	41 92.91	42 95.94	43 98	44 101.07	45 102.91
Rb	**Sr**	**Y**	**Zr**	**Nb**	**Mo**	**Tc**	**Ru**	**Rh**
Rubidium	Strontium	Yttrium	Zirconium	Niobium	Molybdenum	Technetium	Ruthenium	Rhodium

55 132.91	56 137.33	57 138.91	72 178.49	73 180.95	74 183.85	75 186.21	76 190.2	77 192.22
Cs	**Ba**	**La**	**Hf**	**Ta**	**W**	**Re**	**Os**	**Ir**
Caesium	Barium	Lanthanum	Hafnium	Tantalum	Tungsten	Rhenium	Osmium	Iridium

87 223	88 226.03	89 227.03	104 261	105 263	106 266	107 264	108 267	109 268
Fr	**Ra**	**Ac**	**Rh**	**Db**	**Sg**	**Bh**	**Hs**	**Mt**
Francium	Radium	Actinium	Rutherfordium	Dubnium	Seborgium	Bohrium	Hassium	Meitnerium

GROUP I | GROUP II

Lanthanides

58 140.12	59 140.91	60 144.24	61 145	62 150.36	63 151.96	64 157.25
Ce	**Pr**	**Nd**	**Pm**	**Sm**	**Eu**	**Gd**
Cerium	Praseodymium	Neodymium	Promethium	Samarium	Europium	Gadolinium

Actinides

90 232.04	91 231.04	92 238.03	93 237.05	94 244	95 243	96 247
Th	**Pa**	**U**	**Np**	**Pu**	**Am**	**Cm**
Thorium	Protactinium	Uranium	Neptunium	Plutonium	Americium	Curium

BOILING/MELTING POINTS

SOLID   LIQUID   GAS

- Chlorine
- Lead
- Gold
- Sodium
- Oxygen
- Sulphur
- Tungsten

°K   0   1,000   2,000   3,000   4,000   5,000   6,000

Copper

People have used copper to make weapons and tools for 8,000 years. It can be used on its own or mixed with other metals, such as tin or zinc, to form alloys.

Iodine

Iodine is a black solid that turns to gas very easily. Discovered in 1811, it used to be extracted from certain types of seaweed. Iodine compounds, called iodides, are used to make dyes.

NAMING ELEMENTS

The names of many elements are derived from Greek words. They give clues about the elements' properties.

ELEMENT/SYMBOL	GREEK WORD	MEANING
Argon (Ar)	*Argos*	Inactive
Astatine (At)	*Astatos*	Unstable
Barium (Ba)	*Barys*	Heavy
Bromine (Br)	*Brómos*	Stench
Chlorine (Cl)	*Chloros*	Pale green
Dysprosium (Dy)	*Dusprositos*	Hard to get
Hydrogen (H)	*Hydro genes*	Water forming
Mercury (Hg)	*Hydrargyrum*	Liquid silver
Phosphorus (P)	*Phosphoros*	Bringer of light
Technetium (Tc)	*Tekhnétos*	Artificial

Noble gases

The noble gases are helium, neon, argon, krypton, xenon, and radon. They form group 18 (O) of the periodic table and make up one per cent of the air. All noble gases have a full outer shell of electrons, which makes them extremely stable and unreactive.

Helium is the second lightest gas. It cannot catch fire, making it safe to use in balloons and airships.

Helium-filled balloons

ANCIENT ELEMENTS

ELEMENTS	KNOWN SINCE
Carbon	Prehistoric times
Sulphur	Prehistoric times
Gold	Prehistoric times
Lead	Prehistoric times
Copper	c.8000 BC
Silver	c.4000 BC
Iron	c.4000 BC
Tin	c.3500 BC
Mercury	c.1600 BC
Antimony	c.1000 BC

Halogens

The halogens are the gases and solid non-metals of group 17 (VII). They are all poisonous and have a strong smell.

Chlorine, a reactive green gas, is poisonous in large quantities.

Chlorine

Transition metals

The transition metals form the central block of the periodic table. They are less reactive than the alkali and alkaline-earth metals and have higher melting and boiling points.

Zinc is often used as a protective coating that prevents iron or steel from rusting.

The Earth's crust

The bulk of the Earth's crust is oxygen and silicon, mostly combined in rocks or sand (silicon oxide). Clays are made of silicon and oxygen combined with aluminium, the third most common element.

Elements in the Earth's crust

- 9.5% other elements
- 3.5% calcium
- 28% silicon
- 5% iron
- 8% aluminium
- 46% oxygen

Periodic table (main block):

18
2 4 **He** Helium

13	14	15	16	17	
5 10.81 **B** Boron	6 12.01 **C** Carbon	7 14.01 **N** Nitrogen	8 16 **O** Oxygen	9 19 **F** Fluorine	10 20.18 **Ne** Neon
13 26.98 **Al** Aluminium	14 28.09 **Si** Silicon	15 30.97 **P** Phosphorus	16 32.06 **S** Sulphur	17 35.45 **Cl** Chlorine	18 39.95 **Ar** Argon

10	11	12						
28 58.69 **Ni** Nickel	29 63.55 **Cu** Copper	30 65.39 **Zn** Zinc	31 69.72 **Ga** Gallium	32 72.59 **Ge** Germanium	33 74.92 **As** Arsenic	34 78.96 **Se** Selenium	35 79.9 **Br** Bromine	36 83.8 **Kr** Krypton
46 106.42 **Pd** Palladium	47 107.87 **Ag** Silver	48 112.41 **Cd** Cadmium	49 114.82 **In** Indium	50 118.71 **Sn** Tin	51 121.75 **Sb** Antimony	52 127.6 **Te** Tellurium	53 126.91 **I** Iodine	54 131.29 **Xe** Xenon
78 195.08 **Pt** Platinum	79 196.97 **Au** Gold	80 200.59 **Hg** Mercury	81 204.38 **Tl** Thallium	82 207.2 **Pb** Lead	83 208.98 **Bi** Bismuth	84 209 **Po** Polonium	85 210 **At** Astatine	86 222 **Rn** Radon
			GROUP III	GROUP IV	GROUP V	GROUP VI	GROUP VII	GROUP O

Inner transition metals

The inner transition series are the lanthanides and actinides. Uranium is a radioactive metal from the actinide series. Nuclear reactors use the isotope uranium–235 as a fuel.

Uranium fuel rod from a nuclear reactor

Inner transition metals (lanthanides and actinides):

65 158.93 **Tb** Terbium	66 162.5 **Dy** Dysprosium	67 164.93 **Ho** Holmium	68 167.26 **Er** Erbium	69 168.93 **Tm** Thulium	70 173.04 **Yb** Ytterbium	71 174.97 **Lu** Lutetium
97 247 **Bk** Berkelium	98 251 **Cf** Californium	99 252 **Es** Einsteinium	100 257 **Fm** Fermium	101 258 **Md** Mendelevium	102 259 **No** Nobelium	103 256 **Lr** Lawrencium

ELEMENTS PRODUCED ARTIFICIALLY

ELEMENT	YEAR PRODUCED	MAKER
Technetium	1937	C. Perrier & E. Segrè (Italy/USA)
Astatine	1940	D.R. Corson & others (USA)
Neptunium	1940	E.M. McMillan & P. Abelson (USA)
Plutonium	1940	G. Seaborg & others (USA)
Curium	1944	G. Seaborg & others (USA)
Americium	1945	G. Seaborg & others (USA)
Promethium	1945	J.A. Marinsky & others (USA)
Berkelium	1949	S.G. Thompson & others (USA)
Californium	1950	S.G. Thompson & others (USA)
Einsteinium	1952	A. Ghiorso & others (USA)
Fermium	1953	A. Ghiorso & others (USA)
Mendelevium	1958	A. Ghiorso & others (USA/USSR)
Nobelium	1958	A. Ghiorso & others (USA/USSR)
Lawrencium	1961	A. Ghiorso & others (USA/USSR)
Rutherfordium	1964	G. Flerov (USSR)
Dubnium	1968	A. Ghiorso (USA)
Seborgium	1974	A. Ghiorso (USA); G. Flerov (USSR)
Bohrium	1976	G. Munzenburg (Germany)
Meitnerium	1982	P. Armbruster (Germany)
Hassium	1984	P. Armbruster (Germany)

ELEMENT FACTS

- Astatine is the rarest element on Earth. The rarest metal is rhodium.

- At room temperature, osmium is the densest element, and lithium the least dense solid element.

- Hydrogen and helium are the most abundant elements in the universe.

- The tissues of the human body are made up of hydrogen, carbon, oxygen, and nitrogen, and bones contain calcium. Together, these five elements account for 98 per cent of the body's mass.

MATHEMATICS

MATHEMATICS IS THE study of number, shape, and quantity. Arithmetic is the basis of mathematics; it consists of addition, subtraction, division, and multiplication. Geometry is the study of lines, shapes, and angles.

PRIME NUMBERS

A prime number can be divided only by itself and one. For example, 13 is a prime number. Nine is not a prime number; it can be divided by three, as well as by nine and one.

2	3	5	7
11	13	17	19
23	29	31	37
41	43	47	53
59	61	67	71
73	79	83	89
97	101	103	107
109	113	127	131

MATHEMATICAL SYMBOLS

SYMBOL	MEANING
+	Add (plus)
−	Subtract (minus)
x	Multiply (times)
÷	Divided by
=	Equal to
≠	Not equal to
>	Greater than
<	Less than
≥	Greater than or equal to
≤	Less than or equal to
∞	Infinity
%	Per cent
√	Square root of

Anatomy of a circle

A circle is a closed curve on which all points are equidistant from the centre. The diameter passes from one side to the other through the centre point. The ratio of the diameter to the circumference is expressed by pi π (approx. 3.141592).

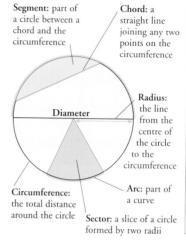

Segment: part of a circle between a chord and the circumference

Chord: a straight line joining any two points on the circumference

Radius: the line from the centre of the circle to the circumference

Diameter

Arc: part of a curve

Circumference: the total distance around the circle

Sector: a slice of a circle formed by two radii

BINARY SYSTEM

The decimal number system is based on ten. From right to left, it increases in multiples of ten. The binary system is based on two. From right to left, it increases in multiples of two. Each digit is twice the value of the digit on its right.

BINARY					DECIMAL	
8	4	2	1		10	1
1	0	1	0		1	0
1	0	0	1			9
1	0	0	0			8
	1	1	1			7
	1	1	0			6
	1	0	1			5
	1	0	0			4
		1	1			3
		1	0			2
			1			1
			0			0

PLANE AND SOLID SHAPES

Triangles

Triangles are three-sided plane figures with interior angles that combine to form 180°. The area of any triangle is: $\frac{1}{2}$ x base x height.

Right-angled triangle: a triangle with one angle of 90°

Obtuse-angled triangle: a triangle with one obtuse (larger than 90°) interior angle

Isosceles triangle: a triangle with two equal sides

Equilateral triangle: a triangle with three equal sides

Plane figures

These are two-dimensional (flat) shapes.

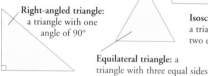

Rhombus: a quadrilateral with sides of equal length

Trapezium: a quadrilateral with only two sides parallel

Rectangle: a quadrilateral with opposite sides of equal length

Parallelogram: a quadrilateral with opposite sides that are parallel and of equal length

Solids

Solids are three-dimensional shapes. Polyhedrons are solids that have plane (flat) faces.

Cube: a polyhedron with six sides of equal length, shape, and area

Cone: a polyhedron with a circular base, narrowing to a point, or apex

Hemisphere: half a sphere

Cylinder: a polygon with two circular faces connected by a tube

Tetrahedron: a polyhedron with four triangles as face

Spheroid: an egg-shaped figure

Rectangular block: a polyhedron with four sides of equal shape and length

Octahedron: a tetrahedron with eight flat sides

Triangular prism: a solid figure with two triangular ends

Square pyramid: a tetrahedron with a square base and four triangular sides

Sphere: a globe-shaped figure with every point equidistant from the centre

Polygons

A polygon is a plane figure with three or more straight sides.

Octagon: a polygon with eight sides

Hexagon: a polygon with six sides

Quadrilateral: a four-sided polygon

Square: a polygon with four equal sides, meeting at right angles

Pentagon: a polygon with five sides

Angles and sides

NAME	NO. OF SIDES	INTERNAL ANGLES	NAME	NO. OF SIDES	INTERNAL ANGLES
Triangle	3	60°	Octagon	8	135°
Quadrilateral	4	90°	Nonagon	9	140°
Pentagon	5	108°	Decagon	10	144°
Hexagon	6	120°	Undecagon	11	147.3°
Heptagon	7	128.6°	Dodecagon	12	150°

WEIGHTS AND MEASURES

THERE ARE TWO major systems of measurement: metric and imperial. Although some countries, such as the United States, still use the older imperial system, scientists and most countries worldwide use metric.

THE SEVEN BASE SI UNITS

The main international system of standard units is called SI units. The seven "base units" are listed below. All other SI units are derived from them.

QUANTITY	UNIT	SYMBOL
Mass	Kilogram	kg
Length	Metre	m
Time	Second	s
Electric current	Ampere	A
Temperature	Kelvin	K
Luminous intensity	Candela	cd
Amount of substance	Mole	mol

NUMBER TERMS

PREFIX (SYMBOL)	EXAMPLE	MEANING
tera (T)	terametre	One million million
giga (G)	gigabyte	One thousand million
mega (M)	megawatt	One million
kilo (k)	kilogram	One thousand
hecto (h)	hectometre	One hundred
deci (d)	decimetre	One-tenth
centi (c)	centimetre	One-hundredth
milli (m)	millimetre	One-thousandth
micro (μ)	microsecond	One-millionth
nano (n)	nanosecond	One-thousand millionth

UNITS OF MEASUREMENT

Length

METRIC
1 millimetre (mm)	
1 centimetre (cm)	= 10 mm
1 metre (m)	= 100 cm
1 kilometre (km)	= 1,000 m

IMPERIAL
1 inch (in)	
1 foot (ft)	= 12 in
1 yard (yd)	= 3 ft
1 mile	= 1,760 yd

Spring balance

Area

METRIC
1 square millimetre (mm^2)	
1 sq centimetre (cm^2)	= 100 mm^2
1 sq metre (m^2)	= 10,000 cm^2
1 hectare (ha)	= 10,000 m^2
1 sq kilometre (km^2)	= 1,000,000 m^2

IMPERIAL
1 sq inch (in^2)	
1 sq foot (ft^2)	= 144 in^2
1 sq yard (yd^2)	= 9 ft^2
1 acre	= 4,840 yd^2
1 sq mile	= 640 acres

Mass and weight

METRIC
1 gram (g)	
1 kilogram (kg)	= 1,000 g
1 tonne (t)	= 1,000 kg

IMPERIAL
1 ounce (oz)	
1 pound (lb)	= 16 oz
1 stone	= 14 lb
1 hundredweight (cwt)	= 8 stones
1 ton	= 20 cwt

Ashanti gold weight

Volume

METRIC
1 cubic millimetre (mm^3)	
1 cubic centimetre (cm^3)	= 1,000 mm^3
1 cubic metre (m^2)	= 1,000,000 cm^3
1 litre	= 1,000 cm^3

IMPERIAL
1 cubic inch (in^3)	
1 cubic foot (ft^3)	= 1,728 in^3
1 cubic yard (yd^3)	= 27 ft^3
1 fluid ounce (fl oz)	
1 UK pint (pt)	= 20 fl oz
1 UK gallon (gal)	= 8 pt

Roman weight

CONVERSION TABLES

Length conversion

TO CONVERT IMPERIAL:	INTO METRIC:	MULTIPLY BY:
Inches	Centimetres	2.54
Feet	Metres	0.3048
Yards	Metres	0.9144
Miles	Kilometres	1.6093

TO CONVERT METRIC:	INTO IMPERIAL:	MULTIPLY BY:
Centimetres	Inches	0.3937
Metres	Feet	3.2808
Metres	Yards	1.0936
Kilometres	Miles	0.6214
Metres	Furlongs	0.005
Metres	Fathoms	0.547
Kilometres	Nautical miles	0.54

Mass and weight conversion

TO CONVERT IMPERIAL:	INTO METRIC:	MULTIPLY BY:
Ounces	Grams	28.3495
Pounds	Kilograms	0.4536
Stones	Kilograms	6.3503
Hundredweights	Kilograms	50.802
Tons	Tonnes	1.0161

TO CONVERT METRIC:	INTO IMPERIAL:	MULTIPLY BY:
Grams	Ounces	0.0352
Kilograms	Pounds	2.2046
Kilograms	Stones	0.1575
Kilograms	Hundredweights	0.0197
Tonnes	Tons	0.9842

Yard stick

Area conversion

TO CONVERT IMPERIAL:	INTO METRIC:	MULTIPLY BY:
Sq inches	Sq centimetres	6.4516
Sq feet	Sq metres	0.0929
Sq yards	Sq metres	0.8361
Acres	Hectares	0.4047
Sq miles	Sq kilometres	2.59

TO CONVERT METRIC:	INTO IMPERIAL:	MULTIPLY BY:
Sq centimetres	Sq inches	0.155
Sq metres	Sq feet	10.7639
Sq metres	Sq yards	1.196
Hectares	Acres	2.4711
Sq kilometres	Sq miles	0.3861

Assyrian weight

Volume conversion

TO CONVERT IMPERIAL:	INTO METRIC:	MULTIPLY BY:
Cubic inches	Cubic cm (ml)	16.3871
Cubic feet	Litres	28.3169
Cubic yards	Cubic metres	0.7646
Fluid ounces	Cubic cm (ml)	28.413
UK pints	Litres	0.5683
UK gallons	Litres	0.4546

TO CONVERT METRIC:	INTO IMPERIAL:	MULTIPLY BY:
Cubic centimetres (millilitres)	Cubic inches	0.061
	Fluid ounces	0.0352
Litres	Cubic feet	0.0353
Cubic metres	Cubic yards	1.308
Litres	UK pints	1.7598
Litres	UK gallons	0.22

Temperature conversions

- To convert °C to °F, multiply by 9, divide by 5, and add 32.
- To convert °F to °C, subtract 32, divide by 9, and multiply by 5.
- To convert °C to kelvin (K), add 273.15.
- To convert kelvin (K) to °C, subtract 273.15.

Celsius	Fahrenheit	Kelvin
100	212	373
90	194	363
80	176	353
70	158	343
60	140	333
50	122	323
40	104	313
30	86	303
20	68	293
10	50	283
0	32	273
-10	14	263
-20	-4	253

POLITICAL WORLD

THE WORLD IS DIVIDED into 193 independent countries. The line that separates one country from another is called a border. Disputed borders are marked on the map by a dotted line.

COUNTRY FACTS

● The world's largest country is the Russian Federation, with an area of 17,075,400 sq km (6,592,810 sq miles).

● The world's smallest country is the Vatican City, with an area of 0.44 sq km (0.17 sq miles).

KEY
1 NETHERLANDS
2 BELGIUM
3 LUXEMBOURG
4 SWITZERLAND
5 LIECHTENSTEIN
6 MOLDOVA
7 ANDORRA
8 MONACO
9 SAN MARINO
10 VATICAN CITY
11 SLOVENIA
12 CROATIA
13 BOSNIA & HERZEGOVINA
14 SERBIA & MONTENEGRO
15 ALBANIA
16 MACEDONIA
17 Ceuta (Spain)
18 Melilla (Spain)

— Country Border
······ Disputed Country Border

Time Zones	23hours	24h	1h	2h	3h	4h	5h	6h	7h	8h	9h

International time zones

The world is divided into 24 time zones, one for each hour of the day. Clocks in each zone are set to a different time. For instance, when it is noon in Greenwich, England, it is 10 p.m. in Sydney, Australia.

GMT
Greenwich Mean Time (GMT) refers to the exact time in Greenwich, England. In each time zone, clocks are set depending on whether they are east or west of Greenwich. The numbers on the map indicate the number of hours that must be added or subtracted to reach GMT.

International Date Line
Lines of longitude and latitude are imaginary lines drawn on the Earth's surface. Meridians (lines of longitude) run from pole to pole. The International Date Line runs along the 180° meridian. When you cross this line from east to west, the date changes. The western side is a day ahead of the eastern side.

KEY
19 *Cayman Is.* (UK)
20 *Navassa Island* (USA)
21 *Virgin Is.* (USA)
22 ST. KITTS & NEVIS
23 *Montserrat* (UK)
24 *Martinique* (France)
25 ST. VINCENT & THE GRENADINES
26 *Netherlands Antilles* (Netherlands)
27 *Aruba* (Netherlands)

11h 12h 13h 14h 15h 16h 17h 18h 19h 20h 21h 22h

WORLD POPULATION

IN 1500, THE WORLD'S POPULATION was about 435 million. Today, it has grown to more than 6 billion, with a million children being born every day. The rapid growth in population since 1800 is largely due to improvements in food production and medical knowledge. In many parts of the world, rapid population growth causes serious problems, such as food shortages and overcrowding in cities.

URBAN POPULATION

In 1900, only 10 per cent of the world's population lived in cities. Today, that figure is about 50 per cent. This table lists the world's most populated urban areas (by administrative division).

URBAN AREA	POPULATION
Toyko	31,036,000
Mexico City	20,965,000
Seoul	19,844,000
New York	19,047,000
São Paulo	18,505,000
Jakarta	17,369,000
Dehli	16,713,000
Mumbai	16,687,000

Tokyo, Japan

World population
The map below shows population figures for the world's main land areas. Between them, China and India account for more than one third of the world's population.

Europe:
704,900,000
11.6 per cent of world population

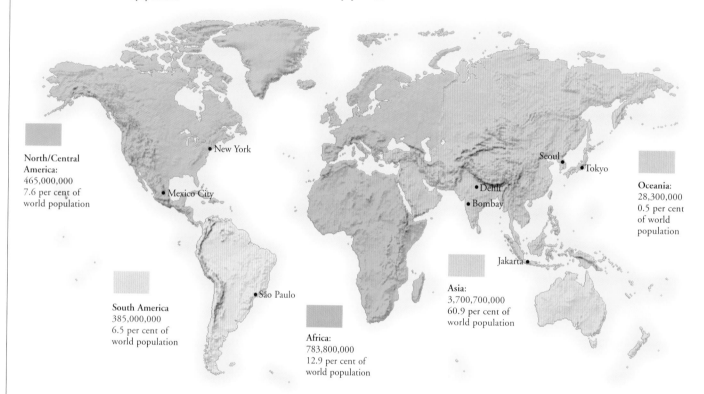

North/Central America:
465,000,000
7.6 per cent of world population

Oceania:
28,300,000
0.5 per cent of world population

South America
385,000,000
6.5 per cent of world population

Africa:
783,800,000
12.9 per cent of world population

Asia:
3,700,700,000
60.9 per cent of world population

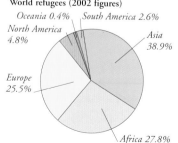

Hutu refugees in Rwanda in 1996

REFUGEES

Throughout history, many millions of people have become refugees. Wars, drought, famine, and poverty are some of the reasons why people leave their homes and families. Today, almost 40 per cent of the world's refugees come from Asia.

World refugees (2002 figures)

Oceania 0.4%   South America 2.6%
North America 4.8%
Asia 38.9%
Europe 25.5%
Africa 27.8%

HIGHEST POPULATION

COUNTRY	POPULATION
China	1,290,000,000
India	1,030,000,000
USA	281,400,000
Indonesia	214,000,000
Brazil	172,600,000

LOWEST POPULATION

COUNTRY	POPULATION
Vatican	542
Tuvalu	11,300
Nauru	12,500
Palau	19,700
San Marino	26,900

FERTILITY RATES

Africa: 5.2
Asia: 2.7
S America: 2.6
Oceania: 2.4
N America: 2
Europe: 1.4

Figures shown are the average number of children per woman.

Fertility rates measure the average number of children born to each woman. Fertility rates are declining rapidly in the industrialized world, and are highest in Africa.

LIVING STANDARDS

IN THE PAST 100 YEARS, living standards have improved greatly across the world. Better health care, even in poorer countries, means that fewer people now die of hunger and disease. Advances in medicine and improved diet and education have helped people to live longer and healthier lives. However, many problems remain, especially in the poorer countries of Africa and Asia.

Slovakian children

ADULT LITERACY

Adult literacy rates show how many adults over the age of 15 can read and write. The table below lists the average literacy rates for a variety of countries.

COUNTRY	PER CENT OF POPULATION
USA	99
UK	99
Brazil	85
China	84
Kuwait	83
India	57
Angola	40
Somalia	24
Niger	16

Shanty school in São Paulo, Brazil

LIFE EXPECTANCY

Life expectancy is the average length of time a person is likely to live. Wealthier countries generally have higher life expectancies than poorer countries. The world average life expectancy is 64.

Highest life expectancy (male)

COUNTRY	AGE
Japan	77.5
Singapore	77.1
Sweden	77
Australia	76.9
Switzerland	76.7

Highest life expectancy (female)

COUNTRY	AGE
Japan	84.1
Singapore	83.2
Canada	83
France	82.9
Australia	82.7

Japanese family

Lowest life expectancy (male)

COUNTRY	AGE
Zambia	37.1
Angola	37.1
Malawi	37.2
Botswana	38.6
Rwanda	38.6

Lowest life expectancy (female)

COUNTRY	AGE
Zimbabwe	36.3
Mozambique	36.7
Zambia	37.4
Malawi	38
Angola	39.6

PEOPLE PER DOCTOR

The table below compares the average number of people per doctor in some developed and developing countries.

COUNTRY	PEOPLE PER DOCTOR
Burkina	20,000
Ghana	16,700
Mali	10,000
Zimbabwe	10,000
Bangladesh	5,000
Thailand	2,500
Guatemala	1,111
USA	370
Austria	333
Georgia	263
Russian Federation	217

Rural hospital, Burkina

SAFE WATER

Almost 2 billion people worldwide do not have access to the minimum level of safe water (20 litres/6 gallons per person per day). The table shows the average number of people with access to safe water in some developed and developing countries.

COUNTRY	PER CENT OF POPULATION
Tunisia	98
Saudi Arabia	93
Iran	90
Mexico	83
Zimbabwe	79
Pakistan	74
Kenya	53
Vietnam	43
Mali	37
Uganda	34
Ethiopia	26

Village well, Vietnam

MAJOR CAUSES OF DEATH

DEATH FACTS

• Worldwide, tuberculosis is the largest single cause of death. Two billion people are infected, just under a third of the total global population.

• Heart disease is the leading cause of death in Europe and North America, followed by depression-related illnesses.

• The UN estimates that more than 36 million people worldwide have HIV, with around 70 per cent of infections concentrated in sub-Saharan Africa.

Nurse administering a vaccine

FOOD SUPPLY

The "Dietary Energy Supply" (DES) is the amount of calories available per person per day. The mimimum amount of calories needed per day is 2,300. This table compares the DES of various countries.

COUNTRY	CALORIES PER DAY
Denmark	3,780
Ireland	3,620
Japan	2,900
Uruguay	2,800
Chad	1,920
Somalia	1,580

WORLD RESOURCES

RAW MATERIALS ARE natural substances that are extracted from water, air, or from the ground. Some energy sources, such as solar or wind power, are renewable. Others, such as oil or coal, are non-renewable and will eventually run out. As world population grows, people are drawing more heavily on the Earth's natural resources.

FOSSIL FUELS

Electricity

This table shows annual production in kilowatt hours.

COUNTRY	KW/HR
USA	3,600,000,000,000
China	1,200,000,000,000
Japan	1,000,000,000,000
Russia	798,000,000,000
Canada	567,000,000,000

Light bulb

Coal

This table shows coal production in tonnes per annum.

COUNTRY	TONNES
USA	570,000,000
China	498,000,000
Australia	155,600,000
India	154,300,000
South Africa	118,800,000

Coal

Oil

This table shows oil production in tonnes per annum.

COUNTRY	TONNES
Saudi Arabia	441,200,000
USA	353,500,000
Russian Federation	323,300,000
Iran	186,600,000
Mexico	172,100,000

Oil plant, Libya

Energy consumption

This table lists the major consumers of coal, oil, electricity, and gas.

COUNTRY	% OF WORLD TOTAL
USA	25%
China	10%
Russia	7%
Japan	5.8%
Germany	3.9%
India	3.1%
UK	2.6%

LEADING AGRICULTURAL PRODUCERS

Today, farming is a major international business, with many countries competing in the export market. This table shows the top producers of a wide range of agricultural products.

PRODUCT	TOP PRODUCERS	PRODUCT	TOP PRODUCERS
Cattle	Australia	Rubber	Thailand
Cocoa	Ivory Coast	Sheep	Australia
Coffee	Brazil	Soya beans	USA
Cotton	China	Tea	India
Corn	USA	Tobacco	China
Cows' milk	India	Wheat	China
Hens' eggs	China	Wood	USA
Potatoes	Russian Federation	Wool	Australia

Tea

Coffee

Cotton

CROP PRODUCERS

Wheat

COUNTRY	TONNES PER ANNUM
China	94,181,100
India	68,458,000
USA	53,276,084
Russian Federation	46,871,000
France	32,065,000
Germany	22,888,608

Emmer

Rice

COUNTRY	TONNES PER ANNUM
China	181,514,992
India	131,900,000
Indonesia	49,400,000
Bangladesh	34,276,000
Vietnam	31,925,000
Thailand	25,200,000

Basmati rice

Maize (Corn)

COUNTRY	TONNES PER ANNUM
USA	239,521,424
China	110,390,000
Brazil	41,411,240
Mexico	18,615,904
France	16,478,000
Argentina	15,350,000

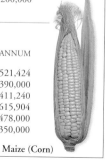
Maize (Corn)

MINERAL PRODUCERS

This table shows the world's major mineral producers.

MINERAL	TOP PRODUCERS	% OF WORLD TOTAL
Bauxite	Australia	30%
Copper	Chile	40%
Iron ore	China	20%
Salt	USA	22%
Uranium	USA	22%

WORLD CONSUMPTION

This table lists the nations with the highest rates of consumption per capita for a variety of commodities.

CEREALS	ROUNDWOOD
Morocco	Finland
Egypt	Guatemala
Algeria	Sweden
Syria	Canada
Turkey	Gabon
Burma	New Zealand

MEAT	PASSENGER CARS
USA	Italy
Cyprus	Germany
New Zealand	Australia
Australia	USA
Spain	Austria
Austria	Switzerland

FISH CATCHES

This table shows the biggest global fish catches per annum in tonnes.

COUNTRY	TONNES
China	39,300,000
Peru	8,437,000
Japan	5,935,000
Chile	5,325,000
India	5,244,000
USA	5,154,000
Indonesia	4,797,000
World total catch	124,448,000

Fishing in the USA

WORLD ECONOMY

THE WEALTH OF A COUNTRY depends on its industrial strength, natural resources, population size, and political stability. Trade creates wealth and jobs by encouraging countries to produce goods that can be sold abroad. However, many poor countries have to borrow money from richer countries to finance their industries.

NATIONAL WEALTH

A country's wealth is measured in two ways. The Gross Domestic Product (GDP) measures the total value of goods and services produced by a national economy. The Gross National Product (GNP) measures GDP and a country's income from abroad. National wealth is measured by dividing either the GDP or the GNP by the country's population.

Richest countries

The countries below have the highest GDP per head.

COUNTRY	AMOUNT IN US$
Luxembourg	33,609
USA	33,586
Monaco	27,451
Switzerland	27,126
Cayman Islands	26,753
Norway	24,837
Jersey	24,743
Denmark	23,930
Belgium	23,766

Zürich, Switzerland

FOREIGN DEBT

Some organizations, such as the World Bank and the International Monetary Fund (IMF), lend developing countries money to finance industry and welfare programmes. The interest charged on these loans is often very high. The countries listed below have the highest foreign debt.

COUNTRY	DEBT (IN MILLIONS OF US$)
USA	862,000
Brazil	232,000
Australia	220,600
Russia	163,000
China	162,000
Mexico	162,000
Argentina	154,000
Indonesia	144,000

International Monetary Fund

World Bank

FOREIGN AID

Some countries depend on foreign aid (in the form of grants or loans) for most of their income. Many countries offer food, tents, medical supplies, and clothing following natural disasters or civil war.

Main aid donors

COUNTRY	AID GIVEN (IN MILLIONS OF US$)
Japan	9,100
USA	6,900
France	6,300
Germany	5,600
Netherlands	3,500
UK	3,400

Main recipients of aid

COUNTRY	AID RECEIVED (IN MILLIONS OF US$)
Indonesia	43,000
Argentina	13,700
Russia	8,523
Greece	5,400
Lebanon	3,500
India	2,900

UN forces supplying food and medical equipment, Sarajevo, Bosnia and Herzegovina, 1996.

Poorest countries

The countries below have the lowest GDP per head.

COUNTRY	AMOUNT IN US$
Sierra Leone	478
Ethiopia	519
Somalia	593
Tanzania	660
Cambodia	671
Dem. Rep. Congo	687
Burundi	694
Eritrea	701
Comoros	709

INTERNATIONAL TRADE

World trade

Five countries dominate world trade. These countries, known as the Big Five, account for almost half of all international trade.

COUNTRY	EXPORTS (MILLIONS OF US$)
USA	776,000
Germany	578,000
Japan	450,000
France	325,000
UK	282,000

World's largest stock markets

The activity of a stock market reflects a country's economic performance. The table below lists the world's most important financial centres.

New York, USA (Wall Street)
Tokyo, Japan
London, UK
Hong Kong, China
Frankfurt, Germany
Zürich, Switzerland
Kuala Lumpur, Malaysia
Paris, France
Toronto, Canada

Export goods

The table below shows the kinds of goods that are traded worldwide. Manufactured goods, such as cars and computers, still dominate the export market, although service industries, such as tourism and banking, are growing rapidly.

GOODS	WORLD TRADE (BILLIONS OF US$)
Automobiles	220
Engines and vehicle parts	160
Data-processing equipment	70
Telecommunications	52
Transistors	49

Car manufacturing plant, Germany

Hong Kong stock market

Addis Ababa, Ethiopia

TRANSPORT AND ENGINEERING

PEOPLE HAVE ALWAYS moved around, and over the centuries have searched for new and more efficient methods of transport. In the past 100 years, advances in technology have led to a huge increase in global travel and trade. Today, vast road and rail networks link countries worldwide. Shipping transports most international goods, and each day airlines carry millions of passengers to every part of the globe.

BUSIEST INTERNATIONAL AIRPORTS

AIRPORT	INTERNATIONAL PASSENGERS PER YEAR
Atlanta, USA	77,939,536
Chicago, USA	72,568,076
Los Angeles, USA	63,876,561
London Heathrow, UK	62,263,710
Dallas, USA	60,000,125
Tokyo, Japan	54,338,212
Frankfurt, Germany	45,858,315
Paris, France	43,596,943
San Francisco, USA	40,387,422
Schipol, Netherlands	39,606,925

Heathrow Airport, UK

MAJOR PORTS

Container ports with volume of goods shown in Twenty Equivalent Units (TEU).

PORT	GOODS (IN MILLION TEU)
Hong Kong, China	16.21
Singapore	15.95
Kaohsiung, Taiwan	6.98
Pusan, Korea	6.44
Rotterdam, Netherlands	6.34

LONGEST SUSPENSION BRIDGES

BRIDGE	COUNTRY	DATE BUILT	LENGTH IN METRES (FEET)
Akashi Kaikyo	Japan	1998	1,990 (6,066)
Great Belt Link	Denmark	1996	1,624 (5,328)
Humber	UK	1980	1,410 (4,626)
Verrazano Narrows	USA	1964	1,298 (4,258)
Golden Gate	USA	1937	1,280 (4,199)
Mackinac Straits	USA	1957	1,158 (3,800)

Golden Gate, San Francisco, USA

ROAD

Countries with most roads

COUNTRY	KM (MILES) OF ROAD
USA	6,370,031 (3,949,419)
India	3,319,644 (2,058,179)
Brazil	1,980,000 (1,227,600)
China	1,400,000 (868,000)
Japan	1,152,217 (714,375)

Top car-owning countries

COUNTRY	NO. OF CARS (PER 1000 PEOPLE)
USA	680
Italy	550
Germany	495
Canada	480
Australia	475

Long Island Expressway, New York, USA

RAIL

Longest rail tunnels

TUNNEL	COUNTRY	DATE OPENED	LENGTH IN KM (MILES)
Seikan	Japan	1988	53.9 (33.5)
Channel Tunnel	France/UK	1994	49.9 (31)
Moscow Metro (Medvedkovo/ Belyaevo section)	Russia	1979	30.7 (19.1)
London Underground (Northern Line)	UK	1939	27.8 (17.3)

Bullet Train, Mt. Fuji, Japan

TRANSPORT AND ENGINEERING RECORDS

LONGEST ROAD: Pan American Highway. It runs from the USA to Brazil and is 24,140 km (15,000 miles) long.

TALLEST DAM: Rogunskaya, Tajikistan. Built in 1989, it is 325 m (1,066 ft) long.

LARGEST RAILWAY STATION: Grand Central Terminal, New York, USA. It has 67 tracks and covers 19 hectares (48 acres).

MOST MOTORWAYS: USA. There are 88,727 km (55,132 miles) of motorway in the USA.

Grand Central Terminal, New York, USA

Longest underground networks

CITY	STATIONS	KM (MILES)
Washington, DC	86	612 (380)
London	275	430 (267)
New York	461	370 (230)
Paris	430	301 (187)
Moscow	115	225 (140)
Tokyo	192	218 (135)

Countries with most rail track

COUNTRY	TOTAL KM (MILES) OF TRACK
USA	270,312 (167,970)
Russia	152,000 (94,455)
Canada	71,000 (44,120)
China	69,400 (43,125)
India	61,850 (38,435)

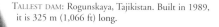

MYTHOLOGY

THE MYTHS OF all cultures throughout history have featured a wide range of gods and goddesses. These mythical creatures were supposed to have special qualities.

NORSE MYTHOLOGY

The Norse people worshipped a large number of gods and goddesses until the 12th century, when Scandinavia became predominantly Christian.

Odin and Thor

Yggdrasil, the Norse family tree

x = union

Frey, god of fertility

EGYPTIAN MYTHOLOGY

Egyptian gods and goddesses often had a human body and the head of an animal or bird.

Eye of Horus

NAME	FORM
Amun-re	Ram-headed god of Thebes
Anubis	Jackal-headed god of the dead
Bastet	Cat goddess of love and fertility
Geb	Earth god; husband of sky goddess Nur
Hathor	Cow-headed goddess of the sky
Horus	Falcon-headed god of light; son of Osiris and Isis
Isis	Goddess of motherhood and fertility
Khnum	Ram-headed creator god
Maat	Goddess of truth, justice, and order
Min	God of fertility and harvest
Mut	Vulture goddess of war
Nephthys	Sister of Isis
Osiris	Supreme god; ruler of the afterlife; husband of Isis
Ptah	God of creation, death, and the afterlife
Ra	Sun god; ancestor of the pharaohs
Seth	God of evil; jealous brother of Osiris
Sobek	Crocodile god; ruler of water
Thoth	Ibis-headed god of wisdom and writing

Bastet   Min   Anubis

JAPANESE MYTHOLOGY

Shinto is the native religion of Japan. It is based on the worship of supernatural spirits or gods, called kami.

NAME	ROLE
Amaterasu	Goddess of the sun
Benten	Goddess of beauty and wealth
Daikoku	God of fortune
Ebisu	God of labour and fishermen
Hachiman	God of war
Inari	God of crops and wealth
Izanagi	Creator god
Izanami	Goddess of the underworld
Kagutsuchi	God of fire
Kamui	God of creation
Ogetsu	Goddess of food
Susanowo	God of tempests
Tsuki-yomi	Goddess of the moon
Uzume	Goddess of the dawn and mirth
Watatsumi	God of the sea`

Daikoku

GREEK AND ROMAN MYTHOLOGY

The ancient Greeks believed that their lives were governed by a great number of gods and goddesses, the most important of whom lived on Mount Olympus. The Romans adopted many Greek gods as their own, but gave them new names.

GREEK	ROMAN	ROLE
Aphrodite	Venus	Goddess of beauty and love
Apollo	Apollo	Sun god; god of prophecy
Ares	Mars	God of war
Artemis	Diana	Goddess of hunting; protector of animals and children
Asclepius	Aesculapius	God of medicine
Athena	Minerva	Goddess of wisdom and war
Demeter	Ceres	Goddess of fertility and crops
Dionysus	Bacchus	God of wine
Eos	Aurora	Goddess of the dawn
Eros	Cupid	God of love

GREEK	ROMAN	ROLE
Hebe	Juventas	Goddess of youth
Helios	Sol	God of the sun
Hephaistos	Vulcan	God of fire and metalwork
Hera	Juno	Queen of the gods; protector of women
Hermes	Mercury	God of travellers
Hestia	Vesta	Goddess of the home
Hygiea	Salus	Goddess of health
Hypnos	Somnus	God of sleep
Kronos	Saturn	God of sowing and seed
Pan	Silvanus	God of the woodland
Persephone	Proserpina	Goddess of the underworld
Poseidon	Neptune	God of the sea
Selene	Luna	Goddess of the moon
Thanatos	Mors	Goddess of night and death
Zeus	Jupiter	King of the gods; god of thunder

Mars

Athena

Jupiter

SPORT

SPORTS ARE GAMES and activities that involve physical ability or skill. Although the origins of competitive sport are unknown, the ancient Greeks first held their Olympic Games in 776 BC. Today, organized sport takes place on both national and global levels.

Basketball ring

OLYMPIC BASKETBALL CHAMPIONS

Basketball became an Olympic event (for men) in 1936. Women began to compete in 1976.

TEAM (MEN)	WINS	YEARS
USA	12	1936, 1948, 1952, 1956, 1960,1964, 1968, 1976, 1984, 1992, 1996, 2000
USSR	2	1972, 1988
Yugoslavia	1	1980

TEAM (WOMEN)	WINS	YEARS
USSR	3	1976, 1980, 1992
USA	4	1984, 1988, 1996, 2000

SUMMER OLYMPICS

The five interlocking colour rings of the Olympic flag represent the continents of Asia, Africa, Europe, America, and Australia.

Olympic rings

YEAR	VENUE
1896	Athens, Greece
1900	Paris, France
1904	St Louis, USA
1908	London, UK
1912	Stockholm, Sweden
1920	Antwerp, Belgium
1924	Paris, France
1928	Amsterdam, Holland
1932	Los Angeles, USA
1936	Berlin, Germany
1948	London, UK
1952	Helsinki, Finland
1956	Melbourne, Australia
1960	Rome, Italy
1964	Tokyo, Japan
1968	Mexico City, Mexico
1972	Munich, Germany
1976	Montreal, Canada
1980	Moscow, USSR
1984	Los Angeles, USA
1988	Seoul, South Korea
1992	Barcelona, Spain
1996	Atlanta, USA
2000	Sydney, Australia
2004	Athens, Greece

FIELD EVENTS

EVENT	MEN'S RECORD HOLDER	RECORD	WOMEN'S RECORD HOLDER	RECORD
Javelin	J. Zelezny (Czech)	98.48 m	O. Menendez (Cuba)	71.52 m
Discus	J. Schult (E. Germany)	74.08 m	G. Reinsch (E. Germany)	76.80 m
Shot put	R. Barnes (USA)	23.12 m	N. Lisovskaya (USSR)	22.63 m
Hammer	Y. Sedykh (USSR)	86.74 m	M. Melinte (Romania)	76.07 m
High jump	J. Sotomayor (Cuba)	2.45 m	S. Kostadinova (Bulgaria)	2.09 m
Pole vault	S. Bubka (Ukraine)	6.14 m	S. Dragila (USA)	4.81 m
Long jump	M. Powell (US)	8.95 m	G. Chistyakova (USSR)	7.52 m
Triple jump	J. Edwards (UK)	18.29 m	I. Kravets (Ukraine)	15.50 m

OLYMPIC SWIMMING EVENTS

EVENT	MEN	WOMEN
Freestyle	50 m	50 m
	100 m	100 m
	200 m	200 m
	400 m	400 m
	1,500 m	800 m
Backstroke	100 m	100 m
	200 m	200 m
Breaststroke	100 m	100 m
	200 m	200 m
Butterfly	100 m	100 m
	200 m	200 m
Individual medleys	200 m	200 m
	400 m	400 m
Freestyle relays	4x100 m	4x100 m
	4x200 m	4x200 m
Medley relay	4x100 m	4x100 m

Swimming goggles

OLYMPIC HOCKEY CHAMPIONS

The table below shows the countries with most Olympic wins in men's and women's hockey.

TEAM (MEN)	WINS	YEARS	TEAM (WOMEN)	WINS	YEARS
India	8	1928, 1932, 1936, 1948, 1952, 1956, 1964, 1980	Australia	3	1988, 1996, 2000
			Zimbabwe	1	1980
Pakistan	3	1960, 1968, 1984	Netherlands	1	1984
Britain	3	1908, 1920, 1988	Spain	1	1992

Hockey stick and ball

Slazenger FLEX

TRACK EVENTS

EVENT (MEN)	DISTANCE	RECORD HOLDER	TIME
Sprints	100 m	M. Greene (USA)	9.79 secs
	200 m	M. Johnson (USA)	19.32 secs
	400 m	M. Johnson (USA)	43.18 secs
Middle distance	800 m	W. Kipketer (Denmark)	1 min 41.11 secs
	1,500 m	H. El Guerrouj (Morocco)	3 mins 26.00 secs
	Mile	H. El Guerrouj (Morocco)	3 mins 43.13 secs
Long distance	5,000 m	H. Gebreselassie (Ethiopia)	12 mins 39.36 secs
	10,000 m	H. Gebreselassie (Ethiopia)	26 mins 22.75 secs
Relays	4x100 m	USA	37.40 secs
	4x400 m	USA	2 mins 54.20 secs
Hurdles	110 m	C. Jackson (UK)	12.91 secs
	400 m	K. Young (USA)	46.78 secs
Steeplechase	3,000 m	B. Boulami (Morocco)	7 mins 55.28 secs
Marathon	42.195 km	K. Khannouchi (Morocco)	2 hrs 5 mins 42 secs
Walks	20 km	B. Segura (Mexico)	1 hr 17 mins 25.6 secs
	50 km	T. Toutain (France)	3 hrs 40 mins 57.9 secs

EVENT (WOMEN)	DISTANCE	RECORD HOLDER	TIME
Sprints	100 m	F. Griffith-Joyner (USA)	10.49 secs
	200 m	F. Griffith-Joyner (USA)	21.34 secs
	400 m	M. Koch (E. Germany)	47.60 secs
Middle distance	800 m	J. Kratochvìlovà (Czech)	1 min 53.28 secs
	1,500 m	J. Qu (China)	3 mins 50.46 secs
	Mile	S. Masterkova (Romania)	4 mins 12.56 secs
Long distance	3,000 m	J. Wang (China)	8 mins 6.11 secs
	5,000 m	B. Jiang (China)	14 mins 28.09 secs
	10,000 m	J. Wang (China)	29 mins 31.78 secs
Relays	4x100 m	E. Germany	41.37 secs
	4x400 m	USSR	3 mins 15.17 secs
Hurdles	100 m	Y. Donkova (Bulgaria)	12.21 secs
	400 m	K. Batten (USA)	52.61 secs
Marathon	42.195 km	C. Ndereba (Kenya)	2 hrs 18 mins 47 secs
Walk	10 km	N. Ryashkina (USSR)	41 mins 56.23 secs

Starting block

ASSOCIATION FOOTBALL

World Cup winners

YEAR	VENUE	WINNING TEAM
1930	Uruguay	Uruguay
1934	Italy	Italy
1938	France	Italy
1950	Brazil	Uruguay
1954	Switzerland	W. Germany
1958	Sweden	Brazil
1962	Chile	Brazil
1966	England	England
1970	Mexico	Brazil
1974	W. Germany	W. Germany
1978	Argentina	Argentina
1982	Spain	Italy
1986	Mexico	Argentina
1990	Italy	W. Germany
1994	USA	Brazil
1998	France	France
2002	Korea/Japan	Brazil

World Cup top scorers

PLAYER	GOALS	YEARS
Gerd Müller (W. Germany)	14	1970–74
Just Fontaine (France)	13	1958
Pelé (Brazil)	12	1958–70

Gerd Müller (centre), W. Germany v. Brazil, 1973

WORLD CUP FACTS

- The World Cup was first held in 1930 and takes place every four years.

- The fastest goal scored in a tournament was by Czech Vaclav Masek, just 16 seconds into the match against Mexico in 1962.

- Russian footballer Oleg Salenko is the highest scorer in any one World Cup game. He scored five goals in the Russia v. Cameroon match (6–1) in 1994.

- The highest score in a World Cup game was 10–1 (Hungary v. El Salvador, 1982).

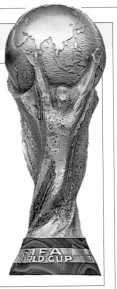

World Cup trophy

TENNIS

Tennis tournaments

TOURNAMENT	PLACE	SURFACE
Wimbledon	London, UK	Grass
US Open	Flushing Meadow, New York, USA	Artificial material
Australian Open	Flinders Park, Melbourne, Australia	Synthetic grass
French Open	Roland Garros Stadium, Paris, France	Clay

To win the grand slam, a player must hold all four major titles simultaneously.

Top winners, major titles (singles)

PLAYER (MALE)	TOTAL	YEARS
P. Sampras (USA)	13	1989–2000
R. Emerson (Australia)	12	1961–67
B. Borg (Sweden)	11	1974–81
R. Laver (Australia)	11	1960–69

Martina Navratilova at Wimbledon, 1986

PLAYER (FEMALE)	TOTAL	YEARS
M. Court (Australia)	24	1960–73
S. Graf (Germany)	22	1989-99
H. Moody (USA)	19	1923–38
M. Navratilova	18	1978–90

RUGBY UNION

World Cup winners

YEAR	VENUE	WINNING TEAM
1987	Australia and New Zealand	New Zealand
1991	British Isles and France	Australia
1995	South Africa	South Africa
1999	Wales	Australia
2003	Australia	England

World Cup top scorers

YEAR	PLAYER	POINTS
1987	Grant Fox (New Zealand)	126
1991	Roger Keyes (Ireland)	68
1995	Thierry Lacroix (France)	116
1999	Gonzalo Quesada (Argentina)	102
2003	Jonny Wilkinson (England)	113

RUGBY FACTS

- Rugby union was developed at Rugby School in England. It was an Olympic sport four times between 1900 and 1924.
- The World Cup is rugby union's most important competition. Sixteen teams entered the first World Cup, which took place in Australia and New Zealand in 1987.

International match rugby ball

MAJOR GOLF TOURNAMENTS

TOURNAMENT	FIRST HELD	TOURNAMENT	FIRST HELD
British Open	1860	Ryder Cup	1927
US Open	1895	US Masters	1934
US PGA	1916	Solheim Cup	1990

The Ryder and Solheim Cups are biennial competitions.

Golf clubs and putters

BASEBALL

TEAM	WINS
New York Yankees	27
St. Louis Cardinals	9
Philadelphia/Kansas City/ Oakland Athletics	9
Brooklyn/Los Angeles Dodgers	6
Boston Red Sox	5
Pittsburgh Pirates	5
New York/San Francisco Giants	5
Cincinnati Reds	5

Baseball bat, glove, and ball

Each year, the top two teams in the USA meet in the World Series, a best-of-seven set of games.

CRICKET

The World Cup is an international one-day tournament. It takes place approximately every four years.

YEAR	VENUE	WINNING TEAM
1975	England	West Indies
1979	England	West Indies
1983	England	India
1987	India/ Pakistan	Australia
1992	Australia/ New Zealand	Pakistan
1996	India/ Pakistan/ Sri Lanka	Sri Lanka
1999	England	Australia
2003	South Africa	Australia

FORMULA 1 CHAMPIONS

YEAR	DRIVER	NATIONALITY
1986	Alain Prost	French
1987	Nelson Piquet	Brazilian
1988	Ayrton Senna	Brazilian
1989	Alain Prost	French
1990	Ayrton Senna	Brazilian
1991	Ayrton Senna	Brazilian
1992	Nigel Mansell	British
1993	Alain Prost	French
1994	Michael Schumacher	German
1995	Michael Schumacher	German
1996	Damon Hill	British
1997	Jacques Villeneuve	Canadian
1998	Mika Hakkinen	Finnish
1999	Mika Hakkinen	Finnish
2000	Michael Schumacher	German
2001	Michael Schumacher	German
2002	Michael Schumacher	German
2003	Michael Schumacher	German

ART AND ARCHITECTURE

Reclining figure, Henry Moore

EVERY CULTURE has produced its own great artists from prehistoric cave painters to pop-art sculptors. In western society, art has become increasingly commercial with many works of art selling for vast sums at auction.

KEY PAINTERS

NAME (NATIONALITY)	DATES	FAMOUS WORK
Sandro Botticelli (Italian)	1444–1510	*Birth of Venus*
Raphael (Italian)	1483–1520	*School of Athens*
Leonardo da Vinci (Italian)	1452–1519	*Mona Lisa*
Peter Rubens (Flemish)	1577–1640	*Descent from the Cross*
Rembrandt van Rijn (Dutch)	1606–1669	*The Anatomy Lesson*
Joseph Turner (English)	1775–1851	*Rain, Steam, and Speed*
Paul Cézanne (French)	1839–1906	*Mont Ste. Victoire*
Claude Monet (French)	1840–1926	*Waterlilies*
Pierre Auguste Renoir (French)	1841–1919	*Umbrellas*
Mary Cassatt (American)	1844–1926	*La Loge*
Paul Gauguin (French)	1848–1903	*Rest*
Vincent Van Gogh (Dutch)	1853–1890	*Sunflowers*
Gustave Klimt (Austrian)	1862–1918	*The Kiss*
Edvard Munch (Norwegian)	1863–1944	*The Scream*
Henri de Toulouse-Lautrec (French)	1864–1901	*Le Moulin Rouge*
Wassili Kandinsky (Russian)	1866–1944	*Shrill-Peaceful Pink*
Henri Matisse (French)	1869–1954	*La Danse*
Pablo Picasso (Spanish)	1881–1973	*Les Demoiselles d'Avignon*
Salvador Dali (Spanish)	1904–1989	*Premonition of a Civil War*
Francis Bacon (English)	1909–1992	*The Screaming Pope*
Jackson Pollock (American)	1912–1956	*Lavender Mist*
Andy Warhol (American)	1926–1987	*Marilyn*

Salvador Dali

SCULPTORS OF THE 20TH CENTURY

NAME (NATIONALITY)	DATES	FAMOUS WORK
Constantin Brancusi (Romanian)	1876–1957	*Torso of a Young Man*
Jacob Epstein (English)	1880–1959	*Ecce Homo*
Hans Jean Arp (French)	1887–1966	*Eggboard*
Henry Moore (English)	1898–1986	*Mother and Child*
Alberto Giacometti (Swiss)	1901–1966	*Suspended Square*
Barbara Hepworth (English)	1903–1975	*Figure of a Woman*
Jean Tinguely (Swiss)	1925–1991	*Homage to New York*
Andy Goldsworthy (English)	b.1956	*Ice Sculptures*

TALLEST BUILDINGS

BUILDING AND LOCATION	HEIGHT
Petronas Twin Towers, KL, Malaysia	452 m (1,483 ft)
Sears Tower, Chicago, USA	443 m (1,453 ft)
Jin Mao Building, Shanghai, China	420 m (1,378 ft)
Citic Plaza, Guangzhou, China	391 m (1,283 ft)
Shun Hing Square, Shenzhen, China	384 m (1,260 ft)
Empire State Building, New York, USA	381 m (1,250 ft)
Central Plaza, Hong Kong, China	374 m (1,227 ft)

Petronas Towers, Malaysia

KEY PHOTOGRAPHERS

Julia Cameron

NAME (NATIONALITY)	DATES	FORM
Julia Cameron (English)	1815–1879	Portraiture
Man Ray (American)	1890–1976	Experimental
Ansel Adams (American)	1902–1984	Landscape
Bill Brandt (English)	1904–1983	Documentary
Henri Cartier-Bresson (French)	b.1908	Photojournalism
Robert Capa (Hungarian)	1913–1954	Photojournalism
Richard Avedon (American)	b.1923	Portraiture

KEY ARCHITECTS

Pompidou Centre

NAME (NATIONALITY)	DATES	FAMOUS BUILDING
Filippo Brunelleschi (Italian)	1377–1446	Dome of Florence Cathedral, Italy
Michelangelo Buonarroti (Italian)	1475–1564	Dome of St. Peters, Vatican City
Inigo Jones (English)	1573–1652	The Queen's House, England
François Mansart (French)	1598–1666	Chateau de Berny, Paris, France
Christopher Wren (English)	1632–1723	St. Paul's Cathedral, London, England
John Vanbrugh (English)	1664–1726	Blenheim Palace, England
Karl Friedrich Schinkel (German)	1781–1841	Altes Museum, Berlin, Germany
Antonio Gaudí (Spanish)	1852–1926	La Sagrada Familia, Barcelona, Spain
Frank Lloyd Wright (American)	1869–1959	Guggenheim Museum, New York, USA
Walter Gropius (German)	1883–1969	Bauhaus, Dessau, Germany
Mies van der Rohe (German)	1886–1969	Seagram Building, New York, USA
Le Corbusier (Swiss)	1887–1965	Notre Dame du Haut, France
Oscar Niemeyer (Brazilian)	b.1907	Government Buildings, Brasília, Brazil
Richard Rogers (English)	b.1933	Pompidou Centre, Paris, France
Kenzo Tange (Japanese)	b.1913	Olympic Games stadium, Tokyo, Japan
Norman Foster (English)	b.1935	Hong Kong and Shanghai Bank, Hong Kong, China

MOST EXPENSIVE PAINTINGS

These famous works of art were sold to the highest bidder at Christie's auction house.

TITLE (ARTIST, DATE SOLD)	PRICE IN US$
Portrait of Dr. Gachet (Van Gogh, 1990)	82,500,000
Au Moulin de la Galette (Renoir, 1990)	78,100,000
Irises (Van Gogh, 1987)	53,900,000
Les Noces de Pierrette (Picasso, 1989)	51,895,000
Yo Picasso (Picasso, 1989)	47,850,000
Au Lapin Agile (Picasso, 1989)	40,700,000
Sunflowers (Van Gogh, 1987)	40,342,500

Au Moulin de la Galette, **Renoir**

THEATRE, MUSIC, AND DANCE

THEATRE HAS ITS roots in ancient Greece, when religious plays included singing and dancing as well as acting. Today, dramatic performances of many kinds continue to entertain audiences around the world.

Viola

Quill pens

KEY DRAMATISTS

NAME (NATIONALIITY)	DATES	FAMOUS PLAY
William Shakespeare (English)	1564–1616	Hamlet
Pierre Corneille (French)	1607–1684	Le Cid
Molière (French)	1622–1673	Tartuffe
Jean Racine (French)	1639–1699	Phèdre
Johann Goethe (German)	1749–1832	Faust
Richard Sheridan (Irish)	1751–1816	The Rivals
Henrik Ibsen (Norwegian)	1828–1906	A Doll's House
George Bernard Shaw (Irish)	1856–1950	Pygmalion
Anton Chekov (Russian)	1860–1904	Uncle Vanya
Luigi Pirandello (Italian)	1867–1936	Six Characters in Search of an Author
Susan Glaspell (American)	1882–1948	Alison's House
Eugene O'Neill (American)	1888–1953	Strange Interlude
Bertolt Brecht (German)	1898–1956	The Threepenny Opera
Samuel Beckett (Irish)	1906–1989	Waiting for Godot
Tennessee Williams (American)	1911–1983	The Glass Menagerie
Eugène Ionesco (French)	1912–1994	The Bald Prima Donna
Arthur Miller (American)	b.1915	Death of a Salesman
John Osborne (English)	1929–1994	Look Back in Anger
Harold Pinter (English)	b.1930	The Caretaker

KEY CLASSICAL COMPOSERS

NAME (NATIONALITY)	DATES	FAMOUS WORK
Antonio Vivaldi (Italian)	1678–1741	The Four Seasons (1725)
Johann Sebastian Bach (German)	1685–1750	Brandenburg Concertos (1721)
George Frederick Händel (German)	1685–1759	Messiah (1742)
Franz Joseph Haydn (Austrian)	1732–1809	London Symphonies (1791–1795)
Wolfgang Amadeus Mozart (Austrian)	1756–1791	The Magic Flute (1791)
Ludwig van Beethoven (German)	1770–1827	Pastoral Symphony (1807–1808)
Franz Schubert (Austrian)	1797–1828	Die Winterreise (1827)
Hector Berlioz (French)	1803–1869	Symphonie Fantastique (1830)
Felix Mendelssohn (German)	1809–1847	A Midsummer Night's Dream (1826)
Frédéric Chopin (Polish)	1810–1849	Piano works
Franz Liszt (Hungarian)	1811–1886	Les Préludes (1854)
Giuseppe Verdi (Italian)	1813–1901	La Traviata (1853)
Richard Wagner (German)	1813–1883	The Flying Dutchman (1843)
Johann Strauss (Austrian)	1825–1899	Die Fledermaus (1874)
Pyotr Ilyich Tchaikovsky (Russian)	1840–1893	Swan Lake (1877)
Antonin Dvorák (Czech)	1841–1904	Slavonic Dances (1878–1886)
Edward Elgar (English)	1857–1934	Enigma Variations (1898–1899)
Giacomo Puccini (Italian)	1858–1924	La Bohème (1896)
Ethel Smyth (English)	1858–1944	The Wreckers (1909)
Gustav Mahler (Austrian)	1860–1911	Resurrection Symphony (1884–1894)
Claude Debussy (French)	1862–1918	La Mer (1903–1905)
Richard Strauss (German)	1864–1949	Der Rosenkavalier (1911)
Sergei Rachmaninov (Russian)	1873–1943	Piano works
Gustav Holst (English)	1874–1934	The Planets (1914–1916)
Maurice Ravel (French)	1875–1937	Boléro (1928)
Igor Stravinsky (Russian)	1882–1971	The Firebird (1910)
Sergei Prokofiev (Russian)	1891–1953	Peter and the Wolf (1936)
Kurt Weill (German)	1900–1950	The Threepenny Opera (1928)
Benjamin Britten (English)	1913–1976	Billy Budd (1951)
Karlheinz Stockhausen (German)	b.1928	Gruppen (1955–1957)
Philip Glass (American)	b.1937	Einstein on the Beach (1976)

Franz Schubert

Philip Glass

FAMOUS BALLETS

Ballet uses dancing, mime, and music to tell a story.

TITLE	CHOREOGRAPHER (NATIONALITY)	FIRST DANCED
La Syphide	Filippo Taglioni (Italian)	1832
Giselle	Jean Coralli/Jules Perot (French/French)	1841
Sleeping Beauty	Marius Petipa (French)	1890
The Nutcracker	Lev Ivanov (Russian)	1892
The Rite of Spring	Vaslav Nijinsky (Russian)	1913
Manon	Kenneth MacMillan (English)	1974
Fait Accompli	Twyla Tharp (American)	1984
Still Life at the Penguin Cafe	David Bintley (English)	1988

BEST-SELLING SINGLES WORLDWIDE

SINGLE	ARTIST
Candle in the Wind 97	Elton John
White Christmas	Bing Crosby
Rock Around The Clock	Bill Haley and His Comets
I Want to Hold Your Hand	Beatles
Hey Jude	Beatles
It's Now or Never	Elvis Presley
I Will Always Love You	Whitney Houston
Don't Be Cruel/Hound Dog	Elvis Presley
Diana	Paul Anka

Whitney Houston

KEY OPERAS

These "musical dramas" use spectacular singers, lavish stage sets, and a full orchestra to dramatic effect.

TITLE	COMPOSER (NATIONALITY)	DATE
The Marriage of Figaro	Wolfgang Mozart (Austrian)	1786
Così fan tutte	Wolfgang Mozart (Austrian)	1790
The Barber of Seville	Gioacchino Rossini (Italian)	1816
Tristan and Isolde	Richard Wagner (German)	1865
Aida	Giuseppe Verdi (Italian)	1871
Carmen	Georges Bizet (French)	1875
The Ring of the Nibelung	Richard Wagner (German)	1876
La Bohème	Giacomo Puccini (Italian)	1896
Madame Butterfly	Giacomo Puccini (Italian)	1904
Peter Grimes	Benjamin Britten (English)	1945

The Marriage of Figaro

BEST-SELLING ALBUMS WORLDWIDE

ALBUM	ARTIST
Thriller	Michael Jackson
The Bodyguard	Soundtrack
Saturday Night Fever	Soundtrack
Sgt. Pepper's Lonely Hearts Club Band	Beatles
Bridge Over Troubled Water	Simon and Garfunkel
Born in the USA	Bruce Springsteen
The Sound of Music	Soundtrack
Rumours	Fleetwood Mac
Brothers in Arms	Dire Straits

Saturday Night Fever

FILM AND THE MEDIA

DURING THE PAST 100 years, advances in modern technology have transformed the media and entertainment industries. Computers create feature-length films with special effects, satellites beam live broadcasts to television sets worldwide, and modern printing presses produce up to four million newspapers every day.

Technicolor camera

KEY FILM DIRECTORS

NAME (NATIONALITY)	DATES	KEY FILM
Cecil De Mille (American)	1881–1959	*The Ten Commandments* (1923)
Jean Cocteau (French)	1889–1963	*La Belle et la Bête* (1946)
Jean Renoir (French)	1894–1979	*La Règle du Jeu* (1939)
John Ford (American)	1895–1973	*Stagecoach* (1939)
Sergei Eisenstein (Russian)	1898–1948	*The Battleship Potemkin* (1925)
Alfred Hitchcock (British)	1899–1980	*Psycho* (1960)
Luis Buñuel (Spanish)	1900–1983	*Un Chien Andalou* (1928)
John Huston (American)	1906–1987	*The African Queen* (1951)
David Lean (British)	1908–1991	*Lawrence of Arabia* (1962)
Elia Kazan (Greek-born American)	b.1909	*On the Waterfront* (1954)
Akira Kurosawa (Japanese)	1910–1998	*Seven Samurai* (1954)
Orson Welles (American)	1915–1985	*Citizen Kane* (1942)
Ingmar Bergman (Swedish)	b.1918–	*The Seventh Seal* (1957)
Federico Fellini (Italian)	1920–1993	*La Dolce Vita* (1960)
Satyajit Ray (Indian)	1921–1992	*Pather Panchali* (1955)
Stanley Kubrick (American)	1928–1999	*A Clockwork Orange* (1971)
Jean-Luc Godard (French)	b.1930	*A Bout de Souffle* (1960)
Woody Allen (American)	b.1935	*Annie Hall* (1977)
Francis Coppola (American)	b.1939	*Apocalypse Now* (1979)
Bernardo Bertolucci (Italian)	b.1940	*The Last Emperor* (1987)
Peter Weir (Australian)	b.1944	*Picnic at Hanging Rock* (1975)
Steven Spielberg (American)	b.1947	*E.T.* (1982)
Claude Berri (French)	b.1954	*Jean de Florette* (1986)
Jane Campion (New Zealand)	b.1955	*The Piano* (1993)

Ingmar Bergman

Scene from *The Piano* (1993)

BEST-SELLING NEWSPAPERS

NAME	COUNTRY	AVERAGE DAILY CIRCULATION
Yomiuri Shimbun	Japan	14,532,000
Asahi Shimbun	Japan	12,601,000
People's Daily	China	8,000,000
Mainichi Shimbun	Japan	5,845,857
Bild Zeitung	Germany	5,674,400
Chunichi Shimbun	Japan	4,323,144
The Sun	UK	3,718,354
Renmin Ribao	China	3,000,000
Sankei Shimbun	Japan	2,890,835
Nihon Keizai Shim.	Japan	2,705,877
Gongren Ribao	China	2,500,000

Asahi Shimbun newspaper

TELEVISION

World television viewing

COUNTRY	NO. OF TELEVISION SETS (IN MILLIONS)
China	400
USA	219
Japan	86.5
India	63
Russia	60.5
Germany	51.4
Brazil	36.5
France	34.8
UK	30.5
Italy	30.3

1980s' television

First countries to have television

COUNTRY	YEAR
UK	1936
USA	1939
USSR	1939
France	1948
Brazil	1950
Cuba	1950
Mexico	1950
Argentina	1951
Denmark	1951
Netherlands	1951

Watching TV in 1948

TELEVISION FACTS

• The worldwide average number of television sets per 1,000 people is 252. Sub-Saharan Africa has an average of 50 sets per 1,000 people, lower than any other region in the world.

• Telstar was the world's first communications satellite. In 1962, it transmitted live television programmes across the globe for the first time.

RADIO

COUNTRY	RADIO SETS PER 1,000 POPULATION
USA	2,068
Finland	1,488
UK	1,417
Australia	1,317
Denmark	1,125
Monaco	1,068
Canada	1,022
Samoa	944
Korea, South	992
Switzerland	975
New Zealand	970

Personal stereo

CINEMA FACTS

• The first feature film was *The Story of the Kelly Gang*, made in Australia in 1906.

• The first "talkie" was *The Jazz Singer*. Released in 1927, it starred Al Jolson (1886–1950).

• The most expensive film ever produced is *Titanic* (USA, 1997). It cost an estimated £133 million ($200 million).

• The highest-grossing film at the box office is *Titanic* (USA, 1997). It earned £1,223 million ($1,835 million).

MOST OSCARS WON

NAME OF FILM	AWARDS
The Return of the King (2003)	11
Titanic (1997)	11
Ben-Hur (1959)	11
West Side Story (1961)	10
The English Patient (1997)	9
The Last Emperor (1987)	9
Gigi (1958)	9
Gandhi (1982)	8
On the Waterfront (1954)	8
From Here to Eternity (1953)	8
Gone With the Wind (1939)	8

OSCAR® FACTS

• The first Oscars® (Academy Awards) were presented in 1929. *Wings* (1927) won the "Best Picture" award.

• The film nominated for the most Oscars was *All About Eve* (USA, 1950). It had 14 nominations and won six awards.

• Katharine Hepburn and Meryl Streep share the honour of more Oscar nominations than any other actor. They have each been nominated 12 times.

Oscar®

GREAT WRITERS AND THINKERS

EVERY SOCIETY HAS produced great writers and thinkers. The tables below list a selection of these influential men and women.

Ludwig Wittgenstein

KEY AUTHORS

Franz Kafka

Gabriel García Márquez

NAME (NATIONALITY)	DATES	FAMOUS WORK
Madame de la Fayette (French)	1634–1693	*La Princesse de Clèves*
Jonathan Swift (Irish)	1667–1745	*Gulliver's Travels*
Johann Wolfgang von Goethe (German)	1749–1832	*Faust*
Jane Austen (English)	1775–1817	*Pride and Prejudice*
Mary Shelley (English)	1797–1851	*Frankenstein*
Victor Hugo (French)	1802–1885	*Les Misérables*
Hans Christian Andersen (Danish)	1805–1875	*The Emperor's New Clothes*
Charles Dickens (English)	1812–1870	*Oliver Twist*
George Eliot (English)	1819–1880	*Middlemarch*
Herman Melville (American)	1819–1891	*Moby Dick*
Fyodor Dostoyevsky (Russian)	1821–1881	*Crime and Punishment*
Leo Tolstoy (Russian)	1828–1910	*War and Peace*
Émile Zola (French)	1840–1902	*Germinal*
Robert Louis Stevenson (Scottish)	1850–1894	*Treasure Island*
James Joyce (Irish)	1882–1941	*Ulysses*
Virginia Woolf (English)	1882–1941	*To the Lighthouse*
Franz Kafka (Czech)	1883–1924	*The Trial*
F. Scott Fitzgerald (American)	1896–1940	*The Great Gatsby*
Ernest Hemingway (American)	1899–1961	*For Whom the Bell Tolls*
Vladimir Nabokov (Russian-born American)	1899–1977	*Lolita*
John Steinbeck (American)	1902–1968	*Of Mice and Men*
George Orwell (English)	1903–1950	*Animal Farm*
Graham Greene (English)	1904–1991	*Brighton Rock*
Albert Camus (French)	1913–1960	*The Outsider*
Italo Calvino (Italian)	1923–1985	*The Path to the Nest of Spiders*
Yukio Mishima (Japanese)	1925–1970	*The Sound of Waves*
Günter Grass (German)	b.1927	*The Tin Drum*
Gabriel García Márquez (Colombian)	b.1928	*One Hundred Years of Solitude*
Toni Morrison (American)	b.1931	*Beloved*
Salman Rushdie (Indian-born British)	b.1947	*Midnight's Children*

KEY PHILOSOPHERS

From the early Greek philosophers to modern thinkers, philosophers have offered opposing theories and beliefs. This table lists some of the world's most important thinkers with a summary of their philosophy.

NAME (NATIONALITY)	DATES	PHILOSOPHY
Confucius (Chinese)	551–479 bc	Emphasized moral order and ancient manners.
Socrates (Greek)	470–399 bc	Taught that morality is based on knowledge.
Aristotle (Greek)	384–322 bc	Believed that logic and reason are most important.
St. Augustine (Roman-born African)	ad 354–430	Outlined his Christian beliefs in his work.
St. Thomas Aquinas (Italian)	1225–1274	Argued to prove the existence of God.
René Descartes (French)	1596–1650	Interpreted the world using mathematical laws.
John Locke (English)	1632–1704	Believed that all knowledge is based on experience.
David Hume (Scottish)	1711–1776	Believed that nothing can be known for certain.
Søren Kierkegaard (Danish)	1813–1855	The founder of existentialism (the belief that the individual must take responsibility for his or her own actions).
Friedrich Nietzsche (German)	1844–1900	Rejected Christianity and argued that people are driven by "the will to power".
Bertrand Russell (English)	1872–1970	Imprisoned for his outspoken pacifism.
Ludwig Wittgenstein (Austrian-born British)	1889–1951	Studied the relationship between language and the world.
Jean-Paul Sartre (French)	1905–1980	Philosopher, novelist, and leading existentialist.
Simone de Beauvoir (French)	1908–1986	Leading feminist philosopher.

NOBEL PEACE PRIZES

Nobel Peace Prize

Established in 1901, Nobel prizes are given annually for outstanding contributions to the fields of economics, physics, chemistry, physiology, literature, and peace. Recent winners of the Nobel Peace Prize are listed below.

NAME (NATIONALITY)	YEAR	WORK
Nelson Mandela and Frederik Willem de Klerk (South African)	1993	Assisting peace between the ANC and the Republic of South Africa.
Yasser Arafat (Palestinian), Shimon Peres, and Yitzhak Rabin (Israelis)	1994	Assisting peace between the PLO and Israel.
Joseph Rotblat (English) and the Pugwash Conferences	1995	Reducing the status of nuclear arms in international politics.
Carlos Filipe Ximenes Belo and José Ramos-Horta (Indonesian)	1996	Helping to bring peace to the conflict in East Timor.
International Campaign to Ban Landmines and Jody Williams (American)	1997	Banning and clearing of anti-personnel mines.
John Hume (Irish) and David Trimble (Irish)	1998	Assisting peace process in Northern Ireland.
Medecins Sans Frontieres	1999	Providing medical aid worldwide.
Kim Dae Jung (South Korean)	2000	Working for democracy in Korea.
UN and Kofi Annan (Ghanaian)	2001	Campaigning for worldwide peace.
Jimmy Carter (American)	2002	Working for social development.
Shirin Ebadi (Iranian)	2003	Campaigning for democracy.

KEY POETS

NAME (NATIONALITY)	DATES	FAMOUS WORK
Homer (Greek)	c.800 bc	*The Iliad*
Virgil (Roman)	70–19 bc	*The Aeneid*
Dante Alighieri (Italian)	1265–1321	*The Divine Comedy*
Geoffrey Chaucer (English)	1340–1400	*The Canterbury Tales*
Luis de Camões (Portuguese)	1524–1580	*The Lusiads*
John Donne (English)	1573–1631	*Divine Sonnets*
John Milton (English)	1608–1674	*Paradise Lost*
Alexander Pope (English)	1688–1744	*An Essay on Man*
William Blake (English)	1757–1827	*Songs of Innocence*
Robert Burns (Scottish)	1759–1796	*Tam o' Shanter*
William Wordsworth (English)	1770–1850	*The Prelude*
George Byron (English)	1788–1824	*Don Juan*
Aleksander Pushkin (Russian)	1799–1837	*Eugene Onegin*
Emily Dickinson (American)	1830–1886	*Bolts of Melody*
Rabindranath Tagore (Indian)	1861–1941	*Gitanjali*
Hagiwava Sakutaro (Japanese)	1886–1942	*Howling at the Moon*
T. S. Eliot (American-born English)	1888–1965	*The Waste Land*
Jorge Luis Borges (Argentinian)	1899–1986	*Labyrinths*
John Betjeman (English)	1906–1984	*Slough*
Octavio Paz (Mexican)	1914–1998	*Sunstone*
Ted Hughes (English)	1930–1998	*Birthday Letters*

Ted Hughes

Emily Dickinson

HISTORY

THIS SECTION describes key events in world history from the earliest civilizations to the present day. Tables list the world's great leaders, and a comparative timeline shows what was happening in each continent at any one time.

Egyptian mummy case

EGYPTIAN PERIODS AND DYNASTIES

PERIOD	DATE	MAIN PHARAOH(S)
Early Dynastic	c.3000–c.2650 BC	Narmer (Menes)
Old Kingdom	c.2650–c.2160 BC	Zoser
		Khufu
First Intermediate Period	c.2160–c.2100 BC	
Middle Kingdom	c.2100–c.1786 BC	Mentuhotep II
Second Intermediate Period	c.1786–c.1550 BC	Hyksos rule
New Kingdom	c.1550–c.1050 BC	Amenhotep I
		Queen Hatshepsut
		Thutmose III
		Tutankhamun
		Rameses II
Third Intermediate Period	c.1050–667 BC	Nubian rule
Late period	c.664–333 BC	Darius III
Foreign rulers	332–30 BC	Alexander the Great
		Ptolemy I Soter
		Queen Cleopatra VII

CHINESE DYNASTIES AND REPUBLICS

DATE (AD)	DYNASTY
220–265	Three Kingdoms
265–316	Western Chin
316–420	Eastern Chin
420–589	Southern
589–618	Sui
618–690	T'ang
690–705	Chou
705–906	T'ang
906–960	Northern Five, Southern Ten
960–1279	Song (Sung)
1279–1368	Yuan (Mongol)
1368–1644	Ming
1644–1911	Manchu (Qing)
1911–1949	Republic (Nationalist)
1949–	People's Republic (Communist)

KEY POPES

REIGN (AD)	POPE
c.42–67	St. Peter
88–97	St. Clement I
254–257	St. Stephen I
440–461	St. Leo I, the Great
590–604	St. Gregory I, the Great
1073–1085	St. Gregory VII
1088–1099	Urban II
1198–1216	Innocent III
1492–1503	Alexander VI
1534–1549	Paul III
1572–1585	Gregory XIII
1846–1878	Pius IX
1958–1963	John XXIII
1978–	John Paul II

JAPANESE PERIODS

Japanese periods began with the introduction of an emperor figure.

DATE (AD)	PERIOD
250–710	Yamato
710–794	Nara
794–1192	Heian
1192–1333	Kamakura
1333–1573	Muromachi
1573–1616	Momoyama
1616–1867	Edo
1868–1912	Meiji
1912–1926	Taisho
1926–1989	Showa
1989–	Heisei

Samurai swords

	40,000 BC	25,000 BC	10,000 BC	7000 BC	3500 BC	2500 BC
AFRICA	30,000 BC Disappearance of the Neanderthals. Neanderthal skull	c.24,000 Cave walls painted at the Apollo site in Namibia, southwest Africa. 18,000 BC Settlement of Zaïre, central Africa	10,000 BC Hunting camps established in Sahara region after Ice Age ends. c.8000 BC Hunter-gatherers paint human figures on rock in North Africa	6000 BC Cattle domesticated, Sahara. Egyptian hieroglyphs	3000 BC Development of hieroglyphic writing. 2590 BC Building of Great Pyramid of Khufu at Giza	2500 BC Sahara region begins to dry out. c.2100 BC–c.1786 BC Middle Kingdom, Egypt. c.1550 BC–c.1050 BC New Kingdom, Egypt
ASIA	40,000 BC Cro-Magnon humans living at Skhül and Kafzel (Israel). 27,000 BC–19,000 BC Female statuettes made at various sites, including locations in Russia	18,000 BC Coldest point of Ice Age. 14,000 BC–11,000 BC El-Kabareh culture, Israel. 12,500 BC Rise of Magdalenian toolmakers. 10,500 BC Earliest pottery, Japan	10,000 BC Ice cap retreats. 9000 BC–8000 BC Cereals grown in Jordan and Syria. 8000 BC Jericho, the world's first known city, is founded. 7500 BC Domestication of pigs, Crimea	5000 BC Rice first cultivated, China. 5000 BC First cities founded in Mesopotamia and Sumer, western Asia. 5000 BC Irrigation systems used, Mesopotamia. 4500 BC Farming begins around River Ganges, India	3500 BC Mesopotamians invent the wheel. 3250 BC First pictographic writing, Mesopotamia. c.3000 BC Development of Sumerian cities	2500 BC Beginning of Indus Valley civilization, Pakistan. 1900 BC Iron Age begins, western Asia. c.1790 BC Hammurabi becomes King of Babylon. Terracotta pig, Indus Valley
EUROPE	40,000 BC Cro-Magnons arrive in Europe from Africa. 35,000 BC Earliest figurative art in the Dordogne, France. 35,000 BC Start of Upper Paleolithic period	15,000 BC Cave paintings, Lascaux, France. 13,000 BC Magdalenian culture; high point of mural art. 11,000 BC Cave paintings, Altamira, Spain	10,000 BC Ice cap retreats. 8300 BC Retreat of glaciers. Ice-Age snow knife	6500 BC Britain separated from mainland Europe as ice melts. 6500 BC First farming communities, southeast Europe. 4500 BC First megalithic tombs, Brittany and Portugal	2900 BC Danubian culture, central Europe. c.2800 BC Building of Stonehenge starts, England. 2600 BC Bronze Age reaches Crete	2500 BC–2200 BC Scandinavian Dolmen period. 2000 BC Beginning of Minoan civilization, Crete. 1600 BC Height of Mycenaean civilization, Greece
AMERICAS	35,000 BC–20,000 BC First humans arrive in North America from Asia	25,000 BC Cave-dwellers present in Brazil. 15,000 BC Cave art begins in Brazil	9000 BC First people reach tip of South America. 8000 BC Semi-permanent settlements, North America	6500 BC Cultivation of potatoes and grain crops, Peru, South America. 5000 BC First settlements in Anáhuac, Mexico	c.3500 BC Maize first cultivated in South America. 3000 BC First pottery in Americas	2500 BC Earliest large settlements in Andes area. 2000 BC Inuits reach northern Greenland
OCEANIA	c.40,000 BC Ancestors of Aboriginals arrive in Australia from Asia	24,000 BC Earliest known cremation, Australia. 16,000 BC Cave art, north coast of Australia		6000 BC New Guinea and Tasmania are separated from Australia as sea level rises	3000 BC Probable introduction of dogs in Australia	2000 BC Beginnings of settlement of Melanesia, South Pacific

942

BRITISH RULERS

The list below details the monarchs of
England from 1042 until 1603, and
subsequent joint British monarchs.

MONARCHS OF ENGLAND

King Henry VIII   **Queen Victoria**

SAXONS
1042–1066	Edward the Confessor
1066	Harold II

NORMANS
1066–1087	William the Conqueror
1087–1100	William II
1100–1135	Henry I
1135–1154	Stephen

PLANTAGENETS
1154–1189	Henry II
1189–1199	Richard I
1199–1216	John
1216–1272	Henry III
1272–1307	Edward I
1307–1327	Edward II
1327–1377	Edward III
1377–1399	Richard II

LANCASTERS
1399–1413	Henry IV
1413–1422	Henry V
1422–1461	Henry VI

YORKS
1461–1483	Edward IV
1483	Edward V
1483–1485	Richard III

TUDORS
1485–1509	Henry VII
1509–1547	Henry VIII
1547–1553	Edward VI
1553–1558	Mary I
1558–1603	Elizabeth I

MONARCHS OF BRITAIN

STUARTS
1603–1625	James I (VI of Scotland)
1625–1649	Charles I

COMMONWEALTH

STUARTS
1660–1685	Charles II
1685–1688	James II
1689–1694	Mary II
1689–1702	William III
1702–1714	Anne

HANOVERS
1714–1727	George I
1727–1760	George II
1760–1820	George III
1820–1830	George IV
1830–1837	William IV

SAXE-COBURG-GOTHAS
1837–1901	Victoria
1901–1910	Edward VII

WINDSORS
1910–1936	George V
1936	Edward VIII
1936–1952	George VI
1952–	Elizabeth II

MONARCHS OF SCOTLAND

The monarchs of Scotland from 1306–1625.

1306–1329	Robert I, the Bruce
1329–1371	David II

STUARTS
1371–1390	Robert II
1390–1406	Robert III
1406–1437	James I
1437–1460	James II
1460–1488	James III
1488–1513	James IV
1513–1542	James V
1542–1567	Mary, Queen of Scots
1567–1625	James VI

BRITISH PRIME MINISTERS

1828–1830	Duke of Wellington
1830–1834	Earl Grey
1834	Viscount Melbourne
1834–1835	Robert Peel
1835–1841	Viscount Melbourne
1841–1846	Robert Peel
1846–1852	Lord John Russell
1852	Earl of Derby
1852–1855	Earl of Aberdeen
1855–1858	Viscount Palmeston
1858–1859	Earl of Derby
1859–1865	Viscount Palmeston
1865–1866	Earl Russell
1866–1868	Earl of Derby
1868	Benjamin Disraeli
1868–1874	William Gladstone
1874–1880	Benjamin Disraeli
1880–1885	William Gladstone
1885–1886	Marquess of Salisbury
1886	William Gladstone
1886–1892	Marquess of Salisbury
1892–1894	William Gladstone
1894–1895	Earl of Rosebery
1895–1902	Marquess of Salisbury
1902–1905	Arthur Balfour
1905–1908	Henry Campbell-Bannerman
1908–1916	Henry Asquith
1916–1922	David Lloyd-George
1922–1923	Andrew Bonar Law
1923–1924	Stanley Baldwin
1924	James Ramsay Macdonald
1924–1929	Stanley Baldwin
1929–1935	James Ramsay Macdonald
1935–1937	Stanley Baldwin
1937–1940	Neville Chamberlain
1940–1945	Winston Churchill
1945–1951	Clement Atlee
1951–1955	Winston Churchill
1955–1957	Anthony Eden
1957–1963	Harold Macmillan
1963–1964	Alec Douglas-Home
1964–1970	Harold Wilson
1970–1974	Edward Heath
1974–1976	Harold Wilson
1976–1979	James Callaghan
1979–1990	Margaret Thatcher
1990–1997	John Major
1997–	Tony Blair

William Gladstone

	1500 BC	1000 BC	600 BC	300 BC	AD 1	AD 300
AFRICA	**1300 BC** Temple of Abu Simbel, Nubia, built for Rameses II **1218 BC** Sea peoples from the Aegean invade Egypt and the eastern Mediterranean	**900 BC** Foundation of kingdom of Kush in Nubia **814 BC** Phoenicians found the city of Carthage, North Africa	**600 BC** Building of Temple of the Sun at Meroë, Sudan **500 BC** Beginning of Nok culture in northern Nigeria **332 BC** Alexander the Great conquers Egypt	**290 BC** Library founded at Alexandria, Egypt **149–146 BC** Rome destroys Carthage in Third Punic War, founding province of Africa	**AD 50** Kingdom of Aksum (Ethiopia) begins to expand **AD 150** Mandingos and Berbers dominate Sudan area **AD 250** Aksum controls trade in Red Sea	**AD 325** Aksum destroys kingdom of Meroë **AD 439** Vandals establish kingdom in northern Africa **Gupta coin**
ASIA	**1400 BC** Chinese capital moved to Anyang **1200 BC** Hittite Empire collapses **1200 BC** Jews settle in Palestine **1100 BC** Phoenicians spread out from eastern Mediterranean	**1000 BC** Kingdom of Israel under King David **721–705 BC** Assyrian Empire at its greatest extent **604 BC** Nebuchadnezzar II rules Babylonian Empire	**563–486 BC** Life of the Buddha **550 BC** Cyrus II founds Persian Empire **322 BC** Chandragupta Maurya founds Mauryan Empire **Buddhist carving**	**221 BC** Qin Shih Huangdi, the first emperor, unites China **185 BC** Bactrians conquer northwest India **112 BC** Silk Road opens, giving West some access to China **64 BC** Roman general Pompey conquers Syria	**AD 30** Jesus Christ is crucified in Jerusalem, Israel **AD 60** Beginning of Kushan Empire, India **AD 105** Paper invented, China **AD 220** End of Han dynasty, China **AD 224** Sassanian dynasty founded in Persia	**AD 320** Chandragupta I founds Gupta Empire in northern India **AD 480** End of Gupta Empire **AD 520** Decimal number system invented in India **AD 550** Buddhism introduced into Japan
EUROPE	**1500 BC** Beginning of Bronze Age in Scandinavia **1450 BC** End of Minoan civilization, Crete **1200 BC** Decline of Mycenaean culture, Greece	**1000 BC** Etruscan people found city-states in Italy **776 BC** First recorded Olympic Games, Greece **753 BC** Rome founded	**509 BC** Roman Republic founded **480 BC** Greeks defeat Persians at Battle of Marathon **431–404 BC** Peloponnesian War, Greece: Sparta defeats Athens	**216 BC** Hannibal defeats Roman army at Cannae **46 BC** Julius Caesar becomes Roman dictator **27 BC** Augustus becomes first Roman Emperor	**AD 43** Romans invade Great Britain **AD 235–284** Period of civil war in Roman Empire **AD 285–305** Emperor Diocletian restores order to Rome	**AD 330** Emperor Constantine founds Constantinople **AD 410** Visigoths sack Rome **AD 486** Franks control France **AD 527** Justinian I becomes Byzantine Emperor
AMERICAS	**1300 BC** Rise of Olmec civilization in Mexico	**800 BC** Zapotec civilization flourishes in central America	**400 BC** Decline of Olmec civilization, Mexico **c.500 BC** Adena people build communal burial mounds, Ohio, USA	**300 BC** Beginning of Early Mayan Period, central America **c.200 BC** Nazca civilization, Peru	**AD 1** Beginning of Moche civilization, northern Peru	**AD 500** Hopewell culture at its peak, North America **AD 600** Height of Mayan civilization, central America
OCEANIA	**1300 BC** Settlers reach Fiji (then western Polynesia) **Olmec mask**	**1000 BC** Most of Polynesian Islands settled	**500 BC** Trading contacts established in South Pacific islands	**Moche stirrup-spout vessel**	**AD 1–100** Hindu-Buddhists from Asia colonize Sumatra and Java	**AD 300** Settlement of eastern Polynesia

943

PRESIDENTS OF THE USA

US presidents are elected to serve a four-year term of office. Since 1951, no president has been allowed to serve more than two terms.

1789–1797	George Washington
1797–1801	John Adams
1801–1809	Thomas Jefferson
1809–1817	James Madison
1817–1825	James Monroe
1825–1829	John Quincy Adams
1829–1837	Andrew Jackson
1837–1841	Martin Van Buren
1841	William H. Harrison
1841–1845	John Tyler
1845–1849	James K. Polk
1849–1850	Zachary Taylor
1850–1853	Millard Fillmore
1853–1857	Franklin Pierce
1857–1861	James Buchanan
1861–1865	Abraham Lincoln

1881	James A. Garfield
1881–1885	Chester A. Arthur
1885–1889	S. Grover Cleveland
1889–1893	Benjamin Harrison
1893–1897	S. Grover Cleveland
1897–1901	William McKinley
1901–1909	Theodore Roosevelt
1909–1913	William H. Taft
1913–1921	Woodrow Wilson
1921–1923	Warren G. Harding
1923–1929	Calvin Coolidge
1929–1933	Herbert Hoover
1933–1945	Franklin D. Roosevelt
1945–1953	Harry S. Truman
1953–1961	Dwight D. Eisenhower
1961–1963	John F. Kennedy

John F. Kennedy

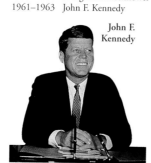

Abraham Lincoln

1865–1869	Andrew Johnson
1869–1877	Ulysses S. Grant
1877–1881	Rutherford B. Hayes

1963–1969	Lyndon B. Johnson
1969–1974	Richard Nixon
1974–1977	Gerald Ford
1977–1981	Jimmy Carter
1981–1989	Ronald Reagan
1989–1993	George Bush
1993–2001	William Clinton
2001–	George W. Bush

RUSSIAN MONARCHS

Until the Bolshevik Revolution in 1917, Russia was a monarchy in which the Tsar or Tsarina held absolute power. Today, supreme power lies with an elected president.

1462–1505	Ivan III, the Great
1505–1533	Basil III
1533–1584	Ivan IV, the Terrible
1584–1598	Fyodor I
1598–1605	Boris Godunov
1605	Fyodor II

1605–1606	Demetrius
1606–1610	Basil IV (Shuiski)
1610–1613	Interregnum (interval in reigns)
1613–1645	Michael Romanov
1645–1676	Alexis
1676–1682	Fyodor III
1682–1689	Ivan V and Peter I, the Great
1689–1725	Peter I, the Great
1725–1727	Catherine I
1727–1730	Peter II
1730–1740	Anna
1740–1741	Ivan VI
1741–1762	Elizabeth
1762	Peter III
1762–1796	Catherine II, the Great
1796–1801	Paul I
1801–1825	Alexander I
1825–1855	Nicholas I
1855–1881	Alexander II
1881–1894	Alexander III
1894–1917	Nicholas II
1917	Bolshevik Revolution

Kremlin Cathedral of the Annunciation

RUSSIAN LEADERS

1917–1922	Vladimir Lenin
1922–1953	Joseph Stalin
1953–1964	Nikita Khrushchev
1964–1982	Leonid Brezhnev
1982–1984	Yuri Andropov
1984–1985	Konstantin Chernenko
1985–1992	Mikhail Gorbachev
1992–1999	Boris Yeltsin
1999–	Vladimir Putin

Mikhail Gorbachev

	600	850	1100	1175	1250	1350
AFRICA	**622** Year One of Islamic calendar **637** Muslims conquer Jerusalem **c.700** Kingdom of Ghana prospers, West Africa	**900** Hausa kingdom of Daura founded in northern Nigeria **1054** Ghana conquered by Muslim Almoravid dynasty	**c.1100** First stone settlements in Zimbabwe **1169** Saladin becomes ruler of Egypt	**1187** Saladin recaptures Jerusalem from Crusaders **1235** Sundiata Keita founds Mali Empire, West Africa	**1250** Mamelukes (rebel slave-soldiers) become rulers of Egypt **1291** Saracens recapture the city of Acre, ending the Crusades	**1352** Moroccan scholar Ibn Battuta makes his great journey across Sahara to Mali **1432** Portuguese explorers reach the Azores
ASIA	**647** Central Asian Hun tribes invade India, causing decline of Gupta Empire **786–809** Harun al-Rashid is caliph of Baghdad **794** Kyoto, ancient capital of Japan, is established	**888** Chola dynasty of Tamil kings replaces the Pallavas in southern India and Sri Lanka **935–41** Civil war in Japan **960** Song dynasty takes over China **Chola statue**	**1104** Christian crusaders capture the city of Acre, Israel **1156** Civil war between rival clans in Japan leads to domination by samurai warlords	**1175** Zen Buddhism introduced to Japan **1206** Genghis Khan founds Mongol Empire **1232** Explosive rockets used in war between Chinese and conquering Mongols **1237** Mongol army begins to conquer Russia	**1290** Ottomans (Turkish Muslims) rise to power **c.1294** Persians convert to Islam **1340** Hindu Kushan Empire in India becomes centre of resistance to Islam **Mongol quiver**	**1368** Hong Wu (Ming) drives Mongols from China **1397** Mongol leader Tamerlane invades Delhi, India **1404** Chinese admiral Zheng Ho sets off on his first voyage **1405** Fall of Mongol Empire
EUROPE	**711** Moors invade Spain and Portugal **732** Frankish leader Charles Martel defeats the Moors and halts Islam's spread to Europe **800** Charlemagne is crowned first Holy Roman Emperor **Peruvian tapestry**	**843** Kenneth MacAlpine unites Scotland **997** Stephen I becomes first King of Hungary **1000** Viking Leif Eriksson reaches North America **1066** William of Normandy invades England to claim throne **1096** First Crusade begins	**1119** Bologna University founded, Italy **1143** Alfonso Henriques becomes first king of Portugal **Toltec pyramid**	**1202–04** Fourth Crusaders sack Constantinople **1209** St. Francis founds Franciscan Order **1215** King John of England seals Magna Carta **1215** St. Dominic founds Dominican Order	**1273** Rudolf Habsburg becomes ruler of Germany, founding the Habsburg dynasty **1337** 100 Years' War begins between England and France **1347** Plague (Black Death) reaches Europe	**1358** The *Jacquerie*: French peasants revolt against raised taxes **1381** Peasants' Revolt in England **1415** Battle of Agincourt: English defeat French **1429** Siege of Orléans, lifted by Joan of Arc's forces
AMERICAS	**700** Peruvians weave wool tapestries	**980** Toltecs set up capital at Tula, Mexico **1000** Chimu civilization founded, Peru	**1151** Fall of Toltec Empire in Mexico	**c.1200** Cuzco, Peru, becomes an Inca centre **c.1200** First farmers settle along Mississippi banks	**c.1250** Mayans build new capital at Mayapán **1325** Aztecs found their capital at Tenochtitlán	**1350** Acamapitzin becomes Aztec ruler **1438** Inca overlord Pachacuti enlarges Inca Empire
OCEANIA	**c.700** Easter Islanders begin to build stone ceremonial platforms	**950** Polynesian navigator Kupe arrives in New Zealand **c.1000** Maoris in New Zealand	**1100s** Giant carved stone statues first erected on Easter Island, South Pacific		**c.1250** Religious assembly platforms built throughout Polynesian Islands	**1350** Maoris create rock art in New Zealand

FRENCH MONARCHS

CAROLINGIAN
936–954 Louis IV
954–986 Lothair
986–987 Louis V

CAPET
987–996 Hugh Capet
996–1031 Robert II
1031–1060 Henry I
1060–1108 Philip I
1108–1137 Louis VI
1137–1180 Louis VII
1180–1223 Philip II
1223–1226 Louis VIII
1226–1270 Louis IX
1270–1285 Philip III
1285–1314 Philip IV
1314–1316 Louis X
1316 John I
1316–1322 Philip V
1322–1328 Charles IV

VALOIS
1328–1350 Philip VI
1350–1364 John II
1364–1380 Charles V
1380–1422 Charles VI
1422–1461 Charles VII
1461–1483 Louis XI
1483–1498 Charles VIII
1498–1515 Louis XII
1515–1547 Francis I
1547–1559 Henry II
1559–1560 Francis II
1560–1574 Charles IX
1574–1589 Henry III

BOURBON
1589–1610 Henry IV
1610–1643 Louis XIII
1643–1715 Louis XIV

1715–1774 Louis XV
1774–1792 Louis XVI

1792–1804 FIRST REPUBLIC

FIRST EMPIRE
1804–1814 Napoleon I

Henry IV

BOURBON
1814–1824 Louis XVIII
1824–1830 Charles X
1830–1848 Louis Philippe

1848–1852 SECOND REPUBLIC

SECOND EMPIRE
1852–1870 Napoleon III

Napoleon I

FRENCH PRESIDENTS

THIRD REPUBLIC
1871–1873 Adolphe Thiers
1873–1879 Patrice de MacMahon
1879–1887 Jules Grévy
1887–1894 Marie François Sadi-Carnot
1894–1895 Jean Casimir-Périer
1895–1899 François Félix Faure
1899–1906 Emile Loubet
1906–1913 Armand Fallières
1913–1920 Raymond Poincaré
1920 Paul Deschanel
1920–1924 Alexandre Millerand
1924–1931 Gaston Doumergue
1931–1932 Paul Doumer
1932–1940 Albert Lebrun

VICHY GOVERNMENT
1940–1944 Henri Philippe Pétain

PROVISIONAL GOVERNMENT
1944–1946 Charles de Gaulle
1946 Félix Gouin
1946 Georges Bidault

FOURTH REPUBLIC
1947–1954 Vincent Auriol
1954–1959 René Coty

FIFTH REPUBLIC
1959–1969 Charles de Gaulle
1969–1974 Georges Pompidou
1974–1981 Valéry Giscard d'Estaing
1981–1995 François Mitterrand
1995– Jacques Chirac

Jacques Chirac

SPANISH MONARCHS

1479–1516 Ferdinand II of Aragon
1474–1504 Isabella of Castile

HABSBURG
1516–1556 Charles I
1556–1598 Philip II
1598–1621 Philip III
1621–1665 Philip IV
1665–1700 Charles II

BOURBON
1700–1724 Philip V (abdicated)
1724 Louis I
1724–1746 Philip V (restored)
1746–1759 Ferdinand VI
1759–1788 Charles III
1788–1808 Charles IV
1808 Ferdinand VII
1808–1813 Joseph Bonaparte
1814–1833 Ferdinand VII
1833–1868 Isabella II
1870–1873 Amadeus of Savoy

1873–1874 FIRST REPUBLIC

BOURBON
1874–1885 Alfonso XII
1885–1886 Maria Cristina (Regent)
1886–1931 Alfonso XIII

1931–1939 SECOND REPUBLIC

1939–1975 Francisco Franco (Dictator)

BOURBON
1975– Juan Carlos

Ferdinand of Aragon and Isabella of Castile

	1450	1500	1550	1600	1640	1700
AFRICA	**1464** Sonni Ali becomes ruler of Songhai, West Africa / **1488** Portuguese navigator Bartholomeu Diaz rounds Cape of Good Hope, South Africa	**1500s** Bantus in southern Africa trade with Europeans / **1500s** Hausa states develop in West Africa / **1517** Egypt and Syria conquered by Ottomans	**1591** Moroccans and European mercenaries destroy Songhai Empire / Ottoman plate	**1600s** All major European powers establish trading posts on African coast	**1651** Dutch found Cape colony in southern Africa / **1690s** Ashanti kingdom established on Gold Coast, Africa / Ashanti golden eagles	**1712** Rise of Futa Jalon kingdom in West Africa
ASIA	**1453** Constantinople falls, ending Byzantine Empire / **1467** Onin War, lasting over 100 years, begins in Japan	**1502** Safavid dynasty begins in Persia / **1520–21** Portuguese traders reach China / **1526** Babur becomes first Mughal Emperor of India / **1546** Burma united under King Tabin Shweti	**1566** Height of Ottoman Empire / **1577** Akbar the Great completes unification of northern India / **1592** Japan invades Korea under commander Hideyoshi	**1603** Tokugawa brings peace to Japan / **1602** Dutch East India company founded / **1632** Building of Taj Mahal begins, India / **1639** Japan closed to foreigners	**1644** Manchu (Qing) dynasty founded, China / **1658** Reign of Aurangzeb, last great Mughal emperor, begins in India / **1688** Genroku period begins, Japan / Louis XIV of France	**1707** Fall of Mughal Empire / **1727** Coffee first grown, Brazil / **1727** Border fixed between Russia and China / **1746** War between British and French colonists, India
EUROPE	Gutenberg Bible / **1450s** Johannes Gutenberg produces first printed books in Europe	**c.1503** Leonardo da Vinci paints Mona Lisa / **1512** Michelangelo completes ceiling of Sistine Chapel / **1517** Protestant Reformation / **1520** Suleiman I begins reign over Ottoman Empire / **1533** Ivan IV, the Terrible begins reign, Russia	**1572** St. Bartholomew's Day massacre of Protestants, France / **1579** Seven provinces unite in Union of Utrecht, Netherlands / **1588** English fleet defeats Spanish Armada / **1598** Edict of Nantes, France, gives Catholics and Huguenots equal rights	**1603** James VI unites Scotland and England / **1604** Russians settle in Siberia / **1610** Assassination of King Henry IV of France / **1618** Beginning of Thirty Years War, Europe	**1642–49** English Civil War, ending in the execution of King Charles I / **1643** Louis XIV begins reign, France / **1677** Ottoman Empire at war with Russia / **1682** Peter the Great begins reign, Russia	**1700** Great Northern War, Scandinavia / **1700s** Enlightenment begins / **1701–13** War of Spanish Succession / **1740** Frederick the Great becomes King of Prussia / **1741** Vitus Bering explores strait between Russia and Alaska
AMERICAS	**1492** Christopher Columbus arrives in the Caribbean / **1499** Amerigo Vespucci explores the Amazon	**1519** Ferdinand Magellan sails across Pacific Ocean / **1534** Jacques Cartier sails St. Lawrence River, Canada	**1579** Francis Drake establishes British claim to west coast of North America	**1609** Henry Hudson sails up Hudson River / **1620** Mayflower sails to America from England	**1675** War between colonists and Native Americans devastates New England	**1709** Mass emigration of Germans to America begins / **1739** Slave uprising in South Carolina
OCEANIA	**c.1450** Tongo people their ceremonial centre, South Pacific	**1526** Portuguese landings in Polynesia	**1567** Spanish explorer Mendaña is first European to reach Soloman Islands	**1606** Luis Vaez de Torres sails between Australia and New Guinea	**1642** Explorer Abel Tasman reaches Tasmania and New Zealand	**1722** Dutch navigator Jacob Roggeveen reaches Samoa and Easter Island

AUSTRALIAN PRIME MINISTERS

1901–1903	Edmund Barton		1941–1945	John J. Curtin
1903–1904	Alfred Deakin		1945	Francis M. Forde
1904	John C. Watson		1945–1949	Joseph B. Chifley
1904–1905	George Houston Reid		1949–1966	Robert G. Menzies
1905–1908	Alfred Deakin		1966–1967	Harold E. Holt
1908–1909	Andrew Fisher		1967–1968	John McEwen
1909–1910	Alfred Deakin		1968–1971	John Grey Gorton
1910–1913	Andrew Fisher		1971–1972	William McMahon
1913–1914	Joseph Cook		1972–1975	E. Gough Whitlam
1914–1915	Andrew Fisher		1975–1983	J. Malcolm Fraser
1915–1923	William M. Hughes		1983–1991	Robert Hawke
1923–1929	Stanley M. Bruce		1991–1996	Paul J. Keating
1929–1932	James H. Scullin		1996–	John Howard
1932–1939	Joseph A. Lyons			
1939	Earle Page			
1939–1941	Robert G. Menzies			
1941	Arthur W. Fadden			

Robert Menzies

CANADIAN PRIME MINISTERS

1867–1873	John A. Macdonald
1873–1878	Alexander Mackenzie
1878–1891	John A. Macdonald
1891–1892	John J.C. Abbott
1892–1894	John S. Thompson
1894–1896	Mackenzie Bowell
1896	Charles Tupper
1896–1911	Wilfred Laurier
1911–1920	Robert Laird Borden
1920–1921	Arthur Meighen
1921–1926	W. L. Mackenzie King
1926	Arthur Meighen
1926–1930	W. L. Mackenzie King
1930–1935	Richard B. Bennett
1935–1948	W. L. Mackenzie King
1948–1957	Louis St. Laurent
1957–1963	John G. Diefenbaker
1963–1968	Lester B. Pearson
1968–1979	Pierre E. Trudeau
1979–1980	C. Joseph Clark
1980–1984	Pierre E. Trudeau
1984	John N. Turner
1984–1993	M. Brian Mulroney
1993	Kim Campbell
1993–2003	Jean Chrétien
2003–	Paul Martin

Pierre Trudeau

NEW ZEALAND PRIME MINISTERS

1856	Henry Sewell		1879–82	John Hall		1935–40	Michael J. Savage
1856	William Fox		1882–83	Frederick Whitaker		1940–49	Peter Fraser
1856–61	Edward W. Stafford		1883–84	Harry A. Atkinson		1949–57	Sidney G. Holland
1861–62	William Fox		1884	Robert Stout		1957	Keith J. Holyoake
1862–63	Alfred Domett		1884	Harry A. Atkinson		1957–60	Walter Nash
1863–64	Frederick Whitaker		1884–87	Robert Stout		1960–72	Keith J. Holyoake
1864–65	Frederick A. Weld		1887–91	Harry A. Atkinson		1972	John Marshall
1865–69	Edward W. Stafford		1891–93	John Ballance		1972–74	Norman Kirk
1869–72	William Fox		1893–06	Richard J. Seddon		1974–75	Wallace E. Rowling
1872	Edward W. Stafford		1906	William Hall-Jones		1975–84	Robert D. Muldoon
1872–73	George M. Waterhouse		1906–12	Joseph G. Ward		1984–89	David Lange
1873	William Fox		1912	Thomas Mackenzie		1989–90	Geoffrey Palmer
1873–75	Julius Vogel		1912–25	William F. Massey		1990	Michael Moore
1875–76	Daniel Pollen		1925	Francis H. Bell		1990–97	James Bolger
1876	Julius Vogel		1925–28	Joseph G. Coates		1997–99	Jenny Shipley
1876–77	Harry A. Atkinson		1928–30	Joseph G. Ward		1999–	Helen Clark
1877–79	George Grey		1930–35	George W. Forbes			

	1750	1790	1830	1845	1860	1880
AFRICA	**1768** Ali Bey becomes ruler of independent Egypt	**1822** Liberia founded as a home for freed slaves **1824–27** First Ashanti War between British and Ashanti of Gold Coast, Ghana	**1830** British and Boers clash in South Africa **1830** French invade Algeria **1836** Great Trek of Boer farmers, South Africa	**1847** British defeat Bantus in southern Africa **1855** David Livingstone arrives in Victoria Falls; this sparks off European exploration of African interior	**1869** Suez Canal opens **1879** Zulu War: British defeat Zulus, South Africa	**1880–81** First Boer War **1895–96** Italy and Ethiopia at war: Ethiopia wins **1899–1902** Second Boer War: Britain wins control of South Africa
ASIA	**1751** China conquers Tibet **1757** Battle of Plassey: British conquer Bengal	**1819** Singapore founded by Stamford Raffles **1824** Britain and Burma at war	**1839** Treaty of Nanking opens Chinese ports to British trade and gives Hong Kong to Britain	**1853** USA forces Japan to open up to foreign trade **1857–58** Indian Mutiny: Indian soldiers in British army rebel against the British	**1861** Empress Tze Hsi begins 47-year rule of China **1872** Samurai's feudal control in Japan ends	**1885** Indian National Congress Party founded **1899–1900** Boxer Rebellion of Chinese peasants
EUROPE	**1756–63** Seven Years' War **1762** Catherine the Great begins reign in Russia **1771** Russia conquers Crimea **1789** Storming of the Bastille; French Revolution underway	**1800** Union of Britain and Ireland **1804** Napoleon Bonaparte becomes Emperor of France **1792–1815** Napoleonic wars **1815** Battle of Waterloo ends Napoleon's reign	**1830** July Revolution overthrows Charles X of France **1832** First Reform Act extends voting rights in Britain **1837** Queen Victoria begins reign, Britain	**1845** Potato famine begins in Ireland **1848** Year of Revolution in Europe **1853–56** Crimean War: Britain and France defeat Russia **1859–61** War of Italian unification	**1864** International Red Cross founded **1866** Austro–Prussian War **1870–71** Franco–Prussian War: France defeated **1871** Britain legalizes trade unions **1871** Otto von Bismarck unites German Empire	**1884** Berlin conference decides colonial divisions in Africa **1896** Modern Olympic Games begin in Greece **1897** Greece and Turkey at war
AMERICAS	**1759** Battle of Quebec **1763** Native American uprising against British, North America **1775–83** American Revolution **1776** Declaration of Independence signed, USA	**1791** Revolution in Haiti led by Pierre Toussaint L'Ouverture **1810–22** Many South American countries gain independence **1812–14** Anglo–American war	**1832** Samuel Morse invents electric telegraph **1836** Texas wins independence from Mexico **1842** General anaesthetic first used by US surgeon Crawford Long	**1846–48** Mexican–American War: USA victorious **1848** Californian Gold Rush **1848** First US women's rights convention, New York State	**1861–65** American Civil War **1867** Dominion of Canada created **1876** Battle of Little Bighorn: Native Americans defeat US Army	**1890** Battle of Wounded Knee: last massacre of Native Americans in USA **1896** Gold struck in Klondike, Canada **1898** Spanish–American War
OCEANIA	**1769** James Cook claims New Zealand & Australia for Britain **1788** British colony of New South Wales founded, Australia	**1817** First European free emigrants arrive to settle Australian grasslands	**1840** British and Maoris in New Zealand sign Treaty of Waitangi	**1850** Australian Colonies Act **1851** Australian Gold Rush	**1860–70** Maoris fight white settlers in New Zealand	**1893** New Zealand becomes first country to give women the right to vote

Tibetan mask

Zulu shield

French soldier's hat

Native American warrior's weapons

MAJOR WARS

DATE	CONFLICT	VICTOR(S)	LOSER(S)
c.1096–1291	Crusades	Muslims	European Christians
c.1337–1453	Hundred Years' War	France	England
1455–1485	Wars of the Roses	House of Lancaster	House of York
1618–1648	Thirty Years' War	European Protestants	European Catholics
1642–1649	English Civil War	Parlimentarians	Royalists
1700–1721	Great Northern War	Russia	Sweden
1701–1713	War of the Spanish Succession	Austria	France
1756–1763	Seven Years War	Britain, Prussia, Hanover	Austria, France Russia, Sweden
1792–1815	Napoleonic Wars	Austria, Britain, Russia, Prussia, Sweden	France
1812–1814	War of 1812	USA	Britain
1846–1848	Mexican–American War	USA	Mexico
1853–1856	Crimean War	Britain, France, Sardinia, Turkey	Russia
1861–1865	American Civil War	Unionists	Confederates
1870–1871	Franco–Prussian War	Prussia	France
1880–1902	Boer Wars	British Commonwealth	Boers
1894–1895	Chinese–Japanese War	Japan	China
1904–1905	Russo–Japanese War	Japan	Russia
1914–1918	World War I	British Commonwealth Belgium, Italy, France, Russia, USA	Germany, Austria, Hungary, Turkey
1931–1933	Chinese–Japanese War	Japan	China
1936–1939	Spanish Civil War	Nationalists	Republicans
1939–1945	World War II	British Commonwealth, USSR, USA	Germany, Italy, Japan
1950–1953	Korean War	South Korea, UN	North Korea
1954–1975	Vietnam War	North Vietnam	South Vietnam, USA
1967	Six-Day War	Israel	Egypt
1967–1970	Nigerian Civil War	Federalists	Biafrans
1973	October War	Israel	Arab Nations
1980–1988	Iran–Iraq War	Negotiated ceasefire	
1990–1991	Gulf War	UN forces	Iraq
1992–1995	Bosnian Civil War	Negotiated ceasefire	
2002	War in Afghanistan	US-led coalition	Taliban
2003	Iraq War	US-led coalition	Iraq

MAJOR REVOLUTIONS

DATE	REVOLUTION	VICTOR(S)	LOSER(S)
1775–1783	American	American colonies	Britain
1789	French	Jacobins	Royalists
1917	Russian	Bolsheviks	Royalists
1945–1949	Chinese	Communists	Nationalists

MAJOR BATTLES

DATE	NAME (COUNTRY)	VICTOR(S)	LOSER(S)
1066	Hastings (England)	Normans	Saxons
1415	Agincourt (France)	England	France
1429	Siege of Orléans (France)	France	England
1571	Lepanto	Christians	Turks
1588	Spanish Armada (England)	England	Spain
1757	Plassey (India)	Britain	India
1777	Saratoga (USA)	USA	Britain
1805	Trafalgar	Britain	France, Spain
1805	Austerlitz (Czech Republic)	France	Austria, Russia
1815	Waterloo (Belgium)	Britain, Holland, Belgium, Prussia	France
1854	Balaclava (Crimea)	Britain	Russia
1863	Gettysburg (USA)	Unionists	Confederates
1940	Britain	Britain	Germany
1942	Midway (Pacific)	USA	Japan
1943	Stalingrad (Russia)	USSR	Germany
1944	Normandy (France)	USA, British Commonwealth	Germany
1954	Dien Bien Phu (Vietnam)	Vietnam	France
1991	Operation Desert Storm (Iraq)	UN forces	Iraq

	1900	1911	1918	1930	1939	1942
AFRICA	**1902** Ovimbundu people of Angola revolt against Portuguese rule **1910** Union of South Africa formed from former Boer republics	**1912** African National Congress formed **1917** Revolt against French rule; Chad forces three-year French withdrawal	**1922** Discovery of tomb of Tutankhamun, Egypt **1922** Egypt wins independence from Britain **1923** Ethiopia joins League of Nations	**1930** Ras Tafari is crowned Haile Selassie in Ethiopia **1935** Italy invades Ethiopia **Haile Selassie**	**1941** Allied troops overrun Italy's African colonies **1941** German troops led by Erwin Rommel arrive in Libya to help Italy	**1942** Allied troops arrive in El Alamein, Egypt, and force Rommel's troops to retreat across North Africa **1945** League of Arab States founded
ASIA	**1901** Peace of Peking ends Boxer Rebellion in China **1904–1905** Japan wins Russo–Japanese War	**1911** Chinese Revolution overthrows Manchu dynasty **1915** Mohandas Gandhi becomes leader of the Indian National Congress Party	**1919** Amritsar Massacre: British fire on peaceful Indian protest **1923** Ottoman Empire ends	**1931–33** Chinese–Japanese War: Japan victorious **1934–35** Long March in China	**1941–42** Japan takes over US, British, and Dutch colonies in Indian and Pacific Oceans	**1944** Japan attacks India but is defeated at Kohima **1945** USA drops first atomic bombs on Japanese cities of Hiroshima and Nagasaki
EUROPE	**1903** Militant women's suffrage. **1904** "Entente Cordiale" (friendly understanding) between Britain and France **1905** Imperial troops crush workers' uprising, Russia **1905** Norway becomes independent	**1912–13** Balkan Wars **1914–18** World War I **1916** Irish rising against British rule **1917** Russian Revolution: Russia becomes first communist state **Russian flag**	**1918–21** Russian Civil War **1923** Ireland wins partial independence from Britain **1924** Stalin becomes leader of USSR **1926** General strike in Britain	**1933** Adolf Hitler becomes German Chancellor **1936** Germany hosts Olympic Games in Berlin **1936** Italy signs alliance with Germany **1936–39** Spanish Civil War **1938** Germany takes over Czechoslovakia	**1939–45** World War II **1940** Germany occupies Denmark, Norway, France, Belgium, and the Netherlands **1940** British air force prevents German invasion of Britain **1941** Germans move into Eastern Europe	**1943** Allies invade Italy **1943–44** Germans driven out of Russia **1944** Allies invade France and drive back Germans **1945** German forces surrender **Nazi flag bearer**
AMERICAS	**1902** British and German fleets seize Venezuelan navy **1906** Earthquake hits San Francisco, USA **1909** US explorer Robert Peary claims to have reached North Pole	**1912–33** US troops occupy Nicaragua **1914** Panama Canal opens **1915–16** US troops put down uprising in Haiti **1917** USA joins Britain and France in World War I	**1920** Women gain vote in USA **1920** Sale of alcohol prohibited in USA **1924** US military planes make first airborne trip around the world **1929** Wall Street Crash	**1931** Canada gains full independence from Britain **1931** Empire State Building built, New York **1933** Alcohol ban lifted, USA **1933** Fulgencio Batista becomes ruler of Cuba	**1940** Xerox machine invented **1941** US navy attacked by Japanese planes at Pearl Harbor, Hawaii **1941** USA joins Allies in war against Germany and Japan	**1942** Enrico Fermi builds first nuclear reactor, USA **1943** Argentine Revolution brings Juan Perón to power **1945** USA tests first atomic bomb in New Mexico
OCEANIA	**1901** Commonwealth of Australia proclaimed **Australian coins, 1910**	**1914** Australia and New Zealand join Allies in World War I	**1919** Australia acquires former German colonies in the Pacific **1927** Canberra becomes the capital of Australia	**1937** Royal New Zealand Air Force formed	**1939** Australia and New Zealand join Allied forces	**1942** Japanese bomb Darwin, Australia, and invade New Guinea and part of Papua

947

BLACK CIVIL RIGHTS

1600–1810 Ten million Africans are taken to the Americas as slaves

1823–1833 Anti-slavery society set up in Britain to end slavery in the colonies

1909 W. E. B. Du Bois (1868–1963) helps found National Association for the Advancement of Coloured People to end racial inequality in the USA

1912 African National Congress (ANC) founded in South Africa to secure racial equality and black representation in parliament

1914 Marcus Garvey (1887–1940) founds Universal Negro Improvement Association in Harlem, New York

1925 A. Philip Randolph (1889–1979) organizes and leads the first successful black trade union

1950–1959 Apartheid laws set up in South Africa. These discriminate against blacks and "coloureds"

1954 US Supreme Court rules that segregated education (by colour) is "inherently unequal"

1955 Martin Luther King (1929–68) organizes campaign to desegregate bus service in Montgomery, Alabama

1960 69 people die in the Sharpeville Massacre during a protest against South Africa's racist "Pass Laws"

1964 Nelson Mandela (b. 1918), leader of military wing of ANC, jailed for life in South Africa

1965–1968 US Congress outlaws discrimination. Martin Luther King is assassinated in 1968

1989 F. W. De Klerk, president of South Africa, lifts ban on ANC and releases Nelson Mandela (1990)

1994 First all-party elections take place in South Africa. Nelson Mandela becomes president

Nelson Mandela, voting in 1994 election in South Africa

WOMEN'S VOTING RIGHTS

Although not a country, the Isle of Man was the first place to give women the vote in 1880. Certain states of the USA gave women the vote at earlier dates (Wyoming in 1869, Colorado in 1894, Utah in 1895, and Idaho in 1896), but it was not given nationally until 1920.

COUNTRY	FIRST VOTE
New Zealand	1893
Australia	1902
Finland	1906
Norway	1913
Denmark	1915
Iceland	1915
Netherlands	1917
USSR	1917
Great Britain	1918
Austria	1918
Canada	1918
Germany	1918
Poland	1918
Czechoslovakia	1920

British suffragette, Emmeline Pankhurst

FIRST WOMEN PRIME MINISTERS AND PRESIDENTS

Indira Gandhi

NAME	COUNTRY	DATES
Sirimavo Bandaranaike (PM)	Ceylon (Sri Lanka)	1960–1965/1970–1977
Indira Gandhi (PM)	India	1966–1977/1980–1984
Golda Meir (PM)	Israel	1969–1974
María Estella Perón (President)	Argentina	1974–1976
Elisabeth Domitien (PM)	Central African Republic	1975
Margaret Thatcher (PM)	UK	1979–1990
Dr. Maria de Lurdes Pintassilgo (PM)	Portugal	1979
Vigdís Finnbogadóttir (President)	Iceland	1980–1996
Mary Eugenia Charles (PM)	Dominica	1980–1993
Gro Harlem Brundtland (PM)	Norway	1981/1986–1989
Corazon Aquino (PM)	Philippines	1986–1992

	1947	1953	1960	1967	1976	1986–Present day
AFRICA	**1950** Group Areas Act legalizes apartheid, South Africa **1951** Libyan independence from Italy sanctioned by UN	**1956** Suez Crisis: Egyptian troops force French and British to withdraw **1957** Pass Laws in South Africa state that all non-whites must carry passes	**1960** 17 African colonies gain independence **1962** UN imposes sanctions on South Africa **1964** ANC leader Nelson Mandela is jailed for life	**1967–70** Civil war in Nigeria **1967** Dr. Christiaan Barnard completes first heart transplant in South Africa	**1976** Riots in black townships across South Africa **1979** Ugandan leader Idi Amin ousted by Tanzanian-backed rebels **1983** Famine in Ethiopia	**1990s** AIDS and HIV-related illness escalates dramatically **1994** ANC wins South Africa's first free elections and Nelson Mandela is first black president **2002** Elections in Zimbabwe spark international controversy
ASIA	**1947** India and Pakistan win independence from Britain **1948** State of Israel founded **1949** Mao proclaims new Communist Republic of China	**1953** Edmund Hillary and Tenzing Norgay climb Everest **1954** Vietnam divided into communist North and US-backed South	**1954–75** Vietnam War **1966** Cultural Revolution begins in China *Model of Vostok I*	**1967** Six-Day War between Israelis and Arabs **1971** Independent state of Bangladesh founded **1973** Arab–Israeli War	**1976** North and South Vietnam reunited **1979** Iranian Revolution **1980–88** Iran–Iraq War	**1989** Pro-democracy movement in Beijing's Tiananmen Square **1990–91** Gulf War **1995** Israel's prime minister Yitzhak Rabin is assassinated
EUROPE	**1948** Communist coup in Czechoslovakia **1949** Germany split into East and West **1949** NATO formed **Nato flag**	**1955** Warsaw Pact signed by Communist nations **1956** Soviet troops put down anti-communist uprising in Hungary **1957** European Economic Community formed	**1961** Berlin Wall built **1961** Russian cosmonaut Yuri Gagarin is first person in space in *Vostok I*	**1968** Anti-communist uprising in Prague crushed **1968** Student riots in Paris **1969** Britain sends troops to Northern Ireland **1971** Women gain the right to vote, Switzerland	**1979** Margaret Thatcher becomes Britain's first woman prime minister **Margaret Thatcher**	**1989** Berlin wall demolished **1989** Communism overthrown in eastern Europe **1991** Break-up of Soviet Union **1992–96** Civil war in former Yugoslavia **2001** Euro launched in 12 EU countries
AMERICAS	**1950** US senator Joseph McCarthy begins anti-communist "witch-hunts"	**1955** Black people in Alabama, USA boycott segregated buses **1955** Military coup in Argentina overthrows President Juan Perón **1959** Revolution in Cuba brings Fidel Castro to power	**1962** Cuban Missile Crisis **1962** Jamaica wins independence from Britain **1963** President John F. Kennedy is assassinated **1965** Civil rights leader Malcolm X is assassinated	**1968** Civil rights leader Martin Luther King is assassinated **1969** Neil Armstrong is the first person to walk on the moon **1974** US president Richard Nixon resigns over Watergate scandal	**1979** Marxist Sandinistas take power in Nicaragua **1982** Falklands War: Britain defeats Argentine forces **1982** Canada creates constitution independent of UK	**1989** USA invades Panama **1993** Canada creates Nunavut, its largest Native territory **2001** Terrorists destroy the World Trade Center, USA
OCEANIA	**1947** South Pacific Commission formed **1951** Australia, New Zealand, and USA sign ANZUS Pact	**1956** British nuclear testing in Maralinga, Australia **1959** Antarctic Treaty preserves area for research	**1960** Aborigines granted the same social security benefits as the rest of Australian society and gain full voting rights two years later	**1967** New Zealand vote extends to 20-year-olds **1975** Papua New Guinea becomes independent	**1985** *Rainbow Warrior*, a Greenpeace ship, is sunk by pro-nuclear protesters in New Zealand	*Rainbow Warrior*

INDEX
AND
CREDITS

GAZETTEER

HOW TO USE THE GAZETTEER

The gazetteer helps you to find places on the maps in the encyclopedia. For identification, all places that are not cities or towns are followed by a brief description.

Grid references help locate the names on the maps. For example, if you look up Nairobi in the gazetteer, you will see the reference 24 D9. The first number, 24, is the page number of the map on which Nairobi appears. The second number, D9, shows that it is in the square D9 of the grid printed over the map. Turn to page 24. Trace down from the letter D at the top of the grid and across from the number 9 along the side of the grid. You will find Nairobi in the square where the letter and number meet.

The following abbreviations have been used in the gazetteer:

abbrev.	=	abbreviation	N	= North
Ben.	=	Bengali	off.	= officially
Cam.	=	Cambodian	prev.	= previously
C	=	Central	Rus.	= Russian
E	=	East	S	= South
Fr.	=	French	St	= Saint
Ger.	=	German	W	= West
L.	=	Lake, Lago, Lac	Wel.	= Welsh
Mts.	=	Mountains		

A

Aachen Germany 379 A6
Aalst Belgium 126 C2
Aarau Switzerland 819 C5
Aare *River* Switzerland 819 B5
Aba Nigeria 33 I9
Ābādān Iran 463 E6
Abashiri Japan 478 G2
Abéché Chad 20 E4
Abengourou Ivory Coast 33 F8
Åbenrå Denmark 258 B6
Abeokuta Nigeria 33 H8
Aberdeen Scotland, UK 858 D4
Aberystwyth Wales, UK 858 C9
Abhā Saudi Arabia 406 C7
Abidjan Ivory Coast 33 F9
Abu Dhabi *Capital* United Arab Emirates 406 H4
Abuja *Capital* Nigeria 33 I7
Abū Kamāl Syria 821 I4
Åbybro Denmark 258 C2
Acapulco Mexico 551 H7
Acarai Mountains *Mountain range* Brazil/Guyana 791 H5
Acarigua Venezuela 791 E2
Accra *Capital* Ghana 33 G9
Achacachi Bolivia 141 B4
Acharnés Greece 403 D7
Acklins Island *Island* Bahamas 172 E3
Aconcagua *Peak* Argentina 787
A Coruña Spain 798 B2
'Adan Yemen *var.* Aden 406 D9 449 B3
Adare, Cape *Coastal feature* Antarctica 56 F7
Ad Dahnā' *Desert region* Saudi Arabia 406 D3
Ad Dakhla Western Sahara 28 A5
Addis Ababa *Capital* Ethiopia 24 E7
Adelaide Australia 95 F7
Adélie, Terre d' *Territory* Antarctica 56 H7

Aden *see* 'Adan
Aden, Gulf of *Sea feature* Indian Ocean 449 B3
Adige *River* Italy 475 D3
Adriatic Sea Mediterranean Sea 475 E4
Aegean Sea Mediterranean Sea 403 E7
Ærø *Island* Denmark 258 C6
Afghanistan *Country* C Asia 80
Africa 15
Afrīn *River* Syria/Turkey 821 E2
'Afula Israel 473 C3
Agadez Niger 33 J5
Agadir Morocco 28 C3
Agartala India 444 H5
Ağcabädi Azerbaijan 186 I5
Ağdam Azerbaijan 186 I5
Agen France 356 D7
Āgra India 444 D4
Agrigento Italy 475 D10
Agrínio Greece 403 B7
Aguarico *River* Ecuador/Peru 285 D2
Aguascalientes Mexico 551 F5
Ahaggar *Mountains* Algeria 28 G6
Ahmadābād India 444 B5
Ahvāz Iran 463 E5
Aïr *Region* Niger 33 J4
Aix-en-Provence France 356 F8
Āīzawl India 444 I5
Ajaccio Corsica, France 356 H9
Ajdābiyā Libya 28 K3
Ajmer India 444 C4
Akanthou Cyprus 821 B3
Akhalts'ikhe Georgia 186 D4
Akita Japan 478 F5
'Akko Israel 473 C2
Akmola Kazakhstan 731 D5
Akola India 444 D6
Akpatok Island *Island* Canada 169 I6
Aksai Chin *Disputed region* China/India 444 D1
Aktau Kazakhstan 731 B5
Alabama *River* Alabama, USA 864 H8

Alabama *State* USA 864 H8
Alajuela Costa Rica 193 G8
Al 'Amārah Iraq 463 D5
Åland Islands *Island group* Finland 333 A9
Al 'Aqabah Jordan 821 D10
Alaska Peninsula *Peninsula* Alaska, USA 864 B3
Alaska Range *Mountain range* Alaska, USA 864 B2
Alaska *State* USA 864 B2
Alaska, Gulf of *Sea feature* Pacific Ocean 611
Alaverdi Armenia 186 F4
Alazani *River* Azerbaijan/Georgia 186 G3
Alba Iulia Romania 727 C6
Albacete Spain 798 F5
Albania *Country* SE Europe 105
Albany Australia 95 B7
Albany New York, USA 864 K6
Albany *River* Canada 169 H8
Al Başrah Iraq 463 D6
Albatross Plateau *Undersea feature* Pacific Ocean 634 J5
Al Baydā' Libya 28 K2
Albert, Lake *Lake* Uganda/Dem. Rep. Congo 20 H8 24 C9
Alberta *Province* Canada 169 D8
Albi France 356 D7
Ålborg Denmark 258 C2
Ålborg Bugt *Sea feature* Denmark 258 D3
Alcácer do Sal Portugal 682 C9
Alcalá de Henares Spain 798 E4
Alchevs'k Ukraine 727 K4
Aldabra Group *Island group* Seychelles 449 B4
Aleg Mauritania 33 B5
Aleksinac Yugoslavia 105 I5
Alençon France 356 D3
Alessandria Italy 475 B3
Ålesund Norway 617 B6
Aleutian Islands *Islands* Alaska, USA 864 B3
Aleutian Trench *Undersea feature* Pacific Ocean 634 F3
Alexandria Egypt 24 C1
Alexandroúpoli Greece 403 F5
Alföld Plain Hungary 312 E10
Algarve *Region* Portugal 682 C11
Algeciras Spain 798 D8
Algeria *Country* N Africa 28
Alghero Italy 475 A6
Algiers *Capital* Algeria 28 F1
Al Hufūf Saudi Arabia 406 F4
Al Ḩasakah Syria 821 H2
Al Hijāz *Region* Saudi Arabia 406 B4
Al Ḩillah Iraq 463 C5
Al Ḩudaydah Yemen 406 D8
Alicante Spain 798 G6
Alice Springs Australia 95 E4
Alīgarh India 444 D4
Al Jaghbūb Libya 28 L3
Al Jawf Saudi Arabia 406 C2
Al Jazirah *Region* Iraq/Syria 821 H3
Al Karak Jordan 821 D8
Alkmaar Netherlands 601 C3
Al Khums Libya 28 I3
Al Kufrah Libya 28 L5
Al Lādhiqīyah Syria 821 D2
Allāhābād India 444 E5
Alma-Ata *Capital* Kazakhstan 731 E7
Al Madīnah Saudi Arabia 406 B4

Al Mafraq Jordan 821 E7
Almalyk Uzbekistan 80 H4
Al Marj Libya 28 K2
Al Mawşil Iraq 463 C3
Almelo Netherlands 601 E4
Almería Spain 798 F7
Al Mukallā Yemen 406 F8
Alofi *Capital* Niue 679 D6
Alor, Kepulauan *Island group* Indonesia 451 H5
Alpi Dolomitiche *Mountains* Italy 475 D2
Alps *Mountain range* C Europe 308
Al Qāmishlī Syria 821 I1
Al Qunayţirah Syria 821 D6
Altai Mountains *Mountain range* C Asia 75
Al Tall al Abyaḑ Syria 821 G2
Altamura Italy 475 G7
Altay Mongolia 566 C3
Altdorf Switzerland 819 D5
Altun Mountains *Mountain range* China 75
Al Wajh Saudi Arabia 406 B3
Alytus Lithuania 112 C6
Amakusa-shotō *Island group* Japan 478 B9
Amami-Ō-shima *Island* Japan 478 B11
Amazon *River* South America 787
Amazon Basin *River feature* Brazil 285 F3
Amazon Delta *Wetland* Brazil 787
Amazonia *Region* C South America 146 C3
Ambanja Madagascar 30 K4
Ambarchik Russian Federation 731 J2
Ambato Ecuador 285 C2
Ambon Indonesia 451 I4
Ambositra Madagascar 30 K6
Ambovombe Madagascar 30 J7
Ambriz Angola 30 A2
Ameland *Island* Netherlands 601 D1
American Samoa *External territory* USA, Pacific Ocean 679 E5
Amersfoort Netherlands 601 D5
Amery Ice Shelf *Coastal feature* Antarctica, Indian Ocean 449 D10
Amiens France 356 D2
Amman *Capital* Jordan 821 D7
Āmol Iran 463 F3
Amorgós *Island* Greece 403 F9
Amritsar India 444 C3
Amsterdam *Capital* Netherland 601 C4
Amstetten Austria 819 J3
Am Timan Chad 20 E5
Amu Darya *River* C Asia 80 F5
Amundsen Gulf *Sea feature* Canada 169 C5
Amundsen Sea Antarctica 56 B6
Amur *River* E Asia 75
Anadyr' Russian Federation 731 K1
Anambas, Kepulauan *Island group* Indonesia 451 D2
Anchorage Alaska, USA 864 C2
Ancona Italy 475 E4
Andalucía *Region* Spain 798 D7
Andaman Islands *Island group* India 449 E3

Andaman Sea Indian Ocean 449 E3
Andes *Mountain range* South America 787
Andizhan Uzbekistan 80 I4
Andong South Korea 497 D6
Andorra *Country* SW Europe 798
Andorra la Vella *Capital* Andorra 798 H2
Ándros *Island* Greece 403 E8
Andros Island *Island* Bahamas 172 D2
Angara *River* C Asia 75
Ángel de la Guarda, Isla *Island* Mexico 551 B2
Angeles Philippines 650 C4
Angel Falls *Waterfall* Venezuela 791 G4
Ångerman *River* Sweden 816 C4
Angers France 356 C4
Anglesey *Island* Wales, UK 858 C8
Angola *Country* C Africa 30
Angola Basin *Undersea feature* Atlantic Ocean 89 F8
Angoulême France 356 D6
Angren Uzbekistan 80 H3
Anguilla *External territory* UK, West Indies 172 K4
Anjouan *Island* Comoros 30 J3
Annaba Algeria 28 G1
An Nafūd *Desert region* Saudi Arabia 406 C2
An Najaf Iraq 463 C5
Annapolis Maryland, USA 864 J7
An Nāşirīyah Iraq 463 D6
Annecy France 356 G6
Anshan China 206 J4
Antalaha Madagascar 30 L4
Antananarivo *Capital* Madagascar 30 K6
Antarctic Peninsula *Peninsula* Antarctica 56 A3
Antarctica 56
Antequera Spain 798 D7
Antigua *Island* Antigua & Barbuda 172 K5
Antigua & Barbuda *Country* West Indies 172
Antofagasta Chile 65 B3
Antsiraňana Madagascar 30 L4
Antsohihy Madagascar 30 K4
Antwerpen Belgium 126 D2
Anyang South Korea 497 C6
Aomori Japan 478 F4
Aosta Italy 475 A2
Aparri Philippines 650 C2
Apeldoorn Netherlands 601 D4
Apennines *Mountain range* Italy 475 C4
Apia *Capital* Samoa 679 D5
Appalachian Mountains *Mountain range* E USA 864 I7
Appenzell Switzerland 819 D5
Apure *River* Venezuela 791 E2
Apurímac *River* Peru 285 E8
Aqaba, Gulf of *Sea feature* Red Sea 473 C12 821 C10
Āqchah Afghanistan 80 F5
Arabah, Wādī al Israel/Jordan 473 D8
Arabian Peninsula *Peninsula* Asia 75
Arabian Sea Indian Ocean 449 C2
Aracaju Brazil 146 I5
'Arad Israel 473 C7

Arad Romania 727 A5

Arafura Sea Asia/Australasia 634 C7

Araguaia *River* Brazil 146 F5

Arāk Iran 463 E4

Aral Sea *Inland sea* Kazakhstan/Uzbekistan 75

Aran Islands *Islands* Ireland 465 B5

Ararat Armenia 186 F6

Ararat, Mount *Peak* Turkey 75

Aras *River* SW Asia 186 I6

Arauca Colombia 791 D4

Arauca *River* Colombia/Venezuela 791 D3

Arbatax Italy 475 B7

Arbil Iraq 463 C3

Arctic Ocean 64

Arda *River* Bulgaria/Greece 403 E4

Ardennes *Region* W Europe 126 E4

Arendal Norway 617 B9

Arequipa Peru 285 G10

Arezzo Italy 475 D4

Argentina *Country* S South America 65

Argentine Basin *Undersea feature* Atlantic Ocean 89 C10

Argentino, Lago *Lake* Argentina 65 B10

Århus Denmark 258 C4

Arica Chile 65 B2

Arizona *State* USA 864 D8

Arkansas *River* C USA 864 G7

Arkansas *State* USA 864 G8

Arkhangel'sk Russian Federation 731 D2

Arles France 356 F8

Arlon Belgium 126 F6

Armenia *Country* SW Asia 186

Armenia Colombia 791 B4

Arnhem Netherlands 601 D5

Arnhem Land *Region* Australia 95 E2

Arno *River* Italy 475 C4

Ar Ramādī Iraq 463 C4

Arran *Island* Scotland, UK 858 B5

Ar Raqqah Syria 821 G3

Arras France 356 F2

Ar Rub' al Khali *Desert* SW Asia 406 F6

Ar Rustāq Oman 406 I4

Artashat Armenia 186 F6

Artigas Uruguay 65 E5

Artyk Turkmenistan 80 D5

Aru, Kepulauan *Island group* Indonesia 451 J4

Arua Uganda 24 C8

Aruba *External territory* Netherlands, West Indies 172 H7

Årup Denmark 258 C5

Arusha Tanzania 24 D10

Arvayheer Mongolia 566 E3

Arvidsjaur Sweden 816 D3

Asadābād Afghanistan 80 H6

Asahikawa Japan 478 F2

Asamankese Ghana 33 G9

Āsānsol India 444 G5

Ascension Island *Island* Atlantic Ocean 89 E8

Ascoli Piceno Italy 475 E5

Aseb Eritrea 24 F6

Ashburton New Zealand 606 D7

Ashdod Israel 473 B5

Ashgabat *Capital* Turkmenistan 80 C5

Ashqelon Israel 473 B6

Ashtarak Armenia 186 F5

Asia 75

Asmara *Capital* Eritrea 24 E5

Assad, Lake *Lake* Syria 821 F3

Assal, Lake *Lake* Djibouti 15

Aş Şalţ Jordan 821 D7

Assen Netherlands 601 E3

Assisi Italy 475 D5

As Sulaymānīyah Iraq 463 C3

As Sulayyil Saudi Arabia 406 E6

As Suwaydā' Syria 821 E6

Astrakhan' Russian Federation 731 B5

Astypálaia *Island* Greece 403 F9

Asunción *Capital* Paraguay 141 G9

Aswân Egypt 24 D3

Asyût Egypt 24 C2

Atacama Desert *Desert* Chile 65 B2

Atakpamé Togo 33 G8

Atâr Mauritania 33 C3

Atbara Sudan 24 D5

Athabasca, Lake *Lake* Canada 169 D7

Athens *Capital* Greece 403 D8

Athlone Ireland 465 D4

Ati Chad 20 D4

Atlanta Georgia, USA 864 I8

Atlantic Ocean 89

Atlantic-Indian Basin *Undersea feature* Atlantic Ocean 89 F12

Atlas Mountains *Mountain range* Morocco 28 D3

Aţ Ţafilah Jordan 821 D8

Aţ Ţā'if Saudi Arabia 406 C5

Attapu Laos 876 F7

Attawapiskat Canada 169 H8

Attawapiskat *River* Canada 169 H8

Atter, L. *Lake* Austria 819 I4

Auch France 356 D7

Auckland Islands *Island group* New Zealand 93

Auckland New Zealand 606 E3

Augsburg Germany 379 E9

Augusta Italy 475 E10

Augusta Maine, USA 864 L5

Aurillac France 356 E7

Austin Texas, USA 864 F9

Australia *Country* Pacific Ocean 95

Australian Territory *Territory* Australia 95 H7

Austria *Country* C Europe 819

Auxerre France 356 F4

Avarua *Capital* Cook Islands 679 F7

Aveiro Portugal 682 C4

Avignon France 356 F8

Ávila Spain 798 D4

Avilés Spain 798 C1

Awbārī Libya 28 I4

Axel Heiberg Island *Island* Canada 169 E2

Axiós *River* Greece/Macedonia 105 I8 403 C4

Ayacucho Peru 285 E8

Aydarkul', Ozero *Lake* Uzbekistan 80 G3

Ayers Rock *see* Uluru

'Ayn ath Tha'lab Libya 28 K4

Ayr Scotland, UK 858 C6

Ayutthaya Thailand 833 E9

Azahar *see* Palau

Azouaou *Physical region* Mali 33 F4

A'zāz Syria 821 E2

Azerbaijan *Country* SW Asia 186

Azores *External territory* Portugal, Atlantic Ocean 89 E5

Azov, Sea of Black Sea 727 J6

Azuero, Peninsula de *Peninsula* Panama 193 I10

Azul Argentina 65 D6

Azur, Côte d' *Coastal region* France 356 G8

Az Zarqā' Jordan 821 E7

Az Zāwiyah Libya 28 I3

B

Ba'abda Lebanon 821 D5

Baalbek Lebanon 821 E5

Bab el Mandeb *Sea feature* Djibouti/Yemen 406 C9

Babahoyo Ecuador 285 B3

Bābol Iran 463 F3

Babuyan Island *Island* Philippines 650 C2

Bacan, Pulau *Island* Indonesia 451 I3

Bacău Romania 727 E6

Bačka Topola Yugoslavia 105 G3

Bacolod Philippines 650 D7

Badajoz Spain 798 C6

Badalona Spain 798 I3

Baden Austria 819 K3

Badgastein Austria 819 H5

Bad Ischl Austria 819 K3

Bafatá Guinea-Bissau 33 B6

Baffin Bay *Sea feature* Atlantic Ocean 89 C2

Baffin Island *Island* Canada 169 G4

Baffin Island *Island* Canada 611

Bafoussam Cameroon 20 B6

Baganuur Mongolia 566 G2

Baghdad *Capital* Iraq 463 C4

Bagherhat Bangladesh 114 I9

Baghlān Afghanistan 80 G6

Baglung Nepal 114 D4

Baguio Philippines 650 C3

Bahamas *Country* West Indies 172

Bahāwalpur Pakistan 639 F5

Bahía Blanca Argentina 65 D7

Bahía, Islas de la *Islands* Honduras 193 E3

Bahir Dar Ethiopia 24 E6

Bahrain *Country* SW Asia 406

Baia Mare Romania 727 C5

Baikal, Lake *Lake* Russian Federation 75

Bairiki *Capital* Kiribati 679 B2

Baitadi Nepal 114 A2

Baja California *Peninsula* Mexico 551 B2

Baja Hungary 312 E10

Baker & Howland Islands *External territory* USA, Pacific Ocean 679 D2

Bakherden Turkmenistan 80 C4

Bākhtarān Iran 463 D4

Baku *Capital* Azerbaijan 186 K4

Balabac Island *Island* Philippines 650 A8

Balabac Strait *Sea feature* South China Sea/Sulu Sea 523 J1

Bālā Morghāb Afghanistan 80 E6

Balaton Lake Hungary 312 D9

Balbina Represa *Reservoir* Brazil 146 D3

Balearic Islands *Island group* Spain 798 I5

Bali *Island* Indonesia 451 F5

Balikpapan Indonesia 451 F3

Balkan Mountains *Mountain range* Bulgaria 403 E3

Balkhash Kazakhstan 731 E6

Balkhash, Ozero *Lake* Kazakhstan 731 D6

Balsas *River* Mexico 551 G6

Baltic Sea Atlantic Ocean 308

Bălţi Moldova 727 E5

Baltiysk Kalingrad, Russian Federation 112 A5

Baluchistan *Region* Pakistan 639 B5

Bamako *Capital* Mali 33 D6

Bambari Central African Republic 20 E6

Bamenda Cameroon 20 B6

Banaba *Island* Kiribati 679 A2

Banda Sea Pacific Ocean 451 I4

Bandaaceh Indonesia 451 A2

Bandar-e 'Abbās Iran 463 H7

Bandar-e Būshehr Iran 463 F7

Bandarlampung Indonesia 451 C4

Bandar Seri Begawan *Capital* Brunei 523 J3

Bandundu Dem. Rep. Congo 20 D9

Bandung Indonesia 451 D5

Bangalore India 444 D9

Banggai, Kepulauan *Island group* Indonesia 451 H3

Banghāzī Libya 28 J2

Bangka, Pulau *Island* Indonesia 451 C3

Bangkok *Capital* Thailand 833 E9

Bangladesh *Country* S Asia 114

Bangor Northern Ireland, UK 858 B6

Bangui *Capital* Central African Republic 20 E7

Bangwelu, Lake *Lake* Zambia 30 F3

Bani *River* Mali 33 E6

Banja Luka Bosnia & Herzegovina 105 D4

Banjarmasin Indonesia 451 F4

Banjul *Capital* Gambia 33 A6

Banks Island *Island* Canada 169 D4

Banks Islands *Island group* Vanuatu 636 F7

Banská Bystrica Slovakia 312 E7

Bantry Bay *Sea feature* Ireland 465 B7

Bantry Ireland 465 B7

Banyo Cameroon 20 C6

Ba'qūbah Iraq 463 C4

Baracaldo Spain 798 E2

Baranavichy Belarus 112 D7

Barbados *Country* West Indies 172

Barbuda *Island* Antigua & Barbuda 172 K5

Barcelona Spain 798 I3

Barcelona Venezuela 791 F2

Bärdä Azerbaijan 186 I5

Bareilly India 444 D4

Barents Sea Arctic Ocean 64 G8

Bari Italy 475 G7

Barinas Venezuela 791 D3

Barisal Bangladesh 114 J9

Barisan, Pegunungan *Mountains* Indonesia 451 B3

Barito *River* Indonesia 451 F3

Bar-le-Duc France 356 G3

Barlee, Lake *Lake* Australia 93

Barnaul Russian Federation 731 F6

Barnstaple England, UK 858 C10

Barquisimeto Venezuela 791 E2

Barra *Island* Scotland, UK 858 A4

Barranquilla Colombia 791 B2

Barreiras Brazil 146 G6

Barrow *River* Ireland 465 E6

Bartang *River* Tajikistan 80 I5

Bartica Guyana 791 I4

Baruun-Urt Mongolia 566 H2

Barysaw Belarus 112 F7

Basarabeasca Moldova 727 F6

Basilan *Island* Philippines 650 D9

Basle Switzerland 819 C4

Basque Provinces *Region* Spain 798 E2

Basse-Terre *Capital* Guadeloupe 172 K5

Bassein Burma 833 B7

Basseterre *Capital* St Kitts & Nevis 172 K5

Bass Strait *Sea feature* Australia 93

Bastia Corsica, France 356 I9

Bastogne Belgium 126 F5

Bata Equatorial Guinea 20 B7

Batan Islands *Islands* Philippines 650 C1

Batangas Philippines 650 C5

Bătdâmbâng Cambodia 876 C9

Bath England, UK 858 D10

Bathurst Canada 169 K8

Bathurst Island *Island* Australia 93

Bathurst Island *Island* Canada 64 B5

Batna Algeria 28 G2

Baton Rouge Louisiana, USA 864 H9

Batterbee, Cape *Coastal feature* Antarctica 449 C10

Batticaloa Sri Lanka 444 E11

Bat'umi Georgia 186 C3

Batu, Kepulauan *Island group* Indonesia 451 A3

Batu Pahat Malaysia 523 C4

Bat Yam Israel 473 B5

Bauchi Nigeria 33 J7

Bavarian Alps *Mountains* Austria/Germany 379 E10

Bayamo Cuba 172 E4

Bayanhongor Mongolia 566 D3

Baydhabo Eritrea 24 F8

Baykal, Ozero *Lake* Russian Federation 731 H6

Bayonne France 356 B7

Bayramaly Turkmenistan 80 E5

Beaufort Sea Arctic Ocean 64 C3

Beauvais France 356 E3

Béchar Algeria 28 E3

Be'ér Sheva' Israel 473 B7

Begamganj Bangladesh 114 K8

Beijing *Capital* China 206 I4

Beira Mozambique 30 H6

Beirut *Capital* Lebanon 821 D5

Beja Portugal 682 C9

Béjaïa Algeria 28 G1

Békéscsaba Hungary 312 G9

Belau *see* Palau

Belarus *see* Belarus

Belcher Islands *Islands* Canada 169 H7

Belém Brazil 146 G3

Belfast Northern Ireland, UK 858 B6

Belfort France 356 H5

Belgaum India 444 C8

Belgium *Country* W Europe 126

Callao Peru 285 D8
Caltagirone Italy 475 E10
Caltanissetta Italy 475 E10
Calvinia South Africa 784 C7
Camagüey Cuba 172 D3
Cambodia *Country* SE Asia *Cam.* Kampuchea 876
Cambridge England, UK 858 F9
Cameron Highlands *Mountain range* Malaysia 523 B3
Cameroon *Country* W Africa 20
Camiri Bolivia 141 D6
Campeche Bahía de *Sea feature* Mexico 551 J5
Campeche Mexico 551 K5
Campina Grande Brazil 146 I4
Campinas Brazil 146 G8
Campo Grande Brazil 146 E8
Canada *Country* North America 169
Canary Basin *Undersea feature* Atlantic Ocean 89 E6
Canary Islands *Islands* Spain 89 E6
Canberra *Capital* Australia 95
Cancún Mexico 551 L4
Caniapiscau, Réservoir *Reservoir* Canada 169 I7
Cannes France 356 G8
Canterbury England, UK 858 G10
Canterbury Bight *Sea feature* Pacific Ocean 606 D7
Canterbury Plains *Plain* New Zealand 606 D7
Cân Thơ Vietnam 876 E11
Cap-Haïtien Haiti 172 G4
Cape Basin *Undersea feature* Atlantic Ocean 89 G9
Cape Coast Ghana 33 G9
Cape Town South Africa 784 B9
Cape Verde *Country* Atlantic Ocean 89 E6
Cape Verde Basin *Undersea feature* Atlantic Ocean 89 E7
Cape York Peninsula *Peninsula* Australia 95 G2
Capri, Isola d' *Island* Italy 475 E7
Caquetá *River* Colombia 791 D7
CAR *see* Central African Republic
Caracas *Capital* Venezuela 791 F2
Caratasca, Laguna de *Coastal feature* Honduras 193 G4
Carcassonne France 356 E8
Cardiff Wales, UK 858 D10
Cardigan Bay *Sea feature* Wales, UK 858 C9
Caribbean Sea Atlantic Ocean 172 H5
Carlisle England, UK 858 D6
Carlow Ireland 465 E5
Carlsberg Ridge *Undersea feature* Indian Ocean 449 C3
Carnarvon South Africa 784 D7
Carnegie, Lake *Lake* Australia 93
Carolina Brazil 146 G4
Caroline Islands *Island group* Micronesia 636 C3
Caroní *River* Venezuela 791 G4
Carpathian Mountains *Mountain range* E Europe 308
Carpaţii Meridionali *Mountain range* Romania 727 C6

Carpentaria, Gulf of *Sea feature* Australia 95 F2
Carra, Lough *Lake* Ireland 465 C3
Carson City Nevada, USA 864 B7
Cartagena Colombia 791 B2
Cartagena Spain 798 G7
Cartago Costa Rica 193 G8
Cartwright Canada 169 K6
Carúpano Venezuela 791 G2
Casablanca Morocco 28 D2
Cascade Range *Mountain range* Canada/USA 611
Cascais Portugal 682 A8
Caspian Sea *Inland sea* Asia/Europe 75 308
Castellón de la Plana Spain 798 G5
Castelo Branco Portugal 682 D6
Castlebar Ireland 465 C3
Castries *Capital* St Lucia 172 L6
Castro Chile 65 B8
Catalonia *Region* Spain 798 H3
Catanduanes Island *Island* Philippines 650 E5
Catania Italy 475 E10
Catanzaro Italy 475 F8
Cat Island *Island* Bahamas 172 E2
Cauca *River* Colombia 791 B3
Caucasus *Mountain range* Asia/Europe 186 E2
Cauquenes Chile 65 B6
Caura *River* Venezuela 791 F4
Cayenne *Capital* French Guiana 791 K4
Cayman Islands *External territory* UK, West Indies 172 C4
Cayman Trench *Undersea feature* Caribbean Sea 172 C4
Cebu *Island* Philippines 650 D7
Cebu Philippines 650 E7
Cedros, Isla *Island* Mexico 551 B3
Cefalù Italy 475 E9
Celebes *Island* Indonesia 449 G4
Celebes Sea Pacific Ocean 634 B6
Celje Slovenia 105 C2
Celtic Sea Atlantic Ocean 465 D8
Central African Republic *Country* C Africa *abbrev.* CAR 20
Central Makran Range *Mountains* Pakistan 639 B6
Central Siberian Plateau *Plateau* Russian Federation . 731 G4
Cerro de Pasco Peru 285 D7
Cēsis Latvia 112 E3
České Budějovice Czech Republic 312 B7
Ceuta *External territory* Spain, N Africa 28 D2
Cévennes *Mountains* France 356 E7
Ceylon *see* Sri Lanka
Chad *Country* C Africa 20
Chad, Lake *Lake* C Africa 15
Chaeryŏng North Korea 497 B5
Chāgai Hills *Mountains* Pakistan 639 B5
Chainpur Nepal 114 B2
Chalándri Greece 403 D8
Chalkída Greece 403 D7

Châlons-sur-Marne France 356 F3
Chaman Pakistan 639 C4
Chambal *River* India 444 D4
Chambéry France 356 G6
Chañaral Chile 65 B4
Chandigarh India 444 D3
Chandpur Bangladesh 114 J8
Chang, Ko *Island* Thailand 833 F10
Chang Jiang *see* Yangtze
Changchun China 206 K3
Changsha China 206 H7
Ch'angwŏn South Korea 497 D7
Changyŏn North Korea 497 A5
Chaniá Greece 403 D10
Channel Islands *Islands* UK 858 D12
Channel Tunnel France/UK 356 E1 858 G10
Chapala, Lago de *Lake* Mexico 551 F6
Chardzhev Turkmenistan 80 E4
Chari *River* C Africa 20 D5
Chārīkār Afghanistan 80 H7
Charleroi Belgium 126 D4
Charleston West Virginia, USA 864 I7
Charleville Australia 95 G5
Charlotte Amalie *Capital* Virgin Islands 172 J4
Charlottetown Canada 169 K8
Chartres France 356 E3
Châteauroux France 356 E5
Chatham Islands *Islands* New Zealand 634 F9
Chauk Burma 833 B5
Chautara Nepal 114 F4
Chaves Portugal 682 D2
Chech'ŏn South Korea 497 C6
Cheju South Korea 497 B9
Cheju-do *Island* South Korea 497 B9
Cheju Strait *Sea feature* South Korea 497 B9
Cheleken Turkmenistan 80 A4
Chelyabinsk Russian Federation 731 D5
Chemnitz Germany 379 F6
Chenāb *River* Pakistan 639 F3
Chengdu China 206 G6
Chennai (Madras) India 444 E9
Cherbourg France 356 C2
Cherepovets Russian Federation 731 C3
Cherkasy Ukraine 727 H3
Chernihiv Ukraine 727 G2
Chernivtsi Ukraine 727 D4
Chernyakhovsk Kaliningrad, Russian Federation 112 B5
Cherskiy Range *Mountains* Russian Federation 75
Chester England, UK 858 D8
Cheyenne Wyoming, USA 864 E6
Chhukha Bhutan 114 I4
Chiang Mai Thailand 833 D6
Chiat'ura Georgia 186 E2
Chiba Japan 478 F7
Chicago Illinois, USA 864 H6
Chiclayo Peru 285 B5
Chidley, Cape *Coastal feature* Canada 169 I5
Chiemsee *Lake* Germany 379 F9
Chihuahua Mexico 551 E2
Chile *Country* S South America 65
Chile Basin *Undersea feature* Pacific Ocean 634 K8
Chile Chico Chile 65 B9

Chillán Chile 65 B6
Chiloé, Isla de *Island* Chile 65 A8
Chimborazo *Peak* Ecuador 787
Chimbote Peru 285 C6
Chimoio Mozambique 30 G5
China *Country* E Asia 206
Chinandega Nicaragua 193 E5
Chindwin *River* Burma 833 B3
Chingola Zambia 30 F3
Chinhae South Korea 497 D8
Chinju South Korea 497 C8
Chíos Greece 403 F7
Chíos *Island* Greece 403 F7
Chirang Bhutan 114 I4
Chirchik Uzbekistan 80 H3
Chiriquí, Golfo de *Sea feature* Panama 193 H9
Chita Russian Federation 731 H6
Chitose Japan 478 F3
Chitré Panama 193 J9
Chittagong Bangladesh 114 K9
Chittagong Hills *Hill region* S Asia 114 L9
Chitungwiza Zimbabwe 30 F5
Chişinău *Capital* Moldova 727 F5
Chojnice Poland 312 D2
Choluteca Honduras 193 E5
Choma Zambia 30 E5
Chomutov Czech Republic 312 B5
Ch'ŏnan South Korea 497 C6
Chon Buri Thailand 833 E9
Ch'ŏngjin North Korea 497 D2
Chŏngju North Korea 497 B4
Chŏngju South Korea 497 C7
Chongqing China 206 G7
Chŏnju South Korea 497 C7
Chonos, Archipiélago de los *Island group* Chile 65 A9
Chornobyl' Ukraine 727 G2
Choybalsan Mongolia 566 H2
Christchurch New Zealand 606 D7
Christmas Island *External territory* Australia, Indian Ocean 449 F5
Chuadanga Bangladesh 114 I8
Chubut *River* Argentina 65 B8
Chūgoku-sanchi *Mountain range* Japan 478 C7
Chukchi Sea Arctic Ocean 64
Chumphon Thailand 833 D10
Ch'unch'ŏn South Korea 497 C5
Ch'ungju South Korea 497 C6
Ch'ungmu South Korea 497 D8
Chuquicamata Chile 65 B3
Chur Switzerland 819 D6
Churchill Canada 169 F7
Churchill Falls Canada 169 J7
Chuuk Islands *Island group* Micronesia 636 C3
Chuy Uruguay 65 F6
Cienfuegos Cuba 172 C3
Cieza Spain 798 F6
Cincinnati Ohio, USA 864 I7
Cirebon Indonesia 451 D5
Ciudad Bolívar Venezuela 791 G3
Ciudad del Este Paraguay 141 H9
Ciudad Guayana Venezuela 791 G3
Ciudad Juárez Mexico 551 E1
Ciudad Obregón Mexico 551 D3
Ciudad Ojeda Venezuela 791 D2

Ciudad Real Spain 798 E6
Ciudad Victoria Mexico 551 G4
Clarenville Canada 169 L6
Clermont-Ferrand France 356 E6
Cleveland Ohio, USA 864 I6
Clipperton Island *External territory* France, Pacific Ocean 634 J5
Clonmel Ireland 465 D6
Cluj-Napoca Romania 727 C5
Coast Ranges *Mountain range* North America 611
Coats Island *Island* Canada 169 G6
Coatzacoalcos Mexico 551 J6
Cobán Guatemala 193 B3
Cochabamba Bolivia 141 C5
Cochin India 444 C10
Cochrane Chile 65 B9
Cochrane Canada 169 I9
Cocos (Keeling) Islands *External territory* Australia, Indian Ocean 449 F5
Cod, Cape *Coastal feature* NE USA 864 L6
Coiba, Isla de *Island* Panama 193 H10
Coihaique Chile 65 B9
Coimbatore India 444 C10
Coimbra Portugal 682 C5
Colbeck, Cape *Coastal feature* Antarctica 56 D6
Colchester England, UK 858 G9
Colhué Huapi, Lago *Lake* Argentina 65 B9
Colima, Nevado de *Peak* Mexico 611
Colmar France 356 H4
Colombia *Country* N South America 791
Colombo *Capital* Sri Lanka 444 E11
Colón Panama 193 J8
Colorado *River* Argentina 65 D7
Colorado Plateau *Upland region* S USA 611
Colorado *River* Argentina 787
Colorado *River* USA 611
Colorado *State* USA 864 E7
Columbia South Carolina, USA 864 I8
Columbus Ohio, USA 864 I6
Comayagua Honduras 193 D4
Comilla Bangladesh 114 K8
Communism Peak *Peak* Tajikistan 75
Como, Lago di *Lake* Italy 475 C2
Comodoro Rivadavia Argentina 65 C9
Comorin, Cape *Cape* India 449 D3
Comoros *Country* Indian Ocean 30
Conakry *Capital* Guinea 33 B7
Concepción Chile 65 B7
Concepción Paraguay 141 G8
Conchos *River* Mexico 551 E3
Concord New Hampshire, USA 864 K6
Concordia Argentina 65 E5
Congo *Country* C Africa 20
Congo, Dem. Rep. *Country* C Africa 20
Congo *River* C Africa *var.* Zaire 20 E8
Congo Basin *Drainage basin* C Africa 15
Connaught *Region* Ireland 465 C4

Connecticut *State* USA 864 K6
Constance, Lake *Lake* C Europe 379 C10
Constantine Algeria 28 G1
Constanța Romania 727 E8
Cook Islands *External territory* New Zealand, Pacific Ocean 679 F6
Cook Strait *Sea feature* New Zealand 606 E5
Cook, Mount *Peak* New Zealand 606 C7
Cooktown Australia 95 G2
Copenhagen *Capital* Denmark 258 F5
Copiapó Chile 65 B4
Coquimbo Chile 65 B5
Corabia Romania 727 C8
Coral Sea Islands *External territory* Australia, Coral Sea 93
Coral Sea Pacific Ocean 634 D7
Corantijn *River* Guyana/Surinam *var.* Courantyne 791 I5
Cordillera Cantábrica *Mountain range* Spain 798 C2
Córdoba Argentina 65 D5
Córdoba Spain 798 D6
Corinth Canal *Waterway* Greece 403 D8
Corinto Nicaragua 193 E6
Cork Ireland 465 C7
Corner Brook Canada 169 K7
Corno Grande, Mount *Mountain* Italy 475 E5
Coro Venezuela 791 D2
Coroico Bolivia 141 B4
Coromandel New Zealand 606 E3
Coronel Oviedo Paraguay 141 G9
Corrib, Lough *Lake* Ireland 465 B4
Corrientes Argentina 65 E4
Corsica *Island* France 356 I9
Corumbá Brazil 146 E6
Cosenza Italy 475 F8
Costa Rica *Country* Central America 193
Côte d'Ivoire *see* Ivory Coast
Cotonou Benin 33 H8
Cotopaxi *Volcano* Ecuador 285 C2
Cottbus Germany 379 G5
Courantyne *River* Guyana/Surinam *var.* Corantijn 791 I5
Courland Lagoon *Sea feature* Baltic Sea 112 B4
Coventry England, UK 858 E9
Covilhã Portugal 682 D5
Cox's Bazar Bangladesh 114 L10
Cozumel, Isla *Island* Mexico 551 L5
Craiova Romania 727 C7
Cremona Italy 475 C3
Cres *Island* Croatia 105 B4
Crete *Island* Greece 403 E11
Crete, Sea of Mediterranean Sea 403 E10
Crimea *Peninsula* Ukraine 727 I7
Croatia *Country* SE Europe 105
Crotone Italy 475 G8
Crozet Basin *Undersea feature* Indian Ocean 449 C8
Crozet Islands *Island group* Indian Ocean 449 B8
Cruzeiro do Sul Brazil 146 A4
Cuanza *River* Angola 30 B3

Cuba *Country* West Indies 172
Cubango *River* southern Africa 30 C5
Cúcuta Colombia 791 C3
Cuenca Ecuador 285 B3
Cuenca Spain 798 F5
Cuernavaca Mexico 551 H6
Cuiabá Brazil 146 E6
Cuito *River* Angola 30 C5
Culiacán Mexico 551 D4
Cumaná Venezuela 791 G2
Cunene *River* Angola/Namibia 30 A5
Curicó Chile 65 B6
Curitiba Brazil 146 F9
Cusco Peru 285 F9
Cuttack India 444 F6
Cuxhaven Germany 379 C3
Cuyuni *River* Guyana/Venezuela 791 I4
Cyprus *Country* Mediterranean Sea 821
Czech Republic *Country* C Europe 312
Częstochowa Poland 312 E5

D

Dadeldhura Nepal 114 B3
Daga Bhutan 114 I4
Dagupan Philippines 650 B4
Dahomey *see* Benin
Dailekh Nepal 114 B3
Dakar *Capital* Senegal 33 A5
Đakovo Croatia 105 F3
Dalandzadgad Mongolia 566 F4
Đa Lat Vietnam 876 G9
Dalian China 206 A4
Dallas Texas, USA 864 F8
Dalmacija *Region* Croatia 105 C5
Daloa Ivory Coast 33 E8
Damān India 444 B6
Damascus *Capital* Syria 821 E5
Damphu Bhutan 114 J4
Dampier Australia 95 A3
Đa Nẵng Vietnam 876 G6
Dandong North Korea 497 A3
Dangara Tajikistan 80 H5
Danube *River* C Europe 308
Danube Delta *Wetland* Romania/Ukraine 727 F7
Danzig, Gulf of *Sea feature* Poland/Russian Federation 312 E2
Dar'ā Syria 821 E6
Dar es Salaam Tanzania 24 E11
Darfur *Mountains* Sudan 24 A6
Darhan Mongolia 566 F2
Darling River *River* Australia 95 G5
Darmstadt Germany 379 C7
Darnah Libya 28 K2
Darnley, Cape *Coastal feature* Antarctica 56 I3
Dartmoor *Region* England, UK 858 C11
Dartmouth Canada 169 K8
Darwin Australia 95 D2
Dashkhovuz Turkmenistan 80 D3
Dasht-e Kavīr *Desert region* Iran 463 G4
Datong China 206 H4
Datu, Telek *Sea feature* Malaysia 523 G4
Daugavpils Latvia 112 E5
Dāvangere India 444 C8

Davao Philippines 650 E8
David Panama 193 H9
Davis Strait *Sea feature* Atlantic Ocean 89 C3
Dawson Canada 169 B6
Dayr az Zawr Syria 821 H3
De Aar South Africa 784 E7
Dead Sea *Salt lake* SW Asia 473 D6 821 D7
Death Valley *Valley* W USA 611
Debre Zeyit Ethiopia 24 E7
Debrecen Hungary 312 G8
Deccan Plateau *Plateau* India 444 D7
Děčín Czech Republic 312 B5
Dehra Dūn India 444 D3
Dej Romania 727 C5
Delaware *State* USA 864 K7
Delémont Switzerland 819 B5
Delft Netherlands 601 B5
Delfzijl Netherlands 601 F2
Demchok *Disputed region* China/India 444 D2
Den Helder Netherlands 601 C3
Denali *Peak* Alaska, USA *prev.* Mount McKinley 864 C2
Denmark *Country* NW Europe 258
Denmark Strait *Sea feature* Greenland/Iceland 89 D3
Denpasar Indonesia 451 F5
Denver Colorado, USA 864 E6
Dera Ghāzi Khān Pakistan 639 E4
Dera Ismāī Khān Pakistan 639 E4
Derby England, UK 858 E8
Derg, Lough *Lake* Ireland 465 C5
Des Moines Iowa, USA 864 G6
Desē Ethiopia 24 E6
Deseado *River* Argentina 65 C9
Dessau Germany 379 E5
Desventurados, Islas de los *Islands* Chile, Pacific Ocean 634 K8
Detroit Michigan, USA 864 I6
Deva Romania 727 B6
Deventer Netherlands 601 E4
Devollit, Lumi i *River* Albania 105 G9
Devon Island *Island* Canada 169 F3
Dezfūl Iran 463 E5
Dhaka *Capital* Bangladesh 114 J8
Dhanbād India 444 G5
Dhankuta Nepal 114 G5
Dhanushkodi India 444 D10
Dharan Nepal 114 G5
Dhārwād India 444 C8
Dhrepanon, Akrotírio *Coastal feature* Greece 403 D5
Dhule India 444 C6
Diamantina River *River* Australia 95 F4
Diekirch Luxembourg 126 F5
Dieppe France 356 E2
Diffa Niger 33 K6
Digul *River* Indonesia 451 L4
Dijon France 356 G5
Dīla Ethiopia 24 E7
Dili Indonesia 451 H5
Dillikot Nepal 114 C3
Dilling Sudan 24 C6
Dilolo Dem. Rep. Congo 20 F11

Dimona Israel 473 C7
Dinagat Island *Island* Philippines 650 F7
Dinajpur Bangladesh 114 H6
Dinant Belgium 126 D4
Dinara *Mountains* Bosnia & Herzegovina 105 D5
Dingle Bay *Sea feature* Ireland 465 B6
Diourbel Senegal 33 B5
Dipayal Nepal 114 B3
Dipolog Philippines 650 D8
Dirē Dawa Ethiopia 24 F7
Disappointment, Lake *Salt lake* Australia 93
Dispur India 444 H4
Djado, Plateau du *Physical region* Niger 33 K4
Djambala Congo 20 C9
Djibouti *Capital* Djibouti 24 F6
Djibouti *Country* E Africa 24
Dnieper *River* E Europe 308
Dniester *River* Moldova/Ukraine 727 E4
Dnipropetrovs'k Ukraine 727 I4
Dobele Latvia 112 D4
Doboj Bosnia & Herzegovina 105 E4
Dobrich Bulgaria 403 G2
Dodekánisos *Islands* Greece 403 G9
Dodoma *Capital* Tanzania 24 D11
Doha *Capital* Qatar 406 G4
Dolores Argentina 65 E6
Dominica *Country* West Indies 172
Dominican Republic *Country* West Indies 172
Domuyo *Peak* Argentina 787
Don *River* Russian Federation 731 B4
Donawitz Austria 819 J5
Dondra Head *Cape* Sri Lanka 449 D3
Donegal Bay *Sea feature* Ireland 465 C2
Donegal Ireland 465 D2
Donets *River* Russian Federation/Ukraine 727 K4
Donets'k Ukraine 727 K5
Dongola Sudan 24 C4
Donna *Island* Norway 617 D4
Dordogne *River* France 356 C6
Dordrecht Netherlands 601 C5
Dornbirn Austria 819 E5
Dortmund Germany 379 B5
Dosso Niger 33 H6
Douai France 356 F2
Douala Cameroon 20 B7
Douglas Isle of Man, UK 858 C7
Douglas South Africa 784 E6
Douro *River* Portugal/Spain 682 C3
Dover Delaware, USA 864 K7
Dover England, UK 858 G10
Dōzen *Island* Japan 478 C7
Dra, Hamada du *Plateau* Algeria 28 D4
Drakensberg *Mountain range* Lesotho/South Africa 784 G7
Dráma Greece 403 E4
Drammen Norway 617 C8
Drau *River* C Europe 819 J6
Drava *River* C Europe 105 F3 312 D10
Dresden Germany 379 F6

Drina *River* Bosnia & Herzegovina/Yugoslavia 105 G5
Drobeta-Turnu Severin Romania 727 B7
Drogheda Ireland 465 F4
Druskininkai Lithuania 112 C6
Dubai United Arab Emirates 406 H4
Dubăsari Moldova 727 F5
Dubawnt *River* Canada 169 E7
Dublin *Capital* Ireland 465 F4
Dubrovnik Croatia 105 E7
Duero *River* Portugal/Spain 798 D3
Dugi Otok *Island* Croatia 105 B5
Duisburg Germany 379 B5
Dumaguete Philippines 650 D7
Dumfries Scotland, UK 858 C6
Dundalk Ireland 465 E3
Dundee Scotland, UK 858 D4
Dunedin New Zealand 606 C8
Dungun Malaysia 523 C3
Dunkerque France 356 F1
Dún Laoghaire Ireland 465 F5
Duqm Oman 406 I6
Durango Mexico 551 E4
Durazno Uruguay 65 E6
Durban South Africa 784 I6
Durrës Albania 105 G8
Dushak Turkmenistan 80 D5
Dushanbe *Capital* Tajikistan 80 H5
Düsseldorf Germany 379 B6
Dutch West Indies *see* Netherlands Antilles
Dvina *River* E Europe 308
Dzhalal-Abad Kyrgyzstan 80 I3
Dzhugdzhur Range *Mountain range* Russian Federation 75
Dzüünharaa Mongolia 566 F2
Dzuunmod Mongolia 566 F3

E

East Cape *Coastal feature* New Zealand 606 G3
East China Sea Pacific Ocean 634 B4
Easter Island *Island* Pacific Ocean 634 J8
Eastern Ghats *Mountain range* India 444 E7
East Falkland *Island* Falkland Islands 65 D11
East Frisian Islands *Islands* Germany 379 B3
East London South Africa 784 G8
Eastmain *River* Canada 169 I8
East Pacific Rise *Undersea feature* Pacific Ocean 634 J7
East Siberian Sea Arctic Ocean 64 F2
Ebeltoft Denmark 258 D4
Ebolowa Cameroon 20 B7
Ebro *River* Spain 798 F3
Ecuador *Country* NW South America 285
Ed Eritrea 24 F6
Ede Netherlands 601 D5
Ede Nigeria 33 H8
Edinburgh Scotland, UK 858 D5

Edmonton Canada 169 D9
Edward, Lake *Lake* Uganda/Dem. Rep. Congo 20 H8 24 C9
Eforie-Nord Romania 727 E8
Egadi, Isole *Island group* Italy 475 D9
Egiyn Gol *River* Mongolia 566 E2
Egypt *Country* NE Africa 24
Eindhoven Netherlands 601 D6
Eisenstadt Austria 819 K4
Eivissa *Island* Spain 798 H5
Ejmiadzin Armenia 186 E5
Elat Israel 473 C12
Elba, Isola d' *Island* Italy 475 C5
Elbasan Albania 105 G9
Elbe *River* Czech Republic/Germany 308
Elbląg Poland 312 E2
El'brus *Peak* Russian Federation 308
Elburz Mountains *Mountain range* Iran 463 E3
El Calafati Argentina 65 B10
Elche Spain 798 G6
Elda Spain 798 G6
Eldoret Kenya 24 D9
Eleuthera *Island* Bahamas 172 E1
El Fasher Sudan 24 B6
Elgin Scotland, UK 858 D3
El Gîza Egypt 24 C2
El Khârga Egypt 24 C3
Ellesmere Island *Island* Canada 169 E2
Ellsworth Land *Region* Antarctica 56 C5
El Minya Egypt 24 C2
El Obeid Sudan 24 C6
El Salvador *Country* Central America 193
El Tigre Venezuela 791 G3
Emden Germany 379 B3
Emmen Netherlands 601 F3
Emperor Seamounts *Undersea feature* Pacific Ocean 634 E3
Ems *River* Germany/Netherlands 379 B4
Encarnación Paraguay 141 G10
Endelave *Island* Denmark 258 C5
Enderby Land *Region* Antarctica 56 H2
England *National region* UK 858 D7
English Channel *Sea feature* Atlantic Ocean 308
Enguri *River* Georgia 186 C2
Ennedi *Plateau* Chad 20 F3
Ennis Ireland 465 C5
Enns *River* Austria 819 I4
Enschede Netherlands 601 F4
Ensenada Mexico 551 A1
Entebbe Uganda 24 C9
Enugu Nigeria 33 I8
Eolie, Isole *Island group* Italy 475 E9
Épinal France 356 G4
Equatorial Guinea *Country* W Africa 20
Erdenet Mongolia 566 F2
Erebus, Mount *Peak* Antarctica 56 F6
Erfurt Germany 379 E6
Erg Chech *Desert region* Algeria/Mali 28 E4 33 E3
Erguig *River* Chad 20 D5
Erie, Lake *Lake* Canada/USA 611

Eritrea *Country* E Africa 24
Erlangen Germany 379 E8
Ernākulam India 444 C10
Esch-sur-Alzette Luxembourg 126 F6
Escuintla Guatemala 193 B4
Eşfahān Iran 463 F5
Esmeraldas Ecuador 285 B1
Espoo Finland 333 C9
Esquel Argentina 65 B8
Essen Germany 379 B5
Essequibo *River* Guyana 791 I5
Estelí Nicaragua 193 E5
Estevan Canada 169 E10
Estonia *Country* E Europe 112
Estrela, Serra da *Mountains* Portugal 682 D5
Ethiopia *Country* E Africa 24
Ethiopian Highlands *Upland* E Africa 24 E7
Etna *Peak* Sicily, Italy 308
Etosha Pan *Salt basin* Namibia 30 B5
Euphrates *River* SW Asia 75
Europe 308
Everest, Mount *Peak* China/Nepal 114 G4
Everglades *Wetlands* Florida, USA 864 I10
Évora Portugal 682 D8
Évvoia *Island* Greece 403 D7
Exeter England, UK 858 D11
Exmoor *Region* England, UK 858 C10
Eyre, Lake *Lake* Australia 95 F5

F

Fåborg Denmark 258 C6
Fada-Ngourma Burkina 33 G6
Faeroe Islands *External territory* Denmark, Atlantic Ocean 89 F3
Faguibine, Lac *Lake* Mali 33 F5
Fairbanks Alaska, USA 864 C2
Faisalābād Pakistan 639 F4
Falkland Islands *External territory* UK, Atlantic Ocean 89 C11
Falster *Island* Denmark 258 E7
Falun Sweden 816 C7
Famagusta Cyprus 821 B4
Farafangana Madagascar 39 K7
Farāh Afghanistan 80 D8
Faridpur Bangladesh 114 I8
Fårö *Island* Sweden 816 D8
Faro Portugal 682 C11
Faya Chad 20 E3
Fazzān *Region* Libya 28 I5
Feira de Santana Brazil 146 I6
Feldkirch Austria 819 E5
Femund, L. *Lake* Norway 617 C7
Feni Bangladesh 114 K8
Fenoarivo Atsinanana Madagascar 30 L5
Fens *Wetland* England, UK 858 F9
Fergana Uzbekistan 80 I4
Fernando de la Mora Paraguay 141 G9
Fernando de Noronha *Island* Brazil 89 D8
Ferrara Italy 475 D3

Ferrol Spain 798 B1
Fès Morocco 28 D2
Feyzābād Afghanistan 80 H5
Fianarantsoa Madagascar 30 K6
Fier Albania 105 G9
Figueira da Foz Portugal 682 B5
Figueres Spain 798 I2
Figuig Morocco 28 E3
Fiji *Country* Pacific Ocean 636
Finisterre, Cabo *Coastal feature* Spain 798 A2
Finland *Country* N Europe 333
Finland, Gulf of *Sea feature* Baltic Sea 308
Fish *River* Namibia 30 C7
Fishguard Wales, UK 858 C9
Fitzroy River *River* Australia 93
Fjerritslev Denmark 258 C2
Flanders *Region* Belgium 126 B2
Flensburg Germany 379 C1
Flinders Island *Island* Australia 93
Flinders Ranges *Mountain range* Australia 95 F6
Flinders River *River* Australia 95 F3
Flin Flon Canada 169 E8
Flint Island *Island* Kiribati 679 G5
Florence Italy 475 D4
Florencia Colombia 791 B6
Flores Guatemala 193 C2
Flores *Island* Indonesia 451 G5
Flores Sea *Pacific Ocean* 451 G5
Florianópolis Brazil 146 F9
Florida *State* USA 864 I9
Florida, Straits of *Sea feature* Bahamas/USA 611
Floridablanca Colombia 791 C4
Flórina Greece 403 B5
Foča Bosnia & Herzegovina 105 F6
Focşani Romania 727 E6
Foggia Italy 475 F6
Foleyet Canada 169 H9
Fongafale *Capital* Tuvalu 679 C4
Fonseca, Gulf of *Sea feature* El Salvador/Honduras 193 D5
Forlì Italy 475 D4
Formentera *Island* Spain 798 H6
Former Yugoslav Republic of Macedonia *see* Macedonia
Formosa Argentina 65 E4
Formosa *see* Taiwan
Fortaleza Brazil 146 I3
Fort-de-France *Capital* Martinique 172 L6
Forth *River* Scotland, UK 858 C5
Forth, Firth of *Inlet* Scotland, UK 858 D5
Foveaux Strait *Sea feature* New Zealand 606 B9
Fort McMurray Canada 169 D8
Fort Peck, Lake *Lake* Montana, USA 864 D4
Fort Smith Canada 169 D7
Fort St. John Canada 169 C8
Fort William Scotland, UK 858 C4
France *Country* W Europe 356
Francistown Botswana 30 F6
Franconian Jura *Mountain range* Germany 379 E8

Frankfort Kentucky, USA 864 I7
Frankfurt am Main Germany 379 C7
Frankfurt an der Oder Germany 379 G4
Frantsa-Iosifa, Zemlya *Islands* Russian Federation 731 F1
Franz Josef Land *Islands* Russian Federation 64 F7
Fraser Island *Island* Australia 93
Frauenfeld Switzerland 819 D4
Fredericia Denmark 258 C5
Fredericton Canada 169 K8
Frederikshavn Denmark 258 D1
Fredrikstad Norway 617 C8
Freetown *Capital* Sierra Leone 33 C8
Freiburg im Breisgau Germany 379 B9
Freistadt Austria 819 I2
Fremantle Australia 95 B6
French Guiana *External territory* France, N South America 791 K5
French Polynesia *External territory* France, Pacific Ocean 679 G6
Fribourg Switzerland 819 B6
Frosinone Italy 475 E6
Fuerteventura *Island* Spain 28 B4
Fuji, Mount *Peak* Japan 478 E7
Fukui Japan 478 D7
Fukuoka Japan 478 B8
Fukushima Japan 478 F4
Fukushima Japan 478 F6
Fulda Germany 379 D6
Furnas Represa *Reservoir* Brazil 146 G8
Fuzhou China 206 J7
Füzuli Azerbaijan 186 I6
Fyn *Island* Denmark 258 C6
FYR Macedonia *see* Macedonia

G

Gaalkacyo Eritrea 24 G7
Gaborone *Capital* Botswana 30 E7
Gabès Tunisia 28 H2
Gabon *Country* W Africa 20
Gabrovo Bulgaria 403 E2
Gaeta, Golfo di *Sea feature* Italy 475 E6
Gafsa Tunisia 28 H2
Gagnoa Ivory Coast 33 E8
Gagra Georgia 186 A1
Gaibanda Bangladesh 114 I6
Gairdner, Lake *Lake* Australia 95 E6
Galápagos Islands *Islands* Ecuador, Pacific Ocean 634 K6
Galaţi Romania 727 E7
Galicia *Region* Spain 798 B2
Galle Sri Lanka 444 E11
Gallipoli Italy 475 G8
Gällivare Sweden 816 D2
Galway Ireland 465 C4
Galway Bay *Sea feature* Ireland 465 C4
Gambia *Country* W Africa 33
Gamgadhi Nepal 114 C2
Gäncä Azerbaijan 186 H4
Gander Canada 169 L6
Gandi Reservoir *Reservoir* India 444 C5
Gandía Spain 798 G5
Ganges *River* S Asia *Ben.* Padma 114 I7 444 G5

Ganges, Mouths of the *Delta* Bangladesh/India 114 J9
Gangtok India 444 G4
Gao Mali 33 G5
Garda, Lago di *Lake* Italy 475 C2
Gardēz Afghanistan 80 H7
Garonne *River* France 356 C7
Garoowe Eritrea 24 G7
Garoua Cameroon 20 C5
Gasa Tashi Thongmen Bhutan 114 I4
Gaspé Canada 169 K7
Gävle Sweden 816 C7
Gaya India 444 F5
Gaza Gaza Strip 473 B6
Gaza Strip *Disputed territory* SW Asia 473 A7
Gazandzhyk Turkmenistan 80 B4
Gdańsk Poland 312 E2
Gdynia Poland 312 E2
Gedaref Sudan 24 D6
Gedser Denmark 258 E7
Geelong Australia 95 G7
Gëkdepe Turkmenistan 80 C4
Gelsenkirchen Germany 379 B5
Gemena Dem. Rep. Congo 20 E7
Geneina Sudan 24 A6
General Eugenio A. Garay Paraguay 141 E6
General Santos Philippines 650 E9
Geneva Switzerland 819 A7
Geneva, L. *Lake* France/Switzerland 356 G6 819 A6
Genk Belgium 126 E2
Genoa Italy 475 B3
Genova, Golfo di *Sea feature* Italy 475 B3
Gent Belgium 126 C2
George Town *Capital* Cayman Islands 172 B4
Georgetown Gambia 33 B6
Georgetown *Capital* Guyana 791 I4
George Town Malaysia 523 A2
Georgia *Country* SW Asia 186
Georgia *Country* SW Asia 75
Georgia *State* USA 864 I8
Gera Germany 379 E6
Geraldton Australia 95 A5
Gereshk Afghanistan 80 F8
Germany *Country* W Europe 379
Getafe Spain 798 E4
Gevgelija Macedonia 105 I9
Geylegphug Bhutan 114 J5
Ghadāmis Libya 28 H3
Ghana *Country* W Africa 33
Ghanzi Botswana 30 D6
Ghardaïa Algeria 28 F3
Gharyān Libya 28 I3
Ghāt Libya 28 H5
Ghaznī Afghanistan 80 G7
Gibraltar *External territory* UK, SW Europe 798 D8
Gibraltar, Strait of *Sea feature* Atlantic Ocean/Mediterranean Sea 798 D8
Gibson Desert *Desert region* Australia 95 D4
Gijón Spain 798 D1
Gilbert Islands *see* Tungaru
Girona Spain 798 I3
Gisborne New Zealand 606 G4
Giurgiu Romania 727 D8
Give Denmark 258 B4

Gjirokastër Albania 105 G10

Gjøvik Norway 617 C7

Glåma *River* Norway 617 C7

Glarus Switzerland 819 D5

Glasgow Scotland, UK 858 C5

Gliwice Poland 312 E6

Gloucester England, UK 858 D9

Gmünd Austria 819 J2

Gmunden Austria 819 I4

Gobi *Desert* China/Mongolia 75

Godåvari *River* India 444 E7

Godoy Cruz Argentina 65 B5

Goiânia Brazil 146 F7

Golan Heights *Disputed territory* SW Asia 473 D1 821 D6

Goma Dem. Rep. Congo 20 H9

Gómez Palacio Mexico 551 F3

Gonaïves Haiti 172 F4

Gonder Ethiopia 24 E6

Good Hope, Cape of *Coastal feature* 784 C9

Gopalpur Bangladesh 114 I7

Gorakhpur India 444 F4

Goré Chad 20 D6

Gorē Ethiopia 24 D7

Gorgān Iran 463 G3

Gori Georgia 186 E3

Goris Armenia 186 H6

Gorontalo Indonesia 451 H3

Gorzów Wielkopolski Poland 312 C3

Gospić Croatia 105 C4

Gostivar Macedonia 105 H8

Göteborg Sweden 816 A8

Gotland *Island* Sweden 816 D9

Gotō-rettō *Island group* Japan 478 A9

Göttingen Germany 379 D5

Gouda Netherlands 601 C5

Gough Island *External territory* UK, Atlantic Ocean 89 F10

Gouin, Réservoir *Reservoir* Canada 169 I8

Govind Ballash Pant Reservoir *Reservoir* India 444 E5

Göyçay Azerbaijan 186 I4

Gozo *Island* Malta 475 E11

Graaf Reinet South Africa 784 E7

Gračanica Bosnia & Herzegovina 105 E4

Graham Land *Region* Antarctica 56 B4

Grahamstown South Africa 784 F8

Grampian Mountains *Mountains* Scotland, UK 858 C4

Granada Nicaragua 193 E6

Granada Spain 798 E7

Gran Canaria *Island* Spain 28 B4

Gran Chaco *Region* C South America 787

Grand Bahama *Island* Bahamas 172 C1

Grand Banks *Undersea feature* Atlantic Ocean 89 C5

Grand Canyon Valley SW USA 864 C7

Grande, Bahía *Sea feature* Argentina 787

Grande, Serra *Mountain range* Brazil 146 H4

Grande Comore *Island* Comoros 30 J3

Grande Prairie Canada 169 C8

Grand Erg Occidental *Desert region* Algeria 28 E3

Grand Erg Oriental *Desert region* Algeria/Tunisia 28 G4

Grand Falls Canada 169 K6

Gråsten Denmark 258 B6

Graz Austria 819 J5

Great Abaco *Island* Bahamas 172 D1

Great Australian Bight *Sea feature* Australia 95 D6

Great Bahama Bank *Undersea feature* Atlantic Ocean 172 D2

Great Barrier Reef *Coral reef* Coral Sea 95 H3

Great Basin *Region* USA 864 B6

Great Bear Lake *Lake* Canada 169 C6

Great Dividing Range *Mountain range* Australia 95 G3

Greater Antarctica *Region* Antarctica 56 G5

Greater Antilles *Island group* West Indies 172 D4

Greater Khingan *Mountain range* China 206 J3

Great Exuma *Island* Bahamas 172 E2

Great Inagua *Island* Bahamas 172 F3

Great Lakes *Lakes* North America 611

Great Man-made River Project Libya 28 K4

Great Plain of China *Region* China 206 I6

Great Plains *Region* N America 864 E5

Great Rift Valley *Valley* E Africa 24 D9

Great Salt Lake *Salt lake* Utah, USA 864 C6

Great Sand Sea *Desert region* Egypt/Libya 28 K3

Great Sandy Desert *Desert* Australia 93

Great Slave Lake *Lake* Canada 169 D7

Great Victoria Desert *Desert* Australia 95 C5

Gredos, Sierra de *Mountains* Spain 798 D4

Greece *Country* SE Europe 403

Greenland *External territory* Denmark, Atlantic Ocean 89 D2

Greenland Basin *Undersea feature* Arctic Ocean 64 D9

Greenland Sea Atlantic Ocean 89 F2

Greenock Scotland, UK 858 C5

Greifswald Germany 379 F2

Grenå Denmark 258 D3

Grenada *Country* West Indies 172

Grenoble France 356 G7

Greymouth New Zealand 606 C6

Grimsby England, UK 858 F8

Grindsted Denmark 258 B5

Groningen Netherlands 601 E2

Grootfontein Namibia 30 C6

Grosseto Italy 475 C5

Groznyy Russian Federation 731 A5

Grudziądz Poland 312 E3

Gstaad Switzerland 819 B6

Guadalajara Mexico 551 F5

Guadalquivir *River* Spain 798 D7

Guadeloupe *External territory* France, West Indies 172 K5

Guadiana *River* Portugal/Spain 682 D9 798 D5

Guainia *River* Colombia 791 E5

Guallatiri *Peak* Chile 787

Guam *External territory* USA, Pacific Ocean 636 C2

Guanare *River* Venezuela 791 E3

Guanare Venezuela 791 D3

Guangzhou China 206 H8

Guantánamo Cuba 172 E4

Guatemala *Country* Central America 193

Guatemala City *Capital* Guatemala 193 B4

Guaviare *River* Colombia 791 E5

Guayaquil Ecuador 285 B3

Guayaquil, Gulf of *Sea feature* Ecuador/Peru 285 B3

Gudenå *River* Denmark 258 C3

Guiana Basin *Undersea feature* Atlantic Ocean 89 D7

Guiana Highlands *Upland* N South America 791 F4

Guider Cameroon 20 C5

Guilin Hills *Hill range* China 206 H7

Guimarães Portugal 682 C3

Guinea *Country* W Africa 33

Guinea, Gulf of *Sea feature* Atlantic Ocean 89 F7

Guinea-Bissau *Country* W Africa 33

Guiyang China 206 G7

Gujrānwāla Pakistan 639 F3

Gujrāt Pakistan 639 F3

Gulariya Nepal 114 B4

Gulf (*formerly* Persian Gulf) *Sea feature* Arabian Sea 449 B2

Gulu Uganda 24 C8

Gunnbjørn Fjeld *Peak* Greenland 611

Guri, Embalse de *Reservoir* Venezuela 791 G3

Gusau Nigeria 33 I6

Gusev Kalingrad, Russian Federation 112 B5

Gushgy Turkmenistan 80 E6

Guwāhati India 444 H4

Guyana *Country* NE South America 791

Gwādar Pakistan 639 A6

Gwalior India 444 D4

Győr Hungary 312 D8

Gyumri Armenia 186 E5

Gyzylarbat Turkmenistan 80 C4

H

Ha Bhutan 114 I4

Ha'apai Group *Islands* Tonga 679 D6

Haapsalu Estonia 112 E1

Haarlem Netherlands 601 C4

Habiganj Bangladesh 114 K7

Habomai Islands *Islands* Japan/Russian Federation (disputed) 478 H2

Hachinohe Japan 478 F4

Hadejia *River* Nigeria 33 J6

Hadera Israel 473 C3

Haderslev Denmark 258 B6

Ḥaḍramawt *Region* Yemen 406 F8

Haeju North Korea 497 B5

Hagåtña Guam 636 C2

Hagen Germany 379 B5

Hague, The *Capital* Netherlands 601 B5

Ḥā'il Saudi Arabia 406 C3

Hailuoto *Island* Finland 333 C5

Hainan *Island* China 206 H9

Hainburg Austria 819 L3

Hai Phong Vietnam 876 F3

Haiti *Country* West Indies 172

Hakodate Japan 478 F3

Ḥalab Syria 821 E2

Halden Norway 617 C8

Halifax Canada 169 K8

Halle Germany 379 E5

Hallein Austria 819 H4

Halmahera *Island* Indonesia 451 I3

Halmstad Sweden 816 B9

Hamada Japan 478 C7

Ḥamah Syria 821 E3

Hamamatsu Japan 478 E7

Hamburg Germany 379 D3

Hämeenlinna Finland 333 C8

Hamersley Range *Mountain range* Australia 95 A4

Hamgyŏng-Sanmaek *Mountain range* North Korea 497 D3

Hamhŭng North Korea 497 C4

Hamilton Canada 169 I10

Hamilton New Zealand 606 E3

Hamm Germany 379 B5

Ḥammār, Hawr al *Lake* Iraq 463 D6

Hammerfest Norway 617 F1

Hampden New Zealand 606 C8

Han *River* South Korea 497 D6

Handan China 206 I5

Hangayn Nuruu *Mountain range* Mongolia 566 D2

Hangzhou China 206 J6

Hannover Germany 379 D4

Hanoi *Capital* Vietnam 876 E3

Hanstholm Denmark 258 B2

Happy Valley-Goose Bay Canada 169 J6

Ḥaraḍ Saudi Arabia 406 F4

Harare *Capital* Zimbabwe 30 F5

Harbin China 206 K3

Hardanger Fjord *Sea feature* Norway 617 B8

Hargeysa Eritrea 24 F7

Hari *River* Indonesia 451 C3

Haringhat *River* Bangladesh 114 I8

Harīrūd *River* C Asia 80 E7

Härnösand Sweden 816 D5

Har Nuur *Lake* Mongolia 566 C2

Harper Liberia 33 D9

Harrisburg Pennsylvania, USA 864 K6

Harstad Norway 617 E3

Hartford Connecticut, USA 864 K6

Har Us Nuur *Lake* Mongolia 566 B2

Hasharon *Plain* Israel 473 C3

Hasselt Belgium 126 E2

Hässleholm Sweden 816 B10

Hastings New Zealand 606 F5

Hatia *River* Bangladesh 114 K8

Hatteras, Cape *Coastal feature* North Carolina, USA 611

Hat Yai Thailand 833 E12

Haugesund Norway 617 A8

Havana *Capital* Cuba 172 B2

Havre-Saint-Pierre Canada 169 K7

Hawaii *Island* Hawaii, USA 864 C10

Hawaii *State* USA 864 B9

Hay *River* Canada 169 D7

Heard & Mcdonald Islands *Dependent territory* Australia, Indian Ocean 449 D9

Hebron West Bank 473 C6

Heerenveen Netherlands 601 D3

Heerlen Netherlands 601 D8

Ḥefa Israel 473 C2

Hefei China 206 I6

Heidelberg Germany 379 C8

Heilbronn Germany 379 C8

Helena Montana, USA 864 D5

Helmand *River* Afghanistan 80 E9

Helmond Netherlands 601 D6

Helsingborg Sweden 816 B10

Helsingør Denmark 258 F4

Helsinki *Capital* Finland 333 C9

Helwân Egypt 24 C2

Hendrik Verwoerdam *Reservoir* South Africa 784 F6

Hengelo Netherlands 601 F4

Henzada Burma 833 B7

Herāt Afghanistan 80 E7

Herisau Switzerland 819 D5

Hermansverk Norway 617 B7

Hermosillo Mexico 551 C2

Herning Denmark 258 B4

Herzliyya Israel 473 B4

Hetauda Nepal 114 E4

Hida-sammyaku *Mountains* Japan 478 E7

Hiiumaa *Island* Estonia 112 D1

Hildesheim Germany 379 D5

Hillerød Denmark 258 F4

Hilversum Netherlands 601 C4

Himalayas *Mountain range* S Asia 75

Himora Ethiopia 24 D6

Ḥims Syria 821 E4

Hindu Kush *Mountain range* C Asia 75

Hinnøya *Island* Norway 617 E3

Hirakud Reservoir *Reservoir* India 444 F6

Hiroshima Japan 478 C8

Hirtshals Denmark 258 C1

Hitachi Japan 478 F6

Hitra *Island* Norway 617 C6

Hjørring Denmark 258 C1

Hlybokaye Belarus 112 E6

Hobart Tasmania 95 G8

Hobro Denmark 258 C3

Hô Chi Minh Vietnam 876 F10

Hoek van Holland Netherlands 601 B5

Hokkaidō *Island* Japan 478 G2

Holguín Cuba 172 E3

Kalinkavichy Belarus 112 F9

Kalisz Poland 312 E4

Kalmar Sweden 816 C9

Kalundborg Denmark 258 D5

Kam"yanets'-Podil's'kyy Ukraine 727 E4

Kama *River* Russian Federation 308

Kamarhati India 444 G5

Kamchatka *Peninsula* Russian Federation 731 K3

Kamchiya *River* Bulgaria 403 G2

Kamina Dem. Rep. Congo 20 F11

Kamloops Canada 169 C9

Kamo Armenia 186 G5

Kampala *Capital* Uganda 24 C9

Kâmpóng Cham Cambodia 876 E10

Kâmpóng Chhnăng Cambodia 876 D9

Kâmpóng Saôm Cambodia 876 D11

Kâmpôt Cambodia 876 D11

Kampuchea *see* Cambodia

Kananga Dem. Rep. Congo 20 F10

Kanazawa Japan 478 E6

Kandahār Afghanistan 80 F8

Kandi Benin 33 H7

Kandla India 444 B5

Kandy Sri Lanka 444 E11

Kanestron, Akrotírio *Coastal feature* Greece 403 D5

Kangaroo Island *Island* Australia 95 F7

Kanggye North Korea 497 B3

Kangnŭng South Korea 497 D5

Kanjiža Yugoslavia 105 G2

Kankan Guinea 33 D7

Kano Nigeria 33 J6

Kanpur India 444 E4

Kansas City Kansas, USA 864 G7

Kansas *State* USA 864 F7

Kansk Russian Federation 731 G5

Kaohsiung Taiwan 206 J8

Kaolack Senegal 33 B6

Kapan Armenia 186 H6

Kapchagay Kazakhstan 731 E7

Kapfenberg Austria 819 J4

Kaposvár Hungary 312 D10

Kapuas *River* Indonesia 451 E3

Kara Kum *see* Karakumy

Kara Sea Arctic Ocean 64 G7

Kara-Balta Kyrgyzstan 80 J3

Kara-Bogaz-Gol, Zaliv *Sea feature* Caspian Sea 80 B3

Karāchi Pakistan 639 C7

Karaganda Kazakhstan 731 E6

Karaj Iran 463 E3

Karakol Kyrgyzstan 80 K3

Karakoram Range *Mountain range* C Asia 639 G1

Karakumskiy Kanal *Canal* Turkmenistan 80 D5

Karakumy *Desert* Turkmenistan *var.* Kara Kum 80 D4

Karamay China 206 C3

Karasburg Namibia 30 C8

Karasjok Norway 617 G2

Karbalā' Iraq 463 C5

Kardítsa Greece 403 C6

Kariba, Lake *Lake* Zambia/Zimbabwe 30 F5

Karkinits'ka Zatoka *Sea feature* Black Sea 727 H6

Karlovac Croatia 105 C3

Karlovy Vary Czech Republic 312 A6

Karlskrona Sweden 816 C9

Karlsruhe Germany 379 C8

Karlstad Sweden 816 B7

Karmi'él Israel 473 C2

Karnali *River* Nepal 114 B3

Karora Eritrea 24 E5

Kárpathos *Island* Greece 403 G10

Karshi Uzbekistan 80 F4

Karskoye More Arctic Ocean 731 F2

Kasai *River* Dem. Rep. Congo 20 E9

Kasama Zambia 30 G3

Kāshān Iran 463 F4

Kashi China 206 B4

Kashmir *Disputed region* India/Pakistan 444 C2 639 G2

Kasongo Dem. Rep. Congo 20 G9

Kaspi Georgia 186 E3

Kassala Sudan 24 D5

Kassel Germany 379 D6

Kateríni Greece 403 C5

Katha Burma 833 C4

Katmandu *Capital* Nepal 114 E4

Katsina Nigeria 33 I6

Kattegat *Sea feature* Denmark/Sweden 816 A9

Kauai *Island* Hawaii, USA 864 B9

Kaunas Lithuania 112 C5

Kavadarci Macedonia 105 I8

Kavála Greece 403 E4

Kawasaki Japan 478 F7

Kayan *River* Indonesia 451 F2

Kayes Mali 33 C6

Kazakhstan *Country* C Asia 731

Kazakh Uplands *Upland* Kazakhstan 75

Kazan' Russian Federation 731 C4

Kazanlŭk Bulgaria 403 F3

Kéa *Island* Greece 403 E8

Kecskemét Hungary 312 F9

Kédainiai Lithuania 112 D5

Keetmanshoop Namibia 30 C8

Kefallinía *Island* Greece 403 A7

Kefar Sava Israel 473 C4

Kelmė Lithuania 112 C4

Kelowna Canada 169 C9

Kemerovo Russian Federation 731 F5

Kemi Finland 333 B4

Kemijärvi Finland 333 C4

Kemijoki *River* Finland 333 C4

Kendari Indonesia 451 H4

Kenema Sierra Leone 33 C8

Këneurgench Turkmenistan 80 D2

Kénitra Morocco 28 D2

Kenora Canada 169 G9

Kentucky *State* USA 864 I7

Kenya *Country* E Africa 24

Keramadec Trench *Undersea feature* Pacific Ocean 93

Kerch Ukraine 727 J7

Kerch Strait *Sea feature* Russian Federation/Ukraine 727 J7

Kerguelen *Island* Indian Ocean 449 D8

Kerguelen Plateau *Undersea feature* Indian Ocean 449 D9

Kerki Turkmenistan 80 F5

Kérkyra Greece 403 A5

Kérkyra *Island* Greece 403 A6

Kermadec Trench *Undersea feature* Pacific Ocean 634 F8

Kermān Iran 463 H6

Kerulen *River* China/Mongolia 566 G3

Khabarovsk Russian Federation 731 K6

Khambhat, Gulf of *Sea feature* India 444 B6

Khān Yūnis Gaza Strip 473 A7

Khanthabouli Laos 876 D6

Kharkiv Ukraine 727 J3

Khartoum *Capital* Sudan 24 C5

Khartoum North Sudan 24 D5

Khāsh Iran 463 J6

Khaskovo Bulgaria 403 F3

Khaydarkan Kyrgyzstan 80 H4

Kherson Ukraine 727 H6

Khmel'-nyts'kyy Ukraine 727 E3

Kholm Afghanistan 80 G6

Khon Kaen Thailand 833 F7

Khorog Tajikistan 80 I5

Khorramshahr Iran 463 E6

Khouribga Morocco 28 D2

Khudzhand Tajikistan 80 H4

Khulna Bangladesh 114 I8

Khvoy Iran 463 C2

Khyber Pass *Mountain pass* Afghanistan/Pakistan 80 H7

Kičevo Macedonia 105 H8

Kiel Germany 379 D2

Kiel Bay *Sea feature* W Germany 258 C7

Kielce Poland 312 F5

Kiev *Capital* Ukraine 727 G3

Kiffa Mauritania 33 C5

Kigali *Capital* Rwanda 20 H9

Kigoma Tanzania 24 C10

Kikwit Dem. Rep. Congo 20 E10

Kilchu North Korea 497 D3

Kilimanjaro *Peak* Tanzania 15

Kilkenny Ireland 465 D5

Kilkís Greece 403 C4

Killarney Ireland 465 B6

Kimberley South Africa 784 F5

Kimch'aek North Korea 497 D3

Kimch'ŏn South Korea 497 C7

Kimje South Korea 497 C7

Kindia Guinea 33 C7

Kindu Dem. Rep. Congo 20 G9

King Island *Island* Australia 93

Kingman Reef *External territory* USA, Pacific Ocean 679 F1

Kingston *Capital* Jamaica 172 D5

Kingston Canada 169 K9

Kingston upon Hull England, UK 858 F7

Kingstown St Vincent & the Grenadines 172 K7

King William Island *Island* Canada 169 E5

Kinshasa *Capital* Dem. Rep. Congo 20 D9

Kirghiz Steppe *Plain* Kazakhstan 731 D5

Kirghizia *see* Kyrgyzstan

Kiribati *Country* Pacific Ocean 679

Kirinyaga *Peak* Kenya 15

Kiritimati *Island* Kiribati 679 G2

Kirkenes Norway 617 H2

Kirkland *Lake* Canada 169 I9

Kirkūk Iraq 463 C3

Kirkwall Scotland, UK 858 D2

Kirov Russian Federation 731 C3

Kirovohrad Ukraine 727 H4

Kīrthar Range *Mountain range* Pakistan 639 C6

Kiruna Sweden 816 D2

Kisangani Dem. Rep. Congo 20 F8

Kishorganj Bangladesh 114 J7

Kismaayo Eritrea 24 F9

Kisumu Kenya 24 D9

Kitakyūshū Japan 478 B8

Kitami Japan 478 G2

Kitchener Canada 169 I10

Kitwe Zambia 30 F3

Kitzbühel Austria 819 G4

Kivu, Lake *Lake* Rwanda/ Dem. Rep. Congo 20 G9

Kladno Czech Republic 312 B6

Klagenfurt Austria 819 I6

Klaipėda Lithuania 112 B4

Klang Malaysia 523 B4

Klerksdorp South Africa 784 G4

Ključ Bosnia & Herzegovina 105 D4

Klosterneuburg Austria 819 K3

Knin Croatia 105 C5

Knittelfeld Austria 819 J5

Knud Rasmussen Land *Region* Greenland 64 C7

Kōbe Japan 478 D7

Koblenz Germany 379 B7

Kobryn Belarus 112 C8

Kočani Macedonia 105 I8

Kōchi Japan 478 C8

Kodiak Island *Island* Alaska, USA 864 B3

Køge Denmark 258 E5

Kōhima India 444 I4

Kohŭng South Korea 497 C8

Koilabas Nepal 114 C4

Kŏje-do *Island* South Korea 497 D8

Kokand Uzbekistan 80 H4

Kokkola Finland 333 B6

Kokshaal-Tau *Mountain range* Kyrgyzstan 80 K3

Kokshetau Kazakhstan 731 D5

Kol'skiy Poluostrov *Peninsula* Russian Federation 731 D2

Kola Peninsula *Peninsula* Russian Federation 308

Kolda Senegal 33 B6

Kolding Denmark 258 C5

Kölen Mountains *Mountain range* Norway/Sweden 617 D5

Kolka Latvia 112 D2

Kolkata (Calcutta) India 444 G5

Köln Germany 379 B6

Kolwezi Dem. Rep. Congo 20 F11

Kolyma Range *Mountain range* Russian Federation 75

Kolymskoye Nagor'ye *Mountain range* Russian Federation 731 K3

Komárno Slovakia 312 E8

Komoé *River* Ivory Coast 33 F8

Komotiní Greece 403 E4

Komsomol'sk Turkmenistan 80 E4

Komsomol'sk-na-Amure Russian Federation 731 K5

Komusan North Korea 497 D2

Kongsberg Norway 617 C8

Konispol Albania 105 G11

Konjic Bosnia & Herzegovina 105 E5

Kopaonik *Mountains* Yugoslavia 105 H6

Koper Slovenia 105 A3

Koprivnica Croatia 105 D2

Korçë Albania 105 H9

Korčula *Island* Croatia 105 D6

Korea Bay *Sea feature* China/North Korea 497 A4

Korea Strait *Sea feature* Japan/South Korea 75

Korhogo Ivory Coast 33 E7

Korinthiakós Kólpos *Sea feature* Greece 403 C7

Kórinthos Greece 403 C8

Kōriyama Japan 478 F6

Korla China 206 D4

Körös *River* Hungary 312 F9

Korosten' Ukraine 727 F2

Korsør Denmark 258 D6

Kortrijk Belgium 126 B3

Kos *Island* Greece 403 G9

Kosan North Korea 497 C4

Kosciuszko, Mount *Peak* Australia 93

Košice Slovakia 312 G7

Kosŏng North Korea 497 C5

Kosovo *Province* Yugoslavia 105 H7

Kosovska Mitrovica Yugoslavia 105 H6

Kosrae *Island* Micronesia 636 E3

Kostanay Kazakhstan 731 D5

Koszalin Poland 312 D2

Kota India 444 C5

Kota Bharu Malaysia 523 C2

Kota Kinabalu Malaysia 523 J2

Kotka Finland 333 D8

Kotto *River* C Africa 20 F6

Koudougou Burkina 33 F6

Kourou French Guiana 791 K4

Kousséri Cameroon 20 C4

Kouvola Finland 333 D8

Kovel' Ukraine 727 D2

Kozáni Greece 403 C5

Kra, Isthmus of *Coastal feature* Burma/Thailand 833 D11

Kragujevac Yugoslavia 105 H5

Krakatau *Peak* Indonesia 75

Kraków Poland 312 F6

Kraljevo Yugoslavia 105 H5

Kranj Slovenia 105 B2

Krasnoyarsk Russian Federation 731 G5

Krasnyy Luch Ukraine 727 K5

Kremenchuk Ukraine 727 H4

Kremenchuts'ke Vodoskhovyshche *Reservoir* Ukraine 727 H4

Krems Austria 819 K3

Kretinga Lithuania 112 B4

Kribi Cameroon 20 B7

Krishna *River* India 444 C7

Kristiansand Norway 617 B9

Kristianstad Sweden 816 B10
Krk *Island* Croatia 105 B3
Kroonstad South Africa 784 G5
Kruševac Yugoslavia 105 H5
Krugersdorp South Africa 784 G4
Krychaw Belarus 112 G8
Kryvyy Rih Ukraine 727 H5
Kuala Lumpur *Capital* Malaysia 523 B3
Kuala Terengganu Malaysia 523 C2
Kuantan Malaysia 523 C3
Kuching Malaysia 523 G4
Kuçovë Albania 105 G9
Kudat Malaysia 523 K1
Kufstein Austria 819 G4
Kugluktuk Canada 169 D5
Kuito Angola 30 C3
Kujang North Korea 497 B4
Kulai Malaysia 523 C4
Kuldīga Latvia 112 C3
Kulyab Tajikistan 80 H5
Kumamoto Japan 478 B9
Kumanovo Macedonia 105 I7
Kumasi Ghana 33 F8
Kumbo Cameroon 20 B6
Kŭmch'ŏn North Korea 497 B5
Kŭmho *River* South Korea 497 D7
Kumi South Korea 497 C7
Kumon Range *Mountain range* Burma 833 C2
Kŭmsong South Korea 497 B8
Kunashir *Island* Japan/Russian Federation *(disputed)* 478 G2
Kunduz Afghanistan 80 G6
Kungar Malaysia 523 A2
Kunlun Shan *Mountain range* China 206 C5
Kunming China 206 G8
Kunsan South Korea 497 B7
Kuopio Finland 333 D6
Kupang Indonesia 451 H5
Kura *River* Azerbaijan/Georgia 186 I5
Kurashiki Japan 478 C8
Kürdämir Azerbaijan 186 J4
Kuressaare Estonia 112 D2
Kurgan-Tyube Tajikistan 80 H5
Kurigram Bangladesh 114 I5
Kurile Islands *Islands* Pacific Ocean 634 D3
Kurile rench *Undersea feature* Pacific Ocean 634 D3
Kurmuk Sudan 24 D6
Kuršėnai Lithuania 112 C4
Kuru *River* Bhutan 114 J4
Kuruman South Africa 784 D5
Kushiro Japan 478 G3
Kushtia Bangladesh 114 I7
Kusŏng North Korea 497 B3
K'ut'aisi Georgia 186 D3
Kuujjuaq Canada 169 I6
Kuujjuarapik Canada 169 H7
Kuŭm North Korea 497 C4
Kuusamo Finland 333 D4
Kuusankoski Finland 333 D8
Kuwait *Capital* Kuwait 406 F2
Kuwait *Country* SW Asia 406
Kværndrup Denmark 258 D6
Kwangju South Korea 497 C8
Kwango *River* Dem. Rep. Congo 20 D10
Kyklades *Islands* Greece 403 E8
Kyŏnggi-man *Sea feature* North Korea/South Korea 497 B6
Kyŏnghŭng North Korea 497 E1

Kyŏngju South Korea 497 D7
Kyōto Japan 478 D7
Kyrenia Cyprus 821 B3
Kyrgyzstan *Country* C Asia *var.* Kirghizia 80
Kýthira *Island* Greece 403 D10
Kyūshū *Island* Japan 478 B9
Kyzyl Kum *Desert* Kazakhstan/Uzbekistan 80 F2
Kyzylorda Kazakhstan 731 C6

L

Laâyoune *Capital* Western Sahara 28 B4
Labé Guinea 33 C7
Laborec *River* Slovakia 312 G7
Labrador City Canada 169 J7
Labrador *Region* Canada 611
Labrador Sea Atlantic Ocean 89 C3
Labuan Malaysia 523 J2
Laccadive Islands *Island group* India 449 D3
La Ceiba Honduras 193 E3
La Chau-de-Fonds Switzerland 819 B5
Ladoga, Lake *Lake* Russian Federation 308
Lae Papua New Guinea 636 C5
Læsø *Island* Denmark 258 E2
La Esperanza Honduras 193 D4
Lågen *River* Norway 617 C7
Laghouat Algeria 28 F2
Lagos Nigeria 33 H8
Lagos Portugal 682 B11
Lagouira Western Sahara 28 A6
Lahore Pakistan 639 F4
Laï Chad 20 D5
Lake District *Region* England, UK 858 D7
Laksham Bangladesh 114 K8
Lakshmipur Bangladesh 114 J8
La Ligua Chile 65 B5
Lalitpur Nepal 114 E4
Lalmanir Hat Bangladesh 114 I5
La Louvière Belgium 126 D3
Lambaré Paraguay 141 G9
Lambaréné Gabon 20 B8
Lambert Glacier *Ice feature* Antarctica 56 I4
Lamía Greece 403 C7
Lampedusa *Island* Italy 475 D11
Lampione *Island* Italy 475 C11
Lanao, L. *Lake* Philippines 650 E8
Lancaster England, UK 858 D7
Lancaster Sound *Sea feature* Canada 169 F4
Land's End *Coastal feature* England, UK 858 B11
Landeck Austria 819 F5
Langeland *Island* Denmark 258 D6
Langkawi, Pulau *Island* Malaysia 523 A2
Lang Sơn Vietnam 876 F2
Länkäran Azerbaijan 186 K7
Lansing Michigan, USA 864 I6
Lanzarote *Island* Spain 28 B3
Lanzhou China 206 G5
Laoag Philippines 650 C2

Laon France 356 F3
La Oroya Peru 285 D8
Laos *Country* SE Asia 876
La Palma *Island* Spain 28 A3
La Paz *Capital* Bolivia 141 B4
La Paz Mexico 551 C4
La Perouse Strait *Sea feature* Japan 478 F1
Lapland *Region* N Europe 308
Lappeenranta Finland 333 D8
Laptev Sea Arctic Ocean *Rus.* Laptevykh, More 64 G4
Laptevykh, More *see* Laptev Sea
L'Aquila Italy 475 E5
La Rioja Argentina 65 C5
Lárisa Greece 403 C6
Lārkāna Pakistan 639 D5
Larnaca Cyprus 821 B4
la Roche-sur-Yon France 356 C5
la Rochelle France 356 C5
La Romana Dominican Republic 172 H4
La Serena Chile 65 B5
La Spezia Italy 475 C4
Las Piedras Uruguay 65 E6
Las Tablas Panama 193 J9
Las Vegas Nevada, USA 864 C7
Latacunga Ecuador 285 C2
Latvia *Country* NE Europe 112
Launceston Australia 95 G8
Laurentian Mountains *Upland* Canada 611
Lausanne Switzerland 819 A6
Laval France 356 C4
Laylá Saudi Arabia 406 E5
Lebanon *Country* SW Asia 821
Lebu Chile 65 A7
Lecce Italy 475 H7
Leduc Canada 169 D9
Leeds England, UK 858 E7
Leeuwarden Netherlands 601 D2
Leeuwin, Cape *Coastal feature* Australia 95 B6
Leeward Islands *Island group* West Indies 172 K4
Lefkáda *Island* Greece 403 B7
Legaspi Philippines 650 D5
Legnica Poland 312 C5
le Havre France 356 D2
Leicester England, UK 858 E9
Leiden Netherlands 601 B5
Leinster *Region* Ireland 465 E5
Leipzig Germany 379 E5
Leivádia Greece 403 C7
Lek *River* Netherlands 601 C5
Lelystad Netherlands 601 D4
le Mans France 356 D4
Lemvig Denmark 258 A3
Lena *River* Russian Federation 731 H3
Leoben Austria 819 J5
León Nicaragua 193 E6
León Mexico 551 E4
León Spain 798 D2
le Puy France 356 F7
Lerwick Scotland, UK 858 A1
Leskovac Yugoslavia 105 I6
Lesotho *Country* southern Africa 784
Lesser Antarctica *Region* Antarctica 56 C6
Lesser Antilles *Island group* West Indies 172 J6
Lesser Caucasus Mountains Asia 186 D3
Lésvos *Island* Greece 403 F6
Lethbridge Canada 169 D9
Leti, Kepulauan *Island group* Indonesia 451 I5

Leuven Belgium 126 D2
Leverkusen Germany 379 B6
Lewis *Island* Scotland, UK 858 A5
Leyte *Island* Philippines 650 E6
Lezhë Albania 105 G8
Lhasa China 206 E7
Lhuntshi Bhutan 114 J4
Liberec Czech Republic 312 C5
Liberia Costa Rica 193 F7
Liberia *Country* W Africa 33
Libreville *Capital* Gabon 20 B8
Libya *Country* N Africa 28
Libyan Desert *Desert* N Africa 15
Liechtenstein *Country* C Europe 819
Liège Belgium 126 F3
Lienz Austria 819 H6
Liepāja Latvia 112 B3
Liestal Switzerland 819 C4
Liezen Austria 819 I4
Liffey *River* Ireland 465 E4
Ligurian Sea Mediterranean Sea 356 H8 475 B4
Likasi Dem. Rep. Congo 20 G11
Lille France 356 F2
Lillebælt *Sea feature* Denmark 258 C6
Lillehammer Norway 617 C7
Lilongwe *Capital* Malawi 30 G4
Lima *Capital* Peru 285 D8
Limassol Cyprus 821 B4
Limerick Ireland 465 C5
Limfjorden *Sea feature* Denmark 258 B2
Límnos *Island* Greece 403 E6
Limoges France 356 D6
Limón Costa Rica 193 H8
Limpopo *River* southern Africa 30 G6 784 G2
Linares Chile 65 B6
Linares Spain 798 E6
Lincoln England, UK 858 F8
Lincoln Nebraska, USA 864 F6
Lincoln Sea Arctic Ocean 64 D6
Linden Guyana 791 I4
Lindi Tanzania 24 E12
Line Islands *Island group* Kiribati 679 G3
Lingga, Kepulauan *Island group* Indonesia 451 C3
Linköping Sweden 816 C8
Linosa *Island* Italy 475 D11
Linz Austria 819 I3
Lion, Golfe du *Sea feature* Mediterranean Sea 356 F9
Lipa Philippines 650 C5
Lipari *Island* Italy 475 E9
Lira Uganda 24 C8
Lisbon *Capital* Portugal 682 B8
Lithuania *Country* E Europe 112
Little Minch *Sea feature* Scotland, UK 858 B3
Little Rock Arkansas, USA 864 G8
Liverpool England, UK 858 D8
Livingstone Zambia 30 E5
Livno Bosnia & Herzegovina 105 D5
Livorno Italy 475 C4
Ljubljana *Capital* Slovenia 308 B2

Ljungan *River* Sweden 816 B5
Ljusnan *River* Sweden 816 C6
Llanos *Region* Colombia/Venezuela 791 F3
Lleida Spain 798 H3
Lobatse Botswana 30 E7
Lobito Angola 30 B3
Locarno Switzerland 819 D7
Lod Israel 473 B5
Lodja Dem. Rep. Congo 20 F9
Łódź Poland 312 E4
Lofoten *Island group* Norway 617 D3
Logan, Mount *Peak* Canada 611
Logroño Spain 798 F2
Loire *River* France 356 D4
Loja Ecuador 285 B4
Lokitaung Kenya 24 D8
Løkken Denmark 258 C2
Loksa Estonia 112 F1
Lolland *Island* Denmark 258 E7
Lombok *Island* Indonesia 451 F5
Lomé *Capital* Togo 33 G8
Lomond, Loch *Lake* Scotland, UK 858 C5
Lomonosov Ridge *Undersea feature* Arctic Ocean *var.* Harris Ridge 64 E5
London Canada 169 I10
London *Capital* UK 858 F10
Londonderry Northern Ireland, UK 858 A6
Londonderry, Cape *Coastal feature* Australia 93
Londrina Brazil 146 F8
Long Beach California, USA 634 I4
Longford Ireland 465 D4
Long Island *Island* Bahamas 172 E2
Long Island *Island* NE USA 864 K6
Longyearbyen Svalbard 64 E8
Lop Nur *Lake* China 206 D4
Lorca Spain 798 F7
Lord Howe Rise *Undersea feature* Pacific Ocean 634 D8
Lorient France 356 B4
Los Angeles California, USA 864 B8
Los Mochis Mexico 551 D4
Lot *River* France 356 D7
Louang Namtha Laos 876 B3
Louangphabang Laos 876 B4
Loubomo Congo 20 C9
Louisiana *State* USA 864 G9
Louisville Kentucky, USA 864 I7
Lovech Bulgaria 403 E2
Loyauté, Îles *Island group* New Caledonia 636 F8
Loznica Yugoslavia 105 F4
Luanda *Capital* Angola 30 A2
Luanshya Zambia 30 F4
Luang *Capital* Angola 30 A2
Lubāns Ezers *Lake* Latvia 112 F4
Lubango Angola 30 B4
Lübeck Germany 379 D3
Lublin Poland 312 G5
Lubny Ukraine 727 H3
Lubumbashi Dem. Rep. Congo 20 G12
Lucan Ireland 465 E4
Lucapa Angola 30 D2
Lucena Philippines 650 C5
Lučenec Slovakia 312 F8
Lucerne Switzerland 819 C5
Lucerne, L. *Lake* Switzerland 819 C5

Lucknow India 444 E4
Lüderitz Namibia 30 B8
Ludhiāna India 444 C3
Lugano Switzerland 819 D7
Lugano, L. *Lake*
  Italy/Switzerland 819 D7
Lugo Spain 798 B2
Luhans'k Ukraine 727 L4
Lule *River* Sweden 816 C2
Luleå Sweden 816 E3
Lumsden New Zealand
  606 B8
Luninyets Belarus 112 D8
Lúrio *River* Mozambique
  30 I4
Lusaka *Capital* Zambia 30 F4
Lushnjë Albania 105 G9
Lūt, Dasht-e *Desert* Iran
  463 I5
Luts'k Ukraine 727 D2
Lutzow-Holm Bay *Sea feature*
  Antarctica 56 H2
Luxembourg *Capital*
  Luxembourg 126 F6
Luxembourg *Country*
  W Europe 126
Luxor Egypt 24 C3
Luzon *Island* Philippines
  650 C3
Luzon Strait *Sea feature*
  Philippines/Taiwan 650 C1
L'viv Ukraine 727 C3
Lyepyel' Belarus 112 F6
Lyon France 356 F6

M

Ma'ān Jordan 821 D9
Maas *River* W Europe 601 E6
Maastricht Netherlands
  601 D8
Macao China 206 H8
Macapá Brazil 146 F2
Macdonnell Ranges *Mountains*
  Australia 93
Macedonia *Country* SE Europe
  off. Former Yugoslav
  Republic of Macedonia
  abbrev. FYR Macedonia 105
Maceió Brazil 146 I5
Machakos Kenya 24 E10
Machala Ecuador 285 B3
Mackay Australia 95 H4
Mackay, Lake *Lake* Australia 93
Mackenzie *River* Canada
  64 B3
Mackenzie Bay *Sea feature*
  Atlantic Ocean 56 I4
Mackenzie *River* Canada
  169 C7
McKinley, Mount *see* Denali
McMurdo Sound *Sea feature*
  Antarctica 56 F7
Mâcon France 356 F6
Madagascar *Country* Indian
  Ocean 30
Madagascar Basin *Undersea
  feature* Indian Ocean
  449 C6
Madagascar Plateau *Undersea
  feature* Indian Ocean 449 B7
Madang Papua New Guinea
  636 C5
Madaripur Bangladesh 114 J8
Madeira *Island group* Portugal
  89 E5
Madeira *River* Bolivia/Brazil
  146 D4
Madison Wisconsin, USA
  864 H6
Madona Latvia 112 E4
Madras (Chennai) India
  444 E9

Madre de Dios *River*
  Bolivia/Peru 141 B2 285 G8
Madrid *Capital* Spain 798 E4
Madurai India 444 D10
Mae Nam Ping *River* Thailand
  833 D7
Mafeteng Lesotho 784 G6
Magadan Russian Federation
  731 K3
Magdalena *River* Colombia
  791 C3
Magdeburg Germany 379 E5
Magellan, Strait of *Sea feature*
  S South America 787
Magerøy *Island* Norway
  617 G1
Maggiore, L. *Lake*
  Italy/Switzerland 475 B2
  819 D7
Magura Bangladesh 114 I8
Māhabalipuram India 444 E9
Mahajanga Madagascar
  30 K5
Mahakali *River* India/Nepal
  114 A2
Mahalapye Botswana 30 E7
Mahanādi *River* India 444 F6
Mahilyow Belarus 112 G7
Maicao Colombia 791 C2
Maiduguri Nigeria 33 K6
Maine *State* USA 864 L5
Mainz Germany 379 C7
Maiquetía Venezuela 791 F2
Maitland Australia 95 H6
Majuro *Capital* Marshall
  Islands 636 F3
Makarska Croatia 105 D6
Makeni Sierra Leone 33 C7
Makgadikgadi *Salt pan*
  Botswana 30 E6
Makhachkala Russian
  Federation 731 B5
Makiyivka Ukraine 727 K5
Makkah Saudi Arabia 406 B5
Makkovik Canada 169 J6
Makurdi Nigeria 33 J8
Malabār Coast *Coastal region*
  India 444 C9
Malabo *Capital* Equatorial
  Guinea 20 B7
Malacca, Strait of *Sea feature*
  Indonesia/Malaysia 451 B2
Maladzyechna Belarus
  112 E6
Málaga Spain 798 D7
Malakal Sudan 24 C7
Malang Indonesia 451 E5
Malanje Angola 30 B3
Malawi *Country* southern
  Africa 30
Malaya Peninsula SE Asia
  523 B3
Malaysia *Country* Asia 523
Maldive Ridge *Undersea feature*
  Indian Ocean 449 D4
Maldives *Country* Indian
  Ocean 449
Mali *Country* W Africa 33
Malindi Kenya 24 E10
Mallorca *Island* Spain 798 J5
Malmö Sweden 816 B10
Malmsbury South Africa
  784 B8
Malta *Country* Mediterranean
  Sea 475
Maluku *Island group* Indonesia
  451 H3
Mamberamo *River* Indonesia
  451 K3
Mamoré *River* Bolivia
  141 C3
Mamoudzou Mayotte 30 K4
Man Ivory Coast 33 D8

Man, Isle of *Island* UK
  858 C7
Manado Indonesia 451 H3
Managua *Capital* Nicaragua
  193 E6
Manama *Capital* Bahrain
  406 F3
Mananjary Madagascar 30 K6
Manaus Brazil 146 D3
Manchester England, UK
  858 D8
Manchuria *Plain* E Asia
  206 J3
Mandalay Burma 833 C5
Mandalgovĭ Mongolia 566 F4
Mangalia Romania 727 E8
Mangalore India 444 C9
Mangla Reservoir *Reservoir*
  India/Pakistan 444 C2
Manguéni, Plateau du *Upland*
  Niger 33 K3
Manicouagan, Réservoir
  Reservoir Canada 169 J7
Manikganj Bangladesh 114 J7
Manila *Capital* Philippines
  650 C4
Manitoba *Province* Canada
  169 F8
Manizales Colombia 791 B4
Mannar Sri Lanka 444 E10
Mannheim Germany 379 C8
Mannu *River* Italy 475 B7
Manono Dem. Rep. Congo
  20 G10
Manp'o North Korea 497 B3
Mansel Island *Island* Canada
  169 G6
Manta Ecuador 285 A2
Mantes-la-Jolie France 356 E3
Mantova Italy 475 C3
Manzanillo Mexico 551 F6
Manzini Swaziland 784 I4
Mao Chad 20 D4
Maoke, Pegunungan
  Mountains Indonesia 451 K4
Maputo *Capital* Mozambique
  30 G7
Mar, Serra do *Mountains*
  Brazil 787
Maracaibo Venezuela 791 D2
Maracaibo, Lago de *Inlet*
  Venezuela 791 D2
Maracay Venezuela 791 E2
Maradi Niger 33 I6
Marajó, Ilha de *Island* Brazil
  787
Maranhão, Barragem do
  Portugal 682 D7
Marañón *River* Peru 285 D4
Marbella Spain 798 D8
Mar Chiquita, Laguna *Salt lake*
  Argentina 65 D5
Mardān Pakistan 639 E2
Mar del Plata Argentina 65 E7
Margarita, Isla de *Island*
  Venezuela 791 G2
Margow, Dasht-e- *Desert*
  Afghanistan 80 E8
Mariana Trench *Undersea
  feature* Pacific Ocean 634 D5
Maribo Denmark 258 E7
Maribor Slovenia 105 C2
Marie Byrd Land *Region*
  Antarctica 56 D5
Mariehamn Finland 333 A9
Mariestad Sweden 816 B8
Marijampolė Lithuania 112 C6
Marinduque *Island* Philippines
  650 C5
Mariscal Estigarribia Paraguay
  141 E7
Maritsa *River* SE Europe
  403 F3

Mariupol' Ukraine 727 K5
Marka Eritrea 24 F9
Marne *River* France 356 F3
Marneuli Georgia 186 F4
Maroua Cameroon 20 C5
Marowijne *River* French
  Guiana/Surinam 791 K5
Marquesas Islands *Island group*
  French Polynesia 679 J4
Marrakech Morocco 28 D3
Marsala Italy 475 D9
Marseille France 356 F8
Marshall Islands *Country*
  Pacific Ocean 636
Martadi Nepal 114 B2
Martigny Switzerland 819 B7
Martin Slovakia 312 E7
Martinique *External territory*
  France, West Indies 172 L6
Mary Turkmenistan 80 E5
Maryland *State* USA 864 J7
Masan South Korea 497 D8
Masbate *Island* Philippines
  650 D6
Masbate Philippines 650 D6
Mascarene Plateau *Undersea
  feature* Indian Ocean 449 C6
Maseru *Capital* Lesotho
  784 G6
Mashhad Iran 463 I3
Masindi Uganda 24 C9
Masinloc Philippines 650 B4
Maşirah, Jazīrat *Island* Oman
  406 J5
Mask, Lough *Lake* Ireland
  465 B4
Massachusetts *State* USA
  864 K6
Massalı Azerbaijan 186 K6
Massawa Eritrea 24 E5
Massif Central *Upland* France
  356 E6
Massoukou Gabon 20 C9
Masterton New Zealand
  606 E5
Matadi Dem. Rep. Congo
  20 C10
Matagalpa Nicaragua 193 F5
Matamoros Mexico 551 H3
Matanzas Cuba 172 B2
Matara Sri Lanka 444 E11
Mataró Spain 798 I3
Mato Grosso *Physical region*
  Brazil 146 E5
Matosinhos Portugal 682 C3
Matrûh Egypt 24 B1
Matsue Japan 478 C7
Matsuyama Japan 478 C8
Matterhorn *Peak* Switzerland
  819 B7
Maturín Venezuela 791 G2
Maui *Island* Hawaii, USA
  864 B9
Maun Botswana 30 D6
Mauna Loa *Peak* Hawaii, USA
  864 C10
Mauritania *Country* W Africa
  33
Mauritius *Country* Indian
  Ocean 449
Mayaguana *Island* Bahamas
  172 F3
Mayotte *External territory*
  France, Indian Ocean
  449 B5
Mazatenango Guatemala
  193 A4
Mazatlán Mexico 551 E5
Mažeikiai Lithuania 112 C4
Mazury *Region* Poland
  312 F3

Mazyr Belarus 112 E9
Mbabane *Capital* Swaziland
  784 I4
Mbala Zambia 30 G2
Mbale Uganda 24 D9
Mbandaka Dem. Rep. Congo
  20 D8
Mbeya Tanzania 24 D11
Mbuji-Mayi Dem. Rep. Congo
  20 F10
Mechelen Belgium 126 D2
Medan Indonesia 451 B2
Medellín Colombia 791 B4
Médenine Tunisia 28 H2
Mediterranean Sea Atlantic
  Ocean 89 G5
Meerut India 444 D3
Meghna *River* Bangladesh
  114 J8
Meherpur Bangladesh
  114 H8
Mek'elē Ethiopia 24 E6
Meknès Morocco 28 D2
Mekong *River* SE Asia 75
Mekong Delta *Wetlands*
  Vietnam 876 F11
Melaka Malaysia 523 C4
Melanesia *Region* Pacific
  Ocean 634 E7
Melbourne Australia 95 G7
Melilla *External territory*
  Spain, N Africa 28 E2
Melitopol' Ukraine 727 I6
Melk Austria 819 J3
Melo Uruguay 65 F5
Melrhir, Chott *Salt lake*
  Algeria 28 G2
Melville Island *Island*
  Australia 95 D1
Melville Island *Island* Canada
  169 D4
Mende France 356 E7
Mendi Papua New Guinea
  636 C5
Mendoza Argentina 65 B5
Menongue Angola 30 C4
Menorca *Island* Spain 798 J4
Mentakap Malaysia 523 C3
Mentawai, Kepulauan *Island
  group* Indonesia 451 B3
Meppel Netherlands 601 E3
Mercedario *Peak* Argentina 787
Mercedes Uruguay 65 E6
Mergui Archipelago *Island
  chain* Burma 833 D10
Mergui Burma 833 D10
Mérida Mexico 551 K5
Mérida Spain 798 C6
Mérida Venezuela 791 D3
Meru Kenya 24 E9
Mesopotamia *Ancient region*
  Iraq 463 E4
Messina Italy 475 F9
Mestia Georgia 186 C1
Mestre Italy 475 D3
Meta *River*
  Colombia/Venezuela 791 D4
Metković Croatia 105 E6
Metz France 356 G3
Meuse *River* W Europe 308
Mexicali Mexico 551 B1
Mexico City *Capital* Mexico
  551 H6
Mexico *Country* North
  America 551
Mexico, Gulf of *Sea feature*
  Atlantic Ocean/Caribbean Sea
  551 I4
Meymaneh Afghanistan 80 F6
Miami Florida, USA 864 J10
Michigan *State* USA 864 I5
Michigan, Lake *Lake* USA
  864 H5

Micronesia *Region* Pacific Ocean 93

Micronesia *Country* Pacific Ocean 636

Micronesia *Region* Pacific Ocean 634 E6

Mid-Atlantic Ridge *Undersea feature* Atlantic Ocean 89 D6

Middelburg South Africa 784 F7

Middelfart Denmark 258 C5

Middlesbrough England, UK 858 E6

Mid-Indian-Ridge *Undersea feature* Indian Ocean 449 D6

Mikkeli Finland 333 D7

Mikuni-sammyaku *Mountains* Japan 478 F6

Milagro Ecuador 285 B3

Milan Italy 475 B2

Mildura Australia 95 G6

Milford Haven Wales, UK 858 C10

Milford Sound New Zealand 606 B8

Millennium Island *Island* Kiribati 679 H4

Mílos *Island* Greece 403 E9

Milwaukee Wisconsin, USA 864 H6

Minatitlán Mexico 551 J6

Minch, The *Sea feature* Scotland, UK 858 B2

Mindanao *Island* Philippines 650 E8

Mindoro *Island* Philippines 650 C5

Mindoro Strait *Sea feature* South China Sea/Sulu Sea 650 C6

Mingäçevir Azerbaijan 186 I4

Mingäçevir Reservoir *Reservoir* Azerbaijan 186 H4

Mingāora Pakistan 639 E2

Minho *River* Portugal/Spain 682 C2 798 B3

Minneapolis Minnesota, USA 864 G5

Minnesota *State* USA 864 G4

Miño *River* Portugal/Spain 798 B2

Minsk *Capital* Belarus 112 E7

Minto, Lake *Lake* Canada 169 H7

Mira *River* Portugal 682 C9

Miranda de Ebro Spain 798 E2

Miri Malaysia 523 I3

Mirim Lagoon *Lagoon* Brazil/Uruguay 65 F6 146 F11

Mirtóo Pelagos *Sea feature* Mediterranean Sea 403 D9

Miryang South Korea 497 D7

Miskolc Hungary 312 F8

Mişrātah Libya 28 I3

Mississippi Delta *Wetlands* USA 864 H9

Mississippi *River* USA 864 G5

Mississippi *State* USA 864 H8

Missouri *River* USA 864 E4

Missouri *State* USA 864 G7

Mito Japan 478 F6

Mittersill Austria 819 G5

Miyazaki Japan 478 C9

Mjøsa, L. *Lake* Norway 617 C7

Mljet *Island* Croatia 105 E7

Mmabatho Botswana 30 E7

Mmabatho South Africa 784 F4

Moçambique Mozambique 30 I4

Mocímboa da Praia Mozambique 30 I3

Mocoa Colombia 791 B6

Mocuba Mozambique 30 H5

Modena Italy 475 C3

Mödling Austria 819 K3

Modriča Bosnia & Herzegovina 105 E4

Mogadishu *Capital* Somalia 24 G9

Mohéli *Island* Comoros 30 J3

Mo i Rana Norway 617 D4

Mokp'o South Korea 497 B8

Moldova *Country* E Europe *var.* Moldova 727

Molde Norway 617 B6

Moldova *see* Moldova

Mollendo Peru 285 F10

Moluccas *Island group* Indonesia 75

Mombasa Kenya 24 E10

Møn *Island* Denmark 258 F6

Monaco *Country* W Europe 356 H8

Monastir Tunisia 28 H2

Monclova Mexico 551 G3

Moncton Canada 169 K8

Mongar Bhutan 114 J4

Mongo Chad 20 E4

Mongolia *Country* NE Asia 566

Monrovia *Capital* Liberia 33 C8

Mons Belgium 126 C4

Mont Blanc *Peak* France/Italy 308

Mont-de-Marsan France 356 C7

Montana *State* USA 864 D5

Montauban France 356 D7

Monte Carlo Monaco 356 H8

Monte Cristi Dominican Republic 172 G4

Montecristi Ecuador 285 B2

Montego Bay Jamaica 172 D4

Montenegro *Republic* Yugoslavia 105 G6

Montería Colombia 791 B3

Montero Bolivia 141 D5

Monterrey Mexico 551 G3

Montevideo *Capital* Uruguay 65 E6

Montgomery Alabama, USA 864 H8

Montpelier Vermont, USA 864 K5

Montpellier France 356 E8

Montréal Canada 169 J9

Montreux Switzerland 819 B6

Montserrat *External territory* UK, West Indies 172 K5

Monument Valley *Valley* SW USA 864 D7

Monywa Burma 833 B5

Monza Italy 475 B2

Moose Factory Canada 169 H8

Mopti Mali 33 F5

Moquegua Peru 285 G11

Mora Sweden 816 B6

Morādābād India 444 D3

Morava *River* C Europe 105 H5 312 D7

Morawhanna Guyana 791 H3

Moray Firth *Inlet* Scotland, UK 858 C3

Morelia Mexico 551 G6

Morena, Sierra *Mountain range* Spain 798 C6

Morghāb *River* Afghanistan/Turkmenistan 80 F6

Morioka Japan 478 F4

Morocco *Country* N Africa 28

Morogoro Tanzania 24 E11

Mörön Mongolia 566 D2

Morondava Madagascar 30 J6

Moroni *Capital* Comoros 30 J3

Morotai, Pulau *Island* Indonesia 451 I2

Mors *Island* Denmark 258 B2

Moscow *Capital* Russian Federation 731 B3

Mosel *River* W Europe *Fr.* Moselle 379 B7

Moselle *River* W Europe *Ger.* Mosel 126 G6 356 G4

Moshi Tanzania 24 E10

Mosquito Coast *Coastal region* Nicaragua 193 G6

Moss Norway 617 C8

Mossendjo Congo 20 C9

Mossoró Brazil 146 I4

Most Czech Republic 312 B5

Mostar Bosnia & Herzegovina 105 E6

Motala Sweden 816 C8

Motril Spain 798 E7

Moulins France 356 E5

Moulmein Burma 833 D7

Moundou Chad 20 D5

Mouscron Belgium 126 B3

Moyale Kenya 24 E8

Moyobamba Peru 285 C5

Mozambique *Country* SE Africa 30

Mozambique Channel *Sea feature* Indian Ocean 30 I6

Mpika Zambia 30 G3

Mtwara Tanzania 24 E12

Muang Không Laos 876 E8

Muang Khôngxédôn Laos 876 E7

Muang Sing Laos 876 B3

Mufulira Zambia 30 F3

Mukacheve Ukraine 727 B4

Mulhacén *Peak* Spain 308

Mulhouse France 356 H4

Mull *Island* Scotland, UK 858 B4

Muller, Pegunungan *Mountains* Indonesia 451 E3

Multān Pakistan 639 E4

Mumbai (Bombay) India 444 B7

Muna, Pulau *Island* Indonesia 451 H4

München Germany 379 E9

Munch'ŏn North Korea 497 C4

Mungla Bangladesh 114 I9

Munshiganj Bangladesh 114 J8

Münster Germany 379 B5

Munster *Region* Ireland 465 C6

Muntinglupa Philippines 650 C4

Muonio *River* Finland/Sweden 333 A2 816 D1

Mur *River* C Europe 819 I5

Murcia Spain 798 G6

Murgab *River* Turkmenistan 80 E5

Murgab Tajikistan 80 J5

Müritz *Lake* Germany 379 F3

Murmansk Russian Federation 731 D2

Murray River *River* Australia 93

Murrumbidgee River *River* Australia 95 G6

Murska Sobota Slovenia 105 D1

Murzuq Libya 28 I4

Muscat *Capital* Oman 406 I4

Mwanza Tanzania 24 D10

Mwene-Ditu Dem. Rep. Congo 20 F10

Mweru, Lake *Lake* Dem. Rep. Congo/Zambia 20 G11 30 F2

Myanmar *see* Burma

Mykolayiv Ukraine 727 H6

Mýkonos *Island* Greece 403 F8

Mymensingh Bangladesh 114 J6

Myŏngch'ŏn North Korea 497 D2

Mysore India 444 C9

Mytilíni Greece 403 F6

Mzuzu Malawi 30 G3

N

Nablus West Bank 473 C4

Nacala Mozambique 30 I4

Næstved Denmark 258 E6

Naga Philippines 650 D5

Nagano Japan 478 E6

Nāgārjuna Reservoir *Reservoir* India 444 D8

Nagasaki Japan 478 B9

Nāgercoil India 444 D10

Nagorno Karabakh *Region* Azerbaijan 186I6

Nagoya Japan 478 E7

Nāgpur India 444 D6

Nagykanizsa Hungary 312 D9

Naha Japan 478 A12

Nahariyya Israel 473 C2

Nain Canada 169 J6

Nairobi *Capital* Kenya 24 D9

Najd *Region* Saudi Arabia 406 D4

Najin North Korea 497 E2

Najrān Saudi Arabia 406 D7

Nakamura Japan 478 C8

Nakhodka Russian Federation 731 F3

Nakhon Ratchasima Thailand 833 F8

Nakhon Sawan Thailand 833 E8

Nakhon Si Thammarat Thailand 833 E12

Nakina Canada 169 H9

Nakskov Denmark 258 D7

Nakuru Kenya 24 D9

Nalayh Mongolia 566 G2

Nal'chik Russian Federation 731 A5

Nam *River* North Korea 497 B4

Namangan Uzbekistan 80 I3

Nam Đinh Vietnam 876 E3

Namib Desert *Desert* Namibia 30 B6

Namibe Angola 30 A4

Namibia *Country* southern Africa 30

Namp'o North Korea 497 B5

Nampula Mozambique 30 I4

Namur Belgium 126 E4

Nanchang China 206 I7

Nancy France 356 G4

Nānded India 444 D7

Nanjing China 206 I6

Nanning China 206 H8

Nantes France 356 C4

Naogaon Bangladesh 114 I7

Napier New Zealand 606 F4

Naples Italy 475 E7

Napo *River* Ecuador/Peru 285 E2

Narayani *River* Nepal 114 E4

Narbonne France 356 E8

Nares Strait *Sea feature* Canada/Greenland 64 C6

Narew *River* Poland 312 G3

Narmada *River* India 444 C6

Narsingdi Bangladesh 114 J7

Narva Estonia 112 G2

Narva *River* Estonia/Russian Federation 112 G2

Narva Bay *Sea feature* Gulf of Finland 112 G1

Narvik Norway 617 E3

Naryn Kyrgyzstan 80 J3

Naryn *River* Kyrgyzstan/Uzbekistan 80 J3

Nashville Tennessee, USA 864 H7

Nāsik India 444 C6

Nâsir, Buḩeiret *Reservoir* Egypt 24 C3

Nassau *Capital* Bahamas 172 D1

Natal Brazil 146 I4

Natitingou Benin 33 G7

Nator Bangladesh 114 I7

Natuna, Kepulauan *Island group* Indonesia 523 F3

Natuna, Kepulauan *Island group* Indonesia 451 D3

Nauru *Country* Pacific Ocean 636

Navapolatsk Belarus 112 F6

Navassa Island *External territory* USA, West Indies 172 E4

Navoi Uzbekistan 80 F4

Nawabganj Bangladesh 114 H7

Nawābshāh Pakistan 639 D6

Naxçivan Azerbaijan 186 G7

Náxos *Island* Greece 403 F9

Nazca Peru 285 E9

Nazrēt Ethiopia 24 E7

Nazerat Israel 473 C3

Nazerat 'Illit Israel 473 C2

N'Dalatando Angola 30 B2

Ndélé Central African Republic 20 E6

Ndjamena *Capital* Chad 20 D4

Ndola Zambia 30 F3

N'Giva Angola 30 B5

N'Guigmi Niger 33 K6

Nebitdag Turkmenistan 80 B4

Nebraska *State* USA 864 F6

Neckar *River* Germany 379 C9

Necochea Argentina 65 E7

Negēlē Ethiopia 24 E8

Negev *Desert region* Israel 473 C9

Negro *River* N South America 787

Negros *Island* Philippines 650 D7

Neiva Colombia 791 B5

Nellore India 444 E8

Nelson New Zealand 606 D6

Neman *River* NE Europe 112 C7

Nemuro Japan 478 G2

Nepal *Country* S Asia 114

Nepalganj Nepal 114 B4

Neretva *River* Bosnia & Herzegovina 105 E6

Neris *River* Belarus/Lithuania 112 D5

Ness, Loch *Lake* Scotland, UK 858 C3

Netanya Israel 473 B4

Netherlands *Country* W Europe *var.* Holland 601

Netherlands Antilles *External territory* Netherlands, West Indies *prev.* Dutch West Indies 172 H7

Netrakona Bangladesh 114 J6

Neubrandenburg Germany 379 F3

Neuchâtel Switzerland 819 B5

Neuchâtel, L. *Lake* Switzerland 819 B5

Neumünster Germany 379 D2

Neunkirchen Austria 819 K4

Neuquén Argentina 65 C7

Neusiedler, L. *Lake* Austria/Hungary 819 L4

Nevada *State* USA 864 C7

Nevada, Sierra *Mountain range* Spain 798 E7

Nevers France 356 E5

New Amsterdam Guyana 791 I4

Newbridge Ireland 465 E5

New Britain *Island* Papua New Guinea 636 D5

New Brunswick *Province* Canada 169 K8

New Caledonia *External territory* France, Pacific Ocean 636 E7

Newcastle Australia 95 H6

Newcastle upon Tyne England, UK 858 E6

New Delhi *Capital* India 444 D3

Newfoundland Basin *Undersea feature* Atlantic Ocean 89 D5

Newfoundland *Province* Canada 169 J6

New Guinea *Island* Pacific Ocean 634 C6

New Hampshire *State* USA 864 K5

New Ireland *Island* Papua New Guinea 636 D5

New Jersey *State* USA 864 K6

New Mexico *State* USA 864 E8

New Orleans Louisiana, USA 864 H9

New Plymouth New Zealand 606 E4

New Providence *Island* Bahamas 172 E1

New Siberian Islands *Islands* Russian Federation 64 F3

New South Wales *State* Australia 95 G6

New York New York, USA 864 K6

New York *State* USA 864 J6

New Zealand *Country* Pacific Ocean 606

Newry Northern Ireland, UK 858 B7

Neyshābūr Iran 463 I3

Ngaoundéré Cameroon 20 C6

Nha Trang Vietnam 876 H9

Niamey *Capital* Niger 33 H6

Niangay, Lac *Lake* Mali 33 F5

Nicaragua *Country* Central America 193

Nicaragua, Lago de *Lake* Nicaragua 193 F6

Nice France 356 H8

Nicobar Islands *Island group* India 449 E3

Nicosia *Capital* Cyprus 821 B4

Nicoya, Golfo de *Sea feature* Costa Rica 193 F7

Nicoya, Península de *Peninsula* Costa Rica 193 F7

Nieuw Amsterdam Surinam 791

Niger *River* W Africa 89 F6

Niger *Country* W Africa 33

Niger Delta *Wetlands* Nigeria 33 I9

Niger *River* W Africa 33 I7

Nigeria *Country* W Africa 33

Niigata Japan 478 E6

Nijmegen Netherlands 601 D5

Nikopol' Ukraine 727 I5

Nile *River* N Africa 24 C4

Nile Delta *Wetlands* Egypt 24 C1

Nilphamari Bangladesh 114 H5

Nîmes France 356 F8

Ninety East Ridge *Undersea feature* Indian Ocean 449 E5

Ningbo China 206 J7

Nioro Mali 33 D5

Nipigon, Lake *Lake* Canada 169 G9

Niš Yugoslavia 105 I6

Nissum Bredning *Sea feature* Denmark 258 B3

Nitra Slovakia 312 E8

Niue *External territory* New Zealand, Pacific Ocean 634 F7

Nizhnevartovsk Russian Federation 731 E4

Nizhniy Novgorod Russian Federation 731 C3

Nizhyn Ukraine 727 H2

Nizwa Oman 406 I5

Nkhotakota Malawi 30 G4

Nkongsamba Cameroon 20 B6

Noakhali Bangladesh 114 K8

Nogales Mexico 551 C1

Nordfjord *Coastal feature* Norway 617 B7

Norfolk Island *External territory* Australia, Pacific Ocean 93

Noril'sk Russian Federation 731 F3

Normandy *Region* France 356 C3

Norrköping Sweden 816 C8

Norrtälje Sweden 816 D7

North Albanian Alps *Mountains* Albania/Yugoslavia 105 G7

North America 611

North American Basin *Undersea feature* Atlantic Ocean 89 C5

North Atlantic Ocean 89 D3

North Bay Canada 169 I9

North Cape *Coastal feature* New Zealand 606 D1

North Cape *Coastal feature* Norway 617 G1

North Carolina *State* USA 864 J8

North Dakota *State* USA 864 F4

Northern Cook Islands *Islands* Cook Islands 679 F5

Northern Dvina *River* Russian Federation 308

Northern Ireland *Province* UK 858 A6

Northern Mariana Islands *External territory* USA, Pacific Ocean 634 D5

Northern Territory *Territory* Australia 95 E3

North European Plain *Region* N Europe 308

North Frisian Islands *Islands* Denmark/Germany 379 C1

North Island *Island* New Zealand 606 E4

North Korea *Country* E Asia 497

North Pole *Ice feature* Arctic Ocean 64 E6

North Sea Atlantic Ocean 89 F4

North Uist *Island* Scotland, UK 858 A3

North West Cape *Coastal feature* Australia 449 G6

Northwest Territory *Territory* Canada 169 C6

Norway *Country* N Europe 617

Norwegian Sea Arctic Ocean 617 C5

Norwich England, UK 858 G9

Noteć *River* Poland 312 D3

Nottingham England, UK 858 E8

Nouâdhibou Mauritania 33 A3

Nouâdhibou, Râs *Coastal feature* Mauritania 33 A3

Nouakchott *Capital* Mauritania 33 B4

Nouméa New Caledonia 636 F8

Nova Gorica Slovenia 105 A2

Nova Gradiška Croatia 105 E3

Nova Kakhovka Ukraine 727 H6

Nova Scotia *Province* Canada 169 K8

Novara Italy 475 B2

Novaya Zemlya *Islands* Russian Federation 731 E2

Nové Zámky Slovakia 312 E8

Novgorod Russian Federation 731 C2

Novi Sad Yugoslavia 105 G3

Novokuznetsk Russian Federation 731 F6

Novo Mesto Slovenia 105 C2

Novosibirsk Russian Federation 731 F5

Novosibirskiye Ostrova *Islands* Russian Federation 731 I2

Nsanje Malawi 30 H5

Nubian Desert *Desert* Sudan 24 C4

Nuevo Laredo Mexico 551 G2

Nuku'alofa *Capital* Tonga 679 C7

Nukus Uzbekistan 80 D2

Nullarbor Plain *Region* Australia 95 C6

Nunavut *Territory* Canada 169 E4

Nunivak Island *Island* Alaska, USA 611

Nuoro Italy 475 B7

Nurek Tajikistan 80 H5

Nürnberg Germany 379 E8

Nyala Sudan 24 B6

Nyasa, Lake *Lake* E Africa 15

Nyeri Kenya 24 D9

Nyíregyháza Hungary 312 G8

Nykøbing Denmark 258 E5

Nykøbing-Falster Denmark 258 E7

Nyköping Sweden 816 C8

Nzérékoré Guinea 33 D8

O

Oahe, Lake *Reservoir* North and South Dakota, USA 864 F5

Oahu *Island* Hawaii, USA 864 B9

Oaxaca Mexico 551 I7

Ob' *River* Russian Federation 731 F5

Oban Scotland, UK 858 B4

Obihiro Japan 478 G3

Obo Central African Republic 20 G7

Och'amch'ire Georgia 186 B2

Odense Denmark 258 D5

Oder *River* C Europe 312 D5 379 F3

Odesa Ukraine 727 G6

Odienné Ivory Coast 33 D7

Ofanto *River* Italy 475 F7

Offenbach Germany 379 C7

Ogaden *Plateau* Ethiopia 24 F7

Ogbomosho Nigeria 33 H8

Ogre Latvia 112 D4

Ogulin Croatia 105 C3

Ohio *River* N USA 864 H7

Ohio *State* USA 864 I6

Ohrid Macedonia 105 H9

Ohrid, Lake *Lake* Albania/Macedonia 105 H9

Ohře *River* Czech Republic/Germany 312 A6

Ōita Japan 478 C8

Ojos del Salado *Peak* Chile 787

Oka *River* Russian Federation 731 G6

Okahandja Namibia 30 C6

Okāra Pakistan 639 F4

Okavango Delta *Wetland* Botswana 30 D5

Okayama Japan 478 D8

Okazaki Japan 478 E7

Okeechobee, Lake *Lake* Florida, USA 864 J10

Okhotsk Russian Federation 731 J4

Okhotsk, Sea of Pacific Ocean 634 D2

Oki-shotō *Island group* Japan 478 C7

Okinawa *Island* Japan 478 A12

Oklahoma City Oklahoma, USA 864 F8

Oklahoma *State* USA 864 F8

Okushiri-tō *Island* Japan 478 E3

Öland *Island* Sweden 816 C9

Olavarría Argentina 65 D6

Olbia Italy 475 B6

Oldenburg Germany 379 C3

Oleksandriya Ukraine 727 H4

Olenëk *River* Russian Federation 731 H3

Ölgiy Mongolia 566 B2

Olhão Portugal 682 D11

Olomouc Czech Republic 312 D6

Olsztyn Poland 312 F2

Olt *River* Romania 727 C8

Olten Switzerland 819 C5

Olympia Washington, USA 864 A4

Omaha Nebraska, USA 864 G6

Oman *Country* SW Asia 406

Oman, Gulf of *Sea feature* Indian Ocean 449 C2

Omdurman Sudan 24 C5

Omsk Russian Federation 731 E5

Ondangwa Namibia 30 B5

Öndörhaan Mongolia 566 H2

Onega, Lake *Lake* Russian Federation 308

Ongjin North Korea 497 B5

Ongole India 444 E8

Onitsha Nigeria 33 I8

Onsŏng North Korea 497 D1

Ontario *Province* Canada 169 G9

Ontario, Lake *Lake* Canada/USA 611

Oostende Belgium 126 B1

Oosterschelde *Inlet* Netherlands 601 B6

Opole Poland 312 D5

Oradea Romania 727 B5

Oran Algeria 28 E2

Orange River *River* southern Africa 15

Oranjestad Aruba 172 H7

Ordubad Azerbaijan 186 H7

Örebro Sweden 816 C7

Oregon *State* USA 864 B5

Orenburg Russian Federation 731 C5

Oreor *Capital* Palau 636 B3

Orestiáda Greece 403 F4

Orhon *River* Mongolia 566 G2

Orinoco *River* Colombia/Venezuela 791 F5

Oristano Italy 475 A7

Orivesi, L. *Lake* Finland 333 D7

Orizaba, Volcán Pico de *Peak* Mexico 611

Orkney Islands *Island group* Scotland, UK 858 D1

Orlando Florida, USA 864 I9

Orléans France 356 E4

Örnsköldsvik Sweden 816 D5

Oro North Korea 497 C3

Orontes *River* SW Asia 821 E3

Orsha Belarus 112 G7

Orsk Russian Federation 731 C5

Orūmīyeh, Daryācheh-ye *Lake* Iran 463 D2

Oruro Bolivia 141 B5

Osa, Península de *Peninsula* Costa Rica 193 G9

Ōsaka Japan 478 D8

Osh Kyrgyzstan 80 I4

Oshawa Canada 169 I9

Osijek Croatia 105 F3

Oskarshamn Sweden 816 C9

Oslo *Capital* Norway 617 C8

Oslo Fjord *Coastal feature* Norway 617 C8

Osnabrück Germany 379 C4

Osorno Chile 65 B8

Oss Netherlands 601 D6

Ossa, Serra d' *Mountains* Portugal 682 D8

Ossora Russian Federation 731 J4

Östersund Sweden 816 C5

Ostrava Czech Republic 312 E6

Ostrołęka Poland 312 G3

Ostrowiec Świętokrzyski Poland 312 G5

Ōsumi-shotō *Island group* Japan 478 B10

Otaru Japan 478 F3

Otra *River* Norway 617 B9

Otranto Italy 475 H7

Otranto, Strait of *Sea feature* Albania/Italy 105 F10 475 G6

Ottawa *Capital* Canada 169 J9

Ottawa *River* Canada 169 I9

Otterup Denmark 258 D5

Ou *River* Laos 876 C3

Ouagadougou *Capital* Burkina 33 F6

Ouahigouya Burkina 33 F6

Ouargla Algeria 28 G3

Oudtshoorn South Africa 784 D8

Ouémé *River* Benin 33 H7

Ouessant, Île d' *Island* France 356 A3

Ouésso Congo 20 D8

Oujda Morocco 28 E2

Oulu Finland 333 C5

Oulujoki *River* Finland 333 D5

Ounasjoki *River* Finland 333 C2

Our *River* W Europe 126 F5

Ourense Spain 798 B2

Ouro Prêto Brazil 146 G8

Ourthe *River* Belgium 126 E4

Outer Hebrides *Island group* Scotland, UK 858 B2

Overflakkee *Island* Netherlands 601 B5

Oviedo Spain 798 D2

Owando Congo 20 D8

Oxford England, UK 858 E10

Oyem Gabon 20 C8

Oyo Nigeria 33 H8

Ózd Hungary 312 F8

P

Pa-an Burma 833 C7

Pabna Bangladesh 114 I7

Pachuca Mexico 551 H5

Pacific Ocean 634

Pacific-Antarctic Ridge *Undersea feature* Pacific Ocean 634 H10

Padang Indonesia 451 B3

Paderborn Germany 379 C5

Padma *see* Ganges

Padova Italy 475 D3

Pag *Island* Croatia 105 B4

Pago Pago *Capital* American Samoa 679 D5

Paide Estonia 112 F2

Pakch'ŏn North Korea 497 B4

Pakistan *Country* S Asia 639

Pakokku Burma 833 B5

Paksey Bangladesh 114 I7

Pakxé Laos 876 E7

Palagruža *Island* Croatia 105 C7

Palau *Country* Pacific Ocean *var.* Belau 636

Palawan *Island* Philippines 650 B7

Paldiski Estonia 112 E1

Palembang Indonesia 451 C4

Palencia Spain 798 D3

Palermo Italy 475 D9

Palikir *Capital* Micronesia 636 E3

Palma Spain 798 I5

Palmas do Tocantins Brazil 146 G5

Palmerston North New Zealand 606 E5

Palmyra Atoll *External territory* USA, Pacific Ocean 679 F1

Palu Indonesia 451 G3

Pamir *River* Afghanistan/Tajikistan 80 I5

Pamirs *Mountains* Tajikistan 80 I5

Pampas *Region* South America 737

Pamplona Spain 798 F2

Panaji India 444 C8

Panama *Country* Central America 193

Panamá, Golfo de *Sea feature* Panama 193 J9

Panama Canal *Canal* Panama 193 J8

Panama City *Capital* Panama 193 J9

Pan American Highway *Road* Central and South America 193 F7

Panay Island *Island* Philippines 650 D6

Pančevo Yugoslavia 105 H4

Panevėžys Lithuania 112 D5

Pangkalpinang Indonesia 451 C3

Panj *River* Afghanistan/Tajikistan 80 G5

Pantanal *Region* Brazil 787

Pantelleria *Island* Italy 475 C10

Pánuco *River* Mexico 551 G5

Papeete *Capital* French Polynesia 679 H6

Paphos Cyprus 821 A4

Papua New Guinea *Country* Pacific Ocean 636

Paraguá *River* Bolivia 141 G8

Paragua *River* Venezuela 791 G4

Paraguay *Country* South America 141

Paraguay *River* C South America 146 E8

Parakou Benin 33 H7

Paramaribo *Capital* Surinam 791 J4

Paraná Argentina 65 D5

Paraná *River* C South America 787

Paranaíba *River* Brazil 146 G4

Pardubice Czech Republic 312 C6

Parecis, Chapada dos *Mountain range* Brazil 146 D6

Parepare Indonesia 451 G4

Paris *Capital* France 356 E3

Parkhar Tajikistan 80 H5

Parma Italy 475 C3

Parnaíba Brazil 146 H3

Pärnu Estonia 112 E2

Paro Bhutan 114 I4

P'aro-ho *Reservoir* South Korea 497 C5

Páros *Island* Greece 403 E9

Parry Islands *Islands* Canada 169 E3

Pasni Pakistan 639 B6

Passo Fundo Brazil 146 F10

Pasto Colombia 791 A6

Patagonia *Region* S South America 65 B10

Patna India 444 F5

Patos Lagoon *Lagoon* Brazil/Uruguay 146 F10

Pátra Greece 403 B7

Pattani Thailand 833 E12

Pattaya Thailand 833 E9

Patuakhali Bangladesh 114 J9

Patuca *River* Honduras 193 F4

Pau France 356 C8

Pavlodar Kazakhstan 731 E6

Pavlohrad Ukraine 727 J4

Paysandú Uruguay 65 E5

Pazardzhik Bulgaria 403 E3

Peć Yugoslavia 105 G7

Pechora *River* Russian Federation 308

Pecos *River* SW USA 864 E8

Pécs Hungary 312 E10

Pegu Burma 833 C7

Peipus, Lake *Lake* Estonia/Russian Federation 112 F2

Peiraías Greece 403 D8

Pèk Laos 876 C4

Pekanbaru Indonesia 451 B3

Pelada, Serra *Mountain range* Brazil 146 F4

Pelagie, Isole *Island group* Italy 475 D11

Pelopónnisos *Region* Greece 403 C8

Pelotas Brazil 146 F10

Pemagatsel Bhutan 114 K4

Pematangsiantar Indonesia 451 B2

Pemba *Island* Tanzania 15

Pennines *Hills* England, UK 858 D6

Pennsylvania *State* USA 864 J6

Penonomé Panama 193 J9

Penzance England, UK 858 B11

Pereira Colombia 791 B4

Périgueux France 356

Perm' Russian Federation 731 D4

Pernik Bulgaria 403 D3

Perpignan France 356 E8

Persian Gulf *see* Gulf

Perth Australia 95 B6

Perth Basin *Undersea feature* Indian Ocean 449 F6

Perth Scotland, UK 858 D4

Peru *Country* C South America 285

Peru Basin *Undersea feature* Pacific Ocean 634 K7

Peru-Chile Trench *Undersea feature* Pacific Ocean 634 L7

Perugia Italy 475 D5

Pescara Italy 475 E5

Peshāwar Pakistan 639 E3

Petah Tiqwa Israel 473 C4

Petaling Jaya Malaysia 523 B4

Peterborough Canada 169 I9

Peterborough England, UK 858 F9

Petra Jordan 821 D9

Petrich Bulgaria 403 D4

Petropavlovsk Kazakhstan 731 G5

Petropavlovsk-Kamchatskiy Russian Federation 731 L4

Pevek Russian Federation 731 J1

Pforzheim Germany 379 C8

Phangan, Ko *Island* Thailand 833 E11

Phichilemu Chile 65 B6

Philadelphia Pennsylvania, USA 864 K6

Philippine Islands *Islands* SE Asia 449 H3

Philippine Sea Pacific Ocean 650 D2

Philippines *Country* Asia 650

Phnom Penh *Capital* Cambodia 876 E10

Phoenix Arizona, USA 864 C8

Phoenix Islands *Island group* Kiribati 679 D3

Phôngsali Laos 876 B2

Phuket Thailand 833 D12

Phuket, Ko *Island* Thailand 833 D12

Phumĭ Kâmpóng Trâbêk Cambodia 876 E9

Phumĭ Sâmraông Cambodia 876 C8

Phuntsholing Bhutan 114 I5

Piacenza Italy 475 C3

Pianosa *Island* Italy 475 F6

Piatra-Neamţ Romania 727 D5

Piave *River* Italy 475 D2

Picos Brazil 146 H4

Pielinen, L. *Lake* Finland 333 F5

Pierre South Dakota, USA 864 F5

Piešťany Slovakia 312 D7

Pietermaritzburg South Africa 784 I6

Pietersburg South Africa 784 H3

Piła Poland 312 D3

Pilar Paraguay 141 F10

Pilcomayo *River* C South America 141 F8

Pinang Pulau *Island* Malaysia 523 A2

Pinar del Río Cuba 172 B2

Pinatubo *Volcano* Philippines 650 C3

Píndos *Mountain range* Greece 403 B6

Pindus Mountains *Mountain range* Greece 308

Pine Island Bay *Sea feature* Antarctica 56 B5

Pineiós *River* Greece 403 B6

Pínnes, Akrotírio *Coastal feature* Greece 403 E5

Pinsk Belarus 112 D8

Pirojpur Bangladesh 114 J9

Pisa Italy 475 C4

Pitcairn Islands *External territory* UK, Pacific Ocean 634 I8

Pite *River* Sweden 816 C2

Piteå Sweden 816 E3

Piteşti Romania 727 C7

Pittsburgh Pennsylvania, USA 864 J6

Piura Peru 285 B4

Pivdennyy Bug *River* Ukraine 727 G5

Plasencia Spain 798 C5

Plate *River* Argentina/Uruguay 65 E6

Platte *River* C USA 611

Plenty, Bay of *Sea feature* New Zealand 606 F3

Pleven Bulgaria 403 E2

Ploieşti Romania 727 D7

Plovdiv Bulgaria 403 E3

Plungė Lithuania 112 C4

Plymouth *Capital* Montserrat 172 K5

Plymouth England, UK 858 C11

Plzeň Czech Republic 312 B6

Po *River* Italy 475 D3

Pobedy, Pik *Peak* China/Kyrgyzstan 75

Po Delta *Wetland* Italy 475 D3

Podgorica Yugoslavia 105 F7

P'ohang South Korea 497 D7

Pohnpei Island *Island* Micronesia 636 E3

Poinsett, Cape *Coastal feature* Antarctica 56 J6

Pointe-Noire Congo 20 C9

Poitiers France 356 D5

Pokhara Nepal 114 D4

Poland *Country* E Europe 312

Polatsk Belarus 112 F6

Pol-e Khomrī Afghanistan 80 G6

Polillo Islands *Island group* Philippines 650 C4

Polis Cyprus 821 A4

Poltava Ukraine 727 I3

Põltsamaa Estonia 112 F2

Polynesia *Region* Pacific Ocean 679 E5

Pomeranian Bay *Sea feature* Germany/Poland 312 C2

Pomorie Bulgaria 403 G3

Pontevedra Spain 798 B2

Pontianak Indonesia 451 D3

Poopó, Lago *Lake* Bolivia 141 B5

Poopó, Lago *Lake* Bolivia 787

Popayán Colombia 791 B5

Popocatépetl *Peak* Mexico 611

Poprad Slovakia 312 F7

Porbandar India 444 A6

Pori Finland 333 B8

Porsangen *Coastal feature* Norway 617 G1

Porsgrunn Norway 617 C8

Portalegre Portugal 682 D7

Port Alice Canada 169 B9

Port-au-Prince *Capital* Haiti 172 F4

Port-de-Paix Haiti 172 F4

Port Elizabeth South Africa 784 F8

Port-Gentil Gabon 20 B8

Port Harcourt Nigeria 33 I9

Port Hope Simpson Canada 169 K6

Portland Oregon, USA 864 B5

Port Laoise Ireland 465 C5

Port Moresby *Capital* Papua New Guinea 636 C6

Port Nolloth South Africa 784 A6

Porto Portugal 682 C3

Pôrto Alegre Brazil 146 F10

Port of Spain *Capital* Trinidad & Tobago 172 L8

Porto-Novo *Capital* Benin 33 H8

Pôrto Velho Brazil 146 C5

Portoviejo Ecuador 285 B2

Port Said Egypt 24 C1

Portsmouth England, UK 858 E11

Port Sudan Sudan 24 D4

Portugal *Country* SW Europe 682

Port-Vila *Capital* Vanuatu 636 F7

Porvenir Chile 65 B11

Posadas Argentina 65 E4

Posŏng *River* South Korea 497 C8

Potenza Italy 475 F7

P'ot'i Georgia 186 C3

Potosí Bolivia 141 C6

Potsdam Germany 379 F4

Potwar Plateau *Plateau* Pakistan 639 F3

Póvoa de Varzim Portugal 682 C3

Poza Rica Mexico 551 H5

Poznań Poland 312 D4

Pozo Colorado Paraguay 141 F8

Præstø Denmark 258 E6

Prague *Capital* Czech Republic 312 B6

Prairies *Region* N America 864 E5

Prato Italy 475 C4

Prešov Slovakia 312 G7

Prespa, Lake *Lake* SE Europe 105 H9 403 B5

Preston England, UK 858 D7

R

Q

S

Pretoria *Capital* South Africa 784 H4
Préveza Greece 403 B6
Prijedor Bosnia & Herzegovina 105 D4
Prilep Macedonia 105 I8
Prince Albert Canada 169 E9
Prince Charles Island *Island* Canada 169 G5
Prince Edward Island *Province* Canada 169 K8
Prince Edward Islands *Island group* Indian Ocean 449 B8
Prince George Canada 169 C8
Prince of Wales Island *Island* Canada 169 E4
Prince Patrick Island *Island* Canada 64 B4
Prince Rupert Canada 169 B8
Princess Elizabeth Land *Region* Antarctica 56 I4
Príncipe *Island* Sao Tome & Principe 20 A8
Pripet *River* Belarus/Ukraine 112 C8 727 D1
Pripet Marshes *Wetlands* Belarus/Ukraine 112 C8 727 E1
Priština Yugoslavia 105 H7
Prizren Yugoslavia 105 H7
Prome Burma 833 B6
Prostějov Czech Republic 312 D7
Provence *Region* France 356 G8
Providence Rhode Island, USA 864 K6
Prudhoe Bay Alaska, USA 864 C1
Prydz Bay *Sea feature* Antarctica 56 I4
Pskov Russian Federation 731 B2
Pskov, Lake *Lake* Estonia/Russian Federation 112 F3
Ptsich *River* Belarus 112 E8
Pucallpa Peru 285 E6
Puebla Mexico 551 H6
Puerto Aisén Chile 65 B9
Puerto Bahía Negra Paraguay 141 G7
Puerto Barrios Guatemala 193 D3
Puerto Busch Bolivia 141 G6
Puerto Cabezas Nicaragua 193 G5
Puerto Carreño Colombia 791 E4
Puerto Cortés Honduras 193 D3
Puerto Deseado Argentina 65 C9
Puerto Montt Chile 65 B8
Puerto Natales Chile 65 B11
Puerto Plata Dominican Republic 172 G4
Puerto Princesa Philippines 650 B7
Puerto Rico *External territory* USA, West Indies 172 I4
Puerto Rico Trench *Undersea feature* Caribbean Sea 172 I4
Puerto Santa Cruz Argentina 65 C10
Puerto Suárez Bolivia 141 G6
Puerto Vallarta Mexico 551 E5
Puerto Williams Chile 65 C11

Pukch'ŏng North Korea 497 D3
Pula Croatia 105 A4
Pulacayo Bolivia 141 B6
Punata Bolivia 141 C5
Pune India 444 C7
Punjab *Region* Pakistan 639 F3
Puno Peru 285 G10
Punta Arenas Chile 65 B11
Puntarenas Costa Rica 193 F8
Purmerend Netherlands 601 C4
Purus *River* Brazil/Peru 146 C4
Pusan South Korea 497 D8
Putumayo *River* NW South America 285 F3 791 C7
Pyapon Burma 833 C8
Pyinmana Burma 833 C6
Pyongyang *Capital* North Korea 497 B4
Pyramid Lake *Lake* Nevada, USA 864 B6
Pyrenees *Mountain range* SW Europe 308
Pyuthan Nepal 114 C4

Qaidam Basin *Physical region* China 206 E5
Qal'eh-ye Now Afghanistan 80 E6
Qatar *Country* SW Asia 406
Qaṭṭâra, Monkhafad el *Desert basin* Egypt 24 B2
Qazax Azerbaijan 186 F4
Qazımämmäd Azerbaijan 186 K5
Qena Egypt 24 C2
Qeshm *Island* Iran 463 H7
Qilian Shan *Mountain range* China 206 E4
Qingdao China 206 J5
Qinghai Hu *Lake* China 206 F5
Qinling *Mountains* China 206 G6
Qiqihar China 206 J2
Qiryat Ata Israel 473 C2
Qiryat Gat Israel 473 B6
Qiryat Motzkin Israel 473 C2
Qiryat Shemona Israel 473 D1
Qom Iran 463 F4
Qondūz *River* Afghanistan 80 G2
Quba Azerbaijan 186 J3
Québec Canada 169 J8
Québec *Province* Canada 169 I8
Queen Charlotte Islands *Islands* Canada 169 A8
Queen Charlotte Sound *Sea feature* Canada 169 A9
Queen Elizabeth Islands *Islands* Canada 169 F3
Queensland *State* Australia 95 G4
Queenstown New Zealand 606 B8
Quelimane Mozambique 30 H5
Querétaro Mexico 551 G5
Quetta Pakistan 639 C4
Quezaltenango Guatemala 193 B3
Quibdó Colombia 791 B4
Quillacollo Bolivia 141 C5
Quimper France 356 A3
Quito *Capital* Ecuador 285 C2
Quy Nhơn Vietnam 876 H8

Ra'ananna Israel 473 B4
Rába *River* Austria/Hungary 312 D9
Rabat *Capital* Morocco 28 D2
Race, Cape *Coastal feature* Canada 169 L7
Rach Gia Vietnam 876 E11
Radom Poland 312 F5
Radstadt Austria 819 H5
Radviliškis Lithuania 112 C4
Rafah Gaza Strip 473 A7
Ragusa Italy 475 E10
Rahīmyār Khān Pakistan 639 E5
Rainier, Mount *Peak* USA 611
Raipur India 444 E6
Rajahmundry India 444 E8
Rajang *River* Malaysia 523 I4
Rajbari Bangladesh 114 I8
Rajbiraj Nepal 114 G5
Rajkot India 444 B6
Rajshahi Bangladesh 114 H7
Rakvere Estonia 112 F2
Raleigh North Carolina, USA 864 J7
Ralik Chain *Islands* Marshall Islands 636 F3
Ramallah West Bank 473 C5
Ramat Gan Israel 473 B4
Ramechhap Nepal 114 F4
Ramla Israel 473 B5
Râmnicu Vâlcea Romania 727 C7
Ramón Castilla Peru 285 G4
Ramree Island *Island* Burma 833 B6
Rancagua Chile 65 B6
Rānchi India 444 F5
Randers Denmark 258 C3
Rangamati Bangladesh 114 K8
Rangoon *Capital* Burma 833 C7
Rangpur Bangladesh 114 I6
Rankin *Inlet* Canada 169 F6
Rankumara Range *Mountain range* New Zealand 606 F4
Rarotonga *Island* Cook Islands 679 F7
Rasht Iran 463 E3
Ratak Chain *Islands* Marshall Islands 636 F2
Ratchaburi Thailand 833 E9
Rauma Finland 333 B8
Raurkela India 444 F6
Ravenna Italy 475 D3
Rāwalpindi Pakistan 639 F3
Rawson Argentina 65 C8
Razgrad Bulgaria 403 F2
Reading England, UK 858 E10
Rebun-tō *Island* Japan 478 F2
Rechytsa Belarus 112 F9
Recife Brazil 146 I5
Red Deer Canada 169 D9
Red River *River* China/Vietnam 876 D2
Red River *River* S USA 864 K7
Red Sea Indian Ocean 449 A2
Ree, Lough *Lake* Ireland 465 D4
Regensburg Germany 379 E8
Reggane Algeria 28 F4
Reggio di Calabria Italy 475 F9
Reggio nell Emilia Italy 475 C3
Regina Canada 169 E9
Rehoboth Namibia 30 C7

Rehovot Israel 473 B5
Reims France 356 F3
Reindeer Lake *Lake* Canada 611
Reni Ukraine 727 E7
Rennes France 356 C3
Resistencia Argentina 65 E4
Reșița Romania 727 B6
Resolute Canada 169 E4
Réunion *External territory* France, Indian Ocean 449 C6
Reus Spain 798 H4
Revillagigedo, Islas *Islands* Mexico 551 C6
Rey, Isla del *Island* Panama 193 K9
Reykjavik *Capital* Iceland 89 E3
Reynosa Mexico 551 H3
Rēzekne Latvia 112 F4
Rhine *River* W Europe 308
Rhode Island *State* USA 864 K6
Rhodope Mountains *Mountain range* Bulgaria/Greece 403 E4
Rhône *River* France/Switzerland 308
Ribe Denmark 258 B5
Ribeirão Prêto Brazil 146 G8
Riberalta Bolivia 141 C2
Rîbnița Moldova 727 F5
Richmond Virginia, USA 864 J7
Riga *Capital* Latvia 112 D3
Riga, Gulf of *Sea feature* Baltic Sea 112 D3
Riihimäki Finland 333 C8
Riiser-Larsen Ice Shelf *Ice feature* Antarctica 56 D2
Rijeka Croatia 105 B3
Rimini Italy 475 D4
Ringe Denmark 258 D6
Ringkøbing Denmark 258 A4
Ringkøbing Fjord *Sea feature* Denmark 258 A4
Ringsted Denmark 258 E5
Ringvassøy *Island* Norway 617 E2
Riobamba Ecuador 285 B2
Rio Branco Brazil 146 B5
Río Cuarto Argentina 65 C5
Rio de Janeiro Brazil 146 G8
Rio de la Plata Argentina 65 E6
Río Gallegos Argentina 65 C11
Rio Grande Brazil 146 F11
Rio Grande Rise *Undersea feature* Atlantic Ocean 89 D9
Río Grande *River* Bolivia 141 D4
Rio Grande *River* North America 611
Río Negro, Embalse del *Reservoir* Uruguay 65 E5
Rishiri-tō *Island* Japan 478 F2
Rivas Nicaragua 193 F6
Rivne Ukraine 727 E2
Riyadh *Capital* Saudi Arabia 406 E4
Rizokarpasso Cyprus 821 C3
Rkîz, Lac *Lake* Mauritania 33 B5
Road Town *Capital* British Virgin Islands 172 J4
Roanne France 356 F6
Rockall *Island* UK 89 E4
Rockhampton Australia 95 H4
Rockstone Guyana 791 I4
Rocky Mountains *Mountain range* Canada/USA 611

Rodez France 356 E7
Ródos Greece 403 H9
Ródos *Island* Greece 403 H10
Roeselare Belgium 126 B2
Romania *Country* SE Europe 727
Romanovka Russian Federation 731 H6
Rome *Capital* Italy 475 D6
Rømø *Island* Denmark 258 A6
Roncador, Serra do *Mountain range* Brazil 146 F5
Rønne Denmark 258 E3
Ronne Ice Shelf *Ice feature* Antarctica 56 C4
Roosendaal Netherlands 601 B6
Røros Norway 617 C6
Rosario Argentina 65 D6
Roseau *Capital* Dominica 172 K6
Roskilde Denmark 258 E5
Ross Dependency *Territory* New Zealand, Antarctica 56 D7
Ross Ice Shelf *Ice feature* Antarctica 56 E6
Rosso Mauritania 33 B5
Ross Sea Antarctica 56 E7
Rostock Germany 379 E2
Rostov-na-Donu Russian Federation 731 B4
Roti *Island* Indonesia 451 H6
Rotorua New Zealand 606 F4
Rotterdam Netherlands 601 B5
Rouen France 356 E3
Rovaniemi Finland 333 C4
Rovuma *River* Mozambique/Tanzania 30 I3
Roxas City Philippines 650 D6
Rožňava Slovakia 312 F7
Rudnyy Kazakhstan 731 D5
Rudolph, Lake *Lake* Ethiopia/Kenya 24 D8
Ruiz *Peak* Colombia 787
Rum, Wadi *Seasonal watercourse* Jordan 821 D10
Rumbek Sudan 24 C7
Rundu Namibia 30 C5
Ruoqiang China 206 D4
Ruse Bulgaria 403 F1
Rushmore, Mount *Peak* South Dakota USA 864 E5
Russian Federation *Country* Europe/Asia 731
Rust'avi Georgia 186 F3
Rwanda *Country* C Africa 20
Ryazan' Russian Federation 731 B3
Rybnik Poland 312 E6
Ryukyu Islands *Island group* Japan 478 A12
Rzeszów Poland 312 G6

Saal *River* Germany 379 E5
Saarbrücken Germany 379 B8
Saaremaa *Island* Estonia 112 D2
Saatlı Azerbaijan 186 J5
Šabac Yugoslavia 105 G4
Sabadell Spain 798 I3
Sabah *Region* Malaysia 523 K3
Şāberī, Hāmūn-e- *Salt pan* Afghanistan/Iran 80 D8

Sabhā Libya 28 I4
Sabirabad Azerbaijan 186 J5
Sable, Cape *Coastal feature* 169 K8
Sabzevār Iran 463 H3
Sacramento California, USA 864 B7
Ṣaʿdah Yemen 406 D7
Sado *Island* Japan 478 E6
Safi Morocco 28 C3
Sahara *Desert* N Africa 15
Sahel *Region* W Africa 15
Sāhīwāl Pakistan 639 F4
Saïda Lebanon 821 D5
Saidpur Bangladesh 114 H6
Saimaa, L. *Lake* Finland 333 D7
Sajama *Peak* Bolivia 787
Sakākah Saudi Arabia 406 C2
Sakakawea, Lake *Lake* North Dakota, USA 864 E4
Sakchu North Korea 497 A3
Sakhalin *Island* Russian Federation 731 K5
Sakskøbing Denmark 258 E7
Salado *River* Argentina 65 D4
Ṣalālah Oman 406 H7
Salamanca Spain 798 D4
Sala y Gómez *Island* Chile, Pacific Ocean 634 J8
Saldanha South Africa 784 B8
Saldus Latvia 112 C3
Salekhard Russian Federation 731 K3
Salem India 444 D9
Salem Oregon, USA 864 A5
Salerno Italy 475 E7
Salerno, Golfo di *Sea feature* Italy 475 E7
Salihorsk Belarus 112 E8
Salima Malawi 30 G4
Salina *Island* Italy 475 E9
Salinas Grandes *Lowpoint* Argentina 65 C5
Salisbury England, UK 858 E10
Salo Finland 333 B9
Salso *River* Italy 475 E10
Salta Argentina 65 C3
Salt Lake City Utah, USA 864 D6
Saltillo Mexico 551 G3
Salto Uruguay 65 E5
Salton Sea *Lake* California, USA 864 C8
Salvador Brazil 146 I6
Salween *River* SE Asia 75
Salyan Azerbaijan 186 K5
Salyan Nepal 114 G5
Salzburg Austria 819 H4
Salzgitter Germany 379 D5
Samaná Dominican Republic 172 H4
Samar *Island* Philippines 650 E6
Samara Russian Federation 731 C4
Samarinda Indonesia 451 F3
Samarkand Uzbekistan 80 G4
Sambre *River* Belgium 126 D4
Samdrup Jongkhar Bhutan 114 K5
Samoa *Country* Pacific Ocean 679
Samobor Croatia 105 C2
Sámos *Island* Greece 403 G8
Samothráki *Island* Greece 403 F5
Samsø *Island* Denmark 258 D5
Samui, Ko *Island group* Thailand 833 E11

San *River* Poland 312 G6
San *River* Cambodia/Vietnam 876 F8
Sana *Capital* Yemen 406 D8
Sanandaj Iran 463 D3
San Antonio Chile 65 B6
San Antonio Oeste Argentina 65 C8
San Antonio Texas, USA 864 F9
Sanāw Yemen 406 F7
San Carlos Uruguay 65 F6
San Carlos de Bariloche 65 B8
San Carlos Philippines 650 B4
San Cristóbal Venezuela 791 C3
Sandakan Malaysia 523 K2
San Diego California, USA 864 C8
Sandnes Norway 617 A8
Sandviken Sweden 816 C7
Sandwip Channel *River* Bangladesh 114 K9
Sandy Desert *Desert* Pakistan 639 B5
San Fernando Chile 65 B6
San Fernando Trinidad & Tobago 172 L8
San Fernando Philippines 650 C5
San Fernando Philippines 650 C4
San Fernando Venezuela 791 E3
San Francisco California, USA 864 B7
San Ignacio Belize 193 C2
San Jorge, Golfo *Sea feature* Argentina 787
San José *Capital* Costa Rica 193 G8
San José del Guaviare Colombia 791 C5
San Juan Argentina 65 B5
San Juan *Capital* Puerto Rico 172 I4
San Juan *River* Costa Rica/Nicaragua 193 G7
San Juan Bautista Paraguay 141 G9
San Juan de los Morros Venezuela 791 E2
San Juan Peru 285 E10
Sankt Gallen Switzerland 819 D4
Sankt Pölten Austria 819 K3
Sankt Veit Austria 819 I6
San Lorenzo Honduras 193 D5
San Luis Potosí Mexico 551 G5
San Marino *Country* S Europe 475
San Matías, Golfo *Sea feature* Argentina 787
San Miguel El Salvador 193 D5
San Miguel *River* Bolivia 141 D4
San Miguel de Tucumán Argentina 65 C4
San Pablo Philippines 650 C5
San Pedro Sula Honduras 193 D3
San Remo Italy 475 A4
San Salvador *Capital* El Salvador 193 C5
San Salvorde Jujuy Argentina 65 C3
San Sebastián Spain 798 F2
Santa Ana El Salvador 193 C4
Santa Ana Bolivia 141 C3

Santander Spain 798 E2
Santa Clara Cuba 172 C3
Santa Cruz Bolivia 141 D5
Santa Cruz Islands *Island group* Solomon Islands 636 F6
Santa Fe Argentina 65 D5
Santa Fe New Mexico, USA 864 E7
Santa Isabel *Island* Solomon Islands 636 E6
Santa Maria Brazil 146 E10
Santa Marta Colombia 791 C2
Santarém Brazil 146 E3
Santarém Portugal 682 B7
Santa Rosa Argentina 65 C6
Santa Rosa de Copán Honduras 193 C4
Santiago *Capital* Chile 65 B6
Santiago Dominican Republic 172 G4
Santiago Panama 193 I9
Santiago de Cuba Cuba 172 E4
Santiago del Estero Argentina 65 C4
Santiago Spain 798 B2
Santo Domingo *Capital* Dominican Republic 172 H4
Santo Domingo de los Colorados Ecuador 285 B2
Santos Brazil 146 G9
São Francisco *River* Brazil 146 G6
São Francisco *River* Brazil 787
São José dos Campos Brazil 146 G8
São Luís Brazil 146 G3
São Manuel *River* Brazil 146 E5
Saône *River* France 356 G5
São Paulo Brazil 146 G8
São Roque, Cabo de *Coastal feature* Brazil 146 I4
São Tomé *Island* Sao Tome & Principe 20 A8
Sao Tome & Principe *Country* W Africa 20
São Tomé *Capital* Sao Tome & Principe 20 A8
São Tomé, Cabo de *Cape* Brazil 146 H8
São Vicente, Cabo de *Coastal feature* Portugal 682 B11
Sapporo Japan 478 F33
Sapta Koshi *River* India/Nepal 114 G5
Sarajevo *Capital* Bosnia & Herzegovina 308 F5
Sarandë Albania 105 G10
Sarawak *Region* Malaysia 523 N4
Sarawak Chamber *Underground feature* Malaysia 523 J3
Sarbhang Bhutan 114 J5
Sardinia *Island* Italy 475 B7
Sargasso Sea Atlantic Ocean 89 C6
Sargodha Pakistan 639 F3
Sarh Chad 20 E5
Sariwŏn North Korea 497 B5
Sarnen Switzerland 819 C5
Sasebo Japan 478 B8
Saskatchewan *Province* Canada 169 E8
Saskatchewan *River* Canada 169 F9
Saskatoon Canada 169 E9
Sassari Italy 475 A6
Satkhira Bangladesh 114 I9
Satu Mare Romania 727 B4
Saudi Arabia *Country* SW Asia 406

Sault Sainte Marie Canada 169 H9
Saurimo Angola 30 C3
Sava *River* SE Europe 105 C3
Savannah Georgia, USA 864 I8
Save *River* Mozambique/Zimbabwe 30 G6
Savona Italy 475 B3
Savonlinna Finland 333 D7
Şawqirah Oman 406 I7
Sayat Turkmenistan 80 F5
Sayḥūt Yemen 406 G8
Saynshand Mongolia 566 G4
Say'ūn Yemen 406 F7
Scandinavia *Region* N Europe 89 G3
Schaffhausen Switzerland 819 D4
Schärding Austria 819 H3
Schefferville Canada J6
Scheldt *River* W Europe 126 D1
Schiermonnikoog *Island* Netherlands 601 E1
Schwerin Germany 379 E3
Schwyz Switzerland 819 D5
Scilly, Isles of *Islands* UK 858 B12
Scotia Ridge *Undersea feature* Atlantic Ocean 89 C11
Scotia Sea Atlantic Ocean 89 C11
Scotland *National region* UK 858 C4
Scutari, Lake *Lake* Albania/Yugoslavia 105 F7
Seattle Washington, USA 864 B4
Segamat Malaysia 523 C4
Ségou Mali 33 E6
Segovia Spain 798 E4
Segura *River* Spain 798 F6
Seikan Tunnel *Tunnel* Japan 478 F4
Seinäjoki Finland 333 B7
Seine *River* France 356 E3
Sejerø *Island* Denmark 258 D5
Sekondi-Takoradi Ghana 33 F9
Semarang Indonesia 451 E5
Semipalatinsk Kazakhstan 731 E6
Sên *River* Cambodia 876 D8
Sendai Japan 478 F5
Senegal *Country* W Africa 33
Senegal *River* Africa 33 B5
Senja *Island* Norway 617 E2
Seoul *Capital* South Korea 497 C6
Sept-Îles Canada 169 J7
Seraing Belgium 126 E3
Seram *Island* Indonesia 451 I4
Serasan, Selat *Sea feature* Malaysia 523 F4
Serbia *Republic* Yugoslavia 105 H4
Seremban Malaysia 523 B4
Serov Russian Federation 731 C4
Serpent's Mouth, The *Sea feature* Trinidad & Tobago/Venezuela 791 H2
Sérres Greece 403 D4
Seti *River* Nepal 114 B2
Sétif Algeria 28 G2
Setúbal Portugal 682 B8
Sevan Armenia 186 F5
Sevan, Lich *Lake* Armenia 186 G5

Sevastopol' Ukraine 727 H8
Severn *River* Canada 169 G8
Severn *River* England/Wales, UK 858 D9
Severnaya Zemlya *Island group* Russian Federation 731 G2
Sevilla Spain 798 C7
Seychelles *Country* Indian Ocean 449
Seydi Turkmenistan 80 E4
Sfax Tunisia 28 H2
Shackleton Ice Shelf *Ice feature* Antarctica 56 J5
Shahbazpur *River* Bangladesh 114 J9
Shāhjāhanpur India 444 E4
Shahzadpur Bangladesh 114 I7
Shandong Peninsula *Coastal feature* China 206 J5
Shanghai China 206 J6
Shannon Ireland 465 C5
Shannon *River* Ireland 465 D4
Shan Plateau *Upland* Burma 833 D5
Shaqrā' Saudi Arabia 406 E4
Sharīn Gol Mongolia 566 F2
Sharjah United Arab Emirates 406 H4
Shebeli *River* Ethiopia/Somalia 24 F8
Sheberghān Afghanistan 80 F6
Shefar'am Israel 473 C2
Sheffield England, UK 858 E8
Shemakha Azerbaijan 186 J4
Shemgang Bhutan 114 J4
Shenyang China 206 J4
Sherbrooke Canada 169 J9
Sherpur Bangladesh 114 I6
's-Hertogenbosch Netherlands 601 D6
Shetland Islands *Island group* Scotland, UK 858 A1
Shijiazhuang China 206 I5
Shikārpur Pakistan 639 D5
Shikoku *Island* Japan 478 C8
Shikotan *Island* Japan/Russian Federation *(disputed)* 478 H2
Shillong India 444 H4
Shimla India 444 D3
Shimonoseki Japan 478 B8
Shinano *River* Japan 478 E6
Shingū Japan 478 D8
Shinyanga Tanzania 24 D10
Shīrāz Iran 463 F6
Shkodër Albania 105 G7
Shrewsbury England, UK 858 D9
Shumen Bulgaria 403 G2
Shymkent Kazakhstan 731 D7
Siaragao Island *Island* Philippines 650 F7
Šiauliai Lithuania 112 C4
Šibenik Croatia 105 C5
Siberia *Region* Russian Federation 731 H4
Sibi Pakistan 639 D5
Sibiu Romania 727 C6
Sibu Malaysia 523 N4
Sibut Central African Republic 20 E6
Sicilian Channel *Sea feature* Mediterranean Sea 475 C10
Sicily *Island* Italy 475 E9
Sidi Bel Abbès Algeria 28 E2
Siegen Germany 379 C6
Siena Italy 475 C4
Sierra Leone *Country* W Africa 33
Sierra Madre *Mountain range* Guatemala/Mexico 634 J5
Sierra Madre del Sur *Mountain range* Mexico 551 H7

Sierra Madre Occidental *Mountain range* Mexico 551 D3

Sierra Madre Oriental *Mountain range* Mexico 551 F3

Sierra Nevada *Mountain range* W USA 864 B7

Sierre Switzerland 819 B6

Siguiri Guinea 33 D7

Sikasso Mali 33 E7

Sikhote-Alin Range *Mountain range* Russian Federation 75

Silgadhi Nepal 114 B3

Silkeborg Denmark 258 C4

Šilutė Lithuania 112 B4

Simferopol' Ukraine 727 I7

Simikot Nepal 114 C2

Simpson Desert *Desert region* Australia 95 E5

Sincelejo Colombia 791 B3

Sind *Region* Pakistan 639 D6

Sindhulimadi Nepal 114 F4

Sines Portugal 682 B9

Singa Sudan 24 D6

Singapore *Country* SE Asia 523

Sinnamary French Guiana 791 K4

Sint-Niklaas Belgium 126 C2

Sintra Portugal 682 A7

Sinŭiju North Korea 497 A3

Sion Switzerland 819 B7

Siracusa Italy 475 E10

Sirajganj Bangladesh 114 I7

Siret *River* Romania/Ukraine 727 E6

Sirikit Reservoir *Reservoir* Thailand 833 E7

Sirte, Gulf of *Sea feature* Mediterranean Sea 28 J3

Sisak Croatia 105 D3

Sīstān, Daryācheh-ye *Lake* Iran 463 J5

Sittang *River* Burma 833 C6

Sittwe Burma 833 A5

Sjælland *Island* Denmark 258 E5

Skagen Denmark 258 D1

Skagerrak *Sea feature* Denmark/Norway 258 B1 617 B9

Skeleton Coast *Coastal feature* Namibia 30 A6

Skellefteå Sweden 816 D4

Skýros *Island* Greece 403 E7

Skive Denmark 258 B3

Skjern Denmark 258 B4

Skjern Å *River* Denmark 258 B4

Skopje *Capital* Macedonia 308 H7

Skövde Sweden 816 B8

Skovorodno Russian Federation 731 I5

Skye *Island* Scotland, UK 858 B3

Slagelse Denmark 258 E5

Slatina Romania 727 C7

Slavonski Brod Croatia 105 E3

Sligo Ireland 465 C3

Sliven Bulgaria 403 F3

Slonim Belarus 112 D7

Slovakia *Country* C Europe 312

Slovenia *Country* SE Europe 105

Slov"yans'k Ukraine 727 K4

Słupsk Poland 312 D2

Slutsk Belarus 112 E8

Smallwood Reservoir *Lake* Canada 169 J6

Smara Western Sahara 28 B4

Smederevo Yugoslavia 105 H4

Smøla *Island* Norway 617 B6

Snake *River* NW USA 864 C6

Snowdonia *Mountains* Wales, UK 858 C8

Sobaek-Sanmaek *Mountain range* South Korea 497 C7

Sobradinho Represa *Reservoir* Brazil 146 H5

Sochi Russian Federation 731 A4

Société, Îles de la *Islands* French Polynesia 679 G6

Socotra *Island* Yemen 49 C3

Sodankylä Finland 333 C3

Sofia *Capital* Bulgaria 403 D3

Sogne Fjord *Coastal feature* Norway 617 B7

Sohâg Egypt 24 C2

Sŏjosŏn-man *Sea feature* North Korea 497 B4

Sokch'o South Korea 497 D5

Sokhumi Georgia 186 B2

Sokodé Togo 33 G7

Sokoto Nigeria 33 I6

Sokoto *River* Nigeria 33 I6

Sol, Costa del *Coastal region* Spain 798 E7

Sōlapur India 444 C7

Solomon Islands *Country* Pacific Ocean 636

Solomon Sea Pacific Ocean 636 D6

Solothurn Switzerland 819 C5

Somali Basin *Undersea feature* Indian Ocean 449 B4

Somalia *Country* E Africa 24

Sombor Yugoslavia 105 F3

Somerset Island *Island* Canada 169 E4

Sŏmjin *River* South Korea 497 C8

Somme *River* France 356 E2

Somoto Nicaragua 193 E5

Son *River* India 444 F5

Sønderborg Denmark 258 C6

Songea Tanzania 24 D12

Songkhla Thailand 833 E12

Songnim North Korea 497 B5

Sonoran Desert *Desert* Mexico/USA 611

Sopron Hungary 312 D8

Soria Spain 798 F3

Sørøya *Island* Norway 617 F1

Sorraia, Rio *River* Portugal 682 C7

Sorrento Italy 475 E7

Sŏsan South Korea 497 B6

Sosnowiec Poland 312 E6

Sound, The *Sea feature* Denmark/Sweden 258 F4

Soûr Lebanon 821 D6

South Africa *Country* southern Africa 784

South America 787

Southampton England, UK 858 E10

Southampton Island *Island* Canada 169 G6

South Atlantic Ocean 89 D10

South Australia *State* Australia 95 E5

South Australian Basin *Undersea feature* Southern Ocean 93

South Carolina *State* USA 864 J8

South China Sea Pacific Ocean 634 B5

South Dakota *State* USA 864 F5

South East Cape, *Coastal feature* Australia 93

Southeast Indian Ridge *Undersea feature* Indian Ocean 449 F8

Southeast Pacific Basin *Undersea feature* Pacific Ocean 634 J9

Southend-on-Sea England, UK 858 F10

Southern Alps *Mountain range* New Zealand 606 C7

Southern Cook Islands *Islands* Cook Islands 93

Southern Cook Islands *Islands* Cook Islands 679 B6

Southern Uplands *Mountain range* Scotland, UK 858 D5

South Fiji Basin *Undersea feature* Pacific Ocean 93

South Georgia *External territory* UK, Atlantic Ocean 89 D11

South Indian Basin *Undersea feature* Indian Ocean 449 F9

South Island *Island* New Zealand 606 B7

South Korea *Country* E Asia 497

South Orkney Islands *Islands* Antarctica 56 B2

South Polar Plateau *Upland* Antarctica 56 E4

South Pole *Ice feature* Antarctica 56 E5

South Sandwich Islands *External territory* UK, Atlantic Ocean 89 E11

South Shetland Islands *Islands* Antarctica 56 A3

South Uist *Island* Scotland, UK 858 A3

Southwest Indian Ridge *Undersea feature* Indian Ocean 449 B7

Sovetsk Kalingrad, Russian Federation 112 B5

Soweto South Africa 784 G4

Spain *Country* SW Europe 798

Spárti Greece 403 C9

Spitak Armenia 186 F4

Spitsbergen *Island* Svalbard 64 E8

Spittal Austria 819 H6

Split Croatia 105 D5

Springbok South Africa 784 B6

Springfield Illinois, USA 864 H6

Srebrenica Bosnia & Herzegovina 105 F5

Sri Aman Malaysia 523 N5

Sri Lanka *Country* S Asia *prev.* Ceylon 444

Srimangal Bangladesh 114 K7

Srinagar India 444 C2

Srinagarind Reservoir *Reservoir* Thailand 833 D8

St. Anton Austria 819 E5

St-Brieuc France 356 B3

St. Catharines Canada 169 I10

St-Chamond France 356 F6

St Christopher & Nevis *see* St Kitts & Nevis

Saintes France 356 C6

St-Étienne France 356 F6

St George's *Capital* Grenada 172 K7

St George's Channel *Sea feature* Ireland/UK 465 F7

St Helena *External territory* UK, Atlantic Ocean 89 F8

St Helens, Mount *Peak* USA 611

Saint John Canada 169 K8

St Johns Antigua & Barbuda 172 K5

St John's Canada 169 L6

St Kitts & Nevis *Country* West Indies *var.* St Christopher & Nevis 172

St-Laurent-du-Maroni French Guiana 791 K4

St. Lawrence *River* Canada 169 J8

St. Lawrence Seaway *Waterway* Canada 169 J9

St. Louis Missouri, USA 864 H7

St-Lô France 356 C3

St Lucia *Country* West Indies 172

St Lucia, Lake *Lake* South Africa 784 J5

St-Malo France 356 C3

St. Moritz Switzerland 819 E6

St-Nazaire France 356 B4

St-Louis Senegal 33 A5

St. Paul Minnesota, USA 864 G5

St Petersburg Russian Federation 731 C2

St Pierre & Miquelon *External territory* France, Atlantic Ocean 169 L7

St Vincent & the Grenadines *Country* West Indies 172

St Vincent, Cape *Coastal feature* Portugal 308

Stanley *Capital* Falkland Islands 65 E11

Stanley, Mount *Peak* Democratic Republic Congo 15

Stanovoy Range *Mountain range* Russian Federation 75

Stans Switzerland 819 C5

Stara Zagora Bulgaria 403 F3

Stavanger Norway 617 A8

Stavropol' Russian Federation 731 A4

Steinkjer Norway 617 C5

Stewart Island *Island* New Zealand 606 B9

Steyr Austria 819 I3

Štip Macedonia 105 I8

Stirling Scotland, UK 858 C5

Stockerau Austria 819 K3

Stockholm *Capital* Sweden 816 D7

Stoke-on-Trent England, UK 858 D8

Store Heddinge Denmark 258 F6

Storebælt *Sea feature* Denmark 258 D5

Stornoway Scotland, UK 858 B2

Storsjön *Lake* Sweden 816 C5

Storuman Sweden 816 C4

Stralsund Germany 379 F2

Stranraer Scotland, UK 858 C6

Strasbourg France 356 H4

Stratford-upon-Avon England, UK 858 E9

Stratonice Czech Republic 312 B7

Stromboli *Island* Italy 475 F9

Struer Denmark 258 B3

Struma *River* Bulgaria/Greece 403 D4

Strumica Macedonia 105 J8

Strymónas *see* Struma

Stuttgart Germany 379 C8

Subotica Yugoslavia 105 G2

Suceava Romania 727 D5

Sucre *Capital* Bolivia 141 C6

Sudan *Country* NE Africa 24

Sudbury Canada 169 I9

Sudd *Region* Sudan 24 C7

Sudeten *Mountains* C Europe 312 D6

Suez Egypt 24 C2

Suez Canal *Canal* Egypt 15

Şuḩār Oman 406 I4

Sühbaatar Mongolia 566 F1

Sukkur Pakistan 639 D6

Sula, Kepulauan *Island group* Indonesia 451 H3

Sulaimān Range *Mountain range* Pakistan 639 D5

Sulawesi *Island* Indonesia 451 G3

Sullana Peru 285 B4

Sulu Archipelago *Island group* Philippines 650 C9

Sulu Sea Pacific Ocean 650 B8

Sulyukta Kyrgyzstan 80 H4

Sumatra *Island* Indonesia 451 B3

Sumba *Island* Indonesia 451 G5

Sumbawa *Island* Indonesia 451 G5

Sumbawanga Tanzania 24 C11

Sumbe Angola 30 B3

Sumqayıt Azerbaijan 186 K4

Sumy Ukraine 727 I2

Sunan North Korea 497 B4

Sunch'ŏn North Korea 497 B4

Sunch'ŏn South Korea 497 C8

Sun City South Africa 784 G3

Sunderland England, UK 858 E6

Sundsvall Sweden 816 C5

Sungai Siput Malaysia 523 B2

Sungari *River* China 206 L2

Sun Koshi *River* Nepal 114 F4

Suntar Russian Federation 731 H4

Sunyani Ghana 33 F8

Superior, Lake *Lake* Canada/USA 611

Sup'ung-ho *Reservoir* China/North Korea 497 B3

Şūr Oman 406 J5

Surabaya Indonesia 451 E5

Sūrat India 444 B6

Surat Thani Thailand 833 D11

Sûre *River* W Europe 126 F5

Surigao Philippines 650 E7

Surinam *Country* NE South America *var.* Suriname 791

Suriname *see* Surinam

Surkhob *River* Tajikistan 80 H4

Surt Libya 28 J3

Sutlej *River* Asia 639 F4

Suva *Capital* Fiji 636 G7

Suwŏn South Korea 497 C6

Svalbard *External territory* Norway, Arctic Ocean 64 E8

Svay Riĕng Cambodia 876 E10

Svendborg Denmark 258 D6

Svyetlahorsk Belarus 112 F9

Swabian Jura *Mountain range* Germany 379 C9

Swakopmund Namibia 30 B6

Swansea Wales, UK 858 C10

Swaziland *Country* southern Africa 784

Sweden *Country* N Europe 816

Swindon England, UK 858 E10

Switzerland *Country* C Europe 819

Syaphrubesi Nepal 114 F4

Sydney Australia 95 H6

Sydney Canada 169 L7

Syktyvkar Russian Federation 731 D3

Sylhet Bangladesh 114 K6

Syr Darya *River* C Asia 75

Syria *Country* SW Asia 821

Syrian Desert *Desert* SW Asia 463 B4 821 G5

Szczecin Poland 312 C3

Szeged Hungary 312 F10

Szekesfehérvár Hungary 312 E9

Szekszárd Hungary 312 E10

Szolnok Hungary 312 F9

Szombathely Hungary 312 D9

T

T'elavi Georgia 186 G3

Tábor Czech Republic 312 C6

Tabora Tanzania 24 C10

Tabrīz Iran 463 D2

Tabuaeran *Island* Kiribati 679 F2

Tabūk Saudi Arabia 406 A2

Tacloban Philippines 650 E6

Tacna Peru 285 G11

Tacuarembó Uruguay 65 E5

T'aebaek-Sanmaek *Mountain range* South Korea 497 D5

Taedong *River* North Korea 497 C3

Taegu South Korea 497 D7

Taejŏn South Korea 497 C7

Tagus *River* Portugal/Spain 682 C6 798 D5

Tahiti *Island* French Polynesia 679 H6

Taipei *Capital* Taiwan 206 J8

Taiping Malaysia 523 B2

Taiwan *Country* E Asia *prev.* Formosa 206

Taiyuan China 206 H5

Ta'izz Yemen 406 D9

Tajikistan *Country* C Asia 80

Taklamakan Desert *Desert region* China 206 C4

Talak *Desert region* Niger 33 I4

Talamanca, Cordillera de *Mountains* Costa Rica 193 G8

Talas Kyrgyzstan 80 I3

Talaud, Kepulauan *Island group* Indonesia 451 I2

Talca Chile 65 B6

Talcahuano Chile 65 B7

Taldykorgan Kazakhstan 731 E7

Tallahassee Florida, USA 864 I9

Tallinn *Capital* Estonia 112 E1

Talsi Latvia 112 D3

Tamale Ghana 33 G7

Tamanrasset Algeria 28 G6

Tampa Florida, USA 864 I9

Tampere Finland 333 C8

Tampico Mexico 551 H5

Tana *River* Finland/Norway 333 B2 617 G2

Tanch'ŏn North Korea 497 D3

Tando Ādam Pakistan 639 D6

Tanega-shima *Island* Japan 478 B10

Tanga Tanzania 24 E10

Tangail Bangladesh 114 I7

Tanganyika, Lake *Lake* E Africa 15

Tanger Morocco 28 D2

Tangshan China 206 I4

Tanimbar, Kepulauan *Island group* Indonesia 451 J4

Tansen Nepal 114 D4

Tanță Egypt 24 C1

Tan-Tan Morocco 28 C4

Tanzania *Country* E Africa 15

Tanzania *Country* E Africa 24

Tapa Estonia 112 F2

Tapachula Mexico 551 J7

Tapajós *River* Brazil 146 E4

Tāpi *River* India 444 C6

Taranto Italy 475 G7

Taranto, Golfo di *Sea feature* Mediterranean Sea 475 G8

Tarapoto Peru 285 C5

Tarawa *Island* Kiribati 679 B2

Taraz Kazakhstan 731 D7

Tarbes France 356 C8

Târgoviște Romania 727 D7

Târgu Mureș Romania 727 C6

Tarija Bolivia 141 C7

Tarim River *River* China 206 C4

Tarlac Philippines 650 C4

Tarn *River* France 356 E7

Tarna Peru 285 D8

Tarnów Poland 312 F6

Tarragona Spain 798 H4

Tartu Estonia 112 F3

Tarțūs Syria 821 D4

Tashi Bhutan 114 K4

Tashigang Bhutan 114 K4

Tashk, Daryācheh-ye *Lake* Iran 463 G6

Tashkent *Capital* Uzbekistan 80 H3

Tasman Plateau *Undersea feature* Pacific Ocean 93

Tasman Sea Pacific Ocean 634 D9

Tasmania *State* Australia 95 G8

Tassili n'Ajjer *Desert plateau* Algeria 28 G5

Tastrup Denmark 258 F5

Tatabánya Hungary 312 E8

Tatra Mountains *Mountains* C Europe 312 F7

Taunggyi Burma 833 C5

Taunton England, UK 858 D10

Taupo New Zealand 606 F4

Taupo, Lake *Lake* New Zealand 606 F4

Tauragė Lithuania 112 C5

Tauranga New Zealand 606 F3

Taurus Mountains *Mountain range* Turkey 75

Tavoy Burma 833 D9

Tawau Malaysia 523 K3

Tawitawi *Island* Philippines 650 C9

Taymyr, Ozero *Lake* Russian Federation 731 G3

Taymyr, Poluostrov *Peninsula* Russian Federation 731 G2

Tbilisi *Capital* Georgia F3

Tegucigalpa *Capital* Honduras 193 E4

Tehran *Capital* Iran 463 F3

Tehuantepec, Golfo de *Sea feature* Mexico 551 J7

Tel Aviv-Yafo Israel 473 B4

Telšiai Lithuania 112 C4

Temuco Chile 65 B7

Ténéré *Region* Niger 33 K4

Tenerife *Island* Spain 28 A4

Tennessee *River* SE USA 864 I7

Tennessee *State* USA 864 I7

Tepelenë Albania 105 G10

Tepic Mexico 551 F5

Teplice Czech Republic 312 B5

Teraina *Island* Kiribati 679 F2

Teresina Brazil 146 H4

Terhathum Nepal 114 G4

Termez Uzbekistan 80 G5

Terneuzen Netherlands 601 B7

Terni Italy 475 D5

Ternopil' Ukraine 727 D3

Terrassa Spain 798 I3

Terschelling *Island* Netherlands 601 D1

Teruel Spain 798 G4

Teseney Eritrea 24 D5

Tete Malawi 30 G5

Tétouan Morocco 28 D2

Tetovo Macedonia 105 H7

Tetulia *River* Bangladesh 114 J9

Tevere *River* Italy 475 D5

Teverya Israel 473 D2

Texas *State* USA 864 F8

Texel *Island* Netherlands 601 C2

Thailand *Country* SE Asia 833

Thailand, Gulf of *Sea feature* South China Sea 833 E10

Tha Khek Laos 876 D6

Thakurgaon Bangladesh 114 H5

Thames *River* England, UK 858 F10

Thane India 444 B7

Thar Desert *Desert* India/Pakistan 444 B4 639 E5

Tharthār, Buhayrat ath *Lake* Iraq 463 C4

Thásos *Island* Greece 403 E5

Thaton Burma 833 C7

Thatta Pakistan 639 D7

The Valley *Capital* Anguilla 172 K4

Thermaïkós Kólpos *Sea feature* Greece 403 C5

Thessaloníki Greece 403 C5

Thiès Senegal 33 A5

Thimpu *Capital* Bhutan 114 I4

Thionville France 356 G3

Thíra *Island* Greece 403 F9

Thisted Denmark 258 B2

Thohoyandou South Africa 784 I2

Thompson Canada 169 E8

Thon Buri Thailand 833 E9

Thracian Sea Greece 403 E5

Thun Switzerland 819 C6

Thunder Bay Canada 169 G9

Thuner, L. *Lake* Switzerland 819 C6

Thuringian Forest *Forested mountains* Germany 379 D6

Thurso Scotland, UK 858 C2

Tianjin China 206 I4

Tiaret Algeria 28 F2

Tiberias, Lake *Lake* Israel 473 D2

Tibesti *Mountains* Chad/Libya 15

Tibet, Plateau of *Plateau* China 206 D6

Tien Shan *Mountain range* C Asia 75

Tienen Belgium 126 E3

Tierra del Fuego *Island* Argentina/Chile 65 C11

Tighina Moldova 727 F6

Tigris *River* SW Asia 463 C3

Tijuana Mexico 551 A1

Tiksi Russian Federation 731 H3

Tilburg Netherlands 601 C6

Tillabéri Niger 33 H6

Timaru New Zealand 606 C7

Timișoara Romania 727 A5

Timor *Island* Indonesia 451 H5

Timor, East *Country* 451 H5

Timor Sea Indian Ocean 449 H5

Tindouf Algeria 28 C4

Tínos *Island* Greece 403 E8

Tioman, Pulau *Island* Malaysia 523 D4

Tipperary Ireland 465 C6

Tirana *Capital* Albania 308 G8

Tiraspol Moldova 727 F6

Tirol *Region* Austria 819 G5

Tirso *River* Italy 475 B7

Tiruchchirāppalli India 444 D10

Tisza *River* E Europe 312 F8

Titicaca, Lake *Lake* Bolivia/Peru 787

Titov Veles Macedonia 105 I8

Tlemcen Algeria 28 E2

Toamasina Madagascar 30 L6

Tobago *Island* Trinidad & Tobago 172 L8

Toba Kākar Range *Mountains* Pakistan 639 D4

Toba, Danau *Lake* Indonesia 451 B2

Tocantins *River* Brazil 146 G6

Tocopilla Chile 65 B3

Toftlund Denmark 258 B6

Togo *Country* W Africa 33

Tokelau *External territory* New Zealand, Pacific Ocean 634 F7

Tokmak Kyrgyzstan 80 J3

Tokuno-shima *Island* Japan 478 B11

Tokushima Japan 478 D8

Tokyo *Capital* Japan 478 F7

Toledo Spain 798 E5

Toliara Madagascar 30 J7

Tomakomai Japan 478 F3

Tombouctou Mali 33 F5

Tombua Angola 30 A4

Tomini, Gulf of *Sea feature* Indonesia 451 G3

Tomsk Russian Federation 731 F5

Tønder Denmark 258 B6

Tonga *Country* Pacific Ocean 679

Tonghae South Korea 497 D6

Tongjosön-man *Sea feature* North Korea 497 D4

Tongking, Gulf of *Sea feature* South China Sea 206 H9

Tongsa Bhutan 114 I4

Tônlé Sap *Lake* Cambodia 876 D9

Toowoomba Australia 95 H5

Topeka Kansas, USA 864 G7

Torkestan, Band-e *Mountain range* Afghanistan 80 F6

Torne *River* Sweden 816 E2

Torneträsk *Lake* Sweden 816 D1

Tornio Finland 333 B4

Toronto Canada 169 I10

Torrens, Lake *Lake* Australia 95 F6

Torreón Mexico 551 F3

Torres Strait *Sea feature* Arafura Sea/Coral Sea 93

Tortosa Spain 798 H4

Toruń Poland 312 E3

Toscana *Region* Italy 475 C4

Toscano, Arcipelago *Island group* Italy 475 C5

Tottori Japan 478 D7

Toubkal *Peak* Morocco 15

Touggourt Algeria 28 G3

Toulon France 356 G8

Toulouse France 356 D8

Toungoo Burma 833 C6

Tournai Belgium 126 B3

Tours France 356 D4

Townsville Australia 95 H3

Towuti, Danau *Lake* Indonesia 451 G4

Toyama Japan 478 E6

Tozeur Tunisia 28 G2

Tqvarch'eli Georgia 186 B2

Tralee Ireland 465 B6

Trang Thailand 833 D12

Transantarctic Mountains *Mountain range* Antarctica 56 D5

Trans-Siberian Railway *Railway* Asia 731 J6

Transylvania *Region* Romania 727 B5

Trapani Italy 475 D9

Trasimeno, Lago *Lake* Italy 475 D5

Traun Austria 819 I3

Traun, L. *Lake* Austria 819 I4

Trebinje Bosnia & Herzegovina 105 E7

Trelew Argentina 65 C8

Tremiti, Isole *Island group* Italy 475 F6

Trenčín Slovakia 312 E7

Trento Italy 475 D2

Trenton New Jersey, USA 864 K6

Tres Arroyos Argentina 65 D7

Tres Marías, Islas *Islands* Mexico 551 E5

Treviso Italy 475 D2

Trier Germany 379 B7

Trieste Italy 475 E3

Tríkala Greece 403 C6

Trincomalee Sri Lanka 444 E10

Trindade, Ilha da *External territory* Brazil, Atlantic Ocean 89 D9

Trinidad Uruguay 65 E6

Trinidad & Tobago *Country* West Indies 172

Trinidad Bolivia 141 C3

Tripoli *Capital* Libya 28 I2

Trípoli Greece 403 C8

Tripoli Lebanon 821 D4

Tristan da Cunha *External territory* UK, Atlantic Ocean 89 E10

Trivandrum India 444 D10

Trnava Slovakia 312 D8

Troense Denmark 258 D6

Trois-Rivières Canada 169 J8

Trollhättan Sweden 816 B8

Tromsø Norway 617 E2

Trondheim Norway 617 C6

Troodos Mountains *Mountains* Cyprus 821 B4

Troyes France 356 F4
Trujillo Honduras 193 F3
Trujillo Peru 285 C6
Tsetserleg Mongolia 566 E3
Tshikapa Dem. Rep. Congo 20 E10
Tskhinvali Georgia 186 E2
Tsumeb Namibia 30 C5
Tsushima *Island* Japan 478 B8
Tubmanburg Liberia 33 C8
Ṭubruq Libya 28 K2
Tucupita Venezuela 791 G3
Tucuruí Reservoir *Reservoir* Brazil 146 F3
Tudmur Syria 821 F4
Tugela *River* South Africa 784 I5
Tuguegarao Philippines 650 C3
Tuktoyaktuk Canada 64 B3
Tula Russian Federation 731 B3
Tulcea Romania 727 F7
Tulkarm West Bank 473 C4
Tulsipur Nepal 114 C4
Tumen *River* E Asia 497 D1
Tundzha *River* Bulgaria 403 F3
Tungaru (*formerly* Gilbert Islands) *Island group* Kiribati 679 B2
Tunis *Capital* Tunisia 28 H1
Tunisia *Country* N Africa 28
Tunja Colombia 791 C4
Tupiza Bolivia 141 C7
Turan Lowland *Lowland* Turkmenistan/Uzbekistan 80 E3
Turin Italy 475 A3
Turkana, Lake *Lake* Ethiopia/Kenya 15
Turkey *Country* SW Asia 75
Turkmenbashi Turkmenistan 80 A3
Turkmenistan *Country* C Asia 80
Turks & Caicos Islands *External territory* UK, West Indies 172 G3
Turku Finland 333 B9
Turnhout Belgium 126 D1
Turpan Depression *Lowland* China 75
Turtkul' Uzbekistan 80 E3
Tuvalu *Country* Pacific Ocean 679
Tuxtla Mexico 551 J6
Tuzla Bosnia & Herzegovina 105 F4
Tweed *River* Scotland, UK 858 D5
Tyrrhenian Sea Mediterranean Sea 475 C7
Tyup Kyrgyzstan 80 K3

U

UAE *see* United Arab Emirates
Ubangi *River* C Africa 20 D7
Uberlândia Brazil 146 G7
Ubon Ratchathani Thailand 833 G8
Ucayali *River* Peru 285 E6
Uchkuduk Uzbekistan 80 F3
Uddaure *Lake* Sweden 816 C3
Uddevalla Sweden 816 B8
Udine Italy 475 E2
Udon Thani Thailand 833 H4
Uele *River* Dem. Rep. Congo 20 F7
Ufa Russian Federation 731 C4

Uganda *Country* E Africa 24
Uíge Angola 30 B2
Ŭijŏngbu South Korea 497 C5
Ujungpandang Indonesia 451 G4
UK *see* United Kingdom
Ukmergė Lithuania 112 D5
Ukraine *Country* E Europe 727
Ulaangom Mongolia 566 B2
Ulan Bator *Capital* Mongolia 566 F2
Ulan-Ude Russian Federation 731 H6
Uldz *River* Mongolia 566 H1
Uliastay Mongolia 566 C3
Ullapool Scotland, UK 858 C3
Ulm Germany 379 D9
Ulsan South Korea 497 D7
Ulster *Region* Ireland, UK 858 A7
Uluru *Peak* Australia *var.* Ayers Rock 95 D4
Ume *River* Sweden 816 D4
Umeå Sweden 816 D4
Umtata South Africa 784 H7
Una *River* Bosnia & Herzegovina/Croatia 105 C4
Ungava Bay *Sea feature* Canada 169 I6
Ungava, Péninsule d' *Peninsula* Canada 169 H6
United Arab Emirates *Country* SW Asia *abbrev.* UAE 406
United Kingdom *Country* NW Europe *abbrev.* UK 858
United States of America *Country* North America *abbrev.* USA 864
Upington South Africa 784 D5
Uppsala Sweden 816 C7
Ural *River* Kazakhstan/Russian Federation 731 C5
Ural Mountains *Mountain range* Russian Federation 731 D4
Ural'sk Kazakhstan 731 C4
Ura-Tyube Tajikistan 80 H4
Urgench Uzbekistan 80 D3
Uroševac Yugoslavia 105 H7
Uruapan Mexico 551 G6
Uruguay *Country* SE South America 65
Uruguay *River* S South America 787
Ürümqi China 206 D3
USA *see* United States of America
Ushuaia Argentina 65 C11
Ust' Chaun Russian Federation 731 J2
Ústí nad Labem Czech Republic 312 B5
Ust'-Kamchatsk Russian Federation 731 L3
Ust'-Kamenogorsk Kazakhstan 731 E6
Ustyurt Plateau *Upland* Kazakhstan/Uzbekistan 80 C2
Usumacinta *River* Guatemala/Mexico 193 B2
Utah *State* USA 864 D7
Utena Lithuania 112 D5
Utrecht Netherlands 601 C5
Uvs Nuur *Lake* Mongolia 566 B2
Uyo Nigeria 33 J9
Uyuni Bolivia 141 B6

Uzbekistan *Country* C Asia 80
Uzhhorod Ukraine 727 B4

V

Vaal *River* South Africa 784 F5
Vaasa Finland 333 B7
Vadodara India 444 B6
Vadsø Norway 617 G2
Vaduz *Capital* Liechtenstein 819 D5
Váh *River* Slovakia 312 D8
Valdés, Península *Peninsula* Argentina 65 D8
Valdez Alaska, USA 864 C2
Valdivia Chile 65 B7
Valence France 356 F7
Valencia *Region* Spain 798 G5
Valencia Spain 798 G5
Valencia Venezuela 791 E2
Valera Venezuela 791 D3
Valga Estonia 112 E3
Valkeakoski Finland 333 C8
Valladolid Spain 798 D3
Valledupar Colombia 791 C2
Vallenar Chile 65 B4
Valletta *Capital* Malta 475 E11
Valmiera Latvia 112 E3
Valparaíso Chile 65 B6
Vanadzor Armenia 186 F4
Vancouver Canada 169 B9
Vancouver Island *Island* Canada 169 B9
Vänern, Lake *Lake* Sweden 816 B8
Vangaindrano Madagascar 30 K7
Vantaa Finland 333 C8
Vanua Levu *Island* Fiji 636 H7
Vanuatu *Country* Pacific Ocean 636
Vārānasi India 444 E5
Varaždin Croatia 105 D2
Varberg Sweden 816 B9
Varde Denmark 258 A5
Vardø Norway 617 H1
Varkaus Finland 333 D7
Varna Bulgaria 403 G2
Västerås Sweden 816 C7
Västervik Sweden 816 C8
Vättern, Lake *Lake* Sweden 816 B8
Vatican City *Country* S Europe 475
Vava'u Group *Island group* Tonga 679 D6
Vawkavysk Belarus 112 C7
Växjö Sweden 816 B9
Vayk' Armenia 186 G6
Vega *Island* Norway 617 D5
Vejle Denmark 258 C5
Velenje Slovenia 105 C2
Velika Plana Yugoslavia 105 H4
Velingrad Bulgaria 403 D3
Venezuela *Country* N South America 791
Venezuela, Gulf of *Sea feature* Caribbean Sea 791 D2
Venezuelan Basin *Undersea feature* Caribbean Sea 172 H6
Venice Italy 475 D3
Venice, Gulf of *Sea feature* Adriatic Sea 475 E3
Venlo Netherlands 601 E6
Venta *River* Latvia/Lithuania 112 C3
Ventspils Latvia 112 C3

Vera Argentina 65 D5
Veracruz Mexico 551 I6
Vereeniging South Africa 784 G4
Verkhoyanskiy Khrebet *Mountains* Russian Federation 731 I4
Vermont *State* USA 864 K5
Véroia Greece 403 C5
Verona Italy 475 D2
Versailles France 356 E3
Verviers Belgium 126 F3
Vesoul France 356 G5
Vestfjorden *Coastal feature* Norway 617 D3
Veszprém Hungary 312 D9
Viana do Castelo Portugal 682 C2
Vianden Luxembourg 126 F5
Viareggio Italy 475 C4
Viborg Denmark 258 C3
Vicenza Italy 475 D2
Vichy France 356 F6
Victoria Canada 169 B9
Victoria *State* Australia 95 G7
Victoria, Lake *Lake* E Africa 15
Victoria Falls *Waterfall* Zambia/Zimbabwe 30 E5
Victoria Island *Island* Canada 169 D5
Victoria Land *Region* Antarctica 56 F7
Victoria River *River* Australia 93
Victoria West South Africa 784 E7
Vidin Bulgaria 403 C1
Viedma Argentina 65 D8
Viekšniai Lithuania 112 C4
Vienna *Capital* Austria 819 K3
Vientiane *Capital* Laos 876 C5
Vietnam *Country* SE Asia 876
Vigan Philippines 650 C3
Vigo Spain 798 B3
Vijayawāda India 444 E8
Vikna *Island* Norway 617 C5
Vila Nova de Gaia Portugal 682 C3
Vila Real Portugal 682 D3
Viljandi Estonia 112 E2
Villa Mercedes Argentina 65 C6
Villach Austria 819 I6
Villahermosa Mexico 551 J6
Villamontes Bolivia 141 D7
Villarrica Paraguay 141 G9
Villavicencio Colombia 791 C5
Vilnius *Capital* Lithuania 112 D6
Viña del Mar Chile 65 B5
Vindel *River* Sweden 816 C3
Vinh Vietnam 876 E5
Vinnytsya Ukraine 727 F4
Vinson Massif *Peak* Antarctica 56 C4
Virgin Islands *External territory* USA, West Indies 172 J4
Virginia *State* USA 864 J7
Virovitica Croatia 105 E2
Virtsu Estonia 112 E2
Visayan Sea Philippines 650 D6
Visby Sweden 816 D9
Viscount Melville Sound *Sea feature* Arctic Ocean 169 D4
Viseu Portugal 682 D4
Vishākhapatnam India 444 F7

Vistula *River* Poland 308
Viterbo Italy 475 D5
Viti Levu *Island* Fiji 636 G7
Vitória Brazil 146 H8
Vitoria Spain 798 F2
Vitsyebsk Belarus 112 G6
Vjosës, Lumi i *River* Albania 105 G10
Vladivostok Russian Federation 731 K6
Vlieland *Island* Netherlands 601 C2
Vlissingen Netherlands 601 A6
Vlorë Albania 105 G9
Vöcklabruck Austria 819 I3
Vojvodina *Region* Yugoslavia 105 G3
Volga *River* Russian Federation 731 B4
Volga Delta *Wetland* Russian Federation 308
Volgograd Russian Federation 731 B4
Vologda Russian Federation 731 C3
Vólos Greece 403 C6
Volta, Lake *Lake* Ghana 33 G8
Volta, Lake *Lake* Ghana 33 G8
Vóreioi Sporádes *Island group* Greece 403 D6
Vorkuta Russian Federation 731 E3
Vormsi *Island* Estonia 112 E1
Voronezh Russian Federation 731 B4
Võrtsjärv *Lake* Estonia 112 F3
Võru Estonia 112 F3
Vosges *Mountain range* France 356 H4
Vostochno-Sibirskoye More Arctic Ocean 731 I1
Vostok Island *Island* Kiribati 679 G4
Vozrozhdeniya, Ostrov *Island* Aral Sea 80 D1
Vršac Yugoslavia 105 H3
Vrangel'ya, Ostrov *Island* Russian Federation 731 J1
Vratsa Bulgaria 403 D2
Vryburg South Africa 784 E4
Vukovar Croatia 105 F3
Vulcano *Island* Italy 475 E9

W

Wa Ghana 33 F7
Waal *River* Netherlands 601 C5
Wad Medani Sudan 24 D5
Waddeneilanden *Island group* Netherlands 601 D1
Waddenzee *Sea feature* Netherlands 6031 D2
Wadi Halfa Sudan 24 C4
Wagga Wagga Australia 95 G7
Waigeo, Pulau *Island* Indonesia 451 J3
Wakayama Japan 478 D8
Wakkanai Japan 478 F1
Wałbrzych Poland 312 C5
Wales *National region* UK *Wel.* Cymru 858 C9
Wallis & Futuna *External territory* France, Pacific Ocean 634 G7
Walvis Bay Namibia 30 B7
Walvis Ridge *Undersea feature* Atlantic Ocean 89 F9
Wandel Sea Arctic Ocean 64 D7
Wanganui New Zealand 606 E5

Wangdi Phodrang Bhutan 114 I4
Wanlaweyn Eritrea 24 F8
Wasrsaw *Capital* Poland 312 F4
Warta *River* Poland 312 E5
Wash, The *Inlet* England, UK 858 F8
Washington *State* USA 864 B4
Washington D.C. *Capital* USA 864 J7
Waterford Ireland 465 E6
Watson *Lake* Canada 169 B7
Wau Sudan 24 B7
Wawa Canada 169 H9
Weddell Sea Antarctica 56 C3
Welkom South Africa 784 G5
Wellington *Capital* New Zealand 606 E6
Wellington, Isla *Island* Chile 65 A10
Wels Austria 819 I3
Weser *River* Germany 379 C4
West Bank *Disputed territory* SW Asia 473 D4
Western Australia *State* Australia 95 B4
Western Dvina *River* E Europe 112 G6
Western Ghats *Mountain range* India 444 C8
Western Sahara *Region* occupied by Morocco N Africa 28
Western Samoa *see* Samoa
Westerschelde *Inlet* Netherlands 601 B6
West European Basin *Undersea feature* Atlantic Ocean 89 E4
West Falkland *Island* Falkland Islands 65 D11
West Indies *Island group* Caribbean Sea 89 B6
Westport New Zealand 606 D6
West Siberian Plain *Region* Russian Federation 731 E4
West Virginia *State* USA 864 I7
Wetar, Pulau *Island* Indonesia 451 H5
Wexford Ireland 465 E6
Whangarei New Zealand 606 E2
Whitehorse Canada 169 B6
White Nile *River* Sudan 24 C7
White Sea Arctic Ocean 308
White Volta *River* Burkina/Ghana 33 G7

Whitney, Mount *Peak* W USA 611
Whyalla Australia 95 F6
Wicklow Mts. *Mountains* Ireland 465 F5
Wiener Neustadt Austria 819 K4
Wiesbaden Germany 379 C7
Wight, Isle of *Island* England, UK 858 E11
Wilhelm, Mount *Peak* Papua New Guinea 93
Wilkes Land *Region* Antarctica 56 H7
Willemstad Netherlands Antilles 172 H7
Windhoek *Capital* Namibia 30 C6
Windsor Canada 169 I10
Windward Islands *Islands* West Indies 172 J6
Winisk Canada 169 G8
Winisk *River* Canada 169 G8
Winnipeg Canada 169 F9
Winnipeg, Lake *Lake* Canada 169 F9
Winnipegosis, Lake *Lake* Canada 169 F9
Winterthur Switzerland 819 D4
Wisconsin *State* USA 864 H5
Wisła *River* Poland 312 F4
Wismar Germany 379 E3
Włocławek Poland 312 E3
Wodzisław Śląski Poland 312 E6
Wolfsberg Austria 819 J5
Wolfsburg Germany 379 D4
Wollongong Australia 95 H6
Wŏnju South Korea 497 C6
Wŏnsan North Korea 497 C4
Worcester England, UK 858 D9
Wrangel Island *Island* Russian Federation 64 E2
Wrocław Poland 312 D5
Wuhan China 206 I6
Wuppertal Germany 379 B6
Würzburg Germany 379 D7
Wuxi China 206 J6
Wyndham Australia 95 D2
Wyoming *State* USA 864 D5

X

Xaignabouli Laos 876 B4
Xi'an China 206 H6
Xai-Xai Mozambique 30 G7
Xalapa Mexico 551 H6
Xam Nua Laos 876 D3
Xánthi Greece 403 E4
Xingu *River* Brazil 146 F4

Y

Yablonovyy Khrebet *Mountains* Russian Federation 731 H5
Yacuiba Bolivia 141 D7
Yafran Libya 28 I3
Yaku-shima *Island* Japan 478 B10
Yakutsk Russian Federation 731 I4
Yala Thailand 833 E13
Yalta Ukraine 727 I8
Yalu *River* China/North Korea 497 B2
Yamaguchi Japan 478 C8
Yamal, Poluostrov *Peninsula* Russian Federation 731 F3
Yambio Sudan 24 B8
Yambol Bulgaria 403 F3
Yamdena, Pulau *Island* Indonesia 451 J5
Yamoussoukro *Capital* Ivory Coast 33 E8
Yamuna *River* India 444 D4
Yanbu' al Baḥr Saudi Arabia 406 B4
Yangdŏk North Korea 497 B4
Yangtze *River* China *var.* Chang Jiang 206 I6
Yaoundé *Capital* Cameroon 20 C7
Yap *Island* Micronesia 636 B3
Yapen, Pulau *Island* Indonesia 451 K3
Yaqui *River* Mexico 551 D2
Yarmouth Canada 169 K8
Yaroslavl' Russian Federation 731 C3
Yazd Iran 463 G5
Yekaterinburg Russian Federation 731 D4
Yellow River *River* China *var.* Huang He 206 I5
Yellow Sea Pacific Ocean 206 J5
Yellowknife Canada 169 D6
Yëloten Turkmenistan 80 E5
Yemen *Country* SW Asia 406
Yenakiyeve Ukraine 727 K4
Yenisey *River* Russian Federation 731 F4
Yerevan *Capital* Armenia 186 F5
Yevlax Azerbaijan 186 I4
Yevpatoriya Ukraine 727 H7
Yinchuan China 206 G5
Yogyakarta Indonesia 451 D5
Yokohama Japan 478 F7
Yola Nigeria 33 K7
Yŏngju South Korea 497 D6
Yopal Colombia 791 C4

York England, UK 858 E7
York, Cape *Coastal feature* Australia 95 G1
Yorkton Canada 169 E9
Yos Sudarso *Island* Indonesia 451 K5
Yŏsu South Korea 497 C8
Young Uruguay 65 E5
Ystad Sweden 816 B10
Yucatan Channel *Sea feature* Mexico 551 K4
Yucatan Peninsula *Peninsula* Mexico 551 K5
Yugoslavia *Country* SE Europe 105
Yukon *River* Canada/USA 611
Yukon Territory *Territory* Canada 169 A6
Yumen China 206 F4
Yuzhno-Sakhalinsk Russian Federation 731 K5
Yverdon Switzerland 819 A6

Z

Zabīd Yemen 406 D8
Zacapa Guatemala 193 C4
Zadar Croatia 105 C5
Zagreb *Capital* Croatia 308 C2
Zagros Mountains *Mountain range* Iran/Iraq 463 F5
Zāhedān Iran 463 J6
Zahlé Lebanon 821 D5
Zaire *see* Congo, Dem. Rep.
Zaječar Yugoslavia 105 I5
Zákynthos *Island* Greece 403 B8
Zalaegerszeg Hungary 312 D9
Zambezi *River* southern Africa 30 D4
Zambezi Zambia 30 D4
Zambia *Country* southern Africa 30
Zamboanga Philippines 650 D8
Zamora Spain 798 D3
Zanzibar *Island* Tanzania 24 E11
Zapala Argentina 65 B7
Zaporizhzhya Ukraine 727 I5
Zaqatala Azerbaijan 186 H3
Zarafshan Uzbekistan 80 F3
Zaragoza Spain 798 G3
Zaranj Afghanistan 80 D8
Zaria Nigeria 33 J7
Zeebrugge Belgium 126 B1
Zefat Israel 473 D2
Zell am See Austria 819 H5
Zenica Bosnia & Herzegovina 105 E5
Zeravshan *River* C Asia 80 H4
Zhengzhou China 206 H5

Zhezkazgan Kazakhstan 731 D6
Zhlobin Belarus 112 F8
Zhodzina Belarus 112 F7
Zhytomyr Ukraine 727 F3
Zibo China 206 I5
Zielona Góra Poland 312 C4
Ziguinchor Senegal 33 A6
Žilina Slovakia 312 E7
Zimbabwe *Country* southern Africa 30
Zinder Niger 33 J6
Zoetermeer Netherlands 601 C5
Zomba Malawi 30 H4
Zouérat Mauritania 33 C3
Zrenjanin Yugoslavia 105 G3
Zug Switzerland 819 C5
Zürich Switzerland 819 C5
Zürich, L. *Lake* Switzerland 819 D5
Zuwārah Libya 28 H2
Zvornik Bosnia & Herzegovina 105 F4
Zwedru Liberia 33 D8
Zwickau Germany 379 F6
Zwolle Netherlands 601 E4

PICTURE SOURCES

The publishers would like to thank the following for permission to use their photographs:

Abbreviations:
l:left, r:right, c:centre, a:above, b:below, t:top

A,B,C

Wallace & Gromit/Aardman Animations Ltd 1995: 181bl **Robert Aberman:** 400crb, bla **ABI Caravans/Kenneth Berry Studios:** 168bla **Action-Plus:** S Bardens: 736ca, bcl, cb Chris Barry: 430cra, 818c, bra R Francis: 88c, 736bla Tony Henshaw: 351bc Glyn Kirk: 88crb, br, 411cb, 818tr P Tarry: 736bl **Advertising Archives:** 14tr **AEA Technology:** 618cbr **AIP Emilio Segre Visual Archives/ Dorothy Davis Locanthi:** 130cl **Airphoto Services:** 59tr **AKG London:** 49bc, 55br, 69c, 72cr, cl, 78crb, 79br, 97cbr, 123br, bcl, bca, 127tc, crb, 138bl, 269tr, ca Disney Enterprises Inc., 294tr, bl, 310cbl, 311cl, cr, 326cr, 359cr, 362tr , 373car, 381c, br, 382tr, br, 386br, 424crb, 428cb, bcl, 439cb, 477cr, br, 484cr, bc, 496cra, 498tcr, 507tr, 521bcr, 535c, cr, cb, 548br, 581tc, 573br, 580tr, bl, bc, br, 588bcl, 589cb, 594cl, cr, 638cr, 649cl, 652bl, 656tr, 671cr, cl, 684cra, crb, 704bl, br, crb, 708bc 724tr, 744br, 745bc, 753tr, 781cbl, 795c, 811tr, tlb, cr, cl, 841bra, 856tr, crb, Erich Lessing: 123trb, 191bc, 192cb, 197bc, 209cla, 228bl, 391tc, 401cl, 428bl, 484bla, c, 498bc, 543ca, cb, 580crb, 594tr, 632br, 648cr, 740br, 753br, 776tr, c Wolfe Fund, 1931, Catherine Lorillard Wolfe Collection, New York, Metropolitan Museum of Art: 776bc **Thanks to Alison/Oilily:** 14crb **Allsport:** 110bra, cra, 351crb, 351bca, 411clb, 430cbr, bcl, 628tr, 803ca, 897bc Agence Vandystadt/ S Cazenove: 736bcr/Richard Martin: 411ccl, 736br /A Patrice: 576cb Frank Baron: 251cr S Botterill: 897cal, cbl H Boylan: 577cbr S Bruly: 937tr Clive Brunskill: 803cr David Canon: 109br Chris Cole: 351crb, 430bl Phil Cole: 110bcl, 251trb Mike Cooper: 128cbr, 577car Stephen Dunn: 628cr Tony Duffy: 88clb S Forster: 577cbl J Gichigi: 736bc Bruce Hazellan: 110trb Mike Hewitt: 351cra, 577br, 829cr Hulton: 109bl, 351cr Info/Billy Stickland: 351br I.O.C.; 628clb D Kidd: 577cr JP Lenfant: 430cb K Levine: 576bc Bob Martin: 577bl R Martin: 897braG Mortimore: 525cra, 628br Adrian Murrell: 109ca D Pensinger: 411cl Mike Powell: 88cr, 251bla Pascal Rondeau: 251crb, 363bl, 576tr, cr, 577tl, tr, 628bl, 897car, bcl, bl Jamie Squire: 818bcra M Stockman: 576bl Mark Thompson: 88bl, 576br Todd Warshaw: 897br **American Museum of Natural History:** 893br, 895br **Ancient Art & Architecture:** 62tc, 71tr, cl, tc, 73cl, 77cb, 103c, 160bra, 197bl, bcl, 198tr, bl, 233c, 247bra, 252ca, bc, 280cl, 288tr, 292bl, bc, 302t, 310cb, 425bl, cr, bra, c, cl, 427clb, bl, 428br, 434bc, 470bra, 477t, 480cr, cb, 498trb, 557cra, cr, bl, 602cla, 627c, 631cr, clb, bra, bl, br, 648bc, 649bla, bcl, bl, bcr, 652car, cbr, bc, 689cra, 691bl, 706bcl, 708cr, 716tr, 735cl, cr, br, cra, 738bl, 743bl, 752br, 762clb, 764tcr, 768bl, 800cr, 809bcr, 813bca L Ellison: 148tr Chris Hellier: 648clb Gianni Tortoli: 140clb **LJ Anderson Collection:** 69tr **Julie & Gillian Andrews:** 636crb **Anglo Australian Observatory:** 370ca, cb, cal **©Apple Corps. Ltd:** 121tr, bla, bca, bc **Aquila:** 260bcl, 779bc Les Baker: 133tr JJ Brooks: 39br Conrad Greaves: 780br Mike Lane:747c Mike Wilkes: 132bra, 345tr, 761bcr **Arcaid:** Esto/Ezra Stoller: 63br Dennis Gilbert: 63bla Ian Lambot: 63bl **Archiv zur Geschichte der Max-Planck-Gesellschaft, Berlin- Dahlem.** Nachlass Otto Hahn, III Abt., Rep. 14B Mappen Nr 15: 548cr **Archive Photos:** 18bc, 632cr **Archives Curie et Joliot-Curie:** 250c **Ardea:** 24ca, 118tl, 136bc, 261tcb, 319cr, 420cr, 492bl, 702tc, 755cl Ian Beames: 58crb, 165cl H&J Beste: 917ca R M Bloomfield: 761br B& S Bottomly: 55clb Coto Donana: 317bc Hans D Dossenbach: 58bl MD England: 512cb Jean Paul Ferrero: 472bc, 488blb, bcb, bcb, 672br, 899c Ferrero-Labat: 512tc Kenneth W Fink: 756tc, 904c R Gibbons: 235bcl Frances Gohier: 83bca, 260bla, 711cb, 912br Nick Gordon: 644bc Clem Haagner: 529crb Don Hadden: 747crb Masahiro Iijima: 472cbAke Lindau: 318c Eric Lindgren: 124clb John Mason: 82bl, 459tl, 687br, 749c B McDairmant: 33tr E Mickleburgh: 917tl P Morris: 58clb, 99c D Parer & E Parer-Cook: 23cla R.F.Porter: 713cl Graham Robertson: 647br Ron & Valerie Taylor: 337crb, 339tr Adrian Warren: 390bl Wardene Weisser: 260clb, 499c **Arxiumas:** 800c **ASAP:** S Uziel: 474tr **Ashmolean Museum, Oxford:** 707bcr **Australian National Maritime Museum, Sydney:** 97bc **Aviation Picture Library:** 225cr Austin J Brown: 278cr, 884bc, bl, c **A-Z Botanical:** A Cooper: 847cla Michael Jones: 585trbLino Pastorelli: 235br **Barnaby's Picture Library:** Brian Gibbs: 904bla Marc Turner: 590bc **BBC Natural History Unit Picture Library:** 257bcra Hans Christoph Kappel: 83cbl EA Kuttapan: 511cb N O'Connor: 154tr Ron O'Connor: 713tr Pete Oxford: 517cb Ian Redwood: 299br **Beethoven Archiv, Bonn:** 123c, bc, 589cl **Bavarian National Museum, Munich:** 653tr **Bibliotheque Nationale, Paris:** 359tc, 562 **Bildarchiv Preussischer Kulturbesitz:** 103bl **Bilderdienst Suddeutscher Verlag:** 224br **Biofotos:** Heather Angel: 74cr, 155cl, 667bc, 672bl Bryn Campbell: 56cr Geoff Moon: 235bcr Jason Venus: 872tr **Biophoto:** Prof GF Leedale: 405bl **Birds Eye/Walls:** 348l, clb, cb **Bodleian Library, Oxford:** 51bl **Thanks to Boots/Mellors:** 14br, bcl, bl **C Bowman (Photoscope):** 601bl **Kelvin Boyes:** 466cr **Bridgeman Art Library:** Albertina Graphic Collection, Vienna: 638cl, cra Alexander Turnbull Library, Wellington, N.Z.: 604cb Alte Pinakothek, Munich: 708br/Giraudon: 874bra Chris Beetles Ltd, London: 238trb Biblioteca Nazionale, Turin: 498bl, 707br Biblioteca Apostolica Vaticana: 546cl Bibliotheque Nationale, Paris: 197bcr, 361cal, 409tr, 447br, 495clb, 566cra Bonhams, London: 746tr British Library, London: 51crb, 138c, 183cla, 242ca, cl, 255cra, 301tr, 329bc, 469br, 495c, 531clb, 532tr, 543bla, 546tr, 566bl, 610crb, 671bcr, 673cr, 707cra, 735bl, 753cr British Museum: 85trb, 301bl, 725tr, 860cbr/Alecto Historical Editions: 238bla, 329bl Burghley House Collection, Lincolnshire: 704c Christie's Images, London: 73cr, 733cl Department of the Environment, London: 860bcl Fitzwilliam Museum, University of Cambridge: 47crb Galleria degli Uffizi, Florence: 477cal Giraudon:/Lauros: Archives Nationales, Paris: 741bla/Musee du Louvre, Paris: 358br/Musee de la Ville de Paris, Musee Carnavalet: 359tl Highgate Cemetry, London: 535br Historisches Museum der Stadt, Vienna: 123tr Imperial War Museum, London: 906bra Index: 768cbl Institute of Mechanical Engineers, London: 842crb Kremlin Museums, Moscow: 391tcr, 732cra Kunsthistorisches Museum: 302tr Lambeth Palace Library, London: 439bcr Maidstone Museum & Art Gallery, Kent: 861cA Meyer Collection, Paris: 811bc Mausoleo do Galla Placidia, Ravenna: 160bl Philip Mould, Historical Portraits Ltd., London: 800bl Mozart Museum, Salzburg/Giraudon: 123bl Musee des Beaux-Arts, Le Havre: 228br Musee Conde Chantilly: 547tr Musee de Picardie, Amiens/Giraudon: 213cr Musee díUnterlinden, Colmar, France: 381cl Musee National DíArt Moderne, paris: 72bc Museo Naval, Madrid/Index, Barcelona: 228tr Museo del Prado, Madrid: 140cra/Index: 334br Museum of Mankind, London: 531cl National Gallery, London: 507c National Library of Australia, Canberra: 238bc National Maritime Museum, London: 78clb, 301c, 631cb National Museum of India, New Dehli: 421bl, 455br, bcr, 493cl Oriental Museum, Durham University: 746tl, 764tcb, Private Collection: 360c, 371br, 498crb, 515bl, 708cra, 811trb, 826cl Rijksmuseum Kroller-Muller, Otterlo: 477cb Royal Asiatic Society, London: 201clb Royal Geographical Society, London: 673cra St Appollonia Museum, Florence: 515crb Santa Maria Novella, Florence: 71c Schloss Charlottenburg, Berlin: 391tr Thyssen Bornemisza Collection: 861tl Tretyakov Gallery, Moscow: 733tr Trinity College Dublin: 466ca Umayyad Mosque, Damascus, Syria: 470cr Vatican Museums & Galleries, Rome: 776cr Victoria and Albert Museum, London: 160cr, 484br, 587cl **Thanks to British Army Recruitment:** 68cl **BFI Stills, Posters & Designs:** 273cla, 331ca, cb, cbl, 332, 373cbl, 491bc, 656br **British Library, London:** 151clb, crb, 381bl, 448crb, 498bcr, 588bl **The British Museum:** 781bl Education Dept/Simon James: 724bc, 725tc **British Nuclear Fuels plc.:** 697bl **British Petroleum Company plc:** 378br, 626tr, 716bc **The Bronte Society:** 149cr, cl, bcl **SG Brown:** 598crb **Brown Brothers:** 658cb, 868cbr **Tony Weller/The Builder Group:** 157cla, cl **Photographie Bulloz:** Bibliotheque de lÍInstitut de France: 507cr, 562 **Michael Busselle:** 116cra **Michael Butler Collection:** 382cb **CADW:** 182tr, cl, c **By Permission of the Syndics of Cambridge University Library:** 607trb, bc **Camera Press:** 254clb, 288bl, 344crb, 376br, 438cr, br, 542tl, 575trb, 775cr, 944cr, cl, 948cr William Carter: 821br A Mamedov: 187br Gavin Smith: 941crb The Times/M Ellidge: 742br Camera Press Ltd: cr **Canon:** 163bl **Canterbury Archaelogical Trust:** 765tr **Mark Carwardine:** 894tl, cl **J Allan Cash Ltd.:** 33c, 76car, 85bc, 209c, 242bca, 312tr, cl, 380c, 404cb, 434br, 473c, 476bc, 490cr, 521bl, 523c, 547cr, 601trc, 610trc, 617bl, 650tr, 683tl, ca, bl, 693br, 706br, 798crb, 799tc, 816clb, 859tl, 823bl, bc **Cephas: Stockfood:** 268br **Channel Four Publicity:** 829br **Mark Chapman:** 152cra, 388tr, 706bcr **Jean Loup Charmet:** 18clb, 205t, 361cbr, 490cla, bc, 566br, 594cra, 781cl Musee Carnavelet: 361ca **Lester Cheeseman:** 25t, 152bc, 833bc **By Permission of the Chelsea Physic Garden:** 510bl **Reproduced by Kind Permission of the Trustees of the Chester Beatty Library, Dublin:** 581cb **Thanks to Chisenhale Castle:** 72bcr **Thanks to the Master & Fellows of Churchill College, Cambridge:** 548tr, bc, cl **CIRCA/Icorec:** 138bra R Beeche: 422tc BJ Mistry: 422bl **Civil Aviation Authority:** 598c **John Cleare/Mountain Camera:** 168cr **"Coca-Cola"** Coke and the design of the contour bottle are registered trademarks of the Coca-Cola Company: 262cl **Stephanie Colasanti:** 450crb **Bruce Coleman:** 118ca, 284br, 761clb, 779bca, br, cr, 822cr Stefano Amantini: 20cla Atlantide: 309cbr, 317bca Trevor Barrett: 234bra Jen & Des Bartlett: 99bcl, 245clb, 384cr, 633br Erwin & Peggy Bauer: 299cb, 512tr, cr, 518br, 699bc, 889cbr, 917clb M Berge: 637tr George Bingham: 96bc E Bjurstrom: 406cr Nigel Blake: 747bl M Borchi: 450br Mark N Boulton: 104cr Fred Bruemmer: 16cra, 674bca, 748bc, 821car Thomas Buchholz: 617t Jane Burton: 74cl, bcr, 82bc, 166bc, 184bla, 420c, 500ca, 622bcl, 699clb, 793crb, 872cr B & C Calhoun: 492tcr, 609bc John Cancalosi: 694bcr, 773tr, 793br Robert P Carr: 155crb Mark Carwardine: 23bl, 518tr Brian J Coates: 55tr Alain Compost: 452bcl, 571bcr, 916cb J Cowan: 665crb, 918cl Gerald Cubitt: 94crb, 235ccr, 524bl, 571bcl, 644br P Davey: 556cr Tony Deane: 258ca Stephen J Doyle: 94ca Francisco J Erize: 57c, 748br Dr P Evans: 472br Jeff Foott: 57clb, 300cl, 751bl, 846bc Christer Fredriksson: 350cra, 816br MPL Fogden: 364clb, 395br, 397tc, 773tl917cr Tor Oddvar Hansen: 747bc BS Henderson: 567cl PA Hinchliffe: 600bl Charles & Sandra Hood: 55bcl, 239cb HPH Photography/Philip vd Berg: 55cl Carol Hughes: 772cl Johnny Johnson: 300cbr, 499t, 675c Janos Jurka: 309car, 674bra, 816ca Dr MP Kahl: 50cl, 343c Steven C Kaufman: 675cr, 694cl Stephen S Krasemann: 117crb, 235bc, 694bl H Lange: 399bc Gordon Langsbury: 74cb Wayne Lankinen: 346bl , 612cal, 761cla Werner Layer: 350crr, 579bc Dr. John Mackinnon: 57br, 640cr Luiz Claudio Marigo: 669cra, 788c McAllister: 406bl, 449br George McCarthy: 90brb, 397tl, 517bl, 585tr Hans Peter Merten: 258ca, 819ca Rinie van Meurs: 674bla, 748clb J Murray: 465br Dr Scott Nielson: 133cr Charlie Ott: 714tcr MR Phicton: 241c Dieter & Mary Plage: 154cr, 647c Dr Eckhart Pott: 136tc, 500bc, 674tr Allan G Potts: 319crb Dr S Prato: 346bla, 472crb Fritz Prenzel: 801bl MP Price: 585cla Andy Purcell: 53bcl Hans Reinhard: 154bla, 235bcl, 513cl, 748bcl, 756tr, 761bcl Dr Frieder Sauer: 500bla, 754bl, 801cra Norbert Schwirtz: 258br John Shaw: 120cl, 714tr Kim Taylor: 54bra, 155br, 158tr, 241bl, 327bl, 342bl, 343bc, 459cl, cbr, 665bc, 780tl, tr, car NO Tomalin: 489bra , 612bla, N de Vore: 449t, 472ca Uwe Walz/GDT: 675tc Rod Williams: 571ca Konrad Wothe: 657tr Gunther Zeisler: 118cl, 556tr, 916bca **Colorific!:** Bill Bachman: 11crb, br Steve Benbow: 268cr, 646cr Randa Bishop: 173bl Pierre Boulat/Cosmos: 29br Catherine Cabrol/GLMR: 790cb Robert Caputo/Matrix: 27clb Mauro Carrara: 503br

E Ferorelli: 194bl Sylvain Grandaden: 11tr A Joyce: 464cl Catherine Karnow: 174bl J Lassila: 862cla Kay Muldoon: 784bl Jim Pickerell: 66bc J Quiggin: 938t Snowden/Hoyer/Focus: 852tc Penny Tweedie: 11tl, 408cra Richard Wilkie/Black Star: 669crb Rod Williams: 423b Konrad Wothe: 283cb Michael Yamashita: 637tl, 877crb G Ziesler: 440tr **Colorsport:** 88bcl, 380tr, 411c, cclb, 430br, 818br, 937tl, cl **Dee Conway:** 108crb, bl, br, 253cr, ccr, br, 254cla **Coo-ee Historical Picture Library:** 604cbr, bl **Steven J Cooling:** 39bc, bcl, 397cbr, 615bra, 616tc, 690br **Donald Cooper, Photostage:** 272bl, 753bc, 939bc **Cooper Hewitt; National Design Museum, Smithsonian Institution, Art Resource, New York, Gift of Gary Loredo:** 382c **Corbis:** 11bra, 131br, 502cr, 531cr, br, 632c, trb, 728bcl, 760br, 845bc Bettmann: 48bc, 255tr, 294bcr, 360cra, 362br, 372tcr, 457bl, 482cbl, 491cr, br, 596cr, 605crb, 760cb, 763cbr, cbl, 768br, 849t, cl, bl 869tr, 886cl, cr, cb, ca/Reuter: 845bl Bettmann/UPI: 244cr, 269bcr, 275bla, 297crb, 368br, 372cr, 438c, 461bcl, bl, 485cra, 491c, bcr, tr, 503cra, 516br, 671bra, 719tcl, 783bl, 818bla, 869cr, cl, 882bca Jan Butchofsky-Houser: 845tr Ecoscene /Sally Morgan: 671br Everett: 373bl R Hamilton Smith: 865br Wolfgang Kaehler: 729cr Library of Congress: 373t Roman Soumar: 210br UPI: 121c Michael Yamashita: 865tc **Sylvia Cordaiy:** Guy Marks: 15crb, 25br **Costas, New York:** 108bc © The George Balanchine Trust **Courtauld Institute Galleries, London:** 161cb **Cray Inc:** 0crb **Croation Catholic Mission:** 575tr **Crown Reserved/Historic Scotland:** 861cl **Culver Pictures Inc.:** 373ca **Mr B J Curtis:** 763br **Cycleurope:** 129tcl

D,E

DACS, 1997: 477cb **Succession Picasso:** 656bl, c, cr, cl **Paul Daion:** 388tcrcl **Dartington Crystal Ltd:** 387clb **James Davis Travel:** 66cal, 175tr, 195cbl, 845ca Sveti Stefan: 107tr **Defence Picture Library:** 885clb **Department of Defense, Pentagon:** 887bl **Deutsches Museum, Munich:** 548c, ccr **Dickens House Museum:** 263cl **Dinodia:** Milind A Ketkar: 444t **Disney Enterprises, Inc.:** 269bl **CM Dixon:** 388tcr, 401clb, br, 447tr, 610br, 613bcl, 724cr, 878bl/National Archaeological Museum, Rome: 776crb **DK Pic Library:** 30cla, 0bcr, Clive Streeter 0ca, Guy Rycart 0br, Joe Cornish 0cb, **Christopher Dobrowolski:** 745cl **Dominic Photography:** 629cbl Catherine Ashmore: 272crb, 629cb Zoe Dominic: 629ca, 836tlb, cl, c **Durban Local History Museum, South Africa:** 372tr **Dyson Ltd:** 262tr, ca, car **Ecoscene:** 523tr Andre DR Brown: 309cal, cbl Donachie: 56br Farmar: 89crb Nick Hawkes: 642br W Lawler: 636bc R Wright: 850blb **EDF Production Transport:** 252cb **Edinburgh University:** 560trb, tr, c **EMI:** 121 **Environmental Images:** Steve Morgan/WIT Wildlife: 234bc **Environmental Picture Library:** Martin Bond: 678br Stewart Boyle: 304ccr Jordi Cami: 883cl David Hoffman: 304tr J Hodson: 883crb Jimmy Holmes: 678cl Steve Morgan: 680br John Novis: 304cr Alex Olah: 353br Peter Rowlands: 894tcPeter Solness: 637crb **Robert Estall Photo Library:** 37br, 170bra, cl, tr,cr Thomas Kelly: 115cb **ET Archive:** 71clb, 116br, 213br, 225cr, 381tr, 469tl, 510tr, 515cl, bc, 588cb, 614cra, 630tr, 738ca, 786tlb, 910bc Archaeological Museum, Venice: 161cl Archive of the Indies, Seville: 789cra British Museum: 320bl, 587tr Chiaramonti Museum, Vatican: 402cb Freer Gallery of Art: 73tc London Museum: 786cl National Museum of History, Lima: 140tr, 790tr National Museum of India: 455cb Plymouth City Art Collection: 659bc Trinity College, Dublin: 214bca Uffizi Gallery, Florence: 214cr Vienna Societa Amici dell Musica : 629cbr **European Space Agency:** 720r **Greg Evans International:** 444ca, 504ca, 505tl, 551crb, 728tr, 784br, 823cb **Mary Evans Picture Library:** , 45bla, 47cb, 49bra, trb, cla, crb, 51ca, cr, 78bc, 97cbl. bca, br, 101br, bc, 116clb, 140bl, 144br, 149bca, 161cbl, bc, 163bca, 166bl, 176bc, 190bl, 191br, 192crb, 197tr, 203br, 210c, cr, 212tr, 227bl, 233tr, bl, 236bra, 238bl, bcr, 247bla, 250tr, cr, bca, trb, 255cb, 263bl, 272trb , 295bl, 296bl, 301ccl, 302cla, bl, crb, br, 303bl, 304bc, 310bc, 311tr, 320cr, clb, 321bl, cr, 326cbr, 352cr, 358car, 359bl, 361bcl, 382cl, 388cbl, bl, 392br, 399tr, 402clb, 413bcl, 416tr, 427crb, br, 439bl, cr, 442bcr, tr, 448tr, cra, 467bl, 470c, 480tr, 481t, 484bl, tr, 485tr, 502bl, 504bra, 509tr, 515cr, 522bl, 526bl, 535cl, 536br, 544cl, bl, 560br, bc, 564t, 582bl, 587cb, 588cr, 594bl, 595cl, cb, 602cbl, 608tr, 610bra, 614tr, 630cbr, 641bc, 645tr, 651cl, 659bl, 673cl, 676tr, 690cl, 704cr, 733tc, 734br, 738bc, 743br, 744tr, 745bl, 753bra, trb, 768car, cbr, bcl, 789cl, 812br, 828bl, 844, 845car, 862tr, 868cb, 882bl, 883tr, 887cl, 898cl, cr, bc, 901tr, 906c, 907bl, 933crb, 941tc, bl, br, 945 acl, cr, Explorer: 108c, 361car, cr Fawcett Library: 641t, tr, cra, cb, cr, c, br, 901ccl Institution of Civil Engineers: 148bra Alexander Meledin Collection: 734tr Smith College Library: 710tr **Eye Ubiquitous:** 112ca Paul Bennett: 93b David Cumming: 173br, 798cr G Hanly: 531crb John Hulme: 799cr Matthew McKee: 636tr

F,G,H

Chris Fairclough Colour Library: 403blb, 705bcr **Ffotograff:** Patricia Aithie: 138br, 706bca **Martin Foote:** 11bl, 94cr, 95tc, crb, 217bcl, 282cr, 653bc, 698crb, br, 808cl, 845cb **Footprints:** 450bc **Ford Motor Company Ltd:** 178cra, 305c, 363cr **Werner Forman Archive:** 17c, 480cl, 481bl, 593tc, 648c, 649br, 705tcr, 743cr, 786tr British Museum: 127bl Dallas Museum of Art, USA: 198bcl , 627l Courtesy Entwistle Gallery, London: 17trb Philip Goldman Collection: 77clb Museum f‚r Volkerkunde, Berlin: 17br, 442c National Museum, Lagos, Nigeria: 73tl Peabody Museum, Harvard University, Cambridge, MA: 613bl Private Collection: 233cb, crb, 480bcr, crb, 738c, cb Schindler Collection, New York: 442c Statens Historiska Museum, Stockholm: 935tr V & A Museum: 480br **Format:** Jacky Chapman: 274bc, 275tl Sheila Gray: 901cr Brenda Prince: 335tr **Fortean Picture Library:** 898bl Janet & Colin Bord: 593cb, bl, 762c Dr ER Gruber: 898cal **Fotomas Index:** 526ca, car, 841tcr **Fototeca:** Cesar Soares : 684tr **French Railways Ltd:** 357crb **Freud Museum, London:** 362ca, cb, cl, trb **Paul Gallagher:** 28car **Garden Picture Library:** John Bethell: 374cr, crb C Fairweather: 374cl **Genesis:** 86bra, 797tl, tr **Geological Society Library:** 279br **Geoscience Features Picture Library:** 222bl, 304tc, 655crb, 697bla, 715cl, 715cr, 777blc, 880cl **Geoslides Photolibrary:** 35cr **Giraudon:** 123cr, 198cr, 546bla, 627cb Bibliotheque Nationale, Paris: 329cl Index: 789crb Musee Carnavalet: 361cb D Corrige: 835bcl National Museum, Bangkok: 490br **Jane Goodall Institute:** 390cr, c, crb David Greybeard: 390cla **Granger Collection, New York:** 287cra, c, 360bl, cr, br, cl, tr, 491cl, bl, 856cra, bc **Ronald Grant Archive:** 149bc, 204ccl, cr, br, 244cla, 331cla, 373bc, 388c, 402crb, 516crb, 593cal, bc, 629bl, 719tl, 738br, 789bl, 869crb BBC Press Service: 516bcl CBS/Fox Video: 516trb (Disney Enterprises, Inc.: 269crb, clb, 331cbb First Independent: 181tr **Guy Gravett/ Glyndebourne, Sussex:** 205clb **Sally & Richard Greenhill:** 14cr, 288crb, 433br, 716cbl, 775ca Kaye Mayers: 213c **Denise Grieg:** 99crb, 100bra Pavel German: 99c, bl, 100br, 488cra, ca, cb, 489bc Nature Focus/GB Baker: 99cl Dominic Chaplin: 100cb/John McCann: 488bla/D Crossman: 489bcr/Gunther Schmida: 99bcr/Tony Stanton: 99tc /AD Trounson: 99cra /Dave Watts: 100cl, cr, clb /Babs & Bert Wells: 99br **Sonia Halliday:** 103br, 160c, bla, 214tc, 427cr, 486tr, 560cr, 605tr, 746bl FHC Birch: 214br Bibliotheque Nationale: 160bca FHC Birch: 401crb Laura Lushington: 669bl, 860bl B Searle: 486cr Jane Taylor: 422br **Hamlyn:** 203clb **Robert Harding Picture Library:** 29tr, 31tl, tc, 77cr, bl, 79cr, 81crb, bc, 101bcl, 153crb, 156t, 157tc, tr, tl, 171tr, bc, 187cla, 194cr, 207cr, bra, 217bcr, 228bc, 288cr, 306cra, 308cl, 315cr, 322bc, 329cr, 356tr, 357bcr, 382clb, 388br, 400cr, 404cl, 406cl, 410cl, 433tr, bcr, 435tl, 442ca, 446cl, t, c, 464c, cbl, 478cl, 490t, clb, 520cr, 526c, 539bl, cr, 547c, 567tr, 587br, 589tl, 612cbl, 614clb, 627cr, 646cb, 689crb, 760tr, 785cl, cr, 792tc, 834cr, 836br, 858cr, 860ca, 868br, 869cb Craig Aurness: 237cr, 559cl Bibliotheque Nationale, Paris: 610cl Bildagenteur Schuster: 847cla, 857cl Alexandre: 17bra /Waldkirch: 380cra N Blythe: 435bcr C Briscoe Knight: 758crb C Bryan: 37tc Camerapix: 19cr Jacky Chapman: 40tr M Chillmaid: 433bl M Collier: 391bl, 635br G & P Corrigan: 206l, 207tr Philip Craven: 610tc, c, A L Durand: 312bl Victor Englebert: 21br, 37bl, cb M Leslie Evans: 27tl Alain Everard: 78cr Explore: 26br FPG International: 48clb, c, 614bca/Icon communications: 869bl Nigel Francis: 681bc Robert Francis: 65tr, 157br, 175cl, 237tr, 476tl Robert Frerck: 66cbr, 516tr, 551ca, 799bl Tony Gervis: 307b, 403cbr K Gillham: 176bra, 404tl, 788cra Gottier: 323cr J Green: 406tr I Griffiths: 520cl Susan Griggs: 650cr Dominic Hanouert-Webster: 816cl Simon Harris: 311br Kim Hart: 90ca G Hellier: 28tr, 77br, 80cra, 152br, 478cra, 481cb, 581tr, crb Walter Hodges,Westlight: 544cra David Martyn Hughes: 681br Uzaemon Ichimura: 836bla IPC Magazines/Womans Journal/James Marrell: 368bl Dave Jacobs/All Rights Reserved: 655crbb F. Jackson: 17cl, 424cla Michael Jenner: 374cra, 408br, 681bl, 760bc, 774bc Victor Kennet: 198c Paolo Koch: 822tl Krafft: 634cr Leimbach: 254tl J Lightfoot: 34bl, 174br R Ian Lloyd: 760cl David Lomax: 208cr, 435tlb, 466br M Long: 214cl T Magor: 424bl Buddy Mays/International Stock: 818crb R McLeod: 923bc HP Merten: 840tr MPH: 684ca L Murray: 403cbl, 404bc Gary Norman/ Operation Raleigh: 792cb David Poole: 27bc, 526cbr Madhya Pradesh: 201bc Rainbird Collection: 94bl Roy Rainford: 126bl, 471bra, 865tlb Walter Rawlings: 63bra, 610tr Geoff Renner: 28tr, 66b, 922trr Chris Rennie: 80tr, cr R Richardson: 392cl, 876t Paul van Riel: 637cra, 763c Jan Robinson: 328c Phil Robinson: 106cl, 314 tcb SADA: 448clb Sasoon: 187ca Sybil Sasson: 447cr JWW Shakespeare: 333ca M Short: 310br James Strachan: 80bl, 682cra S Terry: 475trb Tomlinson: 798tr Adine Tory: 803tr W Westwater: 435tcr JHC Wilson: 448cb Adam Woolfitt: 175tl, 182bl, 183crb, 312bc, 333bl, 524cl, 543bl, 689cr, 799cl, 835br, 838tl, 852cl, tl, 853tr, 859ca 922bl Jim Zuckerman/Westlight: 403br **Harper Collins Publishers Ltd:** 204c, 516bla **Graham Harrison:** 153cra **Harvard University Archives:** 808bc **Hauptstaatsarchiv, Stuttgart:** 400bl **Hencomp Enterprises:** 660br **Jim Henson's Creature Shop:** 331c **Hoa-Qui: Kraft/Explorer:** 880br **Reproduced by Permission of Hodder & Stoughton:** 204cl **Michael Holford:** 51clb, 73cb, 85tr, 116bla, bl, bcl, bcr, 160br, 310bl, 320cl, 424c, 425c, 442bc, 470bl, 495cl, 549clb, 587crb, 593cbr, 649c, 671cl, 738tr, 813cr, cl, ccl, bla, 944cb British Museum: 62t, 253clb, bl, 311bl, 619cl, 652ca, clb, cb, 740tr, 882cr Musee de Bayeux: 860crMusee Guimet: 448bl V & A Museum: 581cblWellcome Collection: 544tr **Thelma Holt/Alastair Muir:** 272cr **Holt Studios International:** 683cl Duncan Smith: 326br **Honda UK:** 128crb **Chris Howes:** 689crb **Christopher Howson:** 375bca **Hulton Getty:** 45cr, 59br, 62bl, 79tl, 98clb, 108clb, bcl, 121cr, 176cl, clb, bca, 158bla, 161tr, 194c, crb, bl, 203bl, 225cb, 248cra, 250bc, 254bl, 255bra, 262br, 266tr, Disney Enterprises, Inc.: 269trb, 272cl, 274bl, 294bc, 331tr, 362bra, bl, 372bl, 373crb, cb, 399bra, cl, cla, bl, 409bl, 415bl, 426cr, br, 448br, 481cla, c, 482bla, 542cl, 560bra, 580cra, cr, 607tr, br, cl, 608cra, bc, bl, 619br, 629tr, 632tr, 645c, bcr, 673bl, 718c, 718crb, 734cl, 740bl, 790cbr, bla, 812tr, 814bl, 829tr, 836bl, 861bl, crb, 868cbl, 869clb, 882cr, 901ca, 905c, cl, 907crb, bra, 908cl, cr, 912tr, 938b, 939bla, 940bra MPI: 399trb **Hunterian Museum:** 354c **Hutchison Library:** 19c, 21t, 30ca, 31cl, 79bl, 308ca, 328cr, 446cra, 463tr, br, 469tcr, 785ccl, 787c, 791l Timothy Beddow: 26clb, 34tc TE Clark: 477car R Constable: 407tr Christine Dodwell: 32bl, 76cl John Downman: 611tr Sarah Errington: 24b, 115tc, 762crb Robert Francis: 65bc, 195tc, cal, c, 859br Melanie Friend: 106cb, 107clb, c, crb B Gerard: 587bl G Goodger: 859bc P Goycolea: 445tr Maurice Harvey: 36cra, 36br, 172bl Nick Haslam: 112br, 727cr J Henderson: 174car Andrew Hill: 32tl Jeremy A Horner: 77bc, 285t, 590c, 790br Eric Lawrie: 792cra Ingrid Hudson: 784tl Crispin Hughes: 105t, 106bl, 526cbl Eric Lawrie: 141c, 286tc, 787t R Ian Lloyd: 208tl, 449cb, 931cl Michael Macintyre: 637cl B Moser: 596br, 877br Trevor Page: 81tr, 187clb, 253ccl, 706bra Edward Parker: 285br, 286c, br, tcb, 552br PE Parker: 21c Christine Pemberton: 649tr S. Pern: 35br, 67cl, 567br Bernard Règent: 22cl,cr, 96cl K Rogers: 669bcr Nigel Sitwell: 78tr A Sole:

497tl, tr A Silvertop: 931c Tony Souter: 477bl Liba Taylor: 933br JC Tordai: 187bc Isabella Tree: 464t David Wason: 107bl Philip Wolmuth: 174cbl Andrey Zvoznikov: 76tr, cal

I,J,K

ICCE/Rob Carlson: 777bc **Photograph with kind permission of ICI Chemicals & Polymers Ltd:** 12br **Ikona:** 228cra **Image Bank:** 208tr, 244br, 381cr, 392ca, 508bcl, 679cl, 682cr, 733br, 741crb, 777brc John Banagon: 680bra A Becker: 859bl P & G Bowater: 156bl Luis Castaneda: 391cla, 799bca G Champlong: 435c, 577cal W Chan: 524tr, tc Gary Cralle: 126tr, 819cl Yves Debay: 25crb Steve Dunwell: 376bl Tom Owen Edmunds: 73br G Gay: 563tr David W.Hamilton: 596cb Hartmann: 588br Peter Hendrie: 635tl Gill C Kenny: 93tc Paul McCormrick: 635cal C Molyneux: 743cra Ghislaine Morel: 304c Kaz Mori: 876crb Robbi Newman: 95bl Marc Romanelli: 452tr, 833cr G Alberto Rossi: 557br, 758br Harold Schoen: 268bra, 819tr Sobel/Klonsky: 564cr W Steinmetz: 799c Stockphotos: 598bl Harald Sund: 90c, 602cb J Szkoolzinski: 435br Paul Trummer: 160tlbAlvis Upitis: 156br Nevada Wier: 876crS Wilkinson: 435bl F Wing: 525bra Hans Wolf: 379br, 380bra **Images Colour Library:** 356br, 603cl, 798br, 837bca Horizon/T Dawes: 603br /Rob Walls: 95cr Charles Walker Collection: 191crb **Images of India:** 493clb, bl **Image Select:** 200bl, 238tr, 371cl/Ann Ronan Picture Library: 12bcl, 13ca, 40br, 47cra, clb, 145br, bl, 163bc, 287bcr, br, 326tc, 371cb, 441bc , 508bl, 655t, 807bl, 911clb, 871cr /Vioujard: 695cl Patrick Piel: 426cbr **Impact:** Mohamed Ansar: 213bc James Barlow: 784tr Martin Black: 314ca, 405br Julian Calder: 658crb M Cator: 479tr Piers Cavendish: 525br, 784tc, 853tcl, crb, 932br Kay Chemush: 638clb A Corbin: 413tcr, 775tr C Cormack: 314cb S Dorantes: 552bc B Edwards: 450cr Alain Evrard: 525cr Alain le Garsmeur: 207bc Ingrid Gaushon: 328br Mark Henley: 422tl, tr, 469tr, 486cla, 525tc, 682br, 853bc, 877clb Colin Jones: 141t P Kokkonen: 333bc Robin Lubbock: 194br A MacNaughton: 438bc Richard McCaig: 194cl, 452br M McQueem: 476br Gavin Milverton: 683cb Guy Moberly: 147ca N Morrison: 442bl Tony Page: 859trCaroline Penn: 187crb, 680tl, 728br Johnathon Pile: 730br Anne Marie Purkiss: 333br Jim Rice: 731t Rahul Sengupta: 21bl Andrew Smith: 288br S Weir: 487bra **Trustees of the Imperial War Museum:** 800cb, 905bl **IMS Bildbyra:** 373tr **The Institute of Social History, Amsterdam:** 602bl **IOC/Olympic Museum Collections:** 632bl, bca **Israel Museum:** D Samuel & Jeane H Gottesman Center for Biblical Manuscripts: 214bc **Italian Tourist Board:** 476bl **Robbie Jack Photography:** 836tl, cr **Lin Jammet:** 857tr **JET, Joint European Torus :** 618cbl **JVZ Picture Library:** T Nilson: 733cb **Hiroshi Kasai:** 455tc **Katz Pictures:** 315cb Nubar Alexarian: 142tcr Bruno Hadjih: 142bra Mark Henley: 153tl, 207bl JB Pictures: 474br Richard McCaig: 153br Saba/Rea/Lehman: 863bl, 933clb/G Smith: 867trb/Ann States: 68br/S Sherbell: 391bra/P Yates: 865bcra Woodfin Camp & Assoc., NY/(G Ludwig: 107tcb **Jorkhi Takamine Kawakami NY:** 429bl **Luke Kelly:** 465t, bl, 466bla **David King Collection:** 0bcr (Reproduced by permission of Hibbert Ralph Entertainment and Silvey Jex Partnership 0cr, Steve Gorton 0cr, 0cbl, 212cra, c, cb, crb, bl, 426ca, 733cr, 734bl, c, cr, 795crb **Kobal Collection:** 717tr Columbia/Tristar Motion Picture Companies 1995 Sony Pictures Entertainment Co. All Rights Reserved/Clive Coote: 516tlb **Kunsthistorisches Museum, Vienna:** 428t

L,M,N,

Labour Movement Library and Archive, Denmark: Jorgen Strohbach: 857trb **Landesdenkmalamt Baden-Wurtemberg, Stuttgart** / Dr J Biel: 192bl **Landesmuseum Trier:** 368t **Frank Lane Picture Agency:** K Aitken/Panda: 772cla Peter Davey: 657crb C Elsey: 511c Tony Hamblin: 669br, 872br H Hautala: 333cr Peggy Heard: 366c John Holmes: 713bl David Hosking: 713crb E & D Hosking: 104c, 234c, 350cl, 459br, 699cl, 817cr, 822tr, 872crb WJ Howes: 844c S Jonasson: 90cra Frank W Lane: 345cbr, cbL Lee Rue: 257bcr Life Science Images: 342ca Mark Newman: 104bc, 366br, 523cr Philip Perry: 256cr F Polkir: 872cra Silvestris: 257cra, 624c T Whittaker: 512br, 556cbl DP Wilson: 623bra, brb, 624br, bl, bla W Wisniewski: 309tr **Cyril Laubscher:** 166cr **Link:** Orde Eliason: 273c, 785c Chandra Kishore Prasad: 372clb, cb, crb, br **David Linley/Debi Treloar:** 369br **By Permission of the Linnean Society of London:** 510cr, cl, c, bcr **London City Ballet:** Peter Teigan: 203cb **London Transport Museum:** 262cbr **Louisanna Army National Guard, Louisiana:** 696cl **Magistrates Association:** 496cbl **Magnum:** Abbas: 877cbBruno Barbey: 478bcl Ian Berry: 506tr Rene Burri: 869br Bruce Davidson: 491trb Stuart Franklin: 479cb PJ Griffiths: 877cla H Gruyaert: 730cl David Hurn: 253bc Richard Kalvar: 853br Wayne Miller: 869c Michael Nichols: 390bcr Steve McCurry: 37cbr Raghu Rai: 575cra, bc, cl C Steele Perkins: 19cbr Dennis Stock: 866bl Alex Webb: 867tr **Manchester Central Local Studies Unit Library:** 641bl **Mander & Mitchenson:** 272ca **Mansell Collection:** 47bc, 161crb, 171cr, cra, 228clb, 233br, 263ca, cra, cb, br, 301cl, tc, 359cl, 383c, 439bc, 487br, 591tr, 593bcr, 594trb, cb, br, 613bcr 740cb, ca, 868tr, 878br, 886b G Marinier: 762cr **MARS:** 225bl **Marx Memorial Library:** 535cra, tr **Mary Rose Trust, Portsmouth:** 59bcra, 60 **S & D Maslowski:** 817crb **Fred Mayer:** 784c **Mayibuye Centre:** 530cl **ME Company/One Little Indian:** 719crb **Courtesy of H Keith Melton:** 225clb, 676cr, bra **Meteorological Office:** 891bl **Metropolitan Museum of Art:** Gift of Mr and Mrs Ira Haupt, 1950, 656cl **Metropolitan Police:** 496clb **Microscopix:** 554bc, 555bla, 655bl **Microsoft:** 457br **Middlesbrough Borough Council:** 238br **Military Picture Library:** 409c, 882br **Mirror Syndications International:** 121bl, 521tr, cr, 901c **Regine Moylett Publicity:** 719crb **Mozart-Archiv:** 580cla **Musee de L'Homme, Phototheque:** 768cal **Musee National d'Art Moderne, Centre Georges Pompidou, Paris:** 589clb, 638bl, 656cr **Museo Arqueologico, Oronoz:** 800tr **Museo Nacional, Centro de Arte Reina Sofia:** 656bl **Museu Picasso:** 656trb **Museum of London:** 334cr, 901cl, bl **The Museum of Modern Art, New York:** 656c **Nardoni Gallery:** 496br **National Blood Service:** 415br **By Courtesy of the Trustees of the National Gallery, London:** 71cr, 800cl **National Library, Dublin:** 466cl **National Medical Slide Bank:** 909bcr, cla **National Meteorogical Library/Ken Woodley:** 221cl **National Motor Museum, Beaulieu:** 179cbl, 577cl, **National Museum of Ireland:** 191bra, 192clb **National Museum, Tokyo:** 320tr **National Palace Museum, Taiwan, Republic of China:** 116cla **By Courtesy of the National Portrait Gallery, London:** 149tr, 263t, 301br **National Trust Photographic Library:** 329br Oliver Benn: 183bl, 704cb Geoffrey Frosh: 671cra **Natural History Museum, London:** 374bl, 437cl, cr **Natural History Picture Agency:** 309cb, 431br Agence Nature: 166tc, 336bca, 622tr B&C Alexander: 675bl, bc, 694bca, 850cla ANT: 83tr, 94tl, 99cr,cb, 100cl, 118cb, 245r, 345br, 489bla, cb, tc, 517cr, 634cra, 635cl, 647c, 675br, 912tc/Martin Harvey: 82tc Henry Ausloos: 423ca Anthony Bannister: 104crb, 300tr, 511tr, 554cb, 568b, 912tcr AP Barnes: 54br GI Bernard: 52cl, 162bc, 165br, 177crb, 459bl, 665cl, 667cb, crb Joe Blossom: 38bl, 912tcl NA Callow: 83cla Laurie Campbell: 276bl, 529bcl, 579cr, 694tcr, 794cl, c Bill Coster: 83cr NR Coulton: 395cb Stephen Dalton: 117tr, br, 118tr, tc, 155cr, 177cl, 316bc, 346bca, 615cbl, 667tr, 872bca917c Manfred Dannegger: 166bra, br, 276bc, 317cbl, 694bla Nigel J Dennis: 39cl, 39cra, 55bl, 245cla, 472c, 918tr Douglas Dickins: 154ca Patrick Fagot: 794cra, 919cbl Martin Garwood: 342clb Melvin Grey: 39crb, 419cl, 633cl Ken Griffiths: 100c Tony Hamblin: 257tl E Hanumantha Rao: 713clb Martin Harvey: 82ccr, 154bcl, 396cbl, 488bra, 533c Brian Hawkes: 90tr, 633bl, 918c P Hermansen: 919br Daniel Heuclin: 54cl, 94tr, 165bcr, 320ccr, 342cl, 568clb, 672tr, 712bl, br Image Quest 3D: 483c Hellio & Van Ingen: 674br EA Janes: 235bca EA Janes: 419r, 902tc B Jones & M Shimlock: 241clb Darek Karp: 154clb R Kirchner: 488clb T Kitchin: 616bra/ & V Hurst: 889bcr Stephen Krasemann: 55cr, 166c, 420bl Gerard Lacz: 317tr, 489cr, 511bc, br Julie Meech: 82c DE Myers: 919tl Haroldo Palo jr: 793bl Peter Parks: 241bra Dr I Poluinin: 847br Dr Eckart Pott: 675bcr Steve Robinson: 54bc Andy Rouse: 165cb, 420bla, 615br Jamy Sauvanet: 794clb Kevin Schafer: 793cr Lady Philippa Scott: 83bl J Shaw: 419crb, 489c, 615bl, tr, trb, 633cb, 665bl Eric Soder: 419c, 579cbr R Sorensen & J Olseirt: 514bc Karl Switak: 636bl, 772bl Roger Tidman: 257cr, 533cr, 534cr Michael Tweedie: 124bra Dave Watts: 894tcb Martin Wendler: 366cr, 793cb, 794br Alan Williams: 534bl, 675tcl Bill Wood: 337cr David Woodfall: 316t, 317ca, 419bcl Norbert Wu: 483t, 622cal **Natural Science Photos:** Carol Farneti Foster: 904br O Meredith: 366cb Photo Safari PVT Ltd: 423cbl C & T Stuart: 423tr John W Warden: 571tc Curtis Williams: 342c **Nature Photographers Ltd:** TD Bonsall: 54tr **NEC Europe:** 875bc **Neff Ltd:** 911crb **Network:** Michael Abrahams: 474c, 804cra Michael Goldwater: 639cr Nikolai Ignatiev: 730tl, 731br Peter Jordan: 605bca K.Kallay/Bilderberg: 81tc, 113tlb J Matthews: 931cr Rapho/W Buss: 567tl, 728c, 866tc/G Sioen: 866tr Barry Lewis: 639b, 804cr Christian Sappa: 113bcl G Sioen: 474bl Anthony Suau: 730cb J Sturrock: 438tr Homer Sykes: 391ca **Peter Newark:** 48cb, br, crb, bra, 49cra, 171cb, 176cr, 224bc, 383br, tr, bc, trb, cb, 481cra, 613br, 614cl, bra, bl, br, 658cla, cra, 868cra, bl, 882bc, 883tc, 887bcl, 905cr **By Permission of the Warden & Fellows, New College, Oxford:** 607cr **Florence Nightingale Museum Trust:** 608cr **Nikon** 164crb **NOAA: National Geophysical Data Center:** 281clb **The Nobel Foundation:** 646bra **JL Nou:** 151bl, cla

O,P,Q

Opec: 626cbr **Robert Opie:** 606tr **Christine Osborne:** 20tr, 25cla, bl, 76c, 408crb, bl, 452bl **Mark O'Shea:** 772cla, 773tcr, 794bl **Oxford Scientific Films:** 118cra, 354cl, 458cr K Atkinson: 624bc T Angermayer: 384c Animals Animals/Breck P Kent: 342cbrZ Leszczynski: 622bl/P Weimann: 317car Doug Allan: 162br, 747clb Kathie Atkinson: 154bcla A Bannister: 568crb, 889bar GI Bernard: 749crb Tony Bomford: 83cb Clive Bromhall: 390bla, 801crb Roger Brown: 289bl Gordon Bull: 239tr Scott Camazine/S Bilotta-Best: 914cr Pat Caulfield: 136cl Dr Mark A Chappell: 235cr Martin Colbeck: 83ca, 283br, 300cb, 657clb Dr JAL Cooke: 58cl, 463cr, 801c,cl,cr, ccr Judd Cooney: 657br Daniel J Cox: 120cl, 256bcr, 622bc, 640cbl, 794car Tony Crabtree: 755cr Stephen Dalton: 124br Richard Day: 640bl Mark Deeble & Victoria Stone: 343br John Downer: 245crb, 916cra Flanagan/Morris: 780cal DB Fleetham: 806br, 920cl Michael Fogden: 50clb, 57crb, cb, 261trb Paul Franklin: 38bcla, 316br, 793cl Max Gibbs: 166cr, 166cla, 599cbl Bob Gibbons: 317cr Laurence Gould: 239cl Howard Hall: 556bl Mark Hamblin: 316bl, 317cl, 384cl, bl Terry Heathcote: 316ca P Henry: 499bl Paul Key: 750bcr Geoff Kidd: 643bl Richard Kirby: 643clb DF Koster: 189crb Rudie Kuiter: 337bl Peter Lack: 39cb Michael Leach: 257clb T Leach: 533bla Zig Leszcynski: 39tlb, 384t, 440bc, 579cbl London Scientific Films: 52cb, 420bra, 751c GA Maclean: 500br Mantis Wildlife Films/Glen Carruthers: 556bca Joe McDonald: 384b Michael McKinnon: 678bl Godfrey Merlen: 747bla John Mitchell: 801t O Newman: 902bcl Okapia/Foot: 423cbr/B&H Kunz: 261bra/ST Myers: 423tl/G Synatzschke: 555bcr Ben Osborne: 316bcr, 916cla Stan Osolinski: 260bcr, 299cbl, 376cr, 396cr, 397br, 440bl, 643crb Richard Packwood: 105br, 260cl, 600tl, 677tr, 713cb Peter Parks: 554cl, c, cr, 555trb, 622cb CM Perrins: 245br Photo Researchers Inc/Tom McHugh: 529bcr JL Pontier: 847ca Prestige Pictures: 640br Robin Redfern: 529cra, 902bl JH Robinson: 396cbr Alan Root: 396bcr Norbert Rosing: 511cr Tui de Roy: 472cl C Sanchez: 397cb Frank Schneidermeyer: 166cl P Sharpe: 512cTim Shepherd: 316cr Survival Anglia: 420br J & D Bartlett: 299ca, 396t Joe B.Blossom: 657bl Frances Furlong: 189cb/WS Paton: 585cra Alan Root: 38cr, 57tr/Maurice Tibbles: 511crb, 750br Harold Taylor: 124bl, 189ca, 241cr, 554bl TC Nature: 459cb David Tipling: 235ca Steve Turner: 39c, 384tr, 423cra, 440cla, 657cb, 713c Tom Ulrich: 889bcl W Wisniewski: 499cr Konrad Wothe: 83c PA Zahl Photo Researchers: 508cra

Oxford University Museum: 255br **P&O Cruises:** 757 **Page One:** Bob Gordon: 193tr, 194tl **Panos Pictures:** 19cb, 29cl, 186bl, 207br, 785bra Martin Adler: 23br, 194bcla Kathie Atkinson: 771cal P Barker: 32br, 106t, 148cra Giuseppe Bizzarri: 252bl Trygue Bolstad: cbl, 785bla JC Callow: 114tr, 115c Ian Cartwright: 36cla Alfredo CedeÒo: 788tr, 851trb David Constantine: 876brNeil Cooper: 115tr, 194trb, cra Rob Cousins: 784cl Jean Leo Dugast: 444b, 524cr, 760bl, 833cra, 834bc, bl N Durrell McKenna: 67t Marc French: 174cal, t CG Gardener: 770tr Ron Giling: 27cr, 33cr, 650bc, bcl Mark Hakansson: 728tc Jeremy Hartley: 34cl, ca, 35bc, 114bc, 323tr, 452tl Jim Holmes:76clb, 449c, 497bl, bc Rhodri Jones: 186c, cr Victoria Keble-Williams: 16cla B Klass: 114bla Pat & Tom Leeson/Photo Researchers: 54cb G Mansfield: 408tc J. Marks: 31bl, 785bl Jon Mitchell: 195bl James Morris: 37cl, c S Murray: 866trb Shanon Nace: 115cbr Zed Nelson: 115tl M O'Brien: 173t Trevor Page: 26cla, 497br Bruce Paton: 323bl N Peachey: 78cla Betty Press: 26t, crb, bl, 35bla, 930bl David Reed: 30cr, 31br Marcus Rose: 77cl, 731cr D Sansoni: 444cb, 446br, 450tl, cl, 524br Marc Schlossman: 20cra, 23ca, cra, 716br J Shanerly 877c Jon Spaull: 731cl,Sean Sprague: 22br, 23bc, 142tl Chris Stowers: 208tc, cl, 451br, 452bc, 525bc, 728tl Tayacon: 523cl Liba Taylor: 23cl, 314tc, 348ca, 727cl, 803bcl, Penny Tweedie: 32tc, 253cl, 408cla Max Whitaker: 218cb, bl, bcl Gregory Wrona: 313cr, 728bcr **Parker Library, Corpus Christie, Cambridge:** 51bra **WR Pashley Ltd:** 129cla **David Paterson:** 473tr, crb **Penguin Children's Books:** 204cb **Ann & Bury Peerless:** 151cr, 214bra, 447cl, 487tcr, 705bl **Performing Arts Library:** Clive Barda: 273cra, crb, 630cra Fritz Curzon: 253tr **Photo Researchers Inc.:** Tom McHugh: 154br **Pictor:** 67cr, 94clb, 126tc, 169l, 175br, 208bl, 379cr, 404bl, 476c, 601cr, 749tr, 822cl **Pictorial Press:** 718bc **Pictures Colour Library:** 314bl, 404cra, 475tr, 617cl, br, 821cal, 822br **Graham Piggott:** 788cr **Ian Pillinger:** 41cra, 45b, 46 **The Planetarium:** 651cra Jill Plank: 283bl **Planet Earth Picture Library:** 217br, bcr, bcl, 241br, 472tr, 810bl, bc, 812cl K & K Ammann: 450tc Kurt Amsler: 194bra Sean T Avery: 38cla Andre Barstchi: 714cr Gary Bell: 635car, 672bcr S Bloom: 440cra Myer S Bornstein: 616tcb John R Bracegirdle: 234br, 317tcr, 353bcr, 533t Philip Chapman: 189cr Mary Clay: 396cb, 756br M Conlin: 556ca Richard Coomber: 616cl, 715c Rob Crandall: 788cl, 794tc Beth Davidson: 616bl, bc Wendy Dennis: 317bra G Douwma: 916ca, cbbr John Downer: 82tr, 299tr, 396br, 609bra J Eastcott: 793bla Ivor Edmonds: 385br, 398cbr John Evans: 162clb Elio Della Ferrera: 39cr Nigel Downer: 316bla Alain Dragesco: 39tl C Farneti: 793ccr D Robert Franz: 616tcr, tr Nick Garbutt: 571bl, bc Roger de la Harpe: 39tr, 785t, bc Steve Hopkin: 750ca K Jayaram: 82cl Adam Jones: 616ca, tc Anthony Joyce: 397bc Brian Kenney: 256br Alex Kerstitch: 770cl David Kjaer: 317cbr Ken Lucas: 39cr, 235bla, 615cbr, 616bcr, 770br D Lyons: 579tr John Lythgoe: 615bcl, 793t David Maitland:802bc Richard Matthews: 57bl, 353bc, 794crb Mark Mattock: 289cal David Jesse McChesney: 777bl Dr Martin Merker: 756bl , cr Jon & Alison Moran: 699br P de Oliveira: 916crb Pete Oxford: 162bl , 640cbr, 794cal David A Panton: 616tl Doug Perrine: 622t, 755bra C Petron: 599cbr Linda Pitkin: 239ccr Rod Planck: 616bca Mike Potts: 615c Mike Read: 316crb Keith Scholey: 794tr, bc Peter Scoones: 38br, 483cr, 534bc Johnathon Scott: 38bcl, 39bl , 165bl, 396bl, 506bc Seaphot/Dick Clarke: 239cr/J & G Lythgoe: 568cl N Sefton: 472cr, 483clb Anup & Manuj Shah: 38c, 82cb M Snyderman: 483bl Peter Stephenson: 83bc Jan Tore Johansson: 317br Mills Tandy: 616br Nigel Tucker: 82cr Peter Velensky: 82bca Tom Walker: 615bcr, cb, 616crb John Waters: 83tc, 787cb JD Watt: 919cr Margaret Welby: 793c Bill Wood: 909bra Andrew Zvoznikov: 729t **Polish Cultural Institute Library:** 313cra **Popperfoto:** Eriko Sugita/Reuters 204cbl; Reuters/Gary Hershorn 0crb, 18cr, bl, bc, 19cl, 45ca, cla, cra, 72bl, 79tr, c, 225tr, cbr, br, 251bl, 301cr, 344cb, 359bra, 372c, 530bl, trb, 628cla, 632bc, 646cl, bl, 659br, 684bl, 719tr, 736cr, 742cl, 786bla, 818bl, 829crb, 831cl, 887crb 905bc, 908tr, cla, clb, 943 tl, tc, cr, 944cla, 945 cl, 946 tc, 947cb, 948br Brunskill: 411cr Liaison/Magani: 582br Reuters: 14cb, cl, 618cbr, 675cl, 857bla/Peter Andrews: 786br **Premaphotos Wildlife:** KG Preston Mafham: 100tc, 794bcr **Pressens Bild:** 520bra, 857crb **Public Record Office:** 247bl Crown: 861bc **Quadrant Picture Library:** 179tr, ca, 180bra, 306tl, 842bcl, bcr, 843cb

R,S,T,

Racal: 695c **RAF Museum, Hendon:** 485cbr, br **Railtrack North West:** 842clb **Redferns:** 121bca, 482c, 587bc Michael Ochs Archives: 482bl Pankaj Shah: 587tc **Renault:** 357clb **Reunion des Musees Nationaux:** 151tr, 835cb **Rex Features:** The Sun 0cr, John Powell 0clb, 68bcr, Julian Simmonds 81bc, 171cbr, Tim Rooke 176 crb, 219cl, 275trb, 331tc, 340br, 391clb, 530br, tr, 581bl, 575bcr, 718clb, 718bl, 719bl, 727t, 790bca, 861crb, 881cl, 884bla, 896tr, 939bcla, bra, 940cra, cr Action Press: 841c Agence DPPI: 897ca, cr ANP Foto: 862trb Jonathon Buckmaster: 40bl Jorgensen: 457tr Clive Dixon: 29bcr, 380bl T Doccon-Gibod: 311cb Fotos International/Frank Edwards: 254br Malcolm Gilson: 311crb Tony Larkin: 219cr Brian Rasic: 719br Sipa Press: 176crb, 210trb, 210crb, 359cb, 411cbr, 530crb, c, 684bc, 834tr, 887bcr, 923bl, 932cr Foulon/Tavernier: 303cl Stills: 254bcl Tom Stockhill: 19bl Greg Williams: 153bl Richard Young: 653br **Roskilde Festival:** 328bc **Rover Group:** 859bca **The Rowland Company/Ariel:** 277trb **The Royal Collection** 1997 Her Majesty Queen Elizabeth II: 507bl, 708cl **Royal College of Music, Junior Department:** 630bl **Royal College of Physicians:** 654br **Royal Geographical Society, London:** 521cl, 810br **Royal Photographic Society, Bath:** 693cra **Charles Russell:** 120bl **The Sainsbury Centre for Visual Arts:** 746bcr, bla **Peter Sanders:** 407tl, cl, cr, 435tr, 468cr, 469c, bl **Hans Sas Fotografie:** 324cl. cr **NJ Saunders:** 73clb **Floyd Sayers:** 282clb, cb, 300t, bcr, 667ca, 916bra **Scala:** 72tr, 215cb, 307cl, 329tc, 401tr, 402ca, 583cr, cl, 708bra, 724c, ccr, 746bc, bra, 813br Accademia, Venice: 707bcl Biblioteca Mariana, Venice: 707cla S Pietra, Vatican: 707bl **Science Photo Library:** 91br, 131cr, 199cl, 226bl, 230c, 278bc, 287tr, 298br, 306bl, 319br, 354br, 363br, 375cra, 376bcr, 378cl, 398cb, 456tr, 501bc, 559cr, 584br, 585bcl, bcr, 598bca, 661bc, 696bl, 743bc, 778bc, 782br, 796bl, 829bc, 838crb Agema Infra Red Systems: 911cr Los Alamos Photo Laboratory: 618br Doug Allan: 56tr Peter Arnold Inc/Volker Steger: 457tc/Szuson J Wong: 542bl Bill Bachman: 230bl Alex Bartel: 296cra A Barrington Brown: 87bra Alex Bartel: 298bcl, 558br, 584br Julian Baum: 814cr Tim Beddow: 542ccl, c Biology Media: 441cl Martin Bond: 12bc, 252car, 387cr, 740bc Dr Tony Brain: 138cl, 916clb Dr Eli Brinks: 744cl BSIP Laurent: 145crb BSIP LECA: 144cl BSIP VEM: 264crb, 769c BSIP Taulin: 441br Dr Jeremy Burgess: 190cl, 231bra, 342cb, 371tr, 584cl, 585bcra, 626cbl, 767c, 815br, 870clb, 871crb Mark Burnett: 45clb CC Studio: 766br 742cr Cern, P.Loiez: 655cbb J Loup Charmet: 697cl, 871cb Pr S Cinti, Universite díAncone: 873clb Mark Clarke: 268clb Clinique Ste Catherine/CNRI: 744bl CNES, 1990 Distribution Spot Image: 259br, 532br CNRI: 376cl, 643tc/RM Tektoff: 555tc Prof C Terlaud: 542ccr Andy Crump, TDR, WHO: 863tr, 933tr W Curtsinger: 912trb Custom Medical Stock Photo: 145tc, 645cr/R Becker: 414bc, 441c Mike Devlin: 376c Luke Dodd: 370clb, 538br Martin Dohrn: 221bl, 268bc, 643br John Durham: 654cra Ralph Eagle: 322bcar Harold Edgerton: 653: lb ESA: 230cl Dr F Espenak: 739ccl Eye of Science: 145cr, 415clb, 555crb, 653bl Sindo Farina: 626bl Dr Gene Feldman, NASA GSFC: 280ca Vaughan Fleming: 717br Sue Ford: 322bla Simon Fraser: 64cl, 199br, 578bra, 625cr/Newcastle University Robotics Group: 717cr A & H Frieder Michler: 554t, 584c D Gifford: 437cra G Gillette: 553bcl Geospace: 471bl Carlos Goldin: 266br Allen Green: 721cbl Alan Greig: 353bl J Greim: 415trb Tony Hallas: 807cr, 870bc Hale Observatories: 370bl, 814tr David Halpern: 378cra Y Hamel, Publiphoto Diffusion: 841cb Adam Hart-Davis: 376blr, 695cr John Heseltine: 710br James Holmes/Hays Chemicals: 13bl/Oxford Centre for Molecular Sciences: 559crb/Rover: 717cb Anthony Howarth: 139br B Iverson: 909blDr WC Keel: 370cbr James King-Holmes: 670br, 697bca Labat/Lanceau, Jerrican: 717cl Gary Ladd: 87tlb Scott Lamazine: 765br Francis Leroy/Biocosmos: 709crb Dr Andrejs Liepins: 190bla Dick Livia: 232cb Bill Longcore: 226cb Dr Kari Lounatmaa: 268cl D Lovegrove: 891tr Dr P Marazzi: 268c Marine Biological Laboratory: 386bl M Marten: 554brW & D McIntyre: 503bcl, 541cr, bc David McLean: 230clb John McMaster: 199cb John Mead: 467br, 828br Peter Menzel: 232crb, 281cla, 306bla, 625br, 810bra, 891cra Dr David Miller: 673br Hank Morgan: 710tc Professor P Motta, Department of Anatomy, University La Sapienza, Rome: 766tl, tcl, tc, 769bl S Nagendra: 931bl Nasa: 86tc, tr, 91bla, 130bc, 236br, 280bra, 471br, 572clb, 660tc, 739cr, 796cr, 797cr, bra, 826bc, 828tcr, 870bcl, cbl, 896bc 922tl /GSFC: 282cbl, 678tl, tcl, tc National Center for Atmospheric Research: 698cr National Institute of Health: 824br National Library of Medicine: 645bc National Snow & Ice Data Centre: 891bra NIBSC: 414bl, 555tlb NOAA: 456bl NOAN: 370bc Novosti Press Agency: 86cl, 698bra, 739bl NRAO/AUI: 370crb NRSC Ltd: 471bc David Nunuk: 13tr Claude Nuridsany & Marie Perennou: 342cra, 346br, 555bcl, 698cl, clb George Olson: 281bl Omikron: 744bc Oxford Molecular Biophysics Laboratory: 744cr Pacific Press Service: 522cr David Parker: 87bl, 232cl, 277bl, 282bl, 416cb, 642bra 716bcl, 796clb /ESA/CNES/Arianespace: 792br P Parvlainen: 572cra Alfred Pasieka: 138cl, 436cl, 553bl, 909br Dr DJ Patterson: 914c Petit Format/Nestle: 709cra Philippe Plailly: 377bc/Eurelios: 298cb, 553br, 850bl Max-Planck Institut fur Extraterrestriche pysik: 870bcr Chris Priest: 697bra J Prince: 413bl Professors PM Motta, T Fujita & M Muto: 190clb Prof. P Motta/Dept of Anatomy, University La Sapienza, Rome: 414br, 582cl Professor Tony Wright, Institute of Laryngology & Otology: 278cl John Radcliffe Hospital: 541ccr J Reader: 506cr, tc Roger Ressmeyer, Starlight: 87tr, bla, 92bc, 812cb, 828bca, 870cla Dr H Rose: 919tc Rosenfeld Images Ltd: 315tr, 456tc, 503bl Royal Greenwich Observatory: 87bca, 663cr, 870br Royal Observatory Edinburgh/AATB: 870cra Rev. Ronald Royer: 230ca, 814bra Peter Ryan: 823br Joe Rychetnik: 739ccr Ph Saada/Eurelios: 695cb J Sanford: 572c, cb, 828tc Tom Van Sant/Geosphere Project, Santa Monica: 279tr, 280tl Francoise Sauze: 716cbr David Scharf: 131bl, 555bra, 643tr, 767cr, cb Dr K Schiller: 544c Secchi-Lecaque/Roussel-Uclaf/CNRI: 144bc, 709cl Blair Seitz: 742bl Dr Seth Shostak: 87tc, 739crb SIU: 873bca D Spears: 909c St Bartholemew's Hospital: 200cb Synaptek: 717bc Andrew Syred: 248tr, 553bra, 584cl Tainturier Jerrican: 200cbr G Tompkinson: 414cb, 744c Alexander Tsiaras: 44cbr US Dept of Energy: 742crb US Library of Congress: 344c USSR Academy of Sciences/Nasa: 797cb Andy Walker/Midland Fertility Services: 710tcl Garry Watson: 541crb X-ray Astronomy Group, Leicester University: 370cr Frank Zullo: 370tr **Science Pictures Ltd:** 554bra **Science & Society Picture Library:** David Parker 86bl, 277br, 287cb, 360bla, 371cr, 485cl, 503crb, 645cl, 695crb, 721c, 825cl, 874bc, 948bcl Bowsfield/BKK: 467crb, ca NMPFT: 695br National Railway Museum: 843bc Science Museum: 178cb, 467cl **Steve Setford:** 352cb **Sewerby Hall Museum/Simon Kench:** 485cr, cb **The Shakespeare Centre Library: Joe Cocks Studio Collection:** 753bl Gill Shaw: 62bcr, 221tc, 605br **Shell UK Ltd:** 262cr **Shiner Ltd:** 129tr **Jamie Simson:** 464cbr **Skoda Auto:** 313bc **Sky Sports:** Kerry Ghais: 875br Sam Teare: 875bcl **Harry Smith Collection:** 393bc **JCD Smith:** 860cbl **Sophia Smith Collection:** 849cr **Smithsonian Institution:** 176tr **Smithsonian Institution Astrophysical Observatory:** 370br **Society for Co--operation in Russian & Soviet Studies:** 424cra, 516tcrb, 732c, 733cra, 795t, cra, bra D Toase: 733cbr **Sony Classical Archives:** 811bl **South American Pictures:** 141bcl, 790cr Nicholas Bright: 792cla Robert Francis: 67ca, 193ca, cb, 521bra Kimball Morrison: 198br Tony Morrison: 65crb, 66cbl, 67cb, 140c, crb, bcr, 142bc, 146c, 147c, br, 194br 198cl, 549cra, 684c, 789cr, br, 791r Chris Sharp: 792c **Southampton Oceanography Centre:** 620trb **The Spanish Tourist Office:** 799tr, tcr **Spectrum:** 94cl, 126br, 148crb, 193bl, 313t,

CREDITS

ILLUSTRATORS

David Ashby: 42tl, tca, 150tl. 216cra, 218tl, 244tl, 291l, 410tl, 455tl, 539tl, 689tl, 693tl, 757c, b, 809tl, 812cr. **Penny Boylan:** 218cl. **Dave Burroughs:** 122tr, 303tl, 395cr, 556bl. **Karen Cochrane:** 71tl, 88tr, 109ca, br, bcl,110tl, 130br, 152cl, 160tl, 184br, 203tl, 210tr, 224tl, 238tl, 250tl, 255tl, 263tl, 272tl, 284br, 287tl, 288tl, 301tl, 323tl, 326tl, 334tl, 348tl, 351acr, c,bl, 371tl, 374tl, 390tl, 399tl, 409tl, 470tl, 480tl, 482tl, 495tl, 530tl, 535tl, 553c, 563acl, 565cr, 587tl, 588tr, ac, c, 608tl, 631tl, 641tl, 646tl, 651tl, 673tl, 685tl, 704tl, 707tl, 718tl, 741tl, 753tl, 760tl, 763tl, 804tl, 808tr, 831acr, bcr, bl, br, 849tl, 874tl, 882tl, 886tl, 887tl, 890r, 911cl, c, bc. **Michael Courtney:** 144l, 415tl, 429r, cr, 441 cr. **Angelika Elsebach:** 57cl, 118br, 132bl, 133tl, bl, 136bl, 154br, 256bl, 337c, 640cl, 702bl, 747cbr. **Simone End:** 52tl, 54tl, 58tl,74tl, 82tl, 99tl, 104tl, 109tl,117tl, bl,120tl,122tl, 124tl,132tl, 135tl,bl,cbr, 154tl, 155tl, 162tl,cr, 165tl, 177tl,184tl, 189tl, 256tl, cl, 265tl, 270tl, 276tl, 283 tl, 289tl, 316tl, 327tl, 336tl, 342tl, 343tl, 345tl, 346tl, 350tl, 351tl, 354tl, 364tl, 366tl, 393tl, 396tl, 411tl, 418tl, ccr, 419 tl, 420tl, 430tl, 431tl, bcl, 458tl, 472tl, 483tl, 488tl, 492tl, 511tl, 517tl, 527tl, 533tl, 556tl, 567tl, 568tl, 573tl, 578tl , 584tl, 599tl, 609tl, 615tl, 624tl, 633tl, 640tl, 643tl, 644tl, 647, 654tl, 657tl, 663tl, 665tl, 667tl, 668tl, 669tl, 672tl, 674tl, 677tl, 687tl, 694tl, 701tl, 711tl, 713tl, 736tl, 737tl, 747tl, 748tl, 751tl, 754tl, 755cl, clb, 756tl, 761tl, 770tl, 772tl, 779tl, cr, 780tr, 801tl, 803tl, 806tl, 817tl, 818tl, 854tl, 872tl, 889tl, 893tl, 894cl, 897tl, 899tl, 902tl, 904tl, cr, 909tl. **Nick Hewetson:** 340 b,752acr, cr, cl, bcl, bcr, bl. **John Houghton/Brighton Illustration:** 85tl, 583 tl, **Chris Lyons:** 757bcl, 828cl. **Pond & Giles:** 57tl,108tl, 144tl, c, bcr, 167tl, 234tl, 245tl, 253tl, 260tl, 264tl, cl, cr, 278tl, cl, 299tl, 322tl, cl, br, 339tl, 362tl, 383tl, 384tl, 386acr, 414tl, 423tl, 429tl, cl, 436tl, b, 437tl, tc, 440tl, 441tl, bcr, cr, 491tl, 498tl, 499tl, 502tl, 506tl, 519tl, tr, 554tl, 555ac, 575tl, 582tl, 596tl, 622tl, 628tl, 643c, 709tl, 715tl, 715b, 749tl, 765tl, 767tl, 769tl, acl, 774tl, 824tl, 873tl, bcr, 909bcr. **Sallie Alane Reason:** 11tc, 17tcr, 18tr, 47tr, 49tc, 51tr, 77tr, 84tr, 101tc, 116tr, 127tr, 138tr, 160tr, 171cl, 176c, 191tr, 196cr, 197cl, 198tc, 209tr, 210bl ,212cl, 213cl, 217tr, 238cra, 247c, 255cl, 259tr, 262tl, 281tr, 291tr, 302c, 307tr, 353cl, 368tl, cr, 386bl, 396tr, 400tr, 401cl, 410acl, 425tr, 426cl, 427tr, 428tr, 439tcl, 442tc, 447c, 455tc, 468tc, tr, 477cl, 480bl, 486c, 490tr, 502c, 526tr, 531tr, 539tr, 540tr, 549tl, 556tl, 557tr, 565tr, 577tr, bc, br, 580tl, 594tr, 596tr, 610tr, 613tr, 614tl, 626cr, 627acr, 631tr, 648tr, 652tr, 658tr, 673acl, tr, 684cl, 687cl, bcr, 688tr, 704tr, 721br, 724tr, 732br, 735tr, 739bc, 740cl, 743tr, 752tr, 781tr, 790tc, 813tr,868cr, 878tc, 905tr, 907cl, cr. **Colin Salmon:** 12tl, 86tl, 87tl, 92tl, cl, br, 101tl, 130tl, bl, 139tl, cr, 196tl, 198tl, 199tl, 226tl, ca, cb, cr, 230tl, 295tl, bcr, 296tl, 298tl, 304bl, 352tl, acl, 363tl, ac, 370tl, 375tl, 398tl, cr, bcl, 416tl, 417tc, 442tl, 508tl, cl, br, 514tl, acr, 520tl, br, 522tl, bcr, 538tl, c, 550tl, 558tl, 571tl, 627tl, tr, 655tl, 660tl, 690tl, 697tl, 717tl, 739tl, 778tl, cl, 782tl, tc, ac, cl, cr, 796 tl, tr, 807tl, 814tl, 815cl, 837tl. **Rodney Shackell:** 182bcl, 183tr, 247tl, 439 tl, 546 tl. **Peter Visscher:** 163tl, cr, 405 tl, 828tl. **John Woodcock:** 11tl, 14tl, 15tr, 16tc, 17tl, 44tl, bl, 47tl, 51tl, 56tl, 59tl, 61tl, 65tl, 66ca, 67ca, 68tl, 69tl, 75tl, 76tc, 77tl, 80tl, br, 81tl, 84tl, 85tl, 89tl, 90tl, 91tl, bl, 93tl, 94tc, 95tl, br, 85r, 89tl, 90tl, 91tl, 93tl, 94tc, 95tl, br, 97tl, 105tl, 114tl, 116tl, 121tl,123tl, 126tl, cr, 127tl, 128tl, 131tl, 138tl, 140tl, 141tl, 143tl, 146tl, 147tl, 148tl, 149tl, 151tl, 152lc, 161tl, 169tl, cra, 170tl, 171tl, 172tl, 178 tl, 181tl, 182tl, 186tl, 188tl, bl, 190tl, ca, cr, 191tl, 193tl,197tl, 206tl, 207tc, cl, 209tl, 212tl, 213tl, 215tl, 216tl, 217tl, 221tl, 222tl, 223tl, 231tl, br, 233tl, 236tl, 242tl, 248tl, 252tl, 259tl, 268tl, 269tl, 274tl, 277tl, 279tl, 280bc, 281bc, 282tl, 285tl, 297tl, 302tl, 305tl, 307tl, 308tl, 309tc, 310tl, 312tl, 315tl, 318tl, 320tl, 328tl, 330tl, 335tl, 340tl, 344tl, 353tl, 356tl, 357acl, 358tl, 360tl, 372tl, 373tl, 376tl, 377cl, 378tl, 379tl, bl, 380tl, 381tl, 387tl, 388tl, 391tl, 392tl, 400tl, 401tl, 406tl, 413tl, 414cl, 415c, cbl, cbr, 421tl, 424tl, 425tl, 426tl, 427tl, 428tl, 429b,cr, 433tl, 434tl, 438tl, 439tl, 441acl, 444tl, 445tc, 447tl, 449tl, 451tl, acr, 452tl, 453tl, 456tl, 461tl, 465tl, bcr, bc, 466tl, 467tl, 468tl, 471tl, 473tl, br, 476tl, 477tl, 479tl, 484tl, 485tl, 486tl, 490tl, 493tl, 497tl, cl, 501tl, 503tl, br, 504tl, 507tl, 510tl, 515tl, 519cl, bc, 521tl, 523tl, 526tl, 531tl, 532tl, 536tl, cl, bl, 540tl, 541tl, 543tl, 548tl, 549tl, 551tl, cr, 552tl, 553tl, 557tl, 560tl, 561tl, 562tl, 565tl, 566tl, c, 572tl, 574tl, 577tl, cl, 579 tl, 580tl, 581tl, 590tl, 593tl, 594tl, 595tl, 598tl, 602tl, tr, 603tl, 606tl, bl, cl, 610tl, 611tl, 612tc, 613tl, 619tl, cr, 620tl, 621tl, c, 625tl, 629tl, 630tl, 638tl, 642tl, 648tl, 650tl, br, 652tl, 653tl, 656tl, 658tl, 670tl, 671tl, 676tl, 679tl, 681c, 683t, 682tl, 683tl, 684tl, 691tl, 695tl, cl, 696tl, 698tl, 699tl, 705tl, 709bl, cl, 710cl, 716tl, 720tl, cl, bl, bc, 722tl, 724tl, 727tl, 729tl, 730t, tl, 731t, tl, 732tl, 734tl, 735tl, 738tl, 739bc, 740tl, 742tl, 743tl, 745tl, 752tl, 757tl, 762tl, 765cr, 766cr, 768tl, 769bcl, 776tl, 781tl, 783tl, bcl, 781tl, 783tl, bcl, 784tl, cl, 785cl, 786tl, 787tl, 788c, 789tl, 791tl, 792c, 793tl, 795tl, 798tl, c, 799tl, 800tl, 808cl, 810tl, 811tl, 812tl, 813tl, 823tl, 824tr, bc, 825tl, bcl, 826tl, c, 829tl, 832tl, 833tl, 835tl, 840tl, 842tl, 843tl, 845tl, 850tl, 851tl, 852tl, acr, 856tl, 857tl,858tl,,bcr, 859tl, 860tl, 862tl, 864tl, bl, bc, 868tl, 875tl, 878tl, 884tl, 885tl, 890tl, 891tl, 896tl, 898tl, 901tl, 905tl, 907tl, 910tl.

Additional illustration by: Luciano Corbello, Peter Serjeant, Mike Saunders

MODEL MAKERS

Mark Beesley: 560c, 572c. **David Donkin Models:** 92 cra, c, cl, cr, 289 c, 434 c, 697acr. **Peter Griffiths:** 15bl, 56bl, 75bl, 91r, 93bl, 130c, 259c, 281c, 308bl, 353c, cl, 505b, 513br, 583b, 611bl, 677c, 681c, 691c, cl, 695tr, 716ac, 732bl, 777c, 787bl, 808cr, 814b, 815c, 825cr, 840b, 841cr, 850c, 862c, 871l, acr. **Paul Holzherr:** 171c, 191c, 400 c, 453 cr, 557 c, 613 bcr, 752c. **Melanie Williams:** 354 ac.

PHOTOGRAPHERS

David Agar: 540 c, cr, cl. **Geoff Brightling:** 122l, 241cra, 567 tc, cr, 806c, cr. **Andy Crawford:** 130c,215c, 247tr, 295 c, cl, cr, 296 tr, cr, 303 cr, 304 bl, 352 cb, 353 c, cl, 363 c, 368 c, 416 tr, br, acr, 417 tl, tr, c, cr, 461 br, 468 bc, b, 504 bl, 508 cl, 509 t, 520 tr, bl, 531 b,c, 598 acl, 603 bl, cc, 655c, 677c, 690cl, cr, 717c, 758cr, 759, 796c, 808cr, 809cr, c, 814b, 815c. **Michael Dunning:** 226tr. **Steve Gorton:** 15bl, 56bl, 75bl, 85cl, br, 93bl,226bc, 227cl, cr, 256c, 296 br, 308 bl, 344 cb, 354 ac, 417 bcr, 434 c, 440acl, 503b, 522tr, c, br, cr, 560c, 583b, 593acr, 603acr, 611bl, 690bc, bcl, 697cr, 748tcr, 756acr, bcr, 767br, 787bl. **Christi Graham:** 443. **Frank Greenaway:** 104c, 117c, 118c, 119, 138c, 177crb, clb, blb, 234cra, 246c, ca, 256tr, 257c, 260 bl, 276t, cra, cr, 283c, 299 cra, cr, 327c, 346tc, tr, 363bcl, 366bl, 393c, cl, cr, 394, 395cl, c, cr, 440c, 513bcl, 573tr, c, cl, bl, 644tr, cl, 647tr, c, 654c, 657c, 663bl, 665c, cr, 667c, 668c, br, 678tr, 701c, 713c, bcb, 770ac, 801c, 847tr, c. **Mark Hamilton:** 41c, 171c, 191c, 203tc, 400 c, 453 cr, 454 c, cr, 515 tr, 557c, 613 bcl, 752c, 836tr, bc. **John Heaver:** 291, 292. **Alan Hills:** 686 **J. Kershaw:** 439, 441, 455 cl, bcl, bcr, 539 r, cra, cl, cr, br. **Simon Miles:** 304 cl, cla. **Gary Ombler:** 163cla, 341 t. **Sam Peckham:** 540 bcl. **Tim Ridley:** 121cl, cr, 362 c, cl, cb, ca. **Janet Pearson:** 293, 410 acr, cr, cbr, b. **Jim Seagar:** 42b. **Clive Streeter:** 164, 199c, bl, cr, 200tl, 226, 296 bl, 375 tc, 398 c, 417 acl, 553 cr, 558 tc, bl, cr. **Mathew Ward:** 91r, 98br, 143c, 202, 218cr, cl, 219tr ,bl, 220cl, c, cr. 221br, 231c, 232tcl, bcr,242tr, 243t, 244cbl, 252cl, 259 c, 277 cl, cr, 281 c, 297 c, 328 tr, bl, 340 tl, 341 b, 348 cb, 438 bcr, 456 c, cr, 457 tc, 502 b, br, 503 c, 536 br, 537 bl, 542 cl, 562 cl, 564, 589 cr, 603 cl, 604 c, cl, 619 cr, 642bl, 646c, 651cl, tr, br, 670cl, 681c, 685c, cl, acr, 691c, cl, br, 695tr, 716ac, 732bl, 742ca, c 760c, 777c, 783cl, c, br, 804c, cl, bcr, 805t, c, 825cr, bc, 826bl, 827, 829acl, 840b, 841cr, 850c.

ACKNOWLEDGEMENTS

Dorling Kindersley would like to thank the following people and organizations for their assistance in the production of this book:

Additional design, editorial, and research assistance: Rachel Foster, Rebecca Johns, Maggie Tingle, Francesca Stich, Sue Copsey, John Mapps, Keith Lye, Nancy Jones
Additional picture research assistance: Ingrid Nilsson, Helen Stallion, Andy Sansom, Joanne Beardwell, Sarah Pownall and Andrea Sadler
Additional DTP design: Tamsin Pender, Tanya Mukajee
Additional cartographic assistance: David Roberts, Roger Bullen, Steve Flanagan, Jane Voss, Sarah Baker-Ede, Jan Clark, Tony Chambers, Michael Martin
Indexers: Hilary Bird, Ruth Duxbury
Proofreader: Marion Dent
Jacket design: Chris Bramfield

All embassies, consulates and high commissions for supplying information; Aga Khan Foundation; American Express; Amnesty International; Angel Sound Recording Studio; Anti-Slavery International; Argyle Diamonds; Arjo Wiggins; Army and Navy Stores; AT&T; Austrian Tourist Board; Barclays Bank; BBC TV, Susie Staples and the Newsround team; Beaties of London Ltd; BECTU; BIFU; Booths Museum; Boots the Chemist; BP; Braemar Antiquea; Birdland; Brighton Sea-Life Centre; British Equity; Cat Survival Trust, Terry Moore; Centre for Information on Language Teaching; Chubb Safe Equipment Company; CILT; City and Guilds of London Arts School; Civil Aviation Authority; Clubb-Chipperfield Ltd; Copec S.A.; Corporation of London; CPSA; Cusden Architects, Wharmsby; Divya Pande; Dudley and West Midlands Zoo, Peter Suddock; Dyson Appliances; Electrox; Gerald Eddy; European Union Information Centre; Finnish Church, Rotherhithe; Food and Agriculture Organization; Food Marketing Institute; Micheal Foreman; Sir Norman Foster and partners; Friends of the Earth; GEC-Marconi Limited; Geffrye Museum; German National Tourist Office; Goethe Institute; Joanna Gough; Greenpeace; HM Prison Service; Sam Hill; Honeywell School, Dick Cooper and Divya Pande; Howard League for Penal Reform; Howletts and Port Lympne Zoo, Jeremy Watson; Imperial War Museum; Institute of Civil Engineering; Italian Cultural Institute; Japan Festival Education Trust; Japan Foundation; Japan Society; Japanese National Tourist Organisation; Jordan Information Bureau; Kew Gardens; Kings College, London; Kit Alsopp Architects; Korea Trade Centre; Lebanon Tourist and Information Office; Lloyds Bank; Hugh Lockhart-Ball; London Patent Office; Gerald Lovell; Makaton Vocabulary Development Programme; Malaysian Tourist Board; Maria Montessori Training Organisation; Mellors Reay and Partners Ltd; Metropolitan Police Force; Middlesex County Court; Midland Bank plc; Museum of Mankind; National Museum of Labour History; National Trust, Clandon Park; Nature Magazine; Daphne Neville; New Forest Nature Quest, Derek Gow; Norwegian Tourist Board; Emma O'Brien; OPEC; OXFAM; Park Beekeeping Supplies, Godfrey Munro; Michael Parsons; Patent Office; Model magazine, Peace Pledge Union; Philippine Tourist Board; Pirelli/Young & Rubicam; Powell/Cotton Museum; Prison Reform Trust; Proctor and Gamble Limited; Professor Cloudesley Thompson; RMT, Laurie Harris; Recline & Sprawl; Renault; Roehampton Golf Course; Royal Institution of Naval Architects; RSPB; Sainsbury's; Genevieve St. Julian-Brown; Scout Association; Sesmarine (International) Ltd; SNCF; Stanley Gibbons Ltd, Mark Peg; Phoebe Fraser Thoms; TUC; Twycross Zoo; UNISON; Viking Society; Frederick Warne for Beatrix Potter; Volkswagen UK; Paul Walsh; Watts, Capt. O M; Whitakers, Malcolm Dyer; Arjo Wiggins; Sarah Wilson; World Wide Fund for Nature; Zanussi; Woolwich Building Society.

CONTRIBUTORS AND CONSULTANTS

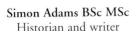

Simon Adams BSc MSc
Historian and writer

Norman Barrett MA
Sports writer and consultant

Dr Martin R. Bates BSc, PhD
Institute of Archaeology
University of London

David Burnie BSc
Science and natural history writer

Jack Challoner BSc, ARCS, PGCE
Science writer, formerly with the Education
Unit, Science Museum, London

Julie Childs BSc
Zoologist and natural history writer,
former Head of Public Affairs, Zoological
Society of London

Neil Clark BSc
Paleontologist, Hunterian Museum and
University of Glasgow

Paul Collins MA
Institute of Archaeology
University College, London

Dr Gordon Daniels
Reader in History,
University of Sheffield

Veronica Doubleday
Lecturer, Historical and Critical Studies,
University of Brighton

John Farndon
Writer and consultant

Roger Few BA
Author on natural history and the
environment

Theresa Greenaway BSc, ARCS
Botanist and natural history writer

Frances Halpin BSc
Science consultant and teacher at
Royal Russell School

Dr Austen Ivereigh D Phil
Lecturer in Latin American History
University of Leeds

Robin Kerrod FRAS
Science writer and consultant

Bruce P. Lenman
Professor of Modern History
University of St Andrews

Nicky Levell
Curator Collections History,
The Horniman Museum

John E. Llewellyn-Jones BSc
Zoologist and botanist; writer and lecturer

Miranda MacQuitty BSc, PhD
Zoologist and natural history writer

Kevin McRae
Writer and consultant

Haydn Middleton MA
Historian and author

Mark O'Shea BSc, FRGS
Curator of Reptiles, West Midland Safari
Park; tropical herpetologist and zoologist;
natural history author

Chris Oxlade BSc
Writer and consultant, specializing in
science and technology

Douglas Palmer BSc, PhD
Writer, lecturer, and Open University tutor
specializing in palaeobiology

Steve Parker BSc
Zoologist, science writer and scientific
fellow of the Zoological Society

Tom Parsons MA
Art historian and writer

James Pickford BA
Writer and
electronic editor FT Mastering

Richard Platt BA
Writer and consultant

Matthew Robertson
Senior invertebrate keeper, Bristol Zoo

Theodore Rowland-Entwistle BA, FRGS
Writer and consultant

Noel Simon
Member emiritus of the Species Survival
Commission of IUCN; original compiler
mammalia volume, Red Data Book

Carole Stott BA, FRAS
Astronomy and space writer;
formerly Head of the Old Royal
Observatory, Greenwich, London

Jonathan Stroud BA
Writer and consultant: literature

Barbara Taylor BSc
Environmental scientist and
natural history writer

Louise Tythacott
Writer and consultant Southeast Asia

Richard Walker BSc PhD
Human biology and natural history writer

Marcus Weeks B Mus
Composer and writer

Philip Wilkinson MA
Historian and writer

Elizabeth Wyse BA
Writer and consultant

Dorling Kindersley Cartography
in conjunction with leading cartographic
consultants, embassies, and consulates